Econometric Analysis of Cross Section and Panel Data

Econometric Analysis of Cross Section and Panel Data

Second Edition

Jeffrey M. Wooldridge

The MIT Press
Cambridge, Massachusetts
London, England

For information about special quantity discounts, please email special_sales@mitpress.mit.edu

This book was set in Times Roman by Asco Typesetters, Hong Kong. Printed and bound in the United States of America.

Library of Congress Cataloging-in-Publication Data

Wooldridge, Jeffrey M.
Econometric analysis of cross section and panel data / Jeffrey M. Wooldridge.—2nd ed.
p. cm.
Includes bibliographical references and index.
ISBN 978-0-262-23258-6 (hardcover : alk. paper)
1. Econometrics—Asymptotic theory. I. Title.
HB139.W663 2010
330.01′5195—dc22 2010020912

10 9 8 7 6 5 4 3 2

Contents

Preface

It has been almost 10 years since the first edition of *Econometric Analysis of Cross Section and Panel Data* was published. The reaction to the first edition was more positive than I could have imagined when I began thinking about the project in the mid-1990s. Of course, as several of you have kindly and constructively pointed out—and as was evident to me the first time I taught out of the book—the first edition was hardly perfect. Issues of organization and gaps in coverage were shortcomings that I wanted to address in a second edition from early on. Plus, there have been some important developments in econometrics that can and should be taught to graduate students in economics.

I doubt this second edition is perfect, either. But I believe it improves the first edition in substantive ways. The structure of this edition is similar to the first edition, but I have made some changes that will contribute to the reader's understanding of several topics. For example, Chapter 11, which covers more advanced topics in linear panel data models, has been rearranged to progress more naturally through situations where instrumental variables are needed in conjuction with methods for accounting for unobserved heterogeneity. Data problems—including censoring, sample selection, attrition, and stratified sampling—are now postponed until Chapters 19 and 20, after popular nonlinear models are presented under random sampling. I think this change will further emphasize a point I tried to make in the first edition: It is critical to distinguish between specifying a population model on the one hand and the method used to sample the data on the other. As an example, consider the Tobit model. In the first edition, I presented the Tobit model as applying to two separate cases: (1) a response variable is a corner solution outcome in the population (with the corner usually at zero) and (2) the underlying variable in the population is continuously distributed but the data collection scheme involves censoring the response in some way. Many readers commented that they were happy I made this distinction, because empirical researchers often seemed to confuse a corner solution due to economic behavior and a corner that is arbitrarily created by a data censoring mechanism. Nevertheless, I still found that beginners did not always fully appreciate the difference, and poor practice in interpreting estimates lingered. Plus, combining the two types of applications of so-called "censored regression models" gave short shrift to true data censoring. In this edition, models for corner solutions in the population are treated in Chapter 17, and a variety of data censoring schemes are covered in more detail in Chapter 19.

As in the first edition, I use the approach of specifying a population model and imposing assumptions on that model. Until Chapter 19, random sampling is assumed to generate the data. Unlike traditional treatments of, say, the linear regression model, my approach forces the student to specify the population of interest, propose a model and assumptions in the population, and then worry about data issues. The last part is easy under random sampling, and so students can focus on various models that are used for populations with different features. The students gain a clear understanding that, under random sampling, our ability to identify parameters (and other quantities of interest) is a product of our assumed model in the population. Later it becomes clear that sampling schemes that depart from random sampling can introduce complications for learning about the underlying population.

The second edition continues to omit some important topics not covered in the first edition. The leading ones are simulation methods of estimation and semiparametric/nonparametric estimation. The book by Cameron and Trivedi (2005) does an admirable job providing accessible introductions to these topics.

I have added several new problems to each of the chapters. As in the first edition, the problems are a blend of methodological questions—some of which lead to tweaking existing methods in useful directions—and empirical work. Several data sets have been added to further illustate how more advanced methods can be applied. The data sets can be accessed by visiting links at the MIT Press website for the book: http://mitpress.mit.edu/9780262232586.

New to the Second Edition

Earlier I mentioned that I have reorganized some of the material from the first edition. I have also added new material, and expanded on some of the existing topics. For example, Chapter 6 (in Part II) introduces control function methods in the context of models linear in parameters, including random coefficient models, and discusses when the method is the same as two-stage least squares and when it differs. Control function methods can be used for certain systems of equations (Chapter 9) and are used regularly for nonlinear models to deal with endogenous explanatory variables, or heterogeneity, or both (Part IV). The control function method is convenient for testing whether certain variables are endogenous, and more tests are included throughout the book. (Examples include Chapter 15 for binary response models and Chapter 18 for count data.) Chapter 6 also contains a more detailed discussion of difference-in-differences methods for independently pooled cross sections.

Chapter 7 now introduces all of the different concepts of exogeneity of the explanatory variables in the context of panel data models, without explicitly introducing unobserved heterogeneity. This chapter also contains a detailed discussion of the properties of generalized least squares when an incorrect variance-covariance structure is imposed. This general discussion is applied in Chapter 10 to models that nominally impose a random effects structure on the variance-covariance matrix.

In this edition, Chapter 8 explicitly introduces and analyzes the so-called "generalized instrumental variables" (GIV) estimator. This estimator, used implicitly in parts of the first edition, is important for discussing efficient estimation. Further, some of the instrumental variables estimators used for panel data models in Chapter 11 are GIV estimators. It is helpful for the reader to understand the general idea underlying GIV, and to see its application to classes of important models.

Chapter 10, while focusing on traditional estimation methods for unobserved effects panel data models, demonstrates more clearly the relationships among random effects, fixed effects, and "correlated random effects" (CRE) models. While the first edition used the CRE approach often—especially for nonlinear models—I never used the phrase "correlated random effects," which I got from Cameron and Trivedi (2005). Chapter 10 also provides a detailed treatment of the Hausman test for comparing the random and fixed effects estimators, including demonstrating that the traditional way of counting degrees of freedom when aggregate time effects are included is wrong and can be very misleading. The important topic of approximating the bias from fixed effects estimation and first differencing estimation, as a function of the number of available time periods, is also fleshed out.

Of the eight chapters in Part II, Chapter 11 has been changed the most. The random effects and fixed effects instrumental variables estimators are introduced and studied in some detail. These estimators form the basis for estimation of panel data models with heterogeneity and endogeneity, such as simultaneous equations models or models with measurement error, as well as models with additional orthogonality restrictions, such as Hausman and Taylor models. The method of first differencing followed by instrumental variables is also given separate treatment. This widely adopted approach can be used to estimate static models with endogeneity and dynamic models, such as those studied by Arellano and Bond (1991). The Arellano and Bond approach, along with several extensions, are now discussed in Section 11.6. Section 11.7 extends the treatment of models with individual-specific slopes, including an analysis of when traditional estimators are consistent for the population averaged effect, and new tests for individual-specific slopes.

As in the first edition, Part III of the book is the most technical, and covers general approaches to estimation. Chapter 12 contains several important additions. There is a new discussion concerning inference when the first-step estimation of a two-step procedure is ignored. Resampling schemes, such as the bootstrap, are discussed in more detail, including how one used the bootstrap in microeconometric applications with a large cross section and relatively few time periods. The most substantive additions are in Sections 12.9 and 12.10, which cover multivariate nonlinear least squares and quantile methods, respectively. An important feature of Section 12.9 is that I make a simple link between mutivariate weighted nonlinear least squares—an estimation method familiar to economists—and the generalized estimating equations (GEE) approach. In effect, these approaches are the same, a point that hopefully allows economists to read other literature that uses the GEE nomenclature.

The section on quantile estimation covers different asymptotic variance estimators and discusses how they compare to violation of assumptions in terms of robustness. New material on estimating and inference when quantile regression is applied to panel data gives researchers simple methods for allowing unobserved effects in quantile estimation, while at the same time offering inference that is fully robust to arbitrary serial correlation.

Chapter 13, on maximum likelihood methods, also includes several additions, including a general discussion of nonlinear unobserved effects models and the different approaches to accounting for the heterogeneity (broadly, random effects, "fixed" effects, and correlated random effects) and different estimation methods (partial maximum likelihood or full maximum likelihood). Two-step maximum likelihood estimators are covered in more detail, including the case where estimating parameters in a first stage can be more efficient than simply plugging in known population values in the second stage. Section 13.11 includes new material on quasi-maximum likelihood estimation (QMLE). This section argues that, for general misspecification, only one form of asymptotic variance can be used. The QMLE perspective is attractive in that it admits that models are almost certainly wrong, thus we should conduct inference on the approximation in a valid way. Vuong's (1988) model selection tests, for nonnested models, is explicitly treated as a way to choose among competing models that are allowed to be misspecified. I show how to extend Vuong's approach to panel data applications (as usual, with a relatively small number of time periods).

Chapter 13 also includes a discussion of QMLE in the linear exponential family (LEF) of likelihoods, when the conditional mean is the object of interest. A general treatment allows me to appeal to the consistency results, and the methods for inference, at several points in Part IV. I emphasize the link between QMLE in the LEF and the so-called "generalized linear models" (GLM) framework. It turns out that GLM is just a special case of QMLE in the LEF, and this recognition should be helpful for studying research conducted from the GLM perspective. A related topic is the GEE approach to estimating panel data models. The starting point for GEE in panel data is to use (for a generic time period) a likelihood in the LEF, but to regain some efficiency that has been lost by not implementing full maximum likelihood by using a generalized least squares approach.

Chapter 14, on generalized method of moments (GMM) and minimum distance (MD) estimation, has been slightly reorganized so that the panel data applications come at the end. These applications have also been expanded to include unobserved effects models with time-varying loads on the heterogeneity.

Perhaps for most readers the changes to Part IV will be most noticeable. The material on discrete response models has been split into two chapters (in contrast to the rather unwieldy single chapter in the first edition). Because Chapter 15 is the first applications-oriented chapter for nonlinear models, I spend more time discussing different ways of measuring the magnitudes of the effects on the response probability. The two leading choices, the partial effects evaluated at the averages and the average partial effect, are discussed in some detail. This discussion carries over for panel data models, too. A new subsection on unobserved effects panel data models with unobserved heterogeneity and a continuous endogenous explanatory variable shows how one can handle both problems in nonlinear models. This chapter contains many more empirical examples than the first edition.

Chapter 16 is new, and covers multinomial and ordered responses. These models are now treated in more detail than in the first edition. In particular, specification issues are fleshed out and the issues of endogeneity and unobserved heterogeneity (in panel data) are now covered in some detail.

Chapter 17, which was essentially Chapter 16 in the first edition, has been given a new title, Corner Solutions Responses, to reflect its focus. In reading Tobin's (1958) paper, I was struck by how he really was talking about the corner solution case—data censoring had nothing to do with his analysis. Thus, this chapter returns to the roots of the Tobit model, and covers several extensions. An important addition is a more extensive treatment of two-part models, which is now in Section 17.6. Hopefully, my unified approach in this section will help clarify the relationships among so-called "hurdle" and "selection" models, and show that the latter are not necessarily superior. Like Chapter 15, this chapter contains several more empirical applications.

Chapter 18 covers other kinds of limited dependent variables, particularly count (nonnegative integer) outcomes and fractional responses. Recent work on panel data methods for fractional responses has been incorporated into this chapter.

Chapter 19 is an amalgamation of material from several chapters in the first edition. The theme of Chapter 19 is data problems. The problem of data censoring—where a random sample of units is obtained from the population, but the response variable is censored in some way—is given a more in-depth treatment. The extreme case of binary censoring is included, along with interval censoring and top coding. Readers are shown how to allow for endogenous explanatory variables and unobserved heterogeneity in panel data.

Chapter 19 also includes the problem of not sampling at all from part of the population (truncated sampling) or not having any information about a response for a subset of the population (incidental truncation). The material on unbalanced panel data sets and the problems of incidental truncation and attrition in panel data are studied in more detail, including the method of inverse probability weighting for correcting for missing data.

Chapter 20 continues the material on nonrandom sampling, providing a separate chapter for stratified sampling and cluster sampling. Stratification and clustering are often features of survey data sets, and it is important to know what adjustments are required to standard econometric methods. The material on cluster sampling summarizes recent work on clustering with a small number of clusters.

The material on treatment effect estimation is now in Chapter 21. While I preserved the setup from the first edition, I have added several more topics. First, I have expanded the discussion of matching estimators. Regression discontinuity designs are covered in a separate section.

The final chapter, Chapter 22, now includes the introductory material on duration analysis. I have included more empirical examples than were in the first edition.

Possible Course Outlines

At Michigan State, I teach a two-semester course to second-year, and some third-year, students that covers the material in my book—plus some additional material. I assume that the graduate students know, or will study on their own, material from Chapters 2 and 3. It helps move my courses along when students are comfortable with the basic algebra of probability (conditional expectations, conditional variances, and linear projections) as well as the basic limit theorems and manipulations. I typically spend a few lectures on Chapters 4, 5, and 6, primarily to provide a bridge between a more traditional treatment of the linear model and one that focuses on a linear population model under random sampling. Chapter 6 introduces control function methods in a simple context and so is worth spending some time on.

In the first semester (15 weeks), I cover the material (selectively) through Chapter 17. But I currently skip, in the first semester, the material in Chapter 12 on multivariate nonlinear regression and quantile estimation. Plus, I do not cover the asymptotic theory underlying M-estimation in much detail, and I pretty much skip Chapter 14 altogether. In effect, the first semester covers the popular linear and nonlinear models, for both cross section and panel data, in the context of random sampling, providing much of the background needed to justify the large-sample approximations.

In the second semester I return to Chapter 12 and cover quantile estimation. I also cover the general quasi-MLE and generalized estimating equations material in

Chapter 13. In Chapter 14, I find the minimum distance approach to estimation is important as a more advanced estimation method. I cover some of the panel data examples from this chapter. I then jump to Chapter 18, which covers count and fractional responses. I spend a fair amount of time on Chapters 19 and 20 because data problems are especially important in practice, and it is important to understand the strengths and weakness of the competing methods. After I cover the main parts of Chapter 21 (including regression discontinuity designs) and Chapter 22 (duration analysis), I sometimes have extra time. (However, if I were to cover some of the more advanced topics in Chapter 21—multivalued and multiple treatments, and dynamic treatement effects in the context of panel data—I likely would run out of time.) If I do have extra time, I like to provide an introduction to nonparametric and semiparametric methods. Cameron and Trivedi (2005) is accessible for the basic methods, while the book by Li and Racine (2007) is comprehensive. Illustrating nonparametric methods using the treatment effects material in Chapter 21 seems particularly effective.

Supplements

A student *Solutions Manual* is available that includes answers to the odd-numbered problems (see http://mitpress.mit.edu/9780262731836). Any instructor who adopts the book for a course may have access to all solutions. In addition, I have created a set of slides for the two-semester course that I teach. They are available as Scientific Word 5.5 files—which can be edited—or as pdf files. For these teaching aids see the web page for the second edition: http://mitpress.mit.edu/9780262232586.

Acknowledgments

The list of people who made inquiries or suggestions for improving the first edition is too long to list. (And, I regret to say, I did not carefully keep track over the past nine years.) I do want to acknowledge Guido Imbens (Harvard University), with whom I have given several short courses over the past three years. Creating material for my lectures with Guido and watching Guido lecture have improved my understanding of certain topics; I hope that is reflected in this edition.

I owe a debt to my colleagues at Michigan State for not just agreeing but encouraging me to develop a second semester course in cross section and panel data methods. The second course has allowed me to teach some material for the first time and has played a role in restructuring the text.

John Covell, Senior Editor at MIT Press, has been remarkably patient throughout what must have been an ordeal for him. John's gentle encouragement during the rough times was especially helpful, and I am grateful he did not give up on me, even when I was ready to give up on myself.

I was very pleased that the folks at P. M. Gordon Associates, Inc. were chosen to edit the manuscript and produce the final text. Nancy Lombardi did a wonderful job with a very messy manuscript.

Finally, as with the first edition, I dedicate the second edition to my wife, Leslie Papke. It was Leslie's early research that sparked my interest in microeconometric methods, and recent joint research of ours appears in the second edition. Most importantly, I treasure the support Leslie has provided during the long process of completing this edition.

I INTRODUCTION AND BACKGROUND

In Part I we introduce the basic approach to econometrics taken throughout the book and cover some background material that is important to master before reading the remainder of the text. Students who have a solid understanding of the algebra of conditional expectations, conditional variances, and linear projections could skip Chapter 2, referring to it only as needed. Chapter 3 contains a summary of the asymptotic analysis needed to read Part II and beyond. In Part III we introduce additional asymptotic tools that are needed to study nonlinear estimation.

1 Introduction

1.1 Causal Relationships and Ceteris Paribus Analysis

The goal of most empirical studies in economics and other social sciences is to determine whether a change in one variable, say w, causes a change in another variable, say y. For example, does having another year of education cause an increase in monthly salary? Does reducing class size cause an improvement in student performance? Does lowering the business property tax rate cause an increase in city economic activity? Because economic variables are properly interpreted as random variables, we should use ideas from probability to formalize the sense in which a change in w causes a change in y.

The notion of **ceteris paribus**—that is, holding all other (relevant) factors fixed—is at the crux of establishing a **causal relationship**. Simply finding that two variables are correlated is rarely enough to conclude that a change in one variable causes a change in another. After all, rarely can we run a controlled experiment that allows a simple correlation analysis to uncover causality. Instead, we can use econometric methods to effectively hold other factors fixed.

If we focus on the average, or expected, response, a ceteris paribus analysis entails estimating $\mathrm{E}(y \mid w, \mathbf{c})$, the expected value of y conditional on w and $\mathbf{c}$. The vector $\mathbf{c}$—whose dimension is not important for this discussion—denotes a set of **control variables** that we would like to explicitly hold fixed when studying the effect of w on the expected value of y. The reason we control for these variables is that we think w is correlated with other factors that also influence y. If w is continuous, interest centers on $\partial \mathrm{E}(y \mid w, \mathbf{c})/\partial w$, which is usually called the **partial effect** of w on $\mathrm{E}(y \mid w, \mathbf{c})$. If w is discrete, we are interested in $\mathrm{E}(y \mid w, \mathbf{c})$ evaluated at different values of w, with the elements of $\mathbf{c}$ fixed at the same specified values. Or, we might average across the distribution of $\mathbf{c}$.

Deciding on the list of proper controls is not always straightforward, and using different controls can lead to different conclusions about a causal relationship between y and w. This is where establishing causality gets tricky: it is up to us to decide which factors need to be held fixed. If we settle on a list of controls, and if all elements of $\mathbf{c}$ can be observed, then estimating the partial effect of w on $\mathrm{E}(y \mid w, \mathbf{c})$ is relatively straightforward. Unfortunately, in economics and other social sciences, many elements of $\mathbf{c}$ are not observed. For example, in estimating the causal effect of education on wage, we might focus on $\mathrm{E}(wage \mid educ, exper, abil)$ where *educ* is years of schooling, *exper* is years of workforce experience, and *abil* is innate ability. In this case, $\mathbf{c} = (exper, abil)$, where *exper* is observed but *abil* is not. (It is widely agreed among labor economists that experience and ability are two factors we should hold fixed to obtain the causal effect of education on wages. Other factors, such as years with the current employer, might belong as well. We can all agree that something such as the last digit of one's social security number need not be included as a control, as it has nothing to do with wage or education.)

As a second example, consider establishing a causal relationship between student attendance and performance on a final exam in a principles of economics class. We might be interested in $\mathrm{E}(score \mid attend, SAT, priGPA)$, where *score* is the final exam score, *attend* is the attendance rate, *SAT* is score on the scholastic aptitude test, and *priGPA* is grade point average at the beginning of the term. We can reasonably collect data on all of these variables for a large group of students. Is this setup enough to decide whether attendance has a causal effect on performance? Maybe not. While *SAT* and *priGPA* are general measures reflecting student ability and study habits, they do not necessarily measure one's interest in or aptitude for econonomics. Such attributes, which are difficult to quantify, may nevertheless belong in the list of controls if we are going to be able to infer that attendance rate has a causal effect on performance.

In addition to not being able to obtain data on all desired controls, other problems can interfere with estimating causal relationships. For example, even if we have good measures of the elements of $\mathbf{c}$, we might not have very good measures of y or w. A more subtle problem—which we study in detail in Chapter 9—is that we may only observe equilibrium values of y and w when these variables are simultaneously determined. An example is determining the causal effect of conviction rates (w) on city crime rates (y).

A first course in econometrics teaches students how to apply multiple regression analysis to estimate ceteris paribus effects of explanatory variables on a response variable. In the rest of this book, we will study how to estimate such effects in a variety of situations. Unlike most introductory treatments, we rely heavily on conditional expectations. In Chapter 2 we provide a detailed summary of properties of conditional expectations.

1.2 Stochastic Setting and Asymptotic Analysis

1.2.1 Data Structures

In order to give proper treatment to modern cross section and panel data methods, we must choose a stochastic setting that is appropriate for the kinds of cross section and panel data sets collected for most econometric applications. Naturally, all else equal, it is best if the setting is as simple as possible. It should allow us to focus on interpreting assumptions with economic content while not having to worry too much about technical regularity conditions. (Regularity conditions are assumptions involving things such as the number of absolute moments of a random variable that must be finite.)

For much of this book we adopt a **random sampling** assumption. More precisely, we assume that (1) a **population model** has been specified and (2) an **independent, identically distributed (i.i.d.)** sample can be drawn from the population. Specifying a population model—which may be a model of $\mathrm{E}(y \mid w, \mathbf{c})$, as in Section 1.1—requires us first to clearly define the population of interest. Defining the relevant population may seem to be an obvious requirement. Nevertheless, as we will see in later chapters, it can be subtle in some cases.

An important virtue of the random sampling assumption is that it allows us to separate the sampling assumption from the assumptions made on the population model. In addition to putting the proper emphasis on assumptions that impinge on economic behavior, stating all assumptions in terms of the population is actually much easier than the traditional approach of stating assumptions in terms of full data matrices.

Because we will rely heavily on random sampling, it is important to know what it allows and what it rules out. Random sampling is often reasonable for **cross section data**, where, at a given point in time, units are selected at random from the population. In this setup, any explanatory variables are treated as random outcomes, along with data on response variables. Fixed regressors cannot be identically distributed across observations, and so the random sampling assumption technically excludes the classical linear model. This feature is actually desirable for our purposes. In Section 1.4 we provide a brief discussion of why it is important to treat explanatory variables as random for modern econometric analysis.

We should not confuse the random sampling assumption with so-called **experimental data**. Experimental data fall under the fixed explanatory variables paradigm. With experimental data, researchers set values of the explanatory variables and then observe values of the response variable. Unfortunately, true experiments are quite rare in economics, and in any case nothing practically important is lost by treating explanatory variables that are set ahead of time as being random. It is safe to say that no one ever went astray by assuming random sampling in place of independent sampling with fixed explanatory variables.

Random sampling does exclude cases of some interest for cross section analysis. For example, the identical distribution assumption is unlikely to hold for a **pooled cross section**, where random samples are obtained from the population at different points in time. This case is covered by **independent, not identically distributed (i.n.i.d.)** observations. Allowing for non-identically distributed observations under independent sampling is not difficult, and its practical effects are easy to deal with. We will mention this case at several points in the book after the analyis is done under random sampling. We do not cover the i.n.i.d. case explicitly in derivations because little is to be gained from the additional complication.

A situation that does require special consideration occurs when cross section observations are not independent of one another. An example is **spatial correlation** models. This situation arises when dealing with large geographical units that cannot be assumed to be independent draws from a large population, such as the 50 states in the United States. It is reasonable to expect that the unemployment rate in one state is correlated with the unemployment rate in neighboring states. While standard estimation methods—such as ordinary least squares and two-stage least squares—can usually be applied in these cases, the asymptotic theory needs to be altered. Key statistics often (although not always) need to be modified. We will briefly discuss some of the issues that arise in this case for single-equation linear models, but otherwise this subject is beyond the scope of this book. For better or worse, spatial correlation is often ignored in applied work because correcting the problem can be difficult.

Cluster sampling also induces correlation in a cross section data set, but in many cases it is relatively easy to deal with econometrically. For example, retirement saving of employees within a firm may be correlated because of common (often unobserved) characteristics of workers within a firm or because of features of the firm itself (such as type of retirement plan). Each firm represents a group or cluster, and we may sample several workers from a large number of firms. As we will see in Chapter 21, provided the number of clusters is large relative to the cluster sizes, standard methods can correct for the presence of within-cluster correlation.

Another important issue is that cross section samples often are, either intentionally or unintentionally, chosen so that they are not random samples from the population of interest. In Chapter 21 we discuss such problems at length, including **sample selection** and **stratified sampling**. As we will see, even in cases of nonrandom samples, the assumptions on the population model play a central role.

For **panel data** (or **longitudinal data**), which consist of repeated observations on the same cross section of, say, individuals, households, firms, or cities over time, the random sampling assumption initially appears much too restrictive. After all, any reasonable stochastic setting should allow for correlation in individual or firm behavior over time. But the random sampling assumption, properly stated, does allow for temporal correlation. What we will do is assume random sampling in the *cross section* dimension. The dependence in the time series dimension can be entirely unrestricted. As we will see, this approach is justified in panel data applications with many cross section observations spanning a relatively short time period. We will also be able to cover panel data sample selection and stratification issues within this paradigm.

A panel data setup that we will not adequately cover—although the estimation methods we cover can usually be used—is seen when the cross section dimension and time series dimension are roughly of the same magnitude, such as when the sample consists of countries over the post–World War II period. In this case it makes little sense to fix the time series dimension and let the cross section dimension grow. The research on asymptotic analysis with these kinds of panel data sets is still in its early stages, and it requires special limit theory. See, for example, Quah (1994), Pesaran and Smith (1995), Kao (1999), Moon and Phillips (2000), Phillips and Moon (2000), and Alvarez and Arellano (2003).

1.2.2 Asymptotic Analysis

Throughout this book we focus on asymptotic properties, as opposed to finite sample properties, of estimators. The primary reason for this emphasis is that finite sample properties are intractable for most of the estimators we study in this book. In fact, most of the estimators we cover will not have desirable finite sample properties such as unbiasedness. Asymptotic analysis allows for a unified treatment of estimation procedures, and it (along with the random sampling assumption) allows us to state all assumptions in terms of the underlying population. Naturally, asymptotic analysis is not without its drawbacks. Occasionally, we will mention when asymptotics can lead one astray. In those cases where finite sample properties can be derived, you are sometimes asked to derive such properties in the problems.

In cross section analysis the asymptotics is as the number of observations, denoted N throughout this book, tends to infinity. Usually what is meant by this statement is obvious. For panel data analysis, the asymptotics is as the cross section dimension gets large while the time series dimension is fixed.

1.3 Some Examples

In this section we provide two examples to emphasize some of the concepts from the previous sections. We begin with a standard example from labor economics.

Example 1.1 (Wage Offer Function): Suppose that the natural log of the *wage offer*, $wage^o$, is determined as

$$\log(wage^o) = \beta_0 + \beta_1 educ + \beta_2 exper + \beta_3 married + u, \tag{1.1}$$

where *educ* is years of schooling, *exper* is years of labor market experience, and *married* is a binary variable indicating marital status. The variable u, called the **error term** or **disturbance**, contains unobserved factors that affect the wage offer. Interest lies in the unknown parameters, the β_j.

We should have a concrete population in mind when specifying equation (1.1). For example, equation (1.1) could be for the population of all *working* women. In this case, it will not be difficult to obtain a random sample from the population.

All assumptions can be stated in terms of the population model. The crucial assumptions involve the relationship between u and the observable explanatory variables, *educ*, *exper*, and *married*. For example, is the expected value of u given the explanatory variables *educ*, *exper*, and *married* equal to zero? Is the variance of u conditional on the explanatory variables constant? There are reasons to think the answer to both of these questions is no, something we discuss at some length in Chapters 4 and 5. The point of raising them here is to emphasize that all such questions are most easily couched in terms of the population model.

What happens if the relevant population is *all* women over age 18? A problem arises because a random sample from this population will include women for whom the wage offer cannot be observed because they are not working. Nevertheless, we can think of a random sample being obtained, but then $wage^o$ is unobserved for women not working.

For deriving the properties of estimators, it is often useful to write the population model for a generic draw from the population. Equation (1.1) becomes

$$\log(wage_i^o) = \beta_0 + \beta_1 educ_i + \beta_2 exper_i + \beta_3 married_i + u_i, \tag{1.2}$$

where i indexes person. Stating assumptions in terms of u_i and $\mathbf{x}_i \equiv (educ_i, exper_i, married_i)$ is the same as stating assumptions in terms of u and $\mathbf{x}$. Throughout this book, the i subscript is reserved for indexing cross section units, such as individual, firm, city, and so on. Letters such as j, g, and h will be used to index variables, parameters, and equations.

Before ending this example, we note that using matrix notation to write equation (1.2) for all N observations adds nothing to our understanding of the model or sampling scheme; in fact, it just gets in the way because it gives the mistaken impression that the matrices tell us something about the assumptions in the underlying population. It is much better to focus on the population model (1.1).

The next example is illustrative of panel data applications.

Example 1.2 (Effect of Spillovers on Firm Output): Suppose that the population is all manufacturing firms in a country operating during a given three-year period. A production function describing output in the population of firms is

$$\log(output_t) = \delta_t + \beta_1 \log(labor_t) + \beta_2 \log(capital_t) + \beta_3\, spillover_t + quality + u_t, \qquad t = 1, 2, 3. \tag{1.3}$$

Here, $spillover_t$ is a measure of foreign firm concentration in the region containing the firm. The term *quality* contains unobserved factors—such as unobserved managerial or worker quality—that affect productivity and are constant over time. The error u_t represents unobserved shocks in each time period. The presence of the parameters δ_t, which represent different intercepts in each year, allows for aggregate productivity to change over time. The coefficients on $labor_t$, $capital_t$, and $spillover_t$ are assumed constant across years.

As we will see when we study panel data methods, there are several issues in deciding how best to estimate the β_j. An important one is whether the unobserved productivity factors (*quality*) are correlated with the observable inputs. Also, can we assume that $spillover_t$ at, say, $t = 3$ is uncorrelated with the error terms in all time periods?

For panel data it is especially useful to add an i subscript indicating a generic cross section observation—in this case, a randomly sampled firm:

$$\log(output_{it}) = \delta_t + \beta_1 \log(labor_{it}) + \beta_2 \log(capital_{it}) + \beta_3\, spillover_{it} + quality_i + u_{it}, \qquad t = 1, 2, 3. \tag{1.4}$$

Equation (1.4) makes it clear that $quality_i$ is a firm-specific term that is constant over time and also has the same effect in each time period, while u_{it} changes across time and firm. Nevertheless, the key issues that we must address for estimation can be discussed for a generic i, since the draws are assumed to be randomly made from the population of all manufacturing firms.

Equation (1.4) is an example of another convention we use throughout the book: the subscript t is reserved to index time, just as i is reserved for indexing the cross section.

1.4 Why Not Fixed Explanatory Variables?

We have seen two examples where, generally speaking, the error in an equation can be correlated with one or more of the explanatory variables. This possibility is so prevalent in social science applications that it makes little sense to adopt an assumption—namely, the assumption of fixed explanatory variables—that rules out such correlation a priori.

In a first course in econometrics, the method of ordinary least squares (OLS) and its extensions are usually learned under the fixed regressor assumption. This is appropriate for understanding the mechanics of least squares and for gaining experience with statistical derivations. Unfortunately, reliance on fixed regressors or, more generally, fixed "exogenous" variables can have unintended consequences, especially in more advanced settings. For example, in Chapters 7 through 11 we will see that assuming fixed regressors or fixed instrumental variables in panel data models imposes often unrealistic restrictions on dynamic economic behavior. This is not just a technical point: estimation methods that are consistent under the fixed regressor assumption, such as generalized least squares, are no longer consistent when the fixed regressor assumption is relaxed in interesting ways.

To illustrate the shortcomings of the fixed regressor assumption in a familiar context, consider a linear model for cross section data, written for each observation i as

$$y_i = \beta_0 + \mathbf{x}_i\boldsymbol{\beta} + u_i, \qquad i = 1, 2, \ldots, N, \tag{1.5}$$

where $\mathbf{x}_i$ is a $1 \times K$ vector and $\boldsymbol{\beta}$ is a $K \times 1$ vector. It is common to see the "ideal" assumptions for this model stated as "The errors $\{u_i\colon i = 1, 2, \ldots, N\}$ are i.i.d. with $\mathrm{E}(u_i) = 0$ and $\mathrm{Var}(u_i) = \sigma^2$." (Sometimes the u_i are also assumed to be normally distributed.) The problem with this statement is that it omits the most important consideration: What is assumed about the relationship between u_i and $\mathbf{x}_i$? If the $\mathbf{x}_i$ are taken as nonrandom—which, evidently, is very often the implicit assumption—then u_i and $\mathbf{x}_i$ are independent of one another. In nonexperimental environments this assumption rules out too many situations of interest. Some important questions, such as efficiency comparisons across models with different explanatory variables, cannot even be asked in the context of fixed regressors. (See Problems 4.5 and 4.15 of Chapter 4 for specific examples.)

In a random sampling context, the u_i are *always* independent and identically distributed, regardless of how they are related to the $\mathbf{x}_i$. Assuming that the population mean of the error is zero is without loss of generality when an intercept is included in the model. Thus, the statement "The errors $\{u_i\colon i = 1, 2, \ldots, N\}$ are i.i.d. with $\mathrm{E}(u_i) = 0$ and $\mathrm{Var}(u_i) = \sigma^2$" is vacuous in a random sampling context. Viewing the $\mathbf{x}_i$ as random draws along with y_i forces us to think about the relationship between the error and the explanatory variables in the *population*. For example, in the population model $y = \beta_0 + \mathbf{x}\boldsymbol{\beta} + u$, is the expected value of u given $\mathbf{x}$ equal to zero? Is u correlated with one or more elements of $\mathbf{x}$? Is the variance of u given $\mathbf{x}$ constant, or does it depend on $\mathbf{x}$? These are the questions that are relevant for estimating $\boldsymbol{\beta}$ and for determining how to perform statistical inference.

Because our focus is on asymptotic analysis, we have the luxury of allowing for random explanatory variables throughout the book, whether the setting is linear models, nonlinear models, single-equation analysis, or system analysis. An incidental but nontrivial benefit is that, compared with frameworks that assume fixed explanatory variables, the unifying theme of random sampling actually simplifies the asymptotic analysis. We will never state assumptions in terms of full data matrices, because such assumptions can be imprecise and can impose unintended restrictions on the population model.

2 Conditional Expectations and Related Concepts in Econometrics

2.1 Role of Conditional Expectations in Econometrics

As we suggested in Section 1.1, the conditional expectation plays a crucial role in modern econometric analysis. Although it is not always explicitly stated, the goal of most applied econometric studies is to estimate or test hypotheses about the expectation of one variable—called the **explained variable**, the **dependent variable**, the **regressand**, or the **response variable**, and usually denoted y—conditional on a set of **explanatory variables**, **independent variables**, **regressors**, **control variables**, or **covariates**, usually denoted $\mathbf{x} = (x_1, x_2, \ldots, x_K)$.

A substantial portion of research in econometric methodology can be interpreted as finding ways to estimate conditional expectations in the numerous settings that arise in economic applications. As we briefly discussed in Section 1.1, most of the time we are interested in conditional expectations that allow us to infer causality from one or more explanatory variables to the response variable. In the setup from Section 1.1, we are interested in the effect of a variable w on the expected value of y, holding fixed a vector of controls, $\mathbf{c}$. The conditional expectation of interest is $\mathrm{E}(y \mid w, \mathbf{c})$, which we will call a **structural conditional expectation**. If we can collect data on y, w, and $\mathbf{c}$ in a random sample from the underlying population of interest, then it is fairly straightforward to estimate $\mathrm{E}(y \mid w, \mathbf{c})$—especially if we are willing to make an assumption about its functional form—in which case the effect of w on $\mathrm{E}(y \mid w, \mathbf{c})$, holding $\mathbf{c}$ fixed, is easily estimated.

Unfortunately, complications often arise in the collection and analysis of economic data because of the nonexperimental nature of economics. Observations on economic variables can contain measurement error, or they are sometimes properly viewed as the outcome of a simultaneous process. Sometimes we cannot obtain a random sample from the population, which may not allow us to estimate $\mathrm{E}(y \mid w, \mathbf{c})$. Perhaps the most prevalent problem is that some variables we would like to control for (elements of $\mathbf{c}$) cannot be observed. In each of these cases there is a conditional expectation (CE) of interest, but it generally involves variables for which the econometrician cannot collect data or requires an experiment that cannot be carried out.

Under additional assumptions—generally called **identification assumptions**—we can sometimes recover the structural conditional expectation originally of interest, even if we cannot observe all of the desired controls, or if we only observe equilibrium outcomes of variables. As we will see throughout this text, the details differ depending on the context, but the notion of conditional expectation is fundamental.

In addition to providing a unified setting for interpreting economic models, the CE operator is useful as a tool for manipulating structural equations into estimable equations. In the next section we give an overview of the important features of the conditional expectations operator. The appendix to this chapter contains a more extensive list of properties.

2.2 Features of Conditional Expectations

2.2.1 Definition and Examples

Let y be a random variable, which we refer to in this section as the *explained variable*, and let $\mathbf{x} \equiv (x_1, x_2, \ldots, x_K)$ be a $1 \times K$ random vector of *explanatory variables*. If $\mathrm{E}(|y|) < \infty$, then there is a function, say μ: $\mathbb{R}^K \to \mathbb{R}$, such that

$$\mathrm{E}(y \mid x_1, x_2, \ldots, x_K) = \mu(x_1, x_2, \ldots, x_K), \tag{2.1}$$

or $\mathrm{E}(y \mid \mathbf{x}) = \mu(\mathbf{x})$. The function $\mu(\mathbf{x})$ determines how the *average* value of y changes as elements of $\mathbf{x}$ change. For example, if y is wage and $\mathbf{x}$ contains various individual characteristics, such as education, experience, and IQ, then $\mathrm{E}(wage \mid educ, exper, IQ)$ is the average value of *wage* for the given values of *educ*, *exper*, and *IQ*. Technically, we should distinguish $\mathrm{E}(y \mid \mathbf{x})$—which is a random variable because $\mathbf{x}$ is a random vector defined in the population—from the conditional expectation when $\mathbf{x}$ takes on a particular value, such as $\mathbf{x}_0$: $\mathrm{E}(y \mid \mathbf{x} = \mathbf{x}_0)$. Making this distinction soon becomes cumbersome and, in most cases, is not overly important; for the most part we avoid it. When discussing probabilistic features of $\mathrm{E}(y \mid \mathbf{x})$, $\mathbf{x}$ is necessarily viewed as a random variable.

Because $\mathrm{E}(y \mid \mathbf{x})$ is an expectation, it can be obtained from the conditional density of y given $\mathbf{x}$ by integration, summation, or a combination of the two (depending on the nature of y). It follows that the conditional expectation operator has the same linearity properties as the unconditional expectation operator, and several additional properties that are consequences of the randomness of $\mu(\mathbf{x})$. Some of the statements we make are proven in the appendix, but general proofs of other assertions require measure-theoretic probabability. You are referred to Billingsley (1979) for a detailed treatment.

Most often in econometrics a model for a conditional expectation is specified to depend on a finite set of parameters, which gives a **parametric model** of $\mathrm{E}(y \mid \mathbf{x})$. This considerably narrows the list of possible candidates for $\mu(\mathbf{x})$.

Example 2.1: For $K = 2$ explanatory variables, consider the following examples of conditional expectations:

$$\mathrm{E}(y \mid x_1, x_2) = \beta_0 + \beta_1 x_1 + \beta_2 x_2, \tag{2.2}$$

$$\mathrm{E}(y \mid x_1, x_2) = \beta_0 + \beta_1 x_1 + \beta_2 x_2 + \beta_3 x_2^2, \tag{2.3}$$

$$\mathrm{E}(y \mid x_1, x_2) = \beta_0 + \beta_1 x_1 + \beta_2 x_2 + \beta_3 x_1 x_2, \tag{2.4}$$

$$\mathrm{E}(y \mid x_1, x_2) = \exp[\beta_0 + \beta_1 \log(x_1) + \beta_2 x_2], \qquad y \geq 0, \; x_1 > 0. \tag{2.5}$$

The model in equation (2.2) is linear in the explanatory variables x_1 and x_2. Equation (2.3) is an example of a conditional expectation nonlinear in x_2, although it is linear in x_1. As we will review shortly, from a statistical perspective, equations (2.2) and (2.3) can be treated in the same framework because they are linear in the *parameters* β_j. The fact that equation (2.3) is nonlinear in $\mathbf{x}$ has important implications for interpreting the β_j, but not for estimating them. Equation (2.4) falls into this same class: it is nonlinear in $\mathbf{x} = (x_1, x_2)$ but linear in the β_j.

Equation (2.5) differs fundamentally from the first three examples in that it is a nonlinear function of the parameters β_j, as well as of the x_j. Nonlinearity in the parameters has implications for estimating the β_j; we will see how to estimate such models when we cover nonlinear methods in Part III. For now, you should note that equation (2.5) is reasonable only if $y \geq 0$.

2.2.2 Partial Effects, Elasticities, and Semielasticities

If y and $\mathbf{x}$ are related in a deterministic fashion, say $y = f(\mathbf{x})$, then we are often interested in how y changes when elements of $\mathbf{x}$ change. In a stochastic setting we cannot assume that $y = f(\mathbf{x})$ for some known function and observable vector $\mathbf{x}$ because there are always unobserved factors affecting y. Nevertheless, we can define the partial effects of the x_j on the conditional expectation $\mathrm{E}(y \mid \mathbf{x})$. Assuming that $\mu(\cdot)$ is appropriately differentiable and x_j is a continuous variable, the partial derivative $\partial\mu(\mathbf{x})/\partial x_j$ allows us to approximate the marginal change in $\mathrm{E}(y \mid \mathbf{x})$ when x_j is increased by a small amount, holding $x_1, \ldots, x_{j-1}, x_{j+1}, \ldots x_K$ constant:

$$\Delta\mathrm{E}(y \mid \mathbf{x}) \approx \frac{\partial\mu(\mathbf{x})}{\partial x_j} \cdot \Delta x_j, \quad \text{holding } x_1, \ldots, x_{j-1}, x_{j+1}, \ldots x_K \text{ fixed.} \tag{2.6}$$

The partial derivative of $\mathrm{E}(y \mid \mathbf{x})$ with respect to x_j is usually called the **partial effect** of x_j on $\mathrm{E}(y \mid \mathbf{x})$ (or, to be somewhat imprecise, the partial effect of x_j on y). Interpreting the magnitudes of coefficients in parametric models usually comes from the approximation in equation (2.6).

If x_j is a discrete variable (such as a binary variable), partial effects are computed by comparing $\mathrm{E}(y \mid \mathbf{x})$ at different settings of x_j (for example, zero and one when x_j is binary), holding other variables fixed.

Example 2.1 (continued): In equation (2.2) we have

$$\frac{\partial \mathrm{E}(y \mid \mathbf{x})}{\partial x_1} = \beta_1, \qquad \frac{\partial \mathrm{E}(y \mid \mathbf{x})}{\partial x_2} = \beta_2.$$

As expected, the partial effects in this model are constant. In equation (2.3),

$$\frac{\partial \mathrm{E}(y \mid \mathbf{x})}{\partial x_1} = \beta_1, \qquad \frac{\partial \mathrm{E}(y \mid \mathbf{x})}{\partial x_2} = \beta_2 + 2\beta_3 x_2,$$

so that the partial effect of x_1 is constant but the partial effect of x_2 depends on the level of x_2. In equation (2.4),

$$\frac{\partial \mathrm{E}(y \mid \mathbf{x})}{\partial x_1} = \beta_1 + \beta_3 x_2, \qquad \frac{\partial \mathrm{E}(y \mid \mathbf{x})}{\partial x_2} = \beta_2 + \beta_3 x_1,$$

so that the partial effect of x_1 depends on x_2, and vice versa. In equation (2.5),

$$\frac{\partial \mathrm{E}(y \mid \mathbf{x})}{\partial x_1} = \exp(\cdot)(\beta_1/x_1), \qquad \frac{\partial \mathrm{E}(y \mid \mathbf{x})}{\partial x_2} = \exp(\cdot)\beta_2, \tag{2.7}$$

where $\exp(\cdot)$ denotes the function $\mathrm{E}(y \mid \mathbf{x})$ in equation (2.5). In this case, the partial effects of x_1 and x_2 both depend on $\mathbf{x} = (x_1, x_2)$.

Sometimes we are interested in a particular function of a partial effect, such as an elasticity. In the determinstic case $y = f(\mathbf{x})$, we define the elasticity of y with respect to x_j as

$$\frac{\partial y}{\partial x_j} \cdot \frac{x_j}{y} = \frac{\partial f(\mathbf{x})}{\partial x_j} \cdot \frac{x_j}{f(\mathbf{x})}, \tag{2.8}$$

again assuming that x_j is continuous. The right-hand side of equation (2.8) shows that the elasticity is a function of $\mathbf{x}$. When y and $\mathbf{x}$ are random, it makes sense to use the right-hand side of equation (2.8), but where $f(\mathbf{x})$ is the conditional mean, $\mu(\mathbf{x})$. Therefore, the (partial) **elasticity** of $\mathrm{E}(y \mid \mathbf{x})$ with respect to x_j, holding $x_1, \ldots, x_{j-1}, x_{j+1}, \ldots, x_K$ constant, is

$$\frac{\partial \mathrm{E}(y \mid \mathbf{x})}{\partial x_j} \cdot \frac{x_j}{\mathrm{E}(y \mid \mathbf{x})} = \frac{\partial \mu(\mathbf{x})}{\partial x_j} \cdot \frac{x_j}{\mu(\mathbf{x})}. \tag{2.9}$$

If $\mathrm{E}(y \mid \mathbf{x}) > 0$ and $x_j > 0$ (as is often the case), equation (2.9) is the same as

$$\frac{\partial \log[\mathrm{E}(y \mid \mathbf{x})]}{\partial \log(x_j)}. \tag{2.10}$$

This latter expression gives the elasticity its interpretation as the approximate percentage change in $\mathrm{E}(y \mid \mathbf{x})$ when x_j increases by 1 percent.

Example 2.1 (continued): In equations (2.2) to (2.5), most elasticities are not constant. For example, in equation (2.2), the elasticity of $\mathrm{E}(y \mid \mathbf{x})$ with respect to x_1 is $(\beta_1 x_1)/(\beta_0 + \beta_1 x_1 + \beta_2 x_2)$, which clearly depends on x_1 and x_2. However, in equation (2.5) the elasticity with respect to x_1 is constant and equal to β_1.

How does equation (2.10) compare with the definition of elasticity based on the expected value of $\log(y)$? If $y > 0$ and $x_j > 0$, we could define the elasticity as

$$\frac{\partial \mathrm{E}[\log(y) \mid \mathbf{x}]}{\partial \log(x_j)}. \tag{2.11}$$

This seems to be a natural definition in a model such as $\log(y) = g(\mathbf{x}) + u$, where $g(\mathbf{x})$ is some function of $\mathbf{x}$ and u is an unobserved disturbance with zero mean conditional on $\mathbf{x}$. How do equations (2.10) and (2.11) compare? Generally, they are different (since the expected value of the log and the log of the expected value can be very different). *If* u is *independent* of $\mathbf{x}$, then equations (2.10) and (2.11) are the same, because then

$$\mathrm{E}(y \mid \mathbf{x}) = \delta \cdot \exp[g(\mathbf{x})],$$

where $\delta \equiv \mathrm{E}[\exp(u)]$. (If u and $\mathbf{x}$ are independent, so are $\exp(u)$ and $\exp[g(\mathbf{x})]$.) As a specific example, if

$$\log(y) = \beta_0 + \beta_1 \log(x_1) + \beta_2 x_2 + u, \tag{2.12}$$

where u has zero mean and is independent of (x_1, x_2), then the elasticity of y with respect to x_1 is β_1 using *either* definition of elasticity. If $\mathrm{E}(u \mid \mathbf{x}) = 0$ but u and $\mathbf{x}$ are not independent, the definitions are generally different.

In many applications with $y > 0$, little is lost by viewing equations (2.10) and (2.11) as the same, and in some later applications we will not make a distinction. Nevertheless, if the error u in a model such as (2.12) is heteroskedastic—that is, $\mathrm{Var}(u \mid \mathbf{x})$ depends on $\mathbf{x}$—then equation (2.10) and equation (2.11) can deviate in nontrivial ways; see Problem 2.8. Although it is partly a matter of taste, equation (2.10) [or, even better, equation (2.9)] is attractive because it applies to any model of $\mathrm{E}(y \mid \mathbf{x})$, and so equation (2.10) allows comparison across many different functional forms. Plus, equation (2.10) applies even when $\log(y)$ is not defined, something that is important in Chapters 17 and 18. Definition (2.10) is more general because sometimes it applies even when $\log(y)$ is not defined. (We will need the general definition of an elasticity in Chapters 17 and 18.)

The percentage change in $E(y \mid \mathbf{x})$ when x_j is increased by one *unit* is approximated as

$$100 \cdot \frac{\partial E(y \mid \mathbf{x})}{\partial x_j} \cdot \frac{1}{E(y \mid \mathbf{x})}, \tag{2.13}$$

which equals

$$100 \cdot \frac{\partial \log[E(y \mid \mathbf{x})]}{\partial x_j} \tag{2.14}$$

if $E(y \mid \mathbf{x}) > 0$. This is sometimes called the **semielasticity** of $E(y \mid \mathbf{x})$ with respect to x_j.

Example 2.1 (continued): In equation (2.5), the semielasticity with respect to x_2 is constant and equal to $100 \cdot \beta_2$. No other semielasticities are constant in these equations.

2.2.3 Error Form of Models of Conditional Expectations

When y is a random variable we would like to explain in terms of observable variables $\mathbf{x}$, it is useful to decompose y as

$$y = E(y \mid \mathbf{x}) + u, \tag{2.15}$$

$$E(u \mid \mathbf{x}) = 0. \tag{2.16}$$

In other words, equations (2.15) and (2.16) are *definitional*: we can always write y as its conditional expectation, $E(y \mid \mathbf{x})$, plus an **error term** or **disturbance term** that has *conditional* mean zero.

The fact that $E(u \mid \mathbf{x}) = 0$ has the following important implications: (1) $E(u) = 0$; (2) u is uncorrelated with *any* function of $x_1, x_2, \ldots, x_K$, and, in particular, u is uncorrelated with each of $x_1, x_2, \ldots, x_K$. That u has zero unconditional expectation follows as a special case of the **law of iterated expectations (LIE)**, which we cover more generally in the next subsection. Intuitively, it is quite reasonable that $E(u \mid \mathbf{x}) = 0$ implies $E(u) = 0$. The second implication is less obvious but very important. The fact that u is uncorrelated with any function of $\mathbf{x}$ is much stronger than merely saying that u is uncorrelated with $x_1, \ldots, x_K$.

As an example, if equation (2.2) holds, then we can write

$$y = \beta_0 + \beta_1 x_1 + \beta_2 x_2 + u, \qquad E(u \mid x_1, x_2) = 0, \tag{2.17}$$

and so

$$E(u) = 0, \qquad \mathrm{Cov}(x_1, u) = 0, \qquad \mathrm{Cov}(x_2, u) = 0. \tag{2.18}$$

But we can say much more: under equation (2.17), u is also uncorrelated with any other function we might think of, such as $x_1^2, x_2^2, x_1x_2, \exp(x_1)$, and $\log(x_2^2 + 1)$. This fact ensures that we have fully accounted for the effects of x_1 and x_2 on the expected value of y; another way of stating this point is that we have the functional form of $E(y \mid \mathbf{x})$ properly specified.

If we only assume equation (2.18), then u can be correlated with nonlinear functions of x_1 and x_2, such as quadratics, interactions, and so on. If we hope to estimate the partial effect of each x_j on $E(y \mid \mathbf{x})$ over a broad range of values for $\mathbf{x}$, we want $E(u \mid \mathbf{x}) = 0$. (In Section 2.3 we discuss the weaker assumption (2.18) and its uses.)

Example 2.2: Suppose that housing prices are determined by the simple model

$$hprice = \beta_0 + \beta_1\, sqrft + \beta_2\, distance + u,$$

where *sqrft* is the square footage of the house and *distance* is the distance of the house from a city incinerator. For β_2 to represent $\partial E(hprice \mid sqrft, distance)/\partial\, distance$, we must assume that $E(u \mid sqrft, distance) = 0$.

2.2.4 Some Properties of Conditional Expectations

One of the most useful tools for manipulating conditional expectations is the law of iterated expectations, which we mentioned previously. Here we cover the most general statement needed in this book. Suppose that $\mathbf{w}$ is a random vector and y is a random variable. Let $\mathbf{x}$ be a random vector that is some function of $\mathbf{w}$, say $\mathbf{x} = \mathbf{f}(\mathbf{w})$. (The vector $\mathbf{x}$ could simply be a subset of $\mathbf{w}$.) This statement implies that if we know the outcome of $\mathbf{w}$, then we know the outcome of $\mathbf{x}$. The most general statement of the LIE that we will need is

$$E(y \mid \mathbf{x}) = E[E(y \mid \mathbf{w}) \mid \mathbf{x}]. \tag{2.19}$$

In other words, if we write $\mu_1(\mathbf{w}) \equiv E(y \mid \mathbf{w})$ and $\mu_2(\mathbf{x}) \equiv E(y \mid \mathbf{x})$, we can obtain $\mu_2(\mathbf{x})$ by computing the expected value of $\mu_1(\mathbf{w})$ given $\mathbf{x}$: $\mu_2(\mathbf{x}) = E[\mu_1(\mathbf{w}) \mid \mathbf{x}]$.

There is another result that looks similar to equation (2.19) but is much simpler to verify. Namely,

$$E(y \mid \mathbf{x}) = E[E(y \mid \mathbf{x}) \mid \mathbf{w}]. \tag{2.20}$$

Note how the positions of $\mathbf{x}$ and $\mathbf{w}$ have been switched on the right-hand side of equation (2.20) compared with equation (2.19). The result in equation (2.20) follows easily from the conditional aspect of the expection: since $\mathbf{x}$ is a function of $\mathbf{w}$, knowing $\mathbf{w}$ implies knowing $\mathbf{x}$; given that $\mu_2(\mathbf{x}) = E(y \mid \mathbf{x})$ is a function of $\mathbf{x}$, the expected value of $\mu_2(\mathbf{x})$ given $\mathbf{w}$ is just $\mu_2(\mathbf{x})$.

Some find a phrase useful for remembering both equations (2.19) and (2.20): "The smaller information set always dominates." Here, $\mathbf{x}$ represents less information than $\mathbf{w}$, since knowing $\mathbf{w}$ implies knowing $\mathbf{x}$, but not vice versa. We will use equations (2.19) and (2.20) almost routinely throughout the book.

For many purposes we need the following special case of the general LIE (2.19). If $\mathbf{x}$ and $\mathbf{z}$ are any random vectors, then

$$\mathrm{E}(y \mid \mathbf{x}) = \mathrm{E}[\mathrm{E}(y \mid \mathbf{x}, \mathbf{z}) \mid \mathbf{x}], \tag{2.21}$$

or, defining $\mu_1(\mathbf{x}, \mathbf{z}) \equiv \mathrm{E}(y \mid \mathbf{x}, \mathbf{z})$ and $\mu_2(\mathbf{x}) \equiv \mathrm{E}(y \mid \mathbf{x})$,

$$\mu_2(\mathbf{x}) = \mathrm{E}[\mu_1(\mathbf{x}, \mathbf{z}) \mid \mathbf{x}]. \tag{2.22}$$

For many econometric applications, it is useful to think of $\mu_1(\mathbf{x}, \mathbf{z}) = \mathrm{E}(y \mid \mathbf{x}, \mathbf{z})$ as a structural conditional expectation, but where $\mathbf{z}$ is unobserved. If interest lies in $\mathrm{E}(y \mid \mathbf{x}, \mathbf{z})$, then we want the effects of the x_j holding the other elements of $\mathbf{x}$ *and* $\mathbf{z}$ fixed. If $\mathbf{z}$ is not observed, we cannot estimate $\mathrm{E}(y \mid \mathbf{x}, \mathbf{z})$ directly. Nevertheless, since y and $\mathbf{x}$ are observed, we can generally estimate $\mathrm{E}(y \mid \mathbf{x})$. The question, then, is whether we can relate $\mathrm{E}(y \mid \mathbf{x})$ to the original expectation of interest. (This is a version of the *identification problem* in econometrics.) The LIE provides a convenient way for relating the two expectations.

Obtaining $\mathrm{E}[\mu_1(\mathbf{x}, \mathbf{z}) \mid \mathbf{x}]$ generally requires integrating (or summing) $\mu_1(\mathbf{x}, \mathbf{z})$ against the conditional density of $\mathbf{z}$ given $\mathbf{x}$, but in many cases the form of $\mathrm{E}(y \mid \mathbf{x}, \mathbf{z})$ is simple enough not to require explicit integration. For example, suppose we begin with the model

$$\mathrm{E}(y \mid x_1, x_2, z) = \beta_0 + \beta_1 x_1 + \beta_2 x_2 + \beta_3 z \tag{2.23}$$

but where z is unobserved. By the LIE, and the linearity of the CE operator,

$$\begin{aligned} \mathrm{E}(y \mid x_1, x_2) &= \mathrm{E}(\beta_0 + \beta_1 x_1 + \beta_2 x_2 + \beta_3 z \mid x_1, x_2) \\ &= \beta_0 + \beta_1 x_1 + \beta_2 x_2 + \beta_3 \mathrm{E}(z \mid x_1, x_2). \end{aligned} \tag{2.24}$$

Now, if we make an assumption about $\mathrm{E}(z \mid x_1, x_2)$, for example, that it is linear in x_1 and x_2,

$$\mathrm{E}(z \mid x_1, x_2) = \delta_0 + \delta_1 x_1 + \delta_2 x_2, \tag{2.25}$$

then we can plug this into equation (2.24) and rearrange:

$$\begin{aligned} &= \beta_0 + \beta_1 x_1 + \beta_2 x_2 + \beta_3(\delta_0 + \delta_1 x_1 + \delta_2 x_2) \\ &= (\beta_0 + \beta_3 \delta_0) + (\beta_1 + \beta_3 \delta_1) x_1 + (\beta_2 + \beta_3 \delta_2) x_2. \end{aligned}$$

This last expression is $E(y \mid x_1, x_2)$; given our assumptions it is necessarily linear in (x_1, x_2).

Now suppose equation (2.23) contains an interaction in x_1 and z:

$$E(y \mid x_1, x_2, z) = \beta_0 + \beta_1 x_1 + \beta_2 x_2 + \beta_3 z + \beta_4 x_1 z. \tag{2.26}$$

Then, again by the LIE,

$$E(y \mid x_1, x_2) = \beta_0 + \beta_1 x_1 + \beta_2 x_2 + \beta_3 E(z \mid x_1, x_2) + \beta_4 x_1 E(z \mid x_1, x_2).$$

If $E(z \mid x_1, x_2)$ is again given in equation (2.25), you can show that $E(y \mid x_1, x_2)$ has terms linear in x_1 and x_2 and, in addition, contains x_1^2 and $x_1 x_2$. The usefulness of such derivations will become apparent in later chapters.

The general form of the LIE has other useful implications. Suppose that for some (vector) function $\mathbf{f}(\mathbf{x})$ and a real-valued function $g(\cdot)$, $E(y \mid \mathbf{x}) = g[\mathbf{f}(\mathbf{x})]$. Then

$$E[y \mid \mathbf{f}(\mathbf{x})] = E(y \mid \mathbf{x}) = g[\mathbf{f}(\mathbf{x})]. \tag{2.27}$$

There is another way to state this relationship: If we define $\mathbf{z} \equiv \mathbf{f}(\mathbf{x})$, then $E(y \mid \mathbf{z}) = g(\mathbf{z})$. The vector $\mathbf{z}$ can have smaller or greater dimension than $\mathbf{x}$. This fact is illustrated with the following example.

Example 2.3: If a wage equation is

$$E(wage \mid educ, exper) = \beta_0 + \beta_1 educ + \beta_2 exper + \beta_3 exper^2 + \beta_4 educ \cdot exper,$$

then

$$E(wage \mid educ, exper, exper^2, educ \cdot exper)$$

$$= \beta_0 + \beta_1 educ + \beta_2 exper + \beta_3 exper^2 + \beta_4 educ \cdot exper.$$

In other words, once *educ* and *exper* have been conditioned on, it is redundant to condition on $exper^2$ and $educ \cdot exper$.

The conclusion in this example is much more general, and it is helpful for analyzing models of conditional expectations that are linear in parameters. Assume that, for some functions $g_1(\mathbf{x}), g_2(\mathbf{x}), \ldots, g_M(\mathbf{x})$,

$$E(y \mid \mathbf{x}) = \beta_0 + \beta_1 g_1(\mathbf{x}) + \beta_2 g_2(\mathbf{x}) + \cdots + \beta_M g_M(\mathbf{x}). \tag{2.28}$$

This model allows substantial flexibility, as the explanatory variables can appear in all kinds of nonlinear ways; the key restriction is that the model is linear in the β_j. If we define $z_1 \equiv g_1(\mathbf{x}), \ldots, z_M \equiv g_M(\mathbf{x})$, then equation (2.27) implies that

$$\mathrm{E}(y \mid z_1, z_2, \ldots, z_M) = \beta_0 + \beta_1 z_1 + \beta_2 z_2 + \cdots + \beta_M z_M. \tag{2.29}$$

This equation shows that any conditional expectation linear in parameters can be written as a conditional expectation linear in parameters and linear in *some* conditioning variables. If we write equation (2.29) in error form as $y = \beta_0 + \beta_1 z_1 + \beta_2 z_2 + \cdots + \beta_M z_M + u$, then, because $\mathrm{E}(u \mid \mathbf{x}) = 0$ and the z_j are functions of $\mathbf{x}$, it follows that u is uncorrelated with $z_1, \ldots, z_M$ (and any functions of them). As we will see in Chapter 4, this result allows us to cover models of the form (2.28) in the same framework as models linear in the original explanatory variables.

We also need to know how the notion of statistical independence relates to conditional expectations. If u is a random variable independent of the random vector $\mathbf{x}$, then $\mathrm{E}(u \mid \mathbf{x}) = \mathrm{E}(u)$, so that if $\mathrm{E}(u) = 0$ and u and $\mathbf{x}$ are independent, then $\mathrm{E}(u \mid \mathbf{x}) = 0$. The converse of this is not true: $\mathrm{E}(u \mid \mathbf{x}) = \mathrm{E}(u)$ does not imply statistical independence between u and $\mathbf{x}$ (just as zero correlation between u and $\mathbf{x}$ does not imply independence).

2.2.5 Average Partial Effects

When we explicitly allow the expectation of the response variable, y, to depend on unobservables—usually called **unobserved heterogeneity**—we must be careful in specifying the partial effects of interest. Suppose that we have in mind the (structural) conditional mean $\mathrm{E}(y \mid \mathbf{x}, q) = \mu_1(\mathbf{x}, q)$, where $\mathbf{x}$ is a vector of observable explanatory variables and q is an unobserved random variable—the unobserved heterogeneity. (We take q to be a scalar for simplicity; the discussion for a vector is essentially the same.) For continuous x_j, the partial effect of immediate interest is

$$\theta_j(\mathbf{x}, q) \equiv \partial \mathrm{E}(y \mid \mathbf{x}, q)/\partial x_j = \partial \mu_1(\mathbf{x}, q)/\partial x_j. \tag{2.30}$$

(For discrete x_j, we would simply look at differences in the regression function for x_j at two different values, when the other elements of $\mathbf{x}$ and q are held fixed.) Because $\theta_j(\mathbf{x}, q)$ generally depends on q, we cannot hope to estimate the partial effects across many different values of q. In fact, even if we could estimate $\theta_j(\mathbf{x}, q)$ for all $\mathbf{x}$ and q, we would generally have little guidance about inserting values of q into the mean function. In many cases we can make a normalization such as $\mathrm{E}(q) = 0$, and estimate $\theta_j(\mathbf{x}, 0)$, but $q = 0$ typically corresponds to a very small segment of the population. (Technically, $q = 0$ corresponds to no one in the population when q is continuously distributed.) Usually of more interest is the partial effect averaged across the population distribution of q; this is called the **average partial effect (APE)**.

For emphasis, let $\mathbf{x}^o$ denote a fixed value of the covariates. The average partial effect evaluated at $\mathbf{x}^o$ is

$$\delta_j(\mathbf{x}^o) \equiv \mathrm{E}_q[\theta_j(\mathbf{x}^o, q)], \tag{2.31}$$

where $\mathrm{E}_q[\cdot]$ denotes the expectation with respect to q. In other words, we simply average the partial effect $\theta_j(\mathbf{x}^o, q)$ across the population distribution of q. Definition (2.31) holds for any population relationship between q and $\mathbf{x}$; in particular, they need not be independent. But remember, in definition (2.31), $\mathbf{x}^o$ is a nonrandom vector of numbers.

For concreteness, assume that q has a continuous distribution with density function $g(\cdot)$, so that

$$\delta_j(\mathbf{x}^o) = \int_{\mathbb{R}} \theta_j(\mathbf{x}^o, \mathfrak{q}) g(\mathfrak{q})\, d\mathfrak{q}, \tag{2.32}$$

where $\mathfrak{q}$ is simply the dummy argument in the integration. The question we answer here is, Is it possible to estimate $\delta_j(\mathbf{x}^o)$ from conditional expectations that depend only on *observable* conditioning variables? Generally, the answer must be no, as q and $\mathbf{x}$ can be arbitrarily related. Nevertheless, if we appropriately restrict the relationship between q and $\mathbf{x}$, we can obtain a very useful equivalance.

One common assumption in nonlinear models with unobserved heterogeneity is that q and $\mathbf{x}$ are independent. We will make the weaker assumption that q and $\mathbf{x}$ are independent *conditional* on a vector of observables, $\mathbf{w}$:

$$\mathrm{D}(q \mid \mathbf{x}, \mathbf{w}) = \mathrm{D}(q \mid \mathbf{w}), \tag{2.33}$$

where $\mathrm{D}(\cdot \mid \cdot)$ denotes conditional distribution. (If we take $\mathbf{w}$ to be empty, we get the special case of independence between q and $\mathbf{x}$.) In many cases, we can interpret equation (2.33) as implying that $\mathbf{w}$ is a vector of good **proxy variables** for q, but equation (2.33) turns out to be fairly widely applicable. We also assume that $\mathbf{w}$ is *redundant* or *ignorable* in the structural expectation

$$\mathrm{E}(y \mid \mathbf{x}, q, \mathbf{w}) = \mathrm{E}(y \mid \mathbf{x}, q). \tag{2.34}$$

As we will see in subsequent chapters, many econometric methods hinge on being able to exclude certain variables from the equation of interest, and equation (2.34) makes this assumption precise. Of course, if $\mathbf{w}$ is empty, then equation (2.34) is trivially true.

Under equations (2.33) and (2.34), we can show the following important result, provided that we can interchange a certain integral and partial derivative:

$$\delta_j(\mathbf{x}^o) = \mathrm{E}_w[\partial \mathrm{E}(y \mid \mathbf{x}^o, \mathbf{w}) / \partial x_j], \tag{2.35}$$

where $\mathrm{E}_w[\cdot]$ denotes the expectation with respect to the distribution of $\mathbf{w}$. Before we verify equation (2.35) for the special case of continuous, scalar q, we must understand its usefulness. The point is that the unobserved heterogeneity, q, has disappeared entirely, and the conditional expectation $E(y \mid \mathbf{x}, \mathbf{w})$ can be estimated quite generally because we assume that a random sample can be obtained on $(y, \mathbf{x}, \mathbf{w})$. (Alternatively, when we write down parametric econometric models, we will be able to derive $E(y \mid \mathbf{x}, \mathbf{w})$.) Then, estimating the average partial effect at any chosen $\mathbf{x}^o$ amounts to averaging $\partial \hat{\mu}_2(\mathbf{x}^o, \mathbf{w}_i)/\partial x_j$ across the random sample, where $\mu_2(\mathbf{x}, \mathbf{w}) \equiv E(y \mid \mathbf{x}, \mathbf{w})$.

Proving equation (2.35) is fairly simple. First, we have

$$\mu_2(\mathbf{x}, \mathbf{w}) = E[E(y \mid \mathbf{x}, q, \mathbf{w}) \mid \mathbf{x}, \mathbf{w}] = E[\mu_1(\mathbf{x}, q) \mid \mathbf{x}, \mathbf{w}] = \int_{\mathbb{R}} \mu_1(\mathbf{x}, q) g(q \mid \mathbf{w}) \, dq,$$

where the first equality follows from the law of iterated expectations, the second equality follows from equation (2.34), and the third equality follows from equation (2.33). If we now take the partial derivative with respect to x_j of the equality

$$\mu_2(\mathbf{x}, \mathbf{w}) = \int_{\mathbb{R}} \mu_1(\mathbf{x}, q) g(q \mid \mathbf{w}) \, dq \tag{2.36}$$

and interchange the partial derivative and the integral, we have, for any $(\mathbf{x}, \mathbf{w})$,

$$\partial \mu_2(\mathbf{x}, \mathbf{w})/\partial x_j = \int_{\mathbb{R}} \theta_j(\mathbf{x}, q) g(q \mid \mathbf{w}) \, dq. \tag{2.37}$$

For fixed $\mathbf{x}^o$, the right-hand side of equation (2.37) is simply $E[\theta_j(\mathbf{x}^o, q) \mid \mathbf{w}]$, and so another application of iterated expectations gives, for any $\mathbf{x}^o$,

$$E_w[\partial \mu_2(\mathbf{x}^o, \mathbf{w})/\partial x_j] = E\{E[\theta_j(\mathbf{x}^o, q) \mid \mathbf{w}]\} = \delta_j(\mathbf{x}^o),$$

which is what we wanted to show.

As mentioned previously, equation (2.35) has many applications in models where unobserved heterogeneity enters a conditional mean function in a nonadditive fashion. We will use this result (in simplified form) in Chapter 4, and also extensively in Part IV. The special case where q is independent of $\mathbf{x}$—and so we do not need the proxy variables $\mathbf{w}$—is very simple: the APE of x_j on $E(y \mid \mathbf{x}, q)$ is simply the partial effect of x_j on $\mu_2(\mathbf{x}) = E(y \mid \mathbf{x})$. In other words, if we focus on average partial effects, there is no need to introduce heterogeneity. If we do specify a model with heterogeneity independent of $\mathbf{x}$, then we simply find $E(y \mid \mathbf{x})$ by integrating $E(y \mid \mathbf{x}, q)$ over the distribution of q.

Our discussion of average partial effects is closely related to Blundell and Powell's (2003) analysis of an **average structural function (ASF)**. Blundell and Powell essentially define the ASF, at a given value $\mathbf{x}^o$, to be $E_q[\mu_1(\mathbf{x}^o, q)]$, where $\mu_1(\mathbf{x}, q) = E(y \mid \mathbf{x}, q)$. In other words, the average structural function takes the conditional expectation of interest—a "structural" conditional expectation—and averages out the unobservable, q. Provided the derivative and expected value can be interchanged—which holds under very general assumptions, see Bartle (1966)—the ASE leads us to the same place as APEs. For further discussion, see Wooldridge (2005c). We will apply equation (2.35) to nonlinear models in several different settings, including panel data models and models with endogenous explanatory variables.

2.3 Linear Projections

In the previous section we saw some examples of how to manipulate conditional expectations. While structural equations are usually stated in terms of CEs, making linearity assumptions about CEs involving unobservables or auxiliary variables is undesirable, especially if such assumptions can be easily relaxed.

By using the notion of a linear projection we can often relax linearity assumptions in auxiliary conditional expectations. Typically this is done by first writing down a structural model in terms of a CE and then using the linear projection to obtain an estimable equation. As we will see in Chapters 4 and 5, this approach has many applications.

Generally, let $y, x_1, \ldots, x_K$ be random variables representing some population such that $\mathrm{E}(y^2) < \infty$, $\mathrm{E}(x_j^2) < \infty$, $j = 1, 2, \ldots, K$. These assumptions place no practical restrictions on the joint distribution of $(y, x_1, x_2, \ldots, x_K)$: the vector can contain discrete and continuous variables, as well as variables that have both characteristics. In many cases y and the x_j are nonlinear functions of some underlying variables that are initially of interest.

Define $\mathbf{x} \equiv (x_1, \ldots, x_K)$ as a $1 \times K$ vector, and make the assumption that the $K \times K$ variance matrix of $\mathbf{x}$ is nonsingular (positive definite). Then the **linear projection** of y on $1, x_1, x_2, \ldots, x_K$ always exists and is unique:

$$\mathrm{L}(y \mid 1, x_1, \ldots x_K) = \mathrm{L}(y \mid 1, \mathbf{x}) = \beta_0 + \beta_1 x_1 + \cdots + \beta_K x_K = \beta_0 + \mathbf{x}\boldsymbol{\beta}, \tag{2.38}$$

where, by definition,

$$\boldsymbol{\beta} \equiv [\mathrm{Var}(\mathbf{x})]^{-1} \,\mathrm{Cov}(\mathbf{x}, y), \tag{2.39}$$

$$\beta_0 \equiv \mathrm{E}(y) - \mathrm{E}(\mathbf{x})\boldsymbol{\beta} = \mathrm{E}(y) - \beta_1 \mathrm{E}(x_1) - \cdots - \beta_K \mathrm{E}(x_K). \tag{2.40}$$

The matrix $\mathrm{Var}(\mathbf{x})$ is the $K \times K$ symmetric matrix with (j,k)th element given by $\mathrm{Cov}(x_j, x_k)$, while $\mathrm{Cov}(\mathbf{x}, y)$ is the $K \times 1$ vector with jth element $\mathrm{Cov}(x_j, y)$. When $K = 1$ we have the familiar results $\beta_1 \equiv \mathrm{Cov}(x_1, y)/\mathrm{Var}(x_1)$ and $\beta_0 \equiv \mathrm{E}(y) -$

$\beta_1 \mathrm{E}(x_1)$. As its name suggests, $\mathrm{L}(y \mid 1, x_1, x_2, \ldots, x_K)$ is always a linear function of the x_j.

Other authors use a different notation for linear projections, the most common being $\mathrm{E}^*(\cdot \mid \cdot)$ and $\mathrm{P}(\cdot \mid \cdot)$. (For example, Chamberlain (1984) and Goldberger (1991) use $\mathrm{E}^*(\cdot \mid \cdot)$.) Some authors omit the 1 in the definition of a linear projection because it is assumed that an intercept is always included. Although this is usually the case, we put unity in explicitly to distinguish equation (2.38) from the case that a zero intercept is intended. The linear projection of y on $x_1, x_2, \ldots, x_K$ is defined as

$$\mathrm{L}(y \mid \mathbf{x}) = \mathrm{L}(y \mid x_1, x_2, \ldots, x_K) = \gamma_1 x_1 + \gamma_2 x_2 + \cdots + \gamma_K x_K = \mathbf{x}\boldsymbol{\gamma},$$

where $\boldsymbol{\gamma} \equiv (\mathrm{E}(\mathbf{x}'\mathbf{x}))^{-1}\mathrm{E}(\mathbf{x}'y)$. Note that $\boldsymbol{\gamma} \neq \boldsymbol{\beta}$ unless $\mathrm{E}(\mathbf{x}) = \mathbf{0}$. Later, we will include unity as an element of $\mathbf{x}$, in which case the linear projection including an intercept can be written as $\mathrm{L}(y \mid \mathbf{x})$.

The linear projection is just another way of writing down a population linear model where the disturbance has certain properties. Given the linear projection in equation (2.38) we can *always* write

$$y = \beta_0 + \beta_1 x_1 + \cdots + \beta_K x_K + u, \tag{2.41}$$

where the error term u has the following properties (by definition of a linear projection): $\mathrm{E}(u^2) < \infty$ and

$$\mathrm{E}(u) = 0, \qquad \mathrm{Cov}(x_j, u) = 0, \qquad j = 1, 2, \ldots, K. \tag{2.42}$$

In other words, u has zero mean and is uncorrelated with every x_j. Conversely, given equations (2.41) and (2.42), the parameters β_j in equation (2.41) must be the parameters in the linear projection of y on $1, x_1, \ldots, x_K$ given by definitions (2.39) and (2.40). Sometimes we will write a linear projection in error form, as in equations (2.41) and (2.42), but other times the notation (2.38) is more convenient.

It is important to emphasize that when equation (2.41) represents the linear projection, all we can say about u is contained in equation (2.42). In particular, it is not generally true that u is independent of $\mathbf{x}$ or that $\mathrm{E}(u \mid \mathbf{x}) = 0$. Here is another way of saying the same thing: equations (2.41) and (2.42) are *definitional*. Equation (2.41) under $\mathrm{E}(u \mid \mathbf{x}) = 0$ is an *assumption* that the conditional expectation is linear.

The linear projection is sometimes called the **minimum mean square linear predictor** or the **least squares linear predictor** because β_0 and $\boldsymbol{\beta}$ can be shown to solve the following problem:

$$\min_{b_0, \mathbf{b} \in \mathbb{R}^K} \mathrm{E}[(y - b_0 - \mathbf{x}\mathbf{b})^2] \tag{2.43}$$

(see Property LP.6 in the appendix). Because the CE is the minimum mean square predictor—that is, it gives the smallest mean square error out of all (allowable) functions (see Property CE.8)—it follows immediately that *if* $\mathrm{E}(y \mid \mathbf{x})$ is linear in $\mathbf{x}$, then the linear projection coincides with the conditional expectation.

As with the conditional expectation operator, the linear projection operator satisfies some important iteration properties. For vectors $\mathbf{x}$ and $\mathbf{z}$,

$$\mathrm{L}(y \mid 1, \mathbf{x}) = \mathrm{L}[\mathrm{L}(y \mid 1, \mathbf{x}, \mathbf{z}) \mid 1, \mathbf{x}]. \tag{2.44}$$

This simple fact can be used to derive omitted variables bias in a general setting as well as proving properties of estimation methods such as two-stage least squares and certain panel data methods.

Another iteration property that is useful involves taking the linear projection of a conditional expectation:

$$\mathrm{L}(y \mid 1, \mathbf{x}) = \mathrm{L}[\mathrm{E}(y \mid \mathbf{x}, \mathbf{z}) \mid 1, \mathbf{x}]. \tag{2.45}$$

Often we specify a structural model in terms of a conditional expectation $\mathrm{E}(y \mid \mathbf{x}, \mathbf{z})$ (which is frequently linear), but, for a variety of reasons, the estimating equations are based on the linear projection $\mathrm{L}(y \mid 1, \mathbf{x})$. If $\mathrm{E}(y \mid \mathbf{x}, \mathbf{z})$ is linear in $\mathbf{x}$ and $\mathbf{z}$, then equations (2.45) and (2.44) say the same thing.

For example, assume that

$$\mathrm{E}(y \mid x_1, x_2) = \beta_0 + \beta_1 x_1 + \beta_2 x_2 + \beta_3 x_1 x_2$$

and define $z_1 \equiv x_1 x_2$. Then, from Property CE.3,

$$\mathrm{E}(y \mid x_1, x_2, z_1) = \beta_0 + \beta_1 x_1 + \beta_2 x_2 + \beta_3 z_1. \tag{2.46}$$

The right-hand side of equation (2.46) is also the linear projection of y on $1, x_1, x_2$, and z_1; it is not generally the linear projection of y on $1, x_1, x_2$.

Our primary use of linear projections will be to obtain estimable equations involving the parameters of an underlying conditional expectation of interest. Problems 2.2 and 2.3 show how the linear projection can have an interesting interpretation in terms of the structural parameters.

Problems

2.1. Given random variables y, x_1, and x_2, consider the model

$$\mathrm{E}(y \mid x_1, x_2) = \beta_0 + \beta_1 x_1 + \beta_2 x_2 + \beta_3 x_2^2 + \beta_4 x_1 x_2.$$

a. Find the partial effects of x_1 and x_2 on $\mathrm{E}(y \mid x_1, x_2)$.

b. Writing the equation as

$$y = \beta_0 + \beta_1 x_1 + \beta_2 x_2 + \beta_3 x_2^2 + \beta_4 x_1 x_2 + u,$$

what can be said about $\mathrm{E}(u \mid x_1, x_2)$? What about $\mathrm{E}(u \mid x_1, x_2, x_2^2, x_1 x_2)$?

c. In the equation of part b, what can be said about $\mathrm{Var}(u \mid x_1, x_2)$?

2.2. Let y and x be scalars such that

$$\mathrm{E}(y \mid x) = \delta_0 + \delta_1 (x - \mu) + \delta_2 (x - \mu)^2,$$

where $\mu = \mathrm{E}(x)$.

a. Find $\partial \mathrm{E}(y \mid x)/\partial x$, and comment on how it depends on x.

b. Show that δ_1 is equal to $\partial \mathrm{E}(y \mid x)/\partial x$ averaged across the distribution of x.

c. Suppose that x has a symmetric distribution, so that $\mathrm{E}[(x - \mu)^3] = 0$. Show that $\mathrm{L}(y \mid 1, x) = \alpha_0 + \delta_1 x$ for some α_0. Therefore, the coefficient on x in the linear projection of y on $(1, x)$ measures something useful in the nonlinear model for $\mathrm{E}(y \mid x)$: it is the partial effect $\partial \mathrm{E}(y \mid x)/\partial x$ averaged across the distribution of x.

2.3. Suppose that

$$\mathrm{E}(y \mid x_1, x_2) = \beta_0 + \beta_1 x_1 + \beta_2 x_2 + \beta_3 x_1 x_2. \tag{2.47}$$

a. Write this expectation in error form (call the error u), and describe the properties of u.

b. Suppose that x_1 and x_2 have zero means. Show that β_1 is the expected value of $\partial \mathrm{E}(y \mid x_1, x_2)/\partial x_1$ (where the expectation is across the population distribution of x_2). Provide a similar interpretation for β_2.

c. Now add the assumption that x_1 and x_2 are independent of one another. Show that the linear projection of y on $(1, x_1, x_2)$ is

$$\mathrm{L}(y \mid 1, x_1, x_2) = \beta_0 + \beta_1 x_1 + \beta_2 x_2. \tag{2.48}$$

(Hint: Show that, under the assumptions on x_1 and x_2, $x_1 x_2$ has zero mean and is uncorrelated with x_1 and x_2.)

d. Why is equation (2.47) generally more useful than equation (2.48)?

2.4. For random scalars u and v and a random vector $\mathbf{x}$, suppose that $\mathrm{E}(u \mid \mathbf{x}, v)$ is a linear function of $(\mathbf{x}, v)$ and that u and v each have zero mean and are uncorrelated with the elements of $\mathbf{x}$. Show that $\mathrm{E}(u \mid \mathbf{x}, v) = \mathrm{E}(u \mid v) = \rho_1 v$ for some ρ_1.

2.5. Consider the two representations

$$y = \mu_1(\mathbf{x}, \mathbf{z}) + u_1, \qquad \mathrm{E}(u_1 \mid \mathbf{x}, \mathbf{z}) = 0.$$

$$y = \mu_2(\mathbf{x}) + u_2, \qquad \mathrm{E}(u_2 \mid \mathbf{x}) = 0.$$

Assuming that $\mathrm{Var}(y \mid \mathbf{x}, \mathbf{z})$ and $\mathrm{Var}(y \mid \mathbf{x})$ are both constant, what can you say about the relationship between $\mathrm{Var}(u_1)$ and $\mathrm{Var}(u_2)$? (Hint: Use Property CV.4 in the appendix.)

2.6. Let $\mathbf{x}$ be a $1 \times K$ random vector, and let q be a random scalar. Suppose that q can be expressed as $q = q^* + e$, where $\mathrm{E}(e) = 0$ and $\mathrm{E}(\mathbf{x}'e) = \mathbf{0}$. Write the linear projection of q^* onto $(1, \mathbf{x})$ as $q^* = \delta_0 + \delta_1 x_1 + \cdots + \delta_K x_K + r^*$, where $\mathrm{E}(r^*) = 0$ and $\mathrm{E}(\mathbf{x}'r^*) = \mathbf{0}$.

a. Show that

$$\mathrm{L}(q \mid 1, \mathbf{x}) = \delta_0 + \delta_1 x_1 + \cdots + \delta_K x_K.$$

b. Find the projection error $r \equiv q - \mathrm{L}(q \mid 1, \mathbf{x})$ in terms of r^* and e.

2.7. Consider the conditional expectation

$$\mathrm{E}(y \mid \mathbf{x}, \mathbf{z}) = g(\mathbf{x}) + \mathbf{z}\boldsymbol{\beta},$$

where $g(\cdot)$ is a general function of $\mathbf{x}$ and $\boldsymbol{\beta}$ is a $1 \times M$ vector. Typically, this is called a **partial linear model**. Show that

$$\mathrm{E}(\tilde{y} \mid \tilde{\mathbf{z}}) = \tilde{\mathbf{z}}\boldsymbol{\beta},$$

where $\tilde{y} \equiv y - \mathrm{E}(y \mid \mathbf{x})$ and $\tilde{\mathbf{z}} \equiv \mathbf{z} - \mathrm{E}(\mathbf{z} \mid \mathbf{x})$. Robinson (1988) shows how to use this result to estimate $\boldsymbol{\beta}$ without specifying $g(\cdot)$.

2.8. Suppose y is a nonnegative continuous variable generated as

$$\log(y) = g(\mathbf{x}) + u,$$

where $\mathrm{E}(u \mid \mathbf{x}) = 0$. Define $a(\mathbf{x}) = \mathrm{E}[\exp(u) \mid \mathbf{x}]$.

a. Show that, using definition (2.9), the elasticity of $\mathrm{E}(y \mid \mathbf{x})$ with respect to x_j is

$$\frac{\partial g(\mathbf{x})}{\partial x_j} \cdot x_j + \frac{\partial a(\mathbf{x})}{\partial x_j} \cdot \frac{x_j}{a(\mathbf{x})}.$$

Note that the second term is the elasticity of $a(\mathbf{x})$ with respect to x_j.

b. If $x_j > 0$, show that the first part of the expression in part a is $\partial g(\mathbf{x})/\partial \log(x_j)$.

c. If you apply equation (2.11) to this model, what would you conclude is the "elasticity of y with respect to x"? How does this compare with part b?

2.9. Let $\mathbf{x}$ be a $1 \times K$ vector with $x_1 \equiv 1$ (to simplify the notation), and define $\mu(\mathbf{x}) \equiv \mathrm{E}(y \mid \mathbf{x})$. Let $\boldsymbol{\delta}$ be the $K \times 1$ vector of linear projection coefficients of y on $\mathbf{x}$, so that $\boldsymbol{\delta} = [\mathrm{E}(\mathbf{x}'\mathbf{x})]^{-1}\mathrm{E}(\mathbf{x}'y)$. Show that $\boldsymbol{\delta}$ is also the vector of coefficients in the linear projection of $\mu(\mathbf{x})$ on $\mathbf{x}$.

2.10. This problem is useful for decomposing the difference in average responses across two groups. It is often used, with specific functional form assumptions, to decompose average wages or earnings across two groups; see, for example, Oaxaca and Ransom (1994). Let y be the response variable, $\mathbf{x}$ a set of explanatory variables, and s a binary group indicator. For example, s could denote gender, union membership status, college graduate versus non-college graduate, and so on. Define $\mu_0(\mathbf{x}) = \mathrm{E}(y \mid \mathbf{x}, s = 0)$ and $\mu_1(\mathbf{x}) = \mathrm{E}(y \mid \mathbf{x}, s = 1)$ to be the regression functions for the two groups.

a. Show that

$$\mathrm{E}(y \mid s = 1) - \mathrm{E}(y \mid s = 0) = \{\mathrm{E}[\mu_1(\mathbf{x}) \mid s = 1] - \mathrm{E}[\mu_0(\mathbf{x}) \mid s = 1]\} + \{\mathrm{E}[\mu_0(\mathbf{x}) \mid s = 1] - \mathrm{E}[\mu_0(\mathbf{x}) \mid s = 0]\}.$$

(Hint: First write $\mathrm{E}(y \mid \mathbf{x}, s) = (1 - s) \cdot \mu_0(\mathbf{x}) + s \cdot \mu_1(\mathbf{x})$ and use iterated expectations. Then use simple algebra.)

b. Suppose both expectations are linear: $\mu_s(\mathbf{x}) = \mathbf{x}\boldsymbol{\beta}_s$, $s = 0, 1$. Show that

$$\mathrm{E}(y \mid s = 1) - \mathrm{E}(y \mid s = 0) = \mathrm{E}(\mathbf{x} \mid s = 1) \cdot (\boldsymbol{\beta}_1 - \boldsymbol{\beta}_0) + [\mathrm{E}(\mathbf{x} \mid s = 1) - \mathrm{E}(\mathbf{x} \mid s = 0)] \cdot \boldsymbol{\beta}_0.$$

Can you interpret this decomposition?

Appendix 2A

2.A.1 Properties of Conditional Expectations

PROPERTY CE.1: Let $a_1(\mathbf{x}), \ldots, a_G(\mathbf{x})$ and $b(\mathbf{x})$ be scalar functions of $\mathbf{x}$, and let $y_1, \ldots, y_G$ be random scalars. Then

$$\mathrm{E}\left(\sum_{j=1}^{G} a_j(\mathbf{x}) y_j + b(\mathbf{x}) \mid \mathbf{x}\right) = \sum_{j=1}^{G} a_j(\mathbf{x}) \mathrm{E}(y_j \mid \mathbf{x}) + b(\mathbf{x})$$

provided that $\mathrm{E}(|y_j|) < \infty$, $\mathrm{E}[|a_j(\mathbf{x})y_j|] < \infty$, and $\mathrm{E}[|b(\mathbf{x})|] < \infty$. This is the sense in which the conditional expectation is a linear operator.

PROPERTY CE.2: $\mathrm{E}(y) = \mathrm{E}[\mathrm{E}(y \mid \mathbf{x})] \equiv \mathrm{E}[\mu(\mathbf{x})]$.

Property CE.2 is the simplest version of the law of iterated expectations. As an illustration, suppose that $\mathbf{x}$ is a discrete random vector taking on values $\mathbf{c}_1, \mathbf{c}_2, \ldots, \mathbf{c}_M$ with probabilities $p_1, p_2, \ldots, p_M$. Then the LIE says

$$\mathrm{E}(y) = p_1 \mathrm{E}(y \mid \mathbf{x} = \mathbf{c}_1) + p_2 \mathrm{E}(y \mid \mathbf{x} = \mathbf{c}_2) + \cdots + p_M \mathrm{E}(y \mid \mathbf{x} = \mathbf{c}_M). \tag{2.49}$$

In other words, $\mathrm{E}(y)$ is simply a weighted average of the $\mathrm{E}(y \mid \mathbf{x} = \mathbf{c}_j)$, where the weight p_j is the probability that $\mathbf{x}$ takes on the value $\mathbf{c}_j$.

PROPERTY CE.3: (1) $\mathrm{E}(y \mid \mathbf{x}) = \mathrm{E}[\mathrm{E}(y \mid \mathbf{w}) \mid \mathbf{x}]$, where $\mathbf{x}$ and $\mathbf{w}$ are vectors with $\mathbf{x} = \mathbf{f}(\mathbf{w})$ for some nonstochastic function $\mathbf{f}(\cdot)$. (This is the general version of the law of iterated expectations.)

(2) As a special case of part 1, $\mathrm{E}(y \mid \mathbf{x}) = \mathrm{E}[\mathrm{E}(y \mid \mathbf{x}, \mathbf{z}) \mid \mathbf{x}]$ for vectors $\mathbf{x}$ and $\mathbf{z}$.

PROPERTY CE.4: If $\mathbf{f}(\mathbf{x}) \in \mathbb{R}^J$ is a function of $\mathbf{x}$ such that $\mathrm{E}(y \mid \mathbf{x}) = g[\mathbf{f}(\mathbf{x})]$ for some scalar function $g(\cdot)$, then $\mathrm{E}[y \mid \mathbf{f}(\mathbf{x})] = \mathrm{E}(y \mid \mathbf{x})$.

PROPERTY CE.5: If the vector $(\mathbf{u}, \mathbf{v})$ is independent of the vector $\mathbf{x}$, then $\mathrm{E}(\mathbf{u} \mid \mathbf{x}, \mathbf{v}) = \mathrm{E}(\mathbf{u} \mid \mathbf{v})$.

PROPERTY CE.6: If $u \equiv y - \mathrm{E}(y \mid \mathbf{x})$, then $\mathrm{E}[\mathbf{g}(\mathbf{x})u] = \mathbf{0}$ for any function $\mathbf{g}(\mathbf{x})$, provided that $\mathrm{E}[|g_j(\mathbf{x})u|] < \infty$, $j = 1, \ldots, J$, and $\mathrm{E}(|u|) < \infty$. In particular, $\mathrm{E}(u) = 0$ and $\mathrm{Cov}(x_j, u) = 0$, $j = 1, \ldots, K$.

Proof: First, note that

$$\mathrm{E}(u \mid \mathbf{x}) = \mathrm{E}[(y - \mathrm{E}(y \mid \mathbf{x})) \mid \mathbf{x}] = \mathrm{E}[(y - \mu(\mathbf{x})) \mid \mathbf{x}] = \mathrm{E}(y \mid \mathbf{x}) - \mu(\mathbf{x}) = 0.$$

Next, by property CE.2, $\mathrm{E}[\mathbf{g}(\mathbf{x})u] = \mathrm{E}(\mathrm{E}[\mathbf{g}(\mathbf{x})u \mid \mathbf{x}]) = \mathrm{E}[\mathbf{g}(\mathbf{x})\mathrm{E}(u \mid \mathbf{x})]$ (by property CE.1) $= \mathbf{0}$ because $\mathrm{E}(u \mid \mathbf{x}) = 0$.

PROPERTY CE.7 (Conditional Jensen's Inequality): If $c\colon \mathbb{R} \to \mathbb{R}$ is a convex function defined on $\mathbb{R}$ and $\mathrm{E}[|y|] < \infty$, then

$$c[\mathrm{E}(y \mid \mathbf{x})] \leq \mathrm{E}[c(y) \mid \mathbf{x}].$$

Technically, we should add the statement "almost surely-$\mathrm{P}_\mathbf{x}$," which means that the inequality holds for all $\mathbf{x}$ in a set that has probability equal to one. As a special case, $[\mathrm{E}(y)]^2 \leq \mathrm{E}(y^2)$. Also, if $y > 0$, then $-\log[\mathrm{E}(y)] \leq \mathrm{E}[-\log(y)]$, or $\mathrm{E}[\log(y)] \leq \log[\mathrm{E}(y)]$.

PROPERTY CE.8: If $\mathrm{E}(y^2) < \infty$ and $\mu(\mathbf{x}) \equiv \mathrm{E}(y \mid \mathbf{x})$, then μ is a solution to

$$\min_{m \in \mathscr{M}} \mathrm{E}[(y - m(\mathbf{x}))^2],$$

where $\mathscr{M}$ is the set of functions $m: \mathbb{R}^K \to \mathbb{R}$ such that $\mathrm{E}[m(\mathbf{x})^2] < \infty$. In other words, $\mu(\mathbf{x})$ is the best mean square predictor of y based on information contained in $\mathbf{x}$.

Proof: By the conditional Jensen's inequality, if follows that $\mathrm{E}(y^2) < \infty$ implies $\mathrm{E}[\mu(\mathbf{x})^2] < \infty$, so that $\mu \in \mathscr{M}$. Next, for any $m \in \mathscr{M}$, write

$$\begin{aligned}\mathrm{E}[(y - m(\mathbf{x}))^2] &= \mathrm{E}[\{(y - \mu(\mathbf{x})) + (\mu(\mathbf{x}) - m(\mathbf{x}))\}^2] \\ &= \mathrm{E}[(y - \mu(\mathbf{x}))^2] + \mathrm{E}[(\mu(\mathbf{x}) - m(\mathbf{x}))^2] + 2\mathrm{E}[(\mu(\mathbf{x}) - m(\mathbf{x}))u],\end{aligned}$$

where $u \equiv y - \mu(\mathbf{x})$. Thus, by CE.6,

$$\mathrm{E}[(y - m(\mathbf{x}))^2] = \mathrm{E}(u^2) + \mathrm{E}[(\mu(\mathbf{x}) - m(\mathbf{x}))^2].$$

The right-hand side is clearly minimized at $m \equiv \mu$.

2.A.2 Properties of Conditional Variances and Covariances

The **conditional variance** of y given $\mathbf{x}$ is defined as

$$\mathrm{Var}(y \mid \mathbf{x}) \equiv \sigma^2(\mathbf{x}) \equiv \mathrm{E}[\{y - \mathrm{E}(y \mid \mathbf{x})\}^2 \mid \mathbf{x}] = \mathrm{E}(y^2 \mid \mathbf{x}) - [\mathrm{E}(y \mid \mathbf{x})]^2.$$

The last representation is often useful for computing $\mathrm{Var}(y \mid \mathbf{x})$. As with the conditional expectation, $\sigma^2(\mathbf{x})$ is a random variable when $\mathbf{x}$ is viewed as a random vector.

PROPERTY CV.1: $\mathrm{Var}[a(\mathbf{x})y + b(\mathbf{x}) \mid \mathbf{x}] = [a(\mathbf{x})]^2 \, \mathrm{Var}(y \mid \mathbf{x})$.

PROPERTY CV.2: $\mathrm{Var}(y) = \mathrm{E}[\mathrm{Var}(y \mid \mathbf{x})] + \mathrm{Var}[\mathrm{E}(y \mid \mathbf{x})] = \mathrm{E}[\sigma^2(\mathbf{x})] + \mathrm{Var}[\mu(\mathbf{x})]$.

Proof:

$$\begin{aligned}\mathrm{Var}(y) &\equiv \mathrm{E}[(y - \mathrm{E}(y))^2] = \mathrm{E}[(y - \mathrm{E}(y \mid \mathbf{x}) + \mathrm{E}(y \mid \mathbf{x}) + \mathrm{E}(y))^2] \\ &= \mathrm{E}[(y - \mathrm{E}(y \mid \mathbf{x}))^2] + \mathrm{E}[(\mathrm{E}(y \mid \mathbf{x}) - \mathrm{E}(y))^2] \\ &\quad + 2\mathrm{E}[(y - \mathrm{E}(y \mid \mathbf{x}))(\mathrm{E}(y \mid \mathbf{x}) - \mathrm{E}(y))].\end{aligned}$$

By CE.6, $\mathrm{E}[(y - \mathrm{E}(y \mid \mathbf{x}))(\mathrm{E}(y \mid \mathbf{x}) - \mathrm{E}(y))] = 0$; so

$$\mathrm{Var}(y) = \mathrm{E}[(y - \mathrm{E}(y \mid \mathbf{x}))^2] + \mathrm{E}[(\mathrm{E}(y \mid \mathbf{x}) - \mathrm{E}(y))^2]$$

$$= \mathrm{E}\{\mathrm{E}[(y - \mathrm{E}(y \mid \mathbf{x}))^2 \mid \mathbf{x}]\} + \mathrm{E}[(\mathrm{E}(y \mid \mathbf{x}) - \mathrm{E}[\mathrm{E}(y \mid \mathbf{x})])^2$$

by the law of iterated expectations

$$\equiv \mathrm{E}[\mathrm{Var}(y \mid \mathbf{x})] + \mathrm{Var}[\mathrm{E}(y \mid \mathbf{x})].$$

An extension of Property CV.2 is often useful, and its proof is similar:

PROPERTY CV.3: $\mathrm{Var}(y \mid \mathbf{x}) = \mathrm{E}[\mathrm{Var}(y \mid \mathbf{x}, \mathbf{z}) \mid \mathbf{x}] + \mathrm{Var}[\mathrm{E}(y \mid \mathbf{x}, \mathbf{z}) \mid \mathbf{x}]$.

Consequently, by the law of iterated expectations CE.2,

PROPERTY CV.4: $\mathrm{E}[\mathrm{Var}(y \mid \mathbf{x})] \geq \mathrm{E}[\mathrm{Var}(y \mid \mathbf{x}, \mathbf{z})]$.

For any function $m(\cdot)$ define the mean squared error as $\mathrm{MSE}(y; m) \equiv \mathrm{E}[(y - m(\mathbf{x}))^2]$. Then CV.4 can be loosely stated as $\mathrm{MSE}[y; \mathrm{E}(y \mid \mathbf{x})] \geq \mathrm{MSE}[y; \mathrm{E}(y \mid \mathbf{x}, \mathbf{z})]$. In other words, in the population one never does worse for predicting y when additional variables are conditioned on. In particular, if $\mathrm{Var}(y \mid \mathbf{x})$ and $\mathrm{Var}(y \mid \mathbf{x}, \mathbf{z})$ are both constant, then $\mathrm{Var}(y \mid \mathbf{x}) \geq \mathrm{Var}(y \mid \mathbf{x}, \mathbf{z})$.

There are also important results relating conditional covariances. The most useful contains Property CV.3 as a special case (when $y_1 = y_2$):

PROPERTY CCOV.1: $\mathrm{Cov}(y_1, y_2 \mid \mathbf{x}) = \mathrm{E}[\mathrm{Cov}(y_1, y_2 \mid \mathbf{x}, \mathbf{z}) \mid \mathbf{x}] + \mathrm{Cov}[\mathrm{E}(y_1 \mid \mathbf{x}, \mathbf{z}), \mathrm{E}(y_2 \mid \mathbf{x}, \mathbf{z}) \mid \mathbf{x}]$.

Proof: By definition, $\mathrm{Cov}(y_1, y_2 \mid \mathbf{x}, \mathbf{z}) = \mathrm{E}\{[y_1 - \mathrm{E}(y_1 \mid \mathbf{x}, \mathbf{z})][y_2 - \mathrm{E}(y_2 \mid \mathbf{x}, \mathbf{z})] \mid \mathbf{x}, \mathbf{z}\}$. Write $\mu_1(\mathbf{x}) = \mathrm{E}(y_1 \mid \mathbf{x})$, $v_1(\mathbf{x}, \mathbf{z}) = \mathrm{E}(y_1 \mid \mathbf{x}, \mathbf{z})$, and similarly for y_2. Then simple algebra gives

$$\begin{aligned}
&\mathrm{Cov}(y_1, y_2 \mid \mathbf{x}, \mathbf{z}) \\
&\quad = \mathrm{E}\{[y_1 - \mu_1(\mathbf{x}) + \mu_1(\mathbf{x}) - v_1(\mathbf{x}, \mathbf{z})] \cdot [y_2 - \mu_2(\mathbf{x}) + \mu_2(\mathbf{x}) - v_2(\mathbf{x}, \mathbf{z})] \mid \mathbf{x}, \mathbf{z}\} \\
&\quad = \mathrm{E}\{[y_1 - \mu_1(\mathbf{x})][y_2 - \mu_2(\mathbf{x})] \mid \mathbf{x}, \mathbf{z}\} + [\mu_1(\mathbf{x}) - v_1(\mathbf{x}, \mathbf{z})][\mu_2(\mathbf{x}) - v_2(\mathbf{x}, \mathbf{z})] \\
&\qquad + \mathrm{E}\{[y_1 - \mu_1(\mathbf{x})][\mu_2(\mathbf{x}) - v_2(\mathbf{x}, \mathbf{z})] \mid \mathbf{x}, \mathbf{z}\} \\
&\qquad + \mathrm{E}\{[y_2 - \mu_2(\mathbf{x})][\mu_1(\mathbf{x}) - v_1(\mathbf{x}, \mathbf{z})] \mid \mathbf{x}, \mathbf{z}\} \\
&\quad = \mathrm{E}\{[y_1 - \mu_1(\mathbf{x})][y_2 - \mu_2(\mathbf{x})] \mid \mathbf{x}, \mathbf{z}\} + [\mu_1(\mathbf{x}) - v_1(\mathbf{x}, \mathbf{z})][\mu_2(\mathbf{x}) - v_2(\mathbf{x}, \mathbf{z})] \\
&\qquad + [v_1(\mathbf{x}, \mathbf{z}) - \mu_1(\mathbf{x})][\mu_2(\mathbf{x}) - v_2(\mathbf{x}, \mathbf{z})] + [v_2(\mathbf{x}, \mathbf{z}) - \mu_2(\mathbf{x})][\mu_1(\mathbf{x}) - v_1(\mathbf{x}, \mathbf{z})] \\
&\quad = \mathrm{E}\{[y_1 - \mu_1(\mathbf{x})][y_2 - \mu_2(\mathbf{x})] \mid \mathbf{x}, \mathbf{z}\} - [v_1(\mathbf{x}, \mathbf{z}) - \mu_1(\mathbf{x})][v_2(\mathbf{x}, \mathbf{z}) - \mu_2(\mathbf{x})],
\end{aligned}$$

because the second and third terms cancel. Therefore, by iterated expectations,

$$\mathrm{E}[\mathrm{Cov}(y_1, y_2 \mid \mathbf{x}, \mathbf{z}) \mid \mathbf{x}] = \mathrm{E}\{[y_1 - \mu_1(\mathbf{x})][y_2 - \mu_2(\mathbf{x})] \mid \mathbf{x}\} \\ - \mathrm{E}\{[\nu_1(\mathbf{x}, \mathbf{z}) - \mu_1(\mathbf{x})][\nu_2(\mathbf{x}, \mathbf{z}) - \mu_2(\mathbf{x})] \mid \mathbf{x}\}$$

or

$$\mathrm{E}[\mathrm{Cov}(y_1, y_2 \mid \mathbf{x}, \mathbf{z}) \mid \mathbf{x}] = \mathrm{Cov}(y_1, y_2 \mid \mathbf{x}) - \mathrm{Cov}[\mathrm{E}(y_1 \mid \mathbf{x}, \mathbf{z}), \mathrm{E}(y_2 \mid \mathbf{x}, \mathbf{z}) \mid \mathbf{x}]$$

because $\mu_1(\mathbf{x}) = \mathrm{E}[\mathrm{E}(y_1 \mid \mathbf{x}, \mathbf{z}) \mid \mathbf{x}]$, and similarly for $\mu_2(\mathbf{x})$. Simple rearrangement completes the proof.

2.A.3 Properties of Linear Projections

In what follows, y is a scalar, $\mathbf{x}$ is a $1 \times K$ vector, and $\mathbf{z}$ is a $1 \times J$ vector. We allow the first element of $\mathbf{x}$ to be unity, although the following properties hold in either case. All of the variables are assumed to have finite second moments, and the appropriate variance matrices are assumed to be nonsingular.

PROPERTY LP.1: If $\mathrm{E}(y \mid \mathbf{x}) = \mathbf{x}\boldsymbol{\beta}$, then $\mathrm{L}(y \mid \mathbf{x}) = \mathbf{x}\boldsymbol{\beta}$. More generally, if

$$\mathrm{E}(y \mid \mathbf{x}) = \beta_1 g_1(\mathbf{x}) + \beta_2 g_2(\mathbf{x}) + \cdots + \beta_M g_M(\mathbf{x}),$$

then

$$\mathrm{L}(y \mid w_1, \ldots, w_M) = \beta_1 w_1 + \beta_2 w_2 + \cdots + \beta_M w_M,$$

where $w_j \equiv g_j(\mathbf{x})$, $j = 1, 2, \ldots, M$. This property tells us that, if $\mathrm{E}(y \mid \mathbf{x})$ is known to be linear in some functions $g_j(\mathbf{x})$, then this linear function also represents a linear projection.

PROPERTY LP.2: Define $u \equiv y - \mathrm{L}(y \mid \mathbf{x}) = y - \mathbf{x}\boldsymbol{\beta}$. Then $\mathrm{E}(\mathbf{x}'u) = \mathbf{0}$.

PROPERTY LP.3: Suppose y_j, $j = 1, 2, \ldots, G$ are each random scalars, and $a_1, \ldots, a_G$ are constants. Then

$$\mathrm{L}\left(\sum_{j=1}^{G} a_j y_j \mid \mathbf{x}\right) = \sum_{j=1}^{G} a_j \mathrm{L}(y_j \mid \mathbf{x}).$$

Thus, the linear projection is a linear operator.

PROPERTY LP.4 (Law of Iterated Projections): $\mathrm{L}(y \mid \mathbf{x}) = \mathrm{L}[\mathrm{L}(y \mid \mathbf{x}, \mathbf{z}) \mid \mathbf{x}]$. More precisely, let

$$\mathrm{L}(y \mid \mathbf{x}, \mathbf{z}) \equiv \mathbf{x}\boldsymbol{\beta} + \mathbf{z}\boldsymbol{\gamma} \quad \text{and} \quad \mathrm{L}(y \mid \mathbf{x}) = \mathbf{x}\boldsymbol{\delta}.$$

For each element of $\mathbf{z}$, write $\mathrm{L}(z_j \mid \mathbf{x}) = \mathbf{x}\boldsymbol{\pi}_j$, $j = 1, \ldots, J$, where $\boldsymbol{\pi}_j$ is $K \times 1$. Then $\mathrm{L}(\mathbf{z} \mid \mathbf{x}) = \mathbf{x}\boldsymbol{\Pi}$, where $\boldsymbol{\Pi}$ is the $K \times J$ matrix $\boldsymbol{\Pi} \equiv (\boldsymbol{\pi}_1, \boldsymbol{\pi}_2, \ldots, \boldsymbol{\pi}_J)$. Property LP.4 implies that

$$\begin{aligned}\mathrm{L}(y \mid \mathbf{x}) = \mathrm{L}(\mathbf{x}\boldsymbol{\beta} + \mathbf{z}\boldsymbol{\gamma} \mid \mathbf{x}) &= \mathrm{L}(\mathbf{x} \mid \mathbf{x})\boldsymbol{\beta} + \mathrm{L}(\mathbf{z} \mid \mathbf{x})\boldsymbol{\gamma} \qquad \text{(by LP.3)} \\ &= \mathbf{x}\boldsymbol{\beta} + (\mathbf{x}\boldsymbol{\Pi})\boldsymbol{\gamma} = \mathbf{x}(\boldsymbol{\beta} + \boldsymbol{\Pi}\boldsymbol{\gamma}). \end{aligned} \tag{2.50}$$

Thus, we have shown that $\boldsymbol{\delta} = \boldsymbol{\beta} + \boldsymbol{\Pi}\boldsymbol{\gamma}$. This is, in fact, the population analogue of the omitted variables bias formula from standard regression theory, something we will use in Chapter 4.

Another iteration property involves the linear projection and the conditional expectation:

PROPERTY LP.5: $\mathrm{L}(y \mid \mathbf{x}) = \mathrm{L}[\mathrm{E}(y \mid \mathbf{x}, \mathbf{z}) \mid \mathbf{x}]$.

Proof: Write $y = \mu(\mathbf{x}, \mathbf{z}) + u$, where $\mu(\mathbf{x}, \mathbf{z}) = \mathrm{E}(y \mid \mathbf{x}, \mathbf{z})$. But $\mathrm{E}(u \mid \mathbf{x}, \mathbf{z}) = 0$; so $\mathrm{E}(\mathbf{x}'u) = \mathbf{0}$, which implies by LP.3 that $\mathrm{L}(y \mid \mathbf{x}) = \mathrm{L}[\mu(\mathbf{x}, \mathbf{z}) \mid \mathbf{x}] + \mathrm{L}(u \mid \mathbf{x}) = \mathrm{L}[\mu(\mathbf{x}, \mathbf{z}) \mid \mathbf{x}] = \mathrm{L}[\mathrm{E}(y \mid \mathbf{x}, \mathbf{z}) \mid \mathbf{x}]$.

A useful special case of Property LP.5 occurs when $\mathbf{z}$ is empty. Then $\mathrm{L}(y \mid \mathbf{x}) = \mathrm{L}[\mathrm{E}(y \mid \mathbf{x}) \mid \mathbf{x}]$.

PROPERTY LP.6: $\boldsymbol{\beta}$ is a solution to

$$\min_{\mathbf{b} \in \mathbb{R}^K} \mathrm{E}[(y - \mathbf{x}\mathbf{b})^2]. \tag{2.51}$$

If $\mathrm{E}(\mathbf{x}'\mathbf{x})$ is positive definite, then $\boldsymbol{\beta}$ is the *unique* solution to this problem.

Proof: For any $\mathbf{b}$, write $y - \mathbf{x}\mathbf{b} = (y - \mathbf{x}\boldsymbol{\beta}) + (\mathbf{x}\boldsymbol{\beta} - \mathbf{x}\mathbf{b})$. Then

$$\begin{aligned}(y - \mathbf{x}\mathbf{b})^2 &= (y - \mathbf{x}\boldsymbol{\beta})^2 + (\mathbf{x}\boldsymbol{\beta} - \mathbf{x}\mathbf{b})^2 + 2(\mathbf{x}\boldsymbol{\beta} - \mathbf{x}\mathbf{b})(y - \mathbf{x}\boldsymbol{\beta}) \\ &= (y - \mathbf{x}\boldsymbol{\beta})^2 + (\boldsymbol{\beta} - \mathbf{b})'\mathbf{x}'\mathbf{x}(\boldsymbol{\beta} - \mathbf{b}) + 2(\boldsymbol{\beta} - \mathbf{b})'\mathbf{x}'(y - \mathbf{x}\boldsymbol{\beta}).\end{aligned}$$

Therefore,

$$\begin{aligned}\mathrm{E}[(y - \mathbf{x}\mathbf{b})^2] &= \mathrm{E}[(y - \mathbf{x}\boldsymbol{\beta})^2] + (\boldsymbol{\beta} - \mathbf{b})'\mathrm{E}(\mathbf{x}'\mathbf{x})(\boldsymbol{\beta} - \mathbf{b}) \\ &\quad + 2(\boldsymbol{\beta} - \mathbf{b})'\mathrm{E}[\mathbf{x}'(y - \mathbf{x}\boldsymbol{\beta})] \\ &= \mathrm{E}[(y - \mathbf{x}\boldsymbol{\beta})^2] + (\boldsymbol{\beta} - \mathbf{b})'\mathrm{E}(\mathbf{x}'\mathbf{x})(\boldsymbol{\beta} - \mathbf{b}),\end{aligned} \tag{2.52}$$

because $\mathrm{E}[\mathbf{x}'(y - \mathbf{x}\boldsymbol{\beta})] = \mathbf{0}$ by LP.2. When $\mathbf{b} = \boldsymbol{\beta}$, the right-hand side of equation

(2.52) is minimized. Further, if $\mathrm{E}(\mathbf{x}'\mathbf{x})$ is positive definite, $(\boldsymbol{\beta} - \mathbf{b})'\mathrm{E}(\mathbf{x}'\mathbf{x})(\boldsymbol{\beta} - \mathbf{b}) > 0$ if $\mathbf{b} \neq \boldsymbol{\beta}$; so in this case $\boldsymbol{\beta}$ is the unique minimizer.

Property LP.6 states that the linear projection is the minimum mean square *linear* predictor. It is not necessarily the minimum mean square predictor: if $\mathrm{E}(y \mid \mathbf{x}) = \mu(\mathbf{x})$ is not linear in $\mathbf{x}$, then

$$\mathrm{E}[(y - \mu(\mathbf{x}))^2] < \mathrm{E}[(y - \mathbf{x}\boldsymbol{\beta})^2]. \tag{2.53}$$

PROPERTY LP.7: This is a partitioned projection formula, which is useful in a variety of circumstances. Write

$$\mathrm{L}(y \mid \mathbf{x}, \mathbf{z}) = \mathbf{x}\boldsymbol{\beta} + \mathbf{z}\boldsymbol{\gamma}. \tag{2.54}$$

Define the $1 \times K$ vector of population residuals from the projection of $\mathbf{x}$ on $\mathbf{z}$ as $\mathbf{r} \equiv \mathbf{x} - \mathrm{L}(\mathbf{x} \mid \mathbf{z})$. Further, define the population residual from the projection of y on $\mathbf{z}$ as $v \equiv y - \mathrm{L}(y \mid \mathbf{z})$. Then the following are true:

$$\mathrm{L}(v \mid \mathbf{r}) = \mathbf{r}\boldsymbol{\beta} \tag{2.55}$$

and

$$\mathrm{L}(y \mid \mathbf{r}) = \mathbf{r}\boldsymbol{\beta}. \tag{2.56}$$

The point is that the $\boldsymbol{\beta}$ in equations (2.55) and (2.56) is the *same* as that appearing in equation (2.54). Another way of stating this result is

$$\boldsymbol{\beta} = [\mathrm{E}(\mathbf{r}'\mathbf{r})]^{-1}\mathrm{E}(\mathbf{r}'v) = [\mathrm{E}(\mathbf{r}'\mathbf{r})]^{-1}\mathrm{E}(\mathbf{r}'y). \tag{2.57}$$

Proof: From equation (2.54) write

$$y = \mathbf{x}\boldsymbol{\beta} + \mathbf{z}\boldsymbol{\gamma} + u, \qquad \mathrm{E}(\mathbf{x}'u) = \mathbf{0}, \qquad \mathrm{E}(\mathbf{z}'u) = \mathbf{0}. \tag{2.58}$$

Taking the linear projection gives

$$\mathrm{L}(y \mid \mathbf{z}) = \mathrm{L}(\mathbf{x} \mid \mathbf{z})\boldsymbol{\beta} + \mathbf{z}\boldsymbol{\gamma}. \tag{2.59}$$

Subtracting equation (2.59) from (2.58) gives $y - \mathrm{L}(y \mid \mathbf{z}) = [\mathbf{x} - \mathrm{L}(\mathbf{x} \mid \mathbf{z})]\boldsymbol{\beta} + u$, or

$$v = \mathbf{r}\boldsymbol{\beta} + u. \tag{2.60}$$

Since $\mathbf{r}$ is a linear combination of $(\mathbf{x}, \mathbf{z})$, $\mathrm{E}(\mathbf{r}'u) = \mathbf{0}$. Multiplying equation (2.60) through by $\mathbf{r}'$ and taking expectations, it follows that

$$\boldsymbol{\beta} = [\mathrm{E}(\mathbf{r}'\mathbf{r})]^{-1}\mathrm{E}(\mathbf{r}'v).$$

(We assume that $\mathrm{E}(\mathbf{r}'\mathbf{r})$ is nonsingular.) Finally, $\mathrm{E}(\mathbf{r}'v) = \mathrm{E}[\mathbf{r}'(y - \mathrm{L}(y \mid \mathbf{z}))] = \mathrm{E}(\mathbf{r}'y)$, since $\mathrm{L}(y \mid \mathbf{z})$ is linear in $\mathbf{z}$ and $\mathbf{r}$ is orthogonal to any linear function of $\mathbf{z}$.

3 Basic Asymptotic Theory

This chapter summarizes some definitions and limit theorems that are important for studying large-sample theory. Most claims are stated without proof, as several require tedious epsilon-delta arguments. We do prove some results that build on fundamental definitions and theorems. A good, general reference for background in asymptotic analysis is White (2001). In Chapter 12 we introduce further asymptotic methods that are required for studying nonlinear models.

3.1 Convergence of Deterministic Sequences

Asymptotic analysis is concerned with the various kinds of convergence of sequences of estimators as the sample size grows. We begin with some definitions regarding nonstochastic sequences of numbers. When we apply these results in econometrics, N is the sample size, and it runs through all positive integers. You are assumed to have some familiarity with the notion of a limit of a sequence.

DEFINITION 3.1: (1) A sequence of nonrandom numbers $\{a_N: N = 1, 2, \ldots\}$ *converges to* a (has limit a) if for all $\varepsilon > 0$, there exists N_ε such that if $N > N_\varepsilon$, then $|a_N - a| < \varepsilon$. We write $a_N \to a$ as $N \to \infty$.

(2) A sequence $\{a_N: N = 1, 2, \ldots\}$ is *bounded* if and only if there is some $b < \infty$ such that $|a_N| \leq b$ for all $N = 1, 2, \ldots$. Otherwise, we say that $\{a_N\}$ is *unbounded.*

These definitions apply to vectors and matrices element by element.

Example 3.1: (1) If $a_N = 2 + 1/N$, then $a_N \to 2$. (2) If $a_N = (-1)^N$, then a_N does not have a limit, but it is bounded. (3) If $a_N = N^{1/4}$, a_N is not bounded. Because a_N increases without bound, we write $a_N \to \infty$.

DEFINITION 3.2: (1) A sequence $\{a_N\}$ is $O(N^\lambda)$ (*at most of order* N^λ) if $N^{-\lambda} a_N$ is bounded. When $\lambda = 0$, $\{a_N\}$ is bounded, and we also write $a_N = O(1)$ (*big oh one*).

(2) $\{a_N\}$ is $o(N^\lambda)$ if $N^{-\lambda} a_N \to 0$. When $\lambda = 0$, a_N converges to zero, and we also write $a_N = o(1)$ (*little oh one*).

From the definitions, it is clear that if $a_N = o(N^\lambda)$, then $a_N = O(N^\lambda)$; in particular, if $a_N = o(1)$, then $a_N = O(1)$. If each element of a sequence of vectors or matrices is $O(N^\lambda)$, we say the sequence of vectors or matrices is $O(N^\lambda)$, and similarly for $o(N^\lambda)$.

Example 3.2: (1) If $a_N = \log(N)$, then $a_N = o(N^\lambda)$ for any $\lambda > 0$. (2) If $a_N = 10 + \sqrt{N}$, then $a_N = O(N^{1/2})$ and $a_N = o(N^{(1/2+\gamma)})$ for any $\gamma > 0$.

3.2 Convergence in Probability and Boundedness in Probability

DEFINITION 3.3: (1) A sequence of random variables $\{x_N: N = 1, 2, \ldots\}$ **converges in probability** to the constant a if for all $\varepsilon > 0$,

$$P[|x_N - a| > \varepsilon] \to 0 \qquad \text{as } N \to \infty.$$

We write $x_N \xrightarrow{p} a$ and say that a is the **probability limit (plim)** of x_N: plim $x_N = a$.

(2) In the special case where $a = 0$, we also say that $\{x_N\}$ is $o_p(1)$ (*little oh p one*). We also write $x_N = o_p(1)$ or $x_N \xrightarrow{p} 0$.

(3) A sequence of random variables $\{x_N\}$ is **bounded in probability** if and only if for every $\varepsilon > 0$, there exists a $b_\varepsilon < \infty$ and an integer N_ε such that

$$P[|x_N| \geq b_\varepsilon] < \varepsilon \qquad \text{for all } N \geq N_\varepsilon.$$

We write $x_N = O_p(1)$ ($\{x_N\}$ is *big oh p one*).

If c_N is a nonrandom sequence, then $c_N = O_p(1)$ if and only if $c_N = O(1)$; $c_N = o_p(1)$ if and only if $c_N = o(1)$. A simple and very useful fact is that if a sequence converges in probability to any real number, then it is bounded in probability.

LEMMA 3.1: If $x_N \xrightarrow{p} a$, then $x_N = O_p(1)$. This lemma also holds for vectors and matrices.

The proof of Lemma 3.1 is not difficult; see Problem 3.1.

DEFINITION 3.4: (1) A random sequence $\{x_N: N = 1, 2, \ldots\}$ is $o_p(a_N)$, where $\{a_N\}$ is a nonrandom, positive sequence, if $x_N/a_N = o_p(1)$. We write $x_N = o_p(a_N)$.

(2) A random sequence $\{x_N: N = 1, 2, \ldots\}$ is $O_p(a_N)$, where $\{a_N\}$ is a nonrandom, positive sequence, if $x_N/a_N = O_p(1)$. We write $x_N = O_p(a_N)$.

We could have started by defining a sequence $\{x_N\}$ to be $o_p(N^\delta)$ for $\delta \in \mathbb{R}$ if $N^{-\delta} x_N \xrightarrow{p} 0$, in which case we obtain the definition of $o_p(1)$ when $\delta = 0$. This is where the one in $o_p(1)$ comes from. A similar remark holds for $O_p(1)$.

Example 3.3: If z is a random variable, then $x_N \equiv \sqrt{N} z$ is $O_p(N^{1/2})$ and $x_N = o_p(N^\delta)$ for any $\delta > \frac{1}{2}$.

LEMMA 3.2: If $w_N = o_p(1)$, $x_N = o_p(1)$, $y_N = O_p(1)$, and $z_N = O_p(1)$, then

(1) $w_N + x_N = o_p(1)$.

(2) $y_N + z_N = O_p(1)$.

(3) $y_N z_N = O_p(1)$.

(4) $x_N z_N = o_p(1)$.

In derivations, we will write relationships 1 to 4 as $o_p(1) + o_p(1) = o_p(1)$, $O_p(1) + O_p(1) = O_p(1)$, $O_p(1) \cdot O_p(1) = O_p(1)$, and $o_p(1) \cdot O_p(1) = o_p(1)$, respectively. Because a $o_p(1)$ sequence is $O_p(1)$, Lemma 3.2 also implies that $o_p(1) + O_p(1) = O_p(1)$ and $o_p(1) \cdot o_p(1) = o_p(1)$.

All of the previous definitions apply element by element to sequences of random vectors or matrices. For example, if $\{\mathbf{x}_N\}$ is a sequence of random $K \times 1$ random vectors, $\mathbf{x}_N \xrightarrow{p} \mathbf{a}$, where $\mathbf{a}$ is a $K \times 1$ nonrandom vector, if and only if $x_{Nj} \xrightarrow{p} a_j$, $j = 1, \ldots, K$. This is equivalent to $\|\mathbf{x}_N - \mathbf{a}\| \xrightarrow{p} 0$, where $\|\mathbf{b}\| \equiv (\mathbf{b}'\mathbf{b})^{1/2}$ denotes the Euclidean length of the $K \times 1$ vector $\mathbf{b}$. Also, $\mathbf{Z}_N \xrightarrow{p} \mathbf{B}$, where $\mathbf{Z}_N$ and $\mathbf{B}$ are $M \times K$, is equivalent to $\|\mathbf{Z}_N - \mathbf{B}\| \xrightarrow{p} 0$, where $\|\mathbf{A}\| \equiv [\text{tr}(\mathbf{A}'\mathbf{A})]^{1/2}$ and $\text{tr}(\mathbf{C})$ denotes the trace of the square matrix $\mathbf{C}$.

A result that we often use for studying the large-sample properties of estimators for linear models is the following. It is easily proven by repeated application of Lemma 3.2 (see Problem 3.2).

LEMMA 3.3: Let $\{\mathbf{Z}_N: N = 1, 2, \ldots\}$ be a sequence of $J \times K$ matrices such that $\mathbf{Z}_N = o_p(1)$, and let $\{\mathbf{x}_N\}$ be a sequence of $J \times 1$ random vectors such that $\mathbf{x}_N = O_p(1)$. Then $\mathbf{Z}_N'\mathbf{x}_N = o_p(1)$.

The next lemma is known as **Slutsky's theorem**.

LEMMA 3.4: Let $\mathbf{g}: \mathbb{R}^K \to \mathbb{R}^J$ be a function continuous at some point $\mathbf{c} \in \mathbb{R}^K$. Let $\{\mathbf{x}_N: N = 1, 2, \ldots\}$ be sequence of $K \times 1$ random vectors such that $\mathbf{x}_N \xrightarrow{p} \mathbf{c}$. Then $\mathbf{g}(\mathbf{x}_N) \xrightarrow{p} \mathbf{g}(\mathbf{c})$ as $N \to \infty$. In other words,

$$\text{plim}\ \mathbf{g}(\mathbf{x}_N) = \mathbf{g}(\text{plim}\ \mathbf{x}_N) \tag{3.1}$$

if $\mathbf{g}(\cdot)$ is continuous at plim $\mathbf{x}_N$.

Slutsky's theorem is perhaps the most useful feature of the plim operator: it shows that the plim passes through nonlinear functions, provided they are continuous. The expectations operator does not have this feature, and this lack makes finite sample analysis difficult for many estimators. Lemma 3.4 shows that plims behave just like regular limits when applying a continuous function to the sequence.

DEFINITION 3.5: Let $(\Omega, \mathscr{F}, \text{P})$ be a probability space. A sequence of events $\{\Omega_N: N = 1, 2, \ldots\} \subset \mathscr{F}$ is said to occur **with probability approaching one (w.p.a.1)** if and only if $\text{P}(\Omega_N) \to 1$ as $N \to \infty$.

Definition 3.5 allows that Ω_N^c, the complement of Ω_N, can occur for each N, but its chance of occurring goes to zero as $N \to \infty$.

COROLLARY 3.1: Let $\{\mathbf{Z}_N: N = 1, 2, \ldots\}$ be a sequence of random $K \times K$ matrices, and let $\mathbf{A}$ be a nonrandom, invertible $K \times K$ matrix. If $\mathbf{Z}_N \xrightarrow{p} \mathbf{A}$, then

(1) $\mathbf{Z}_N^{-1}$ exists w.p.a.1;

(2) $\mathbf{Z}_N^{-1} \xrightarrow{p} \mathbf{A}^{-1}$ or $\operatorname{plim} \mathbf{Z}_N^{-1} = \mathbf{A}^{-1}$ (in an appropriate sense).

Proof: Because the determinant is a continuous function on the space of all square matrices, $\det(\mathbf{Z}_N) \xrightarrow{p} \det(\mathbf{A})$. Because $\mathbf{A}$ is nonsingular, $\det(\mathbf{A}) \neq 0$. Therefore, it follows that $\mathrm{P}[\det(\mathbf{Z}_N) \neq 0] \to 1$ as $N \to \infty$. This completes the proof of part 1.

Part 2 requires a convention about how to define $\mathbf{Z}_N^{-1}$ when $\mathbf{Z}_N$ is nonsingular. Let Ω_N be the set of ω (outcomes) such that $\mathbf{Z}_N(\omega)$ is nonsingular for $\omega \in \Omega_N$; we just showed that $\mathrm{P}(\Omega_N) \to 1$ as $N \to \infty$. Define a new sequence of matrices by

$$\tilde{\mathbf{Z}}_N(\omega) \equiv \mathbf{Z}_N(\omega) \text{ when } \omega \in \Omega_N, \qquad \tilde{\mathbf{Z}}_N(\omega) \equiv \mathbf{I}_K \text{ when } \omega \notin \Omega_N.$$

Then $\mathrm{P}(\tilde{\mathbf{Z}}_N = \mathbf{Z}_N) = \mathrm{P}(\Omega_N) \to 1$ as $N \to \infty$. Then, because $\mathbf{Z}_N \xrightarrow{p} \mathbf{A}$, $\tilde{\mathbf{Z}}_N \xrightarrow{p} \mathbf{A}$. The inverse operator is continuous on the space of invertible matrices, so $\tilde{\mathbf{Z}}_N^{-1} \xrightarrow{p} \mathbf{A}^{-1}$. This is what we mean by $\mathbf{Z}_N^{-1} \xrightarrow{p} \mathbf{A}^{-1}$; the fact that $\mathbf{Z}_N$ can be singular with vanishing probability does not affect asymptotic analysis.

3.3 Convergence in Distribution

DEFINITION 3.6: A sequence of random variables $\{x_N: N = 1, 2, \ldots\}$ **converges in distribution** to the continuous random variable x if and only if

$$F_N(\xi) \to F(\xi) \qquad \text{as } N \to \infty \text{ for all } \xi \in \mathbb{R},$$

where F_N is the cumulative distribution function (c.d.f.) of x_N and F is the (continuous) c.d.f. of x. We write $x_N \xrightarrow{d} x$.

When $x \sim \mathrm{Normal}(\mu, \sigma^2)$, we write $x_N \xrightarrow{d} \mathrm{Normal}(\mu, \sigma^2)$ or $x_N \overset{a}{\sim} \mathrm{Normal}(\mu, \sigma^2)$ (x_N is **asymptotically normal**).

In Definition 3.6, x_N is not required to be continuous for any N. A good example of where x_N is discrete for all N but has an asymptotically normal distribution is the Demoivre-Laplace theorem (a special case of the central limit theorem given in Section 3.4), which says that $x_N \equiv (s_N - Np)/[Np(1-p)]^{1/2}$ has a limiting standard normal distribution, where s_N has the binomial (N, p) distribution.

DEFINITION 3.7: A sequence of $K \times 1$ random vectors $\{\mathbf{x}_N: N = 1, 2, \ldots\}$ converges in distribution to the continuous random vector $\mathbf{x}$ if and only if for any $K \times 1$ nonrandom vector $\mathbf{c}$ such that $\mathbf{c}'\mathbf{c} = 1$, $\mathbf{c}'\mathbf{x}_N \xrightarrow{d} \mathbf{c}'\mathbf{x}$, and we write $\mathbf{x}_N \xrightarrow{d} \mathbf{x}$.

When $\mathbf{x} \sim \text{Normal}(\mathbf{m}, \mathbf{V})$, the requirement in Definition 3.7 is that $\mathbf{c}'\mathbf{x}_N \xrightarrow{d} \text{Normal}(\mathbf{c}'\mathbf{m}, \mathbf{c}'\mathbf{V}\mathbf{c})$ for every $\mathbf{c} \in \mathbb{R}^K$ such that $\mathbf{c}'\mathbf{c} = 1$; in this case we write $\mathbf{x}_N \xrightarrow{d} \text{Normal}(\mathbf{m}, \mathbf{V})$ or $\mathbf{x}_N \overset{a}{\sim} \text{Normal}(\mathbf{m}, \mathbf{V})$. For the derivations in this book, $\mathbf{m} = \mathbf{0}$.

LEMMA 3.5: If $\mathbf{x}_N \xrightarrow{d} \mathbf{x}$, where $\mathbf{x}$ is any $K \times 1$ random vector, then $\mathbf{x}_N = \text{O}_p(1)$.

As we will see throughout this book, Lemma 3.5 turns out to be very useful for establishing that a sequence is bounded in probability. Often it is easiest to first verify that a sequence converges in distribution.

LEMMA 3.6: Let $\{\mathbf{x}_N\}$ be a sequence of $K \times 1$ random vectors such that $\mathbf{x}_N \xrightarrow{d} \mathbf{x}$. If $\mathbf{g}\colon \mathbb{R}^K \to \mathbb{R}^J$ is a continuous function, then $\mathbf{g}(\mathbf{x}_N) \xrightarrow{d} \mathbf{g}(\mathbf{x})$.

The usefulness of Lemma 3.6, which is called the **continuous mapping theorem**, cannot be overstated. It tells us that once we know the limiting distribution of $\mathbf{x}_N$, we can find the limiting distribution of many interesting functions of $\mathbf{x}_N$. This is especially useful for determining the asymptotic distribution of test statistics once the limiting distribution of an estimator is known; see Section 3.5.

The continuity of $\mathbf{g}$ is not necessary in Lemma 3.6, but some restrictions are needed. We will need only the form stated in Lemma 3.6.

COROLLARY 3.2: If $\{\mathbf{z}_N\}$ is a sequence of $K \times 1$ random vectors such that $\mathbf{z}_N \xrightarrow{d} \text{Normal}(\mathbf{0}, \mathbf{V})$, then

(1) For any $K \times M$ nonrandom matrix $\mathbf{A}$, $\mathbf{A}'\mathbf{z}_N \xrightarrow{d} \text{Normal}(\mathbf{0}, \mathbf{A}'\mathbf{V}\mathbf{A})$.
(2) $\mathbf{z}_N'\mathbf{V}^{-1}\mathbf{z}_N \xrightarrow{d} \chi^2_K$ (or $\mathbf{z}_N'\mathbf{V}^{-1}\mathbf{z}_N \overset{a}{\sim} \chi^2_K$).

LEMMA 3.7: Let $\{\mathbf{x}_N\}$ and $\{\mathbf{z}_N\}$ be sequences of $K \times 1$ random vectors. If $\mathbf{z}_N \xrightarrow{d} \mathbf{z}$ and $\mathbf{x}_N - \mathbf{z}_N \xrightarrow{p} \mathbf{0}$, then $\mathbf{x}_N \xrightarrow{d} \mathbf{z}$.

Lemma 3.7 is called the **asymptotic equivalence lemma**. In Section 3.5.1 we discuss generally how Lemma 3.7 is used in econometrics. We use the asymptotic equivalence lemma so frequently in asymptotic analysis that after a while we will not even mention that we are using it.

3.4 Limit Theorems for Random Samples

In this section we state two classic limit theorems for independent, identically distributed (i.i.d.) sequences of random vectors. These apply when sampling is done randomly from a population.

THEOREM 3.1: Let $\{\mathbf{w}_i: i = 1, 2, \ldots\}$ be a sequence of independent, identically distributed $G \times 1$ random vectors such that $E(|w_{ig}|) < \infty$, $g = 1, \ldots, G$. Then the sequence satisfies the **weak law of large numbers (WLLN)**: $N^{-1} \sum_{i=1}^{N} \mathbf{w}_i \xrightarrow{p} \boldsymbol{\mu}_w$, where $\boldsymbol{\mu}_w \equiv \mathrm{E}(\mathbf{w}_i)$.

THEOREM 3.2 (Lindeberg-Levy): Let $\{\mathbf{w}_i: i = 1, 2, \ldots\}$ be a sequence of independent, identically distributed $G \times 1$ random vectors such that $E(w_{ig}^2) < \infty$, $g = 1, \ldots, G$, and $E(\mathbf{w}_i) = \mathbf{0}$. Then $\{\mathbf{w}_i: i = 1, 2, \ldots\}$ satisfies the **central limit theorem (CLT)**; that is,

$$N^{-1/2} \sum_{i=1}^{N} \mathbf{w}_i \xrightarrow{d} \mathrm{Normal}(\mathbf{0}, \mathbf{B})$$

where $\mathbf{B} = \mathrm{Var}(\mathbf{w}_i) = \mathrm{E}(\mathbf{w}_i \mathbf{w}_i')$ is necessarily positive semidefinite. For our purposes, $\mathbf{B}$ is almost always positive definite.

In most of this text, we will only need convergence results for independent, identically distributed observations. Nevertheless, sometimes it will not make sense to assume identical distributions across i. (Cluster sampling and certain kinds of stratified sampling are two examples.) It is important to know that the WLLN and CLT continue to hold for independent, not identically distributed (i.n.i.d.) observations under rather weak assumptions. See Problem 3.11 for a law of large numbers (which contains a condition that is not the weakest possible; White (2001) contains theorems under weaker conditions). Consistency and asymptotic normality arguments for regression and other estimators are more complicated but still fairly straightforward.

3.5 Limiting Behavior of Estimators and Test Statistics

In this section, we apply the previous concepts to sequences of estimators. Because estimators depend on the random outcomes of data, they are properly viewed as random vectors.

3.5.1 Asymptotic Properties of Estimators

DEFINITION 3.8: Let $\{\hat{\boldsymbol{\theta}}_N: N = 1, 2, \ldots\}$ be a sequence of estimators of the $P \times 1$ vector $\boldsymbol{\theta} \in \boldsymbol{\Theta}$, where N indexes the sample size. If

$$\hat{\boldsymbol{\theta}}_N \xrightarrow{p} \boldsymbol{\theta} \tag{3.2}$$

for any value of $\boldsymbol{\theta}$, then we say $\hat{\boldsymbol{\theta}}_N$ is a **consistent estimator** of $\boldsymbol{\theta}$.

Because there are other notions of convergence, in the theoretical literature condition (3.2) is often referred to as *weak consistency*. This is the only kind of consistency we will be concerned with, so we simply call condition (3.2) *consistency*. (See White (2001, Chap. 2) for other kinds of convergence.) Since we do not know $\boldsymbol{\theta}$, the consistency definition requires condition (3.2) for any possible value of $\boldsymbol{\theta}$.

DEFINITION 3.9: Let $\{\hat{\boldsymbol{\theta}}_N: N = 1, 2, \ldots\}$ be a sequence of estimators of the $P \times 1$ vector $\boldsymbol{\theta} \in \boldsymbol{\Theta}$. Suppose that

$$\sqrt{N}(\hat{\boldsymbol{\theta}}_N - \boldsymbol{\theta}) \xrightarrow{d} \text{Normal}(\mathbf{0}, \mathbf{V}), \tag{3.3}$$

where $\mathbf{V}$ is a $P \times P$ positive semidefinite matrix. Then we say that $\hat{\boldsymbol{\theta}}_N$ is $\sqrt{\mathbf{N}}$**-asymptotically normally distributed** and $\mathbf{V}$ is the **asymptotic variance** of $\sqrt{N}(\hat{\boldsymbol{\theta}}_N - \boldsymbol{\theta})$, denoted Avar $\sqrt{N}(\hat{\boldsymbol{\theta}}_N - \boldsymbol{\theta}) = \mathbf{V}$.

Even though $\mathbf{V}/N = \text{Var}(\hat{\boldsymbol{\theta}}_N)$ holds only in special cases, and $\hat{\boldsymbol{\theta}}_N$ rarely has an exact normal distribution, we treat $\hat{\boldsymbol{\theta}}_N$ *as if*

$$\hat{\boldsymbol{\theta}}_N \sim \text{Normal}(\boldsymbol{\theta}, \mathbf{V}/N) \tag{3.4}$$

whenever statement (3.3) holds. For this reason, $\mathbf{V}/N$ is called the **asymptotic variance** of $\hat{\boldsymbol{\theta}}_N$, and we write

$$\text{Avar}(\hat{\boldsymbol{\theta}}_N) = \mathbf{V}/N. \tag{3.5}$$

However, the only sense in which $\hat{\boldsymbol{\theta}}_N$ is approximately normally distributed with mean $\boldsymbol{\theta}$ and variance $\mathbf{V}/N$ is contained in statement (3.3), and this is what is needed to perform inference about $\boldsymbol{\theta}$. Statement (3.4) is a heuristic statement that leads to the appropriate inference.

When we discuss consistent estimation of asymptotic variances—a topic that will arise often—we should technically focus on estimation of $\mathbf{V} \equiv \text{Avar}\ \sqrt{N}(\hat{\boldsymbol{\theta}}_N - \boldsymbol{\theta})$. In most cases, we will be able to find at least one, and usually more than one, consistent estimator $\hat{\mathbf{V}}_N$ of $\mathbf{V}$. Then the corresponding estimator of $\text{Avar}(\hat{\boldsymbol{\theta}}_N)$ is $\hat{\mathbf{V}}_N/N$, and we write

$$\widehat{\text{Avar}}(\hat{\boldsymbol{\theta}}_N) = \hat{\mathbf{V}}_N/N. \tag{3.6}$$

The division by N in equation (3.6) is practically very important. What we call the asymptotic variance of $\hat{\boldsymbol{\theta}}_N$ is estimated as in equation (3.6). Unfortunately, there has not been a consistent usage of the term "asymptotic variance" in econometrics.

Taken literally, a statement such as "$\hat{\mathbf{V}}_N/N$ is consistent for $\text{Avar}(\hat{\boldsymbol{\theta}}_N)$" is not very meaningful because $\mathbf{V}/N$ converges to $\mathbf{0}$ as $N \to \infty$; typically, $\hat{\mathbf{V}}_N/N \xrightarrow{p} \mathbf{0}$ whether or not $\hat{\mathbf{V}}_N$ is consistent for $\mathbf{V}$. Nevertheless, it is useful to have an admittedly imprecise shorthand. In what follows, if we say that "$\hat{\mathbf{V}}_N/N$ consistently estimates $\text{Avar}(\hat{\boldsymbol{\theta}}_N)$," we mean that $\hat{\mathbf{V}}_N$ consistently estimates $\text{Avar}\,\sqrt{N}(\hat{\boldsymbol{\theta}}_N - \boldsymbol{\theta})$.

DEFINITION 3.10: If $\sqrt{N}(\hat{\boldsymbol{\theta}}_N - \boldsymbol{\theta}) \overset{a}{\sim} \text{Normal}(0, \mathbf{V})$ where $\mathbf{V}$ is positive definite with jth diagonal v_{jj}, and $\hat{\mathbf{V}}_N \overset{p}{\to} \mathbf{V}$, then the **asymptotic standard error** of $\hat{\theta}_{Nj}$, denoted $\text{se}(\hat{\theta}_{Nj})$, is $(\hat{v}_{Njj}/N)^{1/2}$.

In other words, the asymptotic standard error of an estimator, which is almost always reported in applied work, is the square root of the appropriate diagonal element of $\hat{\mathbf{V}}_N/N$. The asymptotic standard errors can be loosely thought of as estimating the standard deviations of the elements of $\hat{\boldsymbol{\theta}}_N$, and they are the appropriate quantities to use when forming (asymptotic) t statistics and confidence intervals. Obtaining valid asymptotic standard errors (after verifying that the estimator is asymptotically normally distributed) is often the biggest challenge when using a new estimator.

If statement (3.3) holds, it follows by Lemma 3.5 that $\sqrt{N}(\hat{\boldsymbol{\theta}}_N - \boldsymbol{\theta}) = \text{O}_p(1)$, or $\hat{\boldsymbol{\theta}}_N - \boldsymbol{\theta} = \text{O}_p(N^{-1/2})$, and we say that $\hat{\boldsymbol{\theta}}_N$ is a $\sqrt{\mathbf{N}}$**-consistent estimator** of $\boldsymbol{\theta}$. $\sqrt{N}$-consistency certainly implies that $\text{plim}\,\hat{\boldsymbol{\theta}}_N = \boldsymbol{\theta}$, but it is much stronger because it tells us that the rate of convergence is almost the square root of the sample size N: $\hat{\boldsymbol{\theta}}_N - \boldsymbol{\theta} = \text{o}_p(N^{-c})$ for any $0 \le c < \frac{1}{2}$. In this book, almost every consistent estimator we will study—and every one we consider in any detail—is $\sqrt{N}$-asymptotically normal, and therefore $\sqrt{N}$-consistent, under reasonable assumptions.

If one $\sqrt{N}$-asymptotically normal estimator has an asymptotic variance that is smaller than another's asymptotic variance (in the matrix sense), it makes it easy to choose between the estimators based on asymptotic considerations.

DEFINITION 3.11: Let $\hat{\boldsymbol{\theta}}_N$ and $\tilde{\boldsymbol{\theta}}_N$ be estimators of $\boldsymbol{\theta}$ each satisfying statement (3.3), with asymptotic variances $\mathbf{V} = \text{Avar}\,\sqrt{N}(\hat{\boldsymbol{\theta}}_N - \boldsymbol{\theta})$ and $\mathbf{D} = \text{Avar}\,\sqrt{N}(\tilde{\boldsymbol{\theta}}_N - \boldsymbol{\theta})$ (these generally depend on the value of $\boldsymbol{\theta}$, but we suppress that consideration here). Then

(1) $\hat{\boldsymbol{\theta}}_N$ is **asymptotically efficient relative to** $\tilde{\boldsymbol{\theta}}_N$ if $\mathbf{D} - \mathbf{V}$ is positive semidefinite for all $\boldsymbol{\theta}$,

(2) $\hat{\boldsymbol{\theta}}_N$ and $\tilde{\boldsymbol{\theta}}_N$ are $\sqrt{\mathbf{N}}$**-equivalent** if $\sqrt{N}(\hat{\boldsymbol{\theta}}_N - \tilde{\boldsymbol{\theta}}_N) = \text{o}_p(1)$.

When two estimators are $\sqrt{N}$-equivalent, they have the same limiting distribution (multivariate normal in this case, with the same asymptotic variance). This conclusion follows immediately from the asymptotic equivalence lemma (Lemma 3.7). Sometimes, to find the limiting distribution of, say, $\sqrt{N}(\hat{\boldsymbol{\theta}}_N - \boldsymbol{\theta})$, it is easiest to first find the limiting distribution of $\sqrt{N}(\tilde{\boldsymbol{\theta}}_N - \boldsymbol{\theta})$, and then to show that $\hat{\boldsymbol{\theta}}_N$ and $\tilde{\boldsymbol{\theta}}_N$ are $\sqrt{N}$-equivalent. A good example of this approach is in Chapter 7, where we find the limiting distribution of the feasible generalized least squares estimator, after we have found the limiting distribution of the GLS estimator.

DEFINITION 3.12: Partition $\hat{\boldsymbol{\theta}}_N$ satisfying statement (3.3) into vectors $\hat{\boldsymbol{\theta}}_{N1}$ and $\hat{\boldsymbol{\theta}}_{N2}$. Then $\hat{\boldsymbol{\theta}}_{N1}$ and $\hat{\boldsymbol{\theta}}_{N2}$ are **asymptotically independent** if

$$\mathbf{V} = \begin{pmatrix} \mathbf{V}_1 & \mathbf{0} \\ \mathbf{0} & \mathbf{V}_2 \end{pmatrix},$$

where $\mathbf{V}_1$ is the asymptotic variance of $\sqrt{N}(\hat{\boldsymbol{\theta}}_{N1} - \boldsymbol{\theta}_1)$ and similarly for $\mathbf{V}_2$. In other words, the asymptotic variance of $\sqrt{N}(\hat{\boldsymbol{\theta}}_N - \boldsymbol{\theta})$ is block diagonal.

Throughout this section we have been careful to index estimators by the sample size, N. This is useful to fix ideas on the nature of asymptotic analysis, but it is cumbersome when applying asymptotics to particular estimation methods. After this chapter, an estimator of $\boldsymbol{\theta}$ will be denoted $\hat{\boldsymbol{\theta}}$, which is understood to depend on the sample size N. When we write, for example, $\hat{\boldsymbol{\theta}} \xrightarrow{p} \boldsymbol{\theta}$, we mean convergence in probability as the sample size N goes to infinity.

3.5.2 Asymptotic Properties of Test Statistics

We begin with some important definitions in the large-sample analysis of test statistics.

DEFINITION 3.13: (1) The **asymptotic size** of a testing procedure is defined as the limiting probability of rejecting H_0 when H_0 is true. Mathematically, we can write this as $\lim_{N\to\infty} P_N(\text{reject } H_0 \mid H_0)$, where the N subscript indexes the sample size.

(2) A test is said to be **consistent** against the alternative H_1 if the null hypothesis is rejected with probability approaching one when H_1 is true: $\lim_{N\to\infty} P_N(\text{reject } H_0 \mid H_1) = 1$.

In practice, the asymptotic size of a test is obtained by finding the limiting distribution of a test statistic—in our case, normal or chi-square, or simple modifications of these that can be used as t distributed or F distributed—and then choosing a critical value based on this distribution. Thus, testing using asymptotic methods is practically the same as testing using the classical linear model.

A test is consistent against alternative H_1 if the probability of rejecting H_0 tends to unity as the sample size grows without bound. Just as consistency of an estimator is a minimal requirement, so is consistency of a test statistic. Consistency rarely allows us to choose among tests: most tests are consistent against alternatives that they are supposed to have power against. For consistent tests with the same asymptotic size, we can use the notion of *local power analysis* to choose among tests. We will cover this briefly in Chapter 12 on nonlinear estimation, where we introduce the notion of *local alternatives*—that is, alternatives to H_0 that converge to H_0 at rate $1/\sqrt{N}$. Generally, test statistics will have desirable asymptotic properties when they are based on estimators with good asymptotic properties (such as efficiency). We now derive the limiting distribution of a test statistic that is used very often in econometrics.

LEMMA 3.8: Suppose that statement (3.3) holds, where $\mathbf{V}$ is positive definite. Then for any nonstochastic matrix $Q \times P$ matrix $\mathbf{R}$, $Q \leq P$, with $\text{rank}(\mathbf{R}) = Q$,

$$\sqrt{N}\mathbf{R}(\hat{\boldsymbol{\theta}}_N - \boldsymbol{\theta}) \overset{a}{\sim} \text{Normal}(\mathbf{0}, \mathbf{RVR}')$$

and

$$[\sqrt{N}\mathbf{R}(\hat{\boldsymbol{\theta}}_N - \boldsymbol{\theta})]'[\mathbf{RVR}']^{-1}[\sqrt{N}\mathbf{R}(\hat{\boldsymbol{\theta}}_N - \boldsymbol{\theta})] \overset{a}{\sim} \chi^2_Q.$$

In addition, if $\text{plim}\, \hat{\mathbf{V}}_N = \mathbf{V}$ then

$$[\sqrt{N}\mathbf{R}(\hat{\boldsymbol{\theta}}_N - \boldsymbol{\theta})]'[\mathbf{R}\hat{\mathbf{V}}_N\mathbf{R}']^{-1}[\sqrt{N}\mathbf{R}(\hat{\boldsymbol{\theta}}_N - \boldsymbol{\theta})]$$
$$= (\hat{\boldsymbol{\theta}}_N - \boldsymbol{\theta})'\mathbf{R}'[\mathbf{R}(\hat{\mathbf{V}}_N/N)\mathbf{R}']^{-1}\mathbf{R}(\hat{\boldsymbol{\theta}}_N - \boldsymbol{\theta}) \overset{a}{\sim} \chi^2_Q.$$

For testing the null hypothesis H_0: $\mathbf{R}\boldsymbol{\theta} = \mathbf{r}$, where $\mathbf{r}$ is a $Q \times 1$ nonrandom vector, define the **Wald statistic** for testing H_0 against H_1: $\mathbf{R}\boldsymbol{\theta} \neq \mathbf{r}$ as

$$W_N \equiv (\mathbf{R}\hat{\boldsymbol{\theta}}_N - \mathbf{r})'[\mathbf{R}(\hat{\mathbf{V}}_N/N)\mathbf{R}']^{-1}(\mathbf{R}\hat{\boldsymbol{\theta}}_N - \mathbf{r}). \tag{3.7}$$

Under H_0, $W_N \overset{a}{\sim} \chi^2_Q$. If we abuse the asymptotics and treat $\hat{\boldsymbol{\theta}}_N$ as being distributed as $\text{Normal}(\boldsymbol{\theta}, \hat{\mathbf{V}}_N/N)$, we get equation (3.7) exactly.

LEMMA 3.9: Suppose that statement (3.3) holds, where $\mathbf{V}$ is positive definite. Let $\mathbf{c}$: $\boldsymbol{\Theta} \to \mathbb{R}^Q$ be a continuously differentiable function on the parameter space $\boldsymbol{\Theta} \subset \mathbb{R}^P$, where $Q \leq P$, and assume that $\boldsymbol{\theta}$ is in the interior of the parameter space. Define $\mathbf{C}(\boldsymbol{\theta}) \equiv \nabla_\theta \mathbf{c}(\boldsymbol{\theta})$ as the $Q \times P$ Jacobian of $\mathbf{c}$. Then

$$\sqrt{N}[\mathbf{c}(\hat{\boldsymbol{\theta}}_N) - \mathbf{c}(\boldsymbol{\theta})] \overset{a}{\sim} \text{Normal}[\mathbf{0}, \mathbf{C}(\boldsymbol{\theta})\mathbf{V}\mathbf{C}(\boldsymbol{\theta})'] \tag{3.8}$$

and

$$\{\sqrt{N}[\mathbf{c}(\hat{\boldsymbol{\theta}}_N) - \mathbf{c}(\boldsymbol{\theta})]\}'[\mathbf{C}(\boldsymbol{\theta})\mathbf{V}\mathbf{C}(\boldsymbol{\theta})']^{-1}\{\sqrt{N}[\mathbf{c}(\hat{\boldsymbol{\theta}}_N) - \mathbf{c}(\boldsymbol{\theta})]\} \overset{a}{\sim} \chi^2_Q.$$

Define $\hat{\mathbf{C}}_N \equiv \mathbf{C}(\hat{\boldsymbol{\theta}}_N)$. Then $\text{plim}\, \hat{\mathbf{C}}_N = \mathbf{C}(\boldsymbol{\theta})$. If $\text{plim}\, \hat{\mathbf{V}}_N = \mathbf{V}$, then

$$\{\sqrt{N}[\mathbf{c}(\hat{\boldsymbol{\theta}}_N) - \mathbf{c}(\boldsymbol{\theta})]\}'[\hat{\mathbf{C}}_N\hat{\mathbf{V}}_N\hat{\mathbf{C}}_N']^{-1}\{\sqrt{N}[\mathbf{c}(\hat{\boldsymbol{\theta}}_N) - \mathbf{c}(\boldsymbol{\theta})]\} \overset{a}{\sim} \chi^2_Q. \tag{3.9}$$

Equation (3.8) is very useful for obtaining asymptotic standard errors for nonlinear functions of $\hat{\boldsymbol{\theta}}_N$. The appropriate estimator of $\text{Avar}[\mathbf{c}(\hat{\boldsymbol{\theta}}_N)]$ is $\hat{\mathbf{C}}_N(\hat{\mathbf{V}}_N/N)\hat{\mathbf{C}}_N' =$

$\hat{\mathbf{C}}_N[\text{Avar}(\hat{\boldsymbol{\theta}}_N)]\hat{\mathbf{C}}_N'$. Thus, once $\text{Avar}(\hat{\boldsymbol{\theta}}_N)$ and the estimated Jacobian of $\mathbf{c}$ are obtained, we can easily obtain

$$\text{Avar}[\mathbf{c}(\hat{\boldsymbol{\theta}}_N)] = \hat{\mathbf{C}}_N[\text{Avar}(\hat{\boldsymbol{\theta}}_N)]\hat{\mathbf{C}}_N'. \tag{3.10}$$

The asymptotic standard errors are obtained as the square roots of the diagonal elements of equation (3.10). In the scalar case $\hat{\gamma}_N = c(\hat{\boldsymbol{\theta}}_N)$, the asymptotic standard error of $\hat{\gamma}_N$ is $[\nabla_\theta c(\hat{\boldsymbol{\theta}}_N)[\text{Avar}(\hat{\boldsymbol{\theta}}_N)]\nabla_\theta c(\hat{\boldsymbol{\theta}}_N)']^{1/2}$.

Equation (3.9) is useful for testing nonlinear hypotheses of the form H_0: $\mathbf{c}(\boldsymbol{\theta}) = \mathbf{0}$ against H_1: $\mathbf{c}(\boldsymbol{\theta}) \neq \mathbf{0}$. The Wald statistic is

$$W_N = \sqrt{N}\mathbf{c}(\hat{\boldsymbol{\theta}}_N)'[\hat{\mathbf{C}}_N\hat{\mathbf{V}}_N\hat{\mathbf{C}}_N']^{-1}\sqrt{N}\mathbf{c}(\hat{\boldsymbol{\theta}}_N) = \mathbf{c}(\hat{\boldsymbol{\theta}}_N)'[\hat{\mathbf{C}}_N(\hat{\mathbf{V}}_N/N)\hat{\mathbf{C}}_N']^{-1}\mathbf{c}(\hat{\boldsymbol{\theta}}_N). \tag{3.11}$$

Under H_0, $W_N \overset{a}{\sim} \chi^2_Q$.

The method of establishing equation (3.8), given that statement (3.3) holds, is often called the **delta method**, and it is used very often in econometrics. It gets its name from its use of calculus. The argument is as follows. Because $\boldsymbol{\theta}$ is in the interior of $\boldsymbol{\Theta}$, and because $\text{plim}\ \hat{\boldsymbol{\theta}}_N = \boldsymbol{\theta}$, $\hat{\boldsymbol{\theta}}_N$ is in an open, convex subset of $\boldsymbol{\Theta}$ containing $\boldsymbol{\theta}$ with probability approaching one, therefore w.p.a.1 we can use a mean value expansion $\mathbf{c}(\hat{\boldsymbol{\theta}}_N) = \mathbf{c}(\boldsymbol{\theta}) + \ddot{\mathbf{C}}_N \cdot (\hat{\boldsymbol{\theta}}_N - \boldsymbol{\theta})$, where $\ddot{\mathbf{C}}_N$ denotes the matrix $\mathbf{C}(\boldsymbol{\theta})$ with rows evaluated at mean values between $\hat{\boldsymbol{\theta}}_N$ and $\boldsymbol{\theta}$. Because these mean values are trapped between $\hat{\boldsymbol{\theta}}_N$ and $\boldsymbol{\theta}$, they converge in probability to $\boldsymbol{\theta}$. Therefore, by Slutsky's theorem, $\ddot{\mathbf{C}}_N \xrightarrow{p} \mathbf{C}(\boldsymbol{\theta})$, and we can write

$$\begin{aligned}
\sqrt{N}[\mathbf{c}(\hat{\boldsymbol{\theta}}_N) - \mathbf{c}(\boldsymbol{\theta})] &= \ddot{\mathbf{C}}_N \cdot \sqrt{N}(\hat{\boldsymbol{\theta}}_N - \boldsymbol{\theta}), \\
&= \mathbf{C}(\boldsymbol{\theta})\sqrt{N}(\hat{\boldsymbol{\theta}}_N - \boldsymbol{\theta}) + [\ddot{\mathbf{C}}_N - \mathbf{C}(\boldsymbol{\theta})]\sqrt{N}(\hat{\boldsymbol{\theta}}_N - \boldsymbol{\theta}), \\
&= \mathbf{C}(\boldsymbol{\theta})\sqrt{N}(\hat{\boldsymbol{\theta}}_N - \boldsymbol{\theta}) + \text{o}_p(1) \cdot \text{O}_p(1) = \mathbf{C}(\boldsymbol{\theta})\sqrt{N}(\hat{\boldsymbol{\theta}}_N - \boldsymbol{\theta}) + \text{o}_p(1).
\end{aligned}$$

We can now apply the asymptotic equivalence lemma (Lemma 3.7) and Lemma 3.8 [with $\mathbf{R} \equiv \mathbf{C}(\boldsymbol{\theta})$] to get equation (3.8).

Problems

3.1. Prove Lemma 3.1.

3.2. Using Lemma 3.2, prove Lemma 3.3.

3.3. Explain why, under the assumptions of Lemma 3.4, $\mathbf{g}(\mathbf{x}_N) = \text{O}_p(1)$.

3.4. Prove Corollary 3.2.

3.5. Let $\{y_i: i = 1, 2, \ldots\}$ be an independent, identically distributed sequence with $\mathrm{E}(y_i^2) < \infty$. Let $\mu = \mathrm{E}(y_i)$ and $\sigma^2 = \mathrm{Var}(y_i)$.

a. Let $\bar{y}_N$ denote the sample average based on a sample size of N. Find $\mathrm{Var}[\sqrt{N}(\bar{y}_N - \mu)]$.

b. What is the asymptotic variance of $\sqrt{N}(\bar{y}_N - \mu)$?

c. What is the asymptotic variance of $\bar{y}_N$? Compare this with $\mathrm{Var}(\bar{y}_N)$.

d. What is the asymptotic standard deviation of $\bar{y}_N$?

e. How would you obtain the asymptotic standard error of $\bar{y}_N$?

3.6. Give a careful (albeit short) proof of the following statement: If $\sqrt{N}(\hat{\boldsymbol{\theta}}_N - \boldsymbol{\theta}) = \mathrm{O}_p(1)$, then $\hat{\boldsymbol{\theta}}_N - \boldsymbol{\theta} = \mathrm{o}_p(N^{-c})$ for any $0 \leq c < \frac{1}{2}$.

3.7. Let $\hat{\theta}$ be a $\sqrt{N}$-asymptotically normal estimator for the scalar $\theta > 0$. Let $\hat{\gamma} = \log(\hat{\theta})$ be an estimator of $\gamma = \log(\theta)$.

a. Why is $\hat{\gamma}$ a consistent estimator of γ?

b. Find the asymptotic variance of $\sqrt{N}(\hat{\gamma} - \gamma)$ in terms of the asymptotic variance of $\sqrt{N}(\hat{\theta} - \theta)$.

c. Suppose that, for a sample of data, $\hat{\theta} = 4$ and $\mathrm{se}(\hat{\theta}) = 2$. What is $\hat{\gamma}$ and its (asymptotic) standard error?

d. Consider the null hypothesis H_0: $\theta = 1$. What is the asymptotic t statistic for testing H_0, given the numbers from part c?

e. Now state H_0 from part d equivalently in terms of γ, and use $\hat{\gamma}$ and $\mathrm{se}(\hat{\gamma})$ to test H_0. What do you conclude?

3.8. Let $\hat{\boldsymbol{\theta}} = (\hat{\theta}_1, \hat{\theta}_2)'$ be a $\sqrt{N}$-asymptotically normal estimator for $\boldsymbol{\theta} = (\theta_1, \theta_2)'$, with $\theta_2 \neq 0$. Let $\hat{\gamma} = \hat{\theta}_1/\hat{\theta}_2$ be an estimator of $\gamma = \theta_1/\theta_2$.

a. Show that $\mathrm{plim}\ \hat{\gamma} = \gamma$.

b. Find $\mathrm{Avar}(\hat{\gamma})$ in terms of $\boldsymbol{\theta}$ and $\mathrm{Avar}(\hat{\boldsymbol{\theta}})$ using the delta method.

c. If, for a sample of data, $\hat{\boldsymbol{\theta}} = (-1.5, .5)'$ and $\mathrm{Avar}(\hat{\boldsymbol{\theta}})$ is estimated as $\begin{pmatrix} 1 & -.4 \\ -.4 & 2 \end{pmatrix}$, find the asymptotic standard error of $\hat{\gamma}$.

3.9. Let $\hat{\boldsymbol{\theta}}$ and $\tilde{\boldsymbol{\theta}}$ be two consistent, $\sqrt{N}$-asymptotically normal estimators of the $P \times 1$ parameter vector $\boldsymbol{\theta}$, with $\mathrm{Avar}\ \sqrt{N}(\hat{\boldsymbol{\theta}} - \boldsymbol{\theta}) = \mathbf{V}_1$ and $\mathrm{Avar}\ \sqrt{N}(\tilde{\boldsymbol{\theta}} - \boldsymbol{\theta}) = \mathbf{V}_2$. Define a $Q \times 1$ parameter vector by $\boldsymbol{\gamma} = \mathbf{g}(\boldsymbol{\theta})$, where $\mathbf{g}(\cdot)$ is a continuously differentiable function. Show that, if $\hat{\boldsymbol{\theta}}$ is asymptotically more efficient than $\tilde{\boldsymbol{\theta}}$, then $\hat{\boldsymbol{\gamma}} \equiv \mathbf{g}(\hat{\boldsymbol{\theta}})$ is asymptotically efficient relative to $\tilde{\boldsymbol{\gamma}} \equiv \mathbf{g}(\tilde{\boldsymbol{\theta}})$.

3.10. Let $\{w_i : i = 1, 2, \ldots\}$ be a sequence of independent, identically distributed random variables with $\mathrm{E}(w_i^2) < \infty$ and $\mathrm{E}(w_i) = 0$. Define the standardized partial sum as $x_N = N^{-1/2} \sum_{i=1}^{N} w_i$. Use Chebyshev's inequality (see, for example, Casella and Berger (2002, p. 122)) to prove that $x_N = O_p(1)$. Therefore, we can show directly that a standardized partial sum of i.i.d. random variables with finite second moment is $O_p(1)$, rather than having to appeal to the central limit theorem.

3.11. Let $\{w_i : i = 1, 2, \ldots\}$ be a sequence of independent, not (necessarily) identically distributed random variables with $E(w_i^2) < \infty$, $i = 1, 2, \ldots$ and $E(w_i) = \mu_i$, $i = 1, 2, \ldots$. For each i, define $\sigma_i^2 = Var(w_i)$.

a. Use Chebyshev's inequality to show that a sufficient condition for $N^{-1} \sum_{i=1}^{N} (w_i - \mu_i) \xrightarrow{p} 0$ is $N^{-2} \sum_{i=1}^{N} \sigma_i^2 \to 0$ as $N \to \infty$.

b. Is the condition from part a satisfied if $\sigma_i^2 < b < \infty$, $i = 1, 2, \ldots$? (See White (2001) for weaker conditions under which the WLLN holds for i.n.i.d. sequences.)

II LINEAR MODELS

In Part II we begin our econometric analysis of linear models for cross section and panel data. In Chapter 4 we review the single-equation linear model and discuss ordinary least squares estimation. Although this material is, in principle, review, the approach is likely to be different from an introductory linear models course. In addition, we cover several topics that are not traditionally covered in texts but that have proven useful in empirical work. Chapter 5 discusses instrumental variables estimation of the linear model, and Chapter 6 covers some remaining topics to round out our treatment of the single-equation model.

Chapter 7 begins our analysis of systems of equations. The general setup is that the number of population equations is small relative to the (cross section) sample size. This allows us to cover seemingly unrelated regression models for cross section data as well as begin our analysis of panel data. Chapter 8 builds on the framework from Chapter 7 but considers the case where some explanatory variables may be uncorrelated with the error terms. Generalized method of moments estimation is the unifying theme. Chapter 9 applies the methods of Chapter 8 to the estimation of simultaneous equations models, with an emphasis on the conceptual issues that arise in applying such models.

Chapter 10 explicitly introduces unobserved-effects linear panel data models. Under the assumption that the explanatory variables are strictly exogenous conditional on the unobserved effect, we study several estimation methods, including fixed effects, first differencing, and random effects. The last method assumes, at a minimum, that the unobserved effect is uncorrelated with the explanatory variables in all time periods. Chapter 11 considers extensions of the basic panel data model, including failure of the strict exogeneity assumption and models with individual-specific slopes.

4 Single-Equation Linear Model and Ordinary Least Squares Estimation

4.1 Overview of the Single-Equation Linear Model

This and the next couple of chapters cover what is still the workhorse in empirical economics: the single-equation linear model. Though you are assumed to be comfortable with ordinary least squares (OLS) estimation, we begin with OLS for a couple of reasons. First, it provides a bridge between more traditional approaches to econometrics, which treat explanatory variables as fixed, and the current approach, which is based on random sampling with stochastic explanatory variables. Second, we cover some topics that receive at best cursory treatment in first-semester texts. These topics, such as proxy variable solutions to the omitted variable problem, arise often in applied work.

The population model we study is linear in its parameters,

$$y = \beta_0 + \beta_1 x_1 + \beta_2 x_2 + \cdots + \beta_K x_K + u, \tag{4.1}$$

where $y, x_1, x_2, x_3, \ldots, x_K$ are observable random scalars (that is, we can observe them in a random sample of the population), u is the unobservable random disturbance or error, and $\beta_0, \beta_1, \beta_2, \ldots, \beta_K$ are the parameters (constants) we would like to estimate.

The error form of the model in equation (4.1) is useful for presenting a unified treatment of the statistical properties of various econometric procedures. Nevertheless, the steps one uses for getting to equation (4.1) are just as important. Goldberger (1972) defines a **structural model** as one representing a causal relationship, as opposed to a relationship that simply captures statistical associations. A structural equation can be obtained from an economic model, or it can be obtained through informal reasoning. Sometimes the structural model is directly estimable. Other times we must combine auxiliary assumptions about other variables with algebraic manipulations to arrive at an **estimable model**. In addition, we will often have reasons to estimate nonstructural equations, sometimes as a precursor to estimating a structural equation.

The error term u can consist of a variety of things, including omitted variables and measurement error (we will see some examples shortly). The parameters β_j hopefully correspond to the parameters of interest, that is, the parameters in an underlying structural model. Whether this is the case depends on the application and the assumptions made.

As we will see in Section 4.2, the key condition needed for OLS to consistently estimate the β_j (assuming we have available a random sample from the population) is that the error (in the population) has mean zero and is uncorrelated with each of the regressors:

$$\mathrm{E}(u) = 0, \qquad \mathrm{Cov}(x_j, u) = 0, \qquad j = 1, 2, \ldots, K. \tag{4.2}$$

The zero-mean assumption is for free when an intercept is included, and we will restrict attention to that case in what follows. It is the zero covariance of u with each x_j that is important. From Chapter 2 we know that equation (4.1) and assumption (4.2) are equivalent to defining the linear projection of y onto $(1, x_1, x_2, \ldots, x_K)$ as $\beta_0 + \beta_1 x_1 + \beta_2 x_2 + \cdots + \beta_K x_K$.

Sufficient for assumption (4.2) is the zero conditional mean assumption

$$\mathrm{E}(u \mid x_1, x_2, \ldots, x_K) = \mathrm{E}(u \mid \mathbf{x}) = 0. \tag{4.3}$$

Under equation (4.1) and assumption (4.3), we have the population regression function

$$\mathrm{E}(y \mid x_1, x_2, \ldots, x_K) = \beta_0 + \beta_1 x_1 + \beta_2 x_2 + \cdots + \beta_K x_K. \tag{4.4}$$

As we saw in Chapter 2, equation (4.4) includes the case where the x_j are nonlinear functions of underlying explanatory variables, such as

$$\begin{aligned}\mathrm{E}(savings \mid income, size, age, college) = \beta_0 + \beta_1 \log(income) + \beta_2 size + \beta_3 age \\ + \beta_4 \, college + \beta_5 \, college{\cdot}age.\end{aligned}$$

We will study the asymptotic properties of OLS primarily under assumption (4.2), because it is weaker than assumption (4.3). As we discussed in Chapter 2, assumption (4.3) is natural when a structural model is directly estimable because it ensures that no additional functions of the explanatory variables help to explain y.

An explanatory variable x_j is said to be **endogenous** in equation (4.1) if it is correlated with u. You should not rely too much on the meaning of "endogenous" from other branches of economics. In traditional usage, a variable is endogenous if it is determined within the context of a model. The usage in econometrics, while related to traditional definitions, has evolved to describe any situation where an explanatory variable is correlated with the disturbance. If x_j is uncorrelated with u, then x_j is said to be **exogenous** in equation (4.1). If assumption (4.3) holds, then each explanatory variable is necessarily exogenous.

In applied econometrics, endogeneity usually arises in one of three ways:

Omitted Variables Omitted variables are an issue when we would like to control for one or more additional variables but, usually because of data unavailability, we cannot include them in a regression model. Specifically, suppose that $\mathrm{E}(y \mid \mathbf{x}, q)$ is the conditional expectation of interest, which can be written as a function linear in parameters and additive in q. If q is unobserved, we can always estimate $\mathrm{E}(y \mid \mathbf{x})$, but this need have no particular relationship to $\mathrm{E}(y \mid \mathbf{x}, q)$ when q and $\mathbf{x}$ are allowed to be correlated. One way to represent this situation is to write equation (4.1) where q is part of the error term u. If q and x_j are correlated, then x_j is endogenous. The correlation of explanatory variables with unobservables is often due to *self-selection*: if agents choose the value of x_j, this might depend on factors (q) that are unobservable to the analyst. A good example is omitted ability in a wage equation, where an individual's years of schooling are likely to be correlated with unobserved ability. We discuss the omitted variables problem in detail in Section 4.3.

Measurement Error In this case we would like to measure the (partial) effect of a variable, say x_K^*, but we can observe only an imperfect measure of it, say x_K. When we plug x_K in for x_K^*—thereby arriving at the estimable equation (4.1)—we necessarily put a measurement error into u. Depending on assumptions about how x_K^* and x_K are related, u and x_K may or may not be correlated. For example, x_K^* might denote a marginal tax rate, but we can only obtain data on the average tax rate. We will study the measurement error problem in Section 4.4.

Simultaneity Simultaneity arises when at least one of the explanatory variables is determined simultaneously along with y. If, say, x_K is determined partly as a function of y, then x_K and u are generally correlated. For example, if y is city murder rate and x_K is size of the police force, size of the police force is partly determined by the murder rate. Conceptually, this is a more difficult situation to analyze, because we must be able to think of a situation where we *could* vary x_K exogenously, even though in the data that we collect y and x_K are generated simultaneously. Chapter 9 treats simultaneous equations models in detail.

The distinctions among the three possible forms of endogeneity are not always sharp. In fact, an equation can have more than one source of endogeneity. For example, in looking at the effect of alcohol consumption on worker productivity (as typically measured by wages), we would worry that alcohol usage is correlated with unobserved factors, possibly related to family background, that also affect wage; this is an omitted variables problem. In addition, alcohol demand would generally depend on income, which is largely determined by wage; this is a simultaneity problem. And measurement error in alcohol usage is always a possibility. For an illuminating discussion of the three kinds of endogeneity as they arise in a particular field, see Deaton's (1995) survey chapter on econometric issues in development economics.

4.2 Asymptotic Properties of Ordinary Least Squares

We now briefly review the asymptotic properties of OLS for random samples from a population, focusing on inference. It is convenient to write the population equation of interest in vector form as

$$y = \mathbf{x}\boldsymbol{\beta} + u, \tag{4.5}$$

where $\mathbf{x}$ is a $1 \times K$ vector of regressors and $\boldsymbol{\beta} \equiv (\beta_1, \beta_2, \ldots, \beta_K)'$ is a $K \times 1$ vector. Because most equations contain an intercept, we will just assume that $x_1 \equiv 1$, as this assumption makes interpreting the conditions easier.

We assume that we can obtain a random sample of size N from the population in order to estimate $\boldsymbol{\beta}$; thus, $\{(\mathbf{x}_i, y_i): i = 1, 2, \ldots, N\}$ are treated as independent, identically distributed random variables, where $\mathbf{x}_i$ is $1 \times K$ and y_i is a scalar. For each observation i we have

$$y_i = \mathbf{x}_i\boldsymbol{\beta} + u_i, \tag{4.6}$$

which is convenient for deriving statistical properties of estimators. As for stating and interpreting assumptions, it is easiest to focus on the population model (4.5).

Defining the vector of explanatory variables $\mathbf{x}_i$ as a row vector is less popular than defining it as a column vector, but the row vector notation can be justified along many dimensions, especially when we turn to models with multiple equations or time periods. For now, we can justify the row vector notation by thinking about the most convenient, and by far the most common, method of entering and storing data—in tabular form, where the table has a row for each observation. In other words, if $(\mathbf{x}_i, y_i)$ are the outcomes for unit i, then it makes sense to view $(\mathbf{x}_i, y_i)$ as the ith row of our data matrix or table. Similarly, when we turn to estimation, it makes sense to define $\mathbf{x}_i$ to be the ith row of the matrix of explanatory variables.

4.2.1 Consistency

As discussed in Section 4.1, the key assumption for OLS to consistently estimate $\boldsymbol{\beta}$ is the **population orthogonality condition**:

ASSUMPTION OLS.1: $\mathrm{E}(\mathbf{x}'u) = \mathbf{0}$.

Because $\mathbf{x}$ contains a constant, Assumption OLS.1 is equivalent to saying that u has mean zero and is uncorrelated with each regressor, which is how we will refer to Assumption OLS.1. Sufficient for Assumption OLS.1 is the zero conditional mean assumption (4.3).

It is critical to understand the population nature of Assumption OLS.1. The vector $(\mathbf{x}, u)$ represents a population, and OLS.1 is a restriction on the joint distribution in that population. For example, if $\mathbf{x}$ contains years of schooling and workforce experience, and the main component of u is cognitive ability, then OLS.1 implies that ability is uncorrelated with education and experience in the population; it has nothing to do with relationships in a sample of data.

The other assumption needed for consistency of OLS is that the expected outer product matrix of $\mathbf{x}$ has full rank, so that there are no exact linear relationships among the regressors in the population. This is stated succinctly as follows:

ASSUMPTION OLS.2: rank $\mathrm{E}(\mathbf{x}'\mathbf{x}) = K$.

As with Assumption OLS.1, Assumption OLS.2 is an assumption about the population. Because $\mathrm{E}(\mathbf{x}'\mathbf{x})$ is a symmetric $K \times K$ matrix, Assumption OLS.2 is equivalent to assuming that $\mathrm{E}(\mathbf{x}'\mathbf{x})$ is positive definite. Since $x_1 = 1$, Assumption OLS.2 is also equivalent to saying that the (population) variance matrix of the $K - 1$ nonconstant elements in $\mathbf{x}$ is nonsingular. This is a standard assumption, which fails if and only if at least one of the regressors can be written as a linear function of the other regressors (in the population). Usually Assumption OLS.2 holds, but it can fail if the population model is improperly specified (for example, if we include too many dummy variables in $\mathbf{x}$ or mistakenly use something like $\log(age)$ and $\log(age^2)$ in the same equation).

Under Assumptions OLS.1 and OLS.2, the parameter vector $\boldsymbol{\beta}$ is **identified**. In the context of models that are linear in the parameters under random sampling, identification of $\boldsymbol{\beta}$ simply means that $\boldsymbol{\beta}$ can be written in terms of population moments in observable variables. (Later, when we consider nonlinear models, the notion of identification will have to be more general. Also, special issues arise if we cannot obtain a random sample from the population, something we treat in Chapters 19 and 20.) To see that $\boldsymbol{\beta}$ is identified under Assumptions OLS.1 and OLS.2, premultiply equation (4.5) by $\mathbf{x}'$, take expectations, and solve to get

$$\boldsymbol{\beta} = [\mathrm{E}(\mathbf{x}'\mathbf{x})]^{-1}\mathrm{E}(\mathbf{x}'y).$$

Because $(\mathbf{x}, y)$ is observed, $\boldsymbol{\beta}$ is identified. The **analogy principle** for choosing an estimator says to turn the population problem into its sample counterpart (see Goldberger, 1968; Manski, 1988). In the current application this step leads to the **method of moments**: replace the population moments $\mathrm{E}(\mathbf{x}'\mathbf{x})$ and $\mathrm{E}(\mathbf{x}'y)$ with the corresponding sample averages. Doing so leads to the OLS estimator:

$$\hat{\boldsymbol{\beta}} = \left(N^{-1}\sum_{i=1}^{N}\mathbf{x}_i'\mathbf{x}_i\right)^{-1}\left(N^{-1}\sum_{i=1}^{N}\mathbf{x}_i'y_i\right) = \boldsymbol{\beta} + \left(N^{-1}\sum_{i=1}^{N}\mathbf{x}_i'\mathbf{x}_i\right)^{-1}\left(N^{-1}\sum_{i=1}^{N}\mathbf{x}_i'u_i\right),$$

which can be written in full matrix form as $(\mathbf{X}'\mathbf{X})^{-1}\mathbf{X}'\mathbf{Y}$, where $\mathbf{X}$ is the $N \times K$ data matrix of regressors with ith row $\mathbf{x}_i$ and $\mathbf{Y}$ is the $N \times 1$ data vector with ith element y_i. Under Assumption OLS.2, $\mathbf{X}'\mathbf{X}$ is nonsingular with probability approaching one and $\text{plim}[(N^{-1}\sum_{i=1}^{N}\mathbf{x}_i'\mathbf{x}_i)^{-1}] = \mathbf{A}^{-1}$, where $\mathbf{A} \equiv \text{E}(\mathbf{x}'\mathbf{x})$ (see Corollary 3.1). Further, under Assumption OLS.1, $\text{plim}(N^{-1}\sum_{i=1}^{N}\mathbf{x}_i'u_i) = \text{E}(\mathbf{x}'u) = \mathbf{0}$. Therefore, by Slutsky's theorem (Lemma 3.4), $\text{plim}\,\hat{\boldsymbol{\beta}} = \boldsymbol{\beta} + \mathbf{A}^{-1} \cdot \mathbf{0} = \boldsymbol{\beta}$. We summarize with a theorem:

THEOREM 4.1 (Consistency of OLS): Under Assumptions OLS.1 and OLS.2, the OLS estimator $\hat{\boldsymbol{\beta}}$ obtained from a random sample following the population model (4.5) is consistent for $\boldsymbol{\beta}$.

The simplicity of the proof of Theorem 4.1 should not undermine its usefulness. Whenever an equation can be put into the form (4.5) and Assumptions OLS.1 and OLS.2 hold, OLS using a random sample consistently estimates $\boldsymbol{\beta}$. It does not matter where this equation comes from, or what the β_j actually represent. As we will see in Sections 4.3 and 4.4, often an estimable equation is obtained only after manipulating an underlying structural equation. An important point to remember is that, once the linear (in parameters) equation has been specified with an additive error and Assumptions OLS.1 and OLS.2 are verified, there is no need to reprove Theorem 4.1.

Under the assumptions of Theorem 4.1, $\mathbf{x}\boldsymbol{\beta}$ is the linear projection of y on $\mathbf{x}$. Thus, Theorem 4.1 shows that OLS consistently estimates the parameters in a linear projection, subject to the rank condition in Assumption OLS.2. This is very general, as it places no restrictions on the nature of y—for example, y could be a binary variable or some other variable with discrete characteristics. Because a conditional expectation that is linear in parameters is also the linear projection, Theorem 4.1 also shows that OLS consistently estimates conditional expectations that are linear in parameters. We will use this fact often in later sections.

There are a few final points worth emphasizing. First, if either Assumption OLS.1 or OLS.2 fails, then $\boldsymbol{\beta}$ is not identified (unless we make other assumptions, as in Chapter 5). Usually it is correlation between u and one or more elements of $\mathbf{x}$ that causes lack of identification. Second, the OLS estimator is *not* necessarily unbiased even under Assumptions OLS.1 and OLS.2. However, if we impose the zero conditional mean assumption (4.3), then it can be shown that $\text{E}(\hat{\boldsymbol{\beta}} \mid \mathbf{X}) = \boldsymbol{\beta}$ if $\mathbf{X}'\mathbf{X}$ is nonsingular; see Problem 4.2. By iterated expectations, $\hat{\boldsymbol{\beta}}$ is then also unconditionally unbiased, provided the expected value $\text{E}(\hat{\boldsymbol{\beta}})$ exists.

Finally, we have not made the much more restrictive assumption that u and $\mathbf{x}$ are *independent*. If $\text{E}(u) = 0$ and u is independent of $\mathbf{x}$, then assumption (4.3) holds, but not vice versa. For example, $\text{Var}(u \mid \mathbf{x})$ is entirely unrestricted under assumption (4.3), but $\text{Var}(u \mid \mathbf{x})$ is necessarily constant if u and $\mathbf{x}$ are independent.

4.2.2 Asymptotic Inference Using Ordinary Least Squares

The asymptotic distribution of the OLS estimator is derived by writing

$$\sqrt{N}(\hat{\boldsymbol{\beta}} - \boldsymbol{\beta}) = \left(N^{-1}\sum_{i=1}^{N}\mathbf{x}_i'\mathbf{x}_i\right)^{-1}\left(N^{-1/2}\sum_{i=1}^{N}\mathbf{x}_i'u_i\right).$$

As we saw in Theorem 4.1, $(N^{-1}\sum_{i=1}^{N}\mathbf{x}_i'\mathbf{x}_i)^{-1} - \mathbf{A}^{-1} = o_p(1)$. Also, $\{(\mathbf{x}_i'u_i):i = 1,2,\ldots\}$ is an i.i.d. sequence with zero mean, and we assume that each element has finite variance. Then the central limit theorem (Theorem 3.2) implies that $N^{-1/2}\sum_{i=1}^{N}\mathbf{x}_i'u_i \xrightarrow{d} \text{Normal}(\mathbf{0}, \mathbf{B})$, where $\mathbf{B}$ is the $K \times K$ matrix

$$\mathbf{B} \equiv \mathrm{E}(u^2\mathbf{x}'\mathbf{x}). \tag{4.7}$$

This implies $N^{-1/2}\sum_{i=1}^{N}\mathbf{x}_i'u_i = O_p(1)$, and so we can write

$$\sqrt{N}(\hat{\boldsymbol{\beta}} - \boldsymbol{\beta}) = \mathbf{A}^{-1}\left(N^{-1/2}\sum_{i=1}^{N}\mathbf{x}_i'u_i\right) + o_p(1) \tag{4.8}$$

because $o_p(1) \cdot O_p(1) = o_p(1)$. We can use equation (4.8) to immediately obtain the asymptotic distribution of $\sqrt{N}(\hat{\boldsymbol{\beta}} - \boldsymbol{\beta})$. A **homoskedasticity** assumption simplifies the form of OLS asymptotic variance:

ASSUMPTION OLS.3: $\mathrm{E}(u^2\mathbf{x}'\mathbf{x}) = \sigma^2\mathrm{E}(\mathbf{x}'\mathbf{x})$, where $\sigma^2 \equiv \mathrm{E}(u^2)$.

Because $\mathrm{E}(u) = 0$, σ^2 is also equal to $\mathrm{Var}(u)$. Assumption OLS.3 is the weakest form of the homoskedasticity assumption. If we write out the $K \times K$ matrices in Assumption OLS.3 element by element, we see that Assumption OLS.3 is equivalent to assuming that the squared error, u^2, is uncorrelated with each x_j, x_j^2, and all cross products of the form x_jx_k. By the law of iterated expectations, sufficient for Assumption OLS.3 is $\mathrm{E}(u^2 \mid \mathbf{x}) = \sigma^2$, which is the same as $\mathrm{Var}(u \mid \mathbf{x}) = \sigma^2$ when $\mathrm{E}(u \mid \mathbf{x}) = 0$. The constant conditional variance assumption for u given $\mathbf{x}$ is the easiest to interpret, but it is stronger than needed.

THEOREM 4.2 (Asymptotic Normality of OLS): Under Assumptions OLS.1–OLS.3,

$$\sqrt{N}(\hat{\boldsymbol{\beta}} - \boldsymbol{\beta}) \overset{a}{\sim} \text{Normal}(0, \sigma^2[\mathrm{E}(\mathbf{x}'\mathbf{x})]^{-1}). \tag{4.9}$$

Proof: From equation (4.8) and definition of $\mathbf{B}$, it follows from Lemma 3.7 and Corollary 3.2 that

$$\sqrt{N}(\hat{\boldsymbol{\beta}} - \boldsymbol{\beta}) \overset{a}{\sim} \text{Normal}(0, \mathbf{A}^{-1}\mathbf{B}\mathbf{A}^{-1}),$$

where $\mathbf{A} = \mathrm{E}(\mathbf{x}'\mathbf{x})$. Under Assumption OLS.3, $\mathbf{B} = \sigma^2\mathbf{A}$, which proves the result.

Practically speaking, equation (4.9) allows us to treat $\hat{\boldsymbol{\beta}}$ as approximately normal with mean $\boldsymbol{\beta}$ and variance $\sigma^2[\mathrm{E}(\mathbf{x}'\mathbf{x})]^{-1}/N$. The usual estimator of σ^2, $\hat{\sigma}^2 \equiv \mathrm{SSR}/(N-K)$, where $\mathrm{SSR} = \sum_{i=1}^{N} \hat{u}_i^2$ is the OLS sum of squared residuals, is easily shown to be consistent. (Using N or $N-K$ in the denominator does not affect consistency.) When we also replace $\mathrm{E}(\mathbf{x}'\mathbf{x})$ with the sample average $N^{-1}\sum_{i=1}^{N} \mathbf{x}_i'\mathbf{x}_i = (\mathbf{X}'\mathbf{X}/N)$, we get

$$\widehat{\mathrm{Avar}(\hat{\boldsymbol{\beta}})} = \hat{\sigma}^2(\mathbf{X}'\mathbf{X})^{-1}. \tag{4.10}$$

The right-hand side of equation (4.10) should be familiar: it is the usual OLS variance matrix estimator under the classical linear model assumptions. The bottom line of Theorem 4.2 is that, under Assumptions OLS.1–OLS.3, the usual OLS standard errors, t statistics, and F statistics are asymptotically valid. Showing that the F statistic is approximately valid is done by deriving the Wald test for linear restrictions of the form $\mathbf{R}\boldsymbol{\beta} = \mathbf{r}$ (see Chapter 3). Then the F statistic is simply a degrees-of-freedom-adjusted Wald statistic, which is where the F distribution (as opposed to the chi-square distribution) arises.

4.2.3 Heteroskedasticity-Robust Inference

If Assumption OLS.1 fails, we are in potentially serious trouble, as OLS is not even consistent. In the next chapter we discuss the important method of instrumental variables that can be used to obtain consistent estimators of $\boldsymbol{\beta}$ when Assumption OLS.1 fails. Assumption OLS.2 is also needed for consistency, but there is rarely any reason to examine its failure.

Failure of Assumption OLS.3 has less serious consequences than failure of Assumption OLS.1. As we have already seen, Assumption OLS.3 has nothing to do with consistency of $\hat{\boldsymbol{\beta}}$. Further, the proof of asymptotic normality based on equation (4.8) is still valid without Assumption OLS.3, but the final asymptotic variance is different. We have assumed OLS.3 for deriving the limiting distribution because it implies the asymptotic validity of the usual OLS standard errors and test statistics. Typically, regression packages assume OLS.3 as the default in reporting statistics.

Often there are reasons to believe that Assumption OLS.3 might fail, in which case equation (4.10) is no longer a valid estimate of even the asymptotic variance matrix. If we make the zero conditional mean assumption (4.3), one solution to violation of Assumption OLS.3 is to specify a model for $\mathrm{Var}(y \mid \mathbf{x})$, estimate this model, and apply **weighted least squares** (WLS): for observation i, y_i, and every element of $\mathbf{x}_i$ (including unity) are divided by an estimate of the conditional standard deviation $[\mathrm{Var}(y_i \mid \mathbf{x}_i)]^{1/2}$, and OLS is applied to the weighted data (see Wooldridge (2009a, Chap. 8) for details). This procedure leads to a different estimator of $\boldsymbol{\beta}$. We discuss

WLS in the more general context of nonlinear regression in Chapter 12. Lately, it has become more popular to estimate $\boldsymbol{\beta}$ by OLS even when heteroskedasticity is suspected but to adjust the standard errors and test statistics so that they are valid in the presence of arbitrary heteroskedasticity. Because these standard errors are valid whether or not Assumption OLS.3 holds, this method is easier than a weighted least squares procedure. What we sacrifice is potential efficiency gains from WLS (see Chapter 14). But, efficiency gains from WLS are guaranteed only if the model for $\mathrm{Var}(y \mid \mathbf{x})$ is correct (although gains can often be realized with a misspecified variance model). As a more subtle point, WLS is generally inconsistent if $\mathrm{E}(u \mid \mathbf{x}) \neq 0$ but Assumption OLS.1 holds, so WLS is inappropriate for estimating linear projections. Especially with large sample sizes, the presence of heteroskedasticity need not affect one's ability to perform accurate inference using OLS. But we need to compute standard errors and test statistics appropriately.

The adjustment needed to the asymptotic variance follows from the proof of Theorem 4.2: without OLS.3, the asymptotic variance of $\hat{\boldsymbol{\beta}}$ is $\mathrm{Avar}(\hat{\boldsymbol{\beta}}) = \mathbf{A}^{-1}\mathbf{B}\mathbf{A}^{-1}/N$, where the $K \times K$ matrices $\mathbf{A}$ and $\mathbf{B}$ were defined earlier. We already know how to consistently estimate $\mathbf{A}$. Estimation of $\mathbf{B}$ is also straightforward. First, by the law of large numbers, $N^{-1}\sum_{i=1}^{N} u_i^2 \mathbf{x}_i'\mathbf{x}_i \xrightarrow{p} \mathrm{E}(u^2\mathbf{x}'\mathbf{x}) = \mathbf{B}$. Now, since the u_i are not observed, we replace u_i with the OLS residual $\hat{u}_i = y_i - \mathbf{x}_i\hat{\boldsymbol{\beta}}$. This leads to the consistent estimator $\hat{\mathbf{B}} \equiv N^{-1}\sum_{i=1}^{N} \hat{u}_i^2 \mathbf{x}_i'\mathbf{x}_i$. See White (2001) and Problem 4.4.

The heteroskedasticity-robust variance matrix estimator of $\hat{\boldsymbol{\beta}}$ is $\hat{\mathbf{A}}^{-1}\hat{\mathbf{B}}\hat{\mathbf{A}}^{-1}/N$ or, after cancellations involving the sample sizes,

$$\widehat{\mathrm{Avar}(\hat{\boldsymbol{\beta}})} = (\mathbf{X}'\mathbf{X})^{-1}\left(\sum_{i=1}^{N} \hat{u}_i^2 \mathbf{x}_i'\mathbf{x}_i\right)(\mathbf{X}'\mathbf{X})^{-1}. \tag{4.11}$$

This matrix was introduced in econometrics by White (1980b), although some attribute it to either Eicker (1967) or Huber (1967), statisticians who discovered robust variance matrices. The square roots of the diagonal elements of equation (4.11) are often called the **White standard errors** or **Huber standard errors**, or some hyphenated combination of the names Eicker, Huber, and White. It is probably best to just call them **heteroskedasticity-robust standard errors**, since this term describes their purpose. Remember, these standard errors are asymptotically valid in the presence of any kind of heteroskedasticity, including homoskedasticity.

Robust standard errors are often reported in applied cross-sectional work, especially when the sample size is large. Sometimes they are reported along with the usual OLS standard errors; sometimes they are presented in place of them. Several regression packages now report these standard errors as an option, so it is easy to obtain heteroskedasticity-robust standard errors.

Sometimes, as a degrees-of-freedom correction, the matrix in equation (4.11) is multiplied by $N/(N-K)$. This procedure guarantees that, if the $\hat{u}_i^2$ were constant across i (an unlikely event in practice, but the strongest evidence of homoskedasticity possible), then the usual OLS standard errors would be obtained. There is some evidence that the degrees-of-freedom adjustment improves finite sample performance. There are other ways to adjust equation (4.11) to improve its small-sample properties—see, for example, MacKinnon and White (1985)—but if N is large relative to K, these adjustments typically make little difference.

Once standard errors are obtained, t statistics are computed in the usual way. These are robust to heteroskedasticity of unknown form, and can be used to test single restrictions. The t statistics computed from heteroskedasticity robust standard errors are **heteroskedasticity-robust *t* statistics**. Confidence intervals are also obtained in the usual way.

When Assumption OLS.3 fails, the usual F statistic is not valid for testing multiple linear restrictions, even asymptotically. Many packages allow robust testing with a simple command. If the hypotheses are written as

$$\mathrm{H}_0\colon \mathbf{R}\boldsymbol{\beta} = \mathbf{r}, \tag{4.12}$$

where $\mathbf{R}$ is $Q \times K$ and has rank $Q \leq K$, and $\mathbf{r}$ is $Q \times 1$, then the heteroskedasticity-robust Wald statistic for testing equation (4.12) is

$$W = (\mathbf{R}\hat{\boldsymbol{\beta}} - \mathbf{r})'(\mathbf{R}\hat{\mathbf{V}}\mathbf{R}')^{-1}(\mathbf{R}\hat{\boldsymbol{\beta}} - \mathbf{r}), \tag{4.13}$$

where $\hat{\mathbf{V}}$ is given in equation (4.11). Under H_0, $W \overset{a}{\sim} \chi^2_Q$. The Wald statistic can be turned into an approximate $\mathscr{F}_{Q,N-K}$ random variable by dividing it by Q (and usually making the degrees-of-freedom adjustment to $\hat{\mathbf{V}}$). But there is nothing wrong with using equation (4.13) directly.

4.2.4 Lagrange Multiplier (Score) Tests

In the partitioned model

$$y = \mathbf{x}_1\boldsymbol{\beta}_1 + \mathbf{x}_2\boldsymbol{\beta}_2 + u, \tag{4.14}$$

under Assumptions OLS.1–OLS.3, where $\mathbf{x}_1$ is $1 \times K_1$ and $\mathbf{x}_2$ is $1 \times K_2$, we know that the hypothesis $\mathrm{H}_0\colon \boldsymbol{\beta}_2 = \mathbf{0}$ is easily tested (asymptotically) using a standard F test. There is another approach to testing such hypotheses that is sometimes useful, especially for computing heteroskedasticity-robust tests and for nonlinear models.

Let $\tilde{\boldsymbol{\beta}}_1$ be the estimator of $\boldsymbol{\beta}_1$ under the null hypothesis $\mathrm{H}_0\colon \boldsymbol{\beta}_2 = \mathbf{0}$; this is called the estimator from the **restricted model**. Define the restricted OLS residuals as $\tilde{u}_i =$

$y_i - \mathbf{x}_{i1}\tilde{\boldsymbol{\beta}}_1$, $i = 1, 2, \ldots, N$. Under H_0, $\mathbf{x}_{i2}$ should be, up to sample variation, uncorrelated with $\tilde{u}_i$ in the sample. The Lagrange multiplier or score principle is based on this observation. It turns out that a valid test statistic is obtained as follows: Run the OLS regression

$$\tilde{u} \text{ on } \mathbf{x}_1, \mathbf{x}_2 \tag{4.15}$$

(where the observation index i has been suppressed). Assuming that $\mathbf{x}_1$ contains a constant (that is, the null model contains a constant), let R_u^2 denote the usual R-squared from the regression (4.15). Then the **Lagrange multiplier (LM)** or **score statistic** is $LM \equiv NR_u^2$. These names come from different features of the constrained optimization problem; see Rao (1948), Aitchison and Silvey (1958), and Chapter 12. Because of its form, LM is also referred to as an **N-R-squared test**. Under H_0, $LM \overset{a}{\sim} \chi^2_{K_2}$, where K_2 is the number of restrictions being tested. If NR_u^2 is sufficiently large, then $\tilde{u}$ is significantly correlated with $\mathbf{x}_2$, and the null hypothesis will be rejected.

It is important to include $\mathbf{x}_1$ along with $\mathbf{x}_2$ in regression (4.15). In other words, the OLS residuals from the null model should be regressed on *all* explanatory variables, even though $\tilde{u}$ is orthogonal to $\mathbf{x}_1$ in the sample. If $\mathbf{x}_1$ is excluded, then the resulting statistic generally does *not* have a chi-square distribution when $\mathbf{x}_2$ and $\mathbf{x}_1$ are correlated. If $\mathrm{E}(\mathbf{x}_1'\mathbf{x}_2) = \mathbf{0}$, then we can exclude $\mathbf{x}_1$ from regression (4.15), but this orthogonality rarely holds in applications. If $\mathbf{x}_1$ does not include a constant, R_u^2 should be the **uncentered R-squared**: the total sum of squares in the denominator is obtained without demeaning the dependent variable, $\tilde{u}$. When $\mathbf{x}_1$ includes a constant, the usual centered R-squared and uncentered R-squared are identical because $\sum_{i=1}^N \tilde{u}_i = 0$.

Example 4.1 (Wage Equation for Married, Working Women): Consider a wage equation for married, working women:

$$\log(wage) = \beta_0 + \beta_1 exper + \beta_2 exper^2 + \beta_3 educ$$
$$+ \beta_4 age + \beta_5 kidslt6 + \beta_6 kidsge6 + u, \tag{4.16}$$

where the last three variables are the woman's age, number of children less than six, and number of children at least six years of age, respectively. We can test whether, after the productivity variables experience and education are controlled for, women are paid differently depending on their age and number of children. The F statistic for the hypothesis H_0: $\beta_4 = 0, \beta_5 = 0, \beta_6 = 0$ is $F = [(R_{ur}^2 - R_r^2)/(1 - R_{ur}^2)] \cdot [(N - 7)/3]$, where R_{ur}^2 and R_r^2 are the unrestricted and restricted R-squareds; under H_0 (and homoskedasticity), $F \sim \mathscr{F}_{3, N-7}$. To obtain the LM statistic, we estimate the equation without *age*, *kidslt6*, and *kidsge6*; let $\tilde{u}$ denote the OLS residuals. Then, the *LM* statistic is NR_u^2 from the regression $\tilde{u}$ on 1, *exper*, $exper^2$, *educ*, *age*, *kidslt6*, and *kidsge6*, where the 1 denotes that we include an intercept. Under H_0 and homoskedasticity, $NR_u^2 \overset{a}{\sim} \chi_3^2$.

Using the data on the 428 working, married women in MROZ.RAW (from Mroz, 1987), we obtain the following estimated equation:

$$\begin{aligned}\log(\widehat{wage}) = \underset{\substack{(.317)\\ [.318]}}{-.421} + \underset{\substack{(.013)\\ [.015]}}{.040}\, exper - \underset{\substack{(.00040)\\ [.00041]}}{.00078}\, exper^2 + \underset{\substack{(.014)\\ [.014]}}{.108}\, educ \\ - \underset{\substack{(.0053)\\ [.0059]}}{.0015}\, age - \underset{\substack{(.089)\\ [.106]}}{.061}\, kidslt6 - \underset{\substack{(.028)\\ [.029]}}{.015}\, kidsge6, \qquad R^2 = .158\end{aligned}$$

where the quantities in brackets are the heteroskedasticity-robust standard errors. The *F* statistic for joint significance of *age*, *kidslt6*, and *kidsge6* turns out to be about .24, which gives p-value $\approx .87$. Regressing the residuals $\tilde{u}$ from the restricted model on all exogenous variables gives an R-squared of .0017, so $LM = 428(.0017) = .728$, and p-value $\approx .87$. Thus, the *F* and *LM* tests give virtually identical results.

The test from regression (4.15) maintains Assumption OLS.3 under H_0, just like the usual *F* test. It turns out to be easy to obtain a heteroskedasticity-robust *LM* statistic. To see how to do so, let us look at the formula for the *LM* statistic from regression (4.15) in more detail. After some algebra we can write

$$LM = \left(N^{-1/2}\sum_{i=1}^{N}\hat{\mathbf{r}}_i'\tilde{u}_i\right)'\left(\tilde{\sigma}^2 N^{-1}\sum_{i=1}^{N}\hat{\mathbf{r}}_i'\hat{\mathbf{r}}_i\right)^{-1}\left(N^{-1/2}\sum_{i=1}^{N}\hat{\mathbf{r}}_i'\tilde{u}_i\right),$$

where $\tilde{\sigma}^2 \equiv N^{-1}\sum_{i=1}^{N}\tilde{u}_i^2$ and each $\hat{\mathbf{r}}_i$ is a $1 \times K_2$ vector of OLS residuals from the (multivariate) regression of $\mathbf{x}_{i2}$ on $\mathbf{x}_{i1}$, $i = 1, 2, \ldots, N$. This statistic is not robust to heteroskedasticity because the matrix in the middle is not a consistent estimator of the asymptotic variance of $(N^{-1/2}\sum_{i=1}^{N}\hat{\mathbf{r}}_i'\tilde{u}_i)$ under heteroskedasticity. Following the reasoning in Section 4.2.3, a heteroskedasticity-robust statistic is

$$\begin{aligned}LM &= \left(N^{-1/2}\sum_{i=1}^{N}\hat{\mathbf{r}}_i'\tilde{u}_i\right)'\left(N^{-1}\sum_{i=1}^{N}\tilde{u}_i^2\hat{\mathbf{r}}_i'\hat{\mathbf{r}}_i\right)^{-1}\left(N^{-1/2}\sum_{i=1}^{N}\hat{\mathbf{r}}_i'\tilde{u}_i\right)\\ &= \left(\sum_{i=1}^{N}\hat{\mathbf{r}}_i'\tilde{u}_i\right)'\left(\sum_{i=1}^{N}\tilde{u}_i^2\hat{\mathbf{r}}_i'\hat{\mathbf{r}}_i\right)^{-1}\left(\sum_{i=1}^{N}\hat{\mathbf{r}}_i'\tilde{u}_i\right).\end{aligned}$$

Dropping the i subscript, this is easily obtained, as $N - \mathrm{SSR}_0$ from the OLS regression (without an intercept)

$$1 \text{ on } \tilde{u} \cdot \hat{\mathbf{r}}, \tag{4.17}$$

where $\tilde{u} \cdot \hat{\mathbf{r}} = (\tilde{u} \cdot \hat{r}_1, \tilde{u} \cdot \hat{r}_2, \ldots, \tilde{u} \cdot \hat{r}_{K_2})$ is the $1 \times K_2$ vector obtained by multiplying $\tilde{u}$ by each element of $\hat{\mathbf{r}}$ and SSR_0 is just the usual sum of squared residuals from regression (4.17). Thus, we first regress each element of $\mathbf{x}_2$ onto all of $\mathbf{x}_1$ and collect the residuals in $\hat{\mathbf{r}}$. Then we form $\tilde{u} \cdot \hat{\mathbf{r}}$ (observation by observation) and run the regression in (4.17); $N - \mathrm{SSR}_0$ from this regression is distributed asymptotically as $\chi^2_{K_2}$. (Do not be thrown off by the fact that the dependent variable in regression (4.17) is unity for each observation; a nonzero sum of squared residuals is reported when you run OLS without an intercept.) For more details, see Davidson and MacKinnon (1985, 1993) or Wooldridge (1991a, 1995b).

Example 4.1 (continued): To obtain the heteroskedasticity-robust *LM* statistic for H_0: $\beta_4 = 0, \beta_5 = 0, \beta_6 = 0$ in equation (4.16), we estimate the restricted model as before and obtain $\tilde{u}$. Then we run the regressions (1) *age* on 1, *exper*, *exper*^{2}, *educ*; (2) *kidslt6* on 1, *exper*, *exper*^{2}, *educ*; (3) *kidsge6* on 1, *exper*, *exper*^{2}, *educ*; and obtain the residuals $\hat{r}_1$, $\hat{r}_2$, and $\hat{r}_3$, respectively. The *LM* statistic is $N - \mathrm{SSR}_0$ from the regression 1 on $\tilde{u} \cdot \hat{r}_1$, $\tilde{u} \cdot \hat{r}_2$, $\tilde{u} \cdot \hat{r}_3$, and $N - \mathrm{SSR}_0 \overset{a}{\sim} \chi^2_3$.

When we apply this result to the data in MROZ.RAW we get $LM = .51$, which is very small for a χ^2_3 random variable: p-value $\approx .92$. For comparison, the heteroskedasticity-robust Wald statistic (scaled by Stata to have an approximate F distribution) also yields p-value $\approx .92$.

4.3 Ordinary Least Squares Solutions to the Omitted Variables Problem

4.3.1 Ordinary Least Squares Ignoring the Omitted Variables

Because it is so prevalent in applied work, we now consider the omitted variables problem in more detail. A model that assumes an additive effect of the omitted variable is

$$\mathrm{E}(y \mid x_1, x_2, \ldots, x_K, q) = \beta_0 + \beta_1 x_1 + \beta_2 x_2 + \cdots + \beta_K x_K + \gamma q, \tag{4.18}$$

where q is the omitted factor. In particular, we are interested in the β_j, which are the partial effects of the observed explanatory variables, holding the other explanatory variables constant, *including* the unobservable q. In the context of this additive model, there is no point in allowing for more than one unobservable; any omitted factors are lumped into q. Henceforth we simply refer to q as the omitted variable.

A good example of equation (4.18) is seen when y is log(*wage*) and q includes ability. If x_K denotes a measure of education, β_K in equation (4.18) measures the partial effect of education on wages controlling for—or holding fixed—the level of ability (as well as other observed characteristics). This effect is most interesting from a policy perspective because it provides a causal interpretation of the return to education: β_K is the expected proportionate increase in wage if someone from the working population is exogenously given another year of education.

Viewing equation (4.18) as a structural model, we can always write it in error form as

$$y = \beta_0 + \beta_1 x_1 + \beta_2 x_2 + \cdots + \beta_K x_K + \gamma q + v, \tag{4.19}$$

$$\mathrm{E}(v \mid x_1, x_2, \ldots, x_K, q) = 0, \tag{4.20}$$

where v is the **structural error**. One way to handle the nonobservability of q is to put it into the error term. In doing so, nothing is lost by assuming $\mathrm{E}(q) = 0$, because an intercept is included in equation (4.19). Putting q into the error term means we rewrite equation (4.19) as

$$y = \beta_0 + \beta_1 x_1 + \beta_2 x_2 + \cdots + \beta_K x_K + u, \tag{4.21}$$

$$u \equiv \gamma q + v. \tag{4.22}$$

The error u in equation (4.21) consists of two parts. Under equation (4.20), v has zero mean and is uncorrelated with $x_1, x_2, \ldots, x_K$ (and q). By normalization, q also has zero mean. Thus, $\mathrm{E}(u) = 0$. However, u is uncorrelated with x_j if and only if q is uncorrelated with x_j. If q is correlated with any of the regressors, then so is u, and we have an endogeneity problem. We cannot expect OLS to consistently estimate *any* β_j. Although $\mathrm{E}(u \mid \mathbf{x}) \neq \mathrm{E}(u)$ in equation (4.21), the β_j do have a structural interpretation because they appear in equation (4.19).

It is easy to characterize the plims of the OLS estimators when the omitted variable is ignored; we will call this the **OLS omitted variables inconsistency** or **OLS omitted variables bias** (even though the latter term is not always precise). Write the linear projection of q onto the observable explanatory variables as

$$q = \delta_0 + \delta_1 x_1 + \cdots + \delta_K x_K + r, \tag{4.23}$$

where, by definition of a linear projection, $\mathrm{E}(r) = 0$, $\mathrm{Cov}(x_j, r) = 0$, $j = 1, 2, \ldots, K$. The parameter δ_j measures the relationship between q and x_j after "partialing out" the other x_h. Then we can easily infer the plim of the OLS estimators from regressing y onto $1, x_1, \ldots, x_K$ by finding an equation that does satisfy Assumptions OLS.1 and

OLS.2. Plugging equation (4.23) into equation (4.19) and doing simple algrebra gives

$$y = (\beta_0 + \gamma\delta_0) + (\beta_1 + \gamma\delta_1)x_1 + (\beta_2 + \gamma\delta_2)x_2 + \cdots + (\beta_K + \gamma\delta_K)x_K + v + \gamma r$$

Now, the error $v + \gamma r$ has zero mean and is uncorrelated with each regressor. It follows that we can just read off the plim of the OLS estimators from the regression of y on $1, x_1, \ldots, x_K$: $\text{plim}\,\hat{\beta}_j = \beta_j + \gamma\delta_j$. Sometimes it is assumed that most of the δ_j are zero. When the correlation between q and a particular variable, say x_K, is the focus, a common (usually implicit) assumption is that all δ_j in equation (4.23) except the intercept and coefficient on x_K are zero. Then $\text{plim}\,\hat{\beta}_j = \beta_j$, $j = 1, \ldots, K-1$, and

$$\text{plim}\,\hat{\beta}_K = \beta_K + \gamma[\text{Cov}(x_K, q)/\text{Var}(x_K)] \tag{4.24}$$

(because $\delta_K = \text{Cov}(x_K, q)/\text{Var}(x_K)$ in this case). This formula gives us a simple way to determine the sign, and perhaps the magnitude, of the inconsistency in $\hat{\beta}_K$. If $\gamma > 0$ and x_K and q are positively correlated, the asymptotic bias is positive. The other combinations are easily worked out. If x_K has substantial variation in the population relative to the covariance between x_K and q, then the bias can be small. In the general case of equation (4.23), it is difficult to sign δ_K because it measures a partial correlation. It is for this reason that $\delta_j = 0$, $j = 1, \ldots, K-1$ is often maintained for determining the likely asymptotic bias in $\hat{\beta}_K$ when only x_K is endogenous.

Example 4.2 (Wage Equation with Unobserved Ability): Write a structural wage equation explicitly as

$$\log(wage) = \beta_0 + \beta_1 exper + \beta_2 exper^2 + \beta_3 educ + \gamma\, abil + v,$$

where v has the structural error property $\text{E}(v \mid exper, educ, abil) = 0$. If $abil$ is uncorrelated with $exper$ and $exper^2$ once $educ$ has been partialed out—that is, $abil = \delta_0 + \delta_3 educ + r$ with r uncorrelated with $exper$ and $exper^2$—then $\text{plim}\,\hat{\beta}_3 = \beta_3 + \gamma\delta_3$. Under these assumptions, the coefficients on $exper$ and $exper^2$ are consistently estimated by the OLS regression that omits ability. If $\delta_3 > 0$ then $\text{plim}\,\hat{\beta}_3 > \beta_3$ (because $\gamma > 0$ by definition), and the return to education is likely to be overestimated in large samples.

4.3.2 Proxy Variable–Ordinary Least Squares Solution

Omitted variables bias can be eliminated, or at least mitigated, if a **proxy variable** is available for the unobserved variable q. There are two formal requirements for a proxy variable for q. The first is that the proxy variable should be **redundant** (sometimes called **ignorable**) in the structural equation. If z is a proxy variable for q, then the most natural statement of redundancy of z in equation (4.18) is

$$E(y \mid \mathbf{x}, q, z) = E(y \mid \mathbf{x}, q). \tag{4.25}$$

Condition (4.25) is easy to interpret: z is irrelevant for explaining y, in a conditional mean sense, once $\mathbf{x}$ and q have been controlled for. This assumption on a proxy variable is virtually always made (sometimes only implicitly), and it is rarely controversial: the only reason we bother with z in the first place is that we cannot get data on q. Anyway, we cannot get very far without condition (4.25). In the wage–education example, let q be ability and z be IQ score. By definition it is ability that affects wage: IQ would not matter if true ability were known.

Condition (4.25) is somewhat stronger than needed when unobservables appear additively as in equation (4.18); it suffices to assume that v in equation (4.19) is simply uncorrelated with z. But we will focus on condition (4.25) because it is natural, and because we need it to cover models where q interacts with some observed covariates.

The second requirement of a good proxy variable is more complicated. We require that the correlation between the omitted variable q and each x_j be zero once we *partial out* z. This is easily stated in terms of a linear projection:

$$L(q \mid 1, x_1, \ldots, x_K, z) = L(q \mid 1, z). \tag{4.26}$$

It is also helpful to see this relationship in terms of an equation with an unobserved error. Write q as a linear function of z and an error term as

$$q = \theta_0 + \theta_1 z + r, \tag{4.27}$$

where, by definition, $E(r) = 0$ and $\text{Cov}(z, r) = 0$ because $\theta_0 + \theta_1 z$ is the linear projection of q on 1, z. If z is a reasonable proxy for q, $\theta_1 \neq 0$ (and we usually think in terms of $\theta_1 > 0$). But condition (4.26) assumes much more: it is equivalent to

$$\text{Cov}(x_j, r) = 0, \qquad j = 1, 2, \ldots, K.$$

This condition requires z to be closely enough related to q so that once it is included in equation (4.27), the x_j are not partially correlated with q.

Before showing why these two proxy variable requirements do the trick, we should head off some possible confusion. The definition of proxy variable here is not universal. While a proxy variable is always assumed to satisfy the redundancy condition (4.25), it is not always assumed to have the second property. In Chapter 5 we will use the notion of an *indicator* of q, which satisfies condition (4.25) but not the second proxy variable assumption.

To obtain an estimable equation, replace q in equation (4.19) with equation (4.27) to get

$$y = (\beta_0 + \gamma\theta_0) + \beta_1 x_1 + \cdots + \beta_K x_K + \gamma\theta_1 z + (\gamma r + v). \tag{4.28}$$

Under the assumptions made, the composite error term $u \equiv \gamma r + v$ is uncorrelated with x_j for all j; redundancy of z in equation (4.18) means that z is uncorrelated with v and, by definition, z is uncorrelated with r. It follows immediately from Theorem 4.1 that the OLS regression y on $1, x_1, x_2, \ldots, x_K, z$ produces consistent estimators of $(\beta_0 + \gamma\theta_0), \beta_1, \beta_2, \ldots, \beta_K$, and $\gamma\theta_1$. Thus, we can estimate the partial effect of each of the x_j in equation (4.18) under the proxy variable assumptions.

When z is an **imperfect proxy**, then r in equation (4.27) is correlated with one or more of the x_j. Generally, when we do not impose condition (4.26) and write the linear projection as

$$q = \theta_0 + \rho_1 x_1 + \cdots + \rho_K x_K + \theta_1 z + r,$$

the proxy variable regression gives $\text{plim}\,\hat{\beta}_j = \beta_j + \gamma\rho_j$. Thus, OLS with an imperfect proxy is inconsistent. The hope is that the ρ_j are smaller in magnitude than if z were omitted from the linear projection, and this can usually be argued if z is a reasonable proxy for q; but see the end of this subsection for further discussion.

If including z induces substantial collinearity, it might be better to use OLS without the proxy variable. However, in making these decisions we must recognize that including z reduces the error variance if $\theta_1 \neq 0$: $\text{Var}(\gamma r + v) < \text{Var}(\gamma q + v)$ because $\text{Var}(r) < \text{Var}(q)$, and v is uncorrelated with both r and q. Including a proxy variable can actually reduce asymptotic variances as well as mitigate bias.

Example 4.3 (Using IQ as a Proxy for Ability): We apply the proxy variable method to the data on working men in NLS80.RAW, which was used by Blackburn and Neumark (1992), to estimate the structural model

$$\begin{aligned} \log(wage) = {} & \beta_0 + \beta_1\, exper + \beta_2\, tenure + \beta_3\, married \\ & + \beta_4\, south + \beta_5\, urban + \beta_6\, black + \beta_7\, educ + \gamma\, abil + v, \end{aligned} \tag{4.29}$$

where *exper* is labor market experience, *married* is a dummy variable equal to unity if married, *south* is a dummy variable for the southern region, *urban* is a dummy variable for living in an SMSA, *black* is a race indicator, and *educ* is years of schooling. We assume that *IQ* satisfies the proxy variable assumptions: in the linear projection $abil = \theta_0 + \theta_1 IQ + r$, where r has zero mean and is uncorrelated with *IQ*, we also assume that r is uncorrelated with experience, tenure, education, and other factors appearing in equation (4.29). The estimated equations without and with *IQ* are

$$
\begin{aligned}
\widehat{\log(wage)} = {} & \underset{(0.11)}{5.40} + \underset{(.003)}{.014}\, exper + \underset{(.002)}{.012}\, tenure + \underset{(.039)}{.199}\, married \\
& - \underset{(.026)}{.091}\, south + \underset{(.027)}{.184}\, urban - \underset{(.038)}{.188}\, black + \underset{(.006)}{.065}\, educ.
\end{aligned}
$$

$N = 935, \qquad R^2 = .253$

$$
\begin{aligned}
\widehat{\log(wage)} = {} & \underset{(0.13)}{5.18} + \underset{(.003)}{.014}\, exper + \underset{(.002)}{.011}\, tenure + \underset{(.039)}{.200}\, married \\
& - \underset{(.026)}{.080}\, south + \underset{(.027)}{.182}\, urban - \underset{(.039)}{.143}\, black + \underset{(.007)}{.054}\, educ \\
& + \underset{(.0010)}{.0036}\, IQ.
\end{aligned}
$$

$N = 935, \qquad R^2 = .263$

Notice how the return to schooling has fallen from about 6.5 percent to about 5.4 percent when *IQ* is added to the regression. This is what we expect to happen if ability and schooling are (partially) positively correlated. Of course, these are just the findings from one sample. Adding *IQ* explains only one percentage point more of the variation in log(*wage*), and the equation predicts that 15 more *IQ* points (one standard deviation) increases *wage* by about 5.4 percent. The standard error on the return to education has increased, but the 95 percent confidence interval is still fairly tight.

Often the outcome of the dependent variable from an earlier time period can be a useful proxy variable.

Example 4.4 (Effects of Job Training Grants on Worker Productivity): The data in JTRAIN1.RAW are for 157 Michigan manufacturing firms for the years 1987, 1988, and 1989. These data are from Holzer, Block, Cheatham, and Knott (1993). The goal is to determine the effectiveness of job training grants on firm productivity. For this exercise, we use only the 54 firms in 1988 that reported nonmissing values of the scrap rate (number of items out of 100 that must be scrapped). No firms were awarded grants in 1987; in 1988, 19 of the 54 firms were awarded grants. If the training grant has the intended effect, the average scrap rate should be lower among firms receiving a grant. The problem is that the grants were not randomly assigned: whether or not a firm received a grant could be related to other factors unobservable to the econometrician that affect productivity. In the simplest case, we can write (for the 1988 cross section)

$$\log(scrap) = \beta_0 + \beta_1 grant + \gamma q + v,$$

where v is orthogonal to *grant* but q contains unobserved productivity factors that might be correlated with *grant*, a binary variable equal to unity if the firm received a job training grant. Since we have the scrap rate in the previous year, we can use $\log(scrap_{-1})$ as a proxy variable for q:

$$q = \theta_0 + \theta_1 \log(scrap_{-1}) + r,$$

where r has zero mean and, by definition, is uncorrelated with $\log(scrap_{-1})$. We hope that r has no or little correlation with *grant*. Plugging in for q gives the estimable model

$$\log(scrap) = \delta_0 + \beta_1 grant + \gamma\theta_1 \log(scrap_{-1}) + r + v.$$

From this equation, we see that β_1 measures the proportionate difference in scrap rates for two firms having the *same* scrap rates in the previous year, but where one firm received a grant and the other did not. This is intuitively appealing. The estimated equations are

$$\widehat{\log(scrap)} = \underset{(.240)}{.409} + \underset{(.406)}{.057}\, grant.$$

$$N = 54, \qquad R^2 = .0004$$

$$\widehat{\log(scrap)} = \underset{(.089)}{.021} - \underset{(.147)}{.254}\, grant + \underset{(.044)}{.831}\, \log(scrap_{-1}).$$

$$N = 54, \qquad R^2 = .873$$

Without the lagged scrap rate, we see that the grant appears, if anything, to reduce productivity (by increasing the scrap rate), although the coefficient is statistically insignificant. When the lagged dependent variable is included, the coefficient on grant changes signs, becomes economically large—firms awarded grants have scrap rates about 25.4 percent less than those not given grants—and the effect is significant at the 5 percent level against a one-sided alternative. (The more accurate estimate of the percentage effect is $100 \cdot [\exp(-.254) - 1] = -22.4\%$; see Problem 4.1(a).)

We can always use more than one proxy for x_K. For example, it might be that $\mathrm{E}(q \mid \mathbf{x}, z_1, z_2) = \mathrm{E}(q \mid z_1, z_2) = \theta_0 + \theta_1 z_1 + \theta_2 z_2$, in which case including both z_1 and z_2 as regressors along with $x_1, \ldots, x_K$ solves the omitted variable problem. The weaker condition that the error r in the equation $q = \theta_0 + \theta_1 z_1 + \theta_2 z_2 + r$ is uncorrelated with $x_1, \ldots, x_K$ also suffices.

The data set NLS80.RAW also contains each man's score on the knowledge of the world of work (KWW) test. Problem 4.11 asks you to reestimate equation (4.29) when KWW and IQ are both used as proxies for ability.

Before ending this subsection, it is useful to formally show how not all variables are suitable proxy variables, in the sense that adding them to a regression can actually leave us worse off than excluding them. Intuitively, variables that have low correlation with the omitted variable make poor proxies. For illustration, consider a simple regression model and the extreme case where a proposed proxy variable is uncorrelated with the error term:

$$y = \beta_0 + \beta_1 x + u$$

$$\mathrm{E}(u) = 0, \qquad \mathrm{Cov}(z, u) = 0,$$

where all quantities are scalars and u includes the omitted variable. Let $\tilde{\beta}_1$ denote the OLS slope estimator from regressing y on 1, x and let $\hat{\beta}_1$ be the slope on x from the regression y on 1, x, z (using a random sample of size N in each case). From the omitted variable inconsistency formula (4.24), we know that $\mathrm{plim}(\tilde{\beta}_1) = \beta_1 + \mathrm{Cov}(x, u)/\mathrm{Var}(x)$. Further, from the two-step projection result (Property LP.7 in Chapter 2), we can easily find the plim of $\hat{\beta}_1$. Let $a = x - \mathrm{L}(x \mid 1, z) = x - \pi_0 - \pi_1 z$ be the population residual from linearly projecting x onto z. Then $\mathrm{plim}(\hat{\beta}_1) = \beta_1 + \mathrm{Cov}(a, u)/\mathrm{Var}(a)$. Therefore, the absolute values of the inconsistencies are $|\mathrm{Cov}(x, u)|/\mathrm{Var}(x)$ and $|\mathrm{Cov}(a, u)|/\mathrm{Var}(a)$, respectively. Now, because z is uncorrelated with u, $\mathrm{Cov}(a, u) = \mathrm{Cov}(x, u)$, and so the numerators in the inconsistency terms are the same. Further, by a standard property of a population residual, $\mathrm{Var}(a) \leq \mathrm{Var}(x)$, with strict inequality unless z is also uncorrelated with x. We have shown that $|\mathrm{plim}(\hat{\beta}_1) - \beta_1| > |\mathrm{plim}(\tilde{\beta}_1) - \beta_1|$ whenever $\mathrm{Cov}(z, u) = 0$ and $\mathrm{Cov}(z, x) \neq 0$. In other words, OLS without the proxy has less inconsistency than OLS with the proxy (unless x is uncorrelated with u, too). The proxy variable estimator also has a larger asymptotic variance.

As we will see in Chapter 5, variables uncorrelated with u and correlated with x are very useful for identifying β_1, but they are not used as additional regressors in an OLS regression.

4.3.3 Models with Interactions in Unobservables: Random Coefficient Models

In some cases we might be concerned about interactions between unobservables and observable explanatory variables. Obtaining consistent estimators is more difficult in this case, but a good proxy variable can again solve the problem.

Write the structural model with unobservable q as

$$y = \beta_0 + \beta_1 x_1 + \cdots + \beta_K x_K + \gamma_1 q + \gamma_2 x_K q + v, \tag{4.30}$$

where we make a zero conditional mean assumption on the structural error v:

$$\mathrm{E}(v \mid \mathbf{x}, q) = 0. \tag{4.31}$$

For simplicity we have interacted q with only one explanatory variable, x_K.

Before discussing estimation of equation (4.30), we should have an interpretation for the parameters in this equation, as the interaction $x_K q$ is unobservable. (We discussed this topic more generally in Section 2.2.5.) If x_K is an essentially continuous variable, the partial effect of x_K on $\mathrm{E}(y \mid \mathbf{x}, q)$ is

$$\frac{\partial \mathrm{E}(y \mid \mathbf{x}, q)}{\partial x_K} = \beta_K + \gamma_2 q. \tag{4.32}$$

Thus, the partial effect of x_K actually depends on the level of q. Because q is not observed for anyone in the population, equation (4.32) can never be estimated, even if we could estimate γ_2 (which we cannot, in general). But we can average equation (4.32) across the population distribution of q. Assuming $\mathrm{E}(q) = 0$, the **average partial effect** (**APE**) of x_K is

$$\mathrm{E}(\beta_K + \gamma_2 q) = \beta_K. \tag{4.33}$$

A similar interpretation holds for discrete x_K. For example, if x_K is binary, then $\mathrm{E}(y \mid x_1, \ldots, x_{K-1}, 1, q) - \mathrm{E}(y \mid x_1, \ldots, x_{K-1}, 0, q) = \beta_K + \gamma_2 q$, and β_K is the average of this difference over the distribution of q. In this case, β_K is called the **average treatment effect (ATE)**. This name derives from the case where x_K represents receiving some "treatment," such as participation in a job training program or participation in a school voucher program. We will consider the binary treatment case further in Chapter 21, where we introduce a counterfactual framework for estimating average treatment effects.

It turns out that the assumption $\mathrm{E}(q) = 0$ is without loss of generality. Using simple algebra we can show that, if $\mu_q \equiv \mathrm{E}(q) \neq 0$, then we can consistently estimate $\beta_K + \gamma_2 \mu_q$, which is the average partial effect.

The model in equation (4.30) is sometimes called a **random coefficient model** because (in this case) one of the slope coefficients is "random"—that is, it depends on invidual-specific unobserved heterogeneity. One way to write the equation for a random draw i is $y_i = \beta_0 + \beta_1 x_{i1} + \cdots + \beta_{K-1} x_{i,K-1} + b_{iK} x_{iK} + u_i$, where $b_{iK} = \beta_K + \gamma_2 q_i$ is the random coefficient. Note that all other slope coefficients are assumed to be constant. Regardless of what we label the model, we are typically interested in estimating $\beta_K = \mathrm{E}(b_{iK})$.

If the elements of $\mathbf{x}$ are exogenous in the sense that $\mathrm{E}(q \mid \mathbf{x}) = 0$, then we can consistently estimate each of the β_j by an OLS regression, where q and $x_K q$ are just part of the error term. This result follows from iterated expectations applied to equation (4.30), which shows that $\mathrm{E}(y \mid \mathbf{x}) = \beta_0 + \beta_1 x_1 + \cdots + \beta_K x_K$ if $\mathrm{E}(q \mid \mathbf{x}) = 0$. The resulting equation probably has heteroskedasticity, but this is easily dealt with. Incidentally, this is a case where only assuming that q and $\mathbf{x}$ are uncorrelated would not be enough to ensure consistency of OLS: $x_K q$ and $\mathbf{x}$ can be correlated even if q and $\mathbf{x}$ are uncorrelated.

If q and $\mathbf{x}$ are correlated, we can consistently estimate the β_j by OLS if we have a suitable proxy variable for q. We still assume that the proxy variable, z, satisfies the redundancy condition (4.25). In the current model we must make a stronger proxy variable assumption than we did in Section 4.3.2:

$$\mathrm{E}(q \mid \mathbf{x}, z) = \mathrm{E}(q \mid z) = \theta_1 z, \tag{4.34}$$

where now we assume z has a zero mean in the population. Under these two proxy variable assumptions, iterated expectations gives

$$\mathrm{E}(y \mid \mathbf{x}, z) = \beta_0 + \beta_1 x_1 + \cdots + \beta_K x_K + \gamma_1 \theta_1 z + \gamma_2 \theta_1 x_K z, \tag{4.35}$$

and the parameters are consistently estimated by OLS.

If we do not define our proxy to have zero mean in the population, then estimating equation (4.35) by OLS does not consistently estimate β_K. If $\mathrm{E}(z) \neq 0$, then we would have to write $\mathrm{E}(q \mid z) = \theta_0 + \theta_1 z$, in which case the coefficient on x_K in equation (4.35) would be $\beta_K + \theta_0 \gamma_2$. In practice, we may not know the population mean of the proxy variable, in which case the proxy variable should be demeaned in the sample before interacting it with x_K.

If we maintain homoskedasticity in the structural model—that is, $\mathrm{Var}(y \mid \mathbf{x}, q, z) = \mathrm{Var}(y \mid \mathbf{x}, q) = \sigma^2$—then there must be heteroskedasticity in $\mathrm{Var}(y \mid \mathbf{x}, z)$. Using Property CV.3 in Appendix 2A, it can be shown that

$$\mathrm{Var}(y \mid \mathbf{x}, z) = \sigma^2 + (\gamma_1 + \gamma_2 x_K)^2 \, \mathrm{Var}(q \mid \mathbf{x}, z).$$

Even if $\text{Var}(q \mid \mathbf{x}, z)$ is constant, $\text{Var}(y \mid \mathbf{x}, z)$ depends on x_K. This situation is most easily dealt with by computing heteroskedasticity-robust statistics, which allows for heteroskedasticity of arbitrary form.

Example 4.5 (Return to Education Depends on Ability): Consider an extension of the wage equation (4.29):

$$\log(wage) = \beta_0 + \beta_1 exper + \beta_2 tenure + \beta_3 married + \beta_4 south$$
$$+ \beta_5 urban + \beta_6 black + \beta_7 educ + \gamma_1 abil + \gamma_2 educ{\cdot}abil + v \tag{4.36}$$

so that *educ* and *abil* have separate effects but also have an interactive effect. In this model the return to a year of schooling depends on *abil*: $\beta_7 + \gamma_2 abil$. Normalizing *abil* to have zero population mean, we see that the average of the return to education is simply β_7. We estimate this equation under the assumption that IQ is redundant in equation (4.36) and $\text{E}(abil \mid \mathbf{x}, IQ) = \text{E}(abil \mid IQ) = \theta_1(IQ - 100) \equiv \theta_1 IQ_0$, where IQ_0 is the population-demeaned IQ (IQ is constructed to have mean 100 in the population). We can estimate the β_j in equation (4.36) by replacing *abil* with IQ_0 and $educ{\cdot}abil$ with $educ{\cdot}IQ_0$ and doing OLS.

Using the sample of men in NLS80.RAW gives the following:

$$\widehat{\log(wage)} = \cdots + \underset{(.007)}{.052}\, educ - \underset{(.00516)}{.00094}\, IQ_0 + \underset{(.00038)}{.00034}\, educ \cdot IQ_0$$

$$N = 935, \qquad R^2 = .263$$

where the usual OLS standard errors are reported (if $\gamma_2 = 0$, homoskedasticity may be reasonable). The interaction term $educ{\cdot}IQ_0$ is not statistically significant, and the return to education at the average IQ, 5.2 percent, is similar to the estimate when the return to education is assumed to be constant. Thus there is little evidence for an interaction between education and ability. Incidentally, the F test for joint significance of IQ_0 and $educ{\cdot}IQ_0$ yields a p-value of about .0011, but the interaction term is not needed.

In this case, we happen to know the population mean of IQ, but in most cases we will not know the population mean of a proxy variable. Then, we should use the sample average to demean the proxy before interacting it with x_K; see Problem 4.8. Technically, using the sample average to estimate the population average should be reflected in the OLS standard errors. But, as you are asked to show in Problem 6.10 in Chapter 6, the adjustments generally have very small impacts on the standard errors and can safely be ignored.

In his study on the effects of computer usage on the wage structure in the United States, Krueger (1993) uses computer usage at home as a proxy for unobservables that might be correlated with computer usage at work; he also includes an interaction between the two computer usage dummies. Krueger does not demean the "uses computer at home" dummy before constructing the interaction, so his estimate on "uses a computer at work" does not have an average treatment effect interpretation. However, just as in Example 4.5, Krueger found that the interaction term is insignificant.

4.4 Properties of Ordinary Least Squares under Measurement Error

As we saw in Section 4.1, another way that endogenous explanatory variables can arise in economic applications occurs when one or more of the variables in our model contains **measurement error**. In this section, we derive the consequences of measurement error for ordinary least squares estimation.

The measurement error problem has a statistical structure similar to the omitted variable–proxy variable problem discussed in the previous section. However, they are conceptually very different. In the proxy variable case, we are looking for a variable that is somehow associated with the unobserved variable. In the measurement error case, the variable that we do not observe has a well-defined, quantitative meaning (such as a marginal tax rate or annual income), but our measures of it may contain error. For example, reported annual income is a measure of actual annual income, whereas IQ score is a proxy for ability.

Another important difference between the proxy variable and measurement error problems is that, in the latter case, often the mismeasured explanatory variable is the one whose effect is of primary interest. In the proxy variable case, we cannot estimate the effect of the omitted variable.

Before we turn to the analysis, it is important to remember that measurement error is an issue only when the variables on which we can collect data differ from the variables that influence decisions by individuals, families, firms, and so on. For example, suppose we are estimating the effect of peer group behavior on teenage drug usage, where the behavior of one's peer group is self-reported. Self-reporting may be a mismeasure of actual peer group behavior, but so what? We are probably more interested in the effects of how a teenager perceives his or her peer group.

4.4.1 Measurement Error in the Dependent Variable

We begin with the case where the dependent variable is the only variable measured with error. Let y^* denote the variable (in the population, as always) that we would like to explain. For example, y^* could be annual family saving. The regression model has the usual linear form

$$y^* = \beta_0 + \beta_1 x_1 + \cdots + \beta_K x_K + v \tag{4.37}$$

and we assume that it satisfies at least Assumptions OLS.1 and OLS.2. Typically, we are interested in $\mathrm{E}(y^* \mid x_1, \ldots, x_K)$. We let y represent the observable measure of y^* where $y \neq y^*$.

The population measurement error is defined as the difference between the observed value and the actual value:

$$e_0 = y - y^*. \tag{4.38}$$

For a random draw i from the population, we can write $e_{i0} = y_i - y_i^*$, but what is important is how the measurement error in the population is related to other factors. To obtain an estimable model, we write $y^* = y - e_0$, plug this into equation (4.37), and rearrange:

$$y = \beta_0 + \beta_1 x_1 + \cdots + \beta_K x_K + v + e_0. \tag{4.39}$$

Since $y, x_1, x_2, \ldots, x_K$ are observed, we can estimate this model by OLS. In effect, we just ignore the fact that y is an imperfect measure of y^* and proceed as usual.

When does OLS with y in place of y^* produce consistent estimators of the β_j? Since the original model (4.37) satisfies Assumption OLS.1, v has zero mean and is uncorrelated with each x_j. It is only natural to assume that the measurement error has zero mean; if it does not, this fact only affects estimation of the intercept, β_0. Much more important is what we assume about the relationship between the measurement error e_0 and the explanatory variables x_j. The usual assumption is that the measurement error in y is statistically independent of each explanatory variable, which implies that e_0 is uncorrelated with $\mathbf{x}$. Then, the OLS estimators from equation (4.39) are consistent (and possibly unbiased as well). Further, the usual OLS inference procedures (t statistics, F statistics, LM statistics) are asymptotically valid under appropriate homoskedasticity assumptions.

If e_0 and v are uncorrelated, as is usually assumed, then $\mathrm{Var}(v + e_0) = \sigma_v^2 + \sigma_0^2 > \sigma_v^2$. Therefore, measurement error in the dependent variable results in a larger error variance than when the dependent variable is not measured with error. This result is hardly surprising and translates into larger asymptotic variances for the OLS estimators than if we could observe y^*. But the larger error variance violates none of the assumptions needed for OLS estimation to have its desirable large-sample properties.

Example 4.6 (Saving Function with Measurement Error): Consider a saving function

$$\mathrm{E}(sav^* \mid inc, size, educ, age) = \beta_0 + \beta_1 inc + \beta_2 size + \beta_3 educ + \beta_4 age$$

but where actual saving (sav^*) may deviate from reported saving (sav). The question is whether the measurement error in sav is systematically related to the other variables. It may be reasonable to assume that the measurement error is not correlated with *inc*, *size*, *educ*, and *age*, but we might expect that families with higher incomes or more education report their saving more accurately. Unfortunately, without more information, we cannot know whether the measurement error is correlated with *inc* or *educ*.

When the dependent variable is in logarithmic form, so that $\log(y^*)$ is the dependent variable, a natural measurement error equation is

$$\log(y) = \log(y^*) + e_0. \tag{4.40}$$

This follows from a **multiplicative measurement error** for y: $y = y^* a_0$ where $a_0 > 0$ and $e_0 = \log(a_0)$.

Example 4.7 (Measurement Error in Firm Scrap Rates): In Example 4.4, we might think that the firm scrap rate is mismeasured, leading us to postulate the model $\log(scrap^*) = \beta_0 + \beta_1 grant + v$, where $scrap^*$ is the true scrap rate. The measurement error equation is $\log(scrap) = \log(scrap^*) + e_0$. Is the measurement error e_0 independent of whether the firm receives a grant? Not if a firm receiving a grant is more likely to underreport its scrap rate in order to make it look as if the grant had the intended effect. If underreporting occurs, then, in the estimable equation $\log(scrap) = \beta_0 + \beta_1 grant + v + e_0$, the error $u = v + e_0$ is negatively correlated with *grant*. This result would produce a downward bias in β_1, tending to make the training program look more effective than it actually was.

These examples show that measurement error in the dependent variable *can* cause biases in OLS if the measurement error is systematically related to one or more of the explanatory variables. If the measurement error is uncorrelated with the explanatory variables, OLS is perfectly appropriate.

4.4.2 Measurement Error in an Explanatory Variable

Traditionally, measurement error in an explanatory variable has been considered a much more important problem than measurement error in the response variable. This point was suggested by Example 4.2, and in this subsection we develop the general case.

We consider the model with a single explanatory measured with error:

$$y = \beta_0 + \beta_1 x_1 + \beta_2 x_2 + \cdots + \beta_K x_K^* + v \tag{4.41}$$

where $y, x_1, \ldots, x_{K-1}$ are observable but x_K^* is not. We assume at a minimum that v has zero mean and is uncorrelated with $x_1, x_2, \ldots, x_{K-1}$, x_K^*; in fact, we usually have in mind the structural model $\mathrm{E}(y \mid x_1, \ldots, x_{K-1}, x_K^*) = \beta_0 + \beta_1 x_1 + \beta_2 x_2 + \cdots + \beta_K x_K^*$. If x_K^* were observed, OLS estimation would produce consistent estimators. Instead, we have a measure of x_K^*; call it x_K. A maintained assumption is that v is also uncorrelated with x_K. This follows under the redundancy assumption $\mathrm{E}(y \mid x_1, \ldots, x_{K-1}, x_K^*, x_K) = \mathrm{E}(y \mid x_1, \ldots, x_{K-1}, x_K^*)$, an assumption we used in the proxy variable solution to the omitted variable problem. This means that x_K has no effect on y once the other explanatory variables, including x_K^*, have been controlled for. Because x_K^* is assumed to be the variable that affects y, this assumption is uncontroversial.

The measurement error in the population is simply

$$e_K = x_K - x_K^* \tag{4.42}$$

and this can be positive, negative, or zero. We assume that the average measurement error in the population is zero: $\mathrm{E}(e_K) = 0$, which has no practical consequences because we include an intercept in equation (4.41). Since v is assumed to be uncorrelated with x_K^* and x_K, v is also uncorrelated with e_K.

We want to know the properties of OLS if we simply replace x_K^* with x_K and run the regression of y on $1, x_1, x_2, \ldots, x_K$. These depend crucially on the assumptions we make about the measurement error. An assumption that is almost always maintained is that e_K is uncorrelated with the explanatory variables not measured with error: $\mathrm{E}(x_j e_K) = 0$, $j = 1, \ldots, K-1$.

The key assumptions involve the relationship between the measurement error and x_K^* and x_K. Two assumptions have been the focus in the econometrics literature, and these represent polar extremes. The first assumption is that e_K is uncorrelated with the *observed* measure, x_K:

$$\mathrm{Cov}(x_K, e_K) = 0. \tag{4.43}$$

From equation (4.42), if assumption (4.43) is true, then e_K must be correlated with the unobserved variable x_K^*. To determine the properties of OLS in this case, we write $x_K^* = x_K - e_K$ and plug this into equation (4.41):

$$y = \beta_0 + \beta_1 x_1 + \beta_2 x_2 + \cdots + \beta_K x_K + (v - \beta_K e_K). \tag{4.44}$$

Now, we have assumed that v and e_K both have zero mean and are uncorrelated with each x_j, including x_K; therefore, $v - \beta_K e_K$ has zero mean and is uncorrelated with the x_j. It follows that OLS estimation with x_K in place of x_K^* produces consistent estimators of all of the β_j (assuming the standard rank condition Assumption OLS.2). Since v is uncorrelated with e_K, the variance of the error in equation (4.44) is $\text{Var}(v - \beta_K e_K) = \sigma_v^2 + \beta_K^2 \sigma_{e_K}^2$. Therefore, except when $\beta_K = 0$, measurement error increases the error variance, which is not a surprising finding and violates none of the OLS assumptions.

The assumption that e_K is uncorrelated with x_K is analogous to the proxy variable assumption we made in the Section 4.3.2. Since this assumption implies that OLS has all its nice properties, this is not usually what econometricians have in mind when referring to measurement error in an explanatory variable. The **classical errors-in-variables (CEV)** assumption replaces assumption (4.43) with the assumption that the measurement error is uncorrelated with the *unobserved* explanatory variable:

$$\text{Cov}(x_K^*, e_K) = 0. \tag{4.45}$$

This assumption comes from writing the observed measure as the sum of the true explanatory variable and the measurement error, $x_K = x_K^* + e_K$, and then assuming the two components of x_K are uncorrelated. (This has nothing to do with assumptions about v; we are always maintaining that v is uncorrelated with x_K^* and x_K, and therefore with e_K.)

If assumption (4.45) holds, then x_K and e_K *must* be correlated:

$$\text{Cov}(x_K, e_K) = \text{E}(x_K e_K) = \text{E}(x_K^* e_K) + \text{E}(e_K^2) = \sigma_{e_K}^2. \tag{4.46}$$

Thus, under the CEV assumption, the covariance between x_K and e_K is equal to the variance of the measurement error.

Looking at equation (4.44), we see that correlation between x_K and e_K causes problems for OLS. Because v and x_K are uncorrelated, the covariance between x_K and the composite error $v - \beta_K e_K$ is $\text{Cov}(x_K, v - \beta_K e_K) = -\beta_K \text{Cov}(x_K, e_K) = -\beta_K \sigma_{e_K}^2$. It follows that, in the CEV case, the OLS regression of y on $x_1, x_2, \ldots, x_K$ generally gives inconsistent estimators of *all* of the β_j.

The plims of the $\hat{\beta}_j$ for $j \neq K$ are difficult to characterize except under special assumptions. If x_K^* is uncorrelated with x_j, all $j \neq K$, then so is x_K, and it follows that $\text{plim}\, \hat{\beta}_j = \beta_j$, all $j \neq K$. The plim of $\hat{\beta}_K$ can be characterized in any case. Problem 4.10 asks you to show that

$$\text{plim}(\hat{\beta}_K) = \beta_K \left(\frac{\sigma_{r_K^*}^2}{\sigma_{r_K^*}^2 + \sigma_{e_K}^2} \right), \tag{4.47}$$

where r_K^* is the linear projection error in

$$x_K^* = \delta_0 + \delta_1 x_1 + \delta_2 x_2 + \cdots + \delta_{K-1} x_{K-1} + r_K^*.$$

An important implication of equation (4.47) is that, because the term multiplying β_K is always between zero and one, $|\text{plim}(\hat{\beta}_K)| < |\beta_K|$. This is called the **attenuation bias** in OLS due to CEVs: on average (or in large samples), the estimated OLS effect will be *attenuated* as a result of the presence of CEVs. If β_K is positive, $\hat{\beta}_K$ will tend to underestimate β_K; if β_K is negative, $\hat{\beta}_K$ will tend to overestimate β_K.

In the case of a single explanatory variable ($K = 1$) measured with error, equation (4.47) becomes

$$\text{plim } \hat{\beta}_1 = \beta_1 \left(\frac{\sigma_{x_1^*}^2}{\sigma_{x_1^*}^2 + \sigma_{e_1}^2} \right) \tag{4.48}$$

The term multiplying β_1 in equation (4.48) is $\text{Var}(x_1^*)/\text{Var}(x_1)$, which is always less than unity under the CEV assumption (4.45). As $\text{Var}(e_1)$ shrinks relative to $\text{Var}(x_1^*)$, the attenuation bias disappears.

In the case with multiple explanatory variables, equation (4.47) shows that it is not $\sigma_{x_K^*}^2$ that affects $\text{plim}(\hat{\beta}_K)$ but the variance in x_K^* after netting out the other explanatory variables. Thus, the more collinear x_K^* is with the other explanatory variables, the worse is the attenuation bias.

Example 4.8 (Measurement Error in Family Income): Consider the problem of estimating the causal effect of family income on college grade point average, after controlling for high school grade point average and SAT score:

$$colGPA = \beta_0 + \beta_1 faminc^* + \beta_2 hsGPA + \beta_3 SAT + v,$$

where $faminc^*$ is actual annual family income. Precise data on $colGPA$, $hsGPA$, and SAT are relatively easy to obtain from school records. But family income, especially as reported by students, could be mismeasured. If $faminc = faminc^* + e_1$, and the CEV assumptions hold, then using reported family income in place of actual family income will bias the OLS estimator of β_1 toward zero. One consequence is that a hypothesis test of H_0: $\beta_1 = 0$ will have a higher probability of Type II error.

If measurement error is present in more than one explanatory variable, deriving the inconsistency in the OLS estimators under extensions of the CEV assumptions is complicated and does not lead to very usable results.

In some cases it is clear that the CEV assumption (4.45) cannot be true. For example, suppose that frequency of marijuana usage is to be used as an explanatory variable in a wage equation. Let $smoked^*$ be the number of days, out of the last 30, that a worker has smoked marijuana. The variable *smoked* is the self-reported number of days. Suppose we postulate the standard measurement error model, $smoked = smoked^* + e_1$, and let us even assume that people try to report the truth. It seems very likely that people who do not smoke marijuana at all—so that $smoked^* = 0$—will also report $smoked = 0$. In other words, the measurement error is zero for people who never smoke marijuana. When $smoked^* > 0$ it is more likely that someone miscounts how many days he or she smoked marijuana. Such miscounting almost certainly means that e_1 and $smoked^*$ are correlated, a finding that violates the CEV assumption (4.45).

A general situation where assumption (4.45) is necessarily false occurs when the observed variable x_K has a smaller population variance than the unobserved variable x_K^*. Of course, we can rarely know with certainty whether this is the case, but we can sometimes use introspection. For example, consider actual amount of schooling versus reported schooling. In many cases, reported schooling will be a rounded-off version of actual schooling; therefore, reported schooling is less variable than actual schooling.

Problems

4.1. Consider a standard $\log(wage)$ equation for men under the assumption that all explanatory variables are exogenous:

$$\log(wage) = \beta_0 + \beta_1 married + \beta_2 educ + \mathbf{z}\gamma + u, \tag{4.49}$$

$$\mathrm{E}(u \mid married, educ, \mathbf{z}) = 0,$$

where $\mathbf{z}$ contains factors other than marital status and education that can affect wage. When β_1 is small, $100 \cdot \beta_1$ is approximately the ceteris paribus percentage difference in wages between married and unmarried men. When β_1 is large, it might be preferable to use the exact percentage difference in $\mathrm{E}(wage \mid married, educ, \mathbf{z})$. Call this θ_1.

a. Show that, if u is independent of all explanatory variables in equation (4.49), then $\theta_1 = 100 \cdot [\exp(\beta_1) - 1]$. (Hint: Find $\mathrm{E}(wage \mid married, educ, \mathbf{z})$ for $married = 1$ and $married = 0$, and find the percentage difference.) A natural, consistent, estimator of θ_1 is $\hat{\theta}_1 = 100 \cdot [\exp(\hat{\beta}_1) - 1]$, where $\hat{\beta}_1$ is the OLS estimator from equation (4.49).

b. Use the delta method (see Section 3.5.2) to show that asymptotic standard error of $\hat{\theta}_1$ is $[100 \cdot \exp(\hat{\beta}_1)] \cdot \mathrm{se}(\hat{\beta}_1)$.

c. Repeat parts a and b by finding the exact percentage change in $\mathrm{E}(wage \mid married, educ, \mathbf{z})$ for any given change in *educ*, $\Delta educ$. Call this θ_2. Explain how to estimate θ_2 and obtain its asymptotic standard error.

d. Use the data in NLS80.RAW to estimate equation (4.49), where $\mathbf{z}$ contains the remaining variables in equation (4.29) (except ability, of course). Find $\hat{\theta}_1$ and its standard error; find $\hat{\theta}_2$ and its standard error when $\Delta educ = 4$.

4.2. a. Show that, under random sampling and the zero conditional mean assumption $\mathrm{E}(u \mid \mathbf{x}) = 0$, $\mathrm{E}(\hat{\boldsymbol{\beta}} \mid \mathbf{X}) = \boldsymbol{\beta}$ if $\mathbf{X}'\mathbf{X}$ is nonsingular. (Hint: Use Property CE.5 in the appendix to Chapter 2.)

b. In addition to the assumptions from part a, assume that $\mathrm{Var}(u \mid \mathbf{x}) = \sigma^2$. Show that $\mathrm{Var}(\hat{\boldsymbol{\beta}} \mid \mathbf{X}) = \sigma^2(\mathbf{X}'\mathbf{X})^{-1}$.

4.3. Suppose that in the linear model (4.5), $\mathrm{E}(\mathbf{x}'u) = \mathbf{0}$ (where $\mathbf{x}$ contains unity), $\mathrm{Var}(u \mid \mathbf{x}) = \sigma^2$, but $\mathrm{E}(u \mid \mathbf{x}) \neq \mathrm{E}(u)$.

a. Is it true that $\mathrm{E}(u^2 \mid \mathbf{x}) = \sigma^2$?

b. What relevance does part a have for OLS estimation?

4.4. Show that the estimator $\hat{\mathbf{B}} \equiv N^{-1} \sum_{i=1}^{N} \hat{u}_i^2 \mathbf{x}_i'\mathbf{x}_i$ is consistent for $\mathbf{B} = \mathrm{E}(u^2\mathbf{x}'\mathbf{x})$ by showing that $N^{-1} \sum_{i=1}^{N} \hat{u}_i^2 \mathbf{x}_i'\mathbf{x}_i = N^{-1} \sum_{i=1}^{N} u_i^2 \mathbf{x}_i'\mathbf{x}_i + \mathrm{o}_p(1)$. (Hint: Write $\hat{u}_i^2 = u_i^2 - 2\mathbf{x}_i u_i(\hat{\boldsymbol{\beta}} - \boldsymbol{\beta}) + [\mathbf{x}_i(\hat{\boldsymbol{\beta}} - \boldsymbol{\beta})]^2$, and use the facts that sample averages are $\mathrm{O}_p(1)$ when expectations exist and that $\hat{\boldsymbol{\beta}} - \boldsymbol{\beta} = \mathrm{o}_p(1)$. Assume that all necessary expectations exist and are finite.)

4.5. Let y and z be random scalars, and let $\mathbf{x}$ be a $1 \times K$ random vector, where one element of $\mathbf{x}$ can be unity to allow for a nonzero intercept. Consider the population model

$$\mathrm{E}(y \mid \mathbf{x}, z) = \mathbf{x}\boldsymbol{\beta} + \gamma z, \tag{4.50}$$

$$\mathrm{Var}(y \mid \mathbf{x}, z) = \sigma^2, \tag{4.51}$$

where interest lies in the $K \times 1$ vector $\boldsymbol{\beta}$. To rule out trivialities, assume that $\gamma \neq 0$. In addition, assume that $\mathbf{x}$ and z are orthogonal in the population: $\mathrm{E}(\mathbf{x}'z) = \mathbf{0}$.

Consider two estimators of $\boldsymbol{\beta}$ based on N independent and identically distributed observations: (1) $\hat{\boldsymbol{\beta}}$ (obtained along with $\hat{\gamma}$) is from the regression of y on $\mathbf{x}$ and z; (2) $\tilde{\boldsymbol{\beta}}$ is from the regression of y on $\mathbf{x}$. Both estimators are consistent for $\boldsymbol{\beta}$ under equation (4.50) and $\mathrm{E}(\mathbf{x}'z) = \mathbf{0}$ (along with the standard rank conditions).

a. Show that, without any additional assumptions (except those needed to apply the law of large numbers and the central limit theorem), $\mathrm{Avar}\, \sqrt{N}(\tilde{\boldsymbol{\beta}} - \boldsymbol{\beta}) -$

Avar $\sqrt{N}(\hat{\boldsymbol{\beta}} - \boldsymbol{\beta})$ is always positive semidefinite (and usually positive definite). Therefore, from the standpoint of asymptotic analysis, it is always better under equations (4.50) and (4.51) to include variables in a regression model that are uncorrelated with the variables of interest.

b. Consider the special case where $z = (x_K - \mu_K)^2$, $\mu_K \equiv \mathrm{E}(x_K)$, and x_K is symetrically distributed: $\mathrm{E}[(x_K - \mu_K)^3] = 0$. Then β_K is the partial effect of x_K on $\mathrm{E}(y \mid \mathbf{x})$ evaluated at $x_K = \mu_K$. Is it better to estimate the average partial effect with or without $(x_K - \mu_K)^2$ included as a regressor?

c. Under the setup in Problem 2.3, with $\mathrm{Var}(y \mid \mathbf{x}) = \sigma^2$, is it better to estimate β_1 and β_2 with or without $x_1 x_2$ in the regression?

4.6. Let the variable *nonwhite* be a binary variable indicating race: *nonwhite* = 1 if the person is a race other than white. Given that race is determined at birth and is beyond an individual's control, explain how *nonwhite* can be an endogenous explanatory variable in a regression model. In particular, consider the three kinds of endogeneity discussed in Section 4.1.

4.7. Consider estimating the effect of personal computer ownership, as represented by a binary variable, *PC*, on college GPA, *colGPA*. With data on SAT scores and high school GPA you postulate the model

$$colGPA = \beta_0 + \beta_1 hsGPA + \beta_2 SAT + \beta_3 PC + u.$$

a. Why might u and PC be positively correlated?

b. If the given equation is estimated by OLS using a random sample of college students, is $\hat{\beta}_3$ likely to have an upward or downward asymptotic bias?

c. What are some variables that might be good proxies for the unobservables in u that are correlated with PC?

4.8. Consider a population regression with two explanatory variables, but where they have an interactive effect and x_2 appears as a quadratic:

$$\mathrm{E}(y \mid x_1, x_2) = \beta_0 + \beta_1 x_1 + \beta_2 x_2 + \beta_3 x_1 x_2 + \beta_4 x_2^2.$$

Let $\mu_1 \equiv \mathrm{E}(x_1)$ and $\mu_2 \equiv \mathrm{E}(x_2)$ be the population means of the explanatory variables.

a. Let α_1 denote the average partial effect (across the distribution of the explanatory variables) of x_1 on $\mathrm{E}(y \mid x_1, x_2)$, and let α_2 be the same for x_2. Find α_1 and α_2 in terms of the β_j and μ_j.

b. Rewrite the regression function so that α_1 and α_2 appear directly. (Note that μ_1 and μ_2 will also appear.)

c. Given a random sample, what regression would you run to estimate α_1 and α_2 directly? What if you do not know μ_1 and μ_2?

d. Apply part c to the data in NLS80.RAW, where $y = \log(wage)$, $x_1 = educ$, and $x_2 = exper$. (You will have to plug in the sample averages of *educ* and *exper*.) Compare coefficients and standard errors when the interaction term is *educ·exper* instead, and discuss.

4.9. Consider a linear model where the dependent variable is in logarithmic form, and the lag of $\log(y)$ is also an explanatory variable:

$$\log(y) = \beta_0 + \mathbf{x}\boldsymbol{\beta} + \alpha_1 \log(y_{-1}) + u, \qquad \mathrm{E}(u \mid \mathbf{x}, y_{-1}) = 0,$$

where the inclusion of $\log(y_{-1})$ might be to control for correlation between policy variables in $\mathbf{x}$ and a previous value of y; see Example 4.4.

a. For estimating $\boldsymbol{\beta}$, why do we obtain the same estimator if the *growth* in y, $\log(y) - \log(y_{-1})$, is used instead as the dependent variable?

b. Suppose that there are no covariates $\mathbf{x}$ in the equation. Show that, if the distributions of y and y_{-1} are identical, then $|\alpha_1| < 1$. This is the *regression-to-the-mean* phenomenon in a dynamic setting. (Hint: Show that $\alpha_1 = \mathrm{Corr}[\log(y), \log(y_{-1})]$.)

4.10. Use Property LP.7 from Chapter 2 (particularly equation (2.56)) and Problem 2.6 to derive equation (4.47). (Hint: First use Problem 2.6 to show that the population residual r_K, in the linear projection of x_K on $1, x_1, \ldots, x_{K-1}$, is $r_K^* + e_K$. Then find the projection of y on r_K and use Property LP.7.)

4.11. a. In Example 4.3, use *KWW* and *IQ* simultaneously as proxies for ability in equation (4.29). Compare the estimated return to education without a proxy for ability and with *IQ* as the only proxy for ability.

b. Test *KWW* and *IQ* for joint significance in the estimated equation from part a.

c. When *KWW* and *IQ* are used as proxies for *abil*, does the wage differential between nonblacks and blacks disappear? What is the estimated differential?

d. Add the interactions $educ(IQ - 100)$ and $educ(KWW - \overline{KWW})$ to the regression from part a, where $\overline{KWW}$ is the average score in the sample. Are these terms jointly significant using a standard F test? Does adding them affect any important conclusions?

4.12. Redo Example 4.4, adding the variable *union*—a dummy variable indicating whether the workers at the plant are unionized—as an additional explanatory variable.

4.13. Use the data in CORNWELL.RAW (from Cornwell and Trumball, 1994) to estimate a model of county-level crime rates, using the year 1987 only.

a. Using logarithms of all variables, estimate a model relating the crime rate to the deterrent variables *prbarr*, *prbconv*, *prbpris*, and *avgsen*.

b. Add log(*crmrte*) for 1986 as an additional explanatory variable, and comment on how the estimated elasticities differ from part a.

c. Compute the F statistic for joint significance of all of the wage variables (again in logs), using the restricted model from part b.

d. Redo part c, but make the test robust to heteroskedasticity of unknown form.

4.14. Use the data in ATTEND.RAW to answer this question.

a. To determine the effects of attending lecture on final exam performance, estimate a model relating *stndfnl* (the standardized final exam score) to *atndrte* (the percent of lectures attended). Include the binary variables *frosh* and *soph* as explanatory variables. Interpret the coefficient on *atndrte*, and discuss its significance.

b. How confident are you that the OLS estimates from part a are estimating the causal effect of attendence? Explain.

c. As proxy variables for student ability, add to the regression *priGPA* (prior cumulative GPA) and *ACT* (achievement test score). Now what is the effect of *atndrte*? Discuss how the effect differs from that in part a.

d. What happens to the significance of the dummy variables in part c as compared with part a? Explain.

e. Add the squares of *priGPA* and *ACT* to the equation. What happens to the coefficient on *atndrte*? Are the quadratics jointly significant?

f. To test for a nonlinear effect of *atndrte*, add its square to the equation from part e. What do you conclude?

4.15. Assume that y and each x_j have finite second moments, and write the linear projection of y on $(1, x_1, \ldots, x_K)$ as

$$y = \beta_0 + \beta_1 x_1 + \cdots + \beta_K x_K + u = \beta_0 + \mathbf{x}\boldsymbol{\beta} + u,$$

$$\mathrm{E}(u) = 0, \qquad \mathrm{E}(x_j u) = 0, \qquad j = 1, 2, \ldots, K.$$

a. Show that $\sigma_y^2 = \mathrm{Var}(\mathbf{x}\boldsymbol{\beta}) + \sigma_u^2$.

b. For a random draw i from the population, write $y_i = \beta_0 + \mathbf{x}_i\boldsymbol{\beta} + u_i$. Evaluate the following assumption, which has been known to appear in econometrics textbooks: "$\mathrm{Var}(u_i) = \sigma^2 = \mathrm{Var}(y_i)$ for all i."

c. Define the population R-squared by $\rho^2 \equiv 1 - \sigma_u^2/\sigma_y^2 = \text{Var}(\mathbf{x}\boldsymbol{\beta})/\sigma_y^2$. Show that the R-squared, $R^2 = 1 - \text{SSR}/\text{SST}$, is a consistent estimator of ρ^2, where SSR is the OLS sum of squared residuals and $\text{SST} = \sum_{i=1}^N (y_i - \bar{y})^2$ is the total sum of squares.

d. Evaluate the following statement: "In the presence of heteroskedasticity, the R-squared from an OLS regression is meaningless." (This kind of statement also tends to appear in econometrics texts.)

4.16. Let $\{(\mathbf{x}_i, u_i) : i = 1, 2, \ldots\}$ be a sequence of independent, not identically distributed (i.n.i.d.) random vectors following the linear model $y_i = \mathbf{x}_i\boldsymbol{\beta} + u_i$, $i = 1, 2, \ldots$. Assume that $\text{E}(\mathbf{x}_i'u_i) = \mathbf{0}$ for all i, that $N^{-1}\sum_{i=1}^N \text{E}(\mathbf{x}_i'\mathbf{x}_i) \to \mathbf{A}$, where $\mathbf{A}$ is a $K \times K$ positive definite matrix, and that $\{\mathbf{x}_i'\mathbf{x}_i\}$ satisfies the law of large numbers: $N^{-1}\sum_{i=1}^N [\mathbf{x}_i'\mathbf{x}_i - \text{E}(\mathbf{x}_i'\mathbf{x}_i)] \xrightarrow{p} \mathbf{0}$.

a. If $N^{-1}\sum_{i=1}^N \mathbf{x}_i'u_i$ also satisfies the law of large numbers, prove that the OLS estimator, $\hat{\boldsymbol{\beta}}$, from the regression y_i on $\mathbf{x}_i$, $i = 1, 2, \ldots, N$, is consistent for $\boldsymbol{\beta}$.

b. Define $\mathbf{B}_N = N^{-1}\sum_{i=1}^N \text{E}(u_i^2\mathbf{x}_i'\mathbf{x}_i)$ for each N and assume that $\mathbf{B}_N \to \mathbf{B}$ as $N \to \infty$. Further, assume that $N^{-1/2}\sum_{i=1}^N \mathbf{x}_i'u_i \xrightarrow{d} \text{Normal}(\mathbf{0}, \mathbf{B})$. Show that $\sqrt{N}(\hat{\boldsymbol{\beta}} - \boldsymbol{\beta})$ is asymptotically normal and find its asymptotic variance matrix.

c. Suggest consistent estimators of $\mathbf{A}$ and $\mathbf{B}$; you need not prove consistency.

d. Comment on how the estimators in part c compare with the i.i.d. case.

4.17. Consider the standard linear model $y = \mathbf{x}\boldsymbol{\beta} + u$ under Assumptions OLS.1 and OLS.2. Define $h(\mathbf{x}) \equiv \text{E}(u^2 \mid \mathbf{x})$. Let $\hat{\boldsymbol{\beta}}$ be the OLS estimator, and show that we can always write

$$\text{Avar}\sqrt{N}(\hat{\boldsymbol{\beta}} - \boldsymbol{\beta}) = [\text{E}(\mathbf{x}'\mathbf{x})]^{-1}\text{E}[h(\mathbf{x})\mathbf{x}'\mathbf{x}][\text{E}(\mathbf{x}'\mathbf{x})]^{-1}.$$

This expression is useful when $\text{E}(u \mid \mathbf{x}) = 0$ for comparing the asymptotic variances of OLS and weighted least squares estimators; see, for example, Wooldridge (1994b).

4.18. Describe what is wrong with each of the following two statements:

a. "The central limit theorem implies that, as the sample size grows, the error distribution approaches normality."

b. "The heteroskedasticity-robust standard errors are consistent because $\hat{u}_i^2$ (the squared OLS residual) is a consistent estimator of $\text{E}(u_i^2 \mid \mathbf{x}_i)$ for each i."

5 Instrumental Variables Estimation of Single-Equation Linear Models

In this chapter we treat instrumental variables estimation, which is probably second only to ordinary least squares in terms of methods used in empirical economic research. The underlying population model is the same as in Chapter 4, but we explicitly allow the unobservable error to be correlated with the explanatory variables.

5.1 Instrumental Variables and Two-Stage Least Squares

5.1.1 Motivation for Instrumental Variables Estimation

To motivate the need for the method of instrumental variables, consider a linear population model

$$y = \beta_0 + \beta_1 x_1 + \beta_2 x_2 + \cdots + \beta_K x_K + u, \tag{5.1}$$

$$\mathrm{E}(u) = 0, \qquad \mathrm{Cov}(x_j, u) = 0, \qquad j = 1, 2, \ldots, K-1, \tag{5.2}$$

but where x_K might be correlated with u. In other words, the explanatory variables $x_1, x_2, \ldots, x_{K-1}$ are exogenous, but x_K is potentially endogenous in equation (5.1). The endogeneity can come from any of the sources we discussed in Chapter 4. To fix ideas, it might help to think of u as containing an omitted variable that is uncorrelated with all explanatory variables except x_K. So, we may be interested in a conditional expectation as in equation (4.18), but we do not observe q, and q is correlated with x_K.

As we saw in Chapter 4, OLS estimation of equation (5.1) generally results in inconsistent estimators of *all* the β_j if $\mathrm{Cov}(x_K, u) \neq 0$. Further, without more information, we cannot consistently estimate any of the parameters in equation (5.1).

The method of instrumental variables (IV) provides a general solution to the problem of an endogenous explanatory variable. To use the IV approach with x_K endogenous, we need an observable variable, z_1, *not* in equation (5.1) that satisfies two conditions. First, z_1 must be uncorrelated with u:

$$\mathrm{Cov}(z_1, u) = 0. \tag{5.3}$$

In other words, like $x_1, \ldots, x_{K-1}$, z_1 is exogenous in equation (5.1).

The second requirement involves the relationship between z_1 and the endogenous variable, x_K. A precise statement requires the linear projection of x_K onto *all* the exogenous variables:

$$x_K = \delta_0 + \delta_1 x_1 + \delta_2 x_2 + \cdots + \delta_{K-1} x_{K-1} + \theta_1 z_1 + r_K, \tag{5.4}$$

where, by definition of a linear projection error, $\mathrm{E}(r_K) = 0$ and r_K is uncorrelated with $x_1, x_2, \ldots, x_{K-1}$, and z_1. The key assumption on this linear projection is that the coefficient on z_1 is nonzero:

$$\theta_1 \neq 0. \tag{5.5}$$

This condition is often loosely described as "z_1 is correlated with x_K," but that statement is not quite correct. The condition $\theta_1 \neq 0$ means that z_1 is *partially* correlated with x_K once the other exogenous variables $x_1, \ldots, x_{K-1}$ have been netted out. If x_K is the only explanatory variable in equation (5.1), then the linear projection is $x_K = \delta_0 + \theta_1 z_1 + r_K$, where $\theta_1 = \text{Cov}(z_1, x_K)/\text{Var}(z_1)$, and so condition (5.5) and $\text{Cov}(z_1, x_K) \neq 0$ are the same.

At this point we should mention that we have put no restrictions on the distribution of x_K or z_1. In many cases x_K and z_1 will be both essentially continuous, but sometimes x_K, z_1, or both are discrete. In fact, one or both of x_K and z_1 can be binary variables, or have continuous and discrete characteristics at the same time. Equation (5.4) is simply a linear projection, and this is always defined when second moments of all variables are finite.

When z_1 satisfies conditions (5.3) and (5.5), then it is said to be an **instrumental variable (IV)** candidate for x_K. (Sometimes z_1 is simply called an *instrument* for x_K.) Because $x_1, \ldots, x_{K-1}$ are already uncorrelated with u, they serve as their own instrumental variables in equation (5.1). In other words, the full list of instrumental variables is the same as the list of exogenous variables, but we often just refer to the instrument for the endogenous explanatory variable.

The linear projection in equation (5.4) is called a **reduced-form equation** for the endogenous explanatory variable x_K. In the context of single-equation linear models, a reduced form always involves writing an endogenous variable as a linear projection onto all exogenous variables. The "reduced form" terminology comes from simultaneous equations analysis, and it makes more sense in that context. We use it in all IV contexts because it is a concise way of stating that an endogenous variable has been linearly projected onto the exogenous variables. The terminology also conveys that there is nothing necessarily structural about equation (5.4).

From the structural equation (5.1) and the reduced form for x_K, we obtain a reduced form for y by plugging equation (5.4) into equation (5.1) and rearranging:

$$y = \alpha_0 + \alpha_1 x_1 + \cdots + \alpha_{K-1} x_{K-1} + \lambda_1 z_1 + v, \tag{5.6}$$

where $v = u + \beta_K r_K$ is the reduced-form error, $\alpha_j = \beta_j + \beta_K \delta_j$, and $\lambda_1 = \beta_K \theta_1$. By our assumptions, v is uncorrelated with all explanatory variables in equation (5.6), and so OLS consistently estimates the reduced-form parameters, the α_j and λ_1.

Estimates of the reduced-form parameters are sometimes of interest in their own right, but estimating the structural parameters is generally more useful. For example, at the firm level, suppose that x_K is job training hours per worker and y is a measure of average worker productivity. Suppose that job training grants were randomly assigned to firms. Then it is natural to use for z_1 either a binary variable indicating whether a firm received a job training grant or the actual amount of the grant per worker (if the amount varies by firm). The parameter β_K in equation (5.1) is the effect of job training on worker productivity. If z_1 is a binary variable for receiving a job training grant, then λ_1 is the effect of receiving this particular job training grant on worker productivity, which is of some interest. But estimating the effect of an hour of general job training is more valuable because it can be meaningful in many situations.

We can now show that the assumptions we have made on the IV z_1 solve the **identification problem** for the β_j in equation (5.1). By identification we mean that we can write the β_j in terms of population moments in observable variables. To see how, write equation (5.1) as

$$y = \mathbf{x}\boldsymbol{\beta} + u, \tag{5.7}$$

where the constant is absorbed into $\mathbf{x}$ so that $\mathbf{x} = (1, x_2, \ldots, x_K)$. Write the $1 \times K$ vector of all exogenous variables as

$$\mathbf{z} \equiv (1, x_2, \ldots, x_{K-1}, z_1).$$

Assumptions (5.2) and (5.3) imply the K population orthogonality conditions

$$\mathrm{E}(\mathbf{z}'u) = \mathbf{0}. \tag{5.8}$$

Multiplying equation (5.7) through by $\mathbf{z}'$, taking expectations, and using equation (5.8) gives

$$[\mathrm{E}(\mathbf{z}'\mathbf{x})]\boldsymbol{\beta} = \mathrm{E}(\mathbf{z}'y), \tag{5.9}$$

where $\mathrm{E}(\mathbf{z}'\mathbf{x})$ is $K \times K$ and $\mathrm{E}(\mathbf{z}'y)$ is $K \times 1$. Equation (5.9) represents a system of K linear equations in the K unknowns $\beta_1, \beta_2, \ldots, \beta_K$. This system has a unique solution if and only if the $K \times K$ matrix $\mathrm{E}(\mathbf{z}'\mathbf{x})$ has full rank; that is,

$$\text{rank } \mathrm{E}(\mathbf{z}'\mathbf{x}) = K, \tag{5.10}$$

in which case the solution is

$$\boldsymbol{\beta} = [\mathrm{E}(\mathbf{z}'\mathbf{x})]^{-1}\mathrm{E}(\mathbf{z}'y). \tag{5.11}$$

The expectations $\mathrm{E}(\mathbf{z}'\mathbf{x})$ and $\mathrm{E}(\mathbf{z}'y)$ can be consistently estimated using a random sample on $(\mathbf{x}, y, z_1)$, and so equation (5.11) identifies the vector $\boldsymbol{\beta}$.

It is clear that condition (5.3) was used to obtain equation (5.11). But where have we used condition (5.5)? Let us maintain that there are no linear dependencies among the exogenous variables, so that $E(\mathbf{z}'\mathbf{z})$ has full rank K; this simply rules out perfect collinearity in $\mathbf{z}$ in the population. Then, it can be shown that equation (5.10) holds if and only if $\theta_1 \neq 0$. (A more general case, which we cover in Section 5.1.2, is covered in Problem 5.12.) Therefore, along with the exogeneity condition (5.3), assumption (5.5) is the key identification condition. Assumption (5.10) is the **rank condition** for identification, and we return to it more generally in Section 5.2.1.

Given a random sample $\{(\mathbf{x}_i, y_i, z_{i1}): i = 1, 2, \ldots, N\}$ from the population, the **instrumental variables estimator** of $\boldsymbol{\beta}$ is

$$\hat{\boldsymbol{\beta}} = \left(N^{-1}\sum_{i=1}^{N}\mathbf{z}_i'\mathbf{x}_i\right)^{-1}\left(N^{-1}\sum_{i=1}^{N}\mathbf{z}_i'y_i\right) = (\mathbf{Z}'\mathbf{X})^{-1}\mathbf{Z}'\mathbf{Y},$$

where $\mathbf{Z}$ and $\mathbf{X}$ are $N \times K$ data matrices and $\mathbf{Y}$ is the $N \times 1$ data vector on the y_i. The consistency of this estimator is immediate from equation (5.11) and the law of large numbers. We consider a more general case in Section 5.2.1.

When searching for instruments for an endogenous explanatory variable, conditions (5.3) and (5.5) are equally important in identifying $\boldsymbol{\beta}$. There is, however, one practically important difference between them: condition (5.5) can be tested, whereas condition (5.3) must be maintained. The reason for this disparity is simple: the covariance in condition (5.3) involves the *unobservable* u, and therefore we cannot test anything about $\mathrm{Cov}(z_1, u)$.

Testing condition (5.5) in the reduced form (5.4) is a simple matter of computing a t test after OLS estimation. Nothing guarantees that r_K satisfies the requisite homoskedasticity assumption (Assumption OLS.3), so a heteroskedasticity-robust t statistic for $\hat{\theta}_1$ is often warranted. This statement is especially true if x_K is a binary variable or some other variable with discrete characteristics.

A word of caution is in order here. Econometricians have been known to say that "it is not possible to test for identification." In the model with one endogenous variable and one instrument, we have just seen the sense in which this statement is true: assumption (5.3) cannot be tested. Nevertheless, the fact remains that condition (5.5) can and *should* be tested. In fact, recent work has shown that the strength of the rejection in condition (5.5) (in a p-value sense) is important for determining the finite sample properties, particularly the bias, of the IV estimator. We return to this issue in Section 5.2.6.

In the context of omitted variables, an instrumental variable, like a proxy variable, must be redundant in the structural model (that is, the model that explicitly contains the unobservables; see condition (4.25)). However, unlike a proxy variable, an IV for x_K should be *uncorrelated* with the omitted variable. Remember, we want a proxy variable to be highly correlated with the omitted variable. A proxy variable makes a poor IV and, as we saw in Section 4.3.3, an IV makes a poor proxy variable.

Example 5.1 (Instrumental Variables for Education in a Wage Equation): Consider a wage equation for the U.S. working population:

$$\log(wage) = \beta_0 + \beta_1 exper + \beta_2 exper^2 + \beta_3 educ + u, \tag{5.12}$$

where u is thought to be correlated with *educ* because of omitted ability, as well as other factors, such as quality of education and family background. Suppose that we can collect data on mother's education, *motheduc*. For this to be a valid instrument for *educ* we must assume that *motheduc* is uncorrelated with u and that $\theta_1 \neq 0$ in the reduced-form equation

$$educ = \delta_0 + \delta_1 exper + \delta_2 exper^2 + \theta_1 motheduc + r.$$

There is little doubt that *educ* and *motheduc* are partially correlated, and this assertion is easily tested given a random sample from the population. The potential problem with *motheduc* as an instrument for *educ* is that *motheduc* might be correlated with the omitted factors in u: mother's education is likely to be correlated with child's ability and other family background characteristics that might be in u.

A variable such as the last digit of one's social security number makes a poor IV candidate for the opposite reason. Because the last digit is randomly determined, it is independent of other factors that affect earnings. But it is also independent of education. Therefore, while condition (5.3) holds, condition (5.5) does not.

By being clever it is often possible to come up with more convincing instruments—at least at first glance. Angrist and Krueger (1991) propose using quarter of birth as an IV for education. In the simplest case, let *frstqrt* be a dummy variable equal to unity for people born in the first quarter of the year and zero otherwise. Quarter of birth is arguably independent of unobserved factors such as ability that affect wage (although there is disagreement on this point; see Bound, Jaeger, and Baker (1995)). In addition, we must have $\theta_1 \neq 0$ in the reduced form

$$educ = \delta_0 + \delta_1 exper + \delta_2 exper^2 + \theta_1 frstqrt + r.$$

How can quarter of birth be (partially) correlated with educational attainment? Angrist and Krueger (1991) argue that compulsory school attendence laws induce a relationship between *educ* and *frstqrt*: at least some people are forced, by law, to attend school longer than they otherwise would, and this fact is correlated with quarter of birth. We can determine the strength of this association in a particular sample by estimating the reduced form and obtaining the t statistic for H_0: $\theta_1 = 0$.

This example illustrates that it can be very difficult to find a good instrumental variable for an endogenous explanatory variable because the variable must satisfy two different, often conflicting, criteria. For *motheduc*, the issue in doubt is whether condition (5.3) holds. For *frstqrt*, the initial concern is with condition (5.5). Since condition (5.5) can be tested, *frstqrt* has more appeal as an instrument. However, the partial correlation between *educ* and *frstqrt* is small, and this can lead to finite sample problems (see Section 5.2.6). A more subtle issue concerns the sense in which we are estimating the return to education for the entire population of working people. As we will see in Chapter 18, if the return to education is not constant across people, the IV estimator that uses *frstqrt* as an IV estimates the return to education only for those people induced to obtain more schooling because they were born in the first quarter of the year. These make up a relatively small fraction of the population.

Convincing instruments sometimes arise in the context of program evaluation, where individuals are randomly selected to be eligible for the program. Examples include job training programs and school voucher programs. Actual participation is almost always voluntary, and it may be endogenous because it can depend on unobserved factors that affect the response. However, it is often reasonable to assume that eligibility is exogenous. Because participation and eligibility are correlated, the latter can be used as an IV for the former.

A valid instrumental variable can also come from what is called a **natural experiment**. A natural experiment occurs when some (often unintended) feature of the setup we are studying produces exogenous variation in an otherwise endogenous explanatory variable. The Angrist and Krueger (1991) example seems, at least initially, to be a good natural experiment. Another example is given by Angrist (1990), who studies the effect of serving in the Vietnam war on the earnings of men. Participation in the military is not necessarily exogenous to unobserved factors that affect earnings, even after controlling for education, nonmilitary experience, and so on. Angrist used the following observation to obtain an instrumental variable for the binary Vietnam war participation indicator: men with a lower draft lottery number were more likely to serve in the war. Angrist verifies that the probability of serving in Vietnam is indeed related to draft lottery number. Because the lottery number is randomly determined, it seems like an ideal IV for serving in Vietnam. There are, however, some potential problems. It might be that men who were assigned a low lottery number chose to obtain more education as a way of increasing the chance of obtaining a draft deferment. If we do not control for education in the earnings equation, lottery number could be endogenous. Further, employers may have been willing to invest in job training for men who are unlikely to be drafted. Again, unless we can include measures of job training in the earnings equation, condition (5.3) may be violated. (This reasoning assumes that we are interested in estimating the pure effect of serving in Vietnam, as opposed to including indirect effects such as reduced job training.)

Hoxby (2000) uses topographical features, in particular the natural boundaries created by rivers, as IVs for the concentration of public schools within a school district. She uses these IVs to estimate the effects of competition among public schools on student performance. Cutler and Glaeser (1997) use the Hoxby instruments, as well as others, to estimate the effects of segregation on schooling and employment outcomes for blacks. Levitt (1997) provides another example of obtaining instrumental variables from a natural experiment. He uses the timing of mayoral and gubernatorial elections as instruments for size of the police force in estimating the effects of police on city crime rates. (Levitt actually uses panel data, something we will discuss in Chapter 11.)

Sensible IVs need not come from natural experiments. For example, Evans and Schwab (1995) study the effect of attending a Catholic high school on various outcomes. They use a binary variable for whether a student is Catholic as an IV for attending a Catholic high school, and they spend much effort arguing that religion is exogenous in their versions of equation (5.7). (In this application, condition (5.5) is easy to verify.) Economists often use regional variation in prices or taxes as instruments for endogenous explanatory variables appearing in individual-level equations. For example, in estimating the effects of alcohol consumption on performance in college, the local price of alcohol can be used as an IV for alcohol consumption, provided other regional factors that affect college performance have been appropriately controlled for. The idea is that the price of alcohol, including any taxes, can be assumed to be exogenous to each individual.

Example 5.2 (College Proximity as an IV for Education): Using wage data for 1976, Card (1995) uses a dummy variable that indicates whether a man grew up in the vicinity of a four-year college as an instrumental variable for years of schooling. He also includes several other controls. In the equation with experience and its square, a black indicator, southern and urban indicators, and regional and urban indicators for 1966, the instrumental variables estimate of the return to schooling is .132, or 13.2 percent, while the OLS estimate is 7.5 percent. Thus, for this sample of data, the IV estimate is almost twice as large as the OLS estimate. This result would be counterintuitive if we thought that an OLS analysis suffered from an upward omitted variable bias. One interpretation is that the OLS estimators suffer from the attenuation bias as a result of measurement error, as we discussed in Section 4.4.2. But the classical errors-in-variables assumption for education is questionable. Another interpretation is that the instrumental variable is not exogenous in the wage equation: location is not entirely exogenous. The full set of estimates, including standard errors and t statistics, can be found in Card (1995). Or, you can replicate Card's results in Problem 5.4.

5.1.2 Multiple Instruments: Two-Stage Least Squares

Consider again the model (5.1) and (5.2), where x_K can be correlated with u. Now, however, assume that we have more than one instrumental variable for x_K. Let $z_1, z_2, \dots, z_M$ be variables such that

$$\text{Cov}(z_h, u) = 0, \qquad h = 1, 2, \dots, M, \tag{5.13}$$

so that each z_h is exogenous in equation (5.1). If each of these has some partial correlation with x_K, we could have M different IV estimators. Actually, there are many more than this—more than we can count—since any linear combination of $x_1, x_2, \dots, x_{K-1}, z_1, z_2, \dots, z_M$ is uncorrelated with u. So which IV estimator should we use?

In Section 5.2.3 we show that, under certain assumptions, the **two-stage least squares (2SLS) estimator** is the most efficient IV estimator. For now, we rely on intuition.

To illustrate the method of 2SLS, define the vector of exogenous variables again by $\mathbf{z} \equiv (1, x_1, x_2, \dots, x_{K-1}, z_1, \dots, z_M)$, a $1 \times L$ vector $(L = K + M)$. Out of all possible linear combinations of $\mathbf{z}$ that can be used as an instrument for x_K, the method of 2SLS chooses that which is most highly correlated with x_K. If x_K were exogenous, then this choice would imply that the best instrument for x_K is simply itself. Ruling this case out, the linear combination of $\mathbf{z}$ most highly correlated with x_K is given by the linear projection of x_K on $\mathbf{z}$. Write the reduced form for x_K as

$$x_K = \delta_0 + \delta_1 x_1 + \cdots + \delta_{K-1} x_{K-1} + \theta_1 z_1 + \cdots + \theta_M z_M + r_K, \tag{5.14}$$

where, by definition, r_K has zero mean and is uncorrelated with each right-hand-side variable. As any linear combination of $\mathbf{z}$ is uncorrelated with u,

$$x_K^* \equiv \delta_0 + \delta_1 x_1 + \cdots + \delta_{K-1} x_{K-1} + \theta_1 z_1 + \cdots + \theta_M z_M \tag{5.15}$$

is uncorrelated with u. In fact, x_K^* is often interpreted as the part of x_K that is uncorrelated with u. If x_K is endogenous, it is because r_K is correlated with u.

If we could observe x_K^*, we would use it as an instrument for x_K in equation (5.1) and use the IV estimator from the previous subsection. Since the δ_j and θ_j are population parameters, x_K^* is not a usable instrument. However, as long as we make the standard assumption that there are no exact linear dependencies among the exogenous variables, we can consistently estimate the parameters in equation (5.14) by OLS. The sample analogues of the x_{iK}^* for each observation i are simply the OLS fitted values:

$$\hat{x}_{iK} = \hat{\delta}_0 + \hat{\delta}_1 x_{i1} + \cdots + \hat{\delta}_{K-1} x_{i,K-1} + \hat{\theta}_1 z_{i1} + \cdots + \hat{\theta}_M z_{iM}. \tag{5.16}$$

Now, for each observation i, define the vector $\hat{\mathbf{x}}_i \equiv (1, x_{i1}, \ldots, x_{i,K-1}, \hat{x}_{iK})$, $i = 1, 2, \ldots, N$. Using $\hat{\mathbf{x}}_i$ as the instruments for $\mathbf{x}_i$ gives the IV estimator

$$\hat{\boldsymbol{\beta}} = \left(\sum_{i=1}^{N} \hat{\mathbf{x}}_i' \mathbf{x}_i\right)^{-1} \left(\sum_{i=1}^{N} \hat{\mathbf{x}}_i' y_i\right) = (\hat{\mathbf{X}}'\mathbf{X})^{-1}\hat{\mathbf{X}}'\mathbf{Y}, \tag{5.17}$$

where unity is also the first element of $\mathbf{x}_i$.

The IV estimator in equation (5.17) turns out to be an OLS estimator. To see this fact, note that the $N \times (K+1)$ matrix $\hat{\mathbf{X}}$ can be expressed as $\hat{\mathbf{X}} = \mathbf{Z}(\mathbf{Z}'\mathbf{Z})^{-1}\mathbf{Z}'\mathbf{X} = \mathbf{P}_Z\mathbf{X}$, where the projection matrix $\mathbf{P}_Z = \mathbf{Z}(\mathbf{Z}'\mathbf{Z})^{-1}\mathbf{Z}'$ is idempotent and symmetric. Therefore, $\hat{\mathbf{X}}'\mathbf{X} = \mathbf{X}'\mathbf{P}_Z\mathbf{X} = (\mathbf{P}_Z\mathbf{X})'\mathbf{P}_Z\mathbf{X} = \hat{\mathbf{X}}'\hat{\mathbf{X}}$. Plugging this expression into equation (5.17) shows that the IV estimator that uses instruments $\hat{\mathbf{x}}_i$ can be written as $\hat{\boldsymbol{\beta}} = (\hat{\mathbf{X}}'\hat{\mathbf{X}})^{-1}\hat{\mathbf{X}}'\mathbf{Y}$. The name "two-stage least squares" comes from this procedure.

To summarize, $\hat{\boldsymbol{\beta}}$ can be obtained from the following steps:

1. Obtain the fitted values $\hat{x}_K$ from the regression

$$x_K \text{ on } 1,\ x_1, \ldots, x_{K-1}, z_1, \ldots, z_M, \tag{5.18}$$

where the i subscript is omitted for simplicity. This is called the **first-stage regression.**

2. Run the OLS regression

$$y \text{ on } 1,\ x_1, \ldots, x_{K-1}, \hat{x}_K. \tag{5.19}$$

This is called the **second-stage regression**, and it produces the $\hat{\beta}_j$.

In practice, it is best to use a software package with a 2SLS command rather than explicitly carry out the two-step procedure. Carrying out the two-step procedure explicitly makes one susceptible to harmful mistakes. For example, the following, seemingly sensible, two-step procedure is generally inconsistent: (1) regress x_K on $1, z_1, \ldots, z_M$ and obtain the fitted values, say $\tilde{x}_K$; (2) run the regression in (5.19) with $\tilde{x}_K$ in place of $\hat{x}_K$. Problem 5.11 asks you to show that omitting $x_1, \ldots, x_{K-1}$ in the first-stage regression and then explicitly doing the second-stage regression produces inconsistent estimators of the β_j.

Another reason to avoid the two-step procedure is that the OLS standard errors reported with regression (5.19) will be incorrect, something that will become clear later. Sometimes for hypothesis testing we need to carry out the second-stage regression explicitly (see Section 5.2.4).

The 2SLS estimator and the IV estimator from Section 5.1.1 are identical when there is only one instrument for x_K. Unless stated otherwise, we mean 2SLS whenever we talk about IV estimation of a single equation.

What is the analogue of the condition (5.5) when more than one instrument is available with one endogenous explanatory variable? Problem 5.12 asks you to show that $E(\mathbf{z}'\mathbf{x})$ has full column rank if and only if at least one of the θ_j in equation (5.14) is nonzero. The intuition behind this requirement is pretty clear: we need at least one exogenous variable that does not appear in equation (5.1) to induce variation in x_K that cannot be explained by $x_1, \ldots, x_{K-1}$. Identification of $\boldsymbol{\beta}$ does *not* depend on the values of the δ_h in equation (5.14).

Testing the rank condition with a single endogenous explanatory variable and multiple instruments is straightforward. In equation (5.14) we simply test the null hypothesis

$$\mathrm{H}_0\colon \theta_1 = 0,\ \theta_2 = 0, \ldots, \theta_M = 0 \tag{5.20}$$

against the alternative that at least one of the θ_j is different from zero. This test gives a compelling reason for explicitly running the first-stage regression. If r_K in equation (5.14) satisfies the OLS homoskedasticity assumption OLS.3, a standard F statistic or Lagrange multiplier statistic can be used to test hypothesis (5.20). Often a heteroskedasticity-robust statistic is more appropriate, especially if x_K has discrete characteristics. If we cannot reject hypothesis (5.20) against the alternative that at least one θ_h is different from zero, at a reasonably small significance level, then we should have serious reservations about the proposed 2SLS procedure: the instruments do not pass a minimal requirement.

The model with a single endogenous variable is said to be **overidentified** when $M > 1$ and there are $M - 1$ **overidentifying restrictions**. This terminology comes from the fact that, if each z_h has some partial correlation with x_K, then we have $M - 1$ more exogenous variables than needed to identify the parameters in equation (5.1). For example, if $M = 2$, we could discard one of the instruments and still achieve identification. In Chapter 6 we will show how to test the validity of any overidentifying restrictions.

5.2 General Treatment of Two-Stage Least Squares

5.2.1 Consistency

We now summarize asymptotic results for 2SLS in a single-equation model with perhaps several endogenous variables among the explanatory variables. Write the population model as in equation (5.7), where $\mathbf{x}$ is $1 \times K$ and generally includes unity. Several elements of $\mathbf{x}$ may be correlated with u. As usual, we assume that a random sample is available from the population.

ASSUMPTION 2SLS.1: For some $1 \times L$ vector $\mathbf{z}$, $\mathrm{E}(\mathbf{z}'u) = \mathbf{0}$.

Here we do not specify where the elements of $\mathbf{z}$ come from, but any exogenous elements of $\mathbf{x}$, including a constant, are included in $\mathbf{z}$. Unless every element of $\mathbf{x}$ is exogenous, $\mathbf{z}$ will have to contain variables obtained from outside the model. The zero conditional mean assumption, $\mathrm{E}(u \mid \mathbf{z}) = 0$, implies Assumption 2SLS.1.

The next assumption contains the general rank condition for single-equation analysis.

ASSUMPTION 2SLS.2: (a) rank $\mathrm{E}(\mathbf{z}'\mathbf{z}) = L$; (b) rank $\mathrm{E}(\mathbf{z}'\mathbf{x}) = K$.

Technically, part a of this assumption is needed, but it is not especially important, since the exogenous variables, unless chosen unwisely, will be linearly independent in the population (as well as in a typical sample). Part b is the crucial **rank condition** for identification. In a precise sense it means that $\mathbf{z}$ is sufficiently linearly related to $\mathbf{x}$ so that rank $\mathrm{E}(\mathbf{z}'\mathbf{x})$ has full column rank. We discussed this concept in Section 5.1 for the situation in which $\mathbf{x}$ contains a single endogenous variable. When $\mathbf{x}$ is exogenous, so that $\mathbf{z} = \mathbf{x}$, Assumption 2SLS.1 reduces to Assumption OLS.1 and Assumption 2SLS.2 reduces to Assumption OLS.2.

Necessary for the rank condition is the **order condition**, $L \geq K$. In other words, we must have at least as many instruments as we have explanatory variables. If we do not have as many instruments as right-hand-side variables, then $\boldsymbol{\beta}$ is not identified. However, $L \geq K$ is no guarantee that 2SLS.2b holds: the elements of $\mathbf{z}$ might not be appropriately correlated with the elements of $\mathbf{x}$.

We already know how to test Assumption 2SLS.2b with a single endogenous explanatory variable. In the general case, it is possible to test Assumption 2SLS.2b, given a random sample on $(\mathbf{x}, \mathbf{z})$, essentially by performing tests on the sample analogue of $\mathrm{E}(\mathbf{z}'\mathbf{x})$, $\mathbf{Z}'\mathbf{X}/N$. The tests are somewhat complicated; see, for example Cragg and Donald (1996). Often we estimate the reduced form for each endogenous explanatory variable to make sure that at least one element of $\mathbf{z}$ not in $\mathbf{x}$ is significant. This is not sufficient for the rank condition in general, but it can help us determine if the rank condition fails.

Using linear projections, there is a simple way to see how Assumptions 2SLS.1 and 2SLS.2 identify $\boldsymbol{\beta}$. First, assuming that $\mathrm{E}(\mathbf{z}'\mathbf{z})$ is nonsingular, we can always write the linear projection of $\mathbf{x}$ onto $\mathbf{z}$ as $\mathbf{x}^* = \mathbf{z}\boldsymbol{\Pi}$, where $\boldsymbol{\Pi}$ is the $L \times K$ matrix $\boldsymbol{\Pi} =$

$[\mathrm{E}(\mathbf{z}'\mathbf{z})]^{-1}\mathrm{E}(\mathbf{z}'\mathbf{x})$. Since each column of $\boldsymbol{\Pi}$ can be consistently estimated by regressing the appropriate element of $\mathbf{x}$ onto $\mathbf{z}$, for the purposes of identification of $\boldsymbol{\beta}$, we can treat $\boldsymbol{\Pi}$ as known. Write $\mathbf{x} = \mathbf{x}^* + \mathbf{r}$, where $\mathrm{E}(\mathbf{z}'\mathbf{r}) = \mathbf{0}$ and so $\mathrm{E}(\mathbf{x}^{*\prime}\mathbf{r}) = \mathbf{0}$. Now, the 2SLS estimator is effectively the IV estimator using instruments $\mathbf{x}^*$. Multiplying equation (5.7) by $\mathbf{x}^{*\prime}$, taking expectations, and rearranging gives

$$\mathrm{E}(\mathbf{x}^{*\prime}\mathbf{x})\boldsymbol{\beta} = \mathrm{E}(\mathbf{x}^{*\prime}y), \tag{5.21}$$

since $\mathrm{E}(\mathbf{x}^{*\prime}u) = \mathbf{0}$. Thus, $\boldsymbol{\beta}$ is identified by $\boldsymbol{\beta} = [\mathrm{E}(\mathbf{x}^{*\prime}\mathbf{x})]^{-1}\mathrm{E}(\mathbf{x}^{*\prime}y)$ provided $\mathrm{E}(\mathbf{x}^{*\prime}\mathbf{x})$ is nonsingular. But

$$\mathrm{E}(\mathbf{x}^{*\prime}\mathbf{x}) = \boldsymbol{\Pi}'\mathrm{E}(\mathbf{z}'\mathbf{x}) = \mathrm{E}(\mathbf{x}'\mathbf{z})[\mathrm{E}(\mathbf{z}'\mathbf{z})]^{-1}\mathrm{E}(\mathbf{z}'\mathbf{x})$$

and this matrix is nonsingular if and only if $\mathrm{E}(\mathbf{z}'\mathbf{x})$ has rank K; that is, if and only if Assumption 2SLS.2b holds. If 2SLS.2b fails, then $\mathrm{E}(\mathbf{x}^{*\prime}\mathbf{x})$ is singular and $\boldsymbol{\beta}$ is not identified. (Note that, because $\mathbf{x} = \mathbf{x}^* + \mathbf{r}$ with $\mathrm{E}(\mathbf{x}^{*\prime}\mathbf{r}) = \mathbf{0}$, $\mathrm{E}(\mathbf{x}^{*\prime}\mathbf{x}) = \mathrm{E}(\mathbf{x}^{*\prime}\mathbf{x}^*)$. So $\boldsymbol{\beta}$ is identified if and only if rank $\mathrm{E}(\mathbf{x}^{*\prime}\mathbf{x}^*) = K$.)

The 2SLS estimator can be written as in equation (5.17) or as

$$\hat{\boldsymbol{\beta}} = \left[\left(\sum_{i=1}^{N}\mathbf{x}_i'\mathbf{z}_i\right)\left(\sum_{i=1}^{N}\mathbf{z}_i'\mathbf{z}_i\right)^{-1}\left(\sum_{i=1}^{N}\mathbf{z}_i'\mathbf{x}_i\right)\right]^{-1}\left(\sum_{i=1}^{N}\mathbf{x}_i'\mathbf{z}_i\right)\left(\sum_{i=1}^{N}\mathbf{z}_i'\mathbf{z}_i\right)^{-1}\left(\sum_{i=1}^{N}\mathbf{z}_i'y_i\right). \tag{5.22}$$

We have the following consistency result.

THEOREM 5.1 (Consistency of 2SLS): Under Assumptions 2SLS.1 and 2SLS.2, the 2SLS estimator obtained from a random sample is consistent for $\boldsymbol{\beta}$.

Proof: Write

$$\hat{\boldsymbol{\beta}} = \boldsymbol{\beta} + \left[\left(N^{-1}\sum_{i=1}^{N}\mathbf{x}_i'\mathbf{z}_i\right)\left(N^{-1}\sum_{i=1}^{N}\mathbf{z}_i'\mathbf{z}_i\right)^{-1}\left(N^{-1}\sum_{i=1}^{N}\mathbf{z}_i'\mathbf{x}_i\right)\right]^{-1}$$
$$\cdot\left(N^{-1}\sum_{i=1}^{N}\mathbf{x}_i'\mathbf{z}_i\right)\left(N^{-1}\sum_{i=1}^{N}\mathbf{z}_i'\mathbf{z}_i\right)^{-1}\left(N^{-1}\sum_{i=1}^{N}\mathbf{z}_i'u_i\right)$$

and, using Assumptions 2SLS.1 and 2SLS.2, apply the law of large numbers to each term along with Slutsky's theorem.

5.2.2 Asymptotic Normality of Two-Stage Least Squares

The asymptotic normality of $\sqrt{N}(\hat{\boldsymbol{\beta}} - \boldsymbol{\beta})$ follows from the asymptotic normality of $N^{-1/2}\sum_{i=1}^{N} \mathbf{z}_i' u_i$, which follows from the central limit theorem under Assumption 2SLS.1 and mild finite second-moment assumptions. The asymptotic variance is simplest under a homoskedasticity assumption:

ASSUMPTION 2SLS.3: $\mathrm{E}(u^2\mathbf{z}'\mathbf{z}) = \sigma^2\mathrm{E}(\mathbf{z}'\mathbf{z})$, where $\sigma^2 = \mathrm{E}(u^2)$.

This assumption is the same as Assumption OLS.3 except that the vector of instruments appears in place of $\mathbf{x}$. By the usual LIE argument, sufficient for Assumption 2SLS.3 is the assumption

$$\mathrm{E}(u^2 \mid \mathbf{z}) = \sigma^2, \tag{5.23}$$

which is the same as $\mathrm{Var}(u \mid \mathbf{z}) = \sigma^2$ if $\mathrm{E}(u \mid \mathbf{z}) = 0$. (When $\mathbf{x}$ contains endogenous elements, it makes no sense to make assumptions about $\mathrm{Var}(u \mid \mathbf{x})$.)

THEOREM 5.2 (Asymptotic Normality of 2SLS): Under Assumptions 2SLS.1–2SLS.3, $\sqrt{N}(\hat{\boldsymbol{\beta}} - \boldsymbol{\beta})$ is asymptotically normally distributed with mean zero and variance matrix

$$\sigma^2([\mathrm{E}(\mathbf{x}'\mathbf{z})][\mathrm{E}(\mathbf{z}'\mathbf{z})]^{-1}\mathrm{E}(\mathbf{z}'\mathbf{x})])^{-1} = \sigma^2[\mathrm{E}(\mathbf{x}^{*\prime}\mathbf{x}^*)]^{-1}, \tag{5.24}$$

where $\mathbf{x}^* = \mathbf{z}\boldsymbol{\Pi}$ is the $1 \times K$ vector of linear projections. The right-hand side of equation (5.24) is convenient because it has the same form as the expression for the OLS estimator—see equation (4.9)—but with $\mathbf{x}^*$ replacing $\mathbf{x}$. In particular, we can easily obtain a simple expression for the asymptotic variance for a single coefficient: $\mathrm{Avar}\sqrt{N}(\hat{\beta}_K - \beta_K) = \sigma^2/\mathrm{Var}(r_K^*)$, where r_K^* is the population residual from regressing x_K^* on $x_1^*, \ldots, x_{K-1}^*$ (where, typically, $x_1^* = 1$).

The proof of Theorem 5.2 is similar to Theorem 4.2 for OLS and is therefore omitted.

The matrix in expression (5.24) is easily estimated using sample averages. To estimate σ^2 we will need appropriate estimates of the u_i. Define the **2SLS residuals** as

$$\hat{u}_i = y_i - \mathbf{x}_i\hat{\boldsymbol{\beta}}, \qquad i = 1, 2, \ldots, N. \tag{5.25}$$

Note carefully that these residuals are *not* the residuals from the second-stage OLS regression that can be used to obtain the 2SLS estimates. The residuals from the second-stage regression are $y_i - \hat{\mathbf{x}}_i\hat{\boldsymbol{\beta}}$. Any 2SLS software routine will compute equation (5.25) as the 2SLS residuals, and these are what we need to estimate σ^2.

Given the 2SLS residuals, a consistent (though not unbiased) estimator of σ^2 under Assumptions 2SLS.1–2SLS.3 is

$$\hat{\sigma}^2 \equiv (N - K)^{-1} \sum_{i=1}^{N} \hat{u}_i^2. \tag{5.26}$$

Many regression packages use the degrees-of-freedom adjustment $N - K$ in place of N, but this usage does not affect the consistency of the estimator.

The $K \times K$ matrix

$$\hat{\sigma}^2 \left(\sum_{i=1}^{N} \hat{\mathbf{x}}_i' \hat{\mathbf{x}}_i \right)^{-1} = \hat{\sigma}^2 (\hat{\mathbf{X}}'\hat{\mathbf{X}})^{-1} \tag{5.27}$$

is a valid estimator of the asymptotic variance of $\hat{\boldsymbol{\beta}}$ under Assumptions 2SLS.1–2SLS.3. The (asymptotic) standard error of $\hat{\beta}_j$ is just the square root of the jth diagonal element of matrix (5.27). Asymptotic confidence intervals and t statistics are obtained in the usual fashion.

Example 5.3 (Parents' and Husband's Education as IVs): We use the data on the 428 working, married women in MROZ.RAW to estimate the wage equation (5.12). We assume that experience is exogenous, but we allow *educ* to be correlated with u. The instruments we use for *educ* are *motheduc*, *fatheduc*, and *huseduc*. The reduced form for *educ* is

$$educ = \delta_0 + \delta_1 exper + \delta_2 exper^2 + \theta_1 motheduc + \theta_2 fatheduc + \theta_3 huseduc + r.$$

Assuming that *motheduc*, *fatheduc*, and *huseduc* are exogenous in the log(*wage*) equation (a tenuous assumption), equation (5.12) is identified if at least one of θ_1, θ_2, and θ_3 is nonzero. We can test this assumption using an F test (under homoskedasticity). The F statistic (with 3 and 422 degrees of freedom) turns out to be 104.29, which implies a p-value of zero to four decimal places. Thus, as expected, *educ* is fairly strongly related to *motheduc*, *fatheduc*, and *huseduc*. (Each of the three t statistics is also very significant.)

When equation (5.12) is estimated by 2SLS, we get the following:

$$\begin{aligned} \log(\widehat{wage}) = {} & -.187 + .043\, exper - .00086\, exper^2 + .080\, educ, \\ & \;\;(.285) \quad (.013) \qquad\quad (.00040) \qquad\quad (.022) \end{aligned}$$

where standard errors are in parentheses. The 2SLS estimate of the return to education is about 8 percent, and it is statistically significant. For comparison, when equation (5.12) is estimated by OLS, the estimated coefficient on *educ* is about .107 with a standard error of about .014. Thus, the 2SLS estimate is notably below the OLS estimate and has a larger standard error.

5.2.3 Asymptotic Efficiency of Two-Stage Least Squares

The appeal of 2SLS comes from its efficiency in a class of IV estimators:

THEOREM 5.3 (Relative Efficiency of 2SLS): Under Assumptions 2SLS.1–2SLS.3, the 2SLS estimator is efficient in the class of all instrumental variables estimators using instruments linear in $\mathbf{z}$.

Proof: Let $\hat{\boldsymbol{\beta}}$ be the 2SLS estimator, and let $\tilde{\boldsymbol{\beta}}$ be any other IV estimator using instruments linear in $\mathbf{z}$. Let the instruments for $\tilde{\boldsymbol{\beta}}$ be $\tilde{\mathbf{x}} \equiv \mathbf{z}\boldsymbol{\Gamma}$, where $\boldsymbol{\Gamma}$ is an $L \times K$ nonstochastic matrix. (Note that $\mathbf{z}$ is the $1 \times L$ random vector in the population.) We assume that the rank condition holds for $\tilde{\mathbf{x}}$. For 2SLS, the choice of IVs is effectively $\mathbf{x}^* = \mathbf{z}\boldsymbol{\Pi}$, where $\boldsymbol{\Pi} = [\mathrm{E}(\mathbf{z}'\mathbf{z})]^{-1}\mathrm{E}(\mathbf{z}'\mathbf{x}) \equiv \mathbf{D}^{-1}\mathbf{C}$. (In both cases, we can replace $\boldsymbol{\Gamma}$ and $\boldsymbol{\Pi}$ with $\sqrt{N}$-consistent estimators without changing the asymptotic variances.) Now, under Assumptions 2SLS.1–2SLS.3, we know the asymptotic variance of $\sqrt{N}(\hat{\boldsymbol{\beta}} - \boldsymbol{\beta})$ is $\sigma^2[\mathrm{E}(\mathbf{x}^{*\prime}\mathbf{x}^*)]^{-1}$, where $\mathbf{x}^* = \mathbf{z}\boldsymbol{\Pi}$. It is straightforward to show that $\mathrm{Avar}[\sqrt{N}(\tilde{\boldsymbol{\beta}} - \boldsymbol{\beta})] = \sigma^2[\mathrm{E}(\tilde{\mathbf{x}}'\mathbf{x})]^{-1}[\mathrm{E}(\tilde{\mathbf{x}}'\tilde{\mathbf{x}})][\mathrm{E}(\mathbf{x}'\tilde{\mathbf{x}})]^{-1}$. To show that $\mathrm{Avar}[\sqrt{N}(\tilde{\boldsymbol{\beta}} - \boldsymbol{\beta})] - \mathrm{Avar}[\sqrt{N}(\hat{\boldsymbol{\beta}} - \boldsymbol{\beta})]$ is positive semidefinite (p.s.d.), it suffices to show that $\mathrm{E}(\mathbf{x}^{*\prime}\mathbf{x}^*) - \mathrm{E}(\mathbf{x}'\tilde{\mathbf{x}})[\mathrm{E}(\tilde{\mathbf{x}}'\tilde{\mathbf{x}})]^{-1}\mathrm{E}(\tilde{\mathbf{x}}'\mathbf{x})$ is p.s.d. But $\mathbf{x} = \mathbf{x}^* + \mathbf{r}$, where $\mathrm{E}(\mathbf{z}'\mathbf{r}) = \mathbf{0}$, and so $\mathrm{E}(\tilde{\mathbf{x}}'\mathbf{r}) = \mathbf{0}$. It follows that $\mathrm{E}(\tilde{\mathbf{x}}'\mathbf{x}) = \mathrm{E}(\tilde{\mathbf{x}}'\mathbf{x}^*)$, and so

$$\mathrm{E}(\mathbf{x}^{*\prime}\mathbf{x}^*) - \mathrm{E}(\mathbf{x}'\tilde{\mathbf{x}})[\mathrm{E}(\tilde{\mathbf{x}}'\tilde{\mathbf{x}})]^{-1}\mathrm{E}(\tilde{\mathbf{x}}'\mathbf{x})$$

$$= \mathrm{E}(\mathbf{x}^{*\prime}\mathbf{x}^*) - \mathrm{E}(\mathbf{x}^{*\prime}\tilde{\mathbf{x}})[\mathrm{E}(\tilde{\mathbf{x}}'\tilde{\mathbf{x}})]^{-1}\mathrm{E}(\tilde{\mathbf{x}}'\mathbf{x}^*) = \mathrm{E}(\mathbf{s}^{*\prime}\mathbf{s}^*),$$

where $\mathbf{s}^* = \mathbf{x}^* - \mathrm{L}(\mathbf{x}^* \mid \tilde{\mathbf{x}})$ is the population residual from the linear projection of $\mathbf{x}^*$ on $\tilde{\mathbf{x}}$. Because $\mathrm{E}(\mathbf{s}^{*\prime}\mathbf{s}^*)$ is p.s.d, the proof is complete.

Theorem 5.3 is vacuous when $L = K$ because any (nonsingular) choice of $\boldsymbol{\Gamma}$ leads to the same estimator: the IV estimator derived in Section 5.1.1.

When $\mathbf{x}$ is exogenous, Theorem 5.3 implies that, under Assumptions 2SLS.1–2SLS.3, the OLS estimator is efficient in the class of all estimators using instruments linear in all exogenous variables $\mathbf{z}$. Why? Because $\mathbf{x}$ is a subset of $\mathbf{z}$ and so $\mathrm{L}(\mathbf{x} \mid \mathbf{z}) = \mathbf{x}$.

Another important implication of Theorem 5.3 is that, asymptotically, we always do better by using as many instruments as are available, at least under homoskedasticity. This conclusion follows because using a subset of $\mathbf{z}$ as instruments corresponds to using a particular linear combination of $\mathbf{z}$. For certain subsets we might achieve the same efficiency as 2SLS using all of $\mathbf{z}$, but we can do no better. This observation makes it tempting to add many instruments so that L is much larger than K. Unfortunately, 2SLS estimators based on many overidentifying restrictions can cause finite sample problems; see Section 5.2.6.

Because Assumption 2SLS.3 is assumed for Theorem 5.3, it is not surprising that more efficient estimators are available if Assumption 2SLS.3 fails. If $L > K$, a more efficient estimator than 2SLS exists, as shown by Hansen (1982) and White (1982b, 1984). In fact, even if $\mathbf{x}$ is exogenous and Assumption OLS.3 holds, OLS is not generally asymptotically efficient if, for $\mathbf{x} \subset \mathbf{z}$, Assumptions 2SLS.1 and 2SLS.2 hold but Assumption 2SLS.3 does not. Obtaining the efficient estimator falls under the rubric of generalized method of moments estimation, something we cover in Chapter 8.

5.2.4 Hypothesis Testing with Two-Stage Least Squares

We have already seen that testing hypotheses about a single β_j is straightforward using an asymptotic t statistic, which has an asymptotic normal distribution under the null; some prefer to use the t distribution when N is small. Generally, one should be aware that the normal and t approximations can be poor if N is small. Hypotheses about single linear combinations involving the β_j are also easily carried out using a t statistic. The easiest procedure is to define the linear combination of interest, say $\theta \equiv a_1\beta_1 + a_2\beta_2 + \cdots + a_K\beta_K$, and then to write one of the β_j in terms of θ and the other elements of $\boldsymbol{\beta}$. Then, substitute into the equation of interest so that θ appears directly, and estimate the resulting equation by 2SLS to get the standard error of $\hat{\theta}$. See Problem 5.9 for an example.

To test multiple linear restrictions of the form H_0: $\mathbf{R}\boldsymbol{\beta} = \mathbf{r}$, the Wald statistic is just as in equation (4.13), but with $\hat{\mathbf{V}}$ given by equation (5.27). The Wald statistic, as usual, is a limiting null χ^2_Q distribution. Some econometrics packages, such as Stata, compute the Wald statistic (actually, its F statistic counterpart, obtained by dividing the Wald statistic by Q) after 2SLS estimation using a simple test command.

A valid test of multiple restrictions can be computed using a residual-based method, analogous to the usual F statistic from OLS analysis. Any kind of linear restriction can be recast as exclusion restrictions, and so we explicitly cover exclusion restrictions. Write the model as

$$y = \mathbf{x}_1\boldsymbol{\beta}_1 + \mathbf{x}_2\boldsymbol{\beta}_2 + u, \tag{5.28}$$

where $\mathbf{x}_1$ is $1 \times K_1$ and $\mathbf{x}_2$ is $1 \times K_2$, and interest lies in testing the K_2 restrictions

$$\text{H}_0\text{: } \boldsymbol{\beta}_2 = \mathbf{0} \qquad \text{against} \qquad \text{H}_1\text{: } \boldsymbol{\beta}_2 \neq \mathbf{0}. \tag{5.29}$$

Both $\mathbf{x}_1$ and $\mathbf{x}_2$ can contain endogenous and exogenous variables.

Let $\mathbf{z}$ denote the $L \geq K_1 + K_2$ vector of instruments, and we assume that the rank condition for identification holds. Justification for the following statistic can be found in Wooldridge (1995b).

Let $\hat{u}_i$ be the 2SLS residuals from estimating the unrestricted model using $\mathbf{z}_i$ as instruments. Using these residuals, define the 2SLS unrestricted sum of squared residuals by

$$\text{SSR}_{ur} \equiv \sum_{i=1}^{N} \hat{u}_i^2. \tag{5.30}$$

In order to define the F statistic for 2SLS, we need the sum of squared residuals from the *second*-stage regressions. Thus, let $\hat{\mathbf{x}}_{i1}$ be the $1 \times K_1$ fitted values from the first-stage regression $\mathbf{x}_{i1}$ on $\mathbf{z}_i$. Similarly, $\hat{\mathbf{x}}_{i2}$ are the fitted values from the first-stage regression $\mathbf{x}_{i2}$ on $\mathbf{z}_i$. Define $\widehat{\text{SSR}}_{ur}$ as the usual sum of squared residuals from the unrestricted second-stage regression y on $\hat{\mathbf{x}}_1$, $\hat{\mathbf{x}}_2$. Similarly, $\widehat{\text{SSR}}_r$ is the sum of squared residuals from the restricted second-stage regression, y on $\hat{\mathbf{x}}_1$. It can be shown that, under H_0: $\boldsymbol{\beta}_2 = \mathbf{0}$ (and Assumptions 2SLS.1–2SLS.3), $N \cdot (\widehat{\text{SSR}}_r - \widehat{\text{SSR}}_{ur})/\text{SSR}_{ur} \overset{a}{\sim} \chi^2_{K_2}$. It is just as legitimate to use an F-type statistic:

$$F \equiv \frac{(\widehat{\text{SSR}}_r - \widehat{\text{SSR}}_{ur})}{\text{SSR}_{ur}} \cdot \frac{(N-K)}{K_2} \tag{5.31}$$

is distributed approximately as $\mathcal{F}_{K_2, N-K}$.

Note carefully that $\widehat{\text{SSR}}_r$ and $\widehat{\text{SSR}}_{ur}$ appear in the numerator of (5.31). These quantities typically need to be computed directly from the second-stage regression. In the denominator of F is SSR_{ur}, which is the 2SLS sum of squared residuals. This is what is reported by the 2SLS commands available in popular regression packages.

For 2SLS, it is important not to use a form of the statistic that would work for OLS, namely,

$$\frac{(\text{SSR}_r - \text{SSR}_{ur})}{\text{SSR}_{ur}} \cdot \frac{(N-K)}{K_2}, \tag{5.32}$$

where SSR_r is the 2SLS restricted sum of squared residuals. Not only does expression (5.32) not have a known limiting distribution, but it can also be negative with positive probability even as the sample size tends to infinity; clearly, such a statistic cannot have an approximate F distribution, or any other distribution typically associated with multiple hypothesis testing.

Example 5.4 (Parents' and Husband's Education as IVs, continued): We add the number of young children (*kidslt6*) and older children (*kidsge6*) to equation (5.12) and test for their joint significance using the Mroz (1987) data. The statistic in equation (5.31) is $F = .31$; with 2 and 422 degrees of freedom, the asymptotic p-value is about .737. There is no evidence that number of children affects the wage for working women.

Rather than equation (5.31), we can compute an LM-type statistic for testing hypothesis (5.29). Let $\tilde{u}_i$ be the 2SLS residuals from the restricted model. That is, obtain $\tilde{\boldsymbol{\beta}}_1$ from the model $y = \mathbf{x}_1\beta_1 + u$ using instruments $\mathbf{z}$, and let $\tilde{u}_i \equiv y_i - \mathbf{x}_{i1}\tilde{\boldsymbol{\beta}}_1$. Letting $\hat{\mathbf{x}}_{i1}$ and $\hat{\mathbf{x}}_{i2}$ be defined as before, the LM statistic is obtained as NR_u^2 from the regression

$$\tilde{u}_i \text{ on } \hat{\mathbf{x}}_{i1}, \hat{\mathbf{x}}_{i2}, \qquad i = 1, 2, \ldots, N \tag{5.33}$$

where R_u^2 is generally the uncentered R-squared. (That is, the total sum of squares in the denominator of R-squared is not demeaned.) When $\{\tilde{u}_i\}$ has a zero sample average, the uncentered R-squared and the usual R-squared are the same. This is the case when the null explanatory variables $\mathbf{x}_1$ and the instruments $\mathbf{z}$ both contain unity, the typical case. Under H_0 and Assumptions 2SLS.1–2SLS.3, $LM \overset{a}{\sim} \chi^2_{K_2}$. Whether one uses this statistic or the F statistic in equation (5.31) is primarily a matter of taste; asymptotically, there is nothing that distinguishes the two.

5.2.5 Heteroskedasticity-Robust Inference for Two-Stage Least Squares

Assumption 2SLS.3 can be restrictive, so we should have a variance matrix estimator that is robust in the presence of heteroskedasticity of unknown form. As usual, we need to estimate $\mathbf{B}$ along with $\mathbf{A}$. Under Assumptions 2SLS.1 and 2SLS.2 only, $\mathrm{Avar}(\hat{\boldsymbol{\beta}})$ can be estimated as

$$(\hat{\mathbf{X}}'\hat{\mathbf{X}})^{-1}\left(\sum_{i=1}^{N} \hat{u}_i^2 \hat{\mathbf{x}}_i'\hat{\mathbf{x}}_i\right)(\hat{\mathbf{X}}'\hat{\mathbf{X}})^{-1}. \tag{5.34}$$

Sometimes this matrix is multiplied by $N/(N-K)$ as a degrees-of-freedom adjustment. This heteroskedasticity-robust estimator can be used anywhere the estimator $\hat{\sigma}^2(\hat{\mathbf{X}}'\hat{\mathbf{X}})^{-1}$ is. In particular, the square roots of the diagonal elements of the matrix (5.34) are the heteroskedasticity-robust standard errors for 2SLS. These can be used to construct (asymptotic) t statistics in the usual way. Some packages compute these standard errors using a simple command. For example, using Stata, rounded to three decimal places the heteroskedasticity-robust standard error for *educ* in Example 5.3 is .022, which is the same as the usual standard error rounded to three decimal places. The robust standard error for *exper* is .015, somewhat higher than the nonrobust one (.013).

Sometimes it is useful to compute a robust standard error that can be computed with any regression package. Wooldridge (1995b) shows how this procedure can be carried out using an auxiliary linear regression for each parameter. Consider computing the robust standard error for $\hat{\beta}_j$. Let "se($\hat{\beta}_j$)" denote the standard error computed using the usual variance matrix (5.27); we put this in quotes because it is no longer appropriate if Assumption 2SLS.3 fails. The $\hat{\sigma}$ is obtained from equation (5.26), and $\hat{u}_i$ are the 2SLS residuals from equation (5.25). Let $\hat{r}_{ij}$ be the residuals from the regression

$$\hat{x}_{ij} \text{ on } \hat{x}_{i1}, \hat{x}_{i2}, \ldots, \hat{x}_{i,j-1}, \hat{x}_{i,j+1}, \ldots, \hat{x}_{iK}, \qquad i = 1, 2, \ldots, N$$

and define $\hat{m}_j \equiv \sum_{i=1}^{N} \hat{r}_{ij}\hat{u}_i$. Then, a heteroskedasticity-robust standard error of $\hat{\beta}_j$ can be calculated as

$$\text{se}(\hat{\beta}_j) = [N/(N-K)]^{1/2}[\text{“se}(\hat{\beta}_j)\text{”}/\hat{\sigma}]^2/(\hat{m}_j)^{1/2}. \tag{5.35}$$

Many econometrics packages compute equation (5.35) for you, but it is also easy to compute directly.

To test multiple linear restrictions using the Wald approach, we can use the usual statistic but with the matrix (5.34) as the estimated variance. For example, the heteroskedasticity-robust version of the test in Example 5.4 gives $F = .25$; asymptotically, F can be treated as an $\mathcal{F}_{2,422}$ variate. The asymptotic p-value is .781.

The Lagrange multiplier test for omitted variables is easily made heteroskedasticity-robust. Again, consider the model (5.28) with the null (5.29), but this time without the homoskedasticity assumptions. Using the notation from before, let $\hat{\mathbf{r}}_i \equiv (\hat{r}_{i1}, \hat{r}_{i2}, \ldots, \hat{r}_{iK_2})$ be the $1 \times K_2$ vectors of residuals from the multivariate regression $\hat{\mathbf{x}}_{i2}$ on $\hat{\mathbf{x}}_{i1}$, $i = 1, 2, \ldots, N$. (Again, this procedure can be carried out by regressing each element of $\hat{\mathbf{x}}_{i2}$ on all of $\hat{\mathbf{x}}_{i1}$.) Then, for each observation, form the $1 \times K_2$ vector $\tilde{u}_i \cdot \hat{\mathbf{r}}_i \equiv (\tilde{u}_i \cdot \hat{r}_{i1}, \ldots, \tilde{u}_i \cdot \hat{r}_{iK_2})$. Then, the robust LM test is $N - \text{SSR}_0$ from the regression 1 on $\tilde{u}_i \cdot \hat{r}_{i1}, \ldots, \tilde{u}_i \cdot \hat{r}_{iK_2}$, $i = 1, 2, \ldots, N$. Under H_0, $N - \text{SSR}_0 \overset{a}{\sim} \chi^2_{K_2}$. This procedure can be justified in a manner similar to the tests in the context of OLS. You are referred to Wooldridge (1995b) for details.

5.2.6 Potential Pitfalls with Two-Stage Least Squares

When properly applied, the method of instrumental variables can be a powerful tool for estimating structural equations using nonexperimental data. Nevertheless, there are some problems that one can encounter when applying IV in practice.

One thing to remember is that, unlike OLS under a zero conditional mean assumption, IV methods are never unbiased when at least one explanatory variable is endogenous in the model. In fact, under standard distributional assumptions, the expected value of the 2SLS estimator does not even exist. As shown by Kinal (1980), in the case when all endogenous variables have homoskedastic normal distributions with expectations linear in the exogenous variables, the number of moments of the 2SLS estimator that exist is one fewer than the number of overidentifying restrictions. This finding implies that when the number of instruments equals the number of explanatory variables, the IV estimator does not have an expected value. This is one reason we rely on large-sample analysis to justify 2SLS.

Even in large samples, IV methods can be ill-behaved if we have **weak instruments**. Consider the simple model $y = \beta_0 + \beta_1 x_1 + u$, where we use z_1 as an instrument for x_1. Assuming that $\mathrm{Cov}(z_1, x_1) \neq 0$, the plim of the IV estimator is easily shown to be

$$\mathrm{plim}\ \hat{\beta}_1 = \beta_1 + \mathrm{Cov}(z_1, u)/\mathrm{Cov}(z_1, x_1),$$

which can be written as

$$\mathrm{plim}\ \hat{\beta}_1 = \beta_1 + (\sigma_u/\sigma_{x_1})[\mathrm{Corr}(z_1, u)/\mathrm{Corr}(z_1, x_1)], \tag{5.36}$$

where $\mathrm{Corr}(\cdot\,,\cdot)$ denotes correlation. From this equation we see that if z_1 and u are correlated, the inconsistency in the IV estimator gets arbitrarily large as $\mathrm{Corr}(z_1, x_1)$ gets close to zero. Thus, seemingly small correlations between z_1 and u can cause severe inconsistency—and therefore severe finite sample bias—if z_1 is only weakly correlated with x_1. In fact, it may be better to just use OLS, even if we look only at the inconsistencies in the estimators. To see why, let $\tilde{\beta}_1$ denote the OLS estimator and write its plim as

$$\mathrm{plim}(\tilde{\beta}_1) = \beta_1 + (\sigma_u/\sigma_{x_1})\ \mathrm{Corr}(x_1, u). \tag{5.37}$$

Comparing equations (5.37) and (5.36), the signs of the inconsistency of OLS and IV can be different. Further, the magnitude of the inconsistency in OLS is smaller than that of the IV estimator if $|\mathrm{Corr}(x_1, u)| \cdot |\mathrm{Corr}(z_1, x_1)| < |\mathrm{Corr}(z_1, u)|$. This simple inequality makes it apparent that a weak instrument—captured here by small $|\mathrm{Corr}(z_1, x_1)|$—can easily make IV have more asymptotic bias than OLS. Unfortunately, we never observe u, so we cannot know how large $|\mathrm{Corr}(z_1, u)|$ is relative to $|\mathrm{Corr}(x_1, u)|$. But what is certain is that a small correlation between z_1 and x_1—which we can estimate—should raise concerns, even if we think z_1 is "almost" exogenous.

Another potential problem with applying 2SLS and other IV procedures is that the 2SLS standard errors have a tendency to be "large." What is typically meant by this statement is either that 2SLS coefficients are statistically insignificant or that the 2SLS standard errors are much larger than the OLS standard errors. Not suprisingly, the magnitudes of the 2SLS standard errors depend, among other things, on the quality of the instrument(s) used in estimation.

For the following discussion we maintain the standard 2SLS Assumptions 2SLS.1–2SLS.3 in the model

$$y = \beta_0 + \beta_1 x_1 + \beta_2 x_2 + \cdots + \beta_K x_K + u. \tag{5.38}$$

Let $\hat{\boldsymbol{\beta}}$ be the vector of 2SLS estimators using instruments $\mathbf{z}$. For concreteness, we focus on the asymptotic variance of $\hat{\beta}_K$. Technically, we should study Avar $\sqrt{N}(\hat{\beta}_K - \beta_K)$, but it is easier to work with an expression that contains the same information. In particular, we use the fact that

$$\text{Avar}(\hat{\beta}_K) \approx \frac{\sigma^2}{\widehat{\text{SSR}}_K}, \tag{5.39}$$

where $\widehat{\text{SSR}}_K$ is the sum of squared residuals from the regression

$$\hat{x}_K \text{ on } 1, \; \hat{x}_1, \ldots, \hat{x}_{K-1}. \tag{5.40}$$

(Remember, if x_j is exogenous for any j, then $\hat{x}_j = x_j$.) If we replace σ^2 in regression (5.39) with $\hat{\sigma}^2$, then expression (5.39) is the usual 2SLS variance estimator. For the current discussion we are interested in the behavior of $\widehat{\text{SSR}}_K$.

From the definition of an R-squared, we can write

$$\widehat{\text{SSR}}_K = \widehat{\text{SST}}_K(1 - \hat{R}_K^2), \tag{5.41}$$

where $\widehat{\text{SST}}_K$ is the total sum of squares of $\hat{x}_K$ in the sample, $\widehat{\text{SST}}_K = \sum_{i=1}^N (\hat{x}_{iK} - \bar{\hat{x}}_K)^2$, and $\hat{R}_K^2$ is the R-squared from regression (5.40). In the context of OLS, the term $(1 - \hat{R}_K^2)$ in equation (5.41) is viewed as a measure of multicollinearity, whereas $\widehat{\text{SST}}_K$ measures the total variation in $\hat{x}_K$. We see that, in addition to traditional multicollinearity, 2SLS can have an additional source of large variance: the total variation in $\hat{x}_K$ can be small.

When is $\widehat{\text{SST}}_K$ small? Remember, $\hat{x}_K$ denotes the fitted values from the regression

$$x_K \text{ on } \mathbf{z} \tag{5.42}$$

Therefore, $\widehat{\text{SST}}_K$ is the *same* as the explained sum of squares from the regression (5.42). If x_K is only weakly related to the IVs, then the explained sum of squares from regression (5.42) can be quite small, causing a large asymptotic variance for $\hat{\beta}_K$. If x_K is highly correlated with $\mathbf{z}$, then $\widehat{\text{SST}}_K$ can be almost as large as the total sum of squares of x_K and SST_K, and this fact reduces the 2SLS variance estimate.

When x_K is exogenous—whether or not the other elements of $\mathbf{x}$ are—$\widehat{\text{SST}}_K = \text{SST}_K$. While this total variation can be small, it is determined only by the sample variation in $\{x_{iK}: i = 1, 2, \ldots, N\}$. Therefore, for exogenous elements appearing among $\mathbf{x}$, the quality of instruments has no bearing on the size of the total sum of squares term in equation (5.41). This fact helps explain why the 2SLS estimates on exogenous explanatory variables are often much more precise than the coefficients on endogenous explanatory variables.

In addition to making the term $\widehat{\mathrm{SST}}_K$ small, poor quality of instruments can lead to $\hat{R}_K^2$ close to one. As an illustration, consider a model in which x_K is the only endogenous variable and there is one instrument z_1 in addition to the exogenous variables $(1, x_1, \ldots, x_{K-1})$. Therefore, $\mathbf{z} \equiv (1, x_1, \ldots, x_{K-1}, z_1)$. (The same argument works for multiple instruments.) The fitted values $\hat{x}_K$ come from the regression

$$x_K \text{ on } 1,\ x_1, \ldots, x_{K-1}, z_1. \tag{5.43}$$

Because all other regressors are exogenous (that is, they are included in $\mathbf{z}$), $\hat{R}_K^2$ comes from the regression

$$\hat{x}_K \text{ on } 1,\ x_1, \ldots, x_{K-1}. \tag{5.44}$$

Now, from basic least squares mechanics, if the coefficient on z_1 in regression (5.43) is exactly zero, then the R-squared from regression (5.44) is exactly unity, in which case the 2SLS estimator does not even exist. This outcome virtually never happens, but z_1 could have little explanatory value for x_K once $x_1, \ldots, x_{K-1}$ have been controlled for, in which case $\hat{R}_K^2$ can be close to one. Identification, which only has to do with whether we can consistently estimate $\boldsymbol{\beta}$, requires only that z_1 appear with nonzero coefficient in the population analogue of regression (5.43). But if the explanatory power of z_1 is weak, the asymptotic variance of the 2SLS estimator can be quite large. This is another way to illustrate why nonzero correlation between x_K and z_1 is not enough for 2SLS to be effective: the *partial* correlation is what matters for the asymptotic variance.

Shea (1997) uses equation (5.39) and the analogous formula for OLS to define a measure of "instrument relevance" for x_K (when it is treated as endogenous). The measure is simply $\widehat{\mathrm{SSR}}_K/\mathrm{SSR}_K$, where SSR_K is the sum of squared residuals from the regression x_K on $x_1, \ldots, x_{K-1}$. In other words, the measure is essentially the ratio of the asymptotic variance estimator of OLS (when it is consistent) to the asymptotic variance estimator of the 2SLS estimator. Shea (1997) notes that the measure also can be computed as the squared correlation between two sets of residuals, the first obtained from regressing $\hat{x}_K$ on $\hat{x}_1, \ldots, \hat{x}_{K-1}$ and the second obtained from regressing x_K on $x_1, \ldots, x_{K-1}$. Further, the probability limit of $\widehat{\mathrm{SSR}}_K/\mathrm{SSR}_K$ appears in the inconsistency of the 2SLS estimator (relative to the OLS estimator), but with some other terms that cannot be estimated.

Shea's measure is useful for summarizing the strength of the instruments in a single number. Nevertheless, like measures of multicollinearity, Shea's measure of instrument relevance has its shortcomings. In effect, it uses OLS as a benchmark and records how much larger the 2SLS standard errors are than the OLS standard errors. It says nothing directly about whether the 2SLS estimator is precise enough for inference purposes or whether the asymptotic normal approximation to the actual distribution of the 2SLS is acceptable. And, of course, it is silent on whether the instruments are actually exogenous.

We are in a difficult situation when the 2SLS standard errors are so large that nothing is significant. Often we must choose between a possibly inconsistent estimator that has relatively small standard errors (OLS) and a consistent estimator that is so imprecise that nothing interesting can be concluded (2SLS). One approach is to use OLS unless we can reject exogeneity of the explanatory variables. We show how to test for endogeneity of one or more explanatory variables in Section 6.2.1.

There has been some important recent work on the finite sample properties of 2SLS that emphasizes the potentially large *biases* of 2SLS, even when sample sizes seem to be quite large. Remember that the 2SLS estimator is never unbiased (provided one has at least one truly endogenous variable in $\mathbf{x}$). But we hope that, with a very large sample size, we need only weak instruments to get an estimator with small bias. Unfortunately, this hope is not fulfilled. For example, Bound, Jaeger, and Baker (1995) show that in the setting of Angrist and Krueger (1991), the 2SLS estimator can be expected to behave quite poorly, an alarming finding because Angrist and Krueger use 300,000 to 500,000 observations! The problem is that the instruments—representing quarters of birth and various interactions of these with year of birth and state of birth—are very weak, and they are too numerous relative to their contribution in explaining years of education. One lesson is that, even with a very large sample size and zero correlation between the instruments and error, we should not use too many overidentifying restrictions.

Staiger and Stock (1997) provide a theoretical analysis of the 2SLS estimator (and related estimators) with weak instruments. Formally, they model the weak instrument problem as one where the coefficients on the instruments in the reduced form of the exogenous variables converge to zero as the sample increases at the rate $1/\sqrt{N}$; in the limit, the model is not identified. (This device is not intended to capture the way data are actually generated; its usefulness is in the resulting approximations to the exact distribution of the IV estimators.) For example, in the simple regression model with a single instrument, the reduced form is assumed to be $x_{i1} = \pi_0 + (\rho_1/\sqrt{N})z_{i1} + v_{i1}$, $i = 1, 2, \ldots, N$, where $\rho_1 \neq 0$. Because $\rho_1/\sqrt{N} \to 0$, the resulting asymptotic analysis is much different from the first-order asymptotic theory we have covered in this chapter; in fact, the 2SLS estimator is inconsistent and has a nonnormal limiting distribution not centered at the population parameter value.

One lesson that comes out of the Staiger-Stock work is that we should always compute the F statistics from first-stage regressions (or the t statistic with a single instrumental variable). Staiger and Stock (1997) provide some guidelines about how large the first-stage F statistic should be (equivalently, how small the associated p-value should be) for 2SLS to have acceptable statistical properties. These guidelines should be generally helpful, but they are derived assuming the endogenous explanatory variables have linear conditional expectations and constant variance conditional on the exogenous variables.

5.3 IV Solutions to the Omitted Variables and Measurement Error Problems

In this section, we briefly survey the different approaches that have been suggested for using IV methods to solve the omitted variables problem. Section 5.3.2 covers an approach that applies to measurement error as well.

5.3.1 Leaving the Omitted Factors in the Error Term

Consider again the omitted variable model

$$y = \beta_0 + \beta_1 x_1 + \cdots + \beta_K x_K + \gamma q + v, \tag{5.45}$$

where q represents the omitted variable and $\mathrm{E}(v \mid \mathbf{x}, q) = 0$. The solution that would follow from Section 5.1.1 is to put q in the error term, and then to find instruments for any element of $\mathbf{x}$ that is correlated with q. It is useful to think of the instruments satisfying the following requirements: (1) they are redundant in the structural model $\mathrm{E}(y \mid \mathbf{x}, q)$; (2) they are uncorrelated with the omitted variable, q; and (3) they are sufficiently correlated with the endogenous elements of $\mathbf{x}$ (that is, those elements that are correlated with q). Then 2SLS applied to equation (5.45) with $u \equiv \gamma q + v$ produces consistent and asymptotically normal estimators.

5.3.2 Solutions Using Indicators of the Unobservables

An alternative solution to the omitted variable problem is similar to the OLS proxy variable solution but requires IV rather than OLS estimation. In the OLS proxy variable solution we assume that we have z_1 such that $q = \theta_0 + \theta_1 z_1 + r_1$, where r_1 is uncorrelated with z_1 (by definition) *and* is uncorrelated with $x_1, \ldots, x_K$ (the key proxy variable assumption). Suppose instead that we have two **indicators** of q. Like a proxy variable, an indicator of q must be redundant in equation (5.45). The key difference is that an indicator can be written as

$$q_1 = \delta_0 + \delta_1 q + a_1, \tag{5.46}$$

where

$$\mathrm{Cov}(q, a_1) = 0, \qquad \mathrm{Cov}(\mathbf{x}, a_1) = \mathbf{0}. \tag{5.47}$$

This assumption contains the classical errors-in-variables model as a special case, where q is the unobservable, q_1 is the observed measurement, $\delta_0 = 0$, and $\delta_1 = 1$, in which case γ in equation (5.45) can be identified.

Assumption (5.47) is very different from the proxy variable assumption. Assuming that $\delta_1 \neq 0$—otherwise, q_1 is not correlated with q—we can rearrange equation (5.46) as

$$q = -(\delta_0/\delta_1) + (1/\delta_1)q_1 - (1/\delta_1)a_1, \tag{5.48}$$

where the error in this equation, $-(1/\delta_1)a_1$, is necessarily correlated with q_1; the OLS–proxy variable solution would be inconsistent.

To use the indicator assumption (5.47), we need some additional information. One possibility is to have a second indicator of q:

$$q_2 = \rho_0 + \rho_1 q + a_2, \tag{5.49}$$

where a_2 satisfies the same assumptions as a_1 and $\rho_1 \neq 0$. We still need one more assumption:

$$\mathrm{Cov}(a_1, a_2) = 0. \tag{5.50}$$

This implies that any correlation between q_1 and q_2 arises through their common dependence on q.

Plugging q_1 in for q and rearranging gives

$$y = \alpha_0 + \mathbf{x}\boldsymbol{\beta} + \gamma_1 q_1 + (v - \gamma_1 a_1), \tag{5.51}$$

where $\gamma_1 = \gamma/\delta_1$. Now, q_2 is uncorrelated with v because it is redundant in equation (5.45). Further, by assumption, q_2 is uncorrelated with a_1 (a_1 is uncorrelated with q and a_2). Since q_1 and q_2 are correlated, q_2 can be used as an IV for q_1 in equation (5.51). Of course, the roles of q_2 and q_1 can be reversed. This solution to the omitted variables problem is sometimes called the **multiple indicator solution**.

It is important to see that the multiple indicator IV solution is very different from the IV solution that leaves q in the error term. When we leave q as part of the error, we must decide which elements of $\mathbf{x}$ are correlated with q, and then find IVs for those elements of $\mathbf{x}$. With multiple indicators for q, we need not know which elements of $\mathbf{x}$

are correlated with q; they all might be. In equation (5.51) the elements of $\mathbf{x}$ serve as their own instruments. Under the assumptions we have made, we only need an instrument for q_1, and q_2 serves that purpose.

Example 5.5 (IQ and KWW as Indicators of Ability): We apply the indicator method to the model of Example 4.3, using the 935 observations in NLS80.RAW. In addition to *IQ*, we have a knowledge of the working world (*KWW*) test score. If we write $IQ = \delta_0 + \delta_1 abil + a_1$, $KWW = \rho_0 + \rho_1 abil + a_2$, and the previous assumptions are satisfied in equation (4.29), then we can add *IQ* to the wage equation and use *KWW* as an instrument for *IQ*. We get

$$\begin{aligned}\log(\widehat{wage}) = {} & \underset{(0.33)}{4.59} + \underset{(.003)}{.014}\, exper + \underset{(.003)}{.010}\, tenure + \underset{(.041)}{.201}\, married \\ & - \underset{(.031)}{.051}\, south + \underset{(.028)}{.177}\, urban - \underset{(.074)}{.023}\, black + \underset{(.017)}{.025}\, educ + \underset{(.005)}{.013}\, IQ.\end{aligned}$$

The estimated return to education is about 2.5 percent, and it is not statistically significant at the 5 percent level even with a one-sided alternative. If we reverse the roles of *KWW* and *IQ*, we get an even smaller return to education: about 1.7 percent, with a t statistic of about 1.07. The statistical insignificance is perhaps not too surprising given that we are using IV, but the magnitudes of the estimates are surprisingly small. Perhaps a_1 and a_2 are correlated with each other, or with some elements of $\mathbf{x}$.

In the case of the CEV measurement error model, q_1 and q_2 are measures of q assumed to have uncorrelated measurement errors. Since $\delta_0 = \rho_0 = 0$ and $\delta_1 = \rho_1 = 1$, $\gamma_1 = \gamma$. Therefore, having two measures, where we plug one into the equation and use the other as its instrument, provides consistent estimators of all parameters in the CEV setup.

There are other ways to use indicators of an omitted variable (or a single measurement in the context of measurement error) in an IV approach. Suppose that only one indicator of q is available. Without further information, the parameters in the structural model are not identified. However, suppose we have additional variables that are redundant in the structural equation (uncorrelated with v), are uncorrelated with the error a_1 in the indicator equation, and are correlated with q. Then, as you are asked to show in Problem 5.7, estimating equation (5.51) using this additional set of variables as instruments for q_1 produces consistent estimators. This is almost the method proposed by Griliches and Mason (1972). As discussed by Cardell and Hopkins (1977), Griliches and Mason incorrectly restrict the reduced form for q_1; see Problem 5.11. Blackburn and Neumark (1992) correctly implement the IV method.

Problems

5.1. In this problem you are to establish the algebraic equivalence between 2SLS and OLS estimation of an equation containing an additional regressor. Although the result is completely general, for simplicity consider a model with a single (suspected) endogenous variable:

$$y_1 = \mathbf{z}_1\boldsymbol{\delta}_1 + \alpha_1 y_2 + u_1,$$

$$y_2 = \mathbf{z}\boldsymbol{\pi}_2 + v_2.$$

For notational clarity, we use y_2 as the suspected endogenous variable and $\mathbf{z}$ as the vector of all exogenous variables. The second equation is the reduced form for y_2. Assume that $\mathbf{z}$ has at least one more element than $\mathbf{z}_1$.

We know that one estimator of $(\boldsymbol{\delta}_1, \alpha_1)$ is the 2SLS estimator using instruments $\mathbf{x}$. Consider an alternative estimator of $(\boldsymbol{\delta}_1, \alpha_1)$: (a) estimate the reduced form by OLS, and save the residuals $\hat{v}_2$; (b) estimate the following equation by OLS:

$$y_1 = \mathbf{z}_1\boldsymbol{\delta}_1 + \alpha_1 y_2 + \rho_1 \hat{v}_2 + error. \tag{5.52}$$

Show that the OLS estimates of $\boldsymbol{\delta}_1$ and α_1 from this regression are identical to the 2SLS estimators. (Hint: Use the partitioned regression algebra of OLS. In particular, if $\hat{y} = \mathbf{x}_1\hat{\boldsymbol{\beta}}_1 + \mathbf{x}_2\hat{\boldsymbol{\beta}}_2$ is an OLS regression, $\hat{\boldsymbol{\beta}}_1$ can be obtained by first regressing $\mathbf{x}_1$ on $\mathbf{x}_2$, getting the residuals, say $\ddot{\mathbf{x}}_1$, and then regressing y on $\ddot{\mathbf{x}}_1$; see, for example, Davidson and MacKinnon (1993, Section 1.4). You must also use the fact that $\mathbf{z}_1$ and $\hat{v}_2$ are orthogonal in the sample.)

5.2. Consider a model for the health of an individual:

$$\begin{aligned} health = {} & \beta_0 + \beta_1 age + \beta_2 weight + \beta_3 height \\ & + \beta_4 male + \beta_5 work + \beta_6 exercise + u_1, \end{aligned} \tag{5.53}$$

where *health* is some quantitative measure of the person's *health*; *age*, *weight*, *height*, and *male* are self-explanatory; *work* is weekly hours worked; and *exercise* is the hours of exercise per week.

a. Why might you be concerned about *exercise* being correlated with the error term u_1?

b. Suppose you can collect data on two additional variables, *disthome* and *distwork*, the distances from home and from work to the nearest health club or gym. Discuss whether these are likely to be uncorrelated with u_1.

c. Now assume that *disthome* and *distwork* are in fact uncorrelated with u_1, as are all variables in equation (5.53) with the exception of *exercise*. Write down the reduced form for *exercise*, and state the conditions under which the parameters of equation (5.53) are identified.

d. How can the identification assumption in part c be tested?

5.3. Consider the following model to estimate the effects of several variables, including cigarette smoking, on the weight of newborns:

$$\log(bwght) = \beta_0 + \beta_1 male + \beta_2 parity + \beta_3 \log(faminc) + \beta_4 packs + u, \tag{5.54}$$

where *male* is a binary indicator equal to one if the child is male, *parity* is the birth order of this child, *faminc* is family income, and *packs* is the average number of packs of cigarettes smoked per day during pregnancy.

a. Why might you expect *packs* to be correlated with *u*?

b. Suppose that you have data on average cigarette price in each woman's state of residence. Discuss whether this information is likely to satisfy the properties of a good instrumental variable for packs.

c. Use the data in BWGHT.RAW to estimate equation (5.54). First, use OLS. Then, use 2SLS, where *cigprice* is an instrument for packs. Discuss any important differences in the OLS and 2SLS estimates.

d. Estimate the reduced form for *packs*. What do you conclude about identification of equation (5.54) using *cigprice* as an instrument for *packs*? What bearing does this conclusion have on your answer from part c?

5.4. Use the data in CARD.RAW for this problem.

a. Estimate a log(*wage*) equation by OLS with *educ*, *exper*, $exper^2$, *black*, *south*, *smsa*, *reg661* through *reg668*, and *smsa66* as explanatory variables. Compare your results with Table 2, Column (2) in Card (1995).

b. Estimate a reduced form equation for *educ* containing all explanatory variables from part a and the dummy variable *nearc4*. Do *educ* and *nearc4* have a practically and statistically significant partial correlation? (See also Table 3, Column (1) in Card (1995).)

c. Estimate the log(*wage*) equation by IV, using *nearc4* as an instrument for *educ*. Compare the 95 percent confidence interval for the return to education with that obtained from part a. (See also Table 3, Column (5) in Card (1995).)

d. Now use *nearc2* along with *nearc4* as instruments for *educ*. First estimate the reduced form for *educ*, and comment on whether *nearc2* or *nearc4* is more strongly related to *educ*. How do the 2SLS estimates compare with the earlier estimates?

e. For a subset of the men in the sample, IQ score is available. Regress *iq* on *nearc4*. Is IQ score uncorrelated with *nearc4*?

f. Now regress *iq* on *nearc4* along with *smsa66*, *reg661*, *reg662*, and *reg669*. Are *iq* and *nearc4* partially correlated? What do you conclude about the importance of controlling for the 1966 location and regional dummies in the log(*wage*) equation when using *nearc4* as an IV for *educ*?

5.5. One occasionally sees the following reasoning used in applied work for choosing instrumental variables in the context of omitted variables. The model is

$$y_1 = \mathbf{z}_1\boldsymbol{\delta}_1 + \alpha_1 y_2 + \gamma q + a_1,$$

where q is the omitted factor. We assume that a_1 satisfies the structural error assumption $\mathrm{E}(a_1 \mid \mathbf{z}_1, y_2, q) = 0$, that $\mathbf{z}_1$ is exogenous in the sense that $\mathrm{E}(q \mid \mathbf{z}_1) = 0$, but that y_2 and q may be correlated. Let $\mathbf{z}_2$ be a vector of instrumental variable candidates for y_2. Suppose it is known that $\mathbf{z}_2$ appears in the linear projection of y_2 onto $(\mathbf{z}_1, \mathbf{z}_2)$, and so the requirement that $\mathbf{z}_2$ be partially correlated with y_2 is satisfied. Also, we are willing to assume that $\mathbf{z}_2$ is redundant in the structural equation, so that a_1 is uncorrelated with $\mathbf{z}_2$. What we are unsure of is whether $\mathbf{z}_2$ is correlated with the omitted variable q, in which case $\mathbf{z}_2$ would not contain valid IVs.

To "test" whether $\mathbf{z}_2$ is in fact uncorrelated with q, it has been suggested to use OLS on the equation

$$y_1 = \mathbf{z}_1\boldsymbol{\delta}_1 + \alpha_1 y_2 + \mathbf{z}_2\boldsymbol{\psi}_1 + u_1, \tag{5.55}$$

where $u_1 = \gamma q + a_1$, and test $\mathrm{H}_0\colon \boldsymbol{\psi}_1 = \mathbf{0}$. Why does this method not work?

5.6. Refer to the multiple indicator model in Section 5.3.2.

a. Show that if q_2 is uncorrelated with x_j, $j = 1, 2, \ldots, K$, then the reduced form of q_1 depends only on q_2. (Hint: Use the fact that the reduced form of q_1 is the linear projection of q_1 onto $(1, x_1, x_2, \ldots, x_K, q_2)$ and find the coefficient vector on $\mathbf{x}$ using Property LP.7 from Chapter 2.)

b. What happens if q_2 and $\mathbf{x}$ are correlated? In this setting, is it realistic to assume that q_2 and $\mathbf{x}$ are uncorrelated? Explain.

5.7. Consider model (5.45) where v has zero mean and is uncorrelated with $x_1, \ldots, x_K$ and q. The unobservable q is thought to be correlated with at least some of the x_j. Assume without loss of generality that $\mathrm{E}(q) = 0$.

You have a single indicator of q, written as $q_1 = \delta_1 q + a_1$, $\delta_1 \neq 0$, where a_1 has zero mean and is uncorrelated with each of x_j, q, and v. In addition, $z_1, z_2, \ldots, z_M$ is a set of variables that are (1) redundant in the structural equation (5.45) and (2) uncorrelated with a_1.

a. Suggest an IV method for consistently estimating the β_j. Be sure to discuss what is needed for identification.

b. If equation (5.45) is a $\log(wage)$ equation, q is ability, q_1 is IQ or some other test score, and $z_1, \ldots, z_M$ are family background variables, such as parents' education and number of siblings, describe the economic assumptions needed for consistency of the the IV procedure in part a.

c. Carry out this procedure using the data in NLS80.RAW. Include among the explanatory variables *exper*, *tenure*, *educ*, *married*, *south*, *urban*, and *black*. First use IQ as q_1 and then KWW. Include in the z_h the variables *meduc*, *feduc*, and *sibs*. Discuss the results.

5.8. Consider a model with unobserved heterogeneity (q) and measurement error in an explanatory variable:

$$y = \beta_0 + \beta_1 x_1 + \cdots + \beta_K x_K^* + q + v,$$

where $e_K = x_K - x_K^*$ is the measurement error and we set the coefficient on q equal to one without loss of generality. The variable q might be correlated with any of the explanatory variables, but an indicator, $q_1 = \delta_0 + \delta_1 q + a_1$, is available. The measurement error e_K might be correlated with the observed measure, x_K. In addition to q_1, you also have variables $z_1, z_2, \ldots, z_M$, $M \geq 2$, that are uncorrelated with v, a_1, and e_K.

a. Suggest an IV procedure for consistently estimating the β_j. Why is $M \geq 2$ required? (Hint: Plug in q_1 for q and x_K for x_K^*, and go from there.)

b. Apply this method to the model estimated in Example 5.5, where actual education, say $educ^*$, plays the role of x_K^*. Use IQ as the indicator of $q = ability$, and KWW, *meduc*, *feduc*, and *sibs* as the elements of $\mathbf{z}$.

5.9. Suppose that the following wage equation is for working high school graduates:

$$\log(wage) = \beta_0 + \beta_1 exper + \beta_2 exper^2 + \beta_3 twoyr + \beta_4 fouryr + u,$$

where *twoyr* is years of junior college attended and *fouryr* is years completed at a four-year college. You have distances from each person's home at the time of high school graduation to the nearest two-year and four-year colleges as instruments for *twoyr* and *fouryr*. Show how to rewrite this equation to test $H_0\colon \beta_3 = \beta_4$ against $H_0\colon \beta_4 > \beta_3$, and explain how to estimate the equation. See Kane and Rouse (1995) and Rouse (1995), who implement a very similar procedure.

5.10. Consider IV estimation of the simple linear model with a single, possibly endogenous, explanatory variable, and a single instrument:

$$y = \beta_0 + \beta_1 x + u,$$

$$\mathrm{E}(u) = 0, \qquad \mathrm{Cov}(z, u) = 0, \qquad \mathrm{Cov}(z, x) \neq 0, \qquad \mathrm{E}(u^2 \mid z) = \sigma^2.$$

a. Under the preceding (standard) assumptions, show that Avar $\sqrt{N}(\hat{\beta}_1 - \beta_1)$ can be expressed as $\sigma^2/(\rho_{zx}^2 \sigma_x^2)$, where $\sigma_x^2 = \mathrm{Var}(x)$ and $\rho_{zx} = \mathrm{Corr}(z, x)$. Compare this result with the asymptotic variance of the OLS estimator under Assumptions OLS.1–OLS.3.

b. Comment on how each factor affects the asymptotic variance of the IV estimator. What happens as $\rho_{zx} \to 0$?

5.11. A model with a single endogenous explanatory variable can be written as

$$y_1 = \mathbf{z}_1 \boldsymbol{\delta}_1 + \alpha_1 y_2 + u_1, \qquad \mathrm{E}(\mathbf{z}' u_1) = \mathbf{0},$$

where $\mathbf{z} = (\mathbf{z}_1, \mathbf{z}_2)$. Consider the following two-step method, intended to mimic 2SLS:

a. Regress y_2 on $\mathbf{z}_2$, and obtain fitted values, $\tilde{y}_2$. (That is, $\mathbf{z}_1$ is omitted from the first-stage regression.)

b. Regress y_1 on $\mathbf{z}_1$, $\tilde{y}_2$ to obtain $\tilde{\boldsymbol{\delta}}_1$ and $\tilde{\alpha}_1$. Show that $\tilde{\boldsymbol{\delta}}_1$ and $\tilde{\alpha}_1$ are generally inconsistent. When would $\tilde{\boldsymbol{\delta}}_1$ and $\tilde{\alpha}_1$ be consistent? (Hint: Let y_2^0 be the population linear projection of y_2 on $\mathbf{z}_2$, and let a_2 be the projection error: $y_2^0 = \mathbf{z}_2 \boldsymbol{\lambda}_2 + a_2$, $\mathrm{E}(\mathbf{z}_2' a_2) = \mathbf{0}$. For simplicity, pretend that $\boldsymbol{\lambda}_2$ is known rather than estimated; that is, assume that $\tilde{y}_2$ is actually y_2^0. Then, write

$$y_1 = \mathbf{z}_1 \boldsymbol{\delta}_1 + \alpha_1 y_2^0 + \alpha_1 a_2 + u_1$$

and check whether the composite error $\alpha_1 a_2 + u_1$ is uncorrelated with the explanatory variables.)

5.12. In the setup of Section 5.1.2 with $\mathbf{x} = (x_1, \ldots, x_K)$ and $\mathbf{z} \equiv (x_1, x_2, \ldots, x_{K-1}, z_1, \ldots, z_M)$ (let $x_1 = 1$ to allow an intercept), assume that $\mathrm{E}(\mathbf{z}'\mathbf{z})$ is nonsingular. Prove that rank $\mathrm{E}(\mathbf{z}'\mathbf{x}) = K$ if and only if at least one θ_j in equation (5.15) is different from zero. (Hint: Write $\mathbf{x}^* = (x_1, \ldots, x_{K-1}, x_K^*)$ as the linear projection of each element of $\mathbf{x}$ on $\mathbf{z}$, where $x_K^* = \delta_1 x_1 + \cdots + \delta_{K-1} x_{K-1} + \theta_1 z_1 + \cdots + \theta_M z_M$. Then $\mathbf{x} = \mathbf{x}^* + \mathbf{r}$, where $\mathrm{E}(\mathbf{z}'\mathbf{r}) = \mathbf{0}$, so that $\mathrm{E}(\mathbf{z}'\mathbf{x}) = \mathrm{E}(\mathbf{z}'\mathbf{x}^*)$. Now $\mathbf{x}^* = \mathbf{z}\boldsymbol{\Pi}$, where $\boldsymbol{\Pi}$ is the $L \times K$ matrix whose first $K - 1$ columns are the first $K - 1$ unit vectors in $\mathbb{R}^L$—$(1, 0, 0, \ldots, 0)'$, $(0, 1, 0, \ldots, 0)', \ldots, (0, 0, \ldots, 1, 0, \ldots, 0)'$—and whose last column is $(\delta_1, \delta_2, \ldots, \delta_{K-1}, \theta_1, \ldots, \theta_M)$. Write $\mathrm{E}(\mathbf{z}'\mathbf{x}^*) = \mathrm{E}(\mathbf{z}'\mathbf{z})\boldsymbol{\Pi}$, so that, because $\mathrm{E}(\mathbf{z}'\mathbf{z})$ is nonsingular, $\mathrm{E}(\mathbf{z}'\mathbf{x}^*)$ has rank K if and only if $\boldsymbol{\Pi}$ has rank K.)

5.13. Consider the simple regression model

$y = \beta_0 + \beta_1 x + u$

and let z be a *binary* instrumental variable for x.

a. Show that the IV estimator $\hat{\beta}_1$ can be written as

$\hat{\beta}_1 = (\bar{y}_1 - \bar{y}_0)/(\bar{x}_1 - \bar{x}_0),$

where $\bar{y}_0$ and $\bar{x}_0$ are the sample averages of y_i and x_i over the part of the sample with $z_i = 0$, and $\bar{y}_1$ and $\bar{x}_1$ are the sample averages of y_i and x_i over the part of the sample with $z_i = 1$. This estimator, known as a **grouping estimator**, was first suggested by Wald (1940).

b. What is the intepretation of $\hat{\beta}_1$ if x is also binary, for example, representing participation in a social program?

5.14. Consider the model in (5.1) and (5.2), where we have additional exogenous variables $z_1, \ldots, z_M$. Let $\mathbf{z} = (1, x_1, \ldots, x_{K-1}, z_1, \ldots, z_M)$ be the vector of all exogenous variables. This problem essentially asks you to obtain the 2SLS estimator using linear projections. Assume that $\mathrm{E}(\mathbf{z}'\mathbf{z})$ is nonsingular.

a. Find $\mathrm{L}(y \mid \mathbf{z})$ in terms of the β_j, $x_1, \ldots, x_{K-1}$, and $x_K^* = \mathrm{L}(x_K \mid \mathbf{z})$.

b. Argue that, provided $x_1, \ldots, x_{K-1}, x_K^*$ are not perfectly collinear, an OLS regression of y on $1, x_1, \ldots, x_{K-1}, x_K^*$—using a random sample—consistently estimates all β_j.

c. State a necessary and sufficient condition for x_K^* not to be a perfect linear combination of $x_1, \ldots, x_{K-1}$. What 2SLS assumption is this identical to?

5.15. Consider the model $y = \mathbf{x}\boldsymbol{\beta} + u$, where $x_1, x_2, \ldots, x_{K_1}$, $K_1 \leq K$, are the (potentially) endogenous explanatory variables. (We assume a zero intercept just to simplify the notation; the following results carry over to models with an unknown intercept.) Let $z_1, \ldots, z_{L_1}$ be the instrumental variables available from outside the model. Let $\mathbf{z} = (z_1, \ldots, z_{L_1}, x_{K_1+1}, \ldots, x_K)$ and assume that $\mathrm{E}(\mathbf{z}'\mathbf{z})$ is nonsingular, so that Assumption 2SLS.2a holds.

a. Show that a necessary condition for the rank condition, Assumption 2SLS.2b, is that for each $j = 1, \ldots, K_1$, at least one z_h must appear in the reduced form of x_j.

b. With $K_1 = 2$, give a simple example showing that the condition from part a is not sufficient for the rank condition.

c. If $L_1 = K_1$, show that a sufficient condition for the rank condition is that only z_j appears in the reduced form for x_j, $j = 1, \ldots, K_1$. (As in Problem 5.12, it suffices to study the rank of the $L \times K$ matrix $\boldsymbol{\Pi}$ in $\mathrm{L}(\mathbf{x} \mid \mathbf{z}) = \mathbf{z}\boldsymbol{\Pi}$.)

5.16. Consider the population model

$$y = \alpha + \beta w + u,$$

where all quantities are scalars. Let $\mathbf{g}$ be a $1 \times L$ vector, $L \geq 2$, with $E(\mathbf{g}'u) = 0$; assume the first element of $\mathbf{g}$ is unity. The following is easily extended to the case of a vector $\mathbf{w}$ of endogenous variables.

a. Let $\tilde{\beta}$ denote the 2SLS estimator of β using instruments $\mathbf{g}$. (Of course, the intercept α is estimated along with β.) Argue that, under the rank condition 2SLS.2 and the homoskedasticity Assumption 2SLS.3 (with $\mathbf{z} = \mathbf{g}$),

$$\text{Avar } \sqrt{N}(\tilde{\beta} - \beta) = \sigma_u^2 / \text{Var}(w^*),$$

where $\sigma_u^2 = \text{Var}(u)$ and $w^* = \text{L}(w \mid \mathbf{g})$. (Hint: See the discussion following equation (5.24).)

b. Let $\mathbf{h}$ be a $1 \times J$ vector (with zero mean, to slightly simplify the argument) uncorrelated with $\mathbf{g}$ but generally correlated with u. Write the linear projection of u on $\mathbf{h}$ as $u = \mathbf{h}\gamma + v$, $E(\mathbf{h}'v) = \mathbf{0}$. Explain why $E(\mathbf{g}'v) = \mathbf{0}$.

c. Write the equation

$$y = \alpha + \beta w + \mathbf{h}\gamma + v$$

and let $\hat{\beta}$ be the 2SLS estimator of β using instruments $\mathbf{z} = (\mathbf{g}, \mathbf{h})$. Assuming Assumptions 2SLS.2 and 2SLS.3 for this choice of instruments, show that

$$\text{Avar } \sqrt{N}(\hat{\beta} - \beta) = \sigma_v^2 / \text{Var}(w^*),$$

where $\sigma_v^2 = \text{Var}(v)$. (Hint: Again use the discussion following equation (5.24), but now with $\mathbf{x}^* = (1, \breve{w}, \mathbf{h})$, where $\breve{w} = \text{L}(w \mid \mathbf{g}, \mathbf{h})$. Now, the asymptotic variance can be written $\sigma_v^2 / \text{Var}(\breve{r})$, where $\breve{r}$ is the population residual from the regression $\breve{w}$ on $1, \mathbf{h}$. Show that $\breve{r} = w^*$ when $\text{E}(\mathbf{g}'\mathbf{h}) = \mathbf{0}$.)

d. Argue that for estimating the coefficient on an endogenous explanatory variable, it is always better to include exogenous variables that are orthogonal to the available instruments. For more general results, see Qian and Schmidt (1999). Problem 4.5 covers the OLS case.

6 Additional Single-Equation Topics

6.1 Estimation with Generated Regressors and Instruments

In this section we discuss the large-sample properties of OLS and 2SLS estimators when some regressors or instruments have been estimated in a first step.

6.1.1 Ordinary Least Squares with Generated Regressors

We often need to draw on results for OLS estimation when one or more of the regressors have been estimated from a first-stage procedure. To illustrate the issues, consider the model

$$y = \beta_0 + \beta_1 x_1 + \cdots + \beta_K x_K + \gamma q + u. \tag{6.1}$$

We observe $x_1, \ldots, x_K$, but q is unobserved. However, suppose that q is related to observable data through the function $q = f(\mathbf{w}, \boldsymbol{\delta})$, where f is a known function and $\mathbf{w}$ is a vector of observed variables, but the vector of parameters $\boldsymbol{\delta}$ is unknown (which is why q is not observed). Often, but not always, q will be a linear function of $\mathbf{w}$ and $\boldsymbol{\delta}$. Suppose that we can consistently estimate $\boldsymbol{\delta}$, and let $\hat{\boldsymbol{\delta}}$ be the estimator. For each observation i, $\hat{q}_i = f(\mathbf{w}_i, \hat{\boldsymbol{\delta}})$ effectively estimates q_i. Pagan (1984) calls $\hat{q}_i$ a **generated regressor**. It seems reasonable that, replacing q_i with $\hat{q}_i$ in running the OLS regression

$$y_i \text{ on } 1, x_{i1}, x_{i2}, \ldots, x_{ik}, \hat{q}_i, \qquad i = 1, \ldots, N, \tag{6.2}$$

should produce consistent estimates of all parameters, including γ. The question is, What assumptions are sufficient?

While we do not cover the asymptotic theory needed for a careful proof until Chapter 12 (which treats nonlinear estimation), we can provide some intuition here. Because plim $\hat{\boldsymbol{\delta}} = \boldsymbol{\delta}$, by the law of large numbers it is reasonable that

$$N^{-1} \sum_{i=1}^{N} \hat{q}_i u_i \xrightarrow{p} \mathrm{E}(q_i u_i), \qquad N^{-1} \sum_{i=1}^{N} x_{ij} \hat{q}_i \xrightarrow{p} \mathrm{E}(x_{ij} q_i).$$

From these results it is easily shown that the usual OLS assumption in the population—that u is uncorrelated with $(x_1, x_2, \ldots, x_K, q)$—suffices for the two-step procedure to be consistent (along with the rank condition of Assumption OLS.2 applied to the expanded vector of explanatory variables). In other words, for consistency, replacing q_i with $\hat{q}_i$ in an OLS regression causes no problems.

Things are not so simple when it comes to inference: the standard errors and test statistics obtained from regression (6.2) are generally invalid because they ignore the sampling variation in $\hat{\boldsymbol{\delta}}$. Because $\hat{\boldsymbol{\delta}}$ is also obtained using data—usually the same sample of data—uncertainty in the estimate should be accounted for in the second step. Nevertheless, there is at least one important case where the sampling variation of $\hat{\boldsymbol{\delta}}$ *can* be ignored, at least asymptotically: if

$$\mathrm{E}[\nabla_{\delta} f(\mathbf{w}, \boldsymbol{\delta})' u] = \mathbf{0}, \tag{6.3}$$

$$\gamma = 0, \tag{6.4}$$

then the $\sqrt{N}$-limiting distribution of the OLS estimators from regression (6.2) is the *same* as the OLS estimators when q replaces $\hat{q}$. Condition (6.3) is implied by the zero conditional mean condition,

$$\mathrm{E}(u \mid \mathbf{x}, \mathbf{w}) = 0, \tag{6.5}$$

which frequently holds in generated regressor contexts.

We often want to test the null hypothesis H_0: $\gamma = 0$ before including $\hat{q}$ in the final regression. Fortunately, the usual t statistic on $\hat{q}$ has a limiting standard normal distribution under H_0, so it can be used to test H_0. It simply requires the usual homoskedasticity assumption, $\mathrm{E}(u^2 \mid \mathbf{x}, q) = \sigma^2$. The heteroskedasticity-robust statistic works if heteroskedasticity is present in u under H_0.

Even if condition (6.3) holds, if $\gamma \neq 0$, then an adjustment is needed for the asymptotic variances of *all* OLS estimators that are due to estimation of $\boldsymbol{\delta}$. Thus, standard t statistics, F statistics, and LM statistics will not be asymptotically valid when $\gamma \neq 0$. Using the methods of Chapter 3, it is not difficult to derive an adjustment to the usual variance matrix estimate that accounts for the variability in $\hat{\boldsymbol{\delta}}$ (and also allows for heteroskedasticity). It is *not* true that replacing q_i with $\hat{q}_i$ simply introduces heteroskedasticity into the error term; this is not the correct way to think about the generated regressors issue. Accounting for the fact that $\hat{\boldsymbol{\delta}}$ depends on the same random sample used in the second-stage estimation is much different from having heteroskedasticity in the error. Of course, we might want to use a heteroskedasticity-robust standard error for testing H_0: $\gamma = 0$ because heteroskedasticity in the population error u can always be a problem. However, just as with the usual OLS standard error, this is generally justified only under H_0: $\gamma = 0$.

A general formula for the asymptotic variance of 2SLS in the presence of generated regressors is given in the appendix to this chapter; this covers OLS with generated regressors as a special case. A general framework for handling these problems is given in Newey (1984) and Newey and McFadden (1994), but we must hold off until Chapter 14 to give a careful treatment.

6.1.2 Two-Stage Least Squares with Generated Instruments

In later chapters we will need results on 2SLS estimation when the instruments have been estimated in a preliminary stage. Write the population model as

$$y = \mathbf{x}\boldsymbol{\beta} + u, \tag{6.6}$$

$$\mathrm{E}(\mathbf{z}'u) = \mathbf{0}, \tag{6.7}$$

where $\mathbf{x}$ is a $1 \times K$ vector of explanatory variables and $\mathbf{z}$ is a $1 \times L$ $(L \geq K)$ vector of intrumental variables. Assume that $\mathbf{z} = \mathbf{g}(\mathbf{w}, \boldsymbol{\lambda})$, where $\mathbf{g}(\cdot, \boldsymbol{\lambda})$ is a known function but $\boldsymbol{\lambda}$ needs to be estimated. For each i, define the **generated instruments** $\hat{\mathbf{z}}_i \equiv \mathbf{g}(\mathbf{w}_i, \hat{\boldsymbol{\lambda}})$. What can we say about the 2SLS estimator when the $\hat{\mathbf{z}}_i$ are used as instruments?

By the same reasoning for OLS with generated regressors, consistency follows under weak conditions. Further, under conditions that are met in many applications, we can ignore the fact that the instruments were estimated in using 2SLS for inference. Sufficient are the assumptions that $\hat{\boldsymbol{\lambda}}$ is $\sqrt{N}$-consistent for $\boldsymbol{\lambda}$ and that

$$\mathrm{E}[\nabla_{\lambda}\mathbf{g}(\mathbf{w}, \boldsymbol{\lambda})'u] = \mathbf{0}. \tag{6.8}$$

Under condition (6.8), which holds when $\mathrm{E}(u \mid \mathbf{w}) = 0$, the $\sqrt{N}$-asymptotic distribution of $\hat{\boldsymbol{\beta}}$ is the *same* whether we use $\boldsymbol{\lambda}$ or $\hat{\boldsymbol{\lambda}}$ in constructing the instruments. This fact greatly simplifies calculation of asymptotic standard errors and test statistics. Therefore, if we have a choice, there are practical reasons for using 2SLS with generated instruments rather than OLS with generated regressors. We will see some examples in Section 6.4 and Part IV.

One consequence of this discussion is that, if we add the 2SLS homoskedasticity assumption (2SLS.3), the usual 2SLS standard errors and test statistics are asymptotically valid. If Assumption 2SLS.3 is violated, we simply use the heteroskedasticity-robust standard errors and test statistics. Of course, the finite sample properties of the estimator using $\hat{\mathbf{z}}_i$ as instruments could be notably different from those using $\mathbf{z}_i$ as instruments, especially for small sample sizes. Determining whether this is the case requires either more sophisticated asymptotic approximations or simulations on a case-by-case basis.

6.1.3 Generated Instruments and Regressors

We will encounter examples later where some instruments and some regressors are estimated in a first stage. Generally, the asymptotic variance needs to be adjusted because of the generated regressors, although there are some special cases where the usual variance matrix estimators are valid. As a general example, consider the model

$$y = \mathbf{x}\boldsymbol{\beta} + \gamma f(\mathbf{w}, \boldsymbol{\delta}) + u, \qquad \mathrm{E}(u \mid \mathbf{z}, \mathbf{w}) = 0,$$

and we estimate $\boldsymbol{\delta}$ in a first stage. If $\gamma = 0$, then the 2SLS estimator of $(\boldsymbol{\beta}', \gamma)'$ in the equation

$$y_i = \mathbf{x}_i\boldsymbol{\beta} + \gamma\hat{f}_i + error_i,$$

using instruments $(\mathbf{z}_i, \hat{f}_i)$, has a limiting distribution that does not depend on the limiting distribution of $\sqrt{N}(\hat{\boldsymbol{\delta}} - \boldsymbol{\delta})$ under conditions (6.3) and (6.8). Therefore, the usual 2SLS t statistic for $\hat{\gamma}$, or its heteroskedsticity-robust version, can be used to test H_0: $\gamma = 0$.

6.2 Control Function Approach to Endogeneity

For several reasons, including handling endogeneity in nonlinear models—which we will encounter often in Part IV—it is very useful to have a different approach for dealing with endogenous explanatory variables. Generally, the **control function** approach uses extra regressors to break the correlation between endogenenous explanatory variables and unobservables affecting the response. As we will see, the method still relies on the availability of exogenous variables that do not appear in the structural equation. For notational clarity, y_1 denotes the response variable, y_2 is the endogenous explanatory variable (a scalar for simplicity), and $\mathbf{z}$ is the $1 \times L$ vector of exogenous variables (which includes unity as its first element). Consider the model

$$y_1 = \mathbf{z}_1\boldsymbol{\delta}_1 + \alpha_1 y_2 + u_1, \tag{6.9}$$

where $\mathbf{z}_1$ is a $1 \times L_1$ strict subvector of $\mathbf{z}$ that also includes a constant. The sense in which $\mathbf{z}$ is exogenous is given by the L orthogonality (zero covariance) conditions

$$\mathrm{E}(\mathbf{z}'u_1) = \mathbf{0}. \tag{6.10}$$

Of course, this is the same exogeneity condition we use for consistency of the 2SLS estimator, and we can consistently estimate $\boldsymbol{\delta}_1$ and α_1 by 2SLS under (6.10) and the rank condition, Assumption 2SLS.2.

Just as with 2SLS, the reduced form of y_2—that is, the linear projection of y_2 onto the exogenous variables—plays a critical role. Write the reduced form with an error term as

$$y_2 = \mathbf{z}\boldsymbol{\pi}_2 + v_2, \tag{6.11}$$

$$\mathrm{E}(\mathbf{z}'v_2) = \mathbf{0}, \tag{6.12}$$

where $\boldsymbol{\pi}_2$ is $L \times 1$. From equations (6.11) and (6.12), endogeneity of y_2 arises if and only if u_1 is correlated with v_2. Write the linear projection of u_1 on v_2, in error form, as

$$u_1 = \rho_1 v_2 + e_1, \tag{6.13}$$

where $\rho_1 = \mathrm{E}(v_2 u_1)/\mathrm{E}(v_2^2)$ is the population regression coefficient. By definition, $\mathrm{E}(v_2 e_1) = 0$, and $\mathrm{E}(\mathbf{z}' e_1) = \mathbf{0}$ because u_1 and v_2 are both uncorrelated with $\mathbf{z}$.

Plugging (6.13) into equation (6.9) gives

$$y_1 = \mathbf{z}_1 \boldsymbol{\delta}_1 + \alpha_1 y_2 + \rho_1 v_2 + e_1, \tag{6.14}$$

where we now view v_2 as an explanatory variable in the equation. As just noted, e_1, is uncorrelated with v_2 and $\mathbf{z}$. Plus, y_2 is a linear function of $\mathbf{z}$ and v_2, and so e_1 is also uncorrelated with y_2.

Because e_1 is uncorrelated with $\mathbf{z}_1$, y_2, and v_2, equation (6.14) suggests a simple procedure for consistently estimating $\boldsymbol{\delta}_1$ and α_1 (as well as ρ_1): run the OLS regression of y_1 on $\mathbf{z}_1$, y_2, and v_2 using a random sample. (Remember, OLS consistently estimates the parameters in any equation where the error term is uncorrelated with the right-hand-side variables.) The only problem with this suggestion is that we do not observe v_2; it is the error in the reduced-form equation for y_2. Nevertheless, we can write $v_2 = y_2 - \mathbf{z}\boldsymbol{\pi}_2$, and, because we collect data on y_2 and $\mathbf{z}$, we can consistently estimate $\boldsymbol{\pi}_2$ by OLS. Therefore, we can replace v_2 with $\hat{v}_2$, the OLS residuals from the first-stage regression of y_2 on $\mathbf{z}$. Simple substitution gives

$$y_1 = \mathbf{z}_1 \boldsymbol{\delta}_1 + \alpha_1 y_2 + \rho_1 \hat{v}_2 + error, \tag{6.15}$$

where, for each i, $error_i = e_{i1} + \rho_1 \mathbf{z}_i(\hat{\boldsymbol{\pi}}_2 - \boldsymbol{\pi}_2)$, which depends on the sampling error in $\hat{\boldsymbol{\pi}}_2$ unless $\rho_1 = 0$. We can now use the consistency result for generated regressors from Section 6.1.1 to conclude that the OLS estimators from equation (6.15) will be consistent for $\boldsymbol{\delta}_1$, α_1, and ρ_1.

The OLS estimator from equation (6.15) is an example of a **control function (CF) estimator**. The inclusion of the residuals $\hat{v}_2$ "controls" for the endogeneity of y_2 in the original equation (although it does so with sampling error because $\hat{\boldsymbol{\pi}}_2 \neq \boldsymbol{\pi}_2$).

How does the CF approach compare with the standard instrumental variables (IV) approach, which, for now, means 2SLS? Interestingly, as you are asked to show in Problem 5.1 (using least squares algebra), the OLS estimates of $\boldsymbol{\delta}_1$ and α_1 from equation (6.15) are *identical* to the 2SLS estimates. In other words, the two approaches lead to the same place. Equation (6.15) contains a generated regressor, and so obtaining the appropriate standard errors for the CF estimators requires applying the correction derived in Appendix 6A. Why, then, have we introduced the control function approach when it leads to the same place as 2SLS?

There are a couple of reasons. First, as we will see in the next section, equation (6.15) leads to a straightforward test of the null hypothesis that y_2 is exogenous. Second, and perhaps more important, the CF approach can be adapted to certain nonlinear models in cases where analogues of 2SLS have undesirable properties. In fact, in Part IV we will rely heavily on CF approaches for handling endogeneity in a variety of nonlinear models.

You have perhaps already figured out where the CF approach relies on having at least one element in $\mathbf{z}$ not also in $\mathbf{z}_1$—as also required by 2SLS. We can easily see this from equation (6.15) and the expression $\hat{v}_{i2} = y_{i2} - \mathbf{z}_i\hat{\boldsymbol{\pi}}_2$, $i = 1, \ldots, N$. If $\mathbf{z}_i = \mathbf{z}_{i1}$, then the $\hat{v}_{i2}$ are exact linear functions of y_{i2} and $\mathbf{z}_{i1}$, in which case equation (6.15) suffers from perfect collinearity. If $\mathbf{z}_i$ contains at least one element not in $\mathbf{z}_{i1}$, this breaks the perfect collinearity (at least in the sample). If we write $\mathbf{z} = (\mathbf{z}_1, \mathbf{z}_2)$ and $\boldsymbol{\pi}_{22} = \mathbf{0}$, then, asymptotically, the CF approach suffers from perfect collinearity, and α_1 and $\boldsymbol{\delta}_1$ are not identified, as we already know from our 2SLS analysis.

Although we just argued that the CF approach is identical to 2SLS in a linear model, this equivalence does not carry over to models containing more than one function of y_2. A simple extension of (6.9) is

$$y_1 = \mathbf{z}_1\boldsymbol{\delta}_1 + \alpha_1 y_2 + \gamma_1 y_2^2 + u_1, \tag{6.16}$$

$$\mathrm{E}(u_1 \mid \mathbf{z}) = 0. \tag{6.17}$$

For simplicity, assume that we have a scalar, z_2, that is not also in $\mathbf{z}_1$. Then, under assumption (6.17), we can use, say, z_2^2 as an instrument for y_2^2 because any function of z_2 is uncorrelated with u_1. (We must exclude the case where z_2 is binary, because then $z_2^2 = z_2$.) In other words, we can apply the standard IV estimator with explanatory variables $(\mathbf{z}_1, y_2, y_2^2)$ and instruments $(\mathbf{z}_1, z_2, z_2^2)$; note that we have two endogenous explanatory variables, y_2 and y_2^2.

What would the CF approach entail in this case? To implement the CF approach in equation (6.16), we obtain the conditional expectation $\mathrm{E}(y_1 \mid \mathbf{z}, y_2)$—a linear projection argument no longer works because of the nonlinearity—and that requires an assumption about $\mathrm{E}(u_1 \mid \mathbf{z}, y_2)$. A standard assumption is

$$\mathrm{E}(u_1 \mid \mathbf{z}, y_2) = \mathrm{E}(u_1 \mid \mathbf{z}, v_2) = \mathrm{E}(u_1 \mid v_2) = \rho_1 v_2, \tag{6.18}$$

where the first equality follows because y_2 and v_2 are one-to-one functions of each other (given $\mathbf{z}$) and the second would hold if (u_1, v_2) is independent of $\mathbf{z}$—a nontrivial restriction on the reduced-form error in equation (6.11), not to mention the structural error u_1. The final assumption is linearity of the conditional expectation $\mathrm{E}(u_1 \mid v_2)$, which is more restrictive than simply defining a linear projection. Under (6.18),

$$\begin{aligned}\mathrm{E}(y_1 \mid \mathbf{z}, y_2) &= \mathbf{z}_1\boldsymbol{\delta}_1 + \alpha_1 y_2 + \gamma_1 y_2^2 + \mathrm{E}(u_1 \mid \mathbf{z}, y_2), \\ &= \mathbf{z}_1\boldsymbol{\delta}_1 + \alpha_1 y_2 + \gamma_1 y_2^2 + \rho_1 v_2.\end{aligned} \tag{6.19}$$

Implementing the CF approach means running the OLS regression y_1 on $\mathbf{z}_1$, y_2, y_2^2, $\hat{v}_2$, where $\hat{v}_2$ still represents the reduced-form residuals. The CF estimates are *not* the same as the 2SLS estimates using any choice of instruments for (y_2, y_2^2).

We will study models such as (6.16) in more detail in Chapter 9—in particular, we will discuss identification and choice of instruments—but a few comments are in order. First, if the standard IV and CF approaches no longer lead to the same estimates, do we prefer one over the other? Not surprisingly, there is a trade-off between robustness and efficiency. For the 2SLS estimator using instruments $(\mathbf{z}_1, z_2, z_2^2)$, the key assumption is (6.17), along with partial correlation between y_2 and z_2 in the RF for y_2. (This almost certainly ensures that y_2^2 is appropriately partially correlated with z_2^2.) But the CF estimator requires these two assumptions and, in addition, the last two equalities in (6.18). As shown in Problem 6.13, equations (6.17) and (6.18) imply that $\mathrm{E}(v_2 \mid \mathbf{z}) = 0$, which means that $\mathrm{E}(y_2 \mid \mathbf{z}) = \mathbf{z}\boldsymbol{\pi}_2$. A linear conditional expectation for y_2 is a substantive restriction on the conditional distribution of y_2. Therefore, the CF estimator will be inconsistent in cases where the 2SLS estimator will be consistent. On the other hand, because the CF estimator solves the endogeneity of y_2 and y_2^2 by adding the scalar $\hat{v}_2$ to the regression, it will generally be more precise—perhaps much more precise—than the 2SLS estimator. But a systematic analysis comparing the two approaches in models such as (6.16) has yet to be done. Assumptions such as (6.18) are typically avoided if possible, but this could be costly in terms of inference. In Section 9.5 we will further explore models nonlinear in endogenous variables.

6.3 Some Specification Tests

In Chapters 4 and 5 we covered what is usually called classical hypothesis testing for OLS and 2SLS. We now turn to testing some of the assumptions underlying consistency of either OLS or 2SLS; these are typically called **specification tests**. These tests, including ones robust to arbitrary heteroskedasticity, are easy to obtain and should be routinely reported in applications.

6.3.1 Testing for Endogeneity

There are various ways to motivate tests for whether some explanatory variables are endogenous. If the null hypothesis is that all explanatory variables are exogenous, and we allow one or more to be endogenous under the alternative, then we can base a test on the difference between the 2SLS and OLS estimators, provided we have sufficient exogenous instruments to identify the parameters by 2SLS. Tests for endogeneity have been derived independently by Durbin (1954), Wu (1973), and Hausman

(1978). In the general equation $y = \mathbf{x}\boldsymbol{\beta} + u$ with instruments $\mathbf{z}$, the **Durbin-Wu-Hausman (DWH)** test is based on the difference $\hat{\boldsymbol{\beta}}_{2SLS} - \hat{\boldsymbol{\beta}}_{OLS}$. If all elements of $\mathbf{x}$ are exogenous (and $\mathbf{z}$ is also exogenous—a maintained assumption), then 2SLS and OLS should differ only due to sampling error. Of course, to determine whether this is so, we need to estimate the asymptotic variance of $\sqrt{N}(\hat{\boldsymbol{\beta}}_{2SLS} - \hat{\boldsymbol{\beta}}_{OLS})$. Generally, the calculation is cumbersome, but it simplifies considerably if we maintain homoskedasticity under the null hypothesis. Problem 6.12 asks you to verify that, under the null hypothesis $\mathrm{E}(\mathbf{x}'u) = \mathbf{0}$, and the appropriate homoskedasticity assumption,

$$\mathrm{Avar}[\sqrt{N}(\hat{\boldsymbol{\beta}}_{2SLS} - \hat{\boldsymbol{\beta}}_{OLS})] = \sigma^2[\mathrm{E}(\mathbf{x}^{*\prime}\mathbf{x}^*)]^{-1} - \sigma^2[\mathrm{E}(\mathbf{x}'\mathbf{x})]^{-1}, \tag{6.20}$$

which is simply the difference between the asymptotic variances. (Hausman (1978) shows this kind of result holds more generally when one estimator, OLS in this case, is asymptotically efficient under the null.)

Once we estimate each component in equation (6.20) we can construct a quadratic form in $\hat{\boldsymbol{\beta}}_{2SLS} - \hat{\boldsymbol{\beta}}_{OLS}$ that has an asymptotic chi-square distribution. The estimators of the moment matrices are the usual ones, with the first-stage fitted values $\hat{\mathbf{x}}_i = \mathbf{z}_i\hat{\boldsymbol{\Pi}}$ replacing $\mathbf{x}_i^*$, as usual. For σ^2, there are three possibilities. The first is to estimate the error variances separately for 2SLS and OLS and insert these in the first and second occurrences of σ^2, respectively. Or we can just use the 2SLS estimate or just use the OLS estimate in both places. Using the latter, we obtain one version of the DWH statistic:

$$(\hat{\boldsymbol{\beta}}_{2SLS} - \hat{\boldsymbol{\beta}}_{OLS})'[(\hat{\mathbf{X}}'\hat{\mathbf{X}})^{-1} - (\mathbf{X}'\mathbf{X})^{-1}]^{-}(\hat{\boldsymbol{\beta}}_{2SLS} - \hat{\boldsymbol{\beta}}_{OLS})/\hat{\sigma}^2_{OLS}, \tag{6.21}$$

where we must use a generalized inverse, except in the very unusual case that all elements of $\mathbf{x}$ are allowed to be endogenous under the alternative. In fact, the rank of $\mathrm{Avar}[\sqrt{N}(\hat{\boldsymbol{\beta}}_{2SLS} - \hat{\boldsymbol{\beta}}_{OLS})]$ is equal to the number of elements of $\mathbf{x}$ allowed to be endogenous under the alternative. The singularity of the matrix in expression (6.21) makes computing the statistic cumbersome. Nevertheless, some variant of the statistic is routinely computed by several popular econometrics packages. See Baum, Schaffer, and Stillman (2003) for a detailed survey and recently written software.

A more serious drawback with any statistic based on equation (6.20) is that it is not robust to heteroskedasticity. A robust variance matrix estimator for $\mathrm{Avar}[\sqrt{N}(\hat{\boldsymbol{\beta}}_{2SLS} - \hat{\boldsymbol{\beta}}_{OLS})]$ can be obtained (see Problem 6.12 and Baum, Schaffer, and Stillman (2003)). Unfortunately, calculating robust DWH statistics is done much less frequently than computing standard errors and classical test statistics that are robust to heteroskedasticity. Infrequent use of a fully robust DWH statistic may be partly due to misunderstandings of when the principle of comparing estimators applies. It is commonly thought that one estimator should be asymptotically efficient under the null hypothesis, but this is not necessary—indeed, it is essentially irrelevant. The principle applies whenever two estimators are consistent under the null hypothesis and one estimator, 2SLS in this case, retains consistency under the alternative. Asymptotic efficiency only simplifies the asymptotic variance estimation. In fact, while the standard form of the DWH test maintains OLS.3 and 2SLS.3 in order to have the correct asymptotic size, it has no systematic power for detecting heteroskedasticity.

Regression-based endogeneity tests are very convenient because they are easily computed and almost trivial to make robust to heteroskedasticity. As pointed out by Hausman (1978, 1983), there is a regression-based statistic asymptotically equivalent to equation (6.21). Suppose initially that we have a single potentially endogenous explanatory variable, as in equation (6.9). We maintain assumption (6.10)—that is, each element of $\mathbf{z}$ is exogenous. We want to test

$$\mathrm{H}_0\colon \mathrm{Cov}(y_2, u_1) = 0 \tag{6.22}$$

against the alternative that y_2 is correlated with u_1. Given the reduced-form equation (6.11), equation (6.22) is equivalent to $\mathrm{Cov}(v_2, u_1) = \mathrm{E}(v_2 u_1) = 0$, or $\mathrm{H}_0\colon \rho_1 = 0$, where ρ_1 is the regression coefficient defined in equation (6.13). Even though u_1 and v_2 are not observed, we can use equation (6.15) to test that $\rho_1 = 0$. In fact, when we estimate equation (6.15) by OLS, we obtain an OLS coefficient on $\hat{v}_2$, $\hat{\rho}_1$. Conveniently, using the results from Section 6.1.1, when $\rho_1 = 0$ we do not have to adjust the standard error of $\hat{\rho}_1$ for the first-stage estimation of $\boldsymbol{\pi}_2$. Therefore, if the homoskedasticity assumption $\mathrm{E}(u_1^2 \mid \mathbf{z}, y_2) = \mathrm{E}(u_1^2)$ holds under H_0, we can use the usual t statistic for $\hat{\rho}_1$ as an asymptotically valid test. Conveniently, we can simply use a heteroskedasticity-robust t statistic if heteroskedasticity is suspected under H_0.

We should remember that the OLS standard errors that would be reported from equation (6.15) are not valid unless $\rho_1 = 0$, because $\hat{v}_2$ is a generated regressor. In practice, if we reject $\mathrm{H}_0\colon \rho_1 = 0$, then, to get the appropriate standard errors and other test statistics, we estimate equation (6.9) by 2SLS.

Example 6.1 (Testing for Endogeneity of Education in a Wage Equation): Consider the wage equation

$$\log(wage) = \delta_0 + \delta_1 exper + \delta_2 exper^2 + \alpha_1 educ + u_1 \tag{6.23}$$

for working women, where we believe that *educ* and u_1 may be correlated. The instruments for *educ* are parents' education and husband's education. So, we first regress *educ* on 1, *exper*, $exper^2$, *motheduc*, *fatheduc*, and *huseduc* and obtain the residuals, $\hat{v}_2$. Then we simply include $\hat{v}_2$ along with unity, *exper*, $exper^2$, and *educ* in an OLS regression and obtain the t statistic on $\hat{v}_2$. Using the data in MROZ.RAW gives the result $\hat{\rho}_1 = .047$ and $t_{\hat{\rho}_1} = 1.65$. We find evidence of endogeneity of *educ* at the 10 percent significance level against a two-sided alternative, and so 2SLS is probably a good idea (assuming that we trust the instruments). The correct 2SLS standard errors are given in Example 5.3.

With only a single suspected endogenous explanatory variable, it is straightforward to compute a Hausman (1978) statistic that directly compares 2SLS and OLS, at least when the homoskedasticity assumption holds (for 2SLS and OLS). Then, $\text{Avar}(\hat{\alpha}_{1,2SLS} - \hat{\alpha}_{1,OLS}) = \text{Avar}(\hat{\alpha}_{1,2SLS}) - \text{Avar}(\hat{\alpha}_{1,OLS})$. Therefore, the Hausman t statistic is simply $(\hat{\alpha}_{1,2SLS} - \hat{\alpha}_{1,OLS})/([\text{se}(\hat{\alpha}_{1,2SLS})]^2 - [\text{se}(\hat{\alpha}_{1,OLS})]^2)^{1/2}$. Under the null hypothesis, the t statistic has an asymptotically standard normal distribution. Unfortunately, there is no simple correction if one allows heteroskedasticity: the asymptotic variance of the difference is no longer the difference in asymptotic variances.

Extending the regression-based Hausman test to several potentially endogenous explanatory variables is straightforward. Let $\mathbf{y}_2$ denote a $1 \times G_1$ vector of possible endogenous variables in the population model

$$y_1 = \mathbf{z}_1\boldsymbol{\delta}_1 + \mathbf{y}_2\boldsymbol{\alpha}_1 + u_1, \qquad \text{E}(\mathbf{z}'u_1) = \mathbf{0}, \tag{6.24}$$

where $\boldsymbol{\alpha}_1$ is now $G_1 \times 1$. Again, we assume the rank condition for 2SLS. Write the reduced form as $\mathbf{y}_2 = \mathbf{z}\boldsymbol{\Pi}_2 + \mathbf{v}_2$, where $\boldsymbol{\Pi}_2$ is $L \times G_1$ and $\mathbf{v}_2$ is the $1 \times G_1$ vector of population reduced form errors. For a generic observation, let $\hat{\mathbf{v}}_2$ denote the $1 \times G_1$ vector of OLS residuals obtained from each reduced form. (In other words, take each element of $\mathbf{y}_2$ and regress it on $\mathbf{z}$ to obtain the RF residuals, then collect these in the row vector $\hat{\mathbf{v}}_2$.) Now, estimate the model

$$y_1 = \mathbf{z}_1\boldsymbol{\delta}_1 + \mathbf{y}_2\boldsymbol{\alpha}_1 + \hat{\mathbf{v}}_2\boldsymbol{\rho}_1 + error \tag{6.25}$$

and do a standard F test of H_0: $\boldsymbol{\rho}_1 = \mathbf{0}$, which tests G_1 restrictions in the unrestricted model (6.25). The restricted model is obtained by setting $\boldsymbol{\rho}_1 = \mathbf{0}$, which means we estimate the original model (6.24) by OLS. The test can be made robust to heteroskedasticity in u_1 (since $u_1 = e_1$ under H_0) by applying the heteroskedasticity-robust Wald statistic in Chapter 4. In some regression packages, such as Stata, the robust test is implemented as an F-type test. More precisely, the robust Wald statistic, which has an asymptotic chi-square distribution, is divided by G_1 to give a statistic that can be compared with F critical values.

An alternative to the F test is an LM-type test. Let $\hat{u}_1$ be the OLS residuals from the regression y_1 on $\mathbf{z}_1, \mathbf{y}_2$ (the residuals obtained under the null hypothesis that $\mathbf{y}_2$ is exogenous). Then, obtain the usual R-squared (assuming that $\mathbf{z}_1$ contains a constant), say R_u^2, from the regression

$$\hat{u}_1 \text{ on } \mathbf{z}_1, \mathbf{y}_2, \hat{\mathbf{v}}_2 \tag{6.26}$$

and use NR_u^2 as asymptotically $\chi^2_{G_1}$. This test again maintains homoskedasticity under H_0. The test can be made heteroskedasticity-robust using the method described in equation (4.17): take $\mathbf{x}_1 = (\mathbf{z}_1, \mathbf{y}_2)$ and $\mathbf{x}_2 = \hat{\mathbf{v}}_2$. See also Wooldridge (1995b).

Example 6.2 (Endogeneity of Education in a Wage Equation, continued): We add the interaction term *black·educ* to the log(*wage*) equation estimated by Card (1995); see also Problem 5.4. Write the model as

$$\log(wage) = \alpha_1 educ + \alpha_2 black{\cdot}educ + \mathbf{z}_1\boldsymbol{\delta}_1 + u_1, \tag{6.27}$$

where $\mathbf{z}_1$ contains a constant, *exper*, *exper*^{2}, *black*, *smsa*, 1966 regional dummy variables, and a 1966 SMSA indicator. If *educ* is correlated with u_1, then we also expect *black·educ* to be correlated with u_1. If *nearc4*, a binary indicator for whether a worker grew up near a four-year college, is valid as an instrumental variable for *educ*, then a natural instrumental variable for *black·educ* is *black·nearc4*. Note that *black·nearc4* is uncorrelated with u_1 under the conditional mean assumption $\mathrm{E}(u_1 \mid \mathbf{z}) = 0$, where $\mathbf{z}$ contains all exogenous variables.

The equation estimated by OLS is

$$\begin{aligned}\log(\widehat{wage}) = \underset{(0.75)}{4.81} + \underset{(.004)}{.071}\, educ + \underset{(.006)}{.018}\, black{\cdot}educ - \underset{(.079)}{.419}\, black + \cdots.\end{aligned}$$

Therefore, the return to education is estimated to be about 1.8 percentage points higher for blacks than for nonblacks, even though wages are substantially lower for blacks at all but unrealistically high levels of education. (It takes an estimated 23.3 years of education before a black worker earns as much as a nonblack worker.)

To test whether *educ* is exogenous, we must test whether *educ* and *black·educ* are uncorrelated with u_1. We do so by first regressing *educ* on all instrumental variables: those elements in $\mathbf{z}_1$ plus *nearc4* and *black·nearc4*. (The interaction *black·nearc4* should be included because it might be partially correlated with *educ*.) Let $\hat{v}_{21}$ be the OLS residuals from this regression. Similarly, regress *black·educ* on $\mathbf{z}_1$, *nearc4*, and *black·nearc4*, and save the residuals $\hat{v}_{22}$. By the way, the fact that the dependent variable in the second reduced-form regression, *black·educ*, is zero for a large fraction of the sample has no bearing on how we test for endogeneity.

Adding $\hat{v}_{21}$ and $\hat{v}_{22}$ to the OLS regression and computing the joint F test yields $F = 0.54$ and p-value $= 0.581$; thus we do not reject exogeneity of *educ* and *black·educ*.

Incidentally, the reduced-form regressions confirm that *educ* is partially correlated with *nearc4* (but not *black·nearc4*) and *black·educ* is partially correlated with *black·nearc4* (but not *nearc4*). It is easily seen that these findings mean that the rank condition for 2SLS is satisfied—see Problem 5.15c. Even though *educ* does not appear to be endogenous in equation (6.27), we estimate the equation by 2SLS:

$$\widehat{\log(wage)} = \underset{(0.97)}{3.84} + \underset{(.057)}{.127}\,educ + \underset{(.040)}{.011}\,black\cdot educ - \underset{(.506)}{.283}\,black + \cdots.$$

The 2SLS point estimates certainly differ from the OLS estimates, but the standard errors are so large that the 2SLS and OLS estimates are not statistically different.

Sometimes we may want to test the null hypothesis that a subset of explanatory variables is exogenous while allowing another set of variables to be endogenous. As described in Davidson and MacKinnon (1993, Section 7.9), it is straightforward to obtain the test based on equation (6.25). Write an expanded model as

$$y_1 = \mathbf{z}_1\boldsymbol{\delta}_1 + \mathbf{y}_2\boldsymbol{\alpha}_1 + \mathbf{y}_3\boldsymbol{\gamma}_1 + u_1, \tag{6.28}$$

where $\boldsymbol{\alpha}_1$ is $G_1 \times 1$ and $\boldsymbol{\gamma}_1$ is $J_1 \times 1$. We allow $\mathbf{y}_2$ to be endogenous and test H_0: $\text{E}(\mathbf{y}_3' u_1) = \mathbf{0}$. The relevant equation is now $y_1 = \mathbf{z}_1\boldsymbol{\delta}_1 + \mathbf{y}_2\boldsymbol{\alpha}_1 + \mathbf{y}_3\boldsymbol{\gamma}_1 + \mathbf{v}_3\boldsymbol{\rho}_1 + e_1$, or, when we operationalize it,

$$y_1 = \mathbf{z}_1\boldsymbol{\delta}_1 + \mathbf{y}_2\boldsymbol{\alpha}_1 + \mathbf{y}_3\boldsymbol{\gamma}_1 + \hat{\mathbf{v}}_3\boldsymbol{\rho}_1 + error, \tag{6.29}$$

where $\boldsymbol{\rho}_1$ now represents the vector of population regression coefficients from u_1 on $\mathbf{v}_3$. Because $\mathbf{y}_2$ is allowed to be endogenous under H_0, we cannot estimate equation (6.29) by OLS in order to test H_0: $\boldsymbol{\rho}_1 = \mathbf{0}$. Instead, we apply 2SLS to equation (6.29) with instruments $(\mathbf{z}, \mathbf{y}_3, \hat{\mathbf{v}}_3)$; remember, $(\mathbf{y}_3, \mathbf{v}_3)$ are exogenous in the augmented equation. In effect, we still instrument for $\mathbf{y}_2$, but $\mathbf{y}_3$ and $\hat{\mathbf{v}}_3$ act as their own instruments. Using the results on IV estimation with generated regressors and instruments in Section 6.1.3, the usual Wald statistic (possibly implemented as an F statistic) for testing H_0: $\boldsymbol{\rho}_1 = \mathbf{0}$ is asymptotically valid under H_0. As usual, it may be prudent to allow heteroskedasticity of unknown form under H_0, and this is easily done using econometric software that computes heteroskedasticity-robust tests of exclusion restrictions after 2SLS estimation.

6.3.2 Testing Overidentifying Restrictions

When we have more instruments than we need to identify an equation, we can test whether the additional instruments are valid in the sense that they are uncorrelated with u_1. To explain the various procedures, write the equation in the form

$$y_1 = \mathbf{z}_1\boldsymbol{\delta}_1 + \mathbf{y}_2\boldsymbol{\alpha}_1 + u_1, \tag{6.30}$$

where $\mathbf{z}_1$ is $1 \times L_1$ and $\mathbf{y}_2$ is $1 \times G_1$. The $1 \times L$ vector of all exogenous variables is again $\mathbf{z}$; partition this as $\mathbf{z} = (\mathbf{z}_1, \mathbf{z}_2)$ where $\mathbf{z}_2$ is $1 \times L_2$ and $L = L_1 + L_2$. Because the model is overidentified, $L_2 > G_1$. Under the usual identification conditions we could use any $1 \times G_1$ subset of $\mathbf{z}_2$ as instruments for $\mathbf{y}_2$ in estimating equation (6.30) (remember the elements of $\mathbf{z}_1$ act as their own instruments). Following his general principle, Hausman (1978) suggested comparing the 2SLS estimator using all instruments to 2SLS using a subset that just identifies equation (6.30). If all instruments are valid, the estimates should differ only as a result of sampling error. As with testing for endogeneity, the Hausman (1978) test based on a quadratic form in the coefficient differences can be cumbersome to compute. Fortunately, a regression-based test, originally due to Sargan (1958), is available.

The Sargan test maintains homoskedasticity (Assumption 2SLS.3) under the null hypothesis. It is easily obtained as NR_u^2 from the OLS regression

$$\hat{u}_1 \text{ on } \mathbf{z}, \tag{6.31}$$

where $\hat{u}_1$ are the 2SLS residuals using *all* of the instruments $\mathbf{z}$ and R_u^2 is the usual *R*-squared (assuming that $\mathbf{z}_1$ and $\mathbf{z}$ contain a constant; otherwise it is the uncentered *R*-squared). In other words, simply estimate regression (6.30) by 2SLS and obtain the 2SLS residuals, $\hat{u}_1$. Then regress these on all exogenous variables (including a constant). Under the null that $\mathrm{E}(\mathbf{z}'u_1) = \mathbf{0}$ and Assumption 2SLS.3, $NR_u^2 \stackrel{a}{\sim} \chi^2_{Q_1}$, where $Q_1 \equiv L_2 - G_1$ is the number of overidentifying restrictions.

The usefulness of the Sargan-Hausman test is that, if we reject the null hypothesis, then our logic for choosing the IVs must be reexamined. Unfortunately, the test does not tell us which IVs fail the exogeneity requirement; it could be one of them or all of them. (The symmetric way that all exogenous variables appear in regression in (6.31) makes it clear the test cannot single out faulty instruments.) If we fail to reject the null hypothesis, then we can have some confidence in the set of instruments used—up to a point. Even if we do not reject the null hypothesis, it is possible that more than one instrument is endogenous, and that the 2SLS estimators using a full and reduced set of instruments are asymptotically biased in similar ways. For example, suppose we have a single endogenous explanatory variable, years of schooling (*educ*), in a wage equation, and we propose two instruments, mother's and father's years of schooling, *motheduc* and *fatheduc*. The test of overidentifying restrictions is the same as comparing two IV estimates of the return to schooling: one uses *motheduc* as the only instrument for *educ* and the other uses *fatheduc* as the only instrument. We can easily think neither instrument is truly exogenous, and each is likely to be positively correlated with unobserved cognitive ability. Therefore, we might expect the two IV estimates to give similar answers (and maybe even similar to OLS). But we should not take the similarity in the estimates to mean that the IVs are definitely exogenous; both could be leading us astray in the same direction with roughly the same bias magnitude. Even in cases where the point estimates are practically different, we might fail to reject exogenous instruments simply because the standard errors of the two IV estimates are large.

It is straightforward to obtain a heteroskedasticity-robust test of the overidentifying restrictions, but we need to separate the instrumental variables into two groups. Let $\mathbf{z}_2$ be the $1 \times L_2$ vector of exogenous variables excluded from equation (6.24) and write $\mathbf{z}_2 = (\mathbf{g}_2, \mathbf{h}_2)$, where $\mathbf{g}_2$ is $1 \times G_1$—the same dimension as $\mathbf{y}_2$—and $\mathbf{h}_2$ is $1 \times Q_1$—the number of overidentifying restrictions. It turns out not to matter how we do this division, provided $\mathbf{h}_2$ has Q_1 elements. Wooldridge (1995b) shows that the following procedure is valid. As in equation (6.31), let $\hat{u}_1$ be the 2SLS residuals from estimating equation (6.24), and let $\hat{\mathbf{y}}_2$ denote the fitted values from the first stage regression, $\mathbf{y}_2$ on $\mathbf{z}$ (each element of $\mathbf{y}_2$ onto $\mathbf{z}$). Next, regress each element of $\mathbf{h}_2$ onto $(\mathbf{z}_1, \hat{\mathbf{y}}_2)$ and save the residuals, say $\hat{\mathbf{r}}_2$ ($1 \times Q_1$ for each observation). Then the LM statistic is obtained as $N - \text{SSR}_0$, where SSR_0 is the sum of squared residuals from the regression 1 on $\hat{u}_1\hat{\mathbf{r}}_2$. Under H_0, and without assuming homoskedasticity, $N - \text{SSR}_0 \overset{a}{\sim} \chi^2_{Q_1}$. Alternatively, one may use a heteroskedasticity-robust Wald test of $\text{H}_0 : \boldsymbol{\eta}_1 = \mathbf{0}$ in the auxiliary model

$$\hat{u}_1 = \hat{\mathbf{r}}_2\boldsymbol{\eta}_1 + error. \tag{6.32}$$

This approach differs from the LM statistic in that residuals $\hat{e}_1 \equiv \hat{u}_1 - \hat{\mathbf{r}}_2\hat{\boldsymbol{\eta}}_1$ are used in the implicit variance matrix estimator, rather than $\hat{u}_1$. Under the null hypothesis (and local alternatives), $\hat{\boldsymbol{\eta}}_1 \xrightarrow{p} \mathbf{0}$, and so the statistics are asymptotically equivalent.

Example 6.3 (Overidentifying Restrictions in the Wage Equation): In estimating equation (6.23) by 2SLS, we used (*motheduc, fatheduc, huseduc*) as instruments for *educ*. Therefore, there are two overidentifying restrictions. Letting $\hat{u}_1$ be the 2SLS residuals from equation (6.23) using all instruments, the test statistic is N times the R-squared from the OLS regression

$\hat{u}_1$ on 1, *exper*, *exper*^{2}, *motheduc*, *fatheduc*, *huseduc*

Under H_0 and homoskedasticity, $NR_u^2 \overset{a}{\sim} \chi^2_2$. Using the data on working women in MROZ.RAW gives $R_u^2 = .0026$, and so the overidentification test statistic is about

1.11. The p-value is about .574, so the overidentifying restrictions are not rejected at any reasonable level.

For the heteroskedasticity-robust version, one approach is to obtain the residuals, $\hat{r}_1$ and $\hat{r}_2$, from the OLS regressions *motheduc* on 1, *exper*, $exper^2$, and $\widehat{educ}$ and *fatheduc* on 1, *exper*, $exper^2$, and $\widehat{educ}$, where $\widehat{educ}$ are the first-stage fitted values from the regression *educ* on 1, *exper*, $exper^2$, *motheduc*, *fatheduc*, and *huseduc*. Then obtain $N - \text{SSR}$ from the OLS regression 1 on $\hat{u}_1 \cdot \hat{r}_1$, $\hat{u}_1 \cdot \hat{r}_2$. Using only the 428 observations on working women to obtain $\hat{r}_1$ and $\hat{r}_2$, the value of the robust test statistic is about 1.04 with p-value $= .595$, which is similar to the p-value for the nonrobust test.

6.3.3 Testing Functional Form

Sometimes we need a test with power for detecting neglected nonlinearities in models estimated by OLS or 2SLS. A useful approach is to add nonlinear functions, such as squares and cross products, to the original model. This approach is easy when all explanatory variables are exogenous: F statistics and LM statistics for exclusion restrictions are easily obtained. It is a little tricky for models with endogenous explanatory variables because we need to choose instruments for the additional nonlinear functions of the endogenous variables. We postpone this topic until Chapter 9, when we discuss simultaneous equation models. See also Wooldridge (1995b).

Putting in squares and cross products of all exogenous variables can consume many degrees of freedom. An alternative is Ramsey's (1969) RESET, which has degrees of freedom that do not depend on K. Write the model as

$$y = \mathbf{x}\boldsymbol{\beta} + u, \tag{6.33}$$

$$\mathrm{E}(u \mid \mathbf{x}) = 0. \tag{6.34}$$

(You should convince yourself that it makes no sense to test for functional form if we only assume that $\mathrm{E}(\mathbf{x}'u) = \mathbf{0}$. If equation (6.33) defines a linear projection, then, by definition, functional form is not an issue.) Under condition (6.34) we know that any function of $\mathbf{x}$ is uncorrelated with u (hence the previous suggestion of putting squares and cross products of $\mathbf{x}$ as additional regressors). In particular, if condition (6.34) holds, then $(\mathbf{x}\boldsymbol{\beta})^p$ is uncorrelated with u for any integer p. Since $\boldsymbol{\beta}$ is not observed, we replace it with the OLS estimator, $\hat{\boldsymbol{\beta}}$. Define $\hat{y}_i = \mathbf{x}_i\hat{\boldsymbol{\beta}}$ as the OLS fitted values and $\hat{u}_i$ as the OLS residuals. By definition of OLS, the sample covariance between $\hat{u}_i$ and $\hat{y}_i$ is zero. But we can test whether the $\hat{u}_i$ are sufficiently correlated with low-order polynomials in $\hat{y}_i$, say $\hat{y}_i^2$, $\hat{y}_i^3$, and $\hat{y}_i^4$, as a test for neglected nonlinearity. There are a couple of ways to do so. Ramsey suggests adding these terms to equation (6.33) and doing a standard F test (which would have an approximate $\mathscr{F}_{3,N-K-3}$ distribution under equation (6.33) and the homoskedasticity assumption $\mathrm{E}(u^2 \mid \mathbf{x}) = \sigma^2$). Another possibility is to use an LM test: Regress $\hat{u}_i$ onto $\mathbf{x}_i$, $\hat{y}_i^2$, $\hat{y}_i^3$, and $\hat{y}_i^4$ and use N times the R-squared from this regression as χ_3^2. The methods discussed in Chapter 4 for obtaining heteroskedasticity-robust statistics can be applied here as well. Ramsey's test uses generated regressors, but the null hypothesis is that each generated regressor has zero population coefficient, and so the usual limit theory applies. (See Section 6.1.1.)

There is some misunderstanding in the testing literature about the merits of RESET. It has been claimed that RESET can be used to test for a multitude of specification problems, including omitted variables and heteroskedasticity. In fact, RESET is generally a poor test for either of these problems. It is easy to write down models where an omitted variable, say q, is highly correlated with each $\mathbf{x}$, but RESET has the same distribution that it has under H_0. A leading case is seen when $\mathrm{E}(q \mid \mathbf{x})$ is linear in $\mathbf{x}$. Then $\mathrm{E}(y \mid \mathbf{x})$ is linear in $\mathbf{x}$ [even though $\mathrm{E}(y \mid \mathbf{x}) \neq \mathrm{E}(y \mid \mathbf{x}, q)$], and the asymptotic power of RESET equals its asymptotic size. See Wooldridge (1995b) and Problem 6.4a. The following is an empirical illustration.

Example 6.4 (Testing for Neglected Nonlinearities in a Wage Equation): We use OLS and the data in NLS80.RAW to estimate the equation from Example 4.3:

$$\log(wage) = \beta_0 + \beta_1 exper + \beta_2 tenure + \beta_3 married + \beta_4 south$$
$$+ \beta_5 urban + \beta_6 black + \beta_7 educ + u.$$

The null hypothesis is that the expected value of u given the explanatory variables in the equation is zero. The R-squared from the regression $\hat{u}$ on $\mathbf{x}$, $\hat{y}^2$, and $\hat{y}^3$ yields $R_u^2 = .0004$, so the chi-square statistic is .374 with p-value $\approx .83$. (Adding $\hat{y}^4$ only increases the p-value.) Therefore, RESET provides no evidence of functional form misspecification.

Even though we already know IQ shows up very significantly in the equation (t statistic $= 3.60$; see Example 4.3), RESET does not, and should not be expected to, detect the omitted variable problem. It can only test whether the expected value of y given the variables actually in the regression is linear in those variables.

6.3.4 Testing for Heteroskedasticity

As we have seen for both OLS and 2SLS, heteroskedasticity does not affect the consistency of the estimators, and it is only a minor nuisance for inference. Nevertheless, sometimes we want to test for the presence of heteroskedasticity in order to justify use of the usual OLS or 2SLS statistics. If heteroskedasticity is present, more efficient estimation is possible.

We begin with the case where the explanatory variables are exogenous in the sense that u has zero mean given $\mathbf{x}$:

$$y = \beta_0 + \mathbf{x}\boldsymbol{\beta} + u, \qquad \mathrm{E}(u \mid \mathbf{x}) = 0.$$

The reason we do not assume the weaker assumption $\mathrm{E}(\mathbf{x}'u) = \mathbf{0}$ is that the following class of tests we derive—which encompasses all of the widely used tests for heteroskedasticity—are not valid unless $\mathrm{E}(u \mid \mathbf{x}) = 0$ is maintained under H_0. Thus, we maintain that the mean $\mathrm{E}(y \mid \mathbf{x})$ is correctly specified, and then we test the constant conditional variance assumption. If we do not assume correct specification of $\mathrm{E}(y \mid \mathbf{x})$, a significant heteroskedasticity test might just be detecting misspecified functional form in $\mathrm{E}(y \mid \mathbf{x})$; see Problem 6.4c.

Because $\mathrm{E}(u \mid \mathbf{x}) = 0$, the null hypothesis can be stated as H_0: $\mathrm{E}(u^2 \mid \mathbf{x}) = \sigma^2$. Under the alternative, $\mathrm{E}(u^2 \mid \mathbf{x})$ depends on $\mathbf{x}$ in some way. Thus, it makes sense to test H_0 by looking at covariances

$$\mathrm{Cov}[\mathbf{h}(\mathbf{x}), u^2] \tag{6.35}$$

for some $1 \times Q$ vector function $\mathbf{h}(\mathbf{x})$. Under H_0, the covariance in expression (6.35) should be zero for any choice of $\mathbf{h}(\cdot)$.

Of course, a general way to test zero correlation is to use a regression. Putting i subscripts on the variables, write the model

$$u_i^2 = \delta_0 + \mathbf{h}_i\boldsymbol{\delta} + v_i, \tag{6.36}$$

where $\mathbf{h}_i \equiv \mathbf{h}(\mathbf{x}_i)$; we make the standard rank assumption that $\mathrm{Var}(\mathbf{h}_i)$ has rank Q, so that there is no perfect collinearity in $\mathbf{h}_i$. Under H_0, $\mathrm{E}(v_i \mid \mathbf{h}_i) = \mathrm{E}(v_i \mid \mathbf{x}_i) = 0$, $\boldsymbol{\delta} = \mathbf{0}$, and $\delta_0 = \sigma^2$. Thus, we can apply an F test or an LM test for the null H_0: $\boldsymbol{\delta} = \mathbf{0}$ in equation (6.36). One thing to notice is that v_i cannot have a normal distribution under H_0: because $v_i = u_i^2 - \sigma^2$, $v_i \geq -\sigma^2$. This does not matter for asymptotic analysis; the OLS regression from equation (6.36) gives a consistent, $\sqrt{N}$-asymptotically normal estimator of $\boldsymbol{\delta}$ whether or not H_0 is true. But to apply a standard F or LM test, we must assume that, under H_0, $\mathrm{E}(v_i^2 \mid \mathbf{x}_i)$ is constant—that is, the errors in equation (6.36) are homoskedastic. In terms of the original error u_i, this assumption implies that

$$\mathrm{E}(u_i^4 \mid \mathbf{x}_i) = \mathit{constant} \equiv \kappa^2 \tag{6.37}$$

under H_0. This is called the **homokurtosis** (constant conditional fourth moment) assumption. Homokurtosis always holds when u is independent of $\mathbf{x}$, but there are conditional distributions for which $\mathrm{E}(u \mid \mathbf{x}) = 0$ and $\mathrm{Var}(u \mid \mathbf{x}) = \sigma^2$ but $\mathrm{E}(u^4 \mid \mathbf{x})$ depends on $\mathbf{x}$.

As a practical matter, we cannot test $\boldsymbol{\delta} = \mathbf{0}$ in equation (6.36) directly because u_i is not observed. Since $u_i = y_i - \mathbf{x}_i\boldsymbol{\beta}$ and we have a consistent estimator of $\boldsymbol{\beta}$, it is natural to replace u_i^2 with $\hat{u}_i^2$, where the $\hat{u}_i$ are the OLS residuals for observation i. Doing this step and applying, say, the LM principle, we obtain NR_c^2 from the regression

$$\hat{u}_i^2 \text{ on } 1, \mathbf{h}_i, \qquad i = 1, 2, \ldots, N, \tag{6.38}$$

where R_c^2 is just the usual centered R-squared. Now, if the u_i^2 were used in place of the $\hat{u}_i^2$, we know that, under H_0 and condition (6.37), $NR_c^2 \overset{a}{\sim} \chi_Q^2$, where Q is the dimension of $\mathbf{h}_i$.

What adjustment is needed because we have estimated u_i^2? It turns out that, because of the structure of these tests, no adjustment is needed to the asymptotics. (This statement is not generally true for regressions where the dependent variable has been estimated in a first stage; the current setup is special in that regard.) After tedious algebra, it can be shown that

$$N^{-1/2} \sum_{i=1}^{N} \mathbf{h}_i'(\hat{u}_i^2 - \hat{\sigma}^2) = N^{-1/2} \sum_{i=1}^{N} (\mathbf{h}_i - \boldsymbol{\mu}_h)'(u_i^2 - \sigma^2) + \mathrm{o}_p(1); \tag{6.39}$$

see Problem 6.5. Along with condition (6.37), this equation can be shown to justify the NR_c^2 test from regression (6.38).

Two popular tests are special cases. Koenker's (1981) version of the Breusch and Pagan (1979) test is obtained by taking $\mathbf{h}_i \equiv \mathbf{x}_i$, so that $Q = K$. (The original version of the Breusch-Pagan test relies heavily on normality of the u_i, in particular $\kappa^2 = 3\sigma^2$, so that Koenker's version based on NR_c^2 in regression (6.38) is preferred.) White's (1980b) test is obtained by taking $\mathbf{h}_i$ to be all nonconstant, unique elements of $\mathbf{x}_i$ and $\mathbf{x}_i'\mathbf{x}_i$: the levels, squares, and cross products of the regressors in the conditional mean.

The Breusch-Pagan and White tests have degrees of freedom that depend on the number of regressors in $\mathrm{E}(y \mid \mathbf{x})$. Sometimes we want to conserve on degrees of freedom. A test that combines features of the Breusch-Pagan and White tests but that has only two *dfs* takes $\hat{\mathbf{h}}_i \equiv (\hat{y}_i, \hat{y}_i^2)$, where the $\hat{y}_i$ are the OLS fitted values. (Recall that these are linear functions of the $\mathbf{x}_i$.) To justify this test, we must be able to replace $\mathbf{h}(\mathbf{x}_i)$ with $\mathbf{h}(\mathbf{x}_i, \hat{\boldsymbol{\beta}})$. We discussed the generated regressors problem for OLS in Section 6.1.1 and concluded that, for *testing* purposes, using estimates from earlier stages causes no complications. This is the case here as well: NR_c^2 from $\hat{u}_i^2$ on 1, $\hat{y}_i$, $\hat{y}_i^2$, $i = 1, 2, \ldots, N$ has a limiting χ_2^2 distribution under the null hypothesis, along with condition (6.37). This is easily seen to be a special case of the White test because $(\hat{y}_i, \hat{y}_i^2)$ contains two linear combinations of the squares and cross products of all elements in $\mathbf{x}_i$.

A simple modification is available for relaxing the auxiliary homokurtosis assumption (6.37). Following the work of Wooldridge (1990)—or, working directly from the representation in equation (6.39), as in Problem 6.5—it can be shown that $N - \text{SSR}_0$ from the regression (without a constant)

$$1 \text{ on } (\mathbf{h}_i - \bar{\mathbf{h}})(\hat{u}_i^2 - \hat{\sigma}^2), \qquad i = 1, 2, \ldots, N \tag{6.40}$$

is distributed asymptotically as χ_Q^2 under H_0 (there are Q regressors in regression (6.40)). This test is very similar to the heteroskedasticity-robust LM statistics derived in Chapter 4. It is sometimes called a **heterokurtosis-robust test** for heteroskedasticity.

If we allow some elements of $\mathbf{x}_i$ to be endogenous but assume we have instruments $\mathbf{z}_i$ such that $\text{E}(u_i \mid \mathbf{z}_i) = 0$ and the rank condition holds, then we can test H_0: $\text{E}(u_i^2 \mid \mathbf{z}_i) = \sigma^2$ (which implies Assumption 2SLS.3). Let $\mathbf{h}_i \equiv \mathbf{h}(\mathbf{z}_i)$ be a $1 \times Q$ function of the exogenous variables. The statistics are computed as in either regression (6.38) or (6.40), depending on whether the homokurtosis is maintained, where the $\hat{u}_i$ are the 2SLS residuals. There is, however, one caveat. For the validity of the asymptotic variances that these regressions implicitly use, an additional assumption is needed under H_0: $\text{Cov}(\mathbf{x}_i, u_i \mid \mathbf{z}_i)$ must be constant. This covariance is zero when $\mathbf{z}_i = \mathbf{x}_i$, so there is no additional assumption when the regressors are exogenous. Without the assumption of constant conditional covariance, the tests for heteroskedasticity are more complicated. For details, see Wooldridge (1990). Baum, Schaffer, and Stillman (2003) review tests that do not require the constant conditional covariance assumption.

You should remember that $\mathbf{h}_i$ (or $\hat{\mathbf{h}}_i$) must only be a function of exogenous variables and estimated parameters; it should not depend on endogenous elements of $\mathbf{x}_i$. Therefore, when $\mathbf{x}_i$ contains endogenous variables, it is *not* valid to use $\mathbf{x}_i\hat{\boldsymbol{\beta}}$ and $(\mathbf{x}_i\hat{\boldsymbol{\beta}})^2$ as elements of $\hat{\mathbf{h}}_i$. It *is* valid to use, say, $\hat{\mathbf{x}}_i\hat{\boldsymbol{\beta}}$ and $(\hat{\mathbf{x}}_i\hat{\boldsymbol{\beta}})^2$, where the $\hat{\mathbf{x}}_i$ are the first-stage fitted values from regressing $\mathbf{x}_i$ on $\mathbf{z}_i$.

6.4 Correlated Random Coefficient Models

In Section 4.3.3, we discussed models where unobserved heterogeneity interacts with one or more explanatory variables and mentioned how they can be interpreted as "random coefficient" models. Recall that if the heterogeneity is independent of the covariates, then the usual OLS estimator that ignores the heterogeneity consistently estimates the average partial effect (APE). Or, if we have suitable proxy variables for the unobserved heterogeneity, we can simply add interactions between the covariates and the (demeaned) proxy variables to estimate the APEs.

Consistent estimation of APEs is more difficult if one or more explanatory variables are endogenous (and there are no proxy variables that break the correlation between the unobservable variables and the endogenous variables). In this section, we provide a relatively simple analysis that is suitable for continuous, or roughly continuous, endogenous explanatory variables. We will continue our treatment of such models in Part IV, after we know more about estimation of models for discrete response.

6.4.1 When Is the Usual IV Estimator Consistent?

We study a special case of Wooldridge (2003b), who allows for multiple endogenous explanatory variables. A slight modification of equation (6.9) is

$$y_1 = \eta_1 + \mathbf{z}_1\boldsymbol{\delta}_1 + a_1 y_2 + u_1, \tag{6.41}$$

where $\mathbf{z}_1$ is $1 \times L_1$, y_2 is the endogenous explanatory variable, and a_1 is the "coefficient" on y_2—an unobserved random variable. (The reason we now set apart the intercept in (6.41) will be clear shortly.) We could replace $\boldsymbol{\delta}_1$ with a random vector, say $\mathbf{d}_1$, without substantively changing the following analysis, because we would assume $\mathrm{E}(\mathbf{d}_1 \mid \mathbf{z}) = \mathrm{E}(\mathbf{d}_1) = \boldsymbol{\delta}_1$ for the exogenous variables $\mathbf{z}$. The additional part of the error term, $\mathbf{z}_1(\mathbf{d}_1 - \boldsymbol{\delta}_1)$, has a zero mean conditional on $\mathbf{z}$, and so its presence would not affect our approach to estimation. The interesting feature of equation (6.41) is that the random coefficient, a_1, might be correlated with y_2. Following Heckman and Vytlacil (1998), we refer to (6.41) as a **correlated random coefficient (CRC) model**.

It is convenient to write $a_1 = \alpha_1 + v_1$, where $\alpha_1 = \mathrm{E}(a_1)$ is the object of interest. We can rewrite the equation as

$$y_1 = \eta_1 + \mathbf{z}_1\boldsymbol{\delta}_1 + \alpha_1 y_2 + v_1 y_2 + u_1 \equiv \eta_1 + \mathbf{z}_1\boldsymbol{\delta}_1 + \alpha_1 y_2 + e_1, \tag{6.42}$$

where $e_1 = v_1 y_2 + u_1$. Equation (6.42) shows explicitly a constant coefficient on y_2 (which we hope to estimate) but also an interaction between the unobserved heterogeneity, v_1, and y_2. Remember, equation (6.42) is a population model. For a random draw, we would write $y_{i1} = \eta_1 + \mathbf{z}_{i1}\boldsymbol{\delta}_1 + \alpha_1 y_{i2} + v_{i1} y_{i2} + u_{i1}$, which makes it clear that $\boldsymbol{\delta}_1$ and α_1 are parameters to estimate and v_{i1} is specific to observation i.

As discussed in Wooldridge (1997b, 2003b), the potential problem with applying instrumental variables (2SLS) to (6.42) is that the error term $v_1 y_2 + u_1$ is not necessarily uncorrelated with the instruments $\mathbf{z}$, even if we make the assumptions

$$\mathrm{E}(u_1 \mid \mathbf{z}) = \mathrm{E}(v_1 \mid \mathbf{z}) = 0, \tag{6.43}$$

which we maintain from here on. Generally, the term $v_1 y_2$ can cause problems for IV estimation, but it is important to be clear about the nature of the problem. If we are allowing y_2 to be correlated with u_1, then we also want to allow y_2 and v_1 to be correlated. In other words, $\mathrm{E}(v_1 y_2) = \mathrm{Cov}(v_1, y_2) \equiv \tau_1 \neq 0$. But a nonzero unconditional covariance is *not* a problem with applying IV to equation (6.42); it simply implies that the composite error term, e_1, has (unconditional) mean τ_1 rather than zero. As we know, a nonzero mean for e_1 means that the orginal intercept, η_1, would be inconsistently estimated, but this is rarely a concern.

Therefore, we can allow $\mathrm{Cov}(v_1, y_2)$, the unconditional covariance, to be unrestricted. But the usual IV estimator is generally inconsistent if $\mathrm{E}(v_1 y_2 \mid \mathbf{z})$ depends on $\mathbf{z}$. (There are still cases, which we will cover in Part IV, where the IV estimator is consistent.) Note that, because $\mathrm{E}(v_1 \mid \mathbf{z}) = 0$, $\mathrm{E}(v_1 y_2 \mid \mathbf{z}) = \mathrm{Cov}(v_1, y_2 \mid \mathbf{z})$. Therefore, as shown in Wooldridge (2003b), a sufficient condition for the IV estimator applied to equation (6.42) to be consistent for $\boldsymbol{\delta}_1$ and α_1 is

$$\mathrm{Cov}(v_1, y_2 \mid \mathbf{z}) = \mathrm{Cov}(v_1, y_2). \tag{6.44}$$

The 2SLS intercept estimator is consistent for $\eta_1 + \tau_1$. Condition (6.44) means that the conditional covariance between v_1 and y_2 is not a function of $\mathbf{z}$, but the unconditional covariance is unrestricted.

Because v_1 is unobserved, we cannot generally verify condition (6.44). But it is easy to find situations where it holds. For example, if we write

$$y_2 = m_2(\mathbf{z}) + v_2 \tag{6.45}$$

and assume (v_1, v_2) is independent of $\mathbf{z}$ (with zero mean), then condition (6.44) is easily seen to hold because $\mathrm{Cov}(v_1, y_2 \mid \mathbf{z}) = \mathrm{Cov}(v_1, v_2 \mid \mathbf{z})$, and the latter cannot be a function of $\mathbf{z}$ under independence. Of course, assuming v_2 in equation (6.45) is independent of $\mathbf{z}$ is a strong assumption even if we do not need to specify the mean function, $m_2(\mathbf{z})$. It is much stronger than just writing down a linear projection of y_2 on $\mathbf{z}$ (which is no real assumption at all). As we will see in various models in Part IV, the representation (6.45) with v_2 independent of $\mathbf{z}$ is not suitable for discrete y_2, and generally (6.44) is not a good assumption when y_2 has discrete characteristics. Further, as discussed in Card (2001), condition (6.44) can be violated even if y_2 is (roughly) continuous. Wooldridge (2005c) makes some headway in relaxing condition (6.44), but such methods are beyond the scope of this chapter.

A useful extension of equation (6.41) is to allow observed exogenous variables to interact with y_2. The most convenient formulation is

$$y_1 = \eta_1 + \mathbf{z}_1\boldsymbol{\delta}_1 + \alpha_1 y_2 + (\mathbf{z}_1 - \boldsymbol{\psi}_1)y_2\boldsymbol{\gamma}_1 + v_1 y_2 + u_1, \tag{6.46}$$

where $\boldsymbol{\psi}_1 \equiv \mathrm{E}(\mathbf{z}_1)$ is the $1 \times L_1$ vector of population means of the exogenous variables and $\boldsymbol{\gamma}_1$ is an $L_1 \times 1$ parameter vector. As we saw in Chapter 4, subtracting the mean from $\mathbf{z}_1$ before forming the interaction with y_2 ensures that α_1 is the average partial effect.

Estimation of equation (6.46) is simple if we maintain condition (6.44) (along with (6.43) and the appropriate rank condition). Typically, we would replace the unknown $\boldsymbol{\psi}_1$ with the sample averages, $\bar{\mathbf{z}}_1$, and then estimate

$$y_{i1} = \theta_1 + \mathbf{z}_{i1}\boldsymbol{\delta}_1 + \alpha_1 y_{i2} + (\mathbf{z}_{i1} - \bar{\mathbf{z}}_1)y_{i2}\boldsymbol{\gamma}_1 + error_i \tag{6.47}$$

by instrumental variables, ignoring the estimation error in the population mean (see Problem 6.10 for justification). The only issue is choice of instruments, which is complicated by the interaction term. One possibility is to use interactions between $\mathbf{z}_{i1}$ and all elements of $\mathbf{z}_i$ (including $\mathbf{z}_{i1}$). This results in many overidentifying restrictions, even if we just have one instrument z_{i2} for y_{i2}. Alternatively, we could obtain fitted values from a first-stage linear regression y_{i2} on $\mathbf{z}_i$, $\hat{y}_{i2} = \mathbf{z}_i\hat{\boldsymbol{\pi}}_2$, and then use IVs $[1, \mathbf{z}_i, (\mathbf{z}_{i1} - \bar{\mathbf{z}}_1)\hat{y}_{i2}]$, which results in as many overidentifying restrictions as for the model without the interaction. Note that the use of $(\mathbf{z}_{i1} - \bar{\mathbf{z}}_1)\hat{y}_{i2}$ as IVs for $(\mathbf{z}_{i1} - \bar{\mathbf{z}}_1)y_{i2}$ is asymptotically the same as using instruments $(\mathbf{z}_{i1} - \boldsymbol{\psi}_1) \cdot (\mathbf{z}_i\boldsymbol{\pi}_2)$, where $\mathrm{L}(y_2 \mid \mathbf{z}) = \mathbf{z}\boldsymbol{\pi}_2$ is the linear projection. In other words, consistency of this IV procedure does not in any way restrict the nature of the distribution of y_2 given $\mathbf{z}$. Plus, although we have generated instruments, the assumptions sufficient for ignoring estimation of the instruments hold, and so inference is standard (perhaps made robust to heteroskedasticity, as usual). In Chapter 8 we will develop the tools that allow us to determine when this choice of instruments produces the asymptotically efficient IV estimator.

We can just identify the parameters in equation (6.46) by using a further restricted set of instruments, $[1, \mathbf{z}_{i1}, \hat{y}_{i2}, (\mathbf{z}_{i1} - \bar{\mathbf{z}}_1)\hat{y}_{i2}]$. If so, it is important to use these as instruments and not as regressors. The latter procedure is suggested by Heckman and Vytlacil (1998), which I will refer to as HV (1998), under the assumptions (6.43) and (6.44), along with

$$\mathrm{E}(y_2 \mid \mathbf{z}) = \mathbf{z}\boldsymbol{\pi}_2 \tag{6.48}$$

(where $\mathbf{z}$ includes a constant). Under assumptions (6.43), (6.44), and (6.48), it is easy to show that

$$\mathrm{E}(y_1 \mid \mathbf{z}) = (\eta_1 + \tau_1) + \mathbf{z}_1\boldsymbol{\delta}_1 + \alpha_1(\mathbf{z}\boldsymbol{\pi}_2) + (\mathbf{z}_1 - \boldsymbol{\psi}_1) \cdot (\mathbf{z}\boldsymbol{\pi}_2)\boldsymbol{\gamma}_1. \tag{6.49}$$

HV (1998) use this expression to suggest a two-step regression procedure. In the first step, y_{i2} is regressed on $\mathbf{z}_i$ to obtain the fitted values, $\hat{y}_{i2}$, as before. In the second step, $\eta_1 + \tau_1$, $\boldsymbol{\delta}_1$, α_1, and $\boldsymbol{\gamma}_1$ are estimated from the OLS regression y_{i1} on 1, $\mathbf{z}_{i1}$, $\hat{y}_{i2}$, and $(\mathbf{z}_{i1} - \bar{\mathbf{z}}_1)\hat{y}_{i2}$. Generally, consistency of this procedure hinges on assumption (6.48), and it is important to see that running this regression is not the same as applying IV to equation (6.47) with instruments $[1, \mathbf{z}_{i1}, \hat{y}_{i2}, (\mathbf{z}_{i1} - \bar{\mathbf{z}}_1)\hat{y}_{i2}]$. (The first-stage regressions using the IV approach are, in effect, linear projections of y_2 on $[1, \mathbf{z}_1, \mathbf{z}\boldsymbol{\pi}_2, (\mathbf{z}_1 - \boldsymbol{\psi}_1) \cdot (\mathbf{z}\boldsymbol{\pi}_2)]$ and of $(\mathbf{z}_1 - \boldsymbol{\psi}_1)y_2$ on $[1, \mathbf{z}_1, \mathbf{z}\boldsymbol{\pi}_2, (\mathbf{z}_1 - \boldsymbol{\psi}_1) \cdot (\mathbf{z}\boldsymbol{\pi}_2)]$; no restrictions are made on $\mathrm{E}(y_2 \mid \mathbf{z})$.) In practice, the IV and two-step regression approaches may give similar estimates, but, even if this is the case, the IV standard errors need not be adjusted, whereas the second-step OLS standard errors do, because of the generated regressors problem.

In summary, applying standard IV methods to equation (6.47) provides a consistent estimator of the APE when condition (6.44) holds; no further restrictions on the distribution of y_2 given $\mathbf{z}$ are needed.

6.4.2 Control Function Approach

Garen (1984) studies the model in equation (6.41) (and also allows y_2 to appear as a quadratic and interacted with exogenous variables, but that does not change the control function approach). He proposed a control function approach to estimate the parameters. It is instructive to derive the control function approach here and to contrast it to the IV approaches discussed above.

Like Heckman and Vytlacil (1998), Garen uses a particular model for $\mathrm{E}(y_2 \mid \mathbf{z})$. In fact, Garen makes the assumption $y_2 = \mathbf{z}\boldsymbol{\pi}_2 + v_2$, where (u_1, v_1, v_2) is independent of $\mathbf{z}$ with a mean-zero trivariate normal distribution. The normality and independence assumptions are much stronger than needed. We can get by with

$$\mathrm{E}(u_1 \mid \mathbf{z}, v_2) = \rho_1 v_2, \mathrm{E}(v_1 \mid \mathbf{z}, v_2) = \xi_1 v_2, \tag{6.50}$$

which is the same as equation (6.18). From equation (6.41),

$$\begin{aligned} \mathrm{E}(y_1 \mid \mathbf{z}, y_2) &= \eta_1 + \mathbf{z}_1\boldsymbol{\delta}_1 + \alpha_1 y_2 + \mathrm{E}(v_1 \mid \mathbf{z}, y_2)y_2 + \mathrm{E}(u_1 \mid \mathbf{z}, y_2) \\ &= \eta_1 + \mathbf{z}_1\boldsymbol{\delta}_1 + \alpha_1 y_2 + \xi_1 v_2 y_2 + \rho_1 v_2, \end{aligned} \tag{6.51}$$

and this equation is estimable once we estimate $\boldsymbol{\pi}_2$. So, Garen's (1984) control function procedure is first to regress y_2 on $\mathbf{z}$ and obtain the reduced-form residuals, $\hat{v}_2$, and then to run the OLS regression y_1 on 1, $\mathbf{z}_1$, y_2, $\hat{v}_2 y_2$, $\hat{v}_2$. Under the maintained assumptions, Garen's method consistently estimates $\boldsymbol{\delta}_1$ and α_1. Because the second step uses generated regressors, the standard errors should be adjusted for the estimation of

π_2 in the first stage. Nevertheless, a test that y_2 is exogenous is easily obtained from the usual F test of $H_0: \xi_1 = 0, \rho_1 = 0$ (or a heteroskedasticity-robust version). Under the null hypothesis, no adjustment is needed for the generated standard errors.

Garen's assumptions are more restrictive than those needed for the standard IV estimator to be consistent. For one, it would be a fluke if assumption (6.50) held without the conditional covariance $\text{Cov}(v_1, y_2 \mid z)$ being independent of z. Plus, like HV (1998), Garen relies on a linear model for $\text{E}(y_2 \mid z)$. Further, Garen adds the assumptions that $\text{E}(u_1 \mid v_2)$ and $\text{E}(v_1 \mid v_2)$ are linear functions, something not needed for the IV approach.

If the assumptions needed for Garen's CF estimator to be consistent hold, it is likely more efficient than the IV estimator, although a comparison of the correct asymptotic variances is complicated. As we discussed in Section 6.2, when IV and control function methods lead to different estimators, the CF estimator is likely to be more efficient but less robust.

6.5 Pooled Cross Sections and Difference-in-Differences Estimation

So far our treatment of OLS and 2SLS has been explicitly for the case of random samples. In this section we briefly discuss how random samples from different points in time can be exploited, particularly for policy analysis.

6.5.1 Pooled Cross Sections over Time

A data structure that is useful for a variety of purposes, including policy analysis, is what we will call **pooled cross sections over time**. The idea is that during each year a new random sample is taken from the relevant population. Since distributions of variables tend to change over time, the identical distribution assumption is not usually valid, but the independence assumption is. Sampling a changing population at different points in time gives rise to **independent, not identically distributed (i.n.i.d.)** observations. It is important not to confuse a pooling of independent cross sections with a different data structure, panel data, which we treat starting in Chapter 7. Briefly, in a panel data set we follow the same group of individuals, firms, cities, and so on over time. In a pooling of cross sections over time, there is no replicability over time. (Or, if units appear in more than one time period, their recurrence is treated as coincidental and ignored.)

Every method we have learned for pure cross section analysis can be applied to pooled cross sections, including corrections for heteroskedasticity, specification testing, instrumental variables, and so on. But in using pooled cross sections, we should usually include year (or other time period) dummies to account for aggregate changes over time. If year dummies appear in a model, and it is estimated by 2SLS, the year dummies are their own instruments, as the passage of time is exogenous. For an example, see Problem 6.8. Time dummies can also appear in tests for heteroskedasticity to determine whether the unconditional error variance has changed over time.

In some cases we interact some explanatory variables with the time dummies to allow partial effects to change over time. For example, in estimating a wage equation using data sampled during different years, we might want to allow the return to schooling or union membership to change across time. Or we might want to determine how the gender gap in wages has changed over time. This is easily accomplished by interacting the appropriate variable with a full set of year dummies (less one if we explicitly use the first year as the base year, as is common). Typically, one would include a full set of time period dummies by themselves to allow for secular changes, including inflation and changes in productivity that are not captured by observed covariates. Problems 6.8 and 6.11 ask you to work through some empirical examples, focusing on how the results should be interpreted.

6.5.2 Policy Analysis and Difference-in-Differences Estimation

Much of the recent literature in policy analysis using **natural experiments** can be cast as regression with pooled cross sections with appropriately chosen interactions. In the simplest case, we have two time periods, say year 1 and year 2. There are also two groups, which we will call a **control group** and an **experimental group** or **treatment group**. In the natural experiment literature, people (or firms, or cities, and so on) find themselves in the treatment group essentially by accident. For example, to study the effects of an unexpected change in unemployment insurance on unemployment duration, we choose the treatment group to be unemployed individuals from a state that has a change in unemployment compensation. The control group could be unemployed workers from a neighboring state. The two time periods chosen would straddle the policy change.

As another example, the treatment group might consist of houses in a city undergoing unexpected property tax reform, and the control group would be houses in a nearby, similar town that is not subject to a property tax change. Again, the two (or more) years of data would include the period of the policy change. Treatment means that a house is in the city undergoing the regime change.

To formalize the discussion, call A the control group, and let B denote the treatment group; the dummy variable dB equals unity for those in the treatment group and is zero otherwise. Letting $d2$ denote a dummy variable for the second (post-policy-change) time period, the simplest equation for analyzing the impact of the policy change is

$$y = \beta_0 + \beta_1 dB + \delta_0 d2 + \delta_1 d2 \cdot dB + u, \tag{6.52}$$

where y is the outcome of interest. The dummy variable dB captures possible differences between the treatment and control groups prior to the policy change. The time period dummy, $d2$, captures aggregate factors that would cause changes in y even in the absence of a policy change. The coefficient of interest, δ_1, multiplies the interaction term, $d2 \cdot dB$, which is the same as a dummy variable equal to one for those observations in the treatment group in the second period.

The OLS estimator, $\hat{\delta}_1$, has a very interesting interpretation. Let $\bar{y}_{A,1}$ denote the sample average of y for the control group in the first year, and let $\bar{y}_{A,2}$ be the average of y for the control group in the second year. Define $\bar{y}_{B,1}$ and $\bar{y}_{B,2}$ similarly. Then $\hat{\delta}_1$ can be expressed as

$$\hat{\delta}_1 = (\bar{y}_{B,2} - \bar{y}_{B,1}) - (\bar{y}_{A,2} - \bar{y}_{A,1}) \tag{6.53}$$

This estimator has been labeled the **difference-in-differences (DD)** estimator in the recent program evaluation literature, although it has a long history in analysis of variance.

To see how effective $\hat{\delta}_1$ is for estimating policy effects, we can compare it with some alternative estimators. One possibility is to ignore the control group completely and use the change in the mean over time for the treatment group, $\bar{y}_{B,2} - \bar{y}_{B,1}$, to measure the policy effect. The problem with this estimator is that the mean response can change over time for reasons unrelated to the policy change. Another possibility is to ignore the first time period and compute the difference in means for the treatment and control groups in the second time period, $\bar{y}_{B,2} - \bar{y}_{A,2}$. The problem with this pure cross section approach is that there might be systematic, unmeasured differences in the treatment and control groups that have nothing to do with the treatment; attributing the difference in averages to a particular policy might be misleading.

By comparing the time changes in the means for the treatment and control groups, both group-specific and time-specific effects are allowed for. Nevertheless, unbiasedness of the DD estimator still requires that the policy change not be systematically related to other factors that affect y (and are hidden in u).

In most applications, additional covariates appear in equation (6.52), for example, characteristics of unemployed people or housing characteristics. These account for the possibility that the random samples within a group have systematically different characteristics in the two time periods. The OLS estimator of δ_1 no longer has the simple representation in equation (6.53), but its interpretation is essentially unchanged.

Example 6.5 (Length of Time on Workers' Compensation): Meyer, Viscusi, and Durbin (1995) (hereafter, MVD) study the length of time (in weeks) that an injured worker receives workers' compensation. On July 15, 1980, Kentucky raised the cap on weekly earnings that were covered by workers' compensation. An increase in the cap has no effect on the benefit for low-income workers but makes it less costly for a high-income worker to stay on workers' comp. Therefore, the control group is low-income workers and the treatment group is high-income workers; high-income workers are defined as those for whom the pre-policy-change cap on benefits is binding. Using random samples both before and after the policy change, MVD are able to test whether more generous workers' compensation causes people to stay out of work longer (everything else fixed). MVD start with a difference-in-differences analysis, using log(*durat*) as the dependent variable. The variable *afchnge* is the dummy variable for observations after the policy change, and *highearn* is the dummy variable for high earners. The estimated equation is

$$\begin{aligned}\log(\widehat{durat}) = {} & \underset{(0.031)}{1.126} + \underset{(.0447)}{.0077}\, afchnge + \underset{(.047)}{.256}\, highearn \\ & + \underset{(.069)}{.191}\, afchnge \cdot highearn. \end{aligned} \tag{6.54}$$

$N = 5{,}626, \qquad R^2 = .021$

Therefore, $\hat{\delta}_1 = .191$ $(t = 2.77)$, which implies that the average duration on workers' compensation increased by about 19 percent owing to the higher earnings cap. The coefficient on *afchnge* is small and statistically insignificant: as is expected, the increase in the earnings cap had no effect on duration for low-earnings workers. The coefficient on *highearn* shows that, even in the absence of any change in the earnings cap, high earners spent much more time—on the order of $100 \cdot [\exp(.256) - 1] = 29.2$ percent—on workers' compensation.

MVD also add a variety of controls for gender, marital status, age, industry, and type of injury. These allow for the fact that the kind of people and type of injuries differ systematically in the two years. Perhaps not surprisingly, controlling for these factors has little effect on the estimate of δ_1; see the MVD article and Problem 6.9.

Sometimes the two groups consist of people or cities in different states in the United States, often close geographically. For example, to assess the impact of changing alcohol taxes on alcohol consumption, we can obtain random samples on individuals from two states for two years. In state A, the control group, there was no change in alcohol taxes. In state B, taxes increased between the two years. The outcome variable would be a measure of alcohol consumption, and equation (6.52) can be estimated to determine the effect of the tax on alcohol consumption. Other factors, such as age, education, and gender can be controlled for, although this procedure is not necessary for consistency if sampling is random in both years and in both states.

The basic equation (6.52) can be easily modified to allow for continuous, or at least nonbinary, "treatments." An example is given in Problem 6.7, where the "treatment" for a particular home is its distance from a garbage incinerator site. In other words, there is not really a control group: each unit is put somewhere on a continuum of possible treatments. The analysis is similar because the treatment dummy, dB, is simply replaced with the nonbinary treatment.

In some cases a more convincing analysis of a policy change is available by further refining the definition of treatment and control groups. For example, suppose a state implements a change in health care policy aimed at the elderly, say people 65 and older, and the response variable, y, is a health outcome. One possibility is to use data only on people in the state with the policy change, both before and after the change, with the control group being people under 65 and the treatment group being people 65 and older. This DD strategy is similar to the MVD (1995) application. The potential problem with this DD analysis is that other factors unrelated to the state's new policy might affect the health of the elderly relative to the younger population, such as changes in health care emphasis at the federal level. A different DD analysis would be to use another state as the control group and use the elderly from the non-policy state as the control group. Here the problem is that *changes* in the health of the elderly might be systematically different across states as a result of, say, income and wealth differences rather than the policy change.

A more robust analysis than either of the DD analyses described above can be obtained by using both a different state and a control group within the treatment state. If we again label the two time periods as 1 and 2, let B represent the state implementing the policy, and let E denote the group of elderly, then an expanded version of equation (6.52) is

$$\begin{aligned} y = \beta_0 + \beta_1 dB + \beta_2 dE + \beta_3 dB \cdot dE + \delta_0 d2 + \delta_1 d2 \cdot dB \\ + \delta_2 d2 \cdot dE + \delta_3 d2 \cdot dB \cdot dE + u. \end{aligned} \tag{6.55}$$

The coefficient of interest is now δ_3, the coefficient on the triple interaction term, $d2 \cdot dB \cdot dE$. The OLS estimate $\hat{\delta}_3$ can be expressed as follows:

$$\begin{aligned} \hat{\delta}_3 = [(\bar{y}_{B,E,2} - \bar{y}_{B,E,1}) - (\bar{y}_{B,N,2} - \bar{y}_{B,N,1})] \\ - [(\bar{y}_{A,E,2} - \bar{y}_{A,E,1}) - (\bar{y}_{A,N,2} - \bar{y}_{A,N,1})], \end{aligned} \tag{6.56}$$

where the A subscript means the state not implementing the policy and the N subscript represents the nonelderly. For obvious reasons, the estimator in equation (6.56) is called the **difference-in-difference-in-differences (DDD)** estimate. (The population analogue of equation (6.56) is easily established from equation (6.55) by finding the expected values of the six groups appearing in equation (6.56).) The first term in brackets is the usual DD estimate if we focus only on state B and use nonelderly as the control group. The problem with the usual DD estimate is that the *trend* in health for the elderly could be systematically different from the trend for the nonelderly in the absence of the policy. The second term in brackets is an estimate of the differential trends for state A, and this acts as a further control. If the trend differential—in the absence of the policy—is similar in states, then $\hat{\delta}_3$ is a reliable estimate of the policy effect. When implemented as a regression, a standard error for $\hat{\delta}_3$ is easily obtained, including a heteroskedasticity-robust standard error. As in the DD case, it is straightforward to add additional covariates to equation (6.55).

The DD and DDD methodologies can be applied to more than two time periods. In the first case, a full set of time period dummies is added to (6.53), and a policy dummy replaces $d2 \cdot dB$; the policy dummy is simply defined to be unity for groups and time periods subject to the policy. This imposes the restriction that the policy has the same effect in every year, an assumption that is easily relaxed. In a DDD analysis, a full set of dummies is included for each of the two groups and all time periods, as well as for all pairwise interactions. Then, a policy dummy (or sometimes a continuous policy variable) measures the effect of the policy. See Gruber (1994) for an application to mandated maternity benefits.

Sometimes the treatment and control groups involve multiple geographical or political units, such as states in the United States. For example, Carpenter (2004) considers the effects of state-level zero tolerance alcohol laws for people under age 21 on various drinking behaviors (the outcome variable, y). In each year, a state is defined as a zero tolerance state or not (say, *zerotol*). Carpenter uses young adults aged 21–24 years as an additional control group in a DDD-type analysis. In Carpenter's regressions, a full set of state dummies, year dummies, and monthly dummies are included (the latter to control for seasonal variations in drinking behavior). Carpenter then includes the *zerotol* dummy and the interaction $zerotol \cdot under21$, where $under21$ is a dummy variable for the 18–20 age group. The coefficient on the latter measures the effect of zero tolerance laws. This is in the spirit of a DDD analysis, although Carpenter does not appear to include the pairwise interactions suggested by a full DDD approach.

Problems

6.1. a. In Problem 5.4d, test the null hypothesis that *educ* is exogenous.

b. Test the the single overidentifying restriction in this example.

6.2. In Problem 5.8b, test the null hypothesis that *educ* and *IQ* are exogenous in the equation estimated by 2SLS.

6.3. Consider a model for individual data to test whether nutrition affects productivity (in a developing country):

$$\log(produc) = \delta_0 + \delta_1 exper + \delta_2 exper^2 + \delta_3 educ + \alpha_1 calories + \alpha_2 protein + u_1, \tag{6.57}$$

where *produc* is some measure of worker productivity, *calories* is caloric intake per day, and *protein* is a measure of protein intake per day. Assume here that *exper*, $exper^2$, and *educ* are all exogenous. The variables *calories* and *protein* are possibly correlated with u_1 (see Strauss and Thomas (1995) for discussion). Possible instrumental variables for *calories* and *protein* are regional prices of various goods, such as grains, meats, breads, dairy products, and so on.

a. Under what circumstances do prices make good IVs for *calories* and *proteins*? What if prices reflect quality of food?

b. How many prices are needed to identify equation (6.57)?

c. Suppose we have M prices, $p_1, \ldots, p_M$. Explain how to test the null hypothesis that *calories* and *protein* are exogenous in equation (6.57).

6.4. Consider a structural linear model with unobserved variable q:

$$y = \mathbf{x}\boldsymbol{\beta} + q + v, \qquad \mathrm{E}(v \mid \mathbf{x}, q) = 0.$$

Suppose, in addition, that $\mathrm{E}(q \mid \mathbf{x}) = \mathbf{x}\boldsymbol{\delta}$ for some $K \times 1$ vector $\boldsymbol{\delta}$; thus, q and $\mathbf{x}$ are possibly correlated.

a. Show that $\mathrm{E}(y \mid \mathbf{x})$ is linear in $\mathbf{x}$. What consequences does this fact have for tests of functional form to detect the presence of q? Does it matter how strongly q and $\mathbf{x}$ are correlated? Explain.

b. Now add the assumptions $\mathrm{Var}(v \mid \mathbf{x}, q) = \sigma_v^2$ and $\mathrm{Var}(q \mid \mathbf{x}) = \sigma_q^2$. Show that $\mathrm{Var}(y \mid \mathbf{x})$ is constant. (Hint: $\mathrm{E}(qv \mid \mathbf{x}) = 0$ by iterated expectations.) What does this fact imply about using tests for heteroskedasticity to detect omitted variables?

c. Now write the equation as $y = \mathbf{x}\boldsymbol{\beta} + u$, where $\mathrm{E}(\mathbf{x}'u) = \mathbf{0}$ and $\mathrm{Var}(u \mid \mathbf{x}) = \sigma^2$. If $\mathrm{E}(u \mid \mathbf{x}) \neq \mathrm{E}(u)$, argue that an LM test of the form (6.28) will detect "heteroskedasticity" in u, at least in large samples.

6.5. a. Verify equation (6.39) under the assumptions $\mathrm{E}(u \mid \mathbf{x}) = 0$ and $\mathrm{E}(u^2 \mid \mathbf{x}) = \sigma^2$.

b. Show that, under the additional assumption (6.27),

$$\mathrm{E}[(u_i^2 - \sigma^2)^2(\mathbf{h}_i - \boldsymbol{\mu}_h)'(\mathbf{h}_i - \boldsymbol{\mu}_h)] = \eta^2 \mathrm{E}[(\mathbf{h}_i - \boldsymbol{\mu}_h)'(\mathbf{h}_i - \boldsymbol{\mu}_h)]$$

where $\eta^2 = \mathrm{E}[(u^2 - \sigma^2)^2]$.

c. Explain why parts a and b imply that the LM statistic from regression (6.38) has a limiting χ_Q^2 distribution.

d. If condition (6.37) does not hold, obtain a consistent estimator of $\mathrm{E}[(u_i^2 - \sigma^2)^2(\mathbf{h}_i - \boldsymbol{\mu}_h)'(\mathbf{h}_i - \boldsymbol{\mu}_h)]$. Show how this leads to the heterokurtosis-robust test for heteroskedasticity.

6.6. Using the test for heteroskedasticity based on the auxiliary regression $\hat{u}^2$ on $\hat{y}$, $\hat{y}^2$, test the log(*wage*) equation in Example 6.4 for heteroskedasticity. Do you detect heteroskedasticity at the 5 percent level?

6.7. For this problem use the data in HPRICE.RAW, which is a subset of the data used by Kiel and McClain (1995). The file contains housing prices and characteristics for two years, 1978 and 1981, for homes sold in North Andover, Massachusetts. In 1981, construction on a garbage incinerator began. Rumors about the incinerator being built were circulating in 1979, and it is for this reason that 1978 is used as the base year. By 1981 it was very clear that the incinerator would be operating soon.

a. Using the 1981 cross section, estimate a bivariate, constant elasticity model relating housing price to distance from the incinerator. Is this regression appropriate for determining the causal effects of incinerator on housing prices? Explain.

b. Pooling the two years of data, consider the model

$$\log(price) = \delta_0 + \delta_1 y81 + \delta_2 \log(dist) + \delta_3 y81 \cdot \log(dist) + u.$$

If the incinerator has a negative effect on housing prices for homes closer to the incinerator, what sign is δ_3? Estimate this model and test the null hypothesis that building the incinerator had no effect on housing prices.

c. Add the variables log(*intst*), $[\log(intst)]^2$, log(*area*), log(*land*), *age*, age^2, *rooms*, *baths* to the model in part b, and test for an incinerator effect. What do you conclude?

6.8. The data in FERTIL1.RAW are a pooled cross section on more than a thousand U.S. women for the even years between 1972 and 1984, inclusive; the data set is similar to the one used by Sander (1992). These data can be used to study the relationship between women's education and fertility.

a. Use OLS to estimate a model relating number of children ever born to a woman (*kids*) to years of education, age, region, race, and type of environment reared in. You should use a quadratic in age and should include year dummies. What is the estimated relationship between fertility and education? Holding other factors fixed, has there been any notable secular change in fertility over the time period?

b. Reestimate the model in part a, but use *motheduc* and *fatheduc* as instruments for *educ*. First check that these instruments are sufficiently partially correlated with *educ*. Test whether *educ* is in fact exogenous in the fertility equation.

c. Now allow the effect of education to change over time by including interaction terms such as *y74·educ*, *y76·educ*, and so on in the model. Use interactions of time dummies and parents' education as instruments for the interaction terms. Test that there has been no change in the relationship between fertility and education over time.

6.9. Use the data in INJURY.RAW for this question.

a. Using the data for Kentucky, reestimate equation (6.54) adding as explanatory variables *male*, *married*, and a full set of industry- and injury-type dummy variables. How does the estimate on *afchnge·highearn* change when these other factors are controlled for? Is the estimate still statistically significant?

b. What do you make of the small R-squared from part a? Does this mean the equation is useless?

c. Estimate equation (6.54) using the data for Michigan. Compare the estimate on the interaction term for Michigan and Kentucky, as well as their statistical significance.

6.10. Consider a regression model with interactions and squares of some explanatory variables: $\mathrm{E}(y \mid \mathbf{x}) = \mathbf{z}\boldsymbol{\beta}$, where $\mathbf{z}$ contains a constant, the elements of $\mathbf{x}$, and quadratics and interactions of terms in $\mathbf{x}$.

a. Let $\boldsymbol{\mu} = \mathrm{E}(\mathbf{x})$ be the population mean of $\mathbf{x}$, and let $\bar{\mathbf{x}}$ be the sample average based on the N available observations. Let $\hat{\boldsymbol{\beta}}$ be the OLS estimator of $\boldsymbol{\beta}$ using the N observations on y and $\mathbf{z}$. Show that $\sqrt{N}(\hat{\boldsymbol{\beta}} - \boldsymbol{\beta})$ and $\sqrt{N}(\bar{\mathbf{x}} - \boldsymbol{\mu})$ are asymptotically uncorrelated. (Hint: Write $\sqrt{N}(\hat{\boldsymbol{\beta}} - \boldsymbol{\beta})$ as in equation (4.8), and ignore the $\mathrm{o}_p(1)$ term. You will need to use the fact that $\mathrm{E}(u \mid \mathbf{x}) = 0$.)

b. In the model of Problem 4.8, use part a to argue that

$$\text{Avar}(\hat{\alpha}_1) = \text{Avar}(\tilde{\alpha}_1) + \beta_3^2 \text{ Avar}(\bar{x}_2) = \text{Avar}(\tilde{\alpha}_1) + \beta_3^2(\sigma_2^2/N)$$

where $\alpha_1 = \beta_1 + \beta_3\mu_2$, $\tilde{\alpha}_1$ is the estimator of α_1 *if* we knew μ_2, and $\sigma_2^2 = \text{Var}(x_2)$.

c. How would you obtain the correct asymptotic standard error of $\hat{\alpha}_1$, having run the regression in Problem 4.8d? (Hint: The standard error you get from the regression is really $\text{se}(\tilde{\alpha}_1)$. Thus you can square this to estimate $\text{Avar}(\tilde{\alpha}_1)$, then use the preceding formula. You need to estimate σ_2^2, too.)

d. Apply the result from part c to the model in Problem 4.8; in particular, find the corrected asymptotic standard error for $\hat{\alpha}_1$, and compare it with the uncorrected one from Problem 4.8d. (Both can be nonrobust to heteroskedasticity.) What do you conclude?

6.11. The following wage equation represents the populations of working people in 1978 and 1985:

$$\log(wage) = \beta_0 + \delta_0 y85 + \beta_1 educ + \delta_1 y85 \cdot educ + \beta_2 exper$$
$$+ \beta_3 exper^2 + \beta_4 union + \beta_5 female + \delta_5 y85 \cdot female + u,$$

where the explanatory variables are standard. The variable *union* is a dummy variable equal to one if the person belongs to a union and zero otherwise. The variable *y85* is a dummy variable equal to one if the observation comes from 1985 and zero if it comes from 1978. In the file CPS78_85.RAW, there are 550 workers in the sample in 1978 and a different set of 534 people in 1985.

a. Estimate this equation and test whether the return to education has changed over the seven-year period.

b. What has happened to the gender gap over the period?

c. Wages are measured in nominal dollars. What coefficients would change if we measure *wage* in 1978 dollars in both years? (Hint: Use the fact that for all 1985 observations, $\log(wage_i/P85) = \log(wage_i) - \log(P85)$, where *P85* is the common deflator; $P85 = 1.65$ according to the Consumer Price Index.)

d. Is there evidence that the variance of the error has changed over time?

e. With wages measured nominally, and holding other factors fixed, what is the estimated increase in nominal wage for a male with 12 years of education? Propose a regression to obtain a confidence interval for this estimate. (Hint: You must replace *y85·educ* with something else.)

6.12. In the linear model $y = \mathbf{x}\boldsymbol{\beta} + u$, initially assume that Assumptions 2SLS.1–2SLS.3 hold with $\mathbf{w}$ in place of $\mathbf{z}$, where $\mathbf{w}$ includes all nonredundant elements of $\mathbf{x}$ and $\mathbf{z}$.

a. Show that

$$\begin{aligned}\text{Avar}[\sqrt{N}(\hat{\boldsymbol{\beta}}_{2SLS} - \hat{\boldsymbol{\beta}}_{OLS})] &= \text{Avar}[\sqrt{N}(\hat{\boldsymbol{\beta}}_{2SLS} - \boldsymbol{\beta})] - \text{Avar}[\sqrt{N}(\hat{\boldsymbol{\beta}}_{OLS} - \boldsymbol{\beta})] \\ &= \sigma^2[\text{E}(\mathbf{x}^{*\prime}\mathbf{x}^*)]^{-1} - \sigma^2[\text{E}(\mathbf{x}'\mathbf{x})]^{-1},\end{aligned}$$

where $\mathbf{x}^* = \mathbf{z}\boldsymbol{\Pi}$ is the linear projection of $\mathbf{x}$ on $\mathbf{z}$. (Hint: It will help to write

$$\sqrt{N}(\hat{\boldsymbol{\beta}}_{2SLS} - \boldsymbol{\beta}) = \mathbf{A}_1^{-1}\left(N^{-1/2}\sum_{i=1}^{N}\mathbf{x}_i^{*\prime}u_i\right) + o_p(1)$$

and

$$\sqrt{N}(\hat{\boldsymbol{\beta}}_{OLS} - \boldsymbol{\beta}) = \mathbf{A}_2^{-1}\left(N^{-1/2}\sum_{i=1}^{N}\mathbf{x}_i'u_i\right) + o_p(1),$$

where $\mathbf{A}_1 = E(\mathbf{x}^{*\prime}\mathbf{x}^*)$ and $\mathbf{A}_2 = E(\mathbf{x}'\mathbf{x})$. Then use these two to obtain the joint asymptotic distribution of $\sqrt{N}(\hat{\boldsymbol{\beta}}_{2SLS} - \boldsymbol{\beta})$ and $\sqrt{N}(\hat{\boldsymbol{\beta}}_{OLS} - \boldsymbol{\beta})$ under H_0. Generally, $\text{Avar}[\sqrt{N}(\hat{\boldsymbol{\beta}}_{2SLS} - \hat{\boldsymbol{\beta}}_{OLS})] = \mathbf{V}_1 + \mathbf{V}_2 - (\mathbf{C} + \mathbf{C}')$, where $\mathbf{V}_1 = \text{Avar}[\sqrt{N}(\hat{\boldsymbol{\beta}}_{2SLS} - \boldsymbol{\beta})$, $\mathbf{V}_2 = \text{Avar}[\sqrt{N}(\hat{\boldsymbol{\beta}}_{OLS} - \boldsymbol{\beta})]$, and $\mathbf{C}$ is the asymptotic covariance. Under the given assumptions, you can show $\mathbf{C} = \mathbf{V}_2$.)

b. Show how to estimate $\text{Avar}[\sqrt{N}(\hat{\boldsymbol{\beta}}_{2SLS} - \hat{\boldsymbol{\beta}}_{OLS})$ if Assumption 2SLS.3 (and Assumption OLS.3) do not hold under H_0.

6.13. Referring to equations (6.17) and (6.18), show that if $\text{E}(u_1 \mid \mathbf{z}) = 0$ and $\text{E}(u_1 \mid \mathbf{z}, v_2) = \rho_1 v_2$ for some $\rho_1 \neq 0$, then $\text{E}(v_2 \mid \mathbf{z}) = 0$.

6.14. Let y_1 and y_2 be scalars, and suppose the structural model is

$$y_1 = \mathbf{z}_1\boldsymbol{\delta}_1 + \mathbf{g}(y_2)\boldsymbol{\alpha}_1 + u_1, \qquad \text{E}(u_1 \mid \mathbf{z}) = 0,$$

where $\mathbf{g}(y_2)$ is a $1 \times G_1$ vector of functions of y_2 and $\mathbf{z}$ contains at least one element not in $\mathbf{z}_1$. For example, $\mathbf{g}(y_2) = (y_2, y_2^2)$ allows for a quadratic. Or $\mathbf{g}(y_2)$ might be a vector of dummy variables indicating different intervals that y_2 falls into.

Assume that y_2 has a linear conditional expectation, written as

$$y_2 = \mathbf{z}\boldsymbol{\pi}_2 + v_2, \qquad \text{E}(v_2 \mid \mathbf{z}) = 0.$$

(Remember, this is much stronger than simply writing down a linear projection.)

Further, assume (u_1, v_2) is independent of $\mathbf{z}$. (This pretty much rules out y_2 with discrete characteristics.)

a. Show that

$$\mathrm{E}(y_1 \mid \mathbf{z}, y_2) = \mathrm{E}(y_1 \mid \mathbf{z}, v_2) = \mathbf{z}_1\boldsymbol{\delta}_1 + \mathbf{g}(y_2)\boldsymbol{\alpha}_1 + \mathrm{E}(u_1 \mid v_2).$$

b. Now add the assumption $\mathrm{E}(u_1 \mid v_2) = \rho_1 v_2$. Propose a consistent control function estimator of $\boldsymbol{\delta}_1$, $\boldsymbol{\alpha}_1$ and ρ_1.

c. How would you test the null hypothesis that y_2 is exogenous? Be very specific.

d. How would you modify the CF approach if $\mathrm{E}(u_1 \mid v_2) = \rho_1 v_2 + \xi_1(v_2^2 - \tau_2^2)$, where $\tau_2^2 = \mathrm{E}(v_2^2)$? How would you test the null hypothesis that y_2 is exogenous?

e. Would your general CF approach change if we replace $\mathbf{g}(y_2)$ with $\mathbf{g}(\mathbf{z}_1, y_2)$? Explain.

f. Suggest a more robust method of estimating $\boldsymbol{\delta}_1$ and $\boldsymbol{\alpha}_1$. In particular, suppose you are only willing to assume $E(u_1 \mid \mathbf{z}) = 0$.

6.15. Expand the model from Problem 6.14 to

$$y_1 = \mathbf{z}_1\boldsymbol{\delta}_1 + \mathbf{g}(\mathbf{z}_1, y_2)\boldsymbol{\alpha}_1 + \mathbf{g}(\mathbf{z}_1, y_2)\mathbf{v}_1 + u_1$$

$$\mathrm{E}(u_1 \mid \mathbf{z}) = 0, \qquad E(\mathbf{v}_1 \mid \mathbf{z}) = \mathbf{0},$$

where $\mathbf{g}(\mathbf{z}_1, y_2)$ is a $1 \times J_1$ vector of functions, $\boldsymbol{\alpha}_1$ is a $J_1 \times 1$ parameter vector, and $\mathbf{v}_1$ is a $J_1 \times 1$ vector of unobserved heterogeneity. Make the same assumptions on the reduced form of y_2. Further, assume $\mathrm{E}(u_1 \mid \mathbf{z}, v_2) = \rho_1 v_2$ and $\mathrm{E}(\mathbf{v}_1 \mid \mathbf{z}, v_2) = \boldsymbol{\theta}_1 v_2$ for a $J_1 \times 1$ vector $\boldsymbol{\theta}_1$.

a. Find $\mathrm{E}(y_1 \mid \mathbf{z}, y_2)$.

b. Propose a control function method for consistently estimating $\boldsymbol{\delta}_1$ and $\boldsymbol{\alpha}_1$.

c. How would you test the null hypothesis that y_2 is exogenous?

d. Explain in detail how to appy the CF method to Garen's (1984) model, where only y_2 is interacted with unobserved heterogeneity: $y_1 = \eta_1 + \mathbf{z}_1\boldsymbol{\delta}_1 + \alpha_1 y_2 + \lambda_1 y_2^2 + \mathbf{z}_1 y_2 \boldsymbol{\gamma}_1 + v_1 y_2 + u_1$.

Appendix 6A

We derive the asymptotic distribution of the 2SLS estimator in an equation with generated regressors and generated instruments. The tools needed to make the proof rigorous are introduced in Chapter 12, but the key components of the proof can be given here in the context of the linear model. Write the model as

$$y = \mathbf{x}\boldsymbol{\beta} + u, \qquad \mathrm{E}(u \mid \mathbf{v}) = 0,$$

where $\mathbf{x} = \mathbf{f}(\mathbf{w}, \boldsymbol{\delta})$, $\boldsymbol{\delta}$ is a $Q \times 1$ vector, and $\boldsymbol{\beta}$ is $K \times 1$. Let $\hat{\boldsymbol{\delta}}$ be a $\sqrt{N}$-consistent estimator of $\boldsymbol{\delta}$. The instruments for each i are $\hat{\mathbf{z}}_i = \mathbf{g}(\mathbf{v}_i, \hat{\boldsymbol{\lambda}})$, where $\mathbf{g}(\mathbf{v}, \boldsymbol{\lambda})$ is a $1 \times L$ vector, $\boldsymbol{\lambda}$ is an $S \times 1$ vector of parameters, and $\hat{\boldsymbol{\lambda}}$ is $\sqrt{N}$-consistent for $\boldsymbol{\lambda}$. Let $\hat{\boldsymbol{\beta}}$ be the 2SLS estimator from the equation

$$y_i = \hat{\mathbf{x}}_i\boldsymbol{\beta} + error_i,$$

where $\hat{\mathbf{x}}_i = \mathbf{f}(\mathbf{w}_i, \hat{\boldsymbol{\delta}})$, using instruments $\hat{\mathbf{z}}_i$:

$$\hat{\boldsymbol{\beta}} = \left[\left(\sum_{i=1}^N \hat{\mathbf{x}}_i'\hat{\mathbf{z}}_i\right)\left(\sum_{i=1}^N \hat{\mathbf{z}}_i'\hat{\mathbf{z}}_i\right)^{-1}\left(\sum_{i=1}^N \hat{\mathbf{z}}_i'\hat{\mathbf{x}}_i\right)\right]^{-1}\left(\sum_{i=1}^N \hat{\mathbf{x}}_i'\hat{\mathbf{z}}_i\right)\left(\sum_{i=1}^N \hat{\mathbf{z}}_i'\hat{\mathbf{z}}_i\right)^{-1}\left(\sum_{i=1}^N \hat{\mathbf{z}}_i' y_i\right).$$

Write $y_i = \hat{\mathbf{x}}_i\boldsymbol{\beta} + (\mathbf{x}_i - \hat{\mathbf{x}}_i)\boldsymbol{\beta} + u_i$, where $\mathbf{x}_i = \mathbf{f}(\mathbf{w}_i, \boldsymbol{\delta})$. Plugging this in and multiplying through by $\sqrt{N}$ gives

$$\sqrt{N}(\hat{\boldsymbol{\beta}} - \boldsymbol{\beta}) = (\hat{\mathbf{C}}'\hat{\mathbf{D}}^{-1}\hat{\mathbf{C}})^{-1}\hat{\mathbf{C}}'\hat{\mathbf{D}}^{-1}\left\{N^{-1/2}\sum_{i=1}^N \hat{\mathbf{z}}_i'[(\mathbf{x}_i - \hat{\mathbf{x}}_i)\boldsymbol{\beta} + u_i]\right\},$$

where

$$\hat{\mathbf{C}} \equiv N^{-1}\sum_{i=1}^N \hat{\mathbf{z}}_i'\hat{\mathbf{x}}_i \qquad \text{and} \qquad \hat{\mathbf{D}} = N^{-1}\sum_{i=1}^N \hat{\mathbf{z}}_i'\hat{\mathbf{z}}_i.$$

Now, using Lemma 12.1 in Chapter 12, $\hat{\mathbf{C}} \xrightarrow{p} \mathrm{E}(\mathbf{z}'\mathbf{x})$ and $\hat{\mathbf{D}} \xrightarrow{p} \mathrm{E}(\mathbf{z}'\mathbf{z})$. Further, a mean value expansion of the kind used in Theorem 12.3 gives

$$N^{-1/2}\sum_{i=1}^N \hat{\mathbf{z}}_i'u_i = N^{-1/2}\sum_{i=1}^N \mathbf{z}_i'u_i + \left[N^{-1}\sum_{i=1}^N \nabla_\lambda \mathbf{g}(\mathbf{v}_i, \boldsymbol{\lambda})u_i\right]\sqrt{N}(\hat{\boldsymbol{\lambda}} - \boldsymbol{\lambda}) + \mathrm{o}_p(1),$$

where $\nabla_\lambda \mathbf{g}(\mathbf{v}_i, \boldsymbol{\lambda})$ is the $L \times S$ Jacobian of $\mathbf{g}(\mathbf{v}_i, \boldsymbol{\lambda})'$. Because $\mathrm{E}(u_i \mid \mathbf{v}_i) = 0$, $\mathrm{E}[\nabla_\lambda \mathbf{g}(\mathbf{v}_i, \boldsymbol{\lambda})'u_i] = \mathbf{0}$. It follows that $N^{-1}\sum_{i=1}^N \nabla_\lambda \mathbf{g}(\mathbf{v}_i, \boldsymbol{\lambda})u_i = \mathrm{o}_p(1)$ and, since $\sqrt{N}(\hat{\boldsymbol{\lambda}} - \boldsymbol{\lambda}) = \mathrm{O}_p(1)$, it follows that

$$N^{-1/2}\sum_{i=1}^N \hat{\mathbf{z}}_i'u_i = N^{-1/2}\sum_{i=1}^N \mathbf{z}_i'u_i + \mathrm{o}_p(1).$$

Next, using similar reasoning,

$$N^{-1/2} \sum_{i=1}^{N} \hat{\mathbf{z}}_i'(\mathbf{x}_i - \hat{\mathbf{x}}_i)\boldsymbol{\beta} = -\left[N^{-1} \sum_{i=1}^{N} (\boldsymbol{\beta} \otimes \mathbf{z}_i)' \nabla_\delta \mathbf{f}(\mathbf{w}_i, \boldsymbol{\delta})\right] \sqrt{N}(\hat{\boldsymbol{\delta}} - \boldsymbol{\delta}) + o_p(1)$$

$$= -\mathbf{G}\sqrt{N}(\hat{\boldsymbol{\delta}} - \boldsymbol{\delta}) + o_p(1),$$

where $\mathbf{G} = \mathrm{E}[(\boldsymbol{\beta} \otimes \mathbf{z}_i)' \nabla_\delta \mathbf{f}(\mathbf{w}_i, \boldsymbol{\delta})]$ and $\nabla_\delta \mathbf{f}(\mathbf{w}_i, \boldsymbol{\delta})$ is the $K \times Q$ Jacobian of $\mathbf{f}(\mathbf{w}_i, \boldsymbol{\delta})'$. We have used a mean value expansion and $\hat{\mathbf{z}}_i'(\mathbf{x}_i - \hat{\mathbf{x}}_i)\boldsymbol{\beta} = (\boldsymbol{\beta} \otimes \hat{\mathbf{z}}_i)'(\mathbf{x}_i - \hat{\mathbf{x}}_i)'$. Now, assume that

$$\sqrt{N}(\hat{\boldsymbol{\delta}} - \boldsymbol{\delta}) = N^{-1/2} \sum_{i=1}^{N} \mathbf{r}_i(\boldsymbol{\delta}) + o_p(1),$$

where $\mathrm{E}[\mathbf{r}_i(\boldsymbol{\delta})] = \mathbf{0}$. This assumption holds for all estimators discussed so far, and it also holds for most estimators in nonlinear models; see Chapter 12. Collecting all terms gives

$$\sqrt{N}(\hat{\boldsymbol{\beta}} - \boldsymbol{\beta}) = (\mathbf{C}'\mathbf{D}^{-1}\mathbf{C})^{-1}\mathbf{C}'\mathbf{D}^{-1}\left\{N^{-1/2} \sum_{i=1}^{N} [\mathbf{z}_i'u_i - \mathbf{G}\mathbf{r}_i(\boldsymbol{\delta})]\right\} + o_p(1).$$

By the central limit theorem,

$$\sqrt{N}(\hat{\boldsymbol{\beta}} - \boldsymbol{\beta}) \overset{a}{\sim} \mathrm{Normal}[\mathbf{0}, (\mathbf{C}'\mathbf{D}^{-1}\mathbf{C})^{-1}\mathbf{C}'\mathbf{D}^{-1}\mathbf{M}\mathbf{D}^{-1}\mathbf{C}(\mathbf{C}'\mathbf{D}^{-1}\mathbf{C})^{-1}],$$

where

$$\mathbf{M} = \mathrm{Var}[\mathbf{z}_i'u_i - \mathbf{G}\mathbf{r}_i(\boldsymbol{\delta})].$$

The asymptotic variance of $\hat{\boldsymbol{\beta}}$ is estimated as

$$(\hat{\mathbf{C}}'\hat{\mathbf{D}}^{-1}\hat{\mathbf{C}})^{-1}\hat{\mathbf{C}}'\hat{\mathbf{D}}^{-1}\hat{\mathbf{M}}\hat{\mathbf{D}}^{-1}\hat{\mathbf{C}}(\hat{\mathbf{C}}'\hat{\mathbf{D}}^{-1}\hat{\mathbf{C}})^{-1}/N, \tag{6.58}$$

where

$$\hat{\mathbf{M}} = N^{-1} \sum_{i=1}^{N} (\hat{\mathbf{z}}_i'\hat{u}_i - \hat{\mathbf{G}}\hat{\mathbf{r}}_i)(\hat{\mathbf{z}}_i'\hat{u}_i - \hat{\mathbf{G}}\hat{\mathbf{r}}_i)', \tag{6.59}$$

$$\hat{\mathbf{G}} = N^{-1} \sum_{i=1}^{N} (\hat{\boldsymbol{\beta}} \otimes \hat{\mathbf{z}}_i)' \nabla_\delta \mathbf{f}(\mathbf{w}_i, \hat{\boldsymbol{\delta}}), \tag{6.60}$$

and

$$\hat{\mathbf{r}}_i = \mathbf{r}_i(\hat{\boldsymbol{\delta}}), \qquad \hat{u}_i = y_i - \hat{\mathbf{x}}_i\hat{\boldsymbol{\beta}}. \tag{6.61}$$

A few comments are in order. First, estimation of $\boldsymbol{\lambda}$ does not affect the asymptotic distribution of $\hat{\boldsymbol{\beta}}$. Therefore, if there are no generated regressors, the usual 2SLS inference procedures are valid ($\mathbf{G} = \mathbf{0}$ in this case and so $\mathbf{M} = \mathrm{E}(u_i^2 \mathbf{z}_i' \mathbf{z}_i)$). If $\mathbf{G} = \mathbf{0}$ and $\mathrm{E}(u^2 \mathbf{z}' \mathbf{z}) = \sigma^2 \mathrm{E}(\mathbf{z}' \mathbf{z})$, then the usual 2SLS standard errors and test statistics are valid. If Assumption 2SLS.3 fails, then the heteroskedasticity-robust statistics are valid.

If $\mathbf{G} \neq \mathbf{0}$, then the asymptotic variance of $\hat{\boldsymbol{\beta}}$ depends on that of $\hat{\boldsymbol{\delta}}$ (through the presence of $\mathbf{r}_i(\boldsymbol{\delta})$). Neither the usual 2SLS variance matrix estimator nor the heteroskedasticity-robust form is valid in this case. The matrix $\hat{\mathbf{M}}$ should be computed as in equation (6.59).

In some cases, $\mathbf{G} = \mathbf{0}$ under the null hypothesis that we wish to test. The jth row of $\mathbf{G}$ can be written as $\mathrm{E}[z_{ij} \boldsymbol{\beta}' \nabla_{\delta} \mathbf{f}(\mathbf{w}_i, \boldsymbol{\delta})]$. Now, suppose that $\hat{x}_{ih}$ is the only generated regressor, so that only the hth row of $\nabla_{\delta} \mathbf{f}(\mathbf{w}_i, \boldsymbol{\delta})$ is nonzero. But then if $\beta_h = 0$, $\boldsymbol{\beta}' \nabla_{\delta} \mathbf{f}(\mathbf{w}_i, \boldsymbol{\delta}) = \mathbf{0}$. It follows that $\mathbf{G} = \mathbf{0}$ and $\mathbf{M} = \mathrm{E}(u_i^2 \mathbf{z}_i' \mathbf{z}_i)$, so that no adjustment for the preliminary estimation of $\boldsymbol{\delta}$ is needed. This observation is very useful for a variety of specification tests, including the test for endogeneity in Section 6.3.1. We will also use it in sample selection contexts later on.

7 Estimating Systems of Equations by Ordinary Least Squares and Generalized Least Squares

7.1 Introduction

This chapter begins our analysis of linear systems of equations. The first method of estimation we cover is system ordinary least squares, which is a direct extension of OLS for single equations. In some important special cases the system OLS estimator turns out to have a straightforward interpretation in terms of single-equation OLS estimators. But the method is applicable to very general linear systems of equations.

We then turn to a generalized least squares (GLS) analysis. Under certain assumptions, GLS—or its operationalized version, feasible GLS—will turn out to be asymptotically more efficient than system OLS. Nevertheless, we emphasize in this chapter that the efficiency of GLS comes at a price: it requires stronger assumptions than system OLS in order to be consistent. This is a practically important point that is often overlooked in traditional treatments of linear systems, particularly those that assume the explanatory variables are nonrandom.

As with our single-equation analysis, we assume that a random sample is available from the population. Usually the unit of observation is obvious—such as a worker, a household, a firm, or a city. For example, if we collect consumption data on various commodities for a cross section of families, the unit of observation is the family (not a commodity).

The framework of this chapter is general enough to apply to panel data models. Because the asymptotic analysis is done as the cross section dimension tends to infinity, the results are explicitly for the case where the cross section dimension is large relative to the time series dimension. (For example, we may have observations on N firms over the same T time periods for each firm. Then, we assume we have a random sample of firms that have data in each of the T years.) The panel data model covered here, while having many useful applications, does not fully exploit the replicability over time. In Chapters 10 and 11 we explicitly consider panel data models that contain time-invariant, unobserved effects in the error term.

7.2 Some Examples

We begin with two examples of systems of equations. These examples are fairly general, and we will see later that variants of them can also be cast as a general linear system of equations.

Example 7.1 (Seemingly Unrelated Regressions): The population model is a set of G linear equations,

$$\begin{aligned} y_1 &= \mathbf{x}_1\boldsymbol{\beta}_1 + u_1 \\ y_2 &= \mathbf{x}_2\boldsymbol{\beta}_2 + u_2 \\ &\vdots \\ y_G &= \mathbf{x}_G\boldsymbol{\beta}_G + u_G, \end{aligned} \tag{7.1}$$

where $\mathbf{x}_g$ is $1 \times K_g$ and $\boldsymbol{\beta}_g$ is $K_g \times 1$, $g = 1, 2, \ldots, G$. In many applications $\mathbf{x}_g$ is the same for all g (in which case the $\boldsymbol{\beta}_g$ necessarily have the same dimension), but the general model allows the elements and the dimension of $\mathbf{x}_g$ to vary across equations. Remember, the system (7.1) represents a generic person, firm, city, or whatever from the population. The system (7.1) is often called Zellner's (1962) **seemingly unrelated regressions (SUR) model** (for cross section data in this case). The name comes from the fact that, since each equation in the system (7.1) has its own vector $\boldsymbol{\beta}_g$, it appears that the equations are unrelated. Nevertheless, correlation across the errors in different equations can provide links that can be exploited in estimation; we will see this point later.

As a specific example, the system (7.1) might represent a set of demand functions for the population of families in a country:

$$\begin{aligned} housing &= \beta_{10} + \beta_{11} houseprc + \beta_{12} foodprc + \beta_{13} clothprc + \beta_{14} income \\ &\quad + \beta_{15} size + \beta_{16} age + u_1. \\ food &= \beta_{20} + \beta_{21} houseprc + \beta_{22} foodprc + \beta_{23} clothprc + \beta_{24} income \\ &\quad + \beta_{25} size + \beta_{26} age + u_2. \\ clothing &= \beta_{30} + \beta_{31} houseprc + \beta_{32} foodprc + \beta_{33} clothprc + \beta_{34} income \\ &\quad + \beta_{35} size + \beta_{36} age + u_3. \end{aligned}$$

In this example, $G = 3$ and $\mathbf{x}_g$ (a 1×7 vector) is the same for $g = 1, 2, 3$.

When we need to write the equations for a particular random draw from the population, y_g, $\mathbf{x}_g$, and u_g will also contain an i subscript: equation g becomes $y_{ig} = \mathbf{x}_{ig}\boldsymbol{\beta}_g + u_{ig}$. For the purposes of stating assumptions, it does not matter whether or not we include the i subscript. The system (7.1) has the advantage of being less cluttered while focusing attention on the population, as is appropriate for applications. But for derivations we will often need to indicate the equation for a generic cross section unit i.

When we study the asymptotic properties of various estimators of the $\boldsymbol{\beta}_g$, the asymptotics is done with G fixed and N tending to infinity. In the household demand example, we are interested in a set of three demand functions, and the unit of observation is the family. Therefore, inference is done as the number of families in the sample tends to infinity.

The assumptions that we make about how the unobservables u_g are related to the explanatory variables $(\mathbf{x}_1, \mathbf{x}_2, \ldots, \mathbf{x}_G)$ are crucial for determining which estimators of the $\boldsymbol{\beta}_g$ have acceptable properties. Often, when system (7.1) represents a structural model (without omitted variables, errors-in-variables, or simultaneity), we can assume that

$$\mathrm{E}(u_g \mid \mathbf{x}_1, \mathbf{x}_2, \ldots, \mathbf{x}_G) = 0, \qquad g = 1, \ldots, G. \tag{7.2}$$

One important implication of assumption (7.2) is that u_g is uncorrelated with the explanatory variables in *all* equations, as well as all functions of these explanatory variables. When system (7.1) is a system of equations derived from economic theory, assumption (7.2) is often very natural. For example, in the set of demand functions that we have presented, $\mathbf{x}_g \equiv \mathbf{x}$ is the same for all g, and so assumption (7.2) is the same as $\mathrm{E}(u_g \mid \mathbf{x}_g) = \mathrm{E}(u_g \mid \mathbf{x}) = 0$.

If assumption (7.2) is maintained, and if the $\mathbf{x}_g$ are not the same across g, then any explanatory variables excluded from equation g are assumed to have no effect on expected y_g once $\mathbf{x}_g$ has been controlled for. That is,

$$\mathrm{E}(y_g \mid \mathbf{x}_1, \mathbf{x}_2, \ldots \mathbf{x}_G) = \mathrm{E}(y_g \mid \mathbf{x}_g) = \mathbf{x}_g \boldsymbol{\beta}_g, \qquad g = 1, 2, \ldots, G. \tag{7.3}$$

There are examples of SUR systems where assumption (7.3) is too strong, but standard SUR analysis either explicitly or implicitly makes this assumption.

Our next example involves panel data.

Example 7.2 (Panel Data Model): Suppose that for each cross section unit we observe data on the same set of variables for T time periods. Let $\mathbf{x}_t$ be a $1 \times K$ vector for $t = 1, 2, \ldots, T$, and let $\boldsymbol{\beta}$ be a $K \times 1$ vector. The model in the population is

$$y_t = \mathbf{x}_t \boldsymbol{\beta} + u_t, \qquad t = 1, 2, \ldots, T, \tag{7.4}$$

where y_t is a scalar. For example, a simple equation to explain annual family saving over a five-year span is

$$sav_t = \beta_0 + \beta_1 inc_t + \beta_2 age_t + \beta_3 educ_t + u_t, \qquad t = 1, 2, \ldots, 5,$$

where inc_t is annual income, $educ_t$ is years of education of the household head, and age_t is age of the household head. This is an example of a **linear panel data model**. It is a **static model** because all explanatory variables are dated contemporaneously with sav_t.

The panel data setup is conceptually very different from the SUR example. In Example 7.1, each equation explains a different dependent variable for the same cross section unit. Here we only have one dependent variable we are trying to explain—*sav*—but we observe *sav*, and the explanatory variables, over a five-year period. (Therefore, the label "system of equations" is really a misnomer for panel data applications. At this point, we are using the phrase to denote more than one equation in any context.) As we will see in the next section, the statistical properties of estimators in SUR and panel data models can be analyzed within the same structure.

When we need to indicate that an equation is for a particular cross section unit i during a particular time period t, we write $y_{it} = \mathbf{x}_{it}\boldsymbol{\beta} + u_{it}$. We will omit the i subscript whenever its omission does not cause confusion.

What kinds of exogeneity assumptions do we use for panel data analysis? One possibility is to assume that u_t and $\mathbf{x}_t$ are orthogonal in the conditional mean sense:

$$\mathrm{E}(u_t \mid \mathbf{x}_t) = 0, \qquad t = 1, \ldots, T \tag{7.5}$$

We call this **contemporaneous exogeneity** of $\mathbf{x}_t$ because it only restricts the relationship between the disturbance and explanatory variables in the same time period. Naturally, assumption (7.5) implies that each element of $\mathbf{x}_t$ is uncorrelated with u_t. A stronger assumption on the explanatory variables is

$$\mathrm{E}(u_t \mid \mathbf{x}_t, \mathbf{x}_{t-1}, \ldots, \mathbf{x}_1) = 0, \qquad t = 1, \ldots, T \tag{7.6}$$

(which, of course, implies that $\mathbf{x}_s$ is uncorrelated with u_t for all $s \le t$). When assumption (7.6) holds we say that $\{\mathbf{x}_t\}$ is **sequentially exogenous**. When we combine sequential exogeneity and (7.4), we obtain

$$\mathrm{E}(y_t \mid \mathbf{x}_t, \mathbf{x}_{t-1}, \ldots, \mathbf{x}_1) = \mathrm{E}(y_t \mid \mathbf{x}_t) = \mathbf{x}_t\boldsymbol{\beta}, \tag{7.7}$$

which implies that whatever we have included in $\mathbf{x}_t$, no further lags of $\mathbf{x}_t$ are needed to explain the expected value of y_t. Once lagged variables are included in $\mathbf{x}_t$, it is often desirable (although not necessary) to have assumption (7.7) hold. For example, if y_t is a measure of average worker productivity at the firm level, and $\mathbf{x}_t$ includes a current measure of worker training along with, say, two lags, then we probably hope that two lags are sufficient to capture the distributed lag of productivity on training. However, if we have only a small number of time periods available, we might have to settle for two lags capturing most, but not necessarily all, of the lagged effect.

An even stronger form of exogeneity is that u_t has zero mean conditional on all explanatory variables in all time periods:

$$\mathrm{E}(u_t \mid \mathbf{x}_1, \mathbf{x}_2, \ldots, \mathbf{x}_T) = 0, \qquad t = 1, \ldots, T. \tag{7.8}$$

Under assumption (7.8), we say the $\{\mathbf{x}_t\}$ are **strictly exogenous**. Clearly, condition (7.8) implies that u_t is uncorrelated with all explanatory variables in all time periods, including future time periods. We can write assumption (7.8) under equation (7.4) as $\mathrm{E}(y_t \mid \mathbf{x}_1, \mathbf{x}_2, \ldots, \mathbf{x}_T) = \mathrm{E}(y_t \mid \mathbf{x}_t) = \mathbf{x}_t\boldsymbol{\beta}$. This condition is necessarily false if, say, $\mathbf{x}_{t+1}$ includes y_t.

Contemporaneous exogeneity says nothing about the relationship between $\mathbf{x}_s$ and u_t for any $s \neq t$, sequential exogeneity leaves the relationship unrestricted for $s > t$, but strict exogeneity rules out correlation between the errors and explanatory variables across all time periods. It is critically important to understand that these three assumptions can have different implications for the statistical properties of different estimators.

To illustrate the differences among assumptions (7.5), (7.6), and (7.8), let $\mathbf{x}_t \equiv (1, y_{t-1})$. Then assumption (7.5) holds by construction if $\mathrm{E}(y_t \mid y_{t-1}) = \beta_0 + \beta_1 y_{t-1}$, which just means that $\mathrm{E}(y_t \mid y_{t-1})$ is linear in y_{t-1}. The sequential exogeneity assumption holds if we further assume $\mathrm{E}(y_t \mid y_{t-1}, y_{t-2}, \ldots, y_0) = \mathrm{E}(y_t \mid y_{t-1})$, which means that only one lag of the dependent variable appears in the fully dynamic expectation $\mathrm{E}(y_t \mid y_{t-1}, y_{t-2}, \ldots, y_0)$ (in addition to $\mathrm{E}(y_t \mid y_{t-1})$ being linear in y_{t-1}). Often this is an intended assumption for a dynamic model, but it is an extra assumption compared with assumption (7.5). In this example, the strict exogeneity condition (7.8) *must* fail because $\mathbf{x}_{t+1} = (1, y_t)$, and therefore $\mathrm{E}(u_t \mid \mathbf{x}_1, \mathbf{x}_2, \ldots, \mathbf{x}_T) = \mathrm{E}(u_t \mid y_0, \ldots, y_{T-1}) = u_t \neq 0$ for $t = 1, 2, \ldots, T-1$ (because $u_t = y_t - \beta_0 - \beta_1 y_{t-1}$). Incidentally, it is *not* nearly enough to assume that the unconditional expected value of the error is zero, something that is almost always true in regression models.

Strict exogeneity can fail even if $\mathbf{x}_t$ does not contain lagged dependent variables. Consider a model relating poverty rates to welfare spending per capita, at the city level. A **finite distributed lag (FDL) model** is

$$poverty_t = \theta_t + \delta_0 welfare_t + \delta_1 welfare_{t-1} + \delta_2 welfare_{t-2} + u_t. \tag{7.9}$$

The parameter θ_t simply denotes different aggregate time effects for each year. The contemporaneous exogeneity assumption holds if we assume $\mathrm{E}(poverty_t \mid welfare_t, welfare_{t-1}, welfare_{t-2})$ is linear. In this example, we probably intend that sequential exogeneity holds, too, but this is an empirical question: Is a two-year lag sufficient to capture lagged effects of welfare spending on poverty rates?

Even if two lags of spending suffice to capture the distributed lag dynamics, strict exogeneity generally fails if welfare spending reacts to past poverty rates. An equation that captures this feedback is

$$welfare_t = \eta_t + \rho_1 poverty_{t-1} + r_t. \tag{7.10}$$

Generally, the strict exogeneity assumption (7.8) will be violated if $\rho_1 \neq 0$ because $welfare_{t+1}$ depends on u_t (after substituting (7.9) into (7.10)) and $\mathbf{x}_{t+1}$ contains $welfare_{t+1}$.

As we will see in this and the next several chapters, how we go about estimating $\boldsymbol{\beta}$ depends crucially on whether strict exogeneity holds, or only one of the weaker assumptions. Classical treatments of ordinary least squares and genereralized least squares with panel data tend to treat the $\mathbf{x}_{it}$ as fixed in repeated samples; in practice, this is the same as the strict exogeneity assumption.

7.3 System Ordinary Least Squares Estimation of a Multivariate Linear System

7.3.1 Preliminaries

We now analyze a general multivariate model that contains the examples in Section 7.2, and many others, as special cases. Assume that we have independent, identically distributed cross section observations $\{(\mathbf{X}_i, \mathbf{y}_i): i = 1, 2, \ldots, N\}$, where $\mathbf{X}_i$ is a $G \times K$ matrix and $\mathbf{y}_i$ is a $G \times 1$ vector. Thus, $\mathbf{y}_i$ contains the dependent variables for all G equations (or time periods, in the panel data case). The matrix $\mathbf{X}_i$ contains the explanatory variables appearing anywhere in the system. For notational clarity we include the i subscript for stating the general model and the assumptions.

The multivariate linear model for a random draw from the population can be expressed as

$$\mathbf{y}_i = \mathbf{X}_i\boldsymbol{\beta} + \mathbf{u}_i, \tag{7.11}$$

where $\boldsymbol{\beta}$ is the $K \times 1$ parameter vector of interest and $\mathbf{u}_i$ is a $G \times 1$ vector of unobservables. Equation (7.11) explains the G variables $y_{i1}, \ldots, y_{iG}$ in terms of $\mathbf{X}_i$ and the unobservables $\mathbf{u}_i$. Because of the random sampling assumption, we can state all assumptions in terms of a generic observation; in examples, we will often omit the i subscript.

Before stating any assumptions, we show how the two examples introduced in Section 7.2 fit into this framework.

Example 7.1 (SUR, continued): The SUR model (7.1) can be expressed as in equation (7.11) by defining $\mathbf{y}_i = (y_{i1}, y_{i2}, \ldots, y_{iG})'$, $\mathbf{u}_i = (u_{i1}, u_{i2}, \ldots, u_{iG})'$, and

$$\mathbf{X}_i = \begin{pmatrix} \mathbf{x}_{i1} & \mathbf{0} & \mathbf{0} & \cdots & \mathbf{0} \\ \mathbf{0} & \mathbf{x}_{i2} & & & \mathbf{0} \\ \mathbf{0} & \mathbf{0} & & & \vdots \\ \vdots & & & & \mathbf{0} \\ \mathbf{0} & \mathbf{0} & \mathbf{0} & \cdots & \mathbf{x}_{iG} \end{pmatrix}, \qquad \boldsymbol{\beta} = \begin{pmatrix} \boldsymbol{\beta}_1 \\ \boldsymbol{\beta}_2 \\ \vdots \\ \boldsymbol{\beta}_G \end{pmatrix}. \tag{7.12}$$

Note that the dimension of $\mathbf{X}_i$ is $G \times (K_1 + K_2 + \cdots + K_G)$, so we define $K \equiv K_1 + \cdots + K_G$.

Example 7.2 (Panel Data, continued): The panel data model (7.6) can be expressed as in equation (7.11) by choosing $\mathbf{X}_i$ to be the $T \times K$ matrix $\mathbf{X}_i = (\mathbf{x}_{i1}', \mathbf{x}_{i2}', \ldots, \mathbf{x}_{iT}')'$.

7.3.2 Asymptotic Properties of System Ordinary Least Squares

Given the model in equation (7.11), we can state the key orthogonality condition for consistent estimation of $\boldsymbol{\beta}$ by system ordinary least squares (SOLS).

ASSUMPTION SOLS.1: $\mathrm{E}(\mathbf{X}_i'\mathbf{u}_i) = \mathbf{0}$.

Assumption SOLS.1 appears similar to the orthogonality condition for OLS analysis of single equations. What it implies differs across examples because of the multiple-equation nature of equation (7.11). For most applications, $\mathbf{X}_i$ has a sufficient number of elements equal to unity, so that Assumption SOLS.1 implies that $\mathrm{E}(\mathbf{u}_i) = \mathbf{0}$, and we assume zero mean for the sake of discussion.

It is informative to see what Assumption SOLS.1 entails in the previous examples.

Example 7.1 (SUR, continued): In the SUR case, $\mathbf{X}_i'\mathbf{u}_i = (\mathbf{x}_{i1}u_{i1}, \ldots, \mathbf{x}_{iG}u_{iG})'$, and so Assumption SOLS.1 holds if and only if

$$\mathrm{E}(\mathbf{x}_{ig}'u_{ig}) = \mathbf{0}, \qquad g = 1, 2, \ldots, G. \tag{7.13}$$

Thus, Assumption SOLS.1 does not require $\mathbf{x}_{ih}$ and u_{ig} to be uncorrelated when $h \neq g$.

Example 7.2 (Panel Data, continued): For the panel data setup, $\mathbf{X}_i'\mathbf{u}_i = \sum_{t=1}^{T} \mathbf{x}_{it}'u_{it}$; therefore, a sufficient, and very natural, condition for Assumption SOLS.1 is

$$\mathrm{E}(\mathbf{x}_{it}'u_{it}) = \mathbf{0}, \qquad t = 1, 2, \ldots, T. \tag{7.14}$$

Like assumption (7.5), assumption (7.14) allows $\mathbf{x}_{is}$ and u_{it} to be correlated when $s \neq t$; in fact, assumption (7.14) is weaker than assumption (7.5). Therefore, Assumption SOLS.1 does *not* impose strict exogeneity in panel data contexts.

Assumption SOLS.1 is the weakest assumption we can impose in a regression framework to get consistent estimators of $\boldsymbol{\beta}$. As the previous examples show, Assumption SOLS.1 can hold when some elements of $\mathbf{X}_i$ are correlated with some elements of $\mathbf{u}_i$. Much stronger is the zero conditional mean assumption

$$\mathrm{E}(\mathbf{u}_i \mid \mathbf{X}_i) = \mathbf{0}, \tag{7.15}$$

or $\mathrm{E}(u_{ig} \mid \mathbf{X}_i) = 0$, $g = 1, 2, \ldots, G$. Assumption (7.15) implies, at a minimum, that each element of $\mathbf{X}_i$ is uncorrelated with each element of $\mathbf{u}_i$. For example, in the SUR model, (7.15) implies that $\mathbf{x}_{ih}$ is uncorrelated with u_{ig} for $g = h$ *and* $g \neq h$. In the panel data example, (7.15) is the strict exogeneity assumption (7.8). As we will see later, for large-sample analysis, assumption (7.15) can be relaxed to a zero correlation assumption—all elements of $\mathbf{X}_i$ are uncorrelated with all elements of $\mathbf{u}_i$. The stronger assumption (7.15) is closely linked to traditional treatments of systems of equations under the assumption of nonrandom regressors.

Under Assumption SOLS.1 the vector $\boldsymbol{\beta}$ satisfies

$$\mathrm{E}[\mathbf{X}_i'(\mathbf{y}_i - \mathbf{X}_i\boldsymbol{\beta})] = \mathbf{0}, \tag{7.16}$$

or $\mathrm{E}(\mathbf{X}_i'\mathbf{X}_i)\boldsymbol{\beta} = \mathrm{E}(\mathbf{X}_i'\mathbf{y}_i)$. For each i, $\mathbf{X}_i'\mathbf{y}_i$ is a $K \times 1$ random vector and $\mathbf{X}_i'\mathbf{X}_i$ is a $K \times K$ symmetric, positive semidefinite random matrix. Therefore, $\mathrm{E}(\mathbf{X}_i'\mathbf{X}_i)$ is always a $K \times K$ symmetric, positive semidefinite nonrandom matrix (the expectation here is defined over the population distribution of $\mathbf{X}_i$). To be able to estimate $\boldsymbol{\beta}$, we need to assume that it is the only $K \times 1$ vector that satisfies assumption (7.16).

ASSUMPTION SOLS.2: $\mathbf{A} \equiv \mathrm{E}(\mathbf{X}_i'\mathbf{X}_i)$ is nonsingular (has rank K).

Under Assumptions SOLS.1 and SOLS.2, we can write $\boldsymbol{\beta}$ as

$$\boldsymbol{\beta} = [\mathrm{E}(\mathbf{X}_i'\mathbf{X}_i)]^{-1}\mathrm{E}(\mathbf{X}_i'\mathbf{y}_i), \tag{7.17}$$

which shows that Assumptions SOLS.1 and SOLS.2 identify the vector $\boldsymbol{\beta}$. The analogy principle suggests that we estimate $\boldsymbol{\beta}$ by the sample analogue of assumption (7.17). Define the **system ordinary least squares (SOLS) estimator** of $\boldsymbol{\beta}$ as

$$\hat{\boldsymbol{\beta}} = \left(N^{-1}\sum_{i=1}^{N}\mathbf{X}_i'\mathbf{X}_i\right)^{-1}\left(N^{-1}\sum_{i=1}^{N}\mathbf{X}_i'\mathbf{y}_i\right). \tag{7.18}$$

For computing $\hat{\boldsymbol{\beta}}$ using matrix language programming, it is sometimes useful to write $\hat{\boldsymbol{\beta}} = (\mathbf{X}'\mathbf{X})^{-1}\mathbf{X}'\mathbf{Y}$, where $\mathbf{X} \equiv (\mathbf{X}_1', \mathbf{X}_2', \ldots, \mathbf{X}_N')'$ is the $NG \times K$ matrix of stacked $\mathbf{X}$ and $\mathbf{Y} \equiv (\mathbf{y}_1', \mathbf{y}_2', \ldots, \mathbf{y}_N')'$ is the $NG \times 1$ vector of stacked observations on the $\mathbf{y}_i$. For asymptotic derivations, equation (7.18) is much more convenient. In fact, the consistency of $\hat{\boldsymbol{\beta}}$ can be read off equation (7.18) by taking probability limits. We summarize with a theorem:

THEOREM 7.1 (Consistency of System OLS): Under Assumptions SOLS.1 and SOLS.2, $\hat{\boldsymbol{\beta}} \xrightarrow{p} \boldsymbol{\beta}$.

It is useful to see what the system OLS estimator looks like for the SUR and panel data examples.

Example 7.1 (SUR, continued): For the SUR model,

$$\sum_{i=1}^N \mathbf{X}_i'\mathbf{X}_i = \sum_{i=1}^N \begin{pmatrix} \mathbf{x}_{i1}'\mathbf{x}_{i1} & \mathbf{0} & \mathbf{0} & \cdots & \mathbf{0} \\ \mathbf{0} & \mathbf{x}_{i2}'\mathbf{x}_{i2} & & & \mathbf{0} \\ \mathbf{0} & \mathbf{0} & & & \vdots \\ \vdots & & & & \mathbf{0} \\ \mathbf{0} & \mathbf{0} & \mathbf{0} & \cdots & \mathbf{x}_{iG}'\mathbf{x}_{iG} \end{pmatrix}; \qquad \sum_{i=1}^N \mathbf{X}_i'\mathbf{y}_i = \sum_{i=1}^N \begin{pmatrix} \mathbf{x}_{i1}'y_{i1} \\ \mathbf{x}_{i2}'y_{i2} \\ \vdots \\ \mathbf{x}_{iG}'y_{iG} \end{pmatrix}.$$

Straightforward inversion of a block diagonal matrix shows that the OLS estimator from equation (7.18) can be written as $\hat{\boldsymbol{\beta}} = (\hat{\boldsymbol{\beta}}_1', \hat{\boldsymbol{\beta}}_2', \ldots, \hat{\boldsymbol{\beta}}_G')'$, where each $\hat{\boldsymbol{\beta}}_g$ is just the single-equation OLS estimator from the gth equation. In other words, system OLS estimation of an SUR model (without restrictions on the parameter vectors $\boldsymbol{\beta}_g$) is equivalent to **OLS equation by equation**. Assumption SOLS.2 is easily seen to hold if $\mathrm{E}(\mathbf{x}_{ig}'\mathbf{x}_{ig})$ is nonsingular for all g.

Example 7.2 (Panel Data, continued): In the panel data case,

$$\sum_{i=1}^N \mathbf{X}_i'\mathbf{X}_i = \sum_{i=1}^N \sum_{t=1}^T \mathbf{x}_{it}'\mathbf{x}_{it}; \qquad \sum_{i=1}^N \mathbf{X}_i'\mathbf{y}_i = \sum_{i=1}^N \sum_{t=1}^T \mathbf{x}_{it}'y_{it}.$$

Therefore, we can write $\hat{\boldsymbol{\beta}}$ as

$$\hat{\boldsymbol{\beta}} = \left(\sum_{i=1}^N \sum_{t=1}^T \mathbf{x}_{it}'\mathbf{x}_{it}\right)^{-1} \left(\sum_{i=1}^N \sum_{t=1}^T \mathbf{x}_{it}'y_{it}\right). \tag{7.19}$$

This estimator is called the **pooled ordinary least squares (POLS) estimator** because it corresponds to running OLS on the observations pooled across i and t. We mentioned this estimator in the context of *independent* cross sections in Section 6.5. The estimator in equation (7.19) is for the same cross section units sampled at different points in time. Theorem 7.1 shows that the POLS estimator is consistent under the orthogonality conditions in assumption (7.14) and the mild condition rank $\mathrm{E}(\sum_{t=1}^{T} \mathbf{x}_{it}'\mathbf{x}_{it}) = K$.

In the general system (7.11), the system OLS estimator does not necessarily have an interpretation as OLS equation by equation or as pooled OLS. As we will see in Section 7.7 for the SUR setup, sometimes we want to impose cross equation restrictions on the $\boldsymbol{\beta}_g$, in which case the system OLS estimator has no simple interpretation.

While OLS is consistent under Assumptions SOLS.1 and SOLS.2, it is not necessarily unbiased. Assumption (7.15), and the finite sample assumption $\mathrm{rank}(\mathbf{X}'\mathbf{X}) = K$, *do* ensure unbiasedness of OLS conditional on $\mathbf{X}$. (This conclusion follows because, under independent sampling, $\mathrm{E}(\mathbf{u}_i \mid \mathbf{X}_1, \mathbf{X}_2, \ldots, \mathbf{X}_N) = \mathrm{E}(\mathbf{u}_i \mid \mathbf{X}_i) = \mathbf{0}$ under assumption (7.15).) We focus on the weaker Assumption SOLS.1 because assumption (7.15) is often violated in economic applications, something we already saw for a dynamic panel data model.

For inference, we need to find the asymptotic variance of the OLS estimator under essentially the same two assumptions; technically, the following derivation requires the elements of $\mathbf{X}_i'\mathbf{u}_i\mathbf{u}_i'\mathbf{X}_i$ to have finite expected absolute value. From (7.18) and (7.11), write

$$\sqrt{N}(\hat{\boldsymbol{\beta}} - \boldsymbol{\beta}) = \left(N^{-1}\sum_{i=1}^{N} \mathbf{X}_i'\mathbf{X}_i\right)^{-1} \left(N^{-1/2}\sum_{i=1}^{N} \mathbf{X}_i'\mathbf{u}_i\right).$$

Because $\mathrm{E}(\mathbf{X}_i'\mathbf{u}_i) = \mathbf{0}$ under Assumption SOLS.1, the CLT implies that

$$N^{-1/2}\sum_{i=1}^{N} \mathbf{X}_i'\mathbf{u}_i \xrightarrow{d} \mathrm{Normal}(\mathbf{0}, \mathbf{B}), \tag{7.20}$$

where

$$\mathbf{B} \equiv \mathrm{E}(\mathbf{X}_i'\mathbf{u}_i\mathbf{u}_i'\mathbf{X}_i) \equiv \mathrm{Var}(\mathbf{X}_i'\mathbf{u}_i). \tag{7.21}$$

In particular, $N^{-1/2}\sum_{i=1}^{N} \mathbf{X}_i'\mathbf{u}_i = \mathrm{O}_p(1)$. But $(\mathbf{X}'\mathbf{X}/N)^{-1} = \mathbf{A}^{-1} + \mathrm{o}_p(1)$, so

$$\begin{aligned}\sqrt{N}(\hat{\boldsymbol{\beta}} - \boldsymbol{\beta}) &= \mathbf{A}^{-1}\left(N^{-1/2}\sum_{i=1}^{N}\mathbf{X}_i'\mathbf{u}_i\right) + [(\mathbf{X}'\mathbf{X}/N)^{-1} - \mathbf{A}^{-1}]\left(N^{-1/2}\sum_{i=1}^{N}\mathbf{X}_i'\mathbf{u}_i\right),\\ &= \mathbf{A}^{-1}\left(N^{-1/2}\sum_{i=1}^{N}\mathbf{X}_i'\mathbf{u}_i\right) + o_p(1)\cdot O_p(1),\\ &= \mathbf{A}^{-1}\left(N^{-1/2}\sum_{i=1}^{N}\mathbf{X}_i'\mathbf{u}_i\right) + o_p(1). \end{aligned} \tag{7.22}$$

Therefore, just as with single-equation OLS and 2SLS, we have obtained an asymptotic representation for $\sqrt{N}(\hat{\boldsymbol{\beta}} - \boldsymbol{\beta})$ that is a *nonrandom* linear combination of a partial sum that satisfies the CLT. Equations (7.20) and (7.22) and the asymptotic equivalence lemma imply

$$\sqrt{N}(\hat{\boldsymbol{\beta}} - \boldsymbol{\beta}) \xrightarrow{d} \text{Normal}(\mathbf{0}, \mathbf{A}^{-1}\mathbf{B}\mathbf{A}^{-1}). \tag{7.23}$$

We summarize with a theorem.

THEOREM 7.2 (Asymptotic Normality of SOLS): Under Assumptions SOLS.1 and SOLS.2, equation (7.23) holds.

The asymptotic variance of $\hat{\boldsymbol{\beta}}$ is

$$\text{Avar}(\hat{\boldsymbol{\beta}}) = \mathbf{A}^{-1}\mathbf{B}\mathbf{A}^{-1}/N, \tag{7.24}$$

so that $\text{Avar}(\hat{\boldsymbol{\beta}})$ shrinks to zero at the rate $1/N$, as expected. Consistent estimation of $\mathbf{A}$ is simple:

$$\hat{\mathbf{A}} \equiv \mathbf{X}'\mathbf{X}/N = N^{-1}\sum_{i=1}^{N}\mathbf{X}_i'\mathbf{X}_i. \tag{7.25}$$

A consistent estimator of $\mathbf{B}$ can be found using the analogy principle. First, because $\mathbf{B} = \text{E}(\mathbf{X}_i'\mathbf{u}_i\mathbf{u}_i'\mathbf{X}_i)$, $N^{-1}\sum_{i=1}^{N}\mathbf{X}_i'\mathbf{u}_i\mathbf{u}_i'\mathbf{X}_i \xrightarrow{p} \mathbf{B}$. Since the $\mathbf{u}_i$ are not observed, we replace them with the SOLS residuals:

$$\hat{\mathbf{u}}_i \equiv \mathbf{y}_i - \mathbf{X}_i\hat{\boldsymbol{\beta}} = \mathbf{u}_i - \mathbf{X}_i(\hat{\boldsymbol{\beta}} - \boldsymbol{\beta}). \tag{7.26}$$

Using matrix algebra and the law of large numbers, it can be shown that

$$\hat{\mathbf{B}} \equiv N^{-1}\sum_{i=1}^{N}\mathbf{X}_i'\hat{\mathbf{u}}_i\hat{\mathbf{u}}_i'\mathbf{X}_i \xrightarrow{p} \mathbf{B}. \tag{7.27}$$

(To establish equation (7.27), we need to assume that certain moments involving $\mathbf{X}_i$ and $\mathbf{u}_i$ are finite.) Therefore, Avar $\sqrt{N}(\hat{\boldsymbol{\beta}} - \boldsymbol{\beta})$ is consistently estimated by $\hat{\mathbf{A}}^{-1}\hat{\mathbf{B}}\hat{\mathbf{A}}^{-1}$, and $\text{Avar}(\hat{\boldsymbol{\beta}})$ is estimated as

$$\hat{\mathbf{V}} \equiv \left(\sum_{i=1}^{N} \mathbf{X}_i'\mathbf{X}_i\right)^{-1} \left(\sum_{i=1}^{N} \mathbf{X}_i'\hat{\mathbf{u}}_i\hat{\mathbf{u}}_i'\mathbf{X}_i\right) \left(\sum_{i=1}^{N} \mathbf{X}_i'\mathbf{X}_i\right)^{-1}. \tag{7.28}$$

Under Assumptions SOLS.1 and SOLS.2, we perform inference on $\boldsymbol{\beta}$ as if $\hat{\boldsymbol{\beta}}$ is normally distributed with mean $\boldsymbol{\beta}$ and variance matrix (7.28). The square roots of the diagonal elements of the matrix (7.28) are reported as the asymptotic standard errors. The t ratio, $\hat{\beta}_j/\text{se}(\hat{\beta}_j)$, has a limiting normal distribution under the null hypothesis H_0: $\beta_j = 0$. Sometimes the t statistics are treated as being distributed as t_{NG-K}, which is asymptotically valid because $NG - K$ should be large.

The estimator in matrix (7.28) is another example of a **robust variance matrix estimator** because it is valid without *any* second-moment assumptions on the errors $\mathbf{u}_i$ (except, as usual, that the second moments are well defined). In a multivariate setting it is important to know what this robustness allows. First, the $G \times G$ **unconditional variance matrix**, $\boldsymbol{\Omega} \equiv \text{E}(\mathbf{u}_i\mathbf{u}_i')$, is entirely unrestricted. This fact allows **cross equation correlation** in an SUR system as well as different error variances in each equation. In panel data models, an unrestricted $\boldsymbol{\Omega}$ allows for arbitrary **serial correlation** and **time-varying variances** in the disturbances. A second kind of robustness is that the **conditional variance matrix**, $\text{Var}(\mathbf{u}_i \mid \mathbf{X}_i)$, can depend on $\mathbf{X}_i$ in an arbitrary, unknown fashion. The generality afforded by formula (7.28) is possible because of the $N \to \infty$ asymptotics.

In special cases it is useful to impose more structure on the conditional and unconditional variance matrix of $\mathbf{u}_i$ in order to simplify estimation of the asymptotic variance. We will cover an important case in Section 7.5.2. Essentially, the key restriction will be that the conditional and unconditional variances of $\mathbf{u}_i$ are the same.

There are also some special assumptions that greatly simplify the analysis of the pooled OLS estimator for panel data; see Section 7.8.

7.3.3 Testing Multiple Hypotheses

Testing multiple hypotheses in a fully robust manner is easy once $\hat{\mathbf{V}}$ in matrix (7.28) has been obtained. The robust Wald statistic for testing H_0: $\mathbf{R}\boldsymbol{\beta} = \mathbf{r}$, where $\mathbf{R}$ is $Q \times K$ with rank Q and $\mathbf{r}$ is $Q \times 1$, has its usual form, $W = (\mathbf{R}\hat{\boldsymbol{\beta}} - \mathbf{r})'(\mathbf{R}\hat{\mathbf{V}}\mathbf{R}')^{-1}(\mathbf{R}\hat{\boldsymbol{\beta}} - \mathbf{r})$. Under H_0, $W \overset{a}{\sim} \chi^2_Q$. In the SUR case this is the easiest and most robust way of testing cross equation restrictions on the parameters in different equations using system OLS. In the panel data setting, the robust Wald test provides a way of testing multiple hypotheses about $\boldsymbol{\beta}$ without assuming homoskedasticity or serial independence of the errors.

7.4 Consistency and Asymptotic Normality of Generalized Least Squares

7.4.1 Consistency

System OLS is consistent under fairly weak assumptions, and we have seen how to perform robust inference using OLS. If we strengthen Assumption SOLS.1 and add assumptions on the conditional variance matrix of $\mathbf{u}_i$, we can do better using a generalized least squares procedure. As we will see, GLS is not usually feasible because it requires knowing the variance matrix of the errors up to a multiplicative constant. Nevertheless, deriving the consistency and asymptotic distribution of the GLS estimator is worthwhile because it turns out that the feasible GLS estimator is asymptotically equivalent to GLS.

We are still interested in estimating the parameter vector $\boldsymbol{\beta}$ in equation (7.9), but consistency of GLS generally requires a stronger assumption than Assumption SOLS.1. Although we can, for certain purposes, get by with a weaker assumption, the most straightforward analysis follows from assuming each element of $\mathbf{X}_i$ is uncorrelated with each element $\mathbf{u}_i$. The strengthening of Assumption SOLS.1 is most easily stated using the Kronecker product:

ASSUMPTION SGLS.1: $\mathrm{E}(\mathbf{X}_i \otimes \mathbf{u}_i) = \mathbf{0}$.

Typically, at least one element of $\mathbf{X}_i$ is unity, so in practice Assumption SGLS.1 implies that $\mathrm{E}(\mathbf{u}_i) = \mathbf{0}$. We will assume that $\mathbf{u}_i$ has a zero mean for our dicussion but not in proving any results. A sufficient condition for Assumption SGLS.1 is the zero conditional mean assumption $\mathrm{E}(\mathbf{u}_i \mid \mathbf{X}_i) = \mathbf{0}$, which, of course, also implies $\mathrm{E}(\mathbf{u}_i) = \mathbf{0}$.

The second moment matrix of $\mathbf{u}_i$—which is necessarily constant across i by the random sampling assumption—plays a critical role for GLS estimation of systems of equations. Define the $G \times G$ positive semi-definite matrix $\boldsymbol{\Omega}$ as

$$\boldsymbol{\Omega} \equiv \mathrm{E}(\mathbf{u}_i \mathbf{u}_i'). \tag{7.29}$$

Because $\mathrm{E}(\mathbf{u}_i) = \mathbf{0}$ in the vast majority of applications, we will refer to $\boldsymbol{\Omega}$ as the unconditional variance matrix of $\mathbf{u}_i$. For our general treatment, we assume it is actually positive definite. In applications where the dependent variables satisfy an adding up constraint across equations—such as expenditure shares summing to unity—an equation must be dropped to ensure that $\boldsymbol{\Omega}$ is nonsingular, a topic we return to in Section 7.3.3.

Having defined $\boldsymbol{\Omega}$, and assuming it is nonsingular, we can state a weaker version of Assumption SGLS.1 that is nevertheless sufficient for consistency of the GLS (and feasible GLS) estimator:

$$\mathrm{E}(\mathbf{X}_i'\boldsymbol{\Omega}^{-1}\mathbf{u}_i) = \mathbf{0}, \tag{7.30}$$

which simply says that the linear combination $\boldsymbol{\Omega}^{-1}\mathbf{X}_i$ of $\mathbf{X}_i$ is uncorrelated with $\mathbf{u}_i$. It follows that Assumption SGLS.1 implies (7.30); a concise proof using matrix algebra is

$$\mathrm{vec}\ \mathrm{E}(\mathbf{X}_i'\boldsymbol{\Omega}^{-1}\mathbf{u}_i) = \mathrm{E}(\mathrm{vec}(\mathbf{X}_i'\boldsymbol{\Omega}^{-1}\mathbf{u}_i)] = \mathrm{E}[(\mathbf{u}_i' \otimes \mathbf{X}_i')\ \mathrm{vec}\ \boldsymbol{\Omega}^{-1}] = \mathbf{0}.$$

(Recall that for conformable matrices $\mathbf{D}$, $\mathbf{E}$, and $\mathbf{F}$, $\mathrm{vec}(\mathbf{DEF}) = (\mathbf{F}' \otimes \mathbf{D})\ \mathrm{vec}(\mathbf{E})$, where $\mathrm{vec}(\mathbf{C})$ is the vectorization of the matrix $\mathbf{C}$; see, for example, Theil (1983).)

If (7.30) is sufficient for consistency of GLS, how come we make Assumption SGLS.1? There are a couple of reasons. First, SGLS.1 is more straightforward to interpret, and is independent of the structure of $\boldsymbol{\Omega}$. Second—and this is more subtle—when we turn to feasible GLS estimation in Section 7.5, Assumption SGLS.1 is used to establish the $\sqrt{N}$—equivalance of GLS and feasible GLS. If we knew $\boldsymbol{\Omega}$, (7.30) would be attractive as an assumption, but we almost never know $\boldsymbol{\Omega}$ (even up to a multiplicative constant). Assumption (7.30) will be relevant in Section 7.5.3, where we discuss imposing diagonality on the variance matrix.

In place of Assumption SOLS.2 we assume that a weighted expected outer product of $\mathbf{X}_i$ is nonsingular. Here we insert the assumption of a nonsingular variance matrix for completeness:

Assumption SGLS.2: $\boldsymbol{\Omega}$ is positive definite and $\mathrm{E}(\mathbf{X}_i'\boldsymbol{\Omega}^{-1}\mathbf{X}_i)$ is nonsingular.

The usual motivation for the GLS estimator is to transform a system of equations where the error has a nonscalar variance-covariance matrix into a system where the error vector has a scalar variance-covariance matrix. We obtain this by multiplying equation (7.11) by $\boldsymbol{\Omega}^{-1/2}$:

$$\boldsymbol{\Omega}^{-1/2}\mathbf{y}_i = (\boldsymbol{\Omega}^{-1/2}\mathbf{X}_i)\boldsymbol{\beta} + \boldsymbol{\Omega}^{-1/2}\mathbf{u}_i, \qquad \text{or} \qquad \mathbf{y}_i^* = \mathbf{X}_i^*\boldsymbol{\beta} + \mathbf{u}_i^*. \tag{7.31}$$

Simple algebra shows that $\mathrm{E}(\mathbf{u}_i^*\mathbf{u}_i^{*\prime}) = \mathbf{I}_G$.

Now we estimate equation (7.31) by system OLS. (As yet, we have no real justification for this step, but we know SOLS is consistent under some assumptions.) Call this estimator $\boldsymbol{\beta}^*$. Then

$$\boldsymbol{\beta}^* \equiv \left(\sum_{i=1}^N \mathbf{X}_i^{*\prime}\mathbf{X}_i^*\right)^{-1}\left(\sum_{i=1}^N \mathbf{X}_i^{*\prime}\mathbf{y}_i^*\right) = \left(\sum_{i=1}^N \mathbf{X}_i'\boldsymbol{\Omega}^{-1}\mathbf{X}_i\right)^{-1}\left(\sum_{i=1}^N \mathbf{X}_i'\boldsymbol{\Omega}^{-1}\mathbf{y}_i\right). \tag{7.32}$$

This is the **generalized least squares (GLS) estimator** of $\boldsymbol{\beta}$. Under Assumption SGLS.2, $\boldsymbol{\beta}^*$ exists with probability approaching one as $N \to \infty$.

We can write $\boldsymbol{\beta}^*$ using full matrix notation as $\boldsymbol{\beta}^* = [\mathbf{X}'(\mathbf{I}_N \otimes \boldsymbol{\Omega}^{-1})\mathbf{X}]^{-1} \cdot [\mathbf{X}'(\mathbf{I}_N \otimes \boldsymbol{\Omega}^{-1})\mathbf{Y}]$, where $\mathbf{X}$ and $\mathbf{Y}$ are the data matrices defined in Section 7.3.2 and $\mathbf{I}_N$ is the $N \times N$ identity matrix. But for establishing the asymptotic properties of $\boldsymbol{\beta}^*$, it is most convenient to work with equation (7.32).

We can establish consistency of $\boldsymbol{\beta}^*$ under Assumptions SGLS.1 and SGLS.2 by writing

$$\boldsymbol{\beta}^* = \boldsymbol{\beta} + \left(N^{-1}\sum_{i=1}^{N}\mathbf{X}_i'\boldsymbol{\Omega}^{-1}\mathbf{X}_i\right)^{-1}\left(N^{-1}\sum_{i=1}^{N}\mathbf{X}_i'\boldsymbol{\Omega}^{-1}\mathbf{u}_i\right). \tag{7.33}$$

By the weak law of large numbers (WLLN), $N^{-1}\sum_{i=1}^{N}\mathbf{X}_i'\boldsymbol{\Omega}^{-1}\mathbf{X}_i \xrightarrow{p} \mathrm{E}(\mathbf{X}_i'\boldsymbol{\Omega}^{-1}\mathbf{X}_i)$. By Assumption SGLS.2 and Slutsky's theorem (Lemma 3.4), $\left(N^{-1}\sum_{i=1}^{N}\mathbf{X}_i'\boldsymbol{\Omega}^{-1}\mathbf{X}_i\right)^{-1} \xrightarrow{p} \mathbf{A}^{-1}$, where $\mathbf{A}$ is now defined as

$$\mathbf{A} \equiv \mathrm{E}(\mathbf{X}_i'\boldsymbol{\Omega}^{-1}\mathbf{X}_i). \tag{7.34}$$

Now we must show that $\operatorname{plim} N^{-1}\sum_{i=1}^{N}\mathbf{X}_i'\boldsymbol{\Omega}^{-1}\mathbf{u}_i = \mathbf{0}$, which holds by the WLLN under Assumption SGLS.2. Thus, we have shown that the GLS estimator is consistent under SGLS.1 and SGLS.2.

The proof of consistency that we have sketched fails if we only make Assumption SOLS.1: $\mathrm{E}(\mathbf{X}_i'\mathbf{u}_i) = \mathbf{0}$ does not imply $\mathrm{E}(\mathbf{X}_i'\boldsymbol{\Omega}^{-1}\mathbf{u}_i) = \mathbf{0}$, except when $\boldsymbol{\Omega}$ and $\mathbf{X}_i$ have special structures. If Assumption SOLS.1 holds but Assumption SGLS.1 fails, the transformation in equation (7.31) generally induces correlation between $\mathbf{X}_i^*$ and $\mathbf{u}_i^*$. This can be an important point, especially for certain panel data applications. If we are willing to make the zero conditional mean assumption (7.15), $\boldsymbol{\beta}^*$ can be shown to be unbiased conditional on $\mathbf{X}$.

7.4.2 Asymptotic Normality

We now sketch the asymptotic normality of the GLS estimator under Assumptions SGLS.1 and SGLS.2 and some weak moment conditions. The first step is familiar:

$$\sqrt{N}(\boldsymbol{\beta}^* - \boldsymbol{\beta}) = \left(N^{-1}\sum_{i=1}^{N}\mathbf{X}_i'\boldsymbol{\Omega}^{-1}\mathbf{X}_i\right)^{-1}\left(N^{-1/2}\sum_{i=1}^{N}\mathbf{X}_i'\boldsymbol{\Omega}^{-1}\mathbf{u}_i\right). \tag{7.35}$$

By the CLT, $N^{-1/2}\sum_{i=1}^{N}\mathbf{X}_i'\boldsymbol{\Omega}^{-1}\mathbf{u}_i \xrightarrow{d} \mathrm{Normal}(\mathbf{0}, \mathbf{B})$, where

$$\mathbf{B} \equiv \mathrm{E}(\mathbf{X}_i'\boldsymbol{\Omega}^{-1}\mathbf{u}_i\mathbf{u}_i'\boldsymbol{\Omega}^{-1}\mathbf{X}_i). \tag{7.36}$$

Further, since $N^{-1/2}\sum_{i=1}^{N} \mathbf{X}_i'\boldsymbol{\Omega}^{-1}\mathbf{u}_i = \mathrm{O}_p(1)$ and $(N^{-1}\sum_{i=1}^{N} \mathbf{X}_i'\boldsymbol{\Omega}^{-1}\mathbf{X}_i)^{-1} - \mathbf{A}^{-1} = \mathrm{o}_p(1)$, we can write $\sqrt{N}(\boldsymbol{\beta}^* - \boldsymbol{\beta}) = \mathbf{A}^{-1}(N^{-1/2}\sum_{i=1}^{N} \mathbf{x}_i'\boldsymbol{\Omega}^{-1}\mathbf{u}_i) + \mathrm{o}_p(1)$. It follows from the asymptotic equivalence lemma that

$$\sqrt{N}(\boldsymbol{\beta}^* - \boldsymbol{\beta}) \overset{a}{\sim} \mathrm{Normal}(\mathbf{0}, \mathbf{A}^{-1}\mathbf{B}\mathbf{A}^{-1}). \tag{7.37}$$

Thus,

$$\mathrm{Avar}(\hat{\boldsymbol{\beta}}) = \mathbf{A}^{-1}\mathbf{B}\mathbf{A}^{-1}/N. \tag{7.38}$$

The asymptotic variance in equation (7.38) is not the asymptotic variance usually derived for GLS estimation of systems of equations. Typically the formula is reported as $\mathbf{A}^{-1}/N$. But equation (7.38) is the appropriate expression under the assumptions made so far. The simpler form, which results when $\mathbf{B} = \mathbf{A}$, is not generally valid under Assumptions SGLS.1 and SGLS.2, because we have assumed nothing about the variance matrix of $\mathbf{u}_i$ conditional on $\mathbf{X}_i$. In Section 7.5.2 we make an assumption that simplifies equation (7.38).

7.5 Feasible Generalized Least Squares

7.5.1 Asymptotic Properties

Obtaining the GLS estimator $\boldsymbol{\beta}^*$ requires knowing $\boldsymbol{\Omega}$ up to scale. That is, we must be able to write $\boldsymbol{\Omega} = \sigma^2\mathbf{C}$, where $\mathbf{C}$ is a *known* $G \times G$ positive definite matrix and σ^2 is allowed to be an unknown constant. Sometimes $\mathbf{C}$ is known (one case is $\mathbf{C} = \mathbf{I}_G$), but much more often it is unknown. Therefore, we now turn to the analysis of feasible GLS (FGLS) estimation.

In FGLS estimation we replace the unknown matrix $\boldsymbol{\Omega}$ with a consistent estimator. Because the estimator of $\boldsymbol{\Omega}$ appears highly nonlinearly in the expression for the FGLS estimator, deriving finite sample properties of FGLS is generally difficult. (However, under essentially assumption (7.15) and some additional assumptions, including symmetry of the distribution of $\mathbf{u}_i$, Kakwani (1967) showed that the distribution of the FGLS is symmetric about $\boldsymbol{\beta}$, a property which means that the FGLS is unbiased *if* its expected value exists; see also Schmidt (1976, Section 2.5).) The asymptotic properties of the FGLS estimator are easily established as $N \to \infty$ because, as we will show, its first-order asymptotic properties are *identical* to those of the GLS estimator under Assumptions SGLS.1 and SGLS.2. It is for this purpose that we spent some time on GLS. After establishing the asymptotic equivalence, we can easily obtain the limiting distribution of the FGLS estimator. Of course, GLS is trivially a special case of FGLS where there is no first-stage estimation error.

We initially assume we have a consistent estimator, $\hat{\mathbf{\Omega}}$, of $\mathbf{\Omega}$:

$$\operatorname*{plim}_{N\to\infty} \hat{\mathbf{\Omega}} = \mathbf{\Omega}. \tag{7.39}$$

(Because the dimension of $\hat{\mathbf{\Omega}}$ does not depend on N, equation (7.39) makes sense when defined element by element.) When $\mathbf{\Omega}$ is allowed to be a general positive definite matrix, the following estimation approach can be used. First, obtain the system OLS estimator of $\boldsymbol{\beta}$, which we denote $\check{\boldsymbol{\beta}}$ in this section to avoid confusion. We already showed that $\check{\boldsymbol{\beta}}$ is consistent for $\boldsymbol{\beta}$ under Assumptions SOLS.1 and SOLS.2, and therefore under Assumptions SGLS.1 and SOLS.2. (In what follows, we assume that Assumptions SOLS.2 and SGLS.2 both hold.) By the WLLN, $\operatorname{plim}(N^{-1}\sum_{i=1}^N \mathbf{u}_i\mathbf{u}_i') = \mathbf{\Omega}$, and so a natural estimator of $\mathbf{\Omega}$ is

$$\hat{\mathbf{\Omega}} \equiv N^{-1}\sum_{i=1}^N \check{\mathbf{u}}_i\check{\mathbf{u}}_i', \tag{7.40}$$

where $\check{\mathbf{u}}_i \equiv \mathbf{y}_i - \mathbf{X}_i\check{\boldsymbol{\beta}}$ are the SOLS residuals. We can show that this estimator is consistent for $\mathbf{\Omega}$ under Assumptions SGLS.1 and SOLS.2 and standard moment conditions. First, write

$$\check{\mathbf{u}}_i = \mathbf{u}_i - \mathbf{X}_i(\check{\boldsymbol{\beta}} - \boldsymbol{\beta}), \tag{7.41}$$

so that

$$\check{\mathbf{u}}_i\check{\mathbf{u}}_i' = \mathbf{u}_i\mathbf{u}_i' - \mathbf{u}_i(\check{\boldsymbol{\beta}} - \boldsymbol{\beta})'\mathbf{X}_i' - \mathbf{X}_i(\check{\boldsymbol{\beta}} - \boldsymbol{\beta})\mathbf{u}_i' + \mathbf{X}_i(\check{\boldsymbol{\beta}} - \boldsymbol{\beta})(\check{\boldsymbol{\beta}} - \boldsymbol{\beta})'\mathbf{X}_i'. \tag{7.42}$$

Therefore, it suffices to show that the averages of the last three terms converge in probability to zero. Write the average of the vec of the first term as $N^{-1}\sum_{i=1}^N(\mathbf{X}_i \otimes \mathbf{u}_i)\cdot(\check{\boldsymbol{\beta}} - \boldsymbol{\beta})$, which is $o_p(1)$ because $\operatorname{plim}(\check{\boldsymbol{\beta}} - \boldsymbol{\beta}) = \mathbf{0}$ and $N^{-1}\sum_{i=1}^N(\mathbf{X}_i \otimes \mathbf{u}_i) \xrightarrow{p} \mathbf{0}$. The third term is the transpose of the second. For the last term in equation (7.42), note that the average of its vec can be written as

$$N^{-1}\sum_{i=1}^N(\mathbf{X}_i \otimes \mathbf{X}_i)\cdot \operatorname{vec}\{(\check{\boldsymbol{\beta}} - \boldsymbol{\beta})(\check{\boldsymbol{\beta}} - \boldsymbol{\beta})'\}. \tag{7.43}$$

Now $\operatorname{vec}\{(\check{\boldsymbol{\beta}} - \boldsymbol{\beta})(\check{\boldsymbol{\beta}} - \boldsymbol{\beta})'\} = o_p(1)$. Further, assuming that each element of $\mathbf{X}_i$ has finite second moment, $N^{-1}\sum_{i=1}^N(\mathbf{X}_i \otimes \mathbf{X}_i) = O_p(1)$ by the WLLN. This step takes care of the last term, since $O_p(1)\cdot o_p(1) = o_p(1)$. We have shown that

$$\hat{\mathbf{\Omega}} = N^{-1}\sum_{i=1}^N \mathbf{u}_i\mathbf{u}_i' + o_p(1), \tag{7.44}$$

and so equation (7.39) follows immediately. (In fact, a more careful analysis shows that the $o_p(1)$ in equation (7.44) can be replaced by $o_p(N^{-1/2})$; see Problem 7.4.)

Sometimes the elements of $\boldsymbol{\Omega}$ are restricted in some way. In such cases a different estimator of $\boldsymbol{\Omega}$ is often used that exploits these restrictions. As with $\hat{\boldsymbol{\Omega}}$ in equation (7.40), such estimators typically use the system OLS residuals in some fashion and lead to consistent estimators assuming the structure of $\boldsymbol{\Omega}$ is correctly specified. The advantage of equation (7.40) is that it is consistent for $\boldsymbol{\Omega}$ quite generally. However, if N is not very large relative to G, equation (7.40) can have poor finite sample properties. In Section 7.5.3 we discuss the consequences of using an inconsistent estimator of $\boldsymbol{\Omega}$. For now, we assume (7.39).

Given $\hat{\boldsymbol{\Omega}}$, the **feasible GLS (FGLS) estimator** of $\boldsymbol{\beta}$ is

$$\hat{\boldsymbol{\beta}} = \left(\sum_{i=1}^{N} \mathbf{X}_i' \hat{\boldsymbol{\Omega}}^{-1} \mathbf{X}_i\right)^{-1} \left(\sum_{i=1}^{N} \mathbf{X}_i' \hat{\boldsymbol{\Omega}}^{-1} \mathbf{y}_i\right), \tag{7.45}$$

or, in full matrix notation, $\hat{\boldsymbol{\beta}} = [\mathbf{X}'(\mathbf{I}_N \otimes \hat{\boldsymbol{\Omega}}^{-1})\mathbf{X}]^{-1}[\mathbf{X}'(\mathbf{I}_N \otimes \hat{\boldsymbol{\Omega}}^{-1})\mathbf{Y}]$.

We have already shown that the (infeasible) GLS estimator is consistent under Assumptions SGLS.1 and SGLS.2. Because $\hat{\boldsymbol{\Omega}}$ converges to $\boldsymbol{\Omega}$, it is not surprising that FGLS is also consistent. Rather than show this result separately, we verify the stronger result that FGLS has the same limiting distribution as GLS.

The limiting distribution of FGLS is obtained by writing

$$\sqrt{N}(\hat{\boldsymbol{\beta}} - \boldsymbol{\beta}) = \left(N^{-1}\sum_{i=1}^{N} \mathbf{X}_i' \hat{\boldsymbol{\Omega}}^{-1} \mathbf{X}_i\right)^{-1} \left(N^{-1/2}\sum_{i=1}^{N} \mathbf{X}_i' \hat{\boldsymbol{\Omega}}^{-1} \mathbf{u}_i\right). \tag{7.46}$$

Now

$$N^{-1/2}\sum_{i=1}^{N} \mathbf{X}_i' \hat{\boldsymbol{\Omega}}^{-1} \mathbf{u}_i - N^{-1/2}\sum_{i=1}^{N} \mathbf{X}_i' \boldsymbol{\Omega}^{-1} \mathbf{u}_i = \left[N^{-1/2}\sum_{i=1}^{N} (\mathbf{u}_i \otimes \mathbf{X}_i)'\right] \operatorname{vec}(\hat{\boldsymbol{\Omega}}^{-1} - \boldsymbol{\Omega}^{-1}).$$

Under Assumption SGLS.1, the CLT implies that $N^{-1/2}\sum_{i=1}^{N}(\mathbf{u}_i \otimes \mathbf{X}_i) = O_p(1)$. Because $O_p(1) \cdot o_p(1) = o_p(1)$, it follows that

$$N^{-1/2}\sum_{i=1}^{N} \mathbf{X}_i' \hat{\boldsymbol{\Omega}}^{-1} \mathbf{u}_i = N^{-1/2}\sum_{i=1}^{N} \mathbf{X}_i' \boldsymbol{\Omega}^{-1} \mathbf{u}_i + o_p(1).$$

A similar argument shows that $N^{-1}\sum_{i=1}^{N} \mathbf{X}_i' \hat{\boldsymbol{\Omega}}^{-1} \mathbf{X}_i = N^{-1}\sum_{i=1}^{N} \mathbf{X}_i' \boldsymbol{\Omega}^{-1} \mathbf{X}_i + o_p(1)$. Therefore, we have shown that

$$\sqrt{N}(\hat{\boldsymbol{\beta}} - \boldsymbol{\beta}) = \left(N^{-1}\sum_{i=1}^{N}\mathbf{X}_i'\boldsymbol{\Omega}^{-1}\mathbf{X}_i\right)^{-1}\left(N^{-1/2}\sum_{i=1}^{N}\mathbf{X}_i'\boldsymbol{\Omega}^{-1}\mathbf{u}_i\right) + o_p(1). \tag{7.47}$$

The first term in equation (7.47) is just $\sqrt{N}(\boldsymbol{\beta}^* - \boldsymbol{\beta})$, where $\boldsymbol{\beta}^*$ is the GLS estimator. We can write equation (7.47) as

$$\sqrt{N}(\hat{\boldsymbol{\beta}} - \boldsymbol{\beta}^*) = o_p(1), \tag{7.48}$$

which shows that $\hat{\boldsymbol{\beta}}$ and $\boldsymbol{\beta}^*$ are $\sqrt{N}$-equivalent. Recall from Chapter 3 that this statement is much stronger than simply saying that $\boldsymbol{\beta}^*$ and $\hat{\boldsymbol{\beta}}$ are both consistent for $\boldsymbol{\beta}$. There are many estimators, such as system OLS, that are consistent for $\boldsymbol{\beta}$ but are not $\sqrt{N}$-equivalent to $\boldsymbol{\beta}^*$.

The asymptotic equivalence of $\hat{\boldsymbol{\beta}}$ and $\boldsymbol{\beta}^*$ has practically important consequences. The most important of these is that, for performing asymptotic inference about $\boldsymbol{\beta}$ using $\hat{\boldsymbol{\beta}}$, we do not have to worry that $\hat{\boldsymbol{\Omega}}$ is an estimator of $\boldsymbol{\Omega}$. Of course, whether the asymptotic approximation gives a reasonable approximation to the actual distribution of $\hat{\boldsymbol{\beta}}$ is difficult to tell. With large N, the approximation is usually pretty good. But if N is small relative to G, ignoring estimation of $\boldsymbol{\Omega}$ in performing inference about $\boldsymbol{\beta}$ can be misleading.

We summarize the limiting distribution of FGLS with a theorem.

THEOREM 7.3 (Asymptotic Normality of FGLS): Under Assumptions SGLS.1 and SGLS.2,

$$\sqrt{N}(\hat{\boldsymbol{\beta}} - \boldsymbol{\beta}) \stackrel{a}{\sim} \text{Normal}(\mathbf{0}, \mathbf{A}^{-1}\mathbf{B}\mathbf{A}^{-1}), \tag{7.49}$$

where $\mathbf{A}$ is defined in equation (7.34) and $\mathbf{B}$ is defined in equation (7.36).

In the FGLS context, a consistent estimator of $\mathbf{A}$ is

$$\hat{\mathbf{A}} \equiv N^{-1}\sum_{i=1}^{N}\mathbf{X}_i'\hat{\boldsymbol{\Omega}}^{-1}\mathbf{X}_i. \tag{7.50}$$

A consistent estimator of $\mathbf{B}$ is also readily available after FGLS estimation. Define the FGLS residuals by

$$\hat{\mathbf{u}}_i \equiv \mathbf{y}_i - \mathbf{X}_i\hat{\boldsymbol{\beta}}, \qquad i = 1, 2, \ldots, N. \tag{7.51}$$

(The only difference between the FGLS and SOLS residuals is that the FGLS estimator is inserted in place of the SOLS estimator; in particular, the FGLS residuals are *not* from the transformed equation (7.31).) Using standard arguments, a consistent estimator of $\mathbf{B}$ is

$$\hat{\mathbf{B}} \equiv N^{-1} \sum_{i=1}^{N} \mathbf{X}_i' \hat{\mathbf{\Omega}}^{-1} \hat{\mathbf{u}}_i \hat{\mathbf{u}}_i' \hat{\mathbf{\Omega}}^{-1} \mathbf{X}_i.$$

The estimator of $\text{Avar}(\hat{\boldsymbol{\beta}})$ can be written as

$$\hat{\mathbf{A}}^{-1}\hat{\mathbf{B}}\hat{\mathbf{A}}^{-1}/N = \left(\sum_{i=1}^{N} \mathbf{X}_i'\hat{\mathbf{\Omega}}^{-1}\mathbf{X}_i\right)^{-1} \left(\sum_{i=1}^{N} \mathbf{X}_i'\hat{\mathbf{\Omega}}^{-1}\hat{\mathbf{u}}_i\hat{\mathbf{u}}_i'\hat{\mathbf{\Omega}}^{-1}\mathbf{X}_i\right) \left(\sum_{i=1}^{N} \mathbf{X}_i'\hat{\mathbf{\Omega}}^{-1}\mathbf{X}_i\right)^{-1}. \quad (7.52)$$

This is the extension of the White (1980b) heteroskedasticity-robust asymptotic variance estimator to the case of systems of equations; see also White (2001). This estimator is valid under Assumptions SGLS.1 and SGLS.2; that is, it is completely robust.

Incidentally, if system OLS and feasible GLS have both been used to estimate $\boldsymbol{\beta}$, and both estimators are presumed to be consistent, then it is legitimate to compare the fully robust variance matrices, (7.28) and (7.52), respectively, to determine whether FGLS appears to be asymptotically more efficient—keeping in mind that these are just estimates based on one random sample. The nonrobust OLS variance matrix generally should not be considered because it is valid only under very restrictive assumptions.

7.5.2 Asymptotic Variance of Feasible Generalized Least Squares under a Standard Assumption

Under the assumptions so far, FGLS really has nothing to offer over SOLS. In addition to being computationally more difficult, FGLS is less robust than SOLS. So why is FGLS used? The answer is that, under an additional assumption, FGLS is asymptotically more efficient than SOLS (and other estimators). First, we state the weakest condition that simplifies estimation of the asymptotic variance for FGLS. For reasons to be seen shortly, we call this a **system homoskedasticity assumption**.

ASSUMPTION SGLS.3: $\text{E}(\mathbf{X}_i'\mathbf{\Omega}^{-1}\mathbf{u}_i\mathbf{u}_i'\mathbf{\Omega}^{-1}\mathbf{X}_i) = \text{E}(\mathbf{X}_i'\mathbf{\Omega}^{-1}\mathbf{X}_i)$, where $\mathbf{\Omega} \equiv \text{E}(\mathbf{u}_i\mathbf{u}_i')$.

Another way to state this assumption is $\mathbf{B} = \mathbf{A}$, which, from expression (7.49), simplifies the asymptotic variance. As stated, Assumption SGLS.3 is somewhat difficult to interpret. When $G = 1$, it reduces to Assumption OLS.3. When $\mathbf{\Omega}$ is diagonal and $\mathbf{X}_i$ has either the SUR or panel data structure, Assumption SGLS.3 implies a kind of conditional homoskedasticity in each equation (or time period). Generally, Assumption SGLS.3 puts restrictions on the *conditional* variances and covariances of elements of $\mathbf{u}_i$. A sufficient (though certainly not necessary) condition for Assumption SGLS.3 is easier to interpret:

$$\mathrm{E}(\mathbf{u}_i\mathbf{u}_i' \mid \mathbf{X}_i) = \mathrm{E}(\mathbf{u}_i\mathbf{u}_i'). \tag{7.53}$$

If $\mathrm{E}(\mathbf{u}_i \mid \mathbf{X}_i) = \mathbf{0}$, then assumption (7.53) is the same as assuming $\mathrm{Var}(\mathbf{u}_i \mid \mathbf{X}_i) = \mathrm{Var}(\mathbf{u}_i) = \boldsymbol{\Omega}$, which means that each variance and each covariance of elements involving $\mathbf{u}_i$ must be constant conditional on all of $\mathbf{X}_i$. This is a natural way of stating a system homoskedasticity assumption, but it is sometimes too strong.

When $G = 2$, $\boldsymbol{\Omega}$ contains three distinct elements, $\sigma_1^2 = \mathrm{E}(u_{i1}^2)$, $\sigma_2^2 = \mathrm{E}(u_{i2}^2)$, and $\sigma_{12} = \mathrm{E}(u_{i1}u_{i2})$. These elements are not restricted by the assumptions we have made. (The inequality $|\sigma_{12}| < \sigma_1\sigma_2$ must always hold for $\boldsymbol{\Omega}$ to be a nonsingular covariance matrix.) But assumption (7.53) requires $\mathrm{E}(u_{i1}^2 \mid \mathbf{X}_i) = \sigma_1^2$, $\mathrm{E}(u_{i2}^2 \mid \mathbf{X}_i) = \sigma_2^2$, and $\mathrm{E}(u_{i1}u_{i2} \mid \mathbf{X}_i) = \sigma_{12}$: the conditional variances and covariance must not depend on $\mathbf{X}_i$.

That assumption (7.53) implies Assumption SGLS.3 is a consequence of iterated expectations:

$$\begin{aligned}
\mathrm{E}(\mathbf{X}_i'\boldsymbol{\Omega}^{-1}\mathbf{u}_i\mathbf{u}_i'\boldsymbol{\Omega}^{-1}\mathbf{X}_i) &= \mathrm{E}[\mathrm{E}(\mathbf{X}_i'\boldsymbol{\Omega}^{-1}\mathbf{u}_i\mathbf{u}_i'\boldsymbol{\Omega}^{-1}\mathbf{X}_i \mid \mathbf{X}_i)],\\
&= \mathrm{E}[\mathbf{X}_i'\boldsymbol{\Omega}^{-1}\mathrm{E}(\mathbf{u}_i\mathbf{u}_i' \mid \mathbf{X}_i)\boldsymbol{\Omega}^{-1}\mathbf{X}_i] = \mathrm{E}(\mathbf{X}_i'\boldsymbol{\Omega}^{-1}\boldsymbol{\Omega}\boldsymbol{\Omega}^{-1}\mathbf{X}_i),\\
&= \mathrm{E}(\mathbf{X}_i'\boldsymbol{\Omega}^{-1}\mathbf{X}_i).
\end{aligned}$$

While assumption (7.53) is easier to intepret, we use Assumption SGLS.3 for stating the next theorem because there are cases, including some dynamic panel data models, where Assumption SGLS.3 holds but assumption (7.53) does not.

THEOREM 7.4 (Usual Variance Matrix for FGLS): Under Assumptions SGLS.1–SGLS.3, the asymptotic variance of the FGLS estimator is $\mathrm{Avar}(\hat{\boldsymbol{\beta}}) = \mathbf{A}^{-1}/N \equiv [\mathrm{E}(\mathbf{X}_i'\boldsymbol{\Omega}^{-1}\mathbf{X}_i)]^{-1}/N$.

We obtain an estimator of $\mathrm{Avar}(\hat{\boldsymbol{\beta}})$ by using our consistent estimator of $\mathbf{A}$:

$$\widehat{\mathrm{Avar}(\hat{\boldsymbol{\beta}})} = \hat{\mathbf{A}}^{-1}/N = \left(\sum_{i=1}^{N} \mathbf{X}_i'\hat{\boldsymbol{\Omega}}^{-1}\mathbf{X}_i\right)^{-1}. \tag{7.54}$$

Equation (7.54) is the "usual" formula for the asymptotic variance of FGLS. It is nonrobust in the sense that it relies on Assumption SGLS.3 in addition to Assumptions SGLS.1 and SGLS.2. If system heteroskedasticity in $\mathbf{u}_i$ is suspected, then the robust estimator (7.52) should be used.

Assumption (7.53) has important efficiency implications. One consequence of Problem 7.2 is that, under Assumptions SGLS.1, SOLS.2, SGLS.2, and (7.53), the

FGLS estimator is more efficient than the system OLS estimator. We can actually say much more: FGLS is more efficient than any other estimator that uses the orthogonality conditions $\mathrm{E}(\mathbf{X}_i \otimes \mathbf{u}_i) = \mathbf{0}$. This conclusion will follow as a special case of Theorem 8.4 in Chapter 8, where we define the class of competing estimators. If we replace Assumption SGLS.1 with the zero conditional mean assumption (7.15), then an even stronger efficiency result holds for FGLS, something we treat in Section 8.6.

7.5.3 Properties of Feasible Generalized Least Squares with (Possibly Incorrect) Restrictions on the Unconditional Variance Matrix

Sometimes we might wish to impose restrictions in estimating $\boldsymbol{\Omega}$, possibly because G (in the panel data case, T) is large relative to N (which means an unrestricted estimator of $\boldsymbol{\Omega}$ might result in poor *finite sample* properties of FGLS), or because a particular structure for $\boldsymbol{\Omega}$ suggests itself. For example, in a panel data context with strictly exogenous regressors, an AR(1) model of serial correlation, with variances constant over time, might seem plausible, and greatly conserves on parameters when T is even moderately large. The element (t,s) in $\boldsymbol{\Omega}$ is of the form $\sigma_e^2 \rho^{|t-s|}$ for $|\rho| < 1$; we describe this further in Section 7.8.6. In Chapter 10, we discuss an important panel data model with constant variances over time where the pairwise correlations across any two different time periods are constant.

It is important to know that under Assumption SGLS.1, feasible GLS with an incorrect structure imposed on $\boldsymbol{\Omega}$, is generally consistent and $\sqrt{N}$-asymptotically normal. To see why, let $\hat{\boldsymbol{\Lambda}}$ denote an estimator that may be inconsistent for $\boldsymbol{\Omega}$. Nevertheless, $\hat{\boldsymbol{\Lambda}}$ usually has a well-defined, nonsingular probability limit: $\boldsymbol{\Lambda} \equiv \operatorname{plim} \hat{\boldsymbol{\Lambda}}$. Then, the FGLS estimator of $\boldsymbol{\beta}$ using $\hat{\boldsymbol{\Lambda}}$ as the variance matrix estimator is consistent if

$$\mathrm{E}(\mathbf{X}_i' \boldsymbol{\Lambda}^{-1} \mathbf{u}_i) = \mathbf{0} \tag{7.55}$$

(along with the modification of the rank condition SGLS.2 that inserts $\boldsymbol{\Lambda}$ in place of $\boldsymbol{\Omega}$). Condition (7.55) always holds if Assumption SGLS.1 holds. Therefore, exogeneity of each element of $\mathbf{X}_i$ in each equation (time period) ensures that using an inconsistent estimator of $\boldsymbol{\Omega}$ does not result in inconsistency of FGLS.

The $\sqrt{N}$-asymptotic equivalence between the estimators that use $\hat{\boldsymbol{\Lambda}}$ and $\boldsymbol{\Lambda}$ continues to hold under Assumption SGLS.1, and so we can conduct asymptotic inference ignoring the first stage estimation of $\boldsymbol{\Lambda}$. Nevertheless, the analogue of Assumption SGLS.3, $\mathrm{E}(\mathbf{X}_i' \boldsymbol{\Lambda}^{-1} \mathbf{u}_i \mathbf{u}_i' \boldsymbol{\Lambda}^{-1} \mathbf{X}_i) = \mathrm{E}(\mathbf{X}_i' \boldsymbol{\Lambda}^{-1} \mathbf{X}_i)$, generally fails, even under the system homoskedasticity assumption (7.53). (In fact, it is easy to show $\mathrm{E}(\mathbf{X}_i' \boldsymbol{\Lambda}^{-1} \mathbf{u}_i \mathbf{u}_i' \boldsymbol{\Lambda}^{-1} \mathbf{X}_i)$

$= \mathrm{E}(\mathbf{X}_i'\mathbf{\Lambda}^{-1}\mathbf{\Omega}\mathbf{\Lambda}^{-1}\mathbf{X}_i)$ when (7.53) holds.) Therefore, if we entertain the possibility that the restrictions imposed in obtaining $\hat{\mathbf{\Lambda}}$ are incorrect—as we probably should—the fully robust variance matrix in (7.52) should be used (with the slight notational change of replacing $\hat{\mathbf{\Omega}}$ with $\hat{\mathbf{\Lambda}}$).

We will use the findings in this section in Chapter 10, and we will extend the points made here to estimation of systems of nonlinear equations in Chapter 12. Problem 7.14 asks you to show that using a consistent estimator of $\mathbf{\Omega}$ always leads to an estimator at least as efficient as using an inconsistent estimator, provided the appropriate system homoskedasticity assumption holds.

Before leaving this section, it is useful to point out a case where one *should* use a restricted estimator of $\mathbf{\Omega}$ even if $\mathrm{E}(\mathbf{u}_i\mathbf{u}_i')$ does not satisfy the restrictions. A leading case is a panel data model where the regressors are contemporaneously exogenous but not strictly exogenous, so that Assumption SOLS.1 holds but Assumption SGLS.1 does not. In this case, using an unrestricted estimator of $\mathbf{\Omega}$ generally results in inconsistency of FGLS if $\mathbf{\Omega}$ is not diagonal. Of course, we can always apply pooled OLS in such cases, but POLS ignores the different error variances in the different time periods. We might want to exploit those different variances in estimation whether or not we think $\mathbf{\Omega}$ is diagonal.

If $\hat{\mathbf{\Lambda}}$ is a diagonal matrix containing consistent estimators of the error variances down the diagonals, then $\hat{\mathbf{\Lambda}} \to \mathbf{\Lambda}$, where $\mathbf{\Lambda} = \mathrm{diag}(\sigma_1^2, \ldots, \sigma_T^2)$. It is easily seen that (7.55) holds under $\mathrm{E}(\mathbf{x}_{it}'u_{it}) = \mathbf{0}$, $t = 1, \ldots, T$ regardless of the actual structure of $\mathbf{\Omega}$. In other words, contemporaneous exogeneity is sufficient. As shown in Problem 7.7, the resulting FGLS estimator can be computed from weighted least squares where the weights for different time periods are the inverses of the estimated variances.

Under contemporaneous exogeneity, the FGLS estimator based on diagonal $\hat{\mathbf{\Lambda}}$ can be shown to be $\sqrt{N}$-asymptotically equivalent to the (infeasible) estimator that uses $\mathbf{\Lambda}$, and so asymptotic inference is still straightforward. Of course, without more assumptions, the FGLS estimator that uses $\hat{\mathbf{\Lambda}}$ is not necessarily more efficient than the pooled OLS estimator. Under some additional assumptions given in Problem 7.7 that imply $\mathbf{\Omega}$ is diagonal, and therefore is the same as $\mathbf{\Lambda}$, the FGLS estimator that uses $\mathbf{\Lambda}$ can be shown to be asymptotically more efficient than the POLS estimator.

7.6 Testing the Use of Feasible Generalized Least Squares

Asymptotic standard errors are obtained in the usual fashion from the asymptotic variance estimates. We can use the nonrobust version in equation (7.54) or, even better, the robust version in equation (7.52), to construct t statistics and confidence intervals. Testing multiple restrictions is fairly easy using the Wald test, which always has the same general form. The important consideration lies in choosing the asymptotic variance estimate, $\hat{\mathbf{V}}$. Standard Wald statistics use equation (7.54), and this approach produces limiting chi-square statistics under the homoskedasticity assumption SGLS.3. Completely robust Wald statistics are obtained by choosing $\hat{\mathbf{V}}$ as in equation (7.52).

If Assumption SGLS.3 holds under H_0, we can define a statistic based on the weighted sums of squared residuals. To obtain the statistic, we estimate the model with and without the restrictions imposed on $\boldsymbol{\beta}$, where the same estimator of $\boldsymbol{\Omega}$, usually based on the unrestricted SOLS residuals, is used in obtaining the restricted and unrestricted FGLS estimators. Let $\tilde{\mathbf{u}}_i$ denote the residuals from constrained FGLS (with Q restrictions imposed on $\tilde{\boldsymbol{\beta}}$) using variance matrix $\hat{\boldsymbol{\Omega}}$. It can be shown that, under H_0 and Assumptions SGLS.1–SGLS.3,

$$\left(\sum_{i=1}^{N} \tilde{\mathbf{u}}_i'\hat{\boldsymbol{\Omega}}^{-1}\tilde{\mathbf{u}}_i - \sum_{i=1}^{N} \hat{\mathbf{u}}_i'\hat{\boldsymbol{\Omega}}^{-1}\hat{\mathbf{u}}_i\right) \overset{a}{\sim} \chi_Q^2. \tag{7.56}$$

Gallant (1987) shows expression (7.56) for nonlinear models with fixed regressors; essentially the same proof works here under Assumptions SGLS.1–SGLS.3, as we will show more generally in Chapter 12.

The statistic in expression (7.56) is the difference between the *transformed* sum of squared residuals from the restricted and unrestricted models, but it is just as easy to calculate expression (7.56) directly. Gallant (1987, Chap. 5) has found that an F statistic has better finite sample properties. The F statistic in this context is defined as

$$F = \left[\left(\sum_{i=1}^{N} \tilde{\mathbf{u}}_i'\hat{\boldsymbol{\Omega}}^{-1}\tilde{\mathbf{u}}_i - \sum_{i=1}^{N} \hat{\mathbf{u}}_i'\hat{\boldsymbol{\Omega}}^{-1}\hat{\mathbf{u}}_i\right) \Big/ \left(\sum_{i=1}^{N} \hat{\mathbf{u}}_i'\hat{\boldsymbol{\Omega}}^{-1}\hat{\mathbf{u}}_i\right)\right][(NG-K)]/Q. \tag{7.57}$$

Why can we treat this equation as having an approximate F distribution? First, for $NG-K$ large, $\mathcal{F}_{Q,NG-K} \overset{a}{\sim} \chi_Q^2/Q$. Therefore, dividing expression (7.56) by Q gives us an approximate $\mathcal{F}_{Q,NG-K}$ distribution. The presence of the other two terms in equation (7.57) is to improve the F-approximation. Since $\mathrm{E}(\mathbf{u}_i'\boldsymbol{\Omega}^{-1}\mathbf{u}_i) = \mathrm{tr}\{\mathrm{E}(\boldsymbol{\Omega}^{-1}\mathbf{u}_i\mathbf{u}_i')\} = \mathrm{tr}\{\mathrm{E}(\boldsymbol{\Omega}^{-1}\boldsymbol{\Omega})\} = G$, it follows that $(NG)^{-1}\sum_{i=1}^{N}\mathbf{u}_i'\boldsymbol{\Omega}^{-1}\mathbf{u}_i \xrightarrow{p} 1$; replacing $\mathbf{u}_i'\boldsymbol{\Omega}^{-1}\mathbf{u}_i$ with $\hat{\mathbf{u}}_i'\hat{\boldsymbol{\Omega}}^{-1}\hat{\mathbf{u}}_i$ does not affect this consistency result. Subtracting off K as a degrees-of-freedom adjustment changes nothing asymptotically, and so $(NG-K)^{-1}\sum_{i=1}^{N}\hat{\mathbf{u}}_i'\hat{\boldsymbol{\Omega}}^{-1}\hat{\mathbf{u}}_i \xrightarrow{p} 1$. Multiplying expression (7.56) by the inverse of this quantity does not affect its asymptotic distribution.

7.7 Seemingly Unrelated Regressions, Revisited

We now return to the SUR system in assumption (7.2). We saw in Section 7.3 how to write this system in the form (7.11) if there are no cross equation restrictions on the $\boldsymbol{\beta}_g$. We also showed that the system OLS estimator corresponds to estimating each equation separately by OLS.

As mentioned earlier, in most applications of SUR it is reasonable to assume that $\mathrm{E}(\mathbf{x}_{ig}' u_{ih}) = \mathbf{0}$, $g, h = 1, 2, \ldots, G$, which is just Assumption SGLS.1 for the SUR structure. Under this assumption, FGLS will consistently estimate the $\boldsymbol{\beta}_g$.

OLS equation by equation is simple to use and leads to standard inference for each $\boldsymbol{\beta}_g$ under the OLS homoskedasticity assumption $\mathrm{E}(u_{ig}^2 \mid \mathbf{x}_{ig}) = \sigma_g^2$, which is standard in SUR contexts. So why bother using FGLS in such applications? There are two answers. First, as mentioned in Section 7.5.2, if we can maintain assumption (7.53) in addition to Assumption SGLS.1 (and SGLS.2), FGLS is asymptotically at least as efficient as system OLS. Second, while OLS equation by equation allows us to easily test hypotheses about the coefficients within an equation, it does not provide a convenient way for testing cross equation restrictions. It is possible to use OLS for testing cross equation restrictions by using the variance matrix (7.26), but if we are willing to go through that much trouble, we should just use FGLS.

7.7.1 Comparison between Ordinary Least Squares and Feasible Generalized Least Squares for Seemingly Unrelated Regressions Systems

There are two cases where OLS equation by equation is algebraically equivalent to FGLS. The first case is fairly straightforward to analyze in our setting.

THEOREM 7.5 (Equivalence of FGLS and OLS, I): If $\hat{\boldsymbol{\Omega}}$ is a diagonal matrix, then OLS equation by equation is identical to FGLS.

Proof: If $\hat{\boldsymbol{\Omega}}$ is diagonal, then $\hat{\boldsymbol{\Omega}}^{-1} = \mathrm{diag}(\hat{\sigma}_1^{-2}, \ldots, \hat{\sigma}_G^{-2})$. With $\mathbf{X}_i$ defined as in the matrix (7.10), straightforward algebra shows that

$$\mathbf{X}_i'\hat{\boldsymbol{\Omega}}^{-1}\mathbf{X}_i = \hat{\boldsymbol{\Psi}}^{-1}\mathbf{X}_i'\mathbf{X}_i \qquad \text{and} \qquad \mathbf{X}_i'\hat{\boldsymbol{\Omega}}^{-1}\mathbf{y}_i = \hat{\boldsymbol{\Psi}}^{-1}\mathbf{X}_i'\mathbf{y}_i,$$

where $\hat{\boldsymbol{\Psi}}$ is the block diagonal matrix with $\hat{\sigma}_g^2\mathbf{I}_{k_g}$ as its gth block. It follows that the FGLS estimator can be written as

$$\hat{\boldsymbol{\beta}} = \left(\sum_{i=1}^{N} \hat{\boldsymbol{\Psi}}^{-1}\mathbf{X}_i'\mathbf{X}_i\right)^{-1}\left(\sum_{i=1}^{N} \hat{\boldsymbol{\Psi}}^{-1}\mathbf{X}_i'\mathbf{y}_i\right) = \left(\sum_{i=1}^{N} \mathbf{X}_i'\mathbf{X}_i\right)^{-1}\left(\sum_{i=1}^{N} \mathbf{X}_i'\mathbf{y}_i\right),$$

which is the system OLS estimator.

In applications, $\hat{\boldsymbol{\Omega}}$ would not be diagonal unless we impose a diagonal structure. Nevertheless, we can use Theorem 7.5 to obtain an *asymptotic* equivalance result when $\boldsymbol{\Omega}$ is diagonal. If $\boldsymbol{\Omega}$ is diagonal, then the GLS and OLS are algebraically identical (because GLS uses $\boldsymbol{\Omega}$). We know that FGLS and GLS are $\sqrt{N}$-asymptotically equivalent for any $\boldsymbol{\Omega}$. Therefore, OLS and FGLS are $\sqrt{N}$-asymptotically equivalent if $\boldsymbol{\Omega}$ is diagonal, even though they are not algebraically equivalent (because $\hat{\boldsymbol{\Omega}}$ is not diagonal).

The second algebraic equivalence result holds without any restrictions on $\hat{\boldsymbol{\Omega}}$. It is special in that it assumes that the same regressors appear in each equation.

THEOREM 7.6 (Equivalence of FGLS and OLS, II): If $\mathbf{x}_{i1} = \mathbf{x}_{i2} = \cdots = \mathbf{x}_{iG}$ for all i, that is, if the same regressors show up in each equation (for all observations), then OLS equation by equation and FGLS are identical.

In practice, Theorem 7.6 holds when the population model has the same explanatory variables in each equation. The usual proof of this result groups all N observations for the first equation followed by the N observations for the second equation, and so on (see, for example, Greene (1997, Chap. 17)). Problem 7.5 asks you to prove Theorem 7.6 in the current setup, where we have ordered the observations to be amenable to asymptotic analysis.

It is important to know that when every equation contains the same regressors in an SUR system, there is still a good reason to use a SUR software routine in obtaining the estimates: we may be interested in testing joint hypotheses involving parameters in different equations. In order to do so we need to estimate the variance matrix of $\hat{\boldsymbol{\beta}}$ (not just the variance matrix of each $\hat{\boldsymbol{\beta}}_g$, which only allows tests of the coefficients *within* an equation). Estimating each equation by OLS does not directly yield the covariances between the estimators from different equations. Any SUR routine will perform this operation automatically, then compute F statistics as in equation (7.57) (or the chi-square alternative, the Wald statistic).

Example 7.3 (SUR System for Wages and Fringe Benefits): We use the data on wages and fringe benefits in FRINGE.RAW to estimate a two-equation system for hourly wage and hourly benefits. There are 616 workers in the data set. The FGLS estimates are given in Table 7.1, with asymptotic standard errors in parentheses below estimated coefficients.

The estimated coefficients generally have the signs we expect. Other things equal, people with more education have higher hourly wage and benefits, males have higher predicted wages and benefits ($1.79 and 27 cents higher, respectively), and people with more tenure have higher earnings and benefits, although the effect is diminishing in both cases. (The turning point for *hrearn* is at about 10.8 years, while for *hrbens* it

Table 7.1
An Estimated SUR Model for Hourly Wages and Hourly Benefits

Explanatory Variables	*hrearn*	*hrbens*
educ	.459 (.069)	.077 (.008)
exper	−.076 (.057)	.023 (.007)
exper^2	.0040 (.0012)	−.0005 (.0001)
tenure	.110 (.084)	.054 (.010)
tenure^2	−.0051 (.0033)	−.0012 (.0004)
union	.808 (.408)	.366 (.049)
south	−.457 (.552)	−.023 (.066)
nrtheast	−1.151 (0.606)	−.057 (.072)
nrthcen	−.636 (.556)	−.038 (.066)
married	.642 (.418)	.058 (.050)
white	1.141 (0.612)	.090 (.073)
male	1.785 (0.398)	.268 (.048)
intercept	−2.632 (1.228)	−.890 (.147)

is 22.5 years.) The coefficients on experience are interesting. Experience is estimated to have a dimininshing effect for benefits but an increasing effect for earnings, although the estimated upturn for earnings is not until 9.5 years.

Belonging to a union implies higher wages and benefits, with the benefits coefficient being especially statistically significant ($t \approx 7.5$).

The errors across the two equations appear to be positively correlated, with an estimated correlation of about .32. This result is not surprising: the same unobservables, such as ability, that lead to higher earnings, also lead to higher benefits.

Clearly, there are significant differences between males and females in both earnings and benefits. But what about between whites and nonwhites, and married and unmarried people? The F-type statistic for joint significance of *married* and *white* in both equations is $F = 1.83$. We are testing four restrictions ($Q = 4$), $N = 616$, $G = 2$, and $K = 2(13) = 26$, so the degrees of freedom in the F distribution are 4 and 1,206. The p-value is about .121, so these variables are jointly insignificant at the 10 percent level.

If the regressors are different in different equations, $\boldsymbol{\Omega}$ is not diagonal, and the conditions in Section 7.5.2 hold, then FGLS is generally asymptotically more efficient than OLS equation by equation. One thing to remember is that the efficiency of FGLS comes at the price of assuming that the regressors in each equation are uncorrelated with the errors in each equation. For SOLS and FGLS to be different, the $\mathbf{x}_g$ must vary across g. If $\mathbf{x}_g$ varies across g, certain explanatory variables have been intentionally omitted from some equations. If we are interested in, say, the first equation, but we make a mistake in specifying the second equation, FGLS will generally produce inconsistent estimators of the parameters in all equations. However, OLS estimation of the first equation is consistent if $\mathrm{E}(\mathbf{x}_1' u_1) = \mathbf{0}$.

The previous discussion reflects the trade-off between efficiency and robustness that we often encounter in estimation problems.

7.7.2 Systems with Cross Equation Restrictions

So far we have studied SUR under the assumption that the $\boldsymbol{\beta}_g$ are unrelated across equations. When systems of equations are used in economics, especially for modeling consumer and producer theory, there are often cross equation restrictions on the parameters. Such models can still be written in the general form we have covered, and so they can be estimated by system OLS and FGLS. We still refer to such systems as SUR systems, even though the equations are now obviously related, and system OLS is no longer OLS equation by equation.

Example 7.4 (SUR with Cross Equation Restrictions): Consider the two-equation population model

$$y_1 = \gamma_{10} + \gamma_{11} x_{11} + \gamma_{12} x_{12} + \alpha_1 x_{13} + \alpha_2 x_{14} + u_1 \tag{7.58}$$

$$y_2 = \gamma_{20} + \gamma_{21} x_{21} + \alpha_1 x_{22} + \alpha_2 x_{23} + \gamma_{24} x_{24} + u_2 \tag{7.59}$$

where we have imposed cross equation restrictions on the parameters in the two equations because α_1 and α_2 show up in each equation. We can put this model into the form of equation (7.11) by appropriately defining $\mathbf{X}_i$ and $\boldsymbol{\beta}$. For example, define $\boldsymbol{\beta} = (\gamma_{10}, \gamma_{11}, \gamma_{12}, \alpha_1, \alpha_2, \gamma_{20}, \gamma_{21}, \gamma_{24})'$, which we know must be an 8×1 vector because there are eight parameters in this system. The order in which these elements appear in $\boldsymbol{\beta}$ is up to us, but once $\boldsymbol{\beta}$ is defined, $\mathbf{X}_i$ must be chosen accordingly. For each observation i, define the 2×8 matrix

$$\mathbf{X}_i = \begin{pmatrix} 1 & x_{i11} & x_{i12} & x_{i13} & x_{i14} & 0 & 0 & 0 \\ 0 & 0 & 0 & x_{i22} & x_{i23} & 1 & x_{i21} & x_{i24} \end{pmatrix}.$$

Multiplying $\mathbf{X}_i$ by $\boldsymbol{\beta}$ gives the equations (7.58) and (7.59).

In applications such as the previous example, it is fairly straightforward to test the cross equation restrictions, especially using the sum of squared residuals statistics (equation (7.56) or (7.57)). The unrestricted model simply allows each explanatory variable in each equation to have its own coefficient. We would use the unrestricted estimates to obtain $\hat{\boldsymbol{\Omega}}$, and then obtain the restricted estimates using $\hat{\Omega}$.

7.7.3 Singular Variance Matrices in Seemingly Unrelated Regressions Systems

In our treatment so far we have assumed that the variance matrix $\boldsymbol{\Omega}$ of $\mathbf{u}_i$ is nonsingular. In consumer and producer theory applications this assumption is not always true in the original structural equations, because of additivity constraints.

Example 7.5 (Cost Share Equations): Suppose that, for a given year, each firm in a particular industry uses three inputs, capital (K), labor (L), and materials (M). Because of regional variation and differential tax concessions, firms across the United States face possibly different prices for these inputs: let p_{iK} denote the price of capital to firm i, p_{iL} be the price of labor for firm i, and s_{iM} denote the price of materials for firm i. For each firm i, let s_{iK} be the cost share for capital, let s_{iL} be the cost share for labor, and let s_{iM} be the cost share for materials. By definition, $s_{iK} + s_{iL} + s_{iM} = 1$.

One popular set of cost share equations is

$$s_{iK} = \gamma_{10} + \gamma_{11}\log(p_{iK}) + \gamma_{12}\log(p_{iL}) + \gamma_{13}\log(p_{iM}) + u_{iK} \tag{7.60}$$

$$s_{iL} = \gamma_{20} + \gamma_{12}\log(p_{iK}) + \gamma_{22}\log(p_{iL}) + \gamma_{23}\log(p_{iM}) + u_{iL} \tag{7.61}$$

$$s_{iM} = \gamma_{30} + \gamma_{13}\log(p_{iK}) + \gamma_{23}\log(p_{iL}) + \gamma_{33}\log(p_{iM}) + u_{iM} \tag{7.62}$$

where the symmetry restrictions from production theory have been imposed. The errors u_{ig} can be viewed as unobservables affecting production that the economist cannot observe. For an SUR analysis we would assume that

$$\mathrm{E}(\mathbf{u}_i \mid \mathbf{p}_i) = \mathbf{0}, \tag{7.63}$$

where $\mathbf{u}_i \equiv (u_{iK}, u_{iL}, u_{iM})'$ and $\mathbf{p}_i \equiv (p_{iK}, p_{iL}, p_{iM})$. Because the cost shares must sum to unity for each i, $\gamma_{10} + \gamma_{20} + \gamma_{30} = 1$, $\gamma_{11} + \gamma_{12} + \gamma_{13} = 0$, $\gamma_{12} + \gamma_{22} + \gamma_{23} = 0$, $\gamma_{13} + \gamma_{23} + \gamma_{33} = 0$, and $u_{iK} + u_{iL} + u_{iM} = 0$. This last restriction implies that $\boldsymbol{\Omega} \equiv \mathrm{Var}(\mathbf{u}_i)$ has rank two. Therefore, we can drop one of the equations—say, the equation for materials—and analyze the equations for labor and capital. We can express the restrictions on the gammas in these first two equations as

$$\gamma_{13} = -\gamma_{11} - \gamma_{12} \tag{7.64}$$

$$\gamma_{23} = -\gamma_{12} - \gamma_{22}. \tag{7.65}$$

Using the fact that $\log(a/b) = \log(a) - \log(b)$, we can plug equations (7.64) and (7.65) into equations (7.60) and (7.61) to get

$$s_{iK} = \gamma_{10} + \gamma_{11} \log(p_{iK}/p_{iM}) + \gamma_{12} \log(p_{iL}/p_{iM}) + u_{iK}$$

$$s_{iL} = \gamma_{20} + \gamma_{12} \log(p_{iK}/p_{iM}) + \gamma_{22} \log(p_{iL}/p_{iM}) + u_{iL}.$$

We now have a two-equation system with variance matrix of full rank, with unknown parameters $\gamma_{10}, \gamma_{20}, \gamma_{11}, \gamma_{12}$, and γ_{22}. To write this in the form (7.11), redefine $\mathbf{u}_i = (u_{iK}, u_{iL})'$ and $\mathbf{y}_i \equiv (s_{iK}, s_{iL})'$. Take $\boldsymbol{\beta} \equiv (\gamma_{10}, \gamma_{11}, \gamma_{12}, \gamma_{20}, \gamma_{22})'$ and then $\mathbf{X}_i$ must be

$$\mathbf{X}_i \equiv \begin{pmatrix} 1 & \log(p_{iK}/p_{iM}) & \log(p_{iL}/p_{iM}) & 0 & 0 \\ 0 & 0 & \log(p_{iK}/p_{iM}) & 1 & \log(p_{iL}/p_{iM}) \end{pmatrix}. \tag{7.66}$$

This formulation imposes all the conditions implied by production theory.

This model could be extended in several ways. The simplest would be to allow the intercepts to depend on firm characteristics. For each firm i, let $\mathbf{z}_i$ be a $1 \times J$ vector of observable firm characteristics, where $\mathbf{z}_{i1} \equiv 1$. Then we can extend the model to

$$s_{iK} = \mathbf{z}_i\boldsymbol{\delta}_1 + \gamma_{11} \log(p_{iK}/p_{iM}) + \gamma_{12} \log(p_{iL}/p_{iM}) + u_{iK} \tag{7.67}$$

$$s_{iL} = \mathbf{z}_i\boldsymbol{\delta}_2 + \gamma_{12} \log(p_{iK}/p_{iM}) + \gamma_{22} \log(p_{iL}/p_{iM}) + u_{iL} \tag{7.68}$$

where

$$\mathrm{E}(u_{ig} \mid \mathbf{z}_i, p_{iK}, p_{iL}, p_{iM}) = 0, \qquad g = K, L. \tag{7.69}$$

Because we have already reduced the system to two equations, theory implies no restrictions on $\boldsymbol{\delta}_1$ and $\boldsymbol{\delta}_2$. As an exercise, you should write this system in the form (7.11). For example, if $\boldsymbol{\beta} \equiv (\boldsymbol{\delta}_1', \gamma_{11}, \gamma_{12}, \boldsymbol{\delta}_2', \gamma_{22})'$ is $(2J + 3) \times 1$, how should $\mathbf{X}_i$ be defined?

Under condition (7.69), system OLS and FGLS estimators are both consistent. (In this setup system OLS is *not* OLS equation by equation because γ_{12} shows up in both equations). FGLS is asymptotically efficient if $\mathrm{Var}(\mathbf{u}_i \mid \mathbf{z}_i, \mathbf{p}_i)$ is constant. If $\mathrm{Var}(\mathbf{u}_i \mid \mathbf{z}_i, \mathbf{p}_i)$ depends on $(\mathbf{z}_i, \mathbf{p}_i)$—see Brown and Walker (1995) for a discussion of why we should expect it to—then we should at least use the robust variance matrix estimator for FGLS. In Chapter 12 we will discuss multivariate weighted least squares estimators that can be more efficient.

We can easily test the symmetry assumption imposed in equations (7.67) and (7.68). One approach is to first estimate the system without *any* restrictions on the parameters, in which case FGLS reduces to OLS estimation of each equation. Then, compute the t statistic of the difference in the estimates on $\log(p_{iL}/p_{iM})$ in equation (7.67) and $\log(p_{iK}/p_{iM})$ in equation (7.68). Or, the F statistic from equation (7.57) can be used; $\hat{\mathbf{\Omega}}$ would be obtained from the unrestricted OLS estimation of each equation.

System OLS has no robustness advantages over FGLS in this setup because we cannot relax assumption (7.69) in any useful way.

7.8 Linear Panel Data Model, Revisited

We now study the linear panel data model in more detail. Having data over time for the same cross section units is useful for several reasons. For one, it allows us to look at dynamic relationships, something we cannot do with a single cross section. A panel data set also allows us to control for unobserved cross section heterogeneity, but we will not exploit this feature of panel data until Chapter 10.

7.8.1 Assumptions for Pooled Ordinary Least Squares

We now summarize the properties of pooled OLS and feasible GLS for the linear panel data model

$$y_t = \mathbf{x}_t\boldsymbol{\beta} + u_t, \qquad t = 1, 2, \ldots, T. \tag{7.70}$$

As always, when we need to indicate a particular cross section observation we include an i subscript, such as y_{it}.

This model may appear overly restrictive because $\boldsymbol{\beta}$ is the same in each time period. However, by appropriately choosing $\mathbf{x}_{it}$, we can allow for parameters changing over time. Also, even though we write $\mathbf{x}_{it}$, some of the elements of $\mathbf{x}_{it}$ may not be time-varying, such as gender dummies when i indexes individuals, or industry dummies when i indexes firms, or state dummies when i indexes cities.

Example 7.6 (Wage Equation with Panel Data): Suppose we have data for the years 1990, 1991, and 1992 on a cross section of individuals, and we would like to estimate the effect of computer usage on individual wages. One possible static model is

$$\begin{aligned} \log(wage_{it}) = \theta_0 + \theta_1 d91_t + \theta_2 d92_t + \delta_1 computer_{it} + \delta_2 educ_{it} \\ + \delta_3 exper_{it} + \delta_4 female_i + u_{it}, \end{aligned} \tag{7.71}$$

where $d91_t$ and $d92_t$ are dummy indicators for the years 1991 and 1992 and $computer_{it}$ is a measure of how much person i used a computer during year t. The inclusion of the year dummies allows for aggregate time effects of the kind discussed in the Section 7.2 examples. This equation contains a variable that is constant across t, $female_i$, as well as variables that can change across i and t, such as $educ_{it}$ and $exper_{it}$. The variable $educ_{it}$ is given a t subscript, which indicates that years of education could change from year to year for at least some people. It could also be the case that $educ_{it}$ is the same for all three years for every person in the sample, in which case we could remove the time subscript. The distinction between variables that are time-constant is not very important here; it becomes much more important in Chapter 10.

As a general rule, with large N and small T it is a good idea to allow for separate intercepts for each time period. Doing so allows for aggregate time effects that have the same influence on y_{it} for all i.

Anything that can be done in a cross section context can also be done in a panel data setting. For example, in equation (7.71) we can interact $female_i$ with the time dummy variables to see whether the gender wage gap has changed over time, or we can interact $educ_{it}$ and $computer_{it}$ to allow the return to computer usage to depend on level of education.

The two assumptions sufficient for pooled OLS to consistently estimate $\boldsymbol{\beta}$ are as follows:

ASSUMPTION POLS.1: $\mathrm{E}(\mathbf{x}_t'u_t) = 0,\ t = 1, 2, \ldots, T.$

ASSUMPTION POLS.2: $\operatorname{rank}[\sum_{t=1}^{T} \mathrm{E}(\mathbf{x}_t'\mathbf{x}_t)] = K.$

Remember, Assumption POLS.1 says nothing about the relationship between $\mathbf{x}_s$ and u_t for $s \neq t$. Assumption POLS.2 essentially rules out perfect linear dependencies among the explanatory variables.

To apply the usual OLS statistics from the pooled OLS regression across i and t, we need to add homoskedasticity and no serial correlation assumptions. The weakest forms of these assumptions are the following:

ASSUMPTION POLS.3: (a) $\mathrm{E}(u_t^2\mathbf{x}_t'\mathbf{x}_t) = \sigma^2\mathrm{E}(\mathbf{x}_t'\mathbf{x}_t),\ t = 1, 2, \ldots, T$, where $\sigma^2 = \mathrm{E}(u_t^2)$ for all t; (b) $\mathrm{E}(u_t u_s \mathbf{x}_t'\mathbf{x}_s) = \mathbf{0},\ t \neq s,\ t, s = 1, \ldots, T.$

The first part of Assumption POLS.3 is a fairly strong homoskedasticity assumption; sufficient is $\mathrm{E}(u_t^2 \mid \mathbf{x}_t) = \sigma^2$ for all t. This means not only that the conditional variance does not depend on $\mathbf{x}_t$, but also that the unconditional variance is the same in every time period. Assumption POLS.3b essentially restricts the conditional covariances of the errors across different time periods to be zero. In fact, since $\mathbf{x}_t$ almost always contains a constant, POLS.3b requires *at a minimum* that $\mathrm{E}(u_t u_s) = 0$, $t \neq s$. Sufficient for POLS.3b is $\mathrm{E}(u_t u_s \mid \mathbf{x}_t, \mathbf{x}_s) = 0$, $t \neq s$, $t, s = 1, \ldots, T$.

It is important to remember that Assumption POLS.3 implies more than just a certain form of the *unconditional* variance matrix of $\mathbf{u} \equiv (u_1, \ldots, u_T)'$. Assumption POLS.3 implies $\mathrm{E}(\mathbf{u}_i \mathbf{u}_i') = \sigma^2 \mathbf{I}_T$, which means that the unconditional variances are constant and the unconditional covariances are zero, but it also effectively restricts the *conditional* variances and covariances.

THEOREM 7.7 (Large-Sample Properties of Pooled OLS): Under Assumptions POLS.1 and POLS.2, the pooled OLS estimator is consistent and asymptotically normal. If Assumption POLS.3 holds in addition, then $\mathrm{Avar}(\hat{\boldsymbol{\beta}}) = \sigma^2[\mathrm{E}(\mathbf{X}_i'\mathbf{X}_i)]^{-1}/N$, so that the appropriate estimator of $\mathrm{Avar}(\hat{\boldsymbol{\beta}})$ is

$$\hat{\sigma}^2(\mathbf{X}'\mathbf{X})^{-1} = \hat{\sigma}^2 \left(\sum_{i=1}^{N} \sum_{t=1}^{T} \mathbf{x}_{it}'\mathbf{x}_{it} \right)^{-1}, \tag{7.72}$$

where $\hat{\sigma}^2$ is the usual OLS variance estimator from the pooled regression

$$y_{it} \text{ on } \mathbf{x}_{it}, \qquad t = 1, 2, \ldots, T, \; i = 1, \ldots, N. \tag{7.73}$$

It follows that the usual t statistics and F statistics from regression (7.73) are approximately valid. Therefore, the F statistic for testing Q linear restrictions on the $K \times 1$ vector $\boldsymbol{\beta}$ is

$$F = \frac{(\mathrm{SSR}_r - \mathrm{SSR}_{ur})}{\mathrm{SSR}_{ur}} \cdot \frac{(NT - K)}{Q}, \tag{7.74}$$

where SSR_{ur} is the sum of squared residuals from regression (7.73), and SSR_r is the regression using the NT observations with the restrictions imposed.

Why is a simple pooled OLS analysis valid under Assumption POLS.3? It is easy to show that Assumption POLS.3 implies that $\mathbf{B} = \sigma^2 \mathbf{A}$, where $\mathbf{B} \equiv \sum_{t=1}^{T} \sum_{s=1}^{T} \mathrm{E}(u_t u_s \mathbf{x}_t' \mathbf{x}_s)$, and $\mathbf{A} \equiv \sum_{t=1}^{T} \mathrm{E}(\mathbf{x}_t' \mathbf{x}_t)$. For the panel data case, these are the matrices that appear in expression (7.23).

For computing the pooled OLS estimates and standard statistics, it does not matter how the data are ordered. However, if we put lags of any variables in the equation, it is easiest to order the data in the same way as is natural for studying asymptotic properties: the first T observations should be for the first cross section unit (ordered chronologically), the next T observations are for the next cross section unit, and so on. This procedure gives NT rows in the data set ordered in a very specific way.

Example 7.7 (Effects of Job Training Grants on Firm Scrap Rates): Using the data from JTRAIN1.RAW (Holzer, Block, Cheatham, and Knott, 1993), we estimate a model explaining the firm scrap rate in terms of grant receipt. We can estimate the equation for 54 firms and three years of data (1987, 1988, and 1989). The first grants were given in 1988. Some firms in the sample in 1989 received a grant only in 1988, so we allow for a one-year-lagged effect:

$$\widehat{\log(scrap_{it})} = \underset{(.203)}{.597} - \underset{(.311)}{.239}\, d88_t - \underset{(.338)}{.497}\, d89_t + \underset{(.338)}{.200}\, grant_{it} + \underset{(.436)}{.049}\, grant_{i,t-1},$$

$$N = 54, \qquad T = 3, \qquad R^2 = .0173$$

where we have put i and t subscripts on the variables to emphasize which ones change across firm or time. The R-squared is just the usual one computed from the pooled OLS regression.

In this equation, the estimated grant effect has the wrong sign, and neither the current nor the lagged grant variable is statistically significant. When a lag of $\log(scrap_{it})$ is added to the equation, the estimates are notably different. See Problem 7.9.

7.8.2 Dynamic Completeness

While the homoskedasticity assumption, Assumption POLS.3a, can never be guaranteed to hold, there is one important case where Assumption POLS.3b *must* hold. Suppose that the explanatory variables $\mathbf{x}_t$ are such that, for all t,

$$\mathrm{E}(y_t \mid \mathbf{x}_t, y_{t-1}, \mathbf{x}_{t-1}, \ldots, y_1, \mathbf{x}_1) = \mathrm{E}(y_t \mid \mathbf{x}_t). \tag{7.75}$$

This assumption means that $\mathbf{x}_t$ contains sufficient lags of all variables such that additional lagged values have no partial effect on y_t. The inclusion of lagged y in equation (7.75) is important. For example, if $\mathbf{z}_t$ is a vector of contemporaneous variables such that

$$\mathrm{E}(y_t \mid \mathbf{z}_t, \mathbf{z}_{t-1}, \ldots, \mathbf{z}_1) = \mathrm{E}(y_t \mid \mathbf{z}_t, \mathbf{z}_{t-1}, \ldots, \mathbf{z}_{t-L})$$

and we choose $\mathbf{x}_t = (\mathbf{z}_t, \mathbf{z}_{t-1}, \ldots, \mathbf{z}_{t-L})$, then $\mathrm{E}(y_t \mid \mathbf{x}_t, \mathbf{x}_{t-1}, \ldots, \mathbf{x}_1) = \mathrm{E}(y_t \mid \mathbf{x}_t)$, that is, the sequential exogenecity assumption holds. But equation (7.75) need not hold. Generally, in static and FDL models, there is no reason to expect equation (7.75) to hold, even in the absence of specification problems such as omitted variables.

We call equation (7.75) **dynamic completeness of the conditional mean**, which clearly implies sequential exogenecity. Often, we can ensure that equation (7.75) is at least approximately true by putting sufficient lags of $\mathbf{z}_t$ and y_t into $\mathbf{x}_t$.

In terms of the disturbances, equation (7.75) is equivalent to

$$E(u_t \mid \mathbf{x}_t, u_{t-1}, \mathbf{x}_{t-1}, \ldots, u_1, \mathbf{x}_1) = 0, \tag{7.76}$$

and, by iterated expectations, equation (7.76) implies $E(u_t u_s \mid \mathbf{x}_t, \mathbf{x}_s) = 0$, $s \neq t$. Therefore, equation (7.75) implies Assumption POLS.3b as well as Assumption POLS.1. If equation (7.75) holds along with the homoskedasticity assumption $\text{Var}(y_t \mid \mathbf{x}_t) = \sigma^2$, then Assumptions POLS.1 and POLS.3 both hold, and standard OLS statistics can be used for inference.

The following example is similar in spirit to an analysis of Maloney and McCormick (1993), who use a large random sample of students (including nonathletes) from Clemson University in a cross section analysis.

Example 7.8 (Effect of Being in Season on Grade Point Average): The data in GPA.RAW are on 366 student-athletes at a large university. There are two semesters of data (fall and spring) for each student. Of primary interest is the "in-season" effect on athletes' GPAs. The model—with *i*, *t* subscripts—is

$$\begin{aligned} trmgpa_{it} = {} & \beta_0 + \beta_1 spring_t + \beta_2 cumgpa_{it} + \beta_3 crsgpa_{it} + \beta_4 frstsem_{it} + \beta_5 season_{it} + \beta_6 SAT_i \\ & + \beta_7 verbmath_i + \beta_8 hsperc_i + \beta_9 hssize_i + \beta_{10} black_i + \beta_{11} female_i + u_{it}. \end{aligned}$$

The variable $cumgpa_{it}$ is cumulative GPA at the beginning of the term, and this clearly depends on past-term GPAs. In other words, this model has something akin to a lagged dependent variable. In addition, it contains other variables that change over time (such as $season_{it}$) and several variables that do not (such as SAT_i). We assume that the right-hand side (without u_{it}) represents a conditional expectation, so that u_{it} is necessarily uncorrelated with all explanatory variables and any functions of them. It may or may not be that the model is also dynamically complete in the sense of equation (7.75); we will show one way to test this assumption in Section 7.8.5. The estimated equation is

$$\begin{aligned} \widehat{trmgpa}_{it} = {} & \underset{(0.34)}{-2.07} - \underset{(.046)}{.012}\, spring_t + \underset{(.040)}{.315}\, cumgpa_{it} + \underset{(.096)}{.984}\, crsgpa_{it} \\ & + \underset{(.120)}{.769}\, frstsem_{it} - \underset{(.047)}{.046}\, season_{it} + \underset{(.00015)}{.00141}\, SAT_i - \underset{(.131)}{.113}\, verbmath_i \\ & - \underset{(.0010)}{.0066}\, hsperc_i - \underset{(.000099)}{.000058}\, hssize_i - \underset{(.054)}{.231}\, black_i + \underset{(.051)}{.286}\, female_i. \end{aligned}$$

$N = 366, \quad T = 2, \quad R^2 = .519$

The in-season effect is small—an athlete's GPA is estimated to be .046 points lower when the sport is in season—and it is statistically insignificant as well. The other coefficients have reasonable signs and magnitudes.

Often, once we start putting any lagged values of y_t into $\mathbf{x}_t$, then equation (7.75) is an intended assumption. But this generalization is not always true. In the previous example, we can think of the variable *cumgpa* as another control we are using to hold other factors fixed when looking at an in-season effect on GPA for college athletes: *cumgpa* can proxy for omitted factors that make someone successful in college. We may not care that serial correlation is still present in the error, except that, if equation (7.75) fails, we need to estimate the asymptotic variance of the pooled OLS estimator to be robust to serial correlation (and perhaps heteroskedasticity as well).

In introductory econometrics, students are often warned that having serial correlation in a model with a lagged dependent variable causes the OLS estimators to be inconsistent. While this statement is true in the context of a *specific* model of serial correlation, it is not true in general, and therefore it is very misleading. (See Wooldridge (2009a, Chap. 12) for more discussion in the context of the AR(1) model.) Our analysis shows that, whatever is included in $\mathbf{x}_t$, pooled OLS provides consistent estimators of $\boldsymbol{\beta}$ whenever $\mathrm{E}(y_t \mid \mathbf{x}_t) = \mathbf{x}_t \boldsymbol{\beta}$; it does not matter that the u_t might be serially correlated.

7.8.3 Note on Time Series Persistence

Theorem 7.7 imposes no restrictions on the time series persistence in the data $\{(\mathbf{x}_{it}, y_{it}) \colon t = 1, 2, \ldots, T\}$. In light of the explosion of work in time series econometrics on asymptotic theory with persistent processes [often called *unit root processes*—see, for example, Hamilton (1994)], it may appear that we have not been careful in stating our assumptions. However, we do not need to restrict the dynamic behavior of our data in any way because we are doing fixed-T, large-N asymptotics. It is for this reason that the mechanics of the asymptotic analysis is the same for the SUR case and the panel data case. If T is large relative to N, the asymptotics here may be misleading. Fixing N while T grows or letting N and T both grow takes us into the realm of multiple time series analysis: we would have to know about the temporal dependence in the data, and, to have a general treatment, we would have to assume some form of weak dependence (see Wooldridge, 1994a, for a discussion of weak dependence). Recently, progress has been made on asymptotics in panel data with large T and N when the data have unit roots; see, for example, Pesaran and Smith (1995), Moon and Phillips (2000), and Phillips and Moon (2000).

As an example, consider the simple AR(1) model

$$y_t = \beta_0 + \beta_1 y_{t-1} + u_t, \qquad \mathrm{E}(u_t \mid y_{t-1}, \ldots, y_0) = 0.$$

Assumption POLS.1 holds (provided the appropriate moments exist). Also, Assumption POLS.2 can be maintained. Since this model is dynamically complete, the only potential nuisance is heteroskedasticity in u_t that changes over time or depends on y_{t-1}. In any case, the pooled OLS estimator from the regression y_{it} on 1, $y_{i,t-1}$, $t = 1, \ldots, T$, $i = 1, \ldots, N$, produces consistent, $\sqrt{N}$-asymptotically normal estimators for fixed T as $N \to \infty$, for any values of β_0 and β_1.

In a pure time series case, or in a panel data case with $T \to \infty$ and N fixed, we would have to assume $|\beta_1| < 1$, which is the stability condition for an AR(1) model. Cases where $|\beta_1| \geq 1$ cause considerable complications when the asymptotics is done along the time series dimension (see Hamilton, 1994, Chapter 19). Here, a large cross section and relatively short time series allow us to be agnostic about the amount of temporal persistence.

7.8.4 Robust Asymptotic Variance Matrix

Because Assumption POLS.3 can be restrictive, it is often useful to obtain a robust estimate of $\mathrm{Avar}(\hat{\boldsymbol{\beta}})$ that is valid without Assumption POLS.3. We have already seen the general form of the estimator, given in matrix (7.28). In the case of panel data, this estimator is fully robust to arbitrary heteroskedasticity—conditional or unconditional—and arbitrary serial correlation across time (again, conditional or unconditional). The residuals $\hat{\mathbf{u}}_i$ are the $T \times 1$ pooled OLS residuals for cross section observation i. The fully robust variance matrix estimator can be expressed in the sandwich form as

$$\widehat{\mathrm{Avar}(\hat{\boldsymbol{\beta}})} = \left(\sum_{i=1}^{N} \mathbf{X}_i'\mathbf{X}_i\right)^{-1} \left(\sum_{i=1}^{N}\sum_{t=1}^{T}\sum_{s=1}^{T} \hat{u}_{it}\hat{u}_{is}\mathbf{x}_{it}'\mathbf{x}_{is}\right)\left(\sum_{i=1}^{N} \mathbf{X}_i'\mathbf{X}_i\right)^{-1}, \tag{7.77}$$

where the middle matrix can also be written as

$$\sum_{i=1}^{N}\sum_{t=1}^{T} \hat{u}_{it}^2 \mathbf{x}_{it}'\mathbf{x}_{it} + \sum_{i=1}^{N}\sum_{t=1}^{T}\sum_{s\neq t} \hat{u}_{it}\hat{u}_{is}\mathbf{x}_{it}'\mathbf{x}_{is}. \tag{7.78}$$

This last expression makes it clear that the estimator is robust to arbitrary heteroskedasticity and arbitrary serial correlation. Some statistical packages compute equation (7.77) very easily, although the command may be disguised. (For example, in Stata, equation (7.77) is computed using a cluster sampling option. We cover cluster sampling in Chapter 21.) Whether a software package has this capability or whether it must be programmed by you, the data must be stored as described earlier: The $(\mathbf{y}_i, \mathbf{X}_i)$ should be stacked on top of one another for $i = 1, \ldots, N$.

7.8.5 Testing for Serial Correlation and Heteroskedasticity after Pooled Ordinary Least Squares

Testing for Serial Correlation It is often useful to have a simple way to detect serial correlation after estimation by pooled OLS. One reason to test for serial correlation is that it should not be present if the model is supposed to be dynamically complete in the conditional mean. A second reason to test for serial correlation is to see whether we should compute a robust variance matrix estimator for the pooled OLS estimator.

One interpretation of serial correlation in the errors of a panel data model is that the error in each time period contains a time-constant omitted factor, a case we cover explicitly in Chapter 10. For now, we are simply interested in knowing whether or not the errors are serially correlated.

We focus on the alternative that the error is a first-order autoregressive process; this will have power against fairly general kinds of serial correlation. Write the AR(1) model as

$$u_t = \rho_1 u_{t-1} + e_t \tag{7.79}$$

where

$$\mathrm{E}(e_t \mid \mathbf{x}_t, u_{t-1}, \mathbf{x}_{t-1}, u_{t-2}, \ldots) = 0. \tag{7.80}$$

Under the null hypothesis of no serial correlation, $\rho_1 = 0$.

One way to proceed is to write the dynamic model under AR(1) serial correlation as

$$y_t = \mathbf{x}_t \boldsymbol{\beta} + \rho_1 u_{t-1} + e_t, \qquad t = 2, \ldots, T, \tag{7.81}$$

where we lose the first time period due to the presence of u_{t-1}. If we can observe the u_t, it is clear how we should proceed: simply estimate equation (7.75) by pooled OLS (losing the first time period) and perform a t test on $\hat{\rho}_1$. To operationalize this procedure, we replace the u_t with the pooled OLS residuals. Therefore, we run the regression

$$y_{it} \text{ on } \mathbf{x}_{it}, \hat{u}_{i,t-1}, \qquad t = 2, \ldots, T, \; i = 1, \ldots, N, \tag{7.82}$$

and do a standard t test on the coefficient of $\hat{u}_{i,t-1}$. A statistic that is robust to arbitrary heteroskedasticity in $\mathrm{Var}(y_t \mid \mathbf{x}_t, u_{t-1})$ is obtained by the usual heteroskedasticity-robust t statistic in the pooled regression. This includes Engle's (1982) ARCH model and any other form of static or dynamic heteroskedasticity.

Why is a t test from regression (7.82) valid? Under dynamic completeness, equation (7.81) satisfies Assumptions POLS.1–POLS.3 if we also assume that $\mathrm{Var}(y_t \mid \mathbf{x}_t, u_{t-1})$ is constant. Further, the presence of the generated regressor $\hat{u}_{i,t-1}$ does not affect the limiting distribution of $\hat{\rho}_1$ under the null because $\rho_1 = 0$. Verifying this claim is similar to the pure cross section case in Section 6.1.1.

A nice feature of the statistic computed from regression (7.82) is that it works whether or not $\mathbf{x}_t$ is strictly exogenous. A different form of the test is valid if we assume strict exogeneity: use the t statistic on $\hat{u}_{i,t-1}$ in the regression

$$\hat{u}_{it} \text{ on } \hat{u}_{i,t-1}, \qquad t = 2, \ldots, T, \; i = 1, \ldots, N \tag{7.83}$$

or its heteroskedasticity-robust form. That this test is valid follows by applying Problem 7.4 and the assumptions for pooled OLS with a lagged dependent variable.

Example 7.9 (Athletes' Grade Point Averages, continued): We apply the test from regression (7.82) because *cumgpa* cannot be strictly exogenous (GPA this term affects cumulative GPA after this term). We drop the variables *spring* and *frstsem* from regression (7.82), since these are identically unity and zero, respectively, in the spring semester. We obtain $\hat{\rho}_1 = .194$ and $t_{\hat{\rho}_1} = 3.18$, and so the null hypothesis is rejected. Thus there is still some work to do to capture the full dynamics. But, if we assume that we are interested in the conditional expectation implicit in the estimation, we are getting consistent estimators. This result is useful to know because we are primarily interested in the in-season effect, and the other variables are simply acting as controls. The presence of serial correlation means that we should compute standard errors robust to arbitrary serial correlation (and heteroskedasticity); see Problem 7.10.

Testing for Heteroskedasticity The primary reason to test for heteroskedasticity after running pooled OLS is to detect violation of Assumption POLS.3a, which is one of the assumptions needed for the usual statistics accompanying a pooled OLS regression to be valid. We assume throughout this section that $\mathrm{E}(u_t \mid \mathbf{x}_t) = 0$, $t = 1, 2, \ldots, T$, which strengthens Assumption POLS.1 but does not require strict exogeneity. Then the null hypothesis of homoskedasticity can be stated as $\mathrm{E}(u_t^2 \mid \mathbf{x}_t) = \sigma^2$, $t = 1, 2, \ldots, T$.

Under H_0, u_{it}^2 is uncorrelated with any function of $\mathbf{x}_{it}$; let $\mathbf{h}_{it}$ denote a $1 \times Q$ vector of nonconstant functions of $\mathbf{x}_{it}$. In particular, $\mathbf{h}_{it}$ can, and often should, contain dummy variables for the different time periods.

From the tests for heteroskedasticity in Section 6.3.4. the following procedure is natural. Let $\hat{u}_{it}^2$ denote the squared pooled OLS residuals. Then obtain the usual R-squared, R_c^2, from the regression

$$\hat{u}_{it}^2 \text{ on } 1, \mathbf{h}_{it}, \qquad t = 1, \ldots, T, \; i = 1, \ldots, N \tag{7.84}$$

The test statistic is NTR_c^2, which is treated as asymptotically χ_Q^2 under H_0. (Alternatively, we can use the usual F test of joint significance of $\mathbf{h}_{it}$ from the pooled OLS regression. The degrees of freedom are Q and $NT - K$.) When is this procedure valid?

Using arguments very similar to the cross sectional tests from Chapter 6, it can be shown that the statistic has the same distribution if u_{it}^2 replaces $\hat{u}_{it}^2$; this fact is very convenient because it allows us to focus on the other features of the test. Effectively, we are performing a standard LM test of H_0: $\boldsymbol{\delta} = \mathbf{0}$ in the model

$$u_{it}^2 = \delta_0 + \mathbf{h}_{it}\boldsymbol{\delta} + a_{it}, \qquad t = 1, 2, \ldots, T. \tag{7.85}$$

This test requires that the errors $\{a_{it}\}$ be appropriately serially uncorrelated and requires homoskedasticity; that is, Assumption POLS.3 must hold in equation (7.85). Therefore, the tests based on nonrobust statistics from regression (7.84) essentially require that $\mathrm{E}(a_{it}^2 \mid \mathbf{x}_{it})$ be constant—meaning that $\mathrm{E}(u_{it}^4 \mid \mathbf{x}_{it})$ must be constant under H_0. We also need a stronger homoskedasticity assumption; $\mathrm{E}(u_{it}^2 \mid \mathbf{x}_{it}, u_{i,t-1}, \mathbf{x}_{i,t-1}, \ldots) = \sigma^2$ is sufficient for the $\{a_{it}\}$ in equation (7.85) to be appropriately serially uncorrelated.

A fully robust test for heteroskedasticity can be computed from the pooled regression (7.84) by obtaining a fully robust variance matrix estimator for $\hat{\boldsymbol{\delta}}$ [see equation (7.28)]; this can be used to form a robust Wald statistic.

Since violation of Assumption POLS.3a is of primary interest, it makes sense to include elements of $\mathbf{x}_{it}$ in $\mathbf{h}_{it}$, and possibly squares and cross products of elements of $\mathbf{x}_{it}$. Another useful choice, covered in Chapter 6, is $\hat{\mathbf{h}}_{it} = (\hat{y}_{it}, \hat{y}_{it}^2)$, the pooled OLS fitted values and their squares. Also, Assumption POLS.3a requires the unconditional variances $\mathrm{E}(u_{it}^2)$ to be the same across t. Whether they are can be tested directly by choosing $\mathbf{h}_{it}$ to have $T - 1$ time dummies.

If heteroskedasticity is detected but serial correlation is not, then the usual heteroskedasticity-robust standard errors and test statistics from the pooled OLS regression (7.73) can be used.

7.8.6 Feasible Generalized Least Squares Estimation under Strict Exogeneity

When $\mathrm{E}(\mathbf{u}_i\mathbf{u}_i') \neq \sigma^2\mathbf{I}_T$, it is reasonable to consider a feasible GLS analysis rather than a pooled OLS analysis. In Chapter 10 we will cover a particular FGLS analysis after we introduce unobserved components panel data models. With large N and small T, nothing precludes an FGLS analysis in the current setting. However, we must remember that FGLS is not even guaranteed to produce consistent, let alone efficient, estimators under Assumptions POLS.1 and POLS.2. Unless $\boldsymbol{\Omega} = \mathrm{E}(\mathbf{u}_i\mathbf{u}_i')$ is a diagonal matrix, Assumption POLS.1 should be replaced with the strict exogeneity assumption (7.8). (Problem 7.7 covers the case when $\boldsymbol{\Omega}$ is diagonal.) Sometimes we are willing to assume strict exogeneity in static and finite distributed lag models. As we saw earlier, it cannot hold in models with lagged y_{it}, and it can fail in static models or distributed lag models if there is feedback from y_{it} to future $\mathbf{z}_{it}$.

If we are comfortable with the strict exogeneity assumption, a useful FGLS analysis is obtained when $\{u_{it} : t = 1, 2, \ldots, T\}$ is assumed to follow an AR(1) process, $u_{it} = \rho u_{i,t-1} + e_{it}$. In this case, it is easy to transform the variables and compute the FGLS estimator from a pooled OLS regression. Let $\{\check{u}_{it} : t = 1, \ldots, T; i = 1, \ldots, N\}$ denote the POLS residuals and obtain $\hat{\rho}$ as the coefficient from the regression $\check{u}_{it}$ on $\check{u}_{i,t-1}$, $t = 2, \ldots, T$, $i = 1, \ldots, N$ (where we must be sure to omit the first time period for each i). We can modify the Prais-Winsten approach (for example, Wooldridge, 2009a, Section 12.3) to be applicable on panel data. If the AR(1) process is stable—that is, $|\rho| < 1$—and we assume stationary innovations $\{e_{it}\}$, then $\sigma_u^2 = \sigma_e^2/(1 - \rho^2)$. Therefore, for all $t = 1$ observations, we define $\tilde{y}_{i1} = \sqrt{(1 - \hat{\rho}^2)}y_{i1}$ and $\tilde{\mathbf{x}}_{i1} = \sqrt{(1 - \hat{\rho}^2)}\mathbf{x}_{i1}$. For $t = 2, \ldots, T$, $\tilde{y}_{it} = y_{it} - \hat{\rho}y_{i,t-1}$ and $\tilde{\mathbf{x}}_{it} = \mathbf{x}_{it} - \hat{\rho}\mathbf{x}_{i,t-1}$. Then, the FGLS estimator is obtained from the pooled OLS regression

$$\tilde{y}_{it} \text{ on } \tilde{\mathbf{x}}_{it}, \qquad t = 1, \ldots, T, \ i = 1, \ldots, N. \tag{7.86}$$

If $\boldsymbol{\Omega}$ truly has the AR(1) form and Assumption SGLS.3 holds, then the usual standard errors and test statistics from (7.86) are asymptotically valid. If we have any doubts about the homoskedasticity assumption, or whether the AR(1) assumption sufficiently captures the serial dependence, we can just apply the usual fully robust variance matrix (7.77) and associated statistics to pooled OLS on the transformed variables. This allows us to probably obtain an estimator more efficient than POLS (on the original data) but also guards against the rather simple structure we imposed on $\boldsymbol{\Omega}$. Of course, failure of strict exogeneity generally causes the Prais-Winsten estimator of $\boldsymbol{\beta}$ to be inconsistent.

Notice that the Prais-Winsten approach allows us to use all $t = 1$ observations. With panel data, it is simply too costly to drop the first time period, as in a Cochrane-Orcutt approach. (Indeed, the Cochrane-Orcutt estimator is asymptotically less efficient in the panel data case with fixed $T, N \to \infty$ asymptotics because it drops N observations relative to Prais-Winsten.)

Some statistical packages, including Stata, allow FGLS estimation with a misspecified variance matrix, but often this is under the guise of "generalized estimating equations," a topic we will treat in Chapter 12.

Problems

7.1. Provide the details for a proof of Theorem 7.1.

7.2. In model (7.11), maintain Assumptions SOLS.1 and SOLS.2, and assume $E(\mathbf{X}_i'\mathbf{u}_i\mathbf{u}_i'\mathbf{X}_i) = E(\mathbf{X}_i'\boldsymbol{\Omega}\mathbf{X}_i)$, where $\boldsymbol{\Omega} \equiv E(\mathbf{u}_i\mathbf{u}_i')$. (The last assumption is a different way of stating the homoskedasticity assumption for systems of equations; it always holds if assumption (7.53) holds.) Let $\hat{\boldsymbol{\beta}}_{\text{SOLS}}$ denote the system OLS estimator.

a. Show that $\text{Avar}(\hat{\boldsymbol{\beta}}_{\text{SOLS}}) = [E(\mathbf{X}_i'\mathbf{X}_i)]^{-1}[E(\mathbf{X}_i'\boldsymbol{\Omega}\mathbf{X}_i)][E(\mathbf{X}_i'\mathbf{X}_i)]^{-1}/N$.

b. How would you estimate the asymptotic variance in part a?

c. Now add Assumptions SGLS.1–SGLS.3. Show that $\text{Avar}(\hat{\boldsymbol{\beta}}_{\text{SOLS}}) - \text{Avar}(\hat{\boldsymbol{\beta}}_{\text{FGLS}})$ is positive semidefinite. (Hint: Show that $[\text{Avar}(\hat{\boldsymbol{\beta}}_{\text{FGLS}})]^{-1} - [\text{Avar}(\hat{\boldsymbol{\beta}}_{\text{SOLS}})]^{-1}$ is p.s.d.)

d. If, in addition to the previous assumptions, $\boldsymbol{\Omega} = \sigma^2\mathbf{I}_G$, show that SOLS and FGLS have the same asymptotic variance.

e. Evaluate the following statement: "Under the assumptions of part c, FGLS is never asymptotically worse than SOLS, even if $\boldsymbol{\Omega} = \sigma^2\mathbf{I}_G$."

7.3. Consider the SUR model (7.2) under Assumptions SOLS.1, SOLS.2, and SGLS.3, with $\boldsymbol{\Omega} \equiv \text{diag}(\sigma_1^2, \ldots, \sigma_G^2)$; thus, GLS and OLS estimation equation by equation are the same. (In the SUR model with diagonal $\boldsymbol{\Omega}$, Assumption SOLS.1 is the same as Assumption SGLS.1, and Assumption SOLS.2 is the same as Assumption SGLS.2.)

a. Show that single-equation OLS estimators from any two equations, say, $\hat{\boldsymbol{\beta}}_g$ and $\hat{\boldsymbol{\beta}}_h$, are asymptotically uncorrelated. (That is, show that the asymptotic variance of the system OLS estimator $\hat{\boldsymbol{\beta}}$ is block diagonal.)

b. Under the conditions of part a, assume that $\boldsymbol{\beta}_1$ and $\boldsymbol{\beta}_2$ (the parameter vectors in the first two equations) have the same dimension. Explain how you would test H_0: $\boldsymbol{\beta}_1 = \boldsymbol{\beta}_2$ against H_1: $\boldsymbol{\beta}_1 \neq \boldsymbol{\beta}_2$.

c. Now drop Assumption SGLS.3, maintaining Assumptions SOLS.1 and SOLS.2 and diagonality of $\boldsymbol{\Omega}$. Suppose that $\hat{\boldsymbol{\Omega}}$ is estimated in an unrestricted manner, so that FGLS and OLS are not algebraically equivalent. Show that OLS and FGLS are $\sqrt{N}$-asymptotically equivalent, that is, $\sqrt{N}(\hat{\boldsymbol{\beta}}_{\text{SOLS}} - \hat{\boldsymbol{\beta}}_{\text{FGLS}}) = o_p(1)$. This is one case where FGLS is consistent under Assumption SOLS.1.

7.4. Using the $\sqrt{N}$-consistency of the system OLS estimator $\check{\boldsymbol{\beta}}$ for $\boldsymbol{\beta}$, for $\hat{\boldsymbol{\Omega}}$ in equation (7.40) show that

$$\text{vec}[\sqrt{N}(\hat{\boldsymbol{\Omega}} - \boldsymbol{\Omega})] = \text{vec}\left[N^{-1/2}\sum_{i=1}^{N}(\mathbf{u}_i\mathbf{u}_i' - \boldsymbol{\Omega})\right] + \text{o}_p(1)$$

under Assumptions SGLS.1 and SOLS.2. (Note: This result does not hold when Assumption SGLS.1 is replaced with the weaker Assumption SOLS.1.) Assume that all moment conditions needed to apply the WLLN and CLT are satisfied. The important conclusion is that the asymptotic distribution of vec $\sqrt{N}(\hat{\boldsymbol{\Omega}} - \boldsymbol{\Omega})$ does not depend on that of $\sqrt{N}(\check{\boldsymbol{\beta}} - \boldsymbol{\beta})$, and so any asymptotic tests on the elements of $\boldsymbol{\Omega}$ can ignore the estimation of $\boldsymbol{\beta}$. [Hint: Start from equation (7.42) and use the fact that $\sqrt{N}(\check{\boldsymbol{\beta}} - \boldsymbol{\beta}) = \text{O}_p(1)$.]

7.5. Prove Theorem 7.6, using the fact that when $\mathbf{X}_i = \mathbf{I}_G \otimes \mathbf{x}_i$,

$$\sum_{i=1}^{N}\mathbf{X}_i'\hat{\boldsymbol{\Omega}}^{-1}\mathbf{X}_i = \hat{\boldsymbol{\Omega}}^{-1} \otimes \left(\sum_{i=1}^{N}\mathbf{x}_i'\mathbf{x}_i\right) \quad \text{and} \quad \sum_{i=1}^{N}\mathbf{X}_i'\hat{\boldsymbol{\Omega}}^{-1}\mathbf{y}_i = (\hat{\boldsymbol{\Omega}}^{-1} \otimes \mathbf{I}_K)\begin{pmatrix}\sum_{i=1}^{N}\mathbf{x}_i'y_{i1} \\ \vdots \\ \sum_{i=1}^{N}\mathbf{x}_i'y_{iG}\end{pmatrix}.$$

7.6. Start with model (7.11). Suppose you wish to impose Q linear restrictions of the form $\mathbf{R}\boldsymbol{\beta} = \mathbf{r}$, where $\mathbf{R}$ is a $Q \times K$ matrix and $\mathbf{r}$ is a $Q \times 1$ vector. Assume that $\mathbf{R}$ is partitioned as $\mathbf{R} \equiv [\mathbf{R}_1 \,|\, \mathbf{R}_2]$, where $\mathbf{R}_1$ is a $Q \times Q$ nonsingular matrix and $\mathbf{R}_2$ is a $Q \times (K - Q)$ matrix. Partition $\mathbf{X}_i$ as $\mathbf{X}_i \equiv [\mathbf{X}_{i1} \,|\, \mathbf{X}_{i2}]$, where $\mathbf{X}_{i1}$ is $G \times Q$ and $\mathbf{X}_{i2}$ is $G \times (K - Q)$, and partition $\boldsymbol{\beta}$ as $\boldsymbol{\beta} \equiv (\boldsymbol{\beta}_1', \boldsymbol{\beta}_2')'$. The restrictions $\mathbf{R}\boldsymbol{\beta} = \mathbf{r}$ can be expressed as $\mathbf{R}_1\boldsymbol{\beta}_1 + \mathbf{R}_2\boldsymbol{\beta}_2 = \mathbf{r}$, or $\boldsymbol{\beta}_1 = \mathbf{R}_1^{-1}(\mathbf{r} - \mathbf{R}_2\boldsymbol{\beta}_2)$. Show that the restricted model can be written as

$$\tilde{\mathbf{y}}_i = \tilde{\mathbf{X}}_{i2}\boldsymbol{\beta}_2 + \mathbf{u}_i,$$

where $\tilde{\mathbf{y}}_i = \mathbf{y}_i - \mathbf{X}_{i1}\mathbf{R}_1^{-1}\mathbf{r}$ and $\tilde{\mathbf{X}}_{i2} = \mathbf{X}_{i2} - \mathbf{X}_{i1}\mathbf{R}_1^{-1}\mathbf{R}_2$.

7.7. Consider the panel data model

$$y_{it} = \mathbf{x}_{it}\boldsymbol{\beta} + u_{it}, \qquad t = 1, 2, \ldots, T,$$

$$\text{E}(u_{it} \,|\, \mathbf{x}_{it}, u_{i,t-1}, \mathbf{x}_{i,t-1}, \ldots,) = 0,$$

$$\text{E}(u_{it}^2 \,|\, \mathbf{x}_{it}) = \text{E}(u_{it}^2) = \sigma_t^2, \qquad t = 1, \ldots, T.$$

(Note that $\text{E}(u_{it}^2 \,|\, \mathbf{x}_{it})$ does not depend on $\mathbf{x}_{it}$, but it is allowed to be a different constant in each time period.)

a. Show that $\mathbf{\Omega} = \mathrm{E}(\mathbf{u}_i\mathbf{u}_i')$ is a diagonal matrix.

b. Write down the GLS estimator assuming that $\mathbf{\Omega}$ is known.

c. Argue that Assumption SGLS.1 does not necessarily hold under the assumptions made. (Setting $\mathbf{x}_{it} = y_{i,t-1}$ might help in answering this part.) Nevertheless, show that the GLS estimator from part b *is* consistent for $\boldsymbol{\beta}$ by showing that $\mathrm{E}(\mathbf{X}_i'\mathbf{\Omega}^{-1}\mathbf{u}_i) = \mathbf{0}$. (This proof shows that Assumption SGLS.1 is sufficient, but not necessary, for consistency. Sometimes $\mathrm{E}(\mathbf{X}_i'\mathbf{\Omega}^{-1}\mathbf{u}_i) = \mathbf{0}$ even though Assumption SGLS.1 does not hold.)

d. Show that Assumption SGLS.3 holds under the given assumptions.

e. Explain how to consistently estimate each σ_t^2 (as $N \to \infty$).

f. Argue that, under the assumptions made, valid inference is obtained by weighting each observation $(y_{it}, \mathbf{x}_{it})$ by $1/\hat{\sigma}_t$ and then running pooled OLS.

g. What happens if we assume that $\sigma_t^2 = \sigma^2$ for all $t = 1, \ldots, T$?

7.8. Redo Example 7.3, disaggregating the benefits categories into value of vacation days, value of sick leave, value of employer-provided insurance, and value of pension. Use hourly measures of these along with *hrearn*, and estimate an SUR model. Does marital status appear to affect any form of compensation? Test whether another year of education increases expected pension value and expected insurance by the same amount.

7.9. Redo Example 7.7 but include a single lag of log(*scrap*) in the equation to proxy for omitted variables that may determine grant receipt. Test for AR(1) serial correlation. If you find it, you should also compute the fully robust standard errors that allow for abitrary serial correlation across time and heteroskedasticity.

7.10. In Example 7.9, compute standard errors fully robust to serial correlation and heteroskedasticity. Discuss any important differences between the robust standard errors and the usual standard errors.

7.11. Use the data in CORNWELL.RAW for this question; see Problem 4.13.

a. Using the data for all seven years, and using the logarithms of all variables, estimate a model relating the crime rate to *prbarr*, *prbconv*, *prbpris*, *avgsen*, and *polpc*. Use pooled OLS and include a full set of year dummies. Test for serial correlation assuming that the explanatory variables are strictly exogenous. If there is serial correlation, obtain the fully robust standard errors.

b. Add a one-year lag of log(*crmrte*) to the equation from part a, and compare with the estimates from part a.

c. Test for first-order serial correlation in the errors in the model from part b. If serial correlation is present, compute the fully robust standard errors.

d. Add all of the wage variables (in logarithmic form) to the equation from part b. Which ones are statistically and economically significant? Are they jointly significant? Test for joint significance of the wage variables allowing arbitrary serial correlation and heteroskedasticity.

7.12. If you add wealth at the beginning of year t to the saving equation in Example 7.2, is the strict exogeneity assumption likely to hold? Explain.

7.13. Use the data in NBASAL.RAW to answer this question.

a. Estimate an SUR model for the three response variables *points*, *rebounds*, and *assists*. The explanatory variables in each equation should be *age*, *exper*, $exper^2$, *coll*, *guard*, *forward*, *black*, and *marr*. Does marital status have a positive or negative affect on each variable? Is it statistically significant in the *assists* equation?

b. Test the hypothesis that marital status can be excluded entirely from the system. You may use the test that maintains Assumption SGLS.3.

c. What do you make of the negative, statistically significant coefficients on *coll* in the three equations?

7.14. Consider the system of equations $\mathbf{y}_i = \mathbf{X}_i\boldsymbol{\beta} + \mathbf{u}_i$ under $\mathrm{E}(\mathbf{X}_i \otimes \mathbf{u}_i) = \mathbf{0}$ and $\mathrm{E}(\mathbf{u}_i\mathbf{u}_i' \mid \mathbf{X}_i) = \boldsymbol{\Omega}$. Consider the FGLS estimator with $\hat{\boldsymbol{\Omega}}$ consistent for $\boldsymbol{\Omega}$ and another FGLS estimator using $\hat{\boldsymbol{\Lambda}} \xrightarrow{p} \boldsymbol{\Lambda} \neq \boldsymbol{\Omega}$. Show that the former is at least as asymptotically efficient as the latter.

7.15. In the system of equations $\mathbf{y}_i = \mathbf{X}_i\boldsymbol{\beta} + \mathbf{Z}_i\boldsymbol{\gamma} + \mathbf{u}_i$ under $\mathrm{E}(\mathbf{u}_i \mid \mathbf{X}_i, \mathbf{Z}_i) = \mathbf{0}$ and $\mathrm{Var}(\mathbf{u}_i \mid \mathbf{X}_i, \mathbf{Z}_i) = \boldsymbol{\Omega}$, suppose in addition that each element of $\mathbf{Z}_i$ is uncorrelated with each element of $\mathbf{X}_i$, $\mathrm{E}(\mathbf{X}_i \otimes \mathbf{Z}_i) = \mathbf{0}$. (We are thinking of cases where $\mathbf{X}_i$ includes unity and so $\mathbf{Z}_i$ is standardized to have a zero mean.) Let $\hat{\boldsymbol{\beta}}$ be the FGLS estimator from the full model (obtained along with $\hat{\boldsymbol{\gamma}}$) using a consistent estimator $\hat{\boldsymbol{\Omega}}$ for $\boldsymbol{\Omega}$. Let $\tilde{\boldsymbol{\beta}}$ be the FLGS estimator on the restricted model $\mathbf{y}_i = \mathbf{X}_i\boldsymbol{\beta} + \mathbf{v}_i$ using a consistent estimator of $\mathrm{E}(\mathbf{v}_i\mathbf{v}_i')$. Show that $\mathrm{Avar}[\sqrt{N}(\tilde{\boldsymbol{\beta}} - \boldsymbol{\beta})] - \mathrm{Avar}[\sqrt{N}(\hat{\boldsymbol{\beta}} - \boldsymbol{\beta})]$ is a least positive semidefinite.

8 System Estimation by Instrumental Variables

8.1 Introduction and Examples

In Chapter 7 we covered system estimation of linear equations when the explanatory variables satisfy certain exogeneity conditions. For many applications, even the weakest of these assumptions, Assumption SOLS.1, is violated, in which case instrumental variables procedures are indispensable.

The modern approach to **system instrumental variables (SIV)** estimation is based on the principle of **generalized method of moments (GMM)**. Method of moments estimation has a long history in statistics for obtaining simple parameter estimates when maximum likelihood estimation requires nonlinear optimization. Hansen (1982) and White (1982b) showed how the method of moments can be generalized to apply to a variety of econometric models, and they derived the asymptotic properties of GMM. Hansen (1982), who coined the name "generalized method of moments," treated time series data, and White (1982b) assumed independently sampled observations.

A related class of estimators falls under the heading **generalized instrumental variables (GIV)**. As we will see in Section 8.4, the GIV estimator can be viewed as an extension of the generalized least squares (GLS) method we covered in Chapter 7. We will also see that the GIV estimator, because of its dependence on a GLS-like transformation, is inconsistent in some important cases when GMM remains consistent.

Though the models considered in this chapter are more general than those treated in Chapter 5, the derivations of asymptotic properties of system IV estimators are mechanically similar to the derivations in Chapters 5 and 7. Therefore, the proofs in this chapter will be terse, or omitted altogether.

In econometrics, the most familar application of SIV estimation is to a **simultaneous equations model (SEM)**. We will cover SEMs specifically in Chapter 9, but it is useful to begin with a typical SEM example. System estimation procedures have applications beyond the classical simultaneous equations methods. We will also use the results in this chapter for the analysis of panel data models in Chapter 11.

Example 8.1 (Labor Supply and Wage Offer Functions): Consider the following labor supply function representing the hours of labor supply, h^s, at any wage, w, faced by an individual. As usual, we express this in population form:

$$h^s(w) = \gamma_1 w + \mathbf{z}_1 \boldsymbol{\delta}_1 + u_1 \tag{8.1}$$

where $\mathbf{z}_1$ is a vector of observed labor supply shifters—including such things as education, past experience, age, marital status, number of children, and nonlabor income—and u_1 contains unobservables affecting labor supply. The labor supply function can be derived from individual utility-maximizing behavior, and the notation in equation (8.1) is intended to emphasize that, for given $\mathbf{z}_1$ and u_1, a labor supply function gives the desired hours worked at *any* possible wage (ω) facing the worker. As a practical matter, we can only observe *equilibrium* values of hours worked and hourly wage. But the counterfactual reasoning underlying equation (8.1) is the proper way to view labor supply.

A wage offer function gives the hourly wage that the market will offer as a function of hours worked. (It could be that the wage offer does not depend on hours worked, but in general it might.) For observed productivity attributes $\mathbf{z}_2$ (for example, education, experience, and amount of job training) and unobserved attributes u_2, we write the wage offer function as

$$w^o(\hbar) = \gamma_2 \hbar + \mathbf{z}_2 \boldsymbol{\delta}_2 + u_2. \tag{8.2}$$

Again, for given $\mathbf{z}_2$ and u_2, $w^o(\hbar)$ gives the wage offer for an individual agreeing to work $\hbar$ hours.

Equations (8.1) and (8.2) explain different sides of the labor market. However, rarely can we assume that an individual is given an exogenous wage offer and then, at that wage, decides how much to work based on equation (8.1). A reasonable approach is to assume that observed hours and wage are such that equations (8.1) and (8.2) both hold. In other words, letting (h, w) denote the equilibrium values, we have

$$h = \gamma_1 w + \mathbf{z}_1 \boldsymbol{\delta}_1 + u_1, \tag{8.3}$$

$$w = \gamma_2 h + \mathbf{z}_2 \boldsymbol{\delta}_2 + u_2. \tag{8.4}$$

Under weak restrictions on the parameters, these equations can be solved uniquely for (h, w) as functions of $\mathbf{z}_1$, $\mathbf{z}_2$, u_1, u_2, and the parameters; we consider this topic generally in Chapter 9. Further, if $\mathbf{z}_1$ and $\mathbf{z}_2$ are exogenous in the sense that

$$\mathrm{E}(u_1 \mid \mathbf{z}_1, \mathbf{z}_2) = \mathrm{E}(u_2 \mid \mathbf{z}_1, \mathbf{z}_2) = 0,$$

then, under identification assumptions, we can consistently estimate the parameters of the labor supply and wage offer functions. We consider identification of SEMs in detail in Chapter 9. We also ignore what is sometimes a practically important issue: the equilibrium hours for an individual might be zero, in which case w is not observed for such people. We deal with missing data issues in Chapter 21.

For a random draw from the population, we can write

$$h_i = \gamma_1 w_i + \mathbf{z}_{i1} \boldsymbol{\delta}_1 + u_{i1}, \tag{8.5}$$

$$w_i = \gamma_2 h_i + \mathbf{z}_{i2} \boldsymbol{\delta}_2 + u_{i2}. \tag{8.6}$$

Except under very special assumptions, u_{i1} will be correlated with w_i, and u_{i2} will be correlated with h_i. In other words, w_i is probably endogenous in equation (8.5), and h_i is probably endogenous in equation (8.6). It is for this reason that we study system instrumental variables methods.

An example with the same statistical structure as Example 8.1 but with an omitted variables interpretation is motivated by Currie and Thomas (1995).

Example 8.2 (Student Performance and Head Start): Consider an equation to test the effect of Head Start participation on subsequent student performance:

$$score_i = \gamma_1 HeadStart_i + \mathbf{z}_{i1}\boldsymbol{\delta}_1 + u_{i1}, \tag{8.7}$$

where $score_i$ is the outcome on a test when the child is enrolled in school and $HeadStart_i$ is a binary indicator equal to one if child i participated in Head Start at an early age. The vector $\mathbf{z}_{i1}$ contains other observed factors, such as income, education, and family background variables. The error term u_{i1} contains unobserved factors that affect *score*—such as child's ability—that may also be correlated with *HeadStart*. To capture the possible endogeneity of *HeadStart*, we write a linear reduced form (linear projection) for $HeadStart_i$:

$$HeadStart_i = \mathbf{z}_i\boldsymbol{\delta}_2 + u_{i2}. \tag{8.8}$$

Remember, this projection always exists even though $HeadStart_i$ is a binary variable. The vector $\mathbf{z}_i$ contains $\mathbf{z}_{i1}$ and at least one factor affecting Head Start participation that does not have a direct effect on *score*. One possibility is distance to the nearest Head Start center. In this example we would probably be willing to assume that $\mathrm{E}(u_{i1} \mid \mathbf{z}_i) = 0$, since the test score equation is structural, but we would only want to assume $\mathrm{E}(\mathbf{z}_i' u_{i2}) = \mathbf{0}$, since the Head Start equation is a linear projection involving a binary dependent variable. Correlation between u_1 and u_2 means *HeadStart* is endogenous in equation (8.7).

Both of the previous examples can be written for observation i as

$$y_{i1} = \mathbf{x}_{i1}\boldsymbol{\beta}_1 + u_{i1}, \tag{8.9}$$

$$y_{i2} = \mathbf{x}_{i2}\boldsymbol{\beta}_2 + u_{i2}, \tag{8.10}$$

which looks just like a two-equation SUR system but where $\mathbf{x}_{i1}$ and $\mathbf{x}_{i2}$ can contain endogenous as well as exogenous variables. Because $\mathbf{x}_{i1}$ and $\mathbf{x}_{i2}$ are generally correlated with u_{i1} and u_{i2}, estimation of these equations by OLS or FGLS, as we studied in Chapter 7, will generally produce inconsistent estimators.

We already know one method for estimating an equation such as equation (8.9): if we have sufficient instruments, apply 2SLS. Often 2SLS produces acceptable results, so why should we go beyond single-equation analysis? Not surprisingly, our interest in system methods with endogenous explanatory variables has to do with efficiency. In many cases we can obtain more efficient estimators by estimating $\boldsymbol{\beta}_1$ and $\boldsymbol{\beta}_2$ *jointly*, that is, by using a system procedure. The efficiency gains are analogous to the gains that can be realized by using feasible GLS rather than OLS in an SUR system.

8.2 General Linear System of Equations

We now discuss estimation of a general linear model of the form

$$\mathbf{y}_i = \mathbf{X}_i\boldsymbol{\beta} + \mathbf{u}_i, \tag{8.11}$$

where $\mathbf{y}_i$ is a $G \times 1$ vector, $\mathbf{X}_i$ is a $G \times K$ matrix, and $\mathbf{u}_i$ is the $G \times 1$ vector of errors. This model is identical to equation (7.9), except that we will use different assumptions. In writing out examples, we will often omit the observation subscript i, but for the general analysis, carrying it along is a useful notational device. As in Chapter 7, the rows of $\mathbf{y}_i$, $\mathbf{X}_i$, and $\mathbf{u}_i$ can represent different time periods for the same cross-sectional unit (so $G = T$, the total number of time periods). Therefore, the following analysis applies to panel data models where T is small relative to the cross section sample size, N; for an example, see Problem 8.8. We cover general panel data applications in Chapter 11. (As in Chapter 7, the label "systems of equations" is not especially accurate for basic panel data models because we have only one behavioral equation over T different time periods.)

The following orthogonality condition is the basis for estimating $\boldsymbol{\beta}$:

ASSUMPTION SIV.1: $\mathrm{E}(\mathbf{Z}_i'\mathbf{u}_i) = \mathbf{0}$, where $\mathbf{Z}_i$ is a $G \times L$ matrix of observable instrumental variables.

(The abbreviation SIV stands for "system instrumental variables.") For the purposes of discussion, we assume that $\mathrm{E}(\mathbf{u}_i) = \mathbf{0}$; this assumption is almost always true in practice anyway.

From what we know about IV and 2SLS for single equations, Assumption SIV.1 cannot be enough to identify the vector $\boldsymbol{\beta}$. An assumption sufficient for identification is the **rank condition**:

ASSUMPTION SIV.2: $\operatorname{rank} \mathrm{E}(\mathbf{Z}_i'\mathbf{X}_i) = K$.

Assumption SIV.2 generalizes the rank condition from the single-equation case. (When $G = 1$, Assumption SIV.2 is the same as Assumption 2SLS.2b.) Since $\mathrm{E}(\mathbf{Z}_i'\mathbf{X}_i)$ is an $L \times K$ matrix, Assumption SIV.2 requires the columns of this matrix to be linearly independent. Necessary for the rank condition is the **order condition**: $L \geq K$. We will investigate the rank condition in detail for a broad class of models in Chapter 9. For now, we just assume that it holds.

As in Chapter 7, it is useful to carry along two examples. The first applies to simultaneous equations models and other systems with endogenous explanatory variables. The second is a panel data model where instrumental variables are specified that are not the same as the explanatory variables.

For the first example, write a G equation system for the population as

$$\begin{aligned} y_1 &= \mathbf{x}_1\boldsymbol{\beta}_1 + u_1 \\ &\vdots \\ y_G &= \mathbf{x}_G\boldsymbol{\beta}_G + u_G, \end{aligned} \tag{8.12}$$

where, for each equation g, $\mathbf{x}_g$ is a $1 \times K_g$ vector that can contain both exogenous and endogenous variables. For each g, $\boldsymbol{\beta}_g$ is $K_g \times 1$. Because this looks just like the SUR system from Chapter 7, we will refer to it as an SUR system, keeping in mind the crucial fact that some elements of $\mathbf{x}_g$ are thought to be correlated with u_g for at least some g.

For each equation we assume that we have a set of instrumental variables, a $1 \times L_g$ vector $\mathbf{z}_g$, that are exogenous in the sense that

$$\mathrm{E}(\mathbf{z}_g'u_g) = \mathbf{0}, \qquad g = 1, 2, \ldots, G. \tag{8.13}$$

In most applications, unity is an element of $\mathbf{z}_g$ for each g, so that $\mathrm{E}(u_g) = 0$, all g. As we will see, and as we already know from single-equation analysis, if $\mathbf{x}_g$ contains some elements correlated with u_g, then $\mathbf{z}_g$ must contain more than just the exogenous variables appearing in equation g. Much of the time the same instruments, which consist of *all* exogenous variables appearing anywhere in the system, are valid for every equation, so that $\mathbf{z}_g = \mathbf{w}$ (say), $g = 1, 2, \ldots, G$. Some applications require us to have different instruments for different equations, so we allow that possibility here.

Putting an i subscript on the variables in equations (8.12), and defining

$$\underset{G\times 1}{\mathbf{y}_i} \equiv \begin{pmatrix} y_{i1} \\ y_{i2} \\ \vdots \\ y_{iG} \end{pmatrix}, \qquad \underset{G\times K}{\mathbf{X}_i} \equiv \begin{pmatrix} \mathbf{x}_{i1} & \mathbf{0} & \mathbf{0} & \cdots & \mathbf{0} \\ \mathbf{0} & \mathbf{x}_{i2} & \mathbf{0} & \cdots & \mathbf{0} \\ \vdots & & & & \vdots \\ \mathbf{0} & \mathbf{0} & \mathbf{0} & \cdots & \mathbf{x}_{iG} \end{pmatrix}, \qquad \underset{G\times 1}{\mathbf{u}_i} \equiv \begin{pmatrix} u_{i1} \\ u_{i2} \\ \vdots \\ u_{iG} \end{pmatrix} \tag{8.14}$$

and $\boldsymbol{\beta} = (\boldsymbol{\beta}_1', \boldsymbol{\beta}_2', \ldots, \boldsymbol{\beta}_G')'$, we can write equation (8.12) in the form (8.11). Note that $K = K_1 + K_2 + \cdots + K_G$ is the total number of parameters in the system.

The matrix of instruments has a structure similar to $\mathbf{X}_i$:

$$\mathbf{Z}_i \equiv \begin{pmatrix} \mathbf{z}_{i1} & \mathbf{0} & \mathbf{0} & \cdots & \mathbf{0} \\ \mathbf{0} & \mathbf{z}_{i2} & \mathbf{0} & \cdots & \mathbf{0} \\ \vdots & & & & \vdots \\ \mathbf{0} & \mathbf{0} & \mathbf{0} & \cdots & \mathbf{z}_{iG} \end{pmatrix}, \tag{8.15}$$

which has dimension $G \times L$, where $L = L_1 + L_2 + \cdots + L_G$. Then, for each i,

$$\mathbf{Z}_i'\mathbf{u}_i = (\mathbf{z}_{i1}u_{i1}, \mathbf{z}_{i2}u_{i2}, \ldots, \mathbf{z}_{iG}u_{iG})', \tag{8.16}$$

and so $\mathrm{E}(\mathbf{Z}_i'\mathbf{u}_i) = \mathbf{0}$ reproduces the orthogonality conditions (8.13). Also,

$$\mathrm{E}(\mathbf{Z}_i'\mathbf{X}_i) = \begin{pmatrix} \mathrm{E}(\mathbf{z}_{i1}'\mathbf{x}_{i1}) & \mathbf{0} & \mathbf{0} & \cdots & \mathbf{0} \\ \mathbf{0} & \mathrm{E}(\mathbf{z}_{i2}'\mathbf{x}_{i2}) & \mathbf{0} & \cdots & \mathbf{0} \\ \vdots & & & & \vdots \\ \mathbf{0} & \mathbf{0} & \mathbf{0} & \cdots & \mathrm{E}(\mathbf{z}_{iG}'\mathbf{x}_{iG}) \end{pmatrix}, \tag{8.17}$$

where $\mathrm{E}(\mathbf{z}_{ig}'\mathbf{x}_{ig})$ is $L_g \times K_g$. Assumption SIV.2 requires that this matrix have full column rank, where the number of columns is $K = K_1 + K_2 + \cdots + K_G$. A well-known result from linear algebra says that a block diagonal matrix has full column rank if and only if each block in the matrix has full column rank. In other words, Assumption SIV.2 holds in this example if and only if

$$\operatorname{rank} \mathrm{E}(\mathbf{z}_{ig}'\mathbf{x}_{ig}) = K_g, \qquad g = 1, 2, \ldots, G. \tag{8.18}$$

This is *exactly* the rank condition needed for estimating each equation by 2SLS, which we know is possible under conditions (8.13) and (8.18). Therefore, identification of the SUR system is equivalent to identification equation by equation. This reasoning assumes that the $\boldsymbol{\beta}_g$ are unrestricted across equations. If some prior restrictions are known, then identification is more complicated, something we cover explicitly in Chapter 9.

In the important special case where the same instruments, say $\mathbf{w}_i$, can be used for every equation, we can write definition (8.15) as $\mathbf{Z}_i = \mathbf{I}_G \otimes \mathbf{w}_i$.

For the panel data model

$$y_{it} = \mathbf{x}_{it}\boldsymbol{\beta} + u_{it}, \qquad t = 1, \ldots, T, \tag{8.19}$$

we set $G = T$ and define the $T \times K$ matrix as in Chapter 7:

$$\mathbf{X}_i = \begin{pmatrix} \mathbf{x}_{i1} \\ \mathbf{x}_{i2} \\ \vdots \\ \mathbf{x}_{iT} \end{pmatrix}. \tag{8.20}$$

As the model is written in (8.19), there is a common vector, $\boldsymbol{\beta}$, in each time period. Nevertheless, as we discussed in Chapter 7, this notation allows for different intercepts and slopes because $\mathbf{x}_{it}$ can contain time period dummies and interactions between time dummies and covariates (whether those covariates change over time or not).

If $\mathbf{z}_{it}$ is a $1 \times L_t$ vector of instruments for each time period, in the sense that

$$\mathrm{E}(\mathbf{z}_{it}'u_{it}) = \mathbf{0}, \qquad t = 1, \ldots, T, \tag{8.21}$$

then we can define the matrix of instruments as in (8.15), with the slight notational change $G = T$. When L_t is the same for all t ($L_t = L$, $t = 1, \ldots, T$), a different choice is possible:

$$\mathbf{Z}_i = \begin{pmatrix} \mathbf{z}_{i1} \\ \mathbf{z}_{i2} \\ \vdots \\ \mathbf{z}_{iT} \end{pmatrix}. \tag{8.22}$$

As we will see, generally the choice (8.22) leads to a different estimator than when the IVs are chosen as in (8.15).

8.3 Generalized Method of Moments Estimation

8.3.1 General Weighting Matrix

The orthogonality conditions in Assumption SIV.1 suggest an estimation strategy. Under Assumptions SIV.1 and SIV.2, $\boldsymbol{\beta}$ is the *unique* $K \times 1$ vector solving the linear set population moment conditions

$$\mathrm{E}[\mathbf{Z}_i'(\mathbf{y}_i - \mathbf{X}_i\boldsymbol{\beta})] = \mathbf{0}. \tag{8.23}$$

(That $\boldsymbol{\beta}$ is a solution follows from Assumption SIV.1; that it is unique follows by Assumption SIV.2.) In other words, if $\mathbf{b}$ is any other $K \times 1$ vector (so that at least one element of $\mathbf{b}$ is different from the corresponding element in $\boldsymbol{\beta}$), then

$$\mathrm{E}[\mathbf{Z}_i'(\mathbf{y}_i - \mathbf{X}_i\mathbf{b})] \neq \mathbf{0}. \tag{8.24}$$

This equation shows that $\boldsymbol{\beta}$ is identified. Because sample averages are consistent estimators of population moments, the analogy principle applied to condition (8.23) suggests choosing the estimator $\hat{\boldsymbol{\beta}}$ to solve

$$N^{-1}\sum_{i=1}^{N}\mathbf{Z}_i'(\mathbf{y}_i - \mathbf{X}_i\hat{\boldsymbol{\beta}}) = \mathbf{0}. \tag{8.25}$$

Equation (8.25) is a set of L linear equations in the K unknowns in $\hat{\boldsymbol{\beta}}$. First consider the case $L = K$, so that we have exactly enough IVs for the explanatory variables in the system. Then, if the $K \times K$ matrix $\sum_{i=1}^{N}\mathbf{Z}_i'\mathbf{X}_i$ is nonsingular, we can solve for $\hat{\boldsymbol{\beta}}$ as

$$\hat{\boldsymbol{\beta}} = \left(N^{-1}\sum_{i=1}^{N}\mathbf{Z}_i'\mathbf{X}_i\right)^{-1}\left(N^{-1}\sum_{i=1}^{N}\mathbf{Z}_i'\mathbf{y}_i\right). \tag{8.26}$$

We can write $\hat{\boldsymbol{\beta}}$ using full matrix notation as $\hat{\boldsymbol{\beta}} = (\mathbf{Z}'\mathbf{X})^{-1}\mathbf{Z}'\mathbf{Y}$, where $\mathbf{Z}$ is the $NG \times L$ matrix obtained by stacking $\mathbf{Z}_i$ from $i = 1, 2, \ldots, N$, $\mathbf{X}$ is the $NG \times K$ matrix obtained by stacking $\mathbf{X}_i$ from $i = 1, 2, \ldots, N$, and $\mathbf{Y}$ is the $NG \times 1$ vector obtained from stacking $\mathbf{y}_i$, $i = 1, 2, \ldots, N$. We call equation (8.26) the **system IV (SIV) estimator**. Application of the law of large numbers shows that the SIV estimator is consistent under Assumptions SIV.1 and SIV.2.

When $L > K$—so that we have more columns in the IV matrix $\mathbf{Z}_i$ than we need for identification—choosing $\hat{\boldsymbol{\beta}}$ is more complicated. Except in special cases, equation (8.25) will not have a solution. Instead, we choose $\hat{\boldsymbol{\beta}}$ to make the vector in equation (8.25) as "small" as possible in the sample. One idea is to minimize the squared Euclidean length of the $L \times 1$ vector in equation (8.25). Dropping the $1/N$, this approach suggests choosing $\hat{\boldsymbol{\beta}}$ to make

$$\left[\sum_{i=1}^{N}\mathbf{Z}_i'(\mathbf{y}_i - \mathbf{X}_i\hat{\boldsymbol{\beta}})\right]'\left[\sum_{i=1}^{N}\mathbf{Z}_i'(\mathbf{y}_i - \mathbf{X}_i\hat{\boldsymbol{\beta}})\right]$$

as small as possible. While this method produces a consistent estimator under Assumptions SIV.1 and SIV.2, it rarely produces the best estimator, for reasons we will see in Section 8.3.3.

A more general class of estimators is obtained by using a **weighting matrix** in the quadratic form. Let $\hat{\mathbf{W}}$ be an $L \times L$ symmetric, positive semidefinite matrix, where the "$\wedge$" is included to emphasize that $\hat{\mathbf{W}}$ is generally an estimator. A **generalized method of moments (GMM) estimator** of $\boldsymbol{\beta}$ is a vector $\hat{\boldsymbol{\beta}}$ that solves the problem

$$\min_{\mathbf{b}} \left[\sum_{i=1}^{N} \mathbf{Z}_i'(\mathbf{y}_i - \mathbf{X}_i\mathbf{b}) \right]' \hat{\mathbf{W}} \left[\sum_{i=1}^{N} \mathbf{Z}_i'(\mathbf{y}_i - \mathbf{X}_i\mathbf{b}) \right]. \tag{8.27}$$

Because expression (8.27) is a quadratic function of $\mathbf{b}$, the solution to it has a closed form. Using multivariable calculus or direct substitution, we can show that the unique solution is

$$\hat{\boldsymbol{\beta}} = (\mathbf{X}'\mathbf{Z}\hat{\mathbf{W}}\mathbf{Z}'\mathbf{X})^{-1}(\mathbf{X}'\mathbf{Z}\hat{\mathbf{W}}\mathbf{Z}'\mathbf{Y}), \tag{8.28}$$

assuming that $\mathbf{X}'\mathbf{Z}\hat{\mathbf{W}}\mathbf{Z}'\mathbf{X}$ is nonsingular. To show that this estimator is consistent, we assume that $\hat{\mathbf{W}}$ has a nonsingular probability limit.

ASSUMPTION SIV.3: $\hat{\mathbf{W}} \xrightarrow{p} \mathbf{W}$ as $N \to \infty$, where $\mathbf{W}$ is a nonrandom, symmetric, $L \times L$ positive definite matrix.

In applications, the convergence in Assumption SIV.3 will follow from the law of large numbers because $\hat{\mathbf{W}}$ will be a function of sample averages. The fact that $\mathbf{W}$ is assumed to be positive definite means that $\hat{\mathbf{W}}$ is positive definite with probability approaching one (see Chapter 3). We could relax the assumption of positive definiteness to positive semidefiniteness at the cost of complicating the assumptions. In most applications, we can assume that $\mathbf{W}$ is positive definite.

THEOREM 8.1 (Consistency of GMM): Under Assumptions SIV.1–SIV.3, $\hat{\boldsymbol{\beta}} \xrightarrow{p} \boldsymbol{\beta}$ as $N \to \infty$.

Proof: Write

$$\hat{\boldsymbol{\beta}} = \left[\left(N^{-1} \sum_{i=1}^{N} \mathbf{X}_i'\mathbf{Z}_i \right) \hat{\mathbf{W}} \left(N^{-1} \sum_{i=1}^{N} \mathbf{Z}_i'\mathbf{X}_i \right) \right]^{-1} \left(N^{-1} \sum_{i=1}^{N} \mathbf{X}_i'\mathbf{Z}_i \right) \hat{\mathbf{W}} \left(N^{-1} \sum_{i=1}^{N} \mathbf{Z}_i'\mathbf{y}_i \right).$$

Plugging in $\mathbf{y}_i = \mathbf{X}_i\boldsymbol{\beta} + \mathbf{u}_i$ and doing a little algebra gives

$$\hat{\boldsymbol{\beta}} = \boldsymbol{\beta} + \left[\left(N^{-1} \sum_{i=1}^{N} \mathbf{X}_i'\mathbf{Z}_i \right) \hat{\mathbf{W}} \left(N^{-1} \sum_{i=1}^{N} \mathbf{Z}_i'\mathbf{X}_i \right) \right]^{-1} \left(N^{-1} \sum_{i=1}^{N} \mathbf{X}_i'\mathbf{Z}_i \right) \hat{\mathbf{W}} \left(N^{-1} \sum_{i=1}^{N} \mathbf{Z}_i'\mathbf{u}_i \right).$$

Under Assumption SIV.2, $\mathbf{C} \equiv \mathrm{E}(\mathbf{Z}_i'\mathbf{X}_i)$ has rank K, and combining this with Assumption SIV.3, $\mathbf{C}'\mathbf{W}\mathbf{C}$ has rank K and is therefore nonsingular. It follows by the law of large numbers that plim $\hat{\boldsymbol{\beta}} = \boldsymbol{\beta} + (\mathbf{C}'\mathbf{W}\mathbf{C})^{-1}\mathbf{C}'\mathbf{W}(\text{plim } N^{-1} \sum_{i=1}^{N} \mathbf{Z}_i'\mathbf{u}_i) = \boldsymbol{\beta} + (\mathbf{C}'\mathbf{W}\mathbf{C})^{-1}\mathbf{C}'\mathbf{W} \cdot \mathbf{0} = \boldsymbol{\beta}$.

Theorem 8.1 shows that a large class of estimators is consistent for $\boldsymbol{\beta}$ under Assumptions SIV.1 and SIV.2, provided that we choose $\hat{\mathbf{W}}$ to satisfy modest restrictions.

When $L = K$, the GMM estimator in equation (8.28) becomes equation (8.26), no matter how we choose $\hat{\mathbf{W}}$, because $\mathbf{X}'\mathbf{Z}$ is a $K \times K$ nonsingular matrix.

We can also show that $\hat{\boldsymbol{\beta}}$ is asymptotically normally distributed under these first three assumptions.

THEOREM 8.2 (Asymptotic Normality of GMM): Under Assumptions SIV.1–SIV.3, $\sqrt{N}(\hat{\boldsymbol{\beta}} - \boldsymbol{\beta})$ is asymptotically normally distributed with mean zero and

$$\text{Avar}\,\sqrt{N}(\hat{\boldsymbol{\beta}} - \boldsymbol{\beta}) = (\mathbf{C}'\mathbf{W}\mathbf{C})^{-1}\mathbf{C}'\mathbf{W}\boldsymbol{\Lambda}\mathbf{W}\mathbf{C}(\mathbf{C}'\mathbf{W}\mathbf{C})^{-1}, \tag{8.29}$$

where

$$\boldsymbol{\Lambda} \equiv \mathrm{E}(\mathbf{Z}_i'\mathbf{u}_i\mathbf{u}_i'\mathbf{Z}_i) = \mathrm{Var}(\mathbf{Z}_i'\mathbf{u}_i). \tag{8.30}$$

We will not prove this theorem in detail as it can be reasoned from

$$\sqrt{N}(\hat{\boldsymbol{\beta}} - \boldsymbol{\beta}) = \left[\left(N^{-1}\sum_{i=1}^{N}\mathbf{X}_i'\mathbf{Z}_i\right)\hat{\mathbf{W}}\left(N^{-1}\sum_{i=1}^{N}\mathbf{Z}_i'\mathbf{X}_i\right)\right]^{-1}\left(N^{-1}\sum_{i=1}^{N}\mathbf{X}_i'\mathbf{Z}_i\right)\hat{\mathbf{W}}\left(N^{-1/2}\sum_{i=1}^{N}\mathbf{Z}_i'\mathbf{u}_i\right),$$

where we use the fact that $N^{-1/2}\sum_{i=1}^{N}\mathbf{Z}_i'\mathbf{u}_i \xrightarrow{d} \text{Normal}(\mathbf{0}, \boldsymbol{\Lambda})$. The asymptotic variance matrix in equation (8.29) looks complicated, but it can be consistently estimated. If $\hat{\boldsymbol{\Lambda}}$ is a consistent estimator of $\boldsymbol{\Lambda}$—more on this later—then equation (8.29) is consistently estimated by

$$[(\mathbf{X}'\mathbf{Z}/N)\hat{\mathbf{W}}(\mathbf{Z}'\mathbf{X}/N)]^{-1}(\mathbf{X}'\mathbf{Z}/N)\hat{\mathbf{W}}\hat{\boldsymbol{\Lambda}}\hat{\mathbf{W}}(\mathbf{Z}'\mathbf{X}/N)[(\mathbf{X}'\mathbf{Z}/N)\hat{\mathbf{W}}(\mathbf{Z}'\mathbf{X}/N)]^{-1}. \tag{8.31}$$

As usual, we estimate $\text{Avar}(\hat{\boldsymbol{\beta}})$ by dividing expression (8.31) by N.

While the general formula (8.31) is occasionally useful, it turns out that it is greatly simplified by choosing $\hat{\mathbf{W}}$ appropriately. Since this choice also (and not coincidentally) gives the asymptotically efficient estimator, we hold off discussing asymptotic variances further until we cover the optimal choice of $\hat{\mathbf{W}}$ in Section 8.3.3.

8.3.2 System Two-Stage Least Squares Estimator

A choice of $\hat{\mathbf{W}}$ that leads to a useful and familiar-looking estimator is

$$\hat{\mathbf{W}} = \left(N^{-1}\sum_{i=1}^{N}\mathbf{Z}_i'\mathbf{Z}_i\right)^{-1} = (\mathbf{Z}'\mathbf{Z}/N)^{-1}, \tag{8.32}$$

which is a consistent estimator of $[\mathrm{E}(\mathbf{Z}_i'\mathbf{Z}_i)]^{-1}$. Assumption SIV.3 simply requires that $\mathrm{E}(\mathbf{Z}_i'\mathbf{Z}_i)$ exist and be nonsingular, and these requirements are not very restrictive.

When we plug equation (8.32) into equation (8.28) and cancel N everywhere, we get

$$\hat{\boldsymbol{\beta}} = [\mathbf{X}'\mathbf{Z}(\mathbf{Z}'\mathbf{Z})^{-1}\mathbf{Z}'\mathbf{X}]^{-1}\mathbf{X}'\mathbf{Z}(\mathbf{Z}'\mathbf{Z})^{-1}\mathbf{Z}'\mathbf{Y}. \tag{8.33}$$

This looks just like the single-equation 2SLS estimator, and so we call it the **system 2SLS (S2SLS) estimator**.

When we apply equation (8.33) to the system of equations (8.12), with definitions (8.14) and (8.15), we get something very familiar. As an exercise, you should show that $\hat{\boldsymbol{\beta}}$ produces **2SLS equation by equation**. (The proof relies on the block diagonal structures of $\mathbf{Z}_i'\mathbf{Z}_i$ and $\mathbf{Z}_i'\mathbf{X}_i$ for each i.) In other words, we estimate the first equation by 2SLS using instruments $\mathbf{z}_{i1}$, the second equation by 2SLS using instruments $\mathbf{z}_{i2}$, and so on. When we stack these into one long vector, we get equation (8.33).

The interpretation of the system 2SLS estimator for the panel data model differs depending on the choice of instrument matrix. When the instrument matrix is stacked as in (8.22)—which means that we have the same number of IVs for each time period—the S2SLS estimator reduces to the **pooled 2SLS (P2SLS) estimator**. In other words, one treats the stacked panel data as a long cross section and performs standard 2SLS. If $\mathbf{Z}_i$ takes the form in (8.15), the S2SLS estimator has a different characterization. Namely, we run a first-stage regression separately for each t, $\mathbf{x}_{it}$ on $\mathbf{z}_{it}$, $i = 1, \ldots, N$, and obtain the fitted values, $\hat{\mathbf{x}}_{it} = \mathbf{z}_{it}\hat{\Pi}_t$, where $\hat{\Pi}_t$ is $L_t \times K$. Then we obtain the pooled IV estimator using $\hat{\mathbf{x}}_{it}$ (which is $1 \times K$) as the IVs for $\mathbf{x}_{it}$. The key difference in the two approaches is that the P2SLS estimator pools across time in estimating the reduced form, while the second procedure estimates a separate reduced form for each t. See Problem 8.8 for verification of these claims, or see Wooldridge (2005e).

In the next subsection we will see that the system 2SLS estimator is not necessarily the asymptotically efficient estimator. Still, it is $\sqrt{N}$-consistent and easy to compute given the data matrices $\mathbf{X}$, $\mathbf{Y}$, and $\mathbf{Z}$. This latter feature is important because we need a preliminary estimator of $\boldsymbol{\beta}$ to obtain the asymptotically efficient estimator.

8.3.3 Optimal Weighting Matrix

Given that a GMM estimator exists for any positive definite weighting matrix, it is important to have a way of choosing among all of the possibilities. It turns out that there is a choice of $\mathbf{W}$ that produces the GMM estimator with the smallest asymptotic variance.

We can appeal to expression (8.29) for a hint as to the optimal choice of $\mathbf{W}$. It is this expression we are trying to make as small as possible, in the matrix sense. (See Definition 3.11 for the definition of relative asymptotic efficiency.) The expression

(8.29) simplifies to $(\mathbf{C}'\mathbf{\Lambda}^{-1}\mathbf{C})^{-1}$ if we set $\mathbf{W} \equiv \mathbf{\Lambda}^{-1}$. Using standard arguments from matrix algebra, it can be shown that $(\mathbf{C}'\mathbf{W}\mathbf{C})^{-1}\mathbf{C}'\mathbf{W}\mathbf{\Lambda}\mathbf{W}\mathbf{C}(\mathbf{C}'\mathbf{W}\mathbf{C})^{-1} - (\mathbf{C}'\mathbf{\Lambda}^{-1}\mathbf{C})^{-1}$ is positive semidefinite for any $L \times L$ positive definite matrix $\mathbf{W}$. The easiest way to prove this point is to show that

$$(\mathbf{C}'\mathbf{\Lambda}^{-1}\mathbf{C}) - (\mathbf{C}'\mathbf{W}\mathbf{C})(\mathbf{C}'\mathbf{W}\mathbf{\Lambda}\mathbf{W}\mathbf{C})^{-1}(\mathbf{C}'\mathbf{W}\mathbf{C}) \tag{8.34}$$

is positive semidefinite, and we leave this proof as an exercise (see Problem 8.5). This discussion motivates the following assumption and theorem.

ASSUMPTION SIV.4: $\mathbf{W} = \mathbf{\Lambda}^{-1}$, where $\mathbf{\Lambda}$ is defined by expression (8.30).

THEOREM 8.3 (Optimal Weighting Matrix): Under Assumptions SIV.1–SIV.4, the resulting GMM estimator is efficient among all GMM estimators of the form (8.28).

Provided that we can consistently estimate $\mathbf{\Lambda}$, we can obtain the asymptotically efficient GMM estimator. Any consistent estimator of $\mathbf{\Lambda}$ delivers the efficient GMM estimator, but one estimator is commonly used that imposes no structure on $\mathbf{\Lambda}$.

Procedure 8.1 (GMM with Optimal Weighting Matrix):

a. Let $\check{\boldsymbol{\beta}}$ be an initial consistent estimator of $\boldsymbol{\beta}$. In most cases this is the system 2SLS estimator.

b. Obtain the $G \times 1$ residual vectors

$$\check{\mathbf{u}}_i = \mathbf{y}_i - \mathbf{X}_i\check{\boldsymbol{\beta}}, \qquad i = 1, 2, \ldots, N \tag{8.35}$$

c. A generally consistent estimator of $\mathbf{\Lambda}$ is $\hat{\mathbf{\Lambda}} = N^{-1}\sum_{i=1}^{N} \mathbf{Z}_i'\check{\mathbf{u}}_i\check{\mathbf{u}}_i'\mathbf{Z}_i$.

d. Choose

$$\hat{\mathbf{W}} \equiv \hat{\mathbf{\Lambda}}^{-1} = \left(N^{-1}\sum_{i=1}^{N} \mathbf{Z}_i'\check{\mathbf{u}}_i\check{\mathbf{u}}_i'\mathbf{Z}_i\right)^{-1} \tag{8.36}$$

and use this matrix to obtain the asymptotically optimal GMM estimator.

The estimator of $\mathbf{\Lambda}$ in part c of Procedure 8.1 is consistent for $\mathrm{E}(\mathbf{Z}_i'\mathbf{u}_i\mathbf{u}_i'\mathbf{Z}_i)$ under general conditions. When each row of $\mathbf{Z}_i$ and $\mathbf{u}_i$ represent different time periods—so that we have a single-equation panel data model—the estimator $\hat{\mathbf{\Lambda}}$ allows for arbitrary heteroskedasticity (conditional or unconditional), as well as arbitrary serial dependence (conditional or unconditional). The reason we can allow this generality is that we fix the row dimension of $\mathbf{Z}_i$ and $\mathbf{u}_i$ and let $N \to \infty$. Therefore, we are assuming that N, the size of the cross section, is large enough relative to T to make fixed T asymptotics sensible. (This is the same approach we took in Chapter 7.) With

N very large relative to T, there is no need to downweight correlations between time periods that are far apart, as in the Newey and West (1987) estimator applied to time series problems. Ziliak and Kniesner (1998) do use a Newey-West type procedure in a panel data application with large N. Theoretically, this is not required, and it is not completely general because it assumes that the underlying time series are weakly dependent. (See Wooldridge (1994a) for discussion of weak dependence in time series contexts.) A Newey-West type estimator might improve the finite-sample performance of the GMM estimator.

The asymptotic variance of the optimal GMM estimator is estimated as

$$\left[(\mathbf{X}'\mathbf{Z})\left(\sum_{i=1}^{N}\mathbf{Z}_i'\hat{\mathbf{u}}_i\hat{\mathbf{u}}_i'\mathbf{Z}_i\right)^{-1}(\mathbf{Z}'\mathbf{X})\right]^{-1}, \tag{8.37}$$

where $\hat{\mathbf{u}}_i \equiv \mathbf{y}_i - \mathbf{X}_i\hat{\boldsymbol{\beta}}$; asymptotically, it makes no difference whether the first-stage residuals $\check{\mathbf{u}}_i$ are used in place of $\hat{\mathbf{u}}_i$. The square roots of diagonal elements of this matrix are the asymptotic standard errors of the optimal GMM estimator. This estimator is called a **minimum chi-square estimator**, for reasons that will become clear in Section 8.5.2.

When $\mathbf{Z}_i = \mathbf{X}_i$ and the $\hat{\mathbf{u}}_i$ are the system OLS residuals, expression (8.37) becomes the robust variance matrix estimator for SOLS [see expression (7.28)]. This expression reduces to the robust variance matrix estimator for FGLS when $\mathbf{Z}_i = \hat{\boldsymbol{\Omega}}^{-1}\mathbf{X}_i$ and the $\hat{\mathbf{u}}_i$ are the FGLS residuals [see equation (7.52)].

8.3.4 The Generalized Method of Moments Three-Stage Least Squares Estimator

The GMM estimator using weighting matrix (8.36) places no restrictions on either the unconditional or conditional (on $\mathbf{Z}_i$) variance matrix of $\mathbf{u}_i$: we can obtain the asymptotically efficient estimator without making additional assumptions. Nevertheless, it is still common, especially in traditional simultaneous equations analysis, to assume that the conditional variance matrix of $\mathbf{u}_i$ given $\mathbf{Z}_i$ is constant. This assumption leads to a system estimator that is a middle ground between system 2SLS and the always-efficient minimum chi-square estimator.

The **GMM three-stage least squares (GMM 3SLS) estimator** (or just 3SLS when the context is clear) is a GMM estimator that uses a particular weighting matrix. To define the 3SLS estimator, let $\check{\mathbf{u}}_i = \mathbf{y}_i - \mathbf{X}_i\check{\boldsymbol{\beta}}$ be the residuals from an initial estimation, usually system 2SLS. Define the $G \times G$ matrix

$$\hat{\boldsymbol{\Omega}} \equiv N^{-1}\sum_{i=1}^{N}\check{\mathbf{u}}_i\check{\mathbf{u}}_i'. \tag{8.38}$$

Using the same arguments as in the FGLS case in Section 7.5.1, $\hat{\boldsymbol{\Omega}} \xrightarrow{p} \boldsymbol{\Omega} = \mathrm{E}(\mathbf{u}_i \mathbf{u}_i')$. The weighting matrix used by 3SLS is

$$\hat{\mathbf{W}} = \left(N^{-1} \sum_{i=1}^{N} \mathbf{Z}_i' \hat{\boldsymbol{\Omega}} \mathbf{Z}_i\right)^{-1} = [\mathbf{Z}'(\mathbf{I}_N \otimes \hat{\boldsymbol{\Omega}})\mathbf{Z}/N]^{-1}, \tag{8.39}$$

where $\mathbf{I}_N$ is the $N \times N$ identity matrix. Plugging this into equation (8.28) gives the 3SLS estimator

$$\hat{\boldsymbol{\beta}} = [\mathbf{X}'\mathbf{Z}\{\mathbf{Z}'(\mathbf{I}_N \otimes \hat{\boldsymbol{\Omega}})\mathbf{Z}\}^{-1}\mathbf{Z}'\mathbf{X}]^{-1}\mathbf{X}'\mathbf{Z}\{\mathbf{Z}'(\mathbf{I}_N \otimes \hat{\boldsymbol{\Omega}})\mathbf{Z}\}^{-1}\mathbf{Z}'\mathbf{Y}. \tag{8.40}$$

By Theorems 8.1 and 8.2, $\hat{\boldsymbol{\beta}}$ is consistent and asymptotically normal under Assumptions SIV.1–SIV.3. Assumption SIV.3 requires $\mathrm{E}(\mathbf{Z}_i' \boldsymbol{\Omega} \mathbf{Z}_i)$ to be nonsingular, a standard assumption.

The term "three-stage least squares" is used here for historical reasons, and it will make more sense in Section 8.4. Generally, the GMM 3SLS estimator is simply given by formula equation (8.40); its computation does not require three stages.

Because the 3SLS estimator is simply a GMM estimator with a particular weighting matrix, its consistency follows from Theorem 8.1 without additional assumptions. (And the 3SLS estimator is also $\sqrt{N}$-asymptotically normal.) But a natural question to ask is, When is 3SLS an efficient GMM estimator? The answer is simple. First, note that equation (8.39) always consistently estimates $[\mathrm{E}(\mathbf{Z}_i' \boldsymbol{\Omega} \mathbf{Z}_i)]^{-1}$. Therefore, from Theorem 8.3, equation (8.39) is an efficient weighting matrix provided $\mathrm{E}(\mathbf{Z}_i' \boldsymbol{\Omega} \mathbf{Z}_i) = \boldsymbol{\Lambda} = \mathrm{E}(\mathbf{Z}_i' \mathbf{u}_i \mathbf{u}_i' \mathbf{Z}_i)$.

Assumption SIV.5: $\mathrm{E}(\mathbf{Z}_i' \mathbf{u}_i \mathbf{u}_i' \mathbf{Z}_i) = \mathrm{E}(\mathbf{Z}_i' \boldsymbol{\Omega} \mathbf{Z}_i)$, where $\boldsymbol{\Omega} \equiv \mathrm{E}(\mathbf{u}_i \mathbf{u}_i')$.

Assumption SIV.5 is the system extension of the homoskedasticity assumption for 2SLS estimation of a single equation. A sufficient condition for Assumption SIV.5, and one that is easier to interpret, is

$$\mathrm{E}(\mathbf{u}_i \mathbf{u}_i' \mid \mathbf{Z}_i) = \mathrm{E}(\mathbf{u}_i \mathbf{u}_i'). \tag{8.41}$$

We do not take equation (8.41) as the homoskedasticity assumption because there are interesting applications where Assumption SIV.5 holds but equation (8.41) does not (more on this topic in Chapters 9 and 11). When

$$\mathrm{E}(\mathbf{u}_i \mid \mathbf{Z}_i) = \mathbf{0} \tag{8.42}$$

is assumed in place of Assumption SIV.1, then equation (8.41) is equivalent to $\mathrm{Var}(\mathbf{u}_i \mid \mathbf{Z}_i) = \mathrm{Var}(\mathbf{u}_i)$. Whether we state the assumption as in equation (8.41) or use the weaker form, Assumption SIV.5, it is important to see that the elements of the unconditional variance matrix $\mathbf{\Omega}$ are *not* restricted: $\sigma_g^2 = \text{Var}(u_g)$ can change across g, and $\sigma_{gh} = \text{Cov}(u_g, u_h)$ can differ across g and h.

The system homoskedasticity assumption (8.41) necessarily holds when the instruments $\mathbf{Z}_i$ are treated as nonrandom and $\text{Var}(\mathbf{u}_i)$ is constant across i. Because we are assuming random sampling, we are forced to properly focus attention on the variance of $\mathbf{u}_i$ *conditional* on $\mathbf{Z}_i$.

For the system of equations (8.12) with instruments defined in the matrix (8.15), Assumption SIV.5 reduces to (without the i subscript)

$$\text{E}(u_g u_h \mathbf{z}_g' \mathbf{z}_h) = \text{E}(u_g u_h)\text{E}(\mathbf{z}_g' \mathbf{z}_h), \qquad g, h = 1, 2, \ldots, G. \tag{8.43}$$

Therefore, $u_g u_h$ must be uncorrelated with each of the elements of $\mathbf{z}_g' \mathbf{z}_h$. When $g = h$, assumption (8.43) becomes

$$\text{E}(u_g^2 \mathbf{z}_g' \mathbf{z}_g) = \text{E}(u_g^2)\text{E}(\mathbf{z}_g' \mathbf{z}_g), \tag{8.44}$$

so that u_g^2 is uncorrelated with each element of $\mathbf{z}_g$, along with the squares and cross products of the $\mathbf{z}_g$ elements. This is exactly the homoskedasticity assumption for single-equation IV analysis (Assumption 2SLS.3). For $g \neq h$, assumption (8.43) is new because it involves covariances across different equations.

Assumption SIV.5 implies that Assumption SIV.4 holds (because the matrix (8.39) consistently estimates $\mathbf{\Lambda}^{-1}$ under Assumption SIV.5). Therefore, we have the following theorem:

THEOREM 8.4 (Optimality of 3SLS): Under Assumptions SIV.1, SIV.2, SIV.3, and SIV.5, the 3SLS estimator is an optimal GMM estimator. Further, the appropriate estimator of $\text{Avar}(\hat{\boldsymbol{\beta}})$ is

$$\left[(\mathbf{X}'\mathbf{Z}) \left(\sum_{i=1}^{N} \mathbf{Z}_i' \hat{\mathbf{\Omega}} \mathbf{Z}_i \right)^{-1} (\mathbf{Z}'\mathbf{X}) \right]^{-1} = [\mathbf{X}'\mathbf{Z}\{\mathbf{Z}'(\mathbf{I}_N \otimes \hat{\mathbf{\Omega}})\mathbf{Z}\}^{-1}\mathbf{Z}'\mathbf{X}]^{-1}. \tag{8.45}$$

It is important to understand the implications of this theorem. First, without Assumption SIV.5, the 3SLS estimator is generally less efficient, asymptotically, than the minimum chi-square estimator, and the asymptotic variance estimator for 3SLS in equation (8.45) is inappropriate. Second, even with Assumption SIV.5, the 3SLS estimator is no more asymptotically efficient than the minimum chi-square estimator: expressions (8.36) and (8.39) are both consistent estimators of $\mathbf{\Lambda}^{-1}$ under Assumption SIV.5. In other words, the estimators based on these two different choices for $\hat{\mathbf{W}}$ are $\sqrt{N}$-equivalent under Assumption SIV.5.

Given the fact that the GMM estimator using expression (8.36) as the weighting matrix is never worse, asymptotically, than 3SLS, and in some important cases is strictly better, why is 3SLS ever used? There are at least two reasons. First, 3SLS has a long history in simultaneous equations models, whereas the GMM approach has been around only since the early 1980s, starting with the work of Hansen (1982) and White (1982b). Second, the 3SLS estimator might have better finite-sample properties than the optimal GMM estimator when Assumption SIV.5 holds. However, whether it does or not must be determined on a case-by-case basis.

There is an interesting corollary to Theorem 8.4. Suppose that in the system (8.11) we can assume $\mathrm{E}(\mathbf{X}_i \otimes \mathbf{u}_i) = \mathbf{0}$, which is a strict form of exogenecity from Chapter 7. We can use a method of moments approach to estimating $\boldsymbol{\beta}$, where the instruments for each equation, $\mathbf{x}_i^o$, is the row vector containing every row of $\mathbf{X}_i$. As shown by Im, Ahn, Schmidt, and Wooldridge (1999), the GMM 3SLS estimator using instruments $\mathbf{Z}_i = \mathbf{I}_G \otimes \mathbf{x}_i^o$ is equal to the feasible GLS estimator that uses the same $\hat{\boldsymbol{\Omega}}$. Therefore, if Assumption SIV.5 holds with $\mathbf{Z}_i = \mathbf{I}_G \otimes \mathbf{x}_i^o$, FGLS is asymptotically efficient in the class of GMM estimators that use the orthogonality condition in Assumption SGLS.1. Sufficient for Assumption SIV.5 in the GLS context is the homoskedasticity assumption $\mathrm{E}(\mathbf{u}_i \mathbf{u}_i' \mid \mathbf{X}_i) = \boldsymbol{\Omega}$.

8.4 Generalized Instrumental Variables Estimator

In this section we study a system IV estimator that is based on transforming the original set of moment conditions using a GLS-type transformation. As we will see in Section 8.6, such an approach can lead to an asymptotically efficient estimator. The cost is that, in some cases, the transformation may lead to moment conditions that are no longer valid, leading to inconsistency.

8.4.1 Derivation of the Generalized Instrumental Variables Estimator and Its Asymptotic Properties

Rather than estimating $\boldsymbol{\beta}$ using the moment conditions $\mathrm{E}[\mathbf{Z}_i'(\mathbf{y}_i - \mathbf{X}_i\boldsymbol{\beta})] = 0$, an alternative is to transform the moment conditions in a way analogous to generalized least squares. Typically, a GLS-like transformation is used in the context of a system homoskedasticity assumption such as (8.41), but we can analyze the properties of the estimator without any assumptions other than existence of the second moments. We simply let $\boldsymbol{\Omega} = \mathrm{E}(\mathbf{u}_i \mathbf{u}_i')$ as before, and we assume $\boldsymbol{\Omega}$ is positive definite. Then we transform equation (8.11), just as with a GLS analysis:

$$\boldsymbol{\Omega}^{-1/2}\mathbf{y}_i = \boldsymbol{\Omega}^{-1/2}\mathbf{X}_i\boldsymbol{\beta} + \boldsymbol{\Omega}^{-1/2}\mathbf{u}_i. \tag{8.46}$$

Because we think some elements of $\mathbf{X}_i$ are endogenous, we apply system instrumental variables to equation (8.46). In particular, we use the system 2SLS estimator with instruments $\mathbf{\Omega}^{-1/2}\mathbf{Z}_i$; that is, we transform the instruments in the same way that we transform all other variables in (8.46). The resulting estimator can be written out with full data matrices as

$$\hat{\boldsymbol{\beta}}_{GIV} = \{[\mathbf{X}'(\mathbf{I}_N \otimes \mathbf{\Omega}^{-1})\mathbf{Z}][\mathbf{Z}'(\mathbf{I}_N \otimes \mathbf{\Omega}^{-1})\mathbf{Z}]^{-1}[\mathbf{Z}'(\mathbf{I}_N \otimes \mathbf{\Omega}^{-1})\mathbf{X}]\}^{-1} \cdot [\mathbf{X}'(\mathbf{I}_N \otimes \mathbf{\Omega}^{-1})\mathbf{Z}][\mathbf{Z}'(\mathbf{I}_N \otimes \mathbf{\Omega}^{-1})\mathbf{Z}]^{-1}[\mathbf{Z}'(\mathbf{I}_N \otimes \mathbf{\Omega}^{-1})\mathbf{Y}], \tag{8.47}$$

where, for example, $\mathbf{Z}'(\mathbf{I}_N \otimes \mathbf{\Omega}^{-1})\mathbf{X} = \sum_{i=1}^N \mathbf{Z}_i'\mathbf{\Omega}^{-1}\mathbf{X}_i$. If we plug in $\mathbf{Y} = \mathbf{X}\boldsymbol{\beta} + \mathbf{U}$ and divide the last term by the sample size, then we see that the condition needed for consistency of $\hat{\boldsymbol{\beta}}$ is $N^{-1}\sum_{i=1}^N \mathbf{Z}_i'\mathbf{\Omega}^{-1}\mathbf{u}_i \xrightarrow{p} \mathbf{0}$. For completeness, a set of conditions for consistency and asymptotic normality of the GIV estimator is listed. The first assumption is the key orthogonality condition:

ASSUMPTION GIV.1: $\mathrm{E}(\mathbf{Z}_i \otimes \mathbf{u}_i) = \mathbf{0}$.

Assumption GIV.1 requires that every element of the instrument matrix is uncorrelated with every element of the vector of errors. When $\mathbf{Z}_i = \mathbf{X}_i$, Assumptions GIV.1 and SGLS.1 are identical. For consistency, we can relax Assumption GIV.1 to

$$\mathrm{E}(\mathbf{Z}_i'\mathbf{\Omega}^{-1}\mathbf{u}_i) = \mathbf{0}, \tag{8.48}$$

provided we know $\mathbf{\Omega}$ or use a consistent estimator of $\mathbf{\Omega}$. There are two reasons we adopt the stronger Assumption GIV.1. First, Assumption GIV.1 ensures that replacing $\mathbf{\Omega}$ with a consistent estimator does not affect the $\sqrt{N}$-asymptotic distribution of the GIV estimator. (Essentially the same issue arises with feasible GLS.) Second, Assumption GIV.1 implies that using an inconsistent estimator of $\mathbf{\Omega}$ (for example, if we incorrectly impose restrictions on $\mathbf{\Omega}$) does not cause inconsistency in the GIV estimator. Adopting equation (8.48) would require us to provide separate arguments for asymptotic normality in the realistic case that $\mathbf{\Omega}$ is replaced with $\hat{\mathbf{\Omega}}$, and even for consistency if we allow for inconsistent estimators of $\mathbf{\Omega}$.

An important case where equation (8.48) holds but Assumption GIV.1 might not is when $\mathbf{\Omega}$ (or, at least $\hat{\mathbf{\Omega}}$) is diagonal, in which case we should focus on equation (8.48). See, for example, Problem 8.8. (Because $\hat{\mathbf{\Omega}}$ is diagonal, we do not have to adjust the asymptotic variance of the GIV estimator for the estimation of $\hat{\mathbf{\Omega}}$.) Because Assumption GIV.1 allows for a simpler unified treatment, and because it is often implicit in applications of GIV, we adopt it here.

Naturally, we also need a rank condition:

ASSUMPTION GIV.2: (a) rank $\mathrm{E}(\mathbf{Z}_i'\mathbf{\Omega}^{-1}\mathbf{Z}_i) = L$; (b) rank $\mathrm{E}(\mathbf{Z}_i'\mathbf{\Omega}^{-1}\mathbf{X}_i) = K$.

When $G = 1$, Assumption GIV.2 reduces to Assumption 2SLS.2 from Chapter 5. Typically, GIV.2(a) holds when the instruments exclude exact linear dependencies. Assumption GIV.2(b) requires that, after the GLS-like transformation, there are enough instruments partially correlated with the endogenous elements of $\mathbf{X}_i$.

When $\boldsymbol{\Omega}$ in (8.47) is replaced with a consistent estimator, $\hat{\boldsymbol{\Omega}}$, we obtain the **generalized instrumental variables (GIV) estimator**. Typically, $\hat{\boldsymbol{\Omega}}$ would be chosen as in equation (8.38) after an initial S2SLS estimation. We have argued that the estimator is consistent under Assumptions GIV.1 and GIV.2; the details of replacing $\boldsymbol{\Omega}$ with $\hat{\boldsymbol{\Omega}}$ are very similar to the FGLS case covered in Chapter 7.

Implicit in GIV estimation is the first-stage regression $\hat{\boldsymbol{\Omega}}^{-1/2}\mathbf{X}_i$ on $\hat{\boldsymbol{\Omega}}^{-1/2}\mathbf{Z}_i$, which yields fitted values $\hat{\boldsymbol{\Omega}}^{-1/2}\mathbf{Z}_i\hat{\boldsymbol{\Pi}}^*$, where $\hat{\boldsymbol{\Pi}}^* = [\mathbf{Z}'(\mathbf{I}_N \otimes \hat{\boldsymbol{\Omega}}^{-1})\mathbf{Z}]^{-1}[\mathbf{Z}'(\mathbf{I}_N \otimes \hat{\boldsymbol{\Omega}}^{-1})\mathbf{X}$. Of course, the first-stage regression need not be carried out to compute the GIV estimator, but, in comparing GIV with other estimators, it can be useful to think of GIV as system IV estimation of $\hat{\boldsymbol{\Omega}}^{-1/2}\mathbf{y}_i = \hat{\boldsymbol{\Omega}}^{-1/2}\mathbf{X}_i\boldsymbol{\beta} + \hat{\boldsymbol{\Omega}}^{-1/2}\mathbf{u}_i$ using IVs $\hat{\boldsymbol{\Omega}}^{-1/2}\mathbf{Z}_i\hat{\boldsymbol{\Pi}}^*$.

In Chapter 7, we noted that GLS when $\boldsymbol{\Omega}$ is not a diagonal matrix must be used with caution. Assumption GIV.1 can impose unintended restrictions on the relationships between instruments and errors across equations, or time, or both. Users need to keep in mind that the GIV estimator generally requires stronger assumptions than $\mathrm{E}(\mathbf{Z}_i'\mathbf{u}_i) = \mathbf{0}$ for consistency.

As with FGLS, there is a "standard" assumption under which the GIV estimator has a simplified asymptotic variance. The assumption is an extension of Assumption SGLS.3 in Chapter 7.

ASSUMPTION GIV.3: $\mathrm{E}(\mathbf{Z}_i'\boldsymbol{\Omega}^{-1}\mathbf{u}_i\mathbf{u}_i'\boldsymbol{\Omega}^{-1}\mathbf{Z}_i) = \mathrm{E}(\mathbf{Z}_i'\boldsymbol{\Omega}^{-1}\mathbf{Z}_i)$.

A sufficient condition for GIV.3 is (8.41), the same assumption that is sufficient for the GMM 3SLS estimator to use the optimal weighting matrix. Under Assumptions GIV.1, GIV.2, and GIV.3, it is easy to show

$$\mathrm{Avar}[\sqrt{N}(\hat{\boldsymbol{\beta}}_{GIV} - \boldsymbol{\beta})] = \{\mathrm{E}(\mathbf{X}_i'\boldsymbol{\Omega}^{-1}\mathbf{Z}_i)[\mathrm{E}(\mathbf{Z}_i'\boldsymbol{\Omega}^{-1}\mathbf{Z}_i)]^{-1}\mathrm{E}(\mathbf{Z}_i'\boldsymbol{\Omega}^{-1}\mathbf{X}_i)\}^{-1}, \tag{8.49}$$

and this matrix is easily estimated by the usual process of replacing expectations with sample averages and $\boldsymbol{\Omega}$ with $\hat{\boldsymbol{\Omega}}$.

8.4.2 Comparison of Generalized Method of Moment, Generalized Instrumental Variables, and the Traditional Three-Stage Least Squares Estimator

Especially in estimating standard simultaneous equations models, a different kind of GLS transformation is often used. Rather than use an FGLS estimator in the first stage, as is implicit in GIV, the **traditional 3SLS estimator** is typically motivated as follows. The first stage uses untransformed $\mathbf{X}_i$ and $\mathbf{Z}_i$, giving fitted values $\hat{\mathbf{X}}_i = \mathbf{Z}_i\hat{\Pi}$, where $\hat{\Pi} = (\mathbf{Z}'\mathbf{Z})^{-1}\mathbf{Z}'\mathbf{X}$ is the matrix of first-stage regression coefficients. Then, equation (8.46) is estimated by system IV, but with instruments $\mathbf{\Omega}^{-1/2}\hat{\mathbf{X}}_i$. When we replace $\mathbf{\Omega}$ with its estimate, we arrive at the estimator

$$\hat{\boldsymbol{\beta}}_{T3SLS} = \left(\sum_{i=1}^{N}\hat{\mathbf{X}}_i'\hat{\mathbf{\Omega}}^{-1}\mathbf{X}_i\right)^{-1}\left(\sum_{i=1}^{N}\hat{\mathbf{X}}_i'\hat{\mathbf{\Omega}}^{-1}\mathbf{y}_i\right), \tag{8.50}$$

where the subscript "T3SLS" denotes "traditional" 3SLS. Substituting $\mathbf{y}_i = \mathbf{X}_i\boldsymbol{\beta} + \mathbf{u}_i$ and rearranging shows that the orthogonality condition needed for consistency is

$$\mathrm{E}[(\mathbf{Z}_i\Pi)'\mathbf{\Omega}^{-1}\mathbf{u}_i] = \Pi'\mathrm{E}(\mathbf{Z}_i'\mathbf{\Omega}^{-1}\mathbf{u}_i) = \mathbf{0}, \tag{8.51}$$

where $\Pi = \mathrm{plim}(\hat{\Pi})$. Because of the presence of Π', condition (8.51) is not quite the same as Assumption GIV.1, but it would be a fluke if (8.51) held but GIV.1 did not. Like the GIV estimator, the consistency of the traditional 3SLS estimator does not follow from $\mathrm{E}(\mathbf{Z}_i'\mathbf{u}_i) = \mathbf{0}$.

We have now discussed three different estimators of a system of equations based on estimating the variance matrix $\mathbf{\Omega} = \mathrm{E}(\mathbf{u}_i\mathbf{u}_i')$. Why have seemingly different estimators been given the label "three-stage least squares"? The answer is simple: In the setting that the traditional 3SLS estimator was proposed—system (8.12), with the same instruments used in every equation—all estimates are identical. In fact, the equivalence of all estimates holds if we just impose the common instrument assumption. Let $\mathbf{w}_i$ denote a vector assumed to be exogenous in every equation in the sense that $\mathrm{E}(\mathbf{w}_i'u_{ig}) = \mathbf{0}$ for $g = 1, \ldots, G$. In other words, any variable exogenous in one equation is exogenous in all equations. For a system such as (8.12), this means that the same instruments can be used for every equation. In a panel data setting, it means the chosen instruments are strictly exogenous. In either case, it makes sense to choose the instrument matrix as

$$\mathbf{Z}_i = \mathbf{I}_G \otimes \mathbf{w}_i, \tag{8.52}$$

which is a special case of (8.15). It follows from the results of Im, Ahn, Schmidt, and Wooldridge (1999) that the GMM 3SLS estimator and the GIV estimator (using the same $\hat{\mathbf{\Omega}}$) are identical. Further, it can be shown that the GIV estimator and the traditional 3SLS estimator are identical. (This follows because the first-stage regressions involve the same set of explanatory variables, $\mathbf{w}_i$, and so it does not matter whether the matrix of first-stage regression coefficients is obtained via FGLS, which is what GIV does, or system OLS, which is what T3SLS does.)

In many modern applications of system IV methods to both simultaneous equations and panel data, instruments that are exogenous in one equation are not exogenous in all other equations. In such cases it is important to use the GMM 3SLS estimator once $\mathbf{Z}_i$ has been properly chosen. Of course, the minimum chi-square estimator that does not impose SIV.5 is always available, too. The GIV estimator and the traditional 3SLS estimator generally induce correlation between the transformed instruments and the structural errors. For this reason, we will tend to focus on GMM methods based on the original orthogonality conditions. Nevertheless, particularly in Chapter 11, we will see that the GIV approach can provide insights into the workings of certain panel data estimators while also affording computational simplicity.

8.5 Testing Using Generalized Method of Moments

8.5.1 Testing Classical Hypotheses

Testing hypotheses after GMM estimation is straightforward. Let $\hat{\boldsymbol{\beta}}$ denote a GMM estimator, and let $\hat{\mathbf{V}}$ denote its estimated asymptotic variance. Although the following analysis can be made more general, in most applications we use an optimal GMM estimator. Without Assumption SIV.5, the weighting matrix would be expression (8.36) and $\hat{\mathbf{V}}$ would be as in expression (8.37). This can be used for computing t statistics by obtaining the asymptotic standard errors (square roots of the diagonal elements of $\hat{\mathbf{V}}$). Wald statistics of linear hypotheses of the form H_0: $\mathbf{R}\boldsymbol{\beta} = \mathbf{r}$, where $\mathbf{R}$ is a $Q \times K$ matrix with rank Q, are obtained using the same statistic we have already seen several times. Under Assumption SIV.5 we can use the 3SLS estimator and its asymptotic variance estimate in equation (8.45). For testing general system hypotheses, we would probably not use the 2SLS estimator, because its asymptotic variance is more complicated unless we make very restrictive assumptions.

An alternative method for testing linear restrictions uses a statistic based on the difference in the GMM objective function with and without the restrictions imposed. To apply this statistic, we must assume that the GMM estimator uses the optimal weighting matrix, so that $\hat{\mathbf{W}}$ consistently estimates $[\mathrm{Var}(\mathbf{Z}_i'\mathbf{u}_i)]^{-1}$. Then, from Lemma 3.8,

$$\left(N^{-1/2}\sum_{i=1}^{N}\mathbf{Z}_i'\mathbf{u}_i\right)'\hat{\mathbf{W}}\left(N^{-1/2}\sum_{i=1}^{N}\mathbf{Z}_i'\mathbf{u}_i\right) \overset{a}{\sim} \chi^2_L \tag{8.53}$$

since $\mathbf{Z}_i'\mathbf{u}_i$ is an $L \times 1$ vector with zero mean and variance $\boldsymbol{\Lambda}$. If $\hat{\mathbf{W}}$ does not consistently estimate $[\mathrm{Var}(\mathbf{Z}_i'\mathbf{u}_i)]^{-1}$, then result (8.53) is false, and the following method does not produce an asymptotically chi-square statistic.

Let $\hat{\boldsymbol{\beta}}$ again be the GMM estimator, using optimal weighting matrix $\hat{\mathbf{W}}$, obtained without imposing the restrictions. Let $\tilde{\boldsymbol{\beta}}$ be the GMM estimator using the *same* weighting matrix $\hat{\mathbf{W}}$ but obtained with the Q linear restrictions imposed. The restricted estimator can always be obtained by estimating a linear model with $K - Q$ rather than K parameters. Define the unrestricted and restricted residuals as $\hat{\mathbf{u}}_i \equiv \mathbf{y}_i - \mathbf{X}_i\hat{\boldsymbol{\beta}}$ and $\tilde{\mathbf{u}}_i \equiv \mathbf{y}_i - \mathbf{X}_i\tilde{\boldsymbol{\beta}}$, respectively. It can be shown that, under H_0, the **GMM distance statistic** has a limiting chi-square distribution:

$$\left[\left(\sum_{i=1}^N \mathbf{Z}_i'\tilde{\mathbf{u}}_i\right)'\hat{\mathbf{W}}\left(\sum_{i=1}^N \mathbf{Z}_i'\tilde{\mathbf{u}}_i\right) - \left(\sum_{i=1}^N \mathbf{Z}_i'\hat{\mathbf{u}}_i\right)'\hat{\mathbf{W}}\left(\sum_{i=1}^N \mathbf{Z}_i'\hat{\mathbf{u}}_i\right)\right]\Big/N \overset{a}{\sim} \chi^2_Q. \tag{8.54}$$

See, for example, Hansen (1982) and Gallant (1987). The GMM distance statistic is simply the difference in the criterion function (8.27) evaluated at the restricted and unrestricted estimates, divided by the sample size, N. For this reason, expression (8.54) is called a **criterion function statistic**. Because constrained minimization cannot result in a smaller objective function than unconstrained minimization, expression (8.54) is always nonnegative and usually strictly positive.

Under Assumption SIV.5 we can use the 3SLS estimator, in which case expression (8.54) becomes

$$\left(\sum_{i=1}^N \mathbf{Z}_i'\tilde{\mathbf{u}}_i\right)'\left(\sum_{i=1}^N \mathbf{Z}_i'\hat{\boldsymbol{\Omega}}\mathbf{Z}_i\right)^{-1}\left(\sum_{i=1}^N \mathbf{Z}_i'\tilde{\mathbf{u}}_i\right) - \left(\sum_{i=1}^N \mathbf{Z}_i'\hat{\mathbf{u}}_i\right)'\left(\sum_{i=1}^N \mathbf{Z}_i'\hat{\boldsymbol{\Omega}}\mathbf{Z}_i\right)^{-1}\left(\sum_{i=1}^N \mathbf{Z}_i'\hat{\mathbf{u}}_i\right), \tag{8.55}$$

where $\hat{\boldsymbol{\Omega}}$ would probably be computed using the 2SLS residuals from estimating the unrestricted model. The division by N has disappeared because of the definition of $\hat{\mathbf{W}}$; see equation (8.39).

Testing nonlinear hypotheses is easy once the unrestricted estimator $\hat{\boldsymbol{\beta}}$ has been obtained. Write the null hypothesis as

$$H_0\colon \mathbf{c}(\boldsymbol{\beta}) = \mathbf{0}, \tag{8.56}$$

where $\mathbf{c}(\boldsymbol{\beta}) \equiv [c_1(\boldsymbol{\beta}), c_2(\boldsymbol{\beta}), \ldots, c_Q(\boldsymbol{\beta})]'$ is a $Q \times 1$ vector of functions. Let $\mathbf{C}(\boldsymbol{\beta})$ denote the $Q \times K$ Jacobian of $\mathbf{c}(\boldsymbol{\beta})$. Assuming that rank $\mathbf{C}(\boldsymbol{\beta}) = Q$, the Wald statistic is

$$W = \mathbf{c}(\hat{\boldsymbol{\beta}})'(\hat{\mathbf{C}}\hat{\mathbf{V}}\hat{\mathbf{C}}')^{-1}\mathbf{c}(\hat{\boldsymbol{\beta}}), \tag{8.57}$$

where $\hat{\mathbf{C}} \equiv \mathbf{C}(\hat{\boldsymbol{\beta}})$ is the Jacobian evaluated at the GMM estimate $\hat{\boldsymbol{\beta}}$. Under H_0, the Wald statistic has an asymptotic χ^2_Q distribution.

8.5.2 Testing Overidentification Restrictions

Just as in the case of single-equation analysis with more exogenous variables than explanatory variables, we can test whether overidentifying restrictions are valid in a system context. In the model (8.11) with instrument matrix $\mathbf{Z}_i$, where $\mathbf{X}_i$ is $G \times K$ and $\mathbf{Z}_i$ is $G \times L$, there are overidentifying restrictions if $L > K$. Assuming that $\hat{\mathbf{W}}$ is an optimal weighting matrix, it can be shown that

$$\left(N^{-1/2}\sum_{i=1}^{N}\mathbf{Z}_i'\hat{\mathbf{u}}_i\right)'\hat{\mathbf{W}}\left(N^{-1/2}\sum_{i=1}^{N}\mathbf{Z}_i'\hat{\mathbf{u}}_i\right) \overset{a}{\sim} \chi^2_{L-K} \tag{8.58}$$

under the null hypothesis H_0: $\mathrm{E}(\mathbf{Z}_i'\mathbf{u}_i) = \mathbf{0}$. The asymptotic χ^2_{L-K} distribution is similar to result (8.53), but expression (8.53) contains the unobserved errors, $\mathbf{u}_i$, whereas expression (8.58) contains the residuals, $\hat{\mathbf{u}}_i$. Replacing $\mathbf{u}_i$ with $\hat{\mathbf{u}}_i$ causes the degrees of freedom to fall from L to $L - K$: in effect, K orthogonality conditions have been used to compute $\hat{\boldsymbol{\beta}}$, and $L - K$ are left over for testing.

The **overidentification test statistic** in expression (8.58) is just the objective function (8.27) evaluated at the solution $\hat{\boldsymbol{\beta}}$ and divided by N. It is because of expression (8.58) that the GMM estimator using the optimal weighting matrix is called the minimum chi-square estimator: $\hat{\boldsymbol{\beta}}$ is chosen to make the minimum of the objective function have an asymptotic chi-square distribution. If $\hat{\mathbf{W}}$ is not optimal, expression (8.58) fails to hold, making it much more difficult to test the overidentifying restrictions. When $L = K$, the left-hand side of expression (8.58) is identically zero; there are no overidentifying restrictions to be tested.

Under Assumption SIV.5, the 3SLS estimator is a minimum chi-square estimator, and the overidentification statistic in equation (8.58) can be written as

$$\left(\sum_{i=1}^{N}\mathbf{Z}_i'\hat{\mathbf{u}}_i\right)'\left(\sum_{i=1}^{N}\mathbf{Z}_i'\hat{\boldsymbol{\Omega}}\mathbf{Z}_i\right)^{-1}\left(\sum_{i=1}^{N}\mathbf{Z}_i'\hat{\mathbf{u}}_i\right). \tag{8.59}$$

Without Assumption SIV.5, the limiting distribution of this statistic is not chi square.

In the case where the model has the form (8.12), overidentification test statistics can be used to choose between a systems and a single-equation method. For example, if the test statistic (8.59) rejects the overidentifying restrictions in the entire system, then the 3SLS estimators of the first equation are generally inconsistent. Assuming that the single-equation 2SLS estimation passes the overidentification test discussed in Chapter 6, 2SLS would be preferred. However, in making this judgment it is, as always, important to compare the magnitudes of the two sets of estimates in addition to the statistical significance of test statistics. Hausman (1983, p. 435) shows how to construct a statistic based directly on the 3SLS and 2SLS estimates of a particular equation (assuming that 3SLS is asymptotically more efficient under the null), and this discussion can be extended to allow for the more general minimum chi-square estimator.

8.6 More Efficient Estimation and Optimal Instruments

In Section 8.3.3 we characterized the optimal weighting matrix given the matrix $\mathbf{Z}_i$ of instruments. But this discussion begs the question of how we can best choose $\mathbf{Z}_i$. In this section we briefly discuss two efficiency results. The first has to do with adding valid instruments.

To be precise, let $\mathbf{Z}_{i1}$ be a $G \times L_1$ submatrix of the $G \times L$ matrix $\mathbf{Z}_i$, where $\mathbf{Z}_i$ satisfies Assumptions SIV.1 and SIV.2. We also assume that $\mathbf{Z}_{i1}$ satisfies Assumption SIV.2; that is, $\mathrm{E}(\mathbf{Z}_{i1}'\mathbf{X}_i)$ has rank K. This assumption ensures that $\boldsymbol{\beta}$ is identified using the smaller set of instruments. (Necessary is $L_1 \geq K$.) Given $\mathbf{Z}_{i1}$, we know that the efficient GMM estimator uses a weighting matrix that is consistent for $\boldsymbol{\Lambda}_1^{-1}$, where $\boldsymbol{\Lambda}_1 = \mathrm{E}(\mathbf{Z}_{i1}'\mathbf{u}_i\mathbf{u}_i'\mathbf{Z}_{i1})$. When we use the full set of instruments $\mathbf{Z}_i = (\mathbf{Z}_{i1}, \mathbf{Z}_{i2})$, the optimal weighting matrix is a consistent estimator of $\boldsymbol{\Lambda}$ given in expression (8.30). Can we say that using the full set of instruments (with the optimal weighting matrix) is better than using the reduced set of instruments (with the optimal weighting matrix)? The answer is that, asymptotically, we can do no worse, and often we can do better, using a larger set of valid instruments.

The proof that adding orthogonality conditions generally improves efficiency proceeds by comparing the asymptotic variances of $\sqrt{N}(\tilde{\boldsymbol{\beta}} - \boldsymbol{\beta})$ and $\sqrt{N}(\hat{\boldsymbol{\beta}} - \boldsymbol{\beta})$, where the former estimator uses the restricted set of IVs and the latter uses the full set. Then

$$\text{Avar } \sqrt{N}(\tilde{\boldsymbol{\beta}} - \boldsymbol{\beta}) - \text{Avar } \sqrt{N}(\hat{\boldsymbol{\beta}} - \boldsymbol{\beta}) = (\mathbf{C}_1'\boldsymbol{\Lambda}_1^{-1}\mathbf{C}_1)^{-1} - (\mathbf{C}'\boldsymbol{\Lambda}^{-1}\mathbf{C})^{-1}, \tag{8.60}$$

where $\mathbf{C}_1 = \mathrm{E}(\mathbf{Z}_{i1}'\mathbf{X}_i)$. The difference in equation (8.60) is positive semidefinite if and only if $\mathbf{C}'\boldsymbol{\Lambda}^{-1}\mathbf{C} - \mathbf{C}_1'\boldsymbol{\Lambda}_1^{-1}\mathbf{C}_1$ is p.s.d. The latter result is shown by White (2001, Proposition 4.51) using the formula for partitioned inverse; we will not reproduce it here.

The previous argument shows that we can never do worse asymptotically by adding instruments and computing the minimum chi-square estimator. But we need not always do better. The proof in White (2001) shows that the asymptotic variances of $\tilde{\boldsymbol{\beta}}$ and $\hat{\boldsymbol{\beta}}$ are identical if and only if

$$\mathbf{C}_2 = \mathrm{E}(\mathbf{Z}_{i2}'\mathbf{u}_i\mathbf{u}_i'\mathbf{Z}_{i1})\boldsymbol{\Lambda}_1^{-1}\mathbf{C}_1, \tag{8.61}$$

where $\mathbf{C}_2 = \mathrm{E}(\mathbf{Z}_{i2}'\mathbf{X}_i)$. Generally, this condition is difficult to check. However, if we assume that $\mathrm{E}(\mathbf{Z}_i'\mathbf{u}_i\mathbf{u}_i'\mathbf{Z}_i) = \sigma^2\mathrm{E}(\mathbf{Z}_i'\mathbf{Z}_i)$—the ideal assumption for system 2SLS—then condition (8.61) becomes

$$\mathrm{E}(\mathbf{Z}_{i2}'\mathbf{X}_i) = \mathrm{E}(\mathbf{Z}_{i2}'\mathbf{Z}_{i1})[\mathrm{E}(\mathbf{Z}_{i1}'\mathbf{Z}_{i1})]^{-1}\mathrm{E}(\mathbf{Z}_{i1}'\mathbf{X}_i).$$

Straightforward algebra shows that this condition is equivalent to

$$\mathrm{E}[(\mathbf{Z}_{i2} - \mathbf{Z}_{i1}\mathbf{D}_1)'\mathbf{X}_i] = \mathbf{0}, \tag{8.62}$$

where $\mathbf{D}_1 = [\mathrm{E}(\mathbf{Z}_{i1}'\mathbf{Z}_{i1})]^{-1}\mathrm{E}(\mathbf{Z}_{i1}'\mathbf{Z}_{i2})$ is the $L_1 \times L_2$ matrix of coefficients from the population regression of $\mathbf{Z}_{i2}$ on $\mathbf{Z}_{i1}$. Therefore, condition (8.62) has a simple interpretation: $\mathbf{X}_i$ is orthogonal to the part of $\mathbf{Z}_{i2}$ that is left after netting out $\mathbf{Z}_{i1}$. This statement means that $\mathbf{Z}_{i2}$ is not *partially* correlated with $\mathbf{X}_i$, and so it is not useful as instruments once $\mathbf{Z}_{i1}$ has been included.

Condition (8.62) is very intuitive in the context of 2SLS estimation of a single equation. Under $\mathrm{E}(u_i^2\mathbf{z}_i'\mathbf{z}_i) = \sigma^2\mathrm{E}(\mathbf{z}_i'\mathbf{z}_i)$, 2SLS is the minimum chi-square estimator. The elements of $\mathbf{z}_i$ would include all exogenous elements of $\mathbf{x}_i$, and then some. If, say, x_{iK} is the only endogenous element of $\mathbf{x}_i$, condition (8.62) becomes

$$\mathrm{L}(x_{iK} \mid \mathbf{z}_{i1}, \mathbf{z}_{i2}) = \mathrm{L}(x_{iK} \mid \mathbf{z}_{i1}), \tag{8.63}$$

so that the linear projection of x_{iK} onto $\mathbf{z}_i$ depends only on $\mathbf{z}_{i1}$. If you recall how the IVs for 2SLS are obtained—by estimating the linear projection of x_{iK} on $\mathbf{z}_i$ in the first stage—it makes perfectly good sense that $\mathbf{z}_{i2}$ can be omitted under condition (8.63) without affecting efficiency of 2SLS.

In the general case, if the error vector $\mathbf{u}_i$ contains conditional heteroskedasticity, or correlation across its elements (conditional or otherwise), condition (8.61) is unlikely to be true. As a result, we can keep improving asymptotic efficiency by adding more valid instruments. Whenever the error term satisfies a zero conditional mean assumption, unlimited IVs are available. For example, consider the linear model $\mathrm{E}(y \mid \mathbf{x}) = \mathbf{x}\boldsymbol{\beta}$, so that the error $u = y - \mathbf{x}\boldsymbol{\beta}$ has a zero mean given $\mathbf{x}$. The OLS estimator is the IV estimator using IVs $\mathbf{z}_1 = \mathbf{x}$. The preceding efficiency result implies that, if $\mathrm{Var}(u \mid \mathbf{x}) \neq \mathrm{Var}(u)$, there are unlimited minimum chi-square estimators that are asymptotically more efficient than OLS. Because $\mathrm{E}(u \mid \mathbf{x}) = 0$, $\mathbf{h}(\mathbf{x})$ is a valid set of IVs for any vector function $\mathbf{h}(\cdot)$. (Assuming, as always, that the appropriate moments exist.) Then, the minimum chi-square estimate using IVs $\mathbf{z} = [\mathbf{x}, \mathbf{h}(\mathbf{x})]$ is generally more asymptotically efficient than OLS. (Chamberlain, 1982, and Cragg, 1983, independently obtained this result.) If $\mathrm{Var}(y \mid \mathbf{x})$ is constant, adding functions of $\mathbf{x}$ to the IV list results in no asymptotic improvement because the linear projection of $\mathbf{x}$ onto $\mathbf{x}$ and $\mathbf{h}(\mathbf{x})$ obviously does not depend on $\mathbf{h}(\mathbf{x})$.

Under homoskedasticity, adding moment conditions does not reduce the asymptotic efficiency of the minimum chi-square estimator. Therefore, it may seem that, when we have a linear model that represents a conditional expectation, we cannot lose by adding IVs and performing minimum chi-square. (Plus, we can then test the functional form $\mathrm{E}(y \mid \mathbf{x}) = \mathbf{x}\boldsymbol{\beta}$ by testing the overidentifying restrictions.) Unfortunately, as shown by several authors, including Tauchen (1986), Altonji and Segal (1996), and Ziliak (1997), GMM estimators that use many overidentifying restrictions can have very poor finite sample properties.

The previous discussion raises the following possibility: rather than adding more and more orthogonality conditions to improve on inefficient estimators, can we find a small set of optimal IVs? The answer is yes, provided we replace Assumption SIV.1 with a zero conditional mean assumption.

ASSUMPTION SIV.1′: $\mathrm{E}(u_{ig} \mid \mathbf{w}_i) = 0$, $g = 1, \ldots, G$ for some vector $\mathbf{w}_i$.

Assumption SIV.1′ implies that $\mathbf{w}_i$ is exogenous in *every* equation, and each element of the instrument matrix $\mathbf{Z}_i$ can be *any* function of $\mathbf{w}_i$.

THEOREM 8.5 (Optimal Instruments): Under Assumption SIV.1′ (and sufficient regularity conditions), the optimal choice of instruments is $\mathbf{Z}_i^* = \boldsymbol{\Omega}(\mathbf{w}_i)^{-1}\mathrm{E}(\mathbf{X}_i \mid \mathbf{w}_i)$, where $\boldsymbol{\Omega}(\mathbf{w}_i) \equiv \mathrm{E}(\mathbf{u}_i'\mathbf{u}_i \mid \mathbf{w}_i)$, provided that rank $\mathrm{E}(\mathbf{Z}_i^{*\prime}\mathbf{X}_i) = K$.

We will not prove Theorem 8.5 here. We discuss a more general case in Section 14.5; see also Newey and McFadden (1994, Section 5.4). Theorem 8.5 implies that, if the $G \times K$ matrix $\mathbf{Z}_i^*$ were available, we would use it in equation (8.26) in place of $\mathbf{Z}_i$ to obtain the SIV estimator with the smallest asymptotic variance. This would take the arbitrariness out of choosing additional functions of $\mathbf{z}_i$ to add to the IV list: once we have $\mathbf{Z}_i^*$, all other functions of $\mathbf{w}_i$ are redundant.

Theorem 8.5 implies that if Assumption SIV.1′, the system homoskedasticity assumption (8.41), *and* $\mathrm{E}(\mathbf{X}_i \mid \mathbf{w}_i) = (\mathbf{I}_G \otimes \mathbf{w}_i)\Pi \equiv \mathbf{Z}_i\Pi$ hold, then the optimal instruments are simply $\mathbf{Z}_i^* = \boldsymbol{\Omega}^{-1}(\mathbf{Z}_i\Pi)$. But this choice of instruments leads directly to the traditional 3SLS estimator in equation (8.50) when $\boldsymbol{\Omega}$ and Π are replaced by their $\sqrt{N}$-consistent estimators. As we discussed in Section 8.4.2, this estimator is identical to the GIV estimator and GMM 3SLS estimator.

If $\mathrm{E}(\mathbf{u}_i \mid \mathbf{X}_i) = \mathbf{0}$ and $\mathrm{E}(\mathbf{u}_i\mathbf{u}_i' \mid \mathbf{X}_i) = \boldsymbol{\Omega}$, then the optimal instruments are $\boldsymbol{\Omega}^{-1}\mathbf{X}_i$, which gives the GLS estimator. Replacing $\boldsymbol{\Omega}$ by $\hat{\boldsymbol{\Omega}}$ has no effect asymptotically, and so the FGLS is the SIV estimator with optimal choice of instruments.

Without further assumptions, both $\boldsymbol{\Omega}(\mathbf{w}_i)$ and $\mathrm{E}(\mathbf{X}_i \mid \mathbf{w}_i)$ can be arbitrary functions of $\mathbf{w}_i$, in which case the optimal SIV estimator is not easily obtainable. It is possible to find an estimator that is asymptotically efficient using *nonparametric* estimation methods to estimate $\mathbf{\Omega}(\mathbf{w}_i)$ and $\mathrm{E}(\mathbf{X}_i \mid \mathbf{w}_i)$, but there are many practical hurdles to overcome in applying such procedures. See Newey (1990) for an approach that approximates $\mathrm{E}(\mathbf{X}_i \mid \mathbf{w}_i)$ by parametric functional forms, where the approximation gets better as the sample size grows.

8.7 Summary Comments on Choosing an Estimator

Throughout this chapter we have commented on the robustness and efficiency of different estimators. It is useful here to summarize the considerations behind choosing among estimators for systems or panel data applications.

Generally, if we have started with moment conditions of the form $\mathrm{E}(\mathbf{Z}_i'\mathbf{u}_i) = \mathbf{0}$, GMM estimation based on this set of moment conditions will be more robust than estimators based on a transformed set of moment conditions, such as GIV. If we decide to use GMM, we can use the unrestricted weighting matrix, as in (8.36), or we might use the GMM 3SLS estimator, which uses weighting matrix (8.39). Under Assumption SIV.5, which is a system homoskedasticity assumption, the 3SLS estimator is asymptotically efficient. In an important special case, where the instruments can be chosen as in (8.52), GMM 3SLS, GIV, and traditional 3SLS are identical. When GMM and GIV are both consistent but are not $\sqrt{N}$-asymptotically equivalent, they cannot generally be ranked in terms of asymptotic efficiency.

One of the efficiency results of the previous section is that one can never do worse by adding instruments and using the efficient weighting matrix in GMM. This has implications for panel data applications. For example, if one has the option of choosing the instruments as in equation (8.22) or equation (8.15) (with $G = T$), the efficient GMM estimator using equation (8.15) is no less efficient, asymptotically, than the efficient GMM estimator using equation (8.22). This follows because we can obtain (8.22) as a linear combination of (8.15), and using a linear combination is operationally the same as using a restricted set of instruments.

What about the choice between the S2SLS and the GMM 3SLS estimators? Under the assumptions of Theorem 8.4, GMM 3SLS is asymptotically no less efficient than S2SLS. Nevertheless, it is useful to know that there are situations where S2SLS and GMM 3SLS coincide.

The first is easy: when the general system (8.11) is just identified, that is, $L = K$, all estimators reduce to the IV estimator in equation (8.26). In the case of the SUR system (8.12), the system is just identified if and only if each equation is just identified: $L_g = K_g$, $g = 1, \ldots, G$ and the rank condition holds for each equation.

When estimating system (8.12), there is another case where S2SLS—which, recall, reduces to 2SLS estimation of each equation—coincides with 3SLS, regardless of the degree of overidentification. The 3SLS estimator is equivalent to 2SLS equation by equation when $\hat{\mathbf{\Omega}}$ is a diagonal matrix, that is, $\hat{\mathbf{\Omega}} = \text{diag}(\hat{\sigma}_1^2, \hat{\sigma}_2^2, \ldots, \hat{\sigma}_G^2)$; see Problem 8.7.

The algebraic equivalence of system 2SLS and 3SLS for estimating (8.12) when $\hat{\mathbf{\Omega}}$ is a diagonal matrix allows us to conclude that S2SLS and 3SLS are *asymptotically* equivalent when $\mathbf{\Omega}$ is diagonal. The reason is simple. If we could use $\mathbf{\Omega}$ in the 3SLS estimator, then it would be identical to 2SLS equation by equation. The actual 3SLS estimator, which uses $\hat{\mathbf{\Omega}}$, is $\sqrt{N}$-equivalent to the hypothetical 3SLS estimator that uses $\mathbf{\Omega}$. Therefore, 3SLS and 2SLS are $\sqrt{N}$-equivalent.

Even in cases where 2SLS on each equation is not algebraically or asymptotically equivalent to 3SLS, it is not necessarily true that we should prefer the 3SLS estimator (or the minimum chi-square estimator more generally). Why? Suppose primary interest lies in estimating the parameters of the first equation, $\boldsymbol{\beta}_1$. On the one hand, we know that 2SLS estimation of this equation produces consistent estimators under the orthogonality conditions $\text{E}(\mathbf{z}_1' u_1) = \mathbf{0}$ and the condition rank $\text{E}(\mathbf{z}_1'\mathbf{x}_1) = K_1$. For consistency, we do not care what is happening elsewhere in the system as long as these two assumptions hold. On the other hand, the GMM 3SLS and minimum chi-square estimators of $\boldsymbol{\beta}_1$ are generally inconsistent unless $\text{E}(\mathbf{z}_g' u_g) = \mathbf{0}$ for $g = 1, \ldots, G$. (But we do not need to assume $\text{E}(\mathbf{z}_g' u_h) = 0$ for $g \neq h$ as we would to apply GIV.) Therefore, in using GMM to consistently estimate $\boldsymbol{\beta}_1$, all equations in the system must be properly specified, which means that the instruments must be exogenous in their corresponding equations. Such is the nature of system estimation procedures. As with system OLS and FGLS, there is a trade-off between robustness and efficiency.

Problems

8.1. a. Show that the GMM estimator that solves the problem (8.27) satisfies the first-order condition

$$\left(\sum_{i=1}^{N} \mathbf{Z}_i'\mathbf{X}_i\right)' \hat{\mathbf{W}} \left(\sum_{i=1}^{N} \mathbf{Z}_i'(\mathbf{y}_i - \mathbf{X}_i\hat{\boldsymbol{\beta}})\right) = \mathbf{0}$$

b. Use this expression to obtain formula (8.28).

8.2. Consider the system of equations

$$\mathbf{y}_i = \mathbf{X}_i\boldsymbol{\beta} + \mathbf{u}_i$$

where i indexes the cross section observation, $\mathbf{y}_i$ and $\mathbf{u}_i$ are $G \times 1$, $\mathbf{X}_i$ is $G \times K$, $\mathbf{Z}_i$ is the $G \times L$ matrix of instruments, and $\boldsymbol{\beta}$ is $K \times 1$. Let $\mathbf{\Omega} = \text{E}(\mathbf{u}_i\mathbf{u}_i')$. Make the following four assumptions: (1) $\mathrm{E}(\mathbf{Z}_i'\mathbf{u}_i) = \mathbf{0}$; (2) rank $\mathrm{E}(\mathbf{Z}_i'\mathbf{X}_i) = K$; (3) $\mathrm{E}(\mathbf{Z}_i'\mathbf{Z}_i)$ is nonsingular; and (4) $\mathrm{E}(\mathbf{Z}_i'\boldsymbol{\Omega}\mathbf{Z}_i)$ is nonsingular.

a. What are the asymptotic properties of the 3SLS estimator?

b. Find the asymptotic variance matrix of $\sqrt{N}(\hat{\boldsymbol{\beta}}_{3SLS} - \boldsymbol{\beta})$.

c. How would you estimate $\mathrm{Avar}(\hat{\boldsymbol{\beta}}_{3SLS})$?

8.3. Let $\mathbf{x}$ be a $1 \times K$ random vector and let $\mathbf{z}$ be a $1 \times M$ random vector. Suppose that $\mathrm{E}(\mathbf{x} \mid \mathbf{z}) = \mathrm{L}(\mathbf{x} \mid \mathbf{z}) = \mathbf{z}\boldsymbol{\Pi}$, where $\boldsymbol{\Pi}$ is an $M \times K$ matrix; in other words, the expectation of $\mathbf{x}$ given $\mathbf{z}$ is linear in $\mathbf{z}$. Let $\mathbf{h}(\mathbf{z})$ be any $1 \times Q$ nonlinear function of $\mathbf{z}$, and define an expanded instrument list as $\mathbf{w} \equiv [\mathbf{z}, \mathbf{h}(\mathbf{z})]$.

a. Show that rank $\mathrm{E}(\mathbf{z}'\mathbf{x}) =$ rank $\mathrm{E}(\mathbf{w}'\mathbf{x})$. {Hint: First show that rank $\mathrm{E}(\mathbf{z}'\mathbf{x}) =$ rank $\mathrm{E}(\mathbf{z}'\mathbf{x}^*)$, where $\mathbf{x}^*$ is the linear projection of $\mathbf{x}$ onto $\mathbf{z}$; the same holds with $\mathbf{z}$ replaced by $\mathbf{w}$. Next, show that when $\mathrm{E}(\mathbf{x} \mid \mathbf{z}) = \mathrm{L}(\mathbf{x} \mid \mathbf{z})$, $\mathrm{L}[\mathbf{x} \mid \mathbf{z}, \mathbf{h}(\mathbf{z})] = \mathrm{L}(\mathbf{x} \mid \mathbf{z})$ for any function $\mathbf{h}(\mathbf{z})$ of $\mathbf{z}$.}

b. Explain why the result from part a is important for identification with IV estimation.

8.4. Consider the system of equations (8.12), and let $\mathbf{w}$ be a row vector of variables exogenous in every equation. Assume that the exogeneity assumption takes the stronger form $\mathrm{E}(u_g \mid \mathbf{w}) = 0$, $g = 1, 2, \ldots, G$. This assumption means that $\mathbf{w}$ and nonlinear functions of $\mathbf{w}$ are valid instruments in every equation.

a. Suppose that $\mathrm{E}(\mathbf{x}_g \mid \mathbf{w})$ is linear in $\mathbf{w}$ for all g. Show that adding nonlinear functions of $\mathbf{z}$ to the instrument list cannot help in satisfying the rank condition. (Hint: Apply Problem 8.3.)

b. What happens if $\mathrm{E}(\mathbf{x}_g \mid \mathbf{w})$ is a nonlinear function of $\mathbf{w}$ for some g?

8.5. Verify that the difference $(\mathbf{C}'\boldsymbol{\Lambda}^{-1}\mathbf{C}) - (\mathbf{C}'\mathbf{W}\mathbf{C})(\mathbf{C}'\mathbf{W}\boldsymbol{\Lambda}\mathbf{W}\mathbf{C})^{-1}(\mathbf{C}'\mathbf{W}\mathbf{C})$ in expression (8.34) is positive semidefinite for any symmetric positive definite matrices $\mathbf{W}$ and $\boldsymbol{\Lambda}$. (Hint: Show that the difference can be expressed as

$$\mathbf{C}'\boldsymbol{\Lambda}^{-1/2}[\mathbf{I}_L - \mathbf{D}(\mathbf{D}'\mathbf{D})^{-1}\mathbf{D}']\boldsymbol{\Lambda}^{-1/2}\mathbf{C}$$

where $\mathbf{D} \equiv \boldsymbol{\Lambda}^{1/2}\mathbf{W}\mathbf{C}$. Then, note that for any $L \times K$ matrix $\mathbf{D}$, $\mathbf{I}_L - \mathbf{D}(\mathbf{D}'\mathbf{D})^{-1}\mathbf{D}'$ is a symmetric, idempotent matrix, and therefore positive semidefinite.)

8.6. Consider the system (8.12) in the $G = 2$ case, with an i subscript added:

$$y_{i1} = \mathbf{x}_{i1}\boldsymbol{\beta}_1 + u_{i1},$$

$$y_{i2} = \mathbf{x}_{i2}\boldsymbol{\beta}_2 + u_{i2}.$$

The instrument matrix is

$$\mathbf{Z}_i = \begin{pmatrix} \mathbf{z}_{i1} & \mathbf{0} \\ \mathbf{0} & \mathbf{z}_{i2} \end{pmatrix}.$$

Let $\mathbf{\Omega}$ be the 2×2 variance matrix of $\mathbf{u}_i \equiv (u_{i1}, u_{i2})'$, and write

$$\mathbf{\Omega}^{-1} = \begin{pmatrix} \sigma^{11} & \sigma^{12} \\ \sigma^{12} & \sigma^{22} \end{pmatrix}.$$

a. Find $\mathrm{E}(\mathbf{Z}_i'\mathbf{\Omega}^{-1}\mathbf{u}_i)$ and show that it is not necessarily zero under the orthogonality conditions $\mathrm{E}(\mathbf{z}_{i1}'u_{i1}) = \mathbf{0}$ and $\mathrm{E}(\mathbf{z}_{i2}'u_{i2}) = \mathbf{0}$.

b. What happens if $\mathbf{\Omega}$ is diagonal (so that $\mathbf{\Omega}^{-1}$ is diagonal)?

c. What if $\mathbf{z}_{i1} = \mathbf{z}_{i2}$ (without restrictions on $\mathbf{\Omega}$)?

8.7. With definitions (8.14) and (8.15), show that system 2SLS and 3SLS are numerically identical whenever $\hat{\mathbf{\Omega}}$ is a diagonal matrix.

8.8. Consider the standard panel data model

$$y_{it} = \mathbf{x}_{it}\boldsymbol{\beta} + u_{it}, \tag{8.64}$$

where the $1 \times K$ vector $\mathbf{x}_{it}$ might have some elements correlated with u_{it}. Let $\mathbf{z}_{it}$ be a $1 \times L$ vector of instruments, $L \geq K$, such that $\mathrm{E}(\mathbf{z}_{it}'u_{it}) = \mathbf{0}$, $t = 1, 2, \ldots, T$. (In practice, $\mathbf{z}_{it}$ would contain some elements of $\mathbf{x}_{it}$, including a constant and possibly time dummies.)

a. Write down the system 2SLS estimator if the instrument matrix is $\mathbf{Z}_i = (\mathbf{z}_{i1}', \mathbf{z}_{i2}', \ldots, \mathbf{z}_{iT}')'$ (a $T \times L$ matrix). Show that this estimator is a pooled 2SLS estimator. That is, it is the estimator obtained by 2SLS estimation of equation (8.64) using instruments $\mathbf{z}_{it}$, pooled across all i and t.

b. What is the rank condition for the pooled 2SLS estimator?

c. Without further assumptions, show how to estimate the asymptotic variance of the pooled 2SLS estimator.

d. Without further assumptions, how would you estimate the optimal weighting matrix? Be very specific.

e. Show that the assumptions

$$\mathrm{E}(u_{it} \mid \mathbf{z}_{it}, u_{i,t-1}, \mathbf{z}_{i,t-1}, \ldots, u_{i1}, \mathbf{z}_{i1}) = 0, \qquad t = 1, \ldots, T \tag{8.65}$$

$$\mathrm{E}(u_{it}^2 \mid \mathbf{z}_{it}) = \sigma^2, \qquad t = 1, \ldots, T \tag{8.66}$$

imply that the usual standard errors and test statistics reported from the pooled 2SLS estimation are valid. These assumptions make implementing 2SLS for panel data very simple.

f. What estimator would you use under condition (8.65) but where we relax condition (8.66) to $\mathrm{E}(u_{it}^2 \mid \mathbf{z}_{it}) = \mathrm{E}(u_{it}^2) \equiv \sigma_t^2$, $t = 1, \ldots, T$? This approach will involve an initial pooled 2SLS estimation.

g. Suppose you choose the instrument matrix as $\mathbf{Z}_i = \mathrm{diag}(\mathbf{z}_{i1}, \mathbf{z}_{i2}, \ldots, \mathbf{z}_{iT})$. Show that the system 2SLS estimator can be obtained as follows. (1) For each t, regress $\mathbf{x}_{it}$ on $\mathbf{z}_{it}$, $i = 1, \ldots, T$, and obtain the fitted values, $\hat{\mathbf{x}}_{it}$. (2) Compute the pooled IV estimator using $\hat{\mathbf{x}}_{it}$ as IVs for $\mathbf{x}_{it}$.

h. What is the most efficient way to use the moment conditions $\mathrm{E}(\mathbf{z}_{it}' u_{it}) = \mathbf{0}$, $t = 1, \ldots, T$?

8.9. Consider the single-equation linear model from Chapter 5: $y = \mathbf{x}\boldsymbol{\beta} + u$. Strengthen Assumption 2SLS.1 to $\mathrm{E}(u \mid \mathbf{z}) = 0$ and Assumption 2SLS.3 to $\mathrm{E}(u^2 \mid \mathbf{z}) = \sigma^2$, and keep the rank condition 2SLS.2. Show that if $\mathrm{E}(\mathbf{x} \mid \mathbf{z}) = \mathbf{z}\boldsymbol{\Pi}$ for some $L \times K$ matrix $\boldsymbol{\Pi}$, the 2SLS estimator uses the optimal instruments based on the orthogonality condition $\mathrm{E}(u \mid \mathbf{z}) = 0$. What does this result imply about OLS if $\mathrm{E}(u \mid \mathbf{x}) = 0$ and $\mathrm{Var}(u \mid \mathbf{x}) = \sigma^2$?

8.10. In the model from Problem 8.8, let $\hat{u}_{it} \equiv y_{it} - \mathbf{x}_{it}\hat{\boldsymbol{\beta}}$ be the residuals after pooled 2SLS estimation.

a. Consider the following test for AR(1) serial correlation in $\{u_{it}: t = 1, \ldots, T\}$: estimate the auxiliary equation

$$y_{it} = \mathbf{x}_{it}\boldsymbol{\beta} + \rho\hat{u}_{i,t-1} + error_{it}, \qquad t = 2, \ldots, T, \ i = 1, \ldots, N$$

by 2SLS using instruments $(\mathbf{z}_{it}, \hat{u}_{i,t-1})$, and use the t statistic on $\hat{\rho}$. Argue that, if we strengthen (8.56) to $\mathrm{E}(u_{it} \mid \mathbf{z}_{it}, \mathbf{x}_{i,t-1}, u_{i,t-1}, \mathbf{z}_{i,t-1}, \mathbf{x}_{i,t-2}, \ldots, \mathbf{x}_{i1}, u_{i1}, \mathbf{z}_{i1}) = 0$, then the heteroskedasticity-robust t statistic for $\hat{\rho}$ is asymptotically valid as a test for serial correlation. (Hint: Under the dynamic completeness assumption (8.56), which is effectively the null hypothesis, the fact that $\hat{u}_{i,t-1}$ is used in place of $u_{i,t-1}$ does not affect the limiting distribution of $\hat{\rho}$; see Section 6.1.3.) What is the homoskedasticity assumption that justifies the usual t statistic?

b. What should be done to obtain a heteroskedasticity-robust test?

8.11. a. Use Theorem 8.5 to show that, in the single-equation model

$$y_1 = \mathbf{z}_1\boldsymbol{\delta}_1 + \alpha_1 y_2 + u_1,$$

with $E(u_1 \mid \mathbf{z}) = 0$—where $\mathbf{z}_1$ is a strict subset of $\mathbf{z}$—and $\text{Var}(u_1 \mid \mathbf{z}) = \sigma_1^2$, the optimal instrumental variables are $[\mathbf{z}_1, E(y_2 \mid \mathbf{z})]$.

b. If y_2 is a binary variable with $P(y_2 = 1 \mid \mathbf{z}) = F(\mathbf{z})$ for some known function $F(\cdot)$, $0 \leq F(\mathbf{z}) \leq 1$, what are the optimal IVs?

8.12. Suppose in the system (8.11) we think $\boldsymbol{\Omega}$ has a special form, and so we estimate a restricted version of it. Let $\hat{\boldsymbol{\Lambda}}$ be a $G \times G$ positive semidefinite matrix such that $\text{plim}(\hat{\boldsymbol{\Lambda}}) = \boldsymbol{\Lambda} \neq \boldsymbol{\Omega}$.

a. If we apply GMM 3SLS using $\hat{\boldsymbol{\Lambda}}$, is the resulting estimator generally consistent for $\boldsymbol{\beta}$? Explain.

b. If Assumption SIV.5 holds, but $\boldsymbol{\Lambda} \neq \boldsymbol{\Omega}$, can you use the difference in criterion functions for testing?

c. Let $\hat{\boldsymbol{\Omega}}$ be the unrestricted estimator given by (8.38), and suppose the restrictions imposed in obtaining $\hat{\boldsymbol{\Lambda}}$ hold: $\boldsymbol{\Lambda} = \boldsymbol{\Omega}$. Is there any loss in asymptotic efficiency in using $\hat{\boldsymbol{\Omega}}$ rather than $\hat{\boldsymbol{\Lambda}}$ in a GMM 3SLS analysis? Explain.

8.13. Consider a model where exogenous variables interact with an endogenous explanatory variable:

$$y_1 = \eta_1 + \mathbf{z}_1\boldsymbol{\delta}_1 + \alpha_1 y_2 + \mathbf{z}_1 y_2 \boldsymbol{\gamma}_1 + u_1$$

$$E(u_1 \mid \mathbf{z}) = 0,$$

where $\mathbf{z}$ is the vector of all exogenous variables. Assume, in addition, (1) $Var(u_1 \mid \mathbf{z}) = \sigma_1^2$ and (2) $E(y_2 \mid \mathbf{z}) = \mathbf{z}\boldsymbol{\pi}_2$.

a. Apply Theorem 8.5 to obtain the optimal instrumental variables.

b. How would you operationalize the optimal IV estimator?

8.14. Write a model for panel data with potentially endogenous explanatory variables as

$$y_{it1} = \eta_{t1} + \mathbf{z}_{it1}\boldsymbol{\delta}_1 + \mathbf{y}_{it2}\boldsymbol{\alpha}_2 + u_{it1}, \qquad t = 1, \ldots, T,$$

where η_{t1} denotes a set of intercepts for each t, $\mathbf{z}_{it1}$ is $1 \times L_1$, and $\mathbf{y}_{it2}$ is $1 \times G_1$. Let $\mathbf{z}_{it}$ be the $1 \times L$ vector, $L = L_1 + L_2$, such that $E(\mathbf{z}_{it}' u_{it1}) = \mathbf{0}$, $t = 1, \ldots, T$. We need $L_2 \geq G_1$.

a. A reduced form for $\mathbf{y}_{it2}$ can be written as $\mathbf{y}_{it2} = \mathbf{z}_{it}\boldsymbol{\Pi}_2 + \mathbf{v}_{it2}$. Explain how to use pooled OLS to obtain a fully robust test of $H_0: E(\mathbf{y}_{it2}' u_{it1}) = \mathbf{0}$. (The test should have G_1 degrees of freedom.)

b. Extend the approach based on equation (6.32) to obtain a test of overidentifying restrictions for the pooled 2SLS estimator. You should describe how to make the test fully robust to serial correlation and heteroskedasticity.

8.15. Use the data in AIRFARE.RAW to answer this question.

a. Estimate the passenger demand model

$$\log(passen_{it}) = \beta_0 + \delta_1 y98_t + \delta_2 y99_t + \delta_3 y00_t + \beta_1 \log(fare_{it}) + \beta_2 \log(dist_i) + \beta_3[\log(dist_i)]^2 + u_{it1}$$

by pooled OLS. Obtain the usual standard error and the fully robust standard error for $\hat{\beta}_{1,POLS}$. Interpret the coefficient.

b. Explicitly test $\{u_{it1} : t = 1, \ldots, 4\}$ for AR(1) serial correlation. What do you make of the estimate of ρ?

c. The variable $concen_{it}$ can be used as an IV for $\log(fare_{it})$. Estimate the reduced form for $\log(fare_{it})$ (by pooled OLS) and test whether $\log(fare_{it})$ and $concen_{it}$ are sufficiently partially correlated. You should use a fully robust test.

d. Estimate the model from part a by pooled 2SLS. Is $\hat{\beta}_{1,P2SLS}$ practically different from $\hat{\beta}_{1,POLS}$? How do the pooled and fully robust standard errors for $\hat{\beta}_{1,P2SLS}$ compare?

e. Under what assumptions can you directly compare $\hat{\beta}_{1,P2SLS}$ and $\hat{\beta}_{1,POLS}$ using the usual standard errors to obtain a Hausman statistic? Is it likely these assumptions are satisfied?

f. Use the test from Problem 8.14 to formally test that $\log(fare_{it})$ is exogenous in the demand equation. Use the fully robust version.

9 Simultaneous Equations Models

9.1 Scope of Simultaneous Equations Models

The emphasis in this chapter is on situations where two or more variables are jointly determined by a system of equations. Nevertheless, the population model, the identification analysis, and the estimation methods apply to a much broader range of problems. In Chapter 8, we saw that the omitted variables problem described in Example 8.2 has the same statistical structure as the true simultaneous equations model in Example 8.1. In fact, any or all of simultaneity, omitted variables, and measurement error can be present in a system of equations. Because the omitted variable and measurement error problems are conceptually easier—and it was for this reason that we discussed them in single-equation contexts in Chapters 4 and 5—our examples and discussion in this chapter are geared mostly toward true **simultaneous equations models (SEMs)**.

For effective application of true SEMs, we must understand the kinds of situations suitable for SEM analysis. The labor supply and wage offer example, Example 8.1, is a legitimate SEM application. The labor supply function describes individual behavior, and it is derivable from basic economic principles of individual utility maximization. Holding other factors fixed, the labor supply function gives the hours of labor supply at *any* potential wage facing the individual. The wage offer function describes firm behavior, and, like the labor supply function, the wage offer function is self-contained.

When an equation in an SEM has economic meaning in isolation from the other equations in the system, we say that the equation is **autonomous**. One way to think about autonomy is in terms of counterfactual reasoning, as in Example 8.1. If we know the parameters of the labor supply function, then, for any individual, we can find labor hours given any value of the potential wage (and values of the other observed and unobserved factors affecting labor supply). In other words, we could, in principle, trace out the individual labor supply function for given levels of the other observed and unobserved variables.

Causality is closely tied to the autonomy requirement. An equation in an SEM should represent a causal relationship; therefore, we should be interested in varying each of the explanatory variables—including any that are endogenous—while holding *all* the others fixed. Put another way, each equation in an SEM should represent *some* underlying conditional expectation that has a causal structure. What complicates matters is that the conditional expectations are in terms of counterfactual variables. In the labor supply example, *if* we could run a controlled experiment where we exogenously varied the wage offer across individuals, then the labor supply function could be estimated without ever considering the wage offer function. In fact, in the absence of omitted variables or measurement error, ordinary least squares would be an appropriate estimation method.

Generally, supply and demand examples satisfy the autonomy requirement, regardless of the level of aggregation (individual, household, firm, city, and so on), and simultaneous equations systems were originally developed for such applications. (See, for example, Haavelmo (1943) and Kiefer's (1989) interview of Arthur S. Goldberger.) Unfortunately, many recent applications of SEMs fail the autonomy requirement; as a result, it is difficult to interpret what has actually been estimated. Examples that fail the autonomy requirement often have the same feature: the endogenous variables in the system are all choice variables of the *same* economic unit.

As an example, consider an individual's choice of weekly hours spent in legal market activities and hours spent in criminal behavior. An economic model of crime can be derived from utility maximization; for simplicity, suppose the choice is only between hours working legally (*work*) and hours involved in crime (*crime*). The factors assumed to be exogenous to the individual's choice are things like wage in legal activities, other income sources, probability of arrest, expected punishment, and so on. The utility function can depend on education, work experience, gender, race, and other demographic variables.

Two structural equations fall out of the individual's optimization problem: one has *work* as a function of the exogenous factors, demographics, and unobservables; the other has *crime* as a function of these same factors. Of course, it is always possible that factors treated as exogenous by the individual cannot be treated as exogenous by the econometrician: unobservables that affect the choice of *work* and *crime* could be correlated with the observable factors. But this possibility is an omitted variables problem. (Measurement error could also be an important issue in this example.) Whether or not omitted variables or measurement error are problems, each equation has a causal interpretation.

In the crime example, and many similar examples, it may be tempting to stop before completely solving the model—or to circumvent economic theory altogether—and specify a simultaneous equations system consisting of two equations. The first equation would describe *work* in terms of *crime*, while the second would have *crime* as a function of *work* (with other factors appearing in both equations). While it is often possible to write the first-order conditions for an optimization problem in this way, these equations are *not* the structural equations of interest. Neither equation can stand on its own, and neither has a causal interpretation. For example, what would it mean to study the effect of changing the market wage on hours spent in criminal activity, holding hours spent in legal employment fixed? An individual will generally adjust the time spent in both activities to a change in the market wage.

Often it *is* useful to determine how one endogenous choice variable trades off against another, but in such cases the goal is not—and should not be—to infer causality. For example, Biddle and Hamermesh (1990) present OLS regressions of minutes spent per week sleeping on minutes per week working (controlling for education, age, and other demographic and health factors). Biddle and Hamermesh recognize that there is nothing "structural" about such an analysis. (In fact, the choice of the dependent variable is largely arbitrary.) Biddle and Hamermesh (1990) *do* derive a structural model of the demand for sleep (along with a labor supply function) where a key explanatory variable is the wage offer. The demand for sleep has a causal interpretation, and it does *not* include labor supply on the right-hand side.

Why are SEM applications that do not satisfy the autonomy requirement so prevalent in applied work? One possibility is that there appears to be a general misperception that "structural" and "simultaneous" are synonymous. However, we already know that structural models need not be systems of simultaneous equations. And, as the crime/work example shows, a simultaneous system is not necessarily structural.

9.2 Identification in a Linear System

9.2.1 Exclusion Restrictions and Reduced Forms

Write a system of linear simultaneous equations for the population as

$$\begin{aligned} y_1 &= \mathbf{y}_{(1)}\boldsymbol{\gamma}_{(1)} + \mathbf{z}_{(1)}\boldsymbol{\delta}_{(1)} + u_1 \\ &\vdots \\ y_G &= \mathbf{y}_{(G)}\boldsymbol{\gamma}_{(G)} + \mathbf{z}_{(G)}\boldsymbol{\delta}_{(G)} + u_G, \end{aligned} \tag{9.1}$$

where $\mathbf{y}_{(h)}$ is $1 \times G_h$, $\boldsymbol{\gamma}_{(h)}$ is $G_h \times 1$, $\mathbf{z}_{(h)}$ is $1 \times M_h$, and $\boldsymbol{\delta}_{(h)}$ is $M_h \times 1$, $h = 1, 2, \ldots, G$. These are **structural equations** for the **endogenous variables** $y_1, y_2, \ldots, y_G$. We will assume that, if the system (9.1) represents a true SEM, then equilibrium conditions have been imposed. Hopefully, each equation is autonomous, but, of course, they do not need to be for the statistical analysis.

The vector $\mathbf{y}_{(h)}$ denotes endogenous variables that appear on the right-hand side of the hth structural equation. By convention, $\mathbf{y}_{(h)}$ can contain any of the endogenous variables $y_1, y_2, \ldots, y_G$ *except* for y_h. The variables in $\mathbf{z}_{(h)}$ are the **exogenous variables** appearing in equation h. Usually there is some overlap in the exogenous variables across different equations; for example, except in special circumstances, each $\mathbf{z}_{(h)}$ would contain unity to allow for nonzero intercepts. The restrictions imposed in system (9.1) are called **exclusion restrictions** because certain endogenous and exogenous variables are excluded from some equations.

The $1 \times M$ vector of all exogenous variables $\mathbf{z}$ is assumed to satisfy

$$\mathrm{E}(\mathbf{z}'u_g) = \mathbf{0}, \qquad g = 1, 2, \ldots, G. \tag{9.2}$$

When all of the equations in system (9.1) are truly structural, we are usually willing to assume

$$\mathrm{E}(u_g \mid \mathbf{z}) = 0, \qquad g = 1, 2, \ldots, G. \tag{9.3}$$

However, we know from Chapters 5 and 8 that assumption (9.2) is sufficient for consistent estimation. Sometimes, especially in omitted variables and measurement error applications, one or more of the equations in system (9.1) will simply represent a linear projection onto exogenous variables, as in Example 8.2. It is for this reason that we use assumption (9.2) for most of our identification and estimation analysis. We assume throughout that $\mathrm{E}(\mathbf{z}'\mathbf{z})$ is nonsingular, so that there are no exact linear dependencies among the exogenous variables in the population.

Assumption (9.2) implies that the exogenous variables appearing anywhere in the system are orthogonal to *all* the structural errors. If some elements in, say, $\mathbf{z}_{(1)}$ do not appear in the second equation, then we are explicitly assuming that they do not enter the structural equation for y_2. If there are no reasonable exclusion restrictions in an SEM, it may be that the system fails the autonomy requirement.

Generally, in the system (9.1), the error u_g in equation g will be correlated with $\mathbf{y}_{(g)}$ (we show this correlation explicitly later), and so OLS and GLS will be inconsistent. Nevertheless, under certain identification assumptions, we can estimate this system using the instrumental variables procedures covered in Chapter 8.

In addition to the exclusion restrictions in system (9.1), another possible source of identifying information is on the $G \times G$ variance matrix $\mathbf{\Sigma} \equiv \mathrm{Var}(\mathbf{u})$. For now, $\mathbf{\Sigma}$ is unrestricted and therefore contains no identifying information.

To motivate the general analysis, consider specific labor supply and demand functions for some population:

$$h^s(\omega) = \gamma_1 \log(\omega) + \mathbf{z}_{(1)}\boldsymbol{\delta}_{(1)} + u_1$$

$$h^d(\omega) = \gamma_2 \log(\omega) + \mathbf{z}_{(2)}\boldsymbol{\delta}_{(2)} + u_2,$$

where ω is the dummy argument in the labor supply and labor demand functions. We assume that observed hours, h, and observed wage, w, equate supply and demand:

$$h = h^s(w) = h^d(w).$$

The variables in $\mathbf{z}_{(1)}$ shift the labor supply curve, and $\mathbf{z}_{(2)}$ contains labor demand shifters. By defining $y_1 = h$ and $y_2 = \log(w)$ we can write the equations in equilibrium as a linear simultaneous equations model:

$$y_1 = \gamma_1 y_2 + \mathbf{z}_{(1)}\boldsymbol{\delta}_{(1)} + u_1, \tag{9.4}$$

$$y_1 = \gamma_2 y_2 + \mathbf{z}_{(2)}\boldsymbol{\delta}_{(2)} + u_2. \tag{9.5}$$

Nothing about the general system (9.1) rules out having the same variable on the left-hand side of more than one equation.

What is needed to identify the parameters in, say, the supply curve? Intuitively, since we observe only the equilibrium quantities of hours and wages, we cannot distinguish the supply function from the demand function if $\mathbf{z}_{(1)}$ and $\mathbf{z}_{(2)}$ contain exactly the same elements. If, however, $\mathbf{z}_{(2)}$ contains an element *not* in $\mathbf{z}_{(1)}$—that is, if there is some factor that exogenously shifts the demand curve but not the supply curve—then we can hope to estimate the parameters of the supply curve. To identify the demand curve, we need at least one element in $\mathbf{z}_{(1)}$ that is not also in $\mathbf{z}_{(2)}$.

To formally study identification, assume that $\gamma_1 \neq \gamma_2$; this assumption just means that the supply and demand curves have different slopes. Subtracting equation (9.5) from equation (9.4), dividing by $\gamma_2 - \gamma_1$, and rearranging gives

$$y_2 = \mathbf{z}_{(1)}\boldsymbol{\pi}_{21} + \mathbf{z}_{(2)}\boldsymbol{\pi}_{22} + v_2, \tag{9.6}$$

where $\boldsymbol{\pi}_{21} \equiv \boldsymbol{\delta}_{(1)}/(\gamma_2 - \gamma_1)$, $\boldsymbol{\pi}_{22} = -\boldsymbol{\delta}_{(2)}/(\gamma_2 - \gamma_1)$, and $v_2 \equiv (u_1 - u_2)/(\gamma_2 - \gamma_1)$. This is the **reduced form** for y_2 because it expresses y_2 as a linear function of all of the exogenous variables and an error v_2 which, by assumption (9.2), is orthogonal to all exogenous variables: $\mathrm{E}(\mathbf{z}'v_2) = \mathbf{0}$. Importantly, the reduced form for y_2 is obtained from the two structural equations (9.4) and (9.5).

Given equation (9.4) and the reduced form (9.6), we can now use the identification condition from Chapter 5 for a linear model with a single right-hand-side endogenous variable. This condition is easy to state: the reduced form for y_2 must contain at least one exogenous variable not also in equation (9.4). This means there must be at least one element of $\mathbf{z}_{(2)}$ not in $\mathbf{z}_{(1)}$ with coefficient in equation (9.6) different from zero. Now we use the structural equations. Because $\boldsymbol{\pi}_{22}$ is proportional to $\boldsymbol{\delta}_{(2)}$, the condition is easily restated in terms of the *structural* parameters: in equation (9.5) at least one element of $\mathbf{z}_{(2)}$ not in $\mathbf{z}_{(1)}$ must have nonzero coefficient. In the supply and demand example, identification of the supply function requires at least one exogenous variable appearing in the demand function that does not also appear in the supply function; this conclusion corresponds exactly with our earlier intuition.

The condition for identifying equation (9.5) is just the mirror image: there must be at least one element of $\mathbf{z}_{(1)}$ actually appearing in equation (9.4) that is not also an element of $\mathbf{z}_{(2)}$.

Example 9.1 (Labor Supply for Married Women): Consider labor supply and demand equations for married women, with the equilibrium condition imposed:

$$hours = \gamma_1 \log(wage) + \delta_{10} + \delta_{11} educ + \delta_{12} age + \delta_{13} kids + \delta_{14} othinc + u_1.$$

$$hours = \gamma_2 \log(wage) + \delta_{20} + \delta_{21} educ + \delta_{22} exper + u_2.$$

The supply equation is identified because, by assumption, *exper* appears in the demand function (assuming $\delta_{22} \neq 0$) but not in the supply equation. The assumption that past experience has no direct effect on labor supply can be questioned, but it has been used by labor economists. The demand equation is identified provided that at least one of the three variables *age*, *kids*, and *othinc* actually appears in the supply equation.

We now extend this analysis to the general system (9.1). For concreteness, we study identification of the first equation:

$$y_1 = \mathbf{y}_{(1)}\boldsymbol{\gamma}_{(1)} + \mathbf{z}_{(1)}\boldsymbol{\delta}_{(1)} + u_1 = \mathbf{x}_{(1)}\boldsymbol{\beta}_{(1)} + u_1, \tag{9.7}$$

where the notation used for the subscripts is needed to distinguish an equation with exclusion restrictions from the general equation that we study in Section 9.2.2. Assuming that the reduced forms exist, write the reduced form for $\mathbf{y}_{(1)}$ as

$$\mathbf{y}_{(1)} = \mathbf{z}\boldsymbol{\Pi}_{(1)} + \mathbf{v}_{(1)}, \tag{9.8}$$

where $\mathrm{E}[\mathbf{z}'\mathbf{v}_{(1)}] = \mathbf{0}$. Further, define the $M \times M_1$ matrix *selection matrix* $\mathbf{S}_{(1)}$, which consists of zeros and ones, such that $\mathbf{z}_{(1)} = \mathbf{z}\mathbf{S}_{(1)}$. The rank condition from Chapter 5, Assumption 2SLS.2b, can be stated as

$$\text{rank } \mathrm{E}[\mathbf{z}'\mathbf{x}_{(1)}] = K_1, \tag{9.9}$$

where $K_1 \equiv G_1 + M_1$. But $\mathrm{E}[\mathbf{z}'\mathbf{x}_{(1)}] = \mathrm{E}[\mathbf{z}'(\mathbf{z}\boldsymbol{\Pi}_{(1)}, \mathbf{z}\mathbf{S}_{(1)})] = \mathrm{E}(\mathbf{z}'\mathbf{z})[\boldsymbol{\Pi}_{(1)} \,|\, \mathbf{S}_{(1)}]$. Since we always assume that $\mathrm{E}(\mathbf{z}'\mathbf{z})$ has full rank M, assumption (9.9) is the same as

$$\text{rank}[\boldsymbol{\Pi}_{(1)} \,|\, \mathbf{S}_{(1)}] = G_1 + M_1. \tag{9.10}$$

In other words, $[\boldsymbol{\Pi}_{(1)} \,|\, \mathbf{S}_{(1)}]$ must have full column rank. If the reduced form for $\mathbf{y}_{(1)}$ has been found, this condition can be checked directly. But there is one thing we can conclude immediately: because $[\boldsymbol{\Pi}_{(1)} \,|\, \mathbf{S}_{(1)}]$ is an $M \times (G_1 + M_1)$ matrix, a *necessary* condition for assumption (9.10) is $M \geq G_1 + M_1$, or

$$M - M_1 \geq G_1. \tag{9.11}$$

We have already encountered condition (9.11) in Chapter 5: the number of exogenous variables not appearing in the first equation, $M - M_1$, must be at least as great as the number of endogenous variables appearing on the right-hand side of the first equation (9.7), G_1. This is the **order condition** for identification of the first equation. We have proven the following theorem:

THEOREM 9.1 (Order Condition with Exclusion Restrictions): In a linear system of equations with exclusion restrictions, a *necessary* condition for identifying any particular equation is that the number of excluded exogenous variables from the equation must be at least as large as the number of included right-hand-side endogenous variables in the equation.

It is important to remember that the order condition is only necessary, not sufficient, for identification. If the order condition fails for a particular equation, there is no hope of estimating the parameters in that equation. If the order condition is met, the equation *might* be identified.

9.2.2 General Linear Restrictions and Structural Equations

The identification analysis of the preceding subsection is useful when reduced forms are appended to structural equations. When an entire structural system has been specified, it is best to study identification entirely in terms of the structural parameters.

To this end, we now write the G equations in the population as

$$\begin{aligned} \mathbf{y}\boldsymbol{\gamma}_1 + \mathbf{z}\boldsymbol{\delta}_1 + u_1 &= 0 \\ &\vdots \\ \mathbf{y}\boldsymbol{\gamma}_G + \mathbf{z}\boldsymbol{\delta}_G + u_G &= 0, \end{aligned} \tag{9.12}$$

where $\mathbf{y} \equiv (y_1, y_2, \ldots, y_G)$ is the $1 \times G$ vector of *all* endogenous variables and $\mathbf{z} \equiv (z_1, \ldots, z_M)$ is still the $1 \times M$ vector of all exogenous variables, and probably contains unity. We maintain assumption (9.2) throughout this section and also assume that $\mathrm{E}(\mathbf{z}'\mathbf{z})$ is nonsingular. The notation here differs from that in Section 9.2.1. Here, $\boldsymbol{\gamma}_g$ is $G \times 1$ and $\boldsymbol{\delta}_g$ is $M \times 1$ for all $g = 1, 2, \ldots, G$, so that the system (9.12) is the general linear system without *any* restrictions on the structural parameters.

We can write this system compactly as

$$\mathbf{y}\boldsymbol{\Gamma} + \mathbf{z}\boldsymbol{\Delta} + \mathbf{u} = \mathbf{0}, \tag{9.13}$$

where $\mathbf{u} \equiv (u_1, \ldots, u_G)$ is the $1 \times G$ vector of structural errors, $\boldsymbol{\Gamma}$ is the $G \times G$ matrix with gth column $\boldsymbol{\gamma}_g$, and $\boldsymbol{\Delta}$ is the $M \times G$ matrix with gth column $\boldsymbol{\delta}_g$. So that a reduced form exists, we assume that $\boldsymbol{\Gamma}$ is nonsingular. Let $\boldsymbol{\Sigma} \equiv \mathrm{E}(\mathbf{u}'\mathbf{u})$ denote the $G \times G$ variance matrix of $\mathbf{u}$, which we assume to be nonsingular. At this point, we have placed no other restrictions on $\boldsymbol{\Gamma}$, $\boldsymbol{\Delta}$, or $\boldsymbol{\Sigma}$.

The reduced form is easily expressed as

$$\mathbf{y} = \mathbf{z}(-\boldsymbol{\Delta}\boldsymbol{\Gamma}^{-1}) + \mathbf{u}(-\boldsymbol{\Gamma}^{-1}) \equiv \mathbf{z}\boldsymbol{\Pi} + \mathbf{v}, \tag{9.14}$$

where $\boldsymbol{\Pi} \equiv (-\boldsymbol{\Delta}\boldsymbol{\Gamma}^{-1})$ and $\mathbf{v} \equiv \mathbf{u}(-\boldsymbol{\Gamma}^{-1})$. Define $\boldsymbol{\Lambda} \equiv \mathrm{E}(\mathbf{v}'\mathbf{v}) = \boldsymbol{\Gamma}^{-1\prime}\boldsymbol{\Sigma}\boldsymbol{\Gamma}^{-1}$ as the reduced form variance matrix. Because $\mathrm{E}(\mathbf{z}'\mathbf{v}) = \mathbf{0}$ and $\mathrm{E}(\mathbf{z}'\mathbf{z})$ is nonsingular, $\boldsymbol{\Pi}$ and $\boldsymbol{\Lambda}$ are identified because they can be consistently estimated given a random sample on $\mathbf{y}$ and $\mathbf{z}$ by OLS equation by equation. The question is, under what assumptions can we recover the structural parameters $\boldsymbol{\Gamma}$, $\boldsymbol{\Delta}$, and $\boldsymbol{\Sigma}$ from the reduced form parameters?

It is easy to see that, without some restrictions, we will not be able to identify any of the parameters in the structural system. Let $\mathbf{F}$ be any $G \times G$ nonsingular matrix, and postmultiply equation (9.13) by $\mathbf{F}$:

$$\mathbf{y}\boldsymbol{\Gamma}\mathbf{F} + \mathbf{z}\boldsymbol{\Delta}\mathbf{F} + \mathbf{u}\mathbf{F} = \mathbf{0} \qquad \text{or} \qquad \mathbf{y}\boldsymbol{\Gamma}^* + \mathbf{z}\boldsymbol{\Delta}^* + \mathbf{u}^* = \mathbf{0}, \tag{9.15}$$

where $\boldsymbol{\Gamma}^* \equiv \boldsymbol{\Gamma}\mathbf{F}$, $\boldsymbol{\Delta}^* \equiv \boldsymbol{\Delta}\mathbf{F}$, and $\mathbf{u}^* \equiv \mathbf{u}\mathbf{F}$; note that $\mathrm{Var}(\mathbf{u}^*) = \mathbf{F}'\boldsymbol{\Sigma}\mathbf{F}$. Simple algebra shows that equations (9.15) and (9.13) have *identical* reduced forms. This result means that, without restrictions on the structural parameters, there are many **equivalent structures** in the sense that they lead to the same reduced form. In fact, there is an equivalent structure for each nonsingular $\mathbf{F}$.

Let $\mathbf{B} \equiv \begin{pmatrix} \boldsymbol{\Gamma} \\ \boldsymbol{\Delta} \end{pmatrix}$ be the $(G + M) \times G$ matrix of structural parameters in equation (9.13). If $\mathbf{F}$ is any nonsingular $G \times G$ matrix, then $\mathbf{F}$ represents an **admissible linear transformation** if

1. $\mathbf{BF}$ satisfies all restrictions on $\mathbf{B}$.
2. $\mathbf{F}'\boldsymbol{\Sigma}\mathbf{F}$ satisfies all restrictions on $\boldsymbol{\Sigma}$.

To identify the system, we need enough prior information on the structural parameters $(\mathbf{B}, \boldsymbol{\Sigma})$ so that $\mathbf{F} = \mathbf{I}_G$ is the only admissible linear transformation.

In most applications identification of $\mathbf{B}$ is of primary interest, and this identification is achieved by putting restrictions directly on $\mathbf{B}$. As we will touch on in Section 9.4.2, it is possible to put restrictions on $\boldsymbol{\Sigma}$ in order to identify $\mathbf{B}$, but this approach is somewhat rare in practice. Until we come to Section 9.4.2, $\boldsymbol{\Sigma}$ is an unrestricted $G \times G$ positive definite matrix.

As before, we consider identification of the first equation:

$$\mathbf{y}\boldsymbol{\gamma}_1 + \mathbf{z}\boldsymbol{\delta}_1 + u_1 = 0 \tag{9.16}$$

or $\gamma_{11}y_1 + \gamma_{12}y_2 + \cdots + \gamma_{1G}y_G + \delta_{11}z_1 + \delta_{12}z_2 + \cdots + \delta_{1M}z_M + u_1 = 0$. The first restriction we make on the parameters in equation (9.16) is the **normalization restriction** that one element of $\boldsymbol{\gamma}_1$ is -1. Each equation in the system (9.1) has a normalization restriction because one variable is taken to be the left-hand-side explained variable. In applications, there is usually a natural normalization for each equation. If there is not, we should ask whether the system satisfies the autonomy requirement discussed in Section 9.1. (Even in models that satisfy the autonomy requirement, we often have to choose between reasonable normalization conditions. For example, in Example 9.1, we could have specified the second equation to be a wage offer equation rather than a labor demand equation.)

Let $\boldsymbol{\beta}_1 \equiv (\boldsymbol{\gamma}_1', \boldsymbol{\delta}_1')'$ be the $(G+M) \times 1$ vector of structural parameters in the first equation. With a normalization restriction there are $(G+M) - 1$ unknown elements in $\boldsymbol{\beta}_1$. Assume that prior knowledge about $\boldsymbol{\beta}_1$ can be expressed as

$$\mathbf{R}_1\boldsymbol{\beta}_1 = \mathbf{0}, \tag{9.17}$$

where $\mathbf{R}_1$ is a $J_1 \times (G+M)$ matrix of known constants and J_1 is the number of restrictions on $\boldsymbol{\beta}_1$ (in addition to the normalization restriction). We assume that rank $\mathbf{R}_1 = J_1$, so that there are no redundant restrictions. The restrictions in assumption (9.17) are sometimes called **homogeneous linear restrictions**, but, when coupled with a normalization assumption, equation (9.17) actually allows for nonhomogeneous restrictions.

Example 9.2 (Three-Equation System): Consider the first equation in a system with $G = 3$ and $M = 4$:

$$y_1 = \gamma_{12}y_2 + \gamma_{13}y_3 + \delta_{11}z_1 + \delta_{12}z_2 + \delta_{13}z_3 + \delta_{14}z_4 + u_1$$

so that $\boldsymbol{\gamma}_1 = (-1, \gamma_{12}, \gamma_{13})'$, $\boldsymbol{\delta}_1 = (\delta_{11}, \delta_{12}, \delta_{13}, \delta_{14})'$, and $\boldsymbol{\beta}_1 = (-1, \gamma_{12}, \gamma_{13}, \delta_{11}, \delta_{12}, \delta_{13}, \delta_{14})'$. (We can set $z_1 = 1$ to allow an intercept.) Suppose the restrictions on the structural parameters are $\gamma_{12} = 0$ and $\delta_{13} + \delta_{14} = 3$. Then $J_1 = 2$ and

$$\mathbf{R}_1 = \begin{pmatrix} 0 & 1 & 0 & 0 & 0 & 0 & 0 \\ 3 & 0 & 0 & 0 & 0 & 1 & 1 \end{pmatrix}.$$

Straightforward multiplication gives $\mathbf{R}_1\boldsymbol{\beta}_1 = (\gamma_{12}, \delta_{13} + \delta_{14} - 3)'$, and setting this vector to zero as in equation (9.17) incorporates the restrictions on $\boldsymbol{\beta}_1$.

Given the linear restrictions in equation (9.17), when are these and the normalization restriction enough to identify $\boldsymbol{\beta}_1$? Let $\mathbf{F}$ again be any $G \times G$ nonsingular matrix, and write it in terms of its columns as $\mathbf{F} = (\mathbf{f}_1, \mathbf{f}_2, \ldots, \mathbf{f}_G)$. Define a linear transformation of $\mathbf{B}$ as $\mathbf{B}^* = \mathbf{BF}$, so that the first column of $\mathbf{B}^*$ is $\boldsymbol{\beta}_1^* \equiv \mathbf{Bf}_1$. We need to find a condition so that equation (9.17) allows us to distinguish $\boldsymbol{\beta}_1$ from any other $\boldsymbol{\beta}_1^*$. For the moment, ignore the normalization condition. The vector $\boldsymbol{\beta}_1^*$ satisfies the linear restrictions embodied by $\mathbf{R}_1$ if and only if

$$\mathbf{R}_1\boldsymbol{\beta}_1^* = \mathbf{R}_1(\mathbf{Bf}_1) = (\mathbf{R}_1\mathbf{B})\mathbf{f}_1 = \mathbf{0}. \tag{9.18}$$

Naturally, $(\mathbf{R}_1\mathbf{B})\mathbf{f}_1 = \mathbf{0}$ is true for $\mathbf{f}_1 = \mathbf{e}_1 \equiv (1, 0, 0, \ldots, 0)'$, since then $\boldsymbol{\beta}_1^* = \mathbf{Bf}_1 = \boldsymbol{\beta}_1$. Since assumption (9.18) holds for $\mathbf{f}_1 = \mathbf{e}_1$ it clearly holds for any scalar multiple of $\mathbf{e}_1$. The key to identification is that vectors of the form $c_1\mathbf{e}_1$, for some constant c_1, are the *only* vectors $\mathbf{f}_1$ satisfying condition (9.18). If condition (9.18) holds for vectors $\mathbf{f}_1$ other than scalar multiples of $\mathbf{e}_1$, then we have no hope of identifying $\boldsymbol{\beta}_1$.

Stating that condition (9.18) holds only for vectors of the form $c_1\mathbf{e}_1$ just means that the null space of $\mathbf{R}_1\mathbf{B}$ has dimension unity. Equivalently, because $\mathbf{R}_1\mathbf{B}$ has G columns,

$$\text{rank } \mathbf{R}_1\mathbf{B} = G - 1. \tag{9.19}$$

This is the **rank condition** for identification of $\boldsymbol{\beta}_1$ in the first structural equation under general linear restrictions. Once condition (9.19) is known to hold, the normalization restriction allows us to distinguish $\boldsymbol{\beta}_1$ from any other scalar multiple of $\boldsymbol{\beta}_1$.

THEOREM 9.2 (Rank Condition for Identification): Let $\boldsymbol{\beta}_1$ be the $(G + M) \times 1$ vector of structural parameters in the first equation, with the normalization restriction that one of the coefficients on an endogenous variable is -1. Let the additional information on $\boldsymbol{\beta}_1$ be given by restriction (9.17). Then $\boldsymbol{\beta}_1$ is identified if and only if the rank condition (9.19) holds.

As promised earlier, the rank condition in this subsection depends on the *structural* parameters, $\mathbf{B}$. We can determine whether the first equation is identified by studying the matrix $\mathbf{R}_1\mathbf{B}$. Since this matrix can depend on *all* structural parameters, we must generally specify the entire structural model.

The $J_1 \times G$ matrix $\mathbf{R}_1\mathbf{B}$ can be written as $\mathbf{R}_1\mathbf{B} = [\mathbf{R}_1\boldsymbol{\beta}_1, \mathbf{R}_1\boldsymbol{\beta}_2, \ldots, \mathbf{R}_1\boldsymbol{\beta}_G]$, where $\boldsymbol{\beta}_g$ is the $(G + M) \times 1$ vector of structural parameters in equation g. By assumption (9.17), the first column of $\mathbf{R}_1\mathbf{B}$ is the zero vector. Therefore, $\mathbf{R}_1\mathbf{B}$ cannot have rank larger than $G - 1$. What we must check is whether the columns of $\mathbf{R}_1\mathbf{B}$ other than the first form a linearly independent set.

Using condition (9.19), we can get a more general form of the order condition. Because $\boldsymbol{\Gamma}$ is nonsingular, $\mathbf{B}$ necessarily has rank G (full column rank). Therefore, for condition (9.19) to hold, we must have rank $\mathbf{R}_1 \geq G - 1$. But we have assumed that rank $\mathbf{R}_1 = J_1$, which is the row dimension of $\mathbf{R}_1$.

THEOREM 9.3 (Order Condition for Identification): In system (9.12) under assumption (9.17), a *necessary* condition for the first equation to be identified is

$$J_1 \geq G - 1, \tag{9.20}$$

where J_1 is the row dimension of $\mathbf{R}_1$. Equation (9.20) is the general form of the order condition.

We can summarize the steps for checking whether the first equation in the system is identified.

1. Set one element of γ_1 to -1 as a normalization.
2. Define the $J_1 \times (G + M)$ matrix $\mathbf{R}_1$ such that equation (9.17) captures all restrictions on $\boldsymbol{\beta}_1$.
3. If $J_1 < G - 1$, the first equation is not identified.
4. If $J_1 \geq G - 1$, the equation might be identified. Let $\mathbf{B}$ be the matrix of all structural parameters with only the normalization restrictions imposed, and compute $\mathbf{R}_1\mathbf{B}$. Now impose the restrictions in the entire system and check the rank condition (9.19).

The simplicity of the order condition makes it attractive as a tool for studying identification. Nevertheless, it is not difficult to write down examples where the order condition is satisfied but the rank condition fails.

Example 9.3 (Failure of the Rank Condition): Consider the following three-equation structural model in the population ($G = 3$, $M = 4$):

$$y_1 = \gamma_{12}y_2 + \gamma_{13}y_3 + \delta_{11}z_1 + \delta_{13}z_3 + u_1, \tag{9.21}$$

$$y_2 = \gamma_{21}y_1 + \delta_{21}z_1 + u_2, \tag{9.22}$$

$$y_3 = \delta_{31}z_1 + \delta_{32}z_2 + \delta_{33}z_3 + \delta_{34}z_4 + u_3, \tag{9.23}$$

where $z_1 \equiv 1$, $\mathrm{E}(u_g) = 0$, $g = 1, 2, 3$, and each z_j is uncorrelated with each u_g. Note that the third equation is already a reduced form equation (although it may also have a structural interpretation). In equation (9.21) we have set $\gamma_{11} = -1$, $\delta_{12} = 0$, and $\delta_{14} = 0$. Since this equation contains two right-hand-side endogenous variables and there are two excluded exogenous variables, it passes the order condition.

To check the rank condition, let $\boldsymbol{\beta}_1$ denote the 7×1 vector of parameters in the first equation with only the normalization restriction imposed: $\boldsymbol{\beta}_1 = (-1, \gamma_{12}, \gamma_{13}, \delta_{11}, \delta_{12}, \delta_{13}, \delta_{14})'$. The restrictions $\delta_{12} = 0$ and $\delta_{14} = 0$ are obtained by choosing

$$\mathbf{R}_1 = \begin{pmatrix} 0 & 0 & 0 & 0 & 1 & 0 & 0 \\ 0 & 0 & 0 & 0 & 0 & 0 & 1 \end{pmatrix}.$$

Let $\mathbf{B}$ be the full 7×3 matrix of parameters with only the three normalizations imposed (so that $\boldsymbol{\beta}_2 = (\gamma_{21}, -1, \gamma_{23}, \delta_{21}, \delta_{22}, \delta_{23}, \delta_{24})'$ and $\boldsymbol{\beta}_3 = (\gamma_{31}, \gamma_{32}, -1, \delta_{31}, \delta_{32}, \delta_{33}, \delta_{34})'$). Matrix multiplication gives

$$\mathbf{R}_1\mathbf{B} = \begin{pmatrix} \delta_{12} & \delta_{22} & \delta_{32} \\ \delta_{14} & \delta_{24} & \delta_{34} \end{pmatrix}.$$

Now we impose all of the restrictions in the system. In addition to the restrictions $\delta_{12} = 0$ and $\delta_{14} = 0$ from equation (9.21), we also have $\delta_{22} = 0$ and $\delta_{24} = 0$ from equation (9.22). Therefore, with all restrictions imposed,

$$\mathbf{R}_1\mathbf{B} = \begin{pmatrix} 0 & 0 & \delta_{32} \\ 0 & 0 & \delta_{34} \end{pmatrix}. \tag{9.24}$$

The rank of this matrix is at most unity, and so the rank condition fails because $G - 1 = 2$.

Equation (9.22) easily passes the order condition. What about the rank condition? If $\mathbf{R}_2$ is the 4×7 matrix imposing the restrictions on $\boldsymbol{\beta}_2$, namely, $\gamma_{23} = 0$, $\delta_{22} = 0$, $\delta_{23} = 0$, and $\delta_{24} = 0$, then it is easily seen that, with the restrictions on the entire system imposed,

$$\mathbf{R}_2\mathbf{B} = \begin{pmatrix} \gamma_{13} & 0 & -1 \\ 0 & 0 & \delta_{32} \\ \delta_{13} & 0 & \delta_{33} \\ 0 & 0 & \delta_{34} \end{pmatrix},$$

and we need this matrix to have rank equal to two if (9.22) is identified. A sufficient condition is $\delta_{13} \neq 0$ and at least one of δ_{32} and δ_{34} is different from zero. The rank condition fails if $\gamma_{13} = \delta_{13} = 0$, in which case y_1 and y_2 form a two-equation system with only one exogenous variable, z_1, appearing in both equations. The third equation, (9.23), is identified because it contains no endogenous explanatory variables.

When the restrictions on $\boldsymbol{\beta}_1$ consist entirely of normalization and exclusion restrictions, the order condition (9.20) reduces to the order condition (9.11), as can be seen by the following argument. When all restrictions are exclusion restrictions, the matrix $\mathbf{R}_1$ consists only of zeros and ones, and the number of rows in $\mathbf{R}_1$ equals the number of excluded right-hand-side endogenous variables, $G - G_1 - 1$, plus the number of excluded exogenous variables, $M - M_1$. In other words, $J_1 = (G - G_1 - 1) + (M - M_1)$, and so the order condition (9.20) becomes $(G - G_1 - 1) + (M - M_1) \geq G - 1$, which, upon rearrangement, becomes condition (9.11).

9.2.3 Unidentified, Just Identified, and Overidentified Equations

We have seen that, for identifying a single equation, the rank condition (9.19) is necessary and sufficient. When condition (9.19) fails, we say that the equation is **unidentified**.

When the rank condition holds, it is useful to refine the sense in which the equation is identified. If $J_1 = G - 1$, then we have just enough identifying information. If we were to drop one restriction in $\mathbf{R}_1$, we would necessarily lose identification of the first equation because the order condition would fail. Therefore, when $J_1 = G - 1$, we say that the equation is **just identified**.

If $J_1 > G - 1$, it is often possible to drop one or more restrictions on the parameters of the first equation and still achieve identification. In this case we say the equation is **overidentified**. Necessary but not sufficient for overidentification is $J_1 > G - 1$. It is possible that J_1 is strictly greater than $G - 1$ but the restrictions are such that dropping one restriction loses identification, in which case the equation is not overidentified.

In practice, we often appeal to the order condition to determine the degree of overidentification. While in special circumstances this approach can fail to be accurate, for most applications it is reasonable. Thus, for the first equation, $J_1 - (G - 1)$ is usually intepreted as the number of **overidentifying restrictions**.

Example 9.4 (Overidentifying Restrictions): Consider the two-equation system

$$y_1 = \gamma_{12} y_2 + \delta_{11} z_1 + \delta_{12} z_2 + \delta_{13} z_3 + \delta_{14} z_4 + u_1, \tag{9.25}$$

$$y_2 = \gamma_{21} y_1 + \delta_{21} z_1 + \delta_{22} z_2 + u_2, \tag{9.26}$$

where $\mathrm{E}(z_j u_g) = 0$, all j and g. Without further restrictions, equation (9.25) fails the order condition because every exogenous variable appears on the right-hand side, and the equation contains an endogenous variable. Using the order condition, equation (9.26) is overidentified, with one overidentifying restriction. If z_3 does not actually appear in equation (9.25), then equation (9.26) is just identified, assuming that $\delta_{14} \neq 0$.

9.3 Estimation after Identification

9.3.1 Robustness-Efficiency Trade-off

All SEMs with linearly homogeneous restrictions within each equation can be written with exclusion restrictions as in the system (9.1); doing so may require redefining some of the variables. If we let $\mathbf{x}_{(g)} = (\mathbf{y}_{(g)}, \mathbf{z}_{(g)})$ and $\boldsymbol{\beta}_{(g)} = (\boldsymbol{\gamma}'_{(g)}, \boldsymbol{\delta}'_{(g)})'$, then the system (9.1) is in the general form (8.11) with the slight change in notation. Under assumption (9.2) the matrix of instruments for observation i is the $G \times GM$ matrix

$$\mathbf{Z}_i \equiv \mathbf{I}_G \otimes \mathbf{z}_i. \tag{9.27}$$

If every equation in the system passes the rank condition, a system estimation procedure—such as 3SLS or the more general minimum chi-square estimator—can be used. Alternatively, the equations of interest can be estimated by 2SLS. The bottom line is that the methods studied in Chapters 5 and 8 are directly applicable. All of the tests we have covered apply, including the tests of overidentifying restrictions in Chapters 6 and 8 and the single-equation tests for endogeneity in Chapter 6.

When estimating a simultaneous equations system, it is important to remember the pros and cons of full system estimation. If all equations are correctly specified, system procedures are asymptotically more efficient than a single-equation procedure such as 2SLS. But single-equation methods are more robust. If interest lies, say, in the first equation of a system, 2SLS is consistent and asymptotically normal, provided the first equation is correctly specified and the instruments are exogenous. However, if one equation in a system is misspecified, the 3SLS or GMM estimates of all the parameters are generally inconsistent.

Example 9.5 (Labor Supply for Married, Working Women): Using the data in MROZ.RAW, we estimate a labor supply function for working, married women. Rather than specify a demand function, we specify the second equation as a wage offer function and impose the equilibrium condition:

$$\begin{aligned} hours = {} & \gamma_{12} \log(wage) + \delta_{10} + \delta_{11} educ + \delta_{12} age + \delta_{13} kidslt6 \\ & + \delta_{14} kidsge6 + \delta_{15} nwifeinc + u_1, \end{aligned} \tag{9.28}$$

$$\log(wage) = \gamma_{21} hours + \delta_{20} + \delta_{21} educ + \delta_{22} exper + \delta_{23} exper^2 + u_2, \tag{9.29}$$

where *kidslt6* is number of children less than 6, *kidsge6* is number of children between 6 and 18, and *nwifeinc* is income other than the woman's labor income. We assume that u_1 and u_2 have zero mean conditional on *educ*, *age*, *kidslt6*, *kidsge6*, *nwifeinc*, and *exper*.

The key restriction on the labor supply function is that *exper* (and $exper^2$) have no direct effect on current annual hours. This identifies the labor supply function with one overidentifying restriction, as used by Mroz (1987). We estimate the labor supply function first by OLS (to see what ignoring the endogeneity of log(*wage*) does) and then by 2SLS, using as instruments all exogenous variables in equations (9.28) and (9.29).

There are 428 women who worked at some time during the survey year, 1975. The average annual hours are about 1,303, with a minimum of 12 and a maximum of 4,950.

We first estimate the labor supply function by OLS:

$$\begin{aligned}\widehat{hours} = {} & \underset{(340.1)}{2{,}114.7} - \underset{(54.22)}{17.41}\,\log(wage) - \underset{(17.97)}{14.44}\,educ - \underset{(5.53)}{7.73}\,age \\ & - \underset{(100.01)}{342.50}\,kidslt6 - \underset{(30.83)}{115.02}\,kidsge6 - \underset{(3.66)}{4.35}\,nwifeinc.\end{aligned}$$

The OLS estimates indicate a downward-sloping labor supply function, although the estimate on log(*wage*) is statistically insignificant.

The estimates are much different when we use 2SLS:

$$\begin{aligned}\widehat{hours} = {} & \underset{(594.2)}{2{,}432.2} + \underset{(480.74)}{1{,}544.82}\,\log(wage) - \underset{(58.14)}{177.45}\,educ - \underset{(9.58)}{10.78}\,age \\ & - \underset{(176.93)}{210.83}\,kidslt6 - \underset{(56.92)}{47.56}\,kidsge6 - \underset{(6.48)}{9.25}\,nwifeinc.\end{aligned}$$

The estimated labor supply elasticity is $1{,}544.82/hours$. At the mean *hours* for working women, 1,303, the estimated elasticity is about 1.2, which is quite large.

The supply equation has a single overidentifying restriction. The regression of the 2SLS residuals $\hat{u}_1$ on all exogenous variables produces $R_u^2 = .002$, and so the test statistic is $428(.002) \approx .856$ with p-value $\approx .355$; the overidentifying restriction is not rejected.

Under the exclusion restrictions we have imposed, the wage offer function (9.29) is also identified. Before estimating the equation by 2SLS, we first estimate the reduced form for *hours* to ensure that the exogenous variables excluded from equation (9.29) are jointly significant. The p-value for the F test of joint significance of *age*, *kidslt6*, *kidsge6*, and *nwifeinc* is about .0009. Therefore, we can proceed with 2SLS estimation of the wage offer equation. The coefficient on *hours* is about .00016 (standard error $\approx .00022$), and so the wage offer does not appear to differ by hours worked. The remaining coefficients are similar to what is obtained by dropping *hours* from equation (9.29) and estimating the equation by OLS. (For example, the 2SLS coefficient on education is about .111 with se $\approx$ .015.)

Interestingly, while the wage offer function (9.29) is identified, the analogous labor demand function is apparently unidentified. (This finding shows that choosing the normalization—that is, choosing between a labor demand function and a wage offer function—is not innocuous.) The labor demand function, written in equilibrium, would look like this:

$$hours = \gamma_{22} \log(wage) + \delta_{20} + \delta_{21} educ + \delta_{22} exper + \delta_{23} exper^2 + u_2. \tag{9.30}$$

Estimating the reduced form for log(*wage*) and testing for joint significance of *age*, *kidslt6*, *kidsge6*, and *nwifeinc* yields a *p*-value of about .46, and so the exogenous variables excluded from equation (9.30) would not seem to appear in the reduced form for log(*wage*). Estimation of equation (9.30) by 2SLS would be pointless. (You are invited to estimate equation (9.30) by 2SLS to see what happens.)

It would be more efficient to estimate equations (9.28) and (9.29) by 3SLS, since each equation is overidentified (assuming the homoskedasticity assumption SIV.5). If heteroskedasticity is suspected, we could use the general minimum chi-square estimator. A system procedure is more efficient for estimating the labor supply function because it uses the information that *age*, *kidslt6*, *kidsge6*, and *nwifeinc* do not appear in the log(*wage*) equation. If these exclusion restrictions are wrong, the 3SLS estimators of parameters in *both* equations are generally inconsistent. Problem 9.9 asks you to obtain the 3SLS estimates for this example.

9.3.2 When Are 2SLS and 3SLS Equivalent?

In Section 8.4 we discussed the relationship between system 2SLS and (GMM) 3SLS for a general linear system. Applying that discussion to linear SEMs, we can immediately draw the following conclusions. First, if each equation is just identified, 2SLS equation by equation and 3SLS are identical; in fact, each is identical to the system IV estimator. Basically, there is only one consistent estimator, the IV estimator on each equation. Second, regardless of the degree of overidentification, 2SLS equation by equation and 3SLS are identical when $\hat{\mathbf{\Sigma}}$ is diagonal. (As a practical matter, this occurs only if we force $\hat{\mathbf{\Sigma}}$ to be diagonal.)

There are several other useful algebraic equivalences that have been derived elsewhere. Suppose that the first equation in the system is overidentified but every other equation in the system is just identified. Then the 2SLS estimator of the first equation is identical to its 3SLS estimates of the entire system. (A special case occurs when the first equation is a structural equation and all other equations are unrestricted reduced forms.) As an extension of this result, suppose for an identified system we put each equation in an identified system into two groups, just identified and overidentified. Then for the overidentified set of equations, the 3SLS estimates based on the entire system are identical to the 3SLS estimates obtained using only the overidentified subset. Of course, 3SLS estimation on the just identified set of equations is equivalent to 2SLS estimation on each equation, and this generally differs from the 3SLS estimates based on the entire system. See Schmidt (1976, Theorem 5.2.13) for verification.

9.3.3 Estimating the Reduced Form Parameters

So far, we have discussed estimation of the structural parameters. The usual justifications for focusing on the structural parameters are as follows: (1) we are interested in estimates of "economic parameters" (such as labor supply elasticities) for curiosity's sake; (2) estimates of structural parameters allow us to obtain the effects of a variety of policy interventions (such as changes in tax rates); and (3) even if we want to estimate the reduced form parameters, we often can do so more efficiently by first estimating the structural parameters. Concerning the second reason, if the goal is to estimate, say, the equilibrium change in hours worked given an exogenous change in a marginal tax rate, we must ultimately estimate the reduced form.

As another example, we might want to estimate the effect on county-level alcohol consumption due to an increase in exogenous alcohol taxes. In other words, we are interested in $\partial \mathrm{E}(y_g \mid \mathbf{z})/\partial z_j = \pi_{gj}$, where y_g is alcohol consumption and z_j is the tax on alcohol. Under weak assumptions, reduced form equations exist, and each equation of the reduced form can be estimated by ordinary least squares. Without placing any restrictions on the reduced form, OLS equation by equation is identical to SUR estimation (see Section 7.7). In other words, we do not need to analyze the structural equations at all in order to consistently estimate the reduced form parameters. Ordinary least squares estimates of the reduced form parameters are robust in the sense that they do not rely on any identification assumptions imposed on the structural system.

If the structural model is correctly specified and at least one equation is overidentified, we obtain asymptotically more efficient estimators of the reduced form parameters by deriving the estimates from the structural parameter estimates. In particular, given the structural parameter estimates $\hat{\mathbf{\Delta}}$ and $\hat{\mathbf{\Gamma}}$, we can obtain the reduced form estimates as $\hat{\mathbf{\Pi}} = -\hat{\mathbf{\Delta}}\hat{\mathbf{\Gamma}}^{-1}$ (see equation (9.14)). These are consistent, $\sqrt{N}$-asymptotically normal estimators (although the asymptotic variance matrix is somewhat complicated). From Problem 3.9, we obtain the most efficient estimator of $\mathbf{\Pi}$ by using the most efficient estimators of $\boldsymbol{\Delta}$ and $\boldsymbol{\Gamma}$ (minimum chi-square or, under system homoskedasticity, 3SLS).

Just as in estimating the structural parameters, there is a robustness-efficiency trade-off in estimating the π_{gj}. As mentioned earlier, the OLS estimators of each reduced form are robust to misspecification of any restrictions on the structural equations (although, as always, each element of $\mathbf{z}$ should be exogenous for OLS to be consistent). The estimators of the π_{gj} derived from estimators of $\boldsymbol{\Delta}$ and $\boldsymbol{\Gamma}$—whether the latter are 2SLS or system estimators—are generally nonrobust to incorrect restrictions on the structural system. See Problem 9.11 for a simple illustration.

9.4 Additional Topics in Linear Simultaneous Equations Methods

9.4.1 Using Cross Equation Restrictions to Achieve Identification

So far we have discussed identification of a single equation using only within-equation parameter restrictions (see assumption (9.17)). This is by far the leading case, especially when the system represents a simultaneous equations model with truly autonomous equations. In fact, it is hard to think of a sensible example with true simultaneity where one would feel comfortable imposing restrictions across equations. In supply and demand applications we typically do not think supply and demand parameters, which represent different sides of a market, would satisfy any known restrictions. In studying the relationship between college crime rates and arrest rates, any restrictions on the parameters across the two equations would be arbitrary. Nevertheless, there are examples where endogeneity is caused by omitted variables or measurement error where economic theory imposes cross equation restrictions. An example is a system of expenditure shares when total expenditures or prices are thought to be measured with error: the symmetry condition imposes cross equation restrictions. Not surprisingly, such **cross equation restrictions** are generally useful for identifying equations. A general treatment is beyond the scope of our analysis. Here we just give an example to show how identification and estimation work.

Consider the two-equation system

$$y_1 = \gamma_{12} y_2 + \delta_{11} z_1 + \delta_{12} z_2 + \delta_{13} z_3 + u_1, \tag{9.31}$$

$$y_2 = \gamma_{21} y_1 + \delta_{21} z_1 + \delta_{22} z_2 + u_2, \tag{9.32}$$

where each z_j is uncorrelated with u_1 and u_2 (z_1 can be unity to allow for an intercept). Without further information, equation (9.31) is unidentified, and equation (9.32) is just identified if and only if $\delta_{13} \neq 0$. We maintain these assumptions in what follows.

Now suppose that $\delta_{12} = \delta_{22}$. Because δ_{22} is identified in equation (9.32) we can treat it as known for studying identification of equation (9.31). But $\delta_{12} = \delta_{22}$, and so we can write

$$y_1 - \delta_{12}z_2 = \gamma_{12}y_2 + \delta_{11}z_1 + \delta_{13}z_3 + u_1, \tag{9.33}$$

where $y_1 - \delta_{12}z_2$ is effectively known. Now the right-hand side of equation (9.33) has one endogenous variable, y_2, and the two exogenous variables z_1 and z_3. Because z_2 is excluded from the right-hand side, we can use z_2 as an instrument for y_2, as long as z_2 appears in the reduced form for y_2. This is the case provided $\delta_{12} = \delta_{22} \neq 0$.

This approach to showing that equation (9.31) is identified also suggests a consistent estimation procedure: first, estimate equation (9.32) by 2SLS using (z_1, z_2, z_3) as instruments, and let $\hat{\delta}_{22}$ be the estimator of δ_{22}. Then, estimate

$$y_1 - \hat{\delta}_{22}z_2 = \gamma_{12}y_2 + \delta_{11}z_1 + \delta_{13}z_3 + \mathit{error}$$

by 2SLS using (z_1, z_2, z_3) as instruments. Since $\hat{\delta}_{22} \xrightarrow{p} \delta_{12}$ when $\delta_{12} = \delta_{22} \neq 0$, this last step produces consistent estimators of γ_{12}, δ_{11}, and δ_{13}. Unfortunately, the usual 2SLS standard errors obtained from the final estimation would not be valid because of the preliminary estimation of δ_{22}.

It is easier to use a system procedure when cross equation restrictions are present because the asymptotic variance can be obtained directly. We can always rewrite the system in a linear form with the restrictions imposed. For this example, one way to do so is to write the system as

$$\begin{pmatrix} y_1 \\ y_2 \end{pmatrix} = \begin{pmatrix} y_2 & z_1 & z_2 & z_3 & 0 & 0 \\ 0 & 0 & z_2 & 0 & y_1 & z_1 \end{pmatrix} \boldsymbol{\beta} + \begin{pmatrix} u_1 \\ u_2 \end{pmatrix}, \tag{9.34}$$

where $\boldsymbol{\beta} = (\gamma_{12}, \delta_{11}, \delta_{12}, \delta_{13}, \gamma_{21}, \delta_{21})'$. The parameter δ_{22} does not show up in $\boldsymbol{\beta}$ because we have imposed the restriction $\delta_{12} = \delta_{22}$ by appropriate choice of the matrix of explanatory variables.

The matrix of instruments is $\mathbf{I}_2 \otimes \mathbf{z}$, meaning that we just use all exogenous variables as instruments in each equation. Since $\mathbf{I}_2 \otimes \mathbf{z}$ has six columns, the order condition is exactly satisfied (there are six elements of $\boldsymbol{\beta}$), and we have already seen when the rank condition holds. The system can be consistently estimated using GMM or 3SLS.

9.4.2 Using Covariance Restrictions to Achieve Identification

In most applications of linear SEMs, identification is obtained by putting restrictions on the matrix of structural parameters $\mathbf{B}$. It is also possible to identify the elements of

$\mathbf{B}$ by placing restrictions on the variance matrix $\mathbf{\Sigma}$ of the structural errors. Usually the restrictions come in the form of zero covariance assumptions. In microeconomic applications of models with true simultaneity, it is difficult to think of examples of autonomous systems of equations where it makes sense to assume the errors across the different structural equations are uncorrelated. For example, in individual-level labor supply and demand functions, what would be the justification for assuming that unobserved factors affecting a person's labor supply decisions are uncorrelated with unobserved factors that make the person a more or less desirable worker? In a model of city crime rates and spending on law enforcement, it hardly makes sense to assume that unobserved city features that affect crime rates are uncorrelated with those determining law enforcement expenditures. Nevertheless, there are applications where zero covariance assumptions can make sense, and so we provide a brief treatment here, using examples to illustrate the approach. General analyses of identification with restrictions on $\mathbf{\Sigma}$ are given in Hausman (1983) and Hausman, Newey, and Taylor (1987).

The first example is the two-equation system

$$y_1 = \gamma_{12} y_2 + \delta_{11} z_1 + \delta_{13} z_3 + u_1, \tag{9.35}$$

$$y_2 = \gamma_{21} y_1 + \delta_{21} z_1 + \delta_{22} z_2 + \delta_{23} z_3 + u_2. \tag{9.36}$$

Equation (9.35) is just identified if $\delta_{22} \neq 0$, which we assume, while equation (9.36) is unidentified without more information. Suppose that we have one piece of additional information in terms of a covariance restriction:

$$\mathrm{Cov}(u_1, u_2) = \mathrm{E}(u_1 u_2) = 0. \tag{9.37}$$

In other words, if $\mathbf{\Sigma}$ is the 2×2 structural variance matrix, we are assuming that $\mathbf{\Sigma}$ is diagonal. Assumption (9.37), along with $\delta_{22} \neq 0$, is enough to identify equation (9.36).

Here is a simple way to see how assumption (9.37) identifies equation (9.36). First, because γ_{12}, δ_{11}, and δ_{13} are identified, we can treat them as known when studying identification of equation (9.36). But if the parameters in equation (9.35) are known, u_1 is effectively known. By assumption (9.37), u_1 is uncorrelated with u_2, and u_1 is certainly partially correlated with y_1. Thus, we effectively have (z_1, z_2, z_3, u_1) as instruments available for estimating equation (9.36), and this result shows that equation (9.36) is identified.

We can use this method for verifying identification to obtain consistent estimators. First, estimate equation (9.35) by 2SLS using instruments (z_1, z_2, z_3) and save the 2SLS residuals, $\hat{u}_1$. Then estimate equation (9.36) by 2SLS using instruments $(z_1, z_2, z_3, \hat{u}_1)$. The fact that $\hat{u}_1$ depends on estimates from a prior stage does not affect consistency. But inference is complicated because of the estimation of u_1: condition (6.8) does not hold because u_1 depends on y_2, which is correlated with u_2.

The most efficient way to use covariance restrictions is to write the entire set of orthogonality conditions as $\mathrm{E}[\mathbf{z}'u_1(\boldsymbol{\beta}_1)] = \mathbf{0}$, $\mathrm{E}[\mathbf{z}'u_2(\boldsymbol{\beta}_2)] = \mathbf{0}$, and

$$\mathrm{E}[u_1(\boldsymbol{\beta}_1)u_2(\boldsymbol{\beta}_2)] = 0, \tag{9.38}$$

where the notation $u_1(\boldsymbol{\beta}_1)$ emphasizes that the errors are functions of the structural parameters $\boldsymbol{\beta}_1$—with normalization and exclusion restrictions imposed—and similarly for $u_2(\boldsymbol{\beta}_2)$. For example, from equation (9.35), $u_1(\boldsymbol{\beta}_1) = y_1 - \gamma_{12}y_2 - \delta_{11}z_1 - \delta_{13}z_3$. Equation (9.38), because it is nonlinear in $\boldsymbol{\beta}_1$ and $\boldsymbol{\beta}_2$, takes us outside the realm of linear moment restrictions. In Chapter 14 we will use nonlinear moment conditions in GMM estimation.

A general example with covariance restrictions is a fully recursive system. First, a **recursive system** can be written as

$$\begin{aligned}
y_1 &= \mathbf{z}\boldsymbol{\delta}_1 + u_1,\\
y_2 &= \gamma_{21}y_1 + \mathbf{z}\boldsymbol{\delta}_2 + u_2,\\
y_3 &= \gamma_{31}y_1 + \gamma_{32}y_2 + \mathbf{z}\boldsymbol{\delta}_3 + u_3,\\
&\vdots\\
y_G &= \gamma_{G1}y_1 + \cdots + \gamma_{G,G-1}y_{G-1} + \mathbf{z}\boldsymbol{\delta}_G + u_G,
\end{aligned} \tag{9.39}$$

so that in each equation, only endogenous variables from previous equations appear on the right-hand side. We have allowed all exogenous variables to appear in each equation, and we maintain assumption (9.2).

The first equation in the system (9.39) is clearly identified and can be estimated by OLS. Without further exclusion restrictions none of the remaining equations is identified, but each is identified if we assume that the structural errors are pairwise uncorrelated:

$$\mathrm{Cov}(u_g, u_h) = 0, \qquad g \neq h. \tag{9.40}$$

This assumption means that $\boldsymbol{\Sigma}$ is a $G \times G$ diagonal matrix. Equations (9.39) and (9.40) define a **fully recursive system**. Under these assumptions, the right-hand-side variables in equation g are each uncorrelated with u_g; this fact is easily seen by starting with the first equation and noting that y_1 is a linear function of $\mathbf{z}$ and u_1. Then, in the second equation, y_1 is uncorrelated with u_2 under assumption (9.40). But y_2 is a linear function of $\mathbf{z}$, u_1, and u_2, and so y_2 and y_1 are both uncorrelated with u_3

in the third equation. And so on. It follows that each equation in the system is consistently estimated by ordinary least squares.

It turns out that OLS equation by equation is not necessarily the most efficient estimator in fully recursive systems, even though $\boldsymbol{\Sigma}$ is a diagonal matrix. Generally, efficiency can be improved by adding the zero covariance restrictions to the orthogonality conditions, as in equation (9.38), and applying nonlinear GMM estimation. See Lahiri and Schmidt (1978) and Hausman, Newey, and Taylor (1987).

9.4.3 Subtleties Concerning Identification and Efficiency in Linear Systems

So far we have discussed identification and estimation under the assumption that each exogenous variable appearing in the system, z_j, is *uncorrelated* with each structural error, u_g. It is important to assume only zero correlation in the general treatment because we often add a reduced form equation for an endogenous variable to a structural system, and zero correlation is all we should impose in linear reduced forms.

For entirely structural systems, it is often natural to assume that the structural errors satisfy the zero conditional mean assumption

$$\mathrm{E}(u_g \mid \mathbf{z}) = 0, \qquad g = 1, 2, \ldots, G. \tag{9.41}$$

In addition to giving the parameters in the structural equations the appropriate partial effect interpretations, assumption (9.41) has some interesting statistical implications: *any* function of $\mathbf{z}$ is uncorrelated with each error u_g. Therefore, in the labor supply example (9.28), age^2, $\log(age)$, $educ \cdot exper$, and so on (there are too many functions to list) are all uncorrelated with u_1 and u_2. Realizing this fact, we might ask, why not use nonlinear functions of $\mathbf{z}$ as additional instruments in estimation?

We need to break the answer to this question into two parts. The first concerns identification and the second concerns efficiency. For identification, the bottom line is this: adding nonlinear functions of $\mathbf{z}$ to the instrument list *cannot* help with identification in linear systems. You were asked to show this generally in Problem 8.4, but the main points can be illustrated with a simple model:

$$y_1 = \gamma_{12} y_2 + \delta_{11} z_1 + \delta_{12} z_2 + u_1, \tag{9.42}$$

$$y_2 = \gamma_{21} y_1 + \delta_{21} z_1 + u_2, \tag{9.43}$$

$$\mathrm{E}(u_1 \mid \mathbf{z}) = \mathrm{E}(u_2 \mid \mathbf{z}) = 0. \tag{9.44}$$

From the order condition in Section 9.2.2, equation (9.42) is not identified, and equation (9.43) is identified if and only if $\delta_{12} \neq 0$. Knowing properties of conditional expectations, we might try something clever to identify equation (9.42): since, say, z_1^2 is uncorrelated with u_1 under assumption (9.41), and z_1^2 would appear to be correlated with y_2, we can use it as an instrument for y_2 in equation (9.42). Under this reasoning, we would have enough instruments—z_1, z_2, z_1^2—to identify equation (9.42). In fact, any number of functions of z_1 and z_2 can be added to the instrument list.

The fact that this argument is faulty is fortunate because our identification analysis in Section 9.2.2 says that equation (9.42) is not identified. In this example it is clear that z_1^2 cannot appear in the reduced form for y_2 because z_1^2 appears nowhere in the system. Technically, because $\mathrm{E}(y_2 \mid \mathbf{z})$ is linear in z_1 and z_2 under assumption (9.44), the linear projection of y_2 onto (z_1, z_2, z_1^2) does not depend on z_1^2:

$$\mathrm{L}(y_2 \mid z_1, z_2, z_1^2) = \mathrm{L}(y_2 \mid z_1, z_2) = \pi_{21} z_1 + \pi_{22} z_2. \tag{9.45}$$

In other words, there is no *partial* correlation between y_2 and z_1^2 once z_1 and z_2 are included in the projection.

The zero conditional mean assumptions (9.41) can have some relevance for choosing an efficient estimator, although not always. If assumption (9.41) holds and $\mathrm{Var}(\mathbf{u} \mid \mathbf{z}) = \mathrm{Var}(\mathbf{u}) = \boldsymbol{\Sigma}$, 3SLS using instruments $\mathbf{z}$ for each equation is the asymptotically efficient estimator that uses the orthogonality conditions in assumption (9.41); this conclusion follows from Theorem 8.5. In other words, if $\mathrm{Var}(\mathbf{u} \mid \mathbf{z})$ is constant, it does not help to expand the instrument list beyond the functions of the exogenous variables actually appearing in the system.

If assumption (9.41) holds but $\mathrm{Var}(\mathbf{u} \mid \mathbf{z})$ is not constant, then we know from Chapter 8 that the GMM 3SLS estimator is not an efficient GMM estimator when the system is overidentified. In fact, under (9.41), without homoskedasticity there is no need to stop at instruments $\mathbf{z}$, at least in theory. Why? As we discussed in Section 8.6, one never does worse asymptotically by adding more valid instruments. Under (9.41), any functions of $\mathbf{z}$, collected in the vector $\mathbf{h}(\mathbf{z})$, are uncorrelated with every element of $\mathbf{u}$. Therefore, we can generally improve over the optimal GMM (minimum chi-square) estimator that uses IVs $\mathbf{z}$ by applying optimal GMM with instruments $[\mathbf{z}, \mathbf{h}(\mathbf{z})]$. This result was discovered independently by Hansen (1982) and White (1982b). Expanding the IV list to arbitrary functions of $\mathbf{z}$ and applying full GMM is not used very much in practice: it is usually not clear how to choose $\mathbf{h}(\mathbf{z})$, and, if we use too many additional instruments, the finite sample properties of the GMM estimator can be poor, as we discussed in Section 8.6.

For SEMs linear in the parameters but nonlinear in endogenous variables (in a sense to be made precise), adding nonlinear functions of the exogenous variables to the instruments not only is desirable but is often needed to achieve identification. We turn to this topic next.

9.5 Simultaneous Equations Models Nonlinear in Endogenous Variables

We now study models that are nonlinear in some endogenous variables. While the general estimation methods we have covered are still applicable, identification and choice of instruments require special attention.

9.5.1 Identification

The issues that arise in identifying models nonlinear in endogenous variables are most easily illustrated with a simple example. Suppose that supply and demand are given by

$$\log(q) = \gamma_{12}\log(p) + \gamma_{13}[\log(p)]^2 + \delta_{11}z_1 + u_1, \tag{9.46}$$

$$\log(q) = \gamma_{22}\log(p) + \delta_{22}z_2 + u_2, \tag{9.47}$$

$$\mathrm{E}(u_1 \mid \mathbf{z}) = \mathrm{E}(u_2 \mid \mathbf{z}) = 0, \tag{9.48}$$

where the first equation is the supply equation, the second equation is the demand equation, and the equilibrium condition that supply equals demand has been imposed. For simplicity, we do not include an intercept in either equation, but no important conclusions hinge on this omission. The exogenous variable z_1 shifts the supply function but not the demand function; z_2 shifts the demand function but not the supply function. The vector of exogenous variables appearing somewhere in the system is $\mathbf{z} = (z_1, z_2)$.

It is important to understand why equations (9.46) and (9.47) constitute a "nonlinear" system. This system is still linear in *parameters*, which is important because it means that the IV procedures we have learned up to this point are still applicable. Further, it is *not* the presence of the logarithmic transformations of q and p that makes the system nonlinear. In fact, if we set $\gamma_{13} = 0$, then the model *is* linear for the purposes of identification and estimation: defining $y_1 \equiv \log(q)$ and $y_2 \equiv \log(p)$, we can write equations (9.46) and (9.47) as a standard two-equation system.

When we include $[\log(p)]^2$ we have the model

$$y_1 = \gamma_{12}y_2 + \gamma_{13}y_2^2 + \delta_{11}z_1 + u_1, \tag{9.49}$$

$$y_1 = \gamma_{22}y_2 + \delta_{22}z_2 + u_2. \tag{9.50}$$

With this system there is no way to define *two* endogenous variables such that the system is a two-equation system linear in two endogenous variables. The presence of y_2^2 in equation (9.49) makes this model different from those we have studied up until now. We say that this is a system **nonlinear in endogenous variables**, and this entails a different treatment of identification.

If we used equations (9.49) and (9.50) to obtain y_2 as a function of the z_1, z_2, u_1, u_2, and the parameters, the result would not be linear in $\mathbf{z}$ and $\mathbf{u}$. In this particular case we can find the solution for y_2 using the quadratic formula (assuming a real solution exists). However, $\mathrm{E}(y_2 \mid \mathbf{z})$ would not be linear in $\mathbf{z}$ unless $\gamma_{13} = 0$, and $\mathrm{E}(y_2^2 \mid \mathbf{z})$ would not be linear in $\mathbf{z}$ regardless of the value of γ_{13}. These observations have important implications for identification of equation (9.49) and for choosing instruments.

Before considering equations (9.49) and (9.50) further, consider a second example where closed form expressions for the endogenous variables in terms of the exogenous variables and structural errors do not even exist. Suppose that a system describing crime rates in terms of law enforcement spending is

$$crime = \gamma_{12} \log(spending) + \mathbf{z}_{(1)}\boldsymbol{\delta}_{(1)} + u_1, \tag{9.51}$$

$$spending = \gamma_{21} crime + \gamma_{22} crime^2 + \mathbf{z}_{(2)}\boldsymbol{\delta}_{(2)} + u_2, \tag{9.52}$$

where the errors have zero mean given $\mathbf{z}$. Here, we cannot solve for either *crime* or *spending* (or any other transformation of them) in terms of $\mathbf{z}$, u_1, u_2, and the parameters. And there is no way to define y_1 and y_2 to yield a linear SEM in two endogenous variables. The model is still linear in parameters, but $\mathrm{E}(crime \mid \mathbf{z})$, $\mathrm{E}[\log(spending) \mid \mathbf{z}]$, and $\mathrm{E}(spending \mid \mathbf{z})$ are not linear in $\mathbf{z}$ (nor can we find closed forms for these expectations).

One possible approach to identification in nonlinear SEMs is to ignore the fact that the same endogenous variables show up differently in different equations. In the supply and demand example, define $y_3 \equiv y_2^2$ and rewrite equation (9.49) as

$$y_1 = \gamma_{12} y_2 + \gamma_{13} y_3 + \delta_{11} z_1 + u_1. \tag{9.53}$$

Or, in equations (9.51) and (9.52) define $y_1 = crime$, $y_2 = spending$, $y_3 = \log(spending)$, and $y_4 = crime^2$, and write

$$y_1 = \gamma_{12} y_3 + \mathbf{z}_{(1)}\boldsymbol{\delta}_{(1)} + u_1, \tag{9.54}$$

$$y_2 = \gamma_{21} y_1 + \gamma_{22} y_4 + \mathbf{z}_{(2)}\boldsymbol{\delta}_{(2)} + u_2. \tag{9.55}$$

Defining nonlinear functions of endogenous variables as new endogenous variables turns out to work fairly generally, *provided* we apply the rank and order conditions properly. The key question is, what kinds of equations do we add to the system for the newly defined endogenous variables?

If we add linear projections of the newly defined endogenous variables in terms of the *original* exogenous variables appearing somewhere in the system—that is, the linear projection onto $\mathbf{z}$—then we are being much too restrictive. For example, suppose to equations (9.53) and (9.50) we add the linear equation

$$y_3 = \pi_{31}z_1 + \pi_{32}z_2 + v_3, \tag{9.56}$$

where, by definition, $\mathrm{E}(z_1v_3) = \mathrm{E}(z_2v_3) = 0$. With equation (9.56) to round out the system, the order condition for identification of equation (9.53) clearly fails: we have two endogenous variables in equation (9.53) but only one excluded exogenous variable, z_2.

The conclusion that equation (9.53) is not identified is too pessimistic. There are many other possible instruments available for y_2^2. Because $\mathrm{E}(y_2^2 \mid \mathbf{z})$ is not linear in z_1 and z_2 (even if $\gamma_{13} = 0$), other functions of z_1 and z_2 will appear in a linear projection involving y_2^2 as the dependent variable. To see what the most useful of these are likely to be, suppose that the structural system actually is linear, so that $\gamma_{13} = 0$. Then $y_2 = \pi_{21}z_1 + \pi_{22}z_2 + v_2$, where v_2 is a linear combination of u_1 and u_2. Squaring this reduced form and using $\mathrm{E}(v_2 \mid \mathbf{z}) = 0$ gives

$$\mathrm{E}(y_2^2 \mid \mathbf{z}) = \pi_{21}^2 z_1^2 + \pi_{22}^2 z_2^2 + 2\pi_{21}\pi_{22}z_1z_2 + \mathrm{E}(v_2^2 \mid \mathbf{z}). \tag{9.57}$$

If $\mathrm{E}(v_2^2 \mid \mathbf{z})$ is constant, an assumption that holds under homoskedasticity of the structural errors, then equation (9.57) shows that y_2^2 is correlated with z_1^2, z_2^2, and z_1z_2, which makes these functions natural instruments for y_2^2. The only case where no functions of $\mathbf{z}$ are correlated with y_2^2 occurs when both π_{21} and π_{22} equal zero, in which case the linear version of equation (9.49) (with $\gamma_{13} = 0$) is also unidentified.

Because we derived equation (9.57) under the restrictive assumptions $\gamma_{13} = 0$ and homoskedasticity of v_2, we would not want our linear projection for y_2^2 to omit the exogenous variables that originally appear in the system. (Plus, for simplicity, we omitted intercepts from the equations.) In practice, we would augment equations (9.53) and (9.50) with the linear projection

$$y_3 = \pi_{31}z_1 + \pi_{32}z_2 + \pi_{33}z_1^2 + \pi_{34}z_2^2 + \pi_{35}z_1z_2 + v_3, \tag{9.58}$$

where v_3 is, by definition, uncorrelated with z_1, z_2, z_1^2, z_2^2, and z_1z_2. The system (9.53), (9.50), and (9.58) can now be studied using the usual rank condition.

Adding equation (9.58) to the original system and then studying the rank condition of the first two equations is equivalent to studying the rank condition in the smaller system (9.53) and (9.50). What we mean by this statement is that we do not explicitly add an equation for $y_3 = y_2^2$, but we *do* include y_3 in equation (9.53). Therefore, when applying the rank condition to equation (9.53), we use $G = 2$ (not $G = 3$). The reason this approach is the same as studying the rank condition in the three-equation system (9.53), (9.50), and (9.58) is that adding the third equation increases the rank of

$\mathbf{R}_1\mathbf{B}$ by one whenever at least one additional nonlinear function of $\mathbf{z}$ appears in equation (9.58). (The functions z_1^2, z_2^2, and $z_1 z_2$ appear nowhere else in the system.)

As a general approach to identification in models where the nonlinear functions of the endogenous variables depend only on a single endogenous variable—such as the two examples that we have already covered—Fisher (1965) argues that the following method is sufficient for identification:

1. Relabel the nonredundant functions of the endogenous variables to be new endogenous variables, as in equation (9.53) or in equations (9.54) and (9.55).

2. Apply the rank condition to the original system *without* increasing the number of equations. If the equation of interest satisfies the rank condition, then it is identified.

The proof that this method works is complicated, and it requires more assumptions than we have made (such as $\mathbf{u}$ being *independent* of $\mathbf{z}$). Intuitively, we can expect each additional nonlinear function of the endogenous variables to have a linear projection that depends on new functions of the exogenous variables. Each time we add another function of an endogenous variable, it effectively comes with its own instruments.

Fisher's method can be expected to work in all but the most pathological cases. One case where it does not work is if $\mathrm{E}(v_2^2 \mid \mathbf{z})$ in equation (9.57) is heteroskedastic in such a way as to cancel out the squares and cross product terms in z_1 and z_2; then $\mathrm{E}(y_2^2 \mid \mathbf{z})$ would be constant. Such unfortunate coincidences are not practically important.

It is tempting to think that Fisher's rank condition is also necessary for identification, but this is not the case. To see why, consider the two-equation system

$$y_1 = \gamma_{12} y_2 + \gamma_{13} y_2^2 + \delta_{11} z_1 + \delta_{12} z_2 + u_1, \tag{9.59}$$

$$y_2 = \gamma_{21} y_1 + \delta_{21} z_1 + u_2. \tag{9.60}$$

The first equation clearly fails the modified rank condition because it fails the order condition: there are no restrictions on the first equation except the normalization restriction. However, if $\gamma_{13} \neq 0$ and $\gamma_{21} \neq 0$, then $\mathrm{E}(y_2 \mid \mathbf{z})$ is a nonlinear function of $\mathbf{z}$ (which we cannot obtain in closed form). The result is that functions such as z_1^2, z_2^2, and $z_1 z_2$ (and others) will appear in the linear projections of y_2 and y_2^2 even after z_1 and z_2 have been included, and these can then be used as instruments for y_2 and y_2^2. But if $\gamma_{13} = 0$, the first equation cannot be identified by adding nonlinear functions of z_1 and z_2 to the instrument list: the linear projection of y_2 on z_1, z_2, and any function of (z_1, z_2) will only depend on z_1 and z_2.

Equation (9.59) is an example of a **poorly identified model** because, when it is identified, it is **identified due to a nonlinearity** ($\gamma_{13} \neq 0$ in this case). Such identification is especially tenuous because the hypothesis H_0: $\gamma_{13} = 0$ cannot be tested by estimating the structural equation (since the structural equation is not identified when H_0 holds).

There are other models where identification can be verified using reasoning similar to that used in the labor supply example. Models with interactions between exogenous variables and endogenous variables can be shown to be identified when the model without the interactions is identified (see Example 6.2 and Problem 9.6). Models with interactions among endogenous variables are also fairly easy to handle. Generally, it is good practice to check whether the most general *linear* version of the model would be identified. If it is, then the nonlinear version of the model is probably identified. We saw this result in equation (9.46): if this equation is identified when $\gamma_{13} = 0$, then it is identified for any value of γ_{13}. If the most general linear version of a nonlinear model is not identified, we should be very wary about proceeding, since identification hinges on the presence of nonlinearities that we usually will not be able to test.

9.5.2 Estimation

In practice, it is difficult to know which additional functions we should add to the instrument list for nonlinear SEMs. Naturally, we must always include the exogenous variables appearing somewhere in the system instruments in every equation. After that, the choice is somewhat arbitrary, although the functional forms appearing in the structural equations can be helpful.

A general approach is to always use some squares and cross products of the exogenous variables appearing somewhere in the system. If *exper* and $exper^2$ appear in the system, additional terms such as $exper^3$ and $exper^4$ are natural additions to the instrument list.

Once we decide on a set of instruments, any equation in a nonlinear SEM can be estimated by 2SLS. Because each equation satisfies the assumptions of single-equation analysis, we can use everything we have learned up to now for inference and specification testing for 2SLS. A system method can also be used, where linear projections for the functions of endogenous variables are explicitly added to the system. Then, all exogenous variables included in these linear projections can be used as the instruments for every equation. The minimum chi-square estimator is generally more appropriate than 3SLS because the homoskedasticity assumption will rarely be satisfied in the linear projections.

It is important to apply the instrumental variables procedures directly to the structural equation or equations. In other words, we should directly use the formulas for 2SLS, 3SLS, or GMM. Trying to mimic 2SLS or 3SLS by substituting fitted values for some of the endogenous variables inside the nonlinear functions is usually a mistake: neither the conditional expectation nor the linear projection operator passes through nonlinear functions, and so such attempts rarely produce consistent estimators in nonlinear systems.

Example 9.6 (Nonlinear Labor Supply Function): We add $[\log(wage)]^2$ to the labor supply function in Example 9.5:

$$hours = \gamma_{12}\log(wage) + \gamma_{13}[\log(wage)]^2 + \delta_{10} + \delta_{11}educ + \delta_{12}age + \delta_{13}kidslt6 + \delta_{14}kidsge6 + \delta_{15}nwifeinc + u_1, \tag{9.61}$$

$$\log(wage) = \delta_{20} + \delta_{21}educ + \delta_{22}exper + \delta_{23}exper^2 + u_2, \tag{9.62}$$

where we have dropped *hours* from the wage offer function because it was insignificant in Example 9.5. The natural assumptions in this system are $\mathrm{E}(u_1 \mid \mathbf{z}) = \mathrm{E}(u_2 \mid \mathbf{z}) = 0$, where $\mathbf{z}$ contains all variables other than *hours* and $\log(wage)$.

There are many possibilities as additional instruments for $[\log(wage)]^2$. Here, we add three quadratic terms to the list—age^2, $educ^2$, and $nwifeinc^2$—and we estimate equation (9.61) by 2SLS. We obtain $\hat{\gamma}_{12} = 1{,}873.62$ (se = 635.99) and $\hat{\gamma}_{13} = -437.29$ (se = 350.08). The t statistic on $[\log(wage)]^2$ is about -1.25, so we would be justified in dropping it from the labor supply function. Regressing the 2SLS residuals $\hat{u}_1$ on all variables used as instruments in the supply equation gives R-squared = .0061, and so the N-R-squared statistic is 2.61. With a χ_3^2 distribution this gives p-value = .456. Thus, we fail to reject the overidentifying restrictions.

In the previous example we may be tempted to estimate the labor supply function using a two-step procedure that appears to mimic 2SLS:

1. Regress $\log(wage)$ on all exogenous variables appearing in equations (9.61) and (9.62) and obtain the predicted values. For emphasis, call these $\hat{y}_2$.
2. Estimate the labor supply function from the OLS regression *hours* on 1, $\hat{y}_2$, $(\hat{y}_2)^2$, $educ, \ldots, nwifeinc$.

This two-step procedure is *not* the same as estimating equation (9.61) by 2SLS, and, except in special circumstances, it does *not* produce consistent estimators of the structural parameters. The regression in step 2 is an example of what is sometimes called a **forbidden regression**, a phrase that describes replacing a nonlinear function of an endogenous explanatory variable with the same nonlinear function of fitted values from a first-stage estimation. In plugging fitted values into equation (9.61), our mistake is in thinking that the linear projection of the square is the square of the linear projection. What the 2SLS estimator does in the first stage is project each of y_2 and

y_2^2 onto the original exogenous variables and the additional nonlinear functions of these that we have chosen. The fitted values from the reduced form regression for y_2^2, say $\hat{y}_3$, are not the same as the squared fitted values from the reduced form regression for y_2, $(\hat{y}_2)^2$. This distinction is the difference between a consistent estimator and an inconsistent estimator.

If we apply the forbidden regression to equation (9.61), some of the estimates are very different from the 2SLS estimates. For example, the coefficient on *educ*, when equation (9.61) is properly estimated by 2SLS, is about -87.85 with a t statistic of -1.32. The forbidden regression gives a coefficient on *educ* of about -176.68 with a t statistic of -5.36. Unfortunately, the t statistic from the forbidden regression is generally invalid, even asymptotically. (The forbidden regression will produce consistent estimators in the special case $\gamma_{13} = 0$ if $\mathrm{E}(u_1 \mid \mathbf{z}) = 0$; see Problem 9.12.)

Many more functions of the exogenous variables could be added to the instrument list in estimating the labor supply function. From Chapter 8, we know that efficiency of GMM never falls by adding more nonlinear functions of the exogenous variables to the instrument list (even under the homoskedasticity assumption). This statement is true whether we use a single-equation or system method. Unfortunately, the fact that we do no worse asymptotically by adding instruments is of limited practical help, since we do not want to use too many instruments for a given data set. In Example 9.6, rather than using a long list of additional nonlinear functions, we might use $(\hat{y}_2)^2$ as a single IV for y_2^2. (This method is not the same as the forbidden regression!) If it happens that $\gamma_{13} = 0$ and the structural errors are homoskedastic, this would be the optimal IV. (See Problem 9.12.)

A general system linear in parameters can be written as

$$\begin{aligned} y_1 &= \mathbf{q}_1(\mathbf{y}, \mathbf{z})\boldsymbol{\beta}_1 + u_1 \\ &\vdots \\ y_G &= \mathbf{q}_G(\mathbf{y}, \mathbf{z})\boldsymbol{\beta}_G + u_G, \end{aligned} \tag{9.63}$$

where $\mathrm{E}(u_g \mid \mathbf{z}) = 0$, $g = 1, 2, \ldots, G$. Among other things this system allows for complicated interactions among endogenous and exogenous variables. We will not give a general analysis of such systems because identification and choice of instruments are too abstract to be very useful. Either single-equation or system methods can be used for estimation.

9.5.3 Control Function Estimation for Triangular Systems

A **triangular system** of equations is similar to a recursive system, defined in Section 9.4.2, except that we now allow several endogenous variables to be determined by only exogenous variables (and errors) and then assume those appear in a set of equations for another set of endogenous variables. Allowing for nonlinear functions of endogenous and exogenous variables, we can write

$$\mathbf{y}_1 = \mathbf{F}_1(\mathbf{y}_2, \mathbf{z})\boldsymbol{\beta}_1 + \mathbf{u}_1, \tag{9.64}$$

$$\mathbf{y}_2 = \mathbf{F}_2(\mathbf{z})\boldsymbol{\beta}_2 + \mathbf{u}_2, \tag{9.65}$$

where $\mathbf{y}_1$ is $G_1 \times 1$, $\mathbf{y}_2$ is $G_2 \times 1$, and the functions $\mathbf{F}_1(\cdot)$ and $\mathbf{F}_2(\cdot)$ are known matrix functions. We maintain the exogeneity assumptions

$$\mathrm{E}(\mathbf{u}_1 \mid \mathbf{z}) = \mathbf{0}, \qquad \mathrm{E}(\mathbf{u}_2 \mid \mathbf{z}) = \mathbf{0}, \tag{9.66}$$

without which nonlinear systems are rarely identified. Typically our interest is in (9.64). In fact, (9.65) is often a set of reduced form equations; in any case, $\mathrm{E}(\mathbf{y}_2 \mid \mathbf{z}) = \mathbf{F}_2(\mathbf{z})$. A potentially important point is that a nonlinear structural model, where (9.64) is augmented with an equation where $\mathbf{y}_2$ is a function of $\mathbf{y}_1$, could rarely be solved to produce (9.65) with known $\mathbf{F}_2(\cdot)$ and an additive error with zero conditional mean. Nevertheless, we might simply think of (9.65), with $\mathbf{F}_2(\cdot)$ sufficiently flexible, as a way to approximate $\mathrm{E}(\mathbf{y}_2 \mid \mathbf{z})$.

Without further assumptions, we can estimate (9.64) and (9.65) by GMM methods, provided (9.64) is identified. (Remember, unless $\mathbf{F}_2(\mathbf{z})$ contains exact linear dependencies, (9.65) would always be identified.) Given $\mathbf{F}_1(\cdot)$ and $\mathbf{F}_2(\cdot)$, instruments might suggest themselves, or we might use polynomials of low orders. Here, we discuss a control function approach under an additional assumption, a special case of which we saw in Section 6.2:

$$\mathrm{E}(\mathbf{u}_1 \mid \mathbf{u}_2, \mathbf{z}) = \mathrm{E}(\mathbf{u}_1 \mid \mathbf{u}_2). \tag{9.67}$$

A sufficient condition for (9.67) is that $(\mathbf{u}_1, \mathbf{u}_2)$ is independent of $\mathbf{z}$, but independence is a pretty strong assumption, especially if (9.65) is simply supposed to be a way to specify a model for $\mathrm{E}(\mathbf{y}_2 \mid \mathbf{z})$. Assuming that (9.65) holds with $\mathbf{u}_2$ independent of $\mathbf{z}$ effectively rules out discreteness in the elements of $\mathbf{y}_2$, as will become clear in Part IV of the text. But sometimes (9.67) is reasonable.

The power of (9.67) is that we can write

$$\begin{aligned}\mathrm{E}(\mathbf{y}_1 \mid \mathbf{y}_2, \mathbf{z}) &= \mathrm{E}(\mathbf{y}_1 \mid \mathbf{u}_2, \mathbf{z}) = \mathbf{F}_1(\mathbf{y}_2, \mathbf{z})\boldsymbol{\beta}_1 + \mathrm{E}(\mathbf{u}_1 \mid \mathbf{u}_2, \mathbf{z}) \\ &= \mathbf{F}_1(\mathbf{y}_2, \mathbf{z})\boldsymbol{\beta}_1 + \mathrm{E}(\mathbf{u}_1 \mid \mathbf{u}_2) \equiv \mathbf{F}_1(\mathbf{y}_2, \mathbf{z})\boldsymbol{\beta}_1 + \mathbf{H}_1(\mathbf{u}_2).\end{aligned} \tag{9.68}$$

Therefore, if we knew $\mathbf{H}_1(\cdot)$ and could observe $\mathbf{u}_2$, we could estimate $\boldsymbol{\beta}_1$ by a system estimation method, perhaps system OLS or FGLS. We might be willing to assume

$\mathbf{H}_1(\cdot)$ is linear, so $\mathrm{E}(\mathbf{u}_1 \mid \mathbf{u}_2) = \mathbf{\Lambda}_1 \mathbf{u}_2 = (\mathbf{u}_2' \otimes \mathbf{I}_{G_1}) \operatorname{vec}(\mathbf{\Lambda}_1) \equiv \mathbf{U}_2 \boldsymbol{\lambda}_1$. Then, in a first stage, we can estimate (9.65) by a standard system method and obtain $\hat{\boldsymbol{\beta}}_2$ and the residuals, $\hat{\mathbf{u}}_{i2}$. Next, form $\hat{\mathbf{U}}_{i2} = (\hat{\mathbf{u}}_{i2}' \otimes \mathbf{I}_{G_1})$ and estimate

$$\mathbf{y}_{i1} = \mathbf{F}_{i1} \boldsymbol{\beta}_1 + \hat{\mathbf{U}}_{i2} \boldsymbol{\lambda}_1 + \mathbf{error}_{i1} \tag{9.69}$$

using a system estimation method for exogenous variables (OLS or FGLS), where $\mathbf{F}_{i1} = \mathbf{F}_1(\mathbf{y}_{i2}, \mathbf{z}_i)$ and $\mathbf{error}_{i1}$ includes the estimation error from having to estimate $\boldsymbol{\beta}_2$ in the first stage. As in Chapter 6, the asymptotic variance matrix should be adjusted for the two-step estimation. Alternatively, we will show how to use a more general GMM setup in Chapter 14 to obtain the asymptotic variance from a larger GMM problem.

As a specific example, suppose we are interested in the single equation

$$y_1 = \mathbf{z}_1 \boldsymbol{\delta}_1 + \alpha_{11} y_2 + \alpha_{12} y_3 + \alpha_{13} y_2 y_3 + y_2 \mathbf{z}_1 \boldsymbol{\gamma}_{11} + y_3 \mathbf{z}_1 \boldsymbol{\gamma}_{12} + u_1, \tag{9.70}$$

which allows for interactive effects among endogenous variables and for each endogenous variable and exogenous variables in $\mathbf{z}_1$. We assume that y_2 and y_3 have reduced forms

$$y_2 = \mathbf{z} \boldsymbol{\beta}_2 + u_2, \qquad y_3 = \mathbf{z} \boldsymbol{\beta}_3 + u_3, \tag{9.71}$$

where all errors have zero conditional means. (The vector $\mathbf{z}$ might include nonlinear functions of the exogenous variables.) If, in addition,

$$\mathrm{E}(u_1 \mid \mathbf{z}, u_2, u_3) = \lambda_{11} u_2 + \lambda_{12} u_3 \tag{9.72}$$

then the OLS regression

$$y_{i1} \text{ on } \mathbf{z}_{i1}, y_{i2}, y_{i3}, y_{i2} y_{i3}, y_{i2} \mathbf{z}_{i1}, y_{i3} \mathbf{z}_{i1}, \hat{u}_{i2}, \hat{u}_{i3}, \qquad i = 1, \ldots, N \tag{9.73}$$

consistently estimates the parameters, where $\hat{u}_{i2}$ and $\hat{u}_{i3}$ are the OLS residuals from the first-stage regressions. Notice that we only have to add two control functions to account for the endogeneity of y_2, y_3, $y_2 y_3$, $y_2 \mathbf{z}_1$ and $y_3 \mathbf{z}_1$. Of course, this control function approach uses assumption (9.72); otherwise it is generally inconsistent. The control function approach can be made more flexible by adding, say, the interaction $\hat{u}_{i2} \hat{u}_{i3}$ to (9.73), and maybe even $\hat{u}_{i2}^2$ and $\hat{u}_{i3}^2$ (especially if y_2^2 and y_3^2 were in the model). The standard errors of the structural estimates should generally account for the first-stage estimation, as discussed in Chapter 6. A simple test of the null hypothesis that y_2 and y_3 are exogenous is that all terms involving $\hat{u}_{i2}$ and $\hat{u}_{i3}$ are jointly insignificant; under the null hypothesis, we can ignore the generated regressor problem.

As discussed in Section 6.2, the control function approach for nonlinear models is less robust than applying IV methods directly to equation (9.64) (with equation (9.70) as a special case), but the CF estimator can be more precise, especially if we can get by with few functions of the first-stage residuals. Plus, as shown by Newey, Powell, and Vella (1999), one can extend the CF approach without imposing functional form assumptions at all. Such nonparametric methods are beyond the scope of this text, but they are easily motivated by equation (9.68). In practice, choosing interactions, quadratics, and maybe higher-order polynomials (along with judicious taking of logarithms) might be sufficient.

9.6 Different Instruments for Different Equations

There are general classes of SEMs where the same instruments cannot be used for every equation. We already encountered one such example, the fully recursive system. Another general class of models is SEMs where, in addition to simultaneous determination of some variables, some equations contain variables that are endogenous as a result of omitted variables or measurement error.

As an example, reconsider the labor supply and wage offer equations (9.28) and (9.62), respectively. On the one hand, in the supply function it is not unreasonable to assume that variables other than $\log(wage)$ are uncorrelated with u_1. On the other hand, ability is a variable omitted from the $\log(wage)$ equation, and so *educ* might be correlated with u_2. This is an omitted variable, not a simultaneity, issue, but the statistical problem is the same: correlation between the error and an explanatory variable.

Equation (9.28) is still identified as it was before, because *educ* is exogenous in equation (9.28). What about equation (9.62)? It satisfies the order condition because we have excluded four exogenous variables from equation (9.62): *age*, *kidslt6*, *kidsge6*, and *nwifeinc*. How can we analyze the rank condition for this equation? We need to add to the system the linear projection of *educ* on all exogenous variables:

$$\begin{aligned} educ = {} & \delta_{30} + \delta_{31} exper + \delta_{32} exper^2 + \delta_{33} age \\ & + \delta_{34} kidslt6 + \delta_{35} kidsge6 + \delta_{36} nwifeinc + u_3. \end{aligned} \tag{9.74}$$

Provided the variables other than *exper* and $exper^2$ are sufficiently partially correlated with *educ*, the $\log(wage)$ equation is identified. However, the 2SLS estimators might be poorly behaved if the instruments are not very good. If possible, we would add other exogenous factors to equation (9.74) that are partially correlated with *educ*, such as mother's and father's education. In a system procedure, because we have assumed that *educ* is uncorrelated with u_1, *educ* can, and should, be included in the list of instruments for estimating equation (9.28).

This example shows that having different instruments for different equations changes nothing for single-equation analysis: we simply determine the valid list of instruments for the endogenous variables in the equation of interest and then estimate the equations separately by 2SLS. Instruments may be required to deal with simultaneity, omitted variables, or measurement error, in any combination.

Estimation is more complicated for system methods. First, if 3SLS is to be used, then the GMM 3SLS version must be used to produce consistent estimators of any equation; the more traditional 3SLS estimator discussed in Section 8.3.5 is generally valid only when all instruments are uncorrelated with all errors. When we have different instruments for different equations, the instrument matrix has the form in equation (8.15).

There is a more subtle issue that arises in system analysis with different instruments for different equations. While it is still popular to use 3SLS methods for such problems, it turns out that the key assumption that makes 3SLS the efficient GMM estimator, Assumption SIV.5, is often violated. In such cases the GMM estimator with general weighting matrix enhances asymptotic efficiency and simplifies inference.

As a simple example, consider a two-equation system

$$y_1 = \delta_{10} + \gamma_{12} y_2 + \delta_{11} z_1 + u_1, \tag{9.75}$$

$$y_2 = \delta_{20} + \gamma_{21} y_1 + \delta_{22} z_2 + \delta_{23} z_3 + u_2, \tag{9.76}$$

where (u_1, u_2) has mean zero and variance matrix $\boldsymbol{\Sigma}$. Suppose that z_1, z_2, and z_3 are uncorrelated with u_2 but we can only assume that z_1 and z_3 are uncorrelated with u_1. In other words, z_2 is not exogenous in equation (9.75). Each equation is still identified by the order condition, and we just assume that the rank conditions also hold. The instruments for equation (9.75) are $(1, z_1, z_3)$, and the instruments for equation (9.76) are $(1, z_1, z_2, z_3)$. Write these as $\mathbf{z}_1 \equiv (1, z_1, z_3)$ and $\mathbf{z}_2 \equiv (1, z_1, z_2, z_3)$. Assumption SIV.5 requires the following three conditions:

$$\mathrm{E}(u_1^2 \mathbf{z}_1' \mathbf{z}_1) = \sigma_1^2 \mathrm{E}(\mathbf{z}_1' \mathbf{z}_1). \tag{9.77}$$

$$\mathrm{E}(u_2^2 \mathbf{z}_2' \mathbf{z}_2) = \sigma_2^2 \mathrm{E}(\mathbf{z}_2' \mathbf{z}_2). \tag{9.78}$$

$$\mathrm{E}(u_1 u_2 \mathbf{z}_1' \mathbf{z}_2) = \sigma_{12} \mathrm{E}(\mathbf{z}_1' \mathbf{z}_2). \tag{9.79}$$

The first two conditions hold if $\mathrm{E}(u_1 \mid \mathbf{z}_1) = \mathrm{E}(u_2 \mid \mathbf{z}_2) = 0$ and $\mathrm{Var}(u_1 \mid \mathbf{z}_1) = \sigma_1^2$, $\mathrm{Var}(u_2 \mid \mathbf{z}_2) = \sigma_2^2$. These are standard zero conditional mean and homoskedasticity assumptions. The potential problem comes with condition (9.79). Since u_1 is correlated with one of the elements in $\mathbf{z}_2$, we can hardly just assume condition (9.79). Generally, there is no conditioning argument that implies condition (9.79). One case where condition (9.79) holds is if $\mathrm{E}(u_2 \mid u_1, z_1, z_2, z_3) = 0$, which implies that u_2 and u_1 are uncorrelated. The left-hand side of condition (9.79) is also easily shown to equal zero. But 3SLS with $\sigma_{12} = 0$ imposed is just 2SLS equation by equation. If u_1 and u_2 are correlated, we should not expect condition (9.79) to hold, and therefore the general minimum chi-square estimator should be used for estimation and inference.

Wooldridge (1996) provides a general discussion and contains other examples of cases in which Assumption SIV.5 can and cannot be expected to hold. Whenever a system contains linear projections for nonlinear functions of endogenous variables, we should expect Assumption SIV.5 to fail.

Problems

9.1. Discuss whether each example satisfies the autonomy requirement for true simultaneous equations analysis. The specification of y_1 and y_2 means that each is to be written as a function of the other in a two-equation system.

a. For an employee, $y_1 =$ hourly wage, $y_2 =$ hourly fringe benefits.

b. At the city level, $y_1 =$ per capita crime rate, $y_2 =$ per capita law enforcement expenditures.

c. For a firm operating in a developing country, $y_1 =$ firm research and development expenditures, $y_2 =$ firm foreign technology purchases.

d. For an individual, $y_1 =$ hourly wage, $y_2 =$ alcohol consumption.

e. For a family, $y_1 =$ annual housing expenditures, $y_2 =$ annual savings.

f. For a profit maximizing firm, $y_1 =$ price markup, $y_2 =$ advertising expenditures.

g. For a single-output firm, $y_1 =$ quantity demanded of its good, $y_2 =$ advertising expenditure.

h. At the city level, $y_1 =$ incidence of HIV, $y_2 =$ per capita condom sales.

9.2. Write a two-equation system in the form

$$y_1 = \gamma_1 y_2 + \mathbf{z}_{(1)} \boldsymbol{\delta}_{(1)} + u_1,$$

$$y_2 = \gamma_2 y_1 + \mathbf{z}_{(2)} \boldsymbol{\delta}_{(2)} + u_2.$$

a. Show that reduced forms exist if and only if $\gamma_1\gamma_2 \neq 1$.

b. State in words the rank condition for identifying each equation.

9.3. The following model jointly determines monthly child support payments and monthly visitation rights for divorced couples with children:

$$support = \delta_{10} + \gamma_{12} visits + \delta_{11} finc + \delta_{12} fremarr + \delta_{13} dist + u_1,$$

$$visits = \delta_{20} + \gamma_{21} support + \delta_{21} mremarr + \delta_{22} dist + u_2.$$

For expository purposes, assume that children live with their mothers, so that fathers pay child support. Thus, the first equation is the father's "reaction function": it describes the amount of child support paid for any given level of visitation rights and the other exogenous variables *finc* (father's income), *fremarr* (binary indicator if father remarried), and *dist* (miles currently between the mother and father). Similarly, the second equation is the mother's reaction function: it describes visitation rights for a given amount of child support; *mremarr* is a binary indicator for whether the mother is remarried.

a. Discuss identification of each equation.

b. How would you estimate each equation using a single-equation method?

c. How would you test for endogeneity of *visits* in the father's reaction function?

d. How many overidentification restrictions are there in the mother's reaction function? Explain how to test the overidentifying restriction(s).

9.4. Consider the following three-equation structural model:

$$y_1 = \gamma_{12} y_2 + \delta_{11} z_1 + \delta_{12} z_2 + \delta_{13} z_3 + u_1,$$

$$y_1 = \gamma_{22} y_2 + \gamma_{23} y_3 + \delta_{21} z_1 + u_2,$$

$$y_3 = \delta_{31} z_1 + \delta_{32} z_2 + \delta_{33} z_3 + u_3,$$

where $z_1 \equiv 1$ (to allow an intercept), $\mathrm{E}(u_g) = 0$, all g, and each z_j is uncorrelated with each u_g. You might think of the first two equations as demand and supply equations, where the supply equation depends on a possibly endogenous variable y_3 (such as wage costs) that might be correlated with u_2. For example, u_2 might contain managerial quality.

a. Show that a well-defined reduced form exists as long as $\gamma_{12} \neq \gamma_{22}$.

b. Allowing for the structural errors to be arbitrarily correlated, determine which of these equations is identified. First consider the order condition, and then the rank condition.

9.5. The following three-equation structural model describes a population:

$$y_1 = \gamma_{12} y_2 + \gamma_{13} y_3 + \delta_{11} z_1 + \delta_{13} z_3 + \delta_{14} z_4 + u_1,$$

$$y_2 = \gamma_{21} y_1 + \delta_{21} z_1 + u_2,$$

$$y_3 = \delta_{31} z_1 + \delta_{32} z_2 + \delta_{33} z_3 + \delta_{34} z_4 + u_3,$$

where you may set $z_1 = 1$ to allow an intercept. Make the usual assumptions that $\mathrm{E}(u_g) = 0$, $g = 1, 2, 3$ and that each z_j is uncorrelated with each u_g. In addition to the exclusion restrictions that have already been imposed, assume that $\delta_{13} + \delta_{14} = 1$.

a. Check the order and rank conditions for the first equation. Determine necessary and sufficient conditions for the rank condition to hold.

b. Assuming that the first equation is identified, propose a single-equation estimation method with all restrictions imposed. Be very precise.

9.6. The following two-equation model contains an interaction between an endogenous and exogenous variable (see Example 6.2 for such a model in an omitted variable context):

$$y_1 = \delta_{10} + \gamma_{12} y_2 + \gamma_{13} y_2 z_1 + \delta_{11} z_1 + \delta_{12} z_2 + u_1,$$

$$y_2 = \delta_{20} + \gamma_{21} y_1 + \delta_{21} z_1 + \delta_{23} z_3 + u_2.$$

a. Initially, assume that $\gamma_{13} = 0$, so that the model is a linear SEM. Discuss identification of each equation in this case.

b. For any value of γ_{13}, find the reduced form for y_1 (assuming it exists) in terms of the z_j, the u_g, and the parameters.

c. Assuming that $\mathrm{E}(u_1 \mid \mathbf{z}) = \mathrm{E}(u_2 \mid \mathbf{z}) = 0$, find $\mathrm{E}(y_1 \mid \mathbf{z})$.

d. Argue that, under the conditions in part a, the model is identified regardless of the value of γ_{13}.

e. Suggest a 2SLS procedure for estimating the first equation.

f. Define a matrix of instruments suitable for 3SLS estimation.

g. Suppose that $\delta_{23} = 0$, but we also know that $\gamma_{13} \neq 0$. Can the parameters in the first equation be consistently estimated? If so, how? Can H_0: $\gamma_{13} = 0$ be tested?

9.7. Assume that wage and alcohol consumption are determined by the system

$$wage = \gamma_{12} alcohol + \gamma_{13} educ + \mathbf{z}_{(1)} \boldsymbol{\delta}_{(1)} + u_1,$$

$$alcohol = \gamma_{21} wage + \gamma_{23} educ + \mathbf{z}_{(2)} \boldsymbol{\delta}_{(2)} + u_2,$$

$$educ = \mathbf{z}_{(3)}\boldsymbol{\delta}_{(3)} + u_3.$$

The third equation is a reduced form for years of education.

Elements in $\mathbf{z}_{(1)}$ include a constant, experience, gender, marital status, and amount of job training. The vector $\mathbf{z}_{(2)}$ contains a constant, experience, gender, marital status, and local prices (including taxes) on various alcoholic beverages. The vector $\mathbf{z}_{(3)}$ can contain elements in $\mathbf{z}_{(1)}$ and $\mathbf{z}_{(2)}$ and, in addition, exogenous factors affecting education; for concreteness, suppose one element of $\mathbf{z}_{(3)}$ is distance to nearest college at age 16. Let $\mathbf{z}$ denote the vector containing all nonredundant elements of $\mathbf{z}_{(1)}$, $\mathbf{z}_{(2)}$, and $\mathbf{z}_{(3)}$. In addition to assuming that $\mathbf{z}$ is uncorrelated with each of u_1, u_2, and u_3, assume that *educ* is uncorrelated with u_2, but *educ* might be correlated with u_1.

a. When does the order condition hold for the first equation?

b. State carefully how you would estimate the first equation using a single-equation method.

c. For each observation i define the matrix of instruments for system estimation of all three equations.

d. In a system procedure, how should you choose $\mathbf{z}_{(3)}$ to make the analysis as robust as possible to factors appearing in the reduced form for *educ*?

9.8. a. Extend Problem 5.4b using CARD.RAW to allow $educ^2$ to appear in the $\log(wage)$ equation, without using *nearc2* as an instrument. Specifically, use interactions of *nearc4* with some or all of the other exogenous variables in the $\log(wage)$ equation as instruments for $educ^2$. Compute a heteroskedasticity-robust test to be sure that at least one of these additional instruments appears in the linear projection of $educ^2$ onto your entire list of instruments. Test whether $educ^2$ needs to be in the $\log(wage)$ equation.

b. Start again with the model estimated in Problem 5.4b, but suppose we add the interaction $black \cdot educ$. Explain why $black \cdot z_j$ is a potential IV for $black \cdot educ$, where z_j is any exogenous variable in the system (including *nearc4*).

c. In Example 6.2 we used $black \cdot nearc4$ as the IV for $black \cdot educ$. Now use 2SLS with $black \cdot \widehat{educ}$ as the IV for $black \cdot educ$, where $\widehat{educ}$ are the fitted values from the first-stage regression of *educ* on all exogenous variables (including *nearc4*). What do you find?

d. If $\mathrm{E}(educ \mid \mathbf{z})$ is linear and $\mathrm{Var}(u_1 \mid \mathbf{z}) = \sigma_1^2$, where $\mathbf{z}$ is the set of all exogenous variables and u_1 is the error in the $\log(wage)$ equation, explain why the estimator using $black \cdot \widehat{educ}$ as the IV is asymptotically more efficient than the estimator using $black \cdot nearc4$ as the IV.

9.9. Use the data in MROZ.RAW for this question.

a. Estimate equations (9.28) and (9.29) jointly by 3SLS, and compare the 3SLS estimates with the 2SLS estimates for equations (9.28) and (9.29).

b. Now allow *educ* to be endogenous in equation (9.29), but assume it is exogenous in equation (9.28). Estimate a three-equation system using different instruments for different equations, where *motheduc*, *fatheduc*, and *huseduc* are assumed exogenous in equations (9.28) and (9.29).

9.10. Consider a two-equation system of the form

$$y_1 = \gamma_1 y_2 + \mathbf{z}_1 \boldsymbol{\delta}_1 + u_1,$$

$$y_2 = \mathbf{z}_2 \boldsymbol{\delta}_2 + u_2.$$

Assume that $\mathbf{z}_1$ contains at least one element not also in $\mathbf{z}_2$, and $\mathbf{z}_2$ contains at least one element not in $\mathbf{z}_1$. The second equation is also the reduced form for y_2, but restrictions have been imposed to make it a structural equation. (For example, it could be a wage offer equation with exclusion restrictions imposed, whereas the first equation is a labor supply function.)

a. If we estimate the first equation by 2SLS using all exogenous variables as IVs, are we imposing the exclusion restrictions in the second equation? (Hint: Does the first-stage regression in 2SLS impose any restrictions on the reduced form?)

b. Will the 3SLS estimates of the first equation be the same as the 2SLS estimates? Explain.

c. Explain why 2SLS is more robust than 3SLS for estimating the parameters of the first equation.

9.11. Consider a two-equation SEM:

$$y_1 = \gamma_{12} y_2 + \delta_{11} z_1 + u_1,$$

$$y_2 = \gamma_{21} y_1 + \delta_{22} z_2 + \delta_{23} z_3 + u_2,$$

$$\mathrm{E}(u_1 \mid z_1, z_2, z_3) = \mathrm{E}(u_2 \mid z_1, z_2, z_3) = 0,$$

where, for simplicity, we omit intercepts. The exogenous variable z_1 is a policy variable, such as a tax rate. Assume that $\gamma_{12}\gamma_{21} \neq 1$. The structural errors, u_1 and u_2, may be correlated.

a. Under what assumptions is each equation identified?

b. The reduced form for y_1 can be written in conditional expectation form as $\mathrm{E}(y_1 \mid \mathbf{z}) = \pi_{11} z_1 + \pi_{12} z_2 + \pi_{13} z_3$, where $\mathbf{z} = (z_1, z_2, z_3)$. Find π_{11} in terms of the γ_{gj} and δ_{gj}.

c. How would you estimate the structural parameters? How would you obtain $\hat{\pi}_{11}$ in terms of the structural parameter estimates?

d. Suppose that z_2 should be in the first equation, but it is left out in the estimation from part c. What effect does this omission have on estimating $\partial \mathrm{E}(y_1 \mid \mathbf{z})/\partial z_1$? Does it matter whether you use single-equation or system estimators of the structural parameters?

e. If you are only interested in $\partial \mathrm{E}(y_1 \mid \mathbf{z})/\partial z_1$, what could you do instead of estimating an SEM?

f. Would you say estimating a simultaneous equations model is a robust method for estimating $\partial \mathrm{E}(y_1 \mid \mathbf{z})/\partial z_1$? Explain.

9.12. The following is a two-equation, nonlinear SEM:

$$y_1 = \delta_{10} + \gamma_{12} y_2 + \gamma_{13} y_2^2 + \mathbf{z}_1 \boldsymbol{\delta}_1 + u_1,$$

$$y_2 = \delta_{20} + \gamma_{12} y_1 + \mathbf{z}_2 \boldsymbol{\delta}_2 + u_2,$$

where u_1 and u_2 have zero means conditional on all exogenous variables, $\mathbf{z}$. (For emphasis, we have included separate intercepts.) Assume that both equations are identified when $\gamma_{13} = 0$.

a. When $\gamma_{13} = 0$, $\mathrm{E}(y_2 \mid \mathbf{z}) = \pi_{20} + \mathbf{z}\boldsymbol{\pi}_2$. What is $\mathrm{E}(y_2^2 \mid \mathbf{z})$ under homoskedasticity assumptions for u_1 and u_2?

b. Find $\mathrm{E}(y_1 \mid \mathbf{z})$ when $\gamma_{13} = 0$.

c. Use part b to argue that, when $\gamma_{13} = 0$, the forbidden regression consistently estimates the parameters in the first equation, including $\gamma_{13} = 0$.

d. If u_1 and u_2 have constant variances conditional on $\mathbf{z}$, and γ_{13} happens to be zero, show that the optimal instrumental variables for estimating the first equation are $\{1, \mathbf{z}, [\mathrm{E}(y_2 \mid \mathbf{z})]^2\}$. (Hint: Use Theorem 8.5; for a similar problem, see Problem 8.11.)

e. Reestimate equation (9.61) using IVs $[1, \mathbf{z}, (\hat{y}_2)^2]$, where $\mathbf{z}$ is all exogenous variables appearing in equations (9.61) and (9.62) and $\hat{y}_2$ denotes the fitted values from regressing $\log(wage)$ on 1, $\mathbf{z}$. Discuss the results.

9.13. For this question use the data in OPENNESS.RAW, taken from Romer (1993).

a. A simple simultaneous equations model to test whether "openness" (*open*) leads to lower inflation rates (*inf*) is

$$inf = \delta_{10} + \gamma_{12} open + \delta_{11} \log(pcinc) + u_1,$$

$$open = \delta_{20} + \gamma_{21} inf + \delta_{21} \log(pcinc) + \delta_{22} \log(land) + u_2.$$

Assuming that *pcinc* (per capita income) and *land* (land area) are exogenous, under what assumption is the first equation identified?

b. Estimate the reduced form for *open* to verify that $\log(land)$ is statistically significant.

c. Estimate the first equation from part a by 2SLS. Compare the estimate of γ_{12} with the OLS estimate.

d. Add the term $\gamma_{13} open^2$ to the first equation, and propose a way to test whether it is statistically significant. (Use only one more IV than you used in part c.)

e. With $\gamma_{13} open^2$ in the first equation, use the following method to estimate δ_{10}, γ_{12}, γ_{13}, and δ_{11}: (1) Regress *open* on 1, $\log(pcinc)$ and $\log(land)$, and obtain the fitted values, $\widehat{open}$. (2) Regress *inf* on 1, $\widehat{open}$, $(\widehat{open})^2$, and $\log(pcinc)$. Compare the results with those from part d. Which estimates do you prefer?

9.14. Answer "agree" or "disagree" to each of the following statements, and provide justification.

a. "In the general SEM (9.13), if the matrix of structural parameters $\mathbf{\Gamma}$ is identified, then so is the variance matrix $\mathbf{\Sigma}$ of the structural errors."

b. "Identification in a nonlinear structural equation when the errors are independent of the exogenous variables can always be assured by adding enough nonlinear functions of exogenous variables to the instrument list."

c. "If in a system of equations $E(\mathbf{u} \mid \mathbf{z}) = \mathbf{0}$ but $\text{Var}(\mathbf{u} \mid \mathbf{z}) \neq \text{Var}(\mathbf{u})$, the 3SLS estimator is inconsistent."

d. "In a well-specified simultaneous equations model, any variable exogenous in one equation should be exogenous in all equations."

e. "In a triangular system of three equations, control function methods are preferred to standard IV approaches."

9.15. Consider the triangular system in equations (9.70) and (9.71) under the assumption $E(u_1 \mid \mathbf{z}) = \mathbf{0}$, where $\mathbf{z}$ $(1 \times L)$ contains all exogenous variables in the three equations and $\mathbf{z}_1$ is $1 \times L_1$, with $L_1 \leq L - 2$.

a. Suppose that the model is identified when $\alpha_{13} = 0$, $\gamma_{11} = \mathbf{0}$, and $\gamma_{12} = \mathbf{0}$. Argue that the general model is identified.

b. Let $\hat{y}_{i2}$ and $\hat{y}_{i3}$ be the first-stage fitted values from the regressions y_{i2} on $\mathbf{z}_i$ and y_{i3} on $\mathbf{z}_i$, respectively. Suppose you estimate (9.70) by IV using instruments $(\mathbf{z}_{i1}, \hat{y}_{i2}, \hat{y}_{i3}, \hat{y}_{i2}\hat{y}_{i3}, \hat{y}_{i2}\mathbf{z}_{i1}, \hat{y}_{i3}\mathbf{z}_{i1})$. Are there any overidentification restrictions to test? Explain.

c. Suppose $L > L_1 + 2$ and you estimate (9.70) by 2SLS using instruments $(\mathbf{z}_i, \hat{y}_{i2}\hat{y}_{i3}, \hat{y}_{i2}\mathbf{z}_{i1}, \hat{y}_{i3}\mathbf{z}_{i1})$. How many overidentifying restrictions are there, and how would you test them?

d. Propose a method that gives even more overidentifying restrictions.

e. If you add the assumptions $\mathrm{E}(u_{i2} \mid \mathbf{z}_i) = \mathrm{E}(u_{i3} \mid \mathbf{z}_i) = 0$, $\mathrm{E}(u_{i1}^2 \mid \mathbf{z}_i) = \sigma_1^2$, and $\mathrm{E}(u_{i2}u_{i3} \mid \mathbf{z}_i) = \sigma_{23}$, argue that the estimator from part b is an asymptotically efficient IV estimator. What can you conclude about the estimators from parts c and d?

10 Basic Linear Unobserved Effects Panel Data Models

In Chapter 7 we covered a class of linear panel data models where, at a minimum, the error in each time period was assumed to be uncorrelated with the explanatory variables in the same time period. For certain panel data applications this assumption is too strong. In fact, a primary motivation for using panel data is to solve the omitted variables problem.

In this chapter we study population models that explicitly contain a time-constant, unobserved effect. The treatment in this chapter is "modern" in the sense that unobserved effects are treated as random variables, drawn from the population along with the observed explained and explanatory variables, as opposed to parameters to be estimated. In this framework, the key issue is whether the unobserved effect is uncorrelated with the explanatory variables.

10.1 Motivation: Omitted Variables Problem

It is easy to see how panel data can be used, at least under certain assumptions, to obtain consistent estimators in the presence of omitted variables. Let y and $\mathbf{x} \equiv (x_1, x_2, \ldots, x_K)$ be observable random variables, and let c be an unobservable random variable; the vector $(y, x_1, x_2, \ldots, x_K, c)$ represents the population of interest. As is often the case in applied econometrics, we are interested in the partial effects of the observable explanatory variables x_j in the population regression function

$$\mathrm{E}(y \mid x_1, x_2, \ldots, x_K, c). \tag{10.1}$$

In words, we would like to hold c constant when obtaining partial effects of the observable explanatory variables. We follow Chamberlain (1984) in using c to denote the unobserved variable. Much of the panel data literature uses a Greek letter, such as α or ϕ, but we want to emphasize that the unobservable is a random variable, not a parameter to be estimated. (We discuss this point further in Section 10.2.1.)

Assuming a linear model, with c entering additively along with the x_j, we have

$$\mathrm{E}(y \mid \mathbf{x}, c) = \beta_0 + \mathbf{x}\boldsymbol{\beta} + c, \tag{10.2}$$

where interest lies in the $K \times 1$ vector $\boldsymbol{\beta}$. On the one hand, if c is uncorrelated with each x_j, then c is just another unobserved factor affecting y that is not systematically related to the observable explanatory variables whose effects are of interest. On the other hand, if $\mathrm{Cov}(x_j, c) \neq 0$ for some j, putting c into the error term can cause serious problems. Without additional information we cannot consistently estimate $\boldsymbol{\beta}$, nor will we be able to determine whether there is a problem (except by introspection, or by concluding that the estimates of $\boldsymbol{\beta}$ are somehow "unreasonable").

Under additional assumptions there are ways to address the problem $\mathrm{Cov}(\mathbf{x}, c) \neq \mathbf{0}$. We have covered at least three possibilities in the context of cross section analysis: (1) we might be able to find a suitable proxy variable for c, in which case we can estimate an equation by OLS where the proxy is plugged in for c; (2) for the elements of $\mathbf{x}$ that are correlated with c, we may be able to find instrumental variables, in which case we can use an IV method such as 2SLS; or (3) we may be able to find indicators of c that can then be used in multiple indicator instrumental variables procedure. These solutions are covered in Chapters 4 and 5.

If we have access to only a single cross section of observations, then the three remedies listed, or slight variants of them, largely exhaust the possibilities. However, if we can observe the *same* cross section units at different points in time—that is, if we can collect a panel data set—then other possibilties arise.

For illustration, suppose we can observe y and $\mathbf{x}$ at two different time periods; call these y_t, $\mathbf{x}_t$ for $t = 1, 2$. The population now represents two time periods on the same unit. Also, suppose that the omitted variable c is *time constant*. Then we are interested in the population regression function

$$\mathrm{E}(y_t \mid \mathbf{x}_t, c) = \beta_0 + \mathbf{x}_t\boldsymbol{\beta} + c, \qquad t = 1, 2, \tag{10.3}$$

where $\mathbf{x}_t\boldsymbol{\beta} = \beta_1 x_{t1} + \cdots + \beta_K x_{tK}$ and x_{tj} indicates variable j at time t. Model (10.3) assumes that c has the same effect on the mean response in each time period. Without loss of generality, we set the coefficient on c equal to one. (Because c is unobserved and virtually never has a natural unit of measurement, it would be meaningless to try to estimate its partial effect.)

The assumption that c is constant over time, and has a constant partial effect over time, is crucial to the following analysis. An unobserved, time-constant variable is called an **unobserved effect** in panel data analysis. When t represents different time periods for the same individual, the unobserved effect is often interpreted as capturing features of an individual, such as cognitive ability, motivation, or early family upbringing, that are given and do not change over time. Similarly, if the unit of observation is the firm, c contains unobserved firm characteristics—such as managerial quality or structure—that can be viewed as being (roughly) constant over the period in question. We cover several specific examples of unobserved effects models in Section 10.2.

To discuss the additional assumptions sufficient to estimate $\boldsymbol{\beta}$, it is useful to write model (10.3) in error form as

$$y_t = \beta_0 + \mathbf{x}_t\boldsymbol{\beta} + c + u_t, \tag{10.4}$$

where, by definition,

$$\mathrm{E}(u_t \mid \mathbf{x}_t, c) = 0, \qquad t = 1, 2. \tag{10.5}$$

One implication of condition (10.5) is

$$\mathrm{E}(\mathbf{x}_t' u_t) = \mathbf{0}, \qquad t = 1, 2. \tag{10.6}$$

If we were to assume $\mathrm{E}(\mathbf{x}_t' c) = \mathbf{0}$, we could apply pooled OLS, as we covered in Section 7.8. If c is correlated with any element of $\mathbf{x}_t$, then pooled OLS is biased and inconsistent.

With two years of data we can difference equation (10.4) across the two time periods to eliminate the time-constant unobservable, c. Define $\Delta y = y_2 - y_1$, $\Delta\mathbf{x} = \mathbf{x}_2 - \mathbf{x}_1$, and $\Delta u = u_2 - u_1$. Then, differencing equation (10.4) gives

$$\Delta y = \Delta\mathbf{x}\boldsymbol{\beta} + \Delta u, \tag{10.7}$$

which is just a standard linear model in the differences of all variables (although the intercept has dropped out). Importantly, the parameter vector of interest, $\boldsymbol{\beta}$, appears directly in equation (10.7), and its presence suggests estimating equation (10.7) by OLS. Given a panel data set with two time periods, equation (10.7) is just a standard cross section equation. Under what assumptions will the OLS estimator from equation (10.7) be consistent?

Because we assume a random sample from the population, we can apply the results in Chapter 4 directly to equation (10.7). The key conditions for OLS to consistently estimate $\boldsymbol{\beta}$ are the orthogonality condition (Assumption OLS.1)

$$\mathrm{E}(\Delta\mathbf{x}' \Delta u) = \mathbf{0} \tag{10.8}$$

and the rank condition (Assumption OLS.2)

$$\operatorname{rank} \mathrm{E}(\Delta\mathbf{x}' \Delta\mathbf{x}) = K. \tag{10.9}$$

Consider condition (10.8) first. It is equivalent to $\mathrm{E}[(\mathbf{x}_2 - \mathbf{x}_1)'(u_2 - u_1)] = \mathbf{0}$, or, after simple algebra,

$$\mathrm{E}(\mathbf{x}_2' u_2) + \mathrm{E}(\mathbf{x}_1' u_1) - \mathrm{E}(\mathbf{x}_1' u_2) - \mathrm{E}(\mathbf{x}_2' u_1) = \mathbf{0}. \tag{10.10}$$

The first two terms in equation (10.10) are zero by condition (10.6), which holds for $t = 1, 2$. But condition (10.5) does *not* guarantee that $\mathbf{x}_1$ and u_2 are uncorrelated or that $\mathbf{x}_2$ and u_1 are uncorrelated. It might be reasonable to *assume* that condition (10.8) holds, but we must recognize that it does not follow from condition (10.5). Assuming that the error u_t is uncorrelated with $\mathbf{x}_1$ and $\mathbf{x}_2$ for $t = 1, 2$ is an example of a strict exogeneity assumption on the regressors in unobserved components panel data models. We discuss strict exogeneity assumptions generally in Section 10.2. For now, we emphasize that assuming $\text{Cov}(\mathbf{x}_t, u_s) = \mathbf{0}$ for all t and s puts no restrictions on the correlation between $\mathbf{x}_t$ and the unobserved effect, c.

The second assumption, condition (10.9), also deserves some attention now because the elements of $\mathbf{x}_t$ appearing in structural equation (10.3) have been differenced across time. If $\mathbf{x}_t$ contains a variable that is constant across time for every member of the population, then $\Delta\mathbf{x}$ contains an entry that is identically zero, and condition (10.9) fails. This outcome is not surprising: if c is allowed to be arbitrarily correlated with the elements of $\mathbf{x}_t$, the effect of any variable that is constant across time cannot be distinguished from the effect of c. Therefore, we can consistently estimate β_j only if there is some variation in x_{tj} over time.

In the remainder of this chapter, we cover various ways of dealing with the presence of unobserved effects under different sets of assumptions. We assume we have repeated observations on a cross section of N individuals, families, firms, school districts, cities, or some other economic unit. As in Chapter 7, we assume in this chapter that we have the same time periods, denoted $t = 1, 2, \ldots, T$, for each cross section observation. Such a data set is usually called a **balanced panel** because the same time periods are available for all cross section units. While the mechanics of the unbalanced case are similar to the balanced case, a careful treatment of the unbalanced case requires a formal description of why the panel may be unbalanced, and the sample selection issues can be somewhat subtle. Therefore, we hold off covering unbalanced panels until Chapter 21, where we discuss sample selection and attrition issues.

We still focus on asymptotic properties of estimators, where the time dimension, T, is fixed and the cross section dimension, N, grows without bound. With large-N asymptotics it is convenient to view the cross section observations as independent, identically distributed draws from the population. For any cross section observation i—denoting a single individual, firm, city, and so on—we denote the observable variables for all T time periods by $\{(y_{it}, \mathbf{x}_{it}) : t = 1, 2, \ldots, T\}$. Because of the fixed T assumption, the asymptotic analysis is valid for arbitrary time dependence and distributional heterogeneity across t.

When applying asymptotic analysis to panel data methods, it is important to remember that asymptotics are useful insofar as they provide a reasonable approximation to the finite sample properties of estimators and statistics. For example, a priori it is difficult to know whether $N \to \infty$ asymptotics works well with, say, $N = 50$ states in the United States and $T = 8$ years. But we can be pretty confident that $N \to \infty$ asymptotics are more appropriate than $T \to \infty$ asymptotics, even though N is practically fixed while T can grow. With large geographical regions, the random sampling assumption in the cross section dimension is conceptually flawed. Nevertheless, if N is sufficiently large relative to T, and if we can assume rough independence in the cross section, then our asymptotic analysis should provide suitable approximations.

If T is of the same order as N—for example, $N = 60$ countries and $T = 55$ post–World War II years—an asymptotic analysis that makes explicit assumptions about the nature of the time series dependence is needed. (In special cases, the conclusions about consistent estimation and approximate normality of t statistics will be the same, but not generally.) This area is still relatively new. If T is much larger than N, say $N = 5$ companies and $T = 40$ years, the framework becomes multiple time series analysis: N can be held fixed while $T \to \infty$. We do not cover time series analysis.

10.2 Assumptions about the Unobserved Effects and Explanatory Variables

Before analyzing panel data estimation methods in more detail, it is useful to generally discuss the nature of the unobserved effects and certain features of the observed explanatory variables.

10.2.1 Random or Fixed Effects?

The basic **unobserved effects model (UEM)** can be written, for a randomly drawn cross section observation i, as

$$y_{it} = \mathbf{x}_{it}\boldsymbol{\beta} + c_i + u_{it}, \qquad t = 1, 2, \ldots, T, \tag{10.11}$$

where $\mathbf{x}_{it}$ is $1 \times K$ and can contain observable variables that change across t but not i, variables that change across i but not t, and variables that change across i and t. In addition to unobserved effect, there are many other names given to c_i in applications: **unobserved component, latent variable,** and **unobserved heterogeneity** are common. If i indexes individuals, then c_i is sometimes called an **individual effect** or **individual heterogeneity**; analogous terms apply to families, firms, cities, and other cross-sectional units. The u_{it} are called the **idiosyncratic errors** or **idiosyncratic disturbances** because these change across t as well as across i.

Especially in methodological papers, but also in applications, one often sees a discussion about whether c_i will be treated as a *random effect* or a *fixed effect*. Originally, such discussions centered on whether c_i is properly viewed as a random variable or as a parameter to be estimated. In the traditional approach to panel data models, c_i is called a "random effect" when it is treated as a random variable and a "fixed effect" when it is treated as a parameter to be estimated for each cross section observation i. Our view is that discussions about whether the c_i should be treated as random variables or as parameters to be estimated are wrongheaded for microeconometric panel data applications. With a large number of random draws from the cross section, it almost always makes sense to treat the unobserved effects, c_i, as random draws from the population, along with y_{it} and $\mathbf{x}_{it}$. This approach is certainly appropriate from an omitted variables or neglected heterogeneity perspective. As our discussion in Section 10.1 suggests, the key issue involving c_i is whether or not it is uncorrelated with the observed explanatory variables $\mathbf{x}_{it}$, $t = 1, 2, \ldots, T$. Mundlak (1978) made this argument many years ago, and it still is persuasive.

In modern econometric parlance, a **random effects framework** is synonymous with zero correlation between the observed explanatory variables and the unobserved effect: $\text{Cov}(\mathbf{x}_{it}, c_i) = \mathbf{0}$, $t = 1, 2, \ldots, T$. (Actually, a stronger conditional mean independence assumption, $\text{E}(c_i \mid \mathbf{x}_{i1}, \ldots, \mathbf{x}_{iT}) = \text{E}(c_i)$, will be needed to fully justify statistical inference; more on this subject in Section 10.4.) In applied papers, when c_i is referred to as, say, an "individual random effect," then c_i is probably being assumed to be uncorrelated with the $\mathbf{x}_{it}$.

In most microeconometric applications, a **fixed effects framework** does not actually mean that c_i is being treated as nonrandom; rather, it means that one is allowing for arbitrary dependence between the unobserved effect c_i and the observed explanatory variables $\mathbf{x}_{it}$. So, if c_i is called an "individual fixed effect" or a "firm fixed effect," then, for practical purposes, this terminology means that c_i is allowed to be correlated arbitrarily with $\mathbf{x}_{it}$.

More recently, another concept has cropped up for describing situations where we allow dependence between c_i and $\{\mathbf{x}_{it} : t = 1, \ldots, T\}$, especially, but not only, for nonlinear models. (See, for example, Cameron and Trivedi (2005, pp. 719, 786).) If we *model* the dependence between c_i and $\mathbf{x}_i = (\mathbf{x}_{i1}, \mathbf{x}_{i2}, \ldots, \mathbf{x}_{iT})$—or, more generally, place substantive restrictions on the distribution of c_i given $\mathbf{x}_i$—then we are using a **correlated random effects (CRE) framework**. (The name refers to allowing correlation between c_i and $\mathbf{x}_i$.) Practically, the key difference between a fixed effects approach and a correlated random effects approach is that in the former case the relationship between c_i and $\mathbf{x}_i$ is left entirely unspecified, while in the latter case we restrict this dependence in some way—sometimes rather severely, in the case of nonlinear models (as we will see in Part IV). In Section 10.7.2 we cover Mundlak's (1978) CRE framework in the context of the standard unobserved effects model. Mundlak's approach yields important insights for understanding the difference between the random and fixed effects frameworks, and it is very useful for testing whether c_i is uncorrelated with the regressors (the critical assumption in a traditional random effects analysis). Further, Mundlak's approach is indispensable for analyzing a broad class of nonlinear models with unobserved effects, a topic we cover in Part IV.

In this book, we avoid referring to c_i as a random effect or a fixed effect because of the unwanted connotations of these terms concerning the nature of c_i. Instead, we will mostly refer to c_i as an "unobserved effect" and sometimes as "unobserved heterogeneity." We will refer to "random effects assumptions," "fixed effects assumptions," and "correlated random effects assumptions." Also, we will label different estimation methods as **random effects (RE) estimation**, **fixed effects (FE) estimation**, and, less often for linear models, **correlated random effects (CRE) estimation**. The terminology for estimation methods is so ingrained in econometrics that it would be counterproductive to try to change it now.

10.2.2 Strict Exogeneity Assumptions on the Explanatory Variables

Traditional unobserved components panel data models take the $\mathbf{x}_{it}$ as nonrandom. We will never assume the $\mathbf{x}_{it}$ are nonrandom because potential feedback from y_{it} to $\mathbf{x}_{is}$ for $s > t$ needs to be addressed explicitly.

In Chapter 7 we discussed strict exogeneity assumptions in panel data models that did not explicitly contain unobserved effects. We now provide strict exogeneity assumptions for models with unobserved effects.

In Section 10.1 we stated the strict exogeneity assumption in terms of zero correlation. For inference and efficiency discussions, it is more convenient to state the strict exogeneity assumption in terms of conditional expectations. With an unobserved effect, the most revealing form of the strict exogeneity assumption is

$$\mathrm{E}(y_{it} \mid \mathbf{x}_{i1}, \mathbf{x}_{i2}, \ldots, \mathbf{x}_{iT}, c_i) = \mathrm{E}(y_{it} \mid \mathbf{x}_{it}, c_i) = \mathbf{x}_{it}\boldsymbol{\beta} + c_i \tag{10.12}$$

for $t = 1, 2, \ldots, T$. The second equality is the functional form assumption on $\mathrm{E}(y_{it} \mid \mathbf{x}_{it}, c_i)$. It is the first equality that gives the strict exogeneity its interpretation. It means that, once $\mathbf{x}_{it}$ *and* c_i are controlled for, $\mathbf{x}_{is}$ has no partial effect on y_{it} for $s \neq t$.

When assumption (10.12) holds, we say that the $\{\mathbf{x}_{it} : t = 1, 2, \ldots, T\}$ are **strictly exogenous conditional on the unobserved effect** c_i. Assumption (10.12) and the corresponding terminology were introduced and used by Chamberlain (1982). We will explicitly cover Chamberlain's approach to estimating unobserved effects models in the next chapter, but his manner of stating assumptions is instructive even for traditional panel data analysis.

Assumption (10.12) restricts how the expected value of y_{it} can depend on explanatory variables in other time periods, but it is more reasonable than strict exogeneity without conditioning on the unobserved effect. Without conditioning on an unobserved effect, the strict exogeneity assumption is

$$\mathrm{E}(y_{it} \mid \mathbf{x}_{i1}, \mathbf{x}_{i2}, \ldots, \mathbf{x}_{iT}) = \mathrm{E}(y_{it} \mid \mathbf{x}_{it}) = \mathbf{x}_{it}\boldsymbol{\beta}, \tag{10.13}$$

$t = 1, \ldots, T$. To see that assumption (10.13) is less likely to hold than assumption (10.12), first consider an example. Suppose that y_{it} is output of soybeans for farm i during year t, and $\mathbf{x}_{it}$ contains capital, labor, materials (such as fertilizer), rainfall, and other observable inputs. The unobserved effect, c_i, can capture average quality of land, managerial ability of the family running the farm, and other unobserved, time-constant factors. A natural assumption is that, once current inputs have been controlled for *along with* c_i, inputs used in other years have no effect on output during the current year. However, since the optimal choice of inputs in every year generally depends on c_i, it is likely that some partial correlation between output in year t and inputs in other years will exist if c_i is not controlled for: assumption (10.12) is reasonable while assumption (10.13) is not.

More generally, it is easy to see that assumption (10.13) fails whenever assumption (10.12) holds *and* the expected value of c_i depends on $(\mathbf{x}_{i1}, \ldots, \mathbf{x}_{iT})$. From the law of iterated expectations, if assumption (10.12) holds, then

$$\mathrm{E}(y_{it} \mid \mathbf{x}_{i1}, \ldots, \mathbf{x}_{iT}) = \mathbf{x}_{it}\boldsymbol{\beta} + \mathrm{E}(c_i \mid \mathbf{x}_{i1}, \ldots, \mathbf{x}_{iT}),$$

and so assumption (10.13) fails if $\mathrm{E}(c_i \mid \mathbf{x}_{i1}, \ldots, \mathbf{x}_{iT}) \neq \mathrm{E}(c_i)$. In particular, assumption (10.13) fails if c_i is correlated with any of the $\mathbf{x}_{it}$.

Given equation (10.11), the strict exogeneity assumption can be stated in terms of the idiosyncratic errors as

$$\mathrm{E}(u_{it} \mid \mathbf{x}_{i1}, \ldots, \mathbf{x}_{iT}, c_i) = 0, \qquad t = 1, 2, \ldots, T. \tag{10.14}$$

This assumption, in turn, implies that explanatory variables in each time period are uncorrelated with the idiosyncratic error in each time period:

$$\mathrm{E}(\mathbf{x}_{is}'u_{it}) = \mathbf{0}, \qquad s, t = 1, \ldots, T. \tag{10.15}$$

This assumption is much stronger than assuming zero *contemporaneous* correlation: $\mathrm{E}(\mathbf{x}_{it}'u_{it}) = \mathbf{0}$, $t = 1, \ldots, T$. Nevertheless, assumption (10.15) does allow arbitary correlation between c_i and $\mathbf{x}_{it}$ for all t, something we ruled out in Section 7.8. Later, we will use the fact that assumption (10.14) implies that u_{it} and c_i are uncorrelated.

For examining consistency of panel data estimators, the zero covariance assumption (10.15) generally suffices. Further, assumption (10.15) is often the easiest way to think about whether strict exogeneity is likely to hold in a particular application. But standard forms of statistical inference, as well as the efficiency properties of standard estimators, rely on the stronger conditional mean formulation in assumption (10.14). Therefore, we focus on assumption (10.14).

10.2.3 Some Examples of Unobserved Effects Panel Data Models

Our discussions in Sections 10.2.1 and 10.2.2 emphasize that in any panel data application we should initially focus on two questions: (1) Is the unobserved effect, c_i, uncorrelated with $\mathbf{x}_{it}$ for all t? (2) Is the strict exogeneity assumption (conditional on c_i) reasonable? The following examples illustrate how we might organize our thinking on these two questions.

Example 10.1 (Program Evaluation): A standard model for estimating the effects of job training or other programs on subsequent wages is

$$\log(wage_{it}) = \theta_t + \mathbf{z}_{it}\gamma + \delta_1 prog_{it} + c_i + u_{it}, \tag{10.16}$$

where i indexes individual and t indexes time period. The parameter θ_t denotes a time-varying intercept, and $\mathbf{z}_{it}$ is a set of observable characteristics that affect wage and may also be correlated with program participation.

Evaluation data sets are often collected at two points in time. At $t = 1$, no one has participated in the program, so that $prog_{i1} = 0$ for all i. Then, a subgroup is chosen to participate in the program (or the individuals choose to participate), and subsequent wages are observed for the control and treatment groups in $t = 2$. Model (10.16) allows for any number of time periods and general patterns of program participation.

The reason for including the individual effect, c_i, is the usual omitted ability story: if individuals choose whether or not to participate in the program, that choice could be correlated with ability. This possibility is often called the **self-selection problem**. Alternatively, administrators might assign people based on characteristics that the econometrician cannot observe.

The other issue is the strict exogeneity assumption of the explanatory variables, particularly $prog_{it}$. Typically, we feel comfortable with assuming that u_{it} is uncorrelated with $prog_{it}$. But what about correlation between u_{it} and, say, $prog_{i,t+1}$? Future program participation could depend on u_{it} if people choose to participate in the future based on shocks to their wage in the past, or if administrators choose people as participants at time $t + 1$ who had a low u_{it}. Such feedback might not be very important, since c_i is being allowed for, but it could be. See, for example, Bassi (1984) and Ham and Lalonde (1996). Another issue, which is more easily dealt with, is that the training program could have lasting effects. If so, then we should include lags of $prog_{it}$ in model (10.16). Or, the program itself might last more than one period, in which case $prog_{it}$ can be replaced by a series of dummy variables for how long unit i at time t has been subject to the program.

Example 10.2 (Distributed Lag Model): Hausman, Hall, and Griliches (1984) estimate nonlinear distributed lag models to study the relationship between patents awarded to a firm and current and past levels of R&D spending. A linear, five-lag version of their model is

$$patents_{it} = \theta_t + \mathbf{z}_{it}\gamma + \delta_0 RD_{it} + \delta_1 RD_{i,t-1} + \cdots + \delta_5 RD_{i,t-5} + c_i + u_{it}, \tag{10.17}$$

where RD_{it} is spending on R&D for firm i at time t and $\mathbf{z}_{it}$ contains variables such as firm size (as measured by sales or employees). The variable c_i is a firm heterogeneity term that may influence $patents_{it}$ and that may be correlated with current, past, and future R&D expenditures. Interest lies in the pattern of the δ_j coefficients. As with the other examples, we must decide whether R&D spending is likely to be correlated with c_i. In addition, if shocks to patents today (changes in u_{it}) influence R&D spending at future dates, then strict exogeneity can fail, and the methods in this chapter will not apply.

The next example presents a case where the strict exogeneity assumption is necessarily false, and the unobserved effect and the explanatory variable must be correlated.

Example 10.3 (Lagged Dependent Variable): A simple dynamic model of wage determination with unobserved heterogeneity is

$$\log(wage_{it}) = \beta_1 \log(wage_{i,t-1}) + c_i + u_{it}, \qquad t = 1, 2, \ldots, T. \tag{10.18}$$

Often, interest lies in how persistent wages are (as measured by the size of β_1) *after* controlling for unobserved heterogeneity (individual productivity), c_i. Letting $y_{it} = \log(wage_{it})$, a standard assumption would be

$$\mathrm{E}(u_{it} \mid y_{i,t-1}, \ldots, y_{i0}, c_i) = 0, \tag{10.19}$$

which means that all of the dynamics are captured by the first lag. Let $x_{it} = y_{i,t-1}$. Then, under assumption (10.19), u_{it} is uncorrelated with $(x_{it}, x_{i,t-1}, \ldots, x_{i1})$, but u_{it} cannot be uncorrelated with $(x_{i,t+1}, \ldots, x_{iT})$, as $x_{i,t+1} = y_{it}$. In fact,

$$\mathrm{E}(y_{it}u_{it}) = \beta_1 \mathrm{E}(y_{i,t-1}u_{it}) + \mathrm{E}(c_i u_{it}) + \mathrm{E}(u_{it}^2) = \mathrm{E}(u_{it}^2) > 0, \tag{10.20}$$

because $\mathrm{E}(y_{i,t-1}u_{it}) = 0$ and $\mathrm{E}(c_i u_{it}) = 0$ under assumption (10.19). Therefore, the strict exogeneity assumption never holds in unobserved effects models with lagged dependent variables.

In addition, $y_{i,t-1}$ and c_i are necessarily correlated (since at time $t-1$, $y_{i,t-1}$ is the left-hand-side variable). Not only must strict exogeneity fail in this model, but the exogeneity assumption required for pooled OLS estimation of model (10.18) is also violated. We will study estimation of such models in Chapter 11.

10.3 Estimating Unobserved Effects Models by Pooled Ordinary Least Squares

Under certain assumptions, the pooled OLS estimator can be used to obtain a consistent estimator of $\boldsymbol{\beta}$ in model (10.11). Write the model as

$$y_{it} = \mathbf{x}_{it}\boldsymbol{\beta} + v_{it}, \qquad t = 1, 2, \ldots, T, \tag{10.21}$$

where $v_{it} \equiv c_i + u_{it}$, $t = 1, \ldots, T$ are the **composite errors**. For each t, v_{it} is the sum of the unobserved effect and an idiosyncratic error. From Section 7.8, we know that pooled OLS estimation of this equation is consistent if $\mathrm{E}(\mathbf{x}_{it}'v_{it}) = \mathbf{0}$, $t = 1, 2, \ldots, T$. Practically speaking, no correlation between x_{it} and v_{it} means that we are assuming $\mathrm{E}(\mathbf{x}_{it}'u_{it}) = \mathbf{0}$ and

$$\mathrm{E}(\mathbf{x}_{it}'c_i) = \mathbf{0}, \qquad t = 1, 2, \ldots, T. \tag{10.22}$$

Equation (10.22) is the more restrictive assumption, since $\mathrm{E}(\mathbf{x}_{it}'u_{it}) = \mathbf{0}$ holds if we have successfully modeled $\mathrm{E}(y_{it} \mid \mathbf{x}_{it}, c_i)$.

In static and finite distributed lag models we are sometimes willing to make the assumption (10.22); in fact, we will do so in the next section on random effects estimation. As seen in Example 10.3, models with lagged dependent variables in $\mathbf{x}_{it}$ *must* violate assumption (10.22) because $y_{i,t-1}$ and c_i must be correlated.

Even if assumption (10.22) holds, the composite errors will be serially correlated due to the presence of c_i in each time period. Therefore, inference using pooled OLS requires the robust variance matrix estimator and robust test statistics from Chapter 7. Because v_{it} depends on c_i for all t, the correlation between v_{it} and v_{is} does not generally decrease as the distance $|t - s|$ increases; in time series parlance, the v_{it} are not weakly dependent across time. (We show this property explicitly in the next section when $\{u_{it} : t = 1, \ldots, T\}$ is homoskedastic and serially uncorrelated.) Therefore, it is important that we be able to rely on large-N and fixed-T asymptotics when applying pooled OLS.

As we discussed in Chapter 7, each $(\mathbf{y}_i, \mathbf{X}_i)$ has T rows and should be ordered chronologically, and the $(\mathbf{y}_i, \mathbf{X}_i)$ should be stacked from $i = 1, \ldots, N$. The order of the cross section observations is, as usual, irrelevant.

10.4 Random Effects Methods

10.4.1 Estimation and Inference under the Basic Random Effects Assumptions

As with pooled OLS, a **random effects analysis** puts c_i into the error term. In fact, random effects analysis imposes more assumptions than those needed for pooled

OLS: strict exogeneity in addition to orthogonality between c_i and $\mathbf{x}_{it}$. Stating the assumption in terms of conditional means, we have

ASSUMPTION RE.1:
(a) $\mathrm{E}(u_{it} \mid \mathbf{x}_i, c_i) = 0$, $t = 1, \ldots, T$; (b) $\mathrm{E}(c_i \mid \mathbf{x}_i) = \mathrm{E}(c_i) = 0$

where $\mathbf{x}_i \equiv (\mathbf{x}_{i1}, \mathbf{x}_{i2}, \ldots, \mathbf{x}_{iT})$.

In Section 10.2 we discussed the meaning of the strict exogeneity Assumption RE.1a. Assumption RE.1b is how we will state the orthogonality between c_i and each $\mathbf{x}_{it}$. For obtaining consistency results, we could relax RE.1b to assumption (10.22), but in practice (10.22) affords little more generality, and we will use Assumption RE.1b later to derive the traditional asymptotic variance for the random effects estimator. Assumption RE.1b is always implied by the assumption that the $\mathbf{x}_{it}$ are nonrandom and $\mathrm{E}(c_i) = 0$, or by the assumption that c_i is independent of $\mathbf{x}_i$. The important part is $\mathrm{E}(c_i \mid \mathbf{x}_i) = \mathrm{E}(c_i)$; the assumption $\mathrm{E}(c_i) = 0$ is without loss of generality, provided an intercept is included in $\mathbf{x}_{it}$, as should always be the case.

Why do we maintain Assumption RE.1 when it is more restrictive than needed for a pooled OLS analysis? The random effects approach exploits the serial correlation in the composite error, $v_{it} = c_i + u_{it}$, in a generalized least squares (GLS) framework. In order to ensure that feasible GLS is consistent, we need some form of strict exogeneity between the explanatory variables and the composite error. Under Assumption RE.1 we can write

$$y_{it} = \mathbf{x}_{it}\boldsymbol{\beta} + v_{it}, \tag{10.23}$$

$$\mathrm{E}(v_{it} \mid \mathbf{x}_i) = 0, \qquad t = 1, 2, \ldots, T, \tag{10.24}$$

where

$$v_{it} = c_i + u_{it}. \tag{10.25}$$

Equation (10.24) shows that $\{\mathbf{x}_{it} : t = 1, \ldots, T\}$ satisfies the strict exogeneity assumption SGLS.1 (see Chapter 7) in the model (10.23). Therefore, we can apply GLS methods that account for the particular error structure in equation (10.25).

Write the model (10.23) for all T time periods as

$$\mathbf{y}_i = \mathbf{X}_i\boldsymbol{\beta} + \mathbf{v}_i \tag{10.26}$$

and $\mathbf{v}_i$ can be written as $\mathbf{v}_i = c_i\mathbf{j}_T + \mathbf{u}_i$, where $\mathbf{j}_T$ is the $T \times 1$ vector of ones. Define the (unconditional) variance matrix of $\mathbf{v}_i$ as

$$\boldsymbol{\Omega} \equiv \mathrm{E}(\mathbf{v}_i\mathbf{v}_i'), \tag{10.27}$$

a $T \times T$ matrix that we assume to be positive definite. Remember, this matrix is necessarily the same for all i because of the random sampling assumption in the cross section.

For consistency of GLS, we need the usual rank condition for GLS:

ASSUMPTION RE.2: rank $\mathrm{E}(\mathbf{X}_i'\boldsymbol{\Omega}^{-1}\mathbf{X}_i) = K$.

Applying the results from Chapter 7, we know that GLS and feasible GLS are consistent under Assumptions RE.1 and RE.2. A general FGLS analysis, using an unrestricted variance estimator $\boldsymbol{\Omega}$, is consistent and $\sqrt{N}$-asymptotically normal as $N \to \infty$. But we would not be exploiting the unobserved effects structure of v_{it}. A standard random effects analysis adds assumptions on the idiosyncratic errors that give $\boldsymbol{\Omega}$ a special form. The first assumption is that the idiosyncratic errors u_{it} have a constant unconditional variance across t:

$$\mathrm{E}(u_{it}^2) = \sigma_u^2, \qquad t = 1, 2, \ldots, T. \tag{10.28}$$

The second assumption is that the idiosyncratic errors are serially uncorrelated:

$$\mathrm{E}(u_{it}u_{is}) = 0, \qquad \text{all } t \neq s. \tag{10.29}$$

Under these two assumptions, we can derive the variances and covariances of the elements of $\mathbf{v}_i$. Under Assumption RE.1a, $\mathrm{E}(c_i u_{it}) = 0$, $t = 1, 2, \ldots, T$, and so

$$\mathrm{E}(v_{it}^2) = \mathrm{E}(c_i^2) + 2\mathrm{E}(c_i u_{it}) + \mathrm{E}(u_{it}^2) = \sigma_c^2 + \sigma_u^2,$$

where $\sigma_c^2 = \mathrm{E}(c_i^2)$. Also, for all $t \neq s$,

$$\mathrm{E}(v_{it}v_{is}) = \mathrm{E}[(c_i + u_{it})(c_i + u_{is})] = \mathrm{E}(c_i^2) = \sigma_c^2.$$

Therefore, under assumptions RE.1, (10.28), and (10.29), $\boldsymbol{\Omega}$ takes the special form

$$\boldsymbol{\Omega} = \mathrm{E}(\mathbf{v}_i\mathbf{v}_i') = \begin{pmatrix} \sigma_c^2 + \sigma_u^2 & \sigma_c^2 & \cdots & \sigma_c^2 \\ \sigma_c^2 & \sigma_c^2 + \sigma_u^2 & \cdots & \vdots \\ \vdots & & \ddots & \sigma_c^2 \\ \sigma_c^2 & & & \sigma_c^2 + \sigma_u^2 \end{pmatrix}. \tag{10.30}$$

Because $\mathbf{j}_T\mathbf{j}_T'$ is the $T \times T$ matrix with unity in every element, we can write the matrix (10.30) as

$$\boldsymbol{\Omega} = \sigma_u^2\mathbf{I}_T + \sigma_c^2\mathbf{j}_T\mathbf{j}_T'. \tag{10.31}$$

When $\mathbf{\Omega}$ has the form (10.31), we say it has the **random effects structure**. Rather than depending on $T(T+1)/2$ unrestricted variances and covariances, as would be the case in a general GLS analysis, $\mathbf{\Omega}$ depends only on two parameters, σ_c^2 and σ_u^2, regardless of the size of T. The correlation between the composite errors v_{it} and v_{is} does not depend on the difference between t and s: $\text{Corr}(v_{is}, v_{it}) = \sigma_c^2/(\sigma_c^2 + \sigma_u^2) \geq 0$, $s \neq t$. This correlation is also the ratio of the variance of c_i to the variance of the composite error, and it is useful as a measure of the relative importance of the unobserved effect c_i.

Unlike the stable AR(1) model we briefly discussed in Section 7.8.6, the correlation between the composite errors v_{it} and v_{is} does not tend to zero as t and s get far apart under the RE covariance structure. If $v_{it} = \rho v_{i,t-1} + e_{it}$, where $|\rho| < 1$ and the $\{e_{it}\}$ are serially uncorrelated, then $\text{Cov}(v_{it}, v_{is})$ converges to zero pretty quickly as $|t-s|$ gets large. (Of course, the convergence is faster with smaller $|\rho|$.) Unlike standard models for serial correlation in time series settings, the random effects assumption implies strong persistence in the unobservables over time, due, of course, to the presence of c_i.

Assumptions (10.28) and (10.29) are special to random effects. For efficiency of feasible GLS, we assume that the variance matrix of $\mathbf{v}_i$ conditional on $\mathbf{x}_i$ is constant:

$$\text{E}(\mathbf{v}_i\mathbf{v}_i' \mid \mathbf{x}_i) = \text{E}(\mathbf{v}_i\mathbf{v}_i'). \tag{10.32}$$

Assumptions (10.28), (10.29), and (10.32) are implied by our third RE assumption:

ASSUMPTION RE.3: (a) $\text{E}(\mathbf{u}_i\mathbf{u}_i' \mid \mathbf{x}_i, c_i) = \sigma_u^2\mathbf{I}_T$; (b) $\text{E}(c_i^2 \mid \mathbf{x}_i) = \sigma_c^2$.

Under Assumption RE.3a, $\text{E}(u_{it}^2 \mid \mathbf{x}_i, c_i) = \sigma_u^2$, $t = 1, \ldots, T$, which implies assumption (10.28), and $\text{E}(u_{it}u_{is} \mid \mathbf{x}_i, c_i) = 0$, $t \neq s$, $t, s = 1, \ldots, T$, which implies assumption (10.29) (both by the usual iterated expectations argument). But Assumption RE.3a is stronger because it assumes that the *conditional* variances are constant and the *conditional* covariances are zero. Along with Assumption RE.1b, Assumption RE.3b is the same as $\text{Var}(c_i \mid \mathbf{x}_i) = \text{Var}(c_i)$, which is a homoskedasticity assumption on the unobserved effect c_i. Under Assumption RE.3, assumption (10.32) holds and $\mathbf{\Omega}$ has the form (10.30).

To implement an FGLS procedure, define $\sigma_v^2 = \sigma_c^2 + \sigma_u^2$. For now, assume that we have consistent estimators of σ_u^2 and σ_c^2. Then we can form

$$\hat{\mathbf{\Omega}} \equiv \hat{\sigma}_u^2\mathbf{I}_T + \hat{\sigma}_c^2\mathbf{j}_T\mathbf{j}_T', \tag{10.33}$$

a $T \times T$ matrix that we assume to be positive definite. In a panel data context, the FGLS estimator that uses the variance matrix (10.33) is what is known as the **random effects estimator**.

$$\hat{\boldsymbol{\beta}}_{RE} = \left(\sum_{i=1}^{N} \mathbf{X}_i' \hat{\boldsymbol{\Omega}}^{-1} \mathbf{X}_i\right)^{-1} \left(\sum_{i=1}^{N} \mathbf{X}_i' \hat{\boldsymbol{\Omega}}^{-1} \mathbf{y}_i\right). \tag{10.34}$$

Before we discuss obtaining $\hat{\boldsymbol{\Omega}}$ and performing asymptotic inference under the full set of RE assumptions, it is important to know that the RE estimator is generally consistent with or without Assumption RE.3. Clearly, the form of $\hat{\boldsymbol{\Omega}}$ is motivated by Assumption RE.3. Nevertheless, as we discussed in Section 7.5.3, incorrectly imposing restrictions on $\mathrm{E}(\mathbf{v}_i \mathbf{v}_i')$ does not cause inconsistency of FGLS provided the appropriate strict exogeneity assumption holds, as it does under Assumption RE.1. Of course, we have to insert $\mathrm{plim}(\hat{\boldsymbol{\Omega}})$ (which necessarily has the RE form) in place of $\boldsymbol{\Omega}$ in Assumption RE.2, but that is a minor change. Practically important is that without Assumption RE.3, we need to make inference fully robust, but we hold off on that until Section 10.4.2.

Under Assumption RE.3, the RE estimator is efficient in the class of estimators consistent under $\mathrm{E}(\mathbf{v}_i \mid \mathbf{x}_i) = \mathbf{0}$, including pooled OLS and a variety of weighted least squares estimators, because RE is asymptotically equivalent to GLS under Assumptions RE.1–RE.3. The usual feasible GLS variance matrix—see equation (7.54)—is valid under Assumptions RE.1–RE.3. The only difference from the general analysis is that $\hat{\boldsymbol{\Omega}}$ is chosen as in expression (10.33).

In order to implement the RE procedure, we need to obtain $\hat{\sigma}_c^2$ and $\hat{\sigma}_u^2$. Actually, it is easiest to first find $\hat{\sigma}_v^2 = \hat{\sigma}_c^2 + \hat{\sigma}_u^2$. Under Assumption RE.3a, $\sigma_v^2 = T^{-1} \sum_{t=1}^{T} \mathrm{E}(v_{it}^2)$ for all i; therefore, averaging v_{it}^2 across all i and t would give a consistent estimator of σ_v^2. But we need to estimate $\boldsymbol{\beta}$ to make this method operational. A convenient initial estimator of $\boldsymbol{\beta}$ is the pooled OLS estimator, denoted here by $\check{\boldsymbol{\beta}}$. Let $\check{v}_{it}$ denote the pooled OLS residuals. A consistent estimator of σ_v^2 is

$$\hat{\sigma}_v^2 = \frac{1}{(NT - K)} \sum_{i=1}^{N} \sum_{t=1}^{T} \check{v}_{it}^2, \tag{10.35}$$

which is the usual variance estimator from the OLS regression on the pooled data. The degrees-of-freedom correction in equation (10.35)—that is, the use of $NT - K$ rather than NT—has no effect asymptotically. Under Assumptions RE.1–RE.3, equation (10.35) is a consistent estimator (actually, a $\sqrt{N}$-consistent estimator) of σ_v^2.

To find a consistent estimator of σ_c^2, recall that $\sigma_c^2 = \mathrm{E}(v_{it} v_{is})$, all $t \neq s$. Therefore, for each i, there are $T(T-1)/2$ nonredundant error products that can be used to estimate σ_c^2. If we sum all these combinations and take the expectation, we get, for each i,

$$\mathrm{E}\left(\sum_{t=1}^{T-1}\sum_{s=t+1}^{T} v_{it}v_{is}\right) = \sum_{t=1}^{T-1}\sum_{s=t+1}^{T} \mathrm{E}(v_{it}v_{is}) = \sum_{t=1}^{T-1}\sum_{s=t+1}^{T} \sigma_c^2 = \sigma_c^2 \sum_{t=1}^{T-1}(T-t)$$

$$= \sigma_c^2((T-1) + (T-2) + \cdots + 2 + 1) = \sigma_c^2 T(T-1)/2, \quad (10.36)$$

where we have used the fact that the sum of the first $T-1$ positive integers is $T(T-1)/2$. As usual, a consistent estimator is obtained by replacing the expectation with an average (across i) and replacing v_{it} with its pooled OLS residual. We also make a degrees-of-freedom adjustment as a small-sample correction:

$$\hat{\sigma}_c^2 = \frac{1}{[NT(T-1)/2 - K]} \sum_{i=1}^{N}\sum_{t=1}^{T-1}\sum_{s=t+1}^{T} \check{v}_{it}\check{v}_{is} \quad (10.37)$$

is a $\sqrt{N}$-consistent estimator of σ_c^2 under Assumptions RE.1–RE.3. Equation (10.37), without the degrees-of-freedom adjustment, appears elsewhere—for example, Baltagi (2001, Sect. 2.3). Given $\hat{\sigma}_v^2$ and $\hat{\sigma}_c^2$, we can form $\hat{\sigma}_u^2 = \hat{\sigma}_v^2 - \hat{\sigma}_c^2$. (The idiosyncratic error variance, σ_u^2, can also be estimated using the fixed effects method, which we discuss in Section 10.5. Also, there are other methods of estimating σ_c^2. A common estimator of σ_c^2 is based on the between estimator of $\boldsymbol{\beta}$, which we touch on in Section 10.5; see Hsiao (2003, Sect. 3.3) and Baltagi (2001, Sect. 2.3). Because the RE estimator is a feasible GLS estimator under strict exogeneity, all that we need are consistent estimators of σ_c^2 and σ_u^2 in order to obtain a $\sqrt{N}$-efficient estimator of $\boldsymbol{\beta}$.)

As a practical matter, equation (10.37) is not guaranteed to be positive, although it is in the vast majority of applications. A negative value for $\hat{\sigma}_c^2$ is indicative of negative serial correlation in u_{it}, probably a substantial amount, which means that Assumption RE.3a is violated. Alternatively, some other assumption in the model can be false. We should make sure that time dummies are included in the model if aggregate effects are important; omitting them can induce serial correlation in the implied u_{it}. When the intercepts are allowed to change freely over time, the effects of other aggregate variables will not be identified. If $\hat{\sigma}_c^2$ is negative, unrestricted FGLS may be called for; see Section 10.4.3.

Example 10.4 (RE Estimation of the Effects of Job Training Grants): We now use the data in JTRAIN1.RAW to estimate the effect of job training grants on firm scrap rates, using a random effects analysis. There are 54 firms that reported scrap rates for each of the years 1987, 1988, and 1989. Grants were not awarded in 1987. Some firms received grants in 1988, others received grants in 1989, and a firm could not receive a grant twice. Since there are firms in 1989 that received a grant only in 1988, it is important to allow the grant effect to persist one period. The estimated equation is

$$\widehat{\log(scrap)} = \underset{(.243)}{.415} - \underset{(.109)}{.093}\ d88 - \underset{(.132)}{.270}\ d89 + \underset{(.411)}{.548}\ union$$
$$- \underset{(.148)}{.215}\ grant - \underset{(.205)}{.377}\ grant_{-1}.$$

The lagged value of *grant* has the larger impact and is statistically significant at the 5 percent level against a one-sided alternative. You are invited to estimate the equation without $grant_{-1}$ to verify that the estimated grant effect is much smaller (on the order of 6.7 percent) and statistically insignificant.

Multiple hypotheses tests are carried out as in any FGLS analysis; see Section 7.6, where $G = T$. In computing an F-type statistic based on weighted sums of squared residuals, $\hat{\mathbf{\Omega}}$ in expression (10.33) should be based on the pooled OLS residuals from the unrestricted model. Then, obtain the residuals from the unrestricted random effects estimation as $\hat{\mathbf{v}}_i \equiv \mathbf{y}_i - \mathbf{X}_i\hat{\boldsymbol{\beta}}_{RE}$. Let $\tilde{\boldsymbol{\beta}}_{RE}$ denote the REs estimator with the Q linear restrictions imposed, and define the restricted RE residuals as $\tilde{\mathbf{v}}_i \equiv \mathbf{y}_i - \mathbf{X}_i\tilde{\boldsymbol{\beta}}_{RE}$. Insert these into equation (7.56) in place of $\hat{\mathbf{u}}_i$ and $\tilde{\mathbf{u}}_i$ for a chi-square statistic or into equation (7.57) for an F-type statistic.

In Example 10.4, the Wald test for joint significance of *grant* and $grant_{-1}$ (against a two-sided alternative) yields a χ_2^2 statistic equal to 3.66, with p-value $= .16$. (This test comes from Stata.)

10.4.2 Robust Variance Matrix Estimator

Because failure of Assumption RE.3 does not cause inconsistency in the RE estimator, it is very useful to be able to conduct statistical inference without this assumption. Assumption RE.3 can fail for two reasons. First, $\mathrm{E}(\mathbf{v}_i\mathbf{v}_i' \mid \mathbf{x}_i)$ may not be constant, so that $\mathrm{E}(\mathbf{v}_i\mathbf{v}_i' \mid \mathbf{x}_i) \neq \mathrm{E}(\mathbf{v}_i\mathbf{v}_i')$. This outcome is always a possibility with GLS analysis. Second, $\mathrm{E}(\mathbf{v}_i\mathbf{v}_i')$ may not have the RE structure: the idiosyncratic errors u_{it} may have variances that change over time, or they could be serially correlated. In either case a robust variance matrix is available from the analysis in Chapter 7. We simply use equation (7.52) with $\hat{\mathbf{u}}_i$ replaced by $\hat{\mathbf{v}}_i = \mathbf{y}_i - \mathbf{X}_i\hat{\boldsymbol{\beta}}_{RE}$, $i = 1, 2, \ldots, N$, the $T \times 1$ vectors of RE residuals.

Robust standard errors are obtained in the usual way from the robust variance matrix estimator, and robust Wald statistics are obtained by the usual formula $W = (\mathbf{R}\hat{\boldsymbol{\beta}} - \mathbf{r})'(\mathbf{R}\hat{\mathbf{V}}\mathbf{R}')^{-1}(\mathbf{R}\hat{\boldsymbol{\beta}} - \mathbf{r})$, where $\hat{\mathbf{V}}$ is the robust variance matrix estimator. Remember, if Assumption RE.3 is violated, the sum of squared residuals form of the F statistic is not valid.

The idea behind using a robust variance matrix is the following. Assumptions RE.1–RE.3 lead to a well-known estimation technique whose properties are understood under these assumptions. But it is always a good idea to make the analysis robust whenever feasible. With fixed T and large N asymptotics, we lose nothing in using the robust standard errors and test statistics even if Assumption RE.3 holds. In Section 10.7.2, we show how the RE estimator can be obtained from a particular pooled OLS regression, which makes obtaining robust standard errors and t and F statistics especially easy.

10.4.3 General Feasible Generalized Least Squares Analysis

If the idiosyncratic errors $\{u_{it} : t = 1, 2, \ldots, T\}$ are generally heteroskedastic and serially correlated across t, a more general estimator of $\mathbf{\Omega}$ can be used in FGLS:

$$\hat{\mathbf{\Omega}} = N^{-1} \sum_{i=1}^{N} \check{\mathbf{v}}_i \check{\mathbf{v}}_i', \tag{10.38}$$

where the $\check{\mathbf{v}}_i$ would be the pooled OLS residuals. The FGLS estimator is consistent under Assumptions RE.1 and RE.2, and, if we assume that $\mathrm{E}(\mathbf{v}_i \mathbf{v}_i' \,|\, \mathbf{x}_i) = \mathbf{\Omega}$, then the FGLS estimator is asymptotically efficient and its asymptotic variance estimator takes the usual form.

Using equation (10.38) is more general than the RE analysis. In fact, with large N asymptotics, the general FGLS estimator is just as efficient as the RE estimator under Assumptions RE.1–RE.3. Using equation (10.38) is asymptotically more efficient if $\mathrm{E}(\mathbf{v}_i \mathbf{v}_i' \,|\, \mathbf{x}_i) = \mathbf{\Omega}$, but $\mathbf{\Omega}$ does not have the RE form. So why not always use FGLS with $\hat{\mathbf{\Omega}}$ given in equation (10.38)? There are historical reasons for using RE methods rather than a general FGLS analysis. The structure of $\mathbf{\Omega}$ in the matrix (10.30) was once synonomous with unobserved effects models: any correlation in the composite errors $\{v_{it} : t = 1, 2, \ldots, T\}$ was assumed to be caused by the presence of c_i. The idiosyncratic errors, u_{it}, were, by definition, taken to be serially uncorrelated and homoskedastic.

If N is not several times larger than T, an unrestricted FGLS analysis can have poor finite sample properties because $\hat{\mathbf{\Omega}}$ has $T(T+1)/2$ estimated elements. Even though estimation of $\mathbf{\Omega}$ does not affect the asymptotic distribution of the FGLS estimator, it certainly affects its finite sample properties. Random effects estimation requires estimation of only two variance parameters for any T.

With very large N, using the general estimate of $\mathbf{\Omega}$ is an attractive alternative, especially if the estimate in equation (10.38) appears to have a pattern different from the RE pattern. As a middle ground between a traditional random effects analysis and a full-blown FGLS analysis, we might specify a particular structure for the idiosyncratic error variance matrix $E(\mathbf{u}_i\mathbf{u}_i')$. For example, if $\{u_{it}\}$ follows a stable first-order autoregressive process with autocorrelation coefficient ρ and variance σ_u^2, then $\boldsymbol{\Omega} = E(\mathbf{u}_i\mathbf{u}_i') + \sigma_c^2\mathbf{j}_T\mathbf{j}_T'$ depends in a known way on only three parameters, σ_u^2, σ_c^2, and ρ. These parameters can be estimated after initial pooled OLS estimation, and then an FGLS procedure using the particular structure of $\boldsymbol{\Omega}$ is easy to implement. We do not cover such possibilities explicitly; see, for example, MaCurdy (1982). Some are preprogrammed in statistical packages, but not necessarily with the option of making inference robust to misspecification of $\boldsymbol{\Omega}$ or system heteroskedasticity.

10.4.4 Testing for the Presence of an Unobserved Effect

If the standard random effects assumptions RE.1–RE.3 hold but the model does not actually contain an unobserved effect, pooled OLS is efficient and all associated pooled OLS statistics are asymptotically valid. The absence of an unobserved effect is statistically equivalent to $H_0 : \sigma_c^2 = 0$.

To test $H_0 : \sigma_c^2 = 0$, we can use the simple test for AR(1) serial correlation covered in Chapter 7 (see equation (7.81)). The AR(1) test is valid because the errors v_{it} are serially uncorrelated under the null $H_0 : \sigma_c^2 = 0$ (and we are assuming that $\{\mathbf{x}_{it}\}$ is strictly exogenous). However, a better test is based directly on the estimator of σ_c^2 in equation (10.37).

Breusch and Pagan (1980) derive a statistic using the Lagrange multiplier principle in a likelihood setting (something we cover in Chapter 13). We will not derive the Breusch and Pagan statistic because we are not assuming any particular distribution for the v_{it}. Instead, we derive a similar test that has the advantage of being valid for *any* distribution of $\mathbf{v}_i$ and only states that the v_{it} are uncorrelated under the null. (In particular, the statistic is valid for heteroskedasticity in the v_{it}.)

From equation (10.37), we base a test of H_0: $\sigma_c^2 = 0$ on the null asymptotic distribution of

$$N^{-1/2}\sum_{i=1}^{N}\sum_{t=1}^{T-1}\sum_{s=t+1}^{T}\hat{v}_{it}\hat{v}_{is}, \tag{10.39}$$

which is essentially the estimator $\hat{\sigma}_c^2$ scaled up by $\sqrt{N}$. Because of strict exogeneity, this statistic has the same limiting distribution (as $N \to \infty$ with fixed T) when we replace the pooled OLS residuals $\hat{v}_{it}$ with the errors v_{it} (see Problem 7.4). For any distribution of the v_{it}, $N^{-1/2}\sum_{i=1}^{N}\sum_{t=1}^{T-1}\sum_{s=t+1}^{T} v_{it}v_{is}$ has a limiting normal distribution (under the null that the v_{it} are serially uncorrelated) with variance $E(\sum_{t=1}^{T-1}\sum_{s=t+1}^{T} v_{it}v_{is})^2$. We can estimate this variance in the usual way (take away the expectation, average across i, and replace v_{it} with $\hat{v}_{it}$). When we put expression (10.39) over its asymptotic standard error we get the statistic

$$\frac{\sum_{i=1}^{N}\sum_{t=1}^{T-1}\sum_{s=t+1}^{T}\hat{v}_{it}\hat{v}_{is}}{\left[\sum_{i=1}^{N}\left(\sum_{t=1}^{T-1}\sum_{s=t+1}^{T}\hat{v}_{it}\hat{v}_{is}\right)^2\right]^{1/2}}. \tag{10.40}$$

Under the null hypothesis that the v_{it} are serially uncorrelated, this statistic is distributed asymptotically as standard normal. Unlike the Breusch-Pagan statistic, with expression (10.40) we can reject H_0 for *negative* estimates of σ_c^2, although negative estimates are rare in practice (unless we have already differenced the data, something we discuss in Section 10.6).

The statistic in expression (10.40) can detect many kinds of serial correlation in the composite error v_{it}, and so a rejection of the null should not be interpreted as implying that the RE error structure *must* be true. Finding that the v_{it} are serially uncorrelated is not very surprising in applications, especially since $\mathbf{x}_{it}$ cannot contain lagged dependent variables for the methods in this chapter.

It is probably more interesting to test for serial correlation in the $\{u_{it}\}$, as this is a test of the RE form of $\mathbf{\Omega}$. Baltagi and Li (1995) obtain a test under normality of c_i and $\{u_{it}\}$, based on the Lagrange multiplier principle. In Section 10.7.2, we discuss a simpler test for serial correlation in $\{u_{it}\}$ using a pooled OLS regression on transformed data, which does not rely on normality.

10.5 Fixed Effects Methods

10.5.1 Consistency of the Fixed Effects Estimator

Again consider the linear unobserved effects model for T time periods:

$$y_{it} = \mathbf{x}_{it}\boldsymbol{\beta} + c_i + u_{it}, \qquad t = 1, \ldots, T. \tag{10.41}$$

The RE approach to estimating $\boldsymbol{\beta}$ effectively puts c_i into the error term, under the assumption that c_i is orthogonal to $\mathbf{x}_{it}$, and then accounts for the implied serial correlation in the composite error $v_{it} = c_i + u_{it}$ using a GLS analysis. In many applications the whole point of using panel data is to allow for c_i to be arbitrarily correlated with the $\mathbf{x}_{it}$. A fixed effects analysis achieves this purpose explicitly.

The T equations in the model (10.41) can be written as

$$\mathbf{y}_i = \mathbf{X}_i\boldsymbol{\beta} + c_i\mathbf{j}_T + \mathbf{u}_i, \tag{10.42}$$

where $\mathbf{j}_T$ is still the $T \times 1$ vector of ones. As usual, equation (10.42) represents a single random draw from the cross section.

The first fixed effects (FE) assumption is strict exogeneity of the explanatory variables conditional on c_i:

ASSUMPTION FE.1: $\mathrm{E}(u_{it} \mid \mathbf{x}_i, c_i) = 0, \; t = 1, 2, \ldots, T$.

This assumption is *identical* to the first part of Assumption RE.1. Thus, we maintain strict exogeneity of $\{\mathbf{x}_{it} : t = 1, \ldots, T\}$ conditional on the unobserved effect. The key difference is that we do not assume RE.1b. In other words, for FE analysis, $\mathrm{E}(c_i \mid \mathbf{x}_i)$ is allowed to be any function of $\mathbf{x}_i$.

By relaxing RE.1b we can consistently estimate partial effects in the presence of time-constant omitted variables that can be arbitrarily related to the observables $\mathbf{x}_{it}$. Therefore, FE analysis is more robust than random effects analysis. As we suggested in Section 10.1, this robustness comes at a price: without further assumptions, we cannot include time-constant factors in $\mathbf{x}_{it}$. The reason is simple: if c_i can be arbitrarily correlated with each element of $\mathbf{x}_{it}$, there is no way to distinguish the effects of time-constant observables from the time-constant unobservable c_i. When analyzing individuals, factors such as gender or race cannot be included in $\mathbf{x}_{it}$. For analyzing firms, industry cannot be included in $\mathbf{x}_{it}$ unless industry designation changes over time for at least some firms. For cities, variables describing fixed city attributes, such as whether or not the city is near a river, cannot be included in $\mathbf{x}_{it}$.

The fact that $\mathbf{x}_{it}$ cannot include time-constant explanatory variables is a drawback in certain applications, but when the interest is only on time-varying explanatory variables, it is convenient not to have to worry about modeling time-constant factors that are not of direct interest.

In panel data analysis the term "time-varying explanatory variables" means that each element of $\mathbf{x}_{it}$ varies over time for *some* cross section units. Often there are elements of $\mathbf{x}_{it}$ that are constant across time for a subset of the cross section. For example, if we have a panel of adults and one element of $\mathbf{x}_{it}$ is education, we can allow education to be constant for some part of the sample. But we must have education changing for some people in the sample.

As a general specification, let $d2_t, \ldots, dT_t$ denote time period dummies so that $ds_t = 1$ if $s = t$, and zero otherwise (often these are defined in terms of specific years, such as $d88_t$, but at this level we call them time period dummies). Let $\mathbf{z}_i$ be a vector of time-constant observables, and let $\mathbf{w}_{it}$ be a vector of time-varying variables. Suppose y_{it} is determined by

$$y_{it} = \theta_1 + \theta_2 d2_t + \cdots + \theta_T dT_t + \mathbf{z}_i \boldsymbol{\gamma}_1 + d2_t \mathbf{z}_i \boldsymbol{\gamma}_2 + \cdots + dT_t \mathbf{z}_i \boldsymbol{\gamma}_T + \mathbf{w}_{it} \boldsymbol{\delta} + c_i + u_{it}. \tag{10.43}$$

$$\mathrm{E}(u_{it} \mid \mathbf{z}_i, \mathbf{w}_{i1}, \mathbf{w}_{i2}, \ldots, \mathbf{w}_{iT}, c_i) = 0, \qquad t = 1, 2, \ldots, T. \tag{10.44}$$

We hope that this model represents a causal relationship, where the conditioning on c_i allows us to control for unobserved factors that are time constant. Without further assumptions, the intercept θ_1 cannot be identified and the vector $\boldsymbol{\gamma}_1$ on $\mathbf{z}_i$ cannot be identified, because $\theta_1 + \mathbf{z}_i \boldsymbol{\gamma}_1$ cannot be distinguished from c_i. Note that θ_1 is the intercept for the base time period, $t = 1$, and $\boldsymbol{\gamma}_1$ measures the effects of $\mathbf{z}_i$ on y_{it} in period $t = 1$. Even though we cannot identify the effects of the $\mathbf{z}_i$ in any particular time period, $\boldsymbol{\gamma}_2, \boldsymbol{\gamma}_3, \ldots, \boldsymbol{\gamma}_T$ *are* identified, and therefore we can estimate the *differences* in the partial effects on time-constant variables relative to a base period. In particular, we can test whether the effects of time-constant variables have changed over time. As a specific example, if $y_{it} = \log(wage_{it})$ and one element of $\mathbf{z}_i$ is a female binary variable, then we can estimate how the gender gap has changed over time, even though we cannot estimate the gap in any particular time period.

The idea for estimating $\boldsymbol{\beta}$ under Assumption FE.1 is to transform the equations to eliminate the unobserved effect c_i. When at least two time periods are available, there are several transformations that accomplish this purpose. In this section we study the **fixed effects transformation**, also called the **within transformation**. The FE transformation is obtained by first averaging equation (10.41) over $t = 1, \ldots, T$ to get the cross section equation

$$\bar{y}_i = \bar{\mathbf{x}}_i \boldsymbol{\beta} + c_i + \bar{u}_i, \tag{10.45}$$

where $\bar{y}_i = T^{-1} \sum_{t=1}^{T} y_{it}$, $\bar{\mathbf{x}}_i = T^{-1} \sum_{t=1}^{T} \mathbf{x}_{it}$, and $\bar{u}_i = T^{-1} \sum_{t=1}^{T} u_{it}$. Subtracting equation (10.45) from equation (10.41) for each t gives the FE transformed equation,

$$y_{it} - \bar{y}_i = (\mathbf{x}_{it} - \bar{\mathbf{x}}_i)\boldsymbol{\beta} + u_{it} - \bar{u}_i$$

or

$$\ddot{y}_{it} = \ddot{\mathbf{x}}_{it} \boldsymbol{\beta} + \ddot{u}_{it}, \qquad t = 1, 2, \ldots, T, \tag{10.46}$$

where $\ddot{y}_{it} \equiv y_{it} - \bar{y}_i$, $\ddot{\mathbf{x}}_{it} \equiv \mathbf{x}_{it} - \bar{\mathbf{x}}_i$, and $\ddot{u}_{it} \equiv u_{it} - \bar{u}_i$. The time demeaning of the original equation has removed the individual specific effect c_i.

With c_i out of the picture, it is natural to think of estimating equation (10.46) by pooled OLS. Before investigating this possibility, we must remember that equation (10.46) is an *estimating* equation: the interpretation of $\boldsymbol{\beta}$ comes from the (structural) conditional expectation $\mathrm{E}(y_{it} \mid \mathbf{x}_i, c_i) = \mathrm{E}(y_{it} \mid \mathbf{x}_{it}, c_i) = \mathbf{x}_{it} \boldsymbol{\beta} + c_i$.

To see whether pooled OLS estimation of equation (10.46) will be consistent, we need to show that the key pooled OLS assumption (Assumption POLS.1 from Chapter 7) holds in equation (10.46). That is,

$$\mathrm{E}(\ddot{\mathbf{x}}_{it}'\ddot{u}_{it}) = \mathbf{0}, \qquad t = 1, 2, \ldots, T. \tag{10.47}$$

For each t, the left-hand side of equation (10.47) can be written as $\mathrm{E}[(\mathbf{x}_{it} - \bar{\mathbf{x}}_i)'(u_{it} - \bar{u}_i)]$. Now, under Assumption FE.1, u_{it} is uncorrelated with $\mathbf{x}_{is}$, for all $s, t = 1, 2, \ldots, T$. It follows that u_{it} and $\bar{u}_i$ are uncorrelated with $\mathbf{x}_{it}$ and $\bar{\mathbf{x}}_i$ for $t = 1, 2, \ldots, T$. Therefore, assumption (10.47) holds under Assumption FE.1, and so pooled OLS applied to equation (10.46) can be expected to produce consistent estimators. We can actually say a lot more than condition (10.47): under Assumption FE.1, $\mathrm{E}(\ddot{u}_{it} \mid \mathbf{x}_i) = \mathrm{E}(u_{it} \mid \mathbf{x}_i) - \mathrm{E}(\bar{u}_i \mid \mathbf{x}_i) = 0$, which in turn implies that $\mathrm{E}(\ddot{u}_{it} \mid \ddot{\mathbf{x}}_{i1}, \ldots, \ddot{\mathbf{x}}_{iT}) = 0$, since each $\ddot{\mathbf{x}}_{it}$ is just a function of $\mathbf{x}_i = (\mathbf{x}_{i1}, \ldots, \mathbf{x}_{iT})$. This result shows that the $\ddot{\mathbf{x}}_{it}$ satisfy the conditional expectation form of the strict exogeneity assumption in the model (10.46). Among other things, this conclusion implies that the FE estimator of $\boldsymbol{\beta}$ that we will derive is actually unbiased under Assumption FE.1.

It is important to see that assumption (10.47) fails if we try to relax the strict exogeneity assumption to something weaker, such as $\mathrm{E}(\mathbf{x}_{it}'u_{it}) = \mathbf{0}$, all t, because this assumption does not ensure that $\mathbf{x}_{is}$ is uncorrelated with u_{it}, $s \neq t$. In Chapter 11 we study violations of the strict exogeneity assumption in more detail.

The **FE estimator**, denoted by $\hat{\boldsymbol{\beta}}_{FE}$, is the pooled OLS estimator from the regression

$$\ddot{y}_{it} \text{ on } \ddot{\mathbf{x}}_{it}, \qquad t = 1, 2, \ldots, T;\, i = 1, 2, \ldots, N. \tag{10.48}$$

The FE estimator is simple to compute once the time demeaning has been carried out. Some econometrics packages have special commands to carry out FE estimation (and commands to carry out the time demeaning for all i). It is also fairly easy to program this estimator in matrix-oriented languages.

To study the FE estimator a little more closely, write equation (10.46) for all time periods as

$$\ddot{\mathbf{y}}_i = \ddot{\mathbf{X}}_i\boldsymbol{\beta} + \ddot{\mathbf{u}}_i, \tag{10.49}$$

where $\ddot{\mathbf{y}}_i$ is $T \times 1$, $\ddot{\mathbf{X}}_i$ is $T \times K$, and $\ddot{\mathbf{u}}_i$ is $T \times 1$. This set of equations can be obtained by premultiplying equation (10.42) by a **time-demeaning matrix**. Define $\mathbf{Q}_T \equiv \mathbf{I}_T - \mathbf{j}_T(\mathbf{j}_T'\mathbf{j}_T)^{-1}\mathbf{j}_T'$, which is easily seen to be a $T \times T$ symmetric, idempotent matrix with rank $T - 1$. Further, $\mathbf{Q}_T\mathbf{j}_T = \mathbf{0}$, $\mathbf{Q}_T\mathbf{y}_i = \ddot{\mathbf{y}}_i$, $\mathbf{Q}_T\mathbf{X}_i = \ddot{\mathbf{X}}_i$, and $\mathbf{Q}_T\mathbf{u}_i = \ddot{\mathbf{u}}_i$, and so premultiplying equation (10.42) by $\mathbf{Q}_T$ gives the demeaned equations (10.49).

In order to ensure that the FE estimator is well behaved asymptotically, we need a standard rank condition on the matrix of time-demeaned explanatory variables:

ASSUMPTION FE.2: $\operatorname{rank}\left(\sum_{t=1}^{T} \mathrm{E}(\ddot{\mathbf{x}}_{it}'\ddot{\mathbf{x}}_{it})\right) = \operatorname{rank}[\mathrm{E}(\ddot{\mathbf{X}}_i'\ddot{\mathbf{X}}_i)] = K.$

If $\mathbf{x}_{it}$ contains an element that does not vary over time for any i, then the corresponding element in $\ddot{\mathbf{x}}_{it}$ is identically zero for all t and any draw from the cross section. Since $\ddot{\mathbf{X}}_i$ would contain a column of zeros for all i, Assumption FE.2 could not be true. Assumption FE.2 shows explicitly why time-constant variables are not allowed in fixed effects analysis (unless they are interacted with time-varying variables, such as time dummies).

The FE estimator can be expressed as

$$\hat{\boldsymbol{\beta}}_{FE} = \left(\sum_{i=1}^{N} \ddot{\mathbf{X}}_i'\ddot{\mathbf{X}}_i\right)^{-1} \left(\sum_{i=1}^{N} \ddot{\mathbf{X}}_i'\ddot{\mathbf{y}}_i\right) = \left(\sum_{i=1}^{N}\sum_{t=1}^{T} \ddot{\mathbf{x}}_{it}'\ddot{\mathbf{x}}_{it}\right)^{-1} \left(\sum_{i=1}^{N}\sum_{t=1}^{T} \ddot{\mathbf{x}}_{it}'\ddot{y}_{it}\right). \tag{10.50}$$

It is also called the **within estimator** because it uses the time variation within each cross section. The **between estimator**, which uses only variation between the cross section observations, is the OLS estimator applied to the time-averaged equation (10.45). This estimator is not consistent under Assumption FE.1 because $\mathrm{E}(\bar{\mathbf{x}}_i'c_i)$ is not necessarily zero. The between estimator is consistent under Assumption RE.1 and a standard rank condition, but it effectively discards the time series information in the data set. It is more efficient to use the RE estimator.

Under Assumption FE.1 and the finite sample version of Assumption FE.2, namely, $\operatorname{rank}(\ddot{\mathbf{X}}'\ddot{\mathbf{X}}) = K$, $\hat{\boldsymbol{\beta}}_{FE}$ can be shown to be *unbiased* conditional on $\mathbf{X}$.

10.5.2 Asymptotic Inference with Fixed Effects

Without further assumptions the FE estimator is not necessarily the most efficient estimator based on Assumption FE.1. The next assumption ensures that FE is efficient.

ASSUMPTION FE.3: $\mathrm{E}(\mathbf{u}_i\mathbf{u}_i' \mid \mathbf{x}_i, c_i) = \sigma_u^2\mathbf{I}_T.$

Assumption FE.3 is identical to Assumption RE.3a. Since $\mathrm{E}(\mathbf{u}_i \mid \mathbf{x}_i, c_i) = \mathbf{0}$ by Assumption FE.1, Assumption FE.3 is the same as saying $\operatorname{Var}(\mathbf{u}_i \mid \mathbf{x}_i, c_i) = \sigma_u^2\mathbf{I}_T$ if Assumption FE.1 also holds. As with Assumption RE.3a, it is useful to think of Assumption FE.3 as having two parts. The first is that $\mathrm{E}(\mathbf{u}_i\mathbf{u}_i' \mid \mathbf{x}_i, c_i) = \mathrm{E}(\mathbf{u}_i\mathbf{u}_i')$, which is standard in system estimation contexts (see equation (7.53)). The second is that the unconditional variance matrix $\mathrm{E}(\mathbf{u}_i\mathbf{u}_i')$ has the special form $\sigma_u^2\mathbf{I}_T$. This implies that the idiosyncratic errors u_{it} have a constant variance across t and are serially uncorrelated, just as in assumptions (10.28) and (10.29).

Assumption FE.3, along with Assumption FE.1, implies that the *unconditional* variance matrix of the composite error $\mathbf{v}_i = c_i \mathbf{j}_T + \mathbf{u}_i$ has the RE form. However, without Assumption RE.3b, $\mathrm{E}(\mathbf{v}_i \mathbf{v}_i' \mid \mathbf{x}_i) \neq \mathrm{E}(\mathbf{v}_i \mathbf{v}_i')$. While this result matters for inference with the RE estimator, it has no bearing on a fixed effects analysis.

It is not obvious that Assumption FE.3 has the desired consequences of ensuring efficiency of FE and leading to simple computation of standard errors and test statistics. Consider the demeaned equation (10.46). Normally, for pooled OLS to be relatively efficient, we require that the $\{\ddot{u}_{it} : t = 1, 2, \ldots, T\}$ be homoskedastic across t and serially uncorrelated. The variance of $\ddot{u}_{it}$ can be computed as

$$\begin{aligned} \mathrm{E}(\ddot{u}_{it}^2) &= \mathrm{E}[(u_{it} - \bar{u}_i)^2] = \mathrm{E}(u_{it}^2) + \mathrm{E}(\bar{u}_i^2) - 2\mathrm{E}(u_{it}\bar{u}_i) \\ &= \sigma_u^2 + \sigma_u^2/T - 2\sigma_u^2/T = \sigma_u^2(1 - 1/T). \end{aligned} \tag{10.51}$$

which verifies (unconditional) homoskedasticity across t. However, for $t \neq s$, the covariance between $\ddot{u}_{it}$ and $\ddot{u}_{is}$ is

$$\begin{aligned} \mathrm{E}(\ddot{u}_{it}\ddot{u}_{is}) &= \mathrm{E}[(u_{it} - \bar{u}_i)(u_{is} - \bar{u}_i)] = \mathrm{E}(u_{it}u_{is}) - \mathrm{E}(u_{it}\bar{u}_i) - \mathrm{E}(u_{is}\bar{u}_i) + \mathrm{E}(\bar{u}_i^2) \\ &= 0 - \sigma_u^2/T - \sigma_u^2/T + \sigma_u^2/T = -\sigma_u^2/T < 0. \end{aligned}$$

Combining this expression with the variance in equation (10.51) gives, for all $t \neq s$,

$$\mathrm{Corr}(\ddot{u}_{it}, \ddot{u}_{is}) = -1/(T - 1) \tag{10.52}$$

which shows that the time-demeaned errors $\ddot{u}_{it}$ are negatively serially correlated. (As T gets large, the correlation tends to zero.)

It turns out that, because of the nature of time demeaning, the serial correlation in the $\ddot{u}_{it}$ under Assumption FE.3 causes only minor complications. To find the asymptotic variance of $\hat{\boldsymbol{\beta}}_{FE}$, write

$$\sqrt{N}(\hat{\boldsymbol{\beta}}_{FE} - \boldsymbol{\beta}) = \left(N^{-1}\sum_{i=1}^{N} \ddot{\mathbf{X}}_i'\ddot{\mathbf{X}}_i\right)^{-1}\left(N^{-1/2}\sum_{i=1}^{N} \ddot{\mathbf{X}}_i'\mathbf{u}_i\right),$$

where we have used the important fact that $\ddot{\mathbf{X}}_i'\ddot{\mathbf{u}}_i = \mathbf{X}_i'\mathbf{Q}_T\mathbf{u}_i = \ddot{\mathbf{X}}_i'\mathbf{u}_i$. Under Assumption FE.3, $\mathrm{E}(\mathbf{u}_i\mathbf{u}_i' \mid \ddot{\mathbf{X}}_i) = \sigma_u^2\mathbf{I}_T$. From the system OLS analysis in Chapter 7 it follows that

$$\sqrt{N}(\hat{\boldsymbol{\beta}}_{FE} - \boldsymbol{\beta}) \sim \mathrm{Normal}(\mathbf{0}, \sigma_u^2[\mathrm{E}(\ddot{\mathbf{X}}_i'\ddot{\mathbf{X}}_i)]^{-1}),$$

and so

$$\mathrm{Avar}(\hat{\boldsymbol{\beta}}_{FE}) = \sigma_u^2[\mathrm{E}(\ddot{\mathbf{X}}_i'\ddot{\mathbf{X}}_i)]^{-1}/N. \tag{10.53}$$

Given a consistent estimator $\hat{\sigma}_u^2$ of σ_u^2, equation (10.53) is easily estimated by also replacing $\mathrm{E}(\ddot{\mathbf{X}}_i'\ddot{\mathbf{X}}_i)$ with its sample analogue $N^{-1}\sum_{i=1}^{N}\ddot{\mathbf{X}}_i'\ddot{\mathbf{X}}_i$:

$$\widehat{\mathrm{Avar}}(\hat{\boldsymbol{\beta}}_{FE}) = \hat{\sigma}_u^2\left(\sum_{i=1}^{N}\ddot{\mathbf{X}}_i'\ddot{\mathbf{X}}_i\right)^{-1} = \hat{\sigma}_u^2\left(\sum_{i=1}^{N}\sum_{t=1}^{T}\ddot{\mathbf{x}}_{it}'\ddot{\mathbf{x}}_{it}\right)^{-1}. \tag{10.54}$$

The asymptotic standard errors of the FE estimates are obtained as the square roots of the diagonal elements of the matrix (10.54).

Expression (10.54) is very convenient because it looks just like the usual OLS variance matrix estimator that would be reported from the pooled OLS regression (10.48). However, there is one catch, and this comes in obtaining the estimator $\hat{\sigma}_u^2$ of σ_u^2. The errors in the transformed model are $\ddot{u}_{it}$, and these errors are what the OLS residuals from regression (10.48) estimate. Since σ_u^2 is the variance of u_{it}, we must use a little care.

To see how to estimate σ_u^2, we use equation (10.51) summed across t: $\sum_{t=1}^{T}\mathrm{E}(\ddot{u}_{it}^2) = (T-1)\sigma_u^2$, and so $[N(T-1)]^{-1}\sum_{i=1}^{N}\sum_{t=1}^{T}\mathrm{E}(\ddot{u}_{it}^2) = \sigma_u^2$. Now, define the **fixed effects residuals** as

$$\hat{\ddot{u}}_{it} = \ddot{y}_{it} - \ddot{\mathbf{x}}_{it}\hat{\boldsymbol{\beta}}_{FE}, \qquad t = 1, 2, \ldots, T;\ i = 1, 2, \ldots, N, \tag{10.55}$$

which are simply the OLS residuals from the pooled regression (10.48). Then a consistent estimator of σ_u^2 under Assumptions FE.1–FE.3 is

$$\hat{\sigma}_u^2 = \mathrm{SSR}/[N(T-1) - K], \tag{10.56}$$

where $\mathrm{SSR} = \sum_{i=1}^{N}\sum_{t=1}^{T}\hat{\ddot{u}}_{it}^2$. The subtraction of K in the denominator of equation (10.56) does not matter asymptotically, but it is standard to make such a correction. In fact, under Assumptions FE.1–FE.3, it can be shown that $\hat{\sigma}_u^2$ is actually an unbiased estimator of σ_u^2 conditional on $\mathbf{X}$ (and therefore unconditionally as well).

Pay careful attention to the denominator in equation (10.56). This is not the degrees of freedom that would be obtained from regression (10.48). In fact, the usual variance estimate from regression (10.48) would be $\mathrm{SSR}/(NT - K)$, which has a probability limit less than σ_u^2 as N gets large. The difference between $\mathrm{SSR}/(NT - K)$ and equation (10.56) can be substantial when T is small.

The upshot of all this is that the usual standard errors reported from the regression (10.48) will be too small on average because they use the incorrect estimate of σ_u^2. Of course, computing equation (10.56) directly is pretty trivial. But, if a standard regression package is used after time demeaning, it is perhaps easiest to adjust the usual standard errors directly. Since $\hat{\sigma}_u$ appears in the standard errors, each standard error is simply multiplied by the factor $\{(NT - K)/[N(T-1) - K]\}^{1/2}$. As an example, if $N = 500$, $T = 3$, and $K = 10$, the correction factor is about 1.227.

If an econometrics package has an option for explicitly obtaining fixed effects estimates using panel data, σ_u^2 will be properly estimated, and you do not have to worry about adjusting the standard errors. Many software packages also compute an estimate of σ_c^2, which is useful to determine how large the variance of the unobserved component is to the variance of the idiosyncratic component. Given $\hat{\boldsymbol{\beta}}_{FE}$, $\hat{\sigma}_v^2 = (NT - K)^{-1} \sum_{i=1}^{N} \sum_{t=1}^{T} (y_{it} - \mathbf{x}_{it}\hat{\boldsymbol{\beta}}_{FE})^2$ is a consistent estimator of $\sigma_v^2 = \sigma_c^2 + \sigma_u^2$, and so a consistent estimator of σ_c^2 is $\hat{\sigma}_v^2 - \hat{\sigma}_u^2$. (See Problem 10.14 for a discussion of why the estimated variance of the unobserved effect in an FE analysis is generally larger than that for an RE analysis.)

Example 10.5 (FE Estimation of the Effects of Job Training Grants): Using the data in JTRAIN1.RAW, we estimate the effect of job training grants using the FE estimator. The variable *union* has been dropped because it does not vary over time for any of the firms in the sample. The estimated equation with standard errors is

$$\widehat{\log(scrap)} = \underset{(.109)}{-.080}\ d88 - \underset{(.133)}{.247}\ d89 - \underset{(.151)}{.252}\ grant - \underset{(.210)}{.422}\ grant_{-1}.$$

Compared with the RE estimations the grant is estimated to have a larger effect, both contemporaneously and lagged one year. The t statistics are also somewhat more significant with FE.

Under Assumptions FE.1–FE.3, multiple restrictions are most easily tested using an F statistic, provided the degrees of freedom are appropriately computed. Let SSR_{ur} be the unrestricted SSR from regression (10.48), and let SSR_r denote the restricted sum of squared residuals from a similar regression, but with Q restrictions imposed on $\boldsymbol{\beta}$. Then

$$F = \frac{(\mathrm{SSR}_r - \mathrm{SSR}_{ur})}{\mathrm{SSR}_{ur}} \cdot \frac{[N(T-1) - K]}{Q}$$

is approximately F distributed with Q and $N(T-1) - K$ degrees of freedom. (The precise statement is that $Q \cdot F \sim \chi_Q^2$ as $N \to \infty$ under H_0.) When this equation is applied to Example 10.5, the F statistic for joint significance of *grant* and $grant_{-1}$ is $F = 2.23$, with p-value $= .113$.

10.5.3 Dummy Variable Regression

So far we have viewed the c_i as being unobservable random variables, and for most applications this approach gives the appropriate interpretation of $\boldsymbol{\beta}$. Traditional approaches to fixed effects estimation view the c_i as *parameters* to be estimated along with $\boldsymbol{\beta}$. In fact, if Assumption FE.2 is changed to its finite sample version, $\text{rank}(\ddot{\mathbf{X}}'\ddot{\mathbf{X}}) = K$, then the model under Assumptions FE.1–FE.3 satisfies the Gauss-Markov assumptions conditional on $\mathbf{X}$.

If the c_i are parameters to estimate, how would we estimate each c_i along with $\boldsymbol{\beta}$? One possibility is to define N dummy variables, one for each cross section observation: $dn_i = 1$ if $n = i$, $dn_i = 0$ if $n \neq i$. Then, run the pooled OLS regression

$$y_{it} \text{ on } d1_i, d2_i, \ldots, dN_i, \mathbf{x}_{it}, \qquad t = 1, 2, \ldots, T; i = 1, 2, \ldots, N. \tag{10.57}$$

Then, $\hat{c}_1$ is the coefficient on $d1_i$, $\hat{c}_2$ is the coefficient on $d2_i$, and so on.

It is a nice exercise in least squares mechanics—in particular, partitioned regression (see Davidson and MacKinnon, 1993, Sect. 1.4)—to show that the estimator of $\boldsymbol{\beta}$ obtained from regression (10.57) is, in fact, the FE estimator. This is why $\hat{\boldsymbol{\beta}}_{FE}$ is sometimes referred to as the **dummy variable estimator**. Also, the residuals from regression (10.57) are identical to the residuals from regression (10.48). One benefit of regression (10.57) is that it produces the appropriate estimate of σ_u^2 because it uses $NT - N - K = N(T - 1) - K$ as the degrees of freedom. Therefore, if it can be done, regression (10.57) is a convenient way to carry out FE analysis under Assumptions FE.1–FE.3.

There is an important difference between the $\hat{c}_i$ and $\hat{\boldsymbol{\beta}}_{FE}$. We already know that $\hat{\boldsymbol{\beta}}_{FE}$ is consistent with fixed T as $N \to \infty$. This is not the case with the $\hat{c}_i$. Each time a new cross section observation is added, another c_i is added, and information does not accumulate on the c_i as $N \to \infty$. Each $\hat{c}_i$ *is* an unbiased estimator of c_i when the c_i are treated as parameters, at least if we maintain Assumption FE.1 and the finite sample analogue of Assumption FE.2. When we add Assumption FE.3, the Gauss-Markov assumptions hold (conditional on $\mathbf{X}$), and $\hat{c}_1, \hat{c}_2, \ldots, \hat{c}_N$ are best linear unbiased conditional on $\mathbf{X}$. (The $\hat{c}_i$ give practical examples of estimators that are unbiased but not consistent.)

Econometric software that computes fixed effects estimates rarely reports the "estimates" of the c_i (at least in part because there are typically very many). Sometimes it is useful to obtain the $\hat{c}_i$ even when regression (10.57) is infeasible. Using the OLS first-order conditions for the dummy variable regression, it can be shown that

$$\hat{c}_i = \bar{y}_i - \bar{\mathbf{x}}_i \hat{\boldsymbol{\beta}}_{FE}, \qquad i = 1, 2, \ldots, N, \tag{10.58}$$

which makes sense because $\hat{c}_i$ is the intercept for cross section unit i. We can then focus on specific units—which is more fruitful with larger T—or we can compute the sample average, sample median, or sample quantiles of the $\hat{c}_i$ to get some idea of how heterogeneity is distributed in the population. For example, the sample average

$$\hat{\mu}_c \equiv N^{-1} \sum_{i=1}^{N} \hat{c}_i = N^{-1} \sum_{i=1}^{N} (\bar{y}_i - \bar{\mathbf{x}}_i \hat{\boldsymbol{\beta}}_{FE})$$

is easily seen to be a consistent estimator (as $N \to \infty$) of the population average $\mu_c \equiv \mathrm{E}(c_i) = \mathrm{E}(\bar{y}_i) - \mathrm{E}(\bar{\mathbf{x}}_i)\boldsymbol{\beta}$. So, although we cannot estimate each c_i very well with small T, we can often estimate features of the population distribution of c_i quite well. In fact, many econometrics software packages report $\hat{\mu}_c$ as the "intercept" along with $\hat{\boldsymbol{\beta}}_{FE}$ in fixed effects estimation. In other words, the intercept is simply an estimate of the average heterogeneity. (Seeing an "intercept" with fixed effects output can be a bit confusing because we have seen that the within transformation eliminates any time-constant explanatory variables. But having done that, we can then use the fixed effects estimates of $\boldsymbol{\beta}$ to estimate the mean of the heterogeneity distribution, and this is what is reported as the "intercept.")

As with RE estimation, we can consistently estimate the variance σ_c^2 if we add the assumption that $\{u_{it} : t = 1, 2, \ldots\}$ is serially uncorrelated with constant variance, as implied by Assumption FE.3. First, we can consistently estimate the variance of the composite error, $\sigma_v^2 = \sigma_c^2 + \sigma_u^2$. Because $v_{it} = y_{it} - \mathbf{x}_{it}\boldsymbol{\beta}$ and $\mathrm{E}(v_{it}) = \mathrm{E}(c_i) \equiv \mu_c$,

$$\hat{\sigma}_v^2 = (NT - K)^{-1} \sum_{i=1}^{N} \sum_{t=1}^{T} (y_{it} - \mathbf{x}_{it}\hat{\boldsymbol{\beta}}_{FE} - \hat{\mu}_c)^2 \equiv (NT - K)^{-1} \sum_{i=1}^{N} \sum_{t=1}^{T} (\hat{v}_{it} - \hat{\mu}_v)^2$$

is consistent for σ_v^2 as $N \to \infty$ (where the subtraction of K is a standard degrees-of-freedom adjustment). Then, we can estimate σ_c^2 as $\hat{\sigma}_c^2 = \hat{\sigma}_v^2 - \hat{\sigma}_u^2$, where $\hat{\sigma}_u^2$ is given by (10.56). We can use $\hat{\sigma}_c^2$ (assuming it is positive) to assess the variability in heterogeneity about its mean value. (Incidentally, as shown in Problem 10.14, one must be careful in using FE to estimate σ_c^2 before applying RE because, with time-constant variables, the FE estimate of the heterogeneity variance will be too large. Pooled OLS should be used instead, as we discussed in Section 10.4.1.)

When the c_i are treated as different intercepts, we can compute an exact test of their equality under the classical linear model assumptions (which require, in addition to Assumptions FE.1 to FE.3, normality of the u_{it}). The F statistic has an F distribution with numerator and demoninator degrees of freedom $N - 1$ and $N(T - 1) - K$, respectively. Interestingly, Orme and Yamagata (2005) show that the F statistic is still justified without normality when T is fixed and $N \to \infty$, although they assume the idiosycratic errors are homoskedastic and serially uncorrelated.

Generally, we should view the fact that the dummy variable regression (10.57) produces $\hat{\boldsymbol{\beta}}_{FE}$ as the coefficient vector on $\mathbf{x}_{it}$ as a coincidence. While there are other unobserved effects models where "estimating" the unobserved effects along with the vector $\boldsymbol{\beta}$ results in a consistent estimator of $\boldsymbol{\beta}$, there are many cases where this approach leads to trouble. As we will see in Part IV, many nonlinear panel data models with unobserved effects suffer from an incidental parameters problem, where estimating the incidental parameters, c_i, along with $\boldsymbol{\beta}$ produces an inconsistent estimator of $\boldsymbol{\beta}$.

10.5.4 Serial Correlation and the Robust Variance Matrix Estimator

Recall that the FE estimator is consistent and asymptotically normal under Assumptions FE.1 and FE.2. But without Assumption FE.3, expression (10.54) gives an improper variance matrix estimator. While heteroskedasticity in u_{it} is always a potential problem, serial correlation is likely to be more important in certain applications. When applying the FE estimator, it is important to remember that nothing rules out serial correlation in $\{u_{it} : t = 1, \ldots, T\}$. While it is true that the observed serial correlation in the composite errors, $v_{it} = c_i + u_{it}$, is dominated by the presence of c_i, there can also be serial correlation that dies out over time. Sometimes, $\{u_{it}\}$ can have very strong serial dependence, in which case the usual FE standard errors obtained from expression (10.54) can be very misleading. This possibility tends to be a bigger problem with large T. (As we will see, there is no reason to worry about serial correlation in u_{it} when $T = 2$.)

Testing the idiosyncratic errors, $\{u_{it}\}$, for serial correlation is somewhat tricky. A key point is that we cannot estimate the u_{it}; because of the time demeaning used in FE, we can only estimate the time-demeaned errors, $\ddot{u}_{it}$. As shown in equation (10.52), the time-demeaned errors are negatively correlated if the u_{it} are uncorrelated. When $T = 2$, $\ddot{u}_{i1} = -\ddot{u}_{i2}$ for all i, and so there is perfect negative correlation. This finding shows that for $T = 2$ it is pointless to use the $\ddot{u}_{it}$ to test for any kind of serial correlation pattern.

When $T \geq 3$, we can use equation (10.52) to determine if there is serial correlation in $\{u_{it}\}$. Naturally, we use the fixed effects residuals, $\hat{\ddot{u}}_{it}$. One simplification is obtained by applying Problem 7.4: we can ignore the estimation error in $\boldsymbol{\beta}$ in obtaining the asymptotic distribution of any test statistic based on sample covariances and variances. In other words, it is as if we are using the $\ddot{u}_{it}$, rather than the $\hat{\ddot{u}}_{it}$. The test is complicated by the fact that the $\{\ddot{u}_{it}\}$ are serially correlated under the null hypothesis. There are two simple possibilities for dealing with this. First, we can just use any two time periods (say, the last two), to test equation (10.52) using a simple regression. In other words, run the regression

$$\hat{\ddot{u}}_{iT} \text{ on } \hat{\ddot{u}}_{i,T-1}, \qquad i = 1, \ldots, N,$$

and use $\hat{\delta}$, the coefficient on $\hat{\ddot{u}}_{i,T-1}$, along with its standard error, to test H_0: $\delta = -1/(T-1)$, where $\delta = \mathrm{Corr}(\ddot{u}_{i,T-1}, \ddot{u}_{iT})$. Under Assumptions FE.1–FE.3, the usual t statistic has an asymptotic normal distribution. (It is trivial to make this test robust to heteroskedasticity.)

Alternatively, we can use more time periods if we make the t statistic robust to arbitrary serial correlation. In other words, run the pooled OLS regression

$$\hat{\ddot{u}}_{it} \text{ on } \hat{\ddot{u}}_{i,t-1}, \qquad t = 3, \dots, T; i = 1, \dots, N,$$

and use the fully robust standard error for pooled OLS; see equation (7.26). It may seem a little odd that we make a test for serial correlation robust to serial correlation, but this need arises because the null hypothesis is that the time-demeaned errors are serially correlated. This approach clearly does not produce an optimal test against, say, AR(1) correlation in the u_{it}, but it is very simple and may be good enough to indicate a problem.

Without Assumption FE.3, the asymptotic variance of $\sqrt{N}(\hat{\boldsymbol{\beta}}_{FE} - \boldsymbol{\beta})$ has the sandwich form, $[\mathrm{E}(\ddot{\mathbf{X}}_i'\ddot{\mathbf{X}}_i)]^{-1}\mathrm{E}(\ddot{\mathbf{X}}_i'\ddot{\mathbf{u}}_i\ddot{\mathbf{u}}_i'\ddot{\mathbf{X}}_i)[\mathrm{E}(\ddot{\mathbf{X}}_i'\ddot{\mathbf{X}}_i)]^{-1}$. Thefore, if we suspect or find evidence of serial correlation, we should, at a minimum, compute a fully robust variance matrix estimator (and corresponding test statistics) for the FE estimator. But this is just as in Chapter 7 applied to the time-demeaned set of equations. Let $\hat{\ddot{\mathbf{u}}}_i = \ddot{\mathbf{y}}_i - \ddot{\mathbf{X}}_i\hat{\boldsymbol{\beta}}_{FE}$, $i = 1, 2, \dots, N$, denote the $T \times 1$ vectors of FE residuals. Direct application of equation (7.28) gives

$$\mathrm{Av\hat{a}r}(\hat{\boldsymbol{\beta}}_{FE}) = (\ddot{\mathbf{X}}'\ddot{\mathbf{X}})^{-1}\left(\sum_{i=1}^{N}\ddot{\mathbf{X}}_i'\hat{\ddot{\mathbf{u}}}_i\hat{\ddot{\mathbf{u}}}_i'\ddot{\mathbf{X}}_i\right)(\ddot{\mathbf{X}}'\ddot{\mathbf{X}})^{-1}, \tag{10.59}$$

which was suggested by Arellano (1987) and follows from the general results of White (1984, Chap. 6). The robust variance matrix estimator is valid in the presence of any heteroskedasticity or serial correlation in $\{u_{it} : t = 1, \dots, T\}$, provided that T is small relative to N. (Remember, equation (7.28) is generally justified for fixed T, $N \to \infty$ asymptotics.) The robust standard errors are obtained as the square roots of the diagonal elements of the matrix (10.59), and matrix (10.59) can be used as the $\hat{\mathbf{V}}$ matrix in constructing Wald statistics. Unfortunately, the sum of squared residuals form of the F statistic is no longer asymptotically valid when Assumption FE.3 fails.

Example 10.5 (continued): We now report the robust standard errors for the $\log(scrap)$ equation along with the usual FE standard errors:

$$\widehat{\log(scrap)} = \underset{\substack{(.109)\\ [.096]}}{-.080}\ d88 - \underset{\substack{(.133)\\ [.193]}}{.247}\ d89 - \underset{\substack{(.151)\\ [.140]}}{.252}\ grant - \underset{\substack{(.210)\\ [.276]}}{.422}\ grant_{-1}.$$

The robust standard error on *grant* is actually smaller than the usual standard error, while the robust standard error on $grant_{-1}$ is larger than the usual one. As a result, the absolute value of the t statistic on $grant_{-1}$ drops from about 2 to just over 1.5.

Remember, with fixed T as $N \to \infty$, the robust standard errors are just as valid asymptotically as the nonrobust ones when Assumptions FE.1–FE.3 hold. But the usual standard errors and test statistics may be better behaved under Assumptions FE.1–FE.3 if N is not very large relative to T, especially if u_{it} is normally distributed.

10.5.5 Fixed Effects Generalized Least Squares

Recall that Assumption FE.3 can fail for two reasons. The first is that the conditional variance matrix does not equal the unconditional variance matrix: $\mathrm{E}(\mathbf{u}_i\mathbf{u}_i' \mid \mathbf{x}_i, c_i) \neq \mathrm{E}(\mathbf{u}_i\mathbf{u}_i')$. Even if $\mathrm{E}(\mathbf{u}_i\mathbf{u}_i' \mid \mathbf{x}_i, c_i) = \mathrm{E}(\mathbf{u}_i\mathbf{u}_i')$, the unconditional variance matrix may not be scalar: $\mathrm{E}(\mathbf{u}_i\mathbf{u}_i') \neq \sigma_u^2\mathbf{I}_T$, which means either that the variance of u_{it} changes with t or, probably more important, that there is serial correlation in the idiosyncratic errors. The robust variance matrix (10.59) is valid in any case.

Rather than compute a robust variance matrix for the FE estimator, we can instead relax Assumption FE.3 to allow for an unrestricted, albeit constant, conditional covariance matrix. This is a natural route to follow if the robust standard errors of the FE estimator are too large to be useful and if there is evidence of serial dependence or a time-varying variance in the u_{it}.

ASSUMPTION FEGLS.3: $\mathrm{E}(\mathbf{u}_i\mathbf{u}_i' \mid \mathbf{x}_i, c_i) = \mathbf{\Lambda}$, a $T \times T$ positive definite matrix.

Under Assumption FEGLS.3, $\mathrm{E}(\ddot{\mathbf{u}}_i\ddot{\mathbf{u}}_i' \mid \ddot{\mathbf{x}}_i) = \mathrm{E}(\ddot{\mathbf{u}}_i\ddot{\mathbf{u}}_i')$. Further, using $\ddot{\mathbf{u}}_i = \mathbf{Q}_T\mathbf{u}_i$,

$$\mathrm{E}(\ddot{\mathbf{u}}_i\ddot{\mathbf{u}}_i') = \mathbf{Q}_T\mathrm{E}(\mathbf{u}_i\mathbf{u}_i')\mathbf{Q}_T = \mathbf{Q}_T\mathbf{\Lambda}\mathbf{Q}_T. \tag{10.60}$$

which has rank $T - 1$. The deficient rank in expression (10.60) causes problems for the usual approach to GLS, because the variance matrix cannot be inverted. One way to proceed is to use a *generalized inverse*. A much easier approach—and one that turns out to be algebraically identical—is to drop one of the time periods from the analysis. It can be shown (see Im, Ahn, Schmidt, and Wooldridge, 1999) that it does not matter which of these time periods is dropped: the resulting GLS estimator is the same.

For concreteness, suppose we drop time period T, leaving the equations

$$\begin{aligned} \ddot{y}_{i1} &= \ddot{\mathbf{x}}_{i1}\boldsymbol{\beta} + \ddot{u}_{i1} \\ &\vdots \\ \ddot{y}_{i,T-1} &= \ddot{\mathbf{x}}_{i,T-1}\boldsymbol{\beta} + \ddot{u}_{i,T-1}. \end{aligned} \tag{10.61}$$

So that we do not have to introduce new notation, we write the system (10.61) as equation (10.49), with the understanding that now $\ddot{\mathbf{y}}_i$ is $(T-1) \times 1$, $\ddot{\mathbf{X}}_i$ is $(T-1) \times K$, and $\ddot{\mathbf{u}}_i$ is $(T-1) \times 1$. Define the $(T-1) \times (T-1)$ positive definite matrix $\boldsymbol{\Omega} \equiv \mathrm{E}(\ddot{\mathbf{u}}_i \ddot{\mathbf{u}}_i')$. We do not need to make the dependence of $\boldsymbol{\Omega}$ on $\boldsymbol{\Lambda}$ and $\mathbf{Q}_T$ explicit; the key point is that, if no restrictions are made on $\boldsymbol{\Lambda}$, then $\boldsymbol{\Omega}$ is also unrestricted.

To estimate $\boldsymbol{\Omega}$, we estimate $\boldsymbol{\beta}$ by fixed effects in the first stage. After dropping the last time period for each i, define the $(T-1) \times 1$ residuals $\breve{\ddot{\mathbf{u}}}_i = \ddot{\mathbf{y}}_i - \ddot{\mathbf{X}}_i \hat{\boldsymbol{\beta}}_{FE}$, $i = 1, 2, \ldots, N$. A consistent estimator of $\boldsymbol{\Omega}$ is

$$\hat{\boldsymbol{\Omega}} = N^{-1} \sum_{i=1}^{N} \breve{\ddot{\mathbf{u}}}_i \breve{\ddot{\mathbf{u}}}_i'. \tag{10.62}$$

The **fixed effects GLS (FEGLS)** estimator is defined by

$$\hat{\boldsymbol{\beta}}_{FEGLS} = \left(\sum_{i=1}^{N} \ddot{\mathbf{X}}_i' \hat{\boldsymbol{\Omega}}^{-1} \ddot{\mathbf{X}}_i \right)^{-1} \left(\sum_{i=1}^{N} \ddot{\mathbf{X}}_i' \hat{\boldsymbol{\Omega}}^{-1} \ddot{\mathbf{y}}_i \right),$$

where $\ddot{\mathbf{X}}_i$ and $\ddot{\mathbf{y}}_i$ are defined with the last time period dropped. For consistency of FEGLS, we replace Assumption FE.2 with a new rank condition:

ASSUMPTION FEGLS.2: rank $\mathrm{E}(\ddot{\mathbf{X}}_i' \boldsymbol{\Omega}^{-1} \ddot{\mathbf{X}}_i) = K$.

Under Assumptions FE.1 and FEGLS.2, the FEGLS estimator is consistent. When we add Assumption FEGLS.3, the asymptotic variance is easy to estimate:

$$\widehat{\mathrm{Avar}(\hat{\boldsymbol{\beta}}_{FEGLS})} = \left(\sum_{i=1}^{N} \ddot{\mathbf{X}}_i' \hat{\boldsymbol{\Omega}}^{-1} \ddot{\mathbf{X}}_i \right)^{-1}.$$

The sum of squared residual statistics from FGLS can be used to test multiple restrictions. Note that $G = T - 1$ in the F statistic in equation (7.57).

The FEGLS estimator was proposed by Kiefer (1980) when the c_i are treated as parameters. As we just showed, the procedure consistently estimates $\boldsymbol{\beta}$ when we view c_i as random and allow it to be arbitrarily correlated with $\mathbf{x}_{it}$.

The FEGLS estimator is asymptotically no less efficient than the FE estimator under Assumption FEGLS.3, even when $\boldsymbol{\Lambda} = \sigma_u^2 \mathbf{I}_T$. Generally, if $\boldsymbol{\Lambda} \neq \sigma_u^2 \mathbf{I}_T$, FEGLS is more efficient than FE, but this conclusion relies on the large-N, fixed-T asymptotics. Unfortunately, because FEGLS still uses the fixed effects transformation to remove c_i, it can have large asymptotic standard errors if the matrices $\ddot{\mathbf{X}}_i$ have columns close to zero.

Rather than allowing $\boldsymbol{\Omega}$ to be an unrestricted matrix, we can impose restrictions on $\boldsymbol{\Lambda}$ that imply $\boldsymbol{\Omega}$ has a restricted form. For example, Bhargava, Franzini, and

Narendranathan (1982) (BFN) assume that $\{u_{it}\}$ follows a stable, homoskedastic AR(1) model. This assumption implies that $\mathbf{\Omega}$ depends on only three parameters, σ_c^2, σ_u^2, and the AR coefficient, ρ, no matter how large T is. BFN obtain a transformation that eliminates the unobserved effect, c_i, and removes the serial correlation in u_{it}. They also propose estimators of ρ, so that feasible GLS is possible.

Modeling $\{u_{it}\}$ as a specific time series process is attractive when N is not very large relative to T, as estimating an unrestricted covariance matrix for $\ddot{\mathbf{u}}_i$ (the $(T-1) \times 1$ vector of time-demeaned errors) without large N can lead to poor finite-sample performance of the FGLS estimator. However, the only general statements we can make concern fixed-T, $N \to \infty$ asymptotics. In this scenario, the FGLS estimator that uses unrestricted $\mathbf{\Omega}$ is no less asymptotically efficient than an FGLS estimator that puts restrictions on $\mathbf{\Omega}$. And, if the restrictions on $\mathbf{\Omega}$ are incorrect, the estimator that imposes the restrictions is less asymptotically efficient. Therefore, on purely theoretical grounds, we prefer an estimator of the type in equation (10.62).

As with any FGLS estimator, it is always a good idea to compute a fully robust variance matrix estimator for the FEGLS estimator. The robust variance matrix estimator is still given by equation (7.52), but now we insert the time-demeaned regressors and FEGLS residuals in place of $\mathbf{X}_i$ and $\hat{\mathbf{u}}_i$, respectively. Therefore, the fully robust variance matrix estimator for the FEGLS estimator is

$$\widehat{\text{Avar}}(\hat{\boldsymbol{\beta}}_{FEGLS}) = \left(\sum_{i=1}^{N} \ddot{\mathbf{X}}_i'\hat{\mathbf{\Omega}}^{-1}\ddot{\mathbf{X}}_i\right)^{-1} \left(\sum_{i=1}^{N} \ddot{\mathbf{X}}_i'\hat{\mathbf{\Omega}}^{-1}\hat{\ddot{\mathbf{u}}}_i\hat{\ddot{\mathbf{u}}}_i'\hat{\mathbf{\Omega}}^{-1}\ddot{\mathbf{X}}_i'\right) \left(\sum_{i=1}^{N} \ddot{\mathbf{X}}_i'\hat{\mathbf{\Omega}}^{-1}\ddot{\mathbf{X}}_i\right)^{-1},$$

where $\hat{\ddot{\mathbf{u}}}_i = \ddot{\mathbf{y}}_i - \ddot{\mathbf{X}}_i\hat{\boldsymbol{\beta}}_{FEGLS}$ are the $(T-1) \times 1$ vectors of FEGLS residuals. If $\hat{\mathbf{\Omega}}$ is unrestricted the robust variance matrix estimator is robust to system heteroskedasticity, which is generally present if $\text{E}(\ddot{\mathbf{u}}_i\ddot{\mathbf{u}}_i' \mid \ddot{\mathbf{X}}_i) \neq \text{E}(\ddot{\mathbf{u}}_i\ddot{\mathbf{u}}_i')$. Remember, even if we allow the unconditional variance matrix of $\ddot{\mathbf{u}}_i$ to be unrestricted, we can never guarantee that the conditional variance matrix does not depend on the regressors. When $\hat{\mathbf{\Omega}}$ is restricted, such as in the AR(1) model for $\{u_{it}\}$, the robust estimator is also robust to the retrictions imposed being incorrect. Using an AR(1) model for the idiosyncratic errors might be substantially more efficient than just using the usual FE estimator, and we can guard against incorrect asymptotic inference by using a fully robust variance matrix estimator. As we discussed earlier, if T is somewhat large, for better small-sample properties we may wish to impose restrictions on $\mathbf{\Omega}$ rather than use an unrestricted estimator.

Baltagi and Li (1991) consider FEGLS estimation when $\{u_{it}\}$ follows an AR(1) process. But their estimator of ρ is based on the FE residual—say, from the regression $\hat{\ddot{u}}_{it}$ on $\hat{\ddot{u}}_{i,t-1}$, $t = 2, \ldots, T$—and this estimator is inconsistent for fixed T with

$N \to \infty$. In fact, if $\{u_{it}\}$ is serially uncorrelated, we know from equation (10.52) that $\text{plim}(\hat{\rho}) = -1/(T-1)$. With large T the inconsistency may be small, but what are the consequences generally of using an inconsistent estimator of ρ? We know by now that using an inconsistent estimator of a variance matrix does not lead to inconsistency of a feasible GLS estimator, and this is no exception. But, of course, inference should be made fully robust, because if $\text{plim}(\hat{\rho}) \neq \rho$, GLS does not fully eliminate the serial correlation in $\{u_{it}\}$. Even if $\text{plim}(\hat{\rho})$ is "close" to ρ, we may want to guard against more general forms of serial correlation or violation of system homoskedasticity.

10.5.6 Using Fixed Effects Estimation for Policy Analysis

There are other ways to interpret the FE transformation to illustrate why fixed effects is useful for policy analysis and program evaluation. Consider the model

$$y_{it} = \mathbf{x}_{it}\boldsymbol{\beta} + v_{it} = \mathbf{z}_{it}\gamma + \delta w_{it} + v_{it},$$

where v_{it} may or may not contain an unobserved effect. Let w_{it} be the policy variable of interest; it could be continuous or discrete. The vector $\mathbf{z}_{it}$ contains other controls that might be correlated with w_{it}, including time-period dummy variables.

As an exercise, you can show that sufficient for consistency of fixed effects, along with the rank condition FE.2, is

$$\mathrm{E}[\mathbf{x}_{it}'(v_{it} - \bar{v}_i)] = \mathbf{0}, \qquad t = 1, 2, \ldots, T.$$

This assumption shows that each element of $\mathbf{x}_{it}$, and in particular the policy variable w_{it}, can be correlated with $\bar{v}_i$. What FE requires for consistency is that w_{it} be uncorrelated with deviations of v_{it} from the average over the time period. So a policy variable, such as program participation, can be systematically related to the *persistent* component in the error v_{it} as measured by $\bar{v}_i$. It is for this reason that FE is often superior to pooled OLS or random effects for applications where participation in a program is determined by preprogram attributes that also affect y_{it}.

10.6 First Differencing Methods

10.6.1 Inference

In Section 10.1 we used differencing to eliminate the unobserved effect c_i with $T = 2$. We now study the differencing transformation in the general case of model (10.41). For completeness, we state the first assumption as follows.

ASSUMPTION FD.1: Same as Assumption FE.1.

We emphasize that the model and the interpretation of $\boldsymbol{\beta}$ are *exactly* as in Section 10.5. What differs is our method for estimating $\boldsymbol{\beta}$.

Lagging the model (10.41) one period and subtracting gives

$$\Delta y_{it} = \Delta \mathbf{x}_{it}\boldsymbol{\beta} + \Delta u_{it}, \qquad t = 2, 3, \ldots, T, \tag{10.63}$$

where $\Delta y_{it} = y_{it} - y_{i,t-1}$, $\Delta \mathbf{x}_{it} = \mathbf{x}_{it} - \mathbf{x}_{i,t-1}$, and $\Delta u_{it} = u_{it} - u_{i,t-1}$. As with the FE transformation, this **first-differencing transformation** eliminates the unobserved effect c_i. In differencing we lose the first time period for each cross section: we now have $T - 1$ time periods for each i, rather than T. If we start with $T = 2$, then, after differencing, we arrive at one time period for each cross section: $\Delta y_{i2} = \Delta \mathbf{x}_{i2}\boldsymbol{\beta} + \Delta u_{i2}$.

Equation (10.63) makes it clear that the elements of $\mathbf{x}_{it}$ must be time varying (for at least some cross section units); otherwise $\Delta \mathbf{x}_{it}$ has elements that are identically zero for all i and t. Also, while the intercept in the original equation gets differenced away, equation (10.63) contains changes in time dummies if $\mathbf{x}_{it}$ contains time dummies. In the $T = 2$ case, the coefficient on the second-period time dummy becomes the intercept in the differenced equation. If we difference the general equation (10.43) we get

$$\begin{aligned}\Delta y_{it} &= \theta_2(\Delta d2_t) + \cdots + \theta_T(\Delta dT_t) + (\Delta d2_t)\mathbf{z}_i\boldsymbol{\gamma}_2 \\ &\quad + \cdots + (\Delta dT_t)\mathbf{z}_i\boldsymbol{\gamma}_T + \Delta \mathbf{w}_{it}\boldsymbol{\delta} + \Delta u_{it}.\end{aligned} \tag{10.64}$$

The parameters θ_1 and $\boldsymbol{\gamma}_1$ are not identified because they disappear from the transformed equation, just as with fixed effects.

The **first-difference (FD) estimator**, $\hat{\boldsymbol{\beta}}_{FD}$, is the pooled OLS estimator from the regression

$$\Delta y_{it} \text{ on } \Delta \mathbf{x}_{it}, \qquad t = 2, \ldots, T; i = 1, 2, \ldots, N. \tag{10.65}$$

Under Assumption FD.1, pooled OLS estimation of the first-differenced equations will be consistent because

$$\mathrm{E}(\Delta \mathbf{x}_{it}' \Delta u_{it}) = 0, \qquad t = 2, 3, \ldots, T. \tag{10.66}$$

Therefore, Assumption POLS.1 from Section 7.8 holds. In fact, strict exogeneity holds in the FD equation:

$$\mathrm{E}(\Delta u_{it} \mid \Delta \mathbf{x}_{i2}, \Delta \mathbf{x}_{i3}, \ldots, \Delta \mathbf{x}_{iT}) = 0, \qquad t = 2, 3, \ldots, T,$$

which means the FD estimator is actually unbiased conditional on $\mathbf{X}$.

To arrive at assumption (10.66) we clearly can get by with an assumption weaker than Assumption FD.1. The key point is that assumption (10.66) fails if u_{it} is correlated with $\mathbf{x}_{i,t-1}$, $\mathbf{x}_{it}$, or $\mathbf{x}_{i,t+1}$, and so we just assume that $\mathbf{x}_{is}$ is uncorrelated with u_{it} for all t and s.

For completeness, we state the rank condition for the FD estimator:

ASSUMPTION FD.2: $\operatorname{rank}\left(\sum_{t=2}^{T} \mathrm{E}(\Delta\mathbf{x}_{it}'\Delta\mathbf{x}_{it})\right) = K$.

Assumption FD.2 clearly rules out explanatory variables in $\mathbf{x}_{it}$ that are fixed across time for all i. It also excludes perfect collinearity among the time-varying variables after differencing. There are subtle ways in which perfect collinearity can arise in $\Delta\mathbf{x}_{it}$. For example, suppose that in a panel of individuals working in every year, we collect information on labor earnings, workforce experience ($exper_{it}$), and other variables. Then, because experience increases by one each year for every person in the sample, $\Delta exper_{it} = 1$ for all i and t. If $\mathbf{x}_{it}$ also contains a full set of year dummies, then $\Delta exper_{it}$ is perfectly collinear with the changes in the year dummies. This is easiest to see in the $T = 2$ case, where $\Delta d2_t = 1$ for $t = 2$, and so $\Delta exper_{i2} = \Delta d2_2$ (remember, we only use the second time period in estimation). In the general case, it can be seen that for all $t = 2, \ldots, T$, $\Delta d2_t + 2\Delta d3_t + \cdots + (T-1)\Delta dT_t = 1$, and so $\Delta exper_{it}$ is perfectly collinear with $\Delta d2_t, \Delta d3_t, \ldots, \Delta dT_t$.

Assuming the data have been ordered as we discussed earlier, first differencing is easy to implement provided we keep track of which transformed observations are valid and which are not. Differences for observation numbers 1, $T+1$, $2T+1$, $3T+1, \ldots$, and $(N-1)T+1$ should be set to missing. These observations correspond to the first time period for every cross section unit in the original data set; by definition, there is no first difference for the $t = 1$ observations. A little care is needed so that differences between the first time period for unit $i+1$ and the last time period for unit i are not treated as valid observations. Making sure these are set to missing is easy when a year variable or time period dummies have been included in the data set.

One reason to prefer the FD estimator to the FE estimator is that FD is easier to implement without special software. Are there statistical reasons to prefer FD to FE? Recall that, under Assumptions FE.1–FE.3, the FE estimator is asymptotically efficient in the class of estimators using the strict exogeneity assumption FE.1. Therefore, the FD estimator is less efficient than FE under Assumptions FE.1–FE.3. Assumption FE.3 is key to the efficiency of FE. It assumes homoskedasticity and no serial correlation in u_{it}. Assuming that the $\{u_{it}\colon t = 1, 2, \ldots T\}$ are serially uncorrelated may be too strong. An alternative assumption is that the first differences of the idiosyncratic errors, $\{e_{it} \equiv \Delta u_{it}, t = 2, \ldots, T\}$, are serially uncorrelated (and have constant variance).

ASSUMPTION FD.3: $E(\mathbf{e}_i \mathbf{e}_i' \mid \mathbf{x}_{i1}, \ldots, \mathbf{x}_{iT}, c_i) = \sigma_e^2 \mathbf{I}_{T-1}$, where $\mathbf{e}_i$ is the $(T-1) \times 1$ vector containing e_{it}, $t = 2, \ldots, T$.

Under Assumption FD.3 we can write $u_{it} = u_{i,t-1} + e_{it}$, so that no serial correlation in e_{it} implies that u_{it} is a random walk. A random walk has substantial serial dependence, and so Assumption FD.3 represents an opposite extreme from Assumption FE.3.

Under Assumptions FD.1–FD.3, it can be shown that the FD estimator is most efficient in the class of estimators using the strict exogeneity assumption FE.1. Further, from the pooled OLS analysis in Section 7.8,

$$\widehat{\text{Avar}}(\hat{\boldsymbol{\beta}}_{FD}) = \hat{\sigma}_e^2 (\Delta\mathbf{X}'\Delta\mathbf{X})^{-1}, \tag{10.67}$$

where $\hat{\sigma}_e^2$ is a consistent estimator of σ_e^2. The simplest estimator is obtained by computing the OLS residuals

$$\hat{e}_{it} = \Delta y_{it} - \Delta\mathbf{x}_{it}\hat{\boldsymbol{\beta}}_{FD} \tag{10.68}$$

from the pooled regression (10.65). A consistent estimator of σ_e^2 is

$$\hat{\sigma}_e^2 = [N(T-1) - K]^{-1} \sum_{i=1}^{N} \sum_{t=2}^{T} \hat{e}_{it}^2, \tag{10.69}$$

which is the usual error variance estimator from regression (10.65). These equations show that, under Assumptions FD.1–FD.3, the usual OLS standard errors from the FD regression (10.65) are asymptotically valid.

Unlike in the FE regression (10.48), the denominator in equation (10.69) is correctly obtained from regression (10.65). Dropping the first time period appropriately captures the lost degrees of freedom (N of them).

Under Assumption FD.3, all statistics reported from the pooled regression on the first-differenced data are asymptotically valid, including F statistics based on sums of squared residuals.

10.6.2 Robust Variance Matrix

If Assumption FD.3 is violated, then, as usual, we can compute a robust variance matrix. The estimator in equation (7.26) applied in this context is

$$\widehat{\text{Avar}}(\hat{\boldsymbol{\beta}}_{FD}) = (\Delta\mathbf{X}'\Delta\mathbf{X})^{-1} \left(\sum_{i=1}^{N} \Delta\mathbf{X}_i' \hat{\mathbf{e}}_i \hat{\mathbf{e}}_i' \Delta\mathbf{X}_i \right) (\Delta\mathbf{X}'\Delta\mathbf{X})^{-1}, \tag{10.70}$$

where $\Delta\mathbf{X}$ denotes the $N(T-1) \times K$ matrix of stacked first differences of $\mathbf{x}_{it}$.

Example 10.6 (FD Estimation of the Effects of Job Training Grants): We now estimate the effect of job training grants on log(*scrap*) using first differencing. Specifically, we use pooled OLS on

$$\Delta\log(scrap_{it}) = \delta_1 + \delta_2 d89_t + \beta_1 \Delta grant_{it} + \beta_2 \Delta grant_{i,t-1} + \Delta u_{it}.$$

Rather than difference the year dummies and omit the intercept, we simply include an intercept and a dummy variable for 1989 to capture the aggregate time effects. If we were specifically interested in the year effects from the structural model (in levels), then we should difference those as well.

The estimated equation is

$$\begin{aligned}\Delta\widehat{\log(scrap)} = \; & -.091 \;-\; .096\; d89 \;-\; .223\; \Delta grant \;-\; .351\; \Delta grant_{-1} \\ & \;(.091) \quad (.125) \qquad\quad (.131) \qquad\qquad\quad (.235) \\ & \;[.088] \quad [.111] \qquad\quad [.128] \qquad\qquad\quad [.265]\end{aligned}$$

$$R^2 = .037,$$

where the usual standard errors are in parentheses and the robust standard errors are in brackets. We report R^2 here because it has a useful interpretation: it measures the amount of variation in the growth in the scrap rate that is explained by $\Delta grant$ and $\Delta grant_{-1}$ (and *d89*). The estimates on *grant* and $grant_{-1}$ are fairly similar to the FE estimates, although *grant* is now statistically more significant than $grant_{-1}$. The usual F test for joint significance of $\Delta grant$ and $\Delta grant_{-1}$ is 1.53, with p-value = .222.

In the previous example we used a device that is common when applying FD estimation. Namely, rather than drop an overall intercept and include the differenced time dummies, we estimated an intercept and then included time dummies for $T-2$ of the remaining periods—in Example 10.6, just the third period. Generally, rather than using the $T-1$ regressors $(\Delta d2_t, \Delta d3_t, \ldots, \Delta dT_t)$, it is often more convenient to use, say, $(1, d3_t, \ldots, dT_t)$. Because these sets of regressors involving the time dummies are nonsingular linear transformations of each other, the estimated coefficients on the other variables do not change, nor do their standard errors or any test statistics. In most regression packages, including an overall intercept makes it easier to obtain the appropriate R-squared for the FD equation. Of course, if one is interested in the coefficients on the original time dummies, then it is easiest to simply include all dummies in FD form and omit an overall intercept.

10.6.3 Testing for Serial Correlation

Under Assumption FD.3, the errors $e_{it} \equiv \Delta u_{it}$ should be serially uncorrelated. We can easily test this assumption given the pooled OLS residuals from regression

(10.65). Since the strict exogeneity assumption holds, we can apply the simple form of the test in Section 7.8. The regression is based on $T-2$ time periods:

$$\hat{e}_{it} = \hat{\rho}_1 \hat{e}_{i,t-1} + error_{it}, \qquad t = 3, 4, \ldots, T; i = 1, 2, \ldots, N. \tag{10.71}$$

The test statistic is the usual t statistic on $\hat{\rho}_1$. With $T = 2$ this test is not available, nor is it necessary. With $T = 3$, regression (10.71) is just a cross section regression because we lose the $t = 1$ and $t = 2$ time periods.

If the idiosyncratic errors $\{u_{it} : t = 1, 2, \ldots, T\}$ are uncorrelated to begin with, $\{e_{it} : t = 2, 3, \ldots, T\}$ will be autocorrelated. In fact, under Assumption FE.3 it is easily shown that $\text{Corr}(e_{it}, e_{i,t-1}) = -.5$. In any case, a finding of significant serial correlation in the e_{it} warrants computing the robust variance matrix for the FD estimator.

Example 10.6 (continued): We test for AR(1) serial correlation in the first-differenced equation by regressing $\hat{e}_{it}$ on $\hat{e}_{i,t-1}$ using the year 1989. We get $\hat{\rho}_1 = .237$ with t statistic $= 1.76$. There is marginal evidence of positive serial correlation in the first differences Δu_{it}. Further, $\hat{\rho}_1 = .237$ is very different from $\rho_1 = -.5$, which is implied by the standard random and fixed effects assumption that the u_{it} are serially uncorrelated.

An alternative to computing robust standard errors and test statistics is to use an FDGLS analysis under the assumption that $\text{E}(\mathbf{e}_i \mathbf{e}_i' \mid \mathbf{x}_i)$ is a constant $(T-1) \times (T-1)$ matrix. We omit the details, as they are similar to the FEGLS case in Section 10.5.5. As with FEGLS, we could impose structure on $\text{E}(\mathbf{u}_i \mathbf{u}_i')$, such as a stable, homoskedastic AR(1) model, and then derive $\text{E}(\mathbf{e}_i \mathbf{e}_i')$ in terms of a small set of parameters.

10.6.4 Policy Analysis Using First Differencing

First differencing a structural equation with an unobserved effect is a simple yet powerful method of program evaluation. Many questions can be addressed by having a two-year panel data set with control and treatment groups available at two points in time.

In applying first differencing, we should difference all variables appearing in the structural equation to obtain the estimating equation, including any binary indicators indicating participation in the program. The estimates should be interpreted in the original equation because it allows us to think of comparing different units in the cross section at any point in time, where one unit receives the treatment and the other does not.

In one special case it does not matter whether the policy variable is differenced. Assume that $T = 2$, and let $prog_{it}$ denote a binary indicator set to one if person i was in the program at time t. For many programs, $prog_{i1} = 0$ for all i: no one participated in the program in the initial time period. In the second time period, $prog_{i2}$ is unity for those who participate in the program and zero for those who do not. In this one case, $\Delta prog_i = prog_{i2}$, and the FD equation can be written as

$$\Delta y_{i2} = \theta_2 + \Delta \mathbf{z}_{i2}\gamma + \delta_1 prog_{i2} + \Delta u_{i2}. \tag{10.72}$$

The effect of the policy can be obtained by regressing the change in y on the change in $\mathbf{z}$ and the policy indicator. When $\Delta \mathbf{z}_{i2}$ is omitted, the estimate of δ_1 from equation (10.72) is the **difference-in-differences (DD)** estimator (see Problem 10.4): $\hat{\delta}_1 = \overline{\Delta y}_{treat} - \overline{\Delta y}_{control}$. This is similar to the DD estimator from Section 6.3—see equation (6.53)—but there is an important difference: with panel data, the differences over time are for the *same* cross section units.

If some people participated in the program in the first time period, or if more than two periods are involved, equation (10.72) can give misleading answers. In general, the equation that should be estimated is

$$\Delta y_{it} = \xi_t + \Delta \mathbf{z}_{it}\gamma + \delta_1 \Delta prog_{it} + \Delta u_{it}, \tag{10.73}$$

where the program participation indicator is differenced along with everything else, and the ξ_t are new period intercepts. Example 10.6 is one such case. Extensions of the model, where $prog_{it}$ appears in other forms, are discussed in Chapter 11.

10.7 Comparison of Estimators

10.7.1 Fixed Effects versus First Differencing

When we have only two time periods, FE estimation and FD produce *identical* estimates and inference, as you are asked to show in Problem 10.3. First differencing is easier to implement, and all procedures that can be applied to a single cross section—such as heteroskedasticity-robust inference—can be applied directly.

When $T > 2$ and we are confident the strict exogeneity assumption holds, the choice between FD and FE hinges on the assumptions about the idiosyncratic errors, u_{it}. In particular, the FE estimator is more efficient under Assumption FE.3—the u_{it} are serially uncorrelated—while the FD estimator is more efficient when u_{it} follows a random walk. In many cases, the truth is likely to lie somewhere in between.

If FE and FD estimates differ in ways that cannot be attributed to sampling error, we should worry about violations of the strict exogeneity assumption. If u_{it} is correlated with $\mathbf{x}_{is}$ for any t and s, FE and FD generally have different probability limits. Any of the standard endogeneity problems, including measurement error, time-varying omitted variables, and simultaneity, generally cause correlation between $\mathbf{x}_{it}$ and u_{it}—that is, contemporaneous correlation—which then causes both FD and FE to be inconsistent and to have different probability limits. (We explicitly consider these problems in Chapter 11.) In addition, correlation between u_{it} and $\mathbf{x}_{is}$ for $s \neq t$ causes FD and FE to be inconsistent. When lagged $\mathbf{x}_{it}$ is correlated with u_{it}, we can solve lack of strict exogeneity by including lags and interpreting the equation as a distributed lag model. More problematical is when u_{it} is correlated with *future* $\mathbf{x}_{it}$: only rarely does putting future values of explanatory variables in an equation lead to an interesting economic model. In Chapter 11 we show how to estimate the parameters consistently when there is feedback from u_{it} to $\mathbf{x}_{is}$, $s > t$.

If we maintain contemporaneous exogeneity, that is

$$\mathrm{E}(\mathbf{x}_{it}' u_{it}) = \mathbf{0}, \tag{10.74}$$

then we can show that the FE estimator generally has an inconsistency that shrinks to zero at the rate $1/T$, while the inconsistency of the FD estimator is essentially independent of T. More precisely, we can find the probability limits of the FE and FD estimators (with fixed T and $N \to \infty$) and then study the plims as a function of T. The inconsistency in these estimators is sometimes, rather loosely, called the "asymptotic bias."

Generally, under Assumption FE.1, we can write

$$\operatorname*{plim}_{N\to\infty}(\hat{\boldsymbol{\beta}}_{FE}) = \boldsymbol{\beta} + \left[T^{-1}\sum_{t=1}^{T}\mathrm{E}(\ddot{\mathbf{x}}_{it}'\ddot{\mathbf{x}}_{it})\right]^{-1}\left[T^{-1}\sum_{t=1}^{T}\mathrm{E}(\ddot{\mathbf{x}}_{it}' u_{it})\right]^{-1}, \tag{10.75}$$

where $\ddot{\mathbf{x}}_{it} = \mathbf{x}_{it} - \bar{\mathbf{x}}_i$, as always, and we emphasize that we are taking the plim for fixed T and $N \to \infty$. Under (10.74), $\mathrm{E}(\ddot{\mathbf{x}}_{it}' u_{it}) = \mathrm{E}[(\mathbf{x}_{it} - \bar{\mathbf{x}}_i)' u_{it})] = -\mathrm{E}(\bar{\mathbf{x}}_i' u_{it})$, and so $T^{-1}\sum_{t=1}^{T}\mathrm{E}(\ddot{\mathbf{x}}_{it}' u_{it}) = -T^{-1}\sum_{t=1}^{T}\mathrm{E}(\bar{\mathbf{x}}_i' u_{it}) = -\mathrm{E}(\bar{\mathbf{x}}_i' \bar{u}_i)$. Now, we can easily bound both average moments in (10.75) if we assume that the process $\{(\mathbf{x}_{it}, u_{it}) : t = 1, 2, \ldots\}$, considered as a time series, is stable and weakly dependent. Actually, as will become clear, what we really should assume is that the time-demeaned sequence, $\{\ddot{\mathbf{x}}_{it}\}$, is weakly dependent. This allows for, say, covariate processes such as $\mathbf{x}_{it} = \mathbf{h}_i + \mathbf{r}_{it}$, where $\mathbf{h}_i$ is time-constant heterogeneity and $\{\mathbf{r}_{it}\}$ is weakly dependent, because then $\ddot{\mathbf{x}}_{it} = \ddot{\mathbf{r}}_{it}$; the persistent component, $\mathbf{h}_i$, has been removed. For notational convenience, we just assume that $\{\mathbf{x}_{it}\}$ is weakly dependent. (See Hamilton (1994) and Wooldridge (1994a) for general discussions of weak dependence for time series processes. Weakly dependent processes are commonly, if somewhat misleadingly, referred to as "stationary" processes.)

Under weak dependence of the covariate process, $T^{-1}\sum_{t=1}^{T}\mathrm{E}(\ddot{\mathbf{x}}_{it}'\ddot{\mathbf{x}}_{it})$ is bounded as a function of T, and so is its inverse if we strengthen Assumption FE.2 to hold uniformly in T—a mild restriction that holds under the rank condition if we impose stationarity on $\{\mathbf{x}_{it} : t = 1, 2, \ldots\}$. Further, $\text{Var}(\bar{\mathbf{x}}_i)$ and $\text{Var}(\bar{u}_i)$ are $O(T^{-1})$ under weak dependence. By the Cauchy-Schwartz inequality (for example, Davidson, 1994, Chap. 9) we have, for each $j = 1, \ldots, K$, $|\text{E}(\bar{x}_{ij}\bar{u}_i)| \le [\text{Var}(\bar{x}_{ij})\text{Var}(\bar{u}_i)]^{1/2} = O(T^{-1})$. It follows that

$$\underset{N\to\infty}{\text{plim}}(\hat{\boldsymbol{\beta}}_{FE}) = \boldsymbol{\beta} + O(1) \cdot O(T^{-1}) = \boldsymbol{\beta} + O(T^{-1}) \equiv \boldsymbol{\beta} + \mathbf{r}_{FE}(T), \tag{10.76}$$

where $\mathbf{r}_{FE}(T) = O(T^{-1})$ is the inconsistency as a function of T. It follows that the inconsistency in the FE estimator can be small if we have a reasonably large T, although the exact size of $\mathbf{r}_{FE}(T)$ depends on features of the stochastic process $\{(\mathbf{x}_{it}, u_{it}) : t = 1, 2, \ldots\}$.

Hsiao (2003, Sect. 4.2) derives the exact form of $r_{FE}(T)$ (a scalar) for the stable autoregressive model, that is, with $x_{it} = y_{i,t-1}$ and $|\beta| < 1$. The term $r_{FE}(T)$ is negative and, for fixed T, increases in absolute value as β approaches unity. Unfortunately, finding $\mathbf{r}_{FE}(T)$ in general means modeling $\{(\mathbf{x}_{it}, u_{it}) : t = 1, 2, \ldots\}$, and so we cannot know how close $\mathbf{r}_{FE}(T)$ is to zero for a given T without making specific assumptions. (In the AR(1) model, we effectively modeled the stochastic process of the regressor and error because the former is the lagged dependent variable and the latter is assumed to be serially uncorrelated.)

For the FD estimator, the general probability limit is

$$\underset{N\to\infty}{\text{plim}}(\hat{\boldsymbol{\beta}}_{FD}) = \boldsymbol{\beta} + \left[(T-1)^{-1}\sum_{t=2}^{T}\text{E}(\Delta\mathbf{x}_{it}'\Delta\mathbf{x}_{it})\right]^{-1}\left[(T-1)^{-1}\sum_{t=2}^{T}\text{E}(\Delta\mathbf{x}_{it}'\Delta u_{it})\right]^{-1}. \tag{10.77}$$

If $\{\mathbf{x}_{it} : t = 1, 2, \ldots\}$ is weakly dependent, so is $\Delta\mathbf{x}_{it}$, and so the first average in (10.77) is generally bounded. (In fact, under stationarity this average does not depend on T.) Under (10.74),

$$\text{E}(\Delta\mathbf{x}_{it}'\Delta u_{it}) = -[\text{E}(\mathbf{x}_{it}'u_{i,t-1}) + \text{E}(\mathbf{x}_{i,t-1}'u_{it})],$$

which is generally nonzero. Under stationarity, $\text{E}(\Delta\mathbf{x}_{it}'\Delta u_{it})$ does not depend on t, and so the second average in (10.77) does not depend on T. Even if we assume u_{it} is uncorrelated with past covariates—a sequential exogeneity assumption conditional on c_i—so that $\text{E}(\mathbf{x}_{i,t-1}'u_{it}) = \mathbf{0}$, $\text{E}(\mathbf{x}_{it}'u_{i,t-1})$ does not equal zero if there is feedback from current idiosyncratic errors to future values of the covariates. Therefore, with sequential exogeneity, the second term is $-(T-1)^{-1}\sum_{t=2}^{T}\text{E}(\mathbf{x}_{it}'u_{i,t-1})$, which equals $-\text{E}(\mathbf{x}_{i2}'u_{i1})$ under stationarity, and is generally $O(1)$ even without stationarity.

The previous analysis shows that under contemporaneous exogeneity and weak dependence of the regressors and idiosyncratic errors, the FE estimator has an advantage over the FD estimator when T is large. Interestingly, a more detailed analysis shows that the same order of magnitude holds for $\mathbf{r}_{FE}(T)$ if some regressors have unit roots in their time series representation, that is, they are "integrated of order one," or I(1). (See Hamilton (1994) or Wooldridge (1994a) for more on I(1) processes.) The error process must still be assumed I(0) (weakly dependent). For example, in the scalar case, if $\{x_{it} : t = 1, 2, \ldots\}$ is I(1) without a drift term, then $T^{-2} \sum_{t=1}^{T} \mathrm{E}[(x_{it} - \bar{x}_i)^2] = O(1)$ and $\mathrm{Var}(\bar{x}_i) = O(T)$. If we maintain that $\{u_{it} : t = 1, 2, \ldots\}$ is I(0), then $\mathrm{Var}(\bar{u}_i) = O(T^{-1})$, and simple algebra shows that $r_{FE}(T) = O(T^{-1})$. The orders of magnitude for moments of averages of I(1) series can be inferred from Hamilton (1994, Prop. 17.1), for example, or shown directly. Harris and Tzavalis (1999) established the $O(T^{-1})$ rate for the inconsistency for the autoregressive model with $\beta = 1$—in fact, they show $r_{FE}(T) = -3/(T+1)$—although the process must be without linear trend when $\beta = 1$.

One way to summarize the $O(T^{-1})$ inconsistency for $\hat{\beta}_{FE}$ when $-1 < \beta \le 1$ is that it applies to the model $y_{it} = \beta y_{i,t-1} + (1-\beta)a_i + u_{it}$, so that when $\beta = 1$, $\{y_{it} : t = 0, 1, \ldots\}$ is I(1) without drift (and therefore its mean is $\mathrm{E}(y_{i0})$ for all t). The FD estimator of β has inconsistency $O(1)$ in such models, and more generally with I(1) regressors if strict exogeneity fails.

The previous analysis certainly favors FE estimation when contemporaneous exogeneity holds but strict exogeneity fails, even if $\{y_{it}\}$ and some elements of $\{\mathbf{x}_{it}\}$ have unit roots. Unfortunately, there is a catch: the finding that $\mathbf{r}_{FE}(T) = O(T^{-1})$ depends critically on the idiosyncratic errors $\{u_{it}\}$ being an I(0) sequence. In the terminology of time series econometrics, y_{it} and $\mathbf{x}_{it}$ must be "cointegrated" (see Hamilton, 1994, Chap. 19). If, in a time series sense, our model represents a spurious regression—that is, there is no value of $\boldsymbol{\beta}$ such that $y_{it} - \mathbf{x}_{it}\boldsymbol{\beta} - c_i$ is I(0)—then the FE approach is no longer superior to FD when comparing inconsistencies. In fact, for fixed N, the spurious regression problem for FE becomes more acute as T gets large. By contrast, FD removes any unit roots in y_{it} and $\mathbf{x}_{it}$, and so spurious regression is not an issue (but lack of strict exogeneity might be).

When T and N are similar in magnitude, a more realistic scenario is to let T and N grow at the same time (and perhaps the same rate). In this scenario, convergence results for partial sums of I(1) processes and functions of them are needed to obtain limiting distribution results. Considering large T asymptotics is beyond the scope of this text. Phillips and Moon (1999, 2000) discuss unit roots, spurious regression, cointegration, and a variety of estimation and testing procedures for panel data. See Baltagi (2001, Chap. 12) for a summary.

Because strict exogeneity plays such an important role in FE and FD estimation with small T, it is important to have a way of formally detecting its violation. One possibility is to directly compare $\hat{\boldsymbol{\beta}}_{FE}$ and $\hat{\boldsymbol{\beta}}_{FD}$ via a Hausman test. It could be important to use a robust form of the test that maintains neither Assumption FE.3 nor Assumption FD.3, so that neither estimator is assumed efficient under the null. The Hausman test has no systematic power for detecting violation of the second moment assumptions (either FE.3 or FD.3); it is consistent only against alternatives where $\mathrm{E}(\mathbf{x}_{is}'u_{it}) \neq \mathbf{0}$ for some (s,t) pairs.

Even if we assume that FE or FD is asymptotically efficient under the null, a drawback to the traditional form of the Hausman test is that, with aggregate time effects, the asymptotic variance of $\sqrt{N}(\hat{\boldsymbol{\beta}}_{FE} - \hat{\boldsymbol{\beta}}_{FD})$ is singular. In fact, in a model with only aggregate time effects, it can be shown that the FD and FE estimators are identical. Problem 10.6 asks you to work through the statistic in the case without aggregate time effects. Here, we focus on regression-based tests, which are easy to compute even with time-period dummies and easy to make fully robust.

If $T = 2$, it is easy to test for strict exogeneity. In the equation $\Delta y_i = \Delta\mathbf{x}_i\boldsymbol{\beta} + \Delta u_i$, neither $\mathbf{x}_{i1}$ nor $\mathbf{x}_{i2}$ should be significant as additional explanatory variables in the FD equation. We simply add, say, $\mathbf{x}_{i2}$ to the FD equation and carry out an F test for significance of $\mathbf{x}_{i2}$. With more than two time periods, a test of strict exogeneity is a test of H_0: $\boldsymbol{\gamma} = \mathbf{0}$ in the expanded equation

$$\Delta y_{it} = \Delta\mathbf{x}_{it}\boldsymbol{\beta} + \mathbf{w}_{it}\boldsymbol{\gamma} + \Delta u_{it}, \qquad t = 2, \ldots, T,$$

where $\mathbf{w}_{it}$ is a subset of $\mathbf{x}_{it}$ (that would exclude time dummies). Using the Wald approach, this test can be made robust to arbitrary serial correlation or heteroskedasticity; under Assumptions FD.1–FD.3 the usual F statistic is asymptotically valid.

A test of strict exogeneity using fixed effects, when $T > 2$, is obtained by specifying the equation

$$y_{it} = \mathbf{x}_{it}\boldsymbol{\beta} + \mathbf{w}_{i,t+1}\boldsymbol{\delta} + c_i + u_{it}, \qquad t = 1, 2, \ldots, T-1,$$

where $\mathbf{w}_{i,t+1}$ is again a subset of $\mathbf{x}_{i,t+1}$. Under strict exogeneity, $\boldsymbol{\delta} = \mathbf{0}$, and we can carry out the test using FE estimation. (We lose the last time period by leading $\mathbf{w}_{it}$.) An example is given in Problem 10.12.

Under strict exogeneity, we can use a GLS procedure on either the time-demeaned equation or the FD equation. If the variance matrix of $\mathbf{u}_i$ is unrestricted, it does not matter which transformation we use. Intuitively, this point is pretty clear, since allowing $\mathrm{E}(\mathbf{u}_i\mathbf{u}_i')$ to be unrestricted places no restrictions on $\mathrm{E}(\ddot{\mathbf{u}}_i\ddot{\mathbf{u}}_i')$ or $\mathrm{E}(\Delta\mathbf{u}_i\Delta\mathbf{u}_i')$. Im, Ahn, Schmidt, and Wooldridge (1999) show formally that the FEGLS and FDGLS estimators are asymptotically equivalent under Assumptions FE.1 and FEGLS.3 and the appropriate rank conditions. Of course the system homoskedasticity assumption $E(\mathbf{u}_i\mathbf{u}_i' \mid \mathbf{x}_i, c_i) = E(\mathbf{u}_i\mathbf{u}_i')$ is maintained.

10.7.2 Relationship between the Random Effects and Fixed Effects Estimators

In cases where the key variables in $\mathbf{x}_t$ do not vary much over time, FE and FD methods can lead to imprecise estimates. We may be forced to use random effects estimation in order to learn anything about the population parameters. If an RE analysis is appropriate—that is, if c_i is orthogonal to $\mathbf{x}_{it}$—then the RE estimators can have much smaller variances than the FE or FD estimators. We now obtain an expression for the RE estimator that allows us to compare it with the FE estimator.

Using the fact that $\mathbf{j}_T'\mathbf{j}_T = T$, we can write $\mathbf{\Omega}$ under the random effects structure as

$$\mathbf{\Omega} = \sigma_u^2\mathbf{I}_T + \sigma_c^2\mathbf{j}_T\mathbf{j}_T' = \sigma_u^2\mathbf{I}_T + T\sigma_c^2\mathbf{j}_T(\mathbf{j}_T'\mathbf{j}_T)^{-1}\mathbf{j}_T'$$

$$= \sigma_u^2\mathbf{I}_T + T\sigma_c^2\mathbf{P}_T = (\sigma_u^2 + T\sigma_c^2)(\mathbf{P}_T + \eta\mathbf{Q}_T),$$

where $\mathbf{P}_T \equiv \mathbf{I}_T - \mathbf{Q}_T = \mathbf{j}_T(\mathbf{j}_T'\mathbf{j}_T)^{-1}\mathbf{j}_T'$ and $\eta \equiv \sigma_u^2/(\sigma_u^2 + T\sigma_c^2)$. Next, define $\mathbf{S}_T \equiv \mathbf{P}_T + \eta\mathbf{Q}_T$. Then $\mathbf{S}_T^{-1} = \mathbf{P}_T + (1/\eta)\mathbf{Q}_T$, as can be seen by direct matrix multiplication. Further, $\mathbf{S}_T^{-1/2} = \mathbf{P}_T + (1/\sqrt{\eta})\mathbf{Q}_T$, because multiplying this matrix by itself gives $\mathbf{S}_T^{-1}$ (the matrix is clearly symmetric, since $\mathbf{P}_T$ and $\mathbf{Q}_T$ are symmetric). After simple algebra, it can be shown that $\mathbf{S}_T^{-1/2} = (1-\lambda)^{-1}[\mathbf{I}_T - \lambda\mathbf{P}_T]$, where $\lambda = 1 - \sqrt{\eta}$. Therefore,

$$\mathbf{\Omega}^{-1/2} = (\sigma_u^2 + T\sigma_c^2)^{-1/2}(1-\lambda)^{-1}[\mathbf{I}_T - \lambda\mathbf{P}_T] = (1/\sigma_u)[\mathbf{I}_T - \lambda\mathbf{P}_T],$$

where $\lambda = 1 - [\sigma_u^2/(\sigma_u^2 + T\sigma_c^2)]^{1/2}$. Assume for the moment that we know λ. Then the RE estimator is obtained by estimating the transformed equation $\mathbf{C}_T\mathbf{y}_i = \mathbf{C}_T\mathbf{X}_i\boldsymbol{\beta} + \mathbf{C}_T\mathbf{v}_i$ by system OLS, where $\mathbf{C}_T \equiv [\mathbf{I}_T - \lambda\mathbf{P}_T]$. Write the transformed equation as

$$\check{\mathbf{y}}_i = \check{\mathbf{X}}_i\boldsymbol{\beta} + \check{\mathbf{v}}_i. \tag{10.78}$$

The variance matrix of $\check{\mathbf{v}}_i$ is $E(\check{\mathbf{v}}_i\check{\mathbf{v}}_i') = \mathbf{C}_T\mathbf{\Omega}\mathbf{C}_T = \sigma_u^2\mathbf{I}_T$, which verifies that $\check{\mathbf{v}}_i$ has variance matrix ideal for system OLS estimation.

The tth element of $\check{\mathbf{y}}_i$ is easily seen to be $y_{it} - \lambda\bar{y}_i$, and similarly for $\check{\mathbf{X}}_i$. Therefore, system OLS estimation of equation (10.78) is just pooled OLS estimation of

$$y_{it} - \lambda\bar{y}_i = (\mathbf{x}_{it} - \lambda\bar{\mathbf{x}}_i)\boldsymbol{\beta} + (v_{it} - \lambda\bar{v}_i)$$

over all t and i. The errors in this equation are serially uncorrelated and homoskedastic under Assumption RE.3; therefore, they satisfy the key conditions for pooled OLS analysis. The feasible RE estimator replaces the unknown λ with its estimator, $\hat{\lambda}$, so that $\hat{\boldsymbol{\beta}}_{RE}$ can be computed from the pooled OLS regression

$$\check{y}_{it} \text{ on } \check{\mathbf{x}}_{it}, \qquad t = 1, \ldots, T; i = 1, \ldots, N, \tag{10.79}$$

where now $\check{\mathbf{x}}_{it} = \mathbf{x}_{it} - \hat{\lambda}\bar{\mathbf{x}}_i$ and $\check{y}_{it} = y_{it} - \hat{\lambda}\bar{y}_i$, all t and i. Therefore, we can write

$$\hat{\boldsymbol{\beta}}_{RE} = \left(\sum_{i=1}^{N}\sum_{t=1}^{T}\check{\mathbf{x}}_{it}'\check{\mathbf{x}}_{it}\right)^{-1}\left(\sum_{i=1}^{N}\sum_{t=1}^{T}\check{\mathbf{x}}_{it}'\check{y}_{it}\right). \tag{10.80}$$

The usual variance estimate from the pooled OLS regression (10.79), $\text{SSR}/(NT - K)$, is a consistent estimator of σ_u^2. The usual t statistics and F statistics from the pooled regression are asymptotically valid under Assumptions RE.1–RE.3. For F tests, we obtain $\hat{\lambda}$ from the unrestricted model.

Equation (10.80) shows that the RE estimator is obtained by a **quasi-time demeaning**: rather than removing the time average from the explanatory and dependent variables at each t, RE estimation removes a fraction of the time average. If $\hat{\lambda}$ is close to unity, the RE and FE estimates tend to be close. To see when this result occurs, write $\hat{\lambda}$ as

$$\hat{\lambda} = 1 - \{1/[1 + T(\hat{\sigma}_c^2/\hat{\sigma}_u^2)]\}^{1/2}, \tag{10.81}$$

where $\hat{\sigma}_u^2$ and $\hat{\sigma}_c^2$ are consistent estimators of σ_u^2 and σ_c^2 (see Section 10.4). When $T(\hat{\sigma}_c^2/\hat{\sigma}_u^2)$ is large, the second term in $\hat{\lambda}$ is small, in which case $\hat{\lambda}$ is close to unity. In fact, $\hat{\lambda} \to 1$ as $T \to \infty$ or as $\hat{\sigma}_c^2/\hat{\sigma}_u^2 \to \infty$. For large T, it is not surprising to find similar estimates from FE and RE. Even with small T, RE can be close to FE if the estimated variance of c_i is large relative to the estimated variance of u_{it}, a case often relevant for applications. (As λ approaches unity, the precision of the RE estimator approaches that of the FE estimator, and the effects of time-constant explanatory variables become harder to estimate.)

Example 10.7 (Job Training Grants): In Example 10.4, $T = 3$, $\hat{\sigma}_u^2 \approx .248$, and $\hat{\sigma}_c^2 \approx 1.932$, which gives $\hat{\lambda} \approx .797$. This helps explain why the RE and FE estimates are reasonably close.

Equations (10.80) and (10.81) also show how RE and pooled OLS are related. Pooled OLS is obtained by setting $\hat{\lambda} = 0$, which is never exactly true but could be close. In practice, $\hat{\lambda}$ is not usually close to zero because small values require $\hat{\sigma}_u^2$ to be large relative to $\hat{\sigma}_c^2$.

In Section 10.4 we emphasized that consistency of RE estimation hinges on the orthogonality between c_i and $\mathbf{x}_{it}$. In fact, Assumption POLS.1 is weaker than Assumption RE.1. We now see, because of the particular transformation used by the

RE estimator, that its inconsistency when Assumption RE.1b is violated can be small relative to pooled OLS if σ_c^2 is large relative to σ_u^2 or if T is large.

If we are primarily interested in the effect of a time-constant variable in a panel data study, the robustness of the FE estimator to correlation between the unobserved effect and the $\mathbf{x}_{it}$ is practically useless. Without using an instrumental variables approach—something we take up in Chapter 11—RE estimation is probably our only choice. Sometimes, applications of the RE estimator attempt to control for the part of c_i correlated with $\mathbf{x}_{it}$ by including dummy variables for various groups, assuming that we have many observations within each group. For example, if we have panel data on a group of working people, we might include city dummy variables in a wage equation. Or, if we have panel data at the student level, we might include school dummy variables. Including dummy variables for groups controls for a certain amount of heterogeneity that might be correlated with the (time-constant) elements of $\mathbf{x}_{it}$. By using RE, we can efficiently account for any remaining serial correlation due to unobserved time-constant factors. (Unfortunately, the language used in empirical work can be confusing. It is not uncommon to see school dummy variables referred to as "school fixed effects," even though they appear in an RE analysis at the individual level.)

Regression (10.79) using the quasi-time-demeaned data has several other practical uses. Since it is just a pooled OLS regression that is asymptotically the same as using λ in place of $\hat{\lambda}$, we can easily obtain standard errors that are robust to arbitrary heteroskedasticity in c_i and u_{it}, as well as arbitrary serial correlation in the $\{u_{it}\}$. All that is required is an econometrics package that computes robust standard errors, t, and F statistics for pooled OLS regression, such as Stata. Further, we can use the residuals from regression (10.79), say $\hat{r}_{it}$, to test for serial correlation in $r_{it} \equiv v_{it} - \lambda \bar{v}_i$, which are serially uncorrelated under Assumption RE.3a. If we detect serial correlation in $\{r_{it}\}$, we conclude that Assumption RE.3a is false, which means that the u_{it} are serially correlated. Although the arguments are tedious, it can be shown that estimation of λ and $\boldsymbol{\beta}$ has no effect on the null limiting distribution of the usual (or heteroskedasticity-robust) t statistic from the pooled OLS regression $\hat{r}_{it}$ on $\hat{r}_{i,t-1}$, $t = 2, \ldots, T, i = 1, \ldots, N$.

10.7.3 Hausman Test Comparing Random Effects and Fixed Effects Estimators

Because the key consideration in choosing between an RE and an FE approach is whether c_i and $\mathbf{x}_{it}$ are correlated, it is important to have a method for testing this assumption. Hausman (1978) proposed a test based on the difference between the RE and FE estimates. Since FE is consistent when c_i and $\mathbf{x}_{it}$ are correlated, but RE is inconsistent, a statistically significant difference is interpreted as evidence against the RE assumption RE.1b. This interpretation implicitly assumes that $\{\mathbf{x}_{it}\}$ is strictly exogenous with respect to $\{u_{it}\}$, that is, Assumption RE.1a (FE.1) holds.

Before we obtain the Hausman test, there are three caveats. First, strict exogeneity, Assumption RE.1a, is maintained under the null and the alternative. Correlation between $\mathbf{x}_{is}$ and u_{it} for any s and t causes both FE and RE to be inconsistent, and generally their plims will differ. In order to view the Hausman test as a test of $\text{Cov}(\mathbf{x}_{it}, c_i) = 0$, we must maintain Assumption RE.1a.

A second caveat is that the test is usually implemented assuming that Assumption RE.3 holds under the null. As we will see, this setup implies that the RE estimator is more efficient than the FE estimator, and it simplifies computation of the test statistic. But we must emphasize that Assumption RE.3 is an auxiliary assumption, and it is *not* being tested by the Hausman statistic: the Hausman test has no systematic power against the alternative that Assumption RE.1 is true but Assumption RE.3 is false. Failure of Assumption RE.3 causes the usual Hausman test to have a nonstandard limiting distribution, an issue we return to in a later discussion.

A third caveat concerns the set of parameters that we can compare. Because the FE approach only identifies coefficients on time-varying explanatory variables, we clearly cannot compare FE and RE coefficients on time-constant variables. But there is a more subtle issue: we cannot include in our comparison coefficients on aggregate time effects—that is, variables that change only across t. As with the case of comparing FE and FD estimates, the problem with comparing coefficients on aggregate time effects is not one of identification; we know RE and FE both allow inclusion of a full set of time period dummies. The problem is one of singularity in the asymptotic variance matrix of the difference between $\hat{\boldsymbol{\beta}}_{FE}$ and $\hat{\boldsymbol{\beta}}_{RE}$. Problem 10.17 asks you to show that in the model $y_{it} = \alpha + \mathbf{d}_t\boldsymbol{\eta} + \mathbf{w}_{it}\boldsymbol{\delta} + c_i + u_{it}$, where $\mathbf{d}_t$ is a $1 \times R$ vector of aggregate time effects and $\mathbf{w}_{it}$ is a $1 \times M$ vector of regressors varying across i and t, the asymptotic variance of the difference in the FE and RE estimators of $(\boldsymbol{\eta}', \boldsymbol{\delta}')'$ has rank M, not $R + M$. (In fact, without $\mathbf{w}_{it}$ in the model, the FE and RE estimates of $\boldsymbol{\eta}$ are identical. Problem 10.18 asks you to investigate this algebraic result and some related claims for a particular data set.)

Rather than consider the general case—which is complicated by the singularity of the asymptotic covariance matrix—we assume that there are no aggregate time effects in the model in deriving the traditional form of the Hausman test. Therefore, we write the equation as $y_{it} = \mathbf{x}_{it}\boldsymbol{\beta} + c_i + u_{it} = \mathbf{z}_i\boldsymbol{\gamma} + \mathbf{w}_{it}\boldsymbol{\delta} + c_i + u_{it}$, where $\mathbf{z}_i$ (say, $1 \times J$) includes at least an intercept and often other time-constant variables. The elements of the $1 \times M$ vector $\mathbf{w}_{it}$ vary across i and t (as usual, at least for some units and some time periods), and it is the FE and RE estimators of $\boldsymbol{\delta}$ that we compare. For deriving the traditional form of the test, we maintain Assumptions RE.1 to RE.3 under the null, as well as the rank condition for fixed effects, Assumption FE.2.

A key component of the traditional Hausman test is showing that the asymptotic variance of the FE estimator is never smaller, and is usually strictly larger, than the asymptotic variance of the RE estimator. We already know the asymptotic variance of the FE estimator:

$$\text{Avar}(\hat{\boldsymbol{\delta}}_{FE}) = \sigma_u^2[\text{E}(\ddot{\mathbf{W}}_i'\ddot{\mathbf{W}}_i)]^{-1}/N. \tag{10.82}$$

In the presence of $\mathbf{z}_i$ the derivation of $\text{Avar}(\hat{\boldsymbol{\delta}}_{RE})$ is a little more tedious, but simplified by the pooled OLS characterization of RE using the quasi-time-demeaned data. Define $\breve{\mathbf{w}}_{it} = \mathbf{w}_{it} - \lambda\overline{\mathbf{w}}_i$ as the quasi-time demeaned time-varying regressors. To get $\text{Avar}(\hat{\boldsymbol{\delta}}_{RE})$, we must obtain the population residuals from the pooled regression $\breve{\mathbf{w}}_{it}$ on $(1-\lambda)\mathbf{z}_i$, which, of course, is the same as dropping the $(1-\lambda)$. Call these population residuals $\tilde{\mathbf{w}}_{it}$. Then

$$\text{Avar}(\hat{\boldsymbol{\delta}}_{RE}) = \sigma_u^2[\text{E}(\tilde{\mathbf{W}}_i'\tilde{\mathbf{W}}_i)]^{-1}/N. \tag{10.83}$$

Next, we want to show that $\text{Avar}(\hat{\boldsymbol{\delta}}_{FE}) - \text{Avar}(\hat{\boldsymbol{\delta}}_{RE})$ is positive definite. But this holds if $[\text{Avar}(\hat{\boldsymbol{\delta}}_{RE})]^{-1} - [\text{Avar}(\hat{\boldsymbol{\delta}}_{FE})]^{-1}$ is positive definite, or $\text{E}(\tilde{\mathbf{W}}_i'\tilde{\mathbf{W}}_i) - \text{E}(\ddot{\mathbf{W}}_i'\ddot{\mathbf{W}}_i)$ is positive definite. To demonstrate the latter result, we need to more carefully characterize $\tilde{\mathbf{w}}_{it} = \breve{\mathbf{w}}_{it} - \mathbf{z}_i\boldsymbol{\Pi}$, where $\boldsymbol{\Pi} = [T \cdot \text{E}(\mathbf{z}_i'\mathbf{z}_i)]^{-1}\text{E}[\mathbf{z}_i'(\sum_{t=1}^T \breve{\mathbf{w}}_{it})] = (1-\lambda)[\text{E}(\mathbf{z}_i'\mathbf{z}_i)]^{-1} \cdot \text{E}(\mathbf{z}_i'\overline{\mathbf{w}}_i)$. Straightforward algebra gives $\tilde{\mathbf{w}}_{it} = \breve{\mathbf{w}}_{it} - (1-\lambda)\overline{\mathbf{w}}_i^*$, where $\overline{\mathbf{w}}_i^* = \text{L}(\overline{\mathbf{w}}_i \mid \mathbf{z}_i)$ is the linear projection of $\overline{\mathbf{w}}_i$ on $\mathbf{z}_i$. We can also write

$$\tilde{\mathbf{w}}_{it} = \ddot{\mathbf{w}}_{it} + (1-\lambda)(\overline{\mathbf{w}}_i - \overline{\mathbf{w}}_i^*), \tag{10.84}$$

from which it follows immediately

$$\begin{aligned} \text{E}(\tilde{\mathbf{W}}_i'\tilde{\mathbf{W}}_i) - \text{E}(\ddot{\mathbf{W}}_i'\ddot{\mathbf{W}}_i) &= (1-\lambda)^2\text{E}[(\overline{\mathbf{w}}_i - \overline{\mathbf{w}}_i^*)'(\overline{\mathbf{w}}_i - \overline{\mathbf{w}}_i^*)] \\ &\quad + (1-\lambda)\sum_{t=1}^T \ddot{\mathbf{w}}_{it}'(\overline{\mathbf{w}}_i - \overline{\mathbf{w}}_i^*) + (1-\lambda)\sum_{t=1}^T (\overline{\mathbf{w}}_i - \overline{\mathbf{w}}_i^*)'\ddot{\mathbf{w}}_{it} \\ &= (1-\lambda)^2\text{E}[(\overline{\mathbf{w}}_i - \overline{\mathbf{w}}_i^*)'(\overline{\mathbf{w}}_i - \overline{\mathbf{w}}_i^*)], \end{aligned} \tag{10.85}$$

because $\sum_{t=1}^T \ddot{\mathbf{w}}_{it} = \mathbf{0}$ for all i. For $\lambda < 1$, and provided $\overline{\mathbf{w}}_i - \text{L}(\overline{\mathbf{w}}_i \mid \mathbf{z}_i)$ has variance with full rank—which means the time averages of the time-varying regressors are not perfectly collinear with the time-constant regressors—we have shown that $\text{E}(\tilde{\mathbf{W}}_i'\tilde{\mathbf{W}}_i) - \text{E}(\ddot{\mathbf{W}}_i'\ddot{\mathbf{W}}_i)$ is positive definite.

It can also be shown that, under RE.1 to RE.3, $\text{Avar}(\hat{\boldsymbol{\delta}}_{FE} - \hat{\boldsymbol{\delta}}_{RE}) = \text{Avar}(\hat{\boldsymbol{\delta}}_{FE}) - \text{Avar}(\hat{\boldsymbol{\delta}}_{RE})$; Newey and McFadden (1994, Sect. 5.3) provide general sufficient conditions, which are met by the FE and RE estimators under Assumptions RE.1–RE.3. (We cover these conditions in Chapter 14 in our discussion of general efficiency issues; see Lemma 14.1 and the surrounding discussion.) Therefore, we can compute the Hausman statistic as

$$H = (\hat{\boldsymbol{\delta}}_{FE} - \hat{\boldsymbol{\delta}}_{RE})'[\widehat{\text{Avar}(\hat{\boldsymbol{\delta}}_{FE})} - \widehat{\text{Avar}(\hat{\boldsymbol{\delta}}_{RE})}]^{-1}(\hat{\boldsymbol{\delta}}_{FE} - \hat{\boldsymbol{\delta}}_{RE}), \tag{10.86}$$

which has a χ^2_M distribution under the null hypothesis. The usual estimates of $\text{Avar}(\hat{\boldsymbol{\delta}}_{FE})$ and $\text{Avar}(\hat{\boldsymbol{\delta}}_{RE})$ can be used in equation (10.86), but if different estimates of σ_u^2 are used, the matrix in the middle need not be positive definite, possibly leading to a negative value of H. It is best to use the same estimate of σ_u^2 (based on either FE or RE) in both places.

If we are interested in testing the difference in estimators for a single coefficient, we can use a t statistic form of the Hausman test. In particular, if δ now denotes a scalar on the time-varying variable of interest, we can use $(\hat{\delta}_{FE} - \hat{\delta}_{RE})/\{[\text{se}(\hat{\delta}_{FE})]^2 - [\text{se}(\hat{\delta}_{RE})]^2\}^{1/2}$, provided that we use versions of the standard errors that ensure $\text{se}(\hat{\delta}_{FE}) > \text{se}(\hat{\delta}_{RE})$. Under Assumptions RE.1–RE.3, the t statistic has an asymptotic standard normal distribution.

So far we have stated that the null hypothesis is RE.1–RE.3, but expression (10.84) allows us to characterize the implicit null hypothesis. From (10.84), it is seen that deviations between the RE and FE estimates of $\boldsymbol{\delta}$ are due to correlation between $\overline{\mathbf{w}}_i - \overline{\mathbf{w}}_i^*$ and c_i (where we maintain Assumption RE.1a, which is strict exogeneity conditional on c_i). In other words, the Hausman test is a test of

$$\text{H}_0 : \text{E}[(\overline{\mathbf{w}}_i - \overline{\mathbf{w}}_i^*)'c_i] = \mathbf{0}. \tag{10.87}$$

Equation (10.87) is interesting for several reasons. First, if there are no time-constant variables (except an overall intercept) in the RE estimation, the null hypothesis is $\text{Cov}(\overline{\mathbf{w}}_i, c_i) = \mathbf{0}$, which means we are really testing whether the time-average of the $\mathbf{w}_{it}$ is correlated with the unobserved effect. With time-constant explanatory variables $\mathbf{z}_i$, we first remove the correlation between $\overline{\mathbf{w}}_i$ and $\mathbf{z}_i$ to form the population residuals, $\overline{\mathbf{w}}_i - \overline{\mathbf{w}}_i^*$, before testing for correlation with c_i. An immediate consequence is that, with a rich set of controls in $\mathbf{z}_i$, it is possible for $\overline{\mathbf{w}}_i - \overline{\mathbf{w}}_i^*$ to be uncorrelated with c_i even though $\overline{\mathbf{w}}_i$ is correlated with c_i. Not surprisingly, an RE analysis with good controls in $\mathbf{z}_i$ and an RE analysis that omits such controls can yield very different estimates of $\boldsymbol{\delta}$, and the RE estimate of $\boldsymbol{\delta}$ with $\mathbf{z}_i$ included might be much closer to the FE estimate than if $\mathbf{z}_i$ is excluded. Often, discussions of the Hausman test comparing FE and RE assume that only time-varying explanatory variables are included in the RE estimation, but that is too restrictive for applications with time-constant controls.

Equation (10.87) also suggests a simple regression-based approach to computing a Hausman statistic. In fact, we are led to a regression-based method if we use a particular correlated RE assumption due to Mundlak (1978): $c_i = \psi + \overline{\mathbf{w}}_i \xi + a_i$, where a_i has zero mean and is assumed to be uncorrelated with $\mathbf{w}_i = (\mathbf{w}_{i1}, \ldots, \mathbf{w}_{iT})$ and $\mathbf{z}_i$. Plugging in for c_i gives the expanded equation

$$y_{it} = \mathbf{x}_{it}\boldsymbol{\beta} + \overline{\mathbf{w}}_i \xi + a_i + u_{it}, \tag{10.88}$$

where we absorb ψ into $\boldsymbol{\beta}$ because we assume $\mathbf{x}_{it}$ includes an intercept. In fact, in addition to an intercept, time-constant variables $\mathbf{z}_i$, and $\mathbf{w}_{it}$, $\mathbf{x}_{it}$ can (and usually should) contain a full set of time period dummies. Mundlak (1978) suggested testing $\mathrm{H}_0 : \xi = \mathbf{0}$ to determine if the heterogeneity was correlated with the time averages of the $\mathbf{w}_{it}$. (Incidentally, the formulation in equation (10.88) makes it clear that we cannot include the time average of aggregate time variables in $\overline{\mathbf{w}}_i$ because the time averages simply would be constant across all i.)

How should we estimate the parameters in equation (10.88)? We could estimate the equation by pooled OLS or we could estimate the equation by random effects, which is asymptotically efficient under RE.1–RE.3. As it turns out, the pooled OLS and RE estimates of ξ are identical, and $\hat{\xi} = \hat{\boldsymbol{\delta}}_B - \hat{\boldsymbol{\delta}}_{FE}$, where $\hat{\boldsymbol{\delta}}_B$ (the between estimator) is the coefficient vector on $\overline{\mathbf{w}}_i$ from the cross section regression $\bar{y}_i$ on $\mathbf{z}_i$, $\overline{\mathbf{w}}_i$, $i = 1, \ldots, N$. Further, the coefficient vector on $\mathbf{w}_{it}$ is simply the FE estimate; see Mundlak (1978) and Hsiao (2003, Sect. 3.2) for verification. In other words, the regression-based version of the test explicitly compares the between estimate and the FE estimate of $\boldsymbol{\delta}$. Hausman and Taylor (1981) show that this is the same as basing the test on the RE and FE estimate because the RE estimator is a matrix-weighted average of the between and FE estimators; see also Baltagi (2001, Sect. 2.3).

That the FE estimator of $\boldsymbol{\delta}$—the coefficient on $\mathbf{w}_{it}$—is obtained as the RE estimator in equation (10.88) sheds further light on the source of efficiency of RE over FE. In effect, the RE estimator of $\boldsymbol{\delta}$ sets ξ to zero. Because $\overline{\mathbf{w}}_i$ is correlated with $\mathbf{w}_{it}$—often highly correlated—dropping it from the equation when it is legimate to do so increases efficiency of the remaining parameter estimates by reducing multicollinearity. Of course, inappropriately setting ξ to zero results in inconsistent estimation of $\boldsymbol{\delta}$, and that is the danger of the RE approach.

If we use pooled OLS to test $H_0 : \xi = \mathbf{0}$, the usual pooled OLS test statistic will be inappropriate—at a minimum because of the serial correlation induced by a_i. As we know, it is easy to obtain a fully robust variance matrix estimator, and therefore a fully robust Wald statistic, for pooled OLS. Such a statistic will be fully robust to violations of Assumption RE.3. Alternatively, we can estimate (10.88) by RE, and, if we maintain Assumption RE.3, we can use a standard Wald test computed using the usual RE variance matrix estimator. We also know it is easy to obtain a fully robust Wald statistic, that is, a statistic that does not maintain Assumption RE.3 under the null. If the full set of RE assumptions holds, the RE Wald statistic is asymptotically more efficient than that based on pooled OLS.

Earlier we discussed how the traditional Hausman test maintains Assumption RE.3 under the null. Why should we make the Hausman robust to violations to Assumption RE.3? There is some confusion on this point in the methodolgical and empirical literatures. Hausman (1978) originally presented his testing principle as applying to situations where one estimator is efficient under the null but inconsistent under the alternative—the RE estimator in this case—and the other estimator is consistent under the null and the alternative but inefficient under the null—the FE estimator. While this scenario simplifies calculation of the test statistic—see equation (10.86)—it by no means is required for the test to make sense. In the current context, whether or not the covariates are correlated with c_i (through the time average) has nothing to do with conditional second moment assumptions on c_i or $\mathbf{u}_i = (u_{i1}, \dots, u_{iT})'$—that is, on whether Assumption RE.3 holds. In fact, including Assumption RE.3 in the null hypothesis serves to mask the kinds of misspecification the traditional Hausman test can detect. Certainly the test has power against violations of (10.87)—this is what it is intended to have power against. But the nonrobust Hausman statistic, whether computed in (10.86) or from (10.88)—they are asymptotically equivalent under RE.3—has no systematic power for detecting violation of Assumption RE.3. Specifically, if (10.87) holds and the standard rank conditions hold for FE and RE, the statistic converges in distribution (rather than diverging) whether or not Assumption RE.3 holds. In other words, the test is inconsistent for testing RE.3. This is easily seen from (10.86). The quadratic form will converge in distribution to a quadratic form in a multivariate normal. If Assumption RE.3 holds, that quadratic form has a chi-square distribution with M degrees of freedom, but not otherwise. Without Assumption RE.3, using the χ^2_M distribution to obtain critical values, or p-values, will result in a test that will be undersized or oversized under (10.87)—and we cannot generally tell which is the case. This feature carries over to any Hausman statistic where an auxiliary assumption is maintained that means one estimator is asymptotically efficient under the null. See Wooldridge (1991b) for further discussion in the context of testing conditional mean specifications.

To summarize, we can estimate models that include aggregate time effects, time-constant variables, and regressors that change across both i and t, by RE and FE estimation. But no matter how we compute a test statistic, we can only compare the coefficients on the regressors that change across both i and t. The regression-based version of the test in equation (10.88) makes it easy to obtain a statistic with a nondegenerate asymptotic distribution, and it is also easy to make the regression-based test fully robust to violations of Assumption RE.3.

As in any other context that uses statistical inference, it is possible to get a statistical rejection of RE.1b (say, at the 5 percent level) with the differences between the RE and FE estimates being practically small. The opposite case is also possible: there can be seemingly large differences between the RE and FE estimates but, due to large standard errors, the Hausman statistic fails to reject. What should be done in this case? A typical response is to conclude that the random effects assumptions hold and to focus on the RE estimates. Unfortunately, we may be committing a Type II error: failing to reject Assumption RE.1b when it is false.

Problems

10.1. Consider a model for new capital investment in a particular industry (say, manufacturing), where the cross section observations are at the county level and there are T years of data for each county:

$$\log(invest_{it}) = \theta_t + \mathbf{z}_{it}\boldsymbol{\gamma} + \delta_1 tax_{it} + \delta_2 disaster_{it} + c_i + u_{it}.$$

The variable tax_{it} is a measure of the marginal tax rate on capital in the county, and $disaster_{it}$ is a dummy indicator equal to one if there was a significant natural disaster in county i at time period t (for example, a major flood, a hurricane, or an earthquake). The variables in $\mathbf{z}_{it}$ are other factors affecting capital investment, and the θ_t represent different time intercepts.

a. Why is allowing for aggregate time effects in the equation important?

b. What kinds of variables are captured in c_i?

c. Interpreting the equation in a causal fashion, what sign does economic reasoning suggest for δ_1?

d. Explain in detail how you would estimate this model; be specific about the assumptions you are making.

e. Discuss whether strict exogeneity is reasonable for the two variables tax_{it} and $disaster_{it}$; assume that neither of these variables has a lagged effect on capital investment.

10.2. Suppose you have $T = 2$ years of data on the same group of N working individuals. Consider the following model of wage determination:

$$\log(wage_{it}) = \theta_1 + \theta_2 d2_t + \mathbf{z}_{it}\gamma + \delta_1 female_i + \delta_2 d2_t \cdot female_i + c_i + u_{it}.$$

The unobserved effect c_i is allowed to be correlated with $\mathbf{z}_{it}$ and $female_i$. The variable $d2_t$ is a time period indicator, where $d2_t = 1$ if $t = 2$ and $d2_t = 0$ if $t = 1$. In what follows, assume that

$$\mathrm{E}(u_{it} \mid female_i, \mathbf{z}_{i1}, \mathbf{z}_{i2}, c_i) = 0, \qquad t = 1, 2.$$

a. Without further assumptions, what parameters in the log wage equation can be consistently estimated?

b. Interpret the coefficients θ_2 and δ_2.

c. Write the log wage equation explicitly for the two time periods. Show that the differenced equation can be written as

$$\Delta\log(wage_i) = \theta_2 + \Delta\mathbf{z}_i\gamma + \delta_2 female_i + \Delta u_i,$$

where $\Delta\log(wage_i) = \log(wage_{i2}) - \log(wage_{i1})$, and so on.

d. How would you test $\mathrm{H}_0: \delta_2 = 0$ if $\mathrm{Var}(\Delta u_i \mid \Delta\mathbf{z}_i, female_i)$ is not constant?

10.3. For $T = 2$ consider the standard unoberved effects model

$$y_{it} = \mathbf{x}_{it}\boldsymbol{\beta} + c_i + u_{it}, \qquad t = 1, 2.$$

Let $\hat{\boldsymbol{\beta}}_{FE}$ and $\hat{\boldsymbol{\beta}}_{FD}$ denote the fixed effects and first difference estimators, respectively.

a. Show that the FE and FD estimates are numerically identical.

b. Show that the variance matrix estimates from the FE and FD methods are numerically identical.

10.4. A common setup for program evaluation with two periods of panel data is the following. Let y_{it} denote the outcome of interest for unit i in period t. At $t = 1$, no one is in the program; at $t = 2$, some units are in the control group and others are in the experimental group. Let $prog_{it}$ be a binary indicator equal to one if unit i is in the program in period t; by the program design, $prog_{i1} = 0$ for all i. An unobserved effects model without additional covariates is

$$y_{it} = \theta_1 + \theta_2 d2_t + \delta_1 prog_{it} + c_i + u_{it}, \qquad \mathrm{E}(u_{it} \mid prog_{i2}, c_i) = 0,$$

where $d2_t$ is a dummy variable equal to unity if $t = 2$, and zero if $t = 1$, and c_i is the unobserved effect.

a. Explain why including $d2_t$ is important in these contexts. In particular, what problems might be caused by leaving it out?

b. Why is it important to include c_i in the equation?

c. Using the first differencing method, show that $\hat{\theta}_2 = \overline{\Delta y}_{control}$ and $\hat{\delta}_1 = \overline{\Delta y}_{treat} - \overline{\Delta y}_{control}$, where $\overline{\Delta y}_{control}$ is the average change in y over the two periods for the group with $prog_{i2} = 0$, and $\overline{\Delta y}_{treat}$ is the average change in y for the group where $prog_{i2} = 1$. This formula shows that $\hat{\delta}_1$, the difference-in-differences estimator, arises out of an unobserved effects panel data model.

d. Write down the extension of the model for T time periods.

e. A common way to obtain the DD estimator for two years of panel data is from the model

$$y_{it} = \alpha_1 + \alpha_2 start_t + \alpha_3 prog_i + \delta_1 start_t prog_i + u_{it}, \tag{10.89}$$

where $E(u_{it} \mid start_t, prog_i) = 0$, $prog_i$ denotes whether unit i is in the program in the second period, and $start_t$ is a binary variable indicating when the program starts. In the two-period setup, $start_t = d2_t$ and $prog_{it} = start_t prog_i$. The pooled OLS estimator of δ_1 is the DD estimator from part c. With $T > 2$, the unobserved effects model from part d and pooled estimation of equation (10.89) no longer generally give the same estimate of the program effect. Which approach do you prefer, and why?

10.5. Assume that Assumptions RE.1 and RE.3a hold, but $\text{Var}(c_i \mid \mathbf{x}_i) \neq \text{Var}(c_i)$.

a. Describe the general nature of $E(\mathbf{v}_i \mathbf{v}_i' \mid \mathbf{x}_i)$.

b. What are the asymptotic properties of the random effects estimator and the associated test statistics?

c. How should the random effects statistics be modified?

10.6. For a model where $\mathbf{x}_{it}$ varies across i and t, define the $K \times K$ symmetric matrices $\mathbf{A}_1 \equiv E(\Delta \mathbf{X}_i' \Delta \mathbf{X}_i)$ and $\mathbf{A}_2 \equiv E(\ddot{\mathbf{X}}_i' \ddot{\mathbf{X}}_i)$, and assume both are positive definite. Define $\hat{\boldsymbol{\theta}} \equiv (\hat{\boldsymbol{\beta}}_{FD}', \hat{\boldsymbol{\beta}}_{FE}')'$ and $\boldsymbol{\theta} \equiv (\boldsymbol{\beta}', \boldsymbol{\beta}')'$, both $2K \times 1$ vectors.

a. Under Assumption FE.1 (and the rank conditions we have given), find $\sqrt{N}(\hat{\boldsymbol{\theta}} - \boldsymbol{\theta})$ in terms of $\mathbf{A}_1, \mathbf{A}_2$, $N^{-1/2} \sum_{i=1}^N \Delta \mathbf{X}_i' \Delta \mathbf{u}_i$, and $N^{-1/2} \sum_{i=1}^N \ddot{\mathbf{X}}_i' \ddot{\mathbf{u}}_i$ [with a $o_p(1)$ remainder].

b. Explain how to consistently estimate Avar $\sqrt{N}(\hat{\boldsymbol{\theta}} - \boldsymbol{\theta})$ without further assumptions.

c. Use parts a and b to obtain a robust Hausman statistic comparing the FD and FE estimators. What is the limiting distribution of your statistic under H_0?

d. If $\mathbf{x}_{it} = (\mathbf{d}_t, \mathbf{w}_{it})$, where $\mathbf{d}_t$ is a $\mathbf{1} \times \boldsymbol{R}$ vector of aggregate time variables, can you compare all of the FD and FD estimates of $\boldsymbol{\beta}$? Explain.

10.7. Use the two terms of data in GPA.RAW to estimate an unobserved effects version of the model in Example 7.8. You should drop the variable *cumgpa* (since this variable violates strict exogeneity).

a. Estimate the model by RE, and interpret the coefficient on the in-season variable.

b. Estimate the model by FE; informally compare the estimates to the RE estimates, in particular that on the in-season effect.

c. Construct the nonrobust Hausman test comparing RE and FE. Include all variables in $\mathbf{w}_{it}$ that have some variation across i and t, except for the term dummy.

10.8. Use the data in NORWAY.RAW for the years 1972 and 1978 for a two-year panel data analysis. The model is a simple distributed lag model:

$$\log(crime_{it}) = \theta_0 + \theta_1 d78_t + \beta_1 clrprc_{i,t-1} + \beta_2 clrprc_{i,t-2} + c_i + u_{it}.$$

The variable *clrprc* is the clear-up percentage (the percentage of crimes solved). The data are stored for two years, with the needed lags given as variables for each year.

a. First estimate this equation using a pooled OLS analysis. Comment on the deterrent effect of the clear-up percentage, including interpreting the size of the coefficients. Test for serial correlation in the composite error v_{it} assuming strict exogeneity (see Section 7.8).

b. Estimate the equation by FE, and compare the estimates with the pooled OLS estimates. Is there any reason to test for serial correlation? Obtain heteroskedasticity-robust standard errors for the FE estimates by using the FD equation.

c. Using FE analysis, test the hypothesis $H_0: \beta_1 = \beta_2$. What do you conclude? If the hypothesis is not rejected, what would be a more parsimonious model? Estimate this model.

10.9. Use the data in CORNWELL.RAW for this problem.

a. Estimate both an RE and an FE version of the model in Problem 7.11a. Compute the regression-based version of the Hausman test comparing RE and FE.

b. Add the wage variables (in logarithmic form), and test for joint significance after estimation by FE.

c. Estimate the equation by FD, and comment on any notable changes. Do the standard errors change much between FE and FD?

d. Test the FD equation for AR(1) serial correlation.

10.10. An unobserved effects model explaining current murder rates in terms of the number of executions in the last three years is

$$mrdrte_{it} = \theta_t + \beta_1 exec_{it} + \beta_2 unem_{it} + c_i + u_{it},$$

where $mrdrte_{it}$ is the number of murders in state i during year t, per 10,000 people; $exec_{it}$ is the total number of executions for the current and prior two years; and $unem_{it}$ is the current unemployment rate, included as a control.

a. Using the data in MURDER.RAW, estimate this model by FD. Notice that you should allow different year intercepts. Test the errors in the FD equation for serial correlation.

b. Estimate the model by FE. Are there any important differences from the FD estimates? What about in their fully robust standard errors?

c. Under what circumstances would $exec_{it}$ not be strictly exogenous (conditional on c_i)?

10.11. Use the data in LOWBIRTH.RAW for this question.

a. For 1987 and 1990, consider the state-level equation

$$\begin{aligned} lowbrth_{it} &= \theta_1 + \theta_2 d90_t + \beta_1 afdcprc_{it} + \beta_2 \log(phypc_{it}) \\ &\quad + \beta_3 \log(bedspc_{it}) + \beta_4 \log(pcinc_{it}) + \beta_5 \log(popul_{it}) + c_i + u_{it}, \end{aligned}$$

where the dependent variable is percentage of births that are classified as low birth weight and the key explanatory variable is *afdcprc*, the percentage of the population in the welfare program, Aid to Families with Dependent Children (AFDC). The other variables, which act as controls for quality of health care and income levels, are physicians per capita, hospital beds per capita, per capita income, and population. Interpretating the equation causally, what sign should each β_j have? (Note: Participation in AFDC makes poor women eligible for nutritional programs and prenatal care.)

b. Estimate the preceding equation by pooled OLS, and discuss the results. You should report the usual standard errors and serial correlation–robust standard errors.

c. Difference the equation to eliminate the state FE, c_i, and reestimate the equation. Interpret the estimate of β_1 and compare it to the estimate from part b. What do you make of $\hat{\beta}_2$?

d. Add $afdcprc^2$ to the model, and estimate it by FD. Are the estimates on *afdcprc* and $afdcprc^2$ sensible? What is the estimated turning point in the quadratic?

10.12. The data in WAGEPAN.RAW are from Vella and Verbeek (1998) for 545 men who worked every year from 1980 to 1987. Consider the wage equation

$$\begin{aligned} \log(wage_{it}) &= \theta_t + \beta_1 educ_i + \beta_2 black_i + \beta_3 hisp_i + \beta_4 exper_{it} \\ &\quad + \beta_5 exper_{it}^2 + \beta_6 married_{it} + \beta_7 union_{it} + c_i + u_{it}. \end{aligned}$$

The variables are described in the data set. Notice that education does not change over time.

a. Estimate this equation by pooled OLS, and report the results in standard form. Are the usual OLS standard errors reliable, even if c_i is uncorrelated with all explanatory variables? Explain. Compute appropriate standard errors.

b. Estimate the wage equation by RE. Compare your estimates with the pooled OLS estimates.

c. Now estimate the equation by FE. Why is $exper_{it}$ redundant in the model even though it changes over time? What happens to the marriage and union premiums as compared with the RE estimates?

d. Now add interactions of the form $d81 \cdot educ, d82 \cdot educ, \ldots, d87 \cdot educ$ and estimate the equation by FE. Has the return to education increased over time?

e. Return to the original model estimated by FE in part c. Add a *lead* of the union variable, $union_{i,t+1}$ to the equation, and estimate the model by FE (note that you lose the data for 1987). Is $union_{i,t+1}$ significant? What does your finding say about strict exogeneity of union membership?

f. Return to the original model, but add the interactions $black_i \cdot union_{it}$ and $hisp_i \cdot union_{it}$. Do the union wage premiums differ by race? Obtain the usual FE statistics and those fully robust to heteroskedasticity and serial correlation.

g. Add $union_{i,t+1}$ to the equation from part f, and obtain a fully robust test of the hypothesis that $\{union_{it} : t = 1, \ldots, T\}$ is strictly exogenous. What do you conclude?

10.13. Consider the standard linear unobserved effects model (10.11), under the assumptions

$$\mathrm{E}(u_{it} \mid \mathbf{x}_i, \mathbf{h}_i, c_i) = 0, \ \mathrm{Var}(u_{it} \mid \mathbf{x}_i, \mathbf{h}_i, c_i) = \sigma_u^2 h_{it}, \qquad t = 1, \ldots, T,$$

where $\mathbf{h}_i = (h_{i1}, \ldots, h_{iT})$. In other words, the errors display heteroskedasticity that depends on h_{it}. (In the leading case, h_{it} is a function of $\mathbf{x}_{it}$.) Suppose you estimate $\boldsymbol{\beta}$ by minimizing the weighted sum of squared residuals

$$\sum_{i=1}^{N} \sum_{t=1}^{T} (y_{it} - a_1 d1_i - \cdots - a_N dN_i - \mathbf{x}_{it}\mathbf{b})^2 / h_{it}$$

with respect to the a_i, $i = 1, \ldots, N$ and $\mathbf{b}$, where $dn_i = 1$ if $i = n$. (This would seem to be the natural analogue of the dummy variable regression, modified for known heteroskedasticity. We might call this a **fixed effects weighted least squares** estimator.)

a. Show that the FEWLS estimator is generally consistent for fixed T as $N \to \infty$. Do you need the variance function to be correctly specified in the sense that $\text{Var}(u_{it} \mid \mathbf{x}_i, \mathbf{h}_i, c_i) = \sigma_u^2 h_{it}$, $t = 1, \ldots, T$? Explain.

b. Suppose the variance function is correctly specified and $\text{Cov}(u_{it}, u_{is} \mid \mathbf{x}_i, \mathbf{h}_i, c_i) = 0$, $t \neq s$. Find the asymptotic variance of $\sqrt{N}(\hat{\boldsymbol{\beta}}_{FEWLS} - \boldsymbol{\beta})$.

c. Under the assumptions of part b, how would you estimate σ_u^2 and $\text{Avar}[\sqrt{N}(\hat{\boldsymbol{\beta}}_{FEWLS} - \boldsymbol{\beta})]$?

d. If the variance function is misspecified, or there is serial correlation in u_{it}, or both, how would you estimate $\text{Avar}[\sqrt{N}(\hat{\boldsymbol{\beta}}_{FEWLS} - \boldsymbol{\beta})]$?

10.14. Suppose that we have the unobserved effects model

$$y_{it} = \alpha + \mathbf{x}_{it}\boldsymbol{\beta} + \mathbf{z}_i\boldsymbol{\gamma} + h_i + u_{it}$$

where the $\mathbf{x}_{it}$ $(1 \times K)$ are time-varying, the $\mathbf{z}_i$ $(1 \times M)$ are time-constant, $\text{E}(u_{it} \mid \mathbf{x}_i, \mathbf{z}_i, h_i) = 0$, $t = 1, \ldots, T$, and $\text{E}(h_i \mid \mathbf{x}_i, \mathbf{z}_i) = 0$. Let $\sigma_h^2 = \text{Var}(h_i)$ and $\sigma_u^2 = \text{Var}(u_{it})$. If we estimate $\boldsymbol{\beta}$ by fixed effects, we are estimating the equation $y_{it} = \mathbf{x}_{it}\boldsymbol{\beta} + c_i + u_{it}$, where $c_i = \alpha + \mathbf{z}_i\boldsymbol{\gamma} + h_i$.

a. Find $\sigma_c^2 \equiv \text{Var}(c_i)$. Show that σ_c^2 is at least as large as σ_h^2, and usually strictly larger.

b. Explain why estimation of the model by fixed effects will lead to a larger estimated variance of the unobserved effect than if we estimate the model by random effects. Does this result make intuitive sense?

c. If λ_c is the quasi-time-demeaning parameter without $\mathbf{z}_i$ in the model and λ_h is the quasi-time-demeaning parameter with $\mathbf{z}_i$ in the model, show that $\lambda_c \geq \lambda_h$, with strict inequality if $\boldsymbol{\gamma} \neq \mathbf{0}$.

d. What does part c imply about using pooled OLS versus FE as the first step estimator for estimating the variance of the unobserved heterogeneity in RE estimation?

e. Suppose that, in addition to RE.1–RE.3 holding in the orginal model, $\text{E}(\mathbf{z}_i \mid \mathbf{x}_i) = \mathbf{0}$, $t = 1, \ldots, T$ and $\text{Var}(\mathbf{z}_i \mid \mathbf{x}_i) = \text{Var}(\mathbf{z}_i)$. Show directly—that is, by comparing the two asymptotic variances—that the RE estimator that includes $\mathbf{z}_i$ is asymptotically more efficient than the RE estimator that excludes $\mathbf{z}_i$. (The result also follows from Problem 7.15 without the assumption $\text{Var}(c_i \mid \mathbf{x}_i) = \text{Var}(c_i)$; in fact, we only need to assume $\mathbf{z}_i$ is uncorrelated with $\mathbf{x}_i$.)

10.15. Consider the standard unobserved effects model, first under a stronger version of the RE assumptions. Let $v_{it} = c_i + u_{it}$, $t = 1, \ldots, T$, be the composite errors, as usual. Then, in addition to RE.1–RE.3, assume that the $T \times 1$ vector $\mathbf{v}_i$ is independent of $\mathbf{x}_i$ and that all conditional expectations involving $\mathbf{v}_i$ are linear.

a. Let $\bar{v}_i$ be the time average of the v_{it}. Argue that $E(v_{it} \mid \mathbf{x}_i, \bar{v}_i) = E(v_{it} \mid \bar{v}_i) = \bar{v}_i$. (Hint: To show the second equality, recall that, because the expectation is assumed to be linear, the coefficient on $\bar{v}_i$ is $\mathrm{Cov}(v_{it}, \bar{v}_i)/\mathrm{Var}(\bar{v}_i)$.)

b. Use part a to show that

$$\mathrm{E}(y_{it} \mid \mathbf{x}_i, \bar{y}_i) = \mathbf{x}_{it}\boldsymbol{\beta} + (\bar{y}_i - \bar{\mathbf{x}}\boldsymbol{\beta}).$$

c. Argue that estimation of $\boldsymbol{\beta}$ based on part b leads to the FE estimator.

d. How can you reconcile part d with the fact that the full RE assumptions have been assumed? (Hint: What is the conditional expectation underlying RE estimation?)

e. Show that the arguments leading up to part c carry over using linear projections under RE.1–RE.3 alone.

10.16. Assume that through time periods $T + 1$, the assumptions in Problem 10.15 hold. Suppose you want to forecast $y_{i,T+1}$ at time T, where you know $\mathbf{x}_{i,T+1}$ in addition to all past values on $\mathbf{x}$ and y.

a. It can be shown, under the given assumptions, that $\mathrm{E}(v_{i,T+1} \mid \mathbf{x}_i, \mathbf{x}_{i,T+1}, v_{i1}, \ldots, v_{iT}) = \mathrm{E}(v_{i,T+1} \mid \bar{v}_i)$. Use this to show that $\mathrm{E}(v_{i,T+1} \mid \bar{v}_i) = [\sigma_c^2/(\sigma_c^2 + \sigma_u^2/T)]\bar{v}_i$.

b. Use part a to derive $E(y_{i,T+1} \mid \mathbf{x}_{i1}, \ldots, \mathbf{x}_{iT}, \mathbf{x}_{i,T+1}, y_{i1}, \ldots, y_{iT})$.

c. Compare the expectation in part b with $E(y_{i,T+1} \mid \mathbf{x}_{i1}, \ldots, \mathbf{x}_{iT}, \mathbf{x}_{i,T+1})$.

d. Which of the two expectations in parts b and c leads to a better forecast as defined by smallest variance of the forecast error?

e. How would you forecast $y_{i,T+1}$ if you have to estimate all unknown population parameters?

10.17. Consider a standard unobserved effects model but where we explicitly separate out aggregate time effects, say $\mathbf{d}_t$, a $1 \times R$ vector, where $R \leq T - 1$. (These are usually a full set of time period dummies, but they could be other aggregate time variables, such as specific functions of time.) Therefore, the model is

$$y_{it} = \alpha + \mathbf{d}_t\boldsymbol{\eta} + \mathbf{w}_{it}\boldsymbol{\delta} + c_i + u_{it}, \qquad t = 1, \ldots, T,$$

where $\mathbf{w}_{it}$ is the $1 \times M$ vector of explanatory variables that vary across i and t. Because the $\mathbf{d}_t$ do not change across i, we take them to be nonrandom. Because we have included an intercept in the model, we can assume that $E(c_i) = 0$. Let

$\lambda = 1 - \{1/[1 + T(\sigma_c^2/\sigma_u^2)]\}^{1/2}$ be the usual quasi-time-demeaning parameter for RE estimation. In what follows, we take λ as known because estimating it does not affect the asymptotic distribution results.

a. Show that we can write the quasi-time-demeaned equation for RE estimation as

$$y_{it} - \lambda\bar{y}_i = \mu + (\mathbf{d}_t - \bar{\mathbf{d}})\boldsymbol{\eta} + (\mathbf{w}_{it} - \lambda\bar{\mathbf{w}}_i)\boldsymbol{\delta} + (v_{it} - \lambda\bar{v}_i),$$

where $\mu = (1-\lambda)\alpha + (1-\lambda)\bar{\mathbf{d}}\boldsymbol{\eta}$, $v_{it} = c_i + u_{it}$, and $\bar{\mathbf{d}} = T^{-1}\sum_{t=1}^T \mathbf{d}_t$ is nonrandom.

b. To simplify the algebra without changing the substance of the findings, assume that $\mu = 0$ and that we exclude an intercept in estimating the quasi-time-demeaned equation. Write $\mathbf{g}_{it} = (\mathbf{d}_t - \bar{\mathbf{d}}, \mathbf{w}_{it} - \lambda\bar{\mathbf{w}}_i)$ and $\boldsymbol{\beta} = (\boldsymbol{\eta}', \boldsymbol{\delta}')'$. We will study the asymptotic distribution of the RE estimator by using the pooled OLS estimator from $y_{it} - \lambda\bar{y}_i$ on $\mathbf{g}_{it}$, $t = 1, \ldots, T$; $i = 1, \ldots, N$. Show that under Assumptions RE.1 and RE.2,

$$\sqrt{N}(\hat{\boldsymbol{\beta}}_{RE} - \boldsymbol{\beta}) = \mathbf{A}_1^{-1} N^{-1/2} \sum_{i=1}^N \sum_{t=1}^T \mathbf{g}_{it}'(v_{it} - \lambda\bar{v}_i) + o_p(1),$$

where $\mathbf{A}_1 \equiv \sum_{t=1}^T \mathrm{E}(\mathbf{g}_{it}'\mathbf{g}_{it})$. Further, verify that for any i,

$$\sum_{t=1}^T (\mathbf{d}_t - \bar{\mathbf{d}})(v_{it} - \lambda\bar{v}_i) = \sum_{t=1}^T (\mathbf{d}_t - \bar{\mathbf{d}})u_{it}.$$

c. Show that under FE.1 and FE.2,

$$\sqrt{N}(\hat{\boldsymbol{\beta}}_{FE} - \boldsymbol{\beta}) = \mathbf{A}_2^{-1} N^{-1/2} \sum_{i=1}^N \sum_{t=1}^T \mathbf{h}_{it}' u_{it} + o_p(1),$$

where $\mathbf{h}_{it} \equiv (\mathbf{d}_t - \bar{\mathbf{d}}, \mathbf{w}_{it} - \bar{\mathbf{w}}_i)$ and $\mathbf{A}_2 \equiv \sum_{t=1}^T \mathrm{E}(\mathbf{h}_{it}'\mathbf{h}_{it})$.

d. Under RE.1, FE.1, and FE.2, show that $\mathbf{A}_1\sqrt{N}(\hat{\boldsymbol{\beta}}_{RE} - \boldsymbol{\beta}) - \mathbf{A}_2\sqrt{N}(\hat{\boldsymbol{\beta}}_{FE} - \boldsymbol{\beta})$ has an asymptotic variance matrix of rank M rather than $R + M$.

e. What implications does part d have for a Hausman test that compares FE and RE when the model contains aggregate time variables of any sort? Does it matter whether Assumption RE.3 holds under the null?

10.18. Use the data in WAGEPAN.RAW to answer this question.

a. Using *lwage* as the dependent variable, estimate a model that contains an intercept and the year dummies *d*81 through *d*87. Used pooled OLS, RE, FE, and FD (where in the latter case you difference the year dummies, along with *lwage*, and omit an overall constant in the FD regression). What do you conclude about the coefficients on the dummy variables?

b. Add the time-constant variables *educ*, *black*, and *hisp* to the model, and estimate it by POLS and RE. How do the coefficients compare? What happens if you estimate the equation by FE?

c. Are the POLS and RE standard errors from part b the same? Which ones are probably more reliable?

d. Obtain the fully robust standard errors for POLS. Do you prefer these or the usual RE standard errors?

e. Obtain the fully robust RE standard errors. How do these compare with the fully robust POLS standard errors, and why?

11 More Topics in Linear Unobserved Effects Models

This chapter continues our treatment of linear, unobserved effects panel data models. In Section 11.1 we briefly treat the GMM approach to estimating the standard, additive effect model from Chapter 10, emphasizing some equivalences between the standard estimators and GMM 3SLS estimators. In Section 11.2, we cover estimation of models where, at a minimum, the assumption of strict exogeneity conditional on the unobserved heterogeneity (Assumption FE.1) fails. Instead, we assume we have available instrumental variables (IVs) that are uncorrelated with the idiosyncratic errors in all time periods. Depending on whether these instruments are also uncorrelated with the unobserved effect, we are led to random effects or fixed effects IV methods. Section 11.3 shows how these methods apply to Hausman and Taylor (1981) models, where a subset of explanatory variables is allowed to be endogenous but enough explanatory variables are exogenous so that IV methods can be applied.

Section 11.4 combines first differencing with IV methods. In Section 11.5 we study the properties of fixed effects and first differencing estimators in the presence of measurement error, and propose some IV solutions. We explicitly cover unobserved effects models with sequentially exogenous explanatory variables, including models with lagged dependent variables, in Section 11.6. In Section 11.7, we turn to models with unit-specific slopes, including the important special case of unit-specific time trends.

11.1 Generalized Method of Moments Approaches to the Standard Linear Unobserved Effects Model

11.1.1 Equivalance between GMM 3SLS and Standard Estimators

In Chapter 10, we extensively covered estimation of the unobserved effects model

$$y_{it} = \mathbf{x}_{it}\boldsymbol{\beta} + c_i + u_{it}, \qquad t = 1, \ldots, T, \tag{11.1}$$

which we can write for all T time periods as

$$\mathbf{y}_i = \mathbf{X}_i\boldsymbol{\beta} + c_i\mathbf{j}_T + \mathbf{u}_i = \mathbf{X}_i\boldsymbol{\beta} + \mathbf{v}_i, \tag{11.2}$$

where $\mathbf{j}_T$ is the $T \times 1$ vector of ones, $\mathbf{u}_i$ is the $T \times 1$ vector of idiosyncratic errors, and $\mathbf{v}_i = c_i\mathbf{j}_T + \mathbf{u}_i$ is the $T \times 1$ vector of composite errors. Random effects (RE), fixed effects (FE), and first differencing (FD) are still the most popular approaches to estimating $\boldsymbol{\beta}$ in equation (11.1) with strictly exogenous explanatory variables. As we saw in Chapter 10, each of these estimators is consistent without restrictions on the variance-covariance matrix of the composite ($\mathbf{v}_i$) or idiosyncratic ($\mathbf{u}_i$) errors. We also saw that each estimator is asymptotically efficient under a particular set of assumptions on the conditional second moment matrix of $\mathbf{v}_i$ in the RE case, $\mathbf{u}_i$ in the FE case, and $\Delta\mathbf{u}_i$ in the FD case. Recall that there are two aspects to the second moment assumptions that imply asymptotic efficiency. First, the unconditional variance-covariance matrix is assumed to have a special structure. Second, system homoskedasticity is assumed in all cases. (Loosely, conditional variances and covariances do not depend on the explanatory variables.)

We have already seen how to allow for an unrestricted unconditional variance-covariance matrix in the context of RE, FE, and FD: we simply apply unrestricted FGLS to the appropriately transformed equations. Nevertheless, efficiency of, say, the FEGLS estimator hinges on the system homoskedasticity assumption $\mathrm{E}(\mathbf{u}_i\mathbf{u}_i' \mid \mathbf{x}_i, c_i) = \mathrm{E}(\mathbf{u}_i\mathbf{u}_i')$. Under RE.1, efficiency of the FGLS estimator with unrestricted $\mathrm{Var}(\mathbf{v}_i)$ is ensured only if $\mathrm{E}(\mathbf{v}_i\mathbf{v}_i' \mid \mathbf{x}_i) = \mathrm{E}(\mathbf{v}_i\mathbf{v}_i')$. If this assumption fails, GMM with an optimal weighting matrix is generally more efficient, and so it may be worthwhile to apply GMM methods to (11.2) (or, in the case of FE, a suitably transformed set of equations.)

We first suppose that Assumption RE.1 holds, so that $\mathbf{x}_{is}$ is uncorrelated with the composite error v_{it} for all s and t. (In fact, the zero conditional mean assumptions in Assumption RE.1 imply that $\mathrm{E}(\mathbf{v}_i \mid \mathbf{x}_i) = \mathbf{0}$, and so any function of $\mathbf{x}_i = (\mathbf{x}_{i1}, \mathbf{x}_{i2}, \ldots, \mathbf{x}_{iT})$ is uncorrelated with v_{it}. Here, we limit ourselves to linear functions.)

Let $\mathbf{x}_i^o$ denote the row vector of nonredundant elements of $\mathbf{x}_i$, so that any time-constant elements and aggregate time effects appear only once in $\mathbf{x}_i^o$. Then $\mathrm{E}(\mathbf{x}_i^{o\prime} v_{it}) = \mathbf{0}$, $t = 1, 2, \ldots, T$. This orthogonality condition suggests a system IV procedure, with matrix of instruments

$$\mathbf{Z}_i \equiv \mathbf{I}_T \otimes \mathbf{x}_i^o. \tag{11.3}$$

In other words, use instruments $\mathbf{Z}_i$ to estimate equation (11.2) by 3SLS or, more generally, by minimum chi-square.

The matrix (11.3) can contain many instruments. If $\mathbf{x}_{it}$ contains only variables that change across both i and t, then $\mathbf{Z}_i$ is $T \times T^2K$. With only K parameters to estimate, this choice of instruments implies many overidentifying restrictions even for moderately sized T. Even if computation is not an issue, using many overidentifying restrictions can result in poor finite sample properties.

In some cases, we can reduce the number of moment conditions without sacrificing efficiency. Im, Ahn, Schmidt, and Wooldridge (1999; IASW) show the following result. If $\hat{\mathbf{\Omega}}$ has the random effects structure—which means we impose the RE structure in estimating $\mathbf{\Omega}$—then GMM 3SLS applied to equation (11.2), using instruments

$$\mathbf{Z}_i \equiv (\mathbf{P}_T\mathbf{X}_i, \mathbf{Q}_T\mathbf{W}_i), \tag{11.4}$$

where $\mathbf{P}_T = \mathbf{j}_T(\mathbf{j}_T'\mathbf{j}_T)^{-1}\mathbf{j}_T'$, $\mathbf{Q}_T \equiv \mathbf{I}_T - \mathbf{P}_T$, $\mathbf{j}_T \equiv (1, 1, \ldots, 1)'$, and $\mathbf{W}_i$ is the $T \times M$ submatrix of $\mathbf{X}_i$ obtained by removing the time-constant variables, is identical to the RE estimator. The column dimension of matrix (11.4) is only $K + M$, so there are only M overidentifying restrictions in using the 3SLS estimator.

The algebraic equivalence between 3SLS and RE estimation has some useful applications. First, it provides a different way of testing the orthogonality between c_i and $\mathbf{x}_{it}$ for all t: after 3SLS estimation, we simply apply the GMM overidentification statistic from Chapter 8. (We discussed regression-based tests in Section 10.7.3.) Second, it provides a way to obtain a more efficient estimator when Assumption RE.3 does not hold. If $\boldsymbol{\Omega}$ does not have the RE structure (see equation (10.30)), then the 3SLS estimator that imposes this structure is inefficient; an unrestricted estimator of $\boldsymbol{\Omega}$ should be used instead. Because an unrestricted estimator of $\boldsymbol{\Omega}$ is consistent with or without the RE structure, 3SLS with unrestricted $\hat{\boldsymbol{\Omega}}$ and IVs in matrix (11.4) is no less efficient than the RE estimator. Further, if $\mathrm{E}(\mathbf{v}_i\mathbf{v}_i' \mid \mathbf{x}_i) \neq \mathrm{E}(\mathbf{v}_i\mathbf{v}_i')$, any 3SLS estimator is inefficient relative to GMM with the optimal weighting matrix. Therefore, if Assumption RE.3 fails, minimum chi-square estimation with IVs in matrix (11.4) generally improves on the random effects estimator. In other words, we can gain asymptotic efficiency by using only $M \leq K$ additional moment conditions.

A different 3SLS estimator can be shown to be equivalent to the FE estimator. In particular, IASW (1999, Theorem 4.1) verify an assertion of Arellano and Bover (1995): when $\hat{\boldsymbol{\Omega}}$ has the random effects form, the GMM 3SLS estimator applied to equation (11.2) using instruments $\mathbf{L}_T \otimes \mathbf{x}_i^o$—where $\mathbf{L}_T$ is the $T \times (T-1)$ differencing matrix defined in IASW (1999, eq. (4.1))—is identical to the FE estimator. Therefore, if we intend to use an RE structure for $\hat{\boldsymbol{\Omega}}$ in a GMM 3SLS analysis with instruments $\mathbf{L}_T \otimes \mathbf{x}_i^o$, we might as well just use the usual FE estimator applied to (11.2). But if we use an unrestricted form of $\hat{\boldsymbol{\Omega}}$—presumably because we think $\mathrm{E}(\mathbf{u}_i\mathbf{u}_i') \neq \sigma_u^2\mathbf{I}_T$—the GMM 3SLS estimator that uses instruments $\mathbf{L}_T \otimes \mathbf{x}_i^o$ is generally more efficient than FE if $\boldsymbol{\Omega}$ does not have the RE form. Further, if the system homoskedasticity assumption $\mathrm{E}(\mathbf{u}_i\mathbf{u}_i' \mid \mathbf{x}_i, c_i) = \mathrm{E}(\mathbf{u}_i\mathbf{u}_i')$ fails, GMM with the general optimal weighting matrix would usually increase efficiency over the GMM 3SLS estimator.

11.1.2 Chamberlain's Approach to Unobserved Effects Models

We now study an approach to estimating the linear unobserved effects model (11.1) due to Chamberlain (1982, 1984) and related to Mundlak (1978). We maintain the strict exogeneity assumption on $\mathbf{x}_{it}$ conditional on c_i (see Assumption FE.1), but we allow arbitrary correlation between c_i and $\mathbf{x}_{it}$. Thus we are in the FE environment, and $\mathbf{x}_{it}$ contains only time-varying explanatory variables.

In Chapter 10 we saw that the FE and FD transformations eliminate c_i and produce consistent estimators under strict exogeneity. Chamberlain's approach is to replace the unobserved effect c_i with its linear projection onto the explanatory variables in all time periods (plus the projection error). Assuming c_i and all elements of $\mathbf{x}_i$ have finite second moments, we can always write

$$c_i = \psi + \mathbf{x}_{i1}\boldsymbol{\lambda}_1 + \mathbf{x}_{i2}\boldsymbol{\lambda}_2 + \cdots + \mathbf{x}_{iT}\boldsymbol{\lambda}_T + a_i, \tag{11.5}$$

where ψ is a scalar and $\boldsymbol{\lambda}_1, \ldots, \boldsymbol{\lambda}_T$ are $1 \times K$ vectors. The projection error a_i, by definition, has zero mean and is uncorrelated with $\mathbf{x}_{i1}, \ldots, \mathbf{x}_{iT}$. This equation assumes nothing about the conditional distribution of c_i given $\mathbf{x}_i$. In particular, $\mathrm{E}(c_i \mid \mathbf{x}_i)$ is unrestricted, as in the usual FE analysis. Therefore, although equation (11.5) has the flavor of a correlated random effects specification, it does not restrict the dependence between c_i and $\mathbf{x}_i$ in any way.

Plugging equation (11.5) into equation (11.1) gives, for each t,

$$y_{it} = \psi + \mathbf{x}_{i1}\boldsymbol{\lambda}_1 + \cdots + \mathbf{x}_{it}(\boldsymbol{\beta} + \boldsymbol{\lambda}_t) + \cdots + \mathbf{x}_{iT}\boldsymbol{\lambda}_T + r_{it}, \tag{11.6}$$

where, under Assumption FE.1, the errors $r_{it} \equiv a_i + u_{it}$ satisfy

$$\mathrm{E}(r_{it}) = 0, \; \mathrm{E}(\mathbf{x}_i' r_{it}) = \mathbf{0}, \qquad t = 1, 2, \ldots, T. \tag{11.7}$$

However, unless we assume that $\mathrm{E}(c_i \mid \mathbf{x}_i)$ is linear, it is *not* the case that $\mathrm{E}(r_{it} \mid \mathbf{x}_i) = 0$. Nevertheless, assumption (11.7) suggests a variety of methods for estimating $\boldsymbol{\beta}$ (along with $\psi, \boldsymbol{\lambda}_1, \ldots, \boldsymbol{\lambda}_T$).

Write the system (11.6) for all time periods t as

$$\begin{pmatrix} y_{i1} \\ y_{i2} \\ \vdots \\ y_{iT} \end{pmatrix} = \begin{pmatrix} 1 & \mathbf{x}_{i1} & \mathbf{x}_{i2} & \cdots & \mathbf{x}_{iT} & \mathbf{x}_{i1} \\ 1 & \mathbf{x}_{i1} & \mathbf{x}_{i2} & \cdots & \mathbf{x}_{iT} & \mathbf{x}_{i2} \\ & & & \vdots & & \\ 1 & \mathbf{x}_{i1} & \mathbf{x}_{i2} & \cdots & \mathbf{x}_{iT} & \mathbf{x}_{iT} \end{pmatrix} \begin{pmatrix} \psi \\ \boldsymbol{\lambda}_1 \\ \boldsymbol{\lambda}_2 \\ \vdots \\ \boldsymbol{\lambda}_T \\ \boldsymbol{\beta} \end{pmatrix} + \begin{pmatrix} r_{i1} \\ r_{i2} \\ \vdots \\ r_{iT} \end{pmatrix}, \tag{11.8}$$

or

$$\mathbf{y}_i = \mathbf{W}_i\boldsymbol{\theta} + \mathbf{r}_i, \tag{11.9}$$

where $\mathbf{W}_i$ is $T \times (1 + TK + K)$ and $\boldsymbol{\theta}$ is $(1 + TK + K) \times 1$. From equation (11.7), $\mathrm{E}(\mathbf{W}_i'\mathbf{r}_i) = \mathbf{0}$, and so system OLS is one way to consistently estimate $\boldsymbol{\theta}$. The rank condition requires that rank $\mathrm{E}(\mathbf{W}_i'\mathbf{W}_i) = 1 + TK + K$; essentially, it suffices that the elements of $\mathbf{x}_{it}$ are not collinear and that they vary sufficiently over time. While system OLS is consistent, it is very unlikely to be the most efficient estimator. Not only is the scalar variance assumption $\mathrm{E}(\mathbf{r}_i\mathbf{r}_i') = \sigma_r^2\mathbf{I}_T$ highly unlikely, but also the homoskedasticity assumption

$$\mathrm{E}(\mathbf{r}_i\mathbf{r}_i' \mid \mathbf{x}_i) = \mathrm{E}(\mathbf{r}_i\mathbf{r}_i') \tag{11.10}$$

fails unless we impose further assumptions. Generally, assumption (11.10) is violated if $\mathrm{E}(\mathbf{u}_i\mathbf{u}_i' \mid c_i, \mathbf{x}_i) \neq \mathrm{E}(\mathbf{u}_i\mathbf{u}_i')$, if $\mathrm{E}(c_i \mid \mathbf{x}_i)$ is not linear in $\mathbf{x}_i$, or if $\mathrm{Var}(c_i \mid \mathbf{x}_i)$ is not constant.

If assumption (11.10) does happen to hold, feasible GLS is a natural approach. The matrix $\mathbf{\Omega} = \mathrm{E}(\mathbf{r}_i\mathbf{r}_i')$ can be consistently estimated by first estimating $\boldsymbol{\theta}$ by system OLS, and then proceeding with FGLS as in Section 7.5.

If assumption (11.10) fails, a more efficient estimator is obtained by applying GMM to equation (11.9) with the optimal weighting matrix. Because r_{it} is orthogonal to $\mathbf{x}_i^o = (1, \mathbf{x}_{i1}, \ldots, \mathbf{x}_{iT})$, $\mathbf{x}_i^o$ can be used as instruments for each time period, and so we choose the matrix of instruments (11.3). Interestingly, the 3SLS estimator, which uses $[\mathbf{Z}'(\mathbf{I}_N \otimes \hat{\mathbf{\Omega}})\mathbf{Z}/N]^{-1}$ as the weighting matrix—see Section 8.3.4—is numerically identical to FGLS with the same $\hat{\mathbf{\Omega}}$. Arellano and Bover (1995) showed this result in the special case that $\hat{\mathbf{\Omega}}$ has the random effects structure, and IASW (1999, Theorem 3.1) obtained the general case.

In expression (11.9) there are $1 + TK + K$ parameters, and the matrix of instruments is $T \times T(1 + TK)$; there are $T(1 + TK) - (1 + TK + K) = (T - 1)(1 + TK) - K$ overidentifying restrictions. Testing these restrictions is precisely a test of the strict exogeneity Assumption FE.1, and it is a fully robust test when full GMM is used because no additional assumptions are used.

Chamberlain (1982) works from the system (11.8) under assumption (11.7), but he uses a different estimation approach, known as minimum distance estimation. We cover this approach to estimation in Chapter 14.

11.2 Random and Fixed Effects Instrumental Variables Methods

In this section we study estimation methods when some of the explanatory variables are not strictly exogenous. RE and FE estimations assume strict exogeneity of the instruments conditional on the unobserved effect, and RE estimation adds the assumption that the IVs are actually uncorrelated with the unobserved effect.

We again start with the model (11.1). In Chapter 10 and in Section 11.1, we covered methods that assume, at a minimum,

$$\mathrm{E}(\mathbf{x}_{is}'u_{it}) = \mathbf{0}, \qquad s, t = 1, \ldots, T. \tag{11.11}$$

(The one exception was pooled OLS, but POLS assumes $\mathbf{x}_{it}$ is uncorrelated with c_i.) If we are willing to assume (11.11), but no more, then, as we saw in Chapter 10 and Section 11.1, we can consistently estimate the coefficients on the time-varying elements of $\mathbf{x}_{it}$ by FE, FD, GLS versions of these, or GMM. The next goal is to relax assumption (11.11).

Without assumption (11.11), we generally require IVs in order to consistently estimate the parameters. Let $\{\mathbf{z}_{it} : t = 1, \ldots, T\}$ be a sequence of $1 \times L$ IV candidates, where $L \geq K$. As we discussed in Chapter 8, a simple estimator is the pooled 2SLS estimator (P2SLS). With an unobserved effect explicitly in the error term, consistency of P2SLS essentially relies on

$$\mathrm{E}(\mathbf{z}_{it}'c_i) = \mathbf{0}, \qquad t = 1, \ldots, T \tag{11.12}$$

and

$$\mathrm{E}(\mathbf{z}_{it}'u_{it}) = \mathbf{0}, \qquad t = 1, \ldots, T \tag{11.13}$$

along with a suitable rank condition (which you are invited to supply). Pooled 2SLS estimation is simple, and it is straightforward to make inference robust to arbitrary heteroskedasticity and serial correlation in the composite errors, $\{v_{it} = c_i + u_{it} : t = 1, \ldots, T\}$. But if we are willing to assume (11.12) along with (11.13), we probably are willing to assume that the instruments are actually strictly exogenous (after removing c_i), that is,

$$\mathrm{E}(\mathbf{z}_{is}'u_{it}) = \mathbf{0}, \qquad s, t = 1, \ldots, T. \tag{11.14}$$

Assumptions (11.12) and (11.14) suggest that, under certain assumptions, an RE approach can be more efficient than a pooled 2SLS analysis. The **random effects instrumental variables (REIV) estimator** is simply a generalized IV (GIV) estimator applied to

$$\mathbf{y}_i = \mathbf{X}_i\boldsymbol{\beta} + \mathbf{v}_i, \tag{11.15}$$

where $\mathbf{X}_i$ is $T \times K$, as usual, and the matrix of instruments $\mathbf{Z}_i \equiv (\mathbf{z}_{i1}', \mathbf{z}_{i2}', \ldots, \mathbf{z}_{iT}')'$ is $T \times L$. What makes the REIV estimator special in the class of GIV estimators is that $\boldsymbol{\Omega} \equiv \mathrm{E}(\mathbf{v}_i\mathbf{v}_i')$ is assumed to have the RE form, just as in equation (10.30).

Assuming, for the moment, that $\boldsymbol{\Omega}$ is known, the REIV estimator can be obtained as the system 2SLS estimator (see Chapter 8) of

$$\boldsymbol{\Omega}^{-1/2}\mathbf{y}_i = \boldsymbol{\Omega}^{-1/2}\mathbf{X}_i\boldsymbol{\beta} + \boldsymbol{\Omega}^{-1/2}\mathbf{v}_i \tag{11.16}$$

using transformed instruments $\boldsymbol{\Omega}^{-1/2}\mathbf{Z}_i$. The form of the estimator is given in equation (8.47).

As we discussed in Chapter 8, consistency of the GIV estimator when $\boldsymbol{\Omega}$ is not diagonal—as expected in the current framework because of the presence of c_i, not to mention possible serial correlation in $\{u_{it} : t = 1, \ldots, T\}$—hinges critically on the strict exogeneity of the instruments: $\mathrm{E}(\mathbf{z}_{is}' v_{it}) = \mathbf{0}$ for all $s, t = 1, \ldots, T$. Without this assumption the REIV estimator is inconsistent.

Naturally, we have to estimate $\boldsymbol{\Omega}$—imposing the RE form—but this follows our treatment for the usual RE estimator. The first-stage estimator is pooled 2SLS. Given the P2SLS residuals, we can estimate σ_v^2 and σ_c^2 just as in equations (10.35) and (10.37).

We summarize with a set of assumptions, which are somewhat stronger than necessary for consistency (because we can always get by with zero covariances) but have the advantage of simplifying inference under the full set of assumptions.

ASSUMPTION REIV.1: (a) $\mathrm{E}(u_{it} \mid \mathbf{z}_i, c_i) = 0$, $t = 1, \ldots, T$; (b) $\mathrm{E}(c_i \mid \mathbf{z}_i) = \mathrm{E}(c_i) = 0$, where $\mathbf{z}_i \equiv (\mathbf{z}_{i1}, \ldots, \mathbf{z}_{iT})$.

As usual, the assumption that c_i has a zero mean is without loss of generality provided we include an intercept in the model, which we always assume here.

The rank condition is

ASSUMPTION REIV.2: (a) rank $\mathrm{E}(\mathbf{Z}_i'\boldsymbol{\Omega}^{-1}\mathbf{Z}_i) = L$; (b) rank $\mathrm{E}(\mathbf{Z}_i'\boldsymbol{\Omega}^{-1}\mathbf{X}_i) = K$.

Because Assumption RE.1 implies Assumption GIV.1 and Assumption RE.2 is Assumption GIV.2, the REIV estimator is consistent under these two assumptions. Without further assumptions, a valid asymptotic variance estimator of $\hat{\boldsymbol{\beta}}_{REIV}$ should be fully robust to heteroskedasticity and any pattern of serial correlation in $\{v_{it}\}$. The formula is long but standard; see Problem 11.18.

Typically, the default is to add an assumption that simplifies inference:

ASSUMPTION REIV.3: (a) $\mathrm{E}(\mathbf{u}_i'\mathbf{u}_i \mid \mathbf{Z}_i, c_i) = \sigma_u^2 \mathbf{I}_T$; (b) $\mathrm{E}(c_i^2 \mid \mathbf{Z}_i) = \sigma_c^2$.

As in the case of standard RE, the particular form of $\boldsymbol{\Omega}$ is motivated by Assumption REIV.3 and the estimator is the asymptotically efficient IV estimator under the full set of assumptions. The simplified (nonrobust) form of the asymptotic variance estimator can be expressed as

$$\widehat{\mathrm{Avar}(\hat{\boldsymbol{\beta}}_{REIV})} = \left[\left(\sum_{i=1}^{N} \mathbf{X}_i'\hat{\boldsymbol{\Omega}}^{-1}\mathbf{Z}_i\right)\left(\sum_{i=1}^{N} \mathbf{Z}_i'\hat{\boldsymbol{\Omega}}^{-1}\mathbf{Z}_i\right)^{-1}\left(\sum_{i=1}^{N} \mathbf{Z}_i'\hat{\boldsymbol{\Omega}}^{-1}\mathbf{X}_i\right)\right]^{-1}. \tag{11.17}$$

This matrix can be used to construct asymptotic standard errors and Wald tests, but it does rely on Assumption REIV.3.

Given that the usual RE estimator can be obtained from a pooled OLS regression on quasi-time-demeaned data, it comes as no surprise that a similar result holds for the REIV estimator. Let $\breve{y}_{it} = y_{it} - \hat{\lambda}\bar{y}_i$, $\breve{\mathbf{x}}_{it} = \mathbf{x}_{it} - \hat{\lambda}\bar{\mathbf{x}}_i$, and $\breve{\mathbf{z}}_{it} = \mathbf{z}_{it} - \hat{\lambda}\bar{\mathbf{z}}_i$ be the transform-dependent variable, regressors, and IVs, respectively, where $\hat{\lambda}$ is given as in equation (10.81) (but where the P2SLS residuals, rather than the POLS residuals, are used to obtain $\hat{\sigma}_c^2$ and $\hat{\sigma}_u^2$). Then the REIV estimator can be obtained as the P2SLS estimator on

$$\breve{y}_{it} = \breve{\mathbf{x}}_{it}\boldsymbol{\beta} + error_{it}, \qquad t = 1, \ldots, T; i = 1, \ldots, N, \tag{11.18}$$

using IVs $\breve{\mathbf{z}}_{it}$. This formulation makes fully robust inference especially easy using any econometrics packages that compute heteroskedasticity and serial correlation robust standard errors and test statistics for pooled 2SLS estimation. Because of its interpretation as a pooled 2SLS estimator on transformed data, the REIV estimator is sometimes called the **random effects 2SLS estimator**. Baltagi (1981) calls it the *error components 2SLS estimator*.

It is straightforward to adapt standard specification tests to the REIV framework. For example, we can test the null hypothesis that a set of explanatory variables is exogenous by modifying the control function approach from Chapter 6. Suppose we write an unobserved effects model as

$$y_{it1} = \mathbf{z}_{it1}\boldsymbol{\delta}_1 + \mathbf{y}_{it2}\boldsymbol{\alpha}_1 + \mathbf{y}_{it3}\boldsymbol{\gamma}_1 + c_{i1} + u_{it1}, \tag{11.19}$$

where $v_{it1} \equiv c_{i1} + u_{it1}$ is the composite error, and we want to test $\mathrm{H}_0 : \mathrm{E}(\mathbf{y}_{it3}' v_{it1}) = \mathbf{0}$. Actually, in an RE environment, it only makes sense to maintain strict exogeneity of the $1 \times J_1$ vector $\mathbf{y}_{it3}$ under the null. The variables $\mathbf{y}_{it2}$ are allowed to be endogenous under the null—provided, of course, that we have sufficient instruments excluded from (11.19) that are uncorrelated with the composite errors in every time period. We can write a reduced form for $\mathbf{y}_{it3}$ as

$$\mathbf{y}_{it3} = \mathbf{z}_{it}\boldsymbol{\Pi}_3 + \mathbf{v}_{it3}, \tag{11.20}$$

and then we augment (11.19) by including $\mathbf{v}_{it3}\boldsymbol{\rho}$. Of course, we must decide how to estimate (11.20) to obtain residuals, $\hat{\mathbf{v}}_{it3} = \mathbf{y}_{it3} - \mathbf{z}_{it}\hat{\boldsymbol{\Pi}}_3$, where the columns of $\hat{\boldsymbol{\Pi}}_3$ can be pooled OLS or standard RE estimates. That is, we can estimate the J_1 equations in (11.20) separately by pooled OLS or by RE. Either way, to obtain the test, we simply estimate

$$y_{it1} = \mathbf{z}_{it1}\boldsymbol{\delta}_1 + \mathbf{y}_{it2}\boldsymbol{\alpha}_1 + \mathbf{y}_{it3}\boldsymbol{\gamma}_1 + \hat{\mathbf{v}}_{it3}\boldsymbol{\rho}_1 + error_{it1} \tag{11.21}$$

by REIV, using instruments $(\mathbf{z}_{it}, \mathbf{y}_{it3}, \hat{\mathbf{v}}_{it3})$, and test $\mathrm{H}_0 : \boldsymbol{\rho}_1 = \mathbf{0}$ using a Wald test. Under the null hypothesis that $\mathbf{y}_{is3}$ is strictly exogenous (with respect to $\{v_{it1}\}$), we can ignore the first-stage estimation. (Actually, if we use the usual, nonrobust test, then the null is Assumptions RE.1–RE.3 but with the instruments for time period t given by $(\mathbf{z}_{it}, \mathbf{y}_{it3})$.) We might, of course, want to make the test robust to violation of the RE variance structure as well as to system heteroskedasticity.

Testing overidentifying restrictions is also straightforward. Now write the equation as

$$y_{it1} = \mathbf{z}_{it1}\boldsymbol{\delta}_1 + \mathbf{y}_{it2}\boldsymbol{\alpha}_1 + c_{i1} + u_{it1}, \tag{11.22}$$

where $\mathbf{z}_{it2}$ is the $1 \times L_2$ vector of exogenous variables excluded from (11.19). We assume $L_2 > G_1 = \dim(\mathbf{y}_{it2})$, and write $\mathbf{z}_{it2} = (\mathbf{g}_{it2}, \mathbf{h}_{it2})$, where $\mathbf{g}_{it2}$ is $1 \times G_1$—the same dimension as $\mathbf{y}_{it2}$—and $\mathbf{h}_{it2}$ is $1 \times Q_1$—the number of overidentifying restrictions. As discussed in Section 6.3.1, it does not matter how we choose $\mathbf{h}_{it2}$ provided it has Q_1 elements. (In the case where the model contains separate time period intercepts, these would be included in $\mathbf{z}_{it1}$ and then act as their own instruments. Therefore, $\mathbf{h}_{it2}$ never includes aggregate time effects.)

The test is obtained as follows. Obtain the quasi-time-demeaned RE residuals, $\hat{\breve{u}}_{it1} = \hat{u}_{it} - \hat{\lambda}\bar{\hat{u}}_i$, where $\hat{u}_{it} = y_{it1} - \mathbf{x}_{it1}\hat{\boldsymbol{\beta}}_1$ are the RE residuals (with $\mathbf{x}_{it1} = (\mathbf{z}_{it1}, \mathbf{y}_{it2})$), along with the quasi-time-demeaned explanatory variables and instruments, $\breve{\mathbf{x}}_{it1} = \mathbf{x}_{it1} - \hat{\lambda}\bar{\mathbf{x}}_{i1}$ and $\breve{\mathbf{z}}_{it} = \mathbf{z}_{it} - \hat{\lambda}\bar{\mathbf{z}}_i$. Let $\hat{\breve{\mathbf{y}}}_{it2}$ be the fitted values from the first stage pooled regression $\breve{\mathbf{y}}_{it2}$ on $\breve{\mathbf{z}}_{it}$. Next, use pooled OLS of $\breve{\mathbf{h}}_{it2}$ on $\breve{\mathbf{z}}_{it1}$, $\hat{\breve{\mathbf{y}}}_{it2}$ and obtain the $1 \times Q_1$ residuals, $\hat{\breve{\mathbf{r}}}_{it2}$. Finally, use the augmented equation

$$\breve{u}_{it1} = \hat{\breve{\mathbf{r}}}_{it2}\boldsymbol{\eta}_1 + error_{it1} \tag{11.23}$$

to test $\mathrm{H}_0 : \boldsymbol{\eta}_1 = \mathbf{0}$ by computing a Wald statistic that is robust to both heteroskedasticity and serial correlation. If Assumption REIV.3 is maintained under H_0, the usual F test from the pooled OLS regression in equation (11.23) is asymptotically valid.

As is clear from the preceding analysis, a random effects approach allows some regressors to be correlated with c_i and u_{it} in (11.1), but the instruments are assumed to be strictly exogenous with respect to the idiosyncratic errors *and* to be uncorrelated with c_i. In many applications, instruments are arguably uncorrelated with idiosyncratic shocks in all time periods but might be correlated with historical or immutable factors contained in c_{i1}. In such cases, a fixed effects approach is preferred.

As in the case with regressors satisfying (11.2), we use the within transformation to eliminate c_i from (11.1):

$$y_{it} - \bar{y}_i = (\mathbf{x}_{it} - \bar{\mathbf{x}}_i)\boldsymbol{\beta} + u_{it} - \bar{u}_i, \qquad t = 1, \ldots, T, \tag{11.24}$$

which makes it clear that time-constant explanatory variables are eliminated, as in standard FE analysis. If we estimate equation (11.24) by P2SLS using instruments $\ddot{\mathbf{z}}_{it} \equiv \mathbf{z}_{it} - \bar{\mathbf{z}}_i$ ($1 \times L$ with $L \geq K$), we obtain the **fixed effects instrumental variables (FEIV) estimator** or the **fixed effects 2SLS (FE2SLS) estimator**. Because for each i we have $\sum_{t=1}^{T} \mathbf{z}_{it}'(\mathbf{x}_{it} - \bar{\mathbf{x}}_i) = \sum_{t=1}^{T} (\mathbf{z}_{it} - \bar{\mathbf{z}}_i)'(\mathbf{x}_{it} - \bar{\mathbf{x}}_i)$ and $\sum_{t=1}^{T} \mathbf{z}_{it}'(y_{it} - \bar{y}_i) = \sum_{t=1}^{T} (\mathbf{z}_{it} - \bar{\mathbf{z}}_i)'(y_{it} - \bar{y}_i)$, it does not matter whether or not we time demean the instruments. But using $\ddot{\mathbf{z}}_{it}$ emphasizes that FEIV works only when the instruments vary over time. (For an REIV analysis, instruments can be constant over time provided they satisfy Assumptions REIV.1 and REIV.2.)

Sufficient conditions for consistency of the FE2SLS estimator are immediate. Not surprisingly, a sufficient exogeneity condition for consistency of FEIV is simply the first part of the exogeneity assumption for REIV:

ASSUMPTION FEIV.1: $\mathrm{E}(u_{it} \mid \mathbf{z}_i, c_i) = 0$, $t = 1, \ldots, T$.

In practice, it is important to remember that Assumption FEIV.1 is strict exogeneity of the instruments conditional on c_i; it allows arbitrary correlation between $\mathbf{z}_{it}$ and c_i for all t. The rank condition is

ASSUMPTION FEIV.2: (a) rank $\sum_{t=1}^{T} \mathrm{E}(\ddot{\mathbf{z}}_{it}'\ddot{\mathbf{z}}_{it}) = L$; (b) rank $\sum_{t=1}^{T} \mathrm{E}(\ddot{\mathbf{z}}_{it}'\ddot{\mathbf{x}}_{it}) = K$.

As usual, we can relax FEIV.1 to just assuming $\mathbf{z}_{is}$ and u_{it} are uncorrelated for all s and t. But if we impose Assumptions FEIV.1, FEIV.2, and

ASSUMPTION FEIV.3: $\mathrm{E}(\mathbf{u}_i\mathbf{u}_i' \mid \mathbf{z}_i, c_i) = \sigma_u^2 \mathbf{I}_T$,

then we can apply standard pooled 2SLS inference on the time-demeaned data, provided we take care in estimating σ_u^2. As in Section 10.5, we must use a degrees-of-freedom adjustment for the sum of squared residuals (effectively for the lost time period for each i). See equation (10.56), where we now use the FE2SLS residuals, $\hat{\ddot{u}}_{it} = \ddot{y}_{it} - \ddot{\mathbf{x}}_{it}\hat{\boldsymbol{\beta}}_{FE2SLS}$, in place of the usual FE residuals. Problem 11.9 asks you to work through some of the details.

As with REIV methods, testing a subset of variables for endogeneity and testing overidentification restrictions are immediate. Rather than estimate equation (11.21) by REIV, we use FEIV, where $\hat{\mathbf{v}}_{it3}$ is conveniently replaced with $\hat{\ddot{\mathbf{v}}}_{it3}$, the FE residuals from estimating the reduced form of each element of $\mathbf{y}_{it3}$ by fixed effects. (So, in the scalar case, we estimate $y_{it3} = \mathbf{z}_{it}\boldsymbol{\pi}_3 + a_{i3} + v_{it3}$ by fixed effects and then compute $\hat{\ddot{v}}_{it3} = \ddot{y}_{it3} - \ddot{\mathbf{z}}_{it}\hat{\boldsymbol{\pi}}_3$.) It is important to remember that, unlike the test in the REIV case, the FEIV test does not maintain Assumption REIV.1b under the null. That is, for FE, exogeneity of $\mathbf{y}_{it3}$ does not include that it is uncorrelated with c_{i1}, something we know well from Chapter 10.

To test overidentifying restrictions, we let $\hat{\ddot{u}}_{it1}$ be the FEIV residuals, let $\ddot{\mathbf{z}}_{it}$ denote the time-demeaned instruments, and let $\hat{\ddot{\mathbf{y}}}_{it2}$ be the fitted values from the first-stage pooled OLS regression $\ddot{\mathbf{y}}_{it2}$ on $\ddot{\mathbf{z}}_{it}$. Then, the $1 \times Q_1$ residuals $\hat{\ddot{\mathbf{r}}}_{it2}$ are obtained from the pooled OLS regression $\ddot{\mathbf{h}}_{it2}$ on $\ddot{\mathbf{z}}_{it1}$, $\hat{\ddot{\mathbf{y}}}_{it2}$. To obtain a valid test statistic, we use $\hat{\ddot{u}}_{it1}$ and $\hat{\ddot{\mathbf{r}}}_{it2}$ in place of $\hat{\ddot{u}}_{it1}$ and $\hat{\ddot{\mathbf{r}}}_{it2}$, respectively, in equation (11.23). Again, a fully robust test of $\mathrm{H}_0: \boldsymbol{\eta}_1 = \mathbf{0}$ is preferred. If one maintains Assumption FEIV.3 under the null, some care is needed in estimating $\mathrm{Var}(u_{it1}) = \sigma_1^2$. Implicitly, the variance estimator obtained by using the pooled regression $\hat{\ddot{u}}_{it1}$ on $\hat{\ddot{\mathbf{r}}}_{it2}$, $t = 1, \ldots T$, $i = 1, \ldots, N$ uses the sum of squared residuals divided by $NT - Q_1$, whereas the correct factor is $N(T-1) - Q_1$. Therefore, the nonrobust Wald statistic from pooled OLS should be multiplied by $[N(T-1) - Q_1]/(NT - Q_1)$.

With FEIV, we are testing whether the time-demeaned extra instruments, $\ddot{\mathbf{h}}_{it2}$, are uncorrelated with the idiosyncratic errors, and not that they are also uncorrelated with the unobserved effect. This is as it should be, as consistency of the FEIV estimator does not hinge on $\mathrm{E}(\mathbf{z}_{it}'c_i) = \mathbf{0}$. Now, of course, all instruments—including those in $\mathbf{h}_{it2}$—must vary over time (and the elements of $\mathbf{h}_{it2}$ must vary across i, too).

If $\mathrm{E}(\mathbf{u}_i\mathbf{u}_i') \neq \sigma_u^2\mathbf{I}_T$ but we nominally think $\mathrm{E}(\mathbf{u}_i\mathbf{u}_i' \mid \mathbf{z}_i, c_i) = \mathrm{E}(\mathbf{u}_i\mathbf{u}_i')$, we can obtain a more efficient estimator by applying GIV to the set of equations

$$\ddot{\mathbf{y}}_i = \ddot{\mathbf{X}}_i\boldsymbol{\beta} + \ddot{\mathbf{u}}_i, \tag{11.25}$$

where we drop one time period to avoid singularity of the error variance matrix. We apply the GIV estimator to (11.25) using instruments $\ddot{\mathbf{Z}}_i$. The formula is given by equation (8.47) but with the time-demeaned matrices (minus one time period). Naturally, we would use the FE2SLS estimator in the first stage to estimate $\boldsymbol{\Omega}$. We may want to use a fully robust variance matrix in case system homoskedasticity fails.

The Hausman principle can be applied for comparing the FEIV and REIV estimators, at least for the coefficients on the variables that change across i and t. As in Section 10.7.3, a regression-based test is easiest to carry out (but one should always compare the magnitudes of the FEIV and REIV estimates to see whether they are different in practically important ways). If we maintain Assumption RE.1a—which underlies consistency of both estimators—then we can view the Hausman test as a test of $\mathrm{E}(c_i \mid \mathbf{z}_i) = \mathrm{E}(c_i)$, and this is the usual interpretation of the test. As before, we specify as an alternative a correlated random effects structure, using the subset $\mathbf{w}_{it}$ of $\mathbf{z}_{it}$ that varies across i and t, $c_i = \xi_0 + \bar{\mathbf{z}}_i\boldsymbol{\xi} + a_i$, and then augment the orginal equation (absorbing ξ_0 into the intercept):

$$y_{it} = \mathbf{x}_{it}\boldsymbol{\beta} + \overline{\mathbf{w}}_i\boldsymbol{\xi} + a_i + u_{it}. \tag{11.26}$$

Now, estimate (11.26) by REIV using instruments $(\mathbf{z}_{it}, \overline{\mathbf{w}}_i)$ and test $\xi = 0$. If we make the test robust, then we are not maintaining Assumption REIV.3 under H_0. We can also estimate (11.26) by pooled 2SLS and obtain a fully robust test.

REIV and FEIV methods can be applied to simultaneous equations models for panel data, models with time-varying omitted variables, and panel data models with measurement error. The following example uses airline route concentration ratios to estimate a passenger demand equation.

Example 11.1 (Demand for Air Travel): The data set AIRFARE.RAW contains information on passengers, airfare, and route concentration ratios for 1,149 routes within the United States for the years 1997 through 2000. We estimate a simple demand model

$$\log(passen_{it}) = \theta_{t1} + \alpha_1 \log(fare_{it}) + \delta_1 \log(dist_i) + \delta_2[\log(dist_i)]^2 + c_{i1} + u_{it1}, \tag{11.27}$$

where we allow for separate year intercepts. The variable $dist_i$ is the route distance, in miles; naturally, it does not change over time.

We estimate this equation using four different methods: RE, FE, REIV, and FEIV, where the variable $\log(fare_{it})$ is treated as endogenous in the latter two cases. The IV for $\log(fare_{it})$ is $concen_{it}$, the fraction of route traffic accounted for by the largest carrier. For the REIV estimation, the distance variables are treated as exogenous controls. Of course, they drop out of the FE and FEIV estimation.

For the IV estimation, we can think of the reduced form as being

$$\log(fare_{it}) = \theta_{t2} + \pi_{21} concen_{it} + \pi_{22} \log(dist_i) + \pi_{23}[\log(dist_i)]^2 + c_{i2} + u_{it2}, \tag{11.28}$$

which is (implicitly) estimated by RE or FE, depending on whether (11.27) is estimated by REIV or FEIV. The results of the estimation are given in Table 11.1.

The RE and FE estimated elasticities of passenger demand with respect to airfare are very similar (about -1.1 and -1.2, respectively), and neither is statistically different from -1. The closeness of these estimates is, perhaps, not too surprising, given that $\hat{\lambda} = .915$ for the RE estimation. This indicates that most of the variation in the composite error is estimated to be due to c_{i1}, but, as we remember, that calculation assumes that $\{u_{it1}\}$ is serially uncorrelated.

The large increase in standard errors when we allow for arbitary serial correlation (and, less importantly, heteroskedasticity) suggests the idiosyncratic errors are not serially uncorrelated. The robust standard error for RE, .102, is almost five times as large as the nonrobust standard error, .022. The increase for FE is not quite as dramatic but is still substantial. In either case, the 95 percent confidence intervals are

Table 11.1
Passenger Demand Model, United States Domestic Routes, 1997–2000

Dependent Variable	log(*passen*)			
Explanatory Variable	(1) Random Effects	(2) Fixed Effects	(3) REIV	(4) FEIV
log(*fare*)	−1.102	−1.155	−.508	−.302
	(.022)	(.023)	(.230)	(.277)
	[.102]	[.083]	[.498]	[.613]
log(*dist*)	−1.971	—	−1.505	—
	(.647)		(.693)	
	[.704]		[.784]	
$[\log(dist)]^2$	.171	—	.118	—
	(.049)		(.055)	
	[.054]		[.067]	
$\hat{\lambda}$	.915		.911	
N	1,149	1,149	1,149	1,149

All estimation methods include year dummies for 1998, 1999, and 2000 (not reported).
The usual, nonrobust standard errors are in parentheses below the estimated coefficients. Standard errors robust to arbitrary heteroskedasticity and serial correlation are in brackets.
All standard errors for RE and FE were obtained using the xtreg command in Stata 9.0. The nonrobust standard errors for REIV and FEIV were obtained using the command xtivreg. The fully robust standard errors were obtained using P2SLS on the quasi-time-demeaned and time-demeaned data, respectively.

much wider when we use the more reliable robust standard errors. Clearly, given the closeness of the elasticity estimates, there is no point formally comparing RE and FE via a Hausman test.

Of course, even the FE estimator assumes that $\log(fare_{it})$ is uncorrelated with $\{u_{it1} : t = 1, \ldots, T\}$, and this assumption could easily fail. Columns (3) and (4) use *concen* as an IV for log(*fare*). (The reduced form for log(*fare*) depends positively and in a statistically significant way on *concen*, whether we use RE or FE, and using fully robust standard errors.) The REIV estimator assumes that the concentration ratio is uncorrelated with the idiosyncratic errors as well as the route heterogeneity, c_{i1}. Even so, the estimated elasticity, −.508, is about half the size of the RE estimate. Based on the nonrobust standard error, this elasticity is statistically different from zero (as well as −1) at the 5 percent significance level. But when we use the more realistic robust standard error, the elasticity becomes statistically insignificant; its robust t statistic is about −1.02. Therefore, once we instrument for log(*fare*) and use robust inference, we can say very little about the true elasticity.

The estimated elasticity for FEIV is even smaller in magnitude and even less precisely estimated. The estimated elasticity, −.302, is not even statistically different from zero when we use the overly optimistic nonrobust standard error. The fully robust t statistic is less than .5 in magnitude.

We can use the Hausman test—which is a simple t statistic in this example—to compare the models a few different ways. We consider only two. First, because the FEIV and FE estimates are practically different, we might want to know whether there is statistically significant evidence that $\log(fare_{it})$ is endogenous (correlated with the idiosyncratic errors). Of course, we must maintain strict exogeneity of $concen_{it}$, but only in the sense that it is uncorrelated with $\{u_{it1}\}$. We obtain the FE residuals, $\hat{\ddot{v}}_{it2}$ from the reduced form estimation. Then we add $\hat{\ddot{v}}_{it2}$ to equation (11.27), estimate it by standard FE, and obtain the t statistic on $\hat{\ddot{v}}_{it2}$. Its nonrobust t statistic is -3.68, but the fully robust statistic is only -1.63, which implies a marginal statistical rejection. Given the large differences in elasticity estimates between FE and FEIV, one would not feel comfortable relying on the FE estimates.

We can also check for statistical significance between REIV and FEIV. In this case, the easiest way to implement the test is to estimate the original equation, augmented by the time average $\overline{concen}_i$, by REIV and use the usual t statistic on $\overline{concen}_i$ or the robust form. (A simpler procedure works for obtaining the fully robust statistic: just estimate the augmented equation by pooled IV and use the fully robust t statistic on $\overline{concen}_i$.) The nonrobust t statistic on $\overline{concen}_i$ is -3.08 while the robust t statistic is -2.00. Interestingly, neither estimate is statistically different from zero, but they are statistically different from each other, at least marginally.

Panel data methods combined with IVs have many applications to models with simultaneity or omitted time-varying variables. For example, Foster and Rosenzweig (1995) use the FEIV approach to the effects of adoption of high-yielding seed varieties on household-level profits in rural India. Ayers and Levitt (1998) apply FE2SLS to estimate the effect of Lojack electronic theft prevention devices on city car-theft rates. Papke (2005) applies FE2SLS to building-level panel data on test pass rates and per-student spending. In each of these cases, unit-specific heterogeneity is eliminated, and then IVs are used for the suspected endogenous explanatory variable.

11.3 Hausman and Taylor–Type Models

The results of Section 11.2 apply to a class of unobserved effects models studied by Hausman and Taylor (1981) (HT). The key feature of these models is that the assumptions imply the availability of instrumental variables from within the model; one need not look outside the model for exogenous variables.

The HT model can be written as

$$y_{it} = \mathbf{w}_i\gamma + \mathbf{x}_{it}\boldsymbol{\beta} + c_i + u_{it}, \qquad t = 1, 2, \ldots, T, \tag{11.29}$$

where all elements of $\mathbf{x}_{it}$ display some time variation, and it is convenient to include unity in $\mathbf{w}_i$ and assume that $\mathrm{E}(c_i) = 0$. We assume strict exogeneity conditional on c_i:

$$\mathrm{E}(u_{it} \mid \mathbf{w}_i, \mathbf{x}_{i1}, \ldots, \mathbf{x}_{iT}, c_i) = 0, \qquad t = 1, \ldots, T. \tag{11.30}$$

Estimation of $\boldsymbol{\beta}$ can proceed by FE: the FE transformation eliminates $\mathbf{w}_i \gamma$ and c_i. As usual, this approach places no restrictions on the correlation between c_i and $(\mathbf{w}_i, \mathbf{x}_{it})$.

What about estimation of γ? If in addition to assumption (11.30) we assume

$$\mathrm{E}(\mathbf{w}_i' c_i) = \mathbf{0}, \tag{11.31}$$

then a $\sqrt{N}$-consistent estimator is easy to obtain: average equation (11.29) across t, premultiply by $\mathbf{w}_i'$, take expectations, use the fact that $\mathrm{E}[\mathbf{w}_i'(c_i + \bar{u}_i)] = \mathbf{0}$, and rearrange to get

$$\mathrm{E}(\mathbf{w}_i'\mathbf{w}_i)\gamma = \mathrm{E}[\mathbf{w}_i'(\bar{y}_i - \bar{\mathbf{x}}_i\boldsymbol{\beta})].$$

Now, making the standard assumption that $\mathrm{E}(\mathbf{w}_i'\mathbf{w}_i)$ is nonsingular, it follows by the usual analogy principle argument that

$$\hat{\gamma} = \left(N^{-1}\sum_{i=1}^{N}\mathbf{w}_i'\mathbf{w}_i\right)^{-1}\left[N^{-1}\sum_{i=1}^{N}\mathbf{w}_i'(\bar{y}_i - \bar{\mathbf{x}}_i\hat{\boldsymbol{\beta}}_{FE})\right]$$

is consistent for γ. The asymptotic variance of $\sqrt{N}(\hat{\gamma} - \gamma)$ can be obtained by standard arguments for two-step estimators. Rather than derive this asymptotic variance, we turn to more general assumptions.

Hausman and Taylor (1981) partition $\mathbf{w}_i$ and $\mathbf{x}_{it}$ as $\mathbf{w}_i = (\mathbf{w}_{i1}, \mathbf{w}_{i2})$, $\mathbf{x}_{it} = (\mathbf{x}_{it1}, \mathbf{x}_{it2})$, where $\mathbf{w}_{i1}$ is $1 \times J_1$, $\mathbf{w}_{i2}$ is $1 \times J_2$, $\mathbf{x}_{it1}$ is $1 \times K_1$, $\mathbf{x}_{it2}$ is $1 \times K_2$, and assume that

$$\mathrm{E}(\mathbf{w}_{i1}' c_i) = \mathbf{0} \qquad \text{and} \qquad \mathrm{E}(\mathbf{x}_{it1}' c_i) = \mathbf{0}, \qquad \text{all } t. \tag{11.32}$$

We still maintain assumption (11.30), so that $\mathbf{w}_i$ and $\mathbf{x}_{is}$ are uncorrelated with u_{it} for all t and s.

Assumptions (11.30) and (11.32) provide orthogonality conditions that can be used in a method of moments procedure. Hausman and Taylor actually imposed enough assumptions so that the variance matrix $\boldsymbol{\Omega}$ of the composite error $\mathbf{v}_i = c_i \mathbf{j}_T + \mathbf{u}_i$ has the random effects structure *and* Assumption SIV.5 from Section 8.3.4 holds for the relevant matrix of instruments. Neither of these is necessary, but together they afford some simplifications.

Write equation (11.29) for all T time periods as

$$\mathbf{y}_i = \mathbf{W}_i\gamma + \mathbf{X}_i\boldsymbol{\beta} + \mathbf{v}_i. \tag{11.33}$$

Since $\mathbf{x}_{it}$ is strictly exogenous and $\mathbf{Q}_T\mathbf{v}_i = \mathbf{Q}_T\mathbf{u}_i$ [where $\mathbf{Q}_T \equiv \mathbf{I}_T - \mathbf{j}_T(\mathbf{j}_T'\mathbf{j}_T)^{-1}\mathbf{j}_T'$ is again the $T \times T$ time-demeaning matrix], it follows that $\mathrm{E}[(\mathbf{Q}_T\mathbf{X}_i)'\mathbf{v}_i] = \mathbf{0}$. Thus, the $T \times K$ matrix $\mathbf{Q}_T\mathbf{X}_i$ can be used as instruments in estimating equation (11.33). If these were the only instruments available, then we would be back to FE estimation of $\boldsymbol{\beta}$ without being able to estimate γ.

Additional instruments come from assumption (11.32). In particular, $\mathbf{w}_{i1}$ is orthogonal to v_{it} for all t, and so is $\mathbf{x}_{i1}^o$, the $1 \times TK_1$ vector containing $\mathbf{x}_{it1}$ for all $t = 1, \ldots, T$. Thus, define a set of instruments for equation (11.33) by

$$[\mathbf{Q}_T\mathbf{X}_i, \mathbf{j}_T \otimes (\mathbf{w}_{i1}, \mathbf{x}_{i1}^o)], \tag{11.34}$$

which is a $T \times (K + J_1 + TK_1)$ matrix. Simply put, the vector of IVs for time period t is $(\ddot{\mathbf{x}}_{it}, \mathbf{w}_{i1}, \mathbf{x}_{i1}^o)$. With this set of instruments, the order condition for identification of $(\gamma, \boldsymbol{\beta})$ is that $K + J_1 + TK_1 \geq J + K$, or $TK_1 \geq J_2$. In effect, we must have a sufficient number of elements in $\mathbf{x}_{i1}^o$ to act as instruments for $\mathbf{w}_{i2}$. ($\ddot{\mathbf{x}}_{it}$ are the IVs for $\mathbf{x}_{it}$, and $\mathbf{w}_{i1}$ act as their own IVs.) Whether we do depends on the number of time periods, as well as on K_1.

Actually, matrix (11.34) does not include all possible instruments under assumptions (11.30) and (11.32), even when we focus only on zero covariances. However, under the full set of Hausman-Taylor assumptions mentioned earlier—including the assumption that $\boldsymbol{\Omega}$ has the random effects structure—it can be shown that all instruments other than those in matrix (11.34) are redundant in the sense of Section 8.6; see IASW (1999, Theorem 4.4) for details.

Hausman and Taylor (1981) suggested estimating γ and $\boldsymbol{\beta}$ by REIV. As described in Section 11.2, REIV can be implemented as a P2SLS estimator on transformed data. For the particular choice of instruments in equation (11.34), we first estimate the equation by P2SLS using instruments $\mathbf{z}_{it} \equiv (\ddot{\mathbf{x}}_{it}, \mathbf{w}_{i1}, \mathbf{x}_{i1}^o)$ for time period t. From the P2SLS residuals, the quasi-time-demeaning parameter, $\hat{\lambda}$, is obtained as in equation (10.81), where $\hat{\sigma}_c^2$ and $\hat{\sigma}_u^2$ are gotten from the P2SLS residuals, say $\check{v}_{it} = y_{it} - \mathbf{w}_i\check{\gamma} - \mathbf{x}_{it}\check{\boldsymbol{\beta}}$, rather than the POLS residuals. The quasi-time-demeaning operation is then carried out as in equation (11.18). Some software packages contain specific commands for estimating HT models, but not all allow for fully robust inference (that is, violation of Assumption REIV.3). The P2SLS estimation on the quasi-time-demeaned data makes it easy to obtain fully robust inference for any statistical package that computes heteroskedasticity and serial correlation robust standard errors and test statistics for P2SLS.

If $\boldsymbol{\Omega}$ is not of the random effects form, or if Assumption SIV.5 fails, many more instruments than are in matrix (11.34) can help improve efficiency. Unfortunately, the value of these additional IVs is unclear. For practical purposes, 3SLS with $\hat{\boldsymbol{\Omega}}$ of the

RE form, 3SLS with $\hat{\boldsymbol{\Omega}}$ unrestricted, or GMM with optimal weighting matrix—using the instruments in matrix (11.34)—should be sufficient, with the latter being the most efficient in the presence of conditional heteroskedasticity. The first-stage estimator can be the system 2SLS estimator using matrix (11.34) as instruments. The GMM over-identification test statistic can be used to test the $TK_1 - J_2$ overidentifying restrictions.

In cases where $K_1 \geq J_2$, we can reduce the instrument list even further and still achieve identification: we use $\bar{\mathbf{x}}_{i1}$, rather than $\mathbf{x}_{i1}^o$, as the instruments for $\mathbf{w}_{i2}$. Then, the IVs at time t are $(\ddot{\mathbf{x}}_{it}, \mathbf{w}_{i1}, \bar{\mathbf{x}}_{i1})$. We can then use the GIV estimator with this new set of IVs. Quasi-demeaning leads to an especially simple analysis. Although it generally reduces asymptotic efficiency, replacing $\mathbf{x}_{i1}^o$ with $\bar{\mathbf{x}}_{i1}$ is a reasonable way to reduce the instrument list because much of the partial correlation between $\mathbf{w}_{i2}$ and $\mathbf{x}_{i1}^o$ is likely to be through the time average, $\bar{\mathbf{x}}_{i1}$. Some econometrics packages implement this version of the HT estimator.

HT provide an application of their model to estimating the return to education, where education levels do not vary over the two years in their sample. Initially, HT include as the elements of $\mathbf{x}_{it1}$ all time-varying explanatory variables: experience, an indicator for bad health, and a previous-year unemployment indicator. Race and union status are assumed to be uncorrelated with c_i, and, because these do not change over time, they comprise $\mathbf{w}_{i1}$. The only element of z_{i2} is years of schooling. HT apply the GIV estimator and obtain a return to schooling that is almost twice as large as the pooled OLS estimate. When they allow some of the time-varying explanatory variables to be correlated with c_i, the estimated return to schooling gets even larger. It is difficult to know what to conclude, as the identifying assumptions are not especially convincing. For example, assuming that experience and union status are uncorrelated with the unobserved effect and then using this information to identify the return to schooling seems tenuous.

Breusch, Mizon, and Schmidt (1989) studied the Hausman-Taylor model under the additional assumption that $\mathrm{E}(\mathbf{x}_{it2}'c_i)$ is constant across t. This adds more orthogonality conditions that can be exploited in estimation. See IASW (1999) for a recent analysis.

11.4 First Differencing Instrumental Variables Methods

We now turn to first differencing methods combined with IVs. The model is as in (11.1), but now we remove the unobserved effect by taking the first difference:

$$\Delta y_{it} = \Delta \mathbf{x}_{it}\boldsymbol{\beta} + \Delta u_{it}, \qquad t = 2, \ldots, T, \tag{11.35}$$

or, in matrix form,

$$\Delta \mathbf{y}_i = \Delta \mathbf{X}_i \boldsymbol{\beta} + \Delta \mathbf{u}_i. \tag{11.36}$$

If we have instruments $\mathbf{z}_{it}$ satisfying Assumption FEIV.1, and if the IVs have the same dimension L for all t, then we can apply, say, P2SLS to (11.35) using instruments $\Delta \mathbf{z}_{it}$. Analogous to FD and FE estimation with strictly exogenous $\mathbf{x}_{it}$, we could adopt Assumption FEIV.1 as our first assumption for the **first difference instrumental variables (FDIV) estimator**. But here we are interested in more general cases. Rather than necessarily differencing underlying instruments, we now let $\mathbf{w}_{it}$ denote a $1 \times L_t$ vector of instrumental variables that are contemporaneously exogenous in the FD equation:

ASSUMPTION FDIV.1: For $t = 2, \ldots, T$, $\mathrm{E}(\mathbf{w}_{it}' \Delta u_{it}) = \mathbf{0}$.

The important point about Assumption FDIV.1 is that we can choose the elements of $\mathbf{w}_{it}$ that are not required to be strictly exogenous (conditional on c_i) in the original mode (11.1). We allow the dimension of the instruments to change—usually, grow—as t increases. When the dimension of $\mathbf{w}_{it}$ changes with t, we choose the instrument matrix as the $(T-1) \times L$ matrix

$$\mathbf{W}_i = \mathrm{diag}(\mathbf{w}_{i2}, \mathbf{w}_{i3}, \ldots, \mathbf{w}_{iT}),$$

where $L = L_2 + L_3 + \cdots + L_T$; see also equation (8.15). Sometimes, when $\mathbf{w}_{it}$ has dimension L for all t, we prefer to choose

$$\mathbf{W}_i = (\mathbf{w}_{i2}', \ldots, \mathbf{w}_{iT}')'.$$

In any case, the rank condition for the system IV estimator on the FD equation is

ASSUMPTION FDIV.2: (a) rank $\mathrm{E}(\mathbf{W}_i' \mathbf{W}_i) = L$; (b) rank $\mathrm{E}(\mathbf{W}_i' \Delta \mathbf{X}_i) = K$.

Under FDIV.1 and FDIV.2, we can consistently estimate $\boldsymbol{\beta}$ using the system 2SLS estimator, as described in Section 8.3.2. As discussed there, the S2SLS estimator in the panel data context can be computed rather easily, but its characterization depends on the structure of $\mathbf{W}_i$. The first step is to run separate $T-1$ first-stage regressions,

$$\Delta \mathbf{x}_{it} \text{ on } \mathbf{w}_{it}, \qquad i = 1, 2, \ldots, N, \tag{11.37}$$

and obtain the fitted values, say $\widehat{\Delta \mathbf{x}}_{it}$ (a $1 \times K$ vector for all i and t). Then, estimate (11.35) by pooled IV using instruments $\widehat{\Delta \mathbf{x}}_{it}$ for $\Delta \mathbf{x}_{it}$. Inference is standard because one can compute a variance matrix estimator robust to arbitrary heteroskedasticity and serial correlation in $\{e_{it} \equiv \Delta u_{it} : t = 2, \ldots, T\}$. It is left as an exercise to state the

FD version of FEIV.3 that ensures we can use the standard pooled 2SLS variance matrix.

In many applications of FDIV, the errors in the FD equation (11.35) are necessarily serially correlated, often because the errors in equation (11.1) start off being serially uncorrelated; we cover the leading case in the next section. In such cases, we might wish to apply GMM with an optimal weighting matrix (which could, in some cases, be GMM 3SLS). In a first stage we need to obtain $(T-1) \times 1$ residuals, say $\breve{\mathbf{e}}_i = \Delta\mathbf{y}_i - \Delta\mathbf{X}_i\breve{\boldsymbol{\beta}}$, where $\breve{\boldsymbol{\beta}}$ is probably the system 2SLS estimator described earlier. An optimal weighting matrix is

$$\left(N^{-1}\sum_{i=1}^{N}\mathbf{W}_i'\breve{\mathbf{e}}_i\breve{\mathbf{e}}_i'\mathbf{W}_i\right)^{-1}. \tag{11.38}$$

If $\mathrm{E}(\mathbf{W}_i'\mathbf{e}_i\mathbf{e}_i'\mathbf{W}_i) = \mathrm{E}(\mathbf{W}_i'\boldsymbol{\Omega}\mathbf{W}_i)$, where $\boldsymbol{\Omega} = \mathrm{E}(\mathbf{e}_i\mathbf{e}_i')$, then we can replace $\breve{\mathbf{e}}_i\breve{\mathbf{e}}_i'$ (for all i) in equation (11.38) with the $(T-1) \times (T-1)$ estimator $\breve{\boldsymbol{\Omega}} = N^{-1}\sum_{i=1}^{N}\breve{\mathbf{e}}_i\breve{\mathbf{e}}_i'$. All of the GMM theory we discussed in Chapter 8 applies directly.

For a model with a single endogenous explanatory variable along with some strictly exogenous regressors, a general FD equation is

$$\Delta y_{it1} = \eta_{t1} + \alpha_1 \Delta y_{it2} + \Delta\mathbf{z}_{it1}\boldsymbol{\delta}_1 + \Delta u_{it1}$$

with instruments $\mathbf{w}_{it} = (\Delta\mathbf{z}_{it1}, \mathbf{w}_{it2})$, where $\mathbf{w}_{it2}$ is a set of exogenous variables omitted from the structural equation. These could be differences themselves, that is, $\mathbf{w}_{it2} = \Delta\mathbf{z}_{it2}$, where we may think of the reduced form for y_{it2} being $y_{it2} = \mathbf{z}_{it}\boldsymbol{\pi}_2 + c_{i2} + u_{it2}$ and then we difference to remove c_{i2}. In the next example, from Levitt (1996), the instruments for the endogenous explanatory variable are not obtained by differencing.

Example 11.2 (Effects of Prison Population on Crime Rates): In order to estimate the causal effects of prison population increases on crime rates at the state level, Levitt (1996) uses episodes of prison overcrowding litigation as instruments for the growth in the prison population. Underlying Levitt's FD equation is an unobserved effects model,

$$\log(crime_{it}) = \theta_{t1} + \alpha_1 \log(prison_{it}) + \mathbf{z}_{it1}\boldsymbol{\delta}_1 + c_{i1} + u_{it1}, \tag{11.39}$$

where θ_{t1} represents different time intercepts and both *crime* and *prison* are measured per 100,000 people. (The prison population variable is measured on the last day of the previous year.) The vector $\mathbf{z}_{it1}$ contains the log of police per capita, log of per capita income, proportions of the population in four age categories (with omitted group 35 and older), the unemployment rate (as a proportion), proportion of the population that is black, and proportion of the population living in metropolitan areas. The differenced equation is

$$\Delta \log(crime_{it}) = \eta_{t1} + \alpha_1 \Delta \log(prison_{it}) + \Delta \mathbf{z}_{it1} \boldsymbol{\delta}_1 + \Delta u_{it1}, \tag{11.40}$$

and the instruments are $(\Delta \mathbf{z}_{it1}, final1_{it}, final2_{it})$; the last two variables are binary indicators for whether final decisions were reached on prison overcrowding legislation in the previous year and previous two years, respectively. We estimate this equation using the data in PRISON.RAW.

The first-stage regression POLS regression of $\Delta \log(prison_{it})$ on $\Delta \mathbf{z}_{it1}$, $final1_{it}$, $final2_{it}$, and a full set of year dummies yields fully robust t statistics for $final1_{it}$ and $final2_{it}$ of -4.71 and -3.30, respectively. The robust test of joint significance of the two instruments gives $F = 18.81$ and a p-value of zero to four decimal places. Therefore, assuming the litigation variables are uncorrelated with the idiosyncratic changes Δu_{it1}, a P2SLS estimation on the FD equation is justified. The 2SLS estimate of α_1 is -1.032 (fully robust se $=$ .213). This is a large elasticity. By comparison, the POLS estimates on the FD equation gives a coefficient much smaller in magnitude, $-.181$ (fully robust se $=$ .049). Not surprisingly, the 2SLS estimate is less precise. Levitt (1996) found similar results using a somewhat longer time period (with missing years for some states) and more instruments.

Can we formally reject exogeneity of $\Delta \log(prison_{it})$ in the FD equation? When we estimate the reduced form for $\Delta \log(prison_{it})$, add the reduced-form residual to equation (11.40), and estimate the augmented model by POLS, the fully robust t statistic on the residual is 3.05. Therefore, we strongly reject exogeneity of $\Delta \log(prison_{it})$ in (11.40).

Because it is difficult to find a truly exogenous instrument—even once we remove unobserved heterogeneity by FD or FE—it is prudent to study the properties of panel data IV methods when the instruments might be correlated with the idiosyncrate errors, just as we did with the explanatory variables themselves in Section 10.7.1. Under weak assumptions on the time series dependence, very similar calculations show that the FEIV estimator has inconsistency on the order of T^{-1} if the instruments $\mathbf{z}_{it}$ are contemporaneously exogenous, that is, $\mathrm{E}(\mathbf{z}_{it}' u_{it}) = \mathbf{0}$. By contrast, the inconsistency in the FDIV estimator does not shrink to zero as T grows under contemporaneous exogeneity if either $\mathbf{z}_{i,t-1}$ or $\mathbf{z}_{i,t+1}$ is correlated with u_{it}. Unfortunately, because the inconsistencies in FEIV and FDIV depend on the distribution of $\{\mathbf{z}_{it}\}$, we cannot know for sure which estimator has less inconsistency. Further, as we discussed in Section 10.7.1, there is an important caveat to the $O(T^{-1})$ bias calculation in the FEIV case: it assumes that the idiosyncratic errors $\{u_{it}\}$ are weakly dependent, that is, I(0) (integrated of order zero). By contrast, the differencing transformation eliminates a unit root in $\{u_{it}\}$, and may be preferred when $\{u_{it}\}$ is a persistent process. More research needs to be done on this practically important issue.

11.5 Unobserved Effects Models with Measurement Error

One pitfall in using either FD or FE to eliminate unobserved heterogeneity is that the reduced variation in the explanatory variables can cause severe biases in the presence of measurement error. Measurement error in panel data was studied by Solon (1985) and Griliches and Hausman (1986). It is widely believed in econometrics that the differencing and FE transformations exacerbate measurement error bias (even though they eliminate heterogeneity bias). However, it is important to know that this conclusion rests on the classical errors-in-variables (CEV) model under strict exogeneity, as well as on other assumptions.

To illustrate, consider a model with a single explanatory variable,

$$y_{it} = \beta x_{it}^* + c_i + u_{it}, \tag{11.41}$$

under the strict exogeneity assumption

$$\mathrm{E}(u_{it} \mid \mathbf{x}_i^*, \mathbf{x}_i, c_i) = 0, \qquad t = 1, 2, \ldots, T, \tag{11.42}$$

where x_{it} denotes the observed measure of the unobservable x_{it}^*. Condition (11.42) embodies the standard redundancy condition—that x_{it} does not matter once x_{it}^* is controlled for—in addition to strict exogeneity of the unmeasured and measured regressors. Denote the measurement error as $r_{it} = x_{it} - x_{it}^*$. Assuming that r_{it} is uncorrelated with x_{it}^*—the key CEV assumption—and that variances and covariances are all constant across t, it is easily shown that, as $N \to \infty$, the plim of the POLS estimator is

$$\begin{aligned} \operatorname*{plim}_{N\to\infty} \hat{\beta}_{POLS} &= \beta + \frac{\mathrm{Cov}(x_{it}, c_i + u_{it} - \beta r_{it})}{\mathrm{Var}(x_{it})} \\ &= \beta + \frac{\mathrm{Cov}(x_{it}, c_i) - \beta\sigma_r^2}{\mathrm{Var}(x_{it})}, \end{aligned} \tag{11.43}$$

where $\sigma_r^2 = \mathrm{Var}(r_{it}) = \mathrm{Cov}(x_{it}, r_{it})$; this is essentially the formula derived by Solon (1985).

From equation (11.43), we see that there are two sources of asymptotic bias in the POLS estimator: correlation between x_{it} and the unobserved effect, c_i, and a measurement error bias term, $-\beta\sigma_r^2$. If x_{it} and c_i are positively correlated and $\beta > 0$, the two sources of bias tend to cancel each other out.

Now assume that r_{is} is uncorrelated with x_{it}^* for all t and s, and for simplicity suppose that $T = 2$. If we first difference to remove c_i before performing OLS we obtain

$$\begin{aligned}\operatorname*{plim}_{N\to\infty} \hat{\beta}_{FD} &= \beta + \frac{\operatorname{Cov}(\Delta x_{it}, \Delta u_{it} - \beta \Delta r_{it})}{\operatorname{Var}(\Delta x_{it})} = \beta - \beta\frac{\operatorname{Cov}(\Delta x_{it}, \Delta r_{it})}{\operatorname{Var}(\Delta x_{it})} \\ &= \beta - 2\beta\frac{[\sigma_r^2 - \operatorname{Cov}(r_{it}, r_{i,t-1})]}{\operatorname{Var}(\Delta x_{it})} \\ &= \beta\left(1 - \frac{\sigma_r^2(1-\rho_r)}{\sigma_{x^*}^2(1-\rho_{x^*}) + \sigma_r^2(1-\rho_r)}\right), \qquad (11.44)\end{aligned}$$

where $\rho_{x^*} = \operatorname{Corr}(x_{it}^*, x_{i,t-1}^*)$ and $\rho_r = \operatorname{Corr}(r_{it}, r_{i,t-1})$, where we have used the fact that $\operatorname{Cov}(r_{it}, r_{i,t-1}) = \sigma_r^2\rho_r$ and $\operatorname{Var}(\Delta x_{it}) = 2[\sigma_{x^*}^2(1-\rho_{x^*}) + \sigma_r^2(1-\rho_r)]$; see also Solon (1985) and Hsiao (2003, p. 305). Equation (11.44) shows that, in addition to the ratio $\sigma_r^2/\sigma_{x^*}^2$ being important in determining the size of the measurement error bias, the ratio $(1-\rho_r)/(1-\rho_{x^*})$ is also important. As the autocorrelation in x_{it}^* increases relative to that in r_{it}, the measurement error bias in $\hat{\beta}_{FD}$ increases. In fact, as $\rho_{x^*} \to 1$, the measurement error bias approaches $-\beta$.

Of course, we can never know whether the bias in equation (11.43) is larger than that in equation (11.44), or vice versa. Also, both expressions are based on the CEV assumptions, and then some. If there is little correlation between Δx_{it} and Δr_{it}, the measurement error bias from first differencing may be small, but the small correlation is offset by the fact that differencing can considerably reduce the variation in the explanatory variables.

The FE estimator also has an attenuation bias under similar assumptions. You are asked to derive the probability limit of $\hat{\beta}_{FE}$ in Problem 11.3.

Consistent estimation in the presence of measurement error is possible under certain assumptions. Consider the more general model

$$y_{it} = \mathbf{z}_{it}\gamma + \delta w_{it}^* + c_i + u_{it}, \qquad t = 1, 2, \ldots, T, \qquad (11.45)$$

where w_{it}^* is measured with error. Write $r_{it} = w_{it} - w_{it}^*$, and assume strict exogeneity along with redundancy of w_{it}:

$$\mathrm{E}(u_{it} \mid \mathbf{z}_i, \mathbf{w}_i^*, \mathbf{w}_i, c_i) = 0, \qquad t = 1, 2, \ldots, T. \qquad (11.46)$$

Replacing w_{it}^* with w_{it} and first differencing gives

$$\Delta y_{it} = \Delta \mathbf{z}_{it}\gamma + \delta \Delta w_{it} + \Delta u_{it} - \delta \Delta r_{it}. \tag{11.47}$$

The standard CEV assumption in the current context can be stated as

$$\mathrm{E}(r_{it} \mid \mathbf{z}_i, \mathbf{w}_i^*, c_i) = 0, \qquad t = 1, 2, \ldots, T, \tag{11.48}$$

which implies that r_{it} is uncorrelated with $\mathbf{z}_{is}$, w_{is}^* for all t and s. (As always in the context of linear models, assuming zero correlation is sufficient for consistency, but not for usual standard errors and test statistics to be valid.) Under assumption (11.48) (and other measurement error assumptions), Δr_{it} is correlated with Δw_{it}. To apply an IV method to equation (11.47), we need at least one instrument for Δw_{it}. As in the omitted variables and simultaneity contexts, we may have additional variables outside the model that can be used as instruments. Analogous to the cross section case (as in Chapter 5), one possibility is to use another measure on w_{it}^*, say h_{it}. If the measurement error in h_{it} is orthogonal to the measurement error in w_{is}, all t and s, then Δh_{it} is a natural instrument for Δw_{it} in equation (11.47). Of course, we can use many more instruments in equation (11.47), as any linear combination of $\mathbf{z}_i$ and $\mathbf{h}_i$ is uncorrelated with the composite error under the given assumptions.

Alternatively, a vector of variables $\mathbf{h}_{it}$ may exist that are known to be redundant in equation (11.45), strictly exogenous, and uncorrelated with r_{is} for all s. If $\Delta \mathbf{h}_{it}$ is correlated with Δw_{it}, then an IV procedure, such as P2SLS, is easy to apply. It may be that in applying something like P2SLS to equation (11.47) results in asymptotically valid statistics; this imposes serial independence and homoskedasticity assumptions on Δu_{it}. Generally, however, it is a good idea to use standard errors and test statistics robust to arbitrary serial correlation and heteroskedasticity, or to use a full GMM approach that efficiently accounts for these. An alternative is to use the FE2SLS method. Ziliak, Wilson, and Stone (1999) find that, for a model explaining cyclicality of real wages, the FD and FE estimates are different in important ways. The differences largely disappear when IV methods are used to account for measurement error in the local unemployment rate.

So far, the solutions to measurement error in the context of panel data have assumed nothing about the serial correlation in r_{it}. Suppose that, in addition to assumption (11.46), we assume that the measurement error is serially uncorrelated:

$$\mathrm{E}(r_{it} r_{is}) = 0, \qquad s \neq t \tag{11.49}$$

Assumption (11.49) opens up a solution to the measurement error problem with panel data that is not available with a single cross section or independently pooled cross sections. Under assumption (11.48), r_{it} is uncorrelated with w_{is}^* for all t and s. Thus, if we assume that the measurement error r_{it} is serially uncorrelated, then r_{it} is uncorrelated with w_{is} for all $t \neq s$. Since, by the strict exogeneity assumption, Δu_{it} is uncorrelated with all leads and lags of $\mathbf{z}_{it}$ and w_{it}, we have instruments readily available. For example, $w_{i,t-2}$ and $w_{i,t-3}$ are valid as instruments for Δw_{it} in equation (11.47); so is $w_{i,t+1}$. Again, P2SLS or some other IV procedure can be used once the list of instruments is specified for each time period. However, it is important to remember that this approach requires the r_{it} to be serially uncorrelated, in addition to the other CEV assumptions.

The methods just covered for solving measurement error problems all assume strict exogeneity of all explanatory variables. Naturally, things get harder when measurement error is combined with models with only sequentially exogenous explanatory variables. Nevertheless, differencing away the unobserved effect and then selecting instruments—based on the maintained assumptions—generally works in models with a variety of problems. We now turn explicitly to models under sequential exogeneity assumptions.

11.6 Estimation under Sequential Exogeneity

11.6.1 General Framework

We can also apply the FDIV methods in Section 11.4 to estimate the standard model,

$$y_{it} = \mathbf{x}_{it}\boldsymbol{\beta} + c_i + u_{it}, \qquad t = 1, \ldots, T, \tag{11.50}$$

under a sequential exogeneity assumption, properly modified for the presence of the unobserved effect, c_i. Chamberlain (1992b) calls these **sequential moment restrictions**, which can be written in conditional expectations form as

$$\mathrm{E}(u_{it} \mid \mathbf{x}_{it}, \mathbf{x}_{i,t-1}, \ldots, \mathbf{x}_{i1}, c_i) = 0, \qquad t = 1, \ldots, T. \tag{11.51}$$

When assumption (11.51) holds, we say that $\{\mathbf{x}_{it}\}$ is **sequentially exogenous conditional on the unobserved effect**.

Given equation (11.50), assumption (11.51) is equivalent to

$$\mathrm{E}(y_{it} \mid \mathbf{x}_{it}, \mathbf{x}_{i,t-1}, \ldots, \mathbf{x}_{i1}, c_i) = \mathrm{E}(y_{it} \mid \mathbf{x}_{it}, c_i) = \mathbf{x}_{it}\boldsymbol{\beta} + c_i, \tag{11.52}$$

which provides a simple interpretation of sequential exogeneity conditional on c_i: once $\mathbf{x}_{it}$ and c_i have been controlled for, no *past* values of $\mathbf{x}_{it}$ affect the expected value of y_{it}. Conditioning on the explanatory variables only up through time t is more natural than the strict exogeneity assumption, which requires conditioning on future values of $\mathbf{x}_{it}$ as well. As we proceed, it is important to remember that equation (11.52) is what we should have in mind when interpreting the estimates of $\boldsymbol{\beta}$. Estimating equations in first differences, such as (11.35), do not have natural interpretations when the explanatory variables are only sequentially exogenous.

As we will explicitly show in the next subsection, models with lagged dependent variables are naturally analyzed under sequential exogeneity. Keane and Runkle (1992) argue that panel data models with heterogeneity for testing rational expectations hypotheses do not satisfy the strict exogeneity requirement. But they do satisfy sequential exogeneity; in fact, the conditioning set in assumption (11.51) can include all variables observed at time $t-1$.

As we saw in Section 7.2, in panel data models without unobserved effects, strict exogeneity is sometimes too strong an assumption, even in static and finite distributed lag models. For example, suppose

$$y_{it} = \mathbf{z}_{it}\gamma + \delta h_{it} + c_i + u_{it}, \tag{11.53}$$

where $\{\mathbf{z}_{it}\}$ is strictly exogenous and $\{h_{it}\}$ is sequentially exogenous:

$$\mathrm{E}(u_{it} \mid \mathbf{z}_i, h_{it}, \ldots, h_{i1}, c_i) = 0. \tag{11.54}$$

Further, h_{it} is influenced by past y_{it}, say

$$h_{it} = \mathbf{z}_{it}\xi + \eta y_{i,t-1} + \psi c_i + r_{it}. \tag{11.55}$$

For example, let y_{it} be per capita condom sales in city i during year t, and let h_{it} be the HIV infection rate for city i in year t. Model (11.53) can be used to test whether condom usage is influenced by the spread of HIV. The unobserved effect c_i contains city-specific unobserved factors that can affect sexual conduct, as well as the incidence of HIV. Equation (11.55) is one way of capturing the fact that the spread of HIV depends on past condom usage. Generally, if $\mathrm{E}(r_{i,t+1}u_{it}) = 0$, it is easy to show that $\mathrm{E}(h_{i,t+1}u_{it}) = \eta\mathrm{E}(y_{it}u_{it}) = \eta\mathrm{E}(u_{it}^2) > 0$ if $\eta > 0$ under equations (11.54) and (11.55). Therefore, strict exogeneity fails unless $\eta = 0$.

Sometimes in panel data applications one sees variables that are thought to be contemporaneously endogenous appear with a lag, rather than contemporaneously. So, for example, we might use $h_{i,t-1}$ in place of h_{it} in equation (11.53) because we think h_{it} and u_{it} are correlated. As an example, suppose y_{it} is percentage of flights cancelled by airline i in year t, and h_{it} is profits in the same year. We might specify $y_{it} = \mathbf{z}_{it}\gamma + \delta h_{i,t-1} + c_i + u_{it}$ for strictly exogenous $\mathbf{z}_{it}$. Of course, at $t+1$, the regressors are $\mathbf{x}_{i,t+1} = (\mathbf{z}_{i,t+1}, h_{it})$, which is correlated with u_{it} if h_{it} is. As we discussed in

Section 10.7, the FE estimator arguably has inconsistency of order $1/T$ in this situation. But if we are willing to assume sequential exogeneity, we need not settle for an inconsistent estimator at all.

A general approach to estimation under sequential exogeneity follows in Section 11.4. We take first differences to remove c_i and obtain equation (11.35), written in stacked form as equation (11.36). The only issue is where the instruments come from. Under assumption (11.51),

$$\mathrm{E}(\mathbf{x}_{is}'u_{it}) = \mathbf{0}, \qquad s = 1, \ldots, t; t = 1, \ldots, T, \tag{11.56}$$

which implies the orthogonality conditions

$$\mathrm{E}(\mathbf{x}_{is}'\Delta u_{it}) = \mathbf{0}, \qquad s = 1, \ldots, t-1; t = 2, \ldots, T. \tag{11.57}$$

Therefore, at time t, the available instruments in the FD equation are in the vector $\mathbf{x}_{i,t-1}^o$, where

$$\mathbf{x}_{it}^o \equiv (\mathbf{x}_{i1}, \mathbf{x}_{i2}, \ldots, \mathbf{x}_{it}). \tag{11.58}$$

Therefore, the matrix of instruments is simply

$$\mathbf{W}_i = \mathrm{diag}(\mathbf{x}_{i1}^o, \mathbf{x}_{i2}^o, \ldots, \mathbf{x}_{i,T-1}^o), \tag{11.59}$$

which has $T-1$ rows. Because of sequential exogeneity, the number of valid instruments increases with t.

Given $\mathbf{W}_i$, it is routine to apply GMM estimation. But, as we discussed in Section 11.4, some simpler strategies are available. One useful one is to estimate a reduced form for $\Delta\mathbf{x}_{it}$ separately for each t. So, at time t, run the regression $\Delta\mathbf{x}_{it}$ on $\mathbf{x}_{i,t-1}^o$, $i = 1, \ldots, N$, and obtain the fitted values, $\widehat{\Delta\mathbf{x}}_{it}$. Of course, the fitted values are all $1 \times K$ vectors for each t. Then, estimate the FD equation (11.35) by pooled IV using instruments $\widehat{\Delta\mathbf{x}}_{it}$. It is simple to obtain robust standard errors and test statistics from such a procedure because the first stage estimation to obtain the instruments can be ignored (asymptotically, of course). This is the same set or estimates obtained if we choose $\mathbf{W}_i$ as in (11.59) and choose as the weighting matrix $(\mathbf{W}'\mathbf{W}/N)^{-1}$, that is, we obtain the system 2SLS estimator.

Given an initial consistent estimator, we can obtain the efficient GMM weighting matrix. In most applications, there is a reasonable set of assumptions under which $\mathrm{E}(\mathbf{W}_i'\mathbf{e}_i\mathbf{e}_i'\mathbf{W}_i) = \mathrm{E}(\mathbf{W}_i'\boldsymbol{\Omega}\mathbf{W}_i)$ where $\mathbf{e}_i = \Delta\mathbf{u}_i$ and $\boldsymbol{\Omega} = \mathrm{E}(\mathbf{e}_i\mathbf{e}_i')$, in which case the GMM 3SLS estimator is an efficient GMM estimator. See Wooldridge (1996) and Arellano (2003) for examples.

One potential problem with estimating the FD equation by IVs that are simply lags of $\mathbf{x}_{it}$ is that changes in variables over time are often difficult to predict. In other words, $\Delta \mathbf{x}_{it}$ might have little correlation with $\mathbf{x}_{i,t-1}^o$, in which case we face a problem of weak instruments. In one case, we even lose identification: if $\mathbf{x}_{it} = \boldsymbol{\lambda}_t + \mathbf{x}_{i,t-1} + \mathbf{e}_{it}$ where $\mathrm{E}(\mathbf{e}_{it} \mid \mathbf{x}_{i,t-1}, \ldots, \mathbf{x}_{i1}) = \mathbf{0}$—that is, the elements of $\mathbf{x}_{it}$ are random walks with drift—then $\mathrm{E}(\Delta \mathbf{x}_{it} \mid \mathbf{x}_{i,t-1}, \ldots, \mathbf{x}_{i1}) = \mathbf{0}$, and the rank condition for IV estimation fails. In the next subsection we will study this problem further in the context of the AR(1) model.

As a practical matter, the column dimension of $\mathbf{W}_i$ can be large, especially with large T. Using many overidentifying restrictions is known to contribute to poor finite sample properties of GMM, especially if many of the instruments are weak; see, for example, Tauchen (1986), Altonji and Segal (1996), Ziliak (1997), Stock, Wright, and Yogo (2002), and Han and Phillips (2006). It might be better (even though it is asymptotically less efficient, or no more efficient) to use just a couple of lags, say $\mathbf{w}_{it} = (\mathbf{x}_{i,t-1}, \mathbf{x}_{i,t-2})$, as the instruments at time $t \geq 3$, with $\mathbf{w}_{i2} = \mathbf{x}_{i1}$.

If the model contains strictly exogenous variables, as in equation (11.53), at a minimum the instruments at time t would include $\Delta \mathbf{z}_{it}$—that is, $\Delta \mathbf{z}_{it}$ acts as its own instrument. We can still only include lags of the seqentially exogenous variables. So, at time t in the first difference of (11.53), $\Delta y_{it} = \Delta \mathbf{z}_{it}\boldsymbol{\gamma} + \delta \Delta h_{it} + \Delta u_{it}$, $t = 2, \ldots, T$, the available IVs would be $\mathbf{w}_{it} = (\Delta \mathbf{z}_{it}, h_{i,t-1}, h_{i,t-2}, \ldots, h_{i1})$. Again, either a full GMM procedure or a simple pooled IV procedure (after separate estimation of each reduced form) can be applied, and perhaps only a couple of lags of h_{it} would be included.

11.6.2 Models with Lagged Dependent Variables

A special case of models under sequential exogeneity restrictions are autoregressive models. Here we study the AR(1) model and follow Arellano and Bond (1991). In the model without any other covariates,

$$y_{it} = \rho y_{i,t-1} + c_i + u_{it}, \qquad t = 1, \ldots, T, \tag{11.60}$$

$$\mathrm{E}(u_{it} \mid y_{i,t-1}, y_{i,t-2}, \ldots, y_{i0}, c_i) = 0, \tag{11.61}$$

so that our first observation on y is at $t = 0$. Assumption (11.61) says that we have the dynamics completely specified: once we control for c_i, only one lag of y_{it} is necessary. This is an example of a **dynamic completeness conditional on the unobserved effect** assumption. When we let $x_{it} = y_{i,t-1}$, we see immediately that the AR(1) model satisfies the sequential exogeneity assumptions (conditional on c_i).

One application of model (11.60) is to determine whether $\{y_{it}\}$ exhibits **state dependence**: after controlling for systematic, time-constant differences c_i, does last period's outcome on y help predict this period's outcome? In the AR(1) model, the answer is yes if $\rho \neq 0$.

At time t in the FD equation $\Delta y_{it} = \rho \Delta y_{i,t-1} + \Delta u_{it}$, $t = 2, \ldots, T$, the available instruments are $\mathbf{w}_{it} = (y_{i0}, \ldots, y_{i,t-2})$. Anderson and Hsiao (1982) proposed pooled IV estimation of the FD equation with instrument $y_{i,t-2}$ (in which case all $T - 1$ periods can be used) or $\Delta y_{i,t-2}$ (in which case only $T - 2$ periods can be used). Arellano and Bond (1991) suggested full GMM estimation using all of the available instruments. The pooled IV estimator that uses, say, y_{i0} as the IV at $t = 2$ and then $(y_{i,t-2}, y_{it-3})$ for $t = 3, \ldots, T$, is easy to implement. It is likely more efficient than the Anderson and Hsiao approach but less efficent than the full GMM approach. In this method, $T - 1$ separate reduced forms are estimated for $\Delta y_{i,t-1}$.

As noted by Arellano and Bond (1991), the differenced errors Δu_{it} and $\Delta u_{i,t-1}$ are necessarily correlated under assumption (11.61). Therefore, at a minimum, any estimation method should account for this serial correlation in calculating standard errors and test statistics. GMM handles this serial correlation by using an efficient weighting matrix. Differenced errors two or more periods apart are uncorrelated, and this actually simplifies the optimal weighting matrix. Further, if we add conditional homoskedasticity, $\text{Var}(u_{it} \mid y_{i,t-1}, y_{i,t-2}, \ldots, y_{i0}, c_i) = \sigma_u^2$, then the 3SLS version of the weighting matrix can be used. See Arellano and Bond (1991) and also Wooldridge (1996) for verification. As is usually the case, even after we settle on the instruments, there are a variety of ways to use those instruments.

A more general version of the model is

$$y_{it} = \theta_t + \rho y_{i,t-1} + \mathbf{z}_{it}\gamma + c_i + u_{it}, \qquad t = 1, \ldots, T, \tag{11.62}$$

where θ_t denotes different period intercepts and $\{\mathbf{z}_{it}\}$ is strictly exogenous. When we difference equation (11.62),

$$\Delta y_{it} = \eta_t + \rho \Delta y_{i,t-1} + \Delta \mathbf{z}_{it}\gamma + \Delta u_{it}, \qquad t = 1, \ldots, T, \tag{11.63}$$

the available instruments (in addition to time period dummies) are $(\mathbf{z}_i, y_{i,t-2}, \ldots, y_{i0})$. We might not want to use all of $\mathbf{z}_i$ for every time period. Certainly we would use $\Delta \mathbf{z}_{it}$, and perhaps a lag, $\Delta \mathbf{z}_{i,t-1}$. If we add sequentially exogenous variables, say $\mathbf{h}_{it}$, to (11.62) then $(\mathbf{h}_{i,t-1}, \ldots, \mathbf{h}_{i1})$ would be added to the list (and $\Delta \mathbf{h}_{it}$ would appear in the equation). As always, we might not use the full set of lags in each time period.

Even though our estimating equation is in first differences, it is important to remember that (11.63) is an estimating equation. We should interpret the estimates in light of the original model (11.62). It is equation (11.62) that represents a dynamically complete conditional expectation. Equation (11.63) does not even satisfy $\text{E}(\Delta u_{it} \mid \Delta y_{i,t-1}, \Delta \mathbf{z}_{it}) = 0$, which is why POLS estimation of it is inconsistent. Applying IV to the FD equation is simply a way to estimate the parameters on the original model.

Example 11.3 (Estimating a Dynamic Airfare Equation): Consider an AR(1) model for the log of airfare using the data in AIRFARE.RAW:

$$lfare_{it} = \theta_t + \rho lfare_{i,t-1} + \gamma concen_{it} + c_i + u_{it},$$

where we include a full set of year dummies. We assume the concentration ratio is strictly exogenous and that at most one lag of *lfare* is needed to capture the dynamics. Because we have data for 1997 through 2000, (11.62) is specified for three years. After differencing, we have only two years of data.

The FD equation is

$$\Delta lfare_{it} = \eta_t + \rho \Delta lfare_{i,t-1} + \gamma \Delta concen_{it} + \Delta u_{it}, \qquad t = 1999, 2000.$$

If we estimate this equation by POLS, the estimators are inconsistent because $\Delta lfare_{i,t-1}$ is correlated with Δu_{it}; we include the OLS estimates for comparison. We also apply the simple pooled IV procedure, where separate reduced forms are estimated for $\Delta lfare_{i,t-1}$: one for 1999, with $lfare_{i,t-2}$ and $\Delta concen_{it}$ in the reduced form, and one for 2000, with $lfare_{i,t-2}$, $lfare_{i,t-3}$ and $\Delta concen_{it}$ in the reduced form. The fitted values are used in the pooled IV estimation, with robust standard errors. (We only use $\Delta concen_{it}$ in the IV list at time t.) Finally, we apply the Arellano and Bond (1991) GMM procedure. The results are given in Table 11.2.

As is seen from column (1), the POLS estimate of ρ is actually negative and statistically different from zero. By contrast, the two IV methods give positive and statistically significant estimates. The GMM estimate of ρ is larger, and it also has a smaller standard error (as we would hope for GMM). Compared with the POLS es-

Table 11.2
Dynamic Airfare Model, First Differencing IV Estimation

Dependent Variable Explanatory Variable	*lfare* (1) Pooled OLS	(2) Pooled IV	(3) Arellano-Bond
$lfare_{-1}$	−.126 (.027)	.219 (.062)	.333 (.055)
concen	.076 (.053)	.126 (.056)	.152 (.040)
N	1,149	1,149	1,149

The pooled IV estimates on the FD equation are obtained by first estimating separate reduced forms for $\Delta lfare_{-1}$ for 1999 and 2000, where the IVs for 1999 are $lfare_{-2}$ and $\Delta concen$ and those for 2000 are $lfare_{-2}$, $lfare_{-3}$, and $\Delta concen$.
The POLS and pooled IV standard errors are robust to heteroskedasticity and serial correlation. The GMM standard errors are obtained from an optimal weighting matrix.
Separate year intercepts were estimated for all procedures (not reported).
The Arellano and Bond estimates were obtained using the xtabond command in Stata 9.0.

timate, the IV estimates of the *concen* coefficient are larger and, especially for GMM, much more statistically significant.

In Example 11.3, the estimated ρ is quite far from one, and the IV estimates appear to be well behaved. In some applications, ρ is close to unity, and this leads to a weak instrument problem, as discussed briefly in the previous subsection. The problem is that the lagged change, $\Delta y_{i,t-1}$, is not very highly correlated with $(y_{i,t-2}, \ldots, y_{i0})$. In fact, when $\rho = 1$, so that $\{y_{it}\}$ has a unit root, there is no correlation, and both the pooled IV and Arellano and Bond procedures break down.

Arellano and Bover (1995) and Ahn and Schmidt (1995) suggest adding additional moment conditions that improve the efficiency of the GMM estimator. For example, in the basic model (11.61), Ahn and Schmidt show that assumption (11.62)—and actually weaker versions based on zero correlation—implies the additional set of nonredundant orthogonality conditions

$$\mathrm{E}(v_{iT}\Delta u_{i,t-1}) = 0, \qquad t = 2, \ldots, T-1,$$

where $v_{iT} = c_i + u_{iT}$ is the composite error in the last time period. Then, we can specify the equations

$$\Delta y_{it} = \rho \Delta y_{i,t-1} + \Delta u_{it}, \qquad t = 2, \ldots, T$$

$$y_{iT} = \rho y_{i,T-1} + v_{iT}$$

and combine the original Arellano and Bond orthogonality conditions for the first set of equations with those of Ahn and Schmidt for the latter equation. The resulting moment conditions are nonlinear in ρ, which takes us outside the realm of linear GMM. We cover nonlinear GMM methods in Chapter 14. Blundell and Bond (1998) obtained additional linear moment restrictions in the levels equation $y_{it} = \rho y_{i,t-1} + v_{it}$ based on y_{i0} being drawn from a steady-state distribution. The extra moment conditions are especially helpful for improving the precision (and even reducing the bias) in the GMM estimator when ρ is close to one. See also Hahn (1999). Of course, when $\rho = 1$ it makes no sense to assume the existence of a steady-state distribution (although that condition can be weakened somewhat). See Arellano (2003) and Baltagi (2001, Chapter 8) for further discussion of the AR(1) model, with and without strictly exogenous and sequentially exogenous explanatory variables.

11.7 Models with Individual-Specific Slopes

The unobserved effects models we have studied up to this point all have an additive unobserved effect that has the same partial effect on y_{it} in all time periods. This assumption may be too strong for some applications. We now turn to models that allow for individual-specific slopes.

11.7.1 Random Trend Model

Consider the following extension of the standard unobserved effects model:

$$y_{it} = c_i + g_i t + \mathbf{x}_{it}\boldsymbol{\beta} + u_{it}, \qquad t = 1, 2, \ldots, T. \tag{11.64}$$

This is sometimes called a **random trend model**, as each individual, firm, city, and so on is allowed to have its own time trend. The individual-specific trend is an additional source of heterogeneity. If y_{it} is the natural log of a variable, as is often the case in economic studies, then g_i is (roughly) the average growth rate over a period (holding the explanatory variables fixed). Then equation (11.64) is referred to a **random growth model**; see, for example, Heckman and Hotz (1989).

In many applications of equation (11.64) we want to allow (c_i, g_i) to be arbitrarily correlated with $\mathbf{x}_{it}$. (Unfortunately, allowing this correlation makes the name "random trend model" conflict with our previous usage of random versus fixed effects.) For example, if one element of $\mathbf{x}_{it}$ is an indicator of program participation, equation (11.64) allows program participation to depend on individual-specific trends (or growth rates) in addition to the level effect, c_i. We proceed without imposing restrictions on correlations among $(c_i, g_i, \mathbf{x}_{it})$, so that our analysis is of the fixed effects variety. A random effects approach is also possible, but it is more cumbersome; see Problem 11.5.

For the random trend model, the strict exogeneity assumption on the explanatory variables is

$$\mathrm{E}(u_{it} \mid \mathbf{x}_{i1}, \ldots, \mathbf{x}_{iT}, c_i, g_i) = 0, \tag{11.65}$$

which follows definitionally from the conditional mean specification

$$\mathrm{E}(y_{it} \mid \mathbf{x}_{i1}, \ldots, \mathbf{x}_{iT}, c_i, g_i) = \mathrm{E}(y_{it} \mid \mathbf{x}_{it}, c_i, g_i) = c_i + g_i t + \mathbf{x}_{it}\boldsymbol{\beta}. \tag{11.66}$$

We are still primarily interested in consistently estimating $\boldsymbol{\beta}$.

One approach to estimating $\boldsymbol{\beta}$ is to difference away c_i:

$$\Delta y_{it} = g_i + \Delta\mathbf{x}_{it}\boldsymbol{\beta} + \Delta u_{it}, \qquad t = 2, 3, \ldots, T, \tag{11.67}$$

where we have used the fact that $g_i t - g_i(t-1) = g_i$. Now equation (11.67) is just the standard unobserved effects model we studied in Chapter 10. The key strict exogeneity assumption, $\mathrm{E}(\Delta u_{it} \mid g_i, \Delta\mathbf{x}_{i2}, \ldots, \Delta\mathbf{x}_{iT}) = 0$, $t = 2, 3, \ldots, T$, holds under assumption (11.65). Therefore, we can apply FE or FD methods to equation (11.67) in order to estimate $\boldsymbol{\beta}$.

In differencing the equation to eliminate c_i we lose one time period, so that equation (11.67) applies to $T - 1$ time periods. To apply FE or FD methods to equation (11.67) we must have $T - 1 \geq 2$, or $T \geq 3$. In other words, $\boldsymbol{\beta}$ can be estimated consistently in the random trend model only if $T \geq 3$.

Whether we prefer FE or FD estimation of equation (11.67) depends on the properties of $\{\Delta u_{it}: t = 2, 3, \ldots, T\}$. As we argued in Section 10.6, in some cases it is reasonable to assume that the FD of $\{u_{it}\}$ is serially uncorrelated, in which case the FE method applied to equation (11.67) is attractive. If we make the assumption that the u_{it} are serially uncorrelated and homoskedastic (conditional on $\mathbf{x}_i$, c_i, g_i), then FE applied to equation (11.67) is still consistent and asymptotically normal, but not efficient. The next subsection covers that case explicitly.

Example 11.4 (Random Growth Model for Analyzing Enterprise Zones): Papke (1994) estimates a random growth model to examine the effects of enterprise zones on unemployment claims:

$$\log(uclms_{it}) = \theta_t + c_i + g_i t + \delta_1 ez_{it} + u_{it},$$

so that aggregate time effects are allowed in addition to a jurisdiction-specific growth rate, g_i. She first differences the equation to eliminate c_i and then applies FE estimation to the differences. The data are in EZUNEM.RAW. The estimate of δ_1 is $\hat{\delta}_1 = -.192$ with $\text{se}(\hat{\delta}_1) = .085$. Thus, enterprise zone designation is predicted to lower unemployment claims by about 19.2 percent, and the effect is statistically significant at the 5 percent level.

Friedberg (1998) provides an example, using state-level panel data on divorce rates and divorce laws, that shows how important it can be to allow for state-specific trends. Without state-specific trends, she finds no effect of unilateral divorce laws on divorce rates; with state-specific trends, the estimated effect is large and statistically significant. The estimation method Friedberg uses is the one we discuss in the next subsection.

In using the random trend or random growth model for program evaluation, it may make sense to allow the trend or growth rate to depend on program participation: in addition to shifting the level of y, program participation may also affect the rate of change. In addition to $prog_{it}$, we would include $prog_{it} \cdot t$ in the model:

$$y_{it} = \theta_t + c_i + g_i t + \mathbf{z}_{it}\boldsymbol{\gamma} + \delta_1 prog_{it} + \delta_2 prog_{it} \cdot t + u_{it}.$$

Differencing once, as before, removes c_i,

$$\Delta y_{it} = \xi_t + g_i + \Delta\mathbf{z}_{it}\boldsymbol{\gamma} + \delta_1 \Delta prog_{it} + \delta_2 \Delta(prog_{it} \cdot t) + \Delta u_{it}.$$

We can estimate this differenced equation by FE. An even more flexible specification is to replace $prog_{it}$ and $prog_{it} \cdot t$ with a series of program indicators, $prog1_{it}, \ldots, progM_{it}$, where $progj_{it}$ is one if unit i in time t has been in the program exactly j years, and M is the maximum number of years the program has been around.

If $\{u_{it}\}$ contains substantial serial correlation—more than a random walk—then differencing equation (11.67) might be more attractive. Denote the second difference of y_{it} by

$$\Delta^2 y_{it} \equiv \Delta y_{it} - \Delta y_{i,t-1} = y_{it} - 2y_{i,t-1} + y_{i,t-2},$$

with similar expressions for $\Delta^2 \mathbf{x}_{it}$ and $\Delta^2 u_{it}$. Then

$$\Delta^2 y_{it} = \Delta^2 \mathbf{x}_{it} \boldsymbol{\beta} + \Delta^2 u_{it}, \qquad t = 3, \ldots, T. \tag{11.68}$$

As with the FE transformation applied to equation (11.67), second differencing also eliminates g_i. Because $\Delta^2 u_{it}$ is uncorrelated with $\Delta^2 \mathbf{x}_{is}$, for all t and s, we can estimate equation (11.68) by POLS or a GLS procedure.

When $T = 3$, second differencing is the same as first differencing and then applying FE. Second differencing results in a single cross section on the second-differenced data, so that if the second-difference error is homoskedastic conditional on $\mathbf{x}_i$, the standard OLS analysis on the cross section of second differences is appropriate. Hoxby (1996) uses this method to estimate the effect of teachers' unions on education production using three years of census data.

If $\mathbf{x}_{it}$ contains a time trend, then $\Delta \mathbf{x}_{it}$ contains the same constant for $t = 2, 3, \ldots, T$, which then gets swept away in the FE or FD transformation applied to equation (11.67). Therefore, $\mathbf{x}_{it}$ cannot have time-constant variables *or* variables that have exact linear time trends for all cross section units.

11.7.2 General Models with Individual-Specific Slopes

We now consider a more general model with interactions between time-varying explanatory variables and some unobservable, time-constant variables:

$$y_{it} = \mathbf{w}_{it} \mathbf{a}_i + \mathbf{x}_{it} \boldsymbol{\beta} + u_{it}, \qquad t = 1, 2, \ldots, T, \tag{11.69}$$

where $\mathbf{w}_{it}$ is $1 \times J$, $\mathbf{a}_i$ is $J \times 1$, $\mathbf{x}_{it}$ is $1 \times K$, and $\boldsymbol{\beta}$ is $K \times 1$. The standard unobserved effects model is a special case with $\mathbf{w}_{it} \equiv 1$; the random trend model is a special case with $\mathbf{w}_{it} = \mathbf{w}_t = (1, t)$.

Equation (11.69) allows some time-constant unobserved heterogeneity, contained in the vector $\mathbf{a}_i$, to interact with some of the observable explanatory variables. For example, suppose that $prog_{it}$ is a program participation indicator and y_{it} is an outcome variable. The model

$$y_{it} = a_{i1} + a_{i2} \cdot prog_{it} + \mathbf{x}_{it}\boldsymbol{\beta} + u_{it}$$

allows the effect of the program to depend on the unobserved effect a_{i2} (which may or may not be tied to a_{i1}). While we are interested in estimating $\boldsymbol{\beta}$, we are also interested in the average effect of the program, $\alpha_2 = \mathrm{E}(a_{i2})$. We cannot hope to get good estimators of the a_{i2} in the usual case of small T. Polachek and Kim (1994) study such models, where the return to experience is allowed to be person-specific. Lemieux (1998) estimates a model where unobserved heterogeneity is rewarded differently in the union and nonunion sectors.

In the general model, we initially focus on estimating $\boldsymbol{\beta}$ and then turn to estimation of $\boldsymbol{\alpha} = \mathrm{E}(\mathbf{a}_i)$, which is the vector of average partial effects for the covariates $\mathbf{z}_{it}$. The strict exogeneity assumption is the natural extension of assumption (11.65):

ASSUMPTION FE.1′: $\mathrm{E}(u_{it} \mid \mathbf{w}_i, \mathbf{x}_i, \mathbf{a}_i) = 0$, $t = 1, 2, \ldots, T$.

Along with equation (11.69), Assumption FE.1′ is equivalent to

$$\mathrm{E}(y_{it} \mid \mathbf{w}_{i1}, \ldots, \mathbf{w}_{iT}, \mathbf{x}_{i1}, \ldots, \mathbf{x}_{iT}, \mathbf{a}_i) = \mathrm{E}(y_{it} \mid \mathbf{w}_{it}, \mathbf{x}_{it}, \mathbf{a}_i) = \mathbf{w}_{it}\mathbf{a}_i + \mathbf{x}_{it}\boldsymbol{\beta},$$

which says that, once $\mathbf{w}_{it}$, $\mathbf{x}_{it}$, and $\mathbf{a}_i$ have been controlled for, $(\mathbf{w}_{is}, \mathbf{x}_{is})$ for $s \neq t$ do not help to explain y_{it}.

Define $\mathbf{W}_i$ as the $T \times J$ matrix with tth row $\mathbf{w}_{it}$, and similarly for the $T \times K$ matrix $\mathbf{X}_i$. Then equation (11.69) can be written as

$$\mathbf{y}_i = \mathbf{W}_i\mathbf{a}_i + \mathbf{X}_i\boldsymbol{\beta} + \mathbf{u}_i. \tag{11.70}$$

Assuming that $\mathbf{W}_i'\mathbf{W}_i$ is nonsingular (technically, with probability one), define

$$\mathbf{M}_i \equiv \mathbf{I}_T - \mathbf{W}_i(\mathbf{W}_i'\mathbf{W}_i)^{-1}\mathbf{W}_i', \tag{11.71}$$

the projection matrix onto the null space of $\mathbf{W}_i$ (the matrix $\mathbf{W}_i(\mathbf{W}_i'\mathbf{W}_i)^{-1}\mathbf{W}_i'$ is the projection matrix onto the column space of $\mathbf{W}_i$). In other words, for each cross section observation i, $\mathbf{M}_i\mathbf{y}_i$ is the $T \times 1$ vector of residuals from the time series regression

$$y_{it} \text{ on } \mathbf{w}_{it}, \qquad t = 1, 2, \ldots, T. \tag{11.72}$$

In the basic FE case, regression (11.72) is the regression y_{it} on 1, $t = 1, 2, \ldots, T$, and the residuals are simply the time-demeaned variables. In the random trend case, the regression is y_{it} on 1, t, $t = 1, 2, \ldots, T$, which linearly detrends y_{it} for each i.

The $T \times K$ matrix $\mathbf{M}_i\mathbf{X}_i$ contains as its rows the $1 \times K$ vectors of residuals from the regression $\mathbf{x}_{it}$ on $\mathbf{w}_{it}$, $t = 1, 2, \ldots, T$. The usefulness of premultiplying by $\mathbf{M}_i$ is that it allows us to eliminate the unobserved effect $\mathbf{a}_i$ by premultiplying equation (11.70) through by $\mathbf{M}_i$ and noting that $\mathbf{M}_i\mathbf{W}_i = \mathbf{0}$:

$$\ddot{\mathbf{y}}_i = \ddot{\mathbf{X}}_i\boldsymbol{\beta} + \ddot{\mathbf{u}}_i, \tag{11.73}$$

where $\ddot{\mathbf{y}}_i = \mathbf{M}_i\mathbf{y}_i$, $\ddot{\mathbf{X}}_i = \mathbf{M}_i\mathbf{X}_i$, and $\ddot{\mathbf{u}}_i = \mathbf{M}_i\mathbf{u}_i$. This is an extension of the within transformation used in basic FE estimation.

To consistently estimate $\boldsymbol{\beta}$ by system OLS on equation (11.73), we make the following assumption:

ASSUMPTION FE.2′: rank $\mathrm{E}(\ddot{\mathbf{X}}_i'\ddot{\mathbf{X}}_i) = K$, where $\ddot{\mathbf{X}}_i = \mathbf{M}_i\mathbf{X}_i$.

The rank of $\mathbf{M}_i$ is $T - J$, so a necessary condition for Assumption FE.2′ is $J < T$. In other words, we must have at least one more time period than the number of elements in $\mathbf{a}_i$. In the basic unobserved effects model, $J = 1$, and we know that $T \geq 2$ is needed. In the random trend model, $J = 2$, and we need $T \geq 3$ to estimate $\boldsymbol{\beta}$.

The system OLS estimator of equation (11.73) is

$$\hat{\boldsymbol{\beta}}_{FE} = \left(\sum_{i=1}^{N} \ddot{\mathbf{X}}_i'\ddot{\mathbf{X}}_i\right)^{-1}\left(\sum_{i=1}^{N} \ddot{\mathbf{X}}_i'\ddot{\mathbf{y}}_i\right) = \boldsymbol{\beta} + \left(N^{-1}\sum_{i=1}^{N} \ddot{\mathbf{X}}_i'\ddot{\mathbf{X}}_i\right)^{-1}\left(N^{-1}\sum_{i=1}^{N} \ddot{\mathbf{X}}_i'\mathbf{u}_i\right).$$

Under Assumption FE.1′, $\mathrm{E}(\ddot{\mathbf{X}}_i'\mathbf{u}_i) = \mathbf{0}$, and under Assumption FE.2′, rank $\mathrm{E}(\ddot{\mathbf{X}}_i'\ddot{\mathbf{X}}_i) = K$, and so the usual consistency argument goes through. Generally, it is possible that for some observations, $\ddot{\mathbf{X}}_i'\ddot{\mathbf{X}}_i$ has rank less than K. For example, this result occurs in the standard FE case when $\mathbf{x}_{it}$ does not vary over time for unit i. However, under Assumption FE.2′, $\hat{\boldsymbol{\beta}}_{FE}$ should be well defined unless our cross section sample size is small or we are unlucky in obtaining the sample.

Naturally, the FE estimator is $\sqrt{N}$-asymptotically normally distributed. To obtain the simplest expression for its asymptotic variance, we add the assumptions of constant conditional variance and no (conditional) serial correlation on the idiosyncratic errors $\{u_{it}: t = 1, 2, \ldots, T\}$.

ASSUMPTION FE.3′: $\mathrm{E}(\mathbf{u}_i\mathbf{u}_i' \mid \mathbf{w}_i, \mathbf{x}_i, \mathbf{a}_i) = \sigma_u^2\mathbf{I}_T$.

Under Assumption FE.3′, iterated expectations implies

$$\mathrm{E}(\ddot{\mathbf{X}}_i'\mathbf{u}_i\mathbf{u}_i'\ddot{\mathbf{X}}_i) = \mathrm{E}[\ddot{\mathbf{X}}_i'\mathrm{E}(\mathbf{u}_i\mathbf{u}_i' \mid \mathbf{W}_i, \mathbf{X}_i)\ddot{\mathbf{X}}_i] = \sigma_u^2\mathrm{E}(\ddot{\mathbf{X}}_i'\ddot{\mathbf{X}}_i).$$

Using essentially the same argument as in Section 10.5.2, under Assumptions FE.1′, FE.2′, and FE.3′, Avar $\sqrt{N}(\hat{\boldsymbol{\beta}}_{FE} - \boldsymbol{\beta}) = \sigma_u^2[\mathrm{E}(\ddot{\mathbf{X}}_i'\ddot{\mathbf{X}}_i)]^{-1}$, and so $\mathrm{Avar}(\hat{\boldsymbol{\beta}}_{FE})$ is consistently estimated by

$$\mathrm{Av\hat{a}r}(\hat{\boldsymbol{\beta}}_{FE}) = \hat{\sigma}_u^2\left(\sum_{i=1}^{N}\ddot{\mathbf{X}}_i'\ddot{\mathbf{X}}_i\right)^{-1}, \tag{11.74}$$

where $\hat{\sigma}_u^2$ is a consistent estimator for σ_u^2. As with the standard FE analysis, we must use some care in obtaining $\hat{\sigma}_u^2$. We have

$$\begin{aligned}\sum_{t=1}^{T}\mathrm{E}(\ddot{u}_{it}^2) &= \mathrm{E}(\ddot{\mathbf{u}}_i'\ddot{\mathbf{u}}_i) = \mathrm{E}[\mathrm{E}(\mathbf{u}_i'\mathbf{M}_i\mathbf{u}_i \mid \mathbf{W}_i, \mathbf{X}_i)] = \mathrm{E}\{\mathrm{tr}[\mathrm{E}(\mathbf{u}_i\mathbf{u}_i'\mathbf{M}_i \mid \mathbf{W}_i, \mathbf{X}_i)]\}\\ &= \mathrm{E}\{\mathrm{tr}[\mathrm{E}(\mathbf{u}_i\mathbf{u}_i' \mid \mathbf{W}_i, \mathbf{X}_i)\mathbf{M}_i]\} = \mathrm{E}[\mathrm{tr}(\sigma_u^2\mathbf{M}_i)] = (T-J)\sigma_u^2\end{aligned} \tag{11.75}$$

since $\mathrm{tr}(\mathbf{M}_i) = T - J$. Let $\hat{\ddot{u}}_{it} = \ddot{y}_{it} - \ddot{\mathbf{x}}_{it}\hat{\boldsymbol{\beta}}_{FE}$. Then equation (11.75) and standard arguments imply that an unbiased and consistent estimator of σ_u^2 is

$$\hat{\sigma}_u^2 = [N(T-J) - K]^{-1}\sum_{i=1}^{N}\sum_{t=1}^{T}\hat{\ddot{u}}_{it}^2 = \mathrm{SSR}/[N(T-J) - K]. \tag{11.76}$$

The SSR in equation (11.76) is from the pooled regression

$$\ddot{y}_{it} \text{ on } \ddot{\mathbf{x}}_{it}, \qquad t = 1, 2, \ldots, T;\ i = 1, 2, \ldots, N, \tag{11.77}$$

which can be used to obtain $\hat{\boldsymbol{\beta}}_{FE}$. Division of the SSR from regression (11.77) by $N(T-J) - K$ produces $\hat{\sigma}_u^2$. The standard errors reported from regression (11.77) will be off because the SSR is only divided by $NT - K$; the adjustment factor is $\{(NT-K)/[N(T-J)-K]\}^{1/2}$.

A standard F statistic for testing hypotheses about $\boldsymbol{\beta}$ is also asymptotically valid. Let Q be the number of restrictions on $\boldsymbol{\beta}$ under H_0, and let SSR_r be the restricted sum of squared residuals from a regression like regression (11.77) but with the restrictions on $\boldsymbol{\beta}$ imposed. Let SSR_{ur} be the unrestricted sum of squared residuals. Then

$$F = \frac{(\mathrm{SSR}_r - \mathrm{SSR}_{ur})}{\mathrm{SSR}_{ur}} \cdot \frac{[N(T-J) - K]}{Q} \tag{11.78}$$

can be treated as having an F distribution with Q and $N(T-J) - K$ degrees of freedom. Unless we add a (conditional) normality assumption on $\mathbf{u}_i$, equation (11.78) does not have an exact F distribution, but it is asymptotically valid because $Q \cdot F \overset{a}{\sim} \chi_Q^2$.

Without Assumption FE.3′, equation (11.74) is no longer valid as the variance estimator and equation (11.78) is not a valid test statistic. But the robust variance matrix estimator (10.59) can be used with the new definitions for $\ddot{\mathbf{X}}_i$ and $\hat{\ddot{\mathbf{u}}}_i$. This step leads directly to robust Wald statistics for multiple restrictions.

To obtain a consistent estimator of $\boldsymbol{\alpha} = \mathrm{E}(\mathbf{a}_i)$, premultiply equation (11.72) by $(\mathbf{W}_i'\mathbf{W}_i)^{-1}\mathbf{W}_i'$ and rearrange to get

$$\mathbf{a}_i = (\mathbf{W}_i'\mathbf{W}_i)^{-1}\mathbf{W}_i'(\mathbf{y}_i - \mathbf{X}_i\boldsymbol{\beta}) - (\mathbf{W}_i'\mathbf{W}_i)^{-1}\mathbf{W}_i'\mathbf{u}_i. \tag{11.79}$$

Under Assumption FE.1$'$, $\mathrm{E}(\mathbf{u}_i \mid \mathbf{W}_i) = \mathbf{0}$, and so the second term in equation (11.79) has a zero expected value. Therefore, assuming that the expected value exists,

$$\boldsymbol{\alpha} = \mathrm{E}[(\mathbf{W}_i'\mathbf{W}_i)^{-1}\mathbf{W}_i'(\mathbf{y}_i - \mathbf{X}_i\boldsymbol{\beta})].$$

So a consistent, $\sqrt{N}$-asymptotically normal estimator of $\boldsymbol{\alpha}$ is

$$\hat{\boldsymbol{\alpha}} = N^{-1}\sum_{i=1}^{N}(\mathbf{W}_i'\mathbf{W}_i)^{-1}\mathbf{W}_i'(\mathbf{y}_i - \mathbf{X}_i\hat{\boldsymbol{\beta}}_{FE}). \tag{11.80}$$

With fixed T we cannot consistently estimate the $\mathbf{a}_i$ when they are viewed as parameters. However, for each i, the term in the summand in equation (11.80), call it $\hat{\mathbf{a}}_i$, is an *unbiased* estimator of $\mathbf{a}_i$ under Assumptions FE.1$'$ and FE.2$'$. This conclusion is easy to show: $\mathrm{E}(\hat{\mathbf{a}}_i \mid \mathbf{W}, \mathbf{X}) = (\mathbf{W}_i'\mathbf{W}_i)^{-1}\mathbf{W}_i'[\mathrm{E}(\mathbf{y}_i \mid \mathbf{W}, \mathbf{X}) - \mathbf{X}_i\mathrm{E}(\hat{\boldsymbol{\beta}}_{FE} \mid \mathbf{W}, \mathbf{X})] = (\mathbf{W}_i'\mathbf{W}_i)^{-1}\mathbf{W}_i'[\mathbf{W}_i\mathbf{a}_i + \mathbf{X}_i\boldsymbol{\beta} - \mathbf{X}_i\boldsymbol{\beta}] = \mathbf{a}_i$, where we have used the fact that $\mathrm{E}(\hat{\boldsymbol{\beta}}_{FE} \mid \mathbf{W}, \mathbf{X}) = \boldsymbol{\beta}$. The estimator $\hat{\boldsymbol{\alpha}}$ simply averages the $\hat{\mathbf{a}}_i$ over all cross section observations.

The asymptotic variance of $\sqrt{N}(\hat{\boldsymbol{\alpha}} - \boldsymbol{\alpha})$ can be obtained by expanding equation (11.80) and plugging in $\sqrt{N}(\hat{\boldsymbol{\beta}}_{FE} - \boldsymbol{\beta}) = [\mathrm{E}(\ddot{\mathbf{X}}_i'\ddot{\mathbf{X}}_i)]^{-1}(N^{-1/2}\sum_{i=1}^{N}\ddot{\mathbf{X}}_i'\mathbf{u}_i) + o_p(1)$. A consistent estimator of Avar $\sqrt{N}(\hat{\boldsymbol{\alpha}} - \boldsymbol{\alpha})$ can be shown to be

$$N^{-1}\sum_{i=1}^{N}[(\hat{\mathbf{a}}_i - \hat{\boldsymbol{\alpha}}) - \hat{\mathbf{C}}\hat{\mathbf{A}}^{-1}\ddot{\mathbf{X}}_i'\hat{\ddot{\mathbf{u}}}_i][(\hat{\mathbf{a}}_i - \hat{\boldsymbol{\alpha}}) - \hat{\mathbf{C}}\hat{\mathbf{A}}^{-1}\ddot{\mathbf{X}}_i'\hat{\ddot{\mathbf{u}}}_i]', \tag{11.81}$$

where $\hat{\mathbf{a}}_i \equiv (\mathbf{W}_i'\mathbf{W}_i)^{-1}\mathbf{W}_i'(\mathbf{y}_i - \mathbf{X}_i\hat{\boldsymbol{\beta}}_{FE})$, $\hat{\mathbf{C}} \equiv N^{-1}\sum_{i=1}^{N}(\mathbf{W}_i'\mathbf{W}_i)^{-1}\mathbf{W}_i'\mathbf{X}_i$, $\hat{\mathbf{A}} \equiv N^{-1}\sum_{i=1}^{N}\ddot{\mathbf{X}}_i'\ddot{\mathbf{X}}_i$, and $\hat{\ddot{\mathbf{u}}}_i \equiv \ddot{\mathbf{y}}_i - \ddot{\mathbf{X}}_i\hat{\boldsymbol{\beta}}_{FE}$. This estimator is fully robust in the sense that it does not rely on Assumption FE.3$'$. As usual, asymptotic standard errors of the elements of $\hat{\boldsymbol{\alpha}}$ are obtained by multiplying expression (11.81) by N and taking the square roots of the diagonal elements. As special cases, expression (11.81) can be applied to the traditional unobserved effects and random trend models.

The estimator $\hat{\boldsymbol{\alpha}}$ in equation (11.81) is not necessarily the most efficient. A better approach is to use the moment conditions for $\hat{\boldsymbol{\beta}}_{FE}$ and $\hat{\boldsymbol{\alpha}}$ simultaneously. This leads to nonlinear instrumental variables methods, something we take up in Chapter 14. Chamberlain (1992a) covers the efficient method of moments approach to estimating $\boldsymbol{\alpha}$ and $\boldsymbol{\beta}$; see also Lemieux (1998).

11.7.3 Robustness of Standard Fixed Effects Methods

In the previous two sections, we assumed that a set of slope coefficients, $\boldsymbol{\beta}$, did not vary across unit, and that we know the set of slope coefficients, generally $\mathbf{a}_i$ in (11.69), that might vary across i. Even in this situation, the allowable dimension of the unobserved heterogeneity is restricted by the number of time periods, T. In this subsection we study what happens if we mistakenly treat some random slopes as if they are fixed and apply standard FE methods. We might ignore some heterogeneity because we are ignorant of the scope of heterogeneity in the model or because we simply do not have enough time periods to proceed with a general analysis.

We begin with an extension of the usual model to allow for unit-specific slopes,

$$y_{it} = c_i + \mathbf{x}_{it}\mathbf{b}_i + u_{it} \tag{11.82}$$

$$E(u_{it} \mid \mathbf{x}_i, c_i, \mathbf{b}_i) = 0, \qquad t = 1, \ldots, T, \tag{11.83}$$

where $\mathbf{b}_i$ is $K \times 1$. However, unlike in Section 11.6.2, we now ignore the heterogeneity in the slopes and act as if $\mathbf{b}_i$ is constant all i. We think c_i might be correlated with at least some elements of $\mathbf{x}_{it}$, and therefore we apply the usual FE estimator. The question we address here is, when does the usual FE estimator consistently estimate the population average effect, $\boldsymbol{\beta} = \mathrm{E}(\mathbf{b}_i)$?

In addition to assumption (11.83), we naturally need the usual FE rank condition, Assumption FE.2. But what else is needed for FE to consistently estimate $\boldsymbol{\beta}$? It helps to write $\mathbf{b}_i = \boldsymbol{\beta} + \mathbf{d}_i$ where the unit-specific deviation from the average, $\mathbf{d}_i$, necessarily has a zero mean. Then

$$y_{it} = c_i + \mathbf{x}_{it}\boldsymbol{\beta} + \mathbf{x}_{it}\mathbf{d}_i + u_{it} \equiv c_i + \mathbf{x}_{it}\boldsymbol{\beta} + v_{it}, \tag{11.84}$$

where $v_{it} \equiv \mathbf{x}_{it}\mathbf{d}_i + u_{it}$. As we saw in Section 10.5.6, a sufficient condition for consistency of the FE estimator (along with Assumption FE.2) is

$$\mathrm{E}(\ddot{\mathbf{x}}_{it}'\ddot{v}_{it}) = \mathbf{0}, \qquad t = 1, \ldots, T. \tag{11.85}$$

But $\ddot{v}_{it} = \ddot{\mathbf{x}}_{it}\mathbf{d}_i + \ddot{u}_{it}$ and $\mathrm{E}(\ddot{\mathbf{x}}_{it}'\ddot{u}_{it}) = \mathbf{0}$ by (11.83). Therefore, the extra assumption that ensures (11.85) is $\mathrm{E}(\ddot{\mathbf{x}}_{it}'\ddot{\mathbf{x}}_{it}\mathbf{d}_i) = \mathbf{0}$ for all t. A sufficient condition, and one that is easier to interpret, is

$$\mathrm{E}(\mathbf{b}_i \mid \ddot{\mathbf{x}}_{it}) = \mathrm{E}(\mathbf{b}_i) = \boldsymbol{\beta}, \qquad t = 1, \ldots, T. \tag{11.86}$$

Importantly, condition (11.86) allows the slopes, $\mathbf{b}_i$, to be correlated with the regressors $\mathbf{x}_{it}$ through permanent components. What it rules out is correlation between idiosyncratic movements in $\mathbf{x}_{it}$. We can formalize this statement by writing

$\mathbf{x}_{it} = \mathbf{f}_i + \mathbf{r}_{it}$, $t = 1, \ldots, T$. Then (11.86) holds if $\mathrm{E}(\mathbf{b}_i \mid \mathbf{r}_{i1}, \mathbf{r}_{i2}, \ldots, \mathbf{r}_{iT}) = \mathrm{E}(\mathbf{b}_i)$. So $\mathbf{b}_i$ is allowed to be arbitrarily correlated with the permanent component, $\mathbf{f}_i$. (Of course, $\mathbf{x}_{it} = \mathbf{f}_i + \mathbf{r}_{it}$ is a special representation of the covariates, but it helps to illustrate condition (11.86).)

Wooldridge (2005a) studies a more general class of estimators that includes the usual FE and random trend estimator. Write

$$y_{it} = \mathbf{w}_t \mathbf{a}_i + \mathbf{x}_{it} \mathbf{b}_i + u_{it}, \qquad t = 1, \ldots, T, \tag{11.87}$$

where $\mathbf{w}_t$ is a set of deterministic functions of time. We maintain the standard assumption (11.83) but with $\mathbf{a}_i$ in place of c_i. Now, the "fixed effects" estimator sweeps away $\mathbf{a}_i$ by netting out $\mathbf{w}_t$ from $\mathbf{x}_{it}$. In particular, now let $\ddot{\mathbf{x}}_{it}$ denote the residuals from the regression $\mathbf{x}_{it}$ on $\mathbf{w}_t$, $t = 1, \ldots, T$.

In the random trend model, $\mathbf{w}_t = (1, t)$, and so the elements of $\mathbf{x}_{it}$ have unit-specific linear trends removed in addition to a level effect. Removing even more of the heterogeneity from $\{\mathbf{x}_{it}\}$ makes it even more likely that (11.86) holds. For example, if $\mathbf{x}_{it} = \mathbf{f}_i + \mathbf{h}_i t + \mathbf{r}_{it}$, then $\mathbf{b}_i$ can be arbitrarily correlated with $(\mathbf{f}_i, \mathbf{h}_i)$. Of course, individually detrending the $\mathbf{x}_{it}$ requires at least three time periods, and it decreases the variation in $\ddot{\mathbf{x}}_{it}$ compared to the usual FE estimator. Not surprisingly, increasing the dimension of $\mathbf{w}_t$ (subject to the restriction $\dim(\mathbf{w}_t) < T$), generally leads to less precision of the estimator. See Wooldridge (2005a) for further discussion.

Of course, the FD transformation can be used in place of, or in conjunction with, unit-specific detrending; see Section 11.6.1 for the random growth model. For example, if we use the FD transformation followed by the within transformation, it is easily seen that a condition sufficient for consistency of the resulting estimator for $\boldsymbol{\beta}$ is

$$\mathrm{E}(\mathbf{b}_i \mid \Delta\ddot{\mathbf{x}}_{it}) = \mathrm{E}(\mathbf{b}_i), \qquad t = 2, \ldots, T, \tag{11.88}$$

where $\Delta\ddot{\mathbf{x}}_{it} = \Delta\mathbf{x}_{it} - \overline{\Delta\mathbf{x}}_i$ are the demeaned first differences.

The results for the FE estimator (in the generalized sense of removing unit-specific means and possibly trends) extend to fixed effects IV methods, provided we add a constant conditional covariance assumption of the type introduced in Section 6.4.1, but extended to the panel data case. Murtazashvili and Wooldridge (2008) derive a simple set of sufficient conditions. In the model with general trends, we assume the natural extension of Assumption FEIV.1, that is, $\mathrm{E}(u_{it} \mid \mathbf{z}_i, \mathbf{a}_i, \mathbf{b}_i) = 0$ for all t, along with Assumption FEIV.2. We modify assumption (11.86) in the obvious way: replace $\ddot{\mathbf{x}}_{it}$ with $\ddot{\mathbf{z}}_{it}$, the individual-specific detrended instruments:

$$\mathrm{E}(\mathbf{b}_i \mid \ddot{\mathbf{z}}_{it}) = \mathrm{E}(\mathbf{b}_i) = \boldsymbol{\beta}, \qquad t = 1, \ldots, T. \tag{11.89}$$

But something more is needed. Murtazashvili and Wooldridge (2008) show that, along with the previous assumptions, a sufficient condition is

$$\mathrm{Cov}(\ddot{\mathbf{x}}_{it}, \mathbf{b}_i \mid \ddot{\mathbf{z}}_{it}) = \mathrm{Cov}(\ddot{\mathbf{x}}_{it}, \mathbf{b}_i), \qquad t = 1, \ldots, T. \tag{11.90}$$

Note that the covariance $\mathrm{Cov}(\ddot{\mathbf{x}}_{it}, \mathbf{b}_i)$, a $K \times K$ matrix need not be zero, or even constant across time. In other words, unlike condition (11.86), we can allow the detrended covariates to be correlated with the heterogeneous slopes. But the *conditional* covariance cannot depend on the time-demeaned instruments.

We can easily show why (11.90) suffices with the previous assumptions. First, if $\mathrm{E}(\mathbf{d}_i \mid \ddot{\mathbf{z}}_{it}) = \mathbf{0}$, which follows from $\mathrm{E}(\mathbf{b}_i \mid \ddot{\mathbf{z}}_{it}) = \mathrm{E}(\mathbf{b}_i)$, then $\mathrm{Cov}(\ddot{\mathbf{x}}_{it}, \mathbf{d}_i \mid \ddot{\mathbf{z}}_{it}) = \mathrm{E}(\ddot{\mathbf{x}}_{it}\mathbf{d}_i' \mid \ddot{\mathbf{z}}_{it})$, and so $\mathrm{E}(\ddot{\mathbf{x}}_{it}\mathbf{d}_i \mid \ddot{\mathbf{z}}_{it}) = \mathrm{E}(\ddot{\mathbf{x}}_{it}\mathbf{d}_i) \equiv \gamma_t$ under the previous assumptions. Write $\ddot{\mathbf{x}}_{it}\mathbf{d}_i = \gamma_t + r_{it}$ where $\mathrm{E}(r_{iti} \mid \ddot{\mathbf{z}}_{it}) = 0$, $t = 1, \ldots, T$. Then we can write the transformed equation as

$$\ddot{y}_{it} = \ddot{\mathbf{x}}_{it}\boldsymbol{\beta} + \ddot{\mathbf{x}}_{it}\mathbf{d}_i + \ddot{u}_{it} = \ddot{y}_{it} = \ddot{\mathbf{x}}_{it}\boldsymbol{\beta} + \gamma_t + r_{it} + \ddot{u}_{it}. \tag{11.91}$$

Now, if $\mathbf{x}_{it}$ contains a full set of time period dummies, then we can absorb γ_t into $\ddot{\mathbf{x}}_{it}$, and we assume that here. Then the sufficient condition for consistency of IV estimators applied to the transformed equations is $\mathrm{E}[\ddot{\mathbf{z}}_{it}'(r_{it} + \ddot{u}_{it})] = \mathbf{0}$, and this condition is met under the maintained assumptions. In other words, under (11.89) and (11.90), the FE 2SLS estimator is consistent for the average population effect, $\boldsymbol{\beta}$. (Remember, we use "fixed effects" here in the general sense of eliminating the unit-specific trends, $\mathbf{a}_i$.) We must remember to include a full set of time period dummies if we want to apply this robustness result, something that should be done in any case. Naturally, we can also use GMM to obtain a more efficient estimator. If $\mathbf{b}_i$ truly depends on i, then the composite error $r_{it} + \ddot{u}_{it}$ is likely serially correlated and heteroskedastic. See Murtazashvili and Wooldridge (2008) for further discussion and simulation results on the peformance of the FE2SLS estimator. They also provide examples where the key assumptions cannot be expected to hold, such as when endogenous elements of $\mathbf{x}_{it}$ are discrete.

11.7.4 Testing for Correlated Random Slopes

The findings of the previous subsection suggest that standard panel data methods that remove unit-specific heterogeneity have satisfying robustness properties for estimating the population average effects. Nevertheless, in some cases we want to know whether there is evidence for heterogeneous slopes.

We focus on the model (11.82), first under assumption (11.83). We could consider cases where c_i is assumed to be uncorrelated with $\mathbf{x}_i$, but, in keeping with the spirit of the previous subsection, we allow c_i to be correlated with $\mathbf{x}_i$. Then, allowing for the presence of c_i, the goal is effectively to test $\text{Var}(\mathbf{b}_i) = \text{Var}(\mathbf{d}_i) = \mathbf{0}$. Unfortunately, without additional assumptions, it is not possible to test $\text{Var}(\mathbf{d}_i) = \mathbf{0}$, even if we are very specific about the alternative. Suppose we specify as the alternative

$$\text{Var}(\mathbf{b}_i \mid \mathbf{x}_i) = \text{Var}(\mathbf{b}_i) \equiv \mathbf{\Lambda}, \tag{11.92}$$

so that the conditional variance is not a function of $\mathbf{x}_i$. (We also assume $\text{E}(\mathbf{b}_i \mid \mathbf{x}_i) = \text{E}(\mathbf{b}_i)$ under the alternative.) Unfortunately, even assumption (11.92) is not enough to proceed. We need to restrict the conditional variance matrix of the idiosyncratic errors, and the simplest (and most common) assumption is

$$\text{Var}(\mathbf{u}_i \mid \mathbf{x}_i, c_i, \mathbf{b}_i) = \sigma_u^2 \mathbf{I}_T, \tag{11.93}$$

which is the natural extension of Assumption FE.3 from Chapter 10. Along with (11.83), these assumptions allow us to test $\text{Var}(\mathbf{b}_i) = \mathbf{0}$. To see why, write the time-demeaned equation as $\ddot{\mathbf{y}}_i = \ddot{\mathbf{X}}_i \boldsymbol{\beta} + \ddot{\mathbf{v}}_i$, where

$$\text{E}(\ddot{\mathbf{v}}_i \mid \mathbf{x}_i) = \ddot{\mathbf{X}}_i \text{E}(\mathbf{d}_i \mid \mathbf{x}_i) + \text{E}(\ddot{\mathbf{u}}_i \mid \mathbf{x}_i) = \mathbf{0},$$

$$\text{Var}(\ddot{\mathbf{v}}_i \mid \mathbf{x}_i) = \ddot{\mathbf{X}}_i \mathbf{\Lambda} \ddot{\mathbf{X}}_i' + \sigma_u^2 \mathbf{M}_T,$$

and $\mathbf{M}_T = \mathbf{I}_T - \mathbf{j}_T(\mathbf{j}_T'\mathbf{j}_T)^{-1}\mathbf{j}_T$. The last equation shows that, under the maintained assumptions, $\text{Var}(\ddot{\mathbf{v}}_i \mid \mathbf{x}_i)$ does not depend on $\ddot{\mathbf{X}}_i$ if $\mathbf{\Lambda} = \mathbf{0}$. If $\mathbf{\Lambda} \neq \mathbf{0}$, then the composite error in the time-demeaned equation generally exhibits heteroskedasticity and serial correlation that are quadratic functions of the time-demeaned regressors. So, the method would be to estimate $\boldsymbol{\beta}$ by standard FE methods, obtain the FE residuals, and then test whether the variance matrix is a quadratic function of the $\ddot{\mathbf{x}}_{it}$.

The main problem with the previous test is that it associates system heteroskedasticity—that is, variances and covariances depending on the regressors—with the presence of "random" coefficients. But if $\mathbf{b}_i = \boldsymbol{\beta}$ and $\text{Var}(\mathbf{u}_i \mid \mathbf{x}_i, c_i)$ depends on $\mathbf{x}_i$, $\text{Var}(\ddot{\mathbf{v}}_i \mid \mathbf{x}_i)$ generally depends on $\mathbf{x}_i$. In other words, there is no convincing way to distinguish system heteroskedasticity in $\text{Var}(\mathbf{u}_i \mid \mathbf{x}_i, c_i)$ from nonconstant $\mathbf{b}_i$.

Rather than try to test whether $\text{Var}(\mathbf{b}_i) \neq \mathbf{0}$, we can instead test whether $\mathbf{b}_i$ varies with observable variables; that is, we can test

$$\text{H}_0: \text{E}(\mathbf{b}_i \mid \mathbf{x}_i) = \text{E}(\mathbf{b}_i), \tag{11.94}$$

when the covariates satisfy the strict exogeneity assumption (11.83). A sensible alternative is that $\text{E}(\mathbf{b}_i \mid \mathbf{x}_i)$ depends with the time averages, something we can capture with

$$\mathbf{b}_i = \boldsymbol{\alpha} + \boldsymbol{\Gamma}\bar{\mathbf{x}}_i' + \mathbf{d}_i, \tag{11.95}$$

where $\boldsymbol{\alpha}$ is $K \times 1$ and $\boldsymbol{\Gamma}$ is $K \times L$. Under the null hypothesis, $\boldsymbol{\Gamma} = \mathbf{0}$, and then $\boldsymbol{\alpha} = \boldsymbol{\beta}$. Explicitly allowing for aggregate time effects gives

$$\begin{aligned} y_{it} &= \theta_t + c_i + \mathbf{x}_{it}\boldsymbol{\alpha} + \mathbf{x}_{it}\boldsymbol{\Gamma}\bar{\mathbf{x}}_i' + \mathbf{x}_{it}\mathbf{d}_i + u_{it} \\ &= \theta_t + c_i + \mathbf{x}_{it}\boldsymbol{\alpha} + (\bar{\mathbf{x}}_i \otimes \mathbf{x}_{it}) \operatorname{vec}(\boldsymbol{\Gamma}) + \mathbf{x}_{it}\mathbf{d}_i + u_{it} \\ &\equiv \theta_t + c_i + \mathbf{x}_{it}\boldsymbol{\alpha} + (\bar{\mathbf{x}}_i \otimes \mathbf{x}_{it})\boldsymbol{\gamma} + v_{it}, \end{aligned} \tag{11.96}$$

where $v_{it} = \mathbf{x}_{it}\mathbf{d}_i + u_{it}$ and $\boldsymbol{\gamma} = \operatorname{vec}(\boldsymbol{\Gamma})$. The test of $\mathrm{H}_0: \boldsymbol{\gamma} = \mathbf{0}$ is simple to carry out. It amounts to interacting the time averages with the elements of $\mathbf{x}_{it}$ (or, one can choose a subset of $\bar{\mathbf{x}}_i$ to interact with a subset of $\mathbf{x}_{it}$) and obtaining a fully robust test of joint significance in the context of FE estimation. A failure to reject means that if the $\mathbf{b}_i$ vary by i, they apparently do not do so in a way that depends on the time averages of the covariates. The weakness of this test is that it cannot detect heterogeneity in $\mathbf{b}_i$ that is uncorrelated with $\bar{\mathbf{x}}_i$. (Like the previous test, this test is not intended to determine whether FE is consistent for $\boldsymbol{\beta} = \mathrm{E}(\mathbf{b}_i)$.)

We can easily allow some elements of $\mathbf{x}_{it}$ to be endogenous, in which case we write the alternative as $\mathbf{b}_i = \boldsymbol{\alpha} + \boldsymbol{\Gamma}\bar{\mathbf{z}}_i' + \mathbf{d}_i$. Then, under the assumptions in the previous subsection, we estimate

$$y_{it} = \theta_t + c_i + \mathbf{x}_{it}\boldsymbol{\alpha} + (\bar{\mathbf{z}}_i \otimes \mathbf{x}_{it})\boldsymbol{\gamma} + v_{it} \tag{11.97}$$

by FEIV using instruments $(\mathbf{z}_{it}, \bar{\mathbf{z}}_i \otimes \mathbf{z}_{it})$, which is $1 \times L + L^2$. FE2SLS estimation is equivalent to P2SLS estimation of the equation

$$\ddot{y}_{it} = \eta_t + \ddot{\mathbf{x}}_{it}\boldsymbol{\alpha} + (\bar{\mathbf{z}}_i \otimes \ddot{\mathbf{x}}_{it})\boldsymbol{\gamma} + \ddot{v}_{it} \tag{11.98}$$

using instruments $(\ddot{\mathbf{z}}_{it}, \bar{\mathbf{z}}_i \otimes \ddot{\mathbf{z}}_{it})$, where the double dot denotes time demeaning, as usual. This characterization is convenient for obtaining a fully robust test using software that computes P2SLS estimates with standard errors and test statistics robust to arbitrary serial correlation and heteroskedasticity. (Recall that the usual standard errors from (11.98) are not valid even under homoskedasticity and serial independence because it does not properly account for the lost degrees of freedom due to the time demeaning.) Again, we can be selective about what we actually include in $(\bar{\mathbf{z}}_i \otimes \mathbf{x}_{it})$. For example, perhaps we are interested in one element, say b_{i1}, and one element of $\bar{\mathbf{z}}_i$, say $\bar{z}_{i1}$. Then we would simply add the scalar $\bar{z}_{i1}x_{it1}$ to the equation and compute its t statistic. Generally, if we reject H_0, we can entertain (11.97) as an alternative model, provided we make assumption (11.90). We can explicitly study how the partial effects of $\mathbf{x}_{it}$ depend on $\bar{\mathbf{z}}_i$, and also compute the average partial effects. (Alternatively, we can use $\bar{\mathbf{z}}_i - \bar{\mathbf{z}}$ in place of $\bar{\mathbf{z}}_i$, and then the coefficient on coefficient on $\mathbf{x}_{it}$ effectively would be the APE, $\boldsymbol{\beta} = \mathrm{E}(\mathbf{b}_i)$.) We can also include other time-constant variables that drop out of the FE estimation when they appear by themselves; we just simply interact those variables with elements of $\mathbf{x}_{it}$.

Example 11.5 (Testing for Correlated Random Slopes in a Passenger Demand Equation): Suppose we think the elasticity of passenger demand with respect to airfare differs by route, and so we specify the equation

$$lpassen_{it} = \theta_t + c_i + b_i lfare_{it} + u_{it}$$

and we use $z_{it} = concen_{it}$ as the instrument for $lfare_{it}$, just as in Example 11.1. To test whether b_i is correlated with $\bar{z}_i$, we use the equation

$$lpassen_{it} = \theta_t + c_i + \alpha lfare_{it} + \gamma \overline{concen}_i \cdot lfare_{it} + v_{it},$$

where $v_{it} = x_{it} d_i + u_{it}$. We estimate this equation by FEIV using $concen_{it}$ and $\overline{concen}_i \cdot concen_{it}$ as instruments. As mentioned above, this is equivalent to applying pooled IV to equation (11.98), and that is how we obtain the fully robust t statistic. The estimated γ is very large in magnitude, $\hat{\gamma} = -11.05$, but its robust t statistic is only $-.60$. We conclude that there is little evidence in this data set that b_i varies with the time average of the route concentration.

Problems

11.1. Let y_{it} denote the unemployment rate for city i at time t. You are interested in studying the effects of a federally funded job training program on city unemployment rates. Let $\mathbf{z}_i$ denote a vector of time-constant city-specific variables that may influence the unemployment rate (these could include things like geographic location). Let $\mathbf{x}_{it}$ be a vector of time-varying factors that can affect the unemployment rate. The variable $prog_{it}$ is the dummy indicator for program participation: $prog_{it} = 1$ if city i participated at time t. Any sequence of program participation is possible, so that a city may participate in one year but not the next.

a. Discuss the merits of including $y_{i,t-1}$ in the model

$$y_{it} = \theta_t + \mathbf{z}_i \boldsymbol{\gamma} + \mathbf{x}_{it} \boldsymbol{\beta} + \rho_1 y_{i,t-1} + \delta_1 prog_{it} + u_{it}, \qquad t = 1, 2, \ldots, T.$$

State an assumption that allows you to consistently estimate the parameters by POLS.

b. Evaluate the following statement: "The model in part a is of limited value because the POLS estimators are inconsistent if the $\{u_{it}\}$ are serially correlated."

c. Suppose that it is more realistic to assume that program participation depends on time-constant, unobservable city heterogeneity, but not directly on past unemployment. Write down a model that allows you to estimate the effectiveness of the program in this case. Explain how to estimate the parameters, describing any minimal assumptions you need.

d. Write down a model that allows the features in parts a and c. In other words, $prog_{it}$ can depend on unobserved city heterogeneity as well as on past unemployment history. Explain how to consistently estimate the effect of the program, again stating minimal assumptions.

11.2. Consider the following unobserved components model:

$$y_{it} = \mathbf{z}_{it}\gamma + \delta w_{it} + c_i + u_{it}, \qquad t = 1, 2, \ldots, T,$$

where $\mathbf{z}_{it}$ is a $1 \times K$ vector of time-varying variables (which could include time-period dummies), w_{it} is a time-varying scalar, c_i is a time-constant unobserved effect, and u_{it} is the idiosyncratic error. The $\mathbf{z}_{it}$ are strictly exogenous in the sense that

$$\mathrm{E}(\mathbf{z}_{is}' u_{it}) = \mathbf{0}, \qquad \text{all } s,\ t = 1, 2, \ldots, T, \tag{11.99}$$

but c_i is allowed to be arbitrarily correlated with each $\mathbf{z}_{it}$. The variable w_{it} is endogenous in the sense that it can be correlated with u_{it} (as well as with c_i).

a. Suppose that $T = 2$, and that assumption (11.99) contains the only available orthogonality conditions. What are the properties of the OLS estimators of γ and δ on the differenced data? Support your claim (but do not include asymptotic derivations).

b. Under assumption (11.99), still with $T = 2$, write the linear reduced form for the difference Δw_i as $\Delta w_i = \mathbf{z}_{i1}\boldsymbol{\pi}_1 + \mathbf{z}_{i2}\boldsymbol{\pi}_2 + r_i$, where, by construction, r_i is uncorrelated with both $\mathbf{z}_{i1}$ and $\mathbf{z}_{i2}$. What condition on $(\boldsymbol{\pi}_1, \boldsymbol{\pi}_2)$ is needed to identify γ and δ? (Hint: It is useful to rewrite the reduced form of Δw_i in terms of $\Delta \mathbf{z}_i$ and, say, $\mathbf{z}_{i1}$.) How can you test this condition?

c. Now consider the general T case, where we add to assumption (11.99) the assumption $\mathrm{E}(w_{is} u_{it}) = 0$, $s < t$, so that previous values of w_{it} are uncorrelated with u_{it}. Explain carefully, including equations where appropriate, how you would estimate γ and δ.

d. Again consider the general T case, but now use the fixed effects transformation to eliminate c_i:

$\ddot{y}_{it} = \ddot{\mathbf{z}}_{it}\gamma + \delta\ddot{w}_{it} + \ddot{u}_{it}$

What are the properties of the IV estimators if you use $\ddot{\mathbf{z}}_{it}$ and $w_{i,t-p}$, $p \geq 1$, as instruments in estimating this equation by pooled IV? (You can only use time periods $p+1, \ldots, T$ after the initial demeaning.)

11.3. Show that, in the simple model (11.41) with $T > 2$, under the assumptions (11.42), $\mathrm{E}(r_{it} \mid \mathbf{x}_i^*, c_i) = 0$ for all t, and $\mathrm{Var}(r_{it} - \bar{r}_i)$ and $\mathrm{Var}(x_{it}^* - \bar{x}_i^*)$ constant across t, the plim of the FE estimator is

$$\operatorname*{plim}_{N \to \infty} \hat{\beta}_{FE} = \beta \left\{ 1 - \frac{\mathrm{Var}(r_{it} - \bar{r}_i)}{[\mathrm{Var}(x_{it}^* - \bar{x}_i^*) + \mathrm{Var}(r_{it} - \bar{r}_i)]} \right\}$$

Thus, there is attenuation bias in the FE estimator under these assumptions.

11.4. a. Show that, in the FE model, a consistent estimator of $\mu_c \equiv \mathrm{E}(c_i)$ is $\hat{\mu}_c = N^{-1} \sum_{i=1}^{N} (\bar{y}_i - \bar{\mathbf{x}}_i \hat{\boldsymbol{\beta}}_{FE})$.

b. In the random trend model, how would you estimate $\mu_g = \mathrm{E}(g_i)$?

11.5. An RE analysis of model (11.69) would add $\mathrm{E}(\mathbf{a}_i \mid \mathbf{w}_i, \mathbf{x}_i) = \mathrm{E}(\mathbf{a}_i) = \boldsymbol{\alpha}$ to Assumption FE.1′ and, to Assumption FE.3′, $\mathrm{Var}(\mathbf{a}_i \mid \mathbf{w}_i, \mathbf{x}_i) = \boldsymbol{\Lambda}$, where $\boldsymbol{\Lambda}$ is a $J \times J$ positive semidefinite matrix. (This approach allows the elements of $\mathbf{a}_i$ to be arbitrarily correlated.)

a. Define the $T \times 1$ composite error vector $\mathbf{v}_i \equiv \mathbf{W}_i(\mathbf{a}_i - \boldsymbol{\alpha}) + \mathbf{u}_i$. Find $\mathrm{E}(\mathbf{v}_i \mid \mathbf{w}_i, \mathbf{x}_i)$ and $\mathrm{Var}(\mathbf{v}_i \mid \mathbf{w}_i, \mathbf{x}_i)$. Comment on the conditional variance.

b. If you apply the usual RE procedure to the equation

$$y_{it} = \mathbf{w}_{it}\boldsymbol{\alpha} + \mathbf{x}_{it}\boldsymbol{\beta} + v_{it}, \qquad t = 1, 2, \ldots, T$$

what are the asymptotic properties of the RE estimator and the usual RE standard errors and test statistics?

c. How could you modify your inference from part b to be asymptotically valid?

11.6. Does the measurement error model in equations (11.45) to (11.49) apply when w_{it}^* is a lagged dependent variable? Explain.

11.7. In the Chamberlain model in Section 11.1.2, suppose that $\lambda_t = \lambda/T$ for all t. Show that the POLS coefficient on $\mathbf{x}_{it}$ in the regression y_{it} on 1, $\mathbf{x}_{it}$, $\bar{\mathbf{x}}_i$, $t = 1, \ldots, T$; $i = 1, \ldots, N$, is the FE estimator. (Hint: Use partitioned regression.)

11.8. In model (11.1), first difference to remove c_i:

$$\Delta y_{it} = \Delta \mathbf{x}_{it}\boldsymbol{\beta} + \Delta u_{it}, \qquad t = 2, \ldots, T \tag{11.100}$$

Assume that a vector of instruments, $\mathbf{z}_{it}$, satisfies $\mathrm{E}(\Delta u_{it} \mid \mathbf{z}_{it}) = 0,\ t = 2, \ldots, T$. Typically, several elements in $\Delta\mathbf{x}_{it}$ would be included in $\mathbf{z}_{it}$, provided they are appropriately exogenous. Of course the elements of $\mathbf{z}_{it}$ can be arbitrarily correlated with c_i.

a. State the rank condition that is necessary and sufficient for P2SLS estimation of equation (11.100) using instruments $\mathbf{z}_{it}$ to be consistent (for fixed T).

b. Under what additional assumptions are the usual P2SLS standard errors and test statistics asymptotically valid?

c. How would you test for first-order serial correlation in Δu_{it}?

11.9. Consider model (11.1) under Assumptions FEIV.1 and FEIV.2.

a. Show that, under the additional Assumption FEIV.3, the asymptotic variance of $\sqrt{N}(\hat{\boldsymbol{\beta}} - \boldsymbol{\beta})$ is $\sigma_u^2\{\mathrm{E}(\ddot{\mathbf{X}}_i'\ddot{\mathbf{Z}}_i)[\mathrm{E}(\ddot{\mathbf{Z}}_i'\ddot{\mathbf{Z}}_i)]^{-1}\mathrm{E}(\ddot{\mathbf{Z}}_i'\ddot{\mathbf{X}}_i)\}^{-1}$.

b. Propose a consistent estimator of σ_u^2.

c. Show that the 2SLS estimator of $\boldsymbol{\beta}$ from part a can be obtained by means of a dummy variable approach: estimate

$$y_{it} = c_1\, d1_i + \cdots + c_N\, dN_i + \mathbf{x}_{it}\boldsymbol{\beta} + u_{it}$$

by P2SLS, using instruments $(d1_i, d2_i, \ldots, dN_i, \mathbf{z}_{it})$. (Hint: Use the obvious extension of Problem 5.1 to P2SLS, and repeatedly apply the algebra of partial regression.) This is another case where, even though we cannot estimate the c_i consistently with fixed T, we still get a consistent estimator of $\boldsymbol{\beta}$.

d. In using the 2SLS approach from part c, explain why the usually reported standard errors are valid under Assumption FEIV.3.

e. How would you obtain valid standard errors for 2SLS without Assumption FEIV.3?

11.10. Consider the general model (11.69), where unobserved heterogeneity interacts with possibly several variables. Show that the FE estimator of $\boldsymbol{\beta}$ is also obtained by running the regression

$$y_{it} \text{ on } d1_i\mathbf{w}_{it}, d2_i\mathbf{w}_{it}, \ldots, dN_i\mathbf{w}_{it}, \mathbf{x}_{it}, \qquad t = 1, 2, \ldots, T;\ i = 1, 2, \ldots, N, \qquad (11.101)$$

where $dn_i = 1$ if and only if $n = i$. In other words, we interact $\mathbf{w}_{it}$ in each time period with a full set of cross section dummies, and then include all of these terms in a POLS regression with $\mathbf{x}_{it}$. You should also verify that the residuals from regression (11.101) are identical to those from regression (11.77), and that regression (11.101) yields equation (11.76) directly. This proof extends the material on the basic dummy variable regression from Section 10.5.3.

11.11. Apply the random growth model to the data in JTRAIN1.RAW (see Example 10.6):

$$\log(scrap_{it}) = \theta_t + c_i + g_i t + \beta_1 grant_{it} + \beta_2 grant_{i,t-1} + u_{it}$$

Specifically, difference once and then either difference again or apply fixed effects to the first-differenced equation. Discuss the results.

11.12. An unobserved effects model explaining current murder rates in terms of the number of executions in the last three years is

$$mrdrte_{it} = \theta_t + \beta_1 exec_{it} + \beta_2 unem_{it} + c_i + u_{it},$$

where $mrdrte_{it}$ is the number of murders in state i during year t, per 10,000 people; $exec_{it}$ is the total number of executions for the current and prior two years; and $unem_{it}$ is the current unemployment rate, included as a control.

a. Using the data for 1990 and 1993 in MURDER.RAW, estimate this model by first differencing. Notice that you should allow different year intercepts.

b. Under what circumstances would $exec_{it}$ *not* be strictly exogenous (conditional on c_i)? Assuming that no further lags of *exec* appear in the model and that *unem* is strictly exogenous, propose a method for consistently estimating $\boldsymbol{\beta}$ when *exec* is not strictly exogenous.

c. Apply the method from part b to the data in MURDER.RAW. Be sure to also test the rank condition. Do your results differ much from those in part a?

d. What happens to the estimates from parts a and c if Texas is dropped from the analysis?

11.13. Use the data in PRISON.RAW for this question to estimate equation (11.40).

a. Estimate the reduced form equation for $\Delta\log(prison)$ to ensure that *final1* and *final2* are partially correlated with $\Delta\log(prison)$. The elements of $\Delta\mathbf{x}$ should be the changes in the following variables: log(*polpc*), log(*incpc*), *unem*, *black*, *metro*, *ag0_14*, *ag15_17*, *ag18_24*, and *ag25_34*. Is there serial correlation in this reduced form?

b. Use Problem 11.8c to test for serial correlation in Δu_{it}. What do you conclude?

c. Add an FE to equation (11.40). (This procedure is appropriate if we add a random growth term to equation (11.39).) Estimate the equation in first differences by FEIV.

d. Estimate equation (11.39) using the property crime rate, and test for serial correlation in Δu_{it}. Are there important differences compared with the violent crime rate?

11.14. An extension of the model in Example 11.7 that allows enterprise zone designation to affect the *growth* of unemployment claims is

$$\log(uclms_{it}) = \theta_t + c_i + g_i t + \delta_1 ez_{it} + \delta_2 ez_{it} \cdot t + u_{it}.$$

Notice that each jurisdiction also has a separate growth rate g_i.

a. Use the data in EZUNEM.RAW to estimate this model by FD estimation, followed by FE estimation on the differenced equation. Interpret your estimate of $\hat{\delta}_2$. Is it statistically significant?

b. Reestimate the model setting $\delta_1 = 0$. Does this model fit better than the basic model in Example 11.4?

c. Let w_i be an observed, time-constant variable, and suppose we add $\beta_1 w_i + \beta_2 w_i \cdot t$ to the random growth model. Can either β_1 or β_2 be estimated? Explain.

d. If we add $\eta w_i \cdot ez_{it}$, can η be estimated?

11.15. Use the data in JTRAIN1.RAW for this question.

a. Consider the simple equation

$$\log(scrap_{it}) = \theta_t + \beta_1 hrsemp_{it} + c_i + u_{it},$$

where $scrap_{it}$ is the scrap rate for firm i in year t, and $hrsemp_{it}$ is hours of training per employee. Suppose that you difference to remove c_i, but you still think that $\Delta hrsemp_{it}$ and $\Delta\log(scrap_{it})$ are simultaneously determined. Under what assumption is $\Delta grant_{it}$ a valid IV for $\Delta hrsemp_{it}$?

b. Using the differences from 1987 to 1988 only, test the rank condition for identification for the method described in part a.

c. Estimate the FD equation by IV, and discuss the results.

d. Compare the IV estimates on the first differences with the OLS estimates on the first differences.

e. Use the IV method described in part a, but use all three years of data. How does the estimate of β_1 compare with only using two years of data?

11.16. Consider a Hausman and Taylor–type model with a single time-constant explanatory variable:

$$y_{it} = \gamma w_i + \mathbf{x}_{it}\boldsymbol{\beta} + c_i + u_{it},$$

$$\mathrm{E}(u_{it} \mid w_i, \mathbf{x}_i, c_i) = 0, \qquad t = 1, \ldots, T,$$

where $\mathbf{x}_{it}$ is $1 \times K$ vector of time-varying explanatory variables.

a. If we are interested only in estimating $\boldsymbol{\beta}$, how should we proceed, without making additional assumptions (other than a standard rank assumption)?

b. Let r_i be a time-constant proxy variable for c_i in the sense that

$$\mathrm{E}(c_i \mid r_i, w_i, \mathbf{x}_i) = \mathrm{E}(c_i \mid r_i, \mathbf{x}_i) = \delta_0 + \delta_1 r_i + \overline{\mathbf{x}}_i \boldsymbol{\delta}_2.$$

The key assumption is that, once we condition on r_i and $\mathbf{x}_i$, w_i is not partially related to c_i. Assuming the standard proxy variable redundancy assumption $\mathrm{E}(u_{it} \mid w_i, \mathbf{x}_i, c_i, r_i) = 0$, find $\mathrm{E}(y_{it} \mid w_i, \mathbf{x}_i, r_i)$.

c. Using part b, argue that γ is identified. Suggest a pooled OLS estimator.

d. Assume now that (1) $\mathrm{Var}(u_{it} \mid w_i, \mathbf{x}_i, c_i, r_i) = \sigma_u^2$, $t = 1, \ldots, T$; (2) $\mathrm{Cov}(u_{it}, u_{is} \mid w_i, \mathbf{x}_i, c_i, r_i) = 0$, all $t \neq s$; (3) $\mathrm{Var}(c_i \mid w_i, \mathbf{x}_i, r_i) = \sigma_a^2$. How would you efficiently estimate γ (along with $\boldsymbol{\beta}$, δ_0, δ_1, and $\boldsymbol{\delta}_2$)? [Hint: It might be helpful to write $c_i = \delta_0 + \delta_1 r_i + \overline{\mathbf{x}}_i \boldsymbol{\delta}_2 + a_i$, where $\mathrm{E}(a_i \mid w_i, \mathbf{x}_i, r_i) = 0$ and $\mathrm{Var}(a_i \mid w_i, \mathbf{x}_i, r_i) = \sigma_a^2$.]

11.17. Derive equation (11.81).

11.18. Let $\hat{\boldsymbol{\beta}}$ be the REIV estimator.

a. Derive $\mathrm{Avar}[\sqrt{N}(\hat{\boldsymbol{\beta}}_{REIV} - \boldsymbol{\beta})$ without Assumption REIV.3.

b. Show how to consistently estimate the asymptotic variance in part a.

11.19. Use the data in AIRFARE.RAW for this exercise.

a. Estimate the reduced forms underlying the REIV and FEIV analyses in Example 11.1. Using fully robust t statistics, is *concen* sufficiently (partially) correlated with *lfare*?

b. Redo the REIV estimation, but drop the route distance variables. What happens to the estimated elasticity of passenger demand with respect to *fare*?

c. Now consider a model where the elasticity can depend on route distance:

$$lpassen_{it} = \theta_{t1} + \alpha_1 lfare_{it} + \delta_1 ldist_i + \delta_2 ldist_i^2 + \gamma_1(ldist_i - \mu_1) lfare_{it}$$
$$+ \gamma_2(ldist_i^2 - \mu_2) lfare_{it} + c_{i1} + u_{it1},$$

where $\mu_1 = \mathrm{E}(ldist_i)$ and $\mu_2 = \mathrm{E}(ldist_i^2)$. The means are subtracted before forming the interactions so that α_1 is the average partial effect. In using REIV or FEIV to estimate this model, what should be the IVs for the interaction terms?

d. Use the data in AIRFARE.RAW to estimate the model in part c, replacing μ_1 and μ_2 with their sample averages. How do the REIV and FEIV estimates of α_1 compare with the estimates in Table 11.1?

e. Obtain fully robust standard errors for the FEIV estimation, and obtain a fully robust test of joint significance of the interaction terms. (Ignore the estimation of μ_1 and μ_2.) What is the robust 95 percent confidence interval for α_1?

f. Find the estimated elasticities for $dist = 500$ and $dist = 1{,}500$. What do you conclude?

III GENERAL APPROACHES TO NONLINEAR ESTIMATION

In this part we begin our study of nonlinear econometric methods. What we mean by nonlinear needs some explanation because it does not necessarily mean that the underlying model is what we would think of as nonlinear. For example, suppose the population model of interest can be written as $y = \mathbf{x}\boldsymbol{\beta} + u$, but, rather than assuming $\mathrm{E}(u \mid \mathbf{x}) = 0$, we assume that the *median* of u given $\mathbf{x}$ is zero for all $\mathbf{x}$. This assumption implies $\mathrm{Med}(y \mid \mathbf{x}) = \mathbf{x}\boldsymbol{\beta}$, which is a linear model for the conditional median of y given $\mathbf{x}$. (The conditional mean, $\mathrm{E}(y \mid \mathbf{x})$, may or may not be linear in $\mathbf{x}$.) The standard estimator for a conditional median turns out to be least absolute deviations (LAD), not ordinary least squares. Like OLS, the LAD estimator solves a minimization problem: it minimizes the sum of absolute residuals. However, there is a key difference between LAD and OLS: the LAD estimator cannot be obtained in closed form. The lack of a closed-form expression for LAD has implications not only for obtaining the LAD estimates from a sample of data, but also for the asymptotic theory of LAD.

All the estimators we studied in Part II were obtained in closed form, a feature that greatly facilitates asymptotic analysis: we needed nothing more than the weak law of large numbers, the central limit theorem, and the basic algebra of probability limits. When an estimation method does not deliver closed-form solutions, we need to use more advanced asymptotic theory. In what follows, "nonlinear" describes any problem in which the estimators cannot be obtained in closed form.

The three chapters in this part provide the foundation for asymptotic analysis of most nonlinear models encountered in applications with cross section or panel data. We will make certain assumptions concerning continuity and differentiability, and so problems violating these conditions will not be covered. In the general development of M-estimators in Chapter 12, we will mention some of the applications that are ruled out and provide references.

This part of the book is by far the most technical. We will not dwell on the sometimes intricate arguments used to establish consistency and asymptotic normality in nonlinear contexts. For completeness, we do provide some general results on consistency and asymptotic normality for general classes of estimators. However, for specific estimation methods, such as nonlinear least squares, we will only state assumptions that have real impact for performing inference. Unless the underlying *regularity conditions*—which involve assuming that certain moments of the population random variables are finite, as well as assuming continuity and differentiability of the regression function or log-likelihood function—are obviously false, they are usually just assumed. Where possible, the assumptions will correspond closely with those given previously for linear models.

The analysis of maximum likelihood methods in Chapter 13 is greatly simplified once we have given a general treatment of M-estimators. Chapter 14 contains results for generalized method of moments estimators for models nonlinear in parameters. We also briefly discuss the related topic of minimum distance estimation in Chapter 14.

Readers who are not interested in general approaches to nonlinear estimation might use the more technical material in these chapters only when needed for reference in Part IV.

12 M-Estimation, Nonlinear Regression, and Quantile Regression

12.1 Introduction

We begin our study of nonlinear estimation with a general class of estimators known as M-estimators, a term introduced by Huber (1967). (You might think of the "M" as standing for minimization or maximization.) M-estimation methods include maximum likelihood, nonlinear least squares, least absolute deviations, quasi-maximum likelihood, and many other procedures used by econometricians.

Much of this chapter is somewhat abstract and technical, but it is useful to develop a unified theory early on so that it can be applied in a variety of situations. We will carry along the example of nonlinear least squares for cross section data to motivate the general approach. In Sections 12.9 and 12.10, we study multivariate nonlinear regression and quantile regression, two practically important estimation methods.

In a **nonlinear regression model**, we have a random variable, y, and we would like to model $\mathrm{E}(y \mid \mathbf{x})$ as a function of the explanatory variables $\mathbf{x}$, a K-vector. We already know how to estimate models of $\mathrm{E}(y \mid \mathbf{x})$ when the model is linear in its parameters: OLS produces consistent, asymptotically normal estimators. What happens if the regression function is nonlinear in its parameters?

Generally, let $m(\mathbf{x}, \boldsymbol{\theta})$ be a **parametric model** for $\mathrm{E}(y \mid \mathbf{x})$, where m is a *known* function of $\mathbf{x}$ and $\boldsymbol{\theta}$, and $\boldsymbol{\theta}$ is a $P \times 1$ parameter vector. (This is a parametric model because $m(\cdot, \boldsymbol{\theta})$ is assumed to be known up to a *finite* number of parameters.) The dimension of the parameters, P, can be less than or greater than K. The **parameter space**, $\boldsymbol{\Theta}$, is a subset of $\mathbb{R}^P$. This is the set of values of $\boldsymbol{\theta}$ that we are willing to consider in the regression function. Unlike in linear models, for nonlinear models the asymptotic analysis requires explicit assumptions on the parameter space.

An example of a nonlinear regression function is the **exponential regression function**, $m(\mathbf{x}, \boldsymbol{\theta}) = \exp(\mathbf{x}\boldsymbol{\theta})$, where $\mathbf{x}$ is a row vector and contains unity as its first element. This is a useful functional form whenever $y \geq 0$. A regression model suitable when the response y is restricted to the unit interval is the **logistic function**, $m(\mathbf{x}, \boldsymbol{\theta}) = \exp(\mathbf{x}\boldsymbol{\theta})/[1 + \exp(\mathbf{x}\boldsymbol{\theta})]$. Both the exponential and logistic functions are nonlinear in $\boldsymbol{\theta}$.

In any application, there is no guarantee that our chosen model is adequate for $\mathrm{E}(y \mid \mathbf{x})$. We say that we have a **correctly specified model for the conditional mean**, $\mathrm{E}(y \mid \mathbf{x})$, if, for some $\boldsymbol{\theta}_{\mathrm{o}} \in \boldsymbol{\Theta}$,

$$\mathrm{E}(y \mid \mathbf{x}) = m(\mathbf{x}, \boldsymbol{\theta}_{\mathrm{o}}). \tag{12.1}$$

We introduce the subscript "o" on theta to distinguish the parameter vector appearing in $\mathrm{E}(y \mid \mathbf{x})$ from other candidates for that vector. (Often, the value $\boldsymbol{\theta}_{\mathrm{o}}$ is called "the true value of theta," a phrase that is somewhat loose but still useful as shorthand.) As an example, for $y > 0$ and a single explanatory variable $x > 0$, consider the model $m(x, \boldsymbol{\theta}) = \theta_1 x^{\theta_2}$. If the population regression function is $\mathrm{E}(y \mid x) = 4x^{1.5}$, then $\theta_{o1} = 4$ and $\theta_{o2} = 1.5$. We will never know the actual θ_{o1} and θ_{o2} (unless we somehow control the way the data have been generated), but, if the model is correctly specified, then these values exist, and we would like to estimate them. Generic candidates for θ_{o1} and θ_{o2} are labeled θ_1 and θ_2, and, without further information, θ_1 is any positive number and θ_2 is any real number: the parameter space is $\boldsymbol{\Theta} \equiv \{(\theta_1, \theta_2) : \theta_1 > 0, \theta_2 \in \mathbb{R}\}$. For an exponential regression model, $m(\mathbf{x}, \boldsymbol{\theta}) = \exp(\mathbf{x}\boldsymbol{\theta})$ is a correctly specified model for $\mathrm{E}(y \mid \mathbf{x})$ if and only if there is some K-vector $\boldsymbol{\theta}_o$ such that $\mathrm{E}(y \mid \mathbf{x}) = \exp(\mathbf{x}\boldsymbol{\theta}_o)$.

In our analysis of linear models, there was no need to make the distinction between the parameter vector in the population regression function and other candidates for this vector because the estimators in linear contexts are obtained in closed form, and so their asymptotic properties can be studied directly. As we will see, in our theoretical development we need to distinguish the vector appearing in $\mathrm{E}(y \mid \mathbf{x})$ from a generic element of $\boldsymbol{\Theta}$. We will often drop the subscripting by "o" when studying particular applications because the notation can be cumbersome when there are many parameters.

Equation (12.1) is the most general way of thinking about what nonlinear least squares is intended to do: estimate models of conditional expectations. But, as a statistical matter, equation (12.1) is equivalent to a model with an additive, unobservable error with a zero conditional mean:

$$y = m(\mathbf{x}, \boldsymbol{\theta}_o) + u, \qquad \mathrm{E}(u \mid \mathbf{x}) = 0. \tag{12.2}$$

Given equation (12.2), equation (12.1) clearly holds. Conversely, given equation (12.1), we obtain equation (12.2) by *defining* the error to be $u \equiv y - m(\mathbf{x}, \boldsymbol{\theta}_o)$. In interpreting the model and deciding on appropriate estimation methods, we should not focus on the error form in equation (12.2) because, evidently, the additivity of u has some unintended connotations. In particular, we must remember that, in writing the model in additive error form, the *only* thing implied by equation (12.1) is $\mathrm{E}(u \mid \mathbf{x}) = 0$. Depending on the nature of y, the error u may have some unusual properties. For example, if $y \geq 0$ then $u \geq -m(\mathbf{x}, \boldsymbol{\theta}_o)$, in which case u and $\mathbf{x}$ cannot be independent. Heteroskedasticity in the error—that is, $\mathrm{Var}(u \mid \mathbf{x}) \neq \mathrm{Var}(u)$—is present whenever $\mathrm{Var}(y \mid \mathbf{x})$ depends on $\mathbf{x}$, as is very common when y takes on a restricted range of values. Plus, when we introduce randomly sampled observations $\{(\mathbf{x}_i, y_i) : i = 1, 2, \ldots, N\}$, it is too tempting to write the model and its assumptions as "$y_i = m(\mathbf{x}_i, \boldsymbol{\theta}_o) + u_i$ where the u_i are i.i.d. errors." As we discussed in Section 1.4 for the linear model, under random sampling the $\{u_i\}$ are always i.i.d. What is usually meant is that u_i and $\mathbf{x}_i$ are independent, but, for the reasons we just gave, this assumption is often much too strong. The error form of the model does turn out to be useful for defining estimators of asymptotic variances and for obtaining test statistics.

For later reference, we formalize the first **nonlinear least squares (NLS)** assumption as follows:

ASSUMPTION NLS.1: For some $\boldsymbol{\theta}_o \in \boldsymbol{\Theta}$, $\mathrm{E}(y \mid \mathbf{x}) = m(\mathbf{x}, \boldsymbol{\theta}_o)$.

This form of presentation represents the level at which we will state assumptions for particular econometric methods. In our general development of M-estimators that follows, we will need to add conditions involving moments of $m(\mathbf{x}, \boldsymbol{\theta})$ and y, as well as continuity assumptions on $m(\mathbf{x}, \cdot)$.

If we let $\mathbf{w} \equiv (\mathbf{x}, y)$, then $\boldsymbol{\theta}_o$ indexes a feature of the population distribution of $\mathbf{w}$, namely, the conditional mean of y given $\mathbf{x}$. More generally, let $\mathbf{w}$ be an M-vector of random variables with some distribution in the population. We let $\mathcal{W}$ denote the subset of $\mathbb{R}^M$ representing the possible values of $\mathbf{w}$. Let $\boldsymbol{\theta}_o$ denote a parameter vector describing some feature of the distribution of $\mathbf{w}$. This could be a conditional mean, a conditional mean and conditional variance, a conditional median, or a conditional distribution. As shorthand, we call $\boldsymbol{\theta}_o$ "the true parameter" or "the true value of theta." These phrases simply mean that $\boldsymbol{\theta}_o$ is the parameter vector describing the underlying population, something we will make precise later. We assume that $\boldsymbol{\theta}_o$ belongs to a known parameter space $\boldsymbol{\Theta} \subset \mathbb{R}^P$.

We assume that our data come as a random sample of size N from the population; we label this random sample $\{\mathbf{w}_i : i = 1, 2, \ldots\}$, where each $\mathbf{w}_i$ is an M-vector. This assumption is much more general than it may initially seem. It covers cross section models with many equations, and it also covers panel data settings with small time series dimension. The extension to independently pooled cross sections is almost immediate. In the NLS example, $\mathbf{w}_i$ consists of $\mathbf{x}_i$ and y_i, the ith draw from the population on $\mathbf{x}$ and y.

What allows us to estimate $\boldsymbol{\theta}_o$ when it indexes $\mathrm{E}(y \mid \mathbf{x})$? It is the fact that $\boldsymbol{\theta}_o$ is the value of $\boldsymbol{\theta}$ that minimizes the expected squared error between y and $m(\mathbf{x}, \boldsymbol{\theta})$. That is, $\boldsymbol{\theta}_o$ solves the population problem

$$\min_{\boldsymbol{\theta} \in \boldsymbol{\Theta}} \mathrm{E}\{[y - m(\mathbf{x}, \boldsymbol{\theta})]^2\}, \tag{12.3}$$

where the expectation is over the joint distribution of $(\mathbf{x}, y)$. This conclusion follows immediately from basic properties of conditional expectations (in particular, condition CE.8 in Chapter 2). We will give a slightly different argument here. Write

$$[y - m(\mathbf{x}, \boldsymbol{\theta})]^2 = [y - m(\mathbf{x}, \boldsymbol{\theta}_o)]^2 + 2[m(\mathbf{x}, \boldsymbol{\theta}_o) - m(\mathbf{x}, \boldsymbol{\theta})]u + [m(\mathbf{x}, \boldsymbol{\theta}_o) - m(\mathbf{x}, \boldsymbol{\theta})]^2, \tag{12.4}$$

where u is defined in equation (12.2). Now, since $\mathrm{E}(u \mid \mathbf{x}) = 0$, u is uncorrelated with *any* function of $\mathbf{x}$, including $m(\mathbf{x}, \boldsymbol{\theta}_o) - m(\mathbf{x}, \boldsymbol{\theta})$. Thus, taking the expected value of equation (12.4) gives

$$\mathrm{E}\{[y - m(\mathbf{x}, \boldsymbol{\theta})]^2\} = \mathrm{E}\{[y - m(\mathbf{x}, \boldsymbol{\theta}_o)]^2\} + \mathrm{E}\{[m(\mathbf{x}, \boldsymbol{\theta}_o) - m(\mathbf{x}, \boldsymbol{\theta})]^2\}. \tag{12.5}$$

Since the last term in equation (12.5) is nonnegative, it follows that

$$\mathrm{E}\{[y - m(\mathbf{x}, \boldsymbol{\theta})]^2\} \geq \mathrm{E}\{[y - m(\mathbf{x}, \boldsymbol{\theta}_o)]^2\}, \qquad \text{all } \boldsymbol{\theta} \in \boldsymbol{\Theta}. \tag{12.6}$$

The inequality is strict when $\boldsymbol{\theta} \neq \boldsymbol{\theta}_o$ unless $\mathrm{E}\{[m(\mathbf{x}, \boldsymbol{\theta}_o) - m(\mathbf{x}, \boldsymbol{\theta})]^2\} = 0$; for $\boldsymbol{\theta}_o$ to be identified, we will have to rule this possibility out.

Because $\boldsymbol{\theta}_o$ solves the population problem in expression (12.3), the analogy principle—which we introduced in Chapter 4—suggests estimating $\boldsymbol{\theta}_o$ by solving the sample analogue. In other words, we replace the population moment $\mathrm{E}\{[(y - m(\mathbf{x}, \boldsymbol{\theta})]^2\}$ with the sample average. The **NLS estimator** of $\boldsymbol{\theta}_o$, $\hat{\boldsymbol{\theta}}$, solves

$$\min_{\boldsymbol{\theta} \in \boldsymbol{\Theta}} N^{-1} \sum_{i=1}^{N} [y_i - m(\mathbf{x}_i, \boldsymbol{\theta})]^2. \tag{12.7}$$

For now, we assume that a solution to this problem exists.

The NLS objective function in expression (12.7) is a special case of a more general class of estimators. Let $q(\mathbf{w}, \boldsymbol{\theta})$ be a function of the random vector $\mathbf{w}$ and the parameter vector $\boldsymbol{\theta}$. An **M-estimator** of $\boldsymbol{\theta}_o$ solves the problem

$$\min_{\boldsymbol{\theta} \in \boldsymbol{\Theta}} N^{-1} \sum_{i=1}^{N} q(\mathbf{w}_i, \boldsymbol{\theta}), \tag{12.8}$$

assuming that a solution, call it $\hat{\boldsymbol{\theta}}$, exists. The estimator clearly depends on the sample $\{\mathbf{w}_i : i = 1, 2, \ldots, N\}$, but we suppress that fact in the notation.

The objective function for an M-estimator is a sample average of a function of $\mathbf{w}_i$ and $\boldsymbol{\theta}$. The division by N, while needed for the theoretical development, does not affect the minimization problem. Also, the focus on minimization rather than maximization is without loss of generality because maximization can be trivially turned into minimization.

The parameter vector $\boldsymbol{\theta}_o$ is assumed to uniquely solve the population problem

$$\min_{\boldsymbol{\theta} \in \boldsymbol{\Theta}} \mathrm{E}[q(\mathbf{w}, \boldsymbol{\theta})]. \tag{12.9}$$

Comparing equations (12.8) and (12.9), we see that M-estimators are based on the analogy principle. Once $\boldsymbol{\theta}_o$ has been defined, finding an appropriate function q that delivers $\boldsymbol{\theta}_o$ as the solution to problem (12.9) requires basic results from probability theory. Often there is more than one choice of q such that $\boldsymbol{\theta}_o$ solves problem (12.9), in which case the choice depends on efficiency or computational issues. For the next several sections, we carry along the NLS example; we treat maximum likelihood estimation in Chapter 13.

How do we translate the fact that $\boldsymbol{\theta}_o$ solves the population problem (12.9) into consistency of the M-estimator $\hat{\boldsymbol{\theta}}$ that solves problem (12.8)? Heuristically, the argument is as follows. Since for each $\boldsymbol{\theta} \in \boldsymbol{\Theta}$, $\{q(\mathbf{w}_i, \boldsymbol{\theta}) : i = 1, 2, \ldots\}$ is just an i.i.d. sequence, the law of large numbers implies that

$$N^{-1} \sum_{i=1}^{N} q(\mathbf{w}_i, \boldsymbol{\theta}) \xrightarrow{p} \mathrm{E}[q(\mathbf{w}, \boldsymbol{\theta})] \tag{12.10}$$

under very weak finite moment assumptions. Since $\hat{\boldsymbol{\theta}}$ minimizes the function on the left side of equation (12.10) and $\boldsymbol{\theta}_o$ minimizes the function on the right, it seems plausible that $\hat{\boldsymbol{\theta}} \xrightarrow{p} \boldsymbol{\theta}_o$. This informal argument turns out to be correct, except in pathological cases. There are essentially two issues to address. The first is identifiability of $\boldsymbol{\theta}_o$, which is purely a population issue. The second is the sense in which the convergence in equation (12.10) happens across different values of $\boldsymbol{\theta}$ in $\boldsymbol{\Theta}$.

12.2 Identification, Uniform Convergence, and Consistency

We now present a formal consistency result for M-estimators under fairly weak assumptions. As mentioned previously, the conditions can be broken down into two parts. The first part is the **identification** or **identifiability** of $\boldsymbol{\theta}_o$. For nonlinear regression, we showed how $\boldsymbol{\theta}_o$ solves the population problem (12.3). However, we did not argue that $\boldsymbol{\theta}_o$ is always the *unique* solution to problem (12.3). Whether or not this is the case depends on the distribution of $\mathbf{x}$ and the nature of the regression function:

ASSUMPTION NLS.2: $\mathrm{E}\{[m(\mathbf{x}, \boldsymbol{\theta}_o) - m(\mathbf{x}, \boldsymbol{\theta})]^2\} > 0$, all $\boldsymbol{\theta} \in \boldsymbol{\Theta}$, $\boldsymbol{\theta} \neq \boldsymbol{\theta}_o$.

Assumption NLS.2 plays the same role as Assumption OLS.2 in Chapter 4. It can fail if the explanatory variables $\mathbf{x}$ do not have sufficient variation in the population. In fact, in the linear case $m(\mathbf{x}, \boldsymbol{\theta}) = \mathbf{x}\boldsymbol{\theta}$, Assumption NLS.2 holds if and only if rank $\mathrm{E}(\mathbf{x}'\mathbf{x}) = K$, which is just Assumption OLS.2 from Chapter 4. In nonlinear models, Assumption NLS.2 can fail if $m(\mathbf{x}, \boldsymbol{\theta}_o)$ depends on fewer parameters than are actually in $\boldsymbol{\theta}$. For example, suppose that we choose as our model $m(\mathbf{x}, \boldsymbol{\theta}) = \theta_1 + \theta_2 x_2 + \theta_3 x_3^{\theta_4}$, but the true model is linear in x_2: $\theta_{o3} = 0$. Then $\mathrm{E}[(y - m(\mathbf{x}, \boldsymbol{\theta}))]^2$ is minimized for any $\boldsymbol{\theta}$ with $\theta_1 = \theta_{o1}$, $\theta_2 = \theta_{o2}$, $\theta_3 = 0$, and θ_4 any value. If $\theta_{o3} \neq 0$, Assumption NLS.2 would typically hold provided there is sufficient variation in x_2 and x_3. Because identification fails for certain values of $\boldsymbol{\theta}_o$, this is an example of a **poorly identified model**. (See Section 9.5 for other examples of poorly identified models.)

Identification in commonly used nonlinear regression models, such as exponential and logistic regression functions, holds under weak conditions, provided perfect collinearity in $\mathbf{x}$ can be ruled out. For the most part, we will just assume that, when the model is correctly specified, $\boldsymbol{\theta}_o$ is the unique solution to problem (12.3). For the general M-estimation case, we assume that $q(\mathbf{w}, \boldsymbol{\theta})$ has been chosen so that $\boldsymbol{\theta}_o$ is a solution to problem (12.9). Identification requires that $\boldsymbol{\theta}_o$ be the unique solution:

$$\mathrm{E}[q(\mathbf{w}, \boldsymbol{\theta}_o)] < \mathrm{E}[q(\mathbf{w}, \boldsymbol{\theta})], \qquad \text{all } \boldsymbol{\theta} \in \boldsymbol{\Theta}, \quad \boldsymbol{\theta} \neq \boldsymbol{\theta}_o. \tag{12.11}$$

The second component for consistency of the M-estimator is convergence of the sample average $N^{-1} \sum_{i=1}^{N} q(\mathbf{w}_i, \boldsymbol{\theta})$ to its expected value. It turns out that **pointwise convergence in probability**, as stated in equation (12.10), is not sufficient for consistency. That is, it is not enough to simply invoke the usual weak law of large numbers at each $\boldsymbol{\theta} \in \boldsymbol{\Theta}$. Instead, **uniform convergence in probability** is sufficient. Mathematically,

$$\max_{\boldsymbol{\theta} \in \boldsymbol{\Theta}} \left| N^{-1} \sum_{i=1}^{N} q(\mathbf{w}_i, \boldsymbol{\theta}) - \mathrm{E}[q(\mathbf{w}, \boldsymbol{\theta})] \right| \xrightarrow{p} 0. \tag{12.12}$$

Uniform convergence clearly implies pointwise convergence, but the converse is not true: it is possible for equation (12.10) to hold but equation (12.12) to fail. Nevertheless, under certain regularity conditions, the pointwise convergence in equation (12.10) translates into the uniform convergence in equation (12.12).

To state a formal result concerning uniform convergence, we need to be more careful in stating assumptions about the function $q(\cdot, \cdot)$ and the parameter space $\boldsymbol{\Theta}$. Since we are taking expected values of $q(\mathbf{w}, \boldsymbol{\theta})$ with respect to the distribution of $\mathbf{w}$, $q(\mathbf{w}, \boldsymbol{\theta})$ must be a random variable for each $\boldsymbol{\theta} \in \boldsymbol{\Theta}$. Technically, we should assume that $q(\cdot, \boldsymbol{\theta})$ is a *Borel measurable function* on $\mathcal{W}$ for each $\boldsymbol{\theta} \in \boldsymbol{\Theta}$. Since it is very difficult to write down a function that is not Borel measurable, we spend no further time on it. Rest assured that any objective function that arises in econometrics is Borel measurable. You are referred to Billingsley (1979) and Davidson (1994, Chap. 3).

The next assumption concerning q is practically more important. We assume that, for each $\mathbf{w} \in \mathcal{W}$, $q(\mathbf{w}, \cdot)$ is a *continuous function* over the parameter space $\boldsymbol{\Theta}$. All of the problems we treat in detail have objective functions that are continuous in the parameters, but these do not cover all cases of interest. For example, Manski's (1975) maximum score estimator for binary response models has an objective function that is not continuous in $\boldsymbol{\theta}$. (We cover binary response models in Chapter 15.) It is possible to somewhat relax the continuity assumption in order to handle such cases, but we will not need that generality. See Manski (1988, Sect. 7.3) and Newey and McFadden (1994).

Obtaining uniform convergence is generally difficult for unbounded parameter sets, such as $\boldsymbol{\Theta} = \mathbb{R}^P$. It is easiest to assume that $\boldsymbol{\Theta}$ is a *compact subset* of $\mathbb{R}^P$, which means that $\boldsymbol{\Theta}$ is closed and bounded (see Rudin, 1976, Theorem 2.41). Because the natural parameter spaces in most applications are not bounded (and sometimes not closed), the compactness assumption is untidy for developing a general theory of estimation. However, for most applications it is not an assumption to worry about: $\boldsymbol{\Theta}$ can be defined to be such a large closed and bounded set as to always contain $\boldsymbol{\theta}_o$. Some consistency results for nonlinear estimation without compact parameter spaces are available; see the discussion and references in Newey and McFadden (1994).

We can now state a theorem concerning uniform convergence appropriate for the random sampling environment. This result, known as the **uniform weak law of large numbers (UWLLN)**, dates back to LeCam (1953). See also Newey and McFadden (1994, Lemma 2.4).

THEOREM 12.1 (Uniform Weak Law of Large Numbers): Let $\mathbf{w}$ be a random vector taking values in $\mathcal{W} \subset \mathbb{R}^M$, let $\boldsymbol{\Theta}$ be a subset of $\mathbb{R}^P$, and let $q : \mathcal{W} \times \boldsymbol{\Theta} \to \mathbb{R}$ be a real-valued function. Assume that (a) $\boldsymbol{\Theta}$ is compact; (b) for each $\boldsymbol{\theta} \in \boldsymbol{\Theta}$, $q(\cdot, \boldsymbol{\theta})$ is Borel measurable on $\mathcal{W}$; (c) for each $\mathbf{w} \in \mathcal{W}$, $q(\mathbf{w}, \cdot)$ is continuous on $\boldsymbol{\Theta}$; and (d) $|q(\mathbf{w}, \boldsymbol{\theta})| \le b(\mathbf{w})$ for all $\boldsymbol{\theta} \in \boldsymbol{\Theta}$, where b is a nonnegative function on $\mathcal{W}$ such that $\mathrm{E}[b(\mathbf{w})] < \infty$. Then equation (12.12) holds.

The only assumption we have not discussed is assumption d, which requires the expected absolute value of $q(\mathbf{w}, \boldsymbol{\theta})$ to be bounded across $\boldsymbol{\theta}$. This kind of moment condition is rarely verified in practice, although it can be. For example, for NLS with $0 \le y \le 1$ and the mean function such that $0 \le m(\mathbf{x}, \boldsymbol{\theta}) \le 1$ for all $\mathbf{x}$ and $\boldsymbol{\theta}$, we can take $b(\mathbf{w}) \equiv 1$. See Newey and McFadden (1994) for more complicated examples.

The continuity and compactness assumptions are important for establishing uniform convergence, and they also ensure that both the sample minimization problem (12.8) and the population minimization problem (12.9) actually have solutions. Consider problem (12.8) first. Under the assumptions of Theorem 12.1, the sample average is a continuous function of $\boldsymbol{\theta}$, since $q(\mathbf{w}_i, \boldsymbol{\theta})$ is continuous for each $\mathbf{w}_i$. Since a continuous function on a compact space always achieves its minimum, the M-estimation problem is well defined (there could be more than one solution). As a technical matter, it can be shown that $\hat{\boldsymbol{\theta}}$ is actually a random variable under the measurability assumption on $q(\cdot, \boldsymbol{\theta})$. See, for example, Gallant and White (1988).

It can also be shown that, under the assumptions of Theorem 12.1, the function $\mathrm{E}[q(\mathbf{w}, \boldsymbol{\theta})]$ is continuous as a function of $\boldsymbol{\theta}$. Therefore, problem (12.9) also has at least one solution; identifiability ensures that it has only one solution, which in turn implies consistency of the M-estimator.

THEOREM 12.2 (Consistency of M-Estimators): Under the assumptions of Theorem 12.1, assume that the identification assumption (12.11) holds. Then a random vector, $\hat{\boldsymbol{\theta}}$, solves problem (12.8), and $\hat{\boldsymbol{\theta}} \xrightarrow{p} \boldsymbol{\theta}_{\mathrm{o}}$.

A proof of Theorem 12.2 is given in Newey and McFadden (1994). For nonlinear least squares, once Assumptions NLS.1 and NLS.2 are maintained, the practical requirement is that $m(\mathbf{x}, \cdot)$ be a continuous function over $\boldsymbol{\Theta}$. Since this assumption is almost always true in applications of NLS, we do not list it as a separate assumption. Noncompactness of $\boldsymbol{\Theta}$ is not much of a concern for most applications.

Theorem 12.2 also applies to **median regression**. Suppose that the conditional median of y given $\mathbf{x}$ is $\mathrm{Med}(y \mid \mathbf{x}) = m(\mathbf{x}, \boldsymbol{\theta}_{\mathrm{o}})$, where $m(\mathbf{x}, \boldsymbol{\theta})$ is a known function of $\mathbf{x}$ and $\boldsymbol{\theta}$. The leading case is a linear model, $m(\mathbf{x}, \boldsymbol{\theta}) = \mathbf{x}\boldsymbol{\theta}$, where $\mathbf{x}$ contains unity. The **least absolute deviations (LAD) estimator** of $\boldsymbol{\theta}_{\mathrm{o}}$ solves

$$\min_{\boldsymbol{\theta} \in \boldsymbol{\Theta}} N^{-1} \sum_{i=1}^{N} |y_i - m(\mathbf{x}_i, \boldsymbol{\theta})|.$$

If $\boldsymbol{\Theta}$ is compact and $m(\mathbf{x}, \cdot)$ is continuous over $\boldsymbol{\Theta}$ for each $\mathbf{x}$, a solution always exists. The LAD estimator is motivated by the fact that $\boldsymbol{\theta}_{\mathrm{o}}$ minimizes $\mathrm{E}[|y - m(\mathbf{x}, \boldsymbol{\theta})|]$ over the parameter space $\boldsymbol{\Theta}$; this follows by the fact that for each $\mathbf{x}$, the conditional median is the minimum absolute loss predictor conditional on $\mathbf{x}$. (See, for example, Bassett and Koenker, 1978, and Manski, 1988, Sect. 4.2.2.) If we assume that $\boldsymbol{\theta}_{\mathrm{o}}$ is the unique solution—a standard identification assumption—then the LAD estimator is consistent very generally. In addition to the continuity, compactness, and identification assumptions, it suffices that $\mathrm{E}[|y|] < \infty$ and $|m(\mathbf{x}, \boldsymbol{\theta})| \leq a(\mathbf{x})$ for some function $a(\cdot)$ such that $\mathrm{E}[a(\mathbf{x})] < \infty$. (To see this point, take $b(\mathbf{w}) \equiv |y| + a(\mathbf{x})$ in Theorem 12.2.)

Median regression is a special case of **quantile regression**, where we model quantiles in the distribution of y given $\mathbf{x}$. For example, in addition to the median, we can estimate how the first and third quartiles in the distribution of y given $\mathbf{x}$ change with $\mathbf{x}$. Except for the median (which leads to LAD), the objective function that identifies a conditional quantile is asymmetric about zero. We study quantile regression in Section 12.10.

We end this section with a lemma that we use repeatedly in the rest of this chapter. It follows from Lemma 4.3 in Newey and McFadden (1994).

LEMMA 12.1: Suppose that $\hat{\boldsymbol{\theta}} \xrightarrow{p} \boldsymbol{\theta}_o$, and assume that $r(\mathbf{w}, \boldsymbol{\theta})$ satisfies the same assumptions on $q(\mathbf{w}, \boldsymbol{\theta})$ in Theorem 12.2. Then

$$N^{-1} \sum_{i=1}^{N} r(\mathbf{w}_i, \hat{\boldsymbol{\theta}}) \xrightarrow{p} \mathrm{E}[r(\mathbf{w}, \boldsymbol{\theta}_o)]. \tag{12.13}$$

That is, $N^{-1} \sum_{i=1}^{N} r(\mathbf{w}_i, \hat{\boldsymbol{\theta}})$ is a consistent estimator of $\mathrm{E}[r(\mathbf{w}, \boldsymbol{\theta}_o)]$.

Intuitively, Lemma 12.1 is quite reasonable. We know that $N^{-1} \sum_{i=1}^{N} r(\mathbf{w}_i, \boldsymbol{\theta}_o)$ generally converges in probability to $\mathrm{E}[r(\mathbf{w}, \boldsymbol{\theta}_o)]$ by the law of large numbers. Lemma 12.1 shows that, if we replace $\boldsymbol{\theta}_o$ in the sample average with a consistent estimator, the convergence still holds, at least under standard regularity conditions. In fact, as shown by Newey and McFadden (1994), we need only assume $r(\mathbf{w}, \boldsymbol{\theta})$ is continuous at $\boldsymbol{\theta}_o$ with probability one.

12.3 Asymptotic Normality

Under additional assumptions on the objective function, we can also show that M-estimators are asymptotically normally distributed (and converge at the rate $\sqrt{N}$). It turns out that continuity over the parameter space does not ensure asymptotic normality.

The simplest asymptotic normality proof proceeds as follows. Assume that $\boldsymbol{\theta}_o$ is in the interior of $\boldsymbol{\Theta}$, which means that $\boldsymbol{\Theta}$ must have nonempty interior; this assumption is true in most applications. Then, since $\hat{\boldsymbol{\theta}} \xrightarrow{p} \boldsymbol{\theta}_o$, $\hat{\boldsymbol{\theta}}$ is in the interior of $\boldsymbol{\Theta}$ with probability approaching one. If $q(\mathbf{w}, \cdot)$ is continuously differentiable on the interior of $\boldsymbol{\Theta}$, then (with probability approaching one) $\hat{\boldsymbol{\theta}}$ solves the first-order condition

$$\sum_{i=1}^{N} \mathbf{s}(\mathbf{w}_i, \hat{\boldsymbol{\theta}}) = \mathbf{0}, \tag{12.14}$$

where $\mathbf{s}(\mathbf{w}, \boldsymbol{\theta})$ is the $P \times 1$ vector of partial derivatives of $q(\mathbf{w}, \boldsymbol{\theta}) : \mathbf{s}(\mathbf{w}, \boldsymbol{\theta})' = \nabla_\theta q(\mathbf{w}, \boldsymbol{\theta}) \equiv [\partial q(\mathbf{w}, \boldsymbol{\theta})/\partial \theta_1, \partial q(\mathbf{w}, \boldsymbol{\theta})/\partial \theta_2, \ldots, \partial q(\mathbf{w}, \boldsymbol{\theta})/\partial \theta_P]$. (That is, $\mathbf{s}(\mathbf{w}, \boldsymbol{\theta})$ is the transpose of the gradient of $q(\mathbf{w}, \boldsymbol{\theta})$.) We call $\mathbf{s}(\mathbf{w}, \boldsymbol{\theta})$ the **score of the objective function** $q(\mathbf{w}, \boldsymbol{\theta})$. While condition (12.14) can only be guaranteed to hold with probability approaching one, usually it holds exactly; at any rate, we will drop the qualifier, as it does not affect the derivation of the limiting distribution.

If $q(\mathbf{w}, \cdot)$ is twice continuously differentiable, then each row of the left-hand side of equation (12.14) can be expanded about $\boldsymbol{\theta}_o$ in a mean-value expansion:

$$\sum_{i=1}^{N} \mathbf{s}(\mathbf{w}_i, \hat{\boldsymbol{\theta}}) = \sum_{i=1}^{N} \mathbf{s}(\mathbf{w}_i, \boldsymbol{\theta}_o) + \left(\sum_{i=1}^{N} \ddot{\mathbf{H}}_i\right)(\hat{\boldsymbol{\theta}} - \boldsymbol{\theta}_o). \tag{12.15}$$

The notation $\ddot{\mathbf{H}}_i$ denotes the $P \times P$ **Hessian of the objective function**, $q(\mathbf{w}_i, \boldsymbol{\theta})$, with respect to $\boldsymbol{\theta}$, but with each row of $\mathbf{H}(\mathbf{w}_i, \boldsymbol{\theta}) \equiv \partial^2 q(\mathbf{w}_i, \boldsymbol{\theta})/\partial\boldsymbol{\theta}\partial\boldsymbol{\theta}' \equiv \nabla_\theta^2 q(\mathbf{w}_i, \boldsymbol{\theta})$ evaluated at a different mean value. Each of the P mean values is on the line segment between $\boldsymbol{\theta}_o$ and $\hat{\boldsymbol{\theta}}$. We cannot know what these mean values are, but we do know that each must converge in probability to $\boldsymbol{\theta}_o$ (since each is "trapped" between $\hat{\boldsymbol{\theta}}$ and $\boldsymbol{\theta}_o$).

Combining equations (12.14) and (12.15) and multiplying through by $1/\sqrt{N}$ gives

$$\mathbf{0} = N^{-1/2} \sum_{i=1}^{N} \mathbf{s}(\mathbf{w}_i, \boldsymbol{\theta}_o) + \left(N^{-1} \sum_{i=1}^{N} \ddot{\mathbf{H}}_i\right) \sqrt{N}(\hat{\boldsymbol{\theta}} - \boldsymbol{\theta}_o).$$

Now, we can apply Lemma 12.1 to get $N^{-1} \sum_{i=1}^{N} \ddot{\mathbf{H}}_i \xrightarrow{p} \mathrm{E}[\mathbf{H}(\mathbf{w}, \boldsymbol{\theta}_o)]$ (under some moment conditions). If $\mathbf{A}_o \equiv \mathrm{E}[\mathbf{H}(\mathbf{w}, \boldsymbol{\theta}_o)]$ is nonsingular, then $N^{-1} \sum_{i=1}^{N} \ddot{\mathbf{H}}_i$ is nonsingular w.p.a.1 and $(N^{-1} \sum_{i=1}^{N} \ddot{\mathbf{H}}_i)^{-1} \xrightarrow{p} \mathbf{A}_o^{-1}$. Therefore, we can write

$$\sqrt{N}(\hat{\boldsymbol{\theta}} - \boldsymbol{\theta}_o) = \left(N^{-1} \sum_{i=1}^{N} \ddot{\mathbf{H}}_i\right)^{-1} \left[-N^{-1/2} \sum_{i=1}^{N} \mathbf{s}_i(\boldsymbol{\theta}_o)\right],$$

where $\mathbf{s}_i(\boldsymbol{\theta}_o) \equiv \mathbf{s}(\mathbf{w}_i, \boldsymbol{\theta}_o)$. As we will show, $\mathrm{E}[\mathbf{s}_i(\boldsymbol{\theta}_o)] = \mathbf{0}$. Therefore, $N^{-1/2} \sum_{i=1}^{N} \mathbf{s}_i(\boldsymbol{\theta}_o)$ generally satisfies the central limit theorem because it is the average of i.i.d. random vectors with zero mean, multiplied by the usual $\sqrt{N}$. Since $\mathrm{o}_p(1) \cdot \mathrm{O}_p(1) = \mathrm{o}_p(1)$, we have

$$\sqrt{N}(\hat{\boldsymbol{\theta}} - \boldsymbol{\theta}_o) = \mathbf{A}_o^{-1} \left[-N^{-1/2} \sum_{i=1}^{N} \mathbf{s}_i(\boldsymbol{\theta}_o)\right] + \mathrm{o}_p(1). \tag{12.16}$$

This is an important equation. It shows that $\sqrt{N}(\hat{\boldsymbol{\theta}} - \boldsymbol{\theta}_o)$ inherits its limiting distribution from the average of the scores, evaluated at $\boldsymbol{\theta}_o$. The matrix $\mathbf{A}_o^{-1}$ simply acts as a linear transformation. If we absorb this linear transformation into $\mathbf{s}_i(\boldsymbol{\theta}_o)$, we can write

$$\sqrt{N}(\hat{\boldsymbol{\theta}} - \boldsymbol{\theta}_o) = N^{-1/2} \sum_{i=1}^{N} \mathbf{e}_i(\boldsymbol{\theta}_o) + \mathrm{o}_p(1), \tag{12.17}$$

where $\mathbf{e}_i(\boldsymbol{\theta}_o) \equiv -\mathbf{A}_o^{-1}\mathbf{s}_i(\boldsymbol{\theta}_o)$; this is sometimes called the **influence function representation** of $\hat{\boldsymbol{\theta}}$, where $\mathbf{e}(\mathbf{w}, \boldsymbol{\theta})$ is the influence function.

Equation (12.16) (or (12.17)) allows us to derive the **first-order asymptotic distribution** of $\hat{\boldsymbol{\theta}}$. Higher order representations attempt to reduce the error in the $o_p(1)$ term in equation (12.16); such derivations are much more complicated than equation (12.16) and are beyond the scope of this book.

We have essentially proved the following result:

THEOREM 12.3 (Asymptotic Normality of M-Estimators): In addition to the assumptions in Theorem 12.2, assume (a) $\boldsymbol{\theta}_o$ is in the interior of $\boldsymbol{\Theta}$; (b) $\mathbf{s}(\mathbf{w}, \cdot)$ is continuously differentiable on the interior of $\boldsymbol{\Theta}$ for all $\mathbf{w} \in \mathcal{W}$; (c) Each element of $\mathbf{H}(\mathbf{w}, \boldsymbol{\theta})$ is bounded in absolute value by a function $b(\mathbf{w})$, where $\mathrm{E}[b(\mathbf{w})] < \infty$; (d) $\mathbf{A}_o \equiv \mathrm{E}[\mathbf{H}(\mathbf{w}, \boldsymbol{\theta}_o)]$ is positive definite; (e) $\mathrm{E}[\mathbf{s}(\mathbf{w}, \boldsymbol{\theta}_o)] = \mathbf{0}$; and (f) each element of $\mathbf{s}(\mathbf{w}, \boldsymbol{\theta}_o)$ has finite second moment.

Then

$$\sqrt{N}(\hat{\boldsymbol{\theta}} - \boldsymbol{\theta}_o) \xrightarrow{d} \mathrm{Normal}(0, \mathbf{A}_o^{-1}\mathbf{B}_o\mathbf{A}_o^{-1}), \tag{12.18}$$

where

$$\mathbf{A}_o \equiv \mathrm{E}[\mathbf{H}(\mathbf{w}, \boldsymbol{\theta}_o)] \tag{12.19}$$

and

$$\mathbf{B}_o \equiv \mathrm{E}[\mathbf{s}(\mathbf{w}, \boldsymbol{\theta}_o)\mathbf{s}(\mathbf{w}, \boldsymbol{\theta}_o)'] = \mathrm{Var}[\mathbf{s}(\mathbf{w}, \boldsymbol{\theta}_o)]. \tag{12.20}$$

Thus,

$$\mathrm{Avar}(\hat{\boldsymbol{\theta}}) = \mathbf{A}_o^{-1}\mathbf{B}_o\mathbf{A}_o^{-1}/N. \tag{12.21}$$

Theorem 12.3 implies asymptotic normality of most of the estimators we study in the remainder of the book. A leading example that is not covered by Theorem 12.3 is the LAD estimator. Even if $m(\mathbf{x}, \boldsymbol{\theta})$ is twice continuously differentiable in $\boldsymbol{\theta}$, the objective function for each i, $q(\mathbf{w}_i, \boldsymbol{\theta}) \equiv |y_i - m(\mathbf{x}_i, \boldsymbol{\theta})|$, is not twice continuously differentiable because the absolute value function is nondifferentiable at zero. By itself, nondifferentiability at zero is a minor nuisance. More important, by any reasonable definition, the Hessian of the LAD objective function is the zero matrix in the leading case of a linear conditional median function, and this feature violates assumption d of Theorem 12.3. It turns out that the LAD estimator *is* generally $\sqrt{N}$-asymptotically normal, but Theorem 12.3 cannot be applied. We discuss the asymptotic distribution of LAD and other quantile estimators in Section 12.10.

A key component of Theorem 12.3 is that the score evaluated at $\boldsymbol{\theta}_o$ has expected value zero. In many applications, including NLS, we can show this result directly. But it is also useful to know that it holds in the abstract M-estimation framework, at least if we can interchange the expectation and the derivative. To see this point, note that, if $\boldsymbol{\theta}_o$ is in the interior of $\boldsymbol{\Theta}$, and $\mathrm{E}[q(\mathbf{w}, \boldsymbol{\theta})]$ is differentiable for $\boldsymbol{\theta} \in \operatorname{int} \boldsymbol{\Theta}$, then

$$\nabla_\theta \mathrm{E}[q(\mathbf{w}, \boldsymbol{\theta})]|_{\boldsymbol{\theta}=\boldsymbol{\theta}_o} = \mathbf{0}. \tag{12.22}$$

Now, if the derivative and expectations operator can be interchanged (which is the case quite generally), then equation (12.22) implies

$$\mathrm{E}[\nabla_\theta q(\mathbf{w}, \boldsymbol{\theta}_o)] = \mathrm{E}[\mathbf{s}(\mathbf{w}, \boldsymbol{\theta}_o)] = \mathbf{0}. \tag{12.23}$$

A similar argument shows that, in general, $\mathrm{E}[\mathbf{H}(\mathbf{w}, \boldsymbol{\theta}_o)]$ is positive semidefinite. If $\boldsymbol{\theta}_o$ is identified, $\mathrm{E}[\mathbf{H}(\mathbf{w}, \boldsymbol{\theta}_o)]$ is positive definite.

For the remainder of this chapter, it is convenient to divide the original NLS objective function by two:

$$q(\mathbf{w}, \boldsymbol{\theta}) = [y - m(\mathbf{x}, \boldsymbol{\theta})]^2/2. \tag{12.24}$$

The score of equation (12.24) can be written as

$$\mathbf{s}(\mathbf{w}, \boldsymbol{\theta}) = -\nabla_\theta m(\mathbf{x}, \boldsymbol{\theta})'[y - m(\mathbf{x}, \boldsymbol{\theta})] \tag{12.25}$$

where $\nabla_\theta m(\mathbf{x}, \boldsymbol{\theta})$ is the $1 \times P$ gradient of $m(\mathbf{x}, \boldsymbol{\theta})$, and therefore $\nabla_\theta m(\mathbf{x}, \boldsymbol{\theta})'$ is $P \times 1$. We can show directly that this expression has an expected value of zero at $\boldsymbol{\theta} = \boldsymbol{\theta}_o$ by showing that expected value of $\mathbf{s}(\mathbf{w}, \boldsymbol{\theta}_o)$ conditional on $\mathbf{x}$ is zero:

$$\mathrm{E}[\mathbf{s}(\mathbf{w}, \boldsymbol{\theta}_o) \mid \mathbf{x}] = -\nabla_\theta m(\mathbf{x}, \boldsymbol{\theta}_o)'[\mathrm{E}(y \mid \mathbf{x}) - m(\mathbf{x}, \boldsymbol{\theta}_o)] = \mathbf{0}. \tag{12.26}$$

The variance of $\mathbf{s}(\mathbf{w}, \boldsymbol{\theta}_o)$ is

$$\mathbf{B}_o \equiv \mathrm{E}[\mathbf{s}(\mathbf{w}, \boldsymbol{\theta}_o)\mathbf{s}(\mathbf{w}, \boldsymbol{\theta}_o)'] = \mathrm{E}[u^2 \nabla_\theta m(\mathbf{x}, \boldsymbol{\theta}_o)' \nabla_\theta m(\mathbf{x}, \boldsymbol{\theta}_o)], \tag{12.27}$$

where the error $u \equiv y - m(\mathbf{x}, \boldsymbol{\theta}_o)$ is the difference between y and $\mathrm{E}(y \mid \mathbf{x})$.

The Hessian of $q(\mathbf{w}, \boldsymbol{\theta})$ is

$$\mathbf{H}(\mathbf{w}, \boldsymbol{\theta}) = \nabla_\theta m(\mathbf{x}, \boldsymbol{\theta})' \nabla_\theta m(\mathbf{x}, \boldsymbol{\theta}) - \nabla_\theta^2 m(\mathbf{x}, \boldsymbol{\theta})[y - m(\mathbf{x}, \boldsymbol{\theta})], \tag{12.28}$$

where $\nabla_\theta^2 m(\mathbf{x}, \boldsymbol{\theta})$ is the $P \times P$ Hessian of $m(\mathbf{x}, \boldsymbol{\theta})$ with respect to $\boldsymbol{\theta}$. To find the expected value of $\mathbf{H}(\mathbf{w}, \boldsymbol{\theta})$ at $\boldsymbol{\theta} = \boldsymbol{\theta}_o$, we first find the expectation conditional on $\mathbf{x}$. When evaluated at $\boldsymbol{\theta}_o$, the second term in equation (12.28) is $\nabla_\theta^2 m(\mathbf{x}, \boldsymbol{\theta}_o)u$, and it therefore has a zero mean conditional on $\mathbf{x}$ (since $\mathrm{E}(u \mid \mathbf{x}) = 0$). Therefore,

$$\mathrm{E}[\mathbf{H}(\mathbf{w}, \boldsymbol{\theta}_o) \mid \mathbf{x}] = \nabla_\theta m(\mathbf{x}, \boldsymbol{\theta}_o)' \nabla_\theta m(\mathbf{x}, \boldsymbol{\theta}_o). \tag{12.29}$$

Taking the expected value of equation (12.29) over the distribution of $\mathbf{x}$ gives

$$\mathbf{A}_o = \mathrm{E}[\nabla_\theta m(\mathbf{x}, \boldsymbol{\theta}_o)' \nabla_\theta m(\mathbf{x}, \boldsymbol{\theta}_o)]. \tag{12.30}$$

This matrix plays a fundamental role in nonlinear regression. When $\boldsymbol{\theta}_o$ is identified, $\mathbf{A}_o$ is generally positive definite. In the linear case $m(\mathbf{x}, \boldsymbol{\theta}) = \mathbf{x}\boldsymbol{\theta}$, $\mathbf{A}_o = \mathrm{E}(\mathbf{x}'\mathbf{x})$. In the exponential case $m(\mathbf{x}, \boldsymbol{\theta}) = \exp(\mathbf{x}\boldsymbol{\theta})$, $\mathbf{A}_o = \mathrm{E}[\exp(2\mathbf{x}\boldsymbol{\theta}_o)\mathbf{x}'\mathbf{x}]$, which is generally positive definite whenever $\mathrm{E}(\mathbf{x}'\mathbf{x})$ is. In the example $m(\mathbf{x}, \boldsymbol{\theta}) = \theta_1 + \theta_2 x_2 + \theta_3 x_3^{\theta_4}$ with $\theta_{o3} = 0$, it is easy to show that matrix (12.30) has rank less than four.

For nonlinear regression, $\mathbf{A}_o$ and $\mathbf{B}_o$ appear to be similar in that they both depend on $\nabla_\theta m(\mathbf{x}, \boldsymbol{\theta}_o)' \nabla_\theta m(\mathbf{x}, \boldsymbol{\theta}_o)$. Generally, though, there is no simple relationship between $\mathbf{A}_o$ and $\mathbf{B}_o$ because the latter depends on the distribution of u^2, the squared population error. In Section 12.5 we will show that a homoskedasticity assumption implies that $\mathbf{B}_o$ is proportional to $\mathbf{A}_o$.

The previous analysis of nonlinear regression assumes that the conditional mean function is correctly specified. If we drop this assumption, then we cannot simplify the expected Hessian as in equation (12.30). White (1981, 1994) studies the properties of NLS when the mean function is misspecified. Under weak conditions, the NLS estimator $\hat{\boldsymbol{\theta}}$ converges in probability to a vector $\boldsymbol{\theta}^*$, where $\boldsymbol{\theta}^*$ provides the best mean square approximation to the actual regression function, $\mathrm{E}(y_i \mid \mathbf{x}_i = \mathbf{x})$. More precisely, $\mathrm{E}\{[\mathrm{E}(y_i \mid \mathbf{x}_i) - m(\mathbf{x}_i, \boldsymbol{\theta}^*)]^2\} \le \mathrm{E}\{[\mathrm{E}(y_i \mid \mathbf{x}_i) - m(\mathbf{x}_i, \boldsymbol{\theta})]^2\}$ for $\boldsymbol{\theta} \in \boldsymbol{\Theta}$. The asymptotic normality result in equation (12.18) still holds (with the obvious notational changes). But the second term in equation (12.28), evaluated at $\boldsymbol{\theta}^*$, is no longer guaranteed to be zero: $\nabla_\theta^2 m(\mathbf{x}_i, \boldsymbol{\theta}^*)$ is generally correlated with $y_i - m(\mathbf{x}_i, \boldsymbol{\theta}^*)$, because $\mathrm{E}(y_i \mid \mathbf{x}_i) \neq m(\mathbf{x}_i, \boldsymbol{\theta}^*)$. We have focused on the case of correctly specified conditional mean functions, but one should be aware that the assumption has implications for estimating the asymptotic variance, a topic we return to in Section 12.5.

12.4 Two-Step M-Estimators

Sometimes applications of M-estimators involve a first-stage estimation (an example is OLS with generated regressors, as in Chapter 6). Let $\hat{\gamma}$ be a preliminary estimator, usually based on the random sample $\{\mathbf{w}_i : i = 1, 2, \ldots, N\}$. Where this estimator comes from must be vague for the moment.

A **two-step M-estimator** $\hat{\boldsymbol{\theta}}$ of $\boldsymbol{\theta}_o$ solves the problem

$$\min_{\boldsymbol{\theta} \in \boldsymbol{\Theta}} \sum_{i=1}^{N} q(\mathbf{w}_i, \boldsymbol{\theta}; \hat{\gamma}), \tag{12.31}$$

where q is now defined on $\mathcal{W} \times \mathbf{\Theta} \times \mathbf{\Gamma}$, and $\mathbf{\Gamma}$ is a subset of $\mathbb{R}^J$. We will see several examples of two-step M-estimators in Chapter 13 and the applications in Part IV. An example of a two-step M-estimator is the **weighted nonlinear least squares (WNLS) estimator**, where the weights are estimated in a first stage. The WNLS estimator solves

$$\min_{\boldsymbol{\theta} \in \mathbf{\Theta}} (1/2) \sum_{i=1}^{N} [y_i - m(\mathbf{x}_i, \boldsymbol{\theta})]^2 / h(\mathbf{x}_i, \hat{\boldsymbol{\gamma}}), \tag{12.32}$$

where the weighting function, $h(\mathbf{x}, \boldsymbol{\gamma})$, depends on the explanatory variables and a parameter vector. As with NLS, $m(\mathbf{x}, \boldsymbol{\theta})$ is a model of $\mathrm{E}(y \mid \mathbf{x})$. The function $h(\mathbf{x}, \boldsymbol{\gamma})$ is chosen to be a model of $\mathrm{Var}(y \mid \mathbf{x})$. The estimator $\hat{\boldsymbol{\gamma}}$ comes from a problem used to estimate the conditional variance. We list the key assumptions needed for WNLS to have desirable properties here, but several of the derivations are left for the problems.

ASSUMPTION WNLS.1: Same as Assumption NLS.1.

12.4.1 Consistency

For the general two-step M-estimator, when will $\hat{\boldsymbol{\theta}}$ be consistent for $\boldsymbol{\theta}_{\mathrm{o}}$? In practice, the important condition is the identification assumption. To state the identification condition, we need to know about the asymptotic behavior of $\hat{\boldsymbol{\gamma}}$. A general assumption is that $\hat{\boldsymbol{\gamma}} \xrightarrow{p} \boldsymbol{\gamma}^*$, where $\boldsymbol{\gamma}^*$ is some element in $\mathbf{\Gamma}$. We label this value $\boldsymbol{\gamma}^*$ to allow for the possibility that $\hat{\boldsymbol{\gamma}}$ does not converge to a parameter indexing some interesting feature of the distribution of $\mathbf{w}$. In some cases, the plim of $\hat{\boldsymbol{\gamma}}$ will be of direct interest. In the weighted regression case, if we assume that $h(\mathbf{x}, \boldsymbol{\gamma})$ is a correctly specified model for $\mathrm{Var}(y \mid \mathbf{x})$, then it is possible to choose an estimator such that $\hat{\boldsymbol{\gamma}} \xrightarrow{p} \boldsymbol{\gamma}_{\mathrm{o}}$, where $\mathrm{Var}(y \mid \mathbf{x}) = h(\mathbf{x}, \boldsymbol{\gamma}_{\mathrm{o}})$. (For an example, see Problem 12.2.) If the variance model is misspecified, plim $\hat{\boldsymbol{\gamma}}$ is generally well defined, but $\mathrm{Var}(y \mid \mathbf{x}) \neq h(\mathbf{x}, \boldsymbol{\gamma}^*)$; it is for this reason that we use the notation $\boldsymbol{\gamma}^*$.

The identification condition for the two-step M-estimator is

$$\mathrm{E}[q(\mathbf{w}, \boldsymbol{\theta}_{\mathrm{o}}; \boldsymbol{\gamma}^*)] < \mathrm{E}[q(\mathbf{w}, \boldsymbol{\theta}; \boldsymbol{\gamma}^*)], \qquad \text{all } \boldsymbol{\theta} \in \mathbf{\Theta}, \quad \boldsymbol{\theta} \neq \boldsymbol{\theta}_{\mathrm{o}}.$$

The consistency argument is essentially the same as that underlying Theorem 12.2. If $q(\mathbf{w}_i, \boldsymbol{\theta}; \boldsymbol{\gamma})$ satisfies the UWLLN over $\mathbf{\Theta} \times \mathbf{\Gamma}$ then expression (12.31) can be shown to converge to $\mathrm{E}[q(\mathbf{w}, \boldsymbol{\theta}; \boldsymbol{\gamma}^*)]$ uniformly over $\mathbf{\Theta}$. Along with identification, this result can be shown to imply consistency of $\hat{\boldsymbol{\theta}}$ for $\boldsymbol{\theta}_{\mathrm{o}}$.

In some applications of two-step M-estimation, identification of $\boldsymbol{\theta}_{\mathrm{o}}$ holds for *any* $\boldsymbol{\gamma} \in \mathbf{\Gamma}$. This result can be shown for the WNLS estimator (see Problem 12.4). It is for this reason that WNLS is still consistent even if the function $h(\mathbf{x}, \boldsymbol{\gamma})$ is not correctly specified for $\mathrm{Var}(y \mid \mathbf{x})$. The weakest version of the identification assumption for WNLS is the following:

ASSUMPTION WNLS.2: $\mathrm{E}\{[m(\mathbf{x},\boldsymbol{\theta}_o) - m(\mathbf{x},\boldsymbol{\theta})]^2/h(\mathbf{x},\gamma^*)\} > 0$, all $\boldsymbol{\theta} \in \boldsymbol{\Theta}$, $\boldsymbol{\theta} \neq \boldsymbol{\theta}_o$, where $\gamma^* = \operatorname{plim} \hat{\gamma}$.

As with the case of NLS, we know that weak inequality holds in Assumption WNLS.2 under Assumption WNLS.1. The strict inequality in Assumption WNLS.2 puts restrictions on the distribution of $\mathbf{x}$ and the functional forms of m and h.

In other cases, including several two-step maximum likelihood estimators we encounter in Part IV, the identification condition for $\boldsymbol{\theta}_o$ holds only for $\gamma = \gamma^* = \gamma_o$, where γ_o also indexes some feature of the distribution of $\mathbf{w}$.

12.4.2 Asymptotic Normality

With the two-step M-estimator, there are two cases worth distinguishing. The first occurs when the asymptotic variance of $\sqrt{N}(\hat{\boldsymbol{\theta}} - \boldsymbol{\theta}_o)$ does not depend on the asymptotic variance of $\sqrt{N}(\hat{\gamma} - \gamma^*)$, and the second occurs when the asymptotic variance of $\sqrt{N}(\hat{\boldsymbol{\theta}} - \boldsymbol{\theta}_o)$ should be adjusted to account for the first-stage estimation of γ^*. We first derive conditions under which we can ignore the first-stage estimation error.

Using arguments similar to those in Section 12.3, it can be shown that, under standard regularity conditions,

$$\sqrt{N}(\hat{\boldsymbol{\theta}} - \boldsymbol{\theta}_o) = \mathbf{A}_o^{-1}\left(-N^{-1/2}\sum_{i=1}^{N}\mathbf{s}_i(\boldsymbol{\theta}_o;\hat{\gamma})\right) + o_p(1), \tag{12.33}$$

where now $\mathbf{A}_o = \mathrm{E}[\mathbf{H}(\mathbf{w},\boldsymbol{\theta}_o;\gamma^*)]$. In obtaining the score and the Hessian, we take derivatives only with respect to $\boldsymbol{\theta}$; γ^* simply appears as an extra argument. Now, if

$$N^{-1/2}\sum_{i=1}^{N}\mathbf{s}_i(\boldsymbol{\theta}_o;\hat{\gamma}) = N^{-1/2}\sum_{i=1}^{N}\mathbf{s}_i(\boldsymbol{\theta}_o;\gamma^*) + o_p(1), \tag{12.34}$$

then $\sqrt{N}(\hat{\boldsymbol{\theta}} - \boldsymbol{\theta}_o)$ behaves the same asymptotically whether we used $\hat{\gamma}$ or its plim in defining the M-estimator.

When does equation (12.34) hold? Assuming that $\sqrt{N}(\hat{\gamma} - \gamma^*) = O_p(1)$, which is standard, a mean value expansion similar to the one in Section 12.3 gives

$$N^{-1/2}\sum_{i=1}^{N}\mathbf{s}_i(\boldsymbol{\theta}_o;\hat{\gamma}) = N^{-1/2}\sum_{i=1}^{N}\mathbf{s}_i(\boldsymbol{\theta}_o;\gamma^*) + \mathbf{F}_o\sqrt{N}(\hat{\gamma} - \gamma^*) + o_p(1), \tag{12.35}$$

where $\mathbf{F}_o$ is the $P \times J$ matrix

$$\mathbf{F}_o \equiv \mathrm{E}[\nabla_\gamma \mathbf{s}(\mathbf{w}, \boldsymbol{\theta}_o; \gamma^*)]. \tag{12.36}$$

(Remember, J is the dimension of γ.) Therefore, if

$$\mathrm{E}[\nabla_\gamma \mathbf{s}(\mathbf{w}, \boldsymbol{\theta}_o; \gamma^*)] = \mathbf{0}, \tag{12.37}$$

then equation (12.34) holds, and the asymptotic variance of the two-step M-estimator is the same as if γ^* were plugged in. In other words, under assumption (12.37), we conclude that equation (12.18) holds, where $\mathbf{A}_o$ and $\mathbf{B}_o$ are given in expressions (12.19) and (12.20), respectively, except that γ^* appears as an argument in the score and Hessian. For deriving the asymptotic distribution of $\sqrt{N}(\hat{\boldsymbol{\theta}} - \boldsymbol{\theta}_o)$, we can ignore the fact that $\hat{\gamma}$ was obtained in a first-stage estimation.

One case where assumption (12.37) holds is weighted nonlinear least squares, something you are asked to show in Problem 12.4. Naturally, we must assume that the conditional mean is correctly specified, but, interestingly, assumption (12.37) holds whether or not the conditional variance is correctly specified.

There are many problems for which assumption (12.37) does not hold, including some of the methods for correcting for endogeneity in probit and Tobit models in Part IV. In Chapter 21 we will see that two-step methods for correcting sample selection bias are two-step M-estimators, but assumption (12.37) fails. In such cases we need to make an adjustment to the asymptotic variance of $\sqrt{N}(\hat{\boldsymbol{\theta}} - \boldsymbol{\theta}_o)$. The adjustment is easily obtained from equation (12.35), once we have a first-order representation for $\sqrt{N}(\hat{\gamma} - \gamma^*)$. We assume that

$$\sqrt{N}(\hat{\gamma} - \gamma^*) = N^{-1/2} \sum_{i=1}^{N} \mathbf{r}_i(\gamma^*) + o_p(1), \tag{12.38}$$

where $\mathbf{r}_i(\gamma^*)$ is a $J \times 1$ vector with $\mathrm{E}[\mathbf{r}_i(\gamma^*)] = \mathbf{0}$ (in practice, $\mathbf{r}_i$ depends on parameters other than γ^*, but we suppress those here for simplicity). Therefore, $\hat{\gamma}$ could itself be an M-estimator or, as we will see in Chapter 14, a generalized method of moments estimator. In fact, every estimator considered in this book has a representation as in equation (12.38).

Now we can write

$$\sqrt{N}(\hat{\boldsymbol{\theta}} - \boldsymbol{\theta}_o) = \mathbf{A}_o^{-1} N^{-1/2} \sum_{i=1}^{N} [-\mathbf{g}_i(\boldsymbol{\theta}_o; \gamma^*)] + o_p(1), \tag{12.39}$$

where $\mathbf{g}_i(\boldsymbol{\theta}_o; \gamma^*) \equiv \mathbf{s}_i(\boldsymbol{\theta}_o; \gamma^*) + \mathbf{F}_o \mathbf{r}_i(\gamma^*)$. Since $\mathbf{g}_i(\boldsymbol{\theta}_o; \gamma^*)$ has zero mean, the standardized partial sum in equation (12.39) can be assumed to satisfy the central limit theorem. Define the $P \times P$ matrix

$$\mathbf{D}_o \equiv \mathrm{E}[\mathbf{g}_i(\boldsymbol{\theta}_o;\gamma^*)\mathbf{g}_i(\boldsymbol{\theta}_o;\gamma^*)'] = \mathrm{Var}[\mathbf{g}_i(\boldsymbol{\theta}_o;\gamma^*)]. \tag{12.40}$$

Then

$$\mathrm{Avar}\ \sqrt{N}(\hat{\boldsymbol{\theta}} - \boldsymbol{\theta}_o) = \mathbf{A}_o^{-1}\mathbf{D}_o\mathbf{A}_o^{-1}. \tag{12.41}$$

We will discuss estimation of this matrix in the next section.

Sometimes it is informative to compare the correct asymptotic variance in (12.41) with the asymptotic variance one would obtain by ignoring the sampling error in $\hat{\gamma}$; that is, by using the incorrect formula in equation (12.18). (If $\mathbf{F}_o = \mathbf{0}$, both formulas are the same.) Most often, the concern is that ignoring estimation of γ^* leads one to be too optimistic about the precision in $\hat{\boldsymbol{\theta}}$, which happens when $\mathbf{D}_o - \mathbf{B}_o$ is positive semidefinite (p.s.d.). One case where $\mathbf{D}_o - \mathbf{B}_o$ is unambiguously p.s.d. (but not zero) is when $\mathbf{F}_o \neq \mathbf{0}$ and the scores from the first- and second-step estimation are uncorrelated: $\mathrm{E}[\mathbf{s}_i(\boldsymbol{\theta}_o;\gamma^*)\mathbf{r}_i(\gamma^*)'] = \mathbf{0}$. Then,

$$\mathbf{D}_o = \mathrm{E}[\mathbf{s}_i(\boldsymbol{\theta}_o;\gamma^*)\mathrm{E}[\mathbf{s}_i(\boldsymbol{\theta}_o;\gamma^*)'] + \mathbf{F}_o\mathrm{E}[\mathbf{r}_i(\gamma^*)\mathbf{r}_i(\gamma^*)']\mathbf{F}_o' = \mathbf{B}_o + \mathbf{F}_o\mathrm{E}[\mathbf{r}_i(\gamma^*)\mathbf{r}_i(\gamma^*)']\mathbf{F}_o',$$

and the last term is p.s.d. In other cases, $\mathbf{D}_o - \mathbf{B}_o$ is indefinite, in which case it is not true that the correct asymptotic variances are all larger than the incorrect ones. Perhaps surprisingly, it is also possible that $\mathbf{D}_o - \mathbf{B}_o$ is negative semidefinite. An immediate implication is that it is possible that estimating γ^*, rather than knowing γ^*, can actually lead to a more precise estimator of $\boldsymbol{\theta}_o$. Situations where estimation in a first stage reduces the asymptotic variance in a second stage are special, and when it happens, the estimator of γ^* is usually from a correctly specified maximum likelihood procedure (in which case we would use the notation γ_o rather than γ^*). Therefore, we postpone further discussion until the next chapter, where we explicitly cover maximum likelihood estimation.

12.5 Estimating the Asymptotic Variance

12.5.1 Estimation without Nuisance Parameters

We first consider estimating the asymptotic variance of $\hat{\boldsymbol{\theta}}$ in the case where there are no nuisance parameters. This task requires consistently estimating the matrices $\mathbf{A}_o$ and $\mathbf{B}_o$. One thought is to solve for the expected values of $\mathbf{H}(\mathbf{w},\boldsymbol{\theta}_o)$ and $\mathbf{s}(\mathbf{w},\boldsymbol{\theta}_o)\cdot\mathbf{s}(\mathbf{w},\boldsymbol{\theta}_o)'$ over the distribution of $\mathbf{w}$, and then to plug in $\hat{\boldsymbol{\theta}}$ for $\boldsymbol{\theta}_o$. When we have completely specified the distribution of $\mathbf{w}$, obtaining closed-form expressions for $\mathbf{A}_o$ and $\mathbf{B}_o$ is, in principle, possible. However, except in simple cases, it would be difficult. More important, we rarely specify the entire distribution of $\mathbf{w}$. Even in a maximum likelihood setting, $\mathbf{w}$ is almost always partitioned into two parts: a set of endogenous variables, $\mathbf{y}$, and conditioning variables, $\mathbf{x}$. Rarely do we wish to specify the distribution of $\mathbf{x}$, and so the expected values needed to obtain $\mathbf{A}_o$ and $\mathbf{B}_o$ are not available.

We can always estimate $\mathbf{A}_o$ consistently by taking away the expectation and replacing $\boldsymbol{\theta}_o$ with $\hat{\boldsymbol{\theta}}$. Under regularity conditions that ensure uniform converge of the Hessian, the estimator

$$N^{-1}\sum_{i=1}^{N}\mathbf{H}(\mathbf{w}_i,\hat{\boldsymbol{\theta}}) \equiv N^{-1}\sum_{i=1}^{N}\hat{\mathbf{H}}_i \tag{12.42}$$

is consistent for $\mathbf{A}_o$, by Lemma 12.1. The advantage of the estimator (12.42) is that it is always available in problems with a twice continuously differentiable objective function. This includes cases where $\boldsymbol{\theta}_o$ does not index a feature of an unconditional or conditional distribution (such as nonlinear regression with the conditional mean function misspecified). Its main drawback is computational: it requires calculation of second derivatives, which is a nontrivial task for certain estimation problems.

Because we assume $\hat{\boldsymbol{\theta}}$ solves the minimization problem in equation (12.8), and $\hat{\boldsymbol{\theta}}$ is in the interior of $\boldsymbol{\Theta}$, we know that the Hessian evaluated at $\hat{\boldsymbol{\theta}}$ is at least p.s.d. If the model is well specified in the sense that $\boldsymbol{\theta}_o$ is identified, then the estimator in (12.42) will actually be positive definite with high probability because $\mathrm{E}[\mathbf{H}(\mathbf{w}_i,\boldsymbol{\theta}_o)]$ is positive definite. In some cases, the objective function is strictly convex on $\boldsymbol{\Theta}$, in which case $\sum_{i=1}^{N}\mathbf{H}(\mathbf{w}_i,\boldsymbol{\theta})$ is positive definite for all $\boldsymbol{\theta}\in\boldsymbol{\Theta}$.

In many econometric applications, more structure is available that allows a different estimator. Suppose we can partition $\mathbf{w}$ into $\mathbf{x}$ and $\mathbf{y}$, and that $\boldsymbol{\theta}_o$ indexes some feature of the distribution of $\mathbf{y}$ given $\mathbf{x}$ (such as the conditional mean or, in the case of maximum likelihood, the conditional distribution). Define

$$\mathbf{A}(\mathbf{x},\boldsymbol{\theta}_o) \equiv \mathrm{E}[\mathbf{H}(\mathbf{w},\boldsymbol{\theta}_o)\,|\,\mathbf{x}]. \tag{12.43}$$

While $\mathbf{H}(\mathbf{w},\boldsymbol{\theta}_o)$ is generally a function of $\mathbf{x}$ and $\mathbf{y}$, $\mathbf{A}(\mathbf{x},\boldsymbol{\theta}_o)$ is a function only of $\mathbf{x}$. By the law of iterated expectations, $\mathrm{E}[\mathbf{A}(\mathbf{x},\boldsymbol{\theta}_o)] = \mathrm{E}[\mathbf{H}(\mathbf{w},\boldsymbol{\theta}_o)] = \mathbf{A}_o$. From Lemma 12.1 and standard regularity conditions it follows that

$$N^{-1}\sum_{i=1}^{N}\mathbf{A}(\mathbf{x}_i,\hat{\boldsymbol{\theta}}) \equiv N^{-1}\sum_{i=1}^{N}\hat{\mathbf{A}}_i \xrightarrow{p} \mathbf{A}_o. \tag{12.44}$$

The estimator (12.44) of $\mathbf{A}_o$ is useful in cases where $\mathrm{E}[\mathbf{H}(\mathbf{w},\boldsymbol{\theta}_o)\,|\,\mathbf{x}]$ can be obtained in closed form or is easily approximated. In some leading cases, including NLS and certain maximum likelihood problems, $\mathbf{A}(\mathbf{x},\boldsymbol{\theta}_o)$ depends only on the first derivatives of the conditional mean function.

When the estimator (12.44) is available, it is usually the case that $\boldsymbol{\theta}_o$ actually minimizes $\mathrm{E}[q(\mathbf{w}, \boldsymbol{\theta}) \mid \mathbf{x}]$ for any value of $\mathbf{x}$; from equation (12.4) this is easily seen to be the case for NLS with a correctly specified conditional mean function. Under assumptions that allow the interchange of derivative and expectation, this result implies that $\mathbf{A}(\mathbf{x}, \boldsymbol{\theta}_o)$ is p.s.d. The expected value of $\mathbf{A}(\mathbf{x}, \boldsymbol{\theta}_o)$ over the distribution of $\mathbf{x}$ is positive definite provided $\boldsymbol{\theta}_o$ is identified. Therefore, the estimator (12.44) is usually positive definite in the sample.

Obtaining a p.s.d. estimator of $\mathbf{B}_o$ is straightforward. By Lemma 12.1, under standard regularity conditions we have

$$N^{-1} \sum_{i=1}^{N} \mathbf{s}(\mathbf{w}_i, \hat{\boldsymbol{\theta}}) \mathbf{s}(\mathbf{w}_i, \hat{\boldsymbol{\theta}})' \equiv N^{-1} \sum_{i=1}^{N} \hat{\mathbf{s}}_i \hat{\mathbf{s}}_i' \xrightarrow{p} \mathbf{B}_o. \tag{12.45}$$

Combining the estimator (12.45) with the consistent estimators for $\mathbf{A}_o$, we can consistently estimate Avar $\sqrt{N}(\hat{\boldsymbol{\theta}} - \boldsymbol{\theta}_o)$ by

$$\widehat{\mathrm{Avar}\,\sqrt{N}(\hat{\boldsymbol{\theta}} - \boldsymbol{\theta}_o)} = \hat{\mathbf{A}}^{-1} \hat{\mathbf{B}} \hat{\mathbf{A}}^{-1}, \tag{12.46}$$

where $\hat{\mathbf{A}}$ is one of the estimators (12.42) or (12.44). The asymptotic standard errors are obtained from the matrix

$$\hat{\mathbf{V}} \equiv \widehat{\mathrm{Avar}(\hat{\boldsymbol{\theta}})} = \hat{\mathbf{A}}^{-1} \hat{\mathbf{B}} \hat{\mathbf{A}}^{-1} / N, \tag{12.47}$$

which can be expressed as

$$\left(\sum_{i=1}^{N} \hat{\mathbf{H}}_i \right)^{-1} \left(\sum_{i=1}^{N} \hat{\mathbf{s}}_i \hat{\mathbf{s}}_i' \right) \left(\sum_{i=1}^{N} \hat{\mathbf{H}}_i \right)^{-1} \tag{12.48}$$

or

$$\left(\sum_{i=1}^{N} \hat{\mathbf{A}}_i \right)^{-1} \left(\sum_{i=1}^{N} \hat{\mathbf{s}}_i \hat{\mathbf{s}}_i' \right) \left(\sum_{i=1}^{N} \hat{\mathbf{A}}_i \right)^{-1}, \tag{12.49}$$

depending on the estimator used for $\mathbf{A}_o$. Expressions (12.48) and (12.49) are both at least p.s.d. when they are well defined.

The variance matrix estimators in (12.48) and (12.49) are examples of a **Huber-White sandwich estimator**, after Huber (1967) and White (1982a). When they differ (due to $\mathbf{H}(\mathbf{w}, \boldsymbol{\theta}_o) \neq \mathbf{A}(\mathbf{x}, \boldsymbol{\theta}_o)$), the estimator in equation (12.49) is usually valid only when some feature of the conditional distribution $\mathrm{D}(\mathbf{y}_i \mid \mathbf{x}_i)$ is correctly specified (because otherwise the calculation of $\mathrm{E}[\mathbf{H}(\mathbf{w}, \boldsymbol{\theta}_o) \mid \mathbf{x}]$ would be incorrect). Sometimes it is useful to make a distinction by calling the estimator in (12.49) a **semirobust variance matrix estimator**. The variance matrix estimator that requires the fewest assumptions to produce valid inference is in (12.48) (and so, for emphasis, it might be called a **fully robust variance matrix estimator**).

In the case of NLS, the estimator of $\mathbf{A}_o$ in equation (12.44) is always available when $\mathrm{E}(y_i \mid \mathbf{x}_i) = m(\mathbf{x}_i, \boldsymbol{\theta}_o)$, and it is usually used if we think the mean function is correctly specified:

$$\sum_{i=1}^{N} \hat{\mathbf{A}}_i = \sum_{i=1}^{N} \nabla_\theta \hat{m}_i' \nabla_\theta \hat{m}_i,$$

where $\nabla_\theta \hat{m}_i \equiv \nabla_\theta m(\mathbf{x}_i, \hat{\boldsymbol{\theta}})$ for every observation i. Also, the estimated score for NLS can be written as

$$\hat{\mathbf{s}}_i = -\nabla_\theta \hat{m}_i'[y_i - m(\mathbf{x}_i, \hat{\boldsymbol{\theta}})] = -\nabla_\theta \hat{m}_i' \hat{u}_i, \tag{12.50}$$

where the **nonlinear least squares residuals**, $\hat{u}_i$, are defined as

$$\hat{u}_i \equiv y_i - m(\mathbf{x}_i, \hat{\boldsymbol{\theta}}). \tag{12.51}$$

The estimated asymptotic variance of the NLS estimator is

$$\widehat{\mathrm{Avar}}(\hat{\boldsymbol{\theta}}) = \left(\sum_{i=1}^{N} \nabla_\theta \hat{m}_i' \nabla_\theta \hat{m}_i\right)^{-1} \left(\sum_{i=1}^{N} \hat{u}_i^2 \nabla_\theta \hat{m}_i' \nabla_\theta \hat{m}_i\right) \left(\sum_{i=1}^{N} \nabla_\theta \hat{m}_i' \nabla_\theta \hat{m}_i\right)^{-1}. \tag{12.52}$$

This is called the **heteroskedasticity-robust variance matrix estimator for NLS** because it places no restrictions on $\mathrm{Var}(y \mid \mathbf{x})$. It was first proposed by White (1980a). (Sometimes the expression is multiplied by $N/(N-P)$ as a degrees-of-freedom adjustment, where P is the dimension of $\boldsymbol{\theta}$.) As always, the asymptotic standard error of each element of $\hat{\boldsymbol{\theta}}$ is the square root of the appropriate diagonal element of matrix (12.52).

As a specific example, suppose that $m(\mathbf{x}, \boldsymbol{\theta}) = \exp(\mathbf{x}\boldsymbol{\theta})$. Then $\nabla_\theta \hat{m}_i' \nabla_\theta \hat{m}_i = \exp(2\mathbf{x}_i \hat{\boldsymbol{\theta}}) \mathbf{x}_i' \mathbf{x}_i$, which has dimension $K \times K$. We can plug this equation into expression (12.52) along with $\hat{u}_i = y_i - \exp(\mathbf{x}_i \hat{\boldsymbol{\theta}})$.

Using the previous terminology, the estimator in (12.52) is a semirobust variance matrix estimator because it assumes that the conditional mean is correctly specified. The sense in which (12.52) is robust is that it is valid without any assumptions on $\mathrm{Var}(y_i \mid \mathbf{x}_i)$, but it is not valid if $\mathrm{E}(y_i \mid \mathbf{x}_i)$ is misspecified. If we allow misspecification of $m(\mathbf{x}, \boldsymbol{\theta})$, as in White (1981), the formula (12.52) is no longer valid. Instead, the summands in the outer terms of (12.52) should be replaced with $\nabla_\theta m(\mathbf{x}_i, \hat{\boldsymbol{\theta}}) \nabla_\theta m(\mathbf{x}_i, \hat{\boldsymbol{\theta}})' - \nabla_\theta^2 m(\mathbf{x}_i, \hat{\boldsymbol{\theta}})[y_i - m(\mathbf{x}_i, \hat{\boldsymbol{\theta}})]$, which is simply the $P \times P$ Hessian of $[y_i - m(\mathbf{x}_i, \boldsymbol{\theta})]^2/2$ evaluated at $\hat{\boldsymbol{\theta}}$. In most applications of NLS—and in standard software packages—the conditional mean is assumed to be correctly specified, and equation (12.52) is used as the robust variance matrix estimator.

In many contexts, including NLS and certain quasi-likelihood methods, the asymptotic variance estimator can be simplified under additional assumptions. For our purposes, we state the assumption as follows: For some $\sigma_o^2 > 0$,

$$\mathrm{E}[\mathbf{s}(\mathbf{w}, \boldsymbol{\theta}_o)\mathbf{s}(\mathbf{w}, \boldsymbol{\theta}_o)'] = \sigma_o^2 \mathrm{E}[\mathbf{H}(\mathbf{w}, \boldsymbol{\theta}_o)]. \tag{12.53}$$

This assumption simply says that the expected outer product of the score, evaluated at $\boldsymbol{\theta}_o$, is proportional to the expected value of the Hessian (evaluated at $\boldsymbol{\theta}_o$): $\mathbf{B}_o = \sigma_o^2 \mathbf{A}_o$. Shortly we will provide an assumption under which assumption (12.53) holds for NLS. In the next chapter we will show that assumption (12.53) holds for $\sigma_o^2 = 1$ in the context of maximum likelihood with a correctly specified conditional density. For reasons we will see in Chapter 13, we refer to assumption (12.53) as the **generalized information matrix equality (GIME)**.

LEMMA 12.2: Under regularity conditions of the type contained in Theorem 12.3 and assumption (12.53), $\mathrm{Avar}(\hat{\boldsymbol{\theta}}) = \sigma_o^2 \mathbf{A}_o^{-1}/N$. Therefore, under assumption (12.53), the asymptotic variance of $\hat{\boldsymbol{\theta}}$ can be estimated as

$$\hat{\mathbf{V}} = \hat{\sigma}^2 \left(\sum_{i=1}^{N} \hat{\mathbf{H}}_i \right)^{-1} \tag{12.54}$$

or

$$\hat{\mathbf{V}} = \hat{\sigma}^2 \left(\sum_{i=1}^{N} \hat{\mathbf{A}}_i \right)^{-1}, \tag{12.55}$$

where $\hat{\mathbf{H}}_i$ and $\hat{\mathbf{A}}_i$ are defined as before, and $\hat{\sigma}^2 \xrightarrow{p} \sigma_o^2$.

In the case of nonlinear regression, the parameter σ_o^2 is the variance of y given $\mathbf{x}$, or equivalently $\mathrm{Var}(u \mid \mathbf{x})$, under homoskedasticity:

ASSUMPTION NLS.3: $\mathrm{Var}(y \mid \mathbf{x}) = \mathrm{Var}(u \mid \mathbf{x}) = \sigma_o^2$.

Under Assumption NLS.3, we can show that assumption (12.53) holds with $\sigma_o^2 = \mathrm{Var}(y \mid \mathbf{x})$. First, since $\mathbf{s}(\mathbf{w}, \boldsymbol{\theta}_o)\mathbf{s}(\mathbf{w}, \boldsymbol{\theta}_o)' = u^2 \nabla_\theta m(\mathbf{x}, \boldsymbol{\theta}_o)' \nabla_\theta m(\mathbf{x}, \boldsymbol{\theta}_o)$, it follows that

$$\begin{aligned} \mathrm{E}[\mathbf{s}(\mathbf{w}, \boldsymbol{\theta}_o)\mathbf{s}(\mathbf{w}, \boldsymbol{\theta}_o)' \mid \mathbf{x}] &= \mathrm{E}(u^2 \mid \mathbf{x}) \nabla_\theta m(\mathbf{x}, \boldsymbol{\theta}_o)' \nabla_\theta m(\mathbf{x}, \boldsymbol{\theta}_o) \\ &= \sigma_o^2 \nabla_\theta m(\mathbf{x}, \boldsymbol{\theta}_o)' \nabla_\theta m(\mathbf{x}, \boldsymbol{\theta}_o) \end{aligned} \tag{12.56}$$

under Assumptions NLS.1 and NLS.3. Taking the expected value with respect to $\mathbf{x}$ gives equation (12.53).

Under Assumption NLS.3, a simplified estimator of the asymptotic variance of the NLS estimator exists from equation (12.55). Let

$$\hat{\sigma}^2 = \frac{1}{(N-P)} \sum_{i=1}^{N} \hat{u}_i^2 = \mathrm{SSR}/(N-P), \tag{12.57}$$

where the $\hat{u}_i$ are the NLS residuals (12.51) and SSR is the sum of squared NLS residuals. Using Lemma 12.1, $\hat{\sigma}^2$ can be shown to be consistent very generally. The subtraction of P in the denominator of equation (12.57) is an adjustment that is thought to improve the small sample properties of $\hat{\sigma}^2$.

Under Assumptions NLS.1–NLS.3, the asymptotic variance of the NLS estimator is estimated as

$$\hat{\sigma}^2 \left(\sum_{i=1}^{N} \nabla_\theta \hat{m}_i' \nabla_\theta \hat{m}_i \right)^{-1}. \tag{12.58}$$

This is the default asymptotic variance estimator for NLS, but it is valid only under homoskedasticity; the estimator (12.52) is valid with or without Assumption NLS.3. For an exponential regression function, expression (12.58) becomes $\hat{\sigma}^2 (\sum_{i=1}^{N} \exp(2\mathbf{x}_i\hat{\boldsymbol{\theta}})\mathbf{x}_i'\mathbf{x}_i)^{-1}$. (Remember, if we want to allow Assumption NLS.1 to fail, we should use expression [12.48].)

12.5.2 Adjustments for Two-Step Estimation

In the case of the two-step M-estimator, we may or may not need to adjust the asymptotic variance. If assumption (12.37) holds, estimation is very simple. The most general estimators are expressions (12.48) and (12.49), where $\hat{\mathbf{s}}_i$, $\hat{\mathbf{H}}_i$, and $\hat{\mathbf{A}}_i$ depend on $\hat{\gamma}$, but we only compute derivatives with respect to $\boldsymbol{\theta}$.

In some cases under assumption (12.37), the analogue of assumption (12.53) holds (with $\gamma_o = \operatorname{plim} \hat{\gamma}$ appearing in $\mathbf{H}$ and $\mathbf{s}$). If so, the simpler estimators (12.54) and (12.55) are available. In Problem 12.4 you are asked to show this result for weighted NLS when $\mathrm{Var}(y \mid \mathbf{x}) = \sigma_o^2 h(\mathbf{x}, \gamma_o)$ and $\gamma_o = \operatorname{plim} \hat{\gamma}$. The natural third assumption for WNLS is that the variance function is correctly specified:

ASSUMPTION WNLS.3: For some $\gamma_o \in \boldsymbol{\Gamma}$ and $\sigma_o^2 > 0$, $\mathrm{Var}(y \mid \mathbf{x}) = \sigma_o^2 h(\mathbf{x}, \gamma_o)$. Further, $\sqrt{N}(\hat{\gamma} - \gamma_o) = \mathrm{O}_p(1)$.

Under Assumptions WNLS.1–WNLS.3, the asymptotic variance of the WNLS estimator is estimated as

$$\hat{\sigma}^2 \left(\sum_{i=1}^{N} (\nabla_\theta \hat{m}_i' \nabla_\theta \hat{m}_i)/\hat{h}_i \right)^{-1}, \tag{12.59}$$

where $\hat{h}_i = h(\mathbf{x}_i, \hat{\gamma})$ and $\hat{\sigma}^2$ is as in equation (12.57) except that the residual $\hat{u}_i$ is replaced with the **standardized residual**, $\hat{u}_i/\sqrt{\hat{h}_i}$. The sum in expression (12.59) is simply the outer product of the weighted gradients, $\nabla_\theta \hat{m}_i/\sqrt{\hat{h}_i}$. Thus the NLS formulas can be used but with all quantities weighted by $1/\sqrt{\hat{h}_i}$. It is important to remember that expression (12.59) is not valid without Assumption WNLS.3. Without Assumption WNLS.3, but with correct specification of the conditional mean, the asymptotic variance estimator of the WNLS estimator is

$$\left(\sum_{i=1}^{N} \nabla_\theta \hat{m}_i' \nabla_\theta \hat{m}_i/\hat{h}_i \right)^{-1} \left(\sum_{i=1}^{N} \hat{u}_i^2 \nabla_\theta \hat{m}_i' \nabla_\theta \hat{m}_i/\hat{h}_i^2 \right) \left(\sum_{i=1}^{N} \nabla_\theta \hat{m}_i' \nabla_\theta \hat{m}_i/\hat{h}_i \right)^{-1}, \tag{12.60}$$

where $\hat{u}_i = y_i - m(\mathbf{x}_i, \hat{\boldsymbol{\theta}})$ are the WNLS residuals. Notice that this estimator has the same structure as equation (12.52), but where the residuals are replaced with the standardized residuals, $\hat{u}_i/\sqrt{\hat{h}_i}$, and the gradients are replaced with the weighted gradients, $\nabla_\theta \hat{m}_i/\sqrt{\hat{h}_i}$.

When assumption (12.37) is violated, the asymptotic variance estimator of $\hat{\boldsymbol{\theta}}$ must account for the asymptotic variance of $\hat{\gamma}$; we must estimate equation (12.41). We already know how to consistently estimate $\mathbf{A}_o$: use expression (12.42) or (12.44) where $\hat{\gamma}$ is also plugged in. Estimation of $\mathbf{D}_o$ is also straightforward. First, we need to estimate $\mathbf{F}_o$. An estimator that is always available is the $P \times J$ matrix

$$\hat{\mathbf{F}} = N^{-1} \sum_{i=1}^{N} \nabla_\gamma \mathbf{s}_i(\hat{\boldsymbol{\theta}}; \hat{\gamma}). \tag{12.61}$$

In cases with conditioning variables, such as NLS, a simpler estimator can be obtained by computing $\mathrm{E}[\nabla_\gamma \mathbf{s}(\mathbf{w}_i, \boldsymbol{\theta}_o, \gamma^*) \,|\, \mathbf{x}_i]$, replacing $(\boldsymbol{\theta}_o, \gamma^*)$ with $(\hat{\boldsymbol{\theta}}, \hat{\gamma})$, and using this in place of $\nabla_\gamma \mathbf{s}_i(\hat{\boldsymbol{\theta}}; \hat{\gamma})$. Next, replace $\mathbf{r}_i(\gamma^*)$ with $\hat{\mathbf{r}}_i \equiv \mathbf{r}_i(\hat{\gamma})$. Then

$$\hat{\mathbf{D}} \equiv N^{-1} \sum_{i=1}^{N} \hat{\mathbf{g}}_i \hat{\mathbf{g}}_i' \tag{12.62}$$

is consistent for $\mathbf{D}_o$, where $\hat{\mathbf{g}}_i = \hat{\mathbf{s}}_i + \hat{\mathbf{F}}\hat{\mathbf{r}}_i$. The asymptotic variance of the two-step M-estimator can be obtained as in expression (12.48) or (12.49), but where $\hat{\mathbf{s}}_i$ is replaced with $\hat{\mathbf{g}}_i$.

In some cases, a subtle issue arises in deciding whether adjustment for the presence of $\hat{\gamma}$ is needed. For example, in WNLS with a correctly specified conditional mean (and without any assumption about the conditional variance), $\mathbf{F}_o = \mathbf{0}$, and so no adjustment to the asymptotic variance of $\hat{\boldsymbol{\theta}}$ is needed. But if the mean is misspecified so that $\text{plim}(\hat{\boldsymbol{\theta}}) = \boldsymbol{\theta}^*$, where $\boldsymbol{\theta}^*$ minimizes the weighted mean squared error, then the corresponding matrix, say $\mathbf{F}^* \equiv \text{E}[\nabla_\gamma \mathbf{s}_i(\boldsymbol{\theta}^*; \gamma^*)]$, is not zero. Then, neither (12.59) *nor* (12.60) is valid. Further, it is *not* enough to replace the expected Hessian (under correct specification of the conditional mean) with the Hessian in (12.60). A version that allows the mean to be misspecified must account for the asymptotic variance of $\sqrt{N}(\hat{\gamma} - \gamma^*)$ (which would itself require recognition that the conditional mean is misspecified in the initial NLS estimation). For general two-step M-estimation, we typically require some feature of $\text{D}(\mathbf{y}_i \mid \mathbf{x}_i)$ to be correctly specified (such as the mean in the case of WNLS) in order to justify ignoring the sampling variation in $\hat{\gamma}$. In practice, calculating the variance for two-step methods that allows misspecification of the feature of $\text{D}(\mathbf{y}_i \mid \mathbf{x}_i)$ of interest is rarely done.

12.6 Hypothesis Testing

12.6.1 Wald Tests

Wald tests are easily obtained once we choose a form of the asymptotic variance. To test the Q restrictions $\text{H}_0 : \mathbf{c}(\boldsymbol{\theta}_o) = \mathbf{0}$, we can form the Wald statistic

$$W \equiv \mathbf{c}(\hat{\boldsymbol{\theta}})'(\hat{\mathbf{C}}\hat{\mathbf{V}}\hat{\mathbf{C}}')^{-1}\mathbf{c}(\hat{\boldsymbol{\theta}}), \tag{12.63}$$

where $\hat{\mathbf{V}}$ is an asymptotic variance matrix estimator of $\hat{\boldsymbol{\theta}}$, $\hat{\mathbf{C}} \equiv \mathbf{C}(\hat{\boldsymbol{\theta}})$, and $\mathbf{C}(\boldsymbol{\theta})$ is the $Q \times P$ Jacobian of $\mathbf{c}(\boldsymbol{\theta})$. The estimator $\hat{\mathbf{V}}$ can be chosen to be fully robust, as in expression (12.48) or (12.49); under assumption (12.53), the simpler forms in Lemma 12.2 are available. Also, $\hat{\mathbf{V}}$ can be chosen to account for two-step estimation, when necessary. Provided $\hat{\mathbf{V}}$ has been chosen appropriately, $W \overset{a}{\sim} \chi^2_Q$ under H_0.

A couple of practical restrictions are needed for W to have a limiting χ^2_Q distribution. First, $\boldsymbol{\theta}_o$ must be in the interior of $\boldsymbol{\Theta}$; that is, $\boldsymbol{\theta}_o$ cannot be on the boundary. If, for example, the first element of $\boldsymbol{\theta}$ must be nonnegative—and we impose this restriction in the estimation—then expression (12.63) does not have a limiting chi-square distribution under $\text{H}_0 : \theta_{o1} = 0$. The second condition is that $\mathbf{C}(\boldsymbol{\theta}_o) = \nabla_\theta \mathbf{c}(\boldsymbol{\theta}_o)$ must have rank Q. This rules out cases where $\boldsymbol{\theta}_o$ is unidentified under the null hypothesis, such as the NLS example where $m(\mathbf{x}, \boldsymbol{\theta}) = \theta_1 + \theta_2 x_2 + \theta_3 x_3^{\theta_4}$ and $\theta_{o3} = 0$ under H_0.

One drawback to the Wald statistic is that it is not invariant to how the nonlinear restrictions are imposed. We can change the outcome of a hypothesis test by redefining the constraint function, $\mathbf{c}(\cdot)$. The easiest way to illustrate the lack of invariance of the Wald statistic is to use an aymptotic t statistic. Just as in the classical linear model where the F statistic for a single restriction is the square of the t statistic for that same restriction, the Wald statistic is the square of the corresponding asymptotic t statistic. Suppose that for a parameter $\theta_1 > 0$, the null hypothesis is $\mathrm{H}_0 : \theta_{o1} = 1$. The asymptotic t statistic is $(\hat{\theta}_1 - 1)/\mathrm{se}(\hat{\theta}_1)$, where $\mathrm{se}(\hat{\theta}_1)$ is the asymptotic standard error of $\hat{\theta}_1$. Now define $\phi_1 = \log(\theta_1)$, so that $\phi_{o1} = \log(\theta_{o1})$ and $\hat{\phi}_1 = \log(\hat{\theta}_1)$. The null hypothesis can be stated as $\mathrm{H}_0 : \phi_{o1} = 0$. Using the delta method (see Chapter 3), $\mathrm{se}(\hat{\phi}_1) = \hat{\theta}_1^{-1}\,\mathrm{se}(\hat{\theta}_1)$, and so the t statistic based on $\hat{\phi}_1$ is $\hat{\phi}_1/\mathrm{se}(\hat{\phi}_1) = \log(\hat{\theta}_1)\hat{\theta}_1/\mathrm{se}(\hat{\theta}_1)$ $\neq (\hat{\theta}_1 - 1)/\mathrm{se}(\hat{\theta}_1)$.

The lack of invariance of the Wald statistic is discussed in more detail by Gregory and Veall (1985), Phillips and Park (1988), and Davidson and MacKinnon (1993, Sect. 13.6). The lack of invariance is a cause for concern because it suggests that the Wald statistic can have poor finite sample properties for testing nonlinear hypotheses. What is much less clear is that the lack of invariance has led empirical researchers to search over different statements of the null hypothesis in order to obtain a desired result.

12.6.2 Score (or Lagrange Multiplier) Tests

In cases where the unrestricted model is difficult to estimate but the restricted model is relatively simple to estimate, it is convenient to have a statistic that only requires estimation under the null. Such a statistic is Rao's (1948) **score statistic**, also called the **Lagrange multiplier statistic** in econometrics, based on the work of Aitchison and Silvey (1958). We will focus on Rao's original motivation for the statistic because it leads more directly to test statistics that are used in econometrics. An important point is that, even though Rao, Aitchison and Silvey, Engle (1984), and many others focused on the maximum likelihood setup, the score principle is applicable to any problem where the estimators solve a first-order condition, including the general class of M-estimators.

The score approach is ideally suited for **specification testing**. Typically, the first step in specification testing is to begin with a popular model—one that is relatively easy to estimate and interpret—and nest it within a more complicated model. Then the popular model is tested against the more general alternative to determine if the original model is misspecified. We do not want to estimate the more complicated model unless there is significant evidence against the restricted form of the model. In stating the null and alternative hypotheses, there is no difference between specification testing and classical tests of parameter restrictions. However, in practice, specification testing gives primary importance to the restricted model, and we may have no intention of actually estimating the general model even if the null model is rejected.

We will derive the score test only in the case where no correction is needed for preliminary estimation of nuisance parameters: either there are no such parameters present, or assumption (12.37) holds under H_0. If nuisance parameters are present, we do not explicitly show the score and Hessian depending on $\hat{\gamma}$.

We again assume that there are Q continuously differentiable restrictions imposed on $\boldsymbol{\theta}_o$ under H_0, $\mathbf{c}(\boldsymbol{\theta}_o) = \mathbf{0}$. However, we must also assume that the restrictions define a mapping from $\mathbb{R}^{P-Q}$ to $\mathbb{R}^P$, say, $\mathbf{d} : \mathbb{R}^{P-Q} \to \mathbb{R}^P$. In particular, under the null hypothesis, we can write $\boldsymbol{\theta}_o = \mathbf{d}(\boldsymbol{\lambda}_o)$, where $\boldsymbol{\lambda}_o$ is a $(P - Q) \times 1$ vector. We must assume that $\boldsymbol{\lambda}_o$ is in the interior of its parameter space, $\boldsymbol{\Lambda}$, under H_0. We also assume that $\mathbf{d}$ is twice continuously differentiable on the interior of $\boldsymbol{\Lambda}$.

Let $\tilde{\boldsymbol{\lambda}}$ be the solution to the constrained minimization problem

$$\min_{\boldsymbol{\lambda} \in \boldsymbol{\Lambda}} \sum_{i=1}^{N} q[\mathbf{w}_i, \mathbf{d}(\boldsymbol{\lambda})]. \tag{12.64}$$

The constrained estimator of $\boldsymbol{\theta}_o$ is simply $\tilde{\boldsymbol{\theta}} \equiv \mathbf{d}(\tilde{\boldsymbol{\lambda}})$. In practice, we do not have to explicitly find the function $\mathbf{d}$; solving problem (12.64) is easily done just by directly imposing the restrictions, especially when the restrictions set certain parameters to hypothesized values (such as zero). Then, we just minimize the resulting objective function over the free parameters.

As an example, consider the nonlinear regression model

$$m(\mathbf{x}, \boldsymbol{\theta}) = \exp[\mathbf{x}\boldsymbol{\beta} + \delta_1(\mathbf{x}\boldsymbol{\beta})^2 + \delta_2(\mathbf{x}\boldsymbol{\beta})^3],$$

where $\mathbf{x}$ is $1 \times K$ and contains unity as its first element. The null hypothesis is $H_0 : \delta_1 = \delta_2 = 0$, so that the model with the restrictions imposed is just an exponential regression function, $m(\mathbf{x}, \boldsymbol{\beta}) = \exp(\mathbf{x}\boldsymbol{\beta})$.

The simplest method for deriving the LM test is to use Rao's score principle extended to the M-estimator case. The LM statistic is based on the limiting distribution of

$$N^{-1/2} \sum_{i=1}^{N} \mathbf{s}_i(\tilde{\boldsymbol{\theta}}) \tag{12.65}$$

under H_0. This is the score with respect to the entire vector $\boldsymbol{\theta}$, but we are evaluating it at the restricted estimates. If $\tilde{\boldsymbol{\theta}}$ were replaced by $\hat{\boldsymbol{\theta}}$, then expression (12.65) would be identically zero, which would make it useless as a test statistic. If the restrictions imposed by the null hypothesis are true, then expression (12.65) will not be statistically different from zero.

Assume initially that $\boldsymbol{\theta}_o$ is in the interior of $\boldsymbol{\Theta}$ under H_0; we will discuss how to relax this assumption later. Now $\sqrt{N}(\tilde{\boldsymbol{\theta}} - \boldsymbol{\theta}_o) = \mathrm{O}_p(1)$ by the delta method because $\sqrt{N}(\tilde{\boldsymbol{\lambda}} - \boldsymbol{\lambda}_o) = \mathrm{O}_p(1)$ under the given assumptions. A standard mean value expansion yields

$$N^{-1/2} \sum_{i=1}^{N} \mathbf{s}_i(\tilde{\boldsymbol{\theta}}) = N^{-1/2} \sum_{i=1}^{N} \mathbf{s}_i(\boldsymbol{\theta}_o) + \mathbf{A}_o \sqrt{N}(\tilde{\boldsymbol{\theta}} - \boldsymbol{\theta}_o) + \mathrm{o}_p(1) \tag{12.66}$$

under H_0, where $\mathbf{A}_o$ is given in expression (12.19). But $\mathbf{0} = \sqrt{N}\mathbf{c}(\tilde{\boldsymbol{\theta}}) = \sqrt{N}\mathbf{c}(\boldsymbol{\theta}_o) + \ddot{\mathbf{C}}\sqrt{N}(\tilde{\boldsymbol{\theta}} - \boldsymbol{\theta}_o)$, where $\ddot{\mathbf{C}}$ is the $Q \times P$ Jacobian matrix $\mathbf{C}(\boldsymbol{\theta})$ with rows evaluated at mean values between $\tilde{\boldsymbol{\theta}}$ and $\boldsymbol{\theta}_o$. Under H_0, $\mathbf{c}(\boldsymbol{\theta}_o) = \mathbf{0}$, and plim $\ddot{\mathbf{C}} = \mathbf{C}(\boldsymbol{\theta}_o) \equiv \mathbf{C}_o$. Therefore, under H_0, $\mathbf{C}_o\sqrt{N}(\tilde{\boldsymbol{\theta}} - \boldsymbol{\theta}_o) = \mathrm{o}_p(1)$, and so multiplying equation (12.66) through by $\mathbf{C}_o\mathbf{A}_o^{-1}$ gives

$$\mathbf{C}_o\mathbf{A}_o^{-1} N^{-1/2} \sum_{i=1}^{N} \mathbf{s}_i(\tilde{\boldsymbol{\theta}}) = \mathbf{C}_o\mathbf{A}_o^{-1} N^{-1/2} \sum_{i=1}^{N} \mathbf{s}_i(\boldsymbol{\theta}_o) + \mathrm{o}_p(1). \tag{12.67}$$

By the CLT, $\mathbf{C}_o\mathbf{A}_o^{-1} N^{-1/2} \sum_{i=1}^{N} \mathbf{s}_i(\boldsymbol{\theta}_o) \xrightarrow{d} \mathrm{Normal}(\mathbf{0}, \mathbf{C}_o\mathbf{A}_o^{-1}\mathbf{B}_o\mathbf{A}_o^{-1}\mathbf{C}_o')$, where $\mathbf{B}_o$ is defined in expression (12.20). Under our assumptions, $\mathbf{C}_o\mathbf{A}_o^{-1}\mathbf{B}_o\mathbf{A}_o^{-1}\mathbf{C}_o'$ has full rank Q, and so

$$\left[N^{-1/2} \sum_{i=1}^{N} \mathbf{s}_i(\tilde{\boldsymbol{\theta}})\right]' \mathbf{A}_o^{-1}\mathbf{C}_o'(\mathbf{C}_o\mathbf{A}_o^{-1}\mathbf{B}_o\mathbf{A}_o^{-1}\mathbf{C}_o')^{-1}\mathbf{C}_o\mathbf{A}_o^{-1}\left[N^{-1/2} \sum_{i=1}^{N} \mathbf{s}_i(\tilde{\boldsymbol{\theta}})\right] \xrightarrow{d} \chi_Q^2.$$

The score or LM statistic is given by

$$LM \equiv \left(\sum_{i=1}^{N} \tilde{\mathbf{s}}_i\right)' \tilde{\mathbf{A}}^{-1}\tilde{\mathbf{C}}'(\tilde{\mathbf{C}}\tilde{\mathbf{A}}^{-1}\tilde{\mathbf{B}}\tilde{\mathbf{A}}^{-1}\tilde{\mathbf{C}}')^{-1}\tilde{\mathbf{C}}\tilde{\mathbf{A}}^{-1}\left(\sum_{i=1}^{N} \tilde{\mathbf{s}}_i\right)/N, \tag{12.68}$$

where all quantities are evaluated at $\tilde{\boldsymbol{\theta}}$. For example, $\tilde{\mathbf{C}} \equiv \mathbf{C}(\tilde{\boldsymbol{\theta}})$, $\tilde{\mathbf{B}}$ is given in expression (12.45) but with $\tilde{\boldsymbol{\theta}}$ in place of $\hat{\boldsymbol{\theta}}$, and $\tilde{\mathbf{A}}$ is one of the estimators in expression (12.42) or (12.44), again evaluated at $\tilde{\boldsymbol{\theta}}$. Under H_0, $LM \xrightarrow{d} \chi_Q^2$. Because $\tilde{\mathbf{B}}$ is at least p.s.d., $LM \geq 0$.

For the Wald statistic we assumed that $\boldsymbol{\theta}_o \in \mathrm{int}(\boldsymbol{\Theta})$ under H_0; this assumption is crucial for the statistic to have a limiting chi-square distribution. We will not consider the Wald statistic when $\boldsymbol{\theta}_o$ is on the boundary of $\boldsymbol{\Theta}$ under H_0; see Wolak (1991) for some results. The general derivation of the LM statistic also assumed that $\boldsymbol{\theta}_o \in \mathrm{int}(\boldsymbol{\Theta})$

under H_0. Nevertheless, for certain applications of the LM test we can drop the requirement that $\boldsymbol{\theta}_o$ is in the interior of $\boldsymbol{\Theta}$ under H_0. A leading case occurs when $\boldsymbol{\theta}$ can be partitioned as $\boldsymbol{\theta} \equiv (\boldsymbol{\theta}_1', \boldsymbol{\theta}_2')'$, where $\boldsymbol{\theta}_1$ is $(P - Q) \times 1$ and $\boldsymbol{\theta}_2$ is $Q \times 1$. The null hypothesis is $\mathrm{H}_0 : \boldsymbol{\theta}_{o2} = \mathbf{0}$, so that $\mathbf{c}(\boldsymbol{\theta}) \equiv \boldsymbol{\theta}_2$. It is easy to see that the mean value expansion used to derive the LM statistic is valid provided $\boldsymbol{\lambda}_o \equiv \boldsymbol{\theta}_{o1}$ is in the interior of its parameter space under H_0; $\boldsymbol{\theta}_o \equiv (\boldsymbol{\theta}_{o1}', \mathbf{0})'$ can be on the boundary of $\boldsymbol{\Theta}$. This observation is useful especially when testing hypotheses about parameters that must be either nonnegative or nonpositive.

If we assume the generalized information matrix equality (12.53) with $\sigma_o^2 = 1$, the LM statistic simplifies. The simplification results from the following reasoning: (1) $\tilde{\mathbf{C}}\tilde{\mathbf{D}} = \mathbf{0}$ by the chain rule, where $\tilde{\mathbf{D}} \equiv \nabla_\lambda \mathbf{d}(\tilde{\boldsymbol{\lambda}})$, since $\mathbf{c}[\mathbf{d}(\boldsymbol{\lambda})] \equiv \mathbf{0}$ for $\boldsymbol{\lambda}$ in $\boldsymbol{\Lambda}$. (2) If $\mathbf{E}$ is a $P \times Q$ matrix $\mathbf{E}$ with rank Q, $\mathbf{F}$ is a $P \times (P - Q)$ matrix with rank $P - Q$, and $\mathbf{E}'\mathbf{F} = \mathbf{0}$, then $\mathbf{E}(\mathbf{E}'\mathbf{E})^{-1}\mathbf{E}' = \mathbf{I}_P - \mathbf{F}(\mathbf{F}'\mathbf{F})^{-1}\mathbf{F}'$. (This is simply a statement about projections onto orthogonal subspaces.) Choosing $\mathbf{E} \equiv \tilde{\mathbf{A}}^{-1/2}\tilde{\mathbf{C}}'$ and $\mathbf{F} \equiv \tilde{\mathbf{A}}^{1/2}\tilde{\mathbf{D}}$ gives $\tilde{\mathbf{A}}^{-1/2}\tilde{\mathbf{C}}'(\tilde{\mathbf{C}}\tilde{\mathbf{A}}^{-1}\tilde{\mathbf{C}}')^{-1}\tilde{\mathbf{C}}\tilde{\mathbf{A}}^{-1/2} = \mathbf{I}_P - \tilde{\mathbf{A}}^{1/2}\tilde{\mathbf{D}}(\tilde{\mathbf{D}}'\tilde{\mathbf{A}}\tilde{\mathbf{D}})^{-1}\tilde{\mathbf{D}}'\tilde{\mathbf{A}}^{1/2}$. Now, pre- and post-multiply this equality by $\tilde{\mathbf{A}}^{-1/2}$ to get $\tilde{\mathbf{A}}^{-1}\tilde{\mathbf{C}}'(\tilde{\mathbf{C}}\tilde{\mathbf{A}}^{-1}\tilde{\mathbf{C}}')^{-1}\tilde{\mathbf{C}}\tilde{\mathbf{A}}^{-1} = \tilde{\mathbf{A}}^{-1} - \tilde{\mathbf{D}}(\tilde{\mathbf{D}}'\tilde{\mathbf{A}}\tilde{\mathbf{D}})^{-1}\tilde{\mathbf{D}}'$. (3) Plug $\tilde{\mathbf{B}} = \tilde{\mathbf{A}}$ into expression (12.68) and use step 2, along with the first-order condition $\tilde{\mathbf{D}}'(\sum_{i=1}^N \tilde{\mathbf{s}}_i) = \mathbf{0}$, to get

$$LM = \left(\sum_{i=1}^{N} \tilde{\mathbf{s}}_i\right)' \tilde{\mathbf{M}}^{-1} \left(\sum_{i=1}^{N} \tilde{\mathbf{s}}_i\right), \tag{12.69}$$

where $\tilde{\mathbf{M}}$ can be chosen as $\sum_{i=1}^N \tilde{\mathbf{A}}_i$, $\sum_{i=1}^N \tilde{\mathbf{H}}_i$, or $\sum_{i=1}^N \tilde{\mathbf{s}}_i\tilde{\mathbf{s}}_i'$. (Each of these expressions consistently estimates $\mathbf{A}_o = \mathbf{B}_o$ when divided by N.) The last choice of $\tilde{\mathbf{M}}$ results in a statistic that is N times the uncentered R-squared, say R_0^2, from the regression

$$1 \text{ on } \tilde{\mathbf{s}}_i', \qquad i = 1, 2, \ldots, N. \tag{12.70}$$

(Recall that $\tilde{\mathbf{s}}_i'$ is a $1 \times P$ vector.) Because the dependent variable in regression (12.70) is unity, NR_0^2 is equivalent to $N - \mathrm{SSR}_0$, where SSR_0 is the sum of squared residuals from regression (12.70). This is often called the **outer product of the score LM statistic** because of the estimator it uses for $\mathbf{A}_o$. While this statistic is simple to compute, there is ample evidence that it can have severe size distortions (typically, the null hypothesis is rejected much more often than the nominal size of the test). See, for example, Davidson and MacKinnon (1993), Bera and McKenzie (1986), Orme (1990), and Chesher and Spady (1991).

The **Hessian form of the LM statistic** uses $\tilde{\mathbf{M}} = \sum_{i=1}^N \tilde{\mathbf{H}}_i$, and it has a few drawbacks: (1) because $\tilde{\mathbf{M}}$ is the Hessian for the full model evaluated at the restricted estimates it may not be positive definite, in which case the LM statistic can be negative; (2) it requires computation of the second derivatives; and (3) it is not invariant to reparameterizations. We will discuss the last problem later.

A statistic that always avoids the first problem, and often the second and third problems, is based on $\mathrm{E}[\mathbf{H}(\mathbf{w}, \boldsymbol{\theta}_o) \mid \mathbf{x}]$, assuming that $\mathbf{w}$ partitions into endogenous variables $\mathbf{y}$ and exogenous variables $\mathbf{x}$. We call the LM statistic that uses $\tilde{\mathbf{M}} = \sum_{i=1}^{N} \tilde{\mathbf{A}}_i$ the **expected Hessian form of the LM statistic**. This name comes from the fact that the statistic is based on the *conditional* expectation of $\mathbf{H}(\mathbf{w}, \boldsymbol{\theta}_o)$ given $\mathbf{x}$. When it can be computed, the expected Hessian form is usually preferred because it tends to have the best small sample properties.

The LM statistic in equation (12.69) is valid only when $\mathbf{B}_o = \mathbf{A}_o$, and therefore it is not robust to failures of auxiliary assumptions in some important models. If $\mathbf{B}_o \neq \mathbf{A}_o$, the limiting distribution of equation (12.69) is not chi-square and is not suitable for testing.

In the context of NLS, the expected Hessian form of the LM statistic needs to be modified for the presence of σ_o^2, assuming that Assumption NLS.3 holds under H_0. Let $\tilde{\sigma}^2 \equiv N^{-1} \sum_{i=1}^{N} \tilde{u}_i^2$ be the estimate of σ_o^2 using the restricted estimator of $\boldsymbol{\theta}_o : \tilde{u}_i \equiv y_i - m(\mathbf{x}_i, \tilde{\boldsymbol{\theta}})$, $i = 1, 2, \ldots, N$. It is customary not to make a degrees-of-freedom adjustment when estimating the variance using the null estimates, partly because the sum of squared residuals for the restricted model is always larger than for the unrestricted model. The score evaluated at the restricted estimates can be written as $\tilde{\mathbf{s}}_i = \nabla_\theta \tilde{m}_i' \tilde{u}_i$. Thus the LM statistic that imposes homoskedasticity is

$$LM = \left(\sum_{i=1}^{N} \nabla_\theta \tilde{m}_i' \tilde{u}_i\right)' \left(\sum_{i=1}^{N} \nabla_\theta \tilde{m}_i' \nabla_\theta \tilde{m}_i\right)^{-1} \left(\sum_{i=1}^{N} \nabla_\theta \tilde{m}_i' \tilde{u}_i\right) / \tilde{\sigma}^2. \tag{12.71}$$

A little algebra shows that this expression is identical to N times the uncentered R-squared, R_u^2, from the auxiliary regression

$$\tilde{u}_i \text{ on } \nabla_\theta \tilde{m}_i, \qquad i = 1, 2, \ldots, N. \tag{12.72}$$

In other words, just regress the residuals from the restricted model on the gradient with respect to the *unrestricted* mean function but evaluated at the *restricted* estimates. Under H_0 and Assumption NLS.3, $LM = NR_u^2 \overset{a}{\sim} \chi_Q^2$.

In the nonlinear regression example with $m(\mathbf{x}, \boldsymbol{\theta}) = \exp[\mathbf{x}\boldsymbol{\beta} + \delta_1(\mathbf{x}\boldsymbol{\beta})^2 + \delta_2(\mathbf{x}\boldsymbol{\beta})^3]$, let $\tilde{\boldsymbol{\beta}}$ be the restricted NLS estimator with $\delta_1 = 0$ and $\delta_2 = 0$; in other words, $\tilde{\boldsymbol{\beta}}$ is from a nonlinear regression with an exponential regression function. The restricted residuals are $\tilde{u}_i = y_i - \exp(\mathbf{x}_i\tilde{\boldsymbol{\beta}})$, and the gradient of $m(\mathbf{x}, \boldsymbol{\theta})$ with respect to all parameters, evaluated at the null, is

$$\nabla_\theta m(\mathbf{x}_i, \boldsymbol{\beta}_o, \mathbf{0}) = \{\mathbf{x}_i \exp(\mathbf{x}_i\boldsymbol{\beta}_o), (\mathbf{x}_i\boldsymbol{\beta}_o)^2 \exp(\mathbf{x}_i\boldsymbol{\beta}_o), (\mathbf{x}_i\boldsymbol{\beta}_o)^3 \exp(\mathbf{x}_i\boldsymbol{\beta}_o)\}.$$

Plugging in $\tilde{\boldsymbol{\beta}}$ gives $\nabla_\theta \tilde{m}_i = [\mathbf{x}_i\tilde{m}_i, (\mathbf{x}_i\tilde{\boldsymbol{\beta}})^2\tilde{m}_i, (\mathbf{x}_i\tilde{\boldsymbol{\beta}})^3\tilde{m}_i]$, where $\tilde{m}_i \equiv \exp(\mathbf{x}_i\tilde{\boldsymbol{\beta}})$. Regression (12.72) becomes

$$\tilde{u}_i \text{ on } \mathbf{x}_i\tilde{m}_i,\ (\mathbf{x}_i\tilde{\boldsymbol{\beta}})^2\tilde{m}_i,\ (\mathbf{x}_i\tilde{\boldsymbol{\beta}})^3\tilde{m}_i, \qquad i = 1, 2, \ldots, N. \tag{12.73}$$

Under H_0 and homoskedasticity, $NR_u^2 \sim \chi_2^2$, since there are two restrictions being tested. This is a fairly simple way to test the exponential functional form without ever estimating the more complicated alternative model. Other models that nest the exponential model are discussed in Wooldridge (1992).

This example illustrates an important point: even though $\sum_{i=1}^N (\mathbf{x}_i\tilde{m}_i)'\tilde{u}_i$ is identically zero by the first-order condition for NLS, the term $\mathbf{x}_i\tilde{m}_i$ must generally be included in regression (12.73). The R-squared from the regression without $\mathbf{x}_i\tilde{m}_i$ will be different because the remaining regressors in regression (12.73) are usually correlated with $\mathbf{x}_i\tilde{m}_i$ in the sample. (More important, for $h = 2$ and 3, $(\mathbf{x}_i\boldsymbol{\beta}_o)^h \exp(\mathbf{x}_i\boldsymbol{\beta}_o)$ is probably correlated with $\mathbf{x}_i \exp(\mathbf{x}_i\boldsymbol{\beta}_o)$ in the population.) As a general rule, the entire gradient $\nabla_\theta \tilde{m}_i$ must appear in the auxiliary regression.

In order to be robust against failure of Assumption NLS.3, the more general form of the statistic in expression (12.68) should be used. Fortunately, this statistic also can be easily computed for most hypotheses. Partition $\boldsymbol{\theta}$ into the $(P - Q) \times 1$ vector $\boldsymbol{\beta}$ and the Q vector $\boldsymbol{\delta}$. Assume that the null hypothesis is $\mathrm{H}_0 : \boldsymbol{\delta}_o = \bar{\boldsymbol{\delta}}$, where $\bar{\boldsymbol{\delta}}$ is a prespecified vector (often containing all zeros, but not always). Let $\nabla_\beta \tilde{m}_i$ $[1 \times (P - Q)]$ and $\nabla_\delta \tilde{m}_i$ $(1 \times Q)$ denote the gradients with respect to $\boldsymbol{\beta}$ and $\boldsymbol{\delta}$, respectively, evaluated at $\tilde{\boldsymbol{\beta}}$ and $\bar{\boldsymbol{\delta}}$. After tedious algebra, and using the special structure $\mathbf{C}(\boldsymbol{\theta}) = [\mathbf{0} \,|\, \mathbf{I}_Q]$, where $\mathbf{0}$ is a $Q \times (P - Q)$ matrix of zero, the following procedure can be shown to produce expression (12.68):

1. Run a multivariate regression

$$\nabla_\delta \tilde{m}_i \text{ on } \nabla_\beta \tilde{m}_i, \qquad i = 1, 2, \ldots, N \tag{12.74}$$

and save the $1 \times Q$ vector residuals, say $\tilde{\mathbf{r}}_i$. Then, for each i, form $\tilde{u}_i\tilde{\mathbf{r}}_i$. (That is, multiply $\tilde{u}_i$ by each element of $\tilde{\mathbf{r}}_i$.)

2. $LM = N - \mathrm{SSR}_0 = NR_0^2$ from the regression

$$1 \text{ on } \tilde{u}_i\tilde{\mathbf{r}}_i, \qquad i = 1, 2, \ldots, N \tag{12.75}$$

where SSR_0 is the usual sum of squared residuals and R_0^2 is the uncentered R-squared. This step produces a statistic that has a limiting χ_Q^2 distribution whether or not Assumption NLS.3 holds. See Wooldridge (1991a) for more discussion.

We can illustrate the heteroskedasticity-robust test using the preceding exponential model. Regression (12.74) is the same as regressing each of $(\mathbf{x}_i\tilde{\boldsymbol{\beta}})^2\tilde{m}_i$ and $(\mathbf{x}_i\tilde{\boldsymbol{\beta}})^3\tilde{m}_i$ onto $\mathbf{x}_i\tilde{m}_i$, and saving the residuals $\tilde{r}_{i1}$ and $\tilde{r}_{i2}$, respectively (N each). Then, regression (12.75) is simply 1 on $\tilde{u}_i\tilde{r}_{i1}$, $\tilde{u}_i\tilde{r}_{i2}$. The number of regressors in the final regression of the robust test is always the same as the degrees of freedom of the test.

Finally, these procedures are easily modified for WNLS. Simply multiply both $\tilde{u}_i$ and $\nabla_\theta\tilde{m}_i$ by $1/\sqrt{\tilde{h}_i}$, where the variance estimates $\tilde{h}_i$ are based on the null model (so we use a $\sim$ rather than a $\wedge$). The nonrobust LM statistic that maintains Assumption WNLS.3 is obtained as in regression (12.72). The robust form, which allows $\mathrm{Var}(y \mid \mathbf{x}) \neq \sigma_o^2 h(\mathbf{x}, \boldsymbol{\gamma}_o)$, follows exactly as in regressions (12.74) and (12.75).

In examples like the previous one, there is an alternative, asymptotically equivalent method of obtaining a test statistic that, like the score test, only requires estimation under the null hypothesis. A **variable addition test (VAT)** is obtained by adding (estimated) terms to a standard model. Once the additional variables have been defined, calculation is typically straightforward with existing software, and robust tests—robust to heteroskedasticity in the case of NLS—are easy to obtain.

In the previous example, where we focused on NLS, we again obtain $\tilde{\boldsymbol{\beta}}$ from NLS using the exponential regression function. We then compute $(\mathbf{x}_i\tilde{\boldsymbol{\beta}})^2$ and $(\mathbf{x}_i\tilde{\boldsymbol{\beta}})^3$. Next, we estimate an expanded exponential mean function that includes the original regressors, $\mathbf{x}_i$, and the two additional regressors, say, $\tilde{z}_{i1} \equiv (\mathbf{x}_i\tilde{\boldsymbol{\beta}})^2$ and $\tilde{z}_{i2} \equiv (\mathbf{x}_i\tilde{\boldsymbol{\beta}})^3$. That is, the auxiliary model (used for testing purposes only) is $\exp(\mathbf{x}_i\boldsymbol{\beta} + \alpha_1\tilde{z}_{i1} + \alpha_2\tilde{z}_{i2})$. The VAT is obtained as a standard Wald test for joint exclusion of $\tilde{z}_{i1}$ and $\tilde{z}_{i2}$ (and therefore has an asymptotic χ_2^2 distribution). For the nonrobust test, one difference between the LM test and the VAT is that the latter uses a different variance estimate (because of the additional terms $\tilde{z}_{i1}$ and $\tilde{z}_{i2}$ that have coefficients estimated rather than set to zero). Under the null, both estimators converge to σ_o^2. It is easy to make VAT tests robust to heteroskedasticity whenever one is using an econometrics package that computes heteroskedasticity-robust Wald tests of exclusion restrictions; typically, it simply requires adding a "robust" option to an estimation command such as NLS.

For NLS (and WNLS), the VAT approach can be applied more generally when the mean function has the form $m(\mathbf{x}, \boldsymbol{\beta}, \boldsymbol{\delta}) = R(a(\mathbf{x}\boldsymbol{\beta}, \mathbf{x}, \boldsymbol{\delta}))$, where $a(k, \mathbf{x}, \mathbf{0}) = k$ and $\partial a(k, \mathbf{x}, \mathbf{0})/\partial k = 1$. Then $m(\mathbf{x}, \boldsymbol{\beta}, \mathbf{0}) = R(\mathbf{x}\boldsymbol{\beta})$ and $\nabla_\beta m(\mathbf{x}, \boldsymbol{\beta}, 0) = r(\mathbf{x}\boldsymbol{\beta}) \cdot \mathbf{x}$, where $r(\cdot)$ is the derivative of $R(\cdot)$. The vector of variables to be added is simply $\tilde{\mathbf{z}}_i \equiv \nabla_\delta a(\mathbf{x}_i\tilde{\boldsymbol{\beta}}, \mathbf{x}_i, \mathbf{0})$, a $1 \times Q$ vector, where $\tilde{\boldsymbol{\beta}}$ is the NLS estimator using the mean function $R(\mathbf{x}_i\boldsymbol{\beta})$. In other words, we use the augmented regression function $R(\mathbf{x}_i\boldsymbol{\beta} + \tilde{\mathbf{z}}_i\boldsymbol{\alpha})$ in NLS and test joint exclusion of $\tilde{\mathbf{z}}_i$. Note that this "model" is not correctly specified under the alternative. We estimate the augmented equation to obtain a simple test. The VAT procedure is easy to implement when the mean function $R(\cdot)$ with linear functions inside is easily estimated. (Examples include the exponential and logistic functions, and some others we encounter in Part IV.) We will see how to obtain VAT tests with other estimation methods in future chapters.

The invariance issue for the score statistic is somewhat complicated, but several results are known. First, it is easy to see that the outer product form of the statistic is invariant to differentiable reparameterizations. Write $\boldsymbol{\phi} = \mathbf{g}(\boldsymbol{\theta})$ as a twice continuously differentiable, invertible reparameterization; thus the $P \times P$ Jacobian of $\mathbf{g}$, $\mathbf{G}(\boldsymbol{\theta})$, is nonsingular for all $\boldsymbol{\theta} \in \boldsymbol{\Theta}$. The objective function in terms of $\boldsymbol{\phi}$ is $q^g(\mathbf{w}, \boldsymbol{\phi})$, and we must have $q^g[\mathbf{w}, \mathbf{g}(\boldsymbol{\theta})] = q(\mathbf{w}, \boldsymbol{\theta})$ for all $\boldsymbol{\theta} \in \boldsymbol{\Theta}$. Differentiating and transposing gives $\mathbf{s}(\mathbf{w}, \boldsymbol{\theta}) = \mathbf{G}(\boldsymbol{\theta})'\mathbf{s}^g[\mathbf{w}, \mathbf{g}(\boldsymbol{\theta})]$, where $\mathbf{s}^g(\mathbf{w}, \boldsymbol{\phi})$ is the score of $q^g[\mathbf{w}, \boldsymbol{\phi}]$. If $\tilde{\boldsymbol{\phi}}$ is the restricted estimator of $\boldsymbol{\phi}$, then $\tilde{\boldsymbol{\phi}} = \mathbf{g}(\tilde{\boldsymbol{\theta}})$, and so, for each observation i, $\tilde{\mathbf{s}}_i^g = (\tilde{\mathbf{G}}')^{-1}\tilde{\mathbf{s}}_i$. Plugging this equation into the LM statistic in equation (12.69), with $\tilde{\mathbf{M}}$ chosen as the outer product form, shows that the statistic based on $\tilde{\mathbf{s}}_i^g$ is identical to that based on $\tilde{\mathbf{s}}_i$.

Score statistics based on the estimated Hessian are not generally invariant to reparameterization because they can involve second derivatives of the function $\mathbf{g}(\boldsymbol{\theta})$; see Davidson and MacKinnon (1993, Sect. 13.6) for details. However, when $\mathbf{w}$ partitions as $(\mathbf{x}, \mathbf{y})$, score statistics based on the expected Hessian (conditional on $\mathbf{x}$), $\mathbf{A}(\mathbf{x}, \boldsymbol{\theta})$, *are* often invariant. In Chapter 13 we will see that this is always the case for conditional maximum likelihood estimation. Invariance also holds for NLS and WNLS for both the usual and robust LM statistics because any reparameterization comes through the conditional mean. Predicted values and residuals are invariant to reparameterization, and the statistics obtained from regressions (12.72) and (12.75) only involve the residuals and first derivatives of the conditional mean function. As with the outer product LM statistic, the Jacobian in the first derivative cancels out.

12.6.3 Tests Based on the Change in the Objective Function

When both the restricted and unrestricted models are easy to estimate, a test based on the change in the objective function can greatly simplify the mechanics of obtaining a test statistic: we only need to obtain the value of the objective function with and without the restrictions imposed. However, the computational simplicity comes at a price in terms of robustness. Unlike the Wald and score tests, a test based on the change in the objective function *cannot* be made robust to general failure of assumption (12.53). Therefore, throughout this subsection we assume that the generalized information matrix equality holds. Because the minimized objective function is invariant with respect to any reparameterization, the test statistic is invariant.

In the context of two-step estimators, we must also assume that $\hat{\gamma}$ has no effect on the asymptotic distribution of the M-estimator. That is, we maintain assumption

(12.37) when nuisance parameter estimates appear in the objective function (see Problem 12.8).

We first consider the case where $\sigma_o^2 = 1$, so that $\mathbf{B}_o = \mathbf{A}_o$. Using a second-order Taylor expansion,

$$\sum_{i=1}^{N} q(\mathbf{w}_i, \tilde{\boldsymbol{\theta}}) - \sum_{i=1}^{N} q(\mathbf{w}_i, \hat{\boldsymbol{\theta}}) = \left(\sum_{i=1}^{N} \mathbf{s}_i(\hat{\boldsymbol{\theta}})\right)(\hat{\boldsymbol{\theta}} - \boldsymbol{\theta}_o) + (1/2)(\tilde{\boldsymbol{\theta}} - \hat{\boldsymbol{\theta}})'\left(\sum_{i=1}^{N} \ddot{\mathbf{H}}_i\right)(\tilde{\boldsymbol{\theta}} - \hat{\boldsymbol{\theta}}),$$

where $\ddot{\mathbf{H}}_i$ is the $P \times P$ Hessian evaluate at mean values between $\tilde{\boldsymbol{\theta}}$ and $\hat{\boldsymbol{\theta}}$. Therefore, under H_0 (using the first-order condition for $\hat{\boldsymbol{\theta}}$), we have

$$2\left[\sum_{i=1}^{N} q(\mathbf{w}_i, \tilde{\boldsymbol{\theta}}) - \sum_{i=1}^{N} q(\mathbf{w}_i, \hat{\boldsymbol{\theta}})\right] = [\sqrt{N}(\tilde{\boldsymbol{\theta}} - \hat{\boldsymbol{\theta}})]'\mathbf{A}_0[\sqrt{N}(\tilde{\boldsymbol{\theta}} - \hat{\boldsymbol{\theta}})] + \mathrm{o}_p(1), \tag{12.76}$$

since $N^{-1}\sum_{i=1}^{N} \ddot{\mathbf{H}}_i = \mathbf{A}_o + o_p\ (1)$ and $\sqrt{N}(\tilde{\boldsymbol{\theta}} - \hat{\boldsymbol{\theta}}) = \mathrm{O}_p(1)$. In fact, it follows from equations (12.33) (without $\hat{\gamma}$) and (12.66) that $\sqrt{N}(\tilde{\boldsymbol{\theta}} - \hat{\boldsymbol{\theta}}) = \mathbf{A}_o^{-1} N^{-1/2} \sum_{i=1}^{N} \mathbf{s}_i(\tilde{\boldsymbol{\theta}}) + \mathrm{o}_p(1)$. Plugging this equation into equation (12.76) shows that

$$\begin{aligned} QLR &\equiv 2\left[\sum_{i=1}^{N} q(\mathbf{w}_i, \tilde{\boldsymbol{\theta}}) - \sum_{i=1}^{N} q(\mathbf{w}_i, \hat{\boldsymbol{\theta}})\right] \\ &= \left(N^{-1/2}\sum_{i=1}^{N} \tilde{\mathbf{s}}_i\right)' \mathbf{A}_o^{-1}\left(N^{-1/2}\sum_{i=1}^{N} \tilde{\mathbf{s}}_i\right) + \mathrm{o}_p(1), \end{aligned} \tag{12.77}$$

so that QLR has the same limiting distribution, χ_Q^2, as the LM statistic under H_0. (See equation (12.69), remembering that $\mathrm{plim}(\tilde{\mathbf{M}}/N) = \mathbf{A}_0$.) We call statistic (12.77) the **quasi-likelihood ratio (QLR) statistic**, which comes from the fact that the leading example of equation (12.77) is the likelihood ratio statistic in the context of maximum likelihood estimation, as we will see in Chapter 13. We could also call equation (12.77) a **criterion function statistic**, as it is based on the difference in the criterion or objective function with and without the restrictions imposed.

When nuisance parameters are present, the same estimate, say $\hat{\gamma}$, should be used in obtaining the restricted and unrestricted estimates. This is to ensure that QLR is nonnegative given any sample. Typically, $\hat{\gamma}$ would be based on initial estimation of the unrestricted model.

If $\sigma_o^2 \neq 1$, we simply divide QLR by $\hat{\sigma}^2$, which is a consistent estimator of σ_o^2 obtained from the unrestricted estimation. For example, consider NLS under Assumptions NLS.1–NLS.3. When equation (12.77) is divided by $\hat{\sigma}^2$ in equation (12.57), we obtain $(\mathrm{SSR}_r - \mathrm{SSR}_{ur})/[\mathrm{SSR}_{ur}/(N-P)]$, where SSR_r and SSR_{ur} are the restricted and unrestricted sums of squared residuals. Sometimes an F version of this statistic is used instead, which is obtained by dividing the chi-square version by Q:

$$F = \frac{(\text{SSR}_r - \text{SSR}_{ur})}{\text{SSR}_{ur}} \cdot \frac{(N - P)}{Q}. \tag{12.78}$$

This has exactly the same form as the F statistic from classical linear regression analysis. Under the null hypothesis and homoskedasticity, F can be treated as having an approximate $\mathscr{F}_{Q,N-P}$ distribution. (As always, this association is justified because $Q \cdot \mathscr{F}_{Q,N-P} \overset{a}{\sim} \chi^2_Q$ as $N - P \to \infty$.) Some authors (for example, Gallant, 1987) have found that F has better finite-sample properties than the chi-square version of the statistic.

For weighted NLS, the same statistic works under Assumption WNLS.3 provided the residuals (both restricted and unrestricted) are weighted by $1/\sqrt{\hat{h}_i}$, where the $\hat{h}_i$ are obtained from estimation of the unrestricted model.

12.6.4 Behavior of the Statistics under Alternatives

To keep the notation and assumptions as simple as possible, and to focus on the computation of valid test statistics under various assumptions, we have only derived the limiting distribution of the classical test statistics under the null hypothesis. It is also important to know how the tests behave under alternative hypotheses in order to choose a test with the highest power.

All the tests we have discussed are consistent against the alternatives they are specifically designed against. While test consistency is desirable, it tells us nothing about the likely finite-sample power that a statistic will have against particular alternatives. A framework that allows us to say more uses the notion of a sequence of **local alternatives**. Specifying a local alternative is a device that can approximate the finite-sample power of test statistics for alternatives "close" to H_0. If the null hypothesis is $\text{H}_0 : \mathbf{c}(\boldsymbol{\theta}_o) = \mathbf{0}$, then a sequence of local alternatives is

$$\text{H}_1^N : \mathbf{c}(\boldsymbol{\theta}_{o,N}) = \boldsymbol{\delta}_o/\sqrt{N}, \tag{12.79}$$

where $\boldsymbol{\delta}_o$ is a given $Q \times 1$ vector. As $N \to \infty$, H_1^N approaches H_0, since $\boldsymbol{\delta}_o/\sqrt{N} \to \mathbf{0}$. The division by $\sqrt{N}$ means that the alternatives are local: for given N, equation (12.79) is an alternative to H_0, but as $N \to \infty$, the alternative gets closer to H_0. Dividing $\boldsymbol{\delta}_o$ by $\sqrt{N}$ ensures that each of the statistics has a well-defined limiting distribution under the alternative that differs from the limiting distribution under H_0.

It can be shown that, under equation (12.79), the general forms of the Wald and LM statistics have a limiting *noncentral* chi-square distribution with Q degrees of freedom under the regularity conditions used to obtain their null limiting distributions. The noncentrality parameter depends on $\mathbf{A}_o$, $\mathbf{B}_o$, $\mathbf{C}_o$, and $\boldsymbol{\delta}_o$, and can be estimated by using consistent estimators of $\mathbf{A}_o$, $\mathbf{B}_o$, and $\mathbf{C}_o$. When we add assumption (12.53), then the special versions of the Wald and LM statistics and the QLR statistics have limiting noncentral chi-square distributions. For various $\boldsymbol{\delta}_o$, we can estimate what is known as the **asymptotic local power** of the test statistics by computing probabilities from noncentral chi-square distributions.

Consider the Wald statistic where $\mathbf{B}_o = \mathbf{A}_o$. Denote by $\boldsymbol{\theta}_o$ the limit of $\boldsymbol{\theta}_{o,N}$ as $N \to \infty$. The usual mean value expansion under H_1^N gives

$$\sqrt{N}\mathbf{c}(\hat{\boldsymbol{\theta}}) = \boldsymbol{\delta}_o + \mathbf{C}(\boldsymbol{\theta}_o)\sqrt{N}(\hat{\boldsymbol{\theta}} - \boldsymbol{\theta}_{o,N}) + o_p(1)$$

and, under standard assumptions, $\sqrt{N}(\hat{\boldsymbol{\theta}} - \boldsymbol{\theta}_{o,N}) \overset{a}{\sim} \text{Normal}(\mathbf{0}, \mathbf{A}_o^{-1})$. Therefore, $\sqrt{N}\mathbf{c}(\hat{\boldsymbol{\theta}}) \overset{a}{\sim} \text{Normal}(\boldsymbol{\delta}_o, \mathbf{C}_o\mathbf{A}_o^{-1}\mathbf{C}_o')$ under the sequence (12.79). This result implies that the Wald statistic has a limiting noncentral chi-square distribution with Q degrees of freedom and noncentrality parameter $\boldsymbol{\delta}_o'(\mathbf{C}_o\mathbf{A}_o^{-1}\mathbf{C}_o')^{-1}\boldsymbol{\delta}_o$. This turns out to be the same noncentrality parameter for the LM and QLR statistics when $\mathbf{B}_o = \mathbf{A}_o$. The details are similar to those under H_0; see, for example, Gallant (1987, Sect. 3.6).

The statistic with the largest noncentrality parameter has the largest asymptotic local power. For choosing among the Wald, LM, and QLR statistics, this criterion does not help: they all have the same noncentrality parameters under the local alternatives (12.79) and assumption (12.53). Without assumption (12.53), the robust Wald and LM statistics have the same noncentrality parameter.

The notion of local alternatives is useful when choosing among statistics based on different *estimators*. Not surprisingly, the more efficient estimator produces tests with the best asymptotic local power under standard assumptions. But we should keep in mind the efficiency versus robustness trade-off, especially when efficient test statistics are computed under tenuous assumptions.

General analyses under local alternatives are available in Gallant (1987), Gallant and White (1988), and White (1994). See Andrews (1989) for innovative suggestions for using local power analysis in applied work.

12.7 Optimization Methods

In this section we briefly discuss three iterative schemes that can be used to solve the general minimization problem (12.8) or (12.31). In the latter case, the minimization is only over $\boldsymbol{\theta}$, so the presence of $\hat{\boldsymbol{\gamma}}$ changes nothing. If $\hat{\boldsymbol{\gamma}}$ is present, the score and

Hessian with respect to $\boldsymbol{\theta}$ are simply evaluated at $\hat{\gamma}$. These methods are closely related to the asymptotic variance matrix estimators and test statistics we discussed in Sections 12.5 and 12.6.

12.7.1 Newton-Raphson Method

Iterative methods are defined by an algorithm for going from one iteration to the next. Let $\boldsymbol{\theta}^{\{g\}}$ be the $P \times 1$ vector on the gth iteration, and let $\boldsymbol{\theta}^{\{g+1\}}$ be the value on the next iteration. To motivate how we get from $\boldsymbol{\theta}^{\{g\}}$ to $\boldsymbol{\theta}^{\{g+1\}}$, use a mean value expansion (row by row) to write

$$\sum_{i=1}^{N} \mathbf{s}_i(\boldsymbol{\theta}^{\{g+1\}}) = \sum_{i=1}^{N} \mathbf{s}_i(\boldsymbol{\theta}^{\{g\}}) + \left[\sum_{i=1}^{N} \mathbf{H}_i(\boldsymbol{\theta}^{\{g\}})\right](\boldsymbol{\theta}^{\{g+1\}} - \boldsymbol{\theta}^{\{g\}}) + \mathbf{r}^{\{g\}}, \tag{12.80}$$

where $\mathbf{s}_i(\boldsymbol{\theta})$ is the $P \times 1$ score with respect to $\boldsymbol{\theta}$, evaluated at observation i, $\mathbf{H}_i(\boldsymbol{\theta})$ is the $P \times P$ Hessian, and $\mathbf{r}^{\{g\}}$ is a $P \times 1$ vector of remainder terms. We are trying to find the solution $\hat{\boldsymbol{\theta}}$ to equation (12.14). *If* $\boldsymbol{\theta}^{\{g+1\}} = \hat{\boldsymbol{\theta}}$, then the left-hand side of equation (12.80) is zero. Setting the left-hand side to zero, ignoring $\mathbf{r}^{\{g\}}$, and assuming that the Hessian evaluated at $\boldsymbol{\theta}^{\{g\}}$ is nonsingular, we can write

$$\boldsymbol{\theta}^{\{g+1\}} = \boldsymbol{\theta}^{\{g\}} - \left[\sum_{i=1}^{N} \mathbf{H}_i(\boldsymbol{\theta}^{\{g\}})\right]^{-1} \left[\sum_{i=1}^{N} \mathbf{s}_i(\boldsymbol{\theta}^{\{g\}})\right]. \tag{12.81}$$

Equation (12.81) provides an iterative method for finding $\hat{\boldsymbol{\theta}}$. To begin the iterations we must choose a vector of starting values; call this vector $\boldsymbol{\theta}^{\{0\}}$. Good starting values are often difficult to come by, and sometimes we must experiment with several choices before the problem converges. Ideally, the iterations wind up at the same place regardless of the starting values, but this outcome is not guaranteed. Given the starting values, we plug $\boldsymbol{\theta}^{\{0\}}$ into the right-hand side of equation (12.81) to get $\boldsymbol{\theta}^{\{1\}}$. Then, we plug $\boldsymbol{\theta}^{\{1\}}$ into equation (12.81) to get $\boldsymbol{\theta}^{\{2\}}$, and so on.

If the iterations are proceeding toward the minimum, the increments $\boldsymbol{\theta}^{\{g+1\}} - \boldsymbol{\theta}^{\{g\}}$ will eventually become very small: as we near the solution, $\sum_{i=1}^{N} \mathbf{s}_i(\boldsymbol{\theta}^{\{g\}})$ gets close to zero. Some use as a stopping rule the requirement that the largest absolute change $|\theta_j^{\{g+1\}} - \theta_j^{\{g\}}|$, for $j = 1, 2, \ldots, P$, be smaller than some small constant; others prefer to look at the largest *percentage* change in the parameter values.

Another popular stopping rule is based on the quadratic form

$$\left[\sum_{i=1}^{N} \mathbf{s}_i(\boldsymbol{\theta}^{\{g\}})\right]' \left[\sum_{i=1}^{N} \mathbf{H}_i(\boldsymbol{\theta}^{\{g\}})\right]^{-1} \left[\sum_{i=1}^{N} \mathbf{s}_i(\boldsymbol{\theta}^{\{g\}})\right], \tag{12.82}$$

where the iterations stop when expression (12.82) is less than some suitably small number, say .0001.

The iterative scheme just outlined is usually called the **Newton-Raphson method**. It is known to work in a variety of circumstances. Our motivation here has been heuristic, and we will not investigate situations under which the Newton-Raphson method does not work well. (See, for example, Quandt, 1983, for some theoretical results.) The Newton-Raphson method has some drawbacks. First, it requires computing the second derivatives of the objective function at every iteration. These calculations are not very taxing if closed forms for the second partials are available, but in many cases they are not. A second problem is that, as we saw for the case of nonlinear least squares, the Hessian evaluated at a particular value of $\boldsymbol{\theta}$ may not be positive definite. If the inverted Hessian in expression (12.81) is not positive definite, the procedure may head in the wrong direction.

We should always check that progress is being made from one iteration to the next by computing the difference in the values of the objective function from one iteration to the next:

$$\sum_{i=1}^{N} q_i(\boldsymbol{\theta}^{\{g+1\}}) - \sum_{i=1}^{N} q_i(\boldsymbol{\theta}^{\{g\}}). \tag{12.83}$$

Because we are minimizing the objective function, we should not take the step from g to $g+1$ unless expression (12.83) is negative. (If we are maximizing the function, the iterations in equation (12.81) can still be used because the expansion in equation (12.80) is still appropriate, but then we want expression (12.83) to be positive.)

A slight modification of the Newton-Raphson method is sometimes useful to speed up convergence: multiply the Hessian term in expression (12.81) by a positive number, say r, known as the *step size*. Sometimes the step size $r = 1$ produces too large a change in the parameters. If the objective function does not decrease using $r = 1$, then try, say, $r = \frac{1}{2}$. Again, check the value of the objective function. If it has now decreased, go on to the next iteration (where $r = 1$ is usually used at the beginning of each iteration); if the objective function still has not decreased, replace r with, say, $\frac{1}{4}$. Continue halving r until the objective function decreases. If you have not succeeded in decreasing the objective function after several choices of r, new starting values might be needed. Or, a different optimization method might be needed.

12.7.2 Berndt, Hall, Hall, and Hausman Algorithm

In the context of maximum likelihood estimation, Berndt, Hall, Hall, and Hausman (1974) (hereafter, BHHH) proposed using the outer product of the score in place of the Hessian. This method can be applied in the general M-estimation case (even though the information matrix equality (12.53) that motivates the method need not hold). The BHHH iteration for a minimization problem is

$$\boldsymbol{\theta}^{\{g+1\}} = \boldsymbol{\theta}^{\{g\}} - r\left[\sum_{i=1}^{N} \mathbf{s}_i(\boldsymbol{\theta}^{\{g\}})\mathbf{s}_i(\boldsymbol{\theta}^{\{g\}})'\right]^{-1}\left[\sum_{i=1}^{N} \mathbf{s}_i(\boldsymbol{\theta}^{\{g\}})\right], \tag{12.84}$$

where r is the step size. (If we want to maximize $\sum_{i=1}^{N} q(\mathbf{w}_i, \boldsymbol{\theta})$, the minus sign in equation (12.84) should be replaced with a plus sign.) The term multiplying r, sometimes called the *direction* for the next iteration, can be obtained as the $P \times 1$ OLS coefficients from the regression

$$1 \text{ on } \mathbf{s}_i(\boldsymbol{\theta}^{\{g\}})', \qquad i = 1, 2, \ldots, N. \tag{12.85}$$

The BHHH procedure is easy to implement because it requires computation of the score only; second derivatives are not needed. Further, because the sum of the outer product of the scores is always at least p.s.d., it does not suffer from the potential nonpositive definiteness of the Hessian.

A convenient stopping rule for the BHHH method is obtained as in expression (12.82), but with the sum of the outer products of the score replacing the sum of the Hessians. This is identical to N times the uncentered R-squared from regression (12.85). Interestingly, this is the same regression used to obtain the outer product of the score form of the LM statistic when $\mathbf{B}_o = \mathbf{A}_o$, a feature that suggests a natural method for estimating a complicated model after a simpler version of the model has been estimated. Set the starting value, $\boldsymbol{\theta}^{\{0\}}$, equal to the vector of restricted estimates, $\tilde{\boldsymbol{\theta}}$. Then NR_0^2 from the regression used to obtain the first iteration can be used to test the restricted model against the more general model to be estimated; if the restrictions are not rejected, we could just stop the iterations. Of course, as we discussed in Section 12.6.2, the outer-product form of the LM statistic is often ill-behaved even with fairly large sample sizes.

12.7.3 Generalized Gauss-Newton Method

The final iteration scheme we cover is closely related to the estimator of the expected value of the Hessian in expression (12.44). Let $\mathbf{A}(\mathbf{x}, \boldsymbol{\theta}_o)$ be the expected value of $\mathbf{H}(\mathbf{w}, \boldsymbol{\theta}_o)$ conditional on $\mathbf{x}$, where $\mathbf{w}$ is partitioned into $\mathbf{y}$ and $\mathbf{x}$. Then the **generalized Gauss-Newton method** uses the updating equation

$$\boldsymbol{\theta}^{\{g+1\}} = \boldsymbol{\theta}^{\{g\}} - r\left[\sum_{i=1}^{N} \mathbf{A}_i(\boldsymbol{\theta}^{\{g\}})\right]^{-1}\left[\sum_{i=1}^{N} \mathbf{s}_i(\boldsymbol{\theta}^{\{g\}})\right], \tag{12.86}$$

where $\boldsymbol{\theta}^{\{g\}}$ replaces $\boldsymbol{\theta}_o$ in $\mathbf{A}(\mathbf{x}_i, \boldsymbol{\theta}_o)$. (As before, $\mathbf{A}_i$ and $\mathbf{s}_i$ might also depend on $\hat{\gamma}$.) This scheme works well when $\mathbf{A}(\mathbf{x}, \boldsymbol{\theta}_o)$ can be obtained in closed form.

In the special case of nonlinear least squares, we obtain what is traditionally called the **Gauss-Newton method** (for example, Quandt, 1983). Because $\mathbf{s}_i(\boldsymbol{\theta}) = -\nabla_\theta m_i(\boldsymbol{\theta})'[y_i - m_i(\boldsymbol{\theta})]$, the iteration step is

$$\boldsymbol{\theta}^{\{g+1\}} = \boldsymbol{\theta}^{\{g\}} + r\left(\sum_{i=1}^N \nabla_\theta m_i^{\{g\}\prime} \nabla_\theta m_i^{\{g\}}\right)^{-1} \left(\sum_{i=1}^N \nabla_\theta m_i^{\{g\}\prime} u_i^{\{g\}}\right).$$

The term multiplying the step size r is obtained as the OLS coefficients of the regression of the residuals on the gradient, both evaluated at $\boldsymbol{\theta}^{\{g\}}$. The stopping rule can be based on N times the uncentered R-squared from this regression. Note how closely the Gauss-Newton method of optimization is related to the regression used to obtain the nonrobust LM statistic (see regression (12.72)).

12.7.4 Concentrating Parameters out of the Objective Function

In some cases, it is computationally convenient to *concentrate* one set of parameters out of the objective function. Partition $\boldsymbol{\theta}$ into the vectors $\boldsymbol{\beta}$ and $\boldsymbol{\gamma}$. Then the first-order conditions that define $\hat{\boldsymbol{\theta}}$ are

$$\sum_{i=1}^N \nabla_\beta q(\mathbf{w}_i, \boldsymbol{\beta}, \boldsymbol{\gamma}) = \mathbf{0}, \qquad \sum_{i=1}^N \nabla_\gamma q(\mathbf{w}_i, \boldsymbol{\beta}, \boldsymbol{\gamma}) = \mathbf{0}. \tag{12.87}$$

Rather than solving these for $\hat{\boldsymbol{\beta}}$ and $\hat{\boldsymbol{\gamma}}$, suppose that the second set of equations can be solved for $\boldsymbol{\gamma}$ as a function of $\mathbf{W} \equiv (\mathbf{w}_1, \mathbf{w}_2, \ldots, \mathbf{w}_N)$ and $\boldsymbol{\beta}$ for any outcomes $\mathbf{W}$ and any $\boldsymbol{\beta}$ in the parameter space: $\boldsymbol{\gamma} = \mathbf{g}(\mathbf{W}, \boldsymbol{\beta})$. Then, by construction,

$$\sum_{i=1}^N \nabla_\gamma q[\mathbf{w}_i, \boldsymbol{\beta}, \mathbf{g}(\mathbf{W}, \boldsymbol{\beta})] = \mathbf{0}. \tag{12.88}$$

When we plug $\mathbf{g}(\mathbf{W}, \boldsymbol{\beta})$ into the original objective function, we obtain the **concentrated objective function**,

$$Q^c(\mathbf{W}, \boldsymbol{\beta}) = \sum_{i=1}^N q[\mathbf{w}_i, \boldsymbol{\beta}, \mathbf{g}(\mathbf{W}, \boldsymbol{\beta})]. \tag{12.89}$$

Under standard differentiability assumptions, the minimizer of equation (12.89) is identical to the $\hat{\boldsymbol{\beta}}$ that solves equations (12.87) (along with $\hat{\boldsymbol{\gamma}}$), as can be seen by differentiating equation (12.89) with respect to $\boldsymbol{\beta}$ using the chain rule, setting the result to zero, and using equation (12.88); then $\hat{\boldsymbol{\gamma}}$ can be obtained as $\mathbf{g}(\mathbf{W}, \hat{\boldsymbol{\beta}})$.

As a device for studying asymptotic properties, the concentrated objective function is of limited value because $\mathbf{g}(\mathbf{W}, \boldsymbol{\beta})$ generally depends on all of $\mathbf{W}$, in which case the objective function cannot be written as the sum of independent, identically distributed summands. One setting where equation (12.89) is a sum of i.i.d. functions occurs when we concentrate out individual-specific effects from certain nonlinear panel data models. In addition, the concentrated objective function can be useful for establishing the equivalence of seemingly different estimation approaches.

12.8 Simulation and Resampling Methods

So far we have focused on the asymptotic properties of M-estimators, as these provide a unified framework for inference. But there are a few good reasons to go beyond asymptotic results, at least in some cases. First, the asymptotic approximations need not be very good, especially with small sample sizes, highly nonlinear models, or unusual features of the population distribution of $\mathbf{w}_i$. Simulation methods, while always special, can help determine how well the asymptotic approximations work. Resampling methods can allow us to improve on the asymptotic distribution approximations.

Even if we feel comfortable with asymptotic approximations to the distribution of $\hat{\boldsymbol{\theta}}$, we may not be as confident in the approximations for estimating a nonlinear function of the parameters, say $\gamma_o = \mathbf{g}(\boldsymbol{\theta}_o)$. Under the assumptions in Section 3.5.2, we can use the delta method to approximate the variance of $\hat{\gamma} = \mathbf{g}(\hat{\boldsymbol{\theta}})$. Depending on the nature of $\mathbf{g}(\cdot)$, applying the delta method might be difficult, and it might not result in a very good approximation. Resampling methods can simplify the calculation of standard errors, confidence intervals, and p-values for test statistics, and we can get a good idea of the amount of finite-sample bias in the estimation method. In addition, under certain assumptions and for certain statistics, resampling methods can provide quantifiable improvements to the usual asymptotics.

12.8.1 Monte Carlo Simulation

In a **Monte Carlo simulation**, we attempt to estimate the mean and variance—assuming that these exist—and possibly other features of the distribution of the M-estimator, $\hat{\boldsymbol{\theta}}$. The idea is usually to determine how much bias $\hat{\boldsymbol{\theta}}$ has for estimating $\boldsymbol{\theta}_o$, or to determine the efficiency of $\hat{\boldsymbol{\theta}}$ compared with other estimators of $\boldsymbol{\theta}_o$. In addition, we often want to know how well the asymptotic standard errors approximate the standard deviations of the $\hat{\theta}_j$.

To conduct a simulation, we must choose a population distribution for $\mathbf{w}$, which depends on the finite-dimensional vector $\boldsymbol{\theta}_o$. We must set the values of $\boldsymbol{\theta}_o$, and decide on a sample size, N. We then draw a random sample of size N from this distribution and use the sample to obtain an estimate of $\boldsymbol{\theta}_{\mathrm{o}}$. We draw a new random sample and compute another estimate of $\boldsymbol{\theta}_{\mathrm{o}}$. We repeat the process for several iterations, say M. Let $\hat{\boldsymbol{\theta}}^{(m)}$ be the estimate of $\boldsymbol{\theta}_{\mathrm{o}}$ based on the mth iteration. Given $\{\hat{\boldsymbol{\theta}}^{(m)} : m = 1, 2, \ldots, M\}$, we can compute the sample average and sample variance to estimate $\mathrm{E}(\hat{\boldsymbol{\theta}})$ and $\mathrm{Var}(\hat{\boldsymbol{\theta}})$, respectively. We might also form t statistics or other test statistics to see how well the asymptotic distributions approximate the finite-sample distributions. We can also see how well asymptotic confidence intervals cover the population parameter relative to the nominal confidence level.

A good Monte Carlo study varies the value of $\boldsymbol{\theta}_{\mathrm{o}}$, the sample size, and even the general form of the distribution of $\mathbf{w}$. In fact, it is generally a good idea to check how an estimation method fares when the assumptions on which it is based partially or completely fail. Obtaining a thorough study can be very challenging, especially for a complicated, nonlinear model. First, to get good estimates of the distribution of $\hat{\boldsymbol{\theta}}$, we would like M to be large (perhaps several thousand). But for each Monte Carlo iteration, we must obtain $\hat{\boldsymbol{\theta}}^{(m)}$, and this step can be computationally expensive because it often requires the iterative methods we discussed in Section 12.7. Repeating the simulations for many different sample sizes N, values of $\boldsymbol{\theta}_{\mathrm{o}}$, and distributional shapes can be very time-consuming.

In most economic applications, $\mathbf{w}_i$ is partitioned as $(\mathbf{x}_i, \mathbf{y}_i)$. While we can draw the full vector $\mathbf{w}_i$ randomly in the Monte Carlo iterations, sometimes the $\mathbf{x}_i$ are fixed at the beginning of the iterations, and then $\mathbf{y}_i$ is drawn from the conditional distribution given $\mathbf{x}_i$. This method simplifies the simulations because we do not need to vary the distribution of $\mathbf{x}_i$ along with the distribution of interest, the distribution of $\mathbf{y}_i$ given $\mathbf{x}_i$. If we fix the $\mathbf{x}_i$ at the beginning of the simulations, the distributional features of $\hat{\boldsymbol{\theta}}$ that we estimate from the Monte Carlo simulations are conditional on $\{\mathbf{x}_1, \mathbf{x}_2, \ldots, \mathbf{x}_N\}$. This conditional approach is especially common in linear and nonlinear regression contexts, as well as conditional maximum likelihood.

It is important not to rely too much on Monte Carlo simulations. Many estimation methods, including OLS, IV, and panel data estimators, have asymptotic properties that do not depend on underlying distributions. In the nonlinear regression model, the NLS estimator is $\sqrt{N}$-asymptotically normal, and the usual asymptotic variance matrix (12.58) is valid under Assumptions NLS.1–NLS.3. However, in a typical Monte Carlo simulation, the implied error, u, is assumed to be independent of $\mathbf{x}$, and the distribution of u must be specified. The Monte Carlo results then pertain to this distribution, and it can be misleading to extrapolate to different settings. In addition, we can never try more than just a small part of the parameter space. Because we never know the population value $\boldsymbol{\theta}_{\mathrm{o}}$, we can never be sure how well our Monte Carlo study describes the underlying population. Hendry (1984) discusses how **response surface analysis** can be used to reduce the specificity of Monte Carlo studies. See also Davidson and MacKinnon (1993, Chap. 21).

12.8.2 Bootstrapping

A Monte Carlo simulation, although it is informative about how well the asymptotic approximations can be expected to work in specific situations, does not generally help us refine our inference given a particular sample. (Because we do not know $\boldsymbol{\theta}_o$, we cannot know whether our Monte Carlo findings apply to the population we are studying. Nevertheless, researchers sometimes use the results of a Monte Carlo simulation to obtain rules of thumb for adjusting standard errors or for adjusting critical values for test statistics.) The method of **bootstrapping**, which is a popular **resampling method**, can be used as an alternative to asymptotic approximations for obtaining standard errors, confidence intervals, and p-values for test statistics.

Though there are several variants of the bootstrap, we begin with one that can be applied to general M-estimation. The goal is to approximate the distribution of $\hat{\boldsymbol{\theta}}$ without relying on the usual first-order asymptotic theory. Let $\{\mathbf{w}_1, \mathbf{w}_2, \ldots, \mathbf{w}_N\}$ denote the outcome of the random sample used to obtain the estimate. The **nonparametric bootstrap** is essentially a Monte Carlo simulation where the observed sample is treated as the population. In other words, at each bootstrap iteration, b, a random sample of size N is drawn from $\{\mathbf{w}_1, \mathbf{w}_2, \ldots, \mathbf{w}_N\}$. (That is, we sample *with replacement*.) In practice, we use a random number generator to obtain N integers from the set $\{1, 2, \ldots, N\}$; in the vast majority of iterations some integers will be repeated at least once. These integers index the elements that we draw from $\{\mathbf{w}_1, \mathbf{w}_2, \ldots, \mathbf{w}_N\}$; call these $\{\mathbf{w}_1^{(b)}, \mathbf{w}_2^{(b)}, \ldots, \mathbf{w}_N^{(b)}\}$. Next, we use this bootstrap sample to obtain the M-estimate $\hat{\boldsymbol{\theta}}^{(b)}$ by solving

$$\min_{\boldsymbol{\theta} \in \boldsymbol{\Theta}} \sum_{i=1}^{N} q(\mathbf{w}_i^{(b)}, \boldsymbol{\theta}).$$

We iterate the process B times, obtaining $\hat{\boldsymbol{\theta}}^{(b)}$, $b = 1, \ldots, B$. These estimates can now be used as in a Monte Carlo simulation. Computing the average of the $\hat{\boldsymbol{\theta}}^{(b)}$, say $\bar{\hat{\boldsymbol{\theta}}}$, allows us to estimate the bias in $\hat{\boldsymbol{\theta}}$, called the **bootstrap bias estimate**. The sample variance, $(B-1)^{-1} \sum_{b=1}^{B} [\hat{\boldsymbol{\theta}}^{(b)} - \bar{\hat{\boldsymbol{\theta}}}] \cdot [\hat{\boldsymbol{\theta}}^{(b)} - \bar{\hat{\boldsymbol{\theta}}}]'$, called the **bootstrap variance estimate**, can be used to obtain standard errors for the $\hat{\theta}_j$—the estimates from the original sample. For a scalar estimate $\hat{\gamma}$, we obtain its **bootstrap standard error** as $\text{se}_B(\hat{\gamma}) = [(B-1)^{-1} \sum_{b=1}^{B} (\hat{\gamma}^{(b)} - \bar{\hat{\gamma}})]^{1/2}$. Naturally, we can apply this formula to smooth functions of the original parameter estimates $\hat{\boldsymbol{\theta}}$, say $\hat{\gamma} = g(\hat{\boldsymbol{\theta}})$ for a continuously differentiable function $g : \mathbb{R}^P \to \mathbb{R}$. We can then use $\text{se}_B(\hat{\gamma})$ to construct asymptotic hypotheses tests and confidence intervals for γ_o.

Especially for computing average partial effects—a topic that will arise repeatedly in Part IV—we often need to estimate a parameter that can be written as $\gamma_o = \text{E}[g(\mathbf{w}_i, \boldsymbol{\theta}_o)]$. A natural, consistent estimator is $\hat{\gamma} = N^{-1}\sum_{i=1}^N g(\mathbf{w}_i, \hat{\boldsymbol{\theta}})$. To estimate its asymptotic variance, we must account for the randomness in $\mathbf{w}_i$ as well as $\hat{\boldsymbol{\theta}}$. As before, we draw bootstrap samples, and, for bootstrap sample b, the estimate of γ_o is

$$\hat{\gamma}^{(b)} = N^{-1}\sum_{i=1}^N g(\mathbf{w}_i^{(b)}, \hat{\boldsymbol{\theta}}^{(b)}).$$

Once we have the collection of bootstrap estimates $\{\hat{\gamma}^{(b)} : b = 1, 2, \ldots, B\}$, we can compute the bootstrap bias and, more important, the bootstrap standard error using the previous formulas.

Using the bootstrap standard error to construct statistics and confidence intervals is often much easier than the analytical calculations needed to obtain an asymptotic standard error based on first-order asymptotics. But using the bootstrap standard error to construct test statistics cannot be shown to improve on the approximation provided by the usual asymptotic theory. As it turns out, in many cases the bootstrap *does* improve the approximation of the distribution of test statistics. In other words, the bootstrap can provide an **asymptotic refinement** compared with the usual asymptotic theory, but one must use some care in computing the bootstrap test statistics.

To show that the bootstrap approximation of a distribution converges more quickly than the usual rates associated with first-order asymptotics, the notion of an **asymptotically pivotal statistic** is critical. An asymptotically pivotal statistic is one whose limiting distribution does not depend on unknown parameters. Asymptotic t statistics, Wald statistics, score statistics, and quasi-LR statistics are all asymptotically pivotal when they converge to the standard normal distribution, in the case of a t statistic, and to the chi-square distribution, in the case of the other statistics. One must sometimes use care, though, to ensure a statistic is asymptotically pivotal. For example, for a t statistic to be asymptotically pivotal in the context of nonlinear regression with heteroskedasticity, we must use a heteroskedasticity-robust statistic. The Wald and score statistics must often use robust asymptotic variance estimators to deliver an asymptotic chi-square distribution. The quasi-LR statistic is guaranteed to be asymptotically pivotal only when the generalized information matrix equality holds.

To explain how to bootstrap the critical values for a t statistic, consider testing $\text{H}_0 : \theta_o = c$ for some known value c. The t statistic, $t = (\hat{\theta} - c)/\text{se}(\hat{\theta})$, is asymptotically pivotal if $\text{se}(\hat{\theta})$ is appropriately chosen. To obtain a refinement using the bootstrap, we must obtain the empirical distribution of the statistic

$$t^{(b)} = (\hat{\theta}^{(b)} - \hat{\theta})/\text{se}(\hat{\theta}^{(b)}),$$

where $\hat{\theta}$ is the estimate from the original sample, $\hat{\theta}^{(b)}$ is the estimate for bootstrap sample b, and $\text{se}(\hat{\theta}^{(b)})$ is the standard error estimated from the same bootstrap sample. (So, for example, $\text{se}(\hat{\theta}^{(b)})$ could be a heteroskedasticity-robust standard error for NLS.) Notice how the t statistic for each bootstrap replication is centered at the original estimate, $\hat{\theta}$, not the hypothesized value. As discussed by Horowitz (2001), centering at the estimate is required to ensure asymptotic refinements of the testing procedure.

The way we obtain **bootstrap critical values** for a test depends on the nature of the alternative. For a one-sided alternative, say $\text{H}_0 : \theta_o > c$, we order the statistics $\{t^{(b)} : b = 1, 2, \ldots, B\}$, from smallest to largest, and we pick the value representing the desired quantile of the list of ordered values. For example, to obtain a 5 percent test against a greater than one-sided alternative, we choose the critical value as the 95th percentile in the ordered list of $t^{(b)}$. For a two-sided alternative, we must choose between a **nonsymmetric test** and a **symmetric test**. For the former, a test with size α chooses critical values as the lower and upper $\alpha/2$ quantiles of the ordered bootstrap test statistics, and we reject H_0 if $t > cv_u$ or $t < cv_l$. For the latter, we first order the absolute values of the statistics, $|t^{(b)}|$, and then choose the upper α quantile as the critical value for a test of size α. Naturally, we compare $|t|$ with the critical value. This approach to choosing critical values from bootstrapping is called the **percentile-*t* method**.

We can use the percentile-t method to compute a **bootstrap *p*-value**. For example, against a greater than one-sided alternative, we simply find the fraction of bootstrap t statistics $t^{(b)}$ that exceed t. A symmetric p-value for a two-sided alternative does the same for $|t^{(b)}|$ and $|t|$.

Testing multiple hypotheses is similar. Suppose that for a Q-vector $\boldsymbol{\phi}_o$, we want to test $\text{H}_o : \boldsymbol{\phi}_o = \mathbf{r}$, where $\mathbf{r}$ is a vector of known constants. The Wald statistic computed using the original sample is $W = (\hat{\boldsymbol{\phi}} - \mathbf{r})'\hat{\mathbf{V}}^{-1}(\hat{\boldsymbol{\phi}} - \mathbf{r})$. We compute a series of Wald statistics from bootstrap samples as

$$W^{(b)} = (\hat{\boldsymbol{\phi}}^{(b)} - \hat{\boldsymbol{\phi}})'(\hat{\mathbf{V}}^{(b)})^{-1}(\hat{\boldsymbol{\phi}}^{(b)} - \hat{\boldsymbol{\phi}}), \qquad b = 1, \ldots, B,$$

where we must take care so that the calculation of $\hat{\mathbf{V}}$ (and $\hat{\mathbf{V}}^{(b)}$) delivers an asymptotic chi-square statistic. The bootstrap p-value is the fraction of $W^{(b)}$ that exceed W.

The **parametric bootstrap** is even more similar to a standard Monte Carlo simulation because we assume that the distribution of $\mathbf{w}$ is known up to the parameters $\boldsymbol{\theta}_o$.

Let $f(\cdot, \boldsymbol{\theta})$ denote the parametric density. Then, on each bootstrap iteration, we draw a random sample of size N from $f(\cdot, \hat{\boldsymbol{\theta}})$; this gives $\{\mathbf{w}_1^{(b)}, \mathbf{w}_2^{(b)}, \ldots, \mathbf{w}_N^{(b)}\}$, and the rest of the calculations are the same as in the nonparametric bootstrap. (With the parametric bootstrap, when $f(\cdot, \boldsymbol{\theta})$ is a continuous density, only rarely would we find repeated values among the $\mathbf{w}_i^{(b)}$.)

When $\mathbf{w}_i$ is partitioned into $(\mathbf{x}_i, \mathbf{y}_i)$, where the $\mathbf{x}_i$ are conditioning variables, other resampling schemes are sometimes preferred. In Chapter 13, we study the method of conditional maximum likelihood, where we assume that a model of a conditional density, $f(\mathbf{y} \mid \mathbf{x}; \boldsymbol{\theta})$, is correctly specified. In that case, we can apply a combination of the nonparametric and parametric bootstrap. Because the distribution of $\mathbf{x}_i$ is unspecified, we randomly draw N indexes from $\{1, 2, \ldots, N\}$ to obtain a nonparametric bootstrap sample for the conditioning variables, $\{\mathbf{x}_i^{(b)} : i = 1, \ldots, N\}$. Then, given the estimate $\hat{\boldsymbol{\theta}}$, we obtain $\mathbf{y}_i^{(b)}$ by drawing from the density $f(\cdot \mid \mathbf{x}_i^{(b)}; \hat{\boldsymbol{\theta}})$. We then use the bootstrap samples $(\mathbf{x}_i^{(b)}, \mathbf{y}_i^{(b)})$ as before. Compared with the fully nonparametric bootstrap where we resample the entire vector $\mathbf{w}_i = (\mathbf{x}_i, \mathbf{y}_i)$ from the original data, the method that draws from $f(\cdot \mid \mathbf{x}_i^{(b)}; \hat{\boldsymbol{\theta}})$ is not as widely applicable and is computationally more expensive.

In cases where we have even more structure, other alternatives are available. For example, in a nonlinear regression model with $y_i = m(\mathbf{x}_i, \boldsymbol{\theta}_o) + u_i$, where the error u_i is *independent* of $\mathbf{x}_i$, we first compute the NLS estimate $\hat{\boldsymbol{\theta}}$ and the NLS residuals, $\hat{u}_i = y_i - m(\mathbf{x}_i, \hat{\boldsymbol{\theta}})$, $i = 1, 2, \ldots, N$. Then, using the procedure described for the nonparametric bootstrap, a bootstrap sample of residuals, $\{\hat{u}_i^{(b)} : i = 1, 2, \ldots, N\}$, is obtained, and we compute $y_i^{(b)} = m(\mathbf{x}_i, \hat{\boldsymbol{\theta}}) + \hat{u}_i^{(b)}$. Using the generated data $\{(\mathbf{x}_i, y_i^{(b)}) : i = 1, 2, \ldots, N\}$, we compute the NLS estimate, $\hat{\boldsymbol{\theta}}^{(b)}$. This procedure is called the **nonparametric residual bootstrap**. (We resample the residuals and use these to generate a sample on the dependent variable, but we do not resample the conditioning variables, $\mathbf{x}_i$.) If the model is nonlinear in $\boldsymbol{\theta}$, this method can be computationally demanding because we want B to be several hundred, if not several thousand. Nonetheless, such procedures are becoming more and more feasible as computational speed increases. When u_i has zero conditional mean $[\mathrm{E}(u_i \mid \mathbf{x}_i) = 0]$ but is heteroskedastic $[\mathrm{Var}(u_i \mid \mathbf{x}_i)$ depends on $\mathbf{x}_i]$, alternative sampling methods, in particular the **wild bootstrap**, can be used to obtain heteroskedastic-consistent standard errors. See, for example, Horowitz (2001).

Bootstrapping is easily applied to the kinds of panel data structures that we treat in this text because our sampling assumption for panel data is random sampling in the cross section dimension. For panel data, we simply let $\mathbf{w}_i = (\mathbf{w}_{i1}, \ldots, \mathbf{w}_{iT})$ denote the outcomes across all T time periods for cross section observation i. When we obtain a bootstrap sample, all time periods for a particular unit constitute a single observation. In other words, as with pure cross section applications, we randomly select N integers (with replacement) from $\{1, 2, \ldots, N\}$ and obtain the bootstrap sample $\mathbf{w}_i^{(b)} = (\mathbf{w}_{i1}^{(b)}, \ldots, \mathbf{w}_{iT}^{(b)})$. For emphasis: we do not resample separate time periods within a unit; we only resample units. As with the first-order asymptotic theory based on random samples, this kind of bootstrapping for panel data is realistic for large cross sections and relatively small time periods.

12.9 Multivariate Nonlinear Regression Methods

As with linear regression methods, nonlinear regression methods can be extended to systems of equations. For example, suppose that y_1 and y_2 are fractional variables—say, shares of pension investments put into stocks and bonds, respectively, with a third "other" category—and we wish to account for the bounded nature of these responses in our model. We might specify logistic regression functions of the form

$$\mathrm{E}(y_g \mid \mathbf{x}) = \exp(\mathbf{x}\boldsymbol{\theta}_g)/[1 + \exp(\mathbf{x}\boldsymbol{\theta}_g)], \qquad g = 1, 2,$$

where $\mathbf{x}$ is a row vector of common explanatory variables. We can estimate $\boldsymbol{\theta}_1$ and $\boldsymbol{\theta}_2$ individually, using NLS or WNLS, but we can also estimate them jointly. Not surprisingly, under certain assumptions, a multivariate procedure that accounts for correlation in the unobservables across equations is more efficient than single equation estimation, as we discuss in Section 12.9.2.

We can also apply nonlinear regression to panel data structures. For example, for a nonnegative response variable y_t, a dynamic model is

$$\mathrm{E}(y_t \mid \mathbf{z}_t, y_{t-1}) = \exp(\mathbf{z}_t\boldsymbol{\beta} + \alpha y_{t-1}), \qquad t = 1, \ldots, T.$$

One way to estimate the parameters is by pooled NLS. As we show in the next two subsections, we can cast both system and panel data problems in one framework.

12.9.1 Multivariate Nonlinear Least Squares

A general setup for multivariate nonlinear least squares (MNLS) is to let y_g be the response variable for equation g, which could be a time period. The corresponding explanatory variables are $\mathbf{x}_g$. We assume the model for $\mathrm{E}(y_g \mid \mathbf{x}_g)$ is correctly specified:

$$\mathrm{E}(y_g \mid \mathbf{x}_g) = m_g(\mathbf{x}_g, \boldsymbol{\theta}_{og}), \qquad g = 1, \ldots, G, \tag{12.90}$$

where the parameters in different equations can be distinct or there can be restrictions across g. Given N randomly sampled observations, it should be no surprise that the $\boldsymbol{\theta}_{og}$ can be consistently estimated by solving

$$\min_{\theta} \sum_{i=1}^{N} \sum_{g=1}^{G} [y_{ig} - m_g(\mathbf{x}_{ig}, \boldsymbol{\theta}_g)]^2,$$

or, in vector form,

$$\min_{\theta} \sum_{i=1}^{N} [\mathbf{y}_i - \mathbf{m}(\mathbf{x}_i, \boldsymbol{\theta})]'[\mathbf{y}_i - \mathbf{m}(\mathbf{x}_i, \boldsymbol{\theta})], \tag{12.91}$$

where $\boldsymbol{\theta}$ denotes the vector of all parameters, $\mathbf{y}_i$ is the $G \times 1$ vector of responses for observation i, and $\mathbf{m}(\mathbf{x}_i, \boldsymbol{\theta})$ is the $G \times 1$ vector of conditional mean functions. We call the solution to (12.91) the **multivariate nonlinear least squares estimator**. As with univariate NLS, identification requires that $\boldsymbol{\theta}_o$ is the only solution to the corresponding population problem, and we would assume mean functions twice continuously differentiable in the parameters. Generally, the assumptions are as weak as in the univariate case.

If there are G separate parameter vectors without restrictions across g, then the solutions to (12.91) are the same as NLS on each equation. Sometimes, for example with cost share equations derived from the theory of the firm, the parameters will be restricted across equations. Then the MNLS estimator can be used to estimate the parameters with the restrictions imposed.

In the panel data case, where the conditional mean model is written for a common set of parameters,

$$\mathrm{E}(y_{it} \mid \mathbf{x}_{it}) = m(\mathbf{x}_{it}, \boldsymbol{\theta}_o), \tag{12.92}$$

the MNLS estimator is the **pooled nonlinear least squares (PNLS) estimator**. Problem 12.6 asks you to study this estimator in more detail. Consistency and $\sqrt{N}$-asymptotic normality of the PNLS estimator follows under general assumptions on the smoothness of the mean function, but generally one should use a fully robust variance matrix estimator to account for possible heteroskedasticity and serial correlation. If the conditional mean model is dynamically complete (see Problem 12.6), then one need not worry about serial correlation in the errors when estimating the variance matrix of the PNLS estimator. But heteroskedasticity could still be an issue. If one adds the homoskedasticity assumption $\mathrm{Var}(y_{it} \mid \mathbf{x}_{it}) = \sigma_o^2$ to the appropriate no serial correlation assumption, the usual statistics from the pooled NLS analysis are asymptotically valid.

The PNLS estimator is attractive when one wishes only to impose (12.92), without making the stronger assumption that the covariates are strictly exogenous. Even under strict exogeneity, PNLS is usually needed as a first step in obtaining an asymptotically more efficient estimator. We study that possibility next.

12.9.2 Weighted Multivariate Nonlinear Least Squares

Under certain assumptions, we can use generalized least squares (GLS) methods to more efficiently estimate the parameters appearing in a set of conditional mean functions. Here we focus on the case where the explanatory variables are strictly exogenous. This often applies to systems of equations and sometimes applies to panel data methods. Specifically, we assume

$$\mathrm{E}(\mathbf{y}_i \mid \mathbf{x}_i) = \mathbf{m}(\mathbf{x}_i, \boldsymbol{\theta}_{\mathrm{o}}), \qquad \text{some } \boldsymbol{\theta}_{\mathrm{o}} \in \boldsymbol{\Theta} \subset \mathbb{R}^P, \tag{12.93}$$

where again, $\mathbf{y}_i$ is a $G \times 1$ vector on the dependent variable and $\mathbf{m}(\mathbf{x}_i, \boldsymbol{\theta})$ is a $G \times 1$ vector of conditional mean functions. It is important to note that the entire vector of covariates, $\mathbf{x}_i$, is conditioned on in (12.93). This is the sense in which the explanatory variables are strictly exogenous: if some elements of $\mathbf{x}_i$ are omitted from one of the functions $m_g(\mathbf{x}_i, \boldsymbol{\theta}_{\mathrm{o}})$, then they should have no partial effect on $\mathrm{E}(y_{ig} \mid \mathbf{x}_i)$. As we discussed in Chapter 7, this is often intended in seemingly unrelated regressions (SUR)-type applications; in fact, often the same set of explanatory variables appears in each equation. But assumption (12.93) is violated for panel data models with lagged dependent variables and, as we saw in Chapter 7 for linear models, perhaps in models without lagged dependent variables. Nevertheless, we have seen linear models where strict exogeneity holds after including the time average of the covariates, and we will see this again in later chapters—including Chapters 15, 16, 17, and 18 for nonlinear models.

The most general estimator we consider here is the **weighted multivariate nonlinear least squares (WMNLS) estimator**. We can easily motivate WMNLS. Let $\mathbf{W}(\mathbf{x}_i, \gamma)$ be a model for the $G \times G$ conditional variance matrix $\mathrm{Var}(\mathbf{y}_i \mid \mathbf{x}_i)$. If this model is correctly specified, then, generally, we can obtain a $\sqrt{N}$-consistent estimator of the "true" parameters in the variance matrix, γ_{o}. In fact, we would probably use the residuals from an initial MNLS estimation (more on this shortly). Given $\hat{\gamma}$, and assuming that $\mathbf{W}(\mathbf{x}_i, \hat{\gamma})$ is nonsingular for all i (often true by construction), we can estimate $\boldsymbol{\theta}_{\mathrm{o}}$ by solving

$$\min_{\boldsymbol{\theta}} \sum_{i=1}^{N} [\mathbf{y}_i - \mathbf{m}(\mathbf{x}_i, \boldsymbol{\theta})]' [\mathbf{W}(\mathbf{x}_i, \hat{\gamma})]^{-1} [\mathbf{y}_i - \mathbf{m}(\mathbf{x}_i, \boldsymbol{\theta})]. \tag{12.94}$$

The solution to (12.94) is the WMNLS estimator.

As we will see in later chapters, the WMNLS estimator can be attractive for a broad class of nonlinear models, particularly when we cannot, or do not wish to, specify a complete distribution $\mathrm{D}(\mathbf{y}_i \mid \mathbf{x}_i)$. Of importance, under (12.93), the WMNLS estimator is generally consistent for $\boldsymbol{\theta}_{\mathrm{o}}$ even if the inverse of the weighting matrix is misspecified for $\boldsymbol{\theta}_{\mathrm{o}}$. The intuition for the robustness of the WMNLS estimator is straightforward from the general M-estimation theory. Let γ^* be the probability limit of $\hat{\gamma}$, whether or not the variance is misspecified. Then the WMNLS estimator is consistent for $\boldsymbol{\theta}_{\mathrm{o}}$ if $\boldsymbol{\theta}_{\mathrm{o}}$ uniquely solves the population problem

$$\min_{\boldsymbol{\theta}} \mathrm{E}\{[\mathbf{y}_i - \mathbf{m}(\mathbf{x}_i, \boldsymbol{\theta})]'[\mathbf{W}(\mathbf{x}_i, \gamma^*)]^{-1}[\mathbf{y}_i - \mathbf{m}(\mathbf{x}_i, \boldsymbol{\theta})]\}.$$

But straightforward algebra shows that

$$\begin{aligned}
&[\mathbf{y}_i - \mathbf{m}(\mathbf{x}_i, \boldsymbol{\theta})]'[\mathbf{W}(\mathbf{x}_i, \gamma^*)]^{-1}[\mathbf{y}_i - \mathbf{m}(\mathbf{x}_i, \boldsymbol{\theta})] \\
&\quad = [\mathbf{y}_i - \mathbf{m}(\mathbf{x}_i, \boldsymbol{\theta}_{\mathrm{o}})]'[\mathbf{W}(\mathbf{x}_i, \gamma^*)]^{-1}[\mathbf{y}_i - \mathbf{m}(\mathbf{x}_i, \boldsymbol{\theta}_{\mathrm{o}})] \\
&\qquad - 2[\mathbf{y}_i - \mathbf{m}(\mathbf{x}_i, \boldsymbol{\theta}_{\mathrm{o}})]'[\mathbf{W}(\mathbf{x}_i, \gamma^*)]^{-1}[\mathbf{m}(\mathbf{x}_i, \boldsymbol{\theta}_{\mathrm{o}}) - \mathbf{m}(\mathbf{x}_i, \boldsymbol{\theta})] \\
&\qquad + [\mathbf{m}(\mathbf{x}_i, \boldsymbol{\theta}_{\mathrm{o}}) - \mathbf{m}(\mathbf{x}_i, \boldsymbol{\theta})]'[\mathbf{W}(\mathbf{x}_i, \gamma^*)]^{-1}[\mathbf{m}(\mathbf{x}_i, \boldsymbol{\theta}_{\mathrm{o}}) - \mathbf{m}(\mathbf{x}_i, \boldsymbol{\theta})].
\end{aligned}$$

By the law of interated expectations, the term in the middle has zero conditional mean by (12.93), and so

$$\begin{aligned}
&\mathrm{E}\{[\mathbf{y}_i - \mathbf{m}(\mathbf{x}_i, \boldsymbol{\theta})]'[\mathbf{W}(\mathbf{x}_i, \gamma^*)]^{-1}[\mathbf{y}_i - \mathbf{m}(\mathbf{x}_i, \boldsymbol{\theta})]\} \\
&\quad = \mathrm{E}\{[\mathbf{y}_i - \mathbf{m}(\mathbf{x}_i, \boldsymbol{\theta}_{\mathrm{o}})]'[\mathbf{W}(\mathbf{x}_i, \gamma^*)]^{-1}[\mathbf{y}_i - \mathbf{m}(\mathbf{x}_i, \boldsymbol{\theta}_{\mathrm{o}})]\} \\
&\qquad + \mathrm{E}\{[\mathbf{m}(\mathbf{x}_i, \boldsymbol{\theta}_{\mathrm{o}}) - \mathbf{m}(\mathbf{x}_i, \boldsymbol{\theta})]'[\mathbf{W}(\mathbf{x}_i, \gamma^*)]^{-1}[\mathbf{m}(\mathbf{x}_i, \boldsymbol{\theta}_{\mathrm{o}}) - \mathbf{m}(\mathbf{x}_i, \boldsymbol{\theta})]\}.
\end{aligned} \tag{12.95}$$

The first term on the right-hand side in (12.95) does not depend on $\boldsymbol{\theta}$ and the second term is zero when $\boldsymbol{\theta} = \boldsymbol{\theta}_{\mathrm{o}}$. As always, identification requires that the latter term be zero only when $\boldsymbol{\theta} = \boldsymbol{\theta}_{\mathrm{o}}$.

Not surprisingly, the WMNLS estimator has desirable asymptotic efficiency properties if (12.94) holds, along with

$$\mathrm{Var}(\mathbf{y}_i \mid \mathbf{x}_i) = \mathbf{W}(\mathbf{x}_i, \gamma_{\mathrm{o}}) \qquad \text{for some } \gamma_{\mathrm{o}}. \tag{12.96}$$

Under these assumptions, it is easy to show that the conditional information matrix equality (12.96) holds. Matrix algebra can be used to show directly that the asymptotic variance of Avar $\sqrt{N}(\hat{\boldsymbol{\theta}} - \boldsymbol{\theta}_{\mathrm{o}})$ under correct second moment specification is smaller than that of any other WMNLS estimator using weights that are a function of $\mathbf{x}_i$ (including, of course, constant weights). In particular, the WMNLS estimator is more efficient than MNLS. But remember that MNLS does not require the strict exogeneity assumption for consistency. In Chapter 14, we will develop a general efficiency framework that allows us to conclude that WMNLS is the asymptotically efficient estimator in a broad class of instrumental variables estimators.

Even if we admit the possibility that our model $\mathbf{W}(\mathbf{x}_i, \gamma)$ is misspecified for the conditional variance, there are still good reasons to apply WMNLS, at least under (12.93). As with the linear case, it will often be the case that a misspecified model of the variance matrix that nevertheless captures key features of the conditional second moments might lead to a more efficient estimator of $\boldsymbol{\theta}_o$ than an estimator that ignores variances and covariances: the MNLS estimator. This is the key insight in the **generalized estimating equation (GEE)** literature in statistics—see, for example, Liang and Zeger (1986)—which is typically applied to panel data sets (and cluster samples) but whose insights also apply to SUR-like systems of equations. Borrowing from GEE nomenclature, we refer to $\mathbf{W}(\mathbf{x}, \gamma)$ as a **working variance matrix**, which is allowed, and in many cases is known, to be misspecified. We discuss some ways of choosing this matrix below. The GEE approach is closely related to quasi-maximum likelihood methods, and we cover these, along with GEE for panel data, in Chapter 13.

Given $\hat{\gamma}$ from a first-step estimation, the first-order conditions for the WMNLS estimator, $\hat{\boldsymbol{\theta}}$, are

$$\sum_{i=1}^{N} \nabla_\theta \mathbf{m}(\mathbf{x}_i, \hat{\boldsymbol{\theta}})'[\mathbf{W}(\mathbf{x}_i, \hat{\gamma})]^{-1}[\mathbf{y}_i - \mathbf{m}(\mathbf{x}_i, \hat{\boldsymbol{\theta}})] = \mathbf{0}. \tag{12.97}$$

(The GEE approach works off a very similar set of moment conditions—namely, the first occurrence of $\hat{\boldsymbol{\theta}}$ is replaced with an initial, $\sqrt{N}$-consistent estimator of $\boldsymbol{\theta}_o$—and the GEE estimator is $\sqrt{N}$-equivalent to the WMNLS estimator. Here we focus on equation (12.97).)

With a possibly misspecified conditional variance matrix, the asymptotic variance of $\hat{\boldsymbol{\theta}}$ should be estimated using a Huber-White sandwich form,

$$\left(\sum_{i=1}^{N} \nabla_\theta \mathbf{m}_i(\hat{\boldsymbol{\theta}})'[\mathbf{W}_i(\hat{\gamma})]^{-1}\nabla_\theta \mathbf{m}_i(\hat{\boldsymbol{\theta}})\right)^{-1} \left(\sum_{i=1}^{N} \nabla_\theta \mathbf{m}_i(\hat{\boldsymbol{\theta}})'[\mathbf{W}_i(\hat{\gamma})]^{-1}\hat{\mathbf{u}}_i\hat{\mathbf{u}}_i'[\mathbf{W}_i(\hat{\gamma})]^{-1}\nabla_\theta \mathbf{m}_i(\hat{\boldsymbol{\theta}})\right)$$
$$\cdot \left(\sum_{i=1}^{N} \nabla_\theta \mathbf{m}_i(\hat{\boldsymbol{\theta}})'[\mathbf{W}_i(\hat{\gamma})]^{-1}\nabla_\theta \mathbf{m}_i(\hat{\boldsymbol{\theta}})\right)^{-1}, \tag{12.98}$$

where the notation should be clear. (As usual, saying that (12.98) is valid for $\widehat{\text{Avar}}(\hat{\boldsymbol{\theta}})$ means that Avar $\sqrt{N}(\hat{\boldsymbol{\theta}} - \boldsymbol{\theta}_o)$ is consistently estimated by dividing (12.98) by N.) Problem 12.11 asks you to derive this formula, along with the simplified formula—with the final two terms in (12.98) dropped—that is valid under $\text{Var}(\mathbf{y}_i \mid \mathbf{x}_i) = \mathbf{W}(\mathbf{x}_i, \gamma_o)$ for some γ_o.

When $\mathbf{W}(\mathbf{x}_i, \gamma)$ is chosen to be a diagonal matrix, the WMNLS estimator is typically robust to violations of the strict exogeneity assumption. For example, in a panel data setting where $\text{E}(y_{it} \mid \mathbf{x}_{it}) = m_t(\mathbf{x}_{it}, \boldsymbol{\theta}_o)$, we can choose $\mathbf{W}(\mathbf{x}_i, \gamma)$ to be diagonal where the tth diagonal depends only on $\mathbf{x}_{it}$. The resulting estimator is a **pooled weighted nonlinear least squares (PWNLS)** estimator, which is often useful for dynamic panel data models, or other panel data models without strict exogeneity; see Problem 12.13. In Chapters 13 and 18 we will cover quasi-maximum likelihood estimators that are asymptotically equivalent to PWNLS but can be obtained more easily via one-step estimation.

Sometimes we might choose $\mathbf{W}(\mathbf{x}_i, \gamma) = \boldsymbol{\Omega}$, that is, use a matrix where the variances and covariances do not depend on $\mathbf{x}_i$. A consistent estimator of the unconditional variance matrix of $\mathbf{u}_i \equiv \mathbf{y}_i - \mathbf{m}(\mathbf{x}_i, \boldsymbol{\theta}_o)$ is

$$\hat{\boldsymbol{\Omega}} = N^{-1} \sum_{i=1}^{N} \breve{\mathbf{u}}_i \breve{\mathbf{u}}_i', \tag{12.99}$$

where the $\breve{\mathbf{u}}_i$ are the vectors of MNLS residuals. When we use $\hat{\boldsymbol{\Omega}}$ in (12.99), we have what is sometimes called the **nonlinear SUR estimator**. Equation (12.99) places no restrictions on the unconditional variances and covariances. In panel data cases we might, for example, restrict $\hat{\boldsymbol{\Omega}}$ to have a random effects or an AR(1) structure. The asymptotic analysis of the estimator with constant $\mathbf{W}(\mathbf{x}_i, \gamma)$ follows from the general WMNLS framework. In particular, the nonlinear SUR estimator is consistent and $\sqrt{N}$-asymptotically normal under (12.93) whether or not $\text{Var}(\mathbf{y}_i \mid \mathbf{x}_i)$ is constant. Of course, if $\text{Var}(\mathbf{y}_i \mid \mathbf{x}_i)$ depends on $\mathbf{x}_i$, there could be an alternative WMNLS estimator that is more efficient than the nonlinear SUR estimator, but that hinges on our ability to find $\mathbf{W}(\mathbf{x}_i, \gamma)$ that provides a "better" approximation to $\text{Var}(\mathbf{y}_i \mid \mathbf{x}_i)$ than a constant matrix.

Models for conditional variances $\text{Var}(y_{ig} \mid \mathbf{x}_i)$ are relatively straightforward because we have many univariate distributions to draw on (see Section 13.11.3). Directly specifying models for conditional covariances, when they actually depend on $\mathbf{x}_i$, is more difficult. A fruitful approach is to specify conditional variances for each g but then to nominally assume constant conditional *correlations*. Then, if ρ_{gh} is (nominally) $\text{Corr}(y_{ig}, y_{ih} \mid \mathbf{x}_i)$, we have $\text{Cov}(y_{ig}, y_{ih} \mid \mathbf{x}_i) =$

$\rho_{gh}[\text{Var}(y_{ig} \mid \mathbf{x}_i)\ \text{Var}(y_{ih} \mid \mathbf{x}_i)]^{1/2}$. Let $\mathbf{V}(\mathbf{x}, \boldsymbol{\omega})$ be the $G \times G$ diagonal matrix with the proposed variances down its diagonal, and let $\mathbf{R}(\boldsymbol{\rho})$ denote the $G \times G$ matrix of proposed constant correlations, which depends on the J-vector of parameters $\boldsymbol{\rho}$. In the GEE literature, $\mathbf{R}(\boldsymbol{\rho})$ is called a **working correlation matrix** because there is no presumption that it truly contains the conditional correlations. In fact, there is no presumption that the conditional correlations are even constant.

Given $\mathbf{V}(\mathbf{x}, \boldsymbol{\omega})$ and $\mathbf{R}(\boldsymbol{\rho})$, we can write the working variance matrix as

$$\mathbf{W}(\mathbf{x}_i, \gamma) = \mathbf{V}(\mathbf{x}_i, \boldsymbol{\omega})^{1/2}\mathbf{R}(\boldsymbol{\rho})\mathbf{V}(\mathbf{x}_i, \boldsymbol{\omega})^{1/2}, \tag{12.100}$$

where $\mathbf{V}(\mathbf{x}_i, \boldsymbol{\omega})^{1/2}$ is the matrix square root. Note that γ contains $\boldsymbol{\omega}$ and $\boldsymbol{\rho}$.

To implement WMNLS (GEE) under (12.100), we need to estimate $\boldsymbol{\omega}$ and $\boldsymbol{\rho}$. This typically proceeds by MNLS to first obtain residuals $\check{u}_{ig}$, then by using $\check{u}_{ig}^2$ and the variance models, say $v_g(\mathbf{x}_i, \boldsymbol{\omega})$, to estimate the variances, say $\check{v}_{ig} \equiv v_{ig}(\mathbf{x}_i, \hat{\boldsymbol{\omega}})$. (In many cases, the $v_g(\mathbf{x}, \boldsymbol{\omega})$ functions depend on the mean parameters $\boldsymbol{\theta}$ and a single additional parameter; we will see this explicitly in Section 13.11.3 and Chapter 18.) We can then use the standardized residuals $\check{u}_{ig}/\sqrt{\check{v}_{ig}}$ for all i and g to estimate the parameters in the working correlation matrix $\mathbf{R}(\boldsymbol{\rho})$. The details depend on how $\mathbf{R}(\boldsymbol{\rho})$ is specified.

The most general specification (once we restrict ourselves to a matrix that does not depend on $\mathbf{x}$) is an **unstructured working correlation matrix**, where the elements of $\mathbf{R}(\boldsymbol{\rho})$ are unrestricted (except, of course, for requiring the matrix to be a valid correlation matrix):

$$\mathbf{R}(\boldsymbol{\rho}) = \begin{pmatrix} 1 & \rho_{12} & \rho_{13} & \cdots & \rho_{1G} \\ \rho_{12} & 1 & \rho_{23} & \cdots & \rho_{2G} \\ \rho_{13} & \rho_{23} & \ddots & \ddots & \vdots \\ \vdots & \vdots & \vdots & 1 & \rho_{G-1,G} \\ \rho_{1G} & \rho_{2G} & \cdots & \rho_{G-1,G} & 1 \end{pmatrix}. \tag{12.101}$$

Then, we can estimate each ρ_{gh} as

$$\hat{\rho}_{gh} = \text{Sample Correlation}(\check{u}_{ig}/\sqrt{\check{v}_{ig}}, \check{u}_{ih}/\sqrt{\check{v}_{ih}}). \tag{12.102}$$

Under general conditions, the $\hat{\rho}_{gh}$ converge to, say, ρ_{gh}^* the population correlation between $u_{ig}/\sqrt{v_g(\mathbf{x}_i, \boldsymbol{\omega}^*)}$ and $u_{ih}/\sqrt{v_h(\mathbf{x}_i, \boldsymbol{\omega}^*)}$, where $\boldsymbol{\omega}^* = \text{plim}(\hat{\boldsymbol{\omega}})$.

A common form of $\mathbf{R}(\boldsymbol{\rho})$ in panel data settings is an **exchangeable working correlation matrix**, which introduces a single correlation parameter, ρ, for all pairs. Then, $\hat{\rho}$ is obtained by averaging the $\hat{\rho}_{gh}$ (but where g and h denote different time periods) across all nonredundant pairs with $g \neq h$. An exchangeable correlation matrix allows for a random effects-type correlation structure but with conditional variances changing over time. We will have more to say on this setup in Chapter 13.

Once $\hat{\omega}$ and $\hat{\rho}$ have been obtained, the working variance matrix estimates, $\mathbf{W}_i(\hat{\gamma}) = \mathbf{V}(\mathbf{x}_i, \hat{\omega})^{1/2}\mathbf{R}(\hat{\rho})\mathbf{V}(\mathbf{x}_i, \hat{\omega})^{1/2}$, are easy to obtain, and they can be used in WMNLS. In special cases it may be reasonable to assume $\mathbf{W}(\mathbf{x}, \gamma)$ is correctly specified for $\text{Var}(\mathbf{y}_i \mid \mathbf{x}_i)$, but most of the time one should use equation (12.98) as the variance matrix estimator.

Finally, a final word of caution. The variance matrix estimator (12.98) assumes that the conditional mean is correctly specified, as stated explicitly in equation (12.93). Thus, this estimator is fully robust only if the conditional mean is correctly specified; it is only semirobust if we entertain misspecification of $\text{E}(y_i \mid \mathbf{x}_i)$. Unfortunately, because WMNLS is a two-step estimator, a variance matrix estimator that allows conditional mean misspecification is much more complicated than (12.98) because it depends on the sampling variability of $\hat{\gamma}$. In particular, it is not enough just to replace the outer ends of the sandwich with the unconditional Hessian evaluated at the estimates. (This is why, in the application of WMNLS to GEE, the standard errors from (12.98) are often explicitly labeled as semirobust.)

12.10 Quantile Estimation

The introduction to this chapter included a brief discussion of the problem of estimating a conditional median function, and we discussed how the consistency of LAD follows from Theorem 12.2. Estimation of conditional medians and, more generally, conditional quantiles, is increasingly popular in empirical research. It has been long recognized that while estimating conditional mean functions is valuable, the partial effect of an explanatory variable can have very different effects across different segments of a population. Quantile estimation allows us to study such effects. Koenker and Bassett (1978) developed the theory of quantile regression, and Buchinsky (1998), Peracchi (2001), and Koenker (2005) provide recent treatments. Chamberlain (1994) and Buchinsky (1994) are influential applications of quantile regression to estimate changes in the wage distribution in the United States.

12.10.1 Quantiles, the Estimation Problem, and Consistency

Let y_i denote a random draw from a population. Then, for $0 < \tau < 1$, $q(\tau)$ is a τth quantile of the distribution of y_i if $\text{P}(y_i \leq q(\tau)) \geq \tau$ and $\text{P}(y_i \geq q(\tau)) \geq 1 - \tau$. A special case is the median when $\tau = 1/2$. For notational convenience, we will write the τth quantile of y_i as $\text{Quant}_\tau(y_i)$.

Typically, we are interested in modeling quantiles conditional on a set of covariates $\mathbf{x}_i$. In most applications, the assumption is that the quantiles are linear in parameters (and we will show them linear in $\mathbf{x}_i$, even though we can, as usual, choose $\mathbf{x}_i$ to include nonlinear functions of underlying explanatory variables). Under linearity, we have

$$\text{Quant}_\tau(y_i \mid \mathbf{x}_i) = \alpha_o(\tau) + \mathbf{x}_i \boldsymbol{\beta}_o(\tau), \tag{12.103}$$

where, for reasons to be seen shortly, we explicitly introduce an intercept and explicitly show the intercept and slopes depending on τ.

To estimate the parameters in a conditional quantile function, it is very helpful to know whether a population quantile solves a population extremum problem. We know that the conditional mean minimizes the expected squared error and, in the introduction, we asserted that the conditional median (when $\tau = .5$) minimizes the expected absolute error. Generally, if $q_o(\tau)$ is the τth quantile of y_i, then $q_o(\tau)$ solves

$$\min_{q \in \mathbb{R}} \mathrm{E}\{(\tau 1[y_i - q \geq 0] + (1 - \tau) 1[y_i - q < 0]) |y_i - q|\}, \tag{12.104}$$

where $1[\cdot]$ is the **indicator function** equal to one if the statement in brackets is true and zero otherwise. The function

$$c_\tau(u) = (\tau 1[u \geq 0] + (1 - \tau) 1[u < 0])|u| = (\tau - 1[u < 0])u$$

is called the **asymmetric absolute loss function**, the **τ-absolute loss function**, or the **check function** (because its graph resembles a check mark) (see, for example, Manski, 1988, Sect. 4.2.4). The slope of $c_\tau(u)$ is τ when $u > 0$ and $-(1 - \tau)$ when $u < 0$; the slope is undefined at $u = 0$. When $\tau = .5$, the check function is simply the absolute value divided by two, and so it is symmetric about zero. If $\tau > .5$, the slope of the loss for $u > 0$ is greater than the absolute value of the slope for $u < 0$; the opposite holds if $\tau < .5$.

It follows immediately that a conditional quantile minimizes the asymmetric absolute loss function conditional on $\mathbf{x}_i$. (Of course, when $\tau = .5$, we are back to the fact that the median minimizes the absolute error.) Therefore, we can immediately apply the analogy principle to obtain consistent estimators of the parameters in equation (12.103):

$$\min_{\alpha \in \mathbb{R}, \boldsymbol{\beta} \in \mathbb{R}^K} \sum_{i=1}^{N} c_\tau(y_i - \alpha - \mathbf{x}_i \boldsymbol{\beta}). \tag{12.105}$$

Under the assumption that $\boldsymbol{\theta}_o(\tau) = (\alpha_o(\tau), \boldsymbol{\beta}_o(\tau)')'$ is the unique minimizer of $\mathrm{E}[c_\tau(y_i - \alpha - \mathbf{x}_i\boldsymbol{\beta})]$—it is guaranteed to be a solution—the **quantile regression estimator** is consistent under very weak regularity conditions. Note that $c_\tau(y_i - \alpha - \mathbf{x}_i\boldsymbol{\beta})$ is continuous in the parameters because the check function is continuous. However, the check function is not differentiable at zero.

Before we discuss estimation across different quantiles, it is useful to spend some time on the leading case of the conditional median. In many applications, the LAD estimator is applied along with OLS, often to supposedly demonstrate the sensitivity of OLS to **influential observations**. It is no secret that OLS, because it minimizes the sum of squared residuals, can be sensitive to the inclusion of extreme observations. In the context of specific models of data contamination, one can make precise the notion that OLS is "nonrobust" to influential observations, or "outliers." By contrast, the LAD estimator (and quantile estimators more generally) are "robust" to influential observations. We need not develop a formal framework for defining robustness to outlying data—as in, for example, Huber (1981)—to understand the main point: OLS is sensitive to changes in extreme data points because the mean is sensitive to changes in extreme values; LAD is insensitive to changes in extreme data points because the median is insensitive to changes in extreme values. This point is easy to illustrate by selecting three positive integers, computing the mean and median, multiplying the largest value by 10, and computing the mean and median again. The mean can increase dramatically, while the median will not change.

The insensitivity of the median to changes in extreme values is desirable, but we should not overlook an important point: sometimes, probably more often than not, we are interested in partial effects on the conditional mean. If that is the case, then we must recognize that LAD does not generally consistently estimate parameters in a correctly specified conditional mean. Only least squares does (assuming we rule out error distributions with very thick tails). Therefore, one must be very careful in attributing differences between LAD and OLS to outliers; there are other reasons the estimates may differ significantly. If we define robustness to mean consistently estimating the parameters of the conditional mean, LAD is not a robust estimator of conditional mean parameters because consistency holds only under additional restrictions on the conditional distribution. (Other so-called robust estimators—where "robust" means insensitivity to outlying observations—are not robust for estimating the conditional mean in that they also rely on symmetry for consistency. See Huber (1981) for a general treatment and also Peracchi (2001).)

To study the assumptions under which LAD and OLS estimate the same parameters, it is helpful to write a model for a random draw i as

$$y_i = \alpha_o + \mathbf{x}_i\boldsymbol{\beta}_o + u_i. \tag{12.106}$$

If we assume

$$\mathrm{D}(u_i \mid \mathbf{x}_i) \text{ is symmetric about zero,} \tag{12.107}$$

then $\mathrm{E}(u_i \mid \mathbf{x}_i) = \mathrm{Med}(u_i \mid \mathbf{x}_i) = 0$, which means that the deterministic part of (12.106), $\alpha_o + \mathbf{x}_i\boldsymbol{\beta}_o$, is both the conditional mean and conditional median of y_i (and $\mathrm{D}(y_i \mid \mathbf{x}_i)$ is symmetric about $\alpha_o + \mathbf{x}_i\boldsymbol{\beta}_o$). In discussions of the sensitivity of OLS to outliers, and the superiority of LAD under such circumstances, conditional symmetry is often maintained, if only implicitly. If we maintain conditional symmetry, then the analysis is fairly clean, as the trade-offs between LAD and OLS are readily obtained. Under conditional symmetry, LAD can have a smaller asymptotic variance—see the next section for derivation—than OLS for fat-tailed distributions. But, as is well known, OLS will be more efficient for estimating the mean (median) parameters under certain thin-tailed distributions, such as the normal.

Are there other assumptions under which OLS and LAD are both consistent for the parameters in (12.106)? Yes. Suppose that, instead of (12.107), we assume independence and take as the normalization $\mathrm{E}(u_i) = 0$:

$$\mathrm{D}(u_i \mid \mathbf{x}_i) = \mathrm{D}(u_i) \qquad \text{and} \qquad \mathrm{E}(u_i) = 0. \tag{12.108}$$

Under (12.108), OLS consistently estimates α_o and $\boldsymbol{\beta}_o$. Notice that u_i need not have a symmetric distribution. When it does not, $\mathrm{Med}(u_i) \equiv \eta_o \neq 0$. Nevertheless, by independence,

$$\mathrm{Med}(y_i \mid \mathbf{x}_i) = \alpha_o + \mathbf{x}_i\boldsymbol{\beta}_o + \mathrm{Med}(u_i) = (\alpha_o + \eta_o) + \mathbf{x}_i\boldsymbol{\beta}_o.$$

This equation immediately implies that the LAD slope estimators are consistent for $\boldsymbol{\beta}_o$. Therefore, OLS and LAD should provide similar estimates of the slope parameters. But they will estimate different intercepts.

Unfortunately, in many applications of LAD, the independence assumption is clearly violated. Heteroskedasticity in $\mathrm{Var}(u_i \mid \mathbf{x}_i)$ is common when y_i is a variable such as wealth, income, or pension contributions. In addition, conditional wealth and income distributions tend to be skewed. Therefore, when LAD methods are applied alongside OLS, there are often reasons to think a priori that OLS and LAD will *not* produce similar slope estimates. (In fact, it is unlikely that the conditional mean and conditional median are both linear in $\mathbf{x}_i$.) But important differences in the OLS and LAD estimates need have nothing to do with the presence of outliers.

Sometimes one can use a transformation to ensure conditional symmetry or the independence assumption in (12.108). When $y_i > 0$, the most common transformation is the natural log. Often, the linear model $\log(y_i) = \alpha_o + \mathbf{x}_i\boldsymbol{\beta}_o + u_i$ is more likely to satisfy symmetry or independence. Suppose that symmetry about zero holds in the linear model for $\log(y_i)$. Then, because the median passes through monotonic functions (unlike the expectation), $\text{Med}(y_i \mid \mathbf{x}_i) = \exp(\text{Med}[\log(y_i) \mid \mathbf{x}_i]) = \exp(\alpha_o + \mathbf{x}_i\boldsymbol{\beta}_o)$, and so we can easily recover the partial effects on the median of y_i itself. By contrast, we cannot generally find $\text{E}(y_i \mid \mathbf{x}_i) = \exp(\alpha_o + \mathbf{x}_i\boldsymbol{\beta}_o)\text{E}[\exp(u_i) \mid \mathbf{x}_i]$. If instead we assume (12.108), then $\text{Med}(y_i \mid \mathbf{x}_i)$ and $\text{E}(y_i \mid \mathbf{x}_i)$ are both exponential functions of $\mathbf{x}_i\boldsymbol{\beta}_o$, but with different "intercepts" inside the exponential function.

Incidentally, the fact that the median passes through monotonic functions is very handy for applying LAD to a variety of problems, including some in Chapters 15 and 17. But the expectation operator has useful properties that the median does not: linearity and the law of iterated expectations. For example, suppose we begin with a random coefficient model $y_i = a_i + \mathbf{x}_i\mathbf{b}_i$, where a_i is the heterogeneous intercept and $\mathbf{b}_i$ is a $1 \times K$ vector of heterogeneous slopes ("random coefficients"). If we assume that $(a_i, \mathbf{b}_i)$ is independent of $\mathbf{x}_i$, then

$$\text{E}(y_i \mid \mathbf{x}_i) = \text{E}(a_i \mid \mathbf{x}_i) + \mathbf{x}_i\text{E}(\mathbf{b}_i \mid \mathbf{x}_i) \equiv \alpha_o + \mathbf{x}_i\boldsymbol{\beta}_o,$$

where $\alpha_o = \text{E}(a_i)$ and $\boldsymbol{\beta}_o = \text{E}(\mathbf{b}_i)$. Because OLS consistently estimates the parameters of a conditional mean linear in those parameters, OLS consistently estimates the population averaged effects, or average partial effects, $\boldsymbol{\beta}_o$ (see also Section 4.4.4). Generally, even under independence, there is no way to derive $\text{Med}(y_i \mid \mathbf{x}_i)$, and it cannot be shown that LAD estimation of a linear model estimates average or median partial effects. Angrist, Chernozhukov, and Fernandez-Val (2006) provide a treatment of LAD (and quantile regression) under misspecification and characterize the probability limit of the LAD estimator.

We now turn to general quantile estimation. In many applications, one estimates linear conditional quantile functions for various quantiles. Having a set of estimated linear quantiles allows one to see how various explanatory variables differentially affect different parts of the distribution $\text{D}(y_i \mid \mathbf{x}_i)$. Of course, nothing guarantees that all or even several of the conditional quantiles are actually linear. With additive errors independent of the regressors, we have equation (12.103) but with common slopes, $\boldsymbol{\beta}_o(\tau) = \boldsymbol{\beta}_o$ for all τ. Then, we can estimate the common slopes using any quantile with $0 < \tau < 1$. In most applications of quantile regression, the whole point is to see how the effects of the covariates change with the quantile, and so different linear models are estimated for different quantiles. Practically speaking, the conditions under which the quantile functions do not cross are quite restrictive, and the estimated quantiles often do not show uniformly increasing or decreasing slopes as τ ranges between zero and one. Koenker (2005) provides further discussion.

12.10.2 Asymptotic Inference

As mentioned in Section 12.3, LAD estimation falls outside Theorem 12.3 because the objective function is not twice continuously differentiable with positive definite expected Hessian (at $\boldsymbol{\theta}_o$). For general quantile regression, the nondifferentiability in the check function occurs only at zero. To simplify notation, for a given τ we now write

$$y_i = \mathbf{x}_i\boldsymbol{\theta}_o + u_i, \qquad \text{Quant}_\tau(u_i \mid \mathbf{x}_i) = 0, \tag{12.109}$$

where the first element of $\mathbf{x}_i$ is unity. Provided there is sufficient variation in the distribution of $\mathbf{x}_i$, so that the probability that $y_i - \mathbf{x}_i\hat{\boldsymbol{\theta}}$ is zero is sufficiently small, the nonsmoothness of $c_\tau(u)$ at $u = 0$ does not cause a serious problem. The real complication is that the second derivative of the check function is zero everywhere it is defined, that is, for all $u \neq 0$. Interestingly, although the usual mean value expansion of the score can no longer be applied, it is possible to modify the argument and obtain an influence function representation for the quantile regression estimator. If we write the objective function as

$$q(\mathbf{w}_i, \boldsymbol{\theta}) = \tau 1[y_i - \mathbf{x}_i\boldsymbol{\theta} \geq 0](y_i - \mathbf{x}_i\boldsymbol{\theta}) - (1 - \tau)1[y_i - \mathbf{x}_i\boldsymbol{\theta} < 0](y_i - \mathbf{x}_i\boldsymbol{\theta}),$$

then we can define a score function as

$$\mathbf{s}_i(\boldsymbol{\theta}) = -\mathbf{x}_i'\{\tau 1[y_i - \mathbf{x}_i\boldsymbol{\theta} \geq 0] - (1 - \tau)1[y_i - \mathbf{x}_i\boldsymbol{\theta} < 0]\}. \tag{12.110}$$

We refer to $\mathbf{s}_i(\boldsymbol{\theta})$ as a score function because, for $\boldsymbol{\theta}$ such that $y_i - \mathbf{x}_i\boldsymbol{\theta} \neq 0$, $\mathbf{s}_i(\boldsymbol{\theta})$ is in fact the transpose of the gradient of the objective function, just as before. The hope is that we do not have to worry about what happens when the objective function is nondifferentiable. If u_i has a continuous distribution at zero, then $\text{P}(y_i - \mathbf{x}_i\boldsymbol{\theta}_o = 0) = 0$. In other words, at $\boldsymbol{\theta} = \boldsymbol{\theta}_o$, we can ignore the possibility of observing data where the objective function is nondifferentiable at the true value. Because $\hat{\boldsymbol{\theta}}$ is consistent for $\boldsymbol{\theta}_o$, as the sample size grows there is less and less chance that $q(\mathbf{w}_i, \boldsymbol{\theta})$ is nondifferentiable at $\hat{\boldsymbol{\theta}}$, and so we can use a first-order condition to obtain $\hat{\boldsymbol{\theta}}$.

We can show directly that the score satisfies $\text{E}[\mathbf{s}_i(\boldsymbol{\theta}_o) \mid \mathbf{x}_i] = 0$ because $\text{E}(1[y_i - \mathbf{x}_i\boldsymbol{\theta}_o \geq 0] \mid \mathbf{x}_i) = \text{P}(y_i \geq \mathbf{x}_i\boldsymbol{\theta}_o \mid \mathbf{x}_i) = (1 - \tau)$ by definition of a quantile. Further, $\text{E}(1[y_i - \mathbf{x}_i\boldsymbol{\theta}_o < 0] \mid \mathbf{x}_i) = \text{P}(y_i < \mathbf{x}_i\boldsymbol{\theta}_o \mid \mathbf{x}_i) = \tau$ (when we assume u_i has a continuous distribution at zero), and so

$$\text{E}[\mathbf{s}_i(\boldsymbol{\theta}_o) \mid \mathbf{x}_i] = -\mathbf{x}_i'(\tau(1 - \tau) - (1 - \tau)\tau) = \mathbf{0}.$$

The asymptotic theory requires that we consider solutions that satisfy $N^{-1/2}\sum_{i=1}^N \mathbf{s}_i(\hat{\boldsymbol{\theta}}) = o_p(1)$. (Technically, there is a chance that the solution to the minimization problem does not solve the first-order condition, but it diminishes.) The key to obtaining an influence function representation is to first compute the expected value of the score, then obtain the Jacobian. If we first obtain the Jacobian of the score, then it is identically zero. Therefore, let $\mathbf{a}(\boldsymbol{\theta}) \equiv \mathrm{E}[\mathbf{s}_i(\boldsymbol{\theta})]$ and assume that the $P \times P$ Jacobian of $\mathbf{a}(\cdot)$, say $\mathbf{A}(\cdot)$, exists. Further, assume that $\mathbf{A}(\boldsymbol{\theta}_o)$ is nonsingular; in fact, it will almost always be positive definite. By first taking the expectation of $\mathbf{s}_i(\boldsymbol{\theta})$, we smooth it out, and under weak conditions the expected value of the score is well behaved. The starting point is to find the expectation conditional on $\mathbf{x}_i$:

$$
\begin{aligned}
\mathrm{E}[\mathbf{s}_i(\boldsymbol{\theta}) \mid \mathbf{x}_i] &= -\mathbf{x}_i'\{\tau P[u_i \geq \mathbf{x}_i(\boldsymbol{\theta} - \boldsymbol{\theta}_o) \mid \mathbf{x}_i] - (1 - \tau)P[u_i < \mathbf{x}_i(\boldsymbol{\theta} - \boldsymbol{\theta}_o) \mid \mathbf{x}_i] \\
&= -\mathbf{x}_i'\{\tau[1 - F_u(\mathbf{x}_i(\boldsymbol{\theta} - \boldsymbol{\theta}_o) \mid \mathbf{x}_i)] - (1 - \tau)F_u(\mathbf{x}_i(\boldsymbol{\theta} - \boldsymbol{\theta}_o) \mid \mathbf{x}_i)\} \\
&= -\mathbf{x}_i'[\tau - F_u(\mathbf{x}_i(\boldsymbol{\theta} - \boldsymbol{\theta}_o) \mid \mathbf{x}_i)], \qquad (12.111)
\end{aligned}
$$

where we assume that the conditional cumulative distribution function $F_u(\cdot \mid \mathbf{x})$ is continuous at zero. In fact, we assume that $F_u(\cdot \mid \mathbf{x})$ is continuously differentiable and denote the density $f_u(\cdot \mid \mathbf{x})$. Of course, $\mathrm{E}[\mathbf{s}_i(\boldsymbol{\theta})]$ is just the expected value of (12.111) across the distribution of $\mathbf{x}_i$. Assuming that we can interchange the expectation and the Jacobian—which holds under general conditions, as described in Bartle (1966, Chap. 4)—we can first compute the Jacobian of $\mathrm{E}[\mathbf{s}_i(\boldsymbol{\theta}) \mid \mathbf{x}_i]$ and then obtain its expected value to obtain $\mathbf{A}(\boldsymbol{\theta})$. But from (12.111), $\nabla_{\theta}\mathrm{E}[\mathbf{s}_i(\boldsymbol{\theta}) \mid \mathbf{x}_i] = f_u(\mathbf{x}_i(\boldsymbol{\theta} - \boldsymbol{\theta}_o) \mid \mathbf{x}_i)\mathbf{x}_i'\mathbf{x}_i$, and evaluating this Jacobian at $\boldsymbol{\theta}_o$ and taking the expectation (which we assume can be interchanged with the Jacobian) gives

$$
\mathbf{A}_o \equiv \mathbf{A}(\boldsymbol{\theta}_o) = \mathrm{E}[f_u(0 \mid \mathbf{x}_i)\mathbf{x}_i'\mathbf{x}_i]. \qquad (12.112)
$$

Using the methods of Huber (1967) and Newey and McFadden (1994, Sect. 7), one can derive the representation

$$
\sqrt{N}(\hat{\boldsymbol{\theta}} - \boldsymbol{\theta}_o) = -\mathbf{A}_o^{-1}N^{-1/2}\sum_{i=1}^{N}\mathbf{s}_i(\boldsymbol{\theta}_o) + o_p(1). \qquad (12.113)
$$

Because $\mathbf{s}_i(\boldsymbol{\theta}_o)$ has zero mean, it follows (under mild conditions) that

$$
\sqrt{N}(\hat{\boldsymbol{\theta}} - \boldsymbol{\theta}_o) \xrightarrow{d} \mathrm{Normal}(\mathbf{0}, \mathbf{A}_o^{-1}\mathbf{B}_o\mathbf{A}_o^{-1}), \qquad (12.114)
$$

where

$$
\mathbf{B}_o \equiv \mathrm{E}[\mathbf{s}_i(\boldsymbol{\theta}_o)\mathbf{s}_i(\boldsymbol{\theta}_o)'] = \tau(1 - \tau)\mathrm{E}(\mathbf{x}_i'\mathbf{x}_i). \qquad (12.115)
$$

(Problem 12.14 asks you to derive the expression for $\mathbf{B}_o$.)

The matrix $\mathbf{B}_o$ is simple to estimate (recall that we have chosen τ):

$$\hat{\mathbf{B}} = \tau(1-\tau)\left(N^{-1}\sum_{i=1}^{N}\mathbf{x}_i'\mathbf{x}_i\right). \tag{12.116}$$

We can also use the average outer product of the scores, $\mathbf{s}_i(\hat{\boldsymbol{\theta}})$. This estimator is generally consistent when $\mathrm{P}(y_i - \mathbf{x}_i\boldsymbol{\theta}_o = 0) = 0$ by Lemma 12.1 (allowing the function to be discontinuous at $\boldsymbol{\theta}_o$ with probability zero).

The matrix $\mathbf{A}_o$ is much more difficult to estimate because, at first glance, it seems to require estimation of $f_u(0 \mid \mathbf{x}_i)$, the conditional density of u_i at zero. One approach is to use a **nonparametric density estimator**, but these estimators can be imprecise, especially when the dimension of $\mathbf{x}_i$ is large. It turns out that we can estimate $\mathbf{A}_o$ more simply, using an approach due to Powell (1991). To sketch the approach, we can use the assumption that $f_u(\cdot \mid \mathbf{x}_i)$ is differentiable at zero, along with the definition of a derivative, to approximate $f_u(0 \mid \mathbf{x}_i)$ as

$$\begin{aligned}[F_u(h_N \mid \mathbf{x}_i) - F_u(-h_N \mid \mathbf{x}_i)]/2h_N &= \mathrm{P}(-h_N \le u_i \le h_N \mid \mathbf{x}_i)/2h_N \\ &= \mathrm{P}(|u_i| \le h_N \mid \mathbf{x}_i)/2h_N,\end{aligned}$$

where $\{h_N\}$ is a sequence of positive numbers with $h_N \to 0$. (We will see in a moment why we subscript h_N with the sample size, N.) It is convenient to write the conditional probability as a conditional expectation using indicator functions, $\mathrm{P}(|u_i| \le h_N \mid \mathbf{x}_i) = \mathrm{E}(1[|u_i| \le h_N] \mid \mathbf{x}_i)$. Therefore, an approximation of $\mathrm{E}[f_u(0 \mid \mathbf{x}_i)\mathbf{x}_i'\mathbf{x}_i]$ for "small" h_N is

$$(2h_N)^{-1}\mathrm{E}\{(1[|u_i| \le h_N] \mid \mathbf{x}_i)\mathbf{x}_i'\mathbf{x}_i\} = (2h_N)^{-1}\mathrm{E}(1[|u_i| \le h_N]\mathbf{x}_i'\mathbf{x}_i), \tag{12.117}$$

where the equality holds by iterated expectations. Switching from the conditional to the unconditional expectation of $1[|u_i| \le h_N]$ is an important simplification, and is reminiscent of the argument used to obtain the heteroskedasticity-robust variance matrix estimator. In that case, the matrix to be estimated, in the middle of the sandwich, is $\mathrm{E}[\mathrm{E}(u_i^2 \mid \mathbf{x}_i)\mathbf{x}_i'\mathbf{x}_i] = \mathrm{E}(u_i^2\mathbf{x}_i'\mathbf{x}_i)$. The latter expression is much easier to estimate directly because it circumvents the need to estimate the conditional expectation $\mathrm{E}(u_i^2 \mid \mathbf{x}_i)$.

Proceeding with the quantile regression case, we estimate (12.117) using the sample analogue, as usual:

$$\hat{\mathbf{A}} = (2h_N)^{-1}N^{-1}\sum_{i=1}^{N}1[|\hat{u}_i| \le h_N]\mathbf{x}_i'\mathbf{x}_i = (2Nh_N)^{-1}\sum_{i=1}^{N}1[|\hat{u}_i| \le h_N]\mathbf{x}_i'\mathbf{x}_i, \tag{12.118}$$

where $\hat{u}_i = y_i - \mathbf{x}_i\hat{\boldsymbol{\theta}}$ are the residuals from the quantile regression. Unfortunately, unlike in previous cases, we cannot so easily assert that $\hat{\mathbf{A}}$ is consistent for $\mathbf{A}_o$: we have said nothing about how quickly h_N decreases to zero with the sample size, and the indicator function is not continuous. Powell (1991) (see also Koenker [2005]) shows that, under weak conditions, $h_N \to 0$ such that $\sqrt{N}h_N \to \infty$ are sufficient for consistency. The second condition controls how quickly h_N shrinks to zero. For example, $h_N = aN^{-1/3}$ for any $a > 0$ satisfies these conditions. The practical problem is choosing a (or choosing h_N more generally). Koenker (2005) contains specific recommendations, and also discusses related estimators. In equation (12.118), observation i does not contribute if $|\hat{u}_i| > h_N$. Other methods allow each observation to enter the sum but with a weight that declines as $|\hat{u}_i|$ increases. In practice, one uses the most convenient estimate (that may be programmed into an existing econometrics package that performs quantile regression). The nonparametric bootstrap can be applied to quantile regression, but if the data set is large, the computation using several hundred bootstrap samples can be costly.

If we assume that u_i is independent of $\mathbf{x}_i$ then $f_u(0 \mid \mathbf{x}_i) = f_u(0)$ and the asymptotic variance in equation (12.114) simplifies to

$$\frac{\tau(1-\tau)}{[f_u(0)]^2}[\mathrm{E}(\mathbf{x}_i'\mathbf{x}_i)]^{-1}; \tag{12.119}$$

its estimator has the general form

$$\frac{\tau(1-\tau)}{[\hat{f}_u(0)]^2}\left(N^{-1}\sum_{i=1}^{N}\mathbf{x}_i'\mathbf{x}_i\right)^{-1}, \tag{12.120}$$

and a simple, consistent estimate of $f_u(0)$ is

$$\hat{f}_u(0) = (2Nh_N)^{-1}\sum_{i=1}^{N}1[|\hat{u}_i| \le h_N], \tag{12.121}$$

where h_N satisfies the same conditions as before. The estimator in (12.121) is easily seen to be a simple **histogram estimator** of the density of u_i at $u = 0$, where the bin width is $2h_N$ (and we must use the residuals in place of u_i). Alternatively, one can use a different **kernel density estimator** applied to $\{\hat{u}_i\}$; see, for example, Cameron and Trivedi (2005, Sect. 9.3).

Example 12.1 (Quantile Regression for Financial Wealth): We use the data set on single individuals (*fsize* = 1) in the data file 401KSUBS.RAW (from Abadie (2003))

Table 12.1
Mean and Quantile Regression for Net Total Financial Wealth

Dependent Variable / Explanatory Variable	*nettfa* (1) Mean (OLS)	(2) .10 Quantile	(3) .25 Quantile	(4) Median (LAD)	(5) .75 Quantile	(6) .90 Quantile
inc	.783	−.0179	.0713	.324	.798	1.291
	(.104)	(.0177)	(.0072)	(.012)	(.025)	(.048)
age	−1.568	−.0663	.0336	−.244	−1.386	−3.579
	(1.076)	(.2307)	(.0955)	(.146)	(.287)	(.501)
age^2	.0284	.0024	.0004	.0048	.0242	.0605
	(.0138)	(.0027)	(.0011)		(.0017)	(.0034)
	(.0059)					
*e*401*k*	6.837	.949	1.281	2.598	4.460	6.001
	(2.173)	(.617)	(.263)	(.404)	(.801)	(1.437)
N	2,017	2,017	2,017	2,017	2,017	2,017

The OLS standard errors (in parentheses) are robust to heteroskedasticity.
The quantile regression estimates, along with standard errors (in parentheses), were obtained using Stata 9.0. The variance matrix is of the form in equation (12.120)—that is, it assumes independence between the error and regressors.

to estimate conditional quantiles for net total financial wealth (*nettfa*). The explanatory variables are income, age, and a binary variable indicating eligibility to participate in a 401(k) pension plan through one's employer. The estimates, including OLS estimates of a linear model for the conditional mean, are given in Table 12.1. Financial wealth and income are both measured in thousands of dollars.

There are no surprises in the OLS estimates. The mean relationship between financial wealth and income is strong and very statistically significant. Further, eligibility in a 401(k) plan, holding income and age fixed, is estimated to increase expected financial wealth by about \$6,800. The heteroskedasticity-robust t statistic is over three. The coefficients on *age* and age^2 may appear puzzling at first, but they imply an increasing effect on *nettfa* starting at $age = 27.6$. This makes sense because the youngest person in the sample is 25. (In fact, the fit of the model is hardly changed—the R-squared goes from .1273 to .1272—if we replace *age* and age^2 with the single explanatory variable $(age - 25)^2$, and the restriction certainly cannot be rejected.)

The picture of the effects of income and 401(k) eligibility is very different when we look across the wealth distribution. How do we interpret the coefficient on *inc* for the quantile regressions? Consider the median regression result. Holding *age* and *e*401*k* fixed, the coefficient on *inc* implies that if we compare two groups of people whose income differs by $1,000, the median financial wealth is estimated to be $324 higher for the group with higher income. The effect on the median is less than half of the effect on the mean ($783). The effect of income at the low end of the *nettfa* distribution, the .10 quantile, is nonexistent. Income has a large effect at the upper end of the financial wealth distribution. For example, increasing income by $1,000 dollars increases the .90 quantile of *nettfa* by $1,291, or more than $1,000. The coefficient on *inc* is statistically greater than one.

The effects of 401(k) eligibility on *nettfa* also increase as we move up the wealth distribution, even conditional on income. Wealthy people can afford to contribute the maximums allowable by law, and so the option of contributing to tax-deferred savings plans, such as 401(k) plans, leads to a larger effect as we move up the distribution. (The coefficient on $e401k$ increases to about 9.7 at the .95 quantile.)

12.10.3 Quantile Regression for Panel Data

Quantile regression methods can be applied to panel data, too. For a given quantile $0 < \tau < 1$, suppose we specify

$$\text{Quant}_{\tau}(y_{it} \mid \mathbf{x}_{it}) = \mathbf{x}_{it}\boldsymbol{\theta}_{\text{o}}, \qquad t = 1, \ldots, T, \tag{12.122}$$

where $\mathbf{x}_{it}$ probably allows for a full set of time period intercepts. Of course, we can write $y_{it} = \mathbf{x}_{it}\boldsymbol{\theta}_{\text{o}} + u_{it}$ where $\text{Quant}_{\tau}(u_{it} \mid \mathbf{x}_{it}) = 0$. The natural estimator of $\boldsymbol{\theta}_{\text{o}}$ is the **pooled quantile regression** estimator, $\hat{\boldsymbol{\theta}}$, which solves

$$\min_{\boldsymbol{\theta} \in \Theta} \sum_{i=1}^{N} \sum_{t=1}^{T} c_{\tau}(y_{it} - \mathbf{x}_{it}\boldsymbol{\theta}), \tag{12.123}$$

where $c_{\tau}(\cdot)$ is the check function. Now, when we define a score $\mathbf{s}_i(\boldsymbol{\theta}) = \sum_{t=1}^{T} \mathbf{s}_{it}(\boldsymbol{\theta})$, we generally have to account for serial correlation in $\mathbf{s}_{it}(\boldsymbol{\theta}_{\text{o}})$ (although see Problem 12.15 for the case of dynamically complete quantiles). One technical issue in using the outer product of the score to estimate $\mathbf{B}_{\text{o}}$, that is,

$$\hat{\mathbf{B}} = N^{-1} \sum_{i=1}^{N} \mathbf{s}_i(\hat{\boldsymbol{\theta}})\mathbf{s}_i(\hat{\boldsymbol{\theta}})' = N^{-1} \sum_{i=1}^{N} \sum_{t=1}^{T} \sum_{r=1}^{T} \mathbf{s}_{it}(\hat{\boldsymbol{\theta}})\mathbf{s}_{ir}(\hat{\boldsymbol{\theta}})', \tag{12.124}$$

is that the score function is discontinuous for $\boldsymbol{\theta}$ such that $y_{it} = \mathbf{x}_{it}\boldsymbol{\theta}$, for some $t \in \{1, \ldots, T\}$. Neverthless, if we assume $\text{P}(u_{i1} \neq 0, \ldots, u_{iT} \neq 0) = 1$, then $\mathbf{s}_i(\boldsymbol{\theta})$ is continuous at $\boldsymbol{\theta}_{\text{o}}$ with probability one, and this is enough to apply a slightly generalized version of Lemma 12.1. Because $\hat{\mathbf{B}}$ includes the terms $\mathbf{s}_{it}(\hat{\boldsymbol{\theta}})\mathbf{s}_{ir}(\hat{\boldsymbol{\theta}})'$ for $t \neq r$, $\hat{\mathbf{B}}$ accounts for any kind of neglected dynamics in $\text{Quant}_{\tau}(y_{it} \mid \mathbf{x}_{it})$. The terms

$\mathbf{s}_{it}(\hat{\boldsymbol{\theta}})\mathbf{s}_{it}(\hat{\boldsymbol{\theta}})'$ could be simplified along the lines of (12.116), but it is unecessary and seems pointless when the terms for $t \neq r$ are included.

Estimation of $\mathbf{A}_o$ is similar to the cross section case. A fully robust estimator, one that does not assume independence between u_{it} and $\mathbf{x}_{it}$ and allows the distribution of u_{it} to change across t, is an extension of equation (12.118):

$$\hat{\mathbf{A}} = (2Nh_N)^{-1} \sum_{i=1}^{N} \sum_{t=1}^{T} 1[|\hat{u}_{it}| \leq h_N] \mathbf{x}_{it}' \mathbf{x}_{it}, \tag{12.125}$$

or, we can replace the indicator function with a smoothed version. Rather than using $\hat{\mathbf{A}}^{-1}\hat{\mathbf{B}}\hat{\mathbf{A}}^{-1}/N$ as the estimate of $\text{Avar}(\hat{\boldsymbol{\theta}})$, the bootstrap can be applied using the method for panel data described in Section 12.8.2.

Allowing explicitly for unobserved effects in quantile regression is trickier. For a given quantile $0 < \tau < 1$, a natural specification that incorporates strict exogeneity conditional on c_i is

$$\text{Quant}_\tau(y_{it} \mid \mathbf{x}_i, c_i) = \text{Quant}_\tau(y_{it} \mid \mathbf{x}_{it}, c_i) = \mathbf{x}_{it}\boldsymbol{\theta}_o + c_i, \qquad t = 1, \ldots, T, \tag{12.126}$$

which is reminiscent of the way we specified the conditional mean in Chapter 10. Equivalently, we can write

$$y_{it} = \mathbf{x}_{it}\boldsymbol{\theta}_o + c_i + u_{it}, \qquad \text{Quant}_\tau(u_{it} \mid \mathbf{x}_i, c_i) = 0, \qquad t = 1, \ldots, T.$$

Unfortunately, unlike in the case of estimating effects on the conditional mean, we cannot proceed without further assumptions. A "fixed effects" approach, where we allow $\text{D}(c_i \mid \mathbf{x}_i)$ to be unrestricted, is attractive. Generally, there are no simple transformations to eliminate c_i and estimate $\boldsymbol{\theta}_o$. If we treat the c_i as parameters to estimate along with $\boldsymbol{\theta}_o$, the resulting estimator generally suffers from an incidental parameters problem, a topic that comes up in Chapter 13 and at several places in Part IV. Briefly, if we try to estimate c_i for each i, then, with large N and small T, the poor quality of the estimates of c_i causes the accompanying estimate of $\boldsymbol{\theta}_o$ to be badly behaved. Recall that this was *not* the case when we used the FE estimator for a conditional mean: treating the c_i as parameters led us to the within estimator. Koenker (2004) derives asymptotic properties of this estimation procedure when T grows along with N, but he adds the assumptions that the regressors are fixed and $\{u_{it} : t = 1, \ldots, T\}$ is serially independent.

An alternative approach is suggested by Abrevaya and Dahl (2008) for $T = 2$. Motivated by Chamberlain's approach to linear unobserved effects models (see Section 11.1.2), Abrevaya and Dahl estimate separate quantile regressions $\text{Quant}_\tau(y_{it} \mid \mathbf{x}_{i1}, \mathbf{x}_{i2})$ (with intercepts, of course) for $t = 1, 2$. They define the partial effects in a way that mimics a representation of the partial effects in Chamberlain's correlated random effects (CRE) approach.

For quantile regression, CRE approaches are generically hampered because finding quantiles of sums of random variables is difficult. For example, suppose we impose the Mundlak representation $c_i = \psi_o + \bar{\mathbf{x}}_i \xi_o + a_i$. Then we can write $y_{it} = \psi_o + \mathbf{x}_{it}\boldsymbol{\theta}_o + \bar{\mathbf{x}}_i \xi_o + a_i + u_{it} \equiv y_{it} = \psi_o + \mathbf{x}_{it}\boldsymbol{\theta}_o + \bar{\mathbf{x}}_i \xi_o + v_{it}$, where v_{it} is the composite error. Now, if we assume v_{it} is independent of $\mathbf{x}_i$, then we can estimate $\boldsymbol{\theta}_o$ and ξ_o using pooled quantile regression of y_{it} on 1, $\mathbf{x}_{it}$, and $\bar{\mathbf{x}}_i$. (The intercept does not estimate a quantity of particular interest.) But independence is very strong, and, if we truly believe it, then we probably believe all quantile functions are parallel. Of course, we can always just assert that the effect of interest is the set of coefficients on $\mathbf{x}_{it}$ in the pooled quantile estimation, and we allow these, along with the intercept and coefficients on $\bar{\mathbf{x}}_i$, to change across quantiles. The asymptotic variance matrix estimator discussed for pooled quantile regression applies directly once we define the explanatory variables at time t to be $(1, \mathbf{x}_{it}, \bar{\mathbf{x}}_i)$.

We have more flexibility if we are interested in the median, and a few simple approaches suggest themselves. Write the model $\mathrm{Med}(y_{it} \mid \mathbf{x}_i, c_i) = \mathrm{Med}(y_{it} \mid \mathbf{x}_{it}, c_i) = \mathbf{x}_{it}\boldsymbol{\theta}_o + c_i$ in error form as

$$y_{it} = \mathbf{x}_{it}\boldsymbol{\theta}_o + c_i + u_{it}, \qquad \mathrm{Med}(u_{it} \mid \mathbf{x}_i, c_i) = 0, \qquad t = 1, \ldots, T,$$

and consider the multivariate conditional distribution $\mathrm{D}(\mathbf{u}_i \mid \mathbf{x}_i)$. If this distribution is symmetric about zero in the sense that $\mathrm{D}(\mathbf{u}_i \mid \mathbf{x}_i) = \mathrm{D}(-\mathbf{u}_i \mid \mathbf{x}_i)$—which is sometimes called *centrally symmetric*—then the distribution of $\mathbf{g}'\mathbf{u}_i$ given $\mathbf{x}_i$ is symmetric about zero for any linear combination $\mathbf{g}$ (see, for example, Serfling (2006) for discussion). In particular, the time-demeaned errors $\ddot{u}_{it}$ have (univariate) conditional distributions symmetric about zero, which means we can consistently estimate $\boldsymbol{\theta}_o$ by applying **pooled least absolute deviations** to the time-demeaned equation $\ddot{y}_{it} = \ddot{\mathbf{x}}_{it}\boldsymbol{\theta}_o + \ddot{u}_{it}$, being sure to obtain fully robust standard errors by using equations (12.124) and (12.125) on the time-demeaned data.

Alternatively, under the centrally symmetric assumption, the difference in the errors, $\Delta u_{it} = u_{it} - u_{i,t-1}$, have symmetric distributions about zero, so one can apply pooled LAD to $\Delta y_{it} = \Delta \mathbf{x}_{it}\boldsymbol{\theta}_o + \Delta u_{it}$, $t = 2, \ldots, T$. From Honoré (1992) applied to the uncensored case, LAD on the first differences is consistent when $\{u_{it} : t = 1, \ldots, T\}$ is an i.i.d. sequence conditional on $(\mathbf{x}_i, c_i)$, even if the common distribution is not symmetric, and this may afford robustness for LAD on the first differences rather than on the time-demeaned data. (Interestingly, it follows from the discussion in Honoré (1992, Appendix 1) that when $T = 2$, applying LAD on the first differences is equivalent to estimating the c_i along with $\boldsymbol{\theta}_o$. So, in this case, there is no incidental parameters problem in estimating the c_i as long as $u_{i2} - u_{i1}$ has a symmetric distribution.) Although not an especially weak assumption, central symmetry of $\mathrm{D}(\mathbf{u}_i \mid \mathbf{x}_i)$ allows for serial dependence and heteroskedasticity in the u_{it} (both of which can depend on $\mathbf{x}_i$ or on t). As always, we should be cautious in comparing the pooled OLS and pooled LAD estimates of $\boldsymbol{\theta}_o$ on the demeaned or differenced data because they are only expected to be similar under the conditional symmetry assumption.

If we impose the Mundlak device, we can get by with conditional symmetry of a sequence of bivariate distributions. Write $y_{it} = \psi_o + \mathbf{x}_{it}\boldsymbol{\theta}_o + \bar{\mathbf{x}}_i\xi_o + a_i + u_{it}$, where $\mathrm{Med}(u_{it} \mid \mathbf{x}_i, a_i) = 0$. If $\mathrm{D}(a_i, u_{it} \mid \mathbf{x}_i)$ has a symmetric distribution around zero, then $\mathrm{D}(a_i + u_{it} \mid \mathbf{x}_i)$ is symmetric about zero, and, if this holds for each t, pooled LAD of y_{it} on 1, $\mathbf{x}_{it}$, and $\bar{\mathbf{x}}_i$ consistently estimates $(\psi_o, \boldsymbol{\theta}_o, \xi_o)$. (Therefore, we can estimate the partial effects on $\mathrm{Med}(y_{it} \mid \mathbf{x}_{it}, c_i)$ and also test if c_i is correlated with $\bar{\mathbf{x}}_i$.) The assumptions used for this approach are not as weak as we would like, but, as in using pooled LAD on the time-demeaned data, adding $\bar{\mathbf{x}}_i$ to pooled LAD gives a way to compare with the usual FE estimate of $\boldsymbol{\theta}_o$. (Remember, if we use pooled OLS with $\bar{\mathbf{x}}_i$ included, we obtain the FE estimate.) Fully robust inference can be obtained by computing $\hat{\mathbf{B}}$ and $\hat{\mathbf{A}}$ in (12.124) and (12.125), respectively.

Problems

12.1. a. Use equation (12.4) to show that $\boldsymbol{\theta}_o$ minimizes $\mathrm{E}\{[y - m(\mathbf{x}, \boldsymbol{\theta})]^2 \mid \mathbf{x}\}$ over Θ for any $\mathbf{x}$.

b. Explain why the result in part a is stronger than stating that $\boldsymbol{\theta}_o$ solves problem (12.3).

12.2. Consider the model $\mathrm{E}(y \mid \mathbf{x}) = m(\mathbf{x}, \boldsymbol{\theta}_o)$, $\mathrm{Var}(y \mid \mathbf{x}) = \exp(\alpha_o + \mathbf{x}\boldsymbol{\gamma}_o)$, where $\mathbf{x}$ is $1 \times K$. The vector $\boldsymbol{\theta}_o$ is $P \times 1$ and $\boldsymbol{\gamma}_o$ is $K \times 1$.

a. Define $u \equiv y - \mathrm{E}(y \mid \mathbf{x})$. Show that $\mathrm{E}(u^2 \mid \mathbf{x}) = \exp(\alpha_o + \mathbf{x}\boldsymbol{\gamma}_o)$.

b. Let $\hat{u}_i$ denote the residuals from estimating the conditional mean by NLS. Argue that α_o and $\boldsymbol{\gamma}_o$ can be consistently estimated by a nonlinear regression where $\hat{u}_i^2$ is the dependent variable and the regression function is $\exp(\alpha_o + \mathbf{x}\boldsymbol{\gamma}_o)$. (Hint: Use the results on two-step estimation.)

c. Using part b, propose a (feasible) weighted least squares procedure for estimating $\boldsymbol{\theta}_o$.

d. If the error u is divided by $[\mathrm{Var}(u \mid \mathbf{x})]^{1/2}$, we obtain $v \equiv \exp[-(\alpha_o + \mathbf{x}\boldsymbol{\gamma}_o)/2]u$. Argue that if v is independent of $\mathbf{x}$, then $\boldsymbol{\gamma}_o$ is consistently estimated from the regression $\log(\hat{u}_i^2)$ on 1, $\mathbf{x}_i$, $i = 1, 2, \ldots, N$. (The intercept from this regression will not consistently estimate α_o, but this fact does not matter, since $\exp(\alpha_o + \mathbf{x}\boldsymbol{\gamma}_o) = \sigma_o^2 \exp(\mathbf{x}\boldsymbol{\gamma}_o)$, and σ_o^2 can be estimated from the WNLS regression.)

e. What would you do after running WNLS if you suspect the variance function is misspecified?

12.3. Consider the exponential regression function $m(\mathbf{x}, \boldsymbol{\theta}) = \exp(\mathbf{x}\boldsymbol{\theta})$, where $\mathbf{x}$ is $1 \times K$.

a. Suppose you have estimated a special case of the model, $\hat{\mathrm{E}}(y \mid \mathbf{z}) = \exp[\hat{\theta}_1 + \hat{\theta}_2 \log(z_1) + \hat{\theta}_3 z_2]$, where z_1 and z_2 are the conditioning variables. Show that $\hat{\theta}_2$ is approximately the elasticity of $\hat{\mathrm{E}}(y \mid \mathbf{z})$ with respect to z_1.

b. In the same estimated model from part a, how would you approximate the percentage change in $\hat{\mathrm{E}}(y \mid \mathbf{z})$ given $\Delta z_2 = 1$?

c. Now suppose a square of z_2 is added: $\hat{\mathrm{E}}(y \mid \mathbf{z}) = \exp[\hat{\theta}_1 + \hat{\theta}_2 \log(z_1) + \hat{\theta}_3 z_2 + \hat{\theta}_4 z_2^2]$, where $\hat{\theta}_3 > 0$ and $\hat{\theta}_4 < 0$. How would you compute the value of z_2 where the partial effect of z_2 on $\hat{\mathrm{E}}(y \mid \mathbf{z})$ becomes negative?

d. Now write the general model as $\exp(\mathbf{x}\boldsymbol{\theta}) = \exp(\mathbf{x}_1\boldsymbol{\theta}_1 + \mathbf{x}_2\boldsymbol{\theta}_2)$, where $\mathbf{x}_1$ is $1 \times K_1$ (and probably contains unity as an element) and $\mathbf{x}_2$ is $1 \times K_2$. Derive the usual (nonrobust) and heteroskedasticity-robust LM tests of $\mathrm{H}_0 : \boldsymbol{\theta}_{o2} = \mathbf{0}$, where $\boldsymbol{\theta}_o$ indexes $\mathrm{E}(y \mid \mathbf{x})$.

12.4. a. Show that the score for WNLS is $\mathbf{s}_i(\boldsymbol{\theta}; \boldsymbol{\gamma}) = -\nabla_\theta m(\mathbf{x}_i, \boldsymbol{\theta})' u_i(\boldsymbol{\theta}) / h(\mathbf{x}_i, \boldsymbol{\gamma})$.

b. Show that, under Assumption WNLS.1, $\mathrm{E}[\mathbf{s}_i(\boldsymbol{\theta}_o; \boldsymbol{\gamma}) \mid \mathbf{x}_i] = \mathbf{0}$ for any value of $\boldsymbol{\gamma}$.

c. Show that, under Assumption WNLS.1, $\mathrm{E}[\nabla_\gamma \mathbf{s}_i(\boldsymbol{\theta}_o; \boldsymbol{\gamma})] = \mathbf{0}$ for any value of $\boldsymbol{\gamma}$.

d. How would you estimate $\mathrm{Avar}(\hat{\boldsymbol{\theta}})$ without Assumption WNLS.3?

e. Verify that equation (12.59) is valid under Assumption WNLS.3.

12.5. a. For the regression model

$$m(\mathbf{x}, \boldsymbol{\theta}) = G[\mathbf{x}\boldsymbol{\beta} + \delta_1(\mathbf{x}\boldsymbol{\beta})^2 + \delta_2(\mathbf{x}\boldsymbol{\beta})^3],$$

where $G(\cdot)$ is a known, twice continuously differentiable function with derivative $g(\cdot)$, derive the standard LM test of H_0: $\delta_{o2} = 0$, $\delta_{o3} = 0$ using NLS. Show that, when $G(\cdot)$ is the identity function, the test reduces to RESET from Section 6.2.3.

b. Explain how to implement the variable addition version of the test.

12.6. Consider a panel data model for a random draw i from the population:

$$y_{it} = m(\mathbf{x}_{it}, \boldsymbol{\theta}_o) + u_{it}, \qquad \mathrm{E}(u_{it} \mid \mathbf{x}_{it}) = 0, \qquad t = 1, \ldots, T.$$

a. If you apply pooled nonlinear least squares to estimate $\boldsymbol{\theta}_o$, how would you estimate its asymptotic variance without further assumptions?

b. Suppose that the model is dynamically complete in the conditional mean, so that $\mathrm{E}(u_{it} \mid \mathbf{x}_{it}, u_{i,t-1}, \mathbf{x}_{i,t-1}, \ldots) = 0$ for all t. In addition, $\mathrm{E}(u_{it}^2 \mid \mathbf{x}_{it}) = \sigma_o^2$. Show that the usual statistics from a pooled NLS regression are valid. (Hint: The objective function for each i is $q_i(\boldsymbol{\theta}) = \sum_{t=1}^{T} [y_{it} - m(\mathbf{x}_{it}, \boldsymbol{\theta})]^2/2$ and the score is $\mathbf{s}_i(\boldsymbol{\theta}) = -\sum_{t=1}^{T} \nabla_\theta m(\mathbf{x}_{it}, \boldsymbol{\theta})' u_{it}(\boldsymbol{\theta})$. Now show that $\mathbf{B}_o = \sigma_o^2 \mathbf{A}_o$ and that σ_o^2 is consistently estimated by $(NT - P)^{-1} \sum_{i=1}^{N} \sum_{t=1}^{T} \hat{u}_{it}^2$.)

c. For the mean model $m(\mathbf{x}_{it}, \boldsymbol{\beta}, \boldsymbol{\delta})$, consider testing $\mathrm{H}_0 : \boldsymbol{\delta}_o = \bar{\boldsymbol{\delta}}$. Show that under dynamic completeness and homoskedasticity (under H_0), a valid version of the LM statistic is obtained as NTR_u^2 where R_u^2 is the uncentered R-squared from the pooled OLS regresssion

$$\tilde{u}_{it} \text{ on } \nabla_\beta \tilde{m}_{it}, \nabla_\delta \tilde{m}_{it}, \qquad t = 1, \ldots, T;\ i = 1, \ldots, N,$$

where $\tilde{u}_{it} = y_{it} - m(\mathbf{x}_{it}, \tilde{\boldsymbol{\beta}}, \bar{\boldsymbol{\delta}})$ and the gradients are evaluated at $(\tilde{\boldsymbol{\beta}}, \bar{\boldsymbol{\delta}})$.

12.7. Consider a nonlinear analogue of the SUR system from Chapter 7:

$$\mathrm{E}(y_{ig} \mid \mathbf{x}_i) = \mathrm{E}(y_{ig} \mid \mathbf{x}_{ig}) = m_g(\mathbf{x}_{ig}, \boldsymbol{\theta}_{og}), \qquad g = 1, \ldots, G.$$

Thus, each $\boldsymbol{\theta}_{og}$ can be estimated by NLS using only equation g; call these $\check{\boldsymbol{\theta}}_g$. Suppose also that $\mathrm{Var}(\mathbf{y}_i \mid \mathbf{x}_i) = \boldsymbol{\Omega}_o$, where $\boldsymbol{\Omega}_o$ is $G \times G$ and positive definite.

a. Explain how to consistently estimate $\boldsymbol{\Omega}_o$ (as usual, with G fixed and $N \to \infty$). Call this estimator $\hat{\boldsymbol{\Omega}}$.

b. Let $\hat{\boldsymbol{\theta}}$ be the nonlinear SUR estimator that solves

$$\min_{\boldsymbol{\theta}} \sum_{i=1}^{N} [\mathbf{y}_i - \mathbf{m}(\mathbf{x}_i, \boldsymbol{\theta})]' \hat{\boldsymbol{\Omega}}^{-1} [\mathbf{y}_i - \mathbf{m}(\mathbf{x}_i, \boldsymbol{\theta})]/2,$$

where $\mathbf{m}(\mathbf{x}_i, \boldsymbol{\theta})$ is the $G \times 1$ vector of conditional mean functions and $\mathbf{y}_i$ is $G \times 1$. Show that

$$\mathrm{Avar}\, \sqrt{N}(\hat{\boldsymbol{\theta}} - \boldsymbol{\theta}_o) = \{\mathrm{E}[\nabla_\theta \mathbf{m}(\mathbf{x}_i, \boldsymbol{\theta}_o)' \boldsymbol{\Omega}_o^{-1} \nabla_\theta \mathbf{m}(\mathbf{x}_i, \boldsymbol{\theta}_o)]\}^{-1}.$$

(Hint: Under standard regularity conditions, $N^{-1/2} \sum_{i=1}^{N} \nabla_\theta \mathbf{m}(\mathbf{x}_i, \boldsymbol{\theta}_o)' \hat{\boldsymbol{\Omega}}^{-1} [\mathbf{y}_i - \mathbf{m}(\mathbf{x}_i, \boldsymbol{\theta}_o)] = N^{-1/2} \sum_{i=1}^{N} \nabla_\theta \mathbf{m}(\mathbf{x}_i, \boldsymbol{\theta}_o)' \boldsymbol{\Omega}_o^{-1} [\mathbf{y}_i - \mathbf{m}(\mathbf{x}_i, \boldsymbol{\theta}_o)] + o_p(1)$.)

c. How would you estimate $\mathrm{Avar}(\hat{\boldsymbol{\theta}})$?

d. If $\boldsymbol{\Omega}_o$ is diagonal and if the assumptions stated previously hold, show that NLS equation by equation is just as asymptotically efficient as the nonlinear SUR estimator.

e. Is there a nonlinear analogue of Theorem 7.7 for linear systems in the sense that nonlinear SUR and NLS equation by equation are asymptotically equivalent when the same explanatory variables appear in each equation? (Hint: When would $\nabla_\theta \mathbf{m}(\mathbf{x}_i, \boldsymbol{\theta}_o)$ have the form needed to apply the hint in Problem 7.5? You might try $E(y_g \mid \mathbf{x}) = \exp(\mathbf{x}\boldsymbol{\theta}_{og})$ for all g as an example.)

12.8. Consider the M-estimator with estimated nuisance parameter $\hat{\gamma}$, where $\sqrt{N}(\hat{\gamma} - \gamma_o) = O_p(1)$. If assumption (12.37) holds under the null hypothesis, show that the QLR statistic still has a limiting chi-square distribution, assuming also that $\mathbf{A}_o = \mathbf{B}_o$. (Hint: Start from equation (12.76) but where $\sqrt{N}(\tilde{\boldsymbol{\theta}} - \hat{\boldsymbol{\theta}}) = \mathbf{A}_o^{-1} N^{-1/2} \cdot \sum_{i=1}^N \mathbf{s}_i(\tilde{\boldsymbol{\theta}}; \hat{\gamma}) + o_p(1)$. Now use a mean value expansion of the score about $(\tilde{\boldsymbol{\theta}}, \gamma_o)$ to show that $\sqrt{N}(\tilde{\boldsymbol{\theta}} - \hat{\boldsymbol{\theta}}) = \mathbf{A}_o^{-1} N^{-1/2} \sum_{i=1}^N \mathbf{s}_i(\tilde{\boldsymbol{\theta}}; \gamma_o) + o_p(1)$.)

12.9. For scalar y, suppose that $y = m(\mathbf{x}, \boldsymbol{\beta}_o) + u$, where $\mathbf{x}$ is a $1 \times K$ vector.

a. If $E(u \mid \mathbf{x}) = 0$, what can you say about $\text{Med}(y \mid \mathbf{x})$?

b. Suppose that u and $\mathbf{x}$ are independent. Show that $E(y \mid \mathbf{x}) - \text{Med}(y \mid \mathbf{x})$ does not depend on $\mathbf{x}$.

c. What does part b imply about $\partial E(y \mid \mathbf{x})/\partial x_j$ and $\partial \, \text{Med}(y \mid \mathbf{x})/\partial x_j$?

12.10. For each i, let y_i be a nonnegative integer with a conditional binomial distribution with upper bound n_i (a positive integer) and probability of success $p(\mathbf{x}_i, \boldsymbol{\beta}_o)$, where $0 < p(\mathbf{x}, \boldsymbol{\beta}) < 1$ for all $\mathbf{x}$ and $\boldsymbol{\beta}$. (A leading case is the logistic function.) Therefore, $E(y_i \mid \mathbf{x}_i, n_i) = n_i p(\mathbf{x}_i, \boldsymbol{\beta}_o)$ and $\text{Var}(y_i \mid \mathbf{x}_i, n_i) = n_i p(\mathbf{x}_i, \boldsymbol{\beta}_o)[1 - p(\mathbf{x}_i, \boldsymbol{\beta}_o)]$. Explain in detail how to obtain the weighted nonlinear least squares estimator of $\boldsymbol{\beta}_o$.

12.11. a. Derive equation (12.98) for the WMNLS estimator. You can use equation (12.97) to show that estimation of γ^* can be ignored in obtaining the limiting distribution of $\sqrt{N}(\hat{\boldsymbol{\theta}} - \boldsymbol{\theta}_o)$.

b. If assumption (12.96) holds (and $\hat{\gamma}$ is $\sqrt{N}$-consistent for γ_o), what is the asymptotic variance of $\sqrt{N}(\hat{\boldsymbol{\theta}} - \boldsymbol{\theta}_o)$?

c. Explain how you would compute the QLR statistic for testing hypotheses about $\boldsymbol{\theta}_o$ under assumption (12.96). Naturally, you should assume the mean is correctly specified.

12.12. Let y_i be a scalar response, and let $\mathbf{x}_i$ and $\mathbf{w}_i$ be vectors. Suppose that

$$E(y_i \mid \mathbf{x}_i, \mathbf{w}_i) = m(\mathbf{x}_i, \mathbf{v}(\mathbf{w}_i, \boldsymbol{\delta}_o), \boldsymbol{\theta}_o),$$

where $\mathbf{v}(\mathbf{w}, \boldsymbol{\delta})$ is a known function of $\mathbf{w}$ and the J parameters $\boldsymbol{\delta}$ and $\boldsymbol{\theta}_o$ are a $P \times 1$ vector. Assume that we have a $\sqrt{N}$-asymptotically normal estimator of $\boldsymbol{\delta}_o$ that satisfies

$$\sqrt{N}(\hat{\boldsymbol{\delta}} - \boldsymbol{\delta}_o) = N^{-1/2} \sum_{i=1}^{N} \mathbf{r}(\mathbf{w}_i, \boldsymbol{\delta}_o) + o_p(1).$$

Let $\hat{\boldsymbol{\theta}}$ be the two-step NLS estimator that solves

$$\min_{\theta \in \Theta} \sum_{i=1}^{N} [y_i - m(\mathbf{x}_i, \mathbf{v}(\mathbf{w}_i, \hat{\boldsymbol{\delta}}), \boldsymbol{\theta})]^2/2.$$

a. Show that, under standard regularity conditions, the asymptotic variance of $\sqrt{N}(\hat{\boldsymbol{\theta}} - \theta_o)$ is at least as large as the asymptotic variance if we knew $\boldsymbol{\delta}_o$.

b. Propose a consistent estimator of Avar $\sqrt{N}(\hat{\boldsymbol{\theta}} - \boldsymbol{\theta}_o)$.

12.13. Let $\{(\mathbf{x}_{it}, y_{it}) : t = 1, \ldots, T\}$ be a panel data set, and assume that for some $\boldsymbol{\theta}_o \in \boldsymbol{\Theta} \subset \mathbb{R}^P$, $\mathrm{E}(y_{it} \mid \mathbf{x}_{it}) = m(\mathbf{x}_{it}, \boldsymbol{\theta}_o)$, $t = 1, \ldots, T$. Further, let $h(\mathbf{x}_{it}, \gamma)$ be a model for $\mathrm{Var}(y_{it} \mid \mathbf{x}_{it})$ for each t. Generally, let $\hat{\gamma}$ be a $\sqrt{N}$-consistent estimator for some γ^*, where $h(\mathbf{x}_{it}, \gamma^*)$ need not equal $\mathrm{Var}(y_{it} \mid \mathbf{x}_{it})$.

a. Let $\hat{\boldsymbol{\theta}}$ denote the pooled weighted nonlinear least squares estimator. Is strict exogeneity of $\{\mathbf{x}_{it}\}$ needed for consistency of $\hat{\boldsymbol{\theta}}$ for $\boldsymbol{\theta}_o$? Explain.

b. Propose a consistent estimator of Avar $\sqrt{N}(\hat{\boldsymbol{\theta}} - \boldsymbol{\theta}_o)$ without further assumptions.

c. If the mean is dynamically complete, how would you estimate Avar $\sqrt{N}(\hat{\boldsymbol{\theta}} - \boldsymbol{\theta}_o)$?

d. If the mean is dynamically complete and $\mathrm{Var}(y_{it} \mid \mathbf{x}_{it}) = \sigma_o^2 h(\mathbf{x}_{it}, \gamma_o)$ and $\hat{\gamma}$ is $\sqrt{N}$-consistent for γ_o, how would you estimate Avar $\sqrt{N}(\hat{\boldsymbol{\theta}} - \boldsymbol{\theta}_o)$?

12.14. Derive equation (12.115). (Hint: The product of the two indicator functions appearing in $\mathbf{s}_i(\boldsymbol{\theta}_o)$ is identically zero.)

12.15. Let $\{(\mathbf{x}_{it}, y_{it}) : t = 1, \ldots, T\}$ be a panel data set and assume that, for a given quantile $0 < \tau < 1$, $\mathrm{Quant}_\tau(y_{it} \mid \mathbf{x}_{it}) = \mathbf{x}_{it}\boldsymbol{\theta}_o$, $t = 1, \ldots, T$. Let $\hat{\boldsymbol{\theta}}$ be the pooled quantile regression estimator discussed in Section 12.10.3.

a. Write down the approximate first-order condition solved by $\hat{\boldsymbol{\theta}}$. In particular, define a suitable "score" for each t and then for a random draw i.

b. Show that if the quantile is dynamically complete in the sense that

$$\mathrm{Quant}_\tau(y_{it} \mid \mathbf{x}_{it}, y_{i,t-1}, \mathbf{x}_{i,t-1}, \ldots, y_{i1}, \mathbf{x}_{i1}) = \mathrm{Quant}_\tau(y_{it} \mid \mathbf{x}_{it}) = \mathbf{x}_{it}\boldsymbol{\theta}_o, \qquad t = 1, \ldots, T,$$

then $\mathbf{B}_o \equiv \mathrm{E}[\mathbf{s}_i(\boldsymbol{\theta}_o)\mathbf{s}_i(\boldsymbol{\theta}_o)'] = \tau(1 - \tau) \sum_{t=1}^{T} \mathrm{E}(\mathbf{x}_{it}'\mathbf{x}_{it})$. How would you estimate $\mathbf{B}_o$ in this case?

c. Show that, whether or not the quantile is dynamically complete,

$$\mathbf{A}_o = \sum_{t=1}^{T} \mathrm{E}[f_{u_t}(0 \mid \mathbf{x}_{it})\mathbf{x}_{it}'\mathbf{x}_{it}],$$

where $f_{u_t}(\cdot \mid \mathbf{x}_t)$ is the density of u_{it} given $\mathbf{x}_{it} = \mathbf{x}_t$.

12.16. Consider a linear model with an endogenous explanatory variable, y_2, along with a reduced form for y_2:

$$y_1 = \mathbf{z}_1\boldsymbol{\delta}_1 + \alpha_1 y_2 + u_1$$

$$y_2 = \mathbf{z}\boldsymbol{\pi}_2 + v_2,$$

where $\mathbf{z} = (\mathbf{z}_1, \mathbf{z}_2)$ (with first element of $\mathbf{z}_1$ unity) and $\boldsymbol{\pi}_2 = (\boldsymbol{\pi}_{21}', \boldsymbol{\pi}_{22}')'$; for notational simplicity, we do not use "o" subscripts on the true parameters.

a. Under the assumption $\mathrm{Med}(v_2 \mid \mathbf{z}) = 0$, how would you estimate $\boldsymbol{\pi}_2$?

b. Suppose that $\mathrm{Med}(u_1 \mid y_2, \mathbf{z}) = \mathrm{Med}(u_1 \mid v_2) = \rho_1 v_2$. Propose a two-step consistent estimator of $\boldsymbol{\delta}_1$ and α_1.

c. How would you state the null hypothesis that y_2 is exogenous, and how would you test it?

d. Generally, how would you obtain legitimate standard errors for $\hat{\boldsymbol{\delta}}_1$ and $\hat{\alpha}_1$?

e. If the bivariate conditional distribution $\mathrm{D}(u_1, v_2 \mid \mathbf{z})$ satisfies the centrally symmetric condition $\mathrm{D}(u_1, v_2 \mid \mathbf{z}) = \mathrm{D}(-u_1, -v_2 \mid \mathbf{z})$ (and all variables have at least finite second moments), explain why we should expect the procedure from part b and the usual 2SLS estimator to provide similar estimates in large samples.

12.17. Let $\hat{\boldsymbol{\theta}}$ be an M-estimator of $\boldsymbol{\theta}_o$ with score $\mathbf{s}_i(\boldsymbol{\theta}) \equiv \mathbf{s}(\mathbf{w}_i, \boldsymbol{\theta})$ and expected Hessian $\mathbf{A}_o$ (evaluated at $\boldsymbol{\theta}_o$). Let $\mathbf{g}(\mathbf{w}, \boldsymbol{\theta})$ be an $M \times 1$ function of the random vector $\mathbf{w}$ and the parameter vector, and suppose we wish to estimate $\boldsymbol{\delta}_0 \equiv \mathrm{E}[\mathbf{g}(\mathbf{w}_i, \boldsymbol{\theta}_o)]$. The natural estimator is $\hat{\boldsymbol{\delta}} \equiv N^{-1}\sum_{i=1}^{N} \mathbf{g}(\mathbf{w}_i, \hat{\boldsymbol{\theta}})$. Assume that $\sqrt{N}(\hat{\boldsymbol{\theta}} - \boldsymbol{\theta}_o) \xrightarrow{d} \mathrm{Normal}(\mathbf{0}, \mathbf{A}_o^{-1}\mathbf{B}_o\mathbf{A}_o^{-1})$ where $\mathbf{B}_o \equiv \mathrm{E}[\mathbf{s}_i(\boldsymbol{\theta}_o)\mathbf{s}_i(\boldsymbol{\theta}_o)']$, as usual.

a. Assuming that $\mathbf{g}(\mathbf{w}, \cdot)$ is continuously differentiable on $\mathrm{int}(\boldsymbol{\Theta})$, $\boldsymbol{\theta}_o \in \mathrm{int}(\boldsymbol{\Theta})$, and other regularity conditions, find $\mathrm{Avar}\,\sqrt{N}(\hat{\boldsymbol{\delta}} - \boldsymbol{\delta}_o)$. (Hint: The asymptotic variance depends on $\boldsymbol{\delta}_o$ and $\mathbf{G}_o \equiv \mathrm{E}[\nabla_{\boldsymbol{\theta}}\mathbf{g}(\mathbf{w}_i, \boldsymbol{\theta}_o)]$.)

b. How would you consistently estimate $\mathrm{Avar}\,\sqrt{N}(\hat{\boldsymbol{\delta}} - \boldsymbol{\delta}_o)$?

c. Show that if $\mathbf{g}(\mathbf{w}, \boldsymbol{\theta}) = \mathbf{g}(\mathbf{x}, \boldsymbol{\theta})$, where $\mathbf{x}$ is exogenous in the estimation problem used to obtain $\hat{\boldsymbol{\theta}}$ (so that $\mathrm{E}[\mathbf{s}(\mathbf{w}_i, \boldsymbol{\theta}_o) \mid \mathbf{x}_i] = \mathbf{0}$), then $\mathrm{Avar}\,\sqrt{N}(\hat{\boldsymbol{\delta}} - \boldsymbol{\delta}_o) = \mathrm{Var}[\mathbf{g}(\mathbf{x}_i, \boldsymbol{\theta}_o)] + \mathbf{G}_o[\mathrm{Avar}\,\sqrt{N}(\hat{\boldsymbol{\theta}} - \boldsymbol{\theta}_o)]\mathbf{G}_o'$.

13 Maximum Likelihood Methods

13.1 Introduction

This chapter contains a general treatment of maximum likelihood estimation (MLE) under random sampling. All the models we considered in Part I could be estimated without making full distributional assumptions about the endogenous variables conditional on the exogenous variables: maximum likelihood methods were not needed. Instead, we focused primarily on zero-covariance and zero-conditional-mean assumptions, and secondarily on assumptions about conditional variances and covariances. These assumptions were sufficient for obtaining consistent, asymptotically normal estimators, some of which were shown to be efficient within certain classes of estimators.

Some texts on advanced econometrics take MLE as the unifying theme, and then most models are estimated by maximum likelihood. In addition to providing a unified approach to estimation, MLE has some desirable efficiency properties: it is generally the most efficient estimation procedure in the class of estimators that use information on the distribution of the endogenous variables given the exogenous variables. (We formalize the efficiency of MLE in Section 14.4.) So why not always use MLE?

As we saw in Part I, efficiency usually comes at the price of nonrobustness, and this is certainly the case for maximum likelihood. Maximum likelihood estimators are generally inconsistent if some part of the specified distribution is misspecified. As an example, consider from Section 9.5 a simultaneous equations model that is linear in its parameters but nonlinear in some endogenous variables. There, we discussed estimation by instrumental variables methods. We could estimate SEMs nonlinear in endogenous variables by maximum likelihood if we assumed independence between the structural errors and the exogenous variables and if we assumed a particular distribution for the structural errors, say, multivariate normal. The MLE would be asymptotically more efficient than the best GMM estimator, but failure of normality generally results in inconsistent estimators of all parameters.

As a second example, suppose we wish to estimate $\mathrm{E}(y \mid \mathbf{x})$, where y is bounded between zero and one. The logistic function, $\exp(\mathbf{x}\boldsymbol{\beta})/[1+\exp(\mathbf{x}\boldsymbol{\beta})]$, is a reasonable model for $\mathrm{E}(y \mid \mathbf{x})$, and, as we discussed in Chapter 12, nonlinear least squares provides consistent, $\sqrt{N}$-asymptotically normal estimators under weak regularity conditions. We can easily make inference robust to arbitrary heteroskedasticity in $\mathrm{Var}(y \mid \mathbf{x})$. An alternative approach is to model the density of y given $\mathbf{x}$—which, of course, implies a particular model for $\mathrm{E}(y \mid \mathbf{x})$—and use MLE. As we will see, the strength of MLE is that, under correct specification of the density, we would have the asymptotically efficient estimators, and we would be able to estimate any feature of the conditional distribution, such as $\mathrm{P}(y = 1 \mid \mathbf{x})$. The drawback is that, except in special cases, if we have misspecified the density in any way, we will not be able to consistently estimate the conditional mean.

In most applications, specifying the distribution of the endogenous variables conditional on exogenous variables must have a component of arbitrariness, as economic theory rarely provides guidance. Our perspective is that, for robustness reasons, it is desirable to make as few assumptions as possible—at least until relaxing them becomes practically difficult. There *are* cases in which MLE turns out to be robust to failure of certain assumptions, but these must be examined on a case-by-case basis, a process that detracts from the unifying theme provided by the MLE approach. (One such example is nonlinear regression under a homoskedastic normal assumption; the MLE of the parameters $\boldsymbol{\beta}_o$ is identical to the NLS estimator, and we know the latter is consistent and asymptotically normal quite generally. We will cover some other leading cases in Section 13.11 and Chapter 18.)

Maximum likelihood plays an important role in modern econometric analysis, for good reason. There are many problems for which it is indispensable. For example, in Chapters 15, 16, and 17 we study various limited dependent variable models, and MLE plays a central role.

13.2 Preliminaries and Examples

Traditional maximum likelihood theory for independent, identically distributed observations $\{\mathbf{y}_i \in \mathbb{R}^G : i = 1, 2, \ldots\}$ starts by specifying a family of densities for $\mathbf{y}_i$. This is the framework used in introductory statistics courses, where $\mathbf{y}_i$ is a scalar with a normal or Poisson distribution. But in almost all economic applications, we are interested in estimating parameters of *conditional* distributions. Therefore, we assume that each random draw is partitioned as $(\mathbf{x}_i, \mathbf{y}_i)$, where $\mathbf{x}_i \in \mathbb{R}^K$ and $\mathbf{y}_i \in \mathbb{R}^G$, and we are interested in estimating a model for the conditional distribution of $\mathbf{y}_i$ given $\mathbf{x}_i$. We are not interested in the distribution of $\mathbf{x}_i$, so we will not specify a model for it. Consequently, the method of this chapter is properly called **conditional maximum likelihood estimation (CMLE)**. By taking $\mathbf{x}_i$ to be null we cover unconditional MLE as a special case.

An alternative to viewing $(\mathbf{x}_i, \mathbf{y}_i)$ as a random draw from the population is to treat the conditioning variables $\mathbf{x}_i$ as *nonrandom* vectors that are set ahead of time and that appear in the unconditional distribution of $\mathbf{y}_i$. (This setup is analogous to the fixed regressor assumption in classical regression analysis.) Then the $\mathbf{y}_i$ cannot be identically distributed, and this fact complicates the asymptotic analysis. More important, treating the $\mathbf{x}_i$ as nonrandom is much too restrictive for all uses of maximum likelihood. In fact, later on we will cover methods where $\mathbf{x}_i$ contains what are endogenous variables in a structural model, but where it is convenient to obtain the distribution of one set of endogenous variables conditional on another set. Once we know how to analyze the general CMLE case, applications follow fairly directly.

It is important to understand that the subsequent results apply any time we have random sampling in the cross section dimension. Thus, the general theory applies to system estimation, as in Chapters 7 and 9, provided we are willing to assume a distribution for $\mathbf{y}_i$ given $\mathbf{x}_i$. In addition, panel data settings with large cross sections and relatively small time periods are encompassed, since the appropriate asymptotic analysis is with the time dimension fixed and the cross section dimension tending to infinity.

In order to perform maximum likelihood analysis we need to specify, or derive from an underlying (structural) model, the density of $\mathbf{y}_i$ given $\mathbf{x}_i$. We assume this density is known up to a finite number of unknown parameters, with the result that we have a **parametric model** of a conditional density. The vector $\mathbf{y}_i$ can be continuous or discrete, or it can have both discrete and continuous characteristics. In many of our applications, $\mathbf{y}_i$ is a scalar, but this feature does not simplify the general treatment.

We will carry along two examples to illustrate the general theory of conditional maximum likelihood. The first example is a **binary response model**, specifically the **probit model**. We postpone the uses and interepretation of binary response models until Chapter 15.

Example 13.1 (Probit): Suppose that the **latent variable** y_i^* follows

$$y_i^* = \mathbf{x}_i\boldsymbol{\theta} + e_i \tag{13.1}$$

where e_i is *independent* of $\mathbf{x}_i$ (which is a $1 \times K$ vector with first element equal to unity for all i), $\boldsymbol{\theta}$ is a $K \times 1$ vector of parameters, and $e_i \sim \text{Normal}(0,1)$. Instead of observing y_i^*, we observe only a binary variable indicating the sign of y_i^*:

$$y_i = \begin{cases} 1 & \text{if } y_i^* > 0 \quad (13.2) \\ 0 & \text{if } y_i^* \leq 0 \quad (13.3) \end{cases}$$

To be succinct, it is useful to write equations (13.2) and (13.3) in terms of the indicator function, denoted $1[\cdot]$. Recall that this function is unity whenever the statement in brackets is true, and zero otherwise. Thus, equations (13.2) and (13.3) are equivalently written as $y_i = 1[y_i^* > 0]$. Because e_i is normally distributed, it is irrelevant whether the strict inequality is in equation (13.2) or (13.3).

We can easily obtain the distribution of y_i given $\mathbf{x}_i$:

$$\begin{aligned} \mathrm{P}(y_i = 1 \mid \mathbf{x}_i) &= \mathrm{P}(y_i^* > 0 \mid \mathbf{x}_i) = \mathrm{P}(\mathbf{x}_i\boldsymbol{\theta} + e_i > 0 \mid \mathbf{x}_i) \\ &= \mathrm{P}(e_i > -\mathbf{x}_i\boldsymbol{\theta} \mid \mathbf{x}_i) = 1 - \Phi(-\mathbf{x}_i\boldsymbol{\theta}) = \Phi(\mathbf{x}_i\boldsymbol{\theta}), \end{aligned} \tag{13.4}$$

where $\Phi(\cdot)$ denotes the standard normal cumulative distribution function (cdf). We have used Property CD.4 in the chapter appendix along with the symmetry of the normal distribution. Therefore,

$$\mathrm{P}(y_i = 0 \mid \mathbf{x}_i) = 1 - \Phi(\mathbf{x}_i\boldsymbol{\theta}). \tag{13.5}$$

We can combine equations (13.4) and (13.5) into the density of y_i given $\mathbf{x}_i$:

$$f(y \mid \mathbf{x}_i) = [\Phi(\mathbf{x}_i\boldsymbol{\theta})]^y [1 - \Phi(\mathbf{x}_i\boldsymbol{\theta})]^{1-y}, \qquad y = 0, 1. \tag{13.6}$$

That $f(y \mid \mathbf{x}_i)$ is zero when $y \notin \{0, 1\}$ is obvious, so we will not be explicit about this in the future.

Our second example is useful when the variable to be explained takes on nonnegative integer values. Such a variable is called a **count variable**. We will discuss the use and interpretation of count data models in Chapter 18. For now, it suffices to note that a linear model for $\mathrm{E}(y \mid \mathbf{x})$ when y takes on nonnegative integer values is not ideal because it can lead to negative predicted values. Further, since y can take on the value zero with positive probability, the transformation $\log(y)$ cannot be used to obtain a model with constant elasticities or constant semielasticities. A functional form well suited for $\mathrm{E}(y \mid \mathbf{x})$ is $\exp(\mathbf{x}\boldsymbol{\theta})$. We could estimate $\boldsymbol{\theta}$ by using NLS, but all of the standard distributions for count variables imply heteroskedasticity (see Chapter 18). Thus, we can hope to do better. A traditional approach to regression models with count data is to assume that y_i given $\mathbf{x}_i$ has a Poisson distribution.

Example 13.2 (Poisson Regression): Let y_i be a nonnegative count variable; that is, y_i can take on integer values $0, 1, 2, \ldots$. Denote the conditional mean of y_i given the vector $\mathbf{x}_i$ as $\mathrm{E}(y_i \mid \mathbf{x}_i) = \mu(\mathbf{x}_i)$. A natural distribution for y_i given $\mathbf{x}_i$ is the Poisson distribution:

$$f(y \mid \mathbf{x}_i) = \exp[-\mu(\mathbf{x}_i)]\{\mu(\mathbf{x}_i)\}^y / y!, \qquad y = 0, 1, 2, \ldots. \tag{13.7}$$

(We use y as the dummy argument in the density, not to be confused with the random variable y_i.) Once we choose a form for the conditional mean function, we have completely determined the distribution of y_i given $\mathbf{x}_i$. For example, from equation (13.7), $\mathrm{P}(y_i = 0 \mid \mathbf{x}_i) = \exp[-\mu(\mathbf{x}_i)]$. An important feature of the Poisson distribution is that the variance equals the mean: $\mathrm{Var}(y_i \mid \mathbf{x}_i) = \mathrm{E}(y_i \mid \mathbf{x}_i) = \mu(\mathbf{x}_i)$. The usual choice for $\mu(\cdot)$ is $\mu(\mathbf{x}) = \exp(\mathbf{x}\boldsymbol{\theta})$, where $\boldsymbol{\theta}$ is $K \times 1$ and $\mathbf{x}$ is $1 \times K$ with first element unity.

13.3 General Framework for Conditional Maximum Likelihood Estimation

Let $p_o(\mathbf{y} \mid \mathbf{x})$ denote the conditional density of $\mathbf{y}_i$ given $\mathbf{x}_i = \mathbf{x}$, where $\mathbf{y}$ and $\mathbf{x}$ are dummy arguments. We index this density by "o" to emphasize that it is the true density of $\mathbf{y}_i$ given $\mathbf{x}_i$, and not just one of many candidates. It will be useful to let $\mathcal{X} \subset \mathbb{R}^K$ denote the possible values for $\mathbf{x}_i$ and $\mathcal{Y}$ denote the possible values of $\mathbf{y}_i$; $\mathcal{X}$ and $\mathcal{Y}$ are called the *supports* of the random vectors $\mathbf{x}_i$ and $\mathbf{y}_i$, respectively.

For a general treatment, we assume that, for all $\mathbf{x} \in \mathcal{X}$, $p_o(\cdot \mid \mathbf{x})$ is a density with respect to a *σ-finite measure*, denoted $\nu(d\mathbf{y})$. Defining a σ-finite measure would take us too far afield. We will say little more about the measure $\nu(d\mathbf{y})$ because it does not play a crucial role in applications. It suffices to know that $\nu(d\mathbf{y})$ can be chosen to allow $\mathbf{y}_i$ to be discrete, continuous, or some mixture of the two. When $\mathbf{y}_i$ is discrete, the measure $\nu(d\mathbf{y})$ simply turns all integrals into sums; when $\mathbf{y}_i$ is purely continuous, we obtain the usual Riemann integrals. Even in more complicated cases—where, say, $\mathbf{y}_i$ has both discrete and continuous characteristics—we can get by with tools from basic probability without ever explicitly defining $\nu(d\mathbf{y})$. For more on measures and general integrals, you are referred to Billingsley (1979) and Davidson (1994, Chaps. 3 and 4).

In Chapter 12 we saw how NLS can be motivated by the fact that $\mu_o(\mathbf{x}) \equiv \mathrm{E}(y \mid \mathbf{x})$ minimizes $\mathrm{E}\{[y - m(\mathbf{x})]^2\}$ for all other functions $m(\mathbf{x})$ with $\mathrm{E}\{[m(\mathbf{x})]^2\} < \infty$. Conditional maximum likelihood has a similar motivation. The result from probability that is crucial for applying the analogy principle is the **conditional Kullback-Leibler information inequality.** Although there are more general statements of this inequality, the following suffices for our purpose: for any nonnegative function $f(\cdot \mid \mathbf{x})$ such that

$$\int_{\mathcal{Y}} f(\mathbf{y} \mid \mathbf{x}) \nu(d\mathbf{y}) = 1, \qquad \text{all } \mathbf{x} \in \mathcal{X}, \tag{13.8}$$

Property CD.1 in the chapter appendix implies that

$$\mathcal{K}(f; \mathbf{x}) \equiv \int_{\mathcal{Y}} \log[p_o(\mathbf{y} \mid \mathbf{x}) / f(\mathbf{y} \mid \mathbf{x})] p_o(\mathbf{y} \mid \mathbf{x}) \nu(d\mathbf{y}) \geq 0, \qquad \text{all } \mathbf{x} \in \mathcal{X}. \tag{13.9}$$

Because the integral is identically zero for $f = p_o$, expression (13.9) says that, for each $\mathbf{x}$, $\mathscr{K}(f;\mathbf{x})$ is minimized at $f = p_o$.

We can apply inequality (13.9) to a parametric model for $p_o(\cdot \mid \mathbf{x})$,

$$\{f(\cdot \mid \mathbf{x};\boldsymbol{\theta}),\ \boldsymbol{\theta} \in \boldsymbol{\Theta},\ \boldsymbol{\Theta} \subset \mathbb{R}^P\}, \tag{13.10}$$

which we assume satisfies condition (13.8) for each $\mathbf{x} \in \mathscr{X}$ and each $\boldsymbol{\theta} \in \boldsymbol{\Theta}$; if it does not, then $f(\cdot \mid \mathbf{x};\boldsymbol{\theta})$ does not integrate to unity (with respect to the measure ν), and as a result it is a very poor candidate for $p_o(\mathbf{y} \mid \mathbf{x})$. Model (13.10) is a **correctly specified model of the conditional density**, $p_o(\cdot \mid \cdot)$, if, for some $\boldsymbol{\theta}_o \in \boldsymbol{\Theta}$,

$$f(\cdot \mid \mathbf{x};\boldsymbol{\theta}_o) = p_o(\cdot \mid \mathbf{x}), \qquad \text{all } \mathbf{x} \in \mathscr{X}. \tag{13.11}$$

As we discussed in Chapter 12, it is useful to use $\boldsymbol{\theta}_o$ to distinguish the true value of the parameter from a generic element of $\boldsymbol{\Theta}$. In particular examples, we will not bother making this distinction unless it is needed to make a point.

For each $\mathbf{x} \in \mathscr{X}$, $\mathscr{K}(f,\mathbf{x})$ can be written as $\mathrm{E}\{\log[p_o(\mathbf{y}_i \mid \mathbf{x}_i)] \mid \mathbf{x}_i = \mathbf{x}\} - \mathrm{E}\{\log[f(\mathbf{y}_i \mid \mathbf{x}_i)] \mid \mathbf{x}_i = \mathbf{x}\}$. Therefore, if the parametric model is correctly specified, then $\mathrm{E}\{\log[f(\mathbf{y}_i \mid \mathbf{x}_i;\boldsymbol{\theta}_o)] \mid \mathbf{x}_i\} \geq \mathrm{E}\{\log[f(\mathbf{y}_i \mid \mathbf{x}_i;\boldsymbol{\theta})] \mid \mathbf{x}_i\}$, or

$$\mathrm{E}[\ell_i(\boldsymbol{\theta}_o) \mid \mathbf{x}_i] \geq \mathrm{E}[\ell_i(\boldsymbol{\theta}) \mid \mathbf{x}_i], \qquad \boldsymbol{\theta} \in \boldsymbol{\Theta}, \tag{13.12}$$

where

$$\ell_i(\boldsymbol{\theta}) \equiv \ell(\mathbf{y}_i, \mathbf{x}_i, \boldsymbol{\theta}) \equiv \log f(\mathbf{y}_i \mid \mathbf{x}_i;\boldsymbol{\theta}) \tag{13.13}$$

is the **conditional log likelihood for observation i**. Note that $\ell_i(\boldsymbol{\theta})$ is a *random* function of $\boldsymbol{\theta}$, since it depends on the random vector $(\mathbf{x}_i, \mathbf{y}_i)$. By taking the expected value of expression (13.12) and using iterated expectations, we see that $\boldsymbol{\theta}_o$ solves

$$\max_{\boldsymbol{\theta} \in \boldsymbol{\Theta}} \mathrm{E}[\ell_i(\boldsymbol{\theta})], \tag{13.14}$$

where the expectation is with respect to the joint distribution of $(\mathbf{x}_i, \mathbf{y}_i)$. The sample analogue of expression (13.14) is

$$\max_{\boldsymbol{\theta} \in \boldsymbol{\Theta}} N^{-1} \sum_{i=1}^{N} \log f(\mathbf{y}_i \mid \mathbf{x}_i;\boldsymbol{\theta}). \tag{13.15}$$

A solution to problem (13.15), assuming that one exists, is the **conditional maximum likelihood estimator** of θ_o, which we denote as $\hat{\theta}$. We will sometimes drop "conditional" when it is not needed for clarity.

The CMLE is clearly an M-estimator, since a maximization problem is easily turned into a minimization problem: in the notation of Chapter 12, take $\mathbf{w}_i \equiv (\mathbf{x}_i, \mathbf{y}_i)$

and $q(\mathbf{w}_i, \boldsymbol{\theta}) \equiv -\log f(\mathbf{y}_i \mid \mathbf{x}_i; \boldsymbol{\theta})$. As long as we keep track of the minus sign in front of the log likelihood, we can apply the results in Chapter 12 directly.

The motivation for the conditional MLE as a solution to problem (13.15) may appear backward if you learned about MLE in an introductory statistics course. In a traditional framework, we would treat the $\mathbf{x}_i$ as constants appearing in the distribution of $\mathbf{y}_i$, and we would define $\hat{\boldsymbol{\theta}}$ as the solution to

$$\max_{\boldsymbol{\theta} \in \boldsymbol{\Theta}} \prod_{i=1}^{N} f(\mathbf{y}_i \mid \mathbf{x}_i; \boldsymbol{\theta}). \tag{13.16}$$

Under independence, the product in expression (13.16) is the model for the joint density of $(\mathbf{y}_1, \ldots, \mathbf{y}_N)$, evaluated at the data. Because maximizing the function in (13.16) is the same as maximizing its natural log, we are led to problem (13.15). However, the arguments explaining why solving (13.16) should lead to a good estimator of $\boldsymbol{\theta}_o$ are necessarily heuristic. By contrast, the analogy principle applies directly to problem (13.15), and we need not assume that the $\mathbf{x}_i$ are fixed.

In our two examples, the conditional log likelihoods are fairly simple.

Example 13.1 (continued): In the probit example, the log likelihood for observation i is $\ell_i(\boldsymbol{\theta}) = y_i \log \Phi(\mathbf{x}_i\boldsymbol{\theta}) + (1 - y_i) \log[1 - \Phi(\mathbf{x}_i\boldsymbol{\theta})]$.

Example 13.2 (continued): In the Poisson example, $\ell_i(\boldsymbol{\theta}) = -\exp(\mathbf{x}_i\boldsymbol{\theta}) + y_i\mathbf{x}_i\boldsymbol{\theta} - \log(y_i!)$. Normally, we would drop the last term in defining $\ell_i(\boldsymbol{\theta})$ because it does not affect the maximization problem.

13.4 Consistency of Conditional Maximum Likelihood Estimation

In this section we state a formal consistency result for the CMLE, which is a special case of the M-estimator consistency result Theorem 12.2.

THEOREM 13.1 (Consistency of CMLE): Let $\{(\mathbf{x}_i, \mathbf{y}_i) : i = 1, 2, \ldots\}$ be a random sample with $\mathbf{x}_i \in \mathcal{X} \subset \mathbb{R}^K$, $\mathbf{y}_i \in \mathcal{Y} \subset \mathbb{R}^G$. Let $\boldsymbol{\Theta} \subset \mathbb{R}^P$ be the parameter set, and denote the parametric model of the conditional density as $\{f(\cdot \mid \mathbf{x}; \boldsymbol{\theta}) : \mathbf{x} \in \mathcal{X}, \boldsymbol{\theta} \in \boldsymbol{\Theta}\}$. Assume that (a) $f(\cdot \mid \mathbf{x}; \boldsymbol{\theta})$ is a true density with respect to the measure $\nu(d\mathbf{y})$ for all $\mathbf{x}$ and $\boldsymbol{\theta}$, so that condition (13.8) holds; (b) for some $\boldsymbol{\theta}_o \in \boldsymbol{\Theta}$, $p_o(\cdot \mid \mathbf{x}) = f(\cdot \mid \mathbf{x}; \boldsymbol{\theta}_o)$, all $\mathbf{x} \in \mathcal{X}$, and $\boldsymbol{\theta}_o$ is the *unique* solution to problem (13.14); (c) $\boldsymbol{\Theta}$ is a compact set; (d) for each $\boldsymbol{\theta} \in \boldsymbol{\Theta}$, $\ell(\cdot, \boldsymbol{\theta})$ is a Borel measurable function on $\mathcal{Y} \times \mathcal{X}$; (e) for each $(\mathbf{y}, \mathbf{x}) \in \mathcal{Y} \times \mathcal{X}$, $\ell(\mathbf{y}, \mathbf{x}, \cdot)$ is a continuous function on $\boldsymbol{\Theta}$; and (f) $|\ell(\mathbf{w}, \boldsymbol{\theta})| \leq b(\mathbf{w})$, all $\boldsymbol{\theta} \in \boldsymbol{\Theta}$, and $\mathrm{E}[b(\mathbf{w})] < \infty$. Then there exists a solution to problem (13.15), the CMLE $\hat{\boldsymbol{\theta}}$, and $\operatorname{plim} \hat{\boldsymbol{\theta}} = \boldsymbol{\theta}_o$.

As we discussed in Chapter 12, the measurability assumption in part d is purely technical and does not need to be checked in practice. Compactness of $\boldsymbol{\Theta}$ can be relaxed, but doing so usually requires considerable work. The continuity assumption holds in most econometric applications, but there are cases where it fails, such as when estimating certain models of auctions—see, for example, Donald and Paarsch (1996) and Paarsch and Hong (2006). The moment assumption in part f typically restricts the distribution of $\mathbf{x}_i$ in some way, but such restrictions are rarely a serious concern. For the most part, the key assumptions are that the parametric model is correctly specified, that $\boldsymbol{\theta}_o$ is identified, and that the log-likelihood function is continuous in $\boldsymbol{\theta}$.

For the probit and Poisson examples, the log likelihoods are clearly continuous in $\boldsymbol{\theta}$. We can verify the moment condition (f) if we bound certain moments of $\mathbf{x}_i$ and make the parameter space compact. But our primary concern is that densities are correctly specified. For example, in the probit case, the density for y_i given $\mathbf{x}_i$ will be incorrect if the latent error e_i is not independent of $\mathbf{x}_i$ and normally distributed, or if the latent variable model is not linear to begin with. For identification we must rule out perfect collinearity in $\mathbf{x}_i$. The Poisson CMLE turns out to have desirable properties even if the Poisson distributional assumption does not hold, but we postpone a discussion of the robustness of the Poisson CMLE until Section 13.11 and Chapter 18.

13.5 Asymptotic Normality and Asymptotic Variance Estimation

Under the differentiability and moment assumptions that allow us to apply the theorems in Chapter 12, we can show that the MLE is generally asymptotically normal. Naturally, the computational methods discussed in Section 12.7, including concentrating parameters out of the log likelihood, apply directly.

13.5.1 Asymptotic Normality

We can derive the limiting distribution of the MLE by applying Theorem 12.3. We will have to assume the regularity conditions there; in particular, we assume that $\boldsymbol{\theta}_o$ is in the interior of $\boldsymbol{\Theta}$, and $\ell_i(\boldsymbol{\theta})$ is twice continuously differentiable on the interior of $\boldsymbol{\Theta}$.

The **score of the log likelihood** for observation i is simply

$$\mathbf{s}_i(\boldsymbol{\theta}) \equiv \nabla_{\boldsymbol{\theta}} \ell_i(\boldsymbol{\theta})' = \left(\frac{\partial \ell_i}{\partial \theta_1}(\boldsymbol{\theta}), \frac{\partial \ell_i}{\partial \theta_2}(\boldsymbol{\theta}), \ldots, \frac{\partial \ell_i}{\partial \theta_P}(\boldsymbol{\theta}) \right)', \tag{13.17}$$

a $P \times 1$ vector as in Chapter 12.

Example 13.1 (continued): For the probit case, $\boldsymbol{\theta}$ is $K \times 1$ and

$$\nabla_\theta \ell_i(\boldsymbol{\theta}) = y_i \left[\frac{\phi(\mathbf{x}_i\boldsymbol{\theta})\mathbf{x}_i}{\Phi(\mathbf{x}_i\boldsymbol{\theta})}\right] - (1 - y_i)\left\{\frac{\phi(\mathbf{x}_i\boldsymbol{\theta})\mathbf{x}_i}{[1 - \Phi(\mathbf{x}_i\boldsymbol{\theta})]}\right\}.$$

Transposing this equation, and using a little algebra, gives

$$\mathbf{s}_i(\boldsymbol{\theta}) = \frac{\phi(\mathbf{x}_i\boldsymbol{\theta})\mathbf{x}_i'[y_i - \Phi(\mathbf{x}_i\boldsymbol{\theta})]}{\Phi(\mathbf{x}_i\boldsymbol{\theta})[1 - \Phi(\mathbf{x}_i\boldsymbol{\theta})]}. \tag{13.18}$$

Recall that $\mathbf{x}_i'$ is a $K \times 1$ vector.

Example 13.2 (continued): The score for the Poisson case, where $\boldsymbol{\theta}$ is again $K \times 1$, is

$$\mathbf{s}_i(\boldsymbol{\theta}) = -\exp(\mathbf{x}_i\boldsymbol{\theta})\mathbf{x}_i' + y_i\mathbf{x}_i' = \mathbf{x}_i'[y_i - \exp(\mathbf{x}_i\boldsymbol{\theta})]. \tag{13.19}$$

In the vast majority of cases, the score of the log-likelihood function has an important zero conditional mean property:

$$\mathrm{E}[\mathbf{s}_i(\boldsymbol{\theta}_o) \mid \mathbf{x}_i] = \mathbf{0}. \tag{13.20}$$

In other words, when we evaluate the $P \times 1$ score at $\boldsymbol{\theta}_o$, and take its expectation with respect to $f(\cdot \mid \mathbf{x}_i; \boldsymbol{\theta}_o)$, the expectation is zero. Under condition (13.20), $\mathrm{E}[\mathbf{s}_i(\boldsymbol{\theta}_o)] = \mathbf{0}$, which was a key condition in deriving the asymptotic normality of the M-estimator in Chapter 12.

To show condition (13.20) generally, let $\mathrm{E}_\theta[\cdot \mid \mathbf{x}_i]$ denote conditional expectation with respect to the density $f(\cdot \mid \mathbf{x}_i; \boldsymbol{\theta})$ for any $\boldsymbol{\theta} \in \boldsymbol{\Theta}$. Then, by definition,

$$\mathrm{E}_\theta[\mathbf{s}_i(\boldsymbol{\theta}) \mid \mathbf{x}_i] = \int_{\mathcal{Y}} \mathbf{s}(\mathbf{y}, \mathbf{x}_i, \boldsymbol{\theta}) f(\mathbf{y} \mid \mathbf{x}_i; \boldsymbol{\theta}) \nu(d\mathbf{y}).$$

If integration and differentation can be interchanged on $\mathrm{int}(\boldsymbol{\Theta})$—that is, if

$$\nabla_\theta\left(\int_{\mathcal{Y}} f(\mathbf{y} \mid \mathbf{x}_i; \boldsymbol{\theta}) \nu(d\mathbf{y})\right) = \int_{\mathcal{Y}} \nabla_\theta f(\mathbf{y} \mid \mathbf{x}_i; \boldsymbol{\theta}) \nu(d\mathbf{y}) \tag{13.21}$$

for all $\mathbf{x}_i \in \mathcal{X}$, $\boldsymbol{\theta} \in \mathrm{int}(\boldsymbol{\Theta})$—then

$$\mathbf{0} = \int_{\mathcal{Y}} \nabla_\theta f(\mathbf{y} \mid \mathbf{x}_i; \boldsymbol{\theta}) \nu(d\mathbf{y}), \tag{13.22}$$

since $\int_{\mathcal{Y}} f(\mathbf{y} \mid \mathbf{x}_i; \boldsymbol{\theta}) \nu(d\mathbf{y})$ is unity for all $\boldsymbol{\theta}$, and therefore the partial derivatives with respect to $\boldsymbol{\theta}$ must be identically zero. But the right-hand side of equation (13.22) can be written as $\int_{\mathcal{Y}} [\nabla_\theta \ell(\mathbf{y}, \mathbf{x}_i, \boldsymbol{\theta})] f(\mathbf{y} \mid \mathbf{x}_i; \boldsymbol{\theta}) \nu(d\mathbf{y})$. Putting in $\boldsymbol{\theta}_o$ for $\boldsymbol{\theta}$ and transposing yields condition (13.20).

Example 13.1 (continued): Define $u_i \equiv y_i - \Phi(\mathbf{x}_i\boldsymbol{\theta}_o) = y_i - \mathrm{E}(y_i \mid \mathbf{x}_i)$. Then

$$\mathbf{s}_i(\boldsymbol{\theta}_o) = \frac{\phi(\mathbf{x}_i\boldsymbol{\theta}_o)\mathbf{x}_i' u_i}{\Phi(\mathbf{x}_i\boldsymbol{\theta}_o)[1 - \Phi(\mathbf{x}_i\boldsymbol{\theta}_o)]}$$

and, since $\mathrm{E}(u_i \mid \mathbf{x}_i) = 0$, it follows that $\mathrm{E}[\mathbf{s}_i(\boldsymbol{\theta}_o) \mid \mathbf{x}_i] = \mathbf{0}$.

Example 13.2 (continued): Define $u_i \equiv y_i - \exp(\mathbf{x}_i\boldsymbol{\theta}_o)$. Then $\mathbf{s}_i(\boldsymbol{\theta}_o) = \mathbf{x}_i' u_i$ and so $\mathrm{E}[\mathbf{s}_i(\boldsymbol{\theta}_o) \mid \mathbf{x}_i] = \mathbf{0}$.

Assuming that $\ell_i(\boldsymbol{\theta})$ is twice continuously differentiable on the interior of $\boldsymbol{\Theta}$, let the Hessian for observation i be the $P \times P$ matrix of second partial derivatives of $\ell_i(\boldsymbol{\theta})$:

$$\mathbf{H}_i(\boldsymbol{\theta}) \equiv \nabla_\theta \mathbf{s}_i(\boldsymbol{\theta}) = \nabla_\theta^2 \ell_i(\boldsymbol{\theta}). \tag{13.23}$$

The Hessian is a symmetric matrix that generally depends on $(\mathbf{x}_i, \mathbf{y}_i)$. Since MLE is a maximization problem, the expected value of $\mathbf{H}_i(\boldsymbol{\theta}_o)$ is negative definite. Thus, to apply the theory in Chapter 12, we define

$$\mathbf{A}_o \equiv -\mathrm{E}[\mathbf{H}_i(\boldsymbol{\theta}_o)], \tag{13.24}$$

which is generally a positive definite matrix when $\boldsymbol{\theta}_o$ is identified. Under standard regularity conditions, the asymptotic normality of the CMLE follows from Theorem 12.3: $\sqrt{N}(\hat{\boldsymbol{\theta}} - \boldsymbol{\theta}_o) \overset{a}{\sim} \mathrm{Normal}(\mathbf{0}, \mathbf{A}_o^{-1}\mathbf{B}_o\mathbf{A}_o^{-1})$, where $\mathbf{B}_o \equiv \mathrm{Var}[\mathbf{s}_i(\boldsymbol{\theta}_o)] \equiv \mathrm{E}[\mathbf{s}_i(\boldsymbol{\theta}_o)\mathbf{s}_i(\boldsymbol{\theta}_o)']$. It turns out that this general form of the asymptotic variance matrix is too complicated. We now show that $\mathbf{B}_o = \mathbf{A}_o$.

We must assume enough smoothness such that the following interchange of integral and derivative is valid (see Newey and McFadden, 1994, Sect. 5.1, for the case of unconditional MLE):

$$\nabla_\theta\left(\int_{\mathscr{Y}} \mathbf{s}_i(\boldsymbol{\theta}) f(\mathbf{y} \mid \mathbf{x}_i; \boldsymbol{\theta}) \nu(d\mathbf{y})\right) = \int_{\mathscr{Y}} \nabla_\theta[\mathbf{s}_i(\boldsymbol{\theta}) f(\mathbf{y} \mid \mathbf{x}_i; \boldsymbol{\theta})] \nu(d\mathbf{y}). \tag{13.25}$$

Then, taking the derivative of the identity

$$\int_{\mathscr{Y}} \mathbf{s}_i(\boldsymbol{\theta}) f(\mathbf{y} \mid \mathbf{x}_i; \boldsymbol{\theta}) \nu(d\mathbf{y}) \equiv \mathrm{E}_\theta[\mathbf{s}_i(\boldsymbol{\theta}) \mid \mathbf{x}_i] = \mathbf{0}, \qquad \boldsymbol{\theta} \in \mathrm{int}(\boldsymbol{\Theta}),$$

and using equation (13.25), gives, for all $\boldsymbol{\theta} \in \mathrm{int}(\boldsymbol{\Theta})$,

$$-\mathrm{E}_\theta[\mathbf{H}_i(\boldsymbol{\theta}) \mid \mathbf{x}_i] = \mathrm{Var}_\theta[\mathbf{s}_i(\boldsymbol{\theta}) \mid \mathbf{x}_i],$$

where the indexing by $\boldsymbol{\theta}$ denotes expectation and variance when $f(\cdot \mid \mathbf{x}_i; \boldsymbol{\theta})$ is the density of $\mathbf{y}_i$ given $\mathbf{x}_i$. When evaluated at $\boldsymbol{\theta} = \boldsymbol{\theta}_o$ we get a very important equality:

$$-\mathrm{E}[\mathbf{H}_i(\boldsymbol{\theta}_o) \mid \mathbf{x}_i] = \mathrm{E}[\mathbf{s}_i(\boldsymbol{\theta}_o)\mathbf{s}_i(\boldsymbol{\theta}_o)' \mid \mathbf{x}_i] \tag{13.26}$$

where the expectation and variance are with respect to the true conditional distribution of $\mathbf{y}_i$ given $\mathbf{x}_i$. Equation (13.26) is called the **conditional information matrix equality (CIME)**. Taking the expectation of equation (13.26) (with respect to the distribution of $\mathbf{x}_i$) and using the law of iterated expectations gives

$$-\mathrm{E}[\mathbf{H}_i(\boldsymbol{\theta}_o)] = \mathrm{E}[\mathbf{s}_i(\boldsymbol{\theta}_o)\mathbf{s}_i(\boldsymbol{\theta}_o)'], \tag{13.27}$$

or $\mathbf{A}_o = \mathbf{B}_o$. This relationship is best thought of as the **unconditional information matrix equality (UIME)**.

THEOREM 13.2 (Asymptotic Normality of CMLE): Let the conditions of Theorem 13.1 hold. In addition, assume that (a) $\boldsymbol{\theta}_o \in \mathrm{int}(\boldsymbol{\Theta})$; (b) for each $(\mathbf{y}, \mathbf{x}) \in \mathscr{Y} \times \mathscr{X}$, $\ell(\mathbf{y}, \mathbf{x}, \cdot)$ is twice continuously differentiable on $\mathrm{int}(\boldsymbol{\Theta})$; (c) the interchanges of derivative and integral in equations (13.21) and (13.25) hold for all $\boldsymbol{\theta} \in \mathrm{int}(\boldsymbol{\Theta})$; (d) the elements of $\nabla_\theta^2 \ell(\mathbf{y}, \mathbf{x}, \theta)$ are bounded in absolute value by a function $b(\mathbf{y}, \mathbf{x})$ with finite expectation; and (e) $\mathbf{A}_o$ defined by expression (13.24) is positive definite. Then

$$\sqrt{N}(\hat{\boldsymbol{\theta}} - \boldsymbol{\theta}_o) \xrightarrow{d} \mathrm{Normal}(\mathbf{0}, \mathbf{A}_o^{-1}) \tag{13.28}$$

and therefore

$$\mathrm{Avar}(\hat{\boldsymbol{\theta}}) = \mathbf{A}_o^{-1}/N. \tag{13.29}$$

In standard applications, the log likelihood has many continuous partial derivatives, although there are examples where it does not. Some examples also violate the interchange of the integral and derivative in equation (13.21) or (13.25), such as when the conditional support of $\mathbf{y}_i$ depends on the parameters $\boldsymbol{\theta}_o$. In such cases we cannot expect the CMLE to have a limiting normal distribution; it may not even converge at the rate $\sqrt{N}$. Some progress has been made for specific models when the support of the distribution depends on unknown parameters; see, for example, Donald and Paarsch (1996).

13.5.2 Estimating the Asymptotic Variance

Estimating $\mathrm{Avar}(\hat{\boldsymbol{\theta}})$ requires estimating $\mathbf{A}_o$. From the equalities derived previously, there are at least three possible estimators of $\mathbf{A}_o$ in the CMLE context. In fact, under slight extensions of the regularity conditions in Theorem 13.2, each of the matrices

$$N^{-1}\sum_{i=1}^{N} -\mathbf{H}_i(\hat{\boldsymbol{\theta}}), \qquad N^{-1}\sum_{i=1}^{N} \mathbf{s}_i(\hat{\boldsymbol{\theta}})\mathbf{s}_i(\hat{\boldsymbol{\theta}})', \qquad \text{and} \qquad N^{-1}\sum_{i=1}^{N} \mathbf{A}(\mathbf{x}_i, \hat{\boldsymbol{\theta}}) \tag{13.30}$$

converges to $\mathbf{A}_o = \mathbf{B}_o$, where

$$\mathbf{A}(\mathbf{x}_i, \boldsymbol{\theta}_o) \equiv -\mathrm{E}[\mathbf{H}(\mathbf{y}_i, \mathbf{x}_i, \boldsymbol{\theta}_o) \mid \mathbf{x}_i]. \tag{13.31}$$

Thus, $\widehat{\mathrm{Avar}(\hat{\boldsymbol{\theta}})}$ can be taken to be any of the three matrices

$$\left[-\sum_{i=1}^{N} \mathbf{H}_i(\hat{\boldsymbol{\theta}})\right]^{-1}, \quad \left[\sum_{i=1}^{N} \mathbf{s}_i(\hat{\boldsymbol{\theta}})\mathbf{s}_i(\hat{\boldsymbol{\theta}})'\right]^{-1}, \quad \text{or} \quad \left[\sum_{i=1}^{N} \mathbf{A}(\mathbf{x}_i, \hat{\boldsymbol{\theta}})\right]^{-1} \tag{13.32}$$

and the asymptotic standard errors are the square roots of the diagonal elements of any of the matrices. We discussed each of these estimators in the general M-estimator case in Chapter 12, but a brief review is in order. The first estimator, based on the Hessian of the log likelihood, requires computing second derivatives. When the inverse exists, the estimate is positive definite because $\hat{\boldsymbol{\theta}}$ maximizes the objective function.

The second estimator in equation (13.32), based on the outer product of the score, depends only on first derivatives of the log-likelihood function. This simple estimator was proposed by Berndt, Hall, Hall, and Hausman (1974). Its primary drawback is that it can be poorly behaved in even moderate sample sizes, as we discussed in Section 12.6.2.

If the conditional expectation $\mathbf{A}(\mathbf{x}_i, \boldsymbol{\theta}_o)$ is in closed form (as it is in some leading cases) or can be simulated—as discussed in Porter (2002)—then the estimator based on $\mathbf{A}(\mathbf{x}_i, \hat{\boldsymbol{\theta}})$ has some attractive features. First, it often depends only on first derivatives of a conditional mean or conditional variance function. Second, it is also positive definite when it exists because of the conditional information matrix equality (13.26). Third, this estimator has been found to have significantly better finite-sample properties than the outer product of the score estimator in some situations where $\mathbf{A}(\mathbf{x}_i, \boldsymbol{\theta}_o)$ can be obtained in closed form.

Example 13.1 (continued): The Hessian for the probit log likelihood is a mess. Fortunately, $\mathrm{E}[\mathbf{H}_i(\boldsymbol{\theta}_o) \mid \mathbf{x}_i]$ has a fairly simple form. Taking the derivative of equation (13.18) and using the product rule gives

$$\mathbf{H}_i(\boldsymbol{\theta}) = -\frac{\{\phi(\mathbf{x}_i\boldsymbol{\theta})\}^2 \mathbf{x}_i'\mathbf{x}_i}{\Phi(\mathbf{x}_i\boldsymbol{\theta})[1 - \Phi(\mathbf{x}_i\boldsymbol{\theta})]} + [y_i - \Phi(\mathbf{x}_i\boldsymbol{\theta})]\mathbf{L}(\mathbf{x}_i\boldsymbol{\theta}),$$

where $\mathbf{L}(\mathbf{x}_i\boldsymbol{\theta})$ is a $K \times K$ complicated function of $\mathbf{x}_i\boldsymbol{\theta}$ that we need not find explicitly. Now, when we evaluate this expression at $\boldsymbol{\theta}_o$ and note that $E\{[y_i - \Phi(\mathbf{x}_i\boldsymbol{\theta}_o)]\mathbf{L}(\mathbf{x}_i\boldsymbol{\theta}_o) \mid \mathbf{x}_i\} = [\mathrm{E}(y_i \mid \mathbf{x}_i) - \Phi(\mathbf{x}_i\boldsymbol{\theta}_o)]\mathbf{L}(\mathbf{x}_i\boldsymbol{\theta}_o) = \mathbf{0}$, we have

$$-\mathrm{E}[\mathbf{H}_i(\boldsymbol{\theta}_o) \mid \mathbf{x}_i] = \mathbf{A}_i(\boldsymbol{\theta}_o) = \frac{\{\phi(\mathbf{x}_i\boldsymbol{\theta}_o)\}^2 \mathbf{x}_i'\mathbf{x}_i}{\Phi(\mathbf{x}_i\boldsymbol{\theta}_o)[1 - \Phi(\mathbf{x}_i\boldsymbol{\theta}_o)]}.$$

Thus, $\widehat{\text{Avar}}(\hat{\boldsymbol{\theta}})$ in probit analysis is

$$\left(\sum_{i=1}^{N} \frac{\{\phi(\mathbf{x}_i\hat{\boldsymbol{\theta}})\}^2 \mathbf{x}_i'\mathbf{x}_i}{\Phi(\mathbf{x}_i\hat{\boldsymbol{\theta}})[1-\Phi(\mathbf{x}_i\hat{\boldsymbol{\theta}})]}\right)^{-1}, \tag{13.33}$$

which is always positive definite when the inverse exists. Note that $\mathbf{x}_i'\mathbf{x}_i$ is a $K \times K$ matrix for each i.

Example 13.2 (continued): For the Poisson model with exponential conditional mean, $\mathbf{H}_i(\boldsymbol{\theta}) = -\exp(\mathbf{x}_i\boldsymbol{\theta})\mathbf{x}_i'\mathbf{x}_i$. In this example, the Hessian does not depend on y_i, so there is no distinction between $\mathbf{H}_i(\boldsymbol{\theta}_o)$ and $\mathrm{E}[\mathbf{H}_i(\boldsymbol{\theta}_o) \mid \mathbf{x}_i]$. The positive definite estimate of $\widehat{\text{Avar}}(\hat{\boldsymbol{\theta}})$ is simply

$$\left[\sum_{i=1}^{N} \exp(\mathbf{x}_i\hat{\boldsymbol{\theta}})\mathbf{x}_i'\mathbf{x}_i\right]^{-1}. \tag{13.34}$$

13.6 Hypothesis Testing

Given the asymptotic standard errors, it is easy to form asymptotic t statistics for testing single hypotheses. These t statistics are asymptotically distributed as standard normal.

The three tests covered in Chapter 12 are immediately applicable to the MLE case. Since the information matrix equality holds when the density is correctly specified, we need only consider the simplest forms of the test statistics. The Wald statistic is given in equation (12.63), and the conditions sufficient for it to have a limiting chi-square distribution are discussed in Section 12.6.1.

Define the log-likelihood function for the entire sample by $\mathscr{L}(\boldsymbol{\theta}) \equiv \sum_{i=1}^{N} \ell_i(\boldsymbol{\theta})$. Let $\hat{\boldsymbol{\theta}}$ be the unrestricted estimator, and let $\tilde{\boldsymbol{\theta}}$ be the estimator with the Q nonredundant constraints imposed. Then, under the regularity conditions discussed in Section 12.6.3, the **likelihood ratio (LR) statistic**,

$$LR \equiv 2[\mathscr{L}(\hat{\boldsymbol{\theta}}) - \mathscr{L}(\tilde{\boldsymbol{\theta}})] \tag{13.35}$$

is distributed asymptotically as χ^2_Q under H_0. As with the Wald statistic, we cannot use LR as approximately χ^2_Q when $\boldsymbol{\theta}_o$ is on the boundary of the parameter set. The LR statistic is very easy to compute once the restricted and unrestricted models have been estimated, and the LR statistic is invariant to reparameterizing the conditional density.

The score or LM test is based on the restricted estimation only. Let $\mathbf{s}_i(\tilde{\boldsymbol{\theta}})$ be the $P \times 1$ score of $\ell_i(\boldsymbol{\theta})$ evaluated at the restricted estimates $\tilde{\boldsymbol{\theta}}$. That is, we compute the partial derivatives of $\ell_i($ with respect to each of the P parameters, but then we evaluate this vector of ' 's at the restricted estimates. Then, from Section 12.6.2 and the information r ality, the statistics

$$\left(\sum_{i=1}^{N} \tilde{\mathbf{s}}_i\right)' \left(-\sum_{i=1}^{N} \tilde{\mathbf{H}} \right. \quad , \quad \left(\sum_{i=1}^{N} \tilde{\mathbf{s}}_i\right)' \left(\sum_{i=1}^{N} \tilde{\mathbf{A}}_i\right)^{-1} \left(\sum_{i=1}^{N} \tilde{\mathbf{s}}_i\right), \quad \text{and}$$

$$\left(\sum_{i=1}^{N} \tilde{\mathbf{s}}_i\right)' \left(\sum_{i=1}^{N} \tilde{\mathbf{s}}_i \tilde{\mathbf{s}}_i' \right. \tag{13.36}$$

have limiting χ^2_Q d. ınder H_0. As we know from Section 12.6.2, the first statistic is not guarı ɜ nonnegative (because the matrix in the middle is not necessarily positive (.d is not invariant to reparameterizations, but the outer product statistic is. ˀ ı, using the conditional information matrix equality, it can be shown that t tatistic based on $\tilde{\mathbf{A}}_i$ is invariant to reparameterization. Davidson and MacI 1993, Sect. 13.6) show invariance in the case of unconditional maximum li. ɪ. Invariance holds in the more general conditional ML setup, with $\mathbf{x}_i$ contair y conditioning variables (see Problem 13.5). We have already used the expect ssian form of the LM statistic for nonlinear regression in Section 12.6.2. We wil it in several applications in Part IV, including binary response models and Poi n regression models. In these examples, the statistic can be computed conveniently ısing auxiliary regressions based on weighted residuals.

Because the unconditional information matrix equality holds, we know from Section 12.6.4 that the three classical statistics have the same limiting distribution under local alternatives. Therefore, either small-sample considerations, invariance, or computational issues must be used to choose among the statistics.

13.7 Specification Testing

Because MLE generally relies on its distributional assumptions, it is useful to have available a general class of specification tests that are simple to compute. One general approach is to nest the model of interest within a more general model (which may be much harder to estimate) and obtain the score test against the more general alternative. RESET in a linear model and its extension to exponential regression models in Section 12.6.2 are examples of this approach, albeit in a non-maximum-likelihood setting.

In the context of MLE, it makes sense to test moment conditions implied by the conditional density specification. Let $\mathbf{w}_i = (\mathbf{x}_i, \mathbf{y}_i)$ and suppose that, when $f(\cdot \mid \mathbf{x}; \boldsymbol{\theta})$ is correctly specified,

$$\mathrm{H}_0 : \mathrm{E}[\mathbf{g}(\mathbf{w}_i, \boldsymbol{\theta}_o)] = \mathbf{0}, \tag{13.37}$$

where $\mathbf{g}(\mathbf{w}, \boldsymbol{\theta})$ is a $Q \times 1$ vector. Any application implies innumerable choices for the function $\mathbf{g}$. Since the MLE $\hat{\boldsymbol{\theta}}$ sets the sum of the score to zero, $\mathbf{g}(\mathbf{w}, \boldsymbol{\theta})$ cannot contain elements of $\mathbf{s}(\mathbf{w}, \boldsymbol{\theta})$. Generally, $\mathbf{g}$ should be chosen to test features of a model that are of primary interest, such as first and second conditional moments, or various conditional probabilities.

A test of hypothesis (13.37) is based on how far the sample average of $\mathbf{g}(\mathbf{w}_i, \hat{\boldsymbol{\theta}})$ is from zero. To derive the asymptotic distribution, note that

$$N^{-1/2} \sum_{i=1}^{N} \mathbf{g}_i(\hat{\boldsymbol{\theta}}) = N^{-1/2} \sum_{i=1}^{N} [\mathbf{g}_i(\hat{\boldsymbol{\theta}}) - \boldsymbol{\Pi}_o' \mathbf{s}_i(\hat{\boldsymbol{\theta}})]$$

holds trivially because $\sum_{i=1}^{N} \mathbf{s}_i(\hat{\boldsymbol{\theta}}) = \mathbf{0}$, where

$$\boldsymbol{\Pi}_o \equiv \{\mathrm{E}[\mathbf{s}_i(\boldsymbol{\theta}_o)\mathbf{s}_i(\boldsymbol{\theta}_o)']\}^{-1}\{\mathrm{E}[\mathbf{s}_i(\boldsymbol{\theta}_o)\mathbf{g}_i(\boldsymbol{\theta}_o)']\}$$

is the $P \times Q$ matrix of population regression coefficients from regressing $\mathbf{g}_i(\boldsymbol{\theta}_o)'$ on $\mathbf{s}_i(\boldsymbol{\theta}_o)'$. Using a mean-value expansion about $\boldsymbol{\theta}_o$ and algebra similar to that in Chapter 12, we can write

$$N^{-1/2} \sum_{i=1}^{N} [\mathbf{g}_i(\hat{\boldsymbol{\theta}}) - \boldsymbol{\Pi}_o' \mathbf{s}_i(\hat{\boldsymbol{\theta}})] = N^{-1/2} \sum_{i=1}^{N} [\mathbf{g}_i(\boldsymbol{\theta}_o) - \boldsymbol{\Pi}_o' \mathbf{s}_i(\boldsymbol{\theta}_o)]$$
$$+ \mathrm{E}[\nabla_\theta \mathbf{g}_i(\boldsymbol{\theta}_o) - \boldsymbol{\Pi}_o' \nabla_\theta \mathbf{s}_i(\boldsymbol{\theta}_o)]\sqrt{N}(\hat{\boldsymbol{\theta}} - \boldsymbol{\theta}_o) + \mathrm{o}_p(1). \tag{13.38}$$

The key is that, when the density is correctly specified, the second term on the right-hand side of equation (13.38) is identically zero. Here is the reason: First, equation (13.27) implies that $[\mathrm{E}\nabla_\theta \mathbf{s}_i(\boldsymbol{\theta}_o)]\{\mathrm{E}[\mathbf{s}_i(\boldsymbol{\theta}_o)\mathbf{s}_i(\boldsymbol{\theta}_o)']\}^{-1} = -\mathbf{I}_P$. Second, an extension of the conditional information matrix equality (Newey, 1985; Tauchen, 1985) implies that

$$-\mathrm{E}[\nabla_\theta \mathbf{g}_i(\boldsymbol{\theta}_o) \mid \mathbf{x}_i] = \mathrm{E}[\mathbf{g}_i(\boldsymbol{\theta}_o)\mathbf{s}_i(\boldsymbol{\theta}_o)' \mid \mathbf{x}_i]. \tag{13.39}$$

To show equation (13.39), write

$$\mathrm{E}_\theta[\mathbf{g}_i(\boldsymbol{\theta}) \mid \mathbf{x}_i] = \int_{\mathscr{Y}} \mathbf{g}(\mathbf{y}, \mathbf{x}_i, \boldsymbol{\theta}) f(\mathbf{y} \mid \mathbf{x}_i; \boldsymbol{\theta}) \nu(d\mathbf{y}) = \mathbf{0} \tag{13.40}$$

for all $\boldsymbol{\theta}$. Now, if we take the derivative with respect to $\boldsymbol{\theta}$ and assume that the integrals and derivative can be interchanged, equation (13.40) implies that

$$\int_{\mathscr{Y}} \nabla_\theta \mathbf{g}(\mathbf{y}, \mathbf{x}_i, \boldsymbol{\theta}) f(\mathbf{y} \mid \mathbf{x}_i; \boldsymbol{\theta}) \nu(d\mathbf{y}) + \int_{\mathscr{Y}} \mathbf{g}(\mathbf{y}, \mathbf{x}_i, \boldsymbol{\theta}) \nabla_\theta f(\mathbf{y} \mid \mathbf{x}_i; \boldsymbol{\theta}) \nu(d\mathbf{y}) = \mathbf{0}$$

or $\mathrm{E}_\theta[\nabla_\theta \mathbf{g}_i(\boldsymbol{\theta}) \mid \mathbf{x}_i] + \mathrm{E}_\theta[\mathbf{g}_i(\boldsymbol{\theta})\mathbf{s}_i(\boldsymbol{\theta})' \mid \mathbf{x}_i] = \mathbf{0}$, where we use the fact that $\nabla_\theta f(\mathbf{y} \mid \mathbf{x}; \boldsymbol{\theta}) = \mathbf{s}(\mathbf{y}, \mathbf{x}, \boldsymbol{\theta})' f(\mathbf{y} \mid \mathbf{x}; \boldsymbol{\theta})$. Plugging in $\boldsymbol{\theta} = \boldsymbol{\theta}_o$ and rearranging gives equation (13.39).

What we have shown is that

$$N^{-1/2} \sum_{i=1}^{N} [\mathbf{g}_i(\hat{\boldsymbol{\theta}}) - \boldsymbol{\Pi}_o' \mathbf{s}_i(\hat{\boldsymbol{\theta}})] = N^{-1/2} \sum_{i=1}^{N} [\mathbf{g}_i(\boldsymbol{\theta}_o) - \boldsymbol{\Pi}_o' \mathbf{s}_i(\boldsymbol{\theta}_o)] + o_p(1),$$

which means these standardized partial sums have the same asymptotic distribution. Letting

$$\hat{\boldsymbol{\Pi}} \equiv \left(\sum_{i=1}^{N} \hat{\mathbf{s}}_i \hat{\mathbf{s}}_i' \right)^{-1} \left(\sum_{i=1}^{N} \hat{\mathbf{s}}_i \hat{\mathbf{g}}_i' \right),$$

it is easily seen that plim $\hat{\boldsymbol{\Pi}} = \boldsymbol{\Pi}_o$ under standard regularity conditions. Therefore, the asymptotic variance of $N^{-1/2} \sum_{i=1}^{N} [\mathbf{g}_i(\hat{\boldsymbol{\theta}}) - \boldsymbol{\Pi}_o' \mathbf{s}_i(\hat{\boldsymbol{\theta}})] = N^{-1/2} \sum_{i=1}^{N} \mathbf{g}_i(\hat{\boldsymbol{\theta}})$ is consistently estimated by $N^{-1} \sum_{i=1}^{N} (\hat{\mathbf{g}}_i - \hat{\boldsymbol{\Pi}}' \hat{\mathbf{s}}_i)(\hat{\mathbf{g}}_i - \hat{\boldsymbol{\Pi}}' \hat{\mathbf{s}}_i)'$. When we construct the quadratic form, we get the **Newey-Tauchen-White (NTW) statistic**,

$$NTW = \left[\sum_{i=1}^{N} \mathbf{g}_i(\hat{\boldsymbol{\theta}}) \right]' \left[\sum_{i=1}^{N} (\hat{\mathbf{g}}_i - \hat{\boldsymbol{\Pi}}' \hat{\mathbf{s}}_i)(\hat{\mathbf{g}}_i - \hat{\boldsymbol{\Pi}}' \hat{\mathbf{s}}_i)' \right]^{-1} \left[\sum_{i=1}^{N} \mathbf{g}_i(\hat{\boldsymbol{\theta}}) \right]. \tag{13.41}$$

This statistic was proposed independently by Newey (1985) and Tauchen (1985), and is an extension of White's (1982a) information matrix (IM) test statistic.

For computational purposes it is useful to note that equation (13.41) is identical to $N - \mathrm{SSR}_0 = NR_0^2$ from the regression

$$1 \text{ on } \hat{\mathbf{s}}_i', \hat{\mathbf{g}}_i', \qquad i = 1, 2, \ldots, N, \tag{13.42}$$

where SSR_0 is the usual sum of squared residuals. Under the null that the density is correctly specified, NTW is distributed asymptotically as χ_Q^2, assuming that $\mathbf{g}(\mathbf{w}, \boldsymbol{\theta})$ contains Q nonredundant moment conditions. Unfortunately, the outer product form of regression (13.42) means that the statistic can have poor finite-sample properties. In particular applications—such as nonlinear least squares, binary response analysis, and Poisson regression, to name a few—it is best to use forms of test statistics based on the expected Hessian. We gave the regression-based test for NLS in equation

(12.72), and we will see other examples in later chapters. For the IM test statistic, Davidson and MacKinnon (1992) have suggested an alternative form of the IM statistic that appears to have better finite-sample properties.

Example 13.2 (continued): To test the specification of the conditional mean for Poisson regression, we might take $\mathbf{g}(\mathbf{w}, \boldsymbol{\theta}) = \exp(\mathbf{x}\boldsymbol{\theta})\mathbf{x}'[y - \exp(\mathbf{x}\boldsymbol{\theta})] = \exp(\mathbf{x}\boldsymbol{\theta})\mathbf{s}(\mathbf{w}, \boldsymbol{\theta})$, where the score is given by equation (13.19). If $\mathrm{E}(y \mid \mathbf{x}) = \exp(\mathbf{x}\boldsymbol{\theta}_o)$ then $\mathrm{E}[\mathbf{g}(\mathbf{w}, \boldsymbol{\theta}_o) \mid \mathbf{x}] = \exp(\mathbf{x}\boldsymbol{\theta}_o)\mathrm{E}[\mathbf{s}(\mathbf{w}, \boldsymbol{\theta}_o) \mid \mathbf{x}] = \mathbf{0}$. To test the Poisson variance assumption, $\mathrm{Var}(y \mid \mathbf{x}) = \mathrm{E}(y \mid \mathbf{x}) = \exp(\mathbf{x}\boldsymbol{\theta}_o)$, $\mathbf{g}$ can be of the form $\mathbf{g}(\mathbf{w}, \boldsymbol{\theta}) = \mathbf{a}(\mathbf{x}, \boldsymbol{\theta})\{[y - \exp(\mathbf{x}\boldsymbol{\theta})]^2 - \exp(\mathbf{x}\boldsymbol{\theta})\}$, where $\mathbf{a}(\mathbf{x}, \boldsymbol{\theta})$ is a $Q \times 1$ vector. If the Poisson assumption is true, then $u = y - \exp(\mathbf{x}\boldsymbol{\theta}_o)$ has a zero conditional mean and $\mathrm{E}(u^2 \mid \mathbf{x}) = \mathrm{Var}(y \mid \mathbf{x}) = \exp(\mathbf{x}\boldsymbol{\theta}_o)$. It follows that $\mathrm{E}[\mathbf{g}(\mathbf{w}, \boldsymbol{\theta}_o) \mid \mathbf{x}] = \mathbf{0}$.

Example 13.2 contains examples of what are known as **conditional moment tests**. As the name suggests, the idea is to form orthogonality conditions based on some key conditional moments, usually the conditional mean or conditional variance, but sometimes conditional probabilities or higher order moments. The tests for nonlinear regression in Chapter 12 can be viewed as conditional moment tests, and we will see several other examples in Part IV. For reasons discussed earlier, we will avoid computing the tests using regression (13.42) whenever possible. See Newey (1985), Tauchen (1985), and Pagan and Vella (1989) for general treatments and applications of conditional moment tests. White's (1982a) IM test can often be viewed as a conditional moment test; see Hall (1987) for the linear regression model and White (1994) for a general treatment. White (1994, Chap. 10) shows how to allow the moment function to depend on parameters other than $\boldsymbol{\theta}_o$.

13.8 Partial (or Pooled) Likelihood Methods for Panel Data

Up to this point we have assumed that the parametric model for the density of $\mathbf{y}$ given $\mathbf{x}$ is correctly specified. This assumption is fairly general because $\mathbf{x}$ can contain any observable variable. The leading case occurs when $\mathbf{x}$ contains variables we view as exogenous in a structural model. In other cases, $\mathbf{x}$ will contain variables that are endogenous in a structural model, but putting them in the conditioning set and finding the new conditional density makes estimation of the structural parameters easier.

For studying various panel data models, for estimation using cluster samples, and for various other applications, we need to relax the assumption that the full conditional density of $\mathbf{y}$ given $\mathbf{x}$ is correctly specified. In some examples, such a model is too complicated. Or, for robustness reasons, we do not wish to fully specify the density of $\mathbf{y}$ given $\mathbf{x}$.

13.8.1 Setup for Panel Data

For panel data applications we let $\mathbf{y}$ denote a $T \times 1$ vector, with generic element y_t. Thus, $\mathbf{y}_i$ is a $T \times 1$ random draw vector from the cross section, with tth element y_{it}. As always, we are thinking of T small relative to the cross section sample size. With a slight notational change we can replace y_{it} with, say, a G-vector for each t, an extension that allows us to cover general systems of equations with panel data.

For some vector $\mathbf{x}_t$ containing any set of observable variables, let $\mathrm{D}(y_t \mid \mathbf{x}_t)$ denote the distribution of y_t given $\mathbf{x}_t$. The key assumption is that we have a correctly specified model for the density of y_t given $\mathbf{x}_t$; call it $f_t(y_t \mid \mathbf{x}_t; \boldsymbol{\theta})$, $t = 1, 2, \ldots, T$. The vector $\mathbf{x}_t$ can contain anything, including conditioning variables $\mathbf{z}_t$, lags of these, and lagged values of y. The vector $\boldsymbol{\theta}$ consists of all parameters appearing in f_t for any t; some or all of these may appear in the density for every t, and some may appear only in the density for a single time period.

What distinguishes partial likelihood from maximum likelihood is that we do *not* assume that

$$\prod_{t=1}^{T} \mathrm{D}(y_{it} \mid \mathbf{x}_{it}) \tag{13.43}$$

is a conditional distribution of the vector $\mathbf{y}_i$ given some set of conditioning variables. In other words, even though $f_t(y_t \mid \mathbf{x}_t; \boldsymbol{\theta}_o)$ is the correct density for y_{it} given $\mathbf{x}_{it} = \mathbf{x}_t$ for each t, the product of these is not (necessarily) the density of $\mathbf{y}_i$ given some conditioning variables. Usually, we specify $f_t(y_t \mid \mathbf{x}_t; \boldsymbol{\theta})$ because it is the density of interest for each t.

We define the **partial log likelihood** for each observation i as

$$\ell_i(\boldsymbol{\theta}) \equiv \sum_{t=1}^{T} \log f_t(y_{it} \mid \mathbf{x}_{it}; \boldsymbol{\theta}), \tag{13.44}$$

which is the sum of the log likelihoods across t. What makes partial likelihood methods work is that $\boldsymbol{\theta}_o$ maximizes the expected value of equation (13.44) provided we have the densities $f_t(y_t \mid \mathbf{x}_t; \boldsymbol{\theta})$ correctly specified. We also refer to equation (13.44) as a **pooled log likelihood**.

By the Kullback-Leibler information inequality, $\boldsymbol{\theta}_o$ maximizes $\mathrm{E}[\log f_t(y_{it} \mid \mathbf{x}_{it}; \boldsymbol{\theta})]$ over $\boldsymbol{\Theta}$ for each t, so $\boldsymbol{\theta}_o$ also maximizes the sum of these over t. As usual, identification requires that $\boldsymbol{\theta}_o$ be the unique maximizer of the expected value of equation (13.44). It is sufficient that $\boldsymbol{\theta}_o$ uniquely maximizes $\mathrm{E}[\log f_t(y_{it} \mid \mathbf{x}_{it}; \boldsymbol{\theta})]$ for each t, but this assumption is not necessary.

The **partial (pooled) maximum likelihood estimator (PMLE)** $\hat{\theta}$ solves

$$\max_{\theta \in \Theta} \sum_{i=1}^{N} \sum_{t=1}^{T} \log f_t(y_{it} \mid \mathbf{x}_{it}; \boldsymbol{\theta}), \tag{13.45}$$

which is clearly an M-estimator problem (where the asymptotics are with fixed T and $N \to \infty$). Therefore, from Theorem 12.2, the partial MLE is generally consistent provided $\boldsymbol{\theta}_o$ is identified.

It is also clear that the partial MLE will be asymptotically normal by Theorem 12.3 in Section 12.3. However, unless

$$p_o(\mathbf{y} \mid \mathbf{z}) = \prod_{t=1}^{T} f_t(y_t \mid \mathbf{x}_t; \boldsymbol{\theta}_o) \tag{13.46}$$

for some subvector $\mathbf{z}$ of $\mathbf{x}$, we cannot apply the CIME. A more general asymptotic variance estimator of the type covered in Section 12.5.1 is needed, and we provide such estimators in the next two subsections.

It is useful to discuss at a general level why equation (13.46) does not necessarily hold in a panel data setting. First, suppose $\mathbf{x}_t$ contains only contemporaneous conditioning variables, $\mathbf{z}_t$; in particular, $\mathbf{x}_t$ contains no lagged dependent variables. Then we can always write

$$p_o(\mathbf{y} \mid \mathbf{z}) = p_1^o(y_1 \mid \mathbf{z}) \cdot p_2^o(y_2 \mid y_1, \mathbf{z}) \cdots p_t^o(y_t \mid y_{t-1}, y_{t-2}, \ldots, y_1, \mathbf{z}) \cdots$$
$$p_T^o(y_T \mid y_{T-1}, y_{T-2}, \ldots, y_1, \mathbf{z}),$$

where $p_t^o(y_t \mid y_{t-1}, y_{t-2}, \ldots, y_1, \mathbf{z})$ is the true conditional density of y_t given y_{t-1}, $y_{t-2}, \ldots, y_1$ and $\mathbf{z} \equiv (\mathbf{z}_1, \ldots, \mathbf{z}_T)$. (For $t = 1$, p_1^o is the density of y_1 given $\mathbf{z}$.) For equation (13.46) to hold, we should have

$$p_t^o(y_t \mid y_{t-1}, y_{t-2}, \ldots, y_1, \mathbf{z}) = f_t(y_t \mid \mathbf{z}_t; \boldsymbol{\theta}_o), \qquad t = 1, \ldots, T,$$

which requires that, once $\mathbf{z}_t$ is conditioned on, neither past lags of y_t nor elements of $\mathbf{z}$ from any other time period—past or future—appear in the conditional density $p_t^o(y_t \mid y_{t-1}, y_{t-2}, \ldots, y_1, \mathbf{z})$. Generally, this requirement is very strong, as it requires a combination of strict exogeneity of $\mathbf{z}_t$ and the absense of dynamics in p_t^o.

Equation (13.46) is more likely to hold when $\mathbf{x}_t$ contains lagged dependent variables. In fact, if $\mathbf{x}_t$ contains only lagged values of y_t, then

$$p_o(\mathbf{y}) = \prod_{t=1}^{T} f_t(y_t \mid \mathbf{x}_t; \boldsymbol{\theta}_o)$$

holds if $f_t(y_t \mid \mathbf{x}_t; \boldsymbol{\theta}_o) = p_t^o(y_t \mid y_{t-1}, y_{t-2}, \ldots, y_1)$ for all t (where p_1^o is the unconditional density of y_1), so that all dynamics are captured by f_t. When $\mathbf{x}_t$ contains some variables $\mathbf{z}_t$ in addition to lagged y_t, equation (13.46) requires that the parametric density captures all of the dynamics—that is, that all lags of y_t and $\mathbf{z}_t$ have been properly accounted for in $f(y_t \mid \mathbf{x}_t, \boldsymbol{\theta}_o)$—and strict exogeneity of $\mathbf{z}_t$.

In most treatments of MLE of dynamic models containing additional exogenous variables, the strict exogeneity assumption is maintained, often implicitly by taking $\mathbf{z}_t$ to be nonrandom. In Chapter 7 we saw that strict exogeneity played no role in getting consistent, asymptotically normal estimators in linear panel data models using pooled OLS, and the same is true here. We also allow models where the dynamics have been incompletely specified.

With partial MLE we are interested in fully specifying a density for the conditional distribution $\mathrm{D}(y_{it} \mid \mathbf{x}_{it})$, and it is useful to have a general yet simple way to define strict exogeneity of $\{\mathbf{x}_{it} : t = 1, \ldots, T\}$. The definition is simply stated: the conditioning variables are strictly exogenous if $\mathrm{D}(y_{it} \mid \mathbf{x}_{i1}, \mathbf{x}_{i2}, \ldots, \mathbf{x}_{iT}) = \mathrm{D}(y_{it} \mid \mathbf{x}_{it})$ for $t = 1, \ldots, T$. Naturally, this condition must fail if $\mathbf{x}_{it}$ contains lags of y_{it}, and, just as in linear models, it can fail if $\mathbf{x}_{it}$ contains elements $\mathbf{z}_{it}$ whose future values react to unpredictable changes in y_{it}.

Example 13.3 (Probit with Panel Data): To illustrate the previous discussion, we consider estimation of a panel data binary choice model. The idea is that, for each unit i in the population (individual, firm, and so on) we have a binary outcome, y_{it}, for each of T time periods. For example, if t represents a year, then y_{it} might indicate whether a person was arrested for a crime during year t.

Consider the model in latent variable form:

$$
\begin{aligned}
y_{it}^* &= \mathbf{x}_{it}\boldsymbol{\theta}_o + e_{it} \\
y_{it} &= 1[y_{it}^* > 0] \qquad (13.47) \\
e_{it} \mid \mathbf{x}_{it} &\sim \mathrm{Normal}(0, 1).
\end{aligned}
$$

The vector $\mathbf{x}_{it}$ might contain exogenous variables $\mathbf{z}_{it}$, lags of these, and even lagged y_{it} (not lagged y_{it}^*). Under the assumptions in model (13.47), we have, for each t, $P(y_{it} = 1 \mid \mathbf{x}_{it}) = \Phi(\mathbf{x}_{it}\boldsymbol{\theta}_o)$, and the density of y_{it} given $\mathbf{x}_{it} = \mathbf{x}_t$ is $f(y_t \mid \mathbf{x}_t) = [\Phi(\mathbf{x}_t\boldsymbol{\theta}_o)]^{y_t}[1 - \Phi(\mathbf{x}_t\boldsymbol{\theta}_o)]^{1-y_t}$.

The partial log likelihood for a cross section observation i is

$$
\ell_i(\boldsymbol{\theta}) = \sum_{t=1}^{T} \{y_{it} \log \Phi(\mathbf{x}_{it}\boldsymbol{\theta}) + (1 - y_{it}) \log[1 - \Phi(\mathbf{x}_{it}\boldsymbol{\theta})]\} \qquad (13.48)
$$

and the partial MLE in this case—which simply maximizes $\ell_i(\boldsymbol{\theta})$ summed across all i—is the **pooled probit estimator**. With T fixed and $N \to \infty$, this estimator is consistent and $\sqrt{N}$-asymptotically normal without any assumptions other than identification and standard regularity conditions.

It is very important to know that the pooled probit estimator works without imposing additional assumptions on $\mathbf{e}_i = (e_{i1}, \dots, e_{iT})'$. When $\mathbf{x}_{it}$ contains only exogenous variables $\mathbf{z}_{it}$, it would be standard to assume that

$$e_{it} \text{ is independent of } \mathbf{z}_i \equiv (\mathbf{z}_{i1}, \mathbf{z}_{i2}, \dots, \mathbf{z}_{iT}), \qquad t = 1, \dots, T. \tag{13.49}$$

This is the natural strict exogeneity assumption (and is much stronger than simply assuming that e_{it} and $\mathbf{z}_{it}$ are independent for each t). The crime example can illustrate how strict exogeneity might fail. For example, suppose that $\mathbf{z}_{it}$ measures the amount of time the person has spent in prison prior to the current year. An arrest this year ($y_{it} = 1$) certainly has an effect on expected future values of $\mathbf{z}_{it}$, so that assumption (13.49) is almost certainly false. Fortunately, we do *not* need assumption (13.49) to apply partial likelihood methods.

A second standard assumption is that the e_{it}, $t = 1, 2, \dots, T$ are serially independent. This is especially restrictive in a static model. If we maintain this assumption in addition to assumption (13.49), then equation (13.46) holds (because the y_{it} are then independent conditional on $\mathbf{z}_i$) and the partial MLE is a conditional MLE.

To relax the assumption that the y_{it} are conditionally independent, we can allow the e_{it} to be correlated across t (still assuming that no lagged dependent variables appear). A common assumption is that $\mathbf{e}_i$ has a multivariate normal distribution with a general correlation matrix. Under this assumption, we can write down the joint distribution of $\mathbf{y}_i$ given $\mathbf{z}_i$, but it is complicated, and estimation is very computationally intensive (for discussions see Keane, 1993, and Hajivassilou and Ruud, 1994). We will cover a special case, the random effects probit model, in Chapter 15.

A nice feature of the partial MLE is that $\hat{\boldsymbol{\theta}}$ will be consistent and asymptotically normal even if the e_{it} are arbitrarily serially correlated. This result is entirely analogous to using pooled OLS in linear panel data models when the errors have arbitrary serial correlation.

When $\mathbf{x}_{it}$ contains lagged dependent variables, model (13.47) provides a way of examining dynamic behavior. Or, perhaps $y_{i,t-1}$ is included in $\mathbf{x}_{it}$ as a proxy for unobserved factors, and our focus is on policy variables in $\mathbf{z}_{it}$. For example, if y_{it} is a binary indicator of employment, $y_{i,t-1}$ might be included as a control when studying the effect of a job training program (which may be a binary element of $\mathbf{z}_{it}$) on the employment probability; this method controls for the fact that participation in job training this year might depend on employment last year, and it captures the fact that employment status is persistent. In any case, provided $P(y_{it} = 1 \mid \mathbf{x}_{it})$ follows a probit, the pooled probit estimator is consistent and asymptotically normal. The dynamics may or may not be correctly specified (more on this topic later), and the $\mathbf{z}_{it}$ need not be strictly exogenous (so that whether someone participates in job training in year t can depend on the past employment history).

13.8.2 Asymptotic Inference

The most important practical difference between conditional MLE and partial MLE is in the computation of asymptotic standard errors and test statistics. In many cases, including the pooled probit estimator, the pooled Poisson estimator (see Problem 13.6), and many other pooled procedures, standard econometrics packages can be used to compute the partial MLEs. However, except under certain assumptions, the usual standard errors and test statistics reported from a pooled analysis are not valid. This situation is entirely analogous to the linear model case in Section 7.8 when the errors are serially correlated.

Estimation of the asymptotic variance of the partial MLE is not difficult. In fact, we can combine the M-estimation results from Section 12.5.1 and the results of Section 13.5 to obtain valid estimators.

From Theorem 12.3, we have Avar $\sqrt{N}(\hat{\boldsymbol{\theta}} - \boldsymbol{\theta}_o) = \mathbf{A}_o^{-1}\mathbf{B}_o\mathbf{A}_o^{-1}$, where

$$\mathbf{A}_o = -\mathrm{E}[\nabla_\theta^2 \ell_i(\boldsymbol{\theta}_o)] = -\sum_{t=1}^{T} \mathrm{E}[\nabla_\theta^2 \ell_{it}(\boldsymbol{\theta}_o)] = \sum_{t=1}^{T} \mathrm{E}[\mathbf{A}_{it}(\boldsymbol{\theta}_o)],$$

$$\mathbf{B}_o = \mathrm{E}[\mathbf{s}_i(\boldsymbol{\theta}_o)\mathbf{s}_i(\boldsymbol{\theta}_o)'] = \mathrm{E}\left\{\left[\sum_{t=1}^{T} \mathbf{s}_{it}(\boldsymbol{\theta}_o)\right]\left[\sum_{t=1}^{T} \mathbf{s}_{it}(\boldsymbol{\theta}_o)\right]'\right\},$$

$$\mathbf{A}_{it}(\boldsymbol{\theta}_o) = -\mathrm{E}[\nabla_\theta^2 \ell_{it}(\boldsymbol{\theta}_o) \mid \mathbf{x}_{it}], \qquad \text{and}$$

$$\mathbf{s}_{it}(\boldsymbol{\theta}) = \nabla_\theta \ell_{it}(\boldsymbol{\theta})'.$$

Because we assume that $\boldsymbol{\theta}_o$ is in the interior of the parameter space, and $\boldsymbol{\theta}_o$ maximizes $\mathrm{E}[\boldsymbol{l}_{it}(\boldsymbol{\theta}) \mid \mathbf{x}_{it}]$ over $\boldsymbol{\Theta}$, it is generally true that $\mathrm{E}[\mathbf{s}_{it}(\boldsymbol{\theta}_o) \mid \mathbf{x}_{it}] = \mathbf{0}$ for all t. If $\{\mathbf{x}_{it}\}$ is strictly exogenous, then $\mathrm{E}[\mathbf{s}_{it}(\boldsymbol{\theta}_o) \mid \mathbf{x}_i] = \mathbf{0}$ (because $D(y_{it} \mid \mathbf{x}_i) = D(y_{it} \mid \mathbf{x}_{it})$), but without strict exogeneity we can only say that $\mathbf{s}_{it}(\boldsymbol{\theta}_o)$ has zero mean conditional on $\mathbf{x}_{it}$ (which implies $\mathrm{E}[\mathbf{s}_{it}(\boldsymbol{\theta}_o)] = \mathbf{0}$, of course). The natural definition of sequential exogeneity in this context is $D(y_{it} \mid \mathbf{x}_{it}, \mathbf{x}_{i,t-1}, \ldots, \mathbf{x}_{i1}) = D(y_{it} \mid \mathbf{x}_{it})$, in which case $\mathrm{E}[\mathbf{s}_{it}(\boldsymbol{\theta}_o) \mid \mathbf{x}_{it}, \mathbf{x}_{i,t-1}, \ldots, \mathbf{x}_{i1}] = \mathbf{0}$. As we will see in the next subsection, sequential exogeneity ensures that the scores are serially uncorrelated *if* $\mathbf{x}_{it}$ contains $y_{i,t-1}$. If $\mathbf{x}_{it}$

only includes contemporaneous variables $\mathbf{z}_{it}$, lags of such variables, or both, sequential exogeneity does not imply the scores are serially uncorrelated.

The matrix $\mathbf{A}_o$ is just the sum across t of minus the expected Hessian. The matrix $\mathbf{B}_o$ generally depends on the correlation between the scores at different time periods: $\mathrm{E}[\mathbf{s}_{it}(\boldsymbol{\theta}_o)\mathbf{s}_{ir}(\boldsymbol{\theta}_o)']$, $t \neq r$. For each t, the CIME holds:

$$\mathbf{A}_{it}(\boldsymbol{\theta}_o) = \mathrm{E}[\mathbf{s}_{it}(\boldsymbol{\theta}_o)\mathbf{s}_{it}(\boldsymbol{\theta}_o)' \,|\, \mathbf{x}_{it}].$$

If $\{\mathbf{x}_{it}\}$ is strictly exogenous then $\mathbf{A}_{it}(\boldsymbol{\theta}_o) = \mathrm{E}[\mathbf{s}_{it}(\boldsymbol{\theta}_o)\mathbf{s}_{it}(\boldsymbol{\theta}_o)' \,|\, \mathbf{x}_{it}]$. But strict exogeneity does not help simplify inference because, whether or not strict exogeneity holds, $-\mathrm{E}[\mathbf{H}_i(\boldsymbol{\theta}_o) \,|\, \mathbf{x}_i] = \mathrm{E}[\mathbf{s}_i(\boldsymbol{\theta}_o)\mathbf{s}_i(\boldsymbol{\theta}_o)' \,|\, \mathbf{x}_i]$ likely fails if the scores are serially correlated. More important, serial correlation in the scores causes $\mathbf{B}_o \neq \mathbf{A}_o$. Thus, to perform inference in the context of partial MLE, we generally need separate estimates of $\mathbf{A}_o$ and $\mathbf{B}_o$. Given the structure of the partial MLE, these are easy to obtain. Three possibilities for $\mathbf{A}_o$ are

$$N^{-1}\sum_{i=1}^{N}\sum_{t=1}^{T} -\nabla_\theta^2 \ell_{it}(\hat{\boldsymbol{\theta}}), \qquad N^{-1}\sum_{i=1}^{N}\sum_{t=1}^{T} \mathbf{A}_{it}(\hat{\boldsymbol{\theta}}), \qquad \text{and}$$

$$N^{-1}\sum_{i=1}^{N}\sum_{t=1}^{T} \mathbf{s}_{it}(\hat{\boldsymbol{\theta}})\mathbf{s}_{it}(\hat{\boldsymbol{\theta}})'. \tag{13.50}$$

The validity of the second of these follows from a standard iterated expectations argument, and the last of these follows from the CIME for each t. In most cases, the second estimator is preferred when it is easy to compute.

Since $\mathbf{B}_o$ depends on $\mathrm{E}[\mathbf{s}_{it}(\boldsymbol{\theta}_o)\mathbf{s}_{it}(\boldsymbol{\theta}_o)']$ as well as on cross product terms, there are also at least three estimators available for $\mathbf{B}_o$. The simplest is

$$N^{-1}\sum_{i=1}^{N} \hat{\mathbf{s}}_i\hat{\mathbf{s}}_i' = N^{-1}\sum_{i=1}^{N}\sum_{t=1}^{T} \hat{\mathbf{s}}_{it}\hat{\mathbf{s}}_{it}' + N^{-1}\sum_{i=1}^{N}\sum_{t=1}^{T}\sum_{r\neq t} \hat{\mathbf{s}}_{ir}\hat{\mathbf{s}}_{it}', \tag{13.51}$$

where the second term on the right-hand side accounts for possible serial correlation in the score. The first term on the right-hand side of equation (13.51) can be replaced by one of the other two estimators in equation (13.50). The asymptotic variance of $\hat{\boldsymbol{\theta}}$ is estimated, as usual, by $\hat{\mathbf{A}}^{-1}\hat{\mathbf{B}}\hat{\mathbf{A}}^{-1}/N$ for the chosen estimators $\hat{\mathbf{A}}$ and $\hat{\mathbf{B}}$. The asymptotic standard errors come directly from this matrix, and Wald tests for linear and nonlinear hypotheses can be obtained directly. The robust score statistic discussed in Section 12.6.2 can also be used. When $\mathbf{B}_o \neq \mathbf{A}_o$, the likelihood ratio statistic computed after pooled estimation is *not* valid.

Because the CIME holds for each t, $\mathbf{B}_o = \mathbf{A}_o$ when the scores evaluated at $\boldsymbol{\theta}_o$ are serially uncorrelated, that is, when

$$\mathrm{E}[\mathbf{s}_{it}(\boldsymbol{\theta}_o)\mathbf{s}_{ir}(\boldsymbol{\theta}_o)'] = \mathbf{0}, \qquad t \neq r. \tag{13.52}$$

When the score is serially uncorrelated, inference is very easy: the usual MLE statistics computed from the pooled estimation, including likelihood ratio statistics, are asymptotically valid. Effectively, we can ignore the fact that a time dimension is present. The estimator of $\mathrm{Avar}(\hat{\boldsymbol{\theta}})$ is just $\hat{\mathbf{A}}^{-1}/N$, where $\hat{\mathbf{A}}$ is one of the matrices in equation (13.50).

Example 13.3 (continued): For the pooled probit example, a simple, general estimator of the asymptotic variance is

$$\left[\sum_{i=1}^{N}\sum_{t=1}^{T}\mathbf{A}_{it}(\hat{\boldsymbol{\theta}})\right]^{-1}\left[\sum_{i=1}^{N}\mathbf{s}_i(\hat{\boldsymbol{\theta}})\mathbf{s}_i(\hat{\boldsymbol{\theta}})'\right]\left[\sum_{i=1}^{N}\sum_{t=1}^{T}\mathbf{A}_{it}(\hat{\boldsymbol{\theta}})\right]^{-1}, \tag{13.53}$$

where

$$\mathbf{A}_{it}(\hat{\boldsymbol{\theta}}) = \frac{\{\phi(\mathbf{x}_{it}\hat{\boldsymbol{\theta}})\}^2\mathbf{x}_{it}'\mathbf{x}_{it}}{\Phi(\mathbf{x}_{it}\hat{\boldsymbol{\theta}})[1-\Phi(\mathbf{x}_{it}\hat{\boldsymbol{\theta}})]}$$

and

$$\mathbf{s}_i(\boldsymbol{\theta}) = \sum_{t=1}^{T}\mathbf{s}_{it}(\boldsymbol{\theta}) = \sum_{t=1}^{T}\frac{\phi(\mathbf{x}_{it}\boldsymbol{\theta})\mathbf{x}_{it}'[y_{it}-\Phi(\mathbf{x}_{it}\boldsymbol{\theta})]}{\Phi(\mathbf{x}_{it}\boldsymbol{\theta})[1-\Phi(\mathbf{x}_{it}\boldsymbol{\theta})]}.$$

The estimator (13.53) contains cross product terms of the form $\mathbf{s}_{it}(\hat{\boldsymbol{\theta}})\mathbf{s}_{ir}(\hat{\boldsymbol{\theta}})'$, $t \neq r$, and so it is fully robust. If the score is serially uncorrelated, then the usual probit standard errors and test statistics from the pooled estimation are valid. We will discuss a sufficient condition for the scores to be serially uncorrelated in the next subsection.

13.8.3 Inference with Dynamically Complete Models

There is a very important case where condition (13.52) holds, in which case all statistics obtained by treating $\ell_i(\boldsymbol{\theta})$ as a standard log likelihood are valid. For any definition of $\mathbf{x}_t$, we say that $\{f_t(y_t \mid \mathbf{x}_t; \boldsymbol{\theta}_o) : t = 1, \ldots, T\}$ is a **dynamically complete conditional density** if

$$f_t(y_t \mid \mathbf{x}_t; \boldsymbol{\theta}_o) = p_t^o(y_t \mid \mathbf{x}_t, y_{t-1}, \mathbf{x}_{t-1}, y_{t-2}, \ldots, y_1, \mathbf{x}_1), \qquad t = 1, \ldots, T. \tag{13.54}$$

In other words, $f_t(y_t \mid \mathbf{x}_t; \boldsymbol{\theta}_o)$ must be the conditional density of y_t given $\mathbf{x}_t$ *and* the entire past of $(\mathbf{x}_t, y_t)$. Equation (13.54) implies that the density is correctly specified. We can state the assumption that $\mathbf{x}_{it}$ captures all of the distributional dynamics for y_{it} by writing $\mathrm{D}(y_{it} \mid \mathbf{x}_{it}, y_{i,t-1}, \mathbf{x}_{i,t-1}, \ldots, y_{i1}, \mathbf{x}_{i1}) = \mathrm{D}(y_{it} \mid \mathbf{x}_{it})$, a shorthand that is useful because it is separate from model specification.

When $\mathbf{x}_t = \mathbf{z}_t$ for contemporaneous exogenous variables, assumption (13.54) is very strong: it means that, once $\mathbf{z}_t$ is controlled for, no past values of $\mathbf{z}_t$ *or* y_t appear in the conditional density $p_t^{\mathrm{o}}(y_t \mid \mathbf{z}_t, y_{t-1}, \mathbf{z}_{t-1}, y_{t-2}, \ldots, y_1, \mathbf{z}_1)$. When $\mathbf{x}_t$ contains $\mathbf{z}_t$ and some lags—similar to a finite distributed lag model—then equation (13.54) is perhaps more reasonable, but it still assumes that lagged y_t has no effect on y_t once current and lagged $\mathbf{z}_t$ are controlled for. That assumption (13.54) can be false is analogous to the omnipresence of serial correlation in static and finite distributed lag regression models. One important feature of dynamic completeness is that it does not require strict exogeneity of $\mathbf{z}_t$ [since only current and lagged $\mathbf{x}_t$ appear in equation (13.54)].

Dynamic completeness is more likely to hold when $\mathbf{x}_t$ contains lagged dependent variables. The issue, then, is whether enough lags of y_t (and $\mathbf{z}_t$) have been included in $\mathbf{x}_t$ to fully capture the dynamics. For example, if $\mathbf{x}_t \equiv (\mathbf{z}_t, y_{t-1})$, then equation (13.54) means that, along with $\mathbf{z}_t$, only one lag of y_t is needed to capture all of the dynamics.

Showing that condition (13.52) holds under dynamic completeness is easy. First, for each t, $\mathrm{E}[\mathbf{s}_{it}(\boldsymbol{\theta}_o) \mid \mathbf{x}_{it}] = \mathbf{0}$, since $f_t(y_t \mid \mathbf{x}_t; \boldsymbol{\theta}_o)$ is a correctly specified conditional density. But then, under assumption (13.54),

$$\mathrm{E}[\mathbf{s}_{it}(\boldsymbol{\theta}_o) \mid \mathbf{x}_{it}, y_{i,t-1}, \ldots, y_{i1}, \mathbf{x}_{i1}] = \mathbf{0}. \tag{13.55}$$

Now consider the expected value in condition (13.52) for $r < t$. Since $\mathbf{s}_{ir}(\boldsymbol{\theta}_o)$ is a function of $(\mathbf{x}_{ir}, y_{ir})$, which is in the conditioning set (13.55), the usual iterated expectations argument shows that condition (13.52) holds. It follows that, under dynamic completeness, the usual maximum likelihood statistics from the pooled estimation are asymptotically valid. This result is completely analogous to pooled OLS under dynamic completeness of the conditional mean and homoskedasticity (see Section 7.8).

If the panel data probit model is dynamically complete, any software package that does standard probit can be used to obtain valid standard errors and test statistics, provided the response probability satisfies $\mathrm{P}(y_{it} = 1 \mid \mathbf{x}_{it}) = \mathrm{P}(y_{it} = 1 \mid \mathbf{x}_{it}, y_{i,t-1}, \mathbf{x}_{i,t-1}, \ldots)$. Without dynamic completeness the standard errors and test statistics generally need to be adjusted for serial dependence.

Since dynamic completeness affords nontrivial simplifications, does this fact mean that we should always include lagged values of exogenous and dependent variables until equation (13.54) appears to be satisfied? Not necessarily. Static models are sometimes desirable even if they neglect dynamics. For example, suppose that we have panel data on individuals in an occupation where pay is determined partly by cumulative productivity. (Professional athletes and college professors are two examples.) An equation relating salary to the productivity measures, and possibly demographic variables, is appropriate. Nothing implies that the equation would be dynamically complete; in fact, past salary could help predict current salary, even after controlling for observed productivity. But it does not make much sense to include past salary in the regression equation. As we know from Chapter 10, a reasonable approach is to include an unobserved effect in the equation, and this does not lead to a model with complete dynamics. See also Section 13.9.

We may wish to test the null hypothesis that the density is dynamically complete. White (1994) shows how to test whether the score is serially correlated in a pure time series setting. A similar approach can be used with panel data. A general test for dynamic misspecification can be based on the limiting distribution of (the vectorization of)

$$N^{-1/2}\sum_{i=1}^{N}\sum_{t=2}^{T}\hat{\mathbf{s}}_{it}\hat{\mathbf{s}}_{i,t-1}',$$

where the scores are evaluated at the pooled MLE. Rather than derive a general statistic here, we will study tests of dynamic completeness in particular applications later (see particularly Chapters 15, 16, and 17).

13.9 Panel Data Models with Unobserved Effects

As we saw in Chapters 10 and 11, linear unobserved effects panel data models play an important role in modern empirical research. Nonlinear unobserved effects panel data models are becoming increasingly more important. Although we will cover particular models in Chapters 15 through 18, it is useful to have a general treatment.

13.9.1 Models with Strictly Exogenous Explanatory Variables

For each i, let $\{(\mathbf{y}_{it}, \mathbf{x}_{it}) : t = 1, 2, \ldots, T\}$ be a random draw from the cross section, where $\mathbf{y}_{it}$ and $\mathbf{x}_{it}$ can both be vectors. Associated with each cross section unit i is unobserved heterogeneity, $\mathbf{c}_i$, which could be a vector. We assume interest lies in the distribution of $\mathbf{y}_{it}$ given $(\mathbf{x}_{it}, \mathbf{c}_i)$. The vector $\mathbf{x}_{it}$ can contain lags of contemporaneous variables, say $\mathbf{z}_{it}$ (for example, $\mathbf{x}_{it} = (\mathbf{z}_{it}, \mathbf{z}_{i,t-1}, \mathbf{z}_{i,t-2})$), or even leads of $\mathbf{z}_{it}$ (for example, $\mathbf{x}_{it} = (\mathbf{z}_{it}, \mathbf{z}_{i,t+1})$), but not lags of y_{it}. Whatever the lag structure, we let $t = 1$ denote the first time period available for estimation.

Let $f_t(\mathbf{y}_t \mid \mathbf{x}_t, \mathbf{c}; \boldsymbol{\theta})$ denote a correctly specified density for each t. A key assumption on $\mathbf{x}_{it}$ is **strict exogeneity conditional on the unobserved effects**:

$$\mathrm{D}(\mathbf{y}_{it} \mid \mathbf{x}_{i1}, \mathbf{x}_{i2}, \ldots, \mathbf{x}_{iT}, \mathbf{c}_i) = \mathrm{D}(\mathbf{y}_{it} \mid \mathbf{x}_{it}, \mathbf{c}_i), \qquad t = 1, \ldots, T, \tag{13.56}$$

which means that $\mathbf{x}_{ir}$, $r \neq t$, does not appear in the conditional distribution of $\mathbf{y}_{it}$ once $\mathbf{x}_{it}$ and $\mathbf{c}_i$ have been counted for. In addition to ruling out lagged dependent variables, (13.56) does not allow for general feedback from unanticipated changes in $\mathbf{y}_{it}$ to changes in $\mathbf{x}_{i,t+h}$ for $h > 1$.

A common but restrictive approach to estimating $\boldsymbol{\theta}_o$ (and other quantities of interest, such as average partial effects) is to assume that $\mathbf{c}_i$ is independent of $\mathbf{x}_i = (\mathbf{x}_{i1}, \mathbf{x}_{i2}, \ldots, \mathbf{x}_{iT})$, that is, $\mathrm{D}(\mathbf{c}_i \mid \mathbf{x}_i) = \mathrm{D}(\mathbf{c}_i)$, and to model the distribution of $\mathbf{c}_i$. Such an approach is very similar to the random effects approach to linear panel data models in Chapter 10. There we did not assume full independence (because linear models do not require such a strong assumption), but we assumed conditional mean independence, $\mathrm{E}(\mathbf{c}_i \mid \mathbf{x}_i) = \mathrm{E}(\mathbf{c}_i)$, or, at the very least, zero correlation. In general nonlinear models, it is handy to label $\mathrm{D}(\mathbf{c}_i \mid \mathbf{x}_i) = \mathrm{D}(\mathbf{c}_i)$ as a **random effects (RE)** assumption.

In special cases, which we will address in Chapters 15 and 18, we can consistently estimate $\boldsymbol{\theta}_o$ without imposing any assumptions about $\mathrm{D}(\mathbf{c}_i \mid \mathbf{x}_i)$. Such situations are reminiscent of the **fixed effects (FE)** assumptions from Chapter 10, and we will use that label for nonlinear models, too. As we will see through later examples, in nonlinear models estimation of $\boldsymbol{\theta}_o$ is not always sufficient to calculate the quantities of interest, but it is nevertheless useful when possible.

One way to avoid specifying a model for $\mathrm{D}(\mathbf{c}_i \mid \mathbf{x}_i)$ would be to treat $\{\mathbf{c}_i : i = 1, \ldots, N\}$ as parameters to estimate along with $\boldsymbol{\theta}_o$. However, because the number of $\mathbf{c}_i$ increases with N, attempting to estimate them leads to an **incidental parameters problem** for estimating $\boldsymbol{\theta}_o$. Namely, we cannot consistently estimate $\boldsymbol{\theta}_o$ with fixed T and $N \to \infty$ (except by fluke in a couple of special cases, including the linear model with additive c_i in Chapter 10). For this reason, in this book we reserve the designation "fixed effects" for situations in which we can eliminate the $\mathbf{c}_i$ from a particular conditional distribution that still depends on $\boldsymbol{\theta}_o$, and then apply conditional maximum likelihood methods to consistently estimate $\boldsymbol{\theta}_o$ for fixed T. We do not give a general treatment because the method applies only in special cases, and we cover those in Part IV.

A middle ground between RE and FE approaches is to allow $\mathrm{D}(\mathbf{c}_i \mid \mathbf{x}_i)$ to depend on $\mathbf{x}_i$, but then to model this distribution by specifying a parametric model of the conditional density. In Chapter 10, we mentioned that modeling $\mathrm{E}(\mathbf{c}_i \mid \mathbf{x}_i)$ as a function of $\mathbf{x}_i$ has been called a **correlated random effects (CRE)** approach, and we will use this label subsequently to refer to situations where we model the distribution $\mathrm{D}(\mathbf{c}_i \mid \mathbf{x}_i)$. Often, to impose parsimony we restrict the way in which $\mathrm{D}(\mathbf{c}_i \mid \mathbf{x}_i)$ can depend on the time series $\{\mathbf{x}_{it} : t = 1, 2, \ldots, T\}$. A common restriction is $\mathrm{D}(\mathbf{c}_i \mid \mathbf{x}_i) = \mathrm{D}(\mathbf{c}_i \mid \bar{\mathbf{x}}_i)$, where $\bar{\mathbf{x}}_i$ is the time average. With large enough T, we can allow $\mathrm{D}(\mathbf{c}_i \mid \mathbf{x}_i)$ to depend on other features, such as the individual-specific variance $(T-1)^{-1} \sum_{t=1}^{T} (\mathbf{x}_{it} - \bar{\mathbf{x}}_i)'(\mathbf{x}_{it} - \bar{\mathbf{x}}_i)$ or average growth rates. For the present treatment, there is no gain in considering special cases. Therefore, let $h(\mathbf{c} \mid \mathbf{x}; \boldsymbol{\delta})$ be a correctly specified density for $\mathrm{D}(\mathbf{c}_i \mid \mathbf{x}_i)$.

Once we have specified $h(\mathbf{c} \mid \mathbf{x}; \boldsymbol{\delta})$, there are two common ways to proceed. First, we can make the additional assumption that, conditional on $(\mathbf{x}_i, \mathbf{c}_i)$, the $\mathbf{y}_{it}$ are independent. Then, the joint density of $(\mathbf{y}_{i1}, \ldots, \mathbf{y}_{iT})$, given $(\mathbf{x}_i, \mathbf{c}_i)$, is

$$\prod_{t=1}^{T} f_t(\mathbf{y}_t \mid \mathbf{x}_{it}, \mathbf{c}_i; \boldsymbol{\theta}).$$

We cannot use this density directly to estimate $\boldsymbol{\theta}_o$ because we do not observe the outcomes $\mathbf{c}_i$. Treating the $\mathbf{c}_i$ as parameters to estimate with $\boldsymbol{\theta}_o$ leads to the incidental parameters problem mentioned earlier. Instead, we can use the density of $\mathbf{c}_i$ given $\mathbf{x}_i$ to integrate out the dependence on $\mathbf{c}$. The density of $\mathbf{y}_i$ given $\mathbf{x}_i$ is

$$\int_{\mathbb{R}^J} \left[\prod_{t=1}^{T} f_t(\mathbf{y}_t \mid \mathbf{x}_{it}, \mathbf{c}; \boldsymbol{\theta}_o) \right] h(\mathbf{c} \mid \mathbf{x}_i; \boldsymbol{\delta}_o)\, d\mathbf{c}, \tag{13.57}$$

where J is the dimension of $\mathbf{c}$ and $h(\mathbf{c} \mid \mathbf{x}; \boldsymbol{\delta})$ is the correctly specified model for the density of $\mathbf{c}_i$ given $\mathbf{x}_i = \mathbf{x}$. For concreteness, we assume that $\mathbf{c}$ is a continuous random vector. For each i, the log-likelihood function is

$$\log\left\{ \int_{\mathbb{R}^J} \left[\prod_{t=1}^{T} f_t(\mathbf{y}_{it} \mid \mathbf{x}_{it}, \mathbf{c}; \boldsymbol{\theta}_o) \right] h(\mathbf{c} \mid \mathbf{x}_i; \boldsymbol{\delta}_o)\, d\mathbf{c} \right\}. \tag{13.58}$$

[It is important to see that expression (13.58) does not depend on the $\mathbf{c}_i$; $\mathbf{c}$ has been integrated out.] Assuming identification and standard regularity conditions, we can consistently estimate $\boldsymbol{\theta}_o$ and $\boldsymbol{\delta}_o$ by conditional MLE, where the asymptotics are for fixed T and $N \to \infty$. The CMLE is $\sqrt{N}$-asymptotically normal.

A different approach is often simpler and places no restrictions on the joint distribution of the $\mathbf{y}_{it}$ conditional on $(\mathbf{x}_i, \mathbf{c}_i)$. For each t, we can obtain the density of $\mathbf{y}_{it}$

given $\mathbf{x}_i$ by integrating out $\mathbf{c}_i$:

$$\int_{\mathbb{R}^J} [f_t(\mathbf{y}_t \mid \mathbf{x}_{it}, \mathbf{c}; \boldsymbol{\theta}_o)] h(\mathbf{c} \mid \mathbf{x}_i; \boldsymbol{\delta}_o) \, d\mathbf{c}.$$

Now the problem becomes one of partial MLE. We estimate $\boldsymbol{\theta}_o$ and $\boldsymbol{\delta}_o$ by maximizing

$$\sum_{i=1}^{N} \sum_{t=1}^{T} \log\left\{ \int_{\mathbb{R}^J} [f_t(\mathbf{y}_{it} \mid \mathbf{x}_{it}, \mathbf{c}; \boldsymbol{\theta})] h(\mathbf{c} \mid \mathbf{x}_i; \boldsymbol{\delta}) \, d\mathbf{c} \right\}, \tag{13.59}$$

where the term in braces is a correctly specified model of the density of $\mathrm{D}(\mathbf{y}_{it} \mid \mathbf{x}_i)$. (Actually, using PMLE, $\boldsymbol{\theta}_o$ and $\boldsymbol{\delta}_o$ are not always separately identified, although interesting functions of them, such as average partial effects, are. We will see examples in Chapters 15, 16, and 17.) Across time, the scores for each i will necessarily be serially correlated because the $\mathbf{y}_{it}$ are dependent when we condition only on $\mathbf{x}_i$, and not also on $\mathbf{c}_i$. Therefore, we must make inference robust to serial dependence, as in Section 13.8.2. In Chapter 15, we will study both the conditional MLE and partial MLE approaches for unobserved effects probit models. We do the same for Tobit models in Chapter 17.

13.9.2 Models with Lagged Dependent Variables

Now assume that we are interested in modeling $\mathrm{D}(\mathbf{y}_{it} \mid \mathbf{z}_{it}, \mathbf{y}_{i,t-1}, \mathbf{c}_i)$ where, for simplicity, we include only contemporaneous conditioning variables, $\mathbf{z}_{it}$, and only one lag of $\mathbf{y}_{it}$. Adding lags (or even leads) of $\mathbf{z}_{it}$ or more lags of $\mathbf{y}_{it}$ requires only a notational change.

A key assumption is that we have the dynamics correctly specified and that $\mathbf{z}_i = \{\mathbf{z}_{i1}, \ldots, \mathbf{z}_{iT}\}$ is appropriately strictly exogenous (conditional on $\mathbf{c}_i$). These assumptions are both captured by

$$\mathrm{D}(\mathbf{y}_{it} \mid \mathbf{z}_{it}, \mathbf{y}_{i,t-1}, \mathbf{c}_i) = \mathrm{D}(\mathbf{y}_{it} \mid \mathbf{z}_i, \mathbf{y}_{i,t-1}, \ldots, \mathbf{y}_{i0}, \mathbf{c}_i). \tag{13.60}$$

We assume that $f_t(\mathbf{y}_t \mid \mathbf{z}_t, \mathbf{y}_{t-1}, \mathbf{c}; \boldsymbol{\theta})$ is a correctly specified density for the conditional distribution on the left-hand side of equation (13.60). Given strict exogeneity of $\{\mathbf{z}_{it} : t = 1, \ldots, T\}$ and dynamic completeness, the density of $(\mathbf{y}_{i1}, \ldots, \mathbf{y}_{iT})$ given $(\mathbf{z}_i = \mathbf{z}, \mathbf{y}_{i0} = \mathbf{y}_0, \mathbf{c}_i = \mathbf{c})$ is

$$\prod_{t=1}^{T} f_t(\mathbf{y}_t \mid \mathbf{z}_t, \mathbf{y}_{t-1}, \mathbf{c}; \boldsymbol{\theta}_o). \tag{13.61}$$

(By convention, $\mathbf{y}_{i0}$ is the first observation on $\mathbf{y}_{it}$.) Again, to estimate $\boldsymbol{\theta}_o$, we integrate $\mathbf{c}$ out of this density. To do so, we specify a density for $\mathbf{c}_i$ given $\mathbf{z}_i$ *and* the initial value

$\mathbf{y}_{i0}$ (sometimes called the **initial condition**). Let $h(\mathbf{c} \mid \mathbf{z}, \mathbf{y}_0; \boldsymbol{\delta})$ denote the model for this conditional density. Then, assuming that we have this model correctly specified, the density of $(\mathbf{y}_{i1}, \ldots, \mathbf{y}_{iT})$ given $(\mathbf{z}_i = \mathbf{z}, \mathbf{y}_{i0} = \mathbf{y}_0)$ is

$$\int_{\mathbb{R}^J} \left[\prod_{t=1}^{T} f_t(\mathbf{y}_t \mid \mathbf{z}_t, \mathbf{y}_{t-1}, \mathbf{c}; \boldsymbol{\theta}_o) \right] h(\mathbf{c} \mid \mathbf{z}, \mathbf{y}_0; \boldsymbol{\delta}_o)\, d\mathbf{c}, \tag{13.62}$$

which, for each i, leads to the log-likelihood function conditional on $(\mathbf{z}_i, \mathbf{y}_{i0})$:

$$\log\left\{ \int_{\mathbb{R}^J} \left[\prod_{t=1}^{T} f_t(\mathbf{y}_{it} \mid \mathbf{z}_{it}, \mathbf{y}_{i,t-1}, \mathbf{c}; \boldsymbol{\theta}) \right] h(\mathbf{c} \mid \mathbf{z}_i, \mathbf{y}_{i0}; \boldsymbol{\delta})\, d\mathbf{c} \right\}. \tag{13.63}$$

We sum expression (13.63) across $i = 1, \ldots, N$ and maximize with respect to $\boldsymbol{\theta}$ and $\boldsymbol{\delta}$ to obtain the CMLEs. Provided all functions are sufficiently differentiable and identification holds, the CMLEs are consistent and $\sqrt{N}$-asymptotically normal, as usual. Because we have fully specified the conditional density of $(\mathbf{y}_{i1}, \ldots, \mathbf{y}_{iT})$ given $(\mathbf{z}_i, \mathbf{y}_{i0})$, the general theory of CMLE applies directly. (The fact that the distribution of $\mathbf{y}_{i0}$ given $\mathbf{z}_i$ would typically depend on $\boldsymbol{\theta}_o$ has no bearing on the consistency of the CMLE. The fact that we are conditioning on $\mathbf{y}_{i0}$, rather than basing the analysis on $\mathrm{D}(\mathbf{y}_{i0}, \mathbf{y}_{i1}, \ldots, \mathbf{y}_{iT} \mid \mathbf{z}_i)$, means that we are generally sacrificing efficiency. But by conditioning on $\mathbf{y}_{i0}$ we do not have to find $\mathrm{D}(\mathbf{y}_{i0} \mid \mathbf{z}_i)$, a feat that can be very difficult, if not impossible.) The asymptotic variance of $(\hat{\boldsymbol{\theta}}', \hat{\boldsymbol{\delta}}')'$ can be estimated by any of the formulas in equation (13.32) (properly modified to account for estimation of $\boldsymbol{\theta}_o$ and $\boldsymbol{\delta}_o$).

A weakness of the CMLE approach is that we must specify a density for $\mathbf{c}_i$ given $(\mathbf{z}_i, \mathbf{y}_{i0})$, but this is a price we pay for estimating dynamic, nonlinear models with unobserved effects. The alternative of treating the $\mathbf{c}_i$ as parameters to estimate—which is, unfortunately, often labeled the "fixed effects" approach—does not lead to consistent estimation of $\boldsymbol{\theta}_o$ because of the incidental parameters problem.

In any application, several issues need to be addressed. First, when are the parameters identified? Second, what quantities are we interested in? As we cannot observe $\mathbf{c}_i$, we typically want to average out $\mathbf{c}_i$ when obtaining partial effects. Wooldridge (2005b) shows that average partial effects are generally identified under the assumptions that we have made. Finally, obtaining the CMLE can be very difficult computationally, as can be obtaining the asymptotic variance estimates in equation (13.32). If $\mathbf{c}_i$ is a scalar, estimation is easier, but there is still a one-dimensional integral to approximate for each i. In Chapters 15 through 18 we will see that, under reasonable assumptions, standard software can be used to estimate dynamic models with unobserved effects, including effects that are averaged across the distribution of heterogeneity. See also Problem 13.11 for application to a dynamic linear model.

13.10 Two-Step Estimators Involving Maximum Likelihood

From the results in Chapter 12 on two-step estimation, we know that consistency and asymptotic normality generally apply to two-step estimators that involve maximum likelihood. We provide a brief treatment here, covering two cases. The first is when the second-step estimation is MLE (and the first step may or may not be). Then we cover an interesting situation that can arise when the first-step estimator is MLE.

13.10.1 Second-Step Estimator Is Maximum Likelihood Estimator

Assume that we have a correctly specified density for the conditional distribution $\mathrm{D}(\mathbf{y}_i \mid \mathbf{x}_i)$. Write the model as $f(\mathbf{y} \mid \mathbf{x}; \boldsymbol{\theta}, \gamma)$ for $\boldsymbol{\theta}$ a $P \times 1$ vector and γ a $J \times 1$ vector. The true density is $f(\mathbf{y} \mid \mathbf{x}; \boldsymbol{\theta}_{\mathrm{o}}, \gamma_{\mathrm{o}})$. A preliminary estimator of γ_{o}, say $\hat{\gamma}$, is plugged into the log-likelihood function, and $\hat{\boldsymbol{\theta}}$ solves

$$\max_{\boldsymbol{\theta} \in \boldsymbol{\Theta}} \sum_{i=1}^{N} \log f(\mathbf{y}_i \mid \mathbf{x}_i; \boldsymbol{\theta}, \hat{\gamma}).$$

We call $\hat{\boldsymbol{\theta}}$ a **two-step maximum likelihood estimator**. Consistency of $\hat{\boldsymbol{\theta}}$ follows from results for two-step M-estimators. The practical limitation is that $\log f(\mathbf{y}_i \mid \mathbf{x}_i; \boldsymbol{\theta}, \gamma)$ is continuous on $\boldsymbol{\Theta} \times \boldsymbol{\Gamma}$ and that $\boldsymbol{\theta}_{\mathrm{o}}$ and γ_{o} are identified.

Asymptotic normality of the two-step MLE follows directly from the results on two-step M-estimation in Chapter 12. As we saw there, in general the asymptotic variance of $\sqrt{N}(\hat{\boldsymbol{\theta}} - \boldsymbol{\theta}_{\mathrm{o}})$ depends on the asymptotic variance of $\sqrt{N}(\hat{\gamma} - \gamma_{\mathrm{o}})$ [see equation (12.41)], so we need to know the estimation problem solved by $\hat{\gamma}$. In some cases estimation of γ_{o} can be ignored. An important case is where the expected Hessian, defined with respect to $\boldsymbol{\theta}$ and γ, is block diagonal (the matrix $\mathbf{F}_{\mathrm{o}}$ in equation (12.36) is zero in this case). It can also hold for some values of $\boldsymbol{\theta}_{\mathrm{o}}$, which is important for testing certain hypotheses. We will encounter several examples in Part IV.

Of course, we can also apply two-step methods when the second step is a partial MLE, resulting in a **two-step partial MLE**. As usual, consistency and asymptotic normality hold under correct specification of the marginal (conditional) density for each t and standard regularity conditions. The practical issue is in computing an appropriate asymptotic variance. We will not give a general treatment here, as the general results on M-estimation can be applied directly when we need them in Part IV.

13.10.2 Surprising Efficiency Result When the First-Step Estimator Is Conditional Maximum Likelihood Estimator

We now turn to a case where the conclusion seems counterintuitive: under certain assumptions, estimating parameters in a first stage, by CMLE, can improve the asymptotic efficiency of a second-step M-estimator. To study this phenomenon, assume that the second-step M-estimator, $\hat{\boldsymbol{\theta}}$, solves the problem

$$\min_{\boldsymbol{\theta} \in \boldsymbol{\Theta}} \sum_{i=1}^{N} q(\mathbf{v}_i, \mathbf{w}_i, \mathbf{z}_i, \boldsymbol{\theta}, \hat{\boldsymbol{\gamma}}), \tag{13.64}$$

where we maintain the regularity conditions used in Chapter 12 to apply mean value expansions, the uniform law of large numbers, and the central limit theorem. For reasons we will see, we have separated the data vector in (13.64) into three vectors, $\mathbf{v}_i$, $\mathbf{w}_i$, and $\mathbf{z}_i$. We assume the first-step estimator, $\hat{\boldsymbol{\gamma}}$, comes from a (conditional) MLE problem (that satisfies the appropriate regularity conditions):

$$\max_{\boldsymbol{\gamma} \in \boldsymbol{\Gamma}} \sum_{i=1}^{N} \log h(\mathbf{v}_i \mid \mathbf{z}_i; \boldsymbol{\gamma}),$$

where $h(\cdot \mid \mathbf{z}; \boldsymbol{\gamma})$ is a model of the density underlying $\mathrm{D}(\mathbf{v}_i \mid \mathbf{z}_i)$, and we assume this density is correctly specified with population value $\boldsymbol{\gamma}_o$. By the information matrix equality, we can assume

$$\sqrt{N}(\hat{\boldsymbol{\gamma}} - \boldsymbol{\gamma}_o) = \{\mathrm{E}[\mathbf{d}_i(\boldsymbol{\gamma}_o)\mathbf{d}_i(\boldsymbol{\gamma}_o)']\}^{-1} N^{-1/2} \sum_{i=1}^{N} \mathbf{d}_i(\boldsymbol{\gamma}_o) + o_p(1), \tag{13.65}$$

where $\mathbf{d}_i(\boldsymbol{\gamma}) \equiv \nabla_{\gamma} \log h(\mathbf{v}_i \mid \mathbf{z}_i; \boldsymbol{\gamma})'$ is the $J \times 1$ score of the first-step log likelihood. If we assume nothing further, we would simply have to derive, and estimate, the asymptotic variance of $\sqrt{N}(\hat{\boldsymbol{\theta}} - \boldsymbol{\theta}_o)$ using the methods in Section 12.5.2. But suppose we add the assumption

$$\mathrm{D}(\mathbf{v}_i \mid \mathbf{w}_i, \mathbf{z}_i) = \mathrm{D}(\mathbf{v}_i \mid \mathbf{z}_i), \tag{13.66}$$

which is often called a **conditional independence assumption**: conditional on $\mathbf{z}_i$, $\mathbf{v}_i$ and $\mathbf{w}_i$ are independent. In a sense, assumption (13.66) means that $\mathbf{z}_i$ is such a good explainor of $\mathbf{v}_i$—at least relative to $\mathbf{w}_i$—that once we know $\mathbf{z}_i$, $\mathbf{w}_i$ tells us nothing about the likelihood of outcomes on $\mathbf{v}_i$. This assumption is special, but, as we will see in Part IV, it holds under certain stratified sampling schemes as well as in the context of estimating treatment effects under so-called ignorability of treatment assumptions.

Now, let $\mathbf{s}_i(\boldsymbol{\theta}, \gamma) \equiv \mathbf{s}(\mathbf{v}_i, \mathbf{w}_i, \mathbf{z}_i, \boldsymbol{\theta}, \gamma) \equiv \nabla_\theta q(\mathbf{v}_i, \mathbf{w}_i, \mathbf{z}_i, \boldsymbol{\theta}, \gamma)'$ be the $P \times 1$ score of the second-step objective function, but only with respect to $\boldsymbol{\theta}$. In order to find Avar $\sqrt{N}(\hat{\boldsymbol{\theta}} - \boldsymbol{\theta}_o)$, we need to find the $P \times J$ matrix $\mathbf{F}_o = \mathrm{E}[\nabla_\gamma \mathbf{s}_i(\boldsymbol{\theta}_o, \gamma_o)]$. The key step is to use the generalized CIME in equation (13.39), where it is important to note that, under (13.66), $\mathbf{d}_i(\gamma)$ is the score for the density of $\mathbf{v}_i$ given $(\mathbf{w}_i, \mathbf{z}_i)$, even though it depends only on $\mathbf{z}_i$. Therefore, because $\mathbf{s}_i(\boldsymbol{\theta}_o, \gamma)$ is a function of $(\mathbf{v}_i, \mathbf{w}_i, \mathbf{z}_i)$, we have

$$-\mathrm{E}[\nabla_\gamma \mathbf{s}_i(\boldsymbol{\theta}_o, \gamma_o) \mid \mathbf{w}_i, \mathbf{z}_i] = \mathrm{E}[\mathbf{s}_i(\boldsymbol{\theta}_o, \gamma_o)\mathbf{d}_i(\gamma)' \mid \mathbf{w}_i, \mathbf{z}_i], \tag{13.67}$$

so, using iterated expectations, we conclude that $\mathbf{F}_o = -\mathrm{E}[\mathbf{s}_i(\boldsymbol{\theta}_o, \gamma_o)\mathbf{d}_i(\gamma)']$. But then by equation (12.39) and (13.65),

$$\sqrt{N}(\hat{\boldsymbol{\theta}} - \boldsymbol{\theta}_o) = -\mathbf{A}_o^{-1} N^{-1/2} \sum_{i=1}^{N} \{\mathbf{s}_i^o - \mathrm{E}(\mathbf{s}_i^o \mathbf{d}_i^{o\prime})[\mathrm{E}(\mathbf{d}_i^o \mathbf{d}_i^{o\prime})]^{-1} \mathbf{d}_i^o\} + o_p(1)$$

$$\equiv -\mathbf{A}_o^{-1} N^{-1/2} \sum_{i=1}^{N} \mathbf{g}_i^o + o_p(1),$$

where $\mathbf{A}_o \equiv \mathrm{E}[\nabla_\theta \mathbf{s}_i(\boldsymbol{\theta}_o, \gamma_o)]$ is the $P \times P$ Hessian of the objective function with respect to $\boldsymbol{\theta}$, $\mathbf{g}_i^o \equiv \mathbf{s}_i^o - \mathrm{E}(\mathbf{s}_i^o \mathbf{d}_i^{o\prime})[\mathrm{E}(\mathbf{d}_i^o \mathbf{d}_i^{o\prime})]^{-1} \mathbf{d}_i^o$ are the population residuals from the population system regression of $\mathbf{s}_i^o$ on $\mathbf{d}_i^{o\prime}$, and the "o" superscript denotes evaluation at $\boldsymbol{\theta}_o$ and γ_o or just γ_o. Therefore,

$$\text{Avar } \sqrt{N}(\hat{\boldsymbol{\theta}} - \boldsymbol{\theta}_o) = \mathbf{A}_o^{-1} \mathbf{D}_o \mathbf{A}_o^{-1}, \tag{13.68}$$

where

$$\mathbf{D}_o = \mathrm{E}(\mathbf{g}_i^o \mathbf{g}_i^{o\prime}) = \mathrm{Var}(\mathbf{g}_i^o). \tag{13.69}$$

If we knew γ_o rather than estimating it by CMLE, the asymptotic variance of the estimator, say $\tilde{\boldsymbol{\theta}}$, would be Avar $\sqrt{N}(\tilde{\boldsymbol{\theta}} - \boldsymbol{\theta}_o) = \mathbf{A}_o^{-1} \mathbf{B}_o \mathbf{A}_o^{-1}$ where $\mathbf{B}_o = \mathrm{E}(\mathbf{s}_i^o \mathbf{s}_i^{o\prime})$—the usual expected outer product of the score without accounting for the first-step estimation (because there is none). But $\mathbf{B}_o - \mathbf{D}_o$ is positive semi-definite (p.s.d.), and so the two-step M-estimator is generally more (asymptotically) efficient than the one-step M-estimator that uses knowledge of γ_o. In one case, the two estimators are asymptotically equivalent, namely, when $\mathrm{E}(\mathbf{s}_i^o \mathbf{d}_i^{o\prime}) = \mathbf{0}$ (which implies $\mathbf{F}_o = \mathbf{0}$).

An immediate implication of the improvement in efficiency in estimating γ_o is that if we do use $\hat{\gamma}$ but then ignore the estimation in the second stage, our inference will be conservative. In particular, the standard errors computed from $\hat{\mathbf{A}}^{-1}\hat{\mathbf{B}}\hat{\mathbf{A}}^{-1}/N$ are larger, or no smaller, than they could be. (As usual, the "^" means that we replace all parameters with their estimates.) Consequently, using a standard econometrics package that computes sandwich standard errors but does not easily account for first-step estimation produces conservative inference under assumption (13.66).

It is also easy to compute standard errors that reflect the increased precision from using the MLE, $\hat{\gamma}$, in place of γ_o. Namely, let $\hat{\mathbf{s}}_i = \mathbf{s}_i(\hat{\boldsymbol{\theta}}, \hat{\gamma})$ and $\hat{\mathbf{d}}_i = \mathbf{d}_i(\hat{\gamma})$ be the scores from the second- and first-step estimations, respectively. (Remember, $\mathbf{s}_i(\boldsymbol{\theta}, \gamma)$ is the score with respect to $\boldsymbol{\theta}$ only.) Then, let $\hat{\mathbf{g}}_i'$ be the $1 \times P$ residuals from the multivariate regression of $\hat{\mathbf{s}}_i'$ on $\hat{\mathbf{d}}_i'$, $i = 1, \ldots, N$. Then, we obtain

$$\hat{\mathbf{D}} = N^{-1} \sum_{i=1}^{N} \hat{\mathbf{g}}_i \hat{\mathbf{g}}_i' \tag{13.70}$$

and form the sandwich $\hat{\mathbf{A}}^{-1}\hat{\mathbf{D}}\hat{\mathbf{A}}^{-1}/N$ as $\widehat{\text{Avar}}(\hat{\boldsymbol{\theta}})$.

13.11 Quasi-Maximum Likelihood Estimation

Until now, we have assumed that a (conditional) density function has been correctly specified, although in the panel data case we covered situations where we might only specify a density separately for each time period (see Sections 13.8 and 13.9). As we have seen, if we have a correctly specified density for the conditional distributions $\text{D}(\mathbf{y}_i \mid \mathbf{x}_i)$ or $\text{D}(\mathbf{y}_{it} \mid \mathbf{x}_{it})$, $t = 1, \ldots, T$, then MLE or partial MLE has desirable large-sample properties for estimating the population parameters.

There are situations in which it is important to understand the properties of MLE methods when densities are misspecified, or partly misspecified. Some authors, notably White (1982a, 1994), take the view that all models should be viewed, at least initially, as being misspecified, and inference and interpretation should proceed accordingly. White (1994) also considers an intermediate view in which part of the distribution is correctly specified—the leading case being a conditional mean function—while other aspects might be misspecified. As shown by Gourieroux, Monfort, and Trognon (1984a), this posture is especially useful for the class of densities in the linear exponential family, where often we either suspect or know for certain that the full distribution is not correctly specified, but we pay careful attention to specification of the conditional mean. In the next few subsections, we study the properties of estimators that maximize a log likelihood under various degrees of misspecification.

13.11.1 General Misspecification

In general analyses of maximum likelihood estimation of misspecified models, one typically posits the same setup as in Section 13.3, less the assumption that the conditional density is correctly specified, stated in equation (13.11). Thus, for MLE with a generally misspecified density, there is no "true" value of theta, which we called $\boldsymbol{\theta}_o$. Instead, it is standard to postulate the existence of a unique solution to the population problem (13.14). Following White (1994), we denote this value by $\boldsymbol{\theta}^*$. White (1982a, 1994) also discusses the interpretation of $\boldsymbol{\theta}^*$ as providing the best approximation to the true density in the parametric class $f(\mathbf{y} \mid \mathbf{x}; \boldsymbol{\theta})$, where closeness is measured in terms of the Kullback-Leibler information criterion. This interpretation can be inferred from our discussion in Section 13.3.

When the density is misspecified, we typically call the solution to (13.15), which we still denote by $\hat{\boldsymbol{\theta}}$, a **quasi-maximum likelihood estimator (QMLE)**. Some authors prefer the name **pseudo-maximum likelihood estimator**. We also refer to the log-likelihood function as the **quasi-log-likelihood (pseudo-log-likelihood) function**.

Consistency of $\hat{\boldsymbol{\theta}}$ for $\boldsymbol{\theta}^*$ follows in the same way as when the model is correctly specified: by assumption, $\boldsymbol{\theta}^*$ maximizes $\mathrm{E}[\log f(y_i \mid \mathbf{x}_i; \boldsymbol{\theta})]$ over the parameter space $\boldsymbol{\Theta}$, and then we simply assume enough regularity conditions so that the quasi-log likelihood converges to its expectation uniformly over $\boldsymbol{\Theta}$, just as in Theorem 13.1.

Asymptotic inference concerning $\boldsymbol{\theta}^*$ is more interesting. First, one might legitimately ask: If the model is misspecified, what does it mean to test hypotheses about $\boldsymbol{\theta}^*$? After all, $\boldsymbol{\theta}^*$ does not generally index conditional probabilities or conditional moments. Nevertheless, if we take the realistic stance that models of conditional densities are probably misspecified, the best we can do is to test hypotheses about our best approximation to the true density. And sometimes we assume that the main model we are interested in is correctly specified, but we estimate an auxiliary model as a way to obtain, say, instrumental variables. In such cases, we often do not want to assume that the auxiliary model—which is often chosen for computational convenience—is correctly specified in any sense.

It is fairly straightforward to conduct inference on $\boldsymbol{\theta}^*$. Without further assumptions, there is only one legitimate estimator of $\mathrm{Avar}(\hat{\boldsymbol{\theta}})$:

$$\widehat{\mathrm{Avar}(\hat{\boldsymbol{\theta}})} = \left(\sum_{i=1}^{N} \mathbf{H}_i(\hat{\boldsymbol{\theta}})\right)^{-1} \left(\sum_{i=1}^{N} \mathbf{s}_i(\hat{\boldsymbol{\theta}})\mathbf{s}_i(\hat{\boldsymbol{\theta}})'\right) \left(\sum_{i=1}^{N} \mathbf{H}_i(\hat{\boldsymbol{\theta}})\right)^{-1}, \tag{13.71}$$

where, as before, $\mathbf{s}_i(\boldsymbol{\theta})$ is the $P \times 1$ score vector and $\mathbf{H}_i(\boldsymbol{\theta})$ is the $P \times P$ Hessian. (As usual, this estimator is "legitimate" in the sense that, when divided by N, the right-hand side of (13.71) converges in probability to $\mathrm{Avar}[\sqrt{N}(\hat{\boldsymbol{\theta}} - \boldsymbol{\theta}^*)] = \mathbf{A}^{*-1}\mathbf{B}^*\mathbf{A}^{*-1}$, where $\mathbf{A}^* \equiv -\mathrm{E}[\mathbf{H}_i(\boldsymbol{\theta}^*)]$ and $\mathbf{B}^* \equiv \mathrm{E}[\mathbf{s}_i(\boldsymbol{\theta}^*)\mathbf{s}_i(\boldsymbol{\theta}^*)']$; see Section 12.3.) In some cases—we cover an important one in the next subsection—we can use the expected Hessian conditional on $\mathbf{x}_i$, but, in general, $\mathrm{E}[\mathbf{H}_i(\boldsymbol{\theta}^*) \mid \mathbf{x}_i]$ cannot be computed if $f(\mathbf{y} \mid \mathbf{x}; \boldsymbol{\theta})$ is misspecified.

The estimate in (13.71) requires computing both first and second derivatives, but these calculations can be done numerically, if necessary. Once we have $\widehat{\mathrm{Avar}}(\hat{\boldsymbol{\theta}})$, forming Wald tests for restrictions on $\boldsymbol{\theta}^*$ is straightforward. In particular, individual asymptotic t statistics are easily obtained because the standard errors of the $\hat{\theta}_j$ are the square roots of the diagonal elements of (13.71).

Score testing must be carried out using the fully robust framework in Section 12.6.2 because the information matrix equality cannot be assumed to hold. Plus, the conditional expected value of the Hessian cannot be computed in general, so the score test that uses the Hessian (evaluated at the restricted estimates) is the only statistic that can be relied on. Fortunately, the statistic in equation (12.68) is always nonnegative even though $\tilde{\mathbf{A}}$ might not be positive definite (because $\tilde{\mathbf{B}}$ is always at least p.s.d.). Inference based on the LR statistic is very difficult and not advised: the LR statistic no longer has a limiting chi-square distribution (and its limiting distribution depends on unknown parameters).

As an example, consider the probit model we carried along in earlier sections, but where $\mathrm{P}(y_i = 1 \mid \mathbf{x}_i) \neq \Phi(\mathbf{x}_i\boldsymbol{\theta})$ for all $K \times 1$ vectors $\boldsymbol{\theta}$. In other words, the probit model is misspecified. If we obtain $\hat{\boldsymbol{\theta}}$ by maximizing the probit log likelihood, under very weak conditions $\hat{\boldsymbol{\theta}}$ converges in probability to some $\boldsymbol{\theta}^* \in \mathbb{R}^K$, and $\Phi(\mathbf{x}\boldsymbol{\theta}^*)$ provides the "best" approximation to $\mathrm{P}(y_i = 1 \mid \mathbf{x}_i = \mathbf{x})$ in the sense of minimizing the Kullback-Leibler distance. Based on the probit model, for a continuous conditioning variable, say x_j, we would estimate the partial effect of x_j on $\mathrm{P}(y_i = 1 \mid \mathbf{x}_i = \mathbf{x})$ as the partial derivative $\theta_j^* \phi(\mathbf{x}\boldsymbol{\theta}^*)$. Therefore, having an estimate of the asymptotic variance of $\hat{\boldsymbol{\theta}}$ is critical for obtaining, say, an asymptotic confidence interval for this approximate partial effect. Some econometrics packages include simple options for computing the sandwich estimator in (13.71), in which case inference under misspecification is straightforward.

We can also allow for complete density misspecification in the context of partial (pooled) MLE. We must allow for a general estimate of the Hessian: for each i, $\mathbf{H}_i(\hat{\boldsymbol{\theta}}) = \sum_{t=1}^T \mathbf{H}_{it}(\hat{\boldsymbol{\theta}})$. Further, without assuming that $f_t(\mathbf{y}_t \mid \mathbf{x}_t; \boldsymbol{\theta})$ is correctly specified for each t, we can no longer conclude that $\mathrm{D}(\mathbf{y}_{it} \mid \mathbf{x}_{it}) = \mathrm{D}(\mathbf{y}_{it} \mid \mathbf{x}_{it}, \mathbf{y}_{i,t-1}, \mathbf{x}_{i,t-1}, \ldots, \mathbf{y}_{i1}, \mathbf{x}_{i1})$ is sufficient for the scores of the log likelihood to be serially uncorrelated (when evaluated now at $\boldsymbol{\theta}^*$). Therefore, without further analysis, one must use (13.71) as the estimated asymptotic variance, where $\mathbf{s}_i(\hat{\boldsymbol{\theta}}) = \sum_{t=1}^T \mathbf{s}_{it}(\hat{\boldsymbol{\theta}})$, as in Section 13.8.2. (For commonly used nonlinear models, such as probit models, some econometrics software packages include options to compute the fully robust matrix (13.70) for panel data applications.)

13.11.2 Model Selection Tests

The properties of maximum likelihood under general misspecification can be used to derive a **model selection test** due to Vuong (1989). As the name implies, the test is intended to allow one to choose between competing models. Here we treat the case where the two models are, in a sense to be made precise, nonnested. (When one model is a special case of the other, the score approach provides a much simpler way to test an attractive null model against a more general alternative.)

If we are content with just choosing the model with the "best fit" given the data at hand, then it is legitimate to choose the model with the largest value of the log likelihood. After all, whether or not the model is correctly specified, the average log likelihood consistently estimates the negative of the Kullback-Leibler information criterion (KLIC) for that model. And, we know from Section 13.3, the true density maximizes the KLIC. Therefore, a density model cannot be correctly specified if it delivers (asymptotically) a lower average log likelihood than another model. Comparing log-likelihood values is analogous to comparing R-squareds in a regression context.

As suggested by Vuong (1989), it is useful to attach statistical significance between the difference in log likelihoods. For nonnested models, this turns out to be remarkably easy. Let $f_1(\mathbf{y} \mid \mathbf{x}; \boldsymbol{\theta}_1)$ and $f_2(\mathbf{y} \mid \mathbf{x}; \boldsymbol{\theta}_2)$ be competing models for the density of $\mathrm{D}(\mathbf{y}_i \mid \mathbf{x}_i)$, where both may be misspecified. Let $\hat{\boldsymbol{\theta}}_1$ and $\hat{\boldsymbol{\theta}}_2$ be the QMLEs converging to $\boldsymbol{\theta}_1^*$ and $\boldsymbol{\theta}_2^*$, respectively. Let $\mathscr{L}_m = \sum_{i=1}^N \ell_{im}(\hat{\boldsymbol{\theta}}_m)$ be the quasi-log likelihood evaluated at the relevant estimate for $m = 1, 2$. Then

$$(\mathscr{L}_1 - \mathscr{L}_2)/N \xrightarrow{p} \mathrm{E}[\log f_1(\mathbf{y}_i \mid \mathbf{x}_i; \boldsymbol{\theta}_1^*)] - \mathrm{E}[\log f_2(\mathbf{y}_i \mid \mathbf{x}_i; \boldsymbol{\theta}_2^*)],$$

where the expected values are over the joint distribution $(\mathbf{x}_i, \mathbf{y}_i)$. We can actually say more. Using a mean value expansion and the $\sqrt{N}$-consistency of $\hat{\boldsymbol{\theta}}_m^*$ for $\boldsymbol{\theta}_m^*$, it can be shown that

$$\begin{aligned} N^{-1/2}(\mathscr{L}_1 - \mathscr{L}_2) &= N^{-1/2} \sum_{i=1}^N [\ell_{i1}(\hat{\boldsymbol{\theta}}_1) - \ell_{i2}(\hat{\boldsymbol{\theta}}_2)] \\ &= N^{-1/2} \sum_{i=1}^N [\ell_{i1}(\boldsymbol{\theta}_1^*) - \ell_{i2}(\boldsymbol{\theta}_2^*)] + o_p(1). \end{aligned} \tag{13.72}$$

Equation (13.72) is the key to obtaining a model specification test because it shows that the estimators $\hat{\boldsymbol{\theta}}_1$ and $\hat{\boldsymbol{\theta}}_2$ do not affect that asymptotic distribution of $N^{-1/2}(\mathscr{L}_1 - \mathscr{L}_2)$. Therefore, we can obtain an asymptotic normal distribution for

$N^{-1/2}(\mathscr{L}_1 - \mathscr{L}_2)$ under the null hypothesis

$$\mathrm{H}_0 : \mathrm{E}[\ell_{i1}(\boldsymbol{\theta}_1^*)] = \mathrm{E}[\ell_{i2}(\boldsymbol{\theta}_2^*)]. \tag{13.73}$$

In particular, under (13.73),

$$N^{-1/2} \sum_{i=1}^{N} [\ell_{i1}(\boldsymbol{\theta}_1^*) - \ell_{i2}(\boldsymbol{\theta}_2^*)] \xrightarrow{d} \text{Normal}(0, \eta^2), \tag{13.74}$$

where $\eta^2 = \text{Var}[\ell_{i1}(\boldsymbol{\theta}_1^*) - \ell_{i2}(\boldsymbol{\theta}_2^*)]$. A consistent estimator of η^2 is

$$\hat{\eta}^2 \equiv N^{-1} \sum_{i=1}^{N} [\ell_{i1}(\hat{\boldsymbol{\theta}}_1) - \ell_{i2}(\hat{\boldsymbol{\theta}}_2)]^2. \tag{13.75}$$

Voung's model selection statistic is

$$VMS = N^{-1/2}(\mathscr{L}_1 - \mathscr{L}_2)/\hat{\eta}$$
$$= \frac{N^{-1}\sum_{i=1}^{N}[\ell_{i1}(\hat{\boldsymbol{\theta}}_1) - \ell_{i2}(\hat{\boldsymbol{\theta}}_2)]}{\{N^{-1}\sum_{i=1}^{N}[\ell_{i1}(\hat{\boldsymbol{\theta}}_1) - \ell_{i2}(\hat{\boldsymbol{\theta}}_2)]^2\}^{1/2}/\sqrt{N}} \xrightarrow{d} \text{Normal}(0, 1), \tag{13.76}$$

where the standard normal distribution holds under H_0. Note that, while the numerator is simply the difference in log likelihoods from the two estimated models, the denominator requires computing the squared difference in the log likelihoods for each i. A simple way to obtain a valid test is to define $\hat{d}_i = \ell_{i1}(\hat{\boldsymbol{\theta}}_1) - \ell_{i2}(\hat{\boldsymbol{\theta}}_2)$ for each i and then simply to regress $\hat{d}_i$ on unity to test that its mean is different from zero. (This version of the statistic subtracts off the sample average of $\{\hat{d}_i : i = 1, 2, \ldots N\}$ in forming the variance estimate in the denominator.)

In applying Vuong's approach, it is important to understand the scope of its application, including the underlying null hypothesis. We should not use the VMS statistic and its limiting standard normal distribution for testing nested models under correct specification. Recall that the LR statistic is simply $LR = 2(\mathscr{L}_{ur} - \mathscr{L}_r)$, and, under the null, LR has a limiting χ_Q^2 distribution, where Q is the number of restrictions. The important point is that, if the models are nested and correctly specified, then $\ell_{i1}(\boldsymbol{\theta}_1^*) - \ell_{i2}(\boldsymbol{\theta}_2^*) = \ell_i(\boldsymbol{\theta}_\mathrm{o}) - \ell_i(\boldsymbol{\theta}_\mathrm{o}) = 0$. That is, the difference in log likelihoods evaluated at the plims of the estimators is identically zero under the null. This degeneracy makes the asymptotic equivalence in equation (13.72) useless for deriving a test statistic because the variance η^2 would be identically zero. For nested models, we do not divide the difference in log likelihoods by $\sqrt{N}$ because the result would be a statistic that converges in probability to zero.

The sense in which the models must be nonnested to apply Vuong's approach is that

$$\mathrm{P}[\ell_{i1}(\boldsymbol{\theta}_1^*) \neq \ell_{i2}(\boldsymbol{\theta}_2^*)] > 0. \tag{13.77}$$

In other words, the log likelihoods evaluated at the psuedo-true values $\boldsymbol{\theta}_1^*$ and $\boldsymbol{\theta}_2^*$ must differ for a nontrivial set of outcomes on $(\mathbf{x}_i, \mathbf{y}_i)$. This not only rules out models that are obviously nested, but it rules out other degeneracies, too. For example, if y_i is a count variable, $\mathbf{x}_i = (1, x_{i2}, \ldots, x_{iK})$, and we specify different Poisson distributions—the first with mean function $\exp(\mathbf{x}_i\boldsymbol{\theta})$ and the second with mean function $(\mathbf{x}_i\boldsymbol{\theta})^2$—these models are nonnested provided that the mean of y_i given $\mathbf{x}_i$ actually depends on the nonconstant elements in $\mathbf{x}_i$. But if $\mathrm{E}(y_i \mid \mathbf{x}_i) = \mathrm{E}(y_i)$, then $f_1(y \mid \mathbf{x}; \boldsymbol{\theta}_1^*)$ and $f_2(y \mid \mathbf{x}; \boldsymbol{\theta}_2^*)$ are Poisson distributions with the same (constant) means, and the limiting standard normal distribution for Vuong's statistic fails. On the other hand, if the competing models are Poisson and geometric, even with the same mean function, say $\exp(\mathbf{x}_i\boldsymbol{\theta})$, the models are nonnested no matter what, because the Poisson and geometric distributions differ even if they both have constant means.

Because the models must be nonnested, the null hypothesis in equation (13.73) can only hold if *both* models are misspecified. If one model were correctly specified, yet the densities differed, then we would have a strict inequality in (13.73) in favor of the correctly specified model. We can summarize when it is appropriate to apply Vuong's test: it applies to nonnested models where the null hypothesis is that both models are misspecified yet fit equally well (in the sense that they have the same expected log likelihoods).

If we reject model 2 in favor of model 1 because VMS is statistically greater than zero, then we can only conclude that model 1 fits better in the sense that $\mathrm{E}[\ell_{i1}(\boldsymbol{\theta}_1^*)] > \mathrm{E}[\ell_{i2}(\boldsymbol{\theta}_2^*)]$. It does *not* mean that model 1 is correctly specified (although it could be). There are many models that can fit better than a given model, and clearly not all can be correct.

Naturally, Vuong's approach applies directly to panel data methods when two complete densities have been specified for $\mathrm{D}(\mathbf{y}_{i1}, \ldots, \mathbf{y}_{iT} \mid \mathbf{x}_{i1}, \ldots, \mathbf{x}_{iT})$. But it can also be extended to partial (pooled) MLEs, provided we properly account for the time series dependence. For each t, let $f_{t1}(\mathbf{y}_t \mid \mathbf{x}_t; \boldsymbol{\theta}_1)$ and $f_{t2}(\mathbf{y}_t \mid \mathbf{x}_t; \boldsymbol{\theta}_2)$ be competing models of the conditional density in each time period. As in Sections 13.8 and 13.9, the log likelihoods are

$$\ell_{im}(\boldsymbol{\theta}_m) = \sum_{t=1}^{T} \log f_{tm}(\mathbf{y}_{it} \mid \mathbf{x}_{it}; \boldsymbol{\theta}_m) = \sum_{t=1}^{T} \ell_{itm}(\boldsymbol{\theta}_m), \qquad m = 1, 2. \tag{13.78}$$

The same null hypothesis, (13.73), makes sense in the PMLE setting (and is the weakest sense in which the models fit equally well). Moreover, the convergence result in equation (13.74) still holds under the null. Assuming the nonnested condition (13.77) is satisfied, the variance η^2 is positive. However, in estimating η^2, we must account for the serial dependence in $\{\ell_{it1}(\boldsymbol{\theta}_1^*) - \ell_{it2}(\boldsymbol{\theta}_2^*) : t = 1, \ldots, T\}$. Let $\hat{d}_{it} = \ell_{it1}(\hat{\boldsymbol{\theta}}_1) - \ell_{it2}(\hat{\boldsymbol{\theta}}_2)$ denote the difference in estimated log likelihoods for each t, and let $\hat{\lambda}_t = N^{-1}\sum_{i=1}^N \hat{d}_{it}$. Then $\hat{\eta}^2$ is easily obtained as

$$\hat{\eta}^2 = N^{-1}\sum_{i=1}^N \left\{ \sum_{t=1}^T (\hat{d}_{it} - \hat{\lambda}_t)^2 + \sum_{t=1}^T \sum_{r \neq t}^T (\hat{d}_{it} - \hat{\lambda}_t)(\hat{d}_{ir} - \hat{\lambda}_t) \right\}. \tag{13.79}$$

This variance estimator allows for the possibility that the mean difference in log likelihoods varies across t under the null, but that the averages across t are the same. If the null hypothesis is the stronger version, $\mathrm{E}[\ell_{it1}(\boldsymbol{\theta}_1^*)] = \mathrm{E}[\ell_{it2}(\boldsymbol{\theta}_2^*)]$ for $t = 1, \ldots, T$, then $\hat{\lambda}_t$ can be replaced with the average of $\hat{d}_{it}$ across i and t, say $\hat{\lambda}$. In this case, the test statistic is simply the t statistic $\hat{\lambda}/\mathrm{se}(\hat{\lambda})$, where $\mathrm{se}(\hat{\lambda})$ is the heteroskedasticity and serial correlation robust standard error from the pooled regression $\hat{d}_{it}$ on 1, $t = 1, \ldots, T$; $i = 1, \ldots, N$.

Vuong's model selection test should not be confused with specification tests in the context of nonnested models. For example, the Cox (1961, 1962) approach tests a specified model against a nonnested alternative, and a key component of the test is the average difference in log likelihoods, $(\mathscr{L}_1 - \mathscr{L}_2)/N$. But with Cox's approach, one model is taken to be the correct model under the null hypothesis. (And, in practice, each of two models is taken to be the null model and then tested against the other.) If one model is correct and the models are truly nonnested, then the expected values of the log likelihoods, evaluated at the plims of the MLE (for the null model) and quasi-MLE (for the alternative model), must differ; computation of the Cox statistic requires estimating the mean of the difference in log likelihoods, conditional on $\mathbf{x}_i$, under the null hypothesis. In some cases, including when both distributions are normal but with different means or variances (or both), and binary response models, the Cox statistic is easy to compute. But generally finding the conditional mean difference in the log likelihoods in closed form is intractable. (The mean can be simulated, but how much trouble does one want to go through for a specification test?)

The Cox test can be cast as a conditional moment test when we extend the framework in Section 13.7 to allow for the moment conditions to depend on parameters in addition to $\boldsymbol{\theta}$, as done in White (1994, Chap. 9). For further discussion and several other approaches to testing a model against a nonnested alternative, see Gourieroux and Monfort (1994) and White (1994, Chap. 10).

13.11.3 Quasi-Maximum Likelihood Estimation in the Linear Exponential Family

Section 13.11.1, and the model selection test in the previous subsection, allowed that nothing about the model $f(\mathbf{y} \mid \mathbf{x}; \boldsymbol{\theta})$, or $f_t(\mathbf{y}_t \mid \mathbf{x}_t; \boldsymbol{\theta})$, $t = 1, \ldots, T$, is correctly specified. Sometimes, a useful middle ground between correct specification and complete misspecification is to allow just one or two features of a conditional density to be correctly specified. In this section, we study a class of QMLEs that consistently estimate the parameters in a correctly specified conditional mean.

As one learns in introductory econometrics—although it may not be stated in quite this way—the ordinary least squares (OLS) estimator is a QMLE: OLS can be obtained by maximimizing the Gaussian (normal) log-likelihood function with a conditional mean linear in parameters; in fact, we can arbitrarily set the variance equal to any fixed value without affecting the estimates of the mean parameters. Not surprisingly, the nonlinear least squares estimator we covered in Chapter 12 has the same property: minimizing the sum of squared residuals is the same as maximizing the Gaussian quasi-log likelihood. Therefore, NLS is a QMLE based on the normal density function.

The normal log likelihood is not the only log likelihood that identifies the parameters of a conditional mean despite arbitrary misspecification of the remaining features of the distribution. The Bernoulli log likelihood, the Poisson log likelihood, the exponential log likelihood, and others share these feature. These log likelihoods are all members of the **linear exponential family (LEF)**, and it is useful to provide a somewhat general treatment of this class of QMLEs. For simplicity, we consider the case of a scalar response, even though there are results for multiple responses, too. We draw on Gourieroux, Monfort, and Trognon (1984a), or GMT.

A log likelihood in the LEF can be written as a function of the mean as

$$\log f(y \mid \mu) = a(\mu) + b(y) + yc(\mu), \tag{13.80}$$

for functions $a(\cdot)$, $b(\cdot)$, and $c(\cdot)$, where μ is a candidate value of the mean of y_i and $\mu_o = \mathrm{E}(y_i)$ is the true population mean. Let M denote the set of possible values of the mean. GMT (1984a) show that μ_o solves

$$\max_{\mu \in M} [a(\mu) + \mathrm{E}(y_i)c(\mu)] = \max_{\mu \in M} [a(\mu) + \mu_o c(\mu)]. \tag{13.81}$$

The functions in (13.80) are easily obtained for the normal, Bernoulli, Poisson, exponential, and other cases; GMT (1984a) contains a summary table. For the Bernoulli distribution,

$$\log f(y \mid \mu) = (1-y)\cdot\log(1-\mu) + y\cdot\log(\mu)$$
$$= \log(1-\mu) + y\cdot\log[\mu/(1-\mu)], \qquad 0 < \mu < 1.$$

Therefore, $a(\mu) = \log(1-\mu)$, $b(y) = 0$, and $c(\mu) = \log[\mu/(1-\mu)]$. For some distributions to fit into the LEF, notably the gamma and negative binomial, a nuisance parameter must be fixed at a specific value; see GMT (1984a) for details.

In the most popular examples, it is easy to directly verify that μ_o solves (13.81). We will consider special cases in Part IV. For now, it is important to understand the meaning of the result. Consider the Bernoulli case but, rather than assuming y_i is a zero-one variable, let y_i be any random variable with support in the unit interval, $[0,1]$. y_i can be discrete, continuous, or have both features. For example, we could have $P(y_i = 0) > 0$ but $P(y_i = y) = 0$ for $y \in (0,1]$, or y_i might take on values in $\{0, 1/m_i, 2/m_i, \ldots, 1\}$ for some positive integer m_i. Regardless of the nature of y_i, provided its mean μ_o is in $(0,1)$, μ_o maximizes the expected value of the Bernoulli log likelihood.

In practice, we are interested in conditional rather than unconditional means, which we parameterize as $m(\mathbf{x}, \boldsymbol{\theta})$. Then the conditional quasi-log likelihood function becomes

$$\log f(y \mid m(\mathbf{x},\boldsymbol{\theta})) = a(m(\mathbf{x},\boldsymbol{\theta})) + b(y) + yc(m(\mathbf{x},\boldsymbol{\theta})). \tag{13.82}$$

Because the mean is now assumed to be correctly specified, we assume there is $\boldsymbol{\theta}_o \in \boldsymbol{\Theta}$ such that $E(y_i \mid \mathbf{x}_i) = m(\mathbf{x}_i, \boldsymbol{\theta}_o)$. A simple iterated expectations argument shows that $\boldsymbol{\theta}_o$ solves

$$\max_{\boldsymbol{\theta}\in\boldsymbol{\Theta}} E[a(m(\mathbf{x}_i,\boldsymbol{\theta})) + y_i c(m(\mathbf{x}_i,\boldsymbol{\theta}))], \tag{13.83}$$

regardless of the actual distribution $D(y_i \mid \mathbf{x}_i)$. Again, it is important to understand the meaning of this result. The nature of y_i need not even correspond to the chosen density. For example, y_i could be a nonnegative, continuous variable, and we use the Poisson quasi-log likelihood. The Poisson QMLE is consistent for the conditional mean parameters provided the mean—with the leading case being an exponential function—is correctly specified. The only restriction is that candidates for $E(y_i \mid \mathbf{x}_i = \mathbf{x})$ should have the same range as allowed in the chosen LEF density.

One of the most useful characterizations of QMLE in the LEF is based on the score. It can be shown that the score has the form

$$\mathbf{s}_i(\boldsymbol{\theta}) = \nabla_{\boldsymbol{\theta}} m(\mathbf{x}_i,\boldsymbol{\theta})'[y_i - m(\mathbf{x}_i,\boldsymbol{\theta})]/v(m(\mathbf{x}_i,\boldsymbol{\theta})) \tag{13.84}$$

where $\nabla_\theta m(\mathbf{x}_i, \boldsymbol{\theta})$ is the $1 \times P$ gradient of the mean function and, of importance, $v(\mu)$ is the variance function associated with the chosen LEF density. For the standard normal, $v(\mu) = 1$, for the Bernoulli, $v(\mu) = \mu(1 - \mu)$, for the Poisson, $v(\mu) = \mu$, and for the exponential, $v(\mu) = \mu^2$. The structure in equation (13.84) shows immediately that the QMLE is Fisher consistent: if $\mathrm{E}(y_i \mid \mathbf{x}_i) = m(\mathbf{x}_i, \boldsymbol{\theta}_o)$, then $\mathrm{E}[\mathbf{s}_i(\boldsymbol{\theta}_o) \mid \mathbf{x}_i] = \mathbf{0}$, which in turn implies that the unconditional mean of the score is zero. We derived (13.84) explicitly in the probit example (Example 13.1), and it is also easily seen to be true for the Poisson regression (Example 13.2). But here we emphasize that $\mathrm{E}[\mathbf{s}_i(\boldsymbol{\theta}_o) \mid \mathbf{x}_i] = \mathbf{0}$ holds for arbitrary misspecification of these densities provided the mean is correctly specified.

We can also use the score to compute the expected Hessian conditional on $\mathbf{x}_i$:

$$\mathbf{A}(\mathbf{x}_i, \boldsymbol{\theta}_o) = -\mathrm{E}[\mathbf{H}_i(\boldsymbol{\theta}_o) \mid \mathbf{x}_i] = \nabla_\theta m(\mathbf{x}_i, \boldsymbol{\theta}_o)' \nabla_\theta m(\mathbf{x}_i, \boldsymbol{\theta}_o) / v(m(\mathbf{x}_i, \boldsymbol{\theta}_o)). \tag{13.85}$$

Further,

$$\mathrm{E}[\mathbf{s}_i(\boldsymbol{\theta}_o)\mathbf{s}_i(\boldsymbol{\theta}_o) \mid \mathbf{x}_i] = \mathrm{E}(u_i^2 \mid \mathbf{x}_i) \nabla_\theta m(\mathbf{x}_i, \boldsymbol{\theta}_o)' \nabla_\theta m(\mathbf{x}_i, \boldsymbol{\theta}_o) / [v(m(\mathbf{x}_i, \boldsymbol{\theta}_o))]^2, \tag{13.86}$$

where $u_i \equiv y_i - m(\mathbf{x}_i, \boldsymbol{\theta}_o)$. It follows immediately that the CIME holds if $\mathrm{E}(u_i^2 \mid \mathbf{x}_i) = v(m(\mathbf{x}_i, \boldsymbol{\theta}_o))$, that is,

$$\mathrm{Var}(y_i \mid \mathbf{x}_i) = v(m(\mathbf{x}_i, \boldsymbol{\theta}_o)). \tag{13.87}$$

(In the Bernoulli case, $v(m) = m(1 - m)$, and in the Poisson case, $v(m) = m$.) In other words, *if* the chosen LEF density has a conditional variance equal to the actual $\mathrm{Var}(y_i \mid \mathbf{x}_i)$, then we can use the usual MLE standard errors and inference (even if features of the distribution other than the first two conditional moments are misspecified). So, for example, in a Poisson regression analysis, if $\mathrm{Var}(y_i \mid \mathbf{x}_i) = \mathrm{E}(y_i \mid \mathbf{x}_i)$ and the mean function is correctly specified, we can act as if we are using MLE rather than QMLE, even if higher order conditional moments of y_i do not match up with the Poisson distribution.

If $\mathrm{Var}(y_i \mid \mathbf{x}_i)$ is unrestricted, the IME will not hold, and then the robust sandwich estimator

$$\widehat{\mathrm{Avar}}(\hat{\boldsymbol{\theta}}) = \left(\sum_{i=1}^{N} \mathbf{A}(\mathbf{x}_i, \hat{\boldsymbol{\theta}}) \right)^{-1} \left(\sum_{i=1}^{N} \mathbf{s}_i(\hat{\boldsymbol{\theta}}) \mathbf{s}_i(\hat{\boldsymbol{\theta}})' \right) \left(\sum_{i=1}^{N} \mathbf{A}(\mathbf{x}_i, \hat{\boldsymbol{\theta}}) \right)^{-1}, \tag{13.88}$$

should be used, where $\mathbf{A}(\mathbf{x}_i, \hat{\boldsymbol{\theta}})$ is given in (13.85) with $\hat{\boldsymbol{\theta}}$ replacing $\boldsymbol{\theta}_o$. Because of the particular structure of the log likelihood and the assumption that the conditional mean is correctly specified, we can find $\mathrm{E}[\mathbf{H}_i(\boldsymbol{\theta}_o) \mid \mathbf{x}_i]$. If we did not want to assume correct specification of the conditional mean, we would be in the setup of Section 13.11.1.

QMLE in the LEF is closely related to the so-called **generalized linear model (GLM)** literature in statistics. The terminology and some particulars differ, and the early GLM literature did not recognize the robustness of the approach for estimating conditional mean parameters, but in modern applications the key feature is that they both use QMLE to estimate parameters of a conditional mean. The GLM approach is more restrictive in that the conditional mean is assumed to have an **index structure**. In particular, the mean is assumed to have the form $m(\mathbf{x}, \boldsymbol{\theta}) = r(\mathbf{x}\boldsymbol{\theta})$, where the "index" $\mathbf{x}\boldsymbol{\theta}$ is linear in parameters and $r(\cdot)$ is a function of the index. In addition, an important component of the GLM apparatus is the **link function**, which implicitly defines the mean function. If we let η denote the index $\mathbf{x}\boldsymbol{\theta}$, then the link function $g(\cdot)$ is such that $\eta = g(\mu)$. The link function is strictly monotonic and therefore has an inverse, and so $\mu = g^{-1}(\eta)$ or, in the notation of conditional mean functions, $m(\mathbf{x}, \boldsymbol{\theta}) = g^{-1}(\mathbf{x}\boldsymbol{\theta})$.

The term "generalized linear model" comes from the underlying linearity of the index function, and then the link function introduces nonlinearity. In most applications, it is more natural to specify the conditional mean function because we want the mean function to be consistent with the nature of y_i, and y_i is the outcome we hope to explain. (So, for example, if y_i is nonnegative, we want $m(\mathbf{x}, \boldsymbol{\theta})$ to be positive for all $\mathbf{x}$ and $\boldsymbol{\theta}$; if $0 \leq y_i \leq 1$, we want $m(\mathbf{x}, \boldsymbol{\theta})$ to be in the unit interval.) Once the mean function is specified, we use a suitable LEF density; this is the approach taken by GMT (1984a). Directly specifying $m(\mathbf{x}, \boldsymbol{\theta})$ does not wed one to the index structure, although in most applications, $m(\mathbf{x}, \boldsymbol{\theta})$ has an index form. If, say, $m(\mathbf{x}, \boldsymbol{\theta}) = \exp(\mathbf{x}\boldsymbol{\theta})$ then the link function is $g(\mu) = \log(\mu)$ for $\mu > 0$. If $m(\mathbf{x}, \boldsymbol{\theta}) = \exp(\mathbf{x}\boldsymbol{\theta})/[1 + \exp(\mathbf{x}\boldsymbol{\theta})]$, then $g(\mu) = \log[\mu/(1 - \mu)]$ for $0 < \mu < 1$. McCullagh and Nelder (1989) is a good reference for GLM.

The GLM literature recognized early on that assumption (13.87) was too restrictive for many applications. As we discussed, *no* variance assumption is needed for consistent estimation of $\boldsymbol{\theta}_o$. An assumption that has been used in the GLM literature allows $\mathrm{Var}(y_i \mid \mathbf{x}_i)$ to differ from that implied by the LEF distribution by a constant:

$$\mathrm{Var}(y_i \mid \mathbf{x}_i) = \sigma_o^2 v(m(\mathbf{x}_i, \boldsymbol{\theta}_o)) \tag{13.89}$$

for some $\sigma_o^2 > 0$, which is often called the **dispersion parameter**. Because of its historical role in GLM analysis, we refer to (13.89) as the **GLM variance assumption**. When $\sigma_o^2 > 1$, then we say there is **overdispersion** (relative to the chosen density); **underdispersion** is when $\sigma_o^2 < 1$, and both cases arise in practice.

Under (13.89), it is straightforward to estimate σ_o^2. Let $u_i = y_i - m(\mathbf{x}_i, \boldsymbol{\theta}_o)$ be the additive "errors." Then, because $\mathrm{E}(u_i^2 \mid \mathbf{x}_i) = \sigma_o^2 v(m(\mathbf{x}_i, \boldsymbol{\theta}_o)) \equiv \sigma_o^2 v_i$, it follows by iterated expectations that

$$\mathrm{E}(u_i^2/v_i) = \mathrm{E}[\mathrm{E}(u_i^2/v_i \mid \mathbf{x}_i)] = \mathrm{E}[\mathrm{E}(u_i^2 \mid \mathbf{x}_i)/v_i] = \mathrm{E}(\sigma_o^2 v_i/v_i) = \sigma_o^2. \tag{13.90}$$

Therefore, by the usual analogy principle argument,

$$\hat{\sigma}^2 = (N - P)^{-1} \sum_{i=1}^{N} \hat{u}_i^2/\hat{v}_i \tag{13.91}$$

is consistent for σ_o^2, where $\hat{u}_i \equiv y_i - m(\mathbf{x}_i, \hat{\boldsymbol{\theta}})$ are the residuals, $\hat{v}_i \equiv v(m(\mathbf{x}_i, \hat{\boldsymbol{\theta}}))$ are the estimated conditional variances from the LEF density, and the degrees-of-freedom adjustment is common (but, of course, does not affect consistency). In the GLM literature, the standardized residuals $\hat{u}_i/\sqrt{\hat{v}_i}$ are called the **Pearson residuals** and the estimate in equation (13.91) is the **Pearson dispersion estimator**.

Under the GLM variance assumption, it is easily seen that the generalized IME, given in equation (12.53), is satisfied (once we account for the minor difference between a minimization and maximization problem). In fact, a conditional version holds, which we can call the **generalized conditional information matrix equality (GCIME)**:

$$\mathrm{E}[\mathbf{s}_i(\boldsymbol{\theta}_o)\mathbf{s}_i(\boldsymbol{\theta}_o)' \mid \mathbf{x}_i] = -\sigma_o^2 \mathrm{E}[\mathbf{H}_i(\boldsymbol{\theta}_o) \mid \mathbf{x}_i] = \sigma_o^2 \mathbf{A}(\mathbf{x}_i, \boldsymbol{\theta}_o). \tag{13.92}$$

From Chapter 12, we can take

$$\widehat{\mathrm{Avar}}(\hat{\boldsymbol{\theta}}) = \hat{\sigma}^2 \left(\sum_{i=1}^{N} \mathbf{A}(\mathbf{x}_i, \hat{\boldsymbol{\theta}}) \right)^{-1} = \hat{\sigma}^2 \left(\sum_{i=1}^{N} \nabla_\theta m_i(\hat{\boldsymbol{\theta}})' \nabla_\theta m_i(\hat{\boldsymbol{\theta}})/v_i(\hat{\boldsymbol{\theta}}) \right)^{-1}, \tag{13.93}$$

where the notation should be clear. Most software packages that have GLM commands—typically requiring one to specify the LEF density and the link function—allow computation of the nonrobust variance matrix estimator that assumes (13.87) (which is the same variance estimate under full MLE), the estimator in (13.93), or the fully robust form in (13.88). Therefore, the GLM framework can be used to obtain QMLEs for the LEF for a certain class of mean functions.

Notice how similar the structure of equation (13.93) is to the asymptotic variance of the weighted nonlinear least squares estimator from Chapter 12; see equation (12.59). In fact, the only difference between (13.93) and (12.59) is that with WNLS we allow the parameters in the variance function to be different from $\boldsymbol{\theta}_o$, and, therefore, to be estimated in a separate stage (usually after an initial NLS estimation). The similarity between (13.93) and (12.59) hints at a close link between QMLEs in the LEF and WNLS. In fact, for every QMLE in the LEF, there is an asymptotically equivalent WNLS estimator when the conditional mean is correctly specified: for WNLS, take $h(\mathbf{x}, \gamma) = v(m(\mathbf{x}, \boldsymbol{\theta}))$ and $\hat{\gamma}$ an initial $\sqrt{N}$-consistent estimator of $\boldsymbol{\theta}_o$ (such as NLS). The QMLE and WNLS estimators will be $\sqrt{N}$-equivalent whether or not (13.89) holds.

If we nominally wish to assume (13.89), QMLE is computationally convenient because it is a one-step estimation procedure, and the objective function is usually well behaved; WNLS requires two steps. Therefore, when the variance and mean are thought to be related in a way suggested by an LEF density—more precisely, its GLM extension in (13.89)—QMLE is almost always used. And, of course, we can make inference fully robust to any variance-mean relationship by using the sandwich estimator (13.88).

13.11.4 Generalized Estimating Equations for Panel Data

Naturally, we can extend QMLE in the LEF to panel data. The simplest approach is to specify conditional mean functions $m_t(\mathbf{x}_t, \boldsymbol{\theta})$, $t = 1, \ldots, T$, along with an LEF density, and then to proceed with estimation by ignoring any time dependence. The pooled quasi-likelihood has the same form as equation (13.45), where $f_t(y_t \mid \mathbf{x}_t; \boldsymbol{\theta})$ is in the LEF. (Allowing the mean and density functions to depend on t is probably not necessary, but it reminds us that we often want to allow some parameters to change over t—for example, $m_t(\mathbf{x}_t, \boldsymbol{\theta}) = \exp(\alpha_t + \mathbf{x}_t\boldsymbol{\beta})$. In practice, we would accomplish different "intercepts" within the exponential function by including a full set of time period dummies among the regressors.)

Correct specification of the mean for each t means that, for some $\boldsymbol{\theta}_o$,

$$\mathrm{E}(y_{it} \mid \mathbf{x}_{it}) = m_t(\mathbf{x}_{it}, \boldsymbol{\theta}_o), \qquad t = 1, \ldots, T. \tag{13.94}$$

Notice that (13.94) does *not* assume strict exogeneity of $\{\mathbf{x}_{it} : t = 1, \ldots, T\}$. The score for each t has the same form as equation (13.84):

$$\mathbf{s}_{it}(\boldsymbol{\theta}) = \nabla_{\boldsymbol{\theta}} m_t(\mathbf{x}_{it}, \boldsymbol{\theta})'[y_{it} - m_t(\mathbf{x}_{it}, \boldsymbol{\theta})]/v(m_t(\mathbf{x}_{it}, \boldsymbol{\theta})), \tag{13.95}$$

and the **partial QMLE** (or **pooled QMLE**) is generally found by solving $\sum_{i=1}^{N} \sum_{t=1}^{T} \mathbf{s}_{it}(\hat{\boldsymbol{\theta}}) = \mathbf{0}$.

As we discussed in Section 13.8 for partial MLE, the scores $\{\mathbf{s}_{it}(\boldsymbol{\theta}_o) : t = 1, \ldots, T\}$ are generally serially correlated. However, in Section 13.8.3 we saw an important case in which the scores are not serially correlated: the distribution $\mathrm{D}(\mathbf{y}_{it} \mid \mathbf{x}_{it})$ is dynamically complete in the sense that it also equals $\mathrm{D}(\mathbf{y}_{it} \mid \mathbf{x}_{it}, \mathbf{y}_{i,t-1}, \mathbf{x}_{i,t-1}, \ldots, \mathbf{y}_{i1}, \mathbf{x}_{i1})$.

Here, we are not assuming that we have a full density $f_t(\mathbf{y}_t \mid \mathbf{x}_t; \boldsymbol{\theta})$ correctly specified. Nevertheless, using equation (13.95), we can easily see that if the conditional mean is dynamically complete in the sense that

$$\mathrm{E}(y_{it} \mid \mathbf{x}_{it}) = \mathrm{E}(y_{it} \mid \mathbf{x}_{it}, y_{i,t-1}, \mathbf{x}_{i,t-1}, \dots, y_{i1}, \mathbf{x}_{i1}), \tag{13.96}$$

then

$$\mathrm{E}[\mathbf{s}_{it}(\boldsymbol{\theta}_o) \mid \mathbf{x}_{it}, y_{i,t-1}, \mathbf{x}_{i,t-1}, \dots, y_{i1}, \mathbf{x}_{i1})] = \mathbf{0}, \tag{13.97}$$

and so the scores evaluated at $\boldsymbol{\theta}_o$ are necessarily serially uncorrelated. Importantly, this finding has nothing to do with whether other features of the LEF density, such as the conditional variance, are correctly specified. Without any assumptions on $\mathrm{Var}(y_{it} \mid \mathbf{x}_{it})$, the appropriate asymptotic variance estimator of the pooled QMLE is

$$\left(\sum_{i=1}^{N}\sum_{i=1}^{N} \nabla_\theta \hat{m}_{it}' \nabla_\theta \hat{m}_{it} / \hat{v}_{it}\right)^{-1} \left(\sum_{i=1}^{N}\sum_{i=1}^{N} \hat{u}_{it}^2 \nabla_\theta \hat{m}_{it}' \nabla_\theta \hat{m}_{it} / \hat{v}_{it}^2\right) \left(\sum_{i=1}^{N}\sum_{i=1}^{N} \nabla_\theta \hat{m}_{it}' \nabla_\theta \hat{m}_{it} / \hat{v}_{it}\right)^{-1},$$

where the notation should be clear. This estimator is precisely what is reported from a pooled QMLE analysis—in most cases using a GLM routine—that ignores the time dimension but allows the variance to be misspecified.

If we further add the GLM variance assumption $\mathrm{Var}(y_{it} \mid \mathbf{x}_{it}) = \sigma_o^2 v(m(\mathbf{x}_{it}, \boldsymbol{\theta}_o))$ for all t—including that the scale factor σ_o^2 is constant across t—then the pooled analogue of equation (13.93) is valid (where $\hat{\sigma}^2$ is obtained from the sum of squared standardized residuals across i and t). Some econometrics packages allow computation of these variances as a routine matter, and they also compute the variance matrix that does not assume dynamic completeness in the conditional mean.

Naturally, if the mean is not dynamically complete, then, if we make the stronger assumption of strict exogeneity of the regressors, it is possible to obtain a more efficient estimator. In Section 12.9, we studied the multivariate WNLS estimator, and noted that a common way to choose a nonconstant "working" variance matrix was to specify models for the conditional variances—which may be misspecified—along with a constant "working" correlation matrix. This is common in the generalized estimating equations (GEE) approach to panel data models. For practical purposes, GEE is a special case of WMNLS, where the variance functions are chosen from the LEF of distributions (and the mean functions are commonly chosen from linear, exponential, logistic, and probit, as in standard GLM analysis).

For the $T \times 1$ vector $\mathbf{y}_i$, we assume

$$\mathrm{E}(\mathbf{y}_i \mid \mathbf{x}_i) = \mathbf{m}(\mathbf{x}_i, \boldsymbol{\theta}_o), \qquad \text{some } \boldsymbol{\theta}_o \in \boldsymbol{\Theta}, \tag{13.98}$$

where $\mathbf{x}_i$ is the collection of all regressors across all time periods and $\mathbf{m}(\mathbf{x}, \boldsymbol{\theta})$ is $T \times 1$. Notice that the vector $\mathrm{E}(\mathbf{y}_i \mid \mathbf{x}_i)$ has elements $\mathrm{E}(y_{it} \mid \mathbf{x}_i)$, which means that the regressors are strictly exogenous. When the mean function at time t does not depend on all of $\mathbf{x}_i$, (13.98) implies that the regressors excluded at time t can have no partial effect on $\mathrm{E}(y_{it} \mid \mathbf{x}_i)$. An important case where all elements of $\mathbf{x}_i$ appear for each t is in a correlated random coefficient setup, but then restrictions are obtained using a strict exogeneity assumption conditional on the heterogeneity. We return to this situation below. Generally, one should not apply GEE methods with a nondiagonal working variance matrix (see Section 12.9) unless the regressors satisfy a strict exogeneity assumption.

In the most common applications of GEE, we specify, for each t, a quasi-log likelihood from the LEF. As in the cross section case, this choice is motivated by the nature of y_{it}. Assuming we have a suitable parametric model $m(\mathbf{x}_{it}, \boldsymbol{\theta})$ for the mean, and have chosen an LEF, GEE analysis is straightforward once we choose the working correlation matrix (see Section 12.9). Typically, this correlation matrix is constant, depending on parameters $\boldsymbol{\rho}$, so we can write $\mathbf{R}(\boldsymbol{\rho})$ as the $T \times T$ matrix of proposed correlations. Because we do not allow this matrix to depend on $\mathbf{x}_i$, there can be no presumption that $\mathrm{Corr}(y_{it}, y_{is} \mid \mathbf{x}_i) = r_{ts}(\boldsymbol{\rho}_{\mathrm{o}})$. A key feature of GEE is that we explicitly recognize that the conditional correlations might not be constant—in fact, often we know almost certainly they are not—but we apply weighted multivariate nonlinear least squares anyway to hopefully improve efficiency over just a pooled QMLE analysis.

As mentioned in Section 12.9, the two most common working correlation matrices for panel data are the unstructured and the exchangeable. The latter conserves on parameters in the working variance matrix, but with large N (and not so large T) parsimony might not be necessary. In any case, we need to combine a working correlation matrix with a nominal assumption about the variances. The variances naturally come from the chosen LEF density. So, if we are using the Bernoulli quasi-log likelihood with mean function $m_t(\mathbf{x}_{it}, \boldsymbol{\theta})$, then we use the nominal variance $m_t(\mathbf{x}_{it}, \boldsymbol{\theta})[1 - m_t(\mathbf{x}_{it}, \boldsymbol{\theta})]$. For the Poisson QLL, we use $m_t(\mathbf{x}_{it}, \boldsymbol{\theta})$. The mean parameters are estimated by pooled QMLE in a first stage, say $\check{\boldsymbol{\theta}}$. Then the working correlation matrix can be estimated using standardized residuals $\check{u}_{it}/\sqrt{\check{v}_{it}}$ (see Section 12.9). Then we can form the working variance matrix, $\hat{\mathbf{W}}_i = \hat{\mathbf{V}}_i^{1/2}\hat{\mathbf{R}}\hat{\mathbf{V}}_i^{1/2}$ where $\hat{\mathbf{V}}_i = \mathrm{diag}(v_{i1}(\check{\boldsymbol{\theta}}), \ldots, v_{iT}(\check{\boldsymbol{\theta}}))$ depends on the first-step estimates. We then apply WMNLS, or work off the first-order conditions. It is important to use the asymptotic variance matrix in equation (12.98) that allows the working variance matrix to be misspecified, whether it is due to the variances being misspecified or the working correlation matrix being misspecified. (As we discussed in Section 12.9, equation (12.98) is not valid if the conditional mean is misspecified, and the GEE literature sometimes refers to this estimate as a "semirobust" estimate.) If one believes the variance matrix is correct up to a dispersion factor, then $\hat{\sigma}^2$ is obtained along with other parameter estimates.

Pooled QMLE and GEE methods are attractive for conditional mean models with unobserved heterogeneity, say c_i, and strictly exogenous regressors conditional on c_i: $\mathrm{E}(y_{it} \mid \mathbf{x}_{i1}, \ldots, \mathbf{x}_{iT}, c_i) = \mathrm{E}(y_{it} \mid \mathbf{x}_{it}, c_i)$. When we combine this assumption with a specific correlated RE assumption, such as $c_i = \alpha + \bar{\mathbf{x}}_i \xi + a_i$, where $\bar{\mathbf{x}}_i$ is the vector of time averages and a_i is independent of $(\mathbf{x}_{i1}, \ldots, \mathbf{x}_{iT})$, then we can often find $\mathrm{E}(y_{it} \mid \mathbf{x}_{i1}, \ldots, \mathbf{x}_{iT})$ as a function of $(\mathbf{x}_{it}, \bar{\mathbf{x}}_i)$ (or simply assert that it takes on a convenient form). GEE (including pooled QMLE) becomes an indispensable tool to ensure our inference is robust to misspecification of the serial correlation structure we adopt. We will not provide a general treatment now, but we draw heavily on this idea in several chapters in Part IV.

Problems

13.1. If $f(\mathbf{y} \mid \mathbf{x}; \boldsymbol{\theta})$ is a correctly specified model for the density of $\mathbf{y}_i$ given $\mathbf{x}_i$, does $\boldsymbol{\theta}_o$ solve $\max_{\boldsymbol{\theta} \in \Theta} \mathrm{E}[f(\mathbf{y}_i \mid \mathbf{x}_i; \boldsymbol{\theta})]$?

13.2. Suppose that for a random sample, $y_i \mid \mathbf{x}_i \sim \text{Normal}[m(\mathbf{x}_i, \boldsymbol{\beta}_o), \sigma_o^2]$, where $m(\mathbf{x}, \boldsymbol{\beta})$ is a function of the K-vector of explanatory variables $\mathbf{x}$ and the $P \times 1$ parameter vector $\boldsymbol{\beta}$. Recall that $\mathrm{E}(y_i \mid \mathbf{x}_i) = m(\mathbf{x}_i, \boldsymbol{\beta}_o)$ and $\mathrm{Var}(y_i \mid \mathbf{x}_i) = \sigma_o^2$.

a. Write down the conditional log-likelihood function for observation i. Show that the CMLE of $\boldsymbol{\beta}_o$, $\hat{\boldsymbol{\beta}}$, solves the problem $\min_{\boldsymbol{\beta}} \sum_{i=1}^{N} [y_i - m(\mathbf{x}_i, \boldsymbol{\beta})]^2$. In other words, the CMLE for $\boldsymbol{\beta}_o$ is the nonlinear least squares estimator.

b. Let $\boldsymbol{\theta} \equiv (\boldsymbol{\beta}', \sigma^2)'$ denote the $(P+1) \times 1$ vector of parameters. Find the score of the log likelihood for a generic i. Show directly that $\mathrm{E}[\mathbf{s}_i(\boldsymbol{\theta}_o) \mid \mathbf{x}_i] = \mathbf{0}$. What features of the normal distribution do you need to be correctly specified in order to show that the conditional expectation of the score is zero?

c. Use the first-order condition to find $\hat{\sigma}^2$ in terms of $\hat{\boldsymbol{\beta}}$.

d. Find the Hessian of the log-likelihood function with respect to $\boldsymbol{\theta}$.

e. Show directly that $-\mathrm{E}[\mathbf{H}_i(\boldsymbol{\theta}_o) \mid \mathbf{x}_i] = \mathrm{E}[\mathbf{s}_i(\boldsymbol{\theta}_o)\mathbf{s}_i(\boldsymbol{\theta}_o)' \mid \mathbf{x}_i]$.

f. Propose an estimated asymptotic variance of $\hat{\boldsymbol{\beta}}$, and explain how to obtain the asymptotic standard errors.

13.3. Consider a general binary response model $P(y_i = 1 \mid \mathbf{x}_i) = G(\mathbf{x}_i, \boldsymbol{\theta}_o)$, where $G(\mathbf{x}, \boldsymbol{\theta})$ is strictly between zero and one for all $\mathbf{x}$ and $\boldsymbol{\theta}$. Here, $\mathbf{x}$ and $\boldsymbol{\theta}$ need not have the same dimension; let $\mathbf{x}$ be a K-vector and $\boldsymbol{\theta}$ a P-vector.

a. Write down the log likelihood for observation i.

b. Find the score for each i. Show directly that $\mathrm{E}[\mathbf{s}_i(\boldsymbol{\theta}_o) \mid \mathbf{x}_i] = \mathbf{0}$.

c. When $G(\mathbf{x}, \boldsymbol{\theta}) = \Phi[\mathbf{x}\boldsymbol{\beta} + \delta_1(\mathbf{x}\boldsymbol{\beta})^2 + \delta_2(\mathbf{x}\boldsymbol{\beta})^3]$, find the LM statistic for testing H_0: $\delta_{o1} = 0, \delta_{o2} = 0$.

d. How would you compute a variable addition version of the test in part c?

13.4. In the Newey-Tauchen-White specification-testing context, explain why we can take $\mathbf{g}(\mathbf{w}, \boldsymbol{\theta}) = a(\mathbf{x}, \boldsymbol{\theta})\mathbf{s}(\mathbf{w}, \boldsymbol{\theta})$, where $a(\mathbf{x}, \boldsymbol{\theta})$ is essentially any scalar function of $\mathbf{x}$ and $\boldsymbol{\theta}$.

13.5. In the context of CMLE, consider a reparameterization of the kind in Section 12.6.2: $\boldsymbol{\phi} = \mathbf{g}(\boldsymbol{\theta})$, where the Jacobian of $\mathbf{g}$, $\mathbf{G}(\boldsymbol{\theta})$, is continuous and nonsingular for all $\boldsymbol{\theta} \in \boldsymbol{\Theta}$. Let $\mathbf{s}_i^g(\boldsymbol{\phi}) = \mathbf{s}_i^g[\mathbf{g}(\boldsymbol{\theta})]$ denote the score of the log likelihood in the reparameterized model; thus, from Section 12.6.2, $\mathbf{s}_i^g(\boldsymbol{\phi}) = [\mathbf{G}(\boldsymbol{\theta})']^{-1}\mathbf{s}_i(\boldsymbol{\theta})$.

a. Using the conditional information matrix equality, find $\mathbf{A}_i^g(\boldsymbol{\phi}_o) \equiv \mathrm{E}[\mathbf{s}_i^g(\boldsymbol{\phi}_o)\mathbf{s}_i^g(\boldsymbol{\phi}_o)' \mid \mathbf{x}_i]$ in terms of $\mathbf{G}(\boldsymbol{\theta}_o)$ and $\mathbf{A}_i(\boldsymbol{\theta}_o) \equiv \mathrm{E}[\mathbf{s}_i(\boldsymbol{\theta}_o)\mathbf{s}_i(\boldsymbol{\theta}_o)' \mid \mathbf{x}_i]$.

b. Show that $\tilde{\mathbf{A}}_i^g = \tilde{\mathbf{G}}'^{-1}\tilde{\mathbf{A}}_i\tilde{\mathbf{G}}^{-1}$, where these are all evaluated at the restricted estimate, $\tilde{\boldsymbol{\theta}}$.

c. Use part b to show that the expected Hessian form of the LM statistic is invariant to reparameterization.

13.6. Suppose that for a panel data set with T time periods, y_{it} given $\mathbf{x}_{it}$ has a Poisson distribution with mean $\exp(\mathbf{x}_{it}\boldsymbol{\theta}_o)$, $t = 1, \ldots, T$.

a. Do you have enough information to construct the joint distribution of $\mathbf{y}_i$ given $\mathbf{x}_i$? Explain.

b. Write down the partial log likelihood for each i and find the score, $\mathbf{s}_i(\boldsymbol{\theta})$.

c. Show how to estimate $\mathrm{Avar}(\hat{\boldsymbol{\theta}})$; it should be of the form (13.53).

d. How does the estimator of $\mathrm{Avar}(\hat{\boldsymbol{\theta}})$ simplify if the conditional mean is dynamically complete?

13.7. Suppose that you have two parametric models for conditional densities: $g(y_1 \mid y_2, \mathbf{x}; \boldsymbol{\theta})$ and $h(y_2 \mid \mathbf{x}; \boldsymbol{\theta})$; not all elements of $\boldsymbol{\theta}$ need to appear in both densities. Denote the true value of $\boldsymbol{\theta}$ by $\boldsymbol{\theta}_o$.

a. What is the joint density of (y_1, y_2) given $\mathbf{x}$? How would you estimate $\boldsymbol{\theta}_o$ given a random sample on $(\mathbf{x}, y_1, y_2)$?

b. Suppose now that a random sample is not available on all variables. In particular, y_1 is observed only when $(\mathbf{x}, y_2)$ satisfies a known rule. For example, when y_2 is binary, y_1 is observed only when $y_2 = 1$. We assume $(\mathbf{x}, y_2)$ is always observed. Let r_2 be a binary variable equal to one if y_1 is observed and zero otherwise. A partial MLE is obtained by defining

$$\ell_i(\boldsymbol{\theta}) = r_{i2} \log g(y_{i1} \mid y_{i2}, \mathbf{x}_i; \boldsymbol{\theta}) + \log h(y_{i2} \mid \mathbf{x}_i; \boldsymbol{\theta}) \equiv r_{i2}\ell_{i1}(\boldsymbol{\theta}) + \ell_{i2}(\boldsymbol{\theta})$$

for each i. This formulation ensures that first part of ℓ_i only enters the estimation when y_{i1} is observed. Verify that $\boldsymbol{\theta}_o$ maximizes $\mathrm{E}[\ell_i(\boldsymbol{\theta})]$ over $\boldsymbol{\Theta}$.

c. Show that $-\mathrm{E}[\mathbf{H}_i(\boldsymbol{\theta}_o)] = \mathrm{E}[\mathbf{s}_i(\boldsymbol{\theta}_o)\mathbf{s}_i(\boldsymbol{\theta}_o)']$, even though the problem is not a true conditional MLE problem (and therefore a conditional information matrix equality does not hold).

d. Argue that a consistent estimator of Avar $\sqrt{N}(\hat{\boldsymbol{\theta}} - \boldsymbol{\theta}_o)$ is

$$\left[N^{-1} \sum_{i=1}^{N} (r_{i2}\hat{\mathbf{A}}_{i1} + \hat{\mathbf{A}}_{i2})\right]^{-1}$$

where $\mathbf{A}_{i1}(\boldsymbol{\theta}_o) = -\mathrm{E}[\nabla_\theta^2 \ell_{i1}(\boldsymbol{\theta}_o) \mid y_{i2}, \mathbf{x}_i]$, $\mathbf{A}_{i2}(\boldsymbol{\theta}_o) = -\mathrm{E}[\nabla_\theta^2 \ell_{i2}(\boldsymbol{\theta}_o) \mid \mathbf{x}_i]$, and $\hat{\boldsymbol{\theta}}$ replaces $\boldsymbol{\theta}_o$ in obtaining the estimates.

13.8. Suppose that for random vectors $\mathbf{y}_i$, $\mathbf{x}_i$, and $\mathbf{w}_i$,

$$\mathrm{D}(\mathbf{y}_i \mid \mathbf{x}_i, \mathbf{w}_i) = \mathrm{D}(\mathbf{y}_i \mid \mathbf{x}_i, \mathbf{g}(\mathbf{w}_i, \gamma_o)) \equiv \mathrm{D}(\mathbf{y}_i \mid \mathbf{x}_i, \mathbf{g}_i),$$

where $\mathbf{g}(\mathbf{w}, \gamma)$ is a known function of $\mathbf{w}$ and the J parameters γ and $\mathbf{g}_i \equiv \mathbf{g}(\mathbf{w}_i, \gamma_o)$ (which is unobserved because we generally do not know γ_o). Assume that we have a correctly specified density for $\mathrm{D}(\mathbf{y}_i \mid \mathbf{x}_i, \mathbf{g}_i)$, $f(\mathbf{y} \mid \mathbf{x}, \mathbf{g}; \boldsymbol{\theta})$, and let the $P \times 1$ vector $\boldsymbol{\theta}_o$ denote the true value. Let $\hat{\gamma}$ be an $\sqrt{N}$-asymptotically normal estimator of γ_o that satisfies

$$\sqrt{N}(\hat{\gamma} - \gamma_o) = N^{-1/2} \sum_{i=1}^{N} \mathbf{r}(\mathbf{w}_i, \gamma_o) + o_p(1),$$

and let $\hat{\boldsymbol{\theta}}$ be the two-step nonlinear least squares estimator that solves

$$\max_{\theta \in \Theta} \sum_{i=1}^{N} \log f(\mathbf{y}_i \mid \mathbf{x}_i, \mathbf{g}(\mathbf{w}_i, \hat{\gamma}); \boldsymbol{\theta}).$$

a. Show that, under standard regularity conditions, the asymptotic variance of $\sqrt{N}(\hat{\boldsymbol{\theta}} - \boldsymbol{\theta}_o)$ is at least as large as the asymptotic variance if we knew γ_o.

b. Propose a consistent estimator of Avar $\sqrt{N}(\hat{\boldsymbol{\theta}} - \boldsymbol{\theta}_o)$.

c. Suppose that y_i is a scalar and $\mathrm{P}(y_i = 1 \mid \mathbf{x}_i, \mathbf{w}_i) = \Phi(\mathbf{x}_i\boldsymbol{\beta}_o + \rho_o g_i)$, where $\mathbf{w}_i = (\mathbf{z}_i, h_i)$, $g_i = h_i - \mathbf{z}_i\gamma_o$, and $\mathrm{E}(\mathbf{z}_i' g_i) = \mathbf{0}$. Let $\hat{\boldsymbol{\theta}} = (\hat{\boldsymbol{\beta}}', \hat{\rho})'$ be the two-step probit estimators from probit of y_i on $\mathbf{x}_i$, and $\hat{g}_i$, where $\hat{g}_i = h_i - \mathbf{z}_i\hat{\gamma}$ are OLS residuals from h_i on $\mathbf{z}_i$, $i = 1, \ldots, N$. How does part a apply in this case?

d. Show that, when $\rho_o = 0$, the usual probit variance matrix estimator of $\hat{\boldsymbol{\theta}}$ is asymptotically valid. That is, valid inference is obtained by ignoring the first-stage estimation of γ_o.

e. How would you test $\mathrm{H}_o : \rho_o = 0$?

13.9. Let $\{y_t : t = 0, 1, \ldots, T\}$ be an observable time series representing a population, where we use the convention that $t = 0$ is the first time period for which y is observed. Assume that the sequence follows a *Markov process*: $\mathrm{D}(y_t \mid y_{t-1}, y_{t-2}, \ldots y_0) = \mathrm{D}(y_t \mid y_{t-1})$ for all $t \geq 1$. Let $f_t(y_t \mid y_{t-1}; \boldsymbol{\theta})$ denote a correctly specified model for the density of y_t given y_{t-1}, $t \geq 1$, where $\boldsymbol{\theta}_o$ is the true value of $\boldsymbol{\theta}$.

a. Show that, to obtain the joint distribution of $(y_0, y_2, \ldots, y_T)$, you need to correctly model the density of y_0.

b. Given a random sample of size N from the population, that is, $(y_{i0}, y_{i1}, \ldots, y_{iT})$ for each i, explain how to consistently etimate $\boldsymbol{\theta}_o$ without modeling $\mathrm{D}(y_0)$.

c. How would you estimate the asymptotic variance of the estimator from part b? Be specific.

13.10. Let $\mathbf{y}$ be a $G \times 1$ random vector with elements y_g, $g = 1, 2, \ldots, G$. These could be different response variables for the same cross section unit or responses at different points in time. Let $\mathbf{x}$ be a K-vector of observed conditioning variables, and let c be an unobserved conditioning variable. Let $f_g(\cdot \mid \mathbf{x}, c)$ denote the density of y_g given $(\mathbf{x}, c)$. Further, assume that the $y_1, y_2, \ldots, y_G$ are independent conditional on $(\mathbf{x}, c)$.

a. Write down the joint density of $\mathbf{y}$ given $(\mathbf{x}, c)$.

b. Let $h(\cdot \mid \mathbf{x})$ be the density of c given $\mathbf{x}$. Find the joint density of $\mathbf{y}$ given $\mathbf{x}$.

c. If each $f_g(\cdot \mid \mathbf{x}, c)$ is known up to a P_g-vector of parameters γ_o^g and $h(\cdot \mid \mathbf{x})$ is known up to an M-vector $\boldsymbol{\delta}_o$, find the log likelihood for any random draw $(\mathbf{x}_i, \mathbf{y}_i)$ from the population.

d. Is there a relationship between this setup and a linear SUR model?

13.11. Consider the dynamic, linear unobserved effects model

$$y_{it} = \rho y_{i,t-1} + c_i + e_{it}, \qquad t = 1, 2, \ldots, T$$

$$\mathrm{E}(e_{it} \mid y_{i,t-1}, y_{i,t-2}, \ldots, y_{i0}, c_i) = 0$$

In Section 11.6.2 we discussed estimation of ρ by instrumental variables methods after differencing. The deficiencies of the IV approach for large ρ may be overcome by applying the conditional MLE methods in Section 13.9.2.

a. Make the stronger assumption that $y_{it} \mid (y_{i,t-1}, y_{i,t-2}, \ldots, y_{i0}, c_i)$ is normally distributed with mean $\rho y_{i,t-1} + c_i$ and variance σ_e^2. Find the density of $(y_{i1}, \ldots, y_{iT})$ given (y_{i0}, c_i). Is it a good idea to use the log of this density, summed across i, to estimate ρ and σ_e^2 along with the "fixed effects" c_i?

b. If $c_i \mid y_{i0} \sim \mathrm{Normal}(\alpha_0 + \alpha_1 y_{i0}, \sigma_a^2)$, where $\sigma_a^2 \equiv \mathrm{Var}(a_i)$ and $a_i \equiv c_i - \alpha_0 - \alpha_1 y_{i0}$, write down the density of $(y_{i1}, \ldots, y_{iT})$ given y_{i0}. How would you estimate ρ, α_0, α_1, σ_e^2, and σ_a^2?

c. Under the same assumptions in parts a and b, extend the model to $y_{it} = \rho y_{i,t-1} + c_i + \delta c_i y_{i,t-1} + e_{it}$. Explain how to estimate the parameters of this model, and propose a consistent estimator of the average partial effect of the lag, $\rho + \delta \mathrm{E}(c_i)$.

d. Now extend part b to the case where $\mathbf{z}_{it}\boldsymbol{\beta}$ is added to the conditional mean function, where the $\mathbf{z}_{it}$ are strictly exogenous conditional on c_i. Assume that $c_i \mid y_{i0}, \mathbf{z}_i \sim \mathrm{Normal}(\alpha_0 + \alpha_1 y_{i0} + \bar{\mathbf{z}}_i \boldsymbol{\delta}, \sigma_a^2)$, where $\bar{\mathbf{z}}_i$ is the vector of time averages.

13.12. In the context of GLM, for a given LEF density, there are many ways to characterize what is known as the **canonical link function**. One is that $g(\cdot)$ is the canonical link if the first-order conditions for the QMLE can be expressed as

$$\sum_{i=1}^{n} \mathbf{x}_i'[y_i - g^{-1}(\mathbf{x}_i\hat{\boldsymbol{\theta}})] \equiv \sum_{i=1}^{n} \mathbf{x}_i'[y_i - m(\mathbf{x}_i, \hat{\boldsymbol{\theta}})] = \mathbf{0},$$

where $m(\mathbf{x}, \boldsymbol{\theta})$ is the corresponding mean function and $\hat{\boldsymbol{\theta}}$ is the QMLE. Alternatively, using the canonical link implies that the Hessian of the quasi-log likelihood (QLL) does not depend on y_i; consequently, the Hessian and the expected value of the Hessian given $\mathbf{x}_i$ are identical.

a. Define residuals as usual, $\hat{u}_i = y_i - m(\mathbf{x}_i, \hat{\boldsymbol{\theta}})$. Argue that if $\mathbf{x}_i$ contains a constant—as it almost always does in GLM analysis—then the residuals obtained by using the canonical link always average to zero. (This extends the well-known result for linear regression.)

b. Show that for the Bernoulli QLL, the canonical link function is $g(\mu) = \log[\mu/(1-\mu)]$, so that the mean function is the logistic function, $\exp(\mathbf{x}\boldsymbol{\theta})/[1+\exp(\mathbf{x}\boldsymbol{\theta})]$.

c. Show that for the Poisson QLL, the canonical link is $g(\mu) = \log(\mu)$. What is the mean function?

d. Evaluate the following statement: "In a GLM analysis using the canonical link, our estimate of the asymptotic variance of $\hat{\boldsymbol{\theta}}$ is the same whether or not we assume the mean function is correctly specified."

13.13. Let $\boldsymbol{\theta}^*$ be the solution to the maximization problem

$$\max_{\boldsymbol{\theta} \in \boldsymbol{\Theta}} \mathrm{E}[\ell(\mathbf{w}_i, \boldsymbol{\theta})],$$

where $\ell(\mathbf{w}, \boldsymbol{\theta})$ is a quasi-log likelihood satisfying the conditions of Theorem 12.3 (but with maximization rather than minimization). Assume that $\boldsymbol{\theta}^*$ is in the interior of $\boldsymbol{\Theta}$ and that the gradients and expectation can be interchanged. Let $\hat{\boldsymbol{\theta}}$ be the quasi-MLE. Show that

$$N^{-1/2} \sum_{i=1}^{N} \ell(\mathbf{w}_i, \hat{\boldsymbol{\theta}}) = N^{-1/2} \sum_{i=1}^{N} \ell(\mathbf{w}_i, \boldsymbol{\theta}^*) + o_p(1).$$

Appendix 13A

In this appendix we cover some important properties of conditional distributions and conditional densities. Billingsley (1979) is a good reference for this material. For random vectors $\mathbf{y} \in \mathscr{Y} \subset \mathbb{R}^G$ and $\mathbf{x} \in \mathscr{X} \subset \mathbb{R}^K$, the **conditional distribution** of $\mathbf{y}$ given $\mathbf{x}$ always exists and is denoted $\mathrm{D}(\mathbf{y} \mid \mathbf{x})$. For each $\mathbf{x}$ this distribution is a probability measure and completely describes the behavior of the random vector $\mathbf{y}$ once $\mathbf{x}$ takes on a particular value. In econometrics, we almost always assume that this distribution is described by a **conditional density**, which we denote by $p(\cdot \mid \mathbf{x})$. The density is with respect to a **measure** defined on the support $\mathscr{Y}$ of $\mathbf{y}$. A conditional density makes sense only when this measure does not change with the value of $\mathbf{x}$. In practice, this assumption is not very restrictive, as it means that the nature of $\mathbf{y}$ is not dramatically different for different values of $\mathbf{x}$. Let ν be this measure on $\mathbb{R}^J$. If $\mathrm{D}(\mathbf{y} \mid \mathbf{x})$ is discrete, ν can be the counting measure and all integrals are sums. If $\mathrm{D}(\mathbf{y} \mid \mathbf{x})$ is **absolutely continuous**, then ν is the familiar Lebesgue measure appearing in elementary integration theory. In some cases, $\mathrm{D}(\mathbf{y} \mid \mathbf{x})$ has both discrete and continuous characteristics.

The important point is that all conditional probabilities can be obtained by integration:

$$\mathrm{P}(\mathbf{y} \in \mathscr{A} \mid \mathbf{x} = x) = \int_A p(y \mid x)\nu(\mathrm{d}y),$$

where y is the dummy argument of integration. When $\mathbf{y}$ is discrete, taking on the values $y_1, y_2, \ldots$, then $p(\cdot \mid x)$ is a probability mass function and $\mathrm{P}(\mathbf{y} = y_j \mid \mathbf{x} = x) = p(y_j \mid x)$, $j = 1, 2, \ldots$.

Suppose that f and g are nonnegative functions on $\mathbb{R}^M$, and define $\mathscr{S}_f \equiv \{z \in \mathbb{R}^M : f(z) > 0\}$. Assume that

$$1 = \int_{\mathscr{S}_f} f(z)\nu(dz) \geq \int_{\mathscr{S}_f} g(z)\nu(\mathrm{d}z), \tag{13.99}$$

where ν is a measure on $\mathbb{R}^M$. The equality in expression (13.99) implies that f is a density on $\mathbb{R}^M$, while the inequality holds if g is also a density on $\mathbb{R}^M$. An important result is that

$$\mathscr{I}(f;g) \equiv \int_{\mathscr{S}_f} \log[f(z)/g(z)]f(z)\nu(\mathrm{d}z) \geq 0. \tag{13.100}$$

(Note that $\mathscr{I}(f;g) = \infty$ is allowed; one case where this result can occur is $f(z) > 0$ but $g(z) = 0$ for some z. Also, the integrand is not defined when $f(z) = g(z) = 0$, but such values of z have no effect because the integrand receives zero weight in the integration.) The quantity $\mathscr{I}(f;g)$ is called the **Kullback-Leibler information criterion (KLIC)**. Another way to state expression (13.100) is

$$\mathrm{E}\{\log[f(\mathbf{z})]\} \geq \mathrm{E}\{\log[g(\mathbf{z})]\}, \tag{13.101}$$

where $\mathbf{z} \in \mathscr{Z} \subset \mathbb{R}^M$ is a random vector with density f.

Conditional MLE relies on a conditional version of inequality (13.99):

PROPERTY CD.1: Let $\mathbf{y} \in \mathscr{Y} \subset \mathbb{R}^G$ and $\mathbf{x} \in \mathscr{X} \subset \mathbb{R}^K$ be random vectors. Let $p(\cdot \mid \cdot)$ denote the conditional density of $\mathbf{y}$ given $\mathbf{x}$. For each $\mathbf{x}$, let $\mathscr{Y}(\mathbf{x}) \equiv \{y : p(y \mid \mathbf{x}) > 0\}$ be the *conditional support* of $\mathbf{y}$, and let ν be a measure that does not depend on $\mathbf{x}$. Then, for any other function $g(\cdot \mid \mathbf{x}) \geq 0$ such that

$$1 = \int_{\mathscr{Y}(\mathbf{x})} p(y \mid \mathbf{x})\nu(\mathrm{d}y) \geq \int_{\mathscr{Y}(\mathbf{x})} g(y \mid \mathbf{x})\nu(\mathrm{d}y),$$

the conditional KLIC is nonnegative.

$$\mathcal{I}_{\mathbf{x}}(p;g) \equiv \int_{\mathcal{Y}(\mathbf{x})} \log[p(y \mid \mathbf{x})/g(y \mid \mathbf{x})]p(y \mid \mathbf{x})\nu(\mathrm{d}y) \geq 0.$$

That is,

$$\mathrm{E}\{\log[p(\mathbf{y} \mid \mathbf{x})] \mid \mathbf{x}\} \geq \mathrm{E}\{\log[g(\mathbf{y} \mid \mathbf{x})] \mid \mathbf{x}\}$$

for any $\mathbf{x} \in \mathcal{X}$. The proof uses the conditional Jensen's inequality (Property CE.7 in Chapter 2). See Manski (1988, Sect. 5.1).

PROPERTY CD.2: For random vectors $\mathbf{y}$, $\mathbf{x}$, and $\mathbf{z}$, let $p(y \mid \mathbf{x}, \mathbf{z})$ be the conditional density of $\mathbf{y}$ given $(\mathbf{x}, \mathbf{z})$ and let $p(x \mid \mathbf{z})$ denote the conditional density of $\mathbf{x}$ given $\mathbf{z}$. Then the density of $(\mathbf{y}, \mathbf{x})$ given $\mathbf{z}$ is

$$p(y, x \mid \mathbf{z}) = p(y \mid x, \mathbf{z})p(x \mid \mathbf{z}),$$

where the script variables are placeholders.

PROPERTY CD.3: For random vectors $\mathbf{y}$, $\mathbf{x}$, and $\mathbf{z}$, let $p(y \mid \mathbf{x}, \mathbf{z})$ be the conditional density of $\mathbf{y}$ given $(\mathbf{x}, \mathbf{z})$, let $p(y \mid \mathbf{x})$ be the conditional density of $\mathbf{y}$ given $\mathbf{x}$, and let $p(z \mid \mathbf{x})$ denote the conditional density of $\mathbf{z}$ given $\mathbf{x}$ with respect to the measure $\nu(\mathrm{d}z)$. Then

$$p(y \mid \mathbf{x}) = \int_{\mathcal{Z}} p(y \mid \mathbf{x}, z)p(z \mid \mathbf{x})\nu(\mathrm{d}z).$$

In other words, we can obtain the density of $\mathbf{y}$ given $\mathbf{x}$ by integrating the density of $\mathbf{y}$ given the larger conditioning set, $(\mathbf{x}, \mathbf{z})$, against the density of $\mathbf{z}$ given $\mathbf{x}$.

PROPERTY CD.4: Suppose that the random variable, u, with cdf, F, is independent of the random vector $\mathbf{x}$. Then, for any function $a(\mathbf{x})$ of $\mathbf{x}$, $\mathrm{P}[u \leq a(\mathbf{x}) \mid \mathbf{x}] = F[a(\mathbf{x})]$.

14 Generalized Method of Moments and Minimum Distance Estimation

In Chapter 8 we saw how the generalized method of moments (GMM) approach to estimation can be applied to multiple-equation linear models, including systems of equations, with exogenous or endogenous explanatory variables, and to panel data models. In this chapter we extend GMM to nonlinear estimation problems. This setup allows us to treat various efficiency issues that we have glossed over until now. We also cover the related method of minimum distance estimation. Because the asymptotic analysis has many features in common with Chapters 8 and 12, the analysis is not quite as detailed here as in previous chapters. A good reference for this material, which fills in most of the gaps left here, is Newey and McFadden (1994).

14.1 Asymptotic Properties of Generalized Method of Moments

Let $\{\mathbf{w}_i \in \mathbb{R}^M: i = 1, 2, \ldots\}$ denote a set of independent, identically distributed random vectors, where some feature of the distribution of $\mathbf{w}_i$ is indexed by the $P \times 1$ parameter vector $\boldsymbol{\theta}$. The assumption of identical distribution is mostly for notational convenience; the following methods apply to independently pooled cross sections without modification.

We assume that for some function $\mathbf{g}(\mathbf{w}_i, \boldsymbol{\theta}) \in \mathbb{R}^L$, the parameter $\boldsymbol{\theta}_o \in \boldsymbol{\Theta} \subset \mathbb{R}^P$ satisfies the moment assumptions

$$\mathrm{E}[\mathbf{g}(\mathbf{w}_i, \boldsymbol{\theta}_o)] = 0. \tag{14.1}$$

As we saw in the linear case, where $\mathbf{g}(\mathbf{w}_i, \boldsymbol{\theta})$ was of the form $\mathbf{Z}_i'(\mathbf{y}_i - \mathbf{X}_i\boldsymbol{\theta})$, a minimal requirement for these moment conditions to identify $\boldsymbol{\theta}_o$ is $L \geq P$. If $L = P$, then the analogy principle suggests estimating $\boldsymbol{\theta}_o$ by setting the sample counterpart, $N^{-1}\sum_{i=1}^N \mathbf{g}(\mathbf{w}_i, \boldsymbol{\theta})$, to zero. In the linear case, this step leads to the instrumental variables estimator (see equation (8.22)). When $L > P$, we can choose $\hat{\boldsymbol{\theta}}$ to make the sample average close to zero in an appropriate metric. A **GMM** estimator, $\hat{\boldsymbol{\theta}}$, minimizes a quadratic form in $\sum_{i=1}^N \mathbf{g}(\mathbf{w}_i, \boldsymbol{\theta})$:

$$\min_{\boldsymbol{\theta} \in \boldsymbol{\Theta}} \left[\sum_{i=1}^N \mathbf{g}(\mathbf{w}_i, \boldsymbol{\theta})\right]' \hat{\boldsymbol{\Xi}} \left[\sum_{i=1}^N \mathbf{g}(\mathbf{w}_i, \boldsymbol{\theta})\right], \tag{14.2}$$

where $\hat{\boldsymbol{\Xi}}$ is an $L \times L$ symmetric, positive semidefinite (p.s.d.) weighting matrix.

Consistency of the GMM estimator follows along the lines of consistency of the M-estimator in Chapter 12. Under standard moment conditions, $N^{-1}\sum_{i=1}^N \mathbf{g}(\mathbf{w}_i, \boldsymbol{\theta})$ satisfies the uniform law of large numbers (see Theorem 12.1). If $\hat{\boldsymbol{\Xi}} \xrightarrow{p} \boldsymbol{\Xi}_o$, where $\boldsymbol{\Xi}_o$ is an $L \times L$ positive definite matrix, then the random function

$$Q_N(\boldsymbol{\theta}) \equiv \left[N^{-1}\sum_{i=1}^{N}\mathbf{g}(\mathbf{w}_i,\boldsymbol{\theta})\right]'\hat{\boldsymbol{\Xi}}\left[N^{-1}\sum_{i=1}^{N}\mathbf{g}(\mathbf{w}_i,\boldsymbol{\theta})\right] \tag{14.3}$$

converges uniformly in probability to

$$\{\mathrm{E}[\mathbf{g}(\mathbf{w}_i,\boldsymbol{\theta})]\}'\boldsymbol{\Xi}_o\{\mathrm{E}[\mathbf{g}(\mathbf{w}_i,\boldsymbol{\theta})]\}. \tag{14.4}$$

Because $\boldsymbol{\Xi}_o$ is positive definite, $\boldsymbol{\theta}_o$ *uniquely* minimizes expression (14.4). For completeness, we summarize with a theorem containing regularity conditions:

THEOREM 14.1 (Consistency of GMM): Assume that (a) $\boldsymbol{\Theta}$ is compact; (b) for each $\boldsymbol{\theta} \in \boldsymbol{\Theta}$, $\mathbf{g}(\cdot,\boldsymbol{\theta})$ is Borel measurable on $\mathcal{W}$; (c) for each $\mathbf{w} \in \mathcal{W}$, $\mathbf{g}(\mathbf{w},\cdot)$ is continuous on $\boldsymbol{\Theta}$; (d) $|g_j(\mathbf{w},\boldsymbol{\theta})| \le b(\mathbf{w})$ for all $\boldsymbol{\theta} \in \boldsymbol{\Theta}$ and $j = 1,\ldots,L$, where $b(\cdot)$ is a nonnegative function on $\mathcal{W}$ such that $\mathrm{E}[b(\mathbf{w})] < \infty$; (e) $\hat{\boldsymbol{\Xi}} \xrightarrow{p} \boldsymbol{\Xi}_o$, an $L \times L$ positive definite matrix; and (f) $\boldsymbol{\theta}_o$ is the unique solution to equation (14.1). Then a random vector $\hat{\boldsymbol{\theta}}$ exists that solves problem (14.2), and $\hat{\boldsymbol{\theta}} \xrightarrow{p} \boldsymbol{\theta}_o$.

If we assume only that $\boldsymbol{\Xi}_o$ is p.s.d., then we must directly assume that $\boldsymbol{\theta}_o$ is the unique minimizer of expression (14.4). Occasionally this generality is useful, but we will not need it.

Under the assumption that $\mathbf{g}(\mathbf{w},\cdot)$ is continuously differentiable on $\mathrm{int}(\boldsymbol{\Theta})$, $\boldsymbol{\theta}_o \in \mathrm{int}(\boldsymbol{\Theta})$, and other standard regularity conditions, we can easily derive the limiting distribution of the GMM estimator. The first-order condition for $\hat{\boldsymbol{\theta}}$ can be written as

$$\left[\sum_{i=1}^{N}\nabla_\theta\mathbf{g}(\mathbf{w}_i,\hat{\boldsymbol{\theta}})\right]'\hat{\boldsymbol{\Xi}}\left[\sum_{i=1}^{N}\mathbf{g}(\mathbf{w}_i,\hat{\boldsymbol{\theta}})\right] \equiv \mathbf{0}. \tag{14.5}$$

Define the $L \times P$ matrix

$$\mathbf{G}_o \equiv \mathrm{E}[\nabla_\theta\mathbf{g}(\mathbf{w}_i,\boldsymbol{\theta}_o)], \tag{14.6}$$

which we assume to have full rank P. This assumption essentially means that the moment conditions (14.1) are nonredundant. Then, by the weak law of large numbers (WLLN) and central limit theorem (CLT),

$$N^{-1}\sum_{i=1}^{N}\nabla_\theta\mathbf{g}(\mathbf{w}_i,\boldsymbol{\theta}_o) \xrightarrow{p} \mathbf{G}_o \quad \text{and} \quad N^{-1/2}\sum_{i=1}^{N}\mathbf{g}(\mathbf{w}_i,\boldsymbol{\theta}_o) = \mathrm{O}_p(1), \tag{14.7}$$

respectively. Let $\mathbf{g}_i(\boldsymbol{\theta}) \equiv \mathbf{g}(\mathbf{w}_i,\boldsymbol{\theta})$. A mean value expansion of $\sum_{i=1}^{N}\mathbf{g}(\mathbf{w}_i,\hat{\boldsymbol{\theta}})$ about $\boldsymbol{\theta}_o$, appropriate standardizations by the sample size, and replacing random averages with their plims gives

$$\mathbf{0} = \mathbf{G}_o'\boldsymbol{\Xi}_o N^{-1/2} \sum_{i=1}^{N} \mathbf{g}_i(\boldsymbol{\theta}_o) + \mathbf{A}_o \sqrt{N}(\hat{\boldsymbol{\theta}} - \boldsymbol{\theta}_o) + o_p(1), \tag{14.8}$$

where

$$\mathbf{A}_o \equiv \mathbf{G}_o'\boldsymbol{\Xi}_o\mathbf{G}_o. \tag{14.9}$$

Since $\mathbf{A}_o$ is positive definite under the given assumptions, we have

$$\sqrt{N}(\hat{\boldsymbol{\theta}} - \boldsymbol{\theta}_o) = -\mathbf{A}_o^{-1}\mathbf{G}_o'\boldsymbol{\Xi}_o N^{-1/2} \sum_{i=1}^{N} \mathbf{g}_i(\boldsymbol{\theta}_o) + o_p(1) \xrightarrow{d} \text{Normal}(\mathbf{0}, \mathbf{A}_o^{-1}\mathbf{B}_o\mathbf{A}_o^{-1}), \tag{14.10}$$

where

$$\mathbf{B}_o \equiv \mathbf{G}_o'\boldsymbol{\Xi}_o\boldsymbol{\Lambda}_o\boldsymbol{\Xi}_o\mathbf{G}_o \tag{14.11}$$

and

$$\boldsymbol{\Lambda}_o \equiv \mathrm{E}[\mathbf{g}_i(\boldsymbol{\theta}_o)\mathbf{g}_i(\boldsymbol{\theta}_o)'] = \mathrm{Var}[\mathbf{g}_i(\boldsymbol{\theta}_o)]. \tag{14.12}$$

Expression (14.10) gives the influence function representation for the GMM estimator, and it also gives the limiting distribution of the GMM estimator. We summarize with a theorem, which is essentially given by Newey and McFadden (1994, Theorem 3.4):

THEOREM 14.2 (Asymptotic Normality of GMM): In addition to the assumptions in Theorem 14.1, assume that (a) $\boldsymbol{\theta}_o$ is in the interior of $\boldsymbol{\Theta}$; (b) $\mathbf{g}(\mathbf{w}, \cdot)$ is continuously differentiable on the interior of $\boldsymbol{\Theta}$ for all $\mathbf{w} \in \mathcal{W}$; (c) each element of $\mathbf{g}(\mathbf{w}, \boldsymbol{\theta}_o)$ has finite second moment; (d) each element of $\nabla_\theta \mathbf{g}(\mathbf{w}, \boldsymbol{\theta})$ is bounded in absolute value by a function $b(\mathbf{w})$, where $\mathrm{E}[b(\mathbf{w})] < \infty$; and (e) $\mathbf{G}_o$ in expression (14.6) has rank P. Then expression (14.10) holds, and so $\mathrm{Avar}(\hat{\boldsymbol{\theta}}) = \mathbf{A}_o^{-1}\mathbf{B}_o\mathbf{A}_o^{-1}/N$.

Estimating the asymptotic variance of the GMM estimator is easy once $\hat{\boldsymbol{\theta}}$ has been obtained. A consistent estimator of $\boldsymbol{\Lambda}_o$ is given by

$$\hat{\boldsymbol{\Lambda}} \equiv N^{-1} \sum_{i=1}^{N} \mathbf{g}_i(\hat{\boldsymbol{\theta}})\mathbf{g}_i(\hat{\boldsymbol{\theta}})' \tag{14.13}$$

and $\mathrm{Avar}(\hat{\boldsymbol{\theta}})$ is estimated as $\hat{\mathbf{A}}^{-1}\hat{\mathbf{B}}\hat{\mathbf{A}}^{-1}/N$, where

$$\hat{\mathbf{A}} \equiv \hat{\mathbf{G}}'\hat{\boldsymbol{\Xi}}\hat{\mathbf{G}}, \qquad \hat{\mathbf{B}} \equiv \hat{\mathbf{G}}'\hat{\boldsymbol{\Xi}}\hat{\boldsymbol{\Lambda}}\hat{\boldsymbol{\Xi}}\hat{\mathbf{G}}, \tag{14.14}$$

and

$$\hat{\mathbf{G}} \equiv N^{-1} \sum_{i=1}^{N} \nabla_\theta \mathbf{g}_i(\hat{\boldsymbol{\theta}}). \tag{14.15}$$

As in the linear case in Section 8.3.3, an optimal weighting matrix exists for the given moment conditions: $\hat{\boldsymbol{\Xi}}$ should be a consistent estimator of $\boldsymbol{\Lambda}_o^{-1}$. When $\boldsymbol{\Xi}_o = \boldsymbol{\Lambda}_o^{-1}$, $\mathbf{B}_o = \mathbf{A}_o$ and Avar $\sqrt{N}(\hat{\boldsymbol{\theta}} - \boldsymbol{\theta}_o) = (\mathbf{G}_o'\boldsymbol{\Lambda}_o^{-1}\mathbf{G}_o)^{-1}$. Thus the difference in asymptotic variances between the general GMM estimator and the estimator with plim $\hat{\boldsymbol{\Xi}} = \boldsymbol{\Lambda}_o^{-1}$ is

$$(\mathbf{G}_o'\boldsymbol{\Xi}_o\mathbf{G}_o)^{-1}(\mathbf{G}_o'\boldsymbol{\Xi}_o\boldsymbol{\Lambda}_o\boldsymbol{\Xi}_o\mathbf{G}_o)(\mathbf{G}_o'\boldsymbol{\Xi}_o\mathbf{G}_o)^{-1} - (\mathbf{G}_o'\boldsymbol{\Lambda}_o^{-1}\mathbf{G}_o)^{-1}. \tag{14.16}$$

This expression can be shown to be p.s.d. using the same argument as in Chapter 8 (see Problem 8.5).

To obtain an asymptotically efficient GMM estimator we need a preliminary estimator of $\boldsymbol{\theta}_o$ in order to obtain $\hat{\boldsymbol{\Lambda}}$. Let $\hat{\hat{\boldsymbol{\theta}}}$ be such an estimator, and define $\hat{\boldsymbol{\Lambda}}$ as in expression (14.13) but with $\hat{\hat{\boldsymbol{\theta}}}$ in place of $\hat{\boldsymbol{\theta}}$. Then, an efficient GMM estimator (given the function $\mathbf{g}(\mathbf{w}, \boldsymbol{\theta})$) solves

$$\min_{\boldsymbol{\theta} \in \boldsymbol{\Theta}} \left[\sum_{i=1}^{N} \mathbf{g}(\mathbf{w}_i, \boldsymbol{\theta})\right]' \hat{\boldsymbol{\Lambda}}^{-1} \left[\sum_{i=1}^{N} \mathbf{g}(\mathbf{w}_i, \boldsymbol{\theta})\right], \tag{14.17}$$

and its asymptotic variance is estimated as

$$\widehat{\text{Avar}}(\hat{\boldsymbol{\theta}}) = (\hat{\mathbf{G}}'\hat{\boldsymbol{\Lambda}}^{-1}\hat{\mathbf{G}})^{-1}/N. \tag{14.18}$$

As in the linear case, an optimal GMM estimator is called the **minimum chi-square estimator** because

$$\left[N^{-1/2} \sum_{i=1}^{N} \mathbf{g}_i(\hat{\boldsymbol{\theta}})\right]' \hat{\boldsymbol{\Lambda}}^{-1} \left[\sum_{i=1}^{N} N^{-1/2} \mathbf{g}_i(\hat{\boldsymbol{\theta}})\right] \tag{14.19}$$

has a limiting chi-square distribution with $L - P$ degrees of freedom under the conditions of Theorem 14.2. Therefore, the value of the objective function (properly standardized by the sample size) can be used as a test of any overidentifying restrictions in equation (14.1) when $L > P$. If statistic (14.19) exceeds the relevant critical value in a χ^2_{L-P} distribution, then equation (14.1) must be rejected: at least some of the moment conditions are not supported by the data. For the linear model, this is the same statistic given in equation (8.49).

As always, we can test hypotheses of the form $\text{H}_0 : \mathbf{c}(\boldsymbol{\theta}_o) = \mathbf{0}$, where $\mathbf{c}(\boldsymbol{\theta})$ is a $Q \times 1$ vector, $Q \leq P$, by using the Wald approach and the appropriate variance matrix estimator. A statistic based on the difference in objective functions is also available if the minimum chi-square estimator is used so that $\mathbf{B}_o = \mathbf{A}_o$. Let $\tilde{\boldsymbol{\theta}}$ denote the solution to problem (14.17) subject to the restrictions $\mathbf{c}(\boldsymbol{\theta}) = \mathbf{0}$, and let $\hat{\boldsymbol{\theta}}$ denote the unrestricted estimator-solving problem (14.17); importantly, these both use the same weighting matrix $\hat{\boldsymbol{\Lambda}}^{-1}$. Typically, $\hat{\boldsymbol{\Lambda}}$ is obtained from a first-stage, unrestricted estimator. Assuming that the constraints can be written in implicit form and satisfy the conditions discussed in Section 12.6.2, the **GMM distance statistic** (or **GMM criterion function statistic**) has a limiting χ^2_Q distribution:

$$\left\{\left[\sum_{i=1}^{N}\mathbf{g}_i(\tilde{\boldsymbol{\theta}})\right]'\hat{\boldsymbol{\Lambda}}^{-1}\left[\sum_{i=1}^{N}\mathbf{g}_i(\tilde{\boldsymbol{\theta}})\right]-\left[\sum_{i=1}^{N}\mathbf{g}_i(\hat{\boldsymbol{\theta}})\right]'\hat{\boldsymbol{\Lambda}}^{-1}\left[\sum_{i=1}^{N}\mathbf{g}_i(\hat{\boldsymbol{\theta}})\right]\right\}\Big/N \xrightarrow{d} \chi^2_Q. \tag{14.20}$$

When applied to linear GMM problems, we obtain the statistic in equation (8.45). One nice feature of expression (14.20) is that it is invariant to reparameterization of the null hypothesis, just as the quasi-likelihood ratio (QLR) statistic is invariant for M-estimation. Therefore, we might prefer statistic (14.20) over the Wald statistic (8.48) for testing nonlinear restrictions in linear models. Of course, the computation of expression (14.20) is more difficult because we would actually need to carry out estimation subject to nonlinear restrictions.

A nice application of the GMM methods discussed in this section is two-step estimation procedures, which arose in Chapters 6, 12, and 13. Suppose that the estimator $\hat{\boldsymbol{\theta}}$—it could be an M-estimator or a GMM estimator—depends on a first-stage estimator, $\hat{\boldsymbol{\gamma}}$. A unified approach to obtaining the asymptotic variance of $\hat{\boldsymbol{\theta}}$ is to stack the first-order conditions for $\hat{\boldsymbol{\theta}}$ *and* $\hat{\boldsymbol{\gamma}}$ into the same function $\mathbf{g}(\cdot)$. This is always possible for the estimators encountered in this book. For example, if $\hat{\boldsymbol{\gamma}}$ is an M-estimator solving $\sum_{i=1}^{N}\mathbf{d}(\mathbf{w}_i, \hat{\boldsymbol{\gamma}}) = \mathbf{0}$, and $\hat{\boldsymbol{\theta}}$ is a two-step M-estimator solving

$$\sum_{i=1}^{N}\mathbf{s}(\mathbf{w}_i, \hat{\boldsymbol{\theta}}; \hat{\boldsymbol{\gamma}}) = \mathbf{0}, \tag{14.21}$$

then we can obtain the asymptotic variance of $\hat{\boldsymbol{\theta}}$ by defining

$$\mathbf{g}(\mathbf{w}, \boldsymbol{\theta}, \boldsymbol{\gamma}) = \begin{bmatrix}\mathbf{s}(\mathbf{w}, \boldsymbol{\theta}; \boldsymbol{\gamma}) \\ \mathbf{d}(\mathbf{w}, \boldsymbol{\gamma})\end{bmatrix}$$

and applying the GMM formulas. The first-order condition for the full GMM problem reproduces the first-order conditions for each estimator separately.

In general, either $\hat{\boldsymbol{\gamma}}$, $\hat{\boldsymbol{\theta}}$, or both might themselves be GMM estimators. Then, stacking the orthogonality conditions into one vector can simplify the derivation of the asymptotic variance of the second-step estimator $\hat{\boldsymbol{\theta}}$ while also ensuring efficient estimation when the optimal weighting matrix is used.

Finally, sometimes we want to know whether adding additional moment conditions does not improve the efficiency of the minimum chi-square estimator. (Adding additional moment conditions can never reduce asymptotic efficiency, provided an efficient weighting matrix is used.) In other words, if we start with equation (14.1) but add new moments of the form $\mathrm{E}[\mathbf{h}(\mathbf{w}, \boldsymbol{\theta}_o)] = 0$, when does using the extra moment conditions yield the same asymptotic variance as the original moment conditions? Breusch, Qian, Schmidt, and Wyhowski (1999) prove some general redundancy results for the minimum chi-square estimator. Qian and Schmidt (1999) study the problem of adding moment conditions that do not depend on unknown parameters, and they characterize when such moment conditions improve efficiency.

14.2 Estimation under Orthogonality Conditions

In Chapter 8 we saw how linear systems of equations can be estimated by GMM under certain orthogonality conditions. In general applications, the moment conditions (14.1) almost always arise from assumptions that disturbances are uncorrelated with exogenous variables. For a $G \times 1$ vector $\mathbf{r}(\mathbf{w}_i, \boldsymbol{\theta})$ and a $G \times L$ matrix $\mathbf{Z}_i$, assume that $\boldsymbol{\theta}_o$ satisfies

$$\mathrm{E}[\mathbf{Z}_i'\mathbf{r}(\mathbf{w}_i, \boldsymbol{\theta}_o)] = \mathbf{0}. \tag{14.22}$$

The vector function $\mathbf{r}(\mathbf{w}_i, \boldsymbol{\theta})$ can be thought of as a **generalized residual function**. The matrix $\mathbf{Z}_i$ is usually called the **matrix of instruments**. Equation (14.22) is a special case of equation (14.1) with $\mathbf{g}(\mathbf{w}_i, \boldsymbol{\theta}) \equiv \mathbf{Z}_i'\mathbf{r}(\mathbf{w}_i, \boldsymbol{\theta})$. In what follows, write $\mathbf{r}_i(\boldsymbol{\theta}) \equiv \mathbf{r}(\mathbf{w}_i, \boldsymbol{\theta})$.

Identification requires that $\boldsymbol{\theta}_o$ be the only $\boldsymbol{\theta} \in \boldsymbol{\Theta}$ such that equation (14.22) holds. Condition e of the asymptotic normality result Theorem 14.2 requires that rank $\mathrm{E}[\mathbf{Z}_i'\nabla_\theta \mathbf{r}_i(\boldsymbol{\theta}_o)] = P$ (necessary is $L \geq P$). Thus, while $\mathbf{Z}_i$ must be orthogonal to $\mathbf{r}_i(\boldsymbol{\theta}_o)$, $\mathbf{Z}_i$ must be sufficiently correlated with the $G \times P$ Jacobian, $\nabla_\theta \mathbf{r}_i(\boldsymbol{\theta}_o)$. In the linear case where $\mathbf{r}(\mathbf{w}_i, \boldsymbol{\theta}) = \mathbf{y}_i - \mathbf{X}_i\boldsymbol{\theta}$, this requirement reduces to $\mathrm{E}(\mathbf{Z}_i'\mathbf{X}_i)$ having full column rank, which is simply Assumption SIV.2 in Chapter 8.

Given the instruments $\mathbf{Z}_i$, the efficient estimator can be obtained as in Section 14.1. A preliminary estimator $\hat{\hat{\boldsymbol{\theta}}}$ is usually obtained with

$$\hat{\boldsymbol{\Xi}} \equiv \left(N^{-1} \sum_{i=1}^{N} \mathbf{Z}_i'\mathbf{Z}_i \right)^{-1} \tag{14.23}$$

so that $\hat{\hat{\boldsymbol{\theta}}}$ solves

$$\min_{\theta \in \Theta} \left[\sum_{i=1}^{N} \mathbf{Z}_i' \mathbf{r}_i(\boldsymbol{\theta}) \right]' \left[N^{-1} \sum_{i=1}^{N} \mathbf{Z}_i' \mathbf{Z}_i \right]^{-1} \left[\sum_{i=1}^{N} \mathbf{Z}_i' \mathbf{r}_i(\boldsymbol{\theta}) \right]. \tag{14.24}$$

The solution to problem (14.24) is called the **nonlinear system 2SLS estimator**; it is an example of a **nonlinear instrumental variables estimator**.

From Section 14.1, we know that the nonlinear system 2SLS estimator is guaranteed to be the efficient GMM estimator if for some $\sigma_o^2 > 0$,

$$\mathrm{E}[\mathbf{Z}_i' \mathbf{r}_i(\boldsymbol{\theta}_o) \mathbf{r}_i(\boldsymbol{\theta}_o)' \mathbf{Z}_i] = \sigma_o^2 \mathrm{E}(\mathbf{Z}_i' \mathbf{Z}_i).$$

Generally, this is a strong assumption. Instead, we can obtain the minimum chi-square estimator by obtaining

$$\hat{\boldsymbol{\Lambda}} = N^{-1} \sum_{i=1}^{N} \mathbf{Z}_i' \mathbf{r}_i(\hat{\hat{\boldsymbol{\theta}}}) \mathbf{r}_i(\hat{\hat{\boldsymbol{\theta}}})' \mathbf{Z}_i \tag{14.25}$$

and using this in expression (14.17).

In some cases more structure is available that leads to a three-stage least squares estimator. In particular, suppose that

$$\mathrm{E}[\mathbf{Z}_i' \mathbf{r}_i(\boldsymbol{\theta}_o) \mathbf{r}_i(\boldsymbol{\theta}_o)' \mathbf{Z}_i] = \mathrm{E}(\mathbf{Z}_i' \boldsymbol{\Omega}_o \mathbf{Z}_i), \tag{14.26}$$

where $\boldsymbol{\Omega}_o$ is the $G \times G$ matrix

$$\boldsymbol{\Omega}_o = \mathrm{E}[\mathbf{r}_i(\boldsymbol{\theta}_o) \mathbf{r}_i(\boldsymbol{\theta}_o)']. \tag{14.27}$$

When $\mathrm{E}[\mathbf{r}_i(\boldsymbol{\theta}_o)] = \mathbf{0}$, as is almost always the case under assumption (14.22), $\boldsymbol{\Omega}_o$ is the variance matrix of $\mathbf{r}_i(\boldsymbol{\theta}_o)$. As in Chapter 8, assumption (14.26) is a kind of system homoskedasticity assumption.

By iterated expectations, a sufficient condition for assumption (14.26) is

$$\mathrm{E}[\mathbf{r}_i(\boldsymbol{\theta}_o) \mathbf{r}_i(\boldsymbol{\theta}_o)' \mid \mathbf{Z}_i] = \boldsymbol{\Omega}_o. \tag{14.28}$$

However, assumption (14.26) can hold in cases where assumption (14.28) does not.

If assumption (14.26) holds, then $\boldsymbol{\Lambda}_o$ can be estimated as

$$\hat{\boldsymbol{\Lambda}} = N^{-1} \sum_{i=1}^{N} \mathbf{Z}_i' \hat{\boldsymbol{\Omega}} \mathbf{Z}_i, \tag{14.29}$$

where

$$\hat{\boldsymbol{\Omega}} = N^{-1} \sum_{i=1}^{N} \mathbf{r}_i(\hat{\hat{\boldsymbol{\theta}}}) \mathbf{r}_i(\hat{\hat{\boldsymbol{\theta}}}) \tag{14.30}$$

and $\hat{\hat{\boldsymbol{\theta}}}$ is a preliminary estimator. The resulting GMM estimator is usually called the **nonlinear 3SLS (N3SLS) estimator**. The name is a holdover from the traditional 3SLS estimator in linear systems of equations; there are not really three estimation steps. We should remember that nonlinear 3SLS is generally inefficient when assumption (14.26) fails.

The Wald statistic and the QLR statistic can be computed as in Section 14.1. In addition, a score statistic is sometimes useful. Let $\tilde{\tilde{\boldsymbol{\theta}}}$ be a preliminary inefficient estimator with Q restrictions imposed. The estimator $\tilde{\tilde{\boldsymbol{\theta}}}$ would usually come from problem (14.24) subject to the restrictions $\mathbf{c}(\boldsymbol{\theta}) = \mathbf{0}$. Let $\tilde{\boldsymbol{\Lambda}}$ be the estimated weighting matrix from equation (14.25) or (14.29), based on $\tilde{\tilde{\boldsymbol{\theta}}}$. Let $\tilde{\boldsymbol{\theta}}$ be the minimum chi-square estimator using weighting matrix $\tilde{\boldsymbol{\Lambda}}^{-1}$. Then the score statistic is based on the limiting distribution of the score of the unrestricted objective function evaluated at the restricted estimates, properly standardized:

$$\left[N^{-1}\sum_{i=1}^{N}\mathbf{Z}_i'\nabla_\theta\mathbf{r}_i(\tilde{\boldsymbol{\theta}})\right]'\tilde{\boldsymbol{\Lambda}}^{-1}\left[N^{-1/2}\sum_{i=1}^{N}\mathbf{Z}_i'\mathbf{r}_i(\tilde{\boldsymbol{\theta}})\right]. \tag{14.31}$$

Let $\tilde{\mathbf{s}}_i \equiv \tilde{\mathbf{G}}'\tilde{\boldsymbol{\Lambda}}^{-1}\mathbf{Z}_i'\tilde{\mathbf{r}}_i$, where $\tilde{\mathbf{G}}$ is the first matrix in expression (14.31), and let $\mathbf{s}_i^{\text{o}} \equiv \mathbf{G}_{\text{o}}'\boldsymbol{\Lambda}_{\text{o}}^{-1}\mathbf{Z}_i'\mathbf{r}_i^{\text{o}}$. Then, following the proof in Section 12.6.2, it can be shown that equation (12.67) holds with $\mathbf{A}_{\text{o}} \equiv \mathbf{G}_{\text{o}}'\boldsymbol{\Lambda}_{\text{o}}^{-1}\mathbf{G}_{\text{o}}$. Further, since $\mathbf{B}_{\text{o}} = \mathbf{A}_{\text{o}}$ for the minimum chi-square estimator, we obtain

$$LM = \left(\sum_{i=1}^{N}\tilde{\mathbf{s}}_i\right)'\tilde{\mathbf{A}}^{-1}\left(\sum_{i=1}^{N}\tilde{\mathbf{s}}_i\right)/N, \tag{14.32}$$

where $\tilde{\mathbf{A}} = \tilde{\mathbf{G}}'\tilde{\boldsymbol{\Lambda}}^{-1}\tilde{\mathbf{G}}$. Under H_0 and the usual regularity conditions, LM has a limiting χ_Q^2 distribution.

14.3 Systems of Nonlinear Equations

A leading application of the results in Section 14.2 is to estimation of the parameters in an implicit set of nonlinear equations, such as a nonlinear simultaneous equations model. Partition $\mathbf{w}_i$ as $\mathbf{y}_i \in \mathbb{R}^J$, $\mathbf{x}_i \in \mathbb{R}^K$ and, for $h = 1, \ldots, G$, suppose we have

$$\begin{aligned} q_1(\mathbf{y}_i, \mathbf{x}_i, \boldsymbol{\theta}_{\text{o}1}) &= u_{i1}, \\ &\vdots \\ q_G(\mathbf{y}_i, \mathbf{x}_i, \boldsymbol{\theta}_{\text{o}G}) &= u_{iG} \end{aligned} \tag{14.33}$$

where $\boldsymbol{\theta}_{oh}$ is a $P_h \times 1$ vector of parameters. As an example, write a two-equation SEM in the population as

$$y_1 = \mathbf{x}_1\boldsymbol{\delta}_1 + \gamma_1 y_2^{\gamma_2} + u_1, \tag{14.34}$$

$$y_2 = \mathbf{x}_2\boldsymbol{\delta}_2 + \gamma_3 y_1 + u_2 \tag{14.35}$$

(where we drop "o" to index the parameters). This model, unlike those covered in Section 9.5, is nonlinear in the *parameters* as well as the endogenous variables. Nevertheless, assuming that $\mathrm{E}(u_g \mid \mathbf{x}) = 0$, $g = 1, 2$, the parameters in the system can be estimated by GMM by defining $q_1(\mathbf{y}, \mathbf{x}, \boldsymbol{\theta}_1) = y_1 - \mathbf{x}_1\boldsymbol{\delta}_1 - \gamma_1 y_2^{\gamma_2}$ and $q_2(\mathbf{y}, \mathbf{x}, \boldsymbol{\theta}_2) = y_2 - \mathbf{x}_2\boldsymbol{\delta}_2 - \gamma_3 y_1$.

Generally, the equations (14.33) need not actually determine $\mathbf{y}_i$ given the exogenous variables and disturbances; in fact, nothing requires $J = G$. Sometimes equations (14.33) represent a system of orthogonality conditions of the form $\mathrm{E}[q_g(\mathbf{y}, \mathbf{x}, \boldsymbol{\theta}_{og}) \mid \mathbf{x}] = 0$, $g = 1, \ldots, G$. We will see an example later.

Denote the $P \times 1$ vector of all parameters by $\boldsymbol{\theta}_o$, and the parameter space by $\boldsymbol{\Theta} \subset \mathbb{R}^P$. To identify the parameters, we need the errors u_{ih} to satisfy some orthogonality conditions. A general assumption is, for some subvector $\mathbf{x}_{ih}$ of $\mathbf{x}_i$,

$$\mathrm{E}(u_{ih} \mid \mathbf{x}_{ih}) = \mathbf{0}, \qquad h = 1, 2, \ldots, G. \tag{14.36}$$

This allows elements of $\mathbf{x}_i$ to be correlated with some errors, a situation that sometimes arises in practice (see, for example, Chapter 9 and Wooldridge, 1996). Under assumption (14.36), let $\mathbf{z}_{ih} \equiv \mathbf{f}_h(\mathbf{x}_{ih})$ be a $1 \times L_h$ vector of possibly nonlinear functions of $\mathbf{x}_i$. If there are no restrictions on the $\boldsymbol{\theta}_{oh}$ across equations, we should have $L_h \geq P_h$ so that each $\boldsymbol{\theta}_{oh}$ is identified. By iterated expectations, for all $h = 1, \ldots, G$,

$$\mathrm{E}(\mathbf{z}_{ih}' u_{ih}) = \mathbf{0}, \tag{14.37}$$

provided appropriate moments exist. Therefore, we obtain a set of orthogonality conditions by defining the $G \times L$ matrix $\mathbf{Z}_i$ as the block diagonal matrix with $\mathbf{z}_{ig}$ in the gth block:

$$\mathbf{Z}_i \equiv \begin{bmatrix} \mathbf{z}_{i1} & \mathbf{0} & \mathbf{0} & \cdots & \mathbf{0} \\ \mathbf{0} & \mathbf{z}_{i2} & \mathbf{0} & \cdots & \mathbf{0} \\ \vdots & & & & \vdots \\ \mathbf{0} & \mathbf{0} & \mathbf{0} & \cdots & \mathbf{z}_{iG} \end{bmatrix}, \tag{14.38}$$

where $L \equiv L_1 + L_2 + \cdots + L_G$. Letting $\mathbf{r}(\mathbf{w}_i, \boldsymbol{\theta}) \equiv \mathbf{q}(\mathbf{y}_i, \mathbf{x}_i, \boldsymbol{\theta}) \equiv [q_{i1}(\boldsymbol{\theta}_1), \ldots, q_{iG}(\boldsymbol{\theta}_G)]'$, equation (14.22) holds under assumption (14.36).

When there are no restrictions on the $\boldsymbol{\theta}_g$ across equations and $\mathbf{Z}_i$ is chosen as in matrix (14.38), the system 2SLS estimator reduces to the **nonlinear 2SLS (N2SLS) estimator** (Amemiya, 1974) equation by equation. That is, for each h, the N2SLS estimator solves

$$\min_{\boldsymbol{\theta}_h} \left[\sum_{i=1}^{N} \mathbf{z}_{ih}' q_{ih}(\boldsymbol{\theta}_h)\right]' \left(N^{-1}\sum_{i=1}^{N} \mathbf{z}_{ih}'\mathbf{z}_{ih}\right)^{-1} \left[\sum_{i=1}^{N} \mathbf{z}_{ih}' q_{ih}(\boldsymbol{\theta}_h)\right]. \tag{14.39}$$

Given only the orthogonality conditions (14.37), the N2SLS estimator is the efficient estimator of $\boldsymbol{\theta}_{\text{o}h}$ if

$$\mathrm{E}(u_{ih}^2 \mathbf{z}_{ih}'\mathbf{z}_{ih}) = \sigma_{\text{o}h}^2 \mathrm{E}(\mathbf{z}_{ih}'\mathbf{z}_{ih}), \tag{14.40}$$

where $\sigma_{\text{o}h}^2 \equiv \mathrm{E}(u_{ih}^2)$; sufficient for condition (14.40) is $\mathrm{E}(u_{ih}^2 \mid \mathbf{z}_{ih}) = \sigma_{\text{o}h}^2$. Let $\hat{\hat{\boldsymbol{\theta}}}_h$ denote the N2SLS estimator. Then a consistent estimator of $\sigma_{\text{o}h}^2$ is

$$\hat{\sigma}_h^2 \equiv N^{-1}\sum_{i=1}^{N} \hat{\hat{u}}_{ih}^2, \tag{14.41}$$

where $\hat{\hat{u}}_{ih} \equiv q_h(\mathbf{y}_i, \mathbf{x}_i, \hat{\hat{\boldsymbol{\theta}}}_h)$ are the N2SLS residuals. Under assumptions (14.37) and (14.40), the asymptotic variance of $\hat{\hat{\boldsymbol{\theta}}}_h$ is estimated as

$$\hat{\sigma}_h^2 \left\{ \left[\sum_{i=1}^{N} \mathbf{z}_{ih}' \nabla_{\theta_h} q_{ih}(\hat{\hat{\boldsymbol{\theta}}}_h)\right]' \left(\sum_{i=1}^{N} \mathbf{z}_{ih}'\mathbf{z}_{ih}\right)^{-1} \left[\sum_{i=1}^{N} \mathbf{z}_{ih}' \nabla_{\theta_h} q_{ih}(\hat{\hat{\boldsymbol{\theta}}}_h)\right] \right\}^{-1}, \tag{14.42}$$

where $\nabla_{\theta_h} q_{ih}(\hat{\hat{\boldsymbol{\theta}}}_h)$ is the $1 \times P_h$ gradient.

If assumption (14.37) holds but assumption (14.40) does not, the N2SLS estimator is still $\sqrt{N}$-consistent, but it is not the efficient estimator that uses the orthogonality condition (14.37) whenever $L_h > P_h$ (and expression (14.42) is no longer valid). A more efficient estimator is obtained by solving

$$\min_{\boldsymbol{\theta}_h} \left[\sum_{i=1}^{N} \mathbf{z}_{ih}' q_{ih}(\boldsymbol{\theta}_h)\right]' \left(N^{-1}\sum_{i=1}^{N} \hat{\hat{u}}_{ih}^2 \mathbf{z}_{ih}'\mathbf{z}_{ih}\right)^{-1} \left[\sum_{i=1}^{N} \mathbf{z}_{ih}' q_{ih}(\boldsymbol{\theta}_h)\right]$$

with asymptotic variance estimated as

$$\left\{ \left[\sum_{i=1}^{N} \mathbf{z}_{ih}' \nabla_{\theta_h} q_{ih}(\hat{\hat{\boldsymbol{\theta}}}_h)\right]' \left(\sum_{i=1}^{N} \hat{\hat{u}}_{ih}^2 \mathbf{z}_{ih}'\mathbf{z}_{ih}\right)^{-1} \left[\sum_{i=1}^{N} \mathbf{z}_{ih}' \nabla_{\theta_h} q_{ih}(\hat{\hat{\boldsymbol{\theta}}}_h)\right] \right\}^{-1}.$$

This estimator is asymptotically equivalent to the N2SLS estimator if assumption (14.40) happens to hold.

Rather than focus on one equation at a time, we can increase efficiency if we estimate the equations simultaneously. One reason for doing so is to impose cross equation restrictions on the $\boldsymbol{\theta}_{oh}$. The system 2SLS estimator can be used for these purposes, where $\mathbf{Z}_i$ generally has the form (14.38). But this estimator does not exploit correlation in the errors u_{ig} and u_{ih} in different equations.

The efficient estimator that uses all orthogonality conditions in equation (14.37) is just the GMM estimator with $\hat{\boldsymbol{\Lambda}}$ given by equation (14.25), where $\mathbf{r}_i(\hat{\hat{\boldsymbol{\theta}}})$ is the $G \times 1$ vector of system 2SLS residuals, $\hat{\hat{\mathbf{u}}}_i$. In other words, the efficient GMM estimator solves

$$\min_{\boldsymbol{\theta}\in\boldsymbol{\Theta}} \left[\sum_{i=1}^{N} \mathbf{Z}_i'\mathbf{q}_i(\boldsymbol{\theta})\right]' \left(N^{-1}\sum_{i=1}^{N} \mathbf{Z}_i'\hat{\hat{\mathbf{u}}}_i\hat{\hat{\mathbf{u}}}_i'\mathbf{Z}_i\right)^{-1} \left[\sum_{i=1}^{N} \mathbf{Z}_i'\mathbf{q}_i(\boldsymbol{\theta})\right]. \tag{14.43}$$

The asymptotic variance of $\hat{\boldsymbol{\theta}}$ is estimated as

$$\left\{\left[\sum_{i=1}^{N} \mathbf{Z}_i'\nabla_\theta\mathbf{q}_i(\hat{\boldsymbol{\theta}})\right]' \left(\sum_{i=1}^{N} \mathbf{Z}_i'\hat{\hat{\mathbf{u}}}_i\hat{\hat{\mathbf{u}}}_i'\mathbf{Z}_i\right)^{-1} \left[\sum_{i=1}^{N} \mathbf{Z}_i'\nabla_\theta\mathbf{q}_i(\hat{\boldsymbol{\theta}})\right]\right\}^{-1}.$$

Because this is the efficient GMM estimator, the QLR statistic can be used to test hypotheses about $\boldsymbol{\theta}_o$. The Wald statistic can also be applied.

Under the homoskedasticity assumption (14.26) with $\mathbf{r}_i(\boldsymbol{\theta}_o) = \mathbf{u}_i$, the nonlinear 3SLS estimator, which solves

$$\min_{\boldsymbol{\theta}\in\boldsymbol{\Theta}} \left[\sum_{i=1}^{N} \mathbf{Z}_i'\mathbf{q}_i(\boldsymbol{\theta})\right]' \left(N^{-1}\sum_{i=1}^{N} \mathbf{Z}_i'\hat{\boldsymbol{\Omega}}\mathbf{Z}_i\right)^{-1} \left[\sum_{i=1}^{N} \mathbf{Z}_i'\mathbf{q}_i(\boldsymbol{\theta})\right],$$

is efficient, and its asymptotic variance is estimated as

$$\left\{\left[\sum_{i=1}^{N} \mathbf{Z}_i'\nabla_\theta\mathbf{r}_i(\hat{\boldsymbol{\theta}})\right]' \left(\sum_{i=1}^{N} \mathbf{Z}_i'\hat{\boldsymbol{\Omega}}\mathbf{Z}_i\right)^{-1} \left[\sum_{i=1}^{N} \mathbf{Z}_i'\nabla_\theta\mathbf{r}_i(\hat{\boldsymbol{\theta}})\right]\right\}^{-1}.$$

The N3SLS estimator is used widely for systems of the form (14.33), but, as we discussed in Section 9.6, there are many cases where assumption (14.26) must fail when different instruments are needed for different equations.

As an example, we show how a **hedonic price system** fits into this framework. Consider a linear demand and supply system for G attributes of a good or service (see

Epple, 1987; Kahn and Lang, 1988; and Wooldridge, 1996). The demand and supply system is written as

$$demand_g = \eta_{1g} + \mathbf{w}\boldsymbol{\alpha}_{1g} + \mathbf{x}_1\boldsymbol{\beta}_{1g} + u_{1g}, \qquad g = 1, \ldots, G,$$

$$supply_g = \eta_{2g} + \mathbf{w}\boldsymbol{\alpha}_{2g} + \mathbf{x}_2\boldsymbol{\beta}_{2g} + u_{2g}, \qquad g = 1, \ldots, G,$$

where $\mathbf{w} = (w_1, \ldots, w_G)$ is the $1 \times G$ vector of attribute prices. The demand equations usually represent an individual or household; the supply equations can represent an individual, firm, or employer.

There are several tricky issues in estimating either the demand or supply function for a particular g. First, the attribute prices w_g are not directly observed. What is usually observed are the equilibrium quantities for each attribute and each cross section unit i; call these q_{ig}, $g = 1, \ldots, G$. (In the hedonic systems literature these are often denoted z_{ig}, but we use q_{ig} here because they are endogenous variables, and we have been using $\mathbf{z}_i$ to denote exogenous variables.) For example, the q_{ig} can be features of a house, such as size, number of bathrooms, and so on. Along with these features we observe the equilibrium price of the good, p_i, which we assume follows a quadratic hedonic price function:

$$p_i = \gamma + \mathbf{q}_i\boldsymbol{\psi} + \mathbf{q}_i\boldsymbol{\Pi}\mathbf{q}_i'/2 + \mathbf{x}_{i3}\boldsymbol{\delta} + \mathbf{x}_{i3}\boldsymbol{\Gamma}\mathbf{q}_i' + u_{i3}, \tag{14.44}$$

where $\mathbf{x}_{i3}$ is a vector of variables that affect p_i, $\boldsymbol{\Pi}$ is a $G \times G$ symmetric matrix, and $\boldsymbol{\Gamma}$ is a $G \times G$ matrix.

A key point for identifying the demand and supply functions is that $\mathbf{w}_i = \partial p_i/\partial \mathbf{q}_i$, which, under equation (14.44), becomes $\mathbf{w}_i = \mathbf{q}_i\boldsymbol{\Pi} + \mathbf{x}_{i3}\boldsymbol{\Gamma}$, or $w_{ig} = \mathbf{q}_i\boldsymbol{\pi}_g + \mathbf{x}_{i3}\boldsymbol{\gamma}_g$ for each g. By substitution, the equilibrium estimating equations can be written as equation (14.44) plus

$$q_{ig} = \eta_{1g} + (\mathbf{q}_i\boldsymbol{\Pi} + \mathbf{x}_{i3}\boldsymbol{\Gamma})\boldsymbol{\alpha}_{1g} + \mathbf{x}_{i1}\boldsymbol{\beta}_{1g} + u_{i1g}, \qquad g = 1, \ldots, G, \tag{14.45}$$

$$q_{ig} = \eta_{2g} + (\mathbf{q}_i\boldsymbol{\Pi} + \mathbf{x}_{i3}\boldsymbol{\Gamma})\boldsymbol{\alpha}_{2g} + \mathbf{x}_{i2}\boldsymbol{\beta}_{2g} + u_{i2g}, \qquad g = 1, \ldots, G. \tag{14.46}$$

These two equations are linear in $\mathbf{q}_i, \mathbf{x}_{i1}, \mathbf{x}_{i2}$, and $\mathbf{x}_{i3}$ but nonlinear in the parameters.

Let $\mathbf{u}_{i1}$ be the $G \times 1$ vector of attribute demand disturbances and $\mathbf{u}_{i2}$ the $G \times 1$ vector of attribute supply disturbances. What are reasonable assumptions about $\mathbf{u}_{i1}, \mathbf{u}_{i2}$, and u_{i3}? It is almost always assumed that equation (14.44) represents a conditional expectation with no important unobserved factors; this assumption means $\mathrm{E}(u_{i3} \mid \mathbf{q}_i, \mathbf{x}_i) = 0$, where $\mathbf{x}_i$ contains all elements in $\mathbf{x}_{i1}, \mathbf{x}_{i2}$, and $\mathbf{x}_{i3}$. The properties of $\mathbf{u}_{i1}$ and $\mathbf{u}_{i2}$ are more subtle. It is clear that these cannot be uncorrelated with $\mathbf{q}_i$, and so equations (14.45) and (14.46) contain endogenous explanatory variables if $\boldsymbol{\Pi} \neq \mathbf{0}$.

But there is another problem, pointed out by Bartik (1987), Epple (1987), and Kahn and Lang (1988): because of matching that happens between individual buyers and sellers, $\mathbf{x}_{i2}$ is correlated with u_{i1}, and $\mathbf{x}_{i1}$ is correlated with u_{i2}. Consequently, what would seem to be the obvious IVs for the demand equations (14.45)—the factors shifting the supply curve—are endogenous to equation (14.45). Fortunately, all is not lost: if $\mathbf{x}_{i3}$ contains exogenous factors that affect p_i but do not appear in the structural demand and supply functions, we can use these as instruments in both the demand and supply equations. Specifically, we assume

$$\mathrm{E}(\mathbf{u}_{i1} \mid \mathbf{x}_{i1}, \mathbf{x}_{i3}) = \mathbf{0}, \qquad \mathrm{E}(\mathbf{u}_{i2} \mid \mathbf{x}_{i2}, \mathbf{x}_{i3}) = \mathbf{0}, \qquad \mathrm{E}(u_{i3} \mid \mathbf{q}_i, \mathbf{x}_i) = 0. \tag{14.47}$$

Common choices for $\mathbf{x}_{i3}$ are geographical or industry dummy indicators (for example, Montgomery, Shaw, and Benedict, 1992; Hagy, 1998), where the assumption is that the demand and supply functions do not change across region or industry but the type of matching does, and therefore p_i can differ systematically across region or industry. Bartik (1987) discusses how a randomized experiment can be used to create the elements of $\mathbf{x}_{i3}$.

For concreteness, let us focus on estimating the set of demand functions. If $\mathbf{\Pi} = \mathbf{0}$, so that the quadratic in $\mathbf{q}_i$ does not appear in equation (14.44), a simple two-step procedure is available: (1) estimate equation (14.44) by OLS, and obtain $\hat{w}_{ig} = \hat{\psi}_g + \mathbf{x}_{i3}\hat{\gamma}_g$ for each i and g; (2) run the regression q_{ig} on $1, \hat{\mathbf{w}}_i, \mathbf{x}_{i1}, i = 1, \ldots, N$. Under assumptions (14.47) and identification assumptions, this method produces $\sqrt{N}$-consistent, asymptotically normal estimators of the parameters in demand equation g. Because the second regression involves generated regressors, the standard errors and test statistics should be adjusted.

It is clear that, without restrictions on $\boldsymbol{\alpha}_{1g}$, the order condition necessary for identifying the demand parameters is that the dimension of $\mathbf{x}_{i3}$, say K_3, must exceed G. If $K_3 < G$, then $\mathrm{E}[(\mathbf{w}_i, \mathbf{x}_{i1})'(\mathbf{w}_i, \mathbf{x}_{i1})]$ has less than full rank, and the OLS rank condition fails. If we make exclusion restrictions on $\boldsymbol{\alpha}_{1g}$, fewer elements are needed in $\mathbf{x}_{i3}$. In the case that only w_{ig} appears in the demand equation for attribute g, $\mathbf{x}_{i3}$ can be a scalar, provided its interaction with q_{ig} in the hedonic price system is significant ($\gamma_{gg} \neq 0$). Checking the analogue of the rank condition in general is somewhat complicated; see Epple (1987) for discussion.

When $\mathbf{w}_i = \mathbf{q}_i\mathbf{\Pi} + \mathbf{x}_{i3}\mathbf{\Gamma}$, $\mathbf{w}_i$ is correlated with u_{i1g}, so we must modify the two-step procedure. In the second step, we can use instruments for $\hat{\mathbf{w}}_i$ and perform 2SLS rather than OLS. Assuming that $\mathbf{x}_{i3}$ has enough elements, the demand equations are still identified. If only w_{ig} appears in $demand_{ig}$, sufficient for identification is that an element of $\mathbf{x}_{i3}$ appears in the linear projection of w_{ig} on $\mathbf{x}_{i1}$, $\mathbf{x}_{i3}$. This assumption can hold even if $\mathbf{x}_{i3}$ has only a single element. For the matching reasons we discussed previously, $\mathbf{x}_{i2}$ cannot be used as instruments for $\hat{\mathbf{w}}_i$ in the demand equation.

Whether $\mathbf{\Pi} = \mathbf{0}$ or not, more efficient estimators are obtained from the full demand system and the hedonic price function. Write

$$\mathbf{q}_i' = \boldsymbol{\eta}_1 + (\mathbf{q}_i\mathbf{\Pi} + \mathbf{x}_{i3}\mathbf{\Gamma})\mathbf{A}_1 + \mathbf{x}_{i1}\mathbf{B}_1 + \mathbf{u}_{i1}$$

along with equation (14.44). Then $(\mathbf{x}_{i1}, \mathbf{x}_{i3})$ (and functions of these) can be used as instruments in any of the G demand equations, and $(\mathbf{q}_i, \mathbf{x}_i)$ act as IVs in equation (14.44). (It may be that the supply function is not even specified, in which case $\mathbf{x}_i$ contains only $\mathbf{x}_{i1}$ and $\mathbf{x}_{i3}$.) A first-stage estimator is the nonlinear system 2SLS estimator. Then the system can be estimated by the minimum chi-square estimator that solves problem (14.43). When restricting attention to demand equations plus the hedonic price equation, or supply equations plus the hedonic price equation, nonlinear 3SLS is efficient under certain assumptions. If the demand and supply equations are estimated together, the key assumption (14.26) that makes nonlinear 3SLS asymptotically efficient cannot be expected to hold; see Wooldridge (1996) for discussion.

If one of the demand functions is of primary interest, it may make sense to estimate it along with equation (14.44), by GMM or nonlinear 3SLS. If the demand functions are written in inverse form, the resulting system is linear in the parameters, as shown in Wooldridge (1996).

14.4 Efficient Estimation

In Chapter 8 we obtained the efficient weighting matrix for GMM estimation of linear models, and we extended that to nonlinear models in Section 14.1. In Chapter 13 we asserted that maximum likelihood estimation has some important efficiency properties. We are now in a position to study a framework that allows us to show the efficiency of an estimator within a particular class of estimators, and also to find efficient estimators within a stated class. Our approach is essentially that in Newey and McFadden (1994, Sect. 5.3), although we will not use the weakest possible assumptions. Bates and White (1993) proposed a very similar framework and also considered time series problems.

14.4.1 General Efficiency Framework

Most estimators in econometrics—and all of the ones we have studied—are $\sqrt{N}$-asymptotically normal, with variance matrices of the form

$$\mathbf{V} = \mathbf{A}^{-1}\mathrm{E}[\mathbf{s}(\mathbf{w})\mathbf{s}(\mathbf{w})'](\mathbf{A}')^{-1}, \tag{14.48}$$

where, in most cases, $\mathbf{s}(\mathbf{w})$ is the score of an objective function (evaluated at $\boldsymbol{\theta}_{\text{o}}$) and $\mathbf{A}$ is the expected value of the Jacobian of the score, again evaluated at $\boldsymbol{\theta}_{\text{o}}$. (We suppress an "o" subscript here, as the value of the true parameter is irrelevant.) All M-estimators with twice continuously differentiable objective functions (and even some without) have variance matrices of this form, as do GMM estimators. The following lemma is a useful sufficient condition for showing that one estimator is more efficient than another.

LEMMA 14.1 (Relative Efficiency): Let $\hat{\boldsymbol{\theta}}_1$ and $\hat{\boldsymbol{\theta}}_2$ be two $\sqrt{N}$-asymptotically normal estimators of the $P \times 1$ parameter vector $\boldsymbol{\theta}_{\text{o}}$, with asymptotic variances of the form (14.48) (with appropriate subscripts on $\mathbf{A}$, $\mathbf{s}$, and $\mathbf{V}$). If for some $\rho > 0$,

$$\text{E}[\mathbf{s}_1(\mathbf{w})\mathbf{s}_1(\mathbf{w})'] = \rho\mathbf{A}_1, \tag{14.49}$$

$$\text{E}[\mathbf{s}_2(\mathbf{w})\mathbf{s}_1(\mathbf{w})'] = \rho\mathbf{A}_2, \tag{14.50}$$

then $\mathbf{V}_2 - \mathbf{V}_1$ is p.s.d.

The proof of Lemma 14.1 is given in the chapter appendix.

Condition (14.49) is essentially the generalized information matrix equality (GIME) we introduced in Section 12.5.1 for the estimator $\hat{\boldsymbol{\theta}}_1$. Notice that $\mathbf{A}_1$ is necessarily symmetric and positive definite under condition (14.49). Condition (14.50) is new. In most cases, it says that the expected outer product of the scores $\mathbf{s}_2$ and $\mathbf{s}_1$ equals the expected Jacobian of $\mathbf{s}_2$ (evaluated at $\boldsymbol{\theta}_{\text{o}}$). In Section 12.5.1 we claimed that the GIME plays a role in efficiency, and Lemma 14.1 shows that it does so.

Verifying the conditions of Lemma 14.1 is also very convenient for constructing simple forms of the Hausman (1978) statistic in a variety of contexts. Provided that the two estimators are jointly asymptotically normally distributed—something that is almost always true when each is $\sqrt{N}$-asymptotically normal, and that can be verified by stacking the first-order representations of the estimators—assumptions (14.49) and (14.50) imply that the asymptotic covariance between $\sqrt{N}(\hat{\boldsymbol{\theta}}_2 - \boldsymbol{\theta}_{\text{o}})$ and $\sqrt{N}(\hat{\boldsymbol{\theta}}_1 - \boldsymbol{\theta}_{\text{o}})$ is $\mathbf{A}_2^{-1}\text{E}(\mathbf{s}_2\mathbf{s}_1')\mathbf{A}_1^{-1} = \mathbf{A}_2^{-1}(\rho\mathbf{A}_2)\mathbf{A}_1^{-1} = \rho\mathbf{A}_1^{-1} = \text{Avar}[\sqrt{N}(\hat{\boldsymbol{\theta}}_1 - \boldsymbol{\theta}_{\text{o}})]$. In other words, the asymptotic covariance between the ($\sqrt{N}$-scaled) estimators is equal to the asymptotic variance of the efficient estimator. This equality implies that $\text{Avar}[\sqrt{N}(\hat{\boldsymbol{\theta}}_2 - \hat{\boldsymbol{\theta}}_1)] = \mathbf{V}_2 + \mathbf{V}_1 - \mathbf{C} - \mathbf{C}' = \mathbf{V}_2 + \mathbf{V}_1 - 2\mathbf{V}_1 = \mathbf{V}_2 - \mathbf{V}_1$, where $\mathbf{C}$ is the asymptotic covariance. If $\mathbf{V}_2 - \mathbf{V}_1$ is actually positive definite (rather than just p.s.d.), then $[\sqrt{N}(\hat{\boldsymbol{\theta}}_2 - \hat{\boldsymbol{\theta}}_1)]'(\hat{\mathbf{V}}_2 - \hat{\mathbf{V}}_1)^{-1}[\sqrt{N}(\hat{\boldsymbol{\theta}}_2 - \hat{\boldsymbol{\theta}}_1)] \overset{a}{\sim} \chi^2_P$ under the assumptions of Lemma 14.1, where $\hat{\mathbf{V}}_g$ is a consistent estimator of $\mathbf{V}_g$, $g = 1, 2$. Statistically significant differences between $\hat{\boldsymbol{\theta}}_2$ and $\hat{\boldsymbol{\theta}}_1$ signal some sort of model misspecification. (See Section 6.2.1, where we discussed this form of the Hausman test for comparing

2SLS and OLS to test whether the explanatory variables are exogenous.) If assumptions (14.49) and (14.50) do not hold, this standard form of the Hausman statistic is invalid.

Given Lemma 14.1, we can state a condition that implies efficiency of an estimator in an entire *class* of estimators. It is useful to be somewhat formal in defining the relevant class of estimators. We do so by introducing an index, τ. For each τ in an index set, say, $\mathscr{T}$, the estimator $\hat{\boldsymbol{\theta}}_\tau$ has an associated $\mathbf{s}_\tau$ and $\mathbf{A}_\tau$ such that the asymptotic variance of $\sqrt{N}(\hat{\boldsymbol{\theta}}_\tau - \boldsymbol{\theta}_o)$ has the form (14.48). The index can be very abstract; it simply serves to distinguish different $\sqrt{N}$-asymptotically normal estimators of $\boldsymbol{\theta}_o$. For example, in the class of M-estimators, the set $\mathscr{T}$ consists of objective functions $q(\cdot,\cdot)$ such that $\boldsymbol{\theta}_o$ uniquely minimizes $\mathrm{E}[q(\mathbf{w},\boldsymbol{\theta})]$ over $\boldsymbol{\Theta}$, and q satisfies the twice continuously differentiable and bounded moment assumptions imposed for asymptotic normality. For GMM with *given* moment conditions, $\mathscr{T}$ is the set of all $L \times L$ positive definite matrices. We will see another example in Section 14.4.3. Lemma 14.1 immediately implies the following theorem.

THEOREM 14.3 (Efficiency in a Class of Estimators): Let $\{\hat{\boldsymbol{\theta}}_\tau : \tau \in \mathscr{T}\}$ be a class of $\sqrt{N}$-asymptotically normal estimators with variance matrices of the form (14.48). If for some $\tau^* \in \mathscr{T}$ and $\rho > 0$

$$\mathrm{E}[\mathbf{s}_\tau(\mathbf{w})\mathbf{s}_{\tau^*}(\mathbf{w})'] = \rho\mathbf{A}_\tau, \qquad \text{all } \tau \in \mathscr{T}, \tag{14.51}$$

then $\hat{\boldsymbol{\theta}}_{\tau^*}$ is asymptotically relatively efficient in the class $\{\hat{\boldsymbol{\theta}}_\tau : \tau \in \mathscr{T}\}$.

This theorem has many applications. If we specify a class of estimators by defining the index set $\mathscr{T}$, then the estimator $\hat{\boldsymbol{\theta}}_{\tau^*}$ is more efficient than all other estimators in the class if we can show condition (14.51). (A partial converse to Theorem 14.3 also holds; see Newey and McFadden (1994, Section 5.3).) This is not to say that $\hat{\boldsymbol{\theta}}_{\tau^*}$ is necessarily more efficient than *all* possible $\sqrt{N}$-asymptotically normal estimators. If there is an estimator that falls outside the specified class, then Theorem 14.3 does not help us to compare it with $\hat{\boldsymbol{\theta}}_{\tau^*}$. In this sense, Theorem 14.3 is a more general (and asymptotic) version of the Gauss-Markov theorem from linear regression analysis: while the Gauss-Markov theorem states that OLS has the smallest variance in the class of linear, unbiased estimators, it does not allow us to compare OLS to unbiased estimators that are not linear in the vector of observations on the dependent variable.

14.4.2 Efficiency of Maximum Likelihood Estimator

Students of econometrics are often told that the maximum likelihood estimator is "efficient." Unfortunately, in the context of conditional MLE (CMLE) from Chapter 13, the statement of efficiency is usually ambiguous; Manski (1988, Chap. 8) is a notable exception. Theorem 14.3 allows us to state precisely the class of estimators in which the CMLE is relatively efficient. As in Chapter 13, we let $\mathrm{E}_\theta(\cdot \mid \mathbf{x})$ denote the expectation with respect to the conditional density $f(\mathbf{y} \mid \mathbf{x}; \boldsymbol{\theta})$.

Consider the class of estimators solving the first-order condition

$$N^{-1} \sum_{i=1}^{N} \mathbf{g}(\mathbf{w}_i, \hat{\boldsymbol{\theta}}) \equiv \mathbf{0}, \tag{14.52}$$

where the $P \times 1$ function $\mathbf{g}(\mathbf{w}, \boldsymbol{\theta})$ such that

$$\mathrm{E}_\theta[\mathbf{g}(\mathbf{w}, \boldsymbol{\theta}) \mid \mathbf{x}] = \mathbf{0}, \qquad \text{all } \mathbf{x} \in \mathcal{X}, \quad \text{all } \boldsymbol{\theta} \in \boldsymbol{\Theta}. \tag{14.53}$$

In other words, the class of estimators is indexed by functions $\mathbf{g}$ satisfying a zero conditional moment restriction. We assume the standard regularity conditions from Chapter 12; in particular, $\mathbf{g}(\mathbf{w}, \cdot)$ is continuously differentiable on the interior of $\boldsymbol{\Theta}$.

As we showed in Section 13.7, functions $\mathbf{g}$ satisfying condition (14.53) generally have the property

$$-\mathrm{E}[\nabla_\theta \mathbf{g}(\mathbf{w}, \boldsymbol{\theta}_o) \mid \mathbf{x}] = \mathrm{E}[\mathbf{g}(\mathbf{w}, \boldsymbol{\theta}_o)\mathbf{s}(\mathbf{w}, \boldsymbol{\theta}_o)' \mid \mathbf{x}],$$

where $\mathbf{s}(\mathbf{w}, \boldsymbol{\theta})$ is the score of $\log f(\mathbf{y} \mid \mathbf{x}; \boldsymbol{\theta})$ (as always, we must impose certain regularity conditions on $\mathbf{g}$ and $\log f$). If we take the expectation of both sides with respect to $\mathbf{x}$, we obtain condition (14.51) with $\rho = 1$, $\mathbf{A}_\tau = \mathrm{E}[\nabla_\theta \mathbf{g}(\mathbf{w}, \boldsymbol{\theta}_o)]$, and $\mathbf{s}_{\tau^*}(\mathbf{w}) = -\mathbf{s}(\mathbf{w}, \boldsymbol{\theta}_o)$. It follows from Theorem 14.3 that the conditional MLE is efficient in the class of estimators solving equation (14.52), where $\mathbf{g}(\cdot)$ satisfies condition (14.59) and appropriate regularity conditions. Recall from Section 13.5.1 that the asymptotic variance of the (centered and standardized) CMLE is $\{\mathrm{E}[\mathbf{s}(\mathbf{w}, \boldsymbol{\theta}_o)\mathbf{s}(\mathbf{w}, \boldsymbol{\theta}_o)']\}^{-1}$. This is an example of an **efficiency bound** because no estimator of the form (14.52) under condition (14.53) can have an asymptotic variance smaller than $\{\mathrm{E}[\mathbf{s}(\mathbf{w}, \boldsymbol{\theta}_o)\mathbf{s}(\mathbf{w}, \boldsymbol{\theta}_o)']\}^{-1}$ (in the matrix sense). When an estimator from this class has the same asymptotic variance as the CMLE, we say it *achieves the efficiency bound.*

It is important to see that the efficiency of the CMLE in the class of estimators solving equation (14.52) under condition (14.53) does *not* require $\mathbf{x}$ to be ancillary for $\boldsymbol{\theta}_o$: except for regularity conditions, the distribution of $\mathbf{x}$ is essentially unrestricted, and could depend on $\boldsymbol{\theta}_o$. CMLE simply ignores information on $\boldsymbol{\theta}_o$ that might be contained in the distribution of $\mathbf{x}$, but so do all other estimators that are based on condition (14.53).

By choosing $\mathbf{x}$ to be empty, we conclude that the unconditional MLE is efficient in the class of estimators based on equation (14.52) with $\mathrm{E}_\theta[\mathbf{g}(\mathbf{w}, \boldsymbol{\theta})] = \mathbf{0}$, all $\boldsymbol{\theta} \in \boldsymbol{\Theta}$. This is a very broad class of estimators, including all of the estimators requiring condition

(14.53): if a function $\mathbf{g}$ satisfies condition (14.53), it has zero unconditional mean, too. Consequently, the unconditional MLE is generally more efficient than the conditional MLE. This efficiency comes at the price of having to model the joint density of $(\mathbf{y}, \mathbf{x})$, rather than just the conditional density of $\mathbf{y}$ given $\mathbf{x}$. And, if our model for the density of $\mathbf{x}$ is incorrect, the unconditional MLE generally would be inconsistent.

When is CMLE as efficient as unconditional MLE for estimating $\boldsymbol{\theta}_o$? Assume that the model for the joint density of $(\mathbf{x}, \mathbf{y})$ can be expressed as $f(\mathbf{y} \mid \mathbf{x}; \boldsymbol{\theta})h(\mathbf{x}; \boldsymbol{\delta})$, where $\boldsymbol{\theta}$ is the parameter vector of interest, and $h(\mathbf{x}, \boldsymbol{\delta}_o)$ is the marginal density of $\mathbf{x}$ for some vector $\boldsymbol{\delta}_o$. Then, if $\boldsymbol{\delta}$ does not depend on $\boldsymbol{\theta}$ in the sense that $\nabla_\theta h(\mathbf{x}; \boldsymbol{\delta}) = \mathbf{0}$ for all $\mathbf{x}$ and $\boldsymbol{\delta}$, $\mathbf{x}$ is ancillary for $\boldsymbol{\theta}_o$. In fact, the CMLE is identical to the unconditional MLE. If $\boldsymbol{\delta}$ depends on $\boldsymbol{\theta}$, the term $\nabla_\theta \log[h(\mathbf{x}; \boldsymbol{\delta})]$ generally contains information for estimating $\boldsymbol{\theta}_o$, and unconditional MLE will be more efficient than CMLE.

14.4.3 Efficient Choice of Instruments under Conditional Moment Restrictions

We can also apply Theorem 14.3 to find the optimal set of instrumental variables under general **conditional moment restrictions**. For a $G \times 1$ vector $\mathbf{r}(\mathbf{w}_i, \boldsymbol{\theta})$, where $\mathbf{w}_i \in \mathbb{R}^M$, $\boldsymbol{\theta}_o$ is said to satisfy conditional moment restrictions if

$$\mathrm{E}[\mathbf{r}(\mathbf{w}_i, \boldsymbol{\theta}_o) \mid \mathbf{x}_i] = \mathbf{0}, \tag{14.54}$$

where $\mathbf{x}_i \in \mathbb{R}^K$ is a subvector of $\mathbf{w}_i$. Under assumption (14.54), the matrix $\mathbf{Z}_i$ appearing in equation (14.22) can be any function of $\mathbf{x}_i$. For a *given* matrix $\mathbf{Z}_i$, we obtain the efficient GMM estimator by using the efficient weighting matrix. However, unless $\mathbf{Z}_i$ is the optimal set of instruments, we can generally obtain a more efficient estimator by adding any nonlinear function of $\mathbf{x}_i$ to $\mathbf{Z}_i$. Because the list of potential IVs is endless, it is useful to characterize the optimal choice of $\mathbf{Z}_i$.

The solution to this problem is now pretty well known, and it can be obtained by applying Theorem 14.3. Let

$$\boldsymbol{\Omega}_o(\mathbf{x}_i) \equiv \mathrm{Var}[\mathbf{r}(\mathbf{w}_i, \boldsymbol{\theta}_o) \mid \mathbf{x}_i] \tag{14.55}$$

be the $G \times G$ conditional variance of $\mathbf{r}_i(\boldsymbol{\theta}_o)$ given $\mathbf{x}_i$, and define

$$\mathbf{R}_o(\mathbf{x}_i) \equiv \mathrm{E}[\nabla_\theta \mathbf{r}(\mathbf{w}_i, \boldsymbol{\theta}_o) \mid \mathbf{x}_i]. \tag{14.56}$$

Problem 14.3 asks you to verify that the optimal choice of instruments is

$$\mathbf{Z}^*(\mathbf{x}_i) \equiv \boldsymbol{\Omega}_o(\mathbf{x}_i)^{-1}\mathbf{R}_o(\mathbf{x}_i). \tag{14.57}$$

The optimal instrument matrix is always $G \times P$, and so the efficient method of moments estimator solves

$$\sum_{i=1}^{N} \mathbf{Z}^*(\mathbf{x}_i)'\mathbf{r}_i(\hat{\boldsymbol{\theta}}) = \mathbf{0}.$$

There is no need to use a weighting matrix. Incidentally, by taking $\mathbf{g}(\mathbf{w}, \boldsymbol{\theta}) \equiv \mathbf{Z}^*(\mathbf{x})'\mathbf{r}(\mathbf{w}, \boldsymbol{\theta})$, we obtain a function $\mathbf{g}$ satisfying condition (14.53). From our discussion in Section 14.4.2, it follows immediately that the CMLE is no less efficient than the optimal IV estimator.

In practice, $\mathbf{Z}^*(\mathbf{x}_i)$ is never a known function of $\mathbf{x}_i$. In some cases the function $\mathbf{R}_{\mathrm{o}}(\mathbf{x}_i)$ is a known function of $\mathbf{x}_i$ and $\boldsymbol{\theta}_{\mathrm{o}}$ and can be easily estimated; this statement is true of linear SEMs under conditional mean assumptions (see Chapters 8 and 9) and of multivariate nonlinear regression, which we cover later in this subsection. Rarely do moment conditions imply a parametric form for $\boldsymbol{\Omega}_{\mathrm{o}}(\mathbf{x}_i)$, but sometimes homoskedasticity is assumed:

$$\mathrm{E}[\mathbf{r}_i(\boldsymbol{\theta}_{\mathrm{o}})\mathbf{r}_i(\boldsymbol{\theta}_{\mathrm{o}}) \mid \mathbf{x}_i] = \boldsymbol{\Omega}_{\mathrm{o}} \tag{14.58}$$

and $\boldsymbol{\Omega}_{\mathrm{o}}$ is easily estimated as in equation (14.30), given a preliminary estimate of $\boldsymbol{\theta}_{\mathrm{o}}$.

Since both $\boldsymbol{\Omega}_{\mathrm{o}}(\mathbf{x}_i)$ and $\mathbf{R}_{\mathrm{o}}(\mathbf{x}_i)$ must be estimated, we must know the asymptotic properties of **GMM with generated instruments**. Under conditional moment restrictions, generated instruments have *no* effect on the asymptotic variance of the GMM estimator. Thus, if the matrix of instruments is $\mathbf{Z}(\mathbf{x}_i, \boldsymbol{\gamma}_{\mathrm{o}})$ for some unknown parameter vector $\boldsymbol{\gamma}_{\mathrm{o}}$, and $\hat{\boldsymbol{\gamma}}$ is an estimator such that $\sqrt{N}(\hat{\boldsymbol{\gamma}} - \boldsymbol{\gamma}_{\mathrm{o}}) = \mathrm{O}_p(1)$, then the GMM estimator using the generated instruments $\hat{\mathbf{Z}}_i \equiv \mathbf{Z}(\mathbf{x}_i, \hat{\boldsymbol{\gamma}})$ has the same limiting distribution as the GMM estimator using instruments $\mathbf{Z}(\mathbf{x}_i, \boldsymbol{\gamma}_{\mathrm{o}})$ (using any weighting matrix). This result follows from a mean value expansion, using the fact that the derivative of each element of $\mathbf{Z}(\mathbf{x}_i, \boldsymbol{\gamma})$ with respect to $\boldsymbol{\gamma}$ is orthogonal to $\mathbf{r}_i(\boldsymbol{\theta}_{\mathrm{o}})$ under condition (14.54):

$$N^{-1/2} \sum_{i=1}^{N} \hat{\mathbf{Z}}_i'\mathbf{r}_i(\hat{\boldsymbol{\theta}}) = N^{-1/2} \sum_{i=1}^{N} \mathbf{Z}_i(\boldsymbol{\gamma}_{\mathrm{o}})'\mathbf{r}_i(\boldsymbol{\theta}_{\mathrm{o}}) + \mathrm{E}[\mathbf{Z}_i(\boldsymbol{\gamma}_{\mathrm{o}})'\mathbf{R}_{\mathrm{o}}(\mathbf{x}_i)]\sqrt{N}(\hat{\boldsymbol{\theta}} - \boldsymbol{\theta}_{\mathrm{o}}) + \mathrm{o}_p(1). \tag{14.59}$$

The right-hand side of equation (14.59) is identical to the expansion with $\hat{\mathbf{Z}}_i$ replaced with $\mathbf{Z}_i(\boldsymbol{\gamma}_{\mathrm{o}})$.

Assuming now that $\mathbf{Z}_i(\boldsymbol{\gamma}_{\mathrm{o}})$ is the matrix of efficient instruments, the asymptotic variance of the efficient estimator is

$$\mathrm{Avar}\ \sqrt{N}(\hat{\boldsymbol{\theta}} - \boldsymbol{\theta}_{\mathrm{o}}) = \{\mathrm{E}[\mathbf{R}_{\mathrm{o}}(\mathbf{x}_i)'\boldsymbol{\Omega}_{\mathrm{o}}(\mathbf{x}_i)^{-1}\mathbf{R}_{\mathrm{o}}(\mathbf{x}_i)]\}^{-1}, \tag{14.60}$$

as can be seen from Section 14.1 by noting that $\mathbf{G}_o = \mathrm{E}[\mathbf{R}_o(\mathbf{x}_i)'\boldsymbol{\Omega}_o(\mathbf{x}_i)^{-1}\mathbf{R}_o(\mathbf{x}_i)]$ and $\boldsymbol{\Lambda}_o = \mathbf{G}_o^{-1}$ when the instruments are given by equation (14.57).

Equation (14.60) is another example of an efficiency bound, this time under the conditional moment restrictions (14.48). What we have shown is that any GMM estimator has variance matrix that differs from equation (14.60) by a p.s.d. matrix. Chamberlain (1987) has shown more: *any* estimator that uses only condition (14.54) and satisfies regularity conditions has variance matrix no smaller than equation (14.60).

Estimation of $\mathbf{R}_o(\mathbf{x}_i)$ generally requires nonparametric methods. Newey (1990) describes one approach. Essentially, regress the elements of $\nabla_\theta \mathbf{r}_i(\hat{\hat{\boldsymbol{\theta}}})$ on polynomial functions of $\mathbf{x}_i$ (or other functions with good approximating properties), where $\hat{\hat{\boldsymbol{\theta}}}$ is an initial estimate of $\boldsymbol{\theta}_o$. The fitted values from these regressions can be used as the elements of $\hat{\mathbf{R}}_i$. Other nonparametric approaches are available. See Newey (1990, 1993) for details. Unfortunately, we need a fairly large sample size in order to apply such methods effectively.

As an example of finding the optimal instruments, consider the problem of estimating a conditional mean for a vector $\mathbf{y}_i$:

$$\mathrm{E}(\mathbf{y}_i \mid \mathbf{x}_i) = \mathbf{m}(\mathbf{x}_i, \boldsymbol{\theta}_o). \tag{14.61}$$

Then the residual function is $\mathbf{r}(\mathbf{w}_i, \boldsymbol{\theta}) \equiv \mathbf{y}_i - \mathbf{m}(\mathbf{x}_i, \boldsymbol{\theta})$ and $\boldsymbol{\Omega}_o(\mathbf{x}_i) = \mathrm{Var}(\mathbf{y}_i \mid \mathbf{x}_i)$; therefore, the optimal instruments are $\mathbf{Z}_o(\mathbf{x}_i) \equiv \boldsymbol{\Omega}_o(\mathbf{x}_i)^{-1}\nabla_\theta \mathbf{m}(\mathbf{x}_i, \boldsymbol{\theta}_o)$. This is an important example where $\mathbf{R}_o(\mathbf{x}_i) = -\nabla_\theta \mathbf{m}(\mathbf{x}_i, \boldsymbol{\theta}_o)$ is a known function of $\mathbf{x}_i$ and $\boldsymbol{\theta}_o$. If the homoskedasticity assumption

$$\mathrm{Var}(\mathbf{y}_i \mid \mathbf{x}_i) = \boldsymbol{\Omega}_o \tag{14.62}$$

holds, then the efficient estimator is easy to obtain. First, let $\hat{\hat{\boldsymbol{\theta}}}$ be the multivariate nonlinear least squares (MNLS) estimator, which solves $\min_{\boldsymbol{\theta} \in \Theta} \sum_{i=1}^N [\mathbf{y}_i - \mathbf{m}(\mathbf{x}_i, \boldsymbol{\theta})]' \cdot [\mathbf{y}_i - \mathbf{m}(\mathbf{x}_i, \boldsymbol{\theta})]$. As discussed in Section 12.9, the MNLS estimator is generally consistent and $\sqrt{N}$-asymptotic normal. Define the residuals $\hat{\hat{\mathbf{u}}}_i \equiv \mathbf{y}_i - \mathbf{m}(\mathbf{x}_i, \hat{\hat{\boldsymbol{\theta}}})$, and define a consistent estimator of $\boldsymbol{\Omega}_o$ by $\hat{\boldsymbol{\Omega}} = N^{-1}\sum_{i=1}^N \hat{\hat{\mathbf{u}}}_i \hat{\hat{\mathbf{u}}}_i'$. An efficient estimator, $\hat{\boldsymbol{\theta}}$, solves

$$\sum_{i=1}^N \nabla_\theta \mathbf{m}(\mathbf{x}_i, \hat{\hat{\boldsymbol{\theta}}})'\hat{\boldsymbol{\Omega}}^{-1}[\mathbf{y}_i - \mathbf{m}(\mathbf{x}_i, \hat{\boldsymbol{\theta}})] = \mathbf{0}$$

and the asymptotic variance of $\sqrt{N}(\hat{\boldsymbol{\theta}} - \boldsymbol{\theta}_o)$ is $\{\mathrm{E}[\nabla_\theta \mathbf{m}_i(\boldsymbol{\theta}_o)'\boldsymbol{\Omega}_o^{-1}\nabla_\theta \mathbf{m}_i(\boldsymbol{\theta}_o)]\}^{-1}$. An asymptotically equivalent estimator is the nonlinear SUR estimator described in Section 12.9. In either case, the estimator of $\mathrm{Avar}(\hat{\boldsymbol{\theta}})$ under assumption (14.62) is

$$\widehat{\text{Avar}}(\hat{\boldsymbol{\theta}}) = \left[\sum_{i=1}^{N} \nabla_{\theta}\mathbf{m}_i(\hat{\boldsymbol{\theta}})'\hat{\boldsymbol{\Omega}}^{-1}\nabla_{\theta}\mathbf{m}_i(\hat{\boldsymbol{\theta}})\right]^{-1}.$$

Because the nonlinear SUR estimator is a two-step M-estimator and $\mathbf{B}_o = \mathbf{A}_o$ (in the notation of Chapter 12), the simplest forms of test statistics are valid. If assumption (14.62) fails, the nonlinear SUR estimator is consistent, but robust inference should be used because $\mathbf{A}_o \neq \mathbf{B}_o$. And, the estimator is no longer efficient.

14.5 Classical Minimum Distance Estimation

A method that has features in common with GMM and often is a convenient substitute, is **classical minimum distance (CMD) estimation**.

Suppose that the $P \times 1$ parameter vector of interest, $\boldsymbol{\theta}_o$, which often consists of parameters from a structural model, is known to be related to an $S \times 1$ vector of reduced-form parameters, $\boldsymbol{\pi}_o$, where $S > P$. In particular, $\boldsymbol{\pi}_o = \mathbf{h}(\boldsymbol{\theta}_o)$ for a known, continuously differentiable function $\mathbf{h}: \mathbb{R}^P \to \mathbb{R}^S$, so that $\mathbf{h}$ maps the structural parameters into the reduced-form parameters.

CMD estimation of $\boldsymbol{\theta}_o$ entails first estimating $\boldsymbol{\pi}_o$ by $\hat{\boldsymbol{\pi}}$, and then choosing an estimator $\hat{\boldsymbol{\theta}}$ of $\boldsymbol{\theta}_o$ by making the distance between $\hat{\boldsymbol{\pi}}$ and $\mathbf{h}(\hat{\boldsymbol{\theta}})$ as small as possible. As with GMM estimation, we use a weighted Euclidean measure of distance. While a CMD estimator can be defined for any p.s.d. weighting matrix, we consider only the efficient CMD estimator given our choice of $\hat{\boldsymbol{\pi}}$. As with efficient GMM, the CMD estimator that uses the efficient weighting matrix is also called the **minimum chi-square estimator**.

Assuming that for an $S \times S$ p.s.d. matrix $\boldsymbol{\Xi}_o$

$$\sqrt{N}(\hat{\boldsymbol{\pi}} - \boldsymbol{\pi}_o) \overset{a}{\sim} \text{Normal}(\mathbf{0}, \boldsymbol{\Xi}_o) \tag{14.63}$$

it turns out that an efficient CMD estimator solves

$$\min_{\boldsymbol{\theta} \in \boldsymbol{\Theta}} \{\hat{\boldsymbol{\pi}} - \mathbf{h}(\boldsymbol{\theta})\}'\hat{\boldsymbol{\Xi}}^{-1}\{\hat{\boldsymbol{\pi}} - \mathbf{h}(\boldsymbol{\theta})\}, \tag{14.64}$$

where $\text{plim}_{N\to\infty} \hat{\boldsymbol{\Xi}} = \boldsymbol{\Xi}_o$. In other words, an efficient weighting matrix is the inverse of any consistent estimator of Avar $\sqrt{N}(\hat{\boldsymbol{\pi}} - \boldsymbol{\pi}_o)$.

We can easily derive the asymptotic variance of $\sqrt{N}(\hat{\boldsymbol{\theta}} - \boldsymbol{\theta}_o)$. The first-order condition for $\hat{\boldsymbol{\theta}}$ is

$$\mathbf{H}(\hat{\boldsymbol{\theta}})'\hat{\boldsymbol{\Xi}}^{-1}\{\hat{\boldsymbol{\pi}} - \mathbf{h}(\hat{\boldsymbol{\theta}})\} \equiv \mathbf{0}, \tag{14.65}$$

where $\mathbf{H}(\boldsymbol{\theta}) \equiv \nabla_{\theta}\mathbf{h}(\boldsymbol{\theta})$ is the $S \times P$ Jacobian of $\mathbf{h}(\boldsymbol{\theta})$. Since $\mathbf{h}(\boldsymbol{\theta}_o) = \boldsymbol{\pi}_o$ and

$$\sqrt{N}\{\mathbf{h}(\hat{\boldsymbol{\theta}}) - \mathbf{h}(\boldsymbol{\theta}_o)\} = \mathbf{H}(\boldsymbol{\theta}_o)\sqrt{N}(\hat{\boldsymbol{\theta}} - \boldsymbol{\theta}_o) + o_p(1),$$

by a standard mean value expansion about $\boldsymbol{\theta}_o$, we have

$$\mathbf{0} = \mathbf{H}(\hat{\boldsymbol{\theta}})'\hat{\boldsymbol{\Xi}}^{-1}\{\sqrt{N}(\hat{\boldsymbol{\pi}} - \boldsymbol{\pi}_o) - \mathbf{H}(\boldsymbol{\theta}_o)\sqrt{N}(\hat{\boldsymbol{\theta}} - \boldsymbol{\theta}_o)\} + o_p(1). \tag{14.66}$$

Because $\mathbf{H}(\cdot)$ is continuous and $\hat{\boldsymbol{\theta}} \xrightarrow{p} \boldsymbol{\theta}_o$, $\mathbf{H}(\hat{\boldsymbol{\theta}}) = \mathbf{H}(\boldsymbol{\theta}_o) + o_p(1)$; by assumption $\hat{\boldsymbol{\Xi}} = \boldsymbol{\Xi}_o + o_p(1)$. Therefore,

$$\mathbf{H}(\boldsymbol{\theta}_o)'\boldsymbol{\Xi}_o^{-1}\mathbf{H}(\boldsymbol{\theta}_o)\sqrt{N}(\hat{\boldsymbol{\theta}} - \boldsymbol{\theta}_o) = \mathbf{H}(\boldsymbol{\theta}_o)'\boldsymbol{\Xi}_o^{-1}\sqrt{N}(\hat{\boldsymbol{\pi}} - \boldsymbol{\pi}_o) + o_p(1).$$

By assumption (14.63) and the asymptotic equivalence lemma,

$$\mathbf{H}(\boldsymbol{\theta}_o)'\boldsymbol{\Xi}_o^{-1}\mathbf{H}(\boldsymbol{\theta}_o)\sqrt{N}(\hat{\boldsymbol{\theta}} - \boldsymbol{\theta}_o) \overset{a}{\sim} \text{Normal}[\mathbf{0}, \mathbf{H}(\boldsymbol{\theta}_o)'\boldsymbol{\Xi}_o^{-1}\mathbf{H}(\boldsymbol{\theta}_o)],$$

and so

$$\sqrt{N}(\hat{\boldsymbol{\theta}} - \boldsymbol{\theta}_o) \overset{a}{\sim} \text{Normal}[\mathbf{0}, (\mathbf{H}_o'\boldsymbol{\Xi}_o^{-1}\mathbf{H}_o)^{-1}], \tag{14.67}$$

provided that $\mathbf{H}_o \equiv \mathbf{H}(\boldsymbol{\theta}_o)$ has full-column rank P, as will generally be the case when $\boldsymbol{\theta}_o$ is identified and $\mathbf{h}(\cdot)$ contains no redundancies. The appropriate estimator of $\widehat{\text{Avar}}(\hat{\boldsymbol{\theta}})$ is

$$\widehat{\text{Avar}}(\hat{\boldsymbol{\theta}}) \equiv (\hat{\mathbf{H}}'\hat{\boldsymbol{\Xi}}^{-1}\hat{\mathbf{H}})^{-1}/N = (\hat{\mathbf{H}}'[\widehat{\text{Avar}}(\hat{\boldsymbol{\pi}})]^{-1}\hat{\mathbf{H}})^{-1}. \tag{14.68}$$

The proof that $\hat{\boldsymbol{\Xi}}^{-1}$ is the optimal weighting matrix in expression (14.64) is very similar to the derivation of the optimal weighting matrix for GMM. (It can also be shown by applying Theorem 14.3.) We will simply call the efficient estimator the CMD estimator, where it is understood that we are using the efficient weighting matrix.

There is another efficiency issue that arises when more than one $\sqrt{N}$-asymptotically normal estimator for $\boldsymbol{\pi}_o$ is available: Which estimator of $\boldsymbol{\pi}_o$ should be used? Let $\hat{\boldsymbol{\theta}}$ be the estimator based on $\hat{\boldsymbol{\pi}}$, and let $\tilde{\boldsymbol{\theta}}$ be the estimator based on another estimator, $\tilde{\boldsymbol{\pi}}$. You are asked to show in Problem 14.6 that Avar $\sqrt{N}(\tilde{\boldsymbol{\theta}} - \boldsymbol{\theta}_o)$ – Avar $\sqrt{N}(\hat{\boldsymbol{\theta}} - \boldsymbol{\theta}_o)$ is p.s.d. whenever Avar $\sqrt{N}(\tilde{\boldsymbol{\pi}} - \boldsymbol{\pi}_o)$ – Avar $\sqrt{N}(\hat{\boldsymbol{\pi}} - \boldsymbol{\pi}_o)$ is p.s.d. In other words, we should use the most efficient estimator of $\boldsymbol{\pi}_o$ to obtain the most efficient estimator of $\boldsymbol{\theta}_o$.

A test of overidentifying restrictions is immediately available after estimation, because, under the null hypothesis $\boldsymbol{\pi}_o = \mathbf{h}(\boldsymbol{\theta}_o)$,

$$N[\hat{\boldsymbol{\pi}} - \mathbf{h}(\hat{\boldsymbol{\theta}})]'\hat{\boldsymbol{\Xi}}^{-1}[\hat{\boldsymbol{\pi}} - \mathbf{h}(\hat{\boldsymbol{\theta}})] \overset{a}{\sim} \chi^2_{S-P}. \tag{14.69}$$

To show this result, we use

$$\begin{aligned}\sqrt{N}[\hat{\boldsymbol{\pi}} - \mathbf{h}(\hat{\boldsymbol{\theta}})] &= \sqrt{N}(\hat{\boldsymbol{\pi}} - \boldsymbol{\pi}_o) - \mathbf{H}_o\sqrt{N}(\hat{\boldsymbol{\theta}} - \boldsymbol{\theta}_o) + o_p(1) \\ &= \sqrt{N}(\hat{\boldsymbol{\pi}} - \boldsymbol{\pi}_o) - \mathbf{H}_o(\mathbf{H}_o'\boldsymbol{\Xi}_o^{-1}\mathbf{H}_o)^{-1}\mathbf{H}_o'\boldsymbol{\Xi}_o^{-1}\sqrt{N}(\hat{\boldsymbol{\pi}} - \boldsymbol{\pi}_o) + o_p(1) \\ &= [\mathbf{I}_S - \mathbf{H}_o(\mathbf{H}_o'\boldsymbol{\Xi}_o^{-1}\mathbf{H}_o)^{-1}\mathbf{H}_o'\boldsymbol{\Xi}_o^{-1}]\sqrt{N}(\hat{\boldsymbol{\pi}} - \boldsymbol{\pi}_o) + o_p(1).\end{aligned}$$

Therefore, up to $o_p(1)$,

$$\boldsymbol{\Xi}_o^{-1/2}\sqrt{N}\{\hat{\boldsymbol{\pi}} - \mathbf{h}(\hat{\boldsymbol{\theta}})\} = [\mathbf{I}_S - \boldsymbol{\Xi}_o^{-1/2}\mathbf{H}_o(\mathbf{H}_o'\boldsymbol{\Xi}_o^{-1}\mathbf{H}_o)^{-1}\mathbf{H}_o'\boldsymbol{\Xi}_o^{-1/2}]\mathscr{Z} \equiv \mathbf{M}_o\mathscr{Z},$$

where $\mathscr{Z} \equiv \boldsymbol{\Xi}_o^{-1/2}\sqrt{N}(\hat{\boldsymbol{\pi}} - \boldsymbol{\pi}_o) \xrightarrow{d} \text{Normal}(\mathbf{0}, \mathbf{I}_S)$. But $\mathbf{M}_o$ is a symmetric idempotent matrix with rank $S - P$, so $\{\sqrt{N}[\hat{\boldsymbol{\pi}} - \mathbf{h}(\hat{\boldsymbol{\theta}})]\}'\boldsymbol{\Xi}_o^{-1}\{\sqrt{N}[\hat{\boldsymbol{\pi}} - \mathbf{h}(\hat{\boldsymbol{\theta}})]\} \overset{a}{\sim} \chi^2_{S-P}$. Because $\hat{\boldsymbol{\Xi}}$ is consistent for $\boldsymbol{\Xi}_o$, expression (14.69) follows from the asymptotic equivalence lemma. The statistic can also be expressed as

$$\{\hat{\boldsymbol{\pi}} - \mathbf{h}(\hat{\boldsymbol{\theta}})\}'[\widehat{\text{Avar}(\hat{\boldsymbol{\pi}})}]^{-1}\{\hat{\boldsymbol{\pi}} - \mathbf{h}(\hat{\boldsymbol{\theta}})\}. \tag{14.70}$$

Testing restrictions on $\boldsymbol{\theta}_o$ is also straightforward, assuming that we can express the restrictions as $\boldsymbol{\theta}_o = \mathbf{d}(\boldsymbol{\alpha}_o)$ for an $R \times 1$ vector $\boldsymbol{\alpha}_o$, $R < P$. Under these restrictions, $\boldsymbol{\pi}_o = \mathbf{h}[\mathbf{d}(\boldsymbol{\alpha}_o)] \equiv \mathbf{g}(\boldsymbol{\alpha}_o)$. Thus, $\boldsymbol{\alpha}_o$ can be estimated by minimum distance by solving problem (14.64) with $\boldsymbol{\alpha}$ in place of $\boldsymbol{\theta}$ and $\mathbf{g}(\boldsymbol{\alpha})$ in place of $\mathbf{h}(\boldsymbol{\theta})$. The *same* estimator $\hat{\boldsymbol{\Xi}}$ should be used in both minimization problems. Then it can be shown (under interiority and differentiability) that

$$N[\hat{\boldsymbol{\pi}} - \mathbf{g}(\hat{\boldsymbol{\alpha}})]'\hat{\boldsymbol{\Xi}}^{-1}[\hat{\boldsymbol{\pi}} - \mathbf{g}(\hat{\boldsymbol{\alpha}})] - N[\hat{\boldsymbol{\pi}} - \mathbf{h}(\hat{\boldsymbol{\theta}})]'\hat{\boldsymbol{\Xi}}^{-1}[\hat{\boldsymbol{\pi}} - \mathbf{h}(\hat{\boldsymbol{\theta}})] \overset{a}{\sim} \chi^2_{P-R}, \tag{14.71}$$

when the restrictions on $\boldsymbol{\theta}_o$ are true.

14.6 Panel Data Applications

We now cover several panel data applications of GMM and CMD. The models in Sections 14.6.1 and 14.6.3 are nonlinear in parameters.

14.6.1 Nonlinear Dynamic Models

One increasingly popular use of panel data is to test rationality in economic models of individual, family, or firm behavior (see, for example, Shapiro, 1984; Zeldes, 1989; Keane and Runkle, 1992; Shea, 1995). For a random draw from the population we assume that T time periods are available. Suppose that an economic theory implies that

$$\text{E}[r_t(\mathbf{w}_t, \boldsymbol{\theta}_o) \mid \mathbf{w}_{t-1}, \ldots, \mathbf{w}_1] = 0, \qquad t = 1, \ldots, T, \tag{14.72}$$

where, for simplicity, r_t is a scalar. These conditional moment restrictions are often implied by rational expectations, under the assumption that the decision horizon is the same length as the sampling period. For example, consider a standard life-cycle model of consumption. Let c_{it} denote consumption of family i at time t, let $\mathbf{h}_{it}$ denote taste shifters, let δ_o denote the common rate of time preference, and let a_{it}^j denote the return for family i from holding asset j from period $t-1$ to t. Under the assumption that utility is given by

$$u(c_{it}, \theta_{it}) = \exp(\mathbf{h}_{it}\boldsymbol{\beta}_o)c_{it}^{1-\lambda_o}/(1-\lambda_o), \tag{14.73}$$

the Euler equation is

$$E[(1+a_{it}^j)(c_{it}/c_{i,t-1})^{-\lambda_o} \mid \mathscr{I}_{i,t-1}] = (1+\delta_o)^{-1}\exp(\mathbf{x}_{it}\boldsymbol{\beta}_o), \tag{14.74}$$

where $\mathscr{I}_{it}$ is family i's information set at time t and $\mathbf{x}_{it} \equiv \mathbf{h}_{i,t-1} - \mathbf{h}_{it}$; equation (14.74) assumes that $\mathbf{h}_{it} - \mathbf{h}_{i,t-1} \in \mathscr{I}_{i,t-1}$, an assumption which is often reasonable. Given equation (14.74), we can define a residual function for each t:

$$r_{it}(\boldsymbol{\theta}) = (1+a_{it}^j)(c_{it}/c_{i,t-1})^{-\lambda} - \exp(\mathbf{x}_{it}\boldsymbol{\beta}), \tag{14.75}$$

where $(1+\delta)^{-1}$ is absorbed in an intercept in $\mathbf{x}_{it}$. Let $\mathbf{w}_{it}$ contain c_{it}, $c_{i,t-1}$, a_{it}, and $\mathbf{x}_{it}$. Then condition (14.72) holds, and λ_o and $\boldsymbol{\beta}_o$ can be estimated by GMM.

Returning to condition (14.72), valid instruments at time t are functions of information known at time $t-1$:

$$\mathbf{z}_t = \mathbf{f}_t(\mathbf{w}_{t-1}, \ldots, \mathbf{w}_1). \tag{14.76}$$

The $T \times 1$ residual vector is $\mathbf{r}(\mathbf{w}, \boldsymbol{\theta}) = [r_1(\mathbf{w}_1, \boldsymbol{\theta}), \ldots, r_T(\mathbf{w}_T, \boldsymbol{\theta})]'$, and the matrix of instruments has the same form as matrix (14.38) for each i (with $G = T$). Then, the minimum chi-square estimator can be obtained after using the system 2SLS estimator, although the choice of instruments is a nontrivial matter. A common choice is linear and quadratic functions of variables lagged one or two time periods.

Estimation of the optimal weighting matrix is somewhat simplified under the conditional moment restrictions (14.72). Recall from Section 14.2 that the optimal estimator uses the inverse of a consistent estimator of $\boldsymbol{\Lambda}_o = E[\mathbf{Z}_i'\mathbf{r}_i(\boldsymbol{\theta}_o)\mathbf{r}_i(\boldsymbol{\theta}_o)'\mathbf{Z}_i]$. Under condition (14.72), this matrix is block diagonal. Dropping the i subscript, the (s,t) block is $E[r_s(\boldsymbol{\theta}_o)r_t(\boldsymbol{\theta}_o)\mathbf{z}_s'\mathbf{z}_t]$. For concreteness, assume that $s < t$. Then $\mathbf{z}_t$, $\mathbf{z}_s$, and $r_s(\boldsymbol{\theta}_o)$ are all functions of $\mathbf{w}_{t-1}, \mathbf{w}_{t-2}, \ldots, \mathbf{w}_1$. By iterated expectations it follows that

$$E[r_s(\boldsymbol{\theta}_o)r_t(\boldsymbol{\theta}_o)\mathbf{z}_s'\mathbf{z}_t] = E\{r_s(\boldsymbol{\theta}_o)\mathbf{z}_s'\mathbf{z}_t E[r_t(\boldsymbol{\theta}_o) \mid \mathbf{w}_{t-1}, \ldots, \mathbf{w}_1]\} = 0,$$

and so we only need to estimate the diagonal blocks of $E[\mathbf{Z}_i'\mathbf{r}_i(\boldsymbol{\theta}_o)\mathbf{r}_i(\boldsymbol{\theta}_o)'\mathbf{Z}_i]$:

$$N^{-1}\sum_{i=1}^{N}\hat{\hat{r}}_{it}^{2}\mathbf{z}_{it}'\mathbf{z}_{it} \tag{14.77}$$

is a consistent estimator of the tth block, where the $\hat{\hat{r}}_{it}$ are obtained from an inefficient GMM estimator.

In cases where the data frequency does not match the horizon relevant for decision making, the optimal matrix does not have the block diagonal form: some off-diagonal blocks will be nonzero. See Hansen (1982) for the pure time series case.

The previous model does not allow for unobserved heterogeneity, a feature that can be important in rational expectations types of applications. For example, in addition to having unobserved tastes in the utility function, individuals, families, and firms may have different discount rates. Wooldridge (1997a) shows how to obtain orthogonality conditions when the previous framework allows for unobserved heterogeneity in particular ways. GMM can be applied to the resulting nonlinear moment conditions.

There are many other kinds of dynamic panel data models that result in moment conditions that are nonlinear in parameters, even if the underlying model is linear. For example, for the linear, unobserved effects AR(1) model, Ahn and Schmidt (1995) add to the moment conditions used in the Arellano and Bond (1991) procedure that we covered in Section 11.6.2. Some of these moment conditions are nonlinear in the parameters and can be exploited using nonlinear GMM.

Recently, Wooldridge (2009b) showed how to implement parametric versions of Olley and Pakes (1996) and Levinsohn and Petrin (2003) for estimating firm-level production functions with panel data. The general approach is to replace unobserved productivity with functions of state variables and proxy variables. When the unknown functions are approximated using polynomials, Wooldridge (2009b) shows that the estimation problem can be structured as two equations (for each time period) with different instruments available for the different equations.

14.6.2 Minimum Distance Approach to the Unobserved Effects Model

In Section 11.1.2 we discussed Chamberlain's (1982, 1984) approach to estimating the unobserved effects model $y_{it} = \mathbf{x}_{it}\boldsymbol{\beta} + c_i$ (where we do not index the true value by "o" in this subsection). Rather than eliminate c_i from the equation, Chamberlain replaced it with a linear projection on the entire history of the explanatory variables. In Section 11.1.2, we showed how to estimate the parameters in a GMM framework. It is also useful to see Chamberlain's original suggestion, which was to estimate the parameters using CMD estimation.

Recall that the key equations, after we substitute in the linear projection, are

$$y_{it} = \psi + \mathbf{x}_{i1}\boldsymbol{\lambda}_1 + \cdots + \mathbf{x}_{it}(\boldsymbol{\beta} + \boldsymbol{\lambda}_t) + \cdots + \mathbf{x}_{iT}\boldsymbol{\lambda}_T + v_{it}, \tag{14.78}$$

where

$$\mathrm{E}(v_{it}) = 0, \quad \mathrm{E}(\mathbf{x}_i' v_{it}) = \mathbf{0}, \qquad t = 1, 2, \ldots, T. \tag{14.79}$$

(For notational simplicity we do not index the true parameters by "o".) Equation (14.78) embodies the restrictions on the "structural" parameters $\boldsymbol{\theta} \equiv (\psi, \boldsymbol{\lambda}_1', \ldots, \boldsymbol{\lambda}_T', \boldsymbol{\beta}')'$, a $(1 + TK + K) \times 1$ vector. To apply CMD, write

$$y_{it} = \pi_{t0} + \mathbf{x}_i \boldsymbol{\pi}_t + v_{it}, \qquad t = 1, \ldots, T,$$

so that the vector $\boldsymbol{\pi}$ is $T(1 + TK) \times 1$. When we impose the restrictions,

$$\boldsymbol{\pi}_{t0} = \psi, \ \boldsymbol{\pi}_t = [\boldsymbol{\lambda}_1', \boldsymbol{\lambda}_2', \ldots, (\boldsymbol{\beta} + \boldsymbol{\lambda}_t)', \ldots, \boldsymbol{\lambda}_T']', \qquad t = 1, \ldots, T.$$

Therefore, we can write $\boldsymbol{\pi} = \mathbf{H}\boldsymbol{\theta}$ for a $(T + T^2K) \times (1 + TK + K)$ matrix $\mathbf{H}$. When $T = 2$, $\boldsymbol{\pi}$ can be written with restrictions imposed as $\boldsymbol{\pi} = (\psi, \boldsymbol{\beta}' + \boldsymbol{\lambda}_1', \boldsymbol{\lambda}_2', \psi, \boldsymbol{\lambda}_1', \boldsymbol{\beta}' + \boldsymbol{\lambda}_2')'$, and so

$$\mathbf{H} = \begin{bmatrix} 1 & \mathbf{0} & \mathbf{0} & \mathbf{0} \\ \mathbf{0} & \mathbf{I}_K & \mathbf{0} & \mathbf{I}_K \\ \mathbf{0} & \mathbf{0} & \mathbf{I}_K & \mathbf{0} \\ 1 & \mathbf{0} & \mathbf{0} & \mathbf{0} \\ \mathbf{0} & \mathbf{I}_K & \mathbf{0} & \mathbf{0} \\ \mathbf{0} & \mathbf{0} & \mathbf{I}_K & \mathbf{I}_K \end{bmatrix}.$$

The CMD estimator can be obtained in closed form, once we have $\hat{\boldsymbol{\pi}}$; see Problem 14.7 for the general case.

How should we obtain $\hat{\boldsymbol{\pi}}$, the vector of estimates without the restrictions imposed? There is really only one way, and that is OLS for each time period. Condition (14.79) ensures that OLS is consistent and $\sqrt{N}$-asymptotically normal. Why not use a system method, in particular, SUR? For one thing, we cannot generally assume that $\mathbf{v}_i$ satisfies the requisite homoskedasticity assumption that ensures that SUR is more efficient than OLS equation by equation; see Section 11.1.2. Anyway, because the same regressors appear in each equation and no restrictions are imposed on the $\boldsymbol{\pi}_t$, OLS and SUR are identical. Procedures that might use nonlinear functions of $\mathbf{x}_i$ as instruments are not allowed under condition (14.79).

The estimator $\hat{\boldsymbol{\Xi}}$ of Avar $\sqrt{N}(\hat{\boldsymbol{\pi}} - \boldsymbol{\pi})$ is the robust asymptotic variance for system OLS from Chapter 7.

$$\hat{\boldsymbol{\Xi}} \equiv \left(N^{-1}\sum_{i=1}^{N}\mathbf{X}_i'\mathbf{X}_i\right)^{-1}\left(N^{-1}\sum_{i=1}^{N}\mathbf{X}_i'\hat{\mathbf{v}}_i\hat{\mathbf{v}}_i'\mathbf{X}_i\right)\left(N^{-1}\sum_{i=1}^{N}\mathbf{X}_i'\mathbf{X}_i\right)^{-1}, \tag{14.80}$$

where $\mathbf{X}_i = \mathbf{I}_T \otimes (1, \mathbf{x}_i)$ is $T \times (T + T^2K)$ and $\hat{\mathbf{v}}_i$ is the vector of OLS residuals; see also equation (7.26).

Given the linear model with an additive unobserved effect, the overidentification test statistic (14.69) in Chamberlain's setup is a test of the strict exogeneity assumption. Essentially, it is a test of whether the leads and lags of $\mathbf{x}_t$ appearing in each time period are due to a time-constant unobserved effect c_i. The number of overidentifying restrictions is $(T + T^2K) - (1 + TK + K)$. Perhaps not surprisingly, the minimum distance approach to estimating $\boldsymbol{\theta}$ is asymptotically equivalent to the GMM procedure we described in Section 11.1.2, as can be reasoned from the work of Angrist and Newey (1991).

One hypothesis of interest concerning $\boldsymbol{\theta}$ is that $\boldsymbol{\lambda}_t = 0$, $t = 1, \ldots, T$. Under this hypothesis, the random effects assumption that the unobserved effect c_i is uncorrelated with $\mathbf{x}_{it}$ for all t holds. We discussed a test of this assumption in Chapter 10. A more general test is available in the minimum distance setting. First, estimate $\boldsymbol{\alpha} \equiv (\psi, \boldsymbol{\beta}')'$ by minimum distance, using $\hat{\boldsymbol{\pi}}$ and $\hat{\boldsymbol{\Xi}}$ in equation (14.80). Second, compute the test statistic (14.71). Chamberlain (1984) gives an empirical example.

Minimum distance methods can be applied to more complicated panel data models, including some of the duration models that we cover in Chapter 22. (See Han and Hausman, 1990.) Van der Klaauw (1996) uses minimum distance estimation in a complicated dynamic model of labor force participation and marital status.

14.6.3 Models with Time-Varying Coefficients on the Unobserved Effects

Now we extend the usual linear model to allow the unobserved heterogeneity to have time-varying coefficients:

$$y_{it} = \mathbf{x}_{it}\boldsymbol{\beta} + \eta_t c_i + u_{it}, \qquad t = 1, \ldots, T, \tag{14.81}$$

where, with small T and large N, it makes sense to treat $\{\eta_t : t = 1, \ldots, T\}$ as parameters, like $\boldsymbol{\beta}$. We still view c_i as a random draw that comes with the observed variables for unit i. This model has many applications. Labor economists sometimes think the return to unobserved "talent" might change over time. Those who estimate, say, firm-level production functions like to allow the importance of unobserved factors, such as managerial skill, to change over time.

Because c_i is unobserved, we cannot identify T separate coefficients in (14.81). A convenient normalization is to set the coefficient for $t = 1$ to unity: $\eta_1 \equiv 1$, and we will use this in what follows. Thus, if we seek to estimate the time-varying coefficients—sometimes called the **factor loads**—then we only estimate $\eta_2, \ldots, \eta_T$. Unless otherwise stated, we make the strict exogeneity assumption conditional on c_i:

$$\mathrm{E}(u_{it} \mid \mathbf{x}_{i1}, \mathbf{x}_2, \ldots, \mathbf{x}_{iT}, c_i) = 0, \qquad t = 1, 2, \ldots, T, \tag{14.82}$$

an assumption we used frequently in Chapter 10 for random effects, fixed effects, and first differencing estimation.

Before we discuss estimation of $\boldsymbol{\beta}$ along with the η_t, we can ask how estimators that ignore the time-varying coefficients fare in estimating $\boldsymbol{\beta}$. After all, in some applications we might be primarily interested in $\boldsymbol{\beta}$, but we are concerned that ignoring the time-varying loads causes inconsistency of traditional methods. If we take a random effects approach and assume that c_i is uncorrelated with $\mathbf{x}_{it}$ for all t, what happens if we just apply the usual RE estimator from Chapter 10? Let $\mu_c = \mathrm{E}(c_i)$ and write (14.81) as

$$y_{it} = \alpha_t + \mathbf{x}_{it}\boldsymbol{\beta} + \eta_t d_i + u_{it}, \qquad t = 1, \ldots, T, \tag{14.83}$$

where $\alpha_t = \eta_t \mu_c$ and $d_i = c_i - \mu_c$ has zero mean. In addition, the composite error, $v_{it} \equiv \eta_t d_i + u_{it}$, is uncorrelated with $(\mathbf{x}_{i1}, \mathbf{x}_2, \ldots, \mathbf{x}_{iT})$ (as well as having a zero mean). Of course, v_{it} generally has a time-varying variance as well as serial correlation that is not of the standard RE form found in Assumption RE.3 from Chapter 10. Nevertheless, as we learned there and in Chapter 7, applying feasible GLS to a linear panel data equation is consistent provided v_{it}, the error term, is uncorrelated with $\mathbf{x}_i$, the explanatory variables, across all time periods. The bottom line is, applying the usual RE estimator to (14.83) produces a consistent estimator of $\boldsymbol{\beta}$ even though we have ignored the η_t. Of course, the usual RE variance matrix estimator is inconsistent, so robust inference is needed, but that is straightforward. Further, the usual RE estimator is inefficient relative to the FGLS estimator that does not restrict the variance matrix of the composite error. If we made the standard homoskedasticity and serial independence assumptions on $\{u_{it}\}$ (conditional on $\mathbf{x}_i$, as usual), we could derive the variance matrix of the $T \times 1$ vector $\mathbf{v}_i$ and obtain the appropriate, but restricted, variance matrix. Incidentally, in saying we estimate (14.83) by RE, it is imperative that we include a full set of year intercepts—that is, an overall constant and then $T - 1$ time dummies—to account for the first term. Here we find yet another reason to allow for a different intercept in each time period.

We can also evaluate the usual fixed effects (FE) estimator when we allow correlation between c_i and $\mathbf{x}_i$. The standard FE estimator is consistent provided $\ddot{\mathbf{x}}_{it}$ is uncorrelated with v_{it}. But u_{it} is uncorrelated with $\ddot{\mathbf{x}}_{it}$ by (14.82), and so the key condition is

$$\text{Cov}(\ddot{\mathbf{x}}_{it}, c_i) = \mathbf{0}, \qquad t = 1, \ldots, T. \tag{14.84}$$

In other words, the unobserved effect is uncorrelated with the deviations $\ddot{\mathbf{x}}_{it} = \mathbf{x}_{it} - \bar{\mathbf{x}}_i$. We encountered a similar condition in Section 11.7.3 when we studied the assumptions when the usual FE estimator consistency estimates the population average slope in a model with random slopes.

Because (14.84) allows for correlation between $\bar{\mathbf{x}}_i$ and c_i, we can conclude that the usual FE estimator has some robustness to the presence of η_t for estimating $\boldsymbol{\beta}$. Further, if we use the extended FE estimators for random trend models—see Section 11.7.3—then we can replace $\ddot{\mathbf{x}}_{it}$ with detrended covariates. Then, c_i can be correlated with underlying levels and trends in $\mathbf{x}_{it}$ (provided we have a sufficient number of time periods).

Using the usual RE or FE estimators (with full time period dummies) does not allow us to estimate the η_t, or even determine whether the η_t change over time. Even if we are interested only in $\boldsymbol{\beta}$ when c_i and $\mathbf{x}_{it}$ are allowed to be correlated, being able to detect time-varying factor loads is important because (14.84) is not completely general. It would be very useful to have a simple test of $\text{H}_0 : \eta_2 = \eta_3 = \cdots = \eta_T = 1$ with some power against the alternative of time-varying coefficients. Then we can determine whether a more sophisticated estimation method might be needed.

We can obtain a simple variable addition test that can be computed using linear estimation methods if we specify a particular relationship between c_i and $\mathbf{x}_i$. We use the Mundlak (1978) assumption that we introduced in Chapter 10:

$$c_i = \psi + \bar{\mathbf{x}}_i \boldsymbol{\xi} + a_i. \tag{14.85}$$

Then

$$y_{it} = \eta_t \psi + \mathbf{x}_{it}\boldsymbol{\beta} + \eta_t \bar{\mathbf{x}}_i \boldsymbol{\xi} + \eta_t a_i + u_{it} = \alpha_t + \mathbf{x}_{it}\boldsymbol{\beta} + \bar{\mathbf{x}}_i \boldsymbol{\xi} + \lambda_t \bar{\mathbf{x}}_i \boldsymbol{\xi} + a_i + \lambda_t a_i + u_{it}, \tag{14.86}$$

where $\lambda_t = \eta_t - 1$ for all t. Under the null hypothesis, $\lambda_t = 0$, $t = 2, \ldots, T$. Note that if we impose the null hypothesis, the resulting model is linear, and we can estimate it by pooled OLS of y_{it} on $1, d2_t, \ldots, dT_t, \mathbf{x}_{it}, \bar{\mathbf{x}}_i$ across t and i, where the dr_t are time dummies. As we discussed in Section 10.7.2, the estimate of $\boldsymbol{\beta}$ is the usual FE estimator. More important for our current purposes, we obtain an estimate of $\boldsymbol{\xi}$, which we call $\hat{\boldsymbol{\xi}}$. The following variable addition test can be derived from the score principle in the context of nonlinear regression; we can use an informal derivation directly from equation (14.86). If λ_t is different from zero, then the coefficient on $\bar{\mathbf{x}}_i \boldsymbol{\xi}$ at time t is different from unity, the coefficient on $\bar{\mathbf{x}}_i \boldsymbol{\xi}$ at $t = 1$. Therefore, we add the interaction terms $dr_t(\bar{\mathbf{x}}_i \hat{\boldsymbol{\xi}})$ for $r = 2, \ldots, T$ to the FE estimation. That is, we construct the auxiliary equation

$$y_{it} = \alpha_1 + \alpha_2 d2_t + \cdots + \alpha_T dT_t + \mathbf{x}_{it}\boldsymbol{\beta} + \lambda_2 d2_t(\bar{\mathbf{x}}_i\hat{\xi}) + \cdots + \lambda_T dT_t(\bar{\mathbf{x}}_i\hat{\xi}) + error_{it}, \tag{14.87}$$

estimate this equation by standard FE, and test the joint significance of the $T-1$ terms $d2_t(\bar{\mathbf{x}}_i\hat{\xi}), \ldots, dT_t(\bar{\mathbf{x}}_i\hat{\xi})$. (The term $\bar{\mathbf{x}}_i\hat{\xi}$ would drop out of an FE estimation, so we just omit it.) Note that $\bar{\mathbf{x}}_i\hat{\xi}$ is a scalar, and so the test has $T-1$ degrees of freedom. As always, it is prudent to use a fully robust test (even though, under the null, $\lambda_t a_i$ disappears from the error term).

A few comments about this test are in order. First, although we used the Mundlak device (14.85) to obtain the test, it does not have to represent the actual linear projection because we are simply adding terms to an FE estimation. Under the null, we do not need to restrict the relationshp between c_i and $\mathbf{x}_i$. Of course, the power of the test may be affected by this choice. Second, the test only makes sense if $\xi \neq 0$; in particular, it cannot be used in an RE environment. Third, a rejection of the null does not necessarily mean that the usual FE estimator is inconsistent for $\boldsymbol{\beta}$: assumption (14.84) could still hold. In fact, the change in the estimate of $\boldsymbol{\beta}$ when the interaction terms are added can be indicative of whether accounting for time-varying η_t is likely to be important.

Unfortunately, when we reject constant η_t—that is, $\lambda_t \neq 0$—we cannot simply use the estimate of $\boldsymbol{\beta}$ from (14.87), even under (14.85). The reason is that $\hat{\xi}$ has been estimated under the null, and so $\hat{\xi}$ would not be generally consistent for ξ under the alternative. If we feel comfortable imposing (14.85), then we could estimate (14.86) using minimum distance estimation. The first-stage estimation is linear and estimates, along with separate intercepts and $\boldsymbol{\beta}$, T separate coefficient vectors, say ξ_t, on the time average $\bar{\mathbf{x}}_i$. After pooled OLS estimation, we can impose the restrictions $\xi_t = \eta_t\xi$, $t = 1, \ldots, T$. We can also apply GMM. This becomes a nonlinear GMM problem because the equation is nonlinear in the parameters λ_t and ξ, but the GMM theory we developed in Section 14.1 can be used. If we do not want to use overidentifying restrictions (that would come from the assumption that $\mathbf{x}_{ir}$ is uncorrelated with the error $(1+\lambda_t)a_i + u_{it}$ for all r and t), we could simply estimate (14.86) by NLS. Alternatively, we could use the Chamberlain device and replace $\bar{\mathbf{x}}_i\xi$ with $\mathbf{x}_i\zeta$, where ζ is $TK \times 1$. This would impose no restrictions on the relationship between c_i and $\mathbf{x}_i$.

Typically, when we want to allow arbitrary correlation between c_i and $\mathbf{x}_i$, we work directly from (14.81) and eliminate the c_i. There are several ways to do this. If we maintain that all η_t are different from zero, then we can use a quasi-differencing method to eliminate c_i. In particular, for $t \geq 2$ we can multiply the $t-1$ equation by η_t/η_{t-1} and subtract the result from the time t equation:

$$\begin{aligned} y_{it} - (\eta_t/\eta_{t-1})y_{i,t-1} &= [\mathbf{x}_{it} - (\eta_t/\eta_{t-1})\mathbf{x}_{i,t-1}]\boldsymbol{\beta} + [\eta_t c_i - (\eta_t/\eta_{t-1})\eta_{t-1}c_i] \\ &\quad + [u_{it} - (\eta_t/\eta_{t-1})u_{i,t-1}] \\ &= [\mathbf{x}_{it} - (\eta_t/\eta_{t-1})\mathbf{x}_{i,t-1}]\boldsymbol{\beta} + [u_{it} - (\eta_t/\eta_{t-1})u_{i,t-1}], \qquad t \geq 2. \end{aligned}$$

We define $\theta_t = \eta_t/\eta_{t-1}$ and write

$$y_{it} - \theta_t y_{i,t-1} = (\mathbf{x}_{it} - \theta_t \mathbf{x}_{i,t-1})\boldsymbol{\beta} + e_{it}, \qquad t = 2, \ldots, T, \tag{14.88}$$

where $e_{it} \equiv u_{it} - \theta_t u_{i,t-1}$. Under the strict exogeneity assumption, e_{it} is uncorrelated with every element of $\mathbf{x}_i$, and so we can apply GMM to (14.88) to estimate $\boldsymbol{\beta}$ and $(\theta_2, \ldots, \theta_T)$. Again, this requires using nonlinear GMM methods, and the e_{it} would typically be serially correlated. If we do not impose restrictions on the second moment matrix of $\mathbf{u}_i$, then we would not use any information on the second moments of $\mathbf{e}_i$; we would (eventually) use an unrestricted weighting matrix after an initial estimation.

Using all of $\mathbf{x}_i$ in each time period can result in too many overidentifying restrictions. At time t we might use, say, $\mathbf{z}_{it} = (\mathbf{x}_{it}, \mathbf{x}_{i,t-1})$, and then the instrument matrix $\mathbf{Z}_i$ (with $T - 1$ rows) would be $\operatorname{diag}(\mathbf{z}_{i2}, \ldots, \mathbf{z}_{iT})$. An initial consistent estimator can be gotten by choosing weighting matrix $(N^{-1}\sum_{i=1}^{N}\mathbf{Z}_i'\mathbf{Z}_i)^{-1}$, just as with the system 2SLS estimator in Chapter 8. Then the optimal weighting matrix can be estimated. Ahn, Lee, and Schmidt (2002) provide further discussion.

If $\mathbf{x}_{it}$ contains sequentially but not strictly exogenous explanatory variables—such as a lagged dependent variable—the instruments at time t can only be chosen from $(\mathbf{x}_{i,t-1}, \ldots, \mathbf{x}_{i1})$, just as in Section 11.6.1. Holtz-Eakin, Newey, and Rosen (1988) explicitly consider models with lagged dependent variables.

Other transformations can be used. For example, at time $t \geq 2$ we can use the equation

$$\eta_{t-1} y_{it} - \eta_t y_{i,t-1} = (\eta_{t-1}\mathbf{x}_{it} - \eta_t \mathbf{x}_{i,t-1})\boldsymbol{\beta} + e_{it}, \qquad t = 2, \ldots, T,$$

where now $e_{it} = \eta_{t-1}u_{it} - \eta_t u_{i,t-1}$. This equation has the advantage of allowing $\eta_t = 0$ for some t. The same choices of instruments are available depending on whether $\{\mathbf{x}_{it}\}$ are strictly or sequentially exogenous.

Problems

14.1. Consider the system in equations (14.34) and (14.35).

a. How would you estimate equation (14.35) using single-equation methods? Give a few possibilities, ranging from simple to more complicated. State any additional assumptions relevant for estimating asymptotic variances or for efficiency of the various estimators.

b. Is equation (14.34) identified if $\gamma_1 = 0$?

c. Now suppose that $\gamma_3 = 0$, so that the parameters in equation (14.35) can be consistently estimated by OLS. Let $\hat{y}_2$ be the OLS fitted values. Explain why NLS estimation of

$$y_1 = \mathbf{x}_1\boldsymbol{\delta}_1 + \gamma_1 \hat{y}_2^{\gamma_2} + error$$

does not consistently estimate $\boldsymbol{\delta}_1$, γ_1, and γ_2 when $\gamma_1 \neq 0$ and $\gamma_2 \neq 1$.

14.2. Consider the following labor supply function nonlinear in parameters:

$$hours = \mathbf{z}_1\boldsymbol{\delta}_1 + \gamma_1(wage^{\rho_1} - 1)/\rho_1 + u_1, \qquad \mathrm{E}(u_1 \mid \mathbf{z}) = 0,$$

where $\mathbf{z}_1$ contains unity and $\mathbf{z}$ is the full set of exogenous variables.

a. Show that this model contains the level-level and level-log models as special cases. (Hint: For $w > 0$, $(w^{\rho} - 1)/\rho \to \log(w)$ as $\rho \to 0$.)

b. How would you test H_0: $\gamma_1 = 0$? (Be careful here; ρ_1 cannot be consistently estimated under H_0.)

c. Assuming that $\gamma_1 \neq 0$, how would you estimate this equation if $\mathrm{Var}(u_1 \mid \mathbf{z}) = \sigma_1^2$? What if $\mathrm{Var}(u_1 \mid \mathbf{z})$ is not constant?

d. Find the gradient of the residual function with respect to $\boldsymbol{\delta}_1$, γ_1, and ρ_1. (Hint: Recall that the derivative of w^{ρ} with respect to ρ is $w^{\rho}\log(w)$.)

e. Explain how to obtain the score test of H_0: $\rho_1 = 1$.

14.3. Use Theorem 14.3 to show that the optimal instrumental variables based on the conditional moment restrictions (14.53) are given by equation (14.57).

14.4. a. Show that, under Assumptions WNLS.1–WNLS.3 in Chapter 12, the weighted NLS estimator has asymptotic variance equal to that of the efficient IV estimator based on the orthogonality condition $\mathrm{E}[(y_i - m(\mathbf{x}_i, \boldsymbol{\beta}_o)) \mid \mathbf{x}_i] = 0$.

b. When does the NLS estimator of $\boldsymbol{\beta}_o$ achieve the efficiency bound derived in part a?

c. Suppose that, in addition to $\mathrm{E}(y \mid \mathbf{x}) = m(\mathbf{x}, \boldsymbol{\beta}_o)$, you use the restriction $\mathrm{Var}(y \mid \mathbf{x}) = \sigma_o^2$ for some $\sigma_o^2 > 0$. Write down the two conditional moment restrictions for estimating $\boldsymbol{\beta}_o$ and σ_o^2. What are the efficient instrumental variables?

14.5. Write down $\boldsymbol{\theta}$, $\boldsymbol{\pi}$, and the matrix $\mathbf{H}$ such that $\boldsymbol{\pi} = \mathbf{H}\boldsymbol{\theta}$ in Chamberlain's approach to unobserved effects panel data models when $T = 3$.

14.6. Let $\hat{\pi}$ and $\tilde{\pi}$ be two consistent estimators of π_o, with Avar $\sqrt{N}(\hat{\pi} - \pi_o) = \Xi_o$ and Avar $\sqrt{N}(\tilde{\pi} - \pi_o) = \Lambda_o$. Let $\hat{\theta}$ be the CMD estimator based on $\hat{\pi}$, and let $\tilde{\theta}$ be the CMD estimator based on $\tilde{\pi}$, where $\pi_o = \mathbf{h}(\theta_o)$. Show that, if $\Lambda_o - \Xi_o$ is p.s.d., then so is Avar $\sqrt{N}(\tilde{\theta} - \theta_o)$ – Avar $\sqrt{N}(\hat{\theta} - \theta_o)$. (Hint: Twice use the fact that, for two positive definite matrices $\mathbf{A}$ and $\mathbf{B}$, $\mathbf{A} - \mathbf{B}$ is p.s.d. if and only if $\mathbf{B}^{-1} - \mathbf{A}^{-1}$ is p.s.d.)

14.7. Show that when the mapping from θ_o to π_o is linear, $\pi_o = \mathbf{H}\theta_o$ for a known $S \times P$ matrix $\mathbf{H}$ with rank$(\mathbf{H}) = P$, the CMD estimator $\hat{\theta}$ is

$$\hat{\theta} = (\mathbf{H}'\hat{\Xi}^{-1}\mathbf{H})^{-1}\mathbf{H}'\hat{\Xi}^{-1}\hat{\pi} \tag{14.89}$$

Equation (14.89) *looks* like a generalized least squares (GLS) estimator of $\hat{\pi}$ on $\mathbf{H}$ using variance matrix $\hat{\Xi}$, and this apparent similarity has prompted some to call the minimum chi-square estimator a "generalized least squares" (GLS) estimator. Unfortunately, the association between CMD and GLS is misleading because $\hat{\pi}$ and $\mathbf{H}$ are not data vectors whose row dimension, S, grows with N. The asymptotic properties of the minimum chi-square estimator do *not* follow from those of GLS.

14.8. In Problem 13.9, suppose you model the unconditional distribution of y_0 as $f_0(y_0; \theta)$, which depends on at least some elements of θ appearing in $f_t(y_t \mid y_{t-1}; \theta)$. Discuss the pros and cons of using $f_0(y_0; \theta)$ in a maximum likelihood analysis along with $f_t(y_t \mid y_{t-1}; \theta)$, $t = 1, 2, \ldots, T$.

14.9. Verify that, for the linear unobserved effects model under Assumptions RE.1–RE.3, the conditions of Lemma 14.1 hold for the fixed effects $(\hat{\theta}_2)$ and the random effects $(\hat{\theta}_1)$ estimators, with $\rho = \sigma_u^2$. (Hint: For clarity, it helps to introduce a cross section subscript, i. Then $\mathbf{A}_1 = \mathrm{E}(\check{\mathbf{X}}_i'\check{\mathbf{X}}_i)$, where $\check{\mathbf{X}}_i = \mathbf{X}_i - \lambda\mathbf{j}_T\bar{\mathbf{x}}_i$; $\mathbf{A}_2 = \mathrm{E}(\ddot{\mathbf{X}}_i'\ddot{\mathbf{X}}_i)$, where $\ddot{\mathbf{X}}_i = \mathbf{X}_i - \mathbf{j}_T\bar{\mathbf{x}}_i$; $\mathbf{s}_{i1} = \check{\mathbf{X}}_i'\mathbf{r}_i$, where $\mathbf{r}_i = \mathbf{v}_i - \lambda\mathbf{j}_T\bar{v}_i$; and $\mathbf{s}_{i2} = \ddot{\mathbf{X}}_i'\mathbf{u}_i$; see Chapter 10 for further notation. You should show that $\ddot{\mathbf{X}}_i'\mathbf{u}_i = \ddot{\mathbf{X}}_i'\mathbf{r}_i$ and then $\check{\mathbf{X}}_i'\ddot{\mathbf{X}}_i = \ddot{\mathbf{X}}_i'\ddot{\mathbf{X}}_i$.)

14.10. Consider the model in (14.81) under the strict exogeneity condition (14.82). In addition, assume that $\mathrm{E}(c_i \mid \mathbf{x}_i) = 0$ (and so $\mathbf{x}_{it}$ should contain a constant and a full set of time dummies, but we do not show them explicitly).

a. If $v_{it} = \eta_t c_i + u_{it}$, show that $\mathrm{E}(v_{it} \mid \mathbf{x}_i) = 0$, $t = 1, \ldots, T$.

b. Assume that $\mathrm{Var}(\mathbf{u}_i \mid \mathbf{x}_i, c_i) = \sigma_u^2\mathbf{I}_T$ and $\mathrm{Var}(c_i \mid \mathbf{x}_i) = \sigma_c^2$. Find $\mathrm{Var}(v_{it})$ and $\mathrm{Cov}(v_{it}, v_{is})$, $t \neq s$.

c. Under parts a and b, propose an estimator that is symptotically more efficient than the usual RE estimator.

14.11. Consider a multivariate regression model nonlinear in the parameters,

$$\mathbf{y}_i = \mathbf{X}_i \mathbf{g}(\boldsymbol{\theta}_o) + \mathbf{u}_i, \qquad \mathrm{E}(\mathbf{u}_i \mid \mathbf{X}_i) = \mathbf{0},$$

where $\mathbf{y}_i$ is $G \times 1$, $\mathbf{X}_i$ is $G \times K$, and $\mathbf{g} : \mathbb{R}^P \to \mathbb{R}^K$ is continuously differentiable. Explain how to estimate $\boldsymbol{\theta}_o$ using CMD.

Appendix 14A

Proof of Lemma 14.1: Given condition (14.49), $\mathbf{A}_1 = (1/\rho)\mathrm{E}(\mathbf{s}_1\mathbf{s}_1')$, a $P \times P$ symmetric matrix, and

$$\mathbf{V}_1 = \mathbf{A}_1^{-1}\mathrm{E}(\mathbf{s}_1\mathbf{s}_1')\mathbf{A}_1^{-1} = \rho^2[\mathrm{E}(\mathbf{s}_1\mathbf{s}_1')]^{-1},$$

where we drop the argument $\mathbf{w}$ for notational simplicity. Next, under condition (14.56), $\mathbf{A}_2 = (1/\rho)\mathrm{E}(\mathbf{s}_2'\mathbf{s}_1)$, and so

$$\mathbf{V}_2 = \mathbf{A}_2^{-1}\mathrm{E}(\mathbf{s}_2\mathbf{s}_2')(\mathbf{A}_2')^{-1} = \rho^2[\mathrm{E}(\mathbf{s}_2\mathbf{s}_1')]^{-1}\mathrm{E}(\mathbf{s}_2\mathbf{s}_2')[\mathrm{E}(\mathbf{s}_1\mathbf{s}_2')]^{-1}.$$

Now we use the standard result that $\mathbf{V}_2 - \mathbf{V}_1$ is positive semidefinite if and only if $\mathbf{V}_1^{-1} - \mathbf{V}_2^{-1}$ is p.s.d. But, dropping the term ρ^2 (which is simply a positive constant), we have

$$\mathbf{V}_1^{-1} - \mathbf{V}_2^{-1} = \mathrm{E}(\mathbf{s}_1\mathbf{s}_1') - \mathrm{E}(\mathbf{s}_1\mathbf{s}_2')[\mathrm{E}(\mathbf{s}_2\mathbf{s}_2')]^{-1}\mathrm{E}(\mathbf{s}_2\mathbf{s}_1') \equiv \mathrm{E}(\mathbf{r}_1\mathbf{r}_1'),$$

where $\mathbf{r}_1$ is the $P \times 1$ population residual from the population regression $\mathbf{s}_1$ on $\mathbf{s}_2$. As $\mathrm{E}(\mathbf{r}_1\mathbf{r}_1')$ is necessarily p.s.d., this step completes the proof.

IV NONLINEAR MODELS AND RELATED TOPICS

We now apply the general methods of Part III to study specific nonlinear models that often arise in applications. Many nonlinear econometric models are intended to explain limited dependent variables. Roughly, a **limited dependent variable** is a variable whose range is restricted in some important way. Most variables encountered in economics are limited in range, but not all require special treatment. For example, many variables—wage, population, and food consumption, to name just a few—can only take on positive values. If a strictly positive variable takes on numerous values, we can avoid special econometric tools by taking the log of the variable and then using a linear model.

When the variable to be explained, y, is discrete and takes on a finite number of values, it makes little sense to treat it as an approximately continuous variable. Discreteness of y does not in itself mean that a linear model for $\mathrm{E}(y \mid \mathbf{x})$ is inappropriate. However, in Chapter 15 we will see that linear models have certain drawbacks for modeling binary responses, and we will treat nonlinear models such as probit and logit. We cover basic multinomial response models in Chapter 16, including the case when the response has a natural ordering.

Other kinds of limited dependent variables arise in econometric analysis, especially when modeling choices by individuals, families, or firms. Optimizing behavior often leads to corner solutions for some nontrivial fraction of the population. For example, during any given time, a fairly large fraction of the working age population does not work outside the home. Annual hours worked has a population distribution spread out over a range of values, but with a pileup at the value zero. While it could be that a linear model is appropriate for modeling expected hours worked, a linear model will likely lead to negative predicted hours worked for some people. Taking the natural log is not possible because of the corner solution at zero. In Chapter 17 we discuss econometric models that are better suited for describing these kinds of limited dependent variables.

In Chapter 18 we cover count, fractional, and other nonnegative response variables. Our emphasis is on estimating the conditional mean, and therefore we focus on estimation methods that do not require specific distributional assumptions (although they may nominally specify a distribution in a quasi-maximum likelihood analysis).

In Chapter 19 we shift gears and study several problems concerning missing data, including data censoring, sample selection, and attrition. This is the first chapter where we confront the possibility that the sample we have to work with is not necessarily a random sample on all variables appearing in the underlying population model. Chapter 20 treats additional sampling issues, including stratified sampling and cluster sampling.

Chapter 21 considers estimation of treatment effects, where we explicitly introduce a counterfactual setting that is fundamental to the contemporary literature. This chapter shows how switching regression models and random coefficient models (with endogenous explanatory variables) fits into the treatment effect framework. Chapter 22 concludes with an introduction to modern duration analysis.

15 Binary Response Models

15.1 Introduction

In binary response models, the variable to be explained, y, is a random variable taking on the values zero and one, which indicate whether or not a certain event has occurred. For example, $y = 1$ if a person is employed, $y = 0$ otherwise; $y = 1$ if a family contributes to charity during a particular year, $y = 0$ otherwise; $y = 1$ if a firm has a particular type of pension plan, $y = 0$ otherwise. Regardless of the definition of y, it is traditional to refer to $y = 1$ as a *success* and $y = 0$ as a *failure*.

As in the case of linear models, we often call y the explained variable, the response variable, the dependent variable, or the endogenous variable; $\mathbf{x} \equiv (x_1, x_2, \ldots, x_K)$ is the vector of explanatory variables, regressors, independent variables, exogenous variables, or covariates.

In binary response models, interest lies primarily in the **response probability**,

$$p(\mathbf{x}) \equiv \mathrm{P}(y = 1 \mid \mathbf{x}) = \mathrm{P}(y = 1 \mid x_1, x_2, \ldots, x_K), \tag{15.1}$$

for various values of $\mathbf{x}$. For example, when y is an employment indicator, $\mathbf{x}$ might contain various individual characteristics such as education, age, marital status, and other factors that affect employment status, such as a binary indicator variable for participation in a recent job training program, or measures of past criminal behavior.

For a continuous variable, x_j, the partial effect of x_j on the response probability is

$$\frac{\partial \mathrm{P}(y = 1 \mid \mathbf{x})}{\partial x_j} = \frac{\partial p(\mathbf{x})}{\partial x_j}. \tag{15.2}$$

When multiplied by Δx_j, equation (15.2) gives the approximate change in $\mathrm{P}(y = 1 \mid \mathbf{x})$ when x_j increases by Δx_j, holding all other variables fixed (for "small" Δx_j). Of course if, say, $x_1 \equiv z$ and $x_2 \equiv z^2$ for some variable z (for example, z could be work experience), we would be interested in $\partial p(\mathbf{x})/\partial z$.

If x_K is a binary variable, interest lies in

$$p(x_1, x_2, \ldots, x_{K-1}, 1) - p(x_1, x_2, \ldots, x_{K-1}, 0), \tag{15.3}$$

which is the difference in response probabilities when $x_K = 1$ and $x_K = 0$. For most of the models we consider, whether a variable x_j is continuous or discrete, the partial effect of x_j on $p(\mathbf{x})$ depends on all of $\mathbf{x}$.

In studying binary response models, we need to recall some basic facts about Bernoulli (zero-one) random variables. The only difference between the setup here and that in basic statistics is the conditioning on $\mathbf{x}$. If $\mathrm{P}(y = 1 \mid \mathbf{x}) = p(\mathbf{x})$ then $\mathrm{P}(y = 0 \mid \mathbf{x}) = 1 - p(\mathbf{x})$, $\mathrm{E}(y \mid \mathbf{x}) = p(\mathbf{x})$, and $\mathrm{Var}(y \mid \mathbf{x}) = p(\mathbf{x})[1 - p(\mathbf{x})]$.

15.2 Linear Probability Model for Binary Response

The **linear probability model (LPM)** for binary response y is specified as

$$\mathrm{P}(y = 1 \mid \mathbf{x}) = \beta_0 + \beta_1 x_1 + \beta_2 x_2 + \cdots + \beta_K x_K. \tag{15.4}$$

As usual, the x_j can be functions of underlying explanatory variables, which would simply change the interpretations of the β_j. Assuming that x_1 is not functionally related to the other explanatory variables, $\beta_1 = \partial \mathrm{P}(y = 1 \mid \mathbf{x})/\partial x_1$. Therefore, β_1 is the change in the probability of success given a one-unit increase in x_1. If x_1 is a binary explanatory variable, β_1 is just the difference in the probability of success when $x_1 = 1$ and $x_1 = 0$, holding the other x_j fixed.

Using functions such as quadratics, logarithms, and so on among the independent variables causes no new difficulties. The important point is that the β_j now measures the effects of the explanatory variables x_j on a particular probability.

In deciding on an appropriate estimation technique, it is useful to derive the conditional mean and variance of y. Since y is a Bernoulli random variable, these are simply

$$\mathrm{E}(y \mid \mathbf{x}) = \beta_0 + \beta_1 x_1 + \beta_2 x_2 + \cdots + \beta_K x_K \tag{15.5}$$

$$\mathrm{Var}(y \mid \mathbf{x}) = \mathbf{x}\boldsymbol{\beta}(1 - \mathbf{x}\boldsymbol{\beta}), \tag{15.6}$$

where $\mathbf{x}\boldsymbol{\beta}$ is shorthand for the right-hand side of equation (15.5).

Equation (15.5) implies that, given a random sample, the ordinary least squares (OLS) regression of y on $1, x_1, x_2, \ldots, x_K$ produces consistent and even unbiased estimators of the β_j. Equation (15.6) means that heteroskedasticity is present unless all of the slope coefficients $\beta_1, \ldots, \beta_K$ are zero. A nice way to deal with this issue is to use standard heteroskedasticity-robust standard errors and t statistics. Further, robust tests of multiple restrictions should also be used. There is one case where the usual F statistic can be used, and that is to test for joint significance of all variables (leaving the constant unrestricted). This test is asymptotically valid because $\mathrm{Var}(y \mid \mathbf{x})$ is constant under this particular null hypothesis.

If we operate under the assumption that $\mathrm{P}(y = 1 \mid \mathbf{x})$ is given by equation (15.4), then we can obtain an asymptotically more efficient estimator by applying weighted least squares (WLS). Let $\hat{\boldsymbol{\beta}}$ be the OLS estimator, and let $\hat{y}_i$ denote the OLS fitted values. Then, provided $0 < \hat{y}_i < 1$ for *all* observations i, define the estimated standard deviation as $\hat{\sigma}_i \equiv [\hat{y}_i(1 - \hat{y}_i)]^{1/2}$. Then the WLS estimator, $\boldsymbol{\beta}^*$, is obtained from the OLS regression

$$y_i/\hat{\sigma}_i \text{ on } 1/\hat{\sigma}_i, x_{i1}/\hat{\sigma}_i, \ldots, x_{iK}/\hat{\sigma}_i, \qquad i = 1, 2, \ldots, N. \tag{15.7}$$

The usual standard errors from this regression are valid, as follows from the treatment of weighted least squares in Chapter 12. In addition, all other testing can be done using F statistics or LM statistics using weighted regressions.

If some of the OLS fitted values are not between zero and one, WLS analysis is not possible without ad hoc adjustments to bring deviant fitted values into the unit interval. Further, since the OLS fitted value $\hat{y}_i$ is an estimate of the conditional probability $\mathrm{P}(y_i = 1 \mid \mathbf{x}_i)$, it is somewhat awkward if the predicted probability is negative or above unity.

Aside from the issue of fitted values being outside the unit interval, the LPM implies that a ceteris paribus unit increase in x_j always changes $\mathrm{P}(y = 1 \mid \mathbf{x})$ by the same amount, regardless of the initial value of x_j. This feature of the LPM cannot literally be true because continually increasing one of the x_j would eventually drive $\mathrm{P}(y = 1 \mid \mathbf{x})$ to be less than zero or greater than one.

A sensible posture is to simply view the LPM as the linear projection of y on the explanatory variables. Recall from Chapter 2 that the linear projection provides the best least squares fit among linear functions of $\mathbf{x}$ (although $\mathbf{x}$ itself might include nonlinear functions of underlying explanatory variables). If we operate within this scenario, OLS estimation of the LPM is attractive because it consistently estimates the parameters in the linear projection. The WLS estimator can be viewed as a linear projection on weighted variables, which may not be of as much interest, particularly because the weights are not obtained from $\mathrm{Var}(y \mid \mathbf{x})$ if (15.4) fails.

If the main purpose of estimating a binary response model is to approximate the partial effects of the explanatory variables, averaged across the distribution of $\mathbf{x}$, then the LPM often does a very good job. (Some evidence on how well it does can be obtained by comparing the OLS coefficients with the average partial effects from the nonlinear models we turn to in Section 15.3.) The fact that some predicted probabilities are outside the unit interval need not be a serious concern. But there is no guarantee that the LPM provides good estimates of the partial effects for a wide range of covariate values, especially for extreme values of $\mathbf{x}$.

Example 15.1 (Married Women's Labor Force Participation): We use the data from MROZ.RAW to estimate a linear probability model for labor force participation (*inlf*) of married women. Of the 753 women in the sample, 428 report working nonzero hours during the year. The variables we use to explain labor force participation are age, education, experience, nonwife income in thousands (*nwifeinc*), number of children less than six years of age (*kidslt6*), and number of children between 6 and 18 inclusive (*kidsge6*); 606 women report having no young children, while 118 report having exactly one young child. The usual OLS standard errors are in parentheses, while the heteroskedasticity-robust standard errors are in brackets:

$$\begin{aligned}
\widehat{inlf} = {} & \underset{\substack{(.154)\\ [.151]}}{.586} - \underset{\substack{(.0014)\\ [.0015]}}{.0034}\, nwifeinc + \underset{\substack{(.007)\\ [.007]}}{.038}\, educ + \underset{\substack{(.006)\\ [.006]}}{.039}\, exper - \underset{\substack{(.00018)\\ [.00019]}}{.00060}\, exper^2 \\
& - \underset{\substack{(.002)\\ [.002]}}{.016}\, age - \underset{\substack{(.034)\\ [.032]}}{.262}\, kidslt6 + \underset{\substack{(.013)\\ [.013]}}{.013}\, kidsge6
\end{aligned}$$

$N = 753, \qquad R^2 = .264$

With the exception of *kidsge6*, all coefficients have sensible signs and are statistically significant; *kidsge6* is neither statistically significant nor practically important. The coefficient on *nwifeinc* means that if nonwife income increases by 10 ($10,000), the probability of being in the labor force is predicted to fall by .034. This is a small effect given that an increase in income by $10,000 in 1975 dollars is very large in this sample. (The average of *nwifeinc* is about $20,129 with standard deviation $11,635.) Having one more small child is estimated to reduce the probability of $inlf = 1$ by about .262, which is a fairly large effect.

Of the 753 fitted probabilities, 33 are outside the unit interval. Rather than using some adjustment to those 33 fitted values and applying WLS, we just use OLS and report heteroskedasticity-robust standard errors. Interestingly, these differ in practically unimportant ways from the usual OLS standard errors.

The case for the LPM is even stronger if most of the x_j are discrete and take on only a few values. In the previous example, to allow a diminishing effect of young children on the probability of labor force participation, we can break *kidslt6* into three binary indicators: no young children, one young child, and two or more young children. The last two indicators can be used in place of *kidslt6* to allow the first young child to have a larger effect than subsequent young children. (Interestingly, when this method is used, the marginal effects of the first and second young children are virtually the same. The estimated effect of the first child is about $-.263$, and the additional reduction in the probability of labor force participation for the next child is about $-.274$.)

In the extreme case where the model is *saturated*—that is, $\mathbf{x}$ contains dummy variables for mutually exclusive and exhaustive categories—the LPM is completely general. The fitted probabilities are simply the average y_i within each cell defined by the different values of $\mathbf{x}$; we need not worry about fitted probabilities less than zero or greater than one. See Problem 15.1.

15.3 Index Models for Binary Response: Probit and Logit

We now study binary response models of the form

$$\mathrm{P}(y = 1 \mid \mathbf{x}) = G(\mathbf{x}\boldsymbol{\beta}) \equiv p(\mathbf{x}), \tag{15.8}$$

where $\mathbf{x}$ is $1 \times K$, $\boldsymbol{\beta}$ is $K \times 1$, and we take the first element of $\mathbf{x}$ to be unity. Examples where $\mathbf{x}$ does not contain unity are rare in practice. For the linear probability model, $G(z) = z$ is the identity function, which means that the response probabilities cannot be between 0 and 1 for all $\mathbf{x}$ and $\boldsymbol{\beta}$. In this section we assume that $G(\cdot)$ takes on values in the open unit interval: $0 < G(z) < 1$ for all $z \in \mathbb{R}$.

The model in equation (15.8) is generally called an **index model** because it restricts the way in which the response probability depends on $\mathbf{x}$: $p(\mathbf{x})$ is a function of $\mathbf{x}$ only through the *index* $\mathbf{x}\boldsymbol{\beta} = \beta_1 + \beta_2 x_2 + \cdots + \beta_K x_K$. The function G maps the index into the response probability.

In most applications, G is a cumulative distribution function (cdf) whose specific form can sometimes be derived from an underlying economic model. For example, in Problem 15.2 you are asked to derive an index model from a utility-based model of charitable giving. The binary indicator y equals unity if a family contributes to charity and zero otherwise. The vector $\mathbf{x}$ contains family characteristics, income, and the price of a charitable contribution (as determined by marginal tax rates). Under a normality assumption on a particular unobservable taste variable, G is the standard normal cdf.

Index models where G is a cdf can be derived more generally from an underlying **latent variable model**, as in Example 13.1:

$$y^* = \mathbf{x}\boldsymbol{\beta} + e, \qquad y = 1[y^* > 0], \tag{15.9}$$

where e is a continuously distributed variable independent of $\mathbf{x}$ and the distribution of e is symmetric about zero; recall from Chapter 13 that $1[\cdot]$ is the indicator function. If G is the cdf of e, then, because the pdf of e is symmetric about zero, $1 - G(-z) = G(z)$ for all real numbers z. Therefore,

$$\mathrm{P}(y = 1 \mid \mathbf{x}) = \mathrm{P}(y^* > 0 \mid \mathbf{x}) = \mathrm{P}(e > -\mathbf{x}\boldsymbol{\beta} \mid \mathbf{x}) = 1 - G(-\mathbf{x}\boldsymbol{\beta}) = G(\mathbf{x}\boldsymbol{\beta}),$$

which is exactly equation (15.8).

There is no particular reason for requiring e to be symmetrically distributed in the latent variable model, but this happens to be the case for the binary response models applied most often.

In most applications of binary response models, the primary goal is to explain the effects of the x_j on the response probability $P(y = 1 \mid \mathbf{x})$. The latent variable formulation tends to give the impression that we are primarily interested in the effects of each x_j on y^*. As we will see, the *direction* of the effects of x_j on $E(y^* \mid \mathbf{x}) = \mathbf{x}\boldsymbol{\beta}$ and on $E(y \mid \mathbf{x}) = P(y = 1 \mid \mathbf{x}) = G(\mathbf{x}\boldsymbol{\beta})$ are the same. But the latent variable y^* rarely has a well-defined unit of measurement (for example, y^* might be measured in utility units). Therefore, the magnitude of β_j is not especially meaningful except in special cases.

The **probit model** is the special case of equation (15.8) with

$$G(z) = \Phi(z) \equiv \int_{-\infty}^{z} \phi(v)\, dv, \tag{15.10}$$

where $\phi(z)$ is the standard normal density

$$\phi(z) = (2\pi)^{-1/2} \exp(-z^2/2). \tag{15.11}$$

The probit model can be derived from the latent variable formulation when e has a standard normal distribution.

The **logit model** is a special case of equation (15.8) with

$$G(z) = \Lambda(z) \equiv \exp(z)/[1 + \exp(z)]. \tag{15.12}$$

This model arises from the model (15.9) when e has a standard logistic distribution.

The general specification (15.8) allows us to cover probit, logit, and a number of other binary choice models in one framework. In fact, in what follows we do not even need G to be a cdf, but we do assume that $G(z)$ is strictly between zero and unity for all real numbers z.

In order to successfully apply probit and logit models, it is important to know how to interpret the β_j on both continuous and discrete explanatory variables. First, if x_j is continuous,

$$\frac{\partial p(\mathbf{x})}{\partial x_j} = g(\mathbf{x}\boldsymbol{\beta})\beta_j, \qquad \text{where } g(z) \equiv \frac{dG}{dz}(z). \tag{15.13}$$

Therefore, the partial effect of x_j on $p(\mathbf{x})$ depends on $\mathbf{x}$ through $g(\mathbf{x}\boldsymbol{\beta})$. If $G(\cdot)$ is a strictly increasing cdf, as in the probit and logit cases, $g(z) > 0$ for all z. Therefore, the sign of the effect is given by the sign of β_j. Also, the *relative* effects do not depend on $\mathbf{x}$: for continuous variables x_j and x_h, the ratio of the partial effects is constant and given by the ratio of the corresponding coefficients: $\dfrac{\partial p(\mathbf{x})/\partial x_j}{\partial p(\mathbf{x})/\partial x_h} = \beta_j/\beta_h$. In the typical case that g is a symmetric density about zero, with unique mode at zero, the largest effect is when $\mathbf{x}\boldsymbol{\beta} = 0$. For example, in the probit case with $g(z) = \phi(z)$, $g(0) = \phi(0) = 1/\sqrt{2\pi} \approx .399$. In the logit case, $g(z) = \exp(z)/[1 + \exp(z)]^2$, and so $g(0) = .25$.

If x_K is a binary explanatory variable, then the partial effect from changing x_K from zero to one, holding all other variables fixed, is simply

$$G(\beta_1 + \beta_2 x_2 + \cdots + \beta_{K-1} x_{K-1} + \beta_K) - G(\beta_1 + \beta_2 x_2 + \cdots + \beta_{K-1} x_{K-1}). \tag{15.14}$$

Again, this expression depends on all other values of the other x_j. For example, if y is an employment indicator and x_j is a dummy variable indicating participation in a job training program, then expression (15.14) is the change in the probability of employment due to the job training program; this depends on other characteristics that affect employability, such as education and experience. Knowing the sign of β_K is enough to determine whether the program had a positive or negative effect. But to find the *magnitude* of the effect, we have to estimate expression (15.14).

We can also use the difference in expression (15.14) for other kinds of discrete variables (such as number of children). If x_K denotes this variable, then the effect on the probability of x_K going from c_K to $c_K + 1$ is simply

$$\begin{aligned} &G[\beta_1 + \beta_2 x_2 + \cdots + \beta_{K-1} x_{K-1} + \beta_K(c_K + 1)] \\ &\quad - G(\beta_1 + \beta_2 x_2 + \cdots + \beta_{K-1} x_{K-1} + \beta_K c_K). \end{aligned} \tag{15.15}$$

It is straightforward to include standard functional forms among the explanatory variables. For example, in the model

$$\mathrm{P}(y = 1 \mid \mathbf{z}) = G[\beta_0 + \beta_1 z_1 + \beta_2 z_1^2 + \beta_3 \log(z_2) + \beta_4 z_3],$$

the partial effect of z_1 on $\mathrm{P}(y = 1 \mid \mathbf{z})$ is $\partial \mathrm{P}(y = 1 \mid \mathbf{z})/\partial z_1 = g(\mathbf{x}\boldsymbol{\beta})(\beta_1 + 2\beta_2 z_1)$, where $\mathbf{x}\boldsymbol{\beta} = \beta_0 + \beta_1 z_1 + \beta_2 z_1^2 + \beta_3 \log(z_2) + \beta_4 z_3$. It follows that if the quadratic in z_1 has a hump shape or a **U** shape, the turning point in the response probability is $|\beta_1/(2\beta_2)|$ (because $g(\mathbf{x}\boldsymbol{\beta}) > 0$). Also, $\partial \mathrm{P}(y = 1 \mid \mathbf{z})/\partial \log(z_2) = g(\mathbf{x}\boldsymbol{\beta})\beta_3$, and so $g(\mathbf{x}\boldsymbol{\beta})(\beta_3/100)$ is the approximate change in $\mathrm{P}(y = 1 \mid \mathbf{z})$ given a 1 *percent* increase in z_2. Models with interactions among explanatory variables, including interactions between discrete and continuous variables, are handled similarly. When measuring the effects of discrete variables, we should use expression (15.15).

15.4 Maximum Likelihood Estimation of Binary Response Index Models

Assume we have N independent, identically distributed observations following the model (15.8). Since we essentially covered the case of probit in Chapter 13, the discussion here will be brief. To estimate the model by (conditional) maximum likelihood (MLE), we need the log-likelihood function for each i. The density of y_i given $\mathbf{x}_i$ can be written as

$$f(y \mid \mathbf{x}_i; \boldsymbol{\beta}) = [G(\mathbf{x}_i\boldsymbol{\beta})]^y[1 - G(\mathbf{x}_i\boldsymbol{\beta})]^{1-y}, \qquad y = 0, 1. \tag{15.16}$$

The log likelihood for observation i is a function of the $K \times 1$ vector of parameters and the data $(\mathbf{x}_i, y_i)$:

$$\ell_i(\boldsymbol{\beta}) = y_i \log[G(\mathbf{x}_i\boldsymbol{\beta})] + (1 - y_i) \log[1 - G(\mathbf{x}_i\boldsymbol{\beta})]. \tag{15.17}$$

(Recall from Chapter 13 that, technically speaking, we should distinguish the "true" value of beta, $\boldsymbol{\beta}_o$, from a generic value. For conciseness we do not do so here.) Restricting $G(\cdot)$ to be strictly between zero and one ensures that $\ell_i(\boldsymbol{\beta})$ is well defined for all values of $\boldsymbol{\beta}$.

As usual, the log likelihood for a sample size of N is $\mathscr{L}(\boldsymbol{\beta}) = \sum_{i=1}^{N} \ell_i(\boldsymbol{\beta})$, and the MLE of $\boldsymbol{\beta}$, denoted $\hat{\boldsymbol{\beta}}$, maximizes this log likelihood. If $G(\cdot)$ is the standard normal cdf, then $\hat{\boldsymbol{\beta}}$ is the **probit estimator**; if $G(\cdot)$ is the logistic cdf, then $\hat{\boldsymbol{\beta}}$ is the **logit estimator**. From the general maximum likelihood results we know that $\hat{\boldsymbol{\beta}}$ is consistent and asymptotically normal. We can also easily estimate the asymptotic variance $\hat{\boldsymbol{\beta}}$.

We assume that $G(\cdot)$ is twice continuously differentiable, an assumption that is usually satisfied in applications (and, in particular, for probit and logit). As before, the function $g(z)$ is the derivative of $G(z)$. For the probit model, $g(z) = \phi(z)$, and for the logit model, $g(z) = \exp(z)/[1 + \exp(z)]^2$.

Using the same calculations for the probit example as in Chapter 13, the score of the conditional log likelihood for observation i can be shown to be

$$\mathbf{s}_i(\boldsymbol{\beta}) \equiv \frac{g(\mathbf{x}_i\boldsymbol{\beta})\mathbf{x}_i'[y_i - G(\mathbf{x}_i\boldsymbol{\beta})]}{G(\mathbf{x}_i\boldsymbol{\beta})[1 - G(\mathbf{x}_i\boldsymbol{\beta})]}. \tag{15.18}$$

Similarly, the expected value of the Hessian conditional on $\mathbf{x}_i$ is

$$-\mathrm{E}[\mathbf{H}_i(\boldsymbol{\beta}) \mid \mathbf{x}_i] = \frac{[g(\mathbf{x}_i\boldsymbol{\beta})]^2\mathbf{x}_i'\mathbf{x}_i}{\{G(\mathbf{x}_i\boldsymbol{\beta})[1 - G(\mathbf{x}_i\boldsymbol{\beta})]\}} \equiv \mathbf{A}(\mathbf{x}_i, \boldsymbol{\beta}), \tag{15.19}$$

which is a $K \times K$ positive semidefinite (p.s.d.) matrix for each i. From the general conditional MLE results in Chapter 13, $\mathrm{Avar}(\hat{\boldsymbol{\beta}})$ is estimated as

$$\widehat{\mathrm{Avar}(\hat{\boldsymbol{\beta}})} \equiv \left\{\sum_{i=1}^{N} \frac{[g(\mathbf{x}_i\hat{\boldsymbol{\beta}})]^2\mathbf{x}_i'\mathbf{x}_i}{G(\mathbf{x}_i\hat{\boldsymbol{\beta}})[1 - G(\mathbf{x}_i\hat{\boldsymbol{\beta}})]}\right\}^{-1} \equiv \hat{\mathbf{V}}. \tag{15.20}$$

In most cases the inverse exists, and when it does, $\hat{\mathbf{V}}$ is positive definite. If the matrix in equation (15.20) is not invertible, then perfect collinearity probably exists among the regressors.

As usual, we treat $\hat{\boldsymbol{\beta}}$ as being normally distributed with mean zero and variance matrix in equation (15.20). The (asymptotic) standard error of $\hat{\beta}_j$ is the square root of the jth diagonal element of $\hat{\mathbf{V}}$. These can be used to construct t statistics, which have a limiting standard normal distribution, and to construct approximate confidence intervals for each population parameter. These are reported with the estimates for packages that perform logit and probit. We discuss multiple hypothesis testing in the next section.

Some packages also compute Huber-White standard errors as an option for probit and logit analysis, using the sandwich form (13.71). While the robust variance matrix is consistent, using it in equation (15.20) means we must think that the binary response model is incorrectly specified. Unlike with nonlinear regression, in a binary response model it is not possible to correctly specify $\mathrm{E}(y \mid \mathbf{x})$ but to misspecify $\mathrm{Var}(y \mid \mathbf{x})$. Once we have specified $\mathrm{P}(y = 1 \mid \mathbf{x})$, we have specified all conditional moments of y given $\mathbf{x}$. Nevertheless, as we discussed in Section 13.11, it may be prudent to act as if all models are merely approximations to the truth, in which case inference should be based on the sandwich estimator in equation (13.71). (The sandwich estimator that uses the expected Hessian, as in equation (12.49), makes no sense in the binary response context because the expected Hessian cannot be computed without assumption (15.8).)

In Section 15.8 we will see that, when using binary response models with panel data, it is sometimes important to compute variance matrix estimators that are robust to serial dependence. But this need arises as a result of dependence across time or subgroup, and not because the response probability is misspecified.

15.5 Testing in Binary Response Index Models

Any of the three tests from general MLE analysis—the Wald, likelihood ratio (LR), or Lagrange multiplier (LM) test—can be used to test hypotheses in binary response contexts. Since the tests are all asymptotically equivalent under local alternatives, the choice of statistic usually depends on computational simplicity (since finite sample comparisons must be limited in scope). In the following subsections we discuss some testing situations that often arise in binary choice analysis, and we recommend particular tests for their computational advantages.

15.5.1 Testing Multiple Exclusion Restrictions

Consider the model

$$\mathrm{P}(y = 1 \mid \mathbf{x}, \mathbf{z}) = G(\mathbf{x}\boldsymbol{\beta} + \mathbf{z}\boldsymbol{\gamma}), \tag{15.21}$$

where $\mathbf{x}$ is $1 \times K$ and $\mathbf{z}$ is $1 \times Q$. We wish to test the null hypothesis $\mathrm{H}_0 : \boldsymbol{\gamma} = \mathbf{0}$, so we are testing Q exclusion restrictions. The elements of $\mathbf{z}$ can be functions of $\mathbf{x}$, such as quadratics and interactions—in which case the test is a pure functional form test. Or, the $\mathbf{z}$ can be additional explanatory variables. For example, $\mathbf{z}$ could contain dummy variables for occupation or region. In any case, the form of the test is the same.

Some packages, such as Stata, compute the Wald statistic for exclusion restrictions using a simple command following estimation of the general model. This capability makes it very easy to test multiple exclusion restrictions, provided the dimension of $(\mathbf{x}, \mathbf{z})$ is not so large as to make probit estimation difficult.

The likelihood ratio statistic is also easy to use. Let $\mathscr{L}_{ur}$ denote the value of the log-likelihood function from probit of y on $\mathbf{x}$ and $\mathbf{z}$ (the unrestricted model), and let $\mathscr{L}_r$ denote the value of the likelihood function from probit of y on $\mathbf{x}$ (the restricted model). Then the LR test of $\mathrm{H}_0 : \boldsymbol{\gamma} = \mathbf{0}$ is simply $2(\mathscr{L}_{ur} - \mathscr{L}_r)$, which has an asymptotic χ^2_Q distribution under H_0. This is analogous to the usual F statistic in OLS analysis of a linear model.

The score or LM test is attractive if the unrestricted model is difficult to estimate. In this section, let $\hat{\boldsymbol{\beta}}$ denote the *restricted* estimator of $\boldsymbol{\beta}$, that is, the probit or logit estimator with $\mathbf{z}$ excluded from the model. The LM statistic using the estimated expected Hessian, $\hat{\mathbf{A}}_i$ (see equation (15.20) and Section 12.6.2), can be shown to be numerically identical to the following: (1) Define $\hat{u}_i \equiv y_i - G(\mathbf{x}_i\hat{\boldsymbol{\beta}})$, $\hat{G}_i \equiv G(\mathbf{x}_i\hat{\boldsymbol{\beta}})$, and $\hat{g}_i \equiv g(\mathbf{x}_i\hat{\boldsymbol{\beta}})$. These are all obtainable after estimating the model without $\mathbf{z}$. (2) Use all N observations to run the auxiliary OLS regression

$$\frac{\hat{u}_i}{\sqrt{\hat{G}_i(1 - \hat{G}_i)}} \text{ on } \frac{\hat{g}_i}{\sqrt{\hat{G}_i(1 - \hat{G}_i)}}\mathbf{x}_i, \quad \frac{\hat{g}_i}{\sqrt{\hat{G}_i(1 - \hat{G}_i)}}\mathbf{z}_i. \tag{15.22}$$

The LM statistic is equal to the explained sum of squares from this regression. A test that is asymptotically (but not numerically) equivalent is NR^2_u, where R^2_u is the uncentered R-squared from regression (15.22).

The LM procedure is rather easy to remember. The term $\hat{g}_i\mathbf{x}_i$ is the gradient of the mean function $G(\mathbf{x}_i\boldsymbol{\beta} + \mathbf{z}_i\boldsymbol{\gamma})$ with respect to $\boldsymbol{\beta}$, evaluated at $\boldsymbol{\beta} = \hat{\boldsymbol{\beta}}$ and $\boldsymbol{\gamma} = \mathbf{0}$. Similarly, $\hat{g}_i\mathbf{z}_i$ is the gradient of $G(\mathbf{x}_i\boldsymbol{\beta} + \mathbf{z}_i\boldsymbol{\gamma})$ with respect to $\boldsymbol{\gamma}$, again evaluated at $\boldsymbol{\beta} = \hat{\boldsymbol{\beta}}$ and $\boldsymbol{\gamma} = \mathbf{0}$. Finally, under $\mathrm{H}_0 : \boldsymbol{\gamma} = \mathbf{0}$, the conditional variance of u_i given $(\mathbf{x}_i, \mathbf{z}_i)$ is $G(\mathbf{x}_i\boldsymbol{\beta})[1 - G(\mathbf{x}_i\boldsymbol{\beta})]$; therefore, $[\hat{G}_i(1 - \hat{G}_i)]^{1/2}$ is an estimate of the conditional standard deviation of u_i. The dependent variable in regression (15.22) is often called a **standardized residual** because it is an estimate of $u_i/[G_i(1 - G_i)]^{1/2}$, which has unit conditional (and unconditional) variance. The regressors are simply the gradient of the conditional mean function with respect to both sets of parameters, evaluated under H_0, and weighted by the estimated inverse conditional standard deviation. The first set of regressors in regression (15.22) is $1 \times K$ and the second set is $1 \times Q$.

Under H_0, $LM \sim \chi^2_Q$. The LM approach can be an attractive alternative to the LR statistic if $\mathbf{z}$ has large dimension, since with many explanatory variables probit can be difficult to estimate.

15.5.2 Testing Nonlinear Hypotheses about $\boldsymbol{\beta}$

For testing nonlinear restrictions on $\boldsymbol{\beta}$ in equation (15.8), the Wald statistic is computationally the easiest because the unrestricted estimator of $\boldsymbol{\beta}$, which is just probit or logit, is easy to obtain. Actually imposing nonlinear restrictions in estimation—which is required to apply the score or likelihood ratio methods—can be difficult. However, we must also remember that the Wald statistic for testing nonlinear restrictions is not invariant to reparameterizations, whereas the LM and LR statistics are. (See Sections 12.6 and 13.6; for the LM statistic, we would probably use the expected Hessian.)

Let the restictions on $\boldsymbol{\beta}$ be given by H_0: $\mathbf{c}(\boldsymbol{\beta}) = \mathbf{0}$, where $\mathbf{c}(\boldsymbol{\beta})$ is a $Q \times 1$ vector of possibly nonlinear functions satisfying the differentiability and rank requirements from Chapter 13. Then, from the general MLE analysis, the Wald statistic is simply

$$W = \mathbf{c}(\hat{\boldsymbol{\beta}})'[\nabla_\beta \mathbf{c}(\hat{\boldsymbol{\beta}})\hat{\mathbf{V}}\nabla_\beta \mathbf{c}(\hat{\boldsymbol{\beta}})']^{-1}\mathbf{c}(\hat{\boldsymbol{\beta}}) \tag{15.23}$$

where $\hat{\mathbf{V}}$ is given in equation (15.20) and $\nabla_\beta \mathbf{c}(\hat{\boldsymbol{\beta}})$ is the $Q \times K$ Jacobian of $\mathbf{c}(\boldsymbol{\beta})$ evaluated at $\hat{\boldsymbol{\beta}}$.

15.5.3 Tests against More General Alternatives

In addition to testing for omitted variables, sometimes we wish to test the probit or logit model against a more general functional form. When the alternatives are not standard binary response models, the Wald and LR statistics are cumbersome to apply, whereas the LM approach is convenient because it only requires estimation of the null model.

As an example of a more complicated binary choice model, consider the latent variable model (15.9) but assume that $e \mid \mathbf{x} \sim \text{Normal}[0, \exp(2\mathbf{x}_1\boldsymbol{\delta})]$, where $\mathbf{x}_1$ is $1 \times K_1$ subset of $\mathbf{x}$ that excludes a constant and $\boldsymbol{\delta}$ is a $K_1 \times 1$ vector of additional parameters. (In many cases we would take $\mathbf{x}_1$ to be all nonconstant elements of $\mathbf{x}$.) Therefore, there is heteroskedasticity in the latent variable model, so that e is no longer independent of $\mathbf{x}$. The standard deviation of e given $\mathbf{x}$ is simply $\exp(\mathbf{x}_1\boldsymbol{\delta})$. Define $r = e/\exp(\mathbf{x}_1\boldsymbol{\delta})$, so that r is independent of $\mathbf{x}$ with a standard normal distribution. Then

$$\mathrm{P}(y=1\,|\,\mathbf{x}) = \mathrm{P}(e > -\mathbf{x}\boldsymbol{\beta}\,|\,\mathbf{x}) = \mathrm{P}[\exp(-\mathbf{x}_1\boldsymbol{\delta})e > -\exp(-\mathbf{x}_1\boldsymbol{\delta})\mathbf{x}\boldsymbol{\beta}]$$
$$= \mathrm{P}[r > -\exp(-\mathbf{x}_1\boldsymbol{\delta})\mathbf{x}\boldsymbol{\beta}] = \Phi[\exp(-\mathbf{x}_1\boldsymbol{\delta})\mathbf{x}\boldsymbol{\beta}]. \tag{15.24}$$

The partial effects of x_j on $\mathrm{P}(y=1\,|\,\mathbf{x})$ are much more complicated in equation (15.24) than in equation (15.8). When $\boldsymbol{\delta} = \mathbf{0}$, we obtain the standard probit model. Therefore, a test of the probit functional form for the response probability is a test of $\mathrm{H}_0 : \boldsymbol{\delta} = \mathbf{0}$.

To obtain the LM test of $\boldsymbol{\delta} = \mathbf{0}$ in equation (15.24), it is useful to derive the LM test for an index model against a more general alternative. Consider

$$\mathrm{P}(y=1\,|\,\mathbf{x}) = m(\mathbf{x}\boldsymbol{\beta}, \mathbf{x}, \boldsymbol{\delta}), \tag{15.25}$$

where $\boldsymbol{\delta}$ is a $Q \times 1$ vector of parameters. We wish to test $\mathrm{H}_0 : \boldsymbol{\delta} = \boldsymbol{\delta}_0$, where $\boldsymbol{\delta}_0$ is often (but not always) a vector of zeros. We assume that, under the null, we obtain a standard index model (probit or logit, usually):

$$G(\mathbf{x}\boldsymbol{\beta}) = m(\mathbf{x}\boldsymbol{\beta}, \mathbf{x}, \boldsymbol{\delta}_0). \tag{15.26}$$

In the previous example, $G(\cdot) = \Phi(\cdot)$, $\boldsymbol{\delta}_0 = \mathbf{0}$, and $m(\mathbf{x}\boldsymbol{\beta}, \mathbf{x}, \boldsymbol{\delta}) = \Phi[\exp(-\mathbf{x}_1\boldsymbol{\delta})\mathbf{x}\boldsymbol{\beta}]$.

Let $\hat{\boldsymbol{\beta}}$ be the probit or logit estimator of $\boldsymbol{\beta}$ obtained under $\boldsymbol{\delta} = \boldsymbol{\delta}_0$. Define $\hat{u}_i \equiv y_i - G(\mathbf{x}_i\hat{\boldsymbol{\beta}})$, $\hat{G}_i \equiv G(\mathbf{x}_i\hat{\boldsymbol{\beta}})$, and $\hat{g}_i \equiv g(\mathbf{x}_i\hat{\boldsymbol{\beta}})$. The gradient of the mean function $m(\mathbf{x}_i\boldsymbol{\beta}, \mathbf{x}_i, \boldsymbol{\delta})$ with respect to $\boldsymbol{\beta}$, evaluated at $\boldsymbol{\delta}_0$, is simply $g(\mathbf{x}_i\boldsymbol{\beta})\mathbf{x}_i$. The only other piece we need is the gradient of $m(\mathbf{x}_i\boldsymbol{\beta}, \mathbf{x}_i, \boldsymbol{\delta})$ with respect to $\boldsymbol{\delta}$, evaluated at $\boldsymbol{\delta}_0$. Denote this $1 \times Q$ vector as $\nabla_\delta m(\mathbf{x}_i\boldsymbol{\beta}, \mathbf{x}_i, \boldsymbol{\delta}_0)$. Further, set $\nabla_\delta \hat{m}_i \equiv \nabla_\delta m(\mathbf{x}_i\hat{\boldsymbol{\beta}}, \mathbf{x}_i, \boldsymbol{\delta}_0)$. The *LM* statistic can be obtained as the explained sum of squares from the regression

$$\frac{\hat{u}_i}{\sqrt{\hat{G}_i(1-\hat{G}_i)}} \quad \text{on} \quad \frac{\hat{g}_i}{\sqrt{\hat{G}_i(1-\hat{G}_i)}}\mathbf{x}_i, \quad \frac{\nabla_\delta \hat{m}_i}{\sqrt{\hat{G}_i(1-\hat{G}_i)}}, \tag{15.27}$$

which is quite similar to regression (15.22). The null distribution of the *LM* statistic is χ^2_Q, where Q is the dimension of $\boldsymbol{\delta}$. An asymptotically equivalent statistic is NR_u^2.

When applying this test to the preceding probit example, we have only $\nabla_\delta \hat{m}_i$ left to compute. But $m(\mathbf{x}_i\boldsymbol{\beta}, \mathbf{x}_i, \boldsymbol{\delta}) = \Phi[\exp(-\mathbf{x}_{i1}\boldsymbol{\delta})\mathbf{x}_i\boldsymbol{\beta}]$, and so

$$\nabla_\delta m(\mathbf{x}_i\boldsymbol{\beta}, \mathbf{x}_i, \boldsymbol{\delta}) = -(\mathbf{x}_i\boldsymbol{\beta})\exp(-\mathbf{x}_{i1}\boldsymbol{\delta})\mathbf{x}_{i1}\phi[\exp(-\mathbf{x}_{i1}\boldsymbol{\delta})\mathbf{x}_i\boldsymbol{\beta}].$$

When evaluated at $\boldsymbol{\beta} = \hat{\boldsymbol{\beta}}$ and $\boldsymbol{\delta} = \mathbf{0}$ (the null value), we get $\nabla_\delta \hat{m}_i = -(\mathbf{x}_i\hat{\boldsymbol{\beta}})\phi(\mathbf{x}_i\hat{\boldsymbol{\beta}})\mathbf{x}_{i1}$ $\equiv -(\mathbf{x}_i\hat{\boldsymbol{\beta}})\hat{\phi}_i\mathbf{x}_{i1}$, a $1 \times K_1$ vector. Regression (15.27) becomes

$$\frac{\hat{u}_i}{\sqrt{\hat{\Phi}_i(1-\hat{\Phi}_i)}} \text{ on } \frac{\hat{\phi}_i}{\sqrt{\hat{\Phi}_i(1-\hat{\Phi}_i)}}\mathbf{x}_i, \qquad \frac{(\mathbf{x}_i\hat{\boldsymbol{\beta}})\hat{\phi}_i}{\sqrt{\hat{\Phi}_i(1-\hat{\Phi}_i)}}\mathbf{x}_{i1}. \tag{15.28}$$

(We drop the minus sign because it does not affect the value of the explained sum of squares or R_u^2.) Under the null hypothesis that the probit model is correctly specified, $LM \sim \chi^2_{K_1}$. This statistic is easy to compute after estimation by probit.

For a one-degree-of-freedom test regardless of the dimension of $\mathbf{x}_i$, replace the last term in regression (15.28) with $(\mathbf{x}_i\hat{\boldsymbol{\beta}})^2\hat{\phi}_i/\sqrt{\hat{\Phi}_i(1-\hat{\Phi}_i)}$, and then the explained sum of squares is distributed asymptotically as χ_1^2. See Davidson and MacKinnon (1984) for further examples.

As we discussed briefly in Chapters 12 and 13, variable addition versions of specification tests can be somewhat easier to compute. Rather than running the regression in equation (15.28), we can instead estimate the auxiliary probit model with response probability $\Phi[\mathbf{x}_i\boldsymbol{\beta} + (\mathbf{x}_i\hat{\boldsymbol{\beta}})\mathbf{x}_{i1}\boldsymbol{\delta}]$ and test $\mathrm{H}_0: \boldsymbol{\delta} = \mathbf{0}$ using a standard Wald test. Again, $\hat{\boldsymbol{\beta}}$ denotes the original probit estimates from probit of y_i on $\mathbf{x}_i$. The specification test is obtained from probit of y_i on $\mathbf{x}_i$, $(\mathbf{x}_i\hat{\boldsymbol{\beta}})\mathbf{x}_{i1}$ and testing the last Q terms for joint significance. It is easy to see that the variable addition test (VAT) is asymptotically equivalent to the score test, and the VAT circumvents the need to explicitly obtain the weighted residuals and gradients. The VAT approach also makes it clear that the score test for heteroskedasticity in the error from the latent model is indistinguishable from testing for a particular kind of interactive effect in the covariates. We might have arrived at such a test directly, without modeling $\mathrm{Var}(e \mid \mathbf{x})$.

15.6 Reporting the Results for Probit and Logit

Several statistics should be reported routinely in any probit or logit (or other binary choice) analysis. The $\hat{\beta}_j$, their standard errors, and the value of the likelihood function are reported by all software packages that do binary response analysis. The $\hat{\beta}_j$ give the signs of the partial effects of each x_j on the response probability, and the statistical significance of x_j is determined by whether we can reject $\mathrm{H}_0: \beta_j = 0$.

One measure of goodness of fit that is sometimes reported is the **percent correctly predicted**. The easiest way to describe this statistic is to define a binary predictor of y_i to be one if the predicted probability is at least .5, and zero otherwise. More precisely, define the binary variable $\tilde{y}_i = 1$ if $G(\mathbf{x}_i\hat{\boldsymbol{\beta}}) \geq .5$ and $\tilde{y}_i = 0$ if $G(\mathbf{x}_i\hat{\boldsymbol{\beta}}) < .5$. Given $\{\tilde{y}_i : i = 1, 2, \ldots, N\}$, we can see how well $\tilde{y}_i$ predicts y_i across all observations. There are four possible outcomes on each pair, $(y_i, \tilde{y}_i)$; when both are zero or both are one, we make the correct prediction. In the two cases where one of the pair is zero and the other is one, we make the incorrect prediction. The percent correctly predicted is the percent of times that $\tilde{y}_i = y_i$. (This goodness-of-fit measure can be computed for the linear probability model, too.)

While the percent correctly predicted is useful as a goodness-of-fit measure, it can be misleading. In particular, it is possible to get rather high percentages correctly predicted even when the least likely outcome is very poorly predicted. For example, suppose that $N = 200$, 160 observations have $y_i = 0$, and, out of these 160 observations, 140 of the $\tilde{y}_i$ are also zero (so we correctly predict 87.5 percent of the zero outcomes.) Even if *none* of the predictions is correct when $y_i = 1$, we still correctly predict 70% of all outcomes $(140/200 = .70)$. Often, we hope be able to predict the least likely outcome (such as whether someone is arrested for committing a crime), and we only know how well we do that by obtaining the percent correctly predicted for each outcome. It is easily shown that the overall percent correctly predicted is the weighted average of the percent correctly predicted for $y = 0$ and $y = 1$, with the weights being the fraction of zero and one outcomes on y, respectively.

Some have criticized the prediction rule described above for always using a threshold value of .5, especially when one of the outcomes is unlikely. For example, if $\bar{y} = .08$ (only eight percent "successes" in the sample), it could be that we *never* predict $y_i = 1$ because the estimated probability of success is never greater than .5. One alternative is to use the fraction of successes in the sample as the threshold—.08 in the previous example. In other words, define $\tilde{y}_i = 1$ when $G(\mathbf{x}_i\hat{\boldsymbol{\beta}}) \geq .08$, and zero otherwise. Using this rule will certainly increase the number of predicted successes, but not without cost: we necessarily make more mistakes—perhaps many more—in predicting the zero outcomes ("failures"). In terms of the overall percent correctly predicted, we may actually do worse than when using the traditional .5 threshold.

A third possibility is to choose the threshold such that the fraction of $\tilde{y}_i = 1$ in the sample is the same (or very close) to $\bar{y}$. In other words, search over threshold values τ, $0 < \tau < 1$, such that if we define $\tilde{y}_i = 1$ when $G(\mathbf{x}_i\hat{\boldsymbol{\beta}}) \geq \tau$, then $\sum_{i=1}^{n} \tilde{y}_i \approx \sum_{i=1}^{n} y_i$. (The trial-and-error effort required to find the desired value of τ can be tedious, but it is feasible. In some cases, it will not be possible to make the number of predicted successes exactly the same as the number of successes in the sample.) Now, given the set of binary predictors $\tilde{y}_i$, we can compute the percent correctly predicted for each of the two outcomes, as well as the overall percent correctly predicted.

Various **pseudo-R-squared** measures have been proposed for binary response. McFadden (1974) suggests the measure $1 - \mathscr{L}_{ur}/\mathscr{L}_o$, where $\mathscr{L}_{ur}$ is the log-likelihood function for the estimated model and $\mathscr{L}_o$ is the log-likelihood function in the model with only an intercept. Because the log likelihood for a binary response model is always negative, $|\mathscr{L}_{ur}| \leq |\mathscr{L}_o|$, and so the pseudo-$R$-squared is always between zero and one. Alternatively, we can use a sum of squared residuals measure: $1 - \text{SSR}_{ur}/\text{SSR}_o$, where SSR_{ur} is the sum of squared residuals $\hat{u}_i = y_i - G(\mathbf{x}_i\hat{\boldsymbol{\beta}})$ and SSR_o is the total sum of squares of y_i. Several other measures have been suggested (see, for example, Maddala, 1983, Chap. 2), but goodness of fit is not as important as statistical and economic significance of the explanatory variables. Estrella (1998) contains a recent comparison of goodness-of-fit measures for binary response.

Usually we want to estimate the effects of the variables x_j on the response probabilities $\text{P}(y = 1 \mid \mathbf{x})$. If x_j is (roughly) continuous, then

$$\Delta\widehat{\text{P}(y = 1 \mid \mathbf{x})} \approx [g(\mathbf{x}\hat{\boldsymbol{\beta}})\hat{\beta}_j]\Delta x_j \tag{15.29}$$

for small changes in x_j. (As usual when using calculus, the notion of "small" here is somewhat vague.) Therefore, the estimated partial effect of a continuous variable on the response probability, evaluated at $\mathbf{x}$, is $g(\mathbf{x}\hat{\boldsymbol{\beta}})\hat{\beta}_j$. Because $g(\mathbf{x}\hat{\boldsymbol{\beta}})$ depends on $\mathbf{x}$, we need to decide which partial effects to report. We could report this scale factor at, say, medians of the explanatory variables, or at different quantiles. For summarizing the magnitudes of the effects, it is useful to have a single scale factor that can be used to multiply the coefficients on (roughly) continuous variables. Often the sample averages of the x_j are plugged in to get $g(\bar{\mathbf{x}}\hat{\boldsymbol{\beta}})$, with $\bar{x}_1 \equiv 1$ because we include a constant. We call the resulting partial effect the **partial effect at the average (PEA)**.

The PEA is easy to compute, but it does have drawbacks. First, it need not represent the partial effect for any particular unit in the population. That is, the average of the explanatory variables may not, in any sensible way, represent the average unit in the population. One issue is that, if $\mathbf{x}$ contains nonlinear functions of underlying variables, such as logarithms, we must decide whether to use the average of the nonlinear function or the nonlinear function of the average. The latter has some appeal—for example, if $\log(inc)$ is an explanatory variable, evaluate $\log(inc)$ at $\overline{inc}$, rather than use $\overline{\log(inc)}$—but software packages that support PEA estimation (such as Stata, with its *mfx*, for "marginal effects," command) necessarily use the average of the nonlinear functions (because one must create the nonlinear functions before including them in logit or probit).

If two or more elements of $\mathbf{x}$ are functionally related, such as quadratics or interactions, it is not even clear what the PEAs of individual coefficients mean. For example, suppose $x_{K-1} = age$ and $x_K = age^2$. Then the reported PEAs for age and age^2 are $g(\bar{\mathbf{x}}\hat{\boldsymbol{\beta}})\hat{\beta}_{K-1}$ and $g(\bar{\mathbf{x}}\hat{\boldsymbol{\beta}})\hat{\beta}_K$, respectively, where $\bar{\mathbf{x}} = (1, \bar{x}_2, \ldots, \bar{x}_{K-2}, \overline{age}, \overline{age^2})$. These PEAs do not tell us what we want to know about the partial effect of age on $\text{P}(y = 1 \mid \mathbf{x})$. For any $\mathbf{x}$, the estimated partial effect is $g(\mathbf{x}\hat{\boldsymbol{\beta}})(\hat{\beta}_{K-1} + 2\hat{\beta}_K age)$. Now, we might be interested in evaluating this partial effect at the mean values, but that would entail using $\overline{age}^2$, rather than $\overline{age^2}$, inside $g(\cdot)$. If we are really interested in the effect of *age* on the response probability, we might want to evaluate the partial effect at several different values of *age*, perhaps evaluating the other explanatory variables at their means. If $\hat{\beta}_{K-1}$ and $\hat{\beta}_K$ have different signs, the estimated turning point in the relationship is just as in models linear in the parameters: $\widehat{age}^* = |\hat{\beta}_{K-1}/(2\hat{\beta}_K)|$. The usual turning point calculation works because $g(\mathbf{x}\hat{\boldsymbol{\beta}}) > 0$ for all $\mathbf{x}$. Similar care must be used for obtaining partial effects when interactions are included in $\mathbf{x}$.

For discrete variables, it is well known that the average need not even be a possible outcome of the variable. If, say, x_2 is a binary variable, $\bar{x}_2$ is the fraction of ones in the sample, and therefore cannot correspond to a particular unit (which must have zero or one). For example, if $x_2 = female$ is a gender dummy, then the PEA is the partial effect when *female* is replaced with the fraction of women in the sample. One way to overcome this conceptual problem is to compute partial effects separately for $x_2 = 1$ and $x_2 = 0$, but then we no longer have a single number to report as the partial effect. Similar comments hold for other discrete variables, such as number of children. If the average is 1.5, plugging this value into $g(\cdot)$ does not produce the partial effect for any particular family.

To obtain standard errors of the partial effects in equation (15.29) we can use the delta method. Consider the case $j = K$ for notational simplicity, and for given $\mathbf{x}$, define $\delta_K = \beta_K g(\mathbf{x}\boldsymbol{\beta}) = \partial \mathrm{P}(y = 1 \mid \mathbf{x})/\partial x_K$. Write this relation as $\delta_K = h(\boldsymbol{\beta})$ to denote that this is a (nonlinear) function of the vector $\boldsymbol{\beta}$. We assume $x_1 = 1$. The gradient of $h(\boldsymbol{\beta})$ is

$$\nabla_\beta h(\boldsymbol{\beta}) = \left[\beta_K \frac{dg}{dz}(\mathbf{x}\boldsymbol{\beta}), \beta_K x_2 \frac{dg}{dz}(\mathbf{x}\boldsymbol{\beta}), \ldots, \beta_K x_{K-1} \frac{dg}{dz}(\mathbf{x}\boldsymbol{\beta}), \beta_K x_K \frac{dg}{dz}(\mathbf{x}\boldsymbol{\beta}) + g(\mathbf{x}\boldsymbol{\beta})\right],$$

where dg/dz is simply the derivative of g with respect to its argument. The delta method implies that the asymptotic variance of $\hat{\delta}_K$ is estimated as

$$[\nabla_\beta h(\hat{\boldsymbol{\beta}})]\hat{\mathbf{V}}[\nabla_\beta h(\hat{\boldsymbol{\beta}})]', \tag{15.30}$$

where $\hat{\mathbf{V}}$ is the asymptotic variance estimate of $\hat{\boldsymbol{\beta}}$. The asymptotic standard error of $\hat{\delta}_K$ is simply the square root of expression (15.30). This calculation allows us to obtain a large-sample confidence interval for $\hat{\delta}_K$. The program Stata does this calculation for logit and probit using the *mfx* command. Alternatively, we can apply the bootstrap as discussed in Chapter 12.

If x_K is a discrete variable, then we can estimate the change in the predicted probability in going from c_K to $c_K + 1$ as

$$\begin{aligned}\hat{\delta}_K = {} & G[\hat{\beta}_1 + \hat{\beta}_2\bar{x}_2 + \cdots + \hat{\beta}_{K-1}\bar{x}_{K-1} + \hat{\beta}_K(c_K + 1)] \\ & - G(\hat{\beta}_1 + \hat{\beta}_2\bar{x}_2 + \cdots + \hat{\beta}_{K-1}\bar{x}_{K-1} + \hat{\beta}_K c_K).\end{aligned} \tag{15.31}$$

In particular, when x_K is a binary variable, set $c_K = 0$. Of course, the other x_j's can be evaluated anywhere, but the use of sample averages is typical. The delta method can be used to obtain a standard error of equation (15.31). For probit, Stata does this calculation when x_K is a binary variable. Usually the calculations ignore the fact that $\bar{x}_j$ is an estimate of $\mathrm{E}(x_j)$ in applying the delta method. If we are truly interested in $\beta_K g(\boldsymbol{\mu}_x \boldsymbol{\beta})$, the estimation error in $\bar{\mathbf{x}}$ can be accounted for, but it makes the calculation more complicated, and it is unlikely to have a large effect. The bootstrap would properly account for the sampling variation in $\bar{\mathbf{x}}$ when $\bar{\mathbf{x}}$ is recomputed for each bootstrap replication.

An alternative way to summarize the estimated marginal effects is to estimate the average value of $\beta_K g(\mathbf{x}\boldsymbol{\beta})$ across the population, or $\beta_K \mathrm{E}[g(\mathbf{x}\boldsymbol{\beta})]$. This quantity is the **average partial effect (APE)** that we discussed generally in Chapter 2, and also for linear models with random coefficients in Chapter 4. Here we are averaging across the distribution of all observable covariates. A consistent estimator of the APE is

$$\hat{\beta}_K \left[N^{-1} \sum_{i=1}^{N} g(\mathbf{x}_i \hat{\boldsymbol{\beta}}) \right] \tag{15.32}$$

when x_K is continuous or

$$N^{-1} \sum_{i=1}^{N} [G(\hat{\beta}_1 + \hat{\beta}_2 x_{i2} + \cdots + \hat{\beta}_{K-1} x_{i,K-1} + \hat{\beta}_K) - G(\hat{\beta}_1 + \hat{\beta}_2 x_{i2} + \cdots + \hat{\beta}_{K-1} x_{i,K-1})] \tag{15.33}$$

when x_K is binary. Naturally, we can use equation (15.33) to estimate the APE from changing x_K (continuous or discrete) from any two values, say c_K^0 to c_K^1. Then $\hat{\beta}_K$ is replaced with $\hat{\beta}_K c_K^1$ in the first term and we insert $\hat{\beta}_K c_K^0$ into the second occurrence of $G(\cdot)$. Further, in either equation (15.32) or (15.33), we can fix some of the explanatory variables at specific values and average across the remaining ones. For example, suppose that in a logit or probit model of employment, x_K is a job training binary indicator and x_{K-1} is a race indicator—say, one for nonwhite, zero for white. Then, rather than compute (15.33), we can set $x_{K-1} = 1$ and compute the APE for nonwhites, and then set $x_{K-1} = 0$ to obtain the APE for whites.

As in the case of the PEA, if some elements of $\mathbf{x}$ are functions of each other, obtaining APEs of the form in equation (15.32) is not especially useful. If, say, $x_{K-1} = age$ and $x_K = age^2$, we can estimate the APE of *age* by averaging the individual partial effects, $(\hat{\beta}_{K-1} + 2\hat{\beta}_K age_i) \times g(\mathbf{x}_i \hat{\boldsymbol{\beta}})$, across i. Again, it probably makes more sense to evaluate the partial effect at different values of *age* and then to average these across the other variables, say, $N^{-1} \sum_{i=1}^{N} (\hat{\beta}_{K-1} + 2\hat{\beta}_K age^o) \times g(\hat{\beta}_1 + \hat{\beta}_2 x_{i2} + \cdots + \hat{\beta}_{K-2} x_{i,K-2} + \hat{\beta}_{K-1} age^o + \hat{\beta}_K (age^o)^2)$ for a given value age^o.

Generally, we should not expect the scale factors for the PEAs and APEs to be similar. That is, we should not expect $g(\bar{\mathbf{x}}\hat{\boldsymbol{\beta}})$ to be similar to $N^{-1}\sum_{i=1}^{N} g(\mathbf{x}_i\hat{\boldsymbol{\beta}})$. The reason is simple: the average of a nonlinear function (the APE scale) is not the nonlinear function of the average (the PEA scale). In the population the scales are not the same either, because the expected value does not pass through nonlinear functions: $g[\mathrm{E}(\mathbf{x}\boldsymbol{\beta})] \neq \mathrm{E}[g(\mathbf{x}\boldsymbol{\beta})]$.

Equation (15.33) has a nice interpretation for policy analysis, where x_K is the binary policy indicator (equal to one when the policy is in effect, zero otherwise). We can view each summand in (15.33) as follows. Regardless of whether unit i was subject to the policy, we can obtain the predicted probability in each regime. The term in brackets in equation (15.33) is the difference in the estimated probability that $y_i = 1$ with and without participation. In other words, we compute the (counterfactual) effect of the policy for each cross section unit i, and then average these differences across all i. This gives us an estimate of the average effect of the policy. We will have much more to say about a counterfactual framework for policy analysis in Chapter 21 and the estimation of *average treatment effects*, of which equation (15.33) is an example.

We can obtain standard errors of the estimators in (15.32) and (15.33) by applying the bootstrap to an average, as described in Section 12.8.2, or we can use the delta method; see Problem 15.15.

Unlike the magnitudes of the coefficient estimates, the APEs (and, to a lesser extent, the PEAs) can be compared across models. It is rare to find, say, probit and logit estimates having different signs unless the coefficients are estimated imprecisely. But logit, probit, and the LPM implicitly use different scale factors. The scale for the LPM is unity. For logit and probit, we can look at the functions $g(\cdot)$ at zero to obtain a rough idea of how the $\hat{\beta}_j$—at least the slopes on the continuous variables—may differ. For probit, $g(0) \approx .4$ and for logit $g(0) = .25$. Therefore, we expect the logit slope coefficients to have the largest magnitude, followed by the probit estimates, followed by the LPM estimates. In fact, sometimes some (crude) rules of thumb are adopted: multiply the probit coefficients by 1.6 and the LPM coefficients by 4 to make them roughly comparable to the logit estimates. The LPM estimates are multiplied by 2.5 to make them comparable to the probit estimates. If $\bar{\mathbf{x}}\hat{\boldsymbol{\beta}}$ is close to zero, then $g(\bar{\mathbf{x}}\hat{\boldsymbol{\beta}})$ will be close to .25 for logit and close to .4 for probit, and then the rules of thumb for adjusting coefficients can be justified based on the PEAs. (When one of the outcomes on y is much less likely than the other, it is unlikely that $\bar{\mathbf{x}}\hat{\boldsymbol{\beta}}$ will be close to zero.) Generally, it is a good idea to compute the PEAs and APEs, as well as partial effects at other interesting values of $\mathbf{x}$, or at values that allow us to determine policy effects for different groups in the population.

As a general rule, the estimates from an LPM estimation are more comparable to the APEs than to the PEAs. As mentioned above, the PEAs need not come close to representing an individual in the population. On the other hand, the APE is the partial effect averaged across the population and, in one case, we can show that the LPM estimates are consistent for the APEs *regardless of the actual function* $G(\cdot)$. In fact, using a result of Stoker (1986), we can say much more, for any kind of response variable y. Let $m(\mathbf{x}) = \mathrm{E}(y \mid \mathbf{x})$ be the conditional mean, so that $\boldsymbol{\lambda} = \mathrm{E}[\nabla_{\mathbf{x}} m(\mathbf{x})']$ is the vector of APEs, where now $\mathbf{x}$ just includes continuous covariates and no elements are functionally related. Under assumptions about the distribution of $\mathbf{x}$—which are generally satisified if $\mathbf{x}$ has convex, unbounded support—Stoker shows that $\mathrm{E}[\nabla_{\mathbf{x}} m(\mathbf{x})'] = -\mathrm{E}[m(\mathbf{x}) \times \nabla_{\mathbf{x}} \log f(\mathbf{x})'] = -\mathrm{E}[y \times \nabla_{\mathbf{x}} \log f(\mathbf{x})']$ (where the second equality follows by iterated expectations), and so the vector of APEs is simply $-\mathrm{E}[y \times \nabla_{\mathbf{x}} \log f(\mathbf{x})']$. Now, if $\mathbf{x} \sim \mathrm{Normal}(\boldsymbol{\mu}_{\mathbf{x}}, \boldsymbol{\Sigma}_{\mathbf{x}})$—that is, if $\mathbf{x}$ has a multivariate normal distribution—then it is easily shown that $\nabla_{\mathbf{x}} \log f(\mathbf{x}) = -(\mathbf{x} - \boldsymbol{\mu}_{\mathbf{x}})\boldsymbol{\Sigma}_{\mathbf{x}}^{-1}$. It follows by substitution that

$$\boldsymbol{\lambda} = \mathrm{E}[y \times \boldsymbol{\Sigma}_{\mathbf{x}}^{-1}(\mathbf{x} - \boldsymbol{\mu}_{\mathbf{x}})'] = \{\mathrm{E}[(\mathbf{x} - \boldsymbol{\mu}_{\mathbf{x}})'(\mathbf{x} - \boldsymbol{\mu}_{\mathbf{x}})]\}^{-1}\mathrm{E}[(\mathbf{x} - \boldsymbol{\mu}_{\mathbf{x}})'y],$$

which is simply the vector of slope coefficients from the linear projection of y on $1, \mathbf{x}$. This calculation demonstrates that, regardless of the conditional mean function $m(\mathbf{x})$, if $\mathbf{x}$ has a multivariate normal distribution, then a linear regression consistently estimates the APEs—or, in Stoker's (1986) terminology, the *average derivatives*.

The general result applies to binary responses. In fact, there is no reason to even specify the model in the index form $\mathrm{P}(y = 1 \mid \mathbf{x}) = G(\alpha + \mathbf{x}\boldsymbol{\beta})$. But, in this case—for continuously differentiable functions $G(\cdot)$—the vector of average partial effects is $\mathrm{E}[g(\alpha + \mathbf{x}\boldsymbol{\beta})]\boldsymbol{\beta}$, and we can conclude that $\boldsymbol{\lambda}$ estimates $\boldsymbol{\beta}$ up to the positive scale factor $\mathrm{E}[g(\alpha + \mathbf{x}\boldsymbol{\beta})]$. We discuss results of this sort further in Section 15.7.6.

The result we just derived is of limited practical value because the assumption that $\mathbf{x}$ is multivariate normal is very restrictive. In particular, it rules out discrete variables and continuous variables with asymmetric distributions. In the context of the index model $\mathrm{P}(y = 1 \mid \mathbf{x}) = G(\alpha + \mathbf{x}\boldsymbol{\beta})$, assuming that all elements of $\mathbf{x}$ are normally distributed is very restrictive. (For example, it rules out some staples of empirical work, such as quadratics and interactions, in addition to discrete explanatory variables.) Nevertheless, the result does show that estimation of an LPM can consistently estimate average partial effects, and it may be a good estimator for moderate deviations of $\mathbf{x}$ from normality.

Example 15.2 (Married Women's Labor Force Participation): We now estimate logit and probit models for women's labor force participation. For comparison, we

Table 15.1
LPM, Logit, and Probit Estimates of Labor Force Participation

Dependent Variable: *inlf*			
Independent Variable	LPM (OLS)	Logit (MLE)	Probit (MLE)
nwifeinc	−.0034 (.0015)	−.021 (.008)	−.012 (.005)
educ	.038 (.007)	.221 (.043)	.131 (.025)
exper	.039 (.006)	.206 (.032)	.123 (.019)
exper^2	−.00060 (.00019)	−.0032 (.0010)	−.0019 (.0006)
age	−.016 (.002)	−.088 (.015)	−.053 (.008)
kidslt6	−.262 (.032)	−1.443 (0.204)	−.868 (.119)
kidsge6	.013 (.013)	.060 (.075)	.036 (.043)
constant	.586 (.151)	.425 (.860)	.270 (.509)
Number of observations	753	753	753
Percent correctly predicted	73.4	73.6	73.4
Log-likelihood value	—	−401.77	−401.30
Pseudo-*R*-squared	.264	.220	.221

report the linear probability estimates. The results, with standard errors in parentheses, are given in Table 15.1 (for the LPM, these are heteroskedasticity-robust).

The estimates from the three models tell a consistent story. The signs of the coefficients are the same across models, and the same variables are statistically significant in each model. The pseudo-*R*-squared for the LPM is just the usual *R*-squared reported for OLS; for logit and probit the pseudo-*R*-squared is the measure based on the log likelihoods described previously. In terms of overall percent correctly predicted, the models do equally well. For the probit model, it correctly predicts "out of the labor force" about 63.1 percent of the time, and it correctly predicts "in the labor force" about 81.3 percent of the time. The LPM has the same overall percent correctly predicted, but there are slight differences within each outcome.

As we emphasized earlier, the *magnitudes* of the coefficients are not directly comparable across the models, although the ratios of coefficients on the (roughly) continuous explanatory variables are. For example, the ratios of the *nwifeinc* and *educ* coefficients are about $-.0895$, $-.0950$, and $-.0916$ for the LPM, logit, and probit models, respectively.

If we evaluate the standard normal probability density function, $\phi(\hat{\beta}_0 + \hat{\beta}_1 x_1 + \cdots + \hat{\beta}_k x_k)$, at the average values of the independent variables in the sample (including the average of $exper^2$), we obtain about .391. (This value is close to .4 because the outcomes on *inlf* are fairly balanced: about 56.7% of the women report being in the labor force. When one outcome is much more likely than the other, the scale factor tends to be much smaller.) We can multiply the coefficients on the roughly continuous variables—and maybe even the variables measuring the number of children—to get an estimate of the effect of a one-unit increase on the response probability, starting from the mean values. The scale factor for computing the PEAs for logit is about .243, which is close to .25, the value of the logistic density at zero. If we use these scale factors to compute the PEA for, say, *nwifeinc*, we get about $-.0051$ for logit and about $-.0047$ for probit. Both are somewhat larger in magnitude than the LPM effect, which is $-.0034$.

The scale factors for the APEs are smaller. For probit, the average of $g(\hat{\beta}_0 + \hat{\beta}_1 x_{i1} + \cdots + \hat{\beta}_K x_{iK})$ across i is about .301, and for logit it is .179. When we multiply these scale factors by the *nwifeinc* coefficients we get $-.0038$ for logit and $-.0036$ for probit. A bootstrap standard error for the probit estimate, using 500 bootstrap samples, is about .0016. As expected, the APEs are much closer to the LPM effect, and the bootstrap standard error of the APE is very close to the LPM standard error for the *nwifeinc* coeffcient, .0015. The same is true of the APEs for the other explanatory variables. Even for a discrete variable such as *kidslt*6—of which over 96% of the sample takes on zero or one—the APE for the logit model is about $-.258$, and for the probit it is $-.261$ (bootstrap standard error $= .033$). The partial effect in the LPM is $-.262$ (standard error $= .032$).

Potentially the biggest difference between the LPM model, on the one hand, and the logit and probit models on the other is that the LPM implies *constant* marginal effects for *educ*, *kidlt*6, and so on, while the logit and probit models allow for a diminishing effect—for continuous and discrete variables. For example, in the LPM, one more young child, whether going from zero to one or from one to two, is estimated to reduce the labor force participation of a women by .262, independent of the other income, education, age, and experience of the woman. We just saw that this is a good estimate of the average effect in the sense that it is similar to the estimates for logit and probit (when *kidstlt*6 is treated as a continuous variable). But the effect might differ across the population, and certainly the effect of having the first young child and the second young child might be different. To get an idea of how much a partial effect might differ from the APE, take a women with *nwifeinc* $= 20.13$, *educ* = 12.3, *exper* = 10.6, *age* = 42.5—which are roughly the sample averages—and *kidsge6* = 1. In the probit model, what is the estimated fall in the probability of being in the labor force when going from zero to one small child? We evaluate the standard normal cdf, $\Phi(\hat{\beta}_0 + \hat{\beta}_1 x_1 + \cdots + \hat{\beta}_K x_K)$ at *kidslt6* = 1 and *kidslt6* = 0, with the other explanatory variables set at the values just given. We get, roughly, $.373 - .707 = -.334$, which mean a .334 drop in the probability of being in the labor force. (The scaled coefficient for the PEA is about $-.347$, and so it is not much different.) This estimated effect is substantially larger than the constant effect obtained from the LPM. If the woman goes from one young child to two, the probability falls even more, but the marginal effect is not as large: $.117 - .373 = -.256$.

If we compute the difference in predicted probabilities for each woman at one and zero young children and then average these—that is, if we compute the APE in going from zero to one young child—the estimate is about $-.272$, while the APE in going from one to two is about $-.220$. The LPM estimate is close to the first estimate, which makes sense when interpreting the LPM as estimates of the average partial effect: less than 4 percent of women have more than one young child, and so the estimated effect of moving from one to two (and certainly from two to three) contributes very little to the APE.

Binary response models apply with little modification to independently pooled cross sections or to other data sets where the observations are independent but not necessarily identically distributed. Often year or other time-period dummy variables are included to account for aggregate time effects. Just as with linear models, probit can be used to evaluate the impact of certain policies in the context of a natural experiment; see Problem 15.13. An application is given in Gruber and Poterba (1994).

15.7 Specification Issues in Binary Response Models

We now turn to several issues that can arise in applying binary response models to economic data. All of these topics are relevant for general index models, but features of the normal distribution allow us to obtain concrete results in the context of probit models. Therefore, our primary focus is on probit models.

15.7.1 Neglected Heterogeneity

We begin by studying the consequences of omitting variables when those omitted variables are *independent* of the included explanatory variables. This is also called the **neglected heterogeneity** problem. The (structural) model of interest is

$$P(y = 1 \mid \mathbf{x}, c) = \Phi(\mathbf{x}\boldsymbol{\beta} + \gamma c), \tag{15.34}$$

where $\mathbf{x}$ is $1 \times K$ with $x_1 \equiv 1$ and c is a scalar. We are interested in the partial effects of the x_j on the probability of success, holding c (and the other elements of $\mathbf{x}$) fixed. We can write equation (15.34) in latent variable form as $y^* = \mathbf{x}\boldsymbol{\beta} + \gamma c + e$, where $y = 1[y^* > 0]$ and $e \mid \mathbf{x}, c \sim \text{Normal}(0,1)$. Because $x_1 = 1$, $\text{E}(c) = 0$ without loss of generality.

Now suppose that c is independent of $\mathbf{x}$ and $c \sim \text{Normal}(0, \tau^2)$. (Remember, this assumption is much stronger than $\text{Cov}(\mathbf{x}, c) = \mathbf{0}$ or even $\text{E}(c \mid \mathbf{x}) = 0$: under independence, the distribution of c given $\mathbf{x}$ does not depend on $\mathbf{x}$.) Given these assumptions, the composite term, $\gamma c + e$, is independent of $\mathbf{x}$ and has a $\text{Normal}(0, \gamma^2\tau^2 + 1)$ distribution. Therefore,

$$\text{P}(y = 1 \mid \mathbf{x}) = \text{P}(\gamma c + e > -\mathbf{x}\boldsymbol{\beta} \mid \mathbf{x}) = \Phi(\mathbf{x}\boldsymbol{\beta}/\sigma), \tag{15.35}$$

where $\sigma^2 \equiv \gamma^2\tau^2 + 1$. It follows immediately from equation (15.35) that probit of y on $\mathbf{x}$ consistently estimates $\boldsymbol{\beta}/\sigma$. In other words, if $\hat{\boldsymbol{\beta}}$ is the estimator from a probit of y on $\mathbf{x}$, then $\text{plim}\, \hat{\beta}_j = \beta_j/\sigma$. Because $\sigma = (\gamma^2\tau^2 + 1)^{1/2} > 1$ (unless $\gamma = 0$ or $\tau^2 = 0$), $|\beta_j/\sigma| < |\beta_j|$.

The attenuation bias in estimating β_j in the presence of neglected heterogeneity has prompted statements of the following kind: "In probit analysis, neglected heterogeneity is a much more serious problem than in linear models because, even if the omitted heterogeneity is independent of $\mathbf{x}$, the probit coefficients are inconsistent." We just derived that probit of y on $\mathbf{x}$ consistently estimates $\boldsymbol{\beta}/\sigma$ rather than $\boldsymbol{\beta}$, so the statement is technically correct. However, we should remember that, in nonlinear models, we usually want to estimate partial effects and not just parameters. For the purposes of obtaining the directions of the effects or the relative effects of the continuous explanatory variables, estimating $\boldsymbol{\beta}/\sigma$ is just as good as estimating $\boldsymbol{\beta}$.

To be more precise, the scaled coefficient, β_j/σ, has the same sign as β_j, and so we will correctly (with enough data) determine the direction of the partial effect of any variable—discrete, continuous, or some mixture—by estimating the scaled coefficients. Further, the ratio of any two scaled coefficients, β_j/σ and β_h/σ, is simply β_j/β_h. For a continuous x_j, the partial effect in model (15.34)—which we might call the "structural partial effect"—is

$$\partial \text{P}(y = 1 \mid \mathbf{x}, c)/\partial x_j = \beta_j \phi(\mathbf{x}\boldsymbol{\beta} + \gamma c). \tag{15.36}$$

Therefore, the ratio of partial effects for two continuous variables x_j and x_h is simply β_j/β_h—the same as the ratio of scaled coefficients.

Is there any quantity of interest we cannot estimate by not being able to estimate $\boldsymbol{\beta}$? Yes, although its importance is debatable. Because c is normalized so that $\text{E}(c) = 0$, we might be interested in the partial effect in (15.36) evaluated at $c = 0$, which is simply $\beta_j \phi(\mathbf{x}\boldsymbol{\beta})$. It is clear that we would need to consistently estimate $\boldsymbol{\beta}$ in order to estimate the partial effect at the mean value of heterogeneity (and any value of the covariates). What we consistently estimate from the probit of y on $\mathbf{x}$ is

$$(\beta_j/\sigma)\phi(\mathbf{x}\boldsymbol{\beta}/\sigma). \tag{15.37}$$

This expression shows that, if we are interested in the partial effects evaluated at $c = 0$, then probit of y on $\mathbf{x}$ does not do the trick. An interesting fact about expression (15.37) is that, even though β_j/σ is closer to zero than β_j, $\phi(\mathbf{x}\boldsymbol{\beta}/\sigma)$ is larger than $\phi(\mathbf{x}\boldsymbol{\beta})$ because $\phi(z)$ increases as $|z| \to 0$, and $\sigma > 1$. Therefore, for estimating the partial effects in equation (15.36) at $c = 0$, it is not clear for what values of $\mathbf{x}$ an attenuation bias exists. Plugging other values of c into equation (15.37) makes little sense, as we cannot identify γ, and even if we could, we generally know nothing about the distribution of c other than its mean is zero. Indeed, c is typically meant to capture such nebulous concepts as "ability," "health," or "taste for saving," and without further information we have no hope of estimating the distribution of these unobservable attributes.

With c having a normal distribution in the population, the partial effect evaluated at $c = 0$ describes only a small fraction of the population. (Technically, $\mathrm{P}(c = 0) = 0$.) Instead, we can estimate the average partial effect (APE), where we now average out the unobserved heterogeneity and are left with a function of $\mathbf{x}$. In particular, the APE is obtained, for given $\mathbf{x}$, by averaging equation (15.36) across the distribution of c in the population. For emphasis, let $\mathbf{x}^{\mathrm{o}}$ be a given value of the explanatory variables (which could be, but need not be, the mean value). When we plug $\mathbf{x}^{\mathrm{o}}$ into equation (15.36) and take the expected value with respect to the distribution of c, we get

$$\mathrm{E}[\beta_j \phi(\mathbf{x}^{\mathrm{o}}\boldsymbol{\beta} + \gamma c)] = (\beta_j/\sigma)\phi(\mathbf{x}^{\mathrm{o}}\boldsymbol{\beta}/\sigma). \tag{15.38}$$

In other words, probit of y on $\mathbf{x}$ consistently estimates the average partial effects, which is usually what we want.

The result in equation (15.38) follows from the general treatment of average partial effects in Section 2.2.5. In the current setup, there are no extra conditioning variables, $\mathbf{w}$, and the unobserved heterogeneity is independent of $\mathbf{x}$. It follows from equation (2.35) that the APE with respect to x_j, evaluated at $\mathbf{x}^{\mathrm{o}}$, is simply $\partial \mathrm{E}(y \mid \mathbf{x}^{\mathrm{o}})/\partial x_j$. But from the law of iterated expectations, $\mathrm{E}(y \mid \mathbf{x}) = \mathrm{E}_c[\Phi(\mathbf{x}\boldsymbol{\beta} + \gamma c)] = \Phi(\mathbf{x}\boldsymbol{\beta}/\sigma)$, where $\mathrm{E}_c(\cdot)$ denotes the expectation with respect to the distribution of c. The derivative of $\Phi(\mathbf{x}\boldsymbol{\beta}/\sigma)$ with respect to x_j is $(\beta_j/\sigma)\phi(\mathbf{x}\boldsymbol{\beta}/\sigma)$, which is what we wanted to show.

The bottom line is that omitted heterogeneity in probit models is not a problem when it is independent of $\mathbf{x}$: ignoring it preserves the signs of all partial effects, gives the same relative effects for continuous explanatory variables, and provides consistent estimates of the average partial effects. Of course, the previous arguments hinge on the normality of c and the probit structural equation. If the structural model (15.34) were, say, logit and if c were normally distributed, we would not get a probit or logit for the distribution of y given $\mathbf{x}$; the response probability is more complicated. The lesson from Section 2.2.5 is that we might as well work directly with models for $\mathrm{P}(y=1 \mid \mathbf{x})$ because partial effects of $\mathrm{P}(y=1 \mid \mathbf{x})$ are always the average of the partial effects of $\mathrm{P}(y=1 \mid \mathbf{x}, c)$ over the distribution of c.

If c is correlated with $\mathbf{x}$ or is otherwise dependent on $\mathbf{x}$ (for example, if $\mathrm{Var}(c \mid \mathbf{x})$ depends on $\mathbf{x}$), then omission of c is serious. In this case we cannot get consistent estimates of the average partial effects. For example, if $c \mid \mathbf{x} \sim \mathrm{Normal}(\mathbf{x}\boldsymbol{\delta}, \eta^2)$, then probit of y on $\mathbf{x}$ gives consistent estimates of $(\boldsymbol{\beta} + \gamma\boldsymbol{\delta})/\rho$, where $\rho^2 = \gamma^2\eta^2 + 1$. Unless $\gamma = 0$ or $\boldsymbol{\delta} = \mathbf{0}$, we do not consistently estimate $\boldsymbol{\beta}/\sigma$. This result is not surprising given what we know from the linear case with omitted variables correlated with the x_j. We now study what can be done to account for endogenous variables in probit models.

15.7.2 Continuous Endogenous Explanatory Variables

We now explicitly allow for the case where one of the explanatory variables is correlated with the error term in the latent variable model. One possibility is to estimate an LPM by 2SLS. This procedure is relatively easy and might provide a good estimate of the average effect.

If we want to estimate a probit model with endogenous explanatory variables, we must make some fairly strong assumptions. In this section we consider the case of a continuous endogenous explanatory variable.

Write the model as

$$y_1^* = \mathbf{z}_1\boldsymbol{\delta}_1 + \alpha_1 y_2 + u_1 \tag{15.39}$$

$$y_2 = \mathbf{z}_1\boldsymbol{\delta}_{21} + \mathbf{z}_2\boldsymbol{\delta}_{22} + v_2 = \mathbf{z}\boldsymbol{\delta}_2 + v_2 \tag{15.40}$$

$$y_1 = 1[y_1^* > 0], \tag{15.41}$$

where (u_1, v_2) has a zero mean, bivariate normal distribution, and is independent of $\mathbf{z}$. Equation (15.39), along with equation (15.41), is the structural equation; equation (15.40) is a reduced form for y_2, which is endogenous if u_1 and v_2 are correlated. If u_1 and v_2 are independent, there is no endogeneity problem. Because v_2 is normally distributed, we are assuming that y_2 given $\mathbf{z}$ is normal; thus y_2 should have features of a normal random variable. (For example, y_2 should not be a discrete variable.)

The model is applicable when y_2 is correlated with u_1 because of omitted variables or measurement error. It can also be applied to the case where y_2 is determined jointly with y_1, but with a caveat. If y_1 appears on the right-hand side in a linear structural equation for y_2, then the reduced form for y_2 cannot be found with v_2 having the stated properties. However, if y_1^* appears in a linear structural equation for y_2, then y_2 has the reduced form given by equation (15.40); see Maddala (1983, Chap. 7) for further discussion.

The normalization that gives the parameters in equation (15.39) an average partial effect interpretation, at least in the omitted variable and simultaneity contexts, is $\text{Var}(u_1) = 1$, just as in a probit model with all explanatory variables exogenous. To see this point, consider the outcome on y_1 at two different outcomes of y_2, say y_2^o and $y_2^o + 1$. Holding the observed exogenous factors fixed at $\mathbf{z}_1^o$, and holding u_1 fixed, the difference in responses is

$$1[\mathbf{z}_1^o\boldsymbol{\delta}_1 + \alpha_1(y_2^o + 1) + u_1 \geq 0] - 1[\mathbf{z}_1^o\boldsymbol{\delta}_1 + \alpha_1 y_2^o + u_1 \geq 0].$$

(This difference can take on the values -1, 0, and 1.) Because u_1 is unobserved, we cannot estimate the difference in responses for a given population unit. Nevertheless, if we average across the distribution of u_1, which is $\text{Normal}(0, 1)$, we obtain

$$\Phi[\mathbf{z}_1^o\boldsymbol{\delta}_1 + \alpha_1(y_2^o + 1)] - \Phi(\mathbf{z}_1^o\boldsymbol{\delta}_1 + \alpha_1 y_2^o).$$

Therefore, $\boldsymbol{\delta}_1$ and α_1 are the parameters appearing in the APE. (Alternatively, if we begin by allowing $\sigma_1^2 = \text{Var}(u_1) > 0$ to be unrestricted, the APE would depend on $\boldsymbol{\delta}_1/\sigma_1$ and α_1/σ_1, and so we should just rescale u_1 to have unit variance. The variance and slope parameters are not separately identified, anyway.) The proper normalization for $\text{Var}(u_1)$ should be kept in mind, as two-step procedures, which we cover in the following paragraphs, only consistently estimate $\boldsymbol{\delta}_1$ and α_1 up to scale; we have to do a little more work to obtain estimates of the APE.

The most useful two-step approach is a control function approach due to Rivers and Vuong (1988), as it leads to a simple test for endogeneity of y_2. To derive the procedure, first note that, under joint normality of (u_1, v_2), with $\text{Var}(u_1) = 1$, we can write

$$u_1 = \theta_1 v_2 + e_1, \tag{15.42}$$

where $\theta_1 = \eta_1/\tau_2^2$, $\eta_1 = \text{Cov}(v_2, u_1)$, $\tau_2^2 = \text{Var}(v_2)$, and e_1 is independent of $\mathbf{z}$ *and* v_2 (and therefore of y_2). Because of joint normality of (u_1, v_2), e_1 is also normally distributed with $\text{E}(e_1) = 0$ and $\text{Var}(e_1) = \text{Var}(u_1) - \eta_1^2/\tau_2^2 = 1 - \rho_1^2$, where $\rho_1 = \text{Corr}(v_2, u_1)$. We can now write

$$y_1^* = \mathbf{z}_1\boldsymbol{\delta}_1 + \alpha_1 y_2 + \theta_1 v_2 + e_1, \tag{15.43}$$

$$e_1 \mid \mathbf{z}, y_2, v_2 \sim \text{Normal}(0, 1 - \rho_1^2). \tag{15.44}$$

A standard calculation shows that

$$\mathrm{P}(y_1 = 1 \mid \mathbf{z}, y_2, v_2) = \Phi[(\mathbf{z}_1\boldsymbol{\delta}_1 + \alpha_1 y_2 + \theta_1 v_2)/(1 - \rho_1^2)^{1/2}].$$

Assuming for the moment that we observe v_2, then probit of y_1 on $\mathbf{z}_1$, y_2, and v_2 consistently estimates $\boldsymbol{\delta}_{\rho 1} \equiv \boldsymbol{\delta}_1/(1-\rho_1^2)^{1/2}$, $\alpha_{\rho 1} \equiv \alpha_1/(1-\rho_1^2)^{1/2}$, and $\theta_{\rho 1} \equiv \theta_1/(1-\rho_1^2)^{1/2}$. Notice that because $\rho_1^2 < 1$, each scaled coefficient is greater than its unscaled counterpart unless y_2 is exogenous ($\rho_1 = 0$).

Since we do not know $\boldsymbol{\delta}_2$, we must first estimate it, as in the following procedure:

Procedure 15.1: (a) Run the OLS regression y_2 on $\mathbf{z}$ and save the residuals $\hat{v}_2$.

(b) Run the probit y_1 on $\mathbf{z}_1$, y_2, $\hat{v}_2$ to get consistent estimators of the scaled coefficients $\boldsymbol{\delta}_{\rho 1}$, $\alpha_{\rho 1}$, and $\theta_{\rho 1}$.

A nice feature of Procedure 15.1 is that the usual probit t statistic on $\hat{v}_2$ is a valid test of the null hypothesis that y_2 is exogenous, that is, $\mathrm{H}_0 : \theta_1 = 0$. If $\theta_1 \neq 0$, the usual probit standard errors and test statistics are not strictly valid, and we have only estimated $\boldsymbol{\delta}_1$ and α_1 up to scale. The asymptotic variance of the two-step estimator can be derived using the M-estimator results in Section 12.5.2; see also Rivers and Vuong (1988). Problem 15.15 asks you to obtain the correct variance matrix and to show that it is always greater than the incorrect one, which ignores estimation of $\boldsymbol{\delta}_2$, when $\theta_1 \neq 0$. The bootstrap can be used, but some bootstrap samples may have little variation in y_1 if one outcome is much more likely.

Under $\mathrm{H}_0 : \theta_1 = 0$, $e_1 = u_1$, and so the distribution of v_2 plays no role under the null. Therefore, the *test* of exogeneity is valid without assuming normality or homoskedasticity of v_2, and it can be applied very broadly, even if y_2 is a binary variable. Unfortunately, if y_2 and u_1 are correlated, normality of v_2 is crucial.

Example 15.3 (Testing Exogeneity of Education in the Women's LFP Model): We test the null hypothesis that *educ* is exogenous in the married women's labor force participation equation. We first obtain the reduced form residuals, $\hat{v}_2$, from regressing *educ* on all exogenous variables, including *motheduc*, *fatheduc*, and *huseduc*. Then, we add $\hat{v}_2$ to the probit from Example 15.2. The t statistic on $\hat{v}_2$ is only .867, which is weak evidence against the null hypothesis that *educ* is exogenous. As always, this conclusion hinges on the assumption that the instruments for *educ* are themselves exogenous.

After the two-step estimation, we can easily obtain estimates of the unscaled parameters, $\boldsymbol{\beta}_1 = (\boldsymbol{\delta}_1', \alpha_1)'$, which then allows us to estimate partial effects. From the two-step estimation procedure, we have consistent estimators of $\boldsymbol{\delta}_2$ and τ_2^2 from the first-stage regression, and then $\boldsymbol{\delta}_{\rho 1}$, $\alpha_{\rho 1}$, and $\theta_{\rho 1}$ from the second stage. Straightforward algebra shows that $1 + \theta_{\rho 1}^2 \tau_2^2 = 1/(1 - \rho_1^2)$. Now, because $\boldsymbol{\delta}_1 = (1 - \rho_1^2)^{1/2} \boldsymbol{\delta}_{\rho 1}$ and $\alpha_1 = (1 - \rho_1^2)^{1/2} \alpha_{\rho 1}$, it follows that $\boldsymbol{\beta}_1 = \boldsymbol{\beta}_{\rho 1}/(1 + \theta_{\rho 1}^2 \tau_2^2)^{1/2}$, where $\boldsymbol{\beta}_{\rho 1} = (\boldsymbol{\delta}_{\rho 1}', \alpha_{\rho 1})'$ is the vector of scaled coefficients. Therefore, we can obtain consistent estimators of the original coefficients as

$$\hat{\boldsymbol{\beta}}_1 = \hat{\boldsymbol{\beta}}_{\rho 1}/(1 + \hat{\theta}_{\rho 1}^2 \hat{\tau}_2^2)^{1/2}, \tag{15.45}$$

where all quantities on the right-hand side of equation (15.45) are available from the two-step estimation procedure.

Given $\hat{\boldsymbol{\delta}}_1$ and $\hat{\alpha}_1$, we can compute derivatives and differences in $\Phi(\mathbf{z}_1 \hat{\boldsymbol{\delta}}_1 + \hat{\alpha}_1 y_2)$ at interesting values of $\mathbf{z}_1$ and y_2. Sometimes it is useful to evaluate the partial effects at the mean values. At other times the average partial effects are preferable. For continuous explanatory variables (including y_2), the scale factor for multiplying, say, $\hat{\alpha}_1$ is $N^{-1} \sum_{i=1}^N \phi(\mathbf{z}_{i1} \hat{\boldsymbol{\delta}}_1 + \hat{\alpha}_1 y_{i2})$. We can use the delta method to obtain standard errors for the APEs (or partial effects at the average), but the required calculations are tedious, given the two-step nature of the estimation. The bootstrap is easily applied (but computationally expensive): for each bootstrap sample, one computes the two steps of the procedure and obtains the scaled and unscaled coefficients, and then computes the APEs (or other partial effects of interest). As described in Section 12.8.2, one computes the standard deviation across the bootstrap replications.

An alternative method of computing the APEs does not exploit the normality assumption for v_2. We can use the results in Section 2.2.5 by writing $y_1 = 1[\mathbf{z}_1 \boldsymbol{\delta}_1 + \alpha_1 y_2 + u_1 > 0]$ and setting $q \equiv u_1$, $\mathbf{x} \equiv (\mathbf{z}_1, y_2)$, and $w = v_2$ (a scalar in this case). Because y_1 is a deterministic function of $(\mathbf{z}_1, y_2, u_1)$, v_2 is trivially redundant in $\mathrm{E}(y_1 \mid \mathbf{z}_1, y_2, u_1, v_2)$. Further, we have already used that $\mathrm{D}(u_1 \mid \mathbf{z}_1, y_2, v_2) = \mathrm{D}(u_1 \mid v_2)$, and so assumption (2.33) holds as well. It follows that APEs are obtained by taking derivatives or differences of the average structural function

$$\mathrm{E}_{v_2}[\Phi(\mathbf{z}_1 \boldsymbol{\delta}_{\rho 1} + \alpha_{\rho 1} y_2 + \theta_{\rho 1} v_2)] \tag{15.46}$$

with respect to elements of $(\mathbf{z}_1, y_2)$. Using Lemma 12.1, a consistent estimator of (15.46) is given by

$$N^{-1} \sum_{i=1}^{N} \Phi(\mathbf{z}_1 \hat{\boldsymbol{\delta}}_{\rho 1} + \hat{\alpha}_{\rho 1} y_2 + \hat{\theta}_{\rho 1} \hat{v}_{i2}), \tag{15.47}$$

where the $\hat{v}_{i2}$ are the first-stage OLS residuals from regressing y_{i2} on $\mathbf{z}_i$, $i = 1, \ldots, N$. This approach provides a different strategy for estimating APEs: simply compute partial effects with respect to $\mathbf{z}_1$ and y_2 after the second-stage estimation, but then average these across the $\hat{v}_{i2}$ in the sample. For a continuous explanatory variable, y_2 often being the most important, the estimated APE is $\hat{\alpha}_1[N^{-1}\sum_{i=1}^{N}\phi(\mathbf{z}_{i1}\hat{\boldsymbol{\delta}}_{\rho 1}+\hat{\alpha}_{\rho 1}y_{i2}+\hat{\theta}_{\rho 1}\hat{v}_{i2})]$, and a standard error for this APE can be obtained via the delta method or the bootstrap. Again, the bootstrap is much easier to apply: for each bootstrap sample, one applies the two-step estimation method and computes the APEs for that sample. The process is repeated to obtain a bootstrap standard error for the APEs.

The control function (CF) approach has some decided advantages over another two-step approach—one that appears to mimic the 2SLS estimation of the linear model. Rather than conditioning on v_2 along with $\mathbf{z}$ (and therefore y_2) to obtain $\mathrm{P}(y_1=1\,|\,\mathbf{z},v_2)=\mathrm{P}(y_1=1\,|\,\mathbf{z},y_2,v_2)$, we can obtain $\mathrm{P}(y_1=1\,|\,\mathbf{z})$. To find the latter probability, we plug in the reduced form for y_2 to get $y_1=1[\mathbf{z}_1\boldsymbol{\delta}_1+\alpha_1(\mathbf{z}\boldsymbol{\delta}_2)+\alpha_1 v_2+u_1>0]$. Because $\alpha_1 v_2+u_1$ is independent of $\mathbf{z}$ and (u_1,v_2) has a bivariate normal distribution, $\mathrm{P}(y_1=1\,|\,\mathbf{z})=\Phi\{[\mathbf{z}_1\boldsymbol{\delta}_1+\alpha_1(\mathbf{z}\boldsymbol{\delta}_2)]/\omega_1\}$, where $\omega_1^2\equiv\mathrm{Var}(\alpha_1 v_2+u_1)=\alpha_1^2\tau_2^2+1+2\alpha_1\,\mathrm{Cov}(v_2,u_1)$. (A two-step procedure now proceeds by using the same first-step OLS regression—in this case, to get the fitted values, $\hat{y}_{i2}=\mathbf{z}_i\hat{\boldsymbol{\delta}}_2$—now followed by a probit of y_{i1} on $\mathbf{z}_{i1}$, $\hat{y}_{i2}$. It is easily seen that this method estimates the coefficients up to the common scale factor $1/\omega_1$, which can be any positive value (unlike in the CF case, where we know the scale factor is greater than unity).

As with the CF approach, getting the appropriate standard errors is difficult. A primary drawback of the method that inserts $\hat{y}_2$ for y_2 is that it does not provide a simple test of the null hypothesis that y_2 is exogenous. Plus, the coefficients cannot be directly compared to the usual probit estimates in a Hausman test because of the different scale factors. Additionally, while the APEs can be recovered in much the same way as they can be for the CF approach, equation (15.47) is not available for the fitted values approach. Finally, plugging in fitted values is strictly limited to the structural equation (15.39); adding other functions of y_2 is very cumbersome, and one is prone to making mistakes. See Problem 15.14 and the discussion at the end of this subsection.

Example 15.3 (Endogeneity of Nonwife Income in the Women's LFP Model): We use the data in MROZ.RAW to test the null hypothesis that *nwifeinc* is exogenous in the probit model estimated in Table 15.1. We use as an instrument for *nwifeinc* husband's years of schooling, *huseduc*. Therefore, the identification assumption (perhaps a tenuous one) is that husband's schooling is unrelated to factors that affect a married woman's labor force decision once *nwifeinc* and the other variables (including the woman's education) are accounted for. In the first-stage regression of *nwifeinc* on *huseduc* and the other explanatory variables listed in Table 15.1, the fully robust t

statistic on *huseduc* is about 6.92, which is hardly surprising, because *nwifeinc* is pretty highly correlated with husband's labor earnings, which in turn depends on husband's education. When the reduced form residuals, $\hat{v}_2$, are added to the probit, its coefficient is about .027 with a t statistic of about 1.41—only moderate evidence that *nwifeinc* is endogenous. The coefficient on *nwifeinc* becomes about $-.037$, which is certainly larger in magnitude than the probit estimate in Table 15.1. But we must compare partial effects. If we average the scale factor $\phi(\mathbf{z}_{i1}\hat{\boldsymbol{\delta}}_{\rho 1} + \hat{\alpha}_{\rho 1} y_{i2} + \hat{\theta}_{\rho 1}\hat{v}_{i2})$ across all i (so that we are averaging across the distribution of $(\mathbf{z}_1, y_2)$ in addition to averaging out v_2), we obtain about .300. Therefore, the APE for *nwifeinc* is $.300(-.037) \approx -.011$ with a boostrap standard error, based on 500 bootstrap samples, of about .0058. The estimate, which is marginally statistically significant based on the bootstrap standard error, is about three times larger than the probit estimate that treats *nwifeinc* as exogenous, which was $-.0036$. If we use equation (15.46) to recover the estimates of the original coefficients, $\hat{\alpha}_1 = -.0355$, and this agrees with the joint MLE (as it should because the model is just identified). The scale factor based on $\phi(\mathbf{z}_{i1}\hat{\boldsymbol{\delta}}_1 + \hat{\alpha}_1 y_{i2})$ is about .297, which is very close to the scale factor based on (15.47). For comparision, we estimate a linear probability model by 2SLS. The 2SLS coefficient on *nwifeinc* is about $-.012$ (robust standard error $= .0059$), which, for practical purposes, is the same as the APE for the CF estimate in the probit model.

In the end, we are left in a difficult situation: the evidence against exogeneity of *nwifeinc* is not particularly strong, yet the APE that treats *nwifeinc* as endogenous is quite a bit larger than the APE that treats *nwifeinc* as exogenous.

In the previous example the model is just identified because we have one instrument, *huseduc*, for the endogenous variable *nwifeinc*. If we have overidentifying restrictions, these are easily tested using the CF approach. The key restriction is that $\mathrm{D}(u_1 \mid y_2, \mathbf{z}) = \mathrm{D}(u_1 \mid v_2)$; that is, the conditional distribution depends only on the linear combination $y_2 - \mathbf{z}\boldsymbol{\delta}_2$. If $\mathbf{z}_2$ is the $1 \times L_2$ vector of exogenous variables excluded from the structural equation, then this restriction on $\mathrm{D}(u_1 \mid y_2, \mathbf{z})$ imposes $L_2 - 1$ overidentifying restrictions. We can test these by including any $1 \times (L_2 - 1)$ subvector of $\mathbf{z}_2$, say $\mathbf{h}_2$, as additional explanatory variables in part (b) of Procedure 15.1, and conduct a joint significance test. In effect, we are testing $\mathrm{E}(\mathbf{h}_2' e_1) = \mathbf{0}$, where $u_1 = \rho_1 v_2 + e_1$. (Naturally, if we are allowing y_2 to be endogenous under the null—as we should—then the first-step estimation of $\boldsymbol{\delta}_2$ should be accounted for, either via the delta method or the bootstrap.) It can be shown that the test is invariate to which subset of $\mathbf{z}_2$ we choose for $\mathbf{h}_2$, provided $\mathbf{h}_2$ has $L_2 - 1$ elements.

Rather than use a two-step procedure, we can estimate equations (15.39)–(15.41) by conditional maximum likelihood estimation (CMLE). To obtain the joint distribution of (y_1, y_2), conditional on $\mathbf{z}$, recall that

$$f(y_1, y_2 \mid \mathbf{z}) = f(y_1 \mid y_2, \mathbf{z}) f(y_2 \mid \mathbf{z}) \tag{15.48}$$

(see Property CD.2 in Appendix 13A). Since $y_2 \mid \mathbf{z} \sim \text{Normal}(\mathbf{z}\boldsymbol{\delta}_2, \tau_2^2)$, the density $f(y_2 \mid \mathbf{z})$ is easy to write down. We can also derive the conditional density of y_1 given $(y_2, \mathbf{z})$. Since $v_2 = y_2 - \mathbf{z}\boldsymbol{\delta}_2$ and $y_1 = 1[y_1^* > 0]$,

$$\mathrm{P}(y_1 = 1 \mid y_2, \mathbf{z}) = \Phi\left[\frac{\mathbf{z}_1\boldsymbol{\delta}_1 + \alpha_1 y_2 + (\rho_1/\tau_2)(y_2 - \mathbf{z}\boldsymbol{\delta}_2)}{(1 - \rho_1^2)^{1/2}}\right], \tag{15.49}$$

where we have used the fact that $\theta_1 = \rho_1/\tau_2$.

Let w denote the term in inside $\Phi(\cdot)$ in equation (15.49). Then we have derived

$$f(y_1, y_2 \mid \mathbf{z}) = \{\Phi(w)\}^{y_1}\{1 - \Phi(w)\}^{1-y_1}(1/\tau_2)\phi[(y_2 - \mathbf{z}\boldsymbol{\delta}_2)/\tau_2],$$

and so the log likelihood for observation i (apart from terms not depending on the parameters) is

$$y_{i1} \log \Phi(w_i) + (1 - y_{i1}) \log[1 - \Phi(w_i)] - \tfrac{1}{2} \log(\tau_2^2) - \tfrac{1}{2}(y_{i2} - \mathbf{z}_i\boldsymbol{\delta}_2)^2/\tau_2^2, \tag{15.50}$$

where we understand that w_i depends on the parameters $(\boldsymbol{\delta}_1, \alpha_1, \rho_1, \boldsymbol{\delta}_2, \tau_2)$:

$$w_i \equiv [\mathbf{z}_{i1}\boldsymbol{\delta}_1 + \alpha_1 y_{i2} + (\rho_1/\tau_2)(y_{i2} - \mathbf{z}_i\boldsymbol{\delta}_2)]/(1 - \rho_1^2)^{1/2}.$$

Summing expression (15.50) across all i and maximizing with respect to all parameters gives the MLEs of $\boldsymbol{\delta}_1$, α_1, ρ_1, $\boldsymbol{\delta}_2$, τ_2^2. The general theory of conditional MLE applies, and so standard errors can be obtained using the estimated Hessian, the estimated expected Hessian, or the outer product of the score. MLE applied to this model sometimes goes by the name of **instrumental variables probit**, or **IV probit**.

Maximum likelihood estimation has some decided advantages over two-step procedures. First, MLE is more efficient than any two-step procedure. Second, we get direct estimates of $\boldsymbol{\delta}_1$ and α_1, the parameters of interest for computing partial effects. Evans, Oates, and Schwab (1992) study peer effects on teenage behavior using the full MLE. Of course, obtaining standard errors for the APEs still requires using the delta method or the bootstrap.

Testing that y_2 is exogenous is easy once the MLE has been obtained: just test $\mathrm{H}_0: \rho_1 = 0$ using an asymptotic t test. We could also use a likelihood ratio test.

The drawback to the MLE is computational. Sometimes it can be difficult to get the iterations to converge, as $\hat{\rho}_1$ sometimes tends toward 1 or -1.

Comparing the Rivers-Vuong approach to the MLE shows that the former is a **limited information procedure**. Essentially, Rivers and Vuong focus on $f(y_1 \mid y_2, \mathbf{z})$, where they replace the unknown $\boldsymbol{\delta}_2$ with the OLS estimator $\hat{\boldsymbol{\delta}}_2$ (and they ignore the rescaling problem by taking e_1 in equation (15.43) to have unit variance). MLE estimates the parameters using the information in $f(y_1 \mid y_2, \mathbf{z})$ and $f(y_2 \mid \mathbf{z})$ simultaneously. For the initial test of whether y_2 is exogenous, the Rivers-Vuong approach has significant computational advantages. If exogeneity is rejected, it might be worth doing MLE. As shown by Rivers and Vuong (1988), the two-step estimators and MLEs are identical when the model is just identified.

Another benefit of the MLE approach for this and related problems is that it forces discipline on us in coming up with consistent estimation procedures and correct standard errors. It is easy to abuse two-step procedures if we are not careful in deriving estimating equations. With MLE, although it can be difficult to derive joint distributions of the endogenous variables given the exogenous variables, we know that, if the underlying distributional assumptions hold, consistent and efficient estimators are obtained.

The CF approach has a somewhat subtle robustness property. It is easy to see that the CF approach is consistent if we assume that $\mathrm{D}(u_1 \mid \mathbf{z}, v_2) = \mathrm{D}(u_1 \mid v_2)$ and that $\mathrm{D}(u_1 \mid v_2)$ is normal with mean linear in v_2 and constant variance. Independence between (u_1, v_2) and $\mathbf{z}$ along with bivariate normality of (u_1, v_2) is sufficient but not necessary. It is certainly possible for $\mathrm{D}(u_1 \mid v_2)$ to be normal without v_2 having a normal distribution. In fact, we could even allow the mean $\mathrm{E}(u_1 \mid v_2)$ to be a known, nonlinear function of v_2—say, a quadratic—and then add these functions to the probit in the second-step estimation.

For notational and interpretational simplicity, our previous analysis has assumed that a single endogenous explanatory variable appears additively inside the index function. But a moment's thought shows that the previous analysis goes through much more generally. For example, suppose we specify

$$y_1 = 1[\mathbf{g}_1(\mathbf{z}_1, y_2)\boldsymbol{\beta}_1 + u_1 > 0]$$

$$y_2 = \mathbf{g}_2(\mathbf{z})\boldsymbol{\delta}_2 + v_2,$$

where $\mathbf{g}_1(\cdot)$ and $\mathbf{g}_2(\cdot)$ are known vector functions. As we discussed in Section 6.2, CF approaches offer considerable flexibility in specifying functional form—provided the underlying assumptions hold. Because y_2 is a function of $(\mathbf{z}, v_2)$, if we maintain independence between (u_1, v_2) and $\mathbf{z}$, then $\mathrm{D}(u_1 \mid \mathbf{z}, y_2, v_2) = \mathrm{D}(u_1 \mid \mathbf{z}, v_2) = \mathrm{D}(u_1 \mid v_2)$, and the previous analysis, whether it is the Rivers-Vuong CF approach or MLE—goes through by replacing $\mathbf{x}_1 \equiv (\mathbf{z}_1, y_2)$ with $\mathbf{x}_1 \equiv \mathbf{g}_1(\mathbf{z}_1, y_2)$. For example, we can choose $\mathbf{g}_1(\mathbf{z}_1, y_2) = (\mathbf{z}_1, y_2\mathbf{z}_1)$ to allow full interaction effects (in addition to a main effect, since the first element of $\mathbf{z}_1$ should be unity). Adding a quadratic or other polynomials in y_2 causes no difficulties. Partial effect and APE calculations become more complicated only insofar as derivatives of the function $\mathbf{g}_1(\mathbf{z}_1, y_2)$ must be obtained. So, for example, in a model with $y_1 = 1[\mathbf{z}_1\boldsymbol{\delta}_1 + y_2\mathbf{z}_1\boldsymbol{\alpha}_1 + \gamma_1 y_2^2 + u_1 > 0]$, the partial effect of y_2 is $(\mathbf{z}_1\boldsymbol{\alpha}_1 + 2\gamma_1 y_2)\phi(\mathbf{z}_1\boldsymbol{\delta}_1 + y_2\mathbf{z}_1\boldsymbol{\alpha}_1 + \gamma_1 y_2^2)$. All of the parameters can be estimated using the two-step CF estimator or the MLE. Because of our assumptions, testing for exogeneity proceeds exactly as before: we can use a simple t statistic on $\hat{v}_{i2}$ in the second-step probit (or directly test for zero correlation between u_1 and v_2 in the context of MLE). (Standard software packages that have an "instrumental variables probit" command are easily tricked into estimating general models, provided y_2 appears on its own as an explanatory variable—such as models with quadratics and interactions in y_2. One simply specifies y_2 as the lone endogenous explanatory variable with other functions of y_2 listed as if they were exogenous; the likelihood function will be properly computed.)

Another nice feature of the CF approach is that we can allow for a strictly monotonic transformation of the endogenous explanatory variable in the reduced form. For example, suppose $y_2 = \log(income)$. Then, of course, $income = \exp(y_2)$, and so any function of income—say, its level, quadratic, or interaction terms—can appear in the structural equation if these are deemed better functional forms than $\log(income)$ in the probit. This flexibility is handy because sometimes a variable needs to be transformed before it is reasonable to assume that it has a reduced form with an additive error that is independent of $\mathbf{z}$. As another example, if w_2 is an endogenous variable that is strictly in the unit interval, we might choose $y_2 = \log[w_2/(1 - w_2)]$ as the variable that has a reduced form linear in parameters with an additive error. Then w_2 itself, and any function of it, can appear in the probit model for y_1 because w_2 is a well-defined function of y_2.

That including the reduced form residuals in the CF approach accounts for endogeneity of y_2, even if we have general functions of y_2 and $\mathbf{z}_1$ in the model, hinges crucially on independence between (u_1, v_2) and $\mathbf{z}$. Because of the additivity of v_2 in the reduced form, independence between v_2 and $\mathbf{z}$ pretty much rules out any discreteness in y_2. And, we are assuming at least normality of $\mathrm{D}(u_1 \mid v_2)$ (although that can be relaxed, as we briefly discuss in Section 15.7.5).

If we have multiple exogenous explanatory variables, say a $1 \times G_1$ row vector $\mathbf{y}_2$, we can solve the endogeneity problem in a very similar way. Maximum likelihood estimation becomes much more difficult computationally, but the CF approach is straightforward. The key assumption for the CF approach is $\mathbf{y}_2 = \mathbf{z}\boldsymbol{\Delta}_2 + \mathbf{v}_2$, where $\mathrm{D}(u_1 \mid \mathbf{z}, \mathbf{v}_2) = \mathrm{D}(u_1 \mid \mathbf{v}_2)$ and this latter distribution is normal with constant variance and mean linear in $\mathbf{v}_2$. Calculation of partial effects requires averaging out $\mathbf{v}_2$, either by computing the unscaled coefficients or using the extension of equation (15.47).

Maximum likelihood estimation is also feasible when $(u_1, \mathbf{v}_2)$ is jointly normal and independent of $\mathbf{z}$.

Finally, one should not minimize the usefulness of estimating a linear model for y_1 using standard IV estimation, probably 2SLS. As we discussed in Section 15.6 with exogenous explanatory variables, the OLS estimates of an LPM can provide good estimates of the APEs. The same is true when one (or more) explanatory variable is endogenous. At a minimum, it makes sense to compare 2SLS estimates of an LPM with the APEs obtained from the probit model with endogenous y_2.

15.7.3 Binary Endogenous Explanatory Variable

We now consider the case where the probit model contains a *binary* explanatory variable that is endogenous. We begin with the simplest model,

$$y_1 = 1[\mathbf{z}_1\boldsymbol{\delta}_1 + \alpha_1 y_2 + u_1 > 0] \tag{15.51}$$

$$y_2 = 1[\mathbf{z}\boldsymbol{\delta}_2 + v_2 > 0], \tag{15.52}$$

where (u_1, v_2) is independent of $\mathbf{z}$ and distributed as bivariate normal with mean zero, each has unit variance, and $\rho_1 = \text{Corr}(u_1, v_2)$. If $\rho_1 \neq 0$, then u_1 and y_2 are correlated, and probit estimation of equation (15.51) is inconsistent for $\boldsymbol{\delta}_1$ and α_1.

Model (15.51) and (15.52) applies primarily to omitted variables situations. In particular, we could not obtain the reduced form (15.52) if the structural model has y_1 as a determinant of y_2. Measurement error in binary responses does not lead to this model, either.

As discussed in Section 15.7.2, the normalization $\text{Var}(u_1) = 1$ is the proper one for computing partial effects. Often, the effect of y_2 is of primary interest, especially when y_2 indicates participation in some sort of program, such as job training, and the binary outcome y_1 might denote employment status. The average treatment effect (for a given value of $\mathbf{z}_1$) is $\Phi(\mathbf{z}_1\boldsymbol{\delta}_1 + \alpha_1) - \Phi(\mathbf{z}_1\boldsymbol{\delta}_1)$. This effect can be computed for different subgroups or averaged across the distribution of $\mathbf{z}_1$.

To derive the likelihood function, we again need the joint distribution of (y_1, y_2) given $\mathbf{z}$, which we obtain from equation (15.48). To obtain $\text{P}(y_1 = 1 \mid y_2, \mathbf{z})$, first note that

$$\text{P}(y_1 = 1 \mid v_2, \mathbf{z}) = \Phi[(\mathbf{z}_1\boldsymbol{\delta}_1 + \alpha_1 y_2 + \rho_1 v_2)/(1 - \rho_1^2)^{1/2}]. \tag{15.53}$$

Since $y_2 = 1$ if and only if $v_2 > -\mathbf{z}\boldsymbol{\delta}_2$, we need a basic fact about truncated normal distributions: If v_2 has a standard normal distribution and is independent of $\mathbf{z}$, then the density of v_2 given $v_2 > -\mathbf{z}\boldsymbol{\delta}_2$ is

$$\phi(v_2)/\text{P}(v_2 > -\mathbf{z}\boldsymbol{\delta}_2) = \phi(v_2)/\Phi(\mathbf{z}\boldsymbol{\delta}_2). \tag{15.54}$$

Therefore,

$$\begin{aligned} \mathrm{P}(y_1 = 1 \mid y_2 = 1, \mathbf{z}) &= \mathrm{E}[\mathrm{P}(y_1 = 1 \mid v_2, \mathbf{z}) \mid y_2 = 1, \mathbf{z}] \\ &= \mathrm{E}\{\Phi[(\mathbf{z}_1\boldsymbol{\delta}_1 + \alpha_1 y_2 + \rho_1 v_2)/(1-\rho_1^2)^{1/2}] \mid y_2 = 1, \mathbf{z}\} \\ &= \frac{1}{\Phi(\mathbf{z}\boldsymbol{\delta}_2)} \int_{-\mathbf{z}\boldsymbol{\delta}_2}^{\infty} \Phi[(\mathbf{z}_1\boldsymbol{\delta}_1 + \alpha_1 y_2 + \rho_1 v_2)/(1-\rho_1^2)^{1/2}]\phi(v_2)\,dv_2, \end{aligned} \tag{15.55}$$

where v_2 in the integral is a dummy argument of integration. Of course, $\mathrm{P}(y_1 = 0 \mid y_2 = 1, \mathbf{z})$ is just one minus equation (15.55).

Similarly, $\mathrm{P}(y_1 = 1 \mid y_2 = 0, \mathbf{z})$ is

$$\frac{1}{1-\Phi(\mathbf{z}\boldsymbol{\delta}_2)} \int_{-\infty}^{-\mathbf{z}\boldsymbol{\delta}_2} \Phi[(\mathbf{z}_1\boldsymbol{\delta}_1 + \alpha_1 y_2 + \rho_1 v_2)/(1-\rho_1^2)^{1/2}]\phi(v_2)\,dv_2. \tag{15.56}$$

Combining the four possible outcomes of (y_1, y_2), along with the probit model for y_2, and taking the log gives the log-likelihood function for maximum likelihood analysis. Several authors, for example Greene (2003, Section 21.6), have noted a useful computational feature of the model in equations (15.51) and (15.52). To describe this feature—and to explain the additional flexibility it affords for extending the basic model—we introduce the **bivariate probit model**, typically specified for two binary responses as

$$y_1 = 1[\mathbf{x}_1\boldsymbol{\beta}_1 + e_1 > 0]$$

$$y_2 = 1[\mathbf{x}_2\boldsymbol{\beta}_2 + e_2 > 0],$$

where $\mathbf{x}_1$ is $1 \times K_1$ and $\mathbf{x}_2$ is $1 \times K_2$. In the traditional formulation of bivariate probit, the error term, $\mathbf{e} \equiv (e_1, e_2)$, is assumed to be independent of $(\mathbf{x}_1, \mathbf{x}_2)$ with a bivariate normal distribution. In particular, $\mathbf{e} \mid \mathbf{x} \sim \mathrm{Normal}(\mathbf{0}, \boldsymbol{\Omega})$, where $\mathbf{x}$ consists of all exogenous variables and $\boldsymbol{\Omega}$ is the 2×2 matrix with ones down its diagonal and off-diagonal element $\rho = \mathrm{Corr}(e_1, e_2)$. These assumptions imply that y_1 and y_2 each follow probit models conditional on $\mathbf{x}$. Therefore, $\boldsymbol{\beta}_1$ and $\boldsymbol{\beta}_2$ can be consistently estimated by estimating separate probit models. Not surprisingly, if e_1 and e_2 are correlated, a joint maximum likelihood procedure is more efficient than the separate probits. With exogenous explanatory variables, increased efficiency in estimating $\boldsymbol{\beta}_1$ and $\boldsymbol{\beta}_2$ is the main reason for a joint estimation procedure. (Incidentally, when $\mathbf{x}_1 = \mathbf{x}_2 = \mathbf{x}$, there are generally efficiency gains from joint MLE over probit on each equation. By contrast, as we saw in Chapter 7 for the linear model, OLS on each equation and feasible GLS are identical.)

A simple way to obtain the log-likelihood function is to construct the joint density as $f(y_1 \mid y_2, \mathbf{x}) f(y_2 \mid \mathbf{x})$, and it is here that a useful feature of the bivariate probit as it relates to probit with a binary endogenous variable emerges: the form of the conditional density, $f(y_1 \mid y_2, \mathbf{x})$, is the same even if $\mathbf{x}_1$ includes y_2. In fact, $\mathbf{x}_1$ can be *any* function of $(\mathbf{z}_1, y_2)$. In other words, in expressions (15.55) and (15.56) we can replace $\mathbf{z}_1\boldsymbol{\delta}_1 + \alpha_1 y_2$ with $\mathbf{x}_1\boldsymbol{\beta}_1 = \mathbf{g}_1(\mathbf{z}_1, y_2)\boldsymbol{\beta}_1$. The reason we can allow this generality is simple: when we obtain the density of y_1 given $(y_2, \mathbf{x})$, we are already conditioning on y_2, so the form of the density is the same whether or not y_2 is in $\mathbf{x}_1$. We discussed a similar feature of the log-likelihood function for estimating the model in Section 15.7.2.

The practical implication of our being able to use the bivariate probit log-likelihood function for endogenous explanatory variables is computational: if an econometrics package estimates a bivariate probit, then it can be used directly to estimate the parameters in (15.51) and (15.52). Further, we can use exactly the same routine to estimate a model with interactions in the structural equation, $y_1 = 1[\mathbf{z}_1\boldsymbol{\delta}_1 + y_2\mathbf{z}_1\boldsymbol{\alpha}_1 + u_1 > 0]$, with no more work than defining the interactions and including them in the appropriate command (specifying y_2 as the only endogenous variable but including the interactions with y_2 as additional explanatory variables).

Evans and Schwab (1995) use model (15.51) and (15.52) (and linear probability models) to estimate the causal effect of attending a Catholic high school (y_2) on the probability of attending college (y_1), allowing the Catholic high school indicator to be correlated with unobserved factors that also affect college attendance. As an IV for y_2 they use a binary indicator of whether a student is Catholic. Recently, Altonji, Elder, and Taber (2005) (AET for short) have revisited this question, using affiliation with the Catholic Church and geographic proximity to Catholic schools as instruments. They compare 2SLS estimates of a linear model—which, as always, may provide good approximations to the average partial effects—to those from the bivariate probit. In addition to finding the instruments to be suspect, AET conclude that identification of the parameters can be driven largely by the nonlinearity in the bivariate probit model. Unlike the model in Section 15.7.2, where an exclusion restriction in the structural equation is needed for identification, that is not the case in (15.51) and (15.52). Typically, one would be suspicious if an exclusion restriction is not available. AET's results suggest that even if such restrictions are available, they may have little impact on the estimated average treament effect (the APE of the Catholic high school dummy).

Because computing the MLE requires nonlinear optimization, it is tempting to use some seemingly "obvious" two-step procedures. As an example, we might try to inappropriately mimic 2SLS. Since $\mathrm{E}(y_2 \mid \mathbf{z}) = \Phi(\mathbf{z}\boldsymbol{\delta}_2)$ and $\boldsymbol{\delta}_2$ is consistently estimated by probit of y_2 on $\mathbf{z}$, it is tempting to estimate $\boldsymbol{\delta}_1$ and α_1 from the probit of y_1 on $\mathbf{z}$, $\hat{\Phi}_2$, where $\hat{\Phi}_2 \equiv \Phi(\mathbf{z}\hat{\boldsymbol{\delta}}_2)$. This approach does not produce consistent parameter estimators, for the same reasons the forbidden regression discussed in Section 9.5 for nonlinear simultaneous equations models does not. For this two-step procedure to work, we would have to have $\mathrm{P}(y_1 = 1 \mid \mathbf{z}) = \Phi[\mathbf{z}_1\boldsymbol{\delta}_1 + \alpha_1\Phi(\mathbf{z}\boldsymbol{\delta}_2)]$. But $\mathrm{P}(y_1 = 1 \mid \mathbf{z}) = \mathrm{E}(y_1 \mid \mathbf{z}) = \mathrm{E}(1[\mathbf{z}_1\boldsymbol{\delta}_1 + \alpha_1 y_2 + u_1 > 0] \mid \mathbf{z})$, and since the indicator function $1[\cdot]$ is nonlinear, we cannot pass the expected value through.

Greene (1998), in commenting on Burnett (1997), asserted that the two-step procedure that uses first-stage probit fitted values in place of y_2 in a second-stage probit is consistent but inefficient. As a way to obtain more efficient estimators, he proposed using the full MLE. But it is important to understand that the problem with the two-step procedure is not just a matter of inefficiency and adjusting for the two-step estimation; the procedure does not produce consistent estimators of the parameters, and probably not the APEs either (although a study of this issue would be informative). Burnett (1997) suggested adding the probit residuals, $\hat{r}_{i2} \equiv y_{i2} - \Phi(\mathbf{z}_i\hat{\boldsymbol{\delta}}_2)$, in an attempt to mimic Rivers and Vuong's (1988) method for a continuous y_2, although she applied nonlinear least squares, not MLE, in the second step. Interestingly, the Burnett approach does provide a valid test of the null hypothesis that y_2 is exogenous, although it makes more sense to use probit in the second stage, too. So, do a probit of y_{i1} on $\mathbf{z}_{i1}$, y_{i2}, $\hat{r}_{i2}$ and obtain the usual asymptotic t statistic on $\hat{r}_{i2}$. Under the null hypothesis that y_2 is exogenous, $P(y_1 = 1 \mid \mathbf{z}, y_2) = P(y_1 = 1 \mid \mathbf{z}_1, y_2) = \Phi(\mathbf{z}_1\boldsymbol{\delta}_1 + \alpha_1 y_2)$, and so no additional functions of $(y_{i2}, \mathbf{z}_i)$ should appear. Rather than use the residuals from the linear reduced form for y_2 (which is what the Rivers-Vuong test does), we can use the residuals from a probit. Unfortunately, if y_2 is endogenous, Burnett's suggestion does not appear to consistently estimate the parameters or the APEs.

As mentioned in the previous subsection, we can use the Rivers-Vuong approach to *test* for exogeneity of y_2. This has the virtue of being simple, and, if the test fails to reject, we may not need to compute the MLE. A more efficient test is the score test of $\mathrm{H}_0 : \rho_1 = 0$, and this does not require estimation of the full MLE. Of course, if one has computed the MLE, a t test or LR test can be used.

Example 15.4 (Women's Labor Force Participation and Having More than Two Children): We use a data set from Angrist and Evans (1998), in LABSUP.RAW, to study the effects of having more than two children on women's labor force participation decisions. The population is married women in the United States who have at least two children. The endogenous explanatory variable is $y_2 = morekids$, which is unity if a woman has three or more children (about 49 percent of the sample). The response variable is $y_1 = worked$; roughly 59 percent of the women report being in

Table 15.2
Estimated Effect of Having Three or More Children on Women's Labor Force Participation

Dependent Variable: *worked*

	(1)	(2)	(3)	(4)	(5)
Model	LPM	Probit	LPM	Bivariate probit	Bivariate probit
Estimation method	OLS	MLE	2SLS: *samesex* as IV	MLE: *samesex* as IV	MLE: no IV
Coefficient on *morekids*	−.109 (.006)	−.299 (.015)	−.201 (.096)	−.703 (.204)	−.966 (.243)
APE for *morekids*	−.109 (.006)	−.109 (.006)	−.201 (.096)	−.256 (.072)	−.349 (*)
$\hat{\rho}$	—	—	—	.254 (.131)	.426 (.162)
Number of observations	31,857	31,857	31,857	31,857	31,857

Standard errors for estimated coefficients and APEs are given in parentheses next to coefficients. For the nonlinear models, the APE standard errors were obtained from 500 bootstrap samplings.
A bootstrap standard error could not be obtained for column (5) due to computational problems for some bootstrap samples.

the labor force at the time of the survey. We also include the variables *nonmomi* ("non-mom" income), *educ* (years of schooling), *age*, age^2, and the race indicators *black* and *hispan*; these are all treated as exogenous. As an instrumental variable for *morekids* we use *samesex*, which is a binary variable equal to one if the first two children are of the same sex. (While the outcome of *samesex* is legitimately treated as random, it is not necessarily exogenous to the labor force participation decision: having two children of the same sex can shift a family's budget constraint because, for example, a bedroom is more easily shared and clothes and toys are more easily handed down.) Table 15.2 contains the estimation results from five different approaches: OLS estimation of a linear probability model, probit treating *morekids* as exogenous, 2SLS estimation of an LPM, bivariate probit allowing *morekids* to be endogenous, and bivariate probit that drops *samesex* from the probit for *morekids*. We include the latter primarily to illustrate that the nonlinearity in the model identifies the parameters. For brevity, we only report the coefficients and average partial effects for *morekids*. For the LPMs, the standard errors are robust to arbitrary heteroskedasticity.

When *morekids* is assumed exogenous, the LPM and probit models give the same estimated average partial effect of having more than two children to three decimal places: on average, women with more than two children are about .11 less likely to be in the labor force than women with two children. In addition, the standard errors are the same to three decimal places (and the standard error for probit was obtained from bootstrapping). When *samesex* is used as an IV in the LPM estimation, the effect almost doubles. Column 4 contains the estimates from the bivariate probit where *morekids* is treated as endogenous and *samesex* is excluded from the structural equation but appears in the probit model for *morekids*—the standard case where we impose an exclusion restriction. Now, the nonlinear probit model gives a larger estimated APE than the linear model: $-.256$ versus $-.201$. Interestingly, according to the APE standard error for the bivariate probit, obtained using bootstrapping, the APE is more precisely estimated using the nonlinear model.

If we drop *samesex* from the probit model for *morekids*—which, in a linear context, would lead to a lack of identification—we estimate an even larger effect: the APE is $-.349$. The estimated value of ρ increases substantially when we drop *samesex* from the model for *morekids*, suggesting that including *samesex* in the model for *morekids* helps reduce the correlation between unobservables that affect both *morekids* and *worked*. The large increase in the magnitude of the APE suggests that the nonlinearity in the bivariate probit plays a critical role in determining the APE, a point made by Altonji, Elder, and Taber (2005) when studying the effects of attending a Catholic high school on outcomes such as attending college. Generally, it is dangerous to rely on nonlinearities to identify parameters and partial effects, and one should avoid doing so in bivariate probit models. When bootstrapping was applied to obtain a standard error for the APE in column (5), for some bootstrap samples the computational algorithm would not converge, suggesting that the model without an exclusion restriction is ill specified. In this application, the real issue should be whether the difference in APEs between the linear model estimated by 2SLS and the bivariate probit that uses the same instrument is important.

We can also implement the inconsistent two-step estimation approach where the probit fitted values, say $\widehat{morekids}$, are plugged in for *morekids* in the second-stage probit. The coefficient on $\widehat{morekids}$ is about about $-.843$, which is quite a bit larger in magnitude than the full MLE estimate when *samesex* is used as an IV, $-.703$. The estimated APE for the two-step procedure is about $-.305$, which again is larger in magnitude than the full MLE estimate, $-.256$. The difference in APEs is less than the difference in APEs between the linear 2SLS estimate and full MLE. It is intriguing to think that, somehow, the inconsistent two-step procedure might generally deliver reasonable estimates of the APEs, but there is no evidence on this point.

15.7.4 Heteroskedasticity and Nonnormality in the Latent Variable Model

In applying the probit model it is easy to become confused about the problems of heteroskedasticity and nonnormality. The confusion stems from a failure to distinguish between the underlying latent variable formulation, as in $y^* = \mathbf{x}\boldsymbol{\beta} + e$, and the response probability in equation (15.8). As we have emphasized throughout this chapter, for most purposes we want to estimate $P(y = 1 \mid \mathbf{x})$. The latent variable formulation is convenient for certain manipulations, but we are rarely interested in $E(y^* \mid \mathbf{x})$. (Data censoring cases, where we are only interested in the parameters of an underlying linear model, are treated in Chapter 19.)

Once we focus on the response probability, we can easily see why comparing nonnormality and heteroskedasticity in the latent variable model with the same problems in a linear (or nonlinear) regression requires considerable care. First consider the problem of nonnormality of e in a probit model. If e is independent of $\mathbf{x}$, we can write $P(y = 1 \mid \mathbf{x}) = G(\mathbf{x}\boldsymbol{\beta}) \neq \Phi(\mathbf{x}\boldsymbol{\beta})$, where, generally, $G(z) = 1 - F(-z)$ and $F(\cdot)$ is the cdf of e. One often hears statements such as "nonnormality in a probit model causes bias and inconsistency in the parameter estimates." Technically, this statement is correct, but it largely misses the point. In Section 15.6 we noted that when $\mathbf{x}$ has a multivariate normal distribution, the LPM consistently estimates the APEs for any smooth function $G(\cdot)$. Using a linear model when the response probability is nonlinear is a fairly serious form of misspecification, yet we consistently estimate perhaps the most useful quantities: the APEs. The probit model is likely to do a reasonable job of approximating the APES in lots of cases where $G \neq \Phi$. In fact, the situation that emerges in Example 15.2 is quite common in applications: probit and logit give very similar estimated partial effects. That the logit parameter estimates are larger than the probit estimates by roughly a factor of 1.6 is a consequence of the different implicit scale factors, but the different scalings are easily accounted for by computing partial effects.

Worrying about the choice of G when the response probability is of interest is no different from worrying about the functional form for $E(y \mid \mathbf{x})$ in a regression context. For example, if $y \geq 0$ and we are considering two models for $E(y \mid \mathbf{x})$, a linear model $E(y \mid \mathbf{x}) = \mathbf{x}\boldsymbol{\beta}$ and an exponential model $E(y \mid \mathbf{x}) = \exp(\mathbf{x}\boldsymbol{\beta})$, we do not couch the choice between them in the language of "biased" or "inconsistent" parameter estimation. That OLS estimation of a linear model will not consistently estimate the parameters in $\exp(\mathbf{x}\boldsymbol{\beta})$ is both obvious and not particularly relevant. The issue is whether a linear or exponential function form provides the best fit, and whether the estimated partial effects $E(y \mid \mathbf{x})$ are very different across the models. In some cases, the linear model does provide good estimates of the APEs. We should have the same discussion when deciding on G in the index model $P(y = 1 \mid \mathbf{x}) = E(y \mid \mathbf{x}) = G(\mathbf{x}\boldsymbol{\beta})$: our choice of G is a functional form issue. A nonnormal distribution of u in the linear regression model $y = \mathbf{x}\boldsymbol{\beta} + u$, $E(u \mid \mathbf{x}) = 0$, does not change the functional form of $E(y \mid \mathbf{x})$, and that is why nonnormality is harmless (provided one can rely on asymptotic theory). Nonnormality in e in $y = 1[\mathbf{x}\boldsymbol{\beta} + e > 0]$ means that the probit response probability is incorrect. Even if we could estimate $\boldsymbol{\beta}$ consistently we could not obtain magnitudes of the partial effects. So our focus should be on how well different methods approximate partial effects, and not on whether they estimate parameters consistently. (In the next subsection, we show that relative partial effects of continuous variables can be identified without specifying $G(\cdot)$, and sometimes even if we allow e and $\mathbf{x}$ to have some dependence.)

Once we view nonnormality of e as a functional form problem for $p(\mathbf{x})$, we can evaluate more general parametric models in a sensible way. It can be a good idea to replace $\Phi(\mathbf{x}\boldsymbol{\beta})$ with a function such as $G(\mathbf{x}\boldsymbol{\beta}, \boldsymbol{\gamma})$, where $\boldsymbol{\gamma}$ is an extra set of parameters, especially if $G(\mathbf{x}\boldsymbol{\beta}, \boldsymbol{\gamma})$ is chosen to nest the probit model. (Moon (1988) covers some interesting possibilities in the context of logit models, including asymmetric distributions. See also Problem 15.16.) But generalizing functional form by making the distribution of e more general is not necessarily better than just specifying more flexible models for the response probability directly, as in McDonald (1996). And we definitely should not reject the standard models just because the estimates of $\boldsymbol{\beta}$ seem to change a lot: the basis for comparison should be partial effects at various values of $\mathbf{x}$, APEs, and goodness-of-fit measures such as the values of the log-likelihood functions and the percent correctly predicted.

Similar comments can be made about heteroskedasticity in the latent error e. Traditionally, discussions of its implications tend to suffer from a failure to specify what it is we hope to learn when we estimate binary response models. For example, one often sees reference to Yatchew and Griliches (1984) concerning the inconsistency of the probit MLE when $\text{Var}(e \mid \mathbf{x})$ depends on $\mathbf{x}$, even if $\text{D}(e \mid \mathbf{x})$ is normal. If $\text{D}(e \mid \mathbf{x}) = \text{Normal}(0, h(\mathbf{x}))$, the response probability takes the form $\text{P}(y = 1 \mid \mathbf{x}) = \Phi[\mathbf{x}\boldsymbol{\beta}/h(\mathbf{x})^{1/2}]$, and so it is pretty obvious that probit of y on $\mathbf{x}$ could not consistently estimate $\boldsymbol{\beta}$. Some authors have noted this finding is particularly troubling because "heteroskedasticity is prevalent with microeconomic data." But what does this mean? Even if the usual probit model is correct—so that $\text{Var}(e \mid \mathbf{x}) = 1$—the variance of the response variable, y, is heteroskedastic: $\text{Var}(y \mid \mathbf{x}) = \Phi(\mathbf{x}\boldsymbol{\beta})[1 - \Phi(\mathbf{x}\boldsymbol{\beta})]$. In fact, most observed discrete random variables y will have conditional distributions such that $\text{Var}(y \mid \mathbf{x})$ is not constant, but that is due to the discreteness in y, not necessarily because of heteroskedasticity in an underlying latent error.

Is there any reason we should consider possible heteroskedasticity in $\text{Var}(y^* \mid \mathbf{x})$ when y^* is an unknowable latent variable? There are two reasons. The simplest is for generalizing the functional form of the response probability—just as when we allow for nonnormality in $\text{D}(y^* \mid \mathbf{x})$. In Section 15.5.3 we discussed testing the probit model against an alternative where $\text{Var}(e \mid \mathbf{x}) = \exp(2\mathbf{x}_1\boldsymbol{\delta})$ for $\mathbf{x}_1$ a subset of $\mathbf{x}$ (which, at a minimum, excludes a constant). Then $P(y = 1 \mid \mathbf{x}) = \Phi[\exp(-\mathbf{x}_1\boldsymbol{\delta})\mathbf{x}\boldsymbol{\beta}]$, and so we have potentially allowed a much more flexible response probability. But there is a cost to the more general model: the partial effects, $\partial P(y = 1 \mid \mathbf{x})/\partial x_j$ are more complicated. If δ_j is the coefficient on x_j in the vector $\mathbf{x}_1$, then

$$\frac{\partial\partial P(y = 1 \mid \mathbf{x})}{\partial x_j} = \phi[\exp(-\mathbf{x}_1\boldsymbol{\delta})\mathbf{x}\boldsymbol{\beta}]\exp(-\mathbf{x}_1\boldsymbol{\delta})[\boldsymbol{\beta}_j - \delta_j \cdot (\mathbf{x}\boldsymbol{\beta})], \tag{15.57}$$

and so the sign of the partial effect at $\mathbf{x}$ depends on the sign of $\boldsymbol{\beta}_j - \delta_j \cdot (\mathbf{x}\boldsymbol{\beta})$; it need not be the same sign as β_j. (We can actually find models where the partial effect is always the opposite sign from the coefficient. If $y = 1[\beta_0 + \beta_1 x_1 + e > 0]$ and $D(e \mid \mathbf{x}) = \text{Normal}(0, x_1^2)$, then $P(y = 1 \mid x_1) = \Phi(\beta_0/x_1 + \beta_1)$, and so $\partial P(y = 1 \mid x_1)/\partial x_1 = -(\beta_0/x_1^2)\phi(\beta_0/x_1 + \beta_1)$. If $\beta_0 > 0$ and $\beta_1 > 0$, the partial effect of x_1 on $P(y = 1 \mid x_1)$ is negative while β_1, the partial effect of x_1 on $E(y^* \mid x_1)$, is positive.) These days, estimating a so-called **heteroskedastic probit model** (which usually means an exponential conditional variance for e) is fairly straightforward. The challenge is in intelligently using the resulting estimates. One possibility is to compute partial effects from equation (15.57) and average them across the sample. In any case, it makes no sense to compare the estimates of $\boldsymbol{\beta}$ from a heteroskedastic probit with those from a standard probit. In each case the MLE estimates adjust to fit the data, and this often means that different methods can provide similar partial effects, at least for some values of $\mathbf{x}$.

There is another, more subtle reason to entertain the notion of heteroskedasticity in the latent variable model. As discussed in Wooldridge (2005c), the partial effects in the model $y_i = 1[\mathbf{x}_i\boldsymbol{\beta} + e_i > 0]$, averaged across the distribution of e_i, *are* the same sign as the corresponding β_j. In fact, the ratios of APEs for the continuous variables are equal to the ratios of the coefficients, even when e_i contains heteroskedasticity. To see why, it is easiest to work with the average structural function (ASF) defined by Blundell and Powell (2004); see also Section 2.2.5. For binary response, the ASF as a function of $\mathbf{x}$ is

$$\text{ASF}(\mathbf{x}) = E_{e_i}\{1[\mathbf{x}\boldsymbol{\beta} + e_i > 0]\} = P(e_i > -\mathbf{x}\boldsymbol{\beta}) = 1 - F(-\mathbf{x}\boldsymbol{\beta}), \tag{15.58}$$

where $F(\cdot)$ is the cdf of e_i (which may not be symmetrically distributed about zero), and we put an i subscript on e_i to emphasize it is the random variable that is averaged out. From expression (15.58), we can see that the APE of x_j has the same sign as β_j, and, for a continuous x_j, the APE is simply $\beta_j f(-\mathbf{x}\boldsymbol{\beta})$, assuming that F is continuously differentiable with density f. The relative APEs for two continuous variables x_j and x_h is β_j/β_h—the same conclusion in Section 15.7.1 when we introduced heterogeneity additively inside the probit function that was independent of $\mathbf{x}$.

That the sign of the APE for x_j is given by the sign of β_j, and that the relative APEs for continuous covariates are given by the ratios of elements of $\boldsymbol{\beta}$—whether or not e is independent of $\mathbf{x}$—suggest that $\boldsymbol{\beta}$ is still of some interest. In the next subsection we will discuss estimation of $\boldsymbol{\beta}$ under weaker assumptions (up to a scale factor). But what implications does this discussion about APEs have for heteroskedastic probit? Interestingly, in the heteroskedastic probit model, we can easily recover the APEs. The easiest way is through the ASF. Now, rather than using the unconditional distribution of e_i, we use iterated expectations, because what we have modeled is $\mathrm{D}(e_i \mid \mathbf{x}_i) = \mathrm{D}(e_i \mid \mathbf{x}_{i1})$:

$$\mathrm{ASF}(\mathbf{x}) = \mathrm{E}_{\mathbf{x}_{i1}}(\mathrm{E}\{1[\mathbf{x}\boldsymbol{\beta} + e_i > 0] \mid \mathbf{x}_{i1}\}) = \mathrm{E}_{\mathbf{x}_{i1}}\{\Phi[\exp(-\mathbf{x}_{i1}\boldsymbol{\delta})\mathbf{x}\boldsymbol{\beta}]\}, \tag{15.59}$$

where $\mathrm{E}\{1[\mathbf{x}\boldsymbol{\beta} + e_i > 0] \mid \mathbf{x}_{i1}\} = \Phi[\exp(-\mathbf{x}_{i1}\boldsymbol{\delta})\mathbf{x}\boldsymbol{\beta}]$ follows from $1[\mathbf{x}\boldsymbol{\beta} + e_i > 0] = 1[\exp(-\mathbf{x}_{i1}\boldsymbol{\delta})e_i > -\exp(-\mathbf{x}_{i1}\boldsymbol{\delta})\mathbf{x}\boldsymbol{\beta}]$ along with $\mathrm{D}(\exp(-\mathbf{x}_{i1}\boldsymbol{\delta})e_i \mid \mathbf{x}_{i1}) = \mathrm{Normal}(0, 1)$. It is important to see that $\mathbf{x}$ is just a fixed argument in (15.59), whereas $\mathbf{x}_{i1}$ denotes a random vector that we average out. For a continuous covariate x_j, the partial effect on the ASF is

$$\mathrm{E}_{\mathbf{x}_{i1}}\{\phi[\exp(-\mathbf{x}_{i1}\boldsymbol{\delta})\mathbf{x}\boldsymbol{\beta}]\}\beta_j. \tag{15.60}$$

Given the maximum likelihood estimators $\hat{\boldsymbol{\beta}}$ and $\hat{\boldsymbol{\delta}}$ from heteroskedastic probit, a consistent estimator of (15.60) is $(N^{-1}\sum_{i=1}^{N}\phi[\exp(-\mathbf{x}_{i1}\hat{\boldsymbol{\delta}})\mathbf{x}\hat{\boldsymbol{\beta}}])\hat{\beta}_j$, and then we can insert interesting values of $\mathbf{x}$ or further average out across $\mathbf{x}_i$. Bootstrapping would be a sensible method for obtaining valid standard errors of the APEs.

Now we seem to be in a quandary. We have two ways of computing partial effects, and they can give conflicting answers, not just on magnitude of the effects but also on the direction of the effects. Initially, we discussed how the partial effects based on $\mathrm{P}(y = 1 \mid \mathbf{x})$—given for continuous x_j in equation (15.57)—need not have the same signs as the β_j. But equation (15.60) shows that the APEs obtained from averaging out e_i are, in fact, proportional to the β_j. (Of course, to obtain the partial effects in either case we cannot ignore $\boldsymbol{\delta}$, as it appears directly in both formulas.) Which partial effect is "correct"? Unfortunately, there is a fundamental lack of identification that does not allow us to choose between the two. Equation (15.60) was obtained from $y_i = 1[\mathbf{x}_i\boldsymbol{\beta} + e_i > 0]$ where e_i given $\mathbf{x}_i$ has a heteroskedastic normal distribution. But suppose we start with the model $y_i = 1[\mathbf{x}_i\boldsymbol{\beta} + \exp(\mathbf{x}_{i1}\boldsymbol{\delta})a_i > 0]$, where a_i is independent of $\mathbf{x}_i$ with a standard normal distribution. Now, it is easily shown that the ASF is just the same as the response probability evaluated at $\mathbf{x}$, namely, $\Phi[\exp(-\mathbf{x}_1\boldsymbol{\delta})\mathbf{x}\boldsymbol{\beta}]$, which takes us back to the partial effects in equation (15.57). In fact, the APEs based on (15.57) are commonly reported for heteroskedastic probit, whereas we have just as good a case for using (15.60).

As discussed by Wooldridge (2005a), on aesthetic grounds we might prefer the usual index structure with $\text{Var}(e \mid \mathbf{x})$ heteroskedastic, especially because the APEs are easy to obtain and the β_j give directions of effects and relative effects. But both models nest the usual probit model, and aesthetic considerations cannot change the fact that two observationally equivalent models lead to possibly quite different APEs. Plus, there is nothing unappealing about index models of the form $y_i = 1(\mathbf{x}_i\boldsymbol{\beta} + a_i + a_i\mathbf{x}_{i1}\boldsymbol{\delta} > 0)$ where $\text{D}(a_i \mid \mathbf{x}_i) = \text{Normal}(0, 1)$; in fact, interacting the unobservable a_i with a subset of $\mathbf{x}_i$ makes perfectly good sense, and we studied linear models with this feature in Chapters 4 and 6. Because a_i is independent of $\mathbf{x}_i$, the partial effects defined in terms of the ASF are, like those in equation (15.57), the same as the partial effects on the response probability $p(\mathbf{x})$. The uncomfortable conclusion is that we have no convincing way of choosing between equations (15.57) and (15.60).

15.7.5 Estimation under Weaker Assumptions

Probit, logit, and the extensions of these mentioned in the previous subsection are all parametric models: $\text{P}(y = 1 \mid \mathbf{x})$ depends on a finite number of parameters. There have been many advances in estimation of binary response models that relax parametric assumptions on $\text{P}(y = 1 \mid \mathbf{x})$. We briefly discuss some of those here.

If we are interested in estimating the directions and relative sizes of the partial effects, and not the response probabilities, several results are known. In Section 15.6 we noted a special case—$\mathbf{x}$ is multivariate normal—where the slope coefficients in the linear projection of y on 1, $\mathbf{x}$, say $\boldsymbol{\lambda}$, are the partial effects of $p(\mathbf{x})$ averaged across the distribution of $\mathbf{x}$—regardless of the true response probability! Chung and Goldberger (1984) obtain conditions under which the linear projection identifies the parameters up to scale. In fact, in the index formulation $y = 1[y^* > 0]$ with $y^* = \alpha + \mathbf{x}\boldsymbol{\beta} + e$, Chung and Goldberger simply take α and $\boldsymbol{\beta}$ to be the parameters in the linear projection of y^* on 1, $\mathbf{x}$. Their main result is that if $\text{E}(\mathbf{x} \mid y^*)$ is linear in y^*—sufficient but not necessary is that $(\mathbf{x}, y^*)$ is multivariate normal—then the slope parameters in the linear projection of y on 1, $\mathbf{x}$ are proportional to $\boldsymbol{\beta}$: $\boldsymbol{\lambda} = \tau\boldsymbol{\beta}$, where τ is the slope in the linear projection of y on y^*. (For binary response, it can be shown that $\tau > 0$.) In the standard index model $p(\mathbf{x}) = G(\alpha + \mathbf{x}\boldsymbol{\beta})$, the partial effect for continuous covariates are proportional to their betas, and so the linear projection identifies the relative partial effects of continuous explanatory variables. Unfortunately, we cannot conclude that the $\boldsymbol{\lambda}$ are themselves the APEs unless $\mathbf{x}$ is multivariate normal.

Ruud (1983) obtains similar results for the index models estimated by maximum likelihood, but where we misspecify $G(\cdot)$—thereby employing quasi-MLE. Ruud obtains a result that the slopes in the misspecified MLE are consistent for $\tau\boldsymbol{\beta}$ for an unknown scale factor τ. Ruud's key condition is linearity of the conditional means

$E(\mathbf{x} \mid \mathbf{x}\boldsymbol{\beta})$; multivariate normality of $\mathbf{x}$ is sufficient but not necessary. Of course, this condition is unlikely to be generally satisfied. Ruud (1986) shows how to exploit these results to consistently estimate the slope parameters up to scale fairly generally.

An alternative approach is to explicitly recognize that we do not know the function $G(\cdot)$, but the response probability has the index form in equation (15.8). This arises from the latent variable formulation (15.9) when e is independent of $\mathbf{x}$ but the distribution of e is not known. There are several **semiparametric estimators** of the slope parameters, up to scale, that do not require knowledge of G. Under certain restrictions on the function G and the distribution of $\mathbf{x}$, the semiparametric estimators are consistent and $\sqrt{N}$-asymptotically normal. See, for example, Stoker (1986), Powell, Stock, and Stoker (1989), Ichimura (1993), Klein and Spady (1993), and Ai (1997). Powell (1994) contains a survey of these methods.

Once $\hat{\boldsymbol{\beta}}$ is obtained, the function G can be consistently estimated (in a sense we cannot make precise here, as G is part of an infinite dimensional space). Thus, the response probabilities, as well as the partial effects on these probabilities, can be consistently estimated for unknown G. Obtaining $\hat{G}$ requires **nonparametric regression** of y_i on $\mathbf{x}_i\hat{\boldsymbol{\beta}}$, where $\hat{\boldsymbol{\beta}}$ are the scaled slope estimators. Accessible treatments of the methods used are contained in Stoker (1992), Powell (1994), and Härdle and Linton (1994).

Remarkably, it is possible to estimate $\boldsymbol{\beta}$ up to scale without assuming that e and $\mathbf{x}$ are independent in the model (15.9). In the specification $y = 1[\mathbf{x}\boldsymbol{\beta} + e > 0]$, Manski (1975, 1988) shows how to consistently estimate $\boldsymbol{\beta}$, subject to a scaling, under the assumption that the median of e given $\mathbf{x}$ is zero. Some mild restrictions are needed on the distribution of $\mathbf{x}$; the most important of these is that at least one element of $\mathbf{x}$ with nonzero coefficient is essentially continuous. This allows e to have any distribution, and e and $\mathbf{x}$ can be dependent; for example, $\text{Var}(e \mid \mathbf{x})$ is unrestricted. Manski's estimator, called the **maximum score estimator**, is a least absolute deviations estimator. Since the median of y given $\mathbf{x}$ is $1[\mathbf{x}\boldsymbol{\beta} > 0]$, the maximum score estimator solves

$$\min_{\boldsymbol{\beta}} \sum_{i=1}^{N} |y_i - 1[\mathbf{x}_i\boldsymbol{\beta} > 0]|$$

over all $\boldsymbol{\beta}$ with, say, $\boldsymbol{\beta}'\boldsymbol{\beta} = 1$, or with some element of $\boldsymbol{\beta}$ fixed at unity if the corresponding x_j is known to appear in $\text{Med}(y \mid \mathbf{x})$. (A normalization is needed because if $\text{Med}(y \mid \mathbf{x}) = 1[\mathbf{x}\boldsymbol{\beta} > 0]$ then $\text{Med}(y \mid \mathbf{x}) = 1[\mathbf{x}(\tau\boldsymbol{\beta}) > 0]$ for any $\tau > 0$.) The resulting estimator is consistent—for a recent proof, see Newey and McFadden (1994)—but its limiting distribution is nonnormal. In fact, it converges to its limiting distribution at rate $N^{1/3}$. Horowitz (1992) proposes a smoothed version of the maximum score estimator that converges at a rate close to $\sqrt{N}$.

The maximum score estimator's strength is that it consistently estimates $\boldsymbol{\beta}$ up to scale in cases where the index model (15.8) does not hold. As we saw in the previous subsection, when $y_i = 1[\mathbf{x}_i\boldsymbol{\beta} + e_i > 0]$, the APE for x_j has same sign as β_j and the relative APEs for continuous variables are given by β_j/β_h. Thus, there is some value in estimating the parameters up to a common scale factor. But maximum score estimation does not allow estimation of the APEs for either continuous or discrete covariates because the unconditional distribution of e_i is not identified and, without making further assumptions, we cannot find $\mathrm{P}(y_i = 1 \mid \mathbf{x}_i)$. We should not be too surprised by this state of affairs: if our assumptions are weak, we might not be able to learn everything we would like to know about how $\mathbf{x}$ affects y.

Lewbel (2000) offers a different approach to estimating the coefficients up to scale when e is not independent of $\mathbf{x}$ but e and $\mathbf{x}$ are uncorrelated. The identification results and estimation methods can be found in Lewbel's paper; here we discuss the key assumptions and their applicability. Lewbel's key assumption is the existence of a continuous variable, say x_K, with $\beta_K \neq 0$, such that $\mathrm{D}(e \mid \mathbf{x}) = \mathrm{D}(e \mid x_1, x_2, \ldots, x_{K-1})$. In other words, conditional on $(x_1, \ldots, x_{K-1})$, e and x_K are independent. Applied to the case of heteroskedasticity in the latent variable model, practically speaking the conditional independence assumption means $\mathrm{E}(y^* \mid \mathbf{x})$ must depend on x_K but $\mathrm{Var}(y^* \mid \mathbf{x})$ must not depend on x_K. Therefore, one must be willing to assume that a variable definitely affects the conditional mean of y^* but not its conditional variance. If we parametrically model $\mathrm{D}(e \mid \mathbf{x})$, we need not impose such a restriction, and so the semiparametric approach does not uniformly improve on parametric approaches. (And, as we already know, we can only learn about relative sizes of the coefficients using the semiparametric approach, whereas the parametric approach also delivers APEs.)

As pointed out by Lewbel, one case where his assumption holds is when the latent variable model is a random coefficient model of the form $y_i^* = b_{i1}x_{i1} + \cdots + b_{i,K-1}x_{i,K-1} + \beta_K x_{iK} + a_i$, where $b_{i1}, \ldots, b_{i,K-1}$ are random slopes and $\beta_K \neq 0$. If the vector $(a_i, b_{i1}, \ldots, b_{i,K-1})$ is independent of $\mathbf{x}_i$, then Lewbel's key assumption holds. The problem is that we have arbitrarily restricted x_{iK} to have a constant, nonzero coefficient. Even if x_{iK} is generated randomly and independently of the other covariates and the unobserved heterogeneity, there is no reason to think that its coefficient is constant while other regressors might have heterogeneous coefficients; it is simply an arbitrary restriction. (For example, if y^* is a latent variable measuring propensity to be employed and x_K is a job training indicator, random assignment of x_K has nothing to do with whether job training has differential effects across individuals on the propensity to be employed.) If we focus on partial effects, we can allow the entire vector $\mathbf{b}_i = (b_{i1}, \ldots, b_{iK})'$ to vary along with a_i. Then, we know that the APEs on

$P(y_i = 1 \mid \mathbf{x}_i, a_i, \mathbf{b}_i)$ are easily obtained from $P(y_i = 1 \mid \mathbf{x}_i)$; see Section 2.2.5. Therefore, we can directly specify a flexible model for $P(y_i = 1 \mid \mathbf{x}_i)$ or derive the response probability from $P(y_i = 1 \mid \mathbf{x}_i, a_i, \mathbf{b}_i)$, such as probit, and a distribution for $(a_i, \mathbf{b}_i')'$, such as multivariate normal.

Some progress has been made in estimating parameters up to scale in the model $y_1 = 1[\mathbf{z}_1\boldsymbol{\delta}_1 + \alpha_1 y_2 + u_1 > 0]$, where y_2 might be correlated with u_1 and $\mathbf{z}_1$ is a $1 \times L_1$ vector of exogenous variables. Lewbel's (2000) general approach applies to this situation as well. Let $\mathbf{z}$ be the vector of all exogenous variables uncorrelated with u_1. Then Lewbel requires a continuous element of $\mathbf{z}_1$ with nonzero coefficient—say, the last element, z_{L_1}—that does not appear in $D(u_1 \mid y_2, \mathbf{z})$. (Clearly, y_2 cannot play the role of the variable excluded from $D(u_1 \mid y_2, \mathbf{z})$ if y_2 is thought to be endogenous.) When might Lewbel's exclusion restriction hold? Sufficient is $y_2 = g_2(\mathbf{z}_2) + v_2$, where (u_1, v_2) is independent of $\mathbf{z}$ and $\mathbf{z}_2$ does not contain z_{L_1}. But this means that we have imposed an exclusion restriction on the reduced form of y_2, something usually discouraged in parametric contexts. (Putting restrictions on reduced forms is much different, and less defensible, than putting retrictions on structural equations.) Randomization of z_{L_1} does *not* make its exclusion from the reduced form of y_2 legitimate. In fact, one often hopes that an instrument for y_2 is effectively randomized, which means that z_{L_1} does *not* appear in the structural equation but does appear in the reduced form of y_2—the opposite of Lewbel's assumption. (As a generic example, eligibility is often randomized but participation, y_2, is not, and then one hopes to use an eligibility dummy as an IV for the participation dummy.)

As we have discussed at several points, when we are actually interested in partial effects on response probabilities, estimating coefficients up to an unknown scale is usually unsatisfying. Recently, Blundell and Powell (2004) have shown how to estimate an average structural function—and therefore the APEs—when y_2 is a continuous endogenous explanatory variable. We can think of their method as a nonparametric extension of the model in Section 15.7.2.

Blundell and Powell allow complete flexibility of functional forms, but we can illustrate their general approach using an index model $y_1 = 1[\mathbf{x}_1\boldsymbol{\beta}_1 + u_1 > 0]$, where $\mathbf{x}_1$ can be any function of $(\mathbf{z}_1, y_2)$. The key assumption is that y_2 can be written as $y_2 = g_2(\mathbf{z}) + v_2$, where (u_1, v_2) is independent of $\mathbf{z}$. The independence of the additive error v_2 and $\mathbf{z}$ pretty much rules out discreteness in y_2, even though $g_2(\cdot)$ can be left unspecified. Under the independence assumption,

$$P(y_1 = 1 \mid \mathbf{z}, v_2) = E(y_1 \mid \mathbf{z}, v_2) = H(\mathbf{x}_1\boldsymbol{\beta}_1, v_2)$$

for some (generally unknown) function $H(\cdot, \cdot)$. The average structural function is just $\mathrm{ASF}(\mathbf{z}_1, y_2) = E_{v_{i2}}[H(\mathbf{x}_1\boldsymbol{\beta}_1, v_{i2})]$. We can estimate H and $\boldsymbol{\beta}_1$ quite generally by first estimating the function $g_2(\cdot)$ and then obtaining residuals $\hat{v}_{i2} = y_{i2} - \hat{g}_2(\mathbf{z}_i)$. Then, H and $\boldsymbol{\beta}_1$ can be estimated in a second step by a semiparametric procedure—that is, one that does not assume H is in a parametric family. Then the ASF is estimated by averaging out the reduced form residuals,

$$\widehat{\mathrm{ASF}}(\mathbf{z}_1, y_2) = N^{-1} \sum_{i=1}^{N} \hat{H}(\mathbf{x}_1 \hat{\boldsymbol{\beta}}_1, \hat{v}_{i2}); \tag{15.61}$$

derivatives and changes can be computed with respect to elements of $(\mathbf{z}_1, y_2)$.

Blundell and Powell (2004) actually allow $P(y_1 = 1 \mid \mathbf{z}, y_2)$ to have the general form $H(\mathbf{z}_1, y_2, v_2)$, and then the second-step estimation is entirely nonparametric. They also allow $\hat{g}_2(\cdot)$ to be fully nonparametric. But parametric approximations in each stage might produce good estimates of the APEs. For example, y_{i2} can be regressed on flexible functions of $\mathbf{z}_i$ to obtain $\hat{v}_{i2}$. Then, one can estimate probit or logit models in the second stage that include functions of $\mathbf{z}_1$, y_2, and $\hat{v}_2$ in a flexible way—for example, with levels, quadratics, interactions, and maybe even higher-order polynomials of each. Then, one simply averages out $\hat{v}_{i2}$, as in equation (15.61). Valid standard errors and test statistics can be obtained by bootstrapping or by using the delta method.

Obtaining flexible methods that allow for general discrete y_2, which would extend the parametric approach of Section 15.7.3, is an important task for future research.

15.8 Binary Response Models for Panel Data

When analyzing binary responses in the context of panel data, it is often useful to begin with a linear model with an additive, unobserved effect, and then, just as in Chapters 10 and 11, use the within transformation or first differencing to remove the unobserved effect. A linear probability model for binary outcomes has the same problems as in the cross section case. In fact, it is probably less appealing for unobserved effects models, as it implies the unnatural restrictions $\mathbf{x}_{it}\boldsymbol{\beta} \le c_i \le 1 - \mathbf{x}_{it}\boldsymbol{\beta}, t = 1, \ldots, T$, on the unobserved effects. To see this, note that the response probability for an unobserved effects LPM is $\mathrm{P}(y_{it} = 1 \mid \mathbf{x}_i, c_i) = \mathrm{P}(y_{it} = 1 \mid \mathbf{x}_{it}, c_i) = \mathbf{x}_{it}\boldsymbol{\beta} + c_i$. As in the pure cross section case, the linear functional form is almost certainly false, except in special cases. But FE or FD estimation of the LPM might provide reasonable estimates of APEs. Plus, the LPM has the advantage of not requiring a distributional assumption on $\mathrm{D}(c_i \mid \mathbf{x}_i)$ (which means we do not need to be concerned that c_i is bounded by linear combinations of $\mathbf{x}_{it}$); nor do we have to assume independence of the responses $\{y_{i1}, \ldots, y_{iT}\}$ conditional on $(\mathbf{x}_i, c_i)$ (provided we make our inference robust to serial dependence, as well as heteroskedasticity). The nonlinear methods we cover in this section require one or both of these assumptions. First, we briefly cover estimation when the model is not specified with unobserved heterogeneity and has explanatory variables that may not be strictly exogenous.

15.8.1 Pooled Probit and Logit

In Section 13.8 we used a probit model to illustrate partial likelihood methods with panel data. Naturally, we can use logit or any other binary response function as well. Suppose the model is

$$P(y_{it} = 1 \mid \mathbf{x}_{it}) = G(\mathbf{x}_{it}\boldsymbol{\beta}), \qquad t = 1, 2, \ldots, T \tag{15.62}$$

where $G(\cdot)$ is a known function taking on values in the open unit interval. As we discussed in Chapter 13, $\mathbf{x}_{it}$ can contain a variety of factors, including time dummies, interactions of time dummies with time-constant or time-varying variables, and lagged dependent variables.

In specifying the model (15.62) we have not assumed nearly enough to obtain the distribution of $\mathbf{y}_i \equiv (y_{i1}, \ldots, y_{iT})$ given $\mathbf{x}_i = (\mathbf{x}_{i1}, \ldots, \mathbf{x}_{iT})$, for two reasons. First, we have not assumed $D(y_{it} \mid \mathbf{x}_{i1}, \ldots, \mathbf{x}_{iT}) = D(y_{it} \mid \mathbf{x}_{it})$, so that $\{\mathbf{x}_{it} : t = 1, \ldots, T\}$ is not necessarily strictly exogenous. Second, even if we assume strict exogeneity, we have not restricted the dependence in $\{y_{it} : t = 1, \ldots, T\}$ conditional on $\mathbf{x}_i$. As with many pooled MLE problems, we have only specified a model for $D(y_{it} \mid \mathbf{x}_{it})$. If that model is correctly specified, we can obtain a $\sqrt{N}$-consistent, asymptotically normal estimator by maximizing the partial (pooled) log-likelihood function. For binary response, we maximize the partial log likelihood

$$\sum_{i=1}^{N} \sum_{t=1}^{T} \{y_{it} \log G(\mathbf{x}_{it}\boldsymbol{\beta}) + (1 - y_{it}) \log[1 - G(\mathbf{x}_{it}\boldsymbol{\beta})]\},$$

which is simply an exercise in pooled estimation. Without further assumptions, a robust variance matrix estimator is needed to account for serial correlation in the scores across t; see equation (13.53) with $\hat{\boldsymbol{\beta}}$ in place of $\hat{\boldsymbol{\theta}}$ and G in place of Φ. Wald and score statistics can be computed as in Chapter 12.

In the case that the model (15.62) is dynamically complete, that is,

$$P(y_{it} = 1 \mid \mathbf{x}_{it}, y_{i,t-1}, \mathbf{x}_{i,t-1}, \ldots) = P(y_{it} = 1 \mid \mathbf{x}_{it}), \tag{15.63}$$

or

$$D(y_{it} \mid \mathbf{x}_{it}, y_{i,t-1}, \mathbf{x}_{i,t-1}, \ldots) = D(y_{it} \mid \mathbf{x}_{it}),$$

inference is considerably easier: all the usual statistics from a probit or logit that pools observations and treats the sample as a long independent cross section of size NT are valid, including likelihood ratio statistics. Remember, we are definitely *not* assuming independence across t (for example, $\mathbf{x}_{it}$ can contain lagged dependent variables). Dynamic completeness implies that the scores are serially uncorrelated across t, which is the key condition for the standard inference procedures to be valid. (See the general treatment in Section 13.8.)

To test for dynamic completeness, we can always add a lagged dependent variable and possibly lagged explanatory variables. As an alternative, we can derive a simple one-degree-of-freedom test that works regardless of what is in $\mathbf{x}_{it}$. For concreteness, we focus on the probit case; other index models are handled similarly. Define $u_{it} \equiv y_{it} - \Phi(\mathbf{x}_{it}\boldsymbol{\beta})$, so that, under assumption (15.63), $\mathrm{E}(u_{it} \mid \mathbf{x}_{it}, y_{i,t-1}, \mathbf{x}_{i,t-1}, \ldots) = 0$, all t. It follows that u_{it} is uncorrelated with any function of the variables $(\mathbf{x}_{it}, y_{i,t-1}, \mathbf{x}_{i,t-1}, \ldots)$, including $u_{i,t-1}$. By studying equation (13.53), we can see that it is serial correlation in the u_{it} that makes the usual inference procedures invalid. Let $\hat{u}_{it} = y_{it} - \Phi(\mathbf{x}_{it}\hat{\boldsymbol{\beta}})$. Then a simple test is available by using pooled probit to estimate the artificial model

$$\text{“}\mathrm{P}(y_{it} = 1 \mid \mathbf{x}_{it}, \hat{u}_{i,t-1}) = \Phi(\mathbf{x}_{it}\boldsymbol{\beta} + \gamma_1 \hat{u}_{i,t-1})\text{”} \tag{15.64}$$

using time periods $t = 2, \ldots, T$. The null hypothesis is $\mathrm{H}_0 : \gamma_1 = 0$. If H_0 is rejected, then so is assumption (15.63). This is a case where under the null hypothesis, the estimation of $\boldsymbol{\beta}$ required to obtain $\hat{u}_{i,t-1}$ does not affect the limiting distribution of any of the usual test statistics, Wald, LR, or LM, of $\mathrm{H}_0 : \gamma_1 = 0$. The Wald statistic, that is, the t statistic on $\hat{\gamma}_1$, is the easiest to obtain. For the LM and LR statistics we must be sure to drop the first time period in estimating the restricted model ($\gamma_1 = 0$).

15.8.2 Unobserved Effects Probit Models under Strict Exogeneity

A popular model for binary outcomes with panel data is the **unobserved effects probit model**. A key assumption for many of the estimators for unobserved effects probit models, as well as other nonlinear panel data models, is that the observed covariates are **strictly exogenous conditional on the unobserved effect**. Now, we need this assumption in terms of conditional distributions, which we can state generically as

$$\mathrm{D}(y_{it} \mid \mathbf{x}_i, c_i) \equiv \mathrm{D}(y_{it} \mid \mathbf{x}_{i1}, \mathbf{x}_{i2}, \ldots, \mathbf{x}_{iT}, c_i) = \mathrm{D}(y_{it} \mid \mathbf{x}_{it}, c_i), \qquad t = 1, \ldots, T, \tag{15.65}$$

where c_i is the unobserved effect and $\mathbf{x}_i \equiv (\mathbf{x}_{i1}, \mathbf{x}_{i2}, \ldots, \mathbf{x}_{iT})$. In stating this assumption, we are not restricting in any way the joint distribution conditional on $(\mathbf{x}_i, c_i)$, which we write as $\mathrm{D}(\mathbf{y}_i \mid \mathbf{x}_i, c_i)$ for $\mathbf{y}_i = (y_{i1}, \ldots, y_{iT})$. As in previous chapters, where we stated the strict exogeneity assumption conditional on c_i in terms of the conditional expectation, assumption (15.65) rules out models with lagged dependent variables in $\mathbf{x}_{it}$ and also other situations where one or more elements of $\mathbf{x}_{it}$ may react in the future to idiosyncratic changes in y_{it}. Assumption (15.65) also requires that $\mathbf{x}_{it}$ includes enough lags of underlying explanatory variables if distributed lag dynamics are present.

For the unobserved effects probit model, we specify a response probability that fully determines the conditional distribution $\mathrm{D}(y_{it} \mid \mathbf{x}_{it}, c_i)$:

$$\mathrm{P}(y_{it} = 1 \mid \mathbf{x}_{it}, c_i) = \Phi(\mathbf{x}_{it}\boldsymbol{\beta} + c_i), \qquad t = 1, \ldots, T. \tag{15.66}$$

Most analyses are not convincing unless $\mathbf{x}_{it}$ contains a full set of time dummies. In what follows, we usually leave time dummies implicit to simplify the notation.

Our interest is in the response probability (15.66), and we would like to be able to estimate the parameters and partial effects just by specifying equation (15.66). But we already saw in Chapters 10 and 11 that just specifying a model with contemporaneous conditioning variables is not sufficient for estimating the parameters, and the same is true here: without more assumptions, $\boldsymbol{\beta}$ is not identified. Even adding the strict exogeneity assumption (15.65) is not enough. Unlike with linear models, we face a further difficulty, which has implications both for estimating $\boldsymbol{\beta}$ and for estimating partial effects of interest. Namely, we must specify how c_i relates to the covariates.

What happens if we try to proceed without placing restrictions on $\mathrm{D}(c_i \mid \mathbf{x}_i)$? One possibility is to add, in addition to assumptions (15.65) and (15.66), the assumption that the responses are independent conditional on $(\mathbf{x}_i, c_i)$:

$$y_{i1}, \ldots, y_{iT} \text{ are independent conditional on } (\mathbf{x}_i, c_i). \tag{15.67}$$

Because of the presence of c_i, the y_{it} are dependent across t conditional only on the observables, $\mathbf{x}_i$. (Assumption (15.67) is analogous to the linear model assumption that, conditional on $(\mathbf{x}_i, c_i)$, the y_{it} are serially uncorrelated; see Assumption FE.3 in Chapter 10.) Under assumptions (15.65), (15.66), and (15.67), we can derive the density of $(y_{i1}, \ldots, y_{iT})$ conditional on $(\mathbf{x}_i, c_i)$:

$$f(y_1, \ldots, y_T \mid \mathbf{x}_i, c_i; \boldsymbol{\beta}) = \prod_{t=1}^{T} f(y_t \mid \mathbf{x}_{it}, c_i; \boldsymbol{\beta}), \tag{15.68}$$

where $f(y_t \mid \mathbf{x}_t, c; \boldsymbol{\beta}) = \Phi(\mathbf{x}_t\boldsymbol{\beta} + c)^{y_t}[1 - \Phi(\mathbf{x}_t\boldsymbol{\beta} + c)]^{1-y_t}$. Ideally, we could estimate the quantities of interest without restricting the relationship between c_i and the $\mathbf{x}_{it}$. In this spirit, we might view the c_i as parameters to be estimated along with $\boldsymbol{\beta}$, as this treatment obviates the need to make assumptions about the distribution of c_i given

$\mathbf{x}_i$. The log-likelihood function is $\sum_{i=1}^N \ell_i(c_i, \boldsymbol{\beta})$, where $\ell_i(c_i, \boldsymbol{\beta})$ is the log of equation (15.68) evaluated at the y_{it}. Unfortunately, in addition to being computationally difficult, estimation of the c_i along with $\boldsymbol{\beta}$ introduces an **incidental parameters problem**. Unlike in the linear case, where estimating the c_i along with $\boldsymbol{\beta}$ leads to the $\sqrt{N}$-consistent FE estimator of $\boldsymbol{\beta}$, in the present case estimating the c_i (N of them) along with $\boldsymbol{\beta}$ leads to inconsistent estimation of $\boldsymbol{\beta}$ with T fixed and $N \to \infty$. We discuss the incidental parameters problem in more detail for the unobserved effects logit model in Section 15.8.3.

The estimator of $\boldsymbol{\beta}$ obtained by treating the c_i as parameters has been called the "fixed effects probit" estimator, an unfortunate name. As we saw with linear models, and as we will see with the logit model in the next subsection and with count data models in Chapter 18, in some cases we can consistently estimate the parameters $\boldsymbol{\beta}$ without specifying a distribution for c_i given $\mathbf{x}_i$. This feature is the hallmark of an FE analysis for most microeconometric applications. By contrast, treating the c_i as parameters to estimate can lead to potentially serious biases, as in the probit case.

Here we follow the same approach adopted for linear models: we *always* treat c_i as an unobservable random variable drawn along with $(\mathbf{x}_i, \mathbf{y}_i)$. The question is, under what additional assumptions can we consistently estimate parameters, as well as interesting partial effects? Unfortunately, for the unobserved effects probit model, we must make an assumption about the relationship between c_i and $\mathbf{x}_i$. The **traditional random effects probit model** adds, to assumptions (15.65), (15.66), and (15.67), the assumption

$$c_i \mid \mathbf{x}_i \sim \text{Normal}(0, \sigma_c^2). \tag{15.69}$$

This is a strong assumption, as it implies that c_i and $\mathbf{x}_i$ are independent and that c_i has a normal distribution. It is not enough to assume that c_i and $\mathbf{x}_i$ are uncorrelated, or even that $\mathrm{E}(c_i \mid \mathbf{x}_i) = 0$. The assumption $\mathrm{E}(c_i) = 0$ is without loss of generality provided $\mathbf{x}_{it}$ contains an intercept, as it always should.

Before we discuss estimation of the random effects probit model, we should be sure we know what we want to estimate. As in Section 15.7.1, consistent estimation of $\boldsymbol{\beta}$ means that we can consistently estimate the partial effects of the elements of $\mathbf{x}_t$ on the response probability $\mathrm{P}(y_t = 1 \mid \mathbf{x}_t, c)$ at the average value of c in the population, $c = 0$. (We can also estimate the relative effects of any two elements of $\mathbf{x}_t$ for any value of c, as the relative effects do not depend on c.) For the reasons discussed in Section 15.7.1, APEs are at least as useful. Since $c_i \sim \text{Normal}(0, \sigma_c^2)$, the APE for a continuous x_{tj} is $[\beta_j/(1+\sigma_c^2)^{1/2}]\phi[\mathbf{x}_t\boldsymbol{\beta}/(1+\sigma_c^2)^{1/2}]$, just as in equation (15.38). Therefore, we only need to estimate $\boldsymbol{\beta}_c \equiv \boldsymbol{\beta}/(1+\sigma_c^2)^{1/2}$ to estimate the APEs, for either continuous or discrete explanatory variables. (In other branches of applied statistics, such as biostatistics and education, the coefficients indexing the APEs—$\boldsymbol{\beta}_c$ in our notation—are called the **population-averaged parameters**.)

Under assumptions (15.65), (15.66), (15.67), and (15.69), a conditional maximum likelihood approach is available for estimating $\boldsymbol{\beta}$ and σ_c^2. This is a special case of the approach in Section 13.9. Because the c_i are not observed, they cannot appear in the likelihood function. Instead, we find the joint distribution of $(y_{i1}, \ldots, y_{iT})$ conditional on $\mathbf{x}_i$, a step that requires us to *integrate out* c_i. Since c_i has a Normal$(0, \sigma_c^2)$ distribution,

$$f(y_1, \ldots, y_T \mid \mathbf{x}_i; \boldsymbol{\theta}) = \int_{-\infty}^{\infty} \left[\prod_{t=1}^{T} f(y_t \mid \mathbf{x}_{it}, c; \boldsymbol{\beta}) \right] (1/\sigma_c)\phi(c/\sigma_c)\, \mathrm{d}c, \tag{15.70}$$

where $f(y_t \mid \mathbf{x}_t, c; \boldsymbol{\beta}) = \Phi(\mathbf{x}_t\boldsymbol{\beta} + c)^{y_t}[1 - \Phi(\mathbf{x}_t\boldsymbol{\beta} + c)]^{1-y_t}$ and $\boldsymbol{\theta}$ contains $\boldsymbol{\beta}$ and σ_c^2. Plugging in y_{it} for all t and taking the log of equation (15.70) gives the conditional log likelihood $\ell_i(\boldsymbol{\theta})$ for each i. The log-likelihood function for the entire sample of size N can be maximized with respect to $\boldsymbol{\beta}$ and σ_c^2 (or $\boldsymbol{\beta}$ and σ_c) to obtain $\sqrt{N}$-consistent asymptotically normal estimators; Butler and Moffitt (1982) describe a procedure for approximating the integral in equation (15.70). The conditional MLE in this context is typically called the **random effects probit estimator**, and the theory in Section 13.9 can be applied directly to obtain asymptotic standard errors and test statistics. Since $\boldsymbol{\beta}$ and σ_c^2 can be estimated, the partial effects at $c = 0$ as well as the APEs can be estimated. Since the variance of the idiosyncratic error in the latent variable model is unity, the relative importance of the unobserved effect is measured as $\rho = \sigma_c^2/(\sigma_c^2 + 1)$, which is also the correlation between the composite latent error, say, $c_i + e_{it}$, across any two time periods. Many random effects probit routines report $\hat{\rho}$ and its standard error; these statistics lead to an easy test for the presence of the unobserved effect.

Assumptions (15.67) and (15.69) are fairly strong, and it is possible to relax them. First consider relaxing assumption (15.67). One useful observation is that, under assumptions (15.66) and (15.69) only (even without assumption (15.65)),

$$\mathrm{P}(y_{it} = 1 \mid \mathbf{x}_{it}) = \Phi(\mathbf{x}_{it}\boldsymbol{\beta}_c), \tag{15.71}$$

where $\boldsymbol{\beta}_c = \boldsymbol{\beta}/(1 + \sigma_c^2)^{1/2}$. Therefore, just as in Section 15.8.1, we can estimate $\boldsymbol{\beta}_c$ from pooled probit of y_{it} on $\mathbf{x}_{it}$, $t = 1, \ldots, T$, $i = 1, \ldots, N$, meaning that we directly estimate the APEs. If c_i is truly present, $\{y_{it}: t = 1, \ldots, T\}$ will not be independent conditional on $\mathbf{x}_i$. Robust inference is needed to account for the serial dependence, as discussed in Section 15.8.1.

Rather than simply calculating robust standard errors for $\hat{\boldsymbol{\beta}}_c$ after pooled probit estimation, or using the full random effects (RE) assumptions and obtaining the MLE, we can apply the generalized estimating equation (GEE) approach that we introduced in Section 12.9. As we discussed there, GEE is simply multivariate weighted nonlinear least squares with a correctly specified model for $E(\mathbf{y}_i \mid \mathbf{x}_i)$ but a generally misspecified model for the conditional variance matrix $\text{Var}(\mathbf{y}_i \mid \mathbf{x}_i)$, where $\mathbf{y}_i$ is the T-vector of responses for unit i. In the present application, we have correctly specified each element of $E(\mathbf{y}_i \mid \mathbf{x}_i)$ as $E(y_{it} \mid \mathbf{x}_i) = \Phi(\mathbf{x}_{it}\boldsymbol{\beta}_c)$. Plus, each conditional variance, $\text{Var}(y_{it} \mid \mathbf{x}_i)$, is necessarily equal to $\text{Var}(y_{it} \mid \mathbf{x}_i) = \Phi(\mathbf{x}_{it}\boldsymbol{\beta}_c)[1 - \Phi(\mathbf{x}_{it}\boldsymbol{\beta}_c)]$. What is difficult to obtain, even under the full set of RE probit assumptions, are the conditional correlations, $\text{Corr}(y_{it}, y_{is} \mid \mathbf{x}_i)$. (In fact, there are no closed-form expressions for these correlations.) The most straightforward GEE method is to specify a constant and exchangeable "working" correlation matrix, which means in using WMNLS we act *as if* $\text{Corr}(y_{it}, y_{is} \mid \mathbf{x}_i) = \rho$ for $|\rho| < 1$. This assumption is almost certainly false; the actual conditional correlations likely depend on $\mathbf{x}_i$ in a complicated fashion. Nevertheless, as we explained in Section 12.9, the hope is that allowing a nonzero correlation in the working variance-covariance matrix will produce an estimator asymptotically more efficient than just using pooled probit. At the same time, such a WMNLS estimator will be consistent under assumptions (15.65), (15.66), and (15.69), the same assumptions we use for consistency of pooled probit. Practically, we can think of GEE for RE probit models as a method that has the same robustness as pooled probit yet, ideally, gets back some of the efficiency lost by ignoring the serial dependence in estimation.

The terminology used in the GEE literature when applied to nonlinear unobserved effects models, such as RE probit, can be elusive. We can minimize our confusion by keeping straight the distinctions among a model, the quantities of interest, and an estimation method. The response probability conditional only on $\mathbf{x}_{it}$, $P(y_{it} = 1 \mid \mathbf{x}_{it}) = \Phi(\mathbf{x}_{it}\boldsymbol{\beta}_c)$—for which we only need assumptions (15.66) and (15.69) to derive—is called the **population-averaged (PA) model** in the GEE literature because the parameters, $\boldsymbol{\beta}_c$, index the population-averaged effects. Therefore, using the GEE terminology, the WMNLS estimator is designed to estimate the parameters in the PA model, just as is pooled probit. The model under the full set of RE probit assumptions is called the **subject-specific (SS) model**, primarily because the response probability in equation (15.66), which is conditional on $\mathbf{x}_{it}$ and c_i, allows us, in principle, to compute partial effects for different individuals as described by the heterogeneity, c_i. In actuality, because c_i is not observed (and cannot be estimated with small T), all we can really do is estimate the partial effects on $P(y_{it} = 1 \mid \mathbf{x}_{it} = \mathbf{x}_t, c_i = c)$ for different values of c. These values include the mean (median) value, $c = 0$, but also percentiles in the Normal$(0, \sigma_c^2)$ distribution (because we can estimate σ_c^2 along with $\boldsymbol{\beta}$), but the implication that we can estimate partial effects for specific individuals under the full RE probit assumptions is somewhat misleading.

Rather than act as if there are different models, in the context of unobserved effects probit models it seems better to organize the discussion around quantities that can be estimated under different assumptions on a common model. Much of the time it makes sense to start with equation (15.66) as the model of interest. Then we specify partial effects at different values of c or APEs as the quantities of interest. Finally, we recognize that under (15.66) and (15.69) only, we can estimate the APEs (or PA effects) by pooled probit. If we add the strict exogeneity assumption (15.65), then we can use GEE. If we use the full set of RE probit assumptions and apply MLE, then we can separately estimate $\boldsymbol{\beta}$ and σ_c^2, and therefore the APEs and partial effects at interesting values of c.

A different way to relax assumption (15.67) is to assume a particular correlation structure and then use full CMLE. For example, for each t write the latent variable model as

$$y_{it}^* = \mathbf{x}_{it}\boldsymbol{\beta} + c_i + e_{it}, \qquad y_{it} = 1[y_{it}^* > 0] \tag{15.72}$$

and assume that the $T \times 1$ vector $\mathbf{e}_i$ is multivariate normal, with unit variances, but unrestricted correlation matrix. This assumption, along with assumptions (15.65), (15.66), and (15.69), fully characterizes the distribution of $\mathbf{y}_i$ given $\mathbf{x}_i$. However, even for moderate T, computation of the CMLE can be very difficult. Recent advances in simulation methods of estimation make it possible to estimate such models for fairly large T; see, for example, Keane (1993) and Geweke and Keane (2001). The pooled probit and GEE procedures that we have described are valid for estimating $\boldsymbol{\beta}_c$, the vector that indexes APEs, regardless of the serial dependence in $\{e_{it}\}$, but they are inefficient relative to the full CMLE.

As in the linear case, in many applications the point of introducing the unobserved effect, c_i, is to explicitly allow unobservables to be correlated with some elements of $\mathbf{x}_{it}$. Chamberlain (1980) allowed for correlation between c_i and $\mathbf{x}_i$ by assuming a conditional normal distribution with linear expectation and constant variance. A Mundlak (1978) version of Chamberlain's assumption is

$$c_i \mid \mathbf{x}_i \sim \text{Normal}(\psi + \bar{\mathbf{x}}_i\boldsymbol{\xi}, \sigma_a^2), \tag{15.73}$$

where $\bar{\mathbf{x}}_i$ is the average of $\mathbf{x}_{it}$, $t = 1, \ldots, T$ and σ_a^2 is the variance of a_i in the equation $c_i = \psi + \bar{\mathbf{x}}_i\boldsymbol{\xi} + a_i$. (In other words, σ_a^2 is the conditional variance of c_i, which is assumed not to depend on $\mathbf{x}_i$.) Chamberlain (1980) allowed more generality by having $\mathbf{x}_i$, the vector of all explanatory variables across all time periods, in place of

$\bar{\mathbf{x}}_i$. We will work with assumption (15.73), as it conserves on parameters; the more general model requires a simple notational change. Chamberlain (1980) called model (15.66) under assumptions (15.65) and (15.73) a *random effects probit model*, so we refer to the model as **Chamberlain's correlated random effects probit model**. While assumption (15.73) is restrictive in that it specifies a distribution for c_i given $\mathbf{x}_i$, it at least allows for some dependence between c_i and $\mathbf{x}_i$.

As in the linear case, we can only estimate the effects of time-varying elements in $\mathbf{x}_{it}$. In particular, $\mathbf{x}_{it}$ should no longer contain a constant, as that would be indistinguishable from ψ in assumption (15.73). If our original model contains a time-constant explanatory variable, say w_i, it can be included among the explanatory variables, but we cannot distinguish its effect from c_i unless we assume that the coefficient for w_i in ξ is zero. (That is, unless we assume that c_i is partially uncorrelated with w_i.) Time dummies, which do not vary across i, are omitted from $\bar{\mathbf{x}}_i$.

If assumptions (15.65), (15.66), (15.67), and (15.73) hold, estimation of $\boldsymbol{\beta}$, ψ, ξ, and σ_a^2 is straightforward because we can write the latent variable as $y_{it}^* = \psi + \mathbf{x}_{it}\boldsymbol{\beta} + \bar{\mathbf{x}}_i\xi + a_i + e_{it}$, where the e_{it} are independent Normal(0, 1) variates (conditional on $(\mathbf{x}_i, a_i)$), and $a_i \mid \mathbf{x}_i \sim \text{Normal}(0, \sigma_a^2)$. In other words, by adding $\bar{\mathbf{x}}_i$ to the equation for each time period, we arrive at a traditional RE probit model. (The variance we estimate is σ_a^2 rather than σ_c^2, but, as we will see, this suits our purposes nicely.) Adding $\bar{\mathbf{x}}_i$ as a set of controls for unobserved heterogeneity is very intuitive: we are estimating the effect of changing x_{itj} but holding the time average fixed. A test of the usual RE probit model is easily obtained as a test of $\mathrm{H}_0 : \xi = \mathbf{0}$. Estimation can be carried out using standard RE probit software. Given estimates of ψ and ξ, we can estimate $\mathrm{E}(c_i) = \psi + \mathrm{E}(\bar{\mathbf{x}}_i)\xi$ by $\hat{\mu}_c \equiv \hat{\psi} + \bar{\mathbf{x}}\hat{\xi}$, where $\bar{\mathbf{x}}$ is the sample average of $\bar{\mathbf{x}}_i$. Therefore, for any vector $\mathbf{x}_t$, we can estimate the response probability at $\mathrm{E}(c_i)$ as $\Phi(\hat{\mu}_c + \mathbf{x}_t\hat{\boldsymbol{\beta}})$. Taking differences or derivatives (with respect to the elements of $\mathbf{x}_t$) allows us to estimate the partial effects on the response probabilities for any value of $\mathbf{x}_t$. Further, we can estimate σ_c^2 by using the relationship $\sigma_c^2 = \xi' \operatorname{Var}(\bar{\mathbf{x}}_i)\xi + \sigma_a^2$, and so $\hat{\sigma}_c^2 \equiv \hat{\xi}'[N^{-1}\sum_{i=1}^N (\bar{\mathbf{x}}_i - \bar{\mathbf{x}})'(\bar{\mathbf{x}}_i - \bar{\mathbf{x}})]\hat{\xi} + \hat{\sigma}_a^2$ is consistent for σ_c^2 as $N \to \infty$. Therefore, we can plug in values of c that are a certain number of estimated standard deviations from $\hat{\mu}_c$, say $\hat{\mu}_c \pm \hat{\sigma}_c$. But there is a subtle point at work here: if $\xi \neq \mathbf{0}$, c_i does not generally have an unconditional normal distribution unless $\bar{\mathbf{x}}_i\xi$ is normally distributed; sufficient is that $\bar{\mathbf{x}}_i$ is multivariate normal. With large T and weak dependence in the time series dimension, it might be that $\bar{\mathbf{x}}_i\xi$ has an approximate normal distribution (because it is an average across t). But weak dependence is not necessarily a good assumption, and even if it were, if we had a large T we might proceed by treating the c_i as parameters to estimate. Generally, we should not expect the distribution of c_i to be normal.

If we drop assumption (15.67), we can still estimate scaled versions of ψ, $\boldsymbol{\beta}$, and $\boldsymbol{\xi}$. Under assumptions (15.65), (15.66), and (15.73) we have

$$\begin{aligned} P(y_{it} = 1 \mid \mathbf{x}_i) &= \Phi[(\psi + \mathbf{x}_{it}\boldsymbol{\beta} + \overline{\mathbf{x}}_i\boldsymbol{\xi}) \cdot (1 + \sigma_a^2)^{-1/2}] \\ &\equiv \Phi(\psi_a + \mathbf{x}_{it}\boldsymbol{\beta}_a + \overline{\mathbf{x}}_i\boldsymbol{\xi}_a), \end{aligned} \tag{15.74}$$

where the a subscript means that a parameter vector has been multiplied by $(1 + \sigma_a^2)^{-1/2}$. It follows immediately that ψ_a, $\boldsymbol{\beta}_a$, and $\boldsymbol{\xi}_a$ can be consistently estimated using a pooled probit analysis of y_{it} on 1, $\mathbf{x}_{it}$, $\overline{\mathbf{x}}_i$, $t = 1, \dots, T$, $i = 1, \dots, N$. Because the y_{it} will be dependent condition on $\mathbf{x}_i$, inference that is robust to arbitrary time dependence is required. We can also use GEE.

Conveniently, once we have estimated ψ_a, $\boldsymbol{\beta}_a$, and $\boldsymbol{\xi}_a$, we can estimate the APEs. (We could apply the results from Section 2.2.5 here, but a direct argument is instructive.) To see how, we need to average $P(y_t = 1 \mid \mathbf{x}_t = \mathbf{x}^{\mathrm{o}}, c_i)$ across the distribution of c_i; that is, we need to find $E[P(y_t = 1 \mid \mathbf{x}_t = \mathbf{x}^{\mathrm{o}}, c_i)] = E[\Phi(\mathbf{x}^{\mathrm{o}}\boldsymbol{\beta} + c_i)]$ for any given value $\mathbf{x}^{\mathrm{o}}$ of the explanatory variables. (In what follows, $\mathbf{x}^{\mathrm{o}}$ is a nonrandom vector of numbers that we choose as interesting values of the explanatory variables. For emphasis, we include an i subscript on the random variables appearing in the expectations.) Writing $c_i = \psi + \overline{\mathbf{x}}_i\boldsymbol{\xi} + a_i$ and using iterated expectations, we have $E[\Phi(\psi + \mathbf{x}^{\mathrm{o}}\boldsymbol{\beta} + \overline{\mathbf{x}}_i\boldsymbol{\xi} + a_i)] = E[E\{\Phi(\psi + \mathbf{x}^{\mathrm{o}}\boldsymbol{\beta} + \overline{\mathbf{x}}_i\boldsymbol{\xi} + a_i) \mid \mathbf{x}_i\}]$ [where the first expectation is with respect to $(\mathbf{x}_i, a_i)$]. Using the same argument from Section 15.7.1, $E[\Phi(\psi + \mathbf{x}^{\mathrm{o}}\boldsymbol{\beta} + \overline{\mathbf{x}}_i\boldsymbol{\xi} + a_i) \mid \mathbf{x}_i] = \Phi[\{\psi + \mathbf{x}^{\mathrm{o}}\boldsymbol{\beta} + \overline{\mathbf{x}}_i\boldsymbol{\xi}\} \cdot (1 + \sigma_a^2)^{-1/2}] = \Phi(\psi_a + \mathbf{x}^{\mathrm{o}}\boldsymbol{\beta}_a + \overline{\mathbf{x}}_i\boldsymbol{\xi}_a)$, and so

$$E[\Phi(\mathbf{x}^{\mathrm{o}}\boldsymbol{\beta} + c_i)] = E[\Phi(\psi_a + \mathbf{x}^{\mathrm{o}}\boldsymbol{\beta}_a + \overline{\mathbf{x}}_i\boldsymbol{\xi}_a)]. \tag{15.75}$$

Because the only random variable in the right-hand-side expectation is $\overline{\mathbf{x}}_i$, a consistent estimator of the right-hand side of equation (15.75) is simply

$$N^{-1} \sum_{i=1}^{N} \Phi(\hat{\psi}_a + \mathbf{x}^{\mathrm{o}}\hat{\boldsymbol{\beta}}_a + \overline{\mathbf{x}}_i\hat{\boldsymbol{\xi}}_a). \tag{15.76}$$

APEs can be estimated by evaluating expression (15.76) at two different values for $\mathbf{x}^{\mathrm{o}}$ and forming the difference, or, for continuous variable x_j, by using the average across i of $\hat{\beta}_{aj}\phi(\hat{\psi}_a + \mathbf{x}^{\mathrm{o}}\hat{\boldsymbol{\beta}}_a + \overline{\mathbf{x}}_i\hat{\boldsymbol{\xi}}_a)$ to get the approximate APE of a one-unit increase in x_j. See also Chamberlain (1984, equation (3.4)). If we use Chamberlain's more general version of assumption (15.73), $\mathbf{x}_i$ replaces $\overline{\mathbf{x}}_i$ everywhere.

Our focus on the APEs raises an interesting question: How does treating the c_i's as parameters to estimate—in a "fixed effects probit" analysis—affect estimation of the APEs? Given $\hat{c}_i$, $i = 1, \dots, N$ and $\hat{\boldsymbol{\beta}}$, the APEs could be based on

$N^{-1} \sum_{i=1}^{N} \Phi(\hat{c}_i + \mathbf{x}^{\text{o}} \hat{\boldsymbol{\beta}})$. Even though $\hat{\boldsymbol{\beta}}$ does not consistently estimate $\boldsymbol{\beta}$ and the $\hat{c}_i$ are estimates of the incidental parameters, it could be that the resulting estimates of the APEs have reasonable properties. In fact, recent progress has been made on this question. Fernández-Val (2009) contains theoretical results showing that the inconsistency in APEs constructed using the $\hat{c}_i$ and the accompanying $\hat{\boldsymbol{\beta}}$ is on the order of T^{-1} (and, if there is no heterogeneity, the inconsistency is only $O(T^{-2})$). In simulations, Hahn and Newey (2004) found small biases in the usual probit APEs; they suggested bias-corrected estimators that have inconsistency on the order of T^{-2}. In related work, Greene (2004), using simulations, found that for even moderate T (say, $T \geq 5$), the bias in the partial effects evaluated at the average (as opposed to the average partial effect) can be quite small. All of these papers maintain the conditional independence assumption (15.67) and, in addition, the assumption that the covariates are independent, identically distributed across t. Hopefully, the findings carry over to more realistic scenarios that allow time dependence in the covariates as well as violations of (15.67).

Under assumptions (15.65), (15.66), and the more general version of assumption (15.73), Chamberlain (1980) suggested a minimum distance approach analogous to the linear case (see Section 14.6.2). Namely, obtain $\hat{\boldsymbol{\pi}}_t$ for each t by running a cross-sectional probit of y_{it} on 1, $\mathbf{x}_i$, $i = 1, \ldots, N$. The mapping from the structural parameters $\boldsymbol{\theta}_a \equiv (\psi_a, \boldsymbol{\beta}_a', \boldsymbol{\xi}_a')'$ to the vector $\boldsymbol{\pi}$ is exactly as in the linear case (see Section 14.6.2). The variance matrix estimator for $\hat{\boldsymbol{\pi}}$ is obtained by pooling all T probits and computing the robust variance matrix estimator in equation (13.53), with $\hat{\boldsymbol{\theta}}$ replaced by $\hat{\boldsymbol{\pi}}$; see also Chamberlain (1984, Section 4.5). The minimum distance approach leads to a straightforward test of $\text{H}_0 : \boldsymbol{\xi}_a = \mathbf{0}$, which is a test of assumption (15.69) that does not impose assumption (15.67).

Strict exogeneity of the covariates conditional on c_i is critical for the previous analysis. As mentioned earlier, this assumption rules out lagged dependent variables, a case we consider explicitly in Section 15.8.4. But there are other cases where strict exogeneity is questionable. For example, suppose that y_{it} is an employment indicator for person i in period t and w_{it} is measure of recent arrests. It is possible that whether someone is employed in this period has an effect on future arrests. If so, then shocks that affect employment status could be correlated with future arrests, and such correlation would violate strict exogeneity. Whether this situation is empirically important is largely unknown.

On the one hand, correcting for an explanatory variable that is not strictly exogenous is quite difficult in nonlinear models; Wooldridge (2000) suggests one possible approach. On the other hand, obtaining a test of strict exogeneity is fairly easy. Let $\mathbf{w}_{it}$ denote a $1 \times G$ subset of $\mathbf{x}_{it}$ that we suspect of failing the strict exogeneity requirement. Then a simple test is to add $\mathbf{w}_{i,t+1}$ as an additional set of covariates; under the null hypothesis, $\mathbf{w}_{i,t+1}$ should be insignificant. In implementing this test, we can use either RE probit or pooled probit, where, in either case, we lose the last time period. (In the pooled probit case, we should use a fully robust Wald or score test.) We should still obtain $\bar{\mathbf{x}}_i$ from all T time periods, as the test is either based on the distribution of $(y_{i1}, \ldots, y_{i,T-1})$ given $(\mathbf{x}_{i1}, \ldots, \mathbf{x}_{iT})$ (RE probit) or on the marginal distributions of y_{it} given $(\mathbf{x}_{i1}, \ldots, \mathbf{x}_{iT})$, $t = 1, \ldots, T-1$ (pooled probit). If the test does not reject, it provides at least some justification for the strict exogeneity assumption.

15.8.3 Unobserved Effects Logit Models under Strict Exogeneity

The unobserved effects probit model of the previous subsection has a logit counterpart. In the leading case, the heterogeneity, c_i, is still assumed to satisfy (15.69), but we replace assumption (15.66) with the response probability

$$P(y_{it} = 1 \mid \mathbf{x}_{it}, c_i) = \Lambda(\mathbf{x}_{it}\boldsymbol{\beta} + c_i), \qquad t = 1, \ldots, T, \tag{15.77}$$

where $\Lambda(\cdot)$ is the logistic function. If we maintain the full set of assumptions, given by the strict exogeneity condition (15.65), the conditional independence assumption (15.67), the normality assumption (15.69), and the model in equation (15.77), we arrive at the **random effects logit model**. In the GEE literature, the RE logit model is an example of a subject-specific model (like the RE probit model).

From a computational standpoint, the RE logit model is less desirable than the RE probit model. Even if we focus on a pooled method under assumptions (15.69) and (15.77), estimation is complicated because the response probability obtained by integrating out c_i,

$$P(y_{it} = 1 \mid \mathbf{x}_{it}) = \int_{-\infty}^{\infty} \Lambda(\mathbf{x}_{it}\boldsymbol{\beta} + c)(1/\sigma_c)\phi(c/\sigma_c)\, dc, \tag{15.78}$$

does not have a closed form. In fact, one rarely sees equation (15.78) used as the sole basis for estimating $\boldsymbol{\beta}$ and σ_c^2, whether using a pooled binary response method or a GEE method under assumption (15.65). (Unlike in the probit model, $\boldsymbol{\beta}$ and σ_c^2 are separately identified in (15.78), although that does not mean they are easy to estimate.) Interestingly, although it seems natural to define (15.78), along with the strict exogeneity assumption, as constituting the PA version of the SS model, that is not the designation in the GEE literature. Instead, the PA model is specified as

$$P(y_{it} = 1 \mid \mathbf{x}_i) = P(y_{it} = 1 \mid \mathbf{x}_{it}) = \Lambda(\mathbf{x}_{it}\boldsymbol{\beta}_c), \tag{15.79}$$

where we use the "c" subscript on $\boldsymbol{\beta}_c$ to emphasize that the beta vector in equation (15.79) cannot be the same as $\boldsymbol{\beta}$ in equation (15.77) (and to draw an analogy with probit). In fact, (15.79) is incompatible with (15.77); in specifying (15.79), we are abandoning the more structural model in (15.77) for the sake of expediency. In the GEE literature more generally, a PA model is usually specified to have a convenient functional form for the conditional mean, $\mathrm{E}(y_{it} \mid \mathbf{x}_{it})$ without worrying about whether it can be derived from an underlying unobserved effects model.

If we estimate the model in (15.77) under the full set of RE logit assumptions (or even if we just use equation (15.78)), the partial effects at interesting values of c are easier to obtain than the APEs: we just use differences or derivatives of $\Lambda(\mathbf{x}_t\boldsymbol{\beta} + c)$ with respect to elements of $\mathbf{x}_t$ and plug in interesting values of c, which can be determined because c_i is distributed as $\mathrm{Normal}(0, \sigma_c^2)$. Further, we can apply the Mundlak-Chamberlain device just as in assumption (15.73), and then we can estimate the unconditional mean and variance of c_i as in the probit case. If we want to allow $\mathrm{D}(c_i \mid \mathbf{x}_i)$ to depend on $\bar{\mathbf{x}}_i$ but do not want to use RE logit as the underlying model, we can adopt a strategy that extends the standard PA model strategy. Namely, we just specify

$$\mathrm{P}(y_{it} = 1 \mid \mathbf{x}_i) = \Lambda(\psi_a + \mathbf{x}_{it}\boldsymbol{\beta}_a + \bar{\mathbf{x}}_i\xi_a), \qquad t = 1, \ldots, T, \tag{15.80}$$

where we use the "a" subscript to indicate a new set of parameters (while again drawing an analogy to the probit case). Given equation (15.80), we can estimate the parameters by pooled logit or GEE, and then, to obtain APEs, compute the ASF $N^{-1}\sum_{i=1}^{N}\Lambda(\hat{\psi}_a + \mathbf{x}_t\hat{\boldsymbol{\beta}}_a + \bar{\mathbf{x}}_i\hat{\xi}_a)$ for given $\mathbf{x}_t$. Although equation (15.80) cannot be derived from (15.77), it might provide a good approximation to the APEs.

The real advantage of specifying equation (15.77) in place of (15.66) is that under the logit specification, we can obtain a $\sqrt{N}$-consistent, asymptotically normal estimator of $\boldsymbol{\beta}$ without *any* assumptions on $\mathrm{D}(c_i \mid \mathbf{x}_i)$, provided, of course, that each element of $\mathbf{x}_{it}$ is time varying. In addition to assumption (15.77), we maintain the strict exogeneity assumption (15.65) and the conditional independence assumption (15.67).

How can we allow c_i and $\mathbf{x}_i$ to be arbitrarily related in the unobserved effects logit model? In the linear case we used the FE or FD transformation to eliminate c_i from the estimating equation. It turns out that a similar strategy works in the logit case, although the argument is more subtle. What we do is find the joint distribution of $\mathbf{y}_i \equiv (y_{i1}, \ldots, y_{iT})'$ conditional on $\mathbf{x}_i, c_i,$ *and* $n_i \equiv \sum_{t=1}^{T} y_{it}$. It turns out that this conditional distribution does not depend on c_i, so that it is also the distribution of $\mathbf{y}_i$ given $\mathbf{x}_i$ and n_i. Therefore, we can use standard CMLE methods to estimate $\boldsymbol{\beta}$. (The fact that we can find a conditional distribution that does not depend on the c_i is a feature of the logit functional form. Unfortunately, the same argument does not work for the unobserved effects probit model.)

First consider the $T = 2$ case, where n_i takes a value in $\{0, 1, 2\}$. Intuitively, the conditional distribution of $(y_{i1}, y_{i2})'$ given n_i cannot be informative for $\boldsymbol{\beta}$ when $n_i = 0$ or $n_i = 2$ because these values completely determine the outcome on $\mathbf{y}_i$. However, for $n_i = 1$,

$$\begin{aligned}
\mathrm{P}(y_{i2} = 1 \mid \mathbf{x}_i, c_i, n_i = 1) &= \mathrm{P}(y_{i2} = 1, n_i = 1 \mid \mathbf{x}_i, c_i)/\mathrm{P}(n_i = 1 \mid \mathbf{x}_i, c_i) \\
&= \mathrm{P}(y_{i2} = 1 \mid \mathbf{x}_i, c_i)\mathrm{P}(y_{i1} = 0 \mid \mathbf{x}_i, c_i)/\{\mathrm{P}(y_{i1} = 0, y_{i2} = 1 \mid \mathbf{x}_i, c_i) \\
&\quad + \mathrm{P}(y_{i1} = 1, y_{i2} = 0 \mid \mathbf{x}_i, c_i)\} \\
&= \Lambda(\mathbf{x}_{i2}\boldsymbol{\beta} + c_i)[1 - \Lambda(\mathbf{x}_{i1}\boldsymbol{\beta} + c_i)]/\{[1 - \Lambda(\mathbf{x}_{i1}\boldsymbol{\beta} + c_i)]\Lambda(\mathbf{x}_{i2}\boldsymbol{\beta} + c_i) \\
&\quad + \Lambda(\mathbf{x}_{i1}\boldsymbol{\beta} + c_i)[1 - \Lambda(\mathbf{x}_{i2}\boldsymbol{\beta} + c_i)]\} = \Lambda[(\mathbf{x}_{i2} - \mathbf{x}_{i1})\boldsymbol{\beta}].
\end{aligned}$$

Similarly, $\mathrm{P}(y_{i1} = 1 \mid \mathbf{x}_i, c_i, n_i = 1) = \Lambda[-(\mathbf{x}_{i2} - \mathbf{x}_{i1})\boldsymbol{\beta}] = 1 - \Lambda[(\mathbf{x}_{i2} - \mathbf{x}_{i1})\boldsymbol{\beta}]$. The conditional log likelihood for observation i is

$$\ell_i(\boldsymbol{\beta}) = 1[n_i = 1](w_i \log \Lambda[(\mathbf{x}_{i2} - \mathbf{x}_{i1})\boldsymbol{\beta}] + (1 - w_i) \log\{1 - \Lambda[(\mathbf{x}_{i2} - \mathbf{x}_{i1})\boldsymbol{\beta}]\}), \quad (15.81)$$

where $w_i = 1$ if $(y_{i1} = 0, y_{i2} = 1)$ and $w_i = 0$ if $(y_{i1} = 1, y_{i2} = 0)$. The CMLE is obtained by maximizing the sum of the $\ell_i(\boldsymbol{\beta})$ across i. The indicator function $1[n_i = 1]$ selects out the observations for which $n_i = 1$; as stated earlier, observations for which $n_i = 0$ or $n_i = 2$ do not contribute to the log likelihood. Interestingly, equation (15.81) is just a standard cross-sectional logit of w_i on $(\mathbf{x}_{i2} - \mathbf{x}_{i1})$ using the observations for which $n_i = 1$. (This approach is analogous to differencing in the linear case with $T = 2$.)

The CMLE from equation (15.81) is often called the **fixed effects logit estimator** and sometimes called the **conditional logit estimator**. We must emphasize that the FE logit estimator does *not* arise by treating the c_i as parameters to be estimated along with $\boldsymbol{\beta}$. (This convention is confusing, as the FE probit estimator *does* estimate the c_i along with $\boldsymbol{\beta}$.) As shown recently by Abrevaya (1997), the MLE of $\boldsymbol{\beta}$ that is obtained by maximizing the log likelihood over $\boldsymbol{\beta}$, and the c_i has probability limit $2\boldsymbol{\beta}$. (This finding extends a simple example due to Andersen, 1970; see also Hsiao, 1986, Section 7.3.)

Sometimes the CMLE is described as "conditioning on the unobserved effects in the sample." This description is misleading. What we have done is found a conditional density—which describes the subpopulation with $n_i = 1$—that depends only on observable data and the parameter $\boldsymbol{\beta}$. One should not expend energy worrying about the loss of observations for which $y_{i1} = y_{i2}$. Because $\mathrm{D}(c_i \mid \mathbf{x}_i)$ is unrestricted, c_i is free to vary as much as required to make $\mathrm{P}(y_{it} = 1 \mid \mathbf{x}_{it}, c_i)$ arbitarily close to one (if

$y_{it} = 1$, $t = 1, 2$) or arbitrarily close to zero (if $y_{it} = 0$, $t = 1, 2$). When y_{it} does not change across t, c_i can adjust to make both observed outcomes occur with certainty. Clearly, such data points contain no information for estimating $\boldsymbol{\beta}$, and so they *should* drop out of the estimation.

For general T the log likelihood is more complicated, but it is tractable. First,

$$\mathrm{P}(y_{i1} = y_1, \ldots, y_{iT} = y_T \mid \mathbf{x}_i, c_i, n_i = n)$$
$$= \mathrm{P}(y_{i1} = y_1, \ldots, y_{iT} = y_T \mid \mathbf{x}_i, c_i)/\mathrm{P}(n_i = n \mid \mathbf{x}_i, c_i), \tag{15.82}$$

and the numerator factors as $\mathrm{P}(y_{i1} = y_1 \mid \mathbf{x}_i, c_i) \cdots \mathrm{P}(y_{iT} = y_T \mid \mathbf{x}_i, c_i)$ by the conditional independence assumption. The denominator is the complicated part, but it is easy to describe: $\mathrm{P}(n_i = n \mid \mathbf{x}_i, c_i)$ is the sum of the probabilities of all possible outcomes of $\mathbf{y}_i$ such that $n_i = n$. Using the specific form of the logit function we can write

$$\ell_i(\boldsymbol{\beta}) = \log\left\{\exp\left(\sum_{t=1}^{T} y_{it}\mathbf{x}_{it}\boldsymbol{\beta}\right)\left[\sum_{\mathbf{a} \in R_i} \exp\left(\sum_{t=1}^{T} a_t\mathbf{x}_{it}\boldsymbol{\beta}\right)\right]^{-1}\right\} \tag{15.83}$$

where R_i is the subset of $\mathbb{R}^T$ defined as $\{\mathbf{a} \in \mathbb{R}^T\colon a_t \in \{0, 1\} \text{ and } \sum_{t=1}^{T} a_t = n_i\}$. The log likelihood summed across i can be used to obtain a $\sqrt{N}$-asymptotically normal estimator of $\boldsymbol{\beta}$, and all inference follows from conditional MLE theory. Observations for which equation (15.82) is zero or unity—and which therefore do not depend on $\boldsymbol{\beta}$—drop out of $\mathcal{L}(\boldsymbol{\beta})$. See Chamberlain (1984).

The FE logit estimator $\hat{\boldsymbol{\beta}}$ immediately gives us the effect of each element of $\mathbf{x}_t$ on the log-odds ratio, $\log\{\Lambda(\mathbf{x}_t\boldsymbol{\beta} + c)/[1 - \Lambda(\mathbf{x}_t\boldsymbol{\beta} + c)]\} = \mathbf{x}_t\boldsymbol{\beta} + c$. Unfortunately, we cannot estimate the partial effects on the response probabilities unless we plug in a value for c. Because the distribution of c_i is unrestricted—in particular, $\mathrm{E}(c_i)$ is not necessarily zero—it is hard to know what to plug in for c. In addition, we cannot estimate APEs, as doing so would require finding $\mathrm{E}[\Lambda(\mathbf{x}_t\boldsymbol{\beta} + c_i)]$, a task that apparently requires specifying a distribution for c_i.

The conditional logit approach also has the drawback of apparently requiring the conditional independence assumption (15.67) for consistency. As we saw in Section 15.8.2, if we are willing to make the normality assumption (15.73), the probit approach allows unrestricted serial dependence in y_{it} even after conditioning on $\mathbf{x}_i$ and c_i. This possibility may be especially important when several time periods are available.

Now that we have covered all of the leading estimation methods for unobserved effects models with strictly exogenous explanatory variables, we can provide an example comparing the different approaches. We use a panel data set on the labor force participation of married women from Chay and Hyslop (2001).

Table 15.3
Panel Data Models for Married Women's Labor Force Participation

Model	(1) Linear	(2) Probit		(3) Chamberlain's RE Probit		(4) Chamberlain's RE Probit		(5) FE Logit
Estimation Method	Fixed Effects	Pooled MLE		Pooled MLE		MLE		MLE
	Coefficient	Coefficient	APE	Coefficient	APE	Coefficient	APE	Coefficient
kids	−.0389	−.199	−.0660	−.117	−.0389	−.317	−.0403	−.644
	(.0092)	(.015)	(.0048)	(.027)	(.0085)	(.062)	(.0104)	(.125)
lhinc	−.0089	−.211	−.0701	−.029	−.0095	−.078	−.0099	−.184
	(.0046)	(.024)	(.0079)	(.014)	(.0048)	(.041)	(.0055)	(.083)
$\overline{kids}$	—	—	—	−.086	—	−.210	—	—
	—	—	—	(.031)	—	(.071)	—	—
$\overline{lhinc}$	—	—	—	−.250	—	−.646	—	—
	—	—	—	(.035)	—	(.079)	—	—
$(1+\hat{\sigma}_a^2)^{-1/2}$	—	—		—		.387		—
Log likelihood	—	−16,556.67		−16,516.44		−8,990.09		−2,003.42
Number of women	5,663	5,663		5,663		5,663		1,055

Standard errors are in parentheses below all coefficients or APEs. For the linear model, pooled probit, and Chamberlain's RE probit estimated by pooled MLE, the standard errors are robust to arbitrary serial correlation.
All models include a full set of period dummy variables (unreported).
Columns (2), (3), and (4) also include the time-constant variables *educ*, *black*, *age*, and age^2 (unreported).
Because of prohibitive computation times, bootstrap standard errors were not computed for the RE probit APEs estimated by MLE.

Example 15.5 (Panel Data Models for Women's Labor Force Participation): The data set LFP.RAW contains data on $N = 5,663$ married women over $T = 5$ periods, where the periods are spaced four months apart. The response variable is lfp_{it}, a labor force participation indicator. The key explanatory variables are $kids_{it}$ (number of children under 18) and $lhinc_{it} = \log(hinc_{it})$ (where husband's income, $hinc_{it}$, is in dollars per month and is positive for all i and t). We also include the time-constant variables *educ* (years of schooling in the first period), *black* (a binary race indicator), *age* (age in the first period), and age^2; these drop out of the linear FE and FE logit estimation.

The findings in Table 15.3 reveal a consistent pattern: allowing unobserved heterogeneity to be correlated with $kids_{it}$ and $lhinc_{it}$ has important effects on the estimated APEs. Estimating the LPM by FE gives estimated coefficients of roughly −.039 and −.009 on the $kids_{it}$ and $lhinc_{it}$ variables, respectively, with the coefficient on $lhinc_{it}$

being marginally statistically significant. Each child is estimated to reduce the labor force participation probability by about .039, while a 10% increase in a husband's income lowers the probability by only .0009. If we use probit and assume c_i is independent of $\mathbf{x}_i$, the APEs are much higher, especially on the income variable, which is almost 10 times the LPM coefficient. Could this difference be due to the different functional forms? Column (3) makes it clear that the difference in APEs between columns (1) and (2) is due to the restriction in (2) that c_i is independent of $\mathbf{x}_i$. When we use the Chamberlain-Mundlak device and use pooled probit, we obtain APEs that are very similar to the LPM estimates. In fact, to four decimal places, the APE estimates on $kids_{it}$ are identical. Plus, we can see directly that the coefficients on the time averages are very statistically significant and practically very large; each is much larger than the corresponding coefficient on the time-varying variable.

Using full MLE, rather than PMLE, to estimate Chamberlain's model does not change any conclusions. When we multiply the MLE coefficients by the scale factor .387, the results are very similar to the pooled MLE coefficients ($-.1227$ for $kids_{it}$ and $-.030$ for $lhinc_{it}$). In addition, the APE estimates are very similar to the pooled estimation; interestingly, the bootstrap standard errors for the APEs are actually somewhat higher than for the pooled probit estimates.

Finally, column (5) contains the estimates from FE logit. As we discussed, the coefficient magnitudes are difficult to interpret. But the relative size is $.644/.184 = 3.50$, which is not terribly different from, say, the ratio of coefficients using the pooled MLE estimates of Chamberlain's model, $.117/.029 = 4.03$. But if we do not control for the time averages, the estimated ratios are much different, $.199/.211 = .94$. Because Chamberlain's approach yields APEs, and the estimates in column (3) allow for arbitrary serial dependence, it seems sensible to rely on these estimates (assuming, of course, that we believe $kids_{it}$ and $lhinc_{it}$ are strictly exogenous conditional on c_i).

Because we have covered several different possibilities for modeling and estimation in the context of unobserved effects with binary responses, it is helpful to have a simple summary of the strengths and weaknesses of each approach. Table 15.4 contains such a summary. Each method is evaluated by answers to five questions: (1) Is the response probability contained in the unit interval? (2) Is the distribution of the heterogeneity, given the covariates, restricted? (3) Is serial dependence allowed after accounting for c_i? (4) Are the partial effects at the mean heterogeneity identified? (5) Are the APEs identified?

Table 15.4 reveals a simple but important point that is easily missed: no procedure strictly dominates the others. When deciding on a method or methods, one needs to determine how important each factor is likely to be. For some features, this is easy. For example, hopefully we know whether having consistent parameter estimates is

Table 15.4
Summary of Features of Models and Estimation Methods for Unobserved Effects Binary Response Models

Model, Estimation Method	$P(y_{it} = 1 \mid \mathbf{x}_{it}, c_i)$ Bounded in $(0, 1)$?	Restricts $D(c_i \mid \mathbf{x}_i)$?	Idiosyncratic Serial Dependence?	Partial Effects at $E(c_i)$?	APEs?
RE probit, MLE	Yes	Yes (independence, normal)	No	Yes	Yes
RE probit, pooled MLE	Yes	Yes (independence, normal)	Yes	No	Yes
RE probit, GEE	Yes	Yes (independence, normal)	Yes	No	Yes
Chamberlain's RE probit, MLE	Yes	Yes (linear mean, normal)	No	Yes	Yes
Chamberlain's RE probit, pooled MLE	Yes	Yes (linear mean, normal)	Yes	No	Yes
Chamberlain's RE probit, GEE	Yes	Yes (linear mean, normal)	Yes	No	Yes
LPM, within	No	No	Yes	Yes	Yes
FE logit, MLE	Yes	No	No	No	No

enough for our purposes or whether we want to estimate the magnitudes of effects. Unfortunately, it is difficult to decide issues that are essentially empirical in nature, such as how important functional form restrictions are on $P(y_{it} = 1 \mid \mathbf{x}_{it}, c_i)$ or $D(c_i \mid \mathbf{x}_i)$.

15.8.4 Dynamic Unobserved Effects Models

Dynamic models that also contain unobserved effects are important in testing theories and evaluating policies. Here we cover one class of models that illustrates the important points for general dynamic models and is of considerable interest in its own right. Our treatment follows Wooldridge (2005b).

Suppose we date our observations starting at $t = 0$, so that y_{i0} is the first observation on y. For $t = 1, \ldots, T$ we are interested in the dynamic unobserved effects model

$$P(y_{it} = 1 \mid y_{i,t-1}, \ldots, y_{i0}, \mathbf{z}_i, c_i) = G(\mathbf{z}_{it}\boldsymbol{\delta} + \rho y_{i,t-1} + c_i), \tag{15.84}$$

where $\mathbf{z}_{it}$ is a vector of contemporaneous explanatory variables, $\mathbf{z}_i = (\mathbf{z}_{i1}, \ldots, \mathbf{z}_{iT})$, and G can be the probit or logit function. There are several important points about this model. First, the $\mathbf{z}_{it}$ are assumed to satisfy a strict exogeneity assumption (conditional on c_i), since $\mathbf{z}_i$ appears in the conditioning set on the left-hand side of equation (15.84), but only $\mathbf{z}_{it}$ appears on the right-hand side. Second, the probability of success at time t is allowed to depend on the outcome in $t - 1$ as well as unobserved heterogeneity, c_i. We saw the linear version in Section 11.6.2. Of particular interest is the hypothesis $H_0 : \rho = 0$. Under this null, the response probability at time t does not depend on past outcomes once c_i (and $\mathbf{z}_i$) have been controlled for. Even if $\rho = 0$, $P(y_{it} = 1 \mid y_{i,t-1}, \mathbf{z}_i) \neq P(y_{it} = 1 \mid \mathbf{z}_i)$ owing to the presence of c_i. But economists are interested in whether there is **state dependence**—that is, $\rho \neq 0$ in equation (15.84)—*after* controlling for the unobserved heterogeneity, c_i.

We might also be interested in the effects of $\mathbf{z}_t$, as it may contain policy variables. Then, equation (15.84) simply captures the fact that, in addition to an unobserved effect, behavior may depend on past observed behavior.

How can we estimate $\boldsymbol{\delta}$ and ρ in equation (15.84), in addition to quantities such as APEs? First, we can always write

$$
\begin{aligned}
f(y_1, y_2, \ldots, y_T \mid y_0, \mathbf{z}, c; \boldsymbol{\beta}) &= \prod_{t=1}^{T} f(y_t \mid y_{t-1}, \ldots y_1, y_0, \mathbf{z}_t, c; \boldsymbol{\beta}) \\
&= \prod_{t=1}^{T} G(\mathbf{z}_t\boldsymbol{\delta} + \rho y_{t-1} + c)^{y_t}[1 - G(\mathbf{z}_t\boldsymbol{\delta} + \rho y_{t-1} + c)]^{1-y_t}.
\end{aligned}
\tag{15.85}
$$

With fixed-T asymptotics, this density, because of the unobserved effect c, does not allow us to construct a log-likelihood function that can be used to estimate $\boldsymbol{\beta}$ consistently. Just as in the case with strictly exogenous explanatory variables, treating the c_i as parameters to be estimated does not result in consistent estimators of $\boldsymbol{\delta}$ and ρ as $N \to \infty$. In fact, the simulations in Heckman (1981) show that the incidental parameters problem is even more severe in dynamic models. What we should do is integrate out the unobserved effect c, as we discussed generally in Section 13.9.2.

Our need to integrate c out of the distribution raises the issue of how we treat the initial observations, y_{i0}; this is usually called the **initial conditions problem**. One possibility is to treat each y_{i0} as a nonstochastic starting position for each i. Then, if c_i is assumed to be independent of $\mathbf{z}_i$ (as in a pure RE environment), equation (15.85) can be integrated against the density of c to obtain the density of $(y_1, y_2, \ldots, y_T)$ given $\mathbf{z}$; this density also depends on y_0 through $f(y_1 \mid y_0, c, \mathbf{z}_1; \boldsymbol{\beta})$. We can then apply CMLE. Although treating the y_{i0} as nonrandom simplifies estimation, it is undesirable because it effectively means that c_i and y_{i0} are independent, a very strong assumption.

There seems to be confusion in the literature about when it is plausible to treat the y_{i0} as fixed, and therefore independent of c_i. Some have justified this assumption when one observes the process generating y_{it} from its beginning, as would happen if we follow the employment history of a cohort of high school graduates who do not pursue additional education, with y_{i0} being an employment indicator in the initial postgraduation period. Does it make sense to assume y_{i0} and c_i are independent? Almost certainly not. Because c_i contains unobserved attributes that affect y_{it} in periods $t \geq 1$, it is almost certain that an individual's initial employment status is related to c_i. In this example and most others, treating the y_{i0} as independent of c_i is risky, regardless of when the process underlying the panel data actually started.

Another possibility is to first specify a density for y_{i0} given $(\mathbf{z}_i, c_i)$ and to multiply this density by equation (15.85) to obtain $f(y_0, y_1, y_2, \ldots, y_T \mid \mathbf{z}, c; \boldsymbol{\beta}, \gamma)$. Next, a density for c_i given $\mathbf{z}_i$ can be specified. Finally, $f(y_0, y_1, y_2, \ldots, y_T \mid \mathbf{z}, c; \boldsymbol{\beta}, \gamma)$ is integrated against the density $h(c \mid \mathbf{z}; \boldsymbol{\alpha})$ to obtain the density of $(y_{i0}, y_{i1}, y_{i2}, \ldots, y_{iT})$ given $\mathbf{z}_i$. This density can then be used in an MLE analysis. The problem with this approach is that finding the density of y_{i0} given $(\mathbf{z}_i, c_i)$ is very difficult, if not impossible, even if the process is assumed to be in equilibrium. For discussion, see Hsiao (2003, Section 7.5).

Heckman (1981) suggests approximating the conditional density of y_{i0} given $(\mathbf{z}_i, c_i)$ and then specifying a density for c_i given $\mathbf{z}_i$. For example, we might assume that y_{i0} follows a probit model with success probability $\Phi(\eta + \mathbf{z}_i\boldsymbol{\pi} + \gamma c_i)$ and specify the density of c_i given $\mathbf{z}_i$ as normal. Once these two densities are given, they can be multiplied by equation (15.85), and c can be integrated out to approximate the density of $(y_{i0}, y_{i1}, y_{i2}, \ldots, y_{iT})$ given $\mathbf{z}_i$; see Hsiao (2003, Section 7.5) or Wooldridge (2005b).

Heckman's (1981) approach attempts to find or approximate the joint distribution of $(y_{i0}, y_{i1}, y_{i2}, \ldots, y_{iT})$ given $\mathbf{z}_i$. We discussed an alternative approach in Section 13.9.2: obtain the joint distribution of $(y_{i1}, y_{i2}, \ldots, y_{iT})$ conditional on $(y_{i0}, \mathbf{z}_i)$. This allows us to remain agnostic about the distribution of y_{i0} given $(\mathbf{z}_i, c_i)$, which is the primary source of difficulty in Heckman's approach. If we can find the density of $(y_{i1}, y_{i2}, \ldots, y_{iT})$ given $(y_{i0}, \mathbf{z}_i)$, in terms of $\boldsymbol{\beta}$ and other parameters, then we can use standard CMLE methods: we are simply conditioning on y_{i0} in addition to $\mathbf{z}_i$. It is important to see that using the density of $(y_{i1}, y_{i2}, \ldots, y_{iT})$ given $(y_{i0}, \mathbf{z}_i)$ is *not* the same as treating y_{i0} as nonrandom. Indeed, the model with c_i independent of y_{i0}, given $\mathbf{z}_i$, is a special case.

To obtain $f(y_1, y_2, \ldots, y_T \mid y_{i0}, \mathbf{z}_i)$, we need to propose a density for c_i given $(y_{i0}, \mathbf{z}_i)$. This approach is very much like Chamberlain's (1980) approach to static probit models with unobserved effects, except that we now condition on y_{i0} as well. (Since the density of c_i given $\mathbf{z}_i$ is not restricted by the specification (15.85), our choice of the density of c_i given $(y_{i0}, \mathbf{z}_i)$ is not logically restricted in any way.) Given a density $h(c \mid y_0, \mathbf{z}; \boldsymbol{\gamma})$, which depends on a vector of parameters $\boldsymbol{\gamma}$, we have

$$f(y_1, y_2, \ldots, y_T \mid y_0, \mathbf{z}, \boldsymbol{\theta}) = \int_{-\infty}^{\infty} f(y_1, y_2, \ldots, y_T \mid y_0, \mathbf{z}, c; \boldsymbol{\beta}) h(c \mid y_0, \mathbf{z}; \boldsymbol{\gamma}) \, dc.$$

See Property CD.2 in Chapter 13. The integral can be replaced with a weighted average if the distribution of c is discrete. When $G = \Phi$ in the model (15.84)—the leading case—a very convenient choice for $h(c \mid y_0, \mathbf{z}; \gamma)$ is Normal$(\psi + \xi_0 y_{i0} + \mathbf{z}_i \xi, \sigma_a^2)$, which follows by writing $c_i = \psi + \xi_0 y_{i0} + \mathbf{z}_i \xi + a_i$, where $a_i \sim \text{Normal}(0, \sigma_a^2)$ and independent of $(y_{i0}, \mathbf{z}_i)$. Then we can write

$$y_{it} = 1[\psi + \mathbf{z}_{it}\boldsymbol{\delta} + \rho y_{i,t-1} + \xi_0 y_{i0} + \mathbf{z}_i \xi + a_i + e_{it} > 0],$$

so that y_{it} given $(y_{i,t-1}, \ldots, y_{i0}, \mathbf{z}_i, a_i)$ follows a probit model and a_i given $(y_{i0}, \mathbf{z}_i)$ is distributed as Normal$(0, \sigma_a^2)$. Therefore, the density of $(y_{i1}, \ldots, y_{iT})$ given $(y_{i0}, \mathbf{z}_i)$ has exactly the form in equation (15.70), where $\mathbf{x}_{it} = (1, \mathbf{z}_{it}, y_{i,t-1}, y_{i0}, \mathbf{z}_i)$ and with a and σ_a replacing c and σ_c, respectively. Conveniently, this finding means that we can use standard RE probit software to estimate ψ, $\boldsymbol{\delta}$, ρ, ξ_0, ξ, and σ_a^2: we simply expand the list of explanatory variables to include y_{i0} and $\mathbf{z}_i$ in *each* time period. (The approach that treats y_{i0} and $\mathbf{z}_i$ as fixed omits y_{i0} and $\mathbf{z}_i$ in each time period.) It is simple to test $H_0: \rho = 0$, which means there is no state dependence once we control for an unobserved effect.

We can estimate APEs as in Chamberlain's unobserved effects probit model with strictly exogenous explanatory variables, but now we average out the initial condition along with the leads and lags of all strictly exogenous variables. Let $\mathbf{z}_t$ and y_{t-1} be given values of the explanatory variables. Then the ASF, $\mathrm{E}[\Phi(\mathbf{z}_t\boldsymbol{\delta} + \rho y_{t-1} + c_i)] = \mathrm{E}[\Phi(\psi_a + \mathbf{z}_t\boldsymbol{\delta}_a + \rho_a y_{t-1} + \xi_{a0} y_{i0} + \mathbf{z}_i \xi_a)]$, is consistently estimated as $\widehat{\mathrm{ASF}}(\mathbf{z}_t, y_{t-1}) = N^{-1}\sum_{i=1}^{N} \Phi(\hat{\psi}_a + \mathbf{z}_t\hat{\boldsymbol{\delta}}_a + \hat{\rho}_a y_{t-1} + \hat{\xi}_{a0} y_{i0} + \mathbf{z}_i \hat{\xi}_a)$, where the a subscript denotes that the original coefficients have been multiplied by $(1 + \hat{\sigma}_a^2)^{-1/2}$, and $\hat{\psi}$, $\hat{\boldsymbol{\delta}}$, $\hat{\rho}$, $\hat{\xi}_0$, $\hat{\xi}$, and $\hat{\sigma}_a^2$ are the CMLEs that would be reported directly by any econometrics package that estimates RE probit models. We can take derivatives of this expression with respect to continuous elements of $\mathbf{z}_t$, or take differences with respect to discrete elements. Of particular interest is to alternatively set $y_{t-1} = 1$ and $y_{t-1} = 0$ and obtain the change in the probability that $y_{it} = 1$ when y_{t-1} goes from zero to one. Probably we would average across $\mathbf{z}_{it}$, too. To obtain a single APE, we can also average across all time periods. The key is that we average across $(y_{i0}, \mathbf{z}_i)$ to estimate the ASF, and then from there we decide which partial effects are of interest. Wooldridge (2005b) contains further discussion, and we compute the APE for the lagged dependent variable in the example below.

In estimating the dynamic model just described, it is important to understand that a simpler, pooled estimation method does *not* consistently estimate the scaled parameters or the APEs. In other words, we cannot simply use pooled probit of y_{it} on 1, $\mathbf{z}_{it}$, $y_{i,t-1}$, y_{i0}, $\mathbf{z}_i$. The problem is that, while $\mathrm{P}(y_{it} = 1 \mid \mathbf{z}_i, y_{i,t-1}, \ldots, y_{i0}, a_i) = \Phi(\psi + \mathbf{z}_{it}\boldsymbol{\delta} + \rho y_{i,t-1} + \xi_0 y_{i0} + \mathbf{z}_i \xi + a_i)$, it is not true that $\mathrm{P}(y_{it} = 1 \mid \mathbf{z}_i, y_{i,t-1}, \ldots, y_{i0})$

$= \Phi(\psi_a + \mathbf{z}_{it}\boldsymbol{\delta}_a + \rho_a y_{i,t-1} + \xi_{a0} y_{i0} + \mathbf{z}_i \boldsymbol{\xi}_a)$ unless a_i is identically zero, which means that c_i is a deterministic linear function of $(y_{i0}, \mathbf{z}_i)$. Correlation between $y_{i,t-1}$ and a_i means that $\mathrm{P}(y_{it} = 1 \mid \mathbf{z}_i, y_{i,t-1}, \ldots, y_{i0})$ does not follow a probit model with index that depends on the scaled coefficients of interest. Therefore, we should use the RE probit approach, and not pooled probit (as in Section 15.8.1). For comparison purposes, we can estimate the dynamic model without the unobserved effect, c_i, and then pooled probit is the appropriate estimation method.

Example 15.6 (Dynamic Women's LFP Equation): We now use the data in LFP.RAW to estimate a model for $\mathrm{P}(lfp_{it} = 1 \mid kids_{it}, lhinc_{it}, lfp_{i,t-1}, c_i)$, where one lag of labor force participation is assumed to suffice for the dynamics and $\{(kids_{it}, lhinc_{it}) : t = 1, \ldots, T\}$ is assumed to be strictly exogenous conditional on c_i. Also, we include the time-constant variables *educ*, *black*, *age*, and age^2 and a full set of time-period dummies. (We start with five periods and lose one with the lag. Therefore, we estimate the model using four years of data.) We include among the regressors the initial value, lfp_{i0}, $kids_{i1}$ through $kids_{i4}$, and $lhinc_{i1}$ through $lhinc_{i4}$. (To keep the notation consistent with the previous development, we implicitly relabel the time periods in the data set.) Estimating the model by RE probit gives $\hat{\rho} = 1.541$ (se = .067), and so, even after controlling for unobserved heterogeneity, there is strong evidence of state dependence. But to obtain the size of the effect, we compute the APE for lfp_{t-1}. The calculation involves averaging $\Phi(\hat{\psi}_a + \mathbf{z}_{it}\hat{\boldsymbol{\delta}}_a + \hat{\rho}_a + \hat{\xi}_{a0} y_{i0} + \mathbf{z}_i \hat{\boldsymbol{\xi}}_a) - \Phi(\hat{\psi}_a + \mathbf{z}_{it}\hat{\boldsymbol{\delta}}_a + \hat{\xi}_{a0} y_{i0} + \mathbf{z}_i \hat{\boldsymbol{\xi}}_a)$ across all t and i; we must be sure to scale the original coefficients by $(1 + \hat{\sigma}_a^2)^{-1/2}$, where, in this application, $\hat{\sigma}_a^2 = 1.103$. The APE estimated from this method is about .260 (panel bootstrap standard error is .026 with 500 replications). In other words, averaged across all women and all time periods, the probability of being in the labor force at time t is about .26 higher if the woman was in the labor force at time $t-1$ than if she was not. This estimate controls for unobserved heterogeneity, number of young children, husband's income, and the woman's education, race, and age.

It is instructive to compare the APE with the estimate of a dynamic probit model that ignores c_i. In this case, we just use pooled probit of lfp_{it} on 1, $kids_{it}$, $lhinc_{it}$, $lfp_{i,t-1}$, $educ_i$, $black_i$, age_i, and age_i^2 and include a full set of period dummies. The coefficient on $lfp_{i,t-1}$ is 2.876 (se = .027), which is much higher than in the dynamic RE probit model. More important, the APE for state dependence is about .837 (panel bootstrap se = .005), which is much higher than when heterogeneity is controlled for. Therefore, in this example, much of the persistence in labor force participation of married women is accounted for by the unobserved heterogeneity. There is still some state dependence, but its value is much smaller than a simple dynamic probit indicates.

As mentioned earlier, Wooldridge (2000) proposes an extension of the preceding approach to allow other not strictly exogenous explanatory variables to appear in unobserved effects probit models. Generally, if w_{it} is a variable that is sequentially but not strictly exogenous, we model $\mathrm{P}(y_{it} = 1 \mid w_{it}, \mathbf{z}_{it}, y_{i,t-1}, c_{i1})$ and assume this is the same probability when we include all lags of w_{it}, further lags of y_{it}, and the entire history of the strictly exogenous variables, $\mathbf{z}_{it}$. (Allowing a lagged value of w_{it} only changes the notation.) We then add a model for the density of $\mathrm{D}(w_{it} \mid \mathbf{z}_{it}, w_{i,t-1}, y_{i,t-1}, c_{i2})$, assuming that one lag each of w_{it} and y_{it} is sufficient to capture the dynamics, and that $\mathbf{z}_{it}$ is also strictly exogenous in this distribution. The joint density of (y_{it}, w_{it}) given $(\mathbf{z}_i, w_{i,t-1}, \dots, w_{i0}, y_{i,t-1}, \dots, y_{i0}, \mathbf{c}_i)$ is $f_{t1}(y_t \mid w_t, \mathbf{z}_{it}, y_{i,t-1}, c_{i1}) \cdot f_{t2}(w_t \mid \mathbf{z}_{it}, w_{i,t-1}, y_{i,t-1}, c_{i2}) \equiv g_t(y_t, w_t \mid \mathbf{z}_i, w_{i,t-1}, \dots, w_{i0}, y_{i,t-1}, \dots, y_{i0}, c_{i1}, c_{i2})$. By multiplying these densities from $t = 1$ to T we obtain the density of $(y_{i1}, w_{i1}, \dots, y_{iT}, w_{iT})$ given $(\mathbf{z}_i, y_{i0}, w_{i0}, \mathbf{c}_i)$. Now, as before, if we specify a density for $\mathrm{D}(\mathbf{c}_i \mid \mathbf{z}_i, y_{i0}, w_{i0})$, we can obtain a density for $\mathrm{D}(\mathbf{y}_i, \mathbf{w}_i \mid \mathbf{z}_i, y_{i0}, w_{i0})$ by integrating out $\mathbf{c}_i$. We can construct a log-likelihood function for estimating the parameters in both conditional densities, as well as the parameters in the heterogeneity distribution. The problem is significantly harder if we truly allow two sources of heterogeneity in $\mathbf{c}_i = (c_{i1}, c_{i2})$, especially if we allow them to be correlated, but conditioning on the initial conditions (y_{i0}, w_{i0}) helps simplify the estimation. Wooldridge (2000) provides more details when w_{it} is a binary response that may react to changes in past values of y_{it}, thereby causing it to violate the strict exogeneity assumption.

15.8.5 Probit Models with Heterogeneity and Endogenous Explanatory Variables

The previous methods assumed that the explanatory variables satisfy a strict exogeneity assumption or a sequential exogeneity assumption. We can also use probit models to account for unobserved heterogeneity and contemporaneous endogeneity. We focus on two cases: (1) the endogenous explanatory variable has a conditional normal distribution and (2) the endogenous explanatory variable follows a reduced form probit. The reasons for these restrictions will become clear, as we must adapt the methods from Section 15.7.

We can write the model as

$$y_{it1} = 1[\mathbf{z}_{it1}\boldsymbol{\delta}_1 + \alpha_1 y_{it2} + c_{i1} + u_{it1} \geq 0], \qquad u_{it1} \mid \mathbf{z}_i, c_{i1} \sim \mathrm{Normal}(0, 1), \tag{15.86}$$

where y_{it1} is the binary response, y_{it2} is the endogenous explanatory variable, c_{i1} is the unobserved heterogeneity, $\{u_{it1} : t = 1, \dots, T\}$ is the sequence of idiosyncratic errors, and $\mathbf{z}_i = (\mathbf{z}_{i1}, \dots, \mathbf{z}_{iT})$ is the sequence of strictly exogenous variables (conditional on c_{i1}). Notice that u_{it1} is assumed to be independent of $(\mathbf{z}_i, c_{i1})$. We would want to include a full set of period dummies in $\mathbf{z}_{it}$.

Our focus will be on estimating APEs. Regardless of the nature of y_{t2}, these are easily obtained from the ASF. At time t,

$$\mathrm{ASF}(\mathbf{z}_{t1}, y_{t2}) = \mathrm{E}_{c_{i1}}[\Phi(\mathbf{z}_{t1}\boldsymbol{\delta}_1 + \alpha_1 y_{t2} + c_{i1})], \tag{15.87}$$

where $\mathrm{E}_{c_{i1}}(\cdot)$ denotes the expected value with respect to the distribution of c_{i1}. As we did previously, we specify a model for the conditional distribution $\mathrm{D}(c_{i1} \mid \mathbf{z}_i)$, the distribution conditional only on the strictly exogenous explanatory variables. Not suprisingly, a normal distribution is convenient:

$$c_{i1} = \psi_1 + \bar{\mathbf{z}}_i \boldsymbol{\xi}_1 + a_{i1}, \qquad a_{i1} \mid \mathbf{z}_i \sim \mathrm{Normal}(0, \sigma_{a_1}^2), \tag{15.88}$$

where $\bar{\mathbf{z}}_i$ contains the time averages of *all* strictly exogenous variables (except any aggregate time effects, such as period dummies). In particular, if at time t we have $\mathbf{z}_{it} = (\mathbf{z}_{it1}, \mathbf{z}_{it2})$, then the time averages of $\mathbf{z}_{it2}$ are also in equation (15.88). Plugging into (15.86) and doing simple algebra gives

$$\begin{aligned} y_{it1} &= 1[\mathbf{z}_{it1}\boldsymbol{\delta}_1 + \alpha_1 y_{it2} + \psi_1 + \bar{\mathbf{z}}_i \boldsymbol{\xi}_1 + a_{i1} + u_{it1} \geq 0] \\ &\equiv 1[\mathbf{z}_{it1}\boldsymbol{\delta}_{a1} + \alpha_{a1} y_{it2} + \psi_{a1} + \bar{\mathbf{z}}_i \boldsymbol{\xi}_{a1} + e_{it1} \geq 0], \end{aligned} \tag{15.89}$$

where $e_{it1} \equiv (a_{i1} + u_{it1})/(1 + \sigma_{a_1}^2)^{1/2}$ has a standard normal distribution conditional on $\mathbf{z}_i$. On the parameters, the "a" subscript denotes division by $(1 + \sigma_{a_1}^2)^{1/2}$, for example, $\boldsymbol{\delta}_{a1} \equiv \boldsymbol{\delta}_1/(1 + \sigma_{a_1}^2)^{1/2}$. Now the average structural function can be obtained as

$$\begin{aligned} &\mathrm{E}_{(\bar{\mathbf{z}}_i, e_{it1})}\{1[\mathbf{z}_{t1}\boldsymbol{\delta}_{a1} + \alpha_{a1} y_{t2} + \psi_{a1} + \bar{\mathbf{z}}_i \boldsymbol{\xi}_{a1} + e_{it1} \geq 0]\} \\ &\quad = \mathrm{E}_{\bar{\mathbf{z}}_i}[\Phi(\mathbf{z}_{t1}\boldsymbol{\delta}_{a1} + \alpha_{a1} y_{t2} + \psi_{a1} + \bar{\mathbf{z}}_i \boldsymbol{\xi}_{a1})], \end{aligned}$$

where the equality follows by iterated expectations. It follows that we can consistently estimate the APEs by averaging out $\bar{\mathbf{z}}_i$ if we can estimate the scaled coefficients. But these scaled coefficients are *precisely* what we estimate if we apply one of the MLE methods from Section 15.7.2 or 15.7.3, depending on whether y_{it2} has a conditional normal distribution or follows a probit. In the former case, we can write a reduced form as

$$y_{it2} = \mathbf{z}_{it}\boldsymbol{\delta}_2 + \psi_2 + \bar{\mathbf{z}}_i \boldsymbol{\xi}_2 + v_{it2}, \qquad v_{it2} \mid \mathbf{z}_i \sim \mathrm{Normal}(0, \tau_2^2),\ t = 1, \ldots, T. \tag{15.90}$$

Notice that the instruments for y_{it2} omitted from the estimating equation (15.89) are $\mathbf{z}_{it2}$; all elements of $\bar{\mathbf{z}}_i$ are in equations (15.89) and the reduced form (15.90). Then, we use pooled MLE directly on equations (15.89) and (15.90), and then compute the APEs exactly as we did before, possibly computing them for each time period. (We might call this approach **pooled IV probit**.) Bootstrapping is a simple (though computationally expensive) way to obtain proper standard errors. If y_{it2} is binary, we replace the right hand side of (15.90) with $1[\mathbf{z}_{it}\boldsymbol{\delta}_2 + \psi_2 + \bar{\mathbf{z}}_i\xi_2 + v_{it2} \geq 0]$, set $\tau_2^2 = 1$, and apply **pooled bivariate probit**.

Pooled estimation is very convenient because any routine that allows estimation of the models for cross section data can be used for panel data, provided robust standard errors and test statistics are computed to account for the neglected time dependence. A full MLE method, which would account for the presence of a_{i1} and assume, in addition, that the u_{it1} are serially independent, would be much more computationally intensive and would not be robust to serial correlation in the idiosyncratic errors. More importantly, MLE jointly across time would require specification of the joint distribution of $\{(e_{it1}, v_{it2}) : t = 1, \ldots, T\}$, and not just the bivariate distribution of (e_{it1}, v_{it2}) for each t. Assuming independence across t would be unrealistic, and allowing for realistic correlation over time would be computationally expensive.

When y_{it2} is continuous, a control function approach is also available. Using manipulations similar to those above and in Section 15.7.2, we can write

$$y_{it1} = 1[\mathbf{z}_{it1}\boldsymbol{\delta}_{g1} + \alpha_{g1}y_{it2} + \theta_{g1}v_{it2} + \psi_{g1} + \bar{\mathbf{z}}_i\xi_{g1} + r_{it1} \geq 0],$$

where the coefficients have been scaled by a different variance and so we index the parameters by "g" just to distinguish them from the previous scaled parameters. Now, r_{it1} is independent of $(\mathbf{z}_i, y_{it2}, v_{it2})$ with a standard normal distribution. After obtaining the $\hat{v}_{it2}$ as the residuals from pooled OLS estimation of the reduced form, we use pooled probit of y_{it1} on $\mathbf{z}_{it1}$, y_{it2}, $\hat{v}_{it2}$, 1, and $\bar{\mathbf{z}}_i$. A simple test of the null hypothesis that y_{it2} is contemporaneously endogenous is obtained by a t test of $\mathrm{H}_0 : \theta_{g1} = 0$, which is directly available from the pooled probit provided we make the statistic robust to arbitrary serial dependence.

15.8.6 Semiparametric Approaches

Under strict exogeneity of the explanatory variables, it is possible to consistently estimate $\boldsymbol{\beta}$ up to scale under very weak assumptions. Manski (1987) derives an objective function that identifies $\boldsymbol{\beta}$ up to scale in the $T = 2$ case when e_{i1} and e_{i2} in the model (15.72) are identically distributed conditional on $(\mathbf{x}_{i1}, \mathbf{x}_{i2}, c_i)$ and $\mathbf{x}_{it}$ is strictly exogenous. The estimator is the maximum score estimator applied to the differences Δy_i and $\Delta \mathbf{x}_i$. As in the cross-sectional case, it is not known how to estimate the average response probabilities.

Honoré and Kyriazidou (2000a) show how to estimate the parameters in the unobserved effects logit model with a lagged dependent variable and strictly exogenous explanatory variables without making distributional assumptions about the unobserved effect. Unfortunately, the estimators, which are consistent and asymptotically normal, do not generally converge at the usual $\sqrt{N}$ rate. In addition, as with many semiparametric approaches, discrete explanatory variables such as time dummies are ruled out, and it is not possible to estimate the APEs. See also Arellano and Honoré (2001).

A middle ground between parametrically specifying $\mathrm{D}(c_i \mid \mathbf{x}_i)$ and allowing it to be completely unrestricted is to impose substantive assumptions on $\mathrm{D}(c_i \mid \mathbf{x}_i)$ but without making parametric assumptions. As a special case of Altonji and Matzkin's (2005) "exchangeability" assumption, we might impose the restriction

$$\mathrm{D}(c_i \mid \mathbf{x}_i) = \mathrm{D}(c_i \mid \bar{\mathbf{x}}_i) \tag{15.91}$$

without specifying $\mathrm{D}(c_i \mid \bar{\mathbf{x}}_i)$. Why is this restriction useful? Consider a general specification where the only restriction is strict exogeneity conditional on the heterogeneity:

$$\mathrm{P}(y_{it} = 1 \mid \mathbf{x}_i, \mathbf{c}_i) = \mathrm{P}(y_{it} = 1 \mid \mathbf{x}_{it}, \mathbf{c}_i) = G_t(\mathbf{x}_{it}, \mathbf{c}_i), \tag{15.92}$$

where G_t is an unknown function taking values in $(0, 1)$ and we let $\mathbf{c}_i$ be a vector of unobserved heterogeneity to emphasize the generality of the setup. We allow for a t subscript on G as a general way of allowing aggregate time effects (analogous to including different period dummies in a linear model, probit, or logit). The ASF at time t can be written as

$$\mathrm{ASF}_t(\mathbf{x}_t) = \mathrm{E}_{\mathbf{c}_i}[G_t(\mathbf{x}_t, \mathbf{c}_i)] = \mathrm{E}_{\bar{\mathbf{x}}_i}\{\mathrm{E}[G_t(\mathbf{x}_t, \mathbf{c}_i) \mid \bar{\mathbf{x}}_i]\} \equiv \mathrm{E}_{\bar{\mathbf{x}}_i}[R_t(\mathbf{x}_t, \bar{\mathbf{x}}_i)], \tag{15.93}$$

where $R_t(\mathbf{x}_t, \bar{\mathbf{x}}_i) \equiv \mathrm{E}[G_t(\mathbf{x}_t, \mathbf{c}_i) \mid \bar{\mathbf{x}}_i]$. It follows that, given an estimator $\hat{R}_t(\cdot, \cdot)$ of the function $R_t(\cdot, \cdot)$, the ASF can be estimated as $N^{-1} \sum_{i=1}^N \hat{R}_t(\mathbf{x}_t, \bar{\mathbf{x}}_i)$, and then we can take derivatives or changes with respect to the entries in $\mathbf{x}_t$.

How can we estimate $R_t(\cdot, \cdot)$? This is where assumption (15.91) comes into play. If we combine (15.91) and (15.92) we have

$$\begin{aligned}\mathrm{E}(y_{it} \mid \mathbf{x}_i) &= \mathrm{E}[\mathrm{E}(y_{it} \mid \mathbf{x}_i, \mathbf{c}_i) \mid \mathbf{x}_i] = \mathrm{E}[G_t(\mathbf{x}_{it}, \mathbf{c}_i) \mid \mathbf{x}_i] = \int G_t(\mathbf{x}_{it}, \mathbf{c}) \, \mathrm{d}F(\mathbf{c} \mid \mathbf{x}_i) \\ &= \int G_t(\mathbf{x}_{it}, \mathbf{c}) \, \mathrm{d}F(\mathbf{c} \mid \bar{\mathbf{x}}_i) = R_t(\mathbf{x}_{it}, \bar{\mathbf{x}}_i),\end{aligned}$$

where $F(\mathbf{c} \mid \mathbf{x}_i)$ denotes the cdf of $\mathrm{D}(\mathbf{c}_i \mid \mathbf{x}_i)$ (which can be a discrete, continuous, or mixed distribution), the second equality follows from (15.92), the fourth equality follows from assumption (15.91), and the last equality follows from the definition of $R_t(\cdot, \cdot)$. Of course, because $\mathrm{E}(y_{it} \mid \mathbf{x}_i)$ depends only on $(\mathbf{x}_{it}, \bar{\mathbf{x}}_i)$, we must have

$\mathrm{E}(y_{it} \mid \mathbf{x}_{it}, \bar{\mathbf{x}}_i) = R_t(\mathbf{x}_{it}, \bar{\mathbf{x}}_i)$. Further, $\{\mathbf{x}_{it} : t = 1, \ldots, T\}$ is assumed to have time variation, and so $\mathbf{x}_{it}$ and $\bar{\mathbf{x}}_i$ can be used as separate regressors even in a fully nonparametric setting.

We do not generally treat nonparametric methods in this text, but the preceding discussion suggests some simple yet flexible parametric approaches. The key is that, under specification (15.92) with assumption (15.91), we can specify flexible binary models for $\mathrm{P}(y_{it} = 1 \mid \mathbf{x}_{it}, \bar{\mathbf{x}}_i)$, estimate these models using MLE methods, and then average out $\bar{\mathbf{x}}_i$ to obtain estimated APEs. Without a very large N or with many elements of $\mathbf{x}_{it}$, we probably would economize by assuming that at least some parameters are constant across t. For example, a flexible probit model is

$$\mathrm{P}(y_{it} = 1 \mid \mathbf{x}_{it}, \bar{\mathbf{x}}_i) = \Phi[\theta_t + \mathbf{x}_{it}\boldsymbol{\beta} + \bar{\mathbf{x}}_i\boldsymbol{\gamma} + (\bar{\mathbf{x}}_i \otimes \bar{\mathbf{x}}_i)\boldsymbol{\delta} + (\mathbf{x}_{it} \otimes \bar{\mathbf{x}}_i)\boldsymbol{\eta}], \qquad t = 1, \ldots, T, \tag{15.94}$$

where the Kronecker products simply mean we include all squares and nonredundant interactions among $\bar{\mathbf{x}}_i$ and interactions among $\mathbf{x}_{it}$ and $\bar{\mathbf{x}}_i$. Aggregate time effects are allowed through the θ_t, and we can estimate this model by pooled probit, GEE, or minimum distance methods. Using a logit instead of a probit would likely change very little in terms of estimated partial effects. With large N, one might use a cdf that depends on extra parameters. The point here is that, under (15.91) and (15.92), the focus on APEs liberates one from having to specify specific functional forms in equation (15.92). Because we can only identify APEs anyway, rather than subject-specific effects, we might as well start from models for $\mathrm{P}(y_{it} = 1 \mid \mathbf{x}_{it}, \bar{\mathbf{x}}_i)$.

We can go further. For example, suppose that we think the heterogeneity $\mathbf{c}_i$ is correlated with features of the covariates other than just the time average. Altonji and Matzkin (2005) allow for $\bar{\mathbf{x}}_i$ in equation (15.91) to be replaced by other functions $\mathbf{w}_i$ of $\{\mathbf{x}_{it} : t = 1, \ldots, T\}$, such as sample variances and covariance. These are examples of "exchangeable" functions of $\{\mathbf{x}_{it} : t = 1, \ldots, T\}$—that is, statistics whose value is the same regardless of the ordering of the $\mathbf{x}_{it}$. Nonexchangeable functions can be used, too. For example, we might think that $\mathbf{c}_i$ is correlated with individual-specific trends, and so we obtain $\mathbf{w}_i$ as the intercept and slope from the unit-specific regressions $\mathbf{x}_{it}$ on 1, t, $t = 1, \ldots, T$ (for $T \geq 3$); we can also add the error variance from this individual specific regression if we have sufficient time periods.

Altonji and Matzkin (2005) focus on what they call the **local average response (LAR)** as opposed to the APE. In specification (15.92), the LAR at $\mathbf{x}_t$ for a continuous variable x_{tj} is

$$\int \frac{\partial G_t(\mathbf{x}_t, \mathbf{c})}{\partial x_{tj}} \, \mathrm{d}H_t(\mathbf{c} \mid \mathbf{x}_t), \tag{15.95}$$

where $H_t(\mathbf{c} \mid \mathbf{x}_t)$ denotes the cdf of $\mathrm{D}(\mathbf{c}_i \mid \mathbf{x}_{it} = \mathbf{x}_t)$. This is a "local" partial effect because it averages out the heterogeneity for the slice of the population given by the vector $\mathbf{x}_t$. The APE, which by comparison could be called a "global average response," averages out over the entire distribution of $\mathbf{c}_i$.

When $\mathrm{D}(\mathbf{c}_i \mid \mathbf{x}_i) = \mathrm{D}(\mathbf{c}_i \mid \mathbf{w}_i)$ for $\mathbf{w}_i$ a function of $\mathbf{x}_i$, Altonji and Matzkin show that the LAR can be obtained as

$$\int \frac{\partial R_t(\mathbf{x}_t, \mathbf{w})}{\partial x_{tj}} \mathrm{d}K_t(\mathbf{w} \mid \mathbf{x}_t), \tag{15.96}$$

where $R(\mathbf{x}_t, \mathbf{w}) = \mathrm{E}(y_{it} \mid \mathbf{x}_{it} = \mathbf{x}_t, \mathbf{w}_i = \mathbf{w})$ and $K_t(\mathbf{w} \mid \mathbf{x}_t)$ is the cdf of $\mathrm{D}(\mathbf{w}_i \mid \mathbf{x}_{it} = \mathbf{x}_t)$. Altonji and Matzkin demonstrate how to estimate the LAR based on nonparametric estimation of $\mathrm{E}(y_{it} \mid \mathbf{x}_{it}, \mathbf{w}_i)$ followed by "local" averaging, that is, averaging $\partial \hat{\mathrm{E}}(y_{it} \mid \mathbf{x}_{it} = \mathbf{x}_t, \mathbf{w}_i)/\partial x_{tj}$ over observations i with $\mathbf{x}_{it}$ "close" to $\mathbf{x}_t$. In the binary response context, the expected value is simply $\mathrm{P}(y_{it} = 1 \mid \mathbf{x}_{it}, \mathbf{w}_i)$. Of course, the LAR can even be estimated using parametric models such as that in equation (15.94). For a continuous x_{tj}, we would simply average the derivative of $\Phi[\theta_t + \mathbf{x}_t\boldsymbol{\beta} + \bar{\mathbf{x}}_i\boldsymbol{\gamma} + (\bar{\mathbf{x}}_i \otimes \bar{\mathbf{x}}_i)\boldsymbol{\delta} + (\mathbf{x}_t \otimes \bar{\mathbf{x}}_i)\boldsymbol{\eta}]$ with respect to x_{tj} over i with $\mathbf{x}_{it}$ "close" to $\mathbf{x}_t$. Because defining the appropriate notion of "closeness" requires some care, the LAR is more difficult to estimate than the APE, but LAR is perhaps more relevant because it is the average response to an exogenous change in x_{tj} for units already starting from $\mathbf{x}_t$. See Altonji and Matzkin (2005) for further discussion concerning identification and estimation of LARs.

An interesting possibility is to combine the Blundell and Powell (2004) approach to endogeneity with the Altonji and Matzkin (2005) approach to unobserved heterogeneity, resulting in semiparametric versions of the methods in Section 15.8.5.

Problems

15.1. Suppose that y is a binary outcome and $d1, d2, \ldots, dM$ are dummy variables for exhaustive and mutually exclusive categories; that is, each person in the population falls into one and only one category.

a. Show that the fitted values from the regression (without an intercept)

$$y_i \text{ on } d1_i, d2_i, \ldots, dM_i, \qquad i = 1, 2, \ldots, N$$

are always in the unit interval. In particular, carefully describe the coefficient on each dummy variable and the fitted value for each i.

b. What happens if y_i is regressed on M linearly independent, linear combinations of $d1_i, \ldots, dM_i$, for example, $1, d2_i, d3_i, \ldots, dM_i$?

15.2. Suppose that family i chooses annual consumption c_i (in dollars) and charitable contributions q_i (in dollars) to solve the problem

$$\max_{c,q} \; c + a_i \log(1 + q)$$

$$\text{subject to } c + p_i q \leq m_i, \qquad c, q \geq 0$$

where m_i is income of family i, p_i is the price of one dollar of charitable contributions —where $p_i < 1$ because of the tax deductability of charitable contributions, and this price differs across families because of different marginal tax rates and different state tax codes—and $a_i \geq 0$ determines the marginal utility of charitable contributions. Take m_i and p_i as exogenous to the family in this problem.

a. Show that the optimal solution is $q_i = 0$ if $a_i \leq p_i$, and $q_i = a_i/p_i - 1$ if $a_i > p_i$.

b. Define $y_i = 1$ if $q_i > 0$ and $y_i = 0$ if $q_i = 0$, and suppose that $a_i = \exp(\mathbf{z}_i \gamma + v_i)$, where $\mathbf{z}_i$ is a J-vector of observable family traits and v_i is unobservable. Assume that v_i is independent of $(\mathbf{z}_i, m_i, p_i)$ and v_i/σ has symmetric distribution function $G(\cdot)$, where $\sigma^2 = \text{Var}(v_i)$. Show that

$$\text{P}(y_i = 1 \mid \mathbf{z}_i, m_i, p_i) = G[(\mathbf{z}_i \gamma - \log p_i)/\sigma]$$

so that y_i follows an index model.

15.3. Let $\mathbf{z}_1$ be a vector of variables, let z_2 be a continuous variable, and let d_1 be a dummy variable.

a. In the model

$$\text{P}(y = 1 \mid \mathbf{z}_1, z_2) = \Phi(\mathbf{z}_1 \boldsymbol{\delta}_1 + \gamma_1 z_2 + \gamma_2 z_2^2),$$

find the partial effect of z_2 on the response probability. How would you estimate this partial effect?

b. In the model

$$\text{P}(y = 1 \mid \mathbf{z}_1, z_2, d_1) = \Phi(\mathbf{z}_1 \boldsymbol{\delta}_1 + \gamma_1 z_2 + \gamma_2 d_1 + \gamma_3 z_2 d_1),$$

find the partial effect of z_2. How would you measure the effect of d_1 on the response probability? How would you estimate these effects?

c. Describe how you would obtain the standard errors of the estimated partial effects from parts a and b.

15.4. Evaluate the following statement: "Estimation of a linear probability model is more robust than probit or logit because the LPM does not assume homoskedasticity or a distributional assumption."

15.5. Consider the probit model

$$\mathrm{P}(y = 1 \mid \mathbf{z}, q) = \Phi(\mathbf{z}_1\boldsymbol{\delta}_1 + \gamma_1 z_2 q),$$

where q is independent of $\mathbf{z}$ and distributed as Normal(0, 1); the vector $\mathbf{z}$ is observed but the scalar q is not.

a. Find the partial effect of z_2 on the response probability, namely,

$$\frac{\partial \mathrm{P}(y = 1 \mid \mathbf{z}, q)}{\partial z_2}.$$

b. Show that $\mathrm{P}(y = 1 \mid \mathbf{z}) = \Phi[\mathbf{z}_1\boldsymbol{\delta}_1/(1 + \gamma_1^2 z_2^2)^{1/2}]$.

c. Define $\rho_1 \equiv \gamma_1^2$. How would you test $\mathrm{H}_0 : \rho_1 = 0$?

d. If you have reason to believe $\rho_1 > 0$, how would you estimate $\boldsymbol{\delta}_1$ along with ρ_1?

15.6. Consider taking a large random sample of workers at a given point in time. Let $sick_i = 1$ if person i called in sick during the last 90 days, and zero otherwise. Let $\mathbf{z}_i$ be a vector of individual and employer characteristics. Let $cigs_i$ be the number of cigarettes individual i smokes per day (on average).

a. Explain the underlying experiment of interest when we want to examine the effects of cigarette smoking on workdays lost.

b. Why might $cigs_i$ be correlated with unobservables affecting $sick_i$?

c. One way to write the model of interest is

$$\mathrm{P}(sick = 1 \mid \mathbf{z}, cigs, q_1) = \Phi(\mathbf{z}_1\boldsymbol{\delta}_1 + \gamma_1 cigs + q_1),$$

where $\mathbf{z}_1$ is a subset of $\mathbf{z}$ and q_1 is an unobservable variable that is possibly correlated with $cigs$. What happens if q_1 is ignored and you estimate the probit of $sick$ on $\mathbf{z}_1$, $cigs$?

d. Can $cigs$ have a conditional normal distribution in the population? Explain.

e. Explain how to test whether $cigs$ is exogenous. Does this test rely on $cigs$ having a conditional normal distribution?

f. Suppose that some of the workers live in states that recently implemented no-smoking laws in the workplace. Does the presence of the new laws suggest a good IV candidate for $cigs$?

15.7. Use the data in GROGGER.RAW for this question.

a. Define a binary variable, say *arr86*, equal to unity if a man was arrested at least once during 1986, and zero otherwise. Estimate an LPM relating *arr86* to *pcnv*, *avgsen*, *tottime*, *ptime86*, *inc86*, *black*, *hispan*, and *born60*. Report the usual and heteroskedasticity-robust standard errors. What is the estimated effect on the probability of arrest if *pcnv* goes from .25 to .75?

b. Test the joint significance of *avgsen* and *tottime*, using a nonrobust and robust test.

c. Now estimate the model by probit. At the average values of *avgsen*, *tottime*, *inc86*, and *ptime86* in the sample, and with $black = 1$, $hispan = 0$, and $born60 = 1$, what is the estimated effect on the probability of arrest if *pcnv* goes from .25 to .75? Compare this result with the answer from part a.

d. For the probit model estimated in part c, obtain the percent correctly predicted. What is the percent correctly predicted when $narr86 = 0$? When $narr86 = 1$? What do you make of these findings?

e. In the probit model, add the terms $pcnv^2$, $ptime86^2$, and $inc86^2$ to the model. Are these individually or jointly significant? Describe the estimated relationship between the probability of arrest and *pcnv*. In particular, at what point does the probability of conviction have a negative effect on probability of arrest?

15.8. Use the data set BWGHT.RAW for this problem.

a. Define a binary variable, *smokes*, if the woman smokes during pregnancy. Estimate a probit model relating *smokes* to *motheduc*, *white*, and log(*faminc*). At $white = 0$ and *faminc* evaluated at the average in the sample, what is the estimated difference in the probability of smoking for a woman with 16 years of education and one with 12 years of education?

b. Do you think *faminc* is exogenous in the smoking equation? What about *motheduc*?

c. Assume that *motheduc* and *white* are exogenous in the probit from part a. Also assume that *fatheduc* is exogenous to this equation. Estimate the reduced form for log(*faminc*) to see if *fatheduc* is partially correlated with log(*faminc*).

d. Test the null hypothesis that log(*faminc*) is exogenous in the probit from part a.

15.9. Assume that the binary variable y follows an LPM.

a. Write down the log-likelihood function for observation i.

b. Why might MLE of the LPM be difficult?

c. Assuming that you can estimate the LPM by MLE, explain why it is valid, as a model selection device, to compare the log likelihood from the LPM with that from logit or probit.

15.10. Suppose you wish to use goodness-of-fit measures to compare the LPM with a model such as logit or probit, after estimating the LPM by ordinary least squares. The usual R-squared from OLS estimation measures the proportion of the variance in y that is explained by $\hat{\mathrm{P}}(y = 1 \mid \mathbf{x}) = \mathbf{x}\hat{\boldsymbol{\beta}}$.

a. Explain how to obtain a comparable R-squared measured for the general index model $\mathrm{P}(y = 1 \mid \mathbf{x}) = G(\mathbf{x}\boldsymbol{\beta})$.

b. Compute the R-squared measures using the data in GROGGER.RAW, where the dependent variable is *arr86* and the explanatory variables are *pcnv*, $pcnv^2$, *avgsen*, *tottime*, *ptime86*, $ptime86^2$, *inc86*, $inc86^2$, *black*, *hispan*, and *born60*. Are the R-squareds substantially different?

15.11. List assumptions under which the pooled probit estimator is a conditional MLE based on the distribution of $\mathbf{y}_i$ given $\mathbf{x}_i$, where $\mathbf{y}_i$ is the $T \times 1$ vector of binary outcomes and $\mathbf{x}_i$ is the vector of all explanatory variables across all T time periods.

15.12. Find $\mathrm{P}(y_{i1} = 1, y_{i2} = 0, y_{i3} = 0 \mid \mathbf{x}_i, c_i, n_i = 1)$ in the fixed effects logit model with $T = 3$.

15.13. Suppose that you have a control group, A, and a treatment group, B, and two periods of data. Between the two years, a new policy is implemented that affects group B; see Section 6.5.

a. If your outcome variable is binary (for example, an employment indicator), and you have no covariates, how would you estimate the effect of the policy?

b. If you have covariates, write down a probit model that allows you to estimate the effect of the policy change. Explain in detail how you would estimate this effect.

c. How would you get an asymptotic 95 percent confidence interval for the estimate in part b?

15.14. Consider the binary response model with interactions between the (continuous) endogenous explanatory variable and the exogenous variables:

$$y_1 = 1[\mathbf{z}_1\boldsymbol{\delta}_1 + y_2\mathbf{z}_1\boldsymbol{\alpha}_1 + u_1 > 0],$$

and assume that assumption (15.40) holds with (u_1, v_2) jointly normal and independent of $\mathbf{z}$, with mean zero and $\mathrm{Var}(u_1) = 1$.

a. Find $P(y_1 = 1 \mid \mathbf{z})$ and conclude that it has the form of a particular heteroskedastic probit model.

b. Consider the following two-step procedure. In the first step, regress y_{i2} on $\mathbf{z}_i$ and obtain the fitted values, $\hat{y}_{i2}$. In the second step, estimate probit of y_{i1} on $\mathbf{z}_{i1}$, $\hat{y}_{i2}\mathbf{z}_{i1}$. How come this does not produce consistent estimators of $\boldsymbol{\delta}_1$ and $\boldsymbol{\alpha}_1$?

c. How would you consistently estimate $\boldsymbol{\delta}_1$ and $\boldsymbol{\alpha}_1$?

15.15. Consider the problem of obtaining standard errors for the coefficient and APE estimators in two-step control function estimation of binary response models. For simplicity, let y_2 be a continuous, univariate endogenous variable following the reduced form $y_2 = \mathbf{z}\boldsymbol{\delta}_2 + v_2$, $y_1 = 1[\mathbf{x}_1\boldsymbol{\beta}_1 + u_1 > 0]$, $\mathbf{x}_1 = \mathbf{g}_1(\mathbf{z}_1, y_2)$ is any function of the exogenous and endogenous variables. As usual, we assume that $\mathbf{z} = (\mathbf{z}_1, \mathbf{z}_2)$, where one element of $\mathbf{z}_2$ has nonzero element of $\boldsymbol{\delta}_2$. Assume that the standard Rivers-Vuong assumptions hold, so that

$$P(y_1 = 1 \mid \mathbf{z}, y_2) = \Phi(\mathbf{x}_1\boldsymbol{\beta}_{\rho 1} + \theta_{\rho 1} v_2),$$

where $\boldsymbol{\beta}_{\rho 1}$ and $\theta_{\rho 1}$ are the scaled coefficients that appear in the APEs. For simplicity, let $\boldsymbol{\gamma}_1 = (\boldsymbol{\beta}_{\rho 1}', \theta_{\rho 1})'$, let $\hat{\boldsymbol{\gamma}}_1$ be the second-step Rivers-Vuong estimator, and let $\hat{\boldsymbol{\delta}}_2$ be the first-stage OLS estimator.

a. Find Avar $\sqrt{N}(\hat{\boldsymbol{\gamma}}_1 - \boldsymbol{\gamma}_1)$ using the material in Section 12.4.2.

b. Show that the asymptotic variance that properly accounts for the first-step estimation of $\boldsymbol{\delta}_2$ is no smaller (in the matrix sense) than the asymptotic variance that ignores the estimation error in $\hat{\boldsymbol{\delta}}_2$.

c. Define the vector of estimated average partial effects (based on partial derivatives) as

$$\hat{\boldsymbol{\eta}}_1 = \left[N^{-1} \sum_{i=1}^{N} \Phi(\hat{\mathbf{w}}_{i1}\hat{\boldsymbol{\gamma}}_1) \right] \hat{\boldsymbol{\gamma}}_1,$$

where $\hat{\mathbf{w}}_{i1} = (\mathbf{x}_{i1}, \hat{v}_{i2})$. Find Avar $\sqrt{N}(\hat{\boldsymbol{\eta}}_1 - \boldsymbol{\eta}_1)$. It may help to use Problem 12.17.

d. Show how to consistently estimate the asymptotic variance in part c.

15.16. Suppose that the binary variable y follows the model

$$P(y = 1 \mid \mathbf{x}) = 1 - [1 + \exp(\mathbf{x}\boldsymbol{\beta})]^{-\alpha},$$

where $\alpha > 0$ is a parameter that can be estimated along with the vector $\boldsymbol{\beta}$. The $1 \times K$ vector $\mathbf{x}$ contains unity as its first element. This model is sometimes called the *skewed logit model*. Note that $\alpha = 1$ corresponds to the usual logit model.

a. For a continuous variable x_K, find the partial effect of x_K on $\mathrm{P}(y = 1 \mid \mathbf{x})$.

b. Write down the log-likelihood function for a random draw i.

c. Use the data from MROZ.RAW to estimate the model, using the same explanatory variables in Table 15.1. Using a standard t test, can you reject $\mathrm{H}_0 : \log(\alpha) = 0$?

d. Compute the likelihood ratio test of $\mathrm{H}_0 : \alpha = 1$. How does this compare with the test in part c?

e. Overall, would you say that the more complicated model is justified? What other statistics might you compute to support your answer?

15.17. In Example 15.4, add *samesex* as an explanatory variable to the *worked* equation in bivariate probit, and include *samesex* in the *morekids* probit, too.

a. What is the estimated APE with respect to *morekids*, and how does it compare with those in Table 15.2?

b. Is *samesex* significant in the *worked* equation?

15.18. Consider Chamberlain's random effects probit model under assumptions (15.65), (15.66), and (15.67), but replace assumption (15.73) with

$$c_i \mid \mathbf{x}_i \sim \mathrm{Normal}[\psi + \bar{\mathbf{x}}_i \xi, \sigma_a^2 \exp(\bar{\mathbf{x}}_i \boldsymbol{\lambda})],$$

so that c_i given $\bar{\mathbf{x}}_i$ has exponential heteroskedasticity.

a. Find $\mathrm{P}(y_{it} = 1 \mid \mathbf{x}_i, a_i)$, where $a_i = c_i - \mathrm{E}(c_i \mid \mathbf{x}_i)$. Does this probability differ from the probability under assumption (15.73)? Explain.

b. Derive the log-likelihood function by first finding the density of $(y_{i1}, \ldots, y_{iT})$ given $\mathbf{x}_i$. Does it have similarities with the log-likelihood function under assumption (15.73)?

c. Assuming you have estimated $\boldsymbol{\beta}$, ψ, ξ, σ_a^2, and $\boldsymbol{\lambda}$ by CMLE, how would you estimate the average partial effects? {Hint: First show that $\mathrm{E}[\Phi(\mathbf{x}^{\mathrm{o}}\boldsymbol{\beta} + \psi + \bar{\mathbf{x}}_i \xi + a_i) \mid \mathbf{x}_i]$ $= \Phi(\{\mathbf{x}^{\mathrm{o}}\boldsymbol{\beta} + \psi + \bar{\mathbf{x}}_i \xi\} / \{1 + \sigma_a^2 \exp(\bar{\mathbf{x}}_i \boldsymbol{\lambda})\}^{1/2})$, and then use the appropriate average across i.}

15.19. Use the data in KEANE.RAW for this question, and restrict your attention to black men who are in the sample all 11 years.

a. Use pooled probit to estimate the model $\mathrm{P}(employ_{it} = 1 \mid employ_{i,t-1}) = \Phi(\delta_0 + \rho employ_{i,t-1})$. What assumption is needed to ensure that the usual standard errors and test statistics from pooled probit are asymptotically valid?

b. Estimate $\mathrm{P}(employ_t = 1 \mid employ_{t-1} = 1)$ and $\mathrm{P}(employ_t = 1 \mid employ_{t-1} = 0)$. Explain how you would obtain standard errors of these estimates.

c. Add a full set of year dummies to the analysis in part a, and estimate the probabilities in part b for 1987. Are there important differences with the estimates in part b?

d. Now estimate a dynamic unobserved effects model using the method described in Section 15.8.4. In particular, add $employ_{i,81}$ as an additional explanatory variable, and use random effects probit software. Use a full set of year dummies.

e. Is there evidence of state dependence, conditional on c_i? Explain.

f. Average the estimated probabilities across $employ_{i,81}$ to get the average partial effect for 1987. Compare the estimates with the effects estimated in part c.

16 Multinomial and Ordered Response Models

16.1 Introduction

In this chapter we consider discrete response models with more than two outcomes. Most applications fall into one of two categories. The first is an **unordered response**, sometimes called a **nominal response**, where the values attached to different outcomes are arbitrary and have no effect on estimation, inference, or interpretation. Examples of unordered responses include occupational choice, health plan choice, and transportation mode for commuting to work. For example, if there are four health plans to choose from, we might label these 0, 1, 2, and 3—or 100, 200, 300, 400—and it does not matter which plan we assign to which number (provided, of course, that we use the same labels across across all observations). In Section 16.2 we cover the general class of multinomial response models, which can be used to analyze unordered responses.

For an **ordered response**, the values we assign to each outcome are no longer arbitrary, although the magnitudes (usually) are. An example of an ordered response is a credit rating, where there are seven possible ratings. We might assign each person a rating in the set $\{0, 1, 2, 3, 4, 5, 6\}$, where zero is the lowest rating and six is the highest. The fact that five is a better rating than four conveys important information, but nothing is lost if we use another set of numbers to denote credit rating—provided they maintain the same ordering. We treat ordered response models in Section 16.3.

In addition to covering standard methods devised for cross section data with exogenous explanatory variables, we discuss some simple strategies for handling roughly continuous endogenous explanatory variables as well as unobserved heterogeneity in a panel data context.

16.2 Multinomial Response Models

16.2.1 Multinomial Logit

The first model we cover applies when a unit's response or choice depends on individual characteristics of the unit—but not on attributes of the choices. Thus, it makes sense to define the model in terms of random variables representing the underlying population. Let y denote a random variable taking on the values $\{0, 1, \ldots, J\}$ for J a positive integer, and let $\mathbf{x}$ denote a set of conditioning variables. For example, if y denotes occupational choice, $\mathbf{x}$ can contain things like education, age, gender, race, and marital status. As usual, $(\mathbf{x}_i, y_i)$ is a random draw from the population.

As in the binary response case, we are interested in how ceteris paribus changes in the elements of $\mathbf{x}$ affect the response probabilities, $P(y = j \mid \mathbf{x})$, $j = 0, 1, 2, \ldots, J$.

Since the probabilities must sum to unity, $\mathrm{P}(y = 0 \mid \mathbf{x})$ is determined once we know the probabilities for $j = 1, \ldots, J$.

Let $\mathbf{x}$ be a $1 \times K$ vector with first-element unity. The **multinomial logit (MNL) model** has response probabilities

$$\mathrm{P}(y = j \mid \mathbf{x}) = \exp(\mathbf{x}\boldsymbol{\beta}_j) \Big/ \left[1 + \sum_{h=1}^{J} \exp(\mathbf{x}\boldsymbol{\beta}_h)\right], \qquad j = 1, \ldots, J, \tag{16.1}$$

where $\boldsymbol{\beta}_j$ is $K \times 1$, $j = 1, \ldots, J$. Because the response probabilities must sum to unity,

$$\mathrm{P}(y = 0 \mid \mathbf{x}) = 1 \Big/ \left[1 + \sum_{h=1}^{J} \exp(\mathbf{x}\boldsymbol{\beta}_h)\right].$$

When $J = 1$, $\boldsymbol{\beta}_1$ is the $K \times 1$ vector of unknown parameters, and we get the binary logit model.

The partial effects for this model are complicated. For continuous x_k, we can write

$$\frac{\partial \mathrm{P}(y = j \mid \mathbf{x})}{\partial x_k} = \mathrm{P}(y = j \mid \mathbf{x}) \left\{ \beta_{jk} - \left[\sum_{h=1}^{J} \beta_{hk} \exp(\mathbf{x}\boldsymbol{\beta}_h)\right] \Big/ g(\mathbf{x}, \boldsymbol{\beta}) \right\}, \tag{16.2}$$

where β_{hk} is the kth element of $\boldsymbol{\beta}_h$ and $g(\mathbf{x}, \boldsymbol{\beta}) = 1 + \sum_{h=1}^{J} \exp(\mathbf{x}\boldsymbol{\beta}_h)$. Equation (16.2) shows that even the direction of the effect is not determined entirely by β_{jk}. A simpler interpretation of $\boldsymbol{\beta}_j$ is given by

$$p_j(\mathbf{x}, \boldsymbol{\beta}) / p_0(\mathbf{x}, \boldsymbol{\beta}) = \exp(\mathbf{x}\boldsymbol{\beta}_j), \qquad j = 1, 2, \ldots, J, \tag{16.3}$$

where $p_j(\mathbf{x}, \boldsymbol{\beta})$ denotes the response probability in equation (16.1). Thus the change in $p_j(\mathbf{x}, \boldsymbol{\beta}) / p_0(\mathbf{x}, \boldsymbol{\beta})$ is approximately $\beta_{jk} \exp(\mathbf{x}\boldsymbol{\beta}_j) \Delta x_k$ for roughly continuous x_k. Equivalently, the log-odds ratio is linear in $\mathbf{x}$: $\log[p_j(\mathbf{x}, \boldsymbol{\beta}) / p_0(\mathbf{x}, \boldsymbol{\beta})] = \mathbf{x}\boldsymbol{\beta}_j$. This result extends to general j and h: $\log[p_j(\mathbf{x}, \boldsymbol{\beta}) / p_h(\mathbf{x}, \boldsymbol{\beta})] = \mathbf{x}(\boldsymbol{\beta}_j - \boldsymbol{\beta}_h)$.

Here is another useful fact about the multinomial logit model. Since $\mathrm{P}(y = j$ or $y = h \mid \mathbf{x}) = p_j(\mathbf{x}, \boldsymbol{\beta}) + p_h(\mathbf{x}, \boldsymbol{\beta})$,

$$\mathrm{P}(y = j \mid y = j \text{ or } y = h, \mathbf{x}) = p_j(\mathbf{x}, \boldsymbol{\beta}) / [p_j(\mathbf{x}, \boldsymbol{\beta}) + p_h(\mathbf{x}, \boldsymbol{\beta})] = \Lambda[\mathbf{x}(\boldsymbol{\beta}_j - \boldsymbol{\beta}_h)],$$

where $\Lambda(\cdot)$ is the logistic function. In other words, conditional on the choice being either j or h, the probability that the outcome is j follows a standard logit model with parameter vector $\boldsymbol{\beta}_j - \boldsymbol{\beta}_h$.

Since we have fully specified the density of y given $\mathbf{x}$, estimation of the MNL model is best carried out by maximum likelihood. For each i the conditional log likelihood can be written as

$$\ell_i(\boldsymbol{\beta}) = \sum_{j=0}^{J} 1[y_i = j] \log[p_j(\mathbf{x}_i, \boldsymbol{\beta})],$$

where the indicator function selects out the appropriate response probability for each observation i. As usual, we estimate $\boldsymbol{\beta}$ by maximizing $\sum_{i=1}^{N} \ell_i(\boldsymbol{\beta})$. McFadden (1974) has shown that the log-likelihood function is globally concave, and this fact makes the maximization problem straightforward. The conditions needed to apply Theorems 13.1 and 13.2 for consistency and asymptotic normality are broadly applicable; see McFadden (1984).

Example 16.1 (School and Employment Decisions for Young Men): The data KEANE.RAW (a subset from Keane and Wolpin, 1997) contains employment and schooling history for a sample of men for the years 1981 to 1987. We use the data for 1987. The three possible outcomes are enrolled in school ($status = 0$), not in school and not working ($status = 1$), and working ($status = 2$). The explanatory variables are education, a quadratic in past work experience, and a black binary indicator. The base category is enrolled in school. Out of 1,717 observations, 99 are enrolled in school, 332 are at home, and 1,286 are working. The results are given in Table 16.1.

Another year of education reduces the log-odds between at home and enrolled in school by −.674, and the log-odds between at home and enrolled in school is .813

Table 16.1
Multinomial Logit Estimates of School and Labor Market Decisions

Dependent Variable: *status*		
Explanatory Variable	*Home* ($status = 1$)	*Work* ($status = 2$)
educ	−.674 (.070)	−.315 (.065)
exper	−.106 (.173)	.849 (.157)
$exper^2$	−.013 (.025)	−.077 (.023)
black	.813 (.303)	.311 (.282)
constant	10.28 (1.13)	5.54 (1.09)
Number of observations	1,717	
Percent correctly predicted	79.6	
Log-likelihood value	−907.86	
Pseudo-R-squared	.243	

higher for black men. The magnitudes of these coefficients are difficult to interpret. Instead, we can either compute partial effects, as in equation (16.2), or compute differences in probabilities. For example, consider two black men, each with five years of experience. A black man with 16 years of education has an employment probability that is .042 higher than a man with 12 years of education, and the at-home probability is .072 lower. (Necessarily, the in-school probability is .030 higher for the man with 16 years of education.) These results are easily obtained by comparing fitted probabilities after multinomial logit estimation.

The experience terms are each insignificant in the *home* column, but the Wald test for joint significance of *exper* and $exper^2$ gives p-value $= .047$, and so they are jointly significant at the 5 percent level. We would probably leave their coefficients unrestricted in $\boldsymbol{\beta}_1$ rather than setting them to zero.

The fitted probabilities can be used for prediction purposes: for each observation i, the outcome with the highest estimated probability is the predicted outcome. This can be used to obtain a percent correctly predicted, by category if desired. For the previous example, the overall percent correctly predicted is almost 80 percent, but the model does a much better job of predicting that a man is employed (95.2 percent correct) than in school (12.1 percent) or at home (39.2 percent).

16.2.2 Probabilistic Choice Models

McFadden (1974) showed that a model closely related to the MNL model can be obtained from an underlying utility comparison. Suppose that, for a random draw i from the underlying population (usually, but not necessarily, individuals), the utility from choosing alternative j is

$$y_{ij}^* = \mathbf{x}_{ij}\boldsymbol{\beta} + a_{ij}, \qquad j = 0, \ldots, J, \tag{16.4}$$

where $a_{ij}, j = 0, 1, 2, \ldots, J$ are unobservables affecting tastes. Here, $\mathbf{x}_{ij}$ is a $1 \times K$ vector that differs across alternatives and possibly across individuals as well. For example, $\mathbf{x}_{ij}$ might contain the commute time for individual i using transportation mode j, or the co-payment required by health insurance plan j (which may or may not differ by individual). For reasons we will see, $\mathbf{x}_{ij}$ cannot contain elements that vary only across i and not j; in particular, $\mathbf{x}_{ij}$ does not contain unity. We assume that the $(J+1)$-vector $\mathbf{a}_i$ is independent of $\mathbf{x}_i$, which contains $\{\mathbf{x}_{ij}: j = 0, \ldots, J\}$.

Let y_i denote the choice of individual i that maximizes utility:

$$y_i = \operatorname{argmax}(y_{i0}^*, y_{i2}^*, \ldots, y_{iJ}^*),$$

so that y_i takes on a value in $\{0, 1, \ldots, J\}$. As shown by McFadden (1974), if the a_{ij}, $j = 0, \ldots, J$ are independently distributed with cdf $F(a) = \exp[-\exp(-a)]$—the **type I extreme value distribution**—then

$$P(y_i = j \mid \mathbf{x}_i) = \exp(\mathbf{x}_{ij}\boldsymbol{\beta}) \Big/ \left[\sum_{h=0}^{J} \exp(\mathbf{x}_{ih}\boldsymbol{\beta})\right], \qquad j = 0, \ldots, J. \tag{16.5}$$

The response probabilities in equation (16.5) constitute what is usually called the **conditional logit (CL) model**. Dropping the subscript i and differentiating shows that the marginal effects are given by

$$\partial p_j(\mathbf{x})/\partial x_{jk} = p_j(\mathbf{x})[1 - p_j(\mathbf{x})]\beta_k, \qquad j = 0, \ldots, J, \ k = 1, \ldots, K, \tag{16.6}$$

and

$$\partial p_j(\mathbf{x})/\partial x_{hk} = -p_j(\mathbf{x})p_h(\mathbf{x})\beta_k, \qquad j \neq h, \ k = 1, \ldots, K, \tag{16.7}$$

where $p_j(\mathbf{x})$ is the response probability in equation (16.5) and β_k is the kth element of $\boldsymbol{\beta}$. As usual, if the $\mathbf{x}_j$ contain nonlinear functions of underlying explanatory variables, this fact will be reflected in the partial derivatives.

The CL and MNL models have similar response probabilities, but they differ in some important respects. In the MNL model, the conditioning variables do not change across alternative: for each i, $\mathbf{x}_i$ contains variables specific to the individual but not to the alternatives. This model is appropriate for problems where characteristics of the alternatives are unimportant or are not of interest, or where the data are simply not available. For example, in a model of occupational choice, we do not usually know how much someone could make in every occupation. What we can usually collect data on are things that affect individual productivity and tastes, such as education and past experience. The MNL model allows these characteristics to have different effects on the relative probabilities between any two choices.

The CL model is intended specifically for problems where consumer or firm choices are at least partly based on observable attributes of each alternative. The utility level of each choice is assumed to be a linear function in choice attributes, $\mathbf{x}_{ij}$, with common parameter vector $\boldsymbol{\beta}$. This turns out to actually contain the MNL model as a special case by appropriately choosing $\mathbf{x}_{ij}$. Suppose that $\mathbf{w}_i$ is a vector of individual characteristics and that $P(y_i = j \mid \mathbf{w}_i)$ follows the MNL in equation (16.1) with parameters $\boldsymbol{\delta}_j$, $j = 1, \ldots, J$. We can cast this model as the CL model by defining $\mathbf{x}_{ij} = (d1_j\mathbf{w}_i, d2_j\mathbf{w}_i, \ldots, dJ_j\mathbf{w}_i)$, where dj_h is a dummy variable equal to unity when $j = h$, and $\boldsymbol{\beta} = (\boldsymbol{\delta}_1', \ldots, \boldsymbol{\delta}_J')'$. Consequently, some authors refer to the CL model as the MNL model, with the understanding that alternative-specific characteristics are allowed in the response probability.

Empirical applications of the CL model often include individual-specific variables by allowing them to have separate effects on the latent utilities. A general model is

$$y_{ij}^{*} = \mathbf{z}_{ij}\gamma + \mathbf{w}_i\boldsymbol{\delta}_j + a_{ij}, \qquad j = 0, 1, \ldots, J, \tag{16.8}$$

with $\boldsymbol{\delta}_0 = \mathbf{0}$ as a normalization, where $\mathbf{z}_{ij}$ varies across j and possibly i. If $\boldsymbol{\delta}_j = \boldsymbol{\delta}$ for all j, then $\mathbf{w}_i\boldsymbol{\delta}$ drops out of all response probabilities. The model with both kinds of explanatory variables in (16.8) is called the **mixed logit model**.

The CL model is very convenient for modeling probabilistic choice, but it has some limitations. An important restriction is

$$p_j(\mathbf{x}_j)/p_h(\mathbf{x}_h) = \exp(\mathbf{x}_j\boldsymbol{\beta})/\exp(\mathbf{x}_h\boldsymbol{\beta}) = \exp[(\mathbf{x}_j - \mathbf{x}_h)\boldsymbol{\beta}], \tag{16.9}$$

so that relative probabilities for any two alternatives depend only on the attributes of those two alternatives. This is called the **independence from irrelevant alternatives (IIA) assumption** because it implies that adding another alternative or changing the characteristics of a third alternative does not affect the relative odds between alternatives j and h. This implication is often implausible, especially for applications with similar alternatives. A well-known example is due to McFadden (1974). Consider commuters initially choosing between two modes of transportation, car and red bus. Suppose that a consumer chooses between the buses with equal probability, .5, so that the ratio in equation (16.9) is unity. Now suppose a third mode, blue bus, is added. Assuming bus commuters do not care about the color of the bus, consumers will choose between these with equal probability. But then IIA implies that the probability of each mode is $\frac{1}{3}$; therefore, the fraction of commuters taking a car would fall from $\frac{1}{2}$ to $\frac{1}{3}$, a result that is not very realistic. This example is admittedly extreme—in practice, we would lump the blue bus and red bus into the same category, provided there are no other differences—but it indicates that the IIA property can impose unwanted restrictions in the conditional logit model.

Hausman and McFadden (1984) offer tests of the IIA assumption based on the observation that, if the CL model is true, $\boldsymbol{\beta}$ can be consistently estimated by conditional logit by focusing on any subset of alternatives. They apply the Hausman principle, which compares the estimate of $\boldsymbol{\beta}$ using all alternatives to the estimate using a subset of alternatives.

Several models that relax the IIA assumption have been suggested. In the context of the random utility model, the IIA assumption comes about because the $\{a_{ij} : j =$

$0, 1, \ldots, J\}$ are assumed to be independent Wiebull random variables. A more flexible assumption is that $\mathbf{a}_i$ has a multivariate normal distribution with arbitrary correlations between a_{ij} and a_{ih}, all $j \neq h$. The resulting model is called the **multinomial probit model**. (In keeping with the spirit of the previous names, **conditional probit model** is a better name, which is used by Hausman and Wise (1978) but not by many others.)

Theoretically, the multinomial probit model is attractive, but it has some practical limitations. The response probabilities are very complicated, involving a $(J+1)$-dimensional integral. This complexity not only makes it difficult to obtain the partial effects on the response probabilities, it also makes maximum likelihood estimation (MLE) infeasible for more than about five alternatives. For details, see Maddala (1983, Chap. 3) and Amemiya (1985, Chap. 9). Hausman and Wise (1978) contain an application to transportation mode for three alternatives.

Recent advances in estimation through simulation make multinomial probit estimation feasible for many alternatives. See Hajivassilou and Ruud (1994) and Keane (1993) for recent surveys of simulation estimation. Keane and Moffitt (1998) apply simulation methods to structural multinomial response models, where the econometric model is obtained from utility maximization subject to constraints. Keane and Moffitt study the tax effects of labor force participation allowing for participation in multiple welfare programs.

A different approach to relaxing IIA is to specify a **hierarchical model**. The most popular of these is called the **nested logit model**. McFadden (1984) gives a detailed treatment of these and other models; here we illustrate the basic approach where there are only two hierarchies.

Suppose that the total number of alternatives can be put into S groups of similar alternatives, and let G_s denote the alternatives within group s. Thus the first hierarchy corresponds to which of the S groups y falls into, and the second corresponds to the actual alternative within each group. McFadden (1981) studied the model

$$P(y \in G_s \mid \mathbf{x}) = \left\{\alpha_s \left[\sum_{j \in G_s} \exp(\rho_s^{-1}\mathbf{x}_j\boldsymbol{\beta})\right]^{\rho_s}\right\} \Big/ \left\{\sum_{r=1}^{S} \alpha_r \left[\sum_{j \in G_r} \exp(\rho_r^{-1}\mathbf{x}_j\boldsymbol{\beta})\right]^{\rho_r}\right\} \tag{16.10}$$

and

$$P(y = j \mid y \in G_s, \mathbf{x}) = \exp(\rho_s^{-1}\mathbf{x}_j\boldsymbol{\beta}) \Big/ \left[\sum_{h \in G_s} \exp(\rho_s^{-1}\mathbf{x}_h\boldsymbol{\beta})\right], \tag{16.11}$$

where equation (16.10) is defined for $s = 1, 2, \ldots, S$ while equation (16.11) is defined for $j \in G_s$ and $s = 1, 2, \ldots, S$; of course, if $j \notin G_s$, $P(y = j \mid y \in G_s, \mathbf{x}) = 0$. This model requires a normalization restriction, usually $\alpha_1 = 1$. Equation (16.10) gives the probability that the outcome is in group s (conditional on $\mathbf{x}$); then, conditional on $y \in G_s$, equation (16.11) gives the probability of choosing alternative j within G_s. The response probability $P(y = j \mid \mathbf{x})$, which is ultimately of interest, is obtained by multiplying equations (16.10) and (16.11). This model can be derived by specifying a particular joint distribution for $\mathbf{a}_i$ in equation (16.4); see Amemiya (1985, p. 303).

Equation (16.11) implies that, conditional on choosing group s, the response probabilities take a CL form with parameter vector $\rho_s^{-1}\boldsymbol{\beta}$. This suggests a natural two-step estimation procedure. First, estimate $\boldsymbol{\lambda}_s \equiv \rho_s^{-1}\boldsymbol{\beta}$, $s = 1, 2, \ldots, S$, by applying CL analysis separately to each of the groups. Then, plug the $\hat{\boldsymbol{\lambda}}_s$ into equation (16.10) and estimate α_s, $s = 2, \ldots, S$ and ρ_s, $s = 1, \ldots, S$ by maximizing the log-likelihood function

$$\sum_{i=1}^{N} \sum_{s=1}^{S} 1[y_i \in G_s] \log[q_s(\mathbf{x}_i; \hat{\boldsymbol{\lambda}}, \boldsymbol{\alpha}, \boldsymbol{\rho})],$$

where $q_s(\mathbf{x}; \boldsymbol{\lambda}, \boldsymbol{\alpha}, \boldsymbol{\rho})$ is the probability in equation (16.10) with $\boldsymbol{\lambda}_s = \rho_s^{-1}\boldsymbol{\beta}$. This two-step conditional MLE is consistent and $\sqrt{N}$-asymptotically normal under general conditions, but the asymptotic variance needs to be adjusted for the first-stage estimation of the $\boldsymbol{\lambda}_s$; see Chapters 12 and 13 for more on two-step estimators.

Of course, we can also use full MLE. The log likelihood for observation i can be written as

$$\ell_i(\boldsymbol{\beta}, \boldsymbol{\alpha}, \boldsymbol{\rho}) = \sum_{s=1}^{S} \left(1[y_i \in G_s] \left\{ \log[q_s(\mathbf{x}_i; \boldsymbol{\beta}, \boldsymbol{\alpha}, \boldsymbol{\rho})] + \sum_{j \in G_s} 1[y_i = j] \log[p_{sj}(\mathbf{x}_i; \boldsymbol{\beta}, \rho_s)] \right\} \right), \tag{16.12}$$

where $q_s(\mathbf{x}_i; \boldsymbol{\beta}, \boldsymbol{\alpha}, \boldsymbol{\rho})$ is the probability in equation (16.10) and $p_{sj}(\mathbf{x}_i; \boldsymbol{\beta}, \rho_s)$ is the probability in equation (16.11). The regularity conditions for MLE are satisfied under weak assumptions.

When $\alpha_s = 1$ and $\rho_s = 1$ for all s, the nested logit model reduces to the CL model. Thus, a test of IIA (as well as the other assumptions underlying the CL model) is a test of $H_0: \alpha_2 = \cdots = \alpha_S = \rho_1 = \cdots = \rho_S = 1$. McFadden (1987) suggests a score test, which only requires estimation of the CL model.

Often special cases of the model are used, such as setting each α_s to unity and estimating the ρ_s. In his study of community choice and type of dwelling within a community, McFadden (1978) imposes this restriction along with $\rho_s = \rho$ for all s, so that the model has only one more parameter than the CL model. This approach allows for correlation among the a_j for j belonging to the same community group, but the correlation is assumed to be the same for all communities.

The nested logit model allows different explanatory variables, which can also differ by alternative, to appear in the different levels. For example, one set of variables may be relevant for community choice, such as quality of schools, crime rates, property tax rates, and other measures of community quality. Another set of variables would affect the kind of dwelling, such as the prices of the different kinds of dwellings. Higher-level nested logit models are covered in McFadden (1984) and Amemiya (1985, Chap. 9).

A different approach to modifying CL to arrive at a model that relaxes IIA is to include unobserved heterogeneity in the model—almost always assumed independent of the covariates in cross section applications—and then integrate it out. If c_i represents scalar heterogeneity, we can extend equation (6.8) to

$$y_{ij}^* = \mathbf{x}_{ij}\boldsymbol{\beta} + c_i + a_{ij}, \qquad j = 0, \ldots, J, \tag{16.13}$$

where $\{a_{ij} : j = 0, 1, \ldots, J\}$ conditional on $(\mathbf{x}_i, c_i)$ are independent, identically distributed (i.i.d.) with the type I extreme value distribution, then the presence of c_i allows correlation in the utilities of the different choices conditional only on $\mathbf{x}_i$. Typically, c_i is assumed independent of $\mathbf{x}_i$ with a normal distribution. If c_i has a discrete distribution with a known number of support points, then the resulting model is usually called a **mixture model** or **latent class model**, the idea being that each cross section unit i belongs to an unobserved, or latent, class. Swait (2003) provides a recent example, where $(a_{i0}, \ldots, a_{iJ})$ has the **generalized extreme value** distribution, which contains the CL model and nested logit model as special cases. In addition to discussing parameter estimates, Swait shows how to obtain partial effects after averaging out the heterogeneity.

We can go even further by replacing $\boldsymbol{\beta}$ in equation (16.13) with a random coefficient, say $\mathbf{b}_i$, where $\mathrm{E}(\mathbf{b}_i) = \boldsymbol{\beta}$. In fact, $\mathbf{b}_i$ is typically assumed to be independent of $\mathbf{x}_i$ with a multivariate normal distribution. Such models can add considerable flexibility to the standard models, but they are more difficult to estimate. McFadden and Train (2000) provide a comprehensive treatment, and Cameron and Trividi (2005) provide an overview and additional references.

16.2.3 Endogenous Explanatory Variables

Because explanatory variables can be correlated with unobservables, it is natural to study multinomial response models with endogenous explanatory variables. Rather than start with a linear index with an additive error, as in the derivation of the CL model, we can start with a model for $\mathrm{P}(y_{i1} = j \mid \mathbf{z}_{i1}, \mathbf{y}_{i2}, r_{i1})$, $j = 0, 1, \ldots, J$, where r_{i1} represents unobserved, omitted factors thought to be correlated with the vector $\mathbf{y}_{i2}$. (The vector $\mathbf{z}_{i1}$, and even $\mathbf{y}_{i2}$, can contain variables that change with j, as well as those that change only with i. That is, the exogenous and endogenous variables can be specific to the alternative.) Then, we would use a reduced form for $\mathbf{y}_{i2}$, say $\mathbf{y}_{i2} = \mathbf{z}_i \mathbf{\Pi}_2 + \mathbf{v}_{i2}$, assume that $(r_{i1}, \mathbf{v}_{i2})$ is independent of $\mathbf{z}_i$, and that $(r_{i1}, \mathbf{v}_{i2})$ has a convenient distribution, such as multivariate normal. This approach is similar to the control function approach for probit we covered in Section 15.7.2.

In fact, the approach described in the previous paragraph has been applied when the response probabilities have the CL form. For example, Villas-Boas and Winer (1999) apply this approach to modeling brand choice, where prices are allowed to correlate with unobserved tastes that affect brand choice. The problem in starting with an MNL or CL model for $\mathrm{P}(y_{i1} = j \,|\, \mathbf{z}_{i1}, \mathbf{y}_{i2}, r_{i1})$ in implementing the control function approach is computational: just as the binary logit model does not mix well with normally distributed unobservables, neither does the CL model. Nevertheless, estimation is possible, particularly if one uses simulation methods of estimation briefly mentioned in the previous subsection.

A much simpler control function approach is obtained if we skip the step of modeling $\mathrm{P}(y_{i1} = j \,|\, \mathbf{z}_{i1}, \mathbf{y}_{i2}, r_{i1})$ and jump directly to convenient models for $\mathrm{P}(y_{i1} = j \,|\, \mathbf{z}_{i1}, \mathbf{y}_{i2}, \mathbf{v}_{i2}) = \mathrm{P}(y_{i1} = j \,|\, \mathbf{z}_i, \mathbf{y}_{i2})$. Kuksov and Villas-Boas (2008) and Petrin and Train (2010) are proponents of this solution. The idea is that any parametric model for $\mathrm{P}(y_{i1} = j \,|\, \mathbf{z}_{i1}, \mathbf{y}_{i2}, r_{i1})$ is essentially arbitrary, so, if we can recover quantities of interest directly from $\mathrm{P}(y_{i1} = j \,|\, \mathbf{z}_{i1}, \mathbf{y}_{i2}, \mathbf{v}_{i2})$, why not specify these probabilities directly? If we assume that $\mathrm{D}(r_{i1} \,|\, \mathbf{z}_i, \mathbf{y}_{i2}) = \mathrm{D}(r_{i1} \,|\, \mathbf{v}_{i2})$, and that $\mathrm{P}(y_{i1} = j \,|\, \mathbf{z}_{i1}, \mathbf{y}_{i2}, \mathbf{v}_{i2})$ can be obtained from $\mathrm{P}(y_{i1} = j \,|\, \mathbf{z}_{i1}, \mathbf{y}_{i2}, r_{i1})$ by integrating the latter with respect to $\mathrm{D}(r_{i1} \,|\, \mathbf{v}_{i2})$, then we can apply the results on average partial effects (APEs) that we used in Sections 15.7.2 (because $\mathrm{P}(y_{i1} = j \,|\, \mathbf{z}_{i1}, \mathbf{y}_{i2}, r_{i1}) = \mathrm{E}(1[y_{i1} = j] \,|\, \mathbf{z}_{i1}, \mathbf{y}_{i2}, r_{i1})$ is a conditional expectation). The weakness of this approach is that it implicitly maintains that, say, an MNL model for $\mathrm{P}(y_{i1} = j \,|\, \mathbf{z}_{i1}, \mathbf{y}_{i2}, \mathbf{v}_{i2})$ is consistent with underlying specifications for $\mathrm{P}(y_{i1} = j \,|\, \mathbf{z}_{i1}, \mathbf{y}_{i2}, r_{i1})$ and $\mathrm{D}(r_{i1} \,|\, \mathbf{v}_{i2})$, and those underlying specifications would not have recognizable forms.

Once we have selected a model for $\mathrm{P}(y_{i1} = j \,|\, \mathbf{z}_{i1}, \mathbf{y}_{i2}, \mathbf{v}_{i2})$, which could be CL or nested logit, we can apply a simple two-step procedure. First, we estimate the reduced form for $\mathbf{y}_{i2}$ and obtain the residuals, $\hat{\mathbf{v}}_{i2} = \mathbf{y}_{i2} - \mathbf{z}_i \hat{\mathbf{\Pi}}_2$. (Alternatively, we can use strictly monotonic transformations of the elements of $\mathbf{y}_{i2}$, such as the logarithim if $y_{i2g} > 0$ or $\log[y_{i2g}/(1 - y_{i2g})]$ if $0 < y_{i2g} < 1$, as dependent variables in the reduced forms. As we discussed in the binary response case, using transformations of continuous endogenous explanatory variables allows for more realistic linear reduced forms with additive, independent errors.) Then, we estimate one of the multinomial response models we just covered with explanatory variables $\mathbf{z}_{i1}$, $\mathbf{y}_{i2}$, and $\hat{\mathbf{v}}_{i2}$. As always with control function approaches, we need enough exclusion restrictions in $\mathbf{z}_{i1}$ to identify the parameters and APEs. We can include nonlinear functions of $(\mathbf{z}_{i1}, \mathbf{y}_{i2}, \hat{\mathbf{v}}_{i2})$, including quadratics and interactions.

Given estimates of the probabilities $\mathrm{P}(y_{i1} = j \mid \mathbf{z}_{i1} = \mathbf{z}_1, \mathbf{y}_{i2} = \mathbf{y}_2, \mathbf{v}_{i2} = \mathbf{v}_2) \equiv p_j(\mathbf{z}_1, \mathbf{y}_2, \mathbf{v}_2)$, we can estimate the APEs on the structural probabilities by estimating the average structural function (ASF):

$$\widehat{\mathrm{ASF}}(\mathbf{z}_1, \mathbf{y}_2) = N^{-1} \sum_{i=1}^{N} p_j(\mathbf{z}_1, \mathbf{y}_2, \hat{\mathbf{v}}_{i2}). \tag{16.14}$$

Then, we can take derivatives or changes of $\widehat{\mathrm{ASF}}(\mathbf{z}_1, \mathbf{y}_2)$ with respect to elements of $(\mathbf{z}_1, \mathbf{y}_2)$, as usual. While the delta method can be used to obtain analytical standard errors, the bootstrap is simpler and feasible if one uses, say, CL.

If we adopt a multinomial probit model as the underlying structural model, then we can derive a multinomial probit model in implementing the control function approach. But, as in the case with exogenous explanatory variables, such an approach is computationally much more difficult. Implementing the bootstrap to obtain standard errors for the parameters or APEs would create a computational challenge, even with a small number of alternatives.

16.2.4 Panel Data Methods

We can use reasoning similar to that in the previous subsection to obtain simple strategies for allowing correlated random effects in panel data models. Ideally, we would specify a popular model for the response probabilities conditional on unobserved heterogeneity. However, for the same reasons discussed in Section 16.2.3, such an approach leads to computational difficulties.

To be more precise about the issues, for each time period t, let y_{it} be an unordered response taking values in $\{0, \ldots, J\}$, and let $\mathbf{x}_{it}$ denote a vector of explanatory variables (that includes a constant and can, as usual, include a full set of time dummies and even time-constant variables). Letting $\mathbf{c}_i$ be a vector of unobserved heteogeneity, we would like to start by specifying

$$\mathrm{P}(y_{it} = j \mid \mathbf{x}_{it}, \mathbf{c}_i) = \mathrm{P}(y_{it} = j \mid \mathbf{x}_i, \mathbf{c}_i), \tag{16.15}$$

where the equality of the two probabilities means that we assume strict exogeneity of $\{\mathbf{x}_{it} : t = 1, \ldots, T\}$ conditional on $\mathbf{c}_i$. If we specify equation (16.15) as, say, an MNL, then integrating out $\mathbf{c}_i$, after specifying $\mathrm{D}(\mathbf{c}_i \mid \mathbf{x}_i)$, is typically nontrivial. For example, suppose we start with an MNL model with a single source of heterogeneity,

$$\mathrm{P}(y_{it} = j \mid \mathbf{x}_{it}, c_i) = \exp(\mathbf{x}_{it}\boldsymbol{\beta}_j + \alpha_j c_i) \Bigg/ \left[1 + \sum_{h=1}^{J} \exp(\mathbf{x}_{it}\boldsymbol{\beta}_h + \alpha_h c_i)\right]. \tag{16.16}$$

If we specify

$$c_i \mid \mathbf{x}_i \sim \text{Normal}(\eta + \overline{\mathbf{w}}_i \xi, \sigma_a^2), \tag{16.17}$$

where $\mathbf{w}_{it}$ is the subset of $\mathbf{x}_{it}$ that changes across i and t, then, in principle, we can obtain $\text{P}(y_{it} = j \mid \mathbf{x}_i) = \text{P}(y_{it} = j \mid \mathbf{x}_{it}, \overline{\mathbf{w}}_i)$. But the result is not in closed form and not easy to deal with computationally. Simulation methods of estimation of the kind mentioned in Section 16.2.2 are usually needed.

Instead, if we assume only that $\text{D}(\mathbf{c}_i \mid \mathbf{x}_i) = \text{D}(\mathbf{c}_i \mid \overline{\mathbf{w}}_i)$, then

$$\text{P}(y_{it} = j \mid \mathbf{x}_i) = \text{P}(y_{it} = j \mid \mathbf{x}_{it}, \overline{\mathbf{w}}_i), \qquad j = 0, \ldots, J;\ t = 1, \ldots, T. \tag{16.18}$$

Further, we know that the APEs of $\text{P}(y_{it} = j \mid \mathbf{x}_{it} = \mathbf{x}_t, \mathbf{c}_i)$—that is, the partial effects with $\mathbf{c}_i$ averaged out—can be obtained by averaging out $\overline{\mathbf{w}}_i$ in $\text{P}(y_{it} = j \mid \mathbf{x}_{it} = \mathbf{x}_t, \overline{\mathbf{w}}_i)$. We used this fact several times in Section 15.8; see also Section 2.2.5. Therefore, it may be useful to directly specify models for $\text{P}(y_{it} = j \mid \mathbf{x}_{it}, \overline{\mathbf{w}}_i)$. A simple approach is to specify $\text{P}(y_{it} = j \mid \mathbf{x}_{it}, \overline{\mathbf{w}}_i)$ as, say, MNL:

$$y_{it} \mid (\mathbf{x}_{i1}, \ldots, \mathbf{x}_{iT}) \sim \text{Multinomial}(\mathbf{x}_{it}\boldsymbol{\beta}_1 + \overline{\mathbf{w}}_i \xi_1, \ldots, \mathbf{x}_{it}\boldsymbol{\beta}_J + \overline{\mathbf{w}}_i \xi_J), \tag{16.19}$$

where $\mathbf{x}_{it}$ is assumed to include an intercept (and probably $T - 1$ time period dummies). We can then just apply **pooled multinomial logit** estimation and include the time averages, $\overline{\mathbf{w}}_i$, as additional explanatory variables. Inference should be made robust to arbitrary serial dependence because, at a minimum, part of the heterogeneity is still omitted. Plus, the pooled MNL estimator allows any kind of dependence in $\text{D}(y_{i1}, \ldots, y_{iT} \mid \mathbf{x}_i, \mathbf{c}_i)$. Of course, this approach imposes IIA conditional on $(\mathbf{x}_{it}, \overline{\mathbf{w}}_i)$, but, interestingly, it does not impose IIA on the average response probabilities—the average structural function, in this case—which we would estimate as

$$\widehat{\text{ASF}}_j(\mathbf{x}_t) = N^{-1} \sum_{i=1}^{N} \left\{ \exp(\mathbf{x}_t \hat{\boldsymbol{\beta}}_j + \overline{\mathbf{w}}_i \hat{\xi}_j) \Big/ \left[1 + \sum_{h=1}^{J} \exp(\mathbf{x}_t \hat{\boldsymbol{\beta}}_h + \overline{\mathbf{w}}_i \hat{\xi}_h) \right] \right\}. \tag{16.20}$$

Allowing a mixed model, where some elements of $\mathbf{x}_{it}$ are choice specific, causes no difficulties. We can use the same strategy applied to nested logit models: we simply add the time averages, $\overline{\mathbf{w}}_i$, as additional explanatory variables, used pooled MLE, and make inference robust to arbitrary serial dependence. Many econometrics packages make this approach very straightforward to implement.

We gain even more flexibility by allowing $\mathbf{x}_{it}$ and $\overline{\mathbf{w}}_i$ to interact in the MNL or CL model. In other words, we can add $[\text{vec}(\overline{\mathbf{w}}_i \otimes \mathbf{x}_{it})]'\boldsymbol{\lambda}_j$ to the probabilities implicit in equation (16.19). Other nonlinear functions, such as general polynomials, are easy to include, too.

16.3 Ordered Response Models

16.3.1 Ordered Logit and Ordered Probit

We now turn to models for ordered responses. Let y be an ordered response taking on the values $\{0, 1, 2, \ldots, J\}$ for some known integer J. The **ordered probit model** for y (conditional on explanatory variables $\mathbf{x}$) can be derived from a latent variable model. Assume that a latent variable y^* is determined by

$$y^* = \mathbf{x}\boldsymbol{\beta} + e, \qquad e \mid \mathbf{x} \sim \text{Normal}(0, 1) \tag{16.21}$$

where $\boldsymbol{\beta}$ is $K \times 1$ and, for reasons to be seen, $\mathbf{x}$ does not contain a constant. Let $\alpha_1 < \alpha_2 < \cdots < \alpha_J$ be unknown **cut points** (or **threshold parameters**), and define

$$\begin{aligned}
y &= 0 \qquad \text{if } y^* \leq \alpha_1 \\
y &= 1 \qquad \text{if } \alpha_1 < y^* \leq \alpha_2 \\
&\;\;\vdots \\
y &= J \qquad \text{if } y^* > \alpha_J
\end{aligned} \tag{16.22}$$

For example, if y takes on the values 0, 1, and 2, then there are two cut points, α_1 and α_2.

Given the standard normal assumption for e, it is straightforward to derive the conditional distribution of y given $\mathbf{x}$; we simply compute each response probability:

$$\begin{aligned}
\mathrm{P}(y = 0 \mid \mathbf{x}) &= \mathrm{P}(y^* \leq \alpha_1 \mid \mathbf{x}) = \mathrm{P}(\mathbf{x}\boldsymbol{\beta} + e \leq \alpha_1 \mid \mathbf{x}) = \Phi(\alpha_1 - \mathbf{x}\boldsymbol{\beta}) \\
\mathrm{P}(y = 1 \mid \mathbf{x}) &= \mathrm{P}(\alpha_1 < y^* \leq \alpha_2 \mid \mathbf{x}) = \Phi(\alpha_2 - \mathbf{x}\boldsymbol{\beta}) - \Phi(\alpha_1 - \mathbf{x}\boldsymbol{\beta}) \\
&\;\;\vdots \\
\mathrm{P}(y = J - 1 \mid \mathbf{x}) &= \mathrm{P}(\alpha_{J-1} < y^* \leq \alpha_J \mid \mathbf{x}) = \Phi(\alpha_J - \mathbf{x}\boldsymbol{\beta}) - \Phi(\alpha_{J-1} - \mathbf{x}\boldsymbol{\beta}) \\
\mathrm{P}(y = J \mid \mathbf{x}) &= \mathrm{P}(y^* > \alpha_J \mid \mathbf{x}) = 1 - \Phi(\alpha_J - \mathbf{x}\boldsymbol{\beta}).
\end{aligned} \tag{16.23}$$

You can easily verify that these sum to unity. When $J = 1$ we get the binary probit model: $\mathrm{P}(y = 1 \mid \mathbf{x}) = 1 - \mathrm{P}(y = 0 \mid \mathbf{x}) = 1 - \Phi(\alpha_1 - \mathbf{x}\boldsymbol{\beta}) = \Phi(\mathbf{x}\boldsymbol{\beta} - \alpha_1)$, and so $-\alpha_1$ is the intercept inside Φ. It is for this reason that $\mathbf{x}$ does not contain an intercept in this formulation of the ordered probit model. (When there are only two outcomes, zero and one, we set the single cut point to zero and estimate the intercept; this approach leads to the standard probit model.)

The parameters $\boldsymbol{\alpha}$ and $\boldsymbol{\beta}$ can be estimated by MLE. For each i, the log-likelihood function is

$$\ell_i(\boldsymbol{\alpha}, \boldsymbol{\beta}) = 1[y_i = 0] \log[\Phi(\alpha_1 - \mathbf{x}_i\boldsymbol{\beta})] + 1[y_i = 1] \log[\Phi(\alpha_2 - \mathbf{x}_i\boldsymbol{\beta}) - \Phi(\alpha_1 - \mathbf{x}_i\boldsymbol{\beta})] + \cdots + 1[y_i = J] \log[1 - \Phi(\alpha_J - \mathbf{x}_i\boldsymbol{\beta})] \tag{16.24}$$

This log-likelihood function is well behaved, and many statistical packages routinely estimate ordered probit models.

Other distribution functions can be used in place of Φ. Replacing Φ with the logit function, Λ, gives the **ordered logit model**. In either case we must remember that $\boldsymbol{\beta}$, by itself, is of limited interest. In most cases we are not interested in $\mathrm{E}(y^* \mid \mathbf{x}) = \mathbf{x}\boldsymbol{\beta}$, as y^* is an abstract construct. Instead, we are interested in the response probabilities $\mathrm{P}(y = j \mid \mathbf{x})$, just as in the ordered response case. For the ordered probit model

$$\partial p_0(\mathbf{x})/\partial x_k = -\beta_k \phi(\alpha_1 - \mathbf{x}\boldsymbol{\beta}), \ \partial p_J(\mathbf{x})/\partial x_k = \beta_k \phi(\alpha_J - \mathbf{x}\boldsymbol{\beta})$$

$$\partial p_j(\mathbf{x})/\partial x_k = \beta_k[\phi(\alpha_{j-1} - \mathbf{x}\boldsymbol{\beta}) - \phi(\alpha_j - \mathbf{x}\boldsymbol{\beta})], \qquad 0 < j < J,$$

and the formulas for the ordered logit model are similar. In making comparisons across different models—in particular, comparing ordered probit and ordered logit—we must remember to compare estimated response probabilities at various values of $\mathbf{x}$, such as $\bar{\mathbf{x}}$; the $\hat{\boldsymbol{\beta}}$ are not directly comparable. In particular, the $\hat{\alpha}_j$ are important determinants of the magnitudes of the estimated probabilities and partial effects. (Therefore, treatments of ordered probit that refer to the α_j as ancillary, or secondary, parameters are misleading.)

While the direction of the effect of x_k on the probabilities $\mathrm{P}(y = 0 \mid \mathbf{x})$ and $\mathrm{P}(y = J \mid \mathbf{x})$ is unambiguously determined by the sign of β_k, the sign of β_k does not always determine the direction of the effect for the intermediate outcomes, $1, 2, \ldots,$ $J - 1$. To see this point, suppose there are three possible outcomes, 0, 1, and 2, and that $\beta_k > 0$. Then $\partial p_0(\mathbf{x})/\partial x_k < 0$ and $\partial p_2(\mathbf{x})/\partial x_k > 0$, but $\partial p_1(\mathbf{x})/\partial x_k$ could be either sign. If $|\alpha_1 - \mathbf{x}\boldsymbol{\beta}| < |\alpha_2 - \mathbf{x}\boldsymbol{\beta}|$, the scale factor, $\phi(\alpha_1 - \mathbf{x}\boldsymbol{\beta}) - \phi(\alpha_2 - \mathbf{x}\boldsymbol{\beta})$, is positive; otherwise it is negative. (This conclusion follows because the standard normal pdf is symmetric about zero, reaches its maximum at zero, and declines monotonically as its argument increases in absolute value.)

As with multinomial logit, for ordered responses we can compute the percent correctly predicted, for each outcome as well as overall: our prediction for y is simply the outcome with the highest estimated probability.

Ordered probit and logit can also be applied when y is given quantitative meaning but we wish to acknowledge the discrete, ordered nature of the response. For example, suppose that individuals are asked to give one of three responses on how their pension funds are invested: "mostly bonds," "mixed," and "mostly stocks." One possibility is to assign these outcomes as 0, 1, 2 and apply ordered probit or ordered logit to estimate the effects of various factors on the probability of each outcome. Instead, we could assign the percent invested in stocks as, say, 0, 50, and 100, or 25, 50, and 75. For estimating the probabilities of each category it is irrelevant how we assign the percentages as long as the order is preserved. However, if we give quantitative meaning to y, the expected value of y has meaning. We have

$$E(y \mid \mathbf{x}) = a_0 P(y = a_0 \mid \mathbf{x}) + a_1 P(y = a_1 \mid \mathbf{x}) + \cdots + a_J P(y = a_J \mid \mathbf{x}), \tag{16.25}$$

where $a_0 < a_1 < \cdots < a_J$ are the J values taken on by y. Once we have estimated the response probabilities by ordered probit or ordered logit, we can easily estimate $E(y \mid \mathbf{x})$ for any value of $\mathbf{x}$, for example, $\bar{\mathbf{x}}$. Estimates of the expected values can be compared at different values of the explanatory variables to obtain partial effects for discrete x_j. Alternatively, we can compute average partial effects by averaging the partial derivatives across i or discrete changes.

Example 16.2 (Asset Allocation in Pension Plans): The data in PENSION.RAW are a subset of data used by Papke (1998) in assessing the impact of allowing individuals to choose their own allocations on asset allocation in pension plans. Initially, Papke codes the responses "mostly bonds," "mixed," and "mostly stocks" as 0, 50, and 100, and uses a linear regression model estimated by OLS. The binary explanatory variable *choice* is unity if the person has choice in how his or her pension fund is invested. Controlling for age, education, gender, race, marital status, income (via a set of dummy variables), wealth, and whether the plan is profit sharing gives the OLS estimate $\hat{\beta}_{\text{choice}} = 12.05$ (se $= 6.30$), where $N = 194$. This result means that, other things equal, a person having choice has about 12 percentage points more assets in stocks.

The ordered probit coefficient on *choice* is .371 (se $=$ .184). The magnitude of the ordered probit coefficient does not have a simple interpretation, but its sign and statistical significance agree with the linear regression results. (The estimated cut points are $\hat{\alpha}_1 = -3.087$ and $\hat{\alpha}_2 = -2.054$.) To get an idea of the magnitude of the estimated effect of choice on the expected percent in stocks, we can estimate $E(y \mid \mathbf{x})$ with $choice = 1$ and $choice = 0$, and obtain the difference. However, we need to choose values for the other regressors. For illustration, suppose the person is 60 years old, has 13.5 years of education (roughly the averages in the sample), is a single, nonblack male, has annual income between \$50,000 and \$75,000, had wealth in 1989 of \$200,000 (also close to the sample average), and does not have a profit-sharing plan. Then, for $choice = 1$, $\hat{E}(pctstck \mid \mathbf{x}) \approx 40.0$, and with $choice = 0$, $\hat{E}(pctstck \mid \mathbf{x}) \approx 28.1$. The difference, 11.9, is remarkably close to the linear model estimate of the effect on choice.

For ordered probit, the percentages correctly predicted for each category are 51.6 (mostly bonds), 43.1 (mixed), and 37.9 (mostly stocks). The overall percentage correctly predicted is about 44.3.

16.3.2 Specification Issues in Ordered Models

As with binary probit and logit in Chapter 15, as well as the unordered models discussed in Section 16.1, we can investigate the consequences of various specification problems with ordered probit and logit. Some writers have focused on the **parallel regression assumption**, which arises because of the underlying latent variable formulation with a single unobservable independent of the covariates. In particular, if we write y^* as in equation (16.21), where $\mathrm{D}(e \mid \mathbf{x})$ is standard normal or logistic, then

$$\mathrm{P}(y \leq j \mid \mathbf{x}) = \mathrm{P}(y^* \leq \alpha_j \mid \mathbf{x}) = G(\alpha_j - \mathbf{x}\boldsymbol{\beta}), \qquad j = 0, 1, \ldots, J-1, \tag{16.26}$$

where $G(\cdot) = \Phi(\cdot)$ or $G(\cdot) = \Lambda(\cdot)$, and so the probabilities differ across j only because of the cut parameters, α_j. In effect, an intercept shift inside the nonlinear cdf determines the differences in probabilities. A more general specification allows the vector $\boldsymbol{\beta}$ to change across j, too:

$$\mathrm{P}(y \leq j \mid \mathbf{x}) = G(\alpha_j - \mathbf{x}\boldsymbol{\beta}_j), \qquad j = 0, 1, \ldots, J-1. \tag{16.27}$$

Clearly, equation (16.27) is more general than (16.26), and the vector $(\alpha_j, \boldsymbol{\beta}_j)$ is easily estimated by applying binary reponse MLE to the response variable $w_{ij} = 1[y_i \leq j]$, $j = 0, \ldots, J-1$. As discussed in Long and Freese (2001), estimation of (16.27) and estimation of the ordered response model (which is the restricted model) can be used to obtain the LR statistic for the hypothesis that the $\boldsymbol{\beta}_j$ are all equal.

Testing that the $\boldsymbol{\beta}_j$ are the same in equations (16.27) is certainly a valid specification test of the standard ordered probit or logit model, but it is not clear how to proceed if we reject a common $\boldsymbol{\beta}$. Presumably, logic dictates whether y is an ordered response or an unordered response; if y is an ordered response, the possibility that the estimated probabilities $\hat{\mathrm{P}}(y \leq j \mid \mathbf{x})$ are not increasing in j for all values of $\mathbf{x}$—which can happen if the $\boldsymbol{\beta}_j$ are allowed to differ—does not make sense, and it makes little sense to estimate an unordered model (such as multinomial logit). Furthermore, a statistical rejection need not imply that ordered probit or ordered logit estimates of the response probabilities are poor estimates of the true response probabilities. If we specify the more general model $\mathrm{P}(y \leq j \mid \mathbf{x}) = G(\alpha_j - \mathbf{x}\boldsymbol{\beta}_j)$, then we are left with a bunch of unconnected binary response models for $w_j = 1[y \leq j]$, $j = 0, \ldots, J-1$, and it is not clear what we would learn in the end. (Estimating separate binary response models for the w_j is how one carries out an LR test of the parallel regression function, where the restricted model is just the usual ordered probit or ordered logit; see Long and Freese (2001) for further details.)

Equation (16.26) is useful in its own right. For a continuous variable x_h,

$$\frac{\partial \mathrm{P}(y \leq j \mid \mathbf{x})}{\partial x_h} = -\beta_h g(\alpha_j - \mathbf{x}\boldsymbol{\beta}), \tag{16.28}$$

where $g(\cdot)$ is the density associated with $G(\cdot)$, which means that the signs of the partial effects on $\mathrm{P}(y \leq j \mid \mathbf{x})$ are unambiguously determined by the signs of the coefficients. If $\beta_h > 0$, an increase in x_h decreases the probability that y is less than or equal to any value j.

Other specification issues follow our treatment of binary response models in Chapter 15. For reasons discussed in Section 15.7, these are most easily studied in the context of ordered probit. For example, if we add a normally distributed unobserved heterogeneity term that is independent of $\mathbf{x}$, we consistently estimate the APEs on the response probabilities, and expected value, if we simply ignore the heterogeneity. Just as in the binary response case, we estimate precisely the quantities of interest when we just ignore the heterogeneity. More generally, if we specify $\mathrm{P}(y_i = j \mid \mathbf{x}_i, c_i)$ for heterogeneity c_i independent of $\mathbf{x}_i$, the APEs are obtained by computing partial effects on $\mathrm{P}(y_i = j \mid \mathbf{x}_i)$. Therefore, one can argue that we might as well just specify more flexible models for $\mathrm{P}(y_i = j \mid \mathbf{x}_i)$.

One way to specify more flexible models is to introduce heteroskedasticity or nonnormality in the latent variable equation, just as in the binary response case. So, assume in equation (16.21) that

$$e \mid \mathbf{x} \sim \mathrm{Normal}(0, \exp(2\mathbf{x}_1\boldsymbol{\delta})), \tag{16.29}$$

where $\mathbf{x}_1$ is a subset of $\mathbf{x}$ (possibly $\mathbf{x}_1 = \mathbf{x}$). The response probabilities are obtained by simply multiplying $(\alpha_j - \mathbf{x}\boldsymbol{\beta})$ everywhere in equations (16.23) by $\exp(-\mathbf{x}_1\boldsymbol{\delta})$. A score test of $H_0: \boldsymbol{\delta} = \mathbf{0}$, or a variable addition version of the test, are straightforward to derive; see Problem 16.4. MLE of the unrestricted model is not too difficult, either. But, as in the binary response case, we must remember to compare estimated partial effects across different models, rather than just coefficient estimates. The same issues that arise in the binary case for how to define the APEs arise here, too; see Section 15.7.4.

As in the binary response case, it is possible to relax the normality or logistic assumption on the latent error, e. Again, the key issue in considering such extensions is whether implementing them changes the estimated partial effects in important ways. As usual, it is not necessary or sufficient to consider only the effects on the estimates of $\boldsymbol{\beta}$ and the α_j.

16.3.3 Endogenous Explanatory Variables

Handling one or more continuous endogenous explanatory variables is relatively straightforward in ordered probit models, provided we are willing to make distributional assumptions on the reduced form. In fact, the Rivers and Vuong (1988) approach (see Section 15.7.2) extends immediately to ordered probit. Write the model now as

$$y_1^* = \mathbf{z}_1\boldsymbol{\delta}_1 + \gamma_1 y_2 + u_1 \tag{16.30}$$

$$y_2 = \mathbf{z}\boldsymbol{\delta}_2 + v_2, \tag{16.31}$$

where (u_1, v_2) is independent of $\mathbf{z}$ and jointly normally distributed. (As in the binary case, we can relax these assumptions a bit.) In keeping with the typical ordered probit approach, $\mathbf{z}_1$ does not contain an intercept. Instead, there are cut points, α_j, $j = 1, \ldots, J$. We define the observed ordered response, y_1, in terms of the latent response, y_1^*, just as in equations (16.22).

By now the approach should be clear. If we write $u_1 = \theta_1 v_2 + e_1$ and plug into (16.30) we obtain

$$y_1^* = \mathbf{z}_1\boldsymbol{\delta}_1 + \gamma_1 y_2 + \theta_1 v_2 + e_1, \tag{16.32}$$

where $\theta_1 = \eta_1/\tau_2^2$, $\eta_1 = \mathrm{Cov}(v_2, u_1)$, $\tau_2^2 = \mathrm{Var}(v_2)$, $e_1 \mid \mathbf{z}, v_2 \sim \mathrm{Normal}(0, 1 - \rho_1^2)$, and $\rho_1 = \theta_1^2\tau_2^2 = \eta_1^2/\tau_2^2$. It follows from the standard results on two-step estimation that if we obtain the OLS residuals, $\hat{v}_{i2}$, from the first-stage regression y_{i2} on $\mathbf{z}_i$, $i = 1, \ldots, N$, and then run ordered probit of y_{i1} on $\mathbf{z}_{i1}$, y_{i2}, and $\hat{v}_{i2}$ in a second stage, we consistently estimate the scaled coefficients $\boldsymbol{\delta}_{\rho 1} \equiv \boldsymbol{\delta}_1/(1 - \rho_1^2)^{1/2}$, $\gamma_{\rho 1} \equiv \gamma_1/(1 - \rho_1^2)^{1/2}$, $\theta_{\rho 1} \equiv \theta_1/(1 - \rho_1^2)^{1/2}$, and $\alpha_{\rho j} = \alpha_j/(1 - \rho_1^2)^{1/2}$. A simple test of the null hypothesis that y_2 is exogenous (where we maintain, of course, that $\mathbf{z}$ is exogenous) is just the standard t statistic on $\hat{v}_{i2}$. As in Section 15.7.2, we can estimate the original parameters by dividing each of the scaled coefficients by $(1 + \hat{\theta}_{\rho 1}^2\hat{\tau}_2^2)^{1/2}$. Bootstrapping is a natural way to obtain standard errors; the delta method can also be used.

Alternatively, as in the binary case, we can compute the response probabilities (or expected values) for the second-step ordered probit that includes the residuals, $\hat{v}_{i2}$. Then, the response probabilities, or their derivatives, can be averaged out over $\hat{v}_{i2}$ to obtain consistent estimators of the APEs.

Naturally, allowing endogenous explanatory variables that do not have a conditional, homoskedastic normal distribution is more difficult. One can replace equation (16.31) with $y_2 = 1[\mathbf{z}\boldsymbol{\delta}_2 + v_2 > 0]$ where v_2 has a standard normal distribution, and then use MLE. That requires obtaining $\mathrm{P}(y_1 = j \mid \mathbf{z}, y_2)$, $j = 0, \ldots, J - 1$ for $y_2 = 0$

and $y_2 = 1$, just as in the binary case. The estimation problem is not particularly difficult; see, for example, Adams, Chiang, and Jensen (2003). As discussed in Section 15.7.3, a two-stage approach that replaces y_2 with fitted probabilities from the first-stage probit is not justified; it produces inconsistent estimators of the parameters and (probably) the APEs.

A simpler but more radical solution is to assume that a single (estimable) function of $(\mathbf{z}, y_2)$ is correlated with the unobservables in the structural ordered probit model. This assumption is implicit in all of the control function approaches we have implemented. For example, in the case of equation (16.31), v_2 plays the role of the single, estimable function. To be precise, suppose we explicitly introduce unobservables, r_1, thought to be correlated with y_2. Then, we are interested in the response probabilities

$$\mathrm{P}(y_1 = j \mid \mathbf{z}_1, y_2, r_1) = \mathrm{P}(y_1 = j \mid \mathbf{z}, y_2, r_1), \tag{16.33}$$

where the equality simply implies an exclusion restriction. Because r_1 is not observed, we will integrate r_1 out of the response probabilities when computing partial effects. Define the standardized residual for y_2 as

$$e_2 \equiv [y_2 - \Phi(\mathbf{z}\boldsymbol{\delta}_2)]/\{\Phi(\mathbf{z}\boldsymbol{\delta}_2)[1 - \Phi(\mathbf{z}\boldsymbol{\delta}_2)]\}^{1/2}, \tag{16.34}$$

under the assumption that $D(y_2 \mid \mathbf{z})$ follows a probit model. By construction, $\mathrm{E}(e_2 \mid \mathbf{z}) = 0$ and $\mathrm{Var}(e_2 \mid \mathbf{z}) = 1$. Unlike v_2 in equation (16.31), e_2 cannot be independent of $\mathbf{z}$ because its support depends directly on $\mathbf{z}$. Nevertheless, suppose we simply assert that

$$\mathrm{D}(r_1 \mid \mathbf{z}, y_2) = \mathrm{D}(r_1 \mid e_2). \tag{16.35}$$

Under assumption (16.35), it follows that we can consistently estimate the APEs of $(\mathbf{z}_1, y_2)$ on $\mathrm{P}(y_1 = j \mid \mathbf{z}_1, y_2, r_1)$ by estimating $\mathrm{P}(y_1 = j \mid \mathbf{z}_1, y_2, e_1)$ and then averaging out e_1. In the language of Blundell and Powell (2004), the ASF for the response probabilities is

$$\mathrm{ASF}_j(\mathbf{z}_1, y_2) = \mathrm{E}_{e_{i2}}[p_j(\mathbf{z}_1, y_2, e_{i2})], \tag{16.36}$$

where $p_j(\mathbf{z}_1, y_2, e_2) \equiv \mathrm{P}(y_1 = j \mid \mathbf{z}_1, y_2, e_2)$. Now, the approach to estimating APEs is, in principle, straightforward. In the first stage, we estimate a probit of y_{i2} on $\mathbf{z}_i$ and construct the standardized residuals, $\hat{e}_{i2} \equiv (y_{i2} - \hat{\Phi}_{i2})/[\hat{\Phi}_{i2}(1 - \hat{\Phi}_{i2})]^{1/2}$. Next, we estimate a model for the $p_j(\mathbf{z}_1, y_2, e_2)$ by inserting $\hat{e}_{i2}$ for the unobserved e_{i2}. Because y_1 is an ordered outcome, any estimation approach should recognize the ordered nature. Because ordered probit (and ordered logit) are straightforward, we might, as an approximation, use an ordered probit with $\hat{e}_{i2}$ entered in a flexible way, for example, polynomials, and possibly interacted with $(\mathbf{z}_{i1}, y_{i2})$. The parameter estimates from such an ordered probit would not necessarily mean much, but the APEs would be easy to estimate by averaging out the $\hat{e}_{i2}$ in the estimated response probabilities. At the very least, just adding $\hat{e}_{i2}$ as a single explanatory to the ordered probit and conducting a t test on $\hat{e}_{i2}$ is valid as an endogeneity test; as usual, the null hypothesis is that y_2 is exogenous. (Of course, putting in the residuals from an LPM, or the unstandardized probit residuals, also provides a valid test.) Naturally, because the ordered probit contains binary probit as a special case, the method can be applied to the standard binary probit model.

The key drawback to the computationally simple procedure just described is that there is little basis for assumption (16.35) when y_2 is binary. Nevertheless, it could hold, and then the only issue is choosing functional forms. One could use nonparametric or semiparametric methods in each step, similar to Blundell and Powell (2004), to overcome objections caused by specific functional forms (such as ordered probit in the second stage).

16.3.4 Panel Data Methods

We can easily adapt the correlated random effects (CRE) methods for binary probit (see Section 15.8.2) to ordered probit. We start with the standard latent variable model

$$y_{it}^* = \mathbf{x}_{it}\boldsymbol{\beta} + c_i + e_{it}, \qquad t = 1, \ldots, T, \tag{16.37}$$

where

$$e_{it} \mid \mathbf{x}_i, c_i \sim \text{Normal}(0, 1), \qquad t = 1, \ldots, T, \tag{16.38}$$

and $\mathbf{x}_{it}$ can contain time-period dummies but not an overall intercept. Then, the observed ordered response is $y_{it} = 0$ if $y_{it}^* \leq \alpha_1$, $y_{it1} = 1$ if $\alpha_1 < y_{it}^* \leq \alpha_2$, and so on. We can add the Chamberlain-Mundlak device:

$$c_i = \psi + \bar{\mathbf{x}}_i\boldsymbol{\xi} + a_i, \qquad a_i \mid \mathbf{x}_i \sim \text{Normal}(0, \sigma_a^2). \tag{16.39}$$

Now, if we compute the response probabilities $p_j(\mathbf{x}_{it}, \bar{\mathbf{x}}_i) = P(y_{it} = j \mid \mathbf{x}_{it}, \bar{\mathbf{x}}_i) = P(y_{it} = j \mid \mathbf{x}_i)$, it is easily seen that these have the ordered probit form with parameters $\boldsymbol{\beta}_a$, $\boldsymbol{\xi}_a$, and α_{aj}, $j = 1, \ldots, J$, where the a subscript denotes division by $(1 + \sigma_a^2)^{1/2}$ and ψ_a is absorbed into the cut points. Estimation of the scaled parameters proceeds by **pooled ordered probit**, where we allow for unrestricted serial dependence. Naturally, the APEs of $P(y_{it} = j \mid \mathbf{x}_{it} = \mathbf{x}_t, c_i = c)$ with respect to elements of $\mathbf{x}_t$ are obtained from

$$N^{-1} \sum_{i=1}^{N} p_j(\mathbf{x}_t, \bar{\mathbf{x}}_i, \hat{\boldsymbol{\theta}}_a), \tag{16.40}$$

where $\hat{\boldsymbol{\theta}}_a$ represents the vector of all scaled parameter estimates; the only ones we can obtain without further assumption.

A full MLE approach is possible if we assume that the e_{it} are independent conditional on $(\mathbf{x}_i, c_i)$, but, computationally, full MLE is more difficult than the pooled (partial) MLE. As always, the pooled method identifies only the APEs, but it is more robust than the full MLE.

Wooldridge (2005b) provides a framework to estimate dynamic ordered probit models. An important issue concerns how the dynamics should enter the response probabilities. Wooldridge proposes including a set of dummies indicating the previous period's outcome. Namely, define J dummies, say $w_{i,t-1,1}, \ldots, w_{i,t-1,J}$, where $w_{i,t-1,j} = 1[y_{i,t-1} = j]$, and then $\mathbf{w}_{i,t-1} = (w_{i,t-1,1}, \ldots, w_{i,t-1,J})$ is included among the explanatory variables. So, the latent variable model is

$$y_{it}^* = \mathbf{z}_{it}\boldsymbol{\delta} + \mathbf{w}_{i,t-1}\boldsymbol{\rho} + c_i + u_{it}, \qquad t = 1, \ldots, T. \tag{16.41}$$

To account for the initial conditions problem, the unobserved effect, c_i, is modeled as $c_i = \psi + \mathbf{w}_{i0}\boldsymbol{\eta} + \mathbf{z}_i\boldsymbol{\xi} + a_i$, where $\mathbf{w}_{i0}$ is the J-vector of initial conditions, w_{i0j}, and $\mathbf{z}_i$ is the entire history of the strictly exogenous explanatory variables $\mathbf{z}_{it}$. If a_i is independent of $(\mathbf{w}_{i0}, \mathbf{z}_i)$ and distributed as Normal$(0, \sigma_a^2)$, we can apply **random effects ordered probit** to the latent variable equation

$$y_{it}^* = \mathbf{z}_{it}\boldsymbol{\delta} + \mathbf{w}_{i,t-1}\boldsymbol{\rho} + \mathbf{w}_{i0}\boldsymbol{\eta} + \mathbf{z}_i\boldsymbol{\xi} + a_i + u_{it}, \qquad t = 1, \ldots, T, \tag{16.42}$$

where we absorb the intercept into the cut parameters, α_j. Any software that estimates RE ordered probit models can be applied directly to estimate all parameters, including σ_a^2; we simply specify the explanatory variables at time t as $(\mathbf{z}_{it}, \mathbf{w}_{i,t-1}, \mathbf{w}_{i0}, \mathbf{z}_i)$. (Pooled ordered probit does *not* consistently estimate any interesting parameters; see the discussion in Section 15.8.4 for the binary probit case.) APEs are easily computed, as discussed in Wooldridge (2005b). Not surprisingly, the APEs depend on the coefficients multiplied by $(1 + \hat{\sigma}_a^2)^{-1/2}$.

Problems

16.1. Use the data in KEANE.RAW to answer this question.

a. Estimate the model reported in Table 16.1, using the data for 1981. Do any of the coefficients differ in important ways from those in Table 16.1 (for 1987)?

b. Estimate the model pooled across all years, and include year dummies for 1982 to 1987. Explain why, in general, the standard errors and test statistics should be made robust to arbitrary serial dependence. Do the usual and robust standard errors differ substantially?

c. Should the year dummies be kept in the model? Explain.

d. Using the model estimated in part b, estimate the change in the probability of being employed for a black man with five years of experience when *educ* increases from 12 to 16. Obtain the estimates for both 1981 and 1987, and comment.

e. How would you test whether the coefficients on *exper* and $exper^2$ have changed over time?

16.2. Use the data in PENSION.RAW for this exercise.

a. Estimate a linear model for *pctstck*, where the explanatory variables are *choice*, *age*, *educ*, *female*, *black*, *married*, *finc25*, ..., *finc101*, *wealth89*, and *prftshr*. Why might you compute heteroskedasticity-robust standard errors?

b. The sample contains separate observations for some husband-wife pairs. Compute standard errors of the estimates from the model in part a that account for the cluster correlation within family. (These should also be heteroskedasticity-robust.) Do the standard errors differ much from the usual OLS standard errors, or from the heteroskedasticity-robust standard errors?

c. Estimate the model from part a by ordered probit. Estimate $\mathrm{E}(pctstck \mid \mathbf{x})$ for a single, nonblack female with 12 years of education who is 60 years old. Assume she has net worth (in 1989) equal to \$150,000 and earns \$45,000 a year, and her plan is not profit sharing. Compare this with the estimate of $\mathrm{E}(pctstck \mid \mathbf{x})$ from the linear model.

d. If you want to choose between the linear model and ordered probit based on how well each estimates $\mathrm{E}(y \mid \mathbf{x})$, how would you proceed?

16.3. Consider the ordered probit model under exponential heteroskedasticity, as in (16.29).

a. Derive the response probabilities $\mathrm{P}(y = j \mid \mathbf{x})$.

b. Write down the log likelihood as a function of all parameters, $\boldsymbol{\alpha}$, $\boldsymbol{\beta}$, and $\boldsymbol{\delta}$. Find the gradient of the log likelihood with respect to $\boldsymbol{\delta}$, and evaluate the gradient at $\boldsymbol{\delta} = \mathbf{0}$.

c. What might be a useful variable addition test for $\mathrm{H}_0 : \boldsymbol{\delta} = \mathbf{0}$?

d. For the outcome $y = 1$ (just for concreteness), define the average structural function as

$$\mathrm{ASF}_1(\mathbf{x}) = \mathrm{E}_{e_i}(1[\alpha_1 - \mathbf{x}\boldsymbol{\beta} < e_i \le \alpha_2 - \mathbf{x}\boldsymbol{\beta}]).$$

Find the ASF in terms of the (unconditional) cdf of e_i (and $\mathbf{x}$ and the parameters). Is the cdf of e_i known?

e. Use iterated expectations to show that

$$\mathrm{ASF}_1(\mathbf{x}) = \mathrm{E}_{\mathbf{x}_{i1}}\{\Phi[\exp(-\mathbf{x}_{i1}\boldsymbol{\delta})(\alpha_2 - \mathbf{x}\boldsymbol{\beta})] - \Phi[\exp(-\mathbf{x}_{i1}\boldsymbol{\delta})(\alpha_1 - \mathbf{x}\boldsymbol{\beta})].$$

If you have estimated the parameters by MLE, how would you estimate $\mathrm{ASF}_1(\mathbf{x})$, and how would you use it to estimate APEs?

16.4. Using the data in PENSION.RAW, define a variable *invest* = 0 if *pctstck* = 0, *invest* = 1 if *pctstck* = 50, and *invest* = 2 if *pctstck* = 100.

a. Estimate the ordered probit model in Example 16.2 but with *invest* as the dependent variable. What do you conclude?

b. Are there any interesting quantities that would differ between using *pctstck* and *invest* as the dependent variables?

16.5. Consider the ordered probit model in (16.30) and (16.31), but assume that $v_2 \mid \mathbf{z} \sim \mathrm{Normal}(0, \exp(\mathbf{z}\xi_2))$. In other words, v_2 contains heteroskedasticity. Assume that (u_1, e_2) is jointly normal and independent of $\mathbf{z}$, where $e_2 \equiv \exp(-\mathbf{z}\xi_2/2)v_2$ is the standardized error; in particular, both u_1 and e_2 are independent of $\mathbf{z}$ with a standard normal distribution.

a. Propose $\sqrt{N}$-consistent estimators of $\boldsymbol{\delta}_2$ and ξ_2.

b. Show that $u_1 = \theta_1 e_2 + e_1$, where e_1 is independent of $(\mathbf{z}, e_2)$. Why is e_1 also independent of y_2?

c. Propose a two-step method for consistently estimating the parameters in equation (16.30) and the cut points up to scale.

d. How would you consistently estimate the APEs?

e. If equation (16.30) holds but $y_2 > 0$, and (16.31) holds with $\log(y_2)$ in place of y_2, how would you proceed?

f. Now suppose that $\mathrm{E}(y_2 \mid \mathbf{z}) = \exp(\mathbf{z}\boldsymbol{\delta}_2)$ and $\mathrm{Var}(y_2 \mid \mathbf{z}) = \exp(\mathbf{z}\xi_2)$, and assume that $e_2 \equiv [y_2 - \mathrm{E}(y_2 \mid \mathbf{z})]/[\mathrm{Var}(y_2 \mid \mathbf{z})]^{1/2}$ is independent of $\mathbf{z}$. How would you allow for endogeneity of y_2 in an ordered probit model?

16.6. Write a panel data unobserved effects ordered probit model, with a potentially endogenous explanatory variable, in latent variable form as

$$y_{it1}^* = \mathbf{z}_{it1}\boldsymbol{\delta}_1 + \gamma_1 y_{it2} + c_{i1} + u_{it1}, \qquad u_{it1} \mid \mathbf{z}_i, c_{i1} \sim \mathrm{Normal}(0, 1),$$

where we assume the observed outcome, y_{it1}, is defined to take on values in $\{0, 1, \ldots, J\}$ with cut points $\alpha_1, \ldots, \alpha_J$. The notation extends in a natural way that of Section 15.8.5. Assume, in addition, that

$$c_{i1} = \psi_1 + \bar{\mathbf{z}}_i \boldsymbol{\xi}_1 + a_{i1}, \qquad a_{i1} \mid \mathbf{z}_i \sim \text{Normal}(0, \sigma_{a_1}^2)$$

$$y_{it2} = \mathbf{z}_{it}\boldsymbol{\delta}_2 + \psi_2 + \bar{\mathbf{z}}_i \boldsymbol{\xi}_2 + v_{it2}, \qquad v_{it2} \mid \mathbf{z}_i \sim \text{Normal}(0, \tau_2^2), \qquad t = 1, \ldots, T.$$

a. Propose a two-step control function approach to estimate $\boldsymbol{\delta}_1$, γ_1, and the cut parameters α_j up to scale. Put a g index on the scaled parameters to distinguish them from the original parameters.

b. Show that the average structural function for the probability of outcome $1 \leq j \leq J - 1$ can be written as

$$\begin{aligned} \text{ASF}(\mathbf{z}_{t1}, y_{t2}) = \text{E}_{(\bar{\mathbf{z}}_i, v_{it2})}[&\Phi(\alpha_{gj} - \mathbf{z}_{t1}\boldsymbol{\delta}_{g1} - \gamma_{g1} y_{t2} - \bar{\mathbf{z}}_i \boldsymbol{\xi}_{g1} - \theta_{g1} v_{it2}) \\ &- \Phi(\alpha_{g,j-1} - \mathbf{z}_{t1}\boldsymbol{\delta}_{g1} - \gamma_{g1} y_{t2} - \bar{\mathbf{z}}_i \boldsymbol{\xi}_{g1} - \theta_{g1} v_{it2})], \end{aligned}$$

where $\text{E}_{(\bar{\mathbf{z}}_i, v_{it2})}(\cdot)$ denotes the expected value with respect to the distribution of $(\bar{\mathbf{z}}_i, v_{it2})$.

c. How would you estimate the APEs and obtain valid standard errors?

d. Are the estimators of the parameters and APEs consistent if v_{ir2} is correlated with u_{it1} for some $r \neq t$? Explain.

17 Corner Solution Responses

17.1 Motivation and Examples

We now turn to models for limited dependent variables that have features of both continuous and discrete random variables. In particular, they are continuously distributed over a range of values—sometimes a very wide range—but they take on one or two focal points with positive probability. Such variables arise often in modeling individual, family, or firm behavior, and even when studying outcomes at a more aggregated level, such as the classroom or school level.

The most common case is when the nonnegative response variable, y, has a (roughly) continuous distribution over strictly positive values, but $P(y = 0) > 0$. We call such a variable a **corner solution response** or **corner solution outcome**, where the corner in this case is at zero. Corners can occur at other values, too. For example, consider the population of families making charitable contributions during a given year. If y is the fraction of charitable contributions made to religious organizations, we are likely to see a wide range of values between zero and one, and then pileups at the two endpoints of zero and one. If so, the corners are at zero and one, and it makes sense to treat y as having a continuous distribution over the open interval $(0, 1)$.

Corner solution responses are often called "censored responses," a label that comes from situations with actual data censoring. Consequently, the leading model that we cover in this chapter is sometimes called a "censored regression model." Instead, we use the somewhat unconventional name **corner solution model** because we are trying to capture features of an observed corner solution response. The word "censored" implies that we are not observing the entire possible range of the response variable, but that is not the case for corner solution responses. For example, in a model of charitable contributions, the variable we are interested in explaining, both for theoretical reasons and for the purposes of policy analysis, is the actual amount of charitable contributions. That this outcome might be zero for a nontrivial fraction of the population does not mean that charitable contributions are somehow "censored at zero," a common but misleading phrase that one sees used in the analysis of corner solution responses. The fact that, say, charitable contributions, labor supply, life insurance purchases, and fraction of investments in the stock market pile up at certain focal points means that we might want to use special econometric models. But it is not a problem of data observability.

In Chapter 19, we will study true data-censoring problems, where the underlying variable we would like to explain is censored above or below a threshold. Typically, data censoring arises because of a survey sampling scheme or institutional constraints. There, we will be interested in an underlying response variable that we do not fully observe because it *is* censored above or below certain values. The econometric models for corner solution responses and censored data have similar statistical structures, but the ways one uses the estimates and thinks about violations of underlying assumptions are different. To avoid confusion, and to do justice to both corner solution models and data-censoring mechanisms, we treat data censoring in a separate chapter on data problems.

Before we consider models specifically developed for corner solution responses, it is important to understand that some simple strategies are available, and also to understand the shortcomings of these strategies. Because we are interested in features of $D(y \mid \mathbf{x})$ for observable y, we can model such features directly. If we are interested in the effect of x_j on the mean response $\mathrm{E}(y \mid \mathbf{x})$, it is natural to ask: Why not just assume $\mathrm{E}(y \mid \mathbf{x}) = \mathbf{x}\boldsymbol{\beta}$ (where $x_1 = 1$) and apply OLS on a random sample? Of course, if $\mathrm{E}(y \mid \mathbf{x}) = \mathbf{x}\boldsymbol{\beta}$, then OLS of y_i on $\mathbf{x}_i$, $i = 1, \ldots, N$ is perfectly sensible in that it consistently estimates $\boldsymbol{\beta}$. Consistency holds even though $y_i \geq 0$ and $\mathrm{P}(y_i = 0) > 0$; nothing about consistency of OLS hinges on restricting the probabilistic features of y. The problem with estimating a linear model is the assumption of a mean linear in $\mathbf{x}$: unless the range of $\mathbf{x}$ is fairly limited, $\mathrm{E}(y \mid \mathbf{x})$ cannot truly be linear in $\mathbf{x}$. (In the special case where $\mathbf{x}$ consists of exhaustive and mutually exclusive dummy variables, $\mathrm{E}(y \mid \mathbf{x})$ can always be written as a linear function of $\mathbf{x}$.) A related problem is that the partial effects on $\mathrm{E}(y \mid \mathbf{x})$ cannot really be constant over a wide range of $\mathbf{x}$, and using standard nonlinear transformations of the underlying explanatory variables cannot fully solve the problem. These shortcomings with a linear model for $\mathrm{E}(y \mid \mathbf{x})$ are quite analogous to those for the linear probability model.

As we discussed in Section 15.2 for binary y, it is always valid to view the linear model as the linear projection $\mathrm{L}(y \mid \mathbf{x})$. As we know, regardless of the nature of y (and $\mathbf{x}$), $\mathrm{L}(y \mid \mathbf{x})$ is always well defined, provided all random variables have finite second moments. Further, as we saw in Section 15.7.5, the coefficients in the linear projection can, under restrictive assumptions, equal average partial effects (APEs). Generally, the linear projection may well approximate the APEs. Even so, one may be interested in getting sensible estimates of $\mathrm{E}(y \mid \mathbf{x})$, along with partial effects on the conditional mean, over a wide range of $\mathbf{x}$ values, and the linear projection may provide a poor approximation to the conditional mean, although the approximation is better if $\mathbf{x}$ includes flexible functions of the underlying covariates.

Even though a linear model for $\mathrm{E}(y \mid \mathbf{x})$ usually is not suitable, we have seen other relatively simple functional forms that ensure a positive conditional mean for all values of $\mathbf{x}$ and the parameters. The leading case is an exponential function, $\mathrm{E}(y \mid \mathbf{x}) = \exp(\mathbf{x}\boldsymbol{\beta})$, where again we assume that $x_1 = 1$. (We cannot use $\log(y)$ as the dependent variable in a linear regression because $\log(0)$ is undefined.) It is important to understand that there is nothing wrong with an exponential model for $E(y \mid \mathbf{x})$. It has all of the features we want in a conditional mean model for a nonnegative response. It is true that the exponential mean is not compatible with the Tobit model that we define below. But the Tobit model, as attractive as it is, is just one possibility, and there is nothing logically wrong with directly specifying an exponential model for $E(y \mid \mathbf{x})$. As we will see in Chapter 18, an exponential function also lends itself to relatively simple ways to account for endogenous explanatory variables.

Because $\text{Var}(y \mid \mathbf{x})$ is likely to be heteroskedastic when y is a corner solution, nonlinear least squares (NLS) estimation of an exponential model is likely to be inefficient. As we know from Chapter 12, we can use weighted NLS to obtain more efficient estimators, although that requires specification of a model for the conditional variance that would be arbitrary. However, remember that we can use fully robust inference whether we use NLS or WNLS, and a thoughtfully constructed WNLS estimator might be more efficient than NLS even if we have the conditional variance misspecified.

A more important criticism with modeling $E(y \mid \mathbf{x})$ as an exponential function, or any other function, is that we cannot measure the effect of the x_j on any other feature of $D(y \mid \mathbf{x})$. Often, we are interested in features such as $P(y = 0 \mid \mathbf{x})$ and $E(y \mid \mathbf{x}, y > 0)$. By construction, a model for $E(y \mid \mathbf{x})$ says nothing about other features of $D(y \mid \mathbf{x})$. In this chapter, we are mainly concerned with models that fully specify the conditional distribution, although we will touch on other situations where we specify less than a full conditional distribution.

Before we turn to econometric models, we note that economic models of maximizing or minimizing behavior often lead to the possibility of corner solution outcomes. A good example is annual hours worked for married women. In the population, we see a wide range of hours worked over strictly positive hours, with enough different values to take the distribution as being continuous. But we also see a nontrivial fraction of married women who do not work for a wage or salary.

Generally, utility maximization problems allow for the possibility of a corner solution, as shown by the following simple model of charitable contributions.

Example 17.1 (Charitable Contributions): Problem 15.2 shows how to derive a probit model from a utility maximization problem for charitable giving, using utility function $util_i(c, q) = c + a_i \log(1 + q)$, where c is annual consumption in dollars and q is annual charitable giving. The variable a_i determines the marginal utility of giving for family i. Maximizing subject to the budget constraint $c_i + p_i q_i = m_i$ (where m_i is family income and p_i is the price of a dollar of charitable contributions) and the inequality constraints $c, q \geq 0$, the solution q_i is easily shown to be $q_i = 0$ if $a_i/p_i \leq 1$, and $q_i = a_i/p_i - 1$ if $a_i/p_i > 1$. We can write this relation as $1 + q_i = \max(1, a_i/p_i)$. If $a_i = \exp(\mathbf{z}_i\gamma + u_i)$, where u_i is an unobservable, then charitable contributions are determined by the equation

$$\log(1 + q_i) = \max[0, \mathbf{z}_i\gamma - \log(p_i) + u_i]. \tag{17.1}$$

Because $q_i = 0$ if and only if $\log(1 + q_i) = 0$, equation (17.1) implies that the probability of observing zero charitable contributions is strictly positive. Further, because u_i has a normal distribution, q_i has a continuous distribution over strictly postive values.

The charitable contributions example is a special case of a model that has become a workhorse for corner solution responses when the only corner is at zero—the canonical case. In the population, let y be the corner solution response and let $\mathbf{x}$ be the row vector of covariates (which contains unity as its first element). Assume

$$y = \max(0, \mathbf{x}\boldsymbol{\beta} + u), \tag{17.2}$$

where u is unobservable. Naturally, u could have a variety of distributions, and its conditional distribution $\mathrm{D}(u \mid \mathbf{x})$ could depend on $\mathbf{x}$. But we will mostly work with the assumption

$$u \mid \mathbf{x} \sim \mathrm{Normal}(0, \sigma^2), \tag{17.3}$$

which implies that u is independent of $\mathbf{x}$. Assumptions (17.2) and (17.3) define the **type I Tobit model** (after Tobin, 1958). This model is also called the *standard censored regression model*, but, as we mentioned before, we avoid the word "censored" in this chapter because it connotes some sort of data censoring. Amemiya (1985) gave it the "type I" label, and we use that here because it is neutral with respect to the nature of the application. (Interestingly, Tobin's original application to spending on consumer durables is clearly a corner solution application, and he never uses the word "censored" in his article. Instead, he refers to the response taking on its "limit value." Plus, Tobin was careful to compare the Tobit estimates of the conditional mean with the linear model estimates.) It is handy to have a notation for when a variable follows a Tobit model. If $\mathrm{D}(y \mid \mathbf{x})$ is determined by (17.2) and (17.3), we write $\mathrm{D}(y \mid \mathbf{x}) = \mathrm{Tobit}(\mathbf{x}\boldsymbol{\beta}, \sigma^2)$.

The normality assumption for u means that it has unbounded support, and, because u is independent of $\mathbf{x}$, there is always positive probability (for any $\mathbf{x}$ and any value of $\boldsymbol{\beta}$) that $\mathbf{x}\boldsymbol{\beta} + u < 0$, which means $\mathrm{P}(y = 0 \mid \mathbf{x}) > 0$.

Equation (17.2) has the benefit of directly relating the variable of interest, y, to observed explanatory variables and an unobservable. Nevertheless, sometimes it is useful to write (17.2) as a latent variable model:

$$y^* = \mathbf{x}\boldsymbol{\beta} + u, \qquad u \mid \mathbf{x} \sim \text{Normal}(0, \sigma^2), \tag{17.4}$$

$$y_i = \max(0, y^*). \tag{17.5}$$

The latent variable formulation has the danger of suggesting that we are interested in $\mathrm{E}(y^* \mid \mathbf{x})$, but it will be valuable for certain derivations later on. Given (17.4), the latent variable y^* satisfies the classical linear model assumptions.

We can write the model in Example 17.1 as in equation (17.2) by defining (in the population) $y = \log(1 + q)$ and $\mathbf{x} = [\mathbf{z}, \log(p)]$. This particular transformation of q, along with the restriction that the coefficient on $\log(p)$ is -1, are products of the specific utility function used in the example. In practice, one might just take $y = q$ and not impose restrictions on the vector $\boldsymbol{\beta}$. In such applications, we must be careful not to put too much emphasis on y^*, which some might view as "desired" or "latent" charitable contributions (which can, evidently, be negative). In corner solution applications, we are interested in y, which would be actual charitable contributions.

17.2 Useful Expressions for Type I Tobit

Because y is a nonlinear function of $\mathbf{x}$ and u, we will want to derive various features of its conditional distribution, $\mathrm{D}(y \mid \mathbf{x})$. Given that assumption (17.3) fully specifies $\mathrm{D}(u \mid \mathbf{x})$, we can fully characterize $\mathrm{D}(y \mid \mathbf{x})$. But before doing so, it is useful to derive general features of the conditional mean and median of y that do not require full distributional assumptions.

First, suppose $\mathrm{E}(u \mid \mathbf{x}) = 0$. Then, because the function $g(z) \equiv \max(0, z)$ is convex, it follows from the conditional Jensen's inequality (see Appendix 2A) that

$$\mathrm{E}(y \mid \mathbf{x}) \geq \max(0, \mathrm{E}(\mathbf{x}\boldsymbol{\beta} + u \mid \mathbf{x})) = \max(0, \mathbf{x}\boldsymbol{\beta}). \tag{17.6}$$

Therefore, although we cannot find $\mathrm{E}(y \mid \mathbf{x})$ without further assumptions, we do have a lower bound as a function of $\mathbf{x}\boldsymbol{\beta}$.

Next, assume that rather than a zero mean, $\mathrm{Med}(u \mid \mathbf{x}) = 0$. Unlike the expected value, the median operator passes through monotonic functions, and the function $g(z)$ is monotically increasing (though not strictly so). Therefore,

$$\mathrm{Med}(y \mid \mathbf{x}) = \max(0, \mathrm{Med}(\mathbf{x}\boldsymbol{\beta} + u \mid \mathbf{x})) = \max(0, \mathbf{x}\boldsymbol{\beta}), \tag{17.7}$$

and so, without any restrictions on $\mathrm{D}(u \mid \mathbf{x})$ other than a zero median (and certainly independence between u and $\mathbf{x}$ is not required), we have $\mathrm{Med}(y \mid \mathbf{x})$ as a known function of $\mathbf{x}\boldsymbol{\beta}$. From equations (17.6) and (17.7), if $\mathrm{D}(u \mid \mathbf{x})$ is symmetric about zero, it follows that $\mathrm{E}(y \mid \mathbf{x}) \geq \mathrm{Med}(y \mid \mathbf{x})$. We will return to expression (17.7) in

Section 17.5.4 as a basis for estimating $\boldsymbol{\beta}$ under the zero conditional median assumption for u.

When u is independent of $\mathbf{x}$ and has a normal distribution, we can find an explicit expression for $\mathrm{E}(y \mid \mathbf{x})$. We first derive $\mathrm{P}(y > 0 \mid \mathbf{x})$ and $\mathrm{E}(y \mid \mathbf{x}, y > 0)$, which are of interest in their own right. Then, we use the law of iterated expectations to obtain $\mathrm{E}(y \mid \mathbf{x})$:

$$\begin{aligned}\mathrm{E}(y \mid \mathbf{x}) &= \mathrm{P}(y = 0 \mid \mathbf{x}) \cdot 0 + \mathrm{P}(y > 0 \mid \mathbf{x}) \cdot \mathrm{E}(y \mid \mathbf{x}, y > 0) \\ &= \mathrm{P}(y > 0 \mid \mathbf{x}) \cdot \mathrm{E}(y \mid \mathbf{x}, y > 0). \qquad (17.8)\end{aligned}$$

Deriving $\mathrm{P}(y > 0 \mid \mathbf{x})$ is easy. Define the binary variable $w = 1$ if $y > 0$, $w = 0$ if $y = 0$. Then w follows a probit model:

$$\begin{aligned}\mathrm{P}(w = 1 \mid \mathbf{x}) &= \mathrm{P}(y^* > 0 \mid \mathbf{x}) = \mathrm{P}(u > -\mathbf{x}\boldsymbol{\beta} \mid \mathbf{x}) \\ &= \mathrm{P}(u/\sigma > -\mathbf{x}\boldsymbol{\beta}/\sigma) = \Phi(\mathbf{x}\boldsymbol{\beta}/\sigma). \qquad (17.9)\end{aligned}$$

One implication of equation (17.9) is that $\boldsymbol{\gamma} \equiv \boldsymbol{\beta}/\sigma$, but not $\boldsymbol{\beta}$ and σ separately, can be consistently estimated from a probit of w on $\mathbf{x}$.

To derive $\mathrm{E}(y \mid \mathbf{x}, y > 0)$, we need the following fact about the normal distribution: if $z \sim \mathrm{Normal}(0, 1)$, then, for any constant c,

$$\mathrm{E}(z \mid z > c) = \frac{\phi(c)}{1 - \Phi(c)},$$

where $\phi(\cdot)$ is the standard normal density function. (This is easily shown by noting that the density of z given $z > c$ is $\phi(z)/[1 - \Phi(c)]$, $z > c$, and then integrating $z\phi(z)$ from c to ∞.) Therefore, if $u \sim \mathrm{Normal}(0, \sigma^2)$, then

$$\mathrm{E}(u \mid u > c) = \sigma \mathrm{E}\left(\frac{u}{\sigma} \,\middle|\, \frac{u}{\sigma} > \frac{c}{\sigma}\right) = \sigma\left[\frac{\phi(c/\sigma)}{1 - \Phi(c/\sigma)}\right].$$

We can use this equation to find $\mathrm{E}(y \mid \mathbf{x}, y > 0)$ when y follows a Tobit model:

$$\mathrm{E}(y \mid \mathbf{x}, y > 0) = \mathbf{x}\boldsymbol{\beta} + \mathrm{E}(u \mid u > -\mathbf{x}\boldsymbol{\beta}) = \mathbf{x}\boldsymbol{\beta} + \sigma\left[\frac{\phi(\mathbf{x}\boldsymbol{\beta}/\sigma)}{\Phi(\mathbf{x}\boldsymbol{\beta}/\sigma)}\right] \qquad (17.10)$$

since $1 - \Phi(-\mathbf{x}\boldsymbol{\beta}/\sigma) = \Phi(\mathbf{x}\boldsymbol{\beta}/\sigma)$. Although it is not obvious from looking at equation (17.10), the right-hand side is positive for any values of $\mathbf{x}$ and $\boldsymbol{\beta}$.

For any c, the quantity $\lambda(c) \equiv \phi(c)/\Phi(c)$ is called the **inverse Mills ratio**. Thus, $\mathrm{E}(y \mid \mathbf{x}, y > 0)$ is the sum of $\mathbf{x}\boldsymbol{\beta}$ and σ times the inverse Mills ratio evaluated at $\mathbf{x}\boldsymbol{\beta}/\sigma$.

If x_j is a continuous explanatory variable, then

$$\frac{\partial \mathrm{E}(y \mid \mathbf{x}, y > 0)}{\partial x_j} = \beta_j + \beta_j \left[\frac{\mathrm{d}\lambda}{\mathrm{d}c} (\mathbf{x}\boldsymbol{\beta}/\sigma) \right]$$

assuming that x_j is not functionally related to other regressors. By differentiating $\lambda(c) = \phi(c)/\Phi(c)$, it can be shown that $\frac{\mathrm{d}\lambda}{\mathrm{d}c}(c) = -\lambda(c)[c + \lambda(c)]$, and therefore

$$\frac{\partial \mathrm{E}(y \mid \mathbf{x}, y > 0)}{\partial x_j} = \beta_j \{1 - \lambda(\mathbf{x}\boldsymbol{\beta}/\sigma)[\mathbf{x}\boldsymbol{\beta}/\sigma + \lambda(\mathbf{x}\boldsymbol{\beta}/\sigma)]\}. \tag{17.11}$$

This equation shows that the partial effect of x_j on $\mathrm{E}(y \mid \mathbf{x}, y > 0)$ is not entirely determined by β_j; there is an adjustment factor multiplying β_j, the term in $\{\cdot\}$, that depends on $\mathbf{x}$ through the index $\mathbf{x}\boldsymbol{\beta}/\sigma$. We can use the fact that if $z \sim \text{Normal}(0, 1)$, then $\mathrm{Var}(z \mid z > -c) = 1 - \lambda(c)[c + \lambda(c)]$ for any $c \in \mathbb{R}$, which implies that the adjustment factor in equation (17.11), call it $\theta(\mathbf{x}\boldsymbol{\beta}/\sigma) = (1 - \lambda(\mathbf{x}\boldsymbol{\beta}/\sigma)[\mathbf{x}\boldsymbol{\beta}/\sigma + \lambda(\mathbf{x}\boldsymbol{\beta}/\sigma)])$, is strictly between zero and one. Therefore, the sign of β_j is the same as the sign of the partial effect of x_j.

Other functional forms are easily handled. Suppose that $x_1 = \log(z_1)$ (and that this is the only place z_1 appears in $\mathbf{x}$). Then

$$\frac{\partial \mathrm{E}(y \mid \mathbf{x}, y > 0)}{\partial z_1} = (\beta_1/z_1)\theta(\mathbf{x}\boldsymbol{\beta}/\sigma), \tag{17.12}$$

where β_1 now denotes the coefficient on $\log(z_1)$. Or, suppose that $x_1 = z_1$ and $x_2 = z_1^2$. Then

$$\frac{\partial \mathrm{E}(y \mid \mathbf{x}, y > 0)}{\partial z_1} = (\beta_1 + 2\beta_2 z_1)\theta(\mathbf{x}\boldsymbol{\beta}/\sigma),$$

where β_1 is the coefficient on z_1 and β_2 is the coefficient on z_1^2. Interaction terms are handled similarly. Generally, we compute the partial effect of $\mathbf{x}\boldsymbol{\beta}$ with respect to the variable of interest and multiply this by the factor $\theta(\mathbf{x}\boldsymbol{\beta}/\sigma)$.

All of the usual economic quantities such as elasticities can be computed. The elasticity of y with respect to x_1, conditional on $y > 0$, is

$$\frac{\partial \mathrm{E}(y \mid \mathbf{x}, y > 0)}{\partial x_1} \cdot \frac{x_1}{\mathrm{E}(y \mid \mathbf{x}, y > 0)} \tag{17.13}$$

and equations (17.11) and (17.10) can be used to find the elasticity when x_1 appears in levels form. If z_1 appears in logarithmic form, the elasticity is obtained simply as $\partial \log \mathrm{E}(y \mid \mathbf{x}, y > 0)/\partial \log(z_1)$.

If x_1 is a binary variable, the effect of interest is obtained as the difference between $\mathrm{E}(y \mid \mathbf{x}, y > 0)$ with $x_1 = 1$ and $x_1 = 0$. Other discrete variables (such as number of children) can be handled similarly.

We can also compute $\mathrm{E}(y \mid \mathbf{x})$ from equation (17.8):

$$\begin{aligned}\mathrm{E}(y \mid \mathbf{x}) &= \mathrm{P}(y > 0 \mid \mathbf{x}) \cdot \mathrm{E}(y \mid \mathbf{x}, y > 0) \\ &= \Phi(\mathbf{x}\boldsymbol{\beta}/\sigma)[\mathbf{x}\boldsymbol{\beta} + \sigma\lambda(\mathbf{x}\boldsymbol{\beta}/\sigma)] = \Phi(\mathbf{x}\boldsymbol{\beta}/\sigma)\mathbf{x}\boldsymbol{\beta} + \sigma\phi(\mathbf{x}\boldsymbol{\beta}/\sigma).\end{aligned} \tag{17.14}$$

We can find the partial derivatives of $\mathrm{E}(y \mid \mathbf{x})$ with respect to continuous x_j using the chain rule. In examples where y is some quantity chosen by individuals (labor supply, charitable contributions, life insurance), this derivative accounts for the fact that some people who start at $y = 0$ may switch to $y > 0$ when x_j changes. Formally,

$$\frac{\partial \mathrm{E}(y \mid \mathbf{x})}{\partial x_j} = \frac{\partial \mathrm{P}(y > 0 \mid \mathbf{x})}{\partial x_j} \cdot \mathrm{E}(y \mid \mathbf{x}, y > 0) + \mathrm{P}(y > 0 \mid \mathbf{x}) \cdot \frac{\partial \mathrm{E}(y \mid \mathbf{x}, y > 0)}{\partial x_j}. \tag{17.15}$$

This decomposition is attributed to McDonald and Moffitt (1980). Because $\mathrm{P}(y > 0 \mid \mathbf{x}) = \Phi(\mathbf{x}\boldsymbol{\beta}/\sigma)$, $\partial \mathrm{P}(y > 0 \mid \mathbf{x})/\partial x_j = (\beta_j/\sigma)\phi(\mathbf{x}\boldsymbol{\beta}/\sigma)$. If we plug this along with equation (17.11) into equation (17.15), we get a remarkable simplification:

$$\frac{\partial \mathrm{E}(y \mid \mathbf{x})}{\partial x_j} = \Phi(\mathbf{x}\boldsymbol{\beta}/\sigma)\beta_j. \tag{17.16}$$

The estimated scale factor for a given $\mathbf{x}$ is $\Phi(\mathbf{x}\hat{\boldsymbol{\beta}}/\hat{\sigma})$. This scale factor has a very interesting interpretation: $\Phi(\mathbf{x}\hat{\boldsymbol{\beta}}/\hat{\sigma}) = \hat{\mathrm{P}}(y > 0 \mid \mathbf{x})$; that is, $\Phi(\mathbf{x}\hat{\boldsymbol{\beta}}/\hat{\sigma})$ is the estimated probability of observing a positive response given $\mathbf{x}$. If $\Phi(\mathbf{x}\hat{\boldsymbol{\beta}}/\hat{\sigma})$ is close to one, then it is unlikely we observe $y_i = 0$ when $\mathbf{x}_i = \mathbf{x}$, and the adjustment factor becomes unimportant. We can evaluate $\Phi(\mathbf{x}\hat{\boldsymbol{\beta}}/\hat{\sigma})$ at interesting values of $\mathbf{x}$ to determine how the estimated partial effects change as the covariates change. One possibility is to plug in mean values, although this need not correspond to any particular population unit when $\mathbf{x}$ contains discrete elements (and even sometimes when $\mathbf{x}$ contains all continuous elements). We can use median values, or plug in various quantiles. Often it is useful to have a single scale factor, and the scale factor that delivers APEs is probably the most useful. The APE for a continuous variable x_j is estimated as

$$\left[N^{-1}\sum_{i=1}^{N}\Phi(\mathbf{x}_i\hat{\boldsymbol{\beta}}/\hat{\sigma})\right]\hat{\beta}_j. \tag{17.17}$$

The scale factor in equation (17.17) is the average of $\hat{\mathrm{P}}(y > 0 \mid \mathbf{x})$ across the sample. The delta method can be used to obtain a valid asymptotic standard error for (17.17), but the bootstrap is convenient and feasible because estimation of Tobit models can be done fairly quickly.

Naturally, the scale factor in (17.17) is always between zero and one, and that fact helps explain why Tobit coefficients are typically larger than OLS coefficients from a linear regression. If $\hat{\gamma}_j$ is the OLS estimate on a continuous variable x_j from the regression y_i on $\mathbf{x}_i$, we can compare $\hat{\gamma}_j$ to (17.17) as an indication of whether the linear model gives similar estimates of the APEs. Sometimes it will, but in other cases the linear model APEs can be notably different from the Tobit APEs.

For discrete explanatory variables or for large changes in continuous ones, we can compute the difference in $\mathrm{E}(y \mid \mathbf{x})$ at different values of $\mathbf{x}$. For example, suppose x_K is a binary variable (such as a policy indicator), and define, for each observation i, the two indices $\hat{w}_{i1} = \mathbf{x}_{i(K)}\hat{\boldsymbol{\beta}}_{(K)} + \hat{\beta}_K$ and $\hat{w}_{i0} = \mathbf{x}_{i(K)}\hat{\boldsymbol{\beta}}_{(K)}$, where $\mathbf{x}_{i(K)}$ is the $1 \times (K-1)$ row vector with x_{iK} dropped. Then $\hat{w}_{i1}$ is the estimated index for person i when $x_K = 1$ and $\hat{w}_{i0}$ is the estimated index for person i when $x_K = 0$. (One of these is a counterfactual because x_{iK} is either zero or one for each i.) Then the average difference

$$N^{-1}\sum_{i=1}^{N}\{[\Phi(\hat{w}_{i1}/\hat{\sigma})\hat{w}_{i1} + \hat{\sigma}\phi(\hat{w}_{i1}/\hat{\sigma})] - [\Phi(\hat{w}_{i0}/\hat{\sigma})\hat{w}_{i0} + \hat{\sigma}\phi(\hat{w}_{i0}/\hat{\sigma})]\} \tag{17.18}$$

is the estimated APE of the binary variable x_K. Again, bootstrapping is a convenient method of computing a standard error.

The equations for the partial effects in the type I Tobit model, equations (17.11) and (17.16), and the estimates in (17.17) and (17.18) reveal an important point about the parameters: σ as well as $\boldsymbol{\beta}$ appears in the partial effects. In other words, if we can only estimate $\boldsymbol{\beta}$, we cannot estimate the partial effects of the covariates on $\mathrm{E}(y \mid \mathbf{x}, y > 0)$ and $\mathrm{E}(y \mid \mathbf{x})$. Therefore, treatments of the type I Tobit for corner solutions that refer to σ as "ancillary"—of secondary importance—are misleading. In a linear model, of course, the variance of the errors plays no role in obtaining partial effects on the mean, and so the estimated error variance plays a role only in obtaining the usual OLS standard errors. But the variance of u in equation (17.2) directly enters the conditional means, and so we should not think of σ as ancillary when our interest is in partial effects on the mean. (As we will see in Chapter 20, in true data censoring contexts we are interested in $\boldsymbol{\beta}$, and σ becomes ancillary to estimating partial effects.)

Equations (17.9), (17.11), and (17.14) show that, for continuous variables x_j and x_h, the *relative* partial effects on $\mathrm{P}(y > 0 \mid \mathbf{x})$, $\mathrm{E}(y \mid \mathbf{x}, y > 0)$, and $\mathrm{E}(y \mid \mathbf{x})$ are all equal to β_j/β_h (assuming that $\beta_h \neq 0$). This feature can be a limitation of the Tobit model, and we will study models that relax this implication in Section 17.6.

By taking the log of equation (17.8) and differentiating, we see that the elasticity (or semielasticity) of $E(y \mid \mathbf{x})$ with respect to any x_j is simply the sum of the elasticities (or semielasticities) of $\Phi(\mathbf{x}\boldsymbol{\beta}/\sigma)$ and $E(y \mid \mathbf{x}, y > 0)$, each with respect to x_j.

17.3 Estimation and Inference with the Type I Tobit Model

Let $\{(\mathbf{x}_i, y_i) : i = 1, 2, \ldots N\}$ be a random sample following the censored Tobit model. To use maximum likelihood, we need to derive the density of y_i given $\mathbf{x}_i$. We have already shown that $f(0 \mid \mathbf{x}_i) = P(y_i = 0 \mid \mathbf{x}_i) = 1 - \Phi(\mathbf{x}_i\boldsymbol{\beta}/\sigma)$. Further, for $\mathscr{y} > 0$, $P(y_i \leq \mathscr{y} \mid \mathbf{x}_i) = P(y_i^* \leq \mathscr{y} \mid \mathbf{x}_i)$, which implies that

$$f(\mathscr{y} \mid \mathbf{x}_i) = f^*(\mathscr{y} \mid \mathbf{x}_i), \qquad \text{all } \mathscr{y} > 0,$$

where $f^*(\cdot \mid \mathbf{x}_i)$ denotes the density of y_i^* given $\mathbf{x}_i$. (We use $\mathscr{y}$ as the dummy argument in the density.) By assumption, $y_i^* \mid \mathbf{x}_i \sim \text{Normal}(\mathbf{x}_i\boldsymbol{\beta}, \sigma^2)$, so

$$f^*(\mathscr{y} \mid \mathbf{x}_i) = \frac{1}{\sigma}\phi[(\mathscr{y} - \mathbf{x}_i\boldsymbol{\beta})/\sigma], \qquad -\infty < \mathscr{y} < \infty.$$

(As in recent chapters, we will use $\boldsymbol{\beta}$ and σ^2 to denote the true values as well as dummy arguments in the log-likelihood function and its derivatives.) We can write the density for y_i given $\mathbf{x}_i$ compactly using the indicator function $1[\cdot]$ as

$$f(\mathscr{y} \mid \mathbf{x}_i) = \{1 - \Phi(\mathbf{x}_i\boldsymbol{\beta}/\sigma)\}^{1[\mathscr{y}=0]}\{(1/\sigma)\phi[(\mathscr{y} - \mathbf{x}_i\boldsymbol{\beta})/\sigma]\}^{1[\mathscr{y}>0]}, \tag{17.19}$$

where the density is zero for $\mathscr{y} < 0$. Let $\boldsymbol{\theta} \equiv (\boldsymbol{\beta}', \sigma^2)'$ denote the $(K+1) \times 1$ vector of parameters. The log likelihood is

$$\ell_i(\boldsymbol{\theta}) = 1[y_i = 0] \log[1 - \Phi(\mathbf{x}_i\boldsymbol{\beta}/\sigma)] + 1[y_i > 0]\{\log \phi[(y_i - \mathbf{x}_i\boldsymbol{\beta})/\sigma] - \log(\sigma^2)/2\}. \tag{17.20}$$

Apart from a constant that does not affect the maximization, equation (17.20) can be written as

$$1[y_i = 0] \log[1 - \Phi(\mathbf{x}_i\boldsymbol{\beta}/\sigma)] - 1[y_i > 0]\{(y_i - \mathbf{x}_i\boldsymbol{\beta})^2/2\sigma^2 + \log(\sigma^2)/2\}.$$

Therefore,

$$\partial\ell_i(\boldsymbol{\theta})/\partial\boldsymbol{\beta} = -1[y_i = 0]\phi(\mathbf{x}_i\boldsymbol{\beta}/\sigma)(\mathbf{x}_i/\sigma)[1 - \Phi(\mathbf{x}_i\boldsymbol{\beta}/\sigma)] + 1[y_i > 0](y_i - \mathbf{x}_i\boldsymbol{\beta})\mathbf{x}_i/\sigma^2 \tag{17.21}$$

$$\begin{aligned}\partial\ell_i(\boldsymbol{\theta})/\partial\sigma^2 = {}& 1[y_i = 0]\phi(\mathbf{x}_i\boldsymbol{\beta}/\sigma)(\mathbf{x}_i\boldsymbol{\beta})/\{2\sigma^3[1 - \Phi(\mathbf{x}_i\boldsymbol{\beta}/\sigma)]\} \\ & + 1[y_i > 0]\{(y_i - \mathbf{x}_i\boldsymbol{\beta})^2/(2\sigma^4) - 1/(2\sigma^2)\}.\end{aligned} \tag{17.22}$$

The second derivatives are complicated, but all we need is $\mathbf{A}(\mathbf{x}_i, \boldsymbol{\theta}) \equiv -\mathrm{E}[\mathbf{H}_i(\boldsymbol{\theta}) \mid \mathbf{x}_i]$. After tedious calculations it can be shown that

$$\mathbf{A}(\mathbf{x}_i, \boldsymbol{\theta}) = \begin{bmatrix} a_i \mathbf{x}_i' \mathbf{x}_i & b_i \mathbf{x}_i' \\ b_i \mathbf{x}_i & c_i \end{bmatrix}, \tag{17.23}$$

where

$$a_i = -\sigma^{-2}\{\mathbf{x}_i\gamma\phi_i - [\phi_i^2/(1-\Phi_i)] - \Phi_i\},$$

$$b_i = \sigma^{-3}\{(\mathbf{x}_i\gamma)^2\phi_i + \phi_i - [(\mathbf{x}_i\gamma)\phi_i^2/(1-\Phi_i)]\}/2,$$

$$c_i = -\sigma^{-4}\{(\mathbf{x}_i\gamma)^3\phi_i + (\mathbf{x}_i\gamma)\phi_i - [(\mathbf{x}_i\gamma)\phi_i^2/(1-\Phi_i)] - 2\Phi_i\}/4,$$

$\gamma = \boldsymbol{\beta}/\sigma$, and ϕ_i and Φ_i are evaluated at $\mathbf{x}_i\gamma$. This matrix is used in equation (13.32) to obtain the estimate of $\mathrm{Avar}(\hat{\boldsymbol{\theta}})$. See Amemiya (1973) for details.

Testing is easily carried out in a standard maximum likelihood estimator (MLE) framework. Single exclusion restrictions are tested using asymptotic t statistics once $\hat{\beta}_j$ and its asymptotic standard error have been obtained. Multiple exclusion restrictions are easily tested using the likelihood ratio (LR) statistic, and some econometrics packages routinely compute the Wald statistic. If the unrestricted model has so many variables that computation becomes an issue, the lagrange multiplier (LM) statistic is an attractive alternative.

The Wald statistic is the easiest to compute for testing nonlinear restrictions on $\boldsymbol{\beta}$, just as in binary response analysis, because the unrestricted model is just standard Tobit.

17.4 Reporting the Results

As with any estimation of a parametric model, the parameter estimates $\hat{\boldsymbol{\beta}}$ and $\hat{\sigma}$ and their standard errors should be reported. We saw in Section 17.2 that the $\hat{\beta}_j$ give the direction of the partial effects on the means, and the ratios are the relative partial effects for continuous variables. The value of the log likelihood should be included for testing purposes and also to allow comparisons with other nonnested models. A goodness-of-fit statistic for the conditional mean $\mathrm{E}(y \mid \mathbf{x})$ is often of interest, particularly for comparing with other models of $\mathrm{E}(y \mid \mathbf{x})$ (including linear models). A simple measure is the squared correlation between the actual outcomes, y_i, and fitted values, $\hat{y}_i$, obtained by evaluating equation (17.14) at $\mathbf{x}_i$ and the MLEs, $\hat{\boldsymbol{\beta}}$ and $\hat{\sigma}$.

It is also important to report partial effects. For continuous variables we can use (17.17) and for binary variables we can use (17.18). For discrete variables that are not

Table 17.1
OLS and Tobit Estimation of Annual Hours Worked

Dependent Variable: *hours*		
Independent Variable	Linear (OLS)	Tobit (MLE)
nwifeinc	−3.45 (2.54)	−8.81 (4.46)
educ	28.76 (12.95)	80.65 (21.58)
exper	65.67 (9.96)	131.56 (17.28)
$exper^2$	−.700 (.325)	−1.86 (0.54)
age	−30.51 (4.36)	−54.41 (7.42)
kidslt6	−442.09 (58.85)	−894.02 (111.88)
kidsge6	−32.78 (23.18)	−16.22 (38.64)
constant	1,330.48 (270.78)	965.31 (446.44)
Log-likelihood value	—	−3,819.09
R-squared	.266	.275
$\hat{\sigma}$	750.18	1,122.02

binary it is less obvious how to report a single APE. For key explanatory variables, one might want to evaluate partial effects at a range of values, and then average out across the other explanatory variables. Or, we can evaluate partial effects with each covariate evaluated at its mean or its median, or other quantiles of interest.

Example 17.2 (Annual Hours Equation for Married Women): We use the Mroz (1987) data (MROZ.RAW) to estimate a reduced form annual hours equation for married women. The equation is a reduced form because we do not include hourly wage offer as an explanatory variable. The hourly wage offer is unlikely to be exogenous, and, just as important, we cannot observe it when $hours = 0$. We will show how to deal with both these issues in Chapter 19. For now, the explanatory variables are the same ones appearing in the labor force participation probit in Example 15.2.

Of the 753 women in the sample, 428 worked for a wage outside the home during the year; 325 of the women worked zero hours. For the women who worked positive hours, the range is fairly broad, ranging from 12 to 4,950. Thus, annual hours worked is a reasonable candidate for a Tobit model. We also estimate a linear model (using all 753 observations) by OLS. The results are given in Table 17.1.

Not surprisingly, the Tobit coefficient estimates are the same sign as the corresponding OLS estimates, and the statistical significance of the estimates is similar. (Possible exceptions are the coefficients on *nwifeinc* and *kidsge6*, but the t statistics have similar magnitudes.) Second, though it is tempting to compare the magnitudes of the OLS estimates and the Tobit estimates, such comparisons are not very informative. We must not think that, because the Tobit coefficient on *kidslt6* is roughly twice that of the OLS coefficient, the Tobit model somehow implies a much greater response of hours worked to young children.

The scale factor computed in equation (17.17) is about .589, and we can multiply this by the Tobit coefficients—at least on the roughly continuous variables—to obtain estimated APEs. For example, the APE for *educ* is about $.589(80.65) = 47.5$, and a bootstrap standard error based on 500 replications is about 13. The Tobit estimated APE is well above the comparable OLS estimate, 28.8, and just as precisely estimated.

For the discrete variable *kidslt*6, if we use the calculus definition of an APE, the Tobit APE is about -526.68, which again is much larger in magnitude than the OLS coefficient (-442.1). However, if we compute the difference in estimated expected values at $kidslt6 = 1$ and $kidslt6 = 0$, and average these differences, the result is about -487.2 (bootstrap standard error $= 54$), and this is more in line with the OLS estimate (but still larger in magnitude). The APE in moving from one small child to two small children is about -246.2 (bootstrap standard error $= 12.3$): not surprisingly, the effect on expected hours of having a second young child is less than having a first young child. It makes sense that the OLS estimate is between these two values yet closer to the first partial effect: 118 women in the sample have one small child and only 29 have two or more. If we compute a weighted average of the two APEs, the result is about -439, which is quite close to the OLS estimate and, in some sense, verifies that in some cases OLS can provide a good estimate of APEs, even for a discrete explanatory variable. Interestingly, the APE computed from the Tobit model based on the approximation that *kidslt*6 is continuous is actually worse than the OLS estimate.

We can also evaluate the partial effects at the average values of the covariates, where we plug $\overline{exper}$ into the quadratic rather than using the average of $exper_i^2$. The scale factor evaluated at the means is about .645, which implies partial effects even larger than the APEs. In other words, the PAEs are much larger than the APEs.

We can also compute the partial effects on $\mathrm{E}(y \mid \mathbf{x}, y > 0)$. Again, plugging in the mean values of the explanatory variables, the scale factor in equation (17.11) is about .451, and this number can be multiplied by coefficients to obtain the estimated change in expected hours conditional on hours being positive.

We have reported an R-squared for both the linear regression model and the Tobit model. The R-squared for OLS is the usual one. For Tobit, the R-squared is the square of the correlation coefficient between y_i and $\hat{y}_i$, where $\hat{y}_i = \Phi(\mathbf{x}_i\hat{\boldsymbol{\beta}}/\hat{\sigma})\mathbf{x}_i\hat{\boldsymbol{\beta}} + \hat{\sigma}\phi(\mathbf{x}_i\hat{\boldsymbol{\beta}}/\hat{\sigma})$ is the estimate of $\mathrm{E}(y \mid \mathbf{x} = \mathbf{x}_i)$. This statistic is motivated by the fact that the usual R-squared for OLS is equal to the squared correlation between the y_i and the OLS fitted values.

Based on the R-squared measures, the Tobit conditional mean function fits the hours data somewhat better, although the difference is not overwhelming. However, we should remember that the Tobit estimates are not chosen to maximize an R-squared—they maximize the log-likelihood function—whereas the OLS estimates produce the highest R-squared given the linear functional form for the conditional mean.

When two additional variables, the local unemployment rate and a binary city indicator, are included, the log likelihood becomes about $-3{,}817.89$. The likelihood ratio statistic is about $2(3{,}819.09 - 3{,}817.89) = 2.40$. This is the outcome of a χ^2_2 variate under H_0, and so the p-value is about .30. Therefore, these two variables are jointly insignificant.

17.5 Specification Issues in Tobit Models

17.5.1 Neglected Heterogeneity

Suppose that we are initially interested in the model

$$y = \max(0, \mathbf{x}\boldsymbol{\beta} + \gamma q + u), \qquad u \mid \mathbf{x}, q \sim \mathrm{Normal}(0, \sigma^2), \tag{17.24}$$

where q is an unobserved variable that is assumed to be independent of $\mathbf{x}$ and has a $\mathrm{Normal}(0, \tau^2)$ distribution. It follows immediately that

$$y = \max(0, \mathbf{x}\boldsymbol{\beta} + v), \qquad v \mid \mathbf{x} \sim \mathrm{Normal}(0, \sigma^2 + \gamma^2\tau^2) \tag{17.25}$$

Thus, y conditional on $\mathbf{x}$ follows a Tobit model, and Tobit of y on $\mathbf{x}$ consistently estimates $\boldsymbol{\beta}$ and $\eta^2 \equiv \sigma^2 + \gamma^2\tau^2$.

What about estimating partial effects on $\mathrm{E}(y \mid \mathbf{x}, q)$? As we discussed in Sections 2.2.5 and 15.7.1, we are often interested in the APEs, where, say, $\mathrm{E}(y \mid \mathbf{x}, q)$ is averaged over the population distribution of q, and then derivatives or differences with respect to elements of $\mathbf{x}$ are obtained. From Section 2.2.5 we know that when the heterogeneity is independent of $\mathbf{x}$, the APEs are obtained by finding $\mathrm{E}(y \mid \mathbf{x})$. Naturally, this conditional mean comes from the distribution of y given $\mathbf{x}$. Under the preceding assumptions, it is exactly this distribution that Tobit of y on $\mathbf{x}$ estimates. In other words, we estimate the desired quantities—the APEs—by simply ignoring the heterogeneity. This is the same conclusion we reached for the probit model in Section 15.7.1.

If q is not normal, then these arguments do not carry over because y given $\mathbf{x}$ does not follow a Tobit model. But the flavor of the argument does. A more difficult issue arises when q and $\mathbf{x}$ are correlated, and we address that in the next subsection.

We can also ask what happens if, rather than having heterogeneity appear additively inside the index, as in equation (17.24), the heterogeneity appears multiplicatively: $y = q \cdot \max(0, \mathbf{x}\boldsymbol{\beta} + u)$, where $q \geq 0$ and we assume q is independent of $(\mathbf{x}, u)$. The distribution $\mathrm{D}(y \mid \mathbf{x})$ now depends on the distribution of q, and does not follow a type I Tobit model; generally, finding its distribution would be difficult, even if we specify a simple distribution for q. Nevertheless, if we normalize $\mathrm{E}(q) = 1$, then $\mathrm{E}(y \mid \mathbf{x}, u) = \mathrm{E}(q \mid \mathbf{x}, u) \cdot \max(0, \mathbf{x}\boldsymbol{\beta} + u) = \max(0, \mathbf{x}\boldsymbol{\beta} + u)$ (because $\mathrm{E}(q \mid \mathbf{x}, u) = 1$). It follows immediately from iterated expectations that if assumption (17.3) holds, then $\mathrm{E}(y \mid \mathbf{x})$ has exactly the same form as the type I Tobit model in equation (17.14). That equation (17.14) holds for an extension of the Tobit model means that it makes sense to estimate $\mathrm{E}(y \mid \mathbf{x}) = \Phi(\mathbf{x}\boldsymbol{\beta}/\sigma)\mathbf{x}\boldsymbol{\beta} + \sigma\phi(\mathbf{x}\boldsymbol{\beta}/\sigma)$ by NLS, or a weighted NLS procedure (or a quasi-MLE, which we discuss in Chapter 18). NLS and WNLS approaches are consistent under (17.14) even though $\mathrm{D}(y \mid \mathbf{x})$ does not follow the type I Tobit distribution.

17.5.2 Endogenous Explanatory Variables

Suppose we now allow one of the variables in the Tobit model to be endogenous. The first model we consider has a continuous endogenous explanatory variable:

$$y_1 = \max(0, \mathbf{z}_1\boldsymbol{\delta}_1 + \alpha_1 y_2 + u_1), \tag{17.26}$$

$$y_2 = \mathbf{z}\boldsymbol{\delta}_2 + v_2 = \mathbf{z}_1\boldsymbol{\delta}_{21} + \mathbf{z}_2\boldsymbol{\delta}_{22} + v_2, \tag{17.27}$$

where (u_1, v_2) are zero-mean normally distributed, independent of $\mathbf{z}$. If u_1 and v_2 are correlated, then y_2 is endogenous. For identification we need the usual rank condition $\boldsymbol{\delta}_{22} \neq \mathbf{0}$; $\mathrm{E}(\mathbf{z}'\mathbf{z})$ is assumed to have full rank, as always.

Naturally, we are interested in estimating $\boldsymbol{\delta}_1$ and α_1, but we are also interested in estimating APEs, which depend on $\sigma_1^2 = \mathrm{Var}(u_1)$. The reasoning is just as for the probit model in Section 15.7.2. Holding other factors fixed, the difference in y_1 when y_2 changes from $\bar{y}_2$ to $\bar{y}_2 + 1$ is

$$\max[0, \bar{\mathbf{z}}_1\boldsymbol{\delta}_1 + \alpha_1(\bar{y}_2 + 1) + u_1] - \max[0, \bar{\mathbf{z}}_1\boldsymbol{\delta}_1 + \alpha_1\bar{y}_2 + u_1].$$

Averaging this expression across the distribution of u_1 gives differences in expectations that have the form (17.14), with $\mathbf{x} = [\bar{\mathbf{z}}_1, (\bar{y}_2 + 1)]$ in the first case, $\mathbf{x} = (\bar{\mathbf{z}}_1, \bar{y}_2)$ in the second, and $\sigma = \sigma_1$.

Before estimating this model by MLE, a procedure that requires obtaining the distribution of (y_1, y_2) given $\mathbf{z}$, it is convenient to have a two-step procedure that also delivers a simple test for the endogeneity of y_2. Smith and Blundell (1986) propose a two-step procedure that is analogous to the Rivers-Vuong method (see Section 15.7.2) for binary response models. Under bivariate normality of (u_1, v_2), we can write

$$u_1 = \theta_1 v_2 + e_1, \tag{17.28}$$

where $\theta_1 = \eta_1/\tau_2^2$, $\eta_1 = \text{Cov}(u_1, v_2)$, $\tau_2^2 = \text{Var}(v_2)$, and e_1 is independent of v_2 with a zero-mean normal distribution and variance, say, τ_1^2. Further, because (u_1, v_2) is independent of $\mathbf{z}$, e_1 is independent of $(\mathbf{z}, v_2)$. Now, plugging equation (17.28) into equation (17.26) gives

$$y_1 = \max(0, \mathbf{z}_1\boldsymbol{\delta}_1 + \alpha_1 y_2 + \theta_1 v_2 + e_1), \tag{17.29}$$

where $e_1 \mid \mathbf{z}, v_2 \sim \text{Normal}(0, \tau_1^2)$. Using our previous notation, we can write $\text{D}(y_1 \mid \mathbf{z}, y_2) =$

$$\text{Tobit}(\mathbf{z}_1\boldsymbol{\delta}_1 + \alpha_1 y_2 + \theta_1(y_2 - \mathbf{z}\boldsymbol{\delta}_2), \tau_1^2) = \text{Tobit}(\mathbf{z}_1\boldsymbol{\delta}_1 + \alpha_1 y_2 + \theta_1 v_2, \tau_1^2).$$

It follows that, if we knew v_2, we would just estimate $\boldsymbol{\delta}_1$, α_1, θ_1, and τ_1^2 by type I Tobit. We do not observe v_2 because it depends on the unknown vector $\boldsymbol{\delta}_2$. However, we can easily estimate $\boldsymbol{\delta}_2$ by OLS in a first stage. The Smith-Blundell procedure is as follows:

Procedure 17.1: (a) Estimate the reduced form of y_2 by OLS; this step gives $\hat{\boldsymbol{\delta}}_2$. Define the reduced-form OLS residuals as $\hat{v}_2 = y_2 - \mathbf{z}\hat{\boldsymbol{\delta}}_2$.

(b) Estimate a standard Tobit of y_1 on $\mathbf{z}_1$, y_2, and $\hat{v}_2$. This step gives consistent estimators of $\boldsymbol{\delta}_1$, α_1, θ_1, and τ_1^2.

The usual t statistic on $\hat{v}_2$ reported by Tobit provides a simple test of the null $\text{H}_0: \theta_1 = 0$, which says that y_2 is exogenous. Further, under $\theta_1 = 0$, $e_1 = u_1$, and so normality of v_2 plays no role: as a *test* for endogeneity of y_2, the Smith-Blundell approach is valid without any distributional assumptions on the reduced form of y_2.

Example 17.3 (Testing Exogeneity of Other Income in the Hours Equation): As an illustration, we test for endogeneity of *nwifeinc* in the reduced-form hours equation in Example 17.2. We assume that *huseduc* is exogenous in the hours equation, and so *huseduc* is a valid instrument for *nwifeinc*. We first obtain $\hat{v}_2$ as the OLS residuals from estimating the reduced form for *nwifeinc*. When $\hat{v}_2$ is added to the Tobit model in Example 17.2 (without *unem* and *city*), its coefficient is 24.42 with t statistic =

1.47. Thus, there is marginal evidence that *nwifeinc* is endogenous in the equation. The test is valid under the null hypothesis that *nwifeinc* is exogenous even if *nwifeinc* does not have a conditional normal distribution.

When $\theta_1 \neq 0$, the second-stage Tobit standard errors and test statistics are not asymptotically valid because $\hat{\boldsymbol{\delta}}_2$ has been used in place of $\boldsymbol{\delta}_2$. Smith and Blundell (1986) contain formulas for correcting the asymptotic variances; these can be derived using the formulas for two-step M-estimators in Chapter 12. Alternatively, it is easy to program the two-step procedure in a bootstrap resampling scheme, and the computational time should be reasonable even for larger data sets.

It is easily seen that joint normality of (u_1, v_2) is not necessary for the two-step estimator to consistently estimate the parameters. It suffiices that u_1 conditional on $(\mathbf{z}, v_2)$ is distributed as Normal$(\theta_1 v_2, \tau_1^2)$. Still, this is a fairly restrictive assumption that cannot be expected to hold when v_2 is discrete or partially discrete.

We can recover an estimate σ_1^2 from the estimates obtained from the two-step control function procedure. From equation (17.27) we have $\sigma_1^2 = \theta_1^2\tau_2^2 + \tau_1^2$, and $\hat{\tau}_2^2$ is obtained as the usual estimated error variance from the first-stage regression, whereas $\hat{\theta}_1$ and $\hat{\tau}_1^2$ are obtained from the second-stage Tobit. Forming $\hat{\sigma}_1^2 = \hat{\theta}_1^2\hat{\tau}_2^2 + \hat{\tau}_1^2$ gives us all the estimates we need to obtain the APEs. Generally, it is useful to define the function

$$m(a, \sigma^2) \equiv \Phi(a/\sigma)z + \sigma\phi(a/\sigma). \tag{17.30}$$

Using this notation, the estimated partial effects can be obtained by computing derivatives or differences of $m(\mathbf{z}_1\hat{\boldsymbol{\delta}}_1 + \hat{\alpha}_1 y_2, \hat{\sigma}_1^2)$ with respect to elements of $(\mathbf{z}_1, y_2)$, just as we did in the case of exogenous explanatory variables.

As with all control function procedures, we can easily allow more general functional forms in both the exogenous and endogenous variables (such as squares and interactions). In fact, if we replace $\mathbf{x}_1 = (\mathbf{z}_1, y_2)$ with $\mathbf{x}_1 = \mathbf{g}_1(\mathbf{z}_1, y_2)$, then the estimation procedure is unchanged. Of course, we must believe that y_2 has the reduced form in (17.27) with the error term having the properties already described. Some additional flexibility is gained by allowing $\mathrm{E}(u_1 \mid v_2)$ to be nonlinear—for example, a quadratic function, $\mathrm{E}(u_1 \mid v_2) = \theta_1 v_2 + \psi_1(v_2^2 - \tau_2^2)$ (where the variance of v_2 is subtracted from v_2^2 to ensure $\mathrm{E}(u_1) = 0$)—and then the second step of the procedure adds $\hat{v}_2$ and $\hat{v}_2^2 - \hat{\tau}_2^2$ as the control functions. The easiest way to obtain APEs in this case is to use derivatives and changes with respect to elements of $\mathbf{x}_1$ of

$$N^{-1}\sum_{i=1}^{N} m(\mathbf{x}_1\hat{\boldsymbol{\beta}}_1 + \hat{\theta}_1\hat{v}_{i2} + \hat{\psi}_1(\hat{v}_{i2}^2 - \hat{\tau}_2^2), \hat{\tau}_1^2), \tag{17.31}$$

where $m(a, \sigma)$ is defined in (17.30); that is, we average out the reduced form residuals, $\hat{v}_{i2}$. Of course, (17.31) can be used in the case where $E(u_1 \mid v_2)$ is linear in v_2 and $\mathbf{x}_1 = (\mathbf{z}_1, y_2)$, but it does not exploit the full distributional assumptions.

In extending the usual model by allowing $E(u_1 \mid v_2)$ to be a nonlinear function of v_2, one should be aware that u_1 will likely not have a normal distribution. Practically, we may be as satisfied with a conditional normal distribution for $D(u_1 \mid v_2)$, even if that implies nonnormality of $D(u_1)$.

A full maximum likelihood approach avoids the two-step estimation problem. The joint distribution of (y_1, y_2) given $\mathbf{z}$ is most easily found by using

$$f(y_1, y_2 \mid \mathbf{z}) = f(y_1 \mid y_2, \mathbf{z}) f(y_2 \mid \mathbf{z}) \tag{17.32}$$

just as for the probit case in Section 15.7.2. The density $f(y_2 \mid \mathbf{z})$ is $\text{Normal}(\mathbf{z}\boldsymbol{\delta}_2, \tau_2^2)$. We already know that $D(y_1 \mid \mathbf{z}, y_2) = \text{Tobit}(\mathbf{x}_1\boldsymbol{\beta}_1 + \theta(y_2 - \mathbf{z}\boldsymbol{\delta}_2), \tau_1^2)$, where $\tau_1^2 = \sigma_1^2 - (\eta_1^2/\tau_2^2)$, $\sigma_1^2 = \text{Var}(u_1)$, $\tau_2^2 = \text{Var}(v_2)$, and $\eta_1 = \text{Cov}(v_2, u_1)$. (As in the two-step estimation framework, we can allow $E(u_1 \mid v_2)$ to be a more flexible function of v_2, subject to the caveat that we are implicitly using a nonnormal unconditional distribution for u_1.) Taking the log of equation (17.32), the log-likelihood function for each i is easily constructed as a function of the parameters $(\boldsymbol{\delta}_1, \alpha_1, \boldsymbol{\delta}_2, \sigma_1^2, \tau_2^2, \eta_1)$. The usual conditional maximum likelihood theory can be used for constructing standard errors and test statistics. When the structural equation is just identified, the two-step and MLE estimates are identical (although the two-step inference needs to be adjusted).

Once the MLE has been obtained, we can easily test the null hypothesis of exogeneity of y_2 by using the t statistic for $\hat{\theta}_1$. Because the MLE can be computationally more difficult than the Smith-Blundell procedure, it makes sense to use the Smith-Blundell procedure to test for endogeneity before obtaining the MLE.

If y_2 is a binary variable, then the Smith-Blundell assumptions cannot be expected to hold. Taking equation (17.26) as the structural equation, we could add

$$y_2 = 1[\mathbf{z}\boldsymbol{\pi}_2 + v_2 > 0] \tag{17.33}$$

and assume that (u_1, v_2) has a zero-mean normal distribution and is independent of $\mathbf{z}$; v_2 is standard normal, as always. Equation (17.32) can be used to obtain the log likelihood for each i. Since y_2 given $\mathbf{z}$ is probit, its density is easy to obtain: $f(y_2 \mid \mathbf{z}) = \Phi(\mathbf{z}\boldsymbol{\pi}_2)^{y_2}[1 - \Phi(\mathbf{z}\boldsymbol{\pi}_2)]^{1-y_2}$. The hard part is obtaining the conditional density $f(y_1 \mid y_2, \mathbf{z})$, which is done first for $y_2 = 0$ and then for $y_2 = 1$; see Problem 17.6. Unfortunately, as in the probit case (and nonlinear models generally), the simple strategy of replacing the binary variable y_2, with its fitted value from a probit (or logit, or linear probability model) does not work; it is another example of a forbidden regression. In particular, the distribution of y_1 given $\mathbf{z}$ does not follow a $\text{Tobit}(\mathbf{z}_1\boldsymbol{\delta}_1 + \theta_1\Phi(\mathbf{z}\boldsymbol{\pi}_2), \kappa_1^2)$ model for any variance parameter κ_1^2. Generally, $\mathrm{D}(y_1 \mid \mathbf{z})$ is difficult to characterize, although we could properly use it in a two-step procedure. But better than that, we can obtain $\mathrm{D}(y_1 \mid y_2, \mathbf{z})$ and use it along with a probit specification for $\mathrm{D}(y_2 \mid \mathbf{z})$ to perform joint maximum likelihood estimation.

If y_2 is itself a corner solution and follows a $\text{Tobit}(\mathbf{z}\boldsymbol{\pi}_2, \kappa_2^2)$ model, then the MLE can also be derived. But again, we should not replace y_2 with the estimated expected value $\mathrm{E}(y_2 \mid \mathbf{z})$ obtained from a first-stage Tobit. Such a procedure does not produce consistent estimates and may be very badly biased.

Because properly accounting for endogenous explanatory variables that have nonnormal conditional distributions in Tobit models is challenging, one still sees linear models used when y_1 is a corner, and then standard IV methods, such as 2SLS, can be applied regardless of the nature of y_2. As with binary responses, the linear model has been much maligned for corner solution responses, but a linear model estimated by 2SLS can deliver good estimates of average effects. One of the inappropriate two-step approaches described previously, where fitted probit or Tobit estimates are inserted into a second-stage Tobit, is likely inferior to a linear model that has been properly estimated by instrumental variables. An interesting topic is to find control function methods that can be used for general y_2 that do not suffer from a forbidden regression problem.

The Smith-Blundell control function method extends immediately to more than one endogenous explanatory variables, provided we have sufficient instruments and a vector of reduced form errors $\mathbf{v}_2$ such that $\mathrm{D}(u_1 \mid \mathbf{z}, \mathbf{v}_2) = \mathrm{D}(u_1 \mid \mathbf{v}_2)$, where the latter is homoskedastic normal with linear mean. For example, we might assume $h_g(y_{2g}) = \mathbf{z}\boldsymbol{\pi}_{2g} + v_{2g}$ for a strictly monotonic function $h_g(\cdot)$ for $g = 1, \ldots, G_1$, where G_1 is the number of endogenous explanatory variables. Then $\mathbf{x}_1 = \mathbf{g}_1(\mathbf{z}_1, \mathbf{y}_2)$ is the set of explanatory variables, and we can add the vector of reduced form residuals, obtained from G_1 regressions $h_g(y_{2g})$ on $\mathbf{z}$, to a standard Tobit model in the second stage. See Problem 17.9 for ways to allow more flexibility in $\mathrm{D}(u_1 \mid \mathbf{z}, \mathbf{v}_2)$.

17.5.3 Heteroskedasticity and Nonnormality in the Latent Variable Model

As in the case of probit, both heteroskedasticity and nonnormality result in the Tobit estimator $\hat{\boldsymbol{\beta}}$ being inconsistent for $\boldsymbol{\beta}$. This inconsistency occurs because the derived density of y given $\mathbf{x}$ hinges crucially on $y^* \mid \mathbf{x} \sim \text{Normal}(\mathbf{x}\boldsymbol{\beta}, \sigma^2)$.

Rather than focusing on parameters, we must remember that the presence of heteroskedasticity or nonnormality in the latent variable model entirely changes the functional forms for $E(y \mid \mathbf{x}, y > 0)$ and $E(y \mid \mathbf{x})$. Therefore, it does not make sense to focus only on the inconsistency in estimating $\boldsymbol{\beta}$. We should study how departures from the homoskedastic normal assumption affect the estimated partial derivatives of the conditional mean functions. Allowing for heteroskedasticity or nonnormality in the latent variable model can be useful for generalizing functional form in corner solution applications, and it should be viewed in that light.

Specification tests can be based on the score approach, where the standard Tobit model is nested in a more general alternative. Tests for heteroskedasticity and nonnormality in the latent variable equation are easily constructed if the outer product of the form statistic (see Section 13.6) is used. A useful test for heteroskedasticity is obtained by assuming $\operatorname{Var}(u \mid \mathbf{x}) = \sigma^2 \exp(\mathbf{x}_1 \boldsymbol{\delta})$, where $\mathbf{x}_1$ is a $1 \times Q$ subvector of $\mathbf{x}$ ($\mathbf{x}_1$ does not include a constant). The Q restrictions $H_0 : \boldsymbol{\delta} = \mathbf{0}$ can be tested using the *LM* statistic. The partial derivatives of the log likelihood $\ell_i(\boldsymbol{\beta}, \sigma^2, \boldsymbol{\delta})$ with respect to $\boldsymbol{\beta}$ and σ^2, evaluated at $\boldsymbol{\delta} = \mathbf{0}$, are given exactly as in equations (17.21) and (17.22). Further, we can show that $\partial \ell_i / \partial \boldsymbol{\delta} = \sigma^2 \mathbf{x}_{i1} (\partial \ell_i / \partial \sigma^2)$. Thus the outer product of the score statistic is $N - \mathrm{SSR}_0$ from the regression

$$1 \text{ on } \partial \hat{\ell}_i / \partial \boldsymbol{\beta}, \partial \hat{\ell}_i / \partial \sigma^2, \hat{\sigma}^2 \mathbf{x}_{i1} (\partial \hat{\ell}_i / \partial \sigma^2), \qquad i = 1, \ldots, N,$$

where the derivatives are evaluated at the Tobit estimates (the restricted estimates) and SSR_0 is the usual sum of squared residuals. Under H_0, $N - \mathrm{SSR}_0 \overset{a}{\sim} \chi^2_Q$. Unfortunately, as we discussed in Section 13.6, the outer product form of the statistic can reject much too often when the null hypothesis is true. If MLE of the alternative model is possible, the *LR* statistic is a preferable alternative.

We can also construct tests of nonnormality that require only standard Tobit estimation. The most convenient of these are derived as conditional moment tests, which we discussed in Section 13.7. See Pagan and Vella (1989).

It is not too difficult to estimate Tobit models with u heteroskedastic if a test reveals such a problem. When $E(y \mid \mathbf{x}, y > 0)$ and $E(y \mid \mathbf{x})$ are of interest, we should look at estimates of these expectations with and without heteroskedasticity. The partial effects on $E(y \mid \mathbf{x}, y > 0)$ and $E(y \mid \mathbf{x})$ could be similar even though the estimates of $\boldsymbol{\beta}$ might be very different.

As with the probit model with heteroskedasticity, there is a subtle issue that arises when computing APEs when we introduce heteroskedasticity into the type I Tobit model. Suppose we replace (17.3) with

$$u \mid \mathbf{x} \sim \mathrm{Normal}(0, \sigma^2 \exp(\mathbf{x}_1 \boldsymbol{\delta})).$$

Then, following the same argument in Section 15.7.4, it can be shown that the average structural function is

$$\text{ASF}(\mathbf{x}) = \text{E}_{\mathbf{x}_{i1}}[m(\mathbf{x}\boldsymbol{\beta}, \boldsymbol{\sigma}^2 \exp(\mathbf{x}_{i1}\boldsymbol{\delta}))],$$

where $m(\cdot,\cdot)$ is defined in equation (17.30). This means, for example, that the partial effect of a continuous variable (evaluated at $\mathbf{x}$) is simply estimated as

$$\left[N^{-1}\sum_{i=1}^{N}\Phi(\mathbf{x}\hat{\boldsymbol{\beta}}/[\hat{\sigma}\exp(\mathbf{x}_{i1}\hat{\boldsymbol{\delta}}/2)])\right]\hat{\beta}_j,$$

where all estimates are the MLEs from the heteroskedastic Tobit model. Unfortunately, as we discussed in Section 15.7.4, if the heteroskedasticity arises due to interactions between unobservables that are independent of $\mathbf{x}$ and elements of $\mathbf{x}$, then the APEs are estimated from the partial derivatives of $\text{E}(y \mid \mathbf{x})$, which are more complicated and may have signs that differ from the signs of the $\hat{\beta}_j$.

As a rough idea of the appropriateness of the standard Tobit model, we can compare the probit estimates, say $\hat{\boldsymbol{\gamma}}$, to the Tobit estimate of $\boldsymbol{\gamma} = \boldsymbol{\beta}/\sigma$, namely, $\hat{\boldsymbol{\beta}}/\hat{\sigma}$. These will never be identical, but they should not be statistically different. Statistically significant sign changes are indications of misspecification. For example, if $\hat{\gamma}_j$ is positive and significant but $\hat{\beta}_j$ is negative and perhaps significant, the Tobit model is probably misspecified.

As an illustration, in Example 15.2, we obtained the probit coefficient on *nwifeinc* as $-.012$, and the coefficient on *kidslt6* was $-.868$. When we divide the corresponding Tobit coefficients by $\hat{\sigma} = 1{,}122.02$, we obtain about $-.0079$ and $-.797$, respectively. Though the estimates differ somewhat, the signs are the same and the magnitudes are similar.

It is possible to form a Hausman statistic as a quadratic form in $(\hat{\boldsymbol{\gamma}} - \hat{\boldsymbol{\beta}}/\hat{\sigma})$, but obtaining the appropriate asymptotic variance is somewhat complicated. (See Ruud, 1984, for a formal discussion of this test.) Section 17.6 discusses more flexible models that may be needed for corner solution outcomes.

17.5.4 Estimating Parameters under Weaker Assumptions

It is possible to $\sqrt{N}$-consistently estimate $\boldsymbol{\beta}$ without assuming a particular distribution for u and without even assuming that u and $\mathbf{x}$ are independent. Consider again the latent variable model, but where the *median* of u given $\mathbf{x}$ is zero:

$$y^* = \mathbf{x}\boldsymbol{\beta} + u, \qquad \text{Med}(u \mid \mathbf{x}) = 0. \tag{17.34}$$

As we showed in Section 17.2, assumption (17.34) leads to

$$\text{Med}(y \mid \mathbf{x}) = \max(0, \mathbf{x}\boldsymbol{\beta}). \tag{17.35}$$

In Chapter 12 we showed how the analogy principle leads to least absolute deviations as the appropriate method for estimating the parameters in a conditional median. Therefore, assumption (17.34) suggests estimating $\boldsymbol{\beta}$ by solving

$$\min_{\boldsymbol{\beta}} \sum_{i=1}^{N} |y_i - \max(0, \mathbf{x}_i\boldsymbol{\beta})|. \tag{17.36}$$

This estimator was suggested by Powell (1984). Since $q(\mathbf{w}, \boldsymbol{\beta}) \equiv |y - \max(0, \mathbf{x}\boldsymbol{\beta})|$ is a continuous function of $\boldsymbol{\beta}$, consistency of Powell's estimator follows from Theorem 12.2 under an appropriate identification assumption. Establishing $\sqrt{N}$-asymptotic normality is much more difficult because the objective function is not twice continuously differentiable with nonsingular Hessian. Powell (1984, 1994) and Newey and McFadden (1994) contain applicable theorems.

An attractive feature of Powell's approach is that $\text{Med}(y \mid \mathbf{x})$ can be estimated without specifying $\text{D}(u \mid \mathbf{x})$ beyond its having a zero conditional median. Of course, under (17.34) we cannot estimate other features of $\text{D}(y \mid \mathbf{x})$: if we impose weak assumptions, then often we can learn only about limited features of a distribution. Because y is a corner solution, it is unclear how valuable estimating the conditional median is. For $\mathbf{x}\boldsymbol{\beta} > 0$, $\text{Med}(y \mid \mathbf{x})$ is linear in $\mathbf{x}$, and so the β_j are the partial effects on the median for $\mathbf{x}\boldsymbol{\beta}$. One interesting aspect of equation (17.35) is that if we use the median for predication, we predict $\hat{y}_i = 0$ for all i such that $\mathbf{x}_i\hat{\boldsymbol{\beta}}_i \le 0$. This will not happen if we use the conditional mean, $\text{E}(y \mid \mathbf{x})$, to predict y, as is easily seen for the type I Tobit.

As in the probit case, one consequence of having consistent estimates of the β_j that do not rely on full distributional assumptions is that we can estimate the directions of the APEs on the mean response, and also the relative partial effects for the continuous explanatory variables, under weaker assumptions. But we cannot estimate the magnitude of the partial effects on the means, and there is no easy way to obtain relative effects for discrete explanatory variables. (Because the partial effects of discrete variables cannot be obtained via calculus, relative effects involving a discrete explanatory variable generally depend on $\mathbf{x}$.)

The parametric nature of the Tobit model—that is, it fully specifies $\text{D}(y \mid \mathbf{x})$—is often stated as its major weakness. But for modeling corner solution outcomes, we do not get something for nothing. The Tobit model implies that we can estimate any feature of $\text{D}(y \mid \mathbf{x})$ that we want, including $\text{P}(y > 0 \mid \mathbf{x})$, $\text{E}(y \mid \mathbf{x}, y > 0)$, $\text{E}(y \mid \mathbf{x}, y > 0)$ and, of course, $\text{Med}(y \mid \mathbf{x})$ (which is necessarily given by (17.35)). Therefore, it is difficult to rank Powell's **semiparametric method** and type I Tobit: Powell's method assumes little and delivers estimates of only a single feature of $D(y \mid \mathbf{x})$, the conditional median, while Tobit assumes a lot but delivers the entire conditional distribution. If the type I Tobit model is true, then the MLE estimates of the β_j should not differ significantly from the censored least absolute deviations (CLAD) estimates, and so CLAD can be used as a rough specification check. In the next section we address the idea that perhaps the type I Tobit model is not flexible enough for a wide range of applications.

Interestingly, if we modify the model to allow multiplicative heterogeneity of the form in Section 17.5.1, $y = q \cdot \max(0, \mathbf{x}\boldsymbol{\beta} + u)$, where q is independent of $(\mathbf{x}, u)$, then we cannot determine $\text{Med}(y \mid \mathbf{x})$, and, generally, CLAD estimates nothing of interest—even if $D(u \mid \mathbf{x})$ is homoskedastic normal. Yet, as we showed in Section 17.5.1, $E(y \mid \mathbf{x})$ has the usual Tobit form, and we could consistently estimate the parameters by NLS. Again, by focusing on the features of $D(y \mid \mathbf{x})$ that are identified by different approaches, as opposed to parameters, we find that the choice between seemingly less parametric methods such as CLAD, and an uncommon method such as NLS applied to the Tobit functional form $E(y \mid \mathbf{x}) = \Phi(\mathbf{x}\boldsymbol{\beta}/\sigma)\mathbf{x}\boldsymbol{\beta} + \sigma\phi(\mathbf{x}\boldsymbol{\beta}/\sigma)$, is not as clear-cut as is often presented. The bottom line is that CLAD consistently estimates $\text{Med}(y \mid \mathbf{x})$ if $\text{Med}(y \mid \mathbf{x}) = \max(0, \mathbf{x}\boldsymbol{\beta})$ while NLS consistently estimates $E(y \mid \mathbf{x})$ if $E(y \mid \mathbf{x}) = \Phi(\mathbf{x}\boldsymbol{\beta}/\sigma)\mathbf{x}\boldsymbol{\beta} + \sigma\phi(\mathbf{x}\boldsymbol{\beta}/\sigma)$.

In some cases a quantile other than the median is of interest, and Powell's approach applies when $\text{Quant}_\tau(u \mid \mathbf{x}) = 0$ for a quantile τ, provided the absolute value function is replaced by the asymmetric loss (check) function; see Section 12.10. Buchinsky and Hahn (1998) offer a different approach to estimating quantiles.

The Chung and Goldberger (1984) results on consistent OLS estimation of slope coefficients up to a common scale factor apply when y is given by (17.2) and u and $\mathbf{x}$ are uncorrelated; see also Section 15.7.5. But the assumptions are restrictive, and the OLS estimates at best deliver directions of effects and relative partial effects for the continuous covariates. The Stoker (1986) result also applies: if $\mathbf{x}$ is multivariate normal, then the linear regression y on $\mathbf{x}$ consistently estimates the partial effects averaged across the distribution of $\mathbf{x}$. As in the binary response case, multivariate normality of $\mathbf{x}$ makes Stoker's result of mostly theoretical interest. In Example 17.2 we saw that there is strong evidence that at least one OLS estimate, even on a roughly continuous variable (*educ*), gave a very different estimate of the APE from the Tobit model. Of course, this does not mean that the Tobit model estimate is closer to the population APE, but it does suggest that linear models have limitations for corner solution responses. And Stoker's result cannot be applied to discrete explanatory variables.

17.6 Two-Part Models and Type II Tobit for Corner Solutions

As we saw in Section 17.2, the type I Tobit model implies that the partial effects of an explanatory variable on $P(y > 0 \mid \mathbf{x})$ and $E(y \mid \mathbf{x}, y > 0)$ must have the same signs. It is easy to imagine situations where this implication of the standard Tobit model could be false. For example, if y is amount of life insurance and *age* is an explanatory variable, *age* could have a positive effect, or at least an initially positive effect, on the probability of having a life insurance policy. But after a certain age, the amount of life insurance coverage might decline. Such a situation would violate the type I Tobit model assumptions.

We also showed that the standard Tobit model implies that the relative effects of two continuous explanatory variables, say x_j and x_h, on $P(y > 0 \mid \mathbf{x})$ and $E(y \mid \mathbf{x}, y > 0)$ are identical (and equal to β_j/β_h). For example, in a labor supply model where education and experience appear only in level form, if a year of education has twice the effect as a year of experience on the probability of labor force participation, then education necessarily has twice the effect on the expected hours worked for the subpopulation of those working. Even if we think that the partial effects of a variable on $P(y > 0 \mid \mathbf{x})$ and $E(y \mid \mathbf{x}, y > 0)$ have the same sign, we might not wish to impose the restriction that any two (continuous) explanatory variables have the same relative effects on these two different features of $D(y \mid \mathbf{x})$.

In this section, we consider models that are more flexible than the type I Tobit model. These models allow separate mechanisms to determine what we call the **participation decision** ($y = 0$ versus $y > 0$) and the **amount decision** (the magnitude of y when it is positive). As we will see, such models are fairly easy to estimate. Unfortunately, there is some confusion in the literature about the nature and interpretation of two approaches to extending the type I Tobit model. Fortunately, we can resolve some of the ambiguity in the literature by using a simple, unified setting.

Let s be a binary variable that determines whether y is zero or strictly positive. It is also useful to introduce a continuously distributed, nonnegative latent variable, which we call w^* in this section. Then we assume y is generated as

$$y = s \cdot w^*. \tag{17.37}$$

It is important to remember that y—for example, annual hours worked—is the observed corner solution response, and it is features of $D(y \mid \mathbf{x})$ that we would like to explain. Then, a model like (17.37) can arise if there are fixed costs that affect the decision to enter a particular state. For a married woman out of the labor force, the decision to enter the labor force may depend on a variety of considerations, including whether she has small children. The way that the presence of a small child affects the labor force participation decision may be quite different from how it affects the decision on how much to work. Equation (17.37) is a convenient way to allow different mechanisms for the participation and amount decisions. Other than s being binary and w^* being continuous, there is another important difference between s and w^*: we effectively observe s because s is observationally equivalent to the indicator $1[y > 0]$ (because we assume $P(w^* = 0)$). But w^* is only observed when $s = 1$, in which case $w^* = y$.

To proceed in a parametric setting, we will assume that s and w^* are specific functions of observable covariates and unobservables, and we will make (at least partial) distributional assumptions about the unobservables. But we can discuss, in a general way, different assumptions about how s and w^* are related. As we will see, a useful assumption is that s and w^* are independent conditional on explanatory variables $\mathbf{x}$, which we can write as

$$D(w^* \mid s, \mathbf{x}) = D(w^* \mid \mathbf{x}). \tag{17.38}$$

When assumption (17.38) holds, the resulting model has typically been called a **two-part model** or **hurdle model**. The assumption is basically that, conditional on a set of observed covariates, the mechanisms determining s and w^* are independent. One implication of (17.38) is that the expected value of y conditional on $\mathbf{x}$ and s is easy to obtain:

$$E(y \mid \mathbf{x}, s) = s \cdot E(w^* \mid \mathbf{x}, s) = s \cdot E(w^* \mid \mathbf{x}), \tag{17.39}$$

which, of course, can be derived under the conditional mean version of (17.38),

$$E(w^* \mid \mathbf{x}, s) = E(w^* \mid \mathbf{x}). \tag{17.40}$$

When $s = 1$, (17.39) becomes

$$E(y \mid \mathbf{x}, y > 0) = E(w^* \mid \mathbf{x}), \tag{17.41}$$

so that the so-called conditional expectation of y (where we condition on $y > 0$) is just the expected value of w^* (conditional on $\mathbf{x}$). Further, the so-called unconditional expectation is

$$E(y \mid \mathbf{x}) = E(s \mid \mathbf{x})E(w^* \mid \mathbf{x}) = P(s = 1 \mid \mathbf{x})E(w^* \mid \mathbf{x}). \tag{17.42}$$

Although some, for example, Duan, Manning, Morris, and Newhouse (1984), have argued that two-part models do not impose (17.38), some sort of conditional independence is natural, even if it is only (17.40). This will become clear as our analysis unfolds.

A different class of models explicitly allows correlation between the participation and amount decisions (after conditioning on covariates). Unfortunately, such a model is often called a **selection model**. When attached to corner solution responses, the "selection model" label has shortcomings and has led to considerable confusion. As in other situations—such as treating a corner solution response as a data-censoring problem—the confusion arises because of statistical similarities that models for corner solutions have with missing data models. But, remember, we have no missing data problem here. We are interested in explaining the corner solution response, y, and we assume it is always observable. We may use latent variable models to obtain $\mathrm{D}(y \mid \mathbf{x})$, but in the end, the latent variables are irrelevant. Because of its common use, we will use the selection model label. In Section 17.7.3 we study a version of the **type II Tobit model**.

There has been much discussion in the literature on whether two-part and selection models can be put into a common framework, and whether selection models nest two-part models; see, for example, the survey and discussion in Leung and Yu (1996). Using (17.37) as a unified setting, we will see that, technically speaking, the type II Tobit model (applied to the logarithm of the response) does nest what is probably the most widely used two-part model, the lognormal hurdle model. But the type II Tobit model can be poorly identified without assuming that an exclusion restriction exists. Namely, we will often need to assume that there is at least one element of $\mathbf{x}$ that appears in $\mathrm{P}(s = 1 \mid \mathbf{x})$ that does not appear in $\mathrm{D}(w^* \mid \mathbf{x})$. Therefore, in a practical sense, the models offer two different approaches. We will have more to say on this issue when we cover the specific models.

17.6.1 Truncated Normal Hurdle Model

Cragg (1971) proposed a natural two-part extension of the type I Tobit model. The conditional independence assumption (17.38) is assumed to hold, and the binary variable s is assumed to follow a probit model, that is,

$$\mathrm{P}(s = 1 \mid \mathbf{x}) = \Phi(\mathbf{x}\boldsymbol{\gamma}). \tag{17.43}$$

The unique feature of Cragg's model is that the latent variable w^* is assumed to have a **truncated normal distribution** with parameters that can vary freely from those in (17.43). The support of w^* is $(0, \infty)$, and so there is no possibility that the model predicts negative outcomes on y. We can specify the model in terms of (17.37) by defining $w^* = \mathbf{x}\boldsymbol{\beta} + u$, where u given $\mathbf{x}$ has a truncated normal distribution with lower truncation point $-\mathbf{x}\boldsymbol{\beta}$. Because $y = w^*$ when $y > 0$, we can write the truncated normal assumption in terms of the density of y given $y > 0$ (and $\mathbf{x}$):

$$f(y \mid \mathbf{x}, y > 0) = [\Phi(\mathbf{x}\boldsymbol{\beta}/\sigma)]^{-1}\phi[(y - \mathbf{x}\boldsymbol{\beta})/\sigma]/\sigma, \qquad y > 0, \tag{17.44}$$

where the term $[\Phi(\mathbf{x}\boldsymbol{\beta}/\sigma)]^{-1}$ ensures that the density integrates to unity over $y > 0$. The density of y given $\mathbf{x}$ can be written succinctly as

$$f(y \mid \mathbf{x}) = [1 - \Phi(\mathbf{x}\boldsymbol{\gamma})]^{1[y=0]}\{\Phi(\mathbf{x}\boldsymbol{\gamma})[\Phi(\mathbf{x}\boldsymbol{\beta}/\sigma)]^{-1}\phi[(y - \mathbf{x}\boldsymbol{\beta})/\sigma]/\sigma\}^{1[y>0]}, \tag{17.45}$$

where we must multiply $f(y \mid \mathbf{x}, y > 0)$ by $P(y > 0 \mid \mathbf{x}) = \Phi(\mathbf{x}\boldsymbol{\gamma})$. Equation (17.45), which is how Cragg directly specified the model without introducing s and w^*, makes it clear that the **truncated normal hurdle (TNH) model** reduces to the type I Tobit model when $\boldsymbol{\gamma} = \boldsymbol{\beta}/\sigma$.

As usual, the log-likelihood function for a random draw i is obtained by plugging $(\mathbf{x}_i, y_i)$ into (17.45) and taking the log, so we have

$$\begin{aligned} l_i(\boldsymbol{\theta}) = {} & 1[y_i = 0] \log[1 - \Phi(\mathbf{x}_i\boldsymbol{\gamma})] + 1[y_i > 0] \log[\Phi(\mathbf{x}_i\boldsymbol{\gamma})] \\ & + 1[y_i > 0]\{-\log[\Phi(\mathbf{x}_i\boldsymbol{\beta}/\sigma)] + \log\{\phi[(y_i - \mathbf{x}_i\boldsymbol{\beta})/\sigma]\} - \log(\sigma)\}. \end{aligned}$$

Because the parameters $\boldsymbol{\gamma}$, $\boldsymbol{\beta}$, and σ are allowed to freely vary, it is easily seen that the MLE for $\boldsymbol{\gamma}$, $\hat{\boldsymbol{\gamma}}$, is simply the probit estimator from probit of $s_i \equiv 1[y_i > 0]$ on $\mathbf{x}_i$. The MLEs of $\boldsymbol{\beta}$ and σ (or $\boldsymbol{\beta}$ and σ^2) are also fairly easy to obtain using software that estimates truncated normal regression models. (We return to truncated normal regression in Chapter 19, but in the context of missing data. Here, the truncated normal distribution is convenient for estimating the density of y given $\mathbf{x}$ over strictly positive values.) Inference about the parameters is straightforward using Wald tests. Fin and Schmidt (1984) derive the LM test of the restrictions $\boldsymbol{\gamma} = \boldsymbol{\beta}/\sigma$; naturally, this test only requires estimation of the type I Tobit model. If one estimates Cragg's model, then the *LR* statistic is easy to compute. One must be sure to add the two parts of the log-likelihood function for the hurdle model: that from the probit using all observations and that from the truncated normal using the $y_i > 0$ observations. Of course, one may reject the standard type I Tobit model for other reasons, such as heteroskedasticity or nonnormality in the latent variable model. And, as always, a statistical rejection might not lead to practically different estimates of the partial effects.

As an illustration, we estimate the truncated normal hurdle model for the data in Table 17.1. (The full results are reported in Section 17.6.3.) The log likelihood value is −3,791.95, compared with −3,819.09 for the standard (type I) Tobit model. Therefore, the *LR* statistic is about 54.28. With eight degrees of freedom, the p-value is zero to many decimal places. Therefore, the Tobit model is rejected against Cragg's more general model.

The expected values for the truncated normal hurdle model are straightforward extensions of the standard Tobit model. First, the distribution $\mathrm{D}(y \mid \mathbf{x}, y > 0)$ is identical in the two models, and so

$$\mathrm{E}(y \mid \mathbf{x}, y > 0) = \mathbf{x}\boldsymbol{\beta} + \sigma\lambda(\mathbf{x}\boldsymbol{\beta}/\sigma). \tag{17.46}$$

The difference is that $\mathrm{P}(y > 0 \mid \mathbf{x})$ is allowed to follow an unrestricted probit model. Therefore, for Cragg's model,

$$\mathrm{E}(y \mid \mathbf{x}) = \Phi(\mathbf{x}\boldsymbol{\gamma})[\mathbf{x}\boldsymbol{\beta} + \sigma\lambda(\mathbf{x}\boldsymbol{\beta}/\sigma)]. \tag{17.47}$$

The partial effects no longer have the simple form in (17.16), but they can be computed easily from (17.15). In particular

$$\frac{\partial \mathrm{E}(y \mid \mathbf{x})}{\partial x_j} = \gamma_j \phi(\mathbf{x}\boldsymbol{\gamma})[\mathbf{x}\boldsymbol{\beta} + \sigma\lambda(\mathbf{x}\boldsymbol{\beta}/\sigma)] + \Phi(\mathbf{x}\boldsymbol{\gamma})\beta_j \theta(\mathbf{x}\boldsymbol{\beta}/\sigma), \tag{17.48}$$

where $\theta(z) = 1 - \lambda(z)[z - \lambda(z)]$, as in (17.12). Further, semielasticities on the conditional mean are easily obtained from $\log[\mathrm{E}(y \mid \mathbf{x})] = \log[\Phi(\mathbf{x}\boldsymbol{\gamma})] + \log[\mathrm{E}(y \mid \mathbf{x}, y > 0)]$, which implies $\partial \log[\mathrm{E}(y \mid \mathbf{x})]/\partial x_j = \partial \log[\Phi(\mathbf{x}\boldsymbol{\gamma})]/\partial x_j + \partial \log[\mathrm{E}(y \mid \mathbf{x}, y > 0)]/\partial x_j$. Thus, the semielasticity of $\mathrm{E}(y \mid \mathbf{x})$ with respect to x_j is obtained by multiplying

$$\gamma_j \lambda(\mathbf{x}\boldsymbol{\gamma}) + \beta_j \theta(\mathbf{x}\boldsymbol{\beta}/\sigma)/[\mathbf{x}\boldsymbol{\beta} + \sigma\lambda(\mathbf{x}\boldsymbol{\beta}/\sigma)] \tag{17.49}$$

by 100. If $x_j = \log(z_j)$, then (17.49) is the elasticity of $\mathrm{E}(y \mid \mathbf{x})$ with respect to z_j. We can insert the MLEs into any of the equations and average across $\mathbf{x}_i$ to obtain an APE, average semielastisticity, or average elasticity. As in many nonlinear contexts, the bootstrap is a convenient method for obtaining valid standard errors.

Because we can estimate $\mathrm{E}(y \mid \mathbf{x})$, we can compute the squared correlation between y_i and $\hat{\mathrm{E}}(y_i \mid \mathbf{x}_i) = \Phi(\mathbf{x}_i\hat{\boldsymbol{\gamma}})[\mathbf{x}_i\hat{\boldsymbol{\beta}} + \hat{\sigma}\lambda(\mathbf{x}_i\hat{\boldsymbol{\beta}}/\hat{\sigma})]$ across all i as an R-squared measure. This goodness-of-fit statistic can be compared to the usual Tobit model or the models that we cover subsequently. We can do a similar calculation conditional on $y > 0$ using equation (17.46).

17.6.2 Lognormal Hurdle Model and Exponential Conditional Mean

Cragg (1971) suggested that a lognormal distribution can be used in place of the truncated Tobit, and the resulting hurdle model has been studied in detail by Duan, Manning, Morris, and Newhouse (1984). The participation decision is still governed by a probit model. One way to express y is

$$y = s \cdot w^* = 1[\mathbf{x}\boldsymbol{\gamma} + v > 0] \exp(\mathbf{x}\boldsymbol{\beta} + u), \tag{17.50}$$

where (u, v) is independent of $\mathbf{x}$ with a bivariate normal distribution and u and v are independent. We have already assumed v has a standard normal distribution. Therefore, the assumption that makes (17.50) different from the truncated normal hurdle model is

$$u \mid \mathbf{x} \sim \text{Normal}(0, \sigma^2). \tag{17.51}$$

Assumption (17.51) means that the latent variable $w^* = \exp(\mathbf{x}\boldsymbol{\beta} + u)$ has a lognormal distribution, and, because v and u are independent of $\mathbf{x}$ and each other, y conditional on $(\mathbf{x}, y > 0)$ has a lognormal distribution. Therefore, we call this model the **lognormal hurdle (LH) model**. The expected value conditional on $y > 0$ is

$$\mathrm{E}(y \mid \mathbf{x}, y > 0) = \mathrm{E}(w^* \mid \mathbf{x}, s = 1) = \mathrm{E}(w^* \mid \mathbf{x}) = \exp(\mathbf{x}\boldsymbol{\beta} + \sigma^2/2), \tag{17.52}$$

and so the "unconditional" expectation is

$$\mathrm{E}(y \mid \mathbf{x}) = \Phi(\mathbf{x}\boldsymbol{\gamma}) \exp(\mathbf{x}\boldsymbol{\beta} + \sigma^2/2). \tag{17.53}$$

The semielasticity of $\mathrm{E}(y \mid \mathbf{x})$ with respect to x_j is simply (100 times) $\gamma_j \lambda(\mathbf{x}\boldsymbol{\gamma}) + \beta_j$ where $\lambda(\cdot)$ is the inverse Mills ratio. If $x_j = \log(z_j)$, this expression becomes the elasticity of $\mathrm{E}(y \mid \mathbf{x})$ with respect to z_j.

Estimation of the parameters is particularly straightforward. The density conditional on $\mathbf{x}$ is

$$f(y \mid \mathbf{x}) = [1 - \Phi(\mathbf{x}\boldsymbol{\gamma})]^{1[y=0]} \{\Phi(\mathbf{x}\boldsymbol{\gamma})\phi[(\log(y) - \mathbf{x}\boldsymbol{\beta})/\sigma]/(\sigma y)\}^{1[y>0]}, \tag{17.54}$$

which leads to the log-likelihood function for a random draw:

$$\begin{aligned} l_i(\boldsymbol{\theta}) = {} & 1[y_i = 0] \log[1 - \Phi(\mathbf{x}_i\boldsymbol{\gamma})] + 1[y_i > 0] \log[\Phi(\mathbf{x}_i\boldsymbol{\gamma})] \\ & + 1[y_i > 0]\{\log(\phi[(\log(y_i) - \mathbf{x}_i\boldsymbol{\beta})/\sigma]) - \log(\sigma) - \log(y_i)\}. \end{aligned} \tag{17.55}$$

As with the truncated normal hurdle model, estimation of the parameters can proceed in two steps. The first is probit of s_i on $\mathbf{x}_i$ to estimate $\boldsymbol{\gamma}$, and then $\boldsymbol{\beta}$ is estimated using an OLS regression of $\log(y_i)$ on $\mathbf{x}_i$ for observations with $y_i > 0$. The usual error variance estimator (or without the degrees-of-freedom adjustment), $\hat{\sigma}^2$, is consistent for σ^2. The last term in (17.55), $\log(y_i)$, does not affect estimation of the parameters, but it must be included in comparing log-likelihood values across different models for $\mathrm{D}(y \mid \mathbf{x})$. In particular, in order to compare Cragg's truncated normal hurdle model and the lognormal hurdle model, the log likelihood for each i must be obtained as in (17.55). (Strictly speaking, to compare log-likelihood values, one should use the MLE for σ, which does not use a degrees-of-freedom correction. The difference should be minimal unless N is small.)

The lognormal hurdle model is easy to estimate, the parameters are easy to interpret, and partial effects and elasticities on $\mathrm{P}(y > 0 \mid \mathbf{x})$, $\mathrm{E}(y \mid \mathbf{x}, y > 0)$, and $\mathrm{E}(y \mid \mathbf{x})$ are easy to obtain. Nevertheless, if we are mainly interested in these three features of $\mathrm{D}(y \mid \mathbf{x})$, we can get by with weaker assumptions. Mullahy (1998) pointed out that the linear regression with $\log(y_i)$ as the dependent variable may estimate $\mathrm{E}[\log(y) \mid \mathbf{x}, y > 0]$ consistently, but we may not be uncovering $\mathrm{E}(y \mid \mathbf{x}, y > 0)$ if (17.51) fails. If we assume that u is independent of $\mathbf{x}$ but do not specify a distribution, then we can estimate $\mathrm{E}(y \mid \mathbf{x}, y > 0)$ using Duan's (1983) **smearing estimate**. In the exponential case, we obtain the scale factor, say $\hat{\tau}$, by averaging $\exp(\hat{u}_i)$ over all i with $y_i > 0$, where $\hat{u}_i$ are the OLS residuals from $\log(y_i)$ on $\mathbf{x}_i$ using the $y_i > 0$ data. Then, $\hat{\mathrm{E}}(y \mid \mathbf{x}, y > 0) = \hat{\tau} \exp(\mathbf{x}\hat{\boldsymbol{\beta}})$, where $\hat{\boldsymbol{\beta}}$ is the OLS estimator of $\log(y_i)$ on $\mathbf{x}_i$ using the $y_i > 0$ subsample.

An alternative way to relax (17.51) is to maintain normality but allow heteroskedasticity, say, $\mathrm{Var}(u \mid \mathbf{x}) = \exp(\mathbf{x}\boldsymbol{\delta})$. Then $\hat{\mathrm{E}}(y \mid \mathbf{x}, y > 0) = \exp[\mathbf{x}\hat{\boldsymbol{\beta}} + \exp(\mathbf{x}\hat{\boldsymbol{\delta}})/2]$ where, say, $\hat{\boldsymbol{\beta}}$ and $\hat{\boldsymbol{\delta}}$ are the MLEs based on $\log(y) \mid \mathbf{x}, y > 0 \sim \mathrm{Normal}(\mathbf{x}\boldsymbol{\beta}, \exp(\mathbf{x}\boldsymbol{\delta}))$.

A more direct approach that avoids specific distributional assumptions in the second tier is just to model $\mathrm{E}(y \mid \mathbf{x}, y > 0)$ directly. It is natural to use an exponential function,

$$\mathrm{E}(y \mid \mathbf{x}, y > 0) = \exp(\mathbf{x}\boldsymbol{\beta}), \tag{17.56}$$

and this contains $w^* = \exp(\mathbf{x}\boldsymbol{\beta} + u)$, with u independent of $\mathbf{x}$, as a special case. We need not place any additional restrictions on $\mathrm{D}(y \mid \mathbf{x}, y > 0)$. Given (17.56), we can use NLS using the $y_i > 0$ observations to consistently estimate $\boldsymbol{\beta}$. But NLS is likely to be inefficient because $\mathrm{Var}(y \mid \mathbf{x}, y > 0)$ is unlikely to be constant. We could use a WNLS estimator, but a quasi-MLE in the linear exponential family (LEF), as we discussed in Section 13.11.3, is a nice, simple alternative. Using the gamma quasi-log-likelihood function is especially attractive as it produces a relatively efficient estimator when the variance is proportional to the square of the mean, which holds in the leading case $w^* = \exp(\mathbf{x}\boldsymbol{\beta} + u)$ with u independent of $\mathbf{x}$. We discuss such estimators in more detail in Chapter 18.

Given probit estimates of $\mathrm{P}(y > 0 \mid \mathbf{x}) = \Phi(\mathbf{x}\boldsymbol{\gamma})$ and QMLE estimates of $\mathrm{E}(y \mid \mathbf{x}, y > 0) = \exp(\mathbf{x}\boldsymbol{\beta})$, we can easily estimate $\mathrm{E}(y \mid \mathbf{x}) = \Phi(\mathbf{x}\boldsymbol{\gamma}) \exp(\mathbf{x}\boldsymbol{\beta})$ without additional distributional assumptions. Computation of semielasticities and elasticities follows along the same lines as under the homoskedastic lognormality assumption. If our goal is to estimate partial effects on the two means, an approach that specifies parametric models for the minimal features of $\mathrm{D}(y \mid \mathbf{x})$ is attractive. See Mullahy (1998) for further discussion in the context of health economics.

17.6.3 Exponential Type II Tobit Model

The two-part models in the previous two subsections assume that s and w^* are independent conditional on the observed covariates, $\mathbf{x}$, either in the full distributional sense or in the conditional mean sense. Generally, we might expect some common unobserved factors to affect both the participation decision (whether s is zero or one) and the amount decision (how large w^* is). For example, in a model of married women's labor supply, unobserved factors that affect the decision to enter the workforce might be correlated with factors that affect the hours decision. Fortunately, we can modify the lognormal hurdle model to allow conditional correlation between s and w^*.

We call the model in this subsection the **exponential type II Tobit (ET2T) model**. Before we derive the log-likelihood function, we need to understand where this model fits into the literature. Traditionally, the type II Tobit model has been applied to missing data problems—that is, where we truly have a sample selection issue. We return to this important application in Chapter 19. But, as we emphasized earlier, we do not have a missing data problem in the current setting: we have a corner solution response, and we have been exploring ways to model $\mathrm{D}(y \mid \mathbf{x})$ that are more flexible than the type I Tobit model. Thus far, in the context of equation (17.37), we have assumed conditional independence between s and w^*. Now, we want to relax that assumption. We use the qualifier "exponential" to emphasize that, in (17.37), we should have $w^* = \exp(\mathbf{x}\boldsymbol{\beta} + u)$; it will not make sense to have $w^* = \mathbf{x}\boldsymbol{\beta} + u$, as is often the case in the study of type II Tobit models. After we cover the exponential version of the model, we will explain why a linear model for w^* is inappropriate.

With the model written in equation (17.37), we now allow u and v to be correlated. Because v has variance equal to one, $\mathrm{Cov}(u, v) = \rho\sigma$, where ρ is the correlation between u and v and $\sigma^2 = \mathrm{Var}(u)$. Obtaining the log likelihood in this case is a bit tricky. For simplicity, let $m^* = \log(w^*)$, so that $\mathrm{D}(m^* \mid \mathbf{x})$ is $\mathrm{Normal}(\mathbf{x}\boldsymbol{\beta}, \sigma^2)$. Then $\log(y) = m^*$ when $y > 0$. Of course, we still have $\mathrm{P}(y = 0 \mid \mathbf{x}) = 1 - \Phi(\mathbf{x}\boldsymbol{\gamma})$. To obtain the density of y (conditional on $\mathbf{x}$) over strictly positive values, we find $f(y \mid \mathbf{x}, y > 0)$ and multiply it by $\mathrm{P}(y > 0 \mid \mathbf{x}) = \Phi(\mathbf{x}\boldsymbol{\gamma})$. To find $f(y \mid \mathbf{x}, y > 0)$, we use the change-of-variables formula $f(y \mid \mathbf{x}, y > 0) = g(\log(y) \mid \mathbf{x}, y > 0)/y$, where $g(\cdot \mid \mathbf{x}, y > 0)$ is the density of m^* conditional on $y > 0$ (and $\mathbf{x}$). Obtaining $g(m^* \mid \mathbf{x}, y > 0) = g(m^* \mid \mathbf{x}, s = 1)$ is complicated by the correlation between u and v. One approach is to use Bayes' rule to write $g(m^* \mid \mathbf{x}, s = 1) = \mathrm{P}(s = 1 \mid m^*, \mathbf{x})h(m^* \mid \mathbf{x})/\mathrm{P}(s = 1 \mid \mathbf{x})$ where $h(m^* \mid \mathbf{x})$ is the density of m^* given $\mathbf{x}$. Then, $\mathrm{P}(s = 1 \mid \mathbf{x})g(m^* \mid \mathbf{x}, s = 1) = \mathrm{P}(s = 1 \mid m^*, \mathbf{x})h(m^* \mid \mathbf{x})$, and this is the expression we want to obtain the density of y given $\mathbf{x}$ for strictly positive y. Now, we can write $s = 1[\mathbf{x}\gamma + v > 0] = 1[\mathbf{x}\gamma + (\rho/\sigma)u + e > 0]$, where we use $v = (\rho/\sigma)u + e$ and $e \mid \mathbf{x}, u \sim \text{Normal}(0, (1 - \rho^2))$. Because $u = m^* - \mathbf{x}\boldsymbol{\beta}$, we have

$$P(s = 1 \mid m^*, \mathbf{x}) = \Phi([\mathbf{x}\gamma + (\rho/\sigma)(m^* - \mathbf{x}\boldsymbol{\beta})](1 - \rho^2)^{-1/2}).$$

Further, we have assumed that $h(m^* \mid \mathbf{x})$ is $\text{Normal}(\mathbf{x}\boldsymbol{\beta}, \sigma^2)$. Therefore, the density of y given $\mathbf{x}$ over strictly positive y is

$$f(y \mid \mathbf{x}) = \Phi([\mathbf{x}\gamma + (\rho/\sigma)(m^* - \mathbf{x}\boldsymbol{\beta})](1 - \rho^2)^{-1/2}))\phi((\log(y) - \mathbf{x}\boldsymbol{\beta})/\sigma)/(\sigma y).$$

Combining this expression with the density at $y = 0$ gives the log likelihood as

$$\begin{aligned} l_i(\boldsymbol{\theta}) = {} & 1[y_i = 0] \log[1 - \Phi(\mathbf{x}_i\gamma)] \\ & + 1[y_i > 0]\{\log[\Phi([\mathbf{x}_i\gamma + (\rho/\sigma(\log(y_i) - \mathbf{x}_i\boldsymbol{\beta})](1 - \rho^2)^{-1/2}) \\ & + \log[\phi((\log(y_i) - \mathbf{x}_i\boldsymbol{\beta})/\sigma)] - \log(\sigma) - \log(y_i)\}. \end{aligned} \tag{17.57}$$

Many econometrics packages have this estimator programmed, although the emphasis is on sample selection problems, and one must define $\log(y_i)$ as the variable where the data are missing (when $y_i = 0$). When $\rho = 0$, we obtain the log likelihood for the lognormal hurdle model from the previous subsection. (Incidentally, for a true missing data problem, the last term in (17.57), $\log(y_i)$, is not included. That is because in sample selection problems the log-likelihood function is only a partial log likelihood, where we truly do not observe a response variable for part of the sample. That is not the case here. Inclusion of $\log(y_i)$ does not affect the estimation problem, but it does affect the value of the log-likelihood function, which is needed to compare across different models.)

The ET2T model contains the conditional lognormal model from the previous subsection because both models assume that (u, v) is independent of $\mathbf{x}$ and jointly normally distributed; the conditional lognormal model makes the extra assumption that u and v are independent. This fact seems to imply that we should, at a minimum, always estimate the more general model to see if it is needed. But the issue is not so simple. It turns out that the model with unknown ρ can be poorly identified if the set of explanatory variables that appears in $w^* = \exp(\mathbf{x}\boldsymbol{\beta} + u)$ is the same as the variables in $s = 1[\mathbf{x}\gamma + v > 0]$. One way to see the problem is to derive $E[\log(y) \mid \mathbf{x}, y > 0]$. We do this by first obtaining $E(m^* \mid \mathbf{x}, s = 1)$. By iterated expectations, $E(m^* \mid \mathbf{x}, s) = E[E(m^* \mid \mathbf{x}, v) \mid \mathbf{x}, s]$ because s is a function of $(\mathbf{x}, v)$. But

$$E(m^* \mid \mathbf{x}, v) = \mathbf{x}\boldsymbol{\beta} + E(u \mid \mathbf{x}, v) = \mathbf{x}\boldsymbol{\beta} + E(u \mid v) = \mathbf{x}\boldsymbol{\beta} + \eta v,$$

where $\eta = \rho\sigma$ is the population regression coefficient from u on v. Therefore, $E(m^* \mid \mathbf{x}, s) = \mathbf{x}\boldsymbol{\beta} + \eta E(v \mid \mathbf{x}, s)$, and, as we showed in Section 17.2, $E(v \mid \mathbf{x}, s = 1) =$

$\lambda(\mathbf{x}\gamma)$, where $\lambda(\cdot)$ is the inverse Mills ratio. Therefore, $\mathrm{E}(m^* \mid \mathbf{x}, s = 1) = \mathbf{x}\boldsymbol{\beta} + \eta\lambda(\mathbf{x}\gamma)$, and so

$$\mathrm{E}[\log(y) \mid \mathbf{x}, y > 0] = \mathbf{x}\boldsymbol{\beta} + \eta\lambda(\mathbf{x}\gamma). \tag{17.58}$$

If we know γ—a valid stance for identification analysis because we can estimate it consistently using probit—equation (17.58) nominally identifies $\boldsymbol{\beta}$ and η. But identification is possible only because $\lambda(\cdot)$ is a nonlinear function. If $\boldsymbol{\beta}$ is unrestricted, then $\lambda(\mathbf{x}\gamma)$ is a function of $\mathbf{x}$, just not an exact linear function. This kind of identification can lead to poor estimators in practice because $\lambda(\cdot)$ can be very close to linear over the appropriate range. In fact, if we do not impose a probit model on $\mathrm{P}(y > 0 \mid \mathbf{x})$, identification would be lost because we would have to allow $\lambda(\cdot)$ to be from a class of functions that contain functions arbitrarily close to linear functions.

As a practical matter, the simple two-step procedure suggested by (17.58) can lead to imprecise or unexpected estimates of $\boldsymbol{\beta}$ and η. The two-step procedure obtains $\hat{\gamma}$ from probit of s_i on $\mathbf{x}_i$, and then $\hat{\boldsymbol{\beta}}$ and $\hat{\eta}$ are obtained from OLS of $\log(y_i)$ on $\mathbf{x}_i$, $\lambda(\mathbf{x}_i\hat{\gamma})$ using only observations with $y_i > 0$. Heckman (1976) originally proposed this two-step procedure, although he had the sample selection problem more in mind. Generally, the two-step method is referred to as **Heckman's method** or **Heckit**. We will study the method applied to missing data problems much more fully in Chapter 19.

Of course, the two-step estimation method may poorly identify $\boldsymbol{\beta}$ and η simply because it does not efficiently use all of the information in $\mathrm{D}(y \mid \mathbf{x})$. But there are other indications that the general model is poorly identified. It can be shown that

$$\mathrm{E}(y \mid \mathbf{x}) = \Phi(\mathbf{x}\gamma + \eta)\exp(\mathbf{x}\boldsymbol{\beta} + \sigma^2/2), \tag{17.59}$$

which is exactly of the same form as equation (17.53), where u and v are assumed to be independent. The only difference is the appearance of η. However, because $\mathbf{x}$ always should include a constant, η is not separately identified by $\mathrm{E}(y \mid \mathbf{x})$ (and neither is $\sigma^2/2$). If we based identification entirely on $\mathrm{E}(y \mid \mathbf{x})$, there would be no difference between the lognormal hurdle model and the ET2T model when the same set of regressors appears in the participation and amount equations.

While the previous discussion indicates that the model with ρ unknown may be poorly identified, all of the parameters are technically identified by the log likelihood in (17.57), and MLE is generally feasible. Unfortunately, as with the two-step procedure, the estimates can be difficult to believe when the same set of regressors shows up in both parts of the model.

Example 17.4 (Annual Hours Equation for Married Women): Table 17.1 reports linear model and Tobit estimates for married women's labor supply. We now

Table 17.2
Models for Married Women's Labor Supply

Model	(1) Truncated Normal Hurdle	(2) Lognormal Hurdle	(3) Exponential Type II Tobit
Participation equation			
nwifeinc	−.012 (.005)	−.012 (.005)	−.0097 (.0043)
educ	.131 (.025)	.131 (.025)	.120 (.022)
exper	.123 (.019)	.123 (.019)	.083 (.017)
$exper^2$	−.0019 (.0006)	−.0019 (.0006)	−.0013 (.0005)
age	−.088 (.015)	−.088 (.015)	−.033 (.008)
kidslt6	−.868 (.119)	−.868 (.119)	−.504 (.107)
kidsge6	.036 (.043)	.036 (.043)	.070 (.039)
constant	.270 (.509)	.270 (.509)	−.367 (.448)
Amount equation	*hours*	log(*hours*)	log(*hours*)
nwifeinc	.153 (5.164)	−.0020 (.0044)	.0067 (.0050)
educ	−29.85 (22.84)	−.039 (.020)	−.119 (.024)
exper	72.62 (21.24)	.073 (.018)	−.033 (.020)
$exper^2$	−.944 (.609)	−.0012 (.0005)	.0006 (.0006)
age	−27.44 (8.29)	−.024 (.007)	.014 (.008)
kidslt6	−484.91 (153.79)	−.585 (.119)	.208 (.134)
kidsge6	−102.66 (43.54)	−.069 (.037)	−.092 (.043)
constant	2,123.5 (483.3)	7.90 (.43)	8.67 (.50)
$\hat{\sigma}$	850.77 (43.80)	.884 (.030)	1.209 (.051)
$\hat{\rho}$	—	—	−.972 (.010)
Log likelihood	−3,791.95	−3,894.93	−3,877.88
Number of women	753	753	753

All estimates are from maximum likelihood, with standard errors in parentheses after coefficents.
The headings for the amount equation are intended to emphasize that the log(*hours*) can be expressed as a linear function in the lognormal hurdle and exponential type II Tobit models.

estimate the truncated normal hurdle model, the lognormal hurdle model, and the ET2T model. The results are given in Table 17.2.

There are several interesting features of the estimates in Table 17.2. First, because the lognormal hurdle model is nested within the ET2T model, the log likelihood of the latter is necessarily larger than that of the former. The *LR* test decidedly rejects the null model with $LR = 34.10$ for the test of $H_0 : \rho = 0$. But we should view the very large, negative value $\hat{\rho} = -.972$ with suspicion. It seems very unlikely that the unobserved factors that positively affect the decision to enter the workforce have a strong negative effect on how much to work.

Because of the correlation allowed between u and v in the ET2T model, it is not immediately obvious how each explanatory variable affects $E(y \mid \mathbf{x}, y > 0)$ or $E(y \mid \mathbf{x})$. The positive coefficient on *kidslt6* for the amount equation seems odd, but, because $\hat{\beta}_{kidslt6} > 0$, $\hat{\eta} < 0$, $\hat{\gamma}_{kidslt6} < 0$, and $\lambda(\cdot)$ has a negative slope, the estimated partial effect of *kidslt6* on $E[\log(hours) \mid \mathbf{x}, hours > 0]$ is ambiguous. Equation (17.59) shows that the effect on $E(hours \mid \mathbf{x})$ is ambiguous, and we would have to plug in specific values of $\mathbf{x}$ to determine the sign of the partial effect at interesting values. The experience profile also seems unusual, although, again, it is difficult in the ET2T model to figure out how the inverted U-shape for the participation part and the U-shape for the amount part translate into partial effects. The difficulty in interpreting the estimates in the ET2T model, coupled with the unbelievable estimate of ρ, make this model undesirable for this application. (Unlike with the truncated normal and lognormal hurdle models, the label "amount equation" is less suitable as a label in the ET2T model: equation (17.58) makes it clear that both sets of parameters enter the expectation conditional on $y > 0$.)

Based on the log likelihood, the truncated normal hurdle model fits considerably better than the lognormal hurdle model. We can apply Vuong's (1989) test to see if the difference is statistically significant. Because the participation equations are identical probits in both models, we can only test the "amount" models on the 428 observations with positive *hours*. The simplest way to implement the test is to regress $\hat{\boldsymbol{l}}_{i1} - \hat{\boldsymbol{l}}_{i2}$ on a constant and perform a t test, where, for observation i, $\hat{\boldsymbol{l}}_{i1}$ is the log likelihood for the truncated normal model and $\hat{\boldsymbol{l}}_{i2}$ is the log likelihood for the lognormal model. The average difference in the log likelihoods is .241 with standard error = .033, and so the difference is highly statistically significant. Therefore, we can at least reject the lognormal model as being the true model.

Conditional on $hours > 0$, the truncated normal model fits the conditional mean better than the lognormal model, too. The squared correlation between $hours_i$ and the fitted values for the TNH model is about .138 (computed from (17.46)) and about .128 for the LH model (computed from (17.52)).

We can also easily test the type I Tobit model against the TNH model by using the LR statistic. In this case, the usual Tobit model imposes eight restrictions of the form $\gamma_j = \beta_j/\sigma$. The LR statistic is $LR = 2(3{,}819.09 - 3{,}791.95) = 54.28$, which yields a p-value of essentially zero, and so the standard Tobit model is strongly rejected. However, it is interesting to note that the Tobit model fits better than the ET2T model, even though the latter model contains nine more parameters.

As a practical matter, the TNH model allows certain variables to affect the participation and amount decisions differently. For example, education has a positive effect on the participation decision but appears to have no effect, or maybe a negative effect, on the hours decision conditional on participation. The number of older children does not seem to affect participation—which makes sense because the older children are in school for most of the year, making at least part-time work much more convenient—but having older children has a negative effect on amount of hours worked conditional on working. While having young children has large negative effects on both the participation and amount decisions, the Tobit restriction, $\gamma_{kidslt6} = \beta_{kidslt6}/\sigma$, seems to be rejected, with $\hat{\gamma}_{kidslt6} = -.868$ and $\hat{\beta}_{kidslt6}/\hat{\sigma} = -.570$.

A complete analysis of this example would be to obtain partial effects of some key variables, perhaps *nwifeinc* and *kidslt6*, on the different conditional expectations and to see how the partial effects change across models.

In the example just given, the TNH model provides the best fit and gives sensible estimates. In other cases, one can imagine the lognormal distribution could fit better for the amount distribution conditional on $y > 0$; such issues must be studied for each application.

The ET2T model is more convincing when the covariates determining the participation decision strictly contain those affecting the amount decision. Then, the model can be expressed as

$$y = 1[\mathbf{x}\boldsymbol{\gamma} + v \geq 0] \cdot \exp(\mathbf{x}_1\boldsymbol{\beta}_1 + u), \tag{17.60}$$

where both $\mathbf{x}$ and $\mathbf{x}_1$ contain unity as their first elements but $\mathbf{x}_1$ is a strict subset of $\mathbf{x}$. If we write $\mathbf{x} = (\mathbf{x}_1, \mathbf{x}_2)$, then we are assuming $\boldsymbol{\gamma}_2 \neq \mathbf{0}$. Given at least one exclusion restriction, we can see from $\mathrm{E}[\log(y) \mid \mathbf{x}, y > 0] = \mathbf{x}_1\boldsymbol{\beta}_1 + \eta\lambda(\mathbf{x}\boldsymbol{\gamma})$ that $\boldsymbol{\beta}_1$ and η are likely to be better identified because $\lambda(\mathbf{x}\boldsymbol{\gamma})$ is not an exact function of $\mathbf{x}_1$. (Identification of $\boldsymbol{\gamma}$ is not an issue because it is always identified by the probit model for $\mathrm{P}(y > 0 \mid \mathbf{x})$.) Unfortunately, where the exclusion restriction might come from is often unclear in applications. To use an exclusion restriction in Example 17.4, we need an observed variable that affects the labor force participation decision but not the amount decision. Perhaps a measure of the accessibility of day care can be viewed as affecting fixed costs of participating but not the amount decision. (The price of day care would typically affect the participation and amount decisions.) But such a variable is not available in the Mroz (1987) data set.

In Example 9.5, where we estimated a simultaneous equations model for *hours* and $\log(wage)$, restricting ourselves to working women, we assumed that past workforce experience had no affect on *hours*; this allowed us to identify the *hours* equation. If we make a similar assumption and allow experience to affect participation but exclude it from $\mathbf{x}_1$, we obtain two exclusion restrictions because *exper* appears as a quadratic. Unfortunately, using these exclusion restrictions does not appreciably change the estimated correlation between v and u: $\hat{\rho}$ becomes $-.963$, and the estimated coefficients on the explanatory variables are similar to those in Table 17.2. Therefore, for this application, the ET2T model has some serious shortcomings even if we accept the exclusion restrictions.

Given that the TNH model (and even the Tobit model) fits better than the ET2T model, it is tempting to apply the type II Tobit model to the level, y, rather than

$\log(y)$. After all, the TNH model can be expressed as $y = 1[\mathbf{x}\gamma + v > 0] \cdot (\mathbf{x}\boldsymbol{\beta} + u)$. But in the TNH model, the truncated normal distribution of u at the value $-\mathbf{x}\boldsymbol{\beta}$ ensures that $\mathbf{x}\boldsymbol{\beta} + u > 0$. If we apply the type II Tobit model directly to y, we must assume (u, v) is bivariate normal and *independent* of $\mathbf{x}$. What we gain is that u and v can be correlated, but this comes at the cost of not specifying a proper density because the T2T model allows negative outcomes on y. (This was not a problem when we applied the model to $\log(y)$.) Now, rather than (17.46) or (17.52)—both of which are guaranteed to be positive—we would have

$$E(y \mid \mathbf{x}, y > 0) = \mathbf{x}\boldsymbol{\beta} + \eta\lambda(\mathbf{x}\gamma), \tag{17.61}$$

where $\eta = \rho\sigma$, $\rho = \text{Corr}(u, v)$, and $\sigma^2 = \text{Var}(u)$. When we obtain either two-step estimates or MLEs of γ, $\boldsymbol{\beta}$, and η, nothing guarantees the right-hand side of (17.61) is positive for all $\mathbf{x}$. Especially when $\rho < 0$, it is possible to get negative estimates of $E(y \mid \mathbf{x}, y > 0)$. Clearly negative estimates are possible in the case $\rho = 0$, as nothing guarantees $\mathbf{x}\hat{\boldsymbol{\beta}} > 0$. Therefore, although the T2T model has been applied to corner solution responses—see, for example, Blank (1988) for hours worked and Franses and Paap (2001) for charitable contributions—it is not generally a good idea. As we will see in Chapter 19, the type II Tobit model was originally intended for sample selection problems.

If we (inappropriately) apply the T2T model to *hours*, the value of the "log likelihood"—that is, the value of the partial log likelihood obtained by treating the $hours_i = 0$ observations as missing data—is −3,823.77, which is notably lower than the log likelihood value for the model it is supposed to nest, the TNH model (with log likelihood −3,791.95). This provides verification that the T2T "model" does not nest Cragg's TNH model and in fact fits much worse.

17.7 Two-Limit Tobit Model

As mentioned in the introduction, some corner solution responses take on two values with positive probability. When the response variable is a fraction or a percent, the corners are usually at zero and one or zero and 100, respectively. But it is also possible that institutional constraints impose corners at other values. For example, if workers are allowed to contribute at most 15% of their earnings to a tax-deferred pension plan, and y_i is the fraction of income contributed for worker i, then the corners are at zero and .15.

Generally, let $a_1 < a_2$ be the two limit values of y in the population. Then the **two-limit Tobit** model is most easily defined in terms of an underlying latent variable.

$$
\begin{aligned}
&y^* = \mathbf{x}\boldsymbol{\beta} + u, \qquad u \mid \mathbf{x} \sim \text{Normal}(0, \sigma^2) \\
&y = a_1 \qquad \text{if } y^* \le a_1 \\
&y = y^* \qquad \text{if } a_1 < y^* < a_2 \\
&y = a_2 \qquad \text{if } y^* \ge a_2.
\end{aligned} \tag{17.62}
$$

The specification in equation (17.62) ensures that $\mathrm{P}(y = a_1) > 0$ and $\mathrm{P}(y = a_2) > 0$ but $\mathrm{P}(y = a) = 0$ for $a_1 < a < a_2$. Therefore, this model is applicable only when we actually see pileups at the two endpoints and then a (roughly) continuous distribution in between.

Using similar arguments for the type I Tobit model, the density of y is the same as y^* for values in (a_1, a_2). Further, as you are asked to work out in Problem 17.3,

$$\mathrm{P}(y = a_1 \mid \mathbf{x}) = \Phi((a_1 - \mathbf{x}\boldsymbol{\beta})/\sigma) \tag{17.63}$$

$$\mathrm{P}(y = a_2 \mid \mathbf{x}) = \Phi(-(a_2 - \mathbf{x}\boldsymbol{\beta})/\sigma). \tag{17.64}$$

It follows that the log-likelihood function for a random draw i is

$$
\begin{aligned}
\log f(y_i \mid \mathbf{x}_i; \boldsymbol{\theta}) = {} & 1[y_i = a_1] \log[\Phi((a_1 - \mathbf{x}_i\boldsymbol{\beta})/\sigma)] + 1[y_i = a_2] \log[\Phi(-(a_2 - \mathbf{x}_i\boldsymbol{\beta})/\sigma)] \\
& + 1[a_1 < y_i < a_2] \log[(1/\sigma)\phi((y_i - \mathbf{x}_i\boldsymbol{\beta})/\sigma)].
\end{aligned}
$$

Many econometrics packages that estimate the standard Tobit model also allow specifying any lower and upper limit. The log likelihood is well behaved, and standard asymptotic theory for MLE applies.

As usual with nonlinear models, a difficult aspect is in knowing which estimated features to report. It can be shown (again see Problem 17.3) that

$$
\begin{aligned}
\mathrm{E}(y \mid \mathbf{x}, a_2 < y < a_2) = {} & \mathbf{x}\boldsymbol{\beta} + \sigma[\phi((a_1 - \mathbf{x}\boldsymbol{\beta})/\sigma) - \phi((a_1 - \mathbf{x}\boldsymbol{\beta})/\sigma)]/ \\
& [\Phi((a_2 - \mathbf{x}\boldsymbol{\beta})/\sigma) - \Phi((a_1 - \mathbf{x}\boldsymbol{\beta})/\sigma)],
\end{aligned} \tag{17.65}
$$

where the term after $\mathbf{x}\boldsymbol{\beta}$ is the extension of the inverse Mills ratio. The so-called unconditional expectation can be gotten from

$$
\begin{aligned}
\mathrm{E}(y \mid \mathbf{x}) &= a_1\mathrm{P}(y = a_1 \mid \mathbf{x}) + \mathrm{P}(a_1 < y < a_2 \mid \mathbf{x})\mathrm{E}(y \mid \mathbf{x}, a_1 < y < a_2) + a_2\mathrm{P}(y = a_2 \mid \mathbf{x}) \\
&= a_1\Phi((a_1 - \mathbf{x}\boldsymbol{\beta})/\sigma) + \mathrm{P}(a_1 < y < a_2 \mid \mathbf{x})\mathrm{E}(y \mid \mathbf{x}, a_1 < y < a_2) \\
&\quad + a_2\Phi(-(a_2 - \mathbf{x}\boldsymbol{\beta})/\sigma).
\end{aligned} \tag{17.66}
$$

Equations (17.65) and (17.66) are cumbersome to work with, but they do allow us to obtain predicted values for a vector $\mathbf{x}$, once we have obtained the MLEs.

As with the single corner at zero, the partial effect of a continuous variable x_j on $\mathrm{E}(y \mid \mathbf{x})$ simplifies to a remarkable degree:

$$\frac{\partial \mathrm{E}(y \mid \mathbf{x})}{\partial x_j} = [\Phi((a_2 - \mathbf{x}\boldsymbol{\beta})/\sigma) - \Phi((a_1 - \mathbf{x}\boldsymbol{\beta})/\sigma)]\beta_j. \tag{17.67}$$

This last expression makes partial effects at specific values of $\mathbf{x}$, and APEs, especially easy to compute for continuous explanatory variables. For APEs we have

$$\left(N^{-1}\sum_{i=1}^{N}[\Phi((a_2 - \mathbf{x}_i\hat{\boldsymbol{\beta}})/\hat{\sigma}) - \Phi((a_1 - \mathbf{x}_i\hat{\boldsymbol{\beta}})/\hat{\sigma})]\right)\hat{\beta}_j, \tag{17.68}$$

where the scale factor is, of course, between zero and one. To determine how linear model estimates compare for estimating APEs, we should compare the OLS estimates for continuous variables directly to (17.68). APEs for binary variables should be obtained from equation (17.66), where we difference the two expected values at the two settings of the binary variable, and then average the differences; see (17.18) for the standard Tobit case.

17.8 Panel Data Methods

We now cover panel data methods for corner solution responses. We use the same notation as in previous chapters, namely, y_{it} denotes the response for unit i at time t. The treatment is similar to that given in Section 15.8 for probit models.

17.8.1 Pooled Methods

We begin with the case where $y_{it} \geq 0$ and $\mathrm{P}(y_{it} = 0) > 0$. Before covering the type I Tobit model, it is important to remember that, because we are interested in explaining y_{it}, it is acceptable in some cases to use linear regression methods. Just as in the cross section case, linear regressions are easy to interpret and might provide acceptable approximations to average effects. But the linear model might also not provide good estimates of partial effects at more extreme values.

But it is also easy to apply the type I Tobit model to panel data. We now write

$$y_{it} = \max(0, \mathbf{x}_{it}\boldsymbol{\beta} + u_{it}), \qquad t = 1, 2, \ldots, T \tag{17.69}$$

$$u_{it} \mid \mathbf{x}_{it} \sim \mathrm{Normal}(0, \sigma^2). \tag{17.70}$$

This model has several notable features. First, it does not maintain strict exogeneity of $\mathbf{x}_{it}$: u_{it} is independent of $\mathbf{x}_{it}$, but the relationship between u_{it} and $\mathbf{x}_{is}$, $t \neq s$, is unspecified. As a result, $\mathbf{x}_{it}$ could contain $y_{i,t-1}$ or variables that are affected by feedback. A second important point is that the $\{u_{it} : t = 1, \dots, T\}$ are allowed to be serially dependent, which means that the y_{it} can be dependent after conditioning on the explanatory variables. In short, equations (17.69) and (17.70) only specify a model for $D(y_{it} \mid \mathbf{x}_{it})$, and $\mathbf{x}_{it}$ can contain any conditioning variables (time dummies, interactions of time dummies with time-constant or time-varying variables, lagged dependent variables, and so on).

The pooled estimator maximizes the partial log-likelihood function

$$\sum_{i=1}^{N} \sum_{t=1}^{T} \ell_{it}(\boldsymbol{\beta}, \sigma^2),$$

where $\ell_{it}(\boldsymbol{\beta}, \sigma^2)$ is the log-likelihood function given in equation (17.20). Computationally, we just apply Tobit to the data set *as if* it were one long cross section of size NT. However, while the conditional information matrix equality holds for all t under assumptions (17.69) and (17.70), a robust variance matrix estimator is needed to account for serial correlation in the score across t; see Sections 13.8.2 and 15.8.1. Robust Wald and score statistics can be computed as in Section 12.6. The LR statistic based on the pooled Tobit estimation is not generally valid without further assumptions.

In the case that the panel data model is dynamically complete, that is,

$$D(y_{it} \mid \mathbf{x}_{it}, y_{i,t-1}, \mathbf{x}_{i,t-1}, \dots) = D(y_{it} \mid \mathbf{x}_{it}), \tag{17.71}$$

inference is considerably easier: all the usual statistics from pooled Tobit are valid, including LR statistics. Remember, we are *not* assuming any kind of independence across t; in fact, $\mathbf{x}_{it}$ can contain lagged dependent variables. It just works out that dynamic completeness leads to the same inference procedures one would use on independent cross sections; see the general treatment in Section 13.8.

A general test for dynamic completeness can be based on the scores $\hat{\mathbf{s}}_{it}$, as mentioned in Section 13.8.3, but it is nice to have a simple test that can be computed from pooled Tobit estimation. Under assumption (17.71), variables dated at time $t-1$ and earlier should not affect the distribution of y_{it} once $\mathbf{x}_{it}$ is conditioned on. There are many possibilities, but we focus on just one here. Define $r_{i,t-1} = 1$ if $y_{i,t-1} = 0$ and $r_{i,t-1} = 0$ if $y_{i,t-1} > 0$. Further, define $\hat{u}_{i,t-1} \equiv y_{i,t-1} - \mathbf{x}_{i,t-1}\hat{\boldsymbol{\beta}}$ if $y_{i,t-1} > 0$ and $\hat{u}_{i,t-1} \equiv 0$ if $y_{i,t-1} = 0$. Then estimate the following (artificial) model by pooled Tobit:

$$y_{it} = \max[0, \mathbf{x}_{it}\boldsymbol{\beta} + \gamma_1 r_{i,t-1} + \gamma_2(1 - r_{i,t-1})\hat{u}_{i,t-1} + error_{it}]$$

using time periods $t = 2, \dots, T$, and test the joint hypothesis $H_0 : \gamma_1 = 0,\ \gamma_2 = 0$. Under the null of dynamic completeness, $error_{it} = u_{it}$, and the estimation of $u_{i,t-1}$

does not affect the limiting distribution of the Wald, LR, or LM tests. In computing either the LR or LM test it is important to drop the first time period in estimating the restricted model with $\gamma_1 = \gamma_2 = 0$. Since pooled Tobit is used to estimate both the restricted and unrestricted models, the LR test is fairly easy to obtain.

In some applications it may be important to allow interactions between time dummies and explanatory variables. We might also want to allow the variance of u_{it} to change over time to allow more flexibly for time heterogeneity. If $\sigma_t^2 = \text{Var}(u_{it})$, a pooled approach still works, but $\ell_{it}(\boldsymbol{\beta}, \sigma^2)$ becomes $\ell_{it}(\boldsymbol{\beta}, \sigma_t^2)$, and special software may be needed for estimation.

The exact way that lagged dependent variables should appear in dynamic Tobit models is not clear. We might want to allow different effects of lagged participation and amounts. So, defining $r_{i,t-1} = 1[y_{i,t-1} = 0]$, we might specify

$$y_{it} = \max(0, \mathbf{z}_{it}\boldsymbol{\delta} + \rho_1 r_{i,t-1} + \rho_2(1 - r_{i,t-1})y_{i,t-1} + u_{it}).$$

Any of the two-part models and the selection model we discussed in Section 17.6 are easily adapted to panel data where we use pooled estimation. In Cragg's truncated normal hurdle model and the lognormal hurdle model, we can allow lagged participation and amount decisions to appear separately in the current participation and amount equations. And, of course, we can allow lags of other variables, too. If the model is assumed to be dynamically complete—as it typically would be if we start adding lagged dependent variables—standard inference from the pooled estimation is valid. If we are estimating a static model or finite distributed lag model, serial correlation robust statistics should be used. The two-limit Tobit model from Section 17.7 extends in a straightforward manner, too. Any of these methods is just a special case of the partial MLE results we discussed in Section 13.8: if the distribution is dynamically complete, then we can use the usual standard errors and test statistics; if it is not, all inference should be made robust to serial dependence.

17.8.2 Unobserved Effects Models under Strict Exogeneity

As in the case of probit, allowing for unobserved heterogeneity in Tobit models is tricky. Of course, the simple strategy of specifying a linear model is available. That is, we can write $y_{it} = \mathbf{x}_{it}\boldsymbol{\beta} + c_i + u_{it}$ and, under the assumption that $\mathbf{x}_{ir}$ is uncorrelated with u_{it} for all t and r, estimate $\boldsymbol{\beta}$ by fixed effects. Of course, FE estimation ignores the restriction $u_{it} \geq -(\mathbf{x}_{it}\boldsymbol{\beta} + c_i)$, and, if we think $\text{E}(y_{it} \mid \mathbf{x}_{it}, c_i) = \mathbf{x}_{it}\boldsymbol{\beta} + c_i$, we would be ignoring $c_i \geq -\mathbf{x}_{it}\boldsymbol{\beta}$ for $t = 1, \ldots, T$. Nevertheless, as we discussed in Section 15.8 for binary responses, the linear model has some advantages: we can leave $\text{D}(c_i \mid \mathbf{x}_i)$ unspecified, and we can allow for general serial dependence in $\{u_{it}\}$. Plus, as usual, the $\hat{\boldsymbol{\beta}}$ are easy to interpret, although they are at best approximations to APEs.

To exploit the corner solution nature of y_{it}, we can instead use the **unobserved effects Tobit model**. (We leave the "type I" designation implicit here.) We can write this model as

$$y_{it} = \max(0, \mathbf{x}_{it}\boldsymbol{\beta} + c_i + u_{it}), \qquad t = 1, 2, \ldots, T \tag{17.72}$$

$$u_{it} \mid \mathbf{x}_i, c_i \sim \text{Normal}(0, \sigma_u^2) \tag{17.73}$$

where c_i is the unobserved effect and $\mathbf{x}_i$ contains $\mathbf{x}_{it}$ for all t. Assumption (17.73) is a normality assumption, but it also imples that the $\mathbf{x}_{it}$ are strictly exogenous conditional on c_i. As we have seen in several contexts, this assumption rules out certain kinds of explanatory variables.

Under assumptions (17.72) and (17.73), we can obtain $\mathrm{E}(y_t \mid \mathbf{x}_t, c, y_t > 0)$ and $\mathrm{E}(y_t \mid \mathbf{x}_t, c)$ as in equations (17.10) and (17.14). These expectations, and therefore the partial effects, depend on the parameters $\boldsymbol{\beta}$ and σ_u^2. As in the unobserved effects models for binary responses, the partial effects on $\mathrm{E}(y_t \mid \mathbf{x}_t, c, y_t > 0)$ and $\mathrm{E}(y_t \mid \mathbf{x}_t, c)$ also depend on the unobserved heterogeneity, c. If we can estimate the distribution of c then we can plug in interesting values, such as the mean, median, or various quantiles, in obtaining the partial effects. As we will see, just as in the unobserved effects probit model, we can estimate APEs under weaker assumptions.

Rather than cover a standard random effects version, we consider a more general **correlated random effects Tobit model** that allows c_i and $\mathbf{x}_i$ to be correlated. To this end, assume, just as in the probit case,

$$c_i \mid \mathbf{x}_i \sim \text{Normal}(\psi + \overline{\mathbf{x}}_i\boldsymbol{\xi}, \sigma_a^2), \tag{17.74}$$

where σ_a^2 is the variance of a_i in the equation $c_i = \psi + \overline{\mathbf{x}}_i\boldsymbol{\xi} + a_i$. We could replace $\overline{\mathbf{x}}_i$ with $\mathbf{x}_i$ to be more general, but $\overline{\mathbf{x}}_i$ has at most dimension K. (As usual, $\mathbf{x}_{it}$ would not include a constant, and time dummies would be excluded from $\overline{\mathbf{x}}_i$ because they are already in $\mathbf{x}_{it}$.) Under assumptions (17.42)–(17.44), we can write

$$y_{it} = \max(0, \psi + \mathbf{x}_{it}\boldsymbol{\beta} + \overline{\mathbf{x}}_i\boldsymbol{\xi} + a_i + u_{it}) \tag{17.75}$$

$$u_{it} \mid \mathbf{x}_i, a_i \sim \text{Normal}(0, \sigma_u^2), \qquad t = 1, 2, \ldots, T \tag{17.76}$$

$$a_i \mid \mathbf{x}_i \sim \text{Normal}(0, \sigma_a^2). \tag{17.77}$$

In our previous notation, assumptions (17.75) and (17.76) mean that $\mathrm{D}(y_{it} \mid \mathbf{x}_i, a_i) = \text{Tobit}(\psi + \mathbf{x}_{it}\boldsymbol{\beta} + \overline{\mathbf{x}}_i\boldsymbol{\xi} + a_i, \sigma_u^2)$. The formulation in equations (17.75), (17.76), and (17.77) is very useful, especially if we assume that, conditional on $(\mathbf{x}_i, a_i)$ (equivalently, conditional on $(\mathbf{x}_i, c_i)$), the $\{u_{it}\}$ are serially independent:

$$(u_{i1}, \ldots, u_{iT}) \text{ are independent given } (\mathbf{x}_i, a_i). \tag{17.78}$$

If we set $\xi = \mathbf{0}$, equations (17.75) through (17.78) constitute the traditional **random effects Tobit model**. It is hardly more difficult to estimate the CRE version of the model, because software that estimates random effects Tobit models can be used to obtain consistent and $\sqrt{N}$-asymptotically normal MLEs of ψ, $\boldsymbol{\beta}$, ξ, σ_a^2, and σ_u^2. The log-likelihood function for unit i is obtained first by multiplying the densities for the Tobit$(\psi + \mathbf{x}_{it}\boldsymbol{\beta} + \bar{\mathbf{x}}_i\xi + a_i, \sigma_u^2)$ model across t and then integrating the product with respect to the Normal$(0, \sigma_a^2)$ density—the distribution of a_i. Then, of course, we take the logarithm of the result. The steps are very similar to obtaining the density for the random effects probit model (with the Chamberlain-Mundlak device of adding $\bar{\mathbf{x}}_i$ as a set of regressors).

Although we show the CRE Tobit model with only time-varying regressors—likely including a full set of time dummies—we can always include time-constant regressors, too, just as in the CRE probit model. We might include time-constant controls to proxy for unobserved heterogeneity, or we might actually be interested in the effects of a time-constant variable, say w_i, under the assumption $\mathrm{D}(c_i \mid \mathbf{x}_i, w_i) = \mathrm{D}(c_i \mid \mathbf{x}_i)$. Of course, including time-constant controls can often improve the fit of the model, too. Mechanically, we can include such variables in $\mathbf{x}_{it}$ and simply drop the time averages associated with those variables (just as we do with aggregate time effects). We do not make this explicit in what follows.

As in the probit case, given estimates of all parameters, we can estimate the mean and variance of c_i. A consistent estimator of $\mu_c = \mathrm{E}(c_i)$ is simply $\hat{\mu}_c = \hat{\psi} + \bar{\mathbf{x}}\hat{\xi}$, where $\bar{\mathbf{x}} = N^{-1}\sum_{i=1}^N \bar{\mathbf{x}}_i$. A consistent estimator of σ_c^2 is simply $\hat{\sigma}_c^2 = \hat{\xi}'\hat{\Sigma}_{\bar{\mathbf{x}}_i}\hat{\xi} + \hat{\sigma}_a^2$, where $\hat{\Sigma}_{\bar{\mathbf{x}}_i}$ is the sample variance matrix of $\{\bar{\mathbf{x}}_i : i = 1, \ldots, N\}$. If we define $m(a, \sigma^2) = \Phi(a/\sigma)a + \sigma\phi(a/\sigma)$ as in equation (17.30), then we can compute partial effects at $\hat{\mu}_c$, by taking derivatives and changes of $m(\mathbf{x}_t\hat{\boldsymbol{\beta}} + \hat{\mu}_c, \hat{\sigma}_u^2)$ with respect to elements of $\mathbf{x}_t$. In the case of a derivative, we simply get $\Phi((\mathbf{x}_t\hat{\boldsymbol{\beta}} + \hat{\mu}_c)/\hat{\sigma}_u)\hat{\beta}_j$. Furthermore, we might replace $\hat{\mu}_c$ with $\hat{\mu}_c \pm k\hat{\sigma}_c$ for some value of k, say $k = 1$ or $k = 2$. The bootstrap can be used to obtain valid standard errors where, as always with large N and small T, we resample the cross section units (keeping all T time periods for each i).

Estimating APEs is also relatively simple. APEs (at $\mathbf{x}_t$) are obtained by finding $\mathrm{E}[m(\mathbf{x}_t\boldsymbol{\beta} + c_i, \sigma_u^2)]$ and then computing partial derivatives or changes with respect to elements of $\mathbf{x}_t$. Since $c_i = \psi + \bar{\mathbf{x}}_i\xi + a_i$, we have, by iterated expectations,

$$\mathrm{E}[m(\mathbf{x}_t\boldsymbol{\beta} + c_i, \sigma_u^2)] = \mathrm{E}\{\mathrm{E}[m(\psi + \mathbf{x}_t\boldsymbol{\beta} + \bar{\mathbf{x}}_i\xi + a_i, \sigma_u^2) \mid \mathbf{x}_i]\}, \tag{17.79}$$

where the first expectation is with respect to the distribution of c_i. Since a_i and $\mathbf{x}_i$ are independent and $a_i \sim \text{Normal}(0, \sigma_a^2)$, the conditional expectation in equation (17.79) is obtained by integrating $m(\psi + \mathbf{x}_t\boldsymbol{\beta} + \bar{\mathbf{x}}_i\xi + a_i, \sigma_u^2)$ over a_i with respect to the Normal$(0, \sigma_a^2)$ distribution. Since $m(\psi + \mathbf{x}_t\boldsymbol{\beta} + \bar{\mathbf{x}}_i\xi + a_i, \sigma_u^2)$ is obtained by integrating

$\max(0, \psi + \mathbf{x}_t\boldsymbol{\beta} + \overline{\mathbf{x}}_i\xi + a_i + u_{it})$ with respect to u_{it} over the Normal$(0, \sigma_u^2)$ distribution, it follows that

$$\mathrm{E}[m(\psi + \mathbf{x}_t\boldsymbol{\beta} + \overline{\mathbf{x}}_i\xi + a_i, \sigma_u^2) \,|\, \mathbf{x}_i] = m(\psi + \mathbf{x}_t\boldsymbol{\beta} + \overline{\mathbf{x}}_i\xi, \sigma_a^2 + \sigma_u^2). \tag{17.80}$$

Therefore, the expected value of equation (17.80) (with respect to the distribution of $\overline{\mathbf{x}}_i$) is consistently estimated as

$$N^{-1} \sum_{i=1}^{N} m(\hat{\psi} + \mathbf{x}_t\hat{\boldsymbol{\beta}} + \overline{\mathbf{x}}_i\hat{\xi}, \hat{\sigma}_a^2 + \hat{\sigma}_u^2). \tag{17.81}$$

A similar argument works for $\mathrm{E}(y_t \,|\, \mathbf{x}, c, y_t > 0)$: sum $(\hat{\psi} + \mathbf{x}_t\hat{\boldsymbol{\beta}} + \overline{\mathbf{x}}_i\hat{\xi}) + \hat{\sigma}_v\lambda[(\hat{\psi} + \mathbf{x}_t\hat{\boldsymbol{\beta}} + \overline{\mathbf{x}}_i\hat{\xi})/\hat{\sigma}_v]$ in expression (17.81), where $\lambda(\cdot)$ is the inverse Mills ratio and $\hat{\sigma}_v^2 = \hat{\sigma}_a^2 + \hat{\sigma}_u^2$.

We can relax assumption (17.78) and still obtain consistent, $\sqrt{N}$-asymptotically normal estimates of the APEs. In fact, under assumptions (17.75)–(17.77), we can write

$$y_{it} = \max(0, \psi + \mathbf{x}_{it}\boldsymbol{\beta} + \overline{\mathbf{x}}_i\xi + v_{it}), \tag{17.82}$$

$$v_{it} \,|\, \mathbf{x}_i \sim \text{Normal}(0, \sigma_v^2), \qquad t = 1, 2, \ldots, T, \tag{17.83}$$

where $v_{it} = a_i + u_{it}$. Without further assumptions, the v_{it} are *arbitrarily* serially correlated, and so maximum likelihood analysis using the density of $\mathbf{y}_i$ given $\mathbf{x}_i$ would be computationally demanding. However, we can obtain $\sqrt{N}$-asymptotically normal estimators by a simple pooled Tobit procedure of y_{it} on 1, $\mathbf{x}_{it}$, $\overline{\mathbf{x}}_i$, $t = 1, \ldots, T$, $i = 1, \ldots, N$. While we can only estimate σ_v^2 from this procedure, it is all we need—along with $\hat{\psi}$, $\hat{\boldsymbol{\beta}}$, and $\hat{\xi}$—to obtain the APEs based on expression (17.81). The robust variance matrix for partial MLE derived in Section 13.8.2 should be used for standard errors and inference. A minimum distance approach, analogous to the probit case discussed in Section 15.8.2, is also available.

From equation (17.81), we can easily obtain scale factors for APEs of the continuous explanatory variables. For given $\mathbf{x}_t$, the estimated scale is $N^{-1}\sum_{i=1}^{N}\Phi((\hat{\psi} + \mathbf{x}_t\hat{\boldsymbol{\beta}} + \overline{\mathbf{x}}_i\hat{\xi})/\hat{\sigma}_v)$ where $\hat{\sigma}_v^2 = \hat{\sigma}_a^2 + \hat{\sigma}_u^2$. We can further average across $\mathbf{x}_{it}$ to obtain a scale factor for time period t, or even across all time periods to get a single scale factor. We can use (17.81) directly to estimate APEs for discrete changes. For example, if x_{tK} is binary, we evaluate $m(\hat{\psi} + \mathbf{x}_t\hat{\boldsymbol{\beta}} + \overline{\mathbf{x}}_i\hat{\xi}, \hat{\sigma}_v^2)$ and $x_{tK} = 1$ and $x_{tK} = 0$ and form the difference. Rather than set values for $x_{t1}, \ldots, x_{t,K-1}$, we could average across these as well, and even across all time periods. The next example illustrates how these calculations can be done.

Table 17.3
Panel Data Models for Annual Women's Labor Supply, 1980–1992

Model Estimation Method	(1) Linear Fixed Effects	(2) RE Tobit MLE	(3) CRE Tobit MLE
nwifeinc	−.775 (.343)	−2.251 (.325)	−1.554 (.382)
ch0_2	−342.38 (26.65)	−459.93 (22.67)	−472.09 (23.03)
ch3_5	−254.13 (25.88)	−313.50 (18.82)	−329.39 (19.49)
ch6_17	−42.96 (14.89)	−32.33 (9.82)	−46.12 (10.90)
marr	−634.80 (286.17)	−657.58 (48.93)	−784.18 (155.01)
constant	1,786 (247.30)	1,676.37 (39.28)	1,646.36 (45.26)
	—		
$\hat{\sigma}_a$	—	768.55	756.40
$\hat{\sigma}_u$	—	624.29	621.70
scale factor	—	.811	.826
Log likelihood	—	−70,782.09	−70,733.20
Number of women	898	898	898

All specifications include a full set of time dummies.
The standard errors for FE estimation of the linear model are robust to arbitrary serial correlation and heteroskedasticity.
For RE Tobit, $\hat{\sigma}_a = \hat{\sigma}_c$.
The likelihood ratio test for exclusion of the five time averages in column (3) is 97.78, which gives a p-value of essentially zero.

Example 17.5 (Panel Data Estimation of Annual Hours Equation for Women): We now apply the RE Tobit and CRE Tobit models to an annual hours equation using the Panel Study of Income Dynamics for 1980 to 1992 (PSID80_92.RAW). We include other sources of income (*nwifeinc*), three categories of children (*ch*0_2, *ch*3_5, and *ch*6_17), and a binary marital status indicator (*marr*). We also include a full set of year dummies (not reported). For comparison purposes, a linear model estimated by fixed effects is also reported (Table 17.3).

The three sets of estimates tell the same story in terms of directions of effects. Other income has a negative, statistically significant effect on annual hours, as do number of children—especially young children—and being married. The scale factors for the RE and CRE Tobit models have been computed by averaging across all i and t. Therefore, the APE for *nwifeinc* for RE Tobit is about $.811(-2.25) = -1.82$, and for the CRE Tobit model it is $.826(-1.55) = -1.28$. Both are larger in magnitude than the linear model coefficient obtained from FE, $-.775$. Certainly, including the time averages makes the APE from the Tobit and that from FE closer, but it does not entirely close the gap. The APE for *marr* from the CRE Tobit is about -695.26 (obtained from averaging the differences in estimated means with $marr = 1$ and $marr = 0$). This is almost 10% higher in magnitude than the FE estimate. Of course, we cannot know which estimate is closer to the true APE; each approach has its drawbacks.

A correlated random effects version of the two-limit Tobit model follows in the obvious way. As with the standard Tobit model, partial effects at the mean of c_i and other values are easily obtained under the full set of assumptions, but where equation (17.72) is replaced with the equations that generate two corners. APEs can be estimated without assumption (17.78) because the mean function for a two-limit Tobit conditional on $(\mathbf{x}_{it}, \bar{\mathbf{x}}_i)$ has the same structure as the mean function conditional on $(\mathbf{x}_{it}, c_i)$, provided assumption (17.74) holds. The argument is essentially the same as in the standard unobserved effects Tobit model; see Problem 17.16 for details.

It is also possible to consistently estimate $\boldsymbol{\beta}$ under the conditional median assumption

$$\mathrm{Med}(y_{it} \mid \mathbf{x}_{i1}, \ldots, \mathbf{x}_{iT}, c_i) = \mathrm{Med}(y_{it} \mid \mathbf{x}_{it}, c_i) = \max(0, \mathbf{x}_{it}\boldsymbol{\beta} + c_i), \tag{17.84}$$

which imposes strict exogeneity (for the median) conditional on c_i. Equivalently, we can write

$$y_{it} = \max(0, \mathbf{x}_{it}\boldsymbol{\beta} + c_i + u_{it}), \qquad \mathrm{Med}(u_{it} \mid \mathbf{x}_i, c_i) = 0, \qquad t = 1, \ldots, T. \tag{17.85}$$

Honoré (1992) uses a clever conditioning argument on pairs of time periods, say t and s, that effectively eliminates c_i under the exchangeability assumption that (u_{it}, u_{is}) and (u_{is}, u_{it}) are identically distributed conditional on $(\mathbf{x}_{it}, \mathbf{x}_{is}, c_i)$. The details are too involved to cover here. A nice feature of Honoré's method is that it identifies the parameters in $\mathrm{Med}(y_{it} \mid \mathbf{x}_{it}, c_i)$ without restricting $\mathrm{D}(c_i \mid \mathbf{x}_i)$. However, restrictions are imposed on the joint distribution of $(u_{i1}, \ldots, u_{iT})$, restrictions that rule out, for example, heteroskedasticity that depends on the covariates, unobserved effect, or just time. (Of course, the standard Tobit model imposes homoskedasticity, too, although that is fairly easy to relax in parametric contexts.) A less obvious problem with Honoré's method is that, because we know nothing about the distribution of c_i (either unconditionally or conditional on $\mathbf{x}_i$), we have no idea what are sensible values to plug in for c in the estimated median function $\max(0, \mathbf{x}_t\hat{\boldsymbol{\beta}} + c)$. The estimate $\hat{\beta}_j$ is the estimated partial effect of x_{tj} on the median once $\mathbf{x}_t\boldsymbol{\beta} + c > 0$, but we cannot even estimate the fraction of the population where $\mathbf{x}_t\boldsymbol{\beta} + c > 0$. We might be satisfied by averaging c out of $\max(0, \mathbf{x}_t\boldsymbol{\beta} + c)$—that is, obtain an average structural function but where the median, rather than the mean, is defined as the "structure" of interest—but again, without information about the distribution of c_i, we cannot compute this average. (If c_i has a $\mathrm{Normal}(\mu_c, \sigma_c^2)$ distribution, then $\mathrm{E}_{c_i}(\max(0, \mathbf{x}_t\boldsymbol{\beta} + c_i)) = \Phi((\mu_c + \mathbf{x}_t\boldsymbol{\beta})/\sigma_c)(\mu_c + \mathbf{x}_t\boldsymbol{\beta}) + \sigma_c\phi((\mu_c + \mathbf{x}_t\boldsymbol{\beta})/\sigma_c)$, but we do not have enough information to estimate μ_c and σ_c^2.)

Given the variety of methods for estimating unobserved effects models for corner solution responses, we can produce a table very similar to Table 15.4 for binary response. With Honoré's estimator of $\boldsymbol{\beta}$ playing the role of the fixed effects (FE) logit estimator, the table would only be slightly changed. For example, the CRE Tobit model under the full random effects assumptions allows estimation of partial effects at different values of c, and also estimation of APEs. If we drop the conditional independence assumption, we can only identify APEs (that is, averaged across the distribution of c_i). As we just discussed, Honoré's estimator allows estimation of $\boldsymbol{\beta}$, but not generally partial effects on the median or APEs on the median. Honoré's approach does allow serial correlation in the idiosyncratic errors (unlike the FE logit estimator for binary response), but does impose exchangeability.

17.8.3 Dynamic Unobserved Effects Tobit Models

We now turn to a specific dynamic model,

$$y_{it} = \max(0, \mathbf{z}_{it}\boldsymbol{\delta} + \rho_1 y_{i,t-1} + c_i + u_{it}), \tag{17.86}$$

$$u_{it} \mid (\mathbf{z}_i, y_{i,t-1}, \ldots, y_{i0}, c_i) \sim \text{Normal}(0, \sigma_u^2), \qquad t = 1, \ldots, T. \tag{17.87}$$

We can embellish this model in many ways. For example, the lagged effect of $y_{i,t-1}$ can depend on whether $y_{i,t-1}$ is zero or greater than zero. Thus, we might replace $\rho_1 y_{i,t-1}$ by $\eta_1 r_{i,t-1} + \rho_1(1 - r_{i,t-1})y_{i,t-1}$, where r_{it} is a binary variable equal to unity if $y_{it} = 0$. We can allow a polynomial in $y_{i,t-1}$. Or, we can let the variance of u_{it} change over time. The basic approach does not depend on the particular model.

The discussion in Section 15.8.4 about how to handle the initial value problem also holds here (see Section 13.9.2 for the general case). A fairly general and tractable approach is to specify a distribution for the unobserved effect, c_i, given the initial value, y_{i0}, and the exogenous variables in all time periods, $\mathbf{z}_i$. Let $h(c \mid y_0, \mathbf{z}; \gamma)$ denote such a density. Then the joint density of $(y_1, \ldots, y_T)$ given $(y_0, \mathbf{z})$ is

$$\int_{-\infty}^{\infty} \prod_{t=1}^{T} f(y_t \mid y_{t-1}, \ldots y_1, y_0, \mathbf{z}, c; \boldsymbol{\theta}) h(c \mid y_0, \mathbf{z}; \gamma)\, dc, \tag{17.88}$$

where $f(y_t \mid y_{t-1}, \ldots y_1, y_0, \mathbf{z}, c; \boldsymbol{\theta})$ is the censored-at-zero normal distribution with mean $\mathbf{z}_t\boldsymbol{\delta} + \rho_1 y_{t-1} + c$ and variance σ_u^2. A natural specification for $h(c \mid y_0, \mathbf{z}; \gamma)$ is $\text{Normal}(\psi + \xi_0 y_0 + \mathbf{z}\boldsymbol{\xi}, \sigma_a^2)$, where $\sigma_a^2 = \text{Var}(c \mid y_0, \mathbf{z})$. This leads to a fairly straightforward procedure. To see why, write $c_i = \psi + \xi_0 y_{i0} + \mathbf{z}_i\boldsymbol{\xi} + a_i$, so that

$$y_{it} = \max(0, \psi + \mathbf{z}_{it}\boldsymbol{\delta} + \rho_1 y_{i,t-1} + \xi_0 y_{i0} + \mathbf{z}_i\boldsymbol{\xi} + a_i + u_{it}), \tag{17.89}$$

where the distribution of a_i given $(y_{i0}, \mathbf{z}_i)$ is $\text{Normal}(0, \sigma_a^2)$, and assumption (17.87) holds with a_i replacing c_i. The density in expression (17.88) then has the same form as the random effects Tobit model, where the explanatory variables at time t are

$(\mathbf{z}_{it}, y_{i,t-1}, y_{i0}, \mathbf{z}_i)$. The inclusion of the initial condition in each time period, as well as the entire vector $\mathbf{z}_i$, allows for the unobserved heterogeneity to be correlated with the initial condition and the strictly exogenous variables. Any software that estimates random effects Tobit models can be used to estimate all the parameters; in particular, we can easily test for state dependence ($\rho_1 \neq 0$). APEs can be estimated rather easily. For example, the APEs for $\mathrm{E}(y_t \mid \mathbf{z}_t, y_{t-1}, c)$ are consistently estimated from

$$N^{-1}\sum_{i=1}^{N} m(\hat{\psi}_t + \mathbf{z}_t\hat{\boldsymbol{\delta}} + \hat{\rho}_1 y_{t-1} + \hat{\xi}_0 y_{i0} + \mathbf{z}_i\hat{\boldsymbol{\xi}}, \hat{\sigma}_a^2 + \hat{\sigma}_u^2), \tag{17.90}$$

where different time intercepts, $\hat{\psi}_t$, are explicitly shown for emphasis. (As with linear models and previous nonlinear models, one would usually include time dummies among the regressors.) As usual, we can take derivatives or changes with respect to elements of $(\mathbf{z}_t, y_{t-1})$. Allowing more flexible functions of the initial condition in $\mathrm{E}(c_i \mid y_{i0}, \mathbf{z}_i)$ is straightforward. Allowing heteroskedasticity in $\mathrm{Var}(c_i \mid y_{i0}, \mathbf{z}_i)$, say $\mathrm{Var}(c_i \mid y_{i0}, \mathbf{z}_i) = \exp(\eta + \xi_0 y_{i0} + \mathbf{z}_i\boldsymbol{\xi})$, or with more flexible functions in $(y_{i0}, \mathbf{z}_i)$, should not be too difficult. See Wooldridge (2005b) for further discussion and extensions, including to two-limit Tobit models.

Using a censoring argument, Honoré (1993a) obtains orthogonality conditions that have zero mean at the true values of the parameters without making distributional assumptions about c_i or u_{it} in equation (17.86). Honoré's assumptions put restrictions on the distribution of $\{u_{it} : t = 1, \ldots, T\}$—sufficient is that they are independent, identically distributed conditional on $(\mathbf{z}_i, y_{i0}, c_i)$—but he does not impose a parametric distribution. Therefore, one can test for state dependence fairly generally (although heteroskedasticity in $\{u_{it}\}$ is ruled out). Honoré and Hu (2004) obtained sufficient conditions such that the parameters $\boldsymbol{\delta}$ and ρ_1 are identified by a set of moment conditions similar to those in Honoré (1993a), and they derive the consistency and $\sqrt{N}$-asymptotic normality of a GMM estimator. Unfortunately, the methods used by Honoré (1993a) and Honoré and Hu (2004) do not allow for time dummies, and so it could be difficult to distinguish state dependence from aggregate fluctuations. Further, the censoring arguments hinge critically on $y_{i,t-1}$ appearing linearly in (17.86). It is not clear how to extend their arguments to general functions of $y_{i,t-1}$. At a minimum, one would need to know the signs of the coefficients on the extra functions (such as quadratics, or where we allow a separate effect from zero to a positive value).

As things stand, semiparametric methods for estimating dynamic corner solution models do not uniformly relax assumptions of parametric approaches. Parametric approaches easily handle time dummies, nonlinear functions of $y_{i,t-1}$, and parametric heteroskedasticity. Therefore, it is difficult to know the proper reaction when discrepancies are found in the parameter estimates. Further, as with semiparametric methods for corner solution responses with strictly exogenous explanatory variables, the ability of semiparametric methods to consistently estimate parameters does not result in estimates of partial effects, and so the practical importance of any state dependence is not easily determined.

Problems

17.1. When y is a nonnegative corner solution response with corner at zero, one strategy that has been suggested is to use $\log(1+y)$ as the dependent variable in a linear regression.

a. Does the transformation $\log(1+y)$ solve the problem of a pileup at zero? Explain. Are there other reasons that this transformation might be useful?

b. Suppose we assume the linear model

$$\log(1+y) = \mathbf{x}\boldsymbol{\beta} + r, \qquad \mathrm{E}(r \mid \mathbf{x}) = 0.$$

How would you estimate $\boldsymbol{\beta}$? Generally, can r be independent of $\mathbf{x}$? Explain.

c. Show that

$$\mathrm{E}(y \mid \mathbf{x}) = \exp(\mathbf{x}\boldsymbol{\beta})\mathrm{E}[\exp(r) \mid \mathbf{x}] - 1.$$

If, as an approximation, we assume r and $\mathbf{x}$ are independent with $\eta = \mathrm{E}[\exp(r)]$, find $\mathrm{E}(y \mid \mathbf{x})$.

d. Under the independence assumption in part c, propose a consistent estimate of η. (Hint: Use Duan's (1983) smearing estimate.)

e. Given $\hat{\boldsymbol{\beta}}$ and $\hat{\eta}$, how would you estimate $\mathrm{E}(y \mid \mathbf{x})$? Is the estimate guaranteed to be nonnegative? Explain.

f. Use the data in MROZ.RAW to estimate $\boldsymbol{\beta}$ and η, where $y = hours$. The elements of $\mathbf{x}$ should be the same as in Table 17.1. What is $\hat{\eta}$ for this data set? Compute the fitted values for $hours_i$, say $\widehat{hours}_i$. Do you get any negative fitted values?

g. Using the fitted values from part f, obtain the squared correlation between $hours_i$ and $\widehat{hours}_i$. How does this R-squared measure compare to that for the linear model and the Tobit model in Table 17.1?

h. Test the errors r_i for heteroskedasticity by running the regression $\hat{r}_i^2$ on 1, $(\mathbf{x}_i\hat{\boldsymbol{\beta}})$, $(\mathbf{x}_i\hat{\boldsymbol{\beta}})^2$, where $\mathbf{x}_i\hat{\boldsymbol{\beta}}$ are the fitted values from the OLS regression $\log(1 + hours_i)$ on $\mathbf{x}_i$. (See Section 6.2.4.) Does it appear that r_i is independent of $\mathbf{x}_i$?

17.2. Let y be a response variable taking on values in $[0, 1]$, where $\mathrm{P}(y = 0) = 0$ and $\mathrm{P}(y = 1) > 0$. An example is, for a random sample of markets indexed by i, y_i is the share of the largest firm; by definition, y_i cannot be zero but could be one.

a. Would a two-limit Tobit model be appropriate for y? Explain.

b. Explain why a type I Tobit model applied to $-\log(y)$ makes logical sense.

c. If you apply the suggestion in part b, would it be easy to recover $\mathrm{E}(y \mid \mathbf{x})$? Show what you would have to do.

17.3. Suppose that y given $\mathbf{x}$ follows a two-limit Tobit model as in Section 17.7, with limit points $a_1 < a_2$.

a. Find $\mathrm{P}(y = a_1 \mid \mathbf{x})$ and $\mathrm{P}(y = a_2 \mid \mathbf{x})$ in terms of the standard normal cdf, $\mathbf{x}$, $\boldsymbol{\beta}$, and σ. For $a_1 < \mathscr{y} < a_2$, find $\mathrm{P}(y \leq \mathscr{y} \mid \mathbf{x})$, and use this to find the density of y given $\mathbf{x}$ for $a_1 < \mathscr{y} < a_2$.

b. If $z \sim \mathrm{Normal}(0, 1)$, it can be shown that $\mathrm{E}(z \mid c_1 < z < c_2) = \{\phi(c_1) - \phi(c_2)\}/\{\Phi(c_2) - \Phi(c_1)\}$ for $c_1 < c_2$. Use this fact to find $\mathrm{E}(y \mid \mathbf{x}, a_1 < y < a_2)$ and $\mathrm{E}(y \mid \mathbf{x})$.

c. Consider the following method for estimating $\boldsymbol{\beta}$. Using only the nonlimit observations, that is, observations for which $a_1 < y_i < a_2$, run the OLS regression of y_i on $\mathbf{x}_i$. Explain why this does not generally produce a consistent estimator of $\boldsymbol{\beta}$.

d. Write down the log-likelihood function for observation i; it should consist of three parts.

e. How would you estimate $\mathrm{E}(y \mid \mathbf{x}, a_1 < y < a_2)$ and $\mathrm{E}(y \mid \mathbf{x})$?

f. Show that

$$\frac{\partial \mathrm{E}(y \mid \mathbf{x})}{\partial x_j} = \{\Phi[(a_2 - \mathbf{x}\boldsymbol{\beta})/\sigma] - \Phi[(a_1 - \mathbf{x}\boldsymbol{\beta})/\sigma]\}\beta_j.$$

Why is the scale factor multiplying β_j necessarily between zero and one?

g. Suppose you obtain $\hat{\gamma}$ from a standard OLS regression of y_i on $\mathbf{x}_i$, using all observations. Would you compare $\hat{\gamma}_j$ to the two-limit Tobit estimate, $\hat{\beta}_j$? What would be a sensible comparison?

17.4. Use the data in JTRAIN1.RAW for this question.

a. Using only the data for 1988, estimate a linear equation relating *hrsemp* to $\log(employ)$, *union*, and *grant*. Compute the usual and heteroskedasticity-robust standard errors. Interpret the results.

b. Out of the 127 firms with nonmissing data on all variables, how many have $hrsemp = 0$? Estimate the model from part a by Tobit. Find the estimated average partial effect of *grant* on $\text{E}(hrsemp \mid employ, union, grant, hrsemp > 0)$ for the 127 firms and $union = 1$. What is the APE on $\text{E}(hrsemp \mid employ, union, grant)$?

c. Are $\log(employ)$ and *union* jointly significant in the Tobit model?

d. In terms of goodness of fit for the conditional mean, do you prefer the linear model or Tobit model for estimating $\text{E}(hrsemp \mid employ, union, grant)$?

17.5. Use the data set FRINGE.RAW for this question.

a. Estimate a linear model by OLS relating *hrbens* to *exper, age, educ, tenure, married, male, white, nrtheast, nrthcen, south*, and *union*.

b. Estimate a Tobit model relating the same variables from part a. Why do you suppose the OLS and Tobit estimates are so similar?

c. Add $exper^2$ and $tenure^2$ to the Tobit model from part b. Should these be included?

d. Are there significant differences in hourly benefits across industry, holding the other factors fixed?

17.6. Consider a Tobit model with an endogenous binary explanatory variable:

$$y_1 = \max(0, \mathbf{z}_1\boldsymbol{\delta}_1 + \alpha_1 y_2 + u_1)$$

$$y_2 = 1[\mathbf{z}\boldsymbol{\delta}_2 + v_2 > 0],$$

where (u_1, v_2) is independent of $\mathbf{z}$ with a bivariate normal distribution with mean zero and $\text{Var}(v_2) = 1$. If u_1 and v_2 are correlated, y_2 is endogenous.

a. Find the density of y_1 given $(\mathbf{z}, y_2)$. (Hint: First find the density of y_1 given $(\mathbf{z}, v_2)$, which has the standard Tobit form.)

b. For any observation i, write down the log-likelihood function in terms of the parameters $\boldsymbol{\delta}_1$, α_1, σ_1^2, $\boldsymbol{\delta}_2$, and ρ_1, where $\sigma_1^2 = \text{Var}(u_1)$ and $\rho_1 = \text{Cov}(v_2, u_1)$.

c. Discuss the properties of the following two-step method for estimating $(\boldsymbol{\delta}_1, \alpha_1)$: (1) Run probit of y_{i2} on $\mathbf{z}_i$ and obtain the fitted probabilities, $\Phi(\mathbf{z}_i\hat{\boldsymbol{\delta}}_2)$, $i = 1, \ldots, N$. (2) Run Tobit of y_{i1} on $\mathbf{z}_{i1}$, $\Phi(\mathbf{z}_i\hat{\boldsymbol{\delta}}_2)$, and use the coefficients as estimates of $(\boldsymbol{\delta}_1, \alpha_1)$.

d. For the binary response model $y_2 = 1[\mathbf{z}\boldsymbol{\delta}_2 + v_2 \geq 0]$, the **generalized residual** for a random draw i is defined as $gr_{i2} = \text{E}(v_{i2} \mid y_{i2}, \mathbf{z}_i)$. When v_2 is independent of $\mathbf{z}$ with a standard normal distribution, it can be shown that $gr_{i2} = y_{i2}\phi(\mathbf{z}_i\boldsymbol{\delta}_2)/\Phi(\mathbf{z}_i\boldsymbol{\delta}_2) - (1 - y_{i2})\phi(\mathbf{z}_i\boldsymbol{\delta}_2)/[1 - \Phi(\mathbf{z}_i\boldsymbol{\delta}_2)]$. Show that a variable addition test version of the score test for $\text{H}_0: \rho_1 = 0$ can be obtained from Tobit of y_{i1} on $\mathbf{z}_{i1}$, y_{i2}, $\widehat{gr}_{i2}$ and using a t test on $\widehat{gr}_{i2}$. (Hint: The problem is simplified by reparameterizing the log likelihood by defining $\tau_1^2 = \sigma_1^2 - \rho_1^2$, so that ρ_1 appears only multiplying v_2.)

17.7. Suppose in a two-part model that $P(y > 0 \mid \mathbf{x})$ follows a probit model, $E(y \mid \mathbf{x}, y > 0) = \exp(\mathbf{x}\boldsymbol{\beta})$, and $\text{Var}(y \mid \mathbf{x}, y > 0) = \eta^2[\exp(\mathbf{x}\boldsymbol{\beta})]^2$. Find $\text{Var}(y \mid \mathbf{x})$. (Hint: Write y as in (17.37), where s and w^* are independent conditional on $\mathbf{x}$, with $E(w^* \mid \mathbf{x}) = \exp(\mathbf{x}\boldsymbol{\beta})$ and $\text{Var}(w^* \mid \mathbf{x}) = \eta^2[\exp(\mathbf{x}\boldsymbol{\beta})]^2$.)

17.8. Consider three different approaches for modeling $E(y \mid \mathbf{x})$ when $y \geq 0$ is a corner solution outcome: (1) $E(y \mid \mathbf{x}) = \mathbf{x}\boldsymbol{\beta}$; (2) $E(y \mid \mathbf{x}) = \exp(\mathbf{x}\boldsymbol{\beta})$; and (3) y given $\mathbf{x}$ follows a type I Tobit model.

a. How would you estimate models 1 and 2?

b. Obtain three goodness-of-fit statistics that can be compared across models; each should measure how much sample variation in y_i is explained by $\hat{E}(y_i \mid \mathbf{x}_i)$.

c. Suppose, in your sample, $y_i > 0$ for all i. Show that the OLS and Tobit estimates of $\boldsymbol{\beta}$ are identical. Does the fact that they are identical mean that the linear model for $E(y \mid \mathbf{x})$ and the Tobit model produce the same estimates of $E(y \mid \mathbf{x})$? Explain.

d. If $y > 0$ in the population, does a Tobit model make sense? What is a simple alternative to the three approaches listed at the beginning of this problem? What assumptions are sufficient for estimating $E(y \mid \mathbf{x})$?

17.9. Consider the Tobit model $y_1 = \max(0, \mathbf{x}_1\boldsymbol{\beta}_1 + u_1)$ where $\mathbf{x}_1$ is a function of $(\mathbf{z}_1, y_2)$ and $y_2 = \mathbf{z}\boldsymbol{\delta}_2 + v_2$. Assume that $E(\mathbf{z}'v_2) = \mathbf{0}$ and that $u_1 \mid v_2, \mathbf{z} \sim \text{Normal}(\theta_1 v_2 + \eta_1(v_2^2 - \tau_2^2), \exp(\psi_1 + \omega_1 v_2))$, where $\tau_2^2 = E(v_2^2)$.

a. Find $D(y_1 \mid y_2, \mathbf{z})$.

b. Based on your answer in part a, propose a two-step method for estimating all of the parameters.

c. Show how to estimate the average structural function after the two-step estimation. (Hint: This involves averaging across $\hat{v}_{i2}$.)

d. If $v_2 \mid \mathbf{z} \sim \text{Normal}(0, \tau_2^2)$, what is an alternative method of estimation?

e. Under the assumption on $D(u_1 \mid v_2)$, can u_1 have an unconditional normal distribution? Explain.

17.10. a. Provide a careful derivation of equation (17.16). It will help to use the fact that $d\phi(z)/dz = -z\phi(z)$.

b. Derive equation (17.59).

17.11. Let y be a corner solution response, and let $L(y \mid 1, \mathbf{x}) = \gamma_0 + \mathbf{x}\boldsymbol{\gamma}$ be the linear projection of y onto an intercept and $\mathbf{x}$, where $\mathbf{x}$ is $1 \times K$. If we use a random sample on $(\mathbf{x}, y)$ to estimate γ_0 and $\boldsymbol{\gamma}$ by OLS, are the estimators inconsistent because of the corner solution nature of y? Explain.

17.12. Use the data in APPLE.RAW for this question. These are phone survey data, where each respondent was asked the amount of "ecolabeled" (or "ecologically friendly") apples he or she would purchase at given prices for both ecolabeled apples and regular apples. The prices are cents per pound, and *ecolbs* and *reglbs* are both in pounds.

a. For what fraction of the sample is $ecolbs_i = 0$? Discuss generally whether *ecolbs* is a good candidate for a Tobit model.

b. Estimate a linear regression model for *ecolbs*, with explanatory variables $\log(ecoprc)$, $\log(regprc)$, $\log(faminc)$, *educ*, *hhsize*, and *num5_17*. Are the signs of the coefficient for $\log(ecoprc)$ and $\log(regprc)$ the expected ones? Interpret the estimated coefficient on $\log(ecoprc)$.

c. Test the linear regression in part b for heteroskedasticity by running the regression $\hat{u}^2$ on 1, $\widehat{ecolbs}$, $\widehat{ecolbs}^2$ and carrying out an F test. What do you conclude?

d. Obtain the OLS fitted values. How many are negative?

e. Now estimate a Tobit model for *ecolbs*. Are the signs and statistical significance of the explanatory variables the same as for the linear regression model? What do you make of the fact that the Tobit estimate on $\log(ecoprc)$ is about twice the size of the OLS estimate in the linear model?

f. Obtain the estimated partial effect of $\log(ecoprc)$ for the Tobit model using equation (17.16), where the x_j are evaluated at the mean values. What is the estimated price elasticity (again, at the mean values of the x_j)?

g. Reestimate the Tobit model dropping the variable $\log(regprc)$. What happens to the coefficient on $\log(ecoprc)$? What kind of correlation does this result suggest between $\log(ecoprc)$ and $\log(regprc)$?

h. Reestimate the model from part e, but with *ecoprc* and *regprc* as the explanatory variables, rather than their natural logs. Which functional form do you prefer? (Hint: Compare log-likelihood functions.)

17.13. Suppose that, in the context of an unobserved effects Tobit (or probit) panel data model, the mean of the unobserved effect, c_i, is related to the time average of *detrended* $\mathbf{x}_{it}$. Specifically,

$$c_i = \left[(1/T)\sum_{t=1}^{T}(\mathbf{x}_{it} - \boldsymbol{\pi}_t)\right]\xi + a_i,$$

where $\boldsymbol{\pi}_t = \mathrm{E}(\mathbf{x}_{it})$, $t = 1, \ldots, T$, and $a_i \mid \mathbf{x}_i \sim \mathrm{Normal}(0, \sigma_a^2)$. How does this extension of equation (17.74) affect estimation of the unobserved effects Tobit (or probit) model?

17.14. Consider the correlated random effects Tobit model under assumptions (17.72), (17.73), and (17.78), but replace assumption (17.74) with

$$c_i \mid \mathbf{x}_i \sim \text{Normal}[\psi + \bar{\mathbf{x}}_i \xi, \sigma_a^2 \exp(\bar{\mathbf{x}}_i \boldsymbol{\lambda})]$$

See Problem 15.18 for the probit case.

a. What is the density of y_{it} given $(\mathbf{x}_i, a_i)$, where $a_i = c_i - \text{E}(c_i \mid \mathbf{x}_i)$?

b. Derive the log-likelihood function by first finding the density of $(y_{i1}, \dots, y_{iT})$ given $\mathbf{x}_i$.

c. Assuming you have estimated $\boldsymbol{\beta}$, σ_u^2, ψ, ξ, σ_a^2, and $\boldsymbol{\lambda}$ by CMLE, how would you estimate the APEs?

17.15 Use the data in CPS91.RAW to answer this question.

a. Estimate a Tobit model for *hours* with *nwifeinc*, *educ*, *exper*, *exper*^{2}, *age*, *kidlt6*, and *kidge6* as explanatory variables. What is the value of the log-likelihood function?

b. Estimate Cragg's lognormal hurdle model. Does it fit the conditional distribution of *hours* better than the Tobit model?

c. Estimate the ET2T model (with all explanatory variables in both stages). Discuss how it compares to the model from part b. Do you reject the model from part b in favor of the ET2T model?

d. Estimate Cragg's truncated normal hurdle model. How does its fit compare with the previous models?

17.16. Consider the CRE Tobit model in Section 17.8.2, written with latent variable

$$y_{it}^* = \mathbf{x}_{it}\boldsymbol{\beta} + c_i + u_{it}$$

$$y_{it} = q_1 \qquad \text{if } y_{it}^* \le q_1$$

$$y_{it} = q_2 \qquad \text{if } y_{it}^* \ge q_2$$

$$y_{it} = y_{it}^* \qquad \text{if } q_1 < y_{it}^* < q_2,$$

where $q_1 < q_2$ are the two known limits. Make assumptions (17.73), (17.74), and (17.78).

a. Obtain the log-likelihood function for estimating all of the parameters.

b. How would you estimate $\text{E}(c_i)$ and $\text{Var}(c_i)$?

c. Describe how to obtain the APEs on $\text{E}(y_{it} \mid \mathbf{x}_{it}, c_i)$.

d. How would your analysis change if you dropped assumption (17.78)?

17.17. Consider an unobserved effects Tobit model with a continuous endogenous explanatory variable:

$$y_{it1} = \max(0, \alpha_1 y_{it2} + \mathbf{z}_{it1}\boldsymbol{\delta} + c_{i1} + u_{it1})$$

$$y_{it2} = \mathbf{z}_{it}\boldsymbol{\pi}_2 + c_{i2} + u_{it2}$$

$$c_{i1} = \psi_1 + \bar{\mathbf{z}}_i\xi_1 + a_{i1}$$

$$c_{i2} = \psi_2 + \bar{\mathbf{z}}_i\xi_2 + a_{i2}$$

Although the assumptions can be weakened somewhat, assume that $(u_{it1}, u_{it2}) \mid \mathbf{z}_i, \mathbf{a}_i$ is bivariate normal with mean zero and constant conditional variance matrix (across t, as well as not depending on the conditioning variables). Further, assume $(a_{i1}, a_{i2}) \mid \mathbf{z}_i$ is bivariate normal with mean zero and constant conditional variance matrix. Depending on your approach, y_{it2} may be only contemporaneously exogenous, not strictly exogenous. The mechanics are very similar to those given in Section 15.8.5 for the probit model.

a. Obtain a control function method for consistently estimating α_1 and $\boldsymbol{\delta}_1$. (Hint: It will help to define $v_{it1} = a_{i1} + u_{it1}$ and $v_{it2} = a_{i2} + u_{it2}$.)

b. How would you obtain standard errors for the parameter estimators?

c. How would you consistently estimate the average structural function (which is a function of $(y_{t2}, \mathbf{z}_{t1})$)?

17.18. Consider a standard linear model where the endogenous explanatory variable, y_2, is a corner solution:

$$y_1 = \mathbf{z}_1\boldsymbol{\delta}_1 + \alpha_1 y_2 + u_1$$

$$\mathrm{E}(u_1 \mid \mathbf{z}) = 0,$$

where $\mathbf{z}_1$ is a strict subset of $\mathbf{z}$.

a. What additional assumptions ensure that the 2SLS estimator, using instruments $\mathbf{z}$ and a random sample, is consistent for the parameters? Does it matter that y_2 is a corner solution?

b. Suppose you think $\mathrm{D}(y_2 \mid \mathbf{z})$ follows a Tobit model and $\mathrm{Var}(u_1 \mid \mathbf{z}) = \sigma_1^2$. What might you do instead of 2SLS in part a, and why? State a minimal set of assumptions that ensure the estimator is consistent.

c. Suppose $y_2 = \max(0, \mathbf{z}\boldsymbol{\delta}_2 + v_2)$, $v_2 \mid \mathbf{z} \sim \mathrm{Normal}(0, \tau_2^2)$ and $\mathrm{E}(u_1 \mid \mathbf{z}, v_2) = \rho_1 v_2$. Propose a control function method for estimating $(\boldsymbol{\delta}_1, \alpha_1)$. (For example, see Vella

(1993).) Does the CF approach change if $(\mathbf{z}_1, y_2)$ is replaced by some known function, $\mathbf{x}_1$, of $(\mathbf{z}_1, y_2)$ (for example, including quadratics and interactions)?

d. Compare the merits of the estimation methods from parts a, b, and c.

e. If in the setup of part c you assume (u_1, v_2) is independent of $\mathbf{z}$ with a joint normal distribution, what estimation method would you use? Provide the objective function.

17.19. Let $y_1, y_2, \ldots, y_G$ be a set of limited dependent variables representing a population. These could be outcomes for the same individual, family, firm, and so on. Some elements could be binary outcomes, some could be ordered outcomes, and others might be corner solutions. For a vector of conditioning variables $\mathbf{x}$ and unobserved heterogeneity $\mathbf{c}$, assume that $y_1, y_2, \ldots, y_G$ are independent conditional on $(\mathbf{x}, \mathbf{c})$, where $f_g(\cdot \mid \mathbf{x}, \mathbf{c}; \gamma_0^g)$. For example, if c is a scalar and y_1 is a binary response, $f_1(\cdot \mid \mathbf{x}, \mathbf{c}; \gamma_o^1)$ might represent a probit model with response probability $\Phi(\mathbf{x}\gamma_o^1 + c)$.

a. Write down the density of $\mathbf{y} = (y_1, y_2, \ldots, y_G)$ given $(\mathbf{x}, \mathbf{c})$.

b. Let $h(\cdot \mid \mathbf{x}; \boldsymbol{\delta}_o)$ be the density of $\mathbf{c}$ given $\mathbf{x}$, where $\boldsymbol{\delta}_o$ is the vector of unknown parameters. Find the density of $\mathbf{y}$ given $\mathbf{x}$. Are the y_g independent conditional on $\mathbf{x}$? Explain.

c. Find the log likelihood for any random draw $(\mathbf{x}_i, \mathbf{y}_i)$.

17.20. Use the data in PSID80_92.RAW to answer this question.

a. Estimate the dynamic Tobit model in Section 17.8.3 using $y_{it} = hours_{it}$, with elements of $\mathbf{z}_{it}$ including $nwifeinc_{it}$, $ch0\_2_{it}$, $ch3\_5_{it}$, $ch6\_17_{it}$, and $marr_{it}$. Be sure to include a full set of year dummies, too.

b. Estimate the APE of *nwifeinc* in 1992 when $hours_{t-1} = 0$. Average across the remaining explanatory variables.

c. Estimate the APE of increasing *ch*0_2 from zero to one in 1992, averaging across all other explanatory variables.

18 Count, Fractional, and Other Nonnegative Responses

18.1 Introduction

A **count variable** is a variable that takes on nonnegative integer values. Many variables that we would like to explain in terms of covariates come as counts. A few examples include the number of times someone is arrested during a given year, number of emergency room drug episodes during a given week, number of cigarettes smoked per day, and number of patents applied for by a firm during a year. These examples have two important characteristics in common: there is no natural a priori upper bound, and the outcome will be zero for at least some members of the population. Other count variables do have an upper bound. For example, for the number of children in a family who are high school graduates, the upper bound is number of children in the family.

If y is the count variable and $\mathbf{x}$ is a vector of explanatory variables, we are often interested in the population regression, $\mathrm{E}(y \mid \mathbf{x})$. Throughout this book we have discussed various models for conditional expectations, and we have discussed different methods of estimation. The most straightforward approach is a linear model, $\mathrm{E}(y \mid \mathbf{x}) = \mathbf{x}\boldsymbol{\beta}$, estimated by ordinary least squares (OLS). For count data, linear models have shortcomings very similar to those for binary responses or corner solution responses: because $y \geq 0$, we know that $\mathrm{E}(y \mid \mathbf{x})$ should be nonnegative for all $\mathbf{x}$. If $\hat{\boldsymbol{\beta}}$ is the OLS estimator, there usually will be values of $\mathbf{x}$ such that $\mathbf{x}\hat{\boldsymbol{\beta}} < 0$, so that the predicted value of y is negative. Still, we have seen that the linear model, appropriately viewed as a linear projection, can sometime provide good estimates of average partial effects (APEs) on the conditional mean.

For strictly positive variables, we often use the natural log transformation, $\log(y)$, and use a linear model. This approach is not possible in interesting count data applications, where y takes on the value zero for a nontrivial fraction of the population. Transformations could be applied that are defined for all $y \geq 0$—for example, $\log(1 + y)$—but $\log(1 + y)$ itself is nonnegative, and it is not obvious how to recover $\mathrm{E}(y \mid \mathbf{x})$ from a linear model for $\mathrm{E}[\log(1 + y) \mid \mathbf{x}]$. With count data, it is better to model $\mathrm{E}(y \mid \mathbf{x})$ directly and to choose functional forms that ensure positivity for any value of $\mathbf{x}$ and any parameter values. When y has no upper bound, the most popular of these is the exponential function, $\mathrm{E}(y \mid \mathbf{x}) = \exp(\mathbf{x}\boldsymbol{\beta})$.

In Chapter 12 we discussed nonlinear least squares (NLS) as a general method for estimating nonlinear models of conditional means. NLS can certainly be applied to count data models, but it is not ideal: NLS is relatively inefficient unless $\mathrm{Var}(y \mid \mathbf{x})$ is constant (see Chapter 12), and all of the standard distributions for count data imply heteroskedasticity.

In Section 18.2 we discuss the most popular model for count data, the Poisson regression model. As we will see, the Poisson regression model has some nice features. First, if y given $\mathbf{x}$ has a Poisson distribution—which used to be the maintained assumption in count data contexts—then the conditional maximum likelihood estimators (CMLEs) are fully efficient. Second, the Poisson assumption turns out to be unnecessary for consistent estimation of the conditional mean parameters. As we will see in Section 18.2, the Poisson quasi–maximum likelihood estimator is fully robust to distributional misspecification. It also maintains certain efficiency properties even when the distribution is not Poisson.

In Section 18.3 we discuss other count data models, including the binomial regression model when each count response has a known upper bound. Section 18.4 covers the gamma regression model, which is better suited to nonnegative, continuous responses (but, given the robustness of the quasi-MLE, can be applied to any nonnegative response). In Section 18.5 we discuss how to handle endogenous explanatory variables with an exponential response function; in particular, the methods apply to count data and other nonnegative, unbounded responses.

Fractional response variables are treated in Section 18.6, where again we focus on quasi-likelihood methods. In Section 18.7 we cover panel data extensions of several of the quasi-likelihood methods.

18.2 Poisson Regression

In Chapter 13 we used the basic Poisson regression model to illustrate maximum likelihood estimation. Here we study Poisson regression in much more detail, emphasizing the robustness properties of the estimator when the Poisson distributional assumption is incorrect.

18.2.1 Assumptions Used for Poisson Regression and Quantities of Interest

The basic Poisson regression model assumes that y given $\mathbf{x} \equiv (x_1, \ldots, x_K)$ has a Poisson distribution, as in El Sayyad (1973) and Maddala (1983, Section 2.15). The density of y given $\mathbf{x}$ under the Poisson assumption is completely determined by the conditional mean $\mu(\mathbf{x}) \equiv \mathrm{E}(y \mid \mathbf{x})$:

$$f(y \mid \mathbf{x}) = \exp[-\mu(\mathbf{x})][\mu(\mathbf{x})]^y / y!, \qquad y = 0, 1, \ldots, \tag{18.1}$$

where $y!$ is y factorial. Given a parametric model for $\mu(\mathbf{x})$ [such as $\mu(\mathbf{x}) = \exp(\mathbf{x}\boldsymbol{\beta})$] and a random sample $\{(\mathbf{x}_i, y_i)\colon i = 1, 2, \ldots, N\}$ on $(\mathbf{x}, y)$, it is fairly straightforward to obtain the CMLEs of the parameters. The statistical properties then follow from our treatment of MLE in Chapter 13.

It has long been recognized that the Poisson distributional assumption imposes restrictions on the conditional moments of y that are often violated in applications. The most important of these is equality of the conditional variance and mean:

$$\text{Var}(y \mid \mathbf{x}) = \text{E}(y \mid \mathbf{x}) \tag{18.2}$$

The variance-mean equality has been rejected in numerous applications, and later we show that assumption (18.2) is violated for fairly simple departures from the Poisson model. Importantly, whether or not assumption (18.2) holds has implications for how we carry out statistical inference. In fact, as we will see, it is assumption (18.2), not the Poisson assumption per se, that is important for large-sample inference; this point will become clear in Section 18.2.2. In what follows we refer to assumption (18.2) as the **Poisson variance assumption**.

A weaker assumption allows the variance-mean ratio to be any positive constant:

$$\text{Var}(y \mid \mathbf{x}) = \sigma^2 \text{E}(y \mid \mathbf{x}) \tag{18.3}$$

where $\sigma^2 > 0$ is the variance-mean ratio. This assumption is used in the generalized linear models (GLM) literature that we discussed in Section 13.11.3, and so we will refer to assumption (18.3) as the **Poisson GLM variance assumption**. The GLM literature is concerned with quasi-MLE of a class of nonlinear models that contains Poisson regression as a special case. Here, we work through the details for Poisson regression.

The case $\sigma^2 > 1$ is empirically relevant because it implies that the variance is greater than the mean; this situation is called **overdispersion** (relative to the Poisson case). One distribution for y given $\mathbf{x}$ where assumption (18.3) holds with overdispersion is what Cameron and Trivedi (1986) call NegBin I—a particular parameterization of the negative binomial distribution. When $\sigma^2 < 1$ we say there is **underdispersion**. Underdispersion is less common than overdispersion, but underdispersion has been found in some applications.

There are plenty of count distributions for which assumption (18.3) does not hold—for example, the NegBin II model in Cameron and Trivedi (1986). Therefore, we are often interested in estimating the conditional mean parameters without specifying the conditional variance. As we will see, Poisson regression turns out to be well suited for this purpose.

Given a parametric model $m(\mathbf{x}, \boldsymbol{\beta})$ for $\mu(\mathbf{x})$, where $\boldsymbol{\beta}$ is a $P \times 1$ vector of parameters, the log likelihood for observation i is

$$\ell_i(\boldsymbol{\beta}) = y_i \log[m(\mathbf{x}_i, \boldsymbol{\beta})] - m(\mathbf{x}_i, \boldsymbol{\beta}), \tag{18.4}$$

where we drop the term $\log(y_i!)$ because it does not depend on the parameters $\boldsymbol{\beta}$ (for computational reasons dropping this term is a good idea in practice, too, as $y_i!$ gets very large for even moderate y_i). We let $\mathscr{B} \subset \mathbb{R}^P$ denote the parameter space, which is needed for the theoretical development but is practically unimportant in most cases.

The most common mean function in applications is the exponential:

$$m(\mathbf{x}, \boldsymbol{\beta}) = \exp(\mathbf{x}\boldsymbol{\beta}), \tag{18.5}$$

where $\mathbf{x}$ is $1 \times K$ and contains unity as its first element, and $\boldsymbol{\beta}$ is $K \times 1$. Under assumption (18.5) the log likelihood is $\ell_i(\boldsymbol{\beta}) = y_i \mathbf{x}_i \boldsymbol{\beta} - \exp(\mathbf{x}_i \boldsymbol{\beta})$. The parameters in model (18.5) are easy to interpret. If x_j is continuous, then

$$\frac{\partial \mathrm{E}(y \mid \mathbf{x})}{\partial x_j} = \exp(\mathbf{x}\boldsymbol{\beta})\beta_j.$$

which shows that the partial effects on $\mathrm{E}(y \mid \mathbf{x})$ depend on $\mathbf{x}$. Further,

$$\beta_j = \frac{\partial \mathrm{E}(y \mid \mathbf{x})}{\partial x_j} \cdot \frac{1}{\mathrm{E}(y \mid \mathbf{x})} = \frac{\partial \log[\mathrm{E}(y \mid \mathbf{x})]}{\partial x_j},$$

and so $100\beta_j$ is the semielasticity of $\mathrm{E}(y \mid \mathbf{x})$ with respect to x_j: for small changes Δx_j, the percentage change in $\mathrm{E}(y \mid \mathbf{x})$ is roughly $(100\beta_j)\Delta x_j$. If we replace x_j with $\log(x_j)$, β_j is the elasticity of $\mathrm{E}(y \mid \mathbf{x})$ with respect to x_j. Using equation (18.5) as the model for $\mathrm{E}(y \mid \mathbf{x})$ is analogous to using $\log(y)$ as the dependent variable in linear regression analysis.

Quadratic terms can be added with no additional effort, except in interpreting the parameters. In what follows, we will write the exponential function as in assumption (18.5), leaving transformations of $\mathbf{x}$—such as logs, quadratics, interaction terms, and so on—implicit.

Naturally, $\mathbf{x}$ can also include dummy variables or other discrete variables. The change in the expected value when, say, x_K goes from a_K to $a_K + 1$ is

$$\exp(\beta_1 + \beta_2 x_2 + \cdots + \beta_{K-1} x_{K-1} + \beta_K (a_K + 1))$$
$$- \exp(\beta_1 + \beta_2 x_2 + \cdots + \beta_{K-1} x_{K-1} + \beta a_K),$$

while the proportionate change (starting at $x_K = a_K$) is simply $\exp(\beta_K) - 1$. Therefore, the percentage change in the expected value does not depend on the initial value of x_K or the other covariates, and is simply $100 \cdot [\exp(\beta_K) - 1]$.

Computing average partial effects (APEs) of an explanatory variable on the mean is straightforward with Poisson regression and an exponential mean function. As we saw in Chapter 13—see also equation (18.4)—the first-order condition can be written as $\sum_{i=1}^{N} \mathbf{x}_i'[y_i - \exp(\mathbf{x}_i\hat{\boldsymbol{\beta}})] = \mathbf{0}$, and therefore, when $x_{i1} \equiv 1$ (which should always be the case in practice), the residuals $y_i - \exp(\mathbf{x}_i\hat{\boldsymbol{\beta}})$ sum to zero, or $\bar{y} = \bar{\hat{y}}$, where the fitted values are $\hat{y}_i = \exp(\mathbf{x}_i\hat{\boldsymbol{\beta}})$. Because the estimated partial effect of a continuous variable is $\exp(\mathbf{x}\hat{\boldsymbol{\beta}})\hat{\boldsymbol{\beta}}_j$, the average across the sample is simply $\bar{y}\hat{\beta}_j$. Therefore, as a rough comparison with linear model estimates, the Poisson coefficients can be multiplied by the average outcome, $\bar{y}$. For discrete changes, the differences in predicted values (for the two chosen values of x_K) must be averaged across all i.

Wooldridge (1997c) discusses functional forms other than the exponential that can be used in Poisson regression, including a model that nests the exponential, but an exponential regression function with flexible functions of the explanatory variables is often adequate.

18.2.2 Consistency of the Poisson QMLE

Once we have specified a conditional mean function, we are interested in cases where, other than the conditional mean, the Poisson distribution can be arbitrarily misspecified (subject to regularity conditions). When y_i given $\mathbf{x}_i$ does *not* have a Poisson distribution, we call the estimator $\hat{\boldsymbol{\beta}}$ that solves

$$\max_{\boldsymbol{\beta} \in \mathscr{B}} \sum_{i=1}^{N} \ell_i(\boldsymbol{\beta}) \tag{18.6}$$

the **Poisson quasi-maximum likelihood estimator (QMLE)**. A careful discussion of the consistency of the Poisson QMLE requires introduction of the true value of the parameter, as in Chapters 12 and 13. That is, we assume that for some value $\boldsymbol{\beta}_{\text{o}}$ in the parameter space $\mathscr{B}$,

$$\mathrm{E}(y \mid \mathbf{x}) = m(\mathbf{x}, \boldsymbol{\beta}_{\text{o}}). \tag{18.7}$$

To prove consistency of the Poisson QMLE under assumption (18.7), the key is to show that $\boldsymbol{\beta}_{\text{o}}$ is the unique solution to

$$\max_{\boldsymbol{\beta} \in \mathscr{B}} \mathrm{E}[\ell_i(\boldsymbol{\beta})]. \tag{18.8}$$

Then, under the regularity conditions listed in Theorem 12.2, it follows from this theorem that the solution to equation (18.6) is weakly consistent for $\boldsymbol{\beta}_{\text{o}}$.

Wooldridge (1997c) provides a simple proof that $\boldsymbol{\beta}_{\text{o}}$ is a solution to equation (18.8) when assumption (18.7) holds (see also Problem 18.1). As we discussed in Section 13.11.3, this finding follows from general results on QMLE in the linear exponential family by Gourieroux, Monfort, and Trognon (1984a) (hereafter GMT, 1984a).

Uniqueness of $\boldsymbol{\beta}_o$ must be assumed separately, as it depends on the distribution of $\mathbf{x}_i$. That is, in addition to assumption (18.7), identification of $\boldsymbol{\beta}_o$ requires some restrictions on the distribution of explanatory variables, and these depend on the nature of the regression function m. In the linear regression case, we require full rank of $\mathrm{E}(\mathbf{x}_i'\mathbf{x}_i)$. For Poisson QMLE with an exponential regression function $\exp(\mathbf{x}\boldsymbol{\beta})$, it can be shown that multiple solutions to equation (18.8) exist whenever there is perfect multicollinearity in $\mathbf{x}_i$, just as in the linear regression case. If we rule out perfect multicollinearity, we can usually conclude that $\boldsymbol{\beta}_o$ is identified under assumption (18.7).

It is important to remember that consistency of the Poisson QMLE does not require any additional assumptions concerning the distribution of y_i given $\mathbf{x}_i$. In particular, $\mathrm{Var}(y_i \mid \mathbf{x}_i)$ can be virtually anything (subject to regularity conditions needed to apply the results of Chapter 12), and y_i need not even be a count variable.

18.2.3 Asymptotic Normality of the Poisson QMLE

If the Poission QMLE is consistent for $\boldsymbol{\beta}_o$ without any assumptions beyond (18.7), why did we introduce assumptions (18.2) and (18.3)? It turns out that whether these assumptions hold determines which asymptotic variance matrix estimators and inference procedures are valid, as we now show.

The asymptotic normality of the Poisson QMLE follows from Theorem 12.3. The result is

$$\sqrt{N}(\hat{\boldsymbol{\beta}} - \boldsymbol{\beta}_o) \xrightarrow{d} \mathrm{Normal}(0, \mathbf{A}_o^{-1}\mathbf{B}_o\mathbf{A}_o^{-1}), \tag{18.9}$$

where

$$\mathbf{A}_o \equiv \mathrm{E}[-\mathbf{H}_i(\boldsymbol{\beta}_o)] \tag{18.10}$$

and

$$\mathbf{B}_o \equiv \mathrm{E}[\mathbf{s}_i(\boldsymbol{\beta}_o)\mathbf{s}_i(\boldsymbol{\beta}_o)'] = \mathrm{Var}[\mathbf{s}_i(\boldsymbol{\beta}_o)], \tag{18.11}$$

where we define $\mathbf{A}_o$ in terms of minus the Hessian because the Poisson QMLE solves a maximization rather than a minimization problem. Taking the gradient of equation (18.4) and transposing gives the score for observation i as

$$\mathbf{s}_i(\boldsymbol{\beta}) = \nabla_\beta m(\mathbf{x}_i, \boldsymbol{\beta})'[y_i - m(\mathbf{x}_i, \boldsymbol{\beta})]/m(\mathbf{x}_i, \boldsymbol{\beta}). \tag{18.12}$$

It is easily seen that, under assumption (18.7), $\mathbf{s}_i(\boldsymbol{\beta}_o)$ has a zero mean conditional on $\mathbf{x}_i$. The Hessian is more complicated but, under assumption (18.7), it can be shown that

$$-\mathrm{E}[\mathbf{H}_i(\boldsymbol{\beta}_o) \mid \mathbf{x}_i] = \nabla_\beta m(\mathbf{x}_i, \boldsymbol{\beta}_o)' \nabla_\beta m(\mathbf{x}_i, \boldsymbol{\beta}_o)/m(\mathbf{x}_i, \boldsymbol{\beta}_o). \tag{18.13}$$

Then $\mathbf{A}_o$ is the expected value of this expression (over the distribution of $\mathbf{x}_i$). A fully robust asymptotic variance matrix estimator for $\hat{\boldsymbol{\beta}}$ follows from equation (12.49):

$$\left(\sum_{i=1}^N \hat{\mathbf{A}}_i\right)^{-1} \left(\sum_{i=1}^N \hat{\mathbf{s}}_i \hat{\mathbf{s}}_i'\right) \left(\sum_{i=1}^N \hat{\mathbf{A}}_i\right)^{-1}, \tag{18.14}$$

where $\hat{\mathbf{s}}_i$ is obtained from equation (18.12) with $\hat{\boldsymbol{\beta}}$ in place of $\boldsymbol{\beta}$, and $\hat{\mathbf{A}}_i$ is the right-hand side of equation (18.13) with $\hat{\boldsymbol{\beta}}$ in place of $\boldsymbol{\beta}_o$. This is the fully robust variance matrix estimator in the sense that it requires only assumption (18.7) and the regularity conditions from Chapter 12.

The asymptotic variance of $\hat{\boldsymbol{\beta}}$ simplifies under the GLM assumption (18.3). Maintaining assumption (18.3) (where σ_o^2 now denotes the true value of σ^2) and defining $u_i \equiv y_i - m(\mathbf{x}_i, \boldsymbol{\beta}_o)$, the law of iterated expectations implies that

$$\begin{aligned}\mathbf{B}_o &= \mathrm{E}[u_i^2 \nabla_\beta m_i(\boldsymbol{\beta}_o)' \nabla_\beta m_i(\boldsymbol{\beta}_o)/\{m_i(\boldsymbol{\beta}_o)\}^2] \\ &= \mathrm{E}[\mathrm{E}(u_i^2 \mid \mathbf{x}_i) \nabla_\beta m_i(\boldsymbol{\beta}_o)' \nabla_\beta m_i(\boldsymbol{\beta}_o)/\{m_i(\boldsymbol{\beta}_o)\}^2] = \sigma_o^2 \mathbf{A}_o,\end{aligned}$$

since $\mathrm{E}(u_i^2 \mid \mathbf{x}_i) = \sigma_o^2 m_i(\boldsymbol{\beta}_o)$ under assumptions (18.3) and (18.7). Therefore, $\mathbf{A}_o^{-1}\mathbf{B}_o\mathbf{A}_o^{-1} = \sigma_o^2 \mathbf{A}_o^{-1}$, so we only need to estimate σ_o^2 in addition to obtaining $\hat{\mathbf{A}}$. A consistent estimator of σ_o^2 is obtained from $\sigma_o^2 = \mathrm{E}[u_i^2/m_i(\boldsymbol{\beta}_o)]$, which follows from assumption (18.3) and iterated expectations. The usual analogy principle argument gives the estimator

$$\hat{\sigma}^2 = N^{-1} \sum_{i=1}^N \hat{u}_i^2/\hat{m}_i = N^{-1} \sum_{i=1}^N (\hat{u}_i/\sqrt{\hat{m}_i})^2. \tag{18.15}$$

The last representation shows that $\hat{\sigma}^2$ is simply the average sum of squared weighted residuals, where the weights are the inverse of the estimated nominal standard deviations. (As we discussed in Section 13.11.3, the weighted residuals $\tilde{u}_i \equiv \hat{u}_i/\sqrt{\hat{m}_i}$ are sometimes called the Pearson residuals. In earlier chapters we also called them standardized residuals.) In the GLM literature, a degrees-of-freedom adjustment is usually made by replacing N^{-1} with $(N - P)^{-1}$ in equation (18.15); see also equation (13.91).

Given $\hat{\sigma}^2$ and $\hat{\mathbf{A}}$, it is straightforward to obtain an estimate of $\mathrm{Avar}(\hat{\boldsymbol{\beta}})$ under assumption (18.3). In fact, we can write

$$\widehat{\mathrm{Avar}(\hat{\boldsymbol{\beta}})} = \hat{\sigma}^2 \hat{\mathbf{A}}^{-1}/N = \hat{\sigma}^2 \left(\sum_{i=1}^N \nabla_\beta \hat{m}_i' \nabla_\beta \hat{m}_i / \hat{m}_i\right)^{-1}. \tag{18.16}$$

Note that the matrix is always positive definite when the inverse exists, so it produces well-defined standard errors (given, as usual, by the square roots of the diagonal elements). We call these the **GLM standard errors**.

If the Poisson variance assumption (18.2) holds, things are even easier because σ^2 is known to be unity; the estimated asymptotic variance of $\hat{\boldsymbol{\beta}}$ is given in equation (18.16) but with $\hat{\sigma}^2 \equiv 1$. The same estimator can be derived from the MLE theory in Chapter 13 as the inverse of the estimated information matrix (conditional on the $\mathbf{x}_i$); see Section 13.5.2.

Under assumption (18.3) in the case of overdispersion ($\sigma^2 > 1$), standard errors of the $\hat{\beta}_j$ obtained from equation (18.16) with $\hat{\sigma}^2 = 1$ will systematically underestimate the asymptotic standard deviations, sometimes by a large factor. For example, if $\sigma^2 = 2$, the correct GLM standard errors are, in the limit, 41 percent larger than the incorrect, nominal Poisson standard errors. It is common to see very significant coefficients reported for Poisson regressions—for example, Model (1993)—but we must interpret the standard errors with caution when they are obtained under assumption (18.2). The GLM standard errors are easily obtained by multiplying the Poisson standard errors by $\hat{\sigma} \equiv \sqrt{\hat{\sigma}^2}$. The most robust standard errors are obtained from expression (18.14), as these are valid under *any* conditional variance assumption. In practice, it is a good idea to report the fully robust standard errors along with the GLM standard errors and $\hat{\sigma}$.

If y given $\mathbf{x}$ has a Poisson distribution, it follows from the general efficiency of the conditional MLE—see Section 14.5.2—that the Poisson QMLE is fully efficient in the class of estimators that ignores information on the marginal distribution of $\mathbf{x}$.

A nice property of the Poisson QMLE is that it retains some efficiency for certain departures from the Poisson assumption. The efficiency results of GMT (1984a) can be applied here: if the GLM assumption (18.3) holds for some $\sigma^2 > 0$, the Poisson QMLE is efficient in the class of all QMLEs in the linear exponential family of distributions. In particular, the Poisson QMLE is more efficient than the nonlinear least squares estimator (NLSE), as well as many other QMLEs in the LEF, some of which we cover in Sections 18.3 and 18.4.

Wooldridge (1997c) gives an example of Poisson regression to an economic model of crime, where the response variable is number of arrests of a young man living in California during 1986. Wooldridge finds overdispersion: $\hat{\sigma}$ is either 1.228 or 1.172, depending on the functional form for the conditional mean. The following example shows that underdispersion is possible.

Example 18.1 (Effects of Education on Fertility): We use the data in FERTIL2.RAW to estimate the effects of education on women's fertility in Botswana. The re-

Table 18.1
OLS and Poisson Estimates of a Fertility Equation

Dependent Variable: *children*		
Independent Variable	Linear (OLS)	Exponential (Poisson QMLE)
educ	−.0644 (.0063)	−.0217 (.0025)
age	.272 (.017)	.337 (.009)
age^2	−.0019 (.0003)	−.0041 (.0001)
evermarr	.682 (.052)	.315 (.021)
urban	−.228 (.046)	−.086 (.019)
electric	−.262 (.076)	−.121 (.034)
tv	−.250 (.090)	−.145 (.041)
constant	−3.394 (.245)	−5.375 (.141)
Log-likelihood value	—	−6,497.060
R-squared	.590	.598
$\hat{\sigma}$	1.424	.867
Number of observations	4,358	4,358

sponse variable, *children*, is the number of living children. We use a standard exponential regression function, and the explanatory variables are years of schooling (*educ*), a quadratic in age, and binary indicators for ever married, living in an urban area, having electricity, and owning a television. The results are given in Table 18.1. A linear regression model is also included, with the usual OLS standard errors. For Poisson regression, the standard errors are the GLM standard errors. All of the coefficients are statistically significant at low significance levels. (You are invited to compute the fully robust standard errors in each case. Interestingly, the heteroskedasticity-robust standard errors for OLS do not differ substantively from the usual OLS standard errors, and the fully robust standard errors for the Poisson QMLE are similar to the GLM standard errors.)

Not surprisingly, the signs of the coefficients are the same in the linear and exponential models, but their interpretations differ. For example, the coefficient on *educ* in the linear model implies that each year of education reduces the predicted number of children by about .064. So, if 100 women each get another year of education, we estimate about six fewer children among them. The coefficient on *educ* in the exponential model implies that each year of education is estimated to reduce the expected number of children by 2.2 *percent*. To make the exponential coefficients roughly comparable to the linear model coefficients, we can multiply the former by the sample average of the dependent variable, $\overline{children} = 2.268$, to obtain the APE. For *educ*, the APE is $2.268(-.0217) = -.0492$, which is somewhat smaller in magnitude than the linear model estimate. For the binary variable *tv*, we compute the predicted value for each woman by setting *tv* equal to one and zero and taking the difference. The average across difference across all women is about $-.309$, which means that the average effect of television ownership is almost one-third of a child less; this estimate is somewhat higher in magnitude than the linear model estimate.

The estimate of σ in the Poisson regression implies underdispersion: the variance is less than the mean. (Incidentally, the $\hat{\sigma}$'s for the linear and Poisson models are not comparable.) One implication is that the GLM standard errors are actually less than the corresponding Poisson MLE standard errors.

For the linear model, the R-squared is the usual one. For the exponential model, the R-squared is computed as the squared correlation coefficient between $children_i$ and $\widehat{children}_i = \exp(\mathbf{x}_i\hat{\boldsymbol{\beta}})$. The exponential regression function fits only slightly better.

18.2.4 Hypothesis Testing

Classical hypothesis testing is fairly straightforward in a QMLE setting. Testing hypotheses about individual parameters is easily carried out using asymptotic t statistics after computing the appropriate standard error, as we discussed in Section 18.2.3. Multiple hypotheses tests can be carried out using the Wald, quasi-likelihood ratio (QLR), or score test. We covered these generally in Sections 12.6 and 13.6, and they apply immediately to the Poisson QMLE.

The Wald statistic for testing nonlinear hypotheses is computed as in equation (12.63), where $\hat{\mathbf{V}}$ is chosen appropriately depending on the degree of robustness desired, with expression (18.14) being the most robust. The Wald statistic is convenient for testing multiple exclusion restrictions in a robust fashion.

When the GLM assumption (18.3) holds, the *QLR* statistic can be used. Let $\check{\boldsymbol{\beta}}$ be the restricted estimator, where Q restrictions of the form $\mathbf{c}(\check{\boldsymbol{\beta}}) = \mathbf{0}$ have been imposed. Let $\hat{\boldsymbol{\beta}}$ be the unrestricted QMLE. Let $\mathscr{L}(\boldsymbol{\beta})$ be the quasi-log likelihood for the sample of size N, given in expression (18.6). Let $\hat{\sigma}^2$ be given in equation (18.15) (with or without the degrees-of-freedom adjustment), where the $\hat{u}_i$ are the residuals from the unconstrained maximization. The QLR statistic,

$$QLR \equiv 2[\mathscr{L}(\hat{\boldsymbol{\beta}}) - \mathscr{L}(\check{\boldsymbol{\beta}})]/\hat{\sigma}^2, \tag{18.17}$$

converges in distribution to χ^2_Q under H_0, under the conditions laid out in Section 12.6.3. The division of the usual likelihood ratio statistic by $\hat{\sigma}^2$ provides for some degree of robustness. If we set $\hat{\sigma}^2 = 1$, we obtain the usual LR statistic, which is valid only under assumption (18.2). There is no usable quasi-LR statistic when the GLM assumption (18.3) does not hold.

The score test can also be used to test multiple hypotheses. In this case we estimate only the restricted model. Partition $\boldsymbol{\beta}$ as $(\boldsymbol{\alpha}', \boldsymbol{\gamma}')'$, where $\boldsymbol{\alpha}$ is $P_1 \times 1$ and γ is $P_2 \times 1$, and assume that the null hypothesis is

$$\mathrm{H}_0 : \gamma_o = \bar{\gamma}, \tag{18.18}$$

where $\bar{\gamma}$ is a $P_2 \times 1$ vector of specified constants (often, $\bar{\gamma} = \mathbf{0}$). Let $\check{\boldsymbol{\beta}}$ be the estimator of $\boldsymbol{\beta}$ obtained under the restriction $\gamma = \bar{\gamma}$ [so $\check{\boldsymbol{\beta}} \equiv (\check{\boldsymbol{\alpha}}', \bar{\gamma}')'$], and define quantities under the restricted estimation as $\check{m}_i \equiv m(\mathbf{x}_i, \check{\boldsymbol{\beta}})$, $\check{u}_i \equiv y_i - \check{m}_i$, and $\nabla_\beta \check{m}_i \equiv (\nabla_\alpha \check{m}_i, \nabla_\gamma \check{m}_i) \equiv \nabla_\beta m(\mathbf{x}_i, \check{\boldsymbol{\beta}})$. Now weight the residuals and gradient by the inverse of nominal Poisson standard deviation, estimated under the null, $1/\sqrt{\check{m}_i}$:

$$\tilde{u}_i \equiv \check{u}_i/\sqrt{\check{m}_i}, \qquad \nabla_\beta \tilde{m}_i \equiv \nabla_\beta \check{m}_i/\sqrt{\check{m}_i}, \tag{18.19}$$

so that the $\tilde{u}_i$ here are the Pearson residuals obtained under the null. A form of the score statistic that is valid under the GLM assumption (18.3) (and therefore under assumption (18.2)) is NR^2_u from the regression

$$\tilde{u}_i \text{ on } \nabla_\beta \tilde{m}_i, \qquad i = 1, 2, \ldots, N, \tag{18.20}$$

where R^2_u denotes the uncentered R-squared. Under H_0 and assumption (18.3), $NR^2_u \overset{a}{\sim} \chi^2_{P_2}$. This is identical to the score statistic in equation (12.68) but where we use $\tilde{\mathbf{B}} = \tilde{\sigma}^2 \tilde{\mathbf{A}}$, where the notation is self-explanatory. For more, see Wooldridge (1991a, 1997c).

Following our development for nonlinear regression in Section 12.6.2, it is easy to obtain a test that is completely robust to variance misspecification. Let $\tilde{\mathbf{r}}_i$ denote the $1 \times P_2$ residuals from the regression

$$\nabla_\gamma \tilde{m}_i \text{ on } \nabla_\alpha \tilde{m}_i. \tag{18.21}$$

In other words, regress each element of the weighted gradient with respect to the restricted parameters on the weighted gradient with respect to the unrestricted parameters. The residuals are put into the $1 \times P_2$ vector $\tilde{\mathbf{r}}_i$. The robust score statistic is obtained as $N - \mathrm{SSR}$ from the regression

$$1 \text{ on } \tilde{u}_i\tilde{\mathbf{r}}_i, \qquad i = 1, 2, \ldots, N, \tag{18.22}$$

where $\tilde{u}_i\tilde{\mathbf{r}}_i = (\tilde{u}_i\tilde{r}_{i1}, \tilde{u}_i\tilde{r}_{i2}, \ldots, \tilde{u}_i\tilde{r}_{iP_2})$ is a $1 \times P_2$ vector. Alternatively, we can regress $\tilde{u}_i$ on $\tilde{\mathbf{r}}_i$ and use a heteroskedasticity-robust Wald statistic for joint significance of $\tilde{\mathbf{r}}_i$.

As an example, consider testing $\mathrm{H}_0 : \boldsymbol{\gamma} = \mathbf{0}$ in the exponential model $\mathrm{E}(y \mid \mathbf{x}) = \exp(\mathbf{x}\boldsymbol{\beta}) = \exp(\mathbf{x}_1\boldsymbol{\alpha} + \mathbf{x}_2\boldsymbol{\gamma})$. Then $\nabla_\beta m(\mathbf{x}, \boldsymbol{\beta}) = \exp(\mathbf{x}\boldsymbol{\beta})\mathbf{x}$. Let $\check{\boldsymbol{\alpha}}$ be the Poisson QMLE obtained under $\boldsymbol{\gamma} = \mathbf{0}$, and define $\check{m}_i \equiv \exp(\mathbf{x}_{i1}\check{\boldsymbol{\alpha}})$, with $\check{u}_i$ the residuals. Now $\nabla_\alpha \check{m}_i = \exp(\mathbf{x}_{i1}\check{\boldsymbol{\alpha}})\mathbf{x}_{i1}$, $\nabla_\gamma \check{m}_i = \exp(\mathbf{x}_{i1}\check{\boldsymbol{\alpha}})\mathbf{x}_{i2}$, and $\nabla_\beta \tilde{m}_i = \check{m}_i\mathbf{x}_i/\sqrt{\check{m}_i} = \sqrt{\check{m}_i}\mathbf{x}_i$. Therefore, the test that is valid under the GLM variance assumption is NR_u^2 from the OLS regression $\tilde{u}_i$ on $\sqrt{\check{m}_i}\mathbf{x}_i$, where the $\tilde{u}_i$ are the weighted residuals. For the robust test, first obtain the $1 \times P_2$ residuals $\tilde{\mathbf{r}}_i$ from the regression $\sqrt{\check{m}_i}\mathbf{x}_{i2}$ on $\sqrt{\check{m}_i}\mathbf{x}_{i1}$; then obtain the statistic from regression (18.22).

18.2.5 Specification Testing

Various specification tests have been proposed in the context of Poisson regression. The two most important kinds are conditional mean specification tests and conditional variance specification tests. For conditional mean tests, we usually begin with a fairly simple model whose parameters are easy to interpret—such as $m(\mathbf{x}, \boldsymbol{\beta}) = \exp(\mathbf{x}\boldsymbol{\beta})$—and then test this against other alternatives. Once the set of conditioning variables $\mathbf{x}$ has been specified, all such tests are functional form tests.

A useful class of functional form tests can be obtained using the score principle, where the null model $m(\mathbf{x}, \boldsymbol{\beta})$ is nested in a more general model. Fully robust tests and less robust tests are obtained exactly as in the previous section. Wooldridge (1997c, Section 3.5) contains details and some examples, including an extension of RESET to exponential regression models.

Conditional variance tests are more difficult to compute, especially if we want to maintain only that the first two moments are correctly specified under H_0. For example, it is very natural to test the GLM assumption (18.3) as a way of determining whether the Poisson QMLE is efficient in the class of estimators using only assumption (18.7). Cameron and Trivedi (1986) propose tests of the stronger assumption (18.2) and, in fact, take the null to be that the Poisson distribution is correct in its entirety. These tests are useful if we are interested in whether y given $\mathbf{x}$ truly has a Poisson distribution. However, assumption (18.2) is not necessary for consistency or relative efficiency of the Poisson QMLE.

Wooldridge (1991b) proposes fully robust tests of conditional variances in the context of the linear exponential family, which contains Poisson regression as a special case. To test assumption (18.3), write $u_i = y_i - m(\mathbf{x}_i, \boldsymbol{\beta}_o)$ and note that, under assumptions (18.3) and (18.7), $u_i^2 - \sigma_o^2 m(\mathbf{x}_i, \boldsymbol{\beta}_o)$ is uncorrelated with any function of

$\mathbf{x}_i$. Let $\mathbf{h}(\mathbf{x}_i, \boldsymbol{\beta})$ be a $1 \times Q$ vector of functions of $\mathbf{x}_i$ and $\boldsymbol{\beta}$, and consider the alternative model

$$\mathrm{E}(u_i^2 \mid \mathbf{x}_i) = \sigma_o^2 m(\mathbf{x}_i, \boldsymbol{\beta}_o) + \mathbf{h}(\mathbf{x}_i, \boldsymbol{\beta}_o)\boldsymbol{\delta}_o. \tag{18.23}$$

For example, the elements of $\mathbf{h}(\mathbf{x}_i, \boldsymbol{\beta})$ can be powers of $m(\mathbf{x}_i, \boldsymbol{\beta})$. Popular choices are unity and $\{\mathrm{m}(\mathbf{x}_i, \boldsymbol{\beta})\}^2$. A test of $\mathrm{H}_0 : \boldsymbol{\delta}_o = \mathbf{0}$ is then a test of the GLM assumption. While there are several moment conditions that can be used, a fruitful one is to use the weighted residuals, as we did with the conditional mean tests. We base the test on

$$N^{-1} \sum_{i=1}^{N} (\hat{\mathbf{h}}_i / \hat{m}_i)' \{(\hat{u}_i^2 - \hat{\sigma}^2 \hat{m}_i)/\hat{m}_i\} = N^{-1} \sum_{i=1}^{N} \tilde{\mathbf{h}}_i' (\tilde{u}_i^2 - \hat{\sigma}^2), \tag{18.24}$$

where $\tilde{\mathbf{h}}_i = \hat{\mathbf{h}}_i / \hat{m}_i$ and $\tilde{u}_i = \hat{u}_i / \sqrt{\hat{m}_i}$. (Note that $\hat{\mathbf{h}}_i$ is weighted by $1/\hat{m}_i$, not $1/\sqrt{\hat{m}_i}$.) To turn this equation into a test statistic, we must confront the fact that its standardized limiting distribution depends on the limiting distributions of $\sqrt{N}(\hat{\boldsymbol{\beta}} - \boldsymbol{\beta}_o)$ and $\sqrt{N}(\hat{\sigma}^2 - \sigma_o^2)$. To handle this problem, we use a trick suggested by Wooldridge (1991b) that removes the dependence of the limiting distribution of the test statistic on that of $\sqrt{N}(\hat{\sigma}^2 - \sigma_o^2)$: replace $\tilde{\mathbf{h}}_i$ in equation (18.24) with its demeaned counterpart, $\tilde{\mathbf{r}}_i \equiv \tilde{\mathbf{h}}_i - \bar{\mathbf{h}}$, where $\bar{\mathbf{h}}$ is just the $1 \times Q$ vector of sample averages of each element of $\tilde{\mathbf{h}}_i$. There is an additional purging that then leads to a simple regression-based statistic. Let $\nabla_\beta \hat{m}_i$ be the unweighted gradient of the conditional mean function, evaluated at the Poisson QMLE $\hat{\boldsymbol{\beta}}$, and define $\nabla_\beta \tilde{m}_i \equiv \nabla_\beta \hat{m}_i / \sqrt{\hat{m}_i}$, as before. The following steps come from Wooldridge (1991b, Procedure 4.1):

1. Obtain $\hat{\sigma}^2$ as in equation (18.15) and $\hat{\mathbf{A}}$ as in equation (18.16), and define the $P \times Q$ matrix $\hat{\mathbf{J}} = \hat{\sigma}^2 (N^{-1} \sum_{i=1}^{N} \nabla_\beta \hat{m}_i' \tilde{\mathbf{r}}_i / \hat{m}_i)$.
2. For each i, define the $1 \times Q$ vector

$$\hat{\mathbf{z}}_i \equiv (\tilde{u}_i^2 - \hat{\sigma}^2)\tilde{\mathbf{r}}_i - \hat{\mathbf{s}}_i' \hat{\mathbf{A}}^{-1} \hat{\mathbf{J}}, \tag{18.25}$$

where $\hat{\mathbf{s}}_i \equiv \nabla_\beta \tilde{m}_i' \tilde{u}_i$ is the Poisson score for observation i.

3. Run the regression

$$1 \text{ on } \hat{\mathbf{z}}_i, \qquad i = 1, 2, \ldots, N. \tag{18.26}$$

Under assumptions (18.3) and (18.7), $N - \mathrm{SSR}$ from this regression is distributed asymptotically as χ_Q^2.

The leading case occurs when $\hat{m}_i = \exp(\mathbf{x}_i \hat{\boldsymbol{\beta}})$ and $\nabla_\beta \hat{m}_i = \exp(\mathbf{x}_i \hat{\boldsymbol{\beta}})\mathbf{x}_i = \hat{m}_i \mathbf{x}_i$. The subtraction of $\hat{\mathbf{s}}_i' \hat{\mathbf{A}}^{-1} \hat{\mathbf{J}}$ in equation (18.25) is a simple way of handling the fact that the limiting distribution of $\sqrt{N}(\hat{\boldsymbol{\beta}} - \boldsymbol{\beta}_o)$ affects the limiting distribution of the unadjusted statistic in equation (18.24). This particular adjustment ensures that the tests are just as efficient as any maximum-likelihood-based statistic if $\sigma_o^2 = 1$ and the Poisson assumption is correct. But this procedure is fully robust in the sense that only assumptions (18.3) and (18.7) are maintained under H_0. For further discussion the reader is referred to Wooldridge (1991b).

In practice, it is probably sufficient to choose the number of elements in Q to be small. Setting $\hat{\mathbf{h}}_i = (1, \hat{m}_i^2)$, so that $\tilde{\mathbf{h}}_i = (1/\hat{m}_i, \hat{m}_i)$, is likely to produce a fairly powerful two-degrees-of-freedom test against a fairly broad class of alternatives.

The procedure is easily modified to test the more restrictive assumption (18.2). First, replace $\hat{\sigma}^2$ everywhere with unity. Second, there is no need to demean the auxiliary regressors $\tilde{\mathbf{h}}_i$ (so that now $\tilde{\mathbf{h}}_i$ can contain a constant); thus, wherever $\tilde{\mathbf{r}}_i$ appears, simply use $\tilde{\mathbf{h}}_i$. Everything else is the same. For the reasons discussed earlier, when the focus is on $\mathrm{E}(y \mid \mathbf{x})$, we are more interested in testing assumption (18.3) than assumption (18.2).

18.3 Other Count Data Regression Models

18.3.1 Negative Binomial Regression Models

The Poisson regression model nominally maintains assumption (18.2) but retains some asymptotic efficiency under assumption (18.3). A popular alternative to the Poisson QMLE is full maximum likelihood analysis of the NegBin I model of Cameron and Trivedi (1986). NegBin I is a particular parameterization of the negative binomial distribution. An important restriction in the NegBin I model is that it implies assumption (18.3) with $\sigma^2 > 1$, so that there cannot be underdispersion. (We drop the "o" subscript in this section for notational simplicity.) Typically, NegBin I is parameterized through the mean parameters $\boldsymbol{\beta}$ and an additional parameter, $\eta^2 > 0$, where $\sigma^2 = 1 + \eta^2$.

What are the merits of using NegBin I? On the one hand, when $\boldsymbol{\beta}$ and η^2 are estimated jointly, the MLEs are generally inconsistent if the NegBin I assumption fails. On the other hand, if the NegBin I distribution holds, then the NegBin I MLE is more efficient than the Poisson QMLE (this conclusion follows from Section 14.5.2). Still, under assumption (18.3), the Poisson QMLE is more efficient than any estimator that requires only the conditional mean to be correctly specified for consistency. On balance, because of its robustness, the Poisson QMLE has the edge over NegBin I for estimating the parameters of the conditional mean. If conditional probabilities need to be estimated, then a more flexible model than the Poisson distribution is probably warranted.

Other count data distributions imply a conditional variance other than assumption (18.3). A leading example is the NegBin II model of Cameron and Trivedi (1986). The NegBin II model can be derived from a model of unobserved heterogeneity in a Poisson model. Specifically, let $c_i > 0$ be unobserved heterogeneity, and assume that

$$y_i \mid \mathbf{x}_i, c_i \sim \text{Poisson}[c_i m(\mathbf{x}_i, \boldsymbol{\beta})].$$

If we further assume that c_i is independent of $\mathbf{x}_i$ and has a gamma distribution with unit mean and $\text{Var}(c_i) = \eta^2$, then the distribution of y_i given $\mathbf{x}_i$ can be shown to be negative binomial, with conditional mean and variance

$$\text{E}(y_i \mid \mathbf{x}_i) = m(\mathbf{x}_i, \boldsymbol{\beta}), \tag{18.27}$$

$$\begin{aligned}\text{Var}(y_i \mid \mathbf{x}_i) &= \text{E}[\text{Var}(y_i \mid \mathbf{x}_i, c_i) \mid \mathbf{x}_i] + \text{Var}[\text{E}(y_i \mid \mathbf{x}_i, c_i) \mid \mathbf{x}_i] \\ &= m(\mathbf{x}_i, \boldsymbol{\beta}) + \eta^2 [m(\mathbf{x}_i, \boldsymbol{\beta})]^2,\end{aligned} \tag{18.28}$$

so that the conditional variance of y_i given $\mathbf{x}_i$ is a quadratic in the conditional mean. Because we can write equation (18.28) as $\text{E}(y_i \mid \mathbf{x}_i)[1 + \eta^2 \text{E}(y_i \mid \mathbf{x}_i)]$, NegBin II also implies overdispersion, but where the amount of overdispersion increases with $\text{E}(y_i \mid \mathbf{x}_i)$.

The log-likelihood function for observation i is

$$\begin{aligned}\ell_i(\boldsymbol{\beta}, \eta^2) = \eta^{-2} \log\left[\frac{\eta^{-2}}{\eta^{-2} + m(\mathbf{x}_i, \boldsymbol{\beta})}\right] + y_i \log\left[\frac{m(\mathbf{x}_i, \boldsymbol{\beta})}{\eta^{-2} + m(\mathbf{x}_i, \boldsymbol{\beta})}\right] \\ + \log[\Gamma(y_i + \eta^{-2}) / \Gamma(\eta^{-2})],\end{aligned} \tag{18.29}$$

where $\Gamma(\cdot)$ is the gamma function defined for $r > 0$ by $\Gamma(r) = \int_0^\infty z^{r-1} \exp(-z)\, dz$.

You are referred to Cameron and Trivedi (1986) for details. The parameters $\boldsymbol{\beta}$ and η^2 can be jointly estimated using standard maximum likelihood methods.

It turns out that, for *fixed* η^2, the log likelihood in equation (18.29) is in the linear exponential family; see GMT (1984a). Therefore, if we fix η^2 at any positive value, say $\bar{\eta}^2$, and estimate $\boldsymbol{\beta}$ by maximizing $\sum_{i=1}^N \ell_i(\boldsymbol{\beta}, \bar{\eta}^2)$ with respect to $\boldsymbol{\beta}$, then the resulting QMLE is consistent under the conditional mean assumption (18.27) *only*: for fixed η^2, the negative binomial QMLE has the same robustness properties as the Poisson QMLE. (Notice that when η^2 is fixed, the term involving the gamma function in equation (18.29) does not affect the QMLE.)

The structure of the asymptotic variance estimators and test statistics is very similar to the Poisson regression case. Let

$$\hat{v}_i = \hat{m}_i + \bar{\eta}^2 \hat{m}_i^2 \tag{18.30}$$

be the estimated nominal variance for the given value $\bar{\eta}^2$. We simply weight the residuals $\hat{u}_i$ and gradient $\nabla_\beta \hat{m}_i$ by $1/\sqrt{\hat{v}_i}$:

$$\tilde{u}_i = \hat{u}_i/\sqrt{\hat{v}_i}, \qquad \nabla_\beta \tilde{m}_i = \nabla_\beta \hat{m}_i/\sqrt{\hat{v}_i}. \tag{18.31}$$

For example, under conditions (18.27) and (18.28), a valid estimator of $\text{Avar}(\hat{\boldsymbol{\beta}})$ is

$$\left(\sum_{i=1}^{N} \nabla_\beta \hat{m}_i' \nabla_\beta \hat{m}_i / \hat{v}_i\right)^{-1}.$$

If we drop condition (18.28), the estimator in expression (18.14) should be used but with the standardized residuals and gradients given by equation (18.31). Score statistics are modified in the same way.

When η^2 is set to unity, we obtain the **geometric QMLE**. A better approach is to replace η^2 by a first-stage estimate, say $\hat{\eta}^2$, and then estimate $\boldsymbol{\beta}$ by two-step QMLE. As we discussed in Chapters 12 and 13, sometimes the asymptotic distribution of the first-stage estimator needs to be taken into account. A nice feature of the two-step QMLE in this context is that the key condition, assumption (12.37), can be shown to hold under assumption (18.27). Therefore, we can ignore the first-stage estimation of η^2.

Under assumption (18.28), a consistent estimator of η^2 is easy to obtain, given an initial estimator of $\boldsymbol{\beta}$ (such as the Poisson QMLE or the geometric QMLE). Given $\hat{\hat{\boldsymbol{\beta}}}$, form $\hat{\hat{m}}_i$ and $\hat{\hat{u}}_i$ as the usual fitted values and residuals. One consistent estimator of η^2 is the coefficient on $\hat{\hat{m}}_i^2$ in the regression (through the origin) of $\hat{\hat{u}}_i^2 - \hat{\hat{m}}_i$ on $\hat{\hat{m}}_i^2$; this is the estimator suggested by Gourieroux, Monfort, and Trognon (1984b) and Cameron and Trivedi (1986). An alternative estimator of η^2, which is closely related to the GLM estimator of σ^2 suggested in equation (18.15), is a weighted least squares (WLS) estimate, which can be obtained from the OLS regression $\tilde{\tilde{u}}_i^2 - 1$ on $\hat{\hat{m}}_i$, where the $\tilde{\tilde{u}}_i$ are residuals $\hat{\hat{u}}_i$ weighted by $\hat{\hat{m}}_i^{-1/2}$. The resulting two-step estimator of $\boldsymbol{\beta}$ is consistent under assumption (18.7) only, so it is just as robust as the Poisson QMLE. Because $\hat{\boldsymbol{\beta}}$ is consistent without (18.28), it makes sense to use fully robust standard errors and test statistics. If assumption (18.3) holds, the Poisson QMLE is asymptotically more efficient; if assumption (18.28) holds, the two-step negative binomial estimator is more efficient. Notice that neither variance assumption contains the other as a special case for all parameter values; see Wooldridge (1997c) for additional discussion.

The variance specification tests discussed in Section 18.2.5 can be extended to the negative binomial QMLE; see Wooldridge (1991b).

18.3.2 Binomial Regression Models

Sometimes we wish to analyze count data conditional on a known upper bound. For example, Thomas, Strauss, and Henriques (1990) study child mortality within families conditional on number of children ever born. Another example takes the dependent variable, y_i, to be the number of adult children in family i who are high school graduates; the known upper bound, n_i, is the number of children in family i. By conditioning on n_i we are, presumably, treating it as exogenous.

Let $\mathbf{x}_i$ be a set of exogenous variables. A natural starting point is to assume that y_i given $(n_i, \mathbf{x}_i)$ has a binomial distribution, denoted Binomial $[n_i, p(\mathbf{x}_i, \boldsymbol{\beta})]$, where $p(\mathbf{x}_i, \boldsymbol{\beta})$ is a function bounded between zero and one. In this setup, usually, y_i is viewed as the sum of n_i independent Bernoulli (zero-one) random variables, and $p(\mathbf{x}_i, \boldsymbol{\beta})$ is the (conditional) probability of success on each trial.

The binomial assumption is too restrictive for all applications. The presence of an unobserved effect would invalidate the binomial assumption (after the effect is integrated out). For example, when y_i is the number of children in a family graduating from high school, unobserved family effects may play an important role. Generally, the presence of unobserved heterogeneity within group i violates the independence assumption (conditional on $\mathbf{x}_i$) that is used to derive the binomial distribution.

As in the case of unbounded support, we assume that the conditional mean is correctly specified:

$$\mathrm{E}(y_i \mid \mathbf{x}_i, n_i) = n_i p(\mathbf{x}_i, \boldsymbol{\beta}) \equiv m_i(\boldsymbol{\beta}). \tag{18.32}$$

This formulation ensures that $\mathrm{E}(y_i \mid \mathbf{x}_i, n_i)$ is between zero and n_i. Typically, $p(\mathbf{x}_i, \boldsymbol{\beta}) = G(\mathbf{x}_i\boldsymbol{\beta})$, where $G(\cdot)$ is a cumulative distribution function, such as the standard normal or logistic function.

Given a parametric model $p(\mathbf{x}, \boldsymbol{\beta})$, the binomial quasi-log likelihood for observation i is

$$\ell_i(\boldsymbol{\beta}) = y_i \log[p(\mathbf{x}_i, \boldsymbol{\beta})] + (n_i - y_i) \log[1 - p(\mathbf{x}_i, \boldsymbol{\beta})], \tag{18.33}$$

and the binomial QMLE is obtained by maximizing the sum of $\ell_i(\boldsymbol{\beta})$ over all N observations. From the results of GMT (1984a), the conditional mean parameters are consistently estimated under assumption (18.32) only. This conclusion follows from the general M-estimation results after showing that the true value of $\boldsymbol{\beta}$ maximizes the expected value of equation (18.33) under assumption (18.32) only.

The **binomial GLM variance assumption** is

$$\mathrm{Var}(y_i \mid \mathbf{x}_i, n_i) = \sigma^2 n_i p(\mathbf{x}_i, \boldsymbol{\beta})[1 - p(\mathbf{x}_i, \boldsymbol{\beta})] = \sigma^2 v_i(\boldsymbol{\beta}), \tag{18.34}$$

which generalizes the nominal binomial assumption with $\sigma^2 = 1$. (McCullagh and Nelder [1989, Section 4.5] discuss a model that leads to assumption (18.34) with $\sigma^2 > 1$. But underdispersion is also possible.) Even the GLM assumption can fail if the binary outcomes comprising y_i are not independent conditional on $(\mathbf{x}_i, n_i)$. Therefore, it makes sense to use the fully robust asymptotic variance estimator for the binomial QMLE.

Owing to the structure of LEF densities, and given our earlier analysis of the Poisson and negative binomial cases, it is straightforward to describe the econometric analysis for the binomial QMLE: simply take $\hat{m}_i \equiv n_i p(\mathbf{x}_i, \hat{\boldsymbol{\beta}})$, $\hat{u}_i \equiv y_i - \hat{m}_i$, $\nabla_\beta \hat{m}_i \equiv n_i \nabla_\beta \hat{p}_i$, and $\hat{v}_i \equiv n_i \hat{p}_i(1 - \hat{p}_i)$ in equations (18.31). An estimator of σ^2 under assumption (18.34) is also easily obtained: replace $\hat{m}_i$ in equation (18.15) with $\hat{v}_i$. The structure of asymptotic variances and score tests is identical.

18.4 Gamma (Exponential) Regression Model

It is becoming more popular to directly model the expected value of nonnegative, continuous response variables rather than using a transformation (usually the natural log) and specifying a model linear in parameters with an additive error. Wooldridge (1992) makes the case that if $\mathrm{E}(y \mid \mathbf{x})$ is the quantity of interest when $y \geq 0$, then it makes sense to model this expectation directly. More recently, Blackburn (2007) has suggested estimating models of $\mathrm{E}(wage \mid \mathbf{x})$ directly, where *wage* is a measure of employee compensation, rather than using $\log(wage)$ in a linear regression.

We set out the reasons for directly modeling $\mathrm{E}(y \mid \mathbf{x})$ in Section 2.2.2. For concreteness, assume that $y > 0$, and so $\log(y)$ is well defined. If we postulate the standard linear model $\log(y) = \mathbf{x}\boldsymbol{\beta} + u$, we can ask: when can we recover partial effects, semielasticities, and elasticities on $\mathrm{E}(y \mid \mathbf{x})$? A sufficient condition is to assume u and $\mathbf{x}$ are independent, in which case $\mathrm{E}(y \mid \mathbf{x}) = \alpha \exp(\mathbf{x}\boldsymbol{\beta})$, and α is identified from $\alpha = \mathrm{E}[\exp(u)]$. Duan's (1983) smearing estimate is the most common way to estimate α based on OLS residuals from the regression $\log(y_i)$ on $\mathbf{x}_i$. Alternatively, we can allow dependence between u and $\mathbf{x}$ if we specify $D(u \mid x)$, for example, $u \mid x \sim \mathrm{Normal}(0, \exp(\mathbf{x}\boldsymbol{\gamma}))$, in which case $\mathrm{E}(y \mid \mathbf{x}) = \exp(\mathbf{x}\boldsymbol{\beta} + \exp(\mathbf{x}\boldsymbol{\gamma})/2)$.

Both previous approaches require restrictions on the conditional distribution $D(y \mid \mathbf{x})$ in addition to specifying the conditional mean, and each is a roundabout way of obtaining estimates of $\mathrm{E}(y \mid \mathbf{x})$. Just as when y has some discreteness—for example, it is a count variable—it makes sense to specify simple, logically consistent models for $\mathrm{E}(y \mid \mathbf{x})$. Again, the leading case is an exponential model: $\mathrm{E}(y \mid \mathbf{x}) = \exp(\mathbf{x}\boldsymbol{\beta})$ with $x_1 \equiv 1$. We already know how to interpret the parameters of such a model.

It is important to remember that, regardless of the nature of y—provided it is nonnegative and has no natural upper bound—we can always apply the Poisson QMLE. Thus, even if y is continuous on $(0, \infty)$, Poisson regression delivers consistent, $\sqrt{N}$-asymptotically normal estimators of the parameters in $\mathrm{E}(y \mid \mathbf{x}) = \exp(\mathbf{x}\boldsymbol{\beta})$ (or any other correctly specified mean function). Even for some continuous random variables the Poisson QMLE can be asymptotically efficient in the class of estimators that specify only the mean. Sufficient is that assumption (18.3) holds, and this variance-mean relationship holds for certain parameterizations of the gamma distribution.

Nevertheless, a constant variance-mean ratio is somewhat uncommon for nonnegative continuous variables. In the model $\log(y) = \mathbf{x}\boldsymbol{\beta} + u$ with u independent of $\mathbf{x}$, $\mathrm{Var}(y \mid \mathbf{x}) = \sigma^2[\exp(\mathbf{x}\boldsymbol{\beta})]^2$ where $\sigma^2 = \mathrm{Var}[\exp(u)]$. A natural parameterization of the gamma distribution has the variance proportional to the square of the mean. As shown in GMT (1984a), for a *fixed* value of the variance/mean ratio, the log likelihood is in the LEF. In fact, for estimation purposes, we can set the ratio to unity, which gives us the log likelihood for the exponential distribution. With general mean function $m(\mathbf{x}, \boldsymbol{\beta}) > 0$, we have

$$l_i(\boldsymbol{\beta}) = -y_i/m(\mathbf{x}_i, \boldsymbol{\beta}) - \log[m(\mathbf{x}_i, \boldsymbol{\beta})], \tag{18.35}$$

and the **gamma QMLE** (sometimes called the **exponential QMLE**) is the estimator that maximizes this quasi-log-likelihood function summed across the sample. It is easy to show directly that the score, $\nabla_{\beta} m(\mathbf{x}_i, \boldsymbol{\beta})'\{y_i/[m(\mathbf{x}_i, \boldsymbol{\beta})]^2 - 1/m(\mathbf{x}_i, \boldsymbol{\beta})\} = \nabla_{\beta} m(\mathbf{x}_i, \boldsymbol{\beta})'\{y_i - m(\mathbf{x}_i, \boldsymbol{\beta})\}//[m(\mathbf{x}_i, \boldsymbol{\beta})]^2$ has zero conditional mean (technically, when evaluated at the "true" value of beta) whenever the mean is correctly specified. (Or, one can work with equation (18.35) directly, as in GMT (1984a).) In other words, just as with the Poisson QMLE, the gamma QMLE is fully robust to distributional misspecification other than the conditional mean. Specifying a conditional mean and estimating using the gamma QMLE is often called, as a shorthand, the **gamma regression model**.

The gamma QMLE is efficient in the class of estimators that specify only $\mathrm{E}(y \mid \mathbf{x})$, including NLS and the Poisson QMLE, under the gamma GLM variance assumption, which we write as

$$\mathrm{Var}(y \mid \mathbf{x}) = \sigma^2[\mathrm{E}(y \mid \mathbf{x})]^2. \tag{18.36}$$

When $\sigma^2 = 1$, assumption (18.36) gives the variance-mean relationship for the exponential distribution. Under assumption (18.36), σ is the **coefficient of variation**: it is the ratio of the conditional standard deviation of y to its conditional mean.

Whether or not assumption (18.36) holds, an asymptotic variance matrix can be estimated. The fully robust form is expression (18.14), but, in defining the score and expected Hessian, the residuals and gradients are weighted by $1/\hat{m}_i$ rather than $\hat{m}_i^{-1/2}$. Under assumption (18.36), a valid estimator is

$$\hat{\sigma}^2\left(\sum_{i=1}^{N} \nabla_\beta \hat{m}_i' \nabla_\beta \hat{m}_i / \hat{v}_i\right)^{-1},$$

where $\hat{\sigma}^2 = N^{-1}\sum_{i=1}^{N} \hat{u}_i^2/\hat{m}_i^2$ and $\hat{v}_i = \hat{m}_i^2$. Score tests and QLR tests can be computed just as in the Poisson case. Many statistical packages implement gamma regression with an exponential mean function, often as a feature of a GLM command.

18.5 Endogeneity with an Exponential Regression Function

With all of the previous models, standard econometric problems can arise. In this section, we study the problem of endogenous explanatory variables with an exponential regression function.

We approach the problem of endogenous explanatory variables from an omitted variables perspective. Let y_1 be the nonnegative, in principle unbounded variable to be explained, and let $\mathbf{z}$ and $\mathbf{y}_2$ be observable explanatory variables (of dimension $1 \times L$ and $1 \times G_1$, respectively). Let c_1 be an unobserved latent variable (or unobserved heterogeneity). We assume that the (structural) model of interest is an omitted variables model of exponential form, written in the population as

$$\mathrm{E}(y_1 \mid \mathbf{z}, \mathbf{y}_2, c_1) = \exp(\mathbf{z}_1\boldsymbol{\delta}_1 + \mathbf{y}_2\boldsymbol{\gamma}_1 + c_1), \tag{18.37}$$

where $\mathbf{z}_1$ is a $1 \times L_1$ subset of $\mathbf{z}$ containing unity; thus, the model (18.37) incorporates some exclusion restrictions. On the one hand, the elements in $\mathbf{z}$ are assumed to be exogenous in the sense that they are independent of c_1. On the other hand, $\mathbf{y}_2$ and c_1 are allowed to be correlated, so that $\mathbf{y}_2$ is potentially endogenous.

To use a quasi-likelihood approach, we assume that $\mathbf{y}_2$ has a linear reduced form satisfying certain assumptions. Write

$$\mathbf{y}_2 = \mathbf{z}\boldsymbol{\Pi}_2 + \mathbf{v}_2, \tag{18.38}$$

where $\boldsymbol{\Pi}_2$ is an $L \times G_1$ matrix of reduced form parameters and $\mathbf{v}_2$ is a $1 \times G_1$ vector of reduced form errors. We assume that the rank condition for identification holds, which requires the order condition $L - L_1 \geq G_1$. In addition, we assume that $(c_1, \mathbf{v}_2)$ is independent of $\mathbf{z}$, and that

$$c_1 = \mathbf{v}_2\boldsymbol{\rho}_1 + e_1, \tag{18.39}$$

where e_1 is independent of $\mathbf{v}_2$ (and necessarily of $\mathbf{z}$). (We could relax the independence assumptions to some degree, but we cannot just assume that $\mathbf{v}_2$ is uncorrelated with $\mathbf{z}$ and that e_1 is uncorrelated with $\mathbf{v}_2$.) It is natural to assume that $\mathbf{v}_2$ has zero mean, but it is convenient to assume that $\mathrm{E}[\exp(e_1)] = 1$ rather than $\mathrm{E}(e_1) = 0$. This assumption is without loss of generality whenever a constant appears in $\mathbf{z}_1$, which should almost always be the case.

If $(c_1, \mathbf{v}_2)$ has a multivariate normal distribution, then the representation in equation (18.39) under the stated assumptions always holds. We could also extend equation (18.39) by putting other functions of $\mathbf{v}_2$ on the right-hand side, such as squares and cross products, but we do not show these explicitly. Note that $\mathbf{y}_2$ is exogenous if and only if $\boldsymbol{\rho}_1 = \mathbf{0}$.

Under the maintained assumptions, we have

$$\mathrm{E}(y_1 \mid \mathbf{z}, \mathbf{y}_2, \mathbf{v}_2) = \exp(\mathbf{z}_1\boldsymbol{\delta}_1 + \mathbf{y}_2\boldsymbol{\gamma}_1 + \mathbf{v}_2\boldsymbol{\rho}_1), \tag{18.40}$$

and this equation suggests a strategy for consistently estimating $\boldsymbol{\delta}_1$, $\boldsymbol{\gamma}_1$, and $\boldsymbol{\rho}_1$. If $\mathbf{v}_2$ were observed, we could simply use this regression function in one of the QMLE earlier methods (for example, Poisson, two-step negative binomial, or gamma). Because these methods consistently estimate correctly specified conditional means, we can immediately conclude that the QMLEs would be consistent. (If y_1 conditional on $(\mathbf{z}, \mathbf{y}_2, c_1)$ has a Poisson distribution with mean in equation (18.37), then the distribution of y_1 given $(\mathbf{z}, \mathbf{y}_2, \mathbf{v}_2)$ has overdispersion of the type (18.28), so the two-step negative binomial estimator might be preferred in this context.)

To operationalize this procedure, the unknown quantities $\mathbf{v}_2$ must be replaced with estimates. Let $\hat{\boldsymbol{\Pi}}_2$ be the $L \times G_1$ matrix of OLS estimates from the first-stage estimation of equation (18.38); these are consistent estimates of $\boldsymbol{\Pi}_2$. Define $\hat{\mathbf{v}}_2 = \mathbf{y}_2 - \mathbf{z}\hat{\boldsymbol{\Pi}}_2$ (where the observation subscript is suppressed). Then estimate the exponential regression model using regressors $(\mathbf{z}_1, \mathbf{y}_2, \hat{\mathbf{v}}_2)$ by one of the QMLEs. The estimates $(\hat{\boldsymbol{\delta}}_1, \hat{\boldsymbol{\gamma}}_1, \hat{\boldsymbol{\rho}}_1)$ from this procedure are consistent using standard arguments from two-step estimation in Chapter 12.

This method is similar in spirit to the methods we saw for binary response (Chapter 15) and Tobit regression models (Chapter 17). There is one difference: here, we do not need to make distributional assumptions about y_1 or $\mathbf{y}_2$. However, we do assume that the reduced-form errors $\mathbf{v}_2$ are independent of $\mathbf{z}$. In addition, we assume that c_1 and $\mathbf{v}_2$ are linearly related with e_1 in equation (18.39) independent of $\mathbf{v}_2$.

Because $\hat{\mathbf{v}}_2$ depends on $\hat{\boldsymbol{\Pi}}_2$, the variance matrix estimators for $\hat{\boldsymbol{\delta}}_1$, $\hat{\boldsymbol{\gamma}}_1$, and $\hat{\boldsymbol{\rho}}_1$ should generally be adjusted to account for this dependence, as described in Sections 12.5.2

and 14.1. The bootstrap is also attractive because the two-step procedure takes little computational time (unless the sample size is very large). Using the results from Section 12.5.2, it can be shown that estimation of $\mathbf{\Pi}_2$ does not affect the asymptotic variance of the QMLEs when $\boldsymbol{\rho}_1 = \mathbf{0}$, just as we saw when testing for endogeneity in probit and Tobit models. Therefore, *testing* for endogeneity of $\mathbf{y}_2$ is relatively straightforward: simply test $\mathrm{H}_0 : \boldsymbol{\rho}_1 = \mathbf{0}$ using a Wald or *LM* statistic. When $G_1 = 1$, the most convenient statistic is probably the t statistic on $\hat{v}_2$, with the fully robust form being the most preferred (but the GLM form is also useful). The *LM* test for omitted variables is convenient when $G_1 > 1$ because it can be computed after estimating the null model ($\boldsymbol{\rho}_1 = \mathbf{0}$) and then doing a variable addition test for $\hat{\mathbf{v}}_2$. The test has G_1 degrees of freedom in the chi-square distribution.

There is a final comment worth making about this test. The null hypothesis is the same as $\mathrm{E}(y_1 \mid \mathbf{z}, \mathbf{y}_2) = \exp(\mathbf{z}_1 \boldsymbol{\delta}_1 + \mathbf{y}_2 \boldsymbol{\gamma}_1)$. The test for endogeneity of $\mathbf{y}_2$ simply looks for whether a particular linear combination of $\mathbf{y}_2$ and $\mathbf{z}$ appears in this conditional expectation. For the purposes of getting a limiting chi-square distribution, it does not matter where the linear combination $\hat{\mathbf{v}}_2$ comes from. In other words, under the null hypothesis none of the assumptions we made about $(c_1, \mathbf{v}_2)$ need to hold: $\mathbf{v}_2$ need not be independent of $\mathbf{z}$, and e_1 in equation (18.39) need not be independent of $\mathbf{v}_2$. Therefore, as a test, this procedure is very robust, and it can be applied when $\mathbf{y}_2$ contains binary, count, or other discrete variables. Unfortunately, if $\mathbf{y}_2$ is endogenous, the correction does not work without something like the assumptions made previously.

Example 18.2 (Is Education Endogenous in the Fertility Equation?): We test for endogeneity of *educ* in Example 18.1. The IV for *educ* is a binary indicator for whether the woman was born in the first half of the year (*frsthalf*), which we assume is exogenous in the fertility equation. In the reduced-form equation for *educ*, the coefficient on *frsthalf* is $-.636$ (se $= .104$), and so there is a significant negative partial relationship between years of schooling and being born in the first half of the year.

When we add the first-stage residuals, $\hat{v}_2$, to the Poisson regression, its coefficient is .025, and its GLM standard error is .028. Therefore, there is little evidence against the null hypothesis that *educ* is exogenous. The coefficient on *educ* actually becomes larger in magnitude ($-.046$), but it is much less precisely estimated.

It is straightforward to allow general nonlinear functions of $(\mathbf{z}_1, \mathbf{y}_2)$ in the exponential model because including the control function $\mathbf{v}_2$ accounts for endogeneity quite generally. Further, it might be that $\mathbf{y}_2$, as it appears in equation (18.37), might not have a linear representation as in (18.38), with $\mathbf{v}_2$ having the requisite properties. If the elements of $\mathbf{y}_2$ are continuous, we can often find a strictly monotonic transformation such that a linear reduced form, with an additive error independent of $\mathbf{z}$, is sensible. So, in the scalar case, if $0 < y_2 < 1$, we might use $\log[y_2/(1 - y_2)] = \mathbf{z}\boldsymbol{\pi}_2 + v_2$ as the reduced form, even though y_2 itself appears in the structural equation. Because we can write $y_2 = \exp(\mathbf{z}\boldsymbol{\pi}_2 + v_2)/[1 + \exp(\mathbf{z}\boldsymbol{\pi}_2 + v_2)]$, adding $\hat{v}_2$ to a QMLE analysis controls for the endogeneity of y_2.

In addition to the parameters, one might want the partial effect on the mean, rather than just an elasticity or semielasticity. We can estimate the average partial effects by using the general approach for probit, ordered probit, and Tobit models. The estimated average structural function is

$$\widehat{\mathrm{ASF}}(\mathbf{x}_1) = N^{-1} \sum_{i=1}^{N} \exp(\mathbf{x}_1 \hat{\boldsymbol{\beta}}_1 + \hat{\mathbf{v}}_{i2} \hat{\boldsymbol{\rho}}_1), \tag{18.41}$$

and then we take derivatives or changes with respect to the elements in $\mathbf{x}_1 \equiv \mathbf{g}_1(\mathbf{z}_1, y_2)$ for a known function $\mathbf{g}_1(\cdot)$. The bootstrap can be applied to obtain valid standard errors and confidence intervals.

Recent theoretical work on linear models (for example, Bekker (1994)) as well as simulations (for example, Flores-Lagunes (2007)) suggest a single-step estimation method might have better finite-sample properties than two-step estimation, particularly with weak instruments or many overidentifying restrictions. It is easy to obtain a one-step version of the control function method just described. Suppose we decide to use the Poisson QMLE for the structural part of the model, and assume, for simplicity, that we have a single endogenous explanatory variable and that the linear reduced form is stated in terms of y_2 (the extension to $h_2(y_2)$ is straightforward). Then, we can estimate both sets of parameters simultaneously by solving

$$\min_{\boldsymbol{\theta}} \sum_{i=1}^{N} \{\exp(\mathbf{x}_{i1}\boldsymbol{\beta}_1 + \rho_1(y_{i2} - \mathbf{z}_i\boldsymbol{\pi}_2)) - y_{i1}[\mathbf{x}_{i1}\boldsymbol{\beta}_1 + \rho_1(y_{i2} - \mathbf{z}_i\boldsymbol{\pi}_2)]$$
$$+ (y_{i2} - \mathbf{z}_i\boldsymbol{\pi}_2)^2/\tau_2^2 + \log(\tau_2^2)\},$$

where $\boldsymbol{\theta}$ is the full set of parameters, including the reduced form variance parameter τ_2^2, and $\mathbf{x}_{i1}$ is whatever function of $(\mathbf{z}_{i1}, y_{i2})$ that appears in the model. (If we assume that $y_2 \mid \mathbf{z} \sim \mathrm{Normal}(\mathbf{z}\boldsymbol{\pi}_{o2}, \tau_{o2}^2)$, and $y_1 \mid y_2, \mathbf{z}$ follows a Poisson distribution, then the minimization problem is the same as the **limited information maximum liklelihood (LIML)** estimator. The "limited information" identifier comes from the fact that we use a reduced form for y_2.) This is a standard M-estimation problem, and its consistency holds provided the true values of the parameters solve the corresponding population problem. To this end, we label the population parameters by using the "o"

subscript. Then we know $\boldsymbol{\pi}_{o2}$ minimizes $\mathrm{E}[(y_2 - \mathbf{z}\boldsymbol{\pi}_2)^2/\tau_2^2]$ for any $\tau_2^2 > 0$ (even if $\boldsymbol{\pi}_{o2}$ simply indexes the linear projection), and then the "true" value τ_{o2}^2 is the variance of $y_2 - \mathbf{z}\boldsymbol{\pi}_{o2}$. Further, because we assume $\mathrm{E}(y_1 \mid \mathbf{z}, y_2) = \exp(\mathbf{x}_1\boldsymbol{\beta}_{o1} + \rho_{o1}(y_2 - \mathbf{z}\boldsymbol{\pi}_{o2}))$, it follows that $(\boldsymbol{\beta}_{o1}, \rho_{o1}, \boldsymbol{\pi}_{o2})$ minimize

$$\mathrm{E}\{\exp(\mathbf{x}_{i1}\boldsymbol{\beta}_1 + \rho_1(y_{i2} - \mathbf{z}_i\boldsymbol{\pi}_2)) - y_{i1}[\mathbf{x}_{i1}\boldsymbol{\beta}_1 + \rho_1(y_{i2} - \mathbf{z}_i\boldsymbol{\pi}_2)]\}. \tag{18.42}$$

Therefore, $(\boldsymbol{\beta}_{o1}, \rho_{o1}, \boldsymbol{\pi}_{o2}, \tau_{o2}^2)$ minimizes the sum of the expected values. After M-estimation, we would use a fully robust sandwich estimator for the asymptotic variance because the Poisson distribution for $\mathrm{D}(y_1 \mid \mathbf{z}, y_2)$ is almost certainly wrong. Plus, we may not wish to think v_2 is independent of $\mathbf{z}$ in $y_2 = \mathbf{z}\boldsymbol{\pi}_{o2} + v_2$ (even though obtaining the form of $\mathrm{E}(y_1 \mid \mathbf{z}, y_2)$ uses something like it). If we write $q_{i1}(\boldsymbol{\theta}) = \exp(\mathbf{x}_{i1}\boldsymbol{\beta}_1 + \rho_1(y_{i2} - \mathbf{z}_i\boldsymbol{\pi}_2)) - y_{i1}[\mathbf{x}_{i1}\boldsymbol{\beta}_1 + \rho_1(y_{i2} - \mathbf{z}_i\boldsymbol{\pi}_2)]$ and $q_{i2}(\boldsymbol{\theta}) = (y_{i2} - \mathbf{z}_i\boldsymbol{\pi}_2)^2/\tau_2^2 + \log(\tau_2^2)$, then the scores evaluated at the true parameters are uncorrelated because $\mathrm{E}[\nabla_\theta q_{i1}(\boldsymbol{\theta}_o) \mid y_{i2}, \mathbf{z}_i] = \mathbf{0}$ and $\nabla_\theta q_{i2}(\boldsymbol{\theta}_o)$ depends only on $(y_{i2}, \mathbf{z}_i)$.

The assumption that e_1 in (18.39) is independent of $\mathbf{v}_2$ and $\mathbf{z}$ rules out most cases where $\mathbf{y}_2$ has some discreteness, such as with binary, count, or corner responses. (In particular, the independence assumption likewise fails unless $\mathbf{v}_2$ is independent of $\mathbf{z}$, and it would be very unusual for a discrete variable to be expressible as a linear equation with additive error independent of $\mathbf{z}$.) Terza (1998) considered the case where y_2 is a binary endogenous explanatory variable and follows a reduced form probit:

$$y_2 = 1[\mathbf{z}\boldsymbol{\pi}_2 + v_2 \geq 0], \qquad v_2 \mid \mathbf{z} \sim \mathrm{Normal}(0, 1). \tag{18.43}$$

As shown by Terza (1998), a control function (CF) method can be applied when (a_1, v_2) has a joint normal distribution and is independent of $\mathbf{z}$. To implement a CF approach, we need to find $\mathrm{E}(y_1 \mid \mathbf{z}, y_2) = \exp(\mathbf{x}_1\boldsymbol{\beta}_1)\mathrm{E}[\exp(c_1) \mid \mathbf{z}, y_2]$ where $\mathbf{x}_1$ is a function of $(\mathbf{z}_1, y_2)$, which would almost certainly include y_2 linearly and possibly interact with elements of $\mathbf{z}_1$. Now, suppose (c_1, v_2) is independent of $\mathbf{z}$ with mean zero and jointly normal. Let $\tau_1^2 = \mathrm{Var}(c_1)$ and $\rho_1 = \mathrm{Cov}(v_2, c_1)$, so that $c_1 = \rho_1 v_2 + e_1$, where $e_1 \mid \mathbf{z}, v_2 \sim \mathrm{Normal}(0, \tau_1^2 - \rho_1^2)$. Then

$$\begin{aligned}\mathrm{E}(y_1 \mid \mathbf{z}, v_2) &= \mathrm{E}[\exp(e_1)] \exp(\mathbf{x}_1\boldsymbol{\beta}_1 + \rho_1 v_2) \\ &= \exp((\tau_1^2 - \rho_1^2)/2) \exp(\mathbf{x}_1\boldsymbol{\beta}_1 + \rho_1 v_2) \\ &= \exp((\tau_1^2 - \rho_1^2)/2 + \mathbf{x}_1\boldsymbol{\beta}_1) \exp(\rho_1 v_2).\end{aligned} \tag{18.44}$$

To find $\mathrm{E}(y_1 \mid \mathbf{z}, y_2)$, we have

$$\mathrm{E}(y_1 \mid \mathbf{z}, y_2) = \exp((\tau_1^2 - \rho_1^2)/2) \exp(\mathbf{x}_1\boldsymbol{\beta}_1)\mathrm{E}[\exp(\rho_1 v_2) \mid \mathbf{z}, y_2]. \tag{18.45}$$

As shown by Terza (1998), and as is used in the two-part model in Section 17.6.3,

$$\begin{aligned} \mathrm{E}[\exp(\rho_1 v_2) \mid \mathbf{z}, y_2 = 1] &= \mathrm{E}[\exp(\rho_1 v_2) \mid \mathbf{z}, v_2 > -\mathbf{z}\boldsymbol{\pi}_2] \\ &= \exp(\rho_1^2/2)\Phi(\rho_1 + \mathbf{z}\boldsymbol{\pi}_2)/\Phi(\mathbf{z}\boldsymbol{\pi}_2). \end{aligned} \tag{18.46}$$

Similarly,

$$\mathrm{E}[\exp(\rho_1 v_2) \mid \mathbf{z}, y_2 = 0] = \exp(\rho_1^2/2)[1 - \Phi(\rho_1 + \mathbf{z}\boldsymbol{\pi}_2)]/[1 - \Phi(\mathbf{z}\boldsymbol{\pi}_2)]. \tag{18.47}$$

It follows from (18.45), (18.46), and (18.47) that

$$\begin{aligned} \mathrm{E}(y_1 \mid \mathbf{z}, y_2) = {} & \exp(\tau_1^2/2 + \mathbf{x}_1\boldsymbol{\beta}_1)\{\Phi(\rho_1 + \mathbf{z}\boldsymbol{\pi}_2)/\Phi(\mathbf{z}\boldsymbol{\pi}_2)\}^{y_2} \\ & \cdot \{[1 - \Phi(\rho_1 + \mathbf{z}\boldsymbol{\pi}_2)]/[1 - \Phi(\mathbf{z}\boldsymbol{\pi}_2)]\}^{(1-y_2)}. \end{aligned} \tag{18.48}$$

Notice that, if $\mathbf{x}_1$ contains unity, as it should, then only $\tau_1^2/2 + \beta_{11}$ is identified, along with the other elements of $\boldsymbol{\beta}_1$, ρ_1, and $\boldsymbol{\pi}_2$. This is just fine because the average structural function is $\mathrm{ASF}(\mathbf{z}_1, y_2) = \mathrm{E}_{c_1}[\exp(\mathbf{x}_1\boldsymbol{\beta}_1 + c_1)] = \exp(\tau_1^2/2 + \mathbf{x}_1\boldsymbol{\beta}_1)]$, and so the intercept that is identified is exactly what we want for computing APEs. Thus, in what follows we just absorb $\tau_1^2/2$ into the intercept.

In the first step of Terza's two-step method we estimate the probit model of y_2 on $\mathbf{z}$ to obtain the MLE, $\hat{\boldsymbol{\pi}}_2$. In the second step we estimate the mean function in (18.48) with $\hat{\boldsymbol{\pi}}_2$ in place of $\boldsymbol{\pi}_2$. We can use NLS or a quasi-MLE, such as the Poisson or gamma QMLE. Either way, our inference should account for the two-step estimation, using either the delta method or bootstrap.

A simple test of $H_0: \rho_1 = 0$ is available. The derivative of the mean function with respect to ρ_1, evaluated at $\rho_1 = 0$, is $\exp(\mathbf{x}_1\boldsymbol{\beta}_1)[\lambda(\mathbf{z}\boldsymbol{\pi}_2)]^{y_2}[-\lambda(-\mathbf{z}\boldsymbol{\pi}_2)]^{(1-y_2)}$, where $\lambda(\cdot)$ is the inverse Mills ratio. (We use the fact that $\phi(a)/[1 - \Phi(a)] = \phi(-a)/\Phi(-a)$.) Therefore, a simple variable addition test of $\rho_1 = 0$ can be obtained by adding the variable $y_2 \log[\lambda(\mathbf{z}\hat{\boldsymbol{\pi}}_2)] - (1 - y_2) \log[\lambda(-\mathbf{z}\hat{\boldsymbol{\pi}}_2)]$ to the exponential model $\exp(\mathbf{x}_1\boldsymbol{\beta}_1)$. That is, for each i define $\hat{r}_{i2} = y_{i2} \log[\lambda(\mathbf{z}_i\hat{\boldsymbol{\pi}}_2)] - (1 - y_{i2}) \log[\lambda(-\mathbf{z}_i\hat{\boldsymbol{\pi}}_2)]$, and then use a QMLE or NLS to estimate the artificial mean function $\exp(\mathbf{x}_{i1}\boldsymbol{\beta}_1 + \rho_1\hat{r}_{i2})$, and use a robust t statistic for $\hat{\rho}_1$ (which is not the estimate we obtain from Terza's two-step method).

Mullahy (1997) has shown how to estimate exponential models when some explanatory variables are endogenous without making assumptions about the reduced form of $\mathbf{y}_2$. This approach is especially attractive for dummy endogenous and other discrete explanatory variables, where the linearity in equation (18.39), coupled with independence of $\mathbf{z}$ and $\mathbf{v}_2$, is unrealistic. To sketch Mullahy's approach, write $\mathbf{x}_1 = (\mathbf{z}_1, \mathbf{y}_2)$ and $\boldsymbol{\beta}_1 = (\boldsymbol{\delta}_1', \boldsymbol{\gamma}_1')'$. Then, under the model (18.37), we can write

$$y_1 \exp(-\mathbf{x}_1\boldsymbol{\beta}_1) = \exp(c_1)a_1, \qquad \mathrm{E}(a_1 \mid \mathbf{z}, \mathbf{y}_2, c_1) = 1. \tag{18.49}$$

If we assume that c_1 is independent of $\mathbf{z}$—a standard assumption concerning unobserved heterogeneity and exogenous variables—and use the normalization $\mathrm{E}[\exp(c_1)] = 1$, we have the conditional moment restriction

$$\mathrm{E}[y_1 \exp(-\mathbf{x}_1\boldsymbol{\beta}_1) \mid \mathbf{z}] = 1. \tag{18.50}$$

Because y_1, $\mathbf{x}_1$, and $\mathbf{z}$ are all observable, condition (18.50) can be used as the basis for generalized method of moments (GMM) estimation. The function $g(y_1, \mathbf{y}_2, \mathbf{z}_1; \boldsymbol{\beta}_1) \equiv y_1 \exp(-\mathbf{x}_1\boldsymbol{\beta}_1) - 1$, which depends on observable data and the parameters, is uncorrelated with any function of $\mathbf{z}$ (at the true value of $\boldsymbol{\beta}_1$). GMM estimation can be used as in Section 14.2 once a vector of instrumental variables has been chosen.

An important feature of Mullahy's approach is that no assumptions, other than the standard rank condition for identification in nonlinear models, are made about the distribution of $\mathbf{y}_2$ given $\mathbf{z}$: we need not assume the existence of a linear reduced form for $\mathbf{y}_2$ with errors independent of $\mathbf{z}$. Mullahy's procedure is computationally more difficult, and testing for endogeneity in his framework is harder than in the QMLE approach. Therefore, we might first use the two-step quasi-likelihood method proposed earlier for testing, and if endogeneity seems to be important, Mullahy's GMM estimator can be implemented. See Mullahy (1997) for details and an empirical example.

18.6 Fractional Responses

We now consider models and estimation methods when the response variable, y_i, takes values in the unit interval, $[0, 1]$. Because we have already thoroughly covered binary response models in Chapter 15, we are thinking of cases where y_i is not a binary response.

18.6.1 Exogenous Explanatory Variables

In Section 17.8 we covered the two-limit Tobit model, which can be applied to fractional response variables when the limits are zero and one. Having estimated the two-limit Tobit given a set of explanatory variables, $\mathbf{x}_i$, we can estimate the conditional mean, $\mathrm{E}(y_i \mid \mathbf{x}_i)$, as well as various probabilities. But there are two drawbacks to using Tobit to model fractional responses. First, it does not apply unless there is a pileup at both zero and one. Fractional responses that have continuous distributions in $(0, 1)$ cannot follow at two-limit Tobit, nor can responses that have a mass point at zero or one but not both. Second, the two-limit Tobit imposes a parametric model on the density for $D(y_i \mid \mathbf{x}_i)$. If we are interested primarily in the effects on the conditional mean, then the two-limit Tobit—even when it logically applies—will generally produce inconsistent estimates of $\mathrm{E}(y_i \mid \mathbf{x}_i)$. (How serious the problem might be has not been seriously investigated.)

One can always search for other distributions that are logically consistent with the nature of the response variable. For example, if y_i is a continuous fractional response on $(0, 1)$, a conditional beta distribution is one possibility, and we can apply standard MLE methods for estimation. Kieschnick and McCullough (2003) suggest this approach. Like the two-limit Tobit approach, MLE using the beta distribution is inconsistent for all parameters if any aspect of the distribution is misspecified. Consequently, if one is primarily interested in the conditional mean, specifying a beta distribution is not robust. It not only rules out applications where y_i has a mass point at zero or one, but it is inconsistent when y_i is continuous on $(0, 1)$ but follows a distribution other than the beta distribution.

When y is strictly between zero and one, an alternative approach is to assume the **log-odds transformation** of y, $\log[y/(1-y)]$, has a conditional expectation of the form $\mathbf{x}\boldsymbol{\beta}$. Then, a simple estimator of $\boldsymbol{\beta}$ is the OLS estimator from the regression w_i on $\mathbf{x}_i$, where $w_i \equiv \log[y_i/(1-y_i)]$. While simple, the log-odds approach has a couple of drawbacks. First, it cannot be applied to corner solution responses unless we make some arbitrary adjustments. Because $\log[y/(1-y)] \to -\infty$ as $y \to 0$ and $\log[y/(1-y)] \to \infty$ as $y \to 1$, we might worry that our estimates are sensitive to the adjustment. Second, even if y is strictly in the unit interval, $\boldsymbol{\beta}$ is difficult to interpret: without further assumptions, it is not possible to estimate $\mathrm{E}(y \mid \mathbf{x})$ from a model for $E\{\log[y/(1-y)] \mid \mathbf{x}\}$. See Papke and Wooldridge (1996) for further discussion.

One possibility is to assume the log-odds transformation yields a linear model with an additive error independent of $\mathbf{x}$, so

$$\log[y/(1-y)] = \mathbf{x}\boldsymbol{\beta} + e, \qquad D(e \mid \mathbf{x}) = D(e), \tag{18.51}$$

where we take $\mathrm{E}(e) = 0$ (and assume that $x_1 = 1$). Then, we can write

$$y = \exp(\mathbf{x}\boldsymbol{\beta} + e)/[1 + \exp(\mathbf{x}\boldsymbol{\beta} + e)]. \tag{18.52}$$

Now, if e and $\mathbf{x}$ are independent, then

$$\mathrm{E}(y \mid \mathbf{x}) = \int \exp(\mathbf{x}\boldsymbol{\beta} + e)/[1 + \exp(\mathbf{x}\boldsymbol{\beta} + e)]\, dF(e), \tag{18.53}$$

where $F(\cdot)$ is the distribution function of e (and we use e as the dummy argument in the integration). As shown by Duan (1983) in a general retransformation context, for given $\mathbf{x}$ this expectation can be consistently estimated as

$$\hat{\mathrm{E}}(y \mid \mathbf{x}) = N^{-1} \sum_{i=1}^{N} \exp(\mathbf{x}\hat{\boldsymbol{\beta}} + \hat{e}_i)/[1 + \exp(\mathbf{x}\hat{\boldsymbol{\beta}} + \hat{e}_i)], \tag{18.54}$$

where $\hat{\boldsymbol{\beta}}$ is the OLS estimator from w_i on $\mathbf{x}_i$ and $\hat{e}_i = w_i - \mathbf{x}_i\hat{\boldsymbol{\beta}}$ are the OLS residuals from the log-odds regression. A similar analysis applies if we replace the log-odds transformation in (18.51) with $\Phi^{-1}(y)$, where $\Phi^{-1}(\cdot)$ is the inverse function of the standard normal cdf, in which case we average $\Phi(\mathbf{x}\hat{\boldsymbol{\beta}} + \hat{e}_i)$ across i to estimate $\mathrm{E}(y \mid \mathbf{x})$.

When it is applicable, Duan's method imposes fewer assumptions than a fully parametric model for $D(y \mid \mathbf{x})$. Nevertheless, it still is a roundabout way of estimating partial effects on $\mathrm{E}(y \mid \mathbf{x})$. An alternative is to directly specify models for $\mathrm{E}(y \mid \mathbf{x})$ that ensure predicted values are in $(0, 1)$. For example, we can specify $\mathrm{E}(y \mid \mathbf{x})$ as a logistic function:

$$\mathrm{E}(y \mid \mathbf{x}) = \exp(\mathbf{x}\boldsymbol{\beta})/[1 + \exp(\mathbf{x}\boldsymbol{\beta})], \tag{18.55}$$

or as a probit function,

$$\mathrm{E}(y \mid \mathbf{x}) = \Phi(\mathbf{x}\boldsymbol{\beta}). \tag{18.56}$$

In each case the fitted values will be in $(0, 1)$ and, of course, each allows y to take on any values in $[0, 1]$, including at the endpoints zero and one. Also, just as in logit and probit models for binary responses, the partial effects diminish as $\mathbf{x}\boldsymbol{\beta} \to \infty$. We can compute these partial effects just as in the binary response case, and compute APEs for continuous and discrete variables as in Chapter 15. The difference is that now these are partial effects on the expected value of a fractional response, not on a conditional probability of a binary response. As with the linear probability model for binary response, the APEs in the nonlinear models can be compared with coefficients from a linear regression of y_i on $\mathbf{x}_i$.

Of course, nothing requires us to choose a model for $\mathrm{E}(y \mid \mathbf{x})$ that depends on a cumulative distribution function; any function bounded in $(0, 1)$ would do. But the formulations in (18.55) and (18.56) are convenient for estimation and interpretation. In the next subsection, we will see that (18.56) easily allows certain kinds of endogenous explanatory variables.

Given that (18.55) and (18.56) specify a conditional mean function—say, $G(\mathbf{x}\boldsymbol{\beta})$—one approach to estimation is NLS. NLS is consistent and inference is straightforward, provided we use the fully robust sandwich variance matrix estimator that does not restrict $\mathrm{Var}(y \mid \mathbf{x})$. Nevertheless, as in estimating models of conditional means for unbounded, nonnegative responses, NLS is unlikely to be efficient because common distributions for a fractional response imply heteroskedasticity; this is true of the two-limit Tobit and beta distributions, among others. Instead, we could specify a flexible variance function and use weighted NLS in a two-step procedure, as in Chapter 12. A simpler, one-step strategy is to use a quasi-likelihood approach. Papke and Wooldridge (1996) note that, because the Bernoulli log likelihood is in the linear exponential family, the results of GMT (1984a) can be applied to conclude that the QMLE that solves

$$\max_{\mathbf{b}} \sum_{i=1}^{N} \{(1 - y_i) \log[1 - G(\mathbf{x}_i\mathbf{b})] + y_i \log[G(\mathbf{x}_i\mathbf{b})]\} \tag{18.57}$$

is consistent whenever the conditional mean is correctly specified. (A careful statement of the result requires distinguishing a generic value of the parameter vector from the "true" value.) Notice that (18.57) is well defined for any y_i in $[0, 1]$ and functions $G(\cdot) \in (0, 1)$. Plus, it is a standard estimation problem because it is identical to estimating binary response models. We call estimation of (18.55) by Bernoulli QMLE **fractional logit regression** and (18.56) estimated by Bernoulli QMLE **fractional probit regression**.

There has been some confusion in the literature about the nature of the robustness of the Bernoulli QMLE from (18.57) and how it compares with other methods. For example, when $0 < y < 1$, Kieschnick and McCullough (2003) recommend that researchers choose the fully parametric beta MLE over the Bernoulli QMLE "unless their sample size is large enough to justify the asymptotic arguments underlying the quasi-likelihood approach" (p. 193). This statement is highly misleading. The robustness of the Bernoulli QMLE arises because the population version of the objective function in (18.57) identifies the parameters in a correctly specified conditional mean, without any extra assumptions. By contrast, the beta log-likelihood function does not have this feature unless the full beta distribution is correctly specified. The sample size is irrelevant for choosing between the two approaches because in each case the statistical properties are based on asymptotic analysis, and there is no evidence that the beta MLE is better behaved in small samples than the Bernoulli QMLE. Generally, it is important to remember that the notion of robustness for identifying parameters, with or without various misspecifications, is a population issue.

As we know from Chapter 15, the variance associated with the log likelihood in (18.57) is $G(\mathbf{x}_i\boldsymbol{\beta})[1 - G(\mathbf{x}_i\boldsymbol{\beta})]$. Therefore, it is natural to specify the **Bernoulli GLM variance assumption** as

$$\mathrm{Var}(y \mid \mathbf{x}) = \sigma^2 \mathrm{E}(y \mid \mathbf{x})[1 - \mathrm{E}(y \mid \mathbf{x})]. \tag{18.58}$$

If $\sigma^2 = 1$, then we can actually use the usual estimated inverse information matrix for inference. However, if (18.58) holds, it is often with $\sigma^2 < 1$, and so, in this case, inference based on the usual binary response statistics will be too conservative—often, much too conservative. If assumption (18.58) does hold, we estimate the asymptotic variance as in (18.37) with $\hat{v}_i = G(\mathbf{x}_i\hat{\boldsymbol{\beta}})[1 - G(\mathbf{x}_i\hat{\boldsymbol{\beta}})]$, $\nabla_\beta \hat{m}_i \equiv g(\mathbf{x}_i\hat{\boldsymbol{\beta}})\mathbf{x}_i$ (where $g(\cdot)$ is the derivative of $G(\cdot)$), and

$$\hat{\sigma}^2 = (N - K)^{-1} \sum_{i=1}^{N} \hat{u}_i^2 / \hat{v}_i, \tag{18.59}$$

where K is the number of parameters and $\hat{u}_i = y_i - G(\mathbf{x}_i\hat{\boldsymbol{\beta}})$. Not surprisingly, if (18.58) holds, the Bernoulli QMLE is asymptotically efficient among estimators that specify only $\mathrm{E}(y \mid \mathbf{x})$, assuming, as always, that the mean is correctly specified. (Algebraic properties for the Beroulli log likelihood obtained for the binary case apply in the current situation. In particular, for fractional logit, if $\mathbf{x}_i$ includes a constant, as it almost always should, the residuals $\hat{u}_i$ sum to zero, while this is not true for fractional probit.)

When does (18.58) hold for fractional responses? One case is when y_i is a proportion, say, $y_i = s_i/n_i$, where s_i is the number of "successes" in n_i Bernoulli draws. Suppose that s_i given $(n_i, \mathbf{x}_i)$ follows a binomial distribution, as in Section 18.3.2 with $p(\mathbf{x}, \boldsymbol{\beta}) = G(\mathbf{x}\boldsymbol{\beta})$. Then $\mathrm{E}(y_i \mid n_i, \mathbf{x}_i) = n_i^{-1}\mathrm{E}(s_i \mid n_i, \mathbf{x}_i) = G(\mathbf{x}_i\boldsymbol{\beta})$ and $\mathrm{Var}(y_i \mid n_i, \mathbf{x}_i) = n_i^{-2}\,\mathrm{Var}(s_i \mid n_i, \mathbf{x}_i) = n_i^{-1}G(\mathbf{x}_i\boldsymbol{\beta})[1 - G(\mathbf{x}_i\boldsymbol{\beta})]$. Now, suppose that n_i is independent of $\mathbf{x}_i$. Then

$$\begin{aligned}
\mathrm{Var}(y_i \mid \mathbf{x}_i) &= \mathrm{Var}[\mathrm{E}(y_i \mid n_i, \mathbf{x}_i) \mid \mathbf{x}_i] + \mathrm{E}[\mathrm{Var}(y_i \mid n_i, \mathbf{x}_i) \mid \mathbf{x}_i] \\
&= 0 + \mathrm{E}(n_i^{-1} \mid \mathbf{x}_i) G(\mathbf{x}_i\boldsymbol{\beta})[1 - G(\mathbf{x}_i\boldsymbol{\beta})] \\
&\equiv \sigma^2 G(\mathbf{x}_i\boldsymbol{\beta})[1 - G(\mathbf{x}_i\boldsymbol{\beta})],
\end{aligned} \tag{18.60}$$

where $\sigma^2 \equiv \mathrm{E}(n_i^{-1}) \leq 1$ (with strict inequality unless $n_i = 1$ with probability one). Therefore, if y_i is obtained as a proportion of Bernoulli successes, we can expect underdispersion in (18.58). Further, if we are given data on proportions but do not know n_i, it makes sense to use a fractional logit or probit analysis. If we observe the n_i, we might use a binomial regression model instead.

It is easy to think of cases where the GLM assumption (18.58) fails. For example, it is unlikely that n_i and $\mathbf{x}_i$ are independent in all applications. For example, in Papke and Wooldridge (1996), n_i is number of workers at firm i, y_i is the fraction participation in a 401(k) pension plan, and $\mathbf{x}_i$ includes firm characteristics. Continuing with this example, if the probability of participating in a pension plan depends on unobserved worker and firm characteristics, this within-firm correlation generally invalidates $\text{Var}(s_i \mid n_i, \mathbf{x}_i) = n_i G(\mathbf{x}_i \boldsymbol{\beta})[1 - G(\mathbf{x}_i \boldsymbol{\beta})]$, in which case (18.58) also fails. Therefore, Papke and Wooldridge (1996) recommend fully robust sandwich standard errors and test statistics, which are easy to compute using GLM routines in popular software packages.

Variable addition tests for functional form are easily obtained. For example, after obtaining fractional regression estimates, we can add powers of $\mathbf{x}_i \hat{\boldsymbol{\beta}}$—say, the square and cube—to a subsequent fractional regression and carry out a robust joint test. See Papke and Wooldridge (1996) for further discussion and an application to 401(k) plan participation rates, and also Problem 18.14.

18.6.2 Endogenous Explanatory Variables

The fractional probit model can easily handle certain kinds of continuous endogenous explanatory variables. As in Section 18.5, we consider a specification with an unobserved factor that we would like to condition on:

$$\text{E}(y_1 \mid \mathbf{z}, y_2, c_1) = \text{E}(y_1 \mid \mathbf{z}_1, y_2, c_1) = \Phi(\mathbf{z}_1 \boldsymbol{\delta}_1 + \gamma_1 y_2 + c_1) \tag{18.61}$$

$$y_2 = \mathbf{z}\boldsymbol{\pi}_2 + v_2 = \mathbf{z}_1 \boldsymbol{\pi}_{21} + \mathbf{z}_2 \boldsymbol{\pi}_{22} + v_2, \tag{18.62}$$

where c_1 is an omitted factor thought to be correlated with y_2 but independent of the exogenous variables $\mathbf{z}$. Ideally, we could simply assume that the linear equation for y_2 simply represents a linear projection; unfortunately, we need to assume more, and here we effectively assume that v_2 is independent of $\mathbf{z}$. More specifically, we assume

$$c_1 = \rho_1 v_2 + e_1, \qquad e_1 \mid \mathbf{z}, v_2 \sim \text{Normal}(0, \sigma_{e1}^2), \tag{18.63}$$

where a sufficient, though not necessary, condition is that (c_1, v_2) is bivariate normal and independent of $\mathbf{z}$. Under (18.61), (18.62), and (18.63), we can show that

$$\text{E}(y_1 \mid \mathbf{z}, y_2) = \text{E}(y_1 \mid \mathbf{z}, y_2, v_2) = \Phi(\mathbf{z}_1 \boldsymbol{\delta}_{e1} + \gamma_{e1} y_2 + \rho_{e1} v_2), \tag{18.64}$$

where the "e" subscript denotes multiplication by the scale factor $1/(1 + \sigma_{e1}^2)^{1/2}$. Fortunately, as discussed in Wooldridge (2005a), equation (18.64) can be used as the basis for estimating APEs. The CF approach is now fairly clear. In the first step, obtain the OLS residuals $\hat{v}_{i2}$ from the regression y_{i2} on $\mathbf{z}_i$. Next, use fractional probit of y_{i1} on $\mathbf{z}_{i1}$, y_{i2}, $\hat{v}_{i2}$ to estimate the scaled coefficients.

A simple test of the null hypothesis that y_2 is exogenous is the fully robust t statistic on $\hat{v}_{i2}$; as with other tests based on adding residuals, the first-step estimation can be ignored under the null. If $\rho_1 \neq 0$, then the robust sandwich variance matrix estimator of the scaled coefficients is not valid because it does not account for the first-step estimation. The formulas for two-step estimation from Chapter 12 can be used. Bootstrapping the two-step procedure is quite feasible because computational time for each sample is minimal.

The average structural function is consistently estimated as

$$\widehat{\mathrm{ASF}}(\mathbf{z}_1, y_2) = N^{-1} \sum_{i=1}^{N} \Phi(\mathbf{z}_1 \hat{\boldsymbol{\delta}}_{e1} + \hat{\gamma}_{e1} y_2 + \hat{\rho}_{e1} \hat{v}_{i2}), \tag{18.65}$$

and this can be used to obtain APEs with respect to y_2 or $\mathbf{z}_1$. Bootstrapping the standard errors and test statistics is a sensible way to proceed with inference.

As discussed in Wooldridge (2005c), the basic model can be extended in many ways. For example, if the y_2 we want to appear in (18.65) might not naturally have a linear reduced form with an independent error, we might use a strictly monotonic transformation of it in (18.62): that is, replace y_2 with $h_2(y_2)$. If $y_2 > 0$ then $h_2(y_2) = \log(y_2)$ is natural; if $0 < y_2 < 1$, we might use the log-odds transformation in (18.62), $h_2(y_2) = \log[y_2/(1 - y_2)]$. Unfortunately, if y_2 has a mass point—such as a binary response, or corner response, or count variable—a transformation yielding an additive, independent error probably does not exist.

More generally, we can let $\mathbf{x}_1 = \mathbf{k}_1(\mathbf{z}_1, \mathbf{y}_2)$ for a vector of functions $\mathbf{k}_1(\cdot, \cdot)$, and allow a set of reduced forms for strictly monotonic functions $h_{2g}(y_{2g})$, $g = 1, \ldots, G_1$, where G_1 is the dimension of $\mathbf{y}_2$. Further, if we are willing to assume that $D(c_1 \mid \mathbf{z}, v_2)$ is independent of $\mathbf{z}$ with mean a polynomial in v_2, where v_2 is a scalar for simplicity, then we are justified in adding nonlinear functions of $\hat{v}_2$ to the fractional probit. For example, we could use the control functions $\hat{v}_{i2}$ and $(\hat{v}_{i2}^2 - \hat{\tau}_2^2)$, where $\hat{\tau}_2^2$ is the usual estimated error variance from the first-stage regression. See Wooldridge (2005c) for further discussion and extensions.

The previous method relies on y_2 being continuous because we require that a strictly monotonic transformation of y_2 can be written in a linear fashion with additive error independent of $\mathbf{z}$. We can handle a binary y_2 rather easily if we maintain that $\mathrm{D}(y_2 \mid \mathbf{z})$ follows a probit. In fact, we can maximize the same log likelihood as we derived in Section 15.7.3, even though y_1 is a fractional response. To see why this works, first note that the average structural function in (18.61) is $\Phi(\mathbf{x}_1 \boldsymbol{\beta}_1/(1 + \sigma_{c_1}^2)^{1/2})$, and so we hope to estimate $\boldsymbol{\beta}_{c1} \equiv \boldsymbol{\beta}_1/(1 + \sigma_{c_1}^2)^{1/2}$ (and cannot estimate $\boldsymbol{\beta}_1$ and $\sigma_{c_1}^2$ separately, anyway—see also Section 15.7.1). Next, note that we can obtain $\mathrm{E}(y_1 \mid \mathbf{z}, y_2, c_1)$ as $\mathrm{E}(y_1 \mid \mathbf{z}, y_2, c_1) = E\{1[\mathbf{x}_1\boldsymbol{\beta}_1 + c_1 + r_1 \geq 0] \mid \mathbf{z}, y_2, c_1\}$, where $D(r_1 \mid \mathbf{z}, y_2, c_1) = \text{Normal}(0, 1)$. By iterated expectations,

$$\mathrm{E}(y_1 \mid \mathbf{z}, y_2) = E\{1[\mathbf{x}_1\boldsymbol{\beta}_1 + c_1 + r_1 \geq 0] \mid \mathbf{z}, y_2\}$$

$$= E\{1[\mathbf{x}_1\boldsymbol{\beta}_{c1} + e_1 \geq 0] \mid \mathbf{z}, y_2\}, \tag{18.66}$$

where $e_1 = (c_1 + r_1)/(1 + \sigma_{c_1}^2)^{1/2}$ is independent of $\mathbf{z}$ with a standard normal distribution. If

$$y_2 = 1[\mathbf{z}\boldsymbol{\pi}_2 + v_2 \geq 0], \tag{18.67}$$

and we assume (c_1, v_2) is independent of $\mathbf{z}$ with a zero mean bivariate normal distribution, then (e_1, v_2) is independent of $\mathbf{z}$ with a bivariate normal distribution where each is standard normal. Let $\rho_1 = \text{Corr}(v_2, e_1)$. It follows from (18.66) and (18.67) that $\mathrm{E}(y_1 \mid \mathbf{z}, y_2)$ has exactly the form of $P(w_1 = 1 \mid \mathbf{z}, y_2)$, where $w_1 = 1[\mathbf{x}_1\boldsymbol{\beta}_{c1} + e_1 \geq 0]$. In other words, even though y_1 is not binary, its expected value given $(\mathbf{z}, y_2)$ is the same as the response probability implied by the bivariate probit model from Section 15.7.3. Because the Bernoulli log likelihood is in the linear exponential family, it identifies the correctly specified conditional mean. Further, we are assuming that $\mathrm{D}(y_2 \mid \mathbf{z})$ follows a probit. To be technically precise, if we add "o" subscripts to denote the true population values, $\boldsymbol{\pi}_{o2}$ maximizes $\mathrm{E}[\log f(y_{i2} \mid \mathbf{z}_i; \boldsymbol{\pi}_2)]$ and $(\boldsymbol{\beta}_{oc1}, \rho_{o1}, \boldsymbol{\pi}_{o2})$ maximizes $\mathrm{E}[\log f(y_{i1} \mid y_{i2}, \mathbf{z}_i; \boldsymbol{\beta}_{c1}, \rho_1, \boldsymbol{\pi}_2)]$. It follows that the true parameters maximize

$$\mathrm{E}[\log f(y_{i1} \mid y_{i2}, \mathbf{z}_i; \boldsymbol{\beta}_{c1}, \rho_1, \boldsymbol{\pi}_2)] + \mathrm{E}[\log f(y_{i2} \mid \mathbf{z}_i; \boldsymbol{\pi}_2)],$$

and so the quasi-MLE using the usual bivariate probit log likelihood is consistent and asymptotically normal. The scores for the two quasi-log likelihoods are still uncorrelated, but the information matrix equality would not hold for the first part of the quasi-log likelihood because $\log f(y_{i1} \mid y_{i2}, \mathbf{z}_i; \boldsymbol{\beta}_{c1}, \rho_1, \boldsymbol{\pi}_2)$ is not a true density. An M-estimator sandwich covariance matrix estimator—see equations (12.47) and (12.48)—is required and is straightforward to compute in this setting. Naturally, the bootstrap can be used, too.

18.7 Panel Data Methods

In this final section, we discuss estimation of panel data models, primarily focusing on count data. Our main interest is in models that contain unobserved effects, but we initially cover pooled estimation when the model does not explicitly contain an unobserved effect.

The pioneering work in unobserved effects count data models was done by Hausman, Hall, and Griliches (1984) (HHG), who were interested in explaining patent applications by firms in terms of spending on research and development. HHG developed random and fixed effects (FE) models under full distributional assumptions. Wooldridge (1999a) has shown that one of the approaches suggested by HHG, which is typically called the **fixed effects Poisson model**, has some nice robustness properties. We will study those here.

Other count panel data applications include (with response variable in parentheses) Rose (1990) (number of airline accidents), Papke (1991) (number of firm births in an industry), Downes and Greenstein (1996) (number of private schools in a public school district), and Page (1995) (number of housing units shown to individuals). The time series dimension in each of these studies allows us to control for unobserved heterogeneity in the cross section units, and to estimate certain dynamic relationships.

As with the rest of the book, we explicitly consider the case with N large relative to T, as the asymptotics hold with T fixed and $N \to \infty$.

18.7.1 Pooled QMLE

We begin by discussing pooled estimation after specifying a model for a conditional mean. Let $\{(\mathbf{x}_t, y_t): t = 1, 2, \ldots, T\}$ denote the time series observations for a random draw from the cross section population. We assume that, for some $\boldsymbol{\beta}_o \in \mathscr{B}$,

$$\mathrm{E}(y_t \mid \mathbf{x}_t) = m(\mathbf{x}_t, \boldsymbol{\beta}_o), \qquad t = 1, 2, \ldots, T. \tag{18.68}$$

This assumption simply means that we have a correctly specified parametric model for $\mathrm{E}(y_t \mid \mathbf{x}_t)$. For notational convenience only, we assume that the function m itself does not change over time. Relaxing this assumption just requires a notational change, or we can include time dummies in $\mathbf{x}_t$. For $y_t \geq 0$ and unbounded from above, the most common conditional mean is $\exp(\mathbf{x}_t\boldsymbol{\beta})$. There is no restriction on the time dependence of the observations under assumption (18.68), and $\mathbf{x}_t$ can contain any observed variables. For example, a static model has $\mathbf{x}_t = \mathbf{z}_t$, where $\mathbf{z}_t$ is dated contemporaneously with y_t. A finite distributed lag has $\mathbf{x}_t$ containing lags of $\mathbf{z}_t$. Strict exogeneity of $(\mathbf{x}_1, \ldots, \mathbf{x}_T)$, that is, $\mathrm{E}(y_t \mid \mathbf{x}_1, \ldots, \mathbf{x}_T) = \mathrm{E}(y_t \mid \mathbf{x}_t)$, is not assumed. In particular, $\mathbf{x}_t$ can contain lagged dependent variables, although how these might appear in nonlinear models is not obvious (see Wooldridge (1997c) for some possibilities). A limitation of model (18.68) is that it does not explicitly incorporate an unobserved effect.

For each $i = 1, 2, \ldots, N$, $\{(\mathbf{x}_{it}, y_{it}): t = 1, 2, \ldots, T\}$ denotes the time series observations for cross section unit i. We assume random sampling from the cross section.

One approach to estimating $\boldsymbol{\beta}_o$ is pooled NLS, which was introduced in Section 12.9. When y is a count variable, a Poisson QMLE can be used. This approach is completely analogous to pooled probit and pooled Tobit estimation with panel data. Note, however, that we are not assuming that the Poisson distribution is true.

For each i, the quasi-log likelihood for pooled Poisson estimation is (up to additive constants)

$$\ell_i(\boldsymbol{\beta}) = \sum_{t=1}^{T} \{y_{it} \log[m(\mathbf{x}_{it}, \boldsymbol{\beta})] - m(\mathbf{x}_{it}, \boldsymbol{\beta})\} \equiv \sum_{t=1}^{T} \ell_{it}(\boldsymbol{\beta}). \tag{18.69}$$

The **pooled Poisson QMLE** then maximizes the sum of $\ell_i(\boldsymbol{\beta})$ across $i = 1, \ldots, N$. Consistency and asymptotic normality of this estimator follows from the Chapter 12 results, once we use the fact that $\boldsymbol{\beta}_o$ maximizes $\mathrm{E}[\ell_i(\boldsymbol{\beta})]$; this follows from GMT (1984a). Thus, pooled Poisson estimation is robust in the sense that it consistently estimates $\boldsymbol{\beta}_o$ under assumption (18.68) only.

Without further assumptions we must be careful in estimating the asymptotic variance of $\hat{\boldsymbol{\beta}}$. Let $\mathbf{s}_i(\boldsymbol{\beta})$ be the $P \times 1$ score of $\ell_i(\boldsymbol{\beta})$, which can be written as $\mathbf{s}_i(\boldsymbol{\beta}) = \sum_{t=1}^{T} \mathbf{s}_{it}(\boldsymbol{\beta})$, where $\mathbf{s}_{it}(\boldsymbol{\beta})$ is the score of $\ell_{it}(\boldsymbol{\beta})$; each $\mathbf{s}_{it}(\boldsymbol{\beta})$ has the form (18.12) but with $(\mathbf{x}_{it}, y_{it})$ in place of $(\mathbf{x}_i, y_i)$.

The asymptotic variance of $\sqrt{N}(\hat{\boldsymbol{\beta}} - \boldsymbol{\beta}_o)$ has the usual form $\mathbf{A}_o^{-1}\mathbf{B}_o\mathbf{A}_o^{-1}$, where $\mathbf{A}_o \equiv \sum_{t=1}^{T} \mathrm{E}[\nabla_\beta m_{it}(\boldsymbol{\beta}_o)' \nabla_\beta m_{it}(\boldsymbol{\beta}_o)/m_{it}(\boldsymbol{\beta}_o)]$ and $\mathbf{B}_o \equiv \mathrm{E}[\mathbf{s}_i(\boldsymbol{\beta}_o)\mathbf{s}_i(\boldsymbol{\beta}_o)']$. Consistent estimators are

$$\hat{\mathbf{A}} = N^{-1} \sum_{i=1}^{N} \sum_{t=1}^{T} \nabla_\beta \hat{m}_{it}' \nabla_\beta \hat{m}_{it} / \hat{m}_{it} \tag{18.70}$$

$$\hat{\mathbf{B}} = N^{-1} \sum_{i=1}^{N} \mathbf{s}_i(\hat{\boldsymbol{\beta}}) \mathbf{s}_i(\hat{\boldsymbol{\beta}})', \tag{18.71}$$

and we can use $\hat{\mathbf{A}}^{-1}\hat{\mathbf{B}}\hat{\mathbf{A}}^{-1}/N$ for $\mathrm{Av\hat{a}r}(\hat{\boldsymbol{\beta}})$. This procedure is fully robust to the presence of serial correlation in the score and arbitrary conditional variances. It should be used in the construction of standard errors and Wald statistics. The quasi-*LR* statistic is not usually valid in this setup because of neglected time dependence and possible violations of the Poisson variance assumption.

If the conditional mean is dynamically complete in the sense that

$$\mathrm{E}(y_t \mid \mathbf{x}_t, y_{t-1}, \mathbf{x}_{t-1}, \ldots, y_1, \mathbf{x}_1) = \mathrm{E}(y_t \mid \mathbf{x}_t), \tag{18.72}$$

then $\{\mathbf{s}_{it}(\boldsymbol{\beta}_o)\colon t = 1, 2, \ldots, T\}$ is serially uncorrelated. Consequently, under assumption (18.72), a consistent estimator of $\mathbf{B}$ is

$$\hat{\mathbf{B}} = N^{-1} \sum_{i=1}^{N} \sum_{t=1}^{T} \mathbf{s}_{it}(\hat{\boldsymbol{\beta}}) \mathbf{s}_{it}(\hat{\boldsymbol{\beta}})'. \tag{18.73}$$

Using this equation along with $\hat{\mathbf{A}}$ produces the asymptotic variance that results from treating the observations as one long cross section, but without the Poisson or GLM variance assumptions. Thus, equation (18.73) affords a certain amount of robustness, but it requires the dynamic completeness assumption (18.72).

There are many other possibilities. If we impose the GLM assumption

$$\mathrm{Var}(y_{it} \mid \mathbf{x}_{it}) = \sigma_o^2 m(\mathbf{x}_{it}, \boldsymbol{\beta}_o), \qquad t = 1, 2, \ldots, T, \tag{18.74}$$

along with dynamic completeness, then $\mathrm{Avar}(\hat{\boldsymbol{\beta}})$ can be estimated by

$$\hat{\sigma}^2 \left(\sum_{i=1}^{N} \sum_{t=1}^{T} \nabla_{\beta} \hat{m}_{it}' \nabla_{\beta} \hat{m}_{it} / \hat{m}_{it} \right)^{-1}, \tag{18.75}$$

where $\hat{\sigma}^2 = (NT - P)^{-1} \sum_{i=1}^{N} \sum_{t=1}^{T} \tilde{u}_{it}^2$, $\tilde{u}_{it} = \hat{u}_{it} / \sqrt{\hat{m}_{it}}$, and $\hat{u}_{it} = y_{it} - m_{it}(\hat{\boldsymbol{\beta}})$. This estimator results in a standard GLM analysis on the pooled data.

A very similar analysis holds for pooled gamma QMLE by simply changing the quasi-log likelihood and associated statistics.

18.7.2 Specifying Models of Conditional Expectations with Unobserved Effects

We now turn to models that explicitly contain an unobserved effect. The issues that arise here are similar to those that arose in linear panel data models. First, we must know whether the explanatory variables are strictly exogenous conditional on an unobserved effect. Second, we must decide how the unobserved effect should appear in the conditional mean.

Given conditioning variables $\mathbf{x}_t$, strict exogeneity conditional on the unobserved effect c is defined just as in the linear case:

$$\mathrm{E}(y_t \mid \mathbf{x}_1, \ldots, \mathbf{x}_T, c) = \mathrm{E}(y_t \mid \mathbf{x}_t, c). \tag{18.76}$$

As always, this definition rules out lagged values of y in $\mathbf{x}_t$, and it can rule out feedback from y_t to future explanatory variables. In static models, where $\mathbf{x}_t = \mathbf{z}_t$ for variables $\mathbf{z}_t$ dated contemporaneously with y_t, assumption (18.76) implies that neither past nor future values of $\mathbf{z}$ affect the expected value of y_t, once $\mathbf{z}_t$ and c have been controlled for. This can be too restrictive, but it is often the starting point for analyzing static models.

A finite distributed lag relationship assumes that

$$\mathrm{E}(y_t \mid \mathbf{z}_t, \mathbf{z}_{t-1}, \ldots, \mathbf{z}_1, c) = \mathrm{E}(y_t \mid \mathbf{z}_t, \mathbf{z}_{t-1}, \ldots, \mathbf{z}_{t-Q}, c), \qquad t > Q, \tag{18.77}$$

where Q is the length of the distributed lag. Under assumption (18.77), the strict exogeneity assumption conditional on c becomes

$$\mathrm{E}(y_t \mid \mathbf{z}_1, \mathbf{z}_2, \ldots, \mathbf{z}_T, c) = \mathrm{E}(y_t \mid \mathbf{z}_1, \ldots, \mathbf{z}_t, c), \tag{18.78}$$

which is less restrictive than in the purely static model because lags of $\mathbf{z}_t$ explicitly appear in the model; it still rules out general feedback from y_t to $(\mathbf{z}_{t+1}, \ldots, \mathbf{z}_T)$.

With count variables, a multiplicative unobserved effect is an attractive functional form:

$$\mathrm{E}(y_t \mid \mathbf{x}_t, c) = c \cdot m(\mathbf{x}_t, \boldsymbol{\beta}_o), \tag{18.79}$$

where $m(\mathbf{x}_t, \boldsymbol{\beta})$ is a parametric function known up to the $P \times 1$ vector of parameters $\boldsymbol{\beta}_o$. Equation (18.79) implies that the partial effect of x_{tj} on $\log \mathrm{E}(y_t \mid \mathbf{x}_t, c)$ does not depend on the unobserved effect c. Thus, quantities such as elasticities and semi-elasticities depend only on $\mathbf{x}_t$ and $\boldsymbol{\beta}_o$. The most popular special case is the exponential model $\mathrm{E}(y_t \mid \mathbf{x}_t, a) = \exp(a + \mathbf{x}_t\boldsymbol{\beta})$, which is obtained by taking $c = \exp(a)$.

18.7.3 Random Effects Methods

A **multiplicative random effects model** maintains, at a minimum, two assumptions for a random draw i from the population:

$$\mathrm{E}(y_{it} \mid \mathbf{x}_{i1}, \ldots, \mathbf{x}_{iT}, c_i) = c_i m(\mathbf{x}_{it}, \boldsymbol{\beta}_o), \qquad t = 1, 2, \ldots, T \tag{18.80}$$

$$\mathrm{E}(c_i \mid \mathbf{x}_{i1}, \ldots, \mathbf{x}_{iT}) = \mathrm{E}(c_i) = 1, \tag{18.81}$$

where c_i is the unobserved, time-constant effect and the observed explanatory variables, $\mathbf{x}_{it}$, may be time constant or time varying. Assumption (18.80) is the strict exogeneity assumption of the $\mathbf{x}_{it}$ conditional on c_i, combined with a regression function multiplicative in c_i. When $y_{it} \geq 0$, such as with a count variable, the most popular choice of the parametric regression function is $m(\mathbf{x}_t, \boldsymbol{\beta}) = \exp(\mathbf{x}_t\boldsymbol{\beta})$, in which case $\mathbf{x}_{it}$ would typically contain a full set of time dummies. Assumption (18.81) says that the unobserved effect, c_i, is mean independent of $\mathbf{x}_i$; we normalize the mean to be one, a step which is without loss of generality for common choices of m, including the exponential function with unity in $\mathbf{x}_t$. Under assumptions (18.80) and (18.81), we can "integrate out" c_i by using the law of iterated expectations:

$$\mathrm{E}(y_{it} \mid \mathbf{x}_i) = \mathrm{E}(y_{it} \mid \mathbf{x}_{it}) = m(\mathbf{x}_{it}, \boldsymbol{\beta}_o), \qquad t = 1, 2, \ldots, T. \tag{18.82}$$

Equation (18.82) shows that $\boldsymbol{\beta}_o$ can be consistently estimated by the pooled Poisson method discussed in Section 19.6.1. The robust variance matrix estimator that allows for an arbitrary conditional variance and serial correlation produces valid inference.

Just as in a linear random effects model, the presence of the unobserved heterogeneity causes the y_{it} to be correlated over time, conditional on $\mathbf{x}_i$.

When we introduce an unobserved effect explicitly, a random effects analysis typically accounts for the overdispersion and serial dependence implied by assumptions (18.80) and (18.81). For count data, the **Poisson random effects model** is given by

$$y_{it} \mid \mathbf{x}_i, c_i \sim \text{Poisson}[c_i m(\mathbf{x}_{it}, \boldsymbol{\beta}_o)] \tag{18.83}$$

$$y_{it}, y_{ir} \text{ are independent conditional on } \mathbf{x}_i, c_i, \qquad t \neq r \tag{18.84}$$

$$c_i \text{ is independent of } \mathbf{x}_i \text{ and distributed as Gamma}(\delta_o, \delta_o), \tag{18.85}$$

where we parameterize the gamma distribution so that $\text{E}(c_i) = 1$ and $\text{Var}(c_i) = 1/\delta_o \equiv \eta_o^2$. While $\text{Var}(y_{it} \mid \mathbf{x}_i, c_i) = \text{E}(y_{it} \mid \mathbf{x}_i, c_i)$ under assumption (18.83), by equation (18.28), $\text{Var}(y_{it} \mid \mathbf{x}_i) = \text{E}(y_{it} \mid \mathbf{x}_i)[1 + \eta_o^2 \text{E}(y_{it} \mid \mathbf{x}_i)]$, and so assumptions (18.81) and (18.85) imply overdispersion in $\text{Var}(y_{it} \mid \mathbf{x}_i)$. Although other distributional assumptions for c_i can be used, the gamma distribution leads to a tractable density for $(y_{i1}, \ldots, y_{iT})$ given $\mathbf{x}_i$, which is obtained after c_i has been integrated out. (See HHG, p. 917, and Problem 18.11.) Maximum likelihood analysis (conditional on $\mathbf{x}_i$) is relatively straightforward and is implemented by some econometrics packages.

If assumptions (18.81), (18.82), and (18.83) all hold, the conditional MLE is efficient among all estimators that do not use information on the distribution of $\mathbf{x}_i$; see Section 14.5.2. The main drawback with the random effects Poisson model is that it is sensitive to violations of the maintained assumptions, any of which could be false. (Problem 18.5 covers some ways to allow c_i and $\bar{\mathbf{x}}_i$ to be correlated, but they still rely on stronger assumptions than the FE Poisson estimator, which we cover in Section 18.7.4.)

A **quasi-MLE random effects analysis** keeps some of the key features of assumptions (18.83)–(18.85) but produces consistent estimators under just the conditional mean assumptions (18.80) and (18.81). Nominally, we maintain assumptions (18.83)–(18.85). Define $u_{it} \equiv y_{it} - \text{E}(y_{it} \mid \mathbf{x}_{it}) = y_{it} - m(\mathbf{x}_{it}, \boldsymbol{\beta})$. Then we can write $u_{it} = c_i m_{it}(\boldsymbol{\beta}_o) + e_{it} - m_{it}(\boldsymbol{\beta}_o) = e_{it} + m_{it}(\boldsymbol{\beta}_o)(c_i - 1)$, where $e_{it} \equiv y_{it} - \text{E}(y_{it} \mid \mathbf{x}_{it}, c_i)$. As we showed in Section 19.3.1,

$$\text{E}(u_{it}^2 \mid \mathbf{x}_i) = m_{it}(\boldsymbol{\beta}_o) + \eta_o^2 m_{it}^2(\boldsymbol{\beta}_o). \tag{18.86}$$

Further, for $t \neq r$,

$$\text{E}(u_{it} u_{ir} \mid \mathbf{x}_i) = \text{E}[(c_i - 1)^2] m_{it}(\boldsymbol{\beta}_o) m_{ir}(\boldsymbol{\beta}_o) = \eta_o^2 m_{it}(\boldsymbol{\beta}_o) m_{ir}(\boldsymbol{\beta}_o), \tag{18.87}$$

where $\eta_o^2 = \text{Var}(c_i)$. The serial correlation in equation (18.87) is reminiscent of the serial correlation that arises in linear random effects models under standard assumptions. This shows explicitly that we must correct for serial dependence in computing the asymptotic variance of the pooled Poisson QMLE in Section 18.7.1. The overdispersion in equation (18.86) is analogous to the variance of the composite error in a linear model. A QMLE random effects analysis exploits these nominal variance and covariance expressions but does not rely on either of them for consistency. If we use equation (18.86) while ignoring equation (18.87), we are led to a **pooled negative binomial analysis**, which is very similar to the pooled Poisson analysis except that the quasi-log likelihood for each time period is the negative binomial discussed in Section 18.3.1. See Wooldridge (1997c) for details.

If condition (18.87) holds, it is more efficient—perhaps much more efficient—to use the weighted multivariate nonlinear least squares estimator (WMNLS) discussed in Section 12.9.2. We simply construct an estimate of the conditional variance matrix based on (18.86) and (18.87). To implement the method, we would obtain the pooled Poisson QMLE of $\boldsymbol{\beta}$, say, $\check{\boldsymbol{\beta}}$. We can use this estimator to estimate η_o^2. One possibility is to note that $\mathrm{E}[(u_{it}^2 - m_{it}(\boldsymbol{\beta}_o))/m_{it}(\boldsymbol{\beta}_o) \mid \mathbf{x}_i] = \eta_o^2 m_{it}(\boldsymbol{\beta}_o)$. Let $\check{u}_{it}^2 = (y_{it} - m_{it}(\check{\boldsymbol{\beta}}))^2$ be the squared residuals from the pooled Poisson QMLE. Then obtain $\check{\eta}^2$ from the pooled simple regression (through the origin) $[\check{u}_{it}^2/m_{it}(\check{\boldsymbol{\beta}})] - 1$ on $m_{it}(\check{\boldsymbol{\beta}})]$, $t = 1, \ldots, T$, $i = 1, \ldots, N$. Now, given $\check{\eta}^2$ and $\check{\boldsymbol{\beta}}$, we can estimate the conditional variance and conditional covariances in (18.86) and (18.87). Call the resulting $T \times T$ matrix $\hat{\mathbf{W}}_i$. Then recall that the WMNLS estimator, $\hat{\boldsymbol{\beta}}$, solves

$$\min_{\boldsymbol{\beta}} \sum_{i=1}^{N} [\mathbf{y}_i - \mathbf{m}_i(\boldsymbol{\beta})]' \hat{\mathbf{W}}_i^{-1} [\mathbf{y}_i - \mathbf{m}_i(\boldsymbol{\beta})]'.$$

Under assumptions (18.86) and (18.87), the WMNLS estimator is relatively efficient among estimators that only require a correct conditional mean for consistency, and its asymptotic variance can be estimated as

$$\mathrm{Av\hat{a}r}(\hat{\boldsymbol{\beta}}) = \left(\sum_{i=1}^{N} \nabla_{\beta} \hat{\mathbf{m}}_i' \hat{\mathbf{W}}_i^{-1} \nabla_{\beta} \hat{\mathbf{m}}_i \right)^{-1}.$$

As with the other QMLEs, the WMNLS estimator is consistent under assumptions (18.80) and (18.81) only, but if assumption (18.86) or (18.87) is violated, the variance matrix needs to be made robust. Letting $\hat{\mathbf{u}}_i \equiv \mathbf{y}_i - \mathbf{m}_i(\hat{\boldsymbol{\beta}})$ (a $T \times 1$ vector), the robust estimator is

$$\left(\sum_{i=1}^{N} \nabla_{\beta} \hat{\mathbf{m}}_i' \hat{\mathbf{W}}_i^{-1} \nabla_{\beta} \hat{\mathbf{m}}_i \right)^{-1} \left(\sum_{i=1}^{N} \nabla_{\beta} \hat{\mathbf{m}}_i' \hat{\mathbf{W}}_i^{-1} \hat{\mathbf{u}}_i \hat{\mathbf{u}}_i' \hat{\mathbf{W}}_i^{-1} \nabla_{\beta} \hat{\mathbf{m}}_i \right) \left(\sum_{i=1}^{N} \nabla_{\beta} \hat{\mathbf{m}}_i' \hat{\mathbf{W}}_i^{-1} \nabla_{\beta} \hat{\mathbf{m}}_i \right)^{-1}.$$

This expression gives a way to obtain fully robust inference while having a relatively efficient estimator under the random effects assumptions (18.86) and (18.87).

GMT (1984b) cover a model that suggests an alternative form of $\hat{\mathbf{W}}_i$. The matrix $\hat{\mathbf{W}}_i$ can be modified for other nominal distributional assumptions, such as the gamma (which would be natural to apply to continuous, nonnegative y_{it}.) Further, a typical generalized estimating equation (GEE) approach would choose a different estimator of the variance matrix. The GEE approach associated with the Poisson QMLE would be to maintain the nominal Poisson variance assumption, $\text{Var}(y_{it} \mid \mathbf{x}_i) = \sigma^2 m(\mathbf{x}_{it}, \boldsymbol{\beta}_o)$, along with a constant working correlation matrix. The resulting variance-covariance matrix cannot be derived from an unobserved effects model; generally, it will be inefficient under (18.83) to (18.85). See Section 12.9.2 for further discussion on GEE.

We must remember that none of the suggested WMNLS methods that allow nonzero correlation is consistent if $\text{E}(y_{it} \mid \mathbf{x}_i) \neq m(\mathbf{x}_{it}, \boldsymbol{\beta}_o)$. In the context of an unobserved effects model, we usually think of a misspecified conditional mean as coming either from lack of strict exogeneity of $\{\mathbf{x}_{it} : t = 1, \ldots, T\}$ (conditional on c_i) or from correlation between c_i and $\mathbf{x}_i$.

18.7.4 Fixed Effects Poisson Estimation

HHG first showed how to do an FE type of analysis of count panel data models, which allows for arbitrary dependence between c_i and $\mathbf{x}_i$. Their FE Poisson assumptions are (18.83) and (18.84), with the conditional mean given still by assumption (18.80). The key is that neither assumption (18.85) nor assumption (18.81) is maintained; in other words, arbitrary dependence between c_i and $\mathbf{x}_i$ is allowed. HHG take $m(\mathbf{x}_{it}, \boldsymbol{\beta}) = \exp(\mathbf{x}_{it}\boldsymbol{\beta})$, which is by far the leading case.

HHG use Andersen's (1970) conditional ML methodology to estimate $\boldsymbol{\beta}$. Let $n_i \equiv \sum_{t=1}^{T} y_{it}$ denote the sum across time of the counts across t. Using standard results on obtaining a joint distribution conditional on the sum of its components, HHG show that

$$\mathbf{y}_i \mid n_i, \mathbf{x}_i, c_i \sim \text{Multinomial}\{n_i, p_1(\mathbf{x}_i, \boldsymbol{\beta}_o), \ldots, p_T(\mathbf{x}_i, \boldsymbol{\beta}_o)\}, \tag{18.88}$$

where

$$p_t(\mathbf{x}_i, \boldsymbol{\beta}) \equiv m(\mathbf{x}_{it}, \boldsymbol{\beta}) \Big/ \left[\sum_{r=1}^{T} m(\mathbf{x}_{ir}, \boldsymbol{\beta})\right]. \tag{18.89}$$

Because this distribution does not depend on c_i, equation (18.88) is also the distribution of $\mathbf{y}_i$ conditional on n_i and $\mathbf{x}_i$. Therefore, $\boldsymbol{\beta}_o$ can be estimated by standard conditional MLE techniques using the multinomial log likelihood. The conditional log likelihood for observation i, apart from terms not depending on $\boldsymbol{\beta}$, is

$$\ell_i(\boldsymbol{\beta}) = \sum_{t=1}^{T} y_{it} \log[p_t(\mathbf{x}_i, \boldsymbol{\beta})]. \tag{18.90}$$

The estimator $\hat{\boldsymbol{\beta}}$ that maximizes $\sum_{i=1}^{N} \ell_i(\boldsymbol{\beta})$ will be called the **fixed effects Poisson (FEP) estimator**. (Note that when $y_{it} = 0$ for all t, the cross section observation i does not contribute to the estimation.)

Obtaining the FEP estimator is computationally fairly easy, especially when $m(\mathbf{x}_{it}, \boldsymbol{\beta}) = \exp(\mathbf{x}_{it}\boldsymbol{\beta})$. But the assumptions used to derive the conditional log likelihood in equation (18.90) can be restrictive in practice. Fortunately, the FEP estimator has very strong robustness properties for estimating the parameters in the conditional mean. As shown in Wooldridge (1999a), the FEP estimator is consistent for $\boldsymbol{\beta}_{\mathrm{o}}$ under the conditional mean assumption (18.80) only. Except for the conditional mean, the distribution of y_{it} given $(\mathbf{x}_i, c_i)$ is entirely unrestricted; in particular, there can be overdispersion or underdispersion in the latent variable model. The distribution of y_{it} need not be discrete; it could be continuous or have discrete and continuous features. Also, there is no restriction on the dependence between y_{it} and y_{ir}, $t \neq r$. This is another case where the QMLE derived under fairly strong nominal assumptions turns out to have very desirable robustness properties.

The argument that the FEP estimator is consistent under assumption (18.80) hinges on showing that $\boldsymbol{\beta}_{\mathrm{o}}$ maximizes the expected value of equation (18.90) under assumption (18.80) only. This result is shown in Wooldridge (1999a). Uniqueness holds under general identification assumptions, but certain kinds of explanatory variables are ruled out. For example, when the conditional mean has an exponential form, it is easy to see that the coefficients on time-constant explanatory variables drop out of equation (18.89), just as in the linear case. Interactions between time-constant and time-varying explanatory variables are allowed.

Consistent estimation of the asymptotic variance of $\hat{\boldsymbol{\beta}}$ follows from the results on M-estimation in Chapter 12. The score for observation i can be written as

$$\mathbf{s}_i(\boldsymbol{\beta}) \equiv \nabla_{\beta}\ell_i(\boldsymbol{\beta}) = \sum_{t=1}^{T} y_{it}[\nabla_{\beta} p_t(\mathbf{x}_i, \boldsymbol{\beta})'/p_t(\mathbf{x}_i, \boldsymbol{\beta})]$$

$$\equiv \nabla_{\beta}\mathbf{p}(\mathbf{x}_i, \boldsymbol{\beta})'\mathbf{W}(\mathbf{x}_i, \boldsymbol{\beta})\{\mathbf{y}_i - \mathbf{p}(\mathbf{x}_i, \boldsymbol{\beta})n_i\}, \tag{18.91}$$

where $\mathbf{W}(\mathbf{x}_i, \boldsymbol{\beta}) \equiv [\mathrm{diag}\{p_1(\mathbf{x}_i, \boldsymbol{\beta}), \ldots, p_T(\mathbf{x}_i, \boldsymbol{\beta})\}]^{-1}$, $\mathbf{u}_i(\boldsymbol{\beta}) \equiv \mathbf{y}_i - \mathbf{p}(\mathbf{x}_i, \boldsymbol{\beta})n_i$, $\mathbf{p}(\mathbf{x}_i, \boldsymbol{\beta}) \equiv [p_1(\mathbf{x}_i, \boldsymbol{\beta}), \ldots, p_T(\mathbf{x}_i, \boldsymbol{\beta})]'$, and $p_t(\mathbf{x}_i, \boldsymbol{\beta})$ is given by equation (18.89).

The expected Hessian for observation i can be shown to be

$$\mathbf{A}_o \equiv \mathrm{E}[n_i \nabla_\beta \mathbf{p}(\mathbf{x}_i, \boldsymbol{\beta}_o)' \mathbf{W}(\mathbf{x}_i, \boldsymbol{\beta}_o) \nabla_\beta \mathbf{p}(\mathbf{x}_i, \boldsymbol{\beta}_o)].$$

The asymptotic variance of $\hat{\boldsymbol{\beta}}$ is $\mathbf{A}_o^{-1}\mathbf{B}_o\mathbf{A}_o^{-1}/N$, where $\mathbf{B}_o \equiv \mathrm{E}[\mathbf{s}_i(\boldsymbol{\beta}_o)\mathbf{s}_i(\boldsymbol{\beta}_o)']$. A consistent estimate of $\mathbf{A}$ is

$$\hat{\mathbf{A}} = N^{-1} \sum_{i=1}^{N} n_i \nabla_\beta \mathbf{p}(\mathbf{x}_i, \hat{\boldsymbol{\beta}})' \mathbf{W}(\mathbf{x}_i, \hat{\boldsymbol{\beta}}) \nabla_\beta \mathbf{p}(\mathbf{x}_i, \hat{\boldsymbol{\beta}}) \tag{18.92}$$

and $\mathbf{B}$ is estimated as

$$\hat{\mathbf{B}} = N^{-1} \sum_{i=1}^{N} \mathbf{s}_i(\hat{\boldsymbol{\beta}})\mathbf{s}_i(\hat{\boldsymbol{\beta}})'. \tag{18.93}$$

The robust variance matrix estimator, $\hat{\mathbf{A}}^{-1}\hat{\mathbf{B}}\hat{\mathbf{A}}^{-1}/N$, is valid under assumption (18.80); in particular, it allows for any deviations from the Poisson distribution and arbitrary time dependence. The usual ML estimate, $\hat{\mathbf{A}}^{-1}/N$, is valid under assumptions (18.83) and (18.84). For more details, including methods for specification testing, see Wooldridge (1999a).

Applications of the FEP estimator, which compute the robust variance matrix and some specification test statistics, are given in Papke (1991), Page (1995), and Gordy (1999). We must emphasize that, while the leading application is to count data, the FEP estimator works whenever assumption (18.80) holds. Therefore, y_{it} could be a nonnegative continuous variable, or even a binary response if we believe the unobserved effect is multiplicative (in contrast to the models in Sections 15.8.2 and 15.8.3).

Because the FEP estimator relies heavily on strict exogeneity of $\{\mathbf{x}_{it} : t = 1, \ldots, T\}$, conditional on c_i, it is helpful to have a simple test of this assumption. A straightforward approach is to simply add $\mathbf{w}_{i,t+1}$ to the model, usually an exponential model, where $\mathbf{w}_{it} \subset \mathbf{x}_{it}$. Then, using the FEP estimator, a fully robust joint significance test for $\mathbf{w}_{i,t+1}$ can be used. A significant statistic indicates that the strict exogeneity assumption fails. Naturally, we lose the last time period in carrying out the test. One could even interact $\mathbf{w}_{i,t+1}$ with certain elements of $\mathbf{x}_{it}$ and include these interaction terms in the joint test.

18.7.5 Relaxing the Strict Exogeneity Assumption

If the test in the previous subsection rejects, we probably need to relax the strict exogeneity assumption. In place of assumption (18.80) we assume

$$\mathrm{E}(y_{it} \mid \mathbf{x}_{i1}, \ldots, \mathbf{x}_{it}, c_i) = c_i m(\mathbf{x}_{it}, \boldsymbol{\beta}_o), \qquad t = 1, 2, \ldots, T. \tag{18.94}$$

These are **sequential moment restrictions** of the kind we discussed in Chapter 11. The model (18.94) is applicable to static and distributed lag models with possible feedback, as well as to models with lagged dependent variables. Again, y_{it} need not be a count variable here.

Chamberlain (1992b) and Wooldridge (1997a) have suggested residual functions that lead to conditional moment restrictions. Assuming that $m(\mathbf{x}_{it}, \boldsymbol{\beta}) > 0$, define

$$r_{it}(\boldsymbol{\beta}) \equiv y_{it} - y_{i,t+1}[m(\mathbf{x}_{it}, \boldsymbol{\beta})/m(\mathbf{x}_{i,t+1}, \boldsymbol{\beta})], \qquad t = 1, \dots, T-1. \tag{18.95}$$

Under assumption (18.95), we can use iterated expectations to show that $\mathrm{E}[r_{it}(\boldsymbol{\beta}_o) \mid \mathbf{x}_{i1}, \dots, \mathbf{x}_{it}] = 0$. This expression means that any function of $\mathbf{x}_{i1}, \dots, \mathbf{x}_{it}$ is uncorrelated with $r_{it}(\boldsymbol{\beta}_o)$ and is the basis for a GMM estimation. One can easily test the strict exogeneity assumption in a GMM framework. For further discussion and details on implementation, as well as an alternative residual function, see Wooldridge (1997a).

Blundell, Griffith, and Windmeijer (1998) consider variants of moment conditions in a *linear feedback model*, where the mean function contains a lagged dependent variable, which enters additively, in addition to an exponential regression function in other conditioning variables with a multiplicated unobserved effect. They apply their model to the patents and R&D relationship.

A different approach is conditional maximum likelihood, as we discussed in Sections 15.8.4 and 17.8.3—see Section 13.9 for a general discussion. For example, if we want to estimate a model for y_{it} given $(\mathbf{z}_{it}, y_{i,t-1}, c_i)$, where $\mathbf{z}_{it}$ contains contemporaneous variables, we can model it as a Poisson variable with exponential mean $c_i \exp(\mathbf{z}_{it}\boldsymbol{\beta}_o + \rho_o y_{i,t-1})$. Then, assuming that $\mathrm{D}(y_{it} \mid \mathbf{z}_i, y_{i,t-1}, \dots, y_{i0}, c_i) = \mathrm{D}(y_{it} \mid \mathbf{z}_{it}, y_{i,t-1}, c_i)$, we can obtain the density of $(y_{i1}, \dots, y_{iT})$ given $(y_{i0}, \mathbf{z}_i, c_i)$ by multiplication; see equation (13.60). Given a density specification for $\mathrm{D}(c_i \mid y_{i0}, \mathbf{z}_i)$, we can obtain the conditional log likelihood for each i as in equation (13.62). A very convenient specification is $c_i = \exp(\alpha_o + \xi_o y_{i0} + \mathbf{z}_i\boldsymbol{\gamma}_o)a_i$, where a_i is independent of $(y_{i0}, \mathbf{z}_i)$ and distributed as $\mathrm{Gamma}(\delta_o, \delta_o)$. Then, for each t, y_{it} given $(y_{i,t-1}, \dots, y_{i0}, \mathbf{z}_i, a_i)$ has a Poisson distribution with mean

$$a_i \exp(\alpha_o + \mathbf{z}_{it}\boldsymbol{\beta}_o + \rho_o y_{i,t-1} + \xi_o y_{i0} + \mathbf{z}_i\boldsymbol{\gamma}_o).$$

(As always, we would probably want aggregate time dummies included in this equation.) It is easy to see that the distribution of $(y_{i1}, \dots, y_{iT})$ given $(y_{i0}, \mathbf{z}_i)$ has the random effects Poisson form with gamma heterogeneity; therefore, standard random effects Poisson software can be used to estimate $\alpha_o, \boldsymbol{\beta}_o, \rho_o, \xi_o, \boldsymbol{\gamma}_o$, and δ_o. The usual conditional MLE standard errors, t statistics, Wald statistics, and LR statistics are asymptotically valid for large N. See Wooldridge (2005b) for further details.

With an exponential mean, Windmeijer (2000) shows how to modify the moment conditions in (18.95) to estimate models with contemporaneously endogenous explanatory variables. Alternatively, in some cases a control function method would be available. For example, if we start with $\mathrm{E}(y_{it1} \mid \mathbf{z}_i, y_{it2}, c_{i1}, r_{it1}) = \exp(\mathbf{z}_{it1}\boldsymbol{\delta}_1 + \alpha_1 y_{it2} + c_{i1} + r_{it1})$, where c_{i1} is unobserved heterogeneity and r_{it1} is a time-varying omitted variable, then for continuous y_{it2} we might specify $y_{it2} = \psi_2 + \mathbf{z}_{it}\boldsymbol{\pi}_2 + \bar{\mathbf{z}}_i\xi_2 + v_{it2}$, where we have imposed the Chamberlain-Mundlak device to allow heterogeneity affecting y_{it2} to be correlated with $\mathbf{z}_i$ through the time average, $\bar{\mathbf{z}}_i$. Further, if we specify $c_{i1} = \psi_1 + \bar{\mathbf{z}}_i\xi_1 + a_{i1}$, then we can write $\mathrm{E}(y_{it1} \mid \mathbf{z}_i, y_{it2}, v_{it1}) = \exp(\psi_1 + \mathbf{z}_{it1}\boldsymbol{\delta}_1 + \bar{\mathbf{z}}_i\xi_1 + \alpha_1 y_{it2} + v_{it1})$, where $v_{it1} = a_{i1} + r_{it1}$. While it is hardly general, it is not unreasonable to assume (v_{it1}, v_{it2}) is independent of $\mathbf{z}_i$. If we specify $\mathrm{E}[\exp(v_{it1}) \mid v_{it2}] = \exp(\eta_1 + \rho_1 v_{it2})$ (as would be true under joint normality), we obtain the estimating equation

$$\mathrm{E}(y_{it1} \mid \mathbf{z}_i, y_{it2}, v_{it2}) = \exp(\alpha_1 + z_{it1}\boldsymbol{\delta}_1 + \alpha_1 y_{it2} + \bar{\mathbf{z}}_i\xi_1 + \rho_1 v_{it2}). \tag{18.96}$$

A two-step method is the following: (1) Obtain the residuals $\hat{v}_{it2}$ from the pooled OLS estimation y_{it2} on 1, $\mathbf{z}_{it}$, $\bar{\mathbf{z}}_i$ across t and i. (2) Use a pooled NLS or QMLE (perhaps the Poisson) to estimate the exponential function, where $(\bar{\mathbf{z}}_i, \hat{v}_{it2})$ are explanatory variables along with $(\mathbf{z}_{it1}, y_{it2})$. (As usual, a full set of time period dummies is a good idea in the first and second steps.) Alternatively, WMNLS can be used or GMM. One should adjust for the first-stage estimation, using the delta method or possibly the panel bootstrap, unless $\rho_1 = 0$. Rather than just obtain coefficient estimates, the APEs can be obtained by averaging the exponential function across $(\bar{\mathbf{z}}_i, \hat{v}_{it2})$. The details are quite similar to the probit case in Section 15.8.5.

Terza's (1998) approach when y_{it2} is binary can be modified along similar lines using the Chamberlain-Mundlak device. Once one specifies a probit model of the form $y_{it2} = 1[\psi_2 + \mathbf{z}_{it2}\boldsymbol{\pi}_2 + \bar{\mathbf{z}}_i\xi_2 + v_{it2} \geq 0]$, where v_{it2} is independent of $\mathbf{z}_i$ with a standard normal distribution, and combines this with (18.96), obtaining pooled estimation methods or GMM methods is straightforward.

18.7.6 Fractional Response Models for Panel Data

We can also specify and estimate models with unobserved heterogeneity for fractional response variables. Following Papke and Wooldridge (2008), and for reasons similar to those in Section 18.6.2, it is easiest to work with the probit response function, as specified in

$$\mathrm{E}(y_{it} \mid \mathbf{x}_{it}, c_i) = \Phi(\mathbf{x}_{it}\boldsymbol{\beta} + c_i), \qquad t = 1, \ldots, T. \tag{18.97}$$

The APEs that we are interested in are just as in the probit case, except that these are partial effects on a mean response (not a probability).

Without further assumptions, neither $\boldsymbol{\beta}$ nor the APEs are known to be identified. As with previous nonlinear models, a strict exogeneity assumption, conditional on the unobserved effect, is useful:

$$\mathrm{E}(y_{it} \mid \mathbf{x}_i, c_i) = \mathrm{E}(y_{it} \mid \mathbf{x}_{it}, c_i), \qquad t = 1, \ldots, T, \tag{18.98}$$

where $\mathbf{x}_i \equiv (\mathbf{x}_{i1}, \ldots, \mathbf{x}_{iT})$ is the set of covariates in all time periods. A second useful assumption (which could be made more flexible) is conditional normality using the Chamberlain-Mundlak approach:

$$c_i \mid (\mathbf{x}_{i1}, \mathbf{x}_{i2}, \ldots, \mathbf{x}_{iT}) \sim \mathrm{Normal}(\psi + \bar{\mathbf{x}}_i \boldsymbol{\xi}, \sigma_a^2), \tag{18.99}$$

where, as always, $\bar{\mathbf{x}}_i$ is the $1 \times K$ vector of time averages. For some purposes, it is useful to write $c_i = \psi + \bar{\mathbf{x}}_i \boldsymbol{\xi} + a_i$, where $a_i \mid \mathbf{x}_i \sim \mathrm{Normal}(0, \sigma_a^2)$. (Note that $\sigma_a^2 = \mathrm{Var}(c_i \mid \mathbf{x}_i)$, the *conditional* variance of c_i.) Naturally, if we include time-period dummies in $\mathbf{x}_{it}$, as is usually desirable, we do not include the time averages of these in $\bar{\mathbf{x}}_i$. Also, we may include time-constant variables in $\mathbf{x}_{it}$ (omitting them from $\bar{\mathbf{x}}_i$), provided we understand that we may not be consistently estimating their partial effects.

Assumptions (18.97), (18.98), and (18.99) impose no additional distributional assumptions on $D(y_{it} \mid \mathbf{x}_i, c_i)$, and they place no restrictions on the serial dependence in $\{y_{it}\}$ across time. Nevertheless, the elements of $\boldsymbol{\beta}$ are easily shown to be identified up to a positive scale factor, and the APEs are identified. A simple way to establish identification is to write

$$\mathrm{E}(y_{it} \mid \mathbf{x}_i, a_i) = \Phi(\psi + \mathbf{x}_{it}\boldsymbol{\beta} + \bar{\mathbf{x}}_i \boldsymbol{\xi} + a_i), \tag{18.100}$$

and so

$$\mathrm{E}(y_{it} \mid \mathbf{x}_i) = \mathrm{E}[\Phi(\psi + \mathbf{x}_{it}\boldsymbol{\beta} + \bar{\mathbf{x}}_i \boldsymbol{\xi} + a_i) \mid \mathbf{x}_i] = \Phi[(\psi + \mathbf{x}_{it}\boldsymbol{\beta} + \bar{\mathbf{x}}_i \boldsymbol{\xi})/(1 + \sigma_a^2)^{1/2}]$$

or

$$\mathrm{E}(y_{it} \mid \mathbf{x}_i) \equiv \Phi(\psi_a + \mathbf{x}_{it}\boldsymbol{\beta}_a + \bar{\mathbf{x}}_i \boldsymbol{\xi}_a), \tag{18.101}$$

where the a subscript denotes division of the orginal coefficient by $(1 + \sigma_a^2)^{1/2}$. Because we observe a random sample on $(y_{it}, \mathbf{x}_{it}, \bar{\mathbf{x}}_i)$, (18.101) implies that the scaled coefficients, ψ_a, β_a, and ξ_a are identified, provided there are no perfect linear relationships among the elements of $\mathbf{x}_{it}$ and that there is some time variation in all elements of $\mathbf{x}_{it}$. (The latter requirement ensures that $\mathbf{x}_{it}$ and $\bar{\mathbf{x}}_i$ are not perfectly collinear for all t.) In addition, it follows from the same arguments in Section 15.8.2 that the average structural function is

$$E_{\bar{\mathbf{x}}_i}[\Phi(\psi_a + \mathbf{x}_t \boldsymbol{\beta}_a + \bar{\mathbf{x}}_i \xi_a)] \tag{18.102}$$

with respect to the elements of $\mathbf{x}_t$. A consistent estimator, for given $\mathbf{x}_t$, is

$$\widehat{\mathrm{ASF}}(\mathbf{x}_t) = N^{-1} \sum_{i=1}^{N} \Phi(\hat{\psi}_a + \mathbf{x}_t\hat{\boldsymbol{\beta}}_a + \bar{\mathbf{x}}_i\hat{\xi}_a), \tag{18.103}$$

where $\hat{\boldsymbol{\beta}}_a$ is consistent for $\boldsymbol{\beta}_a$, and so on. APEs are obtained by differentiating or taking differences with respect to elements of $\mathbf{x}_t$. The panel data bootstrap is particularly convenient for obtaining standard errors or confidence intervals for the APEs.

The simplest $\sqrt{N}$-consistent, asymptotically normal estimators are just the pooled Bernoulli quasi-MLEs, where the explanatory variables are a constant, a full set of time dummies (probably), $\mathbf{x}_{it}$, and $\bar{\mathbf{x}}_i$. Alternatively, we could also use pooled NLS. In either case, fully robust inference should be used because the variance associated with the Bernoulli distribution is likely to be wrong, and the variance is unlikely to be constant. More important, there is neglected serial correlation.

Perhaps more efficient estimators can be obtained using the GEE approach as described in Section 12.9.2; see also Section 15.8.2. Papke and Wooldridge (2008) describe implementation in the current setup. An even better strategy is to use a minimum distance approach as described in Section 14.6.2. (And, of course, for additional flexibility, we can replace $\bar{\mathbf{x}}_i\xi_a$ with $\mathbf{x}_i\xi_a$.)

If some elements of $\mathbf{x}_{it}$ are not strictly exogenous, a control function method can be combined with the Chamberlain-Mundlak device. Papke and Wooldridge (2008) show how the same control function estimator described in the binary response probit model in Section 15.8.5 applies to fractional responses with a continuous endogenous explanatory variable. (The consistency of the estimator again relies on the Bernoulli distribution being in the linear exponential family.) Briefly, if we assume that the reduced form of the endogenous explanatory variable, y_{it2}, can be expressed as $y_{it2} = \mathbf{z}_{it}\boldsymbol{\delta}_2 + \psi_2 + \bar{\mathbf{z}}_i\xi_2 + v_{it2}$ (where we impose the Chamberlain-Mundlak device), and we assume joint normality of all unobservables, including v_{it2}, then we can derive an estimating equation of the form

$$\mathrm{E}(y_{it1} \mid \mathbf{z}_i, y_{it2}, v_{it2}) = \Phi(\alpha_{e1} y_{it2} + \mathbf{z}_{it1}\boldsymbol{\delta}_{e1} + \psi_{e1} + \bar{\mathbf{z}}_i\xi_{e1} + \eta_{e1} v_{it2}),$$

where the "e" subscript indicates the original parameters have been scaled—similar to the development in Section 18.6.2. As shown by Papke and Wooldridge (2008), these scaled coefficients appear in the APEs. Therefore, after obtaining the residuals $\hat{v}_{it2}$, these can be inserted in the pooled "probit" estimation in a second step to obtain consistent, $\sqrt{N}$-asymptotically normal estimators. The APEs with respect to $(y_{t2}, \mathbf{z}_{t1})$ are obtained by averaging the derivatives or changes across $(\bar{\mathbf{z}}_i, \hat{v}_{it2})$. Standard errors are easily obtained using the panel data bootstrap. See Papke and Wooldridge (2008) for more discussion.

Problems

18.1. a. For estimating the mean of a nonnegative random variable y, the Poisson quasi-log likelihood for a random draw is

$$\ell_i(\mu) = y_i \log(\mu) - \mu, \qquad \mu > 0$$

(where terms not depending on μ have been dropped). Letting $\mu_o \equiv \mathrm{E}(y_i)$, we have $\mathrm{E}[\ell_i(\mu)] = \mu_o \log(\mu) - \mu$. Show that this function is uniquely maximized at $\mu = \mu_o$. This simple result is the basis for the consistency of the Poisson QMLE in the general case.

b. The gamma (exponential) quasi-log likelihood is

$$\ell_i(\mu) = -y_i/\mu - \log(\mu), \qquad \mu > 0$$

Show that $\mathrm{E}[\ell_i(\mu)]$ is uniquely maximized at $\mu = \mu_o$.

18.2. Carefully write out the robust variance matrix estimator (18.14) when $m(\mathbf{x}, \boldsymbol{\beta}) = \exp(\mathbf{x}\boldsymbol{\beta})$.

18.3. Use the data in SMOKE.RAW to answer this question.

a. Use a linear regression model to explain *cigs*, the number of cigarettes smoked per day. Use as explanatory variables log(*cigpric*), log(*income*), *restaurn*, *white*, *educ*, *age*, and age^2. Are the price and income variables significant? Does using heteroskedasticity-robust standard errors change your conclusions?

b. Now estimate a Poisson regression model for *cigs*, with an exponential conditional mean and the same explanatory variables as in part a. Using the usual MLE standard errors, are the price and income variables each significant at the 5 percent level? Interpret their coefficients.

c. Find $\hat{\sigma}$. Is there evidence of overdispersion? Using the GLM standard errors, discuss the significance of log(*cigpric*) and log(*income*).

d. Compare the usual MLE *LR* statistic for joint significance of log(*cigpric*) and log(*income*) with the *QLR* statistic in equation (18.17).

e. Compute the fully robust standard errors, and compare these with the GLM standard errors.

f. In the model estimated from part b, at what point does the effect of *age* on expected cigarette consumption become negative?

g. Do you think a two-part, or double-hurdle, model for count variables is a better way to model *cigs*?

18.4. Show that under the conditional moment restriction $\mathrm{E}(y \mid \mathbf{x}) = m(\mathbf{x}, \boldsymbol{\beta}_o)$ the Poisson QMLE achieves the efficiency bound in equation (14.60) when the GLM variance assumption holds.

18.5. Consider an unobserved effects model for count data with exponential regression function

$$\mathrm{E}(y_{it} \mid \mathbf{x}_{i1}, \ldots, \mathbf{x}_{iT}, c_i) = c_i \exp(\mathbf{x}_{it}\boldsymbol{\beta}).$$

a. If $\mathrm{E}(c_i \mid \mathbf{x}_{i1}, \ldots, \mathbf{x}_{iT}) = \exp(\alpha + \overline{\mathbf{x}}_i\gamma)$, find $\mathrm{E}(y_{it} \mid \mathbf{x}_{i1}, \ldots, \mathbf{x}_{iT})$.

b. Use part a to derive a test of mean independence between c_i and $\overline{\mathbf{x}}_i$. Assume under H_0 that $\mathrm{Var}(y_{it} \mid \mathbf{x}_i, c_i) = \mathrm{E}(y_{it} \mid \mathbf{x}_i, c_i)$, that y_{it} and y_{ir} are uncorrelated conditional on $(\mathbf{x}_i, c_i)$, and that c_i and $\mathbf{x}_i$ are independent. (Hint: You should devise a test in the context of multivariate weighted nonlinear least squares.)

c. Suppose now that assumptions (18.83) and (18.84) hold, with $m(\mathbf{x}_{it}, \boldsymbol{\beta}) = \exp(\mathbf{x}_{it}\boldsymbol{\beta})$, but assumption (18.85) is replaced by $c_i = a_i \exp(\alpha + \overline{\mathbf{x}}_i\gamma)$, where $a_i \mid \mathbf{x} \sim \mathrm{Gamma}(\delta, \delta)$. Now how would you estimate $\boldsymbol{\beta}$, α, and γ, and how would you test $\mathrm{H}_0 : \gamma = 0$?

18.6. A model with an additive unobserved effect, strictly exogenous regressors, and a nonlinear regression function is

$$\mathrm{E}(y_{it} \mid \mathbf{x}_i, c_i) = c_i + m(\mathbf{x}_{it}, \boldsymbol{\beta}_o), \qquad t = 1, \ldots, T.$$

a. For each i and t define the time-demeaned variables $\ddot{y}_{it} \equiv y_{it} - \bar{y}_i$ and, for each $\boldsymbol{\beta}$, $\ddot{m}_{it}(\boldsymbol{\beta}) = m(\mathbf{x}_{it}, \boldsymbol{\beta}) - (1/T)\sum_{r=1}^{T} m(\mathbf{x}_{ir}, \boldsymbol{\beta})$. Argue that, under standard regularity conditions, the pooled NLS estimator of $\boldsymbol{\beta}_o$ that solves

$$\min_{\boldsymbol{\beta}} \sum_{i=1}^{N} \sum_{t=1}^{T} [\ddot{y}_{it} - \ddot{m}_{it}(\boldsymbol{\beta})]^2 \tag{18.104}$$

is generally consistent and $\sqrt{N}$-asymptotically normal (with T fixed). (Hint: Show that $\mathrm{E}(\ddot{y}_{it} \mid \mathbf{x}_i) = \ddot{m}_{it}(\boldsymbol{\beta}_o)$ for all t.)

b. If $\mathrm{Var}(\mathbf{y}_i \mid \mathbf{x}_i, c_i) = \sigma_o^2 \mathbf{I}_T$, how would you estimate the asymptotic variance of the pooled NLS estimator?

c. If the variance assumption in part b does not hold, how would you estimate the asymptotic variance?

d. Show that the NLS estimator based on time demeaning from part a is in fact *identical* to the pooled NLS estimator that estimates $\{c_1, c_2, \ldots, c_N\}$ along with $\boldsymbol{\beta}_o$:

$$\min_{\{c_1, c_2, \ldots, c_N, \boldsymbol{\beta}\}} \sum_{i=1}^{N} \sum_{t=1}^{T} [y_{it} - c_i - m(\mathbf{x}_{it}, \boldsymbol{\beta})]^2 \tag{18.105}$$

Thus, this is another case where treating the unobserved effects as parameters to estimate does not result in an inconsistent estimator of $\boldsymbol{\beta}_o$. (Hint: It is easiest to concentrate out the c_i from the sum of square residuals; see Section 12.7.4. In the current context, for given $\boldsymbol{\beta}$, find $\hat{c}_i$ as functions of $\mathbf{y}_i, \mathbf{x}_i$, and $\boldsymbol{\beta}$. Then plug these back into equation (18.105) and show that the concentrated sum of squared residuals function is identical to equation (18.104).)

18.7. Assume that the standard FEP assumptions hold, so that, conditional on $(\mathbf{x}_i, c_i), y_{i1}, \ldots, y_{iT}$ are independent Poisson random variables with means $c_i m(\mathbf{x}_{it}, \boldsymbol{\beta}_o)$.

a. Show that, if we treat the c_i as parameters to estimate along with $\boldsymbol{\beta}_o$, then the conditional log likelihood for observation i (apart from terms not depending on c_i or $\boldsymbol{\beta}$) is

$$\begin{aligned}\ell_i(c_i, \boldsymbol{\beta}) &\equiv \log[f(y_{i1}, \ldots, y_{iT} \mid \mathbf{x}_i; c_i, \boldsymbol{\beta})] \\ &= \sum_{t=1}^{T} \{-c_i m(\mathbf{x}_{it}, \boldsymbol{\beta}) + y_{it}[\log(c_i)] + \log[m(\mathbf{x}_{it}, \boldsymbol{\beta})]\},\end{aligned}$$

where we now group c_i with $\boldsymbol{\beta}$ as a parameter to estimate. (Note that $c_i > 0$ is a needed restriction.)

b. Let $n_i = y_{i1} + \cdots + y_{iT}$, and assume that $n_i > 0$. For given $\boldsymbol{\beta}$, maximize $\ell_i(c_i, \boldsymbol{\beta})$ only with respect to c_i. Find the solution, $c_i(\boldsymbol{\beta}) > 0$.

c. Plug the solution from part b into $\ell_i[c_i(\boldsymbol{\beta}), \boldsymbol{\beta}]$, and show that

$$\ell_i[c_i(\boldsymbol{\beta}), \boldsymbol{\beta}] = \sum_{t=1}^{T} y_{it} \log[p_t(\mathbf{x}_i, \boldsymbol{\beta})] + (n_i - 1) \log(n_i).$$

d. Conclude from part c that the log-likelihood function for all N cross section observations, with $(c_1, \ldots, c_N)$ concentrated out, is

$$\sum_{i=1}^{N} \sum_{t=1}^{T} y_{it} \log[p_t(\mathbf{x}_i, \boldsymbol{\beta})] + \sum_{i=1}^{N} (n_i - 1) \log(n_i).$$

What does this mean about the conditional MLE from Section 18.7.4 and the estimator that treats the c_i as parameters to estimate along with $\boldsymbol{\beta}_o$?

18.8. Let y be a fractional response, so that $0 \leq y \leq 1$.

a. Suppose that $0 < y < 1$, so that $w \equiv \log[y/(1-y)]$ is well defined. If we assume the linear model $\mathrm{E}(w \mid \mathbf{x}) = \mathbf{x}\boldsymbol{\alpha}$, does $\mathrm{E}(y \mid \mathbf{x})$ have any simple relationship to $\mathbf{x}\boldsymbol{\alpha}$? What would we need to know to obtain $\mathrm{E}(y \mid \mathbf{x})$? Let $\hat{\boldsymbol{\alpha}}$ be the OLS estimator from the regression w_i on $\mathbf{x}_i$, $i = 1, \ldots, N$.

b. If we estimate the fractional logit model for $\mathrm{E}(y \mid \mathbf{x})$ from Section 18.6.1, should we expect the estimated parameters, $\hat{\boldsymbol{\beta}}$, to be close to $\hat{\boldsymbol{\alpha}}$ from part a? Explain.

c. Now suppose that y takes on the values zero and one with positive probability. To model this population feature we use a latent variable model:

$$y^* \mid \mathbf{x} \sim \mathrm{Normal}(\mathbf{x}\boldsymbol{\gamma}, \sigma^2)$$

$$y = 0, \quad y^* \leq 0$$

$$= y^*, \quad 0 < y^* < 1$$

$$= 1, \quad y^* \geq 1$$

How should we estimate $\boldsymbol{\gamma}$ and σ^2?

d. Given the estimate $\hat{\boldsymbol{\gamma}}$ from part c, does it make sense to compare the magnitude of $\hat{\gamma}_j$ to the corresponding $\hat{\alpha}_j$ from part a or the $\hat{\beta}_j$ from part b? Explain.

e. How might we choose between the models estimated in parts b and c? (Hint: Think about goodness of fit for the conditional mean.)

f. Now suppose that $0 \leq y < 1$. Suppose we apply fractional logit, as in part b, and fractional logit to the subsample with $0 < y_i < 1$. Should we necessarily get similar answers?

g. With $0 \leq y < 1$ suppose that $\mathrm{E}(y_i \mid \mathbf{x}_i, y_i > 0) = \exp(\mathbf{x}_i\boldsymbol{\delta})/[1 + \exp(\mathbf{x}_i\boldsymbol{\delta})]$. How should we estimate $\boldsymbol{\delta}$ in this case?

h. To the assumptions from part g add $\mathrm{P}(y_i = 0 \mid \mathbf{x}_i) = 1 - G(\mathbf{x}_i\boldsymbol{\eta})$, where $G(\cdot)$ is a differentiable, strictly increasing cumulative distribution function. How should we estimate $\mathrm{E}(y_i \mid \mathbf{x}_i)$?

18.9. Use the data in ATTEND.RAW to answer this question.

a. Estimate a linear regression relating *atndrte* to *ACT*, *priGPA*, *frosh*, and *soph*; compute the usual OLS standard errors. Interpret the coefficients on *ACT* and *priGPA*. Are any fitted values outside the unit interval?

b. Model $\mathrm{E}(atndrte \mid \mathbf{x})$ as a logistic function, as in Section 18.6.1. Use the QMLE for the Bernoulli log likelihood, and compute the GLM standard errors. What is $\hat{\sigma}$, and how does it affect the standard errors?

c. For $priGPA = 3.0$ and $frosh = soph = 0$, estimate the effect of increasing ACT from 25 to 30 using the estimated equation from part b. How does the estimate compare with that from the linear model?

d. Does a linear model or a logistic model provide a better fit to $\mathrm{E}(atndrte \mid \mathbf{x})$?

18.10. Use the data in PATENT.RAW for this exercise.

a. Estimate a pooled Poisson regression model relating *patents* to $lsales = \log(sales)$ and current and four lags of $lrnd = \log(1 + rnd)$, where we add one before taking the log to account for the fact that *rnd* is zero for some firms in some years. Use an exponential mean function and include a full set of year dummies. Which lags of *lrnd* are significant using the usual Poisson MLE standard errors?

b. Give two reasons why the usual Poisson MLE standard errors from part a might be invalid.

c. Obtain $\hat{\sigma}$ for the pooled Poisson estimation. Using the GLM standard errors (but without an adjustment for possible serial dependence), which lags of *lrnd* are significant?

d. Obtain the QLR statistic for joint significance of lags one through four of *lrnd*. (Be careful here; you must use the same set of years in estimating the restricted version of the model.) How does it compare to the usual LR statistic?

e. Compute the standard errors that are robust to an arbitrary conditional variance and serial dependence. How do they compare with the standard errors from parts a and c?

f. What is the estimated long-run elasticity of expected patents with respect to R&D spending? (Ignore the fact that one has been added to the R&D numbers before taking the log.) Obtain a fully robust standard error for the long-run elasticity.

g. Now use the FEP estimator, and compare the estimated lag coefficients to those from the pooled Poisson analysis. Estimate the long-run elasticity, and obtain the usual FEP and fully robust standard errors.

18.11. a. For a random draw i from the cross section, assume that (1) for each time period t, $y_{it} \mid \mathbf{x}_i, c_i \sim \text{Poisson}(c_i m_{it})$, where $c_i > 0$ is unobserved heterogeneity and $m_{it} > 0$ is typically a function of only $\mathbf{x}_{it}$; and (2) $(y_{i1}, \ldots, y_{iT})$ are independent conditional on $(\mathbf{x}_i, c_i)$. Derive the density of $(y_{i1}, \ldots, y_{iT})$ conditional on $(\mathbf{x}_i, c_i)$.

b. To the assumptions from part a, add the assumption that $c_i \mid \mathbf{x}_i \sim \text{Gamma}(\delta, \delta)$, so that $\text{E}(c_i) = 1$ and $\text{Var}(c_i) = 1/\delta$. (The density of c_i is $h(c) = [\delta^\delta / \Gamma(\delta)] c^{\delta - 1} \exp(-\delta c)$, where $\Gamma(\delta)$ is the gamma function.) Let $s = y_1 + \cdots + y_T$ and $M_i = m_{i1} + \cdots + m_{iT}$. Show that the density of $(y_{i1}, \ldots, y_{iT})$ given $\mathbf{x}_i$ is

$$\left(\prod_{t=1}^{T} m_{it}^{y_t} / y_t! \right) [\delta^\delta / \Gamma(\delta)][\Gamma(M_i + s) / (M_i + \delta)^{(s+\delta)}].$$

(Hint: The easiest way to show this result is to turn the integral into one involving a $\text{Gamma}(s + \delta, M_i + \delta)$ density and a multiplicative term. Naturally, the density must integrate to unity, and so what is left over is the density we seek.)

18.12. For a random draw i from the cross section, assume that (1) for each t, $y_{it} \mid \mathbf{x}_i, c_i \sim \text{Gamma}(m_{it}, 1/c_i)$, where $c_i > 0$ is unobserved heterogeneity and $m_{it} > 0$; and (2) $(y_{i1}, \ldots, y_{iT})$ are independent conditional on $(\mathbf{x}_i, c_i)$. The gamma distribution is parameterized so that $\text{E}(y_{it} \mid \mathbf{x}_i, c_i) = c_i m_{it}$ and $\text{Var}(y_{it} \mid \mathbf{x}_i, c_i) = c_i^2 m_{it}$.

a. Let $s_i = y_{i1} + \cdots + y_{iT}$. Show that the density of $(y_{i1}, y_{i2}, \ldots, y_{iT})$ conditional on $(s_i, \mathbf{x}_i, c_i)$ is

$$f(y_1, \ldots, y_T \mid s_i, \mathbf{x}_i, c_i) = \left[\Gamma(m_{i1} + \cdots + m_{iT}) / \prod_{t=1}^{T} \Gamma(m_{it}) \right] \times \left[\left(\prod_{t=1}^{T} y_t^{m_{it} - 1} \right) / s_i^{\{(m_{i1} + \cdots + m_{iT}) - 1\}} \right],$$

where $\Gamma(\cdot)$ is the gamma function. Note that the density does not depend on c_i. {Hint: If $Y_1, \ldots, Y_T$ are independent random variables and $S = Y_1 + \cdots + Y_T$, the joint density of $Y_1, \ldots, Y_T$ given $S = s$ is $f_1(y_1) \cdots f_{T-1}(y_{T-1}) f_T(s - y_1 - \cdots - y_{T-1}) / g(s)$, where $g(s)$ is the density of S. When Y_t has a $\text{Gamma}(\alpha_t, \lambda)$ distribution for each t, so that $f_t(y_t) = [\lambda^{\alpha_t} / \Gamma(\alpha_t)] y_t^{(\alpha_t - 1)} \exp(-\lambda y_t)$, $S \sim \text{Gamma}(\alpha_1 + \cdots + \alpha_T, \lambda)$.}

b. Let $m_t(\mathbf{x}_i, \boldsymbol{\beta})$ be a parametric function for m_{it}—for example, $\exp(\mathbf{x}_{it}\boldsymbol{\beta})$. Write down the log-likelihood function for observation i. The conditional MLE in this case is called the **fixed effects gamma estimator**.

18.13 Let y be a continuous fractional response variable, that is, y can take on any value in $(0, 1)$. For a $1 \times K$ vector of conditioning variables $\mathbf{x}$, where $x_1 = 1$, suppose that the conditional density of y_i given $\mathbf{x}_i = \mathbf{x}$ is

$$f(y \mid \mathbf{x}; \boldsymbol{\beta}_o) = \exp(\mathbf{x}\boldsymbol{\beta}_o) y^{[\exp(\mathbf{x}\boldsymbol{\beta}_o) - 1]}, \qquad 0 < y < 1.$$

It can be shown that, for this density, $\mathrm{E}(y_i \mid \mathbf{x}_i) = \exp(\mathbf{x}_i\boldsymbol{\beta}_o)/[1 + \exp(\mathbf{x}_i\boldsymbol{\beta}_o)]$—that is, it is the logistic function evaluated at $\mathbf{x}_i\boldsymbol{\beta}_o$.

a. For a random draw i from the population, write down the log-likelihood function as a function of $\boldsymbol{\beta}$.

b. Find the $K \times 1$ score vector, $\mathbf{s}_i(\boldsymbol{\beta})$.

c. For this density, it can be shown that $\mathrm{E}[\log(y_i) \mid \mathbf{x}_i] = -1/\exp(\mathbf{x}_i\boldsymbol{\beta}_o)$. Why does it makes sense for the conditional expectation to be negative?

d. Verify that $\mathrm{E}[\mathbf{s}_i(\boldsymbol{\beta}_o) \mid \mathbf{x}_i] = 0$.

e. Find $-\mathrm{E}[\mathbf{H}_i(\boldsymbol{\beta}_o) \mid \mathbf{x}_i]$.

f. How would you estimate $Avar\ \sqrt{N}(\hat{\boldsymbol{\beta}} - \boldsymbol{\beta}_o)$? Be very specific.

g. Is the MLE consistent for $\boldsymbol{\beta}_o$ if we only assume the conditional mean is correctly specified, that is, $\mathrm{E}(y_i \mid \mathbf{x}_i) = \exp(\mathbf{x}_i\boldsymbol{\beta}_o)/[1 + \exp(\mathbf{x}_i\boldsymbol{\beta}_o)]$? (Hint: Look at $\mathrm{E}[\mathbf{s}_i(\boldsymbol{\beta}_o) \mid \mathbf{x}_i]$.)

h. If you are only interested in $\mathrm{E}(y_i \mid \mathbf{x}_i)$, what might you do instead of MLE?

18.14. Use data in 401KPART.RAW for this question; it is similar to the data set used in Papke and Wooldridge (1996), except it includes the number of employees eligible to participate in the 401(k) pension plan.

a. Let $y_i = partic_i$ and $n_i = employ_i$, and use binomial QMLE to estimate $\mathrm{E}(y_i \mid n_i, \mathbf{x}_i) = n_i\Lambda(\mathbf{x}_i\boldsymbol{\beta})$, where $\Lambda(\cdot)$ is the logistic function and $\mathbf{x}$ includes a constant, *mrate*, *ltotemp*, *age*, *agesq*, and *sole*. Obtain three sets of standard errors: those based on (18.34) with $\sigma^2 = 1$ (which holds if the distribution is actually binomial), those from (18.34) with σ^2 estimated, and the fully robust standard errors. Comment on how they compare.

b. Now use *prate* in a fractional logit analysis using the same vector $\mathbf{x}$ in part a. Again, compute three sets of standard errors and discuss how they compare.

c. Explain why it makes sense to compare the coefficient estimates from parts a and b. Are their important differences in the coefficients, particularly for the key variable *mrate*? Which approach produces the more precise estimate?

d. Compute the APE for *mrate* on $\mathrm{E}(prate \mid \mathbf{x})$ using the estimates from parts a and b.

e. Using fractional logit, estimate the APE on $\mathrm{E}(prate \mid \mathbf{x})$ when *mrate* goes from .25 to .50.

f. Add $mrate^2$ to the fractional logit estimation. Is there a strong case for including it? Explain.

18.15. For $0 < y_{it} < 1$ consider the model

$$\log[y_{it}/(1 - y_{it})] = \mathbf{x}_{it}\boldsymbol{\beta} + c_i + u_{it}$$

$$\mathrm{E}(u_{it} \mid \mathbf{x}_i, c_i) = 0, \qquad t = 1, \ldots, T.$$

a. Assuming the $\{\mathbf{x}_{it} : t = 1, \ldots, T\}$ are time varying, how would you estimate $\boldsymbol{\beta}$?

b. Let $v_{it} = c_i + u_{it}$ and write y_{it} in terms of $\mathbf{x}_{it}\boldsymbol{\beta} + v_{it}$. Find the average structural function for y_{it} (as a function of $\mathbf{x}_t$) as an expectation over the distribution of v_{it}.

c. Without further assumptions, can you consistently estimate the ASF? Explain.

d. Assume that $c_i = \psi + \bar{\mathbf{x}}_i\boldsymbol{\xi} + a_i$ where $r_{it} \equiv a_i + u_{it}$ is independent of $\mathbf{x}_i$. Explain how to consistently estimate the ASF in this case.

19 Censored Data, Sample Selection, and Attrition

19.1 Introduction

In previous chapters we assumed that we can obtain a random sample from the population of interest. For example, in Part II, where we studied models linear in the parameters, we assumed that data on the dependent variable, the explanatory variables, and instrumental variables can be obtained by means of random sampling—whether in a cross section or panel data context. In earlier chapters of Part IV we studied various nonlinear models for response variables that are limited in some way. Chapter 15 extensively considered binary response models, and we saw that the most commonly used models imply nonconstant partial effects. The same is true for corner solution responses in Chapter 17 and those for count and fractional responses in Chapter 18. It is critical to understand that our reason for looking beyond linear models in those chapters is to obtain functional forms that are more realistic than models that are linear in parameters.

In this chapter we turn to several missing data problems. It is critical—even more so than in the previous chapters—to distinguish between assumptions placed on the population model and assumptions about how the data were generated. Under random sampling, the interesting issues concern the population model and assumptions we make about distributional features in the population. With nonrandom sampling, we must take particular care in stating assumptions about the population and separately stating assumptions on the sampling scheme.

We first study the general problem of **data censoring**. With data censoring we can still randomly sample *units* from the relevant population, but we face the problem that one or more of the variables is censored: we only observe the response over a certain range—sometimes a very limited range and sometimes a broad range. We cover several examples of data censoring in Section 19.2.

In addition to data censoring, we also treat the general problem of sample selection. Section 19.3 begins with a general discussion of examples of missing data schemes, and Section 19.4 establishes when the missing data problem can be ignored without resulting in inconsistent estimators. With sample selection problems, we may or may not be able to randomly sample units from the population. The case of **data truncation**, which we study in Section 19.5, is a situation where we do not randomly draw units from the population; rather, we randomly sample from a subpopulation defined in terms of one or more of the observed variables. Naturally, the population parameters cannot always be identified with such sampling schemes, but they can be under suitable assumptions.

Another sample selection problem is **incidental truncation**, where certain variables are observed only if other variables take on particular values. In such cases, we often can randomly sample units, but we have data missing on key variables (and, unlike in the data censoring case, we have no information on the outcome, or even a range of possible outcomes, of the missing data). We treat this case in Sections 19.6 and 19.7.

Most of the methods that allow for sample selection to be systematically correlated with unobservables rely on linearity or some other simple response function (such as exponential). An alternative approach is **inverse probability weighting**, which can be applied to general missing data problems if we have good enough predictors of selection so that, conditional on those predictors, selection is appropriately exogenous. We cover inverse probability weighting in the context of M-estimation in Section 19.8. Section 19.9 covers sample selection, including the specific problem of attrition, in panel data applications.

Before we treat specific censoring and selection schemes, it is important to understand the notational conventions in this chapter. As in previous chapters, we continue to let y denote the response variable *in the population of interest*. Therefore, we will write population models with y as the dependent variable. The distinction between the underlying response variable of interest, and what we can observe, is critical throughout this chapter. For example, in Section 19.2 we consider the case where we can randomly sample from the population but we only observe a censored version of y. If w denotes the censored outcome, then for a randomly drawn unit i we observe w_i, but this may not equal y_i.

For models with endogenous explanatory variables, we continue to use the conventions of the previous chapters, letting, for example, y_1 and y_2 denote the endogenous variables in the underlying population (where y_1 is typically the response variable and y_2 is an endogenous explanatory variable). In principle, each of these could be censored, and we use w_1 and w_2, respectively, to denote the censored outcomes.

19.2 Data Censoring

Traditionally, data censoring problems are treated within the frameworks of Chapters 15–17—alongside binary responses, multinomial responses, and corner solution responses. The benefit of a parallel treatment is that it economizes on the presentation, but it has significant costs: empirical researchers tend to let the two very different issues of functional form for limited dependent variables and data censoring problems blend together. Thus, although the statistical models used for limited dependent variables and censored dependent variables are similar, their interpretation, as well as the way one views and reacts to violations of standard assumptions, is very different. Because the statistical tools for handling censored data are very similar to specifying and estimating models for limited dependent variables, our coverage of the estimation details can be terse.

As an example, consider the problem of **top coding**, where a variable is reported only up to a specified ceiling. For outcomes above the ceiling, all we know is that the outcome was above the ceiling. Common examples are survey data on wealth and income. In order to elicit responses from wealthy people, some surveys only ask about the amount of wealth up to a given threshold, allowing wealthy people to simply indicate if their wealth is above the threshold. Probably the underlying population model in this case is a standard linear model, but that is a separate issue. To emphasize this point, we might also use top coding when collecting data on charitable contributions. As we saw in Chapter 17, in a large population the charitable contributions is best described as a corner solution outcome, with corner at zero. A sensible population model for charitable contributions is the Tobit model, or perhaps one of the two-part models we covered in Section 17.6. Specification of this population model is separate from the data collection scheme. If we top code contributions at, say, \$10,000 (where contributions are measured in \$1,000s), then the reported contributions data will appear to have two corners: one at zero and one at 10. Of course, these are very different in nature: when we observe a zero, we know that the person had zero charitable contributions. If we observe 10, we only know that the contributions were at least \$10,000. If the top coding were instead at \$20,000, nothing would happen to the population distribution of contributions; it still has a corner at zero. But the top coding changes the upper corner, and by increasing the censoring value we observe more of the population distribution of contributions. As we will see in Section 19.2.3, the statistical model for estimating the parameters when a Type I Tobit variable is top coded is equivalent to a two-limit Tobit; but the underlying model is the standard Type I Tobit model.

Although we will touch on more complicated situations, such as the Tobit model just described, our main focus on this chapter is on a very familiar model: the linear model from introductory econometrics. Let y denote the variable of interest, and assume that it follows a standard linear model in the population:

$$y = \mathbf{x}\boldsymbol{\beta} + u \tag{19.1}$$

$$\mathrm{E}(u \mid \mathbf{x}) = 0, \tag{19.2}$$

where $\mathbf{x}$ is $1 \times K$ with first-element unity. Under assumptions (19.1) and (19.2), if we have random draws $(\mathbf{x}_i, y_i)$ from the population, then OLS is consistent and $\sqrt{N}$-asymptotically normal for the parameters of interest, $\boldsymbol{\beta}$.

The problem we study in this chapter occurs when we observe only a censored version of y. In the top coding example, suppose that wealth is measured in thousands of dollars and is top coded at \$200,000. Then we can define the censored version of wealth (for any unit that can be drawn from the population) as $w = \min(y, 200)$. Of course, for each random draw i, $w_i = \min(y_i, 200)$. If we are presented with the data set on $\mathbf{x}_i$ and w_i, where w_i is called "wealth," we should notice that the maximum value of "wealth" in the sample is 200, with a nontrivial fraction of observations at exactly 200. Because there is no behavioral reason to see a focal point for wealth at 200—let alone, to observe no values greater than 200—we would recognize that the wealth variable has been top coded at 200.

19.2.1 Binary Censoring

We first cover the case where the censoring of the underlying response variable is extreme. As an example, suppose we want to model willingness to pay (WTP) for a proposed public project. Assume that the underlying model is as in equations (19.1) and (19.2) with $y = wtp$. When we draw family (say) i from the population, we would like to observe $(\mathbf{x}_i, wtp_i)$; if we did so for all i, we would estimate $\boldsymbol{\beta}$ by OLS. But willingess to pay can be difficult to elicit, and reported amounts might be noisy. Instead, suppose that each family is presented with a cost of the project, r_i. Presented with this cost, the household either says it is in favor of the project or not. Thus, along with $\mathbf{x}_i$ and r_i, we observe the binary response

$$w_i = 1[y_i > r_i], \tag{19.3}$$

where we assume, for now, that the chance that y_i equals r_i is zero.

What is the most natural way to proceed to estimate $\boldsymbol{\beta}$? If we impose some strong assumptions on the underlying population and the nature of r_i, then we can proceed with maximum likelihood. In particular, assume

$$u_i \mid \mathbf{x}_i, r_i \sim \text{Normal}(0, \sigma^2). \tag{19.4}$$

Assumption (19.4) implies that $y_i = \mathbf{x}_i\boldsymbol{\beta} + u_i$ actually satisfies the classical linear model (CLM). It also requires that r_i is independent of y_i conditional on $\mathbf{x}_i$, that is,

$$\text{D}(y_i \mid \mathbf{x}_i, r_i) = \text{D}(y_i \mid \mathbf{x}_i). \tag{19.5}$$

Assumption (19.5) is satisfied if r_i is randomized or if r_i is chosen as a function of $\mathbf{x}_i$, or some combination of these alternatives.

Given assumption (19.4),

$$\begin{aligned} \text{P}(w_i = 1 \mid \mathbf{x}_i, r_i) &= \text{P}(y_i > r_i \mid \mathbf{x}_i, r_i) = \text{P}[u_i/\sigma > (r_i - \mathbf{x}_i\boldsymbol{\beta})/\sigma \mid \mathbf{x}_i, r_i] \\ &= 1 - \Phi[(r_i - \mathbf{x}_i\boldsymbol{\beta})/\sigma] = \Phi[(\mathbf{x}_i\boldsymbol{\beta} - r_i)/\sigma]. \end{aligned} \tag{19.6}$$

We can see that the binary response, which indicates whether unit i is in favor of the project at cost r_i, follows a probit model with parameter vector $\boldsymbol{\beta}/\sigma$ on $\mathbf{x}_i$ and $-1/\sigma$ on r_i. (In almost all applications $\mathbf{x}_i$ would include an intercept, and we allow that possibility here.) Therefore, all the parameters, including σ, are identified provided $\mathbf{x}_i$ is not perfectly collinear and r_i varies across i in a way not perfectly linearly related to $\mathbf{x}_i$. Given the data censoring, the maximum likelihood estimators (MLEs) are the asymptotically efficient estimators of $\boldsymbol{\beta}$ and σ (or σ^2). Because the underlying population model is linear, we are interested in the slopes, β_j. In the next section we show that the binary censoring problem is a special case of interval censoring with unit-specific thresholds.

The costs of the binary censoring scheme are potentially severe. If we could observe y_i, specifying $\mathrm{E}(y_i \mid \mathbf{x}_i) = \mathbf{x}_i\boldsymbol{\beta}$ would suffice for consistent estimation of $\boldsymbol{\beta}$; in fact, we could just specify a linear projection and use OLS. With censoring, we must add more, and assumption (19.4) implies that the underlying model satisfies the CLM. It is in this setting where discussions of the deleterious effects of nonnormality and heteroskedasticity when using probit models make sense. In Chapter 15 we focused on the case where the binary response is the variable we want to explain, in which case we are interested in estimating the partial effects on the response probability. In that setting, heteroskedasticity and nonnormality in the error of the latent variable model change the functional form of the quantity of interest, and so the relevant issue concerns how those two problems affect the estimated partial effects (and the implications they have for a standard probit model, or even a linear probability model, for estimating the partial effects). With data censoring, we are interested only in the parameters in the underlying linear model. Consequently, it is now legitimate to be concerned about the effects on the parameter estimates of heteroskedasticity or nonnormality in the underlying linear model.

In Section 15.7.6 we discussed various ways of estimating parameters up to scale without placing strong restrictions on $\mathrm{D}(u_i \mid \mathbf{x}_i, r_i)$. Those estimators can be used in the present context. For example, if the distribution of $(\mathbf{x}_i, r_i, y_i)$ implies linear conditional expectations for all elements conditional on y_i, then the Chung and Goldberger (1984) results can be used for OLS. Ruud's (1983, 1986) findings can be applied when u_i is independent of $(\mathbf{x}_i, r_i)$ if the distribution of u_i is misspecified. Manski's (1975, 1988) maximum score estimator requires only symmetry of $\mathrm{D}(u_i \mid \mathbf{x}_i, r_i)$ (around zero), and Horowitz's (1992) smoothed version is more convenient for inference. But in every case these methods only estimate the slope coefficients up to a common scale factor (and the intercept cannot be estimated at all); therefore we cannot learn the magnitude of the effect of any element of $\mathbf{x}$ on willingness to pay, nor do we have a way of predicting willingness to pay for given values of the covariates.

A linear model for willingness to pay is not ideal because $wtp \geq 0$. If wtp is zero for some subset of the population, a sensible population model is the Type I Tobit:

$$y = wtp = \max(0, \mathbf{x}\boldsymbol{\beta} + u), \tag{19.7}$$

under assumption (19.4). If we had a random sample, we would use Type I Tobit MLE to estimate $\boldsymbol{\beta}$ and σ^2 (naturally, r_i would not come into play), and we would use the MLEs to estimate the means, say, from a Type I Tobit. Interestingly, if we have binary censoring, the estimation procedure is identical to that outlined for a linear model for wtp, provided that the r_i are all strictly positive. Because we do not observe y_i, we cannot distinguish between equations (19.1) and (19.7) when $r_i > 0$. But if we believe that y is zero for a nontrivial fraction of the population, any calculations should reflect that belief by using the Type I Tobit formulas for estimating partial effects.

One way to possibly determine whether WTP is ever zero in the population is to set some r_i to zero so that the outcome $w_i = 0$ means $wtp_i = 0$. Or, we might set some r_i sufficiently "close" to zero so that $w_i = 0$ practically means $wtp_i = 0$. Of course, this approach requires a particular survey design before the data have been collected.

If we really think $y = wtp > 0$ in the population—say, everyone in a city would be willing to pay at least a small amount for a new park—then the underlying population model should be something like

$$y = \exp(\mathbf{x}\boldsymbol{\beta} + u), \tag{19.8}$$

under assumption (19.4). Then, $\log(y) = \mathbf{x}\boldsymbol{\beta} + u$, so that the previous analysis applies but with r_i replaced with $\log(r_i)$ (and we are back to assuming $r_i > 0$). Interestingly, the change in the functional form for $P(w_i = 1 \mid \mathbf{x}_i, r_i)$ from equation (19.6) to

$$P(w_i = 1 \mid \mathbf{x}_i, r_i) = \Phi[(\mathbf{x}_i\boldsymbol{\beta} - \log(r_i))/\sigma] \tag{19.9}$$

provides a way to distinguish between assumptions (19.7) and (19.8) as the underlying population models when $r_i > 0$ for all i.

Naturally, the previous models apply to cases other than willingness to pay. But if y cannot take on negative values, the linear model we started with in equation (19.1) is not ideal. Assumption (19.7) leads to the same estimation method but implies a Tobit form for $E(y \mid \mathbf{x})$. If we think $y > 0$ in the population, then equation (19.8) is more attractive, and we can use equations (19.6) and (19.9) to distinguish between them based on values of the log-likelihood functions. In fact, because we know the coefficient on r_i in the first case, and $\log(r_i)$ in the second, must be nonzero, we can use Vuoung's (1989) model selection test to choose between them; see Section 13.11.2.

19.2.2 Interval Coding

We now consider the linear model (19.1) in a scenario where the continuous, quantitative outcome, y, is only recorded to fall into a particular interval. In this case we say we have **interval-coded data** (or **interval-censored data**). We are still interested in the population regression $\mathrm{E}(y \mid \mathbf{x}) = \mathbf{x}\boldsymbol{\beta}$. Let $r_1 < r_2 < \cdots < r_J$ denote the *known* interval limits; these are specified as part of the survey design. For example, rather than asking individuals to report actual annual income, they report the interval that their income falls into.

Under the normality assumption in equation (19.4), we can estimate $\boldsymbol{\beta}$ and σ^2. Not surprisingly, the structure of the problem is similar to the ordered probit model we covered in Section 16.3. In fact, we can define

$$
\begin{aligned}
w &= 0 \quad \text{if } y \le r_1 \\
w &= 1 \quad \text{if } r_1 < y \le r_2 \\
&\ \ \vdots \\
w &= J \quad \text{if } y > r_J
\end{aligned}
\tag{19.10}
$$

and easily obtain the conditional probabilities $\mathrm{P}(w = j \mid \mathbf{x})$ for $j = 0, 1, \ldots, J$. The log likelihood for a random draw i is

$$
\begin{aligned}
l_i(\boldsymbol{\beta}, \sigma) = {}& 1[w_i = 0] \log\{\Phi[(r_1 - \mathbf{x}_i\boldsymbol{\beta})/\sigma]\} + 1[w_i = 1] \log\{\Phi[(r_2 - \mathbf{x}_i\boldsymbol{\beta})/\sigma \\
& - \Phi[(r_1 - \mathbf{x}_i\boldsymbol{\beta})/\sigma]\} + \cdots + 1[w_i = J] \log\{1 - \Phi[(r_J - \mathbf{x}_i\boldsymbol{\beta})/\sigma]\}.
\end{aligned}
\tag{19.11}
$$

The maximum likelihood estimators, $\hat{\boldsymbol{\beta}}$ and $\hat{\sigma}^2$, are often called **interval regression** estimators, with the understanding that the underlying population distribution is homoskedastic normal.

Although equation (19.11) looks a lot like the log likelihood for the ordered probit model, there is an important difference: in ordered probit, the cut points are parameters to estimate, and the parameters $\boldsymbol{\beta}$ do not measure interesting partial effects. With interval regression, the interval endpoints are given (or are themselves data), and $\boldsymbol{\beta}$ contains the partial effects of interest. In particular, as in the case of binary censoring, when we obtain the interval regression estimates, we interpret the $\hat{\boldsymbol{\beta}}$ as if we had been able to run the regression y_i on $\mathbf{x}_i$, $i = 1, \ldots, N$. Imposing the assumptions of the classical linear model allows us to estimate the parameters in the distribution $\mathrm{D}(y \mid \mathbf{x})$, even though the data are interval censored.

Sometimes in applications of interval regression the observed, censored variable, w, is set to some value within the interval that contains y. For example, if y is wealth, we might set w to the midpoint of the interval that y falls into. (Of course, we have to use some other rule if $y < r_1$ or $y > r_J$.) Provided the definition of w determines the proper interval, the maximum likelihood estimators of $\boldsymbol{\beta}$ and σ will be the same.

When w is defined to have the same units as y, it is tempting to ignore the grouping of the data and just to run an OLS regression of w_i on $\mathbf{x}_i$, $i = 1, \ldots, N$. Naturally, such a procedure is generally inconsistent for $\boldsymbol{\beta}$. Nevertheless, the results of Chung and Goldberger apply: if $\mathrm{E}(\mathbf{x} \mid y)$ is linear in y, a linear regression can estimate the slope coefficients up to a common scale factor.

Sometimes the interval limits change across i, a possibility that causes no problems if we assume the limits are exogenous in the following sense:

$$\mathrm{D}(y_i \mid \mathbf{x}_i, r_{i1}, \ldots, r_{iJ}) = \mathrm{D}(y_i \mid \mathbf{x}_i). \tag{19.12}$$

In the binary censoring example from the previous section, assumption (19.12) holds because the one limit value ($J = 1$) is randomly assigned. Generally, the limits can be a function of $\mathbf{x}_i$ (because these are being conditioned on). The resulting log likelihood is exactly as in equation (19.11) with r_j replaced with r_{ij}. Some econometrics packages have "interval regression" commands that allow one to specify the lower and upper endpoints for each unit i, allowing for unit-specific endpoints.

Because of the underlying normality assumption, we can use the Rivers and Vuong (1988) and Smith and Blundell (1986) control function approach to test and correct for endogeneity of explanatory variables. The underlying model is the standard linear model

$$y_1 = \mathbf{z}_1\boldsymbol{\delta}_1 + \alpha_1 y_2 + u_1, \tag{19.13}$$

and we observe the censored variable, w_1. Given the linear reduced form $y_2 = \mathbf{z}\boldsymbol{\delta}_2 + v_2$, we proceed as before: just add the first-stage residuals, $\hat{v}_2$, to the interval regression model, along with $(\mathbf{z}_1, y_2)$. Of course, we are interested in α_1 and $\boldsymbol{\delta}_1$, along with the coefficient on $\hat{v}_2$ to determine whether y_2 is in fact endogenous. Unfortunately, such an approach only works when y_2 is not censored. It is very difficult to account for interval censoring of y_2 along with that for y_1.

Modifying interval regression for linear, unobserved-effects panel data models is straightforward, provided we are willing to rely on the Chamberlain-Mundlak device. We would write

$$y_{it} = \mathbf{x}_{it}\boldsymbol{\beta} + c_i + u_{it}, \qquad t = 1, \ldots, T \tag{19.14}$$

$$c_i = \psi + \bar{\mathbf{x}}_i\boldsymbol{\xi} + a_i, \tag{19.15}$$

where all unobservables have normal distributions and the interval limits, $\{r_{itj}: j = 1, 2, \ldots, J\}$, can vary by i and t. Estimation can be carried out under the assumption of serial independence in $\{u_{it}: t = 1, \dots, T\}$, so that the log likelihood has a random effects structure, or without imposing any assumption on the serial dependence (which leads to pooled estimation of the type we covered in Chapters 15 and 16).

19.2.3 Censoring from Above and Below

Two kinds of censoring are common: one is seen when the value of a variable is observed only when it is below a known cap, the other when it is above a known floor (or, in some cases, both). Consider first the case of **right censoring** (censoring from above). For each i, a censoring threshold, r_i, is observed. When we randomly draw a unit from the population, we observe the explanatory variables, $\mathbf{x}_i$. However, rather than observing the outcome on y_i, we effectively observe

$$w_i = \min(y_i, r_i). \tag{19.16}$$

If the underlying population distribution for y is continuous, the probability that $y_i = r_i$ is zero, and so, if $w_i = r_i$, we know that the observation is censored; if $w_i < r_i$, we know that $w_i = y_i$; that is, we observe y_i. If y_i is (partially) discrete, there can be positive probability that $y_i = r_i$. As a practical matter, when the censoring points change across i, it is helpful in data sets to define a binary variable indicating whether an observation is censored.

For concreteness, we focus on the case where the population distribution of y_i is continuous. Let $f(y \mid \mathbf{x}; \boldsymbol{\theta})$ denote the conditional density. Under $\mathrm{D}(y_i \mid \mathbf{x}_i, r_i) = \mathrm{D}(y_i \mid \mathbf{x}_i)$, we can easily obtain the density of w_i conditional on $(\mathbf{x}_i, r_i)$ because, for $w < r_i$,

$$\mathrm{P}(w_i \le w \mid \mathbf{x}_i, r_i) = \mathrm{P}(y_i \le w \mid \mathbf{x}_i) = F(w \mid \mathbf{x}_i; \boldsymbol{\theta}),$$

where $F(\cdot \mid \mathbf{x}_i; \boldsymbol{\theta})$ is the cdf of y_i conditional on $\mathbf{x}_i$. Therefore, the probability density of w_i given $(\mathbf{x}_i, r_i)$ is simply $f(w \mid \mathbf{x}_i; \boldsymbol{\theta})$ for $w < r_i$, that is, for values strictly less than the censoring point. Further,

$$\mathrm{P}(w_i = r_i \mid \mathbf{x}_i, r_i) = \mathrm{P}(y_i \ge r_i \mid \mathbf{x}_i, r_i) = 1 - F(r_i \mid \mathbf{x}_i; \boldsymbol{\theta}).$$

It follows that we can write the probability density of w_i given $(\mathbf{x}_i, r_i)$ as

$$g(w \mid \mathbf{x}_i, r_i; \boldsymbol{\theta}) = [f(w \mid \mathbf{x}_i; \boldsymbol{\theta})]^{1[w < r_i]} [1 - F(r_i \mid \mathbf{x}_i; \boldsymbol{\theta})]^{1[w = r_i]}. \tag{19.17}$$

The log-likelihood function for a random draw i (where we do not bother to distinguish between the "true" value of theta and a generic value) is

$$\log[g(w \mid \mathbf{x}_i, r_i; \boldsymbol{\theta})] = 1[w_i < r_i] \log[f(w_i \mid \mathbf{x}_i; \boldsymbol{\theta})] + 1[w_i = r_i] \log[1 - F(r_i \mid \mathbf{x}_i; \boldsymbol{\theta})], \tag{19.18}$$

and we sum this expression across all i to obtain the log likelihood for the entire sample. Some authors prefer to write the log likelihood separately for the uncensored and censored observations, but equation (19.18) is actually preferred because it shows that the units are being randomly sampled from a population. Here, we are drawing $(w_i, \mathbf{x}_i, r_i)$. In the vast majority of cases, the conditions sufficient for MLE to be well behaved covered in Chapter 13 hold for censored estimation because the model $f(y \mid \mathbf{x}; \boldsymbol{\theta})$ is smooth in $\boldsymbol{\theta}$.

An interesting feature of equation (19.18) is that we only need to observe the censoring point, r_i, for censored observations. (However, we do need to know which observations are censored and which are not.) This feature of the MLE approach is useful because sometimes in applications to duration models—see Chapter 22—the censoring value is reported only for observations that are actually censored.

In the leading case, y follows a classical linear model in the population of interest, that is,

$$\mathrm{D}(y \mid \mathbf{x}) = \mathrm{Normal}(\mathbf{x}\boldsymbol{\beta}, \sigma^2), \tag{19.19}$$

in which case we have what is typically called the **censored normal regression model**. (In the econometrics literature, this is sometimes called the censored Tobit model or Type I Tobit model, but we are reserving those names for the case of corner solution responses; see Chapter 17.) The log likelihood for the censored normal regression model is

$$l_i(\boldsymbol{\theta}) = 1[w_i < r_i] \log\{\sigma^{-1}\phi[(w_i - \mathbf{x}_i\boldsymbol{\beta})/\sigma]\} + 1[w_i = r_i] \log\{1 - \Phi[(w_i - \mathbf{x}_i\boldsymbol{\beta})/\sigma]\}. \tag{19.20}$$

Many standard econometrics packages estimate this model with little computational difficulty. Often, a transformation, such as taking the natural log, is needed to make equation (19.19) a reasonable assumption. In cases where no such transformation is available that ensures normality, the more general formulation in equation (19.18) can be used to obtain the log likelihood.

Distinguishing between the underlying population model and the censoring scheme can lead to some perhaps surprising implications for econometric practice. For example, suppose that survey data are collected on charitable contributions, where contributions are censored at a fixed cap—let us say \$10,000 a year for concreteness. In the population, there is no natural upper bound for charitable contributions, so one knows immediately that the observed pileup at \$10,000 in the survey data is due to built-in data censoring. It is proper to say that charitable contributions are "censored from above at \$10,000." But the pileup at zero is a different matter: it is due to the fact that some fraction of the population will have zero charitable contributions in a particular year. Therefore, an appropriate course of action is to treat charitable contributions in the population as a corner solution response, with a corner at zero. (We might use a Tobit model, or one of the two-part models discussed in Section 17.6.) Unlike the censoring from above at \$10,000, it makes no sense to say charitable contributions are also "censored from below at zero." There is a corner at zero, but it is not due to data censoring.

Interestingly, in the situation just described, if we assume a Type I Tobit model in the population for charitable contributions, the log-likelihood function for the right-censored charitable contributions is identical to that for the two-limit Tobit model discussed in Section 17.7. Estimation can be done rather straightforwardly by specifying zero and 10,000 as the lower and upper bounds, respectively. The practically important issue concerns what we do with the estimates. In fact, after obtaining the estimates, all calculations—of response probabilities, expected values, and so on—should be based on the Type I Tobit model (ignoring the right censoring). We are interested in features of $\mathrm{D}(y \mid \mathbf{x})$ in the population, where y is actual charitable contributions. Therefore, after accounting for the top coding in estimation by using a two-limit Tobit, we revert to the Type I Tobit for all statements about charitable contributions. The parameters themselves are of interest insofar as they allow us to compute partial effects on probabilities, means, and medians. But the corner at \$10,000 plays no role in such calculations. Similar comments hold for two-part models for corner solutions.

A more subtle example occurs when, say, an upper limit is imposed by law. Consider a stylized case where individuals may contribute no more than 15% of their income to retirement plans. In the population of working people, some individuals will contribute zero, some will contribute at the 15 percent upper limit, and many will contribute a percentage strictly between zero and 15. If we are interested in the effect of explanatory variables—say, taking courses on retirement savings—on the contribution under the current legal regime, a two-limit Tobit model makes sense for the contribution percentage. If we want to know, say, the mean or median difference in the rate between those who have and have not had a retirement savings course, we would use the formulas for the two-limit Tobit model. However, one might want to know the effects of covariates on the contribution percentage in the absence of institutional constraints. Then we would be back to the previous situation: the corner at zero is a corner that arises from utility maximization, but the corner at 15 is imposed—in this case, by law rather than the data collection scheme. In this case, one would use formulas for a Type I Tobit with corner at zero, even though the estimates necessarily are obtained from a two-limit Tobit. In this application, an additional calculation may be of interest: what would be the effect on the average contribution rate if the limit were increased? We can use the formulas for a two-limit Tobit in this case to compute the appropriate derivative.

Not surprisingly, endogenous explanatory variables with censored data can be handled using methods very similar to those for the Type I Tobit model. For example, suppose the population model is

$$y_1 = \mathbf{z}_1\boldsymbol{\delta}_1 + \alpha_1 y_2 + u_1, \tag{19.21}$$

where $\mathrm{D}(u_1 \mid \mathbf{z})$ is $\mathrm{Normal}(0, \sigma_1^2)$. However, the data are right censored. If the reduced form for y_2 is $y_2 = \mathbf{z}\boldsymbol{\delta}_1 + v_2$, where (u_1, v_2) is independent of $\mathbf{z}$ and bivariate normal, we can apply the Smith and Blundell (1986) approach to account for the right censoring. This assumes that y_2 is not censored, so that the first step is OLS of y_2 on $\mathbf{z}$ using a random sample. The residuals, $\hat{v}_2$, are added to the censored normal regression in the second stage. Of course, because the underlying population model is linear, we are interested in α_1 and $\boldsymbol{\delta}_1$. Joint MLE is possible, too, and would be more efficient and avoid the problem of inference after two-step estimation. (Of course, the bootstrap can be applied here by randomly drawing units from the sample. Remember, we have a random sample of units. We simply include the first-step estimation and censored normal estimation within each bootstrap iteration.)

With enough normality, it should not be surprising that the Chamberlain-Mundlak device can be used in the context of right and left censoring. Again, for simplicity consider the linear model $y_{it} = \mathbf{x}_{it}\boldsymbol{\beta} + c_i + u_{it}$, where right censoring is at r_{it}, which can change across i and t. Natural exogeneity assumptions, along with convenient distributional assumptions, are

$$\mathrm{D}(u_{it} \mid \mathbf{x}_i, r_{i1}, \ldots, r_{iT}, c_i) = \mathrm{D}(u_{it}) = \mathrm{Normal}(0, \sigma_u^2), \qquad t = 1, \ldots, T \tag{19.22}$$

$$\mathrm{D}(c_i \mid \mathbf{x}_i, r_{i1}, \ldots, r_{iT}) = \mathrm{D}(c_i \mid \mathbf{x}_i) = \mathrm{Normal}(\psi + \bar{\mathbf{x}}_i\boldsymbol{\xi}, \sigma_a^2). \tag{19.23}$$

As usual, these assumptions mean we can write

$$y_{it} = \psi + \mathbf{x}_{it}\boldsymbol{\beta} + \bar{\mathbf{x}}_i\boldsymbol{\xi} + v_{it}, \qquad \mathrm{D}(v_{it} \mid \mathbf{x}_i, \mathbf{r}_i) = \mathrm{Normal}(0, \sigma_a^2 + \sigma_u^2), \tag{19.24}$$

where $\mathbf{r}_i = (r_{i1}, \ldots, r_{iT})$ is the vector of censoring values for unit i. Now, we can just apply pooled censored normal regression, with censoring points r_{it}, and consistently estimate ψ, $\boldsymbol{\beta}$, $\boldsymbol{\xi}$, and $\sigma_v^2 = \sigma_a^2 + \sigma_u^2$. Because this is a partial likelihood method, we need to make the inference robust to serial correlation. Generally, we cannot separately identify σ_a^2 and σ_u^2 unless we make the further assumption that $\{u_{it}\colon t = 1, \ldots, T\}$ is serially independent, in which case we can use a correlated random effects (CRE) likelihood approach similar in structure to the CRE Tobit model. Naturally, with the underlying population model linear, we are mainly interested in $\boldsymbol{\beta}$ and appropriate inference concerning $\boldsymbol{\beta}$.

All the methods just discussed require a full distributional assumption. (In the panel data case, this statement applies to $\mathrm{D}(y_{it} \mid \mathbf{x}_i, c_i)$, not to a joint distribution across t.) Certainly it is of interest to relax such assumptions when possible. (In Section 19.8, we will discuss ways of using probability weights to relax distributional assumptions.) Powell's (1984) censored least absolute deviations (CLAD) estimator can be applied to censored data without putting strong restrictions on $\mathrm{D}(y \mid \mathbf{x})$. To see how, begin with a linear model for the conditional median,

$$\mathrm{Med}(y \mid \mathbf{x}) = \mathbf{x}\boldsymbol{\beta}. \tag{19.25}$$

(Of course, this may or may not be the conditional mean. Powell's approach applies to the conditional median.) Again, assume that our random sample consists of $(\mathbf{x}_i, r_i, w_i)$, where $w_i = \min(y_i, r_i)$. LAD can be applied to the censoring case because the median passes through the min function:

$$\mathrm{Med}(w_i \mid \mathbf{x}_i, r_i) = \mathrm{Med}[\min(y_i \mid \mathbf{x}_i, r_i), r_i] = \min[\mathrm{Med}(y_i \mid \mathbf{x}_i), r_i] = \min(\mathbf{x}_i\boldsymbol{\beta}, r_i), \tag{19.26}$$

where the second equality holds under the assumption that $\mathrm{Med}(y_i \mid \mathbf{x}_i, r_i) = \mathrm{Med}(y_i \mid \mathbf{x}_i)$—which means censoring is exogenous with respect to y_i in the conditional median sense. As before, the censoring values can be related to $\mathbf{x}_i$. Given equation (19.26), we can use LAD to estimate $\boldsymbol{\beta}$, resulting in the CLAD estimator:

$$\min_{\mathbf{b}} \sum_{i=1}^{N} |w_i - \min(\mathbf{x}_i\mathbf{b}, r_i)|. \tag{19.27}$$

As discussed in Chapter 17, Powell (1984) shows that CLAD is consistent and $\sqrt{N}$-asymptotically normal. His paper contains formulas for estimating the asymptotic variance of the CLAD estimator.

One subtle point concerning the CLAD estimator when applied to censored data is that it requires that the censoring value, r_i, be available even when the observation is not right censored. This data requirement is not much of an issue in top-coding cases, especially when the same value is used. (For example, if wealth is top coded at \$500,000, that information is known, and $r_i = 500{,}000$ for all i.) However, in some duration problems—which we treat explicitly in Chapter 22—only w_i is observed. That is, along with a censoring indicator, we observe either y_i or r_i, but not both. Recall that the maximum likelihood estimator can be applied in situations where r_i is not always observed: we only need to observe r_i when the observation is actually censored.

19.3 Overview of Sample Selection

We now turn to estimation when a sample from subset of the population is used to estimate the unknown parameters. The term **selected sample** is generally used to describe a sample that is not randomly drawn from the underlying population. As mentioned in Section 19.1, there are a variety of **selection mechanisms** that result in selected samples. Some mechanisms are due to sample design, while others are due to the behavior of the units being sampled, including nonresponse on survey questions and attrition from social programs.

Before we launch into specifics, there is an important general point to remember: sample selection can only be an issue once the population of interest has been carefully specified. If we propose a model for a subset of a larger population, it is proper to proceed by obtaining a random sample from that subpopulation and then using the standard econometric methods that we have covered thus far. That we do not have a random sample from the larger population does not affect our ability to consistently estimate the parameters of the model for the subpopulation.

As a specific example that often leads to confusion, consider the conditional lognormal hurdle model that we discussed in Section 17.6.2. In that model, the distribution of $\log(y)$, conditional on $y > 0$ and the covariates $\mathbf{x}$, is normally distributed with a linear conditional mean and constant variance. Therefore, the parameters in the model describing the $y > 0$ subpopulation, $\boldsymbol{\beta}$ and σ^2, are consistently estimated using MLE (which is OLS in this case) on the subsample with $y_i > 0$. Using a linear model for $\log(y)$ on the subsample $y_i > 0$ does not work in the Exponential Type II Tobit model because that model implies that $\log(y)$ conditional on $y > 0$ is not lognormal, nor does it have a linear conditional mean. Some authors prefer to view the failure of the standard $\log(y)$ regression in the ET2T model as a sample selection problem, but that labeling misses the key point: in hurdle models, we are presumably interested in features of $\mathrm{D}(y \mid \mathbf{x})$, and the only issue is whether we have those features correctly specified. In the ET2T model, one often sees discussion of "sample selection bias" in estimating the vector $\boldsymbol{\beta}$ in the formulation $y = 1[\mathbf{x}\boldsymbol{\gamma} + v > 0] \exp(\mathbf{x}\boldsymbol{\beta} + u)$. But $\boldsymbol{\beta}$ does not by itself provide partial effects of any conditional mean involving y, and so, as we discussed in Section 17.6.3, focusing on estimates of $\boldsymbol{\beta}$ in the ET2T model is inappropriate. (In the lognormal hurdle model, $\boldsymbol{\beta}$ indexes the semielasticities and elasticities of $\mathrm{E}(y \mid \mathbf{x}, y > 0)$, which makes the β_j of direct interest.) By contrast, in a sample selection context with a linear regression for the underlying population, the focus on the single set of regression parameters is entirely appropriate, as we wll see in the next several sections.

As a second example, suppose y is a fractional response that takes on the values zero and one with positive probability, and takes on a range of values strictly between zero and one. One possibility is to model $\mathrm{P}(y = 0 \mid \mathbf{x})$ and $\mathrm{P}(y = 1 \mid \mathbf{x})$ along with $\mathrm{E}(y \mid \mathbf{x}, 0 < y < 1)$. Suppose the latter is $\mathrm{E}(y \mid \mathbf{x}, 0 < y < 1) = \Phi(\mathbf{x}\boldsymbol{\beta})$. Then, to consistently estimate $\boldsymbol{\beta}$ we can apply any of the consistent estimators for fractional responses in Section 18.6.1 to the subsample with $0 < y_i < 1$. We do not introduce a sample selection problem by ignoring the data with outcomes $y_i = 0$ or $y_i = 1$.

Now that we know some contexts where sample selection is not an issue, we provide some examples where nonrandom sampling is relevant and can (but does not always) cause serious problems.

Example 19.1 (Saving Function): Suppose we wish to estimate a saving function for all families in a given country, and the population saving function is

$$saving = \beta_0 + \beta_1 income + \beta_2 age + \beta_3 married + \beta_4 kids + u, \tag{19.28}$$

where *age* is the age of the household head and the other variables are self-explanatory. However, we only have access to a survey that included families whose household head was 45 years of age or older. This restricted sampling raises a sample selection issue because we are interested in the saving function for all families, but we can obtain a random sample only for a subset of the population.

Example 19.2 (Truncation Based on Wealth): We are interested in estimating the effect of worker eligibility in a particular pension plan (for example, a 401(k) plan) on family wealth. Let the population model be

$$wealth = \beta_0 + \beta_1 plan + \beta_2 educ + \beta_3 age + \beta_4 income + u, \tag{19.29}$$

where *plan* is a binary indicator for eligibility in the pension plan. However, we can only sample people with a net wealth less than \$200,000, so the sample is selected on the basis of *wealth*. As we will see, sampling based on a response variable is much more serious than sampling based on an exogenous explanatory variable.

In these two examples data were missing on all variables for a subset of the population as a result of survey design. In other cases, units *are* randomly drawn from the population, but data are missing on one or more variables for some units in the sample. Using a subset of a random sample because of missing data can lead to a sample selection problem. As we will see, if the reason the observations are missing is appropriately exogenous, using the subsample has no serious consequences.

Our final example illustrates a more subtle form of a missing data problem.

Example 19.3 (Wage Offer Function): Consider estimating a wage offer equation for people of working age. By definition, this equation is supposed to represent *all* people of working age, whether or not a person is actually working at the time of the survey. Because we can only observe the wage offer for working people, we effectively select our sample on this basis.

This example is not as straightforward as the previous two. We treat it as a sample selection problem because data on a key variable—the wage offer, $wage^o$—are available only for a clearly defined subset of the population. This is sometimes called incidental truncation because $wage^o$ is missing as a result of the outcome of another variable, labor force participation.

The incidental truncation in this example has a strong self-selection component: people self-select into employment, so whether or not we observe $wage^o$ depends on an individual's labor supply decision. Whether we call examples like this sample selection or self-selection is largely irrelevant. The important point is that we must account for the nonrandom nature of the sample we have for estimating the wage offer equation.

In the next several sections we cover a variety of sample selection issues, including tests and corrections.

19.4 When Can Sample Selection Be Ignored?

In Section 19.3 we briefly discussed how there can be no sample selection problem if the model we have specified applies to a subsample of a population for which we can obtain a random sample. Here, we discuss a more substantive question: under what circumstances does using a nonrandom sample from a specified population nevertheless consistently estimate the population parameters?

19.4.1 Linear Models: Estimation by OLS and 2SLS

We begin by obtaining conditions under which estimation of the population model by two-stage least squares (2SLS) using a selected sample is consistent for the population parameters. These results are of interest in their own right, but we will also apply them to several situations later in the chapter.

We assume there is a population represented by the random vector $(\mathbf{x}, y, \mathbf{z})$, where $\mathbf{x}$ is a $1 \times K$ vector of explanatory variables, y is the scalar response variable, and $\mathbf{z}$ is a $1 \times L$ vector of instrumental variables. The population model is the standard single-equation linear model with possibly endogenous explanatory variables:

$$y = \beta_1 + \beta_2 x_2 + \cdots + \beta_K x_K + u = \mathbf{x}\boldsymbol{\beta} + u \tag{19.30}$$

$$\mathrm{E}(\mathbf{z}'u) = \mathbf{0}, \tag{19.31}$$

where we take $x_1 \equiv 1$ for notational simplicity (an assumption that means z_1 is almost certainly equal to unity, too). From Chapter 5 we know that, if we could obtain a random sample from the population, then equation (19.31), along with the rank condition (particularly rank$[\mathrm{E}(\mathbf{z}'\mathbf{x})] = K$), would be sufficient to consistently estimate $\boldsymbol{\beta}$. As we will see, in the context of sample selection, equation (19.31) is rarely sufficient for consistency of the 2SLS estimator on the selected sample.

A leading special case is $\mathbf{z} = \mathbf{x}$, in which case the explanatory variables are assumed to be uncorrelated with the error. Our general treatment allows elements of $\mathbf{x}$ to be correlated with u.

Rather than obtaining a random sample from the population, we only use data points that satisfy certain conditions. The idea is to think of drawing units randomly from the population, but now a random draw for unit i, $(\mathbf{x}_i, y_i, \mathbf{z}_i)$, is supplemented by drawing a **selection indicator**, s_i. By definition, $s_i = 1$ if unit i is used in the estimation, and $s_i = 0$ if we do not use random draw i. Therefore, our "data" consist of $\{(\mathbf{x}_i, y_i, \mathbf{z}_i, s_i)\colon i = 1, \ldots, N\}$, where the value of s_i determines whether we observe all of $(\mathbf{x}_i, y_i, \mathbf{z}_i)$.

Because parameter identification should always be studied in a population, we let s denote a random variable with the distribution of s_i for all i. In other words, $(\mathbf{x}, y, \mathbf{z}, s)$ now represents the population. Therefore, to determine the properties of any estimation procedure using the selected sample, we need to know about the distribution of s and its dependence on $(\mathbf{x}, y, \mathbf{z})$.

To obtain conditions under which 2SLS on the selected sample consistently estimates $\boldsymbol{\beta}$, assume $\{(\mathbf{x}_i, y_i, \mathbf{z}_i, s_i)\colon i = 1, \ldots, N\}$ is a random sample from the population. The 2SLS estimator using the selected sample can be written as

$$\hat{\boldsymbol{\beta}} = \left[\left(N^{-1}\sum_{i=1}^{N} s_i \mathbf{z}_i'\mathbf{x}_i\right)'\left(N^{-1}\sum_{i=1}^{N} s_i \mathbf{z}_i'\mathbf{z}_i\right)^{-1}\left(N^{-1}\sum_{i=1}^{N} s_i \mathbf{z}_i'\mathbf{x}_i\right)\right]^{-1}$$

$$\times \left(N^{-1}\sum_{i=1}^{N} s_i \mathbf{z}_i'\mathbf{x}_i\right)'\left(N^{-1}\sum_{i=1}^{N} s_i \mathbf{z}_i'\mathbf{z}_i\right)^{-1}\left(N^{-1}\sum_{i=1}^{N} s_i \mathbf{z}_i' y_i\right).$$

Substituting $y_i = \mathbf{x}_i\boldsymbol{\beta} + u_i$ gives

$$\hat{\boldsymbol{\beta}} = \boldsymbol{\beta} + \left[\left(N^{-1}\sum_{i=1}^{N} s_i\mathbf{z}_i'\mathbf{x}_i\right)'\left(N^{-1}\sum_{i=1}^{N} s_i\mathbf{z}_i'\mathbf{z}_i\right)^{-1}\left(N^{-1}\sum_{i=1}^{N} s_i\mathbf{z}_i'\mathbf{x}_i\right)\right]^{-1}$$

$$\times\left(N^{-1}\sum_{i=1}^{N} s_i\mathbf{z}_i'\mathbf{x}_i\right)'\left(N^{-1}\sum_{i=1}^{N} s_i\mathbf{z}_i'\mathbf{z}_i\right)^{-1}\left(N^{-1}\sum_{i=1}^{N} s_i\mathbf{z}_i'u_i\right). \tag{19.32}$$

It is easily seen from equation (19.32) that the key condition for consistency is $\mathrm{E}(s_i\mathbf{z}_i'u_i) = \mathbf{0}$, along with the rank condition on the selected sample. Formally, we have the following result:

THEOREM 19.1 (Consistency of 2SLS under Sample Selection): In model (19.30), assume that $\mathrm{E}(u^2) < \infty$, $\mathrm{E}(x_j^2) < \infty$, $j = 1, \ldots, K$, and $\mathrm{E}(z_j^2) < \infty$, $j = 1, \ldots, L$. Further, assume that

$$\mathrm{E}(s\mathbf{z}'u) = \mathbf{0} \tag{19.33}$$

$$\operatorname{rank} \mathrm{E}(\mathbf{z}'\mathbf{z} \mid s = 1) = L \tag{19.34}$$

$$\operatorname{rank} \mathrm{E}(\mathbf{z}'\mathbf{x} \mid s = 1) = K \tag{19.35}$$

Then the 2SLS estimator using the selected sample is consistent for $\boldsymbol{\beta}$ and $\sqrt{N}$-asymptotically normal.

Equation (19.32) essentially proves the consistency result under the assumptions of Theorem 19.1. Conditions (19.34) and (19.35) are fairly straightforward, and imply that the usual rank condition for 2SLS holds in the selected subpopulation. Naturally, it is possible that the rank condition holds on the entire population but not the $s = 1$ subset. For example, if $s = 1$ denotes females in the working population, then neither $\mathbf{x}$ nor $\mathbf{z}$ can include a female dummy variable. Generally, one needs sufficient variation in both the explanatory variables and instruments in the subpopulation in order for the rank condition to hold.

It is worth studying condition (19.33) in some detail. First, it is not generally enough to assume condition (19.31), that is, zero correlation between the instruments and errors in the population. One case where condition (19.31) *is* sufficient occurs when s is independent of $(\mathbf{z}, u)$, so that $\mathrm{E}(s\mathbf{z}'u) = \mathrm{E}(s)\mathrm{E}(\mathbf{z}'u) = \mathbf{0}$ if $\mathrm{E}(\mathbf{z}'u) = \mathbf{0}$. Of course, independence of selection and $(\mathbf{z}, u)$ is a very strong assumption. In the leading case where $\mathbf{z} = \mathbf{x}$, so that estimation is by OLS, the condition is the same as independence between s and $(\mathbf{x}, y)$, which is tantamount to assuming that some observations from an original random sample are dropped randomly, without regard to the values of $(\mathbf{x}_i, y_i)$. In the statistics literature, this has been called the **missing completely at random (MCAR)** assumption; see, for example, Little and Rubin (2002).

More interesting are situations where selection can depend on exogenous variables, but not on the unobserved error. An important sufficient condition for assumption (19.33), easily verified by applying iterated expectations, is

$$\mathrm{E}(u \mid \mathbf{z}, s) = 0. \tag{19.36}$$

Assumption (19.36) allows selection to be correlated with $\mathbf{z}$ but not with u, and has been called **exogenous sampling**. It is easier to interpret this label by looking at a special case, which strengthens the sense in which the instruments are exogenous in the population. Rather than equation (19.31), make the population zero-conditional-mean assumption

$$\mathrm{E}(u \mid \mathbf{z}) = 0. \tag{19.37}$$

By basic properties of conditional expectations, if assumption (19.37) holds and s is a deterministic function of $\mathbf{z}$, then assumption (19.36) holds (which means, of course, that assumption (19.33) holds). In other words, exogenous sampling occurs when $s = h(\mathbf{z})$ for some nonrandom function $h(\cdot)$; that is, s is a nonrandom function of exogenous variables. But we must remember that the sense in which the instruments are exogenous is given by the stronger assumption (19.37).

In the case with exogenous explanatory variables, condition (19.36) is equivalent to

$$\mathrm{E}(y \mid \mathbf{x}, s) = \mathrm{E}(y \mid \mathbf{x}) = \mathbf{x}\boldsymbol{\beta}, \tag{19.38}$$

where the first equality is how we would define exogenous sampling in the context of regression analysis. Notice that assumption (19.38) implies consistency of OLS on the selected sample regardless of whether data are missing on y or elements of $\mathbf{x}$, or both. Assumption (19.38) rules out selection mechanisms that depend on the unobserved factors affecting y in equation (19.30). This assumption is related to (a conditional mean version of) the **missing at random (MAR)** assumption (for example, Little and Rubin, 2002). MAR, which is often stated in terms of conditional distributions, further assumes that the variables determining selection ($\mathbf{x}$ in this case) are always observed. We will have more to say on this kind of assumption in Section 19.8 on inverse probability weighting.

A sufficient condition for assumption (19.36) is that, conditional on $\mathbf{z}$, u and s are independent, which is informatively written as $\mathrm{D}(s \mid \mathbf{z}, u) = \mathrm{D}(s \mid \mathbf{z})$, or, because s is binary,

$$\mathrm{P}(s = 1 \mid \mathbf{z}, u) = \mathrm{P}(s = 1 \mid \mathbf{z}). \tag{19.39}$$

Because $\mathbf{z}$ is observable—at least for part of the population—and u is always unobservable, condition (19.39) is an example of what has been dubbed **selection on observables**, although this concept is usually employed in settings where $\mathbf{z}$ is always observed, something not required for the statement of Theorem 19.1. Again, we will have more to say on this kind of assumption in Section 19.8, where sample selection can also be based on variables that appear outside the model specification.

The asymptotic normality also follows in a fairly straightforward manner from equation (19.32); remember, the summands are i.i.d. random vectors, and the last term has a zero mean by assumption (19.33). Not surprisingly, the usual heteroskedasticity-robust variance matrix estimator, applied to the selected sample, is valid without further assumptions.

If we add the homoskedasticity assumption $\mathrm{E}(u^2 \mid \mathbf{z}, s) = \mathrm{E}(u^2) = \sigma^2$ (which is the same as $\mathrm{Var}(u \mid \mathbf{z}, s) = \sigma^2$ if we maintain assumption (19.36)) to the assumptions of Theorem 19.1, then we can show that the "usual" variance matrix estimator for 2SLS is asymptotically valid. Doing so requires two steps. First, under $\mathrm{E}(u^2 \mid \mathbf{z}, s) = \sigma^2$ the usual iterated expectations argument gives $\mathrm{E}(su^2\mathbf{z}'\mathbf{z}) = \sigma^2\mathrm{E}(s\mathbf{z}'\mathbf{z})$. This equation can be used to show that $\mathrm{Avar}\,\sqrt{N}(\hat{\boldsymbol{\beta}} - \boldsymbol{\beta}) = \sigma^2\{\mathrm{E}(s\mathbf{x}'\mathbf{z})[\mathrm{E}(s\mathbf{z}'\mathbf{z})]^{-1}\mathrm{E}(s\mathbf{z}'\mathbf{x})\}^{-1}$. The second step is to show that the usual 2SLS estimator of σ^2 is consistent. This fact can be seen as follows. Under the homoskedasticity assumption, $\mathrm{E}(su^2) = \mathrm{E}(s)\sigma^2$, where $\mathrm{E}(s)$ is just the fraction of the subpopulation in the overall population. The estimator of σ^2 (without degrees-of-freedom adjustment) is

$$\left(\sum_{i=1}^{N} s_i\right)^{-1} \sum_{i=1}^{N} s_i \hat{u}_i^2, \tag{19.40}$$

since $\sum_{i=1}^{N} s_i$ is simply the number of observations in the selected sample. Removing the "^" from u_i^2 and applying the law of large numbers gives $N^{-1}\sum_{i=1}^{N} s_i \xrightarrow{p} \mathrm{E}(s)$ and $N^{-1}\sum_{i=1}^{N} s_i u_i^2 \xrightarrow{p} \mathrm{E}(su^2) = \mathrm{E}(s)\sigma^2$. Since the N^{-1} terms cancel, expression (19.40) converges in probability to σ^2.

If s is a function only of $\mathbf{z}$, or s is independent of $(\mathbf{z}, u)$, and $\mathrm{E}(u^2 \mid \mathbf{z}) = \sigma^2$—that is, if the homoskedasticity assumption holds in the original population—then $\mathrm{E}(u^2 \mid \mathbf{z}, s) = \sigma^2$. As mentioned previously, without the homoskedasticity assumption we would just use the heteroskedasticity-robust standard errors, just as if a random sample were available with heteroskedasticity present in the population model.

When $\mathbf{x}$ is exogenous and we apply OLS on the selected sample, Theorem 19.1 implies that we can select the sample on the basis of the explanatory variables.

Selection based on y or on endogenous elements of $\mathbf{x}$ is not allowed because then $\mathrm{E}(u \mid \mathbf{x}, s) \neq \mathrm{E}(u)$.

Example 19.4 (Nonrandomly Missing IQ Scores): As an example of how Theorem 19.1 can be applied, consider the analysis in Griliches, Hall, and Hausman (1978) (GHH). The structural equation of interest is

$$\log(wage) = \mathbf{z}_1\boldsymbol{\delta}_1 + abil + v, \qquad \mathrm{E}(v \mid \mathbf{z}_1, abil, IQ) = 0,$$

and we assume that IQ is a valid proxy for $abil$ in the sense that $abil = \theta_1 IQ + e$ and $\mathrm{E}(e \mid \mathbf{z}_1, IQ) = 0$ (see Section 4.3.2). Write

$$\log(wage) = \mathbf{z}_1\boldsymbol{\delta}_1 + \theta_1 IQ + u, \tag{19.41}$$

where $u = v + e$. Under the assumptions made, $\mathrm{E}(u \mid \mathbf{z}_1, IQ) = 0$. It follows immediately from Theorem 19.1 that, if we choose the sample excluding all people with IQs below a fixed value, then OLS estimation of equation (19.41) will be consistent. This problem is not quite the one faced by GHH. Instead, GHH noticed that the *probability* of IQ missing was higher at lower IQs (because people were reluctant to give permission to obtain IQ scores). A simple way to model this situation is $s = 1$ if $IQ + r \geq 0$, $s = 0$ if $IQ + r < 0$, where r is an unobserved random variable. If r is redundant in the structural equation *and* in the proxy variable equation for IQ, that is, if $\mathrm{E}(v \mid \mathbf{z}_1, abil, IQ, r) = 0$ and $\mathrm{E}(e \mid \mathbf{z}_1, IQ, r) = 0$, then $\mathrm{E}(u \mid \mathbf{z}_1, IQ, r) = 0$. Since s is a function of IQ and r, it follows immediately that $\mathrm{E}(u \mid \mathbf{z}_1, IQ, s) = 0$. Therefore, using OLS on the sample for which IQ is observed yields consistent estimators.

If r is correlated with either v or e, $\mathrm{E}(u \mid \mathbf{z}_1, IQ, s) \neq \mathrm{E}(u)$ in general, and OLS estimation of equation (19.41) using the selected sample would not consistently estimate $\boldsymbol{\delta}_1$ and θ_1. Therefore, even though IQ is exogenous in the population equation (19.41), the sample selection is not exogenous. In Section 19.6.2 we cover a method that can be used to correct for sample selection bias.

Theorem 19.1 has other useful applications. Suppose that $\mathbf{x}$ is exogenous in equation (19.30) and that s is a nonrandom function of $(\mathbf{x}, v)$, where v is a variable not appearing in equation (19.30). If (u, v) is independent of $\mathbf{x}$, then $\mathrm{E}(u \mid \mathbf{x}, v) = \mathrm{E}(u \mid v)$, and so

$$\mathrm{E}(y \mid \mathbf{x}) = \mathbf{x}\boldsymbol{\beta} + \mathrm{E}(u \mid \mathbf{x}, v) = \mathbf{x}\boldsymbol{\beta} + \mathrm{E}(u \mid v).$$

If we make an assumption about the functional form of $\mathrm{E}(u \mid v)$, for example, $\mathrm{E}(u \mid v) = \gamma v$, then we can write

$$y = \mathbf{x}\boldsymbol{\beta} + \gamma v + e, \qquad \mathrm{E}(e \mid \mathbf{x}, v) = 0, \tag{19.42}$$

where $e = u - \mathrm{E}(u \mid v)$. Because s is just a function of $(\mathbf{x}, v)$, $\mathrm{E}(e \mid \mathbf{x}, v, s) = 0$, and so $\boldsymbol{\beta}$ and γ can be estimated consistently by the OLS regression y on $\mathbf{x}$, v, using the selected sample. Effectively, including v in the regression on the selected subsample eliminates the sample selection problem and allows us to consistently estimate $\boldsymbol{\beta}$. (Incidentally, because v is independent of $\mathbf{x}$, we would not have to include it in equation (19.30) to consistently estimate $\boldsymbol{\beta}$ *if* we had a random sample from the population. However, including v would result in an asymptotically more efficient estimator of $\boldsymbol{\beta}$ when $\mathrm{Var}(y \mid \mathbf{x}, v)$ is homoskedastic. See problem 4.5.) In Section 19.7 we will see how equation (19.42) can be implemented when v depends on unknown parameters.

19.4.2 Nonlinear Models

Results similar to those in the previous section hold for nonlinear models as well. We will cover explicitly the case of nonlinear regression and maximum likelihood. See problem 19.11 for the GMM case.

In the nonlinear regression case, if $\mathrm{E}(y \mid \mathbf{x}, s) = \mathrm{E}(y \mid \mathbf{x})$—so that selection is exogenous in the conditional mean sense—then NLS on the selected sample is consistent. Sufficient is that s is a deterministic function of $\mathbf{x}$. The consistency argument is simple: NLS on the selected sample solves

$$\min_{\boldsymbol{\beta}} N^{-1} \sum_{i=1}^{N} s_i [y_i - m(\mathbf{x}_i, \boldsymbol{\beta})]^2, \tag{19.43}$$

so it suffices to show that $\boldsymbol{\beta}_{\mathrm{o}}$ in $\mathrm{E}(y \mid \mathbf{x}) = m(\mathbf{x}, \boldsymbol{\beta}_{\mathrm{o}})$ minimizes $\mathrm{E}\{s[y - m(\mathbf{x}, \boldsymbol{\beta})]^2\}$ over $\boldsymbol{\beta}$. By iterated expectations,

$$\mathrm{E}\{s[y - m(\mathbf{x}, \boldsymbol{\beta})]^2\} = \mathrm{E}(s\mathrm{E}\{[y - m(\mathbf{x}, \boldsymbol{\beta})]^2 \mid \mathbf{x}, s\})$$

Next, write $[y - m(\mathbf{x}, \boldsymbol{\beta})]^2 = u^2 + 2[m(\mathbf{x}, \boldsymbol{\beta}_{\mathrm{o}}) - m(\mathbf{x}, \boldsymbol{\beta})]u + [m(\mathbf{x}, \boldsymbol{\beta}_{\mathrm{o}}) - m(\mathbf{x}, \boldsymbol{\beta})]^2$, where $u = y - m(\mathbf{x}, \boldsymbol{\beta}_{\mathrm{o}})$. By assumption, $\mathrm{E}(u \mid \mathbf{x}, s) = 0$. Therefore,

$$\mathrm{E}\{[y - m(\mathbf{x}, \boldsymbol{\beta})]^2 \mid \mathbf{x}, s\} = \mathrm{E}(u^2 \mid \mathbf{x}, s) + [m(\mathbf{x}, \boldsymbol{\beta}_{\mathrm{o}}) - m(\mathbf{x}, \boldsymbol{\beta})]^2,$$

and the second term is clearly minimized at $\boldsymbol{\beta} = \boldsymbol{\beta}_{\mathrm{o}}$. We do have to assume that $\boldsymbol{\beta}_{\mathrm{o}}$ is the *unique* value of $\boldsymbol{\beta}$ that makes $\mathrm{E}\{s[m(\mathbf{x}, \boldsymbol{\beta}) - m(\mathbf{x}, \boldsymbol{\beta}_{\mathrm{o}})]^2\}$ zero. This is the identification condition on the subpopulation.

It can also be shown that, if $\mathrm{Var}(y \mid \mathbf{x}, s) = \mathrm{Var}(y \mid \mathbf{x})$ and $\mathrm{Var}(y \mid \mathbf{x}) = \sigma_{\mathrm{o}}^2$, then the usual, nonrobust NLS statistics are valid. If heteroskedasticity exists either in the population or the subpopulation, standard heteroskedasticity-robust inference can be used. The arguments are very similar to those for 2SLS in the previous subsection.

Another important case is the general conditional maximum likelihood setup. Assume that the distribution of $\mathbf{y}$ given $\mathbf{x}$ and s is the same as the distribution of $\mathbf{y}$ given $\mathbf{x}$: $\mathrm{D}(\mathbf{y} \mid \mathbf{x}, s) = \mathrm{D}(\mathbf{y} \mid \mathbf{x})$. This is a stronger form of ignorability of selection, but it always holds if s is a nonrandom function of $\mathbf{x}$, or if s is independent of $(\mathbf{x}, \mathbf{y})$. In any case, $\mathrm{D}(\mathbf{y} \mid \mathbf{x}, s) = \mathrm{D}(\mathbf{y} \mid \mathbf{x})$ ensures that the MLE on the selected sample is consistent and that the usual MLE statistics are valid. The analogy argument should be familiar by now. Conditional MLE on the selected sample solves

$$\max_{\theta} \; N^{-1} \sum_{i=1}^{N} s_i \ell(\mathbf{y}_i, \mathbf{x}_i; \boldsymbol{\theta}), \tag{19.44}$$

where $\ell(\mathbf{y}_i, \mathbf{x}_i; \boldsymbol{\theta})$ is the log likelihood for observation i. Now for each $\mathbf{x}$, $\boldsymbol{\theta}_o$ maximizes $\mathrm{E}[\ell(\mathbf{y}, \mathbf{x}; \boldsymbol{\theta}) \mid \mathbf{x}]$ over $\boldsymbol{\theta}$. But $\mathrm{E}[s\ell(\mathbf{y}, \mathbf{x}; \boldsymbol{\theta})] = \mathrm{E}\{s\mathrm{E}[\ell(\mathbf{y}, \mathbf{x}; \boldsymbol{\theta}) \mid \mathbf{x}, s]\} = \mathrm{E}\{s\mathrm{E}[\ell(\mathbf{y}, \mathbf{x}; \boldsymbol{\theta}) \mid \mathbf{x}]\}$, since, by assumption, the conditional distribution of $\mathbf{y}$ given $(\mathbf{x}, s)$ does not depend on s. Since $\mathrm{E}[\ell(\mathbf{y}, \mathbf{x}; \boldsymbol{\theta}) \mid \mathbf{x}]$ is maximized at $\boldsymbol{\theta}_o$, so is $\mathrm{E}\{s\mathrm{E}[\ell(\mathbf{y}, \mathbf{x}; \boldsymbol{\theta}) \mid \mathbf{x}]\}$. We must make the stronger assumption that $\boldsymbol{\theta}_o$ is the unique maximum, just as in the previous cases: if the selected subset of the population is too small, we may not be able to identify $\boldsymbol{\theta}_o$. Inference can be carried out using the usual MLE statistics obtained from the selected subsample because the information equality now holds conditional on $\mathbf{x}$ and s under the assumption that $\mathrm{D}(\mathbf{y} \mid \mathbf{x}, s) = \mathrm{D}(\mathbf{y} \mid \mathbf{x})$. We omit the details.

Problem 19.11 asks you to work through the case of GMM estimation of general nonlinear models based on conditional moment restrictions.

19.5 Selection on the Basis of the Response Variable: Truncated Regression

Let $(\mathbf{x}_i, y_i)$ denote a random draw from a population. In this section we explicitly treat the case where the sample is selected on the basis of y_i.

In applying the following methods it is important to remember that there is an underlying population of interest, often described by a linear conditional expectation: $\mathrm{E}(y_i \mid \mathbf{x}_i) = \mathbf{x}_i \boldsymbol{\beta}$. If we could observe a random sample from the population, then we would just use standard regression analysis. The problem comes about because the sample we can observe is chosen at least partly based on the value of y_i. Unlike in the case where selection is based only on $\mathbf{x}_i$, selection based on y_i causes problems for standard OLS analysis on the selected sample.

A classic example of selection based on y_i is Hausman and Wise's (1977) study of the determinants of earnings. Hausman and Wise recognized that their sample from a negative income tax experiment was truncated because only families with income below 1.5 times the poverty level were allowed to participate in the program; no data were available on families with incomes above the threshold value. The truncation rule was known, and so the effects of truncation could be accounted for.

A similar example is example 19.2. We do not observe data on families with wealth above \$200,000. This case is different from the top coding example we discussed in Section 19.2.3. Here, we observe *nothing* about families with high wealth: they are entirely excluded from the sample. In the top coding case, we have a random sample of families, and we always observe $\mathbf{x}_i$; the information on $\mathbf{x}_i$ is useful even if wealth is top coded.

We assume that y_i is a continuous random variable and that the selection rule takes the form

$$s_i = 1[a_1 < y_i < a_2],$$

where a_1 and a_2 are known constants such that $a_1 < a_2$. A good way to think of the sample selection in this case is that we draw $(\mathbf{x}_i, y_i)$ randomly from the population. If y_i falls in the interval (a_1, a_2), then we observe both y_i and $\mathbf{x}_i$. If y_i is outside this interval, then we do not observe y_i or $\mathbf{x}_i$. Thus, all we know is that there is some subset of the population that does not enter our data set because of the selection rule. We know how to characterize the part of the population not being sampled because we know the constants a_1 and a_2.

In most applications we are still interested in estimating $\mathrm{E}(y_i \mid \mathbf{x}_i) = \mathbf{x}_i\boldsymbol{\beta}$. However, because of sample selection based on y_i, we must—at least in a parametric context—specify a full conditional distribution of y_i given $\mathbf{x}_i$. Parameterize the conditional density of y_i given $\mathbf{x}_i$ by $f(\cdot \mid \mathbf{x}_i; \boldsymbol{\beta}, \boldsymbol{\gamma})$, where $\boldsymbol{\beta}$ are the conditional mean parameters and $\boldsymbol{\gamma}$ is a $G \times 1$ vector of additional parameters. The cdf of y_i given $\mathbf{x}_i$ is $F(\cdot \mid \mathbf{x}_i; \boldsymbol{\beta}, \boldsymbol{\gamma})$.

What we can use in estimation is the density of y_i conditional on $\mathbf{x}_i$ *and* the fact that we observe $(y_i, \mathbf{x}_i)$. In other words, we must condition on $a_1 < y_i < a_2$ or, equivalently, $s_i = 1$. The cdf of y_i conditional on $(\mathbf{x}_i, s_i = 1)$ is simply

$$\mathrm{P}(y_i \le y \mid \mathbf{x}_i, s_i = 1) = \frac{\mathrm{P}(y_i \le y, s_i = 1 \mid \mathbf{x}_i)}{\mathrm{P}(s_i = 1 \mid \mathbf{x}_i)}.$$

Because y_i is continuously distributed, $\mathrm{P}(s_i = 1 \mid \mathbf{x}_i) = \mathrm{P}(a_1 < y_i < a_2 \mid \mathbf{x}_i) = F(a_2 \mid \mathbf{x}_i; \boldsymbol{\beta}, \boldsymbol{\gamma}) - F(a_1 \mid \mathbf{x}_i; \boldsymbol{\beta}, \boldsymbol{\gamma}) > 0$ for all possible values of $\mathbf{x}_i$. The case $a_2 = \infty$ corresponds to truncation only from below, in which case $F(a_2 \mid \mathbf{x}_i; \boldsymbol{\beta}, \boldsymbol{\gamma}) \equiv 1$. If $a_1 = -\infty$ (truncation only from above), then $F(a_1 \mid \mathbf{x}_i; \boldsymbol{\beta}, \boldsymbol{\gamma}) = 0$. To obtain the numerator when $a_1 < y < a_2$, we have

$$\mathrm{P}(y_i \le y, s_i = 1 \mid \mathbf{x}_i) = \mathrm{P}(a_1 < y_i \le y \mid \mathbf{x}_i) = F(y \mid \mathbf{x}_i; \boldsymbol{\beta}, \boldsymbol{\gamma}) - F(a_1 \mid \mathbf{x}_i; \boldsymbol{\beta}, \boldsymbol{\gamma}).$$

When we put this equation over $P(s_i = 1 \mid \mathbf{x}_i)$ and take the derivative with respect to the dummy argument $\mathscr{y}$, we obtain the density of y_i given $(\mathbf{x}_i, s_i = 1)$:

$$p(\mathscr{y} \mid \mathbf{x}_i, s_i = 1) = \frac{f(\mathscr{y} \mid \mathbf{x}_i; \boldsymbol{\beta}, \gamma)}{F(a_2 \mid \mathbf{x}_i; \boldsymbol{\beta}, \gamma) - F(a_1 \mid \mathbf{x}_i; \boldsymbol{\beta}, \gamma)} \tag{19.45}$$

for $a_1 < \mathscr{y} < a_2$.

Given a model for $f(y \mid \mathbf{x}; \boldsymbol{\beta}, \gamma)$, the log-likelihood function for any $(\mathbf{x}_i, y_i)$ in the sample can be obtained by plugging y_i into equation (19.45) and taking the log. The CMLEs of $\boldsymbol{\beta}$ and γ using the selected sample are efficient in the class of estimators that do not use information about the distribution of $\mathbf{x}_i$. Standard errors and test statistics can be computed using the general theory of conditional MLE.

In most applications of truncated samples, the population conditional distribution is assumed to be $\text{Normal}(\mathbf{x}\boldsymbol{\beta}, \sigma^2)$, in which case we have the **truncated Tobit model** or **truncated normal regression model**. The truncated Tobit model is related to the censored Tobit model for data-censoring applications (see Section 19.2.3), but there is a key difference: in censored regression, we have a random sample of units and we observe the covariates $\mathbf{x}$ for *all* people, even those for whom the response is not known. If we drop observations entirely when the response is not observed, we obtain the truncated regression model. If in a top coding example we use the information in the top coded observations, we are in the censored regression case. If we drop all top coded observations, we are in the truncated regression case. (Given a choice, we should use a censored regression analysis, as it uses all of the information in the sample.)

From our analysis of the censored regression model in Section 19.2.3, it is not surprising that heteroskedasticity or nonnormality in truncated regression results in inconsistent estimators of $\boldsymbol{\beta}$. This outcome is unfortunate because, if not for the sample selection problem, we could consistently estimate $\boldsymbol{\beta}$ under $E(y \mid \mathbf{x}) = \mathbf{x}\boldsymbol{\beta}$, without specifying $\text{Var}(y \mid \mathbf{x})$ or the conditional distribution. Distribution-free methods for the truncated regression model have been suggested by Powell (1986) under the assumption of a symmetric error distribution; see Powell (1994) for a recent survey.

Truncating a sample on the basis of y is related to **choice-based sampling**. Traditional choice-based sampling applies when y is a discrete response taking on a finite number of values, where sampling frequencies differ depending on the outcome of y. (In the truncation case, the sampling frequency is one when y falls in the interval (a_1, a_2) and zero when y falls outside of the interval.) We do not cover choice-based sampling here; see Manksi and McFadden (1981), Imbens (1992), and Cosslett

(1993). In Section 20.2 we cover some estimation methods for stratified sampling, which can be applied to some choice-based samples.

19.6 Incidental Truncation: A Probit Selection Equation

We now turn to sample selection corrections when selection is determined by a probit model. This setup applies to problems different from those in Section 19.5, where the problem was that a survey or program was designed to intentionally exclude part of the population. We are now interested in selection problems that are due to incidental truncation, attrition in the context of program evalution, and general nonresponse that leads to missing data on the response variable or the explanatory variables.

19.6.1 Exogenous Explanatory Variables

The incidental truncation problem is motivated by Gronau's (1974) model of the wage offer and labor force participation.

Example 19.5 (Labor Force Participation and the Wage Offer): Interest lies in estimating $\mathrm{E}(w_i^o \mid \mathbf{x}_i)$, where w_i^o is the hourly wage offer for a randomly drawn individual i. If w_i^o were observed for everyone in the (working age) population, we would proceed in a standard regression framework. However, a potential sample selection problem arises because w_i^o is observed only for people who work.

We can cast this problem as a weekly labor supply model:

$$\max_h \ \mathrm{util}_i(w_i^o h + a_i, h) \quad \text{subject to } 0 \le h \le 168, \tag{19.46}$$

where h is hours worked per week and a_i is nonwage income of person i. Let $s_i(h) \equiv \mathrm{util}_i(w_i^o h + a_i, h)$, and assume that we can rule out the solution $h_i = 168$. Then the solution can be $h_i = 0$ or $0 < h_i < 168$. If $\mathrm{d}s_i/\mathrm{d}h \le 0$ at $h = 0$, then the optimum is $h_i = 0$. Using this condition, straightforward algebra shows that $h_i = 0$ if and only if

$$w_i^o \le -mu_i^h(a_i, 0)/mu_i^q(a_i, 0), \tag{19.47}$$

where $mu_i^h(\cdot,\cdot)$ is the marginal disutility of working and $mu_i^q(\cdot,\cdot)$ is the marginal utility of income. Gronau (1974) called the right-hand side of equation (19.47) the *reservation wage*, w_i^r, which is assumed to be strictly positive.

We now make the parametric assumptions

$$w_i^o = \exp(\mathbf{x}_{i1}\boldsymbol{\beta}_1 + u_{i1}), \qquad w_i^r = \exp(\mathbf{x}_{i2}\boldsymbol{\beta}_2 + \gamma_2 a_i + u_{i2}) \tag{19.48}$$

where (u_{i1}, u_{i2}) is independent of $(\mathbf{x}_{i1}, \mathbf{x}_{i2}, a_i)$. Here, $\mathbf{x}_{i1}$ contains productivity characteristics, and possibly demographic characteristics, of individual i, and $\mathbf{x}_{i2}$ contains variables that determine the marginal utility of leisure and income; these may overlap with $\mathbf{x}_{i1}$. From equation (19.48) we have the log wage equation

$$\log w_i^{\mathrm{o}} = \mathbf{x}_{i1}\boldsymbol{\beta}_1 + u_{i1}. \tag{19.49}$$

But the wage offer w_i^{o} is observed only if the person works, that is, only if $w_i^{\mathrm{o}} > w_i^r$, or

$$\log w_i^{\mathrm{o}} - \log w_i^r = \mathbf{x}_{i1}\boldsymbol{\beta}_1 - \mathbf{x}_{i2}\boldsymbol{\beta}_2 - \gamma_2 a_i + u_{i1} - u_{i2} \equiv \mathbf{x}_i\boldsymbol{\delta}_2 + v_{i2} > 0.$$

This behavior introduces a potential sample selection problem if we use data only on working people to estimate equation (19.49).

This example differs in an important respect from top coding examples. With top coding, the censoring rule is known for each unit in the population. In Gronau's example, we do not know w_i^r, so we cannot use w_i^{o} in a censored regression analysis. If w_i^r were observed and exogenous and $\mathbf{x}_{i1}$ were always observed, then we would be in the censored regression framework with censoring from below. If w_i^r were observed and exogenous but $\mathbf{x}_{i1}$ were observed only when w_i^{o} is, we would be in the truncated Tobit framework. But w_i^r is allowed to depend on unobservables, and so we need a new framework.

If we drop the i subscript, let $y_1 \equiv \log w^{\mathrm{o}}$, and let y_2 be the binary labor force participation indicator, Gronau's model can be written for a random draw from the population as

$$y_1 = \mathbf{x}_1\boldsymbol{\beta}_1 + u_1, \tag{19.50}$$

$$y_2 = 1[\mathbf{x}\boldsymbol{\delta}_2 + v_2 > 0]. \tag{19.51}$$

We discuss estimation of this model under the following set of assumptions:

ASSUMPTION 19.1: (a) $(\mathbf{x}, y_2)$ are always observed, y_1 is observed only when $y_2 = 1$; (b) (u_1, v_2) is independent of $\mathbf{x}$ with zero mean; (c) $v_2 \sim \text{Normal}(0, 1)$; and (d) $\mathrm{E}(u_1 \mid v_2) = \gamma_1 v_2$.

Assumption 19.1a emphasizes the sample selection nature of the problem. Part b is a strong, but standard, form of exogeneity of $\mathbf{x}$. We will see that assumption 19.1c is needed to derive a conditional expectation given the selected sample. It is probably the most restrictive assumption because it is an explicit distributional assumption. Assuming $\mathrm{Var}(v_2) = 1$ is without loss of generality because y_2 is a binary variable.

Assumption 19.1d requires linearity in the population regression of u_1 on v_2. It always holds if (u_1, v_2) is bivariate normal—a standard assumption in these contexts—but assumption 19.1d holds under weaker assumptions. In particular, we do not need to assume that u_1 itself is normally distributed.

Amemiya (1985) calls equations (19.50) and (19.51) the **Type II Tobit model**. This name is fine as a label, but we must understand that it is a model of sample selection, and it has nothing to do with y_1 being a corner solution outcome. Unfortunately, in almost all treatments of this model, y_1 is set to zero when $y_2 = 0$. Setting y_1 to zero (or any value) when $y_2 = 0$ is misleading and can lead to inappropriate use of the model. For example, it makes no sense to set the wage offer to zero just because we do not observe it. As another example, it makes no sense to set the price per dollar of life insurance (y_1) to zero for someone who did not buy life insurance (so $y_2 = 1$ if and only if a person owns a life insurance policy).

We also have some interest in the parameters of the selection equation (19.51); for example, in Gronau's model it is a reduced-form labor force participation equation. In program evaluation with attrition, the selection equation explains the probability of dropping out of the program.

Because of the similarities in the statistical structures for the Type II Tobit model for sample selection and the exponential Type II Tobit model for corner solutions, now is a good time to review the differences in how one applies these models. Recall that when using the ET2T for a corner solution response, the goal is to model the distribution of the *fully observable outcome* in a flexible way. The possible outcomes include zero—which is a legitimate value and means we need to model the probability of a response at zero, as well as the density for positive values. One can debate about which model is best, but the important point is that there is no missing data problem. (It is for that reason that using the label "selection model" for the hurdle model we discussed in Section 17.6.3 is somewhat misleading.)

The present situation is different from having a corner at zero. In the sample selection setting, the variable y_1 in equation (19.50), which often is in logarithmic form (in which case the setup appears quite similar to the ET2T model), is not always observed. We are interested in the mean response in the population, $E(y_1 \mid \mathbf{x}_1)$, which is assumed to follow a standard linear model. Consequently, once the parameters $\boldsymbol{\beta}_1$ have been consistently estimated, it is trivial to interpret the estimated equation because the elements of $\hat{\boldsymbol{\beta}}_1$ directly measure the partial effects of interest. In other words, in the sample selection context the parameter estimates are directly interpretable as partial effects on $E(y_1 \mid \mathbf{x}_1)$, unlike in the ET2T case, where the various conditional means of the observed response have no simple forms.

We can allow a little more generality in the model by replacing $\mathbf{x}$ in equation (19.51) with $\mathbf{x}_2$; then, as will become clear, $\mathbf{x}_1$ would only need to be observed whenever y_1 is, whereas $\mathbf{x}_2$ must always be observed. This extension is not especially useful for something like Gronau's model because it implies that $\mathbf{x}_1$ contains elements that cannot also appear in $\mathbf{x}_2$. Because the selection equation is not typically a structural equation, it is undesirable to impose exclusion restrictions in equation (19.51). If a variable affecting y_1 is observed only along with y_1, the instrumental variables method that we cover in Section 19.6.2 is more attractive.

To derive an estimating equation, let $(y_1, y_2, \mathbf{x}, u_1, v_2)$ denote a random draw from the population. Since y_1 is observed only when $y_2 = 1$, what we can hope to estimate is $\mathrm{E}(y_1 \mid \mathbf{x}, y_2 = 1)$ [along with $\mathrm{P}(y_2 = 1 \mid \mathbf{x})$]. How does $\mathrm{E}(y_1 \mid \mathbf{x}, y_2 = 1)$ depend on the vector of interest, $\boldsymbol{\beta}_1$? First, under assumption 19.1 and equation (19.50),

$$\mathrm{E}(y_1 \mid \mathbf{x}, v_2) = \mathbf{x}_1\boldsymbol{\beta}_1 + \mathrm{E}(u_1 \mid \mathbf{x}, v_2) = \mathbf{x}_1\boldsymbol{\beta}_1 + \mathrm{E}(u_1 \mid v_2) = \mathbf{x}_1\boldsymbol{\beta}_1 + \gamma_1 v_2, \tag{19.52}$$

where the second equality follows because (u_1, v_2) is independent of $\mathbf{x}$. Equation (19.52) is very useful. The first thing to note is that, if $\gamma_1 = 0$—which implies that u_1 and v_2 are uncorrelated—then $\mathrm{E}(y_1 \mid \mathbf{x}, v_2) = \mathrm{E}(y_1 \mid \mathbf{x}) = \mathrm{E}(y_1 \mid \mathbf{x}_1) = \mathbf{x}_1\boldsymbol{\beta}_1$. Because y_2 is a function of $(\mathbf{x}, v_2)$, it follows immediately that $\mathrm{E}(y_1 \mid \mathbf{x}, y_2) = \mathrm{E}(y_1 \mid \mathbf{x}_1)$. In other words, if $\gamma_1 = 0$, then there is no sample selection problem, and $\boldsymbol{\beta}_1$ can be consistently estimated by OLS using the selected sample.

What if $\gamma_1 \neq 0$? Using iterated expectations on equation (19.52),

$$\mathrm{E}(y_1 \mid \mathbf{x}, y_2) = \mathbf{x}_1\boldsymbol{\beta}_1 + \gamma_1 \mathrm{E}(v_2 \mid \mathbf{x}, y_2) = \mathbf{x}_1\boldsymbol{\beta}_1 + \gamma_1 h(\mathbf{x}, y_2),$$

where $h(\mathbf{x}, y_2) = \mathrm{E}(v_2 \mid \mathbf{x}, y_2)$. If we knew $h(\mathbf{x}, y_2)$, then, from Theorem 19.1, we could estimate $\boldsymbol{\beta}_1$ and γ_1 from the regression y_1 on $\mathbf{x}_1$ and $h(\mathbf{x}, y_2)$, using only the selected sample. Because the selected sample has $y_2 = 1$, we need only find $h(\mathbf{x}, 1)$. But $h(\mathbf{x}, 1) = \mathrm{E}(v_2 \mid v_2 > -\mathbf{x}\boldsymbol{\delta}_2) = \lambda(\mathbf{x}\boldsymbol{\delta}_2)$, where $\lambda(\cdot) \equiv \phi(\cdot)/\Phi(\cdot)$ is the inverse Mills ratio, and so we can write

$$\mathrm{E}(y_1 \mid \mathbf{x}, y_2 = 1) = \mathbf{x}_1\boldsymbol{\beta}_1 + \gamma_1 \lambda(\mathbf{x}\boldsymbol{\delta}_2). \tag{19.53}$$

Equation (19.53), which can be found in numerous places (see, for example, Heckman, 1979, and Amemiya, 1985) makes it clear that an OLS regression of y_1 on $\mathbf{x}_1$ using the selected sample omits the term $\lambda(\mathbf{x}\boldsymbol{\delta}_2)$ and generally leads to inconsistent estimation of $\boldsymbol{\beta}_1$. As pointed out by Heckman (1979), the presence of selection bias can be viewed as an omitted variable problem in the selected sample. An interesting point is that, even though only $\mathbf{x}_1$ appears in the population expectation, $\mathrm{E}(y_1 \mid \mathbf{x})$, other elements of $\mathbf{x}$ appear in the expectation on the subpopulation, $\mathrm{E}(y_1 \mid \mathbf{x}, y_2 = 1)$.

Equation (19.53) also suggests a way to consistently estimate $\boldsymbol{\beta}_1$. Following Heckman (1979), we can consistently estimate $\boldsymbol{\beta}_1$ and γ_1 using the selected sample by regressing y_{i1} on $\mathbf{x}_{i1}$, $\lambda(\mathbf{x}_i\boldsymbol{\delta}_2)$. The problem is that $\boldsymbol{\delta}_2$ is unknown, so we cannot compute the additional regressor $\lambda(\mathbf{x}_i\boldsymbol{\delta}_2)$. Nevertheless, a consistent estimator of $\boldsymbol{\delta}_2$ is available from the first-stage probit estimation of the selection equation.

Procedure 19.1: (a) Obtain the probit estimate $\hat{\boldsymbol{\delta}}_2$ from the model

$$\mathrm{P}(y_{i2} = 1 \mid \mathbf{x}_i) = \Phi(\mathbf{x}_i \boldsymbol{\delta}_2) \tag{19.54}$$

using all N observations. Then obtain the estimated inverse Mills ratios $\hat{\lambda}_{i2} \equiv \lambda(\mathbf{x}_i \hat{\boldsymbol{\delta}}_2)$ (at least for $i = 1, \ldots, N_1$).

(b) Obtain $\hat{\boldsymbol{\beta}}_1$ and $\hat{\gamma}_1$ from the OLS regression on the selected sample,

$$y_{i1} \text{ on } \mathbf{x}_{i1}, \hat{\lambda}_{i2}, \qquad i = 1, 2, \ldots, N_1. \tag{19.55}$$

These estimators are consistent and $\sqrt{N}$-asymptotically normal.

The procedure is sometimes called **Heckit** after Heckman (1976) and the tradition of putting "it" on the end of procedures related to probit (such as Tobit).

A very simple test for selection bias is available from regression (19.55). Under the null of no selection bias, H_0: $\gamma_1 = 0$, we have $\mathrm{Var}(y_1 \mid \mathbf{x}, y_2 = 1) = \mathrm{Var}(y_1 \mid \mathbf{x}) = \mathrm{Var}(u_1)$, and so homoskedasticity holds under H_0. Further, from the results on generated regressors in Chapter 6, the asymptotic variance of $\hat{\gamma}_1$ (and $\hat{\boldsymbol{\beta}}_1$) is not affected by $\hat{\boldsymbol{\delta}}_2$ when $\gamma_1 = 0$. Thus, a standard t test on $\hat{\gamma}_1$ is a valid test of the null hypothsesis of no selection bias.

When $\gamma_1 \neq 0$, obtaining a consistent estimate for the asymptotic variance of $\hat{\boldsymbol{\beta}}_1$ is complicated for two reasons. The first is that, if $\gamma_1 \neq 0$, then $\mathrm{Var}(y_1 \mid \mathbf{x}, y_2 = 1)$ is not constant. As we know, heteroskedasticity itself is easy to correct for using the robust standard errors. However, we should also account for the fact that $\hat{\boldsymbol{\delta}}_2$ is an estimator of $\boldsymbol{\delta}_2$. The adjustment to the variance of $(\hat{\boldsymbol{\beta}}_1, \hat{\gamma}_1)$ because of the two-step estimation is cumbersome—it is *not* enough to simply make the standard errors heteroskedasticity-robust. Some statistical packages now have this feature built in.

As a technical point, we do not need $\mathbf{x}_1$ to be a strict subset of $\mathbf{x}$ for $\boldsymbol{\beta}_1$ to be identified, and procedure 19.1 does carry through when $\mathbf{x}_1 = \mathbf{x}$. However, if $\mathbf{x}_i \hat{\boldsymbol{\delta}}_2$ does not have much variation in the sample, then $\hat{\lambda}_{i2}$ can be approximated well by a linear function of $\mathbf{x}$. If $\mathbf{x} = \mathbf{x}_1$, this correlation can introduce severe collinearity among the regressors in regression (19.55), which can lead to large standard errors of the elements of $\hat{\boldsymbol{\beta}}_1$. When $\mathbf{x}_1 = \mathbf{x}$, $\boldsymbol{\beta}_1$ is identified only due to the nonlinearity of the inverse Mills ratio.

The situation is not quite as bad as in Section 9.5.1. There, identification failed for certain values of the structural parameters. Here, we still have identification for any value of $\boldsymbol{\beta}_1$ in equation (19.50), but it is unlikely we can estimate $\boldsymbol{\beta}_1$ with much precision. Even if we can, we would have to wonder whether a statistically significant inverse Mills ratio term is due to sample selection or functional form misspecification in the population model (19.50).

Table 19.1
Wage Offer Equation for Married Women

Dependent Variable: log(*wage*)		
Independent Variable	OLS	Heckit
educ	.108 (.014)	.109 (.016)
exper	.042 (.012)	.044 (.016)
$exper^2$	−.00081 (.00039)	−.00086 (.00044)
constant	−.522 (.199)	−.578 (.307)
$\hat{\lambda}_2$	—	.032 (.134)
Sample size	428	428
R-squared	.157	.157

Example 19.6 (Wage Offer Equation for Married Women): We use the data in MROZ.RAW to estimate a wage offer function for married women, accounting for potential selectivity bias into the workforce. Of the 753 women, we observe the wage offer for 428 working women. The labor force participation equation contains the variables in Table 15.1, including other income, age, number of young children, and number of older children—in addition to *educ*, *exper*, and $exper^2$. The results of OLS on the selected sample and the Heckit method are given in Table 19.1.

The differences between the OLS and Heckit estimates are practically small, and the inverse Mills ratio term is statistically insignificant. The fact that the intercept estimates differ somewhat is usually unimportant. (The standard errors reported for Heckit are the unadjusted ones from regression (19.55). If $\hat{\lambda}_2$ were statistically significant, we should obtain the corrected standard errors.)

The Heckit results in Table 19.1 use four exclusion restrictions in the structural equation, because *nwifeinc*, *age*, *kidslt6*, and *kidsge6* are all excluded from the wage offer equation. If we allow all variables in the selection equation to also appear in the wage offer equation, the Heckit estimates become very imprecise. The coefficient on *educ* becomes .119 (se = .034), compared with the OLS estimate .100 (se = .015). The coefficient on *kidslt6*—which now appears in the wage offer equation—is −.188 (se = .232) in the Heckit estimation, and −.056 (se = .009) in the OLS estimation. The imprecision of the Heckit estimates is due to the severe collinearity that comes from adding $\hat{\lambda}_2$ to the equation, because $\hat{\lambda}_2$ is now a function only of the explanatory variables in the wage offer equation. In fact, using the selected sample, regressing $\hat{\lambda}_2$ on the seven explanatory variables gives R-squared = .962. Unfortunately, comparing the OLS and Heckit results does not allow us to resolve some important issues. For example, the OLS results suggest that another young child reduces the wage offer by about 5.6 percent (t statistic ≈ -6.2), other things being equal. Is this effect real, or is it simply due to our inability to adequately correct for sample selection bias? Unless we have a variable that affects labor force participation without affecting the wage offer, we cannot answer this question.

If we replace parts c and d in assumption 19.1 with the stronger assumption that (u_1, v_2) is bivariate normal with mean zero, $\text{Var}(u_1) = \sigma_1^2$, $\text{Cov}(u_1, v_2) = \sigma_{12}$, and $\text{Var}(v_2) = 1$, then partial maximum likelihood estimation can be used, as described generally in problem 13.7. Partial MLE will be more efficient than the two-step procedure under joint normality of u_1 and v_2, and it will produce standard errors and likelihood ratio statistics that can be used directly (this conclusion follows from problem 13.7). The drawbacks are that it is less robust than the two-step procedure and that it is sometimes difficult to get the problem to converge.

The reason we cannot perform full conditional MLE—contrast the situation in Section 17.6.3 for the ET2T model—is that y_1 is only observed when $y_2 = 1$. Thus, while we can use the full density of y_2 given $\mathbf{x}$, which is $f(y_2 \mid \mathbf{x}) = [\Phi(\mathbf{x}\boldsymbol{\delta}_2)]^{y_2}[1 - \Phi(\mathbf{x}\boldsymbol{\delta}_2)]^{1-y_2}$, $y_2 = 0, 1$, we can only use the density $f(y_1 \mid y_2, \mathbf{x})$ when $y_2 = 1$. To find $f(y_1 \mid y_2, \mathbf{x})$ at $y_2 = 1$, we can use Bayes' rule to write $f(y_1 \mid y_2, \mathbf{x}) = f(y_2 \mid y_1, \mathbf{x}) f(y_1 \mid \mathbf{x}) / f(y_2 \mid \mathbf{x})$. Therefore, $f(y_1 \mid y_2 = 1, \mathbf{x}) = \text{P}(y_2 = 1 \mid y_1, \mathbf{x}) f(y_1 \mid \mathbf{x}) / \text{P}(y_2 = 1 \mid \mathbf{x})$. But $y_1 \mid \mathbf{x} \sim \text{Normal}(\mathbf{x}_1\boldsymbol{\beta}_1, \sigma_1^2)$. Further, $y_2 = 1[\mathbf{x}\boldsymbol{\delta}_2 + \sigma_{12}\sigma_1^{-2}(y_1 - \mathbf{x}_1\boldsymbol{\beta}_1) + e_2 > 0]$, where e_2 is independent of $(\mathbf{x}, y_1)$ and $e_2 \sim \text{Normal}(0, 1 - \sigma_{12}^2\sigma_1^{-2})$ (this conclusion follows from standard conditional distribution results for joint normal random variables). Therefore,

$$\text{P}(y_2 = 1 \mid y_1, \mathbf{x}) = \Phi\{[\mathbf{x}\boldsymbol{\delta}_2 + \sigma_{12}\sigma_1^{-2}(y_1 - \mathbf{x}_1\boldsymbol{\beta}_1)](1 - \sigma_{12}^2\sigma_1^{-2})^{-1/2}\}.$$

Combining all of these pieces [and noting the cancellation of $\text{P}(y_2 = 1 \mid \mathbf{x})$] we get

$$\ell_i(\boldsymbol{\theta}) = (1 - y_{i2}) \log[1 - \Phi(\mathbf{x}_i\boldsymbol{\delta}_2)] + y_{i2}(\log \Phi\{[\mathbf{x}_i\boldsymbol{\delta}_2 + \sigma_{12}\sigma_1^{-2}(y_{i1} - \mathbf{x}_{i1}\boldsymbol{\beta}_1)] \times (1 - \sigma_{12}^2\sigma_1^{-2})^{-1/2}\} + \log \phi[(y_{i1} - \mathbf{x}_{i1}\boldsymbol{\beta}_1)/\sigma_1] - \log(\sigma_1)).$$

The partial log likelihood is obtained by summing $\ell_i(\boldsymbol{\theta})$ across *all* observations; $y_{i2} = 1$ picks out when y_{i1} is observed and therefore contains information for estimating $\boldsymbol{\beta}_1$.

Ahn and Powell (1993) show how to consistently estimate $\boldsymbol{\beta}_1$ without making any distributional assumptions; in particular, the selection equation need not have the probit form. Vella (1998) contains a useful survey.

19.6.2 Endogenous Explanatory Variables

We now study the sample selection model when one of the elements of $\mathbf{x}_1$ is thought to be correlated with u_1. Or, all the elements of $\mathbf{x}_1$ are exogenous in the population model but data are missing on an element of $\mathbf{x}_1$, and the reason data are missing might be systematically related to u_1. For simplicity, we focus on the case of a single endogenous explanatory variable. Having multiple endogenous explanatory variables adds no complications beyond the usual identification conditions.

The model in the population is

$$y_1 = \mathbf{z}_1\boldsymbol{\delta}_1 + \alpha_1 y_2 + u_1 \tag{19.56}$$

$$y_2 = \mathbf{z}_2\boldsymbol{\delta}_2 + v_2 \tag{19.57}$$

$$y_3 = 1[\mathbf{z}\boldsymbol{\delta}_3 + v_3 > 0]. \tag{19.58}$$

The first equation is the structural equation of interest, the second equation is a linear projection for the potentially endogenous or missing variable y_2, and the third equation is the selection equation. We allow arbitrary correlation among u_1, v_2, and v_3.

The setup in equations (19.56)–(19.58) encompasses at least three cases of interest. The first occurs when y_2 is always observed but is endogenous in equation (19.56). An example is seen when y_1 is $\log(wage^o)$ and y_2 is years of schooling: years of schooling is generally available whether or not someone is in the workforce. The model also applies when y_2 is observed only along with y_1, as would happen if $y_1 = \log(wage^o)$ and y_2 is the ratio of the benefits offer to wage offer. As a second example, let y_1 be the percentage of voters supporting the incumbent in a congressional district, and let y_2 be intended campaign expenditures. Then $y_3 = 1$ if the incumbent runs for reelection, and we only observe (y_1, y_2) when $y_3 = 1$. A third application is to missing data only on y_2, as in example 19.4 where y_2 is IQ score. In the last two cases, y_2 might in fact be exogenous in equation (19.56), but endogenous sample selection effectively makes y_2 endogenous in the selected sample.

If y_1 and y_2 were always observed along with $\mathbf{z}$, we would just estimate equation (19.56) by 2SLS if y_2 is endogenous. We can use the results from Section 19.4.1 to show that 2SLS with the inverse Mills ratio added to the regressors is consistent. Regardless of the data availability on y_1 and y_2, in the second step we use only observations for which both y_1 and y_2 are observed.

ASSUMPTION 19.2: (a) $(\mathbf{z}, y_3)$ is always observed, (y_1, y_2) is observed when $y_3 = 1$; (b) (u_1, v_3) is independent of $\mathbf{z}$; (c) $v_3 \sim \text{Normal}(0, 1)$; (d) $\text{E}(u_1 \mid v_3) = \gamma_1 v_3$; and (e) $\text{E}(\mathbf{z}_2' v_2) = \mathbf{0}$ and, writing $\mathbf{z}_2\boldsymbol{\delta}_2 = \mathbf{z}_1\boldsymbol{\delta}_{22} + \mathbf{z}_{21}\boldsymbol{\delta}_{22}$, $\boldsymbol{\delta}_{22} \neq \mathbf{0}$.

Parts b, c, and d are identical to the corresponding assumptions in assumption 19.1 when all explanatory variables are observed and exogenous. Assumption e is new, resulting from the endogeneity of y_2 in equation (19.56). It is important to see that assumption 19.2e is identical to the rank condition needed for identifying equation (19.56) in the absence of sample selection.

The relationship between $\mathbf{z}_2$ and $\mathbf{z}$ is somewhat subtle. The assumptions allow the possibility that $\mathbf{z}_2 = \mathbf{z}$, but it is helpful to think of $\mathbf{z}$ including at least one factor that "primarily" affects selection that is not also in $\mathbf{z}_2$. This way, we can think of needing at least one instrument for y_2—as in the case without selection—and then at least one more exogenous variable that affects selection. This thinking forces discipline on us when we (potentially) have the problem of an endogenous explanatory variable and sample selection.

One can choose $\mathbf{z}_2 = \mathbf{z}$, but then we should have at least two elements in $\mathbf{z}$ that are not in $\mathbf{z}_1$. As we will see, choosing $\mathbf{z}_2 = \mathbf{z}$ means that the (implicit) reduced form for y_2 will tend to suffer from collinearity because then the inverse Mills ratio will be a function of the same variables, $\mathbf{z}$, appearing linearly as regressors. Unless we are interested in the reduced form parameters, the collinearity introduced by having the same regressors appearing linearly as those appearing in the inverse Mills ratio is not of much concern—remember, 2SLS uses only the fitted values from the reduced form—but it is possible the small-sample performance of the procedure is affected.

Importantly, if we choose $\mathbf{z}_2$ to be a strict subset of $\mathbf{z}$, we are not making exclusion restrictions in the reduced form; we are simply choosing between variables that are viewed as instruments for y_2 versus variables that affect selection. By contrast, we usually do not want to make exclusion restrictions in the selection equation, as the subsequent procedure is inconsistent if those restrictions are violated. Therefore, it is a good idea to choose $\mathbf{z}$ to be the vector of all exogenous variables.

To derive an estimating equation, write (in the population)

$$y_1 = \mathbf{z}_1\boldsymbol{\delta}_1 + \alpha_1 y_2 + g(\mathbf{z}, y_3) + e_1, \tag{19.59}$$

where $g(\mathbf{z}, y_3) \equiv \mathrm{E}(u_1 \mid \mathbf{z}, y_3)$ and $e_1 \equiv u_1 - \mathrm{E}(u_1 \mid \mathbf{z}, y_3)$. By definition, $\mathrm{E}(e_1 \mid \mathbf{z}, y_3) = 0$. If we knew $g(\mathbf{z}, y_3)$ then, from Theorem 19.1, we could just estimate equation (19.59) by 2SLS on the selected sample ($y_3 = 1$) using instruments $[\mathbf{z}, g(\mathbf{z}, 1)]$. It turns out that we do know $g(\mathbf{z}, 1)$ up to some estimable parameters: $\mathrm{E}(u_1 \mid \mathbf{z}, y_3 = 1) = \gamma_1\lambda(\mathbf{z}\boldsymbol{\delta}_3)$. Since $\boldsymbol{\delta}_3$ can be consistently estimated by probit of y_3 on $\mathbf{z}$ (using the entire sample), we have the following:

Procedure 19.2: (a) Obtain $\hat{\boldsymbol{\delta}}_3$ from probit of y_3 on $\mathbf{z}$ using all observations. Obtain the estimated inverse Mills ratios, $\hat{\lambda}_{i3} = \lambda(\mathbf{z}_i\hat{\boldsymbol{\delta}}_3)$.

(b) Using the selected subsample (for which we observe both y_1 and y_2), estimate the equation

$$y_{i1} = \mathbf{z}_{i1}\boldsymbol{\delta}_1 + \alpha_1 y_{i2} + \gamma_1 \hat{\lambda}_{i3} + error_i \tag{19.60}$$

by 2SLS, using instruments $(\mathbf{z}_{i2}, \hat{\lambda}_{i3})$.

The steps in this procedure show that identification actually requires that $\mathbf{z}_{21}$ appear in the linear projection of y_2 onto $\mathbf{z}_1$, $\mathbf{z}_{22}$, *and* $\lambda(\mathbf{z}\boldsymbol{\delta}_3)$ in the selected subpopulation. It would be unusual if this condition were not true when the rank condition 19.2e holds in the population.

The hypothesis-of-no-selection problem (allowing y_2 to be endogenous or not), H_0: $\gamma_1 = 0$, is tested using the usual 2SLS t statistic for $\hat{\gamma}_1$. When $\gamma_1 \neq 0$, standard errors and test statistics should be corrected for the generated regressors problem, as in Chapter 6, or using the bootstrap (with subsamples drawn from the complete list of observations).

Example 19.7 (Education Endogenous and Sample Selection): In example 19.6 we now allow *educ* to be endogenous in the wage offer equation, and we test for sample selection bias. Just as if we did not have a sample selection problem, we need IVs for *educ* that do not appear in the wage offer equation. As in example 5.3, we use parents' education (*motheduc*, *fatheduc*) and husband's education as IVs. In addition, we need some variables that affect labor force participation but not the wage offer; we use the same four variables as in example 19.6. Therefore, all variables except *educ* (and, of course, the wage offer) are treated as exogenous.

We include all of the exogenous variables in the labor force participation equation: *exper*, $exper^2$, *nwifeinc*, *age*, *kidslt6*, *kidsge6*, *motheduc*, *fatheduc*, and *huseduc* (not *educ*). (As it turns out, the three education variables are marginally jointly significant, with p-value = .046.) If we add the inverse Mills ratio, $\hat{\lambda}_3$, to the equation and estimate it by 2SLS, using all of the exogenous variables as instruments—in addition to $\hat{\lambda}_3$—the coefficient on $\hat{\lambda}_3$ is .040 (se = .133). Therefore, there is little evidence of sample selection bias. Further, the estimated coefficient on education is .088 (*se* = .021), which is very close to the estimate when we drop the IMR: the 2SLS coefficient without the IMR included is .087 (se = .021). Thus, there is no practical consequence of correcting for selection bias.

If we use only the parents' and husband's education variables as instruments for *educ*, the coefficient on $\hat{\lambda}_3$ becomes .036 (se = .134), and so the evidence for selection is still nonexistent. The education coefficient changes somewhat, to .081 (*se* = .022), but this is due to the different list of instruments, not the selection correction. Without $\hat{\lambda}_3$ in the equation, the 2SLS estimate using the smaller list of instruments is .080

($se = .022$). Therefore, in this data set, the estimated return to education changes depending on whether education is allowed to be endogenous, and then somewhat depending on the instruments used for it. But whether a sample selection correction is used has essentially no effect.

Importantly, procedure 19.2 applies to any kind of endogenous variable y_2, including binary and other discrete variables, without any additional assumptions. Why? Because the reduced form for y_2 is just a linear projection; we do not have to assume, for example, that v_2 is normally distributed or even independent of $\mathbf{z}$. As an example, we might wish to look at the effects of participation in a job training program on the subsequent wage offer, accounting for the fact that not all who participated in the program will be employed in the following period (y_2 is always observed in this case). If participation is voluntary, an instrument for it might be whether the person was randomly chosen as a potential participant.

In order for the selection correction to work for y_2 with a variety of distributions, it is important to carry out the estimation exactly as described in procedure 19.2. It is tempting to first obtain fitted values, say $\hat{y}_2$, insert these for y_2, and then apply the Heckman regression. (If y_2 is always observed, one would probably just estimate a linear reduced form using all the observations; if y_2 is missing along with y_1, one would probably use a standard Heckman correction on the reduced form.) The problem with using fitted values in place of y_2, and then, say, running the regression y_{i1} on $\mathbf{z}_{i1}$, $\hat{y}_{i2}$, $\hat{\lambda}_{i3}$ on the selected sample, is that this procedure places strong assumptions on the reduced form error, v_2 in equation (19.57). In effect, it adds $-\alpha_1 v_2$ to the structural error, u_1, with the result that we would have to assume, at a minimum, that $u_1 - \alpha_1 v_2$ is independent of $\mathbf{z}$ and that $E(u_1 - \alpha_1 v_2 \mid v_3)$ is linear. Such assumptions are virtually impossible unless y_2 is continuously distributed. Of course, joint normality of (u_1, v_2, v_3) is sufficient, but this approach is much more restrictive than assumption 19.2. Thus, applying 2SLS to equation (19.60) is much preferred to first replacing y_2 with fitted values.

Even if y_2 is exogenous in the population equation (19.56), when y_2 is sometimes missing we generally need an instrument for y_2 when selection is not ignorable (that is, $E(u_1 \mid \mathbf{z}_1, y_2, y_3) \neq E(u_1)$). In example 19.4 we could use family background variables and another test score, such as *KWW*, as IVs for *IQ*, assuming these are always observed. We would generally include all such variables in the reduced-form selection equation. Procedure 19.2 works whether we assume *IQ* is a proxy variable for ability or an indicator of ability (see Chapters 4 and 5).

To illustrate the likely consequences of using the same variable as an instrument for y_2 and to predict selection, reconsider example 19.7. As we already know, the number of young children predicts a lower probability of labor force participation. In this data set, education has a positive and statistically significant partial correlation with *kidslt6*. Therefore, we might try applying procedure 19.2 with *kidslt6* the only element in $\mathbf{z}_2 = \mathbf{z}$ that is not in $\mathbf{z}_1$. That is, the probit for *inlf* includes *exper*, *exper*^{2}, and *kidslt6*, and then the the instrumental variables are *exper*, *exper*^{2}, $\hat{\lambda}_3$, and *kidslt6*. Using this approach, the estimated education coefficient is .329 (*se* = .188), which is much too large to be plausible. Further, the 95% confidence interval (which ignores the two-step estimation) includes zero, showing the effects of the severe collinearity in the IV estimation.

If we make stronger assumptions, it is possible to estimate model (19.56)–(19.58) by partial maximum likelihood of the kind discussed in problem 13.7. One possibility is to assume that (u_1, v_2, v_3) is trivariate normal and independent of $\mathbf{z}$. In addition to ruling out discrete y_2, such a procedure would be computationally difficult. If y_2 is binary, we can model it as $y_2 = 1[\mathbf{z}_2\boldsymbol{\delta}_2 + v_2 > 0]$, where $v_2 \mid \mathbf{z} \sim \text{Normal}(0, 1)$. But maximum likelihood estimation that allows any correlation matrix for (u_1, v_2, v_3) is complicated and less robust than procedure 19.2.

19.6.3 Binary Response Model with Sample Selection

We can estimate binary response models with sample selection if we assume that the latent errors are bivariate normal and independent of the explanatory variables. Write the model as

$$y_1 = 1[\mathbf{x}_1\boldsymbol{\beta}_1 + u_1 > 0] \tag{19.61}$$

$$y_2 = 1[\mathbf{x}\boldsymbol{\delta}_2 + v_2 > 0], \tag{19.62}$$

where the second equation is the sample selection equation and y_1 is observed only when $y_2 = 1$; we assume that $\mathbf{x}$ is always observed. For example, suppose y_1 is an employment indicator and $\mathbf{x}_1$ contains a job training binary indicator (which we assume is exogenous), as well as other human capital and family background variables. We might lose track of some people who are eligible to participate in the program; this is an example of sample attrition. If attrition is systematically related to u_1, estimating equation (19.61) on the sample at hand can result in an inconsistent estimator of $\boldsymbol{\beta}_1$.

If we assume that (u_1, v_2) is independent of $\mathbf{x}$ with a zero-mean normal distribution (and unit variances), we can apply partial maximum likelihood. What we need is the density of y_1 conditional on $\mathbf{x}$ and $y_2 = 1$. We have essentially found this density in Chapter 15: in equation (15.55) set $\alpha_1 = 0$, replace $\mathbf{z}$ with $\mathbf{x}$, and replace $\boldsymbol{\delta}_1$ with $\boldsymbol{\beta}_1$. The parameter ρ_1 is still the correlation between u_1 and v_2. A two-step procedure can be applied: first, estimate $\boldsymbol{\delta}_2$ by probit of y_2 on $\mathbf{x}$. Then, estimate $\boldsymbol{\beta}_1$ and ρ_1 in the second stage using equation (15.55) along with $\mathrm{P}(y_1 = 0 \mid \mathbf{x}, y_2 = 1)$.

A convincing analysis requires at least one variable in $\mathbf{x}$—that is, something that determines selection—that is not also in $\mathbf{x}_1$. Otherwise, identification is off of the nonlinearities in the probit models.

Importantly, some simple strategies for "correcting" for sample selection are not valid. For example, on one hand, it is tempting to estimate the selection equation by probit and then plug the estimated inverse Mills ratio into the second-stage probit, using only the observations with $y_{i2} = 1$. There is no way to justify this as a sample selection correction. On the other hand, inserting the IMR into the second-stage probit is a legitimate test of the null hypothesis of no selection bias. One can start from equation (15.55) with $\alpha_1 = 0$, $\mathbf{z} = \mathbf{x}$, $\mathbf{z}_1 = \mathbf{x}_1$, and $\boldsymbol{\delta}_1 = \boldsymbol{\beta}_1$, which is $\mathrm{E}(y_1 \mid \mathbf{x}, y_2 = 1)$. Fixing $\boldsymbol{\delta}_2$—because we subsequently insert its probit estimate—we can compute the gradient of the mean function with respect to $(\boldsymbol{\beta}_1', \rho_1)'$, and then insert $\rho_1 = 0$ (which holds under the null). If $m(\mathbf{x}, \boldsymbol{\beta}_1, \rho_1; \boldsymbol{\delta}_2)$ denotes the mean function, then it can be shown that $\nabla_{\boldsymbol{\beta}_1} m(\mathbf{x}, \boldsymbol{\beta}_1, 0; \boldsymbol{\delta}_2) = \phi(\mathbf{x}_1\boldsymbol{\beta}_1)\mathbf{x}_1$ and $\nabla_{\rho_1} m(\mathbf{x}, \boldsymbol{\beta}_1, 0; \boldsymbol{\delta}_2) = \phi(\mathbf{x}_1\boldsymbol{\beta}_1)\lambda(\mathbf{x}\boldsymbol{\delta}_2)$, where $\lambda(\cdot)$ is the IMR. If we use these gradients in the score tests developed in Section 15.5.3, we obtain a simple score statistic for sample selection. Actually, the variable addition version of the test is simpler. In the first step, estimate $\boldsymbol{\delta}_2$ by probit of y_{i2} on $\mathbf{x}_i$, using all of the observations. (Under the null, $\hat{\boldsymbol{\delta}}_2$ is the MLE because there is no sample selection.) Construct the IMRs, $\hat{\lambda}_{i2} = \lambda(\mathbf{x}_i\hat{\boldsymbol{\delta}}_2)$. Next, using the observations for which $y_{i2} = 1$ (that is, for which y_{i1} is observed), run probit of y_{i1} on $\mathbf{x}_{i1}$, $\hat{\lambda}_{i2}$ and use the usual t statistic on $\hat{\lambda}_{i2}$ to test the null hypothesis H_0: $\rho_1 = 0$. Because the coefficient on $\hat{\lambda}_{i2}$ is zero under the null, there is no need to adjust the t statistic for the first-stage estimation; see Section 12.4.2.

Allowing for endogenous explanatory variables in equation (19.61) along with sample selection is difficult, and it is a useful area of future research.

19.6.4 An Exponential Response Function

Another nonlinear model for which it is easy to obtain a simple test for selection bias, and relatively easy to correct for sample selection bias, is the exponential response model. The mechanics are very similar to those in Section 18.5 for an exponential response function and a binary endogenous explanatory variable. In particular, we still use equation (18.48) but only for the subsample with $y_{i2} = 1$ (the selected sample). The two-step method proposed by Terza (1998), which consists of estimating a probit in the first stage followed by nonlinear regression (or a quasi-MLE, such as the Poisson or exponential), consistently estimates the parameters. A simple test of sample selection bias is obtained by adding the log of the inverse Mills ratio, $\log[\lambda(\mathbf{z}_i\hat{\boldsymbol{\delta}}_2)]$, to the exponential function, and estimating the resulting "model" by, say, the Poisson QMLE using the selected sample. The robust t statistic for $\log[\lambda(\mathbf{z}_i\hat{\boldsymbol{\delta}}_2)]$ that allows the likelihood to be misspecified is a valid test of the null hypothesis of no selection bias.

19.7 Incidental Truncation: A Tobit Selection Equation

We now study the case where more information is available on sample selection, primarily in the context of incidental truncation. In particular, we assume that selection is based on the outcome of a Tobit, rather than a probit, equation. The model in Section 19.7.1 is a special case of the model studied by Vella (1992) in the context of testing for selectivity bias.

19.7.1 Exogenous Explanatory Variables

We now consider the case where the selection equation is of the censored Tobit form. The population model is

$$y_1 = \mathbf{x}_1\boldsymbol{\beta}_1 + u_1 \tag{19.63}$$

$$y_2 = \max(0, \mathbf{x}\boldsymbol{\delta}_2 + v_2), \tag{19.64}$$

where $(\mathbf{x}, y_2)$ is always observed in the population but y_1 is observed only when $y_2 > 0$. A standard example occurs when y_1 is the log of the hourly wage offer and y_2 is weekly or annual hours of labor supply.

ASSUMPTION 19.3: (a) $(\mathbf{x}, y_2)$ is always observed in the population, but y_1 is observed only when $y_2 > 0$; (b) (u_1, v_2) is independent of $\mathbf{x}$; (c) $v_2 \sim \text{Normal}(0, \tau_2^2)$; and (d) $\mathrm{E}(u_1 \mid v_2) = \gamma_1 v_2$.

These assumptions are very similar to the assumptions for a probit selection equation. The only difference is that v_2 now has an unknown variance, since y_2 is a censored as opposed to binary variable.

Amemiya (1985) calls equations (19.63) and (19.64) the **Type III Tobit model**, but we emphasize that equation (19.63) is the structural population equation of interest and that equation (19.64) simply determines when y_1 is observed. In the labor economics example, we are interested in the wage offer equation, and equation (19.64) is a reduced-form hours equation. As with a probit selection equation, it makes no sense to define y_1 to be, say, zero, just because we do not observe y_1.

The starting point is equation (19.52), just as in the probit selection case. Now define the selection indicator as $s_2 = 1$ if $y_2 > 0$, and $s_2 = 0$ otherwise. Since s_2 is a function of $\mathbf{x}$ and v_2, it follows immediately that

$$\mathrm{E}(y_1 \mid \mathbf{x}, v_2, s_2) = \mathbf{x}_1\boldsymbol{\beta}_1 + \gamma_1 v_2. \tag{19.65}$$

This equation means that, if we could observe v_2, then an OLS regression of y_1 on $\mathbf{x}_1$, v_2 using the selected subsample would consistently estimate $(\boldsymbol{\beta}_1, \gamma_1)$, as we discussed in Section 19.4.1. While v_2 cannot be observed when $y_2 = 0$ (because when $y_2 = 0$, we only know that $v_2 \leq -\mathbf{x}\boldsymbol{\delta}_2$), for $y_2 > 0$, $v_2 = y_2 - \mathbf{x}\boldsymbol{\delta}_2$. Thus, if we knew $\boldsymbol{\delta}_2$, we would know v_2 whenever $y_2 > 0$. It seems reasonable that, because $\boldsymbol{\delta}_2$ can be consistently estimated by Tobit on the whole sample, we can replace v_2 with consistent estimates.

Procedure 19.3: (a) Estimate equation (19.64) by standard Tobit using all N observations. For $y_{i2} > 0$ (say $i = 1, 2, \ldots, N_1$), define

$$\hat{v}_{i2} = y_{i2} - \mathbf{x}_i\hat{\boldsymbol{\delta}}_2. \tag{19.66}$$

(b) Using observations for which $y_{i2} > 0$, estimate $\boldsymbol{\beta}_1$, γ_1 by the OLS regression

$$y_{i1} \text{ on } \mathbf{x}_{i1}, \hat{v}_{i2} \quad i = 1, 2, \ldots, N_1. \tag{19.67}$$

This regression produces consistent, $\sqrt{N}$-asymptotically normal estimators of $\boldsymbol{\beta}_1$ and γ_1 under assumption 19.3.

The statistic to test for selectivity bias is just the usual t statistic on $\hat{v}_{i2}$ in regression (19.67), which was suggested by Vella (1992).

It seems likely that there is an efficiency gain over procedure 19.1. If v_2 were known and we could use regression (19.67) for the entire population, there would definitely be an efficiency gain: the error variance is reduced by conditioning on v_2 along with $\mathbf{x}$, and there would be no heteroskedasticity in the population. See problem 4.5.

Unlike in the probit selection case, $\mathbf{x}_1 = \mathbf{x}$ causes no problems here: v_2 always has separate variation from $\mathbf{x}_1$ because of variation in y_2. We do not need to rely on the nonlinearity of the inverse Mills ratio.

Example 19.8 (Wage Offer Equation for Married Women): We now apply procedure 19.3 to the wage offer equation for married women in example 19.6. (We assume education is exogenous.) The only difference is that the first-step estimation is Tobit, rather than probit, and we include the Tobit residuals as the additional explanatory variables, not the inverse Mills ratio. In regression (19.67), the coefficient on $\hat{v}_2$ is $-.000053$ (se $= .000041$), which is somewhat more evidence of a sample selection problem, but we still do not reject the null hypothesis H_0: $\gamma_1 = 0$ at even the 15 percent level against a two-sided alternative. Further, the coefficient on *educ* is .103 (se $= .015$), which is not much different from the OLS and Heckit estimates. (Again, we use the usual OLS standard error.) When we include all exogenous variables in the wage offer equation, the estimates from procedure 19.3 are much more stable than the Heckit estimates. For example, the coefficient on *educ* becomes .093 (se $= .016$), which is comparable to the OLS estimates discussed in example 19.6.

For partial maximum likelihood estimation, we assume that (u_1, v_2) is jointly normal, and we use the density for $f(y_2 \mid \mathbf{x})$ for the entire sample and the conditional density $f(y_1 \mid \mathbf{x}, y_2, s_2 = 1) = f(y_1 \mid \mathbf{x}, y_2)$ for the selected sample. This approach is fairly straightforward because, when $y_2 > 0$, $y_1 \mid \mathbf{x}, y_2 \sim \text{Normal}[\mathbf{x}_1\boldsymbol{\beta}_1 + \gamma_1(y_2 - \mathbf{x}\boldsymbol{\delta}_2), \eta_1^2]$, where $\eta_1^2 = \sigma_1^2 - \sigma_{12}^2/\tau_2^2$, $\sigma_1^2 = \text{Var}(u_1)$, and $\sigma_{12} = \text{Cov}(u_1, v_2)$. The log likelihood for observation i is

$$\ell_i(\boldsymbol{\theta}) = s_{i2} \log f(y_{i1} \mid \mathbf{x}_i, y_{i2}; \boldsymbol{\theta}) + \log f(y_{i2} \mid \mathbf{x}_i; \boldsymbol{\delta}_2, \tau_2^2), \tag{19.68}$$

where $f(y_{i1} \mid \mathbf{x}_i, y_{i2}; \boldsymbol{\theta})$ is the $\text{Normal}[\mathbf{x}_{i1}\boldsymbol{\beta}_1 + \gamma_1(y_{i2} - \mathbf{x}_i\boldsymbol{\delta}_2), \eta_1^2]$ distribution, evaluated at y_{i1}, and $f(y_{i2} \mid \mathbf{x}_i; \boldsymbol{\delta}_2, \tau_2^2)$ is the standard censored Tobit density (see equation (17.19)). As shown in problem 13.7, the usual MLE theory can be used even though the log-likelihood function is not based on a full conditional density.

It is possible to obtain sample selection corrections and tests for various other nonlinear models when the selection rule is of the Tobit form. For example, suppose that the binary variable y_1 given $\mathbf{z}$ follows a probit model, but it is observed only when $y_2 > 0$. A valid test for selection bias is to include the Tobit residuals, $\hat{v}_2$, in a probit of y_1 on $\mathbf{z}$, $\hat{v}_2$ using the selected sample; see Vella (1992). This procedure also produces consistent estimates (up to scale), as can be seen by applying the maximum likelihood results in Section 19.4.2 along with two-step estimation results.

Honoré, Kyriazidou, and Udry (1997) show how to estimate the parameters of the Type III Tobit model without making distributional assumptions.

19.7.2 Endogenous Explanatory Variables

We explicitly consider the case of a single endogenous explanatory variable, as in Section 19.6.2. We use equations (19.56) and (19.57), and, in place of equation (19.58), we have a Tobit selection equation:

$$y_3 = \max(0, \mathbf{z}\boldsymbol{\delta}_3 + v_3). \tag{19.69}$$

Assumption 19.4: (a) $(\mathbf{z}, y_3)$ is always observed, (y_1, y_2) is observed when $y_3 > 0$; (b) (u_1, v_3) is independent of $\mathbf{z}$; (c) $v_3 \sim \text{Normal}(0, \tau_3^2)$; (d) $\text{E}(u_1 \mid v_3) = \gamma_1 v_3$; and (e) $\text{E}(\mathbf{z}'v_2) = \mathbf{0}$ and, writing $\mathbf{z}\boldsymbol{\delta}_2 = \mathbf{z}_1\boldsymbol{\delta}_{21} + \mathbf{z}_2\boldsymbol{\delta}_{22}$, $\boldsymbol{\delta}_{22} \neq \mathbf{0}$.

Again, these assumptions are very similar to those used with a probit selection mechanism.

To derive an estimating equation, write

$$y_1 = \mathbf{z}_1\delta_1 + \alpha_1 y_2 + \gamma_1 v_3 + e_1, \tag{19.70}$$

where $e_1 \equiv u_1 - \mathrm{E}(u_1 \mid v_3)$. Since (e_1, v_3) is independent of $\mathbf{z}$ by assumption 19.4b, $\mathrm{E}(e_1 \mid \mathbf{z}, v_3) = 0$. From Theorem 19.1, if v_3 were observed, we could estimate equation (19.70) by 2SLS on the selected sample using instruments $(\mathbf{z}, v_3)$. As before, we can estimate v_3 when $y_3 > 0$, since $\boldsymbol{\delta}_3$ can be consistently estimated by Tobit of y_3 on $\mathbf{z}$ (using the entire sample).

Procedure 19.4: (a) Obtain $\hat{\boldsymbol{\delta}}_3$ from Tobit of y_3 on $\mathbf{z}$ using all observations. Obtain the Tobit residuals $\hat{v}_{i3} = y_{i3} - \mathbf{z}_i\hat{\boldsymbol{\delta}}_3$ for $y_{i3} > 0$.

(b) Using the selected subsample, estimate the equation

$$y_{i1} = \mathbf{z}_{i1}\boldsymbol{\delta}_1 + \alpha_1 y_{i2} + \gamma_1 \hat{v}_{i3} + error_i \tag{19.71}$$

by 2SLS, using instruments $(\mathbf{z}_i, \hat{v}_{i3})$. The estimators are $\sqrt{N}$-consistent and asymptotically normal under assumption 19.4.

Comments similar to those after procedure 19.2 hold here as well. Strictly speaking, identification really requires that $\mathbf{z}_2$ appear in the linear projection of y_2 onto $\mathbf{z}_1$, $\mathbf{z}_2$, and v_3 in the selected subpopulation. The null of no selection bias is tested using the 2SLS t statistic (or maybe its heteroskedasticity-robust version) on $\hat{v}_{i3}$. When $\gamma_1 \neq 0$, standard errors should be corrected using two-step methods.

As in the case with a probit selection equation, the endogenous variable y_2 can be continuous, discrete, a corner solution, and so on. Extending the method to multiple endogenous explanatory variables is straightforward. The only restriction is the usual one for linear models: we need enough instruments to identify the structural equation. See problem 19.9 for an application to the Mroz data.

An interesting special case of model (19.56), (19.57), and (19.69) occurs when $y_2 = y_3$. Actually, because we only use observations for which $y_3 > 0$, $y_2 = y_3^*$ is also allowed, where $y_3^* = \mathbf{z}\boldsymbol{\delta}_3 + v_3$. Either way, the variable that determines selection also appears in the structural equation. This special case could be useful when sample selection is caused by a corner solution outcome on y_3 (in which case $y_2 = y_3$ is natural) or because y_3^* is subject to data censoring (in which case $y_2 = y_3^*$ is more realistic). An example of the former occurs when y_3 is hours worked and we assume hours appears in the wage offer function. As a data-censoring example, suppose that y_1 is a measure of growth in an infant's weight starting from birth and that we observe y_1 only if the infant is brought into a clinic within three months. Naturally, birth weight depends on age, and so y_3^*—length of time between the first and second measurements, which has quantitiative meaning—appears as an explanatory variable in the equation for y_1. We have a data-censoring problem for y_3^*, which causes a sample selection problem for y_1. In this case, we would estimate a censored normal regression model for y_3 [or, possibly, $\log(y_3)$] to account for the data censoring. We would include the residuals $\hat{v}_{i3} = y_{i3} - \mathbf{z}_i\hat{\boldsymbol{\delta}}_3$ in equation (19.71) for the noncensored observations. As our extra instrument we might use distance from the child's home to the clinic.

19.7.3 Estimating Structural Tobit Equations with Sample Selection

We briefly show how a structural Tobit model can be estimated using the methods of the previous section. As an example, consider the structural labor supply model

$$\log(w^{o}) = \mathbf{z}_1\boldsymbol{\beta}_1 + u_1 \tag{19.72}$$

$$h = \max[0, \mathbf{z}_2\boldsymbol{\beta}_2 + \alpha_2 \log(w^{o}) + u_2]. \tag{19.73}$$

This system involves simultaneity and sample selection because we observe w^{o} only if $h > 0$.

The general form of the model is

$$y_1 = \mathbf{z}_1\boldsymbol{\beta}_1 + u_1 \tag{19.74}$$

$$y_2 = \max(0, \mathbf{z}_2\boldsymbol{\beta}_2 + \alpha_2 y_1 + u_2). \tag{19.75}$$

ASSUMPTION 19.5: (a) $(\mathbf{z}, y_2)$ is always observed; y_1 is observed when $y_2 > 0$; (b) (u_1, u_2) is independent of $\mathbf{z}$ with a zero-mean bivariate normal distribution; and (c) $\mathbf{z}_1$ contains at least one element whose coefficient is different from zero that is not in $\mathbf{z}_2$.

As always, it is important to see that equations (19.74) and (19.75) constitute a model describing a population. If y_1 were always observed, then equation (19.74) could be estimated by OLS. If, in addition, u_1 and u_2 were uncorrelated, equation (19.75) could be estimated by type I Tobit. Correlation between u_1 and u_2 could be handled by the methods of Section 17.5.2. Now, we require new methods, whether or not u_1 and u_2 are uncorrelated, because y_1 is not observed when $y_2 = 0$.

The restriction in assumption 19.5c is needed to identify the structural parameters $(\boldsymbol{\beta}_2, \alpha_2)$ ($\boldsymbol{\beta}_1$ is always identified). To see that this condition is needed, and for finding the reduced form for y_2, it is useful to introduce the latent variable

$$y_2^* \equiv \mathbf{z}_2\boldsymbol{\beta}_2 + \alpha_2 y_1 + u_2 \tag{19.76}$$

so that $y_2 = \max(0, y_2^*)$. If equations (19.74) and (19.76) make up the system of interest—that is, if y_1 and y_2^* are always observed—then $\boldsymbol{\beta}_1$ is identified without further restrictions, but identification of α_2 and $\boldsymbol{\beta}_2$ requires exactly assumption 19.5c. This turns out to be sufficient even when y_2 follows a Tobit model and we have nonrandom sample selection.

The reduced form for y_2^* is $y_2^* = \mathbf{z}\boldsymbol{\delta}_2 + v_2$. Therefore, we can write the reduced form of equation (19.75) as

$$y_2 = \max(0, \mathbf{z}\boldsymbol{\delta}_2 + v_2). \tag{19.77}$$

But then equations (19.74) and (19.77) constitute the model we studied in Section 17.6.1. The vector $\boldsymbol{\delta}_2$ is consistently estimated by Tobit, and $\boldsymbol{\beta}_1$ is estimated as in procedure 19.3. The only remaining issue is how to estimate the structural parameters of equation (19.75), α_2 and $\boldsymbol{\beta}_2$. In the labor supply case, these are the labor supply parameters.

Assuming identification, estimation of $(\alpha_2, \boldsymbol{\beta}_2)$ is fairly straightforward after having estimated $\boldsymbol{\beta}_1$. To see this point, write the reduced form of y_2 in terms of the structural parameters as

$$y_2 = \max[0, \mathbf{z}_2\boldsymbol{\beta}_2 + \alpha_2(\mathbf{z}_1\boldsymbol{\beta}_1) + v_2]. \tag{19.78}$$

Under joint normality of u_1 and u_2, v_2 is normally distributed. Therefore, if $\boldsymbol{\beta}_1$ were *known*, $\boldsymbol{\beta}_2$ and α_2 could be estimated by standard Tobit using $\mathbf{z}_2$ and $\mathbf{z}_1\boldsymbol{\beta}_1$ as regressors. Operationalizing this procedure requires replacing $\boldsymbol{\beta}_1$ with its consistent estimator. Thus, using all observations, $\boldsymbol{\beta}_2$ and α_2 are estimated from the Tobit equation

$$y_{i2} = \max[0, \mathbf{z}_{i2}\boldsymbol{\beta}_2 + \alpha_2(\mathbf{z}_{i1}\hat{\boldsymbol{\beta}}_1) + error_i]. \tag{19.79}$$

To summarize, we have the following:

Procedure 19.5: (a) Use procedure 19.3 to obtain $\hat{\boldsymbol{\beta}}_1$.
(b) Obtain $\hat{\boldsymbol{\beta}}_2$ and $\hat{\alpha}_2$ from the Tobit in equation (19.79).

In applying this procedure, it is important to note that the explanatory variable in equation (19.79) is $\mathbf{z}_{i1}\hat{\boldsymbol{\beta}}_1$ for all i. These are *not* the fitted values from regression (19.67), which depend on $\hat{v}_{i2}$. Also, it may be tempting to use y_{i1} in place of $\mathbf{z}_{i1}\hat{\boldsymbol{\beta}}_1$ for that part of the sample for which y_{i1} is observed. This approach is not a good idea: the estimators are inconsistent in this case.

The estimation in equation (19.79) makes it clear that the procedure fails if $\mathbf{z}_1$ does not contain at least one variable not in $\mathbf{z}_2$. If $\mathbf{z}_1$ is a subset of $\mathbf{z}_2$, then $\mathbf{z}_{i1}\hat{\boldsymbol{\beta}}_1$ is a linear combination of $\mathbf{z}_{i2}$, and so perfect multicollinearity will exist in equation (19.79).

Estimating $\text{Avar}(\hat{\alpha}_2, \hat{\boldsymbol{\beta}}_2)$ is even messier than estimating $\text{Avar}(\hat{\boldsymbol{\beta}}_1)$, since $(\hat{\alpha}_2, \hat{\boldsymbol{\beta}}_2)$ comes from a three-step procedure. Often just the usual Tobit standard errors and test statistics reported from equation (19.79) are used, even though these are not strictly valid. By setting the problem up as a large GMM problem, as illustrated in Chapter 14, correct standard errors and test statistics can be obtained. Bootstrapping can be used, too.

Under assumption 19.5, a full maximum likelihood approach is possible. In fact, the log-likelihood function can be constructed from equations (19.74) and (19.78), and it has a form very similar to equation (19.68). The only difference is that nonlinear restrictions are imposed automatically on the structural parameters. In addition to making it easy to obtain valid standard errors, MLE is desirable because it allows us to estimate $\sigma_2^2 = \text{Var}(u_2)$, which is needed to estimate average partial effects in equation (19.75).

In examples such as labor supply, it is not clear where the elements of $\mathbf{z}_1$ that are not in $\mathbf{z}_2$ might come from. One possibility is a union binary variable, if we believe that union membership increases wages (other factors accounted for) but has no effect on labor supply once wage and other factors have been controlled for. This approach would require knowing union status for people whether or not they are working in the period covered by the survey. In some studies past experience is assumed to affect wage—which it certainly does—and is assumed not to appear in the labor supply function, a tenuous assumption.

19.8 Inverse Probability Weighting for Missing Data

We now turn to a different method for correcting for general missing data problems, **inverse probability weighting (IPW)**. Compared with Heckman-type approaches, IPW applies very generally to any estimation problem that involves minimization or maximization. However, the assumptions under which IPW produces consistent estimators of the population parameters are quite different from those used in Heckman-type methods. We highlight the differences in this section, which follows the M-estimation setup in Chapter 12 and in Wooldridge (2007).

Again, we characterize missing data using a binary selection indicator, s_i. Therefore, a random draw from the population consists of $(\mathbf{w}_i, s_i)$, and all or part of $\mathbf{w}_i$ is not observed if $s_i = 0$. We are interested in estimating $\boldsymbol{\theta}_o$, the solution to the population problem

$$\min_{\theta \in \Theta} \text{E}[q(\mathbf{w}_i, \boldsymbol{\theta})], \tag{19.80}$$

where $q(\mathbf{w}, \cdot)$ is the objective function for given $\mathbf{w}$. If we use the selected sample to estimate $\boldsymbol{\theta}_o$ we solve

$$\min_{\theta \in \Theta} N^{-1} \sum_{i=1}^{N} s_i q(\mathbf{w}_i, \boldsymbol{\theta}). \tag{19.81}$$

We call the solution to this problem the *unweighted M-estimator*, $\hat{\boldsymbol{\theta}}_u$, to distinguish it from the weighted estimator that will be introduced later. We have already seen examples, particularly for the linear model, where $\hat{\boldsymbol{\theta}}_u$ is not consistent for $\boldsymbol{\theta}_o$.

Inverse probability weighting is a general approach to nonrandom sampling that dates back to Horvitz and Thompson (1952). IPW has been used more recently for regression models with missing data (for example, Robins, Rotnitzky, and Zhou 1995) and in the treatment effects literature (Hirano, Imbens, and Ridder (2003) and Chapter 21). The key is that we have some variables that are "good" predictors of selection, something we make precise in the following assumption.

ASSUMPTION 19.6: (a) The vector $\mathbf{w}_i$ is observed whenever $s_i = 1$.
(b) There is a random vector $\mathbf{z}_i$ such that $P(s_i = 1 \mid \mathbf{w}_i, \mathbf{z}_i) = P(s_i = 1 \mid \mathbf{z}_i) \equiv p(\mathbf{z}_i)$.
(c) For all $\mathbf{z} \in \mathscr{Z} \subset \mathbb{R}^J$, $p(\mathbf{z}) > 0$.
(d) $\mathbf{z}_i$ is observed when $s_i = 1$.

When $\mathbf{z}_i$ is always observed, assumption 19.6 is essentially the missing at random assumption mentioned in Section 19.4. Wooldridge (2007) shows that allowing $\mathbf{z}_i$ to be unobserved when $s_i = 0$ allows coverage of certain stratified sampling schemes, which we treat in Chapter 20, and IPW solutions to censored duration data, which we cover in Chapter 22. One also sees assumption 19.6b described as **ignorable selection** (conditional on $\mathbf{z}_i$). In the treatment effects literature—see Chapter 21—assumption 19.6b is essentially the **unconfoundedness** assumption.

Assumption 19.6 encompasses the selection on observables assumption mentioned in Section 19.4. In the general M-estimation framework, selection on observables typically applies when $\mathbf{w}_i$ partitions as $(\mathbf{x}_i, \mathbf{y}_i)$, $\mathbf{x}_i$ is always observed but $\mathbf{y}_i$ is not, and $\mathbf{z}_i$ is a vector that is always observed and includes $\mathbf{x}_i$. Then, s_i is allowed to be a function of observables $\mathbf{z}_i$, but s_i cannot be related to unobserved factors affecting $\mathbf{y}_i$. Assumption 19.6 does not apply to the selection on unobservables case, at least as that terminology has been used in econometrics. Selection on unobservables is essentially what we covered in Sections 19.5 and 19.6, where we explicitly allowed selection to be correlated with unobservables after conditioning on exogenous variables. Heckman's (1976) solution to the incidental truncation problem, which applies to linear models and a few others, requires at least one exogenous variable that affects selection but does not have a partial effect on the outcome. In assumption 19.6, the $\mathbf{z}_i$ should have properties different from exogenous variables that are used for identification in the Heckman approach. In effect, the $\mathbf{z}_i$ should be good proxies for the unobservables that affect $\mathbf{y}_i$ and also determine selection. Sometimes, $\mathbf{z}_i$ includes outcomes on $\mathbf{y}_i$ and even $\mathbf{x}_i$ from previous time periods.

As an example, consider the linear model for a random draw, $y_i = \mathbf{x}_i\boldsymbol{\beta}_o + u_i$, $\mathrm{E}(\mathbf{x}_i'u_i) = \mathbf{0}$, and suppose data are missing on y_i when $s_i = 0$. Let $\mathbf{z}_i$ be a vector of variables that includes $\mathbf{x}_i$, and, for concreteness, assume that $s_i = 1[\mathbf{z}_i\boldsymbol{\delta}_o + v_i \geq 0]$, where v_i is independent of $\mathbf{z}_i$. To use a Heckman selection correction we would assume $\mathrm{E}(\mathbf{z}_i'u_i) = \mathbf{0}$ but allow arbitrary correlation between v_i and u_i, so that selection is correlated with u_i even after netting out $\mathbf{z}_i$. By contrast, assumption 19.6b is the same as $\mathrm{P}(s_i = 1 \mid \mathbf{z}_i, u_i) = \mathrm{P}(s_i = 1 \mid \mathbf{z}_i)$, which essentially means that u_i and v_i should be independent. Thus, under assumption 19.6b, we assume that $\mathbf{z}_i$ is such a good predictor of selection that, conditional on $\mathbf{z}_i$, s_i is independent of the unobservables in the regression equation, u_i. However, $\mathbf{z}_i$ and u_i can be arbitrarily correlated.

If we could observe the selection probabilities then, under assumption 19.6, solving the missing data problem would be easy. To see why, let $g(\mathbf{w})$ be any scalar function such that the mean, $\mu = \mathrm{E}[g(\mathbf{w}_i)]$, exists. Then, using iterated expectations,

$$\begin{aligned}
\mathrm{E}[s_i g(\mathbf{w}_i)/p(\mathbf{z}_i)] &= \mathrm{E}\{\mathrm{E}[s_i g(\mathbf{w}_i)/p(\mathbf{z}_i) \mid \mathbf{w}_i, \mathbf{z}_i]\} \\
&= \mathrm{E}\{\mathrm{E}(s_i \mid \mathbf{w}_i, \mathbf{z}_i) g(\mathbf{w}_i)/p(\mathbf{z}_i)\} \\
&= \mathrm{E}\{\mathrm{P}(s_i = 1 \mid \mathbf{w}_i, \mathbf{z}_i) g(\mathbf{w}_i)/p(\mathbf{z}_i)\} \\
&= \mathrm{E}\{p(\mathbf{z}_i) g(\mathbf{w}_i)/p(\mathbf{z}_i)\} = \mathrm{E}[g(\mathbf{w}_i)], \qquad (19.82)
\end{aligned}$$

where the last equality follows from $\mathrm{P}(s_i = 1 \mid \mathbf{w}_i, \mathbf{z}_i) = p(\mathbf{z}_i)$. This result shows that the population mean of any function of $\mathbf{w}_i$ can be recovered by weighting the selected observation by the inverse of the probability of selection. It follows immediately that a consistent (actually, unbiased) estimator of μ is $N^{-1}\sum_{i=1}^{n}[s_i g(\mathbf{w}_i)/p(\mathbf{z}_i)]$. Actually, a somewhat more common estimator, based on the fact that $\mathrm{E}[s_i/p(\mathbf{z}_i)] = 1$, is

$$\hat{\mu}_{IPW} = \left(\sum_{i=1}^{N}[s_i/p(\mathbf{z}_i)]\right)^{-1}\left(\sum_{i=1}^{N}[s_i g(\mathbf{w}_i)/p(\mathbf{z}_i)]\right), \qquad (19.83)$$

which is a weighted average of the sampled data where the weights add to one. While equation (19.83) appears to depend on N (the number of times the population was sampled), N is not needed to compute $\hat{\mu}_{IPW}$. The sampling weights implicit in equation (19.83) are often reported in survey data to obtain means in the presence of missing data.

We can now see how to use IPW estimation in the context of M-estimation. The IPW estimator, $\tilde{\boldsymbol{\theta}}_w$, solves

$$\min_{\theta \in \Theta} N^{-1}\sum_{i=1}^{N}[s_i/p(\mathbf{z}_i)]q(\mathbf{w}_i, \boldsymbol{\theta}). \qquad (19.84)$$

From the previous argument, the mean of each summand is $\mathrm{E}[q(\mathbf{w}_i, \boldsymbol{\theta})]$, which is minimized at $\boldsymbol{\theta}_o$, and so, under the mild conditions of the uniform weak law of large numbers, $\tilde{\boldsymbol{\theta}}_w$ is consistent for $\boldsymbol{\theta}_o$; see Theorem 12.2.

In most cases where the selection probabilities $p(\mathbf{z}_i)$ are not known, $\mathbf{z}_i$ is assumed to be always observed, so that a model for $\mathrm{P}(s_i = 1 \mid \mathbf{z}_i)$ can be estimated by binary response maximum likelihood. Here we consider the case where we use a binary response model for $\mathrm{P}(s_i = 1 \mid \mathbf{z}_i)$, which requires that $\mathbf{z}_i$ is always observed.

ASSUMPTION 19.7: (a) $G(\mathbf{z}, \gamma)$ is a parametric model for $p(\mathbf{z})$, where $\gamma \in \boldsymbol{\Gamma} \subset \mathbb{R}^M$ and $G(\mathbf{z}, \gamma) > 0$, all $\mathbf{z}$ and γ.

(b) There there exists $\gamma_o \in \boldsymbol{\Gamma}$ such that $p(\mathbf{z}) = G(\mathbf{z}, \gamma_o)$.

(c) $\hat{\gamma}$ is the binary response maximum likelihood estimator, and the regularity conditions for MLE hold such that

$$\sqrt{N}(\hat{\gamma} - \gamma_o) = \{\mathrm{E}[\mathbf{d}_i(\gamma_o)\mathbf{d}_i(\gamma_o)']\}^{-1}\left(N^{-1/2}\sum_{i=1}^{N}\mathbf{d}_i(\gamma_o)\right) + o_p(1), \tag{19.85}$$

where $\mathbf{d}_i(\gamma) \equiv \nabla_\gamma G(\mathbf{z}, \gamma)'[s_i - G(\mathbf{z}, \gamma)]/\{G(\mathbf{z}, \gamma)[1 - G(\mathbf{z}, \gamma)]\}$ is the $M \times 1$ score vector for the MLE.

Given $\hat{\gamma}$, we can form $G(\mathbf{z}_i, \hat{\gamma})$ for all i with $s_i = 1$, and then obtain the *weighted M-estimator*, $\hat{\boldsymbol{\theta}}_w$, by solving

$$\min_{\theta \in \Theta} N^{-1}\sum_{i=1}^{N}[s_i/G(\mathbf{z}_i, \hat{\gamma})]q(\mathbf{w}_i, \boldsymbol{\theta}). \tag{19.86}$$

Replacing the unknown probability $p(\mathbf{z}) = G(\mathbf{z}, \gamma_o)$ with $G(\mathbf{z}_i, \hat{\gamma})$ does not affect consistency of $\hat{\boldsymbol{\theta}}_w$ under the general conditions for two-step estimators; see Section 12.4.1. More interesting is finding the asymptotic distribution of $\sqrt{N}(\hat{\boldsymbol{\theta}}_w - \boldsymbol{\theta}_o)$.

The following result assumes that the objective function $q(\mathbf{w}, \cdot)$ is twice continuously differentiable on the interior of $\boldsymbol{\Theta}$, as in Section 13.10.2. Write $\mathbf{r}(\mathbf{w}_i, \boldsymbol{\theta}) \equiv \nabla_\theta q(\mathbf{w}_i, \boldsymbol{\theta})'$ as the $P \times 1$ score of the unweighted objective function, $\mathbf{H}(\mathbf{w}, \boldsymbol{\theta}) \equiv \nabla_\theta^2 q(\mathbf{w}, \boldsymbol{\theta})$ as the $P \times P$ Hessian of $q(\mathbf{w}_i, \boldsymbol{\theta})$, and $k(s_i, \mathbf{z}_i, \mathbf{w}_i, \gamma, \boldsymbol{\theta}) \equiv [s_i/G(\mathbf{z}_i, \gamma)]r(\mathbf{w}_i, \boldsymbol{\theta})$ as the selected, weighted score function; in particular, $k(s_i, \mathbf{z}_i, \mathbf{w}_i, \gamma, \boldsymbol{\theta})$ is zero whenever $s_i = 0$.

It is easily shown that the conditions of the "surprising" efficiency result in Section 13.10.2 hold. Therefore,

$$\sqrt{N}(\hat{\boldsymbol{\theta}}_w - \boldsymbol{\theta}_o) \overset{a}{\sim} \mathrm{Normal}(0, \mathbf{A}_o^{-1}\mathbf{D}_o\mathbf{A}_o^{-1}), \tag{19.87}$$

where $\mathbf{A}_o \equiv \mathrm{E}[\mathbf{H}(\mathbf{w}_i, \boldsymbol{\theta}_o)]$, $\mathbf{D}_o \equiv \mathrm{E}(\mathbf{e}_i\mathbf{e}_i')$, $\mathbf{e}_i \equiv \mathbf{k}_i - \mathrm{E}(\mathbf{k}_i\mathbf{d}_i')[\mathrm{E}(\mathbf{d}_i\mathbf{d}_i')]^{-1}\mathbf{d}_i$, and $\mathbf{k}_i$ and $\mathbf{d}_i$ are evaluated at $(\boldsymbol{\gamma}_o, \boldsymbol{\theta}_o)$ and $\boldsymbol{\gamma}_o$, respectively. Further, consistent estimators of $\mathbf{A}_o$ and $\mathbf{D}_o$, respectively, are

$$\hat{\mathbf{A}} \equiv N^{-1}\sum_{i=1}^{N}[s_i/G(\mathbf{z}_i, \hat{\boldsymbol{\gamma}})]\mathbf{H}(\mathbf{w}_i, \hat{\boldsymbol{\theta}}_w) \tag{19.88}$$

and

$$\hat{\mathbf{D}} \equiv N^{-1}\sum_{i=1}^{N}\hat{\mathbf{e}}_i\hat{\mathbf{e}}_i', \tag{19.89}$$

where the $\hat{\mathbf{e}}_i \equiv \hat{\mathbf{k}}_i - (N^{-1}\sum_{i=1}^{N}\hat{\mathbf{k}}_i\hat{\mathbf{d}}_i')(N^{-1}\sum_{i=1}^{N}\hat{\mathbf{d}}_i\hat{\mathbf{d}}_i')^{-1}\hat{\mathbf{d}}_i$ are the $P \times 1$ residuals from the multivariate regression of $\hat{\mathbf{k}}_i$ on $\hat{\mathbf{d}}_i$, $i = 1, \ldots, N$, and all hatted quantities are evaluated at $\hat{\boldsymbol{\gamma}}$ or $\hat{\boldsymbol{\theta}}_w$. The asymptotic variance of $\hat{\boldsymbol{\theta}}_w$ is consistently estimated as $\hat{\mathbf{A}}^{-1}\hat{\mathbf{D}}\hat{\mathbf{A}}^{-1}/N$.

We can compare expression (19.87) with the asymptotic variance that we would obtain by using a known value of $\boldsymbol{\gamma}_o$ in place of the conditional MLE, $\hat{\boldsymbol{\gamma}}$. As before, let $\tilde{\boldsymbol{\theta}}_w$ denote the estimator that uses $1/G(\mathbf{z}_i, \boldsymbol{\gamma}_o)$ as the weights. Then

$$\sqrt{N}(\tilde{\boldsymbol{\theta}}_w - \boldsymbol{\theta}_o) \overset{a}{\sim} \mathrm{Normal}(0, \mathbf{A}_o^{-1}\mathbf{B}_o\mathbf{A}_o^{-1}), \tag{19.90}$$

where $\mathbf{B}_o \equiv \mathrm{E}(\mathbf{k}_i\mathbf{k}_i')$. Because $\mathbf{B}_o - \mathbf{D}_o$ is positive semidefinite, $\mathrm{Avar}\,\sqrt{N}(\tilde{\boldsymbol{\theta}}_w - \boldsymbol{\theta}_o) - \mathrm{Avar}\,\sqrt{N}(\hat{\boldsymbol{\theta}}_w - \boldsymbol{\theta}_o)$ is positive semidefinite.

As an example, consider the linear regression model $y = \mathbf{x}\boldsymbol{\beta}_o + u$, $\mathrm{E}(\mathbf{x}'u) = \mathbf{0}$, and suppose the estimated probabilities $\hat{p}_i = G(\mathbf{z}_i, \hat{\boldsymbol{\gamma}})$ are from a logit estimation. The gradient for the logit estimation is $\hat{\mathbf{d}}_i' = \mathbf{z}_i[s_i - \Lambda(\mathbf{z}_i, \hat{\boldsymbol{\gamma}})]$, a $1 \times M$ vector (the dimension of $\mathbf{z}_i$, which includes a constant). The selected, weighted gradient for the linear regression problem is $\hat{\mathbf{k}}_i' = s_i\mathbf{x}_i\hat{u}_i/\hat{p}_i$, where $\hat{u}_i = y_i - \mathbf{x}_i\hat{\boldsymbol{\beta}}_w$ are the residuals after the IPW estimation. The adjustment to the asymptotic variance is obtained by getting the (row) residuals $\hat{\mathbf{e}}_i'$ from the regression $s_i\mathbf{x}_i\hat{u}_i/\hat{p}_i$ on $\mathbf{z}_i[s_i - \Lambda(\mathbf{z}_i, \hat{\boldsymbol{\gamma}})]$ using all observations. Then, $\hat{\mathbf{D}}$ is constructed as in expression (19.90), and, in this case, $\hat{\mathbf{A}} \equiv N^{-1}\sum_{i=1}^{N}(s_i/\hat{p}_i)\mathbf{x}_i'\mathbf{x}_i$. The asymptotic variance of $\hat{\boldsymbol{\beta}}_w$ is estimated as

$$\left[\sum_{i=1}^{N}(s_i/\hat{p}_i)\mathbf{x}_i'\mathbf{x}_i\right]^{-1}\left(\sum_{i=1}^{N}\hat{\mathbf{e}}_i\hat{\mathbf{e}}_i'\right)\left[\sum_{i=1}^{N}(s_i/\hat{p}_i)\mathbf{x}_i'\mathbf{x}_i\right]^{-1}. \tag{19.91}$$

The conservative estimate would replace $\hat{\mathbf{e}}_i$ with $s_i\mathbf{x}_i'\hat{u}_i/\hat{p}_i$, in which case the estimator looks just like a "heteroskedasticity"-robust sandwich estimator in the context of weighted least squares.

As with all general efficiency results, the conclusion that a difference in asymptotic variances is positive semidefinite does not guarantee an efficiency gain in particular cases: the statement includes the possibility that there is no difference in the asymptotic variances.

One case where there is no efficiency gain from using the estimated probabilities occurs when the missing data mechanism is, in a particular sense, exogenous. Consider the linear regression model. If we impose the assumption

$$\mathrm{E}(u \mid \mathbf{x}, \mathbf{z}) = 0, \tag{19.92}$$

which now means that $\mathrm{E}(y \mid \mathbf{x}, \mathbf{z}) = \mathrm{E}(y \mid \mathbf{x}) = \mathbf{x}\boldsymbol{\beta}$, and $\mathrm{P}(s = 1 \mid \mathbf{x}, y, \mathbf{z}) = \mathrm{P}(s = 1 \mid \mathbf{z})$, then the asymptotic variance is given by expression (19.90) whether or not we estimate the weights. Further, the probability weights can come from a misspecified estimation problem without affecting consistency. For maximum likelihood problems, the exogeneity condition is $\mathrm{D}(y \mid \mathbf{x}, \mathbf{z}) = \mathrm{D}(y \mid \mathbf{x})$. An important situation where this condition and assumption (19.92) hold occurs when $\mathbf{z} = \mathbf{x}$ and the model for $\mathrm{D}(y \mid \mathbf{x})$ or $\mathrm{E}(y \mid \mathbf{x})$ is correctly specified; the exogeneity condition on selection is $\mathrm{P}(s = 1 \mid \mathbf{x}, y) = \mathrm{P}(s = 1 \mid \mathbf{x})$.

Not surprisingly, in the general case of exogenous sampling, the unweighted estimator is also consistent. Along with assumption 19.6b, we generally define exogenous selection in the context of M-estimation as follows. Assume $\boldsymbol{\theta}_o$ satisfies

$$\boldsymbol{\theta}_o = \underset{\boldsymbol{\theta} \in \boldsymbol{\Theta}}{\operatorname{argmin}}\ \mathrm{E}[q(\mathbf{w}, \boldsymbol{\theta}) \mid \mathbf{z}] \tag{19.93}$$

for all outcomes $\mathbf{z}$. This requirement may seem abstract, but it holds for the usual estimation methods when the appropriate underlying feature of the conditional distribution is correctly specified and $\mathbf{z}$ is exogenous in the model. For example, for nonlinear least squares and quasi-MLE in the linear exponential family, assumption (19.93) holds whenever $\mathrm{E}(y \mid \mathbf{x}, \mathbf{z}) = \mathrm{E}(y \mid \mathbf{x})$ and the latter is correctly specified. This condition holds for conditional MLE, too.

Wooldridge (2007, Theorem 4.3) shows that, under exogenous sampling, the unweighted estimator is more efficient than the weighted estimator under a version of the conditional information matrix equality. Generally, the condition is stated as

$$\mathrm{E}[\nabla_{\theta} q(\mathbf{w}, \boldsymbol{\theta}_o)' \nabla_{\theta} q(\mathbf{w}, \boldsymbol{\theta}_o) \mid \mathbf{z}] = \sigma_o^2 \mathrm{E}[\nabla_{\theta}^2 q(\mathbf{w}, \boldsymbol{\theta}_o) \mid \mathbf{z}], \tag{19.94}$$

which holds under assumption (19.93) under suitable regularity conditions for correctly specified CMLE, nonlinear least squares under homoskedasticity, and quasi-MLE under the assumption that the GLM variance assumption holds. The usual nonrobust variance matrix estimators on the selected sample are valid. See Wooldridge (2007) for further discussion.

The previous results help to inform the decision of when weighting should and should not be used. If features of an unconditional distribution, say $\mathrm{D}(\mathbf{w})$, are of interest, unweighted estimators consistently estimate the parameters only if $\mathrm{P}(s = 1 \mid \mathbf{w}) = \mathrm{P}(s = 1)$—that is, the data are **missing completely at random** (Rubin, 1976). Of course, consistency of the weighted estimator relies on the presence of $\mathbf{z}$ such that $\mathrm{P}(s = 1 \mid \mathbf{w}, \mathbf{z}) = \mathrm{P}(s = 1 \mid \mathbf{z})$, but maintaining such an assumption is often one's only recourse.

The decision to weight is more subtle when we begin with the premise that some feature of a conditional distribution, $\mathrm{D}(\mathbf{y} \mid \mathbf{x})$, is of interest. Wooldridge (2007) describes several scenarios concerning both consistent estimation and efficient estimation. Here, we briefly discuss a problem that can arise with weighting if data are missing on some of the conditioning variables, $\mathbf{x}$. The issue arises because, in general, if data are missing on elements of $\mathbf{x}$—due to attrition, say, or nonresponse—these elements generally cannot be included in the selection predictors, $\mathbf{z}$. But then suppose that selection is entirely a function of $\mathbf{x}$: $\mathrm{P}(s = 1 \mid \mathbf{x}, \mathbf{y}) = \mathrm{P}(s = 1 \mid \mathbf{x})$ (even though elements of $\mathbf{x}$ are not observed). Then the unweighted estimator is consistent if (the feature of) $\mathrm{D}(\mathbf{y} \mid \mathbf{x})$ is correctly specified. Generally, if $\mathbf{z}$ omits any element of $\mathbf{x}$, the weighted estimator would actually be inconsistent. In effect, the wrong weights are used because the condition $\mathrm{P}(s = 1 \mid \mathbf{x}, \mathbf{y}, \mathbf{z}) = \mathrm{P}(s = 1 \mid \mathbf{z})$ cannot hold. See Wooldridge (2007) for additional discussion.

When $\mathbf{z}$ can be chosen to include $\mathbf{x}$, the case for weighting is much stronger: if selection does depend only on $\mathbf{x}$, that fact will be picked up in large enough samples if the model for $\mathrm{P}(s = 1 \mid \mathbf{z})$ is sufficiently flexible. Although this approach covers the case of treatment effects estimation—see Chapter 21—it does not cover general missing data problems. Therefore, one has to be cautious when using IPW when some conditioning variables are missing: important differences between the weighted and unweighted estimates cannot necessarily be attributed to a problem with the unweighted estimator, and we can never know why the two estimates are different (unless we have access to a random sample).

When the selection probabilities reflect stratified sampling and are determined from the sample design, the case for weighting is also stronger; see Chapter 20.

19.9 Sample Selection and Attrition in Linear Panel Data Models

In our treatment of panel data models we have assumed that a balanced panel is available—each cross section unit has the same time periods available. Often, some time periods are missing for some units in the population of interest, and we are left with an **unbalanced panel**. Unbalanced panels can arise for several reasons. First, the survey design may simply rotate people or firms out of the sample based on prespecified rules. For example, if a survey of individuals begins at time $t = 1$, at time $t = 2$ some of the original people may be dropped and new people added. At $t = 3$ some additional people might be dropped and others added; and so on. This is an example of a **rotating panel**.

Provided the decision to rotate units out of a panel is made randomly, unbalanced panels are fairly easy to deal with, as we will see shortly. A more complicated problem arises when attrition from a panel is due to units electing to drop out. If this decision is based on factors that are systematically related to the response variable, even after we condition on explanatory variables, a sample selection problem can result—just as in the cross section case. Nevertheless, a panel data set provides us with the means to handle, in a simple fashion, attrition that is based on a time-constant, unobserved effect, provided we use first-differencing methods; we show this in Section 19.9.3.

A different kind of sample selection problem occurs when people do not disappear from the panel but certain variables are unobserved for at least some time periods. This is the incidental truncation problem discussed in Section 19.6. A leading case is estimating a wage offer equation using a panel of individuals. Even if the population of interest is people who are employed in the initial year, some people will become unemployed in subsequent years. For those people we cannot observe a wage offer, just as in the cross-sectional case. This situation is different from the attrition problem where people leave the sample entirely and, usually, do not reappear in later years. In the incidental truncation case we observe some variables on everyone in each time period.

19.9.1 Fixed and Random Effects Estimation with Unbalanced Panels

We begin by studying assumptions under which the usual fixed effects estimator on the unbalanced panel is consistent. The model is the usual linear, unobserved effects model under random sampling in the cross section: for any i,

$$y_{it} = \mathbf{x}_{it}\boldsymbol{\beta} + c_i + u_{it}, \qquad t = 1, \ldots, T \tag{19.95}$$

where $\mathbf{x}_{it}$ is $1 \times K$ and $\boldsymbol{\beta}$ is the $K \times 1$ vector of interest. As before, we assume that N cross section observations are available and the asymptotic analysis is as $N \to \infty$. We first cover the case where c_i is allowed to be correlated with $\mathbf{x}_{it}$, so that all elements of $\mathbf{x}_{it}$ are time varying.

We treated the case where all T time periods are available in Chapters 10 and 11. Now we consider the case where some time periods might be missing for some of the cross section draws. Think of $t = 1$ as the first time period for which data on anyone in the population are available, and $t = T$ as the last possible time period. For a random draw i from the population, let $\mathbf{s}_i \equiv (s_{i1}, \ldots, s_{iT})'$ denote the $T \times 1$ vector of selection indicators: $s_{it} = 1$ if $(\mathbf{x}_{it}, y_{it})$ is observed, and zero otherwise. Generally, we have an unbalanced panel. We can treat $\{(\mathbf{x}_i, \mathbf{y}_i, \mathbf{s}_i): i = 1, 2, \ldots, N\}$ as a random sample from the population; the selection indicators tell us which time periods are missing for each i.

We can easily find assumptions under which the fixed effects estimator on the unbalanced panel is consistent by writing it as

$$\hat{\boldsymbol{\beta}} = \left(N^{-1} \sum_{i=1}^{N} \sum_{t=1}^{T} s_{it} \ddot{\mathbf{x}}_{it}' \ddot{\mathbf{x}}_{it} \right)^{-1} \left(N^{-1} \sum_{i=1}^{N} \sum_{t=1}^{T} s_{it} \ddot{\mathbf{x}}_{it}' \ddot{y}_{it} \right)$$

$$= \boldsymbol{\beta} + \left(N^{-1} \sum_{i=1}^{N} \sum_{t=1}^{T} s_{it} \ddot{\mathbf{x}}_{it}' \ddot{\mathbf{x}}_{it} \right)^{-1} \left(N^{-1} \sum_{i=1}^{N} \sum_{t=1}^{T} s_{it} \ddot{\mathbf{x}}_{it}' u_{it} \right), \tag{19.96}$$

where we define

$$\ddot{\mathbf{x}}_{it} \equiv \mathbf{x}_{it} - T_i^{-1} \sum_{r=1}^{T} s_{ir} \mathbf{x}_{ir}, \qquad \ddot{y}_{it} \equiv y_{it} - T_i^{-1} \sum_{r=1}^{T} s_{ir} y_{ir}, \qquad \text{and} \qquad T_i \equiv \sum_{t=1}^{T} s_{it}$$

That is, T_i is the number of time periods observed for cross section i, and we apply the within transformation on the available time periods.

If fixed effects on the unbalanced panel is to be consistent, we should have $\mathrm{E}(s_{it} \ddot{\mathbf{x}}_{it}' u_{it}) = 0$ for all t. Now, since $\ddot{\mathbf{x}}_{it}$ depends on all of $\mathbf{x}_i$ and $\mathbf{s}_i$, a form of strict exogeneity is needed.

Assumption 19.8: (a) $\mathrm{E}(u_{it} \mid \mathbf{x}_i, \mathbf{s}_i, c_i) = 0$, $t = 1, 2, \ldots, T$; (b) $\sum_{t=1}^{T} \mathrm{E}(s_{it} \ddot{\mathbf{x}}_{it}' \ddot{\mathbf{x}}_{it})$ is nonsingular; and (c) $\mathrm{E}(\mathbf{u}_i \mathbf{u}_i' \mid \mathbf{x}_i, \mathbf{s}_i, c_i) = \sigma_u^2 \mathbf{I}_T$.

Under assumption 19.8a, $\mathrm{E}(s_{it} \ddot{\mathbf{x}}_{it}' u_{it}) = \mathbf{0}$ from the law of iterated expectations (because $s_{it} \ddot{\mathbf{x}}_{it}$ is a function of $(\mathbf{x}_i, \mathbf{s}_i)$). The second assumption is the rank condition on the expected outer product matrix, after accounting for sample selection; naturally, it rules out time-constant elements in $\mathbf{x}_{it}$. These first two assumptions ensure consistency of FE on the unbalanced panel.

In the case of a randomly rotating panel, and in other cases where selection is entirely random, $\mathbf{s}_i$ is independent of $(\mathbf{u}_i, \mathbf{x}_i, c_i)$, in which case assumption 19.8a follows under the standard fixed effects assumption $\mathrm{E}(u_{it} \mid \mathbf{x}_i, c_i) = 0$ for all t. In this case, the natural assumptions on the population model imply consistency and asymptotic normality on the unbalanced panel. Assumption 19.8a also holds under much weaker conditions. In particular, it does not assume anything about the relationship between $\mathbf{s}_i$ and $(\mathbf{x}_i, c_i)$. Therefore, if we think selection in all time periods is correlated with c_i or $\mathbf{x}_i$, but that u_{it} is mean independent of $\mathbf{s}_i$ given $(\mathbf{x}_i, c_i)$ for all t, then FE on the unbalanced panel is consistent and asymptotically normal. This assumption may be a reasonable approximation, especially for short panels. What assumption 19.8a rules out is selection that is partially correlated with the idiosyncratic errors, u_{it}.

When we add assumption 19.8c, standard inference procedures based on FE are valid. In particular, under assumptions 19.8a and 19.8c,

$$\mathrm{Var}\left(\sum_{t=1}^{T} s_{it}\ddot{\mathbf{x}}_{it}' u_{it}\right) = \sigma_u^2 \left[\sum_{t=1}^{T} \mathrm{E}(s_{it}\ddot{\mathbf{x}}_{it}'\ddot{\mathbf{x}}_{it})\right].$$

Therefore, the asymptotic variance of the fixed effects estimator is estimated as

$$\hat{\sigma}_u^2 \left(\sum_{i=1}^{N}\sum_{t=1}^{T} s_{it}\ddot{\mathbf{x}}_{it}'\ddot{\mathbf{x}}_{it}\right)^{-1}. \tag{19.97}$$

The estimator $\hat{\sigma}_u^2$ can be derived from

$$\mathrm{E}\left(\sum_{t=1}^{T} s_{it}\ddot{u}_{it}^2\right) = \mathrm{E}\left[\sum_{t=1}^{T} s_{it}\mathrm{E}(\ddot{u}_{it}^2 \mid \mathbf{s}_i)\right] = \mathrm{E}\{T_i[\sigma_u^2(1 - 1/T_i)]\} = \sigma_u^2 \mathrm{E}[(T_i - 1)].$$

Now, define the FE residuals as $\hat{u}_{it} = \ddot{y}_{it} - \ddot{\mathbf{x}}_{it}\hat{\boldsymbol{\beta}}$ when $s_{it} = 1$. Then, because $N^{-1}\sum_{i=1}^{N}(T_i - 1) \xrightarrow{p} \mathrm{E}(T_i - 1)$,

$$\hat{\sigma}_u^2 = \left[N^{-1}\sum_{i=1}^{N}(T_i - 1)\right]^{-1} N^{-1}\sum_{i=1}^{N}\sum_{t=1}^{T} s_{it}\hat{u}_{it}^2 = \left[\sum_{i=1}^{N}(T_i - 1)\right]^{-1} \sum_{i=1}^{N}\sum_{t=1}^{T} s_{it}\hat{u}_{it}^2$$

is consistent for σ_u^2 as $N \to \infty$. Standard software packages also make a degrees-of-freedom adjustment by subtracting K from $\sum_{i=1}^{N}(T_i - 1)$. It follows that all of the usual test statistics based on an unbalanced fixed effects analysis are valid. In particular, the dummy variable regression discussed in Chapter 10 produces asymptotically valid statistics.

Because the FE estimator uses time demeaning, any unit i for which $T_i = 1$ drops out of the fixed effects estimator. To use these observations we would need to add more assumptions, such as the random effects assumption $\mathrm{E}(c_i \mid \mathbf{x}_i, \mathbf{s}_i) = 0$.

Relaxing assumption 19.8c is easy: just apply the robust variance matrix estimator in equation (10.59) to the unbalanced panel. The only changes are that the rows of $\ddot{\mathbf{X}}_i$ are $s_{it}\ddot{\mathbf{x}}_{it}$ and the elements of $\ddot{\mathbf{u}}_i$ are $s_{it}\ddot{u}_{it}$, $t = 1, \dots, T$.

Under assumption 19.8, it is also valid to used a standard fixed effects analysis on any balanced subset of the unbalanced panel; in fact, we can condition on any outcomes of the s_{it}. For example, if we use unit i only when observations are available in all time periods, we are conditioning on $s_{it} = 1$ for all t. Comparing FE on the unbalanced panel with FE on a balanced panel is a sensible specification check.

Using similar arguments, it can be shown that any kind of differencing method on any subset of the observed panel is consistent. For example, with $T = 3$, we observe cross section units with data for one, two, or three time periods. Those units with $T_i = 1$ drop out, but any other combinations of differences can be used in a pooled OLS analysis. The analogues of assumption 19.8 for first differencing—for example, assumption 19.8c is replaced with $\mathrm{E}(\Delta\mathbf{u}_i\Delta\mathbf{u}_i' \mid \mathbf{x}_i, \mathbf{s}_i, c_i) = \sigma_e^2\mathbf{I}_{T-1}$—ensure that the usual statistics from pooled OLS on the unbalanced first differences are asymptotically valid.

Random effects estimation on an unbalanced panel is somewhat more complicated because of the GLS transformation, and its consistency hinges on stronger assumptions concerning the selection mechanism. In addition to a rank condition, the key extra requirement (compared with FE) is

$$\mathrm{E}(c_i \mid \mathbf{x}_i, \mathbf{s}_i) = \mathrm{E}(c_i), \tag{19.98}$$

so that the heterogeneity is mean independent of the covariates and selection in all time periods. Assumption (19.98) is generally very restrictive. It does allow for units being randomly rotated in and out of a panel or for rotation to depend on the observed factors in $\mathbf{x}_{it}$.

A careful analysis of GLS estimation with unbalanced panels is notationally cumbersome when we explicitly introduce the selection indicators. Nevertheless, the description of the random effects estimator is easy to describe because of the "exchangeable" nature of the random effects covariance structure. In particular, under assumption RE.3 from Section 10.4 (for the balanced case), the covariance between any two time periods is the same. Along with the assumption of constant variance over time, this leads to a straightforward GLS transformation. In the balanced case, the data are quasi-time-demeaned using (an estimate of) the parameter $\lambda = 1 - [\sigma_u^2/(\sigma_u^2 + T\sigma_c^2)]^{1/2}$; see Section 10.7.2. For the unbalanced case, where selection is exogenous in the sense of assumption (19.98), quasi-time-demeaned applies, but the parameter depends on i, namely,

$$\lambda_i = 1 - [\sigma_u^2/(\sigma_u^2 + T_i\sigma_c^2)]^{1/2}, \tag{19.99}$$

where $T_i = \sum_{r=1}^{T} s_{ir}$ is the number of time periods available for unit i. Unlike in the balanced case, λ_i is properly viewed as a random variable because it is a function of T_i. But, under assumption 19.8a and assumption (19.98), T_i is appropriately exogenous because $\mathrm{E}(v_{it} \mid \mathbf{x}_i, T_i) = 0$, where $v_{it} = c_i + u_{it}$. Therefore, transforming the equation using any function of T_i still leads to consistent estimation under assumption (19.98). See Baltagi (2001, Section 9.2) for the case where T_i is treated as nonrandom.

If we knew λ_i, the RE estimator on the unbalanced panel would just be pooled OLS on the quasi-time-demeaned data $\breve{y}_{it} = y_{it} - \lambda_i \bar{y}_i$ and $\breve{\mathbf{x}}_{it} = \mathbf{x}_{it} - \lambda_i \bar{\mathbf{x}}_i$, where, naturally, the time averages are of the observed data. To operationalize the RE estimator, we need initial estimators of σ_u^2 and σ_c^2, but these are obtained by modifying the estimators in the unbalanced case.

With modern software, implementing random effects on an unbalanced panel is straightforward. But one should know that the RE estimator imposes strong assumptions on the nature of the missing data mechanism. Further, as in the balanced case, there are good reasons to believe the RE variance structure should not be taken literally. That is, even if we assume, in addition to assumption 19.8a, assumption 19.8c, and assumption (19.98),

$$\mathrm{Var}(c_i \mid \mathbf{x}_i, \mathbf{s}_i) = \mathrm{Var}(c_i) = \sigma_c^2, \tag{19.100}$$

it is still likely that the composite variance covariance matrix in the population, $\mathrm{Var}(\mathbf{v}_i \mid \mathbf{x}_i)$, does not have the RE structure. We already know in the balanced case that using the incorrect variance matrix in GLS estimation does not cause inconsistency in estimating $\boldsymbol{\beta}$, provided the explanatory variables are strictly exogenous with respect to $v_{it} = c_i + u_{it}$. Not surprisingly, in the unbalanced case we effectively must add strict exogeneity of the selection process. Under this assumption, RE on the unbalanced panel is generally consistent and $\sqrt{N}$-asymptotically normal for any variance structure for $\mathrm{Var}(\mathbf{v}_i \mid \mathbf{x}_i, \mathbf{c}_i)$. But we need to compute a fully robust variance matrix estimator for $\hat{\boldsymbol{\beta}}_{RE}$, which is typically available in modern econometrics packages for the balanced and unbalanced cases.

19.9.2 Testing and Correcting for Sample Selection Bias

The results in the previous subsection imply that sample selection in a fixed effects context is only a problem when selection is related to the idiosyncratic errors, u_{it}. Therefore, any test for selection bias should test only this assumption. A simple test was suggested by Nijman and Verbeek (1992) in the context of random effects estimation, but it works for fixed effects as well: add, say, the lagged selection indicator, $s_{i,t-1}$, to the equation, estimate the model by fixed effects (on the unbalanced panel), and do a t test (perhaps making it fully robust) for the significance of $s_{i,t-1}$. (This method loses the first time period for *all* observations.) Under the null hypothesis, u_{it} is uncorrelated with s_{ir} for all r, and so selection in the previous time period should not be significant in the equation at time t. (Incidentally, it never makes sense to put s_{it} in the equation at time t because $s_{it} = 1$ for all i and t in the selected subsample.)

Putting $s_{i,t-1}$ does not work if $s_{i,t-1}$ is unity whenever s_{it} is unity because then there is no variation in $s_{i,t-1}$ in the selected sample. This is the case in attrition problems if (say) a person can only appear in period t if he or she appeared in $t-1$. An alternative is to include a lead of the selection indicator, $s_{i,t+1}$. For observations i that are in the sample every time period, $s_{i,t+1}$ is always zero. But for attriters, $s_{i,t+1}$ switches from zero to one in the period just before attrition. Alternatively, we can define a variable at t, say $r_{i,t+1}$, which is the number of periods after period t that unit i is in the sample. Either way, if we use fixed effects or first differencing, we need $T > 2$ time periods to carry out the test.

For RE we have other possibilities, such as adding T_i as an additional regressor and using a t test.

For incidental truncation problems it makes sense to extend Heckman's (1976) test to the unobserved effects panel data context. This is done in Wooldridge (1995a). Write the equation of interest as

$$y_{it1} = \mathbf{x}_{it1}\boldsymbol{\beta}_1 + c_{i1} + u_{it1}, \qquad t = 1, \ldots, T \tag{19.101}$$

Initially, suppose that y_{it1} is observed only if the binary selection indicator, s_{it2}, is unity. Let $\mathbf{x}_{it}$ denote the set of all exogenous variables at time t; we assume that these are observed in every time period, and $\mathbf{x}_{it1}$ is a subset of $\mathbf{x}_{it}$. Suppose that, for each t, s_{it2} is determined by the probit equation

$$s_{it2} = 1[\mathbf{x}_i\boldsymbol{\psi}_{t2} + v_{it2} > 0], \qquad v_{it2} \mid \mathbf{x}_i \sim \text{Normal}(0, 1), \tag{19.102}$$

where $\mathbf{x}_i$ contains unity. This is best viewed as a reduced-form selection equation: we let the explanatory variables in all time periods appear in the selection equation at time t to allow for general selection models, including those with unobserved effect and the Chamberlain (1980) device discussed in Section 15.8.2, as well as certain dynamic models of selection. A Mundlak (1978) approach would replace $\mathbf{x}_i$ with $(\mathbf{x}_{it}, \bar{\mathbf{x}}_i)$ at time t and assume that coefficients are constant across time. (See equation (15.68).) Then the parameters can be estimated by pooled probit, greatly conserving on degrees of freedom. Such conservation may be important for small N. For testing purposes, under the null hypothesis it does not matter whether equation (19.102) is the proper model of sample selection, but we will need to assume equation (19.102), or a Mundlak version of it, when correcting for sample selection.

Under the null hypothesis in assumption 19.8a (with the obvious notational changes), the inverse Mills ratio obtained from the sample selection probit should not be significant in the equation estimated by fixed effects. Thus, let $\hat{\lambda}_{it2}$ be the estimated Mills ratios from estimating equation (19.102) by pooled probit across i and t. Then a valid test of the null hypothesis is a t statistic on $\hat{\lambda}_{it2}$ in the FE estimation on the unbalanced panel. Under assumption 19.8c the usual t statistic is valid, but the approach works whether or not the u_{it1} are homoskedastic and serially uncorrelated: just compute the robust standard error. Wooldridge (1995a) shows formally that the first-stage estimation of $\boldsymbol{\psi}_2$ does not affect the limiting distribution of the t statistic under H_0. This conclusion also follows from the results in Chapter 12 on M-estimation.

Correcting for sample selection requires much more care. Unfortunately, under any assumptions that actually allow for an unobserved effect in the underlying selection equation, adding $\hat{\lambda}_{it2}$ to equation (19.101) and using FE does not produce consistent estimators. To see why, suppose

$$s_{it2} = 1[\mathbf{x}_{it}\boldsymbol{\delta}_2 + c_{i2} + a_{it2} > 0], \qquad a_{it2} \mid (\mathbf{x}_i, c_{i1}, c_{i2}) \sim \mathrm{Normal}(0,1). \tag{19.103}$$

Then, to get equation (19.102), v_{it2} depends on a_{it2} and, at least partially, on c_{i2}. Now, suppose we make the strong assumption $\mathrm{E}(u_{it1} \mid \mathbf{x}_i, c_{i1}, c_{i2}, \mathbf{v}_{i2}) = g_{i1} + \rho_1 v_{it2}$, which would hold under the assumption that the (u_{it1}, a_{it2}) are independent across t conditional on $(\mathbf{x}_i, c_{i1}, c_{i2})$. Then we have

$$y_{it1} = \mathbf{x}_{it1}\boldsymbol{\beta}_1 + \rho_1 \mathrm{E}(v_{it2} \mid \mathbf{x}_i, \mathbf{s}_{i2}) + (c_{i1} + g_{i1}) + e_{it1} + \rho_1[v_{it2} - \mathrm{E}(v_{it2} \mid \mathbf{x}_i, \mathbf{s}_{i2})].$$

The composite error, $e_{it1} + \rho_1[v_{it2} - \mathrm{E}(v_{it2} \mid \mathbf{x}_i, \mathbf{s}_{i2})]$, is uncorrelated with any function of $(\mathbf{x}_i, \mathbf{s}_{i2})$. The problem is that $\mathrm{E}(v_{it2} \mid \mathbf{x}_i, \mathbf{s}_{i2})$ depends on all elements in $\mathbf{s}_{i2}$, and this expectation is complicated for even small T.

A method that does work is available using Chamberlain's approach to panel data models, but we need some linearity assumptions on the expected values of u_{it1} and c_{i1} given $\mathbf{x}_i$ and v_{it2}.

ASSUMPTION 19.9: (a) The selection equation is given by equation (19.102); (b) $\mathrm{E}(u_{it1} \mid \mathbf{x}_i, v_{it2}) = \mathrm{E}(u_{it1} \mid v_{it2}) = \rho_{t1} v_{it2}$, $t = 1, \dots, T$; and (c) $\mathrm{E}(c_{i1} \mid \mathbf{x}_i, v_{it2}) = \mathrm{L}(c_{i1} \mid 1, \mathbf{x}_i, v_{it2})$.

The second assumption is standard and follows under joint normality of (u_{it1}, v_{it2}) when this vector is independent of $\mathbf{x}_i$. Assumption 19.9c implies that

$$\mathrm{E}(c_{i1} \mid \mathbf{x}_i, v_{it2}) = \mathbf{x}_i\boldsymbol{\pi}_1 + \phi_{t1} v_{it2},$$

where, by equation (19.102) and iterated expectations, $\mathrm{E}(c_{i1} \mid \mathbf{x}_i) = \mathbf{x}_i \boldsymbol{\pi}_1 + \mathrm{E}(v_{it2} \mid \mathbf{x}_{it}) = \mathbf{x}_i \boldsymbol{\pi}_1$. These assumptions place no restrictions on the serial dependence in (u_{it1}, v_{it2}). They do imply that

$$\mathrm{E}(y_{it1} \mid \mathbf{x}_i, v_{it2}) = \mathbf{x}_{it1}\boldsymbol{\beta}_1 + \mathbf{x}_i\boldsymbol{\pi}_1 + \gamma_{t1} v_{it2}. \tag{19.104}$$

Conditioning on $s_{it2} = 1$ gives

$$\mathrm{E}(y_{it1} \mid \mathbf{x}_i, s_{it2} = 1) = \mathbf{x}_{it1}\boldsymbol{\beta}_1 + \mathbf{x}_i\boldsymbol{\pi}_1 + \gamma_{t1}\lambda(\mathbf{x}_i\boldsymbol{\psi}_{t2}).$$

Therefore, we can consistently estimate $\boldsymbol{\beta}_1$ by first estimating a probit of s_{it2} on $\mathbf{x}_i$ for each t and then saving the inverse Mills ratio, $\hat{\lambda}_{it2}$, all i and t. Next, run the pooled OLS regression using the selected sample:

$$y_{it1} \text{ on } \mathbf{x}_{it1}, \mathbf{x}_i, \hat{\lambda}_{it2}, d2_t\hat{\lambda}_{it2}, \ldots, dT_t\hat{\lambda}_{it2} \quad \text{for all } s_{it2} = 1, \tag{19.105}$$

where $d2_t$ through dT_t are time dummies. If γ_{t1} in equation (19.104) is constant across t, simply include $\hat{\lambda}_{it2}$ by itself in equation (19.105). Again, a simplification that can be practically useful is to replace $\mathbf{x}_i$ with the time average, $\bar{\mathbf{x}}_i$.

The asymptotic variance of $\hat{\boldsymbol{\beta}}_1$ needs to be corrected for general heteroskedasticity and serial correlation, as well as first-stage estimation of the $\boldsymbol{\psi}_{t2}$. These corrections can be made using the formulas for two-step M-estimation from Chapter 12; Wooldridge (1995a) contains the formulas. Alternatively, the panel bootstrap can be used, where the resampling is done using the cross section units.

If the selection equation is of the Tobit form, we have somewhat more flexibility. Write the selection equation now as

$$y_{it2} = \max(0, \mathbf{x}_i\boldsymbol{\psi}_{t2} + v_{it2}), \qquad v_{it2} \mid \mathbf{x}_i \sim \mathrm{Normal}(0, \sigma_{t2}^2), \tag{19.106}$$

where y_{it1} is observed if $y_{it2} > 0$. Then, under assumption 19.8, with the Tobit selection equation in place of equation (19.102), consistent estimation follows from the pooled regression (19.105) where $\hat{\lambda}_{it2}$ is replaced by the Tobit residuals, $\hat{v}_{it2}$ when $y_{it2} > 0$ $(s_{it2} = 1)$. The Tobit residuals are obtained from the T cross section Tobits in equation (19.106); alternatively, especially with small N, we can use a Mundlak-type approach and use pooled Tobit with $\mathbf{x}_i\boldsymbol{\psi}_{t2}$ replaced with $\mathbf{x}_{it}\boldsymbol{\delta}_2 + \bar{\mathbf{x}}_i\boldsymbol{\pi}_2$; see equation (17.82).

It is easy to see that we can add $\alpha_1 y_{it2}$ to the structural equation (19.101), provided we make an explicit exclusion restriction in assumption 19.9. In particular, we must assume that $\mathrm{E}(c_{i1} \mid \mathbf{x}_i, v_{it2}) = \mathbf{x}_{i1}\boldsymbol{\pi}_1 + \phi_{t1} v_{it2}$, and that $\mathbf{x}_{it1}$ is a strict subset of $\mathbf{x}_{it}$. Then, because y_{it2} is a function of $(\mathbf{x}_i, v_{it2})$, we can write $\mathrm{E}(y_{it1} \mid \mathbf{x}_i, v_{it2}) = \mathbf{x}_{it1}\boldsymbol{\beta}_1 + \alpha_1 y_{it2} + \mathbf{x}_{i1}\boldsymbol{\pi}_1 + \gamma_{t1} v_{it2}$. We obtain the Tobit residuals, $\hat{v}_{it2}$ for each t, and then run the regression y_{it1} on $\mathbf{x}_{it1}, y_{it2}, \mathbf{x}_{i1}$, and $\hat{v}_{it2}$ (possibly interacted with time dummies) for the selected sample. If we do not have an exclusion restriction, this regression suffers from perfect multicollinearity. As an example, we can easily include hours worked in a wage offer function for panel data, provided we have a variable affecting labor supply (such as the number of young children) but not the wage offer.

A pure fixed effects approach is more fruitful when the selection equation is of the Tobit form. The following assumption comes from Wooldridge (1995a):

ASSUMPTION 19.10: (a) The selection equation is equation (19.106). (b) For some unobserved effect g_{i1}, $\mathrm{E}(u_{it1} \mid \mathbf{x}_i, c_{i1}, g_{i1}, \mathbf{v}_{i2}) = \mathrm{E}(u_{it1} \mid g_{i1}, v_{it2}) = g_{i1} + \rho_1 v_{it2}$.

Under part b of this assumption,

$$\mathrm{E}(y_{it1} \mid \mathbf{x}_i, \mathbf{v}_{i2}, c_{i1}, g_{i1}) = \mathbf{x}_{it1}\boldsymbol{\beta}_1 + \rho_1 v_{it2} + f_{i1}, \tag{19.107}$$

where $f_{i1} = c_{i1} + g_{i1}$. The same expectation holds when we also condition on $\mathbf{s}_{i2}$ (since $\mathbf{s}_{i2}$ is a function of $\mathbf{x}_i$, $\mathbf{v}_{i2}$). Therefore, estimating equation (19.107) by fixed effects on the unbalanced panel would consistently estimate $\boldsymbol{\beta}_1$ and ρ_1. As usual, we replace v_{it2} with the Tobit residuals $\hat{v}_{it2}$ whenever $y_{it2} > 0$. A t test of H_0: $\rho_1 = 0$ is valid very generally as a test of the null hypothesis of no sample selection. If the $\{u_{it1}\}$ satisfy the standard homoskedasticity and serial uncorrelatedness assumptions, then the usual t statistic is valid. A fully robust test may be warranted. (Again, with an exclusion restriction, we can add y_{it2} as an additional explanatory variable.)

Wooldridge (1995a) discusses an important case where assumption 19.10b holds: in the Tobit version of equation (19.103) with $(\mathbf{u}_{i1}, \mathbf{a}_{i2})$ independent of $(\mathbf{x}_i, c_{i1}, c_{i2})$ and $\mathrm{E}(u_{it1} \mid \mathbf{a}_{i2}) = \mathrm{E}(u_{it1} \mid a_{it2}) = \rho_1 a_{it2}$. The second-to-last equality holds under the common assumption that $\{(u_{it1}, a_{it2}): t = 1, \ldots, T\}$ is serially independent.

The preceding methods assume normality of the errors in the selection equation and, implicitly, the unobserved heterogeneity. Kyriazidou (1997) and Honoré and Kyriazidou (2000b) have proposed methods that do not require distributional assumptions. Dustmann and Rochina-Barrachina (2007) apply Wooldridge's (1995a) and Kyriazidou's (1997) methods to the problem of estimating a wage offer equation with selection into the work force.

Semykina and Wooldridge (in press) show how to extend sample selection corrections for panel data to the case of endogenous explanatory variables. As in the case of cross section corrections, the endogenous explanatory variables need not be observed in all time periods. As shown formally by Semykina and Wooldridge (in press), a simple test for sample selection bias—without taking a stand on endogeneity of the explanatory variables—is obtained by adding inverse Mills ratio terms to the unbalanced panel and using fixed effect 2SLS. Corrections are available by adding time averages of the exogenous variables (both exogenous explanatory variables and the instruments) and applying pooled 2SLS with inverse Mills ratio terms (which, as usual, are estimated in a first stage). See Semykina and Wooldridge (in press) for details.

19.9.3 Attrition

We now turn specifically to testing and correcting for attrition in a linear, unobserved effects panel data model. General attrition, where units may reenter the sample after leaving, is complicated. We analyze a common special case. At $t = 1$ a random sample is obtained from the relevant population—people, for concreteness. In $t = 2$ and beyond, some people drop out of the sample for reasons that may not be entirely random. We assume that, once a person drops out, he or she is out forever: attrition is an *absorbing* state. Any panel data set with attrition can be set up in this way by ignoring any subsequent observations on units after they initially leave the sample. In Section 19.9.2 we discussed one way to test for attrition bias when we assume that attrition is an absorbing state: include $s_{i,t+1}$ as an additional explanatory variable in a fixed effects analysis, or use the number of subsequent periods in the sample.

One method for correcting for attrition bias is closely related to the corrections for incidental truncation covered in the previous subsection. Write the model for a random draw from the population as in equation (19.95), where we assume that $(\mathbf{x}_{it}, y_{it})$ is observed for all i when $t = 1$. Let s_{it} denote the selection indicator for each time period, where $s_{it} = 1$ if $(\mathbf{x}_{it}, y_{it})$ are observed. Because we ignore units once they initially leave the sample, $s_{it} = 1$ implies $s_{ir} = 1$ for $r < t$.

The sequential nature of attrition makes first differencing a natural choice to remove the unobserved effect:

$$\Delta y_{it} = \Delta \mathbf{x}_{it}\boldsymbol{\beta} + \Delta u_{it}, \qquad t = 2, \ldots, T. \tag{19.108}$$

Conditional on $s_{i,t-1} = 1$, write a (reduced-form) selection equation for $t \geq 2$ as

$$s_{it} = 1[\mathbf{w}_{it}\boldsymbol{\delta}_t + v_{it} > 0], \qquad v_{it} \mid \{\Delta \mathbf{x}_{it}, \mathbf{w}_{it}, s_{i,t-1} = 1\} \sim \text{Normal}(0, 1), \tag{19.109}$$

where $\mathbf{w}_{it}$ must contain variables observed at time t for all units with $s_{i,t-1} = 1$. Good candidates for $\mathbf{w}_{it}$ include the variables in $\mathbf{x}_{i,t-1}$ and any variables in $\mathbf{x}_{it}$ that are observed at time t when $s_{i,t-1} = 1$ (for example, if $\mathbf{x}_{it}$ contains lags of variables or a variable such as age). In general, the dimension of $\mathbf{w}_{it}$ can grow with t. For example, if equation (19.95) is dynamically complete, then $y_{i,t-2}$ is orthogonal to Δu_{it}, and so it can be an element of $\mathbf{w}_{it}$. Since $y_{i,t-1}$ is correlated with $u_{i,t-1}$, it should not be included in $\mathbf{w}_{it}$.

Under assumption (19.108), selection in time t, conditional on being in the sample at time $t-1$ ($s_{i,t-1} = 1$), follows a probit model:

$$P(s_{it} = 1 \mid \mathbf{w}_{it}, s_{i,t-1} = 1) = \Phi(\mathbf{w}_{it}\boldsymbol{\delta}_t), \qquad t = 2, \ldots, T. \tag{19.110}$$

Therefore, we can estimate $\boldsymbol{\delta}_t$, $t = 2, \ldots, T$, by a sequence of probits where, in each time period, one uses the units still in the sample in the previous time period.

In order to justify a two-step Heckman correction, we need to assume that, for those still in the sample at $t-1$, $\mathbf{x}_{it}$ does not affect selection in time t once we condition on $\mathbf{w}_{it}$. A natural way to state this condition is

$$P(s_{it} = 1 \mid \Delta\mathbf{x}_{it}, \mathbf{w}_{it}, s_{i,t-1} = 1) = P(s_{it} = 1 \mid \mathbf{w}_{it}, s_{i,t-1} = 1). \tag{19.111}$$

Technically, assumption (19.111) is not strong enough. An assumption that is sufficient—stated in terms of the errors in the first-differenced equation—is that, conditional on $s_{i,t-1} = 1$,

$$(\Delta u_{it}, v_{it}) \text{ is independent of } (\Delta\mathbf{x}_{it}, \mathbf{w}_{it}), \tag{19.112}$$

which, of course, implies that v_{it} is independent of $(\Delta\mathbf{x}_{it}, \mathbf{w}_{it})$ and implies condition (19.111) when v_{it} has a standard normal distribution. We also impose the standard linear functional form assumption:

$$E(\Delta u_{it} \mid v_{it}, s_{i,t-1} = 1) = \rho_t v_{it}, \tag{19.113}$$

in which case

$$E(\Delta y_{it} \mid \Delta\mathbf{x}_{it}, \mathbf{w}_{it}, s_{it} = 1) = \Delta\mathbf{x}_{it}\boldsymbol{\beta} + \rho_t \lambda(\mathbf{w}_{it}\boldsymbol{\delta}_t), \qquad t = 2, \ldots, T, \tag{19.114}$$

where $\lambda(\mathbf{w}_{it}\boldsymbol{\delta}_t)$ is the inverse Mills ratio.

Notice how, because $s_{i,t-1} = 1$ when $s_{it} = 1$, we do not have to condition on $s_{i,t-1}$ in equation (19.113). It now follows from equation (19.113) that pooled OLS of Δy_{it} on $\Delta\mathbf{x}_{it}, d2_t\hat{\lambda}_{it}, \ldots, dT_t\hat{\lambda}_{it}$, $t = 2, \ldots, T$, where the $\hat{\lambda}_{it}$ are from the $T-1$ cross section probits in equation (19.110), is consistent for $\boldsymbol{\beta}_1$ and the ρ_t. A joint test of H_0: $\rho_t = 0$, $t = 2, \ldots, T$, is a fairly simple test for attrition bias, although nothing guarantees serial independence of the errors.

There are two potential problems with this approach. For one, assumption (19.112) is restrictive because it means that $\mathbf{x}_{it}$ does not affect attrition once the elements in $\mathbf{w}_{it}$ have been controlled for. This is a very strong assumption. In fact, in one scenario where this assumption fails, it is actually harmful to apply the Heckman approach. To see how this result can occur, suppose that selection is actually a function of changes in the covariates in the sense that

$$\mathrm{P}(s_{it} = 1 \mid \Delta \mathbf{x}_{it}, \Delta u_{it}) = \mathrm{P}(s_{it} = 1 \mid \Delta \mathbf{x}_{it}). \tag{19.115}$$

Under this condition, pooled OLS estimation of equation (19.108), using the unbalanced panel, is consistent for $\boldsymbol{\beta}$. By contrast, the Heckman method just described is generally inconsistent if $\Delta \mathbf{x}_{it}$ is not included in $\mathbf{w}_{it}$: it is very unlikely that

$$\mathrm{E}(\Delta u_{it} \mid \Delta \mathbf{x}_{it}, \mathbf{w}_{it}, v_{it}, s_{i,t-1} = 1) = \mathrm{E}(\Delta u_{it} \mid v_{it}, s_{i,t-1} = 1)$$

(because v_{it} generally cannot be assumed to be independent of $\Delta \mathbf{x}_{it}$ if $\Delta \mathbf{x}_{it}$ is not included in $\mathbf{w}_{it}$).

A second shortcoming of the Heckman procedure just described is that it requires strict exogeneity of $\{\mathbf{x}_{it}\}$ in the original (levels) equation. Fortunately, in some cases we can apply an instrumental variables approach that is consistent when $\{\mathbf{x}_{it}\}$ is not strictly exogenous or always observed at time t.

Let $\mathbf{z}_{it}$ be a vector of variables such that $\mathbf{z}_{it}$ is redundant in the selection equation (possibly because $\mathbf{w}_{it}$ contains $\mathbf{z}_{it}$) and that $\mathbf{z}_{it}$ is exogenous in the sense that equation (19.112) holds with $\mathbf{z}_{it}$ in place of $\Delta \mathbf{x}_{it}$; for example, $\mathbf{z}_{it}$ should contain $\mathbf{x}_{ir}$ for $r < t$. Now, using an argument similar to the cross section case in Section 19.6.2, we can estimate the equation

$$\Delta y_{it} = \Delta \mathbf{x}_{it} \boldsymbol{\beta} + \rho_2 \, d2_t \hat{\lambda}_{it} + \cdots + \rho_T \, dT_t \hat{\lambda}_{it} + error_{it} \tag{19.116}$$

by instrumental variables with instruments $(\mathbf{z}_{it}, d2_t \hat{\lambda}_{it}, \ldots, dT_t \hat{\lambda}_{it})$, using the selected sample. For example, the pooled 2SLS estimator on the selected sample is consistent and asymptotically normal, and attrition bias can be tested by a joint test of H_0: $\rho_t = 0$, $t = 2, \ldots, T$. Under H_0, only serial correlation and heteroskedasticity adjustments are possibly needed. If H_0 fails we have the usual generated regressors problem for estimating the asymptotic variance. Other IV procedures, such as GMM, can also be used, but they too must account for the generated regressors problem. The panel bootstrap is a simple alternative to the analytical formulas.

Example 19.9 (Dynamic Model with Attrition): Consider the model

$$y_{it} = \mathbf{g}_{it} \boldsymbol{\gamma} + \eta_1 y_{i,t-1} + c_i + u_{it}, \qquad t = 1, \ldots, T, \tag{19.117}$$

where we assume that $(y_{i0}, \mathbf{g}_{i1}, y_{i1})$ are all observed for a random sample from the population. Assume that $\mathrm{E}(u_{it} \mid \mathbf{g}_i, y_{i,t-1}, \ldots, y_{i0}, c_i) = 0$, so that $\mathbf{g}_{it}$ is strictly exogenous. Then the explanatory variables in the probit at time t, $\mathbf{w}_{it}$, can include $\mathbf{g}_{i,t-1}$, $y_{i,t-2}$, and further lags of these. After estimating the selection probit for each t, and differencing, we can estimate

$$\Delta y_{it} = \Delta \mathbf{g}_{it} \boldsymbol{\beta} + \eta_1 \Delta y_{i,t-1} + \rho_3 \, d3_t \hat{\lambda}_{it} + \cdots + \rho_T \, dT_t \hat{\lambda}_{it} + error_{it}$$

by pooled 2SLS on the selected sample starting at $t = 3$, using instruments $(\mathbf{g}_{i,t-1}, \mathbf{g}_{i,t-2}, y_{i,t-2}, y_{i,t-3})$. As usual, there are other possibilities for the instruments.

Although the focus in this section has been on pure attrition, where units disappear entirely from the sample, the methods can also be used in the context of incidental truncation without strictly exogenous explanatory variables. For example, suppose we are interested in the population of men who are employed at $t = 0$ and $t = 1$, and we would like to estimate a dynamic wage equation with an unobserved effect. Problems arise if men become unemployed in future periods. Such events can be treated as an attrition problem if all subsequent time periods are dropped once a man first becomes unemployed. This approach loses information but makes the econometrics relatively straightforward, especially because, in the preceding general model, $\mathbf{x}_{it}$ will always be observed at time t and so can be included in the labor force participation probit (assuming that men do not leave the sample entirely). Things become much more complicated if we are interested in the wage offer for all working age men at $t = 1$ because we have to deal with the sample selection problem into employment at $t = 0$ and $t = 1$.

The methods for attrition and selection just described apply only to linear models, and it is difficult to extend them to general nonlinear models. An alternative approach is based on inverse probability weighting (IPW), which we described in the cross section case in Section 19.8.

Moffitt, Fitzgerald, and Gottschalk (1999) (MFG) propose IPW to estimate linear panel data models under possibly nonrandom attrition. (MFG propose a different set of weights, analogous to those studied by Horowitz and Manski (1998), to solve missing data problems. The weights we use require estimation of only one attrition model, rather than two as in MFG.) IPW must be used with care to solve the attrition problem. As before, we assume that we have a random sample from the population at $t = 1$. We are interested in some feature, such as the conditional mean, or maybe the entire conditional distribution, of y_{it} given $\mathbf{x}_{it}$. Ideally, at each t we would observe $(y_{it}, \mathbf{x}_{it})$ for any unit that was in the random sample at $t = 1$. Instead, we observe $(y_{it}, \mathbf{x}_{it})$ only if $s_{it} = 1$. We can easily solve the attrition problem if we assume that, conditional on observables in the first time period, say, $\mathbf{z}_{i1}$, $(y_{it}, \mathbf{x}_{it})$ is independent of s_{it}:

$$\mathrm{P}(s_{it} = 1 \mid y_{it}, \mathbf{x}_{it}, \mathbf{z}_{i1}) = \mathrm{P}(s_{it} = 1 \mid \mathbf{z}_{i1}), \qquad t = 2, \ldots, T. \tag{19.118}$$

As in the cross section case, assumption (19.118) has been called "selection on observables" in the econometrics literature and "ignorable selection" or "unconfoundedness" in the statistics literature. (The Heckman method we just covered is more like the "selection on unobservables" that we discussed in Section 19.8.) Condition (19.118) is a strong assumption in that it maintains that, in *every* time period, $\mathbf{z}_{i1}$ is such a good predictor of attrition that the distribution of s_{it} given $\{\mathbf{z}_{i1}, (\mathbf{x}_{it}, y_{it})\}$ does not depend on $(\mathbf{x}_{it}, y_{it})$. If we have such an observed set of variables $\mathbf{z}_{i1}$, it is not too surprising that we can account for nonrandom attrition for a large class of estimation problems.

As in the cross section case, IPW estimation typically involves two steps. First, for each t, we estimate a probit or logit of s_{it} on $\mathbf{z}_{i1}$. (A crucial point is that the same cross section units—namely, all units appearing in the first time period—are used in the probit or logit for each time period.) Let $\hat{p}_{it}$ be the fitted probabilities, $t = 2, \ldots, T$, $i = 1, \ldots, N$. In the second step, the objective function for (i, t) is weighted by $1/\hat{p}_{it}$. For general M-estimation, the objective function is

$$\sum_{i=1}^{N} \sum_{t=1}^{T} (s_{it}/\hat{p}_{it}) q_t(\mathbf{w}_{it}, \boldsymbol{\theta}), \tag{19.119}$$

where $\mathbf{w}_{it} \equiv (y_{it}, \mathbf{x}_{it})$ and $q_t(\mathbf{w}_{it}, \boldsymbol{\theta})$ is the objective function in each time period. As usual, the selection indicator s_{it} chooses the observations where we actually observe data. (For $t = 1$, $s_{it} = \hat{p}_{it} = 1$ for all i.) For least squares, $q_t(\mathbf{w}_{it}, \boldsymbol{\theta})$ is simply the squared residual function; for partial MLE, $q_t(\mathbf{w}_{it}, \boldsymbol{\theta})$ is the log-likelihood function.

The argument for why IPW works is similar to the pure cross section case. Let $\boldsymbol{\theta}_o$ denote the value of $\boldsymbol{\theta}$ that solves the population problem $\min_{\boldsymbol{\theta} \in \boldsymbol{\Theta}} \sum_{t=1}^{T} \mathrm{E}[q_t(\mathbf{w}_{it}, \boldsymbol{\theta})]$. Let $\boldsymbol{\delta}_t^o$ denote the true values of the selection response parameters in each time period, so that $\mathrm{P}(s_{it} = 1 \mid \mathbf{z}_{i1}) = p_t(\mathbf{z}_{i1}, \boldsymbol{\delta}_t^o) \equiv p_{it}^o$. Now, under standard regularity conditions, we can replace p_{it}^o with $\hat{p}_{it} \equiv p_t(\mathbf{z}_{i1}, \hat{\boldsymbol{\delta}}_t)$ without affecting the consistency argument. So, apart from regularity conditions, it is sufficient to show that $\boldsymbol{\theta}_o$ minimizes $\sum_{t=1}^{T} \mathrm{E}[(s_{it}/p_{it}^o) q_t(\mathbf{w}_{it}, \boldsymbol{\theta})]$ over $\boldsymbol{\Theta}$. But, from iterated expectations,

$$\begin{aligned} \mathrm{E}[(s_{it}/p_{it}^o) q_t(\mathbf{w}_{it}, \boldsymbol{\theta})] &= \mathrm{E}\{\mathrm{E}[(s_{it}/p_{it}^o) q_t(\mathbf{w}_{it}, \boldsymbol{\theta}) \mid \mathbf{w}_{it}, \mathbf{z}_{i1}]\} \\ &= \mathrm{E}\{[\mathrm{E}(s_{it} \mid \mathbf{w}_{it}, \mathbf{z}_{i1})/p_{it}^o] q_t(\mathbf{w}_{it}, \boldsymbol{\theta})\} = \mathrm{E}[q_t(\mathbf{w}_{it}, \boldsymbol{\theta})] \end{aligned}$$

because $\mathrm{E}(s_{it} \mid \mathbf{w}_{it}, \mathbf{z}_{i1}) = \mathrm{P}(s_{it} = 1 \mid \mathbf{z}_{i1})$ by assumption (19.118). Therefore, the probability limit of the weighted objective function is identical to that of the unweighted function *if* we had no attrition problem. Using this simple analogy argument and standard two-step estimation results from Chapter 12 shows that the inverse probability weighting produces a consistent, $\sqrt{N}$-asymptotically normal estimator. The methods for adjusting the asymptotic variance matrix of two step M-estimators—described in Subsection 12.5.2—can be applied to the IPW M-estimator from equation (19.119). The panel bootstrap that accounts for the two estimation steps is also attractive.

MFG propose an IPW scheme where the conditioning variables in the attrition probits change across time. In particular, at time t an attrition probit is estimated restricting attention to those units still in the sample at time $t-1$. (Out of this group, some are lost to attrition at time t, and some are not.) If we assume that attrition is an absorbing state, we can include in the conditioning variables, $\mathbf{z}_{it}$, all values of y and $\mathbf{x}$ dated at time $t-1$ and earlier (as well as other variables observed for all units in the sample at $t-1$). This approach is appealing because the ignorability assumption is much more plausible if we can condition on both recent responses and covariates. (That is, $\mathrm{P}(s_{it}=1 \mid \mathbf{w}_{it}, \mathbf{w}_{i,t-1}, \ldots, \mathbf{w}_{i1}, s_{i,t-1}=1) = \mathrm{P}(s_{it}=1 \mid \mathbf{w}_{i,t-1}, \ldots, \mathbf{w}_{i1}, s_{i,t-1}=1)$ is more likely than assumption (19.64).) Unfortunately, obtaining the fitted probabilities in this way and using them in an IPW procedure does not generally produce consistent estimators. The problem is that the selection models at each time period are not representative of the population that was originally sampled at $t=1$. Letting $p_{it}^{\mathrm{o}} = \mathrm{P}(s_{it}=1 \mid \mathbf{w}_{i,t-1}, \ldots, \mathbf{w}_{i1}, s_{i,t-1}=1)$, we can no longer use the iterated expectations argument to conclude that $\mathrm{E}[(s_{it}/p_{it}^{\mathrm{o}})q_t(\mathbf{w}_{it}, \boldsymbol{\theta})] = \mathrm{E}[q_t(\mathbf{w}_{it}, \boldsymbol{\theta})]$. Only if $\mathrm{E}[q_t(\mathbf{w}_{it}, \boldsymbol{\theta})] = \mathrm{E}[q_t(\mathbf{w}_{it}, \boldsymbol{\theta}) \mid s_{i,t-1}=1]$ for all $\boldsymbol{\theta}$ does the argument work, but this assumption essentially requires that $\mathbf{w}_{it}$ be independent of $s_{i,t-1}$.

It is possible to allow the covariates in the selection probabilities to increase in richness over time, but the MFG procedure must be modified. For the case where attrition is an absorbing state, we can extend to the M-estimation case the nonlinear regression results of Robins, Rotnitzky, and Zhao (1995) (RRZ). It turns out that in some cases the probabilities to be used in IPW estimation can be constructed sequentially:

$$p_{it}(\boldsymbol{\delta}_t^{\mathrm{o}}) \equiv \pi_{i2}(\gamma_2^{\mathrm{o}})\pi_{i3}(\gamma_3^{\mathrm{o}}) \cdots \pi_{it}(\gamma_t^{\mathrm{o}}), \qquad t = 2, \ldots, T, \tag{19.120}$$

where

$$\pi_{it}(\gamma_t^{\mathrm{o}}) \equiv \mathrm{P}(s_{it}=1 \mid \mathbf{z}_{it}, s_{i,t-1}=1). \tag{19.121}$$

In other words, as in the MFG procedure, we estimate probit models at each time t, restricted to units that are in the sample at $t-1$. The covariates in the probit are essentially everything we can observe for units in the sample at time $t-1$ that might affect attrition. For $t = 2, \ldots, T$, let $\hat{\pi}_{it}$ denote the fitted selection probabilities. Then we construct the probability weights as the product $\hat{p}_{it} \equiv \hat{\pi}_{i2}\hat{\pi}_{i3} \cdots \hat{\pi}_{it}$ and use the objective function (19.119). Naturally, this method only works under certain assumptions. The key ignorability of selection condition can be stated as

$$\mathrm{P}(s_{it}=1 \mid \mathbf{v}_{i1}, \ldots, \mathbf{v}_{iT}, s_{i,t-1}=1) = \mathrm{P}(s_{it}=1 \mid \mathbf{z}_{it}, s_{i,t-1}=1), \tag{19.122}$$

where $\mathbf{v}_{it} \equiv (\mathbf{w}_{it}, \mathbf{z}_{it})$. Now, we must include future values of $\mathbf{w}_{it}$ *and* $\mathbf{z}_{it}$ in the conditioning set on the left-hand side. Assumption (19.122) is fairly strong, but it does allow for attrition to be strongly related to past outcomes on y and $\mathbf{x}$ (which can be included in $\mathbf{z}_{it}$).

It is easy to see how assumption (19.122) leads to equation (19.120). First, with $\mathbf{v}_i = (\mathbf{v}_{i1}, \mathbf{v}_{i2}, \dots, \mathbf{v}_{iT})$, we can always write

$$\begin{aligned} \mathrm{P}(s_{it} = 1 \mid \mathbf{v}_i) &= \mathrm{P}(s_{it} = 1 \mid \mathbf{v}_i, s_{i,t-1} = 1) \cdots \mathrm{P}(s_{i2} = 1 \mid \mathbf{v}_i, s_{i1} = 1)\mathrm{P}(s_{i1} = 1 \mid \mathbf{v}_i) \\ &= \mathrm{P}(s_{it} = 1 \mid \mathbf{v}_i, s_{i,t-1} = 1) \cdots \mathrm{P}(s_{i2} = 1 \mid \mathbf{v}_i) \end{aligned} \tag{19.123}$$

because we assume $s_{i1} \equiv 1$. Under assumption (19.122), $\mathrm{P}(s_{it} = 1 \mid \mathbf{v}_i, s_{i,t-1} = 1) = \mathrm{P}(s_{it} = 1 \mid \mathbf{z}_{it}, s_{i,t-1} = 1)$ for $t \geq 2$, and so

$$p_{it}^o \equiv \mathrm{P}(s_{it} = 1 \mid \mathbf{v}_i) = \mathrm{P}(s_{it} = 1 \mid \mathbf{z}_{it}, s_{i,t-1} = 1) \cdots \mathrm{P}(s_{i2} = 1 \mid \mathbf{z}_{i2}),$$

which is exactly equation (19.121).

As in the cross section case, we can use the "surprising" efficiency result described in Section 13.10.2 to show that, under assumption (19.122), estimating the attrition probabilities is actually more efficient than using the known probabilities (if we could). The key is that we have fully specified $\mathrm{D}(s_{i1}, s_{i2}, \dots, s_{iT} \mid \mathbf{v}_i)$. Because $\{\mathbf{w}_{it}: t = 1, \dots, T\}$ is contained in $\mathbf{v}_i$, the conditional independence assumption (13.66) (with an appropriate change in notation) holds. To realize the efficiency gain in the computed variance matrix estimator, we partial out from the weighted M-estimator score the score from the first-stage MLE. Define

$$k(\mathbf{s}_i, \mathbf{z}_i, \mathbf{w}_i, \gamma, \boldsymbol{\theta}) \equiv \sum_{t=1}^{T} [s_{it}/p_{it}(\boldsymbol{\delta}_t)]\mathbf{r}_t(\mathbf{w}_{it}, \boldsymbol{\theta}),$$

where $\mathbf{r}_t(\mathbf{w}_{it}, \boldsymbol{\theta}) = \nabla_{\theta} q(\mathbf{w}_{it}, \boldsymbol{\theta})$ is the $\mathrm{P} \times 1$ score of the unweighted objective function. Further, let $\mathbf{d}_i(\boldsymbol{\delta})$ denote the score of the conditional log likelihood

$$\sum_{t=2}^{T} s_{i,t-1}\{s_{it} \log(\pi_t(\mathbf{z}_{it}, \gamma_t) + (1 - s_{it}) \log[1 - \pi_t(\mathbf{z}_{it}, \gamma_t)]\},$$

where $\boldsymbol{\delta}$ denotes the vector of γ_t, $t = 2, \dots, T$. Typically, in each time period we would estimate a logit or probit. Then, $\mathbf{d}_i(\boldsymbol{\delta})$ is just the long column vector of stacked scores for each logit or probit, selected at time t so that we use only the units in the sample at $t - 1$. That is,

$$\mathbf{d}_i(\boldsymbol{\delta})' = [s_{i1}\mathbf{g}_2(s_{i2}, \mathbf{z}_{i2}; \gamma_2), s_{i2}\mathbf{g}_3(s_{i3}, \mathbf{z}_{i3}; \gamma_3), \dots, s_{i,T-1}\mathbf{g}_T(s_{iT}, \mathbf{z}_{iT}; \gamma_T)],$$

where $\mathbf{g}_t(s_{it}, \mathbf{z}_{it}; \gamma_t)$ is just the gradient (row vector) for the binary response model at time t, using units in the sample at $t-1$. Then, as in the cross section case, let

$$\hat{\mathbf{e}}_i \equiv \hat{\mathbf{k}}_i - \left(N^{-1}\sum_{i=1}^{N}\hat{\mathbf{k}}_i\hat{\mathbf{d}}_i'\right)\left(N^{-1}\sum_{i=1}^{N}\hat{\mathbf{d}}_i\hat{\mathbf{d}}_i'\right)^{-1}\hat{\mathbf{d}}_i$$

be the $\mathrm{P} \times 1$ residuals from the multivariate regression of $\hat{\mathbf{k}}_i$ on $\hat{\mathbf{d}}_i$, $i = 1, \ldots, N$, where all hatted quantities are evaluated at $\hat{\boldsymbol{\delta}}$ or $\hat{\boldsymbol{\theta}}_w$ (where the latter is the IPW M-estimator). Further, define

$$\hat{\mathbf{D}} \equiv N^{-1}\sum_{i=1}^{N}\hat{\mathbf{e}}_i\hat{\mathbf{e}}_i'$$

and

$$\hat{\mathbf{A}} \equiv N^{-1}\sum_{i=1}^{N}\sum_{t=1}^{T}[s_i/p_{it}(\hat{\boldsymbol{\delta}}_t)]H_t(\mathbf{w}_{it}, \hat{\boldsymbol{\theta}}_w).$$

The asymptotic variance of $\hat{\boldsymbol{\theta}}_w$ is consistently estimated as $\hat{\mathbf{A}}^{-1}\hat{\mathbf{D}}\hat{\mathbf{A}}^{-1}/N$, which allows for general serial dependence in the scores over time as well as violation of the information matrix equality in each time period. (So, for example, with nonlinear regression, or QMLE in the linear exponential family, the conditional variances may be arbitrary.)

An alternative, as usual with large N and small T, is to include both steps of the two-step procedure in a panel bootstrapping routine. The obtained standard errors will properly reflect the increased efficiency from estimating the γ_t.

RRZ (1995) show that, in the case of nonlinear regression where the explanatory variables are always observed—a leading case occurs when the covariates are observed in the first period and do not change over time—condition (19.122) can be relaxed somewhat, and the IPW method still produces consistent, asymptotically normal estimators. When modeling a feature of $\mathrm{D}(\mathbf{y}_{it} \mid \mathbf{x}_{it})$ when the covariates are not always observed, IPW suffers from the same problem we discussed in Section 19.8. Namely, if the feature of $\mathrm{D}(\mathbf{y}_{it} \mid \mathbf{x}_{it})$ is correctly specified (and the objective function has been properly chosen), and if selection is a function of the covariates in the sense that

$$\mathrm{P}(s_{it} = 1 \mid \mathbf{x}_{it}, y_{it}, s_{i,t-1} = 1) = \mathrm{P}(s_{it} = 1 \mid \mathbf{x}_{it}, s_{i,t-1} = 1),$$

then the unweighted pooled M-estimator is consistent. If $\mathbf{x}_{it}$ is not fully observed at time t, then it cannot be included in $\mathbf{z}_{it}$, and condition (19.122) is very likely to fail.

As in the case of the Heckman approach applied to a first-differenced linear equation, the weighting is not innocuous: it would actually lead to inconsistent estimation. Thus, in the case of attrition in the leading case where interest lies in a feature of $\mathrm{D}(\mathbf{y}_{it} \mid \mathbf{x}_{it})$, and some elements of $\mathbf{x}_{it}$ are unobserved in time t for those leaving the sample, one must be careful in interpreting important differences between the weighted and unweighted estimators: the problem might be with the weighted estimator. (Of course, both estimators might be inconsistent, too.)

Problems

19.1. In the setup of Section 19.2.1, suppose that the costs, r_i, do not vary across i. What features of $\mathrm{D}(y_i \mid \mathbf{x}_i)$ can we consistently estimate?

19.2. Some occupations, such as major league baseball, are characterized by salary floors. This situation can be described by

$$y = \exp(\mathbf{x}\boldsymbol{\beta} + u), \qquad u \mid \mathbf{x} \sim \mathrm{Normal}(0, \sigma^2)$$

$$w = \max(f, y),$$

where $f > 0$ is the common salary floor (the minimum wage), y is the person's true worth (productivity), and $\mathbf{x}$ contains human capital and demographic variables.

a. Find the log-likelihood function for a random draw i from the population.

b. How would you estimate $\mathrm{E}(y \mid \mathbf{x})$?

c. Is $\mathrm{E}(w \mid \mathbf{x})$ of much interest in this application? Explain.

19.3. Let y be the percentage of annual income invested in a pension plan, and assume that current law caps this percentage at 10 percent. Therefore, in a sample of data, we observe y_i between zero and 10, with pileups at the two corners, zero and 10.

a. What model would you use for y that recognizes the pileups at zero and 10?

b. Explain the conceptual difference between the outcomes $y = 0$ and $y = 10$. In particular, which limit can be viewed as a form of data censoring?

c. How would you estimate the partial effects on the expected contribution percentage assuming that the current law always will be in effect?

d. Suppose you want to ask, What would be the effect on $\mathrm{E}(y \mid \mathbf{x})$, for any value of $\mathbf{x}$, if the contribution cap were increased from 10 to 11? How would you estimate the effect? [Hint: In the general two-limit Tobit model, call the upper bound, in general,

a_2 (which is known, not a parameter to estimate), and then take the partial derivative with respect to a_2.]

e. If there are no observations at $y = 10$, what does the estimated model reduce to? Does this finding seem sensible?

19.4. a. Suppose you are hired to explain fire damage to buildings in terms of building and neighborhood characteristics. If you use cross section data on reported fires, is there a sample selection problem due to the fact that most buildings do not catch fire during the year?

b. If you want to estimate the relationship between contributions to a 401(k) plan and the match rate of the plan—the rate at which the employer matches employee contributions—is there a sample selection problem if you only use a sample of workers already enrolled in a 401(k) plan?

19.5. In example 19.4, suppose that *IQ* is an indicator of *abil*, and *KWW* is another indicator (see Section 5.3.2). Find assumptions under which IV on the selected sample is valid.

19.6. Let $f(\cdot \mid \mathbf{x}_i; \boldsymbol{\theta})$ denote the density of y_i given $\mathbf{x}_i$ for a random draw from the population. Find the conditional density of y_i given $(\mathbf{x}_i, s_i = 1)$ when the selection rule is $s_i = 1[a_1(\mathbf{x}_i) < y_i < a_2(\mathbf{x}_i)]$, where $a_1(\mathbf{x})$ and $a_2(\mathbf{x})$ are known functions of $\mathbf{x}$. In the Hausman and Wise (1977) example, $a_2(\mathbf{x})$ was a function of family size because the poverty income level depends on family size.

19.7. Suppose in Section 19.6.1 we replace assumption 19.1d with

$$\mathrm{E}(u_1 \mid v_2) = \gamma_1 v_2 + \gamma_2(v_2^2 - 1).$$

(We subtract unity from v_2^2 to ensure that the second term has zero expectation.)

a. Using the fact that $\mathrm{Var}(v_2 \mid v_2 > -a) = 1 - \lambda(a)[\lambda(a) + a]$, show that

$$\mathrm{E}(y_1 \mid \mathbf{x}, y_2 = 1) = \mathbf{x}_1\boldsymbol{\beta}_1 + \gamma_1\lambda(\mathbf{x}\boldsymbol{\delta}_2) - \gamma_2\lambda(\mathbf{x}\boldsymbol{\delta}_2)\mathbf{x}\boldsymbol{\delta}_2.$$

[Hint: Take $a = \mathbf{x}\boldsymbol{\delta}_2$ and use the fact that $\mathrm{E}(v_2^2 \mid v_2 > -a) = \mathrm{Var}(v_2 \mid v_2 > -a) + [\mathrm{E}(v_2 \mid v_2 > -a)]^2$.]

b. Explain how to correct for sample selection in this case.

c. How would you test for the presence of sample selection bias?

19.8. Consider the following alternative to procedure 19.2 when y_2 is always observed. First, run the OLS regression of y_2 on $\mathbf{z}$ and obtain the fitted values, $\hat{y}_2$.

Next, get the inverse Mills ratio, $\hat{\lambda}_3$, from the probit of y_3 on $\mathbf{z}$. Finally, run the OLS regression y_1 on $\mathbf{z}_1, \hat{y}_2, \hat{\lambda}_3$ using the selected sample.

a. Find a set of sufficient conditions that imply consistency of the proposed procedure. (Do not worry about regularity conditions.)

b. Show that the assumptions from part a are more restrictive than those in procedure 19.2, and give some examples that are covered by procedure 19.2 but not by the alternative procedure.

19.9. Apply procedure 19.4 to the data in MROZ.RAW. Use a constant, *exper*, and $exper^2$ as elements of $\mathbf{z}_1$; take $y_2 = educ$. The other elements of $\mathbf{z}$ should include *age*, *kidslt6*, *kidsge6*, *nwifeinc*, *motheduc*, *fatheduc*, and *huseduc*.

19.10. Consider the model

$$y_1 = \mathbf{z}\boldsymbol{\delta}_1 + v_1$$

$$y_2 = \mathbf{z}\boldsymbol{\delta}_2 + v_2$$

$$y_3 = \max(0, \alpha_{31} y_1 + \alpha_{32} y_2 + \mathbf{z}_3\boldsymbol{\delta}_3 + u_3),$$

where $(\mathbf{z}, y_2, y_3)$ are always observed and y_1 is observed when $y_3 > 0$. The first two equations are reduced-form equations, and the third equation is of primary interest. For example, take $y_1 = \log(wage^o)$, $y_2 = educ$, and $y_3 = hours$, and then education and $\log(wage^o)$ are possibly endogenous in the labor supply function. Assume that (v_1, v_2, u_3) are jointly zero-mean normal and independent of $\mathbf{z}$.

a. Find a simple way to consistently estimate the parameters in the third equation allowing for arbitrary correlations among (v_1, v_2, u_3). Be sure to state any identification assumptions needed.

b. Now suppose that y_2 is observed only when $y_3 > 0$; for example, $y_1 = \log(wage^o)$, $y_2 = \log(benefits^o)$, $y_3 = hours$. Now derive a multistep procedure for estimating the third equation under the same assumptions as in part a.

c. How can we estimate the average partial effects?

19.11. Consider the following conditional moment restrictions problem with a selected sample. In the population, $\mathrm{E}[\mathbf{r}(\mathbf{w}, \boldsymbol{\theta}_o) \mid \mathbf{x}] = \mathbf{0}$. Let s be the selection indicator, and assume that

$$\mathrm{E}[\mathbf{r}(\mathbf{w}, \boldsymbol{\theta}_o) \mid \mathbf{x}, s] = \mathbf{0}.$$

Sufficient is that $s = f(\mathbf{x})$ for a nonrandom function f.

a. Let $\mathbf{Z}_i$ be a $G \times L$ matrix of functions of $\mathbf{x}_i$. Show that $\boldsymbol{\theta}_o$ satisfies

$$\mathrm{E}[s_i \mathbf{Z}_i' \mathbf{r}(\mathbf{w}_i, \boldsymbol{\theta}_o)] = \mathbf{0}$$

b. Write down the objective function for the system nonlinear 2SLS estimator based on the selected sample. Argue that, under the appropriate rank condition, the estimator is consistent and $\sqrt{N}$-asymptotically normal.

c. Write down the objective function for a minimum chi-square estimator using the selected sample. Use the estimates from part b to estimate the weighting matrix. Argue that the estimator is consistent and $\sqrt{N}$-asymptotically normal.

19.12. Consider model (19.56), where selection is ignorable in the sense that $\mathrm{E}(u_1 \mid \mathbf{z}, v_3) = 0$. However, data are missing on y_2 when $y_3 = 0$, and $\mathrm{E}(y_2 \mid \mathbf{z}, y_3) \neq \mathrm{E}(y_2 \mid \mathbf{z})$.

a. Find $\mathrm{E}(y_1 \mid \mathbf{z}, y_3)$.

b. If, in addition to assumption 19.2, (v_2, v_3) is independent of $\mathbf{z}$ and $\mathrm{E}(v_2 \mid v_3) = \gamma_2 v_3$, find $\mathrm{E}(y_1 \mid \mathbf{z}, y_3 = 1)$.

c. Suggest a two-step method for consistently estimating $\boldsymbol{\delta}_1$ and α_1.

d. Does this method generally work if $\mathrm{E}(u_1 \mid \mathbf{z}, y_3) \neq 0$?

e. Would you bother with the method from part c if $\mathrm{E}(u_1 \mid \mathbf{z}, y_2, y_3) = 0$? Explain.

19.13. In Section 17.6 we discussed two-part models for a corner solution outcome, say, y. These models have sometimes been studied in the context of incidental truncation.

a. Suppose you have a parametric model for the distribution of y conditional on $\mathbf{x}$ and $y > 0$. (Cragg's model and the lognormal model from Section 17.6 are examples.) If you estimate the parameters of this model by conditional MLE, using only the observations for which $y_i > 0$, do the parameter estimates suffer from sample selection bias? Explain.

b. If instead you specify only $\mathrm{E}(y \mid \mathbf{x}, y > 0) = \exp(\mathbf{x}\boldsymbol{\beta})$ and estimate $\boldsymbol{\beta}$ by nonlinear least squares using observations for which $y_i > 0$, do the estimates suffer from sample selection bias?

c. In addition to the specification from part b, suppose that $\mathrm{P}(y = 0 \mid \mathbf{x}) = 1 - \Phi(\mathbf{x}\boldsymbol{\gamma})$. How would you estimate $\boldsymbol{\gamma}$?

d. Given the assumptions in parts b and c, how would you estimate $\mathrm{E}(y \mid \mathbf{x})$?

e. Given your answers to the first four parts, do you think viewing estimation of two-part models as an incidental truncation problem is appropriate?

19.14. Consider equation (19.30) under the assumption $\mathrm{E}(u \mid \mathbf{z}, s) = \mathrm{E}(u \mid s) = (1 - s)\alpha_0 + s\alpha_1$. The first equality is the assumption; the second is unrestrictive, as it simply allows the mean of u to differ in the selected and unselected subpopulations.

a. Show that 2SLS estimation using the selected subsample consistently estimates the slope parameters, $\beta_2, \ldots, \beta_K$. What is the plim of the intercept estimator? (Hint: Replace u with $(1 - s)\alpha_0 + s\alpha_1 + e$, where $\mathrm{E}(e \mid \mathbf{z}, s) = 0$.)

b. Show that $\mathrm{E}(u \mid \mathbf{z}, s) = \mathrm{E}(u \mid s)$ if (u, s) is independent of $\mathbf{z}$. Does independence of s and $\mathbf{z}$ seem reasonable?

19.15. Suppose that y given $\mathbf{x}$ follows a standard censored Tobit, where y is a corner solution response. However, there is at least one element of $\mathbf{x}$ that we can observe only when $y > 0$. (An example is seen when y is quantity demanded of a good or service, and one element of $\mathbf{x}$ is price, derived as total expenditure on the good divided by y whenever $y > 0$.)

a. Explain why we cannot use standard censored Tobit maximum likelihood estimation to estimate $\boldsymbol{\beta}$ and σ^2. What method can we use instead?

b. How is it that we can still estimate $\mathrm{E}(y \mid \mathbf{x})$, even though we do not observe some elements of $\mathbf{x}$ when $y = 0$?

19.16. Consider a standard linear model with an endogenous explanatory variable:

$$y_1 = \mathbf{z}_1\boldsymbol{\delta}_1 + \alpha_1 y_2 + u_1$$

$$y_2 = \mathbf{z}\boldsymbol{\delta}_2 + v_2,$$

but where y_2 is censored from above. Let r_2 be the censoring variable (which may be random) and define $w_2 = \min(r_2, y_2)$. Assume that (u_1, v_2) is independent of $(\mathbf{z}, r_2)$ and $\mathrm{E}(u_1 \mid v_2) = \rho_1 v_2$.

a. Show that

$$\mathrm{E}(y_1 \mid \mathbf{z}, r_2, v_2) = \mathbf{z}_1\boldsymbol{\delta}_1 + \alpha_1 y_2 + \rho_1 v_2.$$

b. Define $s_2 = 1[y_2 < w_2]$, so $s_2 = 1$ means y_2 is observed. How come

$$\mathrm{E}(y_1 \mid \mathbf{z}, r_2, v_2, s_2) = \mathrm{E}(y_1 \mid \mathbf{z}, r_2, v_2) = \mathbf{z}_1\boldsymbol{\delta}_1 + \alpha_1 y_2 + \rho_1 v_2?$$

c. Propose a two-step estimator that consistently estimates $\boldsymbol{\delta}_1$ and α_1 (along with ρ_1) where only the data with y_{i2} uncensored are used in the second step. How would you obtain valid standard errors?

19.17. Consider an unobserved effects panel data model with binary censoring:

$$y_{it} = \mathbf{x}_{it}\boldsymbol{\beta} + c_i + u_{it}$$

$$w_{it} = 1[y_{it} > r_{it}],$$

where r_{it} is the known censoring value for unit i in time t. Our goal is to estimate $\boldsymbol{\beta}$, which, in the absense of censoring, we could achieve by fixed effects, first difference, random effects (under stronger assumptions), or some variation on these.

a. Maintain that the censoring values are strictly exogenous conditional on c_i (and $\mathbf{x}_i = (\mathbf{x}_{i1}, \ldots, \mathbf{x}_{iT})$) along with normality:

$$\mathrm{D}(u_{it} \mid \mathbf{x}_i, \mathbf{r}_i, c_i) = \mathrm{Normal}(0, \sigma_u^2),$$

where $\mathbf{r}_i = (r_{i1}, r_{i2}, \ldots, r_{iT})$. Explain what kinds of censoring this assumption rules out.

b. Allow censoring to depend on c_i using the Chamberlain-Mundlak device:

$$c_i = \psi + \bar{\mathbf{x}}_i\xi + \eta\bar{r}_i + a_i$$

$$\mathrm{D}(a_i \mid \mathbf{x}_i, \mathbf{r}_i) = \mathrm{Normal}(0, \sigma_a^2),$$

where, as usual, the overbar means time average. In other words, heterogeneity may be (partially) correlated with the average censoring value. Using this assumption with that in part a, show that $\mathrm{P}(w_{it} = 1 \mid \mathbf{x}_i, \mathbf{r}_i)$ follows a probit model and obtain the coefficients on the various explanatory variables.

c. Explain how to consistently estimate $\boldsymbol{\beta}$ without further assumptions (other than that both $\{\mathbf{x}_{it}\}$ and $\{r_{it}\}$ have sufficient time variation).

d. What additional assumption would allow you to also estimate σ_u^2 and σ_a^2? Explain how you would use this assumption in estimation.

19.18. Suppose that in the population, $\mathrm{D}(y \mid \mathbf{x})$ follows a Tobit$(\mathbf{x}\boldsymbol{\beta}, \sigma^2)$ distribution. However, we observe y only when it is strictly positive. (Such a scenario is common for **on-site sampling**, where only individuals known to participate in an activity are sampled. An example is y is annual days spent visiting national parks, and surveys are taken at national parks.)

a. How would you estimate $\boldsymbol{\beta}$ and σ^2 given a random sample from the subpopulation with $y > 0$?

b. How would you estimate partial effects of the x_j on $\mathrm{E}(y \mid \mathbf{x})$? How and why does this approach differ from the usual truncated regression setup?

c. Can you estimate a hurdle model of the kind covered in Section 17.6? Explain.

19.19. Consider a count random variable, y_i, with conditional probability density $f_y(\cdot \mid \mathbf{x})$. Suppose that the integer $r_i \geq 0$ is a right censoring point, and assume that $P(y_i = y \mid \mathbf{x}_i, r_i) = P(y_i = y \mid \mathbf{x}_i)$. For a random draw i from the population, we observe the random variable $w_i = \min(y_i, r_i)$.

a. Let $F_y(\cdot \mid \mathbf{x})$ denote the conditional cdf of y_i given $\mathbf{x}_i = \mathbf{x}$. Find the density of w_i given $(\mathbf{x}_i, r_i)$ for $w = 0, 1, \ldots, r_i$.

b. Find the density from part a if y_i has a conditional Poisson distribution with mean $\exp(\mathbf{x}_i \boldsymbol{\beta})$.

c. If you estimate $\boldsymbol{\beta}$ by maximum likelihood using the right censored data, is the resulting estimator generally robust to failure of the Poisson distribution? Explain.

d. Use your answer to part a to discuss the costs of data censoring for a count variable.

e. What other underlying population distribution might you use, and why?

20 Stratified Sampling and Cluster Sampling

20.1 Introduction

In this chapter we study estimation when the data have been obtained by means of two common nonrandom sampling schemes. **Stratified sampling** occurs when units in a population are sampled with probabilities that do not reflect their frequency in the population. For example, in obtaining a data set on families, low-income families might be oversampled and high-income families undersampled. There are various mechanisms by which stratified samples are obtained, and we will cover the most common ones in this chapter.

The case of truncated sampling covered in Section 19.7 can be viewed as an extreme case of stratified sampling, where part of the population is not sampled at all. For the most part, in this chapter we focus on the case where the entire population is sampled (but where the sampling frequencies differ from the population frequencies). As we will see, in this setup simple weighting methods are available for recovering the underlying population parameters.

Cluster sampling refers to cases where clusters or groups, rather than individual units, are drawn from a population. For example, in evaluating the impact of educational policies on test performance of fourth-graders in Michigan, one might sample classrooms from the entire state (as opposed to randomly drawing fourth-graders from the population of all fourth-graders in Michigan). The classrooms constitute the clusters, and the students within the classrooms are the inividual units. The cluster sampling scheme generally implies that the outcomes of units within a cluster are correlated through unobserved "cluster effects." (In addition, some covariates, such as quality of the teacher, will be perfectly correlated because students in the same class have the same teacher. Other covariates, such as family income, are likely to have substantial correlation but would vary within a classroom.)

When a cluster sample is obtained by randomly drawing clusters from a large population of clusters, the resulting data set has features in common with the panel data sets we have studied throughout the book. Namely, we have many clusters that can be assumed to be independent of each other, but observations within a cluster are correlated. In, say, a firm-level panel data set, the firm plays the role of a cluster and time plays the role of the individual units. Because of their statistical similarity to "large N, small T" panel data sets, most of the statistical methods applied to cluster samples are familiar from our earlier analysis. We treat cluster samples separately because the nature of the within-cluster correlation is generally different from time series correlation, and cluster samples are naturally unbalanced even when there is no sample selection problem. (For example, in the population of fourth-grade classrooms in Michigan, we expect some variation in class size.)

20.2 Stratified Sampling

We begin with an analysis of **stratified samples** where, as mentioned in the introduction, different subsets of the population are sampled with different frequencies. Obtaining samples that are not representative of the underlying population is often done intentionally in obtaining survey data. Some surveys are designed primarily to learn about a particular subset of the population (perhaps based on income, education, age, or race). That group is typically overrepresented in the sample compared with its frequency in the population.

Stratification can be based on exogenous variables or endogenous variables (which are known once a model and assumptions have been specified) or some combination of these. As in the case of the sample selection problems we discussed in Chapter 19, it is important to know which is the case.

We cover the two most common types of stratified sampling in this section (and touch on a third). In Section 20.2.1 we study **standard stratified sampling**, which involves stratifying the population and then drawing random samples from the different strata. A different sampling scheme, **variable probability sampling**, is based on randomly drawing units from a population but then keeping the observations with unequal probabilities.

The section does not provide a detailed treatment of **choice-based sampling**, which occurs in discrete response models when the stratification is based entirely on the response variable. Various methods have been proposed for estimating discrete response models with choice-based samples under different assumptions. Manski and McFadden (1981) and Cosslett (1993) contain general treatments. For a class of discrete response models, Cosslett (1981) proposed an efficient estimation method with choice-based sampling, and Imbens (1992) obtained a computationally simple method-of-moments estimator that also achieves the efficiency bound. Imbens and Lancaster (1996) allow for general response variables in a maximum likelihood setting. In this section, we focus on a convenient weighted-estimation approach that applies to a variety of estimation methods. Not surprisingly, when applied in maximum likelihood contexts, weighted estimators are generally inefficient.

20.2.1 Standard Stratified Sampling and Variable Probability Sampling

The two most common stratification schemes used in obtaining data sets in the social sciences are **standard stratified sampling (SS sampling)** and **variable probability sampling (VP sampling)**. In SS sampling, the population is first partitioned into J groups, $\mathcal{W}_1, \mathcal{W}_2, \ldots, \mathcal{W}_J$, which we assume are nonoverlapping and exhaustive. We let $\mathbf{w}$ denote the random vector representing the population of interest.

STANDARD STRATIFIED SAMPLING: For $j = 1, \ldots, J$, draw a random sample of size N_j from stratum j. For each j, denote this random sample by $\{\mathbf{w}_{ij}: i = 1, 2, \ldots, N_j\}$.

The strata sample sizes N_j are nonrandom. Therefore, the total sample size, $N = N_1 + \cdots + N_J$, is also nonrandom. A randomly drawn observation from stratum $j, \mathbf{w}_{ij}$, has distribution $\mathrm{D}(\mathbf{w} \mid \mathbf{w} \in \mathscr{W}_j)$. Therefore, while observations within a stratum are identically distributed, observations across strata are not. A scheme that is similar in nature to SS sampling is called **multinomial sampling**, where a stratum is first picked at random and then an observation is randomly drawn from the stratum. This *does* result in i.i.d. observations, but it does not correspond to how stratified samples are obtained in practice. It also leads to the same estimators as under SS sampling, so we do not discuss it further; see Cosslett (1993) or Wooldridge (1999b) for further discussion.

Variable probability samples are obtained using a different scheme. First, an observation is drawn at random from the population. If the observation falls into stratum j, it is kept with probability p_j. Thus, random draws from the population are discarded with varying frequencies depending on which stratum they fall into. This kind of sampling is appropriate when information on the variable or variables that determine the strata is relatively easy to obtain compared with the rest of the information. Survey data sets, including initial interviews to collect panel or longitudinal data, are good examples. Suppose we want to oversample individuals from, say, lower income classes. We can first ask an individual her or his income. If the response is in income class j, this person is kept in the sample with probability p_j, and then the remaining information, such as education, work history, family background, and so on can be collected; otherwise, the person is dropped without further interviewing.

A key feature of VP sampling is that observations within a stratum are discarded randomly. As discussed by Wooldridge (1999b), VP sampling is equivalent to the following:

VARIABLE PROBABILITY SAMPLING: Repeat the following steps N times:

1. Draw an observation $\mathbf{w}_i$ at random from the population.
2. If $\mathbf{w}_i$ is in stratum j, toss a (biased) coin with probability p_j of turning up heads. Let $h_{ij} = 1$ if the coin turns up heads and zero otherwise.
3. Keep observation i if $h_{ij} = 1$; otherwise, omit it from the sample.

The number of observations falling into stratum j is denoted N_j, and the number of data points we actually have for estimation is $N_0 = N_1 + N_2 + \cdots + N_J$. Notice that if N—the number of times the population is sampled—is fixed, then N_0 is a random variable: we do not know what each N_j will be prior to sampling.

The assumption that the probability of the coin turning up heads in step 2 depends only on the stratum ensures that sampling is random within each stratum. This roughly reflects how samples are obtained for certain large cross-sectional and panel data sets used in economics, including the panel study of income dynamics and the national longitudinal survey.

To see that a VP sample can be analyzed as a random sample, we construct a population that incorporates the stratification. The VP sampling scheme is equivalent to first tossing all J coins before actually observing which stratum $\mathbf{w}_i$ falls into; this gives $(h_{i1}, \ldots, h_{iJ})$. Next, $\mathbf{w}_i$ is observed to fall into one of the strata. Finally, the outcome is kept or not depending on the coin flip for that stratum. The result is that the vector $(\mathbf{w}_i, \mathbf{h}_i)$, where $\mathbf{h}_i$ is the J-vector of binary indicators h_{ij}, is a random sample from a new population with sample space $\mathcal{W} \times \mathcal{H}$, where $\mathcal{W}$ is the original sample space and $\mathcal{H}$ denotes the sample space associated with outcomes from flipping J coins. Under this alternative way of viewing the sampling scheme, $\mathbf{h}_i$ is independent of $\mathbf{w}_i$. Treating $(\mathbf{w}_i, \mathbf{h}_i)$ as a random draw from the new population is not at odds with the fact that our estimators are based on a nonrandom sample from the original population: we simply use the vector $\mathbf{h}_i$ to determine which observations are kept in the estimation procedure.

20.2.2 Weighted Estimators to Account for Stratification

With variable probability sampling, it is easy to construct weighted objective functions that produce consistent and asymptotically normal estimators of the population parameters. Initially, it is useful to define a set of binary variables that indicate whether a random draw, $\mathbf{w}_i$, is kept in the sample and, if so, which stratum it falls into. Let $z_{ij} = 1[\mathbf{w}_i \in \mathcal{W}_j]$, $j = 1, \ldots, J$ be the binary strata indicators, that is, $z_{ij} = 1$ if and only if $\mathbf{w}_i \in \mathcal{W}_j$. The vector of strata indicators is $\mathbf{z}_i = (z_{i1}, \ldots, z_{iJ})$. Then define

$$r_{ij} = h_{ij} z_{ij}, \qquad j = 1, \ldots, J. \tag{20.1}$$

By definition, $r_{ij} = 1$ for at most one j. If $h_{ij} = 1$ then $r_{ij} = z_{ij}$, so that r_{ij} is the same as the stratum indicator. If $r_{ij} = 0$ for all $j = 1, 2, \ldots, J$, then the random draw $\mathbf{w}_i$ does not appear in the sample (and we probably do not know which stratum the observation fell into).

With these definitions, we can define the **weighted M-estimator**, $\hat{\boldsymbol{\theta}}_w$, as the solution to

$$\min_{\boldsymbol{\theta} \in \boldsymbol{\Theta}} \sum_{i=1}^{N} \sum_{j=1}^{J} p_j^{-1} r_{ij} q(\mathbf{w}_i, \boldsymbol{\theta}), \tag{20.2}$$

where $q(\mathbf{w}, \boldsymbol{\theta})$ is the objective function that is chosen to identify the population parameters $\boldsymbol{\theta}_o$. Note how the outer summation is over all *potential* observations, that is, the observations that *would* appear in a random sample. The indicators r_{ij} simply pick out the observations that actually appear in the available sample, and these indicators also attach each observed data point to its stratum. The objective function (20.2) weights each observed data point in the sample by the inverse of the sampling probability. For implementation it is useful to write the objective function as

$$\min_{\boldsymbol{\theta} \in \boldsymbol{\Theta}} \sum_{i=1}^{N_0} p_{j_i}^{-1} q(\mathbf{w}_i, \boldsymbol{\theta}), \tag{20.3}$$

where, without loss of generality, the data points actually observed are ordered $i = 1, \dots, N_0$. Since j_i is the stratum for observation i, $p_{j_i}^{-1}$ is the weight attached to observation i in the estimation. In practice, the $p_{j_i}^{-1}$ are the **sampling weights** reported with other variables in VP stratified samples.

The objective function $q(\mathbf{w}, \boldsymbol{\theta})$ contains all of the M-estimator examples we have covered so far in the book, including least squares (linear and nonlinear), conditional maximum likelihood, and partial maximum likelihood. In panel data applications, the probability weights are from sampling in an initial year. Weights for later years are intended to reflect both stratification (if any) and possible attrition, as discussed in Section 19.9.3.

In the case of estimating the mean from a population, the resulting weighted M-estimator has a familiar form. Let $\mu_o = \mathrm{E}(w)$ be the population mean. Then the weighted M-estimator solves

$$\min_{\mu \in \mathbb{R}} \sum_{i=1}^{N_0} p_{j_i}^{-1} (w_i - \mu)^2, \tag{20.4}$$

and the solution is easily seen to be the weighted average

$$\hat{\mu}_w = \sum_{i=1}^{N_0} v_{j_i} w_i, \tag{20.5}$$

where

$$v_{j_i} = \left(\sum_{h=1}^{N_0} p_{j_h}^{-1} \right)^{-1} p_{j_i}^{-1}. \tag{20.6}$$

In the general case, Wooldridge (1999b) shows that, under the same assumptions as Theorem 12.2 and the assumption that each sampling probability is positive, the weighted M-estimator consistently estimates $\boldsymbol{\theta}_o$, which is assumed to uniquely minimize $\mathrm{E}[q(\mathbf{w}, \boldsymbol{\theta})]$. Actually, as shown by Wooldridge (2007), consistency follows from our treatment of inverse-probability-weighted M-estimation in Section 19.8. As noted earlier, the vector $\mathbf{z}_i$ is the J-vector of strata indicators, $z_{ij} = 1[w_i \in \mathcal{W}_j]$. Under VP sampling, the sampling probability depends only on the stratum, so Assumption 19.6 holds by design. In particular, define $s_i = h_{i1}z_{i1} + \cdots + h_{iJ}z_{iJ}$ to be the selection indicator. Then

$$\mathrm{P}(s_i = 1 \mid \mathbf{z}_i, \mathbf{w}_i) = \mathrm{P}(s_i = 1 \mid \mathbf{z}_i) = p_1 z_{i1} + p_2 z_{i2} + \cdots + p_J z_{iJ}. \tag{20.7}$$

Therefore, we can use the consistency result for IPW M-estimation directly to establish the consistency of the IPW estimator for VP sampling.

Asymptotic normality also follows under the same regularity conditions as in Chapter 12. Wooldridge (1999b) shows that a valid estimator of the asymptotic variance of $\hat{\boldsymbol{\theta}}_w$ is

$$\left[\sum_{i=1}^{N_0} p_{j_i}^{-1} \nabla_\theta^2 q_i(\hat{\boldsymbol{\theta}}_w)\right]^{-1} \left[\sum_{i=1}^{N_0} p_{j_i}^{-2} \nabla_\theta q_i(\hat{\boldsymbol{\theta}}_w)' \nabla_\theta q_i(\hat{\boldsymbol{\theta}}_w)\right] \left[\sum_{i=1}^{N_0} p_{j_i}^{-1} \nabla_\theta^2 q_i(\hat{\boldsymbol{\theta}}_w)\right]^{-1}, \tag{20.8}$$

which looks like the standard formula for a robust variance matrix estimator except for the presence of the sampling probabilities p_{j_i}.

When $\mathbf{w}$ partitions as $(\mathbf{x}, \mathbf{y})$, an alternative estimator replaces the Hessian $\nabla_\theta^2 q_i(\hat{\boldsymbol{\theta}}_w)$ in expression (20.8) with $\mathbf{A}(\mathbf{x}_i, \hat{\boldsymbol{\theta}}_w)$, where $\mathbf{A}(\mathbf{x}_i, \boldsymbol{\theta}_o) \equiv \mathrm{E}[\nabla_\theta^2 q(\mathbf{w}_i, \boldsymbol{\theta}_o) \mid \mathbf{x}_i]$, as in Chapter 12. Asymptotic standard errors and Wald statistics can be obtained using either estimate of the asymptotic variance.

We can also apply the "surprising" efficiency result concerning estimation of the sampling probabilities to VP stratification—at least if additional information is kept during the sampling. For a random draw i the log likelihood for the density of s_i given $\mathbf{z}_i$ can be written as

$$\ell_i(\mathbf{p}) = \sum_{j=1}^{J} z_{ij}[s_i \log(p_j) + (1 - s_i)\log(1 - p_j)]. \tag{20.9}$$

For each $j = 1, \ldots, J$, the maximum likelihood estimate, $\hat{p}_j$, is easily seen to be the fraction of observations retained out of all of those originally drawn from from stratum j: $\hat{p}_j = M_j/N_j$, where $M_j = \sum_{i=1}^{N} z_{ij}s_i$ and $N_j = \sum_{i=1}^{N} z_{ij}$. In other words, M_j is the number of retained data points from stratum j, and N_j is the number of times stratum j was drawn in the VP sampling scheme. If the N_j, $j = 1, \ldots, J$, are reported along with the VP sample, then we can easily obtain the $\hat{p}_j$ (because the M_j are always known). We do not need to observe the specific strata indicators for observations for which $s_i = 0$. (If the stratification is exogenous, as defined in Section 20.2.3, then it does not matter whether we use the estimated or known sampling probabilities: the asymptotic variance is unchanged in that case.)

Example 20.1 (Linear Model under Stratified Sampling): In estimating the linear model

$$y = \mathbf{x}\boldsymbol{\beta}_{\mathrm{o}} + u, \qquad \mathrm{E}(\mathbf{x}'u) = \mathbf{0} \tag{20.10}$$

by IPW least squares, the asymptotic variance matrix estimator is

$$\left(\sum_{i=1}^{N_0} p_{j_i}^{-1}\mathbf{x}_i'\mathbf{x}_i\right)^{-1}\left(\sum_{i=1}^{N_0} p_{j_i}^{-2}\hat{u}_i^2\mathbf{x}_i'\mathbf{x}_i\right)\left(\sum_{i=1}^{N_0} p_{j_i}^{-1}\mathbf{x}_i'\mathbf{x}_i\right)^{-1}, \tag{20.11}$$

where $\hat{u}_i = y_i - \mathbf{x}_i\hat{\boldsymbol{\beta}}_w$ is the residual after WLS estimation. Interestingly, this is simply the White (1980b) heteroskedasticity-consistent covariance matrix estimator applied to the stratified sample, where all variables for observation i are weighted by $p_{j_i}^{-1/2}$ before performing the regression. This estimator has been suggested by, among others, Hausman and Wise (1981). Hausman and Wise use maximum likelihood to obtain more efficient estimators in the context of the normal linear regression model, that is, $u \mid \mathbf{x} \sim \mathrm{Normal}(\mathbf{x}\boldsymbol{\beta}_{\mathrm{o}}, \sigma_{\mathrm{o}}^2)$. Because of stratification, MLE is not generally robust to failure of the homoskedastic normality assumption.

It is important to remember that the form of expression (20.11) in this example is not due to potential heteroskedasticity in the underlying population model. Even if $\mathrm{E}(u^2 \mid \mathbf{x}) = \sigma_{\mathrm{o}}^2$, the estimator (20.11) is generally needed because of the stratified sampling. This estimator also works in the presence of heteroskedasticity of arbitrary and unknown form in the population, and it is routinely computed by many regression packages.

Example 20.2 (Conditional MLE under Stratified Sampling): When $f(\mathbf{y} \mid \mathbf{x}; \boldsymbol{\theta})$ is a correctly specified model for the density of $\mathbf{y}_i$ given $\mathbf{x}_i$ in the population, the inverse-probability-weighted MLE is obtained with $q_i(\boldsymbol{\theta}) \equiv -\log[f(\mathbf{y}_i \mid \mathbf{x}_i; \boldsymbol{\theta})]$. This estimator is consistent and asymptotically normal, with asymptotic variance estimator given by expression (20.8) [or the form that uses $\mathbf{A}(\mathbf{x}_i, \hat{\boldsymbol{\theta}}_w)$].

A weighting scheme is also available in the standard stratified sampling case, but the weights are different from the VP sampling case. To derive them, let $Q_j = \mathrm{P}(\mathbf{w} \in \mathcal{W}_j)$ denote the population frequency for stratum j; we assume that the Q_j are *known*. By the law of iterated expectations,

$$\mathrm{E}[q(\mathbf{w}, \boldsymbol{\theta})] = Q_1\mathrm{E}[q(\mathbf{w}, \boldsymbol{\theta}) \mid \mathbf{w} \in \mathcal{W}_1] + \cdots + Q_J\mathrm{E}[q(\mathbf{w}, \boldsymbol{\theta}) \mid \mathbf{w} \in \mathcal{W}_J] \tag{20.12}$$

for any $\boldsymbol{\theta}$. For each j, $\mathrm{E}[q(\mathbf{w}, \boldsymbol{\theta}) \mid \mathbf{w} \in \mathscr{W}_j]$ can be consistently estimated using a random sample obtained from stratum j. This scheme leads to the sample objective function

$$Q_1\left[N_1^{-1}\sum_{i=1}^{N_1} q(\mathbf{w}_{i1}, \boldsymbol{\theta})\right] + \cdots + Q_J\left[N_J^{-1}\sum_{i=1}^{N_J} q(\mathbf{w}_{iJ}, \boldsymbol{\theta})\right],$$

where $\mathbf{w}_{ij}$ denotes a random draw i from stratum j and N_j is the nonrandom sample size for stratum j. We can apply the uniform law of large numbers to each term, so that the sum converges uniformly to equation (20.12) under the regularity conditions in Chapter 12. By multiplying and dividing each term by the total number of observations $N = N_1 + \cdots + N_J$, we can write the sample objective function more simply as

$$N^{-1}\sum_{i=1}^{N} (Q_{j_i}/H_{j_i}) q(\mathbf{w}_i, \boldsymbol{\theta}), \tag{20.13}$$

where j_i denotes the stratum for observation i and $H_j \equiv N_j/N$ denotes the fraction of observations in stratum j. Because we have the stratum indicator j_i, we can drop the j subscript on $\mathbf{w}_i$. When we omit the division by N, equation (20.13) has the same form as equation (20.3), but the weights are (Q_{j_i}/H_{j_i}) rather than $p_{j_i}^{-1}$ (and the arguments for why each weighting works are very different). Also, in general, the formula for the asymptotic variance is different in the SS sampling case. In addition to the minor notational change of replacing N_0 with N, the middle matrix in equation (20.8) becomes

$$\sum_{j=1}^{J} (Q_j^2/H_j^2)\left[\sum_{i=1}^{N_j} (\nabla_\theta \hat{q}_{ij} - \overline{\nabla_\theta q_j})'(\nabla_\theta \hat{q}_{ij} - \overline{\nabla_\theta q_j})\right], \tag{20.14}$$

where $\nabla_\theta \hat{q}_{ij} \equiv \nabla_\theta q(\mathbf{w}_{ij}, \hat{\boldsymbol{\theta}}_w)$ and $\overline{\nabla_\theta q_j} \equiv N_j^{-1}\sum_{i=1}^{N_j} \nabla_\theta \hat{q}_{ij}$ (the within-stratum sample average). This approach requires us to explicitly partition observations into their respective strata. See Wooldridge (2001) for a detailed derivation. [If in the VP sampling case the population frequencies Q_j are known, it is better to use as weights $Q_j/(N_j/N_0)$ rather than p_j^{-1}, which makes the analysis look just like the SS sampling case. See Wooldridge (1999b) for details.]

If in Example 20.2 we have standard stratified sampling rather than VP sampling, the weighted MLE is typically called the **weighted exogenous sample MLE (WESMLE)**; this estimator was suggested by Manski and Lerman (1977) in the context of choice-based sampling in discrete response models. (Actually, Manski and Lerman (1977) use multinomial sampling where H_j is the probability of picking stratum j. But Cosslett (1981) showed that a more efficient estimator is obtained by using N_j/N, as one always does in the case of SS sampling; see Wooldridge (1999b) for an extension of Cosslett's result to the M-estimator case.)

Provided that the sampling weights Q_{j_i}/H_{j_i} or $p_{j_i}^{-1}$ are given (along with the stratum), analysis with the weighted M-estimator under SS or VP sampling is fairly straightforward, but it is not likely to be efficient. In the conditional maximum likelihood case it is certainly possible to do better. See Imbens and Lancaster (1996) for a careful treatment.

20.2.3 Stratification Based on Exogenous Variables

When $\mathbf{w}$ partitions as $(\mathbf{x}, \mathbf{y})$, where $\mathbf{x}$ is exogenous in a sense to be made precise, and stratification is based entirely on $\mathbf{x}$, the standard unweighted estimator on the stratified sample is consistent and asymptotically normal. The sense in which $\mathbf{x}$ must be exogenous is that $\boldsymbol{\theta}_o$ solves

$$\min_{\boldsymbol{\theta} \in \boldsymbol{\Theta}} \mathrm{E}[q(\mathbf{w}, \boldsymbol{\theta}) \mid \mathbf{x}] \tag{20.15}$$

for each possible outcome $\mathbf{x}$. This assumption holds in a variety of contexts with conditioning variables and correctly specified models. For example, as we discussed in Chapter 12, the condition holds for nonlinear regression when the conditional mean is correctly specified and $\boldsymbol{\theta}_o$ is the vector of conditional mean parameters; in Chapter 13 we showed that this holds for conditional maximum likelihood when the density of $\mathbf{y}$ given $\mathbf{x}$ is correct. It also holds in other cases, including the quasi–maximum likelihood estimators we discussed in Chapter 18 when the conditional mean is correctly specified. One interesting point—which we will rely on in our treatment of estimating average treatment effects in Chapter 21—is that, in the linear case, it will not be enough for u to be uncorrelated with $\mathbf{x}$. If we want to estimate the linear projection of y on $\mathbf{x}$, we generally need to use the weighted estimator, even if stratification is a function of $\mathbf{x}$.

In the case of VP sampling, a common form of exogenous stratification occurs when the strata are defined in terms of $\mathbf{x}$, and that is the case we treat here. (See Section 19.8 or Wooldridge (2007) for more general situations.) Then, again letting $s_i = h_{i1}z_{i1} + \cdots + h_{iJ}z_{iJ}$ be the selection indicator, where each z_{ij} is a function of $\mathbf{x}_i$, $\mathrm{P}(s_i = 1 \mid \mathbf{w}_i, \mathbf{x}_i) = \mathrm{P}(s_i = 1 \mid \mathbf{x}_i)$. We can immediately apply the results of Section 19.8 to conclude that the unweighted M-estimator is consistent.

A direct proof is also informative. The unweighted M-estimator, using the stratified sample, $\hat{\boldsymbol{\theta}}_u$, minimizes

$$\sum_{i=1}^{N} s_i q(\mathbf{w}_i, \boldsymbol{\theta}) = \sum_{i=1}^{N} \sum_{j=1}^{N} h_{ij} z_{ij} q(\mathbf{w}_i, \boldsymbol{\theta}), \tag{20.16}$$

and consistency generally follows if we can show that the population value, $\boldsymbol{\theta}_o$, uniquely minimizes

$$\sum_{j=1}^{N} \mathrm{E}[h_{ij} z_{ij} q(\mathbf{w}_i, \boldsymbol{\theta})] = \sum_{j=1}^{N} p_j \mathrm{E}[z_{ij} q(\mathbf{w}_i, \boldsymbol{\theta})], \tag{20.17}$$

where the equality follows because h_{ij} is independent of $(z_{ij}, \mathbf{w}_i)$ by the nature of VP sampling, and $p_j = \mathrm{E}(h_{ij})$. Now, because z_{ij} is a function of $\mathbf{x}_i$, it follows by iterated expectations that

$$\mathrm{E}[z_{ij} q(\mathbf{w}_i, \boldsymbol{\theta})] = \mathrm{E}\{\mathrm{E}[z_{ij} q(\mathbf{w}_i, \boldsymbol{\theta}) \mid \mathbf{x}_i]\} = \mathrm{E}\{z_{ij} \mathrm{E}[q(\mathbf{w}_i, \boldsymbol{\theta}) \mid \mathbf{x}_i]\}. \tag{20.18}$$

By assumption, $\boldsymbol{\theta}_o$ minimizes $\mathrm{E}[q(\mathbf{w}_i, \boldsymbol{\theta}) \mid \mathbf{x}_i]$, and, because z_{ij} is a zero-one variable, $\boldsymbol{\theta}_o$ is also a minimizer of $\mathrm{E}[z_{ij} q(\mathbf{w}_i, \boldsymbol{\theta})]$. Now, with $p_j \geq 0$ for all j, $\boldsymbol{\theta}_o$ is also a solution to

$$\min_{\boldsymbol{\theta} \in \boldsymbol{\Theta}} \sum_{j=1}^{N} \mathrm{E}[h_{ij} z_{ij} q(\mathbf{w}_i, \boldsymbol{\theta})], \tag{20.19}$$

which is what we wanted to show.

Unlike in the case of the weighted estimator, uniqueness of $\boldsymbol{\theta}_o$ in the population is no longer sufficient for identification using the unweighted estimator. In particular, if $p_j = 0$ for some j, part of the population is not sampled at all, and this may (but need not) result in lack of identification of $\boldsymbol{\theta}_o$. As discussed in Wooldridge (2001) for the case of SS sampling, $p_j > 0$ for all j ensures identification of $\boldsymbol{\theta}_o$ when it is identified in the population.

Generally, when stratification is based on $\mathbf{x}$, one can make a case for weighting if interest lies in the solution to the population problem

$$\min_{\boldsymbol{\theta} \in \boldsymbol{\Theta}} \mathrm{E}[q(\mathbf{w}, \boldsymbol{\theta})], \tag{20.20}$$

which we have called $\boldsymbol{\theta}_o$. The IPW estimator consistently estimates $\boldsymbol{\theta}_o$ without further assumptions, while the unweighted estimator requires the stronger assumption described surrounding equation (20.15). A special case is the linear regression model discussed in Example 20.1: to consistently estimate the linear projection, we must use weights even if selection is based on $\mathbf{x}$. Consistency of the unweighted estimator requires that we are estimating the conditional mean. In the next chapter, we will see other uses of this fact about the weighted versus unweighted estimator.

Wooldridge (1999b) shows that the usual asymptotic variance estimators (see Section 12.5) are valid when stratification is based on $\mathbf{x}$ and we ignore the stratification problem. For example, the usual conditional maximum likelihood analysis holds. In the case of regression, we can use the usual heteroskedasticity-robust variance matrix estimator. Or, if we assume homoskedasticity in the population, the nonrobust form (see equation (12.58)) is valid with the usual estimator of the error variance.

When a generalized conditional information matrix equality holds, and stratification is based on $\mathbf{x}$, Wooldridge (1999b) shows that the unweighted estimator is more efficient than the weighted estimator. The key assumption is

$$\mathrm{E}[\nabla_\theta q(\mathbf{w}, \boldsymbol{\theta}_o)' \nabla_\theta q(\mathbf{w}, \boldsymbol{\theta}_o) \mid \mathbf{x}] = \sigma_o^2 \mathrm{E}[\nabla_\theta^2 q(\mathbf{w}, \boldsymbol{\theta}_o) \mid \mathbf{x}] \tag{20.21}$$

for some $\sigma_o^2 > 0$. When assumption (20.21) holds and $\boldsymbol{\theta}_o$ solves equation (20.19), the asymptotic variance of the unweighted M-estimator is smaller than that for the weighted M-estimator. This generalization includes conditional maximum likelihood (with $\sigma_o^2 = 1$) and nonlinear regression under homoskedasticity.

Very similar conclusions hold for standard stratified sampling. One useful fact is that, when stratification is based on $\mathbf{x}$, the estimator (20.8) is valid with $p_j = H_j/Q_j$ (and $N_0 = N$); therefore, we need not compute within-strata variation in the estimated score. The unweighted estimator is consistent when stratification is based on $\mathbf{x}$ and the usual asymptotic variance matrix estimators are valid. The unweighted estimator is also more efficient when assumption (20.21) holds. See Wooldridge (2001) for statements of assumptions and proofs of theorems.

As a practical matter, modern statistical packages that have built-in features for analyzing data from stratified samples typically ask for two pieces of information: the sampling weights and the stratum identifier. If one specifies the weights but not the stratum identifier, the middle of the "sandwich" will not be estimated as in equation (20.14). The within-stratum averages will not be subtracted off, resulting in larger estimated asymptotic variances than necessary (except in the case of exogenous sampling under exogeneity of $\mathbf{x}$). In other words, the resulting confidence intervals and inference will be (asymptotically) conservative. It is better to use the information on the strata along with the sampling weights.

20.3 Cluster Sampling

We now turn to the problem of cluster sampling, where individual units are sampled in groups or clusters. As mentioned in the introduction, the problems of cluster sampling and panel data analysis are similar in their statistical structures: each confronts the problem of correlation when observations come with a natural nesting. The similarities are strongest in the case where a large number of clusters, each relatively small, is drawn from a large population of clusters. This case is relatively easy to handle, and we treat it first in Section 20.3.1.

Many data sets have both a panel data and cluster sampling structure. Inference that is robust to serial correlation and cluster correlation is straightforward provided the number of clusters is large. We discuss this case in Section 20.3.2.

Section 20.3.3 summarizes what is known about applying the usual cluster formulas when the cluster sizes are large rather than "small."

Recently, researchers have studied data structures that can be classified as a small number of clusters and many observations per cluster. Section 20.3.4 provides two methods for analyzing such structures.

20.3.1 Inference with a Large Number of Clusters and Small Cluster Sizes

We begin with the problem of estimating linear and nonlinear models when we can sample a large number of clusters from a large population of clusters. For each group or cluster g, let $\{(y_{gm}, \mathbf{x}_g, \mathbf{z}_{gm})\colon m = 1, \ldots, M_g\}$ be the observable data, where M_g is the number of units in cluster g, y_{gm} is a scalar response, $\mathbf{x}_g$ is a $1 \times K$ vector containing explanatory variables that vary only at the cluster level, and $\mathbf{z}_{gm}$ is a $1 \times L$ vector of covariates that vary within (as well as across) groups. In most applications of cluster samples, at least some covariates change only at the group level; earlier we gave the example of teacher characteristics when each cluster is a classroom. In fact, it is probably a sensible rule to at least consider the data as being generated as a cluster sample whenever covariates at a level more aggregated than the individual units are included in an analysis. For example, in analyzing firm-level data, if industry-level covariates are included then we should treat the data as a cluster sample, with each industry acting as a cluster.

Throughout we assume that the sampling scheme generates observations that are independent across g. In other words, we independently draw G clusters from the population of all clusters. This assumption can be restrictive, particularly when the clusters are large geographical units. Nevertheless, in some cases we can define the clusters to allow additional "spatial correlation." For example, if originally we think of sampling fourth-grade classrooms, but then we are worried about correlation in student performance not just within class but also within school, then we can define the clusters to be the schools. What we will not cover is schemes where any two geographical units are allowed to be correlated, with correlation diminishing as the observations are farther apart in space.

The theory with $G \to \infty$ and the group sizes, M_g, fixed is well developed; see, for example, White (1984) and Arellano (1987). Of course, it is up to the researcher to decide whether the sizes of G and the M_g are suitable for this asymptotic framework. Here, we follow Wooldridge (2003a) and summarize these results and emphasize how one might have to use robust inference methods even when it is not so obvious.

Not surprisingly, linear models are easiest to analyze. The standard linear model with an additive error is

$$y_{gm} = \alpha + \mathbf{x}_g \boldsymbol{\beta} + \mathbf{z}_{gm} \boldsymbol{\gamma} + v_{gm}, \qquad m = 1, \ldots, M_g; \; g = 1, \ldots, G. \tag{20.22}$$

As with panel data, our approach to estimation and inference in equation (20.22) depends on several factors, including whether we are interested in the effects of aggregate variables ($\boldsymbol{\beta}$) or individual-specific variables ($\boldsymbol{\gamma}$). In addition, we need to make assumptions about the error terms. An important issue is whether the v_{gm} contain a common group effect that can be separated in an additive fashion, as in

$$v_{gm} = c_g + u_{gm}, \qquad m = 1, \ldots, M_g, \tag{20.23}$$

where c_g is an unobserved cluster effect and u_{gm} is the idiosyncratic error. Another important issue is whether the explanatory variables in equation (20.22) can be taken to be appropriately exogenous. If the covariates satisfy

$$\mathrm{E}(v_{gm} \mid \mathbf{x}_g, \mathbf{z}_{gm}) = 0, \qquad m = 1, \ldots, M_g; \; g = 1, \ldots, G, \tag{20.24}$$

or even a zero-correlation version, the pooled OLS estimator, where we regress y_{gm} on 1, $\mathbf{x}_g$, $\mathbf{z}_{gm}$, $m = 1, \ldots, M_g$; $g = 1, \ldots, G$, is consistent for $\boldsymbol{\theta} \equiv (\alpha, \boldsymbol{\beta}', \boldsymbol{\gamma}')'$ as $G \to \infty$ with M_g fixed. Further, the POLS estimator is $\sqrt{G}$-asymptotically normal.

Without more assumptions, a robust variance matrix is needed to account for correlation within clusters or heteroskedasticity in $\mathrm{Var}(v_{gm} \mid \mathbf{x}_g, \mathbf{z}_{gm})$, or both. When v_{gm} has the form in equation (20.23), the amount of within-cluster correlation can be substantial, with the result that the usual OLS standard errors can be very misleading (and, in most cases, systematically too small). Write $\mathbf{W}_g$ as the $M_g \times (1 + K + L)$ matrix of all regressors for group g. Then the $(1 + K + L) \times (1 + K + L)$ variance matrix estimator is

$$\widehat{\mathrm{Avar}}(\hat{\boldsymbol{\theta}}_{POLS}) = \left(\sum_{g=1}^{G} \mathbf{W}_g' \mathbf{W}_g \right)^{-1} \left(\sum_{g=1}^{G} \mathbf{W}_g' \hat{\mathbf{v}}_g \hat{\mathbf{v}}_g' \mathbf{W}_g \right) \left(\sum_{g=1}^{G} \mathbf{W}_g' \mathbf{W}_g \right)^{-1} \tag{20.25}$$

where $\hat{\mathbf{v}}_g$ is the $M_g \times 1$ vector of pooled OLS residuals for group g. As we discussed for the panel data case, this "sandwich" variance matrix estimator is now computed routinely using "cluster" options in popular statistical packages. One simply needs to specify the cluster identifier.

Pooled OLS estimation of the parameters in equation (20.22) ignores the within-cluster correlation of the v_{gm} in estimation, so that it can be very inefficient if c_g is a part of the error v_{gm}. As we know from panel data analysis, if we strengthen the exogeneity assumption to

$$\mathrm{E}(v_{gm} \mid \mathbf{x}_g, \mathbf{Z}_g) = 0, \qquad m = 1, \ldots, M_g;\ g = 1, \ldots, G, \tag{20.26}$$

where $\mathbf{Z}_g$ is the $M_g \times L$ matrix of unit-specific covariates, then we can exploit the presence of c_g in equation (20.23) in a generalized least squares (GLS) analysis. Assumption (20.26) rules out covariates from one member of the cluster affecting the outcomes on another, holding own covariates fixed. At least nominally, this assumption appears to rule out "peer effects," but such effects can be allowed by including measures of peers in $\mathbf{z}_{gm}$.

The standard random effects approach makes enough assumptions so that the $M_g \times M_g$ variance-covariance matrix of $\mathbf{v}_g = (v_{g1}, v_{g2}, \ldots, v_{g,M_g})'$ has the "random effects" form,

$$\mathrm{Var}(\mathbf{v}_g) = \sigma_c^2 \mathbf{j}_{M_g}' \mathbf{j}_{M_g} + \sigma_u^2 \mathbf{I}_{M_g}, \tag{20.27}$$

where $\mathbf{j}_{M_g}$ is the $M_g \times 1$ vector of ones and $\mathbf{I}_{M_g}$ is the $M_g \times M_g$ identity matrix. In the standard setup, we also make the system homoskedasticity assumption, familiar from the panel data analysis in Chapter 10:

$$\mathrm{Var}(\mathbf{v}_g \mid \mathbf{x}_g, \mathbf{Z}_g) = \mathrm{Var}(\mathbf{v}_g). \tag{20.28}$$

As in the panel data case, it is important to understand the role of assumption (20.28): it implies that the conditional variance-covariance matrix is the same as the unconditional variance-covariance matrix, but it does not restrict $\mathrm{Var}(\mathbf{v}_g)$; it can be any $M_g \times M_g$ matrix under assumption (20.28). The particular random effects structure on $\mathrm{Var}(\mathbf{v}_g)$ is given by assumption (20.27). Under assumptions (20.27) and (20.28), the resulting GLS estimator is the well-known random effects (RE) estimator. The estimator has the same structure as in the unbalanced panel data case; see Section 19.9.1.

The random effects estimator $\hat{\boldsymbol{\theta}}_{RE}$ is asymptotically more efficient than pooled OLS under assumptions (20.26), (20.27), and (20.28) as $G \to \infty$ with the M_g fixed. The RE estimates and test statistics are computed routinely by popular software packages for cluster samples. Nevertheless, an important point is often overlooked in applications of RE: one can, and in many cases should, make inference completely robust to an unknown form of $\mathrm{Var}(\mathbf{v}_g \mid \mathbf{x}_g, \mathbf{Z}_g)$.

The idea in obtaining a fully robust variance matrix for RE is straightforward, as we saw in Chapter 10 for panel data. Even if $\mathrm{Var}(\mathbf{v}_g \mid \mathbf{x}_g, \mathbf{Z}_g)$ does not have the RE form, the RE estimator is still consistent and $\sqrt{G}$-asymptotically normal under assumption (20.26), and it is likely to be more efficient than pooled OLS even if $\mathrm{Var}(\mathbf{v}_g \mid \mathbf{x}_g, \mathbf{Z}_g)$ does not have the RE form. The case for a fully robust variance matrix for RE is somewhat more subtle than in the panel data case, where serial correlation in the idiosyncratic errors generally invalidates assumption (20.27). Of course, heteroskedasticity in $\text{Var}(c_g \mid \mathbf{x}_g, \mathbf{Z}_g)$ or $\text{Var}(u_{gm} \mid \mathbf{x}_g, \mathbf{Z}_g)$ is always a possibility, and either justifies robust inference. As an example, suppose that the coefficients on $\mathbf{z}_{gm}$ vary at the cluster level:

$$y_{gm} = \alpha + \mathbf{x}_g\boldsymbol{\beta} + \mathbf{z}_{gm}\boldsymbol{\gamma}_g + v_{gm}, \qquad m = 1, \ldots, M_g;\ g = 1, \ldots, G. \tag{20.29}$$

By estimating a standard random effects model that assumes common slopes $\boldsymbol{\gamma}$, we effectively include $\mathbf{z}_{gm}(\boldsymbol{\gamma}_g - \boldsymbol{\gamma})$ in the idiosyncratic error; doing so generally creates within-group correlation because $\mathbf{z}_{gm}(\boldsymbol{\gamma}_g - \boldsymbol{\gamma})$ and $\mathbf{z}_{gp}(\boldsymbol{\gamma}_g - \boldsymbol{\gamma})$ will be correlated for $m \neq p$, conditional on $\mathbf{Z}_g$. Also, the idiosyncratic error will have heteroskedasticity that is a function of $\mathbf{z}_{gm}$. Nevertheless, if we assume $\text{E}(\boldsymbol{\gamma}_g \mid \mathbf{X}_g, \mathbf{Z}_g) = \text{E}(\boldsymbol{\gamma}_g) \equiv \boldsymbol{\gamma}$ along with assumption (20.26), the random effects estimator still consistently estimates the average slopes, $\boldsymbol{\gamma}$ (and $\boldsymbol{\beta}$). Therefore, in applying random effects to panel data or cluster samples, it is sensible (with large G) to make the variance estimator of random effects robust to arbitrary heteroskedasticity and within-group correlation.

In applications, one often computes the POLS and RE estimates to see how sensitive the estimates are to choice of variance matrix. Further, one is tempted to compare estimated variance matrices—or, at least, standard errors—to see if RE is more efficient than POLS. It is fine to do so provided one uses fully robust standard errors for POLS and RE. For example, it certainly makes no sense to compare the usual POLS standard errors (which ignore the cluster sampling) with the usual RE standard errors (which account for the clustering, at least to some extent). By comparing the fully robust forms for each set of estimates, one is comparing generally reliable estimates of the sampling variation of the POLS and RE estimates.

If we are only interested in estimating $\boldsymbol{\gamma}$, the fixed effects (FE) or within estimator is attractive. The within transformation subtracts within-group averages from the dependent variable and explanatory variables:

$$y_{gm} - \bar{y}_g = (\mathbf{z}_{gm} - \bar{\mathbf{z}}_g)\boldsymbol{\gamma} + u_{gm} - \bar{u}_g, \qquad m = 1, \ldots, M_g;\ g = 1, \ldots, G, \tag{20.30}$$

and this equation is estimated by pooled OLS. (Of course, the $\mathbf{x}_g$ get swept away by the within-group demeaning.) Under a full set of FE assumptions—which, as in the panel data case, allows arbitrary correlation between c_g and the $\mathbf{z}_{gm}$—inference is straightforward using standard software. Nevertheless, analogous to the random effects case, it is prudent to allow $\text{Var}(\mathbf{u}_g \mid \mathbf{Z}_g)$ to have an arbitrary form, including within-group correlation and heteroskedasticity. For example, if we start with model (20.29), then $(\mathbf{z}_{gm} - \bar{\mathbf{z}}_g)(\boldsymbol{\gamma}_g - \boldsymbol{\gamma})$ appears in the error term. As we discussed in Section 11.7.3, the FE estimator is still consistent if $\text{E}(\boldsymbol{\gamma}_g \mid \mathbf{z}_{gm} - \bar{\mathbf{z}}_g) = \text{E}(\boldsymbol{\gamma}_g) = \boldsymbol{\gamma}$, an assumption that allows $\boldsymbol{\gamma}_g$ to be correlated with $\bar{\mathbf{z}}_g$. Nevertheless, u_{gm} and u_{gp} will be correlated for $m \neq p$. A fully robust variance matrix estimator is

$$\widehat{\text{Avar}}(\hat{\gamma}_{FE}) = \left(\sum_{g=1}^{G} \ddot{\mathbf{Z}}_g'\ddot{\mathbf{Z}}_g\right)^{-1} \left(\sum_{g=1}^{G} \ddot{\mathbf{Z}}_g'\hat{\ddot{\mathbf{u}}}_g\hat{\ddot{\mathbf{u}}}_g'\ddot{\mathbf{Z}}_g\right)\left(\sum_{g=1}^{G} \ddot{\mathbf{Z}}_g'\ddot{\mathbf{Z}}_g\right)^{-1}, \tag{20.31}$$

where $\ddot{\mathbf{Z}}_g$ is the matrix of within-group deviations from means and $\hat{\ddot{\mathbf{u}}}_g$ is the $M_g \times 1$ vector of fixed effects residuals. This estimator is justified with large-G asymptotics. It has exactly the same form as the unbalanced panel data case.

One benefit of a fixed effects approach in the standard model with constant slopes but c_g in the composite error term is that no adjustments are necessary if the c_g are correlated across groups. When the groups represent different geographical units, we might expect correlation across groups close to each other. If we think such correlation is largely captured through the unobserved effect c_g, then its elimination by means of the within transformation effectively solves the problem. If we use pooled OLS or random effects, we would have to deal with spatial correlation across g, in addition to within-group correlation, a difficult statistical problem.

An alternative to FE estimation, and one that leads to a simple Hausman test for comparing FE and RE, is to add the group averages to an RE estimation. Let $\bar{\mathbf{z}}_g$ denote the vector of within-group averages, and write

$$y_{gm} = \alpha + \mathbf{x}_g\boldsymbol{\beta} + \mathbf{z}_{gm}\gamma + \bar{\mathbf{z}}_g\xi + a_g + u_{gm}, \qquad m = 1, \ldots, M_g;\ g = 1, \ldots, G, \tag{20.32}$$

where $c_g = \bar{\mathbf{z}}_g\xi + a_g$ (and we absorb the intercept here into α). Estimating this equation by, say, RE allows us to easily test H_0: $\xi = \mathbf{0}$ in a fully robust way, which tests the null that the RE estimator is consistent. It can be shown that, even though the panel is not balanced, the estimate of γ is the FE estimate. In addition, this approach allows us to estimate coefficients on $\mathbf{x}_g$. (Pooled OLS can also be used, and also delivers the FE estimate of γ.)

Example 20.3 (Cluster Correlation in Teacher Compensation): The data set in BENEFITS.RAW includes average compensation, at the school level, for teachers in Michigan. Interest lies in testing for a trade-off between salary and nonsalary compensation. We view this as a cluster sample of school districts, with the schools within districts representing the individual units.

A standard approach is to estimate the equation

$$\log(avgsal_{gm}) = \alpha + \beta_1 bs_{gm} + \beta_2 \log(staff_{gm}) + \beta_3 \log(enroll_{gm}) + \beta_4 lunch_{gm} + c_g + u_{gm} \tag{20.33}$$

where $avgsal_{gm}$ is the average salary for school m in district g, $bs_{gm} = avgben_{gm}/avgsal_{gm}$, where $avgben_{gm}$ is the average benefits received by teachers, $staff_{gm}$ is the number of staff per 1,000 students, $enroll_{gm}$ is school enrollment, and $lunch_{gm}$ is the

Table 20.1
Salary-Benefits Trade-off for Michigan Teachers

Dependent Variable	log(*avgsal*)		
	(1)	(2)	(3)
Estimation Method	Pooled OLS	Random Effects	Fixed Effects
Explanatory Variable			
bs	−0.177 (0.122) [0.260]	−0.381 (0.112) [0.150]	−0.495 (0.133) [0.194]
log(*staff*)	−0.691 (0.018) [0.035]	−0.617 (0.015) [0.036]	−0.622 (0.017) [0.043]
log(*enroll*)	−0.0292 (0.0085) [0.0257]	−0.0249 (0.0076) [0.0115]	−0.0515 (0.0094) [0.0131]
lunch	−0.00085 (0.00016) [0.00057]	0.00030 (0.00018) [0.00020]	0.00051 (0.00021) [0.00021]
constant	13.724 (0.112) [0.256]	13.367 (0.098) [0.197]	13.618 (0.113) [0.241]
Number of districts	537	537	537
Number of schools	1,848	1,848	1,848

Quantities in parentheses are the nonrobust standard errors; those in brackets are robust to arbitrary within-district correlation as well as heteroskedasticity.
The intercept reported for fixed effects is the average of the estimated district effects.
The fully robust regression based Hausman test, with four degrees-of-freedom in the chi-square distribution, yields $H = 20.70$ and p-value $= 0.0004$.

percentage of students eligible for the federal free or reduced-price lunch program. Using the approximation $\log(1 + x) \approx x$ for "small" x, it can be shown that a dollar-for-dollar trade-off in salary and benefits is the same as $\beta_1 = -1$.

We estimate the equation using three methods: pooled OLS, random effects, and fixed effects. The results are given in Table 20.1. The table contains the nonrobust standard errors for each method—that is, the standard errors computed under the "ideal" set of assumptions for the particular estimator—along with the standard errors that are robust to arbitrary within-district correlation and heteroskedasticity.

The POLS estimates provide little evidence of a trade-off between salary and benefits. The coefficient is negative, but its value, −0.177, is pretty small, and not close to −1 (the hypothesized value for a one-for-one trade-off between salary and benefits). Its fully robust t statistic is less than 0.7 in magnitude. Notice that the robust standard error, which properly accounts for the cluster nature of the data, is more than twice as large as the nonrobust one.

The magnitude of the random effects coefficient *bs* is notably larger than the pooled OLS estimate, and it is statistically different from zero, even using the fully robust standard error. The RE transformation removes a fraction of the district averages. (The fraction depends on the number of schools in a district, and it ranges from about 0.379 to 0.938, with more than 50% of the districts at 0.379.) Even though RE nominally accounts for the cluster (district) effect, the nonrobust standard errors evidently understate the actual sampling variation. The robust 95% confidence interval excludes zero, but it also excludes -1 (and the RE point estimate, -0.381, is far from -1). The robust standard error on $\log(staff)$, 0.036, is more than twice as large as the nonrobust one, 0.015. Again, this finding points to the importance of using robust inference even if we nominally account for the common district effect by means of random effects estimation. Incidentally, the RE robust standard errors are, except in one case, smaller than the robust pooled OLS standard errors, indicating that RE is more efficient than POLS even though RE is evidently not the most efficient estimator (because it appears there is a more complicted pattern of cluster correlation than accounted for by RE).

Column (3) in Table 20.1 contains the fixed effects estimates. The coefficient on *bs* is about -0.50, which is still pretty far from -1, and statistically different from -1 even using the fully robust standard error. Again, allowing for clustering and heteroskedasticity is important for appropriate inference: the usual FE standard errors appear to be too small. Because total compensation varies significantly by district, it is important to allow the district effects to be correlated with the explanatory variables, as FE does.

Not surprisingly, the fully robust RE standard errors are somewhat below the fully robust FE standard errors, a result which makes it tempting to use the RE estimates. But the robust Hausman test, obtained by adding the four group averages to the RE estimation and testing their joint significance, yields a low p-value, about 0.0004. It appears the district effect is systematically related to some of the variables (staff size especially), and so the safest strategy is to use the fixed effects estimates with fully robust inference.

The discussion of the previous methods extends immediately to instrumental variables versions of all estimators. With large G, one can afford to make pooled two-stage least squares (2SLS), random effects 2SLS, and fixed effects 2SLS robust to arbitrary within-cluster correlation and heteroskedasticity. Adding the group averages of the exogenous explanatory variables (including the extra instruments), estimating the resulting equation by RE 2SLS (where the group averages act as their own instruments), and jointly testing the group averages for significance leads to a simple Hausman test comparing RE 2SLS and FE 2SLS.

If the random effects variance matrix structure does not hold, more efficient estimation can be achieved by applying generalized method of moments (GMM); again, GMM is justified with large G.

As we discussed in Section 12.10.3, one might apply least absolute deviations or quantile regression directly to equation (20.32). While difficult to justify in general, adding the group averages and then applying, say, LAD, can be a useful way to approximate the effects of the variables on the median while allowing the group heterogeneity to be correlated with the individual-specific covariates. Under the kinds of symmetry assumptions discussed in Section 12.10.3, this can be a good way to account for outliers in the data.

For a the case where G is much larger than the group sizes, cluster-robust inference is available for nonlinear models, too. A general treatment based on M-estimation is possible, but most of the points can be illustrated with binary response models. Let y_{gm} be a binary response, with $\mathbf{x}_g$ and $\mathbf{z}_{gm}$, $m = 1, \ldots, M_g$, $g = 1, \ldots, G$ defined as before. Assume that

$$y_{gm} = 1[\alpha + \mathbf{x}_g\boldsymbol{\beta} + \mathbf{z}_{gm}\boldsymbol{\gamma} + c_g + u_{gm} \geq 0], \tag{20.34}$$

where c_g is the cluster effect and u_{gm} is the unit-specific error. If, say, we assume

$$u_{gm} \mid \mathbf{x}_g, \mathbf{Z}_g, c_g \sim \text{Normal}(0, 1), \tag{20.35}$$

then

$$\text{P}(y_{gm} = 1 \mid \mathbf{x}_g, \mathbf{z}_{gm}, c_g) = \text{P}(y_{gm} = 1 \mid \mathbf{x}_g, \mathbf{Z}_g, c_g) = \Phi(\alpha + \mathbf{x}_g\boldsymbol{\beta} + \mathbf{z}_{gm}\boldsymbol{\gamma} + c_g), \tag{20.36}$$

where $\Phi(\cdot)$ is the standard normal (cdf), as usual. Alternatively, if u_{gm} follows a logistic distribution, then we replace $\Phi(\cdot)$ with $\Lambda(\cdot)$. Notice that expression (20.35) assumes that, conditional on c_g, $\mathbf{x}_g$, and $\mathbf{z}_{gm}$, $\mathbf{z}_{gp}$ for $p \neq m$ does not affect the outcome. For pooled methods we could relax this restriction (as in the linear case), but, with the presence of c_g, this affords little generality in practice.

As in nonlinear panel data models, the presence of c_g in equation (20.36) raises several important issues, including how we estimate quantities of interest. As in the panel data case, we have some interest in estimating average partial or marginal effects. For example, if the first element of $\mathbf{x}_g$ is continuous,

$$\frac{\partial \text{P}(y_{gm} = 1 \mid \mathbf{x}_g, \mathbf{z}_{gm}, c_g)}{\partial x_{g1}} = \beta_1 \phi(\alpha + \mathbf{x}_g\boldsymbol{\beta} + \mathbf{z}_{gm}\boldsymbol{\gamma} + c_g), \tag{20.37}$$

where $\phi(\cdot)$ is the standard normal density function. If

$$c_g \mid \mathbf{x}_g, \mathbf{Z}_g \sim \text{Normal}(0, \sigma_c^2), \tag{20.38}$$

then the APEs are obtained from the average structural function

$$ASF(\mathbf{x}_g, \mathbf{z}_{gm}) = \Phi[(\alpha + \mathbf{x}_g\boldsymbol{\beta} + \mathbf{z}_{gm}\boldsymbol{\gamma})/(1 + \sigma_c^2)^{1/2}] \equiv \Phi(\alpha_c + \mathbf{x}_g\boldsymbol{\beta}_c + \mathbf{z}_{gm}\boldsymbol{\gamma}_c), \tag{20.39}$$

where $\alpha_c = \alpha/(1 + \sigma_c^2)^{1/2}$, and so on. Because the right-hand side of equation (20.39) is $\mathrm{P}(y_{gm} = 1 \mid \mathbf{x}_g, \mathbf{Z}_g)$, the scaled coefficients are conveniently estimated using pooled probit or a generalized estimating equation (GEE) approach. In either case, inference must be robust to allow general covariance structures $\mathrm{Cov}(y_{gm}, y_{gp} \mid \mathbf{x}_g, \mathbf{Z}_g)$ for $m \neq p$. These certainly will not be zero (as would be required to ignore the clustering using pooled methods), but neither will they be constant. The same formulas used in the panel data case apply to cluster samples, with the small change that the group sizes are generally different.

The pooled and GEE approaches are attractive because they are computationally simple and do not require specification of a joint distribution within clusters. Alternatively, we can impose more assumptions—as in the panel data case—and use full maximimum likelihood (conditional on $\mathbf{x}_g$ and $\mathbf{Z}_{gm}$, of course). If we supplement assumptions (20.34), (20.35), and (20.38) with

$$\{u_{g1}, \ldots, u_{g,M_g}\} \text{ are independent conditional on } (\mathbf{x}_g, \mathbf{Z}_g, c_g), \tag{20.40}$$

then we have the random effects probit model. Details of its estimation are similar to the panel data case, with the minor exception that here we must allow for an unequal number of observations per cluster. Because we can separately identify α, $\boldsymbol{\beta}$, $\boldsymbol{\gamma}$, and σ_c^2, partial effects at various values of c_g are identified in addition to the average partial effects. In one important way, a random effects approach under the conditional independence assumption (20.40) is more attractive for cluster samples than for panel data: in panel data it is often the case that time series innovations are correlated over time. With a cluster sample, independence of individual outcomes after conditioning on a common cluster effect is often more believable. (Nevertheless, we are conditioning only on a scalar heterogeneity, c_g, so such an assumption may still be too restrictive.)

As with panel data, we often want to allow the cluster heterogeneity, c_g, to be correlated with the observed covariates. When the cluster sizes are the same—that is, $M_g = M$ for all g—we can apply the same methods we used for balanced panel, including probit, logit, ordered probit, Tobit, count data, fractional responses, and so on. Calculations of average partial effects are identical, and random effects approaches under conditional independence are attractive. But pooled methods are often computationally simpler and are sufficient for identifying APEs.

A challenging task for CRE approaches using cluster samples is how to model correlation between the unobserved heterogeneity and $\{\mathbf{z}_{gm}: m = 1, \ldots, M_g\}$ when the clusters are not balanced with respect to cluster size. One possible solution is to randomly drop observations from clusters to make them all the same size. Then we could apply the usual approach for balanced panel data. Unfortunately, this approach can be very costly in terms of lost data. For example, if the smallest group has $M_g = 3$, we would have to drop observations from all other groups until we only have three in each group.

The problem with different group sizes is that it is unclear how one should model the correlation between c_g and $(\mathbf{z}_{g1}, \ldots, \mathbf{z}_{g,M_g})$ for each g. Nevertheless, there are several possibilities. We can get some insight by assuming joint normality of $(c_g, \mathbf{z}_{g1}, \ldots, \mathbf{z}_{g,M_g})$ and then assuming that $\mathrm{E}(c_g \mid \mathbf{z}_{g1}, \ldots, \mathbf{z}_{g,M_g}) = \mathrm{E}(c_g \mid \bar{\mathbf{z}}_g) = \eta_g + \bar{\mathbf{z}}_g \xi_g$, that is, assuming $\bar{\mathbf{z}}_g$ is a sufficient statistic for the mean. Then it must follow that

$$\xi_g = [\mathrm{Var}(\bar{\mathbf{z}}_g)]^{-1} \mathrm{Cov}(\bar{\mathbf{z}}_g, c_g)$$

$$\eta_g = \mathrm{E}(c_g) - \mathrm{E}(\bar{\mathbf{z}}_g)\xi_g.$$

For the sake of argument, assume that $\{\mathbf{z}_{gm}: m = 1, \ldots, M_g\}$ has an unobserved effects structure, that is, $\mathbf{z}_{gm} = \mathbf{r}_g + \mathbf{e}_{gm}$ where $\mathbf{r}_g$ is uncorrelated with each $\mathbf{e}_{gm}$ and $\{\mathbf{e}_{gm}: m = 1, \ldots, M_g\}$ are pairwise uncorrelated with zero mean and common variance matrix $\boldsymbol{\Sigma}_{\mathbf{e}}$. Then $\mathrm{E}(\bar{\mathbf{z}}_g) = \boldsymbol{\mu}_{\mathbf{r}}$ and $\mathrm{Var}(\bar{\mathbf{z}}_g) = \boldsymbol{\Sigma}_{\mathbf{r}} + M_g^{-1}\boldsymbol{\Sigma}_{\mathbf{e}}$. Assume that c_g is uncorrelated with the $\mathbf{e}_{gm}$, and let $\boldsymbol{\sigma}_{\mathbf{r}c}$ be the vector of covariances of $\mathbf{r}_g$ with c_g. Then

$$\xi_g = (\boldsymbol{\Sigma}_{\mathbf{r}} + M_g^{-1}\boldsymbol{\Sigma}_{\mathbf{e}})^{-1}\boldsymbol{\sigma}_{\mathbf{r}c} \tag{20.41}$$

$$\eta_g = \mu_c - \boldsymbol{\mu}_{\mathbf{r}}\xi_g, \tag{20.42}$$

where $\mu_c = \mathrm{E}(c_g)$. Further, if we write $c_g = \eta_g + \bar{\mathbf{z}}_g\xi_g + a_g$,

$$\mathrm{Var}(a_g) = \sigma_c^2 - \boldsymbol{\sigma}_{\mathbf{r}c}'(\boldsymbol{\Sigma}_{\mathbf{r}} + M_g^{-1}\boldsymbol{\Sigma}_{\mathbf{e}})^{-1}\boldsymbol{\sigma}_{\mathbf{r}c}. \tag{20.43}$$

These calculations show that, even under fairly strong assumptions, both $\mathrm{E}(c_g \mid \bar{\mathbf{z}}_g)$ and $\mathrm{Var}(c_g \mid \bar{\mathbf{z}}_g)$ depend on the group size, M_g (and $\mathrm{E}(c_g \mid \bar{\mathbf{z}}_g)$ depends on $\bar{\mathbf{z}}_g$, too). If $\boldsymbol{\Sigma}_{\mathbf{r}} = \mathbf{0}$, the mean and variance depend on M_g and $M_g \cdot \bar{\mathbf{z}}_g$. If $\boldsymbol{\Sigma}_{\mathbf{r}}$ is "large" (in a matrix sense), or M_g is large, the mean and variance are almost independent of M_g (but the mean is a linear function of $\bar{\mathbf{z}}_g$). If $\boldsymbol{\Sigma}_{\mathbf{r}}$ and $\boldsymbol{\Sigma}_{\mathbf{e}}$ are both scalar multiples of the identity matrix, the function of M_g has the form $(\sigma_r^2 + M_g^{-1}\sigma_e^2)^{-1}$, which, for large M_g, can be approximated well by a low-order polynomial in M_g^{-1}.

How should we apply these calculations for the conditional mean and variance of c_g? First, we should recognize that they are derived under strong assumptions, so we should not use such specific forms. (Plus, they would not be very easy to handle computationally.) An approach that may be flexible enough is

$$c_g = \psi_0 + \psi_1 M_g + \bar{\mathbf{z}}_g \boldsymbol{\psi}_2 + (M_g \cdot \bar{\mathbf{z}}_g)\boldsymbol{\psi}_3 + a_g \tag{20.44}$$

$$\text{Var}(a_g \mid \mathbf{z}_{g1}, \ldots, \mathbf{z}_{g,M_g}) = \text{Var}(a_g) = \omega_0 + \omega_1 M_g \tag{20.45}$$

(where we expect $\omega_1 < 0$ because the conditional variance of c_g shrinks as the number of explanatory variables increases). If we use these expressions in place of the usual Chamberlain-Mundlak approach (and include $\mathbf{x}_g$, too), we get the following estimating equation:

$$\text{P}(y_{gm} = 1 \mid \mathbf{x}_g, \mathbf{Z}_g) = \Phi\left[\frac{(\alpha + \mathbf{x}_g\boldsymbol{\beta} + \mathbf{z}_{gm}\boldsymbol{\gamma} + \psi_1 M_g + \bar{\mathbf{z}}_g\boldsymbol{\psi}_2 + (M_g \cdot \bar{\mathbf{z}}_g)\boldsymbol{\psi}_3)}{\sqrt{1 + \omega_0 + \omega_1 M_g}}\right]. \tag{20.46}$$

In principle, the parameters here can be estimated by, say, a pooled heteroskedastic probit analysis. To estimate the parameters, a normalization is needed on the variance (because when $\omega_1 = 0$, only the parameters scaled by $1/\sqrt{1 + \omega_0}$ are identified). In fact, using modern software that allows for exponential forms of heteroskedasticity in probit anlaysis, an easy way to estimate the identified parameters, and then obtain average partial effects, is to specify the variance as $\exp[\delta_1 \log(M_g)]$. When $\delta_1 = 0$, the variance is one, and we estimate the scaled coefficients. Notice that specifying the composite variance as $\exp[\delta_1 \log(M_g)]$ also has the benefit of nesting the cases where $\text{Var}(a_g)$ is a linear function of M_g or M_g^{-1}.

A more flexible approach is to let the conditional variance of c_g be as flexible as the conditional mean, but still nesting the preceding simple functional form. For example, a more flexible estimating equation is

$$\text{P}(y_{gm} = 1 \mid \mathbf{x}_g, \mathbf{Z}_g) = \Phi\left[\frac{(\alpha + \mathbf{x}_g\boldsymbol{\beta} + \mathbf{z}_{gm}\boldsymbol{\gamma} + \psi_1 M_g + \bar{\mathbf{z}}_g\boldsymbol{\psi}_2 + (M_g \cdot \bar{\mathbf{z}}_g)\boldsymbol{\psi}_3)}{\exp(\delta_1 \log(M_g) + \bar{\mathbf{z}}_g\boldsymbol{\delta}_2 + \log(M_g)\bar{\mathbf{z}}_g\boldsymbol{\delta}_3)}\right]. \tag{20.47}$$

We could replace M_g in the mean part with M_g^{-1}, or even use both functions. Such an equation is relatively straightforward to estimate using heteroskedastic probit software.

A very attractive alternative with large G and not much variation in the group sizes M_g is to allow a different set of parameters in $\text{D}(c_g \mid M_g, \bar{\mathbf{z}}_g)$ for each value of M_g. This is easily accomplished by including dummies for all but one group size and also interacting the dummies with $\bar{\mathbf{z}}_g$ in the mean and the variance. In equation (20.43) the variance depends only on M_g, and so one might want to simplify the estimation by including only the group-size dummies in the variance.

Regardless of the specific expression we use for $\text{P}(y_{gm} = 1 \mid \mathbf{x}_g, \mathbf{Z}_g)$, it is straightforward to estimate the average partial effects. The conditioning variables that we must average out are $(M_g, \bar{\mathbf{z}}_g)$, and we use, as usual, the discussion in Section 2.2.5.

Let $m(\mathbf{x}_g, \mathbf{z}_{gm}, M_g, \bar{\mathbf{z}}_g, \boldsymbol{\theta})$ be the response probability $\mathrm{P}(y_{gm} = 1 \mid \mathbf{x}_g, \mathbf{Z}_g)$, where $\boldsymbol{\theta}$ is the set of all parameters. Then the ASF, for fixed values of $\mathbf{x}$ and $\mathbf{z}$, is consistently estimated as

$$\widehat{ASF}(\mathbf{x}, \mathbf{z}) = G^{-1} \sum_{g=1}^{G} m(\mathbf{x}, \mathbf{z}, M_g, \bar{\mathbf{z}}_g, \hat{\boldsymbol{\theta}}); \tag{20.48}$$

that is, we average out $(M_g, \bar{\mathbf{z}}_g)$. (As usual, one must use caution in interpreting the effects of the group-level variables if these are partially correlated with c_g.)

Incidentally, the methods proposed here can be applied to unbalanced panel data sets, assuming, of course, that the reason the panel is unbalanced can be ignored. With a large cross section, N (which replaces G), and a small number of time periods, T_i (which replaces M_g) for each observation i, the flexible approach of allowing different parameters for each T_i is attractive.

Rather than adopt a correlated random effects probit approach, we can apply the fixed effects logit approach, assuming that the observations within a cluster are independent conditional on the observed covariates and the cluster effect, c_g. Naturally, the cluster-level variables, $\mathbf{x}_g$, are eliminated, and one can only estimate parameters, not partial effects. The mechanics are essentially identical to the panel data case. Geronimus and Korenman (1992) use sister pairs to study the effects of teenage motherhood on subsequent economic outcomes, so $M_g = 2$ for all g. When the outcome is binary (such as an employment indicator), the authors apply fixed effects logit. CRE probit can also be used to obtain the magnitudes of the effects.

The same CRE approach can be applied to other nonlinear models, such as ordered probit and Tobit models. Generally, if we begin with a density $f(\mathbf{y}_{gm} \mid \mathbf{x}_g, \mathbf{z}_{gm}, \mathbf{c}_g; \boldsymbol{\theta})$, where both $\mathbf{y}_{gm}$ and $\mathbf{c}_g$ can be vectors, and then specify a heterogeneity density, say, $h(\mathbf{c}_g \mid M_g, \bar{\mathbf{z}}_g; \boldsymbol{\delta})$, a partial MLE analysis can be obtained by "integrating out" $\mathbf{c}_g$ to get the density

$$\int f(\mathbf{y}_{gm} \mid \mathbf{x}_g, \mathbf{z}_{gm}, \mathbf{c}; \boldsymbol{\theta}) h(\mathbf{c} \mid M_g, \bar{\mathbf{z}}_g; \boldsymbol{\delta})\, d\mathbf{c}. \tag{20.49}$$

As we know from the panel data case, this density has a simple form for common models, such as Tobit, when c_g is a scalar and $h(\cdot \mid M_g, \bar{\mathbf{z}}_g; \boldsymbol{\delta})$ is chosen to have a simple form, such as normal. However, as for the probit case, one should allow heteroskedasticity in $\mathrm{Var}(c_g \mid M_g, \bar{\mathbf{z}}_g)$, leading to a pooled estimation strategy based on the "heteroskedastic Tobit" model. We also know that using pooled (that is, partial) MLE does not always fully identify the parameters, but it does often identify scaled parameters and average partial effects. Because the observations within clusters are almost certainly correlated, even after conditioning on $(\mathbf{x}_g, \mathbf{Z}_g)$, inference that allows within-cluster correlation is crucial.

Various quasi-MLEs can also be adapted to account for correlated random effects in the context of cluster sampling. In the exponential case, we would be led to a mean function that looks like, say,

$$\mathrm{E}(y_{gm} \mid \mathbf{Z}_g, M_g) = \mathrm{E}(y_{gm} \mid \mathbf{z}_{gm}, M_g, \bar{\mathbf{z}}_g) = \exp(\mathbf{x}_g \boldsymbol{\beta} + \mathbf{z}_{gm}\boldsymbol{\gamma} + \alpha_{M_g} + \bar{\mathbf{z}}_g \boldsymbol{\psi}_{M_g}), \tag{20.50}$$

where α_{M_g} and $\boldsymbol{\psi}_{M_g}$ are specific to the group size, M_g (or we use linear or low-order polynomials in M_g or M_g^{-1}, or both). The parameters can be estimated by, say, pooled Poisson QMLE, or GEE using the Poisson distribution by including a full set of group-size dummies along with $\bar{\mathbf{z}}_g$ and interactions with $\bar{\mathbf{z}}_g$. The elements of $(\boldsymbol{\beta}, \boldsymbol{\gamma})$ measure semielasticities or elasticities on the mean response. The APEs on the mean are obtained by averaging out $(M_g, \bar{\mathbf{z}}_g)$. See Problem 20.8 for the case of a fractional response.

As in the panel data case, the fixed effects Poisson estimator is very convenient when we start with

$$\mathrm{E}(y_{gm} \mid \mathbf{Z}_g, c_g) = \mathrm{E}(y_{gm} \mid \mathbf{z}_{gm}, c_g) = \exp(\mathbf{z}_{gm}\boldsymbol{\gamma} + c_g). \tag{20.51}$$

With arbitrarily unbalanced group sizes, the FE Poisson estimator (viewed as a quasi-MLE) consistently estimates $\boldsymbol{\gamma}$ (and $\mathbf{x}_g$ is eliminated). No other feature of the Poisson distribution needs to be correctly specified, and sources of within-cluster correlation other than c_g are allowed (provided, of course, we use fully robust inference).

20.3.2 Cluster Samples with Unit-Specific Panel Data

Often, cluster samples come with a time component, so that there are two potential sources of correlation across observations: across time within the same individual and across individuals within the same group. The two sources of correlation may also interact: different individuals within the same group or cluster might have unobserved shocks correlated across different time periods.

Generally, accounting for more than two data dimensions is complicated if there is not a natural nesting. Here we consider the case where each unit belongs to a cluster and the cluster identification does not change over time. In other words, we have panel data on each individual or unit, and each unit belongs to a cluster. For example, we might have annual panel data at the firm level where each firm belongs to the same industry (cluster) for all years. Or, we might have panel data for schools that each belong to a district. This is a special case of a **hierarchical linear model (HLM)** setup. Models for data structures involving panel data and clustering are also called **mixed models** (although this latter name typically refers to the situation, which we treat later, in which some slope parameters are constant and others are unobserved heterogeneity). In the HLM/mixed models literature, more levels of nesting are allowed, but we will not consider more general structures; see, for example, Raudenbush and Bryk (2002).

Now we have three data subscripts on at least some variables that we observe. For example, the response variable is y_{gmt}, where g indexes the group or cluster, m is the unit within the group, and t is the time index. Mainly for expository purposes, assume we have a balanced panel with the time periods running from $t = 1, \dots, T$. Within cluster g there are M_g units, and we have sampled G clusters. (In the HLM literature, g is usually called the *first level* and m the *second level.*)

As with a pure cluster sample, we assume that we have many groups, G, and relatively few members of the group. Further, our discussion of asymptotic properties of estimators assumes that T is fixed. In particular, the analysis is with the M_g and T fixed with G getting large. For example, if we can sample, say, several hundred school districts, with a few to maybe a few dozen schools per district, over a handful of years, then we have a data set that can be analyzed in the current framework.

A standard linear model with constant slopes can be written, for $t = 1, \dots, T$, $m = 1, \dots, M_g$, and a random draw g from the population of clusters as

$$y_{gmt} = \eta_t + \mathbf{w}_g \boldsymbol{\alpha} + \mathbf{x}_{gm} \boldsymbol{\beta} + \mathbf{z}_{gmt} \boldsymbol{\delta} + h_g + c_{mg} + u_{gmt}, \tag{20.52}$$

where, say, h_g is the industry or district effect, c_{gm} is the firm effect or school effect (firm or school m in industry or district g), and u_{gmt} is the idiosyncratic effect. In other words, the composite error is

$$v_{gmt} = h_g + c_{gm} + u_{gmt}. \tag{20.53}$$

Generally, the model can include variables that change at any level. In equation (20.52), some elements of $\mathbf{z}_{gmt}$ might change only across g and t, and not by unit. This is an important special case for policy analysis where the policy applies at the group level and changes over time. In such cases it is crucial for obtaining correct inference to recognize the cluster correlation. In effect, if one has observables in the model measured at the group level (whether or not they change over time), it is effectively cheating to then assume there are no group-level unobservables affecting y_{gmt}. This could be the case, but one should not assume it from the outset.

A simple estimation method, assuming v_{gmt} is uncorrelated with $(\mathbf{w}_g, \mathbf{x}_{gm}, \mathbf{z}_{gmt})$, is pooled OLS, which is consistent as $G \to \infty$ for any cluster or serial correlation pattern. The most general inference for pooled OLS—maintaining independence across clusters—is to allow any kind of serial correlation across units or time, or both, within a cluster.

Not surprisingly, one can apply a generalized least squares analysis that makes assumptions about the components of the composite error. Typically, it is assumed that the components are pairwise uncorrelated, the c_{gm} are uncorrelated within cluster (with common variance), and the u_{gmt} are uncorrelated within cluster and across time (with common variance). The resulting feasible GLS estimator is an extension of the usual random effects estimator for panel data. Because of the large-G setting, the estimator is consistent and asymptotically normal whether or not the actual variance structure we use in estimation is the proper one. To guard against heteroskedasticity in any of the errors and serial correlation in the $\{u_{gmt}\}$, one should use fully robust inference that does not rely on the form of the unconditional variance matrix (which may also differ from the conditional variance matrix).

Simple strategies are available, too. For example, one can apply random effects at the individual level, effectively ignoring the clusters in estimation. In other words, treat the data as a standard panel data set in estimation. Such an estimator might be more efficient than pooled OLS yet easier to obtain than a complete GLS analysis that also accounts for the cluster sampling. To account for the cluster sampling in inference, one computes a fully robust variance matrix estimator for the usual random effects estimator. Many statistical packages have options to allow for clustering at a higher level of aggregation than the level at which random effects is applied.

More formally, write the equation for each cluster as

$$\mathbf{y}_g = \mathbf{R}_g\boldsymbol{\theta} + \mathbf{v}_g, \tag{20.54}$$

where a row of $\mathbf{R}_g$ is $(1, d2, \ldots, dT, \mathbf{w}_g, \mathbf{x}_{gm}, \mathbf{z}_{gmt})$ (which includes a full set of period dummies) and $\boldsymbol{\theta}$ is the vector of all regression parameters. For cluster g, $\mathbf{y}_g$ contains M_gT elements (T periods for each unit m). In particular,

$$\mathbf{y}_g = \begin{pmatrix} \mathbf{y}_{g1} \\ \mathbf{y}_{g2} \\ \vdots \\ \mathbf{y}_{g,M_g} \end{pmatrix}, \qquad \mathbf{y}_{gm} = \begin{pmatrix} y_{gm1} \\ y_{gm2} \\ \vdots \\ y_{gmT} \end{pmatrix}, \tag{20.55}$$

so that each $\mathbf{y}_{gm}$ is $T \times 1$; $\mathbf{v}_g$ has an identical structure. Now, we can obtain $\boldsymbol{\Omega}_g = \operatorname{Var}(\mathbf{v}_g)$ under various assumptions and apply feasible GLS.

Random effects estimation at the unit level is obtained by choosing $\boldsymbol{\Omega}_g = \mathbf{I}_{M_g} \otimes \boldsymbol{\Lambda}$, where $\boldsymbol{\Lambda}$ is the $T \times T$ matrix with the RE structure. Of course, if there is within-cluster correlation, this is not the correct form of $\operatorname{Var}(\mathbf{v}_g)$, and that is why robust inference generally is needed after RE estimation. Generally, to allow for an incorrect structure imposed on $\mathbf{\Omega}_g$, or to allow for system heteroskedasticity, that is, $\text{Var}(\mathbf{v}_g \mid \mathbf{R}_g) \neq \text{Var}(\mathbf{v}_g)$, we use fully robust inference. In particular, the robust asymptotic variance of $\hat{\boldsymbol{\theta}}$ is estimated as

$$\widehat{\text{Avar}}(\hat{\boldsymbol{\theta}}) = \left(\sum_{g=1}^{G} \mathbf{R}_g'\hat{\mathbf{\Omega}}_g^{-1}\mathbf{R}_g\right)^{-1} \left(\sum_{g=1}^{G} \mathbf{R}_g'\hat{\mathbf{\Omega}}_g^{-1}\hat{\mathbf{v}}_g\hat{\mathbf{v}}_g'\hat{\mathbf{\Omega}}_g^{-1}\mathbf{R}_g\right)^{-1} \left(\sum_{g=1}^{G} \mathbf{R}_g'\hat{\mathbf{\Omega}}_g^{-1}\mathbf{R}_g\right)^{-1}, \tag{20.56}$$

where $\hat{\mathbf{v}}_g = \mathbf{y}_g - \mathbf{R}_g\hat{\boldsymbol{\theta}}$. Some software packages that allow cluster-robust inference after panel data estimation compute this fully robust asymptotic variance. Unfortunately, routines intended for estimating HLMs (or mixed models) often assume that the structure imposed on $\mathbf{\Omega}_g$ is correct, and that $\text{Var}(\mathbf{v}_g \mid \mathbf{R}_g) = \text{Var}(\mathbf{v}_g)$. The resulting inference could be misleading, especially if serial correlation in $\{u_{gmt}\}$ is not allowed.

Because of the nested data structure, we have available different versions of fixed effects estimators. Subtracting cluster averages from all observations within a cluster eliminates h_g; when $\mathbf{w}_{gt} = \mathbf{w}_g$ for all t, $\mathbf{w}_g$ is also eliminated. But the unit-specific effects, c_{mg}, are still part of the error term. If we are mainly interested in $\boldsymbol{\delta}$, the coefficients on the time-varying variables $\mathbf{z}_{gmt}$, then removing c_{gm} (along with h_g) is attractive. In other words, use a standard fixed effects analysis at the individual level. (If the units were allowed to change groups over time, then we would replace h_g with h_{gt}, and then subtracting off individual-specific means would not remove the time-varying cluster effects.)

Example 20.4 (Effects of Spending on School Performance): The data in MEAP94_98, which are a subset of those used in Papke (2005), contain school-level panel data on student performance and per-pupil spending. The variable to be explained, *math*4, is the percentage of students receiving a satisfactory score on a fourth-grade math test administered by the state of Michigan. The key variable, *lavgrexp* = log(*avgrexp*), is the log of average real per-pupil spending for the current and previous year. The data set is for the years 1994 through 1998; it is unbalanced, with schools having either three, four, or five years of data (in various patterns). The other school-level controls are enrollment, in logarithmic form (*lenroll*), and the percentage of students eligible for the free lunch program (*lunch*). A full set of year dummies is also included.

We can view this as a cluster sample because schools are nested within districts. Certainly much of the variability in spending is across districts, and so it may be important to allow for district-level effects.

The results of fixed effects estimation, at the school level, are given in Table 20.2. Because schools are in the same district in every year, eliminating a school effect also

Table 20.2
Fixed Effects Estimation of Spending on Test Pass Rates

Dependent Variable	*math*4			
	FE Coefficient	Usual FE Standard Error	S.E. Clustered by School	S.E. Clustered by District
Explanatory Variable				
log(*avgrexp*)	6.29	2.10	2.43	3.13
lunch	−0.022	0.031	0.039	0.040
log(*enrol*)	−2.04	1.79	1.79	2.10
*y*95	11.62	0.55	0.54	0.72
*y*96	13.06	0.66	0.69	0.93
*y*97	10.15	0.70	0.73	0.96
*y*98	23.41	0.72	0.77	1.03
Number of districts		467		
Number of schools		1,683		

removes any additive district effect. But within-district correlation can be present if some of the slopes change by district. Along with the FE estimates, three standard errors are provided: the usual FE standard errors that ignore serial correlation and within-district correlation; the standard errors that are robust to arbitrary serial correlation within school but assume no correlation across schools within a district; and the most robust standard errors that allow within-district correlation across schools and time periods. (Remember that we are assuming independence across districts; without this assumption, proper inference becomes much more difficult.)

The FE estimate of $\beta_{lavgrexp}$ is about 6.29, which means that a 10% increase in average real spending is estimated to increase the pass rate by about 0.63 percentage points. Using the usual FE standard error, about 2.10, the t statistic for $\hat{\beta}_{lavgrexp}$ is about 3.0. Therefore, the effect of spending is statistically significant at a low significance level (about 0.3%) using the usual FE inference. The standard error that allows arbitrary serial correlation within schools (and heteroskedasticity, too) is higher, about 2.43. Naturally, this reduces the statistical significance of $\hat{\beta}_{lavgrexp}$. The standard error in column (4) is subtantially higher, about 3.13. Allowing for within-district correlation and serial correlation has practically important effects on the uncertainty associated with the estimate. Using the fully robust standard error, the 95% confidence interval for $\beta_{lavgrexp}$ excludes zero, but only barely.

If the model is given by equations (20.52) and (20.53), the unit-specific time demeaning eliminates all cluster correlation, and the inference need only be made robust to neglected serial correlation in $\{u_{gmt}\}$. But we might want to use cluster-robust inference anyway to allow for more general situations. Suppose the model is

$$
\begin{aligned}
y_{gmt} &= \eta_t + \mathbf{w}_g\boldsymbol{\alpha} + \mathbf{x}_{gm}\boldsymbol{\beta} + \mathbf{z}_{gmt}\mathbf{d}_{mg} + h_g + c_{mg} + u_{gmt} \\
&= \eta_t + \mathbf{w}_{gt}\boldsymbol{\alpha} + \mathbf{x}_{gm}\boldsymbol{\beta} + \mathbf{z}_{gmt}\boldsymbol{\delta} + h_g + c_{mg} + u_{gmt} + \mathbf{z}_{gmt}\mathbf{e}_{gm}, \qquad (20.57)
\end{aligned}
$$

where $\mathbf{d}_{gm} = \boldsymbol{\delta} + \mathbf{e}_{gm}$ is a set of unit-specific intercepts on the individual, time-varying covariates $\mathbf{z}_{gmt}$. The time-demeaned equation within individual m in cluster g is

$$
y_{gmt} - \bar{y}_{gm} = \zeta_t + (\mathbf{z}_{gmt} - \bar{\mathbf{z}}_{gm})\boldsymbol{\delta} + (u_{gmt} - \bar{u}_{gm}) + (\mathbf{z}_{gmt} - \bar{\mathbf{z}}_{gm})\mathbf{e}_{gm}. \qquad (20.58)
$$

Because the $\mathbf{e}_{gm}$ are generally correlated across units within cluster g, the last term generally induces cluster correlation of a heteroskedastic nature within cluster g. From our discussion in Section 11.7.3, we know that FE is still consistent if $\mathrm{E}(\mathbf{d}_{mg} \mid \mathbf{z}_{gmt} - \bar{\mathbf{z}}_{gm}) = \mathrm{E}(\mathbf{d}_{mg})$, $m = 1, \ldots, M_g$, $t = 1, \ldots, T$, and all g, and so cluster-robust inference, which is automatically robust to serial correlation and heteroskedasticity, makes perfectly good sense.

An important feature of the HLM approach is the possibility of allowing the slopes to depend on observed covariates. Often one begins with a model at the unit–time-period level that contains heterogeneity, and then allows the intercept and slopes to depend on higher-level covariates. Write a model for unit m at time t in cluster g as

$$
y_{gmt} = \mathbf{z}_{gmt}\mathbf{d}_{gm} + v_{gmt}, \qquad (20.59)
$$

and then decompose the idiosyncratic error, v_{gmt}, as

$$
v_{gmt} = \eta_t + c_{gm} + u_{gmt}, \qquad (20.60)
$$

where the η_t are aggregate time effects. For notational simplicity, we absorb the group effect, h_{gt}, into u_{gmt}, and allow c_{gm} and u_{gmt} to be correlated within group. For each (g, m) define

$$
\bar{\mathbf{r}}_{gm} = (\mathbf{w}_g, \bar{\mathbf{x}}_g, \mathbf{x}_{gm}, \bar{\mathbf{z}}_{gm}),
$$

where $\bar{\mathbf{x}}_g = M_g^{-1} \sum_{p=1}^{M_g} \mathbf{x}_{gp}$ and $\bar{\mathbf{z}}_{gm} = T^{-1} \sum_{s=1}^{T} \mathbf{z}_{gms}$. In other words, $\bar{\mathbf{r}}_{gm}$ includes the group-level covariates along with group averages of the unit-specific covariates, the unit-specific covariates, and the time averages of the covariates that change over time. Now assume

$$
c_{gm} = \alpha + \bar{\mathbf{r}}_{gm}\gamma + a_{gm} \qquad (20.61)
$$

$$
\mathbf{d}_{gm} = \boldsymbol{\delta} + \boldsymbol{\Pi}(\bar{\mathbf{r}}_{gm} - \boldsymbol{\mu}_{\bar{\mathbf{r}}})' + \mathbf{e}_{gm}, \qquad (20.62)
$$

insert these in the equation, and use basic algebra:

$$
y_{gmt} = \zeta_t + \bar{\mathbf{r}}_{gm}\gamma + \mathbf{z}_{gmt}\boldsymbol{\delta} + [(\bar{\mathbf{r}}_{gm} - \boldsymbol{\mu}_{\bar{\mathbf{r}}}) \otimes \mathbf{z}_{gmt}]\boldsymbol{\pi} + a_{gm} + \mathbf{z}_{gmt}\mathbf{e}_{gm} + u_{gmt},
$$

where $\boldsymbol{\pi} = \text{vec}(\boldsymbol{\Pi})$. Importantly, centering $\bar{\mathbf{r}}_{gm}$ about its average before forming the interactions means that $\boldsymbol{\delta}$ is the average partial effect. If we instead use $\bar{\mathbf{r}}_{gm} \otimes \mathbf{z}_{gmt}$, the coefficients on the level terms, $\mathbf{z}_{gmt}$, may be of little interest because they measure the effects of the $\mathbf{z}_{gmt}$ when $\bar{\mathbf{r}}_{gm}$ is zero, which is unlikely to be an interesting segment of the population. In practice, the population mean, $\boldsymbol{\mu}_{\bar{\mathbf{r}}}$, is replaced with the sample average across m and g. The presence of $\mathbf{z}_{gmt}\mathbf{e}_{gm}$ in the error term, as well as potential serial correlation in $\{u_{gmt}\}$, makes a genuine GLS analysis difficult but possible under simple structures for the variance-covariance matrices. But we can use any of the simpler strategies mentioned earlier. For example, we can act as if $\mathbf{e}_{gm} = 0$ and as if u_{gmt} is serially uncorrelated in estimation. We can apply random effects to account for a cluster-level effect or RE at the individual level, or both. Basically, we include cluster-level variables, averages of unit-specific, time-constant variables, and time averages of the variables that change over time along with the unit-specific variables. For added flexibility, we include a full set of interactions. Regardless of the specifics, we use fully robust inference.

A very similar discussion holds in the context of instrumental variables. Suppose we start with the model

$$y_{gmt} = \eta_t + \mathbf{r}_{gmt}\boldsymbol{\theta} + v_{gmt}, \tag{20.63}$$

where $\mathbf{r}_{gmt}$ contains all covariates and v_{gmt} is the composite error. If we have exogenous variables, say $\mathbf{q}_{gmt}$, such that $\text{E}(\mathbf{q}'_{gmt}v_{gmt}) = \mathbf{0}$ and the rank condition holds, then pooled 2SLS is attractive for its simplicity. It does not matter whether elements of $\mathbf{r}_{gmt}$ or $\mathbf{q}_{gmt}$ contain elements that change only across g, across g and m, across g and t, or across g, m, and t, provided the rank condition holds. Without further assumptions, the 2SLS variance matrix estimator, as well as inference generally, should be robust to arbitrary serial correlation and cluster correlation at the most aggregated level. For example, if g indexes counties and m indexes manufacturing plants operating within a county, then we should cluster at the county level. We may have a policy and instruments that change only at the county level over time, along with exogenous explanatory variables that change at the plant level (either constant or over time). In evaluating whether the rank condition holds—say, for a single endogenous variable w_{gmt}—one can use a pooled OLS regression w_{gmt} on $1, d2_t, \ldots, dT_t$, $\mathbf{q}_{gmt}$ (assuming that $\mathbf{q}_{gmt}$ contains all exogenous variables in equation (20.63)) to test for joint significance of the proposed instruments in $\mathbf{q}_{gmt}$. Naturally, such a test should be made robust to arbitrary cluster and serial correlation to be convincing. The test works even if w_{gmt} does not change across m (or even t for that matter), and the same with $\mathbf{q}_{gmt}$. The inference is valid with large G provided it is made fully robust.

In the previous scenario, if we apply, say, fixed effects 2SLS, where we eliminate a time-constant, plant-level effect, then we need the variables of interest to at least change over time (if not across m); the same is true of the instruments. If we have instruments that change only by g, the FE2SLS estimator—whether we remove a county-level or plant-level effect—does not identify $\boldsymbol{\theta}$.

20.3.3 Should We Apply Cluster-Robust Inference with Large Group Sizes?

Until recently, the "cluster-robust" standard errors and test statistics obtained from pooled OLS, random effects, and fixed effects were known to be valid only as $G \to \infty$ with each M_g fixed. As a practical matter, that fact means that one should have lots of small groups. Recently, because of the structure of many commonly used cluster samples, researchers have become interested in the performance of cluster-robust inference when the number of groups, G, is not substantially larger than the typical group size, M_g.

Consider the basic model without a time structure, for simplicity, and consider formula (20.25), the asymptotic variance for pooled OLS. With a large number of groups and small group sizes, we can get good estimates of the within-cluster correlations—technically, of the cluster correlations of the cross products of the regressors and errors—even if they are unrestricted, and it is for that reason that the robust variance matrix is consistent as $G \to \infty$ with M_g fixed. In fact, in this scenario, one loses nothing in terms of asymptotic local power (with local alternatives shrinking to zero at the rate $G^{-1/2}$) if c_g is not present. In other words, based on first-order asymptotic analysis, there is no cost to being fully robust to any kind of within-group correlation or heteroskedasticity. These arguments apply equally to panel data sets with a large number of cross sections and relatively few time periods, whether or not the idiosyncratic errors are serially correlated, and to the cluster sample/panel data setting considered in Section 20.3.2.

What if one applies robust inference in scenarios where the fixed M_g, $G \to \infty$ asymptotic analysis is not realistic? Hansen (2007) has recently derived properties of the cluster-robust variance matrix and related test statistics under various scenarios that help us more fully understand the properties of cluster-robust inference across different data configurations. Hansen (2007, Theorem 2) shows that, with G and M_g both getting large, the usual inference based on equation (20.25) is valid with arbitrary correlation among the errors, v_{gm}, within each group. Because we usually think of v_{gm} as including the group effect c_g, this means that, with large group sizes, we can obtain valid inference using the cluster-robust variance matrix, provided that G is also large. So, for example, if we have a sample of $G = 100$ schools and roughly $M_g = 100$ students per school, and we use pooled OLS leaving the school effects in the error term, we should expect the inference to have roughly the correct size. Probably we leave the school effects in the error term because we are interested in a school-specific explanatory variable, perhaps indicating a policy change. Adding a short time dimension does not change these conclusions.

Unfortunately, pooled OLS with cluster effects when G is small and group sizes are large falls outside Hansen's theoretical findings: the proper asymptotic analysis would be with G fixed, $M_g \to \infty$, and persistent within-cluster correlation (because of the presence of c_g in the error) causes problems in such cases. Consequently, we should not expect good properties of the cluster-robust inference with small groups and very large group sizes when cluster effects are left in the error term. As an example, suppose that $G = 10$ hospitals have been sampled with several hundred patients per hospital. If the explanatory variable of interest is exogenous and varies only at the hospital level, it is tempting to use pooled OLS with cluster-robust inference. But we have no theoretical justification for doing so, and we have reasons to expect it will not work well—including the simulations in Hansen (2007).

If the explanatory variables of interest vary within group—say, within each hospital a subset of patients were provided with a specific kind of care—fixed effects is attractive for a couple of reasons. The first advantage is the usual one about allowing c_g to be arbitrarily correlated with the $\mathbf{z}_{gm}$. The second advantage is that, with large M_g, we can treat the c_g as parameters to estimate—because we can estimate them precisely—and then assume that the observations are independent across m (as well as g). Therefore, the usual inference is valid, perhaps with adjustments for heteroskedasticity.

In summary, for true cluster sample applications, cluster-robust inference using pooled OLS delivers statistics with proper size when G and M_g are both moderately large, but they should probably be avoided with large M_g and small G. We will discuss some approaches for handling a small number of groups in Section 20.3.4.

20.3.4 Inference When the Number of Clusters Is Small

If the explanatory variable or variables of interest do not change within cluster and the number of clusters is small, none of the previous methods can be used for reliable inference. Fixed effects eliminates the key variables, while for pooled OLS we are not justified in using cluster-robust inference. (Whether a random effects analysis produces valid inference with small G and large M_g appears to be an open, and very interesting, question.)

The problem of proper inference when M_g is large relative to G was brought to light by Moulton (1990), who was interested in studying data on individuals clustered at the state level in the United States. He proposed corrections to the usual OLS standard errors that impose more structure than the usual cluster-robust standard errors studied by Hansen (2007). Either way, the corrections to the usual OLS inference tend to work well provided the M_g are not too much bigger than G. In this subsection we are interested in cases where a large G analysis makes no sense.

Often with small G and large M_g the sampling scheme more resembles that of standard stratified sampling, but without requiring a complete partition of the population. In other words, a small set of populations are defined, and then random samples are obtained from those populations. As an example, a random sample of adults is obtained from each of a handful of cities, some of which received federal aid for a job-training program. Labor market outcomes are recorded, possibly including changes from an early time period. In this scenario, we could analyze the data as independent outcomes across and, more importantly, within group. We will return to this point.

Recent work by Donald and Lang (2007) (hereafter, DL) treats the small G case within the context of cluster sampling. That is, presumably from a large population of clusters, only a handful or so are drawn (and then we may or may not sample every unit within each cluster). As mentioned in the previous subsection, such a scenario causes problems for cluster-robust inference. Therefore, DL propose a different approach.

Before we cover the DL approach, it is important to understand that the structure of data sets in the small G case is the same whether we think of drawing a small number of clusters from a large population or fixing a few clusters and then drawing large random samples from them. Unfortunately, how one proceeds is dependent on how we view the sampling scheme. As we will see, the DL approach is typically much more conservative than the standard approach.

To illustrate the issues considered by DL, consider the simplest case, with a single regressor that varies only by group:

$$y_{gm} = \alpha + \beta x_g + c_g + u_{gm} \tag{20.64}$$

$$= \delta_g + \beta x_g + u_{gm}, \qquad m = 1, \ldots, M_g;\ g = 1, \ldots, G. \tag{20.65}$$

Notice how equation (20.65) is written as a model with common slope, β, but intercept, δ_g, that varies across g. Donald and Lang focus on equation (20.64), where c_g is assumed to be independent of x_g with zero mean. They use this formulation to highlight the problems of applying standard inference to equation (20.64), that is, acting as if c_g is absent. We know this is a bad idea even in the large G, small M_g case, as it ignores the persistent correlation in the errors within each group. Unfortunately, while Hansen (2007) has shown that cluster-robust inference is valid with large G, even if the M_g are also large, it is not valid when G is small. Thus other approaches are needed.

One way to see the problem in applying standard inference is to note that when $M_g = M$ for all $g = 1, \dots, G$, the pooled OLS estimator, $\hat{\beta}$, is identical to the "between" estimator obtained from the regression

$$\bar{y}_g \quad \text{on} \quad 1, x_g, \qquad g = 1, \dots, G. \tag{20.66}$$

Conditional on the x_g, the estimator $\hat{\beta}$ inherits its distribution from $\{\bar{v}_g\colon g = 1, \dots, G\}$, the within-group averages of the composite errors $v_{gm} \equiv c_g + u_{gm}$. The presence of c_g means new observations within group do not provide additional information for estimating β beyond how they affect the group average, $\bar{y}_g$. In effect, we only have G useful pieces of information.

If we add some strong assumptions, there is a solution to the inference problem. In addition to assuming $M_g = M$ for all g, assume $c_g \mid x_g \sim \text{Normal}(0, \sigma_c^2)$ and assume $u_{gm} \mid x_g, c_g \sim \text{Normal}(0, \sigma_u^2)$. Then $\bar{v}_g$ is independent of x_g and $\bar{v}_g \sim \text{Normal}(0, \sigma_c^2 + \sigma_u^2/M)$ for all g. Because we assume independence across g, the equation

$$\bar{y}_g = \alpha + \beta x_g + \bar{v}_g, \qquad g = 1, \dots, G \tag{20.67}$$

satisfies the classical linear model assumptions. Therefore, we can use inference based on the t_{G-2} distribution to test hypotheses about β, provided $G > 2$. When G is very small, the requirements for a significant t statistic using the t_{G-2} distribution are much more stringent than if we use the $t_{M_1+M_2+\cdots+M_G-2}$ distribution—which is what we would be doing if we used the usual pooled OLS statistics.

When $\mathbf{x}_g$ is a $1 \times K$ vector, we need $G > K + 1$ to use the t_{G-K-1} distribution for inference. (In Moulton (1990), $G = 50$ states and $\mathbf{x}_g$ contains 17 elements.)

As pointed out by DL, performing the correct inference in the presence of c_g is *not* just a matter of correcting the pooled OLS standard errors for cluster correlation—something that does not appear to be valid for small G, anyway—or using the RE estimator. In the case of common group sizes, there is only estimator: pooled OLS. Random effects and between regression in equation (20.66) all lead to the *same* $\hat{\beta}$. The regression in equation (20.66), by using the t_{G-2} distribution, yields inference with appropriate size.

We can apply the DL method without normality of the u_{gm} if the common group size M is large: by the central limit theorem, $\bar{u}_g$ will be approximately normally distributed very generally. Then, because c_g is normally distributed, we can treat $\bar{v}_g$ as approximately normal with constant variance. Further, even if the group sizes differ across g, for very large group sizes $\bar{u}_g$ will be a negligible part of $\bar{v}_g$: $\text{Var}(\bar{v}_g) = \sigma_c^2 + \sigma_u^2/M_g$. Provided c_g is normally distributed and it dominates $\bar{v}_g$, a classical linear model analysis on equation (20.67) should be roughly valid.

The broadest applicability of DL's setup occurs when the average of the idiosyncratic errors, $\bar{u}_g$, can be ignored—either because σ_u^2 is small relative to σ_c^2, M_g is large, or both. In fact, applying DL with different group sizes or nonnormality of the u_{gm} is identical to ignoring the estimation error in the sample averages, $\bar{y}_g$. In other words, it is as if we are analyzing the simple regression $\mu_g = \alpha + \beta x_g + c_g$ using the classical linear model assumptions (where we then insert $\bar{y}_g$ in place of the unknown group mean, μ_g, and ignore the estimation error). With small G, we need to further assume that c_g is normally distributed.

If $\mathbf{z}_{gm}$ appears in the model, then we can use the averaged equation

$$\bar{y}_g = \alpha + \mathbf{x}_g\boldsymbol{\beta} + \bar{\mathbf{z}}_g\boldsymbol{\gamma} + \bar{v}_g, \qquad g = 1, \ldots, G, \tag{20.68}$$

provided $G > K + L + 1$. If c_g is independent of $(\mathbf{x}_g, \bar{\mathbf{z}}_g)$ with a homoskedastic normal distribution and the group sizes are large, inference can be carried out using the $t_{G-K-L-1}$ distribution.

The DL solution to the inference problem with small G is pretty common as a strategy to check robustness of results obtained from cluster samples, but often it is implemented with somewhat large G (say, $G = 50$). Often with cluster samples one estimates the parameters using the disaggregated data and also the averaged data. When some covariates vary within cluster, using averaged data is generally inefficient, but when estimating equation (20.68) we need not make standard errors robust to within-cluster correlation. We now know that if G is reasonably large and the group sizes not too large, the cluster-robust inference applied to the disaggregated data can be acceptable. As pointed out by DL, with small G one should use the group averages in a classical linear model analysis.

For small G and large M_g, inference obtained analyzing equation (20.67) as a classical linear model will be very conservative in the absence of a cluster effect. Thus the DL approach can be used in situations where one requires very strong statistical evidence for the effect of a policy. Nevertheless, the DL approach rules out some widely used staples of policy analysis. For example, suppose we have two populations (maybe men and women, two different cities, or a treatment and a control group) with means μ_g, $g = 1, 2$, and we would like to obtain a confidence interval for their difference. In almost all cases, it makes sense to view the data as being two random samples, one from each subgroup of the population. Under random sampling from each group, and assuming normality and equal population variances, the usual comparison-of-means statistic is distributed exactly as $t_{M_1+M_2-2}$ under the null hypothesis of equal population means. (Or, we can construct an exact 95% confidence interval of the difference in population means.) With even moderate sizes for M_1 and M_2, the $t_{M_1+M_2-2}$ distribution is close to the standard normal distribution. Also, we can relax normality to obtain approximately valid inference, and it is easy to adjust the t statistic to allow for different population variances. With a controlled experiment, the standard difference-in-means analysis is often quite convincing. Yet we cannot even study this estimator in the DL setup because $G = 2$.

Donald and Lang criticize Card and Krueger (1994) for comparing mean wage changes of workers at a sample of fast-food restaurants across two states because Card and Krueger fail to account for the state effect (New Jersey or Pennsylvania), c_g, in the composite error, v_{gm}. It is important to remember that the DL criticism of the standard difference-in-differences estimator has nothing to do with whether the increase in the minimum wage in New Jersey (in April 1992) was an exogenous event: DL's framework assumes that x_g, which is an indicator for whether a fast-food restaurant is in New Jersey, is independent of the state effect, c_g. Rather, DL's criticism only concerns inference. (Card and Krueger find a positive, not a negative, employment effect of increasing the minimum wage, so having a confidence interval seems to be less important in this particular case.)

To further study the $G = 2$ case with a binary policy indicator, write the difference in means as

$$\mu_2 - \mu_1 = (\delta_2 + \beta) - \delta_1 = (\alpha + c_2 + \beta) - (\alpha + c_1) = \beta + (c_2 - c_1). \tag{20.69}$$

Under the DL assumptions, $c_2 - c_1$ has mean zero, and so including it as part of the estimate, which is $\bar{y}_2 - \bar{y}_1$, does not result in bias. The authors work under the assumption that β is the parameter of interest, but, if the experiment is properly randomized—as is maintained by DL—it is harmless to include the c_g in the estimated effect, in which case the standard comparison-of-means methodology, using large M_g asymptotics, is appropriate.

Consider now a case where the DL approach to inference can be applied. Assume $G = 4$ with groups 1 and 2 the control groups $(x_1 = x_2 = 0)$ and groups 3 and 4 the treatment groups $(x_3 = x_4 = 1)$. The DL approach would involve computing the averages for each group, $\bar{y}_g$, and running the regression $\bar{y}_g$ on 1, x_g, $g = 1, \ldots, 4$. Inference is based on the t_2 distribution. The estimator $\hat{\beta}$ in this case can be written as

$$\hat{\beta} = (\bar{y}_3 + \bar{y}_4)/2 - (\bar{y}_1 + \bar{y}_2)/2. \tag{20.70}$$

(The pooled OLS regression using the disaggregated data results in the weighted average $(p_3\bar{y}_3 + p_4\bar{y}_4) - (p_1\bar{y}_1 + p_2\bar{y}_2)$, where $p_1 = M_1/(M_1 + M_2)$, $p_2 = M_2/(M_1 + M_2)$, $p_3 = M_3/(M_3 + M_4)$, and $p_4 = M_4/(M_3 + M_4)$ are the relative proportions within the control and treatment groups, respectively.) With $\hat{\beta}$ written as in equation (20.70), we are left to wonder why we need to use the t_2 distribution for, say, constructing a confidence interval. Each $\bar{y}_g$ is usually obtained from a large sample—$M_g = 30$ or so is usually sufficient for approximate normality of the standardized mean—and so $\hat{\beta}$, when properly standardized, has an approximate standard normal distribution quite generally.

In effect, the DL approach rejects the usual large-sample confidence interval based on group means because it may not be the case that $\mu_1 = \mu_2$ and $\mu_3 = \mu_4$. In other words, the control groups may be heterogeneous, as might be the treatment groups. This possibility in itself does not invalidate standard inference applied to equation (20.70). In fact, if we *define* the object of interest as

$$\tau = (\mu_3 + \mu_4)/2 - (\mu_1 + \mu_2)/2, \tag{20.71}$$

which is an average treatment effect of sorts, then $\hat{\beta}$ is consistent for β and (when properly scaled) asymptotically normal as the M_g get large.

The previous example suggests a different way to view the small G, large M_g setup. In this particular setup, we are estimating two parameters, α and β, given four moments that we can estimate with the data. The OLS estimates from $\bar{y}_g$ on 1, x_g, $g = 1, \ldots, G$, are minimum distance (MD) estimates that impose the restrictions $\mu_1 = \mu_2 = \alpha$ and $\mu_3 = \mu_4 = \alpha + \beta$. In particular, using the 4×4 identity matrix as the weight matrix, we get $\hat{\beta}$ as in equation (20.70) and $\hat{\alpha} = (\bar{y}_1 + \bar{y}_2)/2$. Using the MD approach, we see there are two overidentifying restrictions, which are easily tested. But even if we reject them, it simply implies that at least one pair of means within each of the control and treatment groups differs. If, say, we have four cities and random samples of workers from each city, $x_g = 1$ indicates a job-training program in two of the four cities, and y_{gm} is the change in labor market income, then it may simply be the case that the job-training program had differential effects across the two treatment cities, or that the mean change in labor market income differed across the two control cities, or both. Why should we reject the usual large M_g inference simply because the job-training program has heterogeneous effects?

With large group sizes, and whether or not G is especially large, we can put the general problem into an MD framework, as done, for example, by Loeb and Bound (1996), who had $G = 36$ cohort-division groups and many observations per group. For each group g, write

$$y_{gm} = \delta_g + \mathbf{z}_{gm}\boldsymbol{\gamma}_g + u_{gm}, \qquad m = 1, \ldots, M_g, \tag{20.72}$$

where we assume random sampling within group and independent sampling across groups. We make the standard assumptions for OLS to be consistent (as $M_g \to \infty$) and $\sqrt{M_g}$-asymptotically normal, as in Chapter 4. The presence of group-level variables $\mathbf{x}_g$ in a "structural" model can be viewed as putting restrictions on the intercepts, δ_g, in the separate group models in equation (20.72). In particular,

$$\delta_g = \alpha + \mathbf{x}_g\boldsymbol{\beta}, \qquad g = 1, \ldots, G, \tag{20.73}$$

where we think of $\mathbf{x}_g$ as fixed, observed attributes of heterogeneous groups. With K attributes we must have $G \geq K + 1$ to determine α and $\boldsymbol{\beta}$. If M_g is large enough to estimate the δ_g precisely, a simple two-step estimation strategy suggests itself. First, obtain the $\hat{\delta}_g$, along with $\hat{\gamma}_g$, from an OLS regression within each group. If $G = K + 1$, then, typically, we can solve for $\hat{\boldsymbol{\theta}} \equiv (\hat{\alpha}, \hat{\boldsymbol{\beta}}')'$ uniquely in terms of the $G \times 1$ vector $\hat{\boldsymbol{\delta}}$: $\hat{\boldsymbol{\theta}} = \mathbf{X}^{-1}\hat{\boldsymbol{\delta}}$, where $\mathbf{X}$ is the $(K+1) \times (K+1)$ matrix with gth row $(1, \mathbf{x}_g)$. If $G > K + 1$, then, in a second step, we can use a minimum distance approach, as described in Section 14.6. If we use $\mathbf{I}_G$, the $G \times G$ identity matrix, as the weighting matrix, then the minimum distance estimator can be computed from the OLS regression

$$\hat{\delta}_g \quad \text{on} \quad 1, \mathbf{x}_g, \qquad g = 1, \ldots, G. \tag{20.74}$$

Under asymptotics such that $M_g = \rho_g M$ where $0 < \rho_g \leq 1$ and $M \to \infty$, the minimum distance estimator $\hat{\boldsymbol{\theta}}$ is consistent and $\sqrt{M}$-asymptotically normal. Still, this particular MD estimator is asymptotically inefficient except under strong assumptions. Because the samples are assumed to be independent, it is not appreciably more difficult to obtain the efficient MD estimator, also called the "minimum chi-square" estimator.

First consider the case where $\mathbf{z}_{gm}$ does not appear in the first-stage estimation, so that the $\hat{\delta}_g$ is just $\bar{y}_g$, the sample mean for group g. Let $\hat{\sigma}_g^2$ denote the usual sample variance for group g. Because the $\bar{y}_g$ are independent across g, the efficient MD estimator uses a diagonal weighting matrix. As a computational device, the minimum chi-square estimator can be computed by using the weighted least squares (WLS) version of regression (20.74), where group g is weighted by $M_g/\hat{\sigma}_g^2$ (groups that have more data and smaller variance receive greater weight). Conveniently, the reported t statistics from the WLS regression are asymptotically standard normal as the group sizes M_g get large. (With fixed G, the WLS nature of the estimation is just a computational device; the standard asymptotic analysis of the WLS estimator has $G \to \infty$.) The minimum distance approach works with small G provided $G \geq K + 1$ and each M_g is large enough so that normality is a good approximation to the distribution of the (properly scaled) sample average within each group.

If $\mathbf{z}_{gm}$ is present in the first-stage estimation, we use as the minimum chi-square weights the inverses of the asymptotic variances for the g intercepts in the separate G regressions. With large M_g, we might make these fully robust to heteroskedasticity in $\mathrm{E}(u_{gm}^2 \mid \mathbf{z}_{gm})$ using the White (1980a) sandwich variance estimator. At a minimum we would want to allow different σ_g^2 even if we assume homoskedasticity within groups. Once we have the $\widehat{\mathrm{Avar}}(\hat{\delta}_g)$—which are just the squared reported standard errors for the $\hat{\delta}_g$—we use as weights $1/\widehat{\mathrm{Avar}}(\hat{\delta}_g)$ in the computationally simple WLS procedure. We are still using independence across g in obtaining a diagonal weighting matrix in the MD estimation.

An important by-product of the WLS regression is a minimum chi-square statistic that can be used to test the $G - K - 1$ overidentifying restrictions. The statistic is easily obtained as the weighted sum of squared residuals, say, SSR_w. Under the null hypothesis in equation (20.73), $SSR_w \overset{a}{\sim} \chi^2_{G-K-1}$ as the group sizes, M_g, get large. If we reject H_0 at a reasonably small significance level, the $\mathbf{x}_g$ are not sufficient for characterizing the changing intercepts across groups. If we fail to reject H_0, we can have some confidence in our specification and obtain confidence intervals for linear combinations of the population averages using the usual standard normal approximation.

We might also be interested in how one (or more) of the slopes in γ_g depends on the group features, $\mathbf{x}_g$. Then, we simple replace $\hat{\delta}_g$ with, say, $\hat{\gamma}_{g1}$, the slope on the first element of $\mathbf{z}_{gm}$. Naturally, we would use $1/\widehat{\text{Avar}}(\hat{\gamma}_{g1})$ as the weights in the MD estimation.

The minimum distance approach can also be applied if we impose $\gamma_g = \gamma$ for all g, as in the original model. Obtaining the $\hat{\delta}_g$ themselves is easy: run the pooled regression

$$y_{gm} \quad \text{on} \quad d1_g, d2_g, \ldots, dG_g, \mathbf{z}_{gm}, \qquad m = 1, \ldots, M_g;\ g = 1, \ldots, G, \tag{20.75}$$

where $d1_g, d2_g, \ldots, dG_g$ are group dummy variables. Using the $\hat{\delta}_g$ from the pooled regression (20.74) in MD estimation is complicated by the fact that the $\hat{\delta}_g$ are no longer asymptotically independent; in fact, $\hat{\delta}_g = \bar{y}_g - \bar{\mathbf{z}}_g\hat{\gamma}$, where $\hat{\gamma}$ is the vector of common slopes, and the presence of $\hat{\gamma}$ induces correlation among the intercept estimators. Let $\hat{\mathbf{V}}$ be the $G \times G$ estimated (asymptotic) variance matrix of the $G \times 1$ vector $\hat{\boldsymbol{\delta}}$. Then the MD estimator is $\hat{\boldsymbol{\theta}} = (\mathbf{X}'\hat{\mathbf{V}}^{-1}\mathbf{X})^{-1}\mathbf{X}'\hat{\mathbf{V}}^{-1}\hat{\boldsymbol{\delta}}$, and its estimated asymptotic variance is $(\mathbf{X}'\hat{\mathbf{V}}^{-1}\mathbf{X})^{-1}$. If the OLS regression (20.74) is used, or even the WLS version, the resulting standard errors will be incorrect because they ignore the across-group correlation in the estimated intercepts.

Intermediate approaches are available, too. Loeb and Bound (1996) (hereafter, LB) allow different group intercepts and group-specific slopes on education, but impose common slopes on demographic and family background variables. The main group-level covariate is the student-teacher ratio. Thus LB are interested in seeing how the student-teacher ratio affects the relationship between test scores and education levels. They use both the unweighted estimator and the weighted estimator and find that the results differ in unimportant ways. Because they impose common slopes on a set of regressors, the estimated slopes on education (say $\hat{\gamma}_{g1}$) are not asymptotically independent, and perhaps using a nondiagonal estimated variance matrix $\hat{\mathbf{V}}$ (which would be 36×36 in this case) is more appropriate.

If we reject the overidentifying restrictions, we are essentially concluding that $\delta_g = \alpha + \mathbf{x}_g\boldsymbol{\beta} + c_g$, where c_g can be interpreted as the deviation from the restrictions in equation (20.73) for group g. As G increases relative to K, the likelihood of rejecting the restrictions increases. One possibility is to apply the Donald and Lang approach, where the OLS regression (20.74) is analyzed in the context of the classical linear model (CLM) with inference based on the t_{G-K-1} distribution. Why is a CLM analysis justified? Since $\hat{\delta}_g = \delta_g + O_p(M_g^{-1/2})$, we can ingore the estimation error in $\hat{\delta}_g$ for large M_g Then, it is as if we are estimating the equation $\delta_g = \alpha + \mathbf{x}_g\boldsymbol{\beta} + c_g$, $g = 1, \ldots, G$ by OLS. If the c_g are drawn from a normal distribution, classical analysis is applicable because c_g is assumed to be independent of $\mathbf{x}_g$. This approach is desirable when one cannot, or does not want to, find group-level observables that completely determine the δ_g. It is predicated on the assumption that the other factors in c_g are not systematically related to $\mathbf{x}_g$, a reasonable assumption if, say, $\mathbf{x}_g$ is a randomly assigned treatment at the group level, a case considered by Angrist and Lavy (2002).

Unlike in the linear case, for nonlinear models exact inference is unavailable even under the strongest set of assumptions. Nevertheless, if the group sizes M_g are reasonably large, we can extend the DL approach to nonlinear models and obtain approximate inference. In addition, the minimum distance approach carries over essentially without change.

We can apply the methods to any nonlinear model that has an index structure, which includes all the common ones, and many other models besides. Again, it is helpful to study the probit case in some detail. With small G and random sampling of $\{(y_{gm}, \mathbf{z}_{gm})\colon m = 1, \ldots, M_g\}$ within each g, write

$$\mathrm{P}(y_{gm} = 1 \mid \mathbf{z}_{gm}) = \Phi(\delta_g + \mathbf{z}_{gm}\boldsymbol{\gamma}_g), \qquad m = 1, \ldots, M_g \tag{20.76}$$

$$\delta_g = \alpha + \mathbf{x}_g\boldsymbol{\beta}, \qquad g = 1, \ldots, G. \tag{20.77}$$

As with the linear model, we assume the intercept, δ_g in equation (20.76), is a function of the group features $\mathbf{x}_g$. With the M_g moderately large, we can get good estimates of the δ_g. The $\hat{\delta}_g$, $g = 1, \ldots, G$, are easily obtained by estimating a separate probit for each group. Or, we can impose common γ_g and just estimate different group intercepts (sometimes called "group fixed effects").

Under the restrictions in equation (20.77), we can apply the minimum distance approach just as before. Let $\widehat{\mathrm{Avar}}(\hat{\delta}_g)$ denote the estimated asymptotic variances of the $\hat{\delta}_g$ (so these shrink to zero at the rate $1/M_g$). If the $\hat{\delta}_g$ are obtained from G separate probits, they are independent, and the $\widehat{\mathrm{Avar}}(\hat{\delta}_g)$ are all we need. As in the linear case, if a pooled method is used, the $G \times G$ matrix $\widehat{\mathrm{Avar}}(\hat{\boldsymbol{\delta}})$ should be inverted and then used as the weighting matrix. For binary response, we use the usual MLE estimated variance. If we are using fractional probit for a fractional response, these would be from a sandwich estimate of the asymptotic variance. In the case where the $\hat{\delta}_g$ are obtained from separate probits, we can obtain the minimum distance estimates as the WLS estimates from

$$\hat{\delta}_g \quad \text{on} \quad 1, x_g, \qquad g = 1, \ldots, G$$

using weights $1/\widehat{\text{Avar}}(\hat{\delta}_g)$. This is the efficient minimum distance estimator and, conveniently, the proper asymptotic standard errors are reported from the WLS estimation (even though we are doing large M_g, not large G, asymptotics here). Generally, we can write the MD estimator as before: $\hat{\boldsymbol{\theta}} = (\mathbf{X}'\hat{\mathbf{V}}^{-1}\mathbf{X})^{-1}\mathbf{X}'\hat{\mathbf{V}}^{-1}\hat{\boldsymbol{\delta}}$, where $\hat{\boldsymbol{\delta}}$ is the $G \times 1$ vector of $\hat{\delta}_g$ and $\hat{\mathbf{V}} = \widehat{\text{Avar}}(\hat{\boldsymbol{\delta}})$. The overidentification test is obtained exactly as in the linear case: there are $G - K - 1$ degrees of freedom in the chi-square distribution.

If we reject the overidentification restrictions, we can adapt Donald and Lang (2007) and treat

$$\hat{\delta}_g = \alpha + \mathbf{x}_g\boldsymbol{\beta} + error_g, \qquad g = 1, \ldots, G \tag{20.78}$$

as approximately satisfying the classical linear model assumptions, provided $G > K + 1$, just as before. As in the linear case, this approach is justified if $\delta_g = \alpha + \mathbf{x}_g\boldsymbol{\beta} + c_g$ with c_g independent of $\mathbf{x}_g$ and c_g drawn from a homoskedastic normal distribution. It assumes that we can ignore the estimation error in $\hat{\delta}_g$, based on $\hat{\delta}_g = \delta_g + O(1/\sqrt{M_g})$. Because the DL approach ignores the estimation error in $\hat{\delta}_g$, it is unchanged if one imposes some constant slopes across the groups.

Once we have estimated α and $\boldsymbol{\beta}$, the estimated effect on the response probability can be obtained by averaging the response probability for a given $\mathbf{x}$:

$$G^{-1}\sum_{g=1}^{G}\left(M_g^{-1}\sum_{m=1}^{M_g}\Phi(\hat{\alpha} + \mathbf{x}\hat{\boldsymbol{\beta}} + \mathbf{z}_{gm}\hat{\boldsymbol{\gamma}}_g)\right), \tag{20.79}$$

where derivatives or differences with respect to the elements of $\mathbf{x}$ can be computed. Here, the minimum distance approach has an important advantage over the DL approach: the finite sample properties of estimator (20.79) are virtually impossible to obtain, whereas the large-M_g asymptotics underlying minimum distance would be straightforward using the delta method. The bootstrap should also be valid when the sampling scheme generates independent observations within each g.

With binary response problems, the two-step methods described here are problematical when the response does not vary within group. For example, suppose that x_g is a binary treatment—equal to one for receiving a voucher to attend college—and y_{gm} is an indicator of attending college. Each group is a high school class, say. If some high schools have all students attend college, one cannot use probit (or logit) of y_{gm} on $\mathbf{z}_{gm}$, $m = 1, \ldots, M_g$. A linear regression returns zero-slope coefficients and intercept equal to unity. Of course, if randomization occurs at the group level—that is, x_g is independent of group attributes—then it is not necessary to control for the $\mathbf{z}_{gm}$. Instead, the within-group averages can be used in a simple minimum distance approach. In this case, as y_{gm} is binary, the DL approximation will not be valid, as the CLM assumptions will not even approximately hold in the model $\bar{y}_g = \alpha + \mathbf{x}_g\boldsymbol{\beta} + e_g$ (because $\bar{y}_g$ is always a fraction regardless of the size of M_g).

Naturally, there is nothing special about binary response models. It is possible to apply any nonlinear model using the invididual-specific data to obtain group-level estimates. Then, equation (20.78) can be applied.

20.4 Complex Survey Sampling

Often, survey data are characterized by clustering and variable probability sampling. For example, suppose that g represents the **primary sampling unit (PSU)** (say, city) and individuals or families (indexed by m) are **secondary sampling units**, sampled within each PSU with probability p_{gm}. Consider the problem of regression using such a data set. If $\hat{\boldsymbol{\beta}}$ is the IPW estimator pooled across PSUs and individuals, then its variance is estimated as

$$\left(\sum_{g=1}^{G}\sum_{m=1}^{M_g}\mathbf{x}_{gm}'\mathbf{x}_{gm}/p_{gm}\right)^{-1}\left[\sum_{g=1}^{G}\sum_{m=1}^{M_g}\sum_{r=1}^{M_g}\hat{u}_{gm}\hat{u}_{gr}\mathbf{x}_{gm}'\mathbf{x}_{gr}/(p_{gm}p_{gr})\right]\left(\sum_{g=1}^{G}\sum_{m=1}^{M_g}\mathbf{x}_{gm}'\mathbf{x}_{gm}/p_{gm}\right)^{-1}. \tag{20.80}$$

The middle of the sandwich accounts for cluster correlation along with unequal sampling probabilities. If the probabilities are estimated using retention frequencies, expression (20.80) is conservative, as we discussed in Section 20.2.2. A similar expression holds for general M-estimation. Typically, packages that support survey sampling require a variable defining the clusters along with a variable containing the inverse probability weights.

Multistage sampling schemes introduce more complications because standard stratification is often involved. Consider the following setup, closely related to Bhattacharya (2005). Let there be S strata (for example, states in the United States), exhaustive and mutually exclusive. Within stratum s, there are C_s clusters (for example, zip codes). In order to use large-sample approximations, we assume that in each stratum a large number of clusters is sampled. Typically, the sampling of clusters is without replacement, but the resulting dependence across sampled clusters generated is more difficult to study. Instead, we assume sampling with replacement, which is harmless if the number of clusters sampled within each stratum, N_s, is "large." As before, we allow arbitrary correlation across units (say, households) within each cluster (say, zip code).

Within stratum s and cluster c, let there be M_{sc} total units (households or individuals). Therefore, the total number of units in the population is

$$M = \sum_{s=1}^{S} \sum_{c=1}^{C_s} M_{sc}. \tag{20.81}$$

It is convenient to start with the problem of estimating the mean of a variable that describes the population. Let z be a variable, such as family income, whose mean we want to estimate. List all population values as $\{z_{scm}^o: m = 1, \dots, M_{sc},\ c = 1, \dots, C_s,\ s = 1, \dots, S\}$, so the population mean can be written as

$$\mu = M^{-1} \sum_{s=1}^{S} \sum_{c=1}^{C_s} \sum_{m=1}^{M_{sc}} z_{scm}^o. \tag{20.82}$$

Define the total in the population as

$$\tau = \sum_{s=1}^{S} \sum_{c=1}^{C_s} \sum_{m=1}^{M_{sc}} z_{scm}^o = M\mu. \tag{20.83}$$

It is also useful to define the totals within each cluster and stratum, $\tau_{sc} = \sum_{m=1}^{M_{sc}} z_{scm}^o$ and $\tau_s = \sum_{c=1}^{C_s} \tau_{sc}$, respectively.

The specific sampling scheme is as follows: (1) for each stratum s, randomly draw N_s clusters, with replacement; (2) for each cluster c drawn in step (1), randomly sample K_{sc} households with replacement. For each pair (s, c), define the sample average

$$\hat{\mu}_{sc} = K_{sc}^{-1} \sum_{m=1}^{K_{sc}} z_{scm}. \tag{20.84}$$

Because this is an average based on a random sample within (s, c),

$$\mathrm{E}(\hat{\mu}_{sc}) = \mu_{sc} = M_{sc}^{-1} \sum_{m=1}^{M_{sc}} z_{scm}^o. \tag{20.85}$$

To continue up to the cluster level we need the total, $\tau_{sc} = M_{sc}\mu_{sc}$, for which an unbiased estimator is $\hat{\tau}_{sc} = M_{sc}\hat{\mu}_{sc}$ for all $\{(s,c): c = 1, \dots, C_s, s = 1, \dots, S\}$ (even if we eventually do not use some clusters because they are not sampled). Now, for each stratum s, the estimator $N_s^{-1}\sum_{c=1}^{N_s}\hat{\tau}_{sc}$, which is the average of the cluster totals within stratum s, has expected value which is the population average (for stratum s), that is, $C_s^{-1}\sum_{c=1}^{C_s}\tau_{sc} = C_s^{-1}\sum_{c=1}^{C_s}\sum_{m=1}^{M_{sc}} z_{scm}^o = C_s^{-1}\tau_s$. (In general, $C_s^{-1}\tau_s \neq \mu_s = (\sum_{c=1}^{C_s} M_{sc})^{-1}\tau_s$ unless each cluster has only one observation.) It follows that an unbiased estimator of the total τ_s for stratum s is

$$C_s \cdot N_s^{-1}\sum_{c=1}^{N_s}\hat{\tau}_{sc}. \tag{20.86}$$

Finally, the total in the entire population is estimated as

$$\sum_{s=1}^{S}\left(C_s \cdot N_s^{-1}\sum_{c=1}^{N_s}\hat{\tau}_{sc}\right) = \sum_{s=1}^{S}(C_s/N_s)\sum_{c=1}^{N_s}(M_{sc}/K_{sc})\sum_{m=1}^{K_{sc}} z_{scm}$$
$$= \sum_{s=1}^{S}\sum_{c=1}^{N_s}\sum_{m=1}^{K_{sc}}\left(\frac{C_s}{N_s}\cdot\frac{M_{sc}}{K_{sc}}\right)z_{scm} \equiv \sum_{s=1}^{S}\sum_{c=1}^{N_s}\sum_{m=1}^{K_{sc}}\omega_{sc}z_{scm}, \tag{20.87}$$

where

$$\omega_{sc} \equiv \frac{C_s}{N_s}\cdot\frac{M_{sc}}{K_{sc}} \tag{20.88}$$

is the weight for every unit sampled in stratum-cluster pair (s,c). This weight accounts for undersampled or oversampled clusters within strata and undersampled or oversampled units within clusters. Expressions (20.87) and (20.88) appear in the literature on complex survey sampling, sometimes without M_{sc}/K_{sc} when each cluster is sampled as a complete unit, and so $M_{sc}/K_{sc} = 1$. To estimate the population mean, μ, we just divide by M, the total number of units in the population,

$$\hat{\mu} = M^{-1}\left(\sum_{s=1}^{S}\sum_{c=1}^{N_s}\sum_{m=1}^{K_{sc}}\omega_{sc}z_{scm}\right). \tag{20.89}$$

In fact, we do not need to know the population size, M, to obtain an unbiased estimator of μ. We can obtain an alternative estimator that uses a modified set of weights. It falls out naturally from a regression framework, to which we now turn.

To study the asymptotic properties of regression (and many other estimation methods), it is convenient to modify the weights so that they are constant, or converge to a constant. The weights ω_{sc} in expression (20.88) converge to zero at rate N_s^{-1} because C_s and M_{sc} are fixed and K_{sc} is treated as fixed. (We assume a relatively small number of households sampled per cluster.) Let $N = N_1 + N_2 + \cdots + N_S$ be the total number of clusters sampled and define

$$v_{sc} = \frac{C_s}{(N_s/N)} \cdot \frac{M_{sc}}{K_{sc}} = N\omega_{sc}. \tag{20.90}$$

As in Bhattacharya (2005), it is easiest just to assume $N_s = a_s N$ for a_s fixed, $0 < a_s < 1$, $a_1 + \cdots + a_S = 1$. But we can also just assume N_s/N converges to a_s with the same property. Therefore, by writing $v_{sc} = (C_s/a_s)(M_s/K_s)$, we see that v_{sc} is constant. Further, any optimization problem that uses ω_{sc} as weights gives the same answer when v_{sc} is used because the scale factor in equation (20.90) does not depend on s or c. The key in the formulas for the asymptotic variance below is that v_{sc} is (roughly) constant.

While equation (20.90) is the most natural definition of the weights for obtaining the limiting distribution results, we can use different formulations without changing the end formulas. For example, let $C = C_1 + \cdots + C_S$ be the total number of clusters in the population, let M be the total number of units in the population, and let K be the total units samples. Then, for the final formulas, we could use the weights defined as

$$v_{sc} = \frac{(C_s/C)}{(N_s/N)} \cdot \frac{(M_{sc}/M)}{(K_{sc}/K)} = \frac{(NK)}{(CM)}\omega_{sc}. \tag{20.91}$$

Because C, M, and K are fixed, the factor $K/(CM)$ has no effect on estimation or inference. Equation (20.91) has a nice interpretation because it is expressed in terms of frequencies of the population relative to the sample frequencies. For example, if $(C_s/C) > (N_s/N)$, which means that stratum s is underrepresented in terms of number of clusters, equation (20.91) gives more weight to such strata. The same is true of the fractions involving the number of units (say, households).

While we can consider general M-estimation problems, or generalized method of moments as in Bhattacharya (2005), we consider least squares for concreteness. The weighted minimization problem is

$$\min_{\boldsymbol{\beta}} N^{-1} \sum_{s=1}^{S} \sum_{c=1}^{N_s} \sum_{m=1}^{K_{sc}} v_{sc}(y_{scm} - \mathbf{x}_{scm}\boldsymbol{\beta})^2, \tag{20.92}$$

where it is helpful to divide by N to facilitate the asymptotic analysis as $N \to \infty$. The first-order condition is

$$N^{-1}\sum_{s=1}^{S}\sum_{c=1}^{N_s}\sum_{m=1}^{K_{sc}} v_{sc}\mathbf{x}_{scm}'(y_{scm} - \mathbf{x}_{scm}\hat{\boldsymbol{\beta}}) = \mathbf{0}. \tag{20.93}$$

Using arguments similar to the SS sampling case, but accounting for the clustering (by, in effect, treating each cluster as its own observation), we can show that an appropriate estimator of $\text{Avar}(\hat{\boldsymbol{\beta}})$—in the sense that it is consistent for $\text{Avar}[\sqrt{N}(\hat{\boldsymbol{\beta}} - \boldsymbol{\beta})]$ when multiplied by N—is

$$\left(\sum_{s=1}^{S}\sum_{c=1}^{N_s}\sum_{m=1}^{K_{sc}} v_{sc}\mathbf{x}_{scm}'\mathbf{x}_{scm}\right)^{-1}\hat{\mathbf{B}}\left(\sum_{s=1}^{S}\sum_{c=1}^{N_s}\sum_{m=1}^{K_{sc}} v_{sc}\mathbf{x}_{scm}'\mathbf{x}_{scm}\right)^{-1}, \tag{20.94}$$

where $\hat{\mathbf{B}}$ is somewhat complicated:

$$\hat{\mathbf{B}} = \sum_{s=1}^{S}\sum_{c=1}^{N_s}\sum_{m=1}^{K_{sc}} v_{sc}^2\hat{u}_{scm}^2\mathbf{x}_{scm}'\mathbf{x}_{scm} + \sum_{s=1}^{S}\sum_{c=1}^{N_s}\sum_{m=1}^{K_{sc}}\sum_{r\neq m}^{K_{sc}} v_{sc}^2\hat{u}_{scm}\hat{u}_{scr}\mathbf{x}_{scm}'\mathbf{x}_{scr}$$
$$- \sum_{s=1}^{S} N_s^{-1}\left(\sum_{c=1}^{N_s}\sum_{m=1}^{K_{sc}} v_{sc}\mathbf{x}_{scm}'\hat{u}_{scm}\right)\left(\sum_{c=1}^{N_s}\sum_{m=1}^{K_{sc}} v_{sc}\mathbf{x}_{scm}'\hat{u}_{scm}\right)'. \tag{20.95}$$

The first part of $\hat{\mathbf{B}}$ is obtained using the White "heteroskedasticity"-robust form. The second piece accounts for the correlation within clusters; this is typically a positive definite matrix, and it generally increases the asymptotic standard errors. The third piece actually reduces the variance by accounting for the nonzero means of the "score" within strata, just as in the SS sampling case.

If each cluster has just one unit, so $M_{sc} = K_{sc} = 1$, then expression (20.94) reduces to

$$\left(\sum_{s=1}^{S}\sum_{c=1}^{N_s} v_{sc}\mathbf{x}_{sc}'\mathbf{x}_{sc}\right)^{-1}\left[\left(\sum_{s=1}^{S}\sum_{c=1}^{N_s} v_{sc}^2\hat{u}_{sc}^2\mathbf{x}_{sc}'\mathbf{x}_{sc}\right)\right.$$
$$\left. - \sum_{s=1}^{S} N_s^{-1}\left(\sum_{c=1}^{N_s} v_{sc}\mathbf{x}_{sc}'\hat{u}_{sc}\right)\left(\sum_{c=1}^{N_s} v_{sc}\mathbf{x}_{sc}'\hat{u}_{sc}\right)'\right]\cdot\left(\sum_{s=1}^{S}\sum_{c=1}^{N_s} v_{sc}\mathbf{x}_{sc}'\mathbf{x}_{sc}\right)^{-1}, \tag{20.96}$$

which is the formuala for standard stratified sampling with a finite number of units in each stratum.

For general M-estimation, the outer sandwich in (20.94) is replaced with the inverse of the weighted Hessian, $[\sum_{s=1}^{S}\sum_{c=1}^{N_s}\sum_{m=1}^{K_{sc}} v_{sc}\mathbf{H}(\mathbf{w}_{scm}, \hat{\boldsymbol{\theta}})]^{-1}$, while $\mathbf{x}_{scm}'\hat{u}_{scm}$ in equation (20.95) is replaced with the score, $\mathbf{s}(\mathbf{w}_{scm}, \hat{\boldsymbol{\theta}})$. Some econometrics packages have made implementation fairly straightforward for a variety of linear and non-linear models. To obtain the correct asymptotic variance estimator—one that is neither too optimistic nor too conservative—one needs to specify the strata, the clusters, and the sampling weights.

Problems

20.1. Use expressions (20.4) and (20.5) to answer this question.

a. Derive the estimator in equation (20.5) from the minimization problem in expression (20.4).

b. Show directly that the estimator $\tilde{\mu}_w = N^{-1}\sum_{i=1}^{N}(s_i/p_{j_i})w_i$ is unbiased for μ.

c. What practical advantage does $\hat{\mu}_w$ have over $\tilde{\mu}_w$?

20.2. Use the log likelihood in equation (20.9) to derive $\hat{p}_j = M_j/N_j$, $j = 1,\ldots,J$, where M_j is the number of retained observations from stratum j and N_j is the number of times stratum j was drawn.

20.3. Let y be a scalar response variable and $\mathbf{x}$ a vector of explanatory variables, and let $m(\mathbf{x},\boldsymbol{\theta})$ denote a model for $\mathrm{E}(y\,|\,\mathbf{x})$. The parameter space is $\boldsymbol{\Theta}$.

a. Let $\hat{\boldsymbol{\theta}}_w$ be the IPW nonlinear least squaresestimator under VP sampling. Write down the minimization problem solved by $\hat{\boldsymbol{\theta}}_w$.

b. Assume that the model is correctly specified for $\mathrm{E}(y\,|\,\mathbf{x})$, and let $\boldsymbol{\theta}_o$ denote the population value; assume that $\boldsymbol{\theta}_o$ is identified in the population. Provide a set of sufficient conditions for consistency of $\hat{\boldsymbol{\theta}}_w$ for $\boldsymbol{\theta}_o$. (Hint: See Theorem 12.2.)

c. Assuming that $m(\mathbf{x},\cdot)$ is twice continuously differentiable on the interior of $\boldsymbol{\Theta}$ and that $\boldsymbol{\theta}_o \in \mathrm{int}(\boldsymbol{\Theta})$, propose an estimator of the asymptotic variance of $\hat{\boldsymbol{\theta}}_w$ that depends only on the gradient of $m(\mathbf{x},\cdot)$—not its Hessian.

d. If you add the homoskedasticity assumption $\mathrm{Var}(y\,|\,\mathbf{x}) = \sigma_o^2$, does the formula from part c simplify?

e. If $m(\mathbf{x},\boldsymbol{\theta})$ is misspecified, how should you adjust the estimator in part c?

20.4. Consider the problem of standard stratified sampling. Assume that the sample shares, H_j, converge to $\bar{H}_j > 0$ as $N \to \infty$, $j = 1,\ldots,J$. Further, suppose that $\boldsymbol{\theta}_o$ minimizes $\mathrm{E}[q(\mathbf{w},\boldsymbol{\theta})\,|\,\mathbf{x}]$ over $\boldsymbol{\Theta}$ for each $\mathbf{x}$ and that $\boldsymbol{\theta}_o$ uniquely minimizes $\mathrm{E}[q(\mathbf{w},\boldsymbol{\theta})]$ over $\boldsymbol{\Theta}$. Argue that the unweighted estimator is consistent for $\boldsymbol{\theta}_o$. (Hint: Write the unweighted objective function as

$$\sum_{j=1}^{J} H_j \left[N_j^{-1} \sum_{i=1}^{N_j} q(\mathbf{w}_{ij}, \boldsymbol{\theta}) \right]$$

and argue that this function converges uniformly to

$$\bar{H}_1 \mathrm{E}[q(\mathbf{w}, \boldsymbol{\theta}) \mid \mathbf{x} \in \mathscr{X}_1] + \bar{H}_2 \mathrm{E}[q(\mathbf{w}, \boldsymbol{\theta}) \mid \mathbf{x} \in \mathscr{X}_2] + \cdots + \bar{H}_J \mathrm{E}[q(\mathbf{w}, \boldsymbol{\theta}) \mid \mathbf{x} \in \mathscr{X}_J],$$

where the strata are $\mathscr{X}_1, \mathscr{X}_2, \ldots, \mathscr{X}_J$. Then show that $\boldsymbol{\theta}_o$ uniquely minimizes this expression by arguing that it uniquely minimizes $\mathrm{E}[q(\mathbf{w}, \boldsymbol{\theta}) \mid \mathbf{x} \in \mathscr{X}_j]$ for at least one j.)

20.5. Use the data in BENEFITS.RAW to answer this question.

a. To equation (20.33) add the within-district averages of *bs*, *lstaff*, *lenroll*, and *lunch*, where *lstaff* and *lenroll* denote logarithms. Estimate this equation by pooled OLS. How do the coefficients on *bs*, *lstaff*, *lenroll*, and *lunch* compare with the FE coefficients? Are the usual pooled OLS standard errors valid here?

b. Estimate the equation from part a by random effects. (That is, include the district averages along with the original variables.) How do these estimates compare with the FE estimates? How do the cluster-robust standard errors compare with the cluster-robust standard errors for FE?

c. Use the estimation in part b to obtain the value of the fully robust Wald statistic testing the RE assumption that the district effect is uncorrelated with the four district averages.

20.6. Use the data in BENEFITS.RAW to answer this question.

a. How many schools in the sample have a benefits-salary ratio of at least 0.5?

b. Estimate equation (20.33) by fixed effects omitting the observations from part a. Discuss how the estimate of β_{bs} changes, as well as its cluster-robust standard error.

c. Now add the within-district averages of all four variables and estimate the equation by least absolute deviations, using all the observations. How strong is the evidence for a trade-off using LAD?

20.7. Use the data in MEAP94_98 to answer this question.

a. How many schools have all five years of data? Are there any schools with only one year?

b. Obtain the within-school time averages of the variables *lavgrexp*, *lunch*, *lenrol*, and the four-year dummies *y*95 through *y*98. Include these in a pooled OLS regression that includes the other variables in Table 20.2 (including the year dummies themselves). Verify that the coefficients on the original variables are the FE estimates.

What is the coefficient on $\overline{lunch}$ (the time average)? Is it statistically different from zero using a cluster-robust standard error at the district level?

c. Now use RE rather than pooled OLS on the equation in part b. Again verify that you obtain the FE estimates on the original variables. Is the RE coefficient on $\overline{lunch}$ identical to the POLS coefficient? Is it still statistically significant?

d. Redo part c, but do not include the time averages of the year dummies. Do you still get the FE estimates on *lavgrexp*, *lunch*, and *lenrol*? Why, with an unbalanced panel, must we include the time averages of year dummies for RE to equal FE, whereas we did not have to in the balanced case?

e. Now go back to the original FE estimation in Table 20.2, but drop the year dummies. How does the estimated spending effect change from Table 20.2? Which estimate is more reliable?

f. Return to the equation implicit in Table 20.2, but estimate the equation by pooled OLS and RE. (That is, do not include the time averages of the variables.) How do the estimates of the spending effect compare with the FE estimates? How come the *lunch* variable is much more important in the POLS and RE estimation?

g. Considering the various estimates and standard errors in Table 20.2 and obtained for this problem, which estimate of the spending variable and which standard error seem most reliable?

20.8. In the setting of Section 20.3.1, let y_{gm} be a fractional response variable, and consider the model

$$\mathrm{E}(y_{gm} \mid \mathbf{x}_g, \mathbf{Z}_g, c_g) = \Phi(\alpha + \mathbf{x}_g \boldsymbol{\beta} + \mathbf{z}_{gm} \boldsymbol{\gamma} + c_g).$$

a. Assume that $c_g = \eta_g + \bar{\mathbf{z}}_g \boldsymbol{\xi}_g + a_g$. Find $\mathrm{E}(y_{gm} \mid \mathbf{x}_g, \mathbf{Z}_g, a_g)$.

b. Add the assumption $a_g \mid \mathbf{x}_g, \mathbf{Z}_g \sim \mathrm{Normal}(0, \tau_g^2)$ and find $\mathrm{E}(y_{gm} \mid \mathbf{x}_g, \mathbf{Z}_g)$. (Hint: It should have the probit form.)

c. Suppose that η_g, $\boldsymbol{\xi}_g$, and τ_g^2 depend only on the group size, M_g. Suggest a method for estimating all the parameters.

d. How would you perform inference on the parameters estimated in part c?

21 Estimating Average Treatment Effects

21.1 Introduction

We now explicitly cover the problem of estimating an **average treatment effect (ATE)**, sometimes called an **average causal effect**. An ATE is a special case of an average partial effect—it is an APE for a binary explanatory variable—and therefore many of the econometric models and methods that we have used in previous chapters can be applied or adapted to the problem of estimating ATEs.

Estimating ATEs has become important in the program evaluation literature, such as the evaluation of job-training programs or school voucher programs. Many of the early applications of the methods described in this chapter were to medical interventions, and some of the language (such as "treatment group" and "control group") is a carryover from those early applications. But the methods have proven to be useful in situations where experiments are clearly impractical.

The organizing principle of a modern approach to program evaluation is the counterfactual framework pioneered by Rubin (1974)—in fact, the framework has been dubbed the **Rubin causal model (RCM)**—and since adopted by many authors in statistics, econometrics, and many other fields, including Rosenbaum and Rubin (1983), Heckman (1992, 1997), Imbens and Angrist (1994), Angrist, Imbens, and Rubin (1996), Manski (1996), Heckman, Ichimura, and Todd (1997), and Angrist (1998). Research on estimating treatment or causal effects using Rubin's framework continues unabated. This chapter is intended to provide an introduction and a fairly detailed treatment of the most commonly used methods. Recent surveys include Heckman, Lalonde, and Smith (2000), Imbens (2004), Heckman and Vytlacil (2007a, 2007b), and Imbens and Wooldridge (2009), to name a handful.

Counterfactual thinking is not reserved for estimating average treatment effects using the RCM framework. Recall that in Chapter 9 we discussed how sensible applications of simultaneous equations models entail being able to think about each equation in isolation from other equations in the system. (We called this the *autonomy* requirement.) For example, a demand function is defined for each *possible* price, even though when we collect data the prices we observe are (usually assumed to be) equilibrium prices determined by the intersection of supply and demand. Therefore, the reasoning underlying the RCM should be familiar even if the particulars are not.

This chapter mainly focuses on binary treatments, although Section 21.6.2 briefly describes approaches that are available when the treatment takes on more than two values. It is also possible to consider continuous "treatments," which would make coverage of simultaneous equations models and explicit counterfactuals possible. This chapter does not attempt such a unification. Pearl (2000) provides a counterfactual setting that encompasses SEMs.

Most approaches to estimating average treatment effects fall into one of three approaches. The first exploits *ignorability* or *unconfoundedness* of the treatment conditional on a set of observed covariates. As we will see in Section 21.3, this approach is analogous to the proxy variable solution to the omitted variables problem that we discussed in Chapter 4. In fact, one approach to estimating treatment effects is to use linear regression with many controls: in effect, the treatment is exogenous once we control for enough observed factors. As we will see, an important benefit of ignorability of treatment is that no functional form or distributional assumptions are needed to identify the population parameters of interest (even though, as a practical matter, we may make parametric assumptions).

A second approach allows selection into treatment to depend on unobserved (and observed) factors. Traditionally, we would say that the treatment is "endogenous." In this case, we rely on the availability of instrumental variables (IVs) in order to identify and estimate average treatment effects. Sometimes standard IV estimators identify the effects of interest, but in other cases we rely on control function methods. Depending on the quantity we hope to estimate, we generally need to impose restrictions on functional forms or distributions or both. However, we will also discuss the work by Imbens and Angrist (1994) that provides a useful interpretation of IV estimation under very weak assumptions. We discuss IV approaches in Section 21.4.

This chapter also provides an introduction to regression discontinuity designs, where treatment—or the probability of treatment—is a discontinuous function of an observed forcing variable. If underlying regression functions are assumed to be smooth in the forcing variable, the discontinuity of treatment can be used to identify a local treatment effect. Section 21.5 considers both sharp and fuzzy designs.

There is much ongoing research on estimating average treatment effects. Some of these active areas are touched on in Section 21.6. For example, Sections 21.6.2 and 21.6.3 consider multivalued treatments and multiple treatments, respectively.

Section 21.6.4 gives a brief discussion of estimating treatment effects with panel data, showing how standard unobserved effects models can be obtained when one assumes unconfoundedness of the history of treatments conditional on time-constant unobserved heterogeneity (and observed covariates). An alternative approach, which assumes unconfoundedness conditional on the observed past history, is also covered.

21.2 A Counterfactual Setting and the Self-Selection Problem

The modern literature on treatment effects begins with a counterfactual, where each individual (or other agent) has an outcome with and without treatment (where "treatment" is interpreted very broadly). This section draws heavily on Heckman (1992, 1997), Imbens and Angrist (1994), and Angrist, Imbens, and Rubin (1996) (hereafter AIR). Let y_1 denote the outcome with treatment and y_0 the outcome without treatment. Because an individual cannot be in both states, we cannot observe both y_0 and y_1; in effect, the problem we face is one of missing data. In fact, we will show how to apply the inverse probability weighting methods from Section 19.8 to the problem of estimating average treatment effects.

It is important to see that we have made no assumptions about the distributions of y_0 and y_1. In many cases these may be roughly continuously distributed (such as salary), but often y_0 and y_1 are binary outcomes (such as a welfare participation indicator), or even corner solution outcomes (such as married women's labor supply). However, some of the assumptions we make will be less plausible for discontinuous random variables, something we discuss after introducing the assumptions.

The following discussion assumes that we have an independent, identically distributed sample from the population. This assumption rules out cases where the treatment of one unit affects another's outcome (possibly through general equilibrium effects, as in Heckman, Lochner, and Taber, 1998). The assumption that treatment of unit i affects only the outcome of unit i is called the **stable unit treatment value assumption (SUTVA)** in the treatment literature (see, for example, AIR). We are making a stronger assumption because random sampling implies SUTVA.

Let the variable w be a binary treatment indicator, where $w = 1$ denotes treatment and $w = 0$ otherwise. The triple (y_0, y_1, w) represents a random vector from the underlying population of interest. For a random draw i from the population, we write (y_{i0}, y_{i1}, w_i). However, as we have throughout, we state assumptions in terms of the population.

To measure the effect of treatment, we are interested in the difference in the outcomes with and without treatment, $y_1 - y_0$. Because this is a random variable (that is, it is individual specific), we must be clear about what feature of its distribution we want to estimate. Several possibilities have been suggested in the literature. In Rosenbaum and Rubin (1983), the quantity of interest is the **average treatment effect (ATE)**,

$$\tau_{ate} \equiv \mathrm{E}(y_1 - y_0), \tag{21.1}$$

which is the expected effect of treatment on a randomly drawn person from the population. Some have criticized this measure as not being especially relevant for policy purposes: because it averages across the entire population, it includes in the average units who would never be eligible for treatment. Heckman (1997) gives the example of a job training program, where we would not want to include millionaires in computing the average effect of a job training program. This criticism is somewhat misleading, as we can—and would—exclude people from the population who would never be eligible. For example, in evaluating a job training program, we might restrict attention to people whose pretraining income is below a certain threshold; wealthy people would be excluded precisely because we have no interest in how job training affects the wealthy. In evaluating the benefits of a program such as Head Start, we could restrict the population to those who are actually eligible for the program or are likely to be eligible in the future. In evaluating the effectiveness of enterprise zones, we could restrict our analysis to block groups whose unemployment rates are above a certain threshold or whose per capita incomes are below a certain level.

A second quantity of interest, and one that has received much recent attention, is the **average treatment effect on the treated**, which we denote τ_{att}:

$$\tau_{att} \equiv \mathrm{E}(y_1 - y_0 \mid w = 1). \tag{21.2}$$

That is, τ_{att} is the mean effect for those who actually participated in the program. As we will see, in some special cases equations (21.1) and (21.2) are equivalent, but generally they differ.

Imbens and Angrist (1994) define another treatment effect, which they call a **local average treatment effect (LATE)**. LATE has the advantage of being estimable using instrumental variables under very weak conditions. It has two potential drawbacks: (1) it measures the effect of treatment on a generally unidentifiable subpopulation; and (2) the definition of LATE depends on the particular instrumental variable that we have available. We will discuss LATE in the simplest setting in Section 21.4.3.

We can expand the definition of both treatment effects by conditioning on covariates. If x is an observed covariate, the ATE conditional on x is simply $\mathrm{E}(y_1 - y_0 \mid x)$; similarly, equation (21.2) becomes $\mathrm{E}(y_1 - y_0 \mid x, w = 1)$. By choosing x appropriately, we can define ATEs for various subsets of the population. For example, x can be pretraining income or a binary variable indicating poverty status, race, or gender. Recent work by Heckman and Vytlacil (2006) and Heckman, Urzua, and Vytlacil (2006) unifies the various kinds of average treatment effects by defining the marginal treatment effect. In this chapter, we focus on estimating τ_{ate}, τ_{att}, and these effects on various subpopulations.

As noted previously, the difficulty in estimating equation (21.1) or (21.2) is that we observe only y_0 or y_1, not both, for each person. More precisely, along with w, the observed outcome is

$$y = (1 - w)y_0 + wy_1 = y_0 + w(y_1 - y_0). \tag{21.3}$$

Therefore, the question is, How can we estimate τ_{ate} or τ_{att} with a random sample on y and w (and usually some observed covariates)?

First, suppose that the treatment indicator w is statistically independent of (y_0, y_1), as would occur when treatment is *randomized* across agents. One implication of independence between treatment status and the potential outcomes is that τ_{ate} and τ_{att} are identical: $E(y_1 - y_0 \mid w = 1) = E(y_1 - y_0)$. Furthermore, estimation of τ_{ate} is simple. Using equation (21.3), we have

$$E(y \mid w = 1) = E(y_1 \mid w = 1) = E(y_1),$$

where the last equality follows because y_1 and w are independent. Similarly,

$$E(y \mid w = 0) = E(y_0 \mid w = 0) = E(y_0).$$

It follows that

$$\tau_{ate} = \tau_{att} = E(y \mid w = 1) - E(y \mid w = 0). \tag{21.4}$$

The right-hand side is easily estimated by a difference in sample means: the sample average of y for the treated units minus the sample average of y for the untreated units. Thus, randomized treatment guarantees that the difference-in-means estimator from basic statistics is unbiased, consistent, and asymptotically normal. In fact, these properties are preserved under the weaker assumption of **mean independence**: $E(y_0 \mid w) = E(y_0)$ and $E(y_1 \mid w) = E(y_1)$.

Randomization of treatment is often infeasible in program evaluation (although randomization of *eligibility* sometimes is feasible; more on this topic later). In most cases, individuals at least partly determine whether they receive treatment, and their decisions may be related to the benefits of or gain from treatment, $y_1 - y_0$. In other words, there is **self-selection** into treatment.

It turns out that τ_{att} can be consistently estimated as a difference in means under the weaker assumption that w is independent of y_0, without placing any restriction on the relationship between w and y_1. To see this point, note that we can always write

$$\begin{aligned} E(y \mid w = 1) - E(y \mid w = 0) &= E(y_0 \mid w = 1) - E(y_0 \mid w = 0) + E(y_1 - y_0 \mid w = 1) \\ &= [E(y_0 \mid w = 1) - E(y_0 \mid w = 0)] + \tau_{att}. \end{aligned} \tag{21.5}$$

If y_0 is mean independent of w, that is,

$$E(y_0 \mid w) = E(y_0), \tag{21.6}$$

then the first term in equation (21.5) disappears, and so the difference in means estimator is an unbiased estimator of τ_{att}. Unfortunately, condition (21.6) is still a pretty strong assumption. For example, suppose that people are randomly made eligible for a voluntary job training program. Condition (21.6) effectively implies that the participation decision is unrelated to what people would earn in the absence of the program. Nevertheless, the standard difference-in-means estimator is consistent for τ_{att} in some scenarios where it is inconsistent for τ_{ate}.

A useful expression relating τ_{att} and τ_{ate} is obtained by writing $y_0 = \mu_0 + v_0$ and $y_1 = \mu_1 + v_1$, where $\mu_g = \mathrm{E}(y_g)$, $g = 0, 1$. Then

$$y_1 - y_0 = (\mu_1 - \mu_0) + (v_1 - v_0) = \tau_{ate} + (v_1 - v_0).$$

Taking the expectation of this equation conditional on $w = 1$ gives

$$\tau_{att} = \tau_{ate} + \mathrm{E}(v_1 - v_0 \mid w = 1).$$

We can think of $v_1 - v_0$ as the person-specific gain from participation—that is, the deviation from the population mean—and so τ_{att} differs from τ_{ate} by the expected person-specific gain for those who participated. If $y_1 - y_0$ is not mean independent of w, τ_{att} and τ_{ate} generally differ.

Fortunately, we can estimate τ_{ate} and τ_{att} under assumptions less restrictive than independence between (y_0, y_1) and w. In most cases, we can collect data on individual characteristics and relevant pretreatment outcomes—sometimes a substantial amount of data. If, in an appropriate sense, treatment depends on the observables and not on the unobservables determining (y_0, y_1), then we can estimate average treatment effects quite generally, as we show in the next section.

21.3 Methods Assuming Ignorability (or Unconfoundedness) of Treatment

We adopt the framework of the previous section, and, in addition, we let $\mathbf{x}$ denote a vector of observed covariates. Therefore, the population is described by $(y_0, y_1, w, \mathbf{x})$, and we observe y, w, and $\mathbf{x}$, where y is given by equation (21.3). When w and (y_0, y_1) are allowed to be correlated, we need an assumption in order to identify treatment effects. Rosenbaum and Rubin (1983) introduced the following assumption, which they called **ignorability of treatment** (given observed covariates $\mathbf{x}$):

ASSUMPTION ATE.1 (Ignorability): Conditional on $\mathbf{x}$, w and (y_0, y_1) are independent.

Assumption ATE.1 has also been called **unconfoundedness** or simply **conditional independence**. For many purposes, it suffices to assume ignorability in a **conditional mean independence** sense:

ASSUMPTION ATE.1′ (Ignorability in Mean): (a) $E(y_0 \mid \mathbf{x}, w) = E(y_0 \mid \mathbf{x})$; and (b) $E(y_1 \mid \mathbf{x}, w) = E(y_1 \mid \mathbf{x})$.

Naturally, Assumption ATE.1 implies Assumption ATE.1′. In practice, Assumption ATE.1′ might not afford much generality, although it does allow $\text{Var}(y_0 \mid \mathbf{x}, w)$ and $\text{Var}(y_1 \mid \mathbf{x}, w)$ to depend on w. The idea underlying Assumption ATE.1′ is this: if we can observe enough information (contained in $\mathbf{x}$) that determines treatment, then (y_0, y_1) might be mean independent of w, conditional on $\mathbf{x}$. Loosely, even though (y_0, y_1) and w might be correlated, they are uncorrelated once we partial out $\mathbf{x}$.

Assumption ATE.1 certainly holds if w is a deterministic function of $\mathbf{x}$, which has prompted some authors in econometrics to call assumptions like ATE.1 **selection on observables**; see, for example, Barnow, Cain, and Goldberger (1980), Goldberger (1981), Heckman and Robb (1985), and Moffitt (1996). (We discussed a similar assumption in Section 19.9.3 in the context of missing data and attrition.) The name is fine as a label, but we must realize that Assumption ATE.1 does allow w to depend on unobservables, albeit in a restricted fashion. If $w = g(\mathbf{x}, a)$, where a is an unobservable random variable independent of $(\mathbf{x}, y_0, y_1)$, then Assumption ATE.1 holds. But a cannot be arbitrarily correlated with y_0 and y_1.

To proceed, it is helpful to define the two counterfactual conditional means,

$$\mu_0(\mathbf{x}) = E(y_0 \mid \mathbf{x}), \qquad \mu_1(\mathbf{x}) = E(y_1 \mid \mathbf{x}). \tag{21.7}$$

In general, these functions are unknown. But ignorability—in particular, Assumption ATE.1′—along with another assumption that we will discuss shortly, are sufficient to identify $\mu_g(\cdot)$, $g = 0, 1$. We will show this point in the next section. First, it is important to know that, under Assumption ATE.1′, the **average treatment effect conditional on x** and the **average treatment effect on the treated conditional on x** are identical. More precisely, define

$$\tau_{ate}(\mathbf{x}) = E(y_1 - y_0 \mid \mathbf{x}) = \mu_1(\mathbf{x}) - \mu_0(\mathbf{x}) \tag{21.8}$$

$$\tau_{att}(\mathbf{x}) = E(y_1 - y_0 \mid \mathbf{x}, w = 1). \tag{21.9}$$

Then, by Assumption ATE.1′, $E(y_g \mid \mathbf{x}, w) = E(y_g \mid \mathbf{x})$, $w = 0, 1$, and so $\tau_{ate}(\mathbf{x}) = \tau_{att}(\mathbf{x})$. In general, though—even in cases where $\tau_{att}(\mathbf{x})$ is identified—$\tau_{ate}(\mathbf{x})$ and $\tau_{att}(\mathbf{x})$ can be different.

Intuitively, the ignorability assumption seems to have a better chance of holding when the set of control variables, $\mathbf{x}$, is richer. But one must be careful not to include variables in $\mathbf{x}$ that can themselves be affected by treatment. For example, suppose w is a job training indicator, and y is future labor earnings. We would not want to include in $\mathbf{x}$ a measure of, say, education obtained between the time of assignment and the time labor earnings are measured. By doing so, we in effect hold additional education fixed when it varies in reaction to assignment w. Generally, including factors in $\mathbf{x}$ that are affected by w causes ignorability to fail.

Mathematically, Wooldridge (2005d) has shown that ignorability fails when $\mathbf{x}$ is influenced by w in the following setting. Suppose w is actually randomized with respect to (y_0, y_1)—in which case the standard difference-of-means estimator is unbiased and consistent for τ_{ate}. But at least one $\mathbf{x}$ is related to assignment in the sense that $\mathrm{D}(\mathbf{x} \mid w = 1) \neq \mathrm{D}(\mathbf{x} \mid w = 0)$. Using iterated expectations, it can be shown that $\mathrm{E}(y_g \mid \mathbf{x}, w) = \mathrm{E}(y_g \mid \mathbf{x})$, $g = 0, 1$ if and only if $\mathrm{E}(y_g \mid \mathbf{x}) = \mathrm{E}(y_g)$, $g = 0, 1$. That is, ignorability holds only if the covariates do not help to predict the counterfactual outcomes. If $\mathbf{x}$ includes education attained between assignment and measurement of y, $\mathrm{E}(y_g \mid \mathbf{x})$ almost certainly depends on $\mathbf{x}$, and so unconfoundedness fails.

Good candidates for inclusion in $\mathbf{x}$ are variables measured prior to treatment assignment, including past outcomes on y. As shown in Wooldridge (2009c), variables that satisfy instrumental variables assumptions—they are independent of unobservables that affect (y_0, y_1) but help predict w—should be excluded because their inclusion increases bias in standard regression adjustment estimators unless ignorability holds without the instrument-like variables.

Unfortunately, ignorability is fundamentally untestable because we only observe $(y, w, \mathbf{x})$. In some cases, it can be tested indirectly—see, for example, the discussion in Imbens and Wooldridge (2009). An alternative is to perform a sensitivity analysis similar to studying omitted variables. Imbens and Wooldridge (2009) survey some possibilities.

Assuming that ignorability holds, what is the additional assumption we need to identify the unconditional average treatment effect, τ_{ate}? From the law of iterated expectations,

$$\tau_{ate} = \mathrm{E}[\tau_{ate}(\mathbf{x})] = \mathrm{E}[\mu_1(\mathbf{x}) - \mu_0(\mathbf{x})], \tag{21.10}$$

where the expectations are over the distribution of $\mathbf{x}$. As we will see in the next couple of subsections, estimating τ_{ate} will require being able to observe both control and treated units for every outcome on $\mathbf{x}$ (a weaker assumption, to be stated precisely, suffices for τ_{att}). This assumption is typically called the **overlap** assumption.

Assumption ATE.2 (Overlap): For all $\mathbf{x} \in \mathcal{X}$, where $\mathcal{X}$ is the support of the covariates,

$$0 < \mathrm{P}(w = 1 \mid \mathbf{x}) < 1. \tag{21.11}$$

Overlap means that, for any setting of the covariates in the assumed population, there is a chance of seeing units in both the control and treatment groups. If, for example, $P(w = 1 \mid \mathbf{x} = \mathbf{x}_0) = 0$, then units having covariate values $\mathbf{x}_0$ will never be in the treated group. Generally, we will not be able to estimate an average treatment effect over the population that includes units with $\mathbf{x} = \mathbf{x}_0$.

The probability of treatment, as a function of $\mathbf{x}$, plays a very important role in estimating average treatment effects. It is usually called the **propensity score**, and we denote it

$$p(\mathbf{x}) = P(w = 1 \mid \mathbf{x}), \quad \mathbf{x} \in \mathcal{X}. \tag{21.12}$$

The overlap assumption rules out the possibility that the propensity score is ever zero or one.

Rosenbaum and Rubin (1983) call igorability plus overlap **strong ignorability**, an assumption that is critical in all approaches to estimating τ_{ate}. For completeness, we state weaker versions of the ignorability and overlap assumptions that suffice for identifying τ_{att}:

ASSUMPTION ATT.1′ (Ignorability in Mean): $E(y_0 \mid \mathbf{x}, w) = E(y_0 \mid \mathbf{x})$.

ASSUMPTION ATT.2 (Overlap): For all $\mathbf{x} \in \mathcal{X}$, $P(w = 1 \mid \mathbf{x}) < 1$.

21.3.1 Identification

Given the previous ignorability and overlap assumptions, we can establish quite generally that τ_{ate} (and, under the weaker assumptions) τ_{att} are identified. We do so in two ways, each of which motivates subsequent estimation methods.

Our first approach is based directly on the conditional mean $E(y \mid \mathbf{x}, w)$. Recall that we can write $y = y_0 + w(y_1 - y_0)$. Under the mean version of ignorability,

$$\begin{aligned} E(y \mid \mathbf{x}, w) &= E(y_0 \mid \mathbf{x}, w) + w[E(y_1 \mid \mathbf{x}, w) - E(y_0 \mid \mathbf{x}, w)] \\ &= E(y_0 \mid \mathbf{x}) + w[E(y_1 \mid \mathbf{x}) - E(y_0 \mid \mathbf{x})] \\ &\equiv \mu_0(\mathbf{x}) + w[\mu_1(\mathbf{x}) - \mu_0(\mathbf{x})], \end{aligned} \tag{21.13}$$

where getting to equation (21.13) uses Assumption ATE.1′. We have shown

$$E(y \mid \mathbf{x}, w = 0) = \mu_0(\mathbf{x}), \qquad E(y \mid \mathbf{x}, w = 1) = \mu_1(\mathbf{x}). \tag{21.14}$$

Because we observe $(y, \mathbf{x}, w)$, we can, under the overlap assumption, estimate $m_0(\mathbf{x}) \equiv E(y \mid \mathbf{x}, w = 0)$ and $m_1(\mathbf{x}) \equiv E(y \mid \mathbf{x}, w = 1)$ quite generally—and this claim has nothing to do with whether ignorability holds. If Assumption ATE.1′ holds, then

$$\tau_{ate}(\mathbf{x}) = m_1(\mathbf{x}) - m_0(\mathbf{x}). \tag{21.15}$$

In other words, when we add overlap, the functions $m_g(\cdot)$, $g = 0, 1$ that we *can* estimate correspond to the quantities $\mu_g(\cdot)$ that we *need* to estimate in order to estimate $\tau_{ate}(\mathbf{x})$. If we identify $m_g(\cdot)$ for all $\mathbf{x} \in \mathscr{X}$—and this is where overlap comes in—then we can obtain τ_{ate} as

$$\tau_{ate} = \mathrm{E}[m_1(\mathbf{x}) - m_0(\mathbf{x})], \tag{21.16}$$

where again the expected value is over the distribution of $\mathbf{x}$. In practice, with a random sample, we use sample averaging. Details are given in the next subsection.

If we are able to identify $\tau(\mathbf{x})$ at all $\mathbf{x} \in \mathscr{X}$, then we can also identify the average treatment effect on any subset of the population defined by $\mathbf{x}$. For example, if we define

$$\tau_{ate,\mathscr{R}} = \mathrm{E}(y_1 - y_0 \mid \mathbf{x} \in \mathscr{R}), \tag{21.17}$$

then we have

$$\tau_{ate,\mathscr{R}} = \mathrm{E}[\tau_{ate}(\mathbf{x}) \mid \mathbf{x} \in \mathscr{R}],$$

and so we can average $\tau_{ate}(\mathbf{x})$ over the subpopulation with $\mathbf{x} \in \mathscr{R}$.

To see that the weaker ignorability and overlap assumptions, Assumptions ATT.1′ and ATT.2, suffice for identifying τ_{att}, note that we can use $y = y_0 + w(y_1 - y_0)$ to always write

$$\begin{aligned} &\mathrm{E}(y \mid \mathbf{x}, w = 1) - \mathrm{E}(y \mid \mathbf{x}, w = 0) \\ &\quad = \mathrm{E}(y_0 \mid \mathbf{x}, w = 1) - \mathrm{E}(y_0 \mid \mathbf{x}, w = 0) + \mathrm{E}(y_1 - y_0 \mid \mathbf{x}, w = 1) \\ &\quad = [\mathrm{E}(y_0 \mid \mathbf{x}, w = 1) - \mathrm{E}(y_0 \mid \mathbf{x}, w = 0)] + \tau_{att}(\mathbf{x}) \end{aligned} \tag{21.18}$$

If Assumption ATT.1′ holds, then the term in $[\cdot]$ in equation (21.18) is zero, and the difference in estimable means, $m_1(\mathbf{x}) - m_0(\mathbf{x})$, actually identifies $\tau_{att}(\mathbf{x})$:

$$\tau_{att}(\mathbf{x}) = m_1(\mathbf{x}) - m_0(\mathbf{x}). \tag{21.19}$$

Assumption ATT.1′ allows the gain from treatment, $y_1 - y_0$, to be arbitrarily correlated with treatment, even after conditioning on $\mathbf{x}$. It requires ignorability (in mean) only with respect to y_0, the outcome in the absence of treatment. Now τ_{att} is obtained as

$$\tau_{att} = \mathrm{E}[m_1(\mathbf{x}) - m_0(\mathbf{x}) \mid w = 1]. \tag{21.20}$$

We can use this expression to see how the weaker overlap condition, Assumption ATT.2, suffices. By definition, $m_1(\cdot)$ is for the treated subpopulation, $w = 1$, and so we only need to estimate this regression function for values of $\mathbf{x}$ corresponding to units in the treated group. In other words, we do not need a positive probability of treatment for all $\mathbf{x}$. But we still must estimate $m_0(\cdot)$ at values of $\mathbf{x}$ corresponding to the treated subpopulation. If there are values of $\mathbf{x}$ where treatment is certain, we cannot hope to generally estimate $\mathrm{E}(y \mid \mathbf{x}, w = 0)$ for such values because we will not observe control units with the same values of the covariates. The weaker overlap assumption, $\mathrm{P}(w = 1 \mid \mathbf{x}) < 1$, rules out this possibility.

We summarize the previous discussion with a proposition.

PROPOSITION 21.1: Under Assumption ATE.1′, equation (21.15) holds. If we add the overlap Assumption ATE.2, we can obtain τ_{ate} as in equation (21.16). If we assume only Assumption ATT.1′, we have $\tau_{att}(\mathbf{x}) = m_1(\mathbf{x}) - m_0(\mathbf{x})$; under Assumption ATT.2, τ_{att} is identified as in equation (21.20).

A second way to establish identification is to use inverse propensity score weighting. First maintain Assumption ATE.1′. Noting that $wy = wy_1$, we have, by iterated expectations,

$$\mathrm{E}\left[\frac{wy}{p(\mathbf{x})}\,\middle|\,\mathbf{x}\right] = \mathrm{E}\left[\frac{wy_1}{p(\mathbf{x})}\,\middle|\,\mathbf{x}\right] = \mathrm{E}\left\{\mathrm{E}\left[\frac{wy_1}{p(\mathbf{x})}\,\middle|\,\mathbf{x}, w\right]\,\middle|\,\mathbf{x}\right\} = \mathrm{E}\left\{\frac{w\mathrm{E}(y_1 \mid \mathbf{x}, w)}{p(\mathbf{x})}\,\middle|\,\mathbf{x}\right\}$$

$$= \mathrm{E}\left\{\frac{w\mathrm{E}(y_1 \mid \mathbf{x})}{p(\mathbf{x})}\,\middle|\,\mathbf{x}\right\} = \mathrm{E}\left\{\frac{w}{p(\mathbf{x})}\,\middle|\,\mathbf{x}\right\}\mu_1(\mathbf{x}) = \mu_1(\mathbf{x})$$

because $\mathrm{E}(w \mid \mathbf{x}) = p(\mathbf{x})$. A similar argument shows that

$$\mathrm{E}\left[\frac{(1 - w)y}{[1 - p(\mathbf{x})]}\,\middle|\,\mathbf{x}\right] = \mu_0(\mathbf{x}).$$

Combining these two results and using simple algebra gives

$$\mathrm{E}\left\{\frac{[w - p(\mathbf{x})]y}{p(\mathbf{x})[1 - p(\mathbf{x})]}\,\middle|\,\mathbf{x}\right\} = \mu_1(\mathbf{x}) - \mu_0(\mathbf{x}) = \tau_{ate}(\mathbf{x}). \tag{21.21}$$

Of course, this expression only makes sense for $\mathbf{x}$ such that $0 < p(\mathbf{x}) < 1$. If we maintain Assumption ATE.2, and assume that the expectation exists, we can use iterated expectations to write

$$\tau_{ate} = \mathrm{E}\left\{\frac{[w - p(\mathbf{x})]y}{p(\mathbf{x})[1 - p(\mathbf{x})]}\right\}, \tag{21.22}$$

which, because w, y, and $\mathbf{x}$ are all observed, establishes identification of τ_{ate} using the propensity score rather than regression functions.

The argument for τ_{att} is a little different. Write

$$[w - p(\mathbf{x})]y = [w - p(\mathbf{x})][y_0 + w(y_1 - y_0)]$$
$$= [w - p(\mathbf{x})]y_0 + w[w - p(\mathbf{x})](y_1 - y_0)$$
$$= [w - p(\mathbf{x})]y_0 + w[1 - p(\mathbf{x})](y_1 - y_0),$$

where the last equality follows because $w^2 = w$. Therefore,

$$\frac{[w - p(\mathbf{x})]y}{[1 - p(\mathbf{x})]} = \frac{[w - p(\mathbf{x})]y_0}{[1 - p(\mathbf{x})]} + w(y_1 - y_0). \tag{21.23}$$

Consider the numerator of the first term on the right-hand side of equation (21.23):

$$\mathrm{E}\{[w - p(\mathbf{x})]y_0 \mid \mathbf{x}\} = \mathrm{E}(\mathrm{E}\{[w - p(\mathbf{x})]y_0 \mid \mathbf{x}, w\} \mid \mathbf{x}) = \mathrm{E}\{[w - p(\mathbf{x})]\mathrm{E}(y_0 \mid \mathbf{x}, w) \mid \mathbf{x}\}$$
$$= \mathrm{E}\{[w - p(\mathbf{x})]\mathrm{E}(y_0 \mid \mathbf{x}) \mid \mathbf{x}\} = \mathrm{E}\{[w - p(\mathbf{x})] \mid \mathbf{x}\}\mu_0(\mathbf{x}) = 0.$$

Therefore,

$$\mathrm{E}\left\{\frac{[w - p(\mathbf{x})]y}{[1 - p(\mathbf{x})]}\middle|\mathbf{x}\right\} = \mathrm{E}[w(y_1 - y_0) \mid \mathbf{x}] \tag{21.24}$$

and so the unconditional expectations are the same, too. But

$$\mathrm{E}[w(y_1 - y_0)] = \mathrm{P}(w = 0)\mathrm{E}[w(y_1 - y_0) \mid w = 0] + \mathrm{P}(w = 1)\mathrm{E}[w(y_1 - y_0) \mid w = 1]$$
$$= 0 + \mathrm{P}(w = 1)\mathrm{E}[w(y_1 - y_0) \mid w = 1]$$
$$\equiv \rho\tau_{att}, \tag{21.25}$$

where $\rho \equiv \mathrm{P}(w = 1)$ is the unconditional probability of treatment. Putting the pieces together gives

$$\tau_{att} = \mathrm{E}\left\{\frac{[w - p(\mathbf{x})]y}{\rho[1 - p(\mathbf{x})]}\right\}; \tag{21.26}$$

notice that this expression only requires the weaker assumption $p(\mathbf{x}) < 1$ for all $\mathbf{x}$. We summarize with a proposition.

PROPOSITION 21.2: Under Assumptions ATE.1′ and ATE.2, τ_{ate} can be expressed as in equation (21.22). Under the weaker assumptions Assumption ATT.1′ and ATT.2, τ_{att} can be expressed as in equation (21.26).

Wooldridge (1999c) derived expression (21.22) in the context of random coefficient models, while equation (21.26) is essentially due to Dehejia and Wahba (1999), who used the stronger Assumption ATE.1. As we will see, these identification results can be directly turned into estimating equations for τ_{ate} and τ_{att}. We now turn to estimation in the next several subsections.

21.3.2 Regression Adjustment

The identification strategy based on the regression functions $E(y \mid \mathbf{x}, w = 0)$ and $E(y \mid \mathbf{x}, w = 1)$ leads directly to straightforward estimation approaches. Because we have a random sample on $(y, w, \mathbf{x})$ from the relevant population, $m_1(\mathbf{x}) \equiv E(y \mid \mathbf{x}, w = 1)$ and $m_0(\mathbf{x}) \equiv E(y \mid \mathbf{x}, w = 0)$ are **nonparametrically identified**. That is, these are conditional expectations that depend entirely on observables, and so they can be consistently estimated quite generally. (See Härdle and Linton, 1994, or Li and Racine, 2007, for assumptions and methods.) For the purposes of identification, we can just assume $m_1(\mathbf{x})$ and $m_0(\mathbf{x})$ are known, and the fact that they are known means that $\tau(\mathbf{x})$ is identified. If $\hat{m}_1(\mathbf{x})$ and $\hat{m}_0(\mathbf{x})$ are consistent estimators (in an appropriate sense), using the random sample of size N, a consistent estimator of ATE under fairly weak assumptions is

$$\hat{\tau}_{ate,reg} = N^{-1} \sum_{i=1}^{N} [\hat{m}_1(\mathbf{x}_i) - \hat{m}_0(\mathbf{x}_i)] \tag{21.27}$$

while a consistent estimator of ATE_1 is

$$\hat{\tau}_{att,reg} = \left(\sum_{i=1}^{N} w_i \right)^{-1} \left\{ \sum_{i=1}^{N} w_i [\hat{m}_1(\mathbf{x}_i) - \hat{m}_0(\mathbf{x}_i)] \right\} \tag{21.28}$$

The estimators in equations (21.27) and (21.28) are called **regression adjustment** estimators of τ_{ate} and τ_{att}, respectively. Notice that $\hat{\tau}_{att,reg}$ simply averages the differences in predicted values, $\hat{m}_1(\mathbf{x}_i) - \hat{m}_0(\mathbf{x}_i)$, over the subsample of treated units, $w_i = 1$.

The key implementation issue in computing $\hat{\tau}_{ate,reg}$ and $\hat{\tau}_{att,reg}$ is how to obtain $\hat{m}_0(\cdot)$ and $\hat{m}_1(\cdot)$. To be as flexible as possible, one could use nonparametric estimators, such as **kernel estimators** or **series estimators**. Kernel estimators use "local averaging" or "local smoothing" to estimate a function at a particular point. (See Li and Racine, 2007, for a comprehensive treatment of kernel regression with both continuous and discrete covariates.) In addition to being flexible, such local methods have the benefit of forcing us to confront problems with overlap in the covariate distribution. Consider equation (21.27). The function $\hat{m}_0(\cdot)$ is obtained using only those with $w_i = 0$, and $\hat{m}_1(\cdot)$ is obtained using only those with $w_i = 1$. Thus, in obtaining the summand $\hat{m}_1(\mathbf{x}_i) - \hat{m}_0(\mathbf{x}_i)$ for, say, someone in the control group, we must obtain $\hat{m}_1(\mathbf{x}_i)$, where $\hat{m}_1(\cdot)$ was obtained only using those in the treatment group. If $\mathbf{x}_i$ is very different from the covariate values of units in the treated sample, it is pretty hopeless to estimate $\hat{m}_1(\mathbf{x})$ at $\mathbf{x} = \mathbf{x}_i$ using local averaging methods. Similarly, if i denotes a treated unit, we need to evaluate $\hat{m}_0(\cdot)$, which is obtained using control units, at covariate values for a treated unit. Generally, the overlap assumption means that in a large enough data set, we will see both control and treated units for a given set of covariate values (or, at least, for "close" covariate values). If we do not see these units, we cannot hope to estimate τ_{ate} for the original population.

Equation (21.28) makes it clear that the weaker overlap assumption, Assumption ATT, suffices for obtaining a satisfactory estimate, $\hat{\tau}_{att}$. Because $\hat{m}_1(\cdot)$ is obtained using treated units, and equation (21.28) sums only over treated units, we allow the possibility that some units in the control group will have covariates very different from the range of covariate values in the treated subset. But we still need to obtain $\hat{m}_0(\mathbf{x}_i)$ when i is a treated unit. Therefore, for every treated unit, we hopefully have some units in the control group with similar values for the covariates.

Series estimation involves global approximation using flexible parametric models, where the flexibility of the model increases with the sample size. For a recent treatment, see Li and Racine (2007). Hahn (1998) shows that nonparametric regression adjustment using series estimators can achieve the asymptotic efficiency bound for estimating τ_{ate}.

The problem with lack of overlap can be seen in a simpler setting. Suppose there is only one binary covariate, x, and Assumption ATE.1$'$ holds; for concreteness, x could be an indicator for whether pretraining earnings are below a certain threshold. Suppose that everyone in the relevant population with $x = 1$ participates in the program. Then, while we can estimate $\mathrm{E}(y \mid x = 1, w = 1)$ with a random sample from the population, we cannot estimate $\mathrm{E}(y \mid x = 1, w = 0)$ because we have no data on the subpopulation with $x = 1$ and $w = 0$. Intuitively, we only observe the counterfactual y_1 when $x = 1$; we never observe y_0 for any members of the population with $x = 1$. Therefore, $\tau_{ate}(x)$ is not identified at $x = 1$.

If some people with $x = 0$ participate while others do not, we can estimate $\mathrm{E}(y \mid x = 0, w = 1) - \mathrm{E}(y \mid x = 0, w = 0)$ using a simple difference in averages over the group with $x = 0$, and so $\tau_{ate}(x)$ is identified at $x = 0$. But if we cannot estimate $\tau_{ate}(1)$, we cannot estimate the unconditional ATE because $\tau_{ate} = \mathrm{P}(x = 0) \cdot \tau_{ate}(0) + \mathrm{P}(x = 1) \cdot \tau_{ate}(1)$. In effect, we can only estimate the ATE over the subpopulation with $x = 0$, which means that we must redefine the population of interest. This limitation is unfortunate: presumably we would be very interested in the program's effects on the group that always participates.

A similar conclusion holds if the group with $x = 0$ never participates in the program. Then $\tau_{ate}(0)$ is not estimable because $E(y \mid x = 0, w = 1)$ is not estimable. If some people with $x = 1$ participated while others did not, $\tau_{ate}(1)$ would be identified, and then we would view the population of interest as the subgroup with $x = 1$. There is one important difference between this situation and the one where the $x = 1$ group always receives treatment: it may be legitimate to exclude from the population people who have no chance of treatment based on observed covariates. This observation is related to the issue we discussed in Section 21.2 concerning the relevant population for defining τ_{ate}. If, for example, people with very high preprogram earnings $(x = 0)$ have no chance of participating in a job training program, then we would not want to average together $\tau_{ate}(0)$ and $\tau_{ate}(1)$; $\tau_{ate}(1)$ by itself is much more interesting.

Although the previous example is extreme, its consequences can arise in more plausible settings. Suppose that $\mathbf{x}$ is a vector of binary indicators for pretraining income intervals. For most of the intervals, the probability of participating is strictly between zero and one. If the participation probability is zero at the highest income level, we simply exclude the high-income group from the relevant population. (If we specify τ_{att} as the object of interest, we also will exclude high-income people.) Unfortunately, if participation is certain at low-income levels, we must exclude those low-income groups as well.

One can compute simple statistics to judge whether overlap is a problem. As described in Imbens and Rubin (forthcoming), one can compute the **normalized differences**, which take the form

$$\frac{(\bar{x}_{1j} - \bar{x}_{0j})}{(s_{1j}^2 + s_{0j}^2)^{1/2}}, \tag{21.29}$$

where $\bar{x}_{gj}$ is the sample average of covariate j for group $g = 0, 1$ and s_{gj} is the sample standard deviation. Imbens and Rubin suggest that normalized differences above 0.25 are cause for concern. (Notice that the normalized differences are not the t statistic for testing the difference in means. It is the difference in means standardized by a measure of dispersion that is important; the sample size should not play a direct role.) Unfortunately, even if the normalized differences are all small, they only focus on one feature of the marginal distributions. Overlap can still fail in more complicated ways. In the next subsection, we will discuss how to use the estimated propensity score to evaluate overlap. If one or more normalized differences are large, one might need to redefine the population of interest.

It is useful to give a complete treatment of regression adjustment in the parametric case. (It is likely that the same analysis holds when the parametric model is allowed to become more flexible as the sample size grows, at least under standard restrictions.) Let $m_0(\mathbf{x}, \boldsymbol{\delta}_0)$ and $m_1(\mathbf{x}, \boldsymbol{\delta}_1)$ be parametric functions, where $m_0(\mathbf{x}, \boldsymbol{\delta}_0)$ is estimated using the $w_i = 0$ observations and $m_1(\mathbf{x}, \boldsymbol{\delta}_1)$ is estimated using the $w_i = 1$ observations. We have now covered several models and estimation methods that can be used. In the leading case, we can make the functions linear in parameters and use OLS, but we might want to exploit the nature of y; later on, we will discuss this topic further.

Given $\sqrt{N}$-consistent and asymptotically normal estimators $\hat{\boldsymbol{\delta}}_0$ and $\hat{\boldsymbol{\delta}}_1$, we have the following parametric regression adjustment estimate of τ_{ate}:

$$\hat{\tau}_{ate,reg} = N^{-1} \sum_{i=1}^{N} [m_1(\mathbf{x}_i, \hat{\boldsymbol{\delta}}_1) - m_0(\mathbf{x}_i, \hat{\boldsymbol{\delta}}_0)], \tag{21.30}$$

which will be $\sqrt{N}$-consistent and asymptotically normal for τ_{ate}. Using Problem 12.17, it can be shown that

$$\begin{aligned}\text{Avar}\sqrt{N}(\hat{\tau}_{ate,reg} - \tau_{ate}) = {} & \text{E}\{[m_1(\mathbf{x}_i, \boldsymbol{\delta}_1) - m_0(\mathbf{x}_i, \boldsymbol{\delta}_0) - \tau_{ate}]^2\} \\ & + \text{E}[\nabla_{\delta_0} m_0(\mathbf{x}_i, \boldsymbol{\delta}_0)]\mathbf{V}_0 \text{E}[\nabla_{\delta_0} m_0(\mathbf{x}_i, \boldsymbol{\delta}_0)]' \\ & + \text{E}[\nabla_{\delta_1} m_1(\mathbf{x}_i, \boldsymbol{\delta}_1)]\mathbf{V}_1 \text{E}[\nabla_{\delta_1} m_1(\mathbf{x}_i, \boldsymbol{\delta}_1)]',\end{aligned}$$

where $\mathbf{V}_0$ is the asymptotic variance of $\sqrt{N}(\hat{\boldsymbol{\delta}}_0 - \boldsymbol{\delta}_0)$ and similarly for $\mathbf{V}_1$. This formula makes it clear that it is better to use more efficient estimators for $\boldsymbol{\delta}_0$ and $\boldsymbol{\delta}_1$. A variance estimator is simple:

$$\begin{aligned}N \cdot \widehat{\text{Avar}(\hat{\tau}_{ate,reg})} = {} & N^{-1} \sum_{i=1}^{N} [m_1(\mathbf{x}_i, \hat{\boldsymbol{\delta}}_1) - m_0(\mathbf{x}_i, \hat{\boldsymbol{\delta}}_0) - \hat{\tau}_{ate,reg}]^2 \\ & + \left[N^{-1} \sum_{i=1}^{N} \nabla_{\delta_0} m_0(\mathbf{x}_i, \hat{\boldsymbol{\delta}}_0)\right] \hat{\mathbf{V}}_0 \left[N^{-1} \sum_{i=1}^{N} \nabla_{\delta_0} m_0(\mathbf{x}_i, \hat{\boldsymbol{\delta}}_0)\right]' \\ & + \left[N^{-1} \sum_{i=1}^{N} \nabla_{\delta_1} m_1(\mathbf{x}_i, \hat{\boldsymbol{\delta}}_1)\right] \hat{\mathbf{V}}_1 \left[N^{-1} \sum_{i=1}^{N} \nabla_{\delta_1} m_1(\mathbf{x}_i, \hat{\boldsymbol{\delta}}_1)\right]'.\end{aligned} \tag{21.31}$$

An alternative to an analytical expression is to use the bootstrap, which is straightforward in this context. One simply includes the estimation of both mean functions, the calculation of the difference $m_1(\mathbf{x}_i, \hat{\boldsymbol{\delta}}_1) - m_0(\mathbf{x}_i, \hat{\boldsymbol{\delta}}_0)$, and then the averaging of these to obtain $\hat{\tau}_{ate,reg}$ in the same resampling scheme. All three sources of estimation error—in $\hat{\boldsymbol{\delta}}_0$, in $\hat{\boldsymbol{\delta}}_1$, and in replacing the expected value over the distribution of $\mathbf{x}_i$

with the sample average—will be properly accounted for. In fact, as described in Li and Racine (2007), the bootstrap is generally valid for nonparametric procedures, too.

Given the estimated regression functions, it is easy to estimate ATEs over a subset of the population, say $\tau_{ate,\mathcal{R}} = \mathrm{E}(y_1 - y_0 \mid \mathbf{x} \in \mathcal{R})$, as

$$\hat{\tau}_{ate,\mathcal{R},reg} = N_{\mathcal{R}}^{-1} \sum_{i=1}^{N} 1[\mathbf{x}_i \in \mathcal{R}] \cdot [m_1(\mathbf{x}_i, \hat{\boldsymbol{\delta}}_1) - m_0(\mathbf{x}_i, \hat{\boldsymbol{\delta}}_0)].$$

As mentioned earlier, linear regression is still the most popular method of regression adjustment. Suppose that $m_0(\mathbf{x}, \boldsymbol{\delta}_0) = \alpha_0 + \mathbf{x}\boldsymbol{\beta}_0$ and $m_1(\mathbf{x}, \boldsymbol{\delta}_1) = \alpha_1 + \mathbf{x}\boldsymbol{\beta}_1$. Then $(\hat{\alpha}_0, \hat{\boldsymbol{\beta}}_0)$ are from the regression y_i on $1, \mathbf{x}_i$ with $w_i = 0$ and similarly for $(\hat{\alpha}_1, \hat{\boldsymbol{\beta}}_1)$. Then

$$\hat{\tau}_{ate,reg}(\mathbf{x}) = (\hat{\alpha}_1 - \hat{\alpha}_0) + \mathbf{x}(\hat{\boldsymbol{\beta}}_1 - \hat{\boldsymbol{\beta}}_0) \tag{21.32}$$

$$\hat{\tau}_{ate,reg} = (\hat{\alpha}_1 - \hat{\alpha}_0) + \bar{\mathbf{x}}(\hat{\boldsymbol{\beta}}_1 - \hat{\boldsymbol{\beta}}_0) \tag{21.33}$$

$$\hat{\tau}_{att,reg} = (\hat{\alpha}_1 - \hat{\alpha}_0) + \bar{\mathbf{x}}_1(\hat{\boldsymbol{\beta}}_1 - \hat{\boldsymbol{\beta}}_0), \tag{21.34}$$

where $\bar{\mathbf{x}}$ is the sample average over the entire sample and $\bar{\mathbf{x}}_1 = N_1^{-1} \sum_{i=1}^{N} w_i \mathbf{x}_i$ is the average over the treated subsample. The estimate of $\tau_{ate,\mathcal{R}}$ is simply $(\hat{\alpha}_1 - \hat{\alpha}_0) + \bar{\mathbf{x}}_{\mathcal{R}}(\hat{\boldsymbol{\beta}}_1 - \hat{\boldsymbol{\beta}}_0)$, where $\bar{\mathbf{x}}_{\mathcal{R}}$ is the sample average over the restricted sample.

Replacing the vector $\mathbf{x}_i$ with any functions $\mathbf{h}(\mathbf{x}_i)$ is trivial. The only minor point is that we should demean the regressors $\mathbf{h}_i = \mathbf{h}(\mathbf{x}_i)$ using $\bar{\mathbf{h}} = N^{-1} \sum_{i=1}^{N} \mathbf{h}_i$ (or over a subset); it makes no sense to use $\mathbf{h}(\bar{\mathbf{x}})$.

If we ignore the sampling variance in the sample averages, we can obtain a standard error for $\hat{\tau}_{ate,\mathcal{R},reg}$ by using a pooled regression. Using the entire sample, run the regression

$$y_i \quad \text{on} \quad 1, w_i, \mathbf{x}_i, w_i(\mathbf{x}_i - \bar{\mathbf{x}}_{\mathcal{R}}); \tag{21.35}$$

the coefficient on w_i is $\hat{\tau}_{ate,\mathcal{R},reg}$, and we can use the heteroskedasticity-robust standard to form a t statistic or confidence intervals. Technically, we should adjust for the estimation error in $\bar{\mathbf{x}}_{\mathcal{R}}$, but the adjustment may have a small effect (see Problem 6.10). Or, we can use the bootstrap to account for this uncertainty, too. Of course, we get $\hat{\tau}_{ate,reg}$ by using $\bar{\mathbf{x}}_{\mathcal{R}} = \bar{\mathbf{x}}$. If we are mainly interested in the ATE over a subpopulation, it may be better—by way of increasing overlap—to estimate the regression functions on the restricted sample $\mathbf{x}_i \in \mathcal{R}$.

If the range of y is substantively restricted, we may wish to exploit that in estimation. For example, if y is a binary variable, or a fractional response, we can use a logit or probit function and the Bernoulli quasi MLE. If these functions are $G(\alpha_g + \mathbf{x}\boldsymbol{\beta}_g)$,

$g = 0, 1$ with $0 < G(\cdot) < 1$, let $(\hat{\alpha}_g, \hat{\boldsymbol{\beta}}_g)$ be the Bernoulli QMLEs on the two subsamples. Then

$$\hat{\tau}_{ate,reg} = N^{-1} \sum_{i=1}^{N} [G(\hat{\alpha}_1 + \mathbf{x}_i \hat{\boldsymbol{\beta}}_1) - G(\hat{\alpha}_0 + \mathbf{x}_i \hat{\boldsymbol{\beta}}_0)] \tag{21.36}$$

is the estimate of τ_{ate}. As in the general case, $G(\hat{\alpha}_1 + \mathbf{x}_i \hat{\boldsymbol{\beta}}_1) - G(\hat{\alpha}_0 + \mathbf{x}_i \hat{\boldsymbol{\beta}}_0)$ is the difference in average response for unit i, given covariates $\mathbf{x}_i$, in the two treatment states (regardless of unit i's actual treatment status). If $y \geq 0$—such as a count variable, but not restricted to that case—an exponential regression function is sensible, in which case

$$\hat{\tau}_{ate,reg} = N^{-1} \sum_{i=1}^{N} [\exp(\hat{\alpha}_1 + \mathbf{x}_i \hat{\boldsymbol{\beta}}_1) - \exp(\hat{\alpha}_0 + \mathbf{x}_i \hat{\boldsymbol{\beta}}_0)], \tag{21.37}$$

where the parameter estimates can be obtained from a quasi-MLE procedure, such as Poisson or gamma regression, or nonlinear least squares.

Equations (21.33), (21.36), and (21.37) make it clear that when parametric models are used for the means, it is possible to estimate τ_{ate} while essentially ignoring the overlap assumption. When using parametric models we are at least implicitly assuming that, say, $m_1(\cdot, \boldsymbol{\delta}_1)$ holds for all $\mathbf{x} \in \mathcal{X}$, even though we only use the treated subsample to obtain $\hat{\boldsymbol{\delta}}_1$. But as in any regression context, we should be careful in extrapolating the estimated mean functions to values of $\mathbf{x}$ far from those used to obtain $\hat{\boldsymbol{\delta}}_1$. The resulting estimate of τ_{ate} can be sensitive to the exact specification. For example, in the linear case it can be shown (for example, Imbens and Wooldridge, 2009) that

$$\hat{\tau}_{ate,reg} = (\bar{y}_1 - \bar{y}_0) - (\bar{\mathbf{x}}_1 - \bar{\mathbf{x}}_0)(f_0 \hat{\boldsymbol{\beta}}_1 - f_1 \hat{\boldsymbol{\beta}}_0) \tag{21.38}$$

where $f_0 = N_0/(N_0 + N_1)$ is the fraction of control observations and f_1 is the fraction of treated observations. If the difference in means $\bar{\mathbf{x}}_1 - \bar{\mathbf{x}}_0$ is large, changes in the slope estimates can have a large effect on $\hat{\tau}_{ate,reg}$. Therefore, as a general rule, one should not rely on parametric specifications as a way of overcoming poor overlap in the covariate distributions.

21.3.3 Propensity Score Methods

The expressions derived in Section 21.3.1 to establish identification of τ_{ate} and τ_{att} based on the propensity score lead directly to estimators. Practically, though, we need to estimate the propensity score function, $p(\cdot)$. For the moment, let $\hat{p}(\mathbf{x})$ denote such an estimator for any $\mathbf{x} \in \mathcal{X}$ obtained using the random sample $\{(w_i, \mathbf{x}_i) : i =$

$1, \ldots, N\}$. Then equation (21.22) suggests the estimator

$$\hat{\tau}_{ate,psw} = N^{-1} \sum_{i=1}^{N} \left[\frac{w_i y_i}{\hat{p}(\mathbf{x}_i)} - \frac{(1 - w_i) y_i}{1 - \hat{p}(\mathbf{x}_i)} \right] = N^{-1} \sum_{i=1}^{N} \frac{[w_i - \hat{p}(\mathbf{x}_i)] y_i}{\hat{p}(\mathbf{x}_i)[1 - \hat{p}(\mathbf{x}_i)]}, \tag{21.39}$$

while equation (21.26) suggests

$$\hat{\tau}_{att,psw} = N^{-1} \sum_{i=1}^{N} \frac{[w_i - \hat{p}(\mathbf{x}_i)] y_i}{\hat{p}[1 - \hat{p}(\mathbf{x}_i)]}, \tag{21.40}$$

where $\hat{p} = N_1/N$ is the fraction of treated units in the sample. As is evident from the formulas, each estimate is simple to compute given the fitted probabilities of treatment, $\hat{p}(\mathbf{x}_i)$. Interestingly, the estimator in equation (21.39) is the same as an estimator due to Horvitz and Thompson (1952) for handling nonrandom sampling. Not surprisingly, these estimators are generally consistent under Assumptions ATE.1$'$ and ATE.2 or Assumptions ATT.1$'$ and ATT.2, respectively, and suitable regularity conditions. If $\hat{p}(\cdot)$ is obtained via parametric methods, consistency generally follows from Lemma 12.1.

As for estimating the propensity score, Rosenbaum and Rubin (1983) suggest using a flexible logit model, where various functions of $\mathbf{x}$—for example, levels, squares, and interactions—are included. For discrete components of $\mathbf{x}$, one might define a set of dummy variables indicating the different possible values, and then interact these with continuous covariates and other dummy variables defined similarly. Clearly the sample size is important in deciding on how flexible the model can be. If we use a flexible logit or probit, or any index function $G(\cdot)$ with $0 < G(z) < 1$ for all $z \in \mathbb{R}$, then there is no danger of $\hat{p}(\mathbf{x}) = 0$ or $\hat{p}(\mathbf{x}) = 1$, but ruling out zero and one from the fitted probabilities might simply mask the failure of overlap in the population—just as when we use parametric versions of the regression functions and then extrapolate beyond values of $\mathbf{x}$ used to estimate the two functions.

Hirano, Imbens, and Ridder (2003) (HIR for short) study a nonparametric version of the Rosenbaum and Rubin (1983) approach. In particular, they study $\hat{\tau}_{ate,psw}$ when the propensity score is estimated using a flexible logit model, but they explicitly allow the number of functions of the covariates in the logit function to increase as a function of the sample size. Under regularity conditions and an assumption controlling the number of terms in the logit estimation, HIR show that their nonparametric version of the Horvitz-Thompson estimator achieves the semiparametric efficiency bound due to Hahn (1998). Remarkably, the HIR estimator is more efficient—often nontrivially so—than the "estimator" that uses the known propensity scores, $p(\mathbf{x}_i)$, in place of the nonparametric fitted probabilities, $\hat{p}(\mathbf{x}_i)$. Moreover, the HIR estimator is strictly more efficient (except in special cases) than the estimator that uses a maximum likelihood estimator for $\hat{p}(\cdot)$. This fact is related to a result by Robins and Rotnitzky (1995): even if a logit model with a given number of terms is correctly specified for $p(\cdot)$, one generally reduces the asymptotic variance of $\hat{\tau}_{ate,psw}$ by continuing to add terms even though these have no affect on $\mathrm{P}(w = 1 \mid \mathbf{x})$. The HIR estimator essentially takes the Robins and Rotnitzky (1995) result to the limit. (Shortly, we will see how the efficiency gains work in a parametric setting.)

An alternative to global smoothing methods such as the HIR series estimator is to use local smoothing, such as kernel regression. Li, Racine, and Wooldridge (2009) have recently proposed using kernel smoothing that allows both continuous and discrete covariates.

It is informative to show how to obtain the asymptotic variances of $\sqrt{N}(\hat{\tau}_{ate,psw} - \tau_{ate})$ and $\sqrt{N}(\hat{\tau}_{att,psw} - \tau_{att})$ in the parametric cases where we assume a correctly specified model for $p(\mathbf{x})$ and use the Bernoulli MLE. For $\hat{\tau}_{ate,psw}$, we can directly apply the "surprising" efficiency result in Section 13.10.2. The ignorability-of-treatment assumption (conditional on $\mathbf{x}$, of course) is easily shown to imply the key conditional independence assumption in equation (13.66) (with notation properly adjusted). Because $\hat{\tau}_{ate,psw}$ is a sample average, we can work directly off of its "first-order condition." Let $p(\mathbf{x}, \gamma)$ be the correctly specified propensity score model, and define the score from the first-stage propensity score estimation as

$$\mathbf{d}_i = \mathbf{d}(w_i, \mathbf{x}_i, \gamma) = \frac{\nabla_\gamma p(\mathbf{x}_i, \gamma)'[w_i - p(\mathbf{x}_i, \gamma)]}{p(\mathbf{x}_i, \gamma)[1 - p(\mathbf{x}_i, \gamma)]},$$

where γ is used here to also denote the true population value. Further, define

$$k_i = \frac{[w_i - p(\mathbf{x}_i, \gamma)]y_i}{p(\mathbf{x}_i, \gamma)[1 - p(\mathbf{x}_i, \gamma)]}, \tag{21.41}$$

which are the summands in $\hat{\tau}_{ate,psw}$ with the true propensity score inserted. Then the asymptotic variance of $\sqrt{N}(\hat{\tau}_{ate,psw} - \tau_{ate})$ is simply $\mathrm{Var}(e_i)$, where e_i is the population residual from the regression k_i on $\mathbf{d}_i'$. We can easily estimate this variance by using the sample version. Let

$$\hat{\mathbf{d}}_i = \mathbf{d}(w_i, \mathbf{x}_i, \hat{\gamma}) = \frac{\nabla_\gamma p(\mathbf{x}_i, \hat{\gamma})'[w_i - p(\mathbf{x}_i, \hat{\gamma})]}{p(\mathbf{x}_i, \hat{\gamma})[1 - p(\mathbf{x}_i, \hat{\gamma})]} \tag{21.42}$$

be the estimated score, and let

$$\hat{k}_i = \frac{[w_i - \hat{p}(\mathbf{x}_i)]y_i}{\hat{p}(\mathbf{x}_i)[1 - \hat{p}(\mathbf{x}_i)]}. \tag{21.43}$$

Then, obtain the OLS residuals, $\hat{e}_i$, from the regression

$$\hat{k}_i \quad \text{on} \quad 1, \hat{\mathbf{d}}_i', \quad i = 1, \ldots, N, \tag{21.44}$$

where the inclusion of unity ensures that we remove the sample average of $\hat{k}_i$ (which is $\hat{\tau}_{ate,psw}$) in estimating the variance. Given these residuals, the asymptotic standard error of $\hat{\tau}_{ate,psw}$ is

$$\left[N^{-1} \sum_{i=1}^{N} \hat{e}_i^2\right]^{1/2} \bigg/ \sqrt{N}. \tag{21.45}$$

The adjustment is particularly simple in the case of logit estimation of the propensity score because then

$$\hat{\mathbf{d}}_i' = \mathbf{h}_i(w_i - \hat{p}_i), \tag{21.46}$$

where $\mathbf{h}_i \equiv \mathbf{h}(\mathbf{x}_i)$ is the $1 \times R$ vector of covariates (including unity) and $\hat{p}_i = \Lambda(\mathbf{h}_i\hat{\gamma}) = \exp(\mathbf{h}_i\hat{\gamma})/[1 + \exp(\mathbf{h}_i\hat{\gamma})]$. We can also see that, as we add elements to $\mathbf{h}_i$, the population residuals (and the sample conterparts) from the regression k_i on $\mathbf{h}_i(w_i - p_i)$ will shrink provided the extra elements in $\mathbf{h}_i(w_i - p_i)$ are partially correlated with k_i. This is generally the case even though the extra functions in $\mathbf{h}_i$ have zero population coefficients in $\mathrm{P}(w_i = 1 \mid \mathbf{x}_i)$. This was the result noted by Robins and Rotnitzky (1995).

If we ignore estimation of the propensity score, we effectively treat $\{\hat{k}_i : i = 1, \ldots, N\}$ as being drawn from a random sample, and we use its sample average to estimate the population mean, τ_{ate}. The naive standard error that we obtain is

$$\left[N^{-1} \sum_{i=1}^{N} (\hat{k}_i - \hat{\tau}_{ate,psw})^2\right]^{1/2} \bigg/ \sqrt{N}, \tag{21.47}$$

and this is at least as large as expression (21.45), and sometimes much larger. In the population, the comparision is $\mathrm{Var}(k_i)$ versus $\mathrm{Var}[k_i - \mathrm{L}(k_i \mid \mathbf{d}_i')]$, where $\mathrm{L}(k_i \mid \mathbf{d}_i')$ is the linear projection. Netting out $\mathrm{L}(k_i \mid \mathbf{d}_i')$ produces a smaller variance unless k_i and $\mathbf{d}_i$ are uncorrelated.

We can also find an appropriate standard error for $\hat{\tau}_{att,psw}$. Write

$$\hat{\tau}_{att,psw} = \hat{\rho}^{-1} N^{-1} \sum_{i=1}^{N} \hat{q}_i,$$

where $\hat{q}_i = [w_i - p(\mathbf{x}_i, \hat{\gamma})] y_i / [1 - p(\mathbf{x}_i, \hat{\gamma})]$. Now

$$\sqrt{N}(\hat{\tau}_{att,psw} - \tau_{att}) = \hat{\rho}^{-1}N^{-1/2}\sum_{i=1}^{N}(\hat{q}_i - \hat{\rho}\tau_{att}) = \hat{\rho}^{-1}\left[N^{-1/2}\sum_{i=1}^{N}\hat{q}_i - \tau_{att}N^{-1/2}\sum_{i=1}^{N}w_i\right]$$

$$= \hat{\rho}^{-1}\left[N^{-1/2}\sum_{i=1}^{N}r_i - \tau_{att}N^{-1/2}\sum_{i=1}^{N}w_i\right] + o_p(1),$$

where the r_i are the population residuals from regressing q_i on $\mathbf{d}_i'$ (using the same argument as for $\hat{\tau}_{ate,psw}$). Therefore,

$$\sqrt{N}(\hat{\tau}_{att,psw} - \tau_{att}) = \rho^{-1}N^{-1/2}\sum_{i=1}^{N}(r_i - \tau_{att}w_i) + o_p(1),$$

and so estimation of the asymptotic variance is straightforward. The asymptotic standard error of $\hat{\tau}_{att,psw}$ is

$$\hat{\rho}^{-1}\left[N^{-1}\sum_{i=1}^{N}(\hat{r}_i - \hat{\tau}_{att,psw}w_i)^2\right]^{1/2}\Big/\sqrt{N}, \tag{21.48}$$

where $\hat{r}_i$ are the residuals from the regression $\hat{q}_i$ on $\hat{\mathbf{d}}_i'$.

A different use of the estimated propensity scores is in regression adjustment. A simple, still somewhat popular estimate is obtained from the OLS regression

$$y_i \quad \text{on} \quad 1, w_i, \hat{p}(\mathbf{x}_i), \quad i = 1, \ldots, N; \tag{21.49}$$

the coefficient on w_i, say, $\hat{\tau}_{ate,psreg}$, is the estimate of τ_{ate}. The idea is that the estimated propensity score should be sufficient in controlling for correlation between the treatment, w_i, and the covariates, $\mathbf{x}_i$. As it turns out, there is a simple characterization of when $\hat{\tau}_{ate,psreg}$ consistently estimates τ_{ate}. The following is a special case of Wooldridge (1999c, Proposition 3.2).

PROPOSITION 21.3: In addition to Assumptions ATE1.1′ and ATE.2, assume that $\tau_{ate}(\mathbf{x}) = \mathrm{E}(y_1 - y_0 \mid \mathbf{x})$ is *uncorrelated* with $\mathrm{Var}(w \mid \mathbf{x}) = p(\mathbf{x})[1 - p(\mathbf{x})]$. Then, under standard regularity conditions that ensure that $\hat{\gamma}$ (in a parametric estimation problem) is consistent and $\sqrt{N}$-asymptotically normal, $\hat{\tau}_{ate,psreg}$ is consistent for τ_{ate} and $\sqrt{N}$-asymptotically normal.

The assumption that $\tau_{ate}(\mathbf{x}) = \mu_1(\mathbf{x}) - \mu_0(\mathbf{x})$ is uncorrelated with $\mathrm{Var}(w \mid \mathbf{x})$ may appear unlikely, as both are functions of $\mathbf{x}$. However, remember that correlation measures linear dependence. It would not be surprising for $\tau_{ate}(\mathbf{x})$ to be monotonic in many elements of $\mathbf{x}$, while $p(\mathbf{x})[1 - p(\mathbf{x})]$ is a quadratic in the propensity score. If so, the correlation between these two functions of $\mathbf{x}$ might be small. (This comment is analogous to the fact that if z has a symmetric distribution around zero, z and z^2 are uncorrelated even though z^2 is an exact function of z.) In the case where the treatment effect is constant, so that $\tau_{ate}(\mathbf{x}) = \tau_{ate}$, zero correlation holds, and $\hat{\tau}_{ate,psreg}$ consistently estimates τ_{ate} without further assumptions.

The result in Section 13.10.2 can be used to obtain a proper standard error for $\hat{\tau}_{ate,psreg}$—whether or not different slopes are allowed. But we also know that ignoring the propensity-score estimation results in asymptotically conservative inference. Because regression on the propensity score is computationally simple, bootstrapping the propensity score and regression estimation is attractive as a way to obtain proper standard errors and confidence intervals. By resampling the entire vector $(y_i, w_i, \mathbf{x}_i)$, even the estimation error in $\hat{\mu}_p$ is easily accounted for.

Rosenbaum and Rubin (1983) take a different approach to deriving regression on the propensity score and matching methods discussed in the next subsection. A key result is that under Assumption ATE.1, treatment is ignorable conditional only on the propensity score, $p(\mathbf{x})$. For completeness, we provide a simple proof.

PROPOSITION 21.4: Under Assumption ATE.1, w is independent of (y_0, y_1) conditional on $p(\mathbf{x})$. Therefore, $\mathrm{E}[y \mid w = 0, p(\mathbf{x})] = \mathrm{E}[y_0 \mid p(\mathbf{x})]$ and $\mathrm{E}[y \mid w = 1, p(\mathbf{x})] = \mathrm{E}[y_1 \mid p(\mathbf{x})]$.

Proof: Because w is binary, it suffices to show that $P[w = 1 \mid y_0, y_1, p(\mathbf{x})] = P[w = 1 \mid p(\mathbf{x})]$ or $\mathrm{E}[w \mid y_0, y_1, p(\mathbf{x})] = \mathrm{E}[w \mid p(\mathbf{x})]$. But, under Assumption ATE.1, $\mathrm{E}[w \mid y_0, y_1, \mathbf{x}] = \mathrm{E}[w \mid \mathbf{x}] = p(\mathbf{x})$, where the second equality follows because w is binary. By iterated expectations,

$$\mathrm{E}[w \mid y_0, y_1, p(\mathbf{x})] = \mathrm{E}[\mathrm{E}(w \mid y_0, y_1, \mathbf{x}) \mid y_0, y_1, p(\mathbf{x})] = \mathrm{E}[p(\mathbf{x}) \mid y_0, y_1, p(\mathbf{x})] = p(\mathbf{x}),$$

which shows that ignorability of treatment holds conditional on $p(\mathbf{x})$.

Next, write $y = (1 - w)y_0 + wy_1$, as usual. Then

$$\begin{aligned}\mathrm{E}[y \mid w, p(\mathbf{x})] &= (1 - w)\mathrm{E}[y_0 \mid w, p(\mathbf{x})] + w\mathrm{E}[y_1 \mid w, p(\mathbf{x})] \\ &= (1 - w)\mathrm{E}[y_0 \mid p(\mathbf{x})] + w\mathrm{E}[y_1 \mid p(\mathbf{x})].\end{aligned}$$

Inserting $w = 0$ and $w = 1$, respectively, gives the results for the conditional means.

Proposition 21.4 has many uses. For one, it implies that, since $\mathrm{E}[y_g \mid p(\mathbf{x})]$ is identified, $g = 0, 1$, we can identify $\tau_{ate} = \mathrm{E}\{\mathrm{E}[y_1 \mid p(\mathbf{x})] - \mathrm{E}[y_0 \mid p(\mathbf{x})]\}$. In particular, let

$$r_0(p) \equiv \mathrm{E}[y \mid w = 0, p(\mathbf{x}) = p], \qquad r_1(p) \equiv \mathrm{E}[y \mid w = 1, p(\mathbf{x}) = p] \tag{21.50}$$

be the two regression functions that can be identified given the data. Given consistent estimators $\hat{r}_0(\hat{p}_i)$, $\hat{r}_1(\hat{p}_i)$, where $\hat{p}_i \equiv \hat{p}(\mathbf{x}_i)$ are the estimated propensity scores, we get as a general estimate

$$\hat{\tau}_{ate,psreg} = N^{-1} \sum_{i=1}^{N} [\hat{r}_1(\hat{p}_i) - \hat{r}_0(\hat{p}_i)]. \tag{21.51}$$

Generally, this estimator is consistent and $\sqrt{N}$-asymptotically normal provided we have the models for $r_g(\cdot)$, $g = 0, 1$ and the propensity score correctly specified (or we use suitable nonparametric methods). Given the nature of $\hat{\tau}_{ate,psreg}$, bootstrapping is an attractive method for inference.

Heckman, Ichimura, and Todd (1998) propose local smoothers to estimate $r_0(\cdot)$ and $r_1(\cdot)$; this proposal is attractive because these are functions of a scalar. But one must also estimate the propensity score, and this is often a high-dimensional problem. Hahn (1998) proposed series estimation of $r_0(\cdot)$ and $r_1(\cdot)$ along with series estimation of $p(\cdot)$. A simpler approach is just to use parametric functions and parametric asymptotics.

If $r_0(\cdot)$ and $r_1(\cdot)$ are linear, say, $r_g(p) = \eta_g + \pi_g p$, $g = 0, 1$, then estimation is straightforward. Two separate regressions can be run, and then the differences in predicted values, $\hat{r}_1(\hat{p}_i) - \hat{r}_0(\hat{p}_i)$, are averaged to get $\hat{\tau}_{ate,psreg}$. Equivalently, run the regression

$$y_i \quad \text{on} \quad 1, w_i, \hat{p}(\mathbf{x}_i), w_i \cdot [\hat{p}(\mathbf{x}_i) - \hat{p}], \quad i = 1, \ldots, N, \tag{21.52}$$

where $\hat{p}$ is a consistent estimate of $p = \mathrm{E}[p(\mathbf{x}_i)] = \mathrm{P}(w_i = 1)$. If $\hat{p}(\mathbf{x}_i)$ is from a logit that includes an intercept, the two natural estimates, $\bar{w}$ and $N^{-1} \sum_{i=1}^{N} \hat{p}(\mathbf{x}_i)$, are identical. The coefficient on w_i is $\hat{\tau}_{ate,psreg}$. If we ignore estimation of p, the usual heteroskedasticity-robust standard error will be conservative, but bootstrapping can be obtained to get the proper standard error.

The linear models for $\mathrm{E}[y_g \mid p(\mathbf{x})]$ might be too restrictive because $0 < p(\mathbf{x}) < 1$. If y has substantial variation, different functions might be needed. One can always use polynomials in $\hat{p}_i$—as formally studied in a series setting by Hahn (1998). A log-odds transformation might improve the fit, where $\widehat{lodds}_i \equiv \log[\hat{p}_i/(1 - \hat{p}_i)]$ and functions of it (such as polynomials) are used as regressors. It is easy to use two separate regressions and then average the differences in predicted values.

Given that $r_1(\cdot)$ is estimated using the treated subsample and $r_0(\cdot)$ using the control sample, we can see the nature of the overlap assumption. In effect, for each value of the propensity score in the interval $(0, 1)$, we should observe both treated and untreated units. We can easily use the estimated propensity scores to determine whether lack of overlap is a problem. For example, we can compute the normalized difference of the propensity scores (or its log-odds ratio), as in equation (21.29), using the propensity score in place of the covariates. It is also informative to plot histograms of the $\hat{p}_i$ for the control and treatment groups. We hope to rule out situations where the histograms show bins with data on the control units but no or very few data for the corresponding treatment units, and vice versa.

Regression on the propensity score seems attractive because, compared with regression adjustment using $\mathbf{x}$, it reduces the problem of controlling for a possibly large set of covariates, $\mathbf{x}$, to controlling for a single function of them, $p(\mathbf{x})$. But the parsimony afforded by propensity score regressions is somewhat illusory because we should use a flexible model for the propensity score. Even if we settle on logit or probit, we would typically include flexible functions of $\mathbf{x}$, just as if we were doing regression adjustment. One might argue that, because the treatment w_i is binary, we have better leads on suitable models for $\mathrm{P}(w = 1 \mid \mathbf{x})$. Nevertheless, as we discussed in Section 21.3.2, we can account for the nature of y when applying regression adjustment. If we use nonparametric approaches, estimating either $p(\mathbf{x})$ or the regression functions $m_g(\mathbf{x}) = \mathrm{E}(y \mid w = g, \mathbf{x})$ generally requires high-dimensional nonparametric estimation. (Incidentally, if we use a linear probability model for $p(\mathbf{x})$, regressing y_i either on the covariates themselves or the propensity score gives the same estimate of τ_{ate}.)

It is easy to see why regression on the propensity score is generally inefficient. Suppose that assignment is random so that w is independent of $(y_0, y_1, \mathbf{x})$, but $\mathbf{x}$ helps to predict the counterfactual outcomes. Further, assume that we actually know the propensity score, so that regression on the propensity score is y_i on 1, w_i, $p(\mathbf{x}_i)$. Because of random assignment, we do not need to include $p(\mathbf{x}_i)$ in order to obtain a consistent estimator of τ_{ate}: the simple difference in sample averages is consistent. Adding $p(\mathbf{x}_i)$ can actually improve efficiency over the difference-in-means estimator if $p(\mathbf{x})$ appears in the linear projections $\mathrm{L}[y_g \mid 1, p(\mathbf{x})]$: adding $p(\mathbf{x})$ will shrink the error variance. But $p(\mathbf{x})$ is hardly the best function of $\mathbf{x}$ to add to the regression. In the case of a constant treatment effect, the best function of $\mathbf{x}$ to add is $\mu_0(\mathbf{x}) = \mathrm{E}(y_0 \mid \mathbf{x})$ because this approach leads to the smallest possible mean squared error among functions of $\mathbf{x}$. In effect, the error variance is made as small as possible. Of course, we do not know this mean function, but we can approximate it much better using flexible functions of $\mathbf{x}$ than by using a linear function of just the propensity score.

We now show how regression methods and inverse probability weighted (IPW) methods can be used to estimate treatment effects of job training on labor earnings. The underlying data are from Lalonde (1986), although the particular data set used here is from Dehejia and Wahba (1999).

Example 21.1 (Causal Effects of Job Training on Earnings): We will use two data sets for this example, JTRAIN2.RAW and JTRAIN3.RAW. The first data set is from a job training experiment back in the 1970s for men with poor labor market histories. Being in the treatment group, indicated by $train = 1$, was randomly assigned. Out of 445 men, 185 were assigned to the job training program. The response variable is $re78$, real labor market earnings in 1978. (This variable is zero for a nontrivial fraction of the population.) Training began up to two years prior to 1978. The controls that we use here are age (in years), years of education, dummy variables for being black, being Hispanic, and marital status, and real earnings for the two years prior to the start of the program, 1974 and 1975. For simplicity, these all appear in level form without interactions or other functional forms.

JTRAIN3.RAW contains the same information as JTRAIN2.RAW, but the control group in JTRAIN3.RAW was obtained as a random sample from the Panel Study of Income Dynamics. Thus, JTRAIN3.RAW is essentially a nonexperimental version of JTRAIN2.RAW, which allows us to determine how well the nonexperimental methods for estimating treatment effects compare with experimental estimates (Lalonde's original motivation).

We use four estimation methods: a simple comparision of means, regression adjustment pooling across the control and treated groups, regression adjustment using separate regression functions, and IPW estimation using the propensity score. In each case, the controls are (age, $educ$, $black$, $hisp$, $married$, $re74$, $re75$). Note that for the difference-in-means and pooled regression adjustment there is no difference between $\hat{\tau}_{ate}$ and $\hat{\tau}_{att}$.

Before presenting the estimates, we note that there is a severe problem with overlap in JTRAIN3.RAW. For example, for the variable $re75$, the absolute value of the normalized difference in equation (21.29) is about 1.25, well above the Imbens and Rubin rule of 0.25. Other covariates have normalized differences above unity, too. Therefore, unless we think the ATE is constant, we can expect problems in trying to estimate τ_{ate} and, to a lesser degree, τ_{att}, even under ignorability.

Table 21.1 contains the estimates and the standard errors. For the first two estimation methods, we use the heteroskedasticity-robust standard error from the OLS regressions; by assumption, $\tau_{att} = \tau_{ate}$. For regression adjustment using separate regression functions, as well as propensity score weighting, we use 1,000 bootstrap replications in Stata 10. It is slightly more difficult to use the analytical formulas derived in equation (21.31) and expression (21.47).

Not surprisingly, using the experimental data the estimates are consistent across estimation method. Because of random assignment, $\tau_{att} = \tau_{ate}$, so it is also expected that the estimates of these parameters would be similar. The job training program

Table 21.1

Estimation Method	JTRAIN2 $\hat{\tau}_{ate}$	JTRAIN2 $\hat{\tau}_{att}$	JTRAIN3 (Full Sample) $\hat{\tau}_{ate}$	JTRAIN3 (Full Sample) $\hat{\tau}_{att}$	JTRAIN3 (Reduced Sample) $\hat{\tau}_{ate}$	JTRAIN3 (Reduced Sample) $\hat{\tau}_{att}$
Difference in means	1.794	1.794	−15.205	−15.205	−5.005	−5.005
	(0.671)	(0.671)	(0.656)	(0.656)	(0.657)	(0.657)
Pooled regression adjustment	1.683	1.683	0.860	0.860	2.059	2.059
	(0.658)	(0.658)	(0.767)	(0.767)	(0.801)	(0.801)
Separate regression adjustment	1.633	1.774	−8.910	.931	−2.340	2.323
	(0.642)	(0.661)	(3.721)	(0.794)	(1.480)	(0.817)
Propensity score weighting	1.627	1.798	11.029	1.627	7.049	1.649
	(0.637)	(0.660)	(40.809)	(0.835)	(17.295)	(0.986)
Sample size	445	445	2,675	2,675	1,162	1,162

is estimated to increase real labor market earnings in 1978 by between \$1,627 and \$1,798. This is a huge effect considering that the average value of *re*78 for the untreated sample is \$4,554.

The pattern of estimates is very different when the nonexperimental data are used. It is not too surprising that the simple comparison-of-means estimate, which provides no control for self-selection into training, is negative and large. But the other estimates of τ_{ate} also appear unreliable. The estimate of τ_{ate} using propensity score weighting is suspiciously large (though very imprecise). In fact, of the 2,675 observations, the logit model for the propensity score perfectly predicts 158 of the $train = 0$ outcomes. In effect, we are dividing by zero (but in practice it is a very small number). Before one uses propensity score weighting, one should study the distribution of the propensity score. As discussed earlier, one might reduce the sample to observations with, say, $\hat{p}(\mathbf{x}_i)$ between 0.10 and 0.90, or 0.05 and 0.95.

Controlling for the covariates, either through regression adjustment or propensity score weighting, provides sensible estimates of τ_{att}, but the estimates are imprecise. The propensity score weighting is sensible for τ_{att} because small probabilities do not affect $\hat{\tau}_{att}$ (see equation (21.40)). The largest estimated propensity score in the entire sample is about 0.936. It is clear by looking at simple summary statistics of the propensity score that lack of balance is a serious problem: in the treated subsample, the average propensity score is about 0.631; in the control subsample, it is about 0.027.

To address the lack of overlap somewhat crudely, we also use a subset of the data in JTRAIN3.RAW. We use only observations where the average of *re*74 and *re*75 is less than or equal to \$15,000. This choice is essentially arbitrary but provides a mechanism for dropping men who likely have little chance of being part of such a program. The estimates are given in the last two columns of Table 21.1. Restricting the sample produces more sensible estimates, but those for τ_{ate} are still unstable. Again, the three estimates of τ_{att} that account for covariates are fairly stable but not especially precise. A more careful analysis of these data would use more flexible functional forms and cause one to think more carefully about how one might restrict the sample.

21.3.4 Combining Regression Adjustment and Propensity Score Weighting

In the previous two subsections, we described methods for estimating ATEs based on two strategies: the first is based on estimating $\mu_g(x) = \mathrm{E}(y_g \mid \mathbf{x})$ for $g = 0, 1$ and averaging the differences in fitted values, as in equation (21.27), and the second is based on propensity score weighting, as in equation (21.39). For each approach we have discussed estimators that achieve the asymptotic efficiency bound. If we have large sample sizes relative to the dimension of $\mathbf{x}_i$, we might think nonparametric estimators of the conditional means or propensity score are sufficiently accurate to invoke the asymptotic efficiency results.

In other cases we might choose flexible parametric models because full nonparametric estimation is difficult. As shown earlier, one reason for viewing estimators of conditional means or propensity scores as flexible parametric models is that it simplifies standard error calculations for treatment effect estimates. But if we use standard error calculations that rely on parametric models, we should admit the possibility that those parametric models are misspecified. As it turns out, we can combine regression adjustment and propensity score methods to achieve some robustness to misspecification of the parametric models. The resulting estimator of τ_{ate} is said to be **doubly robust** because it only requires either the conditional mean model or the propensity score model to be correctly specified, not both.

The idea behind the doubly robust estimators is developed in Robins and Rotnitzky (1995), Robins, Rotnitzky, and Zhao (1995), and van der Laan and Robins (2003). Wooldridge (2007) provides a simple proof that double robustness holds for certain combinations of conditional mean specifications and estimation methods. To describe the approach, let $m_0(\cdot, \boldsymbol{\delta}_0)$ and $m_1(\cdot, \boldsymbol{\delta}_1)$ be parametric functions for $\mathrm{E}(y_g \mid \mathbf{x})$, $g = 0, 1$, and let $p(\cdot, \gamma)$ be a parametric model for the propensity score. In the first step we estimate γ by Bernoulli maximum likelihood and obtain the estimated propensity scores as $p(\mathbf{x}_i, \hat{\gamma})$ (probably logit or probit). In the second step, we use regression or a quasi-likelihood method, where we weight by the inverse probability. For example, if we use linear functional forms for the conditional mean, to estimate $\boldsymbol{\delta}_1 = (\alpha_1, \boldsymbol{\beta}_1')'$ we would use the IPW linear least squares problem

$$\min_{\alpha_1, \boldsymbol{\beta}_1} \sum_{i=1}^{N} w_i (y_i - \alpha_1 - \mathbf{x}_i \boldsymbol{\beta}_1)^2 / p(\mathbf{x}_i, \hat{\gamma}); \tag{21.53}$$

for $\boldsymbol{\delta}_0$, we weight by $1/[1 - \hat{p}(\mathbf{x}_i)]$ and use the $w_i = 0$ sample. Then, we estimate τ_{ate} as the average of the difference in predicted values,

$$\hat{\tau}_{ate,pswreg} = N^{-1} \sum_{i=1}^{N} [(\hat{\alpha}_1 + \mathbf{x}_i \hat{\boldsymbol{\beta}}_1) - (\hat{\alpha}_0 + \mathbf{x}_i \hat{\boldsymbol{\beta}}_0)]. \tag{21.54}$$

This is the same formula as linear regression adjustment, but we are using different estimates of α_g, $\boldsymbol{\beta}_g$, $g = 0, 1$.

To carefully describe the double robustness result, denote the probability limits of $\hat{\gamma}$, $\hat{\boldsymbol{\delta}}_0$, and $\hat{\boldsymbol{\delta}}_1$ by γ^*, $\boldsymbol{\delta}_0^*$, and $\boldsymbol{\delta}_1^*$, respectively. Now, if the conditional mean functions are truly linear and ignorability holds conditional on $\mathbf{x}_i$, then weighted least squares estimators using *any* function of $\mathbf{x}_i$ consistently estimate $\boldsymbol{\delta}_0^*$ on the control sample and $\boldsymbol{\delta}_1^*$ on the treated sample. We covered the general case for missing data in Section 19.8 (see also Wooldridge, 2007). Therefore, even if $p(\mathbf{x}, \gamma)$ is arbitrarily misspecified, weighting by functions of $p(\mathbf{x}_i, \gamma^*)$ does not cause inconsistency for estimating the parameters of the correctly specified conditional mean. (Replacing γ^* with $\hat{\gamma}$ does not change this claim because $\hat{\gamma}$ converges in probability to γ^*.) Now if $\mathrm{E}(y_g \mid \mathbf{x}) = \alpha_g^* + \mathbf{x}\boldsymbol{\beta}_g^*$, $g = 0, 1$, then $\tau_{ate} = \mathrm{E}[(\alpha_1^* + \mathbf{x}\boldsymbol{\beta}_1^*) - (\alpha_0^* + \mathbf{x}\boldsymbol{\beta}_0^*)]$, which is the usual identification result for τ_{ate} for regression adjustment.

The other half of the double robustness result is more subtle. Now suppose that $p(\mathbf{x}, \gamma)$ is correctly specified for $\mathrm{P}(w = 1 \mid \mathbf{x})$ but allow for the possibility that the conditional means are not linear. As we discussed in Section 19.8, the IPW estimator (under ignorability) recovers the solution to the unweighted minimization problem in the population. In the linear regression case, that means $\boldsymbol{\delta}_g^*$ minimizes $\mathrm{E}[(y_g - \alpha_g - \mathbf{x}\boldsymbol{\beta}_g)^2]$ for $g = 0, 1$. In other words, the $\boldsymbol{\delta}_g^*$ are the parameters in the linear projection $\mathrm{L}(y_g \mid 1, \mathbf{x})$; because we include a constant in this projection, the unconditional mean of y_g is the mean of the linear projection, $\mathrm{E}(y_g) = \mathrm{E}[(\alpha_g^* + \mathbf{x}\boldsymbol{\beta}_g^*)]$. Therefore, $\tau_{ate} = \mathrm{E}[(\alpha_1^* + \mathbf{x}\boldsymbol{\beta}_1^*) - (\alpha_0^* + \mathbf{x}\boldsymbol{\beta}_0^*)]$, just as before, except now we do not need the linear functions to be correctly specified for the conditional means. In other words, linear regression adjustment can still produce a consistent estimator of τ_{ate} when the conditional means are misspecified, but we must use IPW estimation with a correctly specified model for the propensity score. The argument is essentially unchanged when we replace $\mathbf{x}$ with any functions $\mathbf{h}(\mathbf{x})$.

As illustrated for the linear regression case, the key to the second part of the double robustness property—that is, when the conditional means are misspecified—is that we can still recover the counterfactual unconditional means, $\mathrm{E}(y_g)$, as $\mathrm{E}(y_g) = \mathrm{E}[m_g(\mathbf{x}, \boldsymbol{\delta}_g^*)]$. Thus, to extend the double robustness result to nonlinear conditional mean models, we need to find combinations of conditional mean functions and objective functions with this property, where, again, the $\boldsymbol{\delta}_g^*$ solve the population optimization problem. This is a special property, but a couple of very useful cases are known. They turn out to be quasi-maximum likelihood estimators in particular linear exponential family distributions with particular conditional mean functions. We already saw the linear case with the least squares (normal log likelihood) objective function. If y_g is a binary or fractional response, the mean function that delivers double robustness, along with the Bernoulli quasi-log likelihood, is the logistic function

$$m_g(\mathbf{x}, \boldsymbol{\delta}_g) = \Lambda[\alpha_g + \mathbf{h}(\mathbf{x})\boldsymbol{\beta}_g] \tag{21.55}$$

where $\mathbf{h}(\mathbf{x})$ can be any function of $\mathbf{x}$. In other words, for the treated group, we solve the IPW QMLE problem

$$\min_{\alpha_1, \boldsymbol{\beta}_1} \sum_{i=1}^{N} w_i\{(1 - y_i)\log[1 - \Lambda(\alpha_1 + \mathbf{h}_i\boldsymbol{\beta}_1)] + y_i \log[\Lambda(\alpha_1 + \mathbf{h}_i\boldsymbol{\beta}_1)]\}/p(\mathbf{x}_i, \hat{\boldsymbol{\gamma}}),$$

where $\mathbf{h}_i \equiv \mathbf{h}(\mathbf{x}_i)$. Once we have used IPW estimation in each case, the ATE is estimated as before:

$$\hat{\tau}_{ate,pswreg} = N^{-1} \sum_{i=1}^{N} [\Lambda(\hat{\alpha}_1 + \mathbf{h}_i\hat{\boldsymbol{\beta}}_1) - \Lambda(\hat{\alpha}_0 + \mathbf{h}_i\hat{\boldsymbol{\beta}}_0)].$$

If $\mathrm{E}(y_g \mid \mathbf{x}) = \Lambda[\alpha_g^* + \mathbf{h}(\mathbf{x})\boldsymbol{\beta}_g^*]$, $g = 0, 1$ or $\mathrm{P}(w = 1 \mid \mathbf{x}) = p(\mathbf{x}, \boldsymbol{\gamma}^*)$, then $\hat{\tau}_{ate,pswreg} \xrightarrow{p} \tau_{ate}$. We might very well use a logit model for $\mathrm{P}(w = 1 \mid \mathbf{x})$, but that is not necessary. Also, notice that if we replace $\Lambda(\cdot)$ with, say, the standard normal cdf, $\Phi(\cdot)$, in equation (21.55), we lose the double robustness property.

If y_g is a nonnegative response—it could be continuous, discrete, or have both features—an exponential mean function coupled with the Poisson QLL delivers double robustness. With $\mathbf{h}_i = \mathbf{h}(\mathbf{x}_i)$ functions of $\mathbf{x}_i$, we solve an IPW Poisson estimation,

$$\min_{\alpha_1, \boldsymbol{\beta}_1} \sum_{i=1}^{N} w_i[y_i(\alpha_1 + \mathbf{h}_i\boldsymbol{\beta}_1) - \exp(\alpha_1 + \mathbf{h}_i\boldsymbol{\beta}_1)]/p(\mathbf{x}_i, \hat{\boldsymbol{\gamma}}),$$

for the treated sample, and similarly for the control sample. The average treatment effect then has the same form as equation (21.37).

Why do the Bernoulli and Poisson QMLEs with, respectively, the logistic and exponential mean functions yield doubly robust estimators of τ_{ate}? Again, the first half of double robustness is straightforward. The Bernoulli and Poisson QMLEs are fully robust for estimating the parameters of a correctly specified mean regardless of the nature of y_i (and with *any* mean function); weighting by a strictly positive function of $\mathbf{x}_i$, either $1/p(\mathbf{x}_i, \gamma^*)$ or $1/[1 - p(\mathbf{x}_i, \gamma^*)]$, does not change the robustness property when assignment is ignorable. This reasoning gives the first half of the double robustness. For the second half, we need the specific conditional mean functions for the corresponding QLL. When $p(\mathbf{x}, \gamma)$ is correctly specified, so that $\mathrm{P}(w = 1 \mid \mathbf{x}) = p(\mathbf{x}, \gamma^*)$, the IPW estimator consistently estimates the solution to the unweighted population problem—as always. The key is that for the two combinations of mean/QLLs just described, the probability limits satisfy $\mathrm{E}(y_g) = \mathrm{E}[m_g(\mathbf{x}, \boldsymbol{\delta}_g^*)]$. These are easy to establish by studying the first-order conditions for $\boldsymbol{\delta}_g^*$. For example, in the Poisson case, $\boldsymbol{\delta}_g^*$ satisfies (for a random draw i)

$$\mathrm{E}[(1, \mathbf{h}_i)' y_{ig}] = \mathrm{E}[(1, \mathbf{h}_i)' \exp(\alpha_g^* + \mathbf{h}_i \boldsymbol{\beta}_g^*)],$$

and the first of these equations is simply $\mathrm{E}(y_{ig}) = \mathrm{E}[\exp(\alpha_g^* + \mathbf{h}_i \boldsymbol{\beta}_g^*)]$. A similar calculation establishes $\mathrm{E}(y_g) = \mathrm{E}[\Lambda(\alpha_g^* + \mathbf{h}(\mathbf{x}) \boldsymbol{\beta}_g^*)]$ in the logistic/Bernoulli case. (The sample analogue of these population conditions also holds: the sample average of y_i is equal to the average of the fitted values.)

For the previous three cases discussed, the mean functions for the normal (squared residual), Bernoulli, and Poisson quasi-log likelihoods correspond to the "canonical link" functions in the language of generalized linear models. This correspondence is not a coincidence. The mean function associated with a canonical link always has the property $\mathrm{E}(y_g) = \mathrm{E}[m_g(\mathbf{x}, \boldsymbol{\delta}_g^*)]$ provided a constant is included in the index function—as would always be the case in treatment effect applications. It is important to remember that these three conditional mean/QLL combinations can be used for a variety of response variables. As a practical matter, we should ensure that the chosen mean function is logically consistent with the nature of y_g. If y_g has unbounded support and takes on positive and negative values, a linear model seems natural. If y_g is binary or fractional (with possible mass at zero or one), the logit approach seems natural. And if $y_g \geq 0$ and unbounded, the exponential function (combined with the Poisson QLL) seems natural. Remember, the Poisson QMLE can be applied to any kind of y_g.

Because the estimates of τ_{ate} take the form of equation (21.30), we can use equation (21.31)—with proper formulas for $\hat{\mathbf{V}}_0$ and $\hat{\mathbf{V}}_1$—to compute an asymptotic standard error for $\hat{\tau}_{ate,pswreg}$. If the conditional means are correctly specified, the usual robust variance matrix is valid for the parameters using the weighted quasi-MLEs. If the conditional means are misspecified but the propensity score is correctly specified, a better (and smaller) estimate of the asymptotic variances of the $\hat{\boldsymbol{\delta}}_g$ is obtained by netting out the gradient of the propensity score log likelihood from the weighted, selected score for the QMLE, just as in Section 19.8; see also Wooldridge (2007). We might just use the variance matrix that ignores estimation of γ^* because, at worst, it is conservative. However, there is no harm in adjusting for the MLE estimation of γ^* because, if the means are correctly specified, the adjustment will be minimal in large samples. Of course, bootstrapping the two-step procedure and the formula for $\hat{\tau}_{ate,pswreg}$ is easy and provides asymptotically correct inference.

21.3.5 Matching Methods

The motivation for matching estimators is similar to regression adjustment. In particular, for each i, we impute values for the counterfactuals, y_{i0} and y_{i1}. Matching estimators use the observed outcomes when possible. In other words, if we let $\hat{y}_{i0}$ and $\hat{y}_{i1}$ denote the imputed values, $\hat{y}_{i0} = y_i$ when $w_i = 0$ and $\hat{y}_{i1} = y_i$ when $w_i = 1$. Generally, matching estimators take the forms

$$\hat{\tau}_{ate,match} = N^{-1}\sum_{i=1}^{N}(\hat{y}_{i1} - \hat{y}_{i0}) \tag{21.56}$$

$$\hat{\tau}_{att,match} = N_1^{-1}\sum_{i=1}^{N} w_i(y_i - \hat{y}_{i0}), \tag{21.57}$$

where the latter formula uses the fact that $y_{i1} = y_i$ for the treated subsample. (In other words, we never need to impute y_{i1} for the treated subsample.)

The key question in matching is how to impute y_{i0} for the treated units (for both τ_{ate} and τ_{att}) and how to impute y_{i1} for the control units (for τ_{ate}). Abadie and Imbens (2006) consider several approaches, each of which involves finding one or more matches based on the covariate values. In the simplest case, a single match is found for each observation. For concreteness, suppose i is a treated observation ($w_i = 1$). Then $\hat{y}_{i1} = y_i$ and $\hat{y}_{i0} = y_{h(i)}$ for $h(i)$ such that $w_{h(i)} = 0$ and unit $h(i)$ is "closest" to unit i in the sense that $\mathbf{x}_{h(i)}$ is "closest" to $\mathbf{x}_i$ based on a chosen metric (or distance). In other words, for the treated unit i we find the "most similar" untreated observation, and use its response as our best estimate of y_{i0}. Similarly, if $w_i = 0$, $\hat{y}_{i0} = y_i$ and $\hat{y}_{i1} = y_{h(i)}$ where now $w_{h(i)} = 1$. If we choose matches based on the full set of covariates, we call this method **matching on the covariates**. If we settle on a single match for each unit and we have the list of covariates, the only issue is in choosing the distance measure. A common metric is the **Mahalanobis distance**, which for observations h and i is (the square root of) $(\mathbf{x}_h - \mathbf{x}_i)'\hat{\Sigma}_{\mathbf{x}}^{-1}(\mathbf{x}_h - \mathbf{x}_i)$, where $\hat{\Sigma}_{\mathbf{x}}$ is the sample $K \times K$ variance-covariance matrix of the covariates. Some packages use a diagonal version as the default, which gives the weighted average $\sum_{j=1}^{K}(x_{hj} - x_{ij})^2/\hat{\sigma}_j^2$.

Rather than using a single "nearest neighbor," we can impute the missing values using an average of M nearest neighbors. If $w_i = 1$ then

$$\hat{y}_{i0} = M^{-1} \sum_{h \in \aleph_M(i)} y_h \tag{21.58}$$

where $\aleph_M(i)$ contains the M untreated nearest matches to observation i, again based on the covariates. In particular, for all $h \in \aleph_M(i)$, $w_h = 0$. (With ties in the distances, there can be more than M elements in $\aleph_M(i)$, and then M is replaced with the number of elements in $\aleph_M(i)$.) Similarly, if $w_i = 0$,

$$\hat{y}_{i1} = M^{-1} \sum_{h \in \Im_M(i)} y_h \tag{21.59}$$

where $\Im_M(i)$ contains the M treated nearest matches to observation i.

Matching on the full set of covariates can be computationally intensive, but with modern computers the burden is manageable. The method produces a consistent estimator of τ_{ate} under the ignorability-in-mean Assumption ATE.1$'$ along with overlap Assumption ATE.2. (Naturally, the weaker assumptions are sufficient for τ_{att}.) Matching can be motivated by the following thought experiment. Suppose that we draw a value $\mathbf{x}$ from the distribution of covariates in the population. Then, for the given covariate values, we randomly draw a control unit and a treated unit from the subpopulation and record the outcomes. The expected difference in the outcomes is

$$\mathrm{E}(y \mid w = 1, \mathbf{x}) - \mathrm{E}(y \mid w = 0, \mathbf{x}) = \tau_{ate}(\mathbf{x}),$$

where the equality holds under Assumption ATE.1$'$. By iterated expectations, if we average the difference in outcomes across the distribution of $\mathbf{x}$, then we have τ_{ate}. Matching is just the sample analogue of the thought experiment.

It is clear that lack of overlap will cause problems for matching estimators, just as with regression adjustment and propensity score weighting. Suppose i is a control unit and $\mathbf{x}_i$ is very far from all the covariate values in the treated subsample. Then the match used to obtain $\hat{y}_{i0}$ could be very poor, and averaging several poor matched values need not help. Fundamentally, if there are regions in the support $\mathcal{X}$ without both control and treated units, matching can produce poor results.

The large-sample properties of covariate matching have been obtained by Abadie and Imbens (2006); see also Imbens and Wooldridge (2009). Unless $K = 1$ (matching on a single covariate), matching estimators are not $\sqrt{N}$-consistent, and the bias dominates the variance when $K > 3$. See Abadie and Imbens (2006) for bias and variance calculations, and for a bootstrap procedure for conducting valid inference.

Because of Proposition 21.4, matching on the propensity score also produces consistent estimators of τ_{ate} and τ_{att}, which is very convenient because $p(\mathbf{x})$ is a scalar in the unit interval. If we knew the propensity score, we could apply the results of Abadie and Imbens (2006); in particular, the estimator would be $\sqrt{N}$-consistent and variance calculations would be fairly straightforward, as would applying the bootstrap. Rosenbaum and Rubin (1983) first proposed **propensity score matching** using propensity scores obtained from a preliminary logit estimation. Unfortunately, using an estimated propensity score complicates the statistical properties of the matching estimator because matching is an inherently discontinuous operation. In particular, if standard matching methods are used—for example, $h(i)$ is chosen as the match for observation i if $w_{h(i)} = 1 - w_i$ and $h(i) = \text{argmin}_h |\hat{p}(\mathbf{x}_h) - \hat{p}(\mathbf{x}_i)|$—then bootstrapping is no longer justified. (Sometimes a different function of the propensity score, such as the log-odds ratio, is used in the matching, but that in itself does not fix the problems with bootstrapping.) Various methods of smoothing propensity score matching have been proposed; see, for example, Frölich (2004).

Matching methods can also be combined with regression adjustments. See Imbens (2004) and Imbens and Wooldridge (2009) for surveys.

Example 21.2 (Causal Effect of Job Training on Earnings): We now compute matching estimates of the causal effects from Example 21.1. We use a single-match and diagonal-weighting matrix with the inverse of the variances down the diagonal. The standard errors are computed by Stata 10 using the methods in Abadie and Imbens (2006). Table 21.2 contains the results.

Not suprisingly, on the experimental data set, the matching estimates are very similar to the regression-adjustment and propensity-score-weighting estimates obtained in Example 21.1. The estimates are somewhat less precise than the regression and propensity score estimates.

Unfortunately, like the other methods, matching does not work very well on the nonexperimental data—even when the data set is restricted such that $(re74 + re75)/2 \leq 15$. Further work would need to be done to obtain a sample with better overlap.

Table 21.2

	JTRAIN2		JTRAIN3 (Full Sample)		JTRAIN3 (Reduced Sample)	
Estimation Method	$\hat{\tau}_{ate}$	$\hat{\tau}_{att}$	$\hat{\tau}_{ate}$	$\hat{\tau}_{att}$	$\hat{\tau}_{ate}$	$\hat{\tau}_{att}$
Covariate matching	1.628	1.824	−12.869	0.155	−3.846	−0.232
	(0.773)	(0.882)	(3.815)	(1.478)	(2.495)	(1.649)
Sample size	445	445	2,675	2,675	1,162	1,162

21.4 Instrumental Variables Methods

We now turn to instrumental variables estimation of average treatment effects when we suspect failure of the ignorability-of-treatment assumption (ATE.1 or ATE.1′). IV methods for estimating ATEs can be very effective if a good instrument for treatment is available. We need the instrument to predict treatment (after partialing out any controls). As we discussed in Section 5.3.1, the instrument should be redundant in a certain conditional expectation and unrelated to unobserved heterogeneity; we give precise assumptions in the following subsections.

Our primary focus in this section is on the average treatment effect defined in equation (21.1). Section 21.4.1 considers IV estimation, including methods where fitted values from estimation of a binary response model for treatment are used as instruments—and makes the case for preferring fitted values as instruments rather than regressors. Section 21.4.2 provides methods for estimating the ATE that can be used when the gain to treatment depends on unobservables (as well as observables). Two approaches are suggested; one adds a "correction function" and applies IV to the resulting equation. The other is based on a control function approach. In Section 21.4.3 we briefly discuss estimating the local average treatment effect by instrumental variables when we are not willing to make functional form or distributional assumptions.

21.4.1 Estimating the Average Treatment Effect Using IV

In studying IV procedures, it is useful to write the observed outcome y as

$$y = \mu_0 + (\mu_1 - \mu_0)w + v_0 + w(v_1 - v_0), \tag{21.60}$$

where $\mu_g = E(y_g)$ and $v_g = y_g - \mu_g$, $g = 0, 1$. However, unlike in Section 21.3, we do not assume that v_0 and v_1 are mean independent of w, given $\mathbf{x}$. Instead, we assume the availability of instruments, which we collect in the vector $\mathbf{z}$. (Here we separate the extra instruments from the covariates, so that $\mathbf{x}$ and $\mathbf{z}$ do not overlap. In many cases $\mathbf{z}$ is a scalar, but the analysis is no easier in that case.)

If we assume that the stochastic parts of y_1 and y_0 are the same, that is, $v_1 = v_0$, then the interaction term disappears (and $\tau_{ate} = \tau_{att}$). Without the interaction term we can use standard IV methods under weak assumptions.

ASSUMPTION ATEIV.1: (a) In equation (21.60), $v_1 = v_0$; (b) $\mathrm{L}(v_0 \mid \mathbf{x}, \mathbf{z}) = \mathrm{L}(v_0 \mid \mathbf{x})$; and (c) $\mathrm{L}(w \mid \mathbf{x}, \mathbf{z}) \neq \mathrm{L}(w \mid \mathbf{x})$.

All linear projections in this chapter contain unity, which we suppress for notational simplicity.

Under parts a and b of Assumption ATEIV.1, we can write

$$y = \delta_0 + \tau w + \mathbf{x}\boldsymbol{\beta}_0 + u_0, \tag{21.61}$$

where $\tau = \tau_{ate}$ and $u_0 \equiv v_0 - \mathrm{L}(v_0 \mid \mathbf{x}, \mathbf{z})$. By definition, u_0 has zero mean and is uncorrelated with $(\mathbf{x}, \mathbf{z})$, but w and u_0 are generally correlated, which makes OLS estimation of equation (21.61) inconsistent. The redundancy of $\mathbf{z}$ in the linear projection $\mathrm{L}(v_0 \mid \mathbf{x}, \mathbf{z})$ means that $\mathbf{z}$ is appropriately excluded from equation (21.61); this is the part of identification that we cannot test (except indirectly using the overidentification test from Chapter 6). Part c means that $\mathbf{z}$ has predictive power in the linear projection of treatment on $(\mathbf{x}, \mathbf{z})$; this is the standard rank condition for identification from Chapter 5, and we can test it using a first-stage regression and heteroskedasticity-robust tests of exclusion restrictions. Under Assumption ATEIV.1, τ (and the other parameters in equation (21.61)), are identified, and they can be consistently estimated by 2SLS. Because the only endogenous explanatory variable in equation (21.61) is binary, equation (21.60) is called a **dummy endogenous variable model** (Heckman, 1978). As we discussed in Chapter 5, there are no special considerations in estimating equation (21.61) by 2SLS when the endogenous explanatory variable is binary.

Assumption ATEIV.1b holds if the instruments $\mathbf{z}$ are independent of $(y_0, \mathbf{x})$. For example, suppose z is a scalar determining eligibility in a job training program or some other social program. Actual participation, w, might be correlated with v_0, which could contain unobserved ability. If eligibility is randomly assigned, it is often reasonable to assume that z is independent of $(y_0, \mathbf{x})$. Eligibility would positively influence participation, and so Assumption ATEIV.1c should hold.

Random assignment of eligibility is no guarantee that eligibility is a valid instrument for participation. The outcome of z could affect other behavior, which could feed back into u_0 in equation (21.61). For example, consider Angrist's (1990) draft lottery application, where draft lottery number is used as an instrument for enlisting. Lottery number clearly affected enlistment, so Assumption ATEIV.1c is satisfied. Assumption ATEIV.1b is also satisfied *if* men did not change behavior in unobserved ways that affect wage, based on their lottery number. One concern is that men with low lottery numbers may get more education as a way of avoiding service through a deferment. Including years of education in $\mathbf{x}$ effectively solves this problem. But what if men with high draft lottery numbers received more job training because employers did not fear losing them? If a measure of job training status cannot be included in $\mathbf{x}$, lottery number would generally be correlated with u_0. See Angrist, Imbens, and Rubin (1996) and Heckman (1997) for additional discussion.

As the previous discussion implies, the redundancy condition in Assumption ATEIV.1b allows the instruments $\mathbf{z}$ to be correlated with elements of $\mathbf{x}$. For example, in the population of high school graduates, if w is a college degree indicator and the instrument z is distance to the nearest college while attending high school, then z is allowed to be correlated with other controls in the wage equation, such as geographic indicators.

Under $v_1 = v_0$ and the key assumptions on the instruments, 2SLS on equation (21.61) is consistent and asymptotically normal. But if we make stronger assumptions, we can find a more efficient IV estimator.

ASSUMPTION ATEIV.1$'$: (a) In equation (21.60), $v_1 = v_0$; (b) $\mathrm{E}(v_0 \mid \mathbf{x}, \mathbf{z}) = \mathrm{L}(v_0 \mid \mathbf{x})$; (c) $\mathrm{P}(w = 1 \mid \mathbf{x}, \mathbf{z}) \neq \mathrm{P}(w = 1 \mid \mathbf{x})$ and $\mathrm{P}(w = 1 \mid \mathbf{x}, \mathbf{z}) = G(\mathbf{x}, \mathbf{z}; \gamma)$ is a known parametric form (usually probit or logit); and (d) $\mathrm{Var}(v_0 \mid \mathbf{x}, \mathbf{z}) = \sigma_0^2$.

Part b assumes that $\mathrm{E}(v_0 \mid \mathbf{x})$ is linear in $\mathbf{x}$, and so it is more restrictive than Assumption ATEIV.1b. It does not usually hold for discrete response variables y, although it may be a reasonable approximation in some cases. Under parts a and b, the error u_0 in equation (21.61) has a zero conditional mean:

$$\mathrm{E}(u_0 \mid \mathbf{x}, \mathbf{z}) = 0. \tag{21.62}$$

Part d implies that $\mathrm{Var}(u_0 \mid \mathbf{x}, \mathbf{z})$ is constant. From the results on efficient choice of instruments in Section 14.4.3, the optimal IV for w is $\mathrm{E}(w \mid \mathbf{x}, \mathbf{z}) = G(\mathbf{x}, \mathbf{z}; \gamma)$. Therefore, we can use a two-step IV method:

Procedure 21.1 (Under Assumption ATEIV.1$'$): (a) Estimate the binary response model $\mathrm{P}(w = 1 \mid \mathbf{x}, \mathbf{z}) = G(\mathbf{x}, \mathbf{z}; \gamma)$ by maximum likelihood. Obtain the fitted probabilities, $\hat{G}_i$. The leading case occurs when $\mathrm{P}(w = 1 \mid \mathbf{x}, \mathbf{z})$ follows a probit model.

(b) Estimate equation (21.61) by IV using instruments 1, $\hat{G}_i$, and $\mathbf{x}_i$.

There are several nice features of this IV estimator. First, it can be shown that the conditions sufficient to ignore the estimation of γ in the first stage hold; see Section 6.1.2. Therefore, the usual 2SLS standard errors and test statistics are asymptotically valid. Second, under Assumption ATEIV.1$'$, the IV estimator from step b is asymptotically efficient in the class of estimators where the IVs are functions of $(\mathbf{x}_i, \mathbf{z}_i)$; see Problem 8.11. If Assumption ATEIV.1$'$d does not hold, all statistics should be made robust to heteroskedasticity, and we no longer have the efficient IV estimator.

Procedure 21.1 has an important robustness property. Because we are using $\hat{G}_i$ as an instrument for w_i, the model for $\mathrm{P}(w = 1 \mid \mathbf{x}, \mathbf{z})$ does *not* have to be correctly specified. For example, if we specify a probit model for $\mathrm{P}(w = 1 \mid \mathbf{x}, \mathbf{z})$, we do not need the probit model to be correct. Generally, what we need is that the linear projection of w onto $[\mathbf{x}, G(\mathbf{x}, \mathbf{z}; \gamma^*)]$ actually depends on $G(\mathbf{x}, \mathbf{z}; \gamma^*)$, where we use γ^* to denote the plim of the maximum likelihood estimator when the model is misspecified (see White, 1982a, and Section 13.11.1). These requirements are fairly weak when $\mathbf{z}$ is partially correlated with w.

Technically, τ and $\boldsymbol{\beta}$ are identified even if we do not have extra exogenous variables excluded from $\mathbf{x}$. But we can rarely justify the estimator in this case. For concreteness, suppose that w given $\mathbf{x}$ follows a probit model (and we have no $\mathbf{z}$, or $\mathbf{z}$ does not appear in $P(w = 1 \mid \mathbf{x}, \mathbf{z})$). Because $G(\mathbf{x}, \gamma) \equiv \Phi(\gamma_0 + \mathbf{x}\gamma_1)$ is a nonlinear function of $\mathbf{x}$, it is not perfectly correlated with $\mathbf{x}$, so it can be used as an IV for w. This situation is very similar to the one discussed in Section 19.6.1: while identification holds for all values of α and $\boldsymbol{\beta}$ if $\gamma_1 \neq \mathbf{0}$, we are achieving identification off of the nonlinearity of $P(w = 1 \mid \mathbf{x})$. Further, $\Phi(\gamma_0 + \mathbf{x}\gamma_1)$ and $\mathbf{x}$ are typically highly correlated. As we discussed in Section 5.2.6, severe multicollinearity among the IVs can result in very imprecise IV estimators. In fact, if $P(w = 1 \mid \mathbf{x})$ followed a linear probability model, τ would not be identified. See Problem 21.5 for an illustration.

Example 21.3 (Estimating the Effects of Education on Fertility): We use the data in FERTIL2.RAW to estimate the effect of attaining at least seven years of education on fertility. The data are for women of childbearing age in Botswana. Seven years of education is, by far, the modal amount of positive education. (About 21 percent of women report zero years of education. For the subsample with positive education, about 33 percent report seven years of education.) Let $y = children$, the number of living children, and let $w = educ7$ be a binary indicator for at least seven years of education. The elements of $\mathbf{x}$ are *age*, age^2, *evermarr* (ever married), *urban* (lives in an urban area), *electric* (has electricity), and *tv* (has a television).

The OLS estimate of τ is $-.394$ (se $= .050$). We also use the variable *frsthalf*, a binary variable equal to one if the woman was born in the first half of the year, as an IV for *educ7*. It is easily shown that *educ7* and *frsthalf* are significantly negatively related. The usual IV estimate is much larger in magnitude than the OLS estimate, but only marginally significant: -1.131 (se $= .619$). The estimate from Procedure 21.1 is even bigger in magnitude, and very significant: -1.975 (se $= .332$). The standard error that is robust to arbitrary heteroskedasticity is even smaller. Therefore, using the probit fitted values as an IV, rather than the usual linear projection, produces a more precise estimate (and one notably larger in magnitude).

The IV estimate of education effect seems very large. One possible problem is that, because *children* is a nonnegative integer that piles up at zero, the assumptions underlying Procedure 21.1—namely, Assumptions ATEIV.1′a and ATEIV.1′b—

might not be met. We could instead apply methods for exponential response functions in Section 18.5. Both the Terza (1998) and Mullahy (1997) approaches can be derived using a counterfactual framework.

In principle, it is important to recognize that Procedure 21.1 is *not* the same as using $\hat{G}$ as a *regressor* in place of w. That is, IV estimation of equation (21.61) is *not* the same as the OLS estimator from

$$y_i \quad \text{on} \quad 1, \hat{G}_i, \mathbf{x}_i \tag{21.63}$$

Consistency of the OLS estimators from regression (21.63) relies on having the model for $\mathrm{P}(w = 1 \mid \mathbf{x}, \mathbf{z})$ correctly specified. If the first three parts of Assumption ATEIV.1′ hold, then

$$\mathrm{E}(y \mid \mathbf{x}, \mathbf{z}) = \delta_0 + \tau G(\mathbf{x}, \mathbf{z}; \gamma) + \mathbf{x}\boldsymbol{\beta},$$

and, from the results on generated regressors in Chapter 6, the estimators from regression (21.63) are generally consistent. But Procedure 21.1 is more robust because it does not require Assumption ATEIV.1′c for consistency.

A different way to see the robustness of the IV approach compared with the regression approach is to think about the underlying first-stage regression in the population, which is the linear projection of w on $[1, G(\mathbf{x}, \mathbf{z}; \gamma^*), \mathbf{x}]$; write this as $\eta_0 + \eta_1 G(\mathbf{x}, \mathbf{z}; \gamma^*) + \mathbf{x}\boldsymbol{\eta}_2$. The IV estimator is consistent for any values of the etas provided $\eta_1 \neq 0$ because we simply need an exogenous variable that moves around w that is not perfectly correlated with $\mathbf{x}$. By contrast, consistency of the two-step regression estimator for τ requires $\eta_1 = 1$. If $\mathrm{P}(w = 1 \mid \mathbf{x}, \mathbf{z}) = G(\mathbf{x}, \mathbf{z}; \gamma^*)$, then $\eta_0 = 0$, $\eta_1 = 1$, and $\boldsymbol{\eta}_2 = \mathbf{0}$, and so the linear projection of y on $[1, G(\mathbf{x}, \mathbf{z}; \gamma^*), \mathbf{x}]$ is $\delta_0 + \tau G(\mathbf{x}, \mathbf{z}; \gamma^*) + \mathbf{x}\boldsymbol{\beta}$; thus, regression (21.63) consistently estimates all parameters. But if $G(\mathbf{x}, \mathbf{z}; \gamma)$ is misspecified η_1 can differ from unity (and $\boldsymbol{\eta}_2 \neq \mathbf{0}$). Generally, the regression (21.63) consistently estimates $\delta_0 + \tau\eta_0$, $\tau\eta_1$, and $\boldsymbol{\beta} + \tau\boldsymbol{\eta}_2$ as the intercept, coefficient on $\hat{G}_i$, and coefficients on $\mathbf{x}_i$, respectively.

Another problem with regression (21.63) is that the usual OLS standard errors and test statistics are not valid, for two reasons. First, if $\mathrm{Var}(u_0 \mid \mathbf{x}, \mathbf{z})$ is constant, $\mathrm{Var}(y \mid \mathbf{x}, \mathbf{z})$ cannot be constant because $\mathrm{Var}(w \mid \mathbf{x}, \mathbf{z})$ is not constant. By itself this is a minor nuisance because heteroskedasticity-robust standard errors and test statistics are easy to obtain. (However, it does call into question the efficiency of the estimator from regression (21.63).) A more serious problem is that the asymptotic variance of the estimator from regression (21.63) depends on the asymptotic variance of $\hat{\gamma}$ unless $\alpha = 0$, and the heteroskedasticity-robust standard errors do not correct for this.

In summary, using fitted probabilities from a first-stage binary response model, such as probit or logit, as an instrument for w is a nice way to exploit the binary nature of the endogenous explanatory variable. In addition, the asymptotic inference is always standard. Using $\hat{G}_i$ as an instrument does require the assumption that $\mathrm{E}(v_0 \mid \mathbf{x}, \mathbf{z})$ depends only on $\mathbf{x}$ and is linear in $\mathbf{x}$, which can be more restrictive than Assumption ATEIV.1′b.

Allowing for the interaction $w(v_1 - v_0)$ in equation (21.60) is notably harder. In general, when $v_1 \neq v_0$, the IV estimator (using $\mathbf{z}$ or $\hat{G}$ as IVs for w) does not consistently estimate τ_{ate} (or τ_{att}). Nevertheless, it is useful to find assumptions under which IV estimation does consistently estimate *ATE*. This problem has been studied by Angrist (1991), Heckman (1997), and Wooldridge (1997b, 2003b), and we synthesize results from these papers.

Under the conditional mean redundancy assumptions

$$\mathrm{E}(v_0 \mid \mathbf{x}, \mathbf{z}) = \mathrm{E}(v_0 \mid \mathbf{x}) \qquad \text{and} \qquad \mathrm{E}(v_1 \mid \mathbf{x}, \mathbf{z}) = \mathrm{E}(v_1 \mid \mathbf{x}), \tag{21.64}$$

we can always write equation (21.60) as

$$y = \mu_0 + \tau w + g_0(\mathbf{x}) + w[g_1(\mathbf{x}) - g_0(\mathbf{x})] + e_0 + w(e_1 - e_0), \tag{21.65}$$

where $\tau = \tau_{ate}$ and

$$v_0 = g_0(\mathbf{x}) + e_0, \qquad \mathrm{E}(e_0 \mid \mathbf{x}, \mathbf{z}) = 0, \tag{21.66}$$

$$v_1 = g_1(\mathbf{x}) + e_1, \qquad \mathrm{E}(e_1 \mid \mathbf{x}, \mathbf{z}) = 0. \tag{21.67}$$

Given functional form assumptions for g_0 and g_1—which would typically be linear in parameters—we can estimate equation (21.65) by IV, where the error term is $e_0 + w(e_1 - e_0)$. For concreteness, suppose that

$$g_0(\mathbf{x}) = \eta_0 + \mathbf{x}\boldsymbol{\beta}_0, \qquad g_1(\mathbf{x}) - g_0(\mathbf{x}) = (\mathbf{x} - \boldsymbol{\psi})\boldsymbol{\delta}, \tag{21.68}$$

where $\boldsymbol{\psi} = \mathrm{E}(\mathbf{x})$. If we plug these equations into equation (21.65), we need instruments for w *and* $w(\mathbf{x} - \boldsymbol{\psi})$ (note that $\mathbf{x}$ does not contain a constant here). If $q \equiv q(\mathbf{x}, \mathbf{z})$ is the instrument for w (such as the response probability in Procedure 21.1), the natural instrument for $w \cdot \mathbf{x}$ is $q \cdot \mathbf{x}$. (And, if q is the efficient IV for w, $q \cdot \mathbf{x}$ is the efficient instrument for $w \cdot \mathbf{x}$.) When will applying IV to

$$y = \gamma + \tau w + \mathbf{x}\boldsymbol{\beta}_0 + w(\mathbf{x} - \boldsymbol{\psi})\boldsymbol{\delta} + e_0 + w(e_1 - e_0) \tag{21.69}$$

be consistent? If the last term disappears, and, in particular, if

$$e_1 = e_0, \tag{21.70}$$

then the error e_0 has zero mean given $(\mathbf{x}, \mathbf{z})$; this result means that IV estimation of equation (21.69) produces consistent, asymptotically normal estimators.

ASSUMPTION ATEIV.2: With y expressed as in equation (21.60), conditions (21.64), (21.65), and (21.70) hold. In addition, Assumption ATEIV.1′c holds.

We have the following extension of Procedure 21.1:

Procedure 21.2 (Under Assumption ATEIV.2): (a) Same as Procedure 21.1.
(b) Estimate the equation

$$y_i = \gamma + \tau w_i + \mathbf{x}_i \boldsymbol{\beta}_0 + [w_i(\mathbf{x}_i - \overline{\mathbf{x}})]\boldsymbol{\delta} + error_i \tag{21.71}$$

by IV, using instruments 1, $\hat{G}_i$, $\mathbf{x}_i$, and $\hat{G}_i(\mathbf{x}_i - \overline{\mathbf{x}})$.

If we add Assumption ATEIV.1′d, Procedure 21.2 produces the efficient IV estimator (when we ignore estimation of $\mathrm{E}(\mathbf{x})$). As with Procedure 21.1, we do not actually need the binary response model to be correctly specified for identification. As an alternative, we can use $\mathbf{z}_i$ and interactions between $\mathbf{z}_i$ and $\mathbf{x}_i$ as instruments, which generally results in testable overidentifying restrictions.

Technically, the fact that $\overline{\mathbf{x}}$ is an estimator of $\mathrm{E}(\mathbf{x})$ should be accounted for in computing the standard errors of the IV estimators. But, as shown in Problem 6.10, the adjustments for estimating $\mathrm{E}(\mathbf{x})$ often will have a trivial effect on the standard errors; in practice, we can just use the usual or heteroskedasticity-robust standard errors. Alternatively, we can apply the bootstrap.

Example 21.4 (An IV Approach to Evaluating Job Training): To evaluate the effects of a job training program on subsequent wages, suppose that $\mathbf{x}$ includes education, experience, and the square of experience. If z indicates eligibility in the program, we would estimate the equation

$$\begin{aligned}\log(wage) = {} & \mu_0 + \tau\, jobtrain + \beta_{01} educ + \beta_{02} exper + \beta_{03} exper^2 \\ & + \delta_1 jobtrain \cdot (educ - \overline{educ}) + \delta_2 jobtrain \cdot (exper - \overline{exper}) \\ & + \delta_3 jobtrain \cdot (exper^2 - \overline{exper^2}) + error\end{aligned}$$

by IV, using instruments 1, z, $educ$, $exper$, $exper^2$, and interactions of z with all demeaned covariates. Notice that for the last interaction, we subtract off the average of $exper^2$. Alternatively, we could use in place of z the fitted values from a probit of $jobtrain$ on $(\mathbf{x}, z)$.

Procedure 21.2 is easy to carry out, but its consistency generally hinges on condition (21.70), not to mention the functional form assumptions in equation (21.68). We can relax condition (21.70) to

$$\mathrm{E}[w(e_1 - e_0) \mid \mathbf{x}, \mathbf{z}] = \mathrm{E}[w(e_1 - e_0)] \tag{21.72}$$

We do *not* need $w(e_1 - e_0)$ to have zero mean, as a nonzero mean only affects the intercept. It is important to see that correlation between w and $(e_1 - e_0)$ does *not* invalidate the IV estimator of τ from Procedure 21.2. However, we must assume that the covariance conditional on $(\mathbf{x}, \mathbf{z})$ is constant. Even if this assumption is not exactly true, it might be approximately true.

It is easy to see why, along with conditions (21.64) and (21.68), condition (21.72) implies consistency of the IV estimator. We can write equation (21.69) as

$$y = \xi + \tau w + \mathbf{x}\boldsymbol{\beta}_0 + w(\mathbf{x} - \boldsymbol{\psi})\boldsymbol{\delta} + e_0 + r, \tag{21.73}$$

where $r = w(e_1 - e_0) - \mathrm{E}[w(e_1 - e_0)]$ and $\xi = \gamma + \mathrm{E}[w(e_1 - e_0)]$. Under condition (21.72), $\mathrm{E}(r \mid \mathbf{x}, \mathbf{z}) = 0$, and so the composite error $e_0 + r$ has zero mean conditional on $(\mathbf{x}, \mathbf{z})$. Therefore, any function of $(\mathbf{x}, \mathbf{z})$ can be used as instruments in equation (21.73). Under the following modification of Assumption ATEIV.2, Procedure 21.2 is still consistent:

ASSUMPTION ATEIV.2′: With y expressed as in equation (21.60), conditions (21.64), (21.68), and (21.72) hold. In addition, Assumption ATEIV.1′c holds.

Even if Assumption ATEIV.1′d holds in addition to Assumption ATEIV.1′c, the IV estimator is generally not efficient because $\mathrm{Var}(r \mid \mathbf{x}, \mathbf{z})$ would typically be heteroskedastic.

Angrist (1991) provided primitive conditions for assumption (21.72) in the case where $\mathbf{z}$ is independent of $(y_0, y_1, \mathbf{x})$. Then, the covariates can be dropped entirely from the analysis (leading to IV estimation of the simple regression equation $y = \xi + \tau w + error$). We can extend those conditions here to allow $\mathbf{z}$ and $\mathbf{x}$ to be correlated. Assume that

$$\mathrm{E}(w \mid \mathbf{x}, \mathbf{z}, e_1 - e_0) = h(\mathbf{x}, \mathbf{z}) + k(e_1 - e_0) \tag{21.74}$$

for some functions $h(\cdot)$ and $k(\cdot)$ and that

$$e_1 - e_0 \text{ is independent of } (\mathbf{x}, \mathbf{z}). \tag{21.75}$$

Under these two assumptions,

$$\begin{aligned} \mathrm{E}[w(e_1 - e_0) \mid \mathbf{x}, \mathbf{z}] &= h(\mathbf{x}, \mathbf{z})\mathrm{E}(e_1 - e_0 \mid \mathbf{x}, \mathbf{z}) + \mathrm{E}[(e_1 - e_0)k(e_1 - e_0) \mid \mathbf{x}, \mathbf{z}] \\ &= h(\mathbf{x}, \mathbf{z}) \cdot 0 + \mathrm{E}[(e_1 - e_0)k(e_1 - e_0)] \\ &= \mathrm{E}[(e_1 - e_0)k(e_1 - e_0)], \end{aligned} \tag{21.76}$$

which is just an unconditional moment in the distribution of $e_1 - e_0$. We have used the fact that $\mathrm{E}(e_1 - e_0 \mid \mathbf{x}, \mathbf{z}) = 0$ and that any function of $e_1 - e_0$ is independent of $(\mathbf{x}, \mathbf{z})$ under assumption (21.75). If we assume that $k(\cdot)$ is the identity function (as in Wooldridge, 1997b), then equation (21.76) is $\mathrm{Var}(e_1 - e_0)$.

Assumption (21.75) is reasonable for continuously distributed responses, but it would not generally be reasonable when y is a discrete response or corner solution outcome. Further, even if assumption (21.75) holds, assumption (21.74) is violated when w given $\mathbf{x}$, $\mathbf{z}$, and $(e_1 - e_0)$ follows a standard binary response model. For example, a probit model would have

$$\mathrm{P}(w = 1 \mid \mathbf{x}, \mathbf{z}, e_1 - e_0) = \Phi[\pi_0 + \mathbf{x}\boldsymbol{\pi}_1 + \mathbf{z}\boldsymbol{\pi}_2 + \rho(e_1 - e_0)], \tag{21.77}$$

which is not separable in $(\mathbf{x}, \mathbf{z})$ and $(e_1 - e_0)$. Nevertheless, assumption (21.74) might be a reasonable approximation in some cases. Without covariates, Angrist (1991) presents simulation evidence that suggests the simple IV estimator does quite well for estimating the ATE even when assumption (21.74) is violated.

21.4.2 Correction and Control Function Approaches

Rather than assuming that the presence of $w(e_1 - e_0)$ in the error term does not cause inconsistency for IV estimators, we can use functional form and distributional assumptions to directly account for this term. The first approach we consider, proposed by Wooldridge (2008), involves adding a **correction function**, which is a function of the exogenous variables $(\mathbf{x}, \mathbf{z})$, to equation (21.73), and then applying instrumental variables to account for the endogeneity of w and $w(\mathbf{x} - \boldsymbol{\psi})$. To derive the correction function, we add to assumptions (21.75) and (21.77) a normality assumption. Let $c \equiv e_1 - e_0$ and assume

$$c \sim \mathrm{Normal}(0, \omega^2) \tag{21.78}$$

Under assumptions (21.75), (21.77), and (21.78) we can derive an estimating equation to show that τ_{ate} is usually identified.

To derive an estimating equation, note that conditions (21.75), (21.77), and (21.78) imply that

$$\mathrm{P}(w = 1 \mid \mathbf{x}, \mathbf{z}) = \Phi(\theta_0 + \mathbf{x}\boldsymbol{\theta}_1 + \mathbf{z}\boldsymbol{\theta}_2), \tag{21.79}$$

where each theta is the corresponding pi multiplied by $[1 + \rho^2\omega^2]^{-1/2}$. If we let a denote the latent error underlying equation (21.79) (with a standard normal distribution), then conditions (21.75), (21.77), and (21.78) imply that (a, c) has a zero-mean bivariate normal distribution that is independent of $(\mathbf{x}, \mathbf{z})$. Therefore, $\mathrm{E}(c \mid a, \mathbf{x}, \mathbf{z}) = \mathrm{E}(c \mid a) = \xi a$ for some parameter ξ, and

$$\mathrm{E}(wc \mid \mathbf{x}, \mathbf{z}) = \mathrm{E}[w\mathrm{E}(c \mid a, \mathbf{x}, \mathbf{z}) \mid \mathbf{x}, \mathbf{z}] = \xi \mathrm{E}(wa \mid \mathbf{x}, \mathbf{z}).$$

Using the fact that $a \sim \text{Normal}(0, 1)$ and is independent of $(\mathbf{x}, \mathbf{z})$, we have

$$\mathrm{E}(wa \mid \mathbf{x}, \mathbf{z}) = \int_{-\infty}^{\infty} 1[\theta_0 + \mathbf{x}\boldsymbol{\theta}_1 + \mathbf{z}\boldsymbol{\theta}_2 + a \geq 0] a\phi(a) \, \mathrm{d}a$$

$$= \phi(-\{\theta_0 + \mathbf{x}\boldsymbol{\theta}_1 + \mathbf{z}\boldsymbol{\theta}_2\}) = \phi(\theta_0 + \mathbf{x}\boldsymbol{\theta}_1 + \mathbf{z}\boldsymbol{\theta}_2), \tag{21.80}$$

where $\phi(\cdot)$ is the standard normal density. Therefore, we can now write

$$y = \gamma + \tau w + \mathbf{x}\boldsymbol{\beta} + w(\mathbf{x} - \boldsymbol{\psi})\boldsymbol{\delta} + \xi\phi(\theta_0 + \mathbf{x}\boldsymbol{\theta}_1 + \mathbf{z}\boldsymbol{\theta}_2) + e_0 + r, \tag{21.81}$$

where $r = wc - \mathrm{E}(wc \mid \mathbf{x}, \mathbf{z})$. The composite error in equation (21.81) has zero mean conditional on $(\mathbf{x}, \mathbf{z})$, and so we can estimate the parameters using IV methods. One catch is the nonlinear function $\phi(\theta_0 + \mathbf{x}\boldsymbol{\theta}_1 + \mathbf{z}\boldsymbol{\theta}_2)$. We could use nonlinear two-stage least squares, as described in Chapter 14. But a two-step approach is easier. First, we gather together the assumptions:

ASSUMPTION ATEIV.3: With y written as in equation (21.70), maintain assumptions (21.64), (21.68), (21.75), (21.77), (with $\boldsymbol{\pi}_2 \neq \mathbf{0}$), and (21.78).

Procedure 21.3 (Under Assumption ATEIV.3): (a) Estimate θ_0, $\boldsymbol{\theta}_1$, and $\boldsymbol{\theta}_2$ from a probit of w on $(1, \mathbf{x}, \mathbf{z})$. Form the predicted probabilities, $\hat{\Phi}_i$, along with $\hat{\phi}_i = \phi(\hat{\theta}_0 + \mathbf{x}_i\hat{\boldsymbol{\theta}}_1 + \mathbf{z}_i\hat{\boldsymbol{\theta}}_2)$, $i = 1, 2, \ldots, N$.

(b) Estimate the equation

$$y_i = \gamma + \tau w_i + \mathbf{x}_i\boldsymbol{\beta}_0 + w_i(\mathbf{x}_i - \bar{\mathbf{x}})\boldsymbol{\delta} + \xi\hat{\phi}_i + error_i \tag{21.82}$$

by IV, using instruments $[1, \hat{\Phi}_i, \mathbf{x}_i, \hat{\Phi}_i(\mathbf{x}_i - \bar{\mathbf{x}}), \hat{\phi}_i]$.

Wooldridge (2008) calls the extra term $\hat{\phi}_i \equiv \phi(\hat{\theta}_0 + \mathbf{x}_i\hat{\boldsymbol{\theta}}_1 + \mathbf{z}_i\hat{\boldsymbol{\theta}}_2)$ a "correction function" to distinguish it from the more common "control function," which we turn to shortly. Unlike with the control function approach, adding $\phi(\theta_0 + \mathbf{x}_i\boldsymbol{\theta}_1 + \mathbf{z}_i\boldsymbol{\theta}_2)$ does not render w or $w(\mathbf{x} - \boldsymbol{\psi})$ exogenous in equation (21.81). Rather, it ensures that the composite error, $e_0 + r$, is mean independent of $(\mathbf{x}, \mathbf{z})$ when $w(e_1 - e_0)$ is present and not assumed independent of $(\mathbf{x}, \mathbf{z})$. Conveniently, IV estimation of equation (21.82) leads to a simple test of H_0: $\xi = 0$. Under the null, the coefficient on the generated regressor, $\hat{\phi}_i$ is zero. Further, that the IVs are estimated in a first stage does not affect the $\sqrt{N}$-asymptotic distribution of the IV estimators; see Section 6.1.3. Therefore, if we ignore the estimation error in $\bar{\mathbf{x}}$, we can use a standard heteroskedasticity-robust t statistic on $\hat{\phi}_i$ to test whether the correction function is needed. (Note that $r = wc - \mathrm{E}(wc \mid \mathbf{x}, \mathbf{z})$ can be homoskedastic under the null but there is never any harm in making the test robust to heteroskedasticity.) Notice that the only place we used normality of (c, a) is in deriving the correction function. Because $\xi = 0$ under the null, this normality assumption is not needed for the test. (Remember, our use of probit-fitted values as instruments for w does not hinge on the probit model for w being true; it motivates the choice of IVs, but the probit model can be arbitrarily misspecified.)

If we allow the possibility that $\xi \neq 0$, all standard errors need to be adjusted for the two-step estimation. One can use the delta method or express the two-step estimation as a generalized method of moments problem as in Chapter 14. (Either approach can ignore or account for sampling error in $\bar{\mathbf{x}}$.) Because the two-step estimation is computationally simple, the bootstrap is attractive as a way to account for all sampling error in $\hat{\tau}$.

Even if $\xi \neq 0$, adding the correction function $\hat{\phi}_i$ to the equation need not have much effect on the estimate of τ. To see why, consider the version of equation (21.81) when we have no covariates $\mathbf{x}$ and with a scalar IV, z:

$$y = \gamma + \tau w + \xi\phi(\theta_0 + \theta_1 z) + u, \qquad \mathrm{E}(u \mid z) = 0 \tag{21.83}$$

This equation holds, for example, if the instrument z is independent of (v_0, v_1). The simple IV estimator of τ is obtained by omitting $\phi(\theta_0 + \theta_1 z)$. If we use z as an IV for w, the simple IV estimator is consistent provided z and $\phi(\theta_0 + \theta_1 z)$ are uncorrelated. (Remember, having an omitted variable that is uncorrelated with the IV does not cause inconsistency of the IV estimator.) Even though $\phi(\theta_0 + \theta_1 z)$ is a function of z, these two variables might have small correlation because z is monotonic while $\phi(\theta_0 + \theta_1 z)$ is symmetric about $-(\theta_0/\theta_1)$. This discussion shows that condition (21.72) is not necessary for IV to consistently estimate the ATE: It could be that while $\mathrm{E}[w(e_1 - e_0) \mid \mathbf{x}, \mathbf{z}]$ is not constant, it is roughly uncorrelated with $\mathbf{x}$ (or the functions of $\mathbf{x}$) that appear in equation (21.73), as well as with the functions of $\mathbf{z}$ used as instruments.

Equation (21.83) illustrates another important point: If $\xi \neq 0$ and the single instrument z is binary, τ is not identified. Lack of identification occurs because $\phi(\theta_0 + \theta_1 z)$ takes on only two values, which means it is perfectly linearly related to z. So long as z takes on more than two values, τ is generally identified, although the identification is due to the fact that $\phi(\cdot)$ is a different nonlinear function than $\Phi(\cdot)$. With $\mathbf{x}$ in the model $\hat{\phi}_i$ and $\hat{\Phi}_i$ might be collinear, resulting in imprecise IV estimates.

Because r in equation (21.81) is heteroskedastic, the instruments below equation (21.82) are not optimal, and so we might simply use $\mathbf{z}_i$ along with interactions of $\mathbf{z}_i$ with $(\mathbf{x}_i - \bar{\mathbf{x}})$ and $\hat{\phi}_i$ as IVs. If $\mathbf{z}_i$ has dimension greater than one, then we can test the overidentifying restrictions as a partial test of instrument selection and the normality assumptions. Of course, we could use the results of Chapter 14 to characterize and estimate the optimal instruments, but this approach is fairly involved [see, for example, Newey and McFadden (1994)].

We can use a similar set of assumptions to derive a control function (CF) approach for estimating $\tau = \tau_{ate}$. Recall that the CF approach involves finding $\mathrm{E}(y \mid w, \mathbf{x}, \mathbf{z})$ and then using regression methods. (Or, a maximum likelihood approach is often available under a stronger set of assumptions.) Typically, the CF approach is derived in the context of the **endogenous switching regression** model, but it is easily seen that the treatment effect model with heterogeneous treatment, where the treatment is correlated with unobservables even after conditioning on observables, fits that bill when the treatment is defined to be the binary switching variable. In particular, equation (21.69) results by writing $y = (1 - w)y_0 + wy_1$ and imposing the linear, additive structures on y_0 and y_1:

$$\begin{aligned} y &= (1 - w)(\alpha_0 + \mathbf{x}\boldsymbol{\beta}_0 + e_0) + w(\alpha_1 + \mathbf{x}\boldsymbol{\beta}_1 + e_1) \\ &= \alpha_0 + \mathbf{x}\boldsymbol{\beta}_0 + (\alpha_1 - \alpha_0)w + w\mathbf{x}(\boldsymbol{\beta}_1 - \boldsymbol{\beta}_0) + e_0 + w(e_1 - e_0) \\ &\equiv \gamma + \mathbf{x}\boldsymbol{\beta}_0 + \tau w + w(\mathbf{x} - \boldsymbol{\psi})\boldsymbol{\delta} + e_0 + wc, \end{aligned}$$

where $\tau = \tau_{ate} = \mathrm{E}(y_1 - y_0)$ and $\boldsymbol{\psi} = \mathrm{E}(\mathbf{x})$. This particular way of expressing y in terms of the treatment, covariates, and unobservables emphasizes that we are primarily interested in τ, although $\tau_{ate}(\mathbf{x}) = \tau + (\mathbf{x} - \boldsymbol{\psi})\boldsymbol{\delta}$ is of interest for studying how the average treatment effect changes as a function of observables.

We can derive a control function method under the following assumption.

ASSUMPTION ATEIV.4: With y written as in equation (21.70), maintain assumptions (21.64) and (21.68). Furthermore, the treatment can be written as $w = 1[\theta_0 + \mathbf{x}\boldsymbol{\theta}_1 + \mathbf{z}\boldsymbol{\theta}_2 + a \geq 0]$, where (a, e_0, e_1) is independent of $(\mathbf{x}, \mathbf{z})$ with a trivariate normal distribution; in particular, $a \sim \mathrm{Normal}(0, 1)$.

Under Assumption ATEIV.4, we can use calculations very similar to those used in Section 19.6.1 to obtain $\mathrm{E}(y \mid w, \mathbf{x}, \mathbf{z})$. In particular,

$$\begin{aligned} \mathrm{E}(y \mid w, \mathbf{x}, \mathbf{z}) = {} & \gamma + \alpha w + \mathbf{x}\boldsymbol{\beta}_0 + w(\mathbf{x} - \boldsymbol{\psi})\boldsymbol{\delta} + \rho_1 w[\phi(\mathbf{q}\boldsymbol{\theta})/\Phi(\mathbf{q}\boldsymbol{\theta})] \\ & + \rho_2(1 - w)\{\phi(\mathbf{q}\boldsymbol{\theta})/[1 - \Phi(\mathbf{q}\boldsymbol{\theta})]\} \end{aligned} \tag{21.84}$$

where $\mathbf{q}\boldsymbol{\theta} \equiv \theta_0 + \mathbf{x}\boldsymbol{\theta}_1 + \mathbf{z}\boldsymbol{\theta}_2$ and ρ_1 and ρ_2 are additional parameters. Heckman (1978) used this expectation to obtain two-step estimators of the switching regression model. (See Vella and Verbeek (1999) for a recent discussion of the switching regression model in the context of treatment effects.) Not surprisingly, equation (21.84) suggests a simple two-step procedure, where the first step is identical to that in Procedure 21.3:

Procedure 21.4 (Under Assumption ATEIV.4): (a) Estimate θ_0, $\boldsymbol{\theta}_1$, and $\boldsymbol{\theta}_2$ from a probit of w on $(1, \mathbf{x}, \mathbf{z})$. Form the predicted probabilities, $\hat{\Phi}_i$, along with $\hat{\phi}_i = \phi(\hat{\theta}_0 + \mathbf{x}_i\hat{\boldsymbol{\theta}}_1 + \mathbf{z}_i\hat{\boldsymbol{\theta}}_2)$, $i = 1, 2, \ldots, N$.

(b) Run the OLS regression

$$y_i \text{ on } 1, w_i, \mathbf{x}_i, w_i(\mathbf{x}_i - \bar{\mathbf{x}}), w_i(\hat{\phi}_i/\hat{\Phi}_i), (1 - w_i)[\hat{\phi}_i/(1 - \hat{\Phi}_i)] \tag{21.85}$$

using all of the observations. The coefficient on w_i is a consistent estimator of α, the ATE.

When we restrict attention to the $w_i = 1$ subsample, thereby dropping w_i and $w_i(\mathbf{x}_i - \bar{\mathbf{x}})$, we obtain the sample selection correction from Section 19.6.1. (The treatment w_i becomes the sample selection indicator.) But the goal of sample selection corrections is very different from estimating an average treatment effect. For the sample selection problem, the goal is to estimate $\boldsymbol{\beta}_0$, which indexes $\mathrm{E}(y \mid \mathbf{x})$ in the population. By contrast, in estimating an ATE we are interested in the causal effect that w has on y.

It makes sense to check for joint significance of the last two regressors in regression (21.85) as a test of endogeneity of w. Because the coefficients ρ_1 and ρ_2 are zero under H_0, we can use the results from Chapter 6 to justify the usual Wald test (perhaps made robust to heteroskedasticity). If these terms are jointly insignificant at a sufficiently high level, we can justify the usual OLS regression without unobserved heterogeneity. If we reject H_0, we must deal with the generated regressors problem in obtaining a valid standard error for $\hat{\alpha}$.

Technically, Procedure 21.3 is more robust than Procedure 21.4 because the former does not require a trivariate normality assumption. Linear conditional expectations, along with the assumption that w given $(\mathbf{x}, \mathbf{z})$ follows a probit, suffice. In addition, Procedure 21.3 allows us to separate the issues of endogeneity of w and nonconstant treatment effect.

Practically, the extra assumption in Procedure 21.4 is that e_0 is independent of $(\mathbf{x}, \mathbf{z})$ with a normal distribution. We may be willing to make this assumption, especially if the estimates from Procedure 21.3 are too imprecise to be useful. The efficiency issue is a difficult one because of the two-step estimation involved, but, intuitively, Procedure 21.4 is likely to be more efficient because it is based on $\mathrm{E}(y \mid w, \mathbf{x}, \mathbf{z})$. Procedure 21.3 involves replacing the unobserved composite error with its expectation conditional only on $(\mathbf{x}, \mathbf{z})$. In at least one case, Procedure 21.4 gives results when

Procedure 21.3 cannot: when $\mathbf{x}$ is not in the equation and there is a single binary instrument.

So far we have focused on estimating τ_{ate}. Under a variant of Assumption ATEIV.2, we can consistently estimate τ_{att} by IV. As before, we express y as in equation (21.60). First, we show how to consistently estimate $\tau_{att}(\mathbf{x})$, which can be written as

$$\tau_{att}(\mathbf{x}) = \mathrm{E}(y_1 - y_0 \mid \mathbf{x}, w = 1) = (\mu_1 - \mu_0) + \mathrm{E}(v_1 - v_0 \mid \mathbf{x}, w = 1).$$

The following assumption identifies $\tau_{att}(\mathbf{x})$:

ASSUMPTION ATTIV.1: (a) With y expressed as in equation (21.60), the first part of assumption (21.64) holds, that is, $\mathrm{E}(v_0 \mid \mathbf{x}, \mathbf{z}) = \mathrm{E}(v_0 \mid \mathbf{x})$; (b) $\mathrm{E}(v_1 - v_0 \mid \mathbf{x}, \mathbf{z}, w = 1) = \mathrm{E}(v_1 - v_0 \mid \mathbf{x}, w = 1)$; and (c) Assumption ATEIV.1′c holds.

We discussed part a of this assumption earlier, as it also appears in Assumption ATEIV.2′. It can be violated if agents change their behavior based on $\mathbf{z}$. Part b deserves some discussion. Recall that $v_1 - v_0$ is the person-specific gain from participation or treatment. Assumption ATTIV.1 requires that for those in the treatment group, the gain is not predictable given $\mathbf{z}$, once $\mathbf{x}$ is controlled for. Heckman (1997) discusses Angrist's (1990) draft lottery example, where z (a scalar) is draft lottery number. Men who had a large z were virtually certain to escape the draft. But some men with large draft numbers chose to serve anyway. Even with good controls in $\mathbf{x}$, it seems plausible that, for those who chose to serve, a higher z is associated with a higher gain to military service. In other words, for those who chose to serve, $v_1 - v_0$ and z are positively correlated, even after controlling for $\mathbf{x}$. This argument directly applies to estimation of τ_{att}; the effect on estimation of τ_{ate} is less clear.

Assumption ATTIV.1b is plausible when z is a binary indicator for eligibility in a program, which is randomly determined and does not induce changes in behavior other than whether or not to participate.

To see how Assumption ATTIV.1 identifies $\tau_{att}(\mathbf{x})$, rewrite equation (21.60) as

$$\begin{aligned} y &= \mu_0 + g_0(\mathbf{x}) + w[(\mu_1 - \mu_0) + \mathrm{E}(v_1 - v_0 \mid \mathbf{x}, w = 1)] \\ &\quad + w[(v_1 - v_0) - \mathrm{E}(v_1 - v_0 \mid \mathbf{x}, w = 1)] + e_0 \\ &= \mu_0 + g_0(\mathbf{x}) + w \cdot \tau_{att}(\mathbf{x}) + a + e_0, \end{aligned} \tag{21.86}$$

where $a \equiv w[(v_1 - v_0) - \mathrm{E}(v_1 - v_0 \mid \mathbf{x}, w = 1)]$ and e_0 is defined in equation (21.66). Under Assumption ATTIV.1a, $\mathrm{E}(e_0 \mid \mathbf{x}, \mathbf{z}) = 0$. The hard part is dealing with the term a. When $w = 0$, $a = 0$. Therefore, to show that $\mathrm{E}(a \mid \mathbf{x}, \mathbf{z}) = 0$, it suffices to show that $\mathrm{E}(a \mid \mathbf{x}, \mathbf{z}, w = 1) = 0$. (Remember, $\mathrm{E}(a \mid \mathbf{x}, \mathbf{z}) = \mathrm{P}(w = 0) \cdot \mathrm{E}(a \mid \mathbf{x}, \mathbf{z}, w = 0) + \mathrm{P}(w = 1) \cdot \mathrm{E}(a \mid \mathbf{x}, \mathbf{z}, w = 1)$.) But this result follows under Assumption ATTIV.1b:

$$\mathrm{E}(a \mid \mathbf{x}, \mathbf{z}, w = 1) = \mathrm{E}(v_1 - v_0 \mid \mathbf{x}, \mathbf{z}, w = 1) - \mathrm{E}(v_1 - v_0 \mid \mathbf{x}, w = 1) = 0.$$

Now, letting $r \equiv a + e_0$ and assuming that $g_0(\mathbf{x}) = \eta_0 + \mathbf{h}(\mathbf{x})\boldsymbol{\beta}_0$ and $\tau_{att}(\mathbf{x}) = \alpha + \mathbf{f}(\mathbf{x})\boldsymbol{\delta}$ for some row vector of functions $\mathbf{h}(\mathbf{x})$ and $\mathbf{f}(\mathbf{x})$, we can write

$$y = \gamma_0 + \mathbf{h}_0(\mathbf{x})\boldsymbol{\beta}_0 + \alpha w + [w \cdot \mathbf{f}(\mathbf{x})]\boldsymbol{\delta} + r, \qquad \mathrm{E}(r \mid \mathbf{x}, \mathbf{z}) = 0.$$

All the parameters of this equation can be consistently estimated by IV, using any functions of $(\mathbf{x}, \mathbf{z})$ as IVs. (These would include include 1, $\mathbf{h}_0(\mathbf{x})$, $G(\mathbf{x}, \mathbf{z}; \hat{\gamma})$—the fitted treatment probabilities—and $G(\mathbf{x}, \mathbf{z}; \hat{\gamma}) \cdot \mathbf{f}(\mathbf{x})$.) The average treatment effect on the treated for any $\mathbf{x}$ is estimated as $\hat{\alpha} + \mathbf{f}(\mathbf{x})\hat{\boldsymbol{\delta}}$. Averaging over the observations with $w_i = 1$ gives a consistent estimator of τ_{att}.

21.4.3 Estimating the Local Average Treatment Effect by IV

We now discuss estimation of an evaluation parameter introduced by Imbens and Angrist (1994), the local average treatment effect (LATE), in the simplest possible setting. This requires a slightly more complicated notation. (More general cases require even more complicated notation, as in AIR.) As before, we let w be the observed treatment indicator (taking on zero or one), and let the counterfactual outcomes be y_1 with treatment and y_0 without treatment. The observed outcome y can be written as in equation (21.3).

To define τ_{late}, we need to have an instrumental variable, z. In the simplest case z is a binary variable, and we focus attention on that case here. For each unit i in a random draw from the population, z_i is zero or one. Associated with the two possible outcomes on z are counterfactual treatments, w_0 and w_1. These are the treatment statuses we would observe if $z = 0$ and $z = 1$, respectively. For each unit, we observe only one of these. For example, z can denote whether a person is eligible for a particular program, while w denotes actual participation in the program.

Write the observed treatment status as

$$w = (1 - z)w_0 + zw_1 = w_0 + z(w_1 - w_0). \tag{21.87}$$

When we plug this equation into $y = y_0 + w(y_1 - y_0)$ we get

$$y = y_0 + w_0(y_1 - y_0) + z(w_1 - w_0)(y_1 - y_0).$$

A key assumption is

$$z \text{ is independent of } (y_0, y_1, w_0, w_1). \tag{21.88}$$

Under assumption (21.88), all expectations involving functions of (y_0, y_1, w_0, w_1), conditional on z, do not depend on z. Therefore,

$$E(y \mid z = 1) = E(y_0) + E[w_0(y_1 - y_0)] + E[(w_1 - w_0)(y_1 - y_0)],$$

and

$$E(y \mid z = 0) = E(y_0) + E[w_0(y_1 - y_0)].$$

Subtracting the second equation from the first gives

$$E(y \mid z = 1) - E(y \mid z = 0) = E[(w_1 - w_0)(y_1 - y_0)], \tag{21.89}$$

which can be written (see equation (2.49)) as

$$\begin{aligned} &1 \cdot E(y_1 - y_0 \mid w_1 - w_0 = 1)P(w_1 - w_0 = 1) \\ &\qquad + (-1)E(y_1 - y_0 \mid w_1 - w_0 = -1)P(w_1 - w_0 = -1) \\ &\qquad + 0 \cdot E(y_1 - y_0 \mid w_1 - w_0 = 0)P(w_1 - w_0 = 0) \\ &\quad = E(y_1 - y_0 \mid w_1 - w_0 = 1)P(w_1 - w_0 = 1) \\ &\qquad - E(y_1 - y_0 \mid w_1 - w_0 = -1)P(w_1 - w_0 = -1) \end{aligned}$$

To get further, we introduce another important assumption, called *monotonicity* by Imbens and Angrist:

$$w_1 \geq w_0. \tag{21.90}$$

In other words, we are ruling out $w_1 = 0$ and $w_0 = 1$. This assumption has a simple interpretation when z is a dummy variable representing eligibility for treatment: anyone in the population who would be in the treatment group in the absence of eligibility would be in the treatment group if eligible for treatment group. Units of the population who do not satisfy monotonicity are called *defiers*. In many applications, this assumption seems very reasonable. For example, if z denotes randomly assigned eligibility in a job training program, assumption (21.90) simply requires that people who would participate without being eligible would also participate if eligible.

Under assumption (21.90), $P(w_1 - w_0 = -1) = 0$, so assumptions (21.88) and (21.90) imply

$$E(y \mid z = 1) - E(y \mid z = 0) = E(y_1 - y_0 \mid w_1 - w_0 = 1)P(w_1 - w_0 = 1). \tag{21.91}$$

In this setup, Imbens and Angrist (1994) define τ_{late} to be

$$\tau_{late} = E(y_1 - y_0 \mid w_1 - w_0 = 1). \tag{21.92}$$

Because $w_1 - w_0 = 1$ is equivalent to $w_1 = 1$, $w_0 = 0$, τ_{late} has the following interpretation: it is the average treatment effect for those who would be induced to participate by changing z from zero to one. There are two things about τ_{late} that make it different from the other treatment parameters. First, it depends on the instrument, z. If we use a different instrument, then τ_{late} generally changes. The parameters τ_{ate} and τ_{att} are defined without reference to an IV, but only with reference to a population. Second, because we cannot observe both w_1 and w_0, we cannot identify the subpopulation with $w_1 - w_0 = 1$. By contrast, τ_{ate} averages over the entire population, while τ_{att} is the average for those who are actually treated.

Example 21.5 (LATE for Attending a Catholic High School): Suppose that y is a standardized test score, w is an indicator for attending a Catholic high school, and z is an indicator for whether the student is Catholic. Then, generally, τ_{late} is the mean effect on test scores for those individuals who choose a Catholic high school because they are Catholic. Evans and Schwab (1995) use a high school graduation indicator for y, and they estimate a probit model with an endogenous binary explanatory variable, as described in Section 15.7.3. Under the probit assumptions, it is possible to estimate τ_{ate}, whereas the simple IV estimator identifies τ_{late} under weaker assumptions.

Because $\mathrm{E}(y \mid z = 1)$ and $\mathrm{E}(y \mid z = 0)$ are easily estimated using a random sample, τ_{late} is identified if $\mathrm{P}(w_1 - w_0 = 1)$ is estimable *and* nonzero. Importantly, from the monotonicity assumption, $w_1 - w_0$ is a binary variable because $\mathrm{P}(w_1 - w_0 = -1) = 0$. Therefore,

$$\mathrm{P}(w_1 - w_0 = 1) = \mathrm{E}(w_1 - w_0) = \mathrm{E}(w_1) - \mathrm{E}(w_0) = \mathrm{E}(w \mid z = 1) - \mathrm{E}(w \mid z = 0)$$

$$= \mathrm{P}(w = 1 \mid z = 1) - \mathrm{P}(w = 1 \mid z = 0),$$

where the second-to-last equality follows from equations (21.87) and (21.88). Each conditional probability can be consistently estimated given a random sample on (w, z). Therefore, the final assumption is

$$\mathrm{P}(w = 1 \mid z = 1) \neq \mathrm{P}(w = 1 \mid z = 0). \tag{21.93}$$

To summarize, under assumptions (21.88), (21.90), and (21.93),

$$\tau_{late} = [\mathrm{E}(y \mid z = 1) - \mathrm{E}(y \mid z = 0)]/[\mathrm{P}(w = 1 \mid z = 1) - \mathrm{P}(w = 1 \mid z = 0)]. \tag{21.94}$$

Therefore, a consistent estimator is $\hat{\tau}_{late} = (\bar{y}_1 - \bar{y}_0)/(\bar{w}_1 - \bar{w}_0)$, where $\bar{y}_1$ is the sample average of y_i over that part of the sample where $z_i = 1$ and $\bar{y}_0$ is the sample average over $z_i = 0$, and similarly for $\bar{w}_1$ and $\bar{w}_0$ (which are sample proportions).

From Problem 5.13b, we know that $\hat{\tau}_{late}$ is identical to the IV estimator of τ in the simple equation $y = \delta_0 + \tau w + error$, where z is the IV for w.

Our conclusion is that, in the simple case of a binary instrument for the binary treatment, the usual IV estimator consistently estimates τ_{late} under weak assumptions. See Angrist, Imbens, and Rubin (1996) and the discussants' comments for much more, and Imbens and Wooldridge (2009) for a survey of extensions to the basic framework.

21.5 Regression Discontinuity Designs

We now turn to estimating treatment effects in a special situation where certain institutional or logical structures act to determine, or at least affect, treatment assignment. Regression discontinuity (RD) designs have a long history. Important work in bringing the methods into the mainstream in economics includes van der Klaauw (2002) and Hahn, Todd, and van der Klaauw (2001) (or HTV (2001)). Imbens and Lemieux (2008) provide a nice overview and survey of the subject, and this section draws on this work, as well as Imbens and Wooldridge (2009).

Generally, RD designs exploit discontinuities in policy assignment. For example, there might be an age threshold at which one becomes eligible for pension plan vesting, or an income threshold at which one becomes eligible for financial aid. To exploit discontinuities that are often determined by rather ad hoc institutional structures, one assumes that units just on different sides of the discontinuity are essentially the same in unobservables that affect the relevant outcome. The treatment statuses of the two groups differ, say, because of the institutional setup, in which case differences in outcomes can be attributed to the different treatment statuses.

We consider the sharp design RD—where assignment follows a deterministic rule—and the fuzzy design, where the probability of being treated is discontinuous at a known point.

21.5.1 The Sharp Regression Discontinuity Design

As before, let y_0 and y_1 denote the counterfactual outcomes without and with treatment. For a random draw i, these are denoted y_{i0}, y_{i1}. For now, assume there is a single covariate, x_i, determining treatment (sometimes called the *forcing variable*). In the **sharp regression discontinuity (SRD)** design case, treatment is determined as

$$w_i = 1[x_i \geq c]. \tag{21.95}$$

Along with the forcing variable x_i and treatment status w_i, we observe $y_i = (1 - w_i)y_{i0} + w_i y_{i1}$.

Define, as before, the counterfactual conditional means as $\mu_g(x) = \mathrm{E}(y_g \mid x)$, $g = 0, 1$. A critical assumption in RD designs is that these underlying mean functions are continuous. (Technically, they are continuous at $x = c$, but it is hard to imagine how we could ensure that they are without assuming continuity over the range of x.) Now, because w is a deterministic function of x, ignorability necessarily holds. Stated in terms of conditional means,

$$\mathrm{E}(y_g \mid x, w) = \mathrm{E}(y_g \mid x), \quad g = 0, 1,$$

which is exactly Assumption ATE.1′. So, if ignorability holds, why can we not just apply previous methods, such as propensity score weighting? The key is that with a sharp RD design, the overlap assumption fails absolutely: by construction, $p(x) = 0$ for all $x < c$ and $p(x) = 1$ for $x \geq c$. Clearly we cannot use a method such as propensity score weighting.

Technically, we can use regression adjustment, but we would have to rely on extreme forms of extrapolation in using parametric models. For example, if we estimate τ_{ate} using general regression adjustment of the form (21.30)—where $m_1(x, \boldsymbol{\delta}_1) = \mathrm{E}(y \mid x, w = 1)$ and $m_0(x, \boldsymbol{\delta}_0) = \mathrm{E}(y \mid x, w = 0)$—then, say, for control observations we must compute $m_1(x_i, \hat{\boldsymbol{\delta}}_1)$ for $x_i < c$, even though no data points with $x_i < c$ were used in obtaining $\hat{\boldsymbol{\delta}}_1$. If we use local smoothing in a nonparametric setting, we could not convincingly estimate $m_1(x)$ for $x < c$ or $m_0(x)$ for $x \geq c$.

Rather than trying to estimate τ_{ate}, which relies on strong functional form assumptions unless we just assume a constant treatment effect, the RD literature often settles for estimating the average treatment effect at the discontinuity point, defined as

$$\tau_c \equiv \mathrm{E}(y_1 - y_0 \mid x = c) = \mu_1(c) - \mu_0(c). \tag{21.96}$$

This is the average treatment effect for those at the margin of receiving the treatment. By focusing on τ_c we are generally sacrificing external validity of the estimated treatment effect because in different settings the cutoff c may not be particularly relevant.

A leading reason for focusing on τ_c is that it is generally identified without any assumptions other than that the $\mu_g(\cdot)$ functions are continuous at $x = c$. To see why, write

$$y = (1 - w)y_0 + wy_1 = 1[x < c]y_0 + 1[x \geq c]y_1,$$

and so

$$m(x) \equiv \mathrm{E}(y \mid x) = 1[x < c]\mu_0(x) + 1[x \geq c]\mu_1(x). \tag{21.97}$$

Now, using continuity of $\mu_0(\cdot)$ and $\mu_1(\cdot)$ at c,

$$m^-(c) \equiv \lim_{x \uparrow c} m(x) = \mu_0(c)$$

$$m^+(c) \equiv \lim_{x \downarrow c} m(x) = \mu_1(c).$$

It follows that

$$\tau_c = m^+(c) - m^-(c). \tag{21.98}$$

Because we can generally estimate $E(y \mid x, w = 0)$ for all $x < c$ and $E(y \mid x, w = 1)$ for all $x \geq c$, we can estimate the limits of these functions as x approaches c (from the appropriate direction). As a technical point, we must estimate the two regression functions at the boundary value, c, but several strategies have proved useful.

One such strategy is **local linear regression**. Define $\mu_{0c} = \mu_0(c)$, $\mu_{1c} = \mu_1(c)$ and write

$$y_0 = \mu_{0c} + \beta_0(x - c) + u_0 \tag{21.99}$$

$$y_1 = \mu_{1c} + \beta_1(x - c) + u_1 \tag{21.100}$$

so that

$$y = \mu_{0c} + \tau_c w + \beta_0(x - c) + \delta w \cdot (x - c) + r, \tag{21.101}$$

where $r = u_0 + w(u_1 - u_0)$. The estimate of τ_c is just the jump in the linear function at $x = c$. We could use the entire data set to run the regression

$$y_i \quad \text{on} \quad 1, w_i, (x_i - c), w_i \cdot (x_i - c) \tag{21.102}$$

and obtain $\hat{\tau}_c$ as the coefficient on w_i, but this approach would be global estimation to estimate a localized average treatment effect, τ_c. To make this a "local" procedure, choose a "small" value $h > 0$ and only use the data satisfying $c - h < x_i < c + h$. Of course, this is equivalent to estimating two separate regressions: y_i on 1, $(x_i - c)$ for $c - h < x_i < c$ and y_i on 1, $(x_i - c)$ for $c \leq x_i < c + h$, and then $\hat{\tau}_c = \hat{\mu}_{1c} - \hat{\mu}_{0c}$ is the difference in the intercepts. For extra flexibility, we can use a quadratic or cubic in $(x_i - c)$; if a single regression is used, the polynomials should also be interacted with w_i.

If h is viewed as a fixed value chosen ahead of time by the researcher, inference on $\hat{\tau}_c$ is standard: just use a heteroskedasticity-robust t standard error. Imbens and Lemieux (2008) show that if h shrinks to zero quickly enough, the usual inference is still valid. While one can experiment with different choices of h—trading off more bias when h is large versus a smaller variance—one can use a data-based method.

Imbens and Kalyanaraman (2009) explicitly look at choosing h to minimize

$$E\{[\hat{\mu}_0(c) - \mu_0(c)]^2 + [\hat{\mu}_1(c) - \mu_1(c)]^2\}, \tag{21.103}$$

a total mean squared error for the two regression functions at the jump point. The optimal bandwidth choice depends on second derivatives of the regression functions at $x = c$, the density of x_i at $x = c$, the conditional variances, and the kernel used in local linear regression. See Imbens and Kalraynaram (2008) for details.

Adding regressors is no problem: if the regressors are $\mathbf{r}_i$, just run the regression y_i on 1, w_i, $(x_i - c)$, $w_i \cdot (x_i - c)$, $\mathbf{r}_i$, again only using data $c - h < x_i < c + h$. As discussed in Imbens and Lemieux (2008), using extra regressors is likely to have more of an impact when h is large, and it might help reduce the bias arising from the deterioration of the linear approximation. Another reason for adding $\mathbf{r}_i$ is that doing so can reduce the error variance, possibly improving the precision of $\hat{\tau}_c$.

For response variables with limited range, we can use local versions of other estimation methods. For example, suppose the y_g are count variables. Then we might use the observations with $c - h < x_i < c$ to estimate a Poisson regression $E(y \mid x, w = 0) = \exp(\alpha_0 + \beta_0 x)$ and use $c \leq x_i < c + h$ to estimate a Poisson regression $E(y \mid x, w = 1) = \exp(\alpha_1 + \beta_1 x)$. Of course, we could include more flexible functions of x, too. If the exponential regression functions are correctly specified for x "near" c, we can estimate τ_c as

$$\hat{\tau}_c = \exp(\hat{\alpha}_1 + \hat{\beta}_1 c) - \exp(\hat{\alpha}_0 + \hat{\beta}_0 c). \tag{21.104}$$

21.5.2 The Fuzzy Regression Discontinuity Design

In the **fuzzy regression discontinuity (FRD)** design, the probability of treatment changes discontinuously at $x = c$. Define the propensity score as a function of the scalar x as

$$P(w = 1 \mid x) \equiv F(x). \tag{21.105}$$

As in the SRD case, we still assume that the counterfactual conditional mean functions $\mu_0(\cdot)$ and $\mu_1(\cdot)$ are continuous at c. The key assumption for the FRD design is that $F(\cdot)$ is *discontinuous* at c, so that there is a discrete jump in the *probability* of treatment at the cutoff.

There are various ways to identify τ_c. An assumption that leads to a fairly straightforward analysis is that the individual-specific gain, $y_1 - y_0$, is independent of w, conditional on x. Therefore, treatment w is allowed to be correlated with y_0 (after conditioning on x) but not with the unobserved gain from treatment. Compared with identifying other average treatment effects, estimating τ_{att} requires (some version of) ignorability of w with respect to y_0 while τ_{ate} requires that w is ignorable with respect to (y_0, y_1) (which clearly implies the other two assumptions).

To see how τ_c is identified, again write $y = y_0 + w(y_1 - y_0)$ and use conditional independence between w and $(y_1 - y_0)$:

$$\begin{aligned} \mathrm{E}(y \mid x) &= \mathrm{E}(y_0 \mid x) + \mathrm{E}(w \mid x)\mathrm{E}(y_1 - y_0 \mid x) \\ &= \mu_0(x) + \mathrm{E}(w \mid x) \cdot \tau(x). \end{aligned}$$

As in the SRD case, take limits from the right and left and use continuity of $\mu_0(\cdot)$ and $\tau(\cdot)$ at c:

$$m^+(c) = \mu_0(c) + F^+(c)\tau_c$$

$$m^-(c) = \mu_0(c) + F^-(c)\tau_c$$

It follows that, if $F^+(c) \neq F^-(c)$, then

$$\tau_c = \frac{[m^+(c) - m^-(c)]}{[F^+(c) - F^-(c)]}. \tag{21.106}$$

Because the mean and propensity score are generally identified in a neighborhood of c, τ_c is generally identified.

Given consistent estimators of the four quantities in equation (21.106), we have

$$\hat{\tau}_c = \frac{[\hat{m}^+(c) - \hat{m}^-(c)]}{[\hat{F}^+(c) - \hat{F}^-(c)]}. \tag{21.107}$$

Imbens and Lemieux (2008) suggest estimating $m^+(c)$, $m^-(c)$, $F^+(c)$, and $F^-(c)$ all by local linear regression. Namely, $\hat{m}^+(c) = \hat{\alpha}_{1c}$, $\hat{m}^-(c) = \hat{\alpha}_{0c}$, $\hat{F}^+(c) = \hat{\theta}_{1c}$, and $\hat{F}^-(c) = \hat{\theta}_{0c}$ are the intercepts from four local linear regressions. For example, $\hat{\alpha}_{1c}$ is from y_i on 1, $(x_i - c)$, $c \leq x_i < c + h$ and $\hat{\theta}_{1c}$ is from w_i on 1, $(x_i - c)$, $c \leq x_i < c + h$.

As a computational device, and also for simple inference, HTV (2001) show that equation (21.107) is numerically identical to the local IV estimator of τ_c in the equation

$$y_i = \alpha_{0c} + \tau_c w_i + \beta_0(x_i - c) + \delta 1[x_i \geq c] \cdot (x_i - c) + e_i, \tag{21.108}$$

where $z_i \equiv 1[x_i \geq c]$ is the IV for w_i. One uses the data such that $c - h < x_i < c + h$. If h is fixed or is decreasing at a rate described in Imbens and Lemieux (2008), one can use the usual heteroskedasticity-robust IV standard error for $\hat{\tau}_c$.

Rather than using a local linear model for the probability of treatment, we could, say, use a local logit model—for example,

$$P(w = 1 \mid x) = \Lambda(\eta_{c0} + \psi_0(x - c)), \quad x < c$$

$$P(w = 1 \mid x) = \Lambda(\eta_{c1} + \psi_1(x - c)), \quad x \geq c$$

and then use

$$\hat{F}^+(c) - \hat{F}^-(c) = \Lambda(\hat{\eta}_{c1}) - \Lambda(\hat{\eta}_{c0}),$$

where $(\hat{\eta}_{c0}, \hat{\psi}_0)$ are from a logit of w_i on 1, $(x_i - c)$ using $c - h < x_i < c$, and similarly for $(\hat{\eta}_{c1}, \hat{\psi}_1)$.

In the FRD case, we have to choose two bandwidths (even assuming that we use symmetric bandwidths in estimating the regression functions on either side of the jump). We could use the same bandwidth for $P(w = 1 \mid x)$ and $E(y \mid x)$ or choose them separately using, say, Imbens and Kalyanaraman (2009).

21.5.3 Unconfoundedness versus the Fuzzy Regression Discontinuity

Unlike in the SRD case, it is possible that overlap can hold for the FRD (although it might be weak in practice). Therefore, we can compare regression adjustment to estimators that exploit the FRD.

It is useful to return to the linear formulation:

$$y = \mu_{0c} + \tau_c w + \beta_0(x - c) + \delta w \cdot (x - c) + u_0 + w(u_1 - u_0). \tag{21.109}$$

Under the ignorability assumption $D(y_0, y_1 \mid w, x) = D(y_0, y_1 \mid x)$, the composite error has zero mean conditional on (w, x), and so OLS (or local regression) consistently estimates τ_c. In fact, if we believe unconfoundedness and the linear functional form, we can use all the data and average across x_i to estimate τ_{ate}.

If we only assume $D(y_1 - y_0 \mid w, x) = D(y_1 - y_0 \mid x)$—but allow u_0 to be correlated with w—then the OLS estimator is inconsistent. Recall that the estimate of τ_c can be written as

$$\tilde{\tau}_c = \tilde{m}^+(c) - \tilde{m}^-(c),$$

where $\tilde{m}_1(x)$ is estimated using the $w_i = 1$ observations and $\tilde{m}_0(x)$ is estimated using the $w_i = 0$ observations. In other words, the discontinuity in $P(w = 1 \mid x)$ at $x = c$ is essentially ignored. By contrast, the estimator in equation (21.107) is consistent under the weaker version of ignorability, and it directly exploits the jumps in the mean responses and treatment probabilities at $x = c$.

A further benefit of the estimator in equation (21.107) is that it is consistent for ATE for compliers at $x = c$ *without* unconfoundedness, provided we add a monotonicity assumption. See Imbens and Lemieux (2008) for a detailed treatment.

21.6 Further Issues

We now discuss some special considerations and extensions ofthe basic methods previously discussed.

21.6.1 Special Considerations for Responses with Discreteness or Limited Range

We have seen that, when ignorability of selection holds, several methods of estimating average treatment effects are available that depend in no essential way on the nature of y. Propensity score weighting and matching can be applied directly whether the response is continuous or discrete or has both features. Methods that rely on regression adjustment (parametric or even series estimation)—either by itself or in conjunction with other methods—work better when the chosen conditional mean functions are good approximations to $\mathrm{E}(y \mid w = 1, \mathbf{x})$ and $\mathrm{E}(y \mid w = 0, \mathbf{x})$. We already discussed how binary and fractional responses can be modeled using logistic and related functional forms (probably combined with the Bernoulli log likelihood) and how exponential regression functions can be used when y is nonnegative (possibly combined with the Poisson log likelihood). But if y has both discrete and continuous characteristics, we might want to try other models for the conditional expectations. For example, suppose y_0 and y_1 are corner solutions. Under Assumption ATE.1, $\mathrm{D}(y_g \mid w, \mathbf{x}) = \mathrm{D}(y_g \mid \mathbf{x})$, $g = 0, 1$. Therefore, we can estimate models for $\mathrm{D}(y \mid w = 0, \mathbf{x})$ and $\mathrm{D}(y \mid w = 1, \mathbf{x})$ that account for the corner nature of y. This could be the standard Type I Tobit model if the corner is at zero, or a two-limit Tobit model as in Section 17.7 if there are two corners. But we might also try a hurdle model separately for $w = 0$ and $w = 1$. Remember, the idea is to eventually obtain good estimates of the conditional means, and a Tobit or hurdle model might do that better than, say, a linear model, even though the Tobit or hurdle model is itself misspecified. Once we have those estimates of the mean functions, we can use equation (21.30), as always.

When we relaxed ignorability and allowed treatment to be correlated with unobservables even after conditioning on $\mathbf{x}$, the IV, correction function, and control function methods discussed in Section 21.4 relied heavily on linear (in parameters and unobservables) functional forms. Even though the linear functional forms can, under certain assumptions, consistently estimate a local average treatment effect, we may want to use nonlinear functions and try to better approximate τ_{ate} or τ_{att}. If the counterfactual responses are binary, we might specify

$$y_0 = 1[\alpha_0 + \mathbf{x}\boldsymbol{\beta}_0 + e_0 \geq 0] \tag{21.110}$$

$$y_1 = 1[\alpha_1 + \mathbf{x}\boldsymbol{\beta}_1 + e_1 \geq 0], \tag{21.111}$$

where (e_0, e_1) is independent of $(\mathbf{x}, \mathbf{z})$ and each has a standard normal distribution. If we add, as in the linear case,

$$w = 1[\theta_0 + \mathbf{x}\boldsymbol{\theta}_1 + \mathbf{z}\boldsymbol{\theta}_2 + a \geq 0], \tag{21.112}$$

where (e_0, e_1, a) is independent of $(\mathbf{x}, \mathbf{z})$ and trivariate normal, then we can estimate $(\alpha_0, \boldsymbol{\beta}_0')'$ and $(\alpha_1, \boldsymbol{\beta}_1')'$ by "selection" probits on the $w_i = 0$ and $w_i = 1$ subsamples, respectively; see Section 19.6.3. Then $\hat{\tau}_{ate}(\mathbf{x}) = \Phi(\hat{\alpha}_1 + \mathbf{x}\hat{\boldsymbol{\beta}}_1) - \Phi(\hat{\alpha}_0 + \mathbf{x}\hat{\boldsymbol{\beta}}_0)$ and

$$\hat{\tau}_{ate} = N^{-1} \sum_{i=1}^{N} [\Phi(\hat{\alpha}_1 + \mathbf{x}_i\hat{\boldsymbol{\beta}}_1) - \Phi(\hat{\alpha}_0 + \mathbf{x}_i\hat{\boldsymbol{\beta}}_0)]. \tag{21.113}$$

If we impose $\boldsymbol{\beta}_1 = \boldsymbol{\beta}_0$ and $e_1 = e_0$, we obtain the bivariate probit model that we discussed in Section 15.7.3. Naturally, it is better to use the more flexible model unless evidence suggests it is not needed.

If the y_g are corner solutions, we might use the specification $y_g = \max(0, \alpha_g + \mathbf{x}\boldsymbol{\beta}_g + e_g)$ and make the standard assumptions so that y_g follows a Tobit. In fact, we could still assume that (e_0, e_1, a) is independent of $(\mathbf{x}, \mathbf{z})$ and trivariate normal, but now where $\sigma_g^2 = \text{Var}(e_g)$ are variance parameters to be estimated. Although Tobit models with "endogenous switching" are not common, there is no reason they cannot be useful for estimating ATEs with corner solution responses. Statistically, estimation of the parameters for the control and treatment groups is the same as estimating a Tobit model with endogenous sample selection. (The case with $\boldsymbol{\beta}_1 = \boldsymbol{\beta}_0$ and $e_1 = e_0$ is covered in Problem 17.6.) The estimate of τ_{ate} takes the usual form

$$\hat{\tau}_{ate} = N^{-1} \sum_{i=1}^{N} [m(\hat{\alpha}_1 + \mathbf{x}_i\hat{\boldsymbol{\beta}}_1, \hat{\sigma}_1^2) - m(\hat{\alpha}_0 + \mathbf{x}_i\hat{\boldsymbol{\beta}}_0, \hat{\sigma}_0^2)], \tag{21.114}$$

where $m(\cdot, \cdot)$ is the conditional mean function for a Tobit model. Hurdle models could be used, too, but estimation becomes even more complicated.

For exponential response functions we can use the "selection correction" described in Section 19.6.4 on the control and treated samples, and then, as usual, construct an average of the difference in estimated counterfactual means. These can be applied under the assumption $\text{E}(y_g \mid a_g, w, \mathbf{x}, \mathbf{z}) = \exp(a_g + \mathbf{x}\boldsymbol{\beta}_g)$ with a_g independent of $(\mathbf{x}, \mathbf{z})$, $g = 0, 1$ and suitable normality assumptions (at a minimum in the probit model for w). A similar approach can be used for fractional responses when just the counterfactural conditional means are assumed to be correctly specified.

21.6.2 Multivalued Treatments

So far, we have considered the case with a single treatment level, which we indicate as $w_i = 1$ with $w_i = 0$ indicating a control unit. In some cases, program participation can take place at different levels—say, part-time or full-time—or there could be different options for treatment, such as different job training programs. Both cases require an extension of the previous framework and estimation method.

Now suppose that the treatment variable can take on $G+1$ different values, which we label $\{0, 1, 2, \ldots, G\}$. Typically, zero indicates the control group and $1, \ldots, G$ different levels or options for treatment. Thus, w_i takes a value in $\{0, 1, 2, \ldots, G\}$. Now, of course, there are $G+1$ counterfactual outcomes, which we denote, for a random draw i, $\{y_{ig} : g = 0, 1, \ldots, G\}$. The observed response, y_i, can be expressed as

$$y_i = 1[w_i = 0]y_{i0} + 1[w_i = 1]y_{i1} + \cdots + 1[w_i = G]y_{iG}. \tag{21.115}$$

As usual, we have available a set of covariates, $\mathbf{x}_i$. Define $\mu_g = \mathrm{E}(y_{ig})$ as the population means of the counterfactuals. A sufficient ignorability for identifying the means is the conditional mean independence assumption

$$\mathrm{E}(y_{ig} \mid w_i, \mathbf{x}_i) = \mathrm{E}(y_{ig} \mid \mathbf{x}_i), \quad g = 0, 1, \ldots, G. \tag{21.116}$$

Under assumption (21.116) it follows easily that

$$\mathrm{E}(y_i \mid w_i, \mathbf{x}_i) = 1[w_i = 0]\mathrm{E}(y_{i0} \mid \mathbf{x}_i) + 1[w_i = 1]\mathrm{E}(y_{i1} \mid \mathbf{x}_i)$$
$$+ \cdots + 1[w_i = G]\mathrm{E}(y_{iG} \mid \mathbf{x}_i), \tag{21.117}$$

which immediately shows that the mean function $\mathrm{E}(y_g \mid \mathbf{x})$ is identified because

$$\mathrm{E}(y_g \mid \mathbf{x}) = \mathrm{E}(y \mid w = g, \mathbf{x}). \tag{21.118}$$

We can estimate $\mathrm{E}(y \mid w = g, \mathbf{x})$ for each g, given a random sample, by restricting attention to units with $w_i = g$. In other words, regression adjustment in the multiple-treatment case is an obvious extension of the case when w_i is binary. The considerations hold here as in the binary case, including using particular functional forms that account for the nature of y and using nonparametric regression.

Given conditional mean estimates $\{\hat{m}_g(\mathbf{x}) : g = 0, 1, \ldots, G\}$, we can estimate the average treatment effect for treatment level h relative to g, say τ_{gh}, as

$$\hat{\tau}_{gh,reg} = N^{-1} \sum_{i=1}^{N} [\hat{m}_h(\mathbf{x}_i) - \hat{m}_g(\mathbf{x}_i)]. \tag{21.119}$$

Or, if α_{gh} is the average treatment effect for those in either group g or h, $\hat{\alpha}_{gh,reg}$ is obtained by averaging the differences $\hat{m}_h(\mathbf{x}_i) - \hat{m}_g(\mathbf{x}_i)$ across the subsample with $w_i = g$ or $w_i = h$. For example, perhaps g is a lower level of participation in job training than h, and we want to estimate the average treatment effect of going from part-time to full-time for those who were in one of those treated groups. We can define a measure more like the average treatment effect as $\eta_{gh} = \mathrm{E}(y_h - y_g \mid w = h)$, which would be particularly interesting when $g = 0$ is the control group. Now we would simply average $\hat{m}_h(\mathbf{x}_i) - \hat{m}_g(\mathbf{x}_i)$ across the subsample $w_i = h$.

It is pretty clear that overlap is needed to estimate average treatment effects with multiple treatment levels. While we can get by with less for some cases, the most straightforward statement is based on the set of propensity scores (which Imbens, 2000, calls the **generalized propensity score**):

$$\mathrm{P}(w_g = 1 \mid \mathbf{x}) \equiv p_g(\mathbf{x}) > 0, \quad \mathbf{x} \in \mathcal{X}, \quad g = 0, \ldots, G. \tag{21.120}$$

Because the propensity scores must sum to unity, assumption (21.120) rules out the case of unit probabilities for any g.

Propensity score weighting can also be used under the previous ignorability and overlap assumptions. For example, using the same argument in Section 21.3.3, it is easily shown that

$$\mathrm{E}(y_g) = \mathrm{E}\left\{\frac{1[w_i = g]y_i}{p_g(\mathbf{x}_i)}\right\}, \quad g = 0, 1, \ldots, G, \tag{21.121}$$

and so consistent estimates of the counterfactual means take the form

$$\hat{\mu}_{g,ps} = N^{-1} \sum_{i=1}^{N} \left\{\frac{1[w_i = g]y_i}{\hat{p}_g(\mathbf{x}_i)}\right\}, \tag{21.122}$$

where $\hat{p}_g(\cdot)$ are the estimated propensity scores. Given these estimates, we can form differences such as $\hat{\tau}_{gh,ps} = \hat{\mu}_{h,ps} - \hat{\mu}_{g,ps}$. Estimating the other kinds of treament effects mentioned previously requires more care, but is fairly straightforward. See, for example Imbens (2000) and Lechner (2001).

To implement IPW estimation, we have to estimate the propensity scores. A common parametric approach would be to use a multinomial logit (MNL) model with flexible functions in $\mathbf{x}_i$. Because we are just looking for good estimates of the probabilities, the MNL model will often work well, but other approaches—such as nested logit models—can be used. If the treatment categories are obviously ordered—say, w_i is number of years in college for the population of high school graduates—one might try an ordered model, such as ordered logit.

In addition to regression adjustment and propensity score weighting, one can, of course, use matching—either on the covariates or propensity scores. See, for example, Lechner (2001).

21.6.3 Multiple Treatments

The case of multiple treatments is more difficult to handle, and in some cases relies on additional functional form restrictions. Of course, if $\mathbf{w}_i$ is an M-vector of treatment variables and the $\mathbf{x}_i$ are the controls, we can always work with models for $\mathrm{E}(y_i \mid \mathbf{w}_i, \mathbf{x}_i)$ directly, but then we are circumventing the counterfactual framework.

A fairly general framework—which actually encompasses the framework of the previous section—is to use a random coefficient setting. Let $\mathbf{w}_i$ be $1 \times M$ and $\mathbf{c}_i$ an $M \times 1$ vector of unobserved heterogeneity. Assume that

$$y_i = \mathbf{w}_i \mathbf{c}_i = w_{i1} c_{i1} + \cdots + w_{iM} c_{iM}. \tag{21.123}$$

By choosing the c_{im} as counterfactual outcomes and the w_{im} as treatment indicators for each treatment level (including the control), we can put the multivalued treatment framework into the current setting. But we can also allow for truly different treatments. For example, suppose we have two programs, A and B, where participation is allowed in one or both. Then we can define $\mathbf{w}_i$ to have four dummy variables indicating every possible treatment state: participation in neither, participation in A but not B, participation in B but not A, and participation in both. Or, some of the w_{im} can be continuous treatments along with discrete treatments. Further, as described in Wooldridge (2004), the w_{im} can be different functions of the same (nonbinary) treatment in order to make functional forms more flexible. If we want, we can set, say, $w_{i1} \equiv 1$ so that there is an intercept in the equation; in other cases it is more convenient to have a full set of treatment indicators and exclude an intercept.

Given covariates $\mathbf{x}_i$, the goal is to estimate $\mathrm{E}(\mathbf{c}_i \mid \mathbf{x}_i = \mathbf{x})$ and then, eventually, $\boldsymbol{\mu}_{\mathbf{c}} = \mathrm{E}(\mathbf{c}_i)$. When we use appropriate linear combinations, the latter corresponds to average treatment effects across the entire population while $\mathrm{E}(\mathbf{c}_i \mid \mathbf{x}_i = \mathbf{x})$ generally corresponds to conditional average treatment effects.

If we assume ignorability, we can consistently estimate $\mathrm{E}(\mathbf{c}_i \mid \mathbf{x}_i = \mathbf{x})$, and, assuming overlap, we can then average to estimate $\boldsymbol{\mu}_{\mathbf{c}}$. The key assumptions in the population are

$$\mathrm{E}(y \mid \mathbf{w}, \mathbf{c}, \mathbf{x}) = \mathrm{E}(y \mid \mathbf{w}, \mathbf{c}) \tag{21.124}$$

and

$$\mathrm{E}(\mathbf{w}'\mathbf{w} \mid \mathbf{c}, \mathbf{x}) = \mathrm{E}(\mathbf{w}'\mathbf{w} \mid \mathbf{x}). \tag{21.125}$$

In many cases, we would obtain assumption (21.125) from $\mathrm{E}(\mathbf{w} \mid \mathbf{c}, \mathbf{x}) = \mathrm{E}(\mathbf{w} \mid \mathbf{x})$ and $\mathrm{Var}(\mathbf{w} \mid \mathbf{c}, \mathbf{x}) = \mathrm{Var}(\mathbf{w} \mid \mathbf{x})$—in other words, from ignorability conditional on the first two moments of the distribution of $\mathbf{w}$ given $(\mathbf{c}, \mathbf{x})$.

If we also assume that $\mathbf{\Lambda}(\mathbf{x}) \equiv \mathrm{E}(\mathbf{w}'\mathbf{w} \mid \mathbf{x})$ is nonsingular, we can easily find an expression for $\mathrm{E}(\mathbf{c} \mid \mathbf{x})$. Write $y = \mathbf{wc} + u$ where $\mathrm{E}(u \mid \mathbf{w}, \mathbf{c}, \mathbf{x}) = 0$ by assumption (21.124). Then $\mathbf{w}'y = \mathbf{w}'\mathbf{wc} + \mathbf{w}'u$, and so

$$\mathrm{E}(\mathbf{w}'y \mid \mathbf{x}) = \mathrm{E}(\mathbf{w}'\mathbf{wc} \mid \mathbf{x}) + \mathrm{E}(\mathbf{w}'u \mid \mathbf{x}) = \mathrm{E}(\mathbf{w}'\mathbf{wc} \mid \mathbf{x}).$$

Now, by iterated expectations, $\mathrm{E}(\mathbf{w}'\mathbf{wc} \mid \mathbf{x}) = \mathrm{E}[\mathrm{E}(\mathbf{w}'\mathbf{wc} \mid \mathbf{c}, \mathbf{x}) \mid \mathbf{x}]$, and

$$\mathrm{E}[\mathrm{E}(\mathbf{w}'\mathbf{wc} \mid \mathbf{c}, \mathbf{x}) \mid \mathbf{x}] = \mathrm{E}[\mathrm{E}(\mathbf{w}'\mathbf{w} \mid \mathbf{c}, \mathbf{x})\mathbf{c} \mid \mathbf{x}] = \mathrm{E}[\mathrm{E}(\mathbf{w}'\mathbf{w} \mid \mathbf{x})\mathbf{c} \mid \mathbf{x}] = \mathrm{E}(\mathbf{w}'\mathbf{w} \mid \mathbf{x})\mathrm{E}(\mathbf{c} \mid \mathbf{x}),$$

where the second equality follows from assumption (21.125). We have shown that

$$\mathrm{E}(\mathbf{w}'y \mid \mathbf{x}) = \mathrm{E}(\mathbf{w}'\mathbf{w} \mid \mathbf{x})\mathrm{E}(\mathbf{c} \mid \mathbf{x}),$$

and so, assuming invertibility of $\mathrm{E}(\mathbf{w}'\mathbf{w} \mid \mathbf{x})$,

$$\mathrm{E}(\mathbf{c} \mid \mathbf{x}) = [\mathrm{E}(\mathbf{w}'\mathbf{w} \mid \mathbf{x})]^{-1}\mathrm{E}(\mathbf{w}'y \mid \mathbf{x}) \equiv [\mathbf{\Lambda}(\mathbf{x})]^{-1}\mathrm{E}(\mathbf{w}'y \mid \mathbf{x}). \tag{21.126}$$

Because we can collect a random sample on $(y_i, \mathbf{w}_i, \mathbf{x}_i)$, we can estimate all the conditional moments that appear in $\mathrm{E}(\mathbf{c} \mid \mathbf{x})$.

For estimating the unconditional mean $\boldsymbol{\mu}_{\mathbf{c}}$ it suffices to estimate $\mathbf{\Lambda}(\mathbf{x})$ because

$$\boldsymbol{\mu}_{\mathbf{c}} = \mathrm{E}\{[\mathbf{\Lambda}(\mathbf{x})]^{-1}\mathrm{E}(\mathbf{w}'y \mid \mathbf{x})\} = \mathrm{E}\{[\mathbf{\Lambda}(\mathbf{x})]^{-1}\mathbf{w}'y\}, \tag{21.127}$$

which just uses the fact that $\mathbf{w}'y = \mathrm{E}(\mathbf{w}'y \mid \mathbf{x}) + \mathbf{r}$ with $\mathrm{E}(\mathbf{r} \mid \mathbf{x}) \equiv \mathbf{0}$.

Expression (21.127) takes on a simple, recognizable form when $\mathbf{w}$ is a vector of mutually exclusive, exhaustive binary indicators for different treament groups. Then $\mathbf{w}'\mathbf{w} = diag(w_{i1}, \ldots, w_{iM})$ and so $\mathbf{\Lambda}(\mathbf{x})$ is the $M \times M$ diagonal matrix with $\mathrm{E}(w_m \mid \mathbf{x}) = \mathrm{P}(w_m = 1 \mid \mathbf{x})$—that is, the propensity scores—down the diagonal. It is easily seen that the mth element of $\mathrm{E}\{[\mathbf{\Lambda}(\mathbf{x})]^{-1}\mathbf{w}'y)\}$ is simply

$$\mathrm{E}[w_{im}y_i/p_m(\mathbf{x}_i)],$$

which is exactly the expression we derived in the previous subsection to motivate propensity score weighting in the multiple treatment case.

More generally, $\mathbf{\Lambda}(\mathbf{x})$ might not be a diagonal matrix, although it always will be if we choose $\mathbf{w}_i$ to saturate all possible treatment scenarios. In other words, if we have Q possible programs where, for program q there are J_q treatment levels, then $\mathbf{w}_i$ has $\sum_{q=1}^{Q} J_q$ elements. (If certain combinations are impossible, they can just be excluded.) With continuous treatments, or where we, say, let each program have its own set of treatment effects and these do not interact with treatment effects from other programs, then we generally have to estimate conditional covariances along with conditional means (and variances). Assuming we have a consistent estimator $\hat{\mathbf{\Lambda}}(\mathbf{x})$ of $\mathbf{\Lambda}(\mathbf{x})$

for each $\mathbf{x}$, consistent estimators of $\boldsymbol{\mu}_{\mathbf{c}}$ have the form

$$\hat{\boldsymbol{\mu}}_{\mathbf{c}} = N^{-1}\sum_{i=1}^{N}[\hat{\boldsymbol{\Lambda}}(\mathbf{x}_i)]^{-1}\mathbf{w}_i' y_i. \tag{21.128}$$

In many cases it is useful to explicitly separate the random slopes from the random intercept, in which case we can write in the population

$$\mathrm{E}(y \mid \mathbf{w}, \mathbf{c}) = \mathrm{E}(y \mid \mathbf{w}, \mathbf{c}, \mathbf{x}) = a + \mathbf{w}\mathbf{b},$$

where $\mathbf{w}$ is now a set of K treatment variables such that $\boldsymbol{\Omega}(\mathbf{x}) \equiv \mathrm{Var}(\mathbf{w} \mid \mathbf{x})$ is nonsingular for all (relevant) values of $\mathbf{x}$. Then, as can be derived from equation (21.127) using partitioned inverse (see also Wooldridge (2004)),

$$\mathrm{E}(\mathbf{b} \mid \mathbf{x}) = [\mathrm{Var}(\mathbf{w} \mid \mathbf{x})]^{-1}\,\mathrm{Cov}(\mathbf{w}, y \mid \mathbf{x}) \equiv [\boldsymbol{\Omega}(\mathbf{x})]^{-1}\,\mathrm{Cov}(\mathbf{w}, y \mid \mathbf{x})$$

and

$$\boldsymbol{\mu}_{\mathbf{b}} \equiv \mathrm{E}(\mathbf{b}) = \mathrm{E}\{[\boldsymbol{\Omega}(\mathbf{x})]^{-1}[\mathbf{w} - \boldsymbol{\psi}(\mathbf{x})]y\},$$

where $\boldsymbol{\psi}(\mathbf{x}) \equiv \mathrm{E}(\mathbf{w} \mid \mathbf{x})$ is the $1 \times K$ vector of conditional mean functions. In this formulation, we see directly that the conditional mean and conditional variance-covariance matrix of the treatment $\mathbf{w}$ are needed to estimate the average slopes, $\boldsymbol{\mu}_{\mathbf{b}}$. Because we assume a random sample on $(\mathbf{w}, \mathbf{x})$, these moments are generally identified. In practice, we might use parametric models that account for the nature of the elements of $\mathbf{w}$. Naturally, given such estimators, we estimate $\boldsymbol{\mu}_{\mathbf{b}}$ as a sample average, $\hat{\boldsymbol{\mu}}_{\mathbf{b}} = N^{-1}\sum_{i=1}^{N}[\hat{\boldsymbol{\Omega}}(\mathbf{x}_i)]^{-1}[\mathbf{w}_i - \hat{\boldsymbol{\psi}}(\mathbf{x}_i)]y_i$.

When treatment is not ignorable for a set of covariates $\mathbf{x}$, we need to obtain instrumental variables. Linear IV estimation is relatively straightforward provided unobserved heterogeneity is additive, as in Section 21.4.1. But allowing for general heterogeneous treatment effects without ignorability is difficult. Control function approaches would rely on

$$\mathrm{E}(y \mid \mathbf{w}, \mathbf{x}, \mathbf{z}) = \mathbf{w}\mathrm{E}(\mathbf{c} \mid \mathbf{w}, \mathbf{x}, \mathbf{z}),$$

where $\mathbf{z}$ is the vector of instruments, and the latter can be difficult to obtain when $\mathbf{w}$ is a vector. Wooldridge (2008) considered correction function approaches under the assumptions

$$\mathrm{E}(y \mid \mathbf{w}, \mathbf{c}, \mathbf{x}, \mathbf{z}) = \mathrm{E}(y \mid \mathbf{w}, \mathbf{c}) \tag{21.129}$$

(which is not much of an assumption because $\mathbf{c}$ can include lots of factors) and

$$\mathrm{E}(\mathbf{c} \mid \mathbf{x}, \mathbf{z}) = \mathrm{E}(\mathbf{c} \mid \mathbf{x}) = \boldsymbol{\mu}_{\mathbf{c}} + (\mathbf{x} - \boldsymbol{\mu}_{\mathbf{x}})\boldsymbol{\Gamma}, \tag{21.130}$$

which is a standard exclusion restriction on the instruments, $\mathbf{z}$, along with linearity assumption. If we write $c_m = \mu_{cm} + (\mathbf{x} - \boldsymbol{\mu}_{\mathbf{x}})\gamma_m + v_m$, then we have

$$y_i = \mu_{c1} w_{i1} + \mu_{c2} w_{i2} + \cdots + \mu_{cM} w_{im} + w_{i1}(\mathbf{x}_i - \boldsymbol{\mu}_{\mathbf{x}})\gamma_1 + \cdots + w_{iM}(\mathbf{x}_i - \boldsymbol{\mu}_{\mathbf{x}})\gamma_M$$
$$+ w_{i1} v_{i1} + \cdots + w_{iM} v_{iM}.$$

The correction function approach now entails finding $\mathrm{E}(w_{im} u_{im} \mid \mathbf{x}_i, \mathbf{z}_i)$ and inserting these for the $w_{im} v_{im}$, and then applying instrumental variables using functions of $(\mathbf{x}_i, \mathbf{z}_i)$. More specifically, suppose $w_{im} = f_m(\mathbf{x}_i, \mathbf{z}_i, u_{im}, \boldsymbol{\alpha}_m)$ and $\mathrm{E}(v_{im} \mid u_{im}, \mathbf{x}_i, \mathbf{z}_i) = \rho_m u_{im}$. Then, with distributional assumptions on u_{im}, we can estimate $\boldsymbol{\alpha}_m$ and parameters in the distribution of u_{im} to obtain $\mathrm{E}(w_{im} u_{im} \mid \mathbf{x}_i, \mathbf{z}_i) = h_m(\mathbf{x}_i, \mathbf{z}_i, \boldsymbol{\theta}_m)$, where the $\boldsymbol{\theta}_m$ are assumed to be identified and $h_m(\cdot)$ is known. (Section 21.4.2 considered the case where w_i is binary and follows a probit; the correction function was the standard normal pdf evaluated at a linear index.) Now we have the estimating equation

$$y_i = \mu_{c1} w_{i1} + \mu_{c2} w_{i2} + \cdots + \mu_{cM} w_{im} + w_{i1}(\mathbf{x}_i - \boldsymbol{\mu}_{\mathbf{x}})\gamma_1 + \cdots + w_{iM}(\mathbf{x}_i - \boldsymbol{\mu}_{\mathbf{x}})\gamma_M$$
$$+ \rho_1 h_1(\mathbf{x}_i, \mathbf{z}_i, \boldsymbol{\theta}_1) + \cdots + \rho_M h_M(\mathbf{x}_i, \mathbf{z}_i, \boldsymbol{\theta}_M) + r_i \tag{21.131}$$

$\mathrm{E}(r_i \mid \mathbf{x}_i, \mathbf{z}_i) = 0.$

After replacing $\boldsymbol{\mu}_{\mathbf{x}}$ with the sample average $\bar{\mathbf{x}}$, plugging in the $\hat{\boldsymbol{\theta}}_m$, and specifying the instruments, we can estimate the equation by IV. Natural choices for the instruments are $\hat{\mathrm{E}}(w_{im} \mid \mathbf{x}_i, \mathbf{z}_i)$ and $\hat{\mathrm{E}}(w_{im} \mid \mathbf{x}_i, \mathbf{z}_i) \cdot (\mathbf{x}_i - \bar{\mathbf{x}})$, where the $\hat{\mathrm{E}}(w_{im} \mid \mathbf{x}_i, \mathbf{z}_i)$ are obtained from the specified distribution $\mathrm{D}(w_{im} \mid \mathbf{x}_i, \mathbf{z}_i)$. In the simple binary case where w_i follows a probit, we used the probit fitted values, $\hat{\Phi}_i$.

A test for whether all interactions between the treatment variables and heterogeneity have zero coefficients is a standard, heteroskedasticity Wald test of $H_0 : \rho_1 = \cdots = \rho_M = 0$ after IV estimation. If we want to allow some of the ρ_m to be nonzero, the variance matrix of all second-step estimators needs to be adjusted for the estimation of the $\boldsymbol{\theta}_m$, using either the delta method or bootstrapping. Notice that the coefficients on the w_{im} are the estimated counterfactual means, and then we can use these to construct various average treatment effects. We also have direct estimates of how the treatment effects vary with $\mathbf{x}$ (because we have the $\hat{\gamma}_m$).

The correction function method is easy to apply when the marginal models for the treatment indicators are easy to obtain. For example, it is much easier if, say, w_{im} is assumed to follow a probit model than if a collection of indicators follows a multivariate probit. The method applies also when some treatments have discrete and continuous characteristics, such as hours spent in a job training program. If w_{im} follows a Tobit model, then $h_m(\mathbf{x}_i, \mathbf{z}_i, \boldsymbol{\theta}_m)$ is tractable; see Wooldridge (2008).

21.6.4 Panel Data

Using individual panel data with general patterns of treatments is complicated by the different kinds of treatment effects—static and dynamic—that one might like to consider. In this subsection, we consider the case where, in each time period t, unit i is part of a treatment or control group. Thus, w_{it} is a binary variable where $w_{it} = 1$ means treatment in time t. Let $\mathbf{w}_i = (w_{i1}, \ldots, w_{iT})$ denote the entire history of treatment indicators. If we focuse on the ATEs of treatment in a particular time period, it is fairly straightforward to state ignorability assumptions conditional on unobserved heterogeneity. Let $y_{it}(0)$ and $y_{it}(1)$ denote the counterfactual outcomes in the untreated and treated states, respectively. Then ignorability conditional on unobserved heterogeneity $\mathbf{c}_i$ and covariates $\mathbf{x}_i$ is

$$\mathrm{E}[y_{it}(g) \mid \mathbf{w}_i, \mathbf{c}_i, \mathbf{x}_i] = \mathrm{E}[y_{it}(g) \mid \mathbf{c}_i, \mathbf{x}_i], \quad g = 0, 1. \tag{21.132}$$

Notice that this is a strict exogeneity assumption on treatment assignment, conditional on $(\mathbf{c}_i, \mathbf{x}_i)$. Because $y_{it} = y_{it}(0) + w_{it}\mathrm{E}[y_{it}(1) - y_{it}(0)]$, it follows that

$$\begin{aligned}\mathrm{E}(y_{it} \mid \mathbf{w}_i, \mathbf{c}_i, \mathbf{x}_i) &= \mathrm{E}(y_{it} \mid w_{it}, \mathbf{c}_i, \mathbf{x}_i) \\ &= \mathrm{E}[y_{it}(0) \mid \mathbf{c}_i, \mathbf{x}_i] + w_{it}\mathrm{E}[y_{it}(1) - y_{it}(0) \mid \mathbf{c}_i, \mathbf{x}_i]. \end{aligned} \tag{21.133}$$

If the treatment effect $y_{it}(1) - y_{it}(0)$ is constant for each t, say τ_t, and $\mathrm{E}[y_{it}(0) \mid \mathbf{c}_i, \mathbf{x}_i]$ is linear and additive with scalar heterogeneity, and only covariates at time t appear, then

$$\mathrm{E}(y_{it} \mid \mathbf{w}_i, \mathbf{c}_i, \mathbf{x}_i) = c_{i0} + \alpha_{0t} + \mathbf{x}_{it}\boldsymbol{\beta}_{0t} + \tau_t w_{it}, \quad t = 1, \ldots, T,$$

and this leads to a standard fixed-effects or first-differencing analysis (especially if we assume time homogeneity of $\boldsymbol{\beta}_{0t}$ and τ_t).

If we allow $\mathrm{E}[y_{it}(1) - y_{it}(0) \mid \mathbf{c}_i, \mathbf{x}_i]$ to depend on heterogeneity and covariates, we get an estimating equation where w_{it} interacts with $\mathbf{x}_{it}$ as well as with heterogeneity, say a_i. So, assuming time homogeneity except in the intercepts α_{0t} and the means of the covariates, the estimating equation looks like

$$\mathrm{E}(y_{it} \mid \mathbf{w}_i, \mathbf{c}_i, \mathbf{x}_i) = c_{i0} + \alpha_{0t} + \mathbf{x}_{it}\boldsymbol{\beta}_0 + a_i w_{it} + w_{it}(\mathbf{x}_{it} - \boldsymbol{\psi}_t), \quad t = 1, \ldots, T, \tag{21.134}$$

where $\boldsymbol{\psi}_t = \mathrm{E}(\mathbf{x}_{it})$ (which should be replaced by the sample average for each t in estimation). The average treatment effect is $\tau = \mathrm{E}(a_i)$. We discussed how to estimate such models in Section 11.7, and we also noted that there are conditions where setting $a_i = \tau$ in estimation and using the usual FE estimator consistently estimates τ.

If we are willing to assume strictly exogenous treatment, conditional on heterogeneity and covariates, then allowing lagged effects of treatment is straightforward in a regression-type framework. As a practical matter, one just adds lags of treatment indicators to the standard models described previously. Then, one can estimate how long program participation effects last. Explicitly using a counterfactual setting is possible but notationally complicated. For example, suppose we are interested only in contemporaneous effects and effects lagged a year. Then, for each $t \geq 2$, we have counterfactual outcomes $y_{it}(g_{t-1}, g_t)$ where g_{t-1} and g_t can be zero or one, corresponding to treatment in the same time period or one time period earlier. In other words, at time t there are four counterfactuals for unit i: $y_{it}(0,0)$, $y_{it}(1,0)$, $y_{it}(0,1)$, and $y_{it}(1,1)$. We can write the observed outcome as

$$\begin{aligned} y_{it} &= (1 - w_{i,t-1})(1 - w_{it}) y_{it}(0,0) + w_{i,t-1}(1 - w_{it}) y_{it}(1,0) \\ &\quad + (1 - w_{i,t-1}) w_{it} y_{it}(0,1) + w_{i,t-1} w_{it} y_{it}(1,1) \\ &= y_{it}(0,0) + w_{i,t-1}[y_{it}(1,0) - y_{it}(0,0)] + w_{it}[y_{it}(0,1) - y_{it}(0,0)] \\ &\quad + w_{i,t-1} w_{it}[y_{it}(1,1) - y_{it}(1,0) - y_{it}(0,1) + y_{it}(0,0)] \end{aligned}$$

If we modify assumption (21.132) to

$$\mathrm{E}[y_{it}(g_{t-1}, g_t) \mid \mathbf{w}_i, \mathbf{c}_i, \mathbf{x}_i] = \mathrm{E}[y_{it}(g_{t-1}, g_t) \mid \mathbf{c}_i, \mathbf{x}_i], \quad g_{t-1}, g_t = 0, 1, \tag{21.135}$$

then unobserved-effects models fall out naturally. The standard additive model with covariates dated at time t (and possibly earlier time periods) emerges if only $\mathrm{E}[y_{it}(0,0) \mid \mathbf{c}_i, \mathbf{x}_i]$ depends on heterogeneity and covariates, but adding interactions with heterogeneity, and especially with observed covariates (contemporaneous or lagged) is straightforward. If we treat all means as constant over time—$\mu_{gh} = \mathrm{E}[y_{it}(g,h)]$—then it is straightforward to estimate various treatment effects. For example, $\mu_{11} - \mu_{00}$ is the average treatment effect from participating in neither period versus participating in both periods.

We can also adapt an approach due to Altonji and Matzkin (2005); see also Wooldridge (2005a). Under assumption (21.135),

$$\begin{aligned} \mathrm{E}(y_{it} \mid \mathbf{w}_i, \mathbf{c}_i, \mathbf{x}_i) &= \mathrm{E}(y_{it} \mid w_{i,t-1}, w_{it}, \mathbf{c}_i, \mathbf{x}_i) = (1 - w_{i,t-1})(1 - w_{it})\mathrm{E}[y_{it}(0,0) \mid \mathbf{c}_i, \mathbf{x}_i] \\ &\quad + w_{i,t-1}(1 - w_{it})\mathrm{E}[y_{it}(1,0) \mid \mathbf{c}_i, \mathbf{x}_i] \\ &\quad + (1 - w_{i,t-1}) w_{it}\mathrm{E}[y_{it}(0,1) \mid \mathbf{c}_i, \mathbf{x}_i] + w_{i,t-1} w_{it}\mathrm{E}[y_{it}(1,1) \mid \mathbf{c}_i, \mathbf{x}_i] \end{aligned}$$

Unless we make special functional form assumptions of the kind just described, this equation is not directly useful because it depends on the unobserved heterogeneity, $\mathbf{c}_i$. Suppose, however, that we assume that the distribution of $\mathbf{c}_i$ given $(\mathbf{w}_i, \mathbf{x}_i)$ depends on a relatively simple function of the history of treatments, such as the fraction of treated periods, $\bar{w}_i$. (There are more sophisticated possibilities, such as using fractions within various subperiods.) Formally, if $\mathrm{D}(\mathbf{c}_i \mid \mathbf{w}_i, \mathbf{x}_i) = \mathrm{D}(\mathbf{c}_i \mid \bar{w}_i, \mathbf{x}_i)$, then, by iterated expectations and assumption (21.135),

$$\begin{aligned} \mathrm{E}(y_{it} \mid \mathbf{w}_i, \mathbf{x}_i) = \mathrm{E}(y_{it} \mid w_{i,t-1}, w_{it}, \bar{w}_i, \mathbf{x}_i) &= (1 - w_{i,t-1})(1 - w_{it})\mathrm{E}[y_{it}(0,0) \mid \bar{w}_i, \mathbf{x}_i] \\ &+ w_{i,t-1}(1 - w_{it})\mathrm{E}[y_{it}(1,0) \mid \bar{w}_i, \mathbf{x}_i] \\ &+ (1 - w_{i,t-1})w_{it}\mathrm{E}[y_{it}(0,1) \mid \bar{w}_i, \mathbf{x}_i] \\ &+ w_{i,t-1}w_{it}\mathrm{E}[y_{it}(1,1) \mid \bar{w}_i, \mathbf{x}_i] \end{aligned} \tag{21.136}$$

Actually, we could have derived this equation directly if we had just assumed that treatment at $t-1$ and t is unconfounded conditional on $(\bar{w}_i, \mathbf{x}_i)$, but the current derivation makes a link to approaches with unobserved heterogeneity.

It follows now from equation (21.136) that we can estimate $\mathrm{E}[y_{it}(g_{t-1}, g_t) \mid \bar{w}_i, \mathbf{x}_i]$ by estimating $\mathrm{E}(y_{it} \mid w_{i,t-1} = g_{t-1}, w_{it} = g_t, \bar{w}_i, \mathbf{x}_i) \equiv m_t(g_{t-1}, g_t, \bar{w}_i, \mathbf{x}_i)$. That is, for each of the four treatment group combinations, we estimate regressions of y_{it} on $(\bar{w}_i, \mathbf{x}_i)$, or use quasi-MLE. (If $\mathbf{x}_i$ is truly a sequence of covariates that change over time, we might restrict the way $\mathbf{x}_i$ appears, such as $(\mathbf{x}_{it}, \mathbf{x}_{i,t-1}, \bar{\mathbf{x}}_i)$, but this restriction is only intended to conserve on the dimension of the estimation problem.) Given the $\hat{m}_t(g_{t-1}, g_t, \bar{w}_i, \mathbf{x}_i)$, we have

$$\hat{\mathrm{E}}[y_{it}(g_{t-1}, g_t)] = N^{-1} \sum_{i=1}^{N} \hat{m}_t(g_{t-1}, g_t, \bar{w}_i, \mathbf{x}_i), \tag{21.137}$$

that is, we average out the control variables $(\bar{w}_i, \mathbf{x}_i)$. This approach can be made quite flexible and allows estimation of average treatment effects that compare any of the four groups to any other group. And, of course, nothing about the method requires us to focus on only current and one lag of treatment status. The same general approach applies to histories $\mathbf{g}^t = (g_1^t, g_2^t, \ldots, g_t^t)$ where each g_r^t is zero or one.

The previous approaches assume ignorability of treatment conditional on heterogeneity, or a sufficient statistic for the entire treatment history (such as the time average), and a sequence of observed covariates. It may be more realistic to assume ignorability conditional on past observed *outcomes*, treatment assignments, and covariates. For example, if workers are being assigned into job training, an administrator may be more likely to make assignments on the basis of past observed labor market outcomes and past assignment status. General frameworks can be found in Gill and Robins (2001), Lechner and Miquel (2005), and Abbring and Heckman (2007). Here I follow Lechner (2004) and use a **dynamic ignorability** assumption. The setup is that for a total of T time periods we have a balanced panel. For each i, we observe the sequence of binary treatment indicators, $\{w_{it}: t = 1, \ldots, T\}$. Let the $1 \times t$ vector $\mathbf{g}^t$ be defined as in the previous paragraph: a sequence of zeros and ones indicating a treatment regime through time t. We are interested in the counterfactual outcomes $y_{it}(\mathbf{g}^t)$, the outcome under regime $\mathbf{g}^t$. (Incidentally, unlike in some approaches to treatment effect estimation with panel data, we do not have to consider counterfactual outcomes as a function of future treatments. Therefore, we need not put restrictions on the counterfactuals such as the "no anticipation" requirement; see, for example, Abbring and Heckman (2007).) Naturally, we can write the observed outcome, y_{it}, as a function of the $y_{it}(\mathbf{g}^t)$ for $\mathbf{g}^t \in \mathscr{G}^t$, the set of all valid treatment regimes. Further, at each time t we observe a set of covariates, $\mathbf{x}_i^t$ such that $\mathbf{x}_i^{t-1} \subset \mathbf{x}_i^t$, $t = 2, \ldots, T$. At a minimum, $\mathbf{x}_i^t$ would typically include all past observed outcomes, $\{y_{i,t-1}, \ldots, y_{i1}\}$, but it can also include time-constant variables, say, $\mathbf{z}_i$, collected in the intial period. In some cases, $\mathbf{x}_i^t$ can contain variables dated at time t, but one must be sure that such variables are not themselves affected by treatment.

We state the dynamic ignorability assumption (for each t) as

$$\begin{aligned} &\mathrm{D}[w_{ir} \mid y_{it}(\mathbf{g}^t), w_{i,r-1}, \ldots, w_{i1}, \mathbf{x}_i^r] \\ &\quad = \mathrm{D}[w_{ir} \mid w_{i,r-1}, \ldots, w_{i1}, \mathbf{x}_i^r], \quad \mathbf{g}^t \in \mathscr{G}^t, r \leq t. \end{aligned} \tag{21.138}$$

When $r = t$, this condition is

$$\mathrm{D}[w_{it} \mid y_{it}(\mathbf{g}^t), w_{i,t-1}, \ldots, w_{i1}, \mathbf{x}_i^t] = \mathrm{D}[w_{it} \mid w_{i,t-1}, \ldots, w_{i1}, \mathbf{x}_i^t], \quad \mathbf{g}^t \in \mathscr{G}^t,$$

which says that, conditional on past assignments and outcomes (contained in $\mathbf{x}_i^t$), assignment is independent of the counterfactual outcomes. Lechner (2004) refers to this as the weak dynamic conditional independence assumption. Equation (21.138) requires that ignorability of assignment with respect to the counterfactual at time t hold in periods before t.

With a suitable overlap assumption, which will become clear shortly, we can show that equation (21.138) is sufficient to identify the means $\mathrm{E}[y_{it}(\mathbf{g}^t)]$, which we can compare across different $\mathbf{g}^t$ to obtain average treatment effects. To simplify the notation, consider the mean $\mathrm{E}[y_{it}(\mathbf{1}^t)]$ where $\mathbf{1}^t = (1, 1, \ldots, 1)$, a t-vector of ones. This corresponds to treatment in every time period. Define

$$p_{ir}(\mathbf{x}_i^r) \equiv \mathrm{P}(w_{ir} = 1 \mid w_{i,r-1} = 1, \ldots, w_{i1} = 1, \mathbf{x}_i^r), \quad r \leq t \tag{21.139}$$

(which is specific to the particular treatment sequence we are considering). By assumption (21.138), this is also the probability conditional on $y_{it}(\mathbf{1}^t)$. Now, we want to show that a particular kind of inverse probability weighting identifies $\mathrm{E}[y_{it}(\mathbf{1}^t)]$. (This is similar to the attrition problem in Section 19.9.3 except that here we assume that the same units are observed in each time period. Thus, though there is a "missing data" problem in that we do not observe $y_{it}(\mathbf{1}^t)$, we assume that, at a given time period t, for each unit we observe the entire history of past outcomes and other covariates.) The selected, weighted outcome y_{it} for $\mathbf{g}^t = (1, \ldots, 1)$ is

$$\frac{w_{it}w_{i,t-1}\cdots w_{i1}y_{it}}{p_{it}(\mathbf{x}_i^t)\cdots p_{i1}(\mathbf{x}_i^1)} = \frac{w_{it}w_{i,t-1}\cdots w_{i1}y_{it}(\mathbf{1}^t)}{p_{it}(\mathbf{x}_i^t)\cdots p_{i1}(\mathbf{x}_i^1)}, \tag{21.140}$$

where the equality follows because $w_{it}w_{i,t-1}\cdots w_{i1} = 1$ implies that $y_{it} = y_{it}(\mathbf{1}^t)$. Because we have divided by the propensity scores in equation (21.140), we are, of course, assuming they are nonzero. This is the overlap assumption for this particular counterfactual outcome. If, for example, it is impossible to receive treatment in every period, then $\mathrm{E}[y_{it}(\mathbf{1}^t)]$ is generally unidentified. Essentially, we must restrict attention to averages of counterfactual outcomes that correspond to possible treatment sequences.

We now show that the expected value of the second term is $\mathrm{E}[y_{it}(\mathbf{1}^t)]$. We do so sequentially by iterated expectations and assumption (21.138). First,

$$\mathrm{E}\left[\frac{w_{it}w_{i,t-1}\cdots w_{i1}y_{it}(\mathbf{1}^t)}{p_{it}(\mathbf{x}_i^t)\cdots p_{i1}(\mathbf{x}_i^1)}\right] = \mathrm{E}\left\{\mathrm{E}\left[\frac{w_{it}w_{i,t-1}\cdots w_{i1}y_{it}(\mathbf{1}^t)}{p_{it}(\mathbf{x}_i^t)\cdots p_{i1}(\mathbf{x}_i^1)}\,\middle|\, y_{it}(\mathbf{1}^t), w_{i,t-1}, \ldots, w_{i1}, \mathbf{x}_i^t\right]\right\}$$

Now, because $\mathbf{x}_i^{t-1} \subset \mathbf{x}_i^t$, the denominator is a function of the conditioning variables, and the conditional expectation of the numerator is

$$\begin{aligned}
&\mathrm{E}[w_{it} \mid y_{it}(\mathbf{1}^t), w_{i,t-1}, \ldots, w_{i1}, \mathbf{x}_i^t]w_{it}w_{i,t-1}\cdots w_{i1}y_{it}(\mathbf{1}^t) \\
&\quad = \mathrm{P}(w_{it} = 1 \mid w_{i,t-1}, \ldots, w_{i1}, \mathbf{x}_i^t)w_{it}w_{i,t-1}\cdots w_{i1}y_{it}(\mathbf{1}^t) \\
&\quad = \mathrm{P}(w_{it} = 1 \mid w_{i,t-1} = 1, \ldots, w_{i1} = 1, \mathbf{x}_i^t)w_{it}w_{i,t-1}\cdots w_{i1}y_{it}(\mathbf{1}^t) \\
&\quad \equiv p_{it}(\mathbf{x}_i^t)w_{it}w_{i,t-1}\cdots w_{i1}y_{it}(\mathbf{1}^t),
\end{aligned}$$

where the first equality follows from assumption (21.138) and the second follows because the term is zero unless all w_{is}, $s = 1, \ldots, t-1$, are unity. Therefore, we have shown that

$$\mathrm{E}\left[\frac{w_{it}w_{i,t-1}\cdots w_{i1}y_{it}(\mathbf{1}^t)}{p_{it}(\mathbf{x}_i^t)\cdots p_{i1}(\mathbf{x}_i^1)}\,\middle|\, y_{it}(\mathbf{1}^t), w_{i,t-1}, \ldots, w_{i1}, \mathbf{x}_i^t\right] = \frac{w_{i,t-1}\cdots w_{i1}y_{it}(\mathbf{1}^t)}{p_{i,t-1}(\mathbf{x}_i^{t-1})\cdots p_{i1}(\mathbf{x}_i^1)},$$

and so

$$\mathrm{E}\left[\frac{w_{it}w_{i,t-1}\cdots w_{i1}y_{it}(\mathbf{1}^t)}{p_{it}(\mathbf{x}_i^t)\cdots p_{i1}(\mathbf{x}_i^1)}\right] = \mathrm{E}\left[\frac{w_{i,t-1}\cdots w_{i1}y_{it}(\mathbf{1}^t)}{p_{i,t-1}(\mathbf{x}_i^{t-1})\cdots p_{i1}(\mathbf{x}_i^1)}\right] \tag{21.141}$$

Now we can repeat the argument conditioning on $[y_{it}(\mathbf{1}^t), w_{i,t-2}, \ldots, w_{i1}, \mathbf{x}_i^{t-1}]$ and use assumption (21.138) for $r = t-1$. And so on, until we get the expectation to

$$\mathrm{E}\left[\frac{w_{i1}y_{it}(\mathbf{1}^t)}{p_{i1}(\mathbf{x}_i^1)}\right] = \mathrm{E}[y_{it}(\mathbf{1}^t)],$$

where one final application of assumption (21.138) and iterated expectations gets us the desired equality.

Given that

$$\mathrm{E}\left[\frac{w_{it}w_{i,t-1}\cdots w_{i1}y_{it}}{p_{it}(\mathbf{x}_i^t)\cdots p_{i1}(\mathbf{x}_i^1)}\right] = \mathrm{E}[y_{it}(\mathbf{1}^t)], \tag{21.142}$$

where all quantities in the left-hand-side expectation are either observed or estimable, we can consistently estimate $\mathrm{E}[y_{it}(\mathbf{1}^t)]$ by

$$\hat{\mathrm{E}}[y_{it}(\mathbf{1}^t)] = N^{-1}\sum_{i=1}^{N}\frac{w_{it}w_{i,t-1}\cdots w_{i1}y_{it}}{\hat{p}_{it}(\mathbf{x}_i^t)\cdots \hat{p}_{i1}(\mathbf{x}_i^1)}, \tag{21.143}$$

where $\hat{p}_{ir}(\mathbf{x}_i^r)$ is an estimate of $\mathrm{P}(w_{ir} = 1 \mid w_{i,r-1} = 1, \ldots, w_{i1} = 1, \mathbf{x}_i^r)$. We can estimate these probabilities very generally. With lots of data, we might estimate a flexible binary response model for w_{ir} on the subsample with $w_{i,r=1} = 1, \ldots, w_{i1} = 1$ with $\mathbf{x}_i^r$ as the covariates. Or, we might estimate a model for $\mathrm{P}(w_{ir} = 1 \mid w_{i,r-1}, \ldots, w_{i1}, \mathbf{x}_i^r)$ using all i, and then insert $w_{i,r=1} = 1, \ldots, w_{i1} = 1$.

The approach for any sequence of potential treatments $\mathbf{g}^t$ should be clear. We use the treatment indicators to select out the appropriate subsample, and then estimate $\mathrm{P}(w_{ir} = g_r^t \mid w_{i,r-1} = g_{r-1}^t, \ldots, w_{i1} = g_1^t, \mathbf{x}_i^r)$ for $r = 1, \ldots, t$. For example, with $\mathbf{g}^t = (0, 0, \ldots, 0)$ we select out the subsample using $(1 - w_{it})\cdots(1 - w_{i1})$ and then weight by the inverse of the product of the conditional probabilities. By estimating several combinations of treatment patterns we can obtain distributed lag effects of the policy intervention on current and future outcomes.

The two approaches just described—ignorability conditional on unobserved heterogeneity and dynamic ignorability—are generally consistent under different assumptions. Nevertheless, it is sometimes (at least implicitly) claimed that dynamic ignorability is less restrictive. To see that this claim can seem to be true but is not, it is useful to work through a simple case.

Suppose that $T = 2$ and there is no treatment in the first time period, so $w_{i1} \equiv 0$. Consequently, the observed outcome in period one is y_{i1}, and there is no need to distinguish between it and counterfactual outcomes. In period 2 the counterfactual outcomes are $y_{i2}(0)$ and $y_{i2}(1)$, and the observed outcome is $y_{i2} = y_{i2}(0) + w_{i2}[y_{i2}(1) - y_{i2}(0)]$. Assume that the treatment effect is the constant τ. If we assume ignorability conditional on heterogeneity c_i, then we can write $y_{i1} = c_i + u_{i1}$, $y_{i2} = c_i + \eta + \tau w_{i2} + u_{i2}$, where η is the difference in intercepts between the two time periods (assumed to be constant). These simple representations lead to a simple differenced equation:

$$\Delta y_{i2} = \eta + \tau w_{i2} + \Delta u_{i2}, \tag{21.144}$$

where $\Delta y_{i2} = y_{i2} - y_{i1}$ and we use the fact that $w_{i1} = 0$. If we estimate equation (21.144) by OLS, the OLS estimate is the first-difference (FD) estimate,

$$\hat{\tau}_{FD} = \Delta\bar{y}_{treat} - \Delta\bar{y}_{control}, \tag{21.145}$$

which is the difference in average changes over time between the treatment and control groups. This estimator is consistent because treatment is strictly exogenous conditional on the heterogeneity.

A commonly used alternative in the statistics literature is to add the first-period outcome as a control, that is, use the regression

$$\Delta y_{i2} \quad \text{on} \quad 1, w_{i2}, y_{i1}. \tag{21.146}$$

If we add the assumption that the shocks $\{u_{i1}, u_{i2}\}$ are serially uncorrelated—specifically, $\mathrm{E}(u_{i1}u_{i2} \mid w_{i1}, c_i) = 0$—then adding y_{i1} overcontrols and leads to inconsistency. In fact, it can be shown (for example, Angrist and Pischke (2009), Section 5.4) that

$$\text{plim}(\hat{\tau}_{LDV}) = \tau + \pi_1(\sigma_{u_1}^2/\sigma_{r_2}^2), \tag{21.147}$$

where $w_{i2} = \pi_0 + \pi_1 y_{i1} + r_{i2}$ is a linear projection, and so $\pi_1 = \mathrm{Cov}(c_i, w_{i2})/(\sigma_c^2 + \sigma_{u_1}^2)$. We can easily sign the bias given the sign of π_1. For example, if w_{i2} indicates a job training program and less productive workers are more likely to participate ($\pi_1 < 0$), then the regression that controls for y_{i1} underestimates the job training effect. If more productive workers participate, it overestimates the effect of job training. This simple example illustrates a general lesson in estimating treatment effects, whether one uses regression, propensity score weighting, or matching: it is not necessarily true that controlling for more covariates results in less bias. This example shows that adding covariates can actually induce bias when there was none.

Now suppose that ignorability of treatment holds conditional on y_{i1} (and the treatment effect is constant). Then we can write

$$\Delta y_{i2} = \gamma + \tau w_{i2} + \lambda y_{i1} + e_{i2}$$

$$\mathrm{E}(e_{i2}) = 0, \quad \mathrm{Cov}(w_{i2}, e_{i2}) = \mathrm{Cov}(y_{i1}, e_{i2}) = 0.$$

Now, of course, controlling for y_{i1} consistently estimates τ because we are assuming that controlling for y_{i1} (in a linear way) leads to ignorable treatment. On the other hand, the FD estimator suffers from omitted variable "bias":

$$\mathrm{plim}(\hat{\tau}_{FD}) = \tau + \lambda \frac{\mathrm{Cov}(w_{i2}, y_{i1})}{\mathrm{Var}(w_{i2})}. \tag{21.148}$$

Suppose there is regression to the mean, so that $\lambda < 0$. If workers observed with low first-period earnings are more likely to participate, so that $\mathrm{Cov}(w_{i2}, y_{i1}) < 0$, then $\mathrm{plim}(\hat{\tau}_{FD}) > \tau$, and so FD overestimates the effect. In fact, if the correlation between w_{i2} and y_{i1} is negative in the sample, $\hat{\tau}_{FD} > \hat{\tau}_{LDV}$ is an algebraic fact. But this does not allow us to determine which estimator has less inconsistency because the derivations rely on different ignorability assumptions.

Problems

21.1. Consider the difference-in-means estimator, $\bar{d} = \bar{y}_1 - \bar{y}_0$, where $\bar{y}_g$ is the sample average of the y_i with $w_i = g$, $g = 0, 1$.

a. Show that, as an estimator of τ_{att}, the bias in $\bar{y}_1 - \bar{y}_0$ is $\mathrm{E}(y_0 \mid w = 1) - \mathrm{E}(y_0 \mid w = 0)$.

b. Let y_0 be the earnings someone would earn in the absence of job training, and let $w = 1$ denote the job training indicator. Explain the meaning of $\mathrm{E}(y_0 \mid w = 1) < \mathrm{E}(y_0 \mid w = 0)$. Intuitively, does it make sense that $\mathrm{E}(\bar{d}) < \tau_{att}$?

21.2. Explain how you would estimate $\tau_{ate,\mathscr{R}} = \mathrm{E}(y_1 - y_0 \mid \mathbf{x} \in \mathscr{R})$ using propensity score weighting under Assumption ATE.1′.

21.3. Use the data in JTRAIN3.RAW to answer these questions. The response in this case is the binary variable *unem*78.

a. Estimate τ_{ate} from the simple regression of $unem78_i$ on 1, $train_i$. Does the training program have the anticipated effect on being unemployed?

b. Add as controls the variables *age*, *educ*, *black*, *hisp*, *married*, *re74*, *re75*, *unem75*, and *unem74*. How does the estimate of τ_{ate} compare with the simple regression estimate from part a? What is the (heteroskedasticity-robust) 95% confidence interval?

c. Using the same controls as in part b, estimate separate regressions for the treatment and control groups. Now what is $\hat{\tau}_{ate}$? Does it differ much from the estimate in part b? What is $\hat{\tau}_{att}$?

d. Now use regression adjustment with controls *age*, *educ*, *black*, *hisp*, *married*, *re74*, and *re75*, but use only the subsample of men who were unemployed in 1974 or 1975. Again use two separate regression functions. What are $\hat{\tau}_{ate}$ and $\hat{\tau}_{att}$? How do these compare with the estimates from part c?

e. Estimate the propensity score using logit and the explanatory variables in part b. How many outcomes are perfectly predicted? What does this result mean for IPW estimation?

f. Now estimate the propensity score using only observations with $avgre \leq 15$. Use the $\hat{p}(\mathbf{x}_i)$ in IPW estimation to obtain $\hat{\tau}_{ate}$ and $\hat{\tau}_{att}$. Be sure to only use observations with $avgre \leq 15$. Compare these with the corresponding regression adjustment estimates using the $avgre \leq 15$ observations.

21.4. Carefully derive equation (21.80).

21.5. Use the data in JTRAIN2.RAW for this question.

a. As in Example 21.2, run a probit of *train* on 1, $\mathbf{x}$, where $\mathbf{x}$ contains the covariates from Example 21.2. Obtain the probit fitted values, say $\hat{\Phi}_i$.

b. Estimate the equation $re78_i = \gamma_0 + \tau\, train_i + \mathbf{x}_i\boldsymbol{\gamma} + u_i$ by IV, using instruments $(1, \hat{\Phi}_i, \mathbf{x}_i)$. Comment on the estimate of τ and its standard error.

c. Regress $\hat{\Phi}_i$ on $\mathbf{x}_i$ to obtain the R-squared. What do you make of this result?

d. Does the nonlinearity of the probit model for *train* allow us to estimate τ when we do not have an additional instrument? Explain.

21.6. In Procedure 21.2, explain why it is better to estimate equation (21.71) by IV rather than to run the OLS regression y_i on 1, $\hat{G}_i$, $\mathbf{x}_i$, $\hat{G}_i(\mathbf{x}_i - \bar{\mathbf{x}})$, $i = 1, \ldots, N$.

21.7. As a special case of the setup in Section 21.6.3 we can write $y_i = a_i + b_i w_i$ where w_i is a scalar. If we define $\beta = \mathrm{E}(b_i)$, then, under assumptions (21.124) and (21.125),

$$\beta = \mathrm{E}\left\{\frac{[w_i - \psi(\mathbf{x}_i)]y_i}{\omega(\mathbf{x}_i)}\right\},$$

where $\psi(\mathbf{x}_i) = \mathrm{E}(w_i \mid \mathbf{x}_i)$ and $\omega(\mathbf{x}_i) = \mathrm{Var}(w_i \mid \mathbf{x}_i)$.

a. Suppose that the treatment variable w_i is a nonnegative count variable (such as visits to one's family physician during a year) and you think $\mathrm{E}(w \mid \mathbf{x}) = \exp(\gamma_0 + \mathbf{x}\boldsymbol{\gamma})$

and $\text{Var}(w \mid \mathbf{x}) = \exp(\delta_0 + \mathbf{x}\boldsymbol{\delta})$. Propose a method for estimating the mean and variance parameters. [Hint: For the latter, define appropriate errors, say $r = w - \text{E}(w \mid \mathbf{x})$, and note that $\text{E}(r^2 \mid \mathbf{x}) = \text{Var}(w \mid \mathbf{x})$.]

b. Given the estimators from part a, suggest a consistent, $\sqrt{N}$-asymptotically normal estimator of β. How would you conduct inference on β?

c. Apply the method from parts a and b to the data in JTRAIN2.RAW, using as w the variable *mostrn* (months spent in job training) and $y = re78$. Use the same variables in $\mathbf{x}$ as Example 21.1.

d. Now suppose w_i is a proportion (such as proportion of lectures attended) and you think $\text{E}(w \mid \mathbf{x}) = \Lambda(\gamma_0 + \mathbf{x}\boldsymbol{\gamma})$ and $\text{Var}(w \mid \mathbf{x}) = \delta_0 + \delta_1 \text{E}(w \mid \mathbf{x}) + \delta_2 [\text{E}(w \mid \mathbf{x})]^2$, where $\Lambda(\cdot)$ is the logistic function. Now how would you estimate the mean and variance parameters? What practical problem might arise with the estimated variances?

e. Apply the approach from part d to the data set ATTEND.RAW with $w = atndrte$, the proportion (not percentage) of lectures attended. For the response use $y = stndfnl$, for the elements of $\mathbf{x}$ use cubics in *priGPA* and *ACT*, and use the *frosh* and *soph* binary indicators. What is the estimate of β? How does it compare to the multiple regression estimate of *stndfnl* on *atndrte* and the given controls?

21.8. In the IV setup of Section 21.6.3, suppose that $b = \beta$, and therefore we can write

$$y = a + \beta w + e, \qquad \text{E}(e \mid a, \mathbf{x}, \mathbf{z}) = 0.$$

Assume that conditions (21.129) and (21.130) hold for a.

a. Suppose w is a corner solution outcome, such as hours spent in a job training program. If $\mathbf{z}$ is used as IVs for w in $y = \gamma_0 + \beta w + \mathbf{x}\boldsymbol{\gamma} + r$, what is the identification condition?

b. If w given $(\mathbf{x}, \mathbf{z})$ follows a standard Tobit model, propose an IV estimator that uses the Tobit fitted values for w.

c. If $\text{Var}(e \mid a, \mathbf{x}, \mathbf{z}) = \sigma_e^2$ and $\text{Var}(a \mid \mathbf{x}, \mathbf{z}) = \sigma_a^2$, argue that the IV estimator from part b is asymptotically efficient.

d. What is an alternative to IV estimation that would use the Tobit fitted values for w? Which method do you prefer?

e. If $b \neq \beta$, but assumptions (21.129) and (21.130) hold, how would you estimate β?

21.9. a. Using the data in JTRAIN3.RAW, estimate the logit model for the propensity score in Example 21.1, using the same explanatory variables described there.

Plot histograms for the $train_i = 1$ and $train_i = 0$ sample separately. What do you conclude about the overlap assumption?

b. Now use the subsample with $(re74 + re75)/2 \leq 15$, and repeat the exercise from part a. How does the situation compare with the full data set?

21.10. In this problem you are to show that one can improve efficiency in estimating a constant ATE under random assignment by including regressors (provided those regressors are also independent of assignment). Let w_i be the treatment, and assume that w_i is independent of $(y_{i0}, y_{i1}, \mathbf{x}_i)$. Assume that $y_{i1} - y_{i0} = \tau$ for all i. Thus, write

$$y_i = y_{i0} + \tau w_i \equiv \mu_0 + \tau w_i + v_{i0}.$$

a. Derive the asymptotic variance of the simple OLS estimator $\tilde{\tau}$ from the regression of y_i on 1, w_i in terms of $\text{Var}(v_{i0})$, $\rho = \text{P}(w_i = 1)$, and N.

b. Write the linear projection of y_{i0} on $(1, \mathbf{x}_i)$ as

$$y_{i0} = \alpha_0 + \mathbf{x}_i \boldsymbol{\beta}_0 + u_{i0}$$

$$\text{E}(u_{i0}) = 0, \qquad \text{E}(\mathbf{x}_i' u_{i0}) = \mathbf{0}.$$

Show that we can write

$$y_i = \alpha_0 + \tau w_i + \mathbf{x}_i \boldsymbol{\beta}_0 + u_{i0},$$

and explain why w_i is uncorrelated with $\mathbf{x}_i$ and u_{i0}.

c. Using part b, show that the asymptotic variance of $\hat{\tau}$ from the regression y_i on 1, w_i, $\mathbf{x}_i$ is $\text{Var}(u_{i0})/[N\rho(1-\rho)]$.

d. Show that if $\boldsymbol{\beta}_0 \neq \mathbf{0}$, $\text{Var}(u_{i0}) < \text{Var}(v_{i0})$. Conclude that the asymptotic variance of $\hat{\tau}$ is strictly smaller than that of $\tilde{\tau}$ if $\mathbf{x}_i$ helps to predict y_{i0}.

e. Suppose that $\text{E}(y_{i0} \mid \mathbf{x}) \neq \alpha_0 + \mathbf{x}_i \boldsymbol{\beta}_0$—that is, the linear projection differs from the conditional mean. In this situation, why might you use the simple difference-in-means estimator under random assignment. (Hint: Think about small-sample versus large-sample properties.)

21.11. Suppose that we allow full slope, as well as intercept, heterogeneity in a linear representation of two counterfactual outcomes,

$$y_{i0} = a_{i0} + \mathbf{x}_i \mathbf{b}_{i0}$$

$$y_{i1} = a_{i1} + \mathbf{x}_i \mathbf{b}_{i1}.$$

Assume that the vector $(\mathbf{x}_i, \mathbf{z}_i)$ is independent of $(a_{i0}, \mathbf{b}_{i0}, a_{i1}, \mathbf{b}_{i1})$—which makes, as we will see, $\mathbf{z}_i$ instrumental variables candidates in a control function or correction function setting.

a. Define $\alpha_g \equiv \mathrm{E}(a_{ig})$ and $\boldsymbol{\beta}_g \equiv \mathrm{E}(\mathbf{b}_{ig})$, $g = 0, 1$ and $\boldsymbol{\psi} \equiv \mathrm{E}(\mathbf{x}_i)$. Find $\mu_g \equiv \mathrm{E}(y_{ig})$, $g = 0, 1$ in terms of these population parameters.

b. Let $\tau = \tau_{ate} = \mu_1 - \mu_0$ be the ATE. Also, write $a_{ig} = \alpha_g + c_{ig}$ and $\mathbf{b}_{ig} = \boldsymbol{\beta}_g + \mathbf{f}_{ig}$. Show that

$$y_i = \mu_0 + \tau w_i + (\mathbf{x}_i - \boldsymbol{\psi})\boldsymbol{\beta}_0 + w_i(\mathbf{x}_i - \boldsymbol{\psi})\boldsymbol{\delta} + c_{i0} + \mathbf{x}_i\mathbf{f}_{i0} + w_i e_i + w_i\mathbf{x}_i\mathbf{d}_i, \tag{21.149}$$

where $\boldsymbol{\delta} \equiv \boldsymbol{\beta}_1 - \boldsymbol{\beta}_0$, $e_i \equiv c_{i1} - c_{i0}$, and $\mathbf{d}_i \equiv \mathbf{f}_{i1} - \mathbf{f}_{i0}$.

c. Assume that

$$w_i = 1[\theta_0 + \mathbf{x}_i\boldsymbol{\theta}_1 + \mathbf{z}_i\boldsymbol{\theta}_2 + v_i \geq 0] \equiv 1[\mathbf{q}_i\boldsymbol{\theta} + v_i \geq 0],$$

and assume that $\mathrm{E}(c_{i0} \mid v_i, \mathbf{x}_i, \mathbf{z}_i) = \rho_0 v_i$, $\mathrm{E}(\mathbf{f}_{i0} \mid v_i, \mathbf{x}_i, \mathbf{z}_i) = \boldsymbol{\eta}_0 v_i$, $\mathrm{E}(e_i \mid v_i, \mathbf{x}_i, \mathbf{z}_i) = \xi v_i$, and $\mathrm{E}(\mathbf{d}_i \mid v_i, \mathbf{x}_i, \mathbf{z}_i) = \boldsymbol{\theta} a_i$. Find $\mathrm{E}(y_i \mid v_i, \mathbf{x}_i, \mathbf{z}_i)$.

d. Assuming that v_i is independent of $(\mathbf{x}_i, \mathbf{z}_i)$ and has a standard normal distribution, use part c to find $\mathrm{E}(y_i \mid w_i, \mathbf{x}_i, \mathbf{z}_i)$. (Hint: This should depend on the generalized residual $h(w_i, \mathbf{q}_i\boldsymbol{\theta}) = w_i\lambda(\mathbf{q}_i\boldsymbol{\theta}) - (1 - w_i)\lambda(-\mathbf{q}_i\boldsymbol{\theta})$, where $\lambda(\cdot)$ is the inverse Mills ratio.)

e. Propose a two-step control function approach to estimating τ. How does this differ from the method derived in Section 21.4.2?

f. How would you obtain a valid standard error for $\hat{\tau}$ from part e?

g. How would you estimate $\tau_{ate}(\mathbf{x}) = \mathrm{E}(y_1 - y_0 \mid \mathbf{x})$?

21.12. Consider the same setup as Problem 21.11, under the same assumptions.

a. Of the four unobserved terms in equation (21.149), which two have a zero mean conditional on $(\mathbf{x}_i, \mathbf{z}_i)$?

b. Derive the correction functions for the other terms.

c. Propose a two-step correction function estimator of τ (and the other parameters).

d. How would you test whether the correction functions are needed? Be very precise.

21.13. For the sharp regression discontinuity design, what kind of local estimation method might you use if y_i is a fractional response? Specifically describe the model and estimation method, and provide the formula for $\hat{\tau}_c$.

21.14. Consider a treatment effect setup with a binary treatment, w_{it}, in each time period. We are interested in contemporaneous ATEs, $\tau_{t,ate} = \mathrm{E}[y_{it}(1) - y_{it}(0)] \equiv \mu_{t1} - \mu_{t0}$. Assume that for covariates $\mathbf{x}_{it}$, $y_{it}(g) = a_{itg} + \mathbf{x}_{it}\boldsymbol{\beta}_g$, $g = 0, 1$, where a_{itg} are random variables and $\boldsymbol{\beta}_g$ is assumed (for simplicity) to be constant over time. Write $a_{itg} = a_{tg} + c_{itg}$, where $\alpha_{tg} \equiv \mathrm{E}(a_{itg})$. Define $\boldsymbol{\psi}_t \equiv \mathrm{E}(\mathbf{x}_{it})$.

a. Find μ_{t0}, μ_{t1}, and $\tau_{t,ate}$ in terms of the α_{tg}, $\boldsymbol{\beta}_g$, and $\boldsymbol{\psi}_t$.

b. Let $y_{it} = (1 - w_{it}) y_{it}(0) + w_{it} y_{it}(1)$ and let $\tau_t = \tau_{t,ate}$ for notational simplicity. Show that we can write

$$y_{it} = \mu_{t0} + \tau_t w_{it} + (\mathbf{x}_{it} - \boldsymbol{\psi}_t)\boldsymbol{\beta}_0 + w_{it}(\mathbf{x}_{it} - \boldsymbol{\psi}_t)\boldsymbol{\delta} + c_{it0} + w_{it} e_{it}, \tag{21.150}$$

where $\boldsymbol{\delta} \equiv \boldsymbol{\beta}_1 - \boldsymbol{\beta}_0$ and $e_{it} \equiv c_{it1} - c_{it0}$.

c. We think in equation (21.150) that w_{it} is correlated with c_{it0} and e_{it}, possibly because these terms each contain time-constant heterogeneity and idiosyncratic unobservables that are related to treatment. Suppose we have a vector $\mathbf{z}_{it}$ of potential instrumental variables. We allow the time average of the instruments and covariates to be correlated with (c_{it0}, e_{it}). In particular,

$$c_{it0} = (\bar{\mathbf{x}}_i - \boldsymbol{\mu}_{\bar{\mathbf{x}}})\boldsymbol{\xi}_1 + (\bar{\mathbf{z}}_i - \boldsymbol{\mu}_{\bar{\mathbf{z}}})\boldsymbol{\xi}_2 + r_{it0}, \quad \mathrm{E}(r_{it0} \mid \mathbf{x}_i, \mathbf{z}_i) = 0$$

$$e_{it} = (\bar{\mathbf{x}}_i - \boldsymbol{\mu}_{\bar{\mathbf{x}}})\boldsymbol{\eta}_1 + (\bar{\mathbf{z}}_i - \boldsymbol{\mu}_{\bar{\mathbf{z}}})\boldsymbol{\eta}_2 + v_{it}, \quad \mathrm{E}(v_{it} \mid \mathbf{x}_i, \mathbf{z}_i) = 0,$$

where $\mathbf{x}_i$ and $\mathbf{z}_i$ are the entire histories of the covariates and instruments. (Removing the population means of $\bar{\mathbf{x}}_i$ and $\bar{\mathbf{z}}_i$ ensures c_{it0} and e_{it} have zero means.) Rewrite equation (21.150) so that it includes the time averages.

d. Assume that w_{it} can be expressed as

$$w_{it} = 1[\theta_0 + \mathbf{x}_{it}\boldsymbol{\theta}_1 + \mathbf{z}_{it}\boldsymbol{\theta}_2 + \bar{\mathbf{x}}_i\boldsymbol{\theta}_3 + \bar{\mathbf{z}}_i\boldsymbol{\theta}_4 + q_{it} \geq 0]$$

$$\mathrm{D}(q_{it} \mid \mathbf{x}_i, \mathbf{z}_i) = \mathrm{Normal}(0, 1).$$

Further, assume that $\mathrm{E}(c_{it0} \mid q_{it}, \mathbf{x}_i, \mathbf{z}_i) = \alpha_0 q_{it}$ and $\mathrm{E}(e_{it} \mid q_{it}, \mathbf{x}_i, \mathbf{z}_i) = \rho q_{it}$. Find $\mathrm{E}(y_{it} \mid w_{it}, \mathbf{x}_i, \mathbf{z}_i)$.

e. Use the expression from part d to propose a two-step control function approach to estimating the τ_t.

21.15. Use the data in CATHETER.RAW to answer this question. The treatment variable is *rhc*, which is unity if a patient received a right-heart catheterization and zero if not. The response variable is *death*, equal to unity if the patient died within 180 days. The patients were all admitted to the intensive care unit, and so the death rate is very high: almost 65% of the patients died in the first six months. See Li, Racine, and Wooldridge (2008).

a. How many observations are in the sample? What fraction of patients received the RHC treatment?

b. Use the difference in means to estimate the average treatment effect of *rhc*. Does the treatment reduce the probability of death? Is the estimate practically large and statistically significant?

c. Now use regression adjustment, estimating logit models for *death* separately for $rhc = 0$ and $rhc = 1$. As covariates, use *sex*, *race*, *income*, *cat*1, *cat*2, *ninsclas*, and *age*. For all but the age variable include dummy variables for all categories (except, of course, a base category). What is the regression adjustment estimate of τ_{ate}? Of τ_{att}? Obtain standard errors using, say, 1,000 bootstrap replications.

d. Estimate a logit model for *rhc* using the same covariates as in part c. Compare the range and average of the estimated propensity scores for the treated and untreated samples. Plot a histogram in each case, and comment on overlap.

e. Estimate τ_{ate} and τ_{att} by propensity score weighting. Again use 1,000 bootstrap replications to obtain standard errors. How do the estimates compare with those from part d? Overall, does it appear RHC reduces the probability of death?

21.16. Use the data in REGDISC.RAW to answer this question. These are simulated data of a fuzzy regression discontinuity design with forcing variable x. The discontinuity is at $x = 5$.

a. What fraction of the observations have $x_i \geq 5$? What fraction of units are in the treated group (that is, have $w_i = 1$)?

b. Estimate separate linear probability models for $x_i < 5$ and $x_i \geq 5$, and obtain the fitted line. Do the same for logit models, and obtain the fitted logit functions. Graph these functions on the same graph. What is the estimated jump in the probability of treatment in each case?

c. Compute the estimate of τ_c with $c = 5$ in equation (21.107) using linear regression for y and w, and using all the data.

d. Now use the IV estimate described in equation (21.108), again using all the data. Is it the same as the estimate in part c? What is its standard error?

e. Now use a "local" version of the IV method, restricting attention to data with $x_i > 3$ and $x_i < 7$. What happens to the estimated τ_c and its standard error compared with that in part d?

22 Duration Analysis

22.1 Introduction

Some response variables in economics come in the form of a **duration**, which is the time elapsed until a certain event occurs. A few examples include weeks unemployed, months spent on welfare, days until arrest after incarceration, and quarters until an Internet firm files for bankruptcy.

The recent literature on duration analysis is quite rich. In this chapter we focus on the developments that have been used most often in applied work. In addition to providing a rigorous introduction to modern duration analysis, this chapter should prepare you for more advanced treatments, such as Lancaster's (1990) monograph, van den Berg (2001), and Cameron and Trivedi (2005).

Duration analysis has its origins in what is typically called **survival analysis**, where the duration of interest is survival time of a subject. In survival analysis we are interested in how various treatments or demographic characteristics affect survival times. In the social sciences, we are interested in any situation where an individual—or family, or firm, and so on—begins in an initial state and is either observed to exit the state or is censored. (We will discuss the exact nature of censoring in Sections 22.3 and 22.4.) The calendar dates on which units enter the initial state do not have to be the same. (When we introduce covariates in Section 22.2.2, we note how dummy variables for different calendar dates can be included in the covariates, if necessary, to allow for systematic differences in durations by starting date.)

Traditional duration analysis begins by specifying a population distribution for the duration, usually conditional on some explanatory variables (covariates) observed at the beginning of the duration. For example, for the population of people who became unemployed during a particular period, we might observe education levels, experience, marital status—all measured when the person becomes unemployed—wage on prior job, and a measure of unemployment benefits. Then we specify a distribution for the unemployment duration conditional on the covariates. Any reasonable distribution reflects the fact that an unemployment duration is nonnegative. Once a complete conditional distribution has been specified, the same maximum likelihood methods that we studied in Chapter 19 for censored regression models can be used. In this framework, we are typically interested in estimating the effects of the covariates on the expected duration.

Recent treatments of duration analysis tend to focus on the hazard function. The hazard function allows us to approximate the probability of exiting the initial state within a short interval, conditional on having survived up to the starting time of the interval. In econometric applications, hazard functions are usually conditional on some covariates. An important feature for policy analysis is allowing the hazard function to depend on covariates that change over time.

In Section 22.2 we define and discuss hazard functions, and we settle certain issues involved with introducing covariates into hazard functions. In Section 22.3 we show how censored regression models apply to standard duration models with single-cycle flow data, when all covariates are time constant. We also discuss the most common way of introducing unobserved heterogeneity into traditional duration analysis. Given parametric assumptions, we can test for duration dependence—which means that the probability of exiting the initial state depends on the length of time in the state—as well as for the presence of unobserved heterogeneity.

In Section 22.4 we study methods that allow flexible estimation of a hazard function, with both time-constant and time-varying covariates. We assume that we have grouped data; this term means that durations are observed to fall into fixed intervals (often weekly or monthly intervals) and that any time-varying covariates are assumed to be constant within an interval. We focus attention on the case with two states, with everyone in the population starting in the initial state, and single-cycle data, where each person either exits the initial state or is censored before exiting. We also show how heterogeneity can be included when the covariates are strictly exogenous. We touch on some additional issues in Section 22.5.

22.2 Hazard Functions

The hazard function plays a central role in modern duration analysis. In this section, we discuss various features of the hazard function, both with and without covariates, and provide some examples.

22.2.1 Hazard Functions without Covariates

Often in this chapter it is convenient to distinguish random variables from particular outcomes of random variables. Let $T \geq 0$ denote the duration, which has some distribution in the population; t denotes a particular value of T. (As with any econometric analysis, it is important to be very clear about the relevant population, a topic we consider in Section 22.3.) In survival analysis, T is the length of time a subject lives. Much of the current terminology in duration analysis comes from survival applications. For us, T is the time at which a person (or family, firm, and so on) leaves the initial state. For example, if the initial state is unemployment, T would be the time, measured in, say, weeks, until a person becomes employed.

The cumulative distribution function (cdf) of T is defined as

$$F(t) = \mathrm{P}(T \leq t), \qquad t \geq 0 \tag{22.1}$$

The **survivor function** is defined as $S(t) \equiv 1 - F(t) = \text{P}(T > t)$, and this is the probability of "surviving" past time t. We assume in the rest of this section that T is continuous—and, in fact, has a differentiable cdf—because this assumption simplifies statements of certain probabilities. Discreteness in observed durations can be viewed as a consequence of the sampling scheme, as we discuss in Section 22.4. Denote the density of T by $f(t) = \dfrac{dF}{dt}(t)$.

For $h > 0$,

$$\text{P}(t \leq T < t + h \mid T \geq t) \tag{22.2}$$

is the probabilty of leaving the initial state in the interval $[t, t + h)$ given survival up until time t. The **hazard function** for T is defined as

$$\lambda(t) = \lim_{h \downarrow 0} \frac{\text{P}(t \leq T < t + h \mid T \geq t)}{h} \tag{22.3}$$

For each t, $\lambda(t)$ is the instantaneous rate of leaving per unit of time. From equation (22.3) it follows that, for "small" h,

$$\text{P}(t \leq T < t + h \mid T \geq t) \approx \lambda(t)h \tag{22.4}$$

Thus the hazard function can be used to approximate a conditional probability in much the same way that the height of the density of T can be used to approximate an unconditional probability.

Example 22.1 (Unemployment Duration): If T is length of time unemployed, measured in weeks, then $\lambda(20)$ is (approximately) the probability of becoming employed between weeks 20 and 21. The phrase "becoming employed" reflects the fact that the person was unemployed up through week 20. That is, $\lambda(20)$ is roughly the probability of becoming employed between weeks 20 and 21 conditional on having been unemployed through week 20.

Example 22.2 (Recidivism Duration): Suppose T is the number of months before a former prisoner is arrested for a crime. Then $\lambda(12)$ is roughly the probability of being arrested during the 13th month conditional on not having been arrested during the first year.

We can express the hazard function in terms of the density and cdf very simply. First, write

$$\text{P}(t \leq T < t + h \mid T \geq t) = \text{P}(t \leq T < t + h)/\text{P}(T \geq t) = \frac{F(t + h) - F(t)}{1 - F(t)}$$

When the cdf is differentiable, we can take the limit of the right-hand side, divided by h, as h approaches zero from above:

$$\lambda(t) = \lim_{h \downarrow 0} \frac{F(t+h) - F(t)}{h} \cdot \frac{1}{1 - F(t)} = \frac{f(t)}{1 - F(t)} = \frac{f(t)}{S(t)} \tag{22.5}$$

Because the derivative of $S(t)$ is $-f(t)$, we have

$$\lambda(t) = -\frac{d \log S(t)}{dt} \tag{22.6}$$

and, using $F(0) = 0$, we can integrate to get

$$F(t) = 1 - \exp\left[-\int_0^t \lambda(s)\,ds\right], \qquad t \geq 0 \tag{22.7}$$

Straightforward differentiation of equation (22.7) gives the density of T as

$$f(t) = \lambda(t) \exp\left[-\int_0^t \lambda(s)\,ds\right] \tag{22.8}$$

Therefore, all probabilities can be computed using the hazard function. For example, for points $a_1 < a_2$,

$$\mathrm{P}(T \geq a_2 \mid T \geq a_1) = \frac{1 - F(a_2)}{1 - F(a_1)} = \exp\left[-\int_{a_1}^{a_2} \lambda(s)\,ds\right]$$

and

$$\mathrm{P}(a_1 \leq T < a_2 \mid T \geq a_1) = 1 - \exp\left[-\int_{a_1}^{a_2} \lambda(s)\,ds\right] \tag{22.9}$$

This last expression is especially useful for constructing the log-likelihood functions needed in Section 22.4.

The shape of the hazard function is of primary interest in many empirical applications. In the simplest case, the hazard function is constant:

$$\lambda(t) = \lambda, \qquad \text{all } t \geq 0 \tag{22.10}$$

This function means that the process driving T is *memoryless*: the probability of exit in the next interval does not depend on how much time has been spent in the initial state. From equation (22.7), a constant hazard implies

$$F(t) = 1 - \exp(-\lambda t) \tag{22.11}$$

which is the cdf of the **exponential distribution**. Conversely, if T has an exponential distribution, it has a constant hazard.

When the hazard function is not constant, we say that the process exhibits **duration dependence**. Assuming that $\lambda(\cdot)$ is differentiable, there is **positive duration dependence** at time t if $d\lambda(t)/dt > 0$; if $d\lambda(t)/dt > 0$ for all $t > 0$, then the process exhibits positive duration dependence. With positive duration dependence, the probability of exiting the initial state increases the longer one is in the initial state. If the derivative is negative, then there is **negative duration dependence**.

Example 22.3 (Weibull Distribution): If T has a **Weibull distribution**, its cdf is given by $F(t) = 1 - \exp(-\gamma t^{\alpha})$, where γ and α are nonnegative parameters. The density is $f(t) = \gamma\alpha t^{\alpha-1}\exp(-\gamma t^{\alpha})$. By equation (22.5), the hazard function is

$$\lambda(t) = f(t)/S(t) = \gamma\alpha t^{\alpha-1} \tag{22.12}$$

When $\alpha = 1$, the Weibull distribution reduces to the exponential with $\lambda = \gamma$. If $\alpha > 1$, the hazard is monotonically increasing, so the hazard everywhere exhibits positive duration dependence; for $\alpha < 1$, the hazard is monotonically decreasing. Provided we think the hazard is monotonically increasing or decreasing, the Weibull distribution is a relatively simple way to capture duration dependence.

We often want to specify the hazard directly, in which case we can use equation (22.7) to determine the duration distribution.

Example 22.4 (Log-Logistic Hazard Function): The **log-logistic hazard** function is specified as

$$\lambda(t) = \frac{\gamma\alpha t^{\alpha-1}}{1 + \gamma t^{\alpha}} \tag{22.13}$$

where γ and α are positive parameters. When $\alpha = 1$, the hazard is monotonically decreasing from γ at $t = 0$ to zero as $t \to \infty$; when $\alpha < 1$, the hazard is also monotonically decreasing to zero as $t \to \infty$, but the hazard is unbounded as t approaches zero. When $\alpha > 1$, the hazard is increasing until $t = [(\alpha - 1)/\gamma]^{1-\alpha}$, and then it decreases to zero.

Straightforward integration gives

$$\int_0^t \lambda(s)\,ds = \log(1 + \gamma t^{\alpha}) = -\log[(1 + \gamma t^{\alpha})^{-1}]$$

so that, by equation (22.7),

$$F(t) = 1 - (1 + \gamma t^{\alpha})^{-1}, \qquad t \geq 0 \tag{22.14}$$

Differentiating with respect to t gives

$$f(t) = \gamma \alpha t^{\alpha-1}(1 + \gamma t^{\alpha})^{-2}$$

Using this density, it can be shown that $Y \equiv \log(T)$ has density $g(y) = \alpha \exp[\alpha(y - \mu)]/\{1 + \exp[\alpha(y - \mu)]\}^2$, where $\mu = -\alpha^{-1} \log(\gamma)$ is the mean of Y. In other words, $\log(T)$ has a **logistic distribution** with mean μ and variance $\pi^2/(3\alpha^2)$ (hence the name "log-logistic").

22.2.2 Hazard Functions Conditional on Time-Invariant Covariates

Usually in economics we are interested in hazard functions conditional on a set of covariates or regressors. When these do not change over time—as is often the case given the way many duration data sets are collected—then we simply define the hazard (and all other features of T) conditional on the covariates. Thus the conditional hazard is

$$\lambda(t; \mathbf{x}) = \lim_{h \downarrow 0} \frac{\mathrm{P}(t \leq T < t + h \mid T \geq t, \mathbf{x})}{h}$$

where $\mathbf{x}$ is a vector of explanatory variables. All the formulas from the previous subsection continue to hold provided the cdf and density are defined conditional on $\mathbf{x}$. For example, if the conditional cdf $F(\cdot \mid \mathbf{x})$ is differentiable, we have

$$\lambda(t; \mathbf{x}) = \frac{f(t \mid \mathbf{x})}{1 - F(t \mid \mathbf{x})} \tag{22.15}$$

where $f(\cdot \mid \mathbf{x})$ is the density of T given $\mathbf{x}$. Often we are interested in the partial effects of the x_j on $\lambda(t; \mathbf{x})$, which are defined as partial derivatives for continuous x_j and as differences for discrete x_j.

If the durations start at different calendar dates—which is usually the case—we can include indicators for different starting dates in the covariates. These allow us to control for seasonal differences in duration distributions.

An especially important class of models with time-invariant regressors consists of **proportional hazard models**. A proportional hazard can be written as

$$\lambda(t; \mathbf{x}) = \kappa(\mathbf{x})\lambda_0(t) \tag{22.16}$$

where $\kappa(\cdot) > 0$ is a positive function of $\mathbf{x}$ and $\lambda_0(t) > 0$ is called the **baseline hazard**. The baseline hazard is common to all units in the population; individual hazard functions differ proportionately based on a function $\kappa(\mathbf{x})$ of observed covariates.

Typically, $\kappa(\cdot)$ is parameterized as $\kappa(\mathbf{x}) = \exp(\mathbf{x}\boldsymbol{\beta})$, where $\boldsymbol{\beta}$ is a vector of parameters. Then

$$\log \lambda(t; \mathbf{x}) = \mathbf{x}\boldsymbol{\beta} + \log \lambda_0(t) \tag{22.17}$$

and β_j measures the semielasticity of the hazard with respect to x_j. [If x_j is the log of an underlying variable, say $x_j = \log(z_j)$, β_j is the elasticity of the hazard with respect to z_j.]

Occasionally we are interested only in how the covariates shift the hazard function, in which case estimation of λ_0 is not necessary. Cox (1972) obtained a partial maximum likelihood estimator for $\boldsymbol{\beta}$ that does not require estimating $\lambda_0(\cdot)$. We discuss Cox's approach briefly in Section 22.5. In economics, much of the time we are interested in the shape of the baseline hazard. We discuss estimation of proportional hazard models with a flexible baseline hazard in Section 22.4.

If in the Weibull hazard function (22.12) we replace γ with $\exp(\mathbf{x}\boldsymbol{\beta})$, where the first element of $\mathbf{x}$ is unity, we obtain a proportional hazard model with $\lambda_0(t) \equiv \alpha t^{\alpha-1}$. However, if we replace γ in equation (22.13) with $\exp(\mathbf{x}\boldsymbol{\beta})$—which is the most common way of introducing covariates into the log-logistic model—we do not obtain a hazard with the proportional hazard form.

Example 22.1 (continued): If T is an unemployment duration, $\mathbf{x}$ might contain education, labor market experience, marital status, race, and number of children, all measured at the beginning of the unemployment spell. Policy variables in $\mathbf{x}$ might reflect the rules governing unemployment benefits, where these are known before each person's unemployment duration.

Example 22.2 (continued): To explain the length of time before arrest after release from prison, the covariates might include participation in a work program while in prison, years of education, marital status, race, time served, and past number of convictions.

22.2.3 Hazard Functions Conditional on Time-Varying Covariates

Studying hazard functions is more complicated when we wish to model the effects of time-varying covariates on the hazard function. For one thing, it makes no sense to specify the distribution of the duration T conditional on the covariates at only one time period. Nevertheless, we can still define the appropriate conditional probabilities that lead to a conditional hazard function.

Let $\mathbf{x}(t)$ denote the vector of regressors at time t; again, this is the random vector describing the population. For $t \geq 0$, let $\mathbf{X}(t)$, $t \geq 0$, denote the covariate path up through time t: $\mathbf{X}(t) \equiv \{\mathbf{x}(s): 0 \leq s \leq t\}$. Following Lancaster (1990, Chapter 2), we define the conditional hazard function at time t by

$$\lambda[t; \mathbf{X}(t)] = \lim_{h \downarrow 0} \frac{\mathrm{P}[t \leq T < t+h \mid T \geq t, \mathbf{X}(t+h)]}{h} \tag{22.18}$$

assuming that this limit exists. A discussion of assumptions that ensure existence of equation (22.18) is well beyond the scope of this book; see Lancaster (1990, Chapter 2). One case where this limit exists very generally occurs when T is continuous and, for each t, $\mathbf{x}(t+h)$ is constant for all $h \in [0, \eta(t)]$ for some function $\eta(t) > 0$. Then we can replace $\mathbf{X}(t+h)$ with $\mathbf{X}(t)$ in equation (22.18) [because $\mathbf{X}(t+h) = \mathbf{X}(t)$ for h sufficiently small]. For reasons we will see in Section 22.4, we must assume that time-varying covariates are constant over the interval of observation (such as a week or a month), anyway, in which case there is no problem in defining equation (22.18).

For certain purposes, it is important to know whether time-varying covariates are **strictly exogenous**. With the hazard defined as in equation (22.18), Lancaster (1990, Definition 2.1) provides a definition that rules out feedback from the duration to future values of the covariates. Specifically, if $\mathbf{X}(t, t+h)$ denotes the covariate path from time t to $t+h$, then Lancaster's strict exogeneity condition is

$$\mathrm{P}[\mathbf{X}(t, t+h) \mid T \geq t+h, \mathbf{X}(t)] = \mathrm{P}[\mathbf{X}(t, t+h) \mid \mathbf{X}(t)] \tag{22.19}$$

for all $t \geq 0$, $h > 0$. Actually, when condition (22.19) holds, Lancaster says $\{\mathbf{x}(t): t > 0\}$ is "exogenous." We prefer the name "strictly exogenous" because condition (22.19) is closely related to the notions of strict exogeneity that we have encountered throughout this book. Plus, it is important to see that condition (22.19) has nothing to do with contemporaneous endogeneity: by definition, the covariates are **sequentially exogenous** (see Section 7.4) because, by specifying $\lambda[t; \mathbf{X}(t)]$, we are conditioning on current and past covariates.

Equation (22.19) applies to covariates whose entire path is well defined whether or not the agent is in the initial state. One such class of covariates, called **external covariates** by Kalbfleisch and Prentice (1980), has the feature that the covariate path is independent of whether any particular agent has or has not left the initial state. In modeling time until arrest, these covariates might include law enforcement per capita in the person's city of residence or the city unemployment rate.

Other covariates are not external to each agent but have paths that are still defined after the agent leaves the initial state. For example, marital status is well defined before and after someone is arrested, but it is possibly related to whether someone has been arrested. Whether marital status satisfies condition (22.19) is an empirical issue.

The definition of strict exogeneity in condition (22.19) cannot be applied to time-varying covariates whose path is not defined once the agent leaves the initial state. Kalbfleisch and Prentice (1980) call these **internal covariates**. Lancaster (1990, p. 28) gives the example of job tenure duration, where a time-varying covariate is wage paid on the job: if a person leaves the job, it makes no sense to define the future wage path in that job. As a second example, in modeling the time until a former prisoner is arrested, a time-varying covariate at time t might be wage income in the previous month, $t-1$. If someone is arrested and reincarcerated, it makes little sense to define future labor income.

It is pretty clear that internal covariates cannot satisfy any reasonable strict exogeneity assumption. This fact will be important in Section 22.4 when we discuss estimation of duration models with unobserved heterogeneity and grouped duration data. We will actually use a slightly different notion of strict exogeneity that is directly relevant for conditional maximum likelihood estimation. Nevertheless, it is in the same spirit as condition (22.19).

With time-varying covariates there is not, strictly speaking, such a thing as a proportional hazard model. Nevertheless, it has become common in econometrics to call a hazard of the form

$$\lambda[t; \mathbf{x}(t)] = \kappa[\mathbf{x}(t)]\lambda_0(t) \tag{22.20}$$

a **proportional hazard with time-varying covariates**. The function multiplying the baseline hazard is usually $\kappa[\mathbf{x}(t)] = \exp[\mathbf{x}(t)\boldsymbol{\beta}]$; for notational reasons, we show this depending only on $\mathbf{x}(t)$ and not on past covariates [which can always be included in $\mathbf{x}(t)$]. We will discuss estimation of these models, without the strict exogeneity assumption, in Section 22.4.2. In Section 22.4.3, when we multiply equation (22.20) by unobserved heterogeneity, strict exogeneity becomes very important.

The log-logistic hazard is also easily modified to have time-varying covariates. One way to include time-varying covariates parametrically is

$$\lambda[t; \mathbf{x}(t)] = \exp[\mathbf{x}(t)\boldsymbol{\beta}]\alpha t^{\alpha-1}/\{1 + \exp[\mathbf{x}(t)\boldsymbol{\beta}]t^{\alpha}\}$$

We will see how to estimate α and $\boldsymbol{\beta}$ in Section 22.4.2.

22.3 Analysis of Single-Spell Data with Time-Invariant Covariates

We assume that the population of interest is individuals entering the initial state during a given interval of time, say $[0, b]$, where $b > 0$ is a known constant. (Naturally, "individual" can be replaced with any population unit of interest, such as "family" or "firm.") As in all econometric contexts, it is very important to be explicit about the underlying population. By convention, we let zero denote the earliest calendar date that an individual can enter the initial state, and b is the last possible date. For example, if we are interested in the population of U.S. workers who became unemployed at any time during 1998, and unemployment duration is measured in years (with .5 meaning half a year), then $b = 1$. If duration is measured in weeks, then $b = 52$; if duration is measured in days, then $b = 365$; and so on.

In using the methods of this section, we typically ignore the fact that durations are often grouped into discrete intervals—for example, measured to the nearest week or month—and treat them as continuously distributed. If we want to explicitly recognize the discreteness of the measured durations, we should treat them as grouped data, as we do in Section 22.4.

We restrict attention to **single-spell data**. That is, we use, at most, one completed spell per individual. If, after leaving the initial state, an individual subsequently reenters the initial state in the interval $[0, b]$, we ignore this information. In addition, the covariates in the analysis are time invariant, which means we collect covariates on individuals at a given point in time—usually, at the beginning of the spell—and we do not re-collect data on the covariates during the course of the spell. Time-varying covariates are more naturally handled in the context of grouped duration data in Section 22.4.

We study two general types of sampling from the population that we have described. The most common, and the easiest to handle, is flow sampling. In Section 22.3.3 we briefly consider various kinds of stock sampling.

22.3.1 Flow Sampling

With **flow sampling**, we sample individuals who enter the state at some point during the interval $[0, b]$, and we record the length of time each individual is in the initial state. We collect data on covariates known at the time the individual entered the initial state. For example, suppose we are interested in the population of U.S. workers who became unemployed at any time during 1998, and we randomly sample from U.S. male workers who became unemployed during 1998. At the beginning of the unemployment spell we might obtain information on tenure in last job, wage on last job, gender, marital status, and information on unemployment benefits.

There are two common ways to collect flow data on unemployment spells. First, we may randomly sample individuals from a large population, say, all working-age individuals in the United States for a given year, say, 1998. Some fraction of these people will be in the labor force and will become unemployed during 1998—that is, enter the initial state of unemployment during the specified interval—and this group of people who become unemployed is our random sample of all workers who become unemployed during 1998. Another possibility is retrospective sampling. For example, suppose that, for a given state in the United States, we have access to unemployment records for 1998. We can then obtain a random sample of all workers who became unemployed during 1998.

Flow data are usually subject to **right censoring**. That is, after a certain amount of time, we stop following the individuals in the sample, which we must do in order to analyze the data. (Right censoring is the only kind that occurs with flow data, so we will often refer to right censoring as "censoring" in this and the next subsection.) For individuals who have completed their spells in the initial state, we observe the exact duration. But for those still in the initial state, we only know that the duration lasted as long as the tracking period. In the unemployment duration example, we might follow each individual for a fixed length of time, say, two years. If unemployment spells are measured in weeks, we would have right censoring at 104 weeks. Alternatively, we might stop tracking individuals at a fixed calendar date, say, the last week in 1999. Because individuals can become unemployed at any time during 1998, calendar-date censoring results in censoring times that differ across individuals.

22.3.2 Maximum Likelihood Estimation with Censored Flow Data

For a random draw i from the population, let $a_i \in [0, b]$ denote the time at which individual i enters the initial state (the "starting time"), let t_i^* denote the length of time in the initial state (the duration), and let $\mathbf{x}_i$ denote the vector of observed covariates. We assume that t_i^* has a continuous conditional density $f(t \mid \mathbf{x}_i; \boldsymbol{\theta})$, $t \geq 0$, where $\boldsymbol{\theta}$ is the vector of unknown parameters.

Without right censoring we would observe a random sample on $(a_i, t_i^*, \mathbf{x}_i)$, and estimation would be a standard exercise in conditional maximum likelihood. To account for right censoring, we assume that the observed duration, t_i, is obtained as

$$t_i = \min(t_i^*, c_i) \tag{22.21}$$

where c_i is the censoring time for individual i. In some cases, c_i is constant across i. For example, suppose t_i^* is unemployment duration for person i, measured in weeks. If the sample design specifies that we follow each person for at most two years, at which point all people remaining unemployed after two years are censored, then $c = 104$. If we have a fixed calendar date at which we stop tracking individuals, the censoring time differs by individual because the workers typically would become unemployed on different calendar dates. If $b = 52$ weeks and we censor everyone at two years from the start of the study, the censoring times could range from 52 to 104 weeks.

We assume that, conditional on the covariates, the true duration is independent of the starting point, a_i, and the censoring time, c_i:

$$\mathrm{D}(t_i^* \mid \mathbf{x}_i, a_i, c_i) = \mathrm{D}(t_i^* \mid \mathbf{x}_i) \tag{22.22}$$

where $\mathrm{D}(\cdot \mid \cdot)$ denotes conditional distribution. Assumption (22.22) clearly holds when a_i and c_i are constant for all i, but it holds under much weaker assumptions. Sometimes c_i is constant for all i, in which case assumption (22.22) holds when the duration is independent of the starting time, conditional on $\mathbf{x}_i$. If there are seasonal effects on the duration—for example, unemployment durations that start in the summer have a different expected length than durations that start at other times of the year—then we may have to put dummy variables for different starting dates in $\mathbf{x}_i$ to ensure that assumption (22.22) holds. This approach would also ensure that assumption (22.22) holds when a fixed calendar date is used for censoring, implying that c_i is not constant across i. Assumption (22.22) holds for certain nonstandard censoring schemes, too. For example, if an element of $\mathbf{x}_i$ is education, assumption (22.22) holds if, say, individuals with more education are censored more quickly.

Under assumption (22.22), the distribution of t_i^* given $(\mathbf{x}_i, a_i, c_i)$ does not depend on (a_i, c_i). Therefore, if the duration is not censored, the density of $t_i = t_i^*$ given $(\mathbf{x}_i, a_i, c_i)$ is simply $f(t \mid \mathbf{x}_i; \boldsymbol{\theta})$. The probability that t_i is censored is

$$\mathrm{P}(t_i^* \geq c_i \mid \mathbf{x}_i) = 1 - F(c_i \mid \mathbf{x}_i; \boldsymbol{\theta})$$

where $F(t \mid \mathbf{x}_i; \boldsymbol{\theta})$ is the conditional cdf of t_i^* given $\mathbf{x}_i$. Letting d_i be a censoring indicator ($d_i = 1$ if uncensored, $d_i = 0$ if censored), the conditional likelihood for observation i can be written as

$$f(t_i \mid \mathbf{x}_i; \boldsymbol{\theta})^{d_i}[1 - F(t_i \mid \mathbf{x}_i; \boldsymbol{\theta})]^{(1-d_i)} \tag{22.23}$$

Importantly, neither the starting times, a_i, nor the length of the interval, b, plays a role in the analysis. (In fact, in the vast majority of treatments of flow data, b and a_i are not even introduced. However, it is important to know that the reason a_i is not relevant for the analysis of flow data is the conditional independence assumption in equation (22.22).) By contrast, the censoring times c_i do appear in the likelihood for censored observations because then $t_i = c_i$. Given data on $(t_i, d_i, \mathbf{x}_i)$ for a random sample of size N, the maximum likelihood estimator of $\boldsymbol{\theta}$ is obtained by maximizing

$$\sum_{i=1}^{N} \{d_i \log[f(t_i \mid \mathbf{x}_i; \boldsymbol{\theta})] + (1 - d_i) \log[1 - F(t_i \mid \mathbf{x}_i; \boldsymbol{\theta})]\} \tag{22.24}$$

For the choices of $f(\cdot \mid \mathbf{x}; \boldsymbol{\theta})$ used in practice, the conditional MLE regularity conditions—see Chapter 13—hold, and the MLE is $\sqrt{N}$-consistent and asymptotically normal. (If there is no censoring, $d_i = 1$ for all i and the second term in expression (22.24) is simply dropped.)

Because the hazard function can be expressed as in equation (22.15), once we specify f, the hazard function can be estimated once we have the MLE, $\hat{\boldsymbol{\theta}}$. For example, the Weibull distribution with covariates has conditional density

$$f(t \mid \mathbf{x}_i; \boldsymbol{\theta}) = \exp(\mathbf{x}_i \boldsymbol{\beta}) \alpha t^{\alpha-1} \exp[-\exp(\mathbf{x}_i \boldsymbol{\beta}) t^{\alpha}] \tag{22.25}$$

where $\mathbf{x}_i$ contains unity as its first element for all i. (We obtain this density from Example 22.3 with γ replaced by $\exp(\mathbf{x}_i \boldsymbol{\beta})$.) The hazard function in this case is simply $\lambda(t; \mathbf{x}) = \exp(\mathbf{x}\boldsymbol{\beta}) \alpha t^{\alpha-1}$.

Example 22.5 (Weibull Model for Recidivism Duration): Let *durat* be the length of time, in months, until an inmate is arrested after being released from prison. Although the duration is rounded to the nearest month, we treat *durat* as a continuous variable with a Weibull distribution. We are interested in how certain covariates affect the hazard function for recidivism, and also whether there is positive or negative duration dependence, once we have conditioned on the covariates. The variable *workprg*—a binary indicator for participation in a prison work program—is of particular interest.

The data in RECID.RAW, which comes from Chung, Schmidt, and Witte (1991), are flow data because it is a random sample of convicts released from prison during the period July 1, 1977, through June 30, 1978. The data are retrospective in that they were obtained by looking at records in April 1984, which served as the common censoring date. Because of the different starting times, the censoring times, c_i, vary from 70 to 81 months. The results of the Weibull estimation are in Table 22.1.

In interpreting the estimates, we use equation (22.17). For small $\hat{\beta}_j$, we can multiply the coefficient by 100 to obtain the semielasticity of the hazard with respect to x_j. (No covariates appear in logarithmic form, so there are no elasticities among the $\hat{\beta}_j$.) For example, if *tserved* increases by one month, the hazard shifts up by about 1.4 percent, and the effect is statistically significant. Another year of education reduces the hazard by about 2.3 percent, but the effect is insignificant at even the 10 percent level against a two-sided alternative.

The sign of the *workprg* coefficient is unexpected, at least if we expect the work program to have positive benefits after the inmates are released from prison. (The result is not statistically different from zero.) The reason could be that the program is ineffective or that there is self-selection into the program.

Table 22.1
Weibull Estimation of Criminal Recidivism

Explanatory Variable	Coefficient (Standard Error)
workprg	.091 (.091)
priors	.089 (.013)
tserved	.014 (.002)
felon	−.299 (.106)
alcohol	.447 (.106)
drugs	.281 (.098)
black	.454 (.088)
married	−.152 (.109)
educ	−.023 (.019)
age	−.0037 (.0005)
constant	−3.402 (0.301)
$\hat{\alpha}$	.806 (.031)
Observations	1,445
Log likelihood	−1,633.03

For large $\hat{\beta}_j$, we should exponentiate and subtract unity to obtain the proportionate change. For example, at any point in time, the hazard is about 100[exp(.447) – 1] = 56.4 percent greater for someone with an alcohol problem than for someone without.

The estimate of α is .806, and the standard error of $\hat{\alpha}$ leads to a strong rejection of H_0: $\alpha = 1$ against H_0: $\alpha < 1$. Therefore, there is evidence of negative duration dependence, conditional on the covariates. This means that, for a particular ex-convict, the instantaneous rate of being arrested decreases with the length of time out of prison. Figure 22.1 provides a graph of the estimated Weibull hazard.

When the Weibull model is estimated without the covariates, $\hat{\alpha} = .770$ (se = .031), which shows slightly more negative duration dependence. This is a typical finding in

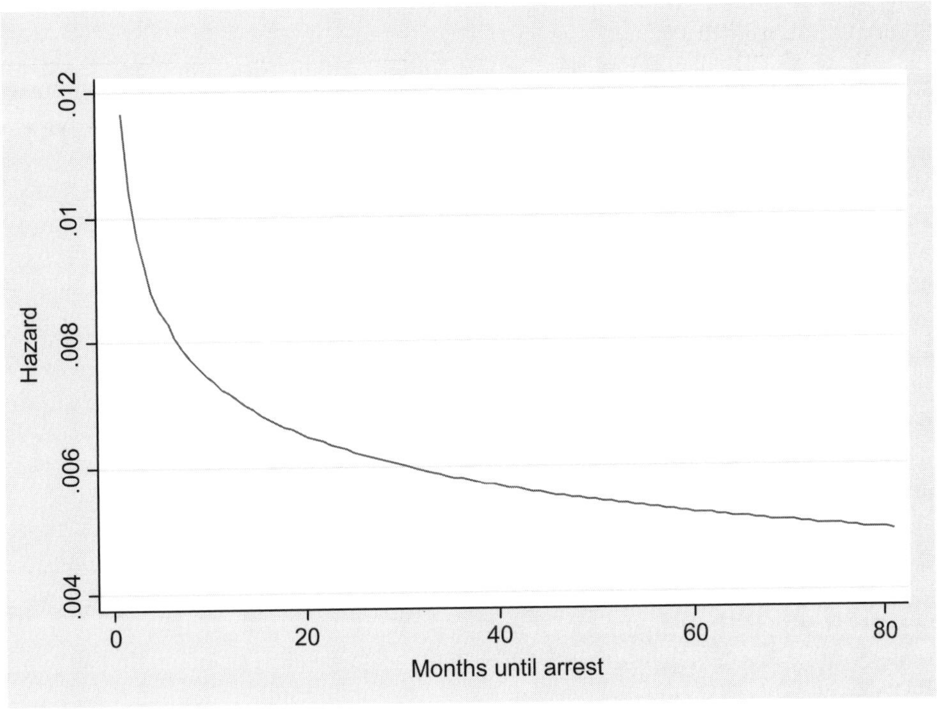

Figure 22.1
Weibull hazard of recidivism

applications of Weibull duration models: estimated α without covariate tends to be less than the estimate with covariates. Lancaster (1990, Section 10.2) contains a theoretical discussion based on unobserved heterogeneity.

When we are primarily interested in the effects of covariates on the expected duration (rather than on the hazard), we can apply a censored Tobit analysis to the log of the duration. A Tobit analysis assumes that, for each random draw i, $\log(t_i^*)$ given $\mathbf{x}_i$ has a Normal$(\mathbf{x}_i\boldsymbol{\delta}, \sigma^2)$ distribution, which implies that t_i^* given $\mathbf{x}_i$ has a lognormal distribution. (The first element of $\mathbf{x}_i$ is unity.) The hazard function for a lognormal distribution, conditional on $\mathbf{x}$, is $\lambda(t; \mathbf{x}) = h[(\log t - \mathbf{x}\boldsymbol{\delta})/\sigma]/\sigma t$, where $h(z) \equiv \phi(z)/[1 - \Phi(z)]$, $\phi(\cdot)$ is the standard normal probability density function (pdf), and $\Phi(\cdot)$ is the standard normal cdf. The lognormal hazard function is not monotonic and does not have the proportional hazard form. Nevertheless, the estimates of the δ_j are easy to interpret because the model is equivalent to

$$\log(t_i^*) = \mathbf{x}_i\boldsymbol{\delta} + e_i \tag{22.26}$$

where e_i is independent of $\mathbf{x}_i$ and normally distributed. Therefore, the δ_j are semielasticities—or elasticities if the covariates are in logarithmic form—of the covariates on the *expected* duration.

The Weibull model can also be represented in regression form. When t_i^* given $\mathbf{x}_i$ has density (22.25), $\exp(\mathbf{x}_i\boldsymbol{\beta})(t_i^*)^\alpha$ is independent of $\mathbf{x}_i$ and has a unit exponential distribution. Therefore, its natural log has a **type I extreme value distribution**; therefore, we can write $\alpha \log(t_i^*) = -\mathbf{x}_i\boldsymbol{\beta} + u_i$, where u_i is independent of $\mathbf{x}_i$ and has density $g(u) = \exp(u)\exp\{\exp(-u)\}$. The mean of u_i is not zero, but, because u_i is independent of $\mathbf{x}_i$, we can write $\log(t_i^*)$ exactly as in equation (22.26), where the slope coefficents are given by $\delta_j = -\beta_j/\alpha$, and the intercept is more complicated. Now, e_i does not have a normal distribution, but it is independent of $\mathbf{x}_i$ with zero mean. Censoring can be handled by maximum likelihood estimation. The estimated coefficients can be compared with the censored Tobit estimates described previously to see if the estimates are sensitive to the distributional assumption.

In Example 22.5, we can obtain the Weibull estimates of the δ_j as $\hat{\delta}_j = -\hat{\beta}_j/\hat{\alpha}$. (Some econometrics packages, such as Stata, allow direct estimation of the δ_j and provide standard errors.) For example, $\hat{\delta}_{\text{drugs}} = -.281/.806 \approx -.349$. When the lognormal model is used, the coefficient on *drugs* is somewhat smaller in magnitude, about $-.298$. As another example, $\hat{\delta}_{\text{age}} = .0046$ in the Weibull estimation and $\hat{\delta}_{\text{age}} = .0039$ in the lognormal estimation. In both cases, the estimates have t statistics greater than six. For obtaining estimates on the expected duration, the Weibull and lognormal models give similar results. The lognormal model fits the data notably better, with log likelihood $= -1{,}597.06$. This result is consistent with the findings of Chung, Schmidt, and Witte (1991).

Importantly, the shapes of the lognormal and Weibull hazards are quite different. The lognormal hazard, which is plotted in Figure 22.2 with the covariates set at their mean values, first increases until about six months and then decreases thereafter. This shape implies that for a short period—roughly six months—the instantaneous probability of being arrested for a new crime increases the longer an ex-convict has been released from prison. After that, the hazard falls to about .001 at 80 months. Therefore, conditional on an ex-convict being out of prison $6\frac{1}{2}$ years, the probability of being arrested for a new crime in the 81st month is roughly .001. The Weibull hazard implies that there is initially a greater than .01 instantaneous probability of being arrested. At 80 months, the probability of being arrested during the 81st month is about .005, or five times larger than that obtained from the lognormal model.

Sometimes we begin by specifying a parametric model for the hazard conditional on $\mathbf{x}$ and then use the formulas from Section 22.2 to obtain the cdf and density. This

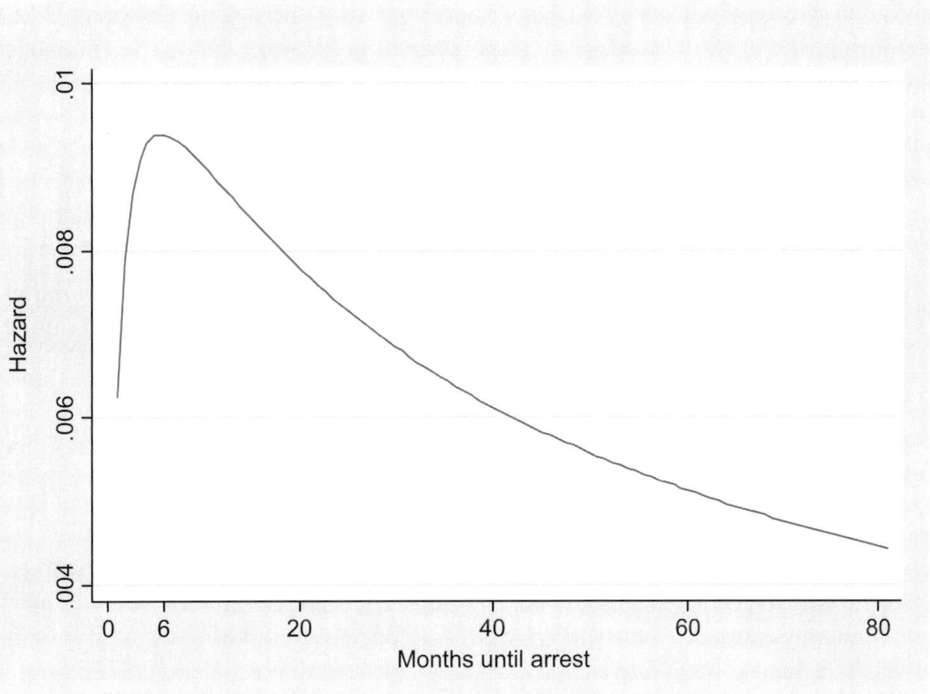

Figure 22.2
Lognormal hazard of recidivism

approach is easiest when the hazard leads to a tractable duration distribution, but there is no reason the hazard function must be of the proportional hazard form.

Example 22.6 (Log-Logistic Hazard with Covariates): A log-logistic hazard function with covariates is

$$\lambda(t;\mathbf{x}) = \exp(\mathbf{x}\boldsymbol{\beta})\alpha t^{\alpha-1}/[1+\exp(\mathbf{x}\boldsymbol{\beta})t^{\alpha}] \tag{22.27}$$

where $x_1 \equiv 1$. From equation (22.14) with $\gamma = \exp(\mathbf{x}\boldsymbol{\beta})$, the cdf is

$$F(t\,|\,\mathbf{x};\boldsymbol{\theta}) = 1 - [1+\exp(\mathbf{x}\boldsymbol{\beta})t^{\alpha}]^{-1}, \qquad t \geq 0 \tag{22.28}$$

The distribution of $\log(t_i^*)$ given $\mathbf{x}_i$ is logistic with mean $-\alpha^{-1}\log\{\exp(\mathbf{x}\boldsymbol{\beta})\} = -\alpha^{-1}\mathbf{x}\boldsymbol{\beta}$ and variance $\pi^2/(3\alpha^2)$. Therefore, $\log(t_i^*)$ can be written as in equation (22.26) where e_i has a zero mean logistic distribution and is *independent* of $\mathbf{x}_i$ and $\boldsymbol{\delta} = -\alpha^{-1}\boldsymbol{\beta}$. This is another example where the effects of the covariates on the mean duration can be obtained by an OLS regression when there is no censoring. With censoring, the distribution of e_i must be accounted for using the log likelihood in expression (22.24).

22.3.3 Stock Sampling

Flow data with right censoring are common, but other sampling schemes are also used. With **stock sampling** we randomly sample from individuals that are in the initial state at a given point in time. The population is again individuals who enter the initial state during a specified interval, $[0, b]$. However, rather than observe a random sample of people flowing into the initial state, we can only obtain a random sample of individuals that are in the initial state at time b. In addition to the possibility of right censoring, we may also face the problem of **left censoring**, which occurs when some or all of the starting times, a_i, are not observed. For now, we assume that (1) we observe the starting times a_i for all individuals we sample at time b and (2) we can follow sampled individuals for a certain length of time after we observe them at time b. We also allow for right censoring.

In the unemployment duration example, where the population comprises workers who became unemployed at some point during 1998, stock sampling would occur if we randomly sampled from workers who were unemployed during the last week of 1998. This kind of sampling causes a clear sample selection problem: we necessarily exclude from our sample any individual whose unemployment spell ended before the last week of 1998. Because these spells were necessarily shorter than a year, we cannot just assume that the missing observations are randomly missing.

The sample selection problem caused by stock sampling is essentially the same situation we faced in Section 19.5, where we covered the truncated regression model. Therefore, we will call this the **left truncation** problem. Kiefer (1988) calls it **length-biased sampling**.

Under the assumptions that we observe the a_i and can observe some spells past the sampling date b, left truncation is fairly easy to deal with. With the exception of replacing flow sampling with stock sampling, we make the same assumptions as in Section 22.3.2.

To account for the truncated sampling, we must modify the density in equation (22.23) to reflect the fact that part of the population is systematically omitted from the sample. Let $(a_i, c_i, \mathbf{x}_i, t_i)$ denote a random draw from the population of all spells starting in $[0, b]$. We observe this vector if and only if the person is still in the initial state at time b, that is, if and only if $a_i + t_i^* \geq b$ or $t_i^* \geq b - a_i$, where t_i^* is the true duration. But, under the conditional independence assumption (22.22),

$$\mathrm{P}(t_i^* \geq b - a_i \mid a_i, c_i, \mathbf{x}_i) = 1 - F(b - a_i \mid \mathbf{x}_i; \boldsymbol{\theta}) \tag{22.29}$$

where $F(\cdot \mid \mathbf{x}_i; \boldsymbol{\theta})$ is the cdf of t_i^* given $\mathbf{x}_i$, as before. The correct conditional density function is obtained by dividing equation (22.23) by equation (22.29). In Problem 22.5 you are asked to adapt the arguments in Section 19.5 to also allow for right censoring. The log-likelihood function can be written as

$$\sum_{i=1}^{N} \{d_i \log[f(t_i \mid \mathbf{x}_i; \boldsymbol{\theta})] + (1 - d_i) \log[1 - F(t_i \mid \mathbf{x}_i; \boldsymbol{\theta})] - \log[1 - F(b - a_i \mid \mathbf{x}_i; \boldsymbol{\theta})]\} \tag{22.30}$$

where, again, $t_i = c_i$ when $d_i = 0$. Unlike in the case of flow sampling, with stock sampling both the starting dates, a_i, and the length of the sampling interval, b, appear in the conditional likelihood function. Their presence makes it clear that specifying the interval $[0, b]$ is important for analyzing stock data. [Lancaster (1990, p. 183) essentially derives equation (22.30) under a slightly different sampling scheme; see also Lancaster (1979).]

Equation (22.30) has an interesting implication. If observation i is right censored at calendar date b—that is, if we do not follow the spell after the initial data collection—then the censoring time is $c_i = b - a_i$. Because $d_i = 0$ for censored observations, the log likelihood for such an observation is $\log[1 - F(c_i \mid \mathbf{x}_i; \boldsymbol{\theta})] - \log[1 - F(b - a_i \mid \mathbf{x}_i; \boldsymbol{\theta})] = 0$. In other words, observations that are right censored at the data collection time provide no information for estimating $\boldsymbol{\theta}$, at least when we use equation (22.30). Consequently, the log likelihood in equation (22.30) does not identify $\boldsymbol{\theta}$ if *all* units are right censored at the interview date: equation (22.30) is identically zero. The intuition for why equation (22.30) fails in this case is fairly clear: our data consist only of $(a_i, \mathbf{x}_i)$, and equation (22.30) is a log likelihood that is conditional on $(a_i, \mathbf{x}_i)$. Effectively, there is no random response variable.

Even when we censor all observed durations at the interview date, we can still estimate $\boldsymbol{\theta}$, provided—at least in a parametric context—we specify a model for the conditional distribution of the starting times, $\mathrm{D}(a_i \mid \mathbf{x}_i)$. (This is essentially the problem analyzed by Nickell, 1979.) We are still assuming that we observe the a_i. So, for example, we randomly sample from the pool of people unemployed in the last week of 1998 and find out when their unemployment spells began (along with covariates). We do not follow any spells past the interview date. (As an aside, if we sample unemployed people during the last week of 1998, we are likely to obtain some observations where spells began before 1998. For the population we have specified, these people would simply be discarded. If we want to include people whose spells began prior to 1998, we need to redefine the interval. For example, if durations are measured in weeks and if we want to consider durations beginning in the five-year period prior to the end of 1998, then $b = 260$.)

For concreteness, we assume that $\mathrm{D}(a_i \mid \mathbf{x}_i)$ is continuous on $[0, b]$ with density $k(\cdot \mid \mathbf{x}_i; \boldsymbol{\eta})$. Let s_i denote a sample selection indicator, which is unity if we observe random draw i, that is, if $t_i^* \geq b - a_i$. Estimation of $\boldsymbol{\theta}$ (and $\boldsymbol{\eta}$) can proceed by applying CMLE to the density of a_i conditional on $\mathbf{x}_i$ *and* $s_i = 1$. (Note that this is the only density we can hope to estimate, as our sample only consists of observations $(a_i, \mathbf{x}_i)$ when $s_i = 1$.) This density is informative for $\boldsymbol{\theta}$ even if $\boldsymbol{\eta}$ is not functionally related to $\boldsymbol{\theta}$ (as would typically be assumed) because there are some durations that started and ended in $[0, b]$; we simply do not observe them. Knowing something about the starting time distribution gives us information about the duration distribution. (In the context of flow sampling, when $\boldsymbol{\eta}$ is not functionally related to $\boldsymbol{\theta}$, the density of a_i given $\mathbf{x}_i$ is uninformative for estimating $\boldsymbol{\theta}$; in other words, a_i is ancillary for $\boldsymbol{\theta}$.)

In Problem 22.6 you are asked to show that the density of a_i conditional on observing $(a_i, \mathbf{x}_i)$ is

$$p(a \mid \mathbf{x}_i, s_i = 1) = k(a \mid \mathbf{x}_i; \boldsymbol{\eta})[1 - F(b - a \mid \mathbf{x}_i; \boldsymbol{\theta})]/\mathrm{P}(s_i = 1 \mid \mathbf{x}_i; \boldsymbol{\theta}, \boldsymbol{\eta}) \tag{22.31}$$

$0 < a < b$, where

$$\mathrm{P}(s_i = 1 \mid \mathbf{x}_i; \boldsymbol{\theta}, \boldsymbol{\eta}) = \int_0^b [1 - F(b - u \mid \mathbf{x}_i; \boldsymbol{\theta})] k(u \mid \mathbf{x}_i; \boldsymbol{\eta}) \, \mathrm{d}u \tag{22.32}$$

(Lancaster (1990, Section 8.3.3) essentially obtains the right-hand side of equation (22.31) but uses the notion of backward recurrence time. The argument in Problem 22.6 is more straightforward because it is based on a standard truncation argument.) Once we have specified the duration cdf, F, and the starting time density, k, we can use conditional MLE to estimate $\boldsymbol{\theta}$ and $\boldsymbol{\eta}$: the log likelihood for observation i is just the log of equation (22.31), evaluated at a_i. If we assume that a_i is independent of $\mathbf{x}_i$ and has a uniform distribution on $[0, b]$, the estimation simplifies somewhat; see Problem 22.6. Allowing for a discontinuous starting time density $k(\cdot \mid \mathbf{x}_i; \boldsymbol{\eta})$ does not materially affect equation (22.31). For example, if the interval [0,1] represents one year, we might want to allow different entry rates over the different seasons. This approach would correspond to a uniform distribution over each subinterval that we choose.

We now turn to the problem of left censoring, which arises with stock sampling when we do not actually know when any spell began. In other words, the a_i are not observed, and therefore neither are the true durations, t_i^*. However, we assume that we can follow spells after the interview date. Without right censoring, this assumption means we can observe the time in the current spell since the interview date, say, r_i, which we can write as $r_i = t_i^* + a_i - b$. We still have a left truncation problem because we only observe r_i when $t_i^* > b - a_i$, that is, when $r_i > 0$. The general approach is the same as with the earlier problems: we obtain the density of the variable that we can at least partially observe, r_i in this case, conditional on observing r_i. Problem 22.8 asks you to fill in the details, accounting also for possible right censoring.

We can easily combine stock sampling and flow sampling. For example, in the case that we observe the starting times, a_i, suppose that, at time $m < b$, we sample a stock of individuals already in the initial state. In addition to following spells of individuals already in the initial state, suppose we can randomly sample individuals flowing into the initial state between times m and b. Then we follow all the individuals appearing in the sample, at least until right censoring. For starting dates after m $(a_i \geq m)$, there is no truncation, and so the log likelihood for these observations is just as in equation (22.24). For $a_i < m$, the log likelihood is identical to equation (22.30) except that m replaces b. Other combinations are easy to infer from the preceding results.

22.3.4 Unobserved Heterogeneity

One way to obtain more general duration models is to introduce unobserved heterogeneity into fairly simple duration models. In addition, we sometimes want to test for duration dependence conditional on observed covariates *and* unobserved heterogeneity. The key assumptions used in most models that incorporate unobserved heterogeneity are that (1) the heterogeneity is *independent* of the observed covariates, as well as starting times and censoring times; (2) the heterogeneity has a distribution known up to a finite number of parameters; and (3) the heterogeneity enters the hazard function multiplicatively. We will make these assumptions. In the context of single-spell flow data, it is difficult to relax any of these assumptions. (In the special case of a lognormal duration distribution, we can relax assumption 1 by using Tobit methods with endogenous explanatory variables; see Section 17.5.2.)

In some fields, particularly those concerned with modeling survival times (such as biostatistics), the unobserved heterogeneity is called *frailty*. Then the hazard conditional on the unobserved frailty is the instantaneous probability of dying conditional on surviving up through time t for an individual with a given frailty. In this chapter, we usually use the term *heterogeneity*. Often, a model that explicitly introduces heterogeneity into a hazard function is called a **mixture model**.

Before we cover the general case, it is useful to cover an example due to Lancaster (1979). For a random draw i from the population, a Weibull hazard function conditional on observed covariates $\mathbf{x}_i$ and unobserved heterogeneity v_i is

$$\lambda(t; \mathbf{x}_i, v_i) = v_i \exp(\mathbf{x}_i \boldsymbol{\beta}) \alpha t^{\alpha - 1} \tag{22.33}$$

where $x_{i1} \equiv 1$ and $v_i > 0$. Lancaster (1990) calls equation (22.33) a **conditional hazard**, because it conditions on the unobserved heterogeneity (or frailty) v_i. Technically, almost all hazards in econometrics are conditional because we almost always condition on observed covariates. Notice how v_i enters equation (22.33) multiplicatively. To identify the parameters α and $\boldsymbol{\beta}$ we need a normalization on the distribution of v_i; we use the most common, $\mathrm{E}(v_i) = 1$. This implies that, for a given vector $\mathbf{x}$, the average hazard is $\exp(\mathbf{x}\boldsymbol{\beta})\alpha t^{\alpha-1}$. An interesting hypothesis is H_0: $\alpha = 1$, which means that, conditional on $\mathbf{x}_i$ *and* v_i, there is no duration dependence.

In the general case where the cdf of t_i^* given $(\mathbf{x}_i, v_i)$ is $F(t \mid \mathbf{x}_i, v_i; \boldsymbol{\theta})$, we can obtain the distribution of t_i^* given $\mathbf{x}_i$ by integrating out the unobserved effect. Because v_i and $\mathbf{x}_i$ are independent, the cdf of t_i^* given $\mathbf{x}_i$ is

$$G(t \mid \mathbf{x}_i; \boldsymbol{\theta}, \boldsymbol{\rho}) = \int_0^\infty F(t \mid \mathbf{x}_i, v; \boldsymbol{\theta}) h(v; \boldsymbol{\rho})\, dv \tag{22.34}$$

where, for concreteness, the density of v_i, $h(\cdot; \boldsymbol{\rho})$, is assumed to be continuous and depends on the unknown parameters $\boldsymbol{\rho}$. From equation (22.34) the density of t_i^* given $\mathbf{x}_i$, $g(t \mid \mathbf{x}_i; \boldsymbol{\theta}, \boldsymbol{\rho})$, is easily obtained. We can now use the methods of Sections 22.3.2 and 22.3.3. For flow data, the log-likelihood function is as in equation (22.24), but with $G(t \mid \mathbf{x}_i; \boldsymbol{\theta}, \boldsymbol{\rho})$ replacing $F(t \mid \mathbf{x}_i; \boldsymbol{\theta})$ and $g(t \mid \mathbf{x}_i; \boldsymbol{\theta}, \boldsymbol{\rho})$ replacing $f(t \mid \mathbf{x}_i; \boldsymbol{\theta})$. We should assume that $\mathrm{D}(t_i^* \mid \mathbf{x}_i, v_i, a_i, c_i) = \mathrm{D}(t_i^* \mid \mathbf{x}_i, v_i)$ and $\mathrm{D}(v_i \mid \mathbf{x}_i, a_i, c_i) = \mathrm{D}(v_i)$; these assumptions ensure that the key condition (22.22) holds. The methods for stock sampling described in Section 22.3.3 also apply to the integrated cdf and density.

If we assume **gamma-distributed heterogeneity**—that is, $v_i \sim \mathrm{Gamma}(\delta, \delta)$, so that $\mathrm{E}(v_i) = 1$ and $\mathrm{Var}(v_i) = 1/\delta$—we can find the distribution of t_i^* given $\mathbf{x}_i$ for a broad class of hazard functions with multiplicative heterogeneity. Suppose that the hazard function is $\lambda(t; \mathbf{x}_i, v_i) = v_i \kappa(t; \mathbf{x}_i)$, where $\kappa(t; \mathbf{x}) > 0$ (and need not have the proportional hazard form). For simplicity, we suppress the dependence of $\kappa(\cdot\,; \cdot)$ on unknown parameters. From equation (22.7), the cdf of t_i^* given $(\mathbf{x}_i, v_i)$ is

$$F(t \mid \mathbf{x}_i, v_i) = 1 - \exp\left[-v_i \int_0^t \kappa(s; \mathbf{x}_i)\, ds\right] \equiv 1 - \exp[-v_i \xi(t; \mathbf{x}_i)] \tag{22.35}$$

where $\xi(t; \mathbf{x}_i) \equiv \int_0^t \kappa(s; \mathbf{x}_i)\, ds$. We can obtain the cdf of t_i^* given $\mathbf{x}_i$ by using equation (22.34). The density of v_i is $h(v) = \delta^\delta v^{\delta-1} \exp(-\delta v)/\Gamma(\delta)$, where $\mathrm{Var}(v_i) = 1/\delta$ and

$\Gamma(\cdot)$ is the gamma function. Let $\xi_i \equiv \xi(t; \mathbf{x}_i)$ for given t. Then

$$\int_0^\infty \exp(-\xi_i v)\delta^\delta v^{\delta-1} \exp(-\delta v)/\Gamma(\delta)\, dv$$

$$= [\delta/(\delta+\xi_i)]^\delta \int_0^\infty (\delta+\xi_i)^\delta v^{\delta-1} \exp[-(\delta+\xi_i)v]/\Gamma(\delta)\, dv$$

$$= [\delta/(\delta+\xi_i)]^\delta = (1+\xi_i/\delta)^{-\delta}$$

where the second-to-last equality follows because the integrand is the Gamma (δ, $\delta+\xi_i$) density and must integrate to unity. Now we use equation (22.34):

$$G(t \mid \mathbf{x}_i) = 1 - [1 + \xi(t; \mathbf{x}_i)/\delta]^{-\delta} \tag{22.36}$$

Taking the derivative of equation (22.36) with respect to t, using the fact that $\kappa(t; \mathbf{x}_i)$ is the derivative of $\xi(t; \mathbf{x}_i)$, yields the density of t_i^* given $\mathbf{x}_i$ as

$$g(t \mid \mathbf{x}_i) = \kappa(t; \mathbf{x}_i)[1 + \xi(t; \mathbf{x}_i)/\delta]^{-\delta-1} \tag{22.37}$$

The function $\kappa(t; \mathbf{x})$ depends on parameters $\boldsymbol{\theta}$, and so $g(t \mid \mathbf{x})$ should be $g(t \mid \mathbf{x}; \boldsymbol{\theta}, \delta)$. With censored data the vector $\boldsymbol{\theta}$ can be estimated along with δ by using the log-likelihood function in equation (22.24) (again, with G replacing F).

The hazard associated with the density $g(t \mid \mathbf{x})$ is typically called the **unconditional hazard** because it does not condition on the unobserved heterogeneity (but, as always, does condition on the observed covariates). It is useful to think of the unconditional hazard as something that can be estimated quite generally because it involves the distribution of an observed outcome conditional on observed covariates. In fact, without censoring, estimation is easily done without making parametric restrictions and without even introducing the notion of unobserved heterogeneity.

When the hazard function has the Weibull form in equation (22.33), $\xi(t; \mathbf{x}) = \exp(\mathbf{x}\boldsymbol{\beta})t^\alpha$, which leads to a very tractable analysis when plugged into equations (22.36) and (22.37). The resulting duration distribution is called the **Burr distribution**. Its hazard function—that is, the unconditional hazard function when the conditional hazard is Weibull and the heterogeneity has a gamma distribution—is $\exp(\mathbf{x}\boldsymbol{\beta})\alpha t^{\alpha-1}[1 + \exp(\mathbf{x}\boldsymbol{\beta})t^\alpha/\delta]^{-1}$. It is useful to reparameterize the Burr distribution by letting $\eta = 1/\delta$ and then writing the hazard as

$$\exp(\mathbf{x}\boldsymbol{\beta})\alpha t^{\alpha-1}/[1 + \eta \exp(\mathbf{x}\boldsymbol{\beta})t^\alpha]$$

Then $\eta = 0$—that is, $Var(v_i) = 0$—leads to the Weibull hazard, as expected. Further, $\eta = 1$ (so that $Var(v_i) = E(v_i)$) gives the log-logistic hazard in equation (22.27).

Therefore, even if we ignore that we derived the Burr distribution using gamma heterogeneity, we see that it nests two important special cases.

If we use a log-logistic hazard for $\kappa(t;\mathbf{x})$—which, recall, implies that $\kappa(t;\mathbf{x})$ is not multiplicatively separable in t and $\mathbf{x}$—and assume gamma heterogeneity, then we plug $\kappa(t;\mathbf{x}) = \exp(\mathbf{x}\boldsymbol{\beta})\alpha t^{\alpha-1}[1+\exp(\mathbf{x}\boldsymbol{\beta})t^{\alpha}]^{-1}$ and $\xi(t;\mathbf{x}) = \log[1+\exp(\mathbf{x}\boldsymbol{\beta})t^{\alpha}]$ into equation (22.37) to obtain the density (as a function of the parameters $\boldsymbol{\beta}$, α, and δ); we plug these expressions into equation (22.36) to obtain the cdf. Again, maximum likelihood estimation with right censoring is fairly straightforward.

Before presenting an example, we should recall why we might want to explicitly introduce unobserved heterogeneity when the heterogeneity is assumed to be independent of the observed covariates. The strongest case is seen when we are interested in testing for duration dependence conditional on observed covariates *and* unobserved heterogeneity, where the unobserved heterogeneity enters the hazard multiplicatively. As carefully exposited by Lancaster (1990, Section 10.2), ignoring multiplicative heterogeneity in the Weibull model results in asymptotically underestimating α. Therefore, we could very well conclude that there is negative duration dependence conditional on $\mathbf{x}$, whereas there is no duration dependence ($\alpha = 1$) conditional on $\mathbf{x}$ and v or even positive duration dependence ($\alpha > 1$).

In a general sense, it is somewhat heroic to think we can distinguish between duration dependence and unobserved heterogeneity when we observe only a single cycle for each agent. The problem is simple to describe: because we can only estimate the distribution of T given $\mathbf{x}$, we cannot uncover the distribution of T given $(\mathbf{x}, v)$ unless we make extra assumptions, a point Lancaster (1990, Section 10.1) illustrates with an example. Therefore, we cannot tell whether the hazard describing T given $(\mathbf{x}, v)$ exhibits duration dependence. But, when the hazard has the proportional hazard form $\lambda(t;\mathbf{x},v) = v\kappa(\mathbf{x})\lambda_0(t)$, it is possible to identify the function $\kappa(\cdot)$ and the baseline hazard $\lambda_0(\cdot)$ quite generally (along with the distribution of v). See Lancaster (1990, Section 7.3) for a presentation of the results of Elbers and Ridder (1982). More recently, Horowitz (1999) demonstrated how to nonparametrically estimate the baseline hazard and the distribution of the unobserved heterogeneity under fairly weak assumptions.

When interest centers on how the observed covariates affect the mean duration, explicitly modeling unobserved heterogeneity is less compelling. Adding unobserved heterogeneity to equation (22.26) does not change the mean effects; it merely changes the error distribution. Without censoring, we would probably estimate $\boldsymbol{\beta}$ in equation (22.26) by OLS (rather than MLE) so that the estimators would be robust to distributional misspecification. With censoring, to perform maximum likelihood, we must know the distribution of t_i^* given $\mathbf{x}_i$, and this depends on the distribution of v_i

Table 22.2
Weibull Hazard with Gamma Heterogeneity, Criminal Recidivism

Explanatory Variable	Coefficient (Standard Error)
workprg	.007 (.204)
priors	.243 (.042)
tserved	.035 (.007)
felon	−.791 (.267)
alcohol	1.174 (.281)
drugs	.285 (.223)
black	.772 (.204)
married	−.806 (.258)
educ	−.027 (.045)
age	−.005 (.001)
constant	−5.394 (.720)
$\hat{\alpha}$	1.708 (.162)
$\hat{\delta}$	5.991 (1.071)
Observations	1,445
Log likelihood	−1,584.92

when we explicitly introduce unobserved heterogeneity. But again introducing unobserved heterogeneity is indistinguishable from simply allowing a more flexible duration distribution.

We now apply a model with a Weibull baseline hazard and gamma heterogeneity to the recidivism data. Individuals with a larger heterogeneity, v_i, have a higher probability of being arrested after release from prison in every interval, conditional on "surviving" up to that point.

The maximum likelihood estimates are given in Table 22.2. Notice how the estimate of α, 1.708, is well above unity. Therefore, the conditional hazard exhibits

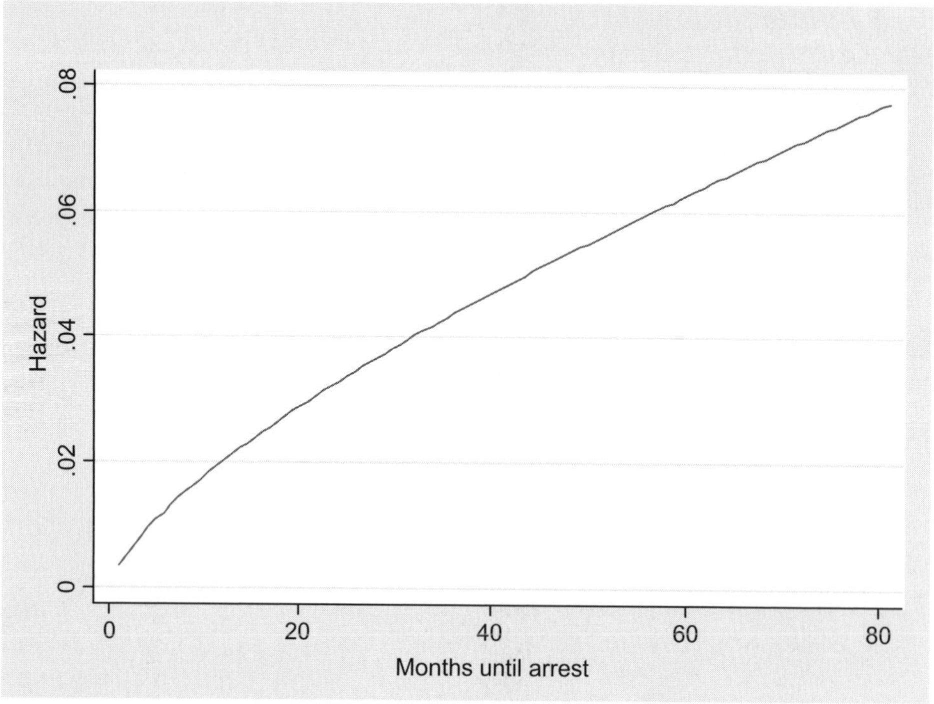

Figure 22.3
Conditional Weibull hazard

positive duration dependence: for a given individual, the instantaneous probability of being arrested after prison release monotonically increases with the time out of prison. The situation is displayed in Figure 22.3. By contrast, in the Weibull model without heterogeneity, we estimated α to be .806.

Allowing for heterogeneity effects an important change on the shape of the hazard. The qualitative effects of the covariates are similar to those in Table 22.1, although the magnitudes of some of the variables—for example, the number of priors, the felon dummy variable, and the marriage dummy variable—increase nontrivially. The estimate of δ is about 6.0, and it is very statistically significant. Thus the Weibull model without heterogeneity is strongly rejected in favor of the Weibull model with heterogeneity.

The unconditional hazard—that is, the hazard for the duration distribution that integrates out the heterogeneity—is plotted in Figure 22.4. The covariates are set at mean values. Its shape is more like that in the lognormal model, although the peak

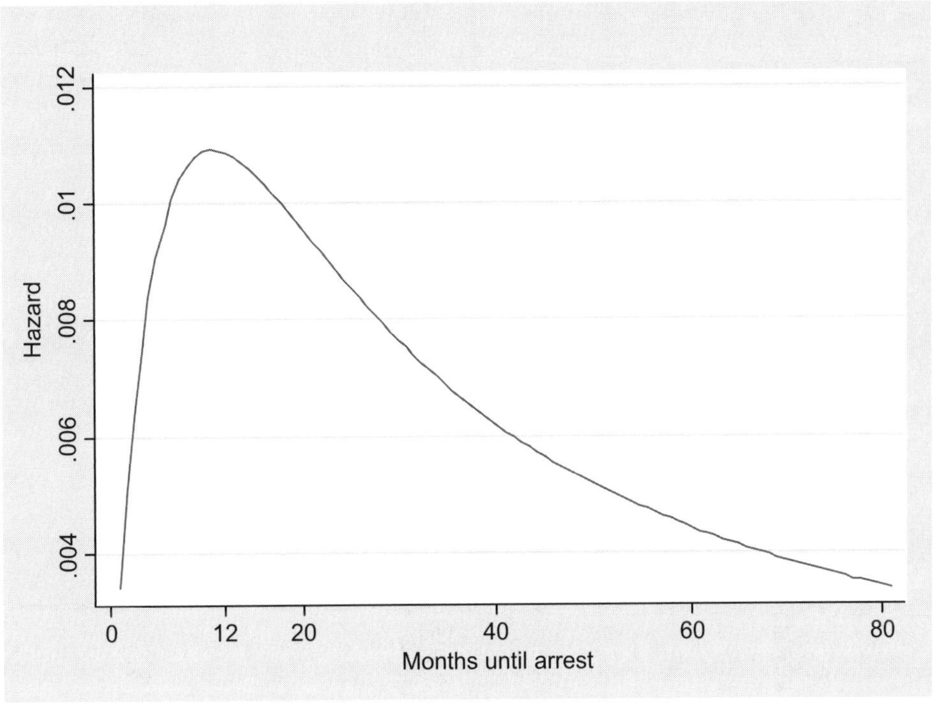

Figure 22.4
Unconditional Burr hazard

of the hazard in Figure 22.4 is at roughly 12 months, rather than six months. The monotonicity of the conditional hazard coupled with the hump shape of the unconditional hazard is common in applications. The reasoning behind the hump shape for the unconditional hazard goes something like this. (For simplicity, assume that there are no observed covariates, or that we are conditioning on a set of values.) Initially, all types of men are in the risk set, and so the shape of the unconditional hazard—that is, the aggregate hazard across the entire population—mimics that of the conditional hazard. But in the early periods, men with high proclivities to commit crimes—that is, with higher v_i—will tend to be arrested. Those arrested drop out of the risk set in subsequent time periods. Therefore, the men left in the risk set in later time periods tend to have the lower predispositions to repeat crimes. As the length of time until arrest increases, men with smaller values of v_i are left in the risk set, and this result translates into a declining unconditional hazard.

As with all applications that assume the proportional hazard form (in both observed covariates and unobserved heterogeneity), we are left with a conundrum: should we accept that the conditional hazard has the shape in Figure 22.3—for any heterogeneity and any value of $\mathbf{x}$—or should the conditional hazard be more complicated? As mentioned earlier, unless we take the multiplicative structure $\lambda(t; \mathbf{x}_i, v_i) = v_i \kappa(\mathbf{x}_i) \lambda_0(t)$ as given, there is a fundamental lack of identification. If we replace $\kappa(\mathbf{x})\lambda_0(t)$ with the general nonseparable function $\kappa(t; \mathbf{x})$, identification of $\kappa(\cdot; \mathbf{x})$ for given values of $\mathbf{x}$ becomes very difficult. Further, more complicated ways of introducing heterogeneity lead into very rough waters. For example, suppose we specify $\lambda(t; \mathbf{x}_i, \mathbf{b}_i) = \exp(\mathbf{x}_i \mathbf{b}_i)\lambda_0(t)$, where $\mathbf{b}_i$ is a $K \times 1$ random vector. (Letting $x_{i1} \equiv 1$ encompasses the usual case of multiplicative heterogeneity.) Even if we assume $\mathbf{b}_i$ is independent of $\mathbf{x}_i$, it is not clear that one can identify $\lambda_0(t)$ without assuming a full distribution for $\mathbf{b}_i$. Even if we took such an approach, we would never be able to distinguish between relatively simple models with unobserved heterogeneity and complicated hazards that cannot be written as a multiple of $\lambda_0(t)$.

22.4 Analysis of Grouped Duration Data

Continuously distributed durations are, strictly speaking, rare in social science applications. Even if an underlying duration is properly viewed as being continuous, measurements are necessarily discrete. When the measurements are fairly precise, it is sensible to treat the durations as continuous random variables. But when the measurements are coarse—such as monthly, or perhaps even weekly—it can be important to account for the discreteness in the estimation.

Grouped duration data arise when each duration is only known to fall into a certain time interval, such as a week, a month, or even a year. For example, unemployment durations are often measured to the nearest week. In Example 22.2 the time until next arrest is measured to the nearest month. Even with grouped data we can generally estimate the parameters of the duration distribution.

The approach we take here to analyzing grouped data summarizes the information on staying in the initial state or exiting in each time interval in a sequence of binary outcomes. (Kiefer, 1988; Han and Hausman, 1990; Meyer, 1990; Lancaster, 1990; McCall, 1994; and Sueyoshi, 1995, all take this approach.) In effect, we have a panel data set where each cross section observation is a vector of binary responses, along with covariates. In addition to allowing us to treat grouped durations, the panel data approach has at least two additional advantages. First, in a proportional hazard specification, it leads to easy methods for estimating flexible hazard functions. Second, because of the sequential nature of the data, time-varying covariates are easily introduced.

We assume flow sampling so that we do not have to address the sample selection problem that arises with stock sampling. We divide the time line into $M+1$ intervals, $[0, a_1), [a_1, a_2), \ldots, [a_{M-1}, a_M), [a_M, \infty)$, where the a_m are known constants. For example, we might have $a_1 = 1, a_2 = 2, a_3 = 3$, and so on, but unequally spaced intervals are allowed. The last interval, $[a_M, \infty)$, is chosen so that any duration falling into it is censored at a_M: no observed durations are greater than a_M. For a random draw from the population, let c_m be a binary censoring indicator equal to unity if the duration is censored in interval m, and zero otherwise. Notice that $c_m = 1$ implies $c_{m+1} = 1$: if the duration was censored in interval m, it is still censored in interval $m+1$. Because durations lasting into the last interval are censored, $c_{M+1} \equiv 1$. Similarly, y_m is a binary indicator equal to unity if the duration ends in the mth interval and zero otherwise. Thus, $y_{m+1} = 1$ if $y_m = 1$. If the duration is censored in interval m ($c_m = 1$), we set $y_m \equiv 1$ by convention.

As in Section 22.3, we allow individuals to enter the initial state at different calendar times. In order to keep the notation simple, we do not explicitly show the conditioning on these starting times, as the starting times play no role under flow sampling when we assume that, conditional on the covariates, the starting times are independent of the duration and any unobserved heterogeneity. If necessary, starting-time dummies can be included in the covariates.

For each person i, we observe $(y_{i1}, c_{i1}), \ldots, (y_{iM}, c_{iM})$, which is a balanced panel data set. To avoid confusion with our notation for a duration (T for the random variable, t for a particular outcome on T), we use m to index the time intervals. The string of binary indicators for any individual is *not* unrestricted: we must observe a string of zeros followed by a string of ones. The important information is the interval in which y_{im} becomes unity for the first time, and whether that represents a true exit from the initial state or censoring.

22.4.1 Time-Invariant Covariates

With time-invariant covariates, each random draw from the population consists of information on $\{(y_1, c_1), \ldots, (y_M, c_M), \mathbf{x}\}$. We assume that a parametric hazard function is specified as $\lambda(t; \mathbf{x}, \boldsymbol{\theta})$, where $\boldsymbol{\theta}$ is the vector of unknown parameters. Let T denote the time until exit from the initial state. While we do not fully observe T, either we know which interval it falls into, or we know whether it was censored in a particular interval. This knowledge is enough to obtain the probability that y_m takes on the value unity given $(y_{m-1}, \ldots, y_1)$, $(c_m, \ldots, c_1)$, and $\mathbf{x}$. In fact, by definition this probability depends only on y_{m-1}, c_m, and $\mathbf{x}$, and only two combinations yield probabilities that are not identically zero or one. These probabilities are

$$\mathrm{P}(y_m = 0 \mid y_{m-1} = 0, \mathbf{x}, c_m = 0) \tag{22.38}$$

$$\mathrm{P}(y_m = 1 \mid y_{m-1} = 0, \mathbf{x}, c_m = 0), \qquad m = 1, \ldots, M \tag{22.39}$$

(We define $y_0 \equiv 0$ so that these equations hold for all $m \geq 1$.) To compute these probabilities in terms of the hazard for T, we assume that the duration is conditionally independent of censoring:

$$T \text{ is independent of } c_1, \ldots, c_M, \text{ given } \mathbf{x} \tag{22.40}$$

This assumption allows the censoring to depend on $\mathbf{x}$ but rules out censoring that depends on unobservables, after conditioning on $\mathbf{x}$. Condition (22.40) holds for fixed censoring or completely randomized censoring. (It may not hold if censoring is due to nonrandom attrition.) Under assumption (22.40) we have, from equation (22.9),

$$\begin{aligned} \mathrm{P}(y_m = 1 \mid y_{m-1} = 0, \mathbf{x}, c_m = 0) &= \mathrm{P}(a_{m-1} \leq T < a_m \mid T \geq a_{m-1}, \mathbf{x}) \\ &= 1 - \exp\left[-\int_{a_{m-1}}^{a_m} \lambda(s; \mathbf{x}, \boldsymbol{\theta})\, ds\right] \equiv 1 - \alpha_m(\mathbf{x}, \boldsymbol{\theta}) \end{aligned} \tag{22.41}$$

for $m = 1, 2, \ldots, M$, where

$$\alpha_m(\mathbf{x}, \boldsymbol{\theta}) \equiv \exp\left[-\int_{a_{m-1}}^{a_m} \lambda(s; \mathbf{x}, \boldsymbol{\theta})\, ds\right] \tag{22.42}$$

Therefore,

$$\mathrm{P}(y_m = 0 \mid y_{m-1} = 0, \mathbf{x}, c_m = 0) = \alpha_m(\mathbf{x}, \boldsymbol{\theta}) \tag{22.43}$$

We can use these probabilities to construct the likelihood function. If, for observation i, uncensored exit occurs in interval m_i, the likelihood is

$$\left[\prod_{h=1}^{m_i - 1} \alpha_h(\mathbf{x}_i, \boldsymbol{\theta})\right][1 - \alpha_{m_i}(\mathbf{x}_i, \boldsymbol{\theta})] \tag{22.44}$$

The first term represents the probability of remaining in the initial state for the first $m_i - 1$ intervals, and the second term is the (conditional) probability that T falls into interval m_i. (Because an uncensored duration must have $m_i \leq M$, expression (22.44) at most depends on $\alpha_1(\mathbf{x}_i, \boldsymbol{\theta}), \ldots, \alpha_M(\mathbf{x}_i, \boldsymbol{\theta})$.) If the duration is censored in interval

m_i, we know only that exit did not occur in the first $m_i - 1$ intervals, and the likelihood consists of only the first term in expression (22.44).

If d_i is a censoring indicator equal to one if duration i is uncensored, the log likelihood for observation i can be written as

$$\sum_{h=1}^{m_i-1} \log[\alpha_h(\mathbf{x}_i, \boldsymbol{\theta})] + d_i \log[1 - \alpha_{m_i}(\mathbf{x}_i, \boldsymbol{\theta})] \tag{22.45}$$

The log likelihood for the entire sample is obtained by summing expression (22.45) across all $i = 1, \ldots, N$. Under the assumptions made, this log likelihood represents the density of $(y_1, \ldots, y_M)$ given $(c_1, \ldots, c_M)$ and $\mathbf{x}$, and so the conditional maximum likelihood theory covered in Chapter 13 applies directly. The various ways of estimating asymptotic variances and computing test statistics are available.

To implement conditional MLE, we must specify a hazard function. One hazard function that has become popular because of its flexibility is a **piecewise-constant proportional hazard**: for $m = 1, \ldots, M$,

$$\lambda(t; \mathbf{x}, \boldsymbol{\theta}) = \kappa(\mathbf{x}, \boldsymbol{\beta})\lambda_m, \qquad a_{m-1} \le t < a_m \tag{22.46}$$

where $\kappa(\mathbf{x}, \boldsymbol{\beta}) > 0$ (and typically $\kappa(\mathbf{x}, \boldsymbol{\beta}) = \exp(\mathbf{x}\boldsymbol{\beta})$). This specification allows the hazard to be different (albeit constant) over each time interval. The parameters to be estimated are $\boldsymbol{\beta}$ and $\boldsymbol{\lambda}$, where the latter is the vector of λ_m, $m = 1, \ldots, M$. (Because durations in $[a_M, \infty)$ are censored at a_M, we cannot estimate the hazard over the interval $[a_M, \infty)$.) As an example, if we have unemployment duration measured in weeks, the hazard can be different in each week. If the durations are sparse, we might assume a different hazard rate for every two or three weeks (this assumption places restrictions on the λ_m). With the piecewise-constant hazard and $\kappa(\mathbf{x}, \boldsymbol{\beta}) = \exp(\mathbf{x}\boldsymbol{\beta})$, for $m = 1, \ldots, M$, we have

$$\alpha_m(\mathbf{x}, \boldsymbol{\theta}) \equiv \exp[-\exp(\mathbf{x}\boldsymbol{\beta})\lambda_m(a_m - a_{m-1})] \tag{22.47}$$

Remember, the a_m are known constants (often $a_m = m$) and not parameters to be estimated. Usually the λ_m are unrestricted, in which case $\mathbf{x}$ does not contain an intercept.

The piecewise-constant hazard implies that the duration distribution is discontinuous at the endpoints, whereas in our discussion in Section 22.2 we assumed that the duration had a continuous distribution. A piecewise-continuous distribution causes no real problems, and the log likelihood is exactly as specified previously. Alternatively, as in Han and Hausman (1990) and Meyer (1990), we can assume that T

has a proportional hazard as in equation (22.16) with continuous baseline hazard, $\lambda_0(\cdot)$. Then, we can estimate $\boldsymbol{\beta}$ along with the parameters

$$\int_{a_{m-1}}^{a_m} \lambda_0(s)\, ds, \qquad m = 1, 2, \ldots, M$$

In practice, the approaches are the same, and it is easiest to just assume a piecewise-constant proportional hazard, as in equation (22.46).

Once the λ_m have been estimated along with $\boldsymbol{\beta}$, an estimated hazard function is easily plotted: graph $\hat{\lambda}_m$ at the midpoint of the interval $[a_{m-1}, a_m)$, and connect the points.

Without covariates, maximum likelihood estimation of the λ_m leads to a well-known estimator of the survivor function. Rather than derive the MLE of the survivor function, it is easier to motivate the estimator from the representation of the survivor function as a product of conditional probabilities. For $m = 1, \ldots, M$, the survivor function at time a_m can be written as

$$S(a_m) = \mathrm{P}(T > a_m) = \prod_{r=1}^{m} \mathrm{P}(T > a_r \mid T > a_{r-1}) \tag{22.48}$$

(Because $a_0 = 0$ and $\mathrm{P}(T > 0) = 1$, the $r = 1$ term on the right-hand side of equation (22.48) is simply $\mathrm{P}(T > a_1)$.) Now, for each $r = 1, 2, \ldots, M$, let N_r denote the number of people in the **risk set** for interval r: N_r is the number of people who have neither left the initial state nor been censored at time a_{r-1}, which is the beginning of interval r. Therefore, N_1 is the number of individuals in the initial random sample; N_2 is the number of individuals who did not exit the initial state in the first interval, less the number of individuals censored in the first interval; and so on. Let E_r be the number of people observed to leave in the rth interval—that is, in the interval $[a_{r-1}, a_r)$. A consistent estimator of $\mathrm{P}(T > a_r \mid T > a_{r-1})$ is $(N_r - E_r)/N_r$, $r = 1, 2, \ldots, M$. (We must use the fact that the censoring is ignorable in the sense of assumption (22.40), so that there is no sample selection bias in using only the uncensored observations.) It follows from equation (22.48) that a consistent estimator of the survivor function at time a_m is

$$\hat{S}(a_m) = \prod_{r=1}^{m} [(N_r - E_r)/N_r], \qquad m = 1, 2, \ldots, M \tag{22.49}$$

This is the **Kaplan-Meier estimator** of the survivor function (at the points $a_1, a_2, \ldots, a_M$). Lancaster (1990, Section 8.2) contains a proof that maximum likelihood estimation of the λ_m (without covariates) leads to the Kaplan-Meier estimator of the survivor function. If there are no censored durations before time a_m, $\hat{S}(a_m)$ is simply the fraction of people who have not left the initial state at time a_m, which is obviously consistent for $\mathrm{P}(T > a_m) = S(a_m)$.

In the general model, we do not need to assume a proportional hazard specification within each interval. For example, we could assume a log-logistic hazard within each interval, with different parameters for each m. Because the hazard in such cases does not depend on the covariates multiplicatively, we must plug in values of $\mathbf{x}$ in order to plot the hazard. Sueyoshi (1995) studies such models in detail.

If the intervals $[a_{m-1}, a_m)$ are coarser than the data—for example, unemployment is measured in weeks, but we choose $[a_{m-1}, a_m)$ to be four weeks for all m—then we can specify nonconstant hazards within each interval. The piecewise-constant hazard corresponds to an exponential distribution within each interval. But we could specify, say, a Weibull distribution within each interval. See Sueyoshi (1995) for details.

22.4.2 Time-Varying Covariates

Deriving the log likelihood is more complicated with time-varying covariates, especially when we do not assume that the covariates are strictly exogenous. Nevertheless, we will show that, if the covariates are constant within each time interval $[a_{m-1}, a_m)$, the form of the log likelihood is the same as expression (22.45), provided $\mathbf{x}_i$ is replaced with $\mathbf{x}_{im}$ in interval m.

For the population, let $\mathbf{x}_1, \mathbf{x}_2, \ldots, \mathbf{x}_M$ denote the outcomes of the covariates in each of the M time intervals, where we assume that the covariates are constant within an interval. This assumption is clearly an oversimplification, but we cannot get very far without it (and it reflects how data sets with time-varying covariates are usually constructed). When the covariates are internal and are not necessarily defined after exit from the initial state, the definition of the covariates in the time intervals is irrelevant; but it is useful to list covariates for all M time periods.

We assume that the hazard at time t conditional on the covariates up through time t depends only on the covariates at time t. If past values of the covariates matter, they can simply be included in the covariates at time t. The conditional independence assumption on the censoring indicators is now stated as

$$\mathrm{D}(T \mid T \geq a_{m-1}, \mathbf{x}_m, c_m) = \mathrm{D}(T \mid T \geq a_{m-1}, \mathbf{x}_m), \qquad m = 1, \ldots, M \tag{22.50}$$

This assumption allows the censoring decision to depend on the covariates during the time interval (as well as past covariates, provided they are either included in $\mathbf{x}_m$ or do not affect the distribution of T given $\mathbf{x}_m$). Under this assumption, the probability of exit (without censoring) is

$$\begin{aligned}\mathrm{P}(y_m = 1 \mid y_{m-1} = 0, \mathbf{x}_m, c_m = 0) &= \mathrm{P}(a_{m-1} \le T < a_m \mid T \ge a_{m-1}, \mathbf{x}_m) \\ &= 1 - \exp\left[-\int_{a_{m-1}}^{a_m} \lambda(s; \mathbf{x}_m, \boldsymbol{\theta})\, ds\right] \equiv 1 - \alpha_m(\mathbf{x}_m, \boldsymbol{\theta})\end{aligned} \tag{22.51}$$

We can use equation (22.51), along with $\mathrm{P}(y_m = 0 \mid y_{m-1} = 0, \mathbf{x}_m, c_m = 0) = \alpha_m(\mathbf{x}_m, \boldsymbol{\theta})$, to build up a partial log likelihood for person i. As we discussed in Section 13.8, this is only a partial likelihood because we are not necessarily modeling the joint distribution of $(y_1, \ldots, y_M)$ given $\{(\mathbf{x}_1, c_1), \ldots, (c_M, \mathbf{x}_M)\}$.

For someone censored in interval m, the information on the duration is contained in $y_{i1} = 0, \ldots, y_{i,m-1} = 0$. For someone who truly exits in interval m, there is additional information in $y_{im} = 1$. Therefore, the partial log likelihood is given by expression (22.45), but, to reflect the time-varying covariates, $\alpha_h(\mathbf{x}_i, \boldsymbol{\theta})$ is replaced by $\alpha_h(\mathbf{x}_{ih}, \boldsymbol{\theta})$ and $\alpha_{m_i}(\mathbf{x}_i, \boldsymbol{\theta})$ is replaced by $\alpha_{m_i}(\mathbf{x}_{i,m_i}, \boldsymbol{\theta})$.

Each term in the partial log likelihood represents the distribution of y_m given $(y_{m-1}, \ldots, y_1)$, $(\mathbf{x}_m, \ldots, \mathbf{x}_1)$, and $(c_m, \ldots, c_1)$. (Most of the probabilities in this conditional distribution are either zero or one; only the probabilities that depend on $\boldsymbol{\theta}$ are shown in expression (22.45).) Therefore, the density is *dynamically complete*, in the terminology of Section 13.8.3. As shown there, the usual maximum likelihood variance matrix estimators and statistics are asymptotically valid, even though we need not have the full conditional distribution of $\mathbf{y}$ given $(\mathbf{x}, \mathbf{c})$. This result would change if, for some reason, we chose not to include past covariates when in fact they affect the current probability of exit even after conditioning on the current covariates. Then the robust forms of the statistics covered in Section 13.8 should be used. In most duration applications we want dynamic completeness.

If the covariates are strictly exogenous and if the censoring is strictly exogenous, then the partial likelihood is the full conditional likelihood. The precise strict exogeneity assumption is

$$\mathrm{D}(T \mid T \ge a_{m-1}, \mathbf{x}, \mathbf{c}) = \mathrm{D}(T \mid T \ge a_{m-1}, \mathbf{x}_m), \qquad m = 1, \ldots, M \tag{22.52}$$

where $\mathbf{x}$ is the vector of covariates across all time periods and $\mathbf{c}$ is the vector of censoring indicators. There are two parts to this assumption. Ignoring the censoring, assumption (22.52) means that neither future nor past covariates appear in the hazard, once current covariates are controlled for. The second implication of assumption (22.52) is that the censoring is also strictly exogenous.

With time-varying covariates, the hazard specification

$$\lambda(t; \mathbf{x}_m, \boldsymbol{\theta}) = \kappa(\mathbf{x}_m, \boldsymbol{\beta})\lambda_m, \qquad a_{m-1} \le t < a_m \tag{22.53}$$

$m = 1, \ldots, M$, is still attractive. It implies that the covariates have a multiplicative effect in each time interval, and it allows the baseline hazard—the part common to all members of the population—to be flexible.

Meyer (1990) essentially uses the specification (22.53) to estimate the effect of unemployment insurance on unemployment spells. McCall (1994) shows how to allow for time-varying coefficients when $\kappa(\mathbf{x}_m, \boldsymbol{\beta}) = \exp(\mathbf{x}_m \boldsymbol{\beta})$. In other words, $\boldsymbol{\beta}$ is replaced with $\boldsymbol{\beta}_m$, $m = 1, \ldots, M$.

22.4.3 Unobserved Heterogeneity

We can also add unobserved heterogeneity to hazards specified for grouped data, even if we have time-varying covariates. With time-varying covariates and unobserved heterogeneity, it is difficult to relax the strict exogeneity assumption. Also, with single-spell data, we cannot allow general correlation between the unobserved heterogeneity and the covariates. Therefore, we assume that the covariates are strictly exogenous conditional on unobserved heterogeneity *and* that the unobserved heterogeneity is independent of the covariates.

The precise assumptions are given by equation (22.52) but where unobserved heterogeneity, v, appears in both conditioning sets. In addition, we assume that v is independent of $(\mathbf{x}, \mathbf{c})$ (which is a further sense in which the censoring is exogenous).

In the leading case of the piecewise-constant baseline hazard, equation (22.53) becomes

$$\lambda(t; v, \mathbf{x}_m, \boldsymbol{\theta}) = v\kappa(\mathbf{x}_m, \boldsymbol{\beta})\lambda_m, \qquad a_{m-1} \le t < a_m \tag{22.54}$$

where $v > 0$ is a continuously distributed heterogeneity term. Using the same reasoning as in Sections 22.4.1 and 22.4.2, the density of $(y_{i1}, \ldots, y_{iM})$ given $(v_i, \mathbf{x}_i, \mathbf{c}_i)$ is

$$\left[\prod_{h=1}^{m_i - 1} \alpha_h(v_i, \mathbf{x}_{ih}, \boldsymbol{\theta})\right][1 - \alpha_{m_i}(v_i, \mathbf{x}_{i,m_i}, \boldsymbol{\theta})]^{d_i} \tag{22.55}$$

where $d_i = 1$ if observation i is uncensored. Because expression (22.55) depends on the unobserved heterogeneity, v_i, we cannot use it directly to consistently estimate $\boldsymbol{\theta}$. However, because v_i is independent of $(\mathbf{x}_i, \mathbf{c}_i)$, with density $g(v; \boldsymbol{\delta})$, we can integrate expression (22.55) against $g(\cdot\,; \boldsymbol{\delta})$ to obtain the density of $(y_{i1}, \ldots, y_{iM})$ given $(\mathbf{x}_i, \mathbf{c}_i)$. This density depends on the observed data—$(m_i, d_i, \mathbf{x}_i)$—and the parameters $\boldsymbol{\theta}$ and $\boldsymbol{\delta}$. From this density, we construct the conditional log likelihood for observation i, and we can obtain the conditional MLE, just as in other nonlinear models with unobserved heterogeneity—see Chapters 15–19. Meyer (1990) assumes that the distribution of v_i is gamma, with unit mean, and obtains the log-likelihood function in closed form. McCall (1994) analyzes a heterogeneity distribution that contains the gamma as a special case.

It is possible to consistently estimate $\boldsymbol{\beta}$ and λ without specifying a parametric form for the heterogeneity distribution; this approach results in a semiparametric maximum likelihood estimator. Heckman and Singer (1984) first showed how to perform this method with a Weibull baseline hazard, and Meyer (1990) proved consistency when the hazard has the form (22.54). The estimated heterogeneity distribution is discrete and, in practice, has relatively few mass points. The consistency argument works by allowing the number of mass points to increase with the sample size. Computation is a difficult issue, and the asymptotic distribution of the semiparametric maximum likelihood estimator has not been worked out.

22.5 Further Issues

The methods we have covered in this chapter have been applied in many contexts. Nevertheless, there are several important topics that we have neglected.

22.5.1 Cox's Partial Likelihood Method for the Proportional Hazard Model

Cox (1972) suggested a partial likelihood method for estimating the parameters $\boldsymbol{\beta}$ in a proportional hazard model without specifying the baseline hazard. The strength of Cox's approach is that the effects of the covariates can be estimated very generally, provided the hazard is of the form (22.16). However, Cox's method is intended to be applied to flow data as opposed to grouped data. If we apply Cox's methods to grouped data, we must confront the practically important issue of individuals with identical observed durations. In addition, with time-varying covariates, Cox's method evidently requires the covariates to be strictly exogenous. Estimation of the hazard function itself is more complicated than the methods for grouped data that we covered in Section 22.4. See Amemiya (1985, Chapter 11) and Lancaster (1990, Chapter 9) for treatments of Cox's partial likelihood estimator.

22.5.2 Multiple-Spell Data

All the methods we have covered assume a single spell for each sample unit. In other words, each individual begins in the initial state and then either is observed leaving the state or is censored. But at least some individuals might have multiple spells, especially if we follow them for long periods. For example, we may observe a person who is initially unemployed, becomes employed, and then after a time becomes unemployed again. If we assume constancy across time about the process driving unemployment duration, we can use multiple spells to aid in identification, particularly in models with heterogeneity that can be correlated with time-varying covariates. Chamberlain (1985) and Honoré (1993b) contain identification results when multiple spells are observed. Chamberlain allowed for correlation between the heterogeneity and the time-varying covariates.

Multiple-spell data are also useful for estimating models with unobserved heterogeneity when the regressors are not strictly exogenous. Ham and Lalonde (1996) give an example in which participation in a job training program can be related to past unemployment duration, even though eligibility is randomly assigned. See also Wooldridge (2000) for a general framework that allows feedback to future explanatory variables in models with unobserved heterogeneity.

22.5.3 Competing Risks Models

Another important topic is allowing for more than two possible states. **Competing risks models** allow for the possibility that an individual may exit into different alternatives. For example, a person working full-time may choose to retire completely or work part-time. Han and Hausman (1990) and Sueyoshi (1992) contain discussions of the assumptions needed to estimate competing risks models, with and without unobserved heterogeneity. See van den Berg (2001) for a detailed treatment.

Problems

22.1. Use the data in RECID.RAW for this problem.

a. Using the covariates in Table 22.1, estimate equation (22.26) by censored Tobit. Verify that the log-likelihood value is $-1{,}597.06$.

b. Plug in the mean values for *priors*, *tserved*, *educ*, and *age*, and the values $workprg = 0$, $felon = 1$, $alcohol = 1$, $drugs = 1$, $black = 0$, and $married = 0$, and plot the estimated hazard for the lognormal distribution. Describe what you find.

c. Using only the uncensored observations, perform an OLS regression of $\log(durat)$ on the covariates in Table 22.1. Compare the estimates on *tserved* and *alcohol* with those from part a. What do you conclude?

d. Now compute an OLS regression using all data—that is, treat the censored observations as if they are uncensored. Compare the estimates on *tserved* and *alcohol* from those in parts a and c.

22.2. Use the data in RECID.RAW to answer these questions:

a. To the Weibull model, add the variables *super* (=1 if release from prison was supervised) and *rules* (number of rules violations while in prison). Do the coefficient estimates on these new variables have the expected signs? Are they statistically significant?

b. Add *super* and *rules* to the lognormal model, and answer the same questions as in part a.

c. Compare the estimated effects of the *rules* variable on the expected duration for the Weibull and lognormal models. Are they practically different?

22.3. Consider the case of flow sampling, as in Section 22.3.2, but suppose that all durations are censored: $d_i = 1$, $i = 1, \ldots, N$.

a. Write down the log-likelihood function when all durations are censored.

b. Find the special case of the Weibull distribution in part a.

c. Consider the Weibull case where $\mathbf{x}_i$ only contains a constant, so that $F(t; \alpha, \beta) = 1 - \exp[-\exp(\beta)t^{\alpha}]$. Show that the Weibull log likelihood cannot be maximized for real numbers $\hat{\beta}$ and $\hat{\alpha}$.

d. From part c, what do you conclude about estimating duration models from flow data when all durations are right censored?

e. If the duration distribution is continuous, $c_i > b > 0$ for some constant b, and $\mathrm{P}(t_i^* < t) > 0$ for all $t > 0$, is it likely, in a large random sample, to find that all durations have been censored?

22.4. Suppose that, in the context of flow sampling, we observe for each i covariates $\mathbf{x}_i$, the censoring time c_i, and the binary indicator d_i (=1 if the observation is uncensored). We never observe t_i^*.

a. Show that the conditional likelihood function has the binary response form. What is the binary "response"?

b. Use the Weibull model to demonstrate the following when we only observe whether durations are censored: if the censoring times c_i are constant, the parameters $\boldsymbol{\beta}$ and α are not identified. (Hint: Consider the same case as in Problem 22.3c, and show that the log likelihood depends only on the constant $\exp(\beta)c^{\alpha}$, where c is the common censoring time.)

c. Use the lognormal model to argue that, provided the c_i vary across i in the population, the parameters are generally identified. (Hint: In the binary response model, what is the coefficient on $\log(c_i)$?)

22.5. In this problem you are to derive the log likelihood in equation (22.30). Assume that $c_i > b - a_i$ for all i, so that we always observe part of each spell after the sampling date, b. In what follows, we supress the parameter vector, $\boldsymbol{\theta}$.

a. For $b - a_i < t < c_i$, show that $\mathrm{P}(t_i^* \le t \mid \mathbf{x}_i, a_i, c_i, s_i = 1) = [F(t \mid \mathbf{x}_i) - F(b - a_i \mid \mathbf{x}_i)]/[1 - F(b - a_i \mid \mathbf{x}_i)]$.

b. Use part a to obtain the density of t_i^* conditional on $(\mathbf{x}_i, a_i, c_i, s_i = 1)$ for $b - a_i < t < c_i$.

c. Show that $\mathrm{P}(t_i = c_i \mid \mathbf{x}_i, a_i, c_i, s_i = 1) = [1 - F(c_i \mid \mathbf{x}_i)]/[1 - F(b - a_i \mid \mathbf{x}_i)]$.

d. Explain why parts b and c lead to equation (22.30).

22.6. Consider the problem of stock sampling where we do not follow spells after the sampling date, b, as described in Section 22.3.3. Let $F(\cdot \mid \mathbf{x}_i)$ denote the cdf of t_i^* given $\mathbf{x}_i$, and let $k(\cdot \mid \mathbf{x}_i)$ denote the continuous density of a_i given $\mathbf{x}_i$. We drop dependence on the parameters for most of the derivations. Assume that t_i^* and a_i are independent conditional on $\mathbf{x}_i$.

a. Let s_i denote a selection indicator, so that $s_i = 1(t_i^* \ge b - a_i)$. For any $0 < a < b$, show that

$$\mathrm{P}(a_i \le a, s_i = 1 \mid \mathbf{x}_i) = \int_0^a k(u \mid \mathbf{x}_i)[1 - F(b - u \mid \mathbf{x}_i)]\, \mathrm{d}u$$

b. Derive equation (22.32). (Hint: $\mathrm{P}(s_i = 1 \mid \mathbf{x}_i) = \mathrm{E}(s_i \mid \mathbf{x}_i) = \mathrm{E}[\mathrm{E}(s_i \mid a_i, \mathbf{x}_i) \mid \mathbf{x}_i]$, and $\mathrm{E}(s_i \mid a_i, \mathbf{x}_i) = \mathrm{P}(t_i^* \ge b - a_i \mid \mathbf{x}_i)$.)

c. For $0 < a < b$, what is the cdf of a_i given $\mathbf{x}_i$ and $s_i = 1$? Now derive equation (22.31).

d. Take $b = 1$, and assume that the starting time distribution is uniform on $[0, 1]$ (independent of $\mathbf{x}_i$). Find the density (22.31) in this case.

e. For the setup in part d, assume that the duration cdf has the Weibull form, $1 - \exp[-\exp(\mathbf{x}_i\boldsymbol{\beta})t^{\alpha}]$. What is the log likelihood for observation i?

22.7. Consider the original stock sampling problem that we covered in Section 22.3.3. There, we derived the log likelihood (22.30) by conditioning on the starting times, a_i. This approach is convenient because we do not have to specify a distribution for the starting times. But suppose we have an acceptable model for $k(\cdot \mid \mathbf{x}_i; \boldsymbol{\eta})$, the (continuous) density of a_i given $\mathbf{x}_i$. Further, we maintain assumption (22.22) and assume $\mathrm{D}(a_i \mid c_i, \mathbf{x}_i) = \mathrm{D}(a_i \mid \mathbf{x}_i)$.

a. Show that the log-likelihood function conditional on $\mathbf{x}_i$, which accounts for truncation, is

$$\sum_{i=1}^{N}\{d_i \log[f(t_i \mid \mathbf{x}_i; \boldsymbol{\theta})] + (1 - d_i) \log[1 - F(t_i \mid \mathbf{x}_i; \boldsymbol{\theta})]$$

$$+ \log[k(a_i \mid \mathbf{x}_i; \boldsymbol{\eta})] - \log[\mathrm{P}(s_i = 1 \mid \mathbf{x}_i; \boldsymbol{\theta}, \boldsymbol{\eta})]\} \tag{22.56}$$

where $\mathrm{P}(s_i = 1 \mid \mathbf{x}_i; \boldsymbol{\theta}, \boldsymbol{\eta})$ is given in equation (22.32).

b. Discuss the trade-offs in using equation (22.30) or the log likelihood in (22.56).

22.8. In the context of stock sampling, where we are interested in the population of durations starting in $[0, b]$, suppose that we interview at date b, as usual, but we do not observe any starting times. (This assumption raises the issue of how we know individual i's starting time is in the specified interval, $[0, b]$. We assume that the interval is defined to make this condition true for all i.) Let $r_i^* = a_i + t_i^* - b$, which can be interpreted as the calendar date at which the spell ends minus the interview date. Even without right censoring, we observe r_i^* only if $r_i^* > 0$, in which case r_i^* is simply the time in the spell since the interview date, b. Assume that t_i^* and a_i are independent conditional on $\mathbf{x}_i$.

a. Show that for $r > 0$, the density of r_i^* given $\mathbf{x}_i$ is

$$h(r \mid \mathbf{x}_i; \boldsymbol{\theta}, \boldsymbol{\eta}) \equiv \int_0^b k(u \mid \mathbf{x}_i; \boldsymbol{\eta}) f(r + b - u \mid \mathbf{x}_i; \boldsymbol{\theta})\, du$$

where, as before, $k(a \mid \mathbf{x}_i; \boldsymbol{\eta})$ is the density of a_i given $\mathbf{x}_i$ and $f(t \mid \mathbf{x}_i; \boldsymbol{\theta})$ is the duration density.

b. Let $q > 0$ be a fixed censoring time after the interview date, and define $r_i = \min(r_i^*, q)$. Find $\mathrm{P}(r_i = q \mid \mathbf{x}_i)$ in terms of the cdf of r_i^*, say, $H(r \mid \mathbf{x}_i; \boldsymbol{\theta}, \boldsymbol{\eta})$.

c. Use parts a and b, along with equation (22.32), to show that the log likelihood conditional on observing $(r_i, \mathbf{x}_i)$ is

$$d_i \log[h(r_i \mid \mathbf{x}_i; \boldsymbol{\theta}, \boldsymbol{\eta})] + (1 - d_i) \log[1 - H(r_i \mid \mathbf{x}_i; \boldsymbol{\theta}, \boldsymbol{\eta})]$$

$$- \log\left\{\int_0^b [1 - F(b - u \mid \mathbf{x}_i; \boldsymbol{\theta})] k(u \mid \mathbf{x}_i; \boldsymbol{\eta})\, \mathrm{d}u\right\} \tag{22.57}$$

where $d_i = 1$ if observation i has not been right censored.

d. Simplify the log likelihood from part c when $b = 1$ and $k(a \mid \mathbf{x}_i; \boldsymbol{\eta})$ is the uniform density on $[0, 1]$.

22.9. Consider the Weibull model with multiplicative heterogeneity, as in equation (22.33), but where v_i takes on only two values. Think of there being two types of people, A and B. Let $0 < \eta < 1$ be the value for type A people with $\rho = P(v_i = \eta)$, $0 < \rho < 1$.

a. Show that to ensure $E(v_i) = 1$, the value of v_i for type B people must be $(1 - \rho\eta)/(1 - \rho)$.

b. Find the cdf of t_i^* conditional on $\mathbf{x}_i$ only. Call this $G(t \mid \mathbf{x}_i; \alpha, \boldsymbol{\beta}, \eta, \rho)$.

c. Find the density of t_i^* conditional on $\mathbf{x}_i$, $g(t \mid \mathbf{x}_i; \alpha, \boldsymbol{\beta}, \eta, \rho)$. How would you estimate the parameters if you have right-censored data?

22.10. Let $0 < a_1 < a_2 < \cdots < a_{M-1} < a_M$ be a positive, increasing set of constants, and let T be a nonnegative random variable with $\mathrm{P}(T > 0) = 1$.

a. Show that, for any $m = 1, \ldots, M$, $\mathrm{P}(T > a_m) = \mathrm{P}(T > a_m \mid T > a_{m-1})\mathrm{P}(T > a_{m-1})$.

b. Use part a to derive equation (22.48).

22.11. Use the data in RECID to answer the following questions.

a. Using the same explanatory variables as in Table 22.2, estimate a model with gamma-distributed heterogeneity and a log-logistic hazard for $\kappa(t; \mathbf{x})$. Does the model fit better or worse than the Weibull/gamma mixture model reported in Table 22.2?

b. Graph the conditional hazard function (with $v = 1$) and at the mean values of the covariates. How does its shape compare with the Weibull/gamma model?

c. Graph the unconditional hazard function and comment on its shape. How do the conditional and unconditional hazards differ?

References

Abadie, A. (2003), "Semiparametric Instrumental Variable Estimation of Treatment Response Models," *Journal of Econometrics* 113, 231–263.

Abadie, A., and G. W. Imbens (2006), "Large Sample Properties of Matching Estimators for Average Treatment Effects," *Econometrica* 74, 235–267.

Abbring, J. H., and J. J. Heckman (2007), "Econometric Evaluation of Social Programs, Part III: Distributional Treatment Effects, Dynamic Treatment Effects and Dynamic Discrete Choice, and General Equilibrium Policy Evaluation," in *Handbook of Econometrics*, Volume 6B, ed. J. J. Heckman and E. Leamer. Amsterdam: North Holland, 5145–5303.

Abrevaya, J. (1997), "The Equivalence of Two Estimators for the Fixed Effects Logit Model," *Economics Letters* 55, 41–43.

Abrevaya, J., and C. Dahl (2008), "The Effects of Birth Inputs on Birthweight: Evidence from Quantile Estimation on Panel Data," *Journal of Business and Economic Statistics* 26, 379–397.

Adams, J. D., E. P. Chiang, and J. L. Jensen (2003), "The Influence of Federal Laboratory R&D on Industrial Research," *Review of Economics and Statistics* 85, 1003–1020.

Ahn, S. C., Y. H. Lee, and P. Schmidt (2002), "GMM Estimation of Linear Panel Data Models with Time-Varying Individual Effects," *Journal of Econometrics* 101, 219–255.

Ahn, H., and J. L. Powell (1993), "Semiparametric Estimation of Censored Selection Models with a Nonparametric Selection Mechanism," *Journal of Econometrics* 58, 3–29.

Ahn, S. C., and P. Schmidt (1995), "Efficient Estimation of Models for Dynamic Panel Data," *Journal of Econometrics* 68, 5–27.

Ai, C. (1997), "A Semiparametric Maximum Likelihood Estimator," *Econometrica* 65, 933–963.

Aitchison, J., and S. D. Silvey (1958), "Maximum-Likelihood Estimation of Parameters Subject to Constraints," *Annals of Mathematical Statistics* 29, 813–828.

Altonji, J. G., T. E. Elder, and C. R. Tabor (2005), "An Evaluation of Instrumental Variable Strategies for Estimating the Effects of Catholic Schooling," *Journal of Human Resources* 40, 791–821.

Altonji, J., and R. L. Matzkin (2005), "Cross Section and Panel Data Estimators for Nonseparable Models with Endogenous Regressors," *Econometrica* 73, 1053–1102.

Altonji, J. G., and L. M. Segal (1996), "Small-Sample Bias in GMM Estimation of Covariance Structures," *Journal of Business and Economic Statistics* 14, 353–366.

Alvarez, J., and M. Arellano (2003), "Time Series and Cross-Section Asymptotics of Dynamic Panel Data Estimators," *Econometrica* 71, 121–159.

Amemiya, T. (1973), "Regression Analysis When the Dependent Variable Is Truncated Normal," *Econometrica* 41, 997–1016.

Amemiya, T. (1974), "The Nonlinear Two-Stage Least-Squares Estimator," *Journal of Econometrics* 2, 105–110.

Amemiya, T. (1985), *Advanced Econometrics*. Cambridge, MA: Harvard University Press.

Andersen, E. B. (1970), "Asymptotic Properties of Conditional Maximum Likelihood Estimators," *Journal of the Royal Statistical Society*, Series B, 32, 283–301.

Anderson, T. W., and C. Hsiao (1982), "Formulation and Estimation of Dynamic Models Using Panel Data," *Journal of Econometrics* 18, 67–82.

Andrews, D. W. K. (1989), "Power in Econometric Applications," *Econometrica* 57, 1059–1090.

Angrist, J. D. (1990), "Lifetime Earnings and the Vietnam Era Draft Lottery: Evidence from Social Security Administrative Records," *American Economic Review* 80, 313–336.

Angrist, J. D. (1991), "Instrumental Variables Estimation of Average Treatment Effects in Econometrics and Epidemiology," National Bureau of Economic Research Technical Working Paper Number 115.

Angrist, J. D. (1998), "Estimating the Labor Market Impact of Voluntary Military Service Using Social Security Data on Military Applicants," *Econometrica* 66, 249–288.

Angrist, J., V. Chernozhukov, and I. Fernandez-Val (2006), "Quantile Regression under Misspecification, with an Application to the U.S. Wage Structure," *Econometrica* 74, 539–563.

Angrist, J. D., and W. N. Evans (1998), "Children and Their Parents' Labor Supply: Evidence from Exogenous Variation in Family Size," *American Economic Review* 88, 450–477.

Angrist, J. D., G. W. Imbens, and D. B. Rubin (1996), "Identification and Causal Effects Using Instrumental Variables," *Journal of the American Statistical Association* 91, 444–455.

Angrist, J. D., and A. B. Krueger (1991), "Does Compulsory School Attendance Affect Schooling and Earnings?" *Quarterly Journal of Economics* 106, 979–1014.

Angrist, J. D., and V. Lavy (2002), "The Effect of High School Matriculation Awards: Evidence from Randomized Trials," National Bureau of Economic Research Working Paper 9389.

Angrist, J. D., and W. K. Newey (1991), "Overidentification Tests in Earnings Functions with Fixed Effects," *Journal of Business and Economic Statistics* 9, 317–323.

Angrist, J. D., and J.-S. Pischke (2009), *Mostly Harmless Econometrics*. Princeton, NJ: Princeton University Press.

Arellano, M. (1987), "Computing Robust Standard Errors for Within-Groups Estimators," *Oxford Bulletin of Economics and Statistics* 49, 431–434.

Arellano, M. (2003), *Panel Data Econometrics*. Oxford: Oxford University Press.

Arellano, M., and S. R. Bond (1991), "Some Specification Tests for Panel Data: Monte Carlo Evidence and an Application to Employment Equations," *Review of Economic Studies* 58, 277–298.

Arellano, M., and O. Bover (1995), "Another Look at the Instrumental Variables Estimation of Error-Component Models," *Journal of Econometrics* 68, 29–51.

Arellano, M., and B. E. Honoré (2001), "Panel Data: Some Recent Developments," in *Handbook of Econometrics*, Volume 5, ed. E. Leamer and J. J. Heckman. Amsterdam: North Holland, 3229–3296.

Ayers, I., and S. D. Levitt (1998), "Measuring Positive Externalities from Unobservable Victim Precaution: An Empirical Analysis of Lojack," *Quarterly Journal of Economics* 108, 43–77.

Baltagi, B. H. (1981), "Simultaneous Equations with Error Components," *Journal of Econometrics* 17, 189–200.

Baltagi, B. H. (2001), *Econometric Analysis of Panel Data*, second edition. West Sussex, UK: Wiley.

Baltagi, B. H., and Q. Li (1991), "A Joint Test for Serial Correlation and Random Individual Effects," *Statistics and Probability Letters* 11, 277–280.

Baltagi, B. H., and Q. Li (1995), "Testing AR(1) Against MA(1) Disturbances in an Error Component Model," *Journal of Econometrics* 68, 133–151.

Barnow, B., G. Cain, and A. Goldberger (1980), "Issues in the Analysis of Selectivity Bias," *Evaluation Studies* 5, 42–59.

Bartik, T. J. (1987), "The Estimation of Demand Parameters in Hedonic Price Models," *Journal of Political Economy* 95, 81–88.

Bartle, R. G. (1966), *The Elements of Integration*. New York: Wiley.

Bassett, G., and R. Koenker (1978), "Asymptotic Theory of Least Absolute Error Regression," *Journal of the American Statistical Association* 73, 618–622.

Bassi, L. J. (1984), "Estimating the Effect of Job Training Programs with Non-Random Selection," *Review of Economics and Statistics* 66, 36–43.

Bates, C. E., and H. White (1993), "Determination of Estimators with Minimum Asymptotic Covariances Matrices," *Econometric Theory* 9, 633–648.

Baum, C. F., M. E. Schaffer, and S. Stillman (2003), "Instrumental Variables and GMM: Estimation and Testing," *The Stata Journal* 3, 1–31.

Bekker, P. A. (1994), "Alternative Approximations to the Distributions of Instrumental Variable Estimators," *Econometrica* 62, 657–681.

Bera, A. K., and C. R. McKenzie (1986), "Alternative Forms and Properties of the Score Test," *Journal of Applied Statistics* 13, 13–25.

Berndt, E. R., B. H. Hall, R. E. Hall, and J. A. Hausman (1974), "Estimation and Inference in Nonlinear Structural Models," *Annals of Economic and Social Measurement* 3, 653–666.

Bhargava, A., L. Franzini, and W. Narendranathan (1982), "Serial Correlation and the Fixed Effects Model," *Review of Economic Studies* 49, 533–549.

Bhattacharya, D. (2005), "Asymptotic Inference from Multi-stage Samples," *Journal of Econometrics* 126, 145–171.

Biddle, J. E., and D. S. Hamermesh (1990), "Sleep and the Allocation of Time," *Journal of Political Economy* 98, 922–943.

Billingsley, P. (1979), *Probability and Measure*. New York: Wiley.

Blackburn, M. (2007), "Estimating Wage Differentials without Logarithms," *Labour Economics* 14, 73–98.

Blackburn, M., and D. Neumark (1992), "Unobserved Ability, Efficiency Wages, and Interindustry Wage Differentials," *Quarterly Journal of Economics* 107, 1421–1436.

Blank, R. M. (1988), "Simultaneously Modeling the Supply of Weeks and Hours among Female Household Heads," *Journal of Labor Economics* 6, 177–204.

Blundell, R., and S. Bond (1998), "Initial Conditions and Moment Restrictions in Dynamic Panel Data Models," *Journal of Econometrics* 87, 115–144.

Blundell, R., R. Griffith, and F. Windmeijer (1998), "Individual Effects and Dynamics in Count Data Models," mimeo, Institute of Fiscal Studies, London.

Blundell, R., and J. L. Powell (2003), "Endogeneity in Nonparametric and Semiparametric Regression Models," in *Advances in Economics and Econometrics*, ed. M. Dewatripont, L. P. Hansen, and S. J. Turnovsky. Cambridge: Cambridge University Press, 312–357.

Blundell, R., and J. L. Powell (2004), "Endogeneity in Semiparametric Binary Response Models," *Review of Economic Studies* 71, 655–679.

Bound, J., D. A. Jaeger, and R. M. Baker (1995), "Problems with Instrumental Variables Estimation When the Correlation between the Instruments and Endogenous Explanatory Variables Is Weak," *Journal of the American Statistical Association* 90, 443–450.

Breusch, T. S., G. E. Mizon, and P. Schmidt (1989), "Efficient Estimation Using Panel Data," *Econometrica* 57, 695–700.

Breusch, T. S., and A. R. Pagan (1979), "A Simple Test for Heteroskedasticity and Random Coefficient Variation," *Econometrica* 50, 987–1007.

Breusch, T. S., and A. R. Pagan (1980), "The LM Test and Its Applications to Model Specification in Econometrics," *Review of Economic Studies* 47, 239–254.

Breusch, T., H. Qian, P. Schmidt, and D. Wyhowski (1999), "Redundancy of Moment Conditions," *Journal of Econometrics* 91, 89–111.

Brown, B. W., and M. B. Walker (1995), "Stochastic Specification in Random Production Models of Cost-Minimizing Firms," *Journal of Econometrics* 66, 175–205.

Buchinsky, M. (1994), "Changes in the U.S. Wage Structure, 1963–1987: Application of Quantile Regression," *Econometrica* 62, 405–458.

Buchinsky, M. (1998), "Recent Advances in Quantile Regression Models: A Practical Guide for Empirical Research," *Journal of Human Resources* 33, 88–126.

Buchinsky, M., and J. Hahn (1998), "An Alternative Estimator for the Censored Quantile Regression Model," *Econometrica* 66, 653–671.

Burnett, N. (1997), "Gender Economics Courses in Liberal Arts Colleges," *Journal of Economic Education* 28, 369–377.

Butler, J. S., and R. A. Moffitt (1982), "A Computationally Efficient Quadrature Procedure for the One-Factor Multinomial Probit Model," *Econometrica* 50, 761–764.

Cameron, A. C., and P. K. Trivedi (1986), "Econometric Models Based on Count Data: Comparisons and Applications of Some Estimators and Tests," *Journal of Applied Econometrics* 1, 29–53.

Cameron, A. C., and P. K. Trivedi (2005), *Microeconometrics: Methods and Applications*. New York: Cambridge University Press.

Card, D. (1995), "Using Geographic Variation in College Proximity to Estimate the Return to Schooling," in *Aspects of Labour Market Behavior: Essays in Honour of John Vanderkamp*, ed. L. N. Christophides, E. K. Grant, and R. Swidinsky. Toronto: University of Toronto Press, 201–222.

Card, D. (2001), "Estimating the Return to Schooling: Progress on Some Persistent Econometric Problems," *Econometrica* 69, 1127–1160.

Card, D., and A. B. Krueger (1994), "Minimum Wages and Employment: A Case Study of the Fast-Food Industry in New Jersey and Pennsylvania," *American Economic Review* 84, 772–793.

Cardell, N. S., and M. M. Hopkins (1977), "Education, Income, and Ability: A Comment," *Journal of Political Economy* 85, 211–215.

Carpenter, C. (2004), "How Do Zero Tolerance Drunk Driving Laws Work?" *Journal of Health Economics* 23, 61–83.

Casella, G., and R. L. Berger (2002), *Statistical Inference*, second edition. Pacific Grove, CA: Duxbury.

Chamberlain, G. (1980), "Analysis of Covariance with Qualitative Data," *Review of Economic Studies* 47, 225–238.

Chamberlain, G. (1982), "Multivariate Regression Models for Panel Data," *Journal of Econometrics* 18, 5–46.

Chamberlain, G. (1984), "Panel Data," in *Handbook of Econometrics*, Volume 2, ed. Z. Griliches and M. D. Intriligator. Amsterdam: North Holland, 1247–1318.

Chamberlain, G. (1985), "Heterogeneity, Omitted Variable Bias, and Duration Dependence," in *Longitudinal Analysis of Labor Market Data*, ed. J. J. Heckman and B. Singer. Cambridge: Cambridge University Press, 3–38.

Chamberlain, G. (1987), "Asymptotic Efficiency in Estimation with Conditional Moment Restrictions," *Journal of Econometrics* 34, 305–334.

Chamberlain, G. (1992a), "Efficiency Bounds for Semiparametric Regression," *Econometrica* 60, 567–596.

Chamberlain, G. (1992b), "Comment: Sequential Moment Restrictions in Panel Data," *Journal of Business and Economic Statistics* 10, 20–26.

Chamberlain, G. (1994), "Quantile Regression, Censoring and the Structure of Wages," in *Proceedings of the Sixth World Congress of the Econometric Society*, ed. C. Sims and J. J. Laffont. New York: Cambridge University Press, 171–209.

Chay, K. Y., and D. R. Hyslop (2001), "Identification and Estimation of Dynamic Binary Response Models: Empirical Evidence Using Alternative Approaches," University of California, Berkeley, Department of Economics Working Paper.

Chesher, A., and R. Spady (1991), "Asymptotic Expansions of the Information Matrix Test Statistic," *Econometrica* 59, 787–815.

Chung, C.-F., and A. Goldberger (1984), "Proportional Projections in Limited Dependent Variable Models," *Econometrica* 52, 531–534.

Chung, C.-F., P. Schmidt, and A. D. Witte (1991), "Survival Analysis: A Survey," *Journal of Quantitative Criminology* 7, 59–98.

Cornwell, C., and D. Trumball (1994), "Estimating the Economic Model of Crime with Panel Data," *Review of Economics and Statistics* 76, 360–366.

Cosslett, S. R. (1981), "Efficient Estimation of Discrete-Choice Models," in *Structural Analysis of Discrete Data with Econometric Applications*, ed. C. F. Manski and D. McFadden. Cambridge, MA: MIT Press, 51–111.

Cosslett, S. R. (1993), "Estimation from Endogenously Stratified Samples," in *Handbook of Statistics*, Volume 11, ed. G. S. Maddala, C. R. Rao, and H. D. Vinod. Amsterdam: North Holland, 1–43.

Cox, D. R. (1961), "Tests of Separate Families of Hypotheses," in *Proceedings of the Fourth Berkeley Symposium on Mathematical Statistics and Probability*. Berkeley: University of California Press, 105–123.

Cox, D. R. (1962), "Further Results on Tests of Separate Families of Hypotheses," *Journal of the Royal Statistical Society*, Series B, 24, 406–424.

Cox, D. R. (1972), "Regression Models and Life Tables," *Journal of the Royal Statistical Society*, Series B, 34, 187–220.

Cragg, J. (1971), "Some Statistical Models for Limited Dependent Variables with Applications to the Demand for Durable Goods," *Econometrica* 39, 829–844.

Cragg, J. (1983), "More Efficient Estimation in the Presence of Heteroskedasticity of Unknown Form," *Econometrica* 51, 751–763.

Cragg, J. G., and S. G. Donald (1996), "Inferring the Rank of a Matrix," *Journal of Econometrics* 76, 223–250.

Currie, J., and D. Thomas (1995), "Does Head Start Make a Difference?" *American Economic Review* 85, 341–364.

Cutler, D. M., and E. L. Glaeser (1997), "Are Ghettos Good or Bad?" *Quarterly Journal of Economics* 112, 827–872.

Davidson, J. (1994), *Stochastic Limit Theory*. Oxford: Oxford University Press.

Davidson, R., and J. G. MacKinnon (1984), "Convenient Specification Tests for Logit and Probit Models," *Journal of Econometrics* 24, 241–262.

Davidson, R., and J. G. MacKinnon (1985), "Heteroskedasticity-Robust Tests in Regression Directions," *Annale de l'INSÉÉ* 59/60, 183–218.

Davidson, R., and J. G. MacKinnon (1992), "A New Form of the Information Matrix Test," *Econometrica* 60, 145–147.

Davidson, R., and J. G. MacKinnon (1993), *Estimation and Inference in Econometrics*. New York: Oxford University Press.

Deaton, A. (1995), "Data and Econometric Tools for Development Analysis," in *Handbook of Development Economics*, Volume 3A, ed. J. Berhman and T. N. Srinivasan. Amsterdam: North Holland, 1785–1882.

Dehejia, R. H., and S. Wahba (1999), "Causal Effects in Non-Experimental Studies: Evaluating the Evaluation of Training Programs," *Journal of the American Statistical Association* 94, 1053–1062.

Donald, S. G., and K. Lang (2007), "Inference with Difference-in-Differences and Other Panel Data," *Review of Economics and Statistics* 89, 221–233.

Donald, S. G., and H. J. Paarsch (1996), "Identification, Estimation, and Testing in Parametric Empirical Models of Auctions within the Independent Private Values Paradigm," *Econometric Theory* 12, 517–567.

Downes, T. M., and S. M. Greenstein (1996), "Understanding the Supply Decisions of Nonprofits: Modeling the Location of Private Schools," *Rand Journal of Economics* 27, 365–390.

Duan, N. (1983), "Smearing Estimate: A Nonparametric Retransformation Method," *Journal of the American Statistical Association* 78, 605–610.

Duan, N., W. G. Manning, C. N. Morris, and J. P. Newhouse (1984), "Choosing between the Sample-Selection Model and the Multi-Part Model," *Journal of Business and Economic Statistics* 2, 283–289.

Durbin, J. (1954), "Errors in Variables," *Review of the International Statistical Institute* 22, 23–32.

Dustmann, C., and M. E. Rochina-Barrachina (2007), "Selection Correction in Panel Data Models: An Application to the Estimation of Females' Wage Equations," *Econometrics Journal* 10, 263–293.

Eicker, F. (1967), "Limit Theorems for Regressions with Unequal and Dependent Errors," *Proceedings of the Fifth Berkeley Symposium on Mathematical Statistics and Probability* 1, 59–82. Berkeley: University of California Press.

Elbers, C., and G. Ridder (1982), "True and Spurious Duration Dependence: The Identifiability of the Proportional Hazard Model," *Review of Economic Studies* 49, 403–410.

El Sayyad, G. M. (1973), "Bayesian and Classical Analysis of Poisson Regression," *Journal of the Royal Statistical Society*, Series B, 35, 445–451.

Engle, R. F. (1982), "Autoregressive Conditional Heteroskedasticity with Estimates of the Variance of U.K. Inflation," *Econometrica* 50, 987–1008.

Engle, R. F. (1984), "Wald, Likelihood Ratio, and Lagrange Multiplier Statistics in Econometrics," in *Handbook of Econometrics*, Volume 2, ed. Z. Griliches and M. D. Intriligator. Amsterdam: North Holland, 776–828.

Epple, D. (1987), "Hedonic Prices and Implicit Markets: Estimated Demand and Supply Functions for Differentiated Products," *Journal of Political Economy* 95, 59–80.

Estrella, A. (1998), "A New Measure of Fit for Equations with Dichotomous Dependent Variables," *Journal of Business and Economic Statistics* 16, 198–205.

Evans, W. N., W. E. Oates, and R. M. Schwab (1992), "Measuring Peer Group Effects: A Study of Teenage Behavior," *Journal of Political Economy* 100, 966–991.

Evans, W. N., and R. M. Schwab (1995), "Finishing High School and Starting College: Do Catholic Schools Make a Difference?" *Quarterly Journal of Economics* 110, 941–974.

Fernández-Val, I. (2009), "Fixed Effects Estimation of Structural Parameters and Marginal Effects in Panel Probit Models," *Journal of Econometrics* 150, 71–85.

Fin, T., and P. Schmidt (1984), "A Test of the Tobit Specification Against an Alternative Suggested by Cragg," *Review of Economics and Statistics* 66, 174–177.

Fisher, F. M. (1965), "Identifiability Criteria in Nonlinear Systems: A Further Note," *Econometrica* 33, 197–205.

Flores-Lagunes, A. (2007), "Finite Sample Evidence of IV Estimators under Weak Instruments," *Journal of Applied Econometrics* 22, 677–694.

Foster, A. D., and M. R. Rosenzweig (1995), "Learning by Doing and Learning from Others: Human Capital and Technical Change in Agriculture," *Journal of Political Economy* 103, 1176–1209.

Franses, P. H., and R. Paap (2001), *Quantitative Models in Marketing Research*. Cambridge: Cambridge University Press.

Friedberg, L. (1998), "Did Unilateral Divorce Raise Divorce Rates? Evidence from Panel Data," *American Economic Review* 88, 608–627.

Frölich, M. (2004), "Finite-Sample Properties of Propensity-Score Matching and Weighting Estimators," *Review of Economics and Statistics* 86, 77–90.

Gallant, A. R. (1987), *Nonlinear Statistical Models*. New York: Wiley.

Gallant, A. R., and H. White (1988), *A Unified Theory of Estimation and Inference for Nonlinear Dynamic Models*. New York: Blackwell.

Garen, J. (1984), "The Returns to Schooling: A Selectivity Bias Approach with a Continuous Choice Variable," *Econometrica* 52, 1199–1218.

Geronimus, A. T., and S. Korenman (1992), "The Socioeconomic Consequences of Teen Childbearing Reconsidered," *Quarterly Journal of Economics* 107, 1187–1214.

Geweke, J., and M. P. Keane (2001), "Computationally Intensive Methods for Integration in Economics," in *Handbook of Econometrics*, Volume 5, ed. E. Leamer and J. J. Heckman. Amsterdam: North Holland, 3463–3568.

Gill, R. D., and J. M. Robins (2001), "Causal Inference for Complex Longitudinal Data: The Continuous Case," *Annals of Statistics* 29, 1785–1811.

Goldberger, A. S. (1968), *Topics in Regression Analysis*. New York: Macmillan.

Goldberger, A. S. (1972), "Structural Equation Methods in the Social Sciences," *Econometrica* 40, 979–1001.

Goldberger, A. S. (1981), "Linear Regression after Selection," *Journal of Econometrics* 15, 357–366.

Goldberger, A. S. (1991), *A Course in Econometrics*. Cambridge, MA: Harvard University Press.

Gordy, M. B. (1999), "Hedging Winner's Curse with Multiple Bids: Evidence from the Portuguese Treasury Bill Auction," *Review of Economics and Statistics* 81, 448–465.

Gourieroux, G., and A. Monfort (1994), "Testing Non-nested Hypotheses," in *Handbook of Econometrics*, Volume 4, ed. R. F. Engle and D. L. McFadden. Amsterdam: North Holland, 2583–2637.

Gourieroux, C., A. Monfort, and C. Trognon (1984a), "Pseudo–Maximum Likelihood Methods: Theory," *Econometrica* 52, 681–700.

Gourieroux, C., A. Monfort, and C. Trognon (1984b), "Pseudo–Maximum Likelihood Methods: Applications to Poisson Models," *Econometrica* 52, 701–720.

Greene, W. (1997), *Econometric Analysis*, third edition. New York: Macmillan.

Greene, W. (1998), "Gender Economics Courses in Liberal Arts Colleges: Further Results," *Journal of Economic Education* 29, 291–300.

Greene, W. (2003), *Econometric Analysis*, fifth edition. Upper Saddle River, NJ: Prentice Hall.

Greene, W. (2004), "The Behaviour of the Maximum Likelihood Estimator of Limited Dependent Variable Models in the Presence of Fixed Effects," *Econometrics Journal* 7, 98–119.

Gregory, A. W., and M. R. Veall (1985), "On Formulating Wald Tests for Nonlinear Restrictions," *Econometrica* 53, 1465–1468.

Griliches, Z., B. H. Hall, and J. A. Hausman (1978), "Missing Data and Self-Selection in Large Panels," *Annale de l'INSÉÉ* 30/31, 137–176.

Griliches, Z., and J. A. Hausman (1986), "Errors in Variables in Panel Data," *Journal of Econometrics* 31, 93–118.

Griliches, Z., and W. M. Mason (1972), "Education, Income and Ability," *Journal of Political Economy*, Part II, 80, S74–S103.

Gronau, R. (1974), "Wage Comparisons—A Selectivity Bias," *Journal of Political Economy* 82, 1119–1143.

Gruber, J. (1994), "The Incidence of Mandated Maternity Benefits," *American Economic Review* 84, 622–641.

Gruber, J., and J. M. Poterba (1994), "Tax Incentives and the Decision to Purchase Health Insurance: Evidence from the Self-Employed," *Quarterly Journal of Economics* 109, 701–733.

Haavelmo, T. (1943), "The Statistical Implications of a System of Simultaneous Equations," *Econometrica* 11, 1–12.

Hagy, A. P. (1998), "The Demand for Child Care Quality: An Hedonic Price Approach," *Journal of Human Resources* 33, 683–710.

Hahn, J. (1998), "On the Role of the Propensity Score in Efficient Semiparametric Estimation of Average Treatment Effects," *Econometrica* 66, 315–331.

Hahn, J. (1999), "How Informative Is the Initial Condition in the Dynamic Panel Data Model with Fixed Effects?" *Journal of Econometrics* 93, 309–326.

Hahn, J., and W. K. Newey (2004), "Jackknife and Analytical Bias Reduction for Nonlinear Panel Models," *Econometrica* 72, 1295–1319.

Hahn, J., P. Tood, and W. van der Klaauw (2001), "Identification and Estimation of Treatment Effects with a Regression-Discontinuity Design," *Econometrica* 69, 201–209.

Hajivassiliou, V. A., and P. A. Ruud (1994), "Classical Estimation Methods for LDV Models Using Simulation," in *Handbook of Econometrics*, Volume 4, ed. R. F. Engle and D. McFadden. Amsterdam: North Holland, 2383–2441.

Hall, A. (1987), "The Information Matrix Test for the Linear Model," *Review of Economic Studies* 54, 257–263.

Ham, J. C., and R. J. Lalonde (1996), "The Effect of Sample Selection and Initial Conditions in Duration Models: Evidence from Experimental Data on Training," *Econometrica* 64, 175–205.

Hamilton, J. D. (1994), *Time Series Analysis*. Princeton, NJ: Princeton University Press.

Han, A. K., and J. A. Hausman (1990), "Flexible Parametric Estimation of Duration and Competing Risk Models," *Journal of Applied Econometrics* 5, 1–28.

Han, C., and P. C. B. Phillips (2006), "GMM with Many Moment Conditions," *Econometrica* 74, 147–192.

Hansen, C. B. (2007), "Asymptotic Properties of a Robust Variance Matrix Estimator for Panel Data When T Is Large," *Journal of Econometrics* 141, 597–620.

Hansen, L. P. (1982), "Large Sample Properties of Generalized Method of Moments Estimators," *Econometrica* 50, 1029–1054.

Härdle, W., and O. Linton (1994), "Applied Nonparametric Methods," in *Handbook of Econometrics*, Volume 4, ed. R. F. Engle and D. McFadden. Amsterdam: North Holland, 2295–2339.

Harris, R. D. F., and E. Tzavalis (1999), "Inference for Unit Roots in Dynamic Panels Where the Time Dimension Is Fixed," *Journal of Econometrics* 91, 201–226.

Hausman, J. A. (1978), "Specification Tests in Econometrics," *Econometrica* 46, 1251–1271.

Hausman, J. A. (1983), "Specification and Estimation of Simultaneous Equations Models," in *Handbook of Econometrics*, Volume 1, ed. Z. Griliches and M. D. Intriligator. Amsterdam: North Holland, 391–448.

Hausman, J. A., B. H. Hall, and Z. Griliches (1984), "Econometric Models for Count Data with an Application to the Patents-R&D Relationship," *Econometrica* 52, 909–938.

Hausman, J. A., and D. L. McFadden (1984), "A Specification Test for the Multinomial Logit Model," *Econometrica* 52, 1219–1240.

Hausman, J. A., W. K. Newey, and W. E. Taylor (1987), "Efficient Estimation and Identification of Simultaneous Equation Models with Covariance Restrictions," *Econometrica* 55, 849–874.

Hausman, J. A., and W. E. Taylor (1981), "Panel Data and Unobservable Individual Effects," *Econometrica* 49, 1377–1398.

Hausman, J. A., and D. A. Wise (1977), "Social Experimentation, Truncated Distributions, and Efficient Estimation," *Econometrica* 45, 319–339.

Hausman, J. A., and D. A., Wise (1978), "A Conditional Probit Model for Qualitative Choice: Discrete Decisions Recognizing Interdependence and Heterogeneous Preferences," *Econometrica* 46, 403–426.

Hausman, J. A., and D. A. Wise (1981), "Stratification on an Endogenous Variable and Estimation: The Gary Income Maintenance Experiment," in *Structural Analysis of Discrete Data with Econometric Applications*, ed. C. F. Manski and D. McFadden. Cambridge, MA: MIT Press, 365–391.

Heckman, J. J. (1976), "The Common Structure of Statistical Models of Truncation, Sample Selection, and Limited Dependent Variables and a Simple Estimator for Such Models," *Annals of Economic and Social Measurement* 5, 475–492.

Heckman, J. J. (1978), "Dummy Endogenous Variables in a Simultaneous Equations System," *Econometrica* 46, 931–960.

Heckman, J. J. (1979), "Sample Selection Bias as a Specification Error," *Econometrica* 47, 153–161.

Heckman, J. J. (1981), "The Incidental Parameters Problem and the Problem of Initial Conditions in Estimating a Discrete Time–Discrete Data Stochastic Process," in *Structural Analysis of Discrete Data with Econometric Applications*, ed. C. F. Manski and D. McFadden. Cambridge, MA: MIT Press, 179–195.

Heckman, J. J. (1992), "Randomization and Social Program Evaluation," in *Evaluating Welfare and Training Programs*, ed. C. F. Manski and I. Garfinkel. Cambridge, MA: Harvard University Press, 201–230.

Heckman, J. J. (1997), "Instrumental Variables: A Study of Implicit Behavioral Assumptions Used in Making Program Evaluations," *Journal of Human Resources* 32, 441–462.

Heckman, J. J., and V. J. Hotz (1989), "Choosing among Alternative Nonexperimental Methods for Estimating the Impact of Social Programs: The Case of Manpower Training," *Journal of the American Statistical Association* 84, 862–875.

Heckman, J. J., H. Ichimura, and P. Todd (1998), "Matching as an Econometric Evaluation Estimator," *Review of Economic Studies* 65, 261–294.

Heckman, J. J., R. Lalonde, and J. Smith (2000), "The Economics and Econometrics of Active Labor Markets Programs," in *Handbook of Labor Economics*, Volume 3, ed. A. Ashenfelter and D. Card. New York: Elsevier Science.

Heckman, J. J., L. Lochner, and C. Taber (1998), "General-Equilibrium Treatment Effects," *American Economic Review* 88, 381–386.

Heckman, J. J., and R. Robb (1985), "Alternative Methods for Evaluating the Impact of Interventions," in *Longitudinal Analysis of Labor Market Data*, ed. J. J. Heckman and B. Singer. New York: Cambridge University Press, 156–245.

Heckman, J. J., and B. Singer (1984), "A Method for Minimizing the Impact of Distributional Assumptions in Econometric Models for Duration Data," *Econometrica* 52, 271–320.

Heckman, J. J., S. Urzua, and E. Vytlacil (2006), "Understanding Instrumental Variables in Models with Essential Heterogeneity," *Review of Economics and Statistics* 88, 389–432.

Heckman, J. J., and E. Vytlacil (1998), "Instrumental Variables Methods for the Correlated Random Coefficient Model," *Journal of Human Resources* 33, 974–987.

Heckman, J. J., and E. Vytlacil (2006), "Structural Equations, Treatment Effects, and Econometric Policy Evaluation," *Econometrica* 73, 669–738.

Heckman, J. J., and E. Vytlacil (2007a), "Econometric Evaluation of Social Programs, Part I: Causal Models, Structural Models and Econometric Policy Evaluation," in *Handbook of Econometrics*, Volume 6B, ed. J. Heckman and E. Leamer. New York: Elsevier Science, Chapter 70, 4779–4874.

Heckman, J. J., and E. Vytlacil (2007b), "Econometric Evaluation of Social Programs, Part II: Using the Marginal Treatment Effect to Organize Alternative Econometric Estimators to Evaluate Social Programs, and to Forecast Their Effects in New Environments," in *Handbook of Econometrics*, Volume 6B, ed. J. Heckman and E. Leamer. New York: Elsevier Science, Chapter 71, 4875–5143.

Hendry, D. F. (1984), "Monte Carlo Experimentation in Econometrics," in *Handbook of Econometrics*, Volume 2, ed. Z. Griliches and M. D. Intriligator. Amsterdam: North Holland, 937–976.

Hirano, K., G. W. Imbens, and G. Ridder (2003), "Efficient Estimation of Average Treatment Effects Using the Estimated Propensity Score," *Econometrica* 71, 1161–1189.

Holtz-Eakin, D., W. Newey, and H. S. Rosen (1988), "Estimating Vector Autoregressions with Panel Data," *Econometrica* 56, 1371–1395.

Holzer, H., R. Block, M. Cheatham, and J. Knott (1993), "Are Training Subsidies Effective? The Michigan Experience," *Industrial and Labor Relations Review* 46, 625–636.

Honoré, B. E. (1992), "Trimmed LAD and Least Squares Estimation of Truncated and Censored Regression Models with Fixed Effects," *Econometrica* 60, 533–565.

Honoré, B. E. (1993a), "Orthogonality Conditions for Tobit Models with Fixed Effects and Lagged Dependent Variables," *Journal of Econometrics* 59, 35–61.

Honoré, B. E. (1993b), "Identification Results for Duration Models with Multiple Spells," *Review of Economic Studies* 60, 241–246.

Honoré, B. E., and L. Hu (2004), "Estimation of Cross Sectional and Panel Data Censored Regression Models with Endogeneity," *Journal of Econometrics* 122, 293–316.

Honoré, B. E., and E. Kyriazidou (2000a), "Panel Data Discrete Choice Models with Lagged Dependent Variables," *Econometrica* 68, 839–874.

Honoré, B. E., and E. Kyriazidou (2000b), "Estimation of Tobit-Type Models with Individual Specific Effects," *Econometric Reviews* 19, 341–366.

Honoré, B. E., E. Kyriazidou, and C. Udry (1997), "Estimation of Type 3 Tobit Models Using Symmetric Trimming and Pairwise Comparisons," *Journal of Econometrics* 76, 107–128.

Horowitz, J. L. (1992), "A Smoothed Maximum Score Estimator for the Binary Response Model," *Econometrica* 60, 505–531.

Horowitz, J. L. (1999), "Semiparametric Estimation of a Proportional Hazard Model with Unobserved Heterogeneity," *Econometrica* 67, 1001–1028.

Horowitz, J. L. (2001), "The Bootstrap," in *Handbook of Econometrics*, Volume 5, ed. J. J. Heckman and E. Leamer. Amsterdam: North Holland, 3159–3228.

Horowitz, J. L., and C. F. Manski (1998), "Censoring of Outcomes and Regressors Due to Survey Nonresponse: Identification and Estimation Using Weights and Imputations," *Journal of Econometrics* 84, 37–58.

Horvitz, D., and D. Thompson (1952), "A Generalization of Sampling without Replacement from a Finite Population," *Journal of the American Statistical Association* 47, 663–685.

Hoxby, C. M. (1996), "How Teachers' Unions Affect Education Production," *Quarterly Journal of Economics* 111, 671–718.

Hoxby, C. M. (2000), "Does Competition among Public Schools Benefit Students and Taxpayers?" *American Economic Review* 90, 1209–1238.

Hsiao, C. (1986), *Analysis of Panel Data*. Cambridge: Cambridge University Press.

Hsiao, C. (2003), *Analysis of Panel Data*, second edition. Cambridge: Cambridge University Press.

Huber, P. J. (1967), "The Behavior of Maximum Likelihood Estimates under Nonstandard Conditions," in *Proceedings of the Fifth Berkeley Symposium in Mathematical Statistics*, Volume 1. Berkeley: University of California Press, 221–233.

Huber, P. J. (1981), *Robust Statistics*. New York: Wiley.

Ichimura, H. (1993), "Semiparametric Least Squares (SLS) and Weighted SLS Estimation of Single-Index Models," *Journal of Econometrics* 58, 71–120.

Im, K. S., S. C. Ahn, P. Schmidt, and J. M. Wooldridge (1999), "Efficient Estimation of Panel Data Models with Strictly Exogenous Explanatory Variables," *Journal of Econometrics* 93, 177–201.

Imbens, G. W. (1992), "An Efficient Method of Moments Estimator for Discrete Choice Models with Choice-Based Sampling," *Econometrica* 60, 1187–1214.

Imbens, G. W. (2000), "The Role of the Propensity Score in Estimating Dose-Response Functions," *Biometrika* 87, 706–710.

Imbens, G. W. (2004), "Nonparametric Estimation of Average Treatment Effects under Exogeneity: A Review," *Review of Economics and Statistics* 86, 4–29.

Imbens, G. W., and J. D. Angrist (1994), "Identification and Estimation of Local Average Treatment Effects," *Econometrica* 62, 467–476.

Imbens, G. W., and K. Kalyanaraman (2009), "Optimal Bandwidth Choice for the Regression Discontinuity Estimator," National Bureau of Economic Research Working Paper Number 14726.

Imbens, G. W., and T. Lancaster (1996), "Efficient Estimation and Stratified Sampling," *Journal of Econometrics* 74, 289–318.

Imbens, G. W., and T. Lemieux (2008), "Regression Discontinuity Designs: A Guide to Practice," *Journal of Econometrics* 142, 615–635.

Imbens, G. W., and D. B. Rubin (forthcoming), *Causal Inference in Statistics*. Cambridge: Cambridge University Press.

Imbens, G. W., and J. M. Wooldridge (2009), "Recent Developments in the Econometrics of Program Evaluation," *Journal of Economic Literature* 47(1), 5–86.

Kahn, S., and K. Lang (1988), "Efficient Estimation of Structural Hedonic Systems," *International Economic Review* 29, 157–166.

Kakwani, N. (1967), "The Unbiasedness of Zellner's Seemingly Unrelated Regressions Equation Estimators," *Journal of the American Statistical Association* 62, 141–142.

Kalbfleisch, J. D., and R. L. Prentice (1980), *The Statistical Analysis of Failure Time Data*. New York: Wiley.

Kane, T. J., and C. E. Rouse (1995), "Labor-Market Returns to Two- and Four-Year Colleges," *American Economic Review* 85, 600–614.

Kao, C. (1999), "Spurious Regression and Residual-Based Tests for Cointegration in Panel Data," *Journal of Econometrics* 90, 1–44.

Keane, M. P. (1993), "Simulation Estimation for Panel Data Models with Limited Dependent Variables," in *Handbook of Statistics*, Volume 11, ed. G. S. Maddala, C. R. Rao, and H. D. Vinod. Amsterdam: North Holland, 545–571.

Keane, M. P., and R. A. Moffitt (1998), "A Structural Model of Multiple Welfare Participation and Labor Supply," *International Economic Review* 39, 553–589.

Keane, M. P., and D. E. Runkle (1992), "On the Estimation of Panel Data Models with Serial Correlation When Instruments Are Not Strictly Exogenous," *Journal of Business and Economic Statistics* 10, 1–9.

Keane, M. P., and K. I. Wolpin (1997), "The Career Decisions of Young Men," *Journal of Political Economy* 105, 473–522.

Kiefer, N. M. (1980), "Estimation of Fixed Effect Models for Time Series of Cross-Sections with Arbitrary Intertemporal Covariance," *Journal of Econometrics* 14, 195–202.

Kiefer, N. M. (1988), "Economic Duration Data and Hazard Functions," *Journal of Economic Literature* 26, 646–679.

Kiefer, N. M. (1989), "The ET Interview: Arthur S. Goldberger," *Econometric Theory* 5, 133–160.

Kiel, K. A., and K. T. McClain (1995), "House Prices during Siting Decision Stages: The Case of an Incinerator from Rumor through Operation," *Journal of Environmental Economics and Management* 28, 241–255.

Kieschnick, R., and B. D. McCullough (2003), "Regression Analysis of Variates Observed on (0,1): Percentages, Proportions and Fractions," *Statistical Modelling* 3, 193–213.

Kinal, T. W. (1980), "The Existence of Moments of k-Class Estimators," *Econometrica* 48, 241–249.

Klein, R. W., and R. H. Spady (1993), "An Efficient Semiparametric Estimator for Discrete Choice Models," *Econometrica* 61, 387–421.

Koenker, R. (1981), "A Note on Studentizing a Test for Heteroskedasticity," *Journal of Econometrics* 17, 107–112.

Koenker, R. (2004), "Quantile Regression for Longitudinal Data," *Journal of Multivariate Analysis* 91, 74–89.

Koenker, R. (2005), *Quantile Regression*. Cambridge: Cambridge University Press.

Koenker, R., and G. Bassett (1978), "Regression Quantiles," *Econometrica* 46, 33–50.

Krueger, A. B. (1993), "How Computers Have Changed the Wage Structure: Evidence from Microdata, 1984–1989," *Quarterly Journal of Economics* 108, 33–60.

Kuksov, D., and J. M. Villas-Boas (2008), "Endogeneity and Individual Consumer Choice," *Journal of Marketing Research* 45, 702–714.

Kyriazidou, E. (1997), "Estimation of a Panel Data Sample Selection Model," *Econometrica* 65, 1335–1364.

Lahiri, K., and P. Schmidt (1978), "On the Estimation of Triangular Structural Systems," *Econometrica* 46, 1217–1221.

Lalonde, R. J. (1986), "Evaluating the Econometric Evaluations of Training Programs with Experimental Data," *American Economic Review* 76, 604–620.

Lancaster, T. (1979), "Econometric Methods for the Duration of Unemployment," *Econometrica* 47, 939–956.

Lancaster, T. (1990), *The Econometric Analysis of Transition Data.* Cambridge: Cambridge University Press.

LeCam, L. (1953), "On Some Asymptotic Properties of Maximum Likelihood Estimates and Related Bayes Estimates," *University of California Publications in Statistics* 1, 277–328.

Lechner, M. (2001), "Identification and Estimation of Causal Effects of Multiple Treatments under the Conditional Independence Assumption," in *Econometric Evaluation of Labour Market Policies*, ed. M. Lechner, and F. Pfeiffer. Heidelberg: Physica, 43–58.

Lechner, M. (2004), "Sequential Matching Estimation of Dynamic Causal Effects," Discussion Paper 2004-06, Department of Economics, University of St. Gallen. St. Gallen, Switzerland.

Lechner, M., and R. Miquel (2005), "Identification of Effects of Dynamic Treatments by Sequential Conditional Independence Assumptions," Discussion Paper 2005-17, Department of Economics, University of St. Gallen. St. Gallen, Switzerland.

Lemieux, T. (1998), "Estimating the Effects of Unions on Wage Inequality in a Panel Data Model with Comparative Advantage and Nonrandom Selection," *Journal of Labor Economics* 16, 261–291.

Leung, S. F., and S. Yu (1996), "On the Choice between Sample Selection and Two-Part Models," *Journal of Econometrics* 72, 197–229.

Levinsohn, J., and A. Petrin (2003), "Estimating Production Functions Using Inputs to Control for Unobservables," *Review of Economic Studies* 70, 317–341.

Levitt, S. D. (1996), "The Effect of Prison Population Size on Crime Rates: Evidence from Prison Overcrowding Legislation," *Quarterly Journal of Economics* 111, 319–351.

Levitt, S. D. (1997), "Using Electoral Cycles in Police Hiring to Estimate the Effect of Police on Crime," *American Economic Review* 87, 270–290.

Lewbel, A. (2000), "Semiparametric Qualitative Response Model Estimation with Unknown Heteroscedasticity or Instrumental Variables," *Journal of Econometrics* 97, 145–177.

Li, Q., and J. S. Racine (2007), *Nonparametric Econometrics*. Princeton, NJ: Princeton University Press.

Li, Q., J. S. Racine, and J. M. Wooldridge (2008), "Estimating Average Treatment Effects with Continuous and Discrete Covariates: The Case of Swan-Ganz Catheterization," *American Economic Review* 98, 357–362.

Li, Q., J. S. Racine, and J. M. Wooldridge (2009), "Efficient Estimation of Average Treatment Effects with Mixed Categorical and Continuous Data," *Journal of Business and Economic Statistics* 27, 206–223.

Liang, Y.-K., and S. L. Zeger (1986), "Longitudinal Data Analysis Using Generalized Linear Models," *Biometrika* 73, 13–22.

Little, R. J. A., and D. B. Rubin (2002), *Statistical Analysis with Missing Data*, second edition. Hoboken, NJ: Wiley.

Loeb, S., and J. Bound (1996), "The Effect of Measured School Inputs on Academic Achievement: Evidence from the 1920s, 1930s and 1940s Birth Cohorts," *Review of Economics and Statistics* 78, 653–664.

Long, J. S., and J. Freese (2001), *Regression Models for Categorical Dependent Variables Using Stata.* College Station, TX: Stata Press.

MacKinnon, J. G., and H. White (1985), "Some Heteroskedasticity Consistent Covariance Matrix Estimators with Improved Finite Sample Properties," *Journal of Econometrics* 29, 305–325.

MaCurdy, T. E. (1982), "The Use of Time Series Processes to Model the Error Structure of Earnings in a Longitudinal Data Analysis," *Journal of Econometrics* 18, 83–114.

Maddala, G. S. (1983), *Limited Dependent and Qualitative Variables in Econometrics*. Cambridge: Cambridge University Press.

Maloney, M. T., and R. E. McCormick (1993), "An Examination of the Role That Intercollegiate Athletic Participation Plays in Academic Achievement: Athlete's Feats in the Classroom," *Journal of Human Resources* 28, 555–570.

Manski, C. F. (1975), "Maximum Score Estimation of the Stochastic Utility Model of Choice," *Journal of Econometrics* 3, 205–228.

Manski, C. F. (1987), "Semiparametric Analysis of Random Effects Linear Models from Binary Panel Data," *Econometrica* 55, 357–362.

Manski, C. F. (1988), *Analog Estimation Methods in Econometrics*. New York: Chapman and Hall.

Manski, C. F. (1996), "Learning about Treatment Effects from Experiments with Random Assignment of Treatments," *Journal of Human Resources* 31, 709–733.

Manski, C. F., and S. Lerman (1977), "The Estimation of Choice Probabilities from Choice-Based Samples," *Econometrica* 45, 1977–1988.

Manski, C. F., and D. McFadden (1981), "Alternative Estimators and Sample Designs for Discrete Choice Analysis," in *Structural Analysis of Discrete Data with Econometric Applications*, ed. C. F. Manski and D. McFadden. Cambridge, MA: MIT Press, 2–50.

McCall, B. P. (1994), "Testing the Proportional Hazards Assumption in the Presence of Unmeasured Heterogeneity," *Journal of Applied Econometrics* 9, 321–334.

McCullagh, P., and J. A. Nelder (1989), *Generalized Linear Models*, second edition. New York: Chapman and Hall.

McDonald, J. B. (1996), "An Application and Comparison of Some Flexible Parametric and Semi-Parametric Qualitative Response Models," *Economics Letters* 53, 145–152.

McDonald, J. F., and R. A. Moffitt (1980), "The Uses of Tobit Analysis," *Review of Economics and Statistics* 62, 318–321.

McFadden, D., and K. Train (2000), "Mixed MNL Models for Discrete Response," *Journal of Applied Econometrics* 15, 447–470.

McFadden, D. L. (1974), "Conditional Logit Analysis of Qualitative Choice Analysis," in *Frontiers in Econometrics*, ed. P. Zarembka. New York: Academic Press, 105–142.

McFadden, D. L. (1978), "Modeling the Choice of Residential Location," in *Spatial Interaction Theory and Residential Location*, ed. A. Karlqvist. Amsterdam: North Holland, 75–96.

McFadden, D. L. (1981), "Econometric Models of Probabilistic Choice," in *Structural Analysis of Discrete Data with Econometric Applications*, ed. C. F. Manski and D. McFadden. Cambridge, MA: MIT Press, 198–272.

McFadden, D. L. (1984), "Econometric Analysis of Qualitative Response Models," in *Handbook of Econometrics*, Volume 2, ed. Z. Griliches and M. D. Intriligator. Amsterdam: North Holland, 1395–1457.

McFadden, D. L. (1987), "Regression Based Specification Tests for the Multinomial Logit Model," *Journal of Econometrics* 34, 63–82.

Meyer, B. D. (1990), "Unemployment Insurance and Unemployment Spells," *Econometrica* 58, 757–782.

Meyer, B. D., W. K. Viscusi, and D. L. Durbin (1995), "Workers' Compensation and Injury Duration: Evidence from a Natural Experiment," *American Economic Review* 85, 322–340.

Model, K. E. (1993), "The Effect of Marijuana Decriminalization on Hospital Emergency Drug Episodes: 1975–1978," *Journal of the American Statistical Association* 88, 737–747.

Moffitt, R. A. (1996), "Identification of Causal Effects Using Instrumental Variables: Comment," *Journal of the American Statistical Association* 91, 462–465.

Moffitt, R., J. Fitzgerald, and P. Gottschalk (1999), "Sample Attrition in Panel Data: The Role of Selection on Observables," *Annale d'Economie et de Statistique* 55/56, 129–152.

Montgomery, E., K. Shaw, and M. E. Benedict (1992), "Pensions and Wages: An Hedonic Price Theory Approach," *International Economic Review* 33, 111–128.

Moon, C.-G. (1988), "Simultaneous Specification Test in a Binary Logit Model: Skewness and Heteroskedasticity," *Communications in Statistics* 17, 3361–3387.

Moon, H. R., and P. C. B. Phillips (2000), "Estimation of Autoregressive Roots Near Unity Using Panel Data," *Econometric Theory* 16, 927–997.

Moulton, B. (1990), "An Illustration of a Pitfall in Estimating the Effects of Aggregate Variables on Micro Units," *Review of Economics and Statistics* 72, 334–338.

Mroz, T. A. (1987), "The Sensitivity of an Empirical Model of Married Women's Hours of Work to Economic and Statistical Assumptions," *Econometrica* 55, 765–799.

Mullahy, J. (1997), "Instrumental-Variable Estimation of Count Data Models: Applications to Models of Cigarette Smoking Behavior," *Review of Economics and Statistics* 79, 586–593.

Mullahy, J. (1998), "Much Ado about Two: Reconsidering Retransformation and the Two-Part Model in Health Econometrics," *Journal of Health Economics* 17, 247–281.

Mundlak, Y. (1978), "On the Pooling of Time Series and Cross Section Data," *Econometrica* 46, 69–85.

Murtazashvili, I., and J. M. Wooldridge (2008), "Fixed Effects Instrumental Variables Estimation in Correlated Random Coefficient Panel Data Models," *Journal of Econometrics* 142, 539–552.

Newey, W. K. (1984), "A Method of Moments Interpretation of Sequential Estimators," *Economics Letters* 14, 201–206.

Newey, W. K. (1985), "Maximum Likelihood Specification Testing and Conditional Moment Tests," *Econometrica* 53, 1047–1070.

Newey, W. K. (1990), "Efficient Instrumental Variables Estimation of Nonlinear Models," *Econometrica* 58, 809–837.

Newey, W. K. (1993), "Efficient Estimation of Models with Conditional Moment Restrictions," in *Handbook of Statistics*, Volume 11, ed. G. S. Maddala, C. R. Rao, and H. D. Vinod. Amsterdam: North Holland, 419–454.

Newey, W. K., and D. McFadden (1994), "Large Sample Estimation and Hypothesis Testing," in *Handbook of Econometrics*, Volume 4, ed. R. F. Engle and D. McFadden. Amsterdam: North Holland, 2111–2245.

Newey, W. K., J. L. Powell, and F. Vella (1999), "Nonparametric Estimation of Triangular Simultaneous Equations Models," *Econometrica* 67, 565–603.

Newey, W. K., and K. D. West (1987), "A Simple, Positive Semi-Definite Heteroskedasticity and Autocorrelation Consistent Covariance Matrix," *Econometrica* 55, 703–708.

Nickell, S. (1979), "Estimating the Probability of Leaving Unemployment," *Econometrica* 47, 1249–1266.

Nijman, T., and M. Verbeek (1992), "Nonresponse in Panel Data: The Impact on Estimates of a Life Cycle Consumption Function," *Journal of Applied Econometrics* 7, 243–257.

Oaxaca, R. L., and M. R. Ransom (1994), "On Discrimination and the Decomposition of Wage Differentials," *Journal of Econometrics* 61, 5–21.

Olley, S., and A. Pakes (1996), "The Dynamics of Productivity in the Telecommunications Equipment Industry," *Econometrica* 64, 1263–1298.

Orme, C. (1990), "The Small Sample Performance of the Information Matrix Test," *Journal of Econometrics* 46, 309–331.

Orme, C. D., and T. Yamagata (2006), "The Asymptotic Distribution of the F-Test Statistic for Individual Effects," *Econometrics Journal* 9, 404–422.

Paarsch, H. J., and H. Hong (2006), *An Introduction to the Structural Econometrics of Auction Data*. Cambridge, MA: MIT Press.

Pagan, A. R. (1984), "Econometric Issues in the Analysis of Regressions with Generated Regressors," *International Economic Review* 25, 221–247.

Pagan, A. R., and F. Vella (1989), "Diagnostic Tests for Models Based on Individual Data: A Survey," *Journal of Applied Econometrics* 4, S29–S59.

Page, M. (1995), "Racial and Ethnic Discrimination in Urban Housing Markets: Evidence from a Recent Audit Study," *Journal of Urban Economics* 38, 183–206.

Papke, L. E. (1991), "Interstate Business Tax Differentials and New Firm Location," *Journal of Public Economics* 45, 47–68.

Papke, L. E. (1994), "Tax Policy and Urban Development: Evidence from the Indiana Enterprise Zone Program," *Journal of Public Economics* 54, 37–49.

Papke, L. E. (1998), "How Are Participants Directing Their Participant-Directed Individual Account Pension Plans?" *American Economic Review* 88, 212–216.

Papke, L. E. (2005), "The Effects of Spending on Test Pass Rates: Evidence from Michigan," *Journal of Public Economics* 89, 821–839.

Papke, L. E., and J. M. Wooldridge (1996), "Econometric Methods for Fractional Response Variables with an Application to 401(k) Plan Participation Rates," *Journal of Applied Econometrics* 11, 619–632.

Papke, L. E., and J. M. Wooldridge (2008), "Panel Data Methods for Fractional Response Variables with an Application to Test Pass Rates," *Journal of Econometrics* 145, 121–133.

Pearl, J. (2000), *Causality: Models, Reasoning, and Inference*. Cambridge: Cambridge University Press.

Perracchi, F. (2001), *Econometrics*. Chichester: Wiley.

Pesaran, M. H., and R. J. Smith (1995), "Estimating Long-Run Relationships from Dynamic Heterogeneous Panels," *Journal of Econometrics* 68, 79–113.

Petrin, A., and K. Train (2010), "A Control Function Approach to Endogeneity in Consumer Choice Models," *Journal of Marketing Research* 47, 3–13.

Phillips, P. C. B., and H. R. Moon (1999), "Linear Regression Limit Theory for Nonstationary Panel Data," *Econometrica* 67, 1057–1111.

Phillips, P. C. B., and H. R. Moon (2000), "Nonstationary Panel Data Analysis: An Overview of Some Recent Developments," *Econometric Reviews* 19, 263–268.

Phillips, P. C. B., and J. Y. Park (1988), "On the Formulation of Wald Tests for Nonlinear Restrictions," *Econometrica* 56, 1065–1083.

Polachek, S., and M.-K. Kim (1994), "Panel Estimates of the Gender Earnings Gap: Individual-Specific Intercepts and Individual-Specific Slope Models," *Journal of Econometrics* 61, 23–42.

Porter, J. (2002), "Efficiency of Covariance Matrix Estimators for Maximum Likelihood Estimation," *Journal of Business and Economic Statistics* 20, 431–440.

Powell, J. L. (1984), "Least Absolute Deviations Estimation for the Censored Regression Model," *Journal of Econometrics* 25, 303–325.

Powell, J. L. (1986), "Symmetrically Trimmed Least Squares Estimation for Tobit Models," *Econometrica* 54, 1435–1460.

Powell, J. L. (1991), "Estimation of Monotonic Regression Models under Quantile Restrictions," in *Nonparametric and Semiparametric Methods in Econometrics and Statistics: Proceedings of the Fifth International Symposium in Economic Theory and Econometrics*, ed. W. A. Barnett, J. L. Powell, and G. E. Cambridge: Cambridge University Press, 357–384.

Powell, J. L. (1994), "Estimation of Semiparametric Models," in *Handbook of Econometrics*, Volume 4, ed. R. F. Engle and D. McFadden. Amsterdam: North Holland, 2443–2521.

Powell, J. L., J. H. Stock, and T. M. Stoker (1989), "Semiparametric Estimation of Weighted Average Derivatives," *Econometrica* 57, 1403–1430.

Qian, H., and P. Schmidt (1999), "Improved Instrumental Variables and Generalized Method of Moments Estimators," *Journal of Econometrics* 91, 145–169.

Quah, D. (1994), "Exploiting Cross-Section Variations for Unit Root Inference in Dynamic Data," *Economics Letters* 44, 9–19.

Quandt, R. E. (1983), "Computational Problems and Methods," in *Handbook of Econometrics*, Volume 1, ed. Z. Griliches and M. D. Intriligator. Amsterdam: North Holland, 699–764.

Ramsey, J. B. (1969), "Tests for Specification Errors in Classical Linear Least Squares Regression Analysis," *Journal of the Royal Statistical Society*, Series B, 31, 350–371.

Rao, C. R. (1948), "Large Sample Tests of Hypotheses Involving Several Parameters with Applications to Problems of Estimation," *Proceedings of the Cambridge Philosophical Society* 44, 50–57.

Raudenbush, S. W., and A. S. Bryk (2002), *Hierarchical Linear Models: Applications and Data Analysis*, second edition. Thousand Oaks, CA: Sage.

Rivers, D., and Q. H. Vuong (1988), "Limited Information Estimators and Exogeneity Tests for Simultaneous Probit Models," *Journal of Econometrics* 39, 347–366.

Robins, J. M., and A. Rotnitzky (1995), "Semiparametric Efficiency in Multivariate Regression Models," *Journal of the American Statistical Association* 90, 122–129.

Robins, J. A., A. Rotnitzky, and L. Zhao (1995), "Analysis of Semiparametric Regression Models for Repeated Outcomes in the Presence of Missing Data," *Journal of the American Statistical Association* 90, 106–121.

Robinson, P. M. (1988), "Root-N-Consistent Semiparametric Regression," *Econometrica* 56, 931–954.

Romer, D. (1993), "Openness and Inflation: Theory and Evidence," *Quarterly Journal of Economics* 108, 869–903.

Rose, N. L. (1990), "Profitability and Product Quality: Economic Determinants of Airline Safety Performance," *Journal of Political Economy* 98, 944–961.

Rosenbaum, P. R., and D. B. Rubin (1983), "The Central Role of the Propensity Score in Observational Studies for Causal Effects," *Biometrika* 70, 41–55.

Rouse, C. E. (1995), "Democratization or Diversion? The Effect of Community Colleges on Educational Attainment," *Journal of Business and Economic Statistics* 13, 217–224.

Rubin, D. B. (1974), "Estimating Causal Effects of Treatments in Randomized and Nonrandomized Studies," *Journal of Educational Psychology* 66, 688–701.

Rubin, D. B. (1976), "Inference and Missing Data," *Biometrika* 63, 581–592.

Rudin, W. (1976), *Principles of Mathematical Analysis*, 3rd edition. New York: McGraw-Hill.

Ruud, P. (1983), "Sufficient Conditions for Consistency of Maximum Likelihood Estimation Despite Misspecification of Distribution," *Econometrica* 51, 225–228.

Ruud, P. (1984), "Tests of Specification in Econometrics," *Econometric Reviews* 3, 211–242.

Ruud, P. (1986), "Consistent Estimation of Limited Dependent Variable Models Despite Misspecification of Distribution," *Journal of Econometrics* 32, 157–187.

Sander, W. (1992), "The Effect of Women's Schooling on Fertility," *Economics Letters* 40, 229–233.

Sargan, J. D. (1958), "The Estimation of Economic Relationships Using Instrumental Variables," *Econometrica* 26, 393–415.

Schmidt, P. (1976), *Econometrics*. New York: Marcel-Dekker.

Semykina, A., and J. M. Wooldridge (in press), "Estimating Panel Data Models in the Presence of Endogeneity and Selection," *Journal of Econometrics*.

Serfling, R. J. (2006), "Multivariate Symmetry and Asymmetry," in *Encyclopedia of Statistical Sciences*, ed. S. Kotz, N. Balakrishnan, C. B. Read, and B. Vidakovic. New York: Wiley, 5338–5345.

Shapiro, M. D. (1984), "The Permanent Income Hypothesis and the Real Interest Rate: Some Evidence from Panel Data," *Economics Letters* 14, 93–100.

Shea, J. (1995), "Union Contracts and the Life-Cycle/Permanent Income Hypothesis," *American Economic Review* 85, 186–200.

Shea, J. (1997), "Instrument Relevance in Multivariate Linear Models: A Simple Measure," *Review of Economics and Statistics* 79, 348–352.

Smith, R., and R. Blundell (1986), "An Exogeneity Test for a Simultaneous Equation Tobit Model with an Application to Labor Supply," *Econometrica* 54, 679–685.

Solon, G. (1985), "Comment on 'Benefits and Limitations of Panel Data' by C. Hsiao," *Econometric Reviews* 4, 183–186.

Staiger, D., and J. H. Stock (1997), "Instrumental Variables Regression with Weak Instruments," *Econometrica* 65, 557–586.

Stock, J. H., J. H. Wright, and M. Yogo (2002), "A Survey of Weak Instruments and Weak Identification in Generalized Method of Moments," *Journal of Business and Economic Statistics* 20, 518–529.

Stoker, T. M. (1986), "Consistent Estimation of Scaled Coefficients," *Econometrica* 54, 1461–1481.

Stoker, T. M. (1992), *Lectures on Semiparametric Econometrics*. Louvain-la-Neuve, Belgium: CORE Lecture Series.

Strauss, J., and D. Thomas (1995), "Human Resources: Empirical Modeling of Household and Family Decisions," in *Handbook of Development Economics*, Volume 3A, ed. J. Berhman and T. N. Srinivasan. Amsterdam: North Holland, 1883–2023.

Sueyoshi, G. T. (1992), "Semiparametric Proportional Hazards Estimation of Competing Risks Models with Time-Varying Covariates," *Journal of Econometrics* 51, 25–58.

Sueyoshi, G. T. (1995), "A Class of Binary Response Models for Grouped Duration Data," *Journal of Applied Econometrics* 10, 411–431.

Swait, J. (2003), "Flexible Covariance Structures for Categorical Dependent Variables through Finite Mixtures of Generalized Extreme Value Models," *Journal of Business and Economic Statistics* 21, 80–87.

Tauchen, G. (1985), "Diagnostic Testing and Evaluation of Maximum Likelihood Models," *Journal of Econometrics* 30, 415–443.

Tauchen, G. (1986), "Statistical Properties of Generalized Method-of-Moments Estimators of Structural Parameters Obtained from Financial Market Data," *Journal of Business and Economic Statistics* 4, 397–416.

Terza, J. V. (1998), "Estimating Count Models with Endogenous Switching: Sample Selection and Endogenous Treatment Effects," *Journal of Econometrics* 84, 129–154.

Theil, H. (1983), "Linear Algebra and Matrix Methods in Econometrics," in *Handbook of Econometrics*, Volume 1, ed. Z. Griliches and M. D. Intriligator. Amsterdam: North Holland, 5–65.

Thomas, D., J. Strauss, and M.-H. Henriques (1990), "Child Survival, Height for Age and Household Characteristics in Brazil," *Journal of Development Economics* 33, 197–234.

Tobin, J. (1958), "Estimation of Relationships for Limited Dependent Variables," *Econometrica* 26, 24–36.

van den Berg, G. (2001), "Duration Models: Specification, Identification, and Multiple Durations," in *Handbook of Econometrics*, Volume 5, ed. J. J. Heckman and E. Leamer. Amsterdam: North Holland, 3381–3460.

van der Klaauw, W. (1996), "Female Labour Supply and Marital Status Decisions: A Life-Cyle Model," *Review of Economic Studies* 63, 199–235.

van der Klaauw, W. (2002), "Estimating the Effect of Financial Aid Offers on College Enrollment: A Regression-Discontinuity Approach," *International Economic Review* 43, 1249–1287.

van der Laan, M. J., and J. M. Robins (2003), *Unified Methods for Censored Longitudinal and Causality*. New York: Springer-Verlag.

Vella, F. (1992), "Simple Tests for Sample Selection Bias in Censored and Discrete Choice Models," *Journal of Applied Econometrics* 7, 413–421.

Vella, F. (1993), "A Simple Estimator for Simultaneous Models with Censored Endogenous Regressors," *International Economic Review* 34, 441–457.

Vella, F. (1998), "Estimating Models with Sample Selection Bias: A Survey," *Journal of Human Resources* 33, 127–169.

Vella, F., and M. Verbeek (1998), "Whose Wages Do Unions Raise? A Dynamic Model of Unionism and Wage Rate Determination for Young Men," *Journal of Applied Econometrics* 13, 163–183.

Vella, F., and M. Verbeek (1999), "Estimating and Interpreting Models with Endogenous Treatment Effects," *Journal of Business and Economic Statistics* 17, 473–478.

Villas-Boas, J. M., and R. S. Winer (1999), "Endogeneity in Brand Choice Models," *Management Science* 10, 1324–1338.

Vuong, Q. (1989), "Likelihood Ratio Tests for Model Selection and Nonnested Hypotheses," *Econometrica* 57, 307–333.

Wald, A. (1940), "The Fitting of Straight Lines if Both Variables Are Subject to Error," *Annals of Mathematical Statistics* 11, 284–300.

White, H. (1980a), "Nonlinear Regression on Cross Section Data," *Econometrica* 48, 721–746.

White, H. (1980b), "A Heteroskedasticity-Consistent Covariance Matrix Estimator and a Direct Test for Heteroskedasticity," *Econometrica* 48, 817–838.

White, H. (1981), "Consequences and Detection of Misspecified Nonlinear Regression Models," *Journal of the American Statistical Association* 76, 419–433.

White, H. (1982a), "Maximum Likelihood Estimation of Misspecified Models," *Econometrica* 50, 1–26.

White, H. (1982b), "Instrumental Variables Regression with Independent Observations," *Econometrica* 50, 483–499.

White, H. (1984), *Asymptotic Theory for Econometricians*. Orlando, FL: Academic Press.

White, H. (1994), *Estimation, Inference and Specification Analysis*. Cambridge: Cambridge University Press.

White, H. (2001), *Asymptotic Theory for Econometricians*, revised edition. San Diego, CA: Academic Press.

Windmeijer, F. (2000), "Moment Conditions for Fixed Effects Count Data Models with Endogenous Regressors," *Economics Letters* 68, 21–24.

Wolak, F. A. (1991), "The Local Nature of Hypothesis Tests Involving Inequality Constraints in Nonlinear Models," *Econometrica* 59, 981–995.

Wooldridge, J. M. (1990), "A Unified Approach to Robust, Regression-Based Specification Tests," *Econometric Theory* 6, 17–43.

Wooldridge, J. M. (1991a), "On the Application of Robust, Regression-Based Diagnostics to Models of Conditional Means and Conditional Variances," *Journal of Econometrics* 47, 5–46.

Wooldridge, J. M. (1991b), "Specification Testing and Quasi-Maximum Likelihood Estimation," *Journal of Econometrics* 48, 29–55.

Wooldridge, J. M. (1992), "Some Alternatives to the Box-Cox Regression Model," *International Economic Review* 33, 935–955.

Wooldridge, J. M. (1994a), "Estimation and Inference for Dependent Processes," in *Handbook of Econometrics*, Volume 4, ed. R. F. Engle and D. L. McFadden. Amsterdam: North-Holland, 2639–2738.

Wooldridge, J. M. (1994b), "Efficient Estimation under Heteroskedasticity," *Econometric Theory* 10, 223.

Wooldridge, J. M. (1995a), "Selection Corrections for Panel Data Models under Conditional Mean Independence Assumptions," *Journal of Econometrics* 68, 115–132.

Wooldridge, J. M. (1995b), "Score Diagnostics for Linear Models Estimated by Two Stage Least Squares," in *Advances in Econometrics and Quantitative Economics*, ed. G. S. Maddala, P. C. B. Phillips, and T. N. Srinivasan. Oxford: Blackwell, 66–87.

Wooldridge, J. M. (1996), "Estimating Systems of Equations with Different Instruments for Different Equations," *Journal of Econometrics* 74, 387–405.

Wooldridge, J. M. (1997a), "Multiplicative Panel Data Models without the Strict Exogeneity Assumption," *Econometric Theory* 13, 667–678.

Wooldridge, J. M. (1997b), "On Two Stage Least Squares Estimation of the Average Treatment Effect in a Random Coefficient Model," *Economics Letters* 56, 129–133.

Wooldridge, J. M. (1997c), "Quasi-Likelihood Methods for Count Data," in *Handbook of Applied Econometrics*, Volume 2, ed. M. H. Pesaran and P. Schmidt. Oxford: Blackwell, 352–406.

Wooldridge, J. M. (1999a), "Distribution-Free Estimation of Some Nonlinear Panel Data Models," *Journal of Econometrics* 90, 77–97.

Wooldridge, J. M. (1999b), "Asymptotic Properties of Weighted M-Estimators for Variable Probability Samples," *Econometrica* 67, 1385–1406.

Wooldridge, J. M. (1999c), "Estimating Average Partial Effects under Conditional Moment Independence Assumptions," mimeo, Michigan State University Department of Economics.

Wooldridge, J. M. (2000), "A Framework for Estimating Dynamic, Unobserved Effects Panel Data Models with Possible Feedback to Future Explanatory Variables," *Economics Letters* 68, 245–250.

Wooldridge, J. M. (2001), "Asymptotic Properties of Weighted M-Estimators for Standard Stratified Samples." *Econometric Theory* 17, 451–470.

Wooldridge, J. M. (2003a), "Cluster-Sample Methods in Applied Econometrics," *American Economic Review* 93 (May), 133–138.

Wooldridge, J. M. (2003b), "Further Results on Instrumental Variables Estimation of Average Treatment Effects in the Correlated Random Coefficient Model," *Economics Letters* 79 (May), 185–191.

Wooldridge, J. M. (2004), "Estimating Average Partial Effects Under Conditional Moment Independence Assumptions," CeMMAP Working Paper Number CWP03/04.

Wooldridge, J. M. (2005a), "Fixed Effects and Related Estimators for Correlated Random-Coefficient and Treatment Effect Panel Data Models," *Review of Economics and Statistics* 87, 385–390.

Wooldridge, J. M. (2005b), "Simple Solutions to the Initial Conditions Problem for Dynamic, Nonlinear Panel Data Models with Unobserved Heterogeneity," *Journal of Applied Econometrics* 20, 39–54.

Wooldridge, J. M. (2005c), "Unobserved Heterogeneity and Estimation of Average Partial Effects," in *Identification and Inference for Econometric Models: Essays in Honor of Thomas Rothenberg*, ed. D. W. K. Andrews and J. H. Stock. Cambridge: Cambridge University Press, 2005, 27–55.

Wooldridge, J. M. (2005d), "Violating Ignorability of Treatment by Controlling for Too Many Factors," *Econometric Theory* 21, 1026–1028.

Wooldridge, J. M. (2005e), "Instrumental Variables Estimation with Panel Data," *Econometric Theory* 21, 865–869.

Wooldridge, J. M. (2007), "Inverse Probability Weighted M-Estimation for General Missing Data Problems," *Journal of Econometrics* 141, 1281–1301.

Wooldridge, J. M. (2008), "Instrumental Variables Estimation of the Average Treatment Effect in Correlated Random Coefficient Models," in *Advances in Econometrics*, Volume 21, ed. D. Millimet, J. Smith, and E. Vytlacil. Amsterdam: Elsevier, 93–117.

Wooldridge, J. M. (2009a), *Introductory Econometrics: A Modern Approach*, fourth edition. Mason, OH: South-Western.

Wooldridge, J. M. (2009b), "On Estimating Firm-Level Production Functions Using Proxy Variables to Control for Unobservables," *Economics Letters* 104, 112–114.

Wooldridge, J. M. (2009c), "Should Instrumental Variables Be Used as Matching Variables?" Mimeo, Michigan State University Department of Economics.

Wu, D. (1973), "Alternative Tests of Independence between Stochastic Regressors and Disturbances," *Econometrica* 41, 733–750.

Yatchew, A., and Z. Griliches (1985), "Specification Error in Probit Models," *Review of Economics and Statistics* 67, 134–39.

Zeldes, S. P. (1989), "Consumption and Liquidity Constraints: An Empirical Investigation," *Journal of Political Economy* 97, 305–346.

Zellner, A. (1962), "An Efficient Method of Estimating Seemingly Unrelated Regressions and Tests of Aggregation Bias," *Journal of the American Statistical Association* 57, 500–509.

Ziliak, J. P. (1997), "Efficient Estimation with Panel Data When Instruments Are Predetermined: An Empirical Comparison of Moment-Condition Estimators," *Journal of Business and Economic Statistics* 15, 419–431.

Ziliak, J. P., and T. J. Kniesner (1998), "The Importance of Sample Attrition in Life Cycle Labor Supply Estimation," *Journal of Human Resources* 33, 507–530.

Ziliak, J. P., B. Wilson, and J. Stone (1999), "Spatial Dynamics and Heterogeneity in the Cyclicality of Real Wages," *Review of Economics and Statistics* 81, 227–236.

Index